TIME
ALMANAC
2010

DISCARDED

POWERED BY

ENCYCLOPÆDIA
Britannica®

www.britannica.com

Jacob E. Safra, *Chairman of the Board*
Jorge Aguilar-Cauz, *President*

Chicago · London · New Delhi · Paris · Seoul · Sydney · Taipei · Tokyo

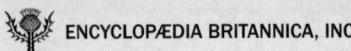

ENCYCLOPÆDIA BRITANNICA, INC.

EDITORIAL
Thad King
Michael J. Anderson
Patricia Bauer
Robert M. Lewis
Kenneth Pletcher
Barbara Schreiber
Melinda C. Shepherd
Karen Jacobs Sparks
Amy Tikkanen

PRODUCTION CONTROL
Marilyn L. Barton

WORLD DATA
Stephen Neher
Mary Kasprzak

CARTOGRAPHY
Michael Nutter
Ken Chmielewski

COPY
Sylvia Wallace
John M. Cunningham
Yvette Charboneau
Kimberly Jeffries
Glenn Jenne
Claire Navarro

ART AND COMPOSITION
Steven N. Kapusta
Nicole DiGiacomo
Carol A. Gaines
Christine McCabe
Cate Nichols
Patrick Riley
Thomas J. Spanos

EDITORIAL LIBRARY
Henry Bolzon
Lars Mahinske

INFORMATION MANAGEMENT
Carmen-Maria Hetrea
Sheila Vasich
Mansur Abdullah
Matthew Heinze

MANUFACTURING
Kim Gerber

MEDIA ASSET MANAGEMENT
Jeannine Deubel
Kimberly Cleary
Kurt Heintz

ENCYCLOPÆDIA BRITANNICA, INC.

Jacob E. Safra
Chairman of the Board

Jorge Aguilar-Cauz
President

Michael Ross
Senior Vice President,
Corporate Development

Dale H. Hoiberg
Senior Vice President
and Editor

Michael Levy
Executive Editor,
Core Reference

Rosaline Jackson-Keys
Director, Almanac and
World Data

Marsha Mackenzie
Executive Director,
Media and Production

HOME ENTERTAINMENT

CONTRIBUTING EDITOR
Kelly Knauer

DESIGN
Anthony Wing Kosner

PICTURES
Patricia Cadley

Richard Fraiman
Publisher

Steven Sandonato
General Manager

Carol Pittard
Executive Director, Marketing
Services

Tom Mifsud
Director, Retail and Special Sales

Peter Harper
Director, New Product Development

Laura Adam
Assistant Director, Newsstand
Marketing

Joy Butts
Assistant Publishing Director,
Brand Marketing

Helen Wan
Associate Counsel

Suzanne Janso
Book Production Manager

Anne-Michelle Gallero
Design and Prepress Manager

Michela Wilde
Associate Brand Manager

Alex Voznesenskiy
Assistant Prepress Manager

Special thanks to: Christine Austin, Glenn Buonocore, Jim Childs, Susan Chodakiewicz, Rose Cirrincione, Jacqueline Fitzgerald, Lauren Hall, Jennifer Jacobs, Brynn Joyce, Mona Li, Robert Marasco, Amy Migliaccio, Brooke Reger, Dave Rozzelle, Ilene Schreider, Adriana Tierno, Sydney Webber

© 2009 BY ENCYCLOPÆDIA BRITANNICA, INC. All rights reserved.

All TIME material copyright © 2009 Time Inc. All rights reserved.

Front cover photography credits: Insets: AP Images (4); Earth: NASA Goddard Space Flight Center Image by Reto Stöckli (land surface, shallow water, clouds). Enhancements by Robert Simmon (ocean color, compositing, 3D globes, animation). Data and technical support: MODIS Land Group; MODIS Science Data Support Team; MODIS Atmosphere Group; MODIS Ocean Group. Additional data: USGS EROS Data Center (topography); USGS Terrestrial Remote Sensing Flagstaff Field Center (Antarctica); Defense Meteorological Satellite Program (city lights). Back cover photography credits: AP Images (3); Boyle: Ken McKay–Rex USA

ISBN 10: 1-60320-091-6; ISBN-13: 978-1-60320-091-2 Hardcover
ISBN 10: 1-60320-825-9; ISBN-13: 978-1-60320-825-3 Paperback
ISSN: 0073-7860

No part of this work may be reproduced or utilized in any form or by any means, electronic or mechanical, including photocopying, recording, or by any information storage and retrieval system, without permission in writing from the publisher.

ENCYCLOPÆDIA BRITANNICA ALMANAC 2010

Britannica.com may be accessed on the Internet at http://www.britannica.com. For information on group and bulk sales, please send an e-mail to books@eb.com.

(Trademark Reg. U.S. Pat. Off.) Printed in U.S.A.

If you would like to order any of our hardcover Collector's Edition books, please call us at 1-800-327-6388 (Monday through Friday, 7:00 A.M.–8:00 P.M. or Saturday, 7:00 A.M.–6:00 P.M. Central Time).

Year in Review

The US in Afghanistan: The Longest War

by Aryn Baker, TIME/Afghanistan

Seven and a half years after US troops arrived in Afghanistan following the attacks of September 11, 2001, the war there is more deadly—and more muddled—than ever. When American troops first went to Afghanistan, they did so to overthrow the Taliban regime, which then ruled the nation and provided a haven for al-Qaeda. In less than three months, the Taliban was defeated, and a US-supported administration, headed by Pres. Hamid Karzai, was installed in Kabul. Yet in 2009, the US is still fighting the Taliban, and al-Qaeda operatives are still plotting from Afghanistan. (Taliban, these days, no longer refers just to the Islamic extremist regime that once ruled the country; the word has become synonymous with any number of antigovernment forces.)

And one part of the region's deadly muddle has gotten worse. In 2001 there were fears that the war in Afghanistan would destabilize Pakistan. (The Pashtun ethnic group, which makes up a large part of the Taliban insurgency, straddles the border between the two countries.) Those fears are now reality; the Pakistani Taliban threatens nuclear-armed Pakistan's viability as a state even more than its cousins jeopardize Afghanistan's.

It is because the war in Afghanistan threatens to destabilize an entire region that it has become America's biggest foreign policy challenge. On 18 Feb 2009, President Obama committed an additional 17,000 troops to Afghanistan; when they all arrive, there will be about 55,000 troops there from the US, plus 37,000 from its allies. The latest Afghan war is now Obama's war. The administration has signaled that it is downsizing expectations about what can still be achieved: the principal goal now is to counter terrorism and bring a degree of stability to Afghanistan—not to turn a poor and fractious nation into a flourishing democratic state.

When Obama laid out his new strategy, he made it clear that the mark of success would be the ability "to disrupt, dismantle, and defeat al-Qaeda in Pakistan and Afghanistan and to prevent their return to either country in the future." But accomplishing even that comparatively limited objective at this stage will require a massive and sustained US commitment—one that involves more than military boots on the ground. Al-Qaeda still thrives in the ungoverned tribal areas along the border between the two countries, and while many of its members have been killed, new recruits quickly take their place. US soldiers have learned that to deny al-Qaeda a foothold in Afghanistan will require the establishment of a government that Afghans can believe in, the security that allows them to support it, and jobs that provide an alternative to fighting. "We are not going to kill our way out of this war," says Lieut. Col. Brett Jenkinson, commander of the US battalion stationed in the Korengal valley. "What we need is a better recruiting pitch for disaffected youth. You can't build hope with military might. You build it through development and good governance."

Other than leading by example, the military can do little to bolster faith in the state. As part of his plan, Obama has proposed a civilian surge—a phalanx of mentors for the Afghans. Much of the more than US$32 billion that the US government has spent in aid to Afghanistan since 2002 has gone through the military or its provincial reconstruction teams. The projects are designed to earn goodwill for foreign forces as much as for local governors, but they also have the unintended consequence of undermining the central government, which never gets a chance to take credit for providing basic services such as roads, electricity, and education. "We aren't here to win hearts and minds," says Jeremy Brenner, a US State Department adviser based in Jalalabad. "What we need is to engender hope and faith in the Afghan government."

The experience of the Americans fighting in the nation's eastern Korengal Valley illustrates how difficult this war is. Over the period from July 2008 to April 2009, Bravo Company, a 150-strong unit of the 1st Battalion, 26th Infantry Regiment, lost seven men in the Korengal while trying to cool down a toxic cauldron of local insurgents, Taliban leaders, foreign jihadis, and al-Qaeda members. Here success cannot be measured in territory gained, schools built, or clinics opened. Irrigation pipes and water pumps are blown up by the insurgents as soon as they are built. Sometimes progress is so slow it feels like a stalemate, admits company commander Capt. James Howell. But, he says, "if we can reach a point where the villagers want to work with us and the Taliban are the only thing stopping them, that's success."

A government in which people have hope would be one that offers them security. The US exit strategy for Afghanistan, according to Adm. Mike Mullen, chairman of the Joint Chiefs of Staff, is to strengthen the Afghan forces so they can protect the fragile advances of the government. To that end, Obama has pledged 4,000 trainers and mentors to help boost the Afghan National Army and police.

But success in Afghanistan will mean nothing if fighters can find sanctuary in Pakistan. Commanders in Afghanistan say the battle next door will be far more complicated than anything they have seen, simply because the Pakistani military doesn't have the skills and resources to conduct an effective counterinsurgency. US-operated Predator drones have successfully targeted al-Qaeda leadership in the border areas, but at the cost of inflaming the Pashtun-led insurgency on the Pakistani side. Stabilizing Afghanistan might well become crucial to preventing the far more terrifying prospect of an Islamic extremist takeover in Pakistan. Says US Army Brig. Gen. John Nicholson, Jr., who commands US and NATO troops in southern Afghanistan: "If the Pashtun population of Pakistan sees a moderate, Islamic and Pashtun-led government in Afghanistan, well, it's hard to argue with. So we have potentially a greater impact in Pakistan with success in the east."

Getting it right in both Afghanistan and Pakistan now, after years of Western drift and inattention, will come at a heavy price in American money and lives. Having doubled down in the hopes of winning in Afghanistan, the Obama administration has no choice but to live with the consequences.

How Twitter Will Change the Way We Live

by Steven Johnson for TIME

The one thing you can say for certain about Twitter is that it makes a terrible first impression. You hear about this new service that lets you send 140-character updates to your "followers," and you think, Why does the world need this, exactly? It's not as if we were all sitting around four years ago scratching our heads and saying, "If only there were a technology that would allow me to send a message to my 50 friends, alerting them in real time about my choice of breakfast cereal."

The basic mechanics of Twitter are remarkably simple. Users publish tweets—those 140-character messages—from a computer or mobile device. As a social network, Twitter revolves around the principle of followers. When you choose to follow another Twitter user, that user's tweets appear in reverse chronological order on your main Twitter page. If you follow 20 people, you'll see a mix of tweets scrolling down the page: breakfast-cereal updates, interesting new links, music recommendations, even musings on the future of education. The mix creates a media experience quite unlike anything that has come before it, strangely intimate and at the same time celebrity-obsessed. You glance at your Twitter feed over that first cup of coffee, and in a few seconds you find out that your nephew got into med school and Shaquille O'Neal just finished a cardio workout in Phoenix.

But the key development with Twitter is how we've jury-rigged the system to do things that its creators never dreamed of. The most fascinating thing about Twitter is not what it's doing to us. It's what we're doing to it.

This is not just a matter of people finding a new use for a tool designed to do something else. In Twitter's case, the users have been redesigning the tool itself. The convention of grouping a topic or event by the "hashtag"—#hackedu or #inauguration—was spontaneously invented by the Twitter user base (as was the convention of replying to another user with the @ symbol). The ability to search a live stream of tweets was developed by another start-up altogether, Summize, which Twitter purchased last year. Thanks to these innovations, following a live feed of tweets about an event—a political debate or a *Lost* episode—has become a central part of the Twitter experience. But as recently as 2008, that mode of interaction would have been technically impossible using Twitter. It's like inventing a toaster oven and then looking around a year later and seeing that your customers have of their own accord turned it into a microwave.

One of the most telling facts about the Twitter platform is that the vast majority of its users interact with the service via software created by third parties. There are dozens of iPhone and BlackBerry applications—all created by enterprising amateur coders or small start-ups—that let you manage Twitter feeds. There are services that help you upload photos and link to them from your tweets and programs that map other Twitizens who are near you geographically.

As the tools have multiplied, we're discovering extraordinary new things to do with them. In June 2009, when Iranians rose up to protest a rigged election, supporters around the world followed the demonstrations in real time on Twitter. Two months earlier, an anticommunist uprising in Moldova was organized via Twitter. Twitter has become so widely used among political activists in China that the government blocked access to it for a period, in an attempt to censor discussion of the 20th anniversary of the Tiananmen Square massacre.

The rapid-fire innovation we're seeing around Twitter is not new, of course. Facebook, whose audience is still several times as large as Twitter's, went from being a way to scope out the most attractive college freshmen to the Social Operating System of the Internet, supporting a vast ecosystem of new applications created by major media companies, individual hackers, game creators, political groups, and charities. The Apple iPhone's long-term competitive advantage may well prove to be the more than 15,000 new applications that have been developed for the device, expanding its functionality in countless ingenious ways.

The history of the Web followed a similar pattern. A platform originally designed to help scholars share academic documents, it now lets you watch television shows, play poker with strangers around the world, publish your own newspaper, rediscover your high-school girlfriend—and, yes, tell the world what you had for breakfast. The speed with which users have extended Twitter's platform points to a larger truth about modern innovation. When we talk about innovation and global competitiveness, we tend to fall back on the easy metric of patents and Ph.D.'s. It turns out the US share of both has been in steady decline since peaking in the early 1970s. Since the mid-1980s, a long progression of doomsayers have warned that our declining market share in the patents-and-Ph.D.'s business augurs dark times for American innovation.

But what actually happened to American innovation during that period? We came up with America Online, Netscape, Amazon, Google, Blogger, Wikipedia, Craigslist, TiVo, Netflix, eBay, the iPod and iPhone, Xbox, Facebook, and Twitter itself. Sure, we didn't build the Prius or the Wii, but if you measure global innovation in terms of actual lifestyle-changing hit products and not just grad students, the US has been lapping the field for the past 20 years.

How could the forecasts have been so wrong? The answer is that we've been tracking only part of the innovation story, ignoring what Massachusetts Institute of Technology professor Eric von Hippel calls "end-user innovation," in which consumers actively modify a product to adapt it to their needs. In its short life, Twitter has been a hothouse of end-user innovation: the hashtag; searching; its 11,000 third-party applications; all those creative new uses of Twitter—some of them banal, some of them spam, and some of them sublime.

This is what I ultimately find most inspiring about the Twitter phenomenon. We are living through the worst economic crisis in generations, with apocalyptic headlines threatening the end of capitalism as we know it, and yet in the middle of this chaos, the engineers at Twitter headquarters are scrambling to keep the servers up, application developers are releasing their latest builds, and ordinary users are figuring out all the ingenious ways to put these tools to use. There's a kind of resilience here that is worth savoring. The weather reports keep announcing that the sky is falling, but here we are—millions of us—sitting around trying to invent new ways to talk to one another.

Skyrocketing Food Prices: A Global Crisis

by Janet H. Clark

As the year 2008 got under way, upwardly spiraling food prices became of increasing concern to international organizations and relief agencies, national governments, and consumers everywhere. UN officials speculated that the crisis could add an additional 100 million hungry people to the billion already living on less than US$1 a day, the common measure of absolute poverty. The impact of rising food prices was greatest in less-developed countries (LDCs), where spending on food accounted for 40–60% of income, compared with about 15% in industrialized countries.

Even in industrialized countries, poor families were being severely affected by a general rise in prices, especially when combined with an economic downturn and higher unemployment. Food prices in the 30 Organisation for Economic Co-operation and Development (OECD) member countries rose by 7.2% year on year in both July and August, the biggest increases since 1990, and in the US the Department of Labor reported that grocery-store food prices rose by 6.6% in 2008, the largest increase since 1980.

With spiking food costs came a growing threat to food security, which provoked political repercussions in many LDCs. In Haiti, for example, food riots led to the ousting of Prime Minister Jacques-Édouard Alexis on 12 April, and the lack of a replacement until July left the government in a state of paralysis while social and economic conditions continued to deteriorate.

Prices of staple foodstuffs escalated alarmingly on world markets. In the first half of the year, the price of internationally traded food commodities, led by grains, rose by 56%. In the first quarter alone, the prices of wheat and corn (maize) rose by 130% and 30%, respectively, over the same period a year earlier, while the cost of rice climbed 10% in both February and March. By midyear the prices of corn, wheat, and soybeans had more than doubled, while that of rice had tripled.

A number of factors contributed to the increases in food prices. One was the economic emergence of China and India, whose populations were becoming increasingly affluent and thus boosting their food consumption; in China annual per capita consumption of meat rose to 54 kg (about 119 lb) from 20 kg (44 lb) in 1985. Another major factor was the increased output of biofuels made from grains and oilseeds in the US and the European Union, where there were generous—and controversial—tax concessions or direct financial support for producers, retailers, or users of biofuels. In July an OECD report strongly criticized these incentives as costly and ineffective and recommended that governments refocus their policies. Partially associated with this was the restrictive and trade-distorting effect of a high level of government support to farmers in many OECD countries, which in 2007 amounted to US$258 billion, or 23% of farm incomes. A surge in petroleum prices led to increased fertilizer and transport costs. In many countries adverse weather led to crop failure, speculation on commodity markets, and hoarding. When Cyclone Nargis struck Myanmar (Burma) on 2 May, it generated a 4-m (12-ft)-high storm surge that devastated the rice-producing Irrawaddy delta. During August and September, Haiti, already suffering from food shortages, was battered by four successive hurricanes. The depreciation of the US dollar against the euro and other currencies early in the year contributed to the rise in dollar-denominated commodity prices. The International Food Policy Research Institute (IFPRI) estimated that 15–27% of the increase was from the dollar's decline. At the same time, countries in Asia and the Middle East that linked their currencies to the weakening dollar experienced overheated economies and suffered higher prices than countries with more flexible exchange rates.

The World Food Programme (WFP) was the main distributor of emergency food relief, with activities in more than 75 countries. In March, however, the organization announced that it was short of money because of the soaring price of cereals and other foodstuffs. At the UN heads of government meeting in June, the WFP reported that it had received US$1.2 billion in aid, including an unexpected US$500 million from Saudi Arabia. Among 60 low-income food-deficit countries surveyed early in the year by the Food and Agriculture Organization (FAO), the most widespread response was to remove or reduce import tariffs on food. This was especially true in South and East Asia, the Middle East, and North Africa. Given that tariff levels on cereals and vegetable oils were already relatively low, however, at 8% and 14%, respectively, only small proportions of the price rises were offset.

In the Middle East, drought reduced the summer harvest, and many major wheat-producing countries, including Iran, Iraq, and Syria, were forced to increase imports. In Saudi Arabia the annual inflation rate soared to 10.6% in June, its highest rate in 30 years, and wheat production was extremely costly because of huge farm subsidies. The Saudi government decided in August that it would make economic sense to outsource its farming and was considering the purchase of rice farms in Thailand through a new investment fund set up to buy agricultural land overseas. United Arab Emirates investors looking for land for agricultural development favored Pakistan, Kazakhstan, and The Sudan.

In early May, Prime Minister Samak Sundaravej of Thailand (the world's biggest rice producer) proposed

> *UN officials speculated that the crisis could add an additional 100 million hungry people to the billion already living on less than US$1 a day, the common measure of absolute poverty.*

the formation of a cartel of Southeast Asian rice-producing countries (including Vietnam, Myanmar, Laos, and Cambodia) to be set up along the lines of OPEC. Laos and Cambodia favored the idea, but there were strong protests in the Philippines, the world's biggest rice importer. In August Thailand announced plans to boost rice production by leasing 160,000 ha (395,000 ac) of unused state land to poor farmers and agribusiness for biofuel crops, sugarcane, palm, and rice. A more novel way of easing food shortages was proposed in July by scientists at the National Autonomous University of Mexico; they asserted that insects, which were nutritious and already provided part of the diet in 113 countries, should be consumed more widely. Thailand, where cricket rearing for food was already practiced by many families, hosted an FAO conference to examine the benefits of insects as a food option.

At an EU summit in July, member countries were divided on trade reform and the need to remove agricultural subsidies and reduce protectionism. For the first time, in 2008 the EU did not use the portion of its agricultural budget designated for buying and stockpiling surplus produce. The resulting unused funds, expected to reach €1 billion (about US$1.4 billion), were to be given to farmers in LDCs through

2009. Cut-price discount stores, which were already popular in the US, were proliferating in Europe and putting pressure on the more costly chains. The search for cheaper food was gathering momentum even in US cities, where there was a resurgence of so-called freegans, who scavenged through supermarket garbage bins and other sources of discarded food.

Despite the widespread fear of a continuing rise in global inflation and the number of people needing food aid, the failure to reach agreement on trade liberalization left agricultural producers in LDCs at a continuing disadvantage. The IFPRI calculated that if export bans by some 40 food-exporting countries were lifted, cereal prices would be 30% lower on average. Two small signs of hope emerged in September. Corporate and government leaders attended the first UN Private Sector Forum on Food Sustainability and the Millennium Development Goals. At the same time, the WFP unveiled Purchase for Progress, an initiative by which governments and private foundations (notably the Bill & Melinda Gates Foundation and the Howard G. Buffett Foundation) would finance WFP purchases of foodstuffs from small farmers in LDCs, which would thus encourage local food production and offer small farmers better access to world markets.

Janet H. Clark is an editor, independent analyst, and writer on international economic and financial topics.

Seed Banks—Preserving Crop Diversity

by Gregory McNamee

On 26 Feb 2008, the most ambitious seed-bank facility ever constructed was inaugurated in Svalbard, a Norwegian archipelago in the Arctic Ocean only about 1,000 km (620 mi) from the North Pole. The Svalbard Global Seed Vault (SGSV), built by the Norwegian government into the side of a permafrost-covered mountain on the island of Spitsbergen, is designed to store in deep freeze the seeds of hundreds of thousands of plant varieties from crops grown on every part of the globe. This high-security "doomsday" conservancy, built far from unrest and civil war, seeks to protect the world's agricultural inheritance against disaster, be it from rising sea levels, an asteroid strike, pestilence, or even the unforeseen consequences of an excessive reliance on crops with single-source genetic modifications.

Established as a backup facility, the SGSV accepts only seed samples that are already held by other seed banks. The deposits are managed by the Global Crop Diversity Trust, an independent international organization that was established in 2004 by the UN Food and Agriculture Organization and the Consultative Group on International Agricultural Research, which operates international seed banks for the most important staple food crops. Seed samples for the SGSV are delivered and stored in sealed boxes and remain the property of the country or organization that deposits them. By late 2008 about 320,000 distinct seed samples, consisting of about 220 million seeds from about 2,900 plant species in more than 200 countries, had been placed in storage. The vault's storage chambers were able to hold 4.5 million seed samples, for a total of 2.25 billion seeds.

> *The organization's seed collectors, often traveling to isolated areas by foot or muleback, have recovered seeds for some 2,000 varieties of plants...*

Since the SGSV safeguards duplicate seed collections, it is not intended to replace any of the roughly 1,400 seed banks that exist worldwide and include national and international institutions, organizations focused on particular types of crops, and regional facilities. In general, these seed banks are intended to preserve the genetic variety of plants, and for this reason they are also referred to as gene banks. Conserving crop varieties and related wild species provides genetic variations that can be useful for developing new varieties with essential traits, such as tolerating new pests or climate conditions.

Among the most important global seed banks is the Millennium Seed Bank (West Sussex, England), which is managed by the Royal Botanic Gardens, Kew. Opened in 2000, the Millennium Seed Bank has succeeded in preserving virtually all of Britain's 1,400 native plants and, in collaboration with seed banks in other parts of the world, seeks to conserve a total of more than 24,000 plant species.

Seed banks that specialize in particular crops include the International Rice Genebank at the International Rice Research Institute (IRRI), based in Los Baños, Philippines, and the International Potato Center (IPC), based in Lima. The IRRI, which was established in 1960, estimates that it has conserved about 100,000 varieties of rice. The IPC, which was established in 1971 and subsequently expanded to include other tubers of Andean origin, counts in its collections about 150 wild potato species.

An example of a regional seed bank is Native Seeds, which was founded in 1983 in the southwestern United States to help Native Americans locate seeds for growing traditional crops. One of the oldest crop conservancies in North America, it aims in part to make poor communities nutritionally self-sufficient. The organization's seed collectors, often traveling to isolated areas by foot or muleback, have recovered seeds for some 2,000 varieties of plants, including amaranth, once widely used for food and fiber in Mexico; tepary beans, a favorite food of the desert peoples of the Southwest; orach, or "mountain spinach," grown in the Rio Grande uplands of New Mexico; panic grass, once a rich source of grain and protein for the Indian peoples of southern California and northern Mexico; and a sunflower grown in the Grand Canyon by the Havasupai Indians—one that is completely resistant to a rust disease that has ravaged commercial sunflower crops.

By selecting single hybrids, industrial agriculture (the source of the stock advertised in most commercial seed catalogs) has diminished the number of varieties of food plants available in the United States and other countries to all but a devoted handful of farmers and experimental gardeners. In the early 1900s, for example, more than 7,000 varieties of apples were grown commercially in the United States; today only a couple of dozen varieties are available to most consumers. The planting of monoculture crops, which increases standardization and efficiency, has replaced traditional crops in plots where they had been grown and bred for centuries. As a consequence, traditional crops, which had acquired the traits that are most suitable for the soils and climate of a given location, have been steadily lost. The preservation of this diversity of crops will help safeguard the future of the food plants upon which humans depend. Seed banks can directly address the concerns raised by a diminishment of genetic diversity among common food crops, and as plant scientists recover varieties of native food plants across the world, they add color to a sadly washed-out genetic palette.

Gregory McNamee is a contributing editor to the Encyclopædia Britannica, *literary critic for the* Hollywood Reporter, *and author of* Moveable Feasts: The History, Science, and Lore of Food.

Combating the Crisis in Darfur

by Alex Meixner

In 2008, five years after conflict broke out in the Darfur region of The Sudan, the prospect seemed dim for a political settlement to end the war that had killed as many as 300,000 people. In early 2003, soon after local rebel groups took up arms against the Khartoum-based regime of Sudanese Pres. Omar al-Bashir, long-standing tensions in Darfur erupted into what the US government later described as the first genocide of the 21st century. The rebels felt marginalized by their government, saw that other rebels in southern Sudan were likely to be granted major economic and political concessions as their own civil war against Khartoum ran down, and realized that they themselves were being left out in the literal and figurative desert with no hope of similar concessions or improved conditions. An oil-fueled economic boom was producing skyscrapers in Khartoum, while Darfur continued to exist largely without roads, hospitals, or a sufficient education system and was suffering through a brutal drought.

Following a few initial conventional battles with new rebel groups in Darfur, the Khartoum regime switched tactics and began to fight a hate-fueled counterinsurgency war in Darfur by funding, arming, and unleashing proxy militias known as Janjaweed— made up of fighters from nomadic groups who identified themselves as "Arab"—on villages whose people identified themselves as "African." This strategy depended on exploiting this self-proclaimed racial divide in Darfur, and it worked, despite the fact that both "Arab" and "African" Darfurians were predominantly Muslim, spoke Arabic, and shared the same skin tone. The result was an undisciplined paramilitary campaign that targeted men, women, and children.

In addition to the hundreds of thousands killed since the beginning of the campaign, approximately 2.5 million more were forced from their homes and into the Sahara. Horrific stories of mass rape, murder, and unspeakable atrocities became commonplace. Survivors gathered in camps for internally displaced persons throughout Darfur and in refugee camps across the border in eastern Chad and in the Central African Republic.

For its part the international community reacted to different aspects of the crisis with varying degrees of success. The biggest bright spot was the Herculean effort put forth by governmental and nongovernmental aid agencies, providing food, medicine, shelter, and basic services to the millions of Darfurians in need. More than 13,000 international and Sudanese aid workers built the world's largest humanitarian life-support system in Darfur, saving countless lives that otherwise would have been lost to starvation and disease.

Less successful were international efforts to reduce the threat of physical violence to Darfurian civilians and to achieve a lasting political solution to end the conflict. To achieve the former, the African Union (AU) in 2004 deployed a 7,400-strong peacekeeping force, the African Union Mission in The Sudan (AMIS). When AMIS went into Darfur, the rest of the international community stood by and watched; once troops had been deployed, they helped protect women from rape, but it soon became clear that AMIS lacked the manpower, equipment, funding, and mandate to truly protect civilians and help restore order to an area as large as Darfur (roughly the size of France). On 31 Aug 2006, the UN Security Council authorized the generation and deployment of a large peacekeeping force with Resolution 1706.

The Sudanese government, however, rejected Resolution 1706, effectively putting the UN between a rock and a hard place: in the entire history of the UN, no peacekeeping mission had ever failed to deploy once authorized by the Security Council. On the other hand, only one mission—the "police action" better known as the Korean War—had ever been deployed over the objection of a sovereign host government. A compromise was sought to bridge the impasse, and the result was a joint peacekeeping force known as the hybrid United Nations/African Union Mission in Darfur (UNAMID), authorized by the Security Council on 31 July 2007. While initial command and control elements of UNAMID began augmenting AMIS in the fall of 2007, UNAMID did not formally take over for AMIS and assume responsibility for peacekeeping in Darfur until 31 Dec 2007. President Bashir initially agreed in writing to accept the new force, but reports soon began to emerge of efforts by the Sudanese government to obstruct the deployment of UNAMID troops and to limit their movements in the province. Also posing an impediment to progress in the region was the fact that the majority of the proposed 26,000 UNAMID peacekeepers and police were not yet on the ground, with

> *In addition to the hundreds of thousands killed since the beginning of the campaign, approximately 2.5 million more were forced from their homes and into the Sahara.*

the force's troop and military personnel level reaching only 12,374 by the close of 2008.

Efforts to arrive at a lasting political solution have arguably fared worse. Several cease-fires were adopted, celebrated, promptly violated, and thus rendered moot. More frustrating still were the nearly 20 months of peace talks that took place in Abuja, Nigeria, culminating on 5 May 2006 in the partial signing of the Darfur Peace Agreement (DPA). The Sudanese government and only one of what were then just three rebel factions signed the agreement, and with the exception of a few initial concessions to the one rebel signer, almost none of the agreement was implemented. After the signing and subsequent collapse of the DPA, the original three rebel factions split into more than a dozen. The international community, operating through a combined UN-AU effort, regrouped, pooled their efforts, and organized new peace talks that began in Surt, Libya, on 27 Oct 2007, but these stalled after representatives of several leading rebel factions refused to participate in the talks. A similar effort in February 2009 to resume peace talks in Doha, Qatar, has thus far yielded no tangible results. Meanwhile, as the international community moved forward, albeit slowly, on fully deploying UNAMID, the violence in Darfur continued, including attacks by rebels and, in some instances, government forces on UNAMID peacekeepers, government and Janjaweed attacks on villages thought to support rebels, and interrebel fighting. As always, Darfurian civilians have been caught in the middle, with the humanitarian life-support system that sustains them growing ever more fragile and the memories of their former, peaceful lives growing ever more faint.

Alex Meixner is director of government relations for the Save Darfur Coalition.

Chronology, July 2008–June 2009

A day-by-day listing of important and interesting events, adapted from
Britannica Book of the Year. See also Disasters.

July 2008

1 Jul The Dow Jones Industrial Average falls 0.8%, crossing the official threshold from a bull stock market to a bear market.

2 Jul In a daring operation, Colombian forces rescue 15 hostages held by the Revolutionary Armed Forces of Colombia (FARC), among them Ingrid Betancourt, a former presidential candidate kidnapped in 2002, and three American contractors seized in 2003.

3 Jul A yearlong celebration of the 400th anniversary of the founding of Canada's Quebec City comes to a climax.

▶ The price of a barrel of oil closes at a record high of US$145.29.

4 Jul Shots are exchanged between Georgian troops and militia members of the country's separatist province of South Ossetia; at least two people are killed.

▶ The first weekend charter flight from China carries tourists across the Taiwan Strait to Taiwan; the flights are expected to expand to carry some 3,000 travelers a day.

5 Jul American Venus Williams defeats her sister Serena Williams to take her fifth All-England (Wimbledon) women's tennis championship; the following day Rafael Nadal of Spain wins the men's title for the first time when he defeats five-time champion Roger Federer of Switzerland.

6 Jul In Mogadishu, Somalia, gunmen kill Osman Ali Ahmed, leader of the United Nations Development Programme for Somalia.

7 Jul In York, England, the General Synod of the Church of England votes to allow the appointment of women as bishops; though some other branches of the Anglican Communion had taken the step several years earlier, the move is controversial.

8 Jul The leaders of the Group of Eight industrialized countries, meeting in Japan, release a document agreeing to cut greenhouse-gas emissions in half by 2050; environmentalists complain that the agreement fails to include targets for the nearer future.

▶ The US and the Czech Republic sign an accord that will allow the US to base part of its antiballistic-missile system in the Czech Republic; ratification of the accord is uncertain.

9 Jul The US Senate gives final approval to a bill that affirms the authority of the Foreign Intelligence Surveillance Act (FISA) court but grants the government latitude in conducting wiretaps outside the court's authority and provides legal immunity to telecommunication companies that complied with earlier wiretapping efforts.

10 Jul Salman Rushdie's 1981 novel *Midnight's Children* wins the Best of the Booker award, as decided by an online poll to celebrate the 40th anniversary of the literature prize.

11 Jul After the announcement of massive layoffs by IndyMac Bancorp prompts a run on the California-based bank by its customers, federal bank regulators seize the bank.

12 Jul American tennis player Michael Chang, the late sports marketer Mark McCormack, and Gene Scott, the late publisher of *Tennis Week* magazine, are inducted into the International Tennis Hall of Fame in a ceremony in Newport RI.

13 Jul The US Federal Reserve announces an emergency short-term loan to shore up the mortgage finance companies Fannie Mae and Freddie Mac, while Pres. George W. Bush asks Congress to approve a larger rescue package.

▶ In Paris the 43-member Union for the Mediterranean is inaugurated, with Pres. Nicolas Sarkozy of France serving as its first northern copresident and Pres. Hosni Mubarak of Egypt as its southern copresident; the union is intended to unify policies on the environment, transportation, immigration, and security.

14 Jul Luis Moreno-Ocampo, the prosecutor of the International Criminal Court, formally requests that the court issue a warrant for the arrest of Sudanese Pres. Omar Hassan al-Bashir on charges of genocide, war crimes, and crimes against humanity relating to the conflict in the Darfur region of The Sudan.

15 Jul US government officials reveal that William J. Burns, undersecretary of state for political affairs, will attend a meeting on Iran's nuclear program with representatives of Iran and other UN Security Council members; this will be the highest-level contact the US has had with Iran since the 1979 Iranian Revolution.

16 Jul Malaysian opposition leader Anwar Ibrahim is arrested on charges of sodomy; his 1998 conviction for sodomy was later overturned.

17 Jul Kuwait names an ambassador to Iraq for the first time since it closed its embassy in Baghdad after the Iraqi invasion of Kuwait in 1990.

▶ James H. Billington, the American librarian of Congress, names Kay Ryan the country's 16th poet laureate; Ryan succeeds Charles Simic.

18 Jul The World Trade Organization rules that China's policy of levying punishing tariffs on carmakers operating in the country unless they use locally made parts violates international trade rules.

▶ The much-anticipated movie *The Dark Knight,* the sequel to *Batman Begins,* opens in theaters across the US at midnight; cinemas in some cities schedule round-the-clock showings to accommodate demand.

19 Jul Iran rejects an international proposal that calls for it to freeze its nuclear program and for the international community to refrain from adding new sanctions as a starting point for negotiations, leaving the talks deadlocked.

20 Jul In Canterbury, England, the Lambeth Conference of the Anglican Communion, held every 10 years, opens with a church service, though more than 200 of the 880 bishops and archbishops invited do not attend; many of the absentees became founding members of the dissident Fellowship of Confessing Anglicans on 29 June.

▶ Padraig Harrington of Ireland wins the British Open golf tournament at the Royal Birkdale Golf Club in Southport, Lancashire, England; Harrington is the first European to have won two consecutive British Opens in over 100 years.

21 Jul Radovan Karadzic, who was indicted by the UN war crimes tribunal on 24 Jul 1995 for his part in the massacre of some 8,000 Muslims in Srebrenica, Bosnia and Herzegovina, earlier that year, is arrested in Belgrade, Serbia, where he had been living in disguise.

▶ Nepal's constituent assembly elects as the country's first president Ram Baran Yadav, who is not a member of the majority Maoist party.

22 Jul The Italian legislature approves a bill granting immunity from prosecution to the prime minister, president, and speakers of the two legislative chambers during their terms of office; the bill benefits Prime Minister Silvio Berlusconi, who is awaiting trial on bribery charges.

23 Jul The US Geological Survey releases an assessment that the Arctic may contain as much as 90 billion bbl of undiscovered oil and 47.29 trillion cu m (about 1.67 quadrillion cu ft) of natural gas, most of it in coastal areas under territorial sovereignty, much of it in Russia.

▶ Cape Verde becomes the 153rd member of the World Trade Organization.

24 Jul A British judge awards £60,000 (about US$120,000) in damages to Max Mosley, president of the governing body of Formula 1 automobile racing, in his lawsuit against a tabloid newspaper that had printed pictures from a video of a sadomasochistic sex gathering Mosley had participated in; the judge ruled that there was no good reason to expose Mosley's private life.

25 Jul The US Office of the Special Inspector General for Iraq Reconstruction reports that oil exports through the country's northern pipeline have increased from 1 million to more than 13 million bbl a month since 2007.

26 Jul Some 22 small bombs explode in crowded neighborhoods in Ahmedabad, India, killing at least 42 people.

27 Jul The National Baseball Hall of Fame in Cooperstown NY inducts pitcher Rich ("Goose") Gossage, managers Dick Williams and Billy Southworth, owners Barney Dreyfuss and Walter O'Malley, and former commissioner Bowie Kuhn.

28 Jul In California, Virgin Galactic head Richard Branson unveils WhiteKnightTwo, the prototype of the booster ship that will carry the company's commercial rocket into space.

29 Jul The Doha round of world trade talks, begun in 2001, reaches an impasse in Geneva as participants are unable to compromise on protections for farmers in less-developed countries.

30 Jul Turkey's Constitutional Court issues a ruling that the governing Justice and Development Party has not violated secular principles of the country to the point that it should be banned but that it has veered too far in an Islamic direction and therefore its public funding must be cut in half.

▶ Zimbabwe's central bank announces that the country's currency will be devalued by dropping 10 zeros, so that a 10-billion-dollar note will become a one-dollar note; on 16 July the inflation rate officially reached 2,200,000%.

31 Jul NASA scientists announce that the Phoenix Mars lander has tested Martian soil and, for the first time, has proved conclusively that it contains water ice.

QUOTE OF THE MONTH

❝ *We've now finally touched it and tasted it. And I'd like to say, from my standpoint, it tastes very fine.* ❞

—William V. Boynton, designer of the Phoenix Mars lander's Thermal and Evolved Gas Analyzer, on the proof that water exists on Mars, 31 July

---

▶ Massachusetts Gov. Deval Patrick signs a bill that will allow same-sex couples living in states that do not permit same-sex marriage to marry in Massachusetts

August 2008

1 Aug Georgian troops enter the separatist province of South Ossetia, and six people die in the fighting between the soldiers and the rebel militia.

2 Aug Bookstores throughout the US hold midnight parties as the fourth novel of the popular Twilight vampire series by Stephenie Meyer, *Breaking Dawn*, goes on sale.

3 Aug At the conclusion of the Lambeth Conference in Canterbury, England, Anglican Archbishop Rowan Williams announces an agreement to negotiate a new covenant between the member churches; in the meantime, liberal members are enjoined to refrain from ordaining gay clergy and blessing same-sex unions, and conservative members are asked not to leave their churches.

▶ South Korean golfer Shin Ji Yai captures the Women's British Open golf tournament; at age 20 years 3 months 6 days, she is the youngest to have won the title.

4 Aug Chinese state media report that two Uighur separatists rammed a truck into a brigade of border-patrol officers outside their barracks in Kashgar, Xinjiang state, and then attacked the officers with knives and several bombs, killing at least 16 of them.

5 Aug The US Government Accountability Office reveals that Iraq has a budget surplus of some US$79 billion, very little of which is being used in the rebuilding of the country's infrastructure; those costs are largely financed by the US.

▶ The Wildlife Conservation Society reports to the International Primatological Society Congress in Edinburgh its discovery of some 125,000 western lowland gorillas in the northern area of the Republic of the Congo; the gorillas are coming under increasing pressure in most parts of the world.

6 Aug The US mortgage finance giant Freddie Mac posts figures for the second quarter that reflect a much deeper loss than had been expected, as does the large insurer American International Group (AIG).

7 Aug Georgian troops take control of several villages in the separatist province of South Ossetia; some 10 people die in the fighting.

8 Aug Russian troops join the battle in Georgia's separatist province of South Ossetia, fighting against Georgia; also, a Russian air strike hits the Georgian port of Poti.

▶ A spectacular opening ceremony featuring some 15,000 performers directed by filmmaker Zhang

Yimou marks the start of the Olympic Games in Beijing.

9 Aug Russian troops enter the separatist province of Abkhazia in Georgia as they continue to pour into South Ossetia and to drop bombs on other parts of Georgia; Georgian Pres. Mikheil Saakashvili asks the outside world for help.

10 Aug At the Oakland Hills Country Club in Bloomfield Hills MI, Padraig Harrington of Ireland defeats Sergio García of Spain and American Ben Curtis by two strokes to become the first European since 1930 to win the Professional Golfers' Association of America championship.

11 Aug Philippine officials say that some 130,000 people have fled the violence in North Cotabato province on the island of Mindanao since a Supreme Court ruling halting the signing of an agreement between the Philippine government and the Moro Islamic Liberation Front caused an outbreak of fighting between rebel and government forces.

12 Aug A Taliban attack on a minibus carrying Pakistani soldiers leaves at least 13 of the troops dead; the soldiers are part of Pakistan's strong military response to Taliban aggressiveness in Bajaur in the Tribal Areas.

13 Aug Lebanon and Syria announce that they will, for the first time since independence, establish diplomatic relations, but the news is overshadowed by a bomb explosion that destroys a bus in Tripoli, Lebanon, killing 15 people.

14 Aug The US reaches an agreement with Poland that will allow placement of an American missile-defense base in the European country.

▶ Nigeria officially cedes the potentially oil-rich Bakassi Peninsula to Cameroon in compliance with a 2002 ruling by the International Court of Justice.

15 Aug Prachanda, leader of the former Maoist insurgency, is elected prime minister of Nepal.

▶ The journal *Science* publishes a study describing the rapid growth of marine dead zones, areas starved of oxygen because of nitrogen from fertilizer runoff in oceanic coastal areas; such zones, frequently in fishing grounds, have doubled every decade since the 1960s.

16 Aug Russian Pres. Dmitry Medvedev signs a revised cease-fire agreement with Georgia, but Russian troops continue operations in Georgia.

17 Aug Iran reports that it has successfully test-fired a rocket that could place a satellite in orbit.

▶ At the Olympics in Beijing, American swimmer Michael Phelps wins a record eighth gold medal, surpassing the previous record for a single Olympiad of seven gold medals won by Mark Spitz in 1972; Phelps has also set four individual world records and one Olympic record and participated in three relays that set world records.

18 Aug Pres. Pervez Musharraf of Pakistan announces his resignation in a nationally televised speech.

▶ The government of Peru declares a state of emergency in response to 10 days of occupation of oil facilities and a hydroelectric plant in the Amazon basin by indigenous people fighting development.

19 Aug In Isser, Algeria, a suicide car bomber kills at least 48 people, many of whom had been waiting in line to take an examination at a police academy.

20 Aug Algeria endures its second bombing in as many days as two bombs go off in Bouira, one of which damages a military compound and the other of which kills at least 12 people on a bus transporting construction workers.

▶ Jamaican sprinter Usain Bolt runs the men's 200-m race in 19.30 sec at the Olympics, breaking the world record by an astonishing two-hundredths of a second.

21 Aug In Wah, Pakistan, outside Pakistan's largest weapons-manufacturing compound, two suicide bombers kill at least 64 people; two days earlier a suicide attack in a hospital emergency room in Dera Ismail Khan left 32 people dead.

22 Aug Aerial bombing in Afghanistan's Herat province by US-led coalition forces after a battle against Taliban insurgents is reported by Afghanistan to have killed 76 civilians, though the coalition forces say that 30 militants were killed; the next day the civilian death toll is raised to 95.

23 Aug South Korea defeats Cuba 3–2 in a stunning upset to win the gold medal in baseball at the Olympic Games in Beijing.

24 Aug Pres. Nicolas Sarkozy of France calls an emergency meeting of the European Union to address relations with Russia and support for Georgia in light of the fact that Russia has failed to comply with the terms of the cease-fire agreement.

▶ The Waipio team from Waipahu, Hawaii, defeats the Matamoros team from Mexico 12–3 to win baseball's 62nd Little League World Series.

25 Aug A government attack on Kalma, a large camp housing some 90,000 internal refugees in the Darfur region of The Sudan, kills dozens of people.

26 Aug Russia officially recognizes the independence of the Georgian provinces of South Ossetia and Abkhazia.

▶ North Korea announces that it has ceased disabling its main nuclear complex at Yongbyon because it has not been removed from a US terrorism blacklist.

27 Aug Democratic Party delegates, meeting at their national convention in Denver, nominate Barack Obama, senator from Illinois, and Joe Biden, senator from Delaware, as the party's candidates for president and vice president, respectively.

28 Aug Iraq signs an agreement with the China National Petroleum Corp. for the development of the Ahdab oil field.

29 Aug Georgia and Russia mutually sever diplomatic relations.

▶ The state-owned airline Alitalia files for bankruptcy protection in Italy.

30 Aug Italy signs an agreement with Libya to provide US$5 billion in aid and projects as compensation for Italy's 1911–42 occupation of Libya; in return, Libya is to take steps to prevent illegal immigration to Italy from Libya.

31 Aug As the intermittently strengthening Hurricane Gustav, having caused destruction in Haiti, the Dominican Republic, Jamaica, and Cuba, heads toward the Gulf Coast in the US, some two million people in Texas, Mississippi, Louisiana, and Alabama evacuate.

September 2008

1 Sep US and Iraqi military officials announce that responsibility for paying and commanding Sunni Awakening Councils in Baghdad and the surrounding area will be taken over by Iraq's government beginning next month, and the US military formally hands over control of once-violent Anbar province to Iraqi armed forces.

2 Sep The US Library of Congress announces that Stevie Wonder is the winner of the Gershwin Prize for Popular Song and that in conjunction with the prize it has commissioned a song from him; the prize will be presented in February 2009.

3 Sep At the Republican National Convention in St. Paul MN, Sen. John McCain of Arizona and Gov. Sarah Palin of Alaska are nominated as the party's candidates for president and vice president, respectively, in the upcoming election in November.

4 Sep The journal *Nature* publishes a study suggesting that the most powerful hurricanes and typhoons, particularly in the Atlantic and Indian oceans, have become stronger over the past 25 years.

5 Sep US Secretary of State Condoleezza Rice meets with Libyan leader Muammar al-Qaddafi in his compound in Tripoli; it is the first visit to the country by a current US secretary of state in more than 50 years.

▶ The US National Snow and Ice Center reports that for the first time since recordings began being taken in the area, both the Northwest Passage above North America and the Northern Sea Route over Europe and Asia were open during the summer, providing a ring of navigable waters in the Arctic.

▶ The Naismith Memorial Basketball Hall of Fame in Springfield MA inducts as members National Basketball Association players Adrian Dantley, Patrick Ewing, and Hakeem Olajuwon and coach Pat Riley, women's college coach Cathy Rush, and broadcaster Dick Vitale.

6 Sep Pakistan's two legislative houses and four provincial assemblies elect Asif Ali Zardari president of the country.

▶ Turkish Pres. Abdullah Gul attends an association football (soccer) match in Armenia after an invitation by Armenian Pres. Serzh Sarkisyan; he is the first Turkish head of state to visit the country.

7 Sep The US government takes over the mortgage finance companies Fannie Mae and Freddie Mac in a rescue package that will all but wipe out their shareholders' stake but will guarantee the corporate debt.

▶ Serena Williams of the US defeats Jelena Jankovic of Serbia to win the women's US Open tennis championship; the following day Roger Federer of Switzerland defeats Andy Murray of Scotland to win the men's title for the fifth straight year.

▶ With his second-place finish behind Helio Castroneves of Brazil in the Indy 300 race in Joliet IL, New Zealand driver Scott Dixon wins the overall IndyCar drivers' championship.

8 Sep Russia agrees to withdraw its troops from Georgia but maintains that Russian troops will remain in the separatist regions of South Ossetia and Abkhazia; it also agrees that observers from the EU may monitor the agreement.

9 Sep Thailand's Constitutional Court rules that Prime Minister Samak Sundaravej's acceptance of payments for hosting the TV cooking show *Tasting and Complaining* violates the country's constitution; he is forced from office.

10 Sep CERN's (the European Organization for Nuclear Research's) Large Hadron Collider, which is intended to create conditions identical to those immediately after the big bang and is the largest particle collider in the world, is activated outside Geneva.

▶ Bolivian Pres. Evo Morales orders the US ambassador to leave, accusing him of assisting those seeking autonomy for Bolivia's eastern provinces.

▶ The US Library of Congress presents its first Award for Lifetime Achievement in the Writing of Fiction to novelist Herman Wouk.

11 Sep Pres. Hugo Chávez of Venezuela expels the US ambassador and recalls the Venezuelan ambassador from Washington DC.

12 Sep A High Court judge in South Africa dismisses corruption charges against Jacob Zuma, leader of the African National Congress (ANC), citing procedural errors in the case.

13 Sep Hurricane Ike goes ashore in Texas, flooding Galveston and Orange and causing considerable damage in Houston; some 51 people are killed throughout the region, 20 of them in Texas.

▶ New Zealand defeats Australia to win the Tri-Nations rugby union title.

14 Sep The American investment firm Merrill Lynch sells itself to Bank of America for about US$50 billion.

▶ In Madrid, Russia defeats Spain four matches to none to win the Fed Cup in tennis.

15 Sep In Zimbabwe, Pres. Robert Mugabe signs a power-sharing agreement with opposition leader Morgan Tsvangirai that makes Tsvangirai prime minister and envisions an even division of power, though many important details remain to be worked out.

▶ As widely expected, the venerable investment bank Lehman Brothers, which received no help from the US government and was unable to find a buyer, files for bankruptcy protection; it is the biggest bankruptcy filing in the country's history.

16 Sep The US government takes over the giant insurer American International Group (AIG), fearing that the company's imminent collapse would send economies worldwide into a tailspin.

▶ Lieut. Gen. Ray Odierno takes over command of US forces in Iraq from Gen. David Petraeus in a ceremony presided over by US Secretary of Defense Robert Gates.

17 Sep In Nalchik, Russia, Aleksandra Kostenyuk of Russia becomes the Fédération Internationale des Échecs (FIDE) women's world chess champion after defeating Hou Yifan of China 2.5–1.5 in the final round of the three-week tournament.

18 Sep In an effort to contain the global credit crisis, the US Federal Reserve joins with the European Central Bank, the Bank of England, and the Bank of Japan as well as the central banks of Canada and Switzerland to make US$180 billion in currency exchanges available.

▶ Two days of legislative elections in Rwanda result in the world's first legislature that has a female majority; women win 45 of 80 seats.

▶ The Dow Jones Industrial Average replaces American International Group (AIG) with Kraft Foods on its listing.

19 Sep North Korea declares that it is no longer interested in being removed from the US government's list of state sponsors of terrorism.

20 Sep Pres. George W. Bush formally proposes a bailout bill that would give the Treasury Department unlimited authority to buy and sell up to US$700 billion in mortgage-related assets; the plan contains few details.

21 Sep The US Federal Reserve approves the requests of investment banks Goldman Sachs and Morgan Stanley to convert themselves into bank holding companies.

▶ The Emmy Awards are presented in Los Angeles; winners include the television shows *30 Rock* and *Mad Men* and the actors Alec Baldwin, Bryan Cranston, Tina Fey, Glenn Close, Jeremy Piven, Zeljko Ivanek, Jean Smart, and Dianne Wiest.

▶ In golf's Ryder Cup competition in Louisville KY, the US defeats Europe for the first time since 1999, with a 16–11 margin of victory.

22 Sep Li Changjiang, the head of China's food and product quality agency, is dismissed in a scandal in which melamine-tainted infant formula has made tens of thousands of babies ill throughout China.

23 Sep The US House of Representatives passes legislation that is intended to prevent the waters of the Great Lakes from being diverted outside the basin and requires conservation measures from the states bordering the lakes; Pres. George W. Bush signs the bill into law the following month.

▶ The world's first wave farm, in which the power of the ocean's waves is harnessed to generate electrical power, begins operation off Aguçadoura, Portugal.

24 Sep US Pres. George W. Bush makes a nationally televised speech to ask for the country's support for a US$700 billion bailout plan to avert financial catastrophe and invites presidential candidates John McCain and Barack Obama to Washington DC to join negotiations on the plan.

25 Sep In the biggest bank failure in American history, the US government takes over the savings and loan bank Washington Mutual and arranges its sale to financial services giant JPMorgan Chase.

▶ French Pres. Nicolas Sarkozy makes a speech in which he asserts that the world's monetary system needs to be overhauled and that, though the economic crisis in the US is having an effect in France, the French government will act to protect bank deposits and taxpayers.

▶ Somali pirates in the Indian Ocean seize the *Faina*, a Ukrainian ship carrying millions of dollars of military weaponry that had been purchased by Kenya; by the following day the US and Russia have sent naval ships in pursuit.

26 Sep Turkmenistan adopts a new constitution that,

among other things, replaces a 2,500-member appointed legislature with a 125-member popularly elected one and sets the presidential term at five years; legislative elections are set for December.

▶ The Global Carbon Project issues an update saying that worldwide emissions of carbon dioxide, a greenhouse gas, had an annual increase in 2000–07 that was nearly four times the rate in the 1990s, largely because of economic growth in less-developed countries.

27 Sep Astronaut Zhai Zhigang of China successfully performs the Chinese space program's first space walk, floating outside the orbital module for 18 minutes.

▶ In the Australian Football League Grand Final in Melbourne, the Hawthorn Hawks defeat the heavily favored Geelong Cats 18.7 (115) to 11.23 (89).

28 Sep Haile Gebrselassie of Ethiopia shatters the world marathon record that he set in 2007 as he wins the Berlin Marathon with a time of 2 hr 3 min 59 sec; Irina Mikitenko of Germany is the fastest woman, with a time of 2 hr 19 min 19 sec.

29 Sep The US House of Representatives rejects the US$700 billion bailout bill supported by US Pres. George W. Bush; as countries around the world struggle to save large banks, the Dow Jones Industrial Average falls nearly 7%, and global stock markets also lose value.

▶ The US Department of Health and Human Services reports that more than 90% of nursing homes in the US have been found to have violated health and safety standards and that for-profit institutions were cited more often for such violations than government or not-for-profit homes.

▶ The World Institute for Nuclear Security is inaugurated in Vienna, with Roger Howsley of Great Britain as its director; the organization seeks to prevent nuclear weapons from falling into the hands of terrorists.

30 Sep London's High Court rules that Nepalese Gurkhas who have served with the British army have the right to live in the UK.

October 2008

1 Oct The US Congress ratifies a nuclear trade agreement made with India in 2005.

2 Oct The Sri Lankan air force bombs the main political offices of the Liberation Tigers of Tamil Eelam in Kilinochhi.

▶ Remains believed to be those of missing adventurer Steve Fossett, who disappeared in September 2007, are found in the Inyo National Forest in California.

3 Oct The US House of Representatives passes a revised version of the US$700 billion financial bailout bill that was rejected in September, and US Pres. George W. Bush signs it into law.

4 Oct Tyler Perry Studios, featuring five soundstages for television and film work, opens in Atlanta; it is the first major film and television studio owned by an African American producer to open in the US.

5 Oct A magnitude-6.6 earthquake strikes Kyrgyzstan, killing at least 72 people and flattening the village of Nura.

▶ The Detroit Shock defeats the San Antonio Silver Stars 76–60 to complete a three-game sweep and win its third Women's National Basketball Association championship.

6 Oct The Russian stock market declines by 19.1%; indexes in London and Frankfurt, Germany, drop more than 7%; Paris stocks lose 9%; and the Dow Jones Industrial Average finishes below 10,000 points for the first time since 2004.

▶ The Nobel Prize for Physiology or Medicine is awarded to Françoise Barré-Sinoussi and Luc Montagnier of France for their discovery of HIV, the virus that causes AIDS, and to Harald zur Hausen of Germany for his discovery of the human papillomavirus, a major cause of cervical cancer.

7 Oct In Stockholm the Nobel Prize for Physics is awarded to Yoichiro Nambu of the US and to Makoto Kobayashi and Toshihide Maskawa of Japan for their work searching for hidden symmetries among elementary particles.

8 Oct British Prime Minister Gordon Brown announces a financial plan to offer recapitalization funds to troubled banks in return for ownership stakes and to provide government guarantees to help banks refinance debt; the government will provide £50 billion (US$75 billion) in this initiative.

▶ The Nobel Prize for Chemistry is awarded to Osamu Shimomura of Japan and to Martin Chalfie and Roger Y. Tsien of the US for their research on the green fluorescent protein produced by the jellyfish *Aequorea victoria* and its use as a marker for observing cells in other animals.

9 Oct Iceland takes over Kaupthing Bank, the last of the country's three major banks to be nationalized, shuts down the stock market, and ceases to support its currency, the króna.

QUOTE OF THE MONTH

❝ *Iceland is bankrupt. The Icelandic króna is history. The only sensible option is for the IMF to come and rescue us.* ❞

—University of Iceland professor Ársæll Valfells, on the collapse of Iceland's economic system, 9 October

---

▶ The Nobel Prize for Literature is awarded to French writer Jean-Marie Gustave Le Clézio.

10 Oct The Nobel Peace Prize is awarded to former Finnish president and international mediator Martti Ahtisaari.

11 Oct US Pres. George W. Bush announces that North Korea is to be removed from the list of state sponsors of terrorism; the following day North Korea indicates that it will resume dismantling its Yongbyon nuclear complex.

12 Oct The Chicago Marathon is won by Evans Cheruiyot of Kenya with a time of 2 hr 6 min 25 sec; the women's victor is Lidiya Grigoryeva of Russia with a time of 2 hr 27 min 17 sec.

13 Oct The Dow Jones Industrial Average gains 936 points, its largest-ever point gain and an increase of 11.1%; the Standard & Poor's 500 index and the Nasdaq composite also rise more than 11%.

▶ The Nobel Memorial Prize in Economic Sciences goes to American Paul Krugman for his work elucidating patterns in world trade and locations of economic activity.

14 Oct The Man Booker Prize for Fiction goes to Indian writer Aravind Adiga for his first novel, *The White Tiger.*

15 Oct The Dow Jones Industrial Average drops a stunning 733 points, losing 7.9% of its value.

▶ The price of a barrel of light, sweet crude oil falls to US$74.54, the first time since August 2007 that it has fallen below US$75.

16 Oct NASA reports that the Fermi Gamma-ray Space Telescope has made a discovery in the constellation Cepheus of a previously unknown type of pulsar that emits only gamma rays.

17 Oct Japan, Austria, Turkey, Mexico, and Uganda are elected to two-year nonpermanent seats on the UN Security Council.

18 Oct A demonstration against the proposed status-of-forces security agreement between Iraq and the US by followers of Shi'ite cleric Muqtada al-Sadr takes place in Baghdad.

▶ Thai Prime Minister Somchai Wongsawat says that he wishes to have face-to-face talks with Cambodian Prime Minister Hun Sen in an attempt to resolve the dispute over a 900-year-old temple on the border between the countries; a firefight on 15 October left three Cambodian soldiers dead.

19 Oct China announces a rural-reform policy that will allow farmers to lease or exchange land-use grants.

▶ At the world open squash championships in Manchester, England, Ramy Ashour of Egypt wins the men's competition and Nicol David of Malaysia the women's title.

20 Oct The genomes and phenotypes of 10 volunteers are made publicly available as part of the Personal Genome Project, which seeks to increase medical knowledge by making this information easily available; the project founders hope to supply the data on 100,000 volunteers.

▶ Festus Mogae, who was president of Botswana from 1998 until April 2008, wins the Mo Ibrahim Prize for Achievement in African Leadership.

21 Oct The inaugural Steinberg Distinguished Playwright Award, which carries an unusually generous prize of US$200,000, is presented to Tony Kushner.

▶ For the first time, trade takes place between India and Pakistan across the Line of Control in Kashmir as 16 Indian trucks carrying apples and walnuts cross into Pakistan; Pakistani trucks loaded with rice and raisins later travel into India.

22 Oct India launches Chandrayaan-1, an unmanned spacecraft that will orbit the Moon, gathering information to create a three-dimensional atlas and searching for mineral resources, particularly uranium; it is India's first scientific spacecraft.

▶ US Secretary of State Condoleezza Rice meets with Mexican Secretary of Foreign Affairs Patricia Espinosa in Puerto Vallarta, Mexico, to discuss cooperation in confronting Mexico's drug cartels.

23 Oct The European Parliament names jailed Chinese human rights activist Hu Jia the winner of the Sakharov Prize for Freedom of Thought.

24 Oct The International Monetary Fund tentatively agrees to grant Iceland a US$2 billion loan over two years to help it rebuild its economy; the last time the IMF made a loan to a Western country was in 1976.

▶ The UN reports that a quickly spreading cholera outbreak in Guinea-Bissau has infected some 12,000 people, 200 of whom have died.

25 Oct Hong Kong's Centre for Food Safety reports that it found eggs from northeastern China to be heavily contaminated with melamine, suggesting that the toxic substance has been deliberately added to animal feed.

▶ The Breeders' Cup Classic Thoroughbred horse race is won by Raven's Pass at Santa Anita Park in Arcadia CA; favorite Curlin finishes fourth.

26 Oct A US Predator drone launches a missile attack on a compound in the village of Manduta in Pakistan's South Waziristan province, killing 20 people; reportedly among the dead are two Taliban leaders who were responsible for attacks against US personnel in Afghanistan.

27 Oct South Korea's central bank holds an emergency meeting and lowers its key interest rate by three-quarters of a percentage point; elsewhere, the Bank of Israel lowers its rate by one-quarter point, and Australia's central bank buys Australian dollars to improve the exchange rate.

▶ Sen. Ted Stevens of Alaska is convicted in the District of Columbia on seven felony counts for having failed to report some US$250,000 in gifts and services he had received; Stevens is running for his seventh term of office.

28 Oct Iran announces that it has opened a new naval base in the port of Jask on the Gulf of Oman.

▶ The online-search company Google announces an agreement with book publishers that will allow it to scan and make available for a fee out-of-print books that are under copyright; the deal will allow both Google and the authors and publishers to be paid for the use of such books.

29 Oct Pakistan formally protests US attacks against Taliban and al-Qaeda militants on its soil and demands a stop to the incursions.

▶ In the World Series, the Philadelphia Phillies defeat the Tampa Bay Rays 4–3 in the final three and a half innings of the fifth game, which began on 27 October and was suspended for two days because of rain and snow, to win the Major League Baseball championship.

30 Oct The oil company Exxon Mobil reports a record US$14.8 billion in profit in its most recent fiscal quarter.

31 Oct US Gen. David Petraeus takes over the Central Command, which oversees military operations in Iraq, Afghanistan, and much of the Middle East, Central Asia, and South Asia.

November 2008

1 Nov Libyan leader Muammar al-Qaddafi meets with Russian Pres. Dmitry Medvedev and Prime Minister Vladimir Putin in Moscow, apparently to discuss closer commercial relations.

2 Nov With a fifth-place finish at the Brazilian Grand Prix, British race-car driver Lewis Hamilton, age 23, becomes the youngest person to have won the Formula 1 drivers' championship.

▶ Sébastien Loeb of France secures a record fifth successive world-rally-championship automobile-racing drivers' title with a third-place finish in the Rally of Japan.

▶ Marílson Gomes dos Santos of Brazil wins the New York City Marathon with a time of 2 hr 8 min 43 sec, while Britain's Paula Radcliffe is the fastest woman, with a time of 2 hr 23 min 56 sec.

3 Nov The US Department of Commerce releases figures showing that the sales of new cars and trucks in October fell to levels not seen since the early 1980s, with figures down almost 32% compared with sales in October 2007.

▶ In a complicated spy and bribery case known as "Suitcasegate"—for the suitcase full of cash found in the airport in Buenos Aires that began the scandal—Venezuelan businessman Franklin Durán is convicted by a court in Miami of having acted as an "unregistered agent" in the US.

4 Nov In a historic presidential election in the US, Democratic candidate Barack Obama wins with 52.9% of the popular vote and 365 electoral votes, against Republican candidate John McCain's 45.7% and 173 electoral votes; Obama celebrates his victory with a rally in Grant Park in Chicago.

▶ Gen. Mario Montoya resigns as head of Colombia's army in a spreading scandal about the apparently pervasive practice of the armed forces' killing of civilians in an attempt to inflate the figures of insurgents killed by security forces.

▶ China and Taiwan sign an agreement that will greatly increase transportation connections as well as trade between the two entities.

5 Nov Officials in Afghanistan complain that a US air strike two days earlier killed at least 40 civilians at a wedding party in Kandahar province.

6 Nov The heads of the automobile companies General Motors, Ford, and Chrysler and the leader of the United Automobile Workers union travel to Washington DC to ask for a second time for government help to prevent the collapse of their industry.

7 Nov US government figures show that 240,000 jobs were lost in October as the unemployment rate rose to 6.5%, its highest level in 14 years.

8 Nov Iraq's executive council ratifies a law setting the composition of provincial councils; the law allots only six seats on the councils to members of religious minorities, half of what the United Nations recommended.

9 Nov At an emergency summit meeting of the Southern African Development Community in Johannesburg, participants call for a cease-fire in the eastern region of the Democratic Republic of the Congo and agree to send military advisers to assist the government.

10 Nov The American electronics retailer Circuit City files for bankruptcy protection.

▶ The 11th annual Mark Twain Prize for American Humor is awarded posthumously to comic George Carlin in a ceremony at the John F. Kennedy Center for the Performing Arts in Washington DC.

11 Nov Food inspectors in Hong Kong report finding high levels of the toxic chemical melamine in fish feed from China.

▶ Peter Eastgate of Denmark wins the World Series of Poker; at 22, he is the youngest winner of the card game tournament.

12 Nov US Secretary of the Treasury Henry Paulson announces that the government no longer plans to use the US$700 billion bailout package to buy bad assets but will rather try to use the money to capitalize banks and to help companies make loans.

▶ The 2008 Dorothy and Lillian Gish Prize is awarded to film actor and director Robert Redford.

13 Nov At the Latin Grammy Awards in Houston, Colombian rock musician Juanes wins five awards, including album of the year for *La vida...es un* *ratico* and both song and record of the year for "Me enamora."

14 Nov With an EU report showing that the economy of the 15-country euro zone shrank 0.2% in the third quarter, the euro zone is officially in recession.

▸ The journal *Science* publishes an article reporting that the Hubble Space Telescope has produced the first visible-light image of a planet in another solar system; the observations are of the planet Fomalhaut b orbiting the star Fomalhaut in the constellation Piscis Australis.

15 Nov California Gov. Arnold Schwarzenegger declares a state of emergency in Los Angeles county as several wildfires, driven by Santa Ana winds, burn hundreds of houses and compel the evacuation of more than 10,000 residents.

16 Nov Iraq's cabinet approves a status-of-forces agreement negotiated with the US; the pact, which must also be approved by the legislature, begins restricting the scope of US combat operations starting on 1 Jan 2009 and calls for a complete US withdrawal by the end of 2011.

▸ After the final auto race of the season, Jimmie Johnson is crowned winner of the NASCAR drivers' championship for the third year in a row.

17 Nov The Saudi-owned supertanker *Sirius Star* is seized by pirates some 450 nautical miles southeast of Mombasa, Kenya, far from the usual area menaced by pirates.

18 Nov A court in Egypt rules that a contract to provide natural gas to Israel signed in 2005 should have been approved by the legislature and so should not be honored.

19 Nov The US Department of Labor reports that the consumer price index for October dropped by 1%, the biggest one-month drop ever measured, and the Dow Jones Industrial Average falls below 8,000 for the first time since 2003.

▸ The US Food and Drug Administration opens a branch in Beijing to screen food and drugs that will be exported to the US; it is intended to be the first of several overseas offices for the agency.

20 Nov At the first habeas corpus hearing on the US government's holding of six detainees at the military detention camp in Guantánamo Bay, Cuba, Judge Richard J. Leon of the Federal District Court in Washington DC rules that five of the men have been illegally held for almost seven years and should be released immediately.

▸ The price of a barrel of oil falls below US$50.

21 Nov The World Health Organization reports that a cholera epidemic that broke out in August in Zimbabwe and has accelerated in November has so far killed 294 people.

▸ After an emergency session, the state legislature of Nebraska revises a safe-haven law to allow only infants up to the age of 30 days to be legally abandoned at hospitals; as originally written, the law had said that all children could be safely abandoned, and since it went into effect on 1 September, 35 older children, several from outside Nebraska, had been left at Nebraska hospitals.

22 Nov On a man-made island in Doha, Qatar, the Museum of Islamic Art celebrates its grand opening with a ceremony attended by heads of state and other luminaries; it will open to the public on 1 December.

▸ New Zealand defeats Australia 34–20 to win the Rugby League World Cup final in an astonishing upset.

23 Nov Spain defeats Argentina 3–1 to win the Davis Cup in international team tennis.

▸ The Columbus Crew wins the Major League Soccer title with a 3–1 victory over the New York Red Bulls in the MLS Cup in Carson CA.

▸ The Calgary Stampeders capture the 96th Canadian Football League Grey Cup, defeating the Montreal Alouettes 22–14.

24 Nov Antigovernment protesters in Bangkok surround the legislative building and cut off its electricity and march on the airport where the government has been meeting since protests began in August.

▸ The US Treasury agrees to inject US$20 billion into the funds of the banking giant Citigroup and to pay for losses on bad assets; it is the second rescue plan from the government for the bank.

25 Nov Voters in Greenland overwhelmingly approve a new law to increase the dependency's autonomy from Denmark, in particular giving it greater rights to profit from local oil resources.

▸ Atlantic Records, a label owned by Warner Music Group, says that it has become the first label to have more than half of its music sales come from digital products, such as MP3 downloads and ringtones.

26 Nov In a brazen strike in Mumbai (Bombay), terrorists attack several public sites, among them train stations, hospitals, and a restaurant, and then take over two luxury hotels and a Jewish community center; at least 82 people are initially reported killed in the siege.

QUOTE OF THE MONTH

❝ I ran into the hotel kitchen, and then we were shunted into a restaurant in the basement. We are now in the dark in this room, and we have barricaded all the doors. It's really bad. ❞

—European Parliament member Sajjad Karim describing his ordeal during the terrorist siege of his hotel in Mumbai (Bombay), 26 November

---

▸ In Alto Minho in northern Portugal, a wind farm made up of 120 wind turbines and five substations officially opens; it is the largest wind farm in Europe.

27 Nov Iraq's legislature ratifies the status-of-forces agreement that mandates the end of US military occupation of Iraq by the end of 2011.

▸ The Perimeter Institute for Theoretical Physics in Ontario announces that physicist Stephen Hawking will hold its first distinguished research chair.

28 Nov Authorities in Mumbai (Bombay) succeed in regaining control of the two luxury hotels and the Jewish center that were attacked by terrorists, ending the siege; at least 174 people are believed to have been killed.

29 Nov Two days of ferocious ethnic and religious violence between Muslims and Christians in Jos, Nigeria, end with the imposition of a curfew; at least 400 people died in fighting.

30 Nov The space shuttle *Endeavour* lands in California after a successful mission to enlarge the capacity of the International Space Station; among those aboard are the space station's outgoing flight engineer, Gregory E. Chamitoff, who had spent six months at the station.

December 2008

1 Dec The National Bureau of Economic Research reports that the US economy has been in recession since December 2007; this is an unusually long recession, and analysts expect it to continue for some time.

▸ The Dow Jones Industrial Average falls 680 points, losing 7.7% of its value, while the Standard & Poor's 500 index drops by 8.9% and the Nasdaq composite loses 9.0%.

▸ Britain's Turner Prize is presented in London to artist Mark Leckey; his work includes the multimedia exhibition *Industrial Light & Magic,* which contains images of the animated characters Felix the Cat and Homer Simpson.

2 Dec The Women's National Basketball Association shuts down the Houston Comets, unable to afford to keep the franchise going or to find a buyer.

3 Dec A group of conservative Episcopal bishops announce that they are forming a new province within the Anglican Communion to serve as an alternative to the Episcopal Church (US); the new province is to be called the Anglican Church in North America.

▸ Against the preferences of the US, Afghan Pres. Hamid Karzai decides to sign the Convention on Cluster Munitions, banning the use of cluster bombs; he participates along with more than 90 other countries' delegates in a signing ceremony in Oslo.

4 Dec Zimbabwe declares its cholera epidemic a national emergency and appeals for international assistance.

▸ The telecommunications company AT&T declares that it plans to lay off 12,000 people over the next year; one difficulty the company is encountering is a decline in the number of subscribers to landline telephones.

5 Dec The US Bureau of Labor Statistics releases a report showing that 533,000 jobs were lost in November; this is the largest monthly total since December 1974.

▸ The Mortgage Bankers Association reports that 1.35 million American homes were in foreclosure in the third quarter, a new record and an increase of 76% over the previous year.

6 Dec In the course of one of the frequent fights between police and leftist youths in Athens, the police shoot to death a 15-year-old boy; ferocious rioting begins within hours and spreads to other cities in Greece.

7 Dec Hundreds of militants attack a lot in Peshawar, Pakistan, and destroy more than 100 trucks fully loaded with supplies for US and NATO armed forces in Afghanistan.

▸ The annual Kennedy Center Honors are presented in Washington DC to musicians George Jones, Pete Townshend, and Roger Daltrey, actor Morgan Freeman, singer and actress Barbra Streisand, and choreographer Twyla Tharp.

8 Dec Belize and Guatemala agree to submit a border disagreement dating from 1821 to the International Court of Justice.

▸ The Tribune Co., which publishes the *Chicago Tribune,* the *Los Angeles Times,* and 10 other newspapers and also owns several television stations, files for bankruptcy protection.

9 Dec Pakistani authorities say that they have arrested some 20 members of Lashkar-e-Taiba, the Islamist militant group believed to be behind the terrorist attacks in Mumbai (Bombay) in November, including its operational leader.

▸ Gov. Rod Blagojevich of Illinois is arrested on federal charges of conspiracy and bribe solicitation; prosecutors say that, among other things, he attempted to sell the Senate seat vacated by President-elect Barack Obama, to which he was empowered to appoint the successor.

10 Dec During six-party talks on North Korea's nuclear program, North Korea refuses to accept a Chinese proposal on nuclear verification; negotiations break down the following day.

▸ In the UK the Channel island of Sark holds its first-ever democratic election after 450 years of feudal government.

11 Dec Bernard L. Madoff, a well-connected and apparently exceptionally successful trader, is arrested by federal agents in New York City; he is believed to have been running an enormous Ponzi scheme, defrauding many individual and institutional customers of some US$50 billion.

12 Dec The day after the US Senate refused to approve a rescue package for automobile manufacturers, officials from the White House and the Treasury Department say that the government is willing to use money from the US$700 billion bailout fund to prevent the collapse of General Motors and Chrysler.

▸ Pres. Rafael Correa of Ecuador declines to make a US$31 million interest payment, declaring his country to be in default on foreign debt.

13 Dec Steer roper Trevor Brazile of Texas wins his sixth all-around cowboy world championship at the 50th annual Wrangler National Finals Rodeo in Las Vegas.

14 Dec The military forces of the Democratic Republic of the Congo, Uganda, and The Sudan start an offensive against the insurgent group the Lord's Resistance Army, seeking to drive it from the Democratic Republic of the Congo back to Uganda, whence it originated.

▸ At a news conference held in Baghdad by Iraqi Pres. Nuri al-Maliki and US Pres. George W. Bush, a journalist from an independent television channel throws both his shoes at Bush, denouncing him for bringing war to Iraq; Bush avoids both shoes.

15 Dec A charter to transform the Association of Southeast Asian Nations (ASEAN) into an entity similar to the EU goes into force.

16 Dec The US Federal Reserve lowers its key interest rate to a range of 0–0.25% and announces new lending programs to get money to businesses and to consumers.

▸ A team of astronomers using NASA's Chandra X-ray Observatory report that they have found that the reason that clusters of galaxies have not grown in the past five billion years may be that their growth is inhibited by the antigravitional force called dark energy.

17 Dec At a meeting in Oran, Algeria, OPEC member countries agree to cut oil production by a record 2.2 million bbl a day.

18 Dec The UN reports that the death toll from the cholera epidemic in Zimbabwe has risen to 1,111, with 133 people dying in the past two days alone.

19 Dec The Palestinian organization Hamas announces that its unwritten truce with Israel is over.

▸ US Pres. George W. Bush announces an emergency bailout of US$17.4 billion for the automobile manufacturers General Motors and Chrysler, in return for which the companies must produce a plan for profitability by 31 March 2009; the money comes from the US$700 billion authorized by Congress to rescue the financial services industry.

20 Dec Canadian Prime Minister Stephen Harper and Premier Dalton McGuinty of Ontario offer the Canadian subsidiaries of the automakers General Motors and Chrysler Can$4 billion (US$3 billion) in emergency loans.

21 Dec Police in Tehran shut down the office of the Center for Protecting Human Rights, headed by Shirin Ebadi, who won the Nobel Peace Prize in 2003.

22 Dec The Organization for Security and Co-operation in Europe announces that its mission in Georgia will be terminated because the organization has been unable to reach a compromise with member country Russia, which insists that the separatist enclaves of South Ossetia and Abkhazia be treated as separate countries.

23 Dec The prestigious but nearly insolvent Museum of Contemporary Art in Los Angeles announces that it will be rescued by arts patron Eli Broad, who will give it US$30 million and require that its management be restructured; Charles Young replaces Jeremy Strick as the museum's director.

24 Dec The Japanese automobile manufacturers Toyota and Nissan report that their worldwide sales of vehicles in November fell 21.8% and 19.8%, respectively, from a year before.

▸ The US Federal Reserve Board allows GMAC, the financing arm of the car manufacturer General Motors, to become a bank holding company.

25 Dec In his annual Christmas message, Pope Benedict XVI calls for peace in the world, particularly in the Middle East, and gives blessings in 64 languages, including, for the first time, Icelandic.

26 Dec Israel opens crossings into the Gaza Strip, allowing relief supplies to reach the area; nonetheless, a dozen rockets and mortar shells are fired toward Israel.

27 Dec Israel launches massive air strikes against Hamas facilities in the Gaza Strip; more than 225 people in Gaza are killed.

28 Dec With a final-game loss to the Green Bay Packers, the Detroit Lions become the first National Football League team ever to lose every game of a 16-game regular season.

29 Dec Israel continues its air assault against Hamas targets in the Gaza Strip; as the death toll passes 350 and Hamas rockets kill three Israelis, Israeli Defense Minister Ehud Barak declares that Israel is engaged in an "all-out war" with Hamas.

30 Dec Ghana's election commission says that the results of the country's presidential runoff are too close to call and that one district that was unable to hold voting on election day will vote on 2 Jan 2009; the results there will determine the winner.

31 Dec As an emergency meeting of the Arab League convenes, Israel rejects a proposed 48-hour ceasefire and continues its bombardment of Gaza.

QUOTE OF THE MONTH

❝ *This terrible massacre would not have happened if the Palestinian people were united behind one leadership, speaking in one voice.* ❞

—Prince Saud al-Faisal of Saudi Arabia, speaking at an emergency Arab League summit, 31 December

---

▸ At the last bell of the year at the New York Stock Exchange, the Dow Jones Industrial Average has lost 33.8% of its value from the beginning of the year, its worst annual loss since 1931; the Standard & Poor's 500-stock index has lost 39.5% of its value.

▸ China and Vietnam announce that they have completed the demarcation of the 1,350-km (840-mi) border between the countries.

January 2009

1 Jan The Green Zone, a 14.5-sq-km (5.6-sq-mi) area in Baghdad that has been the center of the US occupation, is turned over to Iraqi control.

▸ Two newspapers in Mexico report that more than 5,000 people were killed by gangsters in drug-related violence in 2008, more than twice as many as died in 2007.

2 Jan The government of Sri Lanka announces that its military has captured the city of Kilinochchi, the administrative center of the Liberation Tigers of Tamil Eelam.

3 Jan After a week of aerial and naval assaults against Hamas targets in the Gaza Strip, Israeli troops and tanks cross the border into Gaza, initiating a ground war there.

4 Jan A suicide bomber detonates his weapon among a crowd of pilgrims visiting a Shi'ite shrine in Baghdad; at least 40 people, many of them Iranians, are killed.

5 Jan India gives Pakistan evidence that the terrorists who attacked Mumbai (Bombay) in November 2008 were linked to Pakistan; it demands that those responsible be tried in India.

▸ The new US embassy compound in Baghdad is dedicated; it is the largest US embassy in the world.

6 Jan In South Korea opposition lawmakers end a 12-day occupation of the parliament building after successfully blocking a vote on a free-trade agreement with the US as well as other legislation.

▸ US Pres. George W. Bush creates the largest marine reserve in the world, totaling 505,773 sq km (195,280 sq mi) in area, by designating the Mariana Trench, Pacific Remote Islands, and Rose Atoll marine national monuments.

7 Jan Violent protests take place in Oakland CA, where demonstrators are angry over the slow response to an incident in which an unarmed young African American man was shot and killed early on 1 January by a transit policeman on the platform of a Bay Area Rapid Transit station.

▸ The centenary of the UK's domestic intelligence agency, MI5, is marked by the first-ever interview of the agency's head by the press as Jonathan Evans meets with reporters at MI5 headquarters in London.

8 Jan The US Department of Labor releases statistics showing that the number of people receiving unemployment benefits at the end of 2008 reached 4.61 million, the highest number since November 1982.

▶ The University of Florida defeats the University of Oklahoma 24–14 in college football's Bowl Championship Series title game in Miami to win the NCAA Football Bowl Subdivision championship.

9 Jan The *Sirius Star,* a Saudi-owned supertanker that was seized by Somali pirates in November 2008, is released in return for the payment of US$3 million in ransom; however, a boat carrying pirates to shore capsizes, which results in the drowning of five of the pirates and the loss of some of the ransom money.

10 Jan Israel warns residents of the Gaza Strip that it intends to intensify its operations against Hamas, which have so far left some 820 Palestinians dead, while heavy rocket fire from Gaza into Israel continues.

11 Jan At the Golden Globe Awards in Beverly Hills CA, best picture honors go to *Slumdog Millionaire* and *Vicky Cristina Barcelona;* best director goes to Danny Boyle for *Slumdog Millionaire.*

12 Jan Health officials in Minnesota report that they have linked an outbreak of salmonella that has affected some 400 people in 43 states with peanut butter that is sold to institutions.

13 Jan Ethiopian troops complete their withdrawal from Mogadishu, Somalia.

14 Jan After several days of severe flooding in Fiji, the country's sugar farms have been decimated, 9,000 people have been evacuated, and at least 11 people have died.

15 Jan A US Airways A320 jet loses power in both engines because of bird strikes shortly after taking off from New York City's La Guardia Airport; pilot Chesley B. Sullenberger III successfully lands the plane in the Hudson River, and all 155 aboard are safely rescued.

16 Jan Zimbabwe's Reserve Bank issues a new denomination of bank notes denoted at Z$10 trillion; Z$20 trillion, Z$50 trillion, and Z$100 trillion bills are also planned.

▶ The American electronics retailer Circuit City Stores, with 567 outlets and 34,000 employees, announces that it is going out of business.

17 Jan Israel declares that it will begin a cease-fire early the following day in its operations against Hamas in the Gaza Strip; some 1,200 Palestinians and 13 Israelis have died during the 22-day operation.

▶ The organization Human Rights Watch details massacres in which at least 620 people have been slaughtered by the Lord's Resistance Army militia group in the Democratic Republic of the Congo over the past month.

18 Jan Prime Minister Vladimir Putin of Russia and Prime Minister Yuliya Tymoshenko of Ukraine reach an agreement on the price that Ukraine will pay for Russian natural gas; previous accords have fallen through, and at least 12 people have frozen to death while some 20 countries are cut off from gas supplies from Russia.

19 Jan Prominent Russian human rights lawyer Stanislav Markelov and a freelance reporter for the independent newspaper *Novaya Gazeta* are shot down in broad daylight in Moscow.

20 Jan Barack Obama is inaugurated as the 44th president of the United States before what is perhaps the largest crowd ever to attend a presidential inauguration.

▶ A partnership is announced between troubled American car company Chrysler LLC and the Italian automobile manufacturer Fiat, which will acquire a

stake in Chrysler and will sell its Fiat and Alfa Romeo brands of cars in Chrysler dealerships.

21 Jan Hillary Rodham Clinton is confirmed as US secretary of state, and Janet Napolitano is sworn in as US secretary of homeland security.

22 Jan Japan reports that its export rate in December 2008 fell drastically, while China announces a sharp slowdown in growth in the final quarter of the year and South Korea says that its economy shrank in the same period; all these results are related to the economic crisis in the US and Europe.

▶ US Pres. Barack Obama signs executive orders requiring that the military prison at Guantánamo Bay in Cuba be closed within a year, insisting that interrogation methods fall within the guidelines of the Army Field Manual, and ending the CIA's secret overseas prison program.

23 Jan The biggest wind-power complex in Latin America is ceremonially inaugurated along the southern coast of Mexico's Isthmus of Tehuantepec.

24 Jan Pope Benedict XVI revokes the excommunications of four bishops who were consecrated in 1988 without Vatican permission by Archbishop Marcel Lefebvre, who opposed the reforms of the Second Vatican Council; one of the bishops has denied that the Holocaust took place.

25 Jan The Sri Lankan military reports that it has taken control of Mullaittivu, the last major town controlled by the Liberation Tigers of Tamil Eelam.

26 Jan In the field of children's literature, the Newbery Medal is awarded to Neil Gaiman for *The Graveyard Book,* and Beth Krommes wins the Caldecott Medal for her illustrations for *The House in the Night* by Susan Marie Swanson.

▶ A single mother of six in California gives birth to octuplets conceived by in vitro fertilization, arousing controversy; it is only the second time that octuplets have been born alive in the US, the first occasion having taken place in Texas in 1998.

27 Jan The UK offers a package of £2.3 billion (about US$3.2 billion) in aid to the faltering automobile manufacturers Jaguar Land Rover, owned by India's Tata Motors, and Vauxhall, owned by General Motors of the US.

▶ Mexico's central bank reports that for the first time since it began tracking the figure, the amount of money sent in remittances to Mexico fell in 2008, by 3.6%.

28 Jan The US House of Representatives passes a US$819 billion economic stimulus package supported by Pres. Barack Obama.

29 Jan The Illinois state Senate votes unanimously that Gov. Rod Blagojevich is guilty of abuse of power and removes him from office; Pat Quinn becomes governor in his place.

▶ Ford Motor Co. reports that it suffered a net loss of US$14.6 billion in 2008, a record for the company.

30 Jan North Korea announces the nullification of all of its previous agreements with South Korea.

31 Jan In Djibouti, Somalia's transitional legislature elects Sheikh Sharif Sheikh Ahmed, former head of the Islamic Courts Union, president; the news is greeted with exultation in Mogadishu.

▶ Elections to provincial councils are held throughout Iraq in relative peace.

▶ American Serena Williams defeats Dinara Safina of Russia to win the Australian Open women's tennis championship; the following day Rafael Nadal of Spain defeats Roger Federer of Switzerland to win the men's title.

February 2009

1 Feb Jóhanna Sigurðardóttir is sworn in as prime minister of Iceland at the head of a caretaker coalition government.

▶ In Tampa FL the Pittsburgh Steelers defeat the Arizona Cardinals 27–23 to win the National Football League's Super Bowl XLIII.

2 Feb At a meeting in Addis Ababa, Ethiopia, Muammar al-Qaddafi of Libya is elected chairman of the African Union.

▶ Eric Holder is confirmed as US attorney general; he is the first African American to hold that position.

3 Feb Iran announces that it has for the first time launched a satellite into orbit.

▶ In Moscow, Kyrgyz Pres. Kurmanbek Bakiyev announces that he will close the Manas air base used by the US as a staging area for military forces in Afghanistan.

▶ Carmakers report that new-car sales in the US fell 37% in January in the industry's worst January figures since 1963.

4 Feb US Pres. Barack Obama announces new rules that will cap the salary of top executives at companies receiving government financial assistance at US$500,000 and will impose restrictions on bonus and severance pay for such company leaders.

▶ In Puthukkudiyiruppu, Sri Lanka, the last operational hospital in the region where government forces are fighting the remnants of the Liberation Tigers of Tamil Eelam comes under fire, and patients, doctors, and other staff flee; it is thought that as many as 250,000 Tamil civilians are trapped in the war zone.

5 Feb After the payment of US$3.2 million in ransom, the *Faina*, a Ukrainian ship carrying millions of dollars of military weaponry, is released by the Somali pirates who hijacked it in September 2008; the ship, which had been surrounded by US warships to keep the pirates from unloading the weapons, arrives safely at Mombasa, Kenya, on 12 February.

▶ Pat Summitt, coach of the University of Tennessee Lady Vols women's basketball team, becomes the first NCAA Division I college basketball coach to win 1,000 games.

6 Feb The US Department of Labor releases figures showing that job losses in November and December were worse than previously reported and that job losses for January reached 598,000, the worst figure since December 1974; since the recession began in December 2007, 3.6 million jobs have disappeared.

▶ The Aragua Tigers (Tigres) of Venezuela defeat the Mazatlán Deer (Venados) of Mexico 5–3 to win baseball's Caribbean Series.

7 Feb In Ohio, 134 ice fishers stranded when an ice floe under them breaks away on Lake Erie are rescued by local authorities and the US Coast Guard; one man dies.

8 Feb Wildfires race through the Australian state of Victoria for a second day, consuming 1,995 sq km (770 sq mi) of forest and farmland, two towns, and 750 homes and leaving at least 210 people dead;

some of the fires are believed to have been deliberately set.

> **QUOTE OF THE MONTH**
>
> *" Hell in all its fury has visited the good people of Victoria. This is an appalling tragedy. "*
>
> —Australian Prime Minister Kevin Rudd in response to wildfires that have consumed 1,995 sq km (770 sq mi) and left dozens dead, 8 February

▶ 4 At the Grammy Awards in Los Angeles, the top winner is British and American duo Robert Plant and Alison Krauss, who win five awards, including album of the year for Raising Sand and record of the year for "Please Read the Letter"; the award for song of the year goes to Coldplay's "Viva la Vida," and the best new artist is British singer Adele.

9 Feb Star slugger Alex Rodriguez of the New York Yankees Major League Baseball team confesses that he used illegal performance-enhancing drugs when he played for the Texas Rangers in 2001–03.

10 Feb US Secretary of the Treasury Timothy F. Geithner announces a large and complex financial rescue package involving as much as US$2.5 trillion; the markets drop as a result of the lack of details in the presentation.

▶ The US Senate passes a US$838 billion economic stimulus bill and begins talks to reconcile that bill with the one passed by the House of Representatives earlier; the resultant bill is signed into law on 17 February.

▶ Clussexx Three D Grinchy Glee wins Best in Show at the Westminster Kennel Club's 133rd dog show; the Sussex spaniel, known as Stump, is at 10 years of age the oldest dog to win the top award at the premier American dog show.

11 Feb Pres. Robert Mugabe of Zimbabwe swears in Morgan Tsvangirai as prime minister; the previous day Tsvangirai chose Tendai Biti as finance minister.

12 Feb Officials in Pakistan acknowledge that the terrorist attacks that took place in Mumbai (Bombay) in November 2008 were partially planned in Pakistan and announce the arrest of six people in connection with the attack.

13 Feb Somalia's president names Omar Abdirashid Ali Sharmarke to serve as prime minister of the transitional government.

▶ The Peanut Corp. of America, the company whose peanut-butter and peanut-paste products caused an outbreak of salmonella poisoning, goes out of business.

▶ Researchers at the Max Planck Institute for Evolutionary Anthropology in Germany announce that they have reconstructed the genome of Neanderthals using DNA from bone fragments; analysis of the genome is expected to shed light on many areas of human evolution.

14 Feb King Abdullah of Saudi Arabia makes changes to the cabinet that include naming a woman as deputy minister of education and replacing two Wahhabi clerics with members of more-moderate Sunni sects.

▶ The Peruvian film *La teta asustada* (*The Milk of Sorrow*), directed by Claudia Llosa, wins the Golden Bear at the Berlin International Film Festival.

15 Feb Voters in Venezuela approve a ballot measure that will remove term limits for all elected officials, including Pres. Hugo Chávez.

▶ Belgium opens Princess Elisabeth station in East Antarctica; it uses wind and solar power and is the first zero-emission research station on the continent.

▶ In Daytona Beach FL, the 51st running of the Daytona 500 NASCAR race, shortened to 152 laps from 200 because of rain, is won by Matt Kenseth.

16 Feb The government of Pakistan agrees to an accord offered by the Taliban that will allow Shari'ah law in the Swat valley region of the North-West Frontier Province and restrict government military action to responding to attacks, in effect ceding that area to the Taliban.

▶ The US Securities and Exchange Commission declares that the Stanford Group, parent of Stanford International Bank, may have perpetrated a US$8 billion fraud involving certificates of deposit in its bank in Antigua and Barbuda.

17 Feb The UN releases a report saying that the number of civilians killed in the war in Afghanistan in 2008 was 2,118, up from 1,523 the previous year, and that 828 of them had been killed by forces of the US-led coalition and Afghan soldiers.

▶ Kaing Guek Eav, known as Duch, becomes the first defendant to stand trial before a UN-assisted tribunal investigating genocide carried out by members of the Khmer Rouge in Cambodia; he had run a particularly brutal prison during the regime.

▶ The automakers General Motors and Chrysler LLC ask for an additional US$14 billion in assistance from the US government, while promising to cut costs; GM promises to lay off 47,000 workers, close five North American plants, and drop half of its brands.

18 Feb The Swiss bank UBS agrees to reveal the names of American holders of secret bank accounts whom US authorities believe culpable of tax evasion.

▶ US Pres. Barack Obama announces a new US$275 billion plan that is intended to help as many as nine million people save their homes from foreclosure or refinance their mortgages.

▶ At the Brit Awards in London, Welsh singer Duffy wins three prizes, including best British album for *Rockferry;* the award for best international album goes to American band Kings of Leon for *Only by the Night.*

19 Feb The International Atomic Energy Agency reports that it has found that Iran has a third more enriched uranium than the country had disclosed and that the amount of uranium would be sufficient to make an atomic bomb.

▶ LittleBigPlanet, a Sony jumping-and-climbing game for the PlayStation 3 console, wins the prize for game of the year at the 12th annual Interactive Achievement Awards in Las Vegas.

20 Feb A UN-sponsored meeting in Nairobi, Kenya, produces an agreement by 140 countries, including the US, to negotiate a treaty to limit the emissions of mercury into the atmosphere; mercury is a neurotoxin.

▶ A Chinese official complains that Russia has responded inadequately to a situation in which Russian warships on 14 February fired on and sank a Chinese tanker flying a Sierra Leonean flag; seven or eight sailors were lost at sea in the attack.

▶ The Dow Jones Industrial Average falls 100 points, losing 1.3% of its value, to close at 7365.67, its lowest point since 9 Oct 2002.

21 Feb US military officials concede that an air strike in Afghanistan's Herat province by coalition forces on 17 February killed 13 civilians and 3 militants; the US military had initially said that all the dead were militants.

22 Feb A study published in *Nature Structural & Molecular Biology* describes the engineering of antibodies that attack a portion of the influenza virus that does not mutate, suggesting the possibility of a single vaccine effective against all strains of flu.

▶ At the 81st Academy Awards presentation, hosted by Hugh Jackman, Oscars are won by, among others, *Slumdog Millionaire* (best picture) and its director, Danny Boyle, and actors Sean Penn, Kate Winslet, Heath Ledger, and Penélope Cruz.

23 Feb The Liberation Tigers of Tamil Eelam send communications indicating that they would like to participate in an internationally brokered ceasefire.

▶ The US government describes its intention to give US$900 million to nongovernmental organizations to help in rebuilding in the Gaza Strip.

24 Feb NASA launches the Orbiting Carbon Observatory satellite, which is expected to help scientists understand the workings of carbon dioxide in the atmosphere; the launch fails, however.

25 Feb At a conference of the Bangladesh Rifles, a paramilitary border guard organization, in Dhaka, Bangladesh, hundreds of troops mutiny, leading to a lengthy gun battle between the mutineers and army troops in which some 148 people (mostly officers) die.

▶ Indigenous rights activist Mick Dodson, a member of the Yawuru people of Western Australia, is recognized as Australian of the Year.

26 Feb At reconciliation talks in Cairo, leaders of the Palestinian parties Fatah and Hamas announce that committees have been established to find a way to form a unity government and to work out many other issues.

▶ US Pres. Barack Obama proposes a sweeping 10-year budget that would overhaul health care, push back global warming, and reverse a 30-year trend of increasing economic inequality.

▶ The Fox television network declares that it has renewed the animated comedy series *The Simpsons* for two more seasons; *The Simpsons* is currently tied with *Gunsmoke* as the longest-running scripted prime-time show.

27 Feb The US Department of Commerce announces that the country's economy in the final quarter of 2008 contracted at a rate of 6.2%, not 3.8% as previously stated; also, the Department of the Treasury says that it is expanding its stake in the banking giant Citigroup from 8% to 36%.

▶ The final issue of the *Rocky Mountain News* is published in Denver; the newspaper was founded in April 1859 and had been owned by the E.W. Scripps Co. since 1926, but Scripps had been unsuccessfully trying to sell it and felt it could not afford to keep publishing.

28 Feb Two days of military consultations between China and the US conclude with an agreement that high-level discussions between the two countries about military issues will be resumed.

March 2009

1 The US government agrees to allow American International Group (AIG) to draw as much as US$30 billion from the Troubled Asset Relief Program; it is the fourth time the government has had to intervene to save the insurance giant from bankruptcy.

2 Mar Pres. João Bernardo Vieira of Guinea-Bissau is killed by army troops; the previous day the army chief of staff had died in a bomb attack.

▶ The Dow Jones Industrial Average drops below 7,000 for the first time since October 1997, losing 4.2% of its value, while the major British stock index falls 5.3% and that in Italy sinks 6%.

3 Mar Twelve well-armed gunmen ambush a bus carrying the Sri Lankan cricket team to a match in Lahore, Pakistan; six police officers escorting the bus and two bystanders are killed, six cricketers are wounded, and the attackers all escape.

▶ Sales figures for automobiles in the US reveal that sales throughout the industry in February were 4.9% lower than in January and 41% lower than in the previous February.

4 Mar The International Criminal Court issues an international warrant for the arrest of Pres. Omar Hassan al-Bashir of The Sudan to face charges relating to atrocities in the Darfur region; Bashir almost immediately expels several international aid groups working in Darfur.

5 Mar The European Central Bank lowers its key interest rate by half a percentage point, to 1.5%, its lowest level since its inception, and for the first time forecasts that the economy of the 16 eurozone countries is likely to shrink in the coming year.

▶ Relief organizations in Sri Lanka say that some 150,000–200,000 civilians are trapped in a 26-sq-km (10-sq-mi) war zone in northern Sri Lanka.

6 Mar US government data show that the unemployment rate in February reached 8.1%, its highest level in 25 years.

▶ NASA successfully launches its Kepler spacecraft into space; Kepler will scan the cosmos for planets that are about the size of Earth and that are at distances from their stars that would allow water to remain in liquid form.

7 Mar Gunmen attack a British army base in Antrim, Northern Ireland, killing two soldiers and wounding two soldiers and two pizza deliverymen; the dissident group the Real IRA claims responsibility for the first attack on the British military in Northern Ireland since 1997.

8 Mar In London *Black Watch* wins four Laurence Olivier Awards—best new play, best director (John Tiffany), best theater choreographer (Steven Hoggett), and best sound design.

9 Mar The Mamoond, a large clan in the Bajaur region of Pakistan that is connected with the Taliban, signs a peace agreement with the Pakistani government in which, among other things, the Mamoond agree to turn over local Taliban leaders.

10 Mar Somalia's cabinet agrees to base the country's legal system on Shari'ah, the Islamic law; the legislature must approve the plan.

▶ The US$250,000 A.M. Turing Award for excellence in computer science is granted to Barbara Liskov for her contributions to the use of data abstraction to make software easier to create, change, and maintain.

11 Mar Pres. Nicolas Sarkozy of France announces that the country will once again become a full member of NATO; it had withdrawn from the organization's military command in 1966.

▶ *Forbes* magazine releases its annual list of the world's billionaires, which contains 332 fewer names than the previous year's edition; notably, Joaquín Guzmán Loera, head of the drug-trafficking Sinaloa cartel in Mexico, appears on the list.

12 Mar Bernard L. Madoff pleads guilty in US federal court to 11 charges arising from the Ponzi scheme that he ran, which prosecutors say bilked investors of some US$50 billion–US$65 billion over 20 years.

▶ In New York City the winners of the National Book Critics Circle Awards are announced: Roberto Bolaño for *2666* (fiction), Dexter Filkins for *The Forever War* (nonfiction), Patrick French for *The World Is What It Is: The Authorized Biography of V.S. Naipaul* (biography), Ariel Sabar for *My Father's Paradise: A Son's Search for His Jewish Past in Kurdish Iraq* (autobiography), August Kleinzahler for *Sleeping It Off in Rapid City* and Juan Felipe Herrera for *Half the World in Light: New and Selected Poems* (poetry), and Seth Lerer for *Children's Literature: A Reader's History from Aesop to Harry Potter* (criticism).

13 Mar Medet Sadyrkulov, a high-ranking politician in Kyrgyzstan who had recently changed camps to join the opposition, is killed in a car accident that his supporters characterize as highly suspicious.

14 Mar The revelation that executives at the troubled insurer AIG are to receive large bonuses, particularly in the financial products unit that caused the company's difficulties, ignites a firestorm of public criticism.

15 Mar Venezuelan Pres. Hugo Chávez orders the takeover of two key ports in petroleum-exporting states in compliance with a new law shifting control of ports, airports, and highways from the state government to the central government.

▶ French driver Sébastien Loeb's win in the Cyprus Rally makes him the first competitor ever to have achieved 50 victories in World Rally Championship racing.

16 Mar The day after opposition leader Nawaz Sharif broke out of house arrest in Lahore to lead a massive demonstration toward Islamabad, Pakistani Pres. Asif Ali Zardari agrees to restore Iftikhar Muhammad Chaudhry as chief justice.

▶ Bernard d'Espagnat, a French physicist and philosopher, is named the winner of the Templeton Prize for Progress Toward Research or Discoveries About Spiritual Realities.

17 Mar The last print edition of the *Seattle Post-Intelligencer* goes on sale; the newspaper will continue its online presence with a news staff of about 20 people; the previous staff numbered 165.

18 Mar The US Federal Reserve announces plans to buy about US$1 trillion in Treasury bonds and mortgage securities in an attempt to get more money moving in the economy.

▸ US Attorney General Eric H. Holder, Jr., declares that the government will no longer seek to prosecute people distributing marijuana in compliance with state medical marijuana laws.

▸ Lance Mackey wins the Iditarod Trail Sled Dog Race for the third consecutive year, crossing the Burled Arch in Nome AK after a journey of 9 days 21 hours 38 minutes 46 seconds.

19 Mar At a meeting in Tromsø, Norway, representatives of the US, Canada, Russia, Denmark, and Norway—all signatories of a 1973 treaty that limited polar bear hunting—issue a joint statement claiming that the greatest long-term threat to the survival of polar bears is climate change.

▸ Brazil's Supreme Court upholds the creation of the Raposa Serra do Sol indigenous reserve, first established in 2005 by Pres. Luiz Inácio Lula da Silva, in Roraima state; this allows for the removal of rice farmers who petitioned to be permitted to remain in the 1.6 million-ha (4 million-ac) reserve.

20 Mar The African Union suspends Madagascar's membership, saying that the country must restore a constitutional government within the next six months.

21 Mar With its 17–15 defeat of Wales, Ireland wins its first Six Nations rugby union championship, having achieved a won-lost record of 5–0.

22 Mar The 3,100-m (10,200-ft) volcano Mt. Redoubt in Alaska begins erupting, throwing ash on several cities north of Anchorage; it last erupted for a five-month period in 1989–90.

23 Mar In an exciting final game, Japan defeats South Korea 5–3 in 10 innings in Los Angeles to win its second World Baseball Classic championship.

▸ In New Delhi, Tata Motors introduces the much-anticipated Tata Nano, a small four-passenger fuel-efficient car that will sell for about US$2,230.

▸ Workers United, a splinter group of some 150,000 apparel and laundry workers, announces that it will secede from the union coalition Unite Here and join the Service Employees International Union.

24 Mar The Palestinian reading-promotion organization the Tamer Institute is announced as the winner of the Astrid Lindgren Memorial Award for Literature.

25 Mar In a visit to Mexico, US Secretary of State Hillary Rodham Clinton acknowledges that US demand for illegal drugs and its failure to prevent arms from being smuggled from the US into Mexico are significant contributing factors to the drug trade and the violence attending it in Mexico.

26 Mar The Norwegian Academy of Science and Letters awards its annual Abel Prize for outstanding work in mathematics to Russian-born French mathematician Mikhail L. Gromov for his contributions to geometry.

27 Mar Health authorities in China report that an outbreak of hand, foot, and mouth disease has killed 18 children and made some 41,000 people sick since the beginning of the year.

▸ The Grand Palais in Paris opens an exhibition, "Tag," that celebrates graffiti art; among those represented are American graffiti artists Quick, Rammellzee, Seen, and Toxic.

28 Mar Researchers at the Munk Centre for International Studies at the University of Toronto reveal that they have found a sophisticated China-based computer-spying operation that has infiltrated some 1,300 computers in 103 countries; the network seems to be focused on the Dalai Lama, Tibetan exiles, and the governments of countries in South and Southwest Asia.

▸ Well Armed wins the Dubai World Cup, the world's richest horse race, by a record 14 lengths.

29 Mar Oxford defeats Cambridge in the 155th University Boat Race; Cambridge still leads the series, however, by 79–75.

▸ Fiji wins the Hong Kong Sevens rugby title for a record 12th time with its 26–24 defeat of South Africa.

30 Mar At the Arab League's annual summit meeting, in Doha, Qatar, indicted Sudanese Pres. Omar Hassan al-Bashir is among the attendees, and other members express strong support for him.

▸ US Pres. Barack Obama announces that in order to remain eligible for government financial assistance, carmaker Chrysler LLC must complete a merger with Italian automobile company Fiat by 30 April and General Motors must greatly restructure itself, a process that would require major concessions from the United Auto Workers union, within 60 days.

31 Mar Pakistan's Supreme Court restores Shahbaz Sharif to his position as chief minister of Punjab state; he had been removed from office in February, and Punjab had been put under executive rule.

April 2009

1 Apr A protest against capitalism by some 4,000 people in London's financial district turns violent as some demonstrators attack the Royal Bank of Scotland building and fight with riot police.

▸ The television channel CBS announces the cancellation of the soap opera *Guiding Light*, broadcasting's longest-running scripted program; the final episode of the serial, which began on NBC radio in 1937 and moved to television in 1952, will air on 18 September.

2 Apr At the end of a meeting in London of the Group of 20 of the world's major advanced and emerging economies, the members produce an agreement that, among other things, increases the resources available to the IMF by US$1.1 trillion, creates new regulations for hedge funds and rating companies, and sets new rules to govern the pay of bankers.

▸ A US federal judge rules that three people who had been detained for more than four years at the US

" *Taken together, these actions will constitute the largest fiscal and monetary stimulus and the most comprehensive support program for the financial sector in modern times.* "

—statement from the Group of 20 economic meeting, 2 April

air base in Bagram, Afghanistan, have the right to challenge their continued detention in US courts because they neither are from Afghanistan nor were captured there.

3 Apr The US Department of Labor releases a report stating that more than two million jobs were lost in the first quarter of 2009 and that the unemployment rate has reached 8.5%.

4 Apr A summit meeting to celebrate the 60th anniversary of NATO takes place in Strasbourg, France, but near the Bridge of Europe, which links France and Germany, riots break out as thousands of demonstrators, both French and German, rally on either side of the bridge.

‣ An ice bridge that is believed to hold Antarctica's Wilkins Ice Shelf in place shatters at its narrowest point.

‣ In a ceremony in Cleveland, the Rock and Roll Hall of Fame inducts solo musicians Jeff Beck, Bobby Womack, and Wanda Jackson; sidemen Bill Black, D.J. Fontana, and Spooner Oldham; and the groups Little Anthony and the Imperials, Metallica, and Run-DMC.

5 Apr North Korea's test launch of a long-range missile intended to put a satellite into orbit fails, though North Korea declares it a success; on 13 April the UN Security Council responds with a call for sanctions against the country to be strengthened.

6 Apr A magnitude-6.3 earthquake centered on L'Aquila, Italy, causes widespread devastation; at least 295 people are killed, and some 28,000 are left.

‣ The member countries of the EU adopt restrictions on fishing intended to help the endangered bluefin tuna to return to a healthy population size.

‣ The National Collegiate Athletic Association championship in men's basketball is won by the University of North Carolina, which defeats Michigan State University 89–72; the following day the University of Connecticut defeats the University of Louisville 76–54 to win the women's NCAA title, becoming the fifth team in the history of women's college basketball to achieve an undefeated season.

7 Apr Alberto Fujimori, who was president of Peru in 1990–2000, is found guilty by a panel of judges of having ordered kidnappings and death-squad killings of 25 people in the early 1990s and is sentenced to 25 years in prison.

‣ The state legislature of Vermont overrides Gov. Jim Douglas's veto and makes same-sex marriage legal in the state; also, the District of Columbia council votes to recognize same-sex marriages performed in other states as valid marriages.

8 Apr The *Maersk Alabama*, a US container ship carrying agricultural supplies and food for aid agencies, including the World Food Programme, is seized by Somali pirates; after the ship is disabled by its crew, the pirates release the crew in exchange

for the captain, Richard Phillips, and begin ransom negotiations.

‣ For the second consecutive year, the Pacific Fishery Management Council cancels California's commercial chinook salmon fishing season because of the decline in the population of the game fish.

9 Apr The US Central Intelligence Agency declares that its secret overseas prisons will be decommissioned.

10 Apr The day after a court ruling that Fiji's government, installed after a coup in 2006, is illegal, Pres. Ratu Josefa Iloilo abrogates the constitution, appoints himself head of government, and abolishes the judiciary.

11 Apr A summit meeting of leaders of the Association of Southeast Asian Nations (ASEAN) and other Asian countries to discuss the global economic crisis is abruptly canceled and participants evacuated after antigovernment protesters gain access to the convention center in the resort town of Pattaya, Thailand, where the gathering is being held.

‣ Pres. Ratu Josefa Iloilo of Fiji appoints Voreque Bainimarama interim prime minister; Bainimarama, who initially became prime minister after a 2006 coup, reappoints most of the previous cabinet.

12 Apr US Navy snipers aboard the USS *Bainbridge* kill three Somalian pirates who were holding Capt. Richard Phillips of the *Maersk Alabama* hostage on a lifeboat, rescuing Phillips.

‣ Ángel Cabrera of Argentina wins the Masters golf tournament in Augusta GA in a sudden-death playoff over Americans Kenny Perry and Chad Campbell.

13 Apr US Pres. Barack Obama lifts restrictions on travel to Cuba by those with family in that country as well as all restrictions on remittances to ordinary people living in Cuba; in addition, American telecommunications companies are empowered to seek licensing agreements in Cuba.

‣ Swiss architect Peter Zumthor is named winner of the 2009 Pritzker Architecture Prize; among his works are the Kolumba Art Museum in Cologne, Germany, and an art museum in Bregenz, Austria.

‣ Pres. Asif Ali Zardari of Pakistan signs a measure imposing Shar'iah (Islamic law) in the Swat valley, in compliance with an agreement with Taliban militants in power there.

14 Apr After the UN Security Council voted to respond to a trial missile launch by North Korea by tightening sanctions on Pyongyang, the country announces that it will abandon nuclear disarmament talks and will restart its nuclear weapons program.

15 Apr A particularly brutal drug lord, Daniel Rendón Herrera, whose capture was a top priority for Colombian law enforcement, is arrested in northern Colombia.

‣ The first commercial container ship puts in at the new Khalifa bin Salman seaport in Bahrain; the port was built by the Danish ports-management company APM Terminals and the Bahraini government to serve Bahrain, Qatar, Kuwait, Iraq, Iran, and part of Saudi Arabia.

16 Apr The US Department of Justice releases documents that describe in detail the harsh techniques employed by the Central Intelligence Agency in interrogating suspected al-Qaeda operatives in 2002–05.

‣ Russia announces the end of its counterterrorism program in its republic of Chechnya.

17 Apr Leaders of 34 countries in the Western Hemisphere gather for a Summit of the Americas in Port of Spain, Trinidad and Tobago; at the opening ceremony US Pres. Barack Obama declares that the US seeks a positive change in its relations with Cuba.

▶ The US Environmental Protection Agency declares six greenhouse, or heat-trapping, gases to be pollutants that pose a danger to human health.

18 Apr Iranian American journalist Roxana Saberi is convicted of spying on Iran for the US and is sentenced to eight years in prison in Tehran.

19 Apr South Korea agrees to engage in talks with North Korea over the future of a joint industrial complex in Kaesong, North Korea.

▶ After four days of negotiations with Malta, Italy agrees to take in some 140 African migrants who were rescued by a Turkish cargo ship from two sinking boats; the migrants had been bound for the Italian island of Lampedusa when Malta received distress signals from their vessels.

20 Apr It is reported that the first government project to map the Great Wall of China has found that the length of the wall is 8,850 km (5,500 mi), much longer than the previously estimated 5,000 km (3,000 mi); sections of the wall dating to the Ming dynasty (1368–1644) were discovered in Gansu province.

▶ In New York City the winners of the 2009 Pulitzer Prizes are announced; five awards go to the New York Times; winners in letters include Annette Gordon-Reed in history and Lynn Nottage in drama.

▶ The 113th Boston Marathon is won by Deriba Merga of Ethiopia, with a time of 2 hr 8 min 42 sec; the fastest woman is Salina Kosgei of Kenya, who posts a time of 2 hr 32 min 16 sec.

21 Apr The IMF releases a report on the global financial crisis in which it estimates the amount of losses faced by financial establishments throughout the world as US$4.05 trillion.

▶ The World Digital Library, containing some 1,250 books, maps, and works of art from more than 30 national libraries, is inaugurated in a ceremony at UNESCO headquarters in Paris; the international online library is supported by UNESCO and the US Library of Congress.

22 Apr The 16-year civil war in Burundi is declared over as the National Liberation Forces becomes a political party; elections are to take place in 2010.

▶ Turkey and Armenia issue a statement declaring that diplomatic negotiations between the two countries have achieved meaningful progress.

▶ Afghanistan's National Environmental Protection Agency announces the creation of the country's first national park, Band-e-Amir, an area of deep blue lakes separated by natural dams of travertine.

23 Apr The US Centers for Disease Control and Prevention say an unusual strain of swine influenza A (H1N1) that contains gene segments from avian and human flu strains as well as from swine strains has been found in people in California and Texas.

24 Apr Officials in Mexico close museums and schools in and around Mexico City in an attempt to control an outbreak of what is believed to be a new strain of H1N1 swine flu that has killed 61 people and infected as many as 1,004 in the country.

25 Apr North Korea declares that it has begun reprocessing nuclear fuel rods.

26 Apr In response to a declaration of a unilateral cease-fire by the Liberation Tigers of Tamil Eelam, the government of Sri Lanka calls for the organization to surrender.

▶ Samuel Wanjiru of Kenya wins the London Marathon with a time of 2 hr 5 min 9 sec, and Irina Mikitenko of Germany is for the second year in a row the fastest woman in the race, with a time of 2 hr 22 min 11 sec.

▶ At the BAFTA Television Awards in London, winners include the drama series Wallander, the situation comedy The IT Crowd, and the entertainment program The X Factor; the award for entertainment performance goes to Harry Hill.

27 Apr In an attempt to avoid bankruptcy, the American car company General Motors announces a plan to cut 23,000 jobs in the US by 2011, drop 40% of its dealers, close out the Pontiac brand, and offer a swap of company stock for unsecured debt to bondholders.

▶ The international beekeeping organization Apimondia declares that high mortality in beehives throughout Europe threatens the industry with extinction within a decade; about 30% of the hives in Europe died in 2008.

▶ The US National Endowment for the Arts names as the recipients of the 2009 Opera Honors general director Lotfi Mansouri, director and librettist Frank Corsaro, conductor Julius Rudel, composer John Adams, and mezzo-soprano Marilyn Horne.

28 Apr Pakistan's military mobilizes to reverse the Taliban takeover of Buner district in the North-West Frontier Province; it is also reported that some 6,000 Pakistani troops will be moved from the border with India to the border with Afghanistan.

29 Apr The US Department of Commerce releases figures showing that output fell at a 6.1% annual rate in the first quarter of 2009 after having fallen at a 6.3% annual rate the previous quarter, a contraction of a magnitude last seen in 1958, but that consumer spending rose slightly after January.

▶ For the first time ever, the World Health Organization raises its global alert level to Phase 5, meaning that it is highly likely that the new H1N1 swine flu will become a pandemic.

30 Apr The automobile manufacturer Chrysler LLC files for bankruptcy protection after some of its smaller creditors refuse to accept a reduced repayment; an agreement may now be reached with Italian car company Fiat that will allow Chrysler to stay in business.

May 2009

1 May Fiji's military regime misses the deadline to return the country to democratic rule, and the Pacific Islands Forum suspends Fiji's membership on 2 May.

▶ Carol Ann Duffy is named poet laureate of Britain; she is the first woman appointed to the post in its 341-year history.

2 May Fifty-to-one long shot Mine That Bird, ridden by Calvin Borel, wins the Kentucky Derby by six and three-quarters lengths.

3 May Conservative businessman Ricardo Martinelli is elected president of Panama.

4 May Pushpa Kamal Dahal (also called Prachanda) resigns as prime minister of Nepal after the president overruled his attempt to fire the head of the army, who had refused to integrate former Maoist guerrillas from the country's civil war into the armed forces.

▶ LeBron James of the Cleveland Cavaliers is

granted the National Basketball Association's Most Valuable Player award in Akron OH.

5 May Officials in Afghanistan say that US military air strikes the previous day following heavy fighting against Taliban militants in Bala Baluk district killed at least 30 civilians.

▸ *The Legend of Sigurd and Gudrun,* written by J.R.R. Tolkien in the 1920s and '30s and edited by Christopher Tolkien, is published for the first time.

6 May Jacob Zuma is elected president of South Africa by the country's legislature.

7 May The US announces the results of its "stress tests" for banks and tells 10 major institutions, including Bank of America, Citigroup, Wells Fargo, and GMAC, that they must raise US$75 billion more in capital to achieve good financial health.

8 May The Pakistani military offensive against the Taliban in the Swat valley intensifies as some 200,000 civilians flee the area.

▸ The US Department of Labor reveals that the national unemployment rate in April reached 8.9%.

9 May The government of Chad announces that after two days of fighting in which as many as 220 insurgents and 21 Chadian soldiers were killed, it has won conclusive victory over rebels in eastern Chad who sought to overthrow the country's government.

10 May Russia defeats Canada 2–1 to win the International Ice Hockey Federation world championship for the second consecutive year.

11 May US Secretary of Defense Robert M. Gates announces that Gen. David D. McKiernan is being replaced as the top commander of US forces in Afghanistan by Lieut. Gen. Stanley A. McChrystal, who has a stronger background in unconventional warfare.

▸ The space shuttle *Atlantis* takes off on the final mission to make repairs to the Hubble Space Telescope.

12 May In the annual report of the trustees of the US Medicare and Social Security benefit systems, it is projected that the Medicare fund will run out of money in 2017 and Social Security in 2037; this is two years and four years, respectively, earlier than previous estimates.

▸ The Royal Swedish Academy announces that the winners of the Polar Music Prize are British rock musician Peter Gabriel and Venezuelan composer José Antonio Abreu.

13 May Japan's legislature ratifies an agreement signed in February that will see 8,000 US Marines transferred from Okinawa island in Japan to Guam.

▸ NASA's Kepler spacecraft, designed to scan the cosmos for planets similar to Earth and launched in March, begins its mission.

14 May Notice is given to 789 Chrysler dealerships across the US that they will be forced to close the next month.

▸ The Herschel Space Observatory, which will collect long-range radiation and study the creation of galaxies, is launched from French Guiana by the European Space Agency's Ariane 5 rocket.

15 May US government officials announce that some detainees at the military prison at Guantánamo Bay, Cuba, will be tried in military tribunals that have been changed to allow more rights for the defendants than had been earlier permitted.

▸ *The Wall Street Journal* publishes an article describing a fossil found near Darmstadt, Germany, of an Eocene-era primate that may be ancestral to the anthropoid lineage that produced monkeys, apes, and humans; the species has been designated *Darwinius masillae.*

16 May The new 24,500-sq-m (264,000-sq-ft) Modern Wing of the Art Institute of Chicago, designed by Renzo Piano, opens to positive reviews.

▸ In Moscow, Norwegian singer and violinist Alexander Rybak wins the Eurovision Song Contest with his song "Fairytale."

▸ Rachel Alexandra, under jockey Calvin Borel, becomes the first filly since 1924 to win the Preakness Stakes, the second event in US Thoroughbred horse racing's Triple Crown, coming in one length ahead of Kentucky Derby winner Mine That Bird.

17 May In Manchester, England, Usain Bolt of Jamaica runs a 150-m street race in 14.35 sec, a world best in the rarely contested distance.

18 May The Sri Lankan government reports that Liberation Tigers of Tamil Eelam leader Vellupillai Prabhakaran has been killed, and the LTTE acknowledge defeat.

▸ A spokesman for the UN High Commissioner for Refugees declares that some 1.5 million people have been displaced by fighting in Pakistan's North-West Frontier Province since the beginning of the month.

19 May Pres. Mahinda Rajapakse of Sri Lanka in a nationally televised speech declares that the government has defeated the Liberation Tigers of Tamil Eelam; the death of the rebel group's leader, Velupillai Prabhakaran, is confirmed.

▸ The day after the fifth round of reconciliation talks between Fatah and Hamas ended without progress, Salam Fayyad is again appointed prime minister of the Palestinian Authority at the head of a government that contains no Hamas members.

▸ The Ruth Lilly Poetry Prize is presented in Chicago to Fanny Howe.

20 May Iran successfully test-fires a solid-fuel Sejil missile that is believed to have a range greater than 1,930 km (1,200 mi), which suggests a rapidly advancing weapons-development program.

▸ The Whitelee wind farm, south of Glasgow, Scotland, is officially inaugurated; it is the largest onshore wind farm in Europe and is expected to generate 322 MW of electricity, and there are plans to increase its capacity to 452 MW.

▸ The Ukrainian association football (soccer) club FC Shakhtar Donetsk defeats Werder Bremen of Germany 2–1 in overtime to win the final Union of European Football Associations (UEFA) Cup in Istanbul.

21 May The US National Weather Service reports that the Red River in North Dakota has, after a record 61 days, fallen below flood level.

22 May At a summit meeting between the European Union and Russia in Khabarovsk, Russia, no agreement is reached on how to prevent price disputes between Ukraine and Russia from interrupting natural gas supplies to EU countries.

23 May Nepal's interim legislature elects Communist Party of Nepal (Unified Marxist-Leninist) leader Madhav Kumar Nepal prime minister.

24 May A trilateral meeting in Tehran between Iranian Pres. Mahmoud Ahmadinejad, Afghan Pres. Hamid Karzai, and Pakistani Pres. Asif Ali Zardari produces an agreement to work together to fight Islamic extremism and drug smuggling.

▶ The Deccan Chargers defeat the Royal Challengers Bangalore by six runs to win the Indian Premier League championship in cricket.

▶ The 93rd Indianapolis 500 automobile race is won by Helio Castroneves of Brazil as the Indianapolis Motor Speedway, known as the Brickyard, celebrates its centennial.

25 May North Korea conducts its second underground test of a nuclear weapon; its first was in October 2006.

▶ The Organisation for Economic Co-operation and Development reports that the combined economies of its 30 member countries fell 2.1% in the first quarter of the year compared with the previous quarter and fell 2% in the final quarter of 2008; this is the biggest decline since such measurements began in 1960.

26 May Pakistan's Supreme Court overturns a judgment made in February and rules that opposition leader Nawaz Sharif is entitled to run for and hold public office.

▶ US Pres. Barack Obama names Sonia Sotomayor of the Court of Appeals for the 2nd Circuit as his choice to replace the retiring David Souter on the US Supreme Court.

▶ France opens a military base in Abu Dhabi; as many as 500 troops will be stationed there for training and support.

27 May Boubacar Messaoud of Mauritania accepts the 2009 Anti-Slavery International Award for his organization SOS Esclaves; the organization was instrumental in the creation of laws making slavery illegal in Mauritania and continues to fight the practice of slavery in a country in which it is believed that some 600,000 people are still enslaved.

▶ In association football (soccer), FC Barcelona of Spain defeats the English team Manchester United 2–0 to win the UEFA Champions League title in Rome.

28 May The computer software company Microsoft unveils a search service intended to compete with Google; the new service is dubbed Bing.

▶ The media company Time Warner announces plans to spin off its online subsidiary AOL, acquired with much fanfare in 2000.

▶ The 82nd Scripps National Spelling Bee is won by Kavya Shivashankar of California Trail Junior High School in Olathe KS, when she correctly spells *Laodicean.*

29 May At the Lawrence Livermore National Laboratory in California, the National Ignition Facility, which will use lasers to create fusion reactions, is officially dedicated.

▶ The Federal Deposit Insurance Corporation reports that as of the end of March, a record 7.75% of all loans and leases held by American banks were in distress.

▶ The final night of the NBC television show *The Tonight Show* with Jay Leno as host is broadcast; Conan O'Brien will take over as host on 1 June.

30 May Chelsea FC, helmed by Guus Hiddink of The Netherlands, defeats Everton FC 2–1 to win England's FA Cup in association football (soccer).

31 May George Tiller, one of three doctors in the US who performs third-trimester abortions under certain circumstances, is shot to death in Wichita KS; his clinic later closes.

▶ Millvina Dean, the last known person to have survived the sinking of the *Titanic* passenger steamship in 1912, dies at the age of 97 in Southampton, England; she was nine weeks old at the time of the disaster.

June 2009

1 Jun The 101-year-old American automobile company General Motors files for bankruptcy protection and announces the closing of 14 plants.

▶ Air France Flight 447 from Rio de Janeiro to Paris disappears over the Atlantic Ocean; wreckage of the Airbus A330-200 found later shows that it went down and that all 228 aboard perished.

2 Jun It is reported in South Korea that North Korean leader Kim Jong Il has chosen his youngest son, Kim Jong Un, as his successor.

▶ General Motors declares that it has reached a preliminary agreement to sell its Hummer division to the Sichuan Tengzhong Heavy Industrial Machinery Co., based in Chengdu, China; the operations are to remain in the US.

3 Jun Gov. John Lynch of New Hampshire signs legislation making same-sex marriage legal in the state; the law will go into effect on 1 Jan 2010.

4 Jun In Cairo, US Pres. Barack Obama makes a major speech addressing the Muslims of the world, asking for a change in the relationship between the West and the Muslim countries and addressing the conflict between Israel and Palestine.

▶ Two American reporters, Euna Lee and Laura Ling, who were seized in March at North Korea's border with China, go on trial in North Korea for having illegally entered the country "with hostile intent"; on 8 June they are sentenced to 12 years of hard labor.

5 Jun The US Department of Labor reports that the national unemployment rate in May rose to 9.4% but that the rate of job loss has slowed.

6 Jun Svetlana Kuznetsova of Russia defeats her countrywoman Dinara Safina to win the women's French Open tennis title; the following day Roger Federer of Switzerland defeats Robin Söderling of Sweden to capture the men's championship for the first time, making him the sixth man to have won all four Grand Slam titles.

▶ Long shot Summer Bird wins the Belmont Stakes, the last event in Thoroughbred horse racing's US Triple Crown, by two and three-quarters lengths; both Summer Bird and Kentucky Derby winner Mine That Bird, who finished third, were sired by Birdstone.

▶ The Derby, in its 230th year at Epsom Downs in Surrey, England, is won by Sea The Stars, ridden by Mick Kinane; Sea The Stars had previously won the 2,000 Guineas race and was the first horse since 1989 to win both of those British Triple Crown races.

7 Jun The 63rd annual Tony Awards are presented in New York City; winners include *God of Carnage*, *Billy Elliot: the Musical* (which takes 10 awards), *The Norman Conquests,* and *Hair* and the actors

Geoffrey Rush, Marcia Gay Harden, Alice Ripley, and David Alvarez, Trent Kowalik, and Kiril Kulish, who shared a role.

8 Jun Pres. Omar Bongo of Gabon dies in Barcelona; he had been in office since 1967 and was Africa's longest-ruling head of state.

▸ The US Supreme Court rules that the due process clause of the Constitution requires elected judges to recuse themselves from cases in which any of the people involved have donated unusually great amounts of money to their election campaigns.

9 Jun The US government announces that 10 major banks, including JPMorgan Chase, Goldman Sachs, Morgan Stanley, and US Bancorp, will be permitted to return bailout funds to the government and exit from the Troubled Asset Relief Program (TARP).

▸ In the Wisconsin Dells resort area, festivities are held to celebrate the return of Lake Delton, which has been completely refilled a year after heavy rains washed away a dam impounding it and thereby caused it to empty into the Wisconsin River.

10 Jun The permanent members of the UN Security Council agree on a draft resolution to increase sanctions against North Korea; the full Security Council unanimously approves it on 12 June.

11 Jun The World Health Organization declares the outbreak of H1N1 flu a pandemic; it has spread to 74 countries, caused 144 deaths, and sickened at least 27,000 people worldwide.

▸ The US government announces that 4 of the 17 Chinese Uighur detainees at its military base at Guantánamo Bay, Cuba—all of whom had been found not to be enemy combatants—have been released and settled in Bermuda.

▸ American writer Michael Thomas wins the International IMPAC Dublin Literary Award for his first novel, *Man Gone Down.*

12 Jun Shortly after the polls close for what was expected to be a very close presidential election in Iran, Pres. Mahmoud Ahmadinejad is declared the winner by a landslide; opposition candidate Mir Hossein Mousavi insists that in fact he has won the election.

▸ The Pittsburgh Penguins defeat the Detroit Red Wings 2–1 to win the Stanley Cup, the National Hockey League championship trophy.

13 Jun Thousands of people take to the streets of Tehran, enraged by what they believe to be fraudulent results in the previous day's presidential election.

QUOTE OF THE MONTH

❝ *It is our duty to defend people's votes. There is no turning back.* ❞

—Mir Hossein Mousavi, Iranian opposition presidential candidate, after the government declared the election for Pres. Mahmoud Ahmadinejad, 12 June

---

14 Jun For the first time, Israeli Prime Minister Benjamin Netanyahu in a speech endorses the principle of a Palestinian state, but he makes no other changes in his previously stated position.

▸ The Los Angeles Lakers defeat the Orlando Magic 99–86 in game five of the best-of-seven National Basketball Association finals to secure the team's 15th NBA championship.

▸ Anna Nordqvist of Sweden wins the Ladies Professional Golf Association Championship tournament by four strokes over Lindsey Wright of Australia.

15 Jun Russia vetoes an extension of the UN observer mission in the separatist Georgian republic of Abkhazia unless the mission changes its name to recognize Abkhazia as an independent country; only Russia and Nicaragua recognize Abkhazia.

▸ The US Department of State asks the social-networking site Twitter to postpone scheduled maintenance lest it disrupt the flow of information within Iran and from Iran to the West about the political situation there.

16 Jun In Hamilton, Bermuda, some 600 people opposed to the settling in Bermuda of four Chinese Uighur former detainees at the US military prison in Guantánamo Bay, Cuba, demand the resignation of Premier Ewart Brown.

17 Jun For the third consecutive day, tens of thousands of people who demand new elections march in silence in Tehran; demonstrations are also taking place in other cities in Iran.

18 Jun The US Supreme Court rules that convicted prisoners are not constitutionally entitled to DNA testing that could prove their innocence, noting that many state legislatures have conferred that legal right.

▸ NASA launches the Lunar Reconnaissance Orbiter, which will spend a year measuring and mapping the Moon to find suitable landing sites and resources; the mission also includes the Lunar Crater Observation and Sensing Satellite, which will crash a portion of the expended rocket into a crater on the Moon so that subsurface strata can be analyzed.

▸ The 2009 winners of the Kyoto Prize are announced: semiconductor scientist Isamu Akasaki (advanced technology), evolutionary biologists Peter Raymond Grant and Barbara Rosemary Grant (basic sciences), and composer and conductor Pierre Boulez (arts and philosophy).

19 Jun Ayatollah Ali Khamenei, Iran's supreme leader, declares the presidential election results valid and orders an end to demonstrations opposing the reported results.

▸ Near Truth or Consequences NM, Gov. Bill Richardson officially breaks ground on Spaceport America, the country's first commercial spaceport; Virgin Galactic plans to use the facility when it is completed to give tourists rides into suborbital space.

20 Jun Members of Iran's Basij militia use violent beatings and tear gas in Tehran and other cities against thousands of demonstrators demanding new elections.

▸ The long-awaited dramatic new glass-and-concrete Acropolis Museum in Athens celebrates its grand opening.

▸ At the 124th British Amateur Championship tournament in golf, Matteo Manassero of Italy emerges victorious; at age 16 years 2 months, he is by far the youngest golfer to have won the competition.

21 Jun Greenland's new self-governing status within Denmark goes into effect amid ceremony and celebration.

▸ At Lord's Cricket Ground in London, Pakistan defeats Sri Lanka to win the men's World Twenty20 championship; England beats New Zealand for the women's title.

22 Jun Pres. Nicolas Sarkozy becomes the first French president to address the National Assembly and Senate since presidents were barred from Parliament in 1875; in his speech he discusses the economy and also declares that the burka worn by some Muslim women is a sign of subjugation that is not welcome in France.

▶ The American photography company Eastman Kodak Co. announces that it is retiring its iconic color film Kodachrome, which was introduced in 1935.

▶ Lucas Glover holds off Phil Mickelson, David Duval, and Ricky Barnes to win a rain-delayed US Open golf tournament in Farmingdale NY.

23 Jun Kyrgyzstan agrees to allow the US to keep Manas Air Base open in spite of having ordered it closed in February; the US will pay a higher rent, and the base is to be renamed as a transit center.

24 Jun Archaeologists report that a flute made from the bone of a griffon vulture discovered at Hohle Fels cave in southwestern Germany, together with previously found ivory and bone flutes, indicates that music making took place at least 35,000 years ago, far earlier than had previously been believed.

25 Jun Israel agrees to allow Palestinian security forces greater authority in the West Bank towns of Ramallah, Qalqilyah, Bethlehem, and Jericho; also, several Israeli checkpoints in the West Bank have been removed.

▶ UNESCO removes Dresden, Germany, from its World Heritage List of culturally significant sites, citing the impact of a new four-lane bridge over the Elbe River.

26 Jun In Iran, Ayatollah Ahmad Khatami states that leaders of the protests against the presidential election results should be punished, the Council of Guardians reiterates the validity of the results, and opposition leader Mir Hossein Mousavi declares that he will not call for more protests without first applying for permits.

▶ The US Department of Commerce reports that the personal saving rate of Americans in May rose to 6.9%, its highest rate since December 1993.

27 Jun The pro-British militias the Ulster Volunteer Force and the Red Hand Commando state that they have disarmed and put their weapons beyond use, an assertion that the government of Northern Ireland corroborates.

▶ On the American television show *Antiques Roadshow*, in an episode in Raleigh NC, a collection of 18th-century jade and celadon pieces is valued at US$1.07 million; it is the first million-dollar appraisal in the show's 13-year history.

28 Jun The military of Honduras overthrows Pres. Manuel Zelaya in a coup and deports him to Costa Rica; the country's legislature replaces him with Roberto Micheletti.

▶ In Johannesburg, Brazil defeats the US 3–2 to win the Confederations Cup in association football (soccer).

▶ Fame And Glory wins the Irish Derby by five lengths; this is a record seventh victory in the race by horses trained by Aidan O'Brien.

29 Jun The US Supreme Court reaches a decision on a case in which the results of a test for promotion for firefighters were thrown out because nearly all those who did well on the test were white; the court rules that the firefighters who had the top scores on the test but were not promoted were unfairly discriminated against and orders the test results reinstated.

▶ Bernard L. Madoff, convicted of having run the largest Ponzi scheme ever uncovered, is sentenced to 150 years in prison.

30 Jun In accordance with the terms of a security agreement, US troops withdraw from Iraq's cities; the milestone is celebrated in Iraq, though a bomb in Kirkuk kills 33 people.

▶ Some eight months after the US Senate election, Minnesota's Supreme Court dismisses a challenge from Norm Coleman, saying that Al Franken was the winner and can be seated as the state's junior senator.

▶ The wide-circulation hip-hop music magazine *Vibe* goes out of business.

Disasters

Listed here are major disasters between July 2008 and June 2009. The list includes natural and nonmilitary mechanical disasters that claimed 25 or more lives and/or resulted in significant damage to property.

July 2008

8 Jul Southern Bolivia. A truck carrying some 60 people goes off a mountain road, plunging 200 m (650 ft) into a ravine; at least 47 people, including 12 children, die.

16 Jul Northern Egypt. A truck rear-ends a car waiting at a railroad crossing, pushing three vehicles onto the tracks, where they are crushed by a train; at least 40 people are killed.

22 Jul Democratic Republic of the Congo. A motorboat carrying passengers from Mobayi Bongo to the Central African Republic sinks in the Ubangi River; some 47 people drown, with a further 100 missing.

27 Jul Ukraine and Romania. Officials report that five days of heavy storms have left 13 people dead in Ukraine and 5 others dead in Romania; some 8,000 people in the region have been evacuated.

August 2008

1 Aug Balcilar, Turkey. A gas explosion causes the collapse of a three-story girls' dormitory; at least 17 students are crushed to death.

1 Aug Andhra Pradesh state, India. The Secunderabad–Kakinada Gautami Express train is engulfed in flames; at least 30 passengers expire.

2 Aug Bihar state, India. A truck loaded with grain sacks and people goes off a bridge into a nearly dry culvert below; at least 40 people die.

3 Aug Himachel Pradesh state, India. Near the Naina Devi temple, fears of a landslide lead to a stampede in which more than 150 pilgrims, most of them women and children, lose their lives.

8 Aug Near Sherman TX. An illegally operated chartered bus carrying Vietnamese Roman Catholics to a religious gathering in Carthage MO crashes over a guardrail, killing 17 passengers.

9 Aug Boussoukoula, Burkina Faso. At an illegal gold mine, rain causes a mine collapse and mud slide in which at least 34 workers are buried, with dozens more reported missing.

10 Aug Southern India. Officials report that monsoon rains caused the deaths of at least 99 people, including 40 who are swept away when a truck in which they are riding fails to negotiate a flooded bridge in Andhra Pradesh state.

15 Aug Dominican Republic. On the highway between La Romana and Higüey, a passenger bus attempting to go around a parked vehicle hits another passenger bus head-on; at least 20 people are killed.

18 Aug Southeast Asia. It is reported that over the past week, record flooding has devastated much of the region, with thousands of people throughout the area forced from their homes and at least 160 people dead in Vietnam alone.

18 Aug Bihar state, India. As a result of heavy rains that cause the breach of a dam in Nepal, the Kosi River breaks its embankments and changes course, inundating villages in Nepal, Bangladesh, and India, leaving a minimum of two million homeless and at least 90 dead.

20 Aug Spain. An MD-82 airliner operated by the low-cost carrier Spanair and bound for the Canary Islands goes off the end of the runway at Madrid Barajas International Airport on takeoff and bursts into flames; at least 154 of those aboard perish.

24 Aug Kyrgyzstan. A passenger jet bound for Iran crashes shortly after takeoff from Manas International Airport in Bishkek, killing at least 64 passengers.

26 Aug Hispaniola. Hurricane Gustav makes landfall in Haiti and the Dominican Republic; at least 84 people are killed, and thousands of homes are ruined.

27 Aug South of Malta. An overloaded boat that left Zuwarah, Libya, carrying would-be migrants from The Sudan and Eritrea takes on water and sinks; 71 people are feared lost.

28 Aug Limani, Cameroon. After an oil tanker overturns, residents rush to salvage the leaking gasoline, but a spark from a passing bus causes an explosion and fire; dozens of people, including passengers on the bus, are incinerated.

30 Aug Sichuan province, China. A magnitude-5.7 earthquake causes houses to collapse in several villages and leads to the deaths of at least 28 people.

September 2008

1 Sep Democratic Republic of the Congo. A small plane crashes into a mountainside during a thunderstorm; all 17 aboard, most of them aid workers, are feared dead.

6 Sep Egypt. The Muqattam cliffs outside Cairo begin to collapse, loosing hundreds of pounds of rocks and boulders that crush a shantytown in the shadow of the cliffs; dozens of people are killed.

6 Sep Haiti. After a week of flooding caused by Tropical Storm Hanna, at least 529 people have perished, most of them in Gonaïves.

8 Sep Haiti. Hurricane Ike sweeps through Haiti, leaving at least 58 people dead.

12 Sep Los Angeles. A commuter train crashes head-on into a freight train, killing at least 25 people, when the engineer fails to stop at a red signal; it is thought that he may have been distracted by text messaging on his cell phone.

13 Sep Texas. Hurricane Ike spreads heavy flooding throughout Galveston and Orange and causes extensive damage in Houston; some 51 people in the region succumb.

14 Sep Russia. While traveling from Moscow to Perm, a Boeing 737 passenger jet operated by an Aeroflot subsidiary crashes when preparing to land; all 88 aboard die.

20 Sep Guangdong province, China. In Shenzhen ignited fireworks cause a fire in a nightclub that leaves at least 43 people dead.

21 Sep Henan province, China. A gas explosion in a coal mine kills at least 37 miners; 9 are missing.

22 Sep India. The death toll from three days of heavy monsoon rains is reported to have reached 119.

28 Sep Vietnam. Authorities report that Typhoon Hagupit has caused flooding that has left at least 41 people dead; the storm had earlier killed some 8 people in the Philippines and 17 people in China.

30 Sep Jodhpur, Rajasthan state, India. On the first day of a nine-day festival devoted to the Hindu goddess Durga, a stampede causes at least 224 people to be trampled to death.

October 2008

1 Oct Tabora, Tanzania. At an event in a disco hall to celebrate 'Id al-Fitr, overcrowding among the young people attending engenders panic, and 19 children are crushed in the ensuing stampede.

2 Oct Algeria. Torrential rains cause a flash flood in a normally dry river in the Sahara desert; the town of Ghardaia is inundated, with some 600 homes destroyed and at least 33 people killed.

5 Oct Kyrgyzstan. A magnitude-6.6 earthquake strikes, killing at least 72 people and flattening the village of Nura.

8 Oct Nepal. A Yeti Airlines Twin Otter airplane attempting to land at tiny Lukla Airport in the Himalayan mountains catches its wheels on a security fence and crashes; 18 of the 19 people aboard are killed.

10 Oct Eastern Thailand. On an overnight trip to the coast from a technology university in Khon Kaen province, a bus carrying students crashes into a hillside; at least 22 people are killed and 50 badly hurt.

23 Oct Rajasthan state, India. A powerful explosion demolishes an illegal fireworks factory in the village of Deeg; at least 26 people lose their lives in the blast.

25 Oct Yemen. After two days of heavy rain from a tropical storm, massive flooding along the Wadi Hadramawt leaves at least 180 people dead and some 20,000 people displaced.

29 Oct Balochistan province, Pakistan. A shallow magnitude-6.4 earthquake strikes, killing at least 215 people and leaving some 15,000 homeless at the beginning of winter.

November 2008

3 Nov Yemen. The international group Doctors Without Borders reports that 60 bodies have washed up onto the shores over the past two days; the dead had put out from Boosaaso, Somalia, in boats, and some had been forced overboard by smugglers.

4 Nov Philippines. An interisland ferry bound for Sorsogon goes down in bad weather; at least 40 people perish.

7 Nov Vietnam. Authorities report that unseasonal flooding in recent weeks has left at least 82 people dead and led to an outbreak of dengue fever.

7 Nov Pétionville, Haiti. A church-run school collapses, crushing to death at least 91 schoolchildren and teachers.

8 Nov Sea of Japan. A Russian nuclear submarine undergoing testing suffers an accident with its fire-extinguishing system that fills two compartments with Freon gas, asphyxiating at least 20 occupants.

15 Nov Near Boromo, Burkina Faso. A collision occurs between a passenger bus carrying workers to Côte d'Ivoire and a commercial truck, and both vehicles burst into flames; at least 66 of the passengers perish.

24 Nov Southern Brazil. Flooding and landslides have left at least 59 people dead and displaced some 43,000 others; by 1 December the death toll has risen to at least 116.

December 2008

14 Dec Philippines. An overloaded ferry just entering the mouth of the Cagayan River capsizes; at least 23 passengers drown, with 33 others missing.

16 Dec Israel. A bus transporting Russian tour guides to the resort town of Elat goes off the road and rolls down a mountain slope; at least 24 of the passengers are killed.

24 Dec Yevpatoria, Ukraine. An explosion destroys an apartment building, and at least 19 people are killed; it is thought that oxygen tanks stored in the basement may have been the cause of the blast.

27 Dec Tangail, Bangladesh. A truck leaves the road in thick fog and goes into a ditch; at least 24 of the passengers, most of whom were heading home from Dhaka to vote in legislative elections, die.

January 2009

1 Jan Bangkok, Thailand. At Santika, a nightclub, fireworks set off to celebrate the new year cause a fire, which quickly spreads; the conflagration and resulting stampede result in the deaths of at least 59 people.

4 Jan Northern Guatemala. Part of a mountain collapses, creating a large landslide that leaves at least 37 people, mostly coffee workers, dead and a further 50 missing.

8 Jan Costa Rica. A magnitude-6.1 earthquake leaves at least 20 people dead.

9 Jan Karachi, Pakistan. A fire of unknown cause kills at least 40 people in a shantytown.

11 Jan Indonesia. A ferry traveling from Parepare across the Makassar Strait to Samarinda is caught in a storm and sinks; some 300 people are lost.

11 Jan Off Guinea-Bissau. An open wooden boat capsizes in the Atlantic Ocean; more than 40 people, among them members of the National Islamic Council, which runs mosques and schools in the country, are missing.

16 Jan Thailand. Officials in Thailand deny a report in Hong Kong's *South China Morning Post* that the country had turned away ethnic Rohingya people

attempting to migrate from Myanmar (Burma) and Bangladesh and sent them back to sea in unseaworthy vessels; the report said that at least 300 of the Rohingya have disappeared at sea.

24 Jan Spain and France. Ferocious winds cause the collapse of the roof of a sports center in Sant Boi de Llobregat, Spain; four children are killed, which brings the death toll from the windstorm in France and Spain over the past two days to at least 15.

25 Jan Central Vietnam. A wooden boat ferrying shoppers across the Gianh River overturns and sinks; at least 40 passengers drown.

28 Jan US. A winter storm that began the previous day causes power failures and traffic accidents in Texas, Arkansas, Kentucky, Indiana, and Ohio; at least 23 deaths are attributed to the weather system.

31 Jan Near Molo, Kenya. After a tanker transporting gasoline overturns, looters rush to collect the fuel; an explosion, possibly caused by a tossed match, kills at least 115 villagers.

31 Jan Podyelsk, Russia. A fire quickly spreads through a wooden structure housing a nursing home; at least 23 of the residents expire.

February 2009

2 Feb Indonesia. The Indonesian navy rescues some 200 Rohingya men who were spotted after drifting in a wooden boat for close to three weeks, during which time 22 of the boat's passengers had perished.

6 Feb Nigeria. The minister of health reports that at least 84 children in the country have died after ingesting teething medication that contained the industrial solvent diethylene glycol.

7 Feb Brazil. A twin turboprop airplane operated by Manaus Aerotaxi and chartered by a family to fly

from Coari to Manaus goes down in the Manacapuru River; 24 of those aboard die.

8 Feb Victoria, Australia. Wildfires, some of which may have been deliberately set, burn for a second day; two towns and 750 homes are destroyed, and some 173 people lose their lives.

12 Feb Near Buffalo NY. Continental Connection Flight 3407, a turboprop traveling from Newark NJ to Buffalo NY, goes down on its approach and crashes into a house in Clarence Center NY, killing all 49 on board as well as the occupant of the house.

12 Feb Costa Rica. A magnitude-6.1 earthquake with an epicenter about 32 km (20 mi) southwest of San José creates devastation and leaves at least 34 people dead, with more than 60 others missing.

22 Feb Shanxi province, China. An unusually deadly coal mine accident takes place in Guijiao when a gas explosion kills at least 74 miners; a further 114 are hospitalized with carbon monoxide poisoning.

March 2009

12 Mar Off Newfoundland, Canada. A helicopter ferrying workers to offshore oil platforms goes down in the Atlantic Ocean; 17 passengers are lost.

22 Mar Near Butte MT. A single-engine plane carrying passengers to a skiing trip in the Rocky Mountains crashes, killing all 15 aboard.

27 Mar Cireundeu, Indonesia. Heavy rains cause an earthen dam impounding Lake Gintung to collapse, sending a wall of water into the town; at least 100 people drown and some 500 homes are swept away or submerged.

29 Mar Abidjan, Côte d'Ivoire. At a World Cup association football (soccer) qualifying match between the home country's team and that of Malawi, a stampede occurs as crowds try to force their way into the stadium before the start of the game; at least 19 people are crushed to death as a result.

30 Mar Off the coast of Libya. At least one of several boats carrying migrants from various countries in Africa and Asia capsizes; more than 230 people are believed to have lost their lives.

April 2009

1 Apr Scotland. A Super Puma helicopter ferrying workers to Aberdeen from a North Sea oil platform operated by the energy company BP goes down in calm weather; all 16 aboard are lost.

4 Apr Pakistan. A shipping container being trucked from Afghanistan to Iran through Pakistan is stopped by Pakistani police; it is found to be packed with would-be migrants from Afghanistan, at least 62 of whom have perished from suffocation.

6 Apr Indonesia. A military training flight ends in disaster when a Fokker 27 airplane crashes while attempting to land at an air base in West Java; all 24 military personnel aboard are killed.

6 Apr L'Aquila, Italy. A magnitude-6.3 earthquake in the Apennine Mountains devastates the area, killing at least 294 people and leaving some 29,000 homeless.

13 Apr Kamien Pomorski, Poland. A quickly spreading fire at a three-story building housing the homeless results in the deaths of at least 21 residents.

14 Apr Peru. A bus slams into an oil tanker truck near the town of San Vicente de Cañete; at least 20 bus passengers are killed in the resultant fire.

17 Apr Afghanistan. Two earthquakes, of magnitudes 5.5 and 5.1, in Nangarhar province cause the collapse of houses in four villages and leave at least 22 people dead.

19 Apr The Sudan. A passenger bus collides head-on with a truck not far from Khartoum; 21 bus passengers perish.

May 2009

10 May Northern Brazil. Floodwaters fed by two months of heavy rains begin to recede; at least 40 people have died, and some 300,000 have been left homeless.

20 May Indonesia. A C-130 Hercules military transport plane crashes into four houses in the East Java village of Geplak and bursts into flames; at least 98 of the 112 people aboard are killed.

25 May Bangladesh and eastern India. Cyclone Aila makes landfall, displacing half a million people in Bangladesh and leaving some 200 people, most of them in Bangladesh, dead.

June 2009

1 Jun Atlantic Ocean. Air France Flight 447, an Airbus A330-200 that is flying from Rio de Janeiro to Paris, disappears; wreckage and bodies found over the next few weeks indicate that it went down some 970 km (600 mi) off northern Brazil, that all 228 aboard died, and that faulty air speed indicators might have played a role in the disaster.

1 Jun South Africa. The Harmony Gold Mining Co. reports that at least 36 illegal miners were killed in an underground fire on 18 May in the Eland shaft, which had been closed for many years; the bodies of 76 miners are eventually found in the shaft, most of them having died in the fire but others having been killed by poisonous gases.

5 Jun Hermosillo, Mexico. A fire that may have started in a neighboring store sweeps through a day-care center, killing at least 47 babies and small children.

5 Jun China. A landslide buries the Jiwei Mountain iron ore mine and several homes and buildings in Wulong county; at least 26 people, 19 of them miners, are killed, and some 72 people aboveground are missing.

22 Jun Outside Washington DC. A Metro public-transit train slams into the back of a stopped train so hard that the first car rides up on top of the last car of the stopped train; nine people are killed.

29 Jun Viareggio, Italy. Fires caused by the derailment and explosion of a freight train carrying liquefied petroleum gas lead to the collapse of buildings and the deaths of at least 16 residents.

30 Jun Off Comoros. Yemenia Flight 626, which had taken off from Sanaa, Yemen, en route to Moroni, Comoros, goes down in the Indian Ocean; 152 of the 153 aboard perish.

People

The TIME 100, 2009

Each year the editors of TIME designate some 100 individuals as the most influential persons of the year in five categories of endeavor. As with TIME's annual Person of the Year designation, the list includes both heroes and villains; inclusion reflects the power of an individual's impact on history, whether for good or for ill.

LEADERS AND REVOLUTIONARIES

Gordon Brown Britain's PM led the global response to the international economic crisis, insisting on firm regulations over financial firms.

Hillary Clinton The US secretary of state brings wit, brains, courage, and compassion to her new role.

Thomas Dart Cook county's sheriff advocated a more humane approach to foreclosure evictions at the height of the US credit crunch.

Norah al-Faiz The deputy minister for women's education is Saudi Arabia's first female minister, and she says she will work for freedom and equality.

Joaquín Guzmán The Mexican drug lord's war of terror defies his government's power to control crime.

Boris Johnson London's mayor is an eloquent, witty Conservative who is impossible to pigeonhole.

Paul Kagame Rwanda's smart, reforming president is the new face of emerging African leadership.

Ashfaq Kayani Pakistan's army boss kept his word, strongly supporting US antiterrorism efforts.

Edward Kennedy The Senate's veteran liberal icon is a warrior for the less fortunate, filled with energy and passion—even as he fights brain cancer.

Christine Lagarde France's astute finance minister has pursued intelligent economic reforms with zeal.

Avigdor Lieberman Israel's tough-talking foreign minister says, "If you want peace, prepare for war."

Nouri al-Maliki Iraq's PM demanded sovereignty—and got his wish. Now, can he bring his long-divided people together to shape a united future?

David McKiernan The US general convinced President Obama to send more troops to Afghanistan, but he won't lead them; he was replaced there in May 2009.

Angela Merkel Germany's chancellor is a popular, strong voice for her economically challenged nation.

Barack Obama The new US president is a listener who calmly combines both realism and idealism.

Nicolas Sarkozy France's pro-US president is an advocate for women, immigrants, and the weak—even as he has made his nation's voice stronger.

Wang Qishan China's vice-premier is a watchdog for his nation's economic interests worldwide.

Elizabeth Warren As chair of the US congressional committee overseeing the Troubled Asset Relief Program (TARP), she is a leader in reforming markets.

Xi Jinping As vice president, the fix-it specialist is likely to become China's new president in 2012.

Susilo Bambang Yudhoyono Indonesia's president faces poverty, terror—and a reelection campaign.

BUILDERS AND TITANS

Sheila Bair The reform-leading FDIC boss, a firm Republican, gained even more power under a new Democratic president, Barack Obama.

Robin Chase Zipcar's cofounder continues to pioneer an Internet-based sharing culture with GoLoco.

Jamie Dimon Blunt and savvy, the CEO of JPMorgan Chase is one survivor of Wall Street's debacle.

Timothy Geithner After a rocky start, the US treasury secretary has steadied the fragile US economy.

Jack Ma The Internet entrepreneur chased eBay out of China with his successful Taobao.com.

Bernie Madoff Guilty! He stole US$65 billion from investors and became the poster boy for fraud.

Stella McCartney The Brit fashion designer wears tomorrow's face: authentic, chic, green, and vegan.

Alexander Medvedev The head of Gazprom Export is leading Russia's energy industry into the future.

moot The mysterious 21-year-old is the creator of the influential Internet message board 4chan.org.

Alan Mulally He brought Boeing back from near death. Can Ford's new boss work his magic again?

Nandan Nilekani The cofounder of India's Infosys Technologies is leading his nation's rapid growth.

Suze Orman The TV financial advisor is a strong, trusted voice for personal fiscal responsibility.

T. Boone Pickens The energy mogul has become an unlikely, highly effective environmental crusader.

Brad Pitt His passion and labor to rebuild New Orleans have brought life and hope to a unique American city.

Tessa Ross The British television producer claims she only dabbles in movies, but she has helped conjure up such engaging, award-winning films as *In Bruges* and *Slumdog Millionaire*.

Carlos Slim The Mexican media baron fights for change with courage, determination, and vision.

Ted Turner CNN's founder is the biggest landowner in the US and a strong voice for a greener future.

The Twitter Guys American techies Biz Stone, Evan Williams, and Jack Dorsey created a revolutionary form of communication—just ask the demonstrators in Iran.

Meredith Whitney The financial analyst blew the whistle on inflated bank stocks—at the height of the housing bubble—and was proved correct.

Lauren Zalaznick The boss of cable's Bravo network has built a brand with her taste and passion.

ARTISTS & ENTERTAINERS

Penélope Cruz The Spanish star is one of film's leading ladies, brimming with grace and insight.

Elizabeth Diller and Ricardo Scofidio The fearlessly creative husband-and-wife architects excel at making public spaces more welcoming to the public.

Gustavo Dudamel The wunderkind Venezuelan conductor and violinist now wields the principal baton of the LA Philharmonic—and he's only 28.

Zac Efron The teen heartthrob is an entertainer, an artist, and a song-and-dance man for the long run.

Tina Fey Smart, funny, beautiful, the *30 Rock* star also writes, produces, acts, and promotes—wow.

Tom Hanks The popular film star has a wondrous capacity for wonder—and for sharing it with us.

Werner Herzog The German film director, renowned for his early work, continues to find new audiences for his films at age 67.

Sam and Dan Houser The British brothers keep lapping the video-game field with *Grand Theft Auto.*

Judith Jamison For 20 years now, the great dancer has led ballet's Alvin Ailey troupe to new heights.

William Kentridge The South African artist creates riveting images that express ideas words cannot.

Jeff Kinney He writes the popular Diary of a Wimpy Kid books, charting the pulse of young America.

Lang Lang China's popular young pianist opens his heart to audiences, and they return the favor.

John Legend The hardworking singer, rooted in gospel but trained in the classics, is a genius.

Jay Leno Late night's longtime king passed the *Tonight Show* baton to Conan O'Brien and began a prime-time, five-night-a-week show in fall 2009.

Rush Limbaugh When the master of radio intimacy talks, Republicans—and Democrats—must listen.

M.I.A. Sri Lankan refugee Maya Arulpragasam is a citizen of the world whose hit songs speak to all.

A.R. Rahman The prolific hit maker has shaped India's musical sound track for more than a decade.

Tavis Smiley The gifted black communicator heads up an empire devoted to his message: America's unfinished agenda is to heal racial division.

The View Women Our TV family, these five women ask us in, speak their minds—and pull no punches.

Kate Winslet Fearless, risky, honest, and a shapeshifter, she's fast becoming our best screen actor.

HEROES & ICONS

Leonard Abess The Florida banker and community activist made a fortune, survived the economic meltdown—and then did the right thing, sharing his profits with his employees.

Seth Berkley The head of the International AIDS Vaccine Initiative works to alleviate suffering.

Jeff Bezos With his successful introduction of the Kindle e-book reader, Amazon's founder stayed in the lead of the digital revolution.

George Clooney The actor and activist is a pragmatic idealist whose commitment to ending the atrocities in The Sudan is deep, informed, and effective.

Michael Eavis The farmer who founded rock's Glastonbury Festival keeps the music magical by making his annual festival center on the fans.

Brady Gustafson Lance Corporal Gustafson was awarded the Navy Cross after he saved the lives of 20 fellow Marines during an assault in Afghanistan.

Van Jones Barack Obama's special adviser on green labor, a pioneer in fusing social justice and economic opportunity, is helping today's workers master tomorrow's jobs.

Somaly Mam Once sold into sexual slavery, the Cambodian activist now fights for women's rights.

Hadizatou Mani The Nigerian activist, sold as a slave at age 12, fought through the courts to win her freedom and continues to fight for equality.

Rafael Nadal At only 23, the Spaniard has become one of the all-time greats of the tennis court.

Michelle Obama A new first lady inspires and affirms Americans with her intelligence, depth, authenticity, compassion—and gardening shoes.

Manny Pacquiao The Filipino boxing champ is a role model who exemplifies his country's pride.

Suraya Pakzad Her Voice of Women organization is fighting to secure women's rights in Afghanistan.

Sarah Palin Love her or hate her, she remains a volatile force in the Republican Party—and the US—after her resignation as Alaska's governor.

Richard Phillips As skipper of the *Maersk Alabama,* he offered himself as a hostage to Somali pirates in order to save his crew and then was rescued when his captors were killed.

Sister Mary Scullion The nun who cofounded Philadelphia's Project H.O.M.E. has sharply reduced homelessness on the city's streets.

Chesley B. Sullenberger The veteran pilot lost power in both engines but kept his head, saving 155 lives with his quick ditch in the Hudson River.

Rick Warren The maverick megapastor preaches a gospel based on reaching out—and did so by giving the invocation at Barack Obama's inauguration.

Oprah Winfrey The next stop for America's Great Communicator: a cable channel start-up in 2010.

Tiger Woods He respects the greats, wins new fans for golf, is a role model—and keeps winning.

SCIENTISTS AND THINKERS

Shai Agassi His Better Place company aims to make all American cars electric-powered within decades, with a nationwide system of battery-swap sites.

Dan Barber The chef's upstate New York farm and restaurant, Blue Hill at Stone Barns, have become models for the locavore movement.

Nicholas Christakis The Harvard scientist is quantifying what many have long believed, showing how social networks can spread happiness.

Steven Chu Barack Obama's secretary of energy is a scientist, not a politician, who uses his bully pulpit to argue for an energy-independent US.

Paul Ekman The psychologist pioneered the study of facial expression to reveal our inner thoughts.

Jon Favreau At 28, he is Barack Obama's main speechwriter—and thus his words are shaping the future.

Roland Fryer Harvard's young black economist is rigorously rethinking education and race in the US.

Connie Hedegaard Denmark's climate and energy minister is making the world accept the reality of global warming and is crafting a plan to address it.

Barbara Hogan South Africa's minister of health is leading her nation's overdue fight against AIDS.

Paul Krugman The *New York Times* columnist won the Nobel Prize for Economics for his insightful analysis of today's great global depression.

Martin Lindstrom The Dane pioneered the merger of high-tech brain imaging with marketing: ca-ching!

Amory Lovins The green visionary has been preaching environmental responsibility for decades, and he's finally seeing his plans become reality.

Doug Melton The Harvard biologist is using adult stem cells to replace cells lost to diabetes.

Dambisa Moyo The Zambian activist has become a forceful voice against foreign aid to African nations when it serves to prop up corrupt governments.

Yoichiro Nambu The Japanese physicist illuminated the subatomic world—and won the Nobel Prize.

Daniel Nocera The MIT chemist hopes to create hydrogen fuel from water—we hope he succeeds.

Nouriel Roubini The visionary economist warned us of the housing bubble and subprime mess before they hit. Will we listen next time?

Stephan Schuster and Webb Miller The Penn State scientists are pioneers who managed to sequence the DNA of a 20,000-year-old mammoth.

David Sheff His memoir of his son's meth addiction, *Beautiful Boy,* helped redefine the way we view addiction and dependence.

Nate Silver The baseball statistician's FiveThirtyEight.com Web site was the go-to source for poll-based political analysis in the 2008 US presidential campaign.

Celebrities and Newsmakers

These mini-biographies are intended to provide background information about people in the news. See also the Obituaries (below) for recently deceased persons.

50 Cent (Curtis Jackson; 6 Jul 1976, Jamaica, Queens NY), American hard-core rapper.

Eva Aariak (Arctic Bay, NT [now in NU], Canada), Canadian politician; premier of Nunavut from 2008.

Mahmoud (Ridha) Abbas (nom de guerre Abu Mazen; 26 Mar 1935, Zefat, British Palestine), Palestinian politician; secretary-general of the Palestinian Liberation Organization executive committee and cofounder (with Yasir Arafat) of the Fatah movement; he served as the first prime minister of the Palestine Authority and was its president from 2005.

Mohamed Ould Abdel Aziz (1956, Akjoujt, Mauritania), Mauritanian military leader; chairman of the high council of state, 2008–09, and president from 2009.

Paula (Julie) Abdul (19 Jun 1962, San Fernando CA), American pop singer, choreographer, and TV personality.

Abdullah ('Abdullah ibn 'Abd al-'Aziz al-Sa'ud; 1923, Riyadh, Saudi Arabia), Saudi royal; king of Saudi Arabia from 2005.

Datuk Seri Abdullah Ahmad Badawi (26 Nov 1939, Penang state, Malaysia), Malaysian politician; prime minister, 2003–09.

Abdullah II ('Abd Allah ibn al-Husayn; 30 Jan 1962, Amman, Jordan), Jordanian royal; king from 1999.

George Abela (22 Apr 1948, Qormi, Malta), Maltese politician; president from 2009.

Tuanku Mizan Zainal Abidin ibni al-Marhum Sultan Mahmud (22 Jan 1962, Kuala Terengganu, Malaysia), Malaysian politician; *yang di-pertuan agong* (head of state) in 2001 and again from 2006.

J(effrey) J(acob) Abrams (27 Jun 1966, New York NY), American producer and director whose credits include the TV series *Alias* (2001–06) and *Lost* (from 2004) and the film *Star Trek* (2009).

Chinua Achebe (Albert Chinualumogu Achebe; 16 Nov 1930, Ogidi, Nigeria), Nigerian novelist and poet who in 2007 won the second Man Booker International Prize for fiction.

Amy (Lou) Adams (20 Aug 1974, Aviano, Italy), American stage and film actress.

Gerry Adams (Gerard Adams; Irish: Gearóid Mac Ádhaimh; 6 Oct 1948, West Belfast, Northern Ireland), Irish resistance leader; president of Sinn Féin, the political wing of the Irish Republican Army, from 1983.

John (Coolidge) Adams (15 Feb 1947, Worcester MA), American composer.

Thomas Adès (27 Jun 1971, London, England), British composer, pianist, and conductor.

Chimamanda Ngozi Adichie (15 Sep 1977, Enugu, Nigeria), Nigerian novelist; winner of the 2007 Orange Broadband Prize for Fiction.

Aravind Adiga (1974, India), Indian author; recipient of the 2008 Man Booker Prize for *The White Tiger*.

Ben(jamin Geza) Affleck (15 Aug 1972, Berkeley CA), American actor, writer, and director.

(Caleb) Casey Affleck (12 Aug 1975, Falmouth MA), American film actor.

Isaias Afwerki (2 Feb 1946, Asmara, Ethiopia [now in Eritrea]), Eritrean independence leader, secretary-general of the Provisional Government, and first president of Eritrea, from 1993.

Christina (Maria) Aguilera (18 Dec 1980, Staten Island NY), American pop singer.

Bertie Ahern (Bartholomew Patrick Ahern; 12 Sep 1951, Dublin, Ireland), Irish politician; prime minister (*taoiseach*) of Ireland, 1997–2008.

Mahmoud Ahmadinejad (28 Oct 1956, Garmsar, Iran), Iranian politician; president from 2005.

Abdullahi Yusuf Ahmed (15 Dec 1934, Galcaio, Somalia), Somali military officer; nominally president from 2004 to 2008.

Iajuddin Ahmed (1 Feb 1931, Nayagaon, Bengal, British India [now in Bangladesh]), Bangladeshi scientist and educator; president of Bangladesh, 2002–09.

Sheikh Sharif Sheikh Ahmed (25 Jul 1964, Somalia), Somali politician; nominally president from 2009.

Martti Ahtisaari (23 Jun 1937, Viipuri, Finland [now Vyborg, Russia]), Finnish politician; president of Finland, 1994–2000, and winner of the 2008 Nobel Peace Prize.

Akihito (original name Tsugu Akihito; era name Heisei; 23 Dec 1933, Tokyo, Japan), Japanese royal; emperor of Japan from 1989.

Akil Akilov (1944, Tajikistan?), Tajik politician; prime minister from 1999.

Peter Akinola (27 Jan 1944, Abeokuta, Nigeria), Nigerian Anglican churchman; archbishop of Nigeria from 2000.

Jessica (Marie) Alba (28 Apr 1981, Pomona CA), American TV and film actress.

Albert II (Albert Félix Humbert Théodore Christian Eugène Marie of Saxe-Coburg-Gotha; 6 Jun 1934, Brussels, Belgium), Belgian royal; king from 1993.

Albert II (Albert Alexandre Louis Pierre; 14 Mar 1958, Monaco), Monegasque prince and ruler of Monaco from 2005.

Claribel Alegría (12 May 1924, Estelí, Nicaragua), Nicaraguan-born Salvadoran poet, essayist, and journalist; recipient of the 2006 Neustadt Prize.

Sherman J. Alexie, Jr. (7 Oct 1966, Wellpinit, Spokane Indian Reservation, Washington), American poet and novelist who writes of his Native American upbringing.

Monica Ali (20 Oct 1967, Dacca, Pakistan [now Dhaka, Bangladesh]), Bangladeshi-born British writer.

Muhammad Ali (Cassius Marcellus Clay, Jr.; 17 Jan 1942, Louisville KY), American boxer, the first to win the heavyweight championship three separate times.

Samuel A. Alito, Jr. (1 Apr 1950, Trenton NJ), American jurist; associate justice of the US Supreme Court from 2006.

Ilham Aliyev (Ilham Geidar ogly Aliev; 24 Dec 1961, Baku, USSR [now in Azerbaijan]), Azerbaijani politician; prime minister briefly in 2003 and president from October 2003.

Joan Allen (20 Aug 1956, Rochelle IL), American film and theater actress.

Paul G. Allen (21 Jan 1953, Mercer Island WA), American corporate executive; cofounder (1975) of Microsoft Corp. and owner of several professional sports teams.

Woody Allen (Allen Stewart Konigsberg; 1 Dec 1935, Brooklyn NY), American filmmaker and actor.

Isabel Allende (2 Aug 1942, Lima, Peru), Chilean writer in the magic realist tradition.

Pedro Almodóvar (Caballero) (24 Sep 1949, Calzada de Calatrava, Spain), Spanish film director specializing in melodrama.

Alois (Alois Philipp Maria Prince von und zu Liechtenstein; 11 Jun 1968, Zürich, Switzerland), Liechtenstein crown prince.

Marin Alsop (16 Oct 1956, New York NY), American conductor; music director of the Baltimore Symphony Orchestra from 2007; she was the first woman to head a major American orchestra.

Amadou (Amadou Bagayoko; 24 Oct 1954, Bamako, French West Africa [now in Mali]), Malian guitarist (for Amadou and Mariam).

Yukiya Amano (9 May 1947, Japan), Japanese international official; director general of the International Atomic Energy Agency from 2009.

Pamela (Denise) Anderson (1 Jul 1967, Ladysmith, BC, Canada), Canadian-born model and actress.

Paul Thomas Anderson (26 Jun 1970, Studio City CA), American film director.

Wes Anderson (1 May 1969, Houston TX), American film director.

Tadao Ando (13 Sep 1941, Osaka, Japan), Japanese architect; recipient of the 1995 Pritzker Prize.

André 3000 (André Benjamin; Dré; 27 May 1975, Atlanta GA), American hip-hop artist and actor.

Marc Andreessen (9 Jul 1971, Cedar Falls IA), American computer innovator; developer of Netscape.

Andrew (Andrew Albert Christian Edward Mountbatten-Windsor; 19 Feb 1960, Buckingham Palace, London, England), British prince; second son of Queen Elizabeth II and Prince Philip, duke of Edinburgh; and duke of York.

Leif Ove Andsnes (7 Apr 1970, Karmøy, Norway), Norwegian pianist.

Criss Angel (Christopher Nicholas Sarantakos; 19 Dec 1967, Long Island NY), American magician and illusionist.

Maya Angelou (Marguerite Annie Johnson; 4 Apr 1928, St. Louis MO), American poet.

Jennifer Aniston (Jennifer Linn Anistassakis; 11 Feb 1969, Sherman Oaks CA), American TV and film actress.

Kofi (Atta) Annan (18 Apr 1938, Kumasi, Gold Coast [now Ghana]), Ghanaian diplomat; UN secretary-general, 1997–2006; corecipient, with the UN, of the 2001 Nobel Peace Prize.

Anne (Anne Elizabeth Alice Louise Mountbatten-Windsor; 15 Aug 1950, Clarence House, London, England), British princess; daughter of Queen Elizabeth II and Prince Philip, duke of Edinburgh.

Andrus Ansip (1 Oct 1956, Tartu, USSR [now in Estonia]), Estonian politician; prime minister from 2005.

Carmelo Anthony (29 May 1984, New York NY), American pro basketball forward.

Marc Anthony (Marco Antonio Muñiz; 16 Sep 1968, Spanish Harlem, New York NY), American salsa singer.

Judd Apatow (6 Dec 1967, Syosset NY), American filmmaker.

Denys Arcand (25 Jun 1941, Deschambault, QC, Canada), French-Canadian film director, screenwriter, and actor.

Martha Argerich (5 Jun 1941, Buenos Aires, Argentina), Argentine concert pianist.

Óscar Arias (Sánchez) (13 Sep 1941, Heredia, Costa Rica), Costa Rican statesman; president of Costa Rica, 1986–90 and again from 2006; recipient of the 1987 Nobel Peace Prize.

Alan (Wolf) Arkin (26 Mar 1934, Brooklyn NY), American film and TV actor.

Giorgio Armani (11 Jul 1934, Piacenza, Italy), Italian fashion designer.

Billie Joe Armstrong (17 Feb 1972, Rodeo CA), American punk-rock vocalist and guitarist (for Green Day).

Lance Armstrong (18 Sep 1971, Plano TX), American cyclist who won the Tour de France seven years in succession, 1999–2005.

Courteney Cox Arquette (Courteney Bass Cox; 15 Jun 1964, Birmingham AL), American TV and film actress.

Taro Aso (20 Sep 1940, Iizuka, Fukuoka prefecture, Japan), Japanese politician (Liberal Democratic Party); prime minister from 2008.

Bashar al-Assad (11 Sep 1965, Damascus, Syria), Syrian politician; president from 2000.

Alaa Al Aswany (1957, Egypt), Egyptian dentist and popular writer.

Susan Athey (29 Nov 1970, Boston MA), American economist specializing in economic theory, empirical economics, and econometrics.

Kate Atkinson (1951, York, England), British author.

Abdul Rahman ibn Hamad al-Attiyah (1950, Qatar), Qatari international official; secretary-general of the Gulf Cooperation Council from 2002.

Margaret (Eleanor) Atwood (18 Nov 1939, Ottawa, ON, Canada), Canadian poet, novelist, and critic.

Daw Aung San Suu Kyi (19 Jun 1945, Rangoon, Burma [now Yangon, Myanmar]), Burmese human rights activist; recipient in 1991 of the Nobel Peace Prize.

David Axelrod (22 Feb 1953, New York, NY), American political consultant (Democrat); senior adviser to US Pres. Barack Obama.

Hank Azaria (25 Apr 1964, Forest Hills NY), American actor best known for comic film roles and for providing voices for TV's *The Simpsons*.

(Verónica) Michelle Bachelet (Jeria) (29 Sep 1951, Santiago, Chile), Chilean politician (Socialist); president from 2006.

Bob Baffert (13 Jan 1953, Nogales AZ), American trainer of Thoroughbred racehorses.

Jerry D. Bailey (29 Aug 1957, Dallas TX), American jockey.

(Josiah) Voreque ("Frank") Bainimarama (27 Apr 1954, Kiuva, Fiji), Fijian military leader; self-appointed acting prime minister from 2007.

Sheila (Colleen) Bair (3 Apr 1954, Wichita KS), American businesswoman; chair of the Federal Deposit Insurance Corporation (FDIC) from 2006.

Gordon Bajnai (5 Mar 1968, Szeged, Hungary) Hungarian politician; prime minister from 2009.

Kurmanbek Bakiyev (1 Aug 1949, Masadan, Kirghiz SSR, USSR [now Teyyit, Kyrgyzstan]), Kyrgyz politician; president of Kyrgyzstan from 2005.

John E(lias) Baldacci (30 Jan 1955, Bangor ME), American politician (Democrat); governor of Maine from 2003.

Alec Baldwin (Alexander Rae Baldwin III; 3 Apr 1958, Massapequa NY), American film and TV actor.

Christian (Charles Philip) Bale (30 Jan 1974, Haverfordwest, Pembrokeshire, Wales), British film actor.

Jan Peter Balkenende (7 May 1956, Kapelle, Netherlands), Dutch politician (Christian Democratic Appeal); prime minister from 2002.

Steven A. Ballmer (24 Mar 1956, Detroit? MI), American corporate executive; CEO of Microsoft Corp. from 2000.

Ed(ward) Balls (25 Feb 1967, Norwich, England), British public official; secretary of state for children, schools, and families from 2007.

Ban Ki-moon (13 Jun 1944, Umsong, Japanese-occupied Korea [now in South Korea]), Korean government and international official; secretary-general of the United Nations from 2007.

Eric Bana (Eric Banadinovich; 9 Aug 1968, Melbourne, VIC, Australia), Australian actor.

Rupiah Banda (13 Feb 1937, Gwanda, Zimbabwe), Zambian politician; president from 2008.

Russell Banks (28 Mar 1940, Newton MA), American novelist.

Tyra Banks (4 Dec 1973, Los Angeles CA), American model, actress, and TV show host.

Banksy (1974?, Bristol?, England), British graffiti artist.

Haley (Reeves) Barbour (22 Oct 1947, Yazoo City MS), American politician (Republican); governor of Mississippi from 2004.

Javier (Ángel Encinas) Bardem (1 Mar 1969, Las Palmas, Canary Islands, Spain), Spanish film actor.

Daniel Barenboim (15 Nov 1942, Buenos Aires, Argentina), Israeli pianist and conductor; recipient of a Praemium Imperiale in 2007.

Nir Barkat (1959, Israel), Israeli businessman and politician; mayor of Jerusalem from 2008.

Julian Barnes (pseudonyms Edward Pygge and Dan Kavanagh; 19 Jan 1946, Leicester, Leicestershire, England), British author and TV critic.

Sacha (Noam) Baron Cohen (13 Oct 1971, Hammersmith, London, England), British comedian and actor.

Francoise Barre-Sinoussi (30 Jul 1947, Paris, France), French virologist; cowinner of the 2008 Nobel Prize for Physiology or Medicine.

José Manuel Durão Barroso (23 Mar 1956, Lisbon, Portugal), Portuguese politician; prime minister, 2002–04, and president of the European Commission from 2004.

Dean (Oliver) Barrow (2 Mar 1951, Belize City, British Honduras [now Belize]), Belizean politician (United Democratic Party); prime minister from 2008.

John D(avid) Barrow (29 Nov 1952, London, England), British cosmologist, a specialist in the anthropic principle; recipient of the 2006 Templeton Prize.

Dave Barry (3 Jul 1947, Armonk NY), American humorist, newspaper columnist, and author.

Drew Barrymore (Andrew Blythe Barrymore; 22 Feb 1975, Culver City CA), American film actress.

Frederick Barthelme (10 Oct 1943, Houston TX), American writer of short stories and novels.

Bartholomew I (Dimitrios Archontonis; 29 Feb 1940, Imbros [now Gokceada], Turkey), Eastern Orthodox archbishop of Constantinople and ecumenical patriarch from 1991.

Richard Barton (2 Jun 1967, New Canaan CT), American Internet entrepreneur (Expedia.com, Zillow.com).

Jaume Bartumeu Cassany (10 Nov 1954, Andorra), Andorran chief executive from 2009.

Carol (Ann) Bartz (29 Aug 1948, Winona MN), American corporate executive; CEO and president of Yahoo! Inc. from 2009.

Mikhail (Nikolayevich) Baryshnikov (28 Jan 1948, Riga, USSR [now in Latvia]), Soviet-born American ballet dancer, director, and actor.

Traian Basescu (4 Nov 1951, Basarabi, Romania), Romanian politician; president from 2004.

Omar Hassan Ahmad al-Bashir (1944, Hosh Bannaga, Anglo-Egyptian Sudan), Sudanese military leader; president from 1989.

Michael (Benjamin) Bay (17 Feb 1965, Los Angeles CA), American director and producer of action films.

Sanj(aagiyn) Bayar (1956, Ulaanbaatar, Mongolia), Mongolian diplomat; prime minister from 2007.

Beatrix (31 Jan 1938, Soestdijk, Netherlands), Dutch royal; queen of The Netherlands from 1980.

Glenn Beck (10 Feb 1964, Mount Vernon WA), American conservative TV commentator and author.

David (Robert) Beckham (2 May 1975, Leytonstone, East London, England), British association football (soccer) player.

Victoria Beckham (Victoria Caroline Adams; 7 Apr 1975, Goff's Oak, Hertfordshire, England), British pop singer ("Posh Spice" of the Spice Girls) and celebrity.

Kate Beckinsale (26 Jul 1973, London, England), British actress.

Mike Beebe (Michael Dale Beebe; 28 Dec 1946, Amagon AR), American politician (Democrat); governor of Arkansas from 2007.

Kenenisa Bekele (13 Jun 1982, near Bekoji, Ethiopia), Ethiopian cross-country runner.

Bill Belichick (William Stephen Belichick; 16 Apr 1952, Nashville TN), American football coach.

Arden L. Bement, Jr. (22 May 1932, Pittsburgh PA), American materials scientist; director of the National Science Foundation from 2004.

Zine al-Abidine Ben Ali (3 Sep 1936, Hammam-Sousse, French Tunisia), Tunisian politician and president from 1987.

Benedict XVI (Joseph Alois Ratzinger; 16 Apr 1927, Marktl am Inn, Bavaria, Germany), German Roman Catholic churchman; pope from 2005.

Raymond Benjamin (24 Nov 1945, Alexandria, Egypt), French international official; secretary-general of the International Civil Aviation Organization from 2009.

Regina (Marcia) Benjamin (26 Oct 1956, Mobile AL), American physician; nominee for US surgeon general.

Alan Bennett (9 May 1934, Leeds, England), British dramatist and writer.

Gurbanguly Berdymukhammedov (29 Jun 1957, Bararab, USSR [now in Turkmenistan]), Turkmen politician; president from 2006.

Sali (Ram) Berisha (15 Oct 1944, Tropojë, Albania), Albanian cardiologist and politician (Democratic Party); president, 1992–97, and prime minister from 2005.

Silvio Berlusconi (29 Sep 1936, Milan, Italy), Italian businessman and politician; prime minister, 1994–95, 2001–06, and again from 2008.

Ben(jamin Shalom) Bernanke (13 Dec 1953, Augusta GA), American economist; chairman of the Board of Governors of the Federal Reserve System from 2006.

Tim(othy J.) Berners-Lee (8 Jun 1955, London, England), British inventor of the World Wide Web and director of the World Wide Web Consortium (W3C) from 1994.

Halle (Maria) Berry (14 Aug 1968, Cleveland OH), American film actress and model.

Tarcisio Cardinal Bertone (2 Dec 1934, Romano Canavese, Italy), Italian Roman Catholic churchman; secretary of state of the Vatican from 2006.

Steve(n Lynn) Beshear (21 Sep 1944, Dawson Springs KY), American politician (Democrat); governor of Kentucky from 2007.

Beyoncé (Beyoncé Knowles; 4 Sep 1981, Houston TX), American R&B singer and actress.

Jeffrey P. Bezos (12 Jan 1964, Albuquerque NM), American corporate executive; founder and CEO of Amazon.com from 1995.

Bhumibol Adulyadej (Rama IX; 5 Dec 1927, Cambridge MA), Thai royal; king of Thailand from 1946.

Joe Biden (Joseph Robinette Biden, Jr., 20 Nov 1942, Scranton PA), American politician (Democrat); senator from Delaware, 1973–2009, and vice president of the US from 2009.

Jessica (Claire) Biel (3 Mar 1982, Ely MN), American TV and film actress.

Osama bin Laden (also spelled Usamah ibn Ladin; 10 Mar 1957, Riyadh, Saudi Arabia), Saudi Arabian–born terrorist and leader of the al-Qaeda organization.

Harrison Birtwistle (15 Jul 1934, Accrington, Lancashire, England), British composer of operas, chamber music, and orchestral music.

Paul Biya (13 Feb 1933, Mvomeka'a, Cameroon), Cameroonian politician; president from 1982.

Jack Black (28 Aug 1969, Hermosa Beach CA), American film actor and comic rock musician.

Douglas A. Blackmon (6 Sep 1964, Stuttgart AR); American journalist and author; recipient of the 2009 Pulitzer Prize for general nonfiction for *Slavery by Another Name: The Re-Enslavement of Black Americans from the Civil War to World War II.*

Rubén Blades (16 Jul 1948, Panama City, Panama), Panamanian salsa singer and songwriter, actor, and politician.

Rod Blagojevich (Milorad R. Blagojevich; 10 Dec 1956, Chicago IL), American politician (Democrat); governor of Illinois, 2003–09; he was impeached on corruption allegations that included the attempted sale of US Pres. Barack Obama's vacated Senate seat.

Dennis C(utler) Blair (4 Feb 1947, Kittery ME), American military official; US director of national intelligence from 2009.

Tony Blair (Anthony Charles Lynton Blair; 6 May 1953, Edinburgh, Scotland), British politician (Labour); prime minister of the UK, 1997–2007, and special envoy to the Middle East thereafter.

Cate Blanchett (Catherine Elise Blanchett; 14 May 1969, Melbourne, VIC, Australia), Australian film actress.

Kathleen Babineaux Blanco (15 Dec 1942, Coteau LA), American politician (Democrat); governor of Louisiana, 2004–08.

Mary J. Blige (11 Jan 1971, New York NY), American hip-hop soul singer.

Amy Bloom (1953, New York NY), American writer.

Harold (Irving) Bloom (11 Jul 1930, New York NY), American literary critic.

Orlando Bloom (13 Jan 1977, Canterbury, Kent, England), British film actor.

Michael R. Bloomberg (14 Feb 1942, Medford MA), American businessman, philanthropist, and politician (independent); mayor of New York City from 2002.

Matt(hew Roy) Blunt (20 Nov 1970, Springfield MO), American politician (Republican); governor of Missouri, 2005–08.

Emil Boc (6 Sep 1966, Rachitele, Romania), Romanian politician; prime minister from 2008.

Andrea Bocelli (22 Sep 1958, Lajatico, Italy), Italian operatic tenor, blind from childhood.

Samuel (Wright) Bodman (26 Nov 1938, Chicago IL), American chemical engineer, corporate leader, and official; US secretary of energy, 2005–09.

Charles F(rank) Bolden, Jr. (19 Aug 1946, Columbia SC), American astronaut; administrator of NASA from 2009.

Haji Hassanal Bolkiah Mu'izzadin Waddaulah (15 Jul 1946, Brunei Town [now Bandar Seri Begawan], Brunei), Bruneian royal; sultan from 1967.

Usain Bolt (21 Aug 1986, Montego Bay, Jamaica), Jamaican sprinter.

Barry (Lamar) Bonds (24 Jul 1964, Riverside CA), American baseball player who broke the all-time home run record in 2007.

(Thomas) Yayi Boni (1952, Tchaourou, French Dahomey [now Benin]), Beninese politician (independent); president from 2006.

Jon Bon Jovi (John Francis Bongiovi, Jr.; 2 Mar 1962, Perth Amboy NJ), American rock singer, musician, and songwriter.

Bono (Paul David Hewson; also known as Bono Vox; 10 May 1960, Dublin, Ireland), Irish rock vocalist (for U2) as well as a human rights activist and mediator.

Umberto Bossi (19 Sep 1941, Cassano Magnano, Italy), Italian politician and leader of the separatist Northern League from 1991.

Kate Bosworth (Catherine Anne Bosworth; 2 Jan 1983, Los Angeles CA), American film and TV actress.

Bouasone Bouphavanh (3 Jun 1954, Ban Tao Poun, Salavan province, French Indochina [now in Laos]), Laotian politician and prime minister from 2006.

Anthony (Michael) Bourdain (25 Jun 1956, New York NY), American chef, author, and TV personality.

Abdelaziz Bouteflika (2 Mar 1937, Tlemcen, Algeria), Algerian politician, diplomat, and president from 1999.

Danny Boyle (20 Oct 1956, Manchester, England), British film director.

T. Coraghessan Boyle (Thomas John Boyle; 2 Dec 1948, Peekskill NY), American author.

François Bozizé (14 Oct 1946, Mouila, French Equatorial Africa [now in Gabon]), Central African Republic politician; president from 2003.

Tom Brady (Thomas Brady; 3 Aug 1977, San Mateo CA), American professional football quarterback.

Zach(ary Israel) Braff (6 Apr 1975, South Orange NJ), American TV and film actor.

Lakhdar Brahimi (1 Jan 1934, Algeria), Algerian statesman, diplomat, and international official.

Serge Brammertz (17 Feb 1962, Eupen, Belgium), Belgian jurist; deputy prosecutor for the International Criminal Court, 2003–07, and prosecutor for the International Tribunal for the Former Yugoslavia from 2008.

Russell Brand (4 Jun 1975, Grays, Essex, England), British comedian and actor.

Richard (Charles Nicholas) Branson (18 Jul 1950, Shamley Green, Surrey, England), British entrepreneur who founded the Virgin empire in 1973.

Anthony Braxton (4 Jun 1945, Chicago IL), American avant-garde reed player and composer.

Phil(ip Norman) Bredesen (21 Nov 1943, Oceanport NJ), American politician (Democrat); governor of Tennessee from 2003.

Abigail (Kathleen) Breslin (14 Apr 1996, New York NY), American child actress.

Thierry Breton (15 Jan 1955, Paris, France), French businessman and politician; executive chairman of France Télécom, 2002–05, and French economic minister, 2005–07.

Jan(ice K.) Brewer (26 Sep 1944, Hollywood CA), American politician (Republican), governor of Arizona from 2009.

Stephen (Gerald) Breyer (15 Aug 1938, San Francisco CA), American jurist; associate justice of the US Supreme Court from 1994.

Sergey (Mikhaylovich) Brin (21 Aug 1973, Moscow, USSR [now in Russia]), Russian-born computer scientist and Internet entrepreneur who cofounded (1998) the Google Internet search engine.

Matthew Broderick (21 Mar 1962, New York NY), American actor.

Martin Brodeur (6 May 1972, Montreal, QC, Canada), French Canadian ice-hockey player; in 2009 he became the all-time winningest goalie in the National Hockey League.

Wallace S. Broecker (29 Nov 1931, Chicago IL), American geochemist, a specialist in climate change; recipient of a National Medal of Science in 1996 and a Craford Prize in 2006.

Josh (J.) Brolin (12 Feb 1968, Los Angeles CA), American film and TV actor.

Kix Brooks (Leon Eric Brooks; 12 May 1955, Shreveport LA), American country-and-western singer (for Brooks & Dunn).

(Troyal) Garth Brooks (7 Feb 1962, Tulsa OK), American country-and-western singer.

Pierce (Brendan) Brosnan (16 May 1953, Navan, County Meath, Ireland), Irish actor.

Dan Brown (22 Jun 1964, Exeter NH), American novelist.

Ewart (Frederick) Brown, Jr. (1946, Bermuda), Bermudan politician; prime minister from 2006.

(James) Gordon Brown (20 Feb 1951, Glasgow, Scotland), Scottish-born politician (Labour); chancellor of the Exchequer, 1997–2007, and prime minister from 2007.

Jerry Bruckheimer (21 Sep 1945, Detroit MI), American film and TV producer.

Kobe Bryant (23 Aug 1978, Philadelphia PA), American basketball player.

Quentin Bryce (1942, Brisbane, QLD, Australia), Australian politician; governor-general of Australia from 2008.

Bill Bryson (1951, Des Moines IA), American-born journalist and travel writer.

Michael Bublé (9 Sep 1975, Burnaby, BC, Canada), Canadian pop singer.

Patrick J(oseph) Buchanan (2 Nov 1938, Washington DC), American conservative journalist.

Christopher (Taylor) Buckley (1952, New York NY), American satiric novelist and magazine editor.

Mark (Anthony) Buehrle (23 Mar 1979, St. Charles MO), American professional baseball starting pitcher; he pitched a perfect game for the Chicago White Sox in July 2009, only the 18th player in MLB history to do so.

Warren (Edward) Buffett (30 Aug 1930, Omaha NE), American investor; CEO of Berkshire Hathaway Inc. from 1965; named the world's richest person by *Forbes* in 2008.

Sandra (Annette) Bullock (26 Jul 1964, Arlington VA), American film actress.

Gisele (Caroline Nonnenmacher) Bündchen (20 Jul 1980, Horizontina, Rio Grande do Sul state, Brazil), Brazilian fashion model.

Daniel Buren (25 Mar 1938, Paris, France), French conceptual artist; recipient of a 2007 Praemium Imperiale.

Mark Burnett (17 Jul 1960, Myland, East London, England), English-born American reality-TV-show producer.

Ken(neth Lauren) Burns (29 Jul 1953, Brooklyn NY), American documentary filmmaker.

Tim(othy William) Burton (25 Aug 1958, Burbank CA), American film director and writer.

Steve Buscemi (13 Dec 1957, Brooklyn NY), American film actor.

Barbara Bush (Barbara Pierce; 8 Jun 1925, Rye NY), American first lady; wife of US Pres. George W. Bush (married 6 Jan 1945).

George H(erbert) W(alker) Bush (12 Jun 1924, Milton MA), American statesman; vice president of the US, 1981–89, and 41st president, 1989–93; father of US Pres. George W. Bush.

George W(alker) Bush (6 Jul 1946, New Haven CT), American politician (Republican); 43rd president of the US, 2001–09; son of US Pres. George H.W. Bush.

Laura Bush (Laura Lane Welch; 4 Nov 1946, Midland TX), American first lady; wife of US Pres. George W. Bush (married 5 Nov 1977).

Mangosuthu Gatsha Buthelezi (27 Aug 1928, Mahlabatini, Natal, Union of South Africa [now KwaZulu Natal province, South Africa]), South African Zulu chief, the founder (1975) and leader of the Inkatha Freedom Party.

Gerard (James) Butler (13 Nov 1969, Glasgow, Scotland), British actor.

A.S. Byatt (Antonia Susan Drabble; 24 Aug 1936, Sheffield, England), English literary critic and novelist.

Robert C(arlyle) Byrd (20 Nov 1917, North Wilkesboro NC), American politician (Democrat); senator from West Virginia from 1959 and president pro tempore of the Senate from 2007.

(Mary) Rose Byrne (24 Jul 1979, Balmain, Sydney, NSW, Australia), Australian actress.

Nicolas Cage (Nicholas Kim Coppola; 7 Jan 1964, Long Beach CA), American film actor.

Cai Guo Qiang (8 Dec 1957, Quanzhou, Fujian province, China), Chinese installation artist.

Michael Caine (Maurice Joseph Micklewhite, Jr.; 14 Mar 1933, London, England), British actor.

Santiago Calatrava (28 Jul 1951, Valencia, Spain), Spanish architect.

Felipe (de Jesús) Calderón (Hinojosa) (18 Aug 1962, Morelia, Michoacán state, Mexico), Mexican politician (National Action Party); president from 2006.

Felix Perez Camacho (30 Oct 1957, Camp Zama, Japan), Guamanian politician (Republican); governor of Guam from 2003.

Moussa Dadis Camara (1964, Koure, Guinea), Guinean military leader, president from 2008.

David (William Donald) Cameron (9 Oct 1966, London, England), British politician; leader of the Conservative Party from 2005.

Camilla (Camilla Parker Bowles; Camilla Shand; 17 Jul 1947, London, England), British duchess of Cornwall and celebrity; wife of Charles, prince of Wales (married 9 Apr 2005).

Louis C. Camilleri (1955, Alexandria, Egypt), American corporate executive; chairman and CEO of Philip Morris International from 2008.

Gordon Campbell (12 Jan 1948, Vancouver, BC, Canada), Canadian politician (Liberal); premier of British Columbia from 2001.

John D. Campbell (8 Apr 1955, Ailsa Craig, ON, Canada), Canadian harness race driver; he was named 2006 Driver of the Year by the US Harness Writers Association.

Menzies Campbell (22 May 1941, Glasgow, Scotland), British politician; leader of the Liberal Democratic Party, 2006–07.

Naomi Campbell (22 May 1970, London, England), British runway and photographic model.

Fabio Cannavaro (13 Sep 1973, Naples, Italy), Italian association football (soccer) player.

Don(ald L.) Carcieri (16 Dec 1942, East Greenwich RI), American banker and politician (Republican); governor of Rhode Island from 2003.

Drew (Allison) Carey (23 May 1958, Cleveland OH), American comic TV actor and game-show host.

Mariah Carey (27 Mar 1970, Huntington, Long Island, NY), American pop singer.

Peter (Philip) Carey (7 May 1943, Bacchus Marsh, VIC, Australia), Australian author.

Carl XVI Gustaf (Carl Gustaf Folke Hubertus; 30 Apr 1946, Stockholm, Sweden), Swedish royal; king from 1973.

Lennart (Axel Edvard) Carleson (18 Mar 1928, Stockholm, Sweden), Swedish mathematician; recipient of the 2006 Abel Prize.

Robert A. Caro (30 Oct 1935, New York NY), American biographer.

Caroline (Caroline Louise Margaret Grimaldi; 23 Jan 1957, Monte Carlo, Monaco), Monegasque princess, the elder daughter of Prince Rainier III and Princess Grace.

Alain (Frédéric) Carpentier (11 Aug 1933, Toulouse, France), French cardiovascular surgeon; recipient of a 2007 Lasker Medical Prize.

Steve(n John) Carrell (16 Aug 1962, Concord MA), American comic actor.

Jim Carrey (James Eugene Carrey; 17 Jan 1962, Newmarket, ON, Canada), Canadian-born American comic actor.

Edwin W. Carrington (1938, Tobago, British West Indies [now in Trinidad and Tobago]), Trinidadian international official; secretary-general of the Caribbean Community (CARICOM) from 1992.

Jimmy Carter (James Earl Carter, Jr.; 1 Oct 1924, Plains GA), American statesman; 39th president of the US, 1977–81, and recipient of the 2002 Nobel Peace Prize.

Marsh(all N.) Carter (1940, Washington DC?), American corporate executive; chairman of the New York Stock Exchange from 2005.

David Caruso (7 Jan 1956, Forest Hills NY), American actor.

James Carville, Jr. (25 Oct 1944, Carville LA), American political strategist and commentator.

George W. Casey, Jr. (22 Jul 1948, Sendai, Japan), American military officer; chief of staff of the US Army from 2007.

Fidel (Alejandro) Castro (Ruz) (13 Aug 1926, near Birán, Holguín province, Cuba), Cuban revolutionary; leader of Cuba, 1959–2008; he became a symbol of communist revolution in Latin America.

Raúl (Modesto) Castro (Ruz) (3 Jun 1931, near Birán, Holguín province, Cuba), Cuban revolutionary leader and politician; acting president of Cuba from 2006, following the illness of his brother Fidel, and president from 2008.

Helio Castroneves (10 May 1975, São Paulo, Brazil), Brazilian race-car driver.

Kim Cattrall (21 Aug 1956, Liverpool, England), British-born film and TV actress.

Aníbal (António) Cavaco Silva (15 Jul 1939, Boliqueime, Algarve, Portugal), Portuguese politician; prime minister, 1985–95, and president from 2006.

Roberto Cavalli (15 Nov 1940, Florence, Italy), Italian fashion designer.

Michael Cera (7 Jun 1988, Brampton, ON, Canada), Canadian actor.

Vinton G(ray) Cerf (23 Jun 1943, New Haven CT), American computer scientist known as the "father of the Internet"; recipient of a Japan Prize in 2008.

Michael Chabon (24 May 1963, Washington DC), American novelist and short-story writer.

Riccardo Chailly (20 Feb 1953, Milan, Italy), Italian orchestra conductor; music director of the Leipzig Opera, 2005–08, and Leipzig's Gewandhaus Orchestra from 2005.

Martin Chalfie (15? Jan 1947, Chicago IL), American chemist; corecipient of the 2008 Nobel Prize for Chemistry.

John T. Chambers (23 Aug 1949, Cleveland OH), American corporate executive; president and CEO of Cisco Systems, Inc., from 1997.

Jackie Chan (Chan Kwong-Sang; 7 Apr 1954, Hong Kong), Chinese actor and director of martial arts films.

Margaret Chan (1947, Hong Kong), Hong Kong–born public health officer; director general of the World Health Organization from 2006.

Elaine L. Chao (26 Mar 1953, Taipei, Taiwan), American government official; secretary of labor, 2001–09.

Manu Chao (José-Manuel Thomas Arthur Chao; 21 Jun 1961, Paris, France), French-born Spanish rock musician.

Dave Chappelle (David Chappelle; 24 Aug 1973, Washington DC), American film and TV comedian and actor.

Jean Charest (John James Charest; 24 Jun 1958, Sherbrooke, QC, Canada), French Canadian politician; leader of the Quebec Liberal Party from 1998 and premier of Quebec from 2003.

Charles (Charles Philip Arthur George Mountbatten-Windsor; 14 Nov 1948, Buckingham Palace, London, England), British prince of Wales; the eldest son of Queen Elizabeth II and Prince Philip, duke of Edinburgh; and heir apparent to the throne.

David Chase (David DeCesare; 22 Aug 1945, Mount Vernon NY), American TV writer, producer, and director.

Hugo Chávez (Frías) (28 Jul 1954, Sabaneta, Venezuela), Venezuelan military leader and politician; president of Venezuela from 1999.

Don Cheadle (29 Nov 1964, Kansas City MO), American film and TV actor.

Chen Shui-bian (Ch'en Shui-pian; 18 Feb 1951, Hsichuang village, Tainan county, Taiwan), Taiwanese politician and president, 2000–08.

Dick Cheney (Richard Bruce Cheney; 30 Jan 1941, Lincoln NE), American politician (Republican); US secretary of defense, 1989–93, and vice president, 2001–09.

Michael Chertoff (28 Nov 1953, Elizabeth NJ), American attorney; secretary of homeland security, 2005–09.

Robert Kipkoech Cheruiyot (26 Sep 1978, Eldoret, Kenya), Kenyan long-distance runner.

Kenny Chesney (26 Mar 1968, Luttrell TN), American country-and-western singer.

Judy Chicago (Judy Cohen; 20 Jul 1939, Chicago IL), American artist.

Dale Chihuly (20 Sep 1941, Tacoma WA), American glass artist.

Fujio Cho (1937, Tokyo, Japan), Japanese corporate executive; chairman of Toyota Motor Corp. from 2005.

Deepak Chopra (22 Oct 1946, New Delhi, British India), Indian-born American endocrinologist, alternative-medicine advocate, and best-selling author.

Choummaly Sayasone (6 Mar 1936, Attapu province, French Indochina [now in Laos]), Laotian political official; general secretary of the Lao People's Revolutionary Party from 2006, and president from 2006.

Chow Yun-Fat (Zhou Runfa; 18 May 1955, Lamma Island, Hong Kong), Hong Kong actor.

Julie (Frances) Christie (14 Apr 1941, Chukua, Assam, British India), British film actress.

Dimitris Christofias (29 Aug 1946, Kato Dhikomo, British Cyprus), Cypriot politician; president of Cyprus from 2008.

Steven Chu (28 Feb 1948, St. Louis MO), American physicist; corecipient of the 1997 Nobel Prize for Physics; US secretary of energy from 2009.

Ralph J(ohn) Cicerone (2 May 1943, New Castle PA), American electrical engineer and atmospheric scientist; president of the National Academy of Sciences from 2005.

Sandra Cisneros (20 Dec 1954, Chicago IL), American short-story writer and poet.

Tom Clancy (Thomas L. Clancy, Jr.; 12 Apr 1947, Baltimore MD), American best-selling novelist.

Eric Clapton (Eric Patrick Clapp; 30 Mar 1945, Ripley, Surrey, England), British guitarist, singer, and songwriter.

Helen Clark (26 Feb 1950, Hamilton, New Zealand), New Zealand politician (Labour); prime minister, 1999-2008.

Kelly Clarkson (24 Apr 1982, Burleson TX), American pop singer.

Patricia (Davies) Clarkson (29 Dec 1959, New Orleans LA), American stage, film, and TV actress.

John (Marwood) Cleese (27 Oct 1939, Weston-super-Mare, England), British comic actor.

Nick Clegg (Nicholas William Peter Clegg; 7 Jan 1967, Chalfont St. Giles, Buckinghamshire, England), British politician and MP; leader of the Liberal Democrats from 2007.

Van Cliburn (Harvey Lavan Cliburn, Jr.; 12 Jul 1934, Shreveport LA), American pianist.

Lucille Clifton (27 Jun 1936, Depew NY), American poet; recipient of the 2007 Ruth Lilly Poetry Prize.

Bill Clinton (William Jefferson Blythe III; 19 Aug 1946, Hope AR), American statesman; 42nd president of the US, 1993-2001.

Hillary Rodham Clinton (Hillary Diane Rodham; 26 Oct 1947, Chicago IL), American politician (Democrat); senator from New York, 2001-09, unsuccessful candidate for president in 2008, and US secretary of state from 2009; wife of US Pres. Bill Clinton.

George Clooney (6 May 1961, Lexington KY), American film and TV actor.

Chuck Close (Charles Thomas Close; 5 Jul 1940, Monroe WA), American Photo-realist painter.

Glenn Close (19 Mar 1947, Greenwich CT), American actress.

G(erald) Wayne Clough (24 Sep 1941, Douglas GA), American educator and executive; secretary of the Smithsonian Institution from 2008.

Diablo Cody (Brooke Busey; 14 Jun 1978, Chicago IL), American stripper-turned-writer; author of the screenplay for the film *Juno* (2007).

Paulo Coelho (24 Aug 1947, Rio de Janeiro, Brazil), Brazilian novelist.

Ethan Coen (21 Sep 1958, St. Louis Park MN), American filmmaker.

Joel Coen (29 Nov 1955, St. Louis Park MN), American filmmaker.

J(ohn) M(axwell) Coetzee (9 Feb 1940, Cape Town, Union of South Africa), South African novelist and critic; recipient of the 2003 Nobel Prize for Literature.

Leonard Cohen (21 Sep 1934, Montreal, QC, Canada), Canadian singer and songwriter.

Stephen Colbert (13 May 1964, Charleston SC), American TV commentator and satirist; host of *The Colbert Report* from 2005.

Ornette Coleman (9 Mar 1930, Fort Worth TX), American jazz saxophonist, composer, and bandleader; his *Sound Grammar* won the 2007 Pulitzer Prize for music.

Pierluigi Collina (13 Feb 1960, Bologna, Italy), Italian association football (soccer) referee.

Billy Collins (1941, New York NY), American poet; poet laureate of the US, 2001-03.

Francis S. Collins (14 Apr 1950, Staunton VA), American physician, geneticist, and medical administrator; director of the National Institutes of Health from 2009.

Marva Collins (Marva Delores Knight; 31 Aug 1936, Monroeville AL), American educator.

Alan Colmes (24 Sep 1950, Long Island NY), American liberal journalist and commentator on radio and TV.

Álvaro Colom (Caballeros) (15 Jun 1951, Guatemala City, Guatemala), Guatemalan politician (National Union for Hope); president from 2008.

Sean Combs ("Puffy"; Puff Daddy; P. Diddy; Diddy; 4 Nov 1970, Harlem, New York NY), American rap artist, impresario, fashion mogul, and actor.

Common (Lonnie Rashid Lynn, Jr.; Common Sense; 13 Mar 1972, Chicago IL), American hip-hop artist and actor.

Blaise Compaoré (1951, Ziniane, Upper Volta [now Burkina Faso]), Burkinabe politician; president of Burkina Faso from 1987.

Jennifer Connelly (12 Dec 1970, Round Top NY), American fashion model and film actress.

(Thomas) Sean Connery (25 Aug 1930, Edinburgh, Scotland), Scottish film actor.

Alberto Contador (6 Dec 1982, Pinto, Spain), Spanish cyclist; winner of the 2007 and 2009 Tours de France.

James T. Conway (26 Dec 1947, Walnut Ridge AR), American military officer; commandant of the US Marine Corps from 2006.

Dane (Jeffrey) Cook (18 Mar 1972, Boston MA), American comedian and actor.

Anderson (Hays) Cooper (3 Jun 1967, New York NY), American TV journalist.

Bradley Cooper (5 Jan 1975, Philadephia PA), American TV and film actor.

Chris(topher W.) Cooper (9 Jul 1951, Kansas City MO), American film and TV actor.

Cynthia Cooper (14 Apr 1963, Chicago IL), American basketball player and coach.

Francis Ford Coppola (7 Apr 1939, Detroit MI), American film director, writer, and producer.

Sofia Coppola (14 May 1971, New York NY), American film director, writer, actress, and designer; daughter of director Francis Ford Coppola.

Chick Corea (Armando Anthony Corea; 12 Jun 1941, Chelsea MA), American jazz pianist, composer, and bandleader.

Patricia Cornwell (Patricia Daniels; 9 Jun 1956, Miami FL), American author of mystery novels.

Rafael (Vicente) Correa (Delgado) (6 Apr 1963, Guayaquil, Ecuador), Ecuadorian politician; president from 2007.

Carlos Correia (6 Nov 1933, Bissau, Portuguese Guinea [now Guinea-Bissau]), Guinea-Bissauan politician; prime minister, 2008-09.

Jon (Stevens) Corzine (1 Jan 1947, Willey's Station IL), American politician (Democrat); senator from New Jersey, 2001-06, and governor from 2006.

Bill Cosby (William Henry Cosby, Jr.; 12 Jul 1937, Philadelphia PA), American comedian and actor.

Bob Costas (Robert Quinlan Costas; 22 Mar 1952, New York NY), American TV sportscaster and host.

Kevin (Michael) Costner (18 Jan 1955, Lynwood CA), American film actor and director.

Marion Cotillard (30 Sep 1975, Paris, France), French actress.

Pascal Couchepin (5 Apr 1942, Martigny, Switzerland), Swiss politician; president, 2003, and 2008–09.

Tom Coughlin (Thomas Richard Coughlin; 31 Aug 1946, Waterloo NY), American football coach.

David Coulthard (27 Mar 1971, Twynholm, Scotland), British Formula 1 race-car driver.

Katie Couric (7 Jan 1957, Arlington VA), American TV talk-show host and news anchor.

Simon (Phillip) Cowell (7 Oct 1959, Brighton, East Sussex, England), British record producer and TV personality; a judge on the American Idol show (from 2002).

Brian Cowen (Irish: Brian Ó Comhain; 10 Jan 1960, Tullamore, County Offaly, Ireland), Irish politician (Fianna Fáil); prime minister from 2008.

Christopher Cox (16 Oct 1952, St. Paul MN), American politician (Republican); chairman of the US Securities and Exchange Commission, 2005–09.

Tony Cragg (1949, Liverpool, England), British sculptor and installation artist; recipient of a Praemium Imperiale in 2007.

Daniel (Wroughton) Craig (2 Mar 1968, Chester, Cheshire, England), British stage and movie actor who played James Bond in films from 2006.

Bryan Cranston (7 Mar 1956, San Fernando Valley, California), American actor.

Charlie Crist (Charles Joseph Crist, Jr.; 24 Jul 1956, Altoona PA), American politician (Republican); governor of Florida from 2007.

Stanley Crouch (14 Dec 1945, Los Angeles CA), American journalist and critic.

Sheryl Crow (11 Feb 1962, Kennett MO), American singer-songwriter.

Russell (Ira) Crowe (7 Apr 1964, Wellington, New Zealand), New Zealand–born Australian film actor.

Tom Cruise (Thomas Cruise Mapother IV; 3 Jul 1962, Syracuse NY), American actor.

Gastão Cruz (20 Jul 1941, Faro, Portugal), Portuguese poet and literary critic.

Nilo Cruz (1962?, Matanzas, Cuba), Cuban-born American playwright.

Penélope Cruz (Sánchez) (28 Apr 1974, Madrid, Spain), Spanish film actress.

Branko Crvenkovski (12 Oct 1962, Sarajevo, Yugoslavia [now in Bosnia and Herzegovina]), Macedonian politician; prime minister, 1992–98 and 2002–04, and president, 2004–09.

Jamie Cullum (20 Aug 1979, Essex, England), British pop, jazz, and rock pianist and vocalist.

Chet Culver (Chester John Culver; 25 Jan 1966, Washington DC), American politician (Democrat); governor of Iowa from 2007.

Joan Cusack (11 Oct 1962, New York NY), American film and TV actress.

John (Paul) Cusack (28 Jun 1966, Evanston IL), American film actor.

Mirko Cvetkovic (16 Aug 1950, Zajecar, Yugoslavia [now in Serbia]), Serbian politician; prime minister from 2008.

Miley (Ray) Cyrus (Destiny Hope Cyrus; 23 Nov 1992, Franklin TN), American TV (Hannah Montana) and film actress and singer.

Dalai Lama (the 14th Dalai Lama, Tenzin Gyatso; original name Lhamo Dhondrub; 6 Jul 1935, Takster, Amdo province, Tibet [now Tsinghai province, China]), Tibetan spiritual leader (enthroned in 1940) and ruler-in-exile; head of the Tibetan Buddhists; recipient of the 1989 Nobel Peace Prize.

Richard M(ichael) Daley (24 Apr 1942, Chicago IL), American politician (Democrat); mayor of Chicago from 1989.

Matt(hew Page) Damon (8 Oct 1970, Cambridge MA), American film actor.

Claire (Catherine) Danes (12 Apr 1979, New York NY), American actress.

Mitch(ell Elais) Daniels, Jr. (7 Apr 1949, Monongahela PA), American businessman and politician (Republican); director of the US Office of Management and Budget, 2001–03, and governor of Indiana from 2005.

Edwidge Danticat (19 Jan 1969, Port-au-Prince, Haiti), Haitian-born American author.

Larry David (2 Jul 1947, Brooklyn NY), American actor and writer.

Mario Davidovsky (4 Mar 1934, Médanos, Buenos Aires, Argentina), Argentine-born American composer of electronic and electroacoustic works.

Terry Davis (Terence Anthony Gordon Davis; 5 Jan 1938, Stourbridge, West Midlands, England), British politician (Labour) and international executive; secretary-general of the Council of Europe from 2004.

Patrick Day (13 Oct 1953, Brush CO), American jockey.

Daniel (Michael Blake) Day-Lewis (29 Apr 1957, London, England), British film actor.

Jaap de Hoop Scheffer (Jakob Gijsbert de Hoop Scheffer; 3 Apr 1948, Amsterdam, Netherlands), Dutch international official; secretary-general of NATO, 2004–09.

Danielle de Niese (1980, Melbourne, VIC, Australia), Australian-born American operatic soprano.

Robert De Niro (17 Aug 1943, New York NY), American film actor.

Howard (Brush) Dean III (17 Nov 1948, New York NY), American physician and politician (Democrat); governor of Vermont, 1991–2003, and chairman of the Democratic National Committee, 2005–09.

Idriss Déby Itno (1952, Fada, Chad, French Equatorial Africa [now in Chad]), Chadian politician; president from 1990.

Ellen DeGeneres (26 Jan 1958, Metairie LA), American comedian and TV personality.

John P. deJongh, Jr. (13 Nov 1957, St. Thomas, US Virgin Islands), Virgin Islander politician (Democrat); governor of the US Virgin Islands from 2007.

Benicio Del Toro (19 Feb 1967, San Turce, Puerto Rico), American film actor.

Bertrand Delanoë (30 May 1950, Tunis, French Tunisia), French politician (Socialist); mayor of Paris from 2001.

Don DeLillo (20 Nov 1936, New York NY), American postmodernist novelist.

Michael S. Dell (23 Feb 1965, Houston TX), American businessman; founder of Dell Computer Corp. and its CEO, 1984–2004 and again from 2007.

Yelena (Vyacheslavovna) Dementyeva (15 Oct 1981, Moscow, USSR [now in Russia]), Russian tennis player.

Patrick Dempsey (13 Jan 1966, Lewiston ME), American film and TV actor.

Judi Dench (Judith Olivia Dench; 9 Dec 1934, York, England), British stage, TV, and film actress.

Carl Dennis (17 Sep 1939, St. Louis MO), American poet.

Nick Denton (24 Aug 1966, Hampstead, London, England), British founder of Gawker Media.

Johnny Depp (John Christopher Depp II; 9 Jun 1963, Owensboro KY), American film actor.

Kiran Desai (3 Sep 1971, New Delhi, India), Indian-born American novelist; her *The Inheritance of Loss* won the 2006 Booker Prize.

Bernard d'Espagnat (22 Aug 1921, Fourmagnac, France), French physicist and philosopher of science; recipient of the 2009 Templeton Prize.

Frankie Dettori (Lanfranco Dettori; 15 Dec 1970, Milan, Italy), Italian-born English jockey.

Darrell Dexter (10 Sep 1957, Halifax, NS, Canada), Canadian politician (Nova Scotia New Democratic Party); premier of Nova Scotia from 2009.

Cameron (Michelle) Diaz (30 Aug 1972, San Diego CA), American model and actress.

Junot Díaz (31 Dec 1968, Santo Domingo, Dominican Republic), Dominican-born American writer; his novel *The Brief Wondrous Life of Oscar Wao* won the 2008 Pulitzer Prize for fiction.

Kate DiCamillo (25 Mar 1965, Philadelphia PA), American author of children's books.

Leonardo (Wilhelm) DiCaprio (11 Nov 1974, Los Angeles CA), American film actor.

Joan Didion (5 Dec 1934, Sacramento CA), American author and journalist.

Vin Diesel (Mark Vincent; 18 Jul 1967, New York NY), American film actor.

Matt Dillon (18 Feb 1964, New Rochelle NY), American film actor.

Jamie Dimon (James Dimon; 13 Mar 1956, New York NY), American executive; president (from 2004) and CEO (from 2005) of JPMorgan Chase & Co.

Fatou Diome (1968, Niodior island, Senegal), Senegalese French-language novelist.

Céline Dion (30 Mar 1968, Charlemagne, QC, Canada), French Canadian pop singer.

Stéphane Dion (28 Sep 1955, Quebec city, QC, Canada), Canadian politician; leader of the Liberal Party of Canada from 2007.

El Hadj Diouf (15 Jan 1981, Dakar, Senegal), Senegalese association football (soccer) star for French clubs and for the Senegalese national team.

Jacques Diouf (1 Aug 1938, Saint-Louis, French West Africa [now in Senegal]), Senegalese international official; director general of the Food and Agriculture Organization of the UN from 1994.

Milo Djukanovic (15 Feb 1962, Niksic, Yugoslavia [now in Montenegro]), Montenegrin politician; president of Montenegro, 1998–2002, and prime minister, 2003–06 and again from 2008.

Lou Dobbs (24 Sep 1945, Childress TX), American business journalist and TV anchorman.

E(dgar) L(aurence) Doctorow (6 Jan 1931, New York NY), American novelist.

Christopher J(ohn) Dodd (27 May 1944, Willimantic CT), American politician (Democrat); senator from Connecticut from 1981.

Gary Doer (31 Mar 1948, Winnipeg, MB, Canada), Canadian politician (New Democratic Party); premier of Manitoba from 1999.

Timothy M(ichael) Dolan (6 Feb 1950, St. Louis MO), American Roman Catholic church leader; archbishop of New York from 2009.

Domenico Dolce (13 Aug 1958, Polizzi Generosa, near Palermo, Italy), Italian fashion designer and partner of Stefano Gabbana.

Valdis Dombrovskis (5 Aug 1971, Riga, Latvia), Latvian politician; prime minister of Latvia from 2009.

Plácido Domingo (21 Jan 1941, Madrid, Spain), Spanish-born Mexican operatic tenor.

John (Joseph) Donahoe II (1960, US?), American executive; president and CEO of eBay from 2008.

Vincent (Phillip) D'Onofrio (30 Jul 1959, Brooklyn NY), American TV and film actor.

Shaun Donovan (24 Jan 1966, New York NY), American architect and government official; US secretary of housing and urban development from 2009.

Jack Dorsey (4 Apr 1977, St. Louis MO), American entrepreneur; cofounder of Twitter.

José Eduardo dos Santos (28 Aug 1942, Luanda, Portuguese Angola), Angolan statesman and president from 1979.

Denzil L. Douglas (14 Jan 1953, St. Paul's, Saint Kitts, British West Indies [now in Saint Kitts and Nevis]), West Indian politician; prime minister of Saint Kitts and Nevis from 1995.

James H. Douglas (21 Jun 1951, Springfield MA), American politician (Republican); governor of Vermont from 2003.

Michael Douglas (25 Sep 1944, New Brunswick NJ), American film actor and producer.

Rita (Frances) Dove (28 Aug 1952, Akron OH), American writer and teacher; poet laureate of the US, 1993–95.

Maureen Dowd (14 Jan 1952, Washington DC), American journalist and op-ed columnist for the *New York Times*.

Robert Downey, Jr. (4 Apr 1965, New York NY), American actor.

Jim Doyle (James Edward Doyle; 23 Nov 1945, Washington DC), American politician (Democrat); governor of Wisconsin from 2003.

Dr. Dre (Andre Young; 18 Feb 1965, Los Angeles CA), American rap musician and impresario, considered a pioneer of gangsta rap.

Stacy Dragila (Stacy Mikaelson; 25 Mar 1971, Auburn CA), American pole vaulter.

Deborah Drattell (1956, Brooklyn NY), American composer of operas.

Paquito D'Rivera (Francisco Dejesus Rivera; 4 Jun 1948, Havana, Cuba), Cuban-born American jazz reed player and Afro-Cuban bandleader.

Didier Drogba (11 Mar 1978, Abidjan, Côte d'Ivoire), Ivorian association football (soccer) player; he was voted African Footballer of the Year for 2006.

Matt Drudge (27 Oct 1967), American Internet journalist; editor of the Drudge Report.

Nicanor Duarte (Frutos) (11 Oct 1956, Coronel Oviedo, Paraguay), Paraguayan politician; president, 2003–08.

David (William) Duchovny (7 Aug 1960, New York NY), American TV and film actor.

Gustavo (Adolfo) Dudamel (Ramírez) (26 Jan 1981, Barquisimeto, Venezuela), Venezuelan conductor; music director of the Göteborg (Sweden) Symphony Orchestra from 2007 and the Los Angeles Philharmonic from 2009.

Hilary (Ann Lisa) Duff (28 Sep 1987, Houston TX), American TV and film actress and pop singer.

Carol Ann Duffy (23 Dec 1955, Glasgow, Scotland), British poet; first woman to serve as poet laureate of Britain, from 2009.

Mike Duke (Michael T. Duke), American corporate executive; president and CEO of Wal-Mart from 2009.

Sarah Dunant (8 Aug 1950, London, England), British crime and historical novelist, broadcaster, and critic.

Arne Duncan (6 Nov 1964, Chicago IL), American education administrator; US secretary of education from 2009.

Tim(othy Theodore) Duncan (25 Apr 1976, St. Croix, US Virgin Islands), American basketball player.

Ronnie Gene Dunn (1 Jun 1953, Coleman TX), American country-and-western singer (for Brooks & Dunn).

Kirsten (Caroline) Dunst (30 Apr 1982, Point Pleasant NJ), American film actress.

Ann E. Dunwoody (January 1953, Fort Belvoir VA), US general; first woman to reach (2008) four-star status in the US military.

Robert Duvall (5 Jan 1931, San Diego CA), American actor, producer, and screenwriter.

Bob Dylan (Robert Allen Zimmerman; 24 May 1941, Duluth MN), American singer and songwriter; he received a special citation from the Pulitzer Prize committee in 2008.

Esther Dyson (14 Jul 1951, Zürich, Switzerland), American economist and journalist specializing in computer and cyberspace issues.

Freeman (John) Dyson (15 Dec 1923, Crowthorne, Berkshire, England), British-born American physicist and educator; recipient of the 2000 Templeton Prize.

James Dyson (2 May 1947, Cromer, Norfolk, England), British inventor.

Steve Earle (Stephen Fain Earle; 17 Jan 1955, Fort Monroe VA), American country singer, guitarist, and songwriter.

(Ralph) Dale Earnhardt, Jr. (10 Oct 1974, Concord NC), American NASCAR race-car driver.

Michael F(rancis) Easley (23 Mar 1950, Nash county NC), American politician (Democrat); governor of North Carolina, 2001–09.

Clint(on) Eastwood, Jr. (31 May 1930, San Francisco CA), American film actor and moviemaker.

Martin Eberhard (15 May 1960, Berkeley CA), American entrepreneur and cofounder of Tesla Motors.

Roger Ebert (18 Jun 1942, Urbana IL), American film critic.

Marcelo (Luis) Ebrard (Casaubon) (10 Oct 1959, Mexico City, Mexico), Mexican politician (Party of the Democratic Revolution); head of government of the Federal District (mayor of Mexico City) from 2006.

Umberto Eco (5 Jan 1932, Alessandria, Italy), Italian literary critic, novelist, and semiotician.

Marian Wright Edelman (6 Jun 1939, Bennettsville SC), American attorney and civil rights advocate who founded the Children's Defense Fund.

Edward (Edward Anthony Richard Louis Mountbatten-Windsor; 10 Mar 1964, Buckingham Palace, London, England), British prince; third son of Queen Elizabeth II and Prince Philip, duke of Edinburgh; and earl of Wessex.

John Edwards (10 Jun 1953, Seneca SC), American politician (Democrat); senator from North Carolina, 1999–2005.

Tuiatua Tupua Tamasese Efi (1 Mar 1938, Samoa?), Samoan royal; O le Ao o le Malo (elective monarch) from 2007.

Zac Efron (18 Oct 1987, San Luis Obispo CA), American TV and film actor.

Edward Michael Cardinal Egan (2 Apr 1932, Oak Park IL), American Roman Catholic church leader; archbishop of New York, 2000–09, and cardinal from 2001.

Dave Eggers (8 Jan 1970, Chicago IL), American author, screenwriter, and graphic artist; founder and editor of *McSweeney's*, a journal and Web site, from 1998.

Michael D(ammann) Eisner (7 Mar 1942, Mount Kisco NY), American corporate executive; CEO and chairman of the Walt Disney Co., 1984–2004.

Hicham El Guerrouj (14 Sep 1974, Berkane, Morocco), Moroccan distance runner who set several world records.

Mohamed ElBaradei (Muhammad al-Baradei; 17 Jun 1942, Cairo, Egypt), Egyptian international official; director general of the International Atomic Energy Agency, 1997–2009.

Carmen Electra (Tara Leigh Patrick; 20 Apr 1972, Sharonville OH), American model, TV actress, and celebrity.

Olafur Eliasson (1967, Copenhagen, Denmark), Danish installation artist.

Elizabeth II (Elizabeth Alexandra Mary Windsor; 21 Apr 1926, London, England), British royal; queen of the United Kingdom of Great Britain and Northern Ireland from 1952.

George F(rancis) R(ayner) Ellis (11 Aug 1939, Johannesburg, Union of South Africa), South African applied mathematician and professor; recipient of the 2004 Templeton Prize.

Lawrence J(oseph) Ellison (17 Aug 1944, Chicago IL), American corporate executive; founder and CEO of Oracle Corp. from 1977.

James Ellroy (Lee Earle Ellroy; 4 Mar 1948, Los Angeles CA), American mystery writer.

Ernie Els (Theodore Ernest Els; 17 Oct 1969, Johannesburg, South Africa), South African golfer.

Rahm Emanuel (29 Nov 1959, Chicago IL), American politician (Democrat); congressman from Illinois, 2003–09, and White House chief of staff from 2009.

Eminem (Marshall Bruce Mathers III; 17 Oct 1973, St. Joseph MO), American hip-hop artist.

Emmanuel III Delly (Emmanuel-Karim Delly; 6 Oct 1927, Telkaif, Iraq), Iraqi churchman; patriarch of Babylonia and the Chaldeans (leader of the Chaldean Catholic Church) from 2003 and Roman Catholic cardinal from 2007.

Nambaryn Enhbayar (1 Jun 1958, Ulaanbaatar, Mongolia), Mongolian politician (People's Revolutionary Party); prime minister, 2000–04, and president of the Great Hural (parliament) from 2005.

Anne Enright (11 Oct 1962, Dublin, Ireland), Irish writer; her novel *The Gathering* was awarded the 2007 Man Booker Prize.

Enya (Eithne Ní Bhraonáin; 17 May 1961, Gweedore, County Donegal, Ireland), Irish New Age singer.

Recep Tayyip Erdogan (26 Feb 1954, Istanbul, Turkey), Turkish politician (Justice and Development Party); prime minister from 2003.

Patricia Espinosa Cantellano (21 Oct 1958, Mexico City, Mexico), Mexican diplomat and government official; secretary of foreign affairs from 2006.

Melissa Etheridge (29 May 1961, Leavenworth KS), American rock singer and songwriter.

Robin Eubanks (25 Oct 1955, Philadelphia PA), American jazz trombone player.

Richard D. Fairbank (18 Sep 1950, Menlo Park CA), American corporate executive; founder, chairman, and CEO of Capital One Financial Corp. from 1988.

Edie Falco (Edith Falco; 5 Jul 1963, Brooklyn NY), American film and TV actress.

Jimmy Fallon (James Thomas Fallon, Jr.; 19 Sep 1974, Brooklyn NY), American comedian and talk-show host.

(Hannah) Dakota Fanning (23 Feb 1994, Conyers GA), American child film actress.

Abdirahman Mohamed Farole (1945, Italian Somaliland [now in Somalia]), Somali politician; president of the secessionist republic of Puntland from 2009.

Louis (Abdul) Farrakhan (Louis Eugene Walcott; 11 May 1933, Bronx NY), American leader of the Nation of Islam (Black Muslims) from 1978.

Colin (James) Farrell (31 May 1976, Dublin, Ireland), Irish actor.

Suzanne Farrell (Roberta Sue Ficker; 16 Aug 1945, Cincinnati OH), American ballet dancer.

Justin Fatica (1980?, Erie PA), American Catholic youth evangelist; founder (2002) of the Hard as Nails Ministry to bring students to Christ.

Anthony S(tephen) Fauci (24 Dec 1940, Brooklyn NY), American public-health physician and AIDS researcher; director of the National Institute of Allergy and Infectious Diseases from 1984; recipient of a Lasker Medical Award in 2007.

(Catharine) Drew Gilpin Faust (18 Sep 1947, New York NY), American educator and historian; president of Harvard University from 2007.

Brett (Lorenzo) Favre (10 Oct 1969, Kiln MS), American pro football quarterback.

Salam Fayyad (1952, near Tulkarm, Jordan [West Bank]), Palestinian politician (Third Way); prime minister of the Palestinian Authority from 2007.

Roger Federer (8 Aug 1981, Basel, Switzerland), Swiss tennis player who has won the most Grand Slam tournaments in men's professional tennis history.

Russ(ell Dana) Feingold (2 Mar 1953, Janesville WI), American politician (Democrat); senator from Wisconsin from 1993.

Felipe (Felipe de Borbón y Grecia; 30 Jan 1968, Madrid, Spain), Spanish royal, prince of Asturias, and heir to the Spanish throne.

Eddie Fenech Adami (7 Feb 1934, Birkirkara, Malta), Maltese politician; prime minister, 1987–96 and 1998–2004, and president, 2004–09.

Dennis Fentie (8 Nov 1950, Edmonton, AB, Canada), Canadian businessman and politician (Yukon Party); premier of Yukon from 2002.

Craig Ferguson (17 May 1962, Glasgow, Scotland), British film and TV actor; host of TV's The Late Late Show from 2005.

Sarah (Margaret) Ferguson (15 Oct 1959, London, England), British celebrity; duchess of York after her marriage (23 Jul 1986) to Prince Andrew; they divorced in 1996.

Cristina (Elisabet) Fernández (Wilhelm) de Kirchner (19 Feb 1953, La Plata, Argentina), Argentine politician; president, following her husband, Néstor Kirchner, from 2007.

Leonel Fernández (Reyna) (26 Dec 1953, Santo Domingo, Dominican Republic), Dominican politician; president, 1996–2000 and again from 2004.

Gil de Ferran (11 Nov 1967, Paris, France), French-born Brazilian race-car driver.

(John) Will(iam) Ferrell (16 Jul 1967, Irvine CA), American comedian and actor.

America (Georgine) Ferrera (18 Apr 1984, Los Angeles CA), American film and TV actress.

Tina Fey (Elizabeth Stamatina Fey; 18 May 1970, Upper Darby PA), American comedian, writer, and actress.

Robert Fico (15 Sep 1964, Topolcany, Czechoslovakia [now in Slovakia]), Slovak politician (Social Democrat); prime minister from 2006.

Sally (Margaret) Field (6 Nov 1946, Pasadena CA), American comic and dramatic actress.

Ralph (Nathaniel) Fiennes (22 Dec 1962, Suffolk, England), British dramatic actor.

Harvey (Forbes) Fierstein (6 Jun 1954, Brooklyn NY), American playwright and actor.

François Fillon (4 Mar 1954, LeMans, France), French politician; prime minister from 2007.

David (Leo) Fincher (28 Aug 1962, Denver CO), American film director.

Harvey V. Fineberg (15 Sep 1945, Pittsburgh PA), American public-health physician and medical administrator; president of the Institute of Medicine from 2002.

Carly Fiorina (Cara Carleton Sneed; 6 Sep 1954, Austin TX), American corporate executive and political adviser; president and CEO of Hewlett-Packard, 1999–2005, and chairman, 2000–05.

Heinz Fischer (9 Oct 1938, Graz, Austria), Austrian politician (Social Democrat); president from 2004.

Jan Fischer (2 Jan 1951, Prague, Czechoslovakia [now in the Czech Republic]), Czech politician; prime minister from 2009.

Allison Fisher (24 Feb 1968, Cheshunt, Hertfordshire, England), British pocket-billiards champion.

Isla (Lang) Fisher (3 Feb 1976, Muscat, Oman), British film actress.

Benígno (Repeki) Fitial (27 Nov 1945, Saipan, Northern Mariana Islands), Northern Marianas politician (Covenant Party); governor of the Northern Mariana Islands from 2006.

Patrick Fitzgerald (22 Dec 1960, New York NY), American special prosecutor in a number of high-profile cases.

Tim Flannery (28 Jan 1956, Melbourne, VIC, Australia), Australian zoologist and environmentalist; he was named Australian of the Year for 2007.

Leon Fleisher (23 Jul 1928, San Francisco CA), American pianist; recipient of a 2007 Kennedy Center Honor.

Renée Fleming (14 Feb 1959, Indiana PA), American operatic soprano.

Juan Diego Flórez (13 Jan 1973, Lima, Peru), Peruvian bel canto tenor.

Carlisle Floyd (11 Jun 1926, Latta SC), American opera composer and librettist.

Ken Follett (pseudonyms Zachary Stone and Simon Myles; 5 Jun 1949, Cardiff, Wales), British author of political thrillers.

Phil Fontaine (Larry Phillip Fontaine; "Buddy"; 20 Sep 1944, Fort Alexander Reserve, MB, Canada), Canadian Ojibway First Nations activist; national chief of the Assembly of First Nations from 1997.

Harrison Ford (13 Jul 1942, Chicago IL), American film actor.

Richard Ford (16 Feb 1944, Jackson MS), American writer of novels and short stories.

Tom Ford (27 Aug 1961, Austin TX), American fashion designer.

William Clay Ford, Jr. (3 May 1957, Detroit MI), American businessman; executive chairman of Ford Motor Co. from 2006.

William Forsythe (1949, New York NY), American ballet dancer, choreographer, and director.

Luis G. Fortuño (31 Oct 1960, San Juan PR), Puerto Rican politician; governor of Puerto Rico from 2009.

Jodie Foster (Alicia Christian Foster; 19 Nov 1962, Los Angeles CA), American film actress.

Norman (Robert) Foster (1 Jun 1935, near Manchester, England), British architect; recipient of the 1999 Pritzker Prize and a 2002 Praemium Imperiale.

Megan (Denise) Fox (16 May 1986, Rockwood TN), American actress.

Jamie Foxx (Eric Bishop; 13 Dec 1967, Terrell TX), American actor and comedian.

Don Francisco (Mario Kreutzberger; 28 Dec 1940, Talca, Chile), Chilean-born American TV personality; host of the popular show *Sábado Gigante* on the Spanish-language Univision channel.

James (Edward) Franco (19 Apr 1978, Palo Alto CA), American actor.

Al Franken (21 May 1951, New York NY), American comedian, writer, and politician; senator from Minnesota from 2009.

Jonathan Franzen (17 Aug 1959, Western Springs IL), American author.

Frederik (Frederik André Henrik Christian; 26 May 1968, Copenhagen, Denmark), Danish crown prince.

Morgan Freeman (1 Jun 1937, Memphis TN), American theater and film actor.

Dawn French (11 Oct 1957, Holyhead, Wales), British actress, comedian, and writer.

Lucian Freud (8 Dec 1922, Berlin, Germany), German-born British painter.

Dave Freudenthal (David Duane Freudenthal; 12 Oct 1950, Thermopolis WY), American politician (Democrat); governor of Wyoming from 2003.

Saul Friedländer (11 Oct 1932, Prague, Czechoslovakia [now in the Czech Republic]), Czech-born French-Israeli historian and professor whose study *The Years of Extermination: Nazi Germany and the Jews, 1939–1945* won the 2008 Pulitzer Prize for general nonfiction.

Thomas L. Friedman (20 Jul 1953, Minneapolis MN), American journalist and author; foreign-affairs columnist for the *New York Times*.

Janus Friis (1976, Denmark), Danish Internet entrepreneur; codeveloper of Joost, a popular program for receiving TV broadcasts on a personal computer.

Takeo Fukui (28 Nov 1944, Tokyo, Japan), Japanese corporate executive; president and CEO of Honda Motor Co. from 2003.

Richard S. Fuld, Jr. (26 Apr 1946), American corporate executive; the last CEO of Lehman Brothers Holdings, 1993–2008.

(Carlos) Mauricio Funes (Cartagena) (18 Oct 1959, San Salvador, El Salvador), Salvadoran journalist and politician; president from 2009.

Nelly (Kim) Furtado (2 Dec 1978, Victoria, BC, Canada), Canadian singer and songwriter.

Stefano Gabbana (14 Nov 1962, Milan, Italy), Italian fashion designer and partner of Domenico Dolce.

John Galliano (Juan Carlos Antonio Galliano Guillen; 28 Nov 1960, Gibraltar), British fashion designer and designer in chief at Christian Dior.

Sonia Gandhi (Sonia Maino; 9 Dec 1947, Turin, Italy), Italian-born Indian widow of Rajiv Gandhi and a political force in India.

James Gandolfini (18 Sep 1961, Westwood NJ), American TV and film actor.

Mario Garcia (1947?, Cuba), Cuban-born American newspaper designer.

Gael García Bernal (30 Oct 1978, Guadalajara, Jalisco state, Mexico), Mexican actor.

Gabriel (José) García Márquez (6 Mar 1928, Aracataca, Colombia), Colombian novelist and short-story writer, a figure in the magic realism movement in Latin American literature; recipient of the 1972 Neustadt Prize and the 1982 Nobel Prize for Literature.

Alan García (Pérez) (23 May 1949, Lima, Peru), Peruvian politician; president, 1985–90 and again from 2006.

Jennifer (Anne) Garner (17 Apr 1972, Houston TX), American TV and film actress.

Kevin (Maurice) Garnett (19 May 1976, Mauldin SC), American professional basketball player.

Ivan Gasparovic (27 Mar 1941, Poltar, Czechoslovakia [now in Slovakia]), Slovak politician; president from 2004.

Bill Gates (William Henry Gates III; 28 Oct 1955, Seattle WA), American computer programmer, businessman, philanthropist, and cofounder of the Microsoft Corp.; he has been named the world's richest person by *Forbes* numerous times, including in 2009.

Melinda Gates (Melinda French; 15 Aug 1964, Dallas TX), American philanthropist; cofounder of the Bill & Melinda Gates Foundation.

Robert M(ichael) Gates (25 Sep 1943, Wichita KS), American government official; CIA director, 1991–93, and secretary of defense from 2006.

Jean-Paul Gaultier (24 Apr 1952, Arcueil, France), French fashion designer.

Laurent Gbagbo (31 May 1945, Gagnoa, French West Africa [now in Côte d'Ivoire]), Ivorian politician; president of Côte d'Ivoire from 2000.

Haile Gebrselassie (18 Apr 1973, Assela, Ethiopia), Ethiopian runner and world record holder in the marathon.

Frank Gehry (Frank Owen Goldberg; 28 Feb 1929, Toronto, ON, Canada), Canadian-born American architect and designer whose original, sculptural, often audacious work won him worldwide renown; recipient of the 1989 Pritzker Prize.

Timothy (Franz) Geithner (18 Aug 1961, New York NY), American public official; US secretary of the treasury from 2009.

Bob Geldof (Robert Frederick Xenon Geldof; 5 Oct 1954, Dublin, Ireland), Irish singer and songwriter and humanitarian.

Juan Gelman (3 May 1930, Buenos Aires, Argentina), Argentine poet; recipient of the 2007 Cervantes Prize.

Julius Genachowski (19 Aug 1962), American businessman and public official; chairman of the Federal Communications Commission from 2009.

Francis (Eugene) Cardinal George (16 Jan 1937, Chicago IL), American Roman Catholic churchman; archbishop of Chicago from 1997 and cardinal from 1998.

George Tupou V (Tupouto'a; 4 May 1948, Nuku'alofa, British Tonga), Tongan royal; king from 2006.

Leo W. Gerard (1947?, Sudbury, ON, Canada), Canadian labor leader; international president of the United Steelworkers International from 2001.

Richard (Tiffany) Gere (31 Aug 1949, Philadelphia PA), American film actor.

Valery (Abisalovich) Gergiev (2 May 1953, Moscow, USSR [now in Russia]), Russian conductor; artistic and general director of the Mariinsky Theatre from 1996.

Ricky (Dene) Gervais (25 Jun 1961, Reading, Berkshire, England), British comedian and actor.

Ron(ald Anthony) Gettelfinger (1 Aug 1944, near DePauw IN), American labor leader; president of the United Automobile Workers from 2002.

Mohamed Ghannouchi (18 Aug 1941, Al-Hamma, French Tunisia), Tunisian politician; prime minister from 1999.

Robert Ghiz (21 Jan 1974, Charlottetown, PE, Canada), Canadian politician (Liberal); premier of Prince Edward Island from 2007.

Paul (Edward Valentine) Giamatti (6 Jun 1967, New Haven CT), American film actor.

Frida Giannini (1972, Rome, Italy), Italian fashion designer; creative director at Gucci from 2006.

Jim Gibbons (James Arthur Gibbons; 16 Dec 1944, Sparks NV), American politician (Republican); governor of Nevada from 2007.

Robert Gibbs (29 Mar 1971, Auburn AL), American political consultant and media official; White House press secretary from 2009.

Charles (deWolf) Gibson (9 Mar 1943, Evanston IL), American TV journalist and anchorman.

Mel (Columcille Gerard) Gibson (3 Jan 1956, Peekskill NY), Australian American actor, producer, and director.

(Makhdoom Syed) Yousaf Raza Gilani (9 Jun 1952, Karachi, Pakistan), Pakistani politician (PPP); prime minister from 2008.

Melissa Gilbert (8 May 1964, Los Angeles CA), American film and TV actress; president of the Screen Actors Guild, 2002–05.

João Gilberto (do Prado Pereira de Oliveira) (10 Jun 1931, Juazeiro, Bahia state, Brazil), Brazilian bossa-nova singer, songwriter, and guitarist.

Vince Gill (Vincent Grant Gill; 12 Apr 1957, Norman OK), American country and progressive-bluegrass instrumentalist and singer.

Tony Gilroy (Anthony Joseph Gilroy; 11 Sep 1956, New York NY), American screenwriter and director.

Ruth Bader Ginsburg (15 Mar 1933, Brooklyn NY), American jurist; associate justice of the US Supreme Court from 1993.

Dana Gioia (24 Dec 1950, Los Angeles CA), American poet and critic; chairman of the US National Endowment for the Arts, 2003–09.

Nikki Giovanni (Yolande Cornelia Giovanni, Jr.; 7 Jun 1943, Knoxville TN), American poet.

Rudy Giuliani (Rudolph William Giuliani; 28 May 1944, Brooklyn NY), American politician (Republican) and consultant; mayor of New York City, 1994–2002.

Ira Glass (3 Mar 1959, Baltimore MD), American radio broadcaster, creator (1995) and host of This American Life on public radio and later also on cable TV.

Philip Glass (31 Jan 1937, Baltimore MD), American minimalist composer.

Savion Glover (19 Nov 1973, Newark NJ), American dancer and choreographer.

Louise (Elisabeth) Glück (22 Apr 1943, New York NY), American poet; US poet laureate, 2003–04.

Faure (Essozimna) Gnassingbé (Eyadéma) (6 Jun 1966, Afagnan, Togo), Togolese politician; president in February 2005 and again from May 2005.

Jean-Luc Godard (3 Dec 1930, Paris, France), French film director.

Ivars Godmanis (27 Nov 1951, Riga, USSR [now in Latvia]), Latvian politician; prime minister (1990-93, 2007-09).

Whoopi Goldberg (Caryn Elaine Johnson; 13 Nov 1955, New York NY), American comedian, film actress, and TV talk-show host.

(Orette) Bruce Golding (5 Dec 1947, Clarendon, Jamaica, British West Indies), Jamaican politician; prime minister from 2007.

Carlos Gomes, Jr. (19 Dec 1949, Bolama, Portuguese Guinea [now Guinea-Bissau]), Guinea-Bissauan politician; prime minister, 2004–05 and again from 2009.

Ralph E. Gonsalves (8 Aug 1946, Colonarie, Saint Vincent, British West Indies [now in Saint Vincent and the Grenadines]), West Indian politician; prime minister of Saint Vincent and the Grenadines from 2001.

Alejandro González Iñárritu (15 Aug 1963, Mexico City, Mexico), Mexican film director.

Lawrence Gonzi (1 Jul 1953, Valletta, Malta), Maltese politician (Nationalist); prime minister from 2004.

Roger Goodell (19 Feb 1959, Jamestown NY), American sports executive; commissioner of the National Football League from 2006.

Allegra Goodman (1967, Brooklyn NY), American writer, notably on Jewish themes.

Doris Kearns Goodwin (4 Jan 1943, Brooklyn NY), American historian, biographer, and TV commentator.

Annette Gordon-Reed (19 Nov 1958, Livingston TX), American author; recipient of the 2009 Pulitzer Prize for history for The Hemingses of Monticello: An American Family.

Al(bert Arnold) Gore, Jr. (31 Mar 1948, Washington DC), American statesman and environmental advocate; vice president of the US, 1993–2001, and corecipient of the 2007 Nobel Peace Prize.

Ryan (Thomas) Gosling (12 Nov 1980, London, ON, Canada), Canadian TV and film actor.

Jorie Graham (9 May 1951, New York NY), American poet.

Shawn Graham (22 Feb 1968, Rexton, NB, Canada), Canadian politician (Liberal); premier of New Brunswick from 2006.

(Allen) Kelsey Grammer (21 Feb 1955, St. Thomas, US Virgin Islands), American TV actor, writer, and producer.

Michael Grandage (2 May 1962, Yorkshire, England), British theater director; artistic director of London's Donmar Warehouse from 2002.

Jennifer Granholm (Jennifer Mulhern; 5 Feb 1959, Vancouver, BC, Canada), Canadian-born American attorney and politician (Democrat); governor of Michigan from 2003.

Hugh Grant (9 Sep 1960, London, England), British film actor.

Günter (Wilhelm) Grass (16 Oct 1927, Danzig, Germany [now Gdansk, Poland]), German poet, novelist, playwright, sculptor, and printmaker; recipient of the 1999 Nobel Prize for Literature.

Michael Graves (9 July 1934, Indianapolis IN), American postmodernist architect and housewares designer.

Zinaida Greceanii (7 Feb 1956, Tomsk oblast, USSR [now in Russia], Moldovan politician; prime minister from 2008.

Richard Greenberg (1958, Long Island NY), American playwright.

Brian Greene (9 Feb 1963, New York NY), American physicist and expert on string theory.

Paul Greengrass (13 Aug 1955, Cheam, Surrey, England), British film director.

Alan Greenspan (6 Mar 1926, New York NY), American monetary policy maker; chairman of the Board of Governors of the Federal Reserve System, 1987–2006.

Christine Gregoire (Christine O'Grady; 24 Mar 1947, Auburn WA), American politician (Democrat); governor of Washington from 2005.

Grégoire III Laham (Lutfi Laham; 15 Dec 1933, Daraya, Syria), Syrian church leader; patriarch of Antioch in the Greek Melkite Catholic Church from 2000.

Philippa Gregory (9 Jan 1954, Nairobi, Kenya), British historical novelist.

Brad Grey (1958?, Bronx NY), American talent agent, producer, and film executive; chairman and CEO of Paramount Motion Picture Group from 2005.

Ólafur Ragnar Grímsson (14 May 1943, Ísafjörður, Iceland), Icelandic politician; president from 1996.

John Grisham (8 Feb 1955, Jonesboro AR), American lawyer and best-selling novelist.

Matt(hew Abram) Groening (15 Feb 1954, Portland OR), American cartoonist and creator (1989) of TV's *The Simpsons*.

Dave Grohl (David Eric Grohl; 14 Jan 1969, Warren OH), American rock drummer, guitarist, and singer (for Nirvana and Foo Fighters).

Gilbert M. Grosvenor (5 May 1931, Washington DC), American executive; president of the National Geographic Society, 1980–96, and chairman of the board from 1987.

Jon Gruden (17 Aug 1963, Sandusky OH), American professional football coach and TV commentator.

Nikola Gruevski (31 Aug 1970, Skopje, Yugoslavia [now in Macedonia]), Macedonian politician; prime minister from 2006.

Dalia Grybauskaite (1 Mar 1956, Vilnius, USSR [now in Lithuania]), Lithuanian politician; president from 2009.

(Edward Michael) Bear Grylls (7 Jun 1974, Isle of Wight), British survival expert and TV star.

Armando (Emílio) Guebuza (20 Jan 1943, Marrupula, Portuguese Mozambique), Mozambican politician; secretary-general of the Frelimo political party from 2002 and president from 2005.

Ismail Omar Guelleh (27 Nov 1947, Diré-Dawa, Ethiopia), Djiboutian politician; president from 1999.

Guillaume (Guillaume Jean Joseph Marie; 11 Nov 1981, Château de Betzdorf, Luxembourg), Luxembourgian grand duke, prince of Nassau and Bourbon-Parma, and heir to the throne.

Ozzie Guillen (Oswaldo José Guillen Barrios; 20 Jan 1964, Ocumare del Tuy, Venezuela), Venezuelan-born professional baseball manager.

Abdullah Gul (29 Oct 1950, Kayseri, Turkey), Turkish economist and politician; prime minister, 2002–03, and president from 2007.

Natalie (Anne) Gulbis (7 Jan 1983, Sacramento CA), American golfer.

James Edward Gunn (21 Oct 1938, Livingstone TX), American cosmologist; coercipient of the 2005 Crafoord Prize for research into the evolution of the universe.

Tim(othy) Gunn (29 Jul 1953, Washington DC), fashion consultant and TV personality.

José Ángel Gurría Treviño (8 May 1950, Tampico, Tamaulipas state, Mexico), Mexican economist; secretary-general of the Organisation for Economic Co-operation and Development from 2006.

Alfred Gusenbauer (8 Feb 1960, Sankt Pölten, Austria), Austrian politician (Social Democrat); chancellor from 2007.

Xanana Gusmão (José Alexandre Gusmão; 20 Jun 1946, Laleia, Portuguese Timor [now East Timor (Timor-Leste)]), Timorese independence leader; first president of independent East Timor, 2002–07, and prime minister from 2007.

António (Manuel de Oliveira) Guterres (30 Apr 1949, Lisbon, Portugal), Portuguese politician (Socialist); prime minister, 1995–2002, and UN high commissioner for refugees from 2005.

Carlos M. Gutierrez (4 Nov 1953, Havana, Cuba), Cuban-born American corporate executive and government official; CEO of Kellogg Company, 2000–05, and US secretary of commerce, 2005–09.

Buddy Guy (George Guy; 30 Jul 1936, Lettsworth LA), American blues guitarist and singer.

Gyanendra Bir Bikram Shah Dev (7 Jul 1947, Kathmandu, Nepal), Nepalese king, 1950–51 and again in 2001–07.

Jake Gyllenhaal (Jacob Benjamin Gyllenhaal; 19 Dec 1980, Los Angeles CA), American film actor.

Ferenc Gyurcsány (4 Jun 1961, Pápa, Hungary), Hungarian politician; prime minister, 2004–09.

Haakon (Haakon Magnus; 20 Jul 1973, Oslo, Norway), Norwegian crown prince and heir to the throne.

Geir (Hilmar) Haarde (8 Apr 1951, Reykjavík, Iceland), Icelandic politician; prime minister, 2006–09.

Jürgen Habermas (18 Jun 1929, Düsseldorf, Germany), German philosopher, sociologist, and originator of the theory of communication ethics; he won a 2004 Kyoto Prize.

Charlie Haden (6 Aug 1937, Shenandoah IA), American jazz bass player.

Zaha Hadid (31 Oct 1950, Baghdad, Iraq), Iraqi-born architect; recipient of the 2004 Pritzker Prize.

Stephen (John) Hadley (13 Feb 1947, Toledo OH), American security official; US national security advisor, 2005–09.

Hilary Hahn (27 Nov 1979, Lexington VA), American violinist.

Stelios Haji-Ioannou (14 Feb 1967, Athens, Greece), Greek entrepreneur and corporate executive (easyJet and easyGroup).

Donald (Andrew) Hall, Jr. (20 Sep 1928, New Haven CT), American poet, essayist, and critic; US poet laureate, 2006–07.

Tarja (Kaarina) Halonen (24 Dec 1943, Helsinki, Finland), Finnish politician; president from 2000.

Jane Hamilton (13 Jul 1957, Oak Park IL), American novelist.

Richard Hamilton (24 Feb 1922, London, England), British artist; recipient of a 2008 Praemium Imperiale.

Herbie Hancock (Herbert Jeffrey Hancock; 12 Apr 1940, Chicago IL), American jazz keyboardist and composer.

Daniel Handler (pseudonym Lemony Snicket; 28 Feb 1970, San Francisco CA), American children's book author.

Tom Hanks (Thomas Jeffrey Hanks; 9 Jul 1956, Concord CA), American film actor and director.

Sean (Patrick) Hannity (30 Dec 1961, New York NY), American conservative commentator and talk-show host.

Hans Adam II (14 Feb 1945, Vaduz, Liechtenstein), Liechtenstein royal; prince of Liechtenstein from 1989.

Harald V (21 Feb 1937, Skaugum, Norway), Norwegian royal; king from 1991.

Marcia Gay Harden (14 Aug 1959, La Jolla CA), American film, stage, and TV actress.

Roy Hargrove (16 Oct 1969, Waco TX), American jazz trumpeter.

Joy Harjo (9 May 1951, Tulsa OK), American poet, musician, and Native American (Muskogee) activist.

Nikolaus Harnoncourt (6 Dec 1929, Berlin, Germany), Austrian conductor, cellist, and viol player; cofounder in the 1950s of the Concentus Musicus Wien, an early-music group.

Stephen (Joseph) Harper (30 Apr 1959, Toronto, ON, Canada), Canadian politician (Conservative); prime minister of Canada from 2006.

Padraig Harrington (31 Aug 1971, Dublin, Ireland), Irish golfer.

Ed(ward Allen) Harris (28 Nov 1950, Englewood NJ), American film and stage actor and director.

Harry (Henry Charles Albert David Mountbatten-Windsor; 15 Sep 1984, London, England), British prince of Wales; son of Charles and Diana, prince and princess of Wales, and third in line to the British throne.

Mary Hart (Mary Johanna Harum; 8 Nov 1950, Madison SD), American actress and cohost of *Entertainment Tonight* on TV from 1982.

Dominik Hasek (29 Jan 1965, Pardubice, Czechoslovakia [now in the Czech Republic]), Czech ice-hockey goalie.

Sheikh Hasina Wazed (28 Sep 1947, Tungipara, India [now in Bangladesh]), Bangladeshi politician; prime minister, 1996–2001 and again from 2009.

Robert Hass (1 Mar 1941, San Francisco CA), American poet; US poet laureate, 1995–97; his *Time and Materials* won a 2008 Pulitzer Prize for poetry.

Anne (Jacqueline) Hathaway (12 Nov 1982, Brooklyn NY), American film actress.

Tony Hawk (Anthony Frank Hawk; 12 May 1968, San Diego CA), American professional skateboarder.

Stephen W. Hawking (8 Jan 1942, Oxford, Oxfordshire, England), British theoretical physicist, a specialist in cosmology and quantum gravity.

Issa Hayatou (9 Aug 1945, Garoua), Cameroonian association football (soccer) executive.

Michael (Vincent) Hayden (17 Mar 1945, Pittsburgh PA), American director of the National Security Agency, 1999–2005, and director of the CIA, 2006–09.

Salma Hayek (Jiménez) (2 Sep 1966, Coatzacoalcos, Veracruz state, Mexico), Mexican-born actress.

Roy Haynes (13 Mar 1926, Roxbury, Boston MA), American jazz drummer and bandleader.

Todd Haynes (2 Jan 1961, Los Angeles CA), American film director, producer, and screenwriter.

Seamus (Justin) Heaney (13 Apr 1939, near Castledawson, County Londonderry, Northern Ireland), Irish poet; recipient of the 1995 Nobel Prize for Literature.

Hugh M. Hefner (9 Apr 1926, Chicago IL), American magazine publisher (*Playboy*).

Katherine (Marie) Heigl (24 Nov 1978, Washington DC), American model and TV and film actress.

Dave Heineman (David Eugene Heineman; 12 May 1948, Falls City NE), American politician (Republican); governor of Nebraska from 2005.

Michael Heller (Michal Heller; 12 Mar 1936, Tarnow, Poland), Polish cosmologist and Roman Catholic priest; recipient of the 2008 Templeton Prize.

Frederick ("Fritz") Henderson (29 Nov 1958, Detroit MI), American businessman; president and CEO of General Motors from 2009.

Henri (16 Apr 1955, Château de Betzdorf, Luxembourg), Luxembourgian grand duke from 2000.

(Charles) Brad(ford) Henry (10 Jun 1963, Shawnee OK), American politician (Democrat); governor of Oklahoma from 2003.

Thierry (Daniel) Henry (17 Aug 1977, Châtillon, near Paris, France), French association football (soccer) player.

Gary R(ichard) Herbert (7 May 1947, American Fork UT), American politician (Republican); governor of Utah from 2009.

Seymour M(yron) Hersh (8 Apr 1937, Chicago IL), American investigative reporter and writer.

Mohamud Muse Hersi, Somali general; president of the secessionist republic of Puntland, 2005–09.

Jacques Herzog (19 Apr 1950, Basel, Switzerland), Swiss architect; corecipient of the 2001 Pritzker Prize and of a Praemium Imperiale in 2007.

Rosalyn Higgins (Rosalyn Cohen; 2 Jun 1937, London, England), British jurist; president of the International Court of Justice, 2006–09.

Tommy Hilfiger (Thomas Jacob Hilfiger; 24 Mar 1951, Elmira NY), American fashion designer.

Faith Hill (Audrey Faith Perry; 21 Sep 1967, Jackson MS), American country singer.

Julia Butterfly Hill (18 Feb 1974, Mount Vernon MO), American environmental activist.

Paris Hilton (17 Feb 1981, New York NY), American heiress and socialite.

Sam(uel Archibald Anthony) Hinds (27 Dec 1943, Mahaicony, British Guiana [now Guyana]), Guyanese politician; president in 1997 and prime minister, 1992–97, 1997–99, and again from 1999.

Emile (Davenport) Hirsch (13 Mar 1985, Palms CA), American film actor.

Damien Hirst (1965, Bristol, England), British artist.

Christopher Hitchens (26 Apr 1949, Portsmouth, England), American cultural and political critic and journalist.

Stanley Ho (Ho Hung-sun; 25 Nov 1921, Hong Kong), Macanese gaming magnate and multibillionaire.

Susan Hockfield (1951, Chicago IL), American neuroscientist; president of the Massachusetts Institute of Technology from 2004.

David Hockney (9 Jul 1937, Bradford, Yorkshire, England), British painter, draftsman, printmaker, photographer, and stage designer.

John (Henry) Hoeven III (13 Mar 1957, Bismarck ND), American politician (Republican); governor of North Dakota from 2000.

James P(hillip) Hoffa (19 May 1941, Detroit MI), American labor leader; president of the International Brotherhood of Teamsters from 1999.

Dustin Hoffman (8 Aug 1937, Los Angeles CA), American film and stage actor.

Philip Seymour Hoffman (23 Jul 1967, Fairport NY), American stage and film actor and theater director.

Hulk Hogan (Terry Gene Bollea; 11 Aug 1953, Augusta GA), American professional wrestler and actor.

Eric (Himpton) Holder (Jr.) (21 Jan 1951, New York NY), American lawyer; US attorney general from 2009.

John (Paul) Holdren (1 Mar 1944, Sewickley PA), presidential science adviser and director of the Office of Science and Technology Policy from 2009.

Katie Holmes (Kate Noelle Holmes; 18 Dec 1978, Toledo OH), American TV, film, and stage actress.

(Philip) Anthony Hopkins (31 Dec 1937, Margam, West Glamorgan, Wales), British film and stage actor.

Nick Hornby (17 Apr 1957, Redhill, Surrey, England), British novelist and journalist.

Khaled Hosseini (4 Mar 1965, Kabul, Afghanistan), Afghan-born American novelist.

Whitney (Elizabeth) Houston (9 Aug 1963, Newark NJ), American pop singer and film actress.

Dwight Howard (8 Dec 1985, Atlanta GA), American basketball player.

Ron Howard (1 Mar 1954, Duncan OK), American TV and film actor and director.

Terrence (Dashon) Howard (11 Mar 1969, Chicago IL), American TV and film actor.

Daniel Walker Howe (1937, Ogden UT), American historian and professor who won the 2008 Pulitzer Prize for history for his book *What Hath God Wrought*.

Hu Jintao (25 Dec 1942, Jixi, Anhui province, China), Chinese statesman; general secretary of the Communist Party of China, vice chairman of the Military Commission, and president of China from 2003.

Hu Shuli (1953, Beijing, China), Chinese journalist and editor; cofounder of *Caijin*, a business magazine.

Berthold Huber (15 Feb 1950, Ulm, West Germany), German corporate executive; chairman of IG Metall from 2007.

Jan Huber (Johannes Huber; 1947?, The Netherlands), Dutch international official; executive secretary of the Antarctic Treaty system from 2004.

Mike Huckabee (Michael Dale Huckabee; 24 Aug 1955, Hope AR), American politician (Republican) and political commentator; governor of Arkansas, 1996–2007.

Jennifer (Kate) Hudson (12 Sep 1981, Chicago IL), American soul and gospel singer and film actress.

Arianna Huffington (Ariana Stassinopoulos; 1950, Athens, Greece), Greek-born American political commentator, syndicated newspaper columnist, and author.

Felicity (Kendall) Huffman (9 Dec 1962, Bedford NY), American TV and film actress.

Robert (Studley Forrest) Hughes (28 Jul 1938, Sydney, NSW, Australia), Australian art critic and author.

Hun Sen (4 Apr 1951, Kampong Cham province, Cambodia), Cambodian politician; prime minister from 1985.

Holly Hunter (20 Mar 1958, Conyers GA), American film and TV actress.

Jon M(eade) Huntsman, Jr. (26 Mar 1960, Palo Alto CA), American businessman (Huntsman Family Holdings), politician (Republican), and philanthropist; governor of Utah, 2005–09, and US ambassador to China from 2009.

Lubomyr Cardinal Husar (26 Feb 1933, Lwow, Poland [now Lviv, Ukraine]), Ukrainian Greek Catholic Church leader; cardinal from 2001 and major archbishop of Kyiv-Halyc from 2005.

Nicholas Hytner (7 May 1956, Didsbury, near Manchester, England), British theatre director; artistic director of the National Theatre from 2003.

Ice Cube (O'Shea Jackson; 15 Jun 1969), American rapper, songwriter, and actor.

Ice-T (Tracy Morrow; 16 Feb 1958, Newark NJ), American hip-hop artist and actor.

Apisai Ielemia (19 Aug 1955, Vaitupu?, British Ellice Islands [now Tuvalu]), Tuvaluan politician; prime minister from 2006.

Ieronymos II (Ioannis Liapis; 1938, Oinofyta, Greece), Greek Orthodox churchman; archbishop of Athens and all Greece from 2008.

Ekmeleddin Ihsanoglu (26 Dec 1943, Cairo, Egypt), Turkish professor of history; secretary-general of the Organisation of the Islamic Conference from 2005.

Ratu Josefa Iloilo(vatu Uluivuda) (29 Dec 1920, Taveuni island, Fiji), Fijian politician; president, 2000–09.

Toomas Hendrik Ilves (26 Dec 1953, Stockholm, Sweden), Estonian diplomat; president from 2006.

Jeffrey R(obert) Immelt (19 Feb 1956, Cincinnati OH), American corporate executive; CEO of the General Electric Co. from 2001.

Hubert (Alexander) Ingraham (4 Aug 1947, Pine Ridge, Bahamas, British West Indies), Bahamian politician; prime minister, 1992–2002 and again from 2007.

José Miguel Insulza (2 Jun 1943, Santiago, Chile), Chilean government official (Socialist); secretary-general of the Organization of American States from 2005.

Valentin Inzko (22 May 1949, Klagenfurt, Austria) Austrian diplomat; high representative for Bosnia and Herzegovina from 2009.

Bill Irwin (11 Apr 1950, Santa Monica CA), American actor and choreographer.

Walter Isaacson (20 May 1952, New Orleans LA), American corporate executive; chairman and CEO of the Cable News Network (CNN), 2001–03, and president and CEO of the Aspen Institute from 2003.

Riduan Isamuddin (Encep Nurjaman; "Hambali"; 4 Apr 1966, Pamokolan, West Java, Indonesia), Indonesian militant and leader of the Jemaah Islamiyah group; arrested in 2003 by American agents for his alleged involvement in several terrorist attacks.

Kazuo Ishiguro (8 Nov 1954, Nagasaki, Japan), Japanese-born British novelist.

Shintaro Ishihara (30 Sep 1932, Kobe, Japan), Japanese author and nationalist politician; governor of Tokyo from 1999.

Gjorge Ivanov (2 May 1960, Valandovo, Yugoslavia [now in Macedonia]), Macedonian politician, president of Macedonia from 2009.

Allen (Ezail) Iverson (7 Jun 1975, Hampton VA), American basketball player.

James (Francis) Ivory (7 Jun 1928, Berkeley CA), American film director.

Hugh (Michael) Jackman (12 Oct 1968, Sydney, NSW, Australia), Australian film and stage actor.

Alan (Eugene) Jackson (17 Oct 1958, Newnan GA), American country-and-western singer and guitarist.

Janet (Damita Jo) Jackson (16 May 1966, Gary IN), American singer and film and TV actress.

Jesse (Louis) Jackson (8 Oct 1941, Greenville SC), American civil rights leader, minister, and politician.

Lisa P(erez) Jackson (8 Feb 1962, Philadelphia PA), American public official; administrator of the US Environmental Protection Agency from 2009.

Peter Jackson (31 Oct 1961, Pukerua Bay, New Zealand), New Zealand film director and producer.

Phil(ip Douglas) Jackson (17 Sep 1945, Deer Lodge MT), American basketball player and coach.

Samuel L(eroy) Jackson (21 Dec 1948, Washington DC), American film actor.

Marc Jacobs (9 Apr 1963, New York NY), American fashion designer.

Bharrat Jagdeo (23 Jan 1964, Unity village, Demarara, Guyana), Guyanese politician; president from 1999.

Mick Jagger (Michael Philip Jagger; 26 Jul 1943, Dartford, Kent, England), British rock musician and lead singer for the Rolling Stones.

Helmut Jahn (4 Jan 1940, Nürnberg, Germany), German-born architect.

Zsuzsanna Jakab (17 May 1951, Hungary), Hungarian epidemiologist; the first director of the European Centre for Disease Prevention and Control (ECDC), from 2005.

LeBron James (30 Dec 1984, Akron OH), American professional basketball player.

Judith (Ann) Jamison (10 May 1944, Philadelphia PA), American dancer and choreographer (Alvin Ailey American Dance Theater).

Yahya Jammeh (Alphonse Jamus Jebulai Jammeh; 25 May 1965, Kanilai village, Gambia), Gambian politician; president from 1994.

Mariss Jansons (14 Jan 1943, Riga, Latvia), Latvian-born American director; conductor of the Royal Concertgebouw Orchestra of Amsterdam from 2004.

Jim Jarmusch (22 Jan 1953, Akron OH), American avant-garde filmmaker.

Neeme Järvi (7 Jun 1937, Tallinn, Estonia), Estonian conductor; music director of the Detroit Symphony Orchestra, 1990–2005, and of the New Jersey Symphony Orchestra, 2005–09, and chief conductor of the Hague Philharmonic from 2005.

Jay-Z (Shawn Corey Carter; 4 Dec 1970, Brooklyn NY), American rapper.

Michaëlle Jean (6 Sep 1957, Port-au-Prince, Haiti), Haitian-born Canadian journalist; governor-general of Canada from 2005.

Katharine Jefferts Schori (26 Mar 1954, Pensacola FL), American church leader; presiding bishop of the US Episcopal Church from 2006.

Derek (Sanderson) Jeter (26 Jun 1974, Pequannock NJ), American baseball player.

Ha Jin (Xuefei Jin; 21 Feb 1956, Jinzhou, Liaoning province, China), Chinese American novelist.

Bobby Jindal (Piyush Jindal; 10 Jun 1971, Baton Rouge LA), American politician (Republican); governor of Louisiana from 2008.

Steven (Paul) Jobs (24 Feb 1955, San Francisco CA), American inventor and corporate executive; co-founder of Apple Computer and CEO from 1997.

Scarlett Johansson (22 Nov 1984, New York NY), American film actress.

Elton John (Reginald Kenneth Dwight; 25 Mar 1947, Pinner, Middlesex, England), British singer, composer, and pianist.

Jasper Johns (15 May 1930, Augusta GA), American painter and graphic artist, a pioneer of Pop art.

Boris Johnson (Alexander Boris de Pfeffel Johnson; 19 Jun 1964, New York NY), American-born British journalist, editor (*Spectator*), and MP (Conservative); mayor of London from 2008.

Denis Johnson (1949, Munich, West Germany), American novelist, short-story writer, and poet; his *Tree of Smoke* won a National Book Award in 2007.

Dwayne (Douglas) Johnson ("The Rock"; 2 May 1972, Hayward CA), American professional wrestler-turned-actor.

Robert L. Johnson (8 Apr 1946, Hickory MS), American entrepreneur; founder (1980) of BET (Black Entertainment Television) and owner of the Charlotte Bobcats NBA team.

Stephen L. Johnson (21 Mar 1951, Washington DC), American government official; administrator of the US Environmental Protection Agency, 2005–09.

Ellen Johnson-Sirleaf (29 Oct 1938, Monrovia, Liberia), Liberian government and international official; president from 2006.

Angelina Jolie (Angelina Jolie Voight; 4 Jun 1975, Los Angeles CA), American film actress and philanthropist.

Bill T. Jones (William Tass Jones; 15 Feb 1952, Steuben county NY), American dancer, choreographer, and director.

Edward P(aul) Jones (5 Oct 1950, Washington DC), American short-story writer and novelist.

James Earl Jones (Todd Jones; 17 Jan 1931, Arkabutla MS), American actor.

James L(ogan) Jones (19 Dec 1943, Kansas City MO), American military officer; US national security advisor from 2009.

Marion Jones (12 Oct 1975, Los Angeles CA), American sprinter and long jumper.

Norah Jones (30 Mar 1979, New York NY), American jazz-pop vocalist and pianist.

Quincy (Delight) Jones, Jr. (14 Mar 1933, Chicago IL), American jazz and pop arranger, composer, and producer.

Tommy Lee Jones (15 Sep 1946, San Saba TX), American actor.

Michael (Jeffrey) Jordan (17 Feb 1963, Brooklyn NY), American basketball player; he was voted ESPN's Athlete of the Century and is believed by many to be the best basketball player in history.

Juan Carlos I (Juan Carlos Alfonso Victor María de Borbón y Borbón; 5 Jan 1938, Rome, Italy), Spanish royal; king from 1975.

Juanes (Juan Estebán Aristizábal Vásquez; 9 Aug 1972, Medellín, Colombia), Colombian singer, songwriter, and guitarist.

Anerood Jugnauth (29 Mar 1930, Mauritius), Mauritian politician; prime minister, 1982–95 and 2000–03, and president from 2003.

Jean-Claude Juncker (9 Dec 1954, Rédange-sur-Attert, Luxembourg), Luxembourgian politician; prime minister from 1995.

Emilia Kabakov (3 Dec 1945, Dnipropetrovsk, USSR [now in Ukraine]), Ukranian sculptor; recipient of a 2008 Praemium Imperiale.

Ilya Kabakov (30 Sep 1933, Dnipropetrovsk, USSR [now in Ukraine]), Ukranian sculptor; recipient of a 2008 Praemium Imperiale.

Joseph Kabila (4 Jun 1971, Sud-Kivu province, Democratic Republic of the Congo), Congolese politician; president of the Democratic Republic of the Congo from 2001.

Lech Kaczynski (18 Jun 1949, Warsaw, Poland), Polish politician (Law and Justice); president from 2005.

Ismail Kadare (28 Jan 1938, Gjirokastër, Albania), Albanian novelist and poet; recipient of the first Man Booker International Prize, in 2005.

Paul Kagame (23 Oct 1957, Gitarama, Ruanda-Urundi [now Rwanda]), Rwandan politician; president from 2000.

Dahir Riyale Kahin (1952), Somali politician; president of the secessionist Republic of Somaliland from 2002.

Robert E(lliot) Kahn (23 Dec 1938, Brooklyn NY), American computer scientist, a key developer of the network that became the Internet; recipient of a Japan Prize in 2008.

Tim(othy Michael) Kaine (26 Feb 1958, St. Paul MN), American politician (Democrat); governor of Virginia from 2006 and chairman of the Democratic National Committee from 2009.

Kaká (Ricardo Izecson dos Santos Leite; 22 Apr 1982, Brasília, Brazil), Brazilian association football (soccer) player.

Ingvar Kamprad (1926, Småland province, Sweden), Swedish businessman; founder of the home-furnishing company IKEA.

Hiroo Kanamori (17 Oct 1936, Tokyo, Japan), Japanese seismologist; recipient of a 2007 Kyoto Prize.

Radovan Karadzic (19 Jun 1945, Petnjica, Yugoslavia [now in Montenegro]), Bosnian Serb politician and president of Republika Srpska (Bosnia and Herzegovina), 1992–96; he was wanted as a war criminal and was arrested in 2008.

Kostas Karamanlis (Konstantinos Karamanlis; 14 Sep 1956, Athens, Greece); Greek politician (New Democracy); prime minister from 2004.

Donna Karan (Donna Faske; 2 Oct 1948, Forest Hills NY), American fashion designer.

Islam Karimov (30 Jan 1938, Samarkand, USSR [now in Uzbekistan]), Uzbek politician; president from 1990.

Mel(vin Alan) Karmazin (24 Aug 1943, New York NY), American media executive; CEO of Sirius XM Radio (formerly Sirius Satellite Radio) from 2004.

Hamid Karzai (24 Dec 1957, Karz, Afghanistan), Afghan statesman; president of Afghanistan from 2001.

Garry Kasparov (Garri Kimovich Kasparov; original name Garri or Harry Weinstein; 13 Apr 1963, Baku, USSR [now in Azerbaijan]), Azerbaijani-born Russian chess champion of the world, 1985–2000.

Jeffrey Katzenberg (21 Dec 1950, New York NY), American film producer and a cofounder (1994) of DreamWorks SKG.

Takashi Kawamura (19 Dec 1939, Japan?), Japanese businessman; CEO and president of Hitachi Corp. from 2009.

Naomi Kawase (30 May 1969, Nara, Japan), Japanese film director.

Diane Keaton (Diane Hall; 5 Jan 1946, Los Angeles CA), American actress and director.

Keb' Mo' (Kevin Moore; 3 Oct 1951, Los Angeles CA), American blues musician.

Garrison Keillor (Gary Edward Keillor; 7 Aug 1942, Anoka MN), American humorist and writer best known for his long-running radio variety show, *A Prairie Home Companion.*

Toby Keith (Toby Keith Covel; 8 Jul 1961, Clinton OK), American country-and-western singer.

Bill Keller (18 Jan 1949), American journalist; managing editor of the *New York Times,* 1997–2001, and executive editor from 2003.

Tim(othy J.) Keller (1950, Pennsylvania), American churchman and author; founding pastor (1989) of Redeemer Presbyterian Church, New York City.

Ellsworth Kelly (31 May 1923, Newburgh NY), American painter and sculptor.

R. Kelly (Robert S. Kelly; 8 Jan 1969, Chicago IL), American R&B performer.

William M. Kelso (30 Mar 1941, Chicago IL), American archaeologist; director of archaeology for the Jamestown Rediscovery Project.

Thomas (Michael) Keneally (pseudonym William Coyle; 7 Oct 1935, Sydney, NSW, Australia), Australian novelist.

Anthony (McCleod) Kennedy (23 Jul 1936, Sacramento CA), American jurist; associate justice of the US Supreme Court from 1988.

R(ichard) Gil Kerlikowske (1949, Fort Myers FL), American law enforcement official; director of national drug control policy ("drug czar") from 2009.

Lee Kernaghan (15 Apr 1964, Corryong, VIC, Australia), Australian country singer; he was named Australian of the Year for 2008.

John F(orbes) Kerry (11 Dec 1943, Fitzsimmons Army Hospital [now in Aurora CO]), American politician (Democrat) and senator from Massachusetts from 1985; the Democratic candidate for president in 2004.

John (Phillip) Key (9 Aug 1961, Auckland, New Zealand); New Zealand politician (National Party), prime minister from 2008.

Alicia Keys (Alicia Augello Cook; 25 Jan 1981, New York NY), American R&B singer and pianist.

Cheb Khaled (Khaled Hadj Brahim; 29 Feb 1960, Sidi-El-Houri, near Oran, French Algeria), Algerian *rai* performer.

Hamad ibn Isa al-Khalifah (28 Jan 1950, Bahrain), Bahraini sheikh; emir and chief of state from 1999; he proclaimed himself king in 2002.

Zalmay (Mamozy) Khalilzad (22 Mar 1951, Mazar-i-Sharif, Afghanistan), Afghan-born American diplomat; ambassador to Afghanistan, 2003–05, to Iraq, 2005–07, and to the United Nations, 2007–09.

(Seretse Khama) Ian Khama (27 Feb 1953, Bechuanaland [now Botswana]), Botswanan military officer; president from 2008.

Hojatolislam Sayyed Ali Khamenei (15 Jul 1939, Meshed, Iran), Iranian Shiʻite clergyman and politician who served as president, 1981–89, and as that country's *rahbar,* or leader, from 1989.

Mikhail (Borisovich) Khodorkovsky (26 Jun 1963, Moscow, USSR [now in Russia]), Russian businessman, the imprisoned former billionaire head of Yukos Oil Co.

Abbas Kiarostami (22 Jun 1940, Tehran, Iran), Iranian film director.

Mwai Kibaki (15 Nov 1931, Gatuyaini village, Central province, Kenya), Kenyan politician; president from 2002.

Angelique Kidjo (14 Jul 1960, Ouidah, Dahomey [now Benin]), Beninese pop singer.

Nicole (Mary) Kidman (20 Jun 1967, Honolulu HI), American-born Australian actress.

Anselm Kiefer (8 Mar 1945, Donaueschingen, Germany), German Neo-Expressionist painter.

Jakaya (Mrisho) Kikwete (7 Oct 1950, Msoga, British Tanganyika [now in Tanzania]), Tanzanian military officer and government official; president from 2005.

Val (Edward) Kilmer (31 Dec 1959, Los Angeles CA), American film actor.

Jeong H. Kim (1961, Seoul, South Korea), Korean-born American electronics industry executive who was founder (1992) of Yurie Systems, Inc., and president of Alcatel-Lucent's Bell Labs from 2005.

Kim Jong Il (16 Feb 1941, near Khabarovsk, USSR [now in Russia]), North Korean leader and successor to his father, Kim Il-Sung, as general secretary of the Central Committee of the Worker's Party of Korea (North Korea) from 1997.

Jimmy Kimmel (13 Nov 1967, Brooklyn NY), American comedian and TV talk-show host.

Jamaica Kincaid (Elaine Potter Richardson; 25 May 1949, Saint John's, Antigua, British West Indies [now in Antigua and Barbuda]), Antiguan American writer.

B.B. King (Riley B. King; 16 Sep 1925, Itta Bena, near Indianola MS), American blues guitarist and singer.

Larry King (Lawrence Harvey Zeiger; 19 Nov 1933, Brooklyn NY), American TV journalist.

Stephen (Edward) King (pseudonym Richard Bachman; 21 Sep 1947, Portland ME), American writer of novels combining horror, fantasy, and science fiction.

Stephenson King (13 Nov 1958, Saint Lucia, British West Indies?), West Indian politician (United Workers Party); prime minister of Saint Lucia from 2007.

Galway Kinnell (1 Feb 1927, Providence RI), American poet.

Michael Kinsley (9 Mar 1951, Detroit MI), American political commentator and editor.

Kirill I (20 Nov 1946, Leningrad, USSR [now St. Petersburg, Russia]), Russian Orthodox patriarch of Moscow and all Russia from 2009.

Ron Kirk (1954, Austin TX), American politician (Democrat); mayor of Dallas, 1995–2001, and US trade representative from 2009.

Philippe Kirsch (1 Apr 1947, Namur, Belgium), Belgian-born Canadian jurist; president of the International Criminal Court, 2003–09.

Vaclav Klaus (19 Jun 1941, Prague, Czechoslovakia [now in the Czech Republic]), Czech politician who served as prime minister, 1992–97, and president for one month in 1993 and again from 2003.

Calvin (Richard) Klein (19 Nov 1942, Bronx NY), American fashion designer.

August Kleinzahler (1949, Jersey City NJ), American poet.

Heidi Klum (1 Jun 1973, Bergisch Gladbach, West Germany), German American supermodel and TV-show host.

Bobby Knight (Robert Montgomery Knight; 25 Oct 1940, Massillon OH), American basketball coach; the winningest coach in men's collegiate basketball.

Keira Knightley (26 Mar 1985, Teddington, London, England), British film actress.

Ko Un (1 Aug 1933, Kunsan, North Cholla province, Japanese-occupied Korea [now in South Korea]), Korean poet.

Eizo Kobayashi (7 Jan 1949, Fukui prefecture, Japan), Japanese businessman; CEO and president of Itochu Corp. from 2004.

Makoto Kobayashi (7 Apr 1944, Nagoya, Japan), Japanese scientist; cowinner of the 2008 Nobel Prize in Physics.

Samuel Kobia (20 Mar 1947, Miathene, British Kenya), Kenyan Methodist church leader; general secretary of the World Council of Churches from 2004.

Robert (Sedraki) Kocharyan (31 Aug 1954, Stepanakert, Nagorno-Karabakh, USSR [now in Azerbaijan]), Armenian politician; president, 1998–2008.

Horst Köhler (22 Feb 1943, Skierbieszow, Poland), German international economic official; president of Germany from 2004.

Girija Prasad Koirala (1925, Tadi, Bihar, British India), Nepalese politician; prime minister, 1991–94, 1998–99, 2000–01, and 2006–08, and acting head of state, 2007–08.

Yorihiko Kojima (1941, Tokyo, Japan), Japanese businessman; president and CEO of Mitsubishi Corp. from 2004.

Kabine Komara (1950, French West Africa [now in Guinea]), Guinean businessman and politician; prime minister of Guinea from 2009.

Yusef Komunyakaa (29 Apr 1947, Bogalusa LA), American poet.

Zeljko Komsic (20 Jan 1964, Sarajevo, Yugoslavia [now in Bosnia and Herzegovina]), Bosnia and Herzegovinian politician; chairman of the presidency of the republic, 2007–08 and again from 2009.

Alpha Oumar Konaré (2 Feb 1946, Kayes, French West Africa [now in Mali]), Malian statesman; president of Mali, 1992–2002, and chairman of the Commission of the African Union, 2003–08.

Maxim Kontsevich (25 Aug 1964, Khimki, USSR [now in Russia]), Russian mathematician; recipient of the Fields Medal in 1998 and a Crafoord Prize in 2008.

Joseph Kony (1964?, Odek, Uganda), Ugandan rebel commander; leader of the Lord's Resistance Army.

Rem Koolhaas (17 Nov 1944, Rotterdam, Netherlands), Dutch architect; recipient of the 2000 Pritzker Prize.

Jeff Koons (21 Jan 1955, York PA), American Pop-art painter and sculptor.

Dean (Ray) Koontz (9 Jul 1945, Everett PA), American novelist.

Ted Kooser (Theodore Kooser; 25 Apr 1939, Ames IA), American poet; US poet laureate, 2004–06.

Ernest Bai Koroma (2 Oct 1953, Makeni, British Sierra Leone), Sierra Leonean politician; president from 2007.

Michael (David) Kors (Karl Anderson, Jr.; 1959, Merrick, Long Island NY), American fashion designer.

Jadranka Kosor (1 Jul 1953, Pakrac, Yugoslavia [now in Croatia]), Croatian politician; prime minister from 2009.

Vojislav Kostunica (24 Mar 1944, Belgrade, Yugoslavia [now in Serbia]), Serbian politician; president of Yugoslavia, 2000–03; prime minister of Serbia, 2004–08.

Bernard Kouchner (1 Nov 1939, Avignon, France), French foreign minister from 2007.

Lansana Kouyaté (15 Jul 1950, Koba, French West Africa [now in Guinea]), Guinean diplomat and statesman; prime minister, 2007–08.

Jon Krakauer (12 Apr 1954, Brookline MA), American author of nonfiction.

Vladimir (Borisovich) Kramnik (25 Jun 1975, Tuapse, USSR [now in Russia]), Russian chess grand master.

Alison Krauss (23 Jul 1971, Decatur IL), American bluegrass fiddle player and singer.

Lenny Kravitz (26 May 1964, Brooklyn NY), American rock musician.

Gidon Kremer (27 Feb 1947, Riga, USSR [now in Latvia]), Latvian-born violinist and conductor.

William Kristol (23 Dec 1952, New York NY), American editor and columnist.

Paul Krugman (28 Feb 1953, New York NY), American economist and journalist; winner of the 2008 Nobel Prize for Economics.

Andrius Kubilius (8 Dec 1956, Vilnius, USSR [now in Lithuania]), Lithuanian politician; prime minister of Lithuania, 1999–2000 and again from 2008.

Dennis J. Kucinich (8 Oct 1946, Cleveland OH), American politician (Democrat); mayor of Cleveland, 1977–79; congressman from Ohio from 1997.

John (Kofi Agyekum) Kufuor (8 Dec 1938, Kumisi, Gold Coast [now Ghana]), Ghanaian politician; president, 2001–09.

Ted Kulongoski (Theodore R. Kulongoski; 5 Nov 1940 Missouri), American politician (Democrat); governor of Oregon from 2003.

Yayoi Kusama (22 Mar 1929, Matsumoto, Nagano prefecture, Japan), Japanese artist; recipient of a 2006 Praemium Imperiale.

Tony Kushner (16 Jul 1956, New York NY), American playwright.

Shia LaBeouf (11 Jun 1986, Los Angeles CA), American actor.

Lady Gaga (Stefani Joanne Angelina Germanotta; 28 Mar 1986, Yonkers NY), American singer.

Christine Lagarde (1 Jan 1956, Paris, France), French lawyer; minister of finance from 2007.

Emeril (John) Lagasse (15 Oct 1959, Fall River MA), American TV chef, restaurateur, and media personality.

Karl Lagerfeld (10 Sep 1938, Hamburg, Germany), German-born French fashion designer.

Ray LaHood (6 Dec 1945, Peoria IL), American politician (Republican); congressman from Illinois, 1995–2009, and US secretary of transportation from 2009.

Miroslav Lajcak (20 Mar 1963, Poprad, Czechoslovakia [now in Slovakia]), Slovak diplomat and government official; high representative for Bosnia and Herzegovina, 2007–09.

Guy Laliberté (1959, Quebec city, QC, Canada), Canadian circus performer and founder of Cirque du Soleil.

Edward S. Lampert (19 Jul 1962, Roslyn NY), American business executive; founder (1988) of ESL Investments and chairman of Sears Holdings Corp. from 2005.

Pascal Lamy (8 Apr 1947, Levallois-Perret, Paris, France), French financial and government official; EU trade commissioner, 1999–2004, and director general of the World Trade Organization from 2005.

Rocco Landesman (20 Jul 1947, St. Louis MO), American theater producer; chairman of the US National Endowment for the Arts from 2009.

Diane Lane (22 Jan 1965, New York NY), American film actress.

Nathan Lane (Joseph Lane; 3 Feb 1956, Jersey City NJ), American stage and screen actor.

David Lang (8 Jan 1957, Los Angeles CA), American opera composer whose *The Little Match Girl Passion* won the 2008 Pulitzer Prize for music.

Helmut Lang (10 Mar 1956, Vienna, Austria), Austrian fashion designer.

Frank Langella (1 Jan 1940, Bayonne NJ), American film actor.

Anthony M. LaPaglia (31 Jan 1959, Adelaide, SA, Australia), Australian film and TV actor.

Lewis H. Lapham (8 Jan 1935, San Francisco CA), American liberal political commentator and author; editor of *Harper's Magazine*, 1976–81 and 1983–2006.

Lyndon (Hermyle) LaRouche, Jr. (8 Sep 1922, Rochester NH), American economist, populist politician, and perennial presidential candidate.

John Lasseter (12 Jan 1957, Hollywood CA), American animator and director; chief creative officer at Pixar Animation Studios from 2006.

Matt(hew Todd) Lauer (30 Dec 1957, New York NY), American TV journalist and news anchor.

Ralph Lauren (Ralph Lipschitz; 14 Oct 1939, New York NY), American fashion designer.

Hugh Laurie (James Hugh Calum Laurie; 11 Jun 1959, Oxford, England), British TV and film actor.

Sergey (Viktorovich) Lavrov (21 Mar 1950, Moscow, USSR [now in Russia]), Russian politician; foreign minister from 2004.

Jude Law (29 Dec 1972, Blackheath, London, England), British stage and screen actor.

Martin Lawrence (16 Apr 1965, Frankfurt am Main, West Germany), American TV actor and comedian.

Nigella (Lucy) Lawson (6 Jan 1960), British cook and author of food-related books.

John Le Carré (David John Moore Cornwell; 19 Oct 1931, Poole, Dorset, England), English spy novelist.

Jean-Marie Gustave Le Clézio (13 Apr 1940, Nice, France), French author; winner of the 2008 Nobel Prize for Literature.

Ursula K(roeber) Le Guin (21 Oct 1929, Berkeley CA), American science-fiction and fantasy writer.

Meave Leakey (28 Jul 1942, London, England), British-born Kenyan paleoanthropologist.

Richard (Erskine Frere) Leakey (19 Dec 1944, Nairobi, Kenya), Kenyan physical anthropologist, paleontologist, conservationist, and politician.

Michael O. Leavitt (11 Feb 1951, Cedar City UT), American politician (Republican) and official; governor of Utah, 1993–2003, EPA administrator, 2003–05, and US secretary of heath and human services, 2005–09.

Ang Lee (23 Oct 1954, P'ing-Tung county, Taiwan), Taiwanese-born film director.

Jason (Michael) Lee (25 Apr 1970, Orange CA), American skateboarder and film and TV actor.

Spike Lee (Shelton Lee; 20 Mar 1957, Atlanta GA), American film director.

Stan Lee (Stanley Martin Lieber; 28 Dec 1922, New York NY), American comic-book artist; creator of Spider-Man and other superheroes.

Lee Hsien Loong (10 Feb 1952, Singapore), Singaporean politician and economic expert; prime minister from 2004.

Lee Kun Hee (9 Jan 1942, Uiryung, Japanese-occupied Korea [now in South Korea]), South Korean corporate executive; chairman of the Samsung Group, 1987–2008.

Lee Myung-bak (19 Dec 1941, Osaka, Japan), South Korean politician (Grand National Party); mayor of Seoul, 2002–06, and president of South Korea from 2008.

John Leguizamo (22 Jul 1964, Bogotá, Colombia), Colombian-born American comedian and actor.

Dennis Lehane (4 Aug 1966, Dorchester, Boston MA), American crime novelist.

Jim Lehrer (James C. Lehrer; 19 May 1934, Wichita KS), American TV journalist and author.

Annie Leibovitz (Anna-Lou Leibovitz; 2 Oct 1949, Westbury CT), American portrait photographer and photojournalist.

Jean Lemierre (6 Jun 1950, Sainte Adresse, France), French international banking executive and president of the European Bank for Reconstruction and Development from 2000.

Jay Leno (James Douglas Muir Leno; 28 Apr 1950, Short Hills NJ), American comedian and TV talk-show host.

Robert Lepage (12 Dec 1957, Quebec, QC, Canada), Canadian actor, director, and playwright.

Doris Lessing (Doris May Thaler; 22 Oct 1919, Kermanshah, Persia [now Bakhtaran, Iran]), British novelist and short-story writer; recipient of the 2007 Nobel Prize for Literature.

Jonathan (Allen) Lethem (19 Feb 1964, Brooklyn NY), American novelist, short-story writer, and essayist.

Letsie III (David Mohato; 17 Jul 1963, Morija, Basutoland [now Lesotho]), Lesotho royal; king of Lesotho, 1990–95 and again from 1996.

David (Michael) Letterman (12 Apr 1947, Indianapolis IN), American TV talk-show host.

Tracy Letts (4 Jul 1965, Tulsa OK), American playwright and actor whose *August: Osage County* won the 2008 Pulitzer Prize for drama.

Simon Asher Levin (22 Apr 1941, Baltimore MD), American biologist who specializes in the application of mathematics to problems in ecology.

James Levine (23 Jun 1943, Cincinnati OH), American conductor and pianist; music director of the Metropolitan Opera from 1976 and principal conductor of the Boston Symphony Orchestra from 2004.

Bernard-Henri Lévy (5 Nov 1948, Béni-Saf, French Algeria), Algerian-born French media darling and author of best-selling "enhanced nonfiction" books.

Eugene Levy (17 Dec 1946, Hamilton, ON, Canada), Canadian comic actor and writer.

Kenneth D. Lewis (9 Apr 1947, Meridian MS), American corporate executive; CEO of the Bank of America Corp. from 2001.

(Diane) Monique Lhuillier (1971, Cebu, Philippines), American couturier.

Jet Li (Li Lian Jie; 26 Apr 1963, Beijing, China), Chinese-born *wushu* (acrobatic martial arts) champion and film actor.

Li Ka-shing (13 Jun 1928, Chaozhou, Guangdong province, China), Chinese (Hong Kong) corporate executive; chairman of Hutchison Whampoa Ltd. and Cheung Kong Holdings.

Daniel Libeskind (12 May 1946, Lodz, Poland), Polish-born Israeli American architect.

Abu Yahya al-Libi (1963, Libya), Libyan militant Islamic extremist leader associated with the Libyan Islamic Fighting Group and a top strategist for al-Qaeda.

Nicklas (Erik) Lidström (28 Apr 1970, Västerås, Sweden), Swedish ice-hockey defenseman.

Joseph I. Lieberman (24 Feb 1942, Stamford CT), American politician (Independent Democrat); senator from Connecticut from 1989.

Lil' Kim (Kimberly Denise Jones; 11 Jul 1975, Bedford-Stuyvesant, Brooklyn NY), American hip-hop performer.

Rush Limbaugh (12 Jan 1951, Cape Girardeau MO), American radio talk-show host and conservative commentator.

Linda Lingle (Linda Cutter; 4 Jun 1953, St. Louis MO), American politician (Republican); governor of Hawaii from 2002.

Laura Linney (5 Feb 1964, New York NY), American actress.

John Lithgow (19 Oct 1945, Rochester NY), American film and TV actor.

Lucy (Alexis) Liu (2 Dec 1968, Jackson Heights, Queens NY), American TV and film actress.

Liu Chao-shiuan (10 May 1943, Hengyang, Hunan province, China), Taiwanese politician; president of the Executive Yuan (premier) from 2008.

Nicholas (Joseph Orville) Liverpool (9 Sep 1934, Dominica, British West Indies), West Indian politician; president of Dominica from 2003.

Kenneth Livingstone (17 Jun 1945, Lambeth, London, England), British politician (Labour); mayor of London, 2000–08.

Tzipi Livni (Tzipora Malka Livni; 8 Jul 1958, Tel Aviv–Yafo, Israel), Israeli politician (Kadima); foreign minister of Israel, 2006–09, and leader of the Kadima party from 2008.

LL Cool J (James Todd Smith; 14 Jan 1968, Queens NY), American hip-hop artist and actor.

Andrew Lloyd Webber (22 Mar 1948, London, England), British composer of stage musicals; recipient of a Praemium Imperiale in 1995 and a 2006 Kennedy Center Honor.

Gary Locke (21 Jan 1950, Seattle WA), American politician (Democrat); governor of Washington, 1997–2005, and US secretary of commerce from 2009.

Keith Alan Lockhart (7 Nov 1959, Poughkeepsie NY), American conductor of the Boston Pops from 1993.

Lindsay (Morgan) Lohan (2 Jul 1986, New York NY), American actress and film starlet.

Jonah Tali Lomu (12 May 1975, Auckland, New Zealand), New Zealand rugby winger.

Eva (Jacqueline) Longoria Parker (15 Mar 1975, Corpus Christi TX), American TV actress.

Jennifer Lopez (24 Jul 1970, Bronx NY), American pop singer, actress, and fashion designer.

Andrés Manuel López Obrador (13 Nov 1953, Tepetitán, Mexico), Mexican politician (Party of the Democratic Revolution); head of government of the Federal District (mayor of Mexico City), 2000–05; unsuccessful candidate for president in 2006.

Peter Löscher (17 Sep 1957, Villach, Austria), Austrian corporate executive; president and CEO of Siemens AG from 2007.

Trent Lott (9 Oct 1941, Grenada MS), American politician (Republican); senator from Mississippi, 1989–2007, Senate leader, 1996–2003, and Senate whip, 1995–96 and again in 2007.

Christian Louboutin (7 Jan 1963, Paris, France), French high-fashion shoe designer.

Henri Loyrette (31 May 1952, Neuilly-sur-Seine, France), French museum curator; director of the Louvre from 2001.

George (Walton) Lucas, Jr. (14 May 1944, Modesto CA), American film producer.

Susan Lucci (23 Dec 1947, Scarsdale NY), American TV soap opera star.

Fernando (Armindo) Lugo (Méndez) (30 May 1951, San Pedro del Paraná, Paraguay), Paraguayan Roman Catholic bishop and missionary; president from 2008.

Baz(mark Anthony) Luhrmann (17 Sep 1962, near Sydney, NSW, Australia), Australian film and stage director and producer.

Alyaksandr (Hrygorevich) Lukashenka (30 Aug 1954, Kopys, Vitebsk oblast, Belorussian SSR, USSR [now Belarus]), Belarusian politician; president from 1994.

Luiz Inácio Lula da Silva (27 Oct 1945, Garanhuns, Pernambuco state, Brazil), Brazilian labor leader and politician (Workers Party); president from 2003.

Hilary Lunke (7 Jun 1979, Edina MN), American golfer.

John (H.) Lynch (25 Nov 1952, Waltham MA), American businessman and politician (Democrat); governor of New Hampshire from 2005.

Yo-Yo Ma (7 Oct 1955, Paris, France), American cellist.

Ma Ying-jeou (Ma Yingjiu; 13 Jul 1950, Hong Kong), Taiwanese politician and government official; mayor of Taipei, 1998–2006, and president from 2008.

Lorin Maazel (6 Mar 1930, Neuilly, France), French-born American conductor and violinist; music director of the New York Philharmonic from 2002.

Gloria (Macaraeg) Macapagal Arroyo (5 Apr 1947, San Juan, Philippines), Philippine politician; president from 2001.

Rodney (Joseph) MacDonald (2 Jan 1972, Inverness, NS, Canada), Canadian fiddle player and politician (Progressive Conservative); premier of Nova Scotia, 2006–09.

Alistair MacLeod (20 Jul 1936, North Batteford, SK, Canada), Canadian writer.

Rachel Maddow (1 Apr 1973, Castro Valley CA), American liberal television commentator and radio talk-show host.

Bernard L. Madoff (29 Apr 1938, Queens NY), American financier; convicted in 2009 of having operated one of the world's largest Ponzi schemes.

Madonna (Madonna Louise Veronica Ciccone; 16 Aug 1958, Bay City MI), American singer, songwriter, actress, and entrepreneur.

Tobey Maguire (Tobias Vincent Maguire; 27 Jun 1975, Santa Monica CA), American film actor.

Bill Maher (20 Jan 1956, New York NY), American TV comedian and personality.

Roger Michael Cardinal Mahony (27 Feb 1936, Hollywood CA), American Roman Catholic churchman; archbishop of Los Angeles from 1985 and cardinal from 1991.

Natalie Maines (14 Oct 1974, Lubbock TX), American country vocalist (for the Dixie Chicks).

Mohammed ibn Rashid al-Maktum (1949, Dubai, British Trucial States [now in United Arab Emirates]?), UAE sheikh; crown prince from 1995 and ruler of Dubai from 2006.

Tuilaepa Sailele Malielegaoi (14 Apr 1945, Lepa, Samoa), Samoan politician; prime minister of Samoa from 1998.

Nuri (Kamal) al-Maliki (Jawad al-Maliki; Abu Isra; 1 Jul 1950, near Karbala, Iraq), Iraqi politician (Shi'ite); prime minister of Iraq from 2006.

Evgeni Malkin (31 Jul 1986, Magnitogorsk, Russia), Russian ice-hockey player.

John (Gavin) Malkovich (9 Dec 1953, Christopher IL), American film actor and filmmaker.

David (George Joseph) Malouf (20 Mar 1934, Brisbane, QLD, Australia), Australian poet and novelist; recipient of the 2000 Neustadt Prize.

David (Alan) Mamet (30 Nov 1947, Chicago IL), American playwright, director, and screenwriter.

Joe Manchin (Joseph Manchin III; 24 Aug 1947, Farmington WV), American businessman and politician (Democrat); governor of West Virginia from 2005.

Nelson (Rolihlahla) Mandela (18 Jul 1918, Umtata, Cape of Good Hope, Union of South Africa [now Mthatha, South Africa]), South African black nationalist leader and statesman; he was a political prisoner, 1962–90, president of South Africa (1994–99), and corecipient of the 1993 Nobel Peace Prize.

Barry Manilow (Barry Alan Pincus; 17 Jun 1946, Brooklyn NY), American pop singer and songwriter.

Michael (Kenneth) Mann (5 Feb 1943, Chicago IL), American film director.

Eli(sha Nelson) Manning (3 Jan 1981, New Orleans LA), American pro football quarterback.

Patrick (Augustus Merving) Manning (17 Aug 1946, San Fernando, Trinidad, British West Indies [now in Trinidad and Tobago]), Trinidadian politician; prime minister of Trinidad and Tobago, 1991–95 and again from 2001.

Peyton (Williams) Manning (24 Mar 1976, New Orleans LA), American pro football quarterback.

John H. Marburger III (1941?, Staten Island NY), American physicist; presidential science adviser and head of the Office of Science and Technology Policy, 2001–09.

Sergio Marchionne (17 Jun 1952, Chieti, Italy), Italian Canadian businessman; CEO of Chrysler Group LLC.

Brice Marden (15 Oct 1938, Bronxville NY), American minimalist painter and printmaker.

Margrethe II (Margrethe Alexandrine Thorhildur Ingrid; 16 Apr 1940, Copenhagen, Denmark), Danish royal; queen from 1972.

Mariam (Mariam Doumbia; 15 Apr 1958), Malian singer (of Amadou and Mariam).

Mariza (Mariza Nunes; 1974?, Mozambique), Portuguese fado singer.

Mary Ellen Mark (20 Mar 1940, Philadelphia PA), American photojournalist.

Jack Markell (26 Nov 1940, Newark DE), American politician (Democrat); governor of Delaware from 2009.

Branford Marsalis (26 Aug 1960, Breaux Bridge LA), American jazz saxophonist, bandleader, and producer.

Wynton Marsalis (18 Oct 1961, New Orleans LA), American jazz trumpeter and composer.

Yann Martel (25 Jun 1963, Salamanca, Spain), Spanish-born Canadian novelist; recipient of the 2002 Man Booker Prize.

Kevin Martin (14 Dec 1966, Charlotte NC), American politician and chairman of the Federal Communications Commission, 2005–09.

Steve Martin (14 Aug 1945, Waco TX), American comedic actor, screenwriter, playwright, and author; recipient of a 2007 Kennedy Center Honor.

Ricardo (Alberto) Martinelli (Berrocal) (11 Mar 1952, Panama City, Panama), Panamanian politician; president from 2009.

Mel Martinez (Melquíades Rafael Martínez; 23 Oct 1946, Sagua la Grande, Cuba), Cuban-born American politician and official; US secretary of housing and urban development, 2001–03, senator (Republican) from Florida, 2005–09, and general chairman of the Republican National Committee in 2007.

Mary (Mary Donaldson; 5 Feb 1972, Hobart, TAS, Australia), Australian-born marketing executive and crown princess of Denmark; wife of Crown Prince Frederik (married 14 May 2004).

Masako (Masako Owada; 9 Dec 1963, Tokyo, Japan), Japanese royal; princess consort of Crown Prince Naruhito (married 9 Jun 1993).

Toshihide Maskawa (7 Feb 1940, Nagoya, Japan), Japanese physicist; cowinner of the 2008 Nobel Prize for Physics.

Master P (Percy Miller; 29 Apr 1970, New Orleans LA), American gangsta rap performer and producer.

Kalkot Mataskelekele (Mauliliu) (24 Apr 1949, Port Vila?, New Hebrides [now Vanuatu]), Vanuatuan lawyer and politician; president, 2004–09.

Mathilde (Mathilde d'Udekem d'Acoz; 21 Jan 1973, Uccle, Belgium), Belgian royal; princess consort of Prince Philippe (married 4 Dec 1999) and heir to the throne.

Hideki Matsui (12 Jun 1974, Ishikawa prefecture, Japan), Japanese baseball outfielder.

Koichiro Matsuura (29 Sep 1937, Tokyo, Japan), Japanese diplomat and international official; director general of UNESCO from 1999.

Daisuke Matsuzaka (13 Sep 1980, Tokyo, Japan), Japanese baseball player.

Dave Matthews (David John Matthews; 9 Jan 1967, Johannesburg, South Africa), American rock musician (of the Dave Matthews Band).

Máxima (Máxima Zorreguieta Cerruti; 17 May 1971, Buenos Aires, Argentina), Argentine-born Dutch investment banker and princess consort of Crown Prince Willem-Alexander (married 2 Feb 2002).

John (Clayton) Mayer (16 Oct 1977, Bridgeport CT), American singer and songwriter.

Thom Mayne (19 Jan 1944, Waterbury CT), American architect; recipient of the 2005 Pritzker Prize.

Floyd Mayweather, Jr. ("Pretty Boy"; 24 Feb 1977, Grand Rapids MI), American boxing champion in several weight classes, from lightweight to super welterweight.

Kiran Mazumdar-Shaw (1954?, Bangalore [now Bengaluru], India), Indian business executive; founder (1978) of Biocon India, India's first biotechnology company.

Thabo (Mvuyelwa) Mbeki (18 Jun 1942, Idutywa, Cape of Good Hope, Union of South Africa [now in Eastern Cape province, South Africa]), South African politician; president, 1999–2008.

Mary (Patricia) McAleese (27 Jun 1951, Belfast, Northern Ireland), Irish politician; president from 1997.

James (Andrew) McAvoy (21 Apr 1979, Glasgow, Scotland), British actor.

John (Sidney) McCain III (29 Aug 1936, Panama Canal Zone), American politician (Republican); senator from Arizona from 1987; the Republican candidate for president in 2008.

Cormac McCarthy (Charles McCarthy, Jr.; 20 Jul 1933, Providence RI), American novelist in the Southern gothic tradition.

(James) Paul McCartney (18 Jun 1942, Liverpool, England), British singer, songwriter, and former member of the Beatles.

Stella (Nina) McCartney (13 Sep 1971, London, England), British fashion designer.

Matthew McConaughey (4 Nov 1969, Uvalde TX), American film actor.

Mike McConnell (John Michael McConnell; 26 Jul 1943, Greenville SC), American military intelligence officer; director of the National Security Agency, 1992–96, and director of national intelligence, 2007–09.

(Addison) Mitch(ell) McConnell (Jr.) (20 Feb 1942, Tuscumbia, AL), American politician (Republican); senator from Kentucky from 1985, Senate whip, 2003–07, and Senate leader from 2007.

David McCullough (7 Jul 1933, Pittsburgh PA), American biographer and historian.

Audra (Ann) McDonald (3 Jul 1970, West Berlin, West Germany [now in Berlin, Germany], American theater actress.

Frances McDormand (23 Jun 1957, Chicago IL), American film actress.

John (Patrick) McEnroe, Jr. (16 Feb 1959, Wiesbaden, West Germany), American tennis player and TV sportscaster.

Reba McEntire (28 Mar 1954, McAlester OK), American country singer and TV and film actress.

Ian (Russell) McEwan (21 Jun 1948, Aldershot, England), British novelist.

Glenn (Donald) McGrath (9 Feb 1970, Dubbo, NSW, Australia), Australian cricket fast bowler.

Phil(lip C.) McGraw (1 Sep 1950, Vinita OK), American talk-show host, author, and psychologist-educator.

(Samuel) Tim(othy) McGraw (1 May 1967, Delhi LA), American country-and-western singer.

Dalton McGuinty (19 Jul 1955, Ottawa, ON, Canada), Canadian lawyer and politician (Liberal); premier of Ontario from 2003.

Kevin McKenzie (29 Apr 1954, Burlington VT), American ballet dancer, choreographer, and director.

Beverley McLachlin (7 Sep 1943, Pincher Creek, AB, Canada), Canadian Supreme Court justice from 1989 and chief justice from 2000.

Vince McMahon (Vincent Kennedy McMahon, Jr.; 24 Aug 1945, Pinehurst NC), American wrestling promoter; owner of World Wrestling Entertainment, Inc., from 1982.

Larry McMurtry (3 Jun 1936, Wichita Falls TX), American novelist.

W. James McNerney, Jr. (22 Aug 1949, Providence RI), American corporate executive; chairman of the board, president, and CEO of the Boeing Co. from 2005.

Marian McPartland (Margaret Marian Turner; 20 Mar 1918, Slough, England), English-born jazz pianist and composer.

James M. McPherson (11 Oct 1936, Valley City ND), American historian of slavery and the antislavery movement.

Ian McShane (29 Sep 1942, Blackburn, Lancashire, England), British film and TV actor.

Jon Meacham (1969, Chattanooga TN), American author, political commentator, and magazine editor; his American Lion: Andrew Jackson in the White House won the 2009 Pulitzer Prize for biography or autobiography.

Russell (Charles) Means (10 Nov 1939, Pine Ridge SD), American Lakota Sioux activist.

Dmitry (Anatolyevich) Medvedev (14 Sep 1965, Leningrad, USSR [now St. Petersburg, Russia]), Russian lawyer and politician; president of Russia from 2008.

Zubin Mehta (29 Apr 1936, Bombay, British India [now Mumbai, India]), Indian orchestral conductor; music director of the Israel Philharmonic from 1977; recipient of a 2008 Praemium Imperiale.

Cildo Meireles (1948, Rio de Janeiro, Brazil), Brazilian installation artist and sculptor.

John Mellencamp (Johnny Cougar; John Cougar Mellencamp; 7 Oct 1951, Seymour IN), American singer and songwriter.

Eva Mendes (5 Mar 1974, Miami FL), American model and film actress.

Sam(uel Alexander) Mendes (1 Aug 1965, Reading, England), British film director.

Paulo Mendes da Rocha (25 Oct 1928, Vitória, Espírito Santo state, Brazil), Brazilian architect and professor; recipient of the 2006 Pritzker Prize.

Fradique de Menezes (1942), São Tomé and Príncipe politician; president, 2001–03 and again from 2003.

Angela Merkel (Angela Dorothea Kasner; 17 Jul 1954, Hamburg, West Germany), German politician (Christian Democratic Union); chancellor of Germany from 2005.

Hans-Rudolf Merz (10 Nov 1942, Herisau, Switzerland), Swiss politician; president from 2009.

W(illiam) S(tanley) Merwin (30 Sep 1927, New York NY), American poet and translator; his The Shadow of Sirius won the 2009 Pulitzer Prize for poetry.

Stipe Mesic (Stjepan Mesic; 24 Dec 1934, Orahovica, Yugoslavia [now in Croatia]), Croatian politician; president from 2000.

Mette-Marit (Mette-Marit Tjessem Høiby; 19 Aug 1973, Kristiansand, Norway), Norwegian royal; princess consort of Crown Prince Haakon (married 25 Aug 2001).

Pierre de Meuron (8 May 1950, Basel, Switzerland), Swiss architect; corecipient of the 2001 Pritzker Prize and of a Praemium Imperiale in 2007.

Stephenie Meyer (24 Dec 1973, Hartford CT), American author of fiction for young adults.

Jonathan Rhys Meyers (Jonathan Michael Francis O'Keefe; 27 Jul 1977, Dublin, Ireland), Irish film actor.

M.I.A. (Mathangi ["Maya"] Arulpragasam; 18 Jul 1975, London, England), British-born rapper.

Michael (Michael Hohenzollern-Sigmaringen; ruled as Mihai I; 25 Oct 1921, Sinaia, Romania), Romanian king, 1927–30 (under regency) and 1940–47.

Lorne Michaels (Lorne Michael Lipowitz; 17 Nov 1944, Toronto, ON, Canada), Canadian-born TV and film producer.

James (Alix) Michel (16 Aug 1944, Mahe Island, Seychelles), Seychelles politician; president from 2004.

Roberto Micheletti (Baín) (13 Aug 1948, El Progreso, Honduras), Honduran politician; de facto president from 2009, as the result of a military ouster of Pres. Manuel Zelaya.

Michiko (Michiko Shoda; 20 Oct 1934, Tokyo, Japan), Japanese royal; empress consort of Emperor Akihito (married 10 Apr 1959).

Bette Midler (1 Dec 1945, Honolulu HI), American comedian, singer, and actress.

Midori (Midori Goto; 25 Oct 1971, Osaka, Japan), Japanese-born American violinist.

David (Wright) Miliband (15 Jul 1965, London, England), British politician (Labour); foreign secretary from 2007.

David (Raymond) Miller (26 Dec 1958, San Francisco CA), American-born Canadian politician (independent); mayor of Toronto from 2003.

Dennis Miller (3 Nov 1953, Pittsburgh PA), American TV comedian, radio talk-show host, and writer.

(Samuel) Bode Miller (12 Oct 1977, Easton NH), American Alpine skier.

Sienna (Rose) Miller (28 Dec 1981, New York NY), American-born British stage and film actress.

Sue Miller (29 Nov 1943, Chicago IL), American novelist.

John Atta Mills (21 Jul 1944, Tarkwa, Gold Coast [now Ghana]), Ghanaian politician; president from 2009.

Ruth Ann Minner (Ruth Ann Coverdale; 17 Jan 1935, Milford DE), American politician (Democrat); governor of Delaware (2001–09).

Kylie (Ann) Minogue (28 May 1968, Melbourne, VIC, Australia), Australian actress and pop singer.

Helen Mirren (Ilyena Lydia Mironoff; 26 Jul 1945, Chiswick, London, England), British stage, TV, and film actress.

Joni Mitchell (Roberta Joan Anderson; 7 Nov 1943, Fort Macleod, AB, Canada), Canadian singer, songwriter, and painter.

Efthimios E. Mitropoulos (30 May 1939, Piraeus, Greece), Greek international official; secretary-general of the International Maritime Organization from 2004.

Lakshmi (Narayan) Mittal (15 Jun 1950, Sadulpur, Rajasthan state, India), Indian-born British steel magnate.

Satoshi Miura (3 Apr 1944, Japan?), Japanese corporate executive; CEO and president of Nippon Telephone & Telegraph from 2007.

Ratko Mladic (12 Mar 1943, Kalinovik village, Bosnia, Yugoslavia [now in Bosnia and Herzegovina]), Bosnian Serb military officer sought as a war criminal.

N(avarre) Scott Momaday (27 Feb 1934, Lawton OK), American writer of Kiowa heritage.

Thomas S(pencer) Monson (21 Aug 1927, Salt Lake City UT), American church leader; president of the Church of Jesus Christ of Latter-day Saints from 2008.

Luc Montagnier (18 Aug 1932, Chabris, France), French scientist; cowinner of the 2008 Nobel Prize for Physiology or Medicine.

Alan Moore (18 Nov 1953), British author and creator of graphic novels.

Demi Moore (Demetria Gene Guynes; 11 Nov 1962, Roswell NM), American film actress.

Julianne Moore (Julie Anne Smith; 3 Dec 1960, Fayetteville NC), American film actress.

Lorrie Moore (Marie Lorena Moore; 13 Jan 1957, Glens Falls NY), American short-story writer and novelist.

Mandy Moore (Amanda Leigh Moore; 10 Apr 1984, Nashua NH), American pop singer and film actress.

Michael Moore (23 Apr 1954, Davison MI), American film director and author.

(Juan) Evo Morales (Ayma) (26 Oct 1959, Orinoca, Bolivia), Bolivian farm-union leader; president from 2006.

Jason Moran (21 Jan 1975, Houston TX), American jazz pianist and bandleader.

Luis Moreno Ocampo (4 Jun 1952, Buenos Aires, Argentina), Argentine lawyer; the first chief prosecutor of the International Criminal Court, from 2003.

Rhodri Morgan (29 Sep 1939, Cardiff, Wales), Welsh politician (Labour); first minister of Wales from 2000.

Manny Mori (Emanuel Mori; 1948, Chuuk state?, Micronesia), Micronesian politician; president from 2007.

Mark Morris (29 Aug 1956, Seattle WA), American dancer and choreographer.

Toni Morrison (Chloe Anthony Wofford; 18 Feb 1931, Lorain OH), American novelist; recipient of the 1993 Nobel Prize for Literature.

Viggo (Peter) Mortensen (20 Oct 1958, New York NY), American film actor.

Martin Mosebach (31 Jul 1951, Frankfurt am Main, West Germany), German novelist; recipient of the 2007 Georg Büchner Prize.

Walter Mosley (12 Jan 1952, Los Angeles CA), American writer of science fiction and mystery novels.

Kgalema (Petrus) Motlanthe (19 Jul 1949, Johannesburg, Union of South Africa), South African politician (African National Congress); president, 2008–09, and deputy president from 2009.

Andrew Motion (26 Oct 1952, London, England), English poet, teacher, editor, and biographer; poet laureate of England, 1999–2009.

Patrice (Tlhopane) Motsepe (28 Jan 1962, Johannesburg, South Africa), South African mining tycoon and sports club owner; founder (1997) and chairman of African Rainbow Minerals Ltd.

Markos Moulitsas (Zúniga) ("Kos"; 11 Sep 1971, Chicago IL), American populist journalist and blogger; founder and editor of the Daily Kos blog from 2002.

Amr Muhammad Moussa (3 Oct 1936, Cairo, Egypt), Egyptian secretary-general of the League of Arab States from 2001.

Bill Moyers (Billy Don Moyers; 5 Jun 1934, Hugo OK), American TV journalist, former government official, and author.

Mswati III (19 Apr 1968, Swaziland), Swazi royal; king of Swaziland from 1986.

(Muhammed) Hosni Mubarak (4 May 1928, Al-Minufiyah governorate, Egypt), Egyptian politician; president from 1981.

Daniel H. Mudd (1959), American corporate executive; president and CEO of Fannie Mae, 2005–08.

Edward A. Mueller (1947, St. Louis MO), American corporate executive; chairman and CEO of Qwest Communications International Inc. from 2007.

Lisel Mueller (Lisel Neumann; 8 Feb 1924, Hamburg, Germany), German-born American poet.

Robert S(wan) Mueller III (7 Aug 1944, New York NY), American government official; FBI director from 2001.

Robert (Gabriel) Mugabe (21 Feb 1924, Kutama, Southern Rhodesia [now Zimbabwe]), Zimbabwean politician; the first prime minister (1980–87) of the reconstituted state of Zimbabwe and president from 1987.

Muhammad VI (Muhammad ibn al-Hassan; 21 Aug 1963, Rabat, Morocco), Moroccan royal; king from 1999.

Ali Muhammad Mujawar (1953, Shabwah, British-protected Aden [now in Yemen]), Yemeni politician; prime minister from 2007.

Michael (Bernard) Mukasey (28 Jul 1941, Bronx NY), American jurist; US attorney general, 2007–09.

Pranab Mukherjee (11 Dec 1935, Mirati village, West Bengal, British India), Indian politician (Indian National Congress); foreign minister, 1995–96 and 2006–09, and finance minister from 2009.

Alan Mulally (4 Aug 1945, Oakland CA), American businessman; president and CEO of Ford Motor Co.

Paul Muldoon (20 Jun 1951, Portadown, Northern Ireland), Irish-born American poet.

Alice Munro (Alice Anne Laidlaw; 10 Jul 1931, Wingham, ON, Canada), Canadian short-story writer; recipient of the 2009 Man Booker International Prize.

(Keith) Rupert Murdoch (11 Mar 1931, Melbourne, VIC, Australia), Australian-born British newspaper publisher and media entrepreneur; founder of the global media holding company News Corporation Ltd.

Eddie Murphy (3 Apr 1961, Brooklyn NY), American comedian and film actor.

Cormac Cardinal Murphy-O'Connor (24 Aug 1932, Reading, Berkshire, England), British church leader; archbishop of Westminster (leader of the Roman Catholic Church in the UK), 2000–09, and cardinal from 2001.

Narayana Murthy (20 Aug 1946, Kolar, British India), Indian international business executive and pioneer in India's high-tech industry; cofounder and chairman of Infosys Technologies Ltd., a technology and consulting firm.

Yoweri (Kaguta) Museveni (15 Aug 1944, Mbarra district, Uganda), Ugandan politician; president from 1986.

Pervez Musharraf (Pervez Musharraf Nish-i-Imtiaz; 11 Aug 1943, New Delhi, British India), Pakistani military leader and politician; head of Pakistan's government, 1999–2001, and president, 2001–08.

Bingu wa Mutharika (24 Feb 1934, Thyolo district, British Nyasaland [now Malawi]), Malawian politician (United Democratic Front); president from 2004.

Riccardo Muti (28 Jul 1941, Naples, Italy), Italian conductor; music director of La Scala Orchestra in Milan, 1986–2005; named to become music director of the Chicago Symphony Orchestra from 2010.

Anne-Sophie Mutter (29 Jun 1963, Rheinfelden, West Germany), German violinist.

Mike Myers (25 May 1963, Scarborough, ON, Canada), Canadian comedian and actor.

James Nachtwey (14 Mar 1948, Syracuse NY), American news photographer.

Rafael Nadal (Parera) (3 Jun 1986, Manacor, Mallorca, Spain), Spanish tennis player.

Ralph Nader (27 Feb 1934, Winsted CT), American social activist and politician; he was a presidential candidate in 2000, 2004, and 2008.

(Clarence) Ray Nagin, Jr. (11 Jun 1956, New Orleans LA), American politician (Democrat); mayor of New Orleans from 2002.

Parminder K. Nagra (5 Oct 1975, Leicester, Leicestershire, England), British film and TV actress.

Khalifah ibn Zayid Al Nahyan (c. 1948, Al-ʿAyn, Abu Dhabi, British Trucial States [now United Arab Emirates]), UAE sheikh; ruler of Abu Dhabi and president of the United Arab Emirates from 2004.

V(idiadhar) S(urajprasad) Naipaul (17 Aug 1932, Chaguanas, Trinidad, British West Indies [now in Trinidad and Tobago]), Trinidadian-born British writer; recipient of the 2001 Nobel Prize for Literature.

Datuk Seri Najib Tun Razak (23 Jul 1953, Kuala Lipis, Malaysia), Malaysian politician; prime minister from 2009.

Yoichiro Nambu (18 Jan 1921, Tokyo, Japan), American physicist; cowinner of the 2008 Nobel Prize for Physics.

Giorgio Napolitano (29 Jun 1925, Naples, Italy), Italian politician (Communist); president from 2006.

Janet Napolitano (29 Nov 1957, New York NY), American politician (Democrat); governor of Arizona, 2003–09, and US secretary of homeland security from 2009.

Robert (Louis) Nardelli (17 May 1948, Old Forge PA), American corporate executive; CEO of the Home Depot, Inc., 2000–07, and of Chrysler Corp., 2007–09.

Naruhito (23 Feb 1960, Tokyo, Japan), Japanese crown prince.

Nas (Nasir bin Olu Dara Jones; "Nasty Nas"; "Nas Escobar"; 14 Sep 1973, Queens NY), American hip-hop artist.

Milton Nascimento (26 Oct 1942, Rio de Janeiro, Brazil), Brazilian pop singer and songwriter.

Mohamed Nasheed (17 May 1967, Male, Maldives), Maldivian politician; president from 2008.

Sayyed Hassan Nasrallah (31 Aug 1960, Borj Hammoud, Beirut, Lebanon), Lebanese Islamic extremist military leader; secretary-general of Hezbollah from 1992.

Taslima Nasrin (25 Aug 1962, Mymensingh, Bangladesh), Bangladeshi Islamic feminist writer.

S(ellapan) R(amanathan) Nathan (3 Jul 1924, Singapore?), Singaporean politician; president from 1999.

Bruce Nauman (6 Nov 1941, Fort Wayne IN), American sculptor and installation and performance artist.

Nursultan Nazarbayev (6 Jul 1940, Chemolgan, USSR [now in Kazakhstan]), Kazakh politician; president from 1990.

Youssou N'Dour (1 Oct 1959, Dakar, French West Africa [now in Senegal]), Senegalese singer and songwriter.

Liam Neeson (William Neeson; 7 Jun 1952, Ballymena, Northern Ireland), British film actor.

Willie (Hugh) Nelson (30 Apr 1933, Fort Worth TX), American songwriter and guitarist.

Madhav Kumar Nepal (9 Mar 1953, Gaur, Nepal), Nepalese politician; prime minister from 2009.

Nerses Bedros XIX (Boutros Tarmouni; 17 Jan 1940, Cairo, Egypt), Armenian churchman; patriarch of the Catholic Armenians from 1999.

Benjamin Netanyahu (21 Oct 1949, Tel Aviv [now Tel Aviv-Yafo], Israel), Israeli politician; prime minister, 1996–99 and again from 2009.

Randy Newman (Randall Stuart Newman; 28 Nov 1943, Los Angeles CA), American songwriter, singer, and pianist.

Marc Newson (1963, Sydney, NSW, Australia), Australian industrial designer.

Thandie Newton (Thandiwe Newton; 6 Nov 1972, Zambia), Zambian-born British TV and film actress.

Teodoro Obiang Nguema Mbasogo (1942, Acoacan, Río Muni [now Equatorial Guinea]), Equatorial Guinean politician; president of Equatorial Guinea from 1979.

Ngugi wa Thiong'o (James Thiong'o Ngugi; 5 Jan 1938, Limuru, Kenya), Kenyan novelist.

Nguyen Minh Triet (8 Oct 1942, Ben Cat district, French Indochina [now in Vietnam]), Vietnamese politician; president from 2006.

Nguyen Tan Dung (17 Nov 1949, Ca Mau, French Indochina [now in Vietnam]), Vietnamese politician; prime minister from 2006.

Vincent Gerard Nichols (8 Nov 1945, Crosby, Merseyside, England), British church leader; archbishop of Westminster (leader of the Roman Catholic Church in the UK) from 2009.

Jack Nicholson (John Joseph Nicholson; 22 Apr 1937, Neptune NJ), American film actor.

Takashi Nishioka (1936?, Japan?), Japanese corporate executive; chairman of Mitsubishi Motors Corp. from 2005.

Jay Nixon (Jeremiah W. Nixon; 13 Feb 1956, De Soto MO), American politician (Democrat); governor of Missouri from 2008.

Pierre Nkurunziza (18 Dec 1963, Ngozi province, Burundi), Burundian Hutu rebel leader; president from 2005.

Ronald K(enneth) Noble (1957?, New Jersey), American law professor and government official; secretary-general of Interpol from 2000.

Christopher (Jonathan James) Nolan (30 Jul 1970, London, England), British film director.

Indra Nooyi (28 Oct 1955, Madras [now Chennai], Tamil Nadu state, India), Indian-born American businesswoman; chairman and CEO of PepsiCo from 2007.

Norodom Sihamoni (14 May 1953, Phnom Penh, Cambodia), Cambodian royal; king from 2004.

Norodom Sihanouk (Preah Baht Samdach Preah Norodom Sihanuk Varman; 31 Oct 1922, Phnom Penh, Cambodia), Cambodian king, 1941–55 and 1993–2004; head of state, 1960–70 and 1991–93.

Chris Noth (13 Nov 1954, Madison WI), American film and TV actor.

Lynn Nottage (1964, Brooklyn NY), American playwright; her *Ruined* won the 2009 Pulitzer Prize for drama.

Jean Nouvel (12 Aug 1945, Fumel, France), French architect; recipient of a Praemium Imperiale in 2001 and the 2008 Pritzker Prize.

Jim Nussle (James Allen Nussle; 27 Jun 1960, Des Moines IA), American politician (Republican); director of the Office of Management and Budget, 2007–09.

Michael A(nthony) Nutter (29 Jun 1957, Philadelphia PA), American politician (Democrat); mayor of Philadelphia from 2008.

Joyce Carol Oates (16 Jun 1938, Lockport NY), American novelist, short-story writer, and essayist.

Thoraya Obaid (2 Mar 1945, Baghdad, Iraq), Iraqi-born Saudi Arabian civil servant; executive director of the UN Population Fund from 2001.

Barack (Hussein) Obama (II) (4 Aug 1961, Honolulu HI), American politician (Democrat); 44th president of the US, from 2009.

Michelle Obama (Michelle LaVaughn Robinson; 17 Jan 1964, Chicago IL), American first lady; wife of Pres. Barack Obama (married 3 Oct 1992).

Conan O'Brien (18 Apr 1963, Brookline MA), American TV talk-show host.

Lorena Ochoa (15 Nov 1981, Guadalajara, Jalisco state, Mexico), Mexican golfer.

Mark O'Connor (5 Aug 1961, Seattle WA), American country fiddle player.

Sandra Day O'Connor (26 Mar 1930, El Paso TX), American jurist; associate justice of the US Supreme Court, 1981–2005, the first woman appointed to the court.

Piermaria J. Oddone (26 Mar 1944, Arequipa, Peru), Peruvian-born American experimental particle physicist and administrator; director of the Fermi National Accelerator Laboratory from 2005.

Raila (Amollo) Odinga (7 Jan 1945, Maseno, Nyanza province, British Kenya), Kenyan politician (Liberal Democratic); prime minister from 2008.

Nelson O. Oduber (7 Feb 1947), Aruban prime minister, 1989–94 and again from 2001.

Kenzaburo Oe (31 Jan 1935, Ose, Ehime prefecture, Japan), Japanese novelist; recipient of the 1994 Nobel Prize for Literature.

Sadaharu Oh (20 May 1940, Tokyo, Japan), Japanese baseball player.

Keith Olbermann (27 Jan 1959, New York NY), American TV sportscaster and commentator.

Claes (Thure) Oldenburg (28 Jan 1929, Stockholm, Sweden), Swedish-born Pop-art sculptor.

Sharon Olds (19 Nov 1942, San Francisco CA), American poet.

Jamie Oliver (27 May 1975, Essex, England), British chef and TV personality.

Ehud Olmert (30 Sep 1945, Binyamina, British Palestine [now in Israel]), Israeli politician (Kadima); prime minister, 2006–09.

Ashley (Fuller) Olsen (13 Jun 1986, Sherman Oaks CA), American former child star and a marketing phenomenon in modeling, films, TV, and music videos.

Mary-Kate Olsen (13 Jun 1986, Sherman Oaks CA), American former child star and a marketing phenomenon in modeling, films, TV, and music videos.

Martin (Joseph) O'Malley (18 Jan 1963, Washington DC), American politician (Democrat); mayor of Baltimore, 1999–2007, and governor of Maryland from 2007.

Sean Patrick O'Malley (29 Jun 1944, Lakewood OH), American Roman Catholic churchman; archbishop of Boston from 2003; cardinal from 2006.

Marc Ona Essangui (1964?, Gabon?), Gabonese environmental activist; winner of the 2009 Goldman Environmental Prize.

(Philip) Michael Ondaatje (12 Sep 1943, Colombo, British Ceylon [now Sri Lanka]), Canadian novelist and poet.

Shaquille (Rashaun) O'Neal (6 Mar 1972, Newark NJ), American basketball center.

Makoto Ooka (16 Feb 1931, Mishima, Shizuoka prefecture, Japan), Japanese poet and literary critic.

Bill O'Reilly (William James O'Reilly, Jr.; 10 Sep 1949, New York NY), American TV journalist and talk-show host.

David J. O'Reilly (January 1947, Dublin, Ireland), Irish-born American corporate executive; chairman and CEO of ChevronTexaco Corp. from 2000.

Suze Orman (5 Jun 1951, Chicago IL), American financial adviser and best-selling author.

Peter Orszag (16 Dec 1968, Boston MA), American economist; director of the Office of Management and Budget from 2009.

Amancio Ortega Gaona (28 Mar 1936, León, Spain), Spanish textile magnate; founder (1985) and chairman of Inditex Group and of its subsidiary Zara España S.A., a retail and distribution company.

(José) Daniel Ortega (Saavedra) (11 Nov 1945, La Libertad, Nicaragua), Nicaraguan guerrilla leader and politician; president, 1984–90 and again from 2007.

Joel Osteen (5 Mar 1963, Houston TX), American evangelist; head of the Lakewood Church in Houston.

Paul S. Otellini (12 Oct 1950, San Francisco CA), American corporate executive; president of Intel Corp. from 2002 and CEO from 2005.

Peter (Seamus) O'Toole (2 Aug 1932, Connemara, County Galway, Irish Free State), British stage and film actor.

Butch Otter (Clement Leroy Otter; 3 May 1942, Caldwell ID), American politician (Republican); governor of Idaho from 2007.

Alexander (Mikhailovich) Ovechkin (17 Sep 1985, Moscow, USSR [now in Russia]), Russian hockey player.

Hisashi Owada (18 Sep 1932, Niigata, Japan), Japanese jurist; president of the International Court of Justice from 2009.

Clive Owen (3 Oct 1964, Keresley, Coventry, Warwickshire, England), British actor.

Amos Oz (4 May 1939, Jerusalem, British Palestine), Israeli novelist, short-story writer, and essayist.

Mehmet Oz (11 Jun 1960, Cleveland OH), American cardiac surgeon, professor, TV medical expert, and author.

Cynthia Ozick (17 Apr 1928, New York NY), American novelist, short-story writer, and playwright.

Makoto Ozone (25 Mar 1961, Kobe, Japan), Japanese jazz pianist.

Rajendra K. Pachauri (20 Aug 1940, Nainital, Uttar Pradesh [now in Uttarakhand state], British India), Indian businessman; head of the Intergovernmental Panel on Climate Change from 2002.

Al(fredo James) Pacino (25 Apr 1940, New York NY), American film actor.

Larry Page (Lawrence Edward Page; 1972, East Lansing MI), American computer scientist and Internet entrepreneur who cofounded (1998) the Google Internet search engine.

Borut Pahor (2 Nov 1963, Postojna, Yugoslavia [now in Slovenia]), Slovenian politician; prime minister of Slovenia from 2008.

Brad Paisley (28 Oct 1972, Glen Dale WV), American contemporary country-and-western singer.

Ian (Richard Kyle) Paisley (6 Apr 1926, Armagh, County Armagh, Northern Ireland), Northern Irish Protestant leader and politician; first minister for Northern Ireland, 2007–08.

Sarah Palin (Sarah Heath; 11 Feb 1964, Sandpoint ID), American politician (Republican); governor of Alaska, 2006–09, and the Republican nominee for vice president in 2008.

Eddie Palmieri (15 Dec 1936, New York NY), American jazz-salsa pianist.

Samuel J. Palmisano (29 Jul 1951), American corporate executive; president and CEO of the International Business Machines (IBM) Corp. from 2002.

Gwyneth Paltrow (28 Sep 1972, Los Angeles CA), American film and stage actress.

Orhan Pamuk (7 Jun 1952, Istanbul, Turkey), Turkish novelist; winner of the 2006 Nobel Prize for Literature.

Leon Panetta (28 Jun 1938, Monterey CA), American politician; congressman from California, 1977–93, director of the Office of Management and Budget, 1993–94, White House chief of staff, 1994–97, and director of the CIA from 2009.

Paola (Paola dei Principi Ruffo di Calabria; 11 Sep 1937, Forte dei Marmi, Italy), Italian-born Belgian royal; queen consort of King Albert II (married 2 Jul 1959).

Karolos Papoulias (4 Jun 1929, Ioannina, Greece), Greek politician; president from 2005.

Anna (Helene) Paquin (24 Jul 1982, Winnipeg, MB, Canada), New Zealand film actress.

Sara Paretsky (8 Jun 1947, Ames IA), American mystery writer.

Nick Park (Nicholas Wulstan Park; 6 Dec 1958, Preston, Lancashire, England), British film animator.

Alan (William) Parker (14 Feb 1944, Islington, London, England), British advertising copywriter and film director.

Mary-Louise Parker (2 Aug 1964, Fort Jackson SC), American actress on stage, in film, and on TV.

Sarah Jessica Parker (25 Mar 1965, Nelsonville OH), American TV and film actress.

Mark Parkinson (24 Jun 1957, Wichita KS), American politician (Democrat); governor of Kansas from 2009.

Suzan-Lori Parks (10 May 1963, Fort Knox KY), American playwright.

Sean R. Parnell (19 Nov 1962, Hanford CA), American politician (Republican); governor of Alaska from 2009.

Anja Pärson (25 Apr 1981, Umeå, Sweden), Swedish downhill skier.

Richard D(ean) Parsons (4 Apr 1949, Bedford-Stuyvesant, Brooklyn NY), American corporate executive; CEO of Time Warner (formerly AOL Time Warner), 2002–07, and chairman of Citigroup from 2009.

Arvo Pärt (11 Sep 1935, Paide, Estonia), Estonian composer.

Dolly (Rebecca) Parton (19 Jan 1946, Locust Ridge TN), American country-and-western singer, songwriter, and actress; recipient of a 2006 Kennedy Center Honor.

Amy Pascal (1959, Los Angeles CA), American film executive; chairman of Sony Pictures Entertainment Motion Picture Group from 2003 and cochairman of Sony Pictures Entertainment from 2006.

Ann Patchett (2 Dec 1963, Los Angeles CA), American novelist.

David A. Paterson (20 May 1954, Brooklyn NY), American politician (Democrat); governor of New York from 2008.

Pratibha Patil (19 Dec 1934, Jalgaon, British India), Indian politician; the country's first female president, from 2007.

Danica (Sue) Patrick (25 Mar 1982, Beloit WI), American race-car driver.

Deval (Laurdine) Patrick (31 Jul 1956, Chicago IL), American politician (Democrat); governor of Massachusetts from 2007.

Robert Pattinson (13 May 1986, London, England), British actor.

Ron Paul (Ronald Ernest Paul; 20 Aug 1935, Pittsburgh PA), American physician and libertarian politician; congressman from Texas from 1997.

Henry M(erritt) Paulson, Jr. (28 Mar 1946, Palm Beach FL), American corporate executive and government official; CEO of Goldman Sachs Group, 1999–2006, and US secretary of the treasury, 2006–09.

Tim(othy James) Pawlenty (21 Nov 1960, St. Paul MN), American politician (Republican); governor of Minnesota from 2003.

James (Benjamin) Peake (18 Jun 1944, St. Louis MO), American army medical officer; US secretary of veterans affairs, 2007–09.

Amanda Peet (11 Jan 1972, New York NY), American film and TV actress.

Pelé (Edson Arantes do Nascimento; 23 Oct 1940, Três Corações, Minas Gerais state, Brazil), Brazilian association football (soccer) legend.

Cesar Pelli (12 Oct 1926, Tucumán, Argentina), Argentine architect.

Nancy Pelosi (Nancy D'Alesandro; 26 Mar 1940, Baltimore MD), American politician (Democrat); congresswoman from California from 1987, House Democratic leader, 2003–07, and speaker of the House from 2007.

Sean (Justin) Penn (17 Aug 1960, Santa Monica CA), American film actor and director.

Murray Perahia (19 Apr 1947, New York NY), American concert pianist.

Bev(erly Eaves) Perdue (14 Jan 1947, Grundy VA), American politician (Democrat); governor of North Carolina from 2009.

Sonny Perdue (George Ervin Perdue III; 20 Dec 1946, Perry GA), American agribusinessman and politician (Republican); governor of Georgia from 2003.

Shimon Peres (Shimon Perski; 2 Aug 1923, Wolozyn, Poland [now Valozhyn, Belarus]), Israeli statesman, prime minister, 1984–86 and 1995–96, and president from 2007; he won the Nobel Peace Prize in 1994 for his efforts to work with the Palestinian Liberation Organization.

Grayson Perry (24 Mar 1960, Chelmsford, Essex, England), British artist; recipient of the 2003 Turner Prize.

Rick Perry (James Richard Perry; 4 Mar 1950 West Texas), American politician (Republican); governor of Texas from 2000.

Mary E. Peters (4 Dec 1948, Phoenix AZ), American transportation official; US secretary of transportation, 2006–09.

David (Howell) Petraeus (7 Nov 1952, Cornwall-on-Hudson NY), American military leader; commander of Multinational Force Iraq (MNF-I), 2007–08, and of US Central Command from 2008.

Michelle Pfeiffer (29 Apr 1958, Santa Ana CA), American film actress.

Michael Phelps (30 Jun 1985, Baltimore MD), American swimmer.

Regis (Francis Xavier) Philbin (25 Aug 1934, New York NY), American TV personality.

Philip (Prince Philip of Greece and Denmark; 10 Jun 1921, Corfu, Greece), British duke of Edinburgh; prince consort of Queen Elizabeth II (married 20 November 1947).

Philippe (Philippe Leopold Louis Marie; 15 Apr 1960, Brussels, Belgium), Belgian royal; duke of Brabant and crown prince of Belgium.

(Matthew) Ryan Phillippe (10 Sep 1974, New Castle DE), American TV and film actor.

Stone Phillips (2 Dec 1954, Texas City TX), American TV host and anchorman.

Ellen (Philpotts-) Page (21 Feb 1987, Halifax, NS, Canada), Canadian TV and film actress.

Joaquin Phoenix (Joaquin Raphael Bottom; 28 Oct 1974, San Juan, Puerto Rico), American film actor.

Renzo Piano (14 Sep 1937, Genoa, Italy), Italian architect; winner of the 1998 Pritzker Prize and the 2002 UIA Gold Medal for Architecture.

T(homas) Boone Pickens (22 May 1928, Holdenville OK), American billionaire oilman; advocate of aggressive investment in alternative energy.

Jodi Picoult (19 May 1966, Neconset, NY), American author.

DBC Pierre (Peter Warren Finlay; June 1961, Reynella, SA, Australia), Australian-born British novelist; winner of the 2003 Man Booker Prize.

Navanethem Pillay (23 Sep 1941, Durban, Union of South Africa), South African judge; UN high commissioner for human rights (from 2008).

François Pinault (21 Aug 1936, Les Champs-Géraux, Brittany, France), French corporate executive (Pinault-Printemps-Redoute) and art collector.

Laffit Pinçay, Jr. (29 Dec 1946, Panama City, Panama), Panamanian-born American jockey.

Jean Ping (24 Nov 1942, Omboué, French Gabon), Gabonese statesman; UN General Assembly president, 2004, and chairman of the Commission of the African Union from 2008.

Pink (Alecia Beth Moore; 8 Sep 1979, Doylestown PA), American pop singer.

Jada Pinkett Smith (Jada Koren Pinkett; 18 Sep 1971, Baltimore MD), American actress, video director, and clothing designer.

Robert Pinsky (20 Oct 1940, Long Branch NJ), American poet and critic; poet laureate of the US, 1997–2000.

Pedro (Verona Rodrigues) Pires (April 1934, Ilha do Fogo, Cape Verde), Cape Verdean politician; president from 2001.

Surin Pitsuwan (28 Oct 1949, Nakhon Si Thammarat, Thailand), Thai intellectual and government official; secretary-general of the Association of Southeast Asian Nations from 2008.

(William) Brad(ley) Pitt (18 Dec 1963, Shawnee OK), American film actor.

Kira (Sergeyevna) Plastinina (1 Jun 1992, Moscow, Russia), Russian teenage fashion designer.

Yevgeny (Viktorovich) Plushchenko (also spelled Evgeni Plushenko; 3 Nov 1982, Solnechny, USSR [now in Russia]), Russian figure skater.

Amy Poehler (16 Sep 1971, Burlington MA), American actress and comedian on TV and in films.

Hifikepunye (Lucas) Pohamba (18 Aug 1935, Okanghudi, South West Africa [now Namibia]), Namibian independence leader and politician; president from 2005.

Sidney Poitier (20 Feb 1927?, Miami FL), Bahamian American stage and film actor and director.

Roman Polanski (Raimund Liebling; 18 Aug 1933, Paris, France), Polish film director, scriptwriter, and actor.

Judit Polgar (23 Jul 1976, Budapest, Hungary), Hungarian chess grand master.

Sigmar Polke (13 Feb 1941, Oels, Germany [now Olesnica, Poland]), German Pop-art painter of Capitalist Realism.

Gregg Popovich (28 Jan 1949, East Chicago IN), American professional basketball coach.

Natalie Portman (Natalie Hershlag; 9 Jun 1981, Jerusalem, Israel), American film actress.

Zac(hary E.) Posen (24 Oct 1980, Brooklyn NY), American fashion designer.

John E. Potter (1956, Bronx NY), American corporate executive; CEO and postmaster general of the US Postal Service from 2001.

Earl A. ("Rusty") Powell III (24 Oct 1943, Spartanburg SC), American museum official; director of the National Gallery of Art in Washington DC from 1992.

Samantha Power (1970, Ireland), Irish-born American writer and political adviser; foreign-policy adviser to the National Security Council from 2009.

Miuccia Prada (1949, Milan, Italy), Italian fashion designer.

Azim Hasham Premji (24 Jul 1945, Bombay, British India [now Mumbai, India]), Indian corporate executive; chairman of the Wipro Corp. of Bangalore from 1977.

Steve(n Clyde) Preston (1961?, Janesville WI?), American government official; US secretary of housing and urban development, 2008–09.

René (García) Préval (17 Jan 1943, Port-au-Prince, Haiti), Haitian politician; president, 1996–2001 and again from 2006.

André (George) Previn (6 Apr 1929, Berlin, Germany), German-born American pianist, composer, and conductor.

Richard Price (12 Oct 1949, Bronx NY), American novelist and screenwriter.

Prince (Prince Rogers Nelson; 7 Jun 1958, Minneapolis MN), American singer and songwriter.

Birgit Prinz (25 Oct 1977, Frankfurt am Main, West Germany), German association football (soccer) player.

Romano Prodi (9 Aug 1939, Scandiano, Italy), Italian politician and prime minister, 1996–98 and 2006–08.

E(dna) Annie Proulx (22 Aug 1935, Norwich CT), American writer.

Albert Pujols (José Alberto Pujols; 16 Jan 1980, Santo Domingo, Dominican Republic), Dominican baseball player.

Georgi Purvanov (28 Jun 1957, Kovachevtsi, Bulgaria), Bulgarian politician; president from 2002.

Vladimir (Vladimirovich) Putin (7 Oct 1952, Leningrad, USSR [now St. Petersburg, Russia]), Russian intelligence officer; prime minister of Russia, 1999–2000, president, 1999–2008, and prime minister again from 2008.

(Sayyid) Qabus ibn Saʿid (18 Nov 1940, Salalah, Oman), Omani head of state; sultan of Oman from 1970 and prime minister from 1972.

Muammar al-Qaddafi (also spelled Muammar Khadafy, Moammar Gadhafi, or Muʿammar al-Qadhdhafi; spring 1942, near Surt, Libya), Libyan military leader and Arab statesman; de facto chief of state from 1969.

Dennis Quaid (9 Apr 1954, Houston TX), American film actor.

Thomas Quasthoff (9 Nov 1959, Hildesheim, West Germany), German bass-baritone.

Queen Latifah (Dana Elaine Owens; 18 Mar 1970, Newark NJ), American rap musician, film actress, and TV personality.

Anna (Marie) Quindlen (8 Jul 1953, Philadelphia PA), American political commentator and author.

Pat Quinn (16 Dec 1948, Hinsdale IL), American politician (Democrat); governor of Illinois from 2009.

Daniel Radcliffe (23 July 1989, Fulham, London, England), British film and stage actor.

Paula Radcliffe (17 Dec 1973, Northwich, Cheshire, England), British marathon runner.

Nebojsa Radmanovic (1 Oct 1949, Gracanica, Yugoslavia [now in Bosnia and Herzegovina]), Bosnia and Herzegovinian politician; chairman of the presidency of the republic, 2008–09.

Aishwarya Rai (1 Nov 1973, Mangalore, Karnataka state, India), Indian beauty queen and film actress.

Sam(uel M.) Raimi (23 Oct 1959, Franklin MI), American cult filmmaker.

Rain (Jeong Ji-hoon; 25 Jun 1982, Seoul, South Korea), Korean pop singer and actor.

Mahinda Rajapakse (18 Nov 1945, British Ceylon [now Sri Lanka]), Sri Lankan politician; prime minister, 2004–05, and president from 2005.

Andry Rajoelina (30 May 1974, Malagasy politician; president of Madagascar from 2009.

Imomali Rakhmonov (5 Oct 1952, Dangara, Tadzhik SSR, USSR [now Tajikistan]), Tajik politician; president from 1992.

Samuel Ramey (28 Mar 1942, Colby KS), American operatic bass.

José Ramos-Horta (26 Dec 1949, Dili, Portuguese Timor [now East Timor (Timor-Leste)]), Timorese nationalist leader; prime minister, 2006–07, and president from 2007; corecipient of the 1996 Nobel Peace Prize.

Gordon (James) Ramsay (8 Nov 1966, Glasgow, Scotland), British chef and TV personality; proprietor of the London restaurants Aubergine, 1993–98, and Restaurant Gordon Ramsay, from 1998.

Rania al-Abdullah (Rania al-Yaseen; 31 Aug 1970, Kuwait), Kuwaiti-born Jordanian royal; queen consort of King Abdullah II (married 10 Jun 1993).

Ian Rankin (28 Apr 1960, Cardenden, Fife, Scotland), British crime novelist.

Phylicia Rashad (Phylicia Ayers-Allen; 19 Jun 1948, Houston TX), American TV and stage actress.

Anders Fogh Rasmussen (26 Jan 1953, Ginnerup, Denmark), Danish politician; prime minister, 2001–09, and secretary-general of NATO from 2009.

Lars Løkke Rasmussen (15 May 1964, Vejle, Denmark) Danish politician; prime minister from 2009.

Aleksei (Osipovich) Ratmansky (27 Aug 1968, Leningrad, USSR [now St. Petersburg, Russia]), Russian dancer, choreographer, and director.

Simon (Denis) Rattle (19 Jan 1955, Liverpool, England), British orchestra conductor; principal conductor and artistic director of the Berlin Philharmonic from the 2002–03 season.

Marc Ravalomanana (1949, near Atananarivo, French Madagascar), Malagasy politician; president of Madagascar, 2002–09.

Rachael (Domenica) Ray (25 Aug 1968, Cape Cod MA), American TV cook and cookbook author.

(Charles) Robert Redford, Jr. (18 Aug 1937, Santa Monica CA), American film actor and director.

Lynn Redgrave (8 Mar 1943, London, England), British stage, screen, and TV actress.

Vanessa Redgrave (30 Jan 1937, London, England), British stage and screen actress and political activist.

Joshua Redman (1 Feb 1969, Berkeley CA), American jazz saxophone player.

Sumner Redstone (Sumner Murray Rothstein; 27 May 1923, Boston MA), American media executive.

David Rees (1973?), American comic artist.

Martin J(ohn) Rees (23 Jun 1942, Shropshire, England), British astronomer royal; recipient of the Crafoord Prize in 2005.

Keanu (Charles) Reeves (2 Sep 1964, Beirut, Lebanon), American actor.

Steve Reich (3 Oct 1936, New York NY), American composer; his *Double Sextet* won the 2009 Pulitzer Prize for music.

Kathy Reichs (Kathleen Joan Toelle; 1950, Chicago IL), American anthropologist-turned-novelist.

Harry Reid (2 Dec 1939, Searchlight NV), American politician (Democrat); senator from Nevada from 1987, Senate whip, 1998–2005, and Senate leader from 2005.

John C(hristopher) Reilly (24 May 1965, Chicago IL), American stage and film actor.

Rob Reiner (6 Mar 1947, Bronx NY), American actor, director, writer, and producer.

(John) Fredrik Reinfeldt (4 Aug 1965, Österhaninge, Sweden), Swedish politician (Moderate Party); prime minister from 2006.

Jason Reitman (19 Oct 1977, Montreal, QC, Canada), Canadian actor, director, and writer.

M(argaret) Jodi Rell (Mary Carolyn Reavis; 16 Jun 1946, Norfolk VA), American politician (Republican); governor of Connecticut from 2004.

Thomas Esang Remengesau, Jr. (1956), Palauan politician; president, 2001–09.

Edward (Gene) Rendell (5 Jan 1944, New York NY), American politician (Democrat); mayor of Philadelphia, 1992–2000, and governor of Pennsylvania from 2003.

Ruth Rendell (Baroness Rendell of Babergh; pseudonym Barbara Vine; 17 Feb 1930, London, England), British mystery novelist.

Ryan Reynolds (23 Oct 1976, Vancouver, BC, Canada), Canadian film actor.

Yasmina Reza (1 May 1959, Paris, France), French playwright; winner of the 2009 Tony Award for best play for *God of Carnage*.

Christina Ricci (12 Feb 1980, Santa Monica CA), American film actress.

Anne Rice (Howard Allen O'Brien; pseudonyms A.N. Roquelaure and Anne Rampling; 4 Oct 1941, New Orleans LA), American Gothic novelist.

Condoleezza Rice (14 Nov 1954, Birmingham AL), American academic and government official; national security advisor, 2001–05, and US secretary of state, 2005–09.

Adrienne (Cecile) Rich (16 May 1929, Baltimore MD), American poet.

(George) Maxwell Richards (1931, San Fernando, Trinidad, British West Indies [now in Trinidad and Tobago]), Trinidadian chemical engineer and university professor; president of Trinidad and Tobago from 2003.

Keith Richards (18 Dec 1943, Dartford, Kent, England), British rock guitarist and singer (for the Rolling Stones).

Bill Richardson (William Blaine Richardson; 15 Nov 1947, Pasadena CA), American politician (Democrat); governor of New Mexico from 2003.

Nicole Richie (15 Sep 1981, Berkeley CA), American celebrity entertainer.

Gerhard Richter (9 Feb 1932, Dresden, Germany), German Capitalist Realist artist.

Sally K(risten) Ride (26 May 1951, Encino CA), American astronaut and astrophysicist.

Rihanna (Robyn Rihanna Fenty; 20 Feb 1988, Saint Michael parish, Barbados), West Indian pop singer and entertainer.

Robert R. Riley (3 Oct 1944, Ashland AL), American politician (Republican); governor of Alabama from 2003.

LeAnn Rimes (28 Aug 1982, Jackson MS), American country-and-western singer.

Kelly Ripa (2 Oct 1970, Stratford NJ), American talk-show host and actress.

Bill Ritter (August William Ritter, Jr.; 6 Sep 1956, Denver CO), American politician (Democrat); governor of Colorado from 2007.

Rivaldo (Vitor Borba Ferreira; 19 Apr 1972, Recife, Brazil), Brazilian association football (soccer) player.

Geraldo (Miguel) Rivera (4 Jul 1943, Brooklyn NY), American TV journalist and talk-show host.

Tim Robbins (16 Oct 1958, West Covina CA), American actor.

Cecil E(dward) Roberts, Jr. (31 Oct 1946, Kayford WV), American labor leader; president of the United Mine Workers of America from 1995.

John G(lover) Roberts (27 Jan 1955, Buffalo NY), American jurist; chief justice of the US from 2005.

Julia Roberts (Julie Fiona Roberts; 28 Oct 1967, Smyrna GA), American film actress.

Nora Roberts (Eleanor Marie Robertson; 10 Oct 1950, Silver Spring MD), American novelist.

Marilynne Robinson (1947, Sandpoint ID), American author; recipient of the 2009 Orange Prize for Fiction for *Home*.

Peter (David) Robinson (29 Dec 1948, Belfast, Northern Ireland), Northern Irish Protestant loyalist politician; first minister of Northern Ireland from 2008.

Smokey Robinson (William Robinson, Jr.; 19 Feb 1940, Detroit MI), American R&B singer and songwriter; recipient of a 2006 Kennedy Center Honor.

Chris Rock (7 Feb 1966, Georgetown SC), American stand-up comedian and actor.

Kid Rock (Robert James Ritchie; 17 Jan 1971, Romeo MI), American rap-rock artist.

Andy Roddick (30 Aug 1982, Omaha NE), American tennis player.

Alex Rodriguez (27 Jul 1975, New York NY), American baseball shortstop and third baseman.

Narciso Rodríguez (January 1961, New Jersey), American fashion designer.

Robert (Anthony) Rodriguez (20 Jun 1968, San Antonio TX), Mexican American filmmaker.

Seth Rogen (15 Apr 1982, Vancouver, BC, Canada), Canadian film actor.

James E. Rogers (20 Sep 1947, Birmingham AL), American corporate executive; president and CEO (from 2006) and chairman of the board (from 2007) of Duke Energy.

Richard (George) Rogers (23 Jul 1933, Florence, Italy), British architect; recipient of a Praemium Imperiale in 2000 and the Pritzker Prize in 2007.

Jacques Rogge (2 May 1942, Ghent, Belgium), Belgian Olympic yachtsman, surgeon, and sports executive; president of the International Olympic Committee from 2001.

Floyd Roland (23 Nov 1961, Inuvik, NT, Canada), Canadian politician; premier of the Northwest Territories from 2007.

Sonny Rollins (Theodore Walter Rollins; 7 Sep 1930, Harlem, New York NY), American jazz saxophonist.

Ray Romano (21 Dec 1957, Queens NY), American comic actor.

(Willard) Mitt Romney (12 Mar 1947, Bloomfield MI), American businessman, sports executive, and politician (Republican); governor of Massachusetts, 2003–07.

Tony Romo (21 Apr 1980, San Diego CA), American pro football quarterback.

Ronaldo (Ronaldo Luiz Nazario de Lima; 22 Sep 1976, Itaguai, Rio de Janeiro state, Brazil), Brazilian association football (soccer) player.

Cristiano Ronaldo (5 Feb 1985, Madeira, Portugal), Portuguese association football (soccer) player.

Charlie Rose (5 Jan 1942, Henderson NC), American TV journalist and interviewer.

Alan Rosenberg (4 Oct 1950, Passaic NJ), American actor; president of the Screen Actors Guild from 2005.

Diana Ross (Diane Earle; 26 Mar 1944, Detroit MI), American R&B singer and actress; recipient of a 2007 Kennedy Center Honor.

Wilbur Ross (28 Nov 1937, North Bergen NJ), American financier and turnaround specialist..

Philip (Milton) Roth (19 Mar 1933, Newark NJ), American novelist and short-story writer.

Mike Rounds (Marion Michael Rounds; 24 Oct 1954, Huron SD), American politician (Republican); governor of South Dakota from 2003.

Mickey Rourke (16 Sep 1952, Schenectady NY), American actor.

Karl Rove (25 Dec 1950, Denver CO), American right-wing political operative, consultant, and commentator; former chief strategist for Pres. George W. Bush.

J(oanne) K(athleen) Rowling (31 Jul 1965, Chipping Sodbury, near Bristol, Gloucestershire, England), British author, creator of the Harry Potter series.

Rick Rubin (Frederick Jay Rubin; 10 Mar 1963, Lido Beach NY), American record producer.

Kevin (Michael) Rudd (21 Sep 1957, Nambour, QLD, Australia), Australian politician (Labor); prime minister from 2007.

Erkki Ruoslahti (16 Feb 1940, Helsinki, Finland), Finnish-born American cell biologist and distinguished professor at the Burnham Institute for Medical Research, La Jolla CA; corecipient of a 2005 Japan Prize.

Ed(ward Joseph) Ruscha (16 Dec 1937, Omaha NE), American Pop-art artist.

Geoffrey Rush (6 Jul 1951, Toowoomba, QLD, Australia), Australian film actor.

(Ahmed) Salman Rushdie (19 Jun 1947, Bombay, British India [now Mumbai, India]), Anglo-Indian novelist.

Richard Russo (15 Jul 1949, Johnstown NY), American author; winner of the 2002 Pulitzer Prize for fiction.

Burt Rutan (Elbert L. Rutan; 17 Jun 1943, Portland OR), American test pilot, aerospace engineer, and designer of specialized aircraft.

John Rutter (24 Sep 1945, London, England), British composer and conductor; founder (1981) and leader of the Cambridge Singers.

Kay Ryan (11 Sep 1945, San Jose CA), American poet; recipient of the 2004 Ruth Lilly Poetry Prize and US poet laureate from 2008.

Meg Ryan (Margaret Mary Emily Anne Hyra; 19 Nov 1961, Fairfield CT), American film actress.

Alexander Rybak (13 May 1986, Minsk, USSR [now in Belarus]), Norwegian pop singer; winner of the 2009 Eurovision Song Contest.

Winona Ryder (Winona Laura Horowitz; 29 Oct 1971, Winona MN), American film actress.

Mikhail Saakashvili (21 Dec 1967, Tbilisi, USSR [now in Georgia]), Georgian politician; president from 2004.

Charles Saatchi (9 Jun 1943, Baghdad, Iraq), Iraqi-born British advertising executive and art patron.

Sabah al-Ahmad al-Jabir Al Sabah (1929?, Kuwait city, Kuwait), Kuwaiti sheikh; emir from 2006.

Antonio (Elías) Saca (González) (9 Mar 1965, Usulután, El Salvador), Salvadoran politician (Nationalist Republican Alliance); president, 2004–09.

Jeffrey D(avid) Sachs (5 Nov 1954, Detroit MI), American economist; involved in efforts to eradicate poverty on a global scale.

Oliver (Wolf) Sacks (9 Jul 1933, London, England), British-born American neurologist and author of books on medical topics.

Muqtada al-Sadr (1974, Al-Najaf, Iraq), Iraqi Shi'ite Muslim cleric, a charismatic figure in the anti-American and anti-Western insurrection in Iraq following the US-led occupation of March 2003.

Ken Salazar (2 March 1955, Alamosa CO), American lawyer and politician (Democrat); senator from Colorado, 2005–09, and US secretary of the interior from 2009.

Sebastião (Ribeiro) Salgado (8 Feb 1944, Aimorés, Minas Gerais state, Brazil), Brazilian photographer.

'Ali 'Abdallah Salih (21 Mar 1942, Beit al-Ahmar, Yemen), Yemeni politician; president of Yemen (San'a), 1978–90, and of the unified Yemen since.

Alex(ander Elliot Anderson) Salmond (31 Dec 1954, Linlithgow, Scotland), Scottish politician (Scottish National Party); first minister of Scotland from 2007.

Esa-Pekka Salonen (30 Jun 1958, Helsinki, Finland), Finnish conductor; musical director of the Los Angeles Philharmonic, 1992–2009, and principal conductor and artistic adviser of the Philharmonia Orchestra, London, from 2008.

Ahmed Abdallah Sambi (5 Jun 1958, Mutsamudu, Anjouan, French Comoro Islands), Comoran Muslim religious leader; president from 2006.

Ivo Sanader (8 Jun 1953, Split, Yugoslavia [now in Croatia]), Croatian scholar and politician; prime minister, 2003–09.

Adam Sandler (9 Sep 1966, Brooklyn NY), American comic actor.

Mark Sanford (Marshall Clement Sanford, Jr.; 15 Jan 1960, Fort Lauderdale FL), American politician (Republican); governor of South Carolina from 2003.

Malam Bacai Sanhá (5 May 1947, Darsalame, Portuguese Guinea [now Guinea-Bissau]), Guinea-Bissauan politician; president from 2009.

Johan (Alexander) Santana (Araque) (13 Mar 1979, Tovar, Venezuela), Venezuelan pro baseball starting pitcher.

Albert Pintat Santolària (23 Jun 1943, Sant Julià de Lòria, Andorra), Andorran chief executive, 2005–09.

Alejandro Sanz (Alejandro Sánchez Pizarro; 18 Dec 1968, Madrid, Spain), Spanish singer-songwriter and flamenco-pop artist.

Cristina Saralegui (29 Jan 1948, Havana, Cuba), Cuban-born American Spanish-language TV talk-show host.

José Saramago (16 Nov 1922, Azinhaga, Portugal), Portuguese novelist and man of letters; recipient of the 1998 Nobel Prize for Literature.

Susan Sarandon (Susan Abigail Tomalin; 4 Oct 1946, New York NY), American film actress.

Serzh (Azati) Sarkisyan (30 Jun 1954, Stepanakert, Nagorno-Karabakh autonomous oblast, USSR [now in Azerbaijan]), Armenian politician; prime minister, 2007–08, and president from April 2008.

Tigran Sarkisyan (29 Jan 1960, Kirovakan, USSR [now Vanadzor, Armenia]), Armenian economist and politician; prime minister from 2008.

Nicolas Sarkozy (Nicolas Paul-Stéphane Sarközy de Nagy-Bocsa; 28 Jan 1955, Paris, France), French conservative politician; interior minister, 2005–07, and president from 2007.

Denis Sassou-Nguesso (1943, Edou, French Equatorial Africa [now in the Republic of the Congo]), Congolese politician; president of the Republic of Congo, 1979–92 and again from 1997.

Marjane Satrapi (22 Nov 1969, Rasht, Iran), Iranian-born French graphic novelist; author of the Persepolis books, her memoirs of Iran during the last decades of the 20th century.

al-Walid ibn Talal ibn Abdulaziz al-Saud (1954, Riyadh, Saudi Arabia), Saudi prince and billionaire businessman.

Diane K. Sawyer (Lila Sawyer; 22 Dec 1945, Glasgow KY), American TV journalist.

Antonin Scalia (11 Mar 1936, Trehton NJ), American jurist; associate justice of the US Supreme Court from 1986.

Joe Scarborough (Charles Joseph Scarborough; 9 Apr 1963, Atlanta GA), American conservative TV host and commentator.

Marjorie Scardino (Marjorie Morris; 25 Jan 1947, Flagstaff AZ), American-born British media executive; CEO of Pearson PLC from 1997.

Edward T(homas) Schafer (8 Aug 1946, Bismarck ND), American businessman and politician (Republican); US secretary of agriculture, 2008–09.

Mary L. Schapiro (19 June 1955, New York NY), American finance administrator; chairman of the Securities and Exchange Commission from 2009.

Eric E. Schmidt (1955?), American computer scientist and corporate executive; CTO of Sun Microsystems, Inc., 1983–97, chairman and CEO of Novell, Inc., 1997–2001, and chairman and CEO of Google, Inc., from 2001.

Julian Schnabel (26 Oct 1951, Brooklyn NY), American Neo-Expressionist artist and film director.

Daniel Schorr (31 Aug 1916, New York NY), American TV and radio journalist and political commentator.

Howard Schultz (19 Jul 1953, Brooklyn NY), American businessman; CEO of Starbucks Corp. from 1987, and principal owner of the Seattle SuperSonics professional basketball team, 2001–06.

Philip Schultz (1945, Rochester NY), American poet whose Failure won a 2008 Pulitzer Prize for poetry.

Michael Schumacher (3 Jan 1969, Hürth-Hermülheim, West Germany), German Formula 1 race-car driver.

Wolfgang Schüssel (7 Jun 1945, Vienna, Austria), Austrian politician; chancellor, 2000–07.

Susan (Carol) Schwab (23 Mar 1955, Washington DC), American trade official; US trade representative, 2006–09.

Arnold (Alois) Schwarzenegger (30 Jul 1947, Thal bei Graz, Austria), Austrian-born American bodybuilder, film actor, and politician (Republican); governor of California from 2003.

Brian (David) Schweitzer (4 Sep 1955, Havre MT), American politician (Democrat); governor of Montana from 2005.

David Schwimmer (2 Nov 1966, Astoria, Queens NY), American TV and film actor.

Jon Scieszka (8 Sep 1954, Flint MI), American author of books for children.

John Scofield (26 Dec 1951, Dayton OH), American jazz electric guitarist, composer, and bandleader.

Martin Scorsese (17 Nov 1942, Flushing, Long Island NY), American film director, writer, and producer.

H. Lee Scott, Jr. (1949?, Joplin MO), American corporate executive; president and CEO of Wal-Mart Stores, 2000–09.

Ridley Scott (30 Nov 1937, South Shields, Durham, England), British film director and producer.

Kristin Scott Thomas (24 May 1960, Redruth, Cornwall, England), British actress.

Vincent J(ames) Scully, Jr. (1930, New Haven CT), American architectural historian and critic.

Ryan (John) Seacrest (24 Dec 1974, Atlanta GA), American TV program host (American Idol).

Seal (Sealhenry Olusegun Olumide Samuel; 19 Feb 1963, Kilburn, London, England), British soul singer.

Sean Paul (Sean Paul Ryan Francis Henriques; 8 Jan 1973, St. Andrew, Jamaica), Jamaican reggae and rap musician.

Kathleen Sebelius (Kathleen Gilligan; 15 May 1948, Cincinnati OH), American politician (Democrat); governor of Kansas, 2003–09, and US secretary of health and human services from 2009.

Alice Sebold (1963, Madison WI), American novelist.

Amy Sedaris (29 Mar 1961, Endicott NY), American comic actress and writer.

David Sedaris (26 Dec 1956, Johnson City NY), American writer and humorist.

Kyra (Minturn) Sedgwick (19 Aug 1965, New York NY), American film and TV actress.

Ivan G. Seidenberg (1947?, Bronx NY), American corporate executive; CEO of Verizon Communications from 2002.

Jerry Seinfeld (Jerome Seinfeld; 29 Apr 1954, Brooklyn NY), American comic and TV personality.

Fatmir Sejdiu (23 Oct 1951, Pakashtice, Yugoslavia [now in Kosovo]), Kosovar professor and politician; president of Kosovo from 2006.

Bud Selig (Allan H. Selig; 30 Jul 1934, Milwaukee WI), American sports executive; Major League Baseball commissioner from 1998.

Senait (Senait G. Mehari; 3 Dec 1976, Asmara, Ethiopia [now in Eritrea]), Eritrean-born German singer.

Paul Sereno (11 Oct 1957, Aurora IL), American paleontologist.

Marija Serifovic (14 Nov 1984, Kragujevac, Yugoslavia [now in Serbia]), Serbian pop singer; winner of the 2007 Eurovision Song Contest.

Richard Serra (2 Nov 1939, San Francisco CA), American minimalist sculptor of large outdoor works; recipient of a Praemium Imperiale in 1994.

Vikram Seth (20 Jun 1952, Calcutta [now Kolkata], India), Indian poet, novelist, and travel writer.

Nasrallah Pierre Cardinal Sfeir (Nasrallah Boutros Pierre Sfeir; 15 May 1920, Reyfoun, Lebanon), Lebanese (Maronite Catholic) patriarch of Antioch and all the East from 1986 and Roman Catholic cardinal from 1994.

Gil Shaham (19 Feb 1971, Champaign-Urbana IL), American violinist.

Shakira (Shakira Isabel Mebarak Ripoll; 2 Feb 1977, Barranquilla, Colombia), Colombian-born pop singer.

Tony Shalhoub (Anthony Marcus Shalhoub; 9 Oct 1953, Green Bay WI), American TV and film actor.

John Patrick Shanley (1950, Bronx NY), American screenwriter and playwright.

Mariya (Yuryevna) Sharapova (19 Apr 1987, Nyagan, USSR [now in Russia]), Russian tennis player.

Kamalesh Sharma (30 Sep 1941), Indian diplomat; secretary-general of the Commonwealth from 2008.

Al Sharpton (3 Oct 1954, New York NY), American politician (Democrat), political activist, and civil rights leader.

William Shatner (22 Mar 1931, Montreal, QC, Canada), Canadian TV actor.

Charlie Sheen (Carlos Irwin Estevez; 3 Sep 1965, New York NY), American film and TV actor.

Martin Sheen (Ramon Estevez; 3 Aug 1940, Dayton OH), American stage, film, and TV actor.

Judith Sheindlin (21 Oct 1942, Brooklyn NY), American TV judge (of *Judge Judy*).

Sam Shepard (Samuel Shepard Rogers; 5 Nov 1943, Fort Sheridan IL), American playwright and actor.

Cindy Sherman (Cynthia Morris Sherman; 19 Jan 1954, Glen Ridge NJ), American photographer.

Osamu Shimomura (27 Aug 1928, Kyoto, Japan), Japanese chemist; cowinner of the 2008 Nobel Prize for Chemistry.

Eric K. Shinseki (28 Nov 1942, Lihue HI), American army officer; US secretary of veterans affairs from 2009.

Masaaki Shirakawa (27 Sep 1949, Kitakyushu, Japan), Japanese banker; governor of the Bank of Japan from 2008.

Vandana Shiva (5 Nov 1952, Dehra Dun, Uttar Pradesh [now in Uttarakhand] state, India), Indian biologist and social activist against the "biological theft" of the resources of poor countries by the richer ones.

Will Shortz (26 Aug 1952, Crawfordsville IN), American "enigmatologist" and "puzzlemaster"; crossword-puzzle editor at the New York Times.

Than Shwe (2 Feb 1933, Kyaukse, Burma [now Myanmar]), Burmese military officer; head of government in Myanmar, 1992–2003, and chairman of the State Peace and Development Council (head of state) from 1992.

M(anoj) Night Shyamalan (6 Aug 1970, Pondicherry, India), Indian-born film director and screenwriter.

Malick Sidibé (1935/36, Soloba, French Sudan [now Mali]), Malian photographer.

Jóhanna Sigurðardóttir (4 Oct 1942, Reykjavik, Iceland), Icelandic politician; prime minister from 2009.

(David) Derek Sikua (10 Sep 1959, Guadalcanal province, British-protected Solomon Islands), Solomon Islands politician; prime minister from 2007.

Sarah (Kate) Silverman (1 Dec 1970, Bedford NH), American comedian, TV actress, and writer.

Silvia (Silvia Renate Sommerlath; 23 Dec 1943, Heidelberg, Germany), Swedish royal and social activist; queen consort of King Carl XVI Gustaf (married 19 Jun 1976).

Charles Simic (9 May 1938, Belgrade, Yugoslavia [now in Serbia]), Yugoslav-born American poet; US poet laureate, 2007–08.

Russell Simmons (4 Oct 1957, Queens NY), American hip-hop impresario and cofounder of Def Jam Records.

Jessica Simpson (10 Jul 1980, Dallas TX), American pop singer and actress.

Lorna Simpson (13 Aug 1960, Brooklyn NY), American multimedia artist.

Ashlee Simpson-Wentz (3 Oct 1984, Dallas TX), American actress and singer.

Hammerskjoeld Simwinga (17 Nov 1964, Isoka, Zambia), Zambian environmentalist; recipient of the 2007 Goldman Environmental Prize for Africa.

Kushal Pal Singh (15 Aug 1931, Bulandshahr, Uttar Pradesh, British India), Indian real-estate baron.

Manmohan Singh (26 Sep 1932, Gah, Punjab, British India [now in Pakistan]), Indian economist; prime minister from 2004.

Fouad Siniora (July 1943, Sidon, Lebanon), Lebanese banker and Sunni politician; prime minister from 2005 and acting president from 2007–08.

Gary Sinise (17 Mar 1955, Blue Island IL), American TV and film actor and director.

(Sayyid) Alī (Hussaini) al-Sistani (4 Aug 1930?, near Meshed, Iran), Iranian Shi'ite Muslim cleric.

Antonio Skármeta (7 Nov 1940, Antofagasta, Chile), Chilean novelist and screenwriter.

Jeffrey S. Skoll (16 Jan 1965, Montreal, QC, Canada), Canadian entrepreneur; cofounder of eBay and, from 1999, the president of the philanthropic Skoll Foundation.

Leonard (Edward) Slatkin (1 Sep 1944, Los Angeles CA), American conductor; music director of the Detroit Symphony Orchestra from 2008.

Carlos Slim (Helú) (28 Jan 1940, Mexico City, Mexico), Mexican investor; head of Grupo Carso, SA de CV, and longtime chairman and CEO of the national telephone monopoly, Teléfonos de México (Telmex).

Lawrence M. Small (14 Sep 1941, New York NY), American businessman; president and COO of Fannie Mae, 1991–2000, and secretary of the Smithsonian Institution, 2000–07.

Tavis Smiley (13 Sep 1964, Gulfport MS), American advocacy journalist on radio and TV.

Alexander McCall Smith (24 Aug 1948, Bulawayo, Southern Rhodesia [now Zimbabwe]), British author of crime novels and works for children.

Anna Deavere Smith (18 Sep 1950, Baltimore MD), American playwright, actress, professor.

Marc (Kelly) Smith (195?, Chicago IL), American performance poet; originator of the poetry slam.

Michael W. Smith (7 Oct 1957, Kenova WV), American Christian singer.

Patti (Lee) Smith (30 Dec 1946, Chicago IL), American musician, poet, and visual artist.

Stephen Smith (12 Dec 1955, Narrogin, WA, Australia), Australian politician (Labor); foreign minister from 2007.

Will(ard Christopher) Smith, Jr. (25 Sep 1968, Philadelphia PA), American rapper and actor.

Zadie Smith (Sadie Smith; 27 Oct 1975, Willesden Green, London, England), British novelist.

Snoop Dogg (Calvin Broadus; 20 Oct 1972, Long Beach CA), American gangsta rap musician.

Gary (Sherman) Snyder (8 May 1930, San Francisco CA), American poet.

José Sócrates (José Sócrates Carvalho Pinto de Sousa; 6 Sep 1957, Vilar de Maçada, Portugal), Portuguese civil engineer and politician (Socialist); prime minister from 2005.

Steven Soderbergh (14 Jan 1963, Atlanta GA), American film director.

Sofia (Princess Sophie of Greece; Sofia de Grecia y Hannover; 2 Nov 1938, Athens, Greece), Spanish royal; queen consort of King Juan Carlos I (married 12 May 1962).

Javier Solana (Madariaga) (14 Jul 1942, Madrid, Spain), Spanish statesman; NATO secretary-general, 1995–99, and secretary-general of the Council of the European Union from 1999.

Hilda Solis (20 Oct 1957, Los Angeles CA), American politician (Democrat); congresswoman from California, 2001–09, and US secretary of labor from 2009.

László Sólyom (3 Jan 1942, Pécs, Hungary), Hungarian jurist and politician; president from 2005.

Michael (Thomas) Somare (9 Apr 1936, Rabaul, Australian-mandated New Guinea [now Papua New Guinea]), Papua New Guinean politician; prime minister, 1975–80, 1982–85, and again from 2002.

Juan (Octavio) Somavia (21 Apr 1941, Chile), Chilean international official; director general of the International Labour Organization from 1999.

Stephen (Joshua) Sondheim (22 Mar 1930, New York NY), American composer and lyricist for musical theater.

Sang-Hyun Song (21 Dec 1941, Japanese-occupied Korea [now in South Korea]), South Korean jurist; president of the International Criminal Court from 2009.

Sonja (Sonja Haraldsen; 4 Jul 1937, Oslo, Norway), Norwegian royal; queen consort of King Harald V (married 29 Aug 1968).

Sophie (Sophie Helen Rhys-Jones; 20 Jan 1965, Oxford, England), British royal; wife of Prince Edward (married 19 Jun 1999) and countess of Wessex.

Annika Sörenstam (9 Oct 1970, Stockholm, Sweden), Swedish golfer.

Aaron Sorkin (9 Jun 1961, Scarsdale NY), American screenwriter, playwright, and TV producer.

Guillaume Soro (8 May 1972, Kofiplé, Côte d'Ivoire), Ivorian politician; prime minister from 2007.

Sonia (Maria) Sotomayor (25 Jun 1954, Bronx NY), American jurist; associate justice of the US Supreme Court from 2009.

Ahmed Tidiane Souaré (1951, French West Africa?), Guinean economist and statesman; prime minister, 2008–09.

David H(ackett) Souter (17 Sep 1939, Melrose MA), American jurist; associate justice of the US Supreme Court, 1990–2009.

Wole Soyinka (Akinwande Oluwole Soyinka; 13 Jul 1934, Abeokuta, Nigeria), Nigerian playwright, poet, novelist, and critic; recipient of the 1986 Nobel Prize for Literature.

Kevin Spacey (Kevin Matthew Fowler; 26 Jul 1959, South Orange NJ), American stage and film actor and artistic director of the Old Vic theater in London.

Nicholas Sparks (31 Dec 1965, Omaha NE), American novelist.

Britney (Jean) Spears (2 Dec 1981, Kentwood LA), American pop singer and celebrity.

Margaret Spellings (30 Nov 1957, Michigan), American political adviser, education expert, and secretary of education, 2005–09.

W(inston) Baldwin Spencer (8 Oct 1948, West Indian politician; prime minister of Antigua and Barbuda from 2004.

Steven Spielberg (18 Dec 1947, Cincinnati OH), American film director and producer.

Nikola Spiric (4 Sep 1956, Drvar, Yugoslavia [now in Bosnia and Herzegovina]), Bosnia and Herzegovinian politician; chairman of the Council of Ministers (prime minister) from 2007.

Eliot (Laurence) Spitzer (10 Jun 1959, Riverdale, Bronx NY), American attorney and politician (Democrat); governor of New York, 2007–08.

Bruce Springsteen (23 Sep 1949, Freehold NJ), American rock singer and songwriter.

(Michael) Sylvester (Enzio) Stallone ("Sly"; 6 Jul 1946, New York NY), American film actor and director.

Sergey (Dmitriyevich) Stanishev (5 May 1966, Kherson, USSR [now in Ukraine]), Bulgarian politician (Socialist); prime minister from 2005.

Albert Starr (1 Jun 1926, New York NY), American cardiovascular surgeon and inventor of an artificial heart valve; recipient of a 2007 Lasker Medical Prize.

James G. Stavridis (15 Feb 1955, West Palm Beach FL), American military official; Supreme Allied Commander, Europe (SACEUR) from 2009 and commander of the US European Command from 2009.

Danielle (Fernande Schuelein-) Steel (14 Aug 1947, New York NY), American romance novelist.

Michael Steele (19 Oct 1958, Andrews AFB, Prince George's county MD), American politician (Republican); first African American chairman of the Republican National Committee, from 2009.

Gwen Stefani (3 Oct 1969, Fullerton CA), American rock and pop vocalist.

Gregg Steinhafel (1955), American businessman; president of Target Corp. from 1999 and its CEO from 2008.

Ralph M(arvin) Steinman (14 Jan 1943, Montreal, QC, Canada), American immunologist and specialist in immune response in cells; recipient of a 2007 Lasker Medical Prize.

Frank-Walter Steinmeier (5 Jan 1956, Detmold, West Germany), German government official; foreign minister from 2005 and vice-chancellor from 2007.

Frank P(hilip) Stella (12 May 1936, Malden MA), American painter.

Ed Stelmach (11 May 1951, Lamont, AB, Canada), Canadian politician (Progressive Conservative); premier of Alberta from 2006.

Stephanie (Stéphanie Marie Elizabeth Grimaldi; 1 Feb 1965, Monaco), Monegasque princess; the youngest child of Prince Rainier III and Grace Kelly.

Marcus Stephen (1 Oct 1969, Nauru?), Nauruan weight lifter and politician; president from 2007.

Howard Stern (12 Jan 1954, Roosevelt NY), American radio and TV personality.

John Paul Stevens (20 Apr 1920, Chicago IL), American jurist; associate justice of the US Supreme Court from 1975.

Ellen Stewart (7 Nov 1919, Chicago IL), American theater director and producer, the founder (1961) of La MaMa Experimental Theater Club in New York City; recipient of a Praemium Imperiale in 2007.

Jon Stewart (Jonathan Stewart Leibowitz; 28 Nov 1962, New York NY), American actor, writer, and comedian; anchor of TV's *The Daily Show* from 1999.

Kristen Stewart (9 April 1990, Los Angeles CA), American actress.

Patrick Stewart (13 Jul 1940, Mirfield, Yorkshire, England), British actor.

Ben Stiller (30 Nov 1965, New York NY), American comedian, actor, and film director.

Sting (Gordon Matthew Sumner; 2 Oct 1951, Wallsend, Newcastle upon Tyne, England), British singer, songwriter, and actor.

Jens Stoltenberg (16 Mar 1959, Oslo, Norway), Norwegian economist and politician (Norwegian Labor Party); prime minister, 2000–01 and again from 2005.

Biz Stone (Christopher Isaac Stone; 10 Mar 1974, Massachusetts), American entrepreneur; cofounder of Twitter.

Joss Stone (Joscelyn Eve Stoker; 11 Apr 1987, Dover, Kent, England), English soul singer.

Oliver (William) Stone (15 Sep 1946, New York NY), American director, writer, and producer.

Tom Stoppard (Tomas Straussler; 3 Jul 1937, Zlin, Moravia, Czechoslovakia [now in the Czech Republic]), Czech-born British playwright and screenwriter.

Mark Strand (11 Apr 1934, Summerside, PE, Canada), Canadian poet, writer of short fiction, and translator.

Dominique Strauss-Kahn (25 Apr 1949, Neuilly-sur-Seine, France), French politician (Socialist); managing director of the International Monetary Fund from 2007.

Jack Straw (John Whitaker Straw; 3 Aug 1946, Brentwood, Essex, England), British politician; home secretary, 1997–2001, foreign secretary, 2001–06, and secretary of state for justice and lord high chancellor from 2007.

Meryl Streep (Mary Louise Streep; 22 Jun 1949, Summit NJ), American film actress.

Barbra Streisand (Barbara Joan Streisand; 24 Apr 1942, Brooklyn NY), American singer, actress, and film director.

Ted Strickland (4 Aug 1941, Lucasville OH), American politician (Democrat); governor of Ohio from 2007.

Howard Stringer (19 Feb 1942, Cardiff, Wales), Welsh-born business executive; chairman and CEO of Sony Corp. from 2005.

Susan Stroman (17 Oct 1954, Wilmington DE), American theater director.

Elizabeth Strout (6 Jan 1956, Portland ME), American author; winner of the 2009 Pulitzer Prize for fiction for *Olive Kitteridge*.

(Christopher) Ruben Studdard (12 Sep 1978, Frankfurt am Main, West Germany), American singer.

Juan Manuel Suárez del Toro Rivero (1952, Spain), Spanish international official; president of the International Federation of Red Cross and Red Crescent Societies from 2001.

Arthur Ochs Sulzberger, Jr. (22 Sep 1951, Mount Kisco NY), American newspaper executive; publisher of the *New York Times* from 1992 and CEO from 1997.

Pat Summitt (Patricia Head; 14 Jun 1952, Henrietta TN), American women's basketball coach; the winningest coach in NCAA basketball history.

Rashid Sunyaev (Rashid [Aliyevich] Syunyayev; 1 Mar 1943, Tashkent, USSR [now in Uzbekistan]), Uzbek-born Russian astrophysicist, a specialist in cosmological background radiation and black holes; director of the Max Planck Institute for Astrophysics from 1996; recipient of the 2000 Bruce Medal and a 2008 Crafoord Prize.

Kiefer Sutherland (William Frederick Dempsey George Sutherland; 21 Dec 1966, London, England), Canadian film and TV actor.

Ichiro Suzuki (22 Oct 1973, Kasugai, Aichi prefecture, Japan), Japanese baseball player.

Hilary Swank (30 Jul 1974, Lincoln NE), American film actress.

John J. Sweeney (5 May 1934, New York NY), American labor leader; president of the AFL-CIO from 1995.

Taylor Swift (13 Dec 1989, Reading PA), American country singer.

Tilda Swinton (Katherine Matilda Swinton; 5 Nov 1960, London, England), British actress.

Wanda Sykes (7 Mar 1964, Portsmouth VA), American comedian and actress.

Boris Tadic (15 Jan 1958, Sarajevo, Yugoslavia [now in Bosnia and Herzegovina]), Serbian politician and government official; president of Serbia from 2004.

Masatoshi Takeichi (27 Nov 1943, Nagoya, Japan), Japanese developmental biologist, professor, and director of the RIKEN Center for Developmental Biology.

Jalal Talabani (1933, Kalkan, Iraq), Iraqi Kurdish politician; president of Iraq from 2005.

Mehmet Ali Talat (6 Jul 1952, Girne, British Cyprus), Turkish Cypriot politician; prime minister of the Turkish Republic of Northern Cyprus, 2004–05, and president from 2005.

Mamadou Tandja (1938, Maïné-Soroa, French West Africa [now in Niger]), Nigerois politician; president from 1999.

Quentin (Jerome) Tarantino (27 Mar 1963, Knoxville TN), American film director.

Marc Tarpenning (1 Jun 1964, Sacramento CA), American entrepreneur and cofounder of Tesla Motors.

Ratan (Naval) Tata (28 Dec 1937, Bombay, British India [now Mumbai, India]), Indian corporate executive; chairman of the Tata Group and its several subsidiary companies in steel, motors, chemicals, hotels, etc.

Audrey Tautou (9 Aug 1978, Beaumont, France), French film actress.

John Tavener (28 Jan 1944, London, England), British composer.

Charles M(argrave) Taylor (5 Nov 1931, Montreal, QC, Canada), Canadian philosopher and professor; recipient of the 2007 Templeton Prize.

Elizabeth (Rosemond) Taylor (27 Feb 1932, London, England), American film actress.

Julie Taymor (15 Dec 1952, Newton MA), American theater and film director.

Oscar Temaru (1 Nov 1944, Faaa, Tahiti, French Polynesia) French Polynesian politician; president, 2004, 2005–06, 2007–08, and again from 2009.

Mario Testino (1954, Lima, Peru), Peruvian fashion photographer.

Hashim Thaci (24 Apr 1969, Buroja, Yugoslavia [now in Kosovo]), Kosovar politician; prime minister from 2008.

Bal (Keshav) Thackeray (23 Jan 1927), Indian politician who established the Shiv Sena party.

John A. Thain (26 May 1955, Antioch IL), American financial official; CEO of the New York Stock Exchange, 2004–07, and the last CEO of Merrill Lynch, 2007–09.

Hamad ibn Khalifah al-Thani (1950, Doha, Qatar), Qatari sheikh; emir from 1995.

Twyla Tharp (1 Jul 1941, Portland IN), American dancer, director, and choreographer.

Charlize Theron (7 Aug 1975, Benoni, South Africa), South African actress.

Thich Nhat Hanh (11 Oct 1926, central Vietnam), Vietnamese Buddhist monk, pacifist, and teacher.

Lyonchen Jigme (Yoeser) Thinley (1952, Bumthang district, Bhutan), Bhutanese prime minister, 1998–99, 2003–04, and again from 2008.

Clarence Thomas (23 Jun 1948, Pinpoint community, near Savannah GA), American jurist; associate justice of the US Supreme Court from 1991.

Michael Tilson Thomas (21 Dec 1944, Hollywood CA), American conductor and composer; music director of the San Francisco Symphony from 1995.

Tillman (Joseph) Thomas (13 Jun 1945, Hermitage, St. Patrick, Grenada, British West Indies), West Indian politician; prime minister of Grenada from 2008.

David (John Howard) Thompson (December 1961, London, England), Barbadian politician; prime minister from 2008.

Emma Thompson (15 Apr 1959, London, England), British film actress.

Robert Thomson (11 Mar 1961, Echuca, VIC, Australia), Australian journalist; editor of *The Times* of London, 2002–07, and managing editor of *The Wall Street Journal* from 2008.

Billy Bob Thornton (4 Aug 1955, Hot Springs AR), American director and actor.

Uma (Karuna) Thurman (29 Apr 1970, Boston MA), American film actress.

Rex W. Tillerson (23 Mar 1952, Wichita Falls TX), American petroleum company executive; president (from 2004) and CEO (from 2006) of Exxon Mobil Corp.

Timbaland (Timothy Z. Mosley; 10 Mar 1972, Norfolk VA), American R&B and rap composer, record producer, and performer.

Justin (Randall) Timberlake (31 Jan 1981, Memphis TN), American pop singer.

Sakata Tojuro (31 Dec 1931, Kyoto, Japan), Japanese actor; recipient of a 2008 Praemium Imperiale.

Claire Tomalin (Claire Delavenay; 20 Jun 1933, London, England), English biographer and author.

(Iroij) Litokwa Tomeing (14 Oct 1939, Wotje atoll, Japanese-mandated Marshall Islands), Marshallese politician; president of the Marshall Islands from 2008.

Anote Tong (1952), Kiribati politician; president from 2003.

Gaston Tong Sang (7 Aug 1949, Bora-Bora, Tahiti, French Polynesia), French Polynesian politician; president of French Polynesia, 2006–07 and again in 2008–09.

Bamir Topi (24 Apr 1957, Tiranë, Albania), Albanian biologist and politician; president from 2007.

Mirek Topolanek (15 May 1956, Vsetin, Moravia, Czechoslovakia [now in the Czech Republic]), Czech industrial engineer, businessman, and politician; prime minister, 2006–09.

Johnson Toribiong (1946, Airai, US-occupied Palau), Palauan politician, president of Palau from 2009.

Martín Torrijos (Espino) (18 Jul 1963, Panama City, Panama), Panamanian politician (Democratic Revolutionary Party); president, 2004–09.

Amadou Toumani Touré (4 Nov 1948, Mpoti, French Sudan [now in Mali]), Malian politician; president, 1991–92 and again from 2002.

Hamadoun Touré (3 Sep 1953, French Sudan [now Mali]), Malian international official; secretary-general of the International Telecommunication Union from 2007.

Avraham Trahtman (Avraam Trakhtman; 10 Feb 1944, Kalinovo, Sverdlovsk oblast, USSR [now Yekaterinburg, Russia]), Russian-born Israeli mathematician who published a proof of the road-coloring problem in 2007.

Randy Travis (Randy Traywick; 4 May 1959, Marshville NC), American country-and-western singer, songwriter, and actor.

John (Joseph) Travolta (18 Feb 1955, Englewood NJ), American TV and film actor.

Natasha Trethewey (26 Apr 1966, Gulfport MS), American poet whose Native Guard won the 2007 Pulitzer Prize for poetry.

Jean-Claude Trichet (20 Dec 1942, Lyons, France), French banker, governor of the Banque de France, 1993–2003, and president of the European Central Bank from 2003.

Libby Trickett (Lisbeth Lenton; 28 Jan 1985, Townsville, QLD, Australia), Australian swimmer.

Lars von Trier (30 Apr 1956, Copenhagen, Denmark), Danish film director and cinematographer.

Calvin Trillin (5 Dec 1935, Kansas City MO), American author, commentator, and occasional poet.

Travis Tritt (9 Feb 1963, Marietta GA), American country-and-western singer.

Robert L. Trivers (19 Feb 1943, Washington DC), American evolutionary biologist and sociobiologist; recipient of a 2007 Crafoord Prize.

Garry R. Trudeau (21 Jul 1948, New York NY), American cartoonist; creator of the durable Doonesbury syndicated comic strip.

Donald (John) Trump (14 Jun 1946, New York NY), American real-estate developer and reality-TV personality.

Ronald A. Tschetter (4 Oct 1941, Huron SD), American investment executive; director of the Peace Corps from 2006.

Roger Y. Tsien (1 Feb 1952, New York NY), American chemist; cowinner of the 2008 Nobel Prize for Chemistry.

Morgan Tsvangirai (10 Mar 1952, Gutu, Southern Rhodesia [now Zimbabwe]), Zimbabwean labor leader and politician; head of the Movement for Democratic Change (from 1999), main opposition leader to the regime of Pres. Robert Mugabe, and prime minister of Zimbabwe in a historic power-sharing agreement from 2009.

Togiola T(alalei) A. Tulafono (28 Feb 1947, Aunu'u Island, American Samoa), American Samoan politician (Democrat); governor of American Samoa from 2003.

Tommy Tune (28 Feb 1939, Wichita Falls TX), American musical-comedy dancer and actor.

Danilo Turk (19 Feb 1952, Maribor, Yugoslavia [now in Slovenia]), Slovenian law professor and diplomat; president from 2007.

Ted Turner (Robert Edward Turner III; 19 Nov 1938, Cincinnati OH), American TV executive, the founder of Turner Broadcasting System (TBS) and Cable News Network (CNN); sports club owner (of the Atlanta Braves, the Atlanta Hawks, and the Atlanta Thrashers); yachtsman; and philanthropist.

John Turturro (27 Feb 1957, Brooklyn NY), American stage, film, and TV actor.

Donald (Franciszek) Tusk (22 Apr 1957, Gdansk, Poland), Polish politician (Civic Platform); prime minister from 2007.

Desmond (Mpilo) Tutu (7 Oct 1931, Klerksdorp, South Africa), South African Anglican cleric who in 1984 received the Nobel Peace Prize for his role in the opposition to apartheid in South Africa.

Cy Twombly (Edwin Parker Twombly, Jr.; 25 Apr 1928, Lexington VA), American abstract artist and sculptor.

Anne Tyler (25 Oct 1941, Minneapolis MN), American novelist and short-story writer.

Liv Tyler (Liv Rundgren; 1 Jul 1977, Portland ME), American actress and model.

Yuliya (Volodymyrivna) Tymoshenko (27 Nov 1960, Dnipropetrovsk, USSR [now in Ukraine]), Ukrainian businesswoman and politician (Yuliya Tymoshenko Bloc); prime minister in 2005 and again from 2007.

(Alfred) McCoy Tyner (Sulaimon Saud; 11 Dec 1938, Philadelphia PA), American jazz pianist and composer.

João Ubaldo (Osório Pimentel) Ribeiro (23 Jan 1941, Itaparica, Bahia state, Brazil), Brazilian novelist.

Robert J. Ulrich (1944?, Minneapolis MN), American corporate executive; CEO of Target Corp., 1994–2008.

Carrie Underwood (10 Mar 1983, Muskogee OK), American country singer.

Keith (Lionel) Urban (26 Oct 1967, Whangerei, New Zealand), New Zealand–born Australian country singer.

Álvaro Uribe (Vélez) (4 Jul 1952, Medellín, Colombia), Colombian politician; president from 2002.

Usher (Usher Raymond IV; 14 Oct 1978, Chattanooga TN), American R&B singer.

Martine Van Hamel (16 Nov 1945, Brussels, Belgium), Belgian dancer and choreographer for the American Ballet Theatre.

Herman Van Rompuy (31 Oct 1947, Etterbeek, Belgium), Belgian politician (Christian Democratic and Flemish); prime minister from 2008.

Gus van Sant (24 Jul 1952, Louisville KY), American film director.

Matti Vanhanen (4 Nov 1955, Jyväskylä, Finland), Finnish politician; prime minister from 2003.

(Jorge) Mario (Pedro) Vargas Llosa (28 Mar 1936, Arequipa, Peru), Peruvian-born Spanish novelist.

Harold (Eliot) Varmus (18 Dec 1939, Oceanside NY), American virologist; corecipient of 1989 Nobel Prize for Physiology or Medicine; director of the National Institutes of Health, 1993–99, and president of Memorial Sloan-Kettering Cancer Center in New York City from 2000.

Vince Vaughn (Vincent Anthony Vaughn; 28 Mar 1970, Minneapolis MN), American actor.

Tabaré (Ramón) Vázquez (Rosas) (17 Jan 1940, Barrio La Teja, Montevideo, Uruguay), Uruguayan physician and politician (Socialist); president from 2005.

Eddie Vedder (Edward Louis Severson III; 23 Dec 1964, Evanston IL), American rock vocalist and songwriter (for Pearl Jam).

Abhisit Vejjajiva (3 Aug 1964, Newcastle upon Tyne, England), Thai politician; prime minister of Thailand from 2008.

Jaci Velasquez (Jacquelyn Davette Velasquez; 15 Oct 1979, Houston TX), American Latin and gospel singer.

Ann M. Veneman (29 Jun 1949, Modesto CA), American government official; US secretary of agriculture, 2001–05, and executive director of UNICEF from 2005.

(Runaldo) Ronald Venetiaan (18 Jun 1936, Paramaribo, Dutch Guiana [now Suriname]), Surinamese mathematician and politician; president, 1991–96 and again from 2000.

Maxim Vengerov (Maksim Aleksandrovich Vengerov; 20 Aug 1974, Novosibirsk, USSR [now in Russia]), Russian-born concert violinist.

J. Craig Venter (14 Oct 1946, Salt Lake City UT), American geneticist and researcher into the human genome; he was the founder of Celera Genomics.

Guy Verhofstadt (11 Apr 1953, Dendermonde, Belgium), Belgian politician (VLD); prime minister, 1999–2008.

Donatella Versace (2 May 1955, Reggio di Calabria, Italy), Italian fashion designer; creative director at the Versace design house from 1997.

Ben Verwaayen (11 Feb 1952, Driebergen, Netherlands), Dutch corporate executive; CEO of Alcatel-Lucent from 2008.

Charles M. Vest (9 Sep 1941, Morgantown WV), American scientist and educator; president of the Massachusetts Institute of Technology, 1990–2004, and president of the National Academy of Engineering from 2007.

Jack Vettriano (Jack Hoggan; 17 Nov 1951, St. Andrews, Fife, Scotland), British painter.

Victoria (Victoria Ingrid Alice Desirée; 14 Jul 1977, Stockholm, Sweden), Swedish crown princess and duchess of Västergötland.

Antonio Villaraigosa (Antonio Ramón Villar, Jr.; 23 Jan 1953, East Los Angeles CA), American politician (Democrat); mayor of Los Angeles from 2005.

Tom Vilsack (13 Dec 1950, Pittsburgh PA), American politician (Democrat); governor of Iowa, 1999–2007, and US secretary of agriculture from 2009.

Diana Vishneva (Diana Viktorovna Vishnyova; 13 Jun 1976, Leningrad, USSR [now St. Petersburg, Russia]), Russian ballerina with the Mariinsky Ballet and, from 2003, the American Ballet Theatre.

Lindsey Vonn (Lindsey Kildow; 18 Oct 1984, St. Paul MN), American Alpine skier.

Vladimir Voronin (25 May 1941, Corjova, Moldavian SSR, USSR [now Moldova]), Moldovan politician; president from 2001.

Peter Voser (29 Aug 1958, Switzerland), Swiss businessman; CEO of Royal Dutch Shell from 2009.

Filip Vujanovic (1 Sep 1954, Belgrade, Yugoslavia [now in Serbia]), Montenegrin politician; president of the Republic of Montenegro, before and after its independence, 2002–03 (acting) and again from 2003.

Abdoulaye Wade (29 May 1926, Kébémer, French West Africa [now in Senegal]), Senegalese politician; president from 2000.

G. Richard Wagoner, Jr. (9 Feb 1953, Wilmington DE), American corporate executive; CEO of General Motors Corp., 2000–09.

Mark (Robert Michael) Wahlberg (5 Jun 1971, Dorchester, Boston MA), American actor.

Rufus Wainwright (22 Jul 1973, Rhinebeck NY), Canadian singer and songwriter.

Ted Waitt (18 Jan 1963, Sioux City IA), American computer executive and philanthropist; cofounder of Gateway Inc. in 1985 and chairman and CEO of the charitable Waitt Family Foundation from 1993.

Derek (Alton) Walcott (23 Jan 1930, Castries, Saint Lucia, British West Indies), West Indian poet and playwright; recipient of the 1992 Nobel Prize for Literature.

Jimmy (Donal) Wales (7 Aug 1966, Huntsville AL), American Internet publisher; founder of Wikipedia.

Alice (Malsenior) Walker (9 Feb 1944, Eatonton GA), American novelist, poet, and short-story writer.

Brad Wall (24 Nov 1965, Swift Current, SK, Canada), Canadian businessman and politician (Progressive Conservative); premier of Saskatchewan from 2007.

Mike Wallace (Myron Leon Wallace; 9 May 1918, Brookline MA), American TV journalist, interviewer, and coeditor of CBS's 60 Minutes.

Mark J. Walport (1953, England), British immunologist; director of the Wellcome Trust from 2003.

Barbara (Ann) Walters (25 Sep 1931, Boston MA), American broadcast journalist and TV interviewer.

John P. Walters (1951?), American civic and government official; director of national drug control policy ("drug czar"), 2001–09.

Alice L. Walton (c. 1949), American heiress of part of the Wal-Mart fortune.

Jim C. Walton (c. 1948), American business executive; chairman and CEO of the Arvest Group.

Vera Wang (27 Jun 1949, New York NY), American fashion designer.

Jigme Khesar Namgyal Wangchuk (21 Feb 1980, Thimphu, Bhutan), Bhutanese royal; king from 2006.

Shane Keith Warne (13 Sep 1969, Ferntree Gully, VIC, Australia), Australian cricketer, a spin bowler named one of Wisden's Five Cricketers of the Century.

Rick Warren (1954, San Jose CA), American evangelist minister.

Denzel Washington, Jr. (28 Dec 1954, Mount Vernon NY), American film and TV actor.

(Chaudhry) Wasim Akram (3 Jun 1966, Lahore, Pakistan), Pakistani cricket left-handed fast bowler.

Alice Waters (28 Apr 1944, Chatham NJ), American chef and restaurant owner (Chez Panisse, Berkeley CA).

John Waters (22 Apr 1946, Baltimore MD), American filmmaker.

Naomi Watts (28 Sep 1968, Shoreham, Kent, England), Australian film actress.

George (Manneh Oppong Ousman) Weah (1 Oct 1966, Monrovia, Liberia), Liberian-born association football (soccer) star, named in 1998 African Player of the Century.

Hugo Weaving (4 Apr 1960, Austin, Nigeria), Australian film actor.

Karrie Webb (21 Dec 1974, Ayr, QLD, Australia), Australian golfer.

Andrew (Thomas) Weil (8 Jun 1942, Philadelphia PA), American physician and champion of alternative medicine.

Bob Weinstein (18 Oct 1954, Queens NY), American film executive; cofounder of Miramax Films and the Weinstein Co.

Harvey Weinstein (19 Mar 1952, Queens NY), American film executive; cofounder of Miramax Films and the Weinstein Co.

Rachel Weisz (7 Mar 1971, London, England), British film actress.

Gillian Welch (2 Oct 1967, New York NY), American folk and country-and-western singer.

Wen Jiabao (September 1942, Tianjin, China), Chinese geologist and party and state official; premier from 2003.

Jann S. Wenner (7 Jan 1946, New York NY), American journalist; originator (1967) and publisher of *Rolling Stone* magazine.

Kanye West (8 Jun 1977, Atlanta GA), American rapper and music producer.

Randy Weston (Randolph Edward Weston; 6 Apr 1926, Brooklyn NY), American jazz pianist and composer.

Vivienne Westwood (Vivienne Swire; 8 Apr 1941, Tintwistle, Derbyshire, England), British fashion designer.

Christopher Wheeldon (22 Mar 1973, Yeovil, Somerset, England), British dancer and choreographer; founder (2007) of Morphoses/The Wheeldon Company.

Forest (Steven) Whitaker (15 Jul 1961, Longview TX), American film actor and director.

Jack White (John Anthony Gillis; 9 Jul 1975, Detroit MI), American alternative-rock guitarist, drummer, and vocalist (for the White Stripes, the Raconteurs, and the Dead Weather) and record producer.

Shaun White (3 Sep 1986, San Diego CA), American snowboarder.

Ratnasiri Wickremanayake (5 May 1933, British Ceylon [now Sri Lanka]), Sri Lankan politician; prime minister of Sri Lanka, 2000–01 and again from 2005.

John Edgar Wideman (14 Jun 1941, Washington DC), American novelist.

Richard (Purdy) Wilbur (1 Mar 1921, New York NY), American poet associated with the New Formalist movement; poet laureate of the US, 1987–88, and recipient of the 2006 Ruth Lilly Poetry Prize.

Tom Wilkinson (Thomas Jeffery Wilkinson, Jr.; 12 Dec 1948, Leeds, West Yorkshire, England), British character actor.

George F(rederick) Will (4 May 1941, Champaign IL), American conservative political commentator and columnist.

Willem-Alexander (27 Apr 1967, Utrecht, Netherlands), Dutch crown prince.

William (William Arthur Philip Louis Mountbatten-Windsor; 21 Jun 1982, London, England), British prince of Wales; son of Charles and Diana, prince and princess of Wales, and second in line to the British throne.

Brian (Douglas) Williams (5 May 1959, Elmira NY), American TV newsman; anchor of *NBC Nightly News* from 2004.

C(harles) K(enneth) Williams (4 Nov 1936, Newark NJ), American poet.

Danny Williams (4 Aug 1950, St. John's, NF [now NL], Canada), Canadian lawyer and politician (Progressive Conservative); premier of Newfoundland and Labrador from 2003.

Evan Williams (31 Mar 1972, Nebraska), American entrepreneur; cofounder of Twitter.

John Williams (24 Apr 1941, Melbourne, VIC, Australia), Australian-born classical guitarist.

John (Towner) Williams (8 Feb 1932, Queens NY), American conductor and composer of movie sound tracks.

Lucinda Williams (26 Jan 1953, Lake Charles LA), American contemporary folk and country singer and songwriter.

Pharrell Williams ("Skateboard P"; 5 Apr 1973, Virginia Beach VA), American hip-hop artist, songwriter, and producer.

Robbie Williams (Robert Peter Maximillian Williams; 13 Feb 1974, Tunstall, Stoke-on-Trent, Staffordshire, England), British singer.

Robin Williams (21 Jul 1952, Chicago IL), American comedian and actor.

Rowan (Douglas) Williams (14 Jun 1950, Swansea, Wales), Welsh-born Anglican clergyman; archbishop of Canterbury from 2003.

Serena Williams (26 Sep 1981, Saginaw MI), American tennis player and clothing designer.

Vanessa (Lynn) Williams (18 Mar 1963, Tarrytown NY), American singer and actress.

Venus Williams (17 Jun 1980, Lynwood CA), American tennis player.

Bruce Willis (Walter Bruce Willison; 19 Mar 1955, Idar-Oberstein, West Germany [now in Germany]), American actor.

Brian Wilson (20 Jun 1942, Inglewood CA), American pop music songwriter and producer (for the Beach Boys); recipient of a 2007 Kennedy Center Honor.

Lanford Wilson (13 Apr 1937, Lebanon MO), American playwright.

Owen (Cunningham) Wilson (18 Nov 1968, Dallas TX), American actor.

Robert Wilson (4 Oct 1941, Waco TX), American avant-garde theater director.

Amy (Jade) Winehouse (14 Sep 1983, Enfield, Middlesex, England), British singer and songwriter.

Oprah Winfrey (29 Jan 1954, Kosciusko MS), American TV personality; host and producer of *The Oprah Winfrey Show* from 1985.

Kate Winslet (5 Oct 1975, Reading, England), British film actress.

Anna Wintour (3 Nov 1949, London, England), British-born fashion magazine editor, editor in chief of American *Vogue* from 1988.

(Laura Jean) Reese Witherspoon (22 Mar 1976, Baton Rouge LA), American film actress.

Edward Witten (26 Aug 1951, Baltimore MD), American mathematician and specialist in superstring theory; recipient of the 1990 Fields Medal and a 2008 Crafoord Prize.

Patricia A(nn) Woertz (17 Mar 1953, Pittsburgh PA), American corporate executive; CEO of Archer Daniels Midland from 2006.

Girma Wolde-Giorgis (December 1924, Addis Ábaba, Ethiopia), Ethiopian military officer; president from 2001.

Nathan Wolfe (24 Aug 1970, Detroit MI), American virologist and professor, a specialist in the transfer of viruses from animals to humans.

Tom Wolfe (Thomas Kennerly Wolfe, Jr.; 2 Mar 1930, Richmond VA), American novelist, journalist, and social commentator.

Tobias (Jonathan Ansell) Wolff (19 Jun 1945, Birmingham AL), American writer.

Stevie Wonder (Steveland Judkins; Steveland Morris; 13 May 1950, Saginaw MI), American pop songwriter and singer.

Elijah (Jordan) Wood (28 Jan 1981, Cedar Rapids IA), American film actor.

Tiger Woods (Eldrick Woods; 30 Dec 1975, Cypress CA), American golfer.

Klaus Wowereit (1 Oct 1953, West Berlin, West Germany [now in Berlin, Germany]), German politician (Social Democrat); mayor of Berlin from 2001.

Stephen Wozniak (11 Aug 1950, San Jose CA), American electrical engineer, cofounder of Apple Computer Corp., and youth leader.

Ram Baran Yadav (4 Feb 1948, Sapahi, Dhanukha, Nepal), Nepalese politician; the first president of Nepal, from 2008.

Shinya Yamanaka (4 Sep 1962, Osaka, Japan), Japanese physician and stem-cell researcher.

Yang Jiechi (May 1950, Shanghai, China), Chinese foreign minister from 2007.

Yao Ming (12 Sep 1980, Shanghai, China), Chinese basketball player.

Umaru Musa Yar'Adua (1951, Katsina, Nigeria), Nigerian politician; president from 2007.

Catherine Yass (1963, London, England), British photographic artist.

Trisha Yearwood (Patricia Lynn Yearwood; 19 Sep 1964, Monticello GA), American country singer.

Michelle Yeoh (Yang Zi Chong or Yeoh Chu-keng; 6 Aug 1962, Ipoh, Malaysia), Malaysian-born film actress.

Gloria Yerkovich (1942), American child-welfare advocate; founder of Child Find, an organization that helps to locate missing children.

Francis Yip (Yip Lai Yee; 1948, Hong Kong), Hong Kong Chinese pop singer.

Banana Yoshimoto (Yoshimoto Mahoko; 24 Jul 1964, Tokyo, Japan), Japanese writer of best-selling fiction.

Will(iam Robert) Young (20 Jan 1979, Hungerford, Berkshire, England), British pop singer.

Susilo Bambang Yudhoyono (9 Sep 1949, Pacitan, East Java, Indonesia), Indonesian military officer; president from 2004.

Muhammad Yunus (28 Jun 1940, Chittagong, East Bengal, British India [now in Bangladesh]), Bangladeshi economist specializing in microcredit and founder of the Grameen Bank; corecipient of the 2006 Nobel Peace Prize.

Viktor (Andriyovych) Yushchenko (23 Feb 1954, Khoruzhivka, Sumy oblast, USSR [now in Ukraine]), Ukrainian banker and politician (Our Ukraine); prime minister, 1999–2001, and president from 2005.

Sadi Yusuf (1934, near Basra, Iraq), Iraqi-born poet.

Raúl Yzaguirre (22 Jul 1939, south Texas), American Hispanic rights activist.

Adam Zagajewski (21 Jun 1945, Lwow, Poland [now Lviv, Ukraine]), Polish poet, novelist, and essayist; recipient of the 2004 Neustadt Prize.

José Luis Rodríguez Zapatero (4 Aug 1960, Valladolid, Spain), Spanish politician (Socialist Workers Party); prime minister from 2004.

Asif Ali Zardari (21 Jul 1956, Nawabshah, Pakistan), Pakistani politician and widower of Benazir Bhutto; cochairman of the Pakistan People's Party from 2007 and president of Pakistan from 2008.

Valdis Zatlers (22 Mar 1955), Latvian politician; president from 2007.

Ayman al-Zawahiri (19 Jun 1951, Maadi, Egypt), Egyptian-born physician and militant Islamic extremist leader, the chief lieutenant of Osama bin Laden.

(José) Manuel Zelaya (Rosales) (20 Sep 1952, Catacamas, Honduras), Honduran politician (Liberal Party); president, 2006–09.

Sam Zell (Samuel Zielonka; 28 Sep 1941, Chicago IL), American real-estate tycoon.

Renée (Kathleen) Zellweger (25 Apr 1969, Katy TX), American actress.

Robert Zemeckis (14 May 1952, Chicago IL), American film director.

Meles Zenawi (8 May 1955, Adoua, Ethiopia), Ethiopian politician; prime minister from 1995.

Niklas Zennström (1966, Sweden), Swedish Internet entrepreneur; codeveloper of Joost, a popular program for receiving TV broadcasts on a personal computer.

Catherine Zeta-Jones (Catherine Jones; 25 Sep 1969, Swansea, West Glamorgan, Wales), Welsh-born American actress.

Zhang Yimou (14 Nov 1951, Xi'an, Shaanxi province, China), Chinese film director.

Zhang Ziyi (9 Feb 1979, Beijing, China), Chinese actress.

Mary (Alice) Zimmerman (23 Aug 1960, Lincoln NE), American stage director.

Slavoj Zizek (21 Mar 1949, Ljubljana, Yugoslavia [now in Slovenia]), Slovenian political philosopher and social critic.

Robert B. Zoellick (25 Jul 1953, Evergreen Park IL), American businessman and government official; US trade representative, 2001–05, deputy secretary of state, 2005–06, and president of the World Bank from 2007.

Mark Zuckerberg (14 May 1984, Dobbs Ferry NY), American Internet entrepreneur; founder and CEO of Facebook, a social networking Web site.

Mortimer B. Zuckerman (4 Jun 1937, Montreal, QC, Canada), Canadian-born American publisher, columnist, and editor in chief of U.S. News & World Report.

Jacob (Gedleyihlekisa) Zuma (12 Apr 1942, Inkandla, Natal, Union of South Africa [now in KwaZulu Natal province, South Africa]), South African politician; deputy president of South Africa, 1999–2005, president of the African National Congress from 2007, and president of South Africa from 2009.

Peter Zumthor (26 Apr 1943, Basel, Switzerland), Swiss architect; recipient of the 2009 Pritzker Prize.

Harald Zur Hausen (11 Mar 1936, Gelsenkirchen, Germany), German virologist; cowinner of the 2008 Nobel Prize for Physiology or Medicine.

Obituaries

Death of notable people since 1 July 2008

Edie Adams (Elizabeth Edith Enke; 16 Apr 1927, Kingston PA—15 Oct 2008, Los Angeles CA), American singer, a sultry blonde beauty who served as the comic foil for her husband, Ernie Kovacs, in his TV comedy-show sketches; she also found success on Broadway, earning (1957) a Tony Award for her featured (supporting) role as Daisy Mae in *Li'l Abner*.

Aleksey II (Aleksey Mikhailovich Ridiger; 23 Feb 1929, Tallinn, Estonia—5 Dec 2008, near Moscow, Russia), Russian Orthodox prelate who, as the Russian Orthodox patriarch of Moscow and all Russia from 1990, was the spiritual leader of more than 140 million people and the first patriarch in Soviet history to be chosen without government pressure.

Raúl (Ricardo) Alfonsín (Foulkes) (12 Mar 1927, Chascomús, Argentina—31 Mar 2009, Buenos Aires, Argentina), Argentine politician who emerged victorious in the 1983 Argentine presidential elections; his victory marked the first time that the Peronist party had been beaten in a free election, and his term followed eight years of military rule in which at least 9,000 persons "disappeared."

Betty Allen (Elizabeth Louise Allen; 17 Mar 1927, Campbell OH—22 Jun 2009, Valhalla NY), American opera singer who was part of the post-World War II wave of African American singers on the international stage; she sang with many companies, notably the New York City Opera, the Metropolitan Opera, and the New York Philharmonic conducted by Leonard Bernstein, and she was the executive director (1979–92) of the Harlem School of the Arts.

Ken(neth Cooper) Annakin (10 Aug 1914, Beverley, Yorkshire, England—22 Apr 2009, Beverly Hills CA), British film director who was responsible for more than 40 widely varied motion pictures, including the Walt Disney family adventure *Swiss Family Robinson* (1960), the classic war movie *The Longest Day* (1962), and the comedy *Those Magnificent Men in Their Flying Machines or How I Flew from London to Paris in 25 Hours 11 Minutes* (1965); he was made OBE in 2002.

Corazon Aquino (Maria Corazon Cojuangco Aquino; 25 Jan 1933, Tarlac province, Philippines—1 Aug 2009, Makati, Philippines), Philippine political leader who, as president (1986–92) of the Philippines, restored democratic rule in that country after the long dictatorship of Ferdinand Marcos. Her husband, Benigno Simeon Aquino, Jr., a prominent opposition leader, was jailed by Marcos for eight years (1972–80), and her husband's assassination in 1983 galvanized opposition to the Marcos government; when Marcos called for presidential elections in February 1986, Aquino became the unified opposition's candidate, and though she was officially reported to have lost to Marcos, high officials in the military publicly renounced Marcos and proclaimed Aquino the rightful president. She appointed a commission to write a new constitution, which restored the bicameral Congress abolished by Marcos in 1973, held elections to the new Congress, and broke up the monopolies held by Marcos's allies over the economy.

Dave (Lance) Arneson (1 Oct 1947, Hennepin county, Minnesota—7 Apr 2009, St. Paul MN), American inventor who cocreated (1974), with Gary Gygax, the first fantasy role-playing game (RPG), Dungeons & Dragons (D&D), the ancestor to a host of computer-based video RPGs.

Gerald Arpino (Gennaro Peter Arpino; 14 Jan 1923, Staten Island NY—29 Oct 2008, Chicago IL), American ballet choreographer who was a leader of the Joffrey Ballet from its founding in 1956 until 2007; he toured with the Ballet Russe and appeared in Broadway musicals before helping dancer Robert Joffrey found the Joffrey Ballet; Arpino became artistic director after Joffrey's death in 1988, and he moved the company to Chicago in 1995.

Bea Arthur (Bernice Frankel; 13 May 1922, New York NY—25 Apr 2009, Los Angeles CA), American actress who portrayed an acerbic-tongued feminist in the television sitcom *Maude* (1972–78) and a sharp-witted divorcée in *The Golden Girls* (1985–92), which, like *Maude*, often explored such hot-button issues as abortion, homosexuality, infidelity, gun control, and aging; Arthur, who garnered 11 Emmy Award nominations, won an Emmy in 1977 for *Maude*, and in 1988 she was awarded the statuette for her work in *The Golden Girls*. In 1966 she won a Tony Award for best supporting actress for her role in the original production of *Mame*.

Ron(ald Franklin) Asheton (17 Jul 1948, Washington DC—found dead 6 Jan 2009, Ann Arbor MI), American guitarist for the Stooges, an American rock band of the late 1960s and early '70s that helped define punk music; described by one critic as the "godfather of punk guitar," Asheton was included by *Rolling Stone* magazine in 2003 on its list of the 100 greatest guitarists of all time.

J(ames) G(raham) Ballard (15 Nov 1930, Shanghai, China—19 Apr 2009, London, England), British author who was much admired for his science fiction set in ecologically unbalanced landscapes caused by decadent technological excess; to the wider public, however, he was best known for his largely autobiographical novel *Empire of the Sun* (1984; filmed 1987) and for the novel *Crash* (1973; filmed 1996).

Bernard (Leon) Barker (17 Mar 1917, Havana, Cuba—5 Jun 2009, Miami FL), Cuban-born American CIA agent and Watergate burglar who was one of five men arrested for breaking into the Democratic National Committee headquarters in the Watergate complex in Washington DC in 1972; he was recruited by Nixon White House aide E. Howard Hunt, Jr., whom he met in the CIA while planning the 1961 Bay of Pigs invasion of Cuba.

Sammy Baugh (Samuel Adrian Baugh; "Slingin' Sammy"; 17 Mar 1914, Temple TX—17 Dec 2008, Rotan TX), American football player who led the National Football League (NFL) in passing in 6 of his 16 seasons (1937–52) with the Washington Redskins and was considered the first outstanding quarterback in the history of American professional gridiron football—he also excelled as a punter and as a defensive back; in 1943 Baugh led the NFL in passing, punting, and interceptions; he was elected to the Pro Football Hall of Fame in 1963.

Louie Bellson (Luigi Paulino Alfredo Francesco Antonio Balassoni; 6 Jul 1924, Rock Falls IL—14 Feb 2009, Los Angeles CA), American musician, an extraordinary drummer who electrified audiences with his solos and, while still a teenager, invented the double-bass drum kit that became his trademark; he was an accompanist for popular singers such as Tony Bennett and Ella Fitzgerald and for other musicians such as Count Basie, and he achieved celebrity status as drummer with the Duke Ellington Orchestra in the early 1950s.

Estelle Bennett (22 Jul 1941, New York NY—found dead 11 Feb 2009, Englewood NJ), American singer who, with her sister, Veronica (Ronnie) Bennett, and their cousin, Nedra Talley, formed the Ronettes, one of the premier pop girl singing groups of the early 1960s; the Ronettes released a string of hit singles, including "Be My Baby" (1963); the Ronettes were inducted into the Rock and Roll Hall of Fame in 2007.

Jay Bennett (15 Nov 1963, Rolling Meadows IL—found dead 24 May 2009, Urbana IL), American musician and songwriter who was best known for his role in the alternative rock band Wilco.

the Rev. James L(uther) Bevel (19 Oct 1936, Itta Bena MS—19 Dec 2008, Springfield VA), American civil rights leader who, as the project director of the Southern Christian Leadership Conference, became one of the most influential advisers to the Rev. Martin Luther King, Jr.; Bevel was also instrumental in organizing the historic march in Alabama from Selma to Montgomery.

Doc Blanchard (Felix Anthony Blanchard, Jr.; "Mr. Inside"; 11 Dec 1924, McColl SC—19 Apr 2009, Bulverde TX), American football player who was, with Glenn ("Mr. Outside") Davis, part of the famed college football backfield on the undefeated Army teams of 1944–46; in 1945 he rushed for 19 touchdowns and 718 yd, averaging 7.1 yd a carry, and won the Heisman Trophy for the best college player; he also was the first football player to win the Sullivan Award for best amateur athlete; he was inducted into the College Football Hall of Fame in 1959.

Omar Bongo (El Hadj Omar Bongo Ondimba; Albert-Bernard Bongo; 30 Dec 1935, Lewai, French Equatorial Africa [now Bongoville, Gabon]—8 Jun 2009, Barcelona, Spain), Gabonese political leader who was president of Gabon for nearly 42 years; at the time of his death, Bongo was the longest-serving head of government in the world; during his time in office, Bongo preserved economic and political ties with France, the former colonial power, offering privileged oil-drilling rights to the French state-owned petroleum company, and also maintained relative stability in Gabon despite periodic accusations of corruption, money laundering, election rigging, and intimidation of political opponents. Bongo was believed to be one of the richest men in the world, with foreign bank accounts totaling an alleged US$130 million and real estate in France worth some US$190 million.

Luís de Almeida Cabral (11 Apr 1931, Bissau, Portuguese Guinea [now Guinea-Bissau]—30 May 2009, Lisbon, Portugal), Guinea-Bissauan politician who was the first president of independent Guinea-Bissau (1974–80); he participated in the guerrilla war launched in 1960 against the Portuguese colonial government and became president when Guinea-Bissau gained independence in 1974.

Jack Cardiff (18 Sep 1914, Great Yarmouth, Norfolk, England—22 Apr 2009, Ely, Cambridgeshire, England), British cinematographer and director who was known for his dazzling camera work in such films as *Black Narcissus* (1947), for which he won an Academy Award, *War and Peace* (1956), and *The African Queen* (1951); he received the International Award (1993) from the American Society of Cinematographers, a lifetime achievement award (1995) from the British Society of Cinematographers, and an honorary Oscar (2001) for his artistic achievements in cinematography.

David Carradine (John Arthur Carradine; 8 Dec 1936, Hollywood CA—found dead 4 Jun 2009, Bangkok, Thailand), American actor who was best known for his iconic portrayal of Kwai Chang Caine, a Shaolin monk, in the television series *Kung Fu* (1972–75); he also played the title character in Quentin Tarantino's film *Kill Bill: Vol. 1* (2003), a role he reprised in *Kill Bill: Vol. 2* (2004).

Marilyn Chambers (Marilyn Ann Briggs; 22 Apr 1952, Providence RI—found dead 12 Apr 2009, near Santa Clarita CA), American adult-film actress who initially cultivated an image as a fresh-faced blonde, adorning the boxes of Ivory Snow laundry soap, the slogan of which was "99 and 44/100% pure," but whose persona underwent a sensational transformation when she starred in the X-rated film *Behind the Green Door* (1972), which was credited with helping to establish a mainstream market for pornography.

Lansana Conté (1934?, Loumbaya-Moussaya, Dubréka prefecture, French West Africa [now in Guinea]—22 Dec 2008, Conakry, Guinea), Guinean strongman who was the autocratic ruler of his country for almost 25 years; he was reelected three times (1993, 1998, and 2003) in ostensibly multiparty ballots, but he grew increasingly authoritarian amid growing accusations of fraud and intimidation of the opposition.

Hank Crawford (Bennie Ross Crawford, Jr.; 21 Dec 1934, Memphis TN—29 Jan 2009, Memphis TN), American jazz and blues musician who played alto saxophone with a fervently emotional sound that fused gospel music with blues; Crawford was the arranger, pianist, saxophonist, and musical director of Ray Charles's band (1958–63).

(John) Michael Crichton (23 Oct 1942, Chicago IL—4 Nov 2008, Los Angeles CA), American author, physician, and television and motion picture producer-director who used his medical training and vivid imagination to pen wildly popular fictional tales that blended scientific and technological themes amid a fast-paced narrative; among his blockbuster thrillers were the novels *The Andromeda Strain* (1969; filmed 1971; TV miniseries 2008), *Jurassic Park* (1990; cowriter of 1993 screenplay), and, under the name Jeffrey Hudson, the Edgar Award-winning medical detective novel *A Case of Need* (1968; filmed as *The Carey Treatment* [1972]); his screenplays include *The Great Train Robbery* (1979), *Rising Sun* (1993), and *Congo* (1995)—all based on his books—and *Coma* (1978) and *Twister* (1996); he was also the creator of the Emmy Award-winning television series *ER* (1994–2009).

Walter (Leland) Cronkite (Jr.) (4 Nov 1916, St. Joseph MO—17 Jul 2009, New York NY), American journalist who was a pioneer of television news programming and became known as "the most trusted man in America" as the longtime anchor of the *CBS Evening News with Walter Cronkite* (1962–81); from the anchor chair, he reported on the assassination (1963) of US Pres. John F. Kennedy, the Apollo 11 Moon landing (1969), the Watergate Scandal (1972–75), the resignation (1974) of US Pres. Richard M. Nixon, the historic peace negotiations (1977–78) between Egyptian Pres. Anwar el-Sadat and Israeli Prime Minister Menachem Begin, and the Vietnam War, which he famously denounced as unwinnable in 1968. He won several Emmy and Peabody awards, and in 1981 US Pres. Jimmy Carter awarded him the Presidential Medal of Freedom.

Merce Cunningham (Mercier Philip Cunningham; 16 Apr 1919, Centralia WA—26 Jul 2009, New York NY), American dancer and choreographer who made a mark on modern dance in the US and Britain by expanding the potentialities of space, time, and movement in the creation of abstract dance, especially in works for the Merce Cunningham Dance Company, which he founded in 1953; he developed "choreography by chance," a technique in which selected isolated movements are assigned sequence by such random methods as tossing a coin.

Chuck Daly (Charles Jerome Daly; 20 Jul 1930, St. Mary's PA—9 May 2009, Jupiter FL), American basketball coach who led the Detroit Pistons, nicknamed the Bad Boys, to back-to-back NBA championships (1989, 1990) and coached the so-called Dream Team that won the gold medal at the 1992 Olympic Games in Barcelona; known for his ability to work with disparate high-powered strong personalities and make them into a cohesive team, he coached the Pistons for nine years, beginning in 1983, and led them to the playoffs each year, as well as to the Eastern Conference finals from 1987 to 1991; with a regular-season won-lost coaching record of 638–437 over 14 seasons, he was inducted into the Naismith Memorial Basketball Hall of Fame in 1994 and in 1996 was named one of the 10 best coaches in the 50-year history of the NBA.

Glenn (Ashby) Davis ("Jeep"; 12 Sep 1934, Wellsburg WV—28 Jan 2009, Barberton OH), American hurdler who was a world-record holder (1956–62) in the 400-m hurdles and the first man to win the Olympic gold medal twice in that event (1956, 1960); in 1958 he won the James E. Sullivan award; in 1960 he also ran the 200-m hurdles in a world-record time of 22.5 sec.

Michael (Ellis) DeBakey (7 Sep 1908, Lake Charles LA—11 Jul 2008, Houston TX), American cardiovascular surgeon and educator who pioneered surgical procedures for the treatment of defects and diseases of the cardiovascular system; in 1932 he devised the "roller pump," an essential component that permitted open-heart surgery, and he also performed the first successful coronary artery bypass (1964) and the first successful implantation of a ventricular assist device (1966); he was awarded (2008) the Congressional Gold Medal.

Dom(inick) DeLuise (1 Aug 1933, Brooklyn NY—4 May 2009, Santa Monica CA), American comic actor who starred in dozens of movies, especially in association with director Mel Brooks and actor Burt Reynolds; his best-known films include Blazing Saddles (1974), The Cannonball Run (1981), and The Best Little Whorehouse in Texas (1982); DeLuise was also known as a talented cook and wrote two cookbooks as well as several books for children.

Mamadou (Moustapha) Dia (18 Jul 1910, Khombole, Senegal—25 Jan 2009, Dakar, Senegal), Senegalese politician who was a protégé of Léopold Sédar Senghor and served (1959–62) as the first prime minister of Senegal.

Dom(inic Paul) DiMaggio ("The Little Professor"; 12 Feb 1917, San Francisco CA—8 May 2009, Marion MA), American baseball player who enjoyed a stellar career in Major League Baseball as a center fielder for the Boston Red Sox, despite being overshadowed by the prowess of his legendary older brother, Joe; during Dom's 11 seasons (1940–42, 1946–53) with the club, he was selected to the All-Star team seven times; in 1948 he set an American League record by making 503 putouts, and the following year he batted safely in 34 consecutive games, establishing a franchise record that remained unbroken at the time of his death.

David Herbert Donald (1 Oct 1920, Goodman MS—17 May 2009, Boston MA), American historian, an esteemed writer who twice won the Pulitzer Prize for biography, in 1961 for Charles Sumner and the Coming of the Civil War (1960) and in 1988 for Look Homeward: A Life of Thomas Wolfe (1987); he was also well known for his many works on Abraham Lincoln, and in 2005 the Abraham Lincoln Presidential Museum established the David Herbert Donald Prize for "excellence in Lincoln studies."

Ronnie Drew (16 Sep 1934, Dun Laoghaire, Irish Free State—16 Aug 2008, Dublin, Ireland), Irish folk musician who founded (1962) the highly popular and influential musical group the Dubliners and served as its front man for more than 30 years.

Maurice(-Samuel-Roger-Charles) Druon (23 Apr 1918, Paris, France—14 Apr 2009, Paris, France), French author, politician, and man of letters whose Les Grandes Familles (1948) won the 1948 Prix Goncourt; he was perhaps best known for cowriting the lyrics to "Chant des partisans," the unofficial anthem of France's World War II Resistance movement; in 1966 he was elected to the French Academy (the official arbiter of French language and literary standards), of which he was secretary from 1985 to 1999; he was awarded the Grand Cross of the Legion of Honor, and the British government made him honorary CBE in 1988 and KBE in 1999.

Avery (Robert) Cardinal Dulles (24 Aug 1918, Auburn NY—12 Dec 2008, Bronx NY), American prelate who was one of the preeminent Roman Catholic theologians in the United States and an astute liaison between the church's liberal and conservative factions; born to a family of Protestant statesmen (his father was politician John Foster Dulles), Dulles was elevated to cardinal in 2001, thereby becoming the first American to be appointed to that position without first having served as bishop.

Dominick Dunne (29 Oct 1925, Hartford CT—26 Aug 2009, New York NY), American writer who covered high-profile crime trials for the magazine Vanity Fair and wrote popular novels based on true crimes in high society; he was best known for his coverage of the 1995 murder trial of former football star O.J. Simpson.

David Eddings (7 Jul 1931, Spokane WA—2 Jun 2009, Carson City NV), American author who topped best-seller lists with his richly crafted sword-and-sorcery fantasy novels; he broke into the fantasy genre with the epic-length Belgariad series (1982–84), five novels that followed a young farm boy as he uncovered the secrets of his lineage.

Osborn ("Oz") Elliott (25 Oct 1924, New York NY—28 Sep 2008, New York NY), American journalist and editor who advanced Newsweek magazine to a stature rivaling that of its chief competitor, Time, during his tenure (1961–76) as its editor; under his watch Newsweek gave high-profile coverage to civil rights issues, expressing support for the cause of equality, and circulation nearly doubled.

Philip José Farmer (26 Jan 1918, North Terre Haute IN—25 Feb 2009, Peoria IL), American science-fiction author; his short story "The Lovers" (1952) won him a Hugo Award for best new writer, and his novella Riders of the Purple Wage (1967) and novel To Your Scattered Bodies Go (1971) also gained

Hugo Awards; he was honored as a Nebula Award Grand Master by the Science Fiction and Fantasy Writers of America in 2001 and with the World Fantasy Award for Lifetime Achievement in 2001.

(Mary) Farrah (Leni) Fawcett (Farrah Fawcett-Majors; 2 Feb 1947, Corpus Christi TX—25 Jun 2009, Santa Monica CA), American actress who was a glamorous pinup girl—her feathered blonde hair inspired the style adopted by legions of fans in the 1970s, and a poster of her clad in a wet one-piece red bathing suit and flashing her dazzling smile became iconic and sold some six million copies; her beguiling look vaulted her to superstardom in the hit television series *Charlie's Angels,* in which she appeared (1976–77) as a sexy private investigator.

León Febres Cordero (Ribadeneyra) (9 Mar 1931, Guayaquil, Ecuador—15 Dec 2008, Guayaquil, Ecuador), Ecuadoran politician who developed a reputation as a larger-than-life strongman while serving a tumultuous term (1984–88) as president of Ecuador; though his free-market approach to economic policy won him the admiration of US Pres. Ronald Reagan, his relationship with his own legislature was frequently contentious, and his brief kidnapping in 1987 at the hands of rebel commandos underscored Ecuador's political instability.

W(illiam) Mark Felt (Sr.) (17 Aug 1913, Twin Falls ID—18 Dec 2008, Santa Rosa CA), American government official who served as the associate director of the FBI in the early 1970s and in 2005 revealed that he was "Deep Throat," the anonymous informant who secretly cooperated with reporter Bob Woodward in the *Washington Post's* investigation into the abuses of presidential powers stemming from the break-in at the Watergate complex during the 1972 presidential election campaign.

Mark (Steven) Fidrych ("the Bird"; 15 Aug 1954, Worcester MA—13 Apr 2009, Northborough MA), American baseball player who had a phenomenal rookie year as a pitcher for Major League Baseball's Detroit Tigers in 1976, with a won-lost record of 19–9, an earned run average of 2.34, and 97 strikeouts; he was named the American League Rookie of the Year and was the starting pitcher for that season's All-Star game.

(Albert) Horton Foote (Jr.) (14 Mar 1916, Wharton TX—4 Mar 2009, Hartford CT), American playwright and screenwriter who evoked American life in beautifully observed minimal stories frequently set in the early 20th century in the fictional small town of Harrison, Texas; his best-known work, *The Trip to Bountiful,* was broadcast as a television play and staged on Broadway in 1953; he won Oscars for screenwriting for the movies *To Kill a Mockingbird* (1962) and *Tender Mercies* (1983), and he was honored with a Pulitzer Prize for drama in 1995 for *The Young Man from Atlanta.*

Alan (Robert) Ford (7 Dec 1923, Panama Canal Zone—3 Nov 2008, Sarasota FL), American swimmer who became (1944) the first person to break the 50-second barrier in the 100-yd freestyle, and he won the silver medal in the 100-m freestyle at the 1948 Olympics; in 1966 he was inducted into the International Swimming Hall of Fame.

John Hope Franklin (2 Jan 1915, Rentiesville OK—25 Mar 2009, Durham NC), American historian and educator who helped to fashion the legal brief that led to the historic Supreme Court decision outlawing public school segregation, *Brown* v. *Board of Education of Topeka* (1954); in 1995 Pres. Bill Clinton honored him with the Presidential Medal of Freedom.

Marilyn French (Marilyn Edwards; 21 Nov 1929, Brooklyn NY—2 May 2009, New York NY), American author who was a staunch feminist whose works explored her radical beliefs about relationships between the sexes, most notably in her debut novel, *The Women's Room* (1977), in which she maintained that women's identities were lost when they married; it sold more than 20 million copies and was translated into 20 languages.

Millard (Dean) Fuller (3 Jan 1935, Lanett AL—3 Feb 2009, Americus GA), American philanthropist who founded (1976) the Christian charity organization Habitat for Humanity International; the principle of the organization is based on sweat equity—involving future homeowners in the construction of their own homes, which they are then able to purchase through interest-free loans; Pres. Bill Clinton awarded (1996) Fuller the Presidential Medal of Freedom.

Estelle Getty (Estelle Scher Gettleman; 25 Jul 1923, New York NY—22 Jul 2008, Los Angeles CA), American actress who earned a legion of fans and seven straight Emmy Award nominations (1986–92; she won in 1988) for her portrayal of Sophia Petrillo, the sharp-tongued octogenarian in NBC television's situation comedy *The Golden Girls* (1985–92).

William Gibson (13 Nov 1914, Bronx NY—25 Nov 2008, Stockbridge MA), American playwright who won instant acclaim for his play *The Miracle Worker* (1959), which was based on the life of Helen Keller, a deaf and blind child whose determined teacher, Annie Sullivan, taught her to communicate by using sign language; the play ran 719 performances on Broadway and received four Tony Awards, including one for best play.

Robert Giroux (8 Apr 1914, Jersey City NJ—5 Sep 2008, Tinton Falls NJ), American editor and publisher who introduced and guided many of the top authors of the 20th century in a lengthy career in which he ascended to chairman (1973) of the distinguished publishing house Farrar, Straus and Giroux; he published the debut novels of numerous significant writers, including Robert Lowell, Flannery O'Connor, Jack Kerouac, and Susan Sontag.

Robert Graham (19 Aug 1938, Mexico City, Mexico—27 Dec 2008, Santa Monica CA), Mexican-born American sculptor who was celebrated for his bronze civic monuments, many of them massive in scale; among his best-known designs are the Olympic Gateway (1984) in Los Angeles, the Joe Louis Memorial (1986) in Detroit, the Franklin Delano Roosevelt Memorial (1997) in Washington DC, and the Charlie "Bird" Parker Memorial (1999) in Kansas City MO.

Charles Gwathmey (19 Jun 1938, Charlotte NC—3 Aug 2009, New York NY), American architect who was celebrated for his geometric-inspired Modernist architecture; Gwathmey Siegel & Associates, the firm that he founded in 1968 with fellow architect Robert Siegel, was noted for creating massive public buildings (especially museums).

Jörg Haider (26 Jan 1950, Bad Goisern, Austria—11 Oct 2008, near Klagenfurt, Austria), Austrian politician who was the controversial populist leader of the far-right Freedom Party of Austria (FPÖ; 1986–2000) and the governor of the state of Kärnten (1989–91; 1999–2008); he denounced immigration, opposed the expansion of the EU to the east, and exploited the Austrian people's disgust with their scandal-ridden government, but his extreme views and complimentary remarks about Nazi Germany eventually cost him (and the FPÖ) support.

Ned Harkness (Nevin D. Harkness; 19 Sep 1921, Ottawa, ON, Canada–19 Sep 2008, Rochester NY), Canadian hockey and lacrosse coach who became the first coach to win national collegiate championships in two different sports when he led the lacrosse team at Rensselaer Polytechnic Institute, Troy NY, to the NCAA championship in 1952 and the hockey team to a title in 1954; he moved to Cornell University, Ithaca NY (1963–70), where his teams won NCAA ice hockey championships in 1967 and 1970, the latter squad scoring a perfect 29-0-0 record, becoming the only undefeated, untied national championship team in NCAA history; he was inducted into the US Hockey Hall of Fame in 1994 and the National Lacrosse Hall of Fame in 2001.

René (Reynaldo) Harris (11 Nov 1947?, Nauru–5 Jul 2008, Nauru), Nauruan politician who served four times (27 Apr 1999–20 Apr 2000; 30 Mar 2001–9 Jan 2003; 17–18 Jan 2003; 8 Aug 2003–22 Jun 2004) as Nauru's president; his 31 years (1977–2008) as a member of the country's Parliament made him Nauru's longest-serving politician; in 2001 Harris and Australian Prime Minister John Howard negotiated the controversial "Pacific Solution," in which Nauru received millions of dollars in financial aid in exchange for maintaining detention centers for Australia-bound asylum seekers.

Paul Harvey (Aurandt) (4 Sep 1918, Tulsa OK–28 Feb 2009, Phoenix AZ), American radio commentator who enthralled millions of listeners via more than 1,200 radio stations throughout the US with his down-to-earth conservative radio programs during a career that spanned nearly 60 years; he was dubbed "the voice of Middle America" and "the voice of the silent majority"; his no-nonsense approach to news and editorials, laced with long pauses for suspense, along with the genuine warmth and humor that he brought to human-interest stories, created a personal connection with listeners; he also wrote his own commercials and endorsed only products that he trusted. He was awarded the Presidential Medal of Freedom in 2005.

Don(ald L.) Haskins (4 Mar 1930, Enid OK–7 Sep 2008, El Paso TX), American college basketball coach who helped bring racial integration to college basketball when in 1966 he started five African American players on his Texas Western College team that defeated the all-white University of Kentucky team to win the NCAA University Division championship; in his 38-year career, Haskins led 14 teams to the NCAA tournament and had a career won-lost record of 719–353; he was inducted into the Naismith Memorial Basketball Hall of Fame individually in 1997 and in 2007 with his 1965–66 Texas Western team.

Isaac (Lee) Hayes (Jr.) (20 Aug 1942, Covington TN–10 Aug 2008, East Memphis TN), American singer-songwriter, musician, and actor who was a pioneering figure in soul music whose recordings influenced the development of such musical genres as disco, rap, and urban contemporary; he was perhaps best remembered for his compelling sound track for the 1971 film *Shaft*, the title song of which became a number one hit and earned him an Academy Award for best original song; Hayes was inducted in 2002 into the Rock and Roll Hall of Fame.

Jesse (Alexander) Helms (18 Oct 1921, Monroe NC–4 Jul 2008, Raleigh NC), American politician who, as a longtime member (1973–2003) of the US Senate, was a leading figure in the conservative movement; he maintained a staunchly right-wing stance on social issues, leading crusades against abortion, supporting prayer in public schools, and opposing the busing of students for racial integration, but he was perhaps best known for his vehement opposition to civil rights and gay rights. Portrayed by his critics as an extremist and a bigot, he famously opposed the creation of a national holiday in honor of Martin Luther King, Jr.

Don(ald Shepard) Hewitt (14 Dec 1922, New York NY–19 Aug 2009, Bridgehampton NY), American television producer who was best known as the creator and longtime producer (1968–2004) of the compelling television newsmagazine *60 Minutes*, which combined hard-hitting investigative reporting with candid profiles and interviews of celebrities and news makers; he also produced (1960) the first-ever televised US presidential debate; Hewitt won eight Emmy Awards and an Edward R. Murrow Award (2008).

Richard Hickox (5 Mar 1948, Stokenchurch, Buckinghamshire, England–23 Nov 2008, Cardiff, Wales), British conductor who was noted for his success as a choral conductor and for his prodigious output of more than 300 classical recordings; in 1971 he founded the Richard Hickox Orchestra and Richard Hickox Singers (later renamed the City of London Sinfonia and City of London Singers), and his appointments included music director (1976–91) and conductor emeritus (from 1991) of the London Symphony Chorus and music director of Opera Australia (from 2005); he was made CBE in 2002.

Phil(lip Toll) Hill (Jr.) (20 Apr 1927, Miami FL–28 Aug 2008, Monterey CA), American race-car driver who became the first American-born race-car driver to win (1961) the Formula 1 (F1) Grand Prix world championship of drivers; he also won the Le Mans 24-hour endurance race (1958, 1961–62), the Sebring 12-hour race (1958–59, 1961), and the 1964 Daytona Continental 2,000-km road race; in 1991 he was inducted into the International Motorsports Hall of Fame.

Tony Hillerman (Anthony Grove Hillerman; 27 May 1925, Sacred Heart OK–26 Oct 2008, Albuquerque NM), American novelist who produced taut mysteries that brought to light rich American Indian customs and culture and featured Navajo tribal officers as protagonists; these characters use the latest police crime-solving methods coupled with traditional Navajo beliefs (*hozro*, or harmony) in their detection; among his numerous awards were two Edgar Allan Poe Awards from the Mystery Writers of America: best novel (1974) and the Grand Master Award (1991).

Jerome Holtzman (12 Jul 1926, Chicago IL–19 Jul 2008, Evanston IL), American sportswriter who possessed an encyclopedic knowledge of baseball and was dubbed the "dean" of sportswriters; he was responsible for the implementation (1969) of a new baseball rule that designated a "save" to a relief pitcher who took the mound when his team was ahead in scoring and secured the win (the first significant addition to baseball statistics since 1920) and wrote the *Encyclopædia Britannica* entry on baseball; in 1998 he was named baseball's official historian, and he was inducted into the writers' wing of the Baseball Hall of Fame in 1989.

Hua Guofeng (Su Zhu; 16 Feb 1921, Jiaocheng, Shanxi province, China–20 Aug 2008, Beijing, China), Chinese politician who served as premier (1976–80) of China and chairman (1976–81) of the Chinese Communist Party (CCP).

John (Wilden) Hughes (Jr.) (18 Feb 1950, Lansing MI—6 Aug 2009, New York NY), American filmmaker who captured the essence of teen angst in comedic coming-of-age tales; he wrote and directed the iconic films *Sixteen Candles* (1984), *The Breakfast Club* (1985), *Ferris Bueller's Day Off* (1986), and *Planes, Trains, and Automobiles* (1987) and wrote the screenplays for such films as *Mr. Mom* (1983), *Pretty in Pink* (1986), and three of the four Home Alone movies (1990, 1992, 1997).

John Isaacs (15 Sep 1915, Panama City, Panama— 26 Jan 2009, Bronx NY), American basketball player who was a standout point guard for the Harlem Renaissance, a barnstorming all-black professional basketball team that rose to prominence in New York City during the era that preceded the formation of the NBA; he helped lead the Renaissance to a victory in 1939 over the National Basketball League's Oshkosh (WI) All-Stars in a game that was billed as the first world professional basketball championship.

Michael (Joseph) Jackson (29 Aug 1958, Gary IN—25 Jun 2009, Los Angeles CA), American singer, songwriter, and dancer who was the most popular entertainer in the world in the 1980s. Jackson began his lifelong performance career as the youngest and most talented of five brothers known as the Jackson 5, who sported the loudest fashions, the largest Afros, the snappiest choreography, and a youthful, soulful exuberance, and who scored (1969–70) four consecutive number one pop hits for Motown Records: "I Want You Back," "ABC," "The Love You Save," and "I'll Be There." Michael's solo effort *Off the Wall* (1979) became the best-selling album of the year and yielded the international hit singles "Don't Stop 'til You Get Enough" and "Rock with You." Three years later he returned with *Thriller*, a tour de force that elevated him to a worldwide superstar; it captured a record-setting eight Grammys, remained on the charts for more than two years, and sold more than 40 million copies worldwide, long holding the distinction of being the best-selling album in history. The album's second single, "Billie Jean," an electrifying dance track and the vehicle for Jackson's trademark "moonwalk" dance, topped the pop charts, as did "Beat It," which featured a raucous solo from famed guitarist Eddie Van Halen, while the electrifying 14-minute "Thriller" video (1983) became a cultural icon and set a new standard for production values in the genre. In 1997 the Jackson 5 was inducted into the Rock and Roll Hall of Fame, with Michael following in 2001. Despite his professional success, Jackson's eccentric, secluded lifestyle grew increasingly controversial in later years, clouded by allegations of child molestation in 1993, an arrest on child molestation charges in 2003, and finally, a financial collapse that many resulted in the loss of his lavish Neverland ranch.

Janet Jagan (Janet Rosalie Rosenberg; 20 Oct 1920, Chicago IL—28 Mar 2009, Georgetown, Guyana), American-born Guyanese politician who, as president of Guyana from 1997 to 1999, was the country's first white president and the first elected female president in South America.

Betty Jameson (Elizabeth May Jameson; 9 May 1919, Norman OK—31 Jan 2009, Boynton Beach FL), American golfer who shot a 295 to capture the 1947 US Women's Open and thereby became the first female golfer to break 300 in a 72-hole tournament; she had previously won US amateur championships in 1939 and 1940; in 1950 she was one of the founding members of the Ladies Professional Golf Association (LPGA). In 1951 she was inducted into the Hall of Fame of Women's Golf, in 1967 she was one of the six original inductees of the LPGA Tour Hall of Fame, and in 1999 she was named to the Women's Sports Foundation Hall of Fame.

Maurice(-Alexis) Jarre (13 Sep 1924, Lyon, France— 29 Mar 2009, Malibu CA), French composer who wrote the music sound tracks for more than 150 motion pictures, of which 3—*Lawrence of Arabia* (1962), *Doctor Zhivago* (1965, including his best-known work, the balalaika-infused song "Lara's Theme"), and *A Passage to India* (1984)—earned him the Academy Award for best original score; he was an officer of the Legion of Honor, and in February 2009 he was awarded the Berlin Film Festival's Golden Bear for Lifetime Achievement.

(Charles) Van Johnson (25 Aug 1916, Newport RI—12 Dec 2008, Nyack NY), American actor who was one of Hollywood's biggest stars during the early part of his six-decade career, particularly during his 12-year tenure (1942–54) at MGM studios, where he made nearly 50 films (in 1945 he ranked second only to Bing Crosby on the list of top 10 box-office stars).

Uriel Jones (13 Jun 1934, Detroit MI—24 Mar 2009, Dearborn MI), American musician who was the drummer for numerous Motown hits while playing as a member (1963–72) of the label's house studio band, the Funk Brothers; his biggest success came playing drums for such chart-topping hits as "Ain't Too Proud To Beg," "I Heard It Through the Grapevine," "My Girl," "Signed, Sealed, Delivered, I'm Yours," and "Ain't No Mountain High Enough"; the Funk Brothers were honored in 2004 with a Grammy Award for lifetime achievement.

Harry Kalas (26 Mar 1936, Chicago IL—13 Apr 2009, Washington DC), American radio and television sports announcer who was known as the voice of the Philadelphia Phillies Major League Baseball team from 1971; his sonorous voice and his home-run call of "Outta here!" made him popular, and he was honored in 2002 with the National Baseball Hall of Fame's Ford C. Frick Award for broadcasters.

Adrian Kantrowitz (4 Oct 1918, New York NY—14 Nov 2008, Ann Arbor MI), American heart surgeon who was a pioneer in the development of heart surgery and devices to improve heart function; he introduced a pacemaker small enough to implant (1962), and in 1967 he performed the first human heart transplant in the US.

Ephraim Katzir (Ephraim Katchalski; 16 May 1916, Kiev, Russian Empire [now in Ukraine]—30 May 2009, Rehovot, Israel), Russian-born Israeli scientist and politician who, as president of Israel (1973–78), promoted understanding between Israeli Jews and their Arab neighbors; a recognized authority on proteins, he was also the first Israeli elected (1966) to the US National Academy of Sciences.

George (Clyde) Kell (23 Aug 1922, Swifton AR—24 Mar 2009, Swifton AR), American baseball player who, as a slugging third baseman, played for 15 seasons (1943–57) and amassed a career batting average of .306; in 1949 he edged out Ted Williams for the American League batting title; Kell, who also was named to 10 AL All-Star teams, was inducted into the Baseball Hall of Fame in 1983.

Jack (French) Kemp (Jr.) (13 Jul 1935, Los Angeles CA—2 May 2009, Bethesda MD), American politician and football player who, after an illustrious career with the American Football League (AFL), became one of the country's leading conservative politicians following his election in 1970 to the US House of Representatives; he represented suburban Buffalo NY for nine terms (1971–89) and was the Republican nominee for vice president in 1996; he also served (1989–93) as secretary of housing and urban development under Pres. George H.W. Bush. Kemp led the Buffalo Bills to the AFL championship in 1964 and again in 1965, when he also won the league's most valuable player award, and he was named seven times to the AFL All-Star team; he retired from the game in 1969 as the AFL's all-time leader in passing yards, with 21,130.

Ted Kennedy (Edward Moore Kennedy; 22 Feb 1932, Boston MA–25 Aug 2009, Hyannis Port MA), American politician who was a respected US senator (1962–2009), as well as a prominent figure in the Democratic Party and in liberal politics in general for more than four decades. Kennedy, the last surviving brother of Pres. John F. Kennedy, was also a noteworthy spokesman for the policies that had come to be associated with his family name—support for social-welfare legislation and active participation in world affairs; he was known as the "lion of the Senate," serving as a leading advocate for many liberal causes, including voting rights, fair housing, consumer protection, and national health insurance, and at the same time, he was recognized for his willingness to cooperate with Republicans to advance important legislation, such as the No Child Left Behind Act (2001). In the last months of his life, he was granted an honorary British knighthood (KBE) and the US Presidential Medal of Freedom.

Kim Dae-Jung (6 Jan 1924?, Mokp'o, Japanese-occupied Korea [now in South Korea]–18 Aug 2009, Seoul, South Korea), South Korean politician who served (1998–2003) as South Korean president, the first opposition leader to win election to that office; he was awarded (2000) the Nobel Prize for Peace for his efforts to restore democracy in South Korea and to improve relations with North Korea—his "sunshine" policy allowed South Koreans to visit relatives in the North and eased rules governing South Korean investment in the country.

Willie King (8 Mar 1943, Prairie Point MS–8 Mar 2009, near Old Memphis AL), American musician who turned a lifelong love of the blues into a professional career in the last decades of his life; he earned a 2001 *Living Blues* Readers' Award for best blues artist (male), an award he received again in 2003, along with Critics' Awards for best blues artist (male) and best song.

Eartha (Mae) Kitt (17 Jan 1927, North SC–25 Dec 2008, Connecticut), American singer and dancer who seduced audiences with her extraordinary and distinctive sultry voice; she also achieved success as a dramatic stage and film actress, earning two Daytime Emmy Awards (2007 and 2008) for her role in *The Emperor's New School*.

Willem (Johan) Kolff (14 Feb 1911, Leiden, Netherlands–11 Feb 2009, Newtown Square PA), Dutch-born American physician who was a pioneering biomedical engineer who invented the kidney dialysis machine and led the medical team that in 1982 implanted the first artificial human heart.

Max (Emory) Lake (24 Jul 1924, Albany NY–14 Apr 2009, Sydney, NSW, Australia), Australian winemaker, author, and surgeon who in 1963 founded Lake's Folly, the first modern vineyard in New South Wales's Hunter Valley, where he pioneered Australia's boutique wine industry; he received the Order of Australia Medal in 2002.

Dante (Bert Joseph) Lavelli ("Gluefingers"; 23 Feb 1923, Hudson OH–20 Jan 2009, Cleveland OH), American football player who was a star wide receiver (1946–56) for the Cleveland Browns professional football team, helping the Browns capture four All-America Football Conference championships (1946–49) and three National Football League (NFL) championships (1950, 1954, and 1955); he was enshrined in the Pro Football Hall of Fame in 1975; after his retirement, he helped found the charitable NFL Alumni Association.

Andrea Mead Lawrence (19 Apr 1932, Rutland VT–31 Mar 2009, Mammoth Lakes CA), American skier who was the first American Alpine skier to win two gold medals in a single Winter Olympics, winning the slalom and the giant slalom at the 1952 Games in Oslo; her Olympic victories—coupled with her US championship titles in the downhill, slalom, and Alpine combined in 1950, 1952, and 1955 and in the giant slalom in 1953—led to her induction in 1983 into the International Women's Sports Hall of Fame.

Hugh Leonard (John Joseph Byrne; John Keyes Byrne; 9 Nov 1926, Dalkey, County Dublin, Irish Free State–12 Feb 2009, Dublin, Ireland), Irish dramatist who was best known for the play *Da*, which was first produced in 1973 and triumphed on Broadway for almost two years (1978–80), winning the Drama Desk Award for outstanding new play and four Tony Awards, including best play.

Li Ximing (February 1926, Shulu county, Hebei province, China–8 Nov 2008, Beijing, China), Chinese government official who, as the Communist Party of China boss in Beijing during the 1989 Tiananmen Square pro-democracy movement, advocated the military crackdown on the student-led demonstrators that ended in a massacre.

Hank Locklin (Lawrence Hankins Locklin; 15 Feb 1918, McLellan FL–8 Mar 2009, Brewton AL), American country-and-western singer who was known for his tremulous tenor voice on such chart-topping hit singles as "Send Me the Pillow You Dream On" (1949) and "Please Help Me, I'm Falling" (1960); during a career that spanned some five decades, Locklin recorded 65 albums, sold 15 million records, and produced 6 singles that reached number one on the *Billboard* country singles chart.

Huey Long (25 Apr 1904, Sealy TX –10 Jun 2009, Houston TX), American jazz guitarist who played with the influential Ink Spots in a musical career that lasted more than seven decades; he also played alongside innovative jazz and bebop musicians Charlie Parker and Dizzy Gillespie (1943) and as the leader of his own trio.

Orlando López ("Cachaito"; 2 Feb 1933, Havana, Cuba–9 Feb 2009, Havana, Cuba), Cuban musician who was internationally renowned for his virtuoso double-bass playing in the Buena Vista Social Club, the group of veteran Cuban musicians who created a global sensation in 1997 with their self-titled Grammy Award-winning debut album; López was prominently featured in the film *Buena Vista Social Club* (1999), which documented the group.

Karl Malden (Mladen Sekulovich; 22 Mar 1912, Chicago IL–1 Jul 2009, Los Angeles CA), American actor who won critical acclaim for his strong character roles, most notably alongside Marlon Brando in *A Streetcar Named Desire* (1951), a role that won him the Academy Award for best supporting actor (1951), and *On the Waterfront* (1954); he reached a new audience as lead detective Mike Stone in the television show *The Streets of San Francisco* (1972–77) opposite a young Michael Douglas; Malden served (1989–92) as president of the Academy of Motion Picture Arts and Sciences, and he was presented with the 2003 Screen Actors Guild's Life Achievement Award.

Anna Manahan (18 Oct 1924, County Waterford, Irish Free State–8 Mar 2009, Waterford, Ireland), Irish character actress who originated the demanding role of Mag Folan, the controlling mother in playwright Martin McDonagh's fierce family drama *The Beauty Queen of Leenane,* for which she was awarded (1998) a Tony for best featured actress.

Del Martin (Dorothy L. Taliaferro; 5 May 1921, San Francisco CA–27 Aug 2008, San Francisco CA), American activist who was a leader in the battle for lesbian and gay rights for more than 50 years; she and her partner, Phyllis Lyon, founded (1955) the first advocacy group for lesbians, Daughters of Bilitis, and wrote the landmark book *Lesbian/Woman* (1972); Martin was the first avowed lesbian to serve on the board of directors of the National Organization for Women (NOW); in 2008 she and Lyon became the first same-sex couple to be legally wed in California.

Dewey Martin (Walter Milton Dwayne Midkiff; 30 Sep 1940, Chesterville, ON, Canada—found dead 1 Feb 2009, Van Nuys CA), Canadian-born drummer who provided the beat behind the songs of the seminal folk-rock band Buffalo Springfield, of which he was an original member; Buffalo Springfield was inducted into the Rock and Roll Hall of Fame in 1997.

Billy Mays (William Darrell Mays, Jr.; 20 Jul 1958, McKees Rocks PA–28 Jun 2009, Tampa FL), American television pitchman who became a pop-culture icon with his enthusiastic sales of household products in infomercials; he was frequently parodied, including in a series of humorous commercials he did for sports network ESPN, and he also costarred in the reality TV show *Pitchmen* (2009).

George (Anderson) McAfee ("One-Play"; 13 Mar 1918, Corbin KY–4 Mar 2009, Durham NC), American professional gridiron football player who was a phenomenally versatile player for the Chicago Bears during the 1940s, excelling on offense and defense while helping the Bears capture three NFL championships (1940, 1941, and 1946); he was inducted into the Pro Football Hall of Fame in 1966.

Frank McCourt (Francis McCourt; 19 Aug 1930, Brooklyn NY–19 Jul 2009, New York NY), American author and teacher who was perhaps best known for the Pulitzer Prize-winning memoir *Angela's Ashes* (1996), a vivid portrayal of a Dickensian childhood amid the grinding conditions of Irish slum life that also won the National Book Critics Circle Award and was adapted into a well-received film (1999); he taught public school for 29 years.

Ed(ward Peter Leo) McMahon (Jr.) (6 Mar 1923, Detroit MI–23 Jun 2009, Los Angeles CA), American TV personality and actor who was the jovial sidekick of Johnny Carson, the host of *The Tonight Show* (1962–92), and was best remembered for his belly laughs and booming "H-e-e-e-e-ere's Johnny!" which was the nightly tagline used to introduce the late-night star; in the 1980s McMahon joined Dick Clark as a host of *TV's Bloopers & Practical Jokes* and began a long run as the emcee on the TV talent show *Star Search.*

Steve (LaTreal) McNair (14 Feb 1973, Mount Olive MS–4 Jul 2009, Nashville TN), American football player who played 13 NFL seasons (1995–2008) as one of a small number of high-profile African American quarterbacks; he was the third NFL draft pick in 1995, selected by the Houston Oilers (later the Tennessee Titans), whom he led in 2000 to Super Bowl XXXIV; he played in three Pro Bowls and was named joint Most Valuable Player in 2003.

Robert S(trange) McNamara (9 Jun 1916, San Francisco CA–6 Jul 2009, Washington DC), American government official who served (1961–68) as US secretary of defense and played a major role in the country's military involvement in Vietnam—though he initially advocated the deepening military involvement of the US in Vietnam, by 1967 he was openly seeking a way to launch peace negotiations; he later served (1968–81) as president of the World Bank.

Ahmad (Ali) al-Mirghani (16 Aug 1941, Khartoum, Anglo-Egyptian Sudan [now in The Sudan]–2 Nov 2008, Alexandria, Egypt), Sudanese politician who headed a rare democratically elected government in The Sudan as chairman of the Supreme Council from 1986 until he was overthrown by a military coup in 1989; in November 1988 he reached a peace agreement with the Sudan People's Liberation Army (SPLA), headed by John Garang.

Mitch Mitchell (John Mitchell; 9 Jul 1947, Ealing, Middlesex, England—12 Nov 2008, Portland OR), British rock-and-roll musician who was the powerful and innovative drummer of the legendary trio the Jimi Hendrix Experience from 1966; Mitchell backed Hendrix at the Monterey Pop Festival in 1967 and at the Woodstock festival in 1969; the Jimi Hendrix Experience was inducted into the Rock and Roll Hall of Fame in 1992.

Warith Deen Mohammed (Wallace D. Muhammad; 30 Oct 1933, Detroit MI–9 Sep 2008, Markham IL), American religious leader who, after succeeding his father, Elijah Muhammad, as head of the black nationalist Nation of Islam in 1975, reformed the organization and moved it toward inclusion within the worldwide Islamic community, renaming it the World Community of al-Islam in the West (the name was changed to the American Muslim Mission in 1978 and to the Muslim American Society in 1985); in 1992 Mohammed became the first Muslim to give the traditional invocation in the US Senate.

Ricardo Montalbán (Ricardo Gonzalo Pedro Montalbán y Merino; 25 Nov 1920, Mexico City, Mexico—14 Jan 2009, Los Angeles CA), Mexican actor who possessed a distinctive voice and debonair persona and enjoyed a 60-year career appearing onstage; in films such as *Escape from the Planet of the Apes* (1971) and *Star Trek II: The Wrath of Khan* (1982); and on television, where he starred as the suave Mr. Rourke in the hit TV series *Fantasy Island* (1978–84) and earned an Emmy Award for his performance as Indian chief Satangkai in the miniseries *How the West Was Won* (1978).

Charles Morgan, Jr. (11 Mar 1930, Cincinnati OH–8 Jan 2009, Destin FL), American attorney who argued and won several prominent civil rights cases, most notably *Reynolds* v. *Sims,* in which the US Supreme Court required the Alabama state legislature to create voting districts that were equitably apportioned, which was credited with helping to establish the legal doctrine of "one person, one vote" and curtailing voting discrimination in the South; he was the American Civil Liberties Union's Southern director (1964–72) and director of its legislative office (1972–77).

John (Clifford) Mortimer (21 Apr 1923, London, England—16 Jan 2009, near Henley-on-Thames, Oxfordshire, England), British barrister and writer who wrote plays for the stage, television, radio, and motion pictures; he was best known, however, as the creator of the crusty old British barrister Horace Rumpole, whom he featured in numerous stories and on the long-running (1978–92) TV series *Rumpole of the Bailey;* he was knighted in 1998.

Robert (Patrick) Mulligan (23 Aug 1925, Bronx NY—20 Dec 2008, Lyme CT), American film and TV director who earned an Emmy Award for his direction of the TV film *The Moon and the Sixpence* (1959), but who achieved his greatest renown for directing movies that involved complex human relationships, notably *To Kill a Mockingbird* (1962).

Tharon (Myrene) Musser (8 Jan 1925, Roanoke VA—19 Apr 2009, Newtown CT), American lighting designer who illuminated the sets of at least 150 Broadway productions and won Tony Awards for *Follies* (1972), *A Chorus Line* (1976), and *Dreamgirls* (1982).

Levy Patrick Mwanawasa (3 Sep 1948, Mufulira, Northern Rhodesia [now Zambia]—19 Aug 2008, Paris, France), Zambian attorney and politician who, as the third president (2002–08) of Zambia, launched an anticorruption campaign that included stripping his predecessor, Frederick Chiluba, of immunity from prosecution and distinguished himself as one of the few African leaders to publicly criticize Zimbabwean Pres. Robert Mugabe.

Ibrahim Nasir (2 Sep 1926, Male, British Maldives—22 Nov 2008, Singapore), Maldivian politician who dominated life in the Indian Ocean archipelago for more than 20 years; under his control, Maldives was transformed into a modern country.

Peter (Francis) Newell (31 Aug 1915, Vancouver, BC, Canada—17 Nov 2008, Rancho Santa Fe CA), Canadian-born American basketball coach who served as the influential coach of the basketball teams at the University of San Francisco (1946–50), where his 1949 team captured the National Invitation Tournament (NIT) title, and the University of California, Berkeley (1954–60), where he guided his team to triumph in the 1959 NCAA tournament; in 1960 he led the US basketball team to a gold medal in the 1960 Rome Olympic Games; he was inducted into the Basketball Hall of Fame in 1979.

Paul (Leonard) Newman (26 Jan 1925, Cleveland OH—26 Sep 2008, Westport CT), American actor, a matinee idol whose striking good looks and startling blue eyes became hallmarks in a film career in which he was honored for his compelling performances with nine Academy Award nominations and one win; he also won two honorary Oscars, a lifetime achievement (1986) and the Jean Hersholt Humanitarian Award (1994). Newman honed his craft at New York City's Actors Studio, and his impressive portrayal of boxer Rocky Graziano in *Somebody Up There Likes Me* (1956) was followed by *Cat on a Hot Tin Roof* (1958; for which he received his first Academy Award nomination), *The Long, Hot Summer* (1958), and *The Young Philadelphians* (1959). Newman essayed the role that perhaps best defined his screen persona, that of pool shark "Fast" Eddie Felson in *The Hustler* (1961), and earned another Oscar nomination; *Hud* (1963) and *Cool Hand Luke* (1967) further solidified his image as an ingratiating iconoclast. Newman costarred in 11 films with his second wife, actress Joanne Woodward, and directed her in several others. Two enormously popular comedies teamed Newman with costar Robert Redford: the western *Butch Cassidy and the Sundance Kid* (1969) and the Depression-era film *The Sting* (1973), which won the Academy Award for best picture. Newman maintained his star status with such popular films as *The Towering Inferno* (1974), *Slap Shot* (1977), *Fort Apache the Bronx* (1981), *Absence of Malice* (1981), and *The Verdict* (1982). He finally won an Academy Award for his reprise as Felson in *The Color of Money* (1986). In 2005 he starred in the television movie *Empire Falls,* for which he won Emmy, Golden Globe, and Screen Actors Guild awards. In addition to his Hollywood career, Newman launched (1982) the successful Newman's Own line of food products; its profits benefited a number of charitable causes, and in 1988 he founded the Hole in the Wall Gang Camp in south-central Connecticut for children with serious medical conditions.

Gaafar Mohamed el-Nimeiri (Ja'far Muhammad al-Numayri, or Nimeiry; 1 Jan 1930, Wad Nubawi, Omdurman, Sudan—30 May 2009, Omdurman, Sudan), Sudanese military leader and politician who governed The Sudan from 1969 until he was ousted in a bloodless coup in 1985; Nimeiri was credited with the negotiations that led to a settlement of a 10-year conflict in the southern Sudan region, to which he granted autonomy in 1972, but his attempts to promulgate measures of Shari'ah (Islamic law) in The Sudan alienated many in the predominantly Christian southern region.

Thubten Jigme Norbu (Tashi Tsering; Taktser Rinpoche; 16 Aug 1922, Takster, Amdo, Tibet [now in China]—5 Sep 2008, Bloomington IN), Tibetan religious leader, scholar, and activist who was identified as the reincarnation of the Tibetan lama Taktser Rinpoche at age three, 10 years before the birth of his brother, the future 14th Dalai Lama; Norbu, who disagreed with his brother's belief in peaceful resistance to Chinese rule in Tibet, worked as a CIA translator and endorsed guerrilla warfare for Tibetan independence.

Nouhak Phoumsavan (Nouhak Phoumsavanh; 9 Apr 1914, Mukdahan, French Indochina [now in Thailand]—9 Sep 2008, Vientiane, Laos), Laotian resistance leader and politician who was a leader of Laotian resistance to French rule in Indochina and, after independence from France (1954), in the government that replaced it; he was president in 1992–98.

Robert (David Sanders) Novak (26 Feb 1931, Joliet IL—18 Aug 2009, Washington DC), American political journalist and commentator who wrote the syndicated newspaper column "Inside Report" for more than 40 years and from 1980 espoused a conservative viewpoint on a number of political TV talk shows, notably CNN's *Crossfire;* in 2003 he courted controversy when he identified Valerie Plame as a CIA operative in a column after her husband, Joseph Wilson, had publicly asserted that the administration of Pres. George W. Bush had distorted intelligence to justify the 2003 invasion of Iraq.

Odetta (Holmes Felious) (31 Dec 1930, Birmingham AL—2 Dec 2008, New York NY), American folksinger whose renditions of spirituals encapsulated for many the civil rights movement; she sang at the March on Washington led by the Rev. Martin Luther King, Jr. (1963), as well as for US Pres. John F. Kennedy; in 1999 Pres. Bill Clinton awarded her the National Medal of Arts, and in 2003 the Library of Congress named her a Living Legend.

George E(mil) Palade (19 Nov 1912, Iasi, Romania—7 Oct 2008, Del Mar CA), Romanian-born American cell biologist who developed tissue-preparation methods, advanced centrifuging techniques, and conducted electron microscopy studies that resulted in the discovery of several cellular structures; with Albert Claude and Christian de Duve, he was awarded the Nobel Prize for Physiology or Medicine in 1974; he also received the Albert Lasker Award for Basic Medical Research (1966) and the National Medal of Science (1986).

Earl Palmer (25 Oct 1924, New Orleans LA—19 Sep 2008, Banning CA), American drummer who laid the foundations for rock-and-roll drumming on such recordings as Little Richard's "Tutti Frutti," the Righteous Brothers' "You've Lost That Lovin' Feelin'," Sam Cooke's "You Send Me," and Ike and Tina Turner's "River Deep, Mountain High"; Palmer was inducted into the Rock and Roll Hall of Fame in 2000.

Tassos Papadopoulos (7 Jan 1934, Nicosia, British Cyprus—12 Dec 2008, Nicosia, Cyprus), Cypriot politician who in 2003 became the Republic of Cyprus's fifth president, in which position he called on the Greek Cypriot community to reject a UN-sponsored reunification plan and then oversaw the entry of the Greek portion of the island country into the EU in May 2004 and its adoption of the euro currency in January 2008.

Les Paul (Lester William Polsfuss; 9 Jun 1915, Waukesha WI—13 Aug 2009, White Plains NY), American musician and inventor who designed a solid-body electric guitar in 1941 that acquired a devoted following—its versatility and balance made it the favored instrument of such guitarists as Eric Clapton, Jimmy Page, and Peter Frampton; in 1977 Paul earned a Grammy Award for *Chester & Lester* (1976), an instrumental duet album with country legend Chet Atkins, and in 2006 he collected two more Grammys; Paul was inducted into the Grammy Hall of Fame (1978), the Rock and Roll Hall of Fame (1988), and the National Inventors Hall of Fame (2005), and he was awarded a National Medal of Arts by Pres. George W. Bush in 2007.

Tullio Pinelli (24 Jun 1908, Turin, Italy—7 Mar 2009, Rome, Italy), Italian screenwriter who collaborated with filmmaker Federico Fellini on the scripts for more than two dozen motion pictures, 13 of them directed by Fellini, including *La strada* (1954), *La dolce vita* (1960), and *8½* (1963); *La strada, Le notti de Cabiria* (1957; *Nights of Cabiria*), and *8½* won Oscars for best foreign-language film.

Harold Pinter (10 Oct 1930, London, England—24 Dec 2008, London, England), British playwright, director, actor, and screenwriter who won international renown—and the 2005 Nobel Prize for Literature—as one of the most complex post-World War II English-language dramatists. His 29 plays are noted for their use of understatement and subtle underlying menace within deceptively ordinary settings, while his characters' colloquial "Pinteresque" speech consists of disjointed and oddly ambivalent conversation punctuated by resonant hesitations and silences that reveal the many layers of meaning that can be contained in even the most innocuous statements. His reputation as the originator of a unique dramatic idiom was secured by his plays *The Caretaker* (1960; filmed 1963) and *The Homecoming* (1965; filmed 1969); his later successes included *Old Times* (1971), *No Man's Land* (1975), *Betrayal* (1978; filmed 1983), *Moonlight* (1993), and *Celebration* (2000); he was made (2002) a Companion of Honour and named (2007) a chevalier of the French Legion of Honor.

Billy Powell (William Norris Powell; 3 Jun 1952, Corpus Christi TX—28 Jan 2009, Orange Park FL), American rock musician who played keyboards for the Southern-rock band Lynyrd Skynyrd, notably playing the piano introduction to the hit song "Free Bird"; in 1977 Powell survived the crash of a tour plane that killed several members of the band; Lynyrd Skynyrd was inducted into the Rock and Roll Hall of Fame in 2006.

Velupillai Prabhakaran (26 Nov 1954, Velvettithurai, Jaffna Peninsula, Ceylon [now Sri Lanka]—18 May 2009, near Nanthikadal Lagoon, Sri Lanka), Tamil nationalist and guerrilla leader who was dedicated to establishing an independent homeland for the Tamil ethnic minority in northern Sri Lanka and who thus founded (1972) the Liberation Tigers of Tamil Eelam (LTTE) and built that organization, commonly known as the Tamil Tigers, into one of the world's most relentless insurgent groups; over a 30-year period, the Tigers were held responsible for thousands of deaths, including those of former Indian prime minister Rajiv Gandhi in 1991 and Sri Lankan Pres. Ranasinghe Premadasa in 1993; following months of heavy fighting against government troops in early 2009, the Tigers were crushed, and Prabhakaran was killed in action.

Richard Quick (31 Jan 1943, Akron OH—10 Jun 2009, Austin TX), American swim coach who led numerous American swimmers to collegiate and Olympic victory in a career of more than 30 years—beginning in 1984 he coached for six consecutive Olympic Games, working with swimmers such as Matt Biondi, who won eight gold medals, and Janet Evans, who won four; Quick was also a successful college coach with 13 NCAA titles, more than any other Division I swimming coach, and the College Swimming Coaches Association named him the NCAA Coach of the Year six times before honoring him in 2009 with its first Lifetime Achievement Award; in 2000 he was inducted into the International Swimming Hall of Fame.

Mieczyslaw (Franciszek) Rakowski (1 Dec 1926, Kowalewko, Poland—7 Nov 2008, Warsaw, Poland), Polish newspaper editor and politician who, as the last communist prime minister of Poland (September 1988–July 1989), presided over the dissolution of the old regime and the transfer of power to the country's first democratically elected government.

Nick Reynolds (Nicholas Wells Reynolds; 27 Jul 1933, San Diego CA—1 Oct 2008, San Diego CA), American musician who, with Bob Shane and Dave Guard, was a founding member (1957) of the Kingston Trio, one of the groups that helped spark the folk-music revival of the 1960s.

Wendy Richard (Wendy Emerton; 20 Jul 1943, Middleborough, England—26 Feb 2009, London, England), British actress who displayed her versatility on two long-running BBC television shows: the bawdy sitcom *Are You Being Served?* (1972–85; and in the 1977 movie of the same name) and the evening soap opera *EastEnders* (1985–2006); she was made MBE in 2000.

Natasha (Jane) Richardson (11 May 1963, London, England—18 Mar 2009, New York NY), British actress who arose within a renowned acting dynasty to make her own mark in motion pictures and, especially, onstage. She was the elder daughter of director Tony Richardson and actress Vanessa Redgrave—herself the daughter of actors Michael Redgrave and Rachel Kempson, the sister of actors Corin Redgrave and Lynn Redgrave, and the granddaughter of silent-film actor Roy Redgrave; Richardson made her West End debut in 1985 opposite her mother in Anton Chekhov's *The Seagull*, winning a London Drama Critics' Award as most promising newcomer; she captured the attention of American audiences with her starring film roles in *Patty Hearst* (1988), *The Handmaid's Tale* (1990), and *The Comfort of Strangers* (1990). In 1993 Richardson captured a Tony Award nomination for her performance in the revival of Eugene O'Neill's *Anna Christie*, and she returned to Broadway three times: in an acclaimed revival of the musical *Cabaret*, winning the Tony for her star turn as Sally Bowles; as Anna in *Closer* (1999); and as Blanche DuBois in a 2005 revival of *A Streetcar Named Desire*.

Bobby Robson (Robert William Robson; 18 Feb 1933, Sacriston, Durham county, England—31 Jul 2009, Durham county, England), British association football (soccer) player and manager who was one of England's most respected athletes; he played 20 matches with the national team, including appearances in the 1958 and 1962 World Cup finals, and later, as the England manager (1982–90), he steered the team to two World Cup finals tournaments (1986, 1990); he was knighted in 2002 and was inducted into the English Football Hall of Fame in 2003.

Roh Moo Hyun (6 Aug 1946, Gimhae, near Pusan, US-occupied Korea [now in South Korea]—23 May 2009, Pusan, South Korea), South Korean politician who served (2003–08) as president of South Korea during a time in which he faced labor unrest and a faltering economy and found himself in the midst of a financial scandal after several of his aides were accused of having accepted illegal donations.

Karine Ruby (4 Jan 1978, Bonneville, France—29 May 2009, Chamonix, France), French snowboarder who was the most decorated female snowboarder in the world, with two Olympic medals (including the first Olympic medal in the sport of snowboarding awarded to a woman), six Fédération Internationale de Ski (FIS) world championship gold medals, and 67 FIS World Cup victories.

Gerald Schoenfeld (22 Sep 1924, New York NY—25 Nov 2008, New York NY), American producer and theater owner who led a revitalization of theater in New York City, bringing to Broadway such hits as *Equus*, *A Chorus Line*, and *The Phantom of the Opera* and transforming a run-down and sleazy neighborhood into a gleaming attraction for audiences.

Eve Kosofsky Sedgwick (2 May 1950, Dayton OH—12 Apr 2009, New York NY), American author and professor who published the highly influential *Epistemology of the Closet* (1990), a groundbreaking work in the academic field of queer studies, which she was credited with helping to found.

Shi Pei Pu (21 Dec 1938, Shandong, China—30 Jun 2009, Paris, France), Chinese opera singer and spy who engaged in a bizarre love affair and in espionage work with French embassy clerk Bernard Boursicot that became the basis for the Tony Award-winning play *M. Butterfly* (1988; filmed 1993); Shi convinced Boursicot that he was actually a woman disguised as a man, and the two began a love affair that continued for 20 years, during which time Boursicot turned over as many as 150 documents through Shi to the Chinese secret service.

Eunice (Mary) Kennedy Shriver (10 Jul 1921, Brookline MA—11 Aug 2009, Hyannis MA), American social activist who worked to improve the lives of the mentally disabled and founded (1968) the Special Olympics; the sister of Pres. John F. Kennedy and Senators Robert F. Kennedy and Edward M. Kennedy, Shriver became in 1957 the director of the Joseph P. Kennedy, Jr., Foundation, the goals of which were to seek the causes of mental retardation and improve the social treatment of the mentally challenged; she was also a force behind the 1962 creation of the National Institute of Child Health and Human Development, which now bears her name. Shriver was granted the 1966 Albert Lasker Public Service Award, and in 1984 she received the Presidential Medal of Freedom.

Ron(ald Arthur) Silver (Ronald Zimelman; 2 Jul 1946, New York NY—15 Mar 2009, New York NY), American actor and activist who won a Tony Award for his role in David Mamet's *Speed-the-Plow* (1988) and compiled an impressive list of film credits that include *Silkwood* (1983), *Garbo Talks* (1984), and *Reversal of Fortune* (1990).

Naomi (Ruth) Sims (30 Mar 1949, Oxford MS—1 Aug 2009, Newark NJ), American model and business executive who shattered the barrier that had prevented black models from achieving supermodel status when she became (1968) the first black model to adorn the cover of *Ladies' Home Journal*.

V(ishwanath) P(ratap) Singh (25 Jun 1931, Allahabad, Uttar Pradesh, British India—27 Nov 2008, New Delhi, India), Indian politician who was prime minister (1989–1990) of India at the head of a coalition government formed of parties that opposed the powerful Congress (I) Party.

Sister Emmanuelle (Madeleine Cinquin; 16 Nov 1908, Brussels, Belgium—20 Oct 2008, Callian, France), Belgian-born Roman Catholic nun who lived for more than two decades among the *zabbaleen*, the garbage scavengers in the slums of Cairo, where she established schools, clinics, and other social services—her humanitarian work was often compared to that of Mother Teresa in India.

Clint Smith ("Snuffy"; 12 Dec 1913, Assiniboia, SK, Canada—19 May 2009, North Vancouver, BC, Canada), Canadian hockey player who was known during his 11 seasons (1936–47) in the NHL for his playmaking ability as well as for his gentlemanly conduct on the ice; he helped lead the New York Rangers to the Stanley Cup in 1940 and established an NHL record for assists (49) in 1944; in 1945 he became only the third player in league history to score four goals in a single period; he twice received (1939, 1944) the NHL's Lady Byng Trophy, awarded for good sportsmanship, and he was inducted into the Hockey Hall of Fame in 1991.

W(illiam) D(eWitt) Snodgrass (S.S. Gardons; 5 Jan 1926, Wilkinsburg PA—13 Jan 2009, Erieville NY), American poet who composed verse that was distinguished by a careful attention to form and by a relentless yet delicate examination of personal experiences; his first collection, *Heart's Needle* (1959), won the Pulitzer Prize.

Ted Solotaroff (Theodore Solotaroff; 9 Oct 1928, Elizabeth NJ—8 Aug 2008, East Quogue NY), American literary critic who founded (1967) the *New American Review* (later *American Review*), a literary journal that featured writing by such luminaries as E.L. Doctorow, Gabriel García Márquez, and Norman Mailer.

Jo (Elizabeth) Stafford (12 Nov 1917, Coalinga CA—16 Jul 2008, Century City CA), American singer who during the 1940s and '50s became a sensation, hosting and performing on the radio show *The Chesterfield Supper Club* and the television program *The Jo Stafford Show* (1954); she also recorded a succession of charted singles that included the number one hit "You Belong to Me" (1952), which sold two million copies; she won (1960) a Grammy Award for best comedy performance for the album *Jonathan and Darlene Edwards in Paris*.

Gale Storm (Josephine Owaissa Cottle; 5 Apr 1922, Bloomington TX—27 Jun 2009, Danville CA), American actress and singer who was the vivacious star of two popular television sitcoms, *My Little Margie* (1952–55) and *The Gale Storm Show: Oh! Susanna* (1956–60); she also enjoyed a recording career with a number of chart-topping hit songs, including "I Hear You Knockin'" and "Why Do Fools Fall in Love?"

Levi Stubbs (Levi Stubbles; 6 Jun 1936, Detroit MI—17 Oct 2008, Detroit MI), American singer who was the lead vocalist for the Four Tops, one of Motown's most popular acts in the 1960s; his gruff, passionate vocals were set against gentler background harmonies and propelled the group to the pinnacle of fame with such songs as "Baby I Need Your Loving" (1964), "I Can't Help Myself (Sugar Pie, Honey Bunch)" (1965), "It's the Same Old Song" (1965), and "Reach Out I'll Be There" (1966); the Four Tops were inducted into the Rock and Roll Hall of Fame in 1990.

Koko Taylor (Cora Walton; 28 Sep 1928, Bartlett TN—3 Jun 2009, Chicago IL), American blues singer who forged a musical career that spanned nearly half a century and earned her the nickname "Queen of the Blues"; while singing at a blues club in Chicago, she came to the attention of Chess Records producer Willie Dixon, who promptly signed her to that label, and she was soon recording with such blues legends as Buddy Guy, Big Walter Horton, and Robert Nighthawk. Under Dixon's guidance, Taylor released a pair of albums and a number of singles for Chess, most notably the 1965 hit "Wang Dang Doodle," which sold more than a million copies and reached the top five on the *Billboard* rhythm-and-blues singles chart; she garnered eight Grammy Award nominations and collected more than two dozen Blues Music Awards.

Lou(is Milton) Teicher (24 Aug 1924, Wilkes-Barre PA—3 Aug 2008, Highlands NC), American pianist who performed in the 1960s with pianist Arthur Ferrante; the two (billed as Ferrante & Teicher) became a sensation with their florid renditions on twin pianos; during their 50-year association, they sold more than 88 million records.

John M(arks) Templeton (29 Nov 1912, Winchester TN—8 Jul 2008, Nassau, Bahamas), American-born British investor, mutual fund manager, and philanthropist who established (1972) the Templeton Prize for Progress in Religion (from 2003 the Templeton Prize for Progress Toward Research or Discoveries About Spiritual Realities), to be awarded annually to a living person who demonstrated "extraordinary originality in advancing humankind's understanding of God and/or spirituality"; Templeton, who took British citizenship in 1968, was knighted in 1987.

Studs Terkel (Louis Terkel; 16 May 1912, New York NY—31 Oct 2008, Chicago IL), American author and oral historian who chronicled the lives of Americans from the Great Depression to the early 21st century; in 1945 he began his long association with Chicago radio by inaugurating *The Wax Museum*, a program that showcased his knack for engaging people in impromptu interviews; *Studs' Place*, Terkel's nationally broadcast television show (1949–52), comprised songs and stories and used a fictional bar as

its backdrop (its cancellation was due to Terkel's leftist leanings, which got him blacklisted in the early 1950s). In 1967 he published the best-selling *Division Street: America*, a book consisting of conversations he had recorded with people in the Chicago area, and he won a Pulitzer Prize for "*The Good War": An Oral History of World War II* (1984).

Wayman (Lawrence) Tisdale (9 Jun 1964, Tulsa OK—15 May 2009, Tulsa OK), American basketball player who became a top-selling smooth-jazz recording artist. A star basketball player at the University of Oklahoma, where he set a Big Eight conference record for career points (2,661), he was also the leading rebounder on the US team that won the gold medal at the 1984 Olympic Games in Los Angeles, and he went on to play 12 seasons (1985–97) in the NBA, averaging 15.3 points and 6.1 rebounds per game; he was elected to the College Basketball Hall of Fame in 2009. As a bass guitarist he released eight albums, including three that reached number one on the *Billboard* contemporary jazz chart.

John (Hoyer) Updike (18 Mar 1932, Reading PA—27 Jan 2009, Danvers MA), American writer who was renowned for his careful craftsmanship and realistic but subtle depiction of "American, Protestant, small-town, middle-class" life; he began in 1955 an association with *The New Yorker* magazine, to which he contributed editorials, poetry, stories, and criticism throughout his career. *Rabbit, Run* (1960), considered to be one of Updike's best works, was followed by three subsequent novels, *Rabbit Redux* (1971), *Rabbit Is Rich* (1981), and *Rabbit at Rest* (1990) (the latter two of which won Pulitzer Prizes), that follow the same character during later periods of his life—*Rabbit Remembered* (2001) returns to characters from those books in the wake of Rabbit's death; Updike often expounded upon other characters from earlier novels, omitting decades of their lives only to place them in the middle of new adventures—*The Witches of Eastwick* (1984; filmed 1987) was followed by *The Widows of Eastwick* (2008), which trails the women protagonists into old age, and *Bech: A Book* (1970), *Bech Is Back* (1982), and *Bech at Bay* (1998) humorously trace the tribulations of a Jewish writer.

Gene Upshaw (15 Aug 1945, Robstown, Texas—20 Aug 2008, near Lake Tahoe, California), American football player who was a standout offensive lineman for the Oakland Raiders—he led the team to three Super Bowls (1968, 1977, 1981) and was selected to play in seven Pro Bowls (1968, 1972–77); after his retirement he served as the executive director (1983–2008) of the National Football League Players Association; he was inducted into the Pro Football Hall of Fame in 1987.

Jørn Utzon (9 Apr 1918, Copenhagen, Denmark—29 Nov 2008, Copenhagen, Denmark), Danish architect who was best known for his design for the iconic Sydney Opera House, which in 2007 was designated a UNESCO World Heritage site; he was awarded the Pritzker Architectural Prize (2003).

Ramaswamy Venkataraman (4 Dec 1910, Rajamadam, British India—27 Jan 2009, New Delhi, India), Indian politician and lawyer who was president of India from 1987 to 1992; in this largely ceremonial post, he provided relative stability amid a politically turbulent period.

João Bernardo Vieira ("Nino"; 27 Apr 1939, Bissau, Portuguese Guinea [now Guinea-Bissau]—2 Mar 2009, Bissau, Guinea-Bissau), Guinea-Bissauan politician who was president (1980–99 and 2005–09) of his country until ethnic tensions, rivalries within the ruling party, and ongoing conflict between Vieira and the military led to his temporary exile in 1999–2005 and to his eventual assassination; he served as prime minister (1978–80), and in 1980 he took control in a bloodless coup; one day after the army chief of staff died in a bomb attack, Vieira was shot dead by government soldiers.

Sunny von Bülow (Martha Sharp Crawford; 1 Sep 1931, Manassas VA–6 Dec 2008, New York NY), American heiress who spent nearly 28 years in a coma after being found unconscious in her Newport RI mansion in December 1980; her second husband, Claus von Bülow, was initially convicted but then acquitted of having attempted to murder her by injecting her with drugs; the story was the basis of the popular movie *Reversal of Fortune* (1990).

David Foster Wallace (21 Feb 1961, Ithaca NY—found dead 12 Sep 2008, Claremont CA), American novelist, short-story writer, and essayist who produced dense works that provide a dark, often satiric analysis of American culture; his debut novel, *The Broom of the System* (1987), was highly regarded, but he became best known for his second novel, *Infinite Jest* (1996), a massive, multilayered novel that features a sweeping cast of postmodern characters and calendar years that have been named by companies that purchased the rights to promote their products.

Gordon (Trueman Riviere) Waller (4 Jun 1945, Baermar, Aberdeenshire, Scotland—17 Jul 2009, Norwich CT), British singer who was the lower-voiced member of the pop-singing duo Peter and Gordon; between 1964 and 1968, Waller and his singing partner, Peter Asher, racked up eight top 20 hit records.

Thomas H(uckle) Weller (15 Jun 1915, Ann Arbor MI—23 Aug 2008, Needham MA), American physician and virologist who was in 1954 the corecipient (with John Enders and Frederick Robbins) of the Nobel Prize for Physiology or Medicine for the successful cultivation of poliomyelitis virus in tissue cultures, which led to the development of polio vaccines.

Donald E(dwin) Westlake (12 Jul 1933, New York NY—31 Dec 2008, San Tancho, Mexico), American writer who attracted a wide readership as well as great critical acclaim with his stylish crime novels; he won three Edgar Allan Poe Awards from the Mystery Writers of America before being bestowed the title Grand Master—its highest honor—in 1993.

Jerry Wexler (10 Jan 1917, New York NY–15 Aug 2008, Sarasota FL), American record producer and music journalist who coined the phrase "rhythm and blues" in 1949; as an executive for Atlantic Records he guided the careers of such classic performers as Ray Charles, Wilson Pickett, Aretha Franklin, and the British group Led Zeppelin, and he was inducted into the Rock and Roll Hall of Fame in 1987.

James Whitmore (1 Oct 1921, White Plains NY–6 Feb 2009, Malibu CA), American actor who won critical acclaim for his live one-man shows during the 1970s; he famously portrayed Will Rogers, Harry Truman, and Theodore Roosevelt; Whitmore won (2000) an Emmy Award as outstanding guest actor in a drama series for the TV series *The Practice* and earned a Tony Award as best newcomer for his performance in the Broadway production *Command Decision* (1947).

Dingiri Banda Wijetunga (15 Feb 1916, Polgahanga, Ceylon [now Sri Lanka]—21 Sep 2008, Kandy, Sri Lanka), Sri Lankan politician who brought stability to Sri Lanka as the country's head of state (1993–94) during the crucial period immediately following the assassination on 1 May 1993 of Pres. Ranasinghe Premadasa.

the Rev. Abraham (Lincoln) Woods (Jr.) (7 Oct 1928, Birmingham AL–7 Nov 2008, Birmingham AL), American pastor and civil rights activist who led the protesters who staged (1963) the first sit-ins at a whites-only lunch counter in downtown Birmingham, a landmark event in the fight for civil rights; Woods was jailed along with the Rev. Martin Luther King, Jr. (a friend from his Morehouse College days); Woods was also on the scene on 15 Sep 1963, when a dynamite blast claimed the lives of four black girls at the 16th Street Baptist Church, and he was instrumental years later in fighting for a reinvestigation of the bombing.

Rick Wright (Richard William Wright; 28 Jul 1943, Pinner, Middlesex, England—15 Sep 2008, London, England), British singer-songwriter and keyboardist who was a founding member of the rock group Pink Floyd; his atmospheric keyboard work became a central feature of the group's psychedelic sound; he composed songs for several of the group's acclaimed albums, notably *The Dark Side of the Moon* (1973) and *Wish You Were Here* (1975).

Andrew (Newell) Wyeth (12 Jul 1917, Chadds Ford PA–16 Jan 2009, Chadds Ford PA), American watercolorist who was noted primarily for his realistic depictions of the buildings, fields, hills, and people of his personal world, almost entirely from two localities, the Brandywine Valley around Chadds Ford and the area near his summer home in Cushing ME; he was the first painter to receive the Presidential Freedom Award (1963), the first American artist since John Singer Sargent to be elected to the French Académie des Beaux-Arts (1977), the first living American artist to be elected to Britain's Royal Academy (1980), and the first artist to be awarded the US Congressional Gold Medal (1990), and in 2007 he was a recipient of the National Medal of the Arts.

Xiao Ke (14 Jul 1907, Jiahe county, Hunan province, China–24 Oct 2008, Beijing, China), Chinese military official and writer who was the last surviving military leader of the Long March (1934–36), the epic 10,000-km (6,000-mi) trek of the Chinese communists into northwestern China; he later became known for his opposition to the use of troops to suppress the pro-democracy demonstrations in Tiananmen Square in 1989—a position he refused to retract despite political pressure to do so.

Jerry Yang (Yang Xiangzhong; 31 Jul 1959, Weixian, Hebei province, China–5 Feb 2009, Boston MA), Chinese-born American reproductive biologist who, as a pioneer in cloning research, in 1999 succeeded in producing the first cloned farm animal in the US—a Holstein calf named Amy.

(Sandra) Kay Yow (14 Mar 1942, Gibsonville NC–24 Jan 2009, Cary NC), American basketball coach who served (1975–2009) as the head coach at North Carolina State University and became one of the winningest coaches in NCAA Division I history; she tallied a career coaching record of 737–344 over 38 seasons on the collegiate level and, at the time of her death, was one of only six Division I women's basketball coaches to have won at least 700 games; in addition to leading North Carolina State to 20 appearances in the NCAA tournament, she was the head coach of the US women's team that captured a gold medal at the 1988 Olympic Games in Seoul, and she was inducted into the Naismith Memorial Basketball Hall of Fame in 2002.

Awards

TIME's Top 100 Films

There's nothing like a list to stimulate a strong discussion, so in the hopes of striking a few sparks among movie lovers, TIME asked its long-time film critics Richard Corliss and Richard Schickel to compile a list of the 100 greatest films ever made. Of course, the discussions that followed between the two critics were entirely civil at all times. Below, the films and the year they were released.

A–C

Aguirre: The Wrath of God (1972)
The Apu Trilogy (1955, 1956, 1959)
The Awful Truth (1937)
Baby Face (1933)
Bande à part (1964)
Barry Lyndon (1975)
Berlin Alexanderplatz (1980)
Blade Runner (1982)
Bonnie and Clyde (1967)
Brazil (1985)
Bride of Frankenstein (1935)
Camille (1936)
Casablanca (1942)
Charade (1963)
Children of Paradise (1945)
Chinatown (1974)
Chungking Express (1994)
Citizen Kane (1941)
City Lights (1931)
City of God (2002)
Closely Watched Trains (1966)
The Crime of Monsieur Lange (1936)
The Crowd (1928)

D–F

Day for Night (1973)
The Decalogue (1989)
Detour (1945)
The Discreet Charm of the Bourgeoisie (1972)
Dodsworth (1936)
Double Indemnity (1944)
Dr. Strangelove or: How I Learned To Stop Worrying and Love the Bomb (1964)
Drunken Master II (1994)
E.T.: The Extra-Terrestrial (1982)
8 1/2 (1963)
The 400 Blows (1959)
Farewell My Concubine (1993)
Finding Nemo (2003)
The Fly (1986)

G–J

The Godfather, Parts I and II (1972, 1974)
The Good, the Bad, and the Ugly (1966)
Goodfellas (1990)
A Hard Day's Night (1964)
His Girl Friday (1940)
Ikiru (1952)
In a Lonely Place (1950)
Invasion of the Body Snatchers (1956)
It's a Gift (1934)
It's a Wonderful Life (1946)

K–M

Kandahar (2001)
Kind Hearts and Coronets (1949)
King Kong (1933)
The Lady Eve (1941)
The Last Command (1928)
Lawrence of Arabia (1962)
Léolo (1992)
The Lord of the Rings (2001, 2002, 2003)
The Man with a Camera (1929)
The Manchurian Candidate (1962)
Meet Me in St. Louis (1944)
Metropolis (1927)
Miller's Crossing (1990)
Mon oncle d'Amérique (1980)
Mouchette (1967)

N–P

Nayakan (1987)
Ninotchka (1939)
Notorious (1946)
Olympia, Parts 1 and 2 (1938)
On the Waterfront (1954)
Once upon a Time in the West (1968)
Out of the Past (1947)
Persona (1966)
Pinocchio (1940)
Psycho (1960)
Pulp Fiction (1994)
The Purple Rose of Cairo (1985)
Pyaasa (1957)

Q–S

Raging Bull (1980)
Schindler's List (1993)
The Searchers (1956)
Sherlock, Jr. (1924)
The Shop Around the Corner (1940)
Singin' in the Rain (1952)
The Singing Detective (1986)
Smiles of a Summer Night (1955)
Some Like It Hot (1959)
Star Wars (1977)
A Streetcar Named Desire (1951)
Sunrise (1927)
Sweet Smell of Success (1957)
Swing Time (1936)

T–Z

Talk to Her (2002)
Taxi Driver (1976)
Tokyo Story (1953)
A Touch of Zen (1971)
Ugetsu (1953)
Ulysses' Gaze (1995)
Umberto D (1952)
Unforgiven (1992)
White Heat (1949)
Wings of Desire (1987)
Yojimbo (1961)

TIME's Person of the Year, 1927–2008

Every year since 1927, TIME has named a Person of the Year, identifying the individual who has done the most to affect the news in the past twelve months. The designation is often mistaken for an honor, but the magazine has always pointed out that inclusion on the list is not a recognition of good works (like the Nobel Peace prize, for example), but rather a reflection of the sheer power of one's actions, whether for good or for ill. Hence, both Adolf Hitler and Ayatollah Ruhollah Khomeini were chosen Person of the Year at the time when their actions commanded the attention of the world. Below, the complete list of Persons of the Year.

1927	Charles Lindbergh
1928	Walter Chrysler
1929	Owen Young
1930	Mahatma Gandhi
1931	Pierre Laval
1932	Franklin Delano Roosevelt
1933	Hugh Johnson
1934	Franklin Delano Roosevelt
1935	Haile Selassie
1936	Wallis Simpson
1937	Chiang Kai-Shek and Soong Mei-ling
1938	Adolf Hitler
1939	Joseph Stalin
1940	Winston Churchill
1941	Franklin Delano Roosevelt
1942	Joseph Stalin
1943	George Marshall
1944	Dwight Eisenhower
1945	Harry Truman
1946	James F. Byrnes
1947	George Marshall
1948	Harry Truman
1949	Winston Churchill ("Man of the Half-Century")
1950	The American Fighting-Man (representing US troops fighting in the Korean War; first abstract chosen)
1951	Mohammed Mossadegh
1952	Queen Elizabeth II
1953	Konrad Adenauer
1954	John Foster Dulles
1955	Harlow Curtice
1956	Hungarian Freedom Fighter (representing the citizens' uprising against Soviet domination)
1957	Nikita Khrushchev
1958	Charles De Gaulle
1959	Dwight Eisenhower
1960	US Scientists (represented by Linus Pauling, Isidor Rabi, Edward Teller, Joshua Lederberg, Donald A. Glaser, Willard Libby, Robert Woodward, Charles Draper, William Shockley, Emilio Segrè, John Enders, Charles Townes, George Beadle, James Van Allen, and Edward Purcell)
1961	John F. Kennedy
1962	Pope John XXIII
1963	Martin Luther King, Jr.
1964	Lyndon Johnson
1965	William Westmoreland
1966	The Generation Twenty-Five and Under (representing American youth)
1967	Lyndon Johnson
1968	Apollo 8 astronauts Frank Borman, Jim Lovell, and William Anders
1969	The Middle Americans (representing the American electorate's turn to the right)
1970	Willy Brandt
1971	Richard Nixon
1972	Richard Nixon and Henry Kissinger
1973	John Sirica
1974	King Faisal
1975	American Women (represented by Betty Ford, Carla Hills, Ella Grasso, Barbara Jordan, Susie Sharp, Jill Conway, Billie Jean King, Susan Brownmiller, Addie Wyatt, Kathleen Byerly, Carol Sutton, and Alison Cheek)
1976	Jimmy Carter
1977	Anwar el-Sadat
1978	Deng Xiaoping
1979	Ayatollah Ruhollah Khomeini
1980	Ronald Reagan
1981	Lech Walensa
1982	The Computer (first non-human abstract chosen; termed "Machine of the Year")
1983	Ronald Reagan and Yuri Andropov
1984	Peter Ueberroth
1985	Deng Xiaoping
1986	Corazon Aquino
1987	Mikhail Gorbachev
1988	Endangered Earth ("Planet of the Year")
1989	Mikhail Gorbachev ("Man of the Decade")
1990	George H.W. Bush
1991	Ted Turner
1992	Bill Clinton
1993	The Peacemakers (represented by Nelson Mandela and F.W. de Klerk of South Africa and Yasir Arafat and Yitzhak Rabin of the Middle East)
1994	Pope John Paul II
1995	Newt Gingrich
1996	David Ho
1997	Andy Grove
1998	Bill Clinton and Kenneth Starr
1999	Jeffrey P. Bezos
2000	George W. Bush
2001	Rudolph Giuliani
2002	The Whistleblowers (represented by Cynthia Cooper of Worldcom, Sherron Watkins of Enron, and Coleen Rowley of the FBI)
2003	The American Soldier (representing US troops fighting in Iraq and Afghanistan)
2004	George W. Bush
2005	The Good Samaritans (represented by Bono [Paul Hewson], Bill Gates, and Melinda Gates)
2006	You (representing the new age of user-generated Internet content)
2007	Vladimir Putin
2008	Barack Obama

Nobel Prizes

The Alfred B. Nobel Prizes are widely regarded as the world's most prestigious awards given for intellectual achievement. They are awarded annually from a fund bequeathed for that purpose by the Swedish inventor and industrialist Alfred Bernhard Nobel and administered by the Nobel Foundation. Nobel's 1895 established five of the six prizes: those for physics, chemistry, literature, physiology or medicine, and peace. The prize for economic sciences was added in 1969. Each year thousands of invitations are sent out to members of scholarly academies, scientists, university professors, previous Nobel laureates, members of parliaments and other assemblies, and others, requesting nominations for the various prizes. The country given is the citizenship of the recipient at the time that the award was made. Prizes may be withheld or not awarded in years when no worthy recipient can be found or when the world situation (e.g., World Wars I and II) prevents the gathering of information needed to reach a decision. Prizes are announced in mid-October and awarded in December in Stockholm and Oslo. A cash award of SEK 10 million (about US$1,323,000), a personal diploma, and a commemorative medal are given for each prize category.

Nobel Foundation Web site: <http://nobelprize.org>.

Physics

YEAR	WINNER(S)	COUNTRY	ACHIEVEMENT
1901	Wilhelm Conrad Röntgen	Germany	discovery of X-rays
1902	Hendrik Antoon Lorentz	Neth.	} investigation of the influence
	Pieter Zeeman	Neth.	of magnetism on radiation
1903	Henri Becquerel	France	discovery of spontaneous radioactivity
	Marie Curie	France	} investigations of radiation phenomena
	Pierre Curie	France	discovered by Becquerel
1904	John William Strutt, 3rd Baron Rayleigh (of Terling Place)	UK	discovery of argon
1905	Philipp Lenard	Germany	research on cathode rays
1906	J.J. Thomson	UK	research into the electrical conductivity of gases
1907	A.A. Michelson	US	spectroscopic and metrological investigations
1908	Gabriel Lippmann	France	photographic reproduction of colors
1909	Ferdinand Braun	Germany	} development of
	Guglielmo Marconi	Italy	wireless telegraphy
1910	Johannes Diederik van der Waals	Neth.	research concerning the equation of state of gases and liquids
1911	Wilhelm Wien	Germany	discoveries regarding laws governing heat radiation
1912	Nils Dalén	Sweden	invention of automatic regulators for lighting coastal beacons and light buoys
1913	Heike Kamerlingh Onnes	Neth.	investigation into the properties of matter at low temperatures; production of liquid helium
1914	Max von Laue	Germany	discovery of diffraction of X-rays by crystals
1915	Lawrence Bragg	UK	} analysis of crystal structure
	William Bragg	UK	by means of X-rays
1917	Charles Glover Barkla	UK	discovery of the characteristic X-radiation of elements
1918	Max Planck	Germany	discovery of the elemental quanta
1919	Johannes Stark	Germany	discovery of the Doppler effect in positive ion rays and the division of spectral lines in the electric field
1920	Charles Édouard Guillaume	Switz.	discovery of anomalies in alloys
1921	Albert Einstein	Switz.	work in theoretical physics
1922	Niels Bohr	Denmark	investigation of atomic structure and radiation
1923	Robert Andrews Millikan	US	work on the elementary charge of electricity and on the photoelectric effect
1924	Karl Manne Georg Siegbahn	Sweden	work in X-ray spectroscopy
1925	James Franck	Germany	} discovery of the laws governing the
	Gustav Hertz	Germany	impact of an electron upon an atom
1926	Jean Perrin	France	work on the discontinuous structure of matter
1927	Arthur Holly Compton	US	discovery of the wavelength change in diffused X-rays
	C.T.R. Wilson	UK	method of making visible the paths of electrically charged particles
1928	Owen Willans Richardson	UK	work on electron emission by hot metals
1929	Louis-Victor, 7e duc (duke) de Broglie	France	discovery of the wave nature of electrons

Physics (continued)

YEAR	WINNER(S)	COUNTRY	ACHIEVEMENT
1930	Chandrasekhara Venkata Raman	India	work on light diffusion; discovery of Raman effect, light wavelength variation that occurs when a light beam is deflected by molecules
1932	Werner Heisenberg	Germany	creation of quantum mechanics
1933	P.A.M. Dirac	UK	} introduction of wave equations
	Erwin Schrödinger	Austria	} in quantum mechanics
1935	James Chadwick	UK	discovery of the neutron
1936	Carl David Anderson	US	discovery of the positron
	Victor Francis Hess	Austria	discovery of cosmic radiation
1937	Clinton Joseph Davisson	US	} experimental demonstration of the interference
	George Paget Thomson	UK	} phenomenon in crystals irradiated by electrons
1938	Enrico Fermi	Italy	disclosure of artificial radioactive elements produced by neutron irradiation
1939	Ernest Orlando Lawrence	US	invention of the cyclotron
1943	Otto Stern	US	discovery of the magnetic moment of the proton
1944	Isidor Isaac Rabi	US	resonance method for the registration of various properties of atomic nuclei
1945	Wolfgang Pauli	Austria	discovery of the exclusion principle of electrons
1946	Percy Williams Bridgman	US	discoveries in the domain of high-pressure physics
1947	Edward V. Appleton	UK	discovery of the Appleton layer in the upper atmosphere
1948	Patrick M.S. Blackett	UK	discoveries in the domain of nuclear physics and cosmic radiation
1949	Hideki Yukawa	Japan	prediction of the existence of mesons
1950	Cecil Frank Powell	UK	photographic method of studying nuclear processes; discoveries concerning mesons
1951	John D. Cockcroft	UK	} work on the transmutation of atomic nuclei
	Ernest T.S. Walton	Ireland	} by accelerated particles
1952	Felix Bloch	US	} discovery of nuclear magnetic
	E.M. Purcell	US	} resonance in solids
1953	Frits Zernike	Neth.	method of phase-contrast microscopy
1954	Max Born	UK	statistical studies of atomic wave functions
	Walther Bothe	W.Ger.	invention of the coincidence method
1955	Polykarp Kusch	US	measurement of the magnetic moment of the electron
	Willis Eugene Lamb, Jr.	US	discoveries in the hydrogen spectrum
1956	John Bardeen	US	} investigations on
	Walter H. Brattain	US	} semiconductors and the
	William B. Shockley	US	} invention of the transistor
1957	Tsung-Dao Lee	China	} discovery of violations of the principle of parity, the
	Chen Ning Yang	China	} symmetry between phenomena in coordinate systems
1958	Pavel Alexeyevich Cherenkov	USSR	} discovery and interpretation of the Cherenkov effect, which indicates that electrons emit light as they
	Ilya Mikhaylovich Frank	USSR	} pass through a transparent medium at a speed
	Igor Yevgenyevich Tamm	USSR	} higher than the speed of light in that medium
1959	Owen Chamberlain	US	} confirmation of the existence
	Emilio Segrè	US	} of the antiproton
1960	Donald A. Glaser	US	development of the bubble chamber
1961	Robert Hofstadter	US	determination of the shape and size of atomic nucleons
	Rudolf Ludwig Mössbauer	W.Ger.	discovery of the Mössbauer effect, a nuclear process permitting the resonance absorption of gamma rays
1962	Lev Davidovich Landau	USSR	contributions to the understanding of condensed states of matter
1963	J. Hans D. Jensen	W.Ger.	} development of the shell model theory of
	Maria Goeppert Mayer	US	} the structure of the atomic nuclei
	Eugene Paul Wigner	US	principles governing the interaction of protons and neutrons in the nucleus
1964	Nikolay G. Basov	USSR	} work in quantum electronics leading to the
	Aleksandr M. Prokhorov	USSR	} construction of instruments based on
	Charles Hard Townes	US	} maser-laser principles
1965	Richard P. Feynman	US	} work in quantum electrodynamics, which
	Julian Seymour Schwinger	US	} describes mathematically all interactions of light with
	Shin'ichiro Tomonaga	Japan	} matter and of charged particles with one another
1966	Alfred Kastler	France	discovery of optical methods for studying Hertzian resonances in atoms
1967	Hans Albrecht Bethe	US	discoveries concerning the energy production of stars
1968	Luis W. Alvarez	US	work with elementary particles, in particular the discovery of resonance states
1969	Murray Gell-Mann	US	classification of elementary particles and their interactions

Physics (continued)

YEAR	WINNER(S)	COUNTRY	ACHIEVEMENT
1970	Hannes Alfvén	Sweden	work in magnetohydrodynamics and
	Louis-Eugène-Félix Néel	France	in antiferromagnetism and ferrimagnetism
1971	Dennis Gabor	UK	invention of holography
1972	John Bardeen	US	development of the theory of superconductivity, the
	Leon N. Cooper	US	disappearance of electrical resistance in various solids
	John Robert Schrieffer	US	when they are cooled below certain temperatures
1973	Leo Esaki	Japan	experimental discoveries in tunneling in
	Ivar Giaever	US	semiconductors and superconductors
	Brian D. Josephson	UK	predictions of supercurrent properties through a tunnel barrier
1974	Antony Hewish	UK	work in radio
	Martin Ryle	UK	astronomy
1975	Aage N. Bohr	Denmark	work on the atomic nucleus
	Ben R. Mottelson	Denmark	that paved the way for nuclear
	James Rainwater	US	fusion
1976	Burton Richter	US	discovery of new class of
	Samuel C.C. Ting	US	elementary particles (psi, or J)
1977	Philip W. Anderson	US	contributions to understanding the
	Nevill F. Mott	UK	behavior of electrons in
	John H. Van Vleck	US	magnetic, noncrystalline solids
1978	Pyotr L. Kapitsa	USSR	research in magnetism and low-temperature physics
	Arno Penzias	US	discovery of cosmic microwave background
	Robert Woodrow Wilson	US	radiation, providing support for the big-bang theory
1979	Sheldon Lee Glashow	US	contributions to the theory of the
	Abdus Salam	Pakistan	unified weak and electromagnetic
	Steven Weinberg	US	interactions of subatomic particles
1980	James Watson Cronin	US	demonstration of the simultaneous violation of both
	Val Logsdon Fitch	US	charge-conjugation and parity-inversion symmetries
1981	Nicolaas Bloembergen	US	applications of lasers
	Arthur L. Schawlow	US	in spectroscopy
	Kai M.B. Siegbahn	Sweden	development of electron spectroscopy
1982	Kenneth G. Wilson	US	analysis of continuous phase transitions
1983	Subrahmanyan Chandrasekhar	US	contributions to understanding the evolution and devolution of stars
	William A. Fowler	US	studies of nuclear reactions key to the formation of chemical elements
1984	Simon van der Meer	Neth.	discovery of subatomic particles W and Z,
	Carlo Rubbia	Italy	which supports the electroweak theory
1985	Klaus von Klitzing	W.Ger.	discovery of the quantized Hall effect, permitting exact measurements of electrical resistance
1986	Gerd Binnig	W.Ger.	development of the scanning tunneling
	Heinrich Rohrer	Switz.	electron microscope
	Ernst Ruska	W.Ger.	development of the electron microscope
1987	J. Georg Bednorz	W.Ger.	discoveries of superconductivity in
	Karl Alex Müller	Switz.	ceramic materials
1988	Leon Max Lederman	US	research in
	Melvin Schwartz	US	subatomic
	Jack Steinberger	US	particles
1989	Hans Georg Dehmelt	US	development of methods to isolate atoms
	Wolfgang Paul	W.Ger.	and subatomic particles for study
	Norman Foster Ramsey	US	development of the atomic clock
1990	Jerome Isaac Friedman	US	discovery of
	Henry Way Kendall	US	atomic
	Richard E. Taylor	Canada	quarks
1991	Pierre-Gilles de Gennes	France	discovery of general rules for behavior of molecules
1992	Georges Charpak	France	invention of a detector that traces subatomic particles
1993	Russell Alan Hulse	US	identification of
	Joseph H. Taylor, Jr.	US	binary pulsars
1994	Bertram N. Brockhouse	Canada	development of
	Clifford G. Shull	US	neutron-scattering techniques
1995	Martin Lewis Perl	US	discovery of the tau subatomic particle
	Frederick Reines	US	discovery of the neutrino subatomic particle
1996	David M. Lee	US	discovery of
	Douglas D. Osheroff	US	superfluidity in
	Robert C. Richardson	US	isotope helium-3
1997	Steven Chu	US	process of
	Claude Cohen-Tannoudji	France	cooling and trapping atoms with
	William D. Phillips	US	laser light

Physics (continued)

YEAR	WINNER(S)	COUNTRY	ACHIEVEMENT
1998	Robert B. Laughlin	US	discovery of fractional quantum Hall effect, showing
	Horst L. Störmer	US	that electrons in a low-temperature magnetic field can
	Daniel C. Tsui	US	form a quantum fluid with fractional electric charges
1999	Gerardus 't Hooft	Neth.	study of the quantum structure
	Martinus J.G. Veltman	Neth.	of electroweak interactions
2000	Zhores I. Alferov	Russia	development of fast semiconductors
	Herbert Kroemer	Germany	for use in microelectronics
	Jack S. Kilby	US	development of the integrated circuit (microchip)
2001	Eric A. Cornell	US	achievement of Bose-Einstein condensation in dilute
	Wolfgang Ketterle	Germany	gases of alkali atoms; early fundamental studies of
	Carl E. Wieman	US	the properties of the condensates
2002	Raymond Davis, Jr.	US	pioneering contributions to astrophysics,
	Masatoshi Koshiba	Japan	in particular the detection of cosmic neutrinos
	Riccardo Giacconi	US	pioneering contributions to astrophysics, which have led to the discovery of cosmic X-ray sources
2003	Alexei A. Abrikosov	US/Russia	pioneering contributions
	Vitaly L. Ginzburg	Russia	to the theory of superconductors
	Anthony J. Leggett	UK/US	and superfluids
2004	David J. Gross	US	discovery of asymptotic
	H. David Politzer	US	freedom in the theory of
	Frank Wilczek	US	the strong interaction
2005	Roy J. Glauber	US	contributions to quantum theory of optical coherence
	John L. Hall	US	contributions to the development of laser-based
	Theodor W. Hänsch	Germany	precision spectroscopy, including the optical frequency comb technique
2006	John C. Mather	US	discovery of the blackbody form and variability of
	George F. Smoot	US	cosmic microwave background radiation
2007	Albert Fert	France	discovery of Giant Magnetoresistance (large resistance
	Peter Grünberg	Germany	changes in materials composed of alternating layers of various metallic elements), a nanotechnology application
2008	Makoto Kobayashi	Japan	research on the origin of the broken symmetry in
	Toshihide Maskawa	Japan	subatomic physics that predicts three families of quarks
	Yoichiro Nambu	US	discovery of spontaneous broken symmetry in subatomic physics

Chemistry

YEAR	WINNER(S)	COUNTRY	ACHIEVEMENT
1901	Jacobus H. van 't Hoff	Neth.	discovery of the laws of chemical dynamics and osmotic pressure
1902	Emil Fischer	Germany	work on sugar and purine syntheses
1903	Svante Arrhenius	Sweden	theory of electrolytic dissociation
1904	William Ramsay	UK	discovery of inert gas elements and their places in the periodic system
1905	Adolf von Baeyer	Germany	work on organic dyes and hydroaromatic compounds
1906	Henri Moissan	France	isolation of fluorine; introduction of the Moissan furnace
1907	Eduard Buchner	Germany	discovery of noncellular fermentation
1908	Ernest Rutherford	UK	investigations into the disintegration of elements and the chemistry of radioactive substances
1909	Wilhelm Ostwald	Germany	pioneer work on catalysis, chemical equilibrium, and reaction velocities
1910	Otto Wallach	Germany	pioneer work in alicyclic combinations
1911	Marie Curie	France	discovery of radium and polonium; isolation of radium
1912	Victor Grignard	France	discovery of the Grignard reagents
	Paul Sabatier	France	method of hydrogenating organic compounds
1913	Alfred Werner	Switz.	work on the linkage of atoms in molecules
1914	Theodore W. Richards	US	accurate determination of various atomic weights
1915	Richard Willstätter	Germany	research in plant pigments, especially chlorophyll
1918	Fritz Haber	Germany	synthesis of ammonia
1920	Walther Hermann Nernst	Germany	work in thermochemistry
1921	Frederick Soddy	UK	investigation into the chemistry of radioactive substances and the occurrence and nature of isotopes
1922	Francis William Aston	UK	work with mass spectrographs; formulation of the whole-number rule
1923	Fritz Pregl	Austria	method of microanalysis of organic substances
1925	Richard Zsigmondy	Austria	elucidation of the heterogeneous nature of colloidal solutions

Chemistry (continued)

YEAR	WINNER(S)	COUNTRY	ACHIEVEMENT
1926	Theodor H.E. Svedberg	Sweden	work on disperse systems
1927	Heinrich Otto Wieland	Germany	research into the constitution of bile acids
1928	Adolf Windaus	Germany	research into the constitution of sterols and their connection with vitamins
1929	Hans von Euler-Chelpin	Sweden	} investigations into the fermentation of sugars
	Arthur Harden	UK	} and the enzyme action involved
1930	Hans Fischer	Germany	hemin, chlorophyll research; synthesis of hemin
1931	Friedrich Bergius	Germany	} invention and development of
	Carl Bosch	Germany	} chemical high-pressure methods
1932	Irving Langmuir	US	discoveries and investigations in surface chemistry
1934	Harold C. Urey	US	discovery of heavy hydrogen
1935	Frédéric and Irène Joliot-Curie	France	synthesis of new radioactive elements
1936	Peter Debye	Neth.	work on dipole moments and diffraction of X-rays and electrons in gases
1937	Norman Haworth	UK	research on carbohydrates and vitamin C
	Paul Karrer	Switz.	research on carotenoids, flavins, and vitamins
1938	Richard Kuhn (declined)	Germany	carotenoid and vitamin research
1939	Adolf Butenandt (declined)	Germany	work on sexual hormones
	Leopold Ruzicka	Switz.	work on polymethylenes and higher terpenes
1943	Georg Charles von Hevesy	Hungary	use of isotopes as tracers in chemical research
1944	Otto Hahn	Germany	discovery of the fission of heavy nuclei
1945	Artturi Ilmari Virtanen	Finland	invention of the fodder preservation method
1946	John Howard Northrop	US	} preparation of enzymes and
	Wendell M. Stanley	US	} virus proteins in pure form
	James B. Sumner	US	discovery of enzyme crystallization
1947	Robert Robinson	UK	investigation of alkaloids and other plant products
1948	Arne Tiselius	Sweden	research on electrophoresis and adsorption analysis; discoveries concerning serum proteins
1949	William Francis Giauque	US	behavior of substances at extremely low temperatures
1950	Kurt Alder	W.Ger.	} discovery and development of
	Otto Paul Hermann Diels	W.Ger.	} diene synthesis
1951	Edwin M. McMillan	US	} discovery of and research on
	Glenn T. Seaborg	US	} transuranium elements
1952	A.J.P. Martin	UK	} development of partition
	R.L.M. Synge	UK	} chromatography
1953	Hermann Staudinger	W.Ger.	work on macromolecules
1954	Linus Pauling	US	study of the nature of the chemical bond
1955	Vincent du Vigneaud	US	first synthesis of a polypeptide hormone
1956	Cyril N. Hinshelwood	UK	} work on the kinetics of
	Nikolay N. Semyonov	USSR	} chemical reactions
1957	Alexander Robertus Todd, Baron Todd (of Trumpington)	UK	work on nucleotides and nucleotide coenzymes
1958	Frederick Sanger	UK	determination of the structure of the insulin molecule
1959	Jaroslav Heyrovsky	Czecho-slovakia	discovery and development of polarography
1960	Willard Frank Libby	US	development of radiocarbon dating
1961	Melvin Calvin	US	study of chemical steps that take place during photosynthesis
1962	John C. Kendrew	UK	} determination of the structure of
	Max Ferdinand Perutz	UK	} hemoproteins
1963	Giulio Natta	Italy	} research into the structure and synthesis of polymers
	Karl Ziegler	W.Ger.	} in the field of plastics
1964	Dorothy M.C. Hodgkin	UK	determination of the structure of biochemical compounds essential in combating pernicious anemia
1965	R.B. Woodward	US	synthesis of sterols, chlorophyll, and other substances
1966	Robert S. Mulliken	US	work concerning chemical bonds and the electronic structure of molecules
1967	Manfred Eigen	W.Ger.	} studies of
	Ronald G.W. Norrish	UK	} extremely fast
	George Porter	UK	} chemical reactions
1968	Lars Onsager	US	work on the theory of thermodynamics of irreversible processes
1969	Derek H.R. Barton	UK	} work in determining the actual three-dimensional
	Odd Hassel	Norway	} shape of molecules

Chemistry (continued)

YEAR	WINNER(S)	COUNTRY	ACHIEVEMENT
1970	Luis Federico Leloir	Argentina	discovery of sugar nucleotides and their role in the biosynthesis of carbohydrates
1971	Gerhard Herzberg	Canada	research in the structure of molecules
1972	Christian B. Anfinsen	US	fundamental contributions to the study of ribonuclease
	Stanford Moore	US	} fundamental contributions
	William H. Stein	US	to enzyme chemistry
1973	Ernst Otto Fischer	W.Ger.	} organometallic
	Geoffrey Wilkinson	UK	chemistry
1974	Paul J. Flory	US	studies of long-chain molecules
1975	John W. Cornforth	UK	} work in
	Vladimir Prelog	Switz.	stereochemistry
1976	William N. Lipscomb, Jr.	US	studies on the structure of boranes
1977	Ilya Prigogine	Belgium	widening the scope of thermodynamics
1978	Peter Dennis Mitchell	UK	formulation of a theory of energy transfer processes in biological systems
1979	Herbert Charles Brown	US	} introduction of compounds of boron and
	Georg Wittig	W.Ger.	phosphorus in the synthesis of organic substances
1980	Paul Berg	US	first preparation of a hybrid DNA
	Walter Gilbert	US	development of chemical and
	Frederick Sanger	UK	biological analyses of DNA structure
1981	Kenichi Fukui	Japan	} orbital symmetry interpretation
	Roald Hoffmann	US	of chemical reactions
1982	Aaron Klug	UK	determination of the structure of biological substances
1983	Henry Taube	US	study of electron transfer reactions
1984	Bruce Merrifield	US	development of a method of polypeptide synthesis
1985	Herbert A. Hauptman	US	} development of a way to map the
	Jerome Karle	US	chemical structure of small molecules
1986	Dudley R. Herschbach	US	} development of methods
	Yuan T. Lee	US	for analyzing basic
	John C. Polanyi	Canada	chemical reactions
1987	Donald J. Cram	US	} development of molecules
	Jean-Marie Lehn	France	that can link with
	Charles J. Pedersen	US	other molecules
1988	Johann Deisenhofer	W.Ger.	} discovery of structure
	Robert Huber	W.Ger.	proteins needed
	Hartmut Michel	W.Ger.	in photosynthesis
1989	Sidney Altman	US	} discovery of certain
	Thomas Robert Cech	US	basic properties of RNA
1990	Elias James Corey	US	development of retrosynthetic analysis for synthesis of complex molecules
1991	Richard R. Ernst	Switz.	improvements in nuclear magnetic resonance spectroscopy
1992	Rudolph A. Marcus	US	explanation of how electrons transfer between molecules
1993	Kary B. Mullis	US	} invention of techniques for
	Michael Smith	Canada	gene study and manipulation
1994	George A. Olah	US	development of techniques to study hydrocarbon molecules
1995	Paul Crutzen	Neth.	} explanation of processes
	Mario Molina	US	that deplete Earth's
	F. Sherwood Rowland	US	ozone layer
1996	Robert F. Curl, Jr.	US	} discovery of new
	Harold W. Kroto	UK	carbon compounds
	Richard E. Smalley	US	called fullerenes
1997	Paul D. Boyer	US	} explanation of the enzymatic
	John E. Walker	UK	conversion of adenosine triphosphate
	Jens C. Skou	Denmark	discovery of sodium-potassium-activated adenosine triphosphatase
1998	Walter Kohn	US	development of the density-functional theory
	John A. Pople	UK	development of computational methods in quantum chemistry
1999	Ahmed H. Zewail	Egypt/US	study of the transition states of chemical reactions using femtosecond spectroscopy
2000	Alan J. Heeger	US	} discovery of plastics
	Alan G. MacDiarmid	US	that conduct
	Hideki Shirakawa	Japan	electricity

Chemistry (continued)

YEAR	WINNER(S)	COUNTRY	ACHIEVEMENT
2001	William S. Knowles	US	} work on chirally catalyzed
	Ryoji Noyori	Japan	} hydrogenation reactions
	K. Barry Sharpless	US	work on chirally catalyzed oxidation reactions
2002	John B. Fenn	US	development of soft desorption ionization methods
	Koichi Tanaka	Japan	for mass spectrometric analyses of biological macromolecules
	Kurt Wüthrich	Switz.	development of nuclear magnetic resonance spectroscopy for determining the three-dimensional structure of biological macromolecules in solution
2003	Peter Agre	US	} cell membrane channel
	Roderick MacKinnon	US	} discoveries
2004	Aaron Ciechanover	Israel	discovery of
	Avram Hershko	Israel	ubiquitin-mediated
	Irwin Rose	US	protein degradation
2005	Yves Chauvin	France	development of the
	Robert H. Grubbs	US	metathesis method in
	Richard R. Schrock	US	organic synthesis
2006	Roger D. Kornberg	US	studies of the molecular basis of eukaryotic transcription
2007	Gerhard Ertl	Germany	studies of chemical processes on solid surfaces
2008	Martin Chalfie	US	discovery and development
	Osamu Shimomura	US	of GFP, the green
	Roger Y. Tsien	US	fluorescent protein

Physiology or Medicine

YEAR	WINNER(S)	COUNTRY	ACHIEVEMENT
1901	Emil von Behring	Germany	work on serum therapy
1902	Ronald Ross	UK	discovery of how malaria enters an organism
1903	Niels Ryberg Finsen	Denmark	treatment of skin diseases with light
1904	Ivan Petrovich Pavlov	Russia	work on the physiology of digestion
1905	Robert Koch	Germany	tuberculosis research
1906	Camillo Golgi	Italy	} work on the structure
	Santiago Ramón y Cajal	Spain	} of the nervous system
1907	Alphonse Laveran	France	discovery of the role of protozoa in diseases
1908	Paul Ehrlich	Germany	} work on
	Élie Metchnikoff	Russia	} immunity
1909	Emil Theodor Kocher	Switz.	work on aspects of the thyroid gland
1910	Albrecht Kossel	Germany	researches in cellular chemistry
1911	Allvar Gullstrand	Sweden	work on dioptrics of the eye
1912	Alexis Carrel	France	work on the vascular suture; the transplantation of organs
1913	Charles Richet	France	work on anaphylaxis
1914	Robert Bárány	Austria-Hungary	work on vestibular apparatus
1919	Jules Bordet	Belgium	work on immunity factors in blood serum
1920	August Krogh	Denmark	discovery of the capillary motor-regulating mechanism
1922	A.V. Hill	UK	discoveries concerning heat production in muscles
	Otto Meyerhof	Germany	work on metabolism of lactic acid in muscles
1923	Frederick G. Banting	Canada	} discovery of
	J.J.R. Macleod	UK	} insulin
1924	Willem Einthoven	Neth.	discovery of the electrocardiogram mechanism
1926	Johannes Fibiger	Denmark	contributions to cancer research
1927	Julius Wagner-Jauregg	Austria	work on malaria inoculation in dementia paralytica
1928	Charles-Jules-Henri Nicolle	France	work on typhus
1929	Christiaan Eijkman	Neth.	discovery of the antineuritic vitamin
	Frederick Gowland Hopkins	UK	discovery of growth-stimulating vitamins
1930	Karl Landsteiner	US	discovery of human blood groups
1931	Otto Warburg	Germany	discovery of the nature and action of the respiratory enzyme
1932	Edgar Douglas Adrian, 1st Baron Adrian (of Cambridge)	UK	discoveries regarding the functions
	Charles Scott Sherrington	UK	of neurons
1933	Thomas Hunt Morgan	US	discoveries concerning chromosomal heredity functions

Physiology or Medicine (continued)

YEAR	WINNER(S)	COUNTRY	ACHIEVEMENT
1934	George Richards Minot William P. Murphy George H. Whipple	US US US	discoveries concerning liver treatment for anemia
1935	Hans Spemann	Germany	discovery of the organizer effect in embryos
1936	Henry Dale Otto Loewi	UK Germany	work on the chemical transmission of nerve impulses
1937	Albert Szent-Gyorgyi	Hungary	work on biological combustion
1938	Corneille Heymans	Belgium	discovery of the role of sinus and aortic mechanisms in respiration regulation
1939	Gerhard Domagk (declined)	Germany	discovery of the antibacterial effect of Prontosil
1943	Henrik Dam Edward Adelbert Doisy	Denmark US	discovery of vitamin K discovery of the chemical nature of vitamin K
1944	Joseph Erlanger Herbert S. Gasser	US US	research on differentiated functions of nerve fibers
1945	Ernst Boris Chain Alexander Fleming Howard Walter Florey, Baron Florey	UK UK Australia	discovery of penicillin and its curative value
1946	Hermann J. Muller	US	production of mutations by X-ray irradiation
1947	Carl and Gerty Cori Bernardo A. Houssay	US Argentina	discovery of how glycogen is catalytically converted discovery of the pituitary hormone function in sugar metabolism
1948	Paul Hermann Müller	Switz.	discovery of properties of DDT
1949	António Egas Moniz Walter Rudolf Hess	Portugal Switz.	discovery of therapeutic value in leucotomy for psychoses discovery of the function of the interbrain
1950	Philip Showalter Hench Edward Calvin Kendall Tadeus Reichstein	US US Switz.	research on adrenal cortex hormones, their structure, and their biological effects
1951	Max Theiler	South Africa	yellow fever discoveries
1952	Selman A. Waksman	US	discovery of streptomycin
1953	Hans Adolf Krebs Fritz Albert Lipmann	UK US	discovery of the citric-acid cycle discovery of coenzyme A metabolism
1954	John Franklin Enders Frederick C. Robbins Thomas H. Weller	US US US	cultivation of the poliomyelitis virus in tissue cultures
1955	Axel H.T. Theorell	Sweden	discoveries concerning oxidation enzymes
1956	André F. Cournand Werner Forssmann Dickinson W. Richards	US W.Ger. US	discoveries concerning heart catheterization and circulatory changes
1957	Daniel Bovet	Italy	production of synthetic curare
1958	George Wells Beadle Edward L. Tatum Joshua Lederberg	US US US	discovery of the genetic regulation of chemical processes discoveries concerning genetic recombination
1959	Arthur Kornberg Severo Ochoa	US US	work on producing nucleic acids artificially
1960	Macfarlane Burnet Peter B. Medawar	Australia UK	discovery of acquired immunity to tissue transplants
1961	Georg von Békésy	US	discovery of functions of the inner ear
1962	Francis H.C. Crick James Dewey Watson Maurice Wilkins	UK US UK	discoveries concerning the molecular structure of DNA
1963	John Carew Eccles Alan Hodgkin Andrew F. Huxley	Australia UK UK	study of the transmission of impulses along a nerve fiber
1964	Konrad Bloch Feodor Lynen	US W.Ger.	discoveries concerning cholesterol and fatty-acid metabolism
1965	François Jacob André Lwoff Jacques Monod	France France France	discoveries concerning regulatory activities of the body cells
1966	Charles B. Huggins Peyton Rous	US US	research on causes and treatment of cancer
1967	Ragnar Arthur Granit Haldan Keffer Hartline George Wald	Sweden US US	discoveries about chemical and physiological visual processes in the eye
1968	Robert William Holley Har Gobind Khorana Marshall W. Nirenberg	US US US	deciphering of the genetic code

Physiology or Medicine (continued)

YEAR	WINNER(S)	COUNTRY	ACHIEVEMENT
1969	Max Delbrück	US	research and discoveries
	A.D. Hershey	US	concerning viruses and
	Salvador Luria	US	viral diseases
1970	Julius Axelrod	US	discoveries concerning
	Ulf von Euler	Sweden	the chemistry of
	Sir Bernard Katz	UK	nerve transmission
1971	Earl W. Sutherland, Jr.	US	discoveries concerning the action of hormones
1972	Gerald M. Edelman	US	research on the chemical
	Rodney Robert Porter	UK	structure of antibodies
1973	Karl von Frisch	Austria	discoveries in
	Konrad Lorenz	Austria	animal behavior
	Nikolaas Tinbergen	UK	patterns
1974	Albert Claude	US	research on the structural
	Christian René de Duve	Belgium	and functional organization
	George E. Palade	US	of cells
1975	David Baltimore	US	discoveries concerning the interaction between
	Renato Dulbecco	US	tumor viruses and the genetic
	Howard Martin Temin	US	material of the cell
1976	Baruch S. Blumberg	US	studies of the origin and
	D. Carleton Gajdusek	US	spread of infectious diseases
1977	Roger C.L. Guillemin	US	research on pituitary
	Andrew Victor Schally	US	hormones
	Rosalyn S. Yalow	US	development of radioimmunoassay
1978	Werner Arber	Switz.	discovery and application
	Daniel Nathans	US	of enzymes that
	Hamilton O. Smith	US	fragment DNA
1979	Allan M. Cormack	US	development of
	Godfrey N. Hounsfield	UK	the CAT scan
1980	Baruj Benacerraf	US	investigations of genetic
	Jean Dausset	France	control of the response of the
	George Davis Snell	US	immune system to foreign substances
1981	David Hunter Hubel	US	discoveries concerning the processing of visual
	Torsten Nils Wiesel	Sweden	information by the brain
	Roger Wolcott Sperry	US	discoveries concerning cerebral hemisphere functions
1982	Sune K. Bergström	Sweden	discoveries concerning the biochemistry
	Bengt I. Samuelsson	Sweden	and physiology of
	John Robert Vane	UK	of prostaglandins
1983	Barbara McClintock	US	discovery of mobile plant genes that affect heredity
1984	Niels K. Jerne	Denmark	theory and development
	Georges J.F. Köhler	W.Ger.	of a technique
	César Milstein	UK/	for producing
		Argentina	monoclonal antibodies
1985	Michael S. Brown	US	discovery of cell receptors relating to
	Joseph L. Goldstein	US	cholesterol metabolism
1986	Stanley Cohen	US	discovery of chemical agents
	Rita Levi-Montalcini	Italy	that help regulate the growth of cells
1987	Susumu Tonegawa	Japan	study of genetic aspects of antibodies
1988	James Black	UK	development of new
	Gertrude Belle Elion	US	classes of drugs for
	George H. Hitchings	US	combating disease
1989	J. Michael Bishop	US	study of cancer-causing
	Harold Varmus	US	genes called oncogenes
1990	Joseph E. Murray	US	development of kidney and
	E. Donnall Thomas	US	bone-marrow transplants
1991	Erwin Neher	Germany	discovery of how cells
	Bert Sakmann	Germany	communicate, as related to diseases
1992	Edmond H. Fischer	US	discovery of a class of enzymes
	Edwin Gerhard Krebs	US	called protein kinases
1993	Richard J. Roberts	UK	discovery of "split," or
	Phillip A. Sharp	US	interrupted, genetic structure
1994	Alfred G. Gilman	US	discovery of cell signalers
	Martin Rodbell	US	called G-proteins
1995	Edward B. Lewis	US	identification of genes
	Christiane Nüsslein-Volhard	Germany	that control the body's
	Eric F. Wieschaus	US	early structural development
1996	Peter C. Doherty	Australia	discovery of how the immune
	Rolf M. Zinkernagel	Switz.	system recognizes virus-infected cells
1997	Stanley B. Prusiner	US	discovery of the prion, a type of disease-causing protein

Physiology or Medicine (continued)

YEAR	WINNER(S)	COUNTRY	ACHIEVEMENT
1998	Robert F. Furchgott	US	discovery that nitric oxide
	Louis J. Ignarro	US	acts as a signaling molecule in
	Ferid Murad	US	the cardiovascular system
1999	Günter Blobel	US	discovery that proteins help govern cellular organization
2000	Arvid Carlsson	Sweden	discovery of how signals
	Paul Greengard	US	are transmitted between nerve
	Eric Kandel	US	cells in the brain
2001	Leland H. Hartwell	US	discovery of key
	R. Timothy Hunt	UK	regulators of
	Paul M. Nurse	UK	the cell cycle
2002	Sydney Brenner	UK	discoveries concerning how genes
	H. Robert Horvitz	US	regulate and program organ
	John E. Sulston	UK	development and cell death
2003	Paul C. Lauterbur	US	discoveries concerning magnetic
	Peter Mansfield	UK	resonance imaging
2004	Richard Axel	US	discoveries of odorant receptors and the
	Linda B. Buck	US	organization of the olfactory system
2005	Barry J. Marshall	Australia	discovery of the bacterium *Helicobacter pylori* and its
	J. Robin Warren	Australia	role in peptic ulcer disease and gastritis
2006	Andrew Z. Fire	US	discovery of RNA interference: gene silencing
	Craig C. Mello	US	by double-stranded RNA
2007	Mario R. Capecchi	US	discoveries of principles for introducing
	Martin J. Evans	UK	specific gene modifications
	Oliver Smithies	US	using embryonic stem cells
2008	Françoise Barré-Sinoussi	France	discovery of the human
	Luc Montagnier	France	immunodeficiency virus (HIV)
	Harald zur Hausen	Germany	research supporting the theory that human papillomaviruses cause cervical cancer

Literature

YEAR	WINNER(S)	COUNTRY	FIELD
1901	Sully Prudhomme	France	poetry
1902	Theodor Mommsen	Germany	history
1903	Bjørnstjerne Martinus Bjørnson	Norway	prose fiction, poetry, drama
1904	José Echegaray y Eizaguirre	Spain	drama
	Frédéric Mistral	France	poetry
1905	Henryk Sienkiewicz	Poland	prose fiction
1906	Giosuè Carducci	Italy	poetry
1907	Rudyard Kipling	UK	poetry, prose fiction
1908	Rudolf Christoph Eucken	Germany	philosophy
1909	Selma Lagerlöf	Sweden	prose fiction
1910	Paul Johann Ludwig von Heyse	Germany	poetry, prose fiction, drama
1911	Maurice Maeterlinck	Belgium	drama
1912	Gerhart Hauptmann	Germany	drama
1913	Rabindranath Tagore	India	poetry
1915	Romain Rolland	France	prose fiction
1916	Verner von Heidenstam	Sweden	poetry
1917	Karl Gjellerup	Denmark	prose fiction
	Henrik Pontoppidan	Denmark	prose fiction
1918	Erik Axel Karlfeldt (declined)	Sweden	poetry
1919	Carl Spitteler	Switzerland	poetry, prose fiction
1920	Knut Hamsun	Norway	prose fiction
1921	Anatole France	France	prose fiction
1922	Jacinto Benavente y Martínez	Spain	drama
1923	William Butler Yeats	Ireland	poetry
1924	Wladyslaw Stanislaw Reymont	Poland	prose fiction
1925	George Bernard Shaw	Ireland	drama
1926	Grazia Deledda	Italy	prose fiction
1927	Henri Bergson	France	philosophy
1928	Sigrid Undset	Norway	prose fiction
1929	Thomas Mann	Germany	prose fiction
1930	Sinclair Lewis	US	prose fiction
1931	Erik Axel Karlfeldt (posthumously)	Sweden	poetry
1932	John Galsworthy	UK	prose fiction
1933	Ivan Alekseyevich Bunin	USSR	poetry, prose fiction
1934	Luigi Pirandello	Italy	drama

Literature (continued)

YEAR	WINNER(S)	COUNTRY	FIELD
1936	Eugene O'Neill	US	drama
1937	Roger Martin du Gard	France	prose fiction
1938	Pearl Buck	US	prose fiction
1939	Frans Eemil Sillanpää	Finland	prose fiction
1944	Johannes V. Jensen	Denmark	prose fiction
1945	Gabriela Mistral	Chile	poetry
1946	Hermann Hesse	Switzerland	prose fiction
1947	André Gide	France	prose
1948	T.S. Eliot	UK	poetry, criticism
1949	William Faulkner	US	prose fiction
1950	Bertrand Russell	UK	philosophy
1951	Pär Lagerkvist	Sweden	prose fiction
1952	François Mauriac	France	poetry, prose fiction, drama
1953	Winston Churchill	UK	history, oration
1954	Ernest Hemingway	US	prose fiction
1955	Halldór Laxness	Iceland	prose fiction
1956	Juan Ramón Jiménez	Spain	poetry
1957	Albert Camus	France	prose fiction, drama
1958	Boris L. Pasternak (declined)	USSR	prose fiction, poetry
1959	Salvatore Quasimodo	Italy	poetry
1960	Saint-John Perse	France	poetry
1961	Ivo Andric	Yugoslavia	prose fiction
1962	John Steinbeck	US	prose fiction
1963	George Seferis	Greece	poetry
1964	Jean-Paul Sartre (declined)	France	philosophy, drama
1965	Mikhail A. Sholokhov	USSR	prose fiction
1966	S.Y. Agnon	Israel	prose fiction
	Nelly Sachs	Sweden	poetry
1967	Miguel Ángel Asturias	Guatemala	prose fiction
1968	Yasunari Kawabata	Japan	prose fiction
1969	Samuel Beckett	Ireland	prose fiction, drama
1970	Aleksandr I. Solzhenitsyn	USSR	prose fiction
1971	Pablo Neruda	Chile	poetry
1972	Heinrich Böll	West Germany	prose fiction
1973	Patrick White	Australia	prose fiction
1974	Eyvind Johnson	Sweden	prose fiction
	Harry Martinson	Sweden	prose fiction, poetry
1975	Eugenio Montale	Italy	poetry
1976	Saul Bellow	US	prose fiction
1977	Vicente Aleixandre	Spain	poetry
1978	Isaac Bashevis Singer	US	prose fiction
1979	Odysseus Elytis	Greece	poetry
1980	Czeslaw Milosz	US	poetry
1981	Elias Canetti	Bulgaria	prose
1982	Gabriel García Márquez	Colombia	prose fiction, journalism, social criticism
1983	William Golding	UK	prose fiction
1984	Jaroslav Seifert	Czechoslovakia	poetry
1985	Claude Simon	France	prose fiction
1986	Wole Soyinka	Nigeria	drama, poetry
1987	Joseph Brodsky	US	poetry, prose
1988	Naguib Mahfouz	Egypt	prose fiction
1989	Camilo José Cela	Spain	prose fiction
1990	Octavio Paz	Mexico	poetry, prose
1991	Nadine Gordimer	South Africa	prose fiction
1992	Derek Walcott	Saint Lucia	poetry
1993	Toni Morrison	US	prose fiction
1994	Kenzaburo Oe	Japan	prose fiction
1995	Seamus Heaney	Ireland	poetry
1996	Wislawa Szymborska	Poland	poetry
1997	Dario Fo	Italy	drama
1998	José Saramago	Portugal	prose fiction
1999	Günter Grass	Germany	prose fiction
2000	Gao Xingjian	France	prose fiction, drama
2001	V.S. Naipaul	UK	prose fiction
2002	Imre Kertész	Hungary	prose fiction
2003	J.M. Coetzee	South Africa	prose fiction
2004	Elfriede Jelinek	Austria	prose fiction, drama
2005	Harold Pinter	UK	drama

Literature (continued)

YEAR	WINNER(S)	COUNTRY	FIELD
2006	Orhan Pamuk	Turkey	prose fiction
2007	Doris Lessing	UK	prose fiction, social criticism
2008	Jean-Marie Gustave Le Clézio	France/Mauritius	prose fiction, essays

Peace

YEAR	WINNER(S)	COUNTRY	YEAR	WINNER(S)	COUNTRY
1901	Henri Dunant	Switzerland	1951	Léon Jouhaux	France
	Frédéric Passy	France	1952	Albert Schweitzer	France
1902	Élie Ducommun	Switzerland	1953	George C. Marshall	US
	Charles-Albert Gobat	Switzerland	1954	Office of the United Nations	(founded 1951)
1903	Randal Cremer	UK		High Commissioner for	
1904	Institute of International	(founded 1873)		Refugees	
	Law		1957	Lester B. Pearson	Canada
1905	Bertha, Freifrau von	Austria-Hungary	1958	Dominique Pire	Belgium
	Suttner		1959	Philip John Noel-Baker,	UK
1906	Theodore Roosevelt	US		Baron Noel-Baker (of the	
1907	Ernesto Teodoro Moneta	Italy		City of Derby)	
	Louis Renault	France	1960	Albert John Luthuli	South Africa
1908	Klas Pontus Arnoldson	Sweden	1961	Dag Hammarskjöld	Sweden
	Fredrik Bajer	Denmark		(posthumously)	
1909	Auguste-Marie-François	Belgium	1962	Linus Pauling	US
	Beernaert		1963	International Committee of	(founded 1863)
	Paul-H.-B. d'Estournelles	France		the Red Cross	
	de Constant			League of Red Cross	(founded 1919)
1910	International Peace Bureau	(founded 1891)		Societies	
1911	Tobias Michael Carel Asser	The Netherlands	1964	Martin Luther King, Jr.	US
	Alfred Hermann Fried	Austria-Hungary	1965	United Nations Children's	(founded 1946)
1912	Elihu Root	US		Fund	
1913	Henri-Marie Lafontaine	Belgium	1968	René Cassin	France
1917	International Committee of	(founded 1863)	1969	International Labour	(founded 1919)
	the Red Cross			Organisation	
1919	Woodrow Wilson	US	1970	Norman Ernest Borlaug	US
1920	Léon Bourgeois	France	1971	Willy Brandt	West Germany
1921	Karl Hjalmar Branting	Sweden	1973	Henry Kissinger	US
	Christian Lous Lange	Norway		Le Duc Tho (declined)	North Vietnam
1922	Fridtjof Nansen	Norway	1974	Seán MacBride	Ireland
1925	Austen Chamberlain	UK		Eisaku Sato	Japan
	Charles G. Dawes	US	1975	Andrey Dmitriyevich	USSR
1926	Aristide Briand	France		Sakharov	
	Gustav Stresemann	Germany	1976	Mairéad Corrigan	Northern Ireland
1927	Ferdinand-Édouard Buisson	France			
	Ludwig Quidde	Germany		Betty Williams	Northern Ireland
1929	Frank B. Kellogg	US			
1930	Nathan Söderblom	Sweden	1977	Amnesty International	(founded 1961)
1931	Jane Addams	US	1978	Menachem Begin	Israel
	Nicholas Murray Butler	US		Anwar el-Sadat	Egypt
1933	Norman Angell	UK	1979	Mother Teresa	India
1934	Arthur Henderson	UK	1980	Adolfo Pérez Esquivel	Argentina
1935	Carl von Ossietzky	Germany	1981	Office of the United Nations	(founded 1951)
1936	Carlos Saavedra Lamas	Argentina		High Commissioner for	
1937	Robert Gascoyne-Cecil,	UK		Refugees	
	1st Viscount Cecil		1982	Alfonso García Robles	Mexico
	(of Chelwood)			Alva Myrdal	Sweden
1938	Nansen International Office	(founded 1931)	1983	Lech Walesa	Poland
	for Refugees		1984	Desmond Tutu	South Africa
1944	International Committee of	(founded 1863)	1985	International Physicians for	(founded 1980)
	the Red Cross			the Prevention of Nuclear	
1945	Cordell Hull	US		War	
1946	Emily Greene Balch	US	1986	Elie Wiesel	US
	John R. Mott	US	1987	Oscar Arias Sánchez	Costa Rica
1947	American Friends Service	US	1988	United Nations Peace-	
	Committee			keeping Forces	
	Friends Service Council	UK	1989	Dalai Lama	Tibet
1949	John Boyd Orr, Baron Boyd-	UK	1990	Mikhail Gorbachev	USSR
	Orr of Brechin Mearns		1991	Aung San Suu Kyi	Myanmar (Burma)
1950	Ralph Bunche	US			

Peace (continued)

YEAR	WINNER(S)	COUNTRY	YEAR	WINNER(S)	COUNTRY
1992	Rigoberta Menchú	Guatemala	1999	Doctors Without Borders	(founded 1971)
1993	F.W. de Klerk	South Africa	2000	Kim Dae Jung	Republic of
	Nelson Mandela	South Africa			Korea
1994	Yasir Arafat	Palestinian	2001	Kofi Annan	Ghana
		territories		United Nations	(founded 1945)
	Shimon Peres	Israel	2002	Jimmy Carter	US
	Yitzhak Rabin	Israel	2003	Shirin Ebadi	Iran
1995	Pugwash Conferences	(founded 1957)	2004	Wangari Maathai	Kenya
	Joseph Rotblat	UK	2005	Mohamed ElBaradei	Egypt
1996	Carlos Filipe Ximenes Belo	East Timor		International Atomic	(founded 1957)
	José Ramos-Horta	East Timor		Energy Agency	
1997	International Campaign to	(founded 1992)	2006	Muhammad Yunus	Bangladesh
	Ban Landmines			Grameen Bank	(founded 1976)
	Jody Williams	US	2007	Intergovernmental Panel	(founded 1988)
1998	John Hume	Northern		on Climate Change	
		Ireland		Albert Arnold (Al) Gore, Jr.	US
	David Trimble	Northern	2008	Martti Ahtisaari	Finland
		Ireland			

Economics

YEAR	WINNER(S)	COUNTRY	ACHIEVEMENT
1969	Ragnar Frisch	Norway	} work in
	Jan Tinbergen	Neth.	} econometrics
1970	Paul Samuelson	US	work in scientific analysis of economic theory
1971	Simon Kuznets	US	extensive research on the economic growth of nations
1972	Kenneth J. Arrow	US	} contributions to general economic
	John R. Hicks	UK	} equilibrium theory and welfare theory
1973	Wassily Leontief	US	development of input-output analysis
1974	Friedrich von Hayek	UK	} pioneering analysis of the interdependence of
	Gunnar Myrdal	Sweden	} economic, social, and institutional phenomena
1975	Leonid V. Kantorovich	USSR	} contributions to the theory of
	Tjalling C. Koopmans	US	} optimum allocation of resources
1976	Milton Friedman	US	work in consumption analysis, monetary theory, and economic stabilization
1977	James Edward Meade	UK	} contributions to the theory
	Bertil Ohlin	Sweden	} of international trade
1978	Herbert A. Simon	US	research into decision-making processes in economic organizations
1979	Arthur Lewis	UK	} research into analyses of economic processes
	Theodore W. Schultz	US	} in developing nations
1980	Lawrence Robert Klein	US	development and analysis of empirical models of business fluctuations
1981	James Tobin	US	portfolio-selection theory of investment
1982	George J. Stigler	US	studies of economic effects of governmental regulation
1983	Gerard Debreu	US	mathematical proof of the supply-and-demand theory
1984	Richard Stone	UK	development of national income accounting systems
1985	Franco Modigliani	US	analyses of household savings and financial markets
1986	James M. Buchanan	US	public-choice theory bridging economics and political science
1987	Robert Merton Solow	US	contributions to the theory of economic growth
1988	Maurice Allais	France	contributions to the theory of markets and efficient use of resources
1989	Trygve Haavelmo	Norway	development of statistical techniques for economic forecasting
1990	Harry M. Markowitz	US	} study of financial
	Merton H. Miller	US	} markets and investment
	William F. Sharpe	US	} decision making
1991	Ronald Coase	US	application of economic principles to the study of law
1992	Gary S. Becker	US	application of economic theory to social sciences
1993	Robert William Fogel	US	} contributions to
	Douglass C. North	US	} economic history
1994	John C. Harsanyi	US	} development
	John F. Nash	US	} of game
	Reinhard Selten	Germany	} theory
1995	Robert E. Lucas, Jr.	US	incorporation of rational expectations in macroeconomic theory

Economics (continued)

YEAR	WINNER(S)	COUNTRY	ACHIEVEMENT
1996	James A. Mirrlees	UK	} contributions to the theory of incentives under
	William Vickrey (posthumously)	US	conditions of asymmetric information
1997	Robert C. Merton	US	} method for determining the value of
	Myron S. Scholes	US	stock options and other derivatives
1998	Amartya Sen	India	contribution to welfare economics
1999	Robert A. Mundell	Canada	analysis of optimum currency areas and of policy under different exchange-rate regimes
2000	James J. Heckman	US	} development of methods of statistical
	Daniel L. McFadden	US	analysis of individual and household behavior
2001	George A. Akerlof	US	} analyses of
	A. Michael Spence	US	markets with asymmetric
	Joseph E. Stiglitz	US	information
2002	Daniel Kahneman	US/Israel	integration of psychological research into economics, particularly concerning factors in decision making
	Vernon L. Smith	US	establishment of laboratory experiments for empirical economic analysis of alternative market mechanisms
2003	Robert F. Engle	US	methods of analysis of economic time series with time-varying volatility
	Clive W.J. Granger	UK	methods of analysis of economic time series with common trends
2004	Finn E. Kydland	Norway	} macroeconomic analysis of the time consistency of
	Edward C. Prescott	US	economic policy and the driving forces behind business cycles
2005	Robert J. Aumann	Israel/US	} enhancement of the understanding of conflict and
	Thomas C. Schelling	US	cooperation through game-theory analysis
2006	Edmund S. Phelps	US	analysis of intertemporal tradeoffs in macroeconomics
2007	Leonid Hurwicz	US	} research that
	Eric S. Maskin	US	laid the foundations
	Roger B. Myerson	US	of mechanism design theory
2008	Paul Krugman	US	research into trade patterns and location of economic activity

Special Achievement Awards

Kennedy Center Honors

The Kennedy Center Honors are bestowed annually by the John F. Kennedy Center for the Performing Arts in Washington DC. First conferred in 1978, the honors salute several artists each year for lifetime achievement in the performing arts and are celebrated by a televised gala in December. **Web site:** <www.kennedy-center.org/programs/specialevents/honors/>.

YEAR	NAME	FIELD	YEAR	NAME	FIELD
1978	Marian Anderson	opera singer	1982	George Abbott	theater producer, director, writer
	Fred Astaire	dancer, actor		Lillian Gish	actress
	George Balanchine	choreographer		Benny Goodman	swing musician
	Richard Rodgers	composer		Gene Kelly	dancer, actor
	Arthur Rubenstein	pianist		Eugene Ormandy	conductor
1979	Aaron Copland	composer	1983	Katherine Dunham	dancer, choreographer
	Ella Fitzgerald	singer		Elia Kazan	theater and film director
	Henry Fonda	actor			
	Martha Graham	dancer, choreographer		Frank Sinatra	singer, actor
	Tennessee Williams	playwright		James Stewart	actor
1980	Leonard Bernstein	conductor		Virgil Thomson	composer, music critic
	James Cagney	actor	1984	Lena Horne	singer, actress
	Agnes de Mille	dancer, choreographer		Danny Kaye	actor, comedian
	Lynn Fontanne	actress		Gian Carlo Menotti	composer
	Leontyne Price	opera singer		Arthur Miller	playwright
1981	Count Basie	jazz pianist		Isaac Stern	violinist
	Cary Grant	actor	1985	Merce Cunningham	dancer, choreographer
	Helen Hayes	actress		Irene Dunne	actress
	Jerome Robbins	dancer, choreographer		Bob Hope	entertainer, actor
	Rudolf Serkin	pianist			

Kennedy Center Honors (continued)

YEAR	NAME	FIELD
1985	Alan Jay Lerner	playwright, lyricist
(cont.)	Frederick Loewe	composer
	Beverly Sills	opera singer
1986	Lucille Ball	actress
	Ray Charles	soul musician
	Hume Cronyn	actor
	Jessica Tandy	actress
	Yehudi Menuhin	violinist
	Antony Tudor	choreographer
1987	Perry Como	singer
	Bette Davis	actress
	Sammy Davis, Jr.	singer, dancer, entertainer
	Nathan Milstein	violinist
	Alwin Nikolais	choreographer
1988	Alvin Ailey	dancer, choreographer
	George Burns	actor, comedian
	Myrna Loy	actress
	Alexander Schneider	violinist, conductor
	Roger L. Stevens	arts administrator
1989	Harry Belafonte	folk singer, actor
	Claudette Colbert	actress
	Alexandra Danilova	ballet dancer
	Mary Martin	actress, singer
	William Schuman	composer
1990	Dizzy Gillespie	jazz musician
	Katharine Hepburn	actress
	Risë Stevens	opera singer
	Jule Styne	composer
	Billy Wilder	film director
1991	Roy Acuff	country musician
	Betty Comden	theater and film writer
	Adolph Green	theater and film writer
	Fayard Nicholas	dancer
	Harold Nicholas	dancer
	Gregory Peck	actor
	Robert Shaw	conductor
1992	Lionel Hampton	swing musician
	Paul Newman	actor
	Joanne Woodward	actress
	Ginger Rogers	dancer, actress
	Mstislav Rostropovich	musician, conductor
	Paul Taylor	dancer, choreographer
1993	Johnny Carson	television entertainer
	Arthur Mitchell	dancer, choreographer
	George Solti	conductor
	Stephen Sondheim	composer, lyricist
	Marion Williams	gospel singer
1994	Kirk Douglas	actor
	Aretha Franklin	soul singer
	Morton Gould	composer
	Harold Prince	theater director, producer
	Pete Seeger	folk musician
1995	Jacques d'Amboise	dancer, choreographer
	Marilyn Horne	opera singer
	B.B. King	blues musician
	Sidney Poitier	actor
	Neil Simon	playwright
1996	Edward Albee	playwright
	Benny Carter	jazz musician
	Johnny Cash	country musician
	Jack Lemmon	actor
	Maria Tallchief	ballet dancer
1997	Lauren Bacall	actress
	Bob Dylan	singer, songwriter
	Charlton Heston	actor

YEAR	NAME	FIELD
1997	Jessye Norman	opera singer
(cont.)	Edward Villella	dancer, choreographer
1998	Bill Cosby	actor, comedian
	Fred Ebb	lyricist
	John Kander	composer
	Willie Nelson	country musician
	André Previn	pianist, composer, conductor
	Shirley Temple Black	actress, diplomat
1999	Victor Borge	pianist, comedian
	Sean Connery	actor
	Judith Jamison	dancer, choreographer
	Jason Robards	actor
	Stevie Wonder	musician
2000	Mikhail Baryshnikov	dancer
	Chuck Berry	musician
	Plácido Domingo	opera singer
	Clint Eastwood	actor, director
	Angela Lansbury	actress
2001	Julie Andrews	actress
	Van Cliburn	pianist
	Quincy Jones	music producer, composer
	Jack Nicholson	actor
	Luciano Pavarotti	opera singer
2002	James Earl Jones	actor
	James Levine	conductor
	Chita Rivera	musical theater performer
	Paul Simon	singer
	Elizabeth Taylor	actress
2003	James Brown	musician
	Carol Burnett	actress
	Loretta Lynn	musician
	Mike Nichols	director
	Itzhak Perlman	musician
2004	Warren Beatty	film actor, director
	Ossie Davis	actor, writer, producer, director
	Ruby Dee	actress, writer
	Elton John	musician
	Joan Sutherland	opera singer
	John Williams	composer
2005	Tony Bennett	singer
	Suzanne Farrell	dancer, teacher
	Julie Harris	actress
	Robert Redford	film actor, director, producer
	Tina Turner	singer, actress
2006	Zubin Mehta	conductor
	Dolly Parton	singer, actress
	Andrew Lloyd Webber	composer
	Steven Spielberg	film director, producer
	William "Smokey" Robinson	singer
2007	Steve Martin	actor, writer
	Diana Ross	singer, actress
	Leon Fleisher	pianist, conductor
	Martin Scorsese	film director
	Brian Wilson	composer, singer
2008	Morgan Freeman	actor
	George Jones	country musician
	Barbra Streisand	singer, actress, director, producer, writer
	Twyla Tharp	dancer, choreographer
	Pete Townshend	musician, composer
	Roger Daltrey	singer, composer, actor

National Medal of Arts

The National Medal of Arts, awarded annually since 1985 by the National Endowment for the Arts (NEA) and the president of the United States, honors artists and art patrons for remarkable contributions to American arts. Both the NEA and the president choose candidates for the award, and the winners are selected by the president.

Web site: <www.nea.gov/honors/medals/medalists_year.html>.

YEAR	NAME	FIELD
1985	Elliott Carter, Jr.	composer
	Ralph Ellison	writer
	José Ferrer	actor
	Martha Graham	dancer, choreographer
	Louise Nevelson	sculptor
	Georgia O'Keeffe	painter
	Leontyne Price	opera singer
	Dorothy Buffum Chandler	patron
	Lincoln Kirstein	patron
	Paul Mellon	patron
	Alice Tully	patron
	Hallmark Cards, Inc.	patron
1986	Marian Anderson	opera singer
	Frank Capra	film director
	Aaron Copland	composer
	Willem de Kooning	painter
	Agnes de Mille	dancer, choreographer
	Eva Le Gallienne	actress, producer
	Alan Lomax	ethnomusicologist
	Lewis Mumford	architectural critic
	Eudora Welty	writer
	Dominique de Menil	patron
	Exxon Corp.	patron
	Seymour H. Knox	patron
1987	Romare Bearden	painter
	Ella Fitzgerald	singer
	Howard Nemerov	writer, scholar
	Alwin Nikolais	choreographer
	Isamu Noguchi	sculptor
	William Schuman	composer
	Robert Penn Warren	writer
	J.W. Fisher	patron
	Armand Hammer	patron
	Sydney and Frances Lewis	patrons
1988	Saul Bellow	writer
	Helen Hayes	actress
	Gordon Parks	filmmaker, photographer, writer
	I.M. Pei	architect
	Jerome Robbins	dancer, choreographer
	Rudolf Serkin	pianist
	Virgil Thomson	composer, music critic
	Sydney J. Freedberg	art historian, curator
	Roger L. Stevens	arts administrator
	Brooke Astor	patron
	Francis Goelet	patron
	Obert C. Tanner	patron
1989	Leopold Adler	historic preservationist, civic leader
	Katherine Dunham	dancer, choreographer
	Alfred Eisenstaedt	photojournalist
	Martin Friedman	museum director
	Leigh Gerdine	civic leader, patron
	Dizzy Gillespie	jazz musician
	Walker K. Hancock	sculptor
	Vladimir Horowitz[1]	pianist
	Czeslaw Milosz	writer
	Robert Motherwell	painter
	John Updike	writer
	Dayton Hudson Corp.	patron

YEAR	NAME	FIELD
1990	George Abbott	theater producer, director, writer
	Hume Cronyn	actor, director
	Jessica Tandy	actress
	Merce Cunningham	dancer, choreographer
	Jasper Johns	painter, sculptor
	Jacob Lawrence	painter
	B.B. King	blues musician
	Beverly Sills	opera singer
	Ian McHarg	landscape architect
	Harris and Carroll Sterling Masterson	patrons
	David Lloyd Kreeger	patron
	Southeastern Bell Corp.	patron
1991	Maurice Abravanel	conductor, music director
	Roy Acuff	country musician
	Pietro Belluschi	architect
	J. Carter Brown	museum director
	Charles "Honi" Coles	tap dancer
	John O. Crosby	opera director, conductor
	Richard Diebenkorn	painter
	Isaac Stern	violinist
	Kitty Carlisle Hart	actress, singer
	R. Philip Hanes, Jr.	patron
	Pearl Primus	choreographer, anthropologist
	Texaco Inc.	patron
1992	Marilyn Horne	opera singer
	James Earl Jones	actor
	Allan Houser	sculptor
	Minnie Pearl	Grand Ole Opry performer
	Robert Saudek	television producer, museum director
	Earl Scruggs	banjo player
	Robert Shaw	conductor
	Billy Taylor	jazz pianist
	Robert Venturi and Denise Scott Brown	architects
	Robert Wise	film director
	AT&T	patron
	Lila Wallace– Reader's Digest Fund	patron
1993	Cabell "Cab" Calloway	jazz musician
	Ray Charles	soul musician
	Bess Lomax Hawes	folklorist, musician
	Stanley Kunitz	poet
	Robert Merrill	opera singer
	Arthur Miller	playwright
	Robert Rauschenberg	painter
	Lloyd Richards	theater director
	William Styron	writer
	Paul Taylor	dancer, choreographer
	Billy Wilder	film director, writer
	Walter and Leonore Annenberg	patrons
1994	Harry Belafonte	folksinger, actor
	Dave Brubeck	jazz musician

National Medal of Arts (continued)

YEAR	NAME	FIELD	YEAR	NAME	FIELD
1994	Celia Cruz	salsa singer	1999	Aretha Franklin	soul singer
(cont.)	Dorothy DeLay	violin instructor		Michael Graves	architect, designer
	Julie Harris	actress		Odetta	folksinger
	Erick Hawkins	dancer, choreographer		Norman Lear	television producer, writer
	Gene Kelly	dancer, actor			
	Pete Seeger	folk musician		Rosetta LeNoire	actress, theater founder
	Wayne Thiebaud	painter			
	Richard Wilbur	poet		Harvey Lichtenstein	arts administrator
	Young Audiences	arts organization		Lydia Mendoza	Tejano musician
	Catherine Filene Shouse	patron		George Segal	sculptor
				Maria Tallchief	ballet dancer
1995	Licia Albanese	opera singer		The Juilliard School	performing arts school
	Gwendolyn Brooks	poet		Irene Diamond	patron
	Ossie Davis and Ruby Dee	actors	2000	Maya Angelou	poet, writer
	David Diamond	composer		Eddy Arnold	country musician
	James Ingo Freed	architect		Mikhail Baryshnikov	dancer, dance company director
	Bob Hope	entertainer		Benny Carter	jazz musician
	Roy Lichtenstein	painter		Chuck Close	painter
	Arthur Mitchell	dancer, choreographer		Horton Foote	dramatist
	William S. Monroe	bluegrass musician		Claes Oldenburg	sculptor
	Urban Gateways	arts education organization		Itzhak Perlman	violinist
				Harold Prince	theater director
	B. Gerald and Iris Cantor	patrons		Barbra Streisand	singer, actress
				Lewis Manilow	patron
1996	Edward Albee	playwright		National Public Radio cutural programming division	broadcaster
	Sarah Caldwell	opera conductor			
	Harry Callahan	photographer	2001	Alvin Ailey Dance Foundation	modern dance company and school
	Zelda Fichandler	theater founder, director			
				Rudolfo Anaya	writer
	Eduardo "Lalo" Guerrero	Chicano musician		Johnny Cash	country musician
				Kirk Douglas	actor
	Lionel Hampton	swing musician		Helen Frankenthaler	painter
	Bella Lewitzky	dancer, choreographer		Judith Jamison	dancer, choreographer
	Robert Redford	actor, film director		Yo-Yo Ma	cellist
	Maurice Sendak	illustrator, writer		Mike Nichols	theater and film director
	Stephen Sondheim	composer, lyricist			
	Boys Choir of Harlem	choir	2002	Florence Knoll Bassett	designer, architect
	Vera List	patron			
1997	Louise Bourgeois	sculptor		Trisha Brown	dancer, choreographer
	Betty Carter	jazz singer		Philippe de Montebello	museum director
	Daniel Urban Kiley	landscape architect			
	Angela Lansbury	actress		Uta Hagen	actress, educator
	James Levine	opera conductor, pianist		Lawrence Halprin	landscape architect
				Al Hirschfeld[1]	artist, caricaturist
	Tito Puente	jazz and mambo musician		George Jones	singer, songwriter
				Ming Cho Lee	painter, stage designer
	Jason Robards	actor		William "Smokey" Robinson, Jr.	singer, songwriter
	Edward Villella	dancer, choreographer			
	Doc Watson	folk and country musician	2003	Austin City Limits	television show
				Beverly Cleary	children's book author
	MacDowell Colony	artists' colony		Rafe Esquith	arts educator
	Agnes Gund	patron		Suzanne Farrell	dancer, artistic director, arts educator
1998	Jacques d'Amboise	dancer, choreographer			
				Buddy Guy	blues musician
	Antoine "Fats" Domino	rock-and-roll musician		Ron Howard	actor, director, writer
	Ramblin' Jack Elliott	folk musician		Mormon Tabernacle Choir	choir
	Frank O. Gehry	architect			
	Agnes Martin	painter		Leonard Slatkin	conductor
	Gregory Peck	actor		George Strait	singer, songwriter
	Roberta Peters	opera singer		Tommy Tune	director, actor
	Philip Roth	writer	2004	Andrew W. Mellon Foundation	patron
	Gwen Verdon	actress, dancer			
	Steppenwolf Theatre Company	arts organization		Ray Bradbury	writer
				Carlisle Floyd	opera composer
	Sara Lee Corp.	patron		Frederick "Rick" Hart[1]	sculptor
	Barbara Handman	patron		Anthony Hecht[1]	poet

National Medal of Arts (continued)

YEAR	NAME	FIELD
2004 (cont.)	John Ruthven	painter
	Vincent Scully	architectural historian
	Twyla Tharp	dancer, choreographer
2005	Louis Auchincloss	writer
	James DePreist	conductor
	Paquito D'Rivera	musician
	Robert Duvall	actor
	Leonard Garment	arts advocate
	Ollie Johnston	animator, artist
	Wynton Marsalis	musician, educator
	Pennsylvania Academy of the Fine Arts	arts academy
	Tina Ramirez	dancer, choreographer
	Dolly Parton	singer, songwriter
2006	William Bolcom	composer
	Cyd Charisse	dancer
	Roy R. DeCarava	photographer
	Wilhelmina C. Holladay	patron
	Interlochen Center for the Arts	music school
	Erich Kunzel	conductor
	Preservation Hall Jazz Band	jazz ensemble

YEAR	NAME	FIELD
2006 (cont.)	Gregory Rabassa	translator
	Viktor Schreckengost	industrial designer
	Dr. Ralph Stanley	bluegrass musician
2007	Morten Lauridsen	composer
	N. Scott Momaday	author, poet
	Roy R. Neuberger	patron
	R. Craig Noel	theater director
	Les Paul	guitarist, inventor
	Henry Steinway	patron
	George Tooker	painter
	Lionel Hampton International Jazz Festival	music competition, festival
	Andrew Wyeth	painter
2008	Olivia de Havilland	actress
	Fisk Jubilee Singers	choral ensemble
	Ford's Theatre Society	theater, museum
	Hank Jones	jazz musician
	Stan Lee	comic book writer
	José Limón Dance Foundation	dance company
	Jesús Moroles	sculptor
	Presser Foundation	patron
	Sherman Brothers	songwriters

[1]Awarded posthumously.

Spingarn Medal

The National Association for the Advancement of Colored People (NAACP) presents the medal for distinguished achievement among African Americans. The medal is named for early NAACP activist Joel E. Spingarn.

YEAR	NAME	FIELD
1915	Ernest Everett Just	zoologist, marine biologist
1916	Charles Young	army officer
1917	Harry Thacker Burleigh	singer, composer
1918	William Stanley Braithwaite	poet, literary critic
1919	Archibald Henry Grimké	lawyer, diplomat, social activist
1920	W.E.B. Du Bois	sociologist, social activist
1921	Charles S. Gilpin	actor
1922	Mary Burnett Talbert	civil rights activist
1923	George Washington Carver	agricultural chemist
1924	Roland Hayes	singer, composer
1925	James Weldon Johnson	diplomat, anthologist
1926	Carter G. Woodson	historian
1927	Anthony Overton	businessman
1928	Charles W. Chesnutt	writer
1929	Mordecai W. Johnson	minister, university president
1930	Henry Alexander Hunt	educator, government official
1931	Richard B. Harrison	actor
1932	Robert Russa Moton	educator, civil rights leader
1933	Max Yergan	civil rights leader
1934	William T.B. Williams	educator
1935	Mary McLeod Bethune	educator, social activist
1936	John Hope (posthumously)	educator
1937	Walter White	civil rights leader
1938	no medal awarded	
1939	Marian Anderson	opera singer

YEAR	NAME	FIELD
1940	Louis T. Wright	surgeon, civil rights leader
1941	Richard Wright	writer
1942	A. Philip Randolph	labor and civil rights leader
1943	William H. Hastie	lawyer, judge
1944	Charles Richard Drew	surgeon, research scientist
1945	Paul Robeson	actor, singer, social activist
1946	Thurgood Marshall	lawyer, US Supreme Court justice
1947	Percy L. Julian	chemist
1948	Channing H. Tobias	civil rights leader
1949	Ralph Bunche	diplomat, scholar
1950	Charles Hamilton Houston (posthumously)	lawyer
1951	Mabel Keaton Staupers	nurse, social activist
1952	Harry T. Moore (posthumously)	civil rights activist, educator
1953	Paul R. Williams	architect
1954	Theodore K. Lawless	dermatologist, philanthropist
1955	Carl Murphy	journalist, civil rights activist
1956	Jackie Robinson	baseball player
1957	Martin Luther King, Jr.	civil rights leader
1958	Daisy Bates and the Little Rock Nine	school integration activists
1959	Duke Ellington	jazz musician
1960	Langston Hughes	writer
1961	Kenneth Bancroft Clark	educator
1962	Robert C. Weaver	economist, government official
1963	Medgar Evers (posthumously)	civil rights activist

Spingarn Medal (continued)

YEAR	NAME	FIELD
1964	Roy Wilkins	civil rights leader
1965	Leontyne Price	opera singer
1966	John H. Johnson	publisher
1967	Edward W. Brooke III	lawyer, US senator
1968	Sammy Davis, Jr.	singer, dancer, entertainer
1969	Clarence M. Mitchell, Jr.	civil rights lobbyist
1970	Jacob Lawrence	painter
1971	Leon H. Sullivan	minister, civil rights activist
1972	Gordon Parks	filmmaker, photographer, writer
1973	Wilson C. Riles	educator
1974	Damon Keith	lawyer, judge
1975	Hank Aaron	baseball player
1976	Alvin Ailey	dancer, choreogrpher
1977	Alex Haley	writer
1978	Andrew Young	civil rights leader
1979	Rosa Parks	civil rights activist
1980	Rayford W. Logan	educator, writer
1981	Coleman A. Young	labor activist, politician
1982	Benjamin E. Mays	educator, minister
1983	Lena Horne	singer, actress
1984	Thomas Bradley	politician
1985	Bill Cosby	actor, comedian
1986	Benjamin L. Hooks	civil rights leader, government official
1987	Percy Ellis Sutton	civil rights activist, politician
1988	Frederick Douglass Patterson (posthumously)	educator

YEAR	NAME	FIELD
1989	Jesse Jackson	minister, politician, civil rights leader
1990	L. Douglas Wilder	politician
1991	Colin Powell	army general, government official
1992	Barbara Jordan	lawyer, politician
1993	Dorothy I. Height	social activist
1994	Maya Angelou	poet
1995	John Hope Franklin	historian, educator
1996	A. Leon Higginbotham	lawyer, judge, scholar
1997	Carl T. Rowan	journalist, commentator
1998	Myrlie Evers-Williams	civil rights activist
1999	Earl G. Graves	publisher
2000	Oprah Winfrey	television host, media personality
2001	Vernon E. Jordan, Jr.	lawyer, civil rights activist
2002	John Lewis	politician, civil rights activist
2003	Constance Baker Motley	judge, lawyer, civil rights activist
2004	Robert L. Carter	judge, lawyer, civil rights activist
2005	Oliver W. Hill	lawyer, civil rights activist
2006	Benjamin S. Carson	physician
2007	John Conyers, Jr.	politician
2008	Ruby Dee	actress, writer
2009	Julian Bond	statesman, civil rights activist

Did you know? Dalmatians were originally bred as guard dogs for stagecoaches. Because they were used to running long distances and being around horses, and because their bright white coats with black spots were easily visible, they were chosen by fire departments to run ahead of horse-drawn fire engines, barking a warning and clearing the path of onlookers. With the advent of motorized fire trucks, Dalmatians were retained as the official mascot of firehouses everywhere.

Science Honors

Fields Medal

The Fields Medal, officially known as the International Medal for Outstanding Discoveries in Mathematics, is granted every four years to between two and four mathematicians for outstanding or groundbreaking research. It is traditionally given to mathematicians under the age of 40. Prize: Can$15,000 (about US$13,200).

YEAR	NAME	BIRTHPLACE	PRIMARY RESEARCH
1936	Lars Ahlfors	Helsinki, Finland	Riemann surfaces
	Jesse Douglas	New York NY	Plateau problem
1950	Laurent Schwartz	Paris, France	functional analysis
	Atle Selberg	Langesund, Norway	number theory
1954	Kunihiko Kodaira	Tokyo, Japan	algebraic geometry
	Jean-Pierre Serre	Bages, France	algebraic topology
1958	Klaus Roth	Breslau, Germany	number theory
	René Thom	Montbéliard, France	topology
1962	Lars Hörmander	Mjällby, Sweden	partial differential equations
	John Milnor	Orange NJ	differential topology
1966	Michael Atiyah	London, England	topology
	Paul Cohen	Long Branch NJ	set theory
	Alexandre Grothendieck	Berlin, Germany	algebraic geometry
	Stephen Smale	Flint MI	topology

Fields Medal (continued)

YEAR	NAME	BIRTHPLACE	PRIMARY RESEARCH
1970	Alan Baker	London, England	number theory
	Heisuke Hironaka	Yamaguchi prefecture, Japan	algebraic geometry
	Sergey Novikov	Gorky, USSR (now in Russia)	topology
	John Thompson	Ottawa KS	group theory
1974	Enrico Bombieri	Milan, Italy	number theory
	David Mumford	Worth, Sussex, England	algebraic geometry
1978	Pierre Deligne	Brussels, Belgium	algebraic geometry
	Charles Fefferman	Washington DC	classical analysis
	Gregory Margulis	Moscow, USSR (now in Russia)	Lie groups
	Daniel Quillen	Orange NJ	algebraic K-theory
1983	Alain Connes	Darguignan, France	operator theory
	William Thurston	Washington DC	topology
	Shing-Tung Yau	Swatow, China	differential geometry
1986	Simon Donaldson	Cambridge, England	topology
	Gerd Faltings	Gelsenkirchen, West Germany	Mordell conjecture
	Michael Freedman	Los Angeles CA	Poincaré conjecture
1990	Vladimir Drinfeld	Kharkov, USSR (now in Ukraine)	algebraic geometry
	Vaughan Jones	Gisborne, New Zealand	knot theory
	Shigefumi Mori	Nagoya, Japan	algebraic geometry
	Edward Witten	Baltimore MD	superstring theory
1994	Jean Bourgain	Ostend, Belgium	analysis
	Pierre-Louis Lions	Grasse, France	partial differential equations
	Jean-Christophe Yoccoz	Paris, France	dynamical systems
	Yefim Zelmanov	Khabarovsk, USSR (now in Russia)	group theory
1998	Richard Borcherds	Cape Town, South Africa	mathematical physics
	William Gowers	Marlborough, Wiltshire, England	functional analysis
	Maksim Kontsevich	Khimki, USSR (now in Russia)	mathematical physics
	Curt McMullen	Berkeley CA	chaos theory
2002	Laurent Lafforgue	Antony, France	number theory and analysis
	Vladimir Voevodsky	Moscow, USSR (now in Russia)	algebraic geometry
2006	Andrei Okounkov	Moscow, USSR (now in Russia)	algebraic geometry
	Grigory Perelman (declined)	Leningrad, USSR (now in Russia)	Ricci flow
	Terence Tao	Adelaide, SA, Australia	prime numbers, nonlinear equations
	Wendelin Werner	Cologne, West Germany	mathematics of critical phenomena

National Medal of Science

The National Medal of Science was established by Congress in 1959. Awarded annually since 1962 by the National Science Foundation, it recognizes notable achievements in mathematics, engineering, and the physical, natural, and social sciences. A presidentially appointed committee selects the winners from a pool of nominees.

National Science Foundation Web site: <www.nsf.gov/od/nms/medal.jsp>.

YEAR	NAME	FIELD
1962	Theodore von Karman	aerospace engineering
1963	Luis W. Alvarez	physics
	Vannevar Bush	electrical engineering
	John Robinson Pierce	communications engineering
	Cornelius Barnardus van Niel	biology
	Norbert Wiener	mathematics
1964	Roger Adams	chemistry
	Othmar Herman Ammann	civil engineering
	Theodosius Dobzhansky	genetics
	Charles Stark Draper	aerospace engineering
	Solomon Lefschetz	mathematics
	Neal Elgar Miller	psychology
	H. Marston Morse	mathematics
	Marshall Warren Nirenberg	biochemistry
	Julian Seymour Schwinger	physics

YEAR	NAME	FIELD
1964 (cont.)	Harold C. Urey	chemistry
	Robert Burns Woodward	chemistry
1965	John Bardeen	physics
	Peter J.W. Debye	physical chemistry
	Hugh L. Dryden	physics
	Clarence L. Johnson	aerospace engineering
	Leon M. Lederman	physics
	Warren K. Lewis	chemical engineering
	Francis Peyton Rous	pathology
	William W. Rubey	geology
	George Gaylord Simpson	paleontology
	Donald D. Van Slyke	chemistry
	Oscar Zariski	mathematics
1966	Jacob A.B. Bjerknes	meteorology
	Subrahmanyan Chandrasekhar	astrophysics
	Henry Eyring	chemistry
	Edward F. Knipling	entomology
	Fritz Albert Lipmann	biochemistry
	John Willard Milnor	mathematics

National Medal of Science (continued)

YEAR	NAME	FIELD
1966 (cont.)	William C. Rose	biochemistry
	Claude E. Shannon	mathematics, electrical engineering
	John H. Van Vleck	physics
	Sewall Wright	genetics
	Vladimir Kosma Zworykin	electrical engineering
1967	Jesse W. Beams	physics
	Francis Birch	geophysics
	Gregory Breit	physics
	Paul Joseph Cohen	mathematics
	Kenneth S. Cole	biophysics
	Louis P. Hammett	chemistry
	Harry F. Harlow	psychology
	Michael Heidelberger	immunology
	George B. Kistiakowsky	chemistry
	Edwin Herbert Land	physics
	Igor I. Sikorsky	aircraft design
	Alfred H. Sturtevant	genetics
1968	Horace A. Barker	biochemistry
	Paul D. Bartlett	chemistry
	Bernard B. Brodie	pharmacology
	Detlev W. Bronk	biophysics
	J. Presper Eckert, Jr.	engineering, computer science
	Herbert Friedman	astrophysics
	Jay L. Lush	livestock genetics
	Nathan M. Newmark	civil engineering
	Jerzy Neyman	statistics
	Lars Onsager	chemistry
	B.F. Skinner	psychology
	Eugene Paul Wigner	mathematical physics
1969	Herbert C. Brown	chemistry
	William Feller	mathematics
	Robert J. Huebner	virology
	Jack Kilby	electrical engineering
	Ernst Mayr	biology
	Wolfgang K.H. Panofsky	physics
1970	Richard Dagobert Brauer	mathematics
	Robert H. Dicke	physics
	Barbara McClintock	genetics
	George E. Mueller	physics
	Albert Bruce Sabin	medicine, vaccine development
	Allan R. Sandage	astronomy
	John C. Slater	physics
	John Archibald Wheeler	physics
	Saul Winstein	chemistry
1971	no awards given	
1972	no awards given	
1973	Daniel I. Arnon	biochemistry
	Carl Djerassi	chemistry
	Harold E. Edgerton	electrical engineering, photography
	Maurice Ewing	geophysics
	Arie Jan Haagen-Smit	biochemistry
	Vladimir Haensel	chemical engineering
	Frederick Seitz	physics
	Earl W. Sutherland, Jr.	biochemistry
	John Wilder Tukey	statistics
	Richard T. Whitcomb	aerospace engineering
	Robert Rathbun Wilson	particle physics
1974	Nicolaas Bloembergen	physics
	Britton Chance	biophysics
	Erwin Chargaff	biochemistry
	Paul J. Flory	physical chemistry
	William A. Fowler	nuclear astrophysics
	Kurt Gödel	mathematics
	Rudolf Kompfner	physics
	James Van Gundia Neel	genetics
	Linus Pauling	chemistry
	Ralph Brazelton Peck	geotechnical engineering
	Kenneth Sanborn Pitzer	physical chemistry
	James Augustine Shannon	physiology
	Abel Wolman	sanitary engineering
1975	John W. Backus	computer science
	Manson Benedict	nuclear engineering
	Hans Albrecht Bethe	theoretical physics
	Shiing-shen Chern	mathematics
	George B. Dantzig	mathematics
	Hallowell Davis	physiology
	Paul Gyorgy	medicine, vitamin research
	Sterling Brown Hendricks	chemistry
	Joseph O. Hirschfelder	chemistry
	William Hayward Pickering	physics
	Lewis H. Sarett	chemistry
	Frederick Emmons Terman	electrical engineering
	Orville Alvin Vogel	research agronomy
	Wernher von Braun	aerospace engineering
	E. Bright Wilson, Jr.	chemistry
	Chien-Shiung Wu	physics
1976	Morris Cohen	materials science
	Kurt Otto Friedrichs	mathematics
	Peter C. Goldmark	communications engineering
	Samuel Abraham Goudsmit	physics
	Roger Charles Louis Guillemin	physiology
	Herbert S. Gutowsky	chemistry
	Erwin W. Mueller	physics
	Keith Roberts Porter	cell biology
	Efraim Racker	biochemistry
	Frederick D. Rossini	chemistry
	Verner E. Suomi	meteorology
	Henry Taube	chemistry
	George Eugene Uhlenbeck	physics
	Hassler Whitney	mathematics
	Edward O. Wilson	biology
1977	no awards given	
1978	no awards given	
1979	Robert H. Burris	biochemistry
	Elizabeth C. Crosby	neuroanatomy
	Joseph L. Doob	mathematics
	Richard P. Feynman	theoretical physics
	Donald E. Knuth	computer science
	Arthur Kornberg	biochemistry
	Emmett N. Leith	electrical engineering
	Herman F. Mark	chemistry

National Medal of Science (continued)

YEAR	NAME	FIELD	YEAR	NAME	FIELD
1979 (cont.)	Raymond D. Mindlin	mechanical engineering	1986 (cont.)	George Emil Palade	cell biology
	Robert N. Noyce	computer science		Herbert A. Simon	social science
	Severo Ochoa	biochemistry		Joan A. Steitz	molecular biology
	Earl R. Parker	materials science		Frank H. Westheimer	chemistry
	Edward M. Purcell	physics		Chen Ning Yang	theoretical physics
	Simon Ramo	electrical engineering		Antoni Zygmund	mathematics
	John H. Sinfelt	chemical engineering	1987	Philip Hauge Abelson	physical chemistry
	Lyman Spitzer, Jr.	astrophysics		Anne Anastasi	psychology
	Earl Reece Stadtman	biochemistry		Robert Byron Bird	chemical engineering
	George Ledyard Stebbins	botany, genetics		Raoul Bott	mathematics
	Victor F. Weisskopf	physics		Michael E. DeBakey	heart surgery
	Paul Alfred Weiss	biology		Theodor O. Diener	plant pathology
1980	*no awards given*			Harry Eagle	cell biology
1981	Philip Handler	biochemistry		Walter M. Elsasser	physics
1982	Philip W. Anderson	physics		Michael H. Freedman	mathematics
	Seymour Benzer	molecular biology		William S. Johnson	chemistry
	Glenn W. Burton	genetics		Har Gobind Khorana	biochemistry
	Mildred Cohn	biochemistry		Paul C. Lauterbur	chemistry
	F. Albert Cotton	chemistry		Rita Levi-Montalcini	neurology
	Edward H. Heinemann	aerospace engineering		George E. Pake	research, physics
	Donald L. Katz	chemical engineering		H. Bolton Seed	civil engineering
	Yoichiro Nambu	theoretical physics		George J. Stigler	economics
	Marshall H. Stone	mathematics		Walter H. Stockmayer	chemistry
	Gilbert Stork	organic chemistry		Max Tishler	chemistry
	Edward Teller	nuclear physics		James Alfred Van Allen	physics
	Charles Hard Townes	physics		Ernst Weber	electrical engineering
1983	Howard L. Bachrach	biochemistry	1988	William O. Baker	chemistry
	Paul Berg	biochemistry		Konrad E. Bloch	biochemistry
	E. Margaret Burbidge	astronomy		David Allan Bromley	physics
	Maurice Goldhaber	physics		Michael S. Brown	molecular genetics
	Herman H. Goldstine	computer science		Paul C.W. Chu	physics
	William R. Hewlett	electrical engineering		Stanley N. Cohen	genetics
	Roald Hoffmann	chemistry		Elias James Corey	chemistry
	Helmut E. Landsberg	climatology		Daniel C. Drucker	engineering education
	George M. Low	aerospace engineering		Milton Friedman	economics
	Walter H. Munk	oceanography		Joseph L. Goldstein	molecular genetics
	George C. Pimentel	chemistry		Ralph E. Gomory	mathematics, research
	Frederick Reines	physics		Willis M. Hawkins	aerospace engineering
	Wendell L. Roelofs	chemistry, entomology		Maurice R. Hilleman	vaccine research
	Bruno B. Rossi	astrophysics		George W. Housner	earthquake engineering
	Berta V. Scharrer	neuroscience		Eric Kandel	neurobiology
	John Robert Schrieffer	physics		Joseph B. Keller	mathematics
	Isadore M. Singer	mathematics		Walter Kohn	physics
	John G. Trump	electrical engineering		Norman Foster Ramsey	physics
	Richard N. Zare	chemistry		Jack Steinberger	physics
1984	*no awards given*			Rosalyn S. Yalow	medical physics
1985	*no awards given*		1989	Arnold O. Beckman	chemistry
1986	Solomon J. Buchsbaum	physics		Richard B. Bernstein	chemistry
	Stanley Cohen	biochemistry		Melvin Calvin	biochemistry
	Horace R. Crane	physics		Harry G. Drickamer	chemistry, physics
	Herman Feshbach	physics		Katherine Esau	botany
	Harry Gray	chemistry		Herbert E. Grier	aerospace engineering
	Donald A. Henderson	medicine, public health		Viktor Hamburger	biology
	Robert Hofstadter	physics		Samuel Karlin	mathematics
	Peter D. Lax	mathematics		Philip Leder	genetics
	Yuan Tseh Lee	chemistry		Joshua Lederberg	genetics
	Hans Wolfgang Liepmann	aerospace engineering		Saunders Mac Lane	mathematics
	T.Y. Lin	civil engineering		Rudolph A. Marcus	chemistry
	Carl S. Marvel	chemistry		Harden M. McConnell	chemistry
	Vernon B. Mountcastle	neurophysiology		Eugene N. Parker	theoretical astrophysics
	Bernard M. Oliver	electrical engineering			

National Medal of Science (continued)

YEAR	NAME	FIELD
1989	Robert P. Sharp	geology
(cont.)	Donald C. Spencer	mathematics
	Roger Wolcott Sperry	neurobiology
	Henry M. Stommel	oceanography
	Harland G. Wood	biochemistry
1990	Baruj Benacerraf	pathology, immunology
	Elkan R. Blout	chemistry
	Herbert W. Boyer	biochemistry, genetics
	George F. Carrier	mathematics
	Allan MacLeod Cormack	physics
	Mildred S. Dresselhaus	physics
	Karl August Folkers	chemistry
	Nick Holonyak, Jr.	electrical engineering
	Leonid Hurwicz	economics
	Stephen Cole Kleene	mathematics
	Daniel E. Koshland, Jr.	biochemistry
	Edward B. Lewis	genetics
	John McCarthy	computer science
	Edwin Mattison McMillan	nuclear physics
	David G. Nathan	pediatrics
	Robert V. Pound	physics
	Roger R.D. Revelle	oceanography
	John D. Roberts	chemistry
	Patrick Suppes	philosophy, statistics education
	E. Donnall Thomas	medicine
1991	Mary Ellen Avery	pediatrics
	Ronald Breslow	chemistry
	Alberto P. Calderon	mathematics
	Gertrude B. Elion	pharmacology
	George H. Heilmeier	electrical engineering
	Dudley R. Herschbach	chemistry
	G. Evelyn Hutchinson	zoology
	Elvin A. Kabat	immunology
	Robert W. Kates	geography
	Luna B. Leopold	hydrology, geology
	Salvador Luria	biology
	Paul A. Marks	hematology, cancer research
	George A. Miller	psychology
	Arthur L. Schawlow	physics
	Glenn T. Seaborg	nuclear chemistry
	Folke K. Skoog	botany
	H. Guyford Stever	aerospace engineering
	Edward C. Stone	physics
	Steven Weinberg	nuclear physics
	Paul C. Zamecnik	molecular biology
1992	Eleanor J. Gibson	psychology
	Allen Newell	computer science
	Calvin F. Quate	electrical engineering
	Eugene M. Shoemaker	planetary geology
	Howard E. Simmons, Jr.	chemistry
	Maxine F. Singer	biochemistry, administration
	Howard Martin Temin	virology
	John Roy Whinnery	electrical engineering
1993	Alfred Y. Cho	electrical engineering
	Donald J. Cram	chemistry
	Val Logsdon Fitch	particle physics
	Norman Hackerman	chemistry
	Martin D. Kruskal	mathematics
	Daniel Nathans	microbiology

YEAR	NAME	FIELD
1993	Vera C. Rubin	astronomy
(cont.)	Salome G. Waelsch	molecular genetics
1994	Ray W. Clough	civil engineering
	John Cocke	computer science
	Thomas Eisner	chemical ecology
	George S. Hammond	chemistry
	Robert K. Merton	sociology
	Elizabeth F. Neufeld	biochemistry
	Albert W. Overhauser	physics
	Frank Press	geophysics, administration
1995	Thomas Robert Cech	biochemistry
	Hans Georg Dehmelt	physics
	Peter M. Goldreich	astrophysics
	Hermann A. Haus	electrical engineering
	Isabella L. Karle	chemistry
	Louis Nirenberg	mathematics
	Alexander Rich	molecular biology
	Roger N. Shepard	psychology
1996	Wallace S. Broecker	geochemistry
	Norman Davidson	chemistry, molecular biology
	James L. Flanagan	electrical engineering
	Richard M. Karp	computer science
	C. Kumar N. Patel	electrical engineering
	Ruth Patrick	limnology
	Paul Samuelson	economics
	Stephen Smale	mathematics
1997	William K. Estes	psychology
	Darleane C. Hoffman	chemistry
	Harold S. Johnston	chemistry
	Marshall N. Rosenbluth	theoretical plasma physics
	Martin Schwarzschild	astrophysics
	James Dewey Watson	genetics, biophysics
	Robert A. Weinberg	biology, cancer research
	George W. Wetherill	planetary science
	Shing-Tung Yau	mathematics
1998	Bruce N. Ames	biochemistry, cancer research
	Don L. Anderson	geophysics
	John N. Bahcall	astrophysics
	John W. Cahn	materials science
	Cathleen Synge Morawetz	mathematics
	Janet D. Rowley	medicine, cancer research
	Eli Ruckenstein	chemical engineering
	George M. Whitesides	chemistry
	William Julius Wilson	sociology
1999	David Baltimore	virology, administration
	Felix E. Browder	mathematics
	Ronald R. Coifman	mathematics
	James Watson Cronin	particle physics
	Jared Diamond	physiology
	Leo P. Kadanoff	theoretical physics
	Lynn Margulis	microbiology
	Stuart A. Rice	chemistry
	John Ross	chemistry
	Susan Solomon	atmospheric science
	Robert M. Solow	economics
	Kenneth N. Stevens	electrical engineering, speech
2000	Nancy C. Andreasen	psychiatry
	John D. Baldeschwieler	chemistry

National Medal of Science (continued)

YEAR	NAME	FIELD
2000	Gary S. Becker	economics
(cont.)	Yuan-Cheng B. Fung	bioengineering
	Ralph F. Hirschmann	chemistry
	Willis Eugene Lamb, Jr.	physics
	Jeremiah P. Ostriker	astrophysics
	Peter H. Raven	botany
	John Griggs Thompson	mathematics
	Karen K. Uhlenbeck	mathematics
	Gilbert F. White	geography
	Carl R. Woese	microbiology
2001	Andreas Acrivos	chemical engineering
	Francisco J. Ayala	molecular biology
	George F. Bass	nautical archaeology
	Mario R. Capecchi	genetics
	Marvin L. Cohen	materials science
	Ernest R. Davidson	chemistry
	Raymond Davis, Jr.	chemistry, astrophysics
	Ann M. Graybiel	neuroscience
	Charles D. Keéling	oceanography
	Gene E. Likens	ecology
	Victor A. McKusick	medical genetics
	Calyampudi R. Rao	mathematics, statistics
	Gabor A. Somorjai	chemistry
	Elias M. Stein	mathematics
	Harold Varmus	virology, administration
2002	Leo L. Beranek	engineering
	John I. Brauman	chemistry
	James E. Darnell	cell biology
	Richard L. Garwin	physics
	James G. Glimm	mathematics, statistics
	W. Jason Morgan	geophysics
	Evelyn M. Witkin	genetics
	Edward Witten	mathematical physics
2003	J. Michael Bishop	microbiology
	G. Brent Dalrymple	geology
	Carl R. de Boor	mathematics
	Riccardo Giacconi	astrophysics

YEAR	NAME	FIELD
2003	R. Duncan Luce	cognitive science
(cont.)	John M. Prausnitz	chemical engineering
	Solomon H. Snyder	neuroscience
	Charles Yanofsky	molecular biology
2004	Kenneth J. Arrow	economics
	Norman E. Borlaug	agriculture
	Robert N. Clayton	geochemistry
	Edwin N. Lightfoot	engineering
	Stephen J. Lippard	chemistry
	Phillip A. Sharp	molecular biology, biochemistry
	Thomas E. Starzl	medicine
	Dennis P. Sullivan	mathematics
2005	Jan D. Achenbach	mechanical engineering
	Ralph A. Alpher	astronomy
	Gordon H. Bower	psychology
	Bradley Efron	statistics
	Anthony S. Fauci	immunology
	Tobin J. Marks	chemistry
	Lonnie G. Thompson	glaciology
	Torsten N. Wiesel	neurobiology
2006	Hyman Bass	mathematics
	Marvin H. Caruthers	genetic engineering
	Rita R. Colwell	marine microbiology
	Peter B. Dervan	organic chemistry
	Nina V. Fedoroff	molecular biology
	Daniel Kleppner	atomic physics
	Robert S. Langer	medical research
	Lubert Stryer	biochemistry
2007	Fay Ajzenberg-Selove	nuclear physics
	Mostafa A. El-Sayed	laser dynamics
	Leonard Kleinrock	Internet technology
	Robert J. Lefkowitz	receptor biology
	Bert W. O'Malley	molecular biology
	Charles P. Slichter	condensed-matter physics
	Andrew J. Viterbi	wireless communications
	David J. Wineland	ionic physics

Nature, Science, Medicine, & Technology

The New Age of Extinction

by Bryan Walsh, TIME

There have been five extinction waves in the planet's history—including the Permian extinction 250 million years ago, when an estimated 70% of all terrestrial animals and 96% of all marine creatures vanished, and, most recently, the Cretaceous event 65 million years ago, which ended the reign of the dinosaurs. Though scientists have directly assessed the viability of fewer than 3% of the world's described species, the sample polling of animal populations so far suggests that we may have entered what will be the planet's sixth great extinction wave. And this time the cause isn't an errant asteroid or megavolcanoes. It's us.

Through our growing numbers, our thirst for natural resources, and, most of all, climate change—which, by one reckoning, could help carry off 20% to 30% of all species before the end of the century—we're shaping an Earth that will be biologically impoverished. A 2008 assessment by the International Union for Conservation of Nature found that nearly one in four mammals worldwide was at risk for extinction, including endangered species like the famous Tasmanian devil. Overfishing and acidification of the oceans are threatening marine species as diverse as the bluefin tuna and reef-forming corals.

Scary for fishermen, yes, but the question arises, "Why should it matter to the rest of us?" After all, nearly all the species that were ever alive in the past are gone today. Evolution demands extinction. Why should the loss of a few species among millions matter? Answer: for one thing, we're animals too, dependent on this planet like every other form of life. When we pollute and deforest and make a mess of the ecological web, we're taking out mortgages on the Earth that we can't pay back—and those loans will come due. Then there are the undiscovered organisms and animals that could serve as the basis of needed medicines—as the original ingredients of aspirin were derived from the herb meadowsweet—unless we unwittingly destroy them first.

Forests razed can grow back, polluted air and water can be cleaned—but extinction is forever. And we're not talking about losing just a few species. In fact, conservationists quietly acknowledge that we've entered an age of triage, when we might have to decide which species can truly be saved. The worst-case scenarios of habitat loss and climate change show the planet losing hundreds of thousands to millions of species, many of which we haven't even discovered yet. The result could be a virtual genocide of much of the animal world.

So if you care about tigers and tamarins, rhinos and orangutans, if you believe Earth is more than just a home for 6.7 billion human beings and counting, then you should be scared. But fear shouldn't leave us paralyzed. Environmental groups worldwide are responding with new methods to new threats to wildlife.

Conservationists are working with locals on the ground, ensuring that the protection of endangered species is tied to the welfare of the people who live closest to them.

A strategy called avoided deforestation encourages environmental protection by putting a price on the carbon locked in rain forests and allowing countries to trade credits in an international market, provided that the carbon stays in the trees and is not cut or burned. And as global warming forces animals to migrate in order to escape changing climates, conservationists hope to create protected corridors that would give species room to roam. It's uncertain that any of this will stop the sixth extinction wave, let alone preserve the biodiversity we still enjoy, but we have no choice but to try. "We have a window of opportunity," says Kassie Siegel, director of the climate, energy, and air program of the Center for Biological Diversity (CBD). "But it's slamming shut."

Well-run ecotourism can provide support for conservation, but even the best parks might be hard-pressed to compete with the potential revenues from logging, poaching, or mining. The strategy of avoided deforestation, however, offers much more. Rain forests contain billions and billions of tons of carbon; destroying the trees and releasing the carbon not only kills local species but also speeds global warming. Proposals in the global climate negotiations would allow countries to offset some of their greenhouse-gas emissions by paying rain-forest nations to preserve their trees. It's win-win, with both the climate and the critters getting a boost.

As global warming changes the climate, species will try to migrate, often right into the path of development and extinction. What good is a nature reserve—fought for, paid for, and protected—if global warming renders it unlivable? "Climate change could undermine the conservation work of whole generations," says Larry Schweiger, president of the National Wildlife Federation. "It turns out you can't save species without saving the sky."

That will mean reducing carbon emissions as fast as possible. In the US, the CBD has made an art out of using the Endangered Species Act, which mandates that the government prevent the extinction of listed species, to force Washington to act on global warming. The CBD's Siegel led a successful campaign to get the Bush administration to list the polar bear as threatened by climate change, and she expects more species to follow.

In a world where hundreds of millions of human beings still go hungry, it's easy to wonder why we should be concerned about the dwindling of the planet's biodiversity. The answer is that we can't afford not to. We can save life on this special planet—or be its unwitting executioner.

Time

Time Zone Map

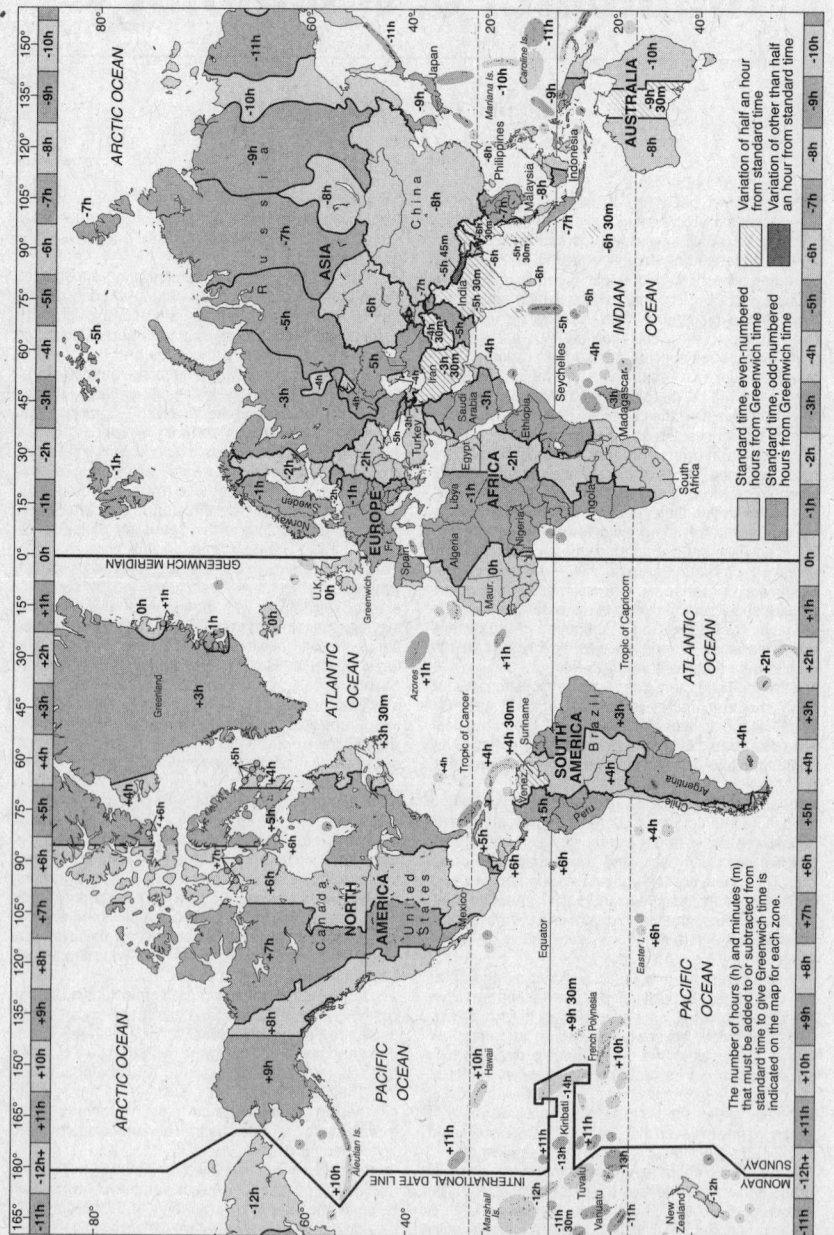

Based on data from the US Defense Mapping Agency Hydrographic/Topographic Center

Daylight Saving Time

Also called **summer time, daylight saving time** is a system for uniformly advancing clocks, especially in summer, so as to extend daylight hours during conventional waking time. In the Northern Hemisphere, clocks are usually set ahead one hour in late March or in April and are set back one hour in late September or in October; most Southern Hemisphere countries that observe daylight saving time set clocks ahead in October or November and reset them in March or April. Equatorial countries do not observe daylight saving time because daylight hours stay about the same from season to season in the lower latitudes.

The practice was first suggested in a whimsical essay by **Benjamin Franklin** in 1784. In 1907 an Englishman, William Willett, campaigned for setting the clock ahead by 80 minutes in four moves of 20 minutes each during the spring and summer months. In 1908 the British House of Commons rejected a bill to advance the clock by one hour in the spring and return to Greenwich Mean (standard) Time in the autumn.

Several countries, including Australia, Great Britain, Germany, and the United States, adopted **summer daylight saving time** during World War I to conserve fuel by reducing the need for artificial light. During World War II, clocks were kept continuously advanced by an hour in some nations—for instance, in the US from 9 Feb 1942 to 30 Sep 1945—and England used "double summer time" during part of the year, advancing clocks two hours from the standard time during the summer and one hour during the winter months.

In 2005 the US Congress changed the law governing daylight saving time, moving the start of daylight saving time from the first Sunday in April to the second Sunday in March, while moving the end date from the last Sunday in October to the first Sunday in November starting in 2007. In most of the countries of Western Europe, daylight saving time starts on the last Sunday in March and ends on the last Sunday in October.

Julian and Gregorian Calendars

The **Julian calendar**, also called the Old Style calendar, is a dating system established by Julius Caesar as a reform of the Roman republican calendar. Caesar, advised by the Alexandrian astronomer Sosigenes, made the new calendar solar, not lunar, and he took the length of the solar year as 365¼ days. The year was divided into 12 months, all of which had either 30 or 31 days except February, which contained 28 days in common (365-day) years and 29 in every fourth year (a leap year, of 366 days). Because of misunderstandings, the calendar was not established in smooth operation until AD 8. Further, Sosigenes had overestimated the length of the year by 11 minutes 14 seconds, and by the mid-1500s, the cumulative effect of this error had shifted the dates of the seasons by about 10 days from Caesar's time.

This inaccuracy led **Pope Gregory XIII** to reform the Julian calendar. His **Gregorian calendar**, also called the New Style calendar, is still in general use. Gregory's proclamation in 1582 restored the calendar to the seasonal dates of AD 325, an adjustment of 10 days. Although the amount of regression was some 14 days by Pope Gregory's time, Gregory based his reform on restoration of the vernal equinox, then falling on 11 March, to the date (21 March) it had in AD 325, the time of the Council of Nicaea. Advancing the calendar 10 days after 4 Oct 1582, the day following being reckoned as 15 October, effected the change.

The Gregorian calendar differs from the Julian only in that no century year is a leap year unless it is exactly divisible by 400 (e.g., 1600, 2000). A further refinement, the designation of years evenly divisible by 4,000 as common (not leap) years, will keep the Gregorian calendar accurate to within one day in 20,000 years.

Jewish Calendar

The **Jewish calendar** is lunisolar—i.e., regulated by the positions of both the Moon and the Sun. It consists usually of 12 alternating lunar months of 29 and 30 days each (except for Heshvan and Kislev, which sometimes have either 29 or 30 days), and totals 353, 354, or 355 days per year. The average lunar year (354 days) is adjusted to the solar year (365¼ days) by the periodic introduction of leap years in order to assure that the major festivals fall in their proper season. The leap year consists of an additional 30-day month called **First Adar**, which always precedes the month of (Second) Adar. (During leap year, the Adar holidays are postponed to Second Adar.) A leap year consists of either 383, 384, or 385 days and occurs seven times during every 19-year period (the so-called Metonic cycle). Among the consequences of the lunisolar structure are these: (1) The number of days in a year may vary considerably, from 353 to 385 days. (2) The first day of a month can fall on any day of the week, that day varying from year to year. Consequently, the days of the week upon which an annual Jewish festival falls vary from year to year despite the festival's fixed position in the Jewish month. The months of the Jewish calendar and their Gregorian equivalents are as follows:

JEWISH MONTH	GREGORIAN MONTH(S)	JEWISH MONTH	GREGORIAN MONTH(S)
Tishri	September–October	Nisan	March–April
Heshvan, or Marheshvan	October–November	Iyyar	April–May
Kislev	November–December	Sivan	May–June
Tevet	December–January	Tammuz	June–July
Shevat	January–February	Av	July–August
Adar	February–March	Elul	August–September

Muslim Calendar

The **Muslim calendar** (also called the **Islamic calendar**, or **Hijrah**) is a dating system used in the Muslim world that is based on a year of 12 months. Each month begins with the sighting of the crescent of the new moon as it emerges from eclipse. The **months** of the Muslim calendar are Muharram, Safar, Rabi I, Rabi II, Jumada I, Jumada II, Rajab, Sha'ban, Ramadan, Shawwal, Dhu al-Qa'dah, and Dhu al-Hijjah.

In the standard Muslim calendar the months are alternately 30 and 29 days long except for the 12th month, Dhu al-Hijjah, the length of which is varied in a 30-year cycle intended to keep the calendar in step with the true phases of the Moon. In 11 years of this cycle, Dhu al-Hijjah has 30 days, and in the other 19 years it has 29. Thus the year has either 354 or 355 days. No months are intercalated, so that the named months do not remain in the same seasons but retrogress through the entire solar, or seasonal, year (of about 365.25 days) every 32.5 solar years.

There are some exceptions to this calendar in the Muslim world. **Turkey** uses the Gregorian calendar, while the **Iranian Muslim calendar** is based on a solar year. The Iranian calendar still begins from the same dating point as other Muslim calendars—that is, some 10 years prior to the death of Muhammad in AD 632. Thus, the Gregorian year AD 2010 corresponds to the Hijrah years of AH 1431–32.

Chinese Calendar

The **Chinese calendar** is a dating system used concurrently with the Gregorian (Western) calendar in China and Taiwan and in neighboring countries (e.g., Japan). The calendar consists of 12 months of alternately 29 and 30 days, equal to 354 or 355 days, or approximately 12 full lunar cycles. Intercalary months have been inserted to keep the calendar year in step with the solar year of about 365 days. **Months** have no names but are instead referred to by numbers within a year and sometimes also by a series of 12 animal names that from ancient times have been attached to years and to hours of the day.

The calendar also incorporates a **meteorologic cycle** that contains 24 points, each beginning one of the periods named. The establishment of this cycle required a fair amount of astronomical understanding of the Earth as a celestial body. Modern scholars acknowledge the superiority of pre-Sung **Chinese astronomy** (at least until about the 13th century AD) over that of other, contemporary nations.

The **24 points** within the meteorologic cycle coincide with points 15° apart on the ecliptic (the plane of the Earth's yearly journey around the Sun or, if it is thought that the Sun turns around the Earth, the apparent journey of the Sun against the stars). It takes about 15.2 days for the Sun to travel from one of these points to another (because the ecliptic is a complete circle of 360°), and the Sun needs 365¼ days to finish its journey in this cycle. Supposedly, each of the 12 months of the year contains two points, but, because a lunar month has only 29½ days and the two points share about 30.4 days, there is always the chance that a lunar month will fail to contain both points, though the distance between any two given points is only 15°. If such an occasion occurs, the intercalation of an extra month takes place. For instance, one may find a year with two "Julys" or with two "Augusts" in the Chinese calendar. In fact, as mentioned above, the exact length of the month in the Chinese calendar is either 30 days or 29 days—a phenomenon that reflects its lunar origin.

SOLAR TERMS—CHINESE (ENGLISH EQUIVALENTS)	GREGORIAN DATE (APPROXIMATE)	LUNAR MONTH (CORRESPONDENCE OF LUNAR AND SOLAR MONTHS APPROXIMATE)
Lichun (spring begins)	5 February	
Yushui (rain water)	19 February	1—tiger
Jingzhe (excited insects)	5 March	
Chunfen (vernal equinox)	20 March	2—rabbit/hare
Qingming (clear and bright)	5 April	
Guyu (grain rains)	20 April	3—dragon
Lixia (summer begins)	5 May	
Xiaoman (grain fills)	21 May	4—snake
Mangzhong (grain in ear)	6 June	
Xiazhi (summer solstice)	21 June	5—horse
Xiaoshu (slight heat)	7 July	
Dashu (great heat)	23 July	6—sheep/ram
Liqiu (autumn begins)	7 August	
Chushu (limit of heat)	23 August	7—monkey
Bailu (white dew)	8 September	
Qiufen (autumn equinox)	23 September	8—chicken/rooster
Hanlu (cold dew)	8 October	
Shuangjiang (hoar frost descends)	24 October	9—dog
Lidong (winter begins)	8 November	
Xiaoxue (little snow)	22 November	10—pig/boar
Daxue (heavy snow)	7 December	
Dongzhi (winter solstice)	22 December	11—rat
Xiaohan (little cold)	6 January	
Dahan (severe cold)	20 January	12—cow/ox

Chinese Calendar (continued)

CHINESE NEW YEAR	GREGORIAN DATE	ANIMAL	CHINESE NEW YEAR	GREGORIAN DATE	ANIMAL
4700	12 Feb 2002	horse	4707	26 Jan 2009	cow/ox
4701	1 Feb 2003	sheep/ram	4708	14 Feb 2010	tiger
4702	22 Jan 2004	monkey	4709	3 Feb 2011	rabbit/hare
4703	9 Feb 2005	chicken/rooster	4710	23 Jan 2012	dragon
4704	29 Jan 2006	dog	4711	10 Feb 2013	snake
4705	18 Feb 2007	pig/boar	4712	31 Jan 2014	horse
4706	7 Feb 2008	rat	4713	19 Feb 2015	sheep/ram

Religious and Traditional Holidays

The word holiday comes from "holy day," and it was originally a day of dedication to religious observance; in modern times a holiday may be of either religious or secular commemoration. All dates in this article are Gregorian.

Jewish holidays—The major holidays are the Pilgrim Festivals: **Pesah** (Passover), **Shavuot** (Feast of Weeks, or Pentecost), and **Sukkoth** (Tabernacles); and the High Holidays: **Rosh Hashana** (New Year) and **Yom Kippur** (Day of Atonement).

Pesah commemorates the Exodus from Egypt and the servitude that preceded it. As such, it is the most significant of the commemorative holidays, for it celebrates the very inception of the Jewish people—i.e., the event that provided the basis for the covenant between God and Israel. The term Pesah refers to the paschal (Passover) lamb sacrificed on the eve of the Exodus, the blood of which marked the Jewish homes to be spared from God's plague. Leaven (se'or) and foods containing leaven (hametz) are neither to be owned nor consumed during Pesah. Aside from meats, fresh fruits, and vegetables, it is customary to consume only those foods prepared under rabbinic supervision and labeled "kosher for Passover." The unleavened bread (matzo) consists entirely of flour and water. On the eve of Pesah families partake of the seder, an elaborate festival meal. The table is bedecked with an assortment of foods symbolizing the passage from slavery (e.g., bitter herbs) into freedom (e.g., wine). Pesah will begin at sundown on 30 March and end on 6 April in 2010. (All Jewish holidays begin at sundown.)

A distinctive **Rosh Hashana** observance is the sounding of the ram's horn (shofar) at the synagogue service. Symbolic ceremonies, such as eating bread and apples dipped in honey, accompanied by prayers for a "sweet" and propitious year, are performed at the festive meals. In 2010 Rosh Hashana will begin at sundown on 8 September and will end on 10 September. **Yom Kippur** is a day when sins are confessed and expiated and man and God are reconciled. It is the holiest and most solemn day of the Jewish year. It is marked by fasting, penitence, and prayer. Working, eating, drinking, washing, anointing one's body, engaging in sexual intercourse, and donning leather shoes are all forbidden. Yom Kippur begins at sundown on 17 September in 2010.

Though not as important theologically, the feast of **Hanukkah** has become socially significant, especially in Western cultures. Hanukkah commemorates the rededication (164 BCE) of the Second Temple of Jerusalem after its desecration three years earlier. Though modern Israel tends to emphasize the military victory of the general Judas Maccabeus, the distinctive rite of lighting the menorah also recalls the Talmud story of how the small supply of nondesecrated oil—enough for one day—miraculously burned in the Temple for eight full days until new oil could be obtained. During Hanukkah, in addition to the lighting of the ceremonial candles, gifts are exchanged and children play holiday games. The festival occurs 11 through 19 Dec 2009, subsequently spanning 1 through 9 Dec 2010.

Christian holidays—The major holidays celebrated by nearly all Christians are **Easter** and **Christmas**.

Easter celebrates the Resurrection of Jesus on the third day after his Crucifixion. In the Christian liturgical year, Easter is preceded by the period of **Lent**, the 40 days (not counting Sundays) before Easter, which traditionally were observed as a period of penance and fasting. Lent begins on **Ash Wednesday**, a day devoted to penitence. Holy Week precedes **Easter Sunday** and includes **Maundy Thursday**, the commemoration of Jesus' last supper with his disciples; **Good Friday**, the day of his Crucifixion; and **Holy Saturday**, the transition between Crucifixion and Resurrection. Easter shares with Christmas the presence of numerous customs, some of which have little to do with the Christian celebration of the resurrection but clearly derive from folk customs. In 2010 the Western churches (nearly all Christian denominations) will observe Ash Wednesday on 17 February and Easter on 4 April. For Eastern Orthodox Christians, Lent begins on 15 February in 2010.

Christmas commemorates the birth of Jesus Christ. Since the early part of the 20th century, Christmas has also become a secular family holiday, observed by non-Christians, devoid of Christian elements, and marked by an increasingly elaborate exchange of gifts. In this secular Christmas celebration, a mythical figure named Santa Claus plays the pivotal role. Christmas is held on 25 December in most Christian cultures but occurs on the following 7 January in some Eastern Orthodox churches.

Islamic holidays—Ramadan is the holy month of fasting for Muslims. The Islamic ordinance prescribes abstention from evil thoughts and deeds as well as from food, drink, and sexual intercourse from dawn until dusk throughout the month. The beginning and end of Ramadan are announced when one trustworthy witness testifies before the authorities that the new moon has been sighted; a cloudy sky may therefore delay or prolong the fast. The end of the fast is celebrated as the feast of **'Id al-Fitr**. Ramadan is scheduled to begin on 11 August in 2010 and 'Id al-Fitr on 10 September of that year (all Islamic holidays begin at sundown). The Muslim New Year, **Hijrah**, is on 18 December in 2009 and 7 December in 2010.

Religious and Traditional Holidays (continued)

After 'Id al-Fitr, the second major Islamic festival is **'Id al-Adha**. Throughout the Muslim world, all who are able sacrifice sheep, goats, camels, or cattle and then divide the flesh equally among themselves, the poor, and friends and neighbors to commemorate the ransom of Ishmael with a ram. This festival falls at the end of the hajj, the pilgrimage to the holy city of Mecca in Saudi Arabia, which every adult Muslim of either sex must make at least once in his or her lifetime. 'Id al-Adha will be observed on 16 November in 2010.

'Ashura was originally designated in AD 622 by Muhammad as a day of fasting from sunset to sunset, probably patterned on the Jewish Day of Atonement, Yom Kippur. Among the Shi'ites, 'Ashura is a major festival that commemorates the death of Husayn (Hussein), son of 'Ali and grandson of Muhammad. It is a period of expressions of grief and of pilgrimage to Karbala (the site of Husayn's death, in present-day Iraq). 'Ashura is on 27 December in 2009 and 16 December in 2010.

Buddhist holidays—Holidays practiced by a large number of Buddhists are *uposatha* days and days that commemorate events in the life of the Buddha.

The four monthly holy days of ancient Buddhism continue to be observed in the Theravada countries of Southeast Asia. These *uposatha* days—the new moon and full moon days of each lunar month and the eighth day following the new and full moons—have their origin, according to some scholars, in the fast days that preceded the Vedic soma sacrifices.

The three major events of the Buddha's life—his birth, Enlightenment, and entrance into final nirvana—are commemorated in all Buddhist countries but not everywhere on the same day. In the Theravada countries the three events are all observed together on **Vesak**, the full moon day of the sixth lunar month, which usually occurs in May. In Japan and other Mahayana countries, the three anniversaries of the Buddha are observed on separate days (in some countries the birth date is 8 April, the Enlightenment date is 8 December, and the death date is 15 February).

Chinese holidays—The **Chinese New Year** is celebrated with a big family meal, and presents of cash are given to children in red envelopes. In 2010 the Chinese New Year will be on 14 February.

During the **Chinese Moon Festival**, on the 15th day of the 8th month of the lunar calendar, people return to their homes to visit with their family. The traditional food is moon cakes, round pastries stuffed with food such as red bean paste. The Moon Festival will occur on 22 September in 2010.

Japanese holidays—The Japanese celebrate **7-5-3 day** (Shichi-go-san no hi), in which parents bring children of those ages to the Shinto shrine to pray for their continued health. This day is held on 15 November.

In mid-July (or mid-August, in some areas) the Japanese celebrate **Bon** (also known as Bon Matsuri, or Urabon). The festival honors the spirits of deceased householders and of the dead generally. Memorial stones are cleaned, community dances are performed, and paper lanterns and fires are lit to welcome the dead and to bid them farewell at the end of their visit. The Shinto New Year, **Gantan-sai**, is celebrated on 1–3 January.

Hindu holidays—**Dussehra** celebrates the victory of Rama over Ravana, the symbol of evil on earth. In 2010 Dussehra falls on 17 October. **Diwali** is a festival of lights devoted to Laksmi, the goddess of wealth. During the festival, small earthenware lamps filled with oil are lit and placed in rows along the parapets of temples and houses and set adrift on rivers and streams. Diwali is on 5 November in 2010. **Maha-sivaratri**, the most important sectarian festival of the year for devotees of the Hindu god Shiva, occurs on 12 February in 2010. **Holi** is a spring festival, probably of ancient origin. Participants throw colored waters and powders on one another, and, on this day, the usual restrictions of caste, sex, status, and age are disregarded. It will be on 1 March in 2010.

Sikh holidays—Sikhs observe all festivals celebrated by the Hindus of northern India. In addition, they celebrate the birthdays of the first and the last Gurus and the martyrdom of the fifth (Arjun) and the ninth (Tegh Bahadur). In 2010 **Guru Nanak Dev Sahib's birthday** is celebrated on 21 November, and that of **Guru Gobind Singh Sahib** is celebrated on 5 January in 2011. On 16 June in 2011 **Arjun's martyrdom** is observed. *Kachi lassi* (sweetened milk) is offered to passersby to commemorate his death. On 24 November in 2011 the **martyrdom of Tegh Bahadur** is observed.

Baha'i holidays—The Baha'i New Year (**Naw Ruz**) in 2010 will fall on 21 March (all Baha'i holidays begin at sundown). Other important observances include the **declaration of the Bab** (23 May), the **Baha Ullah's birth** (12 November), and **Ascension** (29 May).

Zoroastrian holidays—**Noruz** (New Day) is on 21 March for 2010, and the 28th of that month is **Khordad Sal**, the birth of the prophet Zarathustra.

African American holiday—**Kwanzaa** (Swahili for "First Fruits") is celebrated each year from 26 December to 1 January and is patterned after various African harvest festivals. Maulana Karenga, a black-studies professor, created Kwanzaa in 1966 as a nonreligious celebration of family and social values. Each day of Kwanzaa is dedicated to one of seven principles: unity (*umoja*), self-determination (*kujichagulia*), collective responsibility (*ujima*), cooperative economics (*ujamaa*), purpose (*nia*), creativity (*kuumba*), and faith (*imani*).

Did you know?

A small-scale climatic stage that affected most parts of the world and lasted roughly from the beginning of the 16th century until the mid-19th century is known as the Little Ice Age. The harsh winters, moist, cool summers, and advancing ice sheets that characterized the Little Ice Age led to crop failures and the abandonment of the northern villages, and it necessitated the altering of oceanic sailing routes.

Perpetual Calendar

The perpetual calendar is a type of dating system that makes it possible to find the correct day of the week for any date over a wide range of years. Aspects of the perpetual calendar can be found in the Jewish religious and the Julian calendars, and some form of it has appeared in many proposed calendar reforms.

To find the day of the week for any Gregorian or Julian date in the perpetual calendar provided in this table, first find the proper dominical letter (one of the letters A through G) for the year in the upper table. Leap years have two dominical letters, the first applicable to dates in January and February, the second to dates in the remaining months. Then find the same dominical letter in the lower table, in whichever column it appears opposite the month in question. The days then fall as given in the lowest section of the column.

	CENTURY											
YEAR	JULIAN CALENDAR								GREGORIAN CALENDAR			
	0 700 1400	100 800 1500*	200 900	300 1000	400 1100	500 1200	600 1300	1500**	1600 2000	1700 2100	1800 2200	1900 2300
0	DC	ED	FE	GF	AG	BA	CB	...	BA	C	E	G
1 29 57 85	B	C	D	E	F	G	A	F	G	B	D	F
2 30 58 86	A	B	C	D	E	F	G	E	F	A	C	E
3 31 59 87	G	A	B	C	D	E	F	D	E	G	B	D
4 32 60 88	FE	GF	AG	BA	CB	DC	ED	CB	DC	FE	AG	CB
5 33 61 89	D	E	F	G	A	B	C	A	B	D	F	A
6 34 62 90	C	D	E	F	G	A	B	G	A	C	E	G
7 35 63 91	B	C	D	E	F	G	A	F	G	B	D	F
8 36 64 92	AG	BA	CB	DC	ED	FE	GF	ED	FE	AG	CB	ED
9 37 65 93	F	G	A	B	C	D	E	C	D	F	A	C
10 38 66 94	E	F	G	A	B	C	D	B	C	E	G	B
11 39 67 95	D	E	F	G	A	B	C	A	B	D	F	A
12 40 68 96	CB	DC	ED	FE	GF	AG	BA	GF	AG	CB	ED	GF
13 41 69 97	A	B	C	D	E	F	G	E	F	A	C	E
14 42 70 98	G	A	B	C	D	E	F	D	E	G	B	D
15 43 71 99	F	G	A	B	C	D	E	C	D	F	A	C
16 44 72	ED	FE	GF	AG	BA	CB	DC	...	CB	ED	GF	BA
17 45 73	C	D	E	F	G	A	B	...	A	C	E	G
18 46 74	B	C	D	E	F	G	A	...	G	B	D	F
19 47 75	A	B	C	D	E	F	G	...	F	A	C	E
20 48 76	GF	AG	BA	CB	DC	ED	FE	...	ED	GF	BA	DC
21 49 77	E	F	G	A	B	C	D	...	C	E	G	B
22 50 78	D	E	F	G	A	B	C	...	B	D	F	A
23 51 79	C	D	E	F	G	A	B	...	A	C	E	G
24 52 80	BA	CB	DC	ED	FE	GF	AG	...	GF	BA	DC	FE
25 53 81	G	A	B	C	D	E	F	...	E	G	B	D
26 54 82	F	G	A	B	C	D	E	C	D	F	A	C
27 55 83	E	F	G	A	B	C	D	B	C	E	G	B
28 56 84	DC	ED	FE	GF	AG	BA	CB	AG	BA	DC	FE	AG

MONTH	DOMINICAL LETTER						
January, October	A	B	C	D	E	F	G
February, March, November	D	E	F	G	A	B	C
April, July	G	A	B	C	D	E	F
May	B	C	D	E	F	G	A
June	E	F	G	A	B	C	D
August	C	D	E	F	G	A	B
September, December	F	G	A	B	C	D	E
1 8 15 22 29	Sunday	Saturday	Friday	Thursday	Wednesday	Tuesday	Monday
2 9 16 23 30	Monday	Sunday	Saturday	Friday	Thursday	Wednesday	Tuesday
3 10 17 24 31	Tuesday	Monday	Sunday	Saturday	Friday	Thursday	Wednesday
4 11 18 25	Wednesday	Tuesday	Monday	Sunday	Saturday	Friday	Thursday
5 12 19 26	Thursday	Wednesday	Tuesday	Monday	Sunday	Saturday	Friday
6 13 20 27	Friday	Thursday	Wednesday	Tuesday	Monday	Sunday	Saturday
7 14 21 28	Saturday	Friday	Thursday	Wednesday	Tuesday	Monday	Sunday

*On and before 1582, 4 October only.   **On and after 1582, 15 October only.
Source: Smithsonian Physical Tables, 9th edition, rev. 2003.

Civil Holidays

DAY	EVENT
1 January	New Year's Day, the first day of the modern calendar (various countries)
20 January	Inauguration Day, for quadrennial inauguration of US president
26 January	Australia Day, commemorates the establishment of the first British settlement in Australia
3rd Monday in January	Martin Luther King Day, for birth of US civil rights leader
2nd new moon after winter solstice (at the earliest 21 January and at the latest 19 February)	New Year, for Chinese lunar year, inaugurating a 15-day celebration
6 February	Waitangi Day, for Treaty of Waitangi, granting British sovereignty (New Zealand)
11 February	National Foundation Day, for founding by first emperor (Japan)
14 February	St. Valentine's Day, celebrating the exchange of love messages and named for either of two 3rd-century Christian martyrs (various)
3rd Monday in February	Presidents' Day, Washington-Lincoln Day, or Washington's Birthday, for birthdays of US Presidents George Washington and Abraham Lincoln
8 March	International Women's Day, celebration of the women's liberation movement
17 March	St. Patrick's Day, for patron saint of Ireland (Ireland and various)
21 or 22 March	Vernal Equinox Day, for beginning of spring (Japan)
25 March	Independence Day, for proclamation of independence from the Ottoman Empire (Greece)
4th Sunday in Lent	Mothering Day (UK)
1 April	April Fools' Day, or All Fools' Day, day for playing jokes, falling one week after the old New Year's Day of 25 March (various)
5 April	Qingming, for sweeping tombs and honoring the dead (China)
7 April	World Health Day, for founding of World Health Organization
22 April	Earth Day, for conservation and reclaiming of the natural environment (various)
25 April	ANZAC Day, for landing at Gallipoli (Australia/New Zealand/Samoa/Tonga)
29 April	Green Day, national holiday for environment and nature (Japan)
30 April	Queen's Birthday, for Queen Beatrix's investiture and former queen Juliana's birthday (The Netherlands)
1 May	May Day, celebrated as labor day or as festival of flowers (various)
3 May	Constitution Memorial Day, for establishment of democratic government (Japan)
5 May	Children's Day, honoring children (Japan/Republic of Korea)
5 May	Cinco de Mayo, anniversary of Mexico's victory over France in the Battle of Puebla (Mexico)
8/9 May	V-E Day, or Liberation Day, for end of World War II in Europe (various)
2nd Sunday in May	Mother's Day, honoring mothers (US)
Monday on or preceding 25 May	Victoria Day, for Queen Victoria's birthday (Canada)
30 or last Monday in May	Memorial Day, or Decoration Day, in honor of the deceased, especially the war dead (US)
2 June	Anniversary of the Republic, for referendum establishing republic (Italy)
5 June	Constitution Day (Denmark)
6 June	National Day, for Gustav I Vasa's ascension to the throne and adoption of Constitution (Sweden)
10 June	Portugal's Day, or Camões Memorial Day, anniversary of Luis de Camões's death
14 June	Flag Day, honoring flag (US)
3rd Saturday in June	Queen's Official Birthday, for Queen Elizabeth II (UK/New Zealand)
3rd Sunday in June	Father's Day, honoring fathers (US)
23 June	National Day, for Grand Duke Jean's official birthday (Luxembourg)
23–24 June	Midsummer Eve and Midsummer Day, celebrating the return of summer (various European)
last Sunday in June	Gay and Lesbian Pride Day, final day of weeklong advocacy of rights of gay men and lesbians (international)
1 July	Canada Day (formerly Dominion Day), for establishment of dominion
4 July	Independence Day, for Declaration of Independence from Britain (US)
12 July	Orangemen's Day, or Orange Day, anniversary of the Battle of the Boyne (Northern Ireland)
14 July	Bastille Day, for fall of the Bastille and onset of French Revolution (France)
21 July	National Day, for separation from The Netherlands (Belgium)
1 August	National Day, anniversary of the founding of the Swiss Confederation (Switzerland)
6 August	Hiroshima Day, for dropping of atomic bomb (Japan)
full-moon day of 8th lunar month	Chusok, harvest festival (Republic of Korea)
1st Monday in September	Labor Day, tribute to workers (US/Canada)
15 September	Respect-for-the-Aged Day, for the elderly (Japan)
16 September	Independence Day, for independence from Spain (Mexico)
23 or 24 September	Autumnal Equinox Day, for beginning of autumn; in honor of ancestors (Japan)

Civil Holidays (continued)

DAY	EVENT
two weeks ending on 1st Sunday in October	Oktoberfest, festival of food and drink, formerly commemorating marriage of King Louis (Ludwig) I (Germany)
3 October	Day of German Unity, for reunification of Germany
5 October	Republic Day, for founding of the republic (Portugal)
12 or 2nd Monday in October	Hispanic Day, Columbus Day, Discovery Day, or Day of the Race, for Christopher Columbus's discovery of the New World on behalf of Spain (Spain and various)
2nd Monday in October	Thanksgiving Day, harvest festival (Canada)
24 October	United Nations Day, for effective date of UN Charter (international)
26 October	National Day, for end of postwar occupation and return of sovereignty (Austria)
31 October	Halloween, or All Hallows' Eve, festive celebration of ghosts and spirits, on eve of All Saints' Day (various)
5 November	Guy Fawkes Day, anniversary of the Gunpowder Plot to blow up the king and Parliament (UK)
11 November	Armistice Day, Remembrance Day, or Veterans Day, honoring participants in past wars and recalling the Armistice of World War I (various)
23 November	Labor Thanksgiving Day, honoring workers (Japan)
4th Thursday in November	Thanksgiving Day, harvest festival (US)
16 December	Day of Reconciliation, for promoting national unity (South Africa)
23 December	Emperor's Birthday, for birthday of Emperor Akihito (Japan)
26 December	Boxing Day, second day of Christmas, for giving presents to service people (various)
31 December	New Year's Eve, celebration ushering out the old year and in the new year (various)

The Universe

Astronomical Constants

QUANTITY	SYMBOL	VALUE
astronomical unit	AU	length of the semimajor axis of the Earth's orbit around the Sun—149,597,870 km (92,955,808 mi)

measures large distances in space; equals the average distance from the Earth to the Sun

parsec	pc	one parsec equals 3.26 light-years

measures the distance at which the radius of the Earth's orbit subtends an angle of one second of arc

light-year	ly	9.46089×10^{12} km (5.8787×10^{12} mi)

measures the distance traveled by light moving in a vacuum in the course of one year

speed of light (in a vacuum)	c	$2.99792458 \times 10^{10}$ cm per sec (186,282 mi per sec)

mass of the Sun	Sun $M.$	1.989×10^{30} kg (330,000 times the mass of the Earth)

radius of the Sun	Sun $R.$	6.96×10^{8} m (109 times the radius of Earth)

Earth's mean radius		6,378 km (3,963 mi)

mean solar day (on Earth)		24 h 3 min 56.55 sec of mean sideral time

the interval between two successive passages of the Sun across the same meridian is a solar day; in practice, since the rate of the Sun's motion varies with the seasons, use is made of a fictitious Sun that always moves across the sky at an even rate

tropical (or solar) year (on Earth)		365.242 days

the time required for the Earth's orbital motion to return the Sun's position to the spring equinoctial point

synodic month (on Earth)		29.53 days

the time required for the Moon to pass through one complete cycle of phases

Definitions of Astronomical Positions

A **conjunction** is an apparent meeting or passing of two or more celestial bodies. For example, the Moon is in conjunction with the Sun at the phase of new Moon, when it moves between the Earth and Sun and the side turned toward the Earth is dark. Inferior planets—those with orbits smaller than the Earth's (namely, Venus and Mercury)—have two kinds of conjunctions with the Sun. An **inferior conjunction** occurs when the planet passes approximately between Earth and Sun; if it passes exactly between them, moving across the Sun's face as seen from Earth, it is said to be in transit (see below). A **superior conjunction** occurs when Earth and the other planet are on opposite sides of the Sun, but all three bodies are again nearly in a straight line. Superior planets, those having orbits larger than the Earth's can have only superior conjunctions with the Sun.

When celestial bodies appear in opposite directions in the sky they are said to be in **opposition**. The Moon, when full, is said to be in opposition to the Sun (the Earth is then approximately between them). A superior planet (one with an orbit farther from the Sun than Earth's) is in opposition when Earth passes between it and the Sun. The opposition of a planet is a good time to observe it, because the planet is then at its nearest point to the Earth and in its full phase. The inferior planets, Venus and Mercury, can never be in opposition to the Sun.

When a celestial body as seen from the Earth makes a right angle with the direction of the Sun it is said to be in **quadrature**. The Moon at first or last quarter is said to be at east or west quadrature, respectively. A superior planet is at west quadrature when its position is 90° west of the Sun.

The east-west coordinate by which the position of a celestial body is ordinarily measured is known as the **right ascension**. Right ascension in combination with **declination** defines the position of a celestial object. Declination is the angular distance of a body north or south of the celestial equator. North declination is considered positive and south, negative. Thus, +90° declination marks the north celestial pole, 0° the celestial equator, and −90° the south celestial pole. The symbol for right ascension is the Greek letter α (alpha) and for declination the lowercase Greek letter Δ (delta).

The angular distance in celestial longitude separating the Moon or a planet from the Sun is known as **elongation**. The greatest elongation possible for the two inferior planets is about 48° in the case of Venus and about 28° in that of Mercury. Elongation may also refer to the angular distance of any celestial body from another around which it revolves or from a particular point in the sky; e.g., the extreme east or west position of a star with reference to the north celestial pole.

The point at which a planet is closest to the Sun is called the **perihelion**, and the most distant point in that planet's orbit is the **aphelion**. The term helion refers specifically to the Sun as the primary body about which the planet is orbiting.

Occultation refers to the obscuring of the light of an astronomical body, most commonly a star, by another astronomical body, such as a planet or a satellite. Hence, a solar eclipse is the occultation of the Sun by the Moon. From occultations of stars by planets, asteroids, and satellites, astronomers are able to determine the precise sizes and shapes of the latter bodies in addition to the temperatures of planetary atmospheres. For example, astronomers unexpectedly discovered the rings of Uranus during a stellar occultation on 10 Mar 1977.

A complete or partial obscuring of a celestial body by another is an **eclipse**; these occur when three celestial objects become aligned. The Sun is eclipsed when the Moon comes between it and the Earth; the Moon is eclipsed when it moves into the shadow of the Earth cast by the Sun. Eclipses of natural or artificial satellites of a planet occur as the satellites move into the planet's shadow. When the apparent size of the eclipsed body is much smaller than that of the eclipsing body, the phenomenon is known as an **occultation** (see above). Examples are the disappearance of a star, nebula, or planet behind the Moon, or the vanishing of a natural satellite or space probe behind some body of the solar system. A **transit** (see above) occurs when, as viewed from the Earth, a relatively small body passes across the disk of a larger body, usually the Sun or a planet, eclipsing only a very small area: Mercury and Venus periodically transit the Sun, and a satellite may transit its planet.

When an object orbiting the Earth is at the point in its orbit that is the greatest distance from the center of the Earth, this point is known as **apogee**; the term is also used to describe the point farthest from a planet or a satellite (as the Moon) reached by an object orbiting it. **Perigee** is the opposite of apogee.

The difference in direction of a celestial object as seen by an observer from two widely separated points is termed **parallax**. The measurement of parallax is used directly to find the distance of the body from the Earth (geocentric parallax) and from the Sun (heliocentric parallax). The two positions of the observer and the position of the object form a triangle; if the base line between the two observing points is known and the direction of the object as seen from each has been measured, the apex angle (the parallax) and the distance of the object from the observer can be determined.

An **hour angle** is the angle between an observer's meridian (a great circle passing over his head and through the celestial poles) and the hour circle (any other great circle passing through the poles) on which some celestial body lies. This angle, when expressed in hours and minutes, is the time elapsed since the celestial body's last transit of the observer's meridian. The hour angle can also be expressed in degrees, 15° of arc being equal to one hour.

Constellations

F rom the earliest times the star groups known as **constellations**, the smaller groups (parts of constellations) known as **asterisms**, and, also, **individual stars** have received names connoting some meteorological phenomena or symbolizing religious or mythological beliefs. At one time it was held that the constellation names and myths were of Greek origin, but it is now thought that they are primarily of Semitic or even pre-Semitic origin and that they came to the Greeks through the Phoenicians.

Constellations (continued)

The Alexandrian astronomer **Ptolemy** lists the names and orientation of 48 constellations in his *Almagest*, and, with but few exceptions, they are identical with those used at the present time. The majority of the remaining 40 constellations that are now ac- cepted were added by European astronomers in the 17th and 18th centuries. In the 20th century the de- lineation of precise boundaries for all 88 constella- tions was undertaken by a committee of the Interna- tional Astronomical Union.

NAME	GENITIVE	MEANING	NOTES (First-magnitude stars are given in italics in this column)
Constellations described by Ptolemy: the zodiac			
Aries	Arietis	Ram	
Taurus	Tauri	Bull	*Aldebaran* is the constellation's brightest star. Taurus also contains the Pleiades star cluster and the Crab Nebula.
Gemini	Geminorum	Twins	The brightest stars in Gemini are *Castor* and *Pollux*.
Cancer	Cancri	Crab	Cancer contains the well-known star cluster Praesepe.
Leo	Leonis	Lion	*Regulus* is the brightest star in Leo.
Virgo	Virginis	Virgin	*Spica* is the brightest star in Virgo.
Libra	Librae	Balance	
Scorpius	Scorpii	Scorpion	
Sagittarius	Sagittarii	Archer	*Antares* is the brightest star of Scorpius. The center of the Milky Way Galaxy lies in Sagit- tarius, with the densest star clouds of the galaxy.
Capricornus	Capricorni	Sea-goat	
Aquarius	Aquarii	Water-bearer	
Pisces	Piscium	Fishes	
Other Ptolemaic constellations			
Andromeda	Andromedae	Andromeda (an Ethiopian princess of Greek legend)	The constellation's most notable feature is the great spiral galaxy Andromeda (also called M31).
Aquila	Aquilae	Eagle	The brightest star in Aquila is *Altair*.
Ara	Arae	Altar	
Argo Navis	Argus Navis	the ship *Argo*	Argo Navis is now divided into smaller constella- tions that include Carina, Puppis, Pyxis, and Vela.
Auriga	Aurigae	Charioteer	The brightest star in Auriga is *Capella*. The con- stellation also contains open star clusters M36, M37, and M38.
Boötes	Boötis	Herdsman	*Arcturus* is the brightest star in Boötes.
Canis Major	Canis Majoris	Greater Dog	*Sirius* is the brightest star in Canis Major.
Canis Minor	Canis Minoris	Smaller Dog	*Procyon* is the brightest star in Canis Minor.
Cassiopeia	Cassiopeiae	Cassiopeia was a legendary queen of Ethiopia	Tycho's nova, one of the few recorded super- novae in the Galaxy, appeared in Cassiopeia in 1572.
Centaurus	Centauri	Centaur (possibly represents Chiron)	*Alpha Centauri* in Centaurus contains Proxima, the nearest star to the Sun.
Cepheus	Cephei	Cepheus (legendary king of Ethiopia)	Delta Cephei was the prototype for cepheid vari- ables (a class of variable stars).
Cetus	Ceti	Whale	Mira Ceti was the first recognized variable star.
Corona Austrina	Coronae Austrinae	Southern Crown	
Corona Borealis	Coronae Borealis	Northern Crown	
Corvus	Corvi	Raven	
Crater	Crateris	Cup	
Cygnus	Cygni	Swan	Cygnus contains the asterism known as the Northern Cross; the constellation's brightest star is *Deneb*.
Delphinus	Delphini	Dolphin	Delphinus contains the asterism known as Job's Coffin.
Draco	Draconis	Dragon	Draco contains the star Thuban, which was the polestar in 3000 BC.
Equuleus	Equulei	Little Horse	
Eridanus	Eridani	River Eridanus or river god	*Achernar* is the brightest star in Eridanus.
Hercules	Herculis	Hercules (Greek hero)	Hercules contains the great globular star cluster M13.
Hydra	Hydrae	Water Snake	
Lepus	Leporis	Hare	
Lupus	Lupi	Wolf	

Constellations (continued)

NAME	GENITIVE	MEANING	NOTES
Other Ptolemaic constellations (continued)			
Lyra	Lyrae	Lyre	The brightest star in Lyra is *Vega*. In some 10,000 years, *Vega* will become the polestar. Lyra also contains the Ring Nebula (M57).
Ophiuchus	Ophiuchi	Serpent-bearer	
Orion	Orionis	Hunter	*Rigel* is the brightest star in Orion; M42 (the Great Nebula) resides in Orion.
Pegasus	Pegasi	Pegasus (winged horse)	The constellation contains stars of the Great Square of Pegasus.
Perseus	Persei	Perseus (legendary Greek hero)	
Piscis Austrinus	Piscis Austrini	Southern Fish	The brightest star in Piscis Austrinus is *Fomalhaut*.
Sagitta	Sagittae	Arrow	
Serpens	Serpentis	Serpent	
Triangulum	Trianguli	Triangle	The constellation contains M33, a nearby spiral galaxy.
Ursa Major	Ursae Majoris	Great Bear	The seven brightest stars of this constellation are the Big Dipper (also called the Plough).
Ursa Minor	Ursae Minoris	Lesser Bear	Ursa Minor contains Polaris (the north polestar).

NAME	GENITIVE	MEANING	NOTES
Southern constellations, added c. 1600			
Apus	Apodis	Bird of Paradise	
Chamaeleon	Chamaeleontis	Chameleon	
Dorado	Doradus	Swordfish	The most notable object in Dorado is the Large Magellanic Cloud.
Grus	Gruis	Crane	
Hydrus	Hydri	Water Snake	
Indus	Indi	Indian	
Musca	Muscae	Fly	
Pavo	Pavonis	Peacock	
Phoenix	Phoenicis	Phoenix (mythical bird)	
Triangulum Australe	Trianguli Australis	Southern Triangle	
Tucana	Tucanae	Toucan	The most notable object in Tucana is the Small Magellanic Cloud.
Volans	Volantis	Flying Fish	

NAME	GENITIVE	MEANING	NOTES
Constellations of Bartsch, 1624			
Camelopardalis	Camelopardalis	Giraffe	
Columba	Columbae	Dove	
Monoceros	Monocerotis	Unicorn	

NAME	GENITIVE	MEANING	NOTES
Constellations of Hevelius, 1687			
Canes Venatici	Canum Venaticorum	Hunting Dogs	The constellation contains M51 (the Whirlpool Galaxy).
Lacerta	Lacertae	Lizard	
Leo Minor	Leonis Minoris	Lesser Lion	
Lynx	Lyncis	Lynx	
Scutum	Scuti	Shield	Scutum contains the Scutim star cloud in the Milky Way.
Sextans	Sextantis	Sextant	
Vulpecula	Vulpeculae	Fox	Vulpecula contains M27 (the Dumbbell Nebula).

NAME	GENITIVE	MEANING	NOTES
Ancient asterisms that are now separate constellations			
Carina	Carinae	Keel [of the *Argo*, a legendary ship]	The brightest star in Carina is *Canopus*.
Coma Berenices	Comae Berenices	Berenice's Hair	The constellation contains both a coma (star cluster) and the north galactic pole (a point that lies perpendicular to the Milky Way).
Crux	Crucis	[Southern] Cross	
Puppis	Puppis	Stern [of the *Argo*]	
Pyxis	Pyxidis	Compass [of the *Argo*]	
Vela	Velorum	Sails [of the *Argo*]	

Constellations (continued)

NAME	GENITIVE	MEANING	NOTES
Southern constellations of Lacaille, c. 1750			
Antlia	Antliae	Pump	
Caelum	Caeli	[Sculptor's] Chisel	
Circinus	Circini	Drawing Compasses	
Fornax	Fornacis	[Chemical] Furnace	
Horologium	Horologii	Clock	
Mensa	Mensae	Table [Mountain]	
Microscopium	Microscopii	Microscope	
Norma	Normae	Square	
Octans	Octantis	Octant	Octans contains the south celestial pole.
Pictor	Pictoris	Painter's [Easel]	
Reticulum	Reticuli	Reticle	
Sculptor	Sculptoris	Sculptor's [Work-shop]	Sculptor contains the south galactic pole.
Telescopium	Telescopii	Telescope	

Astrology: The Zodiac

Signs of the zodiac are popularly used for divination as well as for designation of constellations.

NAME	SYMBOL	DATES	SEX/NATURE	TRIPLICITY	HOUSE	EXALTATION
Aries the Ram	♈	21 Mar–19 Apr	masculine/moving	fire	Mars	Sun (19°)
Taurus the Bull	♉	20 Apr–20 May	feminine/fixed	earth	Venus	Moon (3°)
Gemini the Twins	♊	21 May–21 Jun	masculine/common	air	Mercury	
Cancer the Crab	♋	22 Jun–22 Jul	feminine/moving	water	Moon	Jupiter (15°)
Leo the Lion	♌	23 Jul–22 Aug	masculine/fixed	fire	Sun	
Virgo the Virgin	♍	23 Aug–22 Sep	feminine/common	earth	Mercury	Mercury (15°)
Libra the Balance	♎	23 Sep–23 Oct	masculine/moving	air	Venus	Saturn (21°)
Scorpius the Scorpion	♏	24 Oct–21 Nov	feminine/fixed	water	Mars	
Sagittarius the Archer	♐	22 Nov–21 Dec	masculine/common	fire	Jupiter	
Capricorn the Goat	♑	22 Dec–19 Jan	feminine/moving	earth	Saturn	Mars (28°)
Aquarius the Water Bearer	♒	20 Jan–18 Feb	masculine/fixed	air	Saturn	
Pisces the Fish	♓	19 Feb–20 Mar	feminine/common	water	Jupiter	Venus (27°)

Classification of Stars

The spectral sequence O–M represents stars of essentially the same chemical composition but of different temperatures and atmospheric pressures. Stars belonging to other, more rare types of spectral classifications differ in chemical composition from those stars classified under the O–M scheme.

Each spectral class is additionally subdivided into 10 spectral types. For example, spectral class A is subdivided into spectral types A0–A9 with 0 being the hottest and 9 the coolest. (Spectral class O is unusual in that it is subdivided into O4–O9.) Between two stars of the same spectral type, the more luminous star will also be larger in diameter. Thus the Yerkes system of luminosity also tells something of a star's radius, with Ia being the largest and V the smallest. Approximately 90% of all stars are main-sequence, or type V, stars.

Based upon these systems, the Sun would be a G2 V star (a yellow, relatively hot dwarf star).

SPECTRAL CLASS	COLOR	APPROXIMATE SURFACE TEMP (°C)	EXAMPLES
O	blue	30,000 or greater	these stars are relatively rare
B	blue-white	20,000 to 30,000	Rigel, Alpha Crucis, Beta Crucis
A	white	10,000 to 20,000	Sirius, Vega, Fomalhaut
F	yellow-white	7,000 to 10,000	Canopus, Procyon
G	yellow	6,000 to 7,000	Sun
K	orange	4,500 to 6,000	Arcturus, Aldebaran
M	red	3,000 to 4,500	Betelgeuse, Antares

LUMINOSITY CLASSES (BASED UPON THE YERKES SYSTEM)

Ia	most luminous supergiants
Ib	luminous supergiants
II	bright giants
III	normal giants
IV	subgiants
V	main-sequence stars (dwarfs)

Astronomical Phenomena for 2010

Source: The Astronomical Almanac for the Year 2010.

MONTH	DAY	HOUR (GMT)	EVENT	MONTH	DAY	HOUR (GMT)	EVENT
January	1	21	Moon at perigee	April	6	10	last quarter
	3	00	Earth at perihelion		7	01	Pluto stationary
	3	12	Mars 7° N of Moon		7	18	Vesta stationary
	4	19	Mercury in inferior conjunction		8	23	Mercury greatest elongation E (19°)
	6	19	Saturn 8° N of Moon		9	03	Moon at apogee
	7	11	last quarter		10	01	Neptune 4° S of Moon
	7	21	Vesta stationary		11	22	Jupiter 6° S of Moon
	11	13	Antares 1°1 S of Moon[1]		12	14	Uranus 6° S of Moon
	11	21	Venus in superior conjunction		14	12	new moon
					15	23	Mercury 1°5 S of Moon
	13	16	Mercury 5° N of Moon		16	13	Venus 4° S of Moon
	14	19	Saturn stationary		18	10	Mercury stationary
	15	07	new moon[2]		21	18	first quarter
	15	16	Mercury stationary		22	09	Mars 5° N of Moon
	17	02	Moon at apogee		24	21	Moon at perigee
	17	23	Neptune 4° S of Moon		26	00	Saturn 8° N of Moon
	18	10	Jupiter 5° S of Moon		28	12	full moon
	20	11	Uranus 6° S of Moon		28	17	Mercury in inferior conjunction
	23	11	first quarter		29	05	Ceres stationary
	27	05	Mercury greatest elongation W (25°)	May	4	04	Pallas at opposition
	27	19	Mars closest approach		4	04	Venus 6° N of Aldebaran
	29	20	Mars at opposition		6	04	last quarter
	30	06	full moon		6	22	Moon at apogee
	30	08	Mars 7° N of Moon		7	10	Neptune 4° S of Moon
	30	09	Moon at perigee		9	18	Jupiter 7° S of Moon
February	3	02	Saturn 8° N of Moon		10	01	Uranus 6° S of Moon
	6	00	last quarter		11	00	Mercury stationary
	7	19	Antares 1°1 S of Moon[1]		12	17	Mercury 8° S of Moon
	12	06	Mercury 2° S of Moon		14	01	new moon
	13	02	Moon at apogee		16	10	Venus 0°08 S of Moon[1]
	14	03	new moon		20	09	Moon at perigee
	14	23	Neptune in conjunction with Sun		20	12	Mars 5° N of Moon
	16	19	Uranus 6° S of Moon		21	00	first quarter
	18	06	Vesta at opposition		23	05	Saturn 8° N of Moon
	22	01	first quarter		26	02	Mercury greatest elongation W (25°)
	26	05	Mars 5° N of Moon		27	23	full moon
	27	22	Moon at perigee		29	22	Ceres 0°09 N of Moon[1]
	28	11	Jupiter in conjunction with Sun		31	16	Saturn stationary
	28	17	full moon	June	1	02	Neptune stationary
March	2	10	Saturn 8° N of Moon		3	17	Moon at apogee
	7	16	last quarter		3	18	Neptune 5° S of Moon
	11	09	Mars stationary		4	22	last quarter
	12	10	Moon at apogee		6	11	Jupiter 7° S of Moon
	13	16	Neptune 4° S of Moon		6	11	Uranus 6° S of Moon
	14	13	Mercury in superior conjunction		6	15	Mars 0°9 N of Regulus
	15	21	new moon		6	19	Jupiter 0°5 S of Uranus
	17	07	Uranus in conjunction with Sun		9	10	Venus 5° S of Pollux
	17	12	Venus 7° S of Moon		11	03	Mercury 5° S of Moon
	20	18	equinox		12	11	new moon
	22	01	Saturn at opposition		15	07	Venus 4° N of Moon
	23	11	first quarter		15	15	Moon at perigee
	25	03	Pallas stationary		16	02	Mercury 5° N of Aldebaran
	25	14	Mars 5° N of Moon		17	19	Mars 6° N of Moon
	28	05	Moon at perigee		18	22	Ceres at opposition
	29	18	Saturn 8° N of Moon		19	04	first quarter
	30	02	full moon		19	11	Saturn 8° N of Moon
					21	11	solstice

Astronomical Phenomena for 2010 (continued)

MONTH	DAY	HOUR (GMT)	EVENT	MONTH	DAY	HOUR (GMT)	EVENT
June	25	19	Ceres 1°0 S of Moon[1]	September	8	10	new moon
(continued)	25	19	Pluto at opposition	(continued)	9	22	Saturn 8° N of Moon
	26	12	full moon[2]		11	08	Mars 5° N of Moon
	28	12	Mercury in superior conjunction		11	13	Venus 0°3 N of Moon[1]
					12	03	Mercury stationary
July	1	01	Neptune 5° S of Moon		14	01	Pluto stationary
	1	10	Moon at apogee		15	06	first quarter
	3	11	Pallas stationary		19	17	Mercury greatest elongation W (18°)
	3	20	Uranus 7° S of Moon		20	16	Neptune 5° S of Moon
	4	01	Jupiter 7° S of Moon		21	08	Moon at apogee
	4	15	last quarter		21	12	Jupiter at opposition
	6	01	Uranus stationary		21	17	Uranus at opposition
	6	11	Earth at aphelion		22	19	Jupiter 0°9 S of Uranus
	9	04	Juno in conjunction with Sun		23	03	equinox
					23	09	full moon
	10	03	Venus 1°1 N of Regulus		23	11	Jupiter 7° S of Moon
					23	11	Uranus 6° S of Moon
	11	20	new moon[2]		23	20	Venus greatest illuminated extent
	13	01	Mercury 4° N of Moon		29	06	Venus 6° S of Mars
	13	11	Moon at perigee				
	15	01	Venus 6° N of Moon	October	1	01	Saturn in conjunction with Sun
	16	05	Mars 6° N of Moon		1	04	last quarter
	16	19	Saturn 8° N of Moon		6	14	Moon at perigee
	18	10	first quarter		7	19	new moon
	24	04	Jupiter stationary		7	19	Venus stationary
	26	02	full moon		9	16	Venus 3° S of Moon
	27	23	Mercury 0°3 S of Regulus[1]		10	02	Mars 4° N of Moon
					14	21	first quarter
	28	07	Neptune 5° S of Moon		17	01	Mercury in superior conjunction
	29	00	Moon at apogee				
	31	03	Uranus 6° S of Moon		17	22	Neptune 5° S of Moon
	31	09	Jupiter 7° S of Moon		18	18	Moon at apogee
					20	11	Jupiter 7° S of Moon
August	1	20	Mars 1°9 S of Saturn		20	15	Uranus 6° S of Moon
	3	05	last quarter		23	02	full moon
	7	01	Mercury greatest elongation E (27°)		29	01	Venus in inferior conjunction
	9	02	Ceres stationary		30	13	last quarter
	10	02	Venus 3° S of Saturn				
	10	03	new moon	November	2	00	Juno 0°7 S of Moon[1]
	10	18	Moon at perigee		3	17	Moon at perigee
	12	02	Mercury 2° N of Moon		4	06	Saturn 8° N of Moon
	13	07	Saturn 8° N of Moon		6	05	new moon
	13	12	Venus 5° N of Moon		7	08	Neptune stationary
	13	17	Mars 6° N of Moon		7	22	Mars 1°6 N of Moon
	16	18	first quarter		10	00	Vesta in conjunction with Sun
	20	04	Mercury stationary		10	04	Mars 4° N of Antares
	20	04	Venus greatest elongation E (46°)		13	17	first quarter
	20	10	Neptune at opposition		14	06	Neptune 5° S of Moon
	23	21	Venus 2° S of Mars		15	11	Mercury 2° N of Antares
	24	12	Neptune 5° S of Moon		15	12	Moon at apogee
	24	17	full moon		16	16	Jupiter 7° S of Moon
	25	06	Moon at apogee		16	16	Venus stationary
	27	07	Uranus 6° S of Moon		16	22	Uranus 6° S of Moon
	27	12	Jupiter 7° S of Moon		19	06	Jupiter stationary
					21	01	Mercury 1°7 S of Mars
September	1	17	last quarter		21	17	full moon
	1	18	Venus 1°2 S of Spica		28	21	last quarter
	3	13	Mercury in inferior conjunction		29	23	Juno 0°5 N of Moon[1]
	4	14	Mars 2° N of Spica		30	19	Moon at perigee
	8	04	Moon at perigee				

Astronomical Phenomena for 2010 (continued)

MONTH	DAY	HOUR (GMT)	EVENT	MONTH	DAY	HOUR (GMT)	EVENT
December	1	16	Mercury greatest elongation E (21°)	December (continued)	14	06	Uranus 7° S of Moon
	1	18	Saturn 8° N of Moon		20	01	Mercury in inferior conjunction
	2	21	Venus 6° N of Moon		21	08	full moon[2]
	4	10	Venus greatest illuminated extent		22	00	solstice
	5	18	new moon		22	17	Pallas in conjunction with Sun
	6	10	Uranus stationary		25	12	Moon at perigee
	7	09	Mercury 1°8 S of Moon		27	01	Pluto in conjunction with Sun
	10	10	Mercury stationary		28	04	last quarter
	11	15	Neptune 5° S of Moon		29	03	Saturn 8° N of Moon
	13	09	Moon at apogee		30	08	Mercury stationary
	13	14	first quarter		31	16	Venus 7° N of Moon
	14	02	Jupiter 7° S of Moon				

[1]Occultation. [2]Eclipse.

Morning and Evening Stars

This table gives the morning and evening stars for autumn 2009 through 2010. The morning and evening stars are actually planets visible to the naked eye during the early morning and at evening twilight.

PLANET	MORNING STAR	EVENING STAR
Mercury	28 Sep–23 Oct 2009; 11 Jan–4 Mar, 8 May–21 Jun, 11 Sep–5 Oct, 26–31 Dec 2010	1–14 Sep, 22 Nov–30 Dec 2009; 24 Mar–20 Apr, 6 Jul–27 Aug, 1 Nov–14 Dec 2010
Venus	1 Sep–1 Dec 2009; 4 Nov–31 Dec 2010	23 Feb–24 Oct 2010
Mars	1 Sep–31 Dec 2009; 1–29 Jan 2010	29 Jan–5 Dec 2010
Jupiter	14 Mar–21 Sep 2010	1 Sep–31 Dec 2009; 1 Jan–15 Feb, 21 Sep–31 Dec 2010
Saturn	6 Oct–31 Dec 2009; 1 Jan–22 Mar, 19 Oct–31 Dec 2010	22 Mar–13 Sep 2010
Uranus	1 Sep–mid-December 2009; early April–mid-December 2010	mid-December 2009–late February 2010, mid-December–31 Dec 2010
Neptune	1 Sep–mid-November 2009; early March–mid-November 2010	mid-November–31 Dec 2009; 1 Jan–late January, mid-November–31 Dec 2010

Characteristics of Celestial Bodies

Mean orbital velocity indicates the average speed at which a planet orbits the Sun unless otherwise specified. **Inclination of orbit to ecliptic** indicates the angle of tilt between a planet's orbit and the plane of Earth's orbit (essentially the plane of the solar system). **Orbital period** indicates the planet's sidereal year (in Earth days except where noted). **Rotation period** indicates the planet's sidereal day (in Earth days except where noted). **Inclination of equator to orbit** indicates the angle of tilt between a planet's orbit and its equator. **Gravitational acceleration** is a measure of the body's gravitational pull on other objects. **Escape velocity** is the speed needed at the surface to escape the planet's gravitational pull. **Eccentricity of orbit** is a measure of the circularity or elongation of an orbit; 0 indicates circular orbits, and closer to 1 more elliptical ones.

Sun
diameter (at equator): 1.39 million km (863,705 mi)

mass (in 10^{20} kg): 19.8 billion

density (mass/volume, in kg/m³): 1,408

mean orbital velocity: the Sun orbits the Milky Way's center at around 220 km/sec (136.7 mi/sec)

orbital period: the Sun takes approximately 250 million Earth years to complete its orbit around the Milky Way's center

rotation period: 25–36 Earth days

gravitational acceleration: 275 m/sec² (902.2 ft/sec²)

escape velocity: 618.02 km/sec (384.01 mi/sec)

mean temperature at visible surface: 5,527 °C (9,980 °F)

probes and space missions: US—Pioneer 5-9, launched 1960-68; Skylab, 1973; Genesis, 2001; Japan—Yohkoh, 1991; US/European Space Agency (ESA)—Ulysses, 1990; SOHO, 1995.

Characteristics of Celestial Bodies (continued)

Mercury
average distance from the Sun: 58 million km (36 million mi)
diameter (at equator): 4,879 km (3,032 mi)
mass (in 10^{20} kg): 3,300
density (mass/volume, in kg/m³): 5,427
eccentricity of orbit: 0.206
mean orbital velocity: 47.9 km/sec (29.7 mi/sec)
inclination of orbit to ecliptic: 7.0°
orbital period: 88 Earth days
rotation period: 58.6 Earth days
inclination of equator to orbit: probably 0°
gravitational acceleration: 3.7 m/sec² (12.1 ft/sec²)
escape velocity: 4.3 km/sec (2.7 mi/sec)
mean temperature at surface†: 167 °C (333 °F)
satellites: none known
probes and space missions: US—Mariner 10, 1973; Messenger, 2004.

Venus
average distance from the Sun: 108.2 million km (67.2 million mi)
diameter (at equator): 12,104 km (7,521 mi)
mass (in 10^{20} kg): 48,700
density (mass/volume, in kg/m³): 5,243
eccentricity of orbit: 0.007
mean orbital velocity: 35.0 km/sec (21.8 mi/sec)
inclination of orbit to ecliptic: 3.4°
orbital period: 224.7 Earth days
rotation period: 243.0 Earth days (retrograde)
inclination of equator to orbit: 177.4°
gravitational acceleration: 8.9 m/sec² (29.1 ft/sec²)
escape velocity: 10.4 km/sec (6.4 mi/sec)
mean temperature at surface†: 464 °C (867 °F)
satellites: none known
probes and space missions: USSR—Venera 1-16, 1961-83; Vega 1 and 2, 1984; US—Mariner 2, 5, and 10, 1962, 1967, and 1973; Pioneer Venus Orbiter and Pioneer Venus Multiprobe, 1978; Galileo, 1989; Magellan, 1989; ESA—Venus Express, 2005.

Earth
average distance from the Sun: 149.6 million km (93 million mi)
diameter (at equator): 12,756 km (7,926 mi)
mass (in 10^{20} kg): 59,700
density (mass/volume, in kg/m³): 5,515
eccentricity of orbit: 0.017
mean orbital velocity: 29.8 km/sec (18.5 mi/sec)
inclination of orbit to ecliptic: 0.00°
orbital period: 365.25 days
rotation period: 23 hours, 56 minutes, and 4 seconds of mean solar time
inclination of equator to orbit: 23.5°
gravitational acceleration: 9.8 m/sec² (32.1 ft/sec²)
escape velocity: 11.2 km/sec (7.0 mi/sec)
mean temperature at surface†: 15 °C (59 °F)
satellites: 1 known—the Moon.

Moon (of Earth)
average distance from Earth: 384,401 km (238,855.7 mi)
diameter (at equator): 3,475 km (2,159 mi)
mass (in 10^{20} kg): 730
density (mass/volume, in kg/m³): 3,340
eccentricity of orbit: orbital eccentricity of Moon around Earth is 0.055
mean orbital velocity: the Moon orbits Earth at 1.0 km/sec (0.64 mi/sec)

inclination of orbit to ecliptic: 5.1°
orbital period: the Moon revolves around Earth in 27.32 Earth days
rotation period: the Moon rotates on its axis every 27.32 Earth days (synchronous with orbital period)
inclination of equator to orbit: 6.7°
gravitational acceleration: 1.6 m/sec² (5.3 ft/sec²)
escape velocity: 2.4 km/sec (1.5 mi/sec)
mean temperature at surface†: daytime: 107 °C (224.6 °F); nighttime: −153 °C (−243.4 °F)
probes and space missions: USSR, US, ESA, Japan—collectively about 70 missions since 1959, including 9 manned missions by the US. On 20 Jul 1969 humans first set foot on the Moon, from NASA's Apollo 11.

Mars
average distance from the Sun: 227.9 million km (141.6 million mi)
diameter (at equator): 6,794 km (4,222 mi)
mass (in 10^{20} kg): 6,420
density (mass/volume, in kg/m³): 3,933
eccentricity of orbit: 0.094
mean orbital velocity: 24.1 km/sec (15 mi/sec)
inclination of orbit to ecliptic: 1.9°
orbital period: 687 Earth days (1.88 Earth years)
rotation period: 24.6 Earth hours
inclination of equator to orbit: 24.9°
gravitational acceleration: 3.7 m/sec² (12.1 ft/sec²)
escape velocity: 5.0 km/sec (3.1 mi/sec)
mean temperature at surface†: −65 °C (−85 °F)
satellites: 2 known—Phobos and Deimos
probes and space missions: US—Mariner 4, 6, 7, and 9, 1964-71; Viking 1 and 2, 1975; Mars Global Surveyor, 1996; Mars Pathfinder, 1996; 2001 Mars Odyssey, 2001; Mars Exploration Rovers, 2003; Mars Reconnaissance Orbiter, 2005; USSR—Mars 2-7, 1971-73; Phobos 1 and 2, 1988; ESA—Mars Express, 2003; Phoenix, 2007.

Jupiter
average distance from the Sun: 778.6 million km (483.8 million mi)
diameter (at equator): 142,984 km (88,846 mi)
mass (in 10^{20} kg): 18.99 million
density (mass/volume, in kg/m³): 1,326
eccentricity of orbit: 0.049
mean orbital velocity: 13.1 km/sec (8.1 mi/sec)
inclination of orbit to ecliptic: 1.3°
orbital period: 11.86 Earth years
rotation period: 9.9 Earth hours
inclination of equator to orbit: 3.1°
gravitational acceleration: 23.1 m/sec² (75.9 ft/sec²)
escape velocity: 59.5 km/sec (37.0 mi/sec)
mean temperature at surface†: −110 °C (−166 °F)
satellites: at least 62 moons—including Callisto, Ganymede, Europa, and Io—plus rings
probes and space missions: US—Pioneer 10 and 11, 1972-73; Voyager 1 and 2, 1977; Galileo, 1989; Ulysses, 1990; US/ESA—Cassini-Huygens, 1997.

Saturn
average distance from the Sun: 1.433 billion km (890.8 million mi)
diameter (at equator): 120,536 km (74,897 mi)
mass (in 10^{20} kg): 5.68 million
density (mass/volume, in kg/m³): 687
eccentricity of orbit: 0.057

Characteristics of Celestial Bodies (continued)

mean orbital velocity: 9.7 km/sec (6 mi/sec)
inclination of orbit to ecliptic: 2.5°
orbital period: 29.43 Earth years
rotation period: 10.66 Earth hours
inclination of equator to orbit: 26.7°
gravitational acceleration: 9.0 m/sec^2 (29.4 ft/sec^2)
escape velocity: 35.5 km/sec (22.1 mi/sec)
mean temperature at surface†: −140 °C (−220 °F)
satellites: at least 61 moons—including Titan—plus
   rings
probes and space missions: US—Pioneer 11, 1973;
   Voyager 1 and 2, 1977; US/ESA—Cassini/Huygens,
   1997.

Uranus
average distance from the Sun: 2.872 billion km
   (1.784 billion miles)
diameter (at equator): 51,118 km (31,763 mi)
mass (in 10^{20} kg): 868,000
density (mass/volume, in kg/m^3): 1,270
eccentricity of orbit: 0.046
mean orbital velocity: 6.8 km/sec (4.2 mi/sec)
inclination of orbit to ecliptic: 0.8°
orbital period: 84.01 Earth years
rotation period: 17.2 Earth hours (retrograde)
inclination of equator to orbit: 97.8°
gravitational acceleration: 8.7 m/sec^2 (28.5 ft/sec^2)
escape velocity: 21.3 km/sec (13.2 mi/sec)
mean temperature at surface†: −195 °C (−320 °F)
satellites: at least 27 moons, plus rings
probes and space missions: US—Voyager 2, 1977.

Neptune
average distance from the Sun: 4.495 billion km
   (2.793 billion mi)
diameter (at equator): 49,528 km (30,775 mi)
mass (in 10^{20} kg): 1.02 million
density (mass/volume, in kg/m^3): 1,638
eccentricity of orbit: 0.009
mean orbital velocity: 5.48 km/sec (3.40 mi/sec)
inclination of orbit to ecliptic: 1.8°
orbital period: 164.79 Earth years
rotation period: 16.1 Earth hours
inclination of equator to orbit: 28.3°
gravitational acceleration: 11.0 m/sec^2 (36.0
   ft/sec^2)
escape velocity: 23.5 km/sec (14.6 mi/sec)
mean temperature at surface†: −200 °C (−330 °F)
satellites: at least 13 moons, plus rings
probes and space missions: US—Voyager 2, 1977.

Pluto
average distance from the Sun: 5.910 billion km
   (3.67 billion mi); Pluto lies within the Kuiper belt
   and can be considered its largest known member
diameter (at equator): 2,344 km (1,485 mi)
mass (in 10^{20} kg): 125
density (mass/volume, in kg/m^3): about 2,000
eccentricity of orbit: 0.249
mean orbital velocity: 4.72 km/sec (2.93 mi/sec)
inclination of orbit to ecliptic: 17.2°
orbital period: 248 Earth years
rotation period: 6.4 Earth days (retrograde)
inclination of equator to orbit: 122.5°
gravitational acceleration: 0.6 m/sec^2 (1.9 ft/sec^2)
escape velocity: 1.1 km/sec (0.7 mi/sec)

mean temperature at surface†: −225 °C (−375 °F)
satellites: 3 known—including Charon
probes and space missions: US—New Horizons, 2006.

asteroids
(several hundred thousand small rocky bodies, about
   1,000 km [610 mi] or less in diameter, that orbit
   the Sun primarily between the orbits of Mars and
   Jupiter)
distance from the Sun: between approximately 300
   million km (190 million mi) and 600 million km
   (380 million mi), with notable outliers
estimated mass (in 10^{21} kg): 2.3
probes and space missions: US—Galileo, 1989;
   Ulysses, 1990; NEAR Shoemaker, 1996; Deep
   Space 1, 1998; Stardust, 1999; Dawn, 2007;
   US/ESA—Cassini-Huygens, 1997; Japan—Hayabusa,
   2003; ESA—Rosetta, 2004.

Comet 1P/Halley
distance from the Sun at closest point of orbit: 87.8
   million km (54 million mi); farthest distance from
   the Sun: 5.2 billion km (3.2 billion mi).
diameter (at equator): 16 x 8 x 8 km (9.9 x 4.9 x 4.9 mi)
density (mass/volume, in kg/m^3): possibly as low
   as 200
eccentricity of orbit: 0.967
inclination of orbit to ecliptic: 18°
orbital period: 76.1 to 79.3 Earth years; the next appearance will be 2061. The comet's orbit is retrograde.
rotation period: 52 Earth hours
probes and space missions: USSR—Vega 1 and 2,
   1984; ESA—Giotto, 1985; Japan—Sakigake and Su-
   isei, 1985.

Comet Hale-Bopp
distance from the Sun at closest point of orbit: 136
   million km (84.5 million mi); farthest distance from
   the Sun: 74.7 billion km (46.4 billion mi).
eccentricity of orbit: 0.995
orbital period: 4,000 Earth years; last closest pass of
   Sun was on 31 Mar 1997.

Kuiper belt
(a huge flat ring located beyond Neptune containing
   residual icy material from the formation of the outer
   planets)
average distance from the Sun (main concentration):
   4.5–7.5 billion km (2.8–4.7 billion mi)
mass: scientists estimate there may be as many as
   100,000 icy, cometlike bodies of a size greater
   than 100 km in the Kuiper belt; the belt is estimated to have a mass of 6,000 x 10^{20} kg.
probes and space missions: US—New Horizons,
   2006.

Oort cloud
(an immense, roughly spherical cloud of icy, cometlike bodies inferred to orbit the Sun at distances
   roughly 1,000 times that of the orbit of Pluto)
average distance from the Sun: 3–7 trillion km
   (1.9–4.3 trillion mi)
mass: some trillions of the cloud's icy objects have an
   estimated total mass of at least 600,000 x 10^{20} kg
   (10 times the mass of Earth).

†For celestial bodies with no surface, temperature given is at a level in the atmosphere equal to 1 bar of
pressure.

Solar System Superlatives

Largest planet: Jupiter (142,984 km [88,846 mi] diameter); all of the other planets in the solar system could fit inside Jupiter.

Largest moon: Jupiter's moon Ganymede (5,268 km [3,273 mi] diameter).

Smallest planet: Mercury (4,879 km [3,032 mi] diameter).

Smallest moons: Saturn and Jupiter both have numerous satellites that are smaller than 10 km (6 mi) in diameter.

Planet closest to the Sun: Mercury (average distance from the Sun 58 million km [36 million mi]).

Planet farthest from the Sun: Neptune (average distance from the Sun 4.50 billion km [2.79 billion mi]); Pluto, demoted to the status of dwarf planet in 2006, was the farthest planet from the Sun for all but 20 years of its 248-year orbital period.

Planet with the most eccentric (least circular) orbit: Mercury (eccentricity of 0.206).

Moon with the most eccentric orbit: Neptune's moon Nereid (eccentricity of 0.75).

Planet with the least eccentric orbit: Venus (eccentricity of 0.007).

Moon with the least eccentric orbit: Saturn's moon Tethys (eccentricity of 0.0001).

Planet most tilted on its axis: Uranus (axial tilt of 98° from its orbital plane).

Planet with the most moons: Jupiter (at least 62).

Planets with the fewest moons: Mercury and Venus (none).

Planet with the longest day: Venus (1 day on Venus equals 243 Earth days).

Planet with the shortest day: Jupiter (1 day on Jupiter equals 9.9 Earth hours).

Planet with the longest year: Neptune (1 year on Neptune equals 165 Earth years).

Planet with the shortest year: Mercury (1 year on Mercury equals 88 Earth days).

Fastest orbiting planet: Mercury (47.9 km/sec [29.7 mi/sec] mean orbital velocity).

Slowest orbiting planet: Neptune (5.48 km/sec [3.40 mi/sec] mean orbital velocity).

Hottest planet: Venus (464 °C [867 °F] average temperature); although Mercury is closer to the Sun, Venus is hotter because Mercury has no atmosphere, whereas the atmosphere of Venus traps heat via a strong greenhouse effect.

Coldest planet: Neptune (−220 °C [−364 °F] average temperature).

Brightest visible star in the night sky: Sirius (apparent visual magnitude −1.46).

Brightest planet in the night sky: Venus (apparent visual magnitude −4.5 to −3.77).

Densest planet: Earth (density of 5,515 kg/m³).

Least dense planet: Saturn (density of 687 kg/m³); Saturn in theory would float in water.

Planet with strongest gravity: Jupiter (more than twice the gravitational force of Earth at an altitude at which one bar of atmospheric pressure is exerted).

Planet with weakest gravity: Mars (slightly more than one-third the gravitational force of Earth).

Planet with the largest mountain: Mars (Olympus Mons, an extinct volcano, stands some 21 km [13 mi] above the planet's mean radius and 540 km [335 mi] across).

Planet with the deepest valley: Mars (Valles Marineris, a system of canyons, is some 4,000 km [2,500 mi] long and from about 2 to 9 km [1 to 5.6 mi] deep).

Largest known impact crater: Valhalla, a crater on Jupiter's moon Callisto, has a bright central area that is about 600 km (370 mi) across, with concentric ridges extending about 1,500 km (900 mi) from the center. (The largest crater on Earth believed to be of impact origin is the Vredefort ring structure in South Africa, which is about 300 km [190 mi] across.)

The Sun

The Sun is the star around which the Earth and the other components of the solar system revolve. It is the dominant body of the system, constituting more than 99% of the system's entire mass. The Sun is the source of an enormous amount of energy, a portion of which provides the Earth with the light and heat necessary to support life. The geologic record of the Earth and Moon reveals that the Sun was formed about 4.5 billion years ago. The energy radiated by the Sun is produced during the conversion of hydrogen atoms to helium. The Sun is at least 90% hydrogen by number of atoms, so the fuel is readily available.

The Sun is classified as a G2 V star, where G2 stands for the second hottest stars of the yellow G class—of surface temperature about 5,500 °C (10,000 °F)—and V represents a main sequence, or dwarf, star, the typical star for this temperature class (see also "Classification of Stars"). The Sun exists in the outer part of the Milky Way Galaxy and was formed from material that had been processed inside other stars and supernovas.

The mass of the Sun is 743 times the total mass of all the planets in the solar system and 330,000 times that of the Earth. All the interesting planetary and in-

terplanetary gravitational phenomena are negligible effects in comparison to the gravitational force exerted by the Sun. Under the force of gravity, the great mass of the Sun presses inward, and to keep the star from collapsing, the central pressure outward must be great enough to support its weight. The Sun's core, which occupies approximately 25% of the star's radius, has a density about 100 times that of water (roughly 6 times that at the center of the Earth), but the temperature at the core is at least 15 million °C (27 million °F), so the central pressure is at least 10,000 times greater than that at the center of the Earth. In this environment atoms are completely stripped of their electrons, and at this high temperature the bare nuclei collide to produce the nuclear reactions that are responsible for generating the energy vital to life on Earth.

The temperature of the Sun's surface is so high that no solid or liquid can exist; the constituent materials are predominantly gaseous atoms, with a very small number of molecules. As a result, there is no fixed surface. The surface viewed from Earth, the photosphere, is approximately 400 km (250 mi) thick and is the layer from which most of the radiation reaches us; the radiation from below the photosphere is ab-

The Sun (continued)

sorbed and reradiated, while the emission from overlying layers drops sharply, by about a factor of six every 200 km (124 mi).

While the temperature of the Sun drops from 15 million °C (27 million °F) at the core to around 5,500 °C (10,000 °F) at the photosphere, a surprising reversal occurs above that point; the temperature begins to rise in the chromosphere, a layer several thousand kilometers thick. Temperatures there range from 4,200 °C (7,600 °F) to 100,000 °C (180,000 °F). Above the chromosphere is a comparatively dim, extended halo called the corona, which has a tem-

perature of 1 million °C (1.8 million °F) and reaches far past the planets. Beyond a distance of around 3.5 million km (2.2 million mi) from the Sun, the corona flows outward at a speed (near the Earth) of 400 km/sec (250 mi/sec); this flow of charged particles is called the solar wind.

The Sun is a very stable source of energy. Superposed on this stability, however, is an interesting 11-year cycle of magnetic activity manifested by regions of transient strong magnetic fields called sunspots. The largest sunspots can be seen on the solar surface even without a telescope.

Mercury

Mercury is the planet closest to the Sun, revolving around it at an average distance of 58 million km (36 million mi). In Sumerian times, some 5,000 years ago, it was already known in the night sky. In classical Greece the planet was called Apollo when it appeared as a morning star and Hermes, for the Greek equivalent of the Roman god Mercury, when it appeared as an evening star.

Mercury's orbit lies inside the orbit of the Earth and is more elliptical than those of most of the other planets. At its closest approach (perihelion), Mercury is only 46 million km (28.5 million mi) from the Sun, while its greatest distance (aphelion) approaches 70 million km (43.5 million mi). Mercury orbits the Sun in 88 Earth days at an average speed of 48 km per second (29.8 mi per sec), allowing it to overtake and pass Earth every 116 Earth days (synodic period).

Because of its proximity to the Sun, the surface of Mercury can become extremely hot. High temperatures at "noon" may reach 400 °C (755 °F) while the "predawn" lowest temperature is −173 °C (−280 °F). Mercury's equator is almost exactly in its orbital plane (its spin-axis inclination is nearly zero), and thus Mercury does not have seasons as does the Earth. Because of its elliptical orbit and a peculiarity of its rotational period (see below), however, certain longitudes experience cyclical variations in temperatures on a "yearly" as well as on a "diurnal" basis.

Mercury is about 4,879 km (3,032 mi) in diameter, the smallest of the planets. Mercury is only a bit larger than the Moon. Its mass, as measured by the gravitational perturbation of the path of the Mariner 10 spacecraft during close flybys in 1974–75, is about one-eighteenth

of the mass of the Earth. Escape velocity, the speed needed to escape from a planet's gravitational field, is about 4.3 km per second (2.7 mi per second)—compared with 11.2 km per sec (7 mi per sec) for the Earth.

The mean density of Mercury, calculated from its mass and radius, is about 5.43 grams per cubic cm, nearly the same as that of the Earth (5.52 grams per cubic cm).

Photographs relayed by the Mariner 10 spacecraft showed that Mercury spins on its axis (rotates) once every 58.646 Earth days, exactly two-thirds of the orbital period of 87.9694 Earth days. This observation confirmed that Mercury is in a 3:2 spin-orbit tidal resonance—i.e., that tides raised on Mercury by the Sun have forced it into a condition that causes it to rotate three times on its axis in the same time it takes to revolve around the Sun twice. The 3:2 spin-orbit coupling combines with Mercury's eccentric orbit to create very unusual temperature effects.

Although Mercury rotates on its axis once every 58.646 Earth days, one rotation does not bring the Sun back to the same part of the sky, because during that time Mercury has moved partway around the Sun. A solar day on Mercury (for example, from one sunrise to another, or one noon to another) is 176 Earth days (exactly two Mercurian years).

Mercury's low escape velocity and high surface temperatures do not permit it to retain a significant atmosphere.

In January 2008 the MESSENGER spacecraft flew by Mercury, revealing previously unseen details in photographs, and scientists approved dozens of new names for surface features such as craters.

Venus

Venus is the second planet from the Sun and the planet whose orbit is closest to that of the Earth. When visible, Venus is the brightest planet in the sky. Viewed through a telescope, it presents a brilliant, yellow-white, essentially featureless face to the observer. The obscured appearance results because the surface of the planet is hidden from sight by a continuous and permanent cover of clouds.

Venus's orbit is the most nearly circular of that of any planet, with a deviation from perfect circularity of only about 1 part in 150. The period of the orbit—that is, the length of the Venusian year—is 224.7 Earth days. The rotation of Venus is unusual in both its direction and speed. Most of the planets in the solar system rotate in a counterclockwise direction when viewed from above their north poles; Venus, however,

rotates in the opposite, or retrograde, direction. Were it not for the planet's clouds, an observer on Venus's surface would see the Sun rise in the west and set in the east.

Venus spins on its axis slowly, taking 243 Earth days to complete one rotation. Venus's spin and orbital periods are nearly synchronized with the Earth's orbit such that Venus presents almost the same face toward the Earth when the two planets are at their closest.

Venus is nearly the Earth's twin in terms of size and mass. Venus's equatorial diameter is about 95% of the Earth's diameter, while its mass is 81.5% that of the Earth. The similarities to the Earth in size and mass also produce a similarity in density; Venus's density is 5.24 grams per cubic cm, as compared with 5.52 for the Earth.

Venus (continued)

In terms of its shape, Venus is more nearly a perfect sphere than are most planets. A planet's rotation generally causes a slight flattening at the poles and bulging at the equator, but Venus's very slow rotation rate allows it to maintain its highly spherical shape.

Venus has the most massive atmosphere of all the terrestrial planets (Mercury, Venus, Earth, and Mars). Its atmosphere is composed of 96.5% carbon dioxide and 3.5% nitrogen. The atmospheric pressure at the planet's surface varies with the surface elevation but averages about 90 bars, or 90 times the atmospheric pressure at the Earth's surface. This is the same pressure found at a depth of about one kilometer in the Earth's oceans. Temperatures range between a minimum temperature of -45 °C (-49 °F) and a maximum temperature of 500 °C (932 °F); the average temperature is 464 °C (867 °F).

Earth

Earth is the third planet in distance outward from the Sun. It is the only planetary body in the solar system that has conditions suitable for life, at least as known to modern science.

The average distance of Earth from the Sun—149.6 million km (93 million mi)—is designated as the distance of the unit of measurement known as the AU (astronomical unit). Earth orbits the Sun at a speed of 29.8 km (18.5 mi) per second, making one complete revolution in 365.25 days. As it revolves around the Sun, Earth spins on its axis and rotates completely once every 23 hr 56 min 4 sec. Earth has a single natural satellite, the Moon.

The fifth largest planet of the solar system, Earth has a total surface area of roughly 509.6 million sq km (197 million sq mi), of which about 29%, or 148 million square km (57 million square mi), is land. Oceans and smaller seas cover the balance of the surface. Earth is the only planet known to have liquid water. Together with ice, the liquid water constitutes the hydrosphere. Seawater makes up more than 98% of the total mass of the hydrosphere and covers about 71% of Earth's surface. Significantly, seawater constituted the environment of the earliest terrestrial life forms.

Earth's atmosphere consists of a mixture of gases, chiefly nitrogen (78%) and oxygen (21%). Argon makes up much of the remainder of the gaseous envelope, with trace amounts of water vapor, carbon dioxide, and various other gases also present.

Earth's structure consists of an inner core of nearly solid iron, surrounded by successive layers of molten metals and solid rock, and a thin layer at the surface comprising the continental crust.

Earth is surrounded by a magnetosphere, a region dominated by Earth's magnetic field and extending upward from about 140 km (90 mi) in the upper atmosphere. In the magnetosphere, the magnetic field of Earth traps rapidly moving charged particles (mainly electrons and protons), the majority of which flow from the Sun (as solar wind). If it were not for this shielding effect, such particles would bombard the terrestrial surface and destroy life. High concentrations of the trapped particles make up two doughnut-shaped zones called the Van Allen radiation belts. These belts play a key role in certain geophysical phenomena, such as auroras.

The Moon

The Moon is the sole natural satellite of the Earth. It revolves around the planet from west to east at a mean distance of about 384,400 km (238,900 mi). The Moon is less than one-third the size of the Earth, having a diameter of only about 3,475 km (2,159 mi) at its equator. The Moon shines by reflecting sunlight, but its albedo—i.e., the fraction of light received that is reflected—is only 0.073.

The Moon rotates about its own axis in about 27.32 days, which is virtually identical to the time it takes to complete its orbit around the Earth. As a result, the Moon always presents nearly the same face to the Earth. The rate of actual rotation is uniform, but the arc through which the Moon moves from day to day varies somewhat, causing the lunar globe (as seen by a terrestrial observer) to oscillate slightly over a period nearly equal to that of revolution.

The surface of the Moon has been a subject of continuous telescopic study from the time of Galileo's first observation in 1609. The Italian Jesuit astronomer Giovanni B. Riccioli designated the dark areas on the Moon as seas (maria), with such fanciful names as Mare Imbrium ("Sea of Showers") and Mare Nectaris ("Sea of Nectar"). This nomenclature continues to be used even though it is now known that the Moon is completely devoid of surface water. During the centuries that followed the publication of these early studies, more detailed maps and, eventually, photographs were produced. A Soviet space probe photographed the side of the Moon facing away from the Earth in 1959. By the late 1960s the US Lunar Orbiter missions had yielded close-up photographs of the entire lunar surface. On 20 Jul 1969, Apollo 11 astronauts Neil Armstrong and Edwin ("Buzz") Aldrin set foot on the Moon.

The most striking formations on the Moon are its craters. These features, which measure up to about 200 km (320 mi) or more in diameter, are scattered over the surface in great profusion and often overlap one another. Meteorites hitting the lunar surface at high velocity produced most of the large craters. Many of the smaller ones—those measuring less than 1 km (0.6 mi) across—appear to have been formed by explosive volcanic activity, however. The Moon's maria have relatively few craters. These lava outpourings spread over vast areas after most of the craters had already been formed.

Various theories for the Moon's origin have been proposed. At the end of the 19th century, the English astronomer Sir George H. Darwin advanced a hypothesis stating that the Moon had been originally part of the Earth but had broken away as a result of tidal gravitational action and receded from the planet. This was proved unlikely in the 1930s. A theory that arose dur-

The Moon (continued)

ing the 1950s postulated that the Moon had formed elsewhere in the solar system and was then later captured by the Earth. This idea was also proved to be physically implausible and was dismissed. Today, most investigators favor an explanation known as the giant-impact hypothesis, which postulates that a Mars-sized body struck the proto-Earth early in the history of the solar system. As a result, a cloud of fragments from both bodies was ejected into orbit around the Earth, and this later accreted into the Moon.

Moon Phases, 2009–2010

As the Moon orbits Earth, more or less of the half of the Moon illuminated by the Sun is visible on Earth. During the lunar month the Moon's appearance changes from dark (the new moon) to being illuminated more and more on the right side (waxing crescent, first quarter, and waxing gibbous) to the full disc being illuminated (the full moon). The phases of the Moon are completed by the Moon being illuminated less and less on the left side (waning gibbous, last quarter, and waning crescent) and end with another new moon. This cycle takes place over a period of around 29 days; the time from new moon to new moon is referred to as a lunation.

The phases of the Moon are caused by the positions of the Sun in relationship to the Moon. Thus, when the Sun and the Moon are close in the sky a dark new moon is the result (the Sun is lighting the half of the Moon not visible to Earth). When the Sun and the Moon are at opposition (in opposite parts of the sky) the full moon occurs (the Sun illuminates fully the half of the Moon seen on Earth). When the Sun and the Moon are at about a 90-degree angle, one sees either a first quarter or a last quarter moon.

The dates for the new moon, first quarter, full moon, and last quarter for late May 2009–December 2010 are given in the table below.

MONTH	NEW MOON	FIRST QUARTER	FULL MOON	LAST QUARTER
May 2009	24	31	(7 June)	(15 June)
June 2009	22	29	(7 July)	(15 July)
July 2009	22	28	(6 August)	(13 August)
August 2009	20	27	(4 September)	(12 September)
September 2009	18	26	(4 October)	(11 October)
October 2009	18	26	(2 November)	(9 November)
November 2009	16	24	(2 December)	(9 December)
December 2009	16	24	31	(7 Jan 2010)
January 2010	15	23	30	(5 February)
February 2010	14	22	28	(7 March)
March 2010	15	23	30	(6 April)
April 2010	14	21	28	(6 May)
May 2010	14	20	27	(4 June)
June 2010	12	19	26	(4 July)
July 2010	11	18	26	(3 August)
August 2010	10	16	24	(1 September)
September 2010	8	15	23	(1 October)
October 2010	7	14	23	30
November 2010	6	13	21	28
December 2010	5	13	21	28

Mars

Mars is the fourth planet in order of average distance from the Sun and the seventh in order of diminishing size and mass. It orbits the Sun once in 687 Earth days and spins on its axis once every 24 Earth hours and 37 minutes.

Because of its blood-red color, Mars has often been associated with warfare and slaughter. It is named for the Roman god of war; as far back as 3,000 years ago, Babylonian astronomer-astrologers called the planet Nergal for their god of death and pestilence. The Greeks called it Ares for their god of battle; the planet's two satellites, Phobos (Fear) and Deimos (Terror), were later named for the two sons of Ares and Aphrodite.

Mars moves around the Sun at a mean distance of approximately 1.52 times that of Earth from the Sun. Because the orbit of Mars is relatively elongated, the distance between Mars and the Sun varies from 206.6 to 249.2 million km (128.4 to 154.8 million mi). Mars completes a single orbit in roughly the time in which Earth completes two. At its closest approach, Mars is less than 56 million km (34.8 million mi) from Earth, but it recedes to almost 400 million km (248.5 million mi). Mars is a small planet. Its equatorial radius is about half that of Earth, and its mass is only one-tenth the terrestrial value.

The axis of rotation is inclined to the orbital plane at an angle of 24.9°, and, as on Earth, the tilt gives rise to seasons. The Martian year consists of 668.6 Martian solar days (called sols). The orientation and eccentricity of the orbit (eccentricity denotes how much the orbit deviates from a perfect circle: the more elongated, the more eccentric) leads to seasons that are quite uneven in length. The Martian atmosphere is mainly composed of carbon dioxide. It is very thin (less than 1% of Earth's atmospheric pressure). Evidence suggests that the atmosphere was much denser in the remote past and that water was once much more abundant at the surface. Only small amounts of water are found in the lower atmosphere today, occasionally forming thin ice clouds at high altitudes and, in several localities, morning ice fogs. Mars's polar caps consist of frozen

Mars (continued)

carbon dioxide and water ice. Intriguing spacecraft observations confirm that water ice also is present under large areas of the Martian surface and hint that liquid water may have flowed in geologically recent times.

The characteristic temperature in the lower atmosphere is about −70 °C (−100 °F). Unlike that of Earth, the total mass (and pressure) of the atmosphere experiences large seasonal variations, as carbon dioxide "snows out" at the winter pole.

The surface of Mars shows some of the most dramatic variation in the solar system: the massive extinct volcano Olympus Mons stands some 21 km (13 mi) above the planet's mean radius and is 540 km (335 mi) across, and Valles Marineris, a system of canyons, is some 4,000 km (2,500 mi) long and from about 2 to 9 km (1 to 5.6 mi) deep.

The two satellites of Mars—Phobos and Deimos—were discovered in 1877 by Asaph Hall of the United States Naval Observatory. Little was known about these bodies until observations were made by NASA's orbiting Mariner 9 spacecraft nearly a century later. The moons of Mars cannot be seen from all locations on the planet because of their small size, proximity to the planet, and near-equatorial orbits.

Two Mars Exploration Rovers—Spirit and Opportunity—landed on Mars in January 2004. In May 2008 the spacecraft Phoenix successfully landed on the planet and began its mission to be the first spacecraft to retrieve and study water (ice) from another planet. In late July it confirmed the presence of water on Mars. In 2009 the Rovers continued to explore features of the planet, notably stratigraphy and volcanic activity, in their fourth Martian winter.

Did you know? The speed of steamboats increased dramatically over the years; the run from New Orleans to Louisville KY, which took 25 days in 1816, required only 4 days by 1853. The average life span of a steamboat was only four to five years because of poor construction and maintenance, exploding boilers, and sinkings due to river construction. Spontaneous races were common and contributed greatly to the approximately 4,000 deaths in steamboat disasters between 1810 and 1850.

Jupiter

Jupiter is the most massive of the planets and is fifth in average distance from the Sun. When ancient astronomers named the planet Jupiter for the ruler of the gods in the Greco-Roman pantheon, they had no idea of the planet's true dimensions, but the name is appropriate, for Jupiter is larger than all the other planets combined. It has a narrow ring system and at least 62 known satellites, 3 larger than Earth's Moon. Jupiter also has an internal heat source—i.e., it emits more energy than it receives from the Sun. This giant has the strongest magnetic field of any planet, with a magnetosphere so large that, if it could be seen from Earth, its apparent diameter would exceed that of the Moon. Jupiter's system is the source of intense bursts of radio noise, at some frequencies occasionally radiating more energy than the Sun.

Of particular interest concerning Jupiter's physical properties is its low mean density of 1.33 grams per cubic cm—in contrast with Earth's 5.52 grams/cm³—coupled with the large dimensions and mass and the short rotational period. The low density and large mass indicate that Jupiter's composition and structure are quite unlike those of Earth and the other inner planets, a deduction that is supported by detailed investigations of the giant planet's atmosphere and interior.

Jupiter has no solid surface; the transition from the atmosphere to its highly compressed core occurs gradually at great depths. The close-up views of Jupiter from the Voyager spacecraft revealed a variety of cloud forms, with a predominance of elliptical features reminiscent of cyclonic and anticyclonic storm systems on Earth. All these systems are in motion, appearing and disappearing on time scales dependent on their sizes and locations. Also observed to vary are the pastel shades of various colors present in the cloud layers—from the tawny yellow that seems to characterize the main layer, through browns and blue-grays, to the well-known salmon-colored Great Red Spot, Jupiter's largest, most prominent, and longest-lived feature.

Because Jupiter has no solid surface, it has no topographic features, and latitudinal currents dominate the planet's large-scale circulation. The lack of a solid surface with physical boundaries and regions with different heat capacities makes the persistence of these currents and their associated cloud patterns all the more remarkable. The Great Red Spot, for example, moves in longitude with respect to Jupiter's rotation, but it does not move in latitude.

The Voyager 1 spacecraft verified the existence of a ring system surrounding Jupiter when it crossed the planet's equatorial plane. Subsequently, images from the Galileo spacecraft revealed that the ring system consists principally of four concentric components whose boundaries are associated with the orbits of Jupiter's four innermost moons. The ring system is composed of large numbers of micrometer-sized particles that produce strong forward scattering of incident sunlight. The presence of such small particles requires a source, and the association of the ring boundaries with the four moons makes the source clear. The particles are thought to be generated by impacts on these moons (and on still smaller bodies within the main part of the ring) by micrometeoroids, cometary debris, and possibly volcanically produced material from Jupiter's moon Io.

Jovian Moons

The satellites orbiting Jupiter are numerous; there are at least 62 Jovian moons and likely additional ones to be discovered.

The first objects in the solar system discovered by means of a telescope (by Galileo in 1610) were the four brightest moons of Jupiter. Now known as the Galilean satellites, they are (in order of increasing distance from Jupiter) Io, Europa, Ganymede, and Callisto. Each is 'a unique world in its own right. Callisto and Ganymede, for example, are as large as or larger than the planet Mercury, but, while Callisto's icy surface is ancient and heavily cratered from impacts, Ganymede's appears to have been extensively modified by internal activity. Europa may still be geologically active and may harbor an ocean of liquid water, and possibly even life, beneath its frozen surface. Io is the most volcanically active body in the solar system; its surface is a vividly colored landscape of erupting vents, pools and solidified flows of lava, and sulfurous deposits.

Data for the first 16 known Jovian moons (discovered 1610–1979) are summarized below. The orbits of the inner eight satellites have low inclinations (they are not tilted relative to the planet's equator) and low èccentricities (their orbits are relatively circular). The orbits of the outer eight have much higher inclinations and eccentricities, and four of them are retrograde (they are opposite to Jupiter's spin and orbital motion around the Sun). The innermost four satellites are thought to be intimately associated with Jupiter's ring and are the sources of the fine particles within the ring itself.

Beginning in 1999 some 47 tiny moons (including one seen in 1975 and then lost) were discovered photographically in observations from Earth. All have high orbital eccentricities and inclinations and large orbital radii; nearly all of the orbits are retrograde. Rough size estimates based on their brightness place them between 2 and 8 km (1.2 and 5 mi) in diameter. They were assigned provisional numerical designations on discovery; many also have received official names.

In the table, "sync" denotes that the orbital period and rotational period are the same, or synchronous; hence, the moon always keeps the same face toward Jupiter. "R" following the orbital period indicates a retrograde orbit. Unspecified quantities are unknown.

NAME (DESIGNATION)	MEAN DISTANCE FROM JUPITER	DIAMETER	MASS (10^{20} KG)	ORBITAL PERIOD (EARTH DAYS)	ROTATIONAL PERIOD (EARTH DAYS)
Metis (JXVI)	128,000 km (79,500 mi)	40 km (25 mi)	0.001	0.295	sync
Adrastea (JXV)	129,000 km (80,000 mi)	20 km (12 mi)	0.0002	0.298	sync
Amalthea (JV)[1]	181,000 km (112,500 mi)	189 km (117 mi)	0.075	0.498	sync
Thebe (JXIV)	222,000 km (138,000 mi)	100 km (62 mi)	0.008	0.675	sync
Io (JI)[1]	422,000 km (262,000 mi)	3,630 km (2,256 mi)	893.2	1.769	sync
Europa (JII)[1]	671,000 km (417,000 mi)	3,130 km (1,945 mi)	480	3.551	sync
Ganymede (JIII)[1]	1,070,000 km (665,000 mi)	5,268 km (3,273 mi)	1,482	7.155	sync
Callisto (JIV)[1]	1,883,000 km (1,170,000 mi)	4,806 km (2,986 mi)	1,076	16.689	sync
Leda (JXIII)	11,127,000 km (6,914,000 mi)	10 km (6 mi)	0.00006	234	
Himalia (JVI)	11,480,000 km (7,133,000 mi)	170 km (106 mi)	0.095	251	0.4
Lysithea (JX)	11,686,000 km (7,261,300 mi)	24 km (15 mi)	0.0008	258	0.5
Elara (JVII)	11,737,000 km (7,293,000 mi)	80 km (50 mi)	0.008	256	0.5
Ananke (JXII)	21,269,000 km (13,216,000 mi)	20 km (12.5 mi)	0.0004	634 R	0.4
Carme (JXI)	23,350,000 km (14,509,000 mi)	30 km (18.6 mi)	0.001	729 R	0.4
Pasiphae (JVIII)	23,500,000 km (14,602,000 mi)	36 km (22.3 mi)	0.003	735 R	
Sinope (JIX)	23,700,000 km (14,726,500 mi)	28 km (17.3 mi)	0.0008	758 R	0.5

[1]Densities are known for these moons: Amalthea (0.86 grams/cm^3), Io (3.53 grams/cm^3), Europa (3.01 grams/cm^8), Ganymede (1.94 grams/cm^3), Callisto (1.83 grams/cm^3).

Jovian Ring

Jupiter's complex ring was discovered and first studied by the twin Voyager spacecraft during their flybys of the giant planet in 1979. It is now known to consist of four main components: an outer gossamer ring, whose outer radius coincides with the orbital radius of the Jovian moon Thebe (222,000 km; 138,000 mi); an inner gossamer ring bounded on its outer edge by the orbit of Amalthea (181,000 km; 112,500 mi); the main ring, extending inward some 6,000 km (3,700 mi) from the orbits of Adrastea (129,000 km; 80,000 mi) and Metis (128,000 km; 79,500 mi); and a halo of particles with a thickness of 25,000 km (15,500 mi) that extends from the main ring inward to a radius of about 95,000 km (59,000 mi). For comparison, Jupiter's visible surface lies at a radius of about 71,500 km (44,400 mi) from its center. The four moons involved with the ring are believed to supply the fine particles that compose it.

Saturn

Saturn is the sixth planet in order of average distance from the Sun and the second largest of the planets in mass and size. Its dimensions are almost equal to those of Jupiter, while its mass is about a third as large; it has the lowest mean density of any object in the solar system.

Both Saturn and Jupiter resemble stellar bodies in that the light gas hydrogen dominates their bulk **chemical composition**. Saturn's atmosphere is 91% hydrogen by mass and is thus the most hydrogen-rich atmosphere in the solar system. Saturn's structure and **evolutionary history**, however, differ significantly from those of its larger counterpart. Like the other giant planets—Jupiter, Uranus, and Neptune—Saturn has extensive satellite and ring systems, which may provide clues to its origin and evolution. The planet has at least 61 moons, including the second largest in the solar system. Saturn's dense and extended rings, which lie in its equatorial plane, are the most impressive in the solar system.

Saturn has no single **rotation period**. Cloud motions in its massive upper atmosphere can be used to trace out a variety of rotation periods, with periods as short as about 10 hours 10 minutes near the equator and increasing with some oscillation to about 30 minutes longer at latitudes higher than 40°. The rotation period of Saturn's deep interior can be determined from the rotation period of the magnetic field, which is presumed to be rooted in an outer core of hydrogen compressed to a metallic state. The "surface" of Saturn that is seen through telescopes and in spacecraft images is actually a complex layer of clouds.

The **atmosphere** of Saturn shows many smaller-scale time-variable features similar to those found in that of Jupiter, such as red, brown, and white spots; bands; eddies; and vortices. The atmosphere generally has a much blander appearance than Jupiter's, however, and is less active on a small scale. A spectacular exception occurred during September–November 1990, when a large white spot appeared near the equator, expanded to a size exceeding 20,000 km (12,400 mi), and eventually spread around the equator before fading.

Saturnian Moons

At least 61 natural satellites are known to circle Saturn. Data for the first 18 Saturnian moons (discovered 1655–1990) are summarized below. As with those of the other giant planets, the satellites closest to Saturn are mostly regular, meaning that their orbits are fairly circular and not greatly inclined (tilted) with respect to the planet's equator. All of the satellites in the table except distant **Phoebe** are regular.

Titan is Saturn's largest moon and the only satellite in the solar system known to have clouds and a dense atmosphere (composed mostly of nitrogen and methane). The moon is also enveloped in a reddish haze, which is thought to be composed of complex organic compounds that are produced by the action of sunlight on its clouds and atmosphere. That organic molecules may have been settling out of the haze onto Titan's surface for much of its history has encouraged some scientists to speculate on the possibility that life may have evolved there. Observations by the Cassini-Huygens spacecraft showed Titan to have a varied surface sculpted by rains of hydrocarbon compounds, flowing liquids, wind, impacts, and possibly volcanic and tectonic activity. Saturn's second largest moon is **Rhea**, followed by **Iapetus** and **Dione**.

An unusual Saturnian satellite is **Hyperion**. Because of its highly irregular shape and eccentric orbit, it does not rotate stably about a fixed axis. Unlike any other known object in the solar system, Hyperion rotates chaotically, alternating unpredictably between periods of tumbling and seemingly regular rotation.

Between 2000 and 2005 about 30 additional tiny moons occupying various (mostly distant) orbits were discovered. Like the numerous outer moons of Jupiter, nearly all of the recent finds around Saturn belong to the irregular class, meaning that their orbits are highly inclined and elliptical. More than half of them, plus Phoebe, are in retrograde orbits (they move opposite to Saturn's spin and orbital motion around the Sun).

In March 2008 it was announced that the Cassini spacecraft had taken images of Rhea in 2005 that appeared to show the first known ring around a moon.

In the table, "sync" denotes that the orbital period and rotational period are the same, or synchronous. Unspecified quantities are unknown.

NAME (DESIGNATION)	MEAN DISTANCE FROM SATURN	DIAMETER	MASS (10²⁰ KG)	DENSITY (GRAMS/CM³)	ORBITAL PERIOD (EARTH DAYS)	ROTATIONAL PERIOD (EARTH DAYS)
Pan (SXVIII)	133,580 km (83,000 mi)	20 km (12 mi)	0.00003	0.63	0.5750	
Atlas (SXV)	137,670 km (85,540 mi)	28 km (17 mi)	0.0001	0.63	0.6019	

Saturnian Moons (continued)

NAME (DESIGNATION)	MEAN DISTANCE FROM SATURN	DIAMETER	MASS (10^{20} KG)	DENSITY (GRAMS/CM^3)	ORBITAL PERIOD (EARTH DAYS)	ROTATIONAL PERIOD (EARTH DAYS)
Prometheus (SXVI)	139,350 km (86,590 mi)	92 km (57 mi)	0.0033	0.63	0.6130	
Pandora (SXVII)	141,700 km (88,050 mi)	92 km (57 mi)	0.002	0.63	0.6285	
Epimetheus (SXI)	151,420 km (94,090 mi)	114 km (71 mi)	0.0054	0.60	0.6942	sync
Janus (SX)	151,470 km (94,120 mi)	178 km (111 mi)	0.0192	0.65	0.6945	sync
Mimas (SI)	185,520 km (115,280 mi)	392 km (244 mi)	0.375	1.14	0.94	sync
Enceladus (SII)	238,020 km (147,900 mi)	520 km (323 mi)	0.7	1.0	1.37	sync
Tethys (SIII)	294,660 km (183,090 mi)	1,060 km (659 mi)	6.27	1.0	1.88	sync
Telesto (SXIII)*	294,660 km (183,090 mi)	30 km (19 mi)	0.00007	1.0	1.88	
Calypso (SXIV)*	294,660 km (183,090 mi)	26 km (16 mi)	0.00004	1.0	1.88	
Dione (SIV)	377,400 km (234,510 mi)	1,120 km (696 mi)	11	1.5	2.73	sync
Helene (SXII)†	377,400 km (234,510 mi)	32 km (20 mi)	0.0003	1.5	2.73	
Rhea (SV)	527,040 km (327,490 mi)	1,530 km (951 mi)	23.1	1.24	4.51	sync
Titan (SVI)	1,221,830 km (759,210 mi)	5,150 km (3,200 mi)	1,350	1.881	15.94	sync
Hyperion (SVII)	1,481,100 km (920,310 mi)	286 km (178 mi)	0.2	1.50	21.27	chaotic
Iapetus (SVIII)	3,561,300 km (2,212,890 mi)	1,460 km (907 mi)	16	1.02	79.33	sync
Phoebe (SIX)	12,952,000 km (8,048,000 mi)	220 km (137 mi)	0.004	1.3	550.5 (retrograde)	0.4

*Telesto and Calypso occupy the same orbit as Tethys but about 60° ahead and behind, respectively.
†Helene occupies the same orbit as Dione but about 60° behind.

Saturnian Rings

Saturn's rings rank among the most spectacular phenomena in the solar system. They have intrigued astronomers ever since they were discovered telescopically by Galileo in 1610, and their mysteries have only deepened since they were photographed and studied by Voyager 1 and 2 in the early 1980s. The **particles** that make up the rings are composed primarily of water ice and range from dust specks to car- and house-sized chunks. The rings exhibit a great amount of structure on many scales, from the broad **A, B, and C rings** visible from Earth down to myriad narrow component ringlets. Odd structures resembling spokes, braids, and spiral waves are also present. Some of this detail is explained by gravitational interaction with a number of Saturn's 61 moons (the orbits of well more than a dozen known moons, from Pan to Dione and Helene, lie within the rings), but much of it remains unaccounted for.

Numerous **divisions** or gaps are seen in the major ring regions. A few of the more prominent ones are named for famous astronomers who were associated with studies of Saturn.

The major rings and divisions, listed outward from Saturn, are given below. For comparison, Saturn's visible surface lies at a radius of about 60,300 km (37,500 mi).

RING (OR DIVISION)	RADIUS OF RING'S INNER EDGE	WIDTH	COMMENTS
D ring	66,970 km (41,610 mi)	7,500 km (4,700 mi)	faint, visible only in reflected light
(Guerin division)			
C ring	74,490 km (46,290 mi)	17,500 km (10,900 mi)	also called Crepe ring
(Maxwell division)			
B ring	91,980 km (57,150 mi)	25,500 km (15,800 mi)	brightest ring
(Cassini division, Huygens gap)			Cassini division is the largest ring gap
A ring	122,050 km (75,840 mi)	14,600 km (9,100 mi)	the outermost ring visible from Earth

Saturnian Rings (continued)

RING (OR DIVISION)	RADIUS OF RING'S INNER EDGE	WIDTH	COMMENTS
(Encke division)			located within the A ring, near its outer edge
F ring	140,220 km (87,130 mi)	30–500 km (20–300 mi)	faint, narrowest major ring
G ring	166,000 km (103,150 mi)	8,000 km (5,000 mi)	faint
E ring	180,000 km (111,850 mi)	300,000 km (186,400 mi)	faint

Uranus

Uranus is the seventh planet in order of distance from the Sun and the first found with the aid of a telescope. Its low density and large size place it among the four giant planets, all of which are composed primarily of hydrogen, helium, water, and other volatile compounds and which thus are without solid surfaces. Absorption of red light by methane gas gives the planet a blue-green color. The planet has at least 27 satellites, ranging up to 789 km (490 mi) in radius, and 13 narrow rings.

Uranus spins on its side; its **rotation axis** is tipped at an angle of 98° relative to its orbit axis. The 98° tilt is thought to have arisen during the final stages of planetary accretion when bodies comparable in size to the present planets collided in a series of violent events that knocked Uranus onto its side.

Although Uranus is nearly featureless, extreme contrast enhancement of images taken by the Voyager spacecraft reveals faint bands oriented parallel to circles of constant latitude. Apparently the rotation of the planet and not the distribution of absorbed sunlight controls the cloud patterns.

Wind is the motion of the atmosphere relative to the rotating planet. At high latitudes on Uranus, as on the Earth, this relative motion is in the direction of the planet's rotation. At low (that is, equatorial) latitudes, the relative motion is in the opposite direction. On the Earth these directions are called east and west, respectively, but the more general terms are prograde and retrograde. The winds that exist on Uranus are several times stronger than are those of the Earth. The wind is 200 m (656 ft) per second (prograde) at a latitude of 55° S and 110 m (360.8 ft) per second (retrograde) at the equator. Neptune's equatorial winds are also retrograde, although those of Jupiter and Saturn are prograde. No satisfactory theory exists to explain these differences.

Uranus has no large **spots** like the Great Red Spot of Jupiter or the Great Dark Spot of Neptune. Since the giant planets have no solid surfaces, the spots represent atmospheric storms. For reasons that are not clear, Uranus seems to have the smallest number of storms of any of the giant planets. Most of the mass of Uranus (roughly 80%) is in the form of a liquid core made primarily of icy materials (water, methane, and ammonia).

Uranus was discovered in 1781 by the English astronomer **William Herschel**, who had undertaken a survey of all stars down to eighth magnitude—i.e., those about five times fainter than stars visible to the naked eye. Herschel suggested naming the new planet the Georgian Planet after his patron, King George III of England, but the planet was eventually named according to the tradition of naming planets for the gods of Greek and Roman mythology; Uranus is the father of Saturn, who is in turn the father of Jupiter.

After the discovery, Herschel continued to observe the planet with larger and better telescopes and eventually discovered its two largest satellites, Titania and Oberon, in 1787. Two more satellites, Ariel and Umbriel, were discovered by the British astronomer William Lassell in 1851. The names of the four satellites come from English literature—they are characters in works by Shakespeare and Pope—and were proposed by Herschel's son, John Herschel. A fifth satellite, Miranda, was discovered by Gerard P. Kuiper in 1948. The tradition of naming the satellites after characters in Shakespeare's and Pope's works continues to the present.

Uranian Moons and Rings

Uranus has 27 known **satellites** forming three distinct groups: 13 small moons orbiting quite close to the planet, 5 large moons located somewhat farther out, and, finally, another 9 small and much more distant moons. The members of the first two groups are in nearly circular orbits with low inclinations with respect to the planet.

The densities of the four largest satellites, **Ariel, Umbriel, Titania**, and **Oberon**, suggest that they are about half (or more) water ice and the rest rock. Oberon and Umbriel are heavily scarred with large impact craters dating back to the very early history of the solar system, evidence that their surfaces probably have been stable since their formation. In contrast, Titania and Ariel have far fewer large craters, indicating relatively young surfaces shaped over time by internal geological activity. **Miranda**, though small compared with the other major moons, has a unique jumbled patchwork of varied surface terrain revealing surprisingly extensive past activity. Data for the major satellites are summarized below.

The 5 major moons were **discovered** telescopically from Earth between 1787 and 1948. Eleven of the 13 innermost moons, with diameters of about 40–160 km (25–100 mi), were found in Voyager 2 images. The rest of the moons, with diameters of 10–200 km (6–120 mi), were detected in Earth-based observations between 1997 and 2003; the orbital motion of nearly all of the outermost moons is retrograde (opposite to the direction of Uranus's spin and revolution around the Sun).

Thirteen narrow rings are known to encircle Uranus, with radii from 39,600 to 97,700 km (24,600 to 60,700 mi), for the most part within the orbits of the innermost moons. For comparison, Uranus's visible surface lies at a radius of about 25,600 km (15,900 mi). The ring system was first detected in 1977 during Earth-based observations of Uranus. Subsequent observations from Earth and images from Voyager 2 and the Hubble Space Telescope clarified the number and other features of the rings.

Uranian Moons and Rings (continued)

NAME (DESIGNATION)	MEAN DISTANCE FROM URANUS	DIAMETER	MASS (10^{20} KG)	DENSITY (GRAMS/CM³)	ORBITAL PERIOD/ ROTATIONAL PERIOD (EARTH DAYS)*
Miranda (V)	129,390 km (80,400 mi)	472 km (293 mi)	0.66	1.2	1.41
Ariel (I)	191,020 km (118,690 mi)	1,158 km (720 mi)	13.5	1.67	2.52
Umbriel (II)	266,300 km (165,470 mi)	1,169 km (726 mi)	11.7	1.4	4.14
Titania (III)	435,910 km (270,860 mi)	1,578 km (981 mi)	35.3	1.71	8.71
Oberon (IV)	583,520 km (362,580 mi)	1,523 km (946 mi)	30.1	1.63	13.46

*The orbital period and rotational period are the same, or synchronous, for the listed moons.

Neptune

Neptune is the eighth planet in average distance from the Sun. It has 13 known satellites. It was named for the Roman god of the sea, whose trident serves as the planet's astronomical symbol.

Neptune's **distance** from the Sun varies between 29.8 and 30.4 astronomical units (AUs). Its **diameter** is about four times that of Earth, but because of its great distance Neptune cannot be seen from Earth without the aid of a telescope. Neptune's deep blue **color** is due to the absorption of red light by methane gas in its atmosphere. It receives less than half as much sunlight as Uranus, but heat escaping from its interior makes Neptune slightly warmer than the latter. The heat released may also be responsible for Neptune's stormier **atmosphere**, which exhibits the fastest winds seen on any planet in the solar system.

Neptune's **orbital period** is 164.8 Earth years. It has not completely circled the Sun since its discovery in 1846, so some refinements in calculations of its orbital size and shape are still expected. The planet's orbital eccentricity of 0.009 means that its orbit is very nearly circular; among the planets in the solar system, only Venus has a smaller eccentricity. Neptune's seasons (and the seasons of its moons) are therefore of nearly equal length, each about 41 Earth years in duration. The length of Neptune's day, as determined by Voyager 2, is 16.11 Earth hours.

As with the other giant planets of the outer solar system, Neptune's atmosphere is composed predominantly of hydrogen and helium. The **temperature** of Neptune's atmosphere varies with altitude. A minimum temperature of about −223 °C (−369 °F) occurs at pressure near 0.1 bar. The temperature increases with altitude to about 477 °C (891 °F) at 2,000 km (1,240 mi, which corresponds to a pressure of 10^{-11} bar) as measured from the one-bar level and remains uniform above that altitude. It also increases with depth to about 6,730 °C (12,140 °F) near the center of the planet.

As is the case with several of the other large planets, the **winds** on Neptune are constrained to blow generally along lines of constant latitude and are relatively invariable with time. Winds on Neptune vary from about 100 m/sec (328 ft/sec) in an easterly (prograde) direction near latitude 70° S to as high as 700 m/sec (2,300 ft/sec) in a westerly (retrograde) direction near latitude 20° S.

The high winds and relatively large contribution of escaping internal heat may be responsible for the observed turbulence in Neptune's visible atmosphere. Two large dark ovals are clearly visible in images of Neptune's southern hemisphere taken by Voyager 2 in 1989, although they are not present in Hubble Space Telescope images made two years later. The largest, called the **Great Dark Spot** because of its similarity in latitude and shape to Jupiter's Great Red Spot, is comparable to the entire Earth in size. It was near this feature that the highest wind speeds were measured. Atmospheric storms such as the Great Dark Spot may be centers where strong upwelling of gases from the interior takes place.

Neptune's mean **density** is about 30% of Earth's; nevertheless, it is the densest of the giant planets. Neptune's greater density implies that a larger percentage of its interior is composed of melted ices and molten rocky materials than is the case for the other gas giants.

Neptunian Moons and Rings

Neptune has at least 13 natural satellites, but Earth-based observations had found only 2 of them, Triton in 1846 and Nereid in 1949, before Voyager 2 flew by the planet. The spacecraft observed 5 small moons orbiting close to Neptune and verified the existence of a 6th that had been detected from Earth in 1981. Data for these 8 moons are summarized in the table below. In 2002–03, 5 additional small moons (diameters roughly 30–60 km [20–40 mi]) were discovered telescopically from Earth; they all occupy highly inclined and elliptical orbits that are comparatively far from Neptune.

Triton is Neptune's only large moon and the only large satellite in the solar system to orbit its planet in the retrograde direction (opposite the planet's rotation and orbital motion around the Sun). Thus, as is also suspected of the solar system's other retrograde moons, Triton likely was captured by its planet rather than formed in orbit with its planet from the solar nebula. Its density (2 grams/cm³) suggests that it is about 25% water ice and the rest rock. Triton has a tenuous atmosphere, mostly of nitrogen. Its varied icy surface, imaged by Voyager 2, contains giant faults and dark markings that have been interpreted as the product of geyserlike

Neptunian Moons and Rings (continued)

"ice volcanoes" in which the eruptive material may be gaseous nitrogen and methane. Nereid has the most elliptical orbit of any planet or moon in the solar system; it also is probably a captured object.

Neptune's system of six faint rings, with radii from about 42,000 to 63,000 km (26,000–39,000 mi), straddles the orbits of its 4 innermost moons. (Neptune's visible surface lies at a radius of 24,800 km, or 15,400 mi.) The outermost ring, named Adams, is

unusual in that it contains several clumps, or concentrations of material, that before Voyager 2's visit had been interpreted incorrectly as independent ring arcs. What created and has maintained this structure has not yet been fully explained; it has been suggested that the clumps resulted from the relatively recent breakup of a small moon and are being temporarily held together by the gravitational effects of the nearby moon Galatea.

NAME (DESIGNATION)	MEAN DISTANCE FROM NEPTUNE	DIAMETER	MASS (10^{20} KG)	ORBITAL PERIOD (EARTH DAYS)
Naiad (III)	48,230 km (29,970 mi)	58 km (36 mi)	0.002	0.294
Thalassa (IV)	50,070 km (31,110 mi)	80 km (50 mi)	0.004	0.311
Despina (V)	52,530 km (32,640 mi)	148 km (92 mi)	0.02	0.335
Galatea (VI)	61,950 km (38,490 mi)	158 km (98 mi)	0.04	0.429
Larissa (VII)	73,550 km (45,700 mi)	192 km (119 mi)	0.05	0.555
Proteus (VIII)	117,640 km (73,100 mi)	416 km (258 mi)	0.5	1.122
Triton (I)*	354,800 km (220,460 mi)	2,700 km (1,678 mi)	214	5.877 (retrograde)
Nereid (II)	5,509,100 km (3,423,200 mi)	340 km (211 mi)	0.2	359.632

*Among the rotational periods of Neptune's moons, only Triton's has been established; it is the same as (synchronous with) the orbital period.

Pluto

Pluto is named for the god of the underworld in Roman mythology. It was long considered the planet normally farthest from the Sun, but on 24 Aug 2006, the International Astronomical Union announced that it was downgrading the status of Pluto to a dwarf planet. The key criterion in this classification was that Pluto, which orbits in the cluttered, icy Kuiper belt, had not cleared the neighborhood around its orbit. This was a controversial decision sure to be revisited.

Pluto has three natural satellites, Charon, Hydra, and Nix. Because Charon's diameter is more than half the size of Pluto's and they orbit around a common center of gravity, it was common to speak of the Pluto-Charon system as a double planet. Charon, named for the boatman in Greek mythology who carried the souls of the dead across the river Styx, was discovered in 1978, while Hydra and Nix were both first seen in 2005. The New Horizons spacecraft, launched in January 2006 and scheduled to arrive at Pluto in 2015, will search for yet more new satellites.

Pluto is so distant (its average distance from the Sun is 39.6 astronomical units, or AU) that sunlight traveling at 299,792 km/sec (186,282.1 mi/sec) takes more than five hours to reach it. An observer standing on the dwarf planet's surface would see the Sun as an extremely bright star in the dark sky, providing Pluto with only 1/1600 the amount of sunlight reaching the Earth.

Pluto has a diameter less than half that of Mercury; it is about two-thirds the size of the Moon. Pluto's physical characteristics are unlike those of any of the planets. Pluto resembles most closely Neptune's icy satellite Triton, which implies a similar origin for these

two bodies. Most scientists now believe that Pluto and Charon are large icy planetesimals left over from the formation of the giant outer planets of the solar system. Accordingly, Pluto can be interpreted to be the largest known member of the Kuiper belt (which, as discussed, includes the outer part of Pluto's orbit). Observations of Pluto show that it appears slightly red, though not as red as Mars or Io. Thus, the surface of Pluto cannot be composed simply of pure ices. Its overall reflectivity, or albedo, ranges from 0.3 to 0.5, as compared with 0.1 for the Moon and 0.8 for Triton.

The surface temperature of Pluto has proved very difficult to measure. Observations made from the Infrared Astronomical Satellite suggest values in the range of −228 to −215 °C (−379 to −355 °F), whereas measurements at radio wavelengths imply a range of −238 to −223 °C (−397 to −370 °F). The temperature certainly must vary over the surface, depending on the local reflectivity and solar zenith angle. There is also expected to be a seasonal decrease in incident solar energy by a factor of roughly three as Pluto moves from perihelion to aphelion.

The detection of methane ice on Pluto's surface made scientists confident that it had an atmosphere before one was actually discovered. The atmosphere was finally detected in 1988 when Pluto passed in front of a star as observed from the Earth. The light of the star was dimmed before disappearing entirely behind Pluto during the occultation. This proved that a thin, greatly distended atmosphere was present. Because that atmosphere must consist of vapors in equilibrium with their ices, small changes in temperature will have a large effect on the amount of gas in the atmosphere.

Measurements and Numbers

The International System of Units (SI)

Rapid advances in science and technology in the 19th and 20th centuries fostered the development of several overlapping systems of units of measurements as scientists improvised to meet the practical needs of their disciplines. The **General Conference on Weights and Measures** was chartered by international convention in 1875 to produce standards of physical measurement based upon an earlier international standard, the meter-kilogram-second (MKS) system. The convention calls for regular General Conference meetings to consider improvements or modifications in standards, an International Committee of Weights and Measures elected by the Conference (meets annually), and several consultative committees. **The International Bureau of Weights and Measures** (Bureau International des Poids et Mesures) at Sèvres, France, serves as a depository for the primary international standards and as a laboratory for certification and intercomparison of national standard copies.

The 1960 **International System** (universally abbreviated as **SI**, from *système international*) builds upon the MKS system. Its **seven basic units**, from which other units are derived, are currently defined as follows: the **meter**, defined as the distance traveled by light in a vacuum in 1/299,792,458 second; the **kilogram** (about 2.2 pounds avoirdupois), which equals 1,000 grams as defined by the international prototype kilogram of platinum-iridium in the keeping of the International Bureau of Weights and Measures; the **second**, the duration of 9,192,631,770 periods of radiation associated with a specified transition of the cesium-133 atom; the **ampere**, which is the current that, if maintained in two wires placed one meter apart in a vacuum, would produce a force of 2×10^{-7} newton per meter of length; the **candela**, defined as the intensity in a given direction of a source emitting radiation of frequency 540×10^{12} hertz and that has a radiant intensity in that direction of 1/683 watt per steradian; the **mole**, defined as containing as many elementary entities of a substance as there are atoms in 0.012 kilogram of carbon-12; and the **kelvin**, which is 1/273.16 of the thermodynamic temperature of the triple point (equilibrium among the solid, liquid, and gaseous phases) of pure water.

International Bureau of Weights and Measures Web site: <www.bipm.fr>.

Elemental and Derived SI Units and Symbols

Quantity	SI Units		
	UNIT	FORMULA/EXPRESSION IN BASE UNITS	SYMBOL
elemental units			
length	meter	—	m
mass	kilogram	—	kg
time	second	—	s
electric current	ampere	—	A
luminous intensity	candela	—	cd
amount of substance	mole	—	mol
thermodynamic temperature	kelvin	—	K
derived units			
acceleration	meter/second squared	m/s^2	
area	square meter	m^2	
charge	coulomb	$A \times s$	C
Celsius temperature	degree Celsius	K	°C
density	kilogram/cubic meter	kg/m^3	
electric field strength	volt/meter	V/m	
electrical potential	volt	W/A	V
energy	joule	$N \times m$	J
force	newton	$kg \times m/s^2$	N
frequency	hertz	s^{-1}	Hz
illumination	lux	lm/m^2	lx
inductance	henry	$V \times s/A$	H
kinematic viscosity	square meter/second	m^2/s	
luminance	candela/square meter	cd/m^2	
luminous flux	lumen	$cd \times sr$	lm
magnetic field strength	ampere/meter	A/m	
magnetic flux	weber	$V \times s$	Wb
magnetic flux density	tesla	Wb/m^2	T
plane angle	radian	$m \times m^{-1}=1$	rad
power	watt	J/s	W
pressure	pascal (newton/square meter)	N/m^2	Pa
resistance	ohm	V/A	Ω
stress	pascal (newton/square meter)	N/m^2	Pa
velocity	meter/second	m/s	
viscosity	newton-second/square meter	$N \times s/m^2$	
volume	cubic meter	m^3	

Conversion of Metric Weights and Measures

conversions accurate within 10 parts per million

inches × 25.4[1] = millimeters; millimeters × 0.0393701 = inches
feet × 0.3048[1] = meters; meters × 3.28084 = feet
yards × 0.9144[1] = meters; meters × 1.09361 = yards
miles (statute) × 1.60934 = kilometers; kilometers × 0.621371 = miles (statute)
square inches × 6.4516[1] = square centimeters; square centimeters × 0.155000 = square inches
square feet × 0.0929030 = square meters; square meters × 10.7639 = square feet
square yards × 0.836127 = square meters; square meters × 1.19599 = square yards
acres × 0.404686 = hectares[2:] hectares[2] × 2.47105 = acres
cubic inches × 16.3871 = cubic centimeters; cubic centimeters × 0.0610237 = cubic inches
cubic feet × 0.0283168 = cubic meters; cubic meters × 35.3147 = cubic feet
cubic yards × 0.764555 = cubic meters; cubic meters × 1.30795 = cubic yards
quarts (liquid) × 0.946353 = liters[2]; liters[2] × 1.05669 = quarts (liq)
gallons × 0.00378541 = cubic meters; cubic meters × 264.172 = gallons
ounces (avdp)[3] × 28.3495 = grams; grams × 0.0352740 = ounces (avdp)[3]
pounds (avdp)[3] × 0.453592 = kilograms; kilograms × 2.20462 = pounds (avdp)[3]
horsepower × 0.745700 = kilowatts; kilowatts × 1.34102 = horsepower

[1]Exact.   [2]Common term not used in SI.   [3]avdp = avoirdupois.
Source: National Institute of Standards and Technology.

Tables of Equivalents: Metric System Prefixes

prefixes designating multiples and submultiples

PREFIX	SYMBOL	FACTOR BY WHICH UNIT IS MULTIPLIED		EXAMPLES
exa-	E	10^{18}	= 1,000,000,000,000,000,000	
peta-	P	10^{15}	= 1,000,000,000,000,000	
tera-	T	10^{12}	= 1,000,000,000,000	
giga-	G	10^{9}	= 1,000,000,000	
mega-	M	10^{6}	= 1,000,000	megaton (Mt)
kilo-	k	10^{3}	= 1,000	kilometer (km)
hecto-, hect-	h	10^{2}	= 100	hectare (ha)
deca- dec-	da	10	= 10	decastere (das)
			1	
deci-	d	10^{-1}	= 0.1	decigram (dg)
centi-, cent-	c	10^{-2}	= 0.01	centimeter (cm)
milli-	m	10^{-3}	= 0.001	milliliter (ml)
micro-, micr-	μ	10^{-6}	= 0.000001	microgram (μg)
nano-	n	10^{-9}	= 0.000000001	
pico-	p	10^{-12}	= 0.000000000001	
femto-	f	10^{-15}	= 0.000000000000001	
atto-	a	10^{-18}	= 0.000000000000000001	

Cooking Measurements

MEASURE	CONVENTIONAL EQUIVALENTS[1]	METRIC EQUIVALENT
drop	1/60 teaspoon	0.08 ml
dash	1/8 teaspoon	0.62 ml
teaspoon	8 dashes; 1/3 tablespoon; 1/6 fluid ounce	4.93 ml
tablespoon	3 teaspoons; 1/2 fluid ounce	14.79 ml
ounce (weight)	1/16 pound	28.35 g
fluid ounce (volume)	2 tablespoons	29.57 ml
cup	8 fluid ounces; 16 tablespoons; 1/2 pint	236.59 ml
pound	16 ounces	453.6 g
pint	16 fluid ounces; 2 cups; 1/2 quart	473.18 ml
quart	32 fluid ounces; 4 cups; 2 pints; 1/4 gallon	946.36 ml
gallon	128 fluid ounces; 16 cups; 8 pints; 4 quarts	3.785 l
peck	2 gallons	7.57 l
bushel	8 gallons; 4 pecks	30.28 l

[1]All ounce measurements are in US ounces or fluid ounces.

Spirits Measures

Many specific volumes have varied over time and from place to place, but the proportional relationships within families of measures have generally remained the same. All ounce measures are in US fluid ounces.

MEASURE	CONVENTIONAL EQUIVALENTS	METRIC EQUIVALENT
pony	0.75 oz = ¾ shot = ½ jigger	22.17 ml
shot/ounce/finger	1 oz = 1⅓ ponies = ⅔ jigger	29.57 ml
jigger	1.5 oz = 2 ponies = 1½ shots	44.36 ml
double	2 oz = 2 shots	59.15 ml
triple	3 oz = 3 shots	88.72 ml
pint	16 oz = ⅝ fifth = ½ quart	473.2 ml
bottle (champagne or other wine)	about 25.5 oz or ⅙ imperial gallon	750 ml (industry standard)
fifth	25.6 oz = ⅘ quart = ⅕ gallon	757.1 ml
quart	32 oz = ½ magnum = ¼ gallon	946.3 ml
magnum	2 bottles (champagne or other wine)	1.5 l
magnum	64 oz = 2 quarts = ½ gallon	1.893 l
yard	80 oz = 5 pints	2.365 l
gallon/double magnum	128 oz = 4 quarts = 5 fifths = 2 magnums	3.785 l
imperial gallon	1.20 gallons = ⅖ barn gallon	4.546 l
ale/beer gallon	1.22 gallons	4.620 l
barn gallon	2½ imperial gallons	11.37 l
half keg	5 gallons (type varies)	varies
keg	10 gallons (type varies)	varies
British bottle	126 bottles = 21 imperial gallons	95.47 l
barrel (wine)	126 quarts = 31½ gallons	119.2 l
barrel (ale/beer)	144 quarts = 36 gallons	136.3 l
British hogshead (ale/beer)	54 imperial gallons = ½ butt (ale/beer) = ¼ tun (ale/beer)	245.5 l
British hogshead (wine)	63 imperial gallons = ½ butt (wine) = ¼ tun (wine)	286.4 l
butt/pipe (ale/beer)	108 imperial gallons = ½ tun (ale/beer)	491.0 l
butt/pipe (wine)	126 imperial gallons = ½ tun (wine)	572.8 l
tun (ale/beer)	216 imperial gallons = 4 British hogsheads (ale/beer) = 2 butts (ale/beer)	982.0 l
tun (wine)	252 imperial gallons = 12 British bottles = 2 butts (wine)	1,146 l

Playing Cards Chances

Blackjack

Number of two-card combinations in a 52-card deck (where aces equal 1 or 11 and face cards equal 10) for each number between 13 and 21

Approximate chances of various hands reaching or exceeding 21

TOTAL WITH TWO CARDS	POSSIBLE COMBINATIONS FROM 52 CARDS	TOTAL IN HAND BEFORE DEAL (TWO OR MORE CARDS)	CHANCE OF REACHING A COUNT OF 17 TO 21 (%)	CHANCE OF EXCEEDING 21	
				ONE CARD (%)	ANY NUMBER OF CARDS (%)
21	64				
20	136				
19	80				
18	86	16	38	62	62
17	96	15	42	54	58
16	86	14	44	46	56
15	96	13	48	38	52
14	102				
13	118				

Poker

Number of ways to reach and odds of reaching various five-card combinations on a single deal (52-card deck, no wild cards)

HAND	NUMBER OF COMBINATIONS	ODDS OF RECEIVING ON A SINGLE DEAL
royal flush	4	1 in 649,740
straight flush	36	1 in 72,193
four of a kind	624	1 in 4,165
full house	3,744	1 in 694
flush	5,108	1 in 509
straight	10,200	1 in 255
three of a kind	54,912	1 in 47
two pairs	123,552	1 in 21
one pair	1,098,240	1 in 2

Roman Numerals

Seven numeral-characters compose the Roman numeral system. When a numeral appears with a line above it, it represents the base value multiplied by 1,000. However, because Roman numerals are now seldom utilized for values beyond 4,999, this convention is no longer in use.

ARABIC	ROMAN	ARABIC	ROMAN	ARABIC	ROMAN	ARABIC	ROMAN
1	I	15	XV	70	LXX	1,000	M
2	II	16	XVI	80	LXXX	1,001	MI
3	III	17	XVII	90	XC	1,002	MII
4	IV	18	XVIII	100	C	1,003	MIII
5	V	19	XIX	101	CI	1,900	MCM
6	VI	20	XX	102	CII	2,000	MM
7	VII	21	XXI	200	CC	2,001	MMI
8	VIII	22	XXII	300	CCC	2,002	MMII
9	IX	23	XXIII	400	CD	2,100	MMC
10	X	24	XXIV	500	D	3,000	MMM
11	XI	30	XXX	600	DC	4,000	MMMM or M$\overline{\text{V}}$
12	XII	40	XL	700	DCC	5,000	$\overline{\text{V}}$
13	XIII	50	L	800	DCCC		
14	XIV	60	LX	900	CM		

Mathematical Formulas

The ratio of the circumference of a circle to its diameter is π (3.14159265358979323846264338 3279..., generally rounded to $^{22}\!/_7$ or 3.1416). It occurs in various mathematical problems involving the lengths of arcs or other curves, the areas of surfaces, and the volumes of many solids.

	SHAPE	ACTION	FORMULA
circumference	circle	multiply diameter by π	πd
area	circle	multiply radius squared by π	πr^2
	rectangle	multiply height by length	hl
	sphere surface	multiply radius squared by π by 4	$4\pi r^2$
	square	length of one side squared	s^2
	trapezoid	parallel side length A + parallel side length B multiplied by height and divided by 2	$(A+B)h/2$
	triangle	multiply base by height and divide by 2	$hb/2$
volume	cone	multiply base radius squared by π by height and divide by 3	$br^2\pi h/3$
	cube	length of one edge cubed	a3
	cylinder	multiply base radius squared by π by height	$br^2\pi h$
	pyramid	multiply base area by height and divide by 3	$hb/3$
	sphere	multiply radius cubed by π by 4 and divide by 3	$4\pi r^3/3$

Large Numbers

The American system of numeration for denominations above one million was modeled on a French system, but subsequently the French system changed to correspond to the German and British systems. In the American system each of the denominations above 1,000 millions (the American *billion*) is 1,000 times the preceding one (one trillion = 1,000 billions; one quadrillion = 1,000 trillions). In the British system the first denomination above 1,000 millions (the British *milliard*) is 1,000 times the preceding one, but each of the denominations above 1,000 milliards (the British *billion*) is 1,000,000 times the preceding one (one billion = 1,000,000 billions; one quadrillion = 1,000,000 trillions). In recent years, however, British usage has reflected widespread and increasing use of the values of the American system.

Source: Merriam-Webster, Inc., *Merriam-Webster's Collegiate Dictionary*, 11th ed., 2003.

AMERICAN NAME	VALUE IN POWERS OF TEN	NUMBER OF ZEROS	BRITISH NAME	VALUE IN POWERS OF TEN	NUMBER OF ZEROS
billion	10^9	9	billion	10^{12}	12
trillion	10^{12}	12	trillion	10^{18}	18
quintillion	10^{18}	18	quintillion	10^{30}	30
septillion	10^{24}	24	septillion	10^{42}	42
quattuordecillion	10^{45}	45	quattuordecillion	10^{84}	84
googol	10^{100}	100	googol	10^{100}	100
centillion	10^{303}	303	centillion	10^{600}	600
googolplex	10^{googol}	googol	googolplex	10^{googol}	googol

Periodic Table of the Elements

The periodic table arranges the elements into groups (vertically) of elements sharing common physical and chemical characteristics and into periods (horizontally) of sequentially increasing atomic number and electron-shell configuration. Elements 113–116 and 118 have been created experimentally and have temporary names. Atomic weights in parentheses indicate the number of the most stable isotope of a radioactive element.

1	2	3	4	5	6	7	8	9	10	11	12	13	14	15	16	17	18
1 H																	2 He
3 Li	4 Be											5 B	6 C	7 N	8 O	9 F	10 Ne
11 Na	12 Mg											13 Al	14 Si	15 P	16 S	17 Cl	18 Ar
19 K	20 Ca	21 Sc	22 Ti	23 V	24 Cr	25 Mn	26 Fe	27 Co	28 Ni	29 Cu	30 Zn	31 Ga	32 Ge	33 As	34 Se	35 Br	36 Kr
37 Rb	38 Sr	39 Y	40 Zr	41 Nb	42 Mo	43 Tc	44 Ru	45 Rh	46 Pd	47 Ag	48 Cd	49 In	50 Sn	51 Sb	52 Te	53 I	54 Xe
55 Cs	56 Ba	57 La	72 Hf	73 Ta	74 W	75 Re	76 Os	77 Ir	78 Pt	79 Au	80 Hg	81 Tl	82 Pb	83 Bi	84 Po	85 At	86 Rn
87 Fr	88 Ra	89 Ac	104 Rf	105 Db	106 Sg	107 Bh	108 Hs	109 Mt	110 Ds	111 Rg	112 Cp	113 Uut	114 Uuq	115 Uup	116 Uuh		118 Uuo

Lanthanide Series

58 Ce	59 Pr	60 Nd	61 Pm	62 Sm	63 Eu	64 Gd	65 Tb	66 Dy	67 Ho	68 Er	69 Tm	70 Yb	71 Lu

Actinide Series

90 Th	91 Pa	92 U	93 Np	94 Pu	95 Am	96 Cm	97 Bk	98 Cf	99 Es	100 Fm	101 Md	102 No	103 Lr

Element	Symbol	Atomic no.	Atomic weight	Element	Symbol	Atomic no.	Atomic weight
Actinium	Ac	89	(227)	Mercury	Hg	80	200.59
Aluminum	Al	13	26.98154	Molybdenum	Mo	42	95.94
Americium	Am	95	(243)	Neodymium	Nd	60	144.242
Antimony	Sb	51	121.760	Neon	Ne	10	20.1797
Argon	Ar	18	39.948	Neptunium	Np	93	(237)
Arsenic	As	33	74.92160	Nickel	Ni	28	58.6934
Astatine	At	85	(210)	Niobium	Nb	41	92.90638
Barium	Ba	56	137.327	Nitrogen	N	7	14.0067
Berkelium	Bk	97	(247)	Nobelium	No	102	(259)
Beryllium	Be	4	9.01218	Osmium	Os	76	190.23
Bismuth	Bi	83	208.98040	Oxygen	O	8	15.9994
Bohrium	Bh	107	(272)	Palladium	Pd	46	106.42
Boron	B	5	10.811	Phosphorus	P	15	30.97376
Bromine	Br	35	79.904	Platinum	Pt	78	195.084
Cadmium	Cd	48	112.411	Plutonium	Pu	94	(244)
Calcium	Ca	20	40.078	Polonium	Po	84	(209)
Californium	Cf	98	(251)	Potassium	K	19	39.0983
Carbon	C	6	12.0107	Praseodymium	Pr	59	140.90765
Cerium	Ce	58	140.116	Promethium	Pm	61	(145)
Cesium	Cs	55	132.90545	Protactinium	Pa	91	231.03588
Chlorine	Cl	17	35.453	Radium	Ra	88	(226)
Chromium	Cr	24	51.9961	Radon	Rn	86	(222)
Cobalt	Co	27	58.93320	Rhenium	Re	75	186.207
Copernicium	Cp	112	(285)	Rhodium	Rh	45	102.90550
Copper	Cu	29	63.546	Roentgenium	Rg	111	(280)
Curium	Cm	96	(247)	Rubidium	Rb	37	85.4678
Darmstadtium	Ds	110	(281)	Ruthenium	Ru	44	101.07
Dubnium	Db	105	(268)	Rutherfordium	Rf	104	(267)
Dysprosium	Dy	66	162.500	Samarium	Sm	62	150.36
Einsteinium	Es	99	(252)	Scandium	Sc	21	44.9559
Erbium	Er	68	167.259	Seaborgium	Sg	106	(271)
Europium	Eu	63	151.964	Selenium	Se	34	78.96
Fermium	Fm	100	(257)	Silicon	Si	14	28.0855
Fluorine	F	9	18.99840	Silver	Ag	47	107.8682
Francium	Fr	87	(223)	Sodium	Na	11	22.98977
Gadolinium	Gd	64	157.25	Strontium	Sr	38	87.62
Gallium	Ga	31	69.723	Sulfur	S	16	32.065
Germanium	Ge	32	72.64	Tantalum	Ta	73	180.94788
Gold	Au	79	196.96657	Technetium	Tc	43	(98)
Hafnium	Hf	72	178.49	Tellurium	Te	52	127.60
Hassium	Hs	108	(270)	Terbium	Tb	65	158.92535
Helium	He	2	4.00260	Thallium	Tl	81	204.3833
Holmium	Ho	67	164.93032	Thorium	Th	90	232.03806
Hydrogen	H	1	1.00794	Thulium	Tm	69	168.93421
Indium	In	49	114.818	Tin	Sn	50	118.710
Iodine	I	53	126.90447	Titanium	Ti	22	47.867
Iridium	Ir	77	192.217	Tungsten (wolfram)	W	74	183.85
Iron	Fe	26	55.845	Ununhexium	Uuh	116	(293)
Krypton	Kr	36	83.798	Ununoctium	Uuo	118	(294)
Lanthanum	La	57	138.90547	Ununpentium	Uup	115	(288)
Lawrencium	Lr	103	(262)	Ununquadium	Uuq	114	(289)
Lead	Pb	82	207.2	Ununtrium	Uut	113	(284)
Lithium	Li	3	6.941	Uranium	U	92	238.02891
Lutetium	Lu	71	174.967	Vanadium	V	23	50.9415
Magnesium	Mg	12	24.3050	Xenon	Xe	54	131.293
Manganese	Mn	25	54.93805	Ytterbium	Yb	70	173.04
Meitnerium	Mt	109	(276)	Yttrium	Y	39	88.90585
Mendelevium	Md	101	(258)	Zinc	Zn	30	65.409
				Zirconium	Zr	40	91.224

Applied Science

Chemistry

Chemistry is the science that deals with the properties, composition, and structure of substances (defined as elements and compounds), the transformations that they undergo, and the energy that is released or absorbed during these processes. Every substance, whether naturally occurring or artificially produced, consists of one or more of the hundred-odd species of atoms that have been identified as elements. Although these atoms, in turn, are composed of more elementary particles, they are the basic building blocks of chemical substances; there is no quantity of oxygen, mercury, or gold, for example, smaller than an atom of that substance. Chemistry, therefore, is concerned not with the subatomic domain but with the properties of atoms and the laws governing their combinations and with how the knowledge of these properties can be used to achieve specific purposes.

Physics

Physics is the science that deals with the structure of matter and the interactions between the fundamental constituents of the observable universe. The basic physical science, its aim is the discovery and formulation of the fundamental laws of nature. In the broadest sense, physics (from the Greek *physikos*) is concerned with all aspects of nature on both the macroscopic and submicroscopic levels. Its scope of study encompasses not only the behavior of objects under the action of given forces but also the nature and origin of gravitational, electromagnetic, and nuclear force fields. Its ultimate objective is the formulation of a few comprehensive principles that bring together and explain all such disparate phenomena. Physics can, at base, be defined as the science of matter, motion, and energy. Its laws are typically expressed with economy and precision in the language of mathematics.

Weight, Mass, and Density

Mass, strictly defined, is the quantitative measure of inertia, the resistance a body offers to a change in its speed or position when force is applied to it. The greater the mass of a body, the smaller the change produced by an applied force. In more practical terms, it is the measure of the amount of material in an object, and in common usage is often expressed as weight. However, the mass of an object is constant regardless of its position, while weight varies according to gravitational pull.

In the International System of Units (SI; the metric system), the kilogram is the standard unit of mass, defined as equaling the mass of the international prototype of the kilogram, currently a platinum-iridium cylinder kept at Sèvres, near Paris, France; it is roughly equal to the mass of 1,000 cubic centimeters of pure water at the temperature of its maximum density. In the US customary system, the unit is the slug, defined as the mass which a one pound force can accelerate at a rate of one foot per second per second, which is the same as the mass of an object weighing 32.17 pounds on the earth's surface.

Weight is the gravitational force of attraction on an object, caused by the presence of a massive second object, such as the Earth or Moon. Weight is the product of an object's mass and the acceleration of gravity at the point where the object is located. A given object will have the same mass on the Earth's surface, on the Moon, or in the absence of gravity, while its weight on the Moon would be about one sixth of its weight on the Earth's surface, because of the Moon's smaller gravitational pull (due in turn to the Moon's smaller mass and radius), and in the absence of gravity the object would have no weight at all.

Weight is measured in units of force, not mass, though in practice units of mass (such as the kilogram) are often substituted because of mass's relatively constant relation to weight on the Earth's surface. The weight of a body can be obtained by multiplying the mass by the acceleration of gravity. In SI, weight is expressed in newtons, or the force required to impart an acceleration of one meter per second per second to a mass of one kilogram. In the US customary system, it is expressed in pounds.

Density is the mass per unit volume of a material substance. It offers a convenient means of obtaining the mass of a body from its volume, or vice versa; the mass is equal to the volume multiplied by the density, while the volume is equal to the mass divided by the density. In SI, density is expressed in kilograms per cubic meter.

Communications

Introduction to the Internet

The Internet is a dynamic collection of computer networks that has revolutionized communications and methods of commerce by enabling those networks around the world to interact with each other. Sometimes referred to as a "network of networks," the Internet was developed in the United States in the 1970s but was not widely used by the general public until the early 1990s. By early 2009 nearly 1.6 billion people, or roughly 24% of the world's population, were estimated to be regular users of the Internet. It is widely assumed that at least half of the world's population will have some

Introduction to the Internet (continued)

form of Internet access by 2010 and that wireless access will play a growing role.

The Internet is so powerful and general that it can be used for almost any purpose that depends on the processing of information, and it is accessible by every individual who connects to one of its constituent networks. It supports human communication via electronic mail (**e-mail**), real-time "chat rooms," instant messaging (IM), newsgroups, and audio and video transmission and allows people to work collaboratively at many different locations. It supports access to information by many applications, including the **World Wide Web**, which uses text and graphical presentations. Publishing has been revolutionized, as whole novels and reference works are available on the Web, and online periodicals, including data prepared daily for an individual subscriber (such as stock market reports or news summaries), are also common. The Internet has attracted a large and growing number of "e-businesses" (including subsidiaries of traditional "brick-and-mortar" companies) that carry out most of their sales and services over the Internet.

While the precise structure of the future Internet is not yet clear, many directions of growth seem apparent. One is the increased availability of wireless access, enabling better real-time use of Web-managed information. Another future development is toward higher backbone and network access speeds. Backbone data rates of 10 billion bits (10 gigabits) per second are readily available today, but data rates of 1 trillion bits (1 terabit) per second or higher will eventually become commercially feasible. At very high data rates, high-resolution video, for example, would occupy only a small fraction of available bandwidth, and remaining bandwidth could be used to transmit auxiliary information about the data being sent, which in turn would enable rapid customization of displays and prompt resolution of certain local queries.

Communications connectivity will be a key function of a future Internet as more machines and devices are interconnected. Since the Internet Engineering Task Force published its 128-bit IP address standard in 1998, the increased number of available addresses (2^{128}, as opposed to 2^{32} under the previous standard) allowed almost every electronic device imaginable to be assigned a unique address. Thus the expressions "wired" office, home, and car may all take on new meanings, even if the access is really wireless.

Growth of Internet Use

Source: International Telecommunication Union, ICT Indicators Database.

YEAR	US USERS	WORLD USERS	YEAR	US USERS	WORLD USERS
1999	102,000,000	279,177,900	2004	194,159,000	934,952,700
2000	124,000,000	393,446,100	2005	205,766,900	1,047,860,400
2001	142,823,000	494,134,400	2006	210,720,400	1,216,976,900
2002	172,834,300	679,819,300	2007	221,724,000	1,402,145,800
2003	183,195,700	790,121,400	2008	220,000,000	1,542,464,500

Worldwide Cellular Mobile Telephone Subscribers, 2008

Source: International Telecommunication Union, ICT Indicators Database.

COUNTRY	SUBSCRIBERS	SUBSCRIBERS PER 1,000 RESIDENTS	COUNTRY	SUBSCRIBERS	SUBSCRIBERS PER 1,000 RESIDENTS
China	634,000,000	474	Vietnam	70,000,000	791
India	346,890,000	292	Philippines	68,101,800	760
United States	270,500,000	876	Turkey	65,824,100	868
Russia	187,500,000	1,323	Nigeria	62,988,500	416
Brazil	150,641,400	776	France	57,972,000	936
Indonesia	140,578,200	600	Ukraine	55,694,500	1,215
Japan	110,395,000	863	Spain	49,681,600	1,114
Germany	107,245,000	1,299	Argentina	46,508,800	1,165
Italy	88,580,000	1,503	Republic of Korea	45,607,000	943
Pakistan	88,019,700	527	South Africa	45,000,000	922
Thailand	79,065,800[1]	1,238[1]	Bangladesh	44,640,000	277
United Kingdom	75,565,400	1,238	Iran	43,000,000	596
Mexico	75,303,500	699	**world**	**4,014,191,800**	**597**

[1]Data for 2007.

Growth of Cell Phone Use in the US

Number of cellular mobile telephone subscribers in the US, 1997–2008. Source: CTIA-The Wireless Association's Annualized Wireless Industry Survey Results, December 1985–December 2008.

YEAR	SUBSCRIBERS	YEAR	SUBSCRIBERS	YEAR	SUBSCRIBERS	YEAR	SUBSCRIBERS
1997	55,312,293	2000	109,478,031	2003	158,721,981	2006	233,040,781
1998	69,209,321	2001	128,374,512	2004	182,140,362	2007	255,395,599
1999	86,047,003	2002	140,766,842	2005	207,896,198	2008	270,333,881

Aerospace Technology

Space Exploration

Three men were the first scientists to conceive pragmatically of spaceflight: the Russian **Konstantin Tsiolkovsky**, the American **Robert Goddard**, and the German **Hermann Oberth**. By the end of World War II, the German development of rocket propulsion for aircraft and guided missiles (notably the V-2) had reached a high level. After the war the US and its allies fell heir to the technical knowledge of rocket power developed by the Germans. The technical director of the German missile effort, **Wernher von Braun**, and some 150 of his top aides surrendered to US troops. Most immigrated to the US, where they assembled and launched V-2 missiles that had been captured and shipped there. The USSR carried out an unpublicized but extensive and likely similar program; Britain and France conducted smaller programs.

In both the US and the USSR the development of **military missile technology** was essential to the achievement of satellite flight. Preparations for the International Geophysical Year (IGY, 1957–58) stimulated discussion of the possibility of launching **artificial Earth satellites** for scientific investigations. Both the US and the USSR became determined to prepare scientific satellites for launching during the IGY. While the US was still developing a space launch vehicle, the USSR startled the world by placing **Sputnik 1** in orbit on 4 Oct 1957. This was followed a month later by **Sputnik 2**, which carried a live dog. The failure by the US to launch its small payload on 6 Dec 1957 heightened that country's political discomfiture in view of its supposed advanced status in science. Following debates on the necessity of achieving parity, the US government established the **National Aeronautics and Space Administration (NASA)** in 1958. Since that time, NASA has conducted virtually all major aspects of the US space program.

The first successful US satellite, **Explorer 1**, was launched about four months after Sputnik 1. During the next decades the two countries participated in a space race, conducting thousands of successful launches of spacecraft of all varieties including scientific-research, communications, meteorological, remote-sensing, military-reconnaissance, early-warning,

and navigation satellites, lunar and planetary probes, and manned craft. The USSR launched the first human, **Yury Gagarin**, into orbit around Earth on 12 Apr 1961. On 20 July 1969, the US landed two men, **Neil Armstrong** and **Edwin ("Buzz") Aldrin**, on the surface of the Moon as part of the **Apollo 11** mission. On 12 Apr 1981, the 20th anniversary of manned space flight, the US launched the first reusable manned space transportation system, the **space shuttle.** Since the 1960s various European countries, Japan, India, China, and other countries have formed their own agencies for space exploration and development. The **European Space Agency (ESA)** consists of 18 member states. Private corporations, too, offer space launches for communications and remote-sensing satellites.

In the post-Apollo decades, while the US focused much of its manned space program on the shuttle, the USSR concentrated on launching a series of increasingly sophisticated Earth-orbiting **space stations**, beginning with the world's first in 1971. Station crews, who were carried up in two- and three-person spacecraft, carried out mostly scientific missions while gaining experience in living and working for long periods in the space environment. After the USSR was dissolved in 1991, its space program was continued by Russia on a much smaller scale owing to economic constraints. The US launched a space station in 1973 using surplus Apollo hardware and conducted shuttle missions to a Russian station, Mir, in the 1990s. In 1998, at the head of a 16-country consortium and with Russia as a major partner, the US began in-orbit assembly of the **International Space Station (ISS)**, using the shuttle and Russian expendable launch vehicles to ferry the facility's modular components and crews into space. In addition to manned and unmanned lunar exploration, space exploration programs have included deep-space robotic missions to the planets, their moons, and smaller bodies such as comets and asteroids. Also important has been the development of unmanned space-based astronomical observatories, which allow observation of near and distant cosmic objects above the filtering and distorting effects of Earth's atmosphere.

Significant space programs and missions:

Sputnik (Russian for "fellow traveler")

Years launched: 1957–58. **Country or space agency:** USSR. **Designation:** 1 through 3 (first series). **Not manned. Events of note:** Sputnik 1 was the first satellite to be successfully launched into space, and Sputnik 2 carried a small dog named Laika ("Barker").

Vanguard

Years launched: 1958–59. **Country or space agency:** US. **Designation:** 1 through 3. **Not manned. Events of note:** The first attempted Vanguard launch, hastily mounted in December 1957 after the USSR's Sputnik successes, failed with the launch vehicle's explosion.

Explorer

Years launched: 1958–75. **Country or space agency:** US. **Designation:** 1 through 55. **Not manned. Events of note:** Explorer 1, the first successful US satellite, discovered Earth's inner radiation belt.

Pioneer

Years launched: 1958–78. **Country or space agency:** US. **Designation:** 1 through 13. **Not manned. Events of note:** Pioneer 10 was the first spacecraft to travel through the asteroid belt, to fly by Jupiter, and to escape the solar system; Pioneer 11 was the first to visit Saturn.

Luna (Russian for "Moon")

Years launched: 1959–76. **Country or space agency:** USSR. **Designation:** 1 through 24. **Not manned. Events of note:** Luna 2 was the first spacecaft to crash-land on the lunar surface; Luna 3 took the first photographs of the Moon's far side; three Lunas (16, 20, and 24) returned with samples of lunar soil.

Vostok (Russian for "east")

Years launched: 1961–63. **Country or space agency:** USSR. **Designation:** 1 through 6. **Manned. Events of note:** The first man in space and to orbit Earth was Soviet cosmonaut Yury Gagarin in Vostok 1, launched on 12 April 1961. Vostok 6 was launched with Valentina Tereshkova, the first woman in space, in 1963.

Mercury
Years launched: 1961–63 (manned missions). **Country or space agency:** US. **Designation:** Mercury spacecraft had program designations, but they were better known by the individual names bestowed on them, such as *Freedom 7*, to honor the seven NASA astronauts chosen for the program. **Events of note:** Some 20 preliminary unmanned Mercury missions took place between 1959 and 1961. Of the six manned missions, *Freedom 7* was launched in 1961 with Alan Shepard (the first American in space) aboard, and *Friendship 7* in 1962 with John Glenn (the first American to orbit Earth).

Ranger
Years launched: 1961–65. **Country or space agency:** US. **Designation:** 1 through 9. **Not manned. Events of note:** Ranger 4 was the first US spacecraft to crashland on the Moon; the last three Rangers returned thousands of images of the lunar surface before crashing on the lunar surface as planned.

Mariner
Years launched: 1962–73. **Country or space agency:** US. **Designation:** 1 through 10. **Not manned. Events of note:** Various Mariners in the program flew by Venus, Mercury, and Mars. Mariner 9 mapped Mars in detail from orbit, becoming the first spacecraft to orbit another planet. Mariner 10 was the first spacecraft to have visited the vicinity of Mercury.

Voskhod (Russian for "sunrise" or "ascent")
Years launched: 1964–65. **Country or space agency:** USSR. **Designation:** 1 and 2. **Manned. Events of note:** Voskhod 1 was the first spacecraft to carry more than one person; Aleksey Leonov performed the first space walk, from the Voskhod 2 spacecraft, on 18 Mar 1965.

Gemini
Years launched: 1965–66. **Country or space agency:** US. **Designation:** 1 through 12. **Manned. Events of note:** Ten two-person manned missions followed two unmanned test flights. Gemini 8 was the first spacecraft to rendezvous and dock with another craft. The Gemini program showed that astronauts could live and work in space for the time needed for a round-trip to the Moon.

Lunar Orbiter
Years launched: 1966–67. **Country or space agency:** US. **Designation:** 1 through 5. **Not manned. Events of note:** Five consecutive spacecraft made detailed photographic surveys of most of the Moon's surface, providing the mapping essential for choosing landing sites for the manned Apollo missions.

Soyuz (Russian for "union")
Years launched: 1967–present. **Country or space agency:** USSR. **Designation:** 1 through 40 (first series). Three subsequent series of upgraded spacecraft received the additional suffix letters T, TM, or TMA and were renumbered from 1. **Manned. Events of note:** On 24 Apr 1967 cosmonaut Vladimir Komarov conducted the inaugural test flight (Soyuz 1) of this multiperson transport craft but died returning to Earth after the parachute system failed, becoming the first fatality during a spaceflight. Soyuz 11 ferried the crew of the first space station, Salyut 1. Soyuz TM-2 made the inaugural manned flight of this TM upgrade while transporting the second crew of the Mir space station. Soyuz TM-31 carried up the International Space Station's first three-man crew.

Apollo
Years launched: 1968–72 (manned missions). **Country or space agency:** US. **Designation:** 7 through 17. **Events of note:** Several unmanned test flights preceded 11 manned Apollo missions, including two in Earth orbit (7 and 9), two in lunar orbit (8 and 10), one lunar flyby (13), and six lunar landings (11, 12, and 14–17) in which a total of 12 astronauts walked on the Moon. Apollo 11, crewed by Neil Armstrong, Michael Collins, and Buzz Aldrin, was the first mission to land humans on the Moon, on 20 Jul 1969. Apollo 13, planned as a lunar landing mission, experienced an onboard explosion en route to the Moon; after a swing around the Moon, the crippled spacecraft made a harrowing but safe return to Earth with its crew, James Lovell, John Swigert, and Fred Haise. The landing missions collectively returned almost 382 kg (842 lb) of lunar rocks and soil for study.

Salyut (Russian for "salute")
Years launched: 1971–82. **Country or space agency:** USSR. **Designation:** 1 through 7 (two designs). **Manned. Events of note:** Salyut 1, launched 19 Apr 1971, was the world's first space station; its crew, cosmonauts Georgy Dobrovolsky, Vladislav Volkov, and Viktor Patsayev, died returning to Earth when their Soyuz spacecraft depressurized. Salyut 6 operated as a highly successful scientific space platform, supporting a series of crews over a four-year period.

Skylab
Year launched: 1973. **Country or space agency:** US. **Manned. Events of note:** Skylab, based on the outfitted and pressurized upper stage of a Saturn V Moon rocket, was the first US space station. Three successive astronaut crews carried out solar astronomy studies, materials-sciences research, and biomedical experiments on the effects of weightlessness.

Apollo-Soyuz
Year launched: 1975. **Countries or space agencies:** US and USSR. **Manned. Events of note:** As a sign of improved US-Soviet relations, an Apollo spacecraft carrying three astronauts docked in Earth orbit with a Soyuz vehicle carrying two cosmonauts. It was the first cooperative multinational space mission.

Viking
Year launched: 1975. **Country or space agency:** US. **Designation:** 1 and 2. **Not manned. Events of note:** Both probes traveled to Mars, released landers, and took photographs of large expanses of Mars from orbit. The Viking 1 lander transmitted the first pictures from the Martian surface; both landers carried experiments designed to detect living organisms or life processes but found no convincing signs of life.

Voyager
Year launched: 1977. **Country or space agency:** US. **Designation:** 1 and 2. **Not manned. Events of note:** Both Voyager spacecraft flew past Jupiter and Saturn, transmitting measurements and photographs; Voyager 2 went on to Uranus in 1986 and then to Neptune. Both craft continued out of the solar system, with Voyager 1 overtaking Pioneer 10 in 1998 to become the most distant human-made object in space.

space shuttle (Space Transportation System, or STS)
Years launched: 1981–present. **Country or space**

agency: US. **Designation:** Individual missions were designated STS with a number (and sometimes letter) suffix, though the orbiter spacecraft themselves were reused. **Manned. Events of note:** The first flight of a manned space shuttle, STS-1, was on 12 Apr 1981 with the orbiter *Columbia*. The other original operational orbiters were *Challenger, Discovery,* and *Atlantis*. During shuttle mission STS-51-L, *Challenger* exploded after liftoff on 28 Jan 1986, killing all seven astronauts aboard, including a private citizen, Christa McAuliffe; the orbiter *Endeavour* was built as a replacement vehicle. Space shuttle missions were used to deploy satellites, space observatories, and planetary probes; to carry out in-space repairs of orbiting spacecraft; and to take US astronauts to the Russian space station Mir. Beginning in 1998 a series of shuttle missions ferried components, supplies, and crews to the International Space Station during its assembly and operation. In 2003 the orbiter *Columbia* disintegrated while returning from a space mission, claiming the lives of its seven-person crew, including Ilan Ramon, the first Israeli astronaut to go into space.

Giotto
Year launched: 1985. **Country or space agency:** ESA. **Not manned. Events of note:** This first deep-space probe launched by ESA made a close flyby of Halley's Comet, collecting data and transmitting images of the icy nucleus. It was then redirected to a second comet, using a gravity-assist flyby of Earth, the first time that a spacecraft coming back from deep space had made such a maneuver.

Mir (Russian for "peace" and "world")
Years launched: 1986–96. **Country or space agency:** USSR/Russia. **Manned. Events of note:** The core of this modular space station was launched on 20 Feb 1986; five additional modules were added over the next decade to create a large, versatile space laboratory. Although intended for a five-year life, it supported human habitation between 1986 and 2000, including an uninterrupted stretch of occupancy of almost 10 years, and it hosted a series of US astronauts as part of a Mir–space shuttle cooperative endeavor. In 1995 Mir cosmonaut Valery Polyakov set a space endurance record of nearly 438 days.

Magellan
Year launched: 1989. **Country or space agency:** US. **Not manned. Events of note:** Magellan was the first deep-space probe deployed by the space shuttle. During four years in orbit above Venus, it mapped some 98% of the surface of the planet with radar at high resolution. At the end of its mission, it was sent on a gradual dive into the Venusian atmosphere, where it measured various properties before burning up.

Galileo
Year launched: 1989. **Country or space agency:** US. **Not manned. Events of note:** Galileo released an atmospheric probe into the Jovian system and then went into orbit around Jupiter for an extended study of the giant planet and its Galilean moons. Among many discoveries, Galileo found evidence of a liquid-water ocean below the moon Europa's icy surface.

NEAR Shoemaker (Near Earth Asteroid Rendezvous)
Year launched: 1996. **Country or space agency:** US. **Not manned. Events of note:** This spacecraft was the first to orbit a small body (the Earth-approaching asteroid Eros) and then to touch down on its surface. It studied Eros for a year with cameras and instruments and then made a soft landing and transmitted gamma-ray data from the surface for more than two weeks.

Mars Pathfinder
Year launched: 1996. **Country or space agency:** US. **Not manned. Events of note:** This was the first spacecraft to land on Mars since the 1976 Viking missions; the lander and its robotic surface rover, Sojourner, together successfully collected 17,000 images and other data.

Cassini-Huygens
Year launched: 1997. **Countries or space agencies:** US and ESA. **Not manned. Events of note:** Consisting of an orbiter (Cassini) and a descent probe (Huygens), the spacecraft traveled to the Saturnian system. En route it flew by Jupiter and returned detailed images. Cassini then established an orbit around Saturn for several years of studies, while the Huygens probe parachuted through the atmosphere of the moon Titan, transmitting data during its descent and from the moon's surface.

International Space Station (ISS)
Years launched: 1998–present. **Countries or space agencies:** US, Russia, ESA, Canada, Japan, and Brazil. **Manned. Events of note:** A large complex of habitat modules and laboratories, the ISS continued to be assembled in Earth orbit by means of space-shuttle and Proton and Soyuz rocket flights that brought components, crews, and supplies. The first component, called Zarya, was launched on 20 Nov 1998. The ISS received its first resident crew on 2 Nov 2000.

Chandra X-Ray Observatory
Year launched: 1999. **Country or space agency:** US. **Not manned. Events of note:** The world's most powerful X-ray telescope, it revolves in an elliptical orbit around Earth, delivering roughly 1,000 observations of the universe annually.

2001 Mars Odyssey
Year launched: 2001. **Country or space agency:** US. **Not manned. Events of note:** This spacecraft was launched to study Mars from orbit and serve as a communications relay for future landers. Some of its data suggested the presence of huge subsurface reservoirs of frozen water in both polar regions.

Mars Express
Year launched: 2003. **Country or space agency:** ESA. **Not manned. Events of note:** The spacecraft's lander, Beagle 2, which was designed to examine the rocks and soil for signs of past or present life, failed to establish radio contact after presumably reaching the Martian surface.

Mars Exploration Rovers
Year launched: 2003. **Country or space agency:** US. **Designation:** Spirit and Opportunity. **Not manned. Events of note:** Twin six-wheeled robotic rovers, each equipped with cameras, a microscopic imager, a rock-grinding tool, and other instruments, landed on opposite sides of Mars. Both rovers found evidence of past water; particularly dramatic was the discovery by Opportunity of rocks that appeared to have been laid down at the shoreline of an ancient body of salty water.

Deep Impact
Year launched: 2005. **Country or space agency:** US. **Not manned. Events of note:** Deep Impact was the first

spacecraft designed to study the interior composition of a comet. It released an instrumented impactor into the path of Comet Tempel 1's icy nucleus. A high-resolution camera and other apparatuses on the flyby portion of the probe studied the impact and the resulting crater.

Mars Reconnaissance Orbiter

Year launched: 2005. **Country or space agency:** US. **Not manned. Events of note:** It carries the most powerful camera ever flown on a space mission. The Orbiter is an important communications link between other spacecraft, Mars, and Earth.

Phoenix

Year launched: 2007. **Country or space agency:** US. **Not manned. Events of note:** Phoenix was the first spacecraft designed to measure water (ice) on a planet other than Earth. It was equipped with robotic arms and sophisticated sensors to dig under the surface of Mars, collect soil samples, and analyze them. It landed on the surface of Mars on 25 May 2008 and quickly established communications with Earth. Before the end of its planned three-month experiment, Phoenix verifed the presence of water (ice) in the Martian subsurface.

Space Exploration Firsts

EVENT	DETAILS	COUNTRY OR AGENCY	DATE ACCOMPLISHED
first person to study in detail the use of rockets for spaceflight	Konstantin Tsiolkovsky	Russia	late 19th–early 20th centuries
first launch of a liquid-fueled rocket	Robert Goddard	US	16 Mar 1926
first launch of the V-2 ballistic missile, the forerunner of modern space rockets	Wernher von Braun	Germany	3 Oct 1942
first artificial Earth satellite	Sputnik 1	USSR	4 Oct 1957
first animal launched into space	dog Laika aboard Sputnik 2	USSR	3 Nov 1957
first spacecraft to hard-land on another celestial object (the Moon)	Luna 2	USSR	14 Sep 1959
first pictures of the far side of the Moon	Luna 3	USSR	7 Oct 1959
first applications satellite launched	TIROS 1 (weather observation)	US	1 Apr 1960
first recovery of a payload from Earth orbit	Discoverer 13	US	11 Aug 1960
first piloted spacecraft to orbit Earth	Vostok 1 (piloted by Yury Gagarin)	USSR	12 Apr 1961
first US citizen in space	Alan Shepard on Freedom 7	US	5 May 1961
first piloted US spacecraft to orbit Earth	Friendship 7 (piloted by John Glenn)	US	20 Feb 1962
first active communications satellite	Telstar 1	US	10 July 1962
first data transmitted to Earth from vicinity of another planet (Venus)	Mariner 2	US	14 Dec 1962
first woman in space	Valentina Tereshkova on Vostok 6	USSR	16 Jun 1963
first satellite to operate in geostationary orbit	Syncom 2 (telecommunications satellite)	US	26 Jul 1963
first space walk	Aleksey Leonov on Voskhod 2	USSR	18 Mar 1965
first spacecraft pictures of Mars	Mariner 4	US	14 Jul 1965
first spacecraft to soft-land on the Moon	Luna 9	USSR	3 Feb 1966
first death during a space mission	Vladimir Komarov on Soyuz 1	USSR	24 Apr 1967
first humans to orbit the Moon	Frank Borman, James Lovell, and William Anders on Apollo 8	US	24 Dec 1968
first human to walk on the Moon	Neil Armstrong on Apollo 11	US	20 Jul 1969
first unmanned spacecraft to carry lunar samples back to Earth	Luna 16	USSR	24 Sep 1970
first soft landing on another planet (Venus)	Venera 7	USSR	15 Dec 1970
first space station launched	Salyut 1	USSR	19 Apr 1971
first spacecraft to orbit another planet (Mars)	Mariner 9	US	13 Nov 1971
first spacecraft to soft-land on Mars	Mars 3	USSR	2 Dec 1971
first spacecraft to fly by Jupiter	Pioneer 10	US	3 Dec 1973
first international docking in space	Apollo and Soyuz spacecraft during Apollo-Soyuz Test Project	US/USSR	17 Jul 1975
first pictures transmitted from the surface of Mars	Viking 1	US	20 Jul 1976
first spacecraft to fly by Saturn	Pioneer 11	US	1 Sep 1979
first reusable spacecraft launched and returned from space	space shuttle Columbia	US	12–14 Apr 1981
first spacecraft to fly by Uranus	Voyager 2	US	24 Jan 1986
first spacecraft to make a close flyby of a comet's nucleus	Giotto at Halley's Comet	European Space Agency (ESA)	13 Mar 1986
first spacecraft to fly by Neptune	Voyager 2	US	24 Aug 1989
first large optical space telescope launched	Hubble Space Telescope	US/ESA	25 Apr 1990
first spacecraft to orbit Jupiter	Galileo	US	7 Dec 1995
first resident crew to occupy the International Space Station	William Shepherd, Yury Gidzenko, and Sergey Krikalev	US/Russia	2 Nov 2000
first spacecraft to orbit and land on an asteroid	NEAR Shoemaker at the asteroid Eros	US	14 Feb 2000– 12 Feb 2001

Space Exploration Firsts (continued)

EVENT	DETAILS	COUNTRY OR AGENCY	DATE ACCOMPLISHED
first piloted Chinese spacecraft to orbit Earth	Shenzhou 5, piloted by Yang Liwei	China	15 Oct 2003
first privately funded human spaceflight (to 100 km [62 mi])	SpaceShipOne, piloted by Michael W. Melvill (private venture)	US	21 Jun 2004
first spacecraft to strike a comet's nucleus and study its interior composition	Deep Impact at Comet Tempel 1	US	4 Jul 2005
first spacecraft designed to measure water (ice) on a planet other than Earth	Phoenix	US	5 Jun 2008

Air Travel

Flight History

Humanity has been fascinated with the possibility of flight for millennia. The history of flight began at least as early as about AD 400 with historical references to a Chinese kite that used a rotary wing as a source of lift. Toys using the principle of the helicopter—in this case a rotary blade turned by the pull of a string—were known during the Middle Ages. During the latter part of the 15th century, Leonardo da Vinci made drawings pertaining to flight. In the 1700s experiments were made with the ornithopter, a machine with flapping wings.

The history of successful flight begins with the hot-air balloon. Two French brothers, Joseph and Étienne Montgolfier, experimented with a large cell contrived of paper in which they could collect heated air. On 19 Sep 1783 the Montgolfiers sent aloft a balloon with a rooster, a duck, and a sheep, and on 21 November the first manned flight was made. Balloons gained importance as their flights increased into hundreds of miles, but they were essentially unsteerable.

Count Ferdinand von Zeppelin, a former military man, spent much of his life after retiring in 1890 working with balloons, particularly on the steering problem. Hydrogen and illuminating gas were eventually substituted for hot air, and a motor was mounted on a bag filled with gas that had been fitted with propellers and rudders. It was Zeppelin who first saw clearly that maintaining a steerable shape was essential. On 2 Jul 1900 Zeppelin undertook the first experimental flight of what he called an airship. The development of the dirigible went well until the docking procedure at Lakehurst NJ on 6 May 1937, when the Hindenburg burst into flames and exploded, with a loss of 36 lives. Public feeling about the craft made further development futile.

It should be remembered, however, that neither balloons nor dirigibles had produced true flight: what they had done was harness the dynamics of the atmosphere to lift a craft off the ground, using what power (if any) they supplied primarily to steer. The first scientific exposition of the principles that ultimately led to the successful flight with a heavier-than-air device came in 1843 from Sir George Cayley, who is regarded by many as the father of fixed-wing flight. He built a successful man-carrying glider that came close to permitting real flight. His work was built upon in the experimentson gliders from the late 1800s by Otto Lilienthal of Germany and Octave Chanute of the United States. The works of Cayley, Lilienthal, and Chanute would inspire the Wright brothers.

The Americans Wilbur and Orville Wright by 1902 had developed a fully practical biplane glider that could be controlled in every direction. Fitting a small engine and two propellers to another biplane, the Wrights on 17 Dec 1903 made the world's first successful flight of a man-carrying, engine-powered, heavier-than-air craft at a site near Kitty Hawk NC.

World War I (1914–18) further accelerated the expansion of aviation. Though initially used for aerial reconnaissance, aircraft were soon fitted with machine guns to shoot at other aircraft and with bombs to drop on ground targets; military aircraft with these types of missions and armaments became known, respectively, as fighters and bombers.

By the 1920s the first small commercial airlines had begun to carry mail, and the increased speed and range of aircraft made nonstop flights over the world's oceans, poles, and continents possible. In the 1930s more efficient monoplane aircraft with all-metal fuselages and retractable undercarriages became standard. Aircraft played a key role in World War II (1939–45), developing in size, weight, speed, power, range, and armament. The war marked the high point of piston-engined propeller craft while also introducing the first aircraft with jet engines, which could fly at higher speeds. Jet-engined craft became the norm for fighters in the late 1940s and proved their superiority as commercial transports beginning in the '50s. The high speeds and low operating costs of jet airliners led to a massive expansion of commercial air travel in the second half of the 20th century.

The next great aviation innovation after the jet engine was aircraft able to fly at supersonic speeds. The first was a Bell XS-1 rocket-powered research plane piloted by Maj. Charles E. Yeager of the US Air Force on 14 Oct 1947. The XS-1 broke the sound barrier at 1,066 km/hr (662 mph) and attained a top speed of 1,126 km/hr (700 mph). Thereafter many military aircraft capable of supersonic flight were built. The first supersonic passenger-carrying commercial airplane, the Concorde, was built jointly by aircraft manufacturers in Great Britain and France and was in regular commercial service between 1976 and 2003. In the 21st century aircraft manufacturers strove to produce larger planes. A huge new passenger airliner, the double-decker Airbus A380, with a passenger capacity of 555 (40% greater than the next largest airplane), began commercial flights in late October 2007. The Boeing 787 Dreamliner, undergoing final tests in 2009, has a capacity of 330 but a range of 3,050 nautical miles, making it more fuel-efficient than the A380.

Airlines in the US: Best On-Time Arrival Performance

Data for 2008.
Source: *US Department of Transportation, February 2009.*

	AIRLINE	% OF ALL FLIGHTS		AIRLINE	% OF ALL FLIGHTS		AIRLINE	% OF ALL FLIGHTS
1	Hawaiian Airlines	90.0	7	Northwest Airlines	76.8	11	Continental Airlines	74.0
2	Southwest Airlines	80.5	8	AirTran Airways	76.7	12	Mesa Airlines	73.0
3	US Airways	80.1	9	Delta Air Lines	76.4	13	American Eagle	72.9
4	Frontier Airlines	79.0	10	Atlantic Southeast	74.2		JetBlue Airways	72.9
	SkyWest Airlines	79.0		Airlines		15	United Airlines	71.6
6	Alaska Airlines	78.3						

World's Busiest Airports

Ranked by total aircraft movement (takeoffs and landings), 2008.
Source: *Airports Council International (preliminary statistics), <www.airports.org>.*

RANK	AIRPORT	SERVES	AIRPORT CODE	TOTAL MOVEMENTS
1	Hartsfield-Jackson Atlanta International Airport	Atlanta GA	ATL	978,824
2	O'Hare International Airport	Chicago IL	ORD	881,566
3	Dallas/Fort Worth International Airport	Dallas/Fort Worth TX	DFW	656,310
4	Denver International Airport	Denver CO	DEN	615,573
5	Los Angeles International Airport	Los Angeles CA	LAX	615,525
6	McCarran International Airport	Las Vegas NV	LAS	578,949
7	George Bush Intercontinental Airport	Houston TX	IAH	576,062
8	Paris Charles de Gaulle International Airport	Paris, France	CDG	559,812
9	Charlotte Douglas International Airport	Charlotte NC	CLT	536,253
10	Phoenix Sky Harbor International Airport	Phoenix AZ	PHX	502,499
11	Philadelphia International Airport	Philadelphia PA	PHL	492,010
12	Frankfurt Airport	Frankfurt, Germany	FRA	485,783
13	Heathrow Airport	London, UK	LHR	478,569
14	Madrid Barajas International Airport	Madrid, Spain	MAD	469,740
15	Detroit Metropolitan Wayne County Airport	Detroit MI	DTW	462,284
16	Minneapolis–St. Paul International Airport	Minneapolis/St. Paul MN	MSP	446,840
17	Amsterdam Airport Schiphol	Amsterdam, Netherlands	AMS	446,626
18	John F. Kennedy International Airport	New York NY	JFK	435,750
19	Newark Liberty International Airport	Newark NJ	EWR	433,463
20	Munich International Airport	Munich, Germany	MUC	432,296
21	Beijing Capital International Airport	Beijing, China	PEK	431,675
22	Toronto Pearson International Airport	Toronto, ON, Canada	YYZ	429,829
23	San Francisco International Airport	San Francisco CA	SFO	387,710
24	Salt Lake City International Airport	Salt Lake City UT	SLC	387,695
25	Van Nuys Airport	Los Angeles CA	VNY	386,706

Meteorology

World Temperature Extremes

	highest recorded air temperature			lowest recorded air temperature		
REGION	PLACE (ELEVATION)	°F	°C	PLACE (ELEVATION)	°F	°C
Africa	Al-'Aziziyah, Libya (112 m [367 ft]; 13 Sep 1922)	136.0	57.8	Ifrane, Morocco (1,635 m [5,364 ft]; 11 Feb 1935)	−11.0	−23.9
Antarctica	Vanda Station, Scott Coast (15 m [49 ft]; 5 Jan 1974)	59.0	15.0	Vostok, 78° 27″ S, 106° 52′ E (3,420 m [11,220 ft]; 21 Jul 1983)	−129.0	−89.4
Asia	Tirat Zevi, Israel (−220 m [−722 ft]; 21 Jun 1942)	129.0	53.9	Oymyakon, Russia (806 m [2,625 ft]; 6 Feb 1933)	−90.0	−67.8
Australia	Cloncurry, Queensland (190 m [622 ft]; 16 Jan 1889)	128.0	53.3	Charlotte Pass, New South Wales (1,755 m [5,758 ft]; 29 Jun 1994)	−9.4	−23.0
Europe	Seville, Spain (8 m [26 ft]; 4 Aug 1881)	122.0	50.0	Ust-Shchuger, Russia (85 m [279 ft]; exact date unknown)	−67.0	−55.0
North America	Greenland Ranch, Death Valley, California (−54 m [−178 ft]; 10 Jul 1913)	134.0	56.7	Snag, Yukon (646 m [2,120 ft]; 3 Feb 1947)	−81.4	−63.0

World Temperature Extremes (continued)

REGION	highest recorded air temperature			lowest recorded air temperature		
	PLACE (ELEVATION)	°F	°C	PLACE (ELEVATION)	°F	°C
South America	Rivadavia, Argentina (206 m [676 ft]; 11 Dec 1905)	120.0	48.9	Colonia, Sarmiento, Argentina (268 m [879 ft]; 1 Jun 1907)	−27.0	−32.8
Tropical Pacific	Tuguegarao, Philippines (22 m [72 ft]; 29 Apr 1912)	108.0	42.2	Haleakala, Hawaii (2,972 m [9,750 ft]; 17 May 1979)	12.0	−11.1

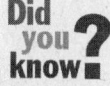

Did you know? The oldest detected meteorite impact on Earth occurred 3.47 billion years ago. The meteor left geochemical evidence of its impact in southern Africa and Australia and is thought to have been about 20 km (12 mi) wide. It would have taken less than two seconds to pass through the atmosphere and slam into the surface of the planet, causing immense tsunamis and devastating erosion to the ocean floor and small continents.

Indexes

Wind Chill Index

The wind chill index is based upon a formula that determines how cold the atmosphere feels by combining the temperature and wind speed and applying other factors. For more information, see <www.nws.noaa.gov/om/windchill/index.shtml>.

	CALM	40	35	30	25	20	15	10	5	0	−5	−10	−15	−20	−25	−30
	5	36	31	25	19	13	7	1	−5	−11	−16	−22	−28	−34	−40	−46
	10	34	27	21	15	9	3	−4	−10	−16	−22	−28	−35	−41	−47	−53
	15	32	25	19	13	6	0	−7	−13	−19	−26	−32	−39	−45	−51	−58
	20	30	24	17	11	4	−2	−9	−15	−22	−29	−35	−42	−48	−55	−61
WIND	25	29	23	16	9	3	−4	−11	−17	−24	−31	−37	−44	−51	−58	−64
SPEED	30	28	22	15	8	1	−5	−12	−19	−26	−33	−39	−46	−53	−60	−67
(MPH)	35	28	21	14	7	0	−7	−14	−21	−27	−34	−41	−48	−55	−62	−69
	40	27	20	13	6	−1	−8	−15	−22	−29	−36	−43	−50	−57	−64	−71
	45	26	19	12	5	−2	−9	−16	−23	−30	−37	−44	−51	−58	−65	−72
	50	26	19	12	4	−3	−10	−17	−24	−31	−38	−45	−52	−60	−67	−74
	55	25	18	11	4	−3	−11	−18	−25	−32	−39	−46	−54	−61	−69	−75
	60	25	17	10	3	−4	−11	−19	−26	−33	−40	−48	−55	−62	−69	−76

TEMPERATURE (°F)

Heat Index

The Heat Index shows the effects of the combination of heat and humidity. Apparent temperature is the temperature as it feels to your body. For more information see <www.jeonet.com/heat.htm>.

relative humidity	70	75	80	85	90	95	100	105	110	115	120
0%	64	69	73	78	83	87	91	95	99	103	107
10%	65	70	75	80	85	90	95	100	105	111	116
20%	66	72	77	82	87	93	99	105	112	120	130
30%	67	73	78	84	90	96	104	113	123	135	148
40%	68	74	79	86	93	101	110	123	137	151	
50%	69	75	81	88	96	107	120	135	150		
60%	70	76	82	90	100	114	132	149			
70%	70	77	85	93	106	124	144				
80%	71	78	86	97	113	136	157				
90%	71	79	88	102	122	150	170				
100%	72	80	91	108	133	166					

AIR TEMPERATURE (°F)

apparent temperature

Ultraviolet (UV) Index

The Ultraviolet (UV) Index predicts the intensity of the sun's ultraviolet rays. It was developed by the National Weather Service and the US Environmental Protection Agency to provide a daily forecast of the expected risk of overexposure to the sun. The Index is calculated on a next-day basis for dozens of cities across the US. Other local conditions, such as cloud cover, are taken into account in determining the UV Index number. UV Index numbers are: 0–2 (minimal exposure); 3–4 (low exposure); 5–6 (moderate exposure); 7–9 (high exposure); and 10 and over (very high exposure).

Some simple precautions can be taken to reduce the risk of sun-related illness: limit time in the sun between 10 AM and 4 PM, when rays are generally the strongest; seek shade whenever possible; use a broad spectrum sunscreen with an SPF of at least 15; wear a wide-brimmed hat and, if possible, tightly woven, full-length clothing; wear UV-protective sunglasses; avoid sunlamps and tanning salons; and watch for the UV Index daily. The UV Index should not be used by seriously sun-sensitive individuals, who should consult their doctors and take additional precautions regardless of the exposure level.

Hurricanes

Hurricane and Tornado Classifications

The **Saffir/Simpson Hurricane Scale**[1] is used to rank tropical cyclones.

Category 1. *Barometric pressure: 28.91 in or more; wind speed: 74–95 mph; storm surge: 4–5 ft; damage: minimal.*

Category 2. *Barometric pressure: 28.50–28.91 in; wind speed: 96–110 mph; storm surge: 6–8 ft; damage: moderate.*

Category 3. *Barometric pressure: 27.91–28.47 in; wind speed: 111–130 mph; storm surge: 9–12 ft; damage: extensive.*

Category 4. *Barometric pressure: 27.17–27.88 in; wind speed: 131–155 mph; storm surge: 13–18 ft; damage: extreme.*

Category 5. *Barometric pressure: less than 27.17 in; wind speed: 155 mph or more; storm surge: 18 ft or more; damage: catastrophic.*

Tornado classifications.
Tornado intensity is commonly estimated after the fact by analyzing damaged structures and then correlating the damage with the wind speeds known to produce various degrees of damage. Tornadoes are assigned specific values on the Fujita Scale, or F-Scale, of tornado intensity established by meteorologist T. Theodore Fujita.

Categories:

F0. *Wind speed: 40–72 mph; damage: light.*

F1. *Wind speed: 73–112 mph; damage: moderate.*

F2. *Wind speed: 113–157 mph; damage: considerable.*

F3. *Wind speed: 158–206 mph; damage: severe.*

F4. *Wind speed: 207–260 mph; damage: devastating.*

F5. *Wind speed: 261–318 mph; damage: incredible.*

[1]*Published by permission of Herbert Saffir, consulting engineer, and Robert Simpson, meteorologist.*

Hurricane Names

Source: National Hurricane Center.

In 1953, the National Hurricane Center developed a list of given names for Atlantic tropical storms. This list is now maintained by the World Meteorological Organization (WMO). Until 1979 only women's names were used, but since then men's and women's names have alternated. There are six lists currently in rotation, so names can be reused every six years. Any country affected by a hurricane, however, can request that its name be retired for ten years. Also, if a storm has been particularly destructive, the WMO can remove it from the list and replace it with a different name.

Deadliest Hurricanes in the US

Listed below, in order of number of deaths, are the 25 deadliest hurricanes to hit the US or its territories in 1851–2006. Hurricane names are given in parentheses after the location, when applicable.

Note: ranking numbers 10 and 20 on the list are repeated due to the equal number of fatalities in separate hurricanes. Source: National Hurricane Center. <www.nhc.noaa.gov/Deadliest_Costliest.shtml>.

	HURRICANE LOCATION	YEAR	CATEGORY	DEATHS
1	Galveston TX	1900	4	8,000[1]
2	NC; SC; Puerto Rico	1899	3	3,419
3	Lake Okeechobee, Florida	1928	4	2,500[2]
4	Cheniere Caminada LA	1893	4	2,000[3]
5	southeastern LA; MS (Katrina)	2005	3	1,500
6	Sea Islands, South Carolina and Georgia	1893	3	1,000[4]
7	Puerto Rico; US Virgin Islands	1867	3	811
8	Puerto Rico	1852	1	800
9	GA; SC	1881	2	700
10	Last Island, Louisiana	1856	4	600[3]

Deadliest Hurricanes in the US (continued)

	HURRICANE LOCATION	YEAR	CATEGORY	DEATHS
10	New Orleans LA	1915	4	600[3]
12	southwestern LA; northern TX (Audrey)	1957	4	416
13	Florida Keys	1935	5	408
14	northeastern US	1944	3	390[3]
15	FL; MS; AL	1926	4	372
16	Grand Isle LA	1909	3	350
17	Puerto Rico (San Felipe)	1928	5	312
18	Florida Keys; southern TX	1919	4	287

	HURRICANE LOCATION	YEAR	CATEGORY	DEATHS
19	Galveston TX	1915	4	275
20	MS; southeastern LA; VA (Camille)	1969	5	256
20	New England	1938	3	256
22	US Virgin Islands; Puerto Rico	1932	2	225
23	northeastern US (Diane)	1955	1	184
24	GA; SC; NC	1898	4	179
25	TX	1875	3	176

[1]Death toll may have been as high as 12,000.   [2]Death toll may have been as high as 3,000.   [3]Including those lost at sea.   [4]Death toll may have been as high as 2,000.

Costliest Hurricanes in the US

Listed below, in order of the highest monetary damage figures in constant 2008 US dollars, are the 25 costliest hurricanes to hit the US or its territories in 1900–2008. Locations of the damaged areas are given in parentheses after the hurricane name. Note that figures for Hurricane Hugo reflect the damage done by that storm both on the US mainland and on its Caribbean territories. Source: National Hurricane Center.
<www.nhc.noaa.gov/Deadliest_Costliest.shtml>.

RANK	HURRICANE (LOCATION)	YEAR	CATEGORY	ESTIMATED DAMAGE (US$), NOT ADJUSTED	DAMAGE IN CONSTANT 2008 US DOLLARS
1	Katrina (southeastern FL; southeastern LA; MS)	2005	3	81,000,000,000	89,296,200,000
2	Andrew (southeastern FL; southeastern LA)	1992	5	26,500,000,000	40,666,600,000
3	Wilma (southern FL)	2005	3	20,600,000,000	22,709,900,000
4	Ike (TX; LA)	2008	2	19,300,000,000	19,300,000,000
5	Charley (southwestern FL)	2004	4	15,000,000,000	17,096,600,000
6	Ivan (AL; northwestern FL)	2004	3	14,200,000,000	16,184,800,000
7	Hugo (SC; US Virgin Islands; Puerto Rico)	1989	4	8,000,000,000	13,890,500,000
8	Rita (southwestern LA; northern TX)	2005	3	11,300,000,000	12,457,400,000
9	Agnes (FL; northeastern US)	1972	1	2,100,000,000	10,816,700,000
10	Frances (FL)	2004	2	8,900,000,000	10,144,000,000
11	Betsy (southeastern FL; southeastern LA)	1965	3	1,420,500,000	9,709,100,000
12	Camille (MS; southeastern LA; VA)	1969	5	1,420,700,000	8,334,600,000
13	Jeanne (FL)	2004	3	6,900,000,000	7,864,400,000
14	Frederic (AL; MS)	1979	3	2,300,000,000	6,820,900,000
15	Diane (northeastern US)	1955	1	831,700,000	6,681,600,000
16	Allison (northern TX)	2001	TS[1]	5,000,000,000	6,078,600,000
17	Floyd (mid-Atlantic US; northeastern US)	1999	2	4,500,000,000	5,815,500,000
18	(New England)	1938	3	300,000,000	4,580,900,000
19	Fran (NC)	1996	3	3,200,000,000	4,391,100,000
20	Alicia (northern TX)	1983	3	2,000,000,000	4,323,400,000
21	Gustav (LA)	2008	2	4,300,000,000	4,300,000,000
22	Opal (northwestern FL; AL)	1995	3	3,000,000,000	4,238,300,000
23	Isabel (mid-Atlantic US)	2003	2	3,370,000,000	3,943,300,000
24	Carol (northeastern US)	1954	3	460,000,000	3,681,800,000
25	Juan (LA)	1985	1	1,500,000,000	3,001,400,000

[1]Of tropical storm intensity but included because of high damage.

Did you know? The amount of water in river systems at any given time is but a tiny fraction of the Earth's total water. The oceans contain 97% of all water. About three-quarters of all fresh water is stored as land ice; nearly all of the remainder occurs as groundwater. Lakes account for less than 0.5% of all fresh water, soil moisture 0.05%, and water in river channels only 0.025%, or about one four-thousandth of the Earth's total fresh water.

Geologic Disasters

Measuring Earthquakes

The seismologists Beno Gutenberg and Charles Francis Richter introduced measurement of the seismic energy released by earthquakes on a magnitude scale in 1935. Each increase of one unit on the scale represents a 10-fold increase in the magnitude of an earthquake. Seismographs are designed to measure the different components of seismic waves, such as wave type, intensity, and duration. This table shows the typical effects of earthquakes in various magnitude ranges. For further information, see <www.seismo.unr.edu/ftp/pub/louie/class/100/magnitude.html>.

MAGNITUDE	EARTHQUAKE EFFECTS
Less than 3.5	Generally not felt, but recorded.
3.5–5.4	Often felt, but rarely causes damage.
Less than 6.0	At most, slight damage to well-designed buildings. Can cause major damage to poorly constructed buildings over small regions.
6.1–6.9	Can be destructive in areas up to about 100 km (61 mi) across where people live.
7.0–7.9	Major earthquake. Can cause serious damage over larger areas.
8 or greater	Great earthquake. Can cause serious damage in areas several hundred km across.

Major Historical Earthquakes

Magnitudes given for pre-20th-century events are generally estimations from intensity data. In cases where no magnitude is available, the earthquake's maximum intensity, written as a Roman numeral from I to XII, is given.

YEAR (AD)	AFFECTED AREA	MAGNITUDE OR INTENSITY	DEATHS
365	Knossos, Crete, Greece	XI	50,000
526	Antioch, Syria	unknown	250,000
844	Damascus, Syria	VIII	50,000
847	Damascus, Syria	X	70,000
847	Mosul, Iraq	unknown	50,000
856	Damghan, Iran	unknown	200,000
893	Daipur, India	unknown	180,000
893	Ardabil, Iran	unknown	150,000
893	Caucasus	unknown	82,000
1042	Palmyra, Syria	X	50,000
1138	Aleppo, Syria	unknown	230,000
1201	Upper Egypt or Syria	IX	1,100,000
1268	Cilicia, Turkey	unknown	60,000
1290	Chihli, China	unknown	100,000
1556	Shaanxi province, China	8.0	830,000
1667	Shemakha, Azerbaijan	unknown	80,000
1668	Shandong province, China	XII	50,000
1693	Sicily, Italy	7.5	60,000
1703	Jeddo, Japan	unknown	200,000
1727	Tabriz, Iran	unknown	77,000
1730	Hokkaido, Japan	unknown	137,000
1731	Beijing, China	unknown	100,000
1739	China	X	50,000
1755	Lisbon, Portugal; Spain; Morocco	8.7	70,000
1755	Kashan, Iran	unknown	40,000
1780	Tabriz, Iran	unknown	100,000
1783	Calabria, Italy	unknown	50,000
1811	New Madrid MO	8.6	unknown
1812	Caracas, Venezuela	7.7	26,000
1835	northern Japan	7.6	28,300
1857	Tejon Pass, California	7.9	1
1868	Arica, Chile	9.0	25,000
1868	Ecuador; Colombia	7.7	70,000
1883	Java, Indonesia	unknown	100,000
1896	Sanriku, Japan	8.5	27,000

YEAR (AD)	AFFECTED AREA	MAGNITUDE OR INTENSITY	DEATHS
1905	Calabria, Italy	7.9	557
1905	Kangra, India	7.5	19,000
1906	off the coast of Ecuador	8.8	1,000
1906	Valparaíso, Chile	8.2	20,000
1906	San Francisco CA	7.8	c. 3,000
1907	southwestern Tajikistan	8.0	12,000
1908	Messina, Italy	7.2	70,000
1912	Sea of Marmara, Turkey	7.8	2,800
1915	Avezzano, Italy	7.0	32,610
1920	Ningxia province, China	7.8	200,000
1923	Tokyo; Yokohama, Japan	7.9	143,000
1927	Qinghai province, China	7.6	40,900
1932	Gansu province, China	7.6	unknown
1933	Sanriku, Japan	8.4	2,990
1935	Quetta, Pakistan	7.5	30,000
1939	Erzincan, Turkey	7.8	32,700
1939	Chillán, Chile	7.8	28,000
1944	Tonankai, Japan	8.1	998
1944	San Juan, Argentina	7.4	c. 8,000
1945	off the coast of Pakistan	8.0	4,000
1946	Nankaido, Japan	8.1	1,362
1948	Ashgabat, Turkmenistan	7.3	110,000
1950	China-India border, near Myanmar (Burma)	8.6	1,526
1960	Puerto Montt, Chile	9.5	1,655–5,700
1960	Agadir, Morocco	5.7	10,000–15,000
1964	Prince William Sound, Alaska	9.2	128
1968	Khorasan, Iran	7.3	12,000
1970	northern Peru	7.9	66,000
1970	Yunnan province, China	7.5	10,000
1972	Fars, Iran	7.1	5,054
1972	Managua, Nicaragua	6.2	5,000
1974	Yunnan province, China	6.8	20,000
1974	North-West Frontier Province, Pakistan	6.2	5,300
1975	Liaoning province, China	7.0	2,000
1976	Mindanao, Philippines	7.9	8,000

Major Historical Earthquakes (continued)

YEAR (AD)	AFFECTED AREA	MAGNITUDE OR INTENSITY	DEATHS	YEAR (AD)	AFFECTED AREA	MAGNITUDE OR INTENSITY	DEATHS
1976	Tangshan, China	7.5	255,000–655,000	1998	Feyzabad, Afghanistan	6.6	4,000
1976	Guatemala City, Guatemala	7.5	23,000	1999	Taiwan	7.6	2,400
				1999	Golcuk, Turkey	7.6	17,118
1976	Turkey-Iran border	7.3	5,000	2001	El Salvador	7.7	852
1977	Bucharest, Romania	7.2	1,500	2001	Gujarat state, India	7.6	20,023
1978	Khorasan, Iran	7.8	15,000	2003	northern Algeria	6.8	2,266
1979	Colombia; Ecuador	7.9	579	2003	Bam, Iran	6.6	31,000
1980	Ech-Chéliff (El-Asnam), Algeria	7.7	5,000	2004	off the western coast of Sumatra, Indonesia	9.1	227,898
1980	southern Italy	6.5	3,114	2005	northern Sumatra, Indonesia	8.6	1,313
1985	Michoacán state, Mexico	8.0	9,500–35,000	2005	Kashmir, Pakistan	7.6	c. 86,000
1988	Gyumri (Leninakan), Armenia	6.8	25,000	2006	Kuril Islands, Russia	8.3	unknown
				2006	Tonga	7.9	unknown
1990	Luzon, Philippines	7.7	1,621	2006	Bantul, Indonesia	6.3	5,749
1990	Rasht, Iran	7.4	50,000	2007	southern Sumatra, Indonesia	8.5	25
1991	northern India	6.8	2,000				
1992	Flores, Indonesia	7.5	2,500	2007	Solomon Islands	8.1	54
1993	Latur, India	6.2	9,748	2007	off the coast of central Peru	8.0	514
1995	Sakhalin Island, Russia	7.1	1,989				
1995	Kobe, Japan	6.9	5,502	2008	eastern Sichuan province, China	7.9	69,000–87,000
1997	eastern Iran	7.3	1,567	2009	central Italy	6.3	295

Tsunami

A tsunami is a catastrophic ocean wave, usually caused by a submarine earthquake occurring less than 30 mi (50 km) beneath the seafloor, with a magnitude greater than 6.5. Underwater or coastal landslides or volcanic eruptions also may cause a tsunami. The often-used term tidal wave is a misnomer: the wave has no connection with the tides. After the earthquake or other generating impulse, a train of simple, progressive oscillatory waves is propagated great distances at the ocean surface in ever-widening circles, much like the waves produced by a pebble falling into a shallow pool. In deep water, the wavelengths are enormous, about 60 to 125 mi (100 to 200 km), and the wave heights are very small, only 1 to 2 ft (0.3 to 0.6 m). The resulting wave steepness is extremely low; coupled with the waves' long periods that vary from five minutes to an hour, this enables normal wind waves and swell to completely obscure the waves in deep water. Thus, a ship in the open ocean experiences the passage of a tsunami as an insignificant rise and fall. As the waves approach the continental coasts, friction with the increasingly shallow bottom reduces the velocity of the waves. The period must remain constant; consequently, as the velocity lessens, the wavelengths become shortened and the wave amplitudes increase, coastal waters rising as high as 100 feet (30 m) in 10 to 15 minutes. By a poorly understood process, the continental shelf waters begin to oscillate after the rise in sea level. Between three and five major oscillations generate most of the damage; the oscillations cease, however, only several days after they begin. Occasionally, the first arrival of a tsunami at a coast may be a trough, the water receding and exposing the shallow seafloor.

Deadly Volcano Eruptions
Casualty figures are approximate.

VOLCANO (LOCATION)	YEAR	CASUALTIES	VOLCANO (LOCATION)	YEAR	CASUALTIES
Tambora (Indonesia)	1815	92,000[1]	Raung (Indonesia)	1730	3,000
Krakatoa (Indonesia)	1883	36,000[1]	Lamington (Papua New Guinea)	1951	3,000
Pelée (Martinique)	1902	30,000	Awu (Indonesia)	1856	2,800
Ruiz (Colombia)	1985	25,000[2]	Taal (Philippines)	1906	1,500
Etna (Italy)	1669	20,000	Taal (Philippines)	1911	1,300
Unzen (Japan)	1792	15,000	Etna (Italy)	1536	1,000
Kelud (Indonesia)	1586	10,000	Paricutín (Mexico)	1949	1,000
Laki (Iceland)	1783	9,000	Purace (Colombia)	1949	1,000
Kelud (Indonesia)	1919	5,000	Pinatubo (Philippines)	1991	350
Vesuvius (Italy)	79	3,360	El Chichón (Mexico)	1982	100
Awu (Indonesia)	1711	3,200	St. Helens (Washington)	1980	57
Raung (Indonesia)	1638	3,000			

[1]Includes tsunami triggered by eruption.   [2]Includes mudflow triggered by eruption.

Civil Engineering

The Seven Wonders of the Ancient World

The seven wonders of the ancient world were considered to be the preeminent architectural and sculptural achievements of the Mediterranean and Middle East. Although different lists exist, the classic list contains the following:

Pyramids of Giza. The oldest of the wonders and the only one substantially in existence today, the pyramids of Giza were erected c. 2575–c. 2465 BC on the west bank of the Nile River in northern Egypt. The designations of the pyramids—Khufu, Khafre, and Menkaure—correspond to the kings for whom they were built. Khufu (also called the Great Pyramid) is the largest of the three, the length of each side at the base averaging 230 m (755 ¾ ft). According to Herodotus, the Great Pyramid took 20 years to construct and demanded the labor of 100,000 men.

Hanging Gardens of Babylon. A series of landscaped terraces ascribed to either Queen Sammu-ramat (810–783 BC) or King Nebuchadrezzar II (c. 605–c. 561 BC), the gardens were built within the walls of the royal palace at Babylon (in present-day southern Iraq). They did not actually "hang" but were instead roof gardens laid out on a series of ziggurat terraces that were irrigated by pumps from the Euphrates River.

Statue of Zeus. An ornate figure of Zeus on his throne, this wonder was completed about 430 BC by Phidias of Athens after eight years of work. It was placed in the huge Temple of Zeus at Olympia in western Greece. The statue, almost 12 m (40 ft) high and plated with gold and ivory, represented the god sitting on an elaborate throne ornamented with ebony, ivory, gold, and precious stones. On his outstretched right hand was a statue of Nike (Victory), and in the god's left hand was a scepter on which an eagle was perched.

Temple of Artemis. The great temple was built by Croesus, king of Lydia, in about 550 BC and was rebuilt after being burned by a madman named Herostratus in 356 BC. The artemesium was famous not only for its great size (over 110 by 55 m [350 by 80 ft]) but also for the magnificent works of art that adorned it. It was destroyed by invading Goths in AD 262, and though it was never rebuilt, copies survive of the famous statue of Artemis in it. This early representation stands stiffly straight, with her hands extended outward. The original was made of gold, ebony, silver, and black stone.

Mausoleum of Halicarnassus. This monumental tomb of Mausolus, the tyrant of Caria in southwestern Asia Minor, was built between about 353 and 351 BC by Mausolus' sister and widow, Artemisia. According to the description of Pliny the Elder, the monument, designed by the architect Pythius (Pytheos), was almost square, with a total periphery of 125 m (411 ft). It was bounded by 36 columns, and the top formed a pyramid surmounted by a marble chariot. Fragments of the mausoleum's sculpture are preserved in the British Museum. The mausoleum was probably destroyed by an earthquake, and the stones were reused in local buildings.

Colossus of Rhodes. This huge bronze statue was built at the harbor of Rhodes in ancient Greece in commemoration of the raising of the siege of Rhodes (305–304 BC). The sculptor was Chares of Lyndus. The Colossus was said to be 32 m (105 ft) high, making it technically impossible that it could have straddled the harbor entrance, as was popularly believed. The Colossus took 12 years to build (c. 294–282 BC) and was toppled by an earthquake about 225 BC.

Pharos of Alexandria. This lighthouse, the most famous of the ancient world, was built by Sostratus of Cnidus about 280 BC on the island of Pharos off Alexandria, and it is said to have been more than 100 m (350 ft) high. It is the archetype of all lighthouses since. The lighthouse was destroyed by an earthquake in the 1300s. In 1994 a large amount of masonry blocks and statuary, thought to be wreckage from the lighthouse, was found in the waters off Pharos.

Tallest Buildings in the World

Building height equals the distance from the sidewalk level of the main entrance to the structural top of the building, including spires but not including antennae, signage, or flag poles. Only buildings that have been completed are included here.
Source: Council on Tall Buildings and Urban Habitat.

RANK	BUILDING	CITY	YEAR COMPLETED	HEIGHT IN FT/M	STORIES
1	Taipei 101	Taipei, Taiwan	2004	1,670/509	101
2	Shanghai World Finance Center	Shanghai, China	2008	1,614/492	101
3	Petronas Tower 1	Kuala Lumpur, Malaysia	1998	1,483/452	88
4	Petronas Tower 2	Kuala Lumpur, Malaysia	1998	1,483/452	88
5	Willis Tower (Sears Tower)	Chicago IL	1974	1,451/442	110
6	Jin Mao Building	Shanghai, China	1999	1,381/421	88
7	Two International Finance Centre	Hong Kong, China	2003	1,362/415	88
8	CITIC Plaza	Guangzhou, China	1996	1,283/391	80
9	Shun Hing Square	Shenzhen, China	1996	1,260/384	69
10	Empire State Building	New York NY	1931	1,250/381	102
11	Central Plaza	Hong Kong, China	1992	1,227/374	78
12	Bank of China	Hong Kong, China	1989	1,205/367	70
13	Almas Tower	Dubai, UAE	2008	1,191/363	68
14	Emirates Tower One	Dubai, UAE	1999	1,165/355	54
15	Tuntex Sky Tower	Kaohsiung, Taiwan	1997	1,140/348	85

Tallest Buildings in the World (continued)

RANK	BUILDING	CITY	YEAR COMPLETED	HEIGHT IN FT/M	STORIES
16	Aon Centre	Chicago IL	1973	1,136/346	83
17	The Center	Hong Kong, China	1998	1,135/346	73
18	John Hancock Center	Chicago IL	1969	1,127/344	100
19	Rose Rotana Tower	Dubai, UAE	2007	1,093/333	72
20	Shimao International Plaza	Shanghai, China	2006	1,093/333	60
21	Minsheng Bank Building	Wuhan, China	2008	1,087/331	68
22	Q1	Gold Coast, QLD, Australia	2005	1,058/323	78
23	Burj Al Arab	Dubai, UAE	1999	1,053/321	60
24	Nina Tower I	Hong Kong, China	2006	1,046/319	80
25	Chrysler Building	New York NY	1930	1,046/319	77

Longest Span Structures in the World by Type

Bridges

SUSPENSION	LOCATION	YEAR OF COMPLETION	MAIN SPAN (M)
Akashi Kaikyo	Kobe–Awaji Island, Japan	1998	1,991
part of eastern link between islands of Honshu and Shikoku			
Xihoumen	Zhoushan archipelago, China	2007	1,650
links Jintang and Cezi islands			
Store Baelt (Great Belt)	Zealand–Funen, Denmark	1998	1,624
part of link between Copenhagen and mainland Europe			
Nancha	Zhenjiang, China	2005	1,490
world's third longest suspension bridge			
Humber	near Kingston upon Hull, England	1981	1,410
crosses Humber estuary between Yorkshire and Lincolnshire			

CABLE-STAYED (STEEL)			
Sutong	Nantong, China	2008	1,088
longest main span, highest main-bridge tower, and deepest foundation piers for a cable-stayed bridge			
Stonecutters (Angchuanzhou)	Tsing Yi–Sha Tin, Hong Kong	2009	1,018
links growing areas of Northeast New Territories and Kowloon, Hong Kong			
Edong	Huangshi–Huanggang, China	2009	926
alleviates congestion on Huangshi Yangtze Bridge			
Tatara	Onomichi–Imabari, Japan	1999	890
part of western link between islands of Honshu and Shikoku			
Normandie	near Le Havre, France	1995	856
crosses Seine estuary between upper and lower Normandy			

ARCH steel			
Chaotianmen	Chongqing, China (across the Yangtze)	2009	552
world's longest steel-arch bridge			
Lupu	Shanghai, China	2003	550
crosses Huangpujiang (Huangpu River) between central Shanghai and Pudong New District			
New River Gorge	Fayetteville WV	1977	518
provides road link through scenic New River Gorge National River area			
concrete			
Wanxian	Sichuan province, China	1997	425
crosses Chang Jiang (Yangtze River) in Three Gorges area			
Krk I	Krk island, Croatia	1980	390
links scenic Krk island with mainland Croatia			
Jiangjiehe	Guizhou province, China	1995	330
spans gorge of Wujiang (Wu River)			

CANTILEVER steel truss			
Québec	Quebec City, QC, Canada	1917	549
provides rail crossing over St. Lawrence River			
Forth	Edinburgh–North Queensferry, Scotland	1890	2 spans, each 521
provides rail crossing over Firth of Forth			
Minato	Osaka–Amagasaki, Japan	1974	510
carries road traffic across Osaka's harbor			

Longest Span Structures in the World by Type (continued)

CANTILEVER (CONTINUED)
prestressed concrete

Shibanpo-2	Chongqing, China	2006	336
world's longest prestressed-concrete box girder bridge			
Stolmasundet	Austevoll, Norway	1998	301
links islands of Stolmen and Sjelbörn south of Bergen			
Raftsundet	Lofoten, Norway	1998	298
crosses Raft Sound in arctic Lofoten islands			

BEAM
steel truss

Ikitsuki Ohashi	Nagasaki prefecture, Japan	1991	400
connects islands of Iki and Hirado off northwest Kyushu			
Astoria	Astoria OR	1966	376
carries Pacific Coast Highway across Columbia River between Oregon and Washington			
Francis Scott Key	Baltimore MD	1977	366
spans Patapsco River at Baltimore harbor			

steel plate and box girder

Presidente Costa e Silva	Rio de Janeiro state, Brazil	1974	300
crosses Guanabara Bay between Rio de Janeiro and suburb of Niterói			
Neckartalbrücke-1	Weitingen, Germany	1978	263
carries highway across Neckar River valley			
Brankova	Belgrade, Serbia	1956	261
provides road crossing of Sava River between Old and New Belgrade			

MOVABLE
vertical lift

Arthur Kill	Elizabeth NJ–New York NY	1959	170
provides rail link between port of Elizabeth and Staten Island			
Cape Cod Canal	Cape Cod MA	1935	166
provides rail crossing over waterway near Buzzard's Bay			
Delair	Delair NJ–Philadelphia PA	1960	165
provides rail link across Delaware River between Philadelphia and southern Jersey Shore			

swing span

Al-Firdan (El-Ferdan)	Suez Canal, Egypt	2001	340
provides road and rail link between Sinai Peninsula and eastern Nile delta region			
Santa Fe	Fort Madison IA–Niota IL	1927	160
provides road and rail crossing of Mississippi River			
Kaiser-Wilhelm-Brücke	Wilhelmshaven, Germany	1907	159
crosses the Wupper River			

BASCULE

South Capitol Street/Frederick Douglass Memorial	Washington DC	1949	118
carries road traffic over Anacostia River			
Sault Sainte Marie	Sault Sainte Marie MI–Ontario, Canada	1941	102
connects rail systems of United States and Canada			
Charles Berry	Lorain OH	1940	101
carries road traffic over Black River			
Market Street/Chief John Ross	Chattanooga TN	1917	94
carries road traffic over Tennessee River			

Causeways (fixed link over water only)

Lake Pontchartrain-2	Metairie–Mandeville LA	1969	38,422
carries northbound road traffic from suburbs of New Orleans to north lakeshore			
Lake Pontchartrain-1	Mandeville–Metairie LA	1956	38,352
carries southbound road traffic from north lakeshore to suburbs of New Orleans			
Hangzhou Bay Transoceanic	near Jiaxing–near Cixi, China	2008	36,000
world's longest transoceanic bridge or causeway			
King Fahd	Bahrain–Saudi Arabia	1986	24,950
carries road traffic across Gulf of Bahrain in Persian Gulf			
Confederation	Borden-Carleton, PE–Cape Jourimain, NB, Canada	1997	12,900
carries road traffic over Northumberland Strait			

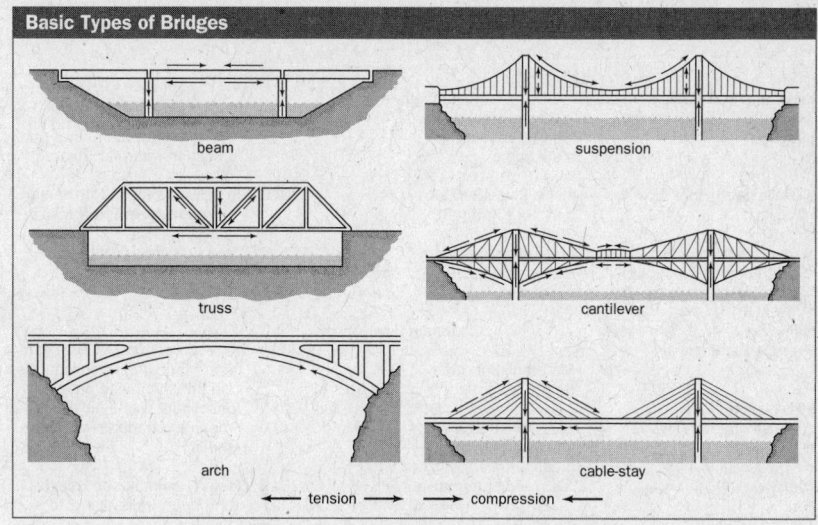

Basic Types of Bridges

beam

suspension

truss

cantilever

arch

cable-stay

⟵ tension ⟶   ⟶ compression ⟵

Notable Civil Engineering Projects (in progress or completed as of July 2009)

NAME	LOCATION		YEAR OF COMPLETION	NOTES
airports		terminal area (sq m)		
Beijing Capital (new Terminal 3)	northeast of Beijing	986,000	2008	Opened 29 February; is the world's largest airport terminal
Dubai International (new Terminal 3)	near Dubai, UAE	532,000	2008	Opened 14 October; total area including concourse and car park is 1,459,000 sq m; 40 km from Al Maktoum International Airport
Changi (new Terminal 3)	mostly on landfill at eastern tip of Singapore	380,000	2008	Opened 9 January; new terminal in Asia's sixth busiest airport in passenger traffic
bridges		length (main span; m)		
Manifa Causeway	in Persian Gulf, offshore of Manifa, Saudi Arabia	41,000 (total causeway length)	2011	Includes 20 km of laterals from main causeway to drilling islands; will enable massive oil field redevelopment
Hangzhou Bay Transoceanic	near Jiaxing, China–near Cixi, China	36,000	2008	Opened to traffic 1 May; world's longest transoceanic bridge/causeway
I-95 (Woodrow Wilson #2)	Alexandria VA–Maryland suburbs of Washington DC	1,852 (length of each span)	2008	Two bascule spans forming wider inverted V shape for ships; outer span opened 10 Jun 2006, inner span on 30 May 2008
buildings		height (m)		
Burj Dubai (Dubai Tower)	Dubai, UAE	800* (*as of June 2009; final height with spire is undisclosed)	2009	Claimed to be world's tallest building on 21 July 2007
Pentominium	Dubai, UAE	618	2012	Will be world's tallest residential tower
Freedom Tower or 1 World Trade Center	New York City	1,776 ft (541.3 m)	2013	Complex to include six new buildings, a memorial, and a museum

Notable Civil Engineering Projects (in progress or completed as of July 2009) (continued)

NAME	LOCATION		YEAR OF COMPLETION	NOTES
dams and hydrologic projects		**crest length (m)**		
Sardar Sarovar (Narmada) Project	Narmada River, Madhya Pradesh state, India	1,210	2009	Largest dam of controversial 30-dam project; drinking and irrigation water for Gujarat state
Merowe (earth core rockfill) Dam	on Nile River, 350 km north of Khartoum, Sudan	841	2010	To contain 20% of Nile annual flow; to double The Sudan's power capacity
Manuel Piar (Tocoma) (fourth of four-dam Lower Caroní Development scheme)	Caroní River, northern Bolívar state, Venezuela	?	2010	Final unit of world's third largest hydroelectric complex
highways		**length (km)**		
Interoceanic Highway	Iñapari–Ilo/ Matarani/San Juan de Marcona, Peru	c. 3,100	2010	To be paved road for Brazilian imports/exports from/to Asia via three Peruvian ports
East-West Highway (across northern Algeria)	Tunisian border (near Annaba)– Moroccan border (near Tlemcen)	1,216	2010	To facilitate economic develop- ment and trade across North Africa
Transylvanian Motorway	Brasov–Bors, Romania	415	2013	To link Romania and Hungary and open Transylvania to tourism
canals and floodgates		**length (m)**		
Arabian Canal	Dubai, UAE	75,000	2010	Largest civil engineering project in the history of the UAE; 150-m-wide waterway to turn arid interior into exclu- sive waterfront property
New Orleans Surge Barrier	Gulf Intercoastal Waterway–Mississippi River Gulf Outlet, New Orleans	2,283	2011	Central component of 3-km- long project to prevent storm- surge flooding using barrier walls and floodgates
Panama Canal Expansion	between Panama City and Colón, Panama	—	2014	Will include new wider and longer three-chamber locks, doubling the canal's capacity and allowing the passage of the world's biggest container ships
railways (heavy)		**length (km)**		
Benguela Railway (rehabilitation; closed by civil war 1975–2002)	Benguela–Luau, Angola (at DR Congo border)	1,314	2011	Will enable resumption of copper exports from DR Congo and Zambia
Xinqiu–Bayan Ul Railway	Xinqiu, Liaoning prov- ince–Bayan Ul, Inner Mongolia, China	487	2010	To be important for coal trans- port; future link to Mongolia expected
North-South Railway (in part)	Araguaína, Tocantins– Palmas, Tocantins, Brazil	361	2009	Rail exports of agriculture, forestry, and mineral prod- ucts from vast area of interior of northern Brazil is expected
railways (high speed)		**length (km)**		
Beijing–Shanghai Express Railway	Beijing–Shanghai	1,318	2013	To halve travel time between capital and financial center
Spanish high speed	Madrid–France (via Barcelona)	719	2012	Madrid to Barcelona link opened 20 Feb 2008
Turkish high speed	Ankara–Istanbul	533	2010	To connect capital with largest city
subways/metros/light rails		**length (km)**		
New Mexico Rail Runner Express (commuter rail service)	Belen–Santa Fe NM (via Albuquerque)	c. 141	2008	Operational in Albuquerque area in 2006; final c. 67-km extension to Santa Fe in ser- vice from 17 December

Notable Civil Engineering Projects (in progress or completed as of July 2009) (continued)

NAME	LOCATION		YEAR OF COMPLETION	NOTES
subways/metros/light rails (continued)		length (km)		
Delhi Metro	Delhi	124.8	2010	Many extensions of lines under construction between 2008 and 2010
Dubai Metro (Red/Green lines)	Dubai, UAE	69.7	2009/2010	To be world's longest fully automated driverless transport system
tunnels		length (m)		
Apennine Range tunnels (9)	Bologna, Italy–Florence (high-speed railway)	73,400	2010	Longest tunnel (Vaglia) to be 18.7 km; tunnels to cover 93% of railway
Marmaray railroad project tunnels	connecting European and Asian portions of Istanbul	13,600	2011	To include 1.4-km-long bored tunnel, world's deepest sunken-tube tunnel (56 m under the Bosporus strait)
Eiksund Undersea	Ørsta–Hareidlandet (Heroy Island), Norway	7,765	2008	Opened to traffic 23 February; world's deepest underwater tunnel (287 m under water surface)
miscellaneous		length (km)		
Eastern Africa Submarine Cable System	western Indian Ocean between South Africa and The Sudan	13,700	2010	To be first underwater fiber-optic cable in Indian Ocean, providing Internet and communications services to 250 million people in Africa
Svalbard Global Seed Vault	near Longyearbyen Spitsbergen, in the Norwegian Arctic	—	2008	Capable of storing three million seeds in perpetuity and guarding them against disease, war, and other catastrophes; opened 26 February

1 m=3.28 ft; 1 km=0.62 mi

Life on Earth

Taxonomy

Taxonomy is the classification of living and extinct organisms. The term is derived from the Greek *taxis* ("arrangement") and *nomos* ("law") and refers to the methodology and principles of systematic botany and zoology by which the various kinds of plants and animals are arranged in hierarchies of superior and subordinate groups.

Popularly, classifications of living organisms arise according to need and are often superficial; for example, although the term fish is common to the names shellfish, crayfish, and starfish, there are more anatomical differences between a shellfish and a starfish than there are between a bony fish and a human. Also, vernacular names vary widely. Biologists have attempted to view all living organisms with equal thoroughness and thus have devised a formal classification. A formal classification supports a relatively uniform and internationally understood nomenclature, thereby simplifying cross-referencing and retrieval of information.

Carolus Linnaeus, who is usually regarded as the founder of modern taxonomy and whose books are considered the beginning of modern botanical and zoological nomenclature, drew up rules for assigning names to plants and animals and was the first to use binomial nomenclature consistently, beginning in 1758. Classification since Linnaeus has incorporated newly discovered information and more closely approaches a natural system, and the process of clarifying relationships continues to this day. The table below shows the seven ranks that are accepted as obligatory by zoologists and botanists and sample listings for animals and plants.

	ANIMALS	PLANTS
Kingdom	Animalia	Plantae
Phylum/Division	Chordata	Tracheophyta
Class	Mammalia	Pteropsida
Order	Primates	Coniferales

Taxonomy (continued)

	ANIMALS	PLANTS
Family	Hominidae	Pinaceae
Genus	*Homo*	*Pinus*
Species	*Homo sapiens* (human)	*Pinus strobus* (white pine)

Names of the Male, Female, Young, and Group of Selected Animals

ANIMAL	MALE	FEMALE	YOUNG	GROUP
ape	male	female	baby	shrewdness
bear	boar	sow	cub	sleuth, sloth
deer	buck, stag	doe	fawn	herd
donkey	jack, jackass	jennet, jenny	colt, foal	drove, herd
ferret	hob	jill	kit	business, fesynes
fox	reynard	vixen	kit, cub, pup	skulk, leash
giraffe	bull	doe	calf	herd, corps, tower
hamster	buck	doe	pup	horde
hippopotamus	bull	cow	calf	herd, bloat
horse	stallion, stud	mare, dam	foal, colt (male), filly (female)	stable, harras, herd, team (working) string or field (racing)
human	man	woman	baby, infant, toddler	clan (related), crowd, family (closely related), community, tribe
lion	lion	lioness	cub	pride
mouse	buck	doe	pup, pinkie, kitten	horde, mischief
pig	boar	sow	piglet, shoat, farrow	drove, herd, litter (of pups), sounder
quail	cock	hen	chick	bevy, covey, drift
rhinoceros	bull	cow	calf	crash
seal	bull	cow	pup	herd, pod, rookery, harem
sheep	buck, ram	ewe, dam	lamb, lambkin, cosset	drift, drove, flock, herd, mob, trip
turkey	tom	hen	poult	rafter
whale	bull	cow	calf	gam, grind, herd, pod, school

Forests of the World

*This table shows the 20 countries or dependencies that lost the most forest area between 1990 and 2005 and those that gained the most, as well as forest losses or gains by continent. 1 hectare (ha) = .01 sq km, .004 sq mi. Source: State of the World's Forests 2009. **Web site:** <www.fao.org/forestry>.*

COUNTRY/AREA	LAND AREA ('000 HA)	TOTAL FOREST IN 1990 ('000 HA)	TOTAL FOREST IN 2005 ('000 HA)	PERCENTAGE OF LAND AREA IN 2005 (%)	% CHANGE 1990-2005
Kiribati	81	28	2	3.0	−92.86
Kazakhstan	269,970	9,758	3,337	1.2	−65.80
Comoros	186	12	5	2.9	−58.33
Togo	5,439	719	386	7.1	−46.31
Lesotho	3,035	14	8	0.3	−42.86
The Bahamas	1,001	842	515	51.5	−38.84
Brunei	527	452	278	52.8	−38.50
Mozambique	78,638	31,238	19,262	24.6	−38.34
Burundi	2,568	241	152	5.9	−36.93
Nigeria	91,077	17,501	11,089	12.2	−36.64
Afghanistan	65,209	1,351	867	1.3	−35.83
Mauritania	103,070	415	267	0.3	−35.66
Niger	126,670	1,945	1,266	1.0	−34.91
Haiti	2,756	158	105	3.8	−33.54
Pakistan	77,088	2,755	1,902	2.5	−30.96
Libya	175,954	311	217	0.1	−30.23
Benin	11,062	3,349	2,351	21.3	−29.80
Uganda	19,710	5,103	3,627	18.4	−28.92
Ghana	22,754	7,535	5,517	24.2	−26.78
Albania	2,740	1,069	794	29.0	−25.72
Lebanon	1,023	37	137	13.3	+270.27
Federated States of Micronesia	70	24	63	90.6	+162.50
Ethiopia	100,000	4,996	13,000	11.9	+160.21
Cape Verde	403	35	84	20.7	+140.00
Northern Mariana Islands	46	14	33	72.4	+135.71

Forests of the World (continued)

COUNTRY/AREA	LAND AREA ('000 HA)	TOTAL FOREST IN 1990 ('000 HA)	TOTAL FOREST IN 2005 ('000 HA)	PERCENTAGE OF LAND AREA IN 2005 (%)	% CHANGE 1990–2005
Mauritius	203	17	37	18.2	+117.65
Tunisia	15,536	499	1,056	6.8	+111.62
Kuwait	1,782	3	6	0.3	+100.00
Oman	30,950	1	2	[1]	+100.00
Sierra Leone	7,162	1,416	2,754	38.5	+94.49
Uruguay	17,502	791	1,506	8.6	+90.39
Iceland	10,025	25	46	[1]	+84.00
Saudi Arabia	214,969	1,504	2,728	1.3	+81.38
Puerto Rico	887	234	408	46.0	+74.36
Uzbekistan	42,540	1,923	3,295	8.0	+71.35
St. Vincent and the Grenadines	39	7	11	27.4	+57.14
El Salvador	2,072	193	298	14.4	+54.40
Iran	162,855	7,299	11,075	6.8	+51.73
East Timor	1,487	541	798	53.7	+47.50
Cyprus	924	119	174	18.9	+46.22
South America	1,760,726	922,731	831,540	47.7	−9.88
Africa	2,963,666	702,502	635,412	21.4	−9.55
Europe	2,208,811	1,030,475	1,001,394	44.3	−2.82
North and Central America	2,112,080	555,002	699,875	33.1	+26.10
Asia	3,096,597	551,448	571,576	18.5	+3.65
Oceania	849,091	201,271	206,254	24.3	+2.48
World	13,013,868	3,963,429	3,952,025	30.3	−0.29

[1]Negligible.

Geology

The Continents

Figures given are approximate. Area and population as of 2008. Highest and lowest points listed are all given in relation to sea level.

CONTINENT	POPULATION	AREA	% OF TOTAL LAND AREA[1]	HIGHEST/LOWEST POINT
Africa	955,761,100	30,247,722 sq km 11,678,801 sq mi	20.2	Mt. Kilimanjaro (Tanzania): 5,895 m (19,340 ft) Lake Assal (Djibouti): −157 m (−515 ft)
Antarctica	N/A	14,200,000 sq km 5,500,000 sq mi	9.5	Vinson Massif: 4,892 m (16,050 ft) Bentley Subglacial Trench: −2,500 m (−8,200 ft)
Asia	4,018,522,000	31,700,654 sq km 12,239,721 sq mi	21.1	Mt. Everest (China/Nepal): 8,850 m (29,035 ft) Dead Sea (Israel/Jordan): −400 m (−1,312 ft)
Europe	735,213,700	23,041,330 sq km 8,896,305 sq mi	15.4	Mont Blanc (France/Italy/Switzerland); 4,807 m (15,771 ft) Caspian Sea (Russia): −27 m (−90 ft)
North America	526,827,700	24,393,718 sq km 9,418,467 sq mi	16.3	Mt. McKinley (Alaska): 6,194 m (20,320 ft) Death Valley (California): −86 m (−282 ft)
Australia (and Oceania)	35,120,640	8,515,146 sq km 3,287,718 sq mi	5.7	Jaya Peak (Indonesia): 5,030 m (16,500 ft) Lake Eyre (Australia): −15 m (−50 ft)
South America	378,448,500	17,824,370 sq km 6,882,027 sq mi	11.9	Mt. Aconcagua (Argentina/Chile): 6,959 m (22,834 ft) Valdés Peninsula (Argentina): −40 m (−131 ft)

[1]Together, the continents make up about 29.2% of the Earth's surface.

Geologic Time Scale

Eon	Era	Period	Epoch	Age	mya[1]
Phanerozoic	Cenozoic	Quaternary	Holocene		
			Pleistocene	Tarantian	0.0117
				"Ionian"	0.126
				Calabrian	0.781
				Gelasian	1.806
		Neogene	Pliocene	Piacenzian	2.588
				Zanclean	3.600
			Miocene	Messinian	5.332
				Tortonian	7.246
				Serravallian	11.608
				Langhian	13.82
				Burdigalian	15.97
				Aquitanian	20.43
		Paleogene	Oligocene	Chattian	23.03
				Rupelian	28.4 ± 0.1
			Eocene	Priabonian	33.9 ± 0.1
				Bartonian	37.2 ± 0.1
				Lutetian	40.4 ± 0.2
				Ypresian	48.6 ± 0.2
			Paleocene	Thanetian	55.8 ± 0.2
				Selandian	58.7 ± 0.2
				Danian	61.1
	Mesozoic	Cretaceous	Upper	Maastrichtian	65.5 ± 0.3
				Campanian	70.6 ± 0.6
				Santonian	83.5 ± 0.7
				Coniacian	85.8 ± 0.7
				Turonian	88.6
				Cenomanian	93.6 ± 0.8
			Lower	Albian	99.6 ± 0.9
				Aptian	112.0 ± 1.0
				Barremian	125.0 ± 1.0
				Hauterivian	130.0 ± 1.5
				Valanginian	~133.9
				Berriasian	145.5 ± 4.0

Eon	Era	Period	Epoch	Age	mya[1]
Phanerozoic	Mesozoic	Jurassic	Upper	Tithonian	145.5 ± 4.0
				Kimmeridgian	150.8 ± 4.0
				Oxfordian	~155.6
			Middle	Callovian	161.2 ± 4.0
				Bathonian	164.7 ± 4.0
				Bajocian	167.7 ± 3.5
				Aalenian	171.6 ± 3.0
			Lower	Toarcian	175.6 ± 2.0
				Pliensbachian	183.0 ± 1.5
				Sinemurian	189.6 ± 1.5
				Hettangian	196.5 ± 1.0
		Triassic	Upper	Rhaetian	199.6 ± 0.6
				Norian	203.6 ± 1.5
				Carnian	216.5 ± 2.0
			Middle	Ladinian	~228.7
				Anisian	237.0 ± 2.0
			Lower	Olenekian	~245.9
				Induan	249.5
	Paleozoic	Permian	Lopingian	Changhsingian	251.0 ± 0.4
				Wuchiapingian	253.8 ± 0.7
			Guadalupian	Capitanian	260.4 ± 0.7
				Wordian	265.8 ± 0.7
				Roadian	268.0 ± 0.7
			Cisuralian	Kungurian	270.6 ± 0.7
				Artinskian	275.6 ± 0.7
				Sakmarian	284.4 ± 0.7
				Asselian	294.6 ± 0.8
		Carboniferous	Pennsylvanian[2] Upper	Gzhelian	299.0 ± 0.8
				Kasimovian	303.9 ± 0.9
				Moscovian	306.5 ± 1.0
			Middle	Bashkirian	311.7 ± 1.1
			Mississippian[2] Upper	Serpukhovian	318.1 ± 1.3
			Middle	Visean	326.4 ± 1.6
			Lower	Tournaisian	345.3 ± 2.1
					359.2 ± 2.5

Eon	Era	Period	Epoch	Age	mya[1]
Phanerozoic	Paleozoic	Devonian	Upper	Famennian	359.2 ± 2.5
				Frasnian	374.5 ± 2.6
			Middle	Givetian	385.3 ± 2.6
				Eifelian	391.8 ± 2.7
			Lower	Emsian	397.5 ± 2.7
				Pragian	407.0 ± 2.8
				Lochkovian	411.2 ± 2.8
		Silurian	Pridoli		416.0 ± 2.8
			Ludlow	Ludfordian	418.7 ± 2.7
				Gorstian	421.3 ± 2.6
			Wenlock	Homerian	422.9 ± 2.5
				Sheinwoodian	426.2 ± 2.4
			Llandovery	Telychian	428.2 ± 2.3
				Aeronian	436.0 ± 1.9
				Rhuddanian	439.0 ± 1.8
		Ordovician	Upper	Hirnantian	443.7 ± 1.5
				Katian	445.6 ± 1.5
				Sandbian	455.8 ± 1.6
			Middle	Darriwilian	460.9 ± 1.6
				Dapingian	468.1 ± 1.6
			Lower	Floian	471.8 ± 1.6
				Tremadocian	478.6 ± 1.7
		Cambrian[3]	Furongian	Stage 10	488.3 ± 1.7
				Stage 9	~492.0
				Paibian	~496.0
			Series 3	Guzhangian	~499.0
				Drumian	~503.0
				Stage 5	~506.5
			Series 2	Stage 4	~510.0
				Stage 3	~515.0
			Terreneuvian	Stage 2	~521.0
				Fortunian	~528.0
					542.0 ± 1.0

Eon	Era	Period	mya[1]
Proterozoic	Neoproterozoic	Ediacaran	542.0
		Cryogenian	~635.0
		Tonian	850.0
		Stenian	1,000.0
	Mesoproterozoic	Ectasian	1,200.0
		Calymmian	1,400.0
		Statherian	1,600.0
	Paleoproterozoic	Orosirian	1,800.0
		Rhyacian	2,050.0
		Siderian	2,300.0
			2,500.0
Archean	Neoarchean		2,800.0
	Mesoarchean		3,200.0
	Paleoarchean		3,600.0
	Eoarchean		4,000.0
	Hadean (informal)		4,600.0

Precambrian

1 Millions of years ago.
2 Both the Mississippian and Pennsylvanian time units are formally designated as subperiods within the Carboniferous Period.
3 Several Cambrian unit age boundaries are informal and are awaiting ratified definitions.

Published with permission from the International Commission on Stratigraphy (ICS). International chronostratigraphic units, ranks, names, and formal status are approved by the ICS and ratified by the International Union of Geological Sciences (IUGS).
Source: 2009 International Stratigraphic Chart produced by the ICS.

Geography

Largest Islands of the World

NAME AND LOCATION	REGION	AREA[1] SQ MI	SQ KM
Greenland	North America	836,330	2,166,086
New Guinea, Papua New Guinea/Indonesia	Oceania	309,000	800,000
Borneo, Indonesia/Malaysia/Brunei	Asia	292,000	755,000
Madagascar	Africa	226,662	587,051
Baffin, Nunavut, Canada	North America	195,928	507,451
Sumatra, Indonesia	Asia	170,233	446,687
Great Britain, UK	Europe	88,394	228,938
Honshu, Japan	Asia	87,992	227,898
Victoria, Northwest Territories/Nunavut, Canada	North America	83,896	217,291
Ellesmere, Nunavut, Canada	North America	75,767	196,236
Celebes, Indonesia	Asia	74,845	193,847
South Island, New Zealand	Oceania	58,776	152,229
Java, Indonesia	Asia	49,926	129,307
North Island, New Zealand	Oceania	44,872	116,219
Cuba	North America	42,427	109,886
Newfoundland, Canada	North America	42,031	108,860
Luzon, Philippines	Asia	40,420	104,688
Iceland	Europe	39,769	103,000
Mindanao, Philippines	Asia	36,537	94,630
Ireland, Ireland/UK	Europe	32,590	84,408

[1]Area given may include small adjoining islands. Conversions for rounded figures may be rounded to the nearest hundred.

Highest Mountains of the World by Region

"I" in the name of a peak refers to the highest in a group of numbered peaks of the same name.

NAME AND LOCATION	HEIGHT IN M	HEIGHT IN FT	YEAR FIRST CLIMBED
Africa			
Kilimanjaro (Kibo peak), Tanzania	5,895	19,340	1889
Kenya (Batian peak), Kenya	5,199	17,058	1899
Margherita, Ruwenzori Range, Dem. Rep. of the Congo/Uganda	5,119	16,795	1906
Ras Dejen, Simen Mtns., Ethiopia	4,533	14,872	1841
Antarctica			
Vinson Massif, Sentinel Range, Ellsworth Mtns.	4,892	16,050	1966
Tyree, Sentinel Range, Ellsworth Mtns.	4,852	15,918	1967
Shinn, Sentinel Range, Ellsworth Mtns.	4,660	15,289	1966
Gardner, Sentinel Range, Ellsworth Mtns.	4,573	15,003	1966
Asia			
Everest (Chomolungma), Himalayas, China/Nepal	8,850	29,035	1953
K2 (Godwin Austen) (Chogori), Karakoram Range, Pakistan/China	8,611	28,251	1954
Kanchenjunga I, Himalayas, Nepal/India	8,586	28,169	1955
Lhotse I, Himalayas, Nepal/China	8,501	27,890	1956
Caucasus			
Elbrus, Russia	5,642	18,510	1874
Dykhtau, Russia	5,204	17,073	1888
Koshtantau, Russia	5,151	16,900	1889
Shkhara, Russia/Georgia	5,068	16,627	1888
Europe			
Mont Blanc, Alps, France/Italy/Switzerland	4,807	15,771	1786
Dufourspitze, Monte Rosa Massif, Alps, Switzerland/Italy	4,634	15,203	1855
Dom (Mischabel), Alps, Switzerland	4,545	14,912	1858
Weisshorn, Alps, Switzerland	4,505	14,780	1861

Highest Mountains of the World by Region (continued)

NAME AND LOCATION	HEIGHT IN M	HEIGHT IN FT	YEAR FIRST CLIMBED
North America			
McKinley, Alaska Range, Alaska	6,194	20,320	1913
Logan, St. Elias Mtns., Yukon, Canada	5,951	19,524	1925
Citlaltépetl (Orizaba), Cordillera Neo-Volcánica, Mexico	5,610	18,406	1848
St. Elias, St. Elias Mtns., Alaska/Canada	5,489	18,008	1897
Oceania			
Jaya (Sukarno) (Carstensz), Sudirman Range, Indonesia	5,030	16,500[1]	1962
Pilimsit (Idenburg), Sudirman Range, Indonesia	4,800	15,750[1]	1962
Trikora (Wilhelmina), Jayawijaya Mtns., Indonesia	4,750	15,580[1]	1912
Mandala (Juliana), Jayawijaya Mtns., Indonesia	4,700	15,420[1]	1959
South America			
Aconcagua, Andes, Argentina/Chile	6,959	22,834	1897
Ojos del Salado, Andes, Argentina/Chile	6,893	22,614	1937
Bonete, Andes, Argentina	6,872	22,546	1913
Mercedario, Andes, Argentina/Chile	6,770	22,211	1934

[1]Conversions rounded to the nearest 10 ft.

Major Caves and Cave Systems of the World by Continent

Source: Bob Gulden, National Speleological Society.

NAME AND LOCATION	DEPTH[1]		LENGTH[2]	
	FT	M	MI	KM
Africa				
Ifflis, Algeria	3,839	1,170	1.2	2.0
Boussouil, Algeria	2,641	805	2.0	3.2
Tafna (Bou Ma'za), Algeria	N/A	N/A	11.4	18.4
Tamdoun, Morocco	N/A	N/A	11.4	18.4
Asia				
Krubera, Georgia	7,188	2,191	8.2	13.2
Illyuzia-Mezhonnogo-Snezhnaya, Georgia	5,751	1,753	15.0	24.1
Air Jernih, Malaysia	1,165	355	109.2	175.7
Shuanghe Dongqun, China	1,946	593	74.4	119.8
Australia (and Oceania)				
Neide-Muruk, Papua New Guinea	4,127	1,258	10.6	17.0
Nettlebed, New Zealand	2,917	889	15.1	24.3
Bullita, Northern Territory, Australia	75	23	68.1	109.6
Mamo Kananda, Papua New Guinea	1,732	528	34.1	54.8
Europe				
Lamprechtsofen Vogelschacht, Austria	5,354	1,632	31.7	51.0
Gouffre Mirolda–Lucien Bouclier, France	5,335	1,626	8.1	13.0
Optimisticheskaya, Ukraine	49	15	143.0	230.1
Hölloch, Switzerland	3,079	939	120.9	194.5
North America				
Cuicateco, Mexico	4,869	1,484	16.3	26.2
Huautla, Mexico	4,839	1,475	38.6	62.1
Mammoth–Flint Ridge, Kentucky	379	116	367.0	590.6
Jewel, South Dakota	632	193	144.8	233.1
South America				
Kaukiran, Peru	1,335	407	1.3	2.1
Aonda, Venezuela	1,188	362	N/A	N/A
Boa Vista, Brazil	164	50	63.7	102.5
Barriguda, Brazil	200	61	18.6	30.0

[1]Below highest entrance.   [2]Explored portion of cave.

Major Deserts of the World by Continent

NAME AND LOCATION	AREA SQ KM	AREA SQ MI	NAME AND LOCATION	AREA SQ KM	AREA SQ MI
Africa			**Australia (continued)**		
Sahara, northern Africa	8,600,000	3,320,000	Great Sandy, northern Western Australia	400,000	150,000
Kalahari, southwestern Africa	930,000	360,000	Gibson, Western Australia	156,000	60,000
Namib, southwestern Africa	135,000	52,000	Simpson, Northern Territory	143,000	55,000
Libyan, Libya, Egypt, and Sudan	N/A	N/A	**North America**		
			Great Basin, southwestern US	492,000	190,000
Asia			Chihuahuan, northern Mexico	450,000	175,000
Arabian, southwestern Asia	2,330,000	900,000	Sonoran, southwestern US and Baja California	310,800	120,000
Gobi, Mongolia and northeastern China	1,300,000	500,000	Mojave, southwestern US	65,000	25,000
Rubʿ al-Khali, southern Arabian Peninsula	650,000	250,000	**South America**		
Karakum, Turkmenistan	350,000	135,000	Patagonian, southern Argentina	673,000	260,000
Australia			Atacama, northern Chile	140,000	54,000
Great Victoria, Western and South Australia	647,000	250,000			

Major Volcanoes of the World by Continent

NAME AND LOCATION	ELEVATION M	ELEVATION FT	FIRST RECORDED ERUPTION	MOST RECENT ERUPTION
Africa				
Kilimanjaro, Tanzania[1]	5,895	19,340	N/A	N/A
Cameroon, Cameroon	4,095	13,435	1650	2000
Teide (Tenerife), Canary Islands	3,715	12,188	N/A	1909
Nyiragongo, Democratic Republic of the Congo	3,470	11,384	1884	2009
Antarctica				
Erebus, Ross Island	3,794	12,447	1841	2009
Melbourne, Victoria Land	2,732	8,963	N/A	c. 1750
Belinda, Montagu Island	1,370	4,495	N/A	2007
Darnley, Sandwich Islands	1,100	3,609	1823	1956
Asia and Australia (and Oceania)				
Klyuchevskaya, Kamchatka, Russia	4,835	15,863	1697	2009
Mauna Kea, Hawaii	4,205	13,796	N/A	c. 2460 BC
Mauna Loa, Hawaii	4,170	13,681	1750	1984
Kerinci, Sumatra, Indonesia	3,800	12,467	1838	2009
Europe				
Etna, Italy	3,330	10,925	N/A	2009
Askja, Iceland	1,516	4,974	1875	1961
Hekla, Iceland	1,491	4,892	1104	2000
Vesuvius, Italy	1,281	4,203	79	1944
North America				
Citlaltépetl (Orizaba), Mexico	5,675	18,619	N/A	1846
Popocatépetl, Mexico	5,426	17,802	1347	2009
Rainier, Washington	4,392	14,409	N/A	1894
Shasta, California	4,317	14,163	1786	1786
South America				
Guallatiri, Chile	6,071	19,918	1825	1960
Tupungatito, Chile	6,000	19,685	1829	1987
Cotopaxi, Ecuador	5,911	19,393	1532	1940
Láscar, Chile	5,592	18,346	1848	2007

[1]Includes three dormant volcanoes (Kibo, Mawensi, and Shira) that have not erupted in historic times.

Oceans and Seas

	AREA		VOLUME	
	SQ KM	SQ MI	CU KM	CU MI
Pacific Ocean				
without marginal seas	165,250,000	63,800,000	707,600,000	169,900,000
with marginal seas	179,680,000	69,370,000	723,700,000	173,700,000
Atlantic Ocean				
without marginal seas	82,440,000	31,830,000	324,600,000	77,900,000
with marginal seas	106,460,000	41,100,000	354,700,000	85,200,000
Indian Ocean				
without marginal seas	73,440,000	28,360,000	291,000,000	69,900,000
with marginal seas	74,920,000	28,930,000	291,900,000	70,100,000
Arctic Ocean	14,090,000	5,440,000	17,000,000	4,100,000
Gulf of Mexico and Caribbean Sea	4,320,000	1,670,000	9,600,000	2,300,000
Mediterranean and Black Seas	2,970,000	1,150,000	4,200,000	100,000
Bering Sea	2,304,000	890,000	3,330,000	80,000
Hudson Bay	1,230,000	470,000	160,000	40,000
North Sea	570,000	220,000	50,000	10,000
Baltic Sea	420,000	160,000	20,000	5,000
Irish Sea	100,000	40,000	6,000	1,000
English Channel	75,000	29,000	4,000	1,000

	AVERAGE DEPTH		
	M	FT	DEEPEST POINT
Pacific Ocean			
without marginal seas	4,280	14,040	Mariana Trench
with marginal seas	4,030	13,220	(11,034 m; 36,201 ft)
Atlantic Ocean			
without marginal seas	3,930	12,890	Puerto Rico Trench
with marginal seas	3,330	10,920	(8,380 m; 27,493 ft)
Indian Ocean			
without marginal seas	3,960	10,040	Sunda Deep of the Java
with marginal seas	3,900	12,790	Trench (7,450 m; 24,442 ft)
Arctic Ocean	1,205	3,950	(5,502 m; 18,050 ft)
Gulf of Mexico and Caribbean Sea	2,220	7,280	Cayman Trench (7,686 m; 25,216 ft)
Mediterranean and Black Seas	1,430	4,690	Ionian Basin (4,900 m; 16,000 ft)
Bering Sea	1,440	4,720	Bowers Basin (4,097 m; 13,442 ft)
Hudson Bay	128	420	(867 m; 2,846 ft)
North Sea	94	310	Skagerrak (700 m; 2,300 ft)
Baltic Sea	55	180	Landsort Deep (459 m; 1,506 ft)
Irish Sea	60	200	Mull of Galloway (175 m; 576 ft)
English Channel	54	180	Hurd Deep (172 m; 565 ft)

Major Natural Lakes of the World

Conversions for figures may have been rounded, thousands to the nearest hundred and hundreds to the nearest ten.

NAME	LOCATION	AREA		NAME	LOCATION	AREA	
		SQ MI	SQ KM			SQ MI	SQ KM
Caspian Sea	Central Asia	149,200	386,400	Tanganyika	eastern Africa	12,700	32,900
Superior	Canada/US	31,700	82,100	Great Bear	Canada	12,096	31,328
Victoria	eastern Africa	26,828	69,484	Nyasa (Malawi)	eastern Africa	11,430	29,604
Huron	Canada/US	23,000	59,600	Great Slave	Canada	11,030	28,568
Michigan	US	22,300	57,800	Erie	Canada/US	9,910	25,667

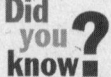
Did you know? Wall Street, which was recognized even before the Civil War as the financial capital of the US, is narrow and short, extending only about seven blocks across part of southern Manhattan in New York City. It was named for an earthen wall built by Dutch settlers in 1653 to repel an expected English invasion.

Longest Rivers of the World by Continent

This list includes both rivers and river systems. Conversions of rounded figures may be rounded to the nearest 10 or 100 miles or kilometers.

NAME	OUTFLOW	LENGTH	
		MI	KM
Africa			
Nile	Mediterranean Sea	4,132	6,650
Congo	South Atlantic Ocean	2,900	4,700
Niger	Gulf of Guinea	2,600	4,200
Zambezi	Mozambique Channel	2,200	3,540
Asia			
Yangtze	East China Sea	3,915	6,300
Yenisey-Baikal-Selenga	Kara Sea	3,442	5,539
Huang He (Yellow)	Gulf of Chihli	3,395	5,464
Ob-Irtysh	Gulf of Ob	3,362	5,410
Europe			
Volga	Caspian Sea	2,193	3,530
Danube	Black Sea	1,770	2,850
Ural	Caspian Sea	1,509	2,428
Dnieper	Black Sea	1,367	2,200
North America			
Mississippi-Missouri-Jefferson	Gulf of Mexico	3,710	5,971
Mackenzie-Slave-Peace	Beaufort Sea	2,635	4,241
Missouri-Jefferson	Mississippi River	2,540	4,088
St. Lawrence–Great Lakes	Gulf of St. Lawrence	2,500	4,000
Australia			
Darling	Murray River	1,702	2,739
Murray	Great Australian Bight	1,572	2,530
Murrumbidgee	Murray River	1,050	1,690
Lachlan	Murrumbidgee River	930	1,500
South America			
Amazon-Ucayali-Apurímac	South Atlantic Ocean	4,000	6,400
Paraná	Río de la Plata	3,032	4,880
Madeira-Mamoré-Guaporé	Amazon River	2,082	3,352
Juruá	Amazon River	2,040	3,283

Preserving Nature

US National Parks

Dates in parentheses indicate when the area was first designated a park, in most cases under a different name. Web site: <www.nps.gov/parks.html>.

PARK	LOCATION	DESIGNATION DATE	SQ MI	SQ KM
Acadia	Bar Harbor ME	1929 (1916)	74	192
American Samoa	American Samoa	1993 (1988)	14	36
Arches	Moab UT	1971 (1929)	120	311
Badlands	southwestern South Dakota	1978 (1939)	379	982
Big Bend	curve of the Rio Grande river, Texas	1944	1,252	3,243
Biscayne	near Miami FL	1980 (1968)	270	699
Black Canyon of the Gunnison	near Montrose CO	1999 (1933)	43	112
Bryce Canyon	Bryce Canyon, Utah	1928 (1923)	56	145
Canyonlands	near Moab UT	1964	527	1,366
Capitol Reef	near Torrey UT	1971 (1937)	379	982
Carlsbad Caverns	near Carlsbad NM	1930 (1923)	73	189
Channel Islands	Ventura CA	1980 (1938)	75	194
Congaree	Hopkins SC	2003	34	88
Crater Lake	Crater Lake OR	1902	286	741
Cuyahoga Valley	near Cleveland and Akron OH	2000 (1974)	51	133
Death Valley	Death Valley, California	1994 (1933)	5,219	13,518
Denali	central Alaska	1980 (1917)	9,492	24,584
Dry Tortugas	Key West FL	1992 (1935)	101	262
Everglades	southern Florida	1947	2,358	6,107

US National Parks (continued)

PARK	LOCATION	DESIGNATION DATE	SQ MI	SQ KM
Gates of the Arctic	Bettles AK	1980 (1978)	13,238	34,287
Glacier	northwest Montana	1910	1,584	4,102
Glacier Bay	Gustavus AK	1980 (1925)	5,130	13,287
Grand Canyon	Grand Canyon, Arizona	1919 (1908)	1,902	4,927
Grand Teton	Moose WY	1950 (1929)	484	1,255
Great Basin	near Baker NV	1986 (1922)	121	313
Great Sand Dunes	Mosca CO	2000 (1932)	132	343
Great Smoky Mountains	Tennessee and North Carolina	1934	815	2,110
Guadalupe Mountains	Salt Flat TX	1972	135	350
Haleakala	Kula, Maui HI	1960 (1916)	47	121
Hawaii Volcanoes	near Hilo HI	1961 (1916)	328	849
Hot Springs	Hot Springs AR	1921 (1832)	9	22
Isle Royale	Houghton MI	1940 (1931)	893	2,314
Joshua Tree	near Palm Springs CA	1994 (1936)	1,591	4,120
Katmai	near King Salmon AK	1980 (1918)	7,385	19,128
Kenai Fjords	Seward AK	1980 (1978)	1,047	2,711
Kobuk Valley	Kotzebue AK	1980 (1978)	2,672	6,920
Lake Clark	Port Alsworth AK	1980 (1978)	6,297	16,309
Lassen Volcanic	Mineral CA	1916 (1907)	166	430
Mammoth Cave	Mammoth Cave, Kentucky	1941	83	214
Mesa Verde	near Cortez and Mancos CO	1906	81	211
Mount Rainier	near Ashford WA	1899	368	954
North Cascades	near Marblemount WA	1968	1,069	2,769
Olympic	near Port Angeles WA	1938	1,442	3,734
Petrified Forest	Arizona	1962 (1906)	146	379
Redwood	Crescent City CA	1994	172	445
Rocky Mountain	near Estes Park and Grand Lake CO	1915	415	1,076
Saguaro	Tucson AZ	1994 (1933)	143	370
Sequoia & Kings Canyon	near Three Rivers CA	1940 (1890)	1,351	3,498
Shenandoah	near Luray VA	1935	311	805
Theodore Roosevelt	Medora ND (south unit); near Watford City ND (north unit)	1978 (1947)	110	285
Virgin Islands	St. John, US Virgin Islands	1956	23	59
Voyageurs	International Falls MN	1975	341	883
Wind Cave	near Hot Springs SD	1903	44	115
Wolf Trap	Vienna VA	2002 (1966)	130 acres	
Wrangell–St. Elias	near Copper Center AK	1980	20,587	53,320
Yellowstone	Idaho, Montana, and Wyoming	1872	3,468	8,983
Yosemite	in the Sierra Nevada, California	1890 (1864)	1,189	3,081
Zion	Springdale UT	1919 (1909)	229	593

Health

Worldwide Health Indicators

*Column data as follows: **Life expectancy** in 2005; **Doctors** = persons per doctor[1]; **Infant mortality** per 1,000 births in 2005; **Water** = percentage (%) of population with access to safe drinking water in 2004; **Food** = percentage (%) of the FAO recommended minimum in 2004[2].*

REGION/BLOC	LIFE EXPECTANCY MALE	LIFE EXPECTANCY FEMALE	DOCTORS	INFANT MORTALITY	WATER	FOOD
World	66.0	70.0	730	38.3	83	118
Africa	51.8	53.8	2,560	78.4	64[3]	103
Central Africa	49.8	50.2	12,890	96.1	46[3]	80
East Africa	46.9	48.2	13,620	86.7	50[3]	86
North Africa	67.2	71.0	890	39.2	91	125
Southern Africa	47.8	51.2	1,610	55.1	85[3]	119
West Africa	47.7	49.7	6,260	94.3	65[3]	109
Americas	71.5	77.6	520	17.1	91[3]	129
Anglo-America[4]	75.0	80.4	370	6.2	100[3]	140
Canada	76.7	83.6	540	4.8	100	136
United States	74.8	80.1	360	6.4	100	141

Worldwide Health Indicators (continued)

REGION/BLOC	LIFE EXPECTANCY MALE	LIFE EXPECTANCY FEMALE·	DOCTORS	INFANT MORTALITY	WATER	FOOD
Americas (continued)						
Latin America	69.4	76.0	690	23.6	91	123
Caribbean	67.5	71.6	380	29.4	79[3]	118
Central America	67.9	73.7	950	21.4	88[3]	106
Mexico	72.7	77.6	810	12.6	97	134
South America	68.9	76.2	710	26.3	86[3]	122
Andean Group	69.4	75.6	830	23.5	86[3]	108
Brazil	67.7	75.9	770	30.7	90	132
Other South America	72.1	79.4	410	17.5	82[3]	120
Asia	**67.2**	**70.3**	**970**	**39.6**	**81[3]**	**116**
Eastern Asia	71.2	75.0	610	22.3	78[5]	121
China	70.4	73.7	620	25.2	77	123
Japan	78.6	85.6	530	2.7	100	110
Republic of Korea	71.7	79.3	740	6.4	92	123
Other Eastern Asia	71.7	77.3	500	13.8	94[3]	93
South Asia	63.3	64.6	2,100	60.5	85[6]	108
India	63.6	65.2	1,920	56.3	86	112
Pakistan	64.7	65.5	1,840	76.2	91	100
Other South Asia	60.4	60.5	5,080	71.0	85[3]	97
Southeast Asia	66.8	71.9	3,120	33.9	82	123
Southwest Asia	67.3	71.9	610	35.5	85[3]	118
Central Asia	61.0	68.9	330	54.0	82[3]	99
Gulf Cooperation Council	73.4	77.5	620	12.7	95[3]	117
Iran	68.6	71.4	1,200	41.6	94	131
Other Southwest Asia	67.6	71.9	690	31.6	82[3]	119
Europe	**71.0**	**79.1**	**300**	**7.2**	**98[3]**	**130**
European Union (EU)	75.5	81.8	290	4.8	100[3]	137
France	76.7	83.8	330	3.6	100	142
Germany	75.8	82.0	290	4.1	100	131
Italy	77.6	83.2	180	5.9	100[3]	151
Spain	76.7	83.2	240	4.4	100	138
United Kingdom	75.9	81.0	720	5.1	100	137
Other EU	73.6	80.3	320	5.2	100[3]	133
Non-EU[7]	78.5	83.5	480	3.8	100[3]	131
Eastern Europe	62.3	73.8	290	11.7	95[3]	119
Russia	59.9	73.3	240	11.5	97	117
Ukraine	62.2	74.0	330	10.0	96	120
Other Eastern Europe	67.3	74.7	370	13.4	84[3]	121
Australia	**78.5**	**83.3**	**400**	**4.7**	**100**	**116**
Oceania	**74.5**	**79.4**	**480**	**14.7**	**50[8]**	**117**
Pacific Ocean Islands	68.3	73.3	770	30.1	67[3]	118

[1]Latest data available for individual countries. [2]The Food and Agriculture Organization of the United Nations (FAO) calculates this percentage by dividing the caloric equivalent to the known average daily supply of foodstuffs for human consumption in a given country by its population, thus arriving at a minimum daily per capita caloric intake. The higher the percentage, the more calories consumed. [3]Data for 2000. [4]Includes Canada, the US, Greenland, Bermuda, and St. Pierre and Miquelon. [5]Does not include Japan. [6]Includes Iran. [7]Western Europe only; includes Andorra, Faroe Islands, Gibraltar, Guernsey, Iceland, Isle of Man, Jersey, Liechtenstein, Monaco, Norway, San Marino, and Switzerland. [8]Does not include New Zealand.

Causes of Death, Worldwide, by Region

Global estimates for 2002 as published in the World Health Organization (WHO) World Health Report 2004. Regions are as defined by the WHO. Numbers are in thousands ('000).

LEADING CAUSES OF DEATH	ALL CATE-GORIES (%)	ALL CATE-GORIES	REGION AFRI-CA	REGION AMER-ICAS	REGION EASTERN MEDITER-RANEAN	REGION EUROPE	REGION SOUTHEAST ASIA	REGION WESTERN PACIFIC
1 Ischemic heart disease	12.6	7,208	332	921	538	2,373	2,039	993
2 Cerebrovascular disease	9.7	5,509	359	452	227	1,447	1,059	1,957
3 Lower respiratory infections	6.8	3,884	1,104	223	348	280	1,453	471

Causes of Death, Worldwide, by Region (continued)

LEADING CAUSES OF DEATH	ALL CATEGORIES (%)	ALL CATEGORIES	AFRICA	AMERICAS	EASTERN MEDITERRANEAN	EUROPE	SOUTHEAST ASIA	WESTERN PACIFIC
4 HIV disease	4.9	2,777	2,095	103	44	36	436	61
5 Chronic obstructive pulmonary disease	4.8	2,748	117	241	95	261	656	1,375
6 Perinatal conditions	4.3	2,462	554	175	303	65	1,012	349
7 Diarrheal diseases	3.2	1,798	707	57	259	16	604	154
8 Tuberculosis	2.7	1,566	348	46	138	69	599	366
9 Malaria	2.2	1,272	1,136	1	59	0	65	11
10 Trachea, bronchus, and lung cancers	2.2	1,243	17	231	27	366	174	427
11 Road traffic accidents	2.1	1,192	195	135	133	127	296	304
12 Diabetes mellitus	1.7	988	80	253	55	142	263	192
13 Hypertensive heart disease	1.6	911	60	135	97	179	152	284
14 Self-inflicted injuries	1.5	873	34	63	34	163	246	331
15 Stomach cancer	1.5	850	34	74	21	157	63	500
16 Cirrhosis of the liver	1.4	786	54	105	67	171	204	185
17 Nephritis and nephrosis	1.2	677	99	102	65	76	169	165
18 Colon and rectum cancers	1.1	622	20	109	15	228	63	186
19 Liver cancer	1.1	618	45	37	15	66	61	394
20 Measles	1.1	611	311	0	70	6	196	28
21 Violence	1.0	559	134	146	26	73	113	66
22 Congenital anomalies	0.9	493	56	58	83	38	149	108
23 Breast cancer	0.8	477	35	89	27	150	93	82
24 Esophagus cancer	0.8	446	22	32	16	48	82	245
25 Inflammatory heart disease	0.7	404	42	67	37	101	76	81

Ten Leading Causes of Death in the US, by Age

Preliminary data for 2006. Numbers in thousands. Rates per 100,000 population. Numbers are based on weighted data rounded to the nearest individual, so category percentages and rates may not add to totals given. Source: National Vital Statistics Report, <www.cdc.gov/nchs>.

CAUSE	NUMBER	RATE	%
ALL AGES			
1 Diseases of heart	629,121	210.2	25.9
Ischemic heart disease	424,892	141.9	17.5
Heart failure	60,315	20.1	2.5
2 Malignant neoplasms	560,102	187.1	23.1
Neoplasms of the trachea, bronchus, and lung	158,525	52.9	6.5
Neoplasms of the colon, rectum, and anus	53,465	17.9	2.2
Neoplasms of the breast	41,223	13.8	1.7
3 Cerebrovascular diseases	137,265	45.8	5.7
4 Chronic lower respiratory diseases	124,614	41.6	5.1
5 Accidents	117,748	39.3	4.9
Motor-vehicle accidents	44,572	14.9	1.8
6 Diabetes mellitus	72,507	24.2	3.0
7 Alzheimer disease	72,914	24.4	3.0
8 Pneumonia	55,387	18.5	2.3
9 Nephritis, nephrotic syndrome, and nephrosis	44,791	15.0	1.8
10 Septicemia	34,031	11.4	1.4
All other causes	455,333	152.1	18.8
All causes, all ages	**2,425,901**	**810.3**	**100**

CAUSE	NUMBER	RATE	%
1–4 YEARS			
1 Accidents	1,591	9.8	34.3
Motor-vehicle accidents	586	3.6	12.6
All other accidents	1,005	6.2	21.7
2 Congenital malformations, deformations, and chromosomal abnormalities	501	3.1	10.8
3 Malignant neoplasms	372	2.3	8.0

CAUSE	NUMBER	RATE	%
1–4 YEARS (CONTINUED)			
4 Assault (homicide)	350	2.1	7.5
5 Diseases of heart	160	1.0	3.5
6 Influenza and pneumonia	114	0.7	2.5
7 Septicemia	88	0.5	1.9
8 Conditions of perinatal origin	67	0.4	1.4
9 Nonmalignant/unknown neoplasms	63	0.4	1.4
10 Cerebrovascular diseases	53	0.3	1.1
All other causes	1,277	7.8	27.5
All causes, 1–4 years	**4,636**	**28.5**	**100**

CAUSE	NUMBER	RATE	%
5–14 YEARS			
1 Accidents	2,228	5.5	36.3
Motor-vehicle accidents	1,323	3.3	21.6
All other accidents	905	2.2	14.7
2 Malignant neoplasms	916	2.3	14.9
3 Assault (homicide)	387	1.0	6.3
4 Congenital malformations, deformations, and chromosomal abnormalities	330	0.8	5.4
5 Diseases of heart	242	0.6	3.9
6 Intentional self-harm (suicide)	213	0.5	3.5
7 Chronic lower respiratory diseases	113	0.3	1.8
8 Cerebrovascular diseases	93	0.2	1.5
9 Septicemia	78	0.2	1.3
10 Nonmalignant/unknown neoplasms	76	0.2	1.2
All other causes	1,460	3.6	23.8
All causes, 5–14 years	**6,136**	**15.2**	**100**

Ten Leading Causes of Death in the US, by Age (continued)

CAUSE	NUMBER	RATE	%
15–24 YEARS			
1 Accidents	15,859	37.4	45.8
Motor-vehicle accidents	10,845	25.6	31.3
All other accidents	5,014	11.8	14.5
2 Assault (homicide)	5,596	13.2	16.2
3 Intentional self-harm (suicide)	4,097	9.7	11.8
4 Malignant neoplasms	1,643	3.9	4.7
5 Diseases of heart	1,021	2.4	2.9
6 Congenital malformations, deformations, and chromosomal abnormalities	456	1.1	1.3
7 Cerebrovascular diseases	206	0.5	0.6
8 HIV disease	198	0.5	0.6
9 Influenza and pneumonia	180	0.4	0.5
10 Pregnancy and childbirth	172	0.4	0.5
All other causes	5,204	12.3	15.0
All causes, 15–24 years	**34,632**	**81.6**	**100**
25–44 YEARS			
1 Accidents	30,949	36.8	24.7
Motor-vehicle accidents	13,779	16.4	11.0
All other accidents	17,170	20.4	13.7
2 Malignant neoplasms	17,604	20.9	14.1
3 Diseases of heart	14,873	17.7	11.9
4 Intentional self-harm (suicide)	11,240	13.4	9.0
5 Assault (homicide)	7,525	8.9	6.0
6 HIV disease	5,150	6.1	4.1
7 Chronic liver disease and cirrhosis	2,805	3.3	2.2
8 Diabetes mellitus	2,705	3.2	2.2
9 Cerebrovascular diseases	2,703	3.2	2.2
10 Septicemia	1,131	1.3	0.9
All other causes	28,488	33.9	22.8
All causes, 25–44 years	**125,173**	**148.9**	**100**
45–64 YEARS			
1 Malignant neoplasms	151,654	202.6	32.7
2 Diseases of heart	101,588	135.7	21.9

CAUSE	NUMBER	RATE	%
45–64 YEARS (CONTINUED)			
3 Accidents	29,505	39.4	6.4
Motor-vehicle accidents	10,939	14.6	2.4
All other accidents	18,566	24.8	4.0
4 Diabetes mellitus	17,012	22.7	3.7
5 Cerebrovascular diseases	16,779	22.4	3.6
6 Chronic lower respiratory diseases	16,181	21.6	3.5
7 Chronic liver disease and cirrhosis	14,725	19.7	3.2
8 Intentional self-harm (suicide)	11,492	15.4	2.5
9 Nephritis, nephrotic syndrome, and nephrosis	6,495	8.7	1.4
10 Septicemia	6,184	8.3	1.3
All other causes	92,848	124.0	20.0
All causes, 45–64 years	**464,463**	**620.4**	**100**
65 YEARS AND OVER			
1 Diseases of heart	510,934	1,371.3	29.0
2 Malignant neoplasms	387,828	1,040.9	22.0
3 Cerebrovascular diseases	117,284	314.8	6.7
4 Chronic lower respiratory diseases	107,058	287.3	6.1
5 Alzheimer disease	72,135	193.6	4.1
6 Diabetes mellitus	52,599	141.2	3.0
7 Influenza and pneumonia	49,459	132.7	2.8
8 Nephritis, nephrotic syndrome, and nephrosis	36,960	99.2	2.1
9 Accidents	36,436	97.8	2.1
Motor-vehicle accidents	6,953	18.7	0.4
All other accidents	29,483	79.1	1.7
10 Septicemia	26,125	70.1	1.5
All other causes	365,186	980.1	20.7
All causes, 65 years and over	**1,762,004**	**4,728.9**	**100**

HIV/AIDS

Acquired immunodeficiency syndrome, or AIDS, is a fatal transmissable disorder of the immune system that is caused by the human immunodeficiency virus (HIV). HIV was first isolated in 1983. In most cases, HIV slowly attacks and destroys the **immune system**, leaving the infected individual vulnerable to malignancies and infections that eventually cause death. AIDS is the last stage of HIV infection, during which time these diseases arise. An average interval of 10 years exists between infection with HIV and development of the conditions typical of AIDS. **Pneumonia** and **Kaposi sarcoma** are two of the most common diseases seen in AIDS patients.

HIV is contracted through semen, vaginal fluid, breast milk, blood, or other body fluids containing blood. Health care workers may come into contact with other body fluids that may transmit the HIV virus, including amniotic and synovial fluids. Although it is a transmiss-

able virus, it is not contagious and cannot be spread through coughing, sneezing, or casual physical contact. Other **sexually transmitted diseases**, such as genital herpes, may increase the risk of contracting HIV through sexual contact.

The main **cellular target** of HIV is a special class of white blood cells critical to the immune system known as T4 helper cells. Once HIV has entered, it can cause these cells to function poorly or to die. A hallmark of the onset of AIDS is a drastic reduction in the number of helper T cells in the body. Two predominant strains of the virus, designated HIV-1 and HIV-2, are known. Worldwide the most common strain is HIV-1, with HIV-2 more common primarily in western Africa; the two strains act in a similar manner, but the latter causes a form of AIDS that progresses much more slowly.

Diagnosis is made on the basis of blood tests approved by the Centers for Disease Control and Pre-

HIV/AIDS (continued)

vention that may be administered by a health professional. Alternately, a home collection kit may be purchased. No vaccine or cure has yet been developed that can prevent HIV infection. Several **drugs** are now used to slow the development of AIDS, including azidothymidine (AZT). **Protease inhibitors,** such as ritonavir and indinavir, have been shown to block the development of AIDS, at least temporarily. Protease inhibitors are most effective when used in conjunction with two different reverse transcriptase inhibitors—the so-called triple-drug therapy.

HIV/AIDS is a major problem in developing countries, particularly sub-Saharan Africa. The most recent UN report states that at the end of 2007, as many as 36.1 million people were estimated to be living with HIV. In 2007 alone, as many as 4.1 million contracted the disease and up to 2.4 million died of it.

For confidential information on HIV/AIDS, call 1-800-342-AIDS.

Internet resources: <www.cdc.gov/hiv>.

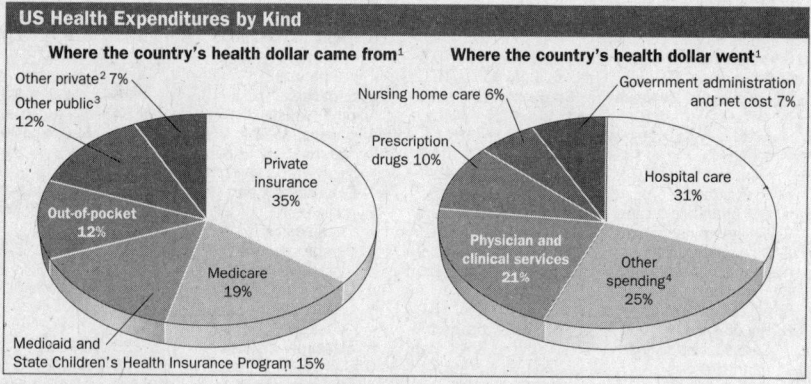

US Health Expenditures by Kind

Where the country's health dollar came from[1]

- Other private[2] 7%
- Other public[3] 12%
- Out-of-pocket 12%
- Private insurance 35%
- Medicare 19%
- Medicaid and State Children's Health Insurance Program 15%

Where the country's health dollar went[1]

- Nursing home care 6%
- Prescription drugs 10%
- Government administration and net cost 7%
- Hospital care 31%
- Physician and clinical services 21%
- Other spending[4] 25%

[1] Calendar year 2007. Detail may not add to 100% because of rounding.
[2] Other private includes industrial in-plant, privately funded construction, and non-patient revenues, including philanthropy.
[3] Other public includes programs such as workers' compensation, public health activity, US Department of Defense, US Department of Veterans Affairs, Indian Health Service, state and local hospital subsidies, and school health.
[4] Other spending includes dentist and other professional services, home health care, durable medical equipment, over-the-counter medicines and sundries, other nondurable medical products, government public health activities, and research and construction.
Source: Centers for Medicare and Medicaid Services, Office of the Actuary, National Health Statistics Group.

Sexually Transmitted Diseases (STDs)

Sexually transmitted diseases (STDs) are usually passed from person to person by direct sexual contact. They may also be transmitted from a mother to her child before or at birth or, less frequently, may be passed from person to person in nonsexual contact. STDs usually initially affect the genitals, the reproductive tract, the urinary tract, the oral cavity, the anus, or the rectum, but they may mature in the body to attack various organs and systems. Following are some of the major STDs:

Syphilis was first widely reported by European writers in the 16th century, and a virtual epidemic swept Europe around the year 1500. Syphilis is spread through direct contact with a syphilis sore (chancre); development of this sore is the first stage of the disease. The second stage manifests itself as a rash on the palms and the bottoms of the feet. In the last stage, symptoms disappear, but the disease remains in the body and may damage internal organs and lead to paralysis, blindness, dementia, and even death. For individuals infected less than a year, a single dose of penicillin will cure the disease. Larger doses are needed for those who have had it for a longer period of time.

Gonorrhea, a form of urethritis (an infection and inflammation of the urethra), is one of the most common STDs. Although spread through sexual contact, the gonorrhea infection can also be spread to other parts of the body after touching the infected area. Men manifest symptoms, which include discharge and a burning sensation when urinating, more often than women. If gonorrhea is left untreated, women may develop pelvic inflammatory disease (PID) and men may become infertile. The disease can also spread to the blood or joints and is potentially life threatening.

Chlamydia, another form of urethritis, can be transmitted during vaginal, anal, or oral sex. Since there are frequently no symptoms, most infected individuals do not know they have the disease until complications develop. Untreated chlamydia can cause pain during urination or sex in men and PID in women. Antibiotics can successfully cure the disease.

Genital herpes, a disease that became especially widespread in the 1960s and 1970s, often presents minimal symptoms upon infection. The most common sign, however, is blistering in the genital area; outbreaks can occur over many years but generally decrease in severity and number. Genital herpes is

Sexually Transmitted Diseases (STDs) (continued)

caused by the herpes simplex viruses type 1 (HSV-1) and type 2 (HSV-2). The former causes infections on and around the mouth but may be spread through the saliva to the genitals; the latter is transmitted during sexual contact with someone who has a genital infection. The HSV-2 infection can cause problems for people with suppressed immune systems and for infants who contract the disease upon delivery. Herpes can also leave individuals more susceptible to HIV infection and make those carrying the disease more infectious. A variety of treatments, including antiviral medications, have been used to help manage genital herpes, but currently there is no cure for the disease.

Internet resources:
<www.cdc.gov/nchstp/od/nchstp.html>.

Diet and Exercise

The Food and Drug Administration (FDA)

The FDA is a division of the US Department of Health and Human Services. **FDA Web site:** *<www.fda.gov>.*

Mission: To promote and protect the public health by helping safe and effective products reach the market in a timely way and monitoring products for continued safety after they are in use. **History:** The FDA celebrated its 100th anniversary in 2006, having been created by the passing of the Food and Drugs Act, or Wiley Act, in 1906. The Food, Drug, and Cosmetic Act of 1938 then brought cosmetics and medical devices under the authority of the FDA. The Food and Drug Administration Act of 1988 officially established the body as an agency of the Department of Health and Human Services, with a commissioner of food and drugs appointed by the president with the consent of the Senate. **Location:** Rockville MD (with a transfer to Silver Spring MD in progress and scheduled to be completed in 2012). **Commissioner of Food and**

Drugs: Margaret Hamburg. **Budget:** FY 2010 (requested) US$3.2 billion. **Functions:** The FDA is the agency of the US federal government authorized by Congress to inspect, test, approve, and set safety standards for foods and food additives, drugs, chemicals, cosmetics, and household and medical devices. Generally, the FDA is empowered to prevent untested products from being sold and to take legal action to halt the sale of undoubtedly harmful products or of products that involve a health or safety risk. Through court procedure, the FDA can seize products and prosecute the persons or firms responsible for legal violation. FDA authority is limited to interstate commerce. The agency cannot control prices nor directly regulate advertising except of prescription drugs and medical devices.

Body Mass Index (BMI)

The BMI is a measure expressing the relationship of weight to height determined by dividing body weight in kilograms by the square of height in meters (for convenience, the information has been converted to standard US measurements in the table below). It is more highly correlated with body fat than any other indicator of height and weight. The National Institutes of Health recommend using the BMI scale to help assess the risk of diseases and disabilities associated with an unhealthy weight. The BMI may overestimate body fat in athletes and others who have a muscular build, and it may underestimate body fat in older persons and others who have lost muscle mass.
Source: <www.nhlbi.nih.gov>.

HEIGHT (INCHES)	BODY WEIGHT (POUNDS)																				
58	91	96	100	105	110	115	119	124	129	134	138	143	148	153	158	162	167	172	177	181	186
59	94	99	104	109	114	119	124	128	133	138	143	148	153	158	163	168	173	178	183	188	193
60	97	102	107	112	118	123	128	133	138	143	148	153	158	163	168	174	179	184	189	194	199
61	100	106	111	116	122	127	132	137	143	148	153	158	164	169	174	180	185	190	195	201	206
62	104	109	115	120	126	131	136	142	147	153	158	164	169	175	180	186	191	196	202	207	213
63	107	113	118	124	130	135	141	146	152	158	163	169	175	180	186	191	197	203	208	214	220
64	110	116	122	128	134	140	145	151	157	163	169	174	180	186	192	197	204	209	215	221	227
65	114	120	126	132	138	144	150	156	162	168	174	180	186	192	198	204	210	216	222	228	234
66	118	124	130	136	142	148	155	161	167	173	179	186	192	198	204	210	216	223	229	235	241
67	121	127	134	140	146	153	159	166	172	178	185	191	198	204	211	217	223	230	236	242	249
68	125	131	138	144	151	158	164	171	177	184	190	197	203	210	216	223	230	236	243	249	256
69	128	135	142	149	155	162	169	176	182	189	196	203	209	216	223	230	236	243	250	257	263
70	132	139	146	153	160	167	174	181	188	195	202	209	216	222	229	236	243	250	257	264	271
71	136	143	150	157	165	172	179	186	193	200	208	215	222	229	236	243	250	257	265	272	279
72	140	147	154	162	169	177	184	191	199	206	213	221	228	235	242	250	258	265	272	279	287
73	144	151	159	166	174	182	189	197	204	212	219	227	235	242	250	257	265	272	280	288	295
74	148	155	163	171	179	186	194	202	210	218	225	233	241	249	256	264	272	280	287	295	303
75	152	160	168	176	184	192	200	208	216	224	232	240	248	256	264	272	279	287	295	303	311
BMI	19	20	21	22	23	24	25	26	27	28	29	30	31	32	33	34	35	36	37	38	39
			NORMAL					OVERWEIGHT								OBESE					

Food Guide Pyramid

In 2005 the USDA released an update of its food-pyramid guide to a healthy diet. It is designed to help individuals get proper nutrients while at the same time consuming the appropriate amount of calories necessary to maintain healthy weight. The 2005 pyramid also provides information about exercise and weight loss. Diets should be low in added sugars, salt, saturated fat and cholesterol and moderate in overall fat.

Find your balance between food and physical activity:

- Be sure to stay within your daily calorie needs.
- Be physically active for at least 30 minutes most days of the week.
- About 60 minutes a day of physical activity may be needed to prevent weight gain.
- For sustaining weight loss, at least 60 to 90 minutes a day of physical activity may be required.
- Children and teenagers should be physically active for 60 minutes every day or most days.

Recommended daily intake
These amounts are appropriate for individuals who get less than 30 minutes per day of moderate physical activity, beyond normal daily activities. Those who are more physically active may be able to consume more because they may have greater calorie needs.

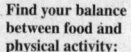

MyPyramid.gov

	Grains	Vegetables	Fruits	Fats and Oils—limit your intake	Milk	Meat and Beans
Children 2–3 years old	3 ounce equivalents[1]	1 cup[2]	1 cup[3]		2 cups[4]	2 ounce equivalents[5]
Children 4–8 years old	4–5 ounce equivalents[1]	1.5 cups[2]	1–1.5 cups[3]		2 cups[4]	3–4 ounce equivalents[5]
Girls 9–13 years old	5 ounce equivalents[1]	2 cups[2]	1.5 cups[3]		3 cups[4]	5 ounce equivalents[5]
Boys 9–13 years old	6 ounce equivalents[1]	2.5 cups[2]	1.5 cups[3]		3 cups[4]	5 ounce equivalents[5]
Girls 14–18 years old	6 ounce equivalents[1]	2.5 cups[2]	1.5 cups[3]		3 cups[4]	5 ounce equivalents[5]
Boys 14–18 years old	7 ounce equivalents[1]	3 cups[2]	2 cups[3]		3 cups[4]	6 ounce equivalents[5]
Women 19–30 years old	6 ounce equivalents[1]	2.5 cups[2]	2 cups[3]		3 cups[4]	5.5 ounce equivalents[5]
Men 19–30 years old	8 ounce equivalents[1]	3 cups[2]	2 cups[3]		3 cups[4]	6.5 ounce equivalents[5]
Women 31–50 years old	6 ounce equivalents[1]	2.5 cups[2]	1.5 cups[3]		3 cups[4]	5 ounce equivalents[5]
Men 31–50 years old	7 ounce equivalents[1]	3 cups[2]	2 cups[3]		3 cups[4]	6 ounce equivalents[5]
Women 51+ years old	5 ounce equivalents[1]	2 cups[2]	1.5 cups[3]		3 cups[4]	5 ounce equivalents[5]
Men 51+ years old	6 ounce equivalents[1]	2.5 cups[2]	2 cups[3]		3 cups[4]	5.5 ounce equivalents[5]

[1] 1 slice of bread, 1 cup of ready-to-eat cereal, or ½ cup of cooked rice, cooked pasta, or cooked cereal can be considered as 1 ounce equivalent from the grains group.
[2] 1 cup of raw or cooked vegetables or vegetable juice or 2 cups of raw leafy greens can be considered as 1 cup from the vegetable group.
[3] 1 cup of fruit or 100% fruit juice or ½ cup of dried fruit can be considered as 1 cup from the fruit group.
[4] 1 cup of milk or yogurt, 1½ ounces of natural cheese, or 2 ounces of processed cheese can be considered as 1 cup from the milk group.
[5] 1 ounce of meat, poultry, or fish, ¼ cup cooked dry beans, 1 egg, 1 tablespoon of peanut butter, or ½ ounce of nuts or seeds can be considered as 1 ounce equivalent from the meat and beans group.

Source: USDA.

Nutrient Composition of Selected Fruits and Vegetables

Values shown are approximations for 100 grams (3.57 oz.). Foods are raw unless otherwise noted. Source: USDA Nutrient Data Laboratory. kcal: kilocalorie; g: gram; mg: milligram; IU: international unit.

	ENERGY (KCAL)	WATER (G)	CARBO-HYDRATE (G)	PROTEIN (G)	FAT (G)	VITAMIN A (IU)	VITAMIN C (MG)	THIAMINE (MG)	RIBO-FLAVIN (MG)	NIACIN (MG)
Fruits										
Apple	59	83.93	15.25	0.19	0.36	53	5.7	0.017	0.014	0.077
Avocado	161	74.27	7.39	1.98	15.32	61	7.9	0.108	0.122	1.921
Banana	92	74.26	23.43	1.03	0.48	81	9.1	0.045	0.100	0.540
Blueberries	56	84.61	14.13	0.67	0.38	100	13.0	0.048	0.050	0.359
Cherries (sweet)	72	80.76	16.55	1.20	0.96	214	7.0	0.050	0.060	0.400
Grapes	67	81.30	17.15	0.63	0.35	100	4.0	0.092	0.057	0.300
Grapefruit	32	90.89	8.08	0.63	0.10	124	34.4	0.036	0.020	0.250
Lemon	29	88.98	9.32	1.10	0.30	29	53.0	0.040	0.020	0.100
Orange	47	86.75	11.75	0.94	0.12	205	53.2	0.087	0.040	0.282
Peach	43	87.66	11.10	0.70	0.09	535	6.6	0.017	0.041	0.990
Pear	59	83.81	15.11	0.39	0.40	20	4.0	0.020	0.040	0.100
Pineapple	49	86.50	12.39	0.39	0.43	23	15.4	0.092	0.036	0.420
Plum	55	85.20	13.01	0.79	0.62	323	9.5	0.043	0.096	0.500
Raspberries	49	86.57	11.57	0.91	0.55	130	25.0	0.030	0.090	0.900
Strawberries	30	91.57	7.02	0.61	0.37	27	56.7	0.020	0.066	0.230
Vegetables										
Asparagus[1]	24	92.20	4.23	2.59	0.31	539	10.8	0.123	0.126	1.082
Beans (snap, green)	31	90.27	7.14	1.82	0.12	668	16.3	0.084	0.105	0.752
Broccoli	28	90.69	5.24	2.98	0.35	1,542	93.2	0.065	0.119	0.638
Cabbage	25	92.15	5.43	1.44	0.27	133	32.2	0.050	0.040	0.300
Carrot	43	87.79	10.14	1.03	0.19	28,129	9.3	0.097	0.059	0.928
Cauliflower	25	91.91	5.20	1.98	0.21	19	46.4	0.057	0.063	0.526
Collards[1]	26	91.86	4.90	2.11	0.36	3,129	18.2	0.040	0.106	0.575
Corn (sweet, yellow)[1]	108	69.57	25.11	3.32	1.28	217	6.2	0.215	0.072	1.614
Mushroom[1]	27	91.08	5.14	2.17	0.47	0	4.0	0.073	0.300	4.460
Onion[1]	44	87.86	10.15	1.36	0.19	0	5.2	0.042	0.023	0.165
Pepper (sweet, red)	27	92.19	6.43	0.89	0.19	5,700	190.0	0.066	0.030	0.509
Potato[2]	93	75.42	21.56	1.96	0.10	0	12.8	0.105	0.021	1.395
Spinach	22	91.58	3.50	2.86	0.35	6,715	28.1	0.078	0.189	0.724
Sweet potato[2]	103	72.85	24.27	1.72	0.11	21,822	24.6	0.073	0.127	0.604
Tomato (red)	21	93.76	4.64	0.85	0.33	623	19.1	0.059	0.048	0.628

[1]Boiled. [2]Baked.

Nutritional Value of Selected Foods

Values shown are approximations. Source: Home and Garden Bulletin No. 72, USDA. kcal: kilocalorie; g: gram; mg: milligram; oz: ounce; fl oz: fluid ounce.

FOOD	AMOUNT	GRAMS	ENERGY (KCAL)	CARBO-HYDRATE (G)	PROTEIN (G)	TOTAL FAT (G)	SATU-RATED FAT (G)	CALCIUM (MG)	IRON (MG)	SODIUM (MG)
Beverages										
Beer	12 fl oz	360	150	13	1	0	0	14	0.1	18
Cola, regular	12 fl oz	369	160	41	0	0	0	11	0.2	18
Cola, diet (w/aspartame and saccharine)	12 fl oz	355	0	0	0	0	0	14	0.2	32
Coffee, brewed	6 fl oz	180	0	0	0	0	0	4	0	2
Wine, table, red	3.5 fl oz	102	75	3	0	0	0	8	0.4	5
Dairy										
Butter, salted	4 oz	113	810	0	1	92	57.1	27	0.2	933
Cheese, American (pasteurized, processed)	1 oz	28.35	105	0	6	9	5.6	174	0.1	406
Cottage cheese, small curd	8 oz	210	215	6	26	9	6	126	0.3	850
Cream cheese	1 oz	28.35	100	1	2	10	6.2	23	0.3	84
Cream, sour	8 oz	230	495	10	7	48	30	268	0.1	123
Eggs, cooked, fried	1 egg	46	90	1	6	7	1.9	25	0.7	162
Ice cream, vanilla, 11% fat	8 oz	133	270	32	5	14	8.9	176	0.1	116
Milk, whole, 3.3% fat	8 oz	244	150	11	8	8	5.1	291	0.1	120

Nutritional Value of Selected Foods (continued)

FOOD	AMOUNT	GRAMS	ENERGY (KCAL)	CARBO-HYDRATE (G)	PROTEIN (G)	TOTAL FAT (G)	SATU-RATED FAT (G)	CALCIUM (MG)	IRON (MG)	SODIUM (MG)
Dairy (continued)										
Milk, low fat, 2% fat	8 oz	244	120	12	8	5	2.9	297	0.1	122
Milk, skim	8 oz	245	85	12	8	0	0.3	302	0.1	126
Yogurt, plain, low fat	8 oz	227	145	16	12	4	2.3	415	0.2	159
Fats, oils										
Margarine, hard, 80% fat	0.5 oz	14	100	0	0	11	2.2	4	0	132
Olive oil	0.5 oz	14	125	0	0	14	1.9	0	0	0
Vegetable shortening	0.5 oz	13	115	0	0	13	3.3	0	0	0
Fish										
Fish sticks, frozen	1 piece	28	70	4	6	3	0.8	11	0.3	53
Ocean perch, breaded, fried	1 piece	85	185	7	16	11	2.6	31	1.2	138
Oysters, raw	8 oz	240	160	8	20	4	1.4	226	15.6	175
Salmon, baked, red	3 oz	85	140	0	21	5	1.2	26	0.5	55
Shrimp, fried	3 oz	85	200	11	16	10	2.5	61	2	384
Tuna, canned, white, in water	3 oz	85	135	0	30	1	0.3	17	0.6	468
Fruits, fruit products										
Applesauce, canned, sweetened	8 oz	255	195	51	0	0	0.1	10	0.9	8
Pineapple, canned, heavy syrup	8 oz	255	200	52	1	0	0	36	1	3
Raisins	8 oz	145	435	115	5	1	0.2	71	3	17
Watermelon	1 piece	482	155	35	3	2	0.3	39	0.8	10
Grains										
Bagels, plain	1 bagel	68	200	38	7	2	0.3	29	1.8	245
Bread, rye, light	1 slice	25	65	12	2	1	0.2	20	0.7	175
Bread, white	1 slice	25	65	12	2	1	0.3	32	0.7	129
Bread, whole wheat	1 slice	28	70	13	3	1	0.4	20	1	180
Cereal, Cheerios	1 oz	28.35	110	20	4	2	0.3	48	4.5	307
Cereal, Kellogg's Corn Flakes	1 oz	28.35	110	24	2	0	0	1	1.8	351
Cereal, Lucky Charms	1 oz	28.35	110	23	3	1	0.2	32	4.5	201
Cereal, Post Raisin Bran	1 oz	28.35	85	21	3	1	0.1	13	4.5	185
Cake, white, w/white frosting, commercial	1 piece	71	260	42	3	9	2.1	33	1	176
Cheesecake	1 piece	92	280	26	5	18	9.9	52	0.4	204
Chocolate chip cookies, commercial	4 cookies	42	180	28	2	9	2.9	13	0.8	140
Doughnuts, cake, plain	1 doughnut	50	210	24	3	12	2.8	22	1	192
English muffins, plain	1 muffin	57	140	27	5	1	0.3	96	1.7	378
Oatmeal, instant, cooked, w/salt	8 oz	234	145	25	6	2	0.4	19	1.6	374
Popcorn, air-popped, unsalted	8 oz	8	30	6	1	0	0	1	0.2	0
Rice, brown, cooked	8 oz	195	230	50	5	1	0.3	23	1	0
Rice, white, instant, cooked	8 oz	165	180	40	4	0	0.1	5	1.3	0
Meat, poultry										
Bacon, regular, cooked	3 slices	19	110	0	6	9	3.3	2	0.3	303
Chicken, breast, roasted	3 oz	86	140	0	27	3	0.9	13	0.9	64
Chicken, drumstick, floured, fried	1.7 oz	49	120	1	13	7	1.8	6	0.7	44
Ham, roasted, lean and fat	3 oz	85	205	0	18	14	5.1	6	0.7	1009
Hamburger	4-oz patty	174	445	38	25	21	7.1	75	4.8	763
Lamb chops, braised, lean	1.7 oz	48	135	0	17	7	2.9	12	1.3	36
Turkey, roasted	8 oz	140	240	0	41	7	2.3	35	2.5	98
Nuts, legumes, seeds										
Peanuts, oil-roasted, unsalted	8 oz	145	840	27	39	71	9.9	125	2.8	22
Peanut butter	0.5 oz	16	95	3	5	8	1.4	5	0.3	75
Tofu	1 piece	120	85	3	9	5	0.7	108	2.3	8

Nutritional Value of Selected Foods (continued)

FOOD	AMOUNT	GRAMS	ENERGY (KCAL)	CARBO-HYDRATE (G)	PROTEIN (G)	TOTAL FAT (G)	SATU-RATED FAT (G)	CALCIUM (MG)	IRON (MG)	SODIUM (MG)
Sauces, dressings, condiments										
Catsup	0.5 oz	15	15	4	0	0	0	3	0.1	156
Cheese sauce w/milk, from mix	8 fl oz	279	305	23	16	17	9.3	569	0.3	1565
Mayonnaise	0.5 oz	14	100	0	0	11	1.7	3	0.1	80
Mustard, yellow	0.17 oz	5	5	0	0	0	0	4	0.1	63
Salad dressing, French	0.5 oz	16	85	1	0	9	1.4	2	0	188
Salad dressing, Italian, low calorie	0.5 oz	15	5	2	0	0	0	1	0	136
Sugars, sweets, miscellaneous snacks										
Chocolate, dark, sweet	1 oz	28.35	150	16	1	10	5.9	7	0.6	5
Potato chips	10 chips	20	105	10	1	7	1.8	5	0.2	94
Pudding, chocolate, instant	4 oz	130	155	27	4	4	2.3	130	0.3	440
Sugar, brown	8 oz	220	820	212	0	0	0	187	4.8	97
Sugar, white, granulated	8 oz	200	770	199	0	0	0	3	0.1	5

Reading Food Labels

The FDA requires most food manufacturers to provide standardized information about certain nutrients. Within strict guidelines the nutritional labels are designed to aid the consumer in making informed dietary decisions as well as to regulate claims made by manufacturers about their products.

The percent daily value is based on a 2,000-calorie-per-day diet. Some larger packages will have listings for both 2,000-calorie and 2,500-calorie diets. For products that require additional preparation before eating, such as dry cake mixes, manufacturers often provide two columns of nutritional information, one with the values of the food as purchased, the other with the values of the food as prepared.

The FDA selects mandatory label components (see sample label at right) based on current understanding of nutrition concerns, and component order on the label is consistent with the priority of dietary recommendations. Components that may appear in addition to the mandatory components are limited to the following: calories from saturated fat, polyunsaturated fat, monounsaturated fat, potassium, soluble fiber, insoluble fiber, sugar alcohol (for example, sugar substitutes xylitol, mannitol, and sorbitol), other carbohydrate (the difference between total carbohydrate and the sum of dietary fiber, sugars, and sugar alcohol if declared), percent of vitamin A present as beta-carotene, and other essential vitamins and minerals. Any of these optional components that form the basis of product claims, fortification, or enrichment must appear in the nutrition facts. In 2006 labels were required to specify amounts of trans fatty acids.

Certain key descriptions are also regulated by the FDA. They include the following, in amounts per serving:

Low fat: 3 g or less
Low saturated fat: 1 g or less
Low sodium: 140 mg or less
Low cholesterol: 20 mg or less and 2 g or less of saturated fat
Low calorie: 40 calories or less

Dietary Guidelines for Americans, 2005
Web site: <www.health.gov/dietaryguidelines>.

Nutrition Facts

Serving Size 1 cup (228g)
Servings Per Container 2

Amount Per Serving

Calories 250   Calories from Fat 110

%Daily Value*

Total Fat 12g	**18%**
Saturated Fat 3g	**15%**
Trans Fat 3g	
Cholesterol 30mg	**10%**
Sodium 470mg	**20%**
Potassium 700mg	**20%**
Total Carbohydrate 31g	**10%**
Dietary Fiber 0g	**0%**
Sugars 5g	
Protein 5g	

Vitamin A	**4%**
Vitamin C	**2%**
Calcium	**20%**
Iron	**4%**

* Percent Daily Values are based on a 2,000 calorie diet. Your Daily Values may be higher or lower depending on your calorie needs:

	Calories	2,000	2,500
Total Fat	Less than	65g	80g
Sat Fat	Less than	20g	25g
Cholesterol	Less than	300mg	300mg
Sodium	Less than	2,400mg	2,400mg
Total Carbohydrate		300g	375g
Dietary Fiber		25g	30g

Ways To Burn 150 Calories

Values shown are approximations. Activities are listed from more to less vigorous—the more vigorous an activity, the less time it takes to burn a calorie. When specific distances are given, the activity must be performed in the time shown (for example, one must run 1.5 miles in 15 minutes to burn 150 calories).

ACTIVITY	DURATION (MINUTES)
Climbing stairs	15
Shoveling snow	15
Running 1.5 miles (10 minutes/mile)	15
Jumping rope	15
Bicycling 4 miles	15
Playing basketball	15–20
Playing wheelchair basketball	20
Swimming laps	20
Performing water aerobics	30
Walking 2 miles (15 minutes/mile)	30

ACTIVITY	DURATION (MINUTES)
Raking leaves	30
Pushing a stroller 1.5 miles	30
Dancing fast	30
Shooting baskets	30
Walking 1.75 miles (20 minutes/mile)	35
Gardening (standing)	30–45
Playing touch football	30–45
Playing volleyball	45
Washing windows or floors	45–60
Washing and waxing a car or boat	45–60

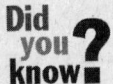
Did you know?

In 17th-century Holland a speculative frenzy erupted over the sale of tulip bulbs. Tulips had been introduced into Europe from Turkey shortly after 1550. Demand for new varieties soon exceeded the supply, and prices rose to astonishing heights. The craze, known as the tulip mania, reached its peak in Holland in 1633–37. Homes, estates, and industries were mortgaged so that bulbs could be purchased; bulbs of rare varieties sold for the equivalent of hundreds of dollars each. The crash came in 1637, when almost overnight the price structure collapsed, sweeping away fortunes and leaving behind financial ruin for many Dutch families.

Iran: Power of the People

by Nahid Siamdoust, TIME/Tehran

After sitting Pres. Mahmoud Ahmadinejad was hastily declared the winner in Iran's 12 June national election, the nation, and especially the capital city of Tehran, erupted in street demonstrations against Iran's regime, which is led by Muslim clerics. TIME's Nahid Siamdoust reported on the first days of the uprising.

When a million people showed up on Revolution Avenue in downtown Tehran to protest the results of the 12 June presidential election, most of them wore sneakers, in case they had to run for their lives. The crowd included people of all walks and ages. Students holding posters that read "Lies forbidden" walked side by side with chadori housewives, heavily made-up young girls, manual laborers, middle-aged government workers, and the elderly. The marchers didn't chant insulting slogans, and there were few police in sight. Beneath the placid surface simmered frustration and anger—but also traces of hope. "People have come out because they've finally had enough. They're tired of all the lies that Ahmadinejad has dished out," said Massoumeh, 46, who brought her two young daughters to the march. (Like most other Iranians I talked to, she did not want to give her full name.)

The popular revolt that spread across the country in the days after the election has been as startling to ordinary Iranians as to the authorities trying to suppress it. Not since the Islamic Revolution of 1979 has Tehran seen such spontaneous outpourings of emotion. Within hours of the announcement of the election results, Tehranis developed their own sign language of dissent. People passing one another stretched hands in peace signs. Drivers on jam-packed streets honked their horns in protest. Apartment dwellers climbed to their rooftops to shout "Allahu akbar" and "Death to dictator!"—a gesture last seen three decades ago.

When the regime blocked the Internet and cell-phone networks, demonstrators organized their rallies by word of mouth. It was democracy in action. "The amazing thing is that this movement has no leader," said Sima, 40, a book editor in Tehran. "Sure, people support [opposition presidential candidate Mir-Hossein] Mousavi, but the real reason they're here is to protest against the fraud."

It's not yet clear where the movement is headed. The regime has crushed challenges to its authority before, most recently in 1999, when students poured into the streets to protest the closing of a reformist newspaper, prompting the government to unleash vigilantes on them. The state deployed its shock troops again this time: members of the Basij, a pro-Ahmadinejad paramilitary group, stormed dormitories at Tehran University, reportedly killing five students and detaining hundreds. At least one demonstrator was killed when a Basiji opened fire on a crowd. There are eyewitness reports of deaths from clashes across Iran. Yet no matter what transpires—whether the government bows to the demands for change or launches a bloodier crackdown—Iran will never be the same. The election and its aftermath exposed the cynicism of the country's leaders but also revealed the determination of millions of Iranians to reach for a future that suddenly seems within their grasp.

The mood on the streets of Tehran has been a mix of anger, exhilaration, and dread. The day after Ahmadinejad was declared the victor in a landslide, people emptied into the streets in rage. Downtown, groups of demonstrators set several buses, a building, and hundreds of garbage bins on fire, smashed the windows of state banks, and destroyed ATMs. On Ghaem-Magham Street, I watched a lone woman dressed in a head-to-toe black chador standing on the side of the road, flashing the peace sign to passing cars and yelling, "Only Mousavi." The woman, a 36-year-old bank employee named Maryam, had told her children to find dinner for themselves. "What I'm doing here is more important for their future," she said. When people driving by warned her that she might get beaten for speaking so openly, she said, "Let them beat me. My country is going to waste. What am I worth in comparison?"

Just then, a Basiji charged at her from nowhere carrying a metal rod. As he prepared to strike her, a group of men got out of their cars, tackled the man, and started beating him. Maryam got up from the ground, composed herself, and went right back to her spot to continue her mission. I watched as seven more people joined her, until they were chased away by police special forces wielding batons.

Despite the initial postelection mayhem, the government had some reason to believe that the fury would subside. Since Ahmadinejad's victory in 2005, when many voters stayed away from the polls, the reform movement had been largely dormant. So when Mousavi called for a demonstration on 15 June, no one was sure how many people would show up—until Ahmadinejad's victory speech, in which he compared the protesters to fans upset about losing a soccer match and called them a minority of "twigs and mote." A number of people I talked to at the pro-Mousavi march on Revolution Avenue cited the President's comments as reason to keep up the fight. "What he said drove me crazy," said a 26-year-old mechanic from Hashemiye, in south Tehran.

That people are now willing to risk their lives and take action shows that Iran has crossed a threshold. The nature of the demonstrations has reminded the state that people do, after all, care as much about democratic rights as they do about the economy. Ahmadinejad has done poorly on both counts, but as long as the state respected the vote, Iranians were willing to overlook other shortcomings. Now that trust is gone. "This time they went too far," says Mohsen, a 32-year-old government employee. "We already deposed one of the strongest dictatorships in the world 30 years ago. They should know that we won't tolerate another."

Countries of the World

The information about the countries of the world that follows has been assembled and analyzed by *Encyclopædia Britannica* editors from hundreds of private, national, and international sources. Included are all the sovereign states of the world. The historical background sketches have been adapted, augmented, and updated from *Britannica Concise Encyclopedia* and the statistical sections from *Britannica World Data,* which is published annually in conjunction with the *Britannica Book of the Year.* The section called Recent Developments also has been adapted from material appearing in recent issues of the yearbook, as well as from other sources inside and outside Britannica. The locator maps have been prepared by Britannica's cartography department. Several countries, including those with the largest economies, are given expanded coverage in this section.

All information is the latest available to Britannica. It must be understood that in many cases it takes several years for the various countries or agencies to gather and process statistics—the most current data available will normally be dated several years earlier.

A few definitions of terms used in the articles may be useful. **GDP** (gross domestic product) is the total value of goods and services produced in a country during a given accounting period, usually a year. Typically the value is given in current prices of the year indicated. **GNI** (gross national income) is essentially GDP plus income from foreign transactions minus payments made outside the country. **Imports** are material goods legally entering a country (or customs area) and subject to customs regulations. The value of goods imported is given free on board (**f.o.b.**) unless otherwise specified; the value of goods exported and imported f.o.b. is calculated from the cost of production and excludes the cost of transport. The principal alternate basis for valuation of goods in international trade is that of cost, insurance, and freight (**c.i.f.**); its use is restricted to imports, as it comprises the principal charges needed to bring the goods to the customs house in the country of destination. **Exports** are material goods legally leaving a country and subject to customs regulations. Valuation of goods exported is virtually always f.o.b.

Afghanistan

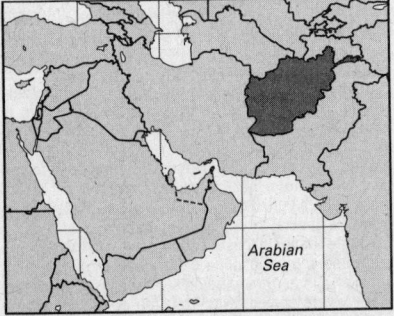

Arabian
Sea

Official name: Islamic Republic of Afghanistan (Jomhuri-ye Eslami-ye Afghanestan [Dari (Persian)]; Da Afghanestan Eslami Jamhuriyat [Pashto]). **Form of government:** Islamic republic with two legislative bodies (House of Elders [102]; House of the People [249]). **Chief of state and head of government:** President Hamid Karzai (from 2002). **Capital:** Kabul. **Official languages:** Dari (Persian); Pashto; six additional languages have local official status per the 2004 constitution. **Official religion:** Islam. **Monetary unit:** 1 (new) afghani (Af) = 100 puls; valuation (1 Jul 2009) US$1 = Af 47.30.

Demography

Area: 249,347 sq mi, 645,807 sq km. **Population** (2008): 28,266,000. **Density** (2008): persons per sq mi 113.4, persons per sq km 43.8. **Urban** (2006) 21.5%. **Sex distribution** (2006): male 51.14%; female 48.86%. **Age breakdown** (2006): under 15,

44.6%; 15–29, 26.7%; 30–44, 16.0%; 45–59, 8.6%; 60–74, 3.5%; 75 and over, 0.6%. **Ethnolinguistic composition** (2004): Pashtun 42%; Tajik 27%; Hazara 9%; Uzbek 9%; Chahar Aimak 4%; Turkmen 3%; other 6%. **Religious affiliation** (2004): Sunni Muslim 82%; Shiʻi Muslim 17%; other 1%. **Major cities** (2006): Kabul 2,536,300; Herat 349,000; Kandahar (Qandahar) 324,800; Mazar-e Sharif 300,600; Jalalabad 168,600. **Location:** southern Asia, bordering Uzbekistan, Tajikistan, China, Pakistan, Iran, and Turkmenistan.

Vital statistics

Birth rate per 1,000 population (2006): 46.6 (world avg. 20.3). **Death rate** per 1,000 population (2006): 20.3 (world avg. 8.6). **Total fertility rate** (avg. births per childbearing woman; 2006): 6.69. **Life expectancy** at birth (2006): male 43.2 years; female 43.5 years.

National economy

Budget (2005–06). *Revenue:* Af 67,531,000,000 (grants for development revenue 51.3%; grants for current revenue 24.8%; domestic revenue 23.9%, of which taxes 18.2%). *Expenditures:* Af 91,417,-000,000 (development expenditures 64.0%; current expenditures 36.0%). **Gross national income** (2007): US$10,137,000,000 (US$373 per capita). **Public debt** (external, outstanding; 2006): US$1,761,-000,000. **Production** (metric tons except as noted). *Agriculture and fishing* (2006–07): wheat 3,363,000, barley 364,000, rice 361,000, opium poppy (2007) 8,200 (93% of world production); livestock (number of live animals) 9,259,000 sheep, 6,746,000 goats, 174,000 camels; fisheries production (2005) 1,000 (from aquaculture, none). *Mining and quarrying:* salt (2005) 34,000. *Manufacturing*

---

1 metric ton = about 1.1 short tons;　1 kilometer = 0.6 mi (statute);　1 metric ton-km cargo = about 0.68 short ton-mi cargo;　c.i.f.: cost, insurance, and freight;　f.o.b.: free on board

(value added in Af '000,000; 2005–06): food products 48,575; chemical products 1,206; cement, bricks, and ceramics 809. *Energy production (consumption):* electricity (kW-hr; 2006–07) 916,900,000 (483,600,000); hard coal (metric tons; 2005) 33,000 (33,000); petroleum products (metric tons; 2005) none (186,000); natural gas (cu m; 2005) 2,600,000 (2,600,000). **Population economically active** (2005): total 4,296,300; activity rate of total population 18.0% (participation rates: female 47.0%; unemployed 8.5%). **Selected balance of payments data.** Receipts from (US$'000,000): tourism (1998) 1.0; foreign direct investment (2004–06 avg.) 2; official development assistance (2006) 3,000.

Foreign trade

Imports (2006–07; c.i.f.): US$2,744,000,000 (machinery and equipment 19.4%; household items and medicine 12.0%; food products 12.0%; base and fabricated metals 10.0%; mineral fuels 9.3%). *Major import sources* (2005–06): Japan 16.8%; Pakistan 15.9%; China 12.8%; Russia 9.2%; Uzbekistan 8.3%. **Exports** (2006–07; f.o.b.): US$416,000,000 (carpets and handicrafts 45.0%; dried fruits 30.3%; fresh fruits 9.4%; skins 5.5%). *Major export destinations* (2005–06): Pakistan 77.6%; India 6.0%; Russia 3.4%; UAE 2.9%.

Transport and communications

Transport. *Railroads* (2006): none. *Roads* (2005): total length 34,782 km (paved 7%). *Vehicles* (2004–05): passenger cars 197,449; trucks and buses 123,964. *Air transport* (2004–05): passenger-km 681,000,000; metric ton-km cargo 20,624,000. **Communications,** in total units (units per 1,000 persons). Telephone landlines (2007): 81,000 (3); cellular telephone subscribers (2007): 4,668,000 (172); total Internet users (2007): 580,000 (21); broadband Internet subscribers (2005): 220 (0.01).

Education and health

Literacy (2006): total population ages 15 and over literate 28.1%; males 43.1%; females 12.6%. **Health:** physicians (2005) 4,747 (1 per 5,000 persons); hospital beds (2004) 9,667 (1 per 2,381 persons); infant mortality rate (2006) 160.2.

Military

Total active duty personnel (2008): 76,000 (army 100%); foreign troops (2008): 41-country NATO-sponsored security and development force 50,700, of which US 20,600, UK 8,300, Germany 3,300, France 2,700, Canada 2,500, Italy 2,400; other combat operations along Pakistan border 20,000 troops, of which US 18,000. **Military expenditure as percentage of GDP** (2005): 9.9%; per capita expenditure US$31.

Background

The area was part of the Persian empire in the 6th century BC and was conquered by Alexander the Great in the 4th century BC. Hindu influence entered with the Hephthalites and Sasanians; Islam became entrenched during the rule of the Saffarids, c. AD 870. Afghanistan was divided between the Mughal empire of India and the Safavid empire of Persia until the 18th century, when other Persians under Nadir Shah took control. Great Britain and Russia fought several wars in the area in the 19th century. From the 1930s Afghanistan had a stable monarchy; it was overthrown in the 1970s. The rebels' intention was to institute Marxist reforms, but the reforms sparked rebellion, and troops from the USSR invaded to establish order. Afghan guerrillas prevailed, and the Soviet Union withdrew in 1988–89. In 1992 an Islamic republic was established, and in 1996 the Taliban militia took power and enforced a harsher Islamic order. The militia's unwillingness to extradite Osama bin Laden and members of his al-Qaeda militant organization following the September 11 attacks in 2001 led to military conflict with the US and allied nations and the overthrow of the Taliban, and a multinational force continued to occupy the country in the early 21st century.

Recent Developments

Afghanistan in 2008 saw a surge of violence from militants relentlessly attacking the US-backed Kabul government. The number of roadside bombs in Afghanistan doubled from a year earlier, to some 2,000, and the increased use of suicide attacks and roadside bombs suggested that the Taliban was adopting strategies from fighting in Iraq. Bold operations in Afghanistan reflected more aggressive Taliban and al-Qaeda activity inside areas in northwestern Pakistan that were being used as a base and sanctuary. An assassination attempt on Pres. Hamid Karzai at a public ceremony in Kabul occurred in April. In June a prison in Kandahar was blown open, freeing almost 400 Taliban fighters. In September US forces adopted an aggressive strategy, including the launch of commando raids and unmanned drone attacks inside Pakistan's tribal areas. In mid-2009 US Pres. Barack Obama began his stated goal of sending an additional 20,000 US troops to the country to aid in the stabilization efforts. The death toll for foreign troops by the middle of July, however, had already made it the deadliest month of the conflict.

Internet resources: <www.afghan-web.com>.

Albania

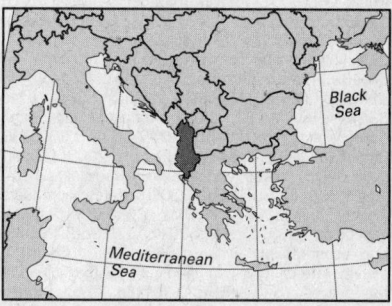

Official name: Republika e Shqipërisë (Republic of Albania). **Form of government:** unitary multiparty republic with one legislative house (Assembly [140]). **Chief of state:** President Bamir Topi (from 2007). **Head of government:** Prime Minister Sali Berisha (from 2005). **Capital:** Tirana (Tiranë). **Official language:** Albanian. **Official religion:** none. **Monetary**

unit: 1 lek = 100 qindarka; valuation (1 Jul 2009) US$1 = 93.59 leks.

Demography

Area: 11,082 sq mi, 28,703 sq km. **Population** (2008): 3,194,000. **Density** (2008): persons per sq mi 288.2, persons per sq km 111.3. **Urban** (2004): 44.5%. **Sex distribution** (2004): male 49.82%; female 50.18%. **Age breakdown** (2005): under 15, 26.9%; 15–29, 25.3%; 30–44, 19.8%; 45–59, 16.0%; 60–74, 9.3%; 75–84, 2.4%; 85 and over, 0.3%. **Ethnic composition** (2000): Albanian 91.7%; Greek 2.3%; Aromanian 1.8%; Rom 1.8%; other 2.4%. **Traditional religious groups** (2005): Muslim 68%, of which Sunni 51%, Bektashi 17%; Orthodox 22%; Roman Catholic 10%. **Major cities** (2001): Tirana (Tiranë) 343,078; Durrës 99,546; Elbasan 87,797; Shkodër 82,455; Vlorë 77,691. **Location:** southeastern Europe, bordering Montenegro, Kosovo, Macedonia, Greece, and the Mediterranean Sea.

Vital statistics

Birth rate per 1,000 population (2007): 10.7 (world avg. 20.3). **Death rate** per 1,000 population (2007): 4.8 (world avg. 8.6). **Natural increase rate** per 1,000 population (2007): 5.9 (world avg. 11.7). **Total fertility rate** (avg. births per childbearing woman; 2006): 2.03. **Life expectancy** at birth (2006): male 74.8 years; female 80.3 years.

National economy

Budget (2005). *Revenue:* 199,600,000,000 leks (tax revenue 91.3%, of which turnover tax/VAT 31.7%, social security contributions 18.4%, customs duties and excise taxes 17.0%; other revenue 8.7%). *Expenditures:* 245,100,000,000 leks (current expenditures 79.4%, of which social security and welfare 22.5%, wages and salaries 22.5%, debt service 12.2%; development expenditures 20.6%). **Gross national income** (2007): US$10,456,000,000 (US$3,290 per capita). **Public debt** (external, outstanding; 2006): US$1,588,000,000. **Production** (metric tons except as noted). *Agriculture and fishing* (2006): alfalfa for forage and silage 2,962,000, corn (maize) 245,400, wheat 230,900; livestock (number of live animals) 1,830,000 sheep, 940,000 goats, 634,000 cattle; fisheries production (2005) 5,275 (from aquaculture 28%). *Mining and quarrying* (2005): chromium ore 50,000. *Manufacturing* (value added in US$'000,000; 2005): basic chemicals 33; textiles 33; base metals 32. *Energy production (consumption):* electricity (kW-hr; 2005) 5,443,000,000 (5,814,000,000); lignite (metric tons; 2005) 92,000 (105,000); crude petroleum (barrels; 2007) 1,820,000 ([2005] 2,950,000); petroleum products (metric tons; 2005) 222,000 (1,048,000); natural gas (cu m; 2005) 17,170,000 (17,170,000). **Population economically active** (2006): total 1,084,000; activity rate of total population 34.6% (participation rates: ages 15–64, 53.7%; female 39.6%; unemployed 13.8%). **Selected balance of payments data.** Receipts from (US$'000,000): tourism (2005) 854; remittances (2006) 1,359; foreign direct investment (FDI) (2004–06 avg.) 313; official development assistance (2006) 321. Disbursements for (US$'000,000): tourism (2005) 786; remittances (2006) 27; FDI (2004–06 avg.) 10.

Foreign trade

Imports (2007; c.i.f.): 376,796,000,000 leks (non-electrical and electrical machinery 20.8%; mineral fuels and electricity 16.7%; food, beverages, and tobacco 16.6%; construction materials and base and fabricated metals 15.8%; textiles and footwear 10.4%). *Major import sources:* Italy 27.1%; Greece 14.6%; China 8.0%; Turkey 7.3%; Germany 5.5%. **Exports** (2007; f.o.b.): 96,688,000,000 leks (textiles and footwear 48.4%; construction materials and base and fabricated metals 15.8%; mineral fuels and electricity 15.4%; food, beverages, and tobacco 7.3%). *Major export destinations:* Italy 68.1%; Greece 8.3%; Germany 2.4%; Macedonia 2.3%; Turkey 2.3%.

Transport and communications

Transport. *Railroads* (2004): length (2005) 447 km; passenger-km 89,000,000; metric ton-km cargo 32,000,000. *Roads* (2002): total length 18,000 km (paved 39%). *Vehicles* (2004): passenger cars 190,004; trucks and buses 71,875. *Air transport* (2005; Albanian Air only): passenger-km 152,000,000; metric ton-km, none. **Communications,** in total units (units per 1,000 persons). Telephone landlines (2007): 81,000 (3); cellular telephone subscribers (2007): 2,300,000 (721); personal computers (2002): 36,000 (12); total Internet users (2006): 471,000 (150); broadband Internet subscribers (2006): 300,000 (95).

Education and health

Educational attainment (2001). Population ages 20 and over having: no formal schooling/incomplete primary education 7.8%; primary 55.6%; lower secondary 2.7%; upper secondary 17.9%; vocational 8.8%; university 7.2%. **Literacy** (2006): total population ages 15 and over literate 98.7%; males 99.2%; females 98.3%. **Health:** physicians (2004) 3,699 (1 per 845 persons); hospital beds (2005) 9,284 (1 per 339 persons); infant mortality rate per 1,000 live births (2006) 20.8; undernourished population (2002–04) 200,000 (6% of total population based on the consumption of a minimum daily requirement of 1,980 calories).

Military

Total active duty personnel (2007): 11,020 (army 56.3%, navy 10.0%, air force 12.4%, other [includes command structure] 21.3%). **Military expenditure as percentage of GDP** (2005): 1.4%; per capita expenditure US$37.

Background

The Albanians are descended from the Illyrians, an ancient Indo-European people who lived in central Europe and migrated south by the beginning of the Iron Age. Of the two major Illyrian migrating groups, the Ghegs settled in the north and the Tosks in the south, along with Greek colonizers. The area was under

---

1 metric ton = about 1.1 short tons; 1 kilometer = 0.6 mi (statute); 1 metric ton-km cargo = about 0.68 short ton-mi cargo; c.i.f.: cost, insurance, and freight; f.o.b.: free on board

Roman rule by the 1st century BC; after AD 395 it was connected administratively to Constantinople. Turkish invasion began in the 14th century and continued into the 15th century; though the national hero, Skanderbeg, was able to resist them for a time, after his death (1468) the Turks consolidated their rule. The country achieved independence in 1912 and was admitted into the League of Nations in 1920. It was briefly a republic in 1925–28 and then became a monarchy under Zog I, whose initial alliance with Benito Mussolini led to Italy's invasion of Albania in 1939. After the war a socialist government under Enver Hoxha was installed. Gradually Albania cut itself off from the nonsocialist international community and eventually from all nations, including China, its last political ally. By 1990 economic hardship had produced antigovernment demonstrations, and in 1992 a noncommunist government was elected and Albania's international isolation ended. In the late 20th and early 21st centuries, Albania continued to experience economic uncertainty and ethnic turmoil, the latter involving Albanian minorities in Serbia and Macedonia.

Recent Developments

In April 2009 Albania (along with Croatia) joined NATO, reflecting both Albania's progress in developing stable democratic institutions and its achievements in transforming the military into a small professional force able to contribute to NATO's collective defense. Albania also continued to pursue EU integration, with plans to apply for membership in 2009.

Internet resources: <www.instat.gov.al>.

Algeria

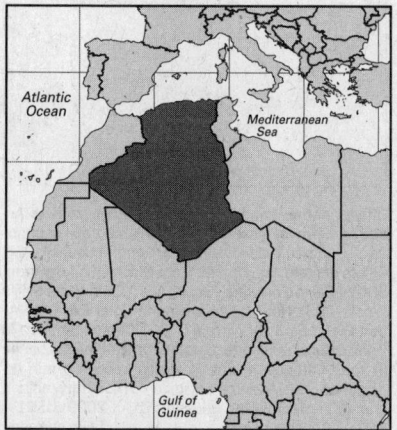

Official name: Al-Jumhuriyah al-Jazairiyah al-Dimuqratiyah al-Sha'biyah (Arabic) (People's Democratic Republic of Algeria). Form of government: multiparty republic with two legislative bodies (Council of the Nation [144; includes 48 nonelected seats appointed by the president]; National People's Assembly [389]). Chief of state: President Abdelaziz Bouteflika (from 1999). Head of government: Prime Minister Ahmed Ouyahia (from 2008). Capital: Algiers. Official languages: Arabic; Tamazight is designated as a national language. Official religion: Islam. Monetary unit: 1 Algerian dinar (DA) = 100 centimes; valuation (1 Jul 2009) US$1 = DA 71.58.

Demography

Area: 919,595 sq mi, 2,381,741 sq km. Population (2008): 34,574,000. Density (2008): persons per sq mi 37.6, persons per sq km 14.5. Urban (2005): 60.0%. Sex distribution (2005): male 50.46%; female 49.54%. Age breakdown (2005): under 15, 29.7%; 15–29, 32.1%; 30–44, 21.0%; 45–59, 10.8%; 60–74, 5.0%; 75–84, 1.2%; 85 and over, 0.2%. Ethnic composition (2000): Algerian Arab 59.1%; Berber 26.2%, of which Arabized Berber 3.0%; Bedouin Arab 14.5%; other 0.2%. Religious affiliation (2000): Muslim 99.7%, of which Sunni 99.1%, Ibadiyah 0.6%; Christian 0.3%. Major cities (1998): Algiers 1,519,570 (urban agglomeration [2007] 3,354,000); Oran 692,516; Constantine 462,187; Annaba 348,554; Batna 242,514. Location: northern Africa, bordering the Mediterranean Sea, Tunisia, Libya, Niger, Mali, Mauritania, Western Sahara, and Morocco.

Vital statistics

Birth rate per 1,000 population (2006): 17.1 (world avg. 20.3). Death rate per 1,000 population (2006): 4.6 (world avg. 8.6). Natural increase rate per 1,000 population (2006): 12.5 (world avg. 11.7). Total fertility rate (avg. births per childbearing woman; 2006): 1.89. Life expectancy at birth (2006): male 71.7 years; female 74.9 years.

National economy

Budget (2006). Revenue: DA 3,639,900,000,000 (hydrocarbon revenue 76.9%; nonhydrocarbon revenue 23.1%). Expenditures: DA 2,452,700,000,000 (current expenditures 58.5%; capital expenditures 41.5%). Public debt (external, outstanding; 2006): US$3,738,000,000. Production (metric tons except as noted). Agriculture and fishing (2006): wheat 2,687,930, potatoes 2,180,961, barley 1,235,880, dates 491,188, olives 364,733; livestock (number of live animals) 19,615,730 sheep, 3,754,590 goats; fisheries production (2005) 126,627 (from aquaculture, negligible). Mining and quarrying (2006): iron ore 1,996,000; phosphate rock 1,510,000; zinc (metal content) 572. Manufacturing (value added in US$'000,000; 2005): food and beverages 1,230; fabricated metal products 880; refined petroleum/manufactured gas 720. Energy production (consumption): electricity (kW-hr; 2005) 32,873,000,000 (32,846,000,000); hard coal (metric tons; 2005) none (779,000); crude petroleum (barrels; 2006) 524,700,000 ([2005] 142,200,000); petroleum products (metric tons; 2005) 37,994,000 (10,393,000); natural gas (cu m; 2006) 84,900,000,000 ([2005] 31,450,000,000). Gross national income (2007): US$122,465,-000,000 (US$3,620 per capita). Population economically active (2006): total 10,109,600; activity rate of population 30% (participation rates: ages 15–64 [1998] 52.6%; female 16.9%; unemployed 12.3%). Selected balance of payments data. Receipts from (US$'000,000): tourism (2005) 184; remittances (2006) 2,527; foreign direct investment

(FDI) (2004–06 avg.) 1,253; official development assistance (2006) 209. Disbursements for (US$'000,000): tourism (2005) 370; FDI (2004–06 avg.) 117.

Foreign trade

Imports (2006; c.i.f.): US$21,456,000,000 (food and live animals 16.9%; nonelectrical machinery 16.0%; base metals 12.9%). *Major import sources:* France 20.4%; Italy 8.8%; China 8.0%; Germany 6.9%; US 6.6%. **Exports** (2006; f.o.b): US$54,613,000,000 (crude petroleum 55.6%; natural gas 27.7%; manufactured gas 7.4%; refined petroleum 7.2%). *Major export destinations:* US 27.2%; Italy 17.1%; Spain 11.0%; France 8.4%; Canada 6.6%.

Transport and communications

Transport. *Railroads* (2004): route length 3,973 km; (2000) passenger-km 1,142,000,000; metric ton-km cargo 2,029,000,000. *Roads* (2004): total length 108,302 km (paved 70%). *Vehicles* (2005): passenger cars 1,905,892; trucks and buses 1,068,520. *Air transport* (2005; Air Algérie only): passenger-km 3,101,000,000; metric ton-km cargo 36,177,000. **Communications,** in total units (units per 1,000 persons). Telephone landlines (2007): 2,923,000 (86); cellular telephone subscribers (2007): 21,446,000 (633); personal computers (2005): 1,920,000 (58); total Internet users (2007): 3,500,000 (103); broadband Internet subscribers (2005): 195,000 (5.9).

Education and health

Educational attainment (1998). Percentage of economically active population ages 6 and over having: no formal schooling 30.1%; primary education 29.9%; lower secondary 20.7%; upper secondary 13.4%; higher 4.3%; other 1.6%. **Literacy** (2005): total population ages 15 and over literate 72.1%; males literate 80.6%; females literate 63.4%. **Health:** physicians (2003) 36,347 (1 per 877 persons); hospital beds (1999) 57,796 (1 per 520 persons); infant mortality rate per 1,000 live births (2006) 29.9; undernourished population (2002–04) 1,400,000 (4% of total population based on the consumption of a minimum daily requirement of 1,870 calories).

Military

Total active duty personnel (2007): 147,000 (army 86.4%, navy 4.1%, air force 9.5%). **Military expenditure as percentage of GDP** (2005): 2.9%; per capita expenditure US$89.

Background

Phoenician traders settled the area early in the 1st millennium BC; several centuries later the Romans invaded, and by AD 40 they had control of the Mediterranean coast. The fall of Rome in the 5th century led to invasion by the Vandals and later by Byzantium. The Islamic invasion began in the 7th century; by 711 all of northern Africa was under the control of the Umayyad caliphate. Several Islamic Berber empires

followed, most prominently the Almoravid (c. 1054–1130), which extended its domain to Spain, and the Almohad (c. 1130–1269). The Barbary Coast pirates, operating in the area, had menaced Mediterranean trade for centuries, and France seized this pretext to enter Algeria in 1830. By 1847 France had established control in the region, and by the late 19th century it had instituted civil rule. Popular movements resulted in the bloody Algerian War (1954–62); independence was achieved following a referendum in 1962. Beginning in the 1990s, Islamic fundamentalists opposing secular rule brought Algeria to a state of civil war.

Recent Developments

The parliament in 2008 approved constitutional amendments allowing more than two presidential terms for an incumbent, lengthening each term to seven years, and making the government answerable to the president rather than to the parliament. This was precipitated partly by the worsening security situation. Although there was relative calm following the devastating bombings in December 2007, the summer of 2008 was violent, with several serious bomb attacks in June and August and at least 68 deaths.

Internet resources: <www.algeria.com>.

Andorra

Official name: Principat d'Andorra (Principality of Andorra). **Form of government:** parliamentary coprincipality with one legislative house (General Council [28]). **Chiefs of state:** French President Nicolas Sarkozy (from 2007); Bishop of Urgell, Spain, Joan Enric Vives Sicília (from 2003). **Head of government:** Chief Executive Albert Pintat Santolària (from 2005). **Capital:** Andorra la Vella. **Official language:** Catalan. **Official religion:** none (Roman Catholicism enjoys special recognition in accordance with Andorran tradition). **Monetary unit:** 1 euro (€) = 100 cents; valuation (1 Jul 2009) US$1 = €0.71 (Andorra uses the euro as its official currency, even though it is not a member of the EU).

Demography

Area: 179 sq mi, 464 sq km. **Population** (2008): 84,100. **Density** (2008): persons per sq mi 469.8,

---

1 metric ton = about 1.1 short tons;   *1 kilometer = 0.6 mi (statute);*   *1 metric ton-km cargo = about 0.68 short ton-mi cargo;*   *c.i.f.: cost, insurance, and freight;*   *f.o.b.: free on board*

persons per sq km 181.3. **Urban** (2003): 93%. **Sex distribution** (2005): male 52.16%; female 47.84%. **Age breakdown** (2004): under 15, 14.8%; 15–29, 19.4%; 30–44, 29.3%; 45–59, 20.2%; 60–74, 10.3%; 75–84, 4.2%; 85 and over, 1.8%. **Ethnic composition** (by nationality; 2004): Spanish 37.4%; Andorran 35.7%; Portuguese 13.0%; French 6.6%; British 1.3%; Moroccan 0.7%; Argentine 0.5%; other 4.8%. **Religious affiliation** (2000): Roman Catholic 89.1%; other Christian 4.3%; Muslim 0.6%; Hindu 0.5%; nonreligious 5.0%; other 0.5%. **Major urban areas** (2007): Andorra la Vella 24,574; Escaldes-Engordany 16,475; Encamp 14,029. **Location:** southwestern Europe, between France and Spain.

Vital statistics

Birth rate per 1,000 population (2007): 10.0 (world avg. 20.3). **Death rate** per 1,000 population (2007): 2.8 (world avg. 8.6). **Natural increase rate** per 1,000 population (2007): 7.2 (world avg. 11.7). **Total fertility rate** (avg. births per childbearing woman; 2006): 1.30. **Life expectancy** at birth (2006): male 80.6 years; female 86.6 years.

National economy

Budget (2005). *Revenue:* €308,500,000 (indirect taxes 70.9%; investment income 7.1%; taxes and other income 22.0%). *Expenditures:* €308,500,000 (current expenditures 52.6%; development expenditures 47.2%; financial operations 0.2%). **Public debt** (2004): US$278,000,000. **Production.** *Agriculture* (metric tons except as noted; 2006): tobacco 315; other traditional crops include potatoes, grapes, and grasses for feed; livestock (number of live animals; 2006) 2,524 sheep, 1,434 cattle, 508 goats. *Quarrying:* small amounts of marble are quarried. *Manufacturing* (value of recorded exports in €'000; 2003): transportation equipment 17,513; electrical machinery and apparatus 11,433; optical, photographic, and measuring apparatus 10,658; perfumery and cosmetic preparations 5,008. *Energy production (consumption):* electricity (kW-hr; 2005) 83,900,000 (568,000,000); petroleum products (metric tons; 1998) none (nearly 100,000). **Population economically active** (2007): total 43,234; activity rate of total population 55% (participation rates: ages 15–64 [2003] 75.1%; female 46.6%; unemployed, n.a.). **Gross national income** (at current market prices; 2007): US$3,250,000,000 (US$43,504 per capita). **Selected balance of payments data.** Disbursements for (US$'000,000): remittances (2001–02) 12.

Foreign trade

Imports (2005): €1,442,000,000 (food and beverages 16.6%; electrical machinery 13.0%; motor vehicles 11.3%; clothing and knitwear 7.8%; perfumes, cosmetics, and soaps 7.4%). *Major import sources* (2007): Spain 58.7%; France 18.8%; Germany 5.1%; Italy 3.3%; Japan 2.7%. **Exports** (2005): €114,000,-000 (food and beverages 28.7%; electrical machinery 18.7%; motor vehicles 16.3%; optical, photographic, and measuring apparatus 6.3%; perfumes, cosmetics, and soaps 3.0%). *Major export destinations* (2007): Spain 61.6%; France 16.2%; Germany 15.7%; Italy 2.2%.

Transport and communications

Transport. *Railroads:* none. *Roads* (1999): total length 269 km (paved 74%). *Vehicles* (2006): passenger cars 50,952; trucks and buses 4,463. **Communications,** in total units (units per 1,000 persons). Telephone landlines (2006): 36,000 (457); cellular telephone subscribers (2006): 69,000 (864); total Internet users (2005): 27,000 (284); broadband Internet subscribers (2006): 15,000 (183).

Education and health

Literacy: resident population literate, virtually 100%. **Health** (2003): physicians 244 (1 per 296 persons); hospital beds 233 (1 per 310 persons); infant mortality rate per 1,000 live births (2006) 4.0.

Military

Total active duty personnel: none. France and Spain are responsible for Andorra's external security; the police force is assisted in alternate years by either French gendarmerie or Barcelona police. Andorra has no defense budget.

Background

Andorra's independence is traditionally ascribed to Charlemagne, who recovered the region from the Muslims in 803. It was placed under the joint suzerainty of the French counts of Foix and the Spanish bishops of the See of Urgell in 1278, and it was subsequently governed jointly by the Spanish bishop of Urgell and the French head of state. This feudal system of government, the last in Europe, lasted until 1993, when a constitution was adopted that transferred most of the coprinces' powers to the Andorran General Council, a body elected by universal suffrage. Andorra has long had a strong affinity with Catalonia; its institutions are based in Catalonian law, and it is part of the diocese of the See of Urgell (Spain). The traditional economy was based on sheep raising, but tourism has been very important since the 1950s.

Recent Developments

A principal goal of Andorra was to institute reforms needed to remove the country from the Organisation for Economic Co-operation and Development's list of tax havens. To that end, in early 2009 plans to implement tax information exchange protocols by November were announced.

Internet resources: <www.estadistica.ad>.

Angola

Official name: República de Angola (Republic of Angola). **Form of government:** unitary multiparty republic with one legislative house (National Assembly [220, excluding 3 unfilled seats reserved for Angolans living abroad]). **Head of state and government:** President José Eduardo dos Santos (from 1979), assisted by Prime Minister Paulo Kassoma (from 2008). **Capital:** Luanda. **Official language:** Portuguese. **Official religion:** none. **Monetary unit:** 1 kwanza (AOA) = 100 cêntimos; valuation (1 Jul 2009) US$1 = kwanza 74.78.

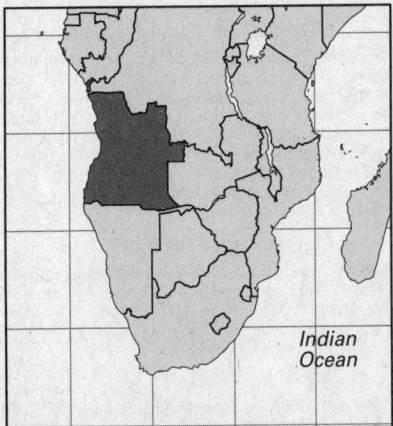

Indian Ocean

Demography

Area: 481,354 sq mi, 1,246,700 sq km. **Population** (2008): 12,531,000. **Density** (2008): persons per sq mi 26.0, persons per sq km 10.1. **Urban** (2006): 55.8%. **Sex distribution** (2005): male 50.48%; female 49.52%. **Age breakdown** (2005): under 15, 43.8%; 15–29, 26.5%; 30–44, 16.7%; 45–59, 8.5%; 60–74, 3.9%; 75 and over, 0.6%. **Ethnic composition** (2000): Ovimbundu 25.2%; Kimbundu 23.1%; Kongo 12.6%; Lwena (Luvale) 8.2%; Chokwe 5.0%; Kwanyama 4.1%; Nyaneka 3.9%; Luchazi 2.3%; Ambo (Ovambo) 2.0%; Mbwela 1.7%; Nyemba 1.7%; mixed race (Eur-african) 1.0%; white 0.9%; other 8.3%. **Religious affiliation** (2001): Christian 94.1%, of which Roman Catholic 62.1%, Protestant 15.0%; traditional beliefs 5.0%; other 0.9%. **Major cities** (2004): Luanda (urban agglomeration; 2005) 2,766,000; Huambo 173,600; Lobito 137,400; Benguela 134,500; Namibe 132,900. **Location:** southern Africa, bordering the Democratic Republic of the Congo (DRC), Zambia, Namibia, and the Atlantic Ocean; the exclave of Cabinda on the Atlantic Ocean borders the Republic of the Congo and the DRC.

Vital statistics

Birth rate per 1,000 population (2006): 45.0 (world avg. 20.3). **Death rate** per 1,000 population (2006): 25.2 (world avg. 8.6). **Natural increase rate** per 1,000 population (2006): 19.8 (world avg. 11.7). **Total fertility rate** (avg. births per childbearing woman; 2006): 6.35. **Life expectancy** at birth (2006): male 36.5 years; female 38.2 years.

National economy

Budget (2006). *Revenue:* US$20,966,000,000 (petroleum revenue 80.1%, nonpetroleum revenue 19.9%). *Expenditures:* US$14,269,000,000 (current expenditures 71.8%; development expenditures 28.2%). **Production** (metric tons except as noted). *Agriculture and fishing* (2006): cassava 8,810,000, sweet potatoes 685,000, potatoes 593,000, oil palm fruit 291,233; livestock (number of live animals)

4,150,000 cattle, 2,050,000 goats, 780,000 pigs; fisheries production (2005) 240,000 (from aquaculture, none). *Mining and quarrying* (2006): diamonds 9,175,000 carats. *Manufacturing* (2003): fuel oil 639,319; cement 500,620; diesel fuel 407,542. *Energy production (consumption):* electricity (kW-hr; 2005) 2,653,000,000 (2,653,000,000); crude petroleum (barrels; 2007) 627,000,000 ([2005] 13,500,000); petroleum products (metric tons; 2005) 1,595,000 (1,834,000); natural gas (cu m; 2005) 730,000,000 (730,000,000). **Selected balance of payments data.** Receipts from (US$'000,000): tourism (2005) 88; foreign direct disinvestment (2004–06 avg.) −331; official development assistance (2006) 171. Disbursements for (US$'000,000): tourism (2005) 74; remittances (2006) 413; foreign direct investment (2004–06 avg.) 138. **Gross national income** (2007): US$43,635,000,000 (US$2,560 per capita). **Public debt** (external, outstanding; 2006): US$7,398,-000,000. **Population economically active** (1999): total 5,729,000; activity rate of total population 57.7% (participation rates: ages 11 and over [1991] 60.1%; female 38.4%; unemployed [2002] 70%).

Foreign trade

Imports (2006): US$10,776,000,000 (consumer goods 60.3%; capital goods 28.8%; intermediate goods 10.9%). *Major import sources* (2005): South Korea 20.5%; Portugal 13.4%; US 12.5%; South Africa 7.4%; Brazil 7.0%. **Exports** (2006): US$31,817,000,000 (crude petroleum 94.2%; diamonds 3.6%; refined petroleum 0.9%). *Major export destinations* (2005): US 39.8%; China 29.6%; France 7.8%; Chile 5.4%; Taiwan 4.4%.

Transport and communications

Transport. *Railroads* (2004): route length of lines in operation 850 km; passenger-km (2001) 3,722,300,000. *Roads* (2001): total length 51,429 km (paved 10%). *Vehicles* (2001): passenger cars 117,200; trucks and buses 118,300. *Air transport:* passenger-km (TAAG airline only; 2001) 732,-968,000; metric ton-km cargo (2004) 64,000,000. **Communications,** in total units (units per 1,000 persons). Telephone landlines (2005): 94,000 (7.9); cellular telephone subscribers (2007): 3,307,000 (194); personal computers (2004): 27,000 (2.3); total Internet users (2007): 100,000 (5.9).

Education and health

Literacy (2006): percentage of population ages 15 and over literate 67.4%; males literate 82.9%; females literate 54.2%. **Health:** physicians (2004) 1,165 (1 per 9,890 persons); hospital beds (2001) 13,810 (1 per 769 persons); infant mortality rate per 1,000 live births (2006) 186.6; undernourished population (2002–04) 4,800,000 (35% of total population based on the consumption of a minimum daily requirement of 1,800 calories).

Military

Total active duty personnel (2007): 107,000 (army 93.5%, navy 0.9%, air force 5.6%). **Military expendi-**

1 metric ton = about 1.1 short tons; 1 kilometer = 0.6 mi (statute); 1 metric ton-km cargo = about 0.68 short ton-mi cargo; c.i.f.: cost, insurance, and freight; f.o.b.: free on board

ture as percentage of GDP (2005): 5.7%; per capita expenditure US$140.

Background

An influx of Bantu-speaking peoples in the 1st millennium AD led to their dominance in the area by c. 1500. The most important Bantu kingdom was the Kongo; south of the Kongo was the Ndongo kingdom of the Mbundu people. Portuguese explorers arrived in 1483 and over time gradually extended their rule. Angola's frontiers were largely determined with other European nations in the 19th century, but not without severe resistance by the indigenous peoples. Its status as a Portuguese colony was changed to that of an overseas province in 1951. Resistance to colonial rule led to the outbreak of fighting in 1961, which led ultimately to independence in 1975. Rival factions continued fighting after independence; although a peace accord was reached in 1994, forces led by Jonas M. Savimbi continued to resist government control. The killing of Savimbi in February 2002 changed the political balance and led to the signing of a cease-fire agreement in Luanda in April that effectively ended the civil war.

Recent Developments

In early 2008 the discovery of another extensive offshore oil field was announced, which boosted Angola's prospects of remaining among the world's top 10 fastest-growing economies. The wealth accrued from sales of oil remained in the hands of a small number of people, however, and had not brought noticeable benefit to the population as a whole—countrywide, unemployment remained extremely high, and poverty was a continuing problem.

Internet resources: <www.angola.org>.

Antigua and Barbuda

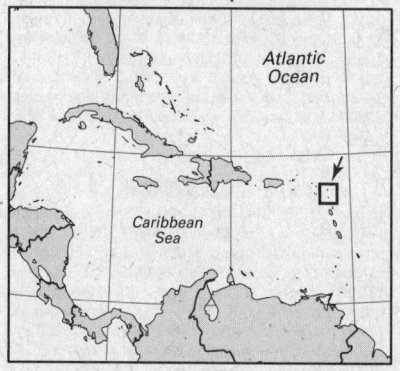

Atlantic
Ocean

Caribbean
Sea

Official name: Antigua and Barbuda. Form of government: constitutional monarchy with two legislative houses (Senate [17]; House of Representatives [17]). Chief of state: British Queen Elizabeth II (from 1952), represented by Governor-General Louise Lake-Tack (from 2007). Head of government: Prime Minister Baldwin Spencer (from 2004). Capital: Saint John's.

Official language: English. Official religion: none. Monetary unit: 1 Eastern Caribbean dollar (EC$) = 100 cents; valuation (1 Jul 2009) US$1 = EC$2.67.

Demography

Area: 171 sq mi, 442 sq km. Population (2008): 87,500. Density (2008): persons per sq mi 513.2, persons per sq km 198.1. Urban (2003): 37.7%. Sex distribution (2001): male 46.96%; female 53.04%. Age breakdown (2001): under 15, 28.3%; 15–29, 24.4%; 30–44, 25.0%; 45–59, 13.0%; 60–74, 6.2%; 75–84, 2.3%; 85 and over, 0.8%. Ethnic composition (2000): black 82.4%; US white 12.0%; mulatto 3.5%; British 1.3%; other 0.8%. Religious affiliation (2001): Christian 74%, of which Anglican 23%, independent Christian 23%, other Protestant (including Methodist, Moravian, and Seventh-day Adventist) 28%; Rastafarian 2%; atheist/nonreligious 5%; other/unknown 19%. Major settlements (2001): Saint John's (2004) 23,600; All Saints 3,412; Liberta 2,239. Location: islands in the eastern Caribbean Sea.

Did you know? Antigua, the "gateway to the Caribbean," is home to Nelson's Dockyard, constructed by British Adm. Horatio Nelson. The collection of buildings, most built between 1785 and 1792, is considered an architectural treasure and is a major tourist attraction.

Vital statistics

Birth rate per 1,000 population (2006): 16.9 (world avg. 20.3); (2001) within marriage 25.7%; outside of marriage 74.3%. Death rate per 1,000 population (2006): 5.4 (world avg. 8.6). Natural increase rate per 1,000 population (2006): 11.5 (world avg. 11.7). Total fertility rate (avg. births per childbearing woman; 2006): 2.24. Life expectancy at birth (2006): male 69.8 years; female 74.7 years.

National economy

Budget (2007). Revenue: EC$718,300,000 (tax revenue 91.4%, of which taxes on international transactions 38.3%, taxes on income and profits 14.0%; current nontax revenue 5.1%; grants 2.8%; development revenue 0.7%). Expenditures: EC$923,800,000 (current expenditures 78.3%, of which transfers and subsidies 21.7%; development expenditures 21.7%). Production (metric tons except as noted). Agriculture and fishing (2005): tropical fruit (including papayas, guavas, soursops, and oranges) 7,900, mangoes 1,430, "Antiguan Black" pineapples 210; livestock (number of live animals) 19,000 sheep, 14,300 cattle; fisheries production 2,999 (from aquaculture, none). Mining and quarrying: crushed stone for local use. Manufacturing: manufactures include cement, handicrafts, and furniture, as well as electronic components for export. Energy production (consumption): electricity (kW-hr; 2005) 109,000,000 (109,000,-000); petroleum products (metric tons; 2005) none (134,000). Population economically active (2001): total 39,564; activity rate of total population 51.5% (participation rates: ages 15–64, 77.0%; female 50%; unemployed 8.4%). Gross national income (2007): US$977,000,000 (US$11,520 per capita).

Public debt (external, outstanding; 2004): US$519,-900,000. **Selected balance of payments data.** Receipts from (US$'000,000): tourism (2005) 327; remittances (2006) 11; foreign direct investment (2004–06 avg.) 145; official development assistance (2006) 3.3. Disbursements for (US$'000, 000): tourism (2005) 40.

Foreign trade

Imports (2005): US$525,000,000 (refined petroleum products 33.8%; food and live animals 13.3%; machinery and apparatus 11.5%; transport equipment 9.5%). *Major import sources:* US 48.9%; Trinidad and Tobago 10.9%; Netherlands Antilles 10.2%; UK 6.8%; Japan 2.8%. **Exports** (2005): US$121,000,000 (refined petroleum products 69.9%; yachts, sailboats, and other boats 10.4%; telecommunications equipment 5.1%). *Major export destinations:* Netherlands Antilles 23.4%; UK 16.7%; Saint Kitts and Nevis 10.3%; US 7.7%; Anguilla 7.0%.

Transport and communications

Transport. *Roads* (2002): total length 1,165 km (paved 33%). *Vehicles:* passenger cars (1998) 24,000; trucks and buses (1995) 1,342. *Air transport* (2001): passenger-km 304,000,000; metric ton-km cargo 200,000. **Communications,** in total units (units per 1,000 persons). Telephone landlines (2004): 38,000 (494); cellular telephone subscribers (2004): 54,000 (701); total Internet users (2007): 60,000 (723).

Education and health

Educational attainment (2001). Percentage of population ages 25 and over having: no formal schooling 0.6%; incomplete primary education 2.6%; complete primary 27.9%; secondary 43.6%; higher (not university) 14.4%; university 10.9%. **Literacy** (2003): percentage of total population ages 15 and over literate 85.8%. **Health:** physicians (1999) 76 (1 per 867 persons); hospital beds (1996) 255 (1 per 269 persons); infant mortality rate per 1,000 live births (2006) 18.9.

Military

Total active duty personnel (2007): a 170-member defense force (army 73.5%, navy 26.5%) is part of the Eastern Caribbean regional security system. **Military expenditure as percentage of GDP** (2004): 0.6%; per capita expenditure US$57.

Background

Christopher Columbus visited Antigua in 1493 and named it after a church in Seville, Spain. It was colonized in 1632 by English settlers, who imported African slaves to grow tobacco and sugarcane. Barbuda was colonized by the English in 1678. In 1834 its slaves were emancipated. Antigua (with Barbuda) was part of the British colony of the Leeward Islands from 1871 until that colony was defederated in 1956. The islands achieved full independence in 1981.

Recent Developments

The country was rocked in 2009 by allegations that local banks owned by billionaire Texan R. Allen Stanford had been involved in a US$8 billion fraud. Regulators took over businesses run by Stanford, the country's largest private employer, leading to fears not only of problems related to unemployment but also of attacks on the nation's reputation as a financial center.

Internet resources: <www.ab.gov.ag>.

Argentina

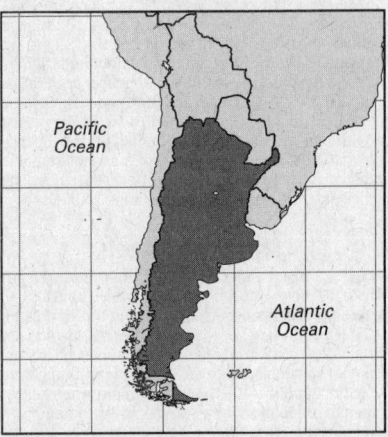

Official name: República Argentina (Argentine Republic). **Form of government:** federal republic with two legislative houses (Senate [72]; Chamber of Deputies [257]). **Head of state and government:** President Cristina Fernández de Kirchner (from 2007), assisted by Cabinet Chief Sergio Massa (from 2008). **Capital:** Buenos Aires. **Official language:** Spanish. **Official religion:** none (Roman Catholicism has special status and receives financial support from the state). **Monetary unit:** 1 peso (ARS) = 100 centavos; valuation (1 Jul 2009) US$1 = ARS 3.80.

Demography

Area: 1,073,519 sq mi, 2,780,403 sq km. **Population** (2008): 39,737,000. **Density** (2008): persons per sq mi 37.0, persons per sq km 14.3. **Urban** (2003): 90.1%. **Sex distribution** (2007): male 49.23%; female 50.77%. **Age breakdown** (2005): under 15, 26.4%; 15–29, 25.5%; 30–44, 19.1%; 45–59, 15.0%; 60–74, 9.6%; 75–84, 3.5%; 85 and over, 0.9%. **Ethnic composition** (2000): European extraction 86.4%; mestizo 6.5%; Amerindian 3.4%; Arab 3.3%; other 0.4%. **Religious affiliation** (2000): Roman Catholic 79.8%; Protestant 5.4%; Muslim 1.9%; Jewish 1.3%; other 11.6%. **Major cities** (2001): Buenos Aires 2,776,138 (metropolitan area 11,460,575); Córdoba 1,267,521; San Justo

---

1 metric ton = about 1.1 short tons;   1 kilometer = 0.6 mi (statute);   1 metric ton-km cargo = about 0.68 short ton-mi cargo;   c.i.f.: cost, insurance, and freight;   f.o.b.: free on board

1,253,921; Rosario 908,163; La Plata 563,943. **Location:** southern South America, bordering Bolivia, Paraguay, Brazil, Uruguay, the South Atlantic Ocean, and Chile.

Vital statistics

Birth rate per 1,000 population (2007): 18.3 (world avg. 20.3). **Death rate** per 1,000 population (2007): 7.5 (world avg. 8.6). **Natural increase rate** per 1,000 population (2007): 10.8 (world avg. 11.7). **Total fertility rate** (avg. births per childbearing woman; 2007): 2.39. **Life expectancy** at birth (2007): male 72.9 years; female 79.6 years.

National economy

Budget (2005). *Revenue:* ARS 82,106,000,000 (tax revenue 77.4%; social security contributions 16.2%; nontax revenue 2.3%; other 4.1%). *Expenditures:* ARS 77,531,000,000 (current expenditures 88.2%, of which interest on debt 13.0%; capital expenditures 11.8%). **Public debt** (external, outstanding; 2006): US$64,711,000,000. **Gross national income** (2007): US$238,853,000,000 (US$6,050 per capita). **Production** (metric tons except as noted). *Agriculture and fishing* (2006): soybeans 40,467,100, sugarcane 18,799,056, corn (maize) 14,445,538, sunflower seeds 3,797,836, maté 265,181; livestock (number of live animals; 2006) 50,768,000 cattle, 12,450,000 sheep, 3,655,000 horses; fisheries production (2005) 933,902 (from aquaculture, negligible). *Mining and quarrying* (2006): copper (metal content) 180,144; silver 248,227 kg; gold 44,131 kg. *Manufacturing* (value added in US$'000,000; 2002): food products 10,152, of which vegetable oils and fats 3,864; base metals 4,031; industrial and agricultural chemicals 2,770; refined petroleum products 2,514. *Energy production (consumption):* electricity (kW-hr; 2007) 104,448,000,000 ([2005] 110,930,-000,000); coal (metric tons; 2005) 25,000 (1,380,000); crude petroleum (barrels; 2007) 238,200,000 ([2005] 188,100,000); petroleum products (metric tons; 2005) 25,370,000 (20,-303,000); natural gas (cu m; 2007) 59,484,000,000 ([2005] 42,992,000,000). **Selected balance of payments data.** Receipts from (US$'000,000): tourism (2006) 3,308; remittances (2006) 542; foreign direct investment (FDI) (2004–06 avg.) 4,800; official development assistance (2006) 114. Disbursements for (US$'000,-000): tourism (2006) 3,131; remittances (2006) 367; FDI (2004–06 avg.) 1,200. **Population economically active** (2006): total 11,089,700; activity rate of total population 46.2% (participation rates: ages 15 and over 68.5%; female 43.4%; unemployed 9.5%).

Foreign trade

Imports (2006): US$34,160,000,000 (machinery and apparatus 31.1%; chemical products 18.8%; road vehicles 15.1%; mineral fuels 4.7%). *Major import sources:* Brazil 34.4%; US 12.6%; China 9.1%; Germany 4.5%; Mexico 3.3%. **Exports** (2006): US$46,423,000,000 (soybeans [all forms] 19.2%; mineral fuels 14.6%; road vehicles 8.6%; chemical products 8.1%; cereals 7.0%; copper 4.0%). *Major export destinations:* Brazil 17.3%; Chile 9.4%; US 8.7%; China 7.5%; Spain 4.1%.

Transport and communications

Transport. *Railroads:* route length (2003) 35,753 km; passenger-km (2004) 7,526,000,000; metric ton-km cargo (2001) 11,603,000,000. *Roads* (2003): total length 233,000 km (paved 31%). *Vehicles:* passenger cars (2000) 5,386,700; trucks and buses (1998) 1,496,567. *Air transport* (2005): passenger-km 14,916,000,000; metric ton-km cargo 132,444,000. **Communications,** in total units (units per 1,000 persons). Telephone landlines (2007): 9,500,000 (240); cellular telephone subscribers (2007): 40,402,000 (1,022); personal computers (2005): 3,500,000 (90); total Internet users (2007): 9,309,000 (236); broadband Internet subscribers (2007): 2,600,000 (66).

Education and health

Educational attainment (2001). Percentage of population ages 15 and over having: no formal schooling 3.7%; incomplete primary education 14.2%; complete primary 28.0%; secondary 37.1%; some higher 8.3%; complete higher 8.7%. **Literacy** (2001): percentage of total population ages 10 and over literate 97.4%; males literate 97.4%; females literate 97.4%. **Health:** physicians (2004) 122,706 (1 per 312 persons); hospital beds (2000) 150,813 (1 per 244 persons); infant mortality rate (2007) 12.1; undernourished population (2002–04) 1,200,000 (3% of total population based on the consumption of a minimum daily requirement of 1,940 calories).

Military

Total active duty personnel (2007): 76,000 (army 54.5%, navy 26.3%, air force 19.2%). **Military expenditure as percentage of GDP** (2005): 1.0%; per capita expenditure US$50.

Background

Little is known of Argentina's indigenous population before the Europeans' arrival. The area was explored for Spain by Sebastian Cabot in 1526–30; by 1580, Asunción, Santa Fe, and Buenos Aires had been settled. At first attached to the Viceroyalty of Peru (1620), it was later included with regions of modern Uruguay, Paraguay, and Bolivia in the Viceroyalty of the Río de la Plata, or Buenos Aires (1776). With the establishment of the United Provinces of the Río de la Plata in 1816, Argentina achieved its independence from Spain, but its boundaries were not set until the early 20th century. In 1943 the government was overthrown by the military; Col. Juan Perón took control in 1946. He in turn was overthrown in 1955. He returned to power in 1973 after two decades of turmoil. His second wife, Isabel, became president on his death in 1974 but lost power after a military coup in 1976. The military government tried to take the Falkland Islands (Islas Malvinas) in 1982 but was defeated by the British, with the result that the government returned to civilian rule in 1983. The government of Raúl Alfonsín worked to end the human rights abuses that characterized the former regimes. Hyperinflation led to public riots and Alfonsín's electoral defeat in 1989; his Peronist successor, Carlos Menem, instituted laissez-faire economic policies. In 1999 Fernando de la Rúa of the Alliance coalition was elected president, and his administration struggled with rising unemployment, foreign debt, and government corruption until the collapse of the government late in 2001.

Recent Developments

Argentina faced serious economic challenges in 2008, including an annual inflation rate of about 25% and a decelerating economic growth rate of 7% (with a 5% growth rate projected for 2009). In an effort to spur foreign investment, the government announced in September that Argentina would begin paying back the country's overdue loans from the Paris Club of creditor nations. In April 2009 the Argentine government laid claim to some 1,700,000 sq km (660,000 sq mi) of seabed stretching to the Antarctic and to the Falkland, South Sandwich, and South Georgia islands, all territories of the UK. The UK rejected these claims. A similar disagreement was the cause of the Falkland Islands War between the two countries in 1982.

Internet resources: <www.turismo.gov.ar/eng/menu.htm>.

Armenia

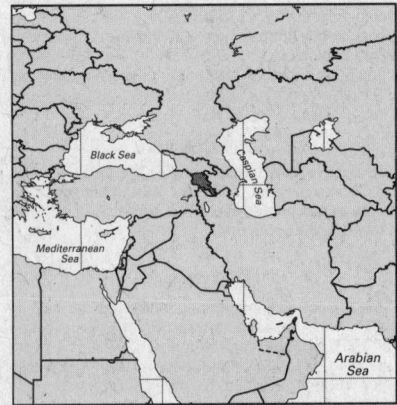

Official name: Hayastani Hanrape-toutioun (Republic of Armenia). **Form of government:** unitary multiparty republic with a single legislative body (National Assembly [131]). **Head of state:** President Serzh Sarkisyan (from 2008). **Head of government:** Prime Minister Tigran Sarkisyan (from 2008). **Capital:** Yerevan. **Official language:** Armenian. **Official religion:** none (the Armenian Apostolic Church [Armenian Orthodox Church] has special status per 1991 religious law). **Monetary unit:** 1 dram (AMD) = 100 luma; valuation (1 Jul 2009) US$1 = 360.06 drams.

Demography

Area: 11,484 sq mi, 29,743 sq km; in addition, about 16% of neighboring Azerbaijan (including the 1,700-sq mi [4,400-sq km] geographic region of Nagorno-Karabakh [Armenian: Artsakh]) has been occupied by Armenian forces since 1993. **Population** (2008):

2,996,000. **Density** (2008): persons per sq mi 260.9, persons per sq km 100.7. **Urban** (2006): 64.1%. **Sex distribution** (2006): male 48.32%; female 51.68%. **Age breakdown** (2005): under 15, 20.9%; 15–29, 27.2%; 30–44, 19.5%; 45–59, 17.9%; 60–74, 10.2%; 75–84, 3.8%; 85 and over, 0.5%. **Ethnic composition** (2001): Armenian 97.9%; Kurdish 1.3%; Russian 0.5%; other 0.3%. **Religious affiliation** (2005): Armenian Apostolic (Orthodox) 72.9%; Roman Catholic 4.0%; Sunni Muslim 2.4%; other Christian 1.3%; Yazidi 1.3%; other/nonreligious 18.1%. **Major cities** (2005): Yerevan 1,103,800; Gyumri 148,300; Vanadzor 105,500; Vagharshapat 56,700; Hrazdan 52,800. **Location:** western Transcaucasia, bordering Georgia, Azerbaijan, Iran, and Turkey.

Vital statistics

Birth rate per 1,000 population (2006): 11.7 (world avg. 20.3); (2005) within marriage 88.5%; outside of marriage 11.5%. **Death rate** per 1,000 population (2006): 8.5 (world avg. 8.6). **Natural increase rate** per 1,000 population (2006): 3.2 (world avg. 11.7). **Total fertility rate** (avg. births per childbearing woman; 2006): 1.33. **Life expectancy** at birth (2006): male 70.0 years; female 76.4 years.

National economy

Budget (2005). *Revenue:* AMD 374,746,900,000 (tax revenue 81.2%, of which VAT 39.2%, tax on profits 12.4%; nontax revenue 18.8%). *Expenditures:* AMD 417,505,900,000 (defense 15.4%; education and science 14.6%; public administration 10.6%; social security 10.6%; police 8.4%). **Public debt** (external, outstanding; 2006): US$1,037,000,000. **Gross national income** (2007): US$7,925,000,000 (US$2,640 per capita). **Production** (metric tons except as noted). *Agriculture and fishing* (2007): potatoes 540,000, tomatoes 250,000, grapes 200,000; livestock (number of live animals) 620,200 cattle, 587,200 sheep, 3,870,000 chickens; fisheries production (2005) 1,033 (from aquaculture 79%). *Mining and quarrying* (2005): copper (metal content) 16,256; molybdenum (metal content) 3,030; gold (metal content) 1,400 kg. *Manufacturing* (value of production in AMD '000,000; 2005): base and fabricated metals 259,305; food products and beverages 202,057; construction materials 23,648; wood and paper products 4,688; 320,000 carats of cut diamonds were processed in 2004. *Energy production (consumption):* electricity (kW-hr; 2007) 5,896,000,000 ([2005] 5,537,000,000); coal (metric tons; 2005), none (negligible); petroleum products (metric tons; 2005) none (320,000); natural gas (cu m; 2005) none (1,596,000,000). **Population economically active:** total (2006) 1,181,300; activity rate of total population (2001) 49.5% (participation rates: ages 15–64 [2001] 72.1%; female 45.7%; officially unemployed 7.5%). **Selected balance of payments data.** Receipts from (US$'000,000): tourism (2006) 271; remittances (2006) 1,175; foreign direct investment (FDI) (2004–06 avg.) 273; official development assistance (2006) 213. Disbursements for (US$'000,000): tourism (2006) 286; remittances (2006) 148; FDI (2004–06 avg.) 4.

Foreign trade

Imports (2006; c.i.f.): US$2,194,000,000 (machinery and apparatus 14.0%; food products 10.6%; diamonds 10.2%; chemical products 8.6%; refined petroleum products 7.9%; natural gas 7.2%). *Major import sources:* Russia 13.7%; Turkmenistan 7.7%; Ukraine 7.5%; Belgium 5.5%; Iran 5.1%. **Exports** (2006; f.o.b.): US$1,004,000,000 (cut diamonds 23.6%; ferroalloys 16.0%; copper 14.4%; grape brandy 7.2%; gold 3.7%;). *Major export destinations:* Germany 14.7%; The Netherlands 12.6%; Russia 11.6%; Belgium 10.8%; Israel 10.6%.

Transport and communications

Transport (2005). *Railroads:* length 732 km; passenger-km 26,600,000; metric ton-km cargo 654,100,000. *Roads:* length 7,515 km (paved 69%). *Air transport:* passenger-km 959,500,000; metric ton-km cargo 10,700,000. **Communications,** in total units (units per 1,000 persons). Telephone landlines (2005): 537,000 (180); cellular telephone subscribers (2006): 318,000 (105); personal computers (2004): 200,000 (67); total Internet users (2006): 173,000 (57); broadband Internet subscribers (2006): 2,000 (0.3).

Education and health

Educational attainment (2001). Percentage of population ages 25 and over having: no formal schooling 0.7%; primary education 13.0%; completed secondary and some postsecondary 66.0%; higher 20.3%. **Literacy** (2006): percentage of total population ages 15 and over literate, virtually 100%. **Health** (2005): physicians 12,307 (1 per 242 persons); hospital beds 14,353 (1 per 208 persons); infant mortality rate per 1,000 live births (2006) 13.9; undernourished population (2002–04) 700,000 (24% of total population based on the consumption of a minimum daily requirement of 1,980 calories).

Military

Total active duty personnel (2007): 42,080 (army 94.7%, air force 5.3%); Russian troops (2007) 3,170. **Military expenditure as percentage of GDP** (2005): 2.7%; per capita expenditure US$46.

Background

Armenia is a successor state to a historical region in southwestern Asia. Historical Armenia's boundaries have varied considerably, but the region extended over what is now northeastern Turkey and the Republic of Armenia. The area was later conquered by the Medes and the Macedonians and still later allied with the Roman Empire. Armenia adopted Christianity as its national religion in AD 303. It came under the rule of the Ottoman Turks in 1514. Over the next centuries, as parts were ceded to other rulers, nationalism arose among the scattered Armenians; by the late 19th century it was causing widespread disruption. Fighting between Turks and Russians escalated when part of Armenia was ceded to Russia in 1878, and it continued through World War I, leading to Armenian deaths on a genocidal scale. With the Turkish defeat, the Russian-controlled part of Armenia was set up as a Soviet republic in 1921. Armenia became a constituent republic of the USSR in 1936. With the latter's dissolution in the late 1980s, Armenia de-

clared its independence in 1991. It fought Azerbaijan for control over Nagorno-Karabakh until a cease-fire in 1994. About one-fifth of the population left the country beginning in 1993 because of an energy crisis. Political tension escalated, and in 1999 the prime minister and some legislators were killed in a terrorist attack on the legislature.

Recent Developments

Armenia's GDP grew by 10.3% during the first six months of 2008, but the August war between Russia and Georgia caused serious short-term economic disruptions; growth for the whole year was cut to 6.8%. In the realm of foreign affairs, Turkish Pres. Abdullah Gul accepted an invitation from Pres. Serzh Sarkisyan to attend a September soccer match between the Armenian and Turkish national teams.

Internet resources: <www.armstat.am/en/>.

Australia

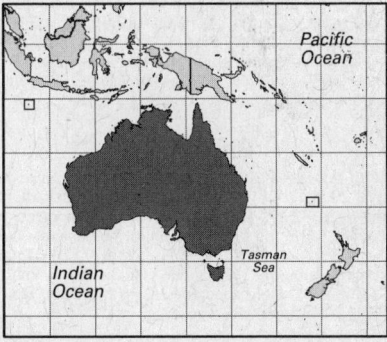

Official name: Commonwealth of Australia. **Form of government:** federal parliamentary state (formally a constitutional monarchy) with two legislative houses (Senate [76]; House of Representatives [150]). **Chief of state:** British Queen Elizabeth II (from 1952), represented by Governor-General Quentin Bryce (from 2008). **Head of government:** Prime Minister Kevin Rudd (from 2007). **Capital:** Canberra. **Official language:** English. **Official religion:** none. **Monetary unit:** 1 Australian dollar ($A) = 100 cents; valuation (1 Jul 2009) US$1 = $A 1.24.

Demography

Area: 2,969,978 sq mi, 7,692,208 sq km. **Population** (2008): 21,338,000. **Density** (2008): persons per sq mi 7.2, persons per sq km 2.8. **Urban** (2005): 88.2%. **Sex distribution** (2006): male 49.35%; female 50.65%. **Age breakdown** (2006): under 15, 19.8%; 15–29, 20.1%; 30–44, 21.9%; 45–59, 20.1%; 60–74, 11.7%; 75–84, 4.8%; 85 and over, 1.6%. **Ethnic composition** (2001): white 92%; Asian 6%; Aboriginal 2%. **Religious affiliation** (2006): Christian 63.9%, of which Roman Catholic 25.6%, Anglican Church of Australia 18.7%, other Christian 19.6% (Uniting Church 5.7%, Presbyterian 2.9%, Orthodox 2.6%, Baptist 1.6%, Lutheran 1.3%); Buddhist 2.1%; Muslim 1.7%; Hindu 0.7%; Jewish 0.4%; no religion 18.7%; other 12.5%. **Major urban centers (urban ag-**

glomerations) (2001 [2006]): Sydney 3,502,301 (4,293,105); Melbourne 3,160,171 (3,684,461); Brisbane 1,508,161 (1,820,375); Perth 1,176,542 (1,507,949); Adelaide 1,002,127 (1,138,833); Gold Coast 421,557 ([2005] 482,000); Canberra 339,727 (328,441); Newcastle 279,975 (512,131); Gosford (Central Coast) 255,429; Wollongong 228,846 (276,155); Sunshine Coast 169,931 (220,199); Geelong 130,194 (167,781); Hobart 126,048 (205,510); Townsville 119,504 (153,631); Cairns 98,981 (127,856); Toowoomba 89,338 (121,612). **Place of birth** (2006): 70.9% native-born; 29.1% foreign-born, of which Europe 10.5% (UK 5.2%, Italy 1.0%, Greece 0.6%, Germany 0.5%, The Netherlands 0.4%, Poland 0.3%), Asia and Middle East 7.3% (China [including Hong Kong] 1.4%, Vietnam 0.8%, India 0.7%), New Zealand 2.0%, Africa, the Americas, and other 9.3%. **Location:** Oceania, continent between the Indian Ocean and the South Pacific Ocean. **Mobility** (1999). Population ages 15 and over living in the same residence as in 1998: 84.4%; different residence between states, regions, and neighborhoods 15.6%. **Migration** (2004–05): permanent immigrants admitted 123,400, from UK 14.7%, New Zealand 14.0%, China 9.0%, India 7.6%, Sudan 4.6%, South Africa 3.7%, Philippines 3.4%, Malaysia 2.4%, Singapore 2.4%, Sri Lanka 1.9%, Vietnam 1.8%, Iraq 1.5%; refugee arrivals 13,200; emigration 59,200.

Vital statistics

Birth rate per 1,000 population (2006): 12.8 (world avg. 20.3); (2005) within marriage 67.8%; outside of marriage 32.2%. **Death rate** per 1,000 population (2006): 6.5 (world avg. 8.6). **Natural increase rate** per 1,000 population (2006): 6.3 (world avg. 11.7). **Total fertility rate** (avg. births per childbearing woman; 2005): 1.81. **Life expectancy** at birth (2005): male 78.5 years; female 83.3 years.

Social indicators

Quality of working life. Average workweek (2006): 33.2 hours. Working 50 hours a week or more (2006) 22.5%. Annual rate per 100,000 workers (2004) for: accidental injury and industrial disease 1,220; death 1.0. Proportion of employed persons insured for damages or income loss resulting from: injury 100%; permanent disability 100%; death 100%. Working days lost to industrial disputes per 1,000 employees (2006): 22. Means of transportation to work (2003): private automobile 74.5%; public transportation 12.0%; motorcycle, bicycle, and on foot 5.7%. Discouraged job seekers (2006): 52,900 (0.5% of labor force). **Educational attainment** (2005). Percentage of population ages 15–64 having: no formal schooling through incomplete secondary education 48.5%; completed secondary and postsecondary, technical, or other certificate/diploma 28.9%; bachelor's degree 14.2%; incomplete graduate and graduate degree or diploma 5.4%; unknown 3.0%. **Social participation.** Trade union membership in total workforce (2006): 20.3%. **Social deviance** (2005). Offense rate per 100,000 population for: murder 1.3; sexual assault (2003) 92; assault (2003) 798; auto theft 419; burglary and housebreaking (2004) 1,534; robbery 69. Incidence per 100,000 in general population of:

prisoners 124; suicide 10.3. **Material well-being** (2005). Households possessing: refrigerator 99.9%; washing machine 96.4%; dishwasher 41.5%; automobiles per 1,000 population (2006) 544.

National economy

Gross national income (2007): US$755,795,-000,000 (US$35,960 per capita). **Budget** (2005–06). *Revenue:* $A 225,513,000,000 (tax revenue 91.6%, of which income tax 50.7%, corporate taxes 21.7%; nontax revenue 8.4%). *Expenditures:* $A 209,797,000,000 (social security and welfare 41.2%; health 17.9%; economic services 8.0%; public services 8.0%; education 7.9%; defense 7.5%). **Public debt** (2002–03): $A 69,926,000,000. **Production** (gross value in $A '000 except as noted). *Agriculture and fishing* (2006–07): livestock (slaughtered value) 12,339,100 (cattle 7,987,900, sheep and lambs 2,055,900, poultry 1,301,500, pigs 943,600); wheat 2,522,300, wool 2,278,400, sugarcane 1,182,700, grapes 1,140,800, barley 1,012,800, seed cotton 514,400, potatoes 513,700, apples 475,000, bananas (2004–05) 327,000, oranges (2004–05) 310,000, tomatoes 293,800, sorghum 291,700, canola 201,600, oats 174,200, carrots (2004–05) 166,000; livestock (number of live animals; 2006) 92,728,000 sheep, 28,846,000 cattle, 2,755,000 pigs, 93,600,000 chickens; fisheries production (2005) 293,022 (from aquaculture 16%); aquatic plants production 14,167 (from aquaculture, none). *Mining and quarrying* (metric tons except as noted; 2006): iron ore (metal content) 170,933,000 (world rank: 2), bauxite 62,307,000 (world rank: 1), ilmenite 2,377,000 (world rank: 1), zinc (metal content) 1,362,000 (world rank: 2), copper (metal content) 879,000 (world rank: 5), lead (metal content) 686,000 (world rank: 2), rutile 232,000 (world rank: 1), nickel (metal content) 185,000 (world rank: 3), cobalt (metal content) 7,400 (world rank: 3), opal (value of production) $A 50,000,000 (world rank: 1), diamonds 21,915,000 carats (world rank by volume: 2), gold 247,000 kilograms (world rank: 4). *Manufacturing* (gross value added in $A '000,000; 2004–05): food, beverages, and tobacco 19,076; machinery and apparatus 18,185; fabricated metal products 17,483; mineral fuels 12,817; printing and publishing 10,095; wood and paper products 6,924; cement, bricks, and ceramics 4,852; textiles and wearing apparel 2,621. *Energy production (consumption):* electricity (kW-hr; 2007) 227,496,000,000 ([2005] 251,120,000,000); hard coal (metric tons; 2005) 265,426,000 (35,830,000); lignite (metric tons; 2005) 110,160,000 (108,617,000); crude petroleum (barrels; 2006–07) 171,900,000 ([2005] 224,000,000); petroleum products (metric tons; 2005) 32,306,000 (36,423,000); natural gas (cu m; 2007) 37,211,000,000 ([2005] 28,779,000,000). **Population economically active** (July 2007): total 10,952,000; activity rate of total population 52.5% (participation rates: ages 15 and over, 65.0%; female [2006] 45.0%; unemployed [June 2008] 4.2%). **Selected balance of payments data.** Receipts from (US$'000,000): tourism (2006) 17,854; remittances (2006) 3,064; foreign direct investment (2004–06 avg.) 8,290. Disbursements for (US$'000,000): tourism (2006) 11,690; remittances (2006) 2,681; foreign direct disinvestment (2004–06 avg.) –4.

1 metric ton = about 1.1 short tons;   1 kilometer = 0.6 mi (statute);   1 metric ton-km cargo = about 0.68 short ton-mi cargo;   c.i.f.: cost, insurance, and freight;   f.o.b.: free on board

Foreign trade

Imports (2005–06; f.o.b.): $A 167,603,000,000 (machinery and apparatus 29.3%, of which telecommunications equipment 5.8%; office machines and automatic data-processing equipment 5.3%, electrical machinery 4.8%; transportation equipment 15.8%, of which motor vehicles 12.2%; crude and refined petroleum 12.7%; chemical products 6.1%, of which medicines and pharmaceuticals 4.3%; textiles and wearing apparel 3.9%). *Major import sources* (2006–07): China 15.0%; US 13.8%; Japan 9.6%; Singapore 5.6%; Germany 5.1%; UK 4.1%; Thailand 4.0%; Malaysia 3.7%; South Korea 3.3%; New Zealand 3.1%. **Exports** (2005–06; f.o.b.): $A 151,792,000,000 (mineral fuels 24.9%, of which coal [all forms] 16.0%, petroleum products and natural gas 8.9%; food and beverages 12.0%, of which meat and meat preparations 4.4%, cereals and cereal preparations 3.2%; iron ore 8.2%; aluminum and aluminum ore 6.9%; gold 4.8%; machinery and apparatus 4.1%; transportation equipment 3.5%). *Major export destinations* (2006–07): Japan 19.4%; China 13.6%; South Korea 7.8%; US 5.8%; New Zealand 5.6%; UK 3.7%; Taiwan 3.7%; Singapore 2.7%; Indonesia 2.5%; Thailand 2.5%.

Transport and communications

Transport. *Railroads* (2006): route length 38,550 km; passengers carried (2004–05) 616,270,000; passenger-km (2004–05) 11,200,000,000; metric ton-km cargo (2004–05) 182,990,000,000. *Roads* (2004): total length 810,641 km (paved 42%). *Vehicles* (2006): passenger cars 11,189,000; trucks and buses 2,665,000. *Merchant marine* (2006): vessels (1,000 gross tons and over) 53; total deadweight tonnage 1,532,874. *Air transport* (domestic carriers only; 2006): passenger-km 88,173,000,000; metric ton-km cargo 2,633,000,000. **Communications**, in total units (units per 1,000 persons). Telephone landlines (2007): 9,760,000 (471); cellular telephone subscribers (2007): 21,260,000 (1,025); personal computers (2005): 14,007,000 (689); total Internet users (2007): 11,200,000 (540); broadband Internet subscribers (2007): 4,830,000 (232).

Education and health

Literacy (2006): percentage of total population literate, virtually 100%. **Health** (2005–06): physicians 63,300 (1 per 322 persons); hospital beds (2005) 83,349 (1 per 244 persons); infant mortality rate per 1,000 live births 5.0; undernourished population (2002–04) less than 2.5% of total population.

Military

Total active duty personnel (2007): 51,293 (army 49.2%, navy 24.9%, air force 25.9%). **Military expenditure as percentage of GDP** (2005): 1.8%; per capita expenditure US$645.

Background

Australia has long been inhabited by Aborigines, who arrived on the continent 40,000–60,000 years ago. Estimates of the population at the time of European settlement in 1788 range from 300,000 to more than 1,000,000. Widespread European knowledge of Australia began with 17th-century explorations. The Dutch landed in 1616 and the British in 1688, but the first large-scale expedition was that of James Cook in 1770, which established Britain's claim to Australia. The first English settlement, at Port Jackson (1788), consisted mainly of convicts and seamen; convicts were to make up a large proportion of the incoming settlers. By 1859 the colonial nuclei of all Australia's states had been formed, but with devastating effects on the Aborigines, whose population declined sharply with the introduction of European diseases and weaponry. Britain granted its colonies limited self-government in the mid-19th century, and Australia achieved federation in 1901. Australia fought alongside the British in World War I, notably at Gallipoli, and again in World War II, preventing the occupation of Australia by the Japanese. It joined the US in the Korean and Vietnam wars. Since the 1960s the government has sought to deal more fairly with the Aborigines, and a loosening of immigration restrictions has led to a more heterogeneous population. Constitutional links allowing British interference in government were formally abolished in 1968, and Australia has assumed a leading role in Asian and Pacific affairs. During the 1990s it experienced several debates about giving up its British ties and becoming a republic.

Recent Developments

The government of Kevin Rudd, the Australian prime minister elected in late 2007, began well, and the country celebrated in February 2008 when Prime Minister Rudd apologized to the country's indigenous citizens, declaring that "business as usual" was not working and pledging that within five years Aboriginal mortality would be halved to close the massive 17-year gap in life expectancy between Aboriginal and non-Aboriginal Australians. Rudd chose Ross Garnaut to shed expert light on the issues of climate change and global warming, and Garnaut issued a report in which he proposed that the government set limits on the level of carbon emissions that companies could generate and recommended the introduction of a "carbon tax." Action to begin the political process of combating global warming, by reducing emissions by 60% by 2050, began at the end of 2008. By signing the Kyoto Protocol and withdrawing Australian troops from Iraq, Prime Minister Rudd distanced himself from the policies of his predecessor, John Howard. The government trod carefully, however, stressing its pivotal relationship with the US. Maintaining the crucial alliance with the US was such a priority that the prime minister visited Washington DC at the beginning of a 17-day overseas tour aimed at explaining Australian foreign policy under the new administration. During Rudd's talks with US Pres. George W. Bush in March, both leaders agreed on the approach to take in Afghanistan, and in April 2009 Australia announced that it was nearly doubling the size of its force there. In early 2009, forest fires swept through Victoria state. The fires, at least some of which were blamed on arson, claimed an estimated 173 lives. Many in Australia counted such fires, as well as what some were calling the worst drought in a century, as proof of the perils of global warming.

Internet resources: <www.abs.gov.au>.

Austria

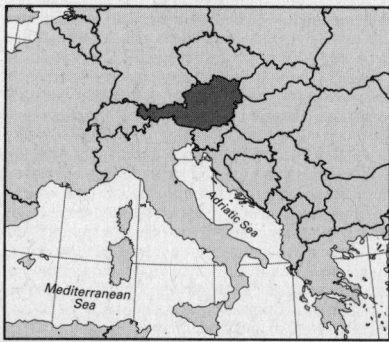

Official name: Republik Österreich (Republic of Austria). **Form of government:** federal state with two legislative houses (Federal Council [64]; National Council [183]). **Chief of state:** President Heinz Fischer (from 2004). **Head of government:** Chancellor Werner Faymann (from 2008). **Capital:** Vienna. **Official language:** German. **Official religion:** none. **Monetary unit:** 1 euro (€) = 100 cents; valuation (1 Jul 2009) US$1 = €0.71.

Demography

Area: 32,386 sq mi, 83,879 sq km. **Population** (2008): 8,338,000. **Density** (2008): persons per sq mi 257.5, persons per sq km 99.4. **Urban** (2003): 65.8%. **Sex distribution** (2007): male 48.66%; female 51.34%. **Age breakdown** (2005): under 15, 16.0%; 15–29, 18.5%; 30–44, 24.1%; 45–59, 19.4%; 60–74, 14.3%; 75–84, 6.1%; 85 and over, 1.6%. **Ethnic composition** (2000): Austrian 86.5%; German Swiss 4.0%; German 3.5%; Bosniac 0.9%; Turkish 0.9%; Polish 0.5%; other 3.7%. **Religious affiliation** (2001): Christian 81.5%, of which Roman Catholic 73.7%, Protestant (mostly Lutheran) 4.7%, Orthodox 2.2%; Muslim 4.2%; nonreligious 12.0%; other 0.3%; unknown 2.0%. **Major cities** (2006): Vienna 1,664,146 (urban agglomeration 1,954,964); Graz 247,698; Linz 188,894; Salzburg 149,018; Innsbruck 117,693. **Location:** central Europe, bordering the Czech Republic, Slovakia, Hungary, Slovenia, Italy, Switzerland, Liechtenstein, and Germany.

Vital statistics

Birth rate per 1,000 population (2007): 9.2 (world avg. 20.3); within marriage 61.8%; outside of marriage 38.2%. **Death rate** per 1,000 population (2007): 9.0 (world avg. 8.6). **Natural increase rate** per 1,000 population (2007): 0.2 (world avg. 11.7). **Total fertility rate** (avg. births per childbearing woman; 2007): 1.38. **Life expectancy** at birth (2007): male 77.3 years; female 82.9 years.

National economy

Budget (2004). *Revenue:* €59,237,000,000 (tax revenue 97.3%, of which turnover tax 32.0%, individual income taxes 29.2%, corporate income tax

7.3%; nontax revenue 2.7%). *Expenditures:* €62,667,000,000 (social security, health, and welfare 34.4%; education 14.3%; interest on debt 13.3%; transportation 9.6%). **Public debt** (December 2006): US$194,118,000,000. **Production** (metric tons except as noted). *Agriculture and fishing* (2006): sugar beets 2,493,097, corn (maize) 1,471,668, wheat 1,396,300; livestock (number of live animals) 3,160,382 pigs, 2,002,143 cattle; fisheries production (2005) 2,790 (from aquaculture 87%). *Mining and quarrying* (2006): iron ore (metal content) 650,000; manganese (metal content) 16,000; tungsten 1,300. *Manufacturing* (value added in €'000,000; 2004): nonelectrical machinery and apparatus 5,034; electrical machinery and electronics 4,060; fabricated metal products 3,979. *Energy production (consumption):* electricity (kW-hr; 2007) 63,744,000,000 ([2005] 68,346,000,000); hard coal (metric tons; 2005) none (4,039,000); lignite (metric tons; 2005) none (1,270,000); crude petroleum (barrels; 2006) 6,500,000 ([2005] 64,100,000); petroleum products (metric tons; 2005) 7,776,000 (12,450,000); natural gas (cu m; 2006) 1,700,000,000 ([2005] 10,531,000,000). **Population economically active** (2005): total 4,032,200; activity rate of total population 49.7% (participation rates: ages 15–64, 72.4%; female 45.4%; unemployed 7.2%). **Gross national income** (2007): US$355,088,000,000 (US$42,700 per capita). **Selected balance of payments data.** Receipts from (US$'000,000): tourism (2006) 17,854; remittances (2006) 2,941; foreign direct investment (FDI) (2004–06 avg.) 4,394. Disbursements for (US$'000,000): tourism (2006) 11,690; remittances (2006) 2,543; FDI (2004–06 avg.) 7,470.

Foreign trade

Imports (2005; c.i.f.): €96,499,000,000 (machinery and transportation equipment 36.8%, of which nonelectrical machinery and apparatus 11.5%, road vehicles 11.5%; mineral fuels 12.2%; chemical products 10.9%; food products 5.2%). *Major import sources:* Germany 42.2%; Italy 6.6%; France 4.0%; Switzerland 3.3%; Czech Republic 3.3%. **Exports** (2005; f.o.b.): €94,705,000,000 (machinery and transportation equipment 41.6%, of which nonelectrical machinery and apparatus 17.2%, road vehicles 11.8%, electrical machinery and apparatus 7.3%; chemical products 9.8%; base metals 5.7%). *Major export destinations:* Germany 31.8%; Italy 8.6%; US 5.6%; Switzerland 4.5%; France 4.2%.

Transport and communications

Transport. *Railroads* (federal railways only; 2004) route length 5,629 km; passenger-km (2003) 8,248,700,000; metric ton-km cargo 17,931,100,000. *Roads* (2003): total length 133,718 km (paved 100%). *Vehicles* (2004): passenger cars 4,109,129; trucks and buses 342,384. *Air transport* (2007): passenger-km 17,412,000,000; metric ton-km cargo 453,756,000. **Communications,** in total units (units per 1,000 persons). Telephone landlines (2007): 3,374,000 (404); cellular telephone subscribers (2007): 9,768,000 (1,168); personal computers (2005): 4,000,000 (489); total Internet users

1 metric ton = about 1.1 short tons;　1 kilometer = 0.6 mi (statute);　1 metric ton-km cargo = about 0.68 short ton-mi cargo;　c.i.f.: cost, insurance, and freight;　f.o.b.: free on board

(2007): 4,277,000 (512); broadband Internet subscribers (2007): 1,577,000 (190).

Education and health

Educational attainment (2002). Percentage of population ages 25 and over having: no formal schooling through lower-secondary education 22%; upper secondary/higher vocational 63%; university 14%, **Literacy:** virtually 100%. **Health:** physicians (2005) 39,750 (1 per 208 persons); hospital beds (2004) 65,053 (1 per 133 persons); infant mortality rate per 1,000 live births (2007) 3.7; undernourished population (2002–04) less than 2.5% of total population.

Military

Total active duty personnel (2007): 39,600 (army 83.1%; air force 16.9%). **Military expenditure as percentage of GDP** (2005): 0.9%; per capita expenditure US$329.

Background

Settlement in Austria goes back some 3,000 years, when Illyrians were probably the main inhabitants. The Celts invaded c. 400 BC and established Noricum. The Romans arrived after 200 BC and established the provinces of Raetia, Noricum, and Pannonia; prosperity followed and the population became Romanized. With the fall of Rome in the 5th century AD, many tribes invaded, including the Slavs; they were eventually subdued by Charlemagne, and the area became ethnically Germanic. The distinct political entity that would become Austria emerged in 976 with Leopold I of Babenberg as margrave. In 1278 Rudolf I of the Holy Roman Empire (formerly Rudolf IV of Habsburg) conquered the area; Habsburg rule lasted until 1918. While in power the Habsburgs created a kingdom centered on Austria, Bohemia, and Hungary. The Napoleonic Wars brought about the creation of the Austrian Empire (1804) and the end of the Holy Roman Empire (1806). Count von Metternich tried to assure Austrian supremacy among Germanic states, but war with Prussia led Austria to divide the empire into the Dual Monarchy of Austria-Hungary. Nationalist sentiment plagued the kingdom, and the assassination of Francis Ferdinand by a Serbian nationalist in 1914 triggered World War I, which destroyed the Austro-Hungarian Empire. In the postwar carving up of Austria-Hungary, Austria became an independent republic. It was annexed by Nazi Germany in 1938 and joined the Axis powers in World War II. The republic was restored in 1955 after 10 years of Allied occupation. Austria became a member of the European Union in 1995.

Recent Developments

In March 2008 the Austrian government earmarked €10.7 billion (US$16.4 billion) for railway improvements and €8.1 billion (US$12.4 billion) for motorway expansion and renovation projects. The largest infrastructure project was the creation of a tunnel under the Brenner Pass, linking Italy with southern Tyrol, which would help to shift some of the transport between Germany and Italy from roads to railways and thereby reduce Austria's carbon dioxide emissions, a significant concern since Austria was

on track to miss its Kyoto Protocol targets. In October a set of measures to shore up liquidity in the banking sector was agreed upon, offering up to €100 billion (US$133 billion) in aid to commercial banks.

Internet resources: <www.statistik.at/web_en>.

Azerbaijan

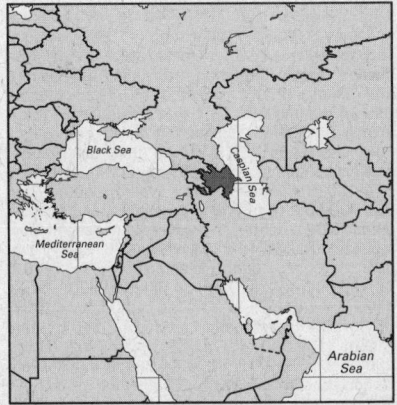

Official name: Azerbaycan Respublikasi (Republic of Azerbaijan). **Form of government:** unitary multiparty republic with a single legislative body (National Assembly [125]). **Head of state and government:** President Ilham Aliyev (from 2003), assisted by Prime Minister Artur Rasizade (from 2003). **Capital:** Baku. **Official language:** Azerbaijani. **Official religion:** none. **Monetary unit:** 1 (new) manat (AZN) = 100 gopik; valuation (1 Jul 2009) free rate, US$1 = AZN 0.80 (the [new] manat replaced the [old] manat [AZM] 1 Jan 2006, at the rate of 1 AZN = 4,500 AZM).

Demography

Area: 33,400 sq mi, 86,600 sq km. **Population** (2008): 8,178,000. **Density** (2008): persons per sq mi 244.8, persons per sq km 94.5. **Urban** (2007): 51.7%. **Sex distribution** (2006): male 49.16%; female 50.84%. **Age breakdown** (2006): under 15, 26.3%; 15–29, 27.9%; 30–44, 22.7%; 45–59, 14.1%; 60–74, 6.7%; 75–84, 1.9%; 85 and over, 0.4%. **Ethnic composition** (1999): Azerbaijani 90.6%; Lezgian (Dagestani) 2.2%; Russian 1.8%; Armenian 1.5%; other 3.9%. **Religious affiliation** (2005): Muslim 87.0%, of which Shi'i 52.8%, Sunni 34.2%; nonreligious/other 13.0%. **Major cities** (2005): Baku 1,132,800 (urban agglomeration 1,856,000); Ganca 305,600; Sumqayit (Sumgait) 266,600; Mingacevir (Mingechaur) 95,300; Ali Bayramli 68,700. **Location:** eastern Transcaucasia, bordering Russia, the Caspian Sea, Iran, Turkey, Armenia, and Georgia.

Vital statistics

Birth rate per 1,000 population (2006): 17.8 (world avg. 20.3); within marriage 85.2%; outside of marriage 14.8%. **Death rate** per 1,000 population

(2006): 6.2 (world avg. 8.6). **Natural increase rate** per 1,000 population (2006): 11.6 (world avg. 11.7). **Total fertility rate** (avg. births per childbearing woman; 2005): 2.33. **Life expectancy** at birth (2006): male 69.6 years; female 75.1 years.

National economy

Budget (2005). *Revenue:* AZN 2,055,200,000 (tax revenue 86.0%, of which VAT 29.2%, taxes on profits 17.3%, personal income tax 15.5%; nontax revenue 14.0%). *Expenditures:* AZN 2,140,700,000 (national economy 21.6%; education 18.1%; social security/welfare 14.8%; defense/police 10.0%). **Production** (metric tons except as noted). *Agriculture and fishing* (2006): wheat 1,460,303, potatoes 999,343, barley 399,737; livestock (number of live animals) 7,304,431 sheep, 2,148,108 cattle; fisheries production (2005) 9,016 (from aquaculture, negligible). *Mining and quarrying* (2004): limestone 800,000. *Manufacturing* (value added in US$'000,000; 2005): food, beverages, and tobacco products 301; petroleum products 251; base metals, fabricated metals, and machinery 126. *Energy production (consumption):* electricity (kW-hr; 2007) 20,337,000,000 ([2005] 24,074,000,000); crude petroleum (barrels; 2007) 303,000,000 ([2005] 56,800,000); petroleum products (metric tons; 2005) 7,152,000 (4,898,000); natural gas (cu m; 2007) 9,606,000,000 ([2005] 9,687,000,000). **Population economically active** (2005): total 3,906,500; activity rate of total population 46.3% (participation rates: ages 15–61 [male], 15–56 [female] 71.8%; female 47.7%; officially unemployed 1.4%). **Gross national income** (2007): US$21,872,000,000 (US$2,550 per capita). **Public debt** (external, outstanding; 2006): US$1,359,000,000. **Selected balance of payments data.** Receipts from (US$'000,000): tourism (2006) 117; remittances (2007) 1,287; foreign direct investment (FDI) (2004–06 avg.) 1,537; official development assistance (2006) 206. Disbursements for (US$'000,000): tourism (2006) 201; remittances (2007) 435; FDI (2004–06 avg.) 1,044.

Foreign trade

Imports (2006; c.i.f.): US$5,268,000,000 (machinery and apparatus 29.8%; natural gas 8.8%; base metals 7.7%; food and live animals 7.6%; road vehicles 7.5%; drilling/production platforms 5.0%). *Major import sources:* Russia 22.4%; UK 8.6%; Germany 7.7%; Turkey 7.3%; Turkmenistan 7.0%. **Exports** (2006; f.o.b.): US$6,372,000,000 (crude petroleum 60.4%; refined petroleum products 23.6%; aluminum oxide 2.4%; fruits and nuts 1.5%; ships and boats 1.1%). *Major export destinations:* Italy 44.7%; Israel 10.7%; Turkey 6.1%; France 5.5%; Russia 5.4%.

Transport and communications

Transport. *Railroads* (2005): length 2,122 km; passenger-km 881,000,000; metric ton-km cargo 9,524,000,000. *Roads* (2004): total length 59,141 km (paved 49%). *Vehicles* (2005): passenger cars 479,447; trucks and buses 117,587. *Air transport* (2007): passenger-km 1,764,000,000; metric ton-km

cargo 11,892,000. **Communications,** in total units (units per 1,000 persons). Telephone landlines (2007): 1,254,000 (148); cellular telephone subscribers (2007): 4,300,000 (508); personal computers (2005): 195,000 (23); total Internet users (2007): 1,036,000 (122); broadband Internet subscribers (2006): 2,200 (0.3).

Education and health

Educational attainment (1999). Percentage of population ages 25 and over having: primary education 4.1%; some secondary 9.3%; secondary 50.1%; vocational 4.2%; some higher 0.9%; higher 13.3%. **Literacy** (1999): 98.8%. **Health** (2006): physicians 30,800 (1 per 264 persons); hospital beds 68,400 (1 per 119 persons); infant mortality rate per 1,000 live births 10.1; undernourished population (2002–04) 600,000 (7% of total population based on the consumption of a minimum daily requirement of 1,940 calories).

Military

Total active duty personnel (2007): 66,740 (army 85.2%, navy 3.0%, air force 11.8%). **Military expenditure as percentage of GDP** (2005): 2.5%; per capita expenditure US$37.

Background

Azerbaijan adjoins the Iranian region of the same name, and the origin of their respective inhabitants is the same. By the 9th century AD the area had come under Turkish influence, and in ensuing centuries it was fought over by Arabs, Mongols, Turks, and Iranians. Russia acquired the territory of what is now independent Azerbaijan in the early 19th century. After the Russian Revolution of 1917, Azerbaijan declared its independence; it was subdued by the Red Army in 1920 and became a Soviet Socialist Republic. It declared independence from the collapsing Soviet Union in 1991. Azerbaijan has two geographic peculiarities. The exclave Nakhichevan is separated from the rest of Azerbaijan by Armenian territory. Nagorno-Karabakh, which lies within Azerbaijan and is administered by it, has a Christian Armenian majority. Azerbaijan and Armenia went to war over both territories in the 1990s, causing great economic disruption. Though a cease-fire was declared in 1994, the political situation remained unresolved.

Recent Developments

In October 2008 Azerbaijan's prosecutor general announced the arrest of 25 suspects who were identified as belonging to a group of militants with links to neighboring Dagestan, a republic in southern Russia. Following visits in January and June to Armenia and Azerbaijan by Minsk Group mediators of the Organization for Security and Co-operation in Europe, Pres. Ilham Aliyev and his Armenian counterpart, Serzh Sarkisyan, on 2 November signed a declaration in Moscow affirming their shared commitment to a peaceful solution to the Nagorno-Karabakh conflict.

Internet resources: <www.azstat.org/indexen.php>.

---

1 metric ton = about 1.1 short tons; 1 kilometer = 0.6 mi (statute); 1 metric ton-km cargo = about 0.68 short ton-mi cargo; c.i.f.: cost, insurance, and freight; f.o.b.: free on board

Bahamas, The

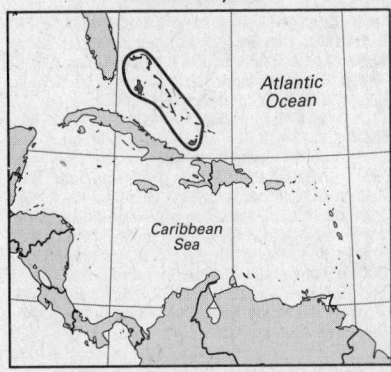

Atlantic
Ocean

Caribbean
Sea

Official name: The Commonwealth of The Bahamas.
Form of government: constitutional monarchy with
two legislative houses (Senate [16]; House of Assembly [41]). **Chief of state:** British Queen Elizabeth II
(from 1952), represented by Governor-General Arthur
Dion Hanna (from 2006). **Head of government:** Prime
Minister Hubert Ingraham (from 2007). **Capital:** Nassau. **Official language:** English. **Official religion:**
none. **Monetary unit:** 1 Bahamian dollar (B$) = 100
cents; valuation (1 Jul 2009) US$1 = B$1.00.

Demography

Area: 5,382 sq mi, 13,939 sq km. **Population**
(2008): 335,000. **Density** (2008): persons per sq mi
86.1, persons per sq km 33.3. **Urban** (2003): 89.5%.
Sex distribution (2007): male 48.62%; female
51.38%. **Age breakdown** (2006): under 15, 27.6%;
15–29, 26.0%; 30–44, 22.2%; 45–59, 14.9%;
60–74, 7.1%; 75 and over, 2.2%. **Ethnic composition**
(2000): local black 67.5%; mulatto 14.2%; British
12.0%; Haitian black 3.0%; US white 2.4%; other
0.9%. **Religious affiliation** (2000): Baptist 35.4%; Anglican 15.1%; Roman Catholic 13.5%; other Protestant/independent Christian 32.3%; other/nonreligious 3.7%. **Major cities** (2002): Nassau 179,300;
Freeport 42,600; West End 7,800; Cooper's Town
5,700; Marsh Harbour 3,600. **Location:** chain of islands in the Caribbean Sea, southeast of Florida.

Vital statistics

Birth rate per 1,000 population (2006): 13.9 (world
avg. 20.3); (2000) within marriage 43.2%; outside of
marriage 56.8%. **Death rate** per 1,000 population
(2006): 5.3 (world avg. 8.6). **Natural increase rate** per
1,000 population (2006): 8.6 (world avg. 11.7). **Total
fertility rate** (avg. births per childbearing woman;
2006): 2.18. **Life expectancy** at birth (2006): male
62.2 years; female 69.0 years.

National economy

Budget (2004–05). *Revenue:* B$1,039,376,000 (tax
revenue 89.0%, of which import taxes 39.7%, stamp
taxes from imports 10.8%; nontax revenue 11.0%).
Expenditures: B$1,143,469,000 (education 18.7%,
health 16.9%, public order 12.3%, interest on public
debt 10.3%, tourism 6.0%). **Public debt** (external, outstanding; 2007): US$324,300,000. **Production** (met-

ric tons except as noted). *Agriculture and fishing*
(2006): sugarcane 55,500, fruits 33,472; livestock
(number of live animals; 2005) 3,000,000 chickens;
fisheries production (2005) 11,357 (mainly lobsters,
crayfish, and conch; from aquaculture, negligible).
Mining and quarrying (2006): salt 1,150,000; aragonite 1,100. *Manufacturing* (value of export production in B$'000; 2004): rum 31,344; chemical products (2001) 13,842. *Energy production
(consumption):* electricity (kW-hr; 2006–07)
2,149,000,000 ([2005] 2,090,000,000); petroleum
products (metric tons; 2005) none (684,000). **Gross
national income** (2006): US$6,077,000,000
(US$18,570 per capita). **Population economically active** (2007): total 186,105; activity rate of total population 56.2% (participation rates: ages 15–64,
76.2%; female [2004] 48.8%; unemployed 7.9%). **Selected balance of payments data.** Receipts from
(US$'000,000): tourism (2006) 2,069; foreign direct
investment (2004–06 avg.) 571. Disbursements for
(US$'000,000): tourism (2006) 385; remittances
(2007) 164.

Foreign trade

Imports (2005; c.i.f.): B$2,567,000,000 (machinery
and transportation equipment 22.1%; mineral fuels
19.8%; food products 13.2%; chemical products
7.0%). *Major import sources:* US 83.9%; Curaçao
7.1%; Puerto Rico 1.9%; Japan 1.2%. **Exports** (2005;
f.o.b.): B$450,800,000 (domestic exports 60.1%, of
which plastics 25.7%, fish, crustaceans, and mollusks [mainly crayfish] 17.2%, alcoholic beverages
[mainly rum] 3.7%; reexports 39.9%, of which petroleum 9.0%). *Major export destinations:* US 68.9%;
France 8.3%; Germany 7.0%; UK 4.6%; Canada 4.5%.

Transport and communications

Transport. *Railroads:* none. *Roads* (2000): total
length 2,693 km (paved 57%). *Vehicles:* passenger
cars (2002) 90,000; trucks and buses (2001)
25,000. *Air transport* (Bahamasair only; 2001): passenger-km 374,000,000; short ton-mi ' cargo
1,208,000, metric ton-km cargo 1,764,000. **Communications,** in total units (units per 1,000 persons).
Telephone landlines (2007): 133,000 (401); cellular
telephone subscribers (2007): 374,000 (1,129);
total Internet users (2007): 120,000 (362); broadband Internet subscribers (2007): 13,000 (39).

Education and health

Educational attainment (2000). Percentage of population ages 15 and over having: no formal schooling/unknown 2.5%; primary education 8.7%; incomplete secondary 19.9%; complete secondary 53.7%;
incomplete higher 8.1%; complete higher 7.1%. *Literacy* (2005): percentage of total population ages 15
and over literate 95.8%; males literate 95.0%; females
literate 96.7%. **Health** (2001): physicians 458 (1 per
672 persons); hospital beds 1,540 (1 per 200 persons); infant mortality rate per 1,000 live births (2006)
16.3; undernourished population (2002–04) 25,000
(8% of total population based on the consumption of
a minimum daily requirement of 1,940 calories).

Military

Total active duty personnel (2007): 860 (paramilitary
coast guard 100%). **Military expenditure as percent-**

age of GDP (2005): 0.7%; per capita expenditure US$121.

Background

The islands were inhabited by Lucayan Indians when Christopher Columbus sighted them on 12 Oct 1492. He is thought to have landed on San Salvador (Watling) Island. The Spaniards made no attempt to settle but carried out slave raids that depopulated the islands; when English settlers arrived in 1648 from Bermuda, the islands were uninhabited. They became a haunt of pirates, and few of the ensuing settlements prospered. The islands enjoyed some prosperity following the American Revolution, when Loyalists fled the US and established cotton plantations. The islands were a center for blockade runners during the American Civil War. Not until the development of tourism after World War II did permanent economic prosperity arrive. The Bahamas was granted internal self-government in 1964 and became independent in 1973.

Recent Developments

In early 2009 the Organisation for Economic Co-operation and Development announced that The Bahamas was on its so-called "gray list" of countries; these nations have agreed to improve financial transparency standards but have not signed the necessary international accords to do so.

Internet resources:
<http://statistics.bahamas.gov.bs>.

Bahrain

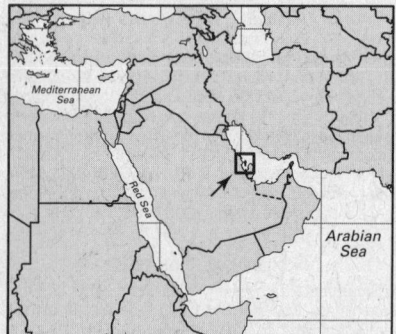

Official name: Mamlakat al-Bahrayn (Kingdom of Bahrain). Form of government: constitutional monarchy with a parliament comprising two legislative houses (Shura Council [40] and Council of Representatives [40]). Chief of state: King Sheikh Hamad ibn ʿIsa al-Khalifah (from 2002). Head of government: Prime Minister Sheikh Khalifah ibn Sulman al-Khalifah (from 1970). Capital: Manama. Official language: Arabic. Official religion: Islam. Monetary unit: 1 Bahrain dinar (BD) = 1,000 fils; valuation (1 Jul 2009) US$1 = BD 0.38.

Demography

Area: 290 sq mi, 750 sq km. Population (2008): 1,084,000. Density (2008): persons per sq mi 3,857.7, persons per sq km 1,489.0. Urban (2005): 96.4%. Sex distribution (2005): male 57.52%; female 42.48%. Age breakdown (2005): under 15, 27.2%; 15–29, 23.2%; 30–44, 29.9%; 45–59, 15.2%; 60–74, 3.6%; 75–84, 0.8%; 85 and over, 0.1%. Ethnic composition (2000): Bahraini Arab 63.9%; Indo-Pakistani 14.8%, of which Urdu 4.5%, Malayali 3.5%; Persian 13.0%; Filipino 4.5%; British 2.1%; other 1.7%. Religious affiliation (2000): Muslim 82.4%, of which Shiʿi 58%, Sunni 24%; Christian 10.5%; Hindu 6.3%; other 0.8%. Major urban areas (2001): Manama 143,035; Muharraq 91,307; Al-Rifaʿ 79,550; Madinat Hamad 52,718; Al-ʿAli 47,529. Location: the Middle East, archipelago in the Persian Gulf, east of Saudi Arabia.

Vital statistics

Birth rate per 1,000 population (2005): 21.0 (world avg. 20.3). Death rate per 1,000 population (2005): 3.1 (world avg. 8.6). Natural increase rate per 1,000 population (2005): 17.9 (world avg. 11.7). Total fertility rate (avg. births per childbearing woman; 2005): 2.63. Life expectancy at birth (2005): male 71.7 years; female 76.8 years.

National economy

Budget (2005). Revenue: BD 1,671,400,000 (petroleum and natural gas revenue 75.7%; other 24.3%). Expenditures: BD 1,289,200,000 (current expenditures 79.4%; development expenditures 20.6%). Production (metric tons except as noted). Agriculture and fishing (2005): dates 15,000, vegetables 7,703 (of which tomatoes 2,100, onions 1,149), fruit (excluding dates) 5,010; livestock (number of live animals) 40,000 sheep, 26,000 goats, 470,000 chickens, 930 camels; fisheries production 11,857 (from aquaculture, negligible). Manufacturing (barrels; 2005): jet fuel 19,956,000; distillate fuel oil 19,278,000; gasoline 7,309,000; naphtha 1,783,000. Energy production (consumption): electricity (kW-hr; 2005–06) 9,567,000,000 ([2005] 8,698,000,000); crude petroleum (barrels; 2005–06) 66,400,000 ([2005] 97,300,000); petroleum products (metric tons; 2005) 11,437,000 (1,192,000); natural gas (cu m; 2006) 10,700,000,000 ([2005] 7,447,000,000). Gross national income (2007): US$14,022,000,000 (US$12,935 per capita). Population economically active (2005): total 350,000; activity rate of total population 48.3% (participation rates: ages 15 and over 67%; female 23.2%; unemployed [citizens only; early 2006] 16–18%). Public debt (December 2004): US$3,866,000,000. Selected balance of

Did you know? The first petroleum well in the Middle East was drilled in Bahrain, beginning in 1931, near the highest point in Jebel Dukhan. At a drilling depth of 2,008 feet, 70 tons of petroleum flowed naturally from the well.

---

1 metric ton = about 1.1 short tons;   1 kilometer = 0.6 mi (statute);   1 metric ton-km cargo = about 0.68 short ton-mi cargo;   c.i.f.: cost, insurance, and freight;   f.o.b.: free on board

payments data. Receipts from (US$'000,000): tourism (2006) 1,048; foreign direct investment (FDI) (2004–06 avg.) 1,609. Disbursements for (US$'000,000): tourism (2006) 455; remittances (2007) 1,531; FDI (2004–06 avg.) 1,046.

Foreign trade

Imports (2006; c.i.f.): US$8,957,000,000 (crude petroleum 54.7%, machinery and apparatus 9.3%, road vehicles 7.0%, metal and metal scrap 4.6%, food and live animals 4.5%). *Major import sources* (2004): Saudi Arabia 47.7%; Japan 6.2%; UK 3.7%; Germany 3.6%; France 3.6%. Exports (2006; f.o.b.): US$11,662,000,000 (refined petroleum products 79.1%, aluminum [all forms] 12.1%, iron ore agglomerates 1.2%, urea 1.1%). *Major export destinations* (2004): unknown destinations for petroleum exports 76.5%; Saudi Arabia 6.4%; US 3.2%; Taiwan 2.7%.

Transport and communications

Transport. *Railroads:* none. *Roads* (2003): total length 3,498 km (paved 79%). *Vehicles* (private vehicles only; 2005): passenger cars 241,813; trucks and buses 44,811. *Air transport* (Gulf Air, the national airline of both Bahrain and Oman, only; 2007): passenger-km 13,999,000,000; metric ton-km cargo 498,000,000. Communications, in total units (units per 1,000 persons). Telephone landlines (2006): 190,000 (262); cellular telephone subscribers (2007): 1,116,000 (1,483); personal computers (2004): 121,000 (164); total Internet users (2007): 250,000 (332); broadband Internet subscribers (2006): 39,000 (52).

Education and health

Educational attainment (2001). Percentage of population ages 15 and over having: no formal education 24.0%; primary education 37.1%; secondary 26.4%; higher 12.5%. Literacy (2005): percentage of population ages 15 and over literate 90.0%; males literate 92.6%; females literate 86.4%. Health (2005): physicians 1,973 (1 per 362 persons); hospital beds 2,033 (1 per 352 persons); infant mortality rate per 1,000 live births 17.3.

Military

Total active duty personnel (2007): 8,200 (army 73.2%, navy 8.5%, air force 18.2%); US troops in Bahrain (2006): 3,000. Military expenditure as percentage of GDP (2005): 3.6%; per capita expenditure US$675.

Background

The area has long been an important trading center and is mentioned in Persian, Greek, and Roman references. It was ruled by Arabs from the 7th century AD but was then occupied by the Portuguese in 1521–1602. Since 1783 it has been ruled by the Khalifah family, though through a series of treaties its defense remained a British responsibility from 1820 to 1971. After Britain withdrew its forces from the Persian Gulf (1968), Bahrain declared its independence in 1971. It served as a center for the allies in the Persian Gulf War (1990–91). Since 1994 it has experienced bouts of political unrest, mainly among

its large Shi'ite population. Constitutional revisions, ratified in 2002, made Bahrain a constitutional monarchy and enfranchised women.

Recent Developments

In July 2008 Huda Nonoo, a Bahraini Jew, was appointed ambassador to the US—the first Jewish person ever appointed ambassador by an Arab country. Bahrain's usually robust economy was damaged by the global recession beginning in the fall of 2008.

- Internet resources: <www.cio.gov.bh/en/>.

Bangladesh

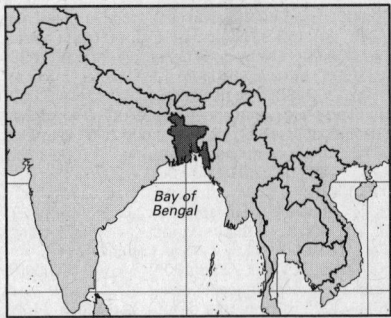

Official name: Gana Prajatantri Bangladesh (People's Republic of Bangladesh). Form of government: unitary multiparty republic with one legislative house (Parliament [300]). Chief of state: President Zillur Rahman (from 2009). Head of government: Prime Minister Sheikh Hasina Wazed (from 2009). Capital: Dhaka. Official language: Bengali. Official religion: Islam. Monetary unit: 1 Bangladesh taka (Tk) = 100 paisa; valuation (1 Jul 2009) US$1 = Tk 68.70.

Demography

Area: 56,977 sq mi, 147,570 sq km. Population (2008): 142,547,000. Density (2008): persons per sq mi 2,649.7, persons per sq km 1,023.1. Urban (2006): 24.6%. Sex distribution (2006): male 51.21%; female 48.79%. Age breakdown (2005): under 15, 35.5%; 15–29, 28.6%; 30–44, 19.5%; 45–59, 10.8%; 60–74, 4.6%; 75–84, 0.9%; 85 and over, 0.1%. Ethnic composition (1997): Bengali 97.7%; tribal 1.9%, of which Chakma 0.4%, Saontal 0.2%, Marma 0.1%; other 0.4%. Religious affiliation (2005): Muslim (nearly all Sunni) 88.3%; Hindu 10.5%; Buddhist 0.6%; Christian (mostly Roman Catholic) 0.3%; other 0.3%. Major cities (metropolitan areas) (2006): Dhaka 6,479,751 (11,813,728); Chittagong 2,438,403 (4,090,809); Khulna 830,454 (1,323,071); Rajshahi 447,031 (737,336); Comilla 404,200. Location: South Asia, bordering India, Myanmar (Burma), and the Bay of Bengal.

Vital statistics

Birth rate per 1,000 population (2006): 29.8 (world avg. 20.3). Death rate per 1,000 population (2006): 8.3 (world avg. 8.6). Total fertility rate (avg. births per childbearing woman; 2006): 3.11. **Life expectancy** at birth (2006): male 64.4 years; female 66.0 years.

National economy

Budget (2005–06). *Revenue:* Tk 448,700,000,000 (tax revenue 80.6%, of which VAT 27.6%, import duties 18.4%, taxes on income and profits 15.5%; nontax revenue 19.4%). *Expenditures:* Tk 610,600,-000,000 (current expenditures 57.0%, of which education 10.4%, domestic interest payments 10.2%; development expenditures 35.2%; other 7.8%). **Public debt** (external, outstanding; 2006): US$18,866,000,000. **Production** (metric tons except as noted). *Agriculture and fishing* (2007): rice 43,729,000, sugarcane 6,423,440, jute 801,000, rapeseed 234,865, tea 57,580, sesame seeds 50,000, ginger 49,405; livestock (number of live animals) 36,900,000 goats, 24,500,000 cattle, 142,000,000 chickens; fisheries production (2005) 2,215,957 (from aquaculture 40%). *Mining and quarrying* (2005–06): marine salt 350,000; kaolin 8,500. *Manufacturing* (value added in US$'000,000; 1998): wearing apparel 839; tobacco products 634; textiles 567. *Energy production. (consumption):* electricity (kW-hr; 2007) 22,572,000,000 ([2005] 22,643,-000,000); coal (metric tons; 2005) n.a. (700,000); crude petroleum (barrels; 2006) 2,000,000 ([2005] 10,100,000); petroleum products (metric tons; 2005) 884,000 (3,617,000); natural gas (cu m; 2007) 15,225,000,000 ([2005] 14,340,000,000). **Population economically active** (2002–03): total 46,324,000; activity rate of total population 34.7% (participation rates: ages 15–64, 58.6%; female 22.3%; officially unemployed 4.3%). **Gross national income** (2007): US$75,047,000,000 (US$470 per capita). **Selected balance of payments data.** Receipts from (US$'000,000): tourism (2006) 80; remittances (2007) 6,560; foreign direct investment (2004–06 avg.) 592; official development assistance (2006) 1,223. Disbursements for (US$'000,000): tourism (2006) 140; remittances (2007) 6.

Foreign trade

Imports (2005–06): US$14,746,000,000 (textile yarn, fabrics, and made-up articles 15.1%; machinery and aparatus 10.4%; imports for export processing zone 7.2%; base metals 6.6%; cotton 5.0%). *Major import sources* (2004): India 18.5%; China 13.1%; Singapore 10.5%; Japan 5.4%; Hong Kong 5.0%. **Exports** (2005–06): US$10,526,300,000 (woven garments 38.8%; hosiery and knitwear 36.3%; frozen fish and shrimp 4.4%; jute manufactures 3.4%). *Major export destinations* (2004): US 25.6%; Germany 17.6%; UK 12.0%; France 7.5%; Italy 4.6%.

Transport and communications

Transport. *Railroads* (2002): route length 2,768 km; passenger-km 3,970,000,000; metric ton-km cargo 908,000,000. *Roads* (2003): total length 239,226 km (paved 10%). *Vehicles* (2004): passenger cars 185,000; trucks and buses 88,000. *Air transport* (Biman Bangladesh only; 2005): passenger-km 5,163,000,000; metric ton-km cargo 181,034,000. **Communications,** in total units (units per 1,000 persons). Telephone landlines (2007): 1,187,000 (7.5);

cellular telephone subscribers (2007): 34,370,000 (217); personal computers (2004): 1,650,000 (12); total Internet users (2007): 500,000 (3.2).

Education and health

Educational attainment (2004). Percentage of population ages 25 and over having: no formal schooling 48.8%; incomplete primary education 17.9%; complete primary 7.7%; incomplete secondary 15.1%; complete secondary or higher 10.5%. **Literacy** (2002) total population ages 15 and over literate 41.1%; males literate 50.3%; females literate 31.4%. **Health** (2002): physicians 32,498 (1 per 4,049 persons); hospital beds 45,607 (1 per 2,886 persons);·infant mortality rate per 1,000 live births (2006) 60.8; undernourished population (2002–04) 44,000,000 (30% of total population based on the consumption of a minimum daily requirement of 1,780 calories).

Military

Total active duty personnel (2007): 150,000 (army 80.0%, navy 10.7%, air force 9.3%). **Military expenditure as percentage of GDP** (2005): 1.0%; per capita expenditure US$5.

Background

In its early years Bangladesh was known as Bengal. When the British left the subcontinent in 1947, the area that was East Bengal became the part of Pakistan called East Pakistan. Bengali nationalist sentiment increased after the creation of an independent Pakistan. In 1971 violence erupted; some one million Bengalis were killed, and millions more fled to India, which finally entered the war on the side of the Bengalis, ensuring West Pakistan's defeat. East Pakistan became the independent nation of Bangladesh. Little of the devastation caused by the war has been repaired, and political instability, including the assassinations of two presidents, has continued. In addition, the low-lying country has been repeatedly battered by natural disasters, notably tropical storms and flooding.

Recent Developments

A huge blow was dealt to the US$8 billion "manpower" export as Bangladeshi workers in a number of Middle Eastern countries protested violently against low wages and exploitation. Several of these countries decided to stop taking in any more workers from selective sectors in Bangladesh, and thousands were also deported. In February 2009, soldiers from the Bangladesh Rifles mutinied in protest over poor treatment and pay, killing more than 140 army officers and 20 civilians.

Internet resources:
<www.discoverybangladesh.com>.

Barbados

Official name: Barbados. **Form of government:** constitutional monarchy with two legislative houses (Senate [21]; House of Assembly [30]). **Chief of state:**

---

1 metric ton = about 1.1 short tons;   1 kilometer = 0.6 mi (statute);   1 metric ton-km cargo = about 0.68 short ton-mi cargo;   c.i.f.: cost, insurance, and freight;   f.o.b.: free on board

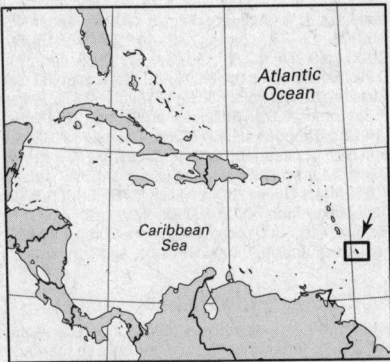

Atlantic Ocean

Caribbean Sea

British Queen Elizabeth II (from 1952), represented by Governor-General Sir Clifford Husbands (from 1996). **Head of government:** Prime Minister David Thompson (from 2008). **Capital:** Bridgetown. **Official language:** English. **Official religion:** none. **Monetary unit:** 1 Barbados dollar (BDS$) = 100 cents; valuation (1 Jul 2009) US$1 = BDS$1.98.

Demography

Area: 166 sq mi, 430 sq km. **Population** (2008): 282,000. **Density** (2008): persons per sq mi 1,698.8, persons per sq km 655.8. **Urban** (2005): 52.6%. **Sex distribution** (2005): male 48.26%; female 51.74%. **Age breakdown** (2005): under 15, 19.0%; 15–29, 22.8%; 30–44, 26.1%; 45–59, 19.0%; 60–74, 8.2%; 75–84, 3.8%; 85 and over, 1.1%. **Ethnic composition** (2000): local black 87.1%; mulatto 6.0%; British expatriates 4.3%; US white 1.2%; Indo-Pakistani 1.1%; other 0.3%. **Religious affiliation** (2000): Christian 72.5%, of which Anglican 28.3%, Pentecostal 18.7%, Adventist 5.5%, Methodist 5.1%, Rastafarian 1.1%; Muslim 0.7%; Hindu 0.3%; nonreligious 17.3%; other/unknown 8.1%. **Major urban areas** (2004): Bridgetown 99,100; Speightstown 3,600; Oistins (2000) 1,203. **Location:** island at the eastern edge of the Caribbean Sea where it adjoins the North Atlantic Ocean, northeast of Venezuela.

Vital statistics

Birth rate per 1,000 population (2006): 12.7 (world avg. 20.3). **Death rate** per 1,000 population (2006): 8.7 (world avg. 8.6). **Natural increase rate** per 1,000 population (2006): 4.0 (world avg. 11.7). **Total fertility rate** (avg. births per childbearing woman; 2006): 1.65. **Life expectancy** at birth (2006): male 70.8 years; female 74.8 years.

National economy

Budget (2005–06). *Revenue:* Bds$2,145,000,000 (tax revenue 95.2%, of which VAT 31.8%, corporate taxes 16.8%, personal income taxes 14.3%; nontax revenue 4.8%). *Expenditures:* Bds$2,328,500,000 (current expenditures 85.2%, of which education 18.3%, debt payments 12.8%, health 11.3%; development expenditures 14.8%). **Public debt** (external, outstanding; December 2005): US$763,500,000. **Production** (metric tons except as noted). *Agriculture*

and fishing (2006): raw sugar 33,701, sweet potatoes 2,000, coconuts 1,950, okra 1,550; livestock (number of live animals) 19,000 pigs, 10,800 sheep, 3,400,000 chickens; fisheries production (2005) 1,869 (from aquaculture, none). Manufacturing (value added in US$'000,000; 1997): industrial chemicals 87; food products 63; beverages (significantly rum and beer) 58. *Energy production (consumption):* electricity (kW-hr; 2007) 924,000,000 (924,000,000); crude petroleum (barrels; 2007) 303,000 ([2005] negligible); petroleum products (metric tons; 2005) 1,000 (360,000); natural gas (cu m; 2007) 21,100,000 ([2005] 26,300,000). **Population economically active** (December 2005): total 145,800; activity rate of total population 53.1% (participation rates: ages 15 and over, 69.0%; female 49.5%; unemployed [January–March 2008] 7.9%). **Gross national income** (2006): US$3,307,000,000 (US$11,291 per capita). **Selected balance of payments data.** Receipts from (US$'000,000): tourism (2006) 978; remittances (2007) 140; foreign direct investment (FDI) (2004–06 avg.) 29. Disbursements for (US$'000,000): tourism (2005) 96; remittances (2007) 40; FDI (2004–06 avg.) 6.

Foreign trade

Imports (2006; c.i.f.): Bds$3,257,000,000 (machinery and apparatus 19.8%; refined petroleum products 17.4%; food products 11.5%; chemical products 9.5%). *Major import sources:* US 37.6%; Trinidad and Tobago 22.5%; UK 5.8%; Japan 3.7%; Canada 3.7%. **Exports** (2006; f.o.b.): Bds$882,000,000 (refined petroleum products 25.9%; food products 10.2%, of which raw sugar 4.4%; crude petroleum 5.2%; rum 5.0%; medicines 4.9%). *Major export destinations:* US 20.1%; Trinidad and Tobago 11.0%; UK 7.5%; Saint Lucia 5.1%; ships' stores and bunkers 25.9%.

Transport and communications

Transport. *Railroads:* none. *Roads* (2004): total length 1,600 km (paved 100%). *Vehicles* (2004): passenger cars 92,195; trucks and buses 8,597. *Air transport* (2003): metric ton-km cargo 200,000. **Communications,** in total units (units per 1,000 persons). Telephone landlines (2005): 135,000 (501); cellular telephone subscribers (2005): 206,000 (766); personal computers (2005): 40,000 (148); total Internet users (2007): 280,000 (953); broadband Internet subscribers (2005): 32,000 (118).

Education and health

Educational attainment (2003). Percentage of employed labor force having: no formal schooling/unknown 1.4%; primary education 14.9%; secondary 58.7%; technical/vocational 5.4%; university 19.6%. **Literacy** (2002): total population ages 15 and over literate 99.7%. **Health** (2002): physicians 376 (1 per 721 persons); hospital beds 501 (1 per 541 persons); infant mortality rate per 1,000 live births (2006) 11.8; undernourished population (2002–04) less than 2.5% of total population.

Military

Total active duty personnel (2007): 610 (army 82.0%, navy 18.0%). **Military expenditure as percentage of GDP** (2005): 0.5%; per capita expenditure US$52.

Background

The island of Barbados was probably inhabited by Arawak Indians who originally came from South America. Spaniards may have landed by 1518, and by 1536 they had apparently wiped out the Indian population. Barbados was settled by the English in the 1620s. Slaves were brought in to work the sugar plantations, which were especially prosperous in the 17th–18th centuries. The British Empire abolished slavery in 1834, and all the slaves in Barbados were freed by 1838. In 1958 Barbados joined the West Indies Federation. When the latter dissolved in 1962, Barbados sought independence from Britain; it achieved it and joined the Commonwealth in 1966.

Recent Developments

Barbados reaffirmed in February 2008 its decision not to join Venezuela's PetroCaribe initiative, under which Caracas provided petroleum products and crude oil to Caricom countries on a deferred-payment basis.

Internet resources: <www.barstats.gov.bb>.

Belarus

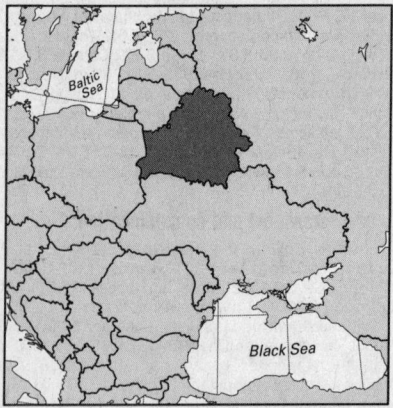

Official name: Respublika Belarus (Republic of Belarus). **Form of government:** republic with two legislative bodies (Council of the Republic [64]; House of Representatives [110]). **Head of state and government:** President Alyaksandr H. Lukashenka (from 1994), assisted by Prime Minister Syarhey Sidorski (from 2003). **Capital:** Minsk. **Official languages:** Belarusian; Russian. **Official religion:** none. **Monetary unit:** Belarusian ruble (Br); valuation (1 Jul 2009) US$1 = Br 2,825.00.

Demography

Area: 80,153 sq mi, 207,595 sq km. **Population** (2008): 9,675,000. **Density** (2008): persons per sq mi 120.7, persons per sq km 46.6. **Urban** (2006): 72.8%. **Sex distribution** (2006): male 46.69%; fe-

male 53.31%. **Age breakdown** (2005): under 15, 15.2%; 15–29, 24.1%; 30–44, 22.0%; 45–59, 20.2%; 60–74, 12.8%; 75–84, 5.0%; 85 and over, 0.7%. **Ethnic composition** (1999): Belarusian 81.2%; Russian 11.4%; Polish 3.9%; Ukrainian 2.4%; Jewish 0.3%; other 0.8%. **Religious affiliation** (2000): Belarusian Orthodox 48.7%; Roman Catholic 13.2%; unaffiliated Christian 5.9%; other Christian 2.4%; Jewish 0.6%; Muslim 0.3%; nonreligious 24.0%; atheist 4.9%. **Major cities** (2004): Minsk 1,765,800; Homyel 481,200; Mahilyow 366,900; Vitsyebsk 342,700; Hrodna 316,700. **Location:** eastern Europe, bordering Latvia, Russia, Ukraine, Poland, and Lithuania.

Vital statistics

Birth rate per 1,000 population (2005): 9.2 (world avg. 20.3); within marriage 75.9%; outside marriage 24.1%. **Death rate** per 1,000 population (2005): 14.5 (world avg. 8.6). **Natural increase rate** per 1,000 population (2005): −5.3 (world avg. 11.7). **Total fertility rate** (avg. births per childbearing woman; 2005): 1.21. **Life expectancy** at birth (2005): male 62.9 years; female 75.1 years.

National economy

Budget (2004). *Revenue:* Br 17,417,000,000 (tax revenue 72.7%, of which VAT 21.9%, tax on profits 9.3%, personal income tax 8.1%; nontax revenue 5.7%; other 21.6%). *Expenditures:* Br 17,595,-000,000 (current expenditure 75.1%; development expenditure 4.6%; other 20.3%). **Public debt** (external, outstanding; 2006): US$846,000,000. **Population economically active** (2005): 4,426,300; activity rate of total population 45.4% (participation rate [1999]: ages 15–64, 69.7%; female 53.1%; officially unemployed [December 2006] 1.2%). **Production** (metric tons except as noted). *Agriculture and fishing* (2007): potatoes 8,744,000, corn (maize) 5,410,000, sugar beets 3,624,000, flax fiber and tow 39,000; livestock (number of live animals) 3,988,900 cattle, 3,641,800 pigs, 27,900,000 chickens; fisheries production (2006) 5,050 (from aquaculture 82%). *Mining and quarrying* (2005): potash 4,844,000; peat 2,408,000. *Manufacturing* (2006): fertilizers 5,469,000; cement 3,495,000; steel (2002) 1,607,000. *Energy production (consumption):* electricity (kW-hr; 2006) 31,800,000,000 ([2005] 34,999,000,000); coal (metric tons; 2005) none (168,000); crude petroleum (barrels; 2007) 12,800,000 ([2005] 145,400,000); petroleum products (metric tons; 2005) 17,137,000 (4,850,000); natural gas (cu m; 2005) 228,000,000 (20,407,-000,000). **Gross national income** (2007): US$40,-897,000,000 (US$4,220 per capita). **Selected balance of payments data.** Receipts from (US$'000,-000): tourism (2006) 272; remittances (2007) 363; foreign direct investment (2004–06 avg.) 274. Disbursements for (US$'000,000): tourism (2006) 735; remittances (2007) 111.

Foreign trade

Imports (2006; c.i.f.): US$22,323,000,000 (crude petroleum 25.1%; nonelectrical machinery 10.6%; chemical products 9.9%; food products 6.7%; base metals 6.5%). *Major import sources:* Russia 58.6%;

1 metric ton = about 1.1 short tons;   1 kilometer = 0.6 mi (statute);   1 metric ton-km cargo = about 0.68 short ton-mi cargo;   c.i.f.: cost, insurance, and freight;   f.o.b.: free on board

Germany 7.5%; Ukraine 5.5%; Poland 3.4%; China 2.5%. **Exports** (2006; f.o.b.): US$19,739,000,000 (refined petroleum products 34.1%; machinery and apparatus 11.4%; road vehicles 7.2%; food products 6.9%, of which dairy products 3.2%; potassium chloride 5.1%). *Major export destinations:* Russia 34.7%; The Netherlands 17.7%; UK 7.5%; Ukraine 6.3%; Poland 5.2%.

Transport and communications

Transport. *Railroads* (2007): length (2002) 5,533 km; passenger-km 9,366,000,000; metric ton-km cargo 47,933,000,000. *Roads* (2005): total length 94,797 km (paved 89%). *Vehicles:* passenger cars (2005) 1,771,398; trucks and buses (2001) 85,791. *Air transport* (2007): passenger-km 975,000,000; metric ton-km cargo 66,000,000. **Communications**, in total units (units per 1,000 persons). Telephone landlines (2007): 3,672,000 (379); cellular telephone subscribers (2006): 5,960,000 (614); total Internet users (2007): 6,000,000 (619); broadband Internet subscribers (2006): 11,000 (1.2).

Education and health

Literacy (2001): total population ages 15 and over literate 99.7%; males literate 99.8%; females literate 99.6%. **Health** (2007): physicians 46,900 (1 per 207 persons); hospital beds 108,900 (1 per 89 persons); infant mortality rate per 1,000 live births (2005) 6.3; undernourished population (2002–04) 400,000 (4% of total population based on the consumption of a minimum daily requirement of 1,970 calories).

Military

Total active duty personnel (2007): 72,940 (army 40.6%, air force and air defense 24.9%, centrally controlled units 34.5%). **Military expenditure as percentage of GDP** (2005): 7.2%; per capita expenditure US$38.

Background

While Belarusians share a distinct identity and language, they did not enjoy political sovereignty until the late 20th century. The territory that is now Belarus underwent partition and changed hands often; as a result its history is entwined with those of its neighbors. In medieval times the region was ruled by Lithuanians and Poles. Following the Third Partition of Poland, it was ruled by Russia. After World War I, the western part was assigned to Poland, and the eastern part became Soviet Russian territory. After World War II, the Soviets expanded what had been the Belorussian SSR by annexing more of Poland. Much of the area suffered radiation contamination from the Chernobyl accident in 1986, forcing many to evacuate. Belarus declared its independence in 1991 and later joined the Commonwealth of Independent States. Amid increasing political turmoil in the 1990s, it proposed a union with Russia in 1997 that was still being debated at the start of the 21st century.

Recent Developments

Relations with the US soured in 2008 as Belarus refused to release all designated political prisoners. In March US Ambassador Karen Stewart left the country, and the respective embassies were reduced to a skeleton staff. The Belarusian economy performed well in 2008, however. GDP rose by 10.0%, and the value of industrial output increased by 10.8% and agriculture output by 8.9%. Official unemployment dropped by 15.4%. Nonetheless, during a period of international economic uncertainty, Belarus was forced to negotiate a new US$2 billion loan from Russia, and Moscow continued to demand that Belarus begin using the Russian ruble as a common currency.

Internet resources:
<http://belstat.gov.by/homep/en/main.html>.

Belgium

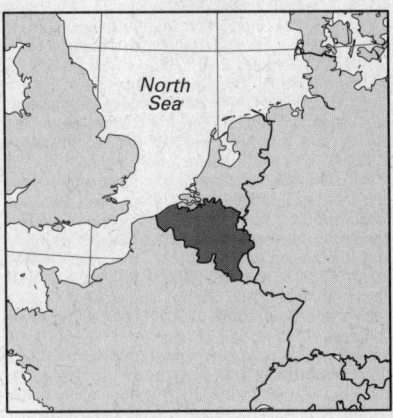

Official name: Koninkrijk België (Dutch); Royaume de Belgique (French); Königreich Belgien (German) (Kingdom of Belgium). **Form of government:** federal constitutional monarchy with two legislative chambers (Senate [71]; House of Representatives [150]). **Chief of state:** King Albert II (from 1993). **Head of government:** Prime Minister Herman Van Rompuy (from 2008). **Capital:** Brussels. **Official languages:** Dutch; French; German. **Official religion:** none. **Monetary unit:** 1 euro (€) = 100 cents; US$1 = €0.71 (1 Jul 2009).

Demography

Area: 11,787 sq mi, 30,528 sq km. **Population** (2008): 10,697,000. **Density** (2008): persons per sq mi 907.5, persons per sq km 350.4. **Urban** (2005): 97.2%. **Sex distribution** (2005): male 48.94%; female 51.06%. **Age breakdown** (2005): under 15, 16.8%; 15–29, 18.1%; 30–44, 21.9%; 45–59, 20.8%; 60–74, 14.1%; 75–84, 6.5%; 85 and over, 1.8%. **Ethnic composition** (2000): Flemish 53.7%; Walloon (French) 31.6%; Italian 2.6%; French 2.0%; Arab 1.8%; German 1.5%; Berber 0.9%; other 5.9%. **Religious affiliation** (2001): self-identified Roman Catholic 46.7%; other Christian 2.6%; Muslim 3.9%; nonreligious/secular/other 46.8%. **Major cities** (2007): Brussels (population of capital region) 1,809,242; Antwerp 466,203; Gent (Ghent) 235,143; Charleroi 201,550; Liège 188,907. **Location:** western Europe, bordering The Netherlands, Germany, Luxembourg, France, and the North Sea.

Vital statistics

Birth rate per 1,000 population (2007): 11.4 (world avg. 20.3); within marriage 61.0%; outside of marriage 39.0%. **Death rate** per 1,000 population (2007): 9.7 (world avg. 8.6). **Total fertility rate** (avg. births per childbearing woman; 2005): 1.72. **Life expectancy** at birth (2006): male 76.6 years; female 82.3 years.

National economy

Budget (2005). *Revenue:* €149,218,000,000 (social security contributions 28.2%; income tax 24.3%; taxes on goods and services 23.0%). *Expenditures:* €149,504,000,000 (social insurance benefits 46.3%, of which health 12.6%; wages 24.1%; interest on debt 9.1%). **Production** (metric tons except as noted). *Agriculture and fishing* (2007): sugar beets 5,746,892, potatoes 2,877,685, wheat 1,480,710, chicory roots 361,305; livestock (number of live animals) 6,270,000 pigs, 2,639,700 cattle; fisheries production (2005) 25,767 (from aquaculture 5%). *Mining and quarrying* (2005): Belgian bluestone 1,200,000 cu m. *Manufacturing* (value added in €'000,000; 2005): chemical products 8,903; base and fabricated metals 7,116; food, beverages, and tobacco 6,046; value of traded polished diamonds handled in Antwerp (2005) US$15,900,000,000. *Energy production (consumption):* electricity (kW-hr; 2007) 88,278,000,000 ([2005] 93,248,000,000); hard coal (metric tons; 2005) none (7,474,000); lignite (metric tons; 2005) 109,000 (283,000); crude petroleum (barrels; 2005) none (235,000,000); petroleum products (metric tons; 2005) 27,934,000 (17,176,000); natural gas (cu m; 2005) none, (16,825,000,000). **Population economically active** (2006): total 4,647,200; activity rate 44.2% (participation rates: ages 15–64, 58.8%; female 44.4%; unemployed [2007] 6.9%). **Gross national income** (2007): US$432,540,000,000 (US$40,710 per capita). **Public debt** (December 2006): US$357,000,-000,000. **Selected balance of payments data.** Receipts from (US$'000,000): tourism (2006) 10,242; remittances (2007) 8,027; foreign direct investment (FDI) (2004–06 avg.) 49,824. Disbursements for (US$'000,000): tourism (2006) 15,482; remittances (2007) 3,156; FDI (2004–06 avg.) 42,918.

Foreign trade

Imports (2006; c.i.f.): US$353,790,000,000 (mineral fuels 13.5%; road vehicles 10.6%; medicine and pharmaceuticals 8.9%; organic chemicals 7.6%; nonelectrical machinery 6.3%). *Major import sources:* The Netherlands 18.4%; Germany 17.5%; France 11.3%; UK 6.6%; Ireland 5.8%. **Exports** (2006; f.o.b.): US$369,256,000,000 (road vehicles 11.9%; medicines and pharmaceuticals 8.9%; mineral fuels 7.7%; food products 6.9%; organic chemicals 6.8%; diamonds 4.2%). *Major export destinations:* Germany 19.9%; France 17.0%; The Netherlands 12.0%; UK 8.0%.

Transport and communications

Transport. *Railroads* (2005): route length 3,536 km; passenger-km 9,117,000,000; metric ton-km cargo 8,130,000,000. *Roads* (2004): total length 150,567 km (paved 78%). *Vehicles* (2006): passenger cars 4,976,286; trucks and buses 638,579. *Air transport* (Brussels Airlines only; 2007): passenger-km 7,069,000,000; metric ton-km cargo 80,000,000. **Communications,** in total units (units per 1,000 persons). Telephone landlines (2006): 4,719,000 (452); cellular telephone subscribers (2006): 9,660,000 (926); personal computers (2004) 3,627,000 (351); total Internet users (2005): 4,800,000 (458); broadband Internet subscribers (2005): 2,005,000 (191).

Education and health

Educational attainment (2002). Percentage of population ages 25 and over having: no formal schooling through lower-secondary education 39%; upper secondary/higher vocational 33%; university 28%. **Health:** physicians (2005) 42,176 (1 per 248 persons); hospital beds (2004) 70,865 (1 per 147 persons); infant mortality rate per 1,000 live births (2007) 3.1; undernourished population (2002–04) less than 2.5% of total population.

Military

Total active duty personnel (2007): 39,690 (army 31.7%, navy 4.0%, air force 18.8%, medical service 4.6%, joint service 40.9%). **Military expenditure as percentage of GDP** (2005): 1.1%; per capita expenditure US$403.

Background

Inhabited in ancient times by the Belgae, a Celtic people, the area was conquered by Caesar in 57 BC; under Augustus it became the Roman province of Gallia Belgica. Conquered by the Franks, it later broke up into semi-independent territories, including Brabant and Luxembourg. By the late 15th century AD, the territories of The Netherlands, of which the future Belgium was a part, had gradually united and passed to the Habsburgs. In the 16th century, it was a center for European commerce. The basis of modern Belgium was laid in the southern Catholic provinces that split from the northern provinces after the Union of Utrecht in 1579. Overrun by the French and incorporated into France in 1801, it was reunited to Holland and with it became the independent Kingdom of The Netherlands in 1815. After the revolt of its citizens in 1830, it became the independent Kingdom of Belgium. Under Léopold II it acquired vast lands in Africa. Overrun by the Germans in World Wars I and II, Belgium was the scene of the Battle of the Bulge. Internal discord led to legislation in the 1970s and 1980s that created three nearly autonomous regions in accordance with language distribution: Flemish Flanders, French Wallonia, and bilingual Brussels. In 1993 it became a federation comprising the three regions, which gained greater autonomy at the outset of the 21st century. It is a member of the European Union.

Recent Developments

The longest-running political crisis in Belgium's history formally ended in March 2008 when Flemish Christian Democrat Yves Leterme's five-party coalition government was sworn in—nine months after the

---

1 metric ton = about 1.1 short tons;   1 kilometer = 0.6 mi (statute);   1 metric ton-km cargo = about 0.68 short ton-mi cargo;   c.i.f.: cost, insurance, and freight;   f.o.b.: free on board

country's general election in June 2007. The partnership between the French- and Dutch-speaking Christian Democrats and Liberals and the French-speaking Socialists was far from smooth, however, as the parties negotiated possible constitutional reforms that would affect the future status of the bilingual Brussels-Halle-Vilvoorde constituency and devolve more power to the country's three regions. King Albert II accepted the prime minister's resignation, however, on 22 December after aides to Leterme were accused of having tried to influence a ruling by the country's appeals court.

Internet resources: <www.visitbelgium.com>.

Belize

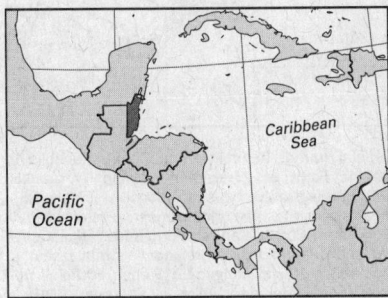

Pacific Ocean

Caribbean Sea

Official name: Belize. **Form of government:** constitutional monarchy with two legislative houses (Senate [12]; House of Representatives [32]). **Chief of state:** British Queen Elizabeth II (from 1952), represented by Governor-General Sir Colville Young (from 1993). **Head of government:** Prime Minister Dean Barrow (from 2008). **Capital:** Belmopan. **Official language:** English. **Official religion:** none. **Monetary unit:** 1 Belize dollar (BZ$) = 100 cents; valuation (1 Jul 2009) US$1 = BZ$1.93.

Demography

Area: 8,867 sq mi, 22,965 sq km. **Population** (2008): 323,000. **Density** (2008): persons per sq mi 36.4, persons per sq km 14.1. **Urban** (2005): 50.2%. **Sex distribution** (2007): male 50.66%; female 49.34%. **Age breakdown** (2007): under 15, 38.9%; 15–29, 29.4%; 30–44, 17.7%; 45–59, 8.9%; 60–74, 3.8%; 75–84, 1.1%; 85 and over, 0.2%. **Ethnic composition** (2000): mestizo (Spanish-Indian) 48.7%; Creole (predominantly black) 24.9%; Mayan Indian 10.6%; Garifuna (black–Carib Indian) 6.1%; white 4.3%; East Indian 3.0%; other or not stated 2.4%. **Religious affiliation** (2000): Roman Catholic 49.6%; Protestant 31.8%, of which Pentecostal 7.4%, Anglican 5.3%, Seventh-day Adventist 5.2%, Mennonite 4.1%; other Christian 1.9%; nonreligious 9.4%; other 7.3%. **Major cities** (2007): Belize City 63,670; San Ignacio/Santa Elena 18,265; Belmopan 16,435; Orange Walk 15,990; Dangriga 11,600. **Location:** Central America, bordering Mexico, the Caribbean Sea, and Guatemala.

Vital statistics

Birth rate per 1,000 population (2007): 28.3 (world avg. 20.3); (1997) within marriage 40.3%; outside of marriage 59.7%. **Death rate** per 1,000 population (2007): 5.7 (world avg. 8.6). **Natural increase rate** per 1,000 population (2007): 22.6 (world avg. 11.7). **Total fertility rate** (avg. births per childbearing woman; 2007): 3.52. **Life expectancy** at birth (2007): male 66.4 years; female 70.1 years.

National economy

Budget (2006–07). *Revenue:* BZ$598,048,000 (tax revenue 85.9%, of which taxes on goods and services 33.8%, taxes on international trade 28.5%, taxes on income and profits 22.6%; other revenue 14.1%). *Expenditures:* BZ$667,943,000 (current expenditures 84.1%; capital expenditures 15.9%). **Production** (metric tons except as noted). *Agriculture and fishing* (2007): sugarcane 1,250,000, oranges 225,000, bananas 90,000; livestock (number of live animals) 58,500 cattle, 1,600,000 chickens; fisheries production (2005) 14,548 (from aquaculture 73%). *Mining and quarrying* (2005): limestone 600,000; sand and gravel 160,000. *Manufacturing* (value added in US'000,000; 2004): food products and beverages (significantly citrus concentrate, flour, sugar, and beer) 69.2; textiles, clothing, and footwear 7.2. *Energy production (consumption):* electricity (kW-hr; 2005) 174,000,000 (204,000,000); crude petroleum (barrels; 2007) 1,100,000 (n.a.); petroleum products (metric tons; 2005) none (266,000). **Population economically active** (2005): total 110,786; activity rate of total population 38.2% (participation rates: ages 14 and over 59.4%; female 36.7%; unemployed 11.0%). **Gross national income** (2007): US$1,157,000,000 (US$3,800 per capita). **Public debt** (external, outstanding; September 2006): US$929,600,000. **Selected balance of payments data.** Receipts from (US'000,000): tourism (2006) 253; remittances (2007) 75; foreign direct investment (2004–06 avg.) 104; official development assistance (2006) 7.6. Disbursements for (US'000,000): tourism (2006) 41; remittances (2007) 22.

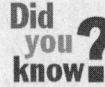

Did you know? Belize's waters contain the world's second-largest barrier reef, making the country a popular destination for underwater sports enthusiasts. Ecotourists also come to visit the rainforests and view the abundant wildlife.

Foreign trade

Imports (2005): BZ$1,226,200,000 (mineral fuels and electricity 19.2%; machinery and transportation equipment 16.3%; direct imports to commercial free zone 15.0%; food and live animals 9.8%; chemical products 7.2%). *Major import sources:* US 39%; Central American countries 19%; Mexico 9%; EU 7%; Caricom (Caribbean Community) 2%. **Exports** (2005): BZ$643,800,000 (domestic exports 60.4%, of which seafood products [significantly shrimp] 14.1%, citrus [mostly oranges] concentrate 11.9%, raw sugar 10.8%, bananas 7.9%; reexports [principally to Mexico] 39.6%). *Major export destinations* (domestic exports only): US 52%; UK 22%; other EU 7%; Caricom 11%; Mexico 4%.

Transport and communications

Transport. *Railroads:* none. *Roads* (2000): total length 2,984 km (paved 14%). *Vehicles* (2003): passenger cars 36,952; trucks and buses 7,380. *Air transport* (Belize international airport only; 2001): passenger arrivals 256,564, passenger departures 240,900; cargo loaded 186 metric tons, cargo unloaded 1,272 metric tons. **Communications,** in total units (units per 1,000 persons). Telephone landlines (2007): 34,000 (118); cellular telephone subscribers (2007): 118,000 (411); personal computers (2002): 35,000 (132); total Internet users (2007): 32,000 (111); broadband Internet subscribers (2007): 6,500 (21).

Education and health

Educational attainment (2000). Percentage of population ages 25 and over having: no formal schooling/unknown 37.2%; primary education 40.9%; secondary 11.7%; postsecondary/advanced vocational 6.4%; university 3.8%. **Literacy** (2001): total population ages 14 and over literate 93.4%; males 93.6%; females 93.3%. **Health** (2004): physicians 221 (1 per 1,279 persons); hospital beds 650 (1 per 435 persons); infant mortality rate per 1,000 live births (2007) 21.2; undernourished population (2002–04) 10,000 (4% of total population based on the consumption of a minimum daily requirement of 1,810 calories).

Military

Total active duty personnel (2007): 1,050 (army 100%); foreign troops (2006): British army 30. **Military expenditure as percentage of GDP** (2004): 1.4%; per capita expenditure US$55.

Background

The area was inhabited by the Maya c. 300 BC–AD 900; the ruins of their ceremonial centers, including Caracol and Xunantunich, can still be seen. The Spanish claimed sovereignty from the 16th century but never tried to settle Belize, though they regarded as interlopers the British who did. British logwood cutters arrived in the mid-17th century; Spanish opposition was finally overcome in 1798. When settlers began to penetrate the interior they met with Indian resistance. In 1871 British Honduras became a crown colony, but an unfulfilled provision of an 1859 British-Guatemalan treaty led Guatemala to claim the territory. The situation had not been resolved when Belize was granted its independence in 1981. A British force, stationed there to ensure the new nation's security, was withdrawn after Guatemala officially recognized the territory's independence in 1991.

Recent Developments

Although petroleum exports to the US outpaced tourism and agriculture as the primary source of foreign exchange in 2008, Belize's vulnerability to world economic shocks led during the first half of 2008 to a record increase (6.9%) in the consumer price index (which dropped to 6.4% for the twelve-month figure).

Internet resources: <www.statisticsbelize.org.bz>.

Benin

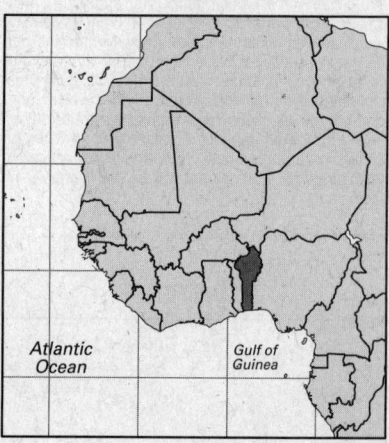

Atlantic Ocean

Gulf of Guinea

Official name: République du Bénin (Republic of Benin). **Form of government:** multiparty republic with one legislative house (National Assembly [83]). **Head of state and government:** President Yayi Boni (from 2006). **Capital:** Porto-Novo (official capital and seat of legislature; administrative seat in Cotonou). **Official language:** French. **Official religion:** none. **Monetary unit:** 1 CFA franc (CFAF) = 100 centimes; valuation (1 Jul 2009) US$1 = CFAF 462.89.

Demography

Area: 43,484 sq mi, 112,622 sq km. **Population** (2008): 8,295,000. **Density** (2008): persons per sq mi 190.8, persons per sq km 73.7. **Urban** (2005): 38.8%. **Sex distribution** (2007): male 49.90%; female 50.10%. **Age breakdown** (2007): under 15, 45.7%; 15–29, 27.3%; 30–44, 15.5%; 45–59, 7.4%; 60–74, 3.4%; 75–84, 0.6%; 85 and over, 0.1%. **Ethnic composition** (2002): Fon 39.2%; Adjara 15.2%; Yoruba (Nago) 12.3%; Bariba 9.2%; Fulani 7.0%; Somba (Otomary) 6.1%; Yoa-Lokpa 4.0%; other 7.0%. **Religious affiliation** (2002): Christian 42.8%, of which Roman Catholic 27.1%, Protestant 5.4%, indigenous Christian 5.3%; Muslim 24.4%; traditional beliefs 23.3%, of which voodoo 17.3%; nonreligious 6.5%; other 3.0%. **Major cities** (2004): Cotonou 818,100; Porto-Novo 234,300; Parakou 227,900; Djougou 206,500; Abomey 126,800. **Location:** western Africa, bordering Burkina Faso, Niger, Nigeria, the Atlantic Ocean, and Togo.

Vital statistics

Birth rate per 1,000 population (2007): 40.4 (world avg. 20.3). **Death rate** per 1,000 population (2007): 10.0 (world avg. 8.6). **Natural increase rate** per 1,000 population (2007): 30.4 (world avg. 11.7). **Total fertility rate** (avg. births per childbearing woman; 2007): 5.66. **Life expectancy** at birth (2007): male 57.0 years; female 59.2 years.

---

1 metric ton = about 1.1 short tons;   1 kilometer = 0.6 mi (statute);   1 metric ton-km cargo = about 0.68 short ton-mi cargo;   c.i.f.: cost, insurance, and freight;   f.o.b.: free on board

National economy

Budget (2005). *Revenue:* CFAF 422,100,000,000 (tax revenue 79.2%; nontax revenue 11.7%; grants 9.1%). *Expenditures:* CFAF 455,300,000,000 (current expenditures 73.4%, of which interest on public debt 1.5%; development expenditures 26.8%; net lending –0.2%). **Public debt** (external, outstanding; 2005): US$1,762,000,000. **Gross national income** (2007): US$5,120,000,000 (US$570 per capita). **Production** (metric tons except as noted). *Agriculture and fishing* (2007): cassava 2,525,000, yams 2,240,000, corn (maize) 900,000, seed cotton 313,500, oil palm fruit 275,000; livestock (number of live animals) 1,900,000 cattle, 1,439,600 goats, 811,200 sheep; fisheries production (2005) 38,407 (from aquaculture, negligible). *Mining* (2006): insignificant production of clay and gold. *Manufacturing* (value added in US$'000,000; 1999): food products 74; textiles 42; beverages 36. *Energy production (consumption):* electricity (kW-hr; 2005) 107,000,000 (702,000,000); crude petroleum (barrels; 2005) 137,000 (negligible); petroleum products (metric tons; 2005) none (796,000). **Population economically active** (2002): total 2,830,900; activity rate of total population 41.4% (participation rates: ages 15–64 [1997] 84.3%; female [1998] 50.8%; unemployed in Cotonou [April 2003] 6.8%). **Selected balance of payments data.** *Receipts from* (US$'000,000): tourism (2005) 103; remittances (2007) 173; foreign direct investment (2004–06 avg.) 60; official development assistance (2006) 375. *Disbursements for* (US$'000,000): tourism (2005) 27; remittances (2007) 40.

Foreign trade

Imports (2005): CFAF 454,600,000,000 (food products 31.2%; refined petroleum products 14.7%; machinery and transportation equipment 13.6%). *Major import sources* (2004): China 32%; France 13%; Thailand 7%; Côte d'Ivoire 5%. **Exports** (2005): CFAF 300,000,000,000 (domestic exports 59.5%, of which cotton 30.4%; reexports 40.5%). *Major export destinations* (2004): China 30%; India 19%; Ghana 6%; Niger 6%; Nigeria 4%.

Transport and communications

Transport. *Railroads* (2002): length (2004) 578 km; passenger-km 62,194,000; metric ton-km cargo 88,832,000. *Roads* (2004): total length 19,000 km (paved 9.5%). *Vehicles:* passenger cars (2002) 103,000; trucks and buses (1996) 8,058. *Air transport* (2003): passengers carried 46,000; metric ton-km cargo 7,000,000. **Communications,** in total units (units per 1,000 persons). Telephone landlines (2007): 110,000 (12); cellular telephone subscribers (2007): 1,895,000 (210); personal computers (2005): 32,000 (4.2); total Internet users (2007): 150,000 (17); broadband Internet subscribers (2007): 2,000 (0.2).

Education and health

Educational attainment (2002). Percentage of population ages 15 and over having: no formal schooling 63.5%; primary education 18.7%; secondary 15.9%; postsecondary 1.9%. **Literacy** (2005): percentage of total population ages 15 and over literate 43.2%; males literate 58.8%; females literate 28.4%. **Health**

(2001): physicians 923 (1 per 7,183 persons); hospital beds 590 (1 per 11,238 persons); infant mortality rate per 1,000 live births (2007) 67.8; undernourished population (2002–04) 800,000 (12% of total population based on the consumption of a minimum daily requirement of 1,800 calories).

Military

Total active duty personnel (2007): 4,750 (army 90.5%, navy 2.1%, air force 7.4%). **Military expenditure as percentage of GNI** (2005): 1.7%; per capita expenditure US$10.

Background

In southern Benin, the Dahomey, or Fon, established the Abomey kingdom in 1625. In the 18th century, the kingdom became known as Dahomey when it expanded to include Allada and Ouidah, where French forts had been established in the 17th century. In 1857 the French reestablished themselves in the area, and eventually fighting ensued. In 1894 Dahomey became a French protectorate; it was incorporated into the federation of French West Africa in 1904. It achieved independence in 1960. The area called Dahomey was renamed Benin in 1975. Its chronically weak economy produced tension between laborers and the government into the 21st century.

Recent Developments

In March 2008, ministers from Benin and Burkina Faso reached an agreement on lowering tensions in a 68-sq-km (26-sq-mi) border area claimed by both. Meeting at Porga in northern Benin, the delegations agreed that neither would attempt to establish sovereignty over the disputed region and that joint border patrols would operate to maintain security.

Internet resources: <http://benintourisme.com/?lang=en>.

Bhutan

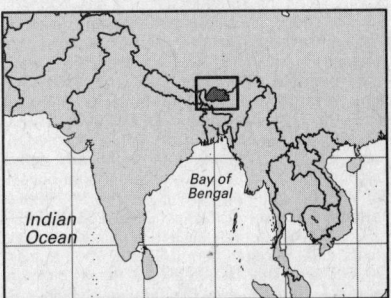

Official name: Druk-Yul (Kingdom of Bhutan). **Form of government:** constitutional monarchy with two legislative houses (National Council [25]; National Assembly [47]). **Chief of state:** King Jigme Khesar Namgyal Wangchuk (from 2006). **Head of government:** Prime Minister Lyonchen Jigmi Thinley (from 2008). **Capital:** Thimphu. **Official language:** Dzongkha (a Tibetan dialect). **Official religion:** Mahayana Buddhism. **Monetary unit:** 1 ngultrum (Nu) = 100 chetrum; valuation (1 Jul 2009) US$1 = Nu 47.85 (the Indian rupee is also accepted as legal tender).

Demography

Area: 14,824 sq mi, 38,394 sq km. **Population** (2008): 682,000. **Density** (2008): persons per sq mi 46.0, persons per sq km 17.8. **Urban** (2005): 30.9%. **Sex distribution** (2005): male 54.20%; female 45.80%. **Age breakdown** (2005): under 15, 33.1%; 15–29, 32.0%; 30–44, 17.5%; 45–59, 10.4%; 60–74, 5.5%; 75–84, 1.3%; 85 and over, 0.2%. **Ethnic composition** (2005): Bhutia (Ngalops) 50%; Nepalese (Gurung) 35%; Sharchops 15%. **Religious affiliation** (2005): Buddhist 74%; Hindu 25%; Christian 1%. **Major towns** (2001): Thimphu 50,510; Phuentsholing 13,292; Gedu 7,826; Gelaphu 6,384; Samtse 3,703. **Location:** southern Asia, bordering China and India.

Vital statistics

Birth rate per 1,000 population (2005): 20.5 (world avg. 20.3). **Death rate** per 1,000 population (2005): 7.5 (world avg. 8.6). **Natural increase rate** per 1,000 population (2005): 13.0 (world avg. 11.7). **Total fertility rate** (avg. births per childbearing woman; 2005): 2.55. **Life expectancy** at birth (2005): male 62.9 years; female 66.4 years.

National economy

Budget (2005–06). *Revenue:* Nu 13,534,000,000 (grants 47.2%; tax revenue 27.8%; nontax revenue 22.5%; other 2.5%). *Expenditures:* Nu 16,151,-000,000 (capital expenditures 55.1%; current expenditures 44.9%). **Public debt** (external, outstanding; September 2007): US$756,200,000. **Production** (metric tons except as noted). *Agriculture and fishing* (2007): corn (maize) 94,500, rice 69,000, potatoes 57,000, ginger 7,350, nutmeg, mace, and cardamom 5,800, mustard seed 4,500; livestock (number of live animals) 385,000 cattle, 35,000 pigs, 26,000 horses; fisheries production (2005) 300 (from aquaculture, negligible). *Mining and quarrying* (2006): limestone 550,000; dolomite 410,000; gypsum 160,000; ferrosilicon 20,000. *Manufacturing* (value of sales in Nu '000,000; 2005): chemical products 857; cement 807; ferroalloys 651; wood board products 158. *Energy production (consumption):* electricity (kW-hr; 2005) 2,355,000,000 (739,000,000); coal (metric tons; 2005) 51,000 (65,000); petroleum products (metric tons; 2005) none (51,000). **Population economically active** (2005): total 257,000; activity rate of total population 38.2% (officially unemployed 3.1%). **Gross national income** (2007): US$1,166,000,000 (US$1,770 per capita). **Selected balance of payments data.** Receipts from (US$'000,000): tourism (2006) 24; remittances (2005) 1.5; foreign direct investment (2004–06 avg.) 6; official development assistance (2006) 94.

Foreign trade

Imports (2005; c.i.f.): Nu 17,035,000,000 (machinery, transportation equipment, and base and fabricated metals 45.5%; mineral fuels 16.1%; food and beverages 14.9%; textiles 4.2%). *Major import sources:* India 75.1%; Japan 3.8%; Singapore 2.6%; Thailand 1.6%; South Korea 1.5%. **Exports** (2005; f.o.b.): Nu 11,386,000,000 (electricity 30.2%; copper wire and cable 9.6%; calcium carbide 6.2%; ferroalloys 6.0%; cement 5.4%). *Major export destinations:* India 87.6%; Hong Kong 6.0%; Bangladesh 4.9%.

Transport and communications

Transport. *Railroads:* none. *Roads* (2004): total length 4,153 km (paved 59%). *Vehicles* (2003): passenger cars 10,574; trucks and buses 3,852. *Air transport* (2002): passenger-km 61,000,000; metric ton-km cargo 5,700,000. **Communications,** in total units (units per 1,000 persons). Telephone landlines (2007): 30,000 (34); cellular telephone subscribers (2007): 149,000 (172); personal computers (2005): 13,000 (16); total Internet users (2007): 40,000 (46).

Education and health

Literacy (2005): total population ages 6 and over literate 59.5%; males literate 69.1%; females literate 48.7%. **Health** (2003): physicians 140 (1 per 5,245 persons); hospital beds 1,093 (1 per 672 persons); infant mortality rate per 1,000 live births (2005) 48.8.

Military

Total active duty personnel (2002): about 6,000 (army 100%). **Military expenditure as percentage of GDP** (2005): 1.0%; per capita expenditure US$11.

Background

Bhutan's mountains and forests long made it inaccessible to the outside world, and its feudal rulers banned foreigners until well into the 20th century. In 1865 it came under British influence, and in 1910 it agreed to be guided by Britain in its foreign affairs. India took over Britain's role in 1949, and China's 1950 occupation of neighboring Tibet further strengthened Bhutan's ties with India. The apparent Chinese threat made Bhutan's rulers aware of the need to modernize, and it embarked on a program to build roads and hospitals and to create a system of secular education. The transition from an absolute monarchy to a parliamentary democracy was completed in March 2008, and a new constitution was promulgated in July.

Recent Developments

Thanks to a boom in tourism and hydropower, Bhutan's economic growth rate stood at 8% in 2008. Living standards were among the region's highest, with an average per capita income of more than US$1,400. Hydropower exports to India drove GDP growth, and total exports to India in 2006–07 amounted to about US$200 million. Indian Prime Minister Manmohan Singh visited Bhutan in May 2008 and addressed a joint session of the parliament.

Internet resources: <www.rma.org.bt>.

---

1 metric ton = about 1.1 short tons; 1 kilometer = 0.6 mi (statute); 1 metric ton-km cargo = about 0.68 short ton-mi cargo; c.i.f.: cost, insurance, and freight; f.o.b.: free on board

Bolivia

Caribbean Sea

Atlantic Ocean

Pacific Ocean

Official name: República de Bolivia (Republic of Bolivia). **Form of government:** unitary multiparty republic with two legislative houses (Chamber of Senators [27]; Chamber of Deputies [130]). **Head of state and government:** President Evo Morales (from 2006). **Capitals:** La Paz (executive and legislative); Sucre (judicial). **Official languages:** Spanish and 36 indigenous languages. **Official religion:** none. **Monetary unit:** 1 boliviano (Bs) = 100 centavos; valuation (1 Jul 2009) US$1 = Bs 6.89.

Demography

Area: 424,164 sq mi, 1,098,581 sq km. **Population** (2008): 9,694,000. **Density** (2008): persons per sq mi 22.9, persons per sq km 8.8. **Urban** (2005): 64.2%. **Sex distribution** (2006): male 49.85%; female 50.15%. **Age breakdown** (2005): under 15, 38.1%; 15–29, 27.1%; 30–44, 17.6%; 45–59, 10.4%; 60–74, 5.3%; 75–84, 1.3%; 85 and over, 0.2%. **Ethnic composition** (2001): Amerindian 62%, of which Quechua 31%, Aymara 25%; mestizo 28%; white 10%, of which German 3%. **Religious affiliation** (2001): Roman Catholic 78%; Protestant/independent Christian 16%; other Christian 3%, of which Mormon 1.8%; nonreligious 2.5%; other 0.5%. **Major cities** (2001): Santa Cruz 1,116,059 (urban agglomeration [2005] 1,320,000); La Paz 789,585 (urban agglomeration [2005] 1,527,000); El Alto 647,350; Cochabamba 516,683; Oruro 201,230. **Location:** central South America, bordering Brazil, Paraguay, Argentina, Chile, and Peru.

Did you know? The Bolivian national bird is the Andean condor. The largest flying bird in the world, it has a wingspan that has been measured at 3.2 meters (10.5 feet).

Vital statistics

Birth rate per 1,000 population (2007): 27.9 (world avg. 20.3). **Death rate** per 1,000 population (2007): 7.6 (world avg. 8.6). **Natural increase rate** per 1,000 population (2007): 20.3 (world avg. 11.7). **Total fertility rate** (avg. births per childbearing woman; 2007): 3.54. **Life expectancy** at birth (2007): male 63.3 years; female 67.5 years.

National economy

Budget (2006). *Revenue:* Bs 30,071,900,000 (taxes on hydrocarbons 35.4%; other tax income 49.5%; other 15.1%). *Expenditures:* Bs 26,876,500,000 (current expenditures 65.3%; capital expenditures 34.7%). **Public debt** (external, outstanding; 2006): US$3,203,000,000. **Production** (metric tons except as noted). *Agriculture and fishing* (2007): sugarcane 6,200,000, soybeans 1,900,000, potatoes 755,000 (Bolivia was the third largest producer of coca in the world in 2005); livestock (number of live animals) 8,990,000 sheep, 7,515,000 cattle, 2,490,000 pigs, (2004) 1,900,000 llamas and alpacas; fisheries production (2006) 7,130 (from aquaculture 6%). *Mining and quarrying* (metal content; 2005): zinc 157,019; tin 18,694; silver 420; gold 8,906 kg. *Manufacturing* (value added in Bs '000,000; 2004): food products 1,545; beverages and tobacco products 581; refined petroleum products 497. *Energy production (consumption):* electricity (kW-hr; 2005) 5,230,000,000 (5,235,000,000); crude petroleum (barrels; 2005) 16,600,000 (15,800,000); petroleum products (metric tons; 2005) 1,639,000 (1,849,000); natural gas (cu m; 2005) 11,875,000,000 (997,000,000). **Population economically active** (2000): total 3,823,937; activity rate of total population 46.2% (participation rates: ages 15–64, 71.8%; female 44.6%; unemployed [2006] 8% in urban areas; underemployment widespread). **Gross national income** (2007): US$11,964,000,000 (US$1,260 per capita). **Selected balance of payments data.** Receipts from (US$'000,000): tourism (2006) 201; remittances (2007) 870; foreign direct investment (FDI) (2004–06 avg.) 22; official development assistance (2006) 581. Disbursements for (US$'000,000): tourism (2006) 226; remittances (2007) 73; FDI (2004–06 avg.) 3.

Foreign trade

Imports (2006; c.i.f.): US$2,824,200,000 (chemical products 17.6%; road vehicles 10.5%; refined petroleum products 9.4%; specialized industrial machinery 9.1%; base metals 7.1%). *Major import sources:* Brazil 20.4%; Argentina 15.8%; US 12.1%; Chile 8.3%; Japan 7.9%. **Exports** (2006; f.o.b.): US$4,223,300,000 (natural gas 39.5%; zinc 13.0%; crude petroleum 8.2%; soybeans 8.2%; silver 3.9%; gold 3.0%). *Major export destinations:* Brazil 37.7%; US 9.8%; Argentina 9.3%; Japan 9.0%; Peru 5.9%.

Transport and communications

Transport. *Railroads* (1997): route length (2004) 3,519 km; passenger-km 224,900,000; metric ton-km cargo 838,900,000. *Roads* (2004): total length 62,479 km (paved 7%). *Vehicles* (2004): passenger cars 171,642; trucks and buses 173,864. *Air transport* (2006): passenger-km 1,056,000,000; metric ton-km cargo 7,668,000. **Communications,** in total units (units per 1,000 persons). Telephone landlines (2007): 678,000 (71); cellular telephone subscribers (2007): 3,254,000 (342); personal computers (2004): 210,000 (23); total Internet users (2007): 198,000 (21); broadband Internet subscribers (2007): 34,000 (3.6).

Education and health

Educational attainment (2003). Percentage of population ages 19 and over having: no formal schooling/unknown 14.8%; some to complete primary education 44.9%; some to complete secondary 24.8%; some to complete higher 15.5%. **Literacy** (2003): percentage of total population ages 15 and over literate 87.2%; males literate 93.1%; females literate 81.6%. **Health:** physicians (2002) 2,987 (1 per 2,827 persons); hospital beds (2005) 9,886 (1 per 954 persons); infant mortality rate per 1,000 live births (2007) 46.5; undernourished population (2002–04) 2,000,000 (23% of total population based on the consumption of a minimum daily requirement of 1,780 calories).

Military

Total active duty personnel (2007): 46,100 (army 75.5%, navy 10.4%, air force 14.1%). **Military expenditure as percentage of GDP** (2005): 1.6%; per capita expenditure US$16.

Background

The Bolivian highlands were the location of the advanced Tiwanaku culture in the 7th–11th centuries and, with its passing, became the home of the Aymara, an Indian group conquered by the Incas in the 15th century. The Incas were overrun by the invading Spanish under Francisco Pizarro in the 1530s. By 1600 Spain had established the cities of Charcas (now Sucre), La Paz, Santa Cruz, and what would become Cochabamba and had begun to exploit the silver wealth of Potosí. Bolivia flourished in the 17th century, and for a time Potosí was the largest city in the Americas. By the end of the century, the mineral wealth had dried up. Talk of independence began as early as 1809, but not until 1825 were Spanish forces finally defeated. Bolivia shrank in size when it lost Atacama province to Chile in 1884 at the end of the War of the Pacific and again in 1939 when it lost most of Gran Chaco to Paraguay. One of South America's poorest countries, it was plagued by governmental instability for much of the 20th century. Social and economic tension continued in the early 21st century, fueled by resistance to government efforts to eradicate the growth of coca (from which the narcotic cocaine is derived), by unrest among Bolivia's Indians, and by disagreements over how to exploit the country's vast natural gas reserves.

Recent Developments

Pres. Evo Morales, who had nationalized most of the petroleum industry in 2006, remained determined in 2008 to distribute export revenues widely among Bolivians. The resulting stimulus at a time of high world energy prices led Bolivia's GDP to grow by 6.2%. His willingness to nationalize key industries was predicted to prove controversial in the future, as Bolivia possessed half of the world's known reserves of lithium, a key component in battery production and the growing field of electric-car manufacturing.

Internet resources: <www.ine.gov.bo>.

Bosnia and Herzegovina

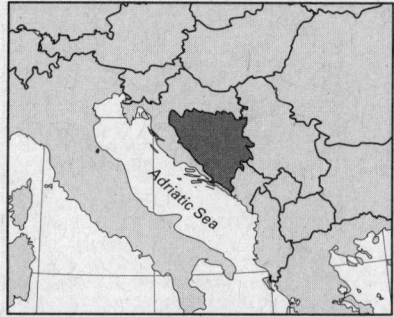

Official name: Bosna i Hercegovina (Bosnia and Herzegovina). **Form of government:** emerging republic with bicameral legislature (House of Peoples [15]; House of Representatives [42]). **Chiefs of state:** tripartite presidency with 8-month-long rotating chairmanship (final authority rests with International High Representative Miroslav Lajčák [from 2007]). **Head of government:** Prime Minister Nebojsa Radmanovic (from 2008). **Capital:** Sarajevo. **Official language:** Bosnian; Croatian; Serbian. **Official religion:** none. **Monetary unit:** 1 convertible marka (KM; plural maraka) = 100 feninga; valuation (1 Jul 2009) US$1 = KM 1.39 (the euro [€] also circulates as semiofficial legal tender).

Demography

Area: 19,772 sq mi, 51,209 sq km. **Population** (2008): 3,858,000. **Density** (2008): persons per sq mi 195.1, persons per sq km 75.3. **Urban** (2005): 45.7%. **Sex distribution** (2005): male 48.63%; female 51.37%. **Age breakdown** (2005): under 15, 17.6%; 15–29, 21.6%; 30–44, 22.8%; 45–59, 18.9%; 60–74, 15.5%; 75–84, 3.3%; 85 and over, 0.3%. **Ethnic composition** (1999): Bosniac 44.0%; Serb 31.0%; Croat 17.0%; other 8.0%. **Religious affiliation** (2002): Sunni Muslim 40%; Serbian Orthodox 31%; Roman Catholic 15%; Protestant 4%; nonreligious/other 10%. **Major cities** (2005): Sarajevo 380,000 (urban agglomeration [2004] 602,500); Banja Luka 165,100; Zenica 84,300; Tuzla 84,100; Mostar 63,500. **Location:** southeastern Europe, bordered by Croatia, Serbia, Montenegro, and the Adriatic Sea.

Vital statistics

Birth rate per 1,000 population (2007): 8.8 (world avg. 20.3); (2005) within marriage 88.8%; outside of marriage 11.2%. **Death rate** per 1,000 population (2007): 8.6 (world avg. 8.6). **Natural increase rate** per 1,000 population (2007): 0.2 (world avg. 11.7). **Total fertility rate** (avg. births per childbearing woman; 2005): 1.19. **Life expectancy** at birth (2005): male 71 years; female 77 years.

National economy

Budget (2004). *Revenue:* KM 6,191,000,000 (indirect taxes 42.1%; social security contributions 30.1%;

---

1 metric ton = about 1.1 short tons; 1 kilometer = 0.6 mi (statute); 1 metric ton-km cargo = about 0.68 short ton-mi cargo; c.i.f.: cost, insurance, and freight; f.o.b.: free on board

taxes on trade 8.1%; other 19.7%). *Expenditures:* KM 6,601,000,000 (current expenditures 87.3%; development expenditures 12.3%). **Gross national income** (2007): US$14,051,000,000 (US$3,580 per capita). **Production** (metric tons except as noted). *Agriculture and fishing* (2007): corn (maize) 635,344, potatoes 387,239, wheat 257,112; livestock (number of live animals) 1,000,000 sheep, 712,000 pigs, 515,000 cattle, in addition, 285,000 beehives; fisheries production (2006) 9,626 (from aquaculture 79%). *Mining* (2005): bauxite 900,000; iron ore (metal content) 150,000; lime 120,000. *Manufacturing* (value of exports in KM '000,000; 2003): base metals and fabricated metal products 498.3; wood products 398.9; machinery and apparatus 286.1. *Energy production (consumption):* electricity (kW-hr; 2005) 12,718,-000,000 (11,312,000,000); hard coal (metric tons; 2005) 3,550,000 (3,550,000); lignite (metric tons; 2005) 9,040,000 (9,380,000); petroleum products (metric tons; 2005) none (1,165,000); natural gas (cu m; 2005) none (437,000,000). **Public debt** (external, outstanding; 2006): US$2,830,000,000. **Population economically active** (2006): total 1,177,000; activity rate of total population 30.6% (participation rates: ages 15–64, 51.3%; female 36%; unemployed 31.1%). **Selected balance of payments data.** Receipts from (US$'000,000): tourism (2006) 592; remittances (2007) 2,514; foreign direct investment (2004–06 avg.) 537; official development assistance (2006) 494. Disbursements for (US$'000,000): tourism (2006) 158; remittances (2007) 65.

Foreign trade

Imports (2006; c.i.f.): US$7,559,000,000 (machinery and apparatus 16.2%; food products 12.4%; crude petroleum 11.5%; chemical products 10.7%; road vehicles 6.4%). *Major import sources:* Croatia 17.1%; Germany 12.4%; Serbia 9.8%; Italy 9.0%; Slovenia 7.6%. **Exports** (2006; f.o.b.): US$3,428,-000,000 (aluminum 10.2%; base metals 7.0%; fabricated metal products 6.6%; engine parts 6.1%; footwear 5.7%). *Major export destinations:* Croatia 18.7%; Italy 13.8%; Serbia 13.2%; Germany 12.9%; Slovenia 12.2%.

Transport and communications

Transport. *Railroads* (2004): length 1,021 km; passenger-km (2005) 51,396,000; metric ton-km cargo (2005) 1,159,000,000. *Roads* (2005) total length 22,419 km (paved [2001] 64%). *Vehicles* (1996): passenger cars 96,182; trucks and buses 10,919. *Air transport* (2001) passenger-km 44,000,000; metric ton-km (2003) 1,000,000. **Communications,** in total units (units per 1,000 persons). Telephone landlines (2007) 1,065,000 (271); cellular telephone subscribers (2007): 2,450,000 (623); total Internet users (2007): 1,055,000 (268); broadband Internet subscribers (2007): 85,000 (22).

Education and health

Educational attainment (2004). Percentage of population ages 18 and over having: no formal schooling 8.0%; some to complete primary education 31.9%; lower secondary 24.4%; upper secondary 26.6%; higher 4.9%; advanced 4.2%. **Literacy** (2002): total population ages 15 and over literate 94.6%; males literate 98.4%; females literate 91.1%. **Health:** physicians (2004) 5,004 (1 per 769 persons); hospital beds (2003) 11,981 (1 per 322 persons); infant mortality rate per 1,000 live births (2007) 5.3; undernourished population (2002–04) 350,000 (9% of total population based on the consumption of a minimum daily requirement of 2,000 calories).

Military

Total active duty personnel: EU-sponsored (EUFOR) peacekeeping troops (November 2007) 2,450. **Military expenditure as percentage of GDP** (2005): 1.9%; per capita expenditure US$46.

Background

Habitation long predates the era of Roman rule, when much of the country was included in the province of Dalmatia. Slav settlement began in the 6th century AD. For the next several centuries, parts of the region fell under the rule of Serbs, Croats, Hungarians, Venetians, and Byzantines. The Ottoman Turks invaded Bosnia in the 14th century, and after many battles it became a Turkish province in 1463. Herzegovina, then known as Hum, was taken in 1482. In the 16th–17th centuries the area was an important Turkish outpost, constantly at war with the Habsburgs and Venice. During this period much of the native population converted to Islam. At the Congress of Berlin after the Russo-Turkish War of 1877–78, Bosnia and Herzegovina was assigned to Austria-Hungary, and it was fully annexed in 1908. Growing Serb nationalism resulted in the 1914 assassination of the Austrian archduke Francis Ferdinand at Sarajevo by a Bosnian Serb, an event that precipitated World War I. After the war the area was annexed to Serbia. Following World War II the twin territory became a republic of communist Yugoslavia. With the collapse of communist regimes in Eastern Europe, Bosnia and Herzegovina declared its independence in 1992; its Serb population objected, and conflict ensued among Serbs, Croats, and Muslims. The 1995 peace accord established a loosely federated government roughly divided between a Muslim-Croat Federation and a Serb Republic (Republika Srpska). From 1996 to 2002 an EU peacekeeping force was installed there.

Recent Developments

Bosnia and Herzegovina's June 2008 signing of the Stabilization and Association Agreement (SAA) signaled the first concrete step in the country's path toward EU membership. Both the Muslim-Croatian Federation and the Republika Srpska approved laws for police reform, a requirement that needed to occur prior to the SAA signing. Agreement on state property law, another key requirement for EU integration, was reached in April 2009.

Internet resources: <www.bhas.ba/eng>.

Botswana

Official name: Republic of Botswana. **Form of government:** multiparty republic with one legislative body (National Assembly [63]). **Head of state and government:** President Ian Khama (from 2008). **Capital:** Gaborone. **Official language:** English (Tswana is the national language). **Official religion:** none. **Monetary unit:** 1 pula (P) = 100 thebe; valuation (1 Jul 2009) US$1 = P 6.66.

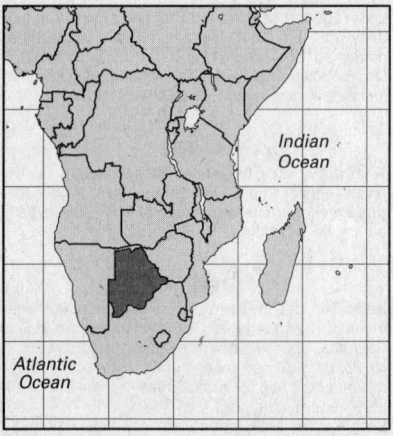

(2007): sorghum 33,000, corn (maize) 12,000, sunflower seeds 7,000; livestock (number of live animals) 3,100,000 cattle, 1,960,000 goats, 300,000 sheep; fisheries production (2005) 132 (from aquaculture, none). *Mining and quarrying* (2006): soda ash 255,677; nickel ore (metal content) 38,000; copper ore (metal content) 24,300; diamonds 34,293,000 carats (about 70% gem and near-gem quality; Botswana is the world's leading producer of diamonds by value). *Manufacturing* (value added in US$'000,000; 2004): beverages 50; motor vehicles (1997) 33; textiles 12. *Energy production (consumption):* electricity (kW-hr; 2005) 912,000,000 (2,602,000,000); hard coal (metric tons; 2006) 962,000 ([2004] 916,000). **Gross national income** (2007): US$10,991,000,000 (US$5,840 per capita). **Selected balance of payments data.** Receipts from (US$'000,000): tourism (2006) 537; remittances (2007) 117; foreign direct investment (2004–06 avg.) 316; official development assistance (2006) 65. Disbursements for (US$'000,000): tourism (2006) 277; remittances (2007) 118.

Demography

Area: 224,848 sq mi, 582,356 sq km. **Population** (2008): 1,842,000. **Density** (2008): persons per sq mi 8.2, persons per sq km 3.2. **Urban** (2005): 53.6%. **Sex distribution** (2007): male 50.07%; female 49.93%. **Age breakdown** (2007): under 15, 35.8%; 15–29, 33.7%; 30–44, 16.3%; 45–59, 8.7%; 60–74, 3.9%; 75–84, 1.2%; 85 and over, 0.4%. **Ethnic composition** (2000): Tswana 66.8%; Kalanga 14.8%; Ndebele 1.7%; Herero 1.4%; San (Bushman) 1.3%; Afrikaner 1.3%; other 12.7%. **Religious affiliation** (2005): independent Christian 41.7%; traditional beliefs 35.0%; Protestant 12.8%; Muslim 0.3%; Hindu 0.2%; other 10.0%. **Major cities** (2004): Gaborone 199,600; Francistown 89,100; Molepolole 58,600; Selebi-Pikwe 53,500; Maun 47,000. **Location:** southern Africa, bordered by Namibia, Zimbabwe, and South Africa.

Vital statistics

Birth rate per 1,000 population (2007): 23.2 (world avg. 20.3). **Death rate** per 1,000 population (2007): 13.6 (world avg. 8.6). **Total fertility rate** (avg. births per childbearing woman; 2007): 2.73. **Life expectancy** at birth (2007): male 51.6 years; female 49.6 years.

National economy

Budget (2005–06). *Revenue:* P 21,697,300,000 (tax revenue 88.2%, of which mineral royalties 50.2%, customs duties and excise tax 16.1%; nontax revenue 10.8%; grants 1.0%). *Expenditures:* P 20,122,200,000 (general government services including defense 27.7%; education 24.5%; economic services 15.4%; health 12.4%; transfers 9.0%). **Public debt** (external, outstanding; 2006): US$384,000,000. **Population economically active** (2001): total 587,882; activity rate of total population 35.0% (participation rates: ages 15–64, 57.6%; female 43.8%; unemployed, [2004] more than 20%). **Production** (metric tons except as noted). *Agriculture and fishing*

Foreign trade

Imports (2005; c.i.f.): US$3,247,000,000 (machinery and apparatus 16.3%; food, beverages, and tobacco 13.7%; mineral fuels 13.3%; transportation equipment 12.5%; chemical and rubber products 11.9%). *Major import sources:* Customs Union of Southern Africa (CUSA) 85.1%; Europe 6.5%; Zimbabwe 1.5%. **Exports** (2005; f.o.b.): US$4,395,000,000 (diamonds 75.1%; copper-nickel matte 10.3%; textiles 5.0%; meat products 1.7%). *Major export destinations:* Europe 77.0%, of which UK 75.7%; CUSA 9.0%; Zimbabwe 4.1%.

Transport and communications

Transport. *Railroads* (2001): route length (2002) 888 km; passenger-km 106,000,000; metric ton-km cargo 747,000,000. *Roads* (2004): total length 24,455 km (paved 33%). *Vehicles* (2005): passenger cars 82,056; trucks and buses 74,387. *Air transport* (Air Botswana only; 2002): passenger-km 96,000,000; metric ton-km cargo 300,000. **Communications,** in total units (units per 1,000 persons). Telephone landlines (2006): 137,000 (78); cellular telephone subscribers (2007): 1,427,000 (758); personal computers (2005): 86,000 (49); total Internet users (2007): 80,000 (43); broadband Internet subscribers (2005): 1,600.

Education and health

Educational attainment (1993). Percentage of population ages 25 and over having: no formal schooling 34.7%; primary education 44.1%; some secondary 19.8%; postsecondary 1.4%. **Literacy** (2005): percentage of total population ages 16 and over literate 81.4%; males literate 78.6%; females literate 84.1%. **Health** (2006): physicians 526 (1 per 3,346 persons); hospital beds 3,911 (1 per 450 persons); infant mortality rate per 1,000 live births (2007) 44.0; undernourished population (2002–04) 600,000 (32% of total population based on the consumption of a minimum daily requirement of 1,860 calories).

---

1 metric ton = about 1.1 short tons;   1 kilometer = 0.6 mi (statute);   1 metric ton-km cargo = about 0.68 short ton-mi cargo;   c.i.f.: cost, insurance, and freight;   f.o.b.: free on board

Military

Total active duty personnel (2007): 9,000 (army 94.4%, air force 5.6%). Military expenditure as percentage of GDP (2005): 3.0%; per capita expenditure US$177.

Background

The region's earliest inhabitants were the Khoekhoe and San (Bushmen). Sites were settled as early as AD 190 during the southerly migration of Bantu-speaking farmers. Tswana dynasties, which developed in the western Transvaal in the 13th–14th centuries, moved into Botswana in the 18th century and established several powerful states. European missionaries arrived in the early 19th century, but it was the discovery of gold in 1867 that excited European interest. In 1885 the area became the British Bechuanaland Protectorate. The next year the region south of the Molopo River became a crown colony, and it was annexed by the Cape Colony 10 years later. Bechuanaland itself continued as a British protectorate until the 1960s. In 1966 the Republic of Bechuanaland (later Botswana) was proclaimed an independent member of the British Commonwealth. Independent Botswana tried to maintain a delicate balance between its economic dependence on South Africa and its relations with the surrounding black countries; the independence of Namibia in 1990 and South Africa's rejection of apartheid eased tensions.

Recent Developments

Botswana, the world's leading producer of diamonds by value, opened a new rough-diamond sorting center in March 2008. The center, created in partnership with the De Beers diamond conglomeration, increased manufacturing employment in the country by some 10%. It also marked the first instance in which the entire diamond trade process—from mining to marketing—took place within the country.

Internet resources: <www.cso.gov.bw>.

Brazil

Official name: República Federativa do Brasil (Federative Republic of Brazil). Form of government: multiparty federal republic with two legislative houses (Federal Senate [81]; Chamber of Deputies [513]). Chief of state and government: President Luiz Inácio Lula da Silva (from 2003). Capital: Brasília. Official language: Portuguese. Official religion: none. Monetary unit: 1 real (R$; plural reais) = 100 centavos; valuation (1 Jul 2009) US$1 = 1.93 reais.

Demography

Area: 3,287,612 sq mi, 8,514,877 sq km. Population (2008): 187,163,000. Density (2008): persons per sq mi 56.9, persons per sq km 22.0. Urban (2005): 82.8%. Sex distribution (2005): male 49.34%; female 50.66%. Age breakdown (2005): under 15, 27.8%; 15–29, 27.6%; 30–44, 21.7%; 45–59, 14.1%; 60–74, 6.5%; 75–84, 1.8%; 85 and over, 0.5%. Racial composition (2000): white 53.7%; mulatto and mestizo 39.1%; black and black/Amerindian 6.2%; Asian 0.5%; Amerindian 0.4%. Religious affiliation (2005): Roman Catholic 65.1%; Protestant 12.7%, of which Assemblies of God 9.2%; independent Christian 10.7%, of which Universal Church of the Kingdom of God 2.2%; Spiritist (Kardecist) 1.3%; Jehovah's Witness 0.7%; African and syncretic religions 0.4%; Muslim 0.4%; nonreligious/other 8.7%. Major cities (metropolitan areas) (2007): São Paulo 10,238,500 (19,226,426); Rio de Janeiro 6,093,500 (11,563,302); Belo Horizonte 2,412,900 (5,450,084); Porto Alegre 1,379,100 (3,896,515); Recife 1,533,600 (3,654,534); Salvador 2,891,400 (3,598,454); Brasília 2,348,600 (3,507,662); Fortaleza 2,431,400 (3,436,515); Curitiba 1,797,400 (3,124,596); Campinas 1,022,000 (2,635,261); Belém 1,399,800 (2,043,543); Goiânia 1,236,400 (1,973,892); Manaus 1,602,100 (1,612,475); Vitória 314,000 (1,609,532). Location: eastern South America, bordered by Venezuela, Guyana, Suriname, French Guiana, Uruguay, Argentina, Paraguay, Bolivia, Peru, and Colombia. Families. Average family size (2005) 3.2; (1996) 1–2 persons 25.2%, 3 persons 20.3%, 4 persons 22.2%, 5–6 persons 23.3%, 7 or more persons 9.0%. Migration (2000). Brazilian emigrants living abroad 1,887,895; in the US 42.3%, in Paraguay 23.4%, in Japan 12.0%. Foreign-born immigrants living in Brazil 683,830; from Europe 56.3%, of which Portugal 31.2%; South/Central America 21.0%; Asia 17.8%, of which Japan 10.4%.

Vital statistics

Birth rate per 1,000 population (2006): 17.3 (world avg. 20.3). Death rate per 1,000 population (2006): 6.2 (world avg. 8.6). Natural increase rate per 1,000 population (2006): 11.1 (world avg. 11.7). Total fertility rate (avg. births per childbearing woman; 2005): 2.30. Life expectancy at birth (2006): male 68.7 years; female 76.2 years.

Social indicators

Educational attainment (2005). Percentage of population ages 25 and over having: no formal schooling/unknown or less than one year of primary education 15.5%; 1 to 3 years of primary education 13.7%; complete primary/incomplete secondary 40.2%; complete secondary 18.8%; 1 to 3 years of higher education 3.8%; 4 years or more of higher education

8.0%. **Quality of working life.** Proportion of employed population receiving minimum wage (2002) 53.5%. Number and percentage of children (ages 5–17) working 5,400,000 (12.6% of age group). **Access to services** (1999). Proportion of households having access to: electricity (2002) 96.0%, of which urban households having access 98.8%, rural households having access 73.2%; safe public (piped) water supply 79.8%, of which urban households having access 92.3%, rural households having access 24.9%; public (piped) sewage system 43.6%, of which urban households having access 52.5%, rural households having access 4.5%; no sewage disposal 8.5%, of which urban households having no disposal 2.9%, rural households having no disposal 32.9%. **Social participation.** Trade union membership in total workforce (2001) 19,500,000. **Social deviance.** Annual murder rate per 100,000 population (2002): Brazil 28; Rio de Janeiro only, 56; São Paulo only, 54. **Material well-being** (2003). Households possessing: television receiver 89.9%, of which urban 94.5%, rural 69.4%; refrigerator 86.7%, of which urban 91.7%, rural 60.0%; washing machine 34.0%, of which urban 38.1%, rural 10.0%.

National economy

Gross national income (2007): US$1,133,030,-000,000 (US$5,910 per capita). **Budget** (2004): *Revenue:* R$422,450,000,000 (tax revenue 76.4%, of which income tax 24.3%, social security contributions 18.2%; social welfare contributions 22.2%; other 1.4%). *Expenditures:* R$372,730,000,000 (social security and welfare 33.8%; personnel 23.5%; transfers to state and local governments 18.1%; other 24.6%). **Public debt** (external, outstanding; 2005): US$94,497,000,000. **Production** ('000 metric tons except as noted). *Agriculture and fishing* (2007): sugarcane 514,080, soybeans 58,197, corn (maize) 51,590, cassava 27,313, oranges 18,279, rice 11,080, bananas 6,972, wheat 3,998, seed cotton 3,854, potatoes 3,394, tomatoes 3,364, dry beans 3,330, coconuts 2,771, pineapples 2,666, coffee 2,178, papayas 1,898, cashew apples (2006) 1,660, mangoes and guavas 1,546, sorghum 1,386, grapes 1,342, dry onions 1,302, apples 1,094, lemons and limes 1,060, tobacco 919, oil palm fruit 590, maté 435, peanuts (groundnuts) 225, cacao beans 221, cashews 176, natural rubber 106, garlic 93, Brazil nuts (2006) 30; livestock (number of live animals) 207,170,000 cattle, 34,080,000 pigs, 15,600,000 sheep, 5,800,000 horses; fisheries production (2005) 1,008,066 (from aquaculture 26%). *Mining and quarrying* (metric tons; 2004): iron ore (metal content) 169,300,000 (world rank: 1); columbium (niobium) 39,741 of pyrochlore in concentrates (world rank: 1); bauxite 19,700,000 (world rank: 2); manganese (metal content in concentrate) 3,143,000 (world rank: 2); tantalum 277 (world rank: 2); asbestos fiber 231,115 (world rank: 4); tin (mine output; metal content) 12,468 (world rank: 5); kaolin (marketable product) 2,148,000; copper (metal content) 103,153; nickel (metal content in ore) 51,886; gold 47,596 kg; diamonds 300,000 carats. *Energy production (consumption):* electricity (kW·hr; 2006) 412,159,000,000 ([2005] 441,980,000,000); hard coal (metric tons; 2005) 6,250,000 (20,000,000); crude petroleum (barrels; 2007) 645,800,000 ([2005] 627,500,000); petroleum products (metric tons; 2005) 79,814,000 (73,452,000); natural gas (cu m; 2007) 18,151,000,000 ([2005] 17,776,-000,000); ethanol (litres; 2007) 19,000,000,000 (16,700,000,000). **Population economically active** (2004): total 92,860,100; activity rate of total population 51.1% (participation rates: ages 15–64, 73.2%; female 43.1%; unemployed [February 2006–January 2007] 10.0%). **Selected balance of payments data.** Receipts from (US$'000,000): tourism (2006) 4,316; remittances (2007) 4,382; foreign direct investment (FDI) (2004–06 avg.) 17,331; official development assistance (2006) 82. Disbursements for (US$'000,000): tourism (2006) 5,764; remittances (2007) 896; FDI (2004–06 avg.) 13,509.

Foreign trade

Imports (2006): US$91,343,000,000 (mineral fuels 18.8%, of which crude petroleum 9.9%, refined petroleum products 4.7%; chemical products 18.0%, of which organic chemicals 4.9%, medicines and pharmaceuticals 3.3%; road vehicles 6.2%; general industrial machinery 5.1%; microcircuits/transistors 4.3%; telecommunications equipment 4.1%; power-generating machinery 3.8%; food products 3.8%). *Major import sources* (2006): US 16.2%; Argentina 8.8%; China 8.7%; Germany 7.1%; Japan 4.2%; South Korea 3.4%; Chile 3.2%; France 3.1%. **Exports** (2006): US$137,806,000,000 (food products 18.4%, of which meat 6.2%, raw sugar 2.9%, coffee 2.1%; road vehicles 8.6%; base metals 6.9%; chemical products 6.7%, of which organic chemicals 2.7%; iron ore and concentrates 6.5%; soybeans [all forms] 5.0%; crude petroleum 5.0%; power-generating machinery 3.3%; refined petroleum products 2.6%; aircraft/spacecraft 2.5%; specialized industrial machinery 2.5%; telecommunications equipment 2.3%; aluminum 2.0%; wood pulp and waste paper 1.8%). *Major export destinations* (2006): US 18.0%; Argentina 8.5%; China 6.1%; The Netherlands 4.2%; Germany 4.1%; Mexico 3.2%; Japan 2.8%; Italy 2.8%; Chile 2.8%.

Transport and communications

Transport. *Railroads* (2005): route length 29,605 km; passenger-km 5,852,000,000; metric ton-km cargo 154,870,000,000. *Roads* (2004): total length 1,751,868 km (paved [2000] 6%). *Vehicles* (2004): passenger cars 24,936,541; trucks and buses 6,294,502. *Air transport* (2005): passenger-km 50,689,000,000; metric ton-km cargo 1,530,700,000. **Communications,** in total units (units per 1,000 persons). Telephone landlines (2007): 39,400,000 (205); cellular telephone subscribers (2007): 120,980,000 (631); personal computers (2005): 32,130,000 (174); total Internet users (2007): 50,000,000 (261); broadband Internet subscribers (2007): 8,100,000 (44).

Education and health

Literacy (2005): total population ages 15 and over literate (functionally literate) 89.0% (76.5%); males literate (functionally literate) 88.7% (75.9%); females literate (functionally literate) 89.2% (77.0%). **Health:**

---

1 metric ton = about 1.1 short tons;   1 kilometer = 0.6 mi (statute);   1 metric ton-km cargo = about 0.68 short ton-mi cargo;   c.i.f.: cost, insurance, and freight;   f.o.b.: free on board

physicians (2001) 357,888 (1 per 485 persons); hospital beds (2005) 443,210 (1 per 416 persons); infant mortality rate per 1,000 live births (2006) 25.1; undernourished population (2002–04) 13,100,000 (7% of total population based on the consumption of a minimum daily requirement of 1,900 calories).

Military

Total active duty personnel (2007): 367,901 (army 64.7%, navy 16.9%, air force 18.4%). **Military expenditure as percentage of GDP** (2005): 1.6%; per capita expenditure US$68.

Background

Little is known about Brazil's early indigenous inhabitants. Though the area was theoretically allotted to Portugal by the 1494 Treaty of Tordesillas, it was not formally claimed by discovery until Pedro Álvares Cabral accidentally touched land in 1500. It was first settled by the Portuguese in the early 1530s on the southeastern coast and at São Vicente (near modern São Paulo); the French and Dutch created small settlements over the next century. A viceroyalty was established in 1640, and Rio de Janeiro became the capital in 1763. In 1808 Brazil became the refuge and the seat of the government of John VI of Portugal when Napoleon invaded Portugal; ultimately the Kingdom of Portugal, Brazil, and the Algarves was proclaimed, and John ruled from Brazil in 1815–21. On John's return to Portugal, his son Pedro I proclaimed Brazilian independence. In 1889 his successor, Pedro II, was deposed, and a constitution mandating a federal republic was adopted. The 20th century saw increased immigration and growth in manufacturing along with frequent military coups and suspensions of civil liberties. Construction of a new capital at Brasília, intended to spur development of the country's interior, worsened the inflation rate. After 1979 the military government began a gradual return to democratic practices, and in 1989 the first popular presidential election in 29 years was held.

Recent Developments

In 2008 Brazil benefited from a wave of high commodity prices, new infrastructure investment programs, a burgeoning domestic market, and record state and federal revenues. In April Standard & Poor's became the first rating agency to upgrade Brazil to investment-grade status. After riding the commodity boom to its peak in July, however, Brazil witnessed declining liquidity and tighter credit markets as the global economy began its downturn. Notwithstanding this global financial crisis, the Brazilian economy showed continued signs of growth. GDP grew an estimated 11.2% and accumulated inflation reached only 5.9%. Global volatility, however, did affect the Brazilian stock market, which fell nearly 60% in late October from its highest close of 2008. Severe flooding wreaked havoc in the south in late November. The flooding resulted in the deaths of more than 130 people and left tens of thousands homeless and more than one million without power. Flooding occurred in the north in April and May 2009, leaving at least 40 dead and more than 300,000 homeless.

Internet resources: <www.ibge.gov.br/english/default.php>.

Brunei

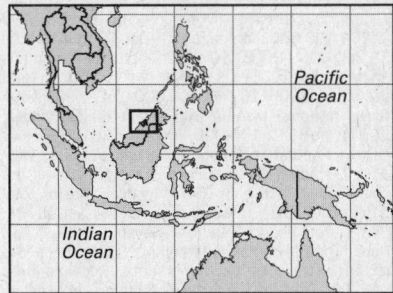

Official name: Negara Brunei Darussalam (State of Brunei, Abode of Peace). **Form of government:** monarchy (sultanate) with one advisory body (Legislative Council [29]). **Head of state and government:** Sultan and Prime Minister Haji Hassanal Bolkiah Mu'izzadin Waddaulah (from 1967). **Capital:** Bandar Seri Begawan. **Official language:** Malay. **Official religion:** Islam. **Monetary unit:** 1 Brunei dollar (B$) = 100 sen; valuation (1 Jul 2009) US$1 = B$1.43.

Demography

Area: 2,226 sq mi, 5,765 sq km. **Population** (2008): 400,000. **Density** (2008): persons per sq mi 179.7, persons per sq km 69.4. **Urban** (2005): 73.5%. **Sex distribution** (2005): male 52.77%; female 47.23%. **Age breakdown** (2005): under 15, 29.5%; 15–29, 28.4%; 30–44, 24.1%; 45–59, 13.2%; 60–74, 4.0%; 75 and over, 0.8%. **Ethnic composition** (2003): Malay 66.6%; Chinese 10.9%; other indigenous 3.6%; other 18.9%. **Religious affiliation** (2004): Muslim 67%; Buddhist 13%; Christian 10%; traditional beliefs/other 10%. **Major cities** (2004): Bandar Seri Begawan (urban agglomeration) 81,500; Kuala Belait 28,400; Seria 23,500. **Location:** southeastern Asia, bordering the South China Sea and Malaysia.

Vital statistics

Birth rate per 1,000 population (2005): 19.9 (world avg. 20.3). **Death rate** per 1,000 population (2005): 2.8 (world avg. 8.6). **Natural increase rate** per 1,000 population (2005): 17.1 (world avg. 11.7). **Total fertility rate** (avg. births per childbearing woman; 2005): 2.10. **Life expectancy** at birth (2005): male 74.6 years; female 77.5 years.

National economy

Budget (2005–06). *Revenue:* B$8,441,000,000 (tax revenue 62.2%, of which taxes on petroleum and natural gas companies 59.1%; nontax revenue 37.8%, of which dividends paid by petroleum companies 22.9%, petroleum and natural gas royalties 10.0%). *Expenditures:* B$5,086,000,000 (current expenditures 80.1%; capital expenditures 19.9%). **Production** (metric tons except as noted). *Agriculture and fishing* (2007): cassava 1,800, rice 1,200, pineapples 990; livestock (number of live animals) 4,580 buffalo, 15,500,000 chickens; fisheries production (2005) 3,108 (from aquaculture 23%). *Mining and quarrying:* sand and gravel for construction. *Manufacturing* (value added in B$'000,000; 2005): liquefied natural gas 1,672; textiles and apparel 197; other manufactures 83. *Energy production (consumption):* electricity (kW-hr; 2005) 3,264,000,000 (3,264,000,000); crude petroleum (barrels; 2006) 72,300,000 ([2005] 100,000); petroleum products (metric tons; 2005) 1,115,000 (1,136,000); natural gas (cu m; 2005) 10,364,000,000 (1,476,000,000). **Gross national income** (at current market prices; 2007): US$12,400,000,000 (US$31,523 per capita). **Population economically active** (2001): total 157,594 (foreign workers accounted for 70% of the economically active in 2004); activity rate of total population 45.2% (participation rates: ages 15–64, 65.9%; female 41.2%; unemployed [2005] 4.3%). **Public debt** (external, outstanding; 2005): none. **Selected balance of payments data.** Receipts from (US$'000,000): tourism (2006) 224; foreign direct investment (FDI) (2004–06 avg.) 352. Disbursements for (US$'000,000): tourism (2006) 408; remittances (2003) 139; FDI (2004–06 avg.) 26.

Foreign trade

Imports (2006; c.i.f.): US$1,676,000,000 (food and live animals 14.1%; road vehicles 10.5%; chemical products 10.5%; base metals 7.6%; power-generating machinery 6.0%). *Major import sources:* Malaysia 21.6%; Singapore 17.4%; Japan 12.8%; US 9.0%; China 7.9%. **Exports** (2006; f.o.b.): US$7,636,000,-000 (crude petroleum 67.3%; liquefied natural gas 29.0%; apparel and clothing accessories 1.7%). *Major export destinations:* Japan 30.6%; Indonesia 19.8%; South Korea 15.1%; Australia 12.2%; US 6.7%.

Transport and communications

Transport. *Railroads* (2004): length 19 km. *Roads* (2005): total length 3,650 km (paved 77%). *Vehicles* (2003): passenger cars 212,000; trucks and buses (2002) 20,000. *Air transport* (2007): passenger-km 3,720,000,000; metric ton-km cargo 115,536,000. **Communications,** in total units (units per 1,000 persons). Telephone landlines (2006): 80,000 (210); cellular telephone subscribers (2006): 254,000 (665); personal computers (2004): 31,000 (87); total Internet users (2006): 166,000 (434); broadband Internet subscribers (2006): 11,000 (28).

Education and health

Educational attainment (1991). Percentage of population ages 25 and over having: no formal schooling/unknown 17.5%; primary education 43.3%; secondary 26.3%; postsecondary and higher 12.9%. **Literacy** (2002): percentage of total population ages 15 and over literate 93.9%; males literate 96.3%; females literate 91.4%. **Health** (2004): physicians 463 (1 per 773 persons); hospital beds 943 (1 per 379 persons); infant mortality rate per 1,000 live births (2005) 8.8; undernourished population (2002–04) 15,000 (4% of total population based on the consumption of a minimum daily requirement of 1,910 calories).

Military

Total active duty personnel (2007): 7,000 (army 70.0%, navy 14.3%, air force 15.7%); British troops

110; Singaporean troops 500. **Military expenditure as percentage of GDP** (2005): 3.9%; per capita expenditure US$684.

Background

Brunei traded with China in the 6th century AD. Through allegiance to the Javanese Majapahit kingdom (13th–15th centuries), it came under Hindu influence. In the early 15th century, with the decline of the Majapahit kingdom, many people converted to Islam, and Brunei became an independent sultanate. When Ferdinand Magellan's ships visited in 1521, the sultan of Brunei controlled almost all of Borneo and its neighboring islands. Beginning in the late 16th century, Brunei lost power because of the Portuguese, Dutch, and, later, British activities in the region. By the 19th century, the sultanate of Brunei included Sarawak (present-day Brunei) and part of North Borneo (now part of Sabah). In 1841 a revolt took place against the sultan, and a British soldier, James Brooke, helped put it down; he was later proclaimed governor. In 1847 the sultanate entered into a treaty with Great Britain and by 1906 had yielded all administration to a British resident. Brunei rejected membership in the Federation of Malaysia in 1963, negotiated a new treaty with Britain in 1979, and achieved independence in 1984, with membership in the Commonwealth.

Recent Developments

In a bid to promote industrial investment in nonenergy sectors, Brunei signed an agreement in early 2008 with the American company Alcoa to study the feasibility of building an aluminum-smelting plant. Brunei also inaugurated Wawasan Brunei 2035, a strategic economic-development plan with the goal of seeing the sultanate rank in the top 10 countries in the world in terms of GDP per capita by the year 2035. It envisioned coordinated educational, employment, and environmental plans, among others, creating a diversified, sustainable economy.

Internet resources: <www.tourismbrunei.com>.

Bulgaria

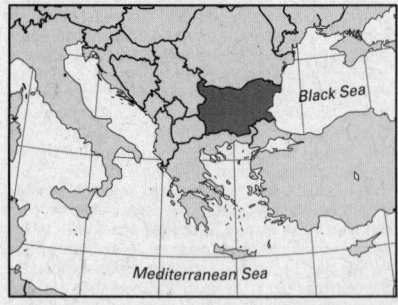

Official name: Republika Bulgariya (Republic of Bulgaria). **Form of government:** unitary multiparty republic with one legislative body (National Assembly

---

1 metric ton = about 1.1 short tons;   1 kilometer = 0.6 mi (statute);   1 metric ton-km cargo = about 0.68 short ton-mi cargo;   c.i.f.: cost, insurance, and freight;   f.o.b.: free on board

[240]). **Chief of state:** President Georgi Purvanov (from 2002). **Head of government:** Prime Minister Boiko Borisov (from 2009). **Capital:** Sofia. **Official language:** Bulgarian. **Official religion:** none. **Monetary unit:** 1 lev (Lw; plural leva) = 100 stotinki; valuation (1 Jul 2009) US$1 = 1.38 leva.

Demography

Area: 42,858 sq mi, 111,002 sq km. **Population** (2008): 7,569,000. **Density** (2008): persons per sq mi 176.6, persons per sq km 68.2. **Urban** (2007): 70.7%. **Sex distribution** (2007): male 48.42%; female 51.58%. **Age breakdown** (2007): under 15, 13.4%; 15–29, 20.4%; 30–44, 21.5%; 45–59, 21.2%; 60–74, 16.1%; 75–84, 6.3%; 85 and over, 1.1%. **Ethnic composition** (2001): Bulgarian 83.9%; Turkish 9.4%; Rom (Gypsy) 4.7%; other 2.0%. **Religious affiliation** (2005): Bulgarian Orthodox 81%; Sunni Muslim 12%; Evangelical Protestant 2%; Catholic 1%; other 4%. **Major cities** (2007): Sofia 1,240,788; Plovdiv 341,464; Varna 312,026; Burgas 189,529; Ruse 158,201. **Location:** southeastern Europe, bordering Romania, the Black Sea, Turkey, Greece, Macedonia, and Serbia.

Vital statistics

Birth rate per 1,000 population (2007): 9.8 (world avg. 20.3); (2005) within marriage 51.0%; outside of marriage 49.0%. **Death rate** per 1,000 population (2007): 14.8 (world avg. 8.6). **Natural increase rate** per 1,000 population (2007): 5.0 (world avg. 11.7). **Total fertility rate** (avg. births per childbearing woman; 2007): 1.42. **Life expectancy** at birth (2007): male 69.2 years; female 76.3 years.

National economy

Budget (2005). *Revenue:* 17,030,000,000 leva (tax revenue 79.7%, of which VAT 28.2%, social insurance 20.6%; nontax revenue 20.3%). *Expenditures:* 17,008,000,000 leva (social insurance 33.1%; economic services 14.4%; defense and security 12.2%; health 11.8%; education 10.7%). **Public debt** (external, outstanding; January 2007): US$7,253,300,-000. **Gross national income** (2007): US$35,062,-000,000 (US$4,590 per capita). **Production** (metric tons except as noted). *Agriculture and fishing* (2007): wheat 2,390,000, corn (maize) 1,312,900, sunflower seeds 564,447; livestock (number of live animals) 1,635,410 sheep, 1,012,655 pigs, 628,271 cattle; fisheries production (2005) 8,579 (from aquaculture 37%). *Mining and quarrying* (2004): copper (metal content) 107,000; iron (metal content) 27,000; gold 2,431 kg. *Manufacturing* (value added in US$'000,000; 2004): refined petroleum products, n.a.; wearing apparel 359; food products 320. *Energy production (consumption):* electricity (kW-hr; 2007) 43,392,000,000 ([2005] 36,781,000,000); hard coal (metric tons; 2005) 9,000 (4,361,000); lignite (metric tons; 2007) 28,308,000 ([2005] 24,870,000); crude petroleum (barrels; 2005) 220,000 (45,400,000); petroleum products (metric tons; 2005) 5,268,000 (3,821,000); natural gas (cu m; 2007) 312,000,000 ([2005] 3,343,000,000). **Population economically active** (2005): total 3,314,200; activity rate of total population 49.7% (participation rates: ages 15–64 [2003] 60.9%; female 44.4%; unemployed [January–March 2008] 6.5%). **Selected balance of payments data.** Receipts from (US$'000,000): tourism (2006) 2,610; remittances (2007) 2,087; foreign direct investment (FDI) (2004–06 avg.) 4,162. Disbursements for (US$'000,-000): tourism (2006) 1,474; remittances (2007) 86; FDI (2004–06 avg.) 82.

Foreign trade

Imports (2006; c.i.f.): €18,375,000,000 (crude petroleum and natural gas 17.4%; transportation equipment 13.8%; machinery and apparatus 12.1%; textiles 7.7%; base and fabricated metals 6.6%). *Major import sources:* Russia 17.3%; Germany 12.4%; Italy 8.7%; Turkey 6.0%; Greece 4.9%. **Exports** (2006): €11,982,600,000 (base and fabricated metals 21.6%, of which iron and steel 7.4%; mineral fuels 15.5%, of which refined petroleum products 13.3%; machinery and transportation equipment 14.3%; clothing and footwear 13.4%). *Major export destinations:* Turkey 11.4%; Italy 10.1%; Germany 9.6%; Greece 8.9%; Belgium 6.5%.

Transport and communications

Transport. *Railroads* (2004): track length 6,238 km; passenger-km 2,404,000,000; metric ton-km cargo 5,212,000,000. *Roads* (2004): length 44,033 km (paved 99%). *Vehicles* (2004): cars 2,438,383; trucks and buses 353,681. *Air transport* (2003): passenger-km 3,005,000,000; metric ton-km cargo 21,000,000. **Communications,** in total units (units per 1,000 persons). Telephone landlines (2007): 2,300,000 (301); cellular telephone subscribers (2007): 9,897,000 (1,296); personal computers (2004): 461,000 (59); total Internet users (2006): 1,870,000 (244); broadband Internet subscribers (2007): 563,000 (50).

Education and health

Educational attainment (2004). Percentage of population ages 25–64 having: no formal schooling to complete primary education 28%; secondary 50%; higher 22%. **Literacy** (2003): percentage of total population ages 15 and over literate 98.6%; males literate 99.1%; females literate 98.2%. **Health** (2005): physicians 28,030 (1 per 274 persons); hospital beds 50,688 (1 per 152 persons); infant mortality rate per 1,000 live births (2007) 9.2; undernourished population (2002–04) 600,000 (8% of total population based on the consumption of a minimum daily requirement of 1,990 calories).

Military

Total active duty personnel (2007): 40,747 (army 46.1%, navy 10.1%, air force 22.9%, other 20.9%). **Military expenditure as percentage of GDP** (2005): 2.4%; per capita expenditure US$74.

Background

Evidence of human habitation in Bulgaria dates from prehistoric times. Thracians were its first recorded inhabitants, dating from c. 3500 BC, and their first state dates from about the 5th century BC; the area was subdued by the Romans, who divided it into the provinces of Moesia and Thrace. In the 7th century AD the Bulgars took the region to the south of the Danube. The Byzantine Empire in 681 formally recognized Bulgar control over the area between the

Balkans and the Danube. In the second half of the 14th century, Bulgaria fell to the Turks and ultimately lost its independence. At the end of the Russo-Turkish War (1877–78), Bulgaria rebelled. The ensuing Treaty of San Stefano was unacceptable to the Great Powers, and the Congress of Berlin (1878) resulted. In 1908 the Bulgarian ruler, Ferdinand, declared Bulgaria's independence. After its involvement in the Balkan Wars (1912–13), Bulgaria lost territory. It sided with the Central Powers in World War I and with Germany in World War II. A communist coalition seized power in 1944, and in 1946 a people's republic was declared. Like other Eastern European countries in the late 1980s, Bulgaria experienced political unrest; its communist leader resigned in 1989. A new constitution proclaiming a republic was implemented in 1991. Bulgaria joined NATO in 2004 and the EU in 2007.

Recent Developments

In 2008 Bulgaria's GDP rose 6.0%, largely fueled by the services and construction sectors; tourism boomed by 10.4%, and real-estate prices were valued 24.9% higher than in 2007. Nevertheless, experts pointed to the slowdown in health care reform as one of the biggest risk factors for Bulgaria's long-term economic development. Moreover, the country continued to face a large trade deficit and a persisting pattern of emigration among young professionals. The energy sector made some long-term investments, including participation in the South Stream project, a gas pipeline that would supply natural gas to Romania, Hungary, the Czech Republic, Italy, Austria, and Serbia, starting in 2013.

Internet resources: <www.nsi.bg/Index_e.htm>.

Burkina Faso

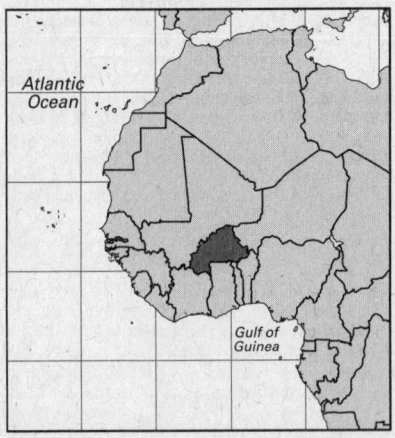

Official name: Burkina Faso. **Form of government:** multiparty republic with one legislative body (National Assembly [111]). **Chief of state:** President Blaise Compaoré (from 1987). **Head of government:** Prime Minister Tertius Zongo (from 2007). **Capital:** Ouagadougou. **Official language:** French. **Official religion:** none. **Monetary unit:** 1 CFA franc (CFAF) = 100 centimes; valuation (1 Jul 2009) US$1 = CFAF 462.89.

Demography

Area: 103,456 sq mi, 267,950 sq km. **Population** (2008): 14,391,000. **Density** (2008): persons per sq mi 139.1, persons per sq km 53.7. **Urban** (2007): 19.2%. **Sex distribution** (2006): male 48.33%; female 51.67%. **Age breakdown** (2006): under 15, 46.7%; 15–29, 28.0%; 30–44, 14.8%; 45–59, 6.5%; 60–74, 3.3%; 75 and over, 0.7%. **Ethnic composition** (1995): Mossi 47.9%; Fulani 10.3%; Lobi 6.9%; Bobo 6.9%; Mande 6.7%; Senufo 5.3%; Grosi 5.0%; Gurma 4.8%; Tuareg 3.1%. **Religious affiliation** (2005): Muslim 48%; traditional beliefs 32%; Roman Catholic 12%; Protestant/independent Christian 8%. **Major cities** (2006): Ouagadougou 1,181,702; Bobo-Dioulasso 435,543; Koudougou 82,720; Banfora 72,144; Ouahigouya 70,957. **Location:** western Africa, bordering Mali, Niger, Benin, Togo, Ghana, and Côte d'Ivoire.

Vital statistics

Birth rate per 1,000 population (2006): 45.6 (world avg. 20.3). **Death rate** per 1,000 population (2006): 15.6 (world avg. 8.6). **Natural increase rate** per 1,000 population (2006): 30.0 (world avg. 11.7). **Total fertility rate** (avg. births per childbearing woman; 2006): 6.47. **Life expectancy** at birth (2006): male 47.3 years; female 50.4 years.

National economy

Budget (2006). *Revenue:* CFAF 793,000,000,000 (tax revenue 52.3%, of which taxes on goods and services 29.3%; loans 23.2%; grants 18.5%; nontax revenue 3.6%; other 2.4%). *Expenditures:* CFAF 892,-100,000,000 (current expenditures 50.1%; development expenditures 49.9%). **Public debt** (external; 2006): US$1,022,000,000. **Production** (metric tons except as noted). *Agriculture and fishing* (2007): sorghum 1,619,590, millet 1,104,010, seed cotton 690,000, shea nuts (2005) 70,000, bambara beans 40,500, sesame 35,600; livestock (number of live animals) 11,427,500 goats, 8,764,100 cattle, 7,321,200 sheep; fisheries production (2005) 9,006 (from aquaculture, negligible). *Mining and quarrying* (2006): gold 1,571 kg. *Manufacturing* (value added in CFAF '000,000; 1999): food products, beverages, and tobacco 126,125; textiles 46,217; chemical products 9,335; cement, bricks, and ceramics 3,484; paper products 2,150. *Energy production (consumption):* electricity (kW-hr; 2005) 417,000,000 (417,000,000); petroleum products (metric tons; 2005) none (237,000). **Population economically active** (2003): total 5,417,000; activity rate 43.6% (participation rates: ages 15–64, 84.7%; female 46.6%; unemployed, n.a.). **Gross national income** (2007): US$6,384,000,000 (US$430 per capita). **Selected balance of payments data.** Receipts from (US$'000,000): tourism (2005) 45; remittances (2007) 50; foreign direct investment (2004–06 avg.) 25; official development assistance (2006) 871. Disbursements for (US$'000,000): tourism (2005) 46; remittances (2007) 44.

1 metric ton = about 1.1 short tons;   1 kilometer = 0.6 mi (statute);   1 metric ton-km cargo = about 0.68 short ton-mi cargo;   c.i.f.: cost, insurance, and freight;   f.o.b.: free on board

Foreign trade

Imports (2005): CFAF 619,000,000,000 (mineral fuels 24.6%; machinery and apparatus 14.3%; chemical products 14.1%; transportation equipment 9.1%). *Major import sources:* France 18.7%; Côte d'Ivoire 18.0%; Togo 11.4%; Benin 6.8%; Ghana 5.9%. **Exports** (2005): CFAF 175,000,000,000 (raw cotton 74.5%, sesame 2.9%, cigarettes 2.1%, sugar 1.5%). *Major export destinations:* Togo 41.1%; Ghana 16.7%; Côte d'Ivoire 10.5%; France 9.8%; Switzerland 9.4%.

Transport and communications

Transport. *Railroads:* route length (2004) 622 km; passenger-km (2003) 9,980,000; metric ton-km cargo (2005) 674,900,000. *Roads* (2006): total length 15,272 km (paved 17%). *Vehicles* (2005): passenger cars 84,161; trucks and buses 38,261. *Air transport* (Ouagadougou and Bobo-Dioulasso airports only; 2005): passenger arrivals 134,247, passenger departures 137,373; cargo unloaded 2,837 metric tons, cargo loaded 1,347 metric tons. **Communications,** in total units (units per 1,000 persons). Telephone landlines (2006): 95,000 (7); cellular telephone subscribers (2007): 1,611,000 (109); personal computers (2005): 31,000 (2.4); total Internet users (2006): 80,000 (5.9); broadband Internet subscribers (2006): 1,700 (0.1).

Education and health

Educational attainment (2003). Percentage of population ages 25 and over having: no formal schooling/unknown 85.4%; incomplete to complete primary education 7.9%; incomplete to complete secondary 5.5%; higher 1.2%. **Literacy** (2003): percentage of total population ages 15 and over literate 26.6%; males literate 36.8%; females literate 16.6%. **Health:** physicians (2004) 369 (1 per 35,439 persons); hospital beds (2001) 15,801 (1 per 735 persons); infant mortality rate per 1,000 live births (2006) 91.4; undernourished population (2002–04) 2,000,000 (15% of total population based on the consumption of a minimum daily requirement of 1,800 calories).

Military

Total active duty personnel (2007): 10,800 (army 98.1%, air force 1.9%). **Military expenditure as percentage of GDP** (2005): 1.3%; per capita expenditure US$6.

Background

Probably in the 14th century, the Mossi and Gurma peoples established themselves in eastern and central areas of what is now Burkina Faso. The Mossi kingdoms of Yatenga and Ouagadougou existed into the early 20th century. A French protectorate was established over the region (1895–97), and its southern boundary was demarcated through an Anglo-French agreement. It was part of the Upper Senegal–Niger colony and then became a separate colony in 1919. Named Upper Volta, it was constituted an overseas territory within the French Union in 1947, became an autonomous republic within the French Community in 1958, and achieved total independence in 1960. Since then, the country has been ruled primarily by the military and has experienced several coups; following one in 1983, the country received its present name. A new constitution, adopted in 1991, restored multiparty rule.

Recent Developments

In late February 2008 popular discontent over rapidly increasing food prices erupted into serious riots in the Burkina Faso capital and in the cities of Bobo-Dioulasso, Banfora, and Ouahigouya. Security forces arrested at least 180 people for organizing the protests. Import taxes on basic necessities were suspended that month, and in March the government announced that food prices were to be artificially cut by 5–15%. These actions were reversed late in the year as pressure on food prices eased. Economic growth was nonetheless estimated at 4.5% for the year.

Internet resources: <www.burkina.com/>.

Burundi

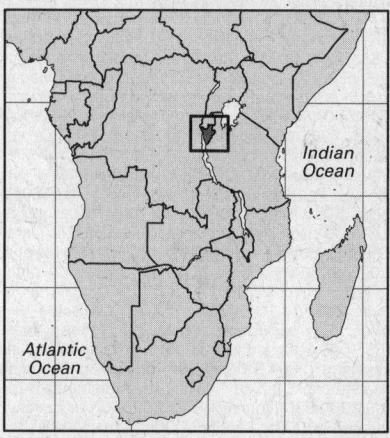

Indian Ocean

Atlantic Ocean

Official name: Republika y'u Burundi (Rundi); République du Burundi (French) (Republic of Burundi). **Form of government:** republic with two legislative bodies (Senate [49]; National Assembly [100]). **Head of state and government:** President Pierre Nkurunziza (from 2005). **Capital:** Bujumbura. **Official languages:** Rundi; French. **Official religion:** none. **Monetary unit:** 1 Burundi franc (FBu) = 100 centimes; valuation (1 Jul 2009) US$1 = FBu 1,193.00.

Demography

Area: 10,740 sq mi, 27,816 sq km. **Population** (2008): 8,691,000. **Density** (2008): persons per sq mi 867.5, persons per sq km 334.9. **Urban** (2007): 9.9%. **Sex distribution** (2005): male 48.82%; female 51.18%. **Age breakdown** (2005): under 15, 45.1%; 15–29, 29.0%; 30–44, 13.7%; 45–59, 8.2%; 60–74, 3.2%; 75–84, 0.7%; 85 and over, 0.1%. **Ethnic composition** (2000): Hutu 80.9%; Tutsi 15.6%; Lingala 1.6%; Twa Pygmy 1.0%; other 0.9%. **Religious affiliation** (2004): Christian 67%, of which Roman Catholic 62%, Protestant 5%; traditional beliefs 23%; Muslim 10%. **Major cities** (2004): Bujumbura

340,300; Gitega 46,900; Muyinga 45,300; Ngozi 40,200; Ruyigi 36,800. **Location:** central Africa, bordering Rwanda, Tanzania, Lake Tanganyika, and the Democratic Republic of the Congo.

Vital statistics

Birth rate per 1,000 population (2005): 45.6 (world avg. 20.3). **Death rate** per 1,000 population (2005): 16.1 (world avg. 8.6). **Natural increase rate** per 1,000 population (2005): 29.5 (world avg. 11.7). **Total fertility rate** (avg. births per childbearing woman; 2005): 6.80. **Life expectancy** at birth (2005): male 47.0 years; female 49.8 years.

National economy

Budget (2006). *Revenue:* FBu 220,170,000,000 (tax revenue 71.3%, of which sales tax 37.8%, taxes on international trade 11.7%, corporate taxes 11.1%, income tax 8.7%; grants 18.8%; nontax revenue 6.9%; other 3.0%). *Expenditures:* FBu 319,061,000,000 (current expenditures 70.1%, of which debt service 6.4%; capital expenditures 27.9%; other 2.0%). **Public debt** (external, outstanding; September 2006): US$1,227,000,000. **Production** (metric tons except as noted). *Agriculture and fishing* (2007): bananas 1,600,000, sweet potatoes 835,000, cassava 710,000; livestock (number of live animals) 750,000 goats, 400,000 cattle, 250,000 sheep; fisheries production (2005) 14,200 (from aquaculture 1%). *Mining and quarrying* (2006): columbite-tantalite ore 16,177 kg; gold 4,313 kg. *Manufacturing* (2005): beer 1,012,500 hectoliters; carbonated beverages 143,600 hectoliters; cottonseed oil 135,900 liters. *Energy production (consumption):* electricity (kW-hr; 2005) 101,000,000 (172,000,000); petroleum products (metric tons; 2005) none (71,000); peat (metric tons; 2005) 4,700 ([2000] 12,000). **Selected balance of payments data.** Receipts from (US$'000,000): tourism (2006) 1.3; foreign direct investment (2004–06 avg.) 97; official development assistance (2006) 415. Disbursements for (US$'000,000): tourism (2006) 125. **Gross national income** (2007): US$923,000,000 (US$110 per capita). **Population economically active** (2003): total 3,464,000; activity rate of total population 49.2% (participation rates: ages 15–64, 92.2%; female 52.1%; unemployed, n.a.).

Foreign trade

Imports (2006): FBu 442,500,000,000 (machinery and apparatus 21.3%; transportation equipment 15.7%; mineral fuels 13.4%; fabricated metal products 7.2%; pharmaceuticals 6.6%). *Major import sources:* Saudi Arabia 12.6%; Belgium and Luxembourg 11.7%; Kenya 8.2%; Japan 7.8%; Russia 4.7%. **Exports** (2006): FBu 60,400,000,000 (coffee 67.7%; tea 17.0%; hides and skins 2.6%; cotton fabric 1.9%). *Major export destinations:* Switzerland 34.4%; UK 12.3%; Pakistan 7.8%; Rwanda 5.1%; other EU 24.6%.

Transport and communications

Transport. *Railroads:* none. *Roads* (2004): total length 12,322 km (paved 7%). *Vehicles:* passenger cars (2003) 7,000; trucks and buses (2002) 14,400. *Air transport* (Bujumbura airport only; 2005): passenger arrivals 73,072, passenger departures 63,908; cargo unloaded 3,093 metric tons, cargo loaded 188 metric tons. **Communications,** in total units (units per 1,000 persons). Telephone landlines (2005): 31,000 (4.1); cellular telephone subscribers (2007): 250,000 (29); personal computers (2004): 34,000 (4.8); total Internet users (2006): 60,000 (7.7).

Education and health

Literacy (2007): percentage of total population ages 15 and over literate 56.1%; males literate 61.4%; females literate 51.1%. **Health** (2004): physicians 200 (1 per 37,581 persons); hospital beds (1999) 3,380 (1 per 1,657 persons); infant mortality rate per 1,000 live births (2005) 64.4; undernourished population (2002–04) 4,500,000 (66% of total population based on the consumption of a minimum daily requirement of 1,800 calories).

Military

Total active duty personnel (2007): 35,000 (army 100%); South African peacekeeping troops (November 2007) 862. **Military expenditure as percentage of GDP** (2005): 6.2%; per capita expenditure US$6.

Background

Original settlement by the Twa people was followed by Hutu settlement, which occurred gradually and was completed by the 11th century. The Tutsi arrived 300–400 years later; though a minority, they established the kingdom of Burundi in the 16th century. In the 19th century the area came within the German sphere of influence, but the Tutsi remained in power. Following World War I the Belgians took control of the area, which became a UN trusteeship after World War II. Colonial-period conditions had intensified Hutu-Tutsi ethnic animosities, and as independence neared, hostilities flared. Independence was granted in 1962 in the form of a kingdom ruled by the Tutsi. In 1965 the Hutu rebelled but were brutally repressed. The rest of the 20th century saw violent clashes between the two groups. In 2001 a power-sharing transitional government was established, paving the way to the promulgation of a new constitution and the installation of a new government in 2005.

Recent Developments

The National Liberation Forces (FNL), the last rebel group in Burundi following a 14-year civil war, launched several deadly attacks in April 2008 before signing a peace agreement in June. The removal of an ethnic term from the FNL's official name, its registration as a political party, and the release of more than 100 former child soldiers in April 2009 led to greater hopes for peace.

Internet resources: <www.burunditourisme.com/index.php?id=10&L=1>.

1 metric ton = about 1.1 short tons;   1 kilometer = 0.6 mi (statute);   1 metric ton-km cargo = about 0.68 short ton-mi cargo;   c.i.f.: cost, insurance, and freight;   f.o.b.: free on board

Cambodia

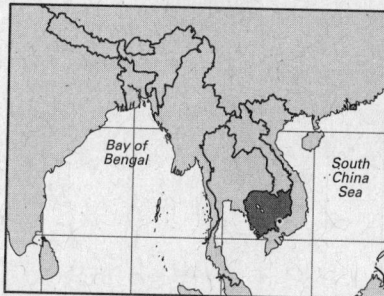

Bay of
Bengal

South
China
Sea

Official name: Preahreacheanachakr Kampuchea (Kingdom of Cambodia). **Form of government:** constitutional monarchy with two legislative houses (Senate [61]; National Assembly [123]). **Chief of state:** King Norodom Sihamoni (from 2004). **Head of government:** Prime Minister Samdech Hun Sen (from 1998). **Capital:** Phnom Penh. **Official language:** Khmer. **Official religion:** Buddhism. **Monetary unit:** 1 riel (KHR) = 100 sen; valuation (1 Jul 2009) US$1 = 4,124.10 riels.

Demography

Area: 69,898 sq mi, 181,035 sq km. **Population** (2008): 14,242,000. **Density** (2008): persons per sq mi 207.2, persons per sq km 80.0. **Urban** (2004): 15.0%. **Sex distribution** (2005): male 48.75%; female 51.25%. **Age breakdown** (2005): under 15, 36.6%; 15–29, 30.5%; 30–44, 18.4%; 45–59, 9.4%; 60–74, 4.1%; 75–84, 0.9%; 85 and over, 0.1%. **Ethnic composition** (2000): Khmer 85.2%; Chinese 6.4%; Vietnamese 3.0%; Cham 2.5%; Lao 0.6%; other 2.3%. **Religious affiliation** (2000): Buddhist 84.7%; Chinese folk religionist 4.7%; traditional beliefs 4.3%; Muslim 2.3%; Christian 1.1%; other 2.9%. **Major urban areas** (1998): Phnom Penh (2005) 1,364,000; Battambang 124,290; Sisophon 85,382; Siemreap 83,715; Sihanoukville 66,723. **Location:** southeastern Asia, bordering Thailand, Laos, Vietnam, and the Gulf of Thailand.

Vital statistics

Birth rate per 1,000 population (2007): 25.5 (world avg. 20.3). **Death rate** per 1,000 population (2007): 8.2 (world avg. 8.6). **Natural increase rate** per 1,000 population (2007): 17.3 (world avg. 11.7). **Total fertility rate** (avg. births per childbearing woman; 2007): 3.12. **Life expectancy** at birth (2007): male 59.3 years; female 63.4 years.

National economy

Budget (2005). *Revenue:* KHR 3,280,300,000,000 (tax revenue 58.3%; nontax revenue 17.2%; grants 20.0%; other 4.5%). *Expenditures:* KHR 3,294,700,-000,000 (current expenditure 59.7%; development expenditure 40.3%). **Production** (metric tons except as noted). *Agriculture and fishing* (2007): rice 5,995,000, cassava 2,000,000, corn (maize) 380,-000, rubber 22,000; livestock (number of live animals) 3,500,000 cattle, 2,790,000 pigs, 775,000 buffalo, (2005) 120,000 crocodiles; fisheries production (2005) 410,000 (from aquaculture 6%); aquatic plants production 16,000 (from aquaculture 100%). *Mining and quarrying* (2007): gold, n.a.; gemstones, n.a.; salt 76,700. *Manufacturing* (value added in KHR '000,000,000; 2002): wearing apparel 1,808; food products 392; base and fabricated metals 120. *Energy production (consumption):* electricity (kW-hr; 2005) 764,000,000 (846,000,000); petroleum products (metric tons; 2005) none (176,000). **Selected balance of payments data.** Receipts from (US$'000,-000): tourism (2006) 963; remittances (2007) 353; foreign direct investment (2004–06 avg.) 332; official development assistance (2006) 529. Disbursements for (US$'000,000): tourism (2006) 122; remittances (2007) 157. **Gross national income** (2007): US$7,858,000,000 (US$540 per capita). **Public debt** (external, outstanding; 2006): US$3,318,000,000. **Population economically active** (2004): total 7,557,600; activity rate of total population 55% (participation rates: ages 15–64, 82.6%; female 49.4%; registered unemployed [November 2001] 1.8%).

Foreign trade

Imports (2005): US$4,254,000,000 (retained imports 97.3%; imports for reexport 2.7%). *Major import sources* (2004): Thailand 23.9%; Hong Kong 15.0%; China 13.5%; Singapore 11.5%; Vietnam 7.6%. **Exports** (2005): US$2,910,000,000 (domestic exports 95.3%, of which garments 77.7%, rice 6.1%, rubber 4.1%, fish 2.6%; reexports 4.7%). *Major export destinations* (2004): US 56.2%; Germany 11.5%; UK 7.0%; Canada 4.3%; Vietnam 3.7%.

Transport and communications

Transport. *Railroads:* length (2004) 602 km; passenger-km (2000) 45,000,000; metric ton-km (1999) 76,171,000. *Roads* (2004): total length 38,257 km (paved 6%). *Vehicles* (2004): passenger cars 235,298; trucks and buses 35,448. *Air transport* (2005–06): passenger-km 198,000,000; metric ton-km cargo 1,214,000. **Communications,** in total units (units per 1,000 persons). Telephone landlines (2007): 38,000 (2.6); cellular telephone subscribers (2007): 2,583,000 (179); personal computers (2004): 38,000 (2.6); total Internet users (2007): 70,000 (4.8); broadband Internet subscribers (2007): 5,000 (0.4).

Education and health

Educational attainment (2004). Percentage of literate population ages 25 and over having: no formal schooling/unknown 4.6%; incomplete primary education 54.0%; complete primary 23.7%; incomplete secondary 11.3%; secondary/vocational 5.3%; higher 1.1%. **Literacy** (2004): percentage of total population ages 15 and over literate 74.4%; males literate 82.1%; females literate 67.4%. **Health:** physicians (2004) 2,122 (1 per 6,169 persons); hospital beds (2002) 9,800 (1 per 1,405 persons); infant mortality rate per 1,000 live births (2007) 58.5; undernourished population (2002–04) 4,600,000 (33% of total population based on the consumption of a minimum daily requirement of 1,770 calories).

Military

Total active duty personnel (2007): 124,300 (army 60.3%, navy 2.3%, air force 1.2%, provincial forces

36.2%). **Military expenditure as percentage of GDP** (2005): 1.8%; per capita expenditure US$8.

Background

In the early Christian era, what is now Cambodia was under Hindu and, to a lesser extent, Buddhist influence. The Khmer state gradually spread in the early 7th century and reached its height under Jayavarman II and his successors in the 9th–12th centuries, when it ruled the Mekong Valley and the tributary Shan states and built Angkor. Widespread adoption of Buddhism occurred in the 13th century, resulting in a script change from Sanskrit to Pali. From the 13th century Cambodia was attacked by Annam and Siamese city-states and was alternately a province of one or the other. The area became a French protectorate in 1863. It was occupied by the Japanese in World War II and became independent in 1954. Cambodia's borders were the scene of fighting in the Vietnam War from 1961, and in 1970 its northeastern and eastern areas were occupied by the North Vietnamese and penetrated by US and South Vietnamese forces. An indiscriminate US bombing campaign alienated much of the population, enabling the communist Khmer Rouge under Pol Pot to seize power in 1975. Their regime of terror resulted in the deaths of at least one million Cambodians. Vietnam invaded in 1979 and drove the Khmer Rouge into the western hinterlands, but it was unable to effect reconstruction of the country, and Cambodian infighting continued. A peace accord was reached by most Cambodian factions under UN auspices in 1991, and elections were held in 1993. In 2004 King Norodom Sihanouk abdicated, and his son Sihamoni was named his successor.

Did you know? The Kizuna Bridge became the first bridge ever to span the Mekong River when it opened to the public on 4 Dec 2001. The Mekong flows through Cambodia for about 500 km (300 mi) and is considered the country's most important river.

Recent Developments

A major crisis in Cambodia was a standoff between Thai and Cambodian troops in the area around the ancient temple of Preah Vihear. A 1962 World Court decision that had declared the temple site Cambodian territory was never popularly accepted among Thais, and Preah Vihear carried great symbolic weight in both countries. In July 2008 UNESCO declared Preah Vihear a World Heritage site; a troop buildup began, and soon there were reportedly thousands of troops from both countries along the disputed border. Actual fighting broke out in October, when three Cambodian soldiers were killed and several Thai troops captured. Despite continuing talks, three Thai soldiers were killed in fighting in April 2009.

Internet resources: <www.nbc.org.kh/index.asp>.

Cameroon

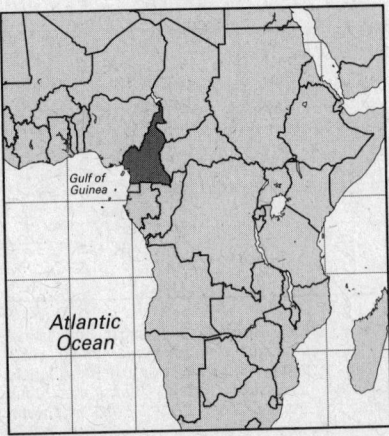

Official name: République du Cameroun (French); Republic of Cameroon (English). **Form of government:** unitary multiparty republic with one legislative house (National Assembly [180]). **Chief of state:** President Paul Biya (from 1982). **Head of government:** Prime Minister Ephraïm Inoni (from 2004). **Capital:** Yaoundé. **Official languages:** French; English. **Official religion:** none. **Monetary unit:** 1 CFA franc (CFAF) = 100 centimes; valuation (1 Jul 2009) US$1 = CFAF 462.89.

Demography

Area: 183,920 sq mi, 476,350 sq km (includes the 270-sq-mi [699-sq-km] area of Bakassi Peninsula, which was formally ceded by Nigeria to Cameroon in August 2008). **Population** (2008): 18,468,000. **Density** (2008): persons per sq mi 102.6, persons per sq km 39.6. **Urban** (2007): 56.0%. **Sex distribution** (2006): male 50.15%; female 49.85%. **Age breakdown** (2006): under 15, 41.5%; 15–29, 29.0%; 30–44, 15.7%; 45–59, 8.8%; 60–74, 4.1%; 75–84, 0.8%; 85 and over, 0.1%. **Ethnic composition** (1983): Fang 19.6%; Bamileke and Bamum 18.5%; Duala, Luanda, and Basa 14.7%; Fulani 9.6%; Tikar 7.4%; Mandara 5.7%; Maka 4.9%; Chamba 2.4%; Mbum 1.3%; Hausa 1.2%; French 0.2%; other 14.5%. **Religious affiliation** (2005): Roman Catholic 27.4%; traditional beliefs 22.2%; Protestant 20.2%; Sunni Muslim 20.0%; nonreligious/other 10.2%. **Major urban areas** (2004): Douala 1,532,800; Yaoundé 1,434,700; Garoua 409,000; Kousséri 332,900; Bamenda 298,500. **Location:** western Africa, bordering Chad, the Central African Republic, the Republic of the Congo, Gabon, Equatorial Guinea, the Bight of Biafra, and Nigeria.

Vital statistics

Birth rate per 1,000 population (2006): 35.6 (world avg. 20.3). **Death rate** per 1,000 population (2006): 13.0 (world avg. 8.6). **Natural increase rate** per

---

1 metric ton = about 1.1 short tons;   1 kilometer = 0.6 mi (statute);   1 metric ton-km cargo = about 0.68 short ton-mi cargo;   c.i.f.: cost, insurance, and freight;   f.o.b.: free on board

1,000 population (2006): 22.6 (world avg. 11.7). **Total fertility rate** (avg. births per childbearing woman; 2006): 4.58. **Life expectancy** at birth (2006): male 51.7 years; female 53.0 years.

National economy

Budget (2005). *Revenue:* CFAF 1,590,000,000,000 (non-oil revenue 69.4%, of which VAT 22.0%, direct taxes 16.5%, customs duties 11.9%, nontax revenue 7.9%; oil revenue 27.6%; grants 3.0%). *Expenditures:* CFAF 1,278,000,000,000 (current expenditure 82.6%, of which interest on public debt 10.1%; capital expenditure 16.1%; other 1.3%). **Gross national income** (2007): US$19,447,-000,000 (US$1,050 per capita). **Population economically active** (2003): total 6,093,000; activity rate of total population 38.7% (participation rates: ages 15–64, 68.4%; female 39.6%; unemployed, n.a.). **Public debt** (external, outstanding; 2006): US$2,078,000,000. **Production** (metric tons except as noted). *Agriculture and fishing* (2007): cassava 2,076,000, sugarcane 1,430,000, plantains 1,317,000, oil palm fruit 1,300,000; livestock (number of live animals) 6,000,000 cattle, 4,400,000 goats, 3,800,000 sheep; fisheries production (2005) 142,682 (from aquaculture, negligible). *Mining and quarrying* (2006): pozzolana 600,000; limestone 100,000; gold 20,000 kg. *Manufacturing* (value added in US$'000,000; 2002): food products 97; refined petroleum products 88; beverages 78. *Energy production (consumption):* electricity (kW-hr; 2005) 4,145,000,000 (4,145,000,000); crude petroleum (barrels; 2005) 43,500,000 (13,920,000); petroleum products (metric tons; 2005) 1,784,000 (932,000). **Selected balance of payments data.** Receipts from (US$'000,000): tourism (2005) 36; remittances (2007) 103; foreign direct investment (2004–06 avg.) 284; official development assistance (2006) 1,684. Disbursements for (US$'000,000): tourism (2004) 323; remittances (2007) 42.

Foreign trade

Imports (2005): CFAF 1,524,200,000,000 (crude petroleum 27.8%; machinery and apparatus 11.6%; chemical products 11.1%; cereals 7.4%; motor vehicles 6.1%). *Major import sources:* Nigeria 21.0%; France 17.7%; China 5.0%; US 4.6%; Japan 3.9%. **Exports** (2005): CFAF 1,476,000,000,000 (crude petroleum 44.8%; fuels and lubricants 12.2%; sawn wood 12.0%; cocoa beans 7.5%; aluminum 4.7%). *Major export destinations:* Spain 19.7%; France 12.7%; Italy 11.7%; The Netherlands 7.6%; US 6.7%.

Transport and communications

Transport. *Railroads* (2005): route length 1,016 km; passenger-km 323,000,000; metric ton-km cargo 1,119,000,000. *Roads* (2004): total length 50,000 km (paved 10%). *Vehicles* (2005): passenger cars 175,981; trucks and buses 59,399. *Air transport* (2001): passenger-km 796,567,000; metric ton-km cargo 23,255,000. **Communications**, in total units (units per 1,000 persons). Telephone landlines (2005): 100,000 (6.1); cellular telephone subscribers (2007): 4,536,000 (245); personal computers (2005): 200,000 (12); total Internet users (2006): 370,000 (22).

Education and health

Educational attainment (2004). Percentage of population ages 25 and over having: no formal schooling/unknown 34.3%; primary education 35.3%; secondary 26.2%; higher 4.2%. **Literacy** (2007): percentage of total population ages 15 and over literate 78.8%; males literate 84.6%; females literate 73.2%. **Health** (2004): physicians 2,966 (1 per 5,609 persons); hospital beds 38,067 (1 per 437 persons); infant mortality rate per 1,000 live births (2006) 67.2; undernourished population (2002–04) 4,200,000 (26% of total population based on the consumption of a minimum daily requirement of 1,860 calories).

Military

Total active duty personnel (2007): 14,100 (army 88.7%, navy 9.2%, air force 2.1%). **Military expenditure as percentage of GDP** (2005): 1.3%; per capita expenditure US$13.

Background

The Cameroon area had long been inhabited before European colonization. Bantu speakers from equatorial Africa settled in the south, followed by Muslim Fulani from the Niger River basin, who settled in the north. Portuguese explorers visited in the late 15th century and established a foothold, but they lost control to the Dutch in the 17th century. In 1884 the Germans took control and extended their protectorate over Cameroon. In World War I joint French-British action forced the Germans to retreat, and after the war the region was divided into French and British administrative zones. After World War II the two areas became UN trusteeships. In 1960 the French trust territory became an independent republic. In 1961 the southern part of the British trust territory voted for union with the new republic of Cameroon, and the northern part voted for union with Nigeria. In recent decades economic problems have produced unrest in the country.

Recent Developments

On 14 August 2008, Nigeria officially relinquished the Bakassi Peninsula to Cameroon, six years after the World Court decision to uphold Cameroon's claims to the oil-rich area. In the months before the handover, more than 50 people died in clashes between the mainly Nigerian residents and the Cameroonian army. Despite promises of security for all, an estimated 100,000 people fled Bakassi for Akwa Ibom state in Nigeria.

Internet resources: <www.spm.gov.cm/acceuil.php ?lang=en>.

Canada

Official name: Canada. **Form of government:** federal multiparty parliamentary state with two legislative houses (Senate [105]; House of Commons [308]). **Chief of state:** British Queen Elizabeth II (from 1952), represented by Governor-General Michaëlle Jean (from 2005). **Head of government:** Prime Minister Stephen Harper (from 2006). **Capital:** Ottawa.

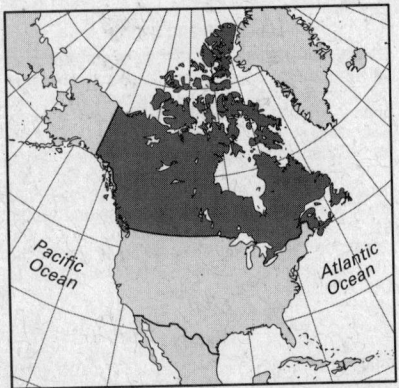

Official languages: English; French. **Official religion:** none. **Monetary unit:** 1 Canadian dollar (Can$) = 100 cents; valuation (1 Jul 2009) US$1 = Can$1.14.

Demography

Area: 3,855,103 sq mi, 9,984,670 sq km. **Population** (2008): 33,213,000. **Density** (2008): persons per sq mi 9.5, persons per sq km 3.7. **Urban** (2005): 80.1%. **Sex distribution** (2006): male 48.95%; female 51.05%. **Age breakdown** (2006): under 15, 17.7%; 15–29, 19.6%; 30–44, 21.6%; 45–59, 22.3%; 60–74, 12.3%; 75–84, 4.8%; 85 and over, 1.7%. **Ethnic origin** (2000): Anglo-Canadian 45.5%; French Canadian 23.5%; Chinese 3.4%; British expatriates 3.3%; Indo-Pakistani 2.6%, of which Punjabi 2.3%; German 2.4%; Italian 2.2%; US white 1.8%; Métis (part Indian) 1.8%; Indian 1.5%; Jewish 1.4%; Arab 1.3%; Ukrainian 1.2%; Eskimo (Inuit) 0.1%; other 8.0%. **Religious affiliation** (2001): Christian 77.1%, of which Roman Catholic 43.2%, Protestant 28.3%, unspecified Christian 2.6%, Orthodox 1.7%, other Christian 1.3%; Muslim 2.0%; Jewish 1.1%; Hindu 1.0%; Buddhist 1.0%; Sikh 0.9%; nonreligious 16.5%; other 0.4%. **Major metropolitan areas** (2006): Toronto 5,113,149; Montreal 3,635,571; Vancouver 2,116,581; Ottawa-Hull 1,130,761; Calgary 1,079,310; Edmonton 1,034,945; Quebec 715,515; Winnipeg 694,668; Hamilton 692,911; London 457,720. **Location:** northern North America, bordering the Arctic Ocean, the North Atlantic Ocean, the US, and the North Pacific Ocean. **Place of birth** (2001): 81.6% native-born; 18.4% foreign-born, of which in the UK 2.0%, elsewhere in Europe 5.7%, Asia 5.8%, US 0.8%, other 4.1%. **Mobility** (2001). Population living in the same residence as in 1996: 58.1%; different residence, same municipality 22.4%; same province, different municipality 3.3%; different province 12.7%; different country 3.5%. **Immigration** (2004): permanent immigrants admitted 235,824; from Asia 48.6%, of which China 15.4%, India 10.8%, Philippines 5.6%; Europe 17.8%, of which UK 2.6%, France 2.1%; US 3.2%; refugee arrivals 26,526; overall refugee population (end of 2004) 141,398.

Vital statistics

Birth rate per 1,000 population (2005–06): 10.6 (world avg. 20.3); (1997) within marriage 72.3%; outside of marriage 27.7%. **Death rate** per 1,000 population (2005–06): 7.2 (world avg. 8.6). **Natural increase rate** per 1,000 population (2005–06): 3.4 (world avg. 11.7). **Total fertility rate** (avg. births per childbearing woman; 2006): 1.61. **Life expectancy** at birth (2006): male 76.9 years; female 83.7 years.

Social indicators

Educational attainment (2004). Percentage of population ages 15 and over having: incomplete primary and complete primary education 8.8%; incomplete secondary 15.7%; complete secondary 19.3%; some university/higher vocational 39.0%; bachelor's degree or higher 17.2%. **Quality of working life.** Average workweek (2005): 35.2 hours. Annual rate per 100,000 workers (2005) for: injury, accident, or industrial illness 2,090; death 6.8. Average days lost to labor stoppages per 1,000 employee-workdays (2001): 0.7. Average commuting distance (2001): 7.2 km; mode of transportation: automobile 80.7%, public transportation 10.5%, walking 6.6%, other 2.2%. Labor force covered by a pension plan (2001): 33.6%. **Access to services.** Proportion of households having access to: electricity (2002) 100%; public water supply (1996) 99.8%; public sewage collection (1996) 99.3%. **Social participation.** Population ages 19 and over participating in voluntary work (2000): 26.7%. Union membership as percentage of civilian labor force (2003) 25.0%. Attendance at religious services on a weekly basis (2006): 17%. **Social deviance** (2004). Offense rate per 100,000 population for: violent crime 946.1, of which assault 731.8, sexual assault 73.7, homicide 2.0; property crime 3,990.9, of which auto theft 530.7, breaking and entering 859.9. **Material well-being** (2003). Households possessing: automobile 62.4%; telephone 96.3%; cellular phone 53.9%; color television 99.0%; central air conditioner 39.3%; cable television 65.1%; home computers 66.8%; Internet access 56.9%.

National economy

Gross national income (2007): US$1,300,025,-000,000 (US$39,420 per capita). **Budget** (2005–06). *Revenue:* Can$229,660,000,000 (income tax 62.9%; sales tax 15.4%; contributions to social security 9.6%; other 12.1%). *Expenditures:* Can$216,-156,000,000 (social services and welfare 37.1%; defense and social protection 11.2%; health 10.0%; public debt interest 9.9%; resource conservation and industrial development 3.8%; education 2.3%). **Public debt** (January 2007): US$582,601,000,000. **Production** (metric tons except as noted). *Agriculture and fishing* (2007): wheat 20,641,100, barley 11,822,-100, corn (maize) 10,554,500, rapeseed 8,864,200, oats 5,009,100, potatoes 4,970,938, dry peas 3,023,600, soybeans 2,785,400, lentils 669,700, linseed 633,500, tomatoes 607,852, apples 405,089, canary seed 169,200, cranberries and blueberries (2005) 139,099, mustard seed 112,000, mushrooms 81,500; livestock (number of live animals; 2006) 14,329,000 pigs, 14,315,000 cattle, 590,500 sheep; fisheries production (2005)

---

1 metric ton = about 1.1 short tons; 1 kilometer = 0.6 mi (statute); 1 metric ton-km cargo = about 0.68 short ton-mi cargo; c.i.f.: cost, insurance, and freight; f.o.b.: free on board

1,235,065 (from aquaculture 13%). *Mining and quarrying* (value of production in Can$'000,000; 2005): nickel 3,302 (world rank: 3); potash 2,839 (world rank: 1); copper 2,455 (world rank: 8); gold 2,041 (world rank: 8); diamonds (gemstones) 1,684 (world rank: 4); iron ore 1,496 (world rank: 9); zinc 998 (world rank: 4); silver 299 (world rank: 6); lime 262 (world rank: 10); gypsum 100 (world rank: 3); cobalt 91 (world rank: 4). *Manufacturing* (value added in Can$'000,000,000 at prices of 1997; 2005): transportation equipment 28.1; food products 17.6; chemical products 17.2; fabricated metal products 14.2; wood industries 13.7; machinery and apparatus 12.5; base metals 12.3; paper products 11.4; rubber and plastic products 10.3; computers and electronic products 10.3. *Energy production (consumption)*: electricity (kW-hr; 2005) 628,194,000,000 (604,343,000,000); hard coal (metric tons; 2005) 28,586,000 (15,107,000); lignite (metric tons; 2005) 36,759,000 (45,413,000); crude petroleum produced from the Alberta oil sands (barrels; 2007) 914,000,000 ([2005] 670,900,000) (in 2006 there were 411,000,000 barrels of marketable crude petroleum [47% of total production]); petroleum products (metric tons; 2005) 88,583,000 (80,070,000); natural gas (cu m; 2007) 166,467,000,000 ([2005] 96,376,000,000). **Population economically active** (2006): total 17,825,800; activity rate of total population 55.6% (participation rates: ages 15 and over, 67.5%; female 46.7%; unemployed [February 2007] 6.1%). **Selected balance of payments data.** Receipts from (US$'000,000): tourism (2006) 14,678; foreign direct investment (FDI) (2004–06 avg.) 32,533. Disbursements for (US$'000,000): tourism (2006) 20,538; FDI (2004–06 avg.) 40,825.

Foreign trade

Imports (2006): Can$404,535,000,000 (machinery and apparatus 24.7%; transportation equipment 23.4%, of which road vehicles and parts 19.7%; chemical products 7.3%; base metals 6.9%; food products 5.8%; crude petroleum 5.6%. *Major import sources* (2006): US 65.5%; Japan 2.9%; UK 2.4%; other European Economic Community countries 8.0%. **Exports** (2006): Can$458,166,900,000 (transportation equipment 22.7%, of which road vehicles and parts 18.1%; machinery and apparatus 16.4%; base metals and alloys 9.9%; crude petroleum 8.4%; food products 6.9%; chemical products 6.8%; natural gas 6.0%; wood and wood pulp 4.9%; paper products 2.4%). *Major export destinations* (2006): US 78.9%; UK 2.6%; Japan 2.3%; other European Economic Community countries 4.7%.

Transport and communications

Transport. *Railroads* (2005): length 72,168 km; passenger-km 1,472,781,000; metric ton-km cargo 352,133,000,000. *Roads* (2004): total length 1,408,900 km (paved 35%). *Vehicles* (2005): passenger cars 18,123,885; trucks and buses 785,649. *Air transport* (Air Canada only; 2007): passenger-km 74,400,000,000; metric ton-km cargo 1,184,-868,000. **Communications**, in total units (units per 1,000 persons). Telephone landlines (2006): 21,000,000 (645); cellular telephone subscribers (2006): 18,749,000 (576); personal computers (2004): 22,390,000 (701); total Internet users (2007): 28,000,000 (852); broadband Internet subscribers (2006): 7,676,000 (236).

Education and health

Literacy (2005): percentage of total population ages 15 and over literate, virtually 100%. **Health**: physicians (2004) 67,087 (1 per 476 persons); hospital beds (2002–03) 115,120 (1 per 274 persons); infant mortality rate per 1,000 live births (2005) 5.4; undernourished population (2002–04) less than 2.5% of total population.

Military

Total active duty personnel (2007): 64,000 (army 52.0%, navy 17.3%, air force 30.7%). **Military expenditure as percentage of GDP** (2005): 1.1%; per capita expenditure US$403.

Background

Originally inhabited by American Indians and Inuit, Canada was visited c. AD 1000 by Scandinavian explorers, whose discovery is confirmed by archaeological evidence from Newfoundland. Fishing expeditions off Newfoundland by the English, French, Spanish, and Portuguese began as early as 1500. The French claim to Canada was made in 1534 when Jacques Cartier entered the Gulf of St. Lawrence. A small settlement was made in Nova Scotia (Acadia) in 1605, and in 1608 Samuel de Champlain founded Quebec. Fur trading was the impetus behind the early colonizing efforts. In response to French activity, the English in 1670 formed the Hudson's Bay Company.

The British-French rivalry for the interior of upper North America lasted almost a century. The first French loss occurred in 1713 at the conclusion of Queen Anne's War (War of the Spanish Succession) when Nova Scotia and Newfoundland were ceded to the British. The Seven Years' War (French and Indian War) resulted in France's expulsion from continental North America in 1763. After the US War of Independence, the population was augmented by Loyalists fleeing the US, and the increasing number arriving in Quebec led the British to divide the colony into Upper and Lower Canada in 1791. The British reunited the two provinces in 1841. Canadian expansionism resulted in the confederation movement of the mid-19th century, and in 1867 the Dominion of Canada, comprising Nova Scotia, New Brunswick, Quebec, and Ontario, came into existence. After confederation, Canada entered a period of westward expansion.

The prosperity that accompanied Canada into the 20th century was marred by continuing conflict between the English and French communities. Through the Statute of Westminster (1931), Canada was recognized as an equal of Great Britain. With the Constitution Act of 1982, the British gave Canada total control over its constitution and severed the remaining legal connections between the two countries. French Canadian unrest continued to be a major concern, with a movement growing for Quebec separatism in the late 20th century. Referendums for more political autonomy for Quebec were rejected in 1992 and 1995, but the issue remained unresolved. In 1999 Canada formed the new territory of Nunavut, and in December 2001 Newfoundland was renamed Newfoundland and Labrador.

Recent Developments

Although Prime Minister Stephen Harper's Conservative Party won reelection in October, 2008 was an otherwise difficult year for the Conservatives, who faced several scandals. Harper came under fire in February after an audiotape interview from 2005 was released in which the Conservative leader seemed to indicate that his party had offered financial incentives to Independent MP Chuck Cadman in an effort to persuade him to cast a vote of no confidence in the previous Liberal government. Foreign Affairs Minister Maxime Bernier—who had previously been criticized for promising to fly aid to hurricane-ravaged Myanmar (Burma) on military planes that were actually unavailable and for not knowing the name of the president of Haiti—resigned in May, hours before news leaked that he had left confidential NATO documents at the home of a woman with whom he had been involved and had asked her to dispose of them. In June the prime minister made a formal apology on behalf of the country to former students of residential schools that were operated by the government and numerous Christian churches from the 19th century until 1996. The schools, often sites of physical, emotional, and sexual abuse, removed aboriginal children from their families as part of an aggressive assimilation policy that sought to destroy First Nations culture. Approximately 86,000 of the former students were still living in 2008; they would share in a Can$2 billion government compensation package.

Finance Minister Jim Flaherty in February presented Canada's smallest budget in 11 years. Major spending announcements included Can$1 billion over three years and Can$250 million over five years to assist the struggling manufacturing and auto industries, respectively; a Can$2 billion infrastructure investment fund; a tax savings account in which Canadians could deposit or invest up to Can$5,000 tax free each year; and Can$500 million for public transit. Spending increased by only 3.4%—a significant reduction from the 14.8% rise from two previous Conservative budgets. The outlook had changed by the end of the year in the wake of a global credit and financial crisis. In August and September 2008 Canada's stock market lost 20% of its value and was off by almost 40% from record highs set the previous year. The federal government was expected to have a deficit of Can$40 billion in fiscal year 2009, while Ontario announced the largest deficit in its history, Can$14.2 billion. The Canadian dollar was valued below US$0.90 in May 2009, following a 30-year high in 2007 in which it had closed above parity with the US dollar.

Arctic initiatives, particularly those strengthening Canada's claim of sovereignty over its territorial waters for security and resource-extraction purposes, were high priorities. In August 2008 the government announced a state-of-the-art mapping program to identify energy- and mineral-development potential in the area and a series of large-scale rehearsals for emergencies involving cruise ships and commercial vessels. In April 2009 the government announced the composition of a new 500-soldier Arctic force that would be formed in the next several years. The following month soldiers underwent extreme-weather training at the site of the new Arctic base under construction at Resolute Bay.

Internet resources: <www.statcan.gc.ca>.

Cape Verde

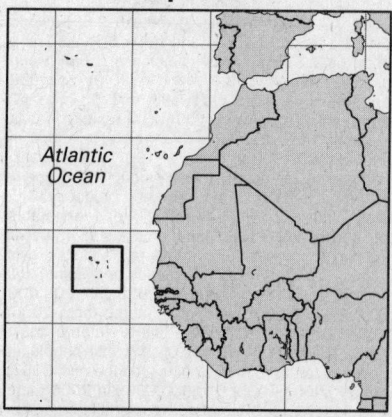

Official name: República de Cabo Verde (Republic of Cape Verde). **Form of government:** multiparty republic with one legislative house (National Assembly [72]). **Chief of state:** President Pedro Pires (from 2001). **Head of government:** Prime Minister José Maria Neves (from 2001). **Capital:** Praia. **Official language:** Portuguese. **Official religion:** none. **Monetary unit:** 1 escudo (C.V.Esc.) = 100 centavos; valuation (1 Jul 2009) US$1 = C.V.Esc. 78.28.

Demography

Area: 1,557 sq mi, 4,033 sq km. **Population** (2008): 500,000. **Density** (2008): persons per sq mi 321.1, persons per sq km 124.0. **Urban** (2007): 58.9%. **Sex distribution** (2005): male 48.47%; female 51.53%. **Age breakdown** (2005): under 15, 39.4%; 15–29, 31.0%; 30–44, 16.6%; 45–59, 7.5%; 60–74, 4.1%; 75–84, 1.2%; 85 and over, 0.2%. **Ethnic composition** (2000): Cape Verdean *mestico* (black-white admixture) 69.6%; Fulani 12.2%; Balanta 10.0%; Mandyako 4.6%; Portuguese white 2.0%; other 1.6%. **Religious affiliation** (2000): Christian 95.1%, of which Roman Catholic 88.1%, Protestant 3.3%, independent Christian 2.7%; Muslim 2.8%; other 2.1%. **Major cities** (2005): Praia 111,500; Mindelo 70,000; Santa Maria (2000) 13,220; Assomada 11,900; Pedra Badejo 10,700. **Location:** islands in the North Atlantic Ocean, off the coast of western Africa.

Vital statistics

Birth rate per 1,000 population (2006): 24.9 (world avg. 20.3). **Death rate** per 1,000 population (2006): 6.6 (world avg. 8.6). **Natural increase rate** per 1,000 population (2006): 18.3 (world avg. 11.7). **Total fertility rate** (avg. births per childbearing woman; 2005): 2.90. **Life expectancy** at birth (2006): male 68.3 years; female 76.1 years.

National economy

Budget (2006). *Revenue:* C.V.Esc. 34,603,000,000 (tax revenue 68.1%, of which consumption taxes

28.6%, taxes on income and profits 22.0%; grants 20.2%; nontax revenue 11.0%; net lending 0.7%). *Expenditures:* C.V.Esc. 36,309,000,000 (current expenditures 59.7%; capital expenditures 34.8%; other 5.5%). **Public debt** (external, outstanding; 2005): US$545,800,000. **Gross national income** (2007): US$1,287,000,000 (US$2,430 per capita). **Production** (metric tons except as noted). *Agriculture and fishing* (2007): sugarcane 15,400, corn (maize) 12,000, bananas 6,800; livestock (number of live animals) 217,000 pigs, 115,400 goats; fisheries production (2005) 7,742 (from aquaculture, none). *Mining and quarrying* (2006): salt 1,600. *Manufacturing* (1999): flour 15,901; soap 1,371; frozen fish (2002) 900. *Energy production (consumption):* electricity (kW-hr; 2005) 237,000,000 (237,000,000); petroleum products (metric tons; 2005) none (93,000). **Population economically active** (2003): total 157,000; activity rate of total population 32.5% (participation rates: ages 15–64, 58%; female 34%; unemployed [2006] 21.1%). **Selected balance of payments data.** Receipts from (US$'000,000): tourism (2006) 215; remittances (2007) 143; foreign direct investment (2004–06 avg.) 73; official development assistance (2006) 138. Disbursements for (US$'000,000): tourism (2006) 82; remittances (2007) 6.

Foreign trade

Imports (2006): C.V.Esc. 47,578,000,000 (food and agricultural products 27.2%; machinery and apparatus 10.7%; mineral fuels 8.6%; transportation equipment 5.4%, base metals 5.2%). *Major import sources:* Portugal 30.9%; The Netherlands and Belgium 13.3%; US 12.8%; Spain 7.6%; Brazil 5.4%. **Exports** (2006): C.V.Esc. 7,286,000,000 (reexports [significantly resold fuel (bunkering) to passing ships and aircraft] 75.9%; domestic exports 24.1%, of which fresh fish 10.5%, clothing 6.7%, footwear 3.3%). *Major export destinations:* Portugal 49.8%; Spain 27.3%.

Transport and communications

Transport. *Railroads:* none. *Roads* (2001): total length 1,400 km (paved [2000] 69%). *Vehicles* (2003): passenger cars 23,811; trucks and buses 5,032. *Air transport* (2002): passenger-km 279,000,000. **Communications**, in total units (units per 1,000 persons). Telephone landlines (2006): 72,000 (138); cellular telephone subscribers (2007): 148,000 (279); personal computers (2004): 48,000 (102); total Internet users (2007): 37,000 (70); broadband Internet subscribers (2006): 1,800 (3.7).

Education and health

Educational attainment (1990). Percentage of population ages 25 and over having: no formal schooling/unknown 52.3%; primary 40.9%; incomplete secondary 3.9%; complete secondary 1.4%; higher 1.5%. **Literacy** (2007): total population ages 15 and over literate 79.4%; males literate 87.5%; females literate 72.6%. **Health** (2005): physicians 241 (1 per 1,976 persons); hospital beds 950 (1 per 501 persons); infant mortality rate per 1,000 live births 30.0.

Military

Total active duty personnel (2007): 1,200 (army 83.3%, air force 8.3%, coast guard 8.4%). **Military ex-**

penditure as percentage of GDP** (2004): 0.7%; per capita expenditure US$15.

Background

When visited by the Portuguese in 1456–60, the islands were uninhabited. In 1460 Diogo Gomes sighted and named Maio and São Tiago, and in 1462 the first settlers landed on São Tiago, founding the city of Ribeira Grande. The city's importance grew with the development of the slave trade, but its wealth attracted pirates so often that it was abandoned after 1712. The prosperity of the Portuguese-controlled islands vanished with the decline of the slave trade in the 19th century but later improved because of their position on the great trade routes between Europe, South America, and southern Africa. In 1951 the colony became an overseas province of Portugal. Many islanders preferred independence, and it was granted in 1975. At one time associated politically with Guinea-Bissau, Cape Verde split from it in the wake of a 1980 coup there.

Recent Developments

In 2008 Cape Verde continued to enjoy political stability and annual economic growth of more than 6%, thanks in part to new infrastructure development and increased tourism. In January, Cape Verde was upgraded by the United Nations from a lower-income country to a middle-income country, joining only 13 other African countries with that status. On 23 July Cape Verde became the 153rd member of the World Trade Organization.

Internet resources: <www. governo.cv/index.php?lang=en>.

Central African Republic

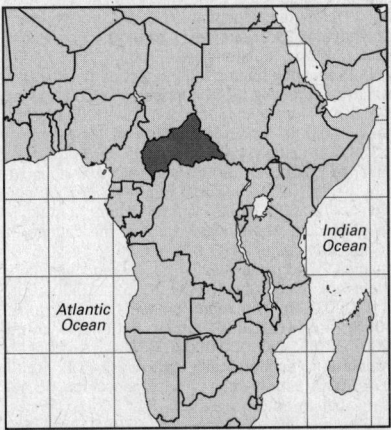

Official name: République Centrafricaine (Central African Republic). **Form of government:** multiparty republic with one legislative body (National Assembly [105]). **Chief of state:** President François Bozizé (from 2003). **Head of government:** Prime Minister Faustin Archange Touadéra (from 2008). **Capital:** Bangui. **Official languages:** French; Sango. **Official religion:**

none. **Monetary unit:** 1 CFA franc (CFAF) = 100 centimes; valuation (1 Jul 2009) US$1 = CFAF 462.89.

Demography

Area: 240,324 sq mi, 622,436 sq km. **Population** (2008): 4,424,000. **Density** (2008): persons per sq mi 18.4, persons per sq km 7.1. **Urban** (2007): 38.3%. **Sex distribution** (2005): male 48.72%; female 51.28%. **Age breakdown** (2005): under 15, 42.7%; 15–29, 28.1%; 30–44, 14.7%; 45–59, 8.8%; 60–74, 4.6%; 75–84, 1.0%; 85 and over, 0.1%. **Ethnolinguistic composition** (2004): Gbaya (Baya) 33%; Banda 27%; Mandjia 13%; Sara 10%; Mbum 7%; Ngbaka 4%; other 6%. **Religious affiliation** (2005): independent Christian 20.2%; Roman Catholic 19.8%; traditional beliefs 19.5%; Protestant 16.4%; Sunni Muslim 14.5%; nonreligious/other 9.6%. **Major cities** (2003): Bangui 622,771; Bimbo 124,176; Berbérati 76,918; Carnot 45,421; Bambari 41,356. **Location:** central Africa, bordering Chad, The Sudan, the Democratic Republic of the Congo, the Republic of the Congo, and Cameroon.

Vital statistics

Birth rate per 1,000 population (2006): 33.9 (world avg. 20.3). **Death rate** per 1,000 population (2006): 18.7 (world avg. 8.6). **Natural increase rate** per 1,000 population (2006): 15.1 (world avg. 11.7). **Total fertility rate** (avg. births per childbearing woman; 2006): 4.41. **Life expectancy** at birth (2006): male 43.5 years; female 43.6 years.

National economy

Budget (2005). *Revenue:* CFAF 88,000,000,000 (taxes 57.5%, of which indirect domestic taxes 30.0%, direct taxes on income and profits 16.7%, taxes on international trade 10.8%; grants 33.5%; nontax revenue 9.0%). *Expenditures:* CFAF 120,400,-000,000 (current expenditures 62.6%; development expenditures 31.9%; interest payments 5.5%). **Public debt** (external, outstanding; 2006): US$863,000,-000. **Production** (metric tons except as noted). *Agriculture and fishing* (2007): cassava 565,000, yams 346,000, peanuts (groundnuts) 137,000, sesame seeds 40,000; livestock (number of live animals) 3,378,000 cattle, 3,087,000 goats, 805,000 pigs; fisheries production (2005) 15,000 (from aquaculture, negligible). *Mining and quarrying* (2006): diamonds 420,000 carats (official figure; a roughly equal amount was smuggled out of the country in 2006). *Manufacturing* (2002): refined sugar 10,570; palm oil 2,743; soap 1,625. *Energy production (consumption):* electricity (kW-hr; 2005) 110,000,000 (110,000,000); petroleum products (metric tons; 2005) none (82,000). **Gross national income** (2007): US$1,667,000,000 (US$380 per capita). **Population economically active** (2003): total 1,786,000; activity rate of total population 45.4% (participation rates: ages 15–64, 80.4%; female 46.2%; unemployed [Bangui only; 2001] 23%). **Selected balance of payments data.** Receipts from (US$'000,000): tourism (2005) 4.0; foreign direct investment (2004–06 avg.) 26; official development assistance (2006) 134. Disbursements for (US$'000,000): tourism (2004) 32.

Foreign trade

Imports (2005): CFAF 90,300,000,000 (petroleum products 19.6%; unspecified 80.4%). *Major import sources:* France 17%; The Netherlands 10%; Cameroon 10%; US 7%. **Exports** (2005): CFAF 67,400,000,000 (diamonds 48.7%; wood products 38.3%; cotton 1.6%; coffee 1.3%). *Major export destinations:* Belgium 35%; France 10%; Spain 9%; Italy 8%; China 7%.

Transport and communications

Transport. *Railroads:* none. *Roads* (national roads only; much of the 9,700-mi [15,600-km] local road network is unusable; 2005): total length 10,000 km (paved 7%). *Vehicles:* passenger cars (2002) 5,000; trucks and buses (2001) 6,300. *Air transport* (2003): passenger arrivals 19,250, passenger departures 19,107; metric ton-km cargo 7,000,000. **Communications,** in total units (units per 1,000 persons). Telephone landlines (2005): 10,000 (2.5); cellular telephone subscribers (2007): 130,000 (30); personal computers (2005): 12,000 (3); total Internet users (2006): 13,000 (3.2).

Education and health

Educational attainment (1994–95). Percentage of population ages 25 and over having: no formal schooling/unknown 55.1%; at least some primary education 30.5%; at least some secondary education 14.4%. **Literacy** (2007): total population ages 15 and over literate 56.6%; males literate 67.6%; females literate 46.4%. **Health:** physicians (2004) 331 (1 per 11,867 persons); hospital beds (2001) 4,365 (1 per 879 persons); infant mortality rate per 1,000 live births (2006) 85.6; undernourished population (2002–04) 1,700,000 (44% of total population based on the consumption of a minimum daily requirement of 1,800 calories).

Military

Total active duty personnel (2007): 3,150 (army 63.5%, air force 4.8%, paramilitary [gendarmerie] 31.7%); deployment of 3,700 troops from 14 EU nations to protect refugees and displaced persons in both the Central African Republic and Chad began in March 2008. **Military expenditure as percentage of GDP** (2005): 1.1%; per capita expenditure US$2.

Background

For several centuries before the arrival of Europeans, the territory was subjected to slave traders. The French explored and claimed central Africa and in 1889 established a post at Bangui. In 1898 they partitioned the colony among commercial concessionaires. United with Chad in 1906 to form the French colony of Ubangi-Shari, it later became part of French Equatorial Africa. It was separated from Chad in 1920 and became an overseas territory in 1946. Named an autonomous republic within the French Community in 1958, the country achieved independence in 1960. In 1966 the military overthrew a civilian government and installed Jean-Bédel Bokassa, who in 1976 declared himself Emperor Bokassa I

---

1 metric ton = about 1.1 short tons;   1 kilometer = 0.6 mi (statute);   1 metric ton-km cargo = about 0.68 short ton-mi cargo;   c.i.f.: cost, insurance, and freight;   f.o.b.: free on board

and renamed the country the Central African Empire. The military again seized power in the 1980s. A new constitution was promulgated in 2004, and a democratically elected government was installed in 2005.

Recent Developments

By early 2008, 100,000 Central Africans had fled from the north to neighboring countries, while an additional 200,000 had been driven from their homes by continuing violent confrontations between the army and various rebel groups. An EU force of more than 3,000 was mobilized in March of that year to the Central African Republic and Chad to protect displaced people fleeing from the strife in Darfur, a region in The Sudan. As violence continued, a UN peacekeeping mission, with a mandate for up to 5,200 soldiers, took over from the EU force in March 2009.

Internet resources: <www.stat-centrafrique.com/>.

Chad

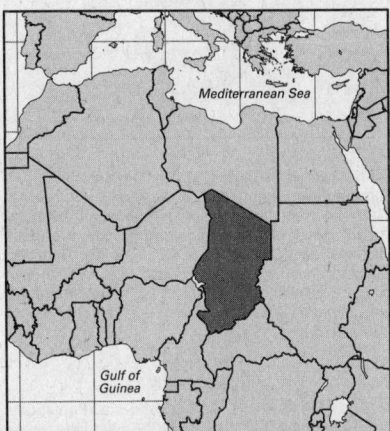

Official name: Jumhuriyah Tshad (Arabic); République du Tchad (French) (Republic of Chad). **Form of government:** unitary republic with one legislative body (National Assembly [155]). **Chief of state:** President Idriss Déby (from 1990). **Head of government:** Prime Minister Youssouf Saleh Abbas (from 2008). **Capital:** N'Djamena. **Official languages:** Arabic; French. **Official religion:** none. **Monetary unit:** 1 CFA franc (CFAF) = 100 centimes; valuation (1 Jul 2009) US$1 = CFAF 462.89.

Demography

Area: 495,755 sq mi, 1,284,000 sq km. **Population** (2008): 10,111,000. **Density** (2008): persons per sq mi 20.4, persons per sq km 7.9. **Urban** (2007): 26.3%. **Sex distribution** (2005): male 48.82%; female 51.18%. **Age breakdown** (2005): under 15, 48.0%; 15–29, 26.7%; 30–44, 13.7%; 45–59, 7.3%; 60–74, 3.5%; 75 and over, 0.8%. **Ethnolinguistic composition** (1993): Sara 27.7%; Sudanic Arab 12.3%; Mayo-Kebbi peoples 11.5%; Kanem-Bornu peoples 9.0%; Ouaddaï peoples 8.7%; Hadjeray (Had-

jaraï) 6.7%; Tangale (Tandjilé) peoples 6.5%; Gorane peoples 6.3%; Fitri-Batha peoples 4.7%; Fulani (Peul) 2.4%; other 4.2%. **Religious affiliation** (2005): Sunni Muslim 57.0%; animist 18.8%; Protestant 10.5%; other (significantly Roman Catholic and nonreligious) 13.7%. **Major cities** (2000): N'Djamena (urban agglomeration; 2005) 888,000; Moundou 108,728; Sarh 95,050; Abéché 63,165; Kelo 36,643. **Location:** central Africa, bordered by Libya, The Sudan, the Central African Republic, Cameroon, Nigeria, and Niger.

Vital statistics

Birth rate per 1,000 population (2007): 42.4 (world avg. 20.3). **Death rate** per 1,000 population (2007): 16.7 (world avg. 8.6). **Natural increase rate** per 1,000 population (2007): 25.7 (world avg. 11.7). **Total fertility rate** (avg. births per childbearing woman; 2007): 5.56. **Life expectancy** at birth (2007): male 46.2 years; female 48.3 years.

National economy

Budget (2005). *Revenue:* CFAF 311,100,000,000 (tax revenue 45.9%; petroleum revenue 43.7%; nontax revenue 10.4%). *Expenditures:* CFAF 482,000,000,000 (capital expenditures 61.9%; current expenditures 38.1%, of which wages and salaries 13.9%, materials and supply 7.8%, transfer payments 7.1%, defense 6.3%). **Public debt** (external, outstanding; 2006): US$1,686,000,000. **Production** (metric tons except as noted). *Agriculture and fishing* (2007): rice 1,290,000, sorghum 700,000, millet 550,000, gum arabic (2006) 20,000; livestock (number of live animals) 6,820,300 cattle, 6,096,390 goats, 2,981,800 sheep, 749,500 camels; fisheries production (2005) 70,000 (from aquaculture, none). *Mining and quarrying* (2006): natron 12,000; salt 10,000; gold 150 kg. *Manufacturing* (2004–05): cotton fiber 88,158; refined sugar 51,823; woven cotton fabrics (2000) 1,000,000 meters. *Energy production (consumption):* electricity (kW-hr; 2005) 100,000,-000 (100,000,000); crude petroleum (barrels; 2006) 55,900,000 (n.a.); petroleum products (metric tons; 2005) none (61,000). **Selected balance of payments data.** Receipts from (US$'000,000): tourism (2005) 14; foreign direct investment (2004–06 avg.) 603; official development assistance (2006) 284. Disbursements for (US$'000,000): tourism (2002) 80. **Population economically active** (2003): total 3,385,000; activity rate of total population 37.1% (participation rates: ages 15–64, 70.2%; female 47.3%). **Gross national income** (2007): US$5,760,000,000 (US$540 per capita).

Foreign trade

Imports (2005): CFAF 323,500,000,000 (nonpetroleum private sector 42.7%; public sector 19.3%; petroleum sector 15.6%). *Major import sources:* France 21%; Cameroon 15%; US 12%; Belgium 7%; Portugal 5%. **Exports** (2004): CFAF 1,152,300,000,000 (crude petroleum 84.5%; live cattle 10.4%; cotton 3.3%). *Major export destinations:* US 78%; China 10%; Taiwan 4%.

Transport and communications

Transport. *Railroads:* none. *Roads* (2002): total length 33,400 km (paved 1%). *Vehicles* (2002): passenger cars 8,900; trucks and buses 12,400. *Air transport:* passenger-km (2001) 130,000,000; metric ton-km cargo (2004) 7,000,000. **Communications,** in total units (units per 1,000 persons). Telephone landlines (2006): 13,000 (1.3); cellular telephone subscribers (2007): 918,000 (85); personal computers (2004): 15,000 (1.6); total Internet users (2006): 60,000 (6).

Education and health

Educational attainment (2003). Percentage of population ages 25 and over having: no formal schooling 74.5%; primary education 17.4%; secondary education 6.8%; higher education 1.3%. **Literacy** (2007): percentage of total population ages 15 and over literate 53.7%; males literate 61.5%; females literate 46.3%. **Health:** physicians (2004) 345 (1 per 27,180 persons); hospital beds (1998) 4,105 (1 per 1,908 persons); infant mortality rate per 1,000 live births (2007) 102.1; undernourished population (2002–04) 3,000,000 (35% of total population based on the consumption of a minimum daily requirement of 1,810 calories).

Military

Total active duty personnel (2007): 25,350 (army 78.9%; air force 1.4%; other 19.7%); deployment of 3,700 troops from 14 EU nations to protect refugees and displaced persons in both Chad and the Central African Republic began in March 2008. **Military expenditure as percentage of GDP** (2005): 1.0%; per capita expenditure US$6.

Background

About AD 800 the kingdom of Kanem was founded in north-central Africa, and by the early 1200s its borders had expanded to form a new kingdom, Kanem-Bornu, in the northern regions of the area. Its power peaked in the 16th century with its command of the southern terminus of the trans-Sahara trade route to Tripoli. Around this time the rival kingdoms of Baguirmi and Wadai evolved in the south. In the years 1883–93 all three kingdoms fell to the Sudanese adventurer Rabih al-Zubayr, who was in turn pushed out by the French in 1900. Extending their power, the French in 1910 made Chad a part of French Equatorial Africa. Chad became a separate colony in 1920 and was made an overseas territory in 1946. The country achieved independence in 1960. This was followed by decades of civil war and frequent intervention by France and Libya.

Recent Developments

An EU military force of 3,700 troops (EUFOR) was deployed to Chad in early 2008 to help protect humanitarian personnel providing services mainly to refugees streaming in from Darfur, a war-torn region in The Sudan, as well as to some 180,000 internally displaced people. In February the long-standing conflict in eastern Chad between the government and rebels reached the capital, and heavy fighting occurred there before the rebels were expelled. Chad retained its reputation as one of the most corrupt countries in the world, and much of the money that flowed

to the government in the form of new oil revenues seemed to disappear. In March 2009 a UN peacekeeping force with a mandate for 5,200 troops replaced EUFOR.

Internet resources: <www.inseed-tchad.org>.

Chile

Official name: República de Chile (Republic of Chile). **Form of government:** multiparty republic with two legislative houses (Senate [38]; Chamber of Deputies [120]). **Head of state and government:** President Michelle Bachelet (from 2006). **Capital:** Santiago (legislative bodies meet in Valparaíso). **Official language:** Spanish. **Official religion:** none. **Monetary unit:** 1 peso (Ch$) = 100 centavos; valuation (1 Jul 2009) US$1 = Ch$529.10.

Demography

Area: 291,930 sq mi, 756,096 sq km. **Population** (2008): 16,454,000. **Density** (2008): persons per sq mi 56.4, persons per sq km 21.8. **Urban** (2003): 87.0%. **Sex distribution** (2005): male 49.47%; female 50.53%. **Age breakdown** (2005): under 15, 24.9%; 15–29, 24.3%; 30–44, 23.0%; 45–59, 16.2%; 60–74, 8.3%; 75–84, 2.5%; 85 and over, 0.8%. **Ethnic composition** (2002): mestizo 72%; white 22%; Amerindian 5%, of which Araucanian (Mapuche) 4%; other 1%. **Religious affiliation** (2002): Roman Catholic 70.0%; Protestant/independent Christian 15.1%; other Christian 2.0%; atheist/nonreligious 8.3%. **Major urban agglomerations** (2002): Santiago 5,428,590; Valparaíso/Viña del Mar 803,683; Concepción 666,381; La Serena/Coquimbo 296,253; Antofagasta 285,255. **Location:** southern South America, bordering Peru, Bolivia, Argentina, the South Atlantic Ocean, and the South Pacific Ocean.

Vital statistics

Birth rate per 1,000 population (2006): 15.2 (world avg. 20.3). **Death rate** per 1,000 population (2006):

5.8 (world avg. 8.6). **Total fertility rate** (avg. births per childbearing woman; 2006): 2.00. **Life expectancy** at birth (2006): male 73.5 years; female 80.2 years.

National economy

Budget (2005). *Revenue:* Ch$15,680,877,000,000 (tax revenue 71.3%; copper revenue 15.6%; other 13.1%). *Expenditures:* Ch$10,582,361,000,000 (subsidies and grants 31.0%; pension payments 28.7%; wages and salaries 23.8%; goods and services 11.1%). **Public debt** (external, outstanding; 2006): US$9,454,000,000. **Population economically active** (2005): total 6,345,400; activity rate of total population 39.2% (participation rates: ages 15–64, 59.3%; female 35.6%; unemployed [2006] 7.8%). **Production** (metric tons except as noted). *Agriculture and fishing* (2007): grapes 2,350,000, sugar beets 1,806,600, corn (maize) 1,557,100; livestock (number of live animals) 4,350,000 cattle, 3,480,000 pigs, 3,420,000 sheep; fisheries production (2005) 5,028,539 (from aquaculture 14%); aquatic plants production 425,343 (from aquaculture 4%). *Mining* (2005): copper (metal content) 5,321,000; iron ore (metal content) 4,707,000; molybdenum (metal content) 47,748; lithium carbonate 43,595; silver (metal content) 1,400,000 kg; gold (metal content) 40,447 kg. *Manufacturing* (value added in US$'000,000; 2003): food products 2,041; nonferrous base metals 1,877; beverages 962; refined petroleum products 845. *Energy production (consumption):* electricity (kW-hr; 2007) 57,576,-000,000 ([2005] 56,535,000,000); hard coal (metric tons; 2007) 192,000 ([2005] 4,426,000); crude petroleum (barrels; 2006) 1,210,000 ([2005] 74,600,000); petroleum products (metric tons; 2005) 9,747,000 (11,066,000); natural gas (cu m; 2007) 1,999,000,000 ([2005] 8,311,000,000). **Gross national income** (2007): US$138,630,-000,000 (US$8,350 per capita). **Selected balance of payments data.** Receipts from (US$'000,000): tourism (2006) 1,214; remittances (2007) 3; foreign direct investment (FDI) (2004–06 avg.) 7,362; official development assistance (2006) 83. Disbursements for (US$'000,000): tourism (2006) 1,252; remittances (2007) 6; FDI (2004–06 avg.) 2,216.

Foreign trade

Imports (2005): US$32,021,400,000 (capital goods 22.3%; consumer goods 14.7%; crude petroleum 11.8%; free zone imports 5.1%). *Major import sources* (2006): US 16.0%; Argentina 12.9%; Brazil 12.2%; China 10.0%. **Exports** (2005): US$39,881,400,000 (copper 45.9%; food products 12.0%, of which salmon and trout 4.2%; wood and wooden furniture 4.5%; paper products 4.2%). *Major export destinations* (2006): US 16.0%; Japan 10.8%; China 8.8%; The Netherlands 6.8%; South Korea 6.1%.

Transport and communications

Transport. *Railroads* (2002): route length 8,707 km; (2004) passenger-km 830,259,000; metric ton-km cargo 3,899,000,000. *Roads* (2003): total length 80,505 km (paved 22%). *Vehicles* (2005): passenger cars 1,406,796; trucks and buses 681,974. *Air transport* (2007): passenger-km 16,056,000,000; metric ton-km cargo 1,294,968,000. **Communications,** in total units (units per 1,000 persons). Tele-

phone landlines (2007): 3,379,000 (203); cellular telephone subscribers (2007): 13,955,000 (839); personal computers (2005): 2,800,000 (172); total Internet users (2007): 5,570,000 (335); broadband Internet subscribers (2007): 1,198,000 (72).

Education and health

Educational attainment (2002). Percentage of population ages 25 and over having: no formal schooling/other 5.4%; incomplete primary education 24.6%; complete primary 8.7%; secondary 43.9%; higher technical 4.9%; university 12.5%. **Literacy** (2002): total population ages 15 and over literate 95.7%; males literate 95.8%; females literate 95.6%. **Health:** physicians (2004) 20,726 (1 per 778 persons); hospital beds (2003) 39,782 (1 per 401 persons); infant mortality rate per 1,000 live births (2006) 8.6; undernourished population (2002–04) 600,000 (4% of total population based on the consumption of a minimum daily requirement of 1,920 calories).

Military

Total active duty personnel (2007): 64,966 (army 55.4%, navy 31.5%, air force 13.1%). **Military expenditure as percentage of GDP** (2005): 3.8%; per capita expenditure US$270.

Background

Originally inhabited by native peoples, including the Mapuche, the Chilean coast was invaded by the Spanish in 1536. A settlement begun at Santiago in 1541 was governed under the Viceroyalty of Peru but became a separate captaincy general in 1778. It revolted against Spanish rule in 1810; its independence was finally assured by the victory of José de San Martín in 1818, and the area was then governed by Bernardo O'Higgins to 1823. In the War of the Pacific against Peru and Bolivia, it won the rich nitrate fields on the coast of Bolivia, effectively forcing that country into a landlocked position. Chile remained neutral in World War I and World War II but severed diplomatic ties with the Axis powers in 1943. In 1970 Salvador Allende was elected president, becoming the first avowed Marxist to be elected chief of state in Latin America. Following economic upheaval, he was ousted in 1973 in a coup led by Gen. Augusto Pinochet, whose military junta for many years harshly suppressed all internal opposition. A national referendum in 1988 rejected Pinochet, and elections held in 1989 returned the country to civilian rule.

Recent Developments

Chile's economy in 2008 continued to thrive, with yearly growth estimated at 4%, though inflation was up, running at 9%. Ironically, the consequences of the US financial crisis for Chile had positive as well as negative aspects. For example, the US dollar, which had dropped markedly in recent years, gained significant ground in late 2008. This, coupled with the decline in the price of oil, helped boost the Chilean export sector, one of the most vibrant sectors of Chile's economy. The price of copper, Chile's longtime leading export, declined in the later part of the year, however, as the global slowdown reduced demand for the metal. The spread of a virus among Chile's farmed salmon caused concern in the aquaculture industry.

Although dozens of salmon farms were affected, the volume of Chile's exports of farmed fish remained strong, with most going to the US and Japan, the country's largest export markets.

Internet resources: <www.bcentral.cl/eng/index.htm>.

China

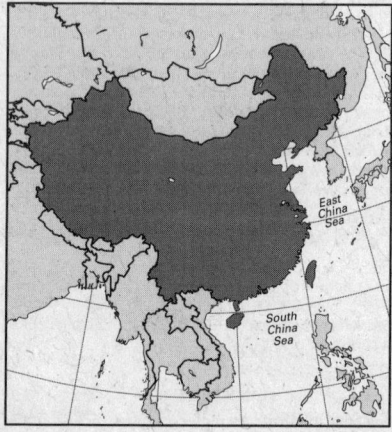

Official name: Zhonghua Renmin Gongheguo (People's Republic of China). **Form of government:** single-party people's republic with one legislative house (National People's Congress [3,000]). **Chief of state:** President Hu Jintao (from 2003). **Head of government:** Premier Wen Jiabao (from 2003). **Capital:** Beijing (Peking). **Official language:** Mandarin Chinese. **Official religion:** none. **Monetary unit:** 1 renminbi (yuan) (Y) = 10 jiao = 100 fen; valuation (1 Jul 2009) US$1 = Y 6.83.

Demography

Area: 3,696,100 sq mi, 9,572,900 sq km. **Population** (2008): 1,324,681,000. **Density** (2008): persons per sq mi 358.4, persons per sq km 138.4. **Urban** (2006): 43.9%. **Sex distribution** (2006): male 51.52%; female 48.48%. **Age breakdown** (2004): under 15, 19.3%; 15–29, 22.1%; 30–44, 27.2%; 45–59, 19.0%; 60–74, 9.6%; 75–84, 2.4%; 85 and over, 0.4%. **Ethnic composition** (2000): Han (Chinese) 91.53%; Chuang 1.30%; Manchu 0.86%; Hui 0.79%; Miao 0.72%; Uighur 0.68%; Tuchia 0.65%; Yi 0.62%; Mongolian 0.47%; Tibetan 0.44%; Puyi 0.24%; Tung 0.24%; Yao 0.21%; Korean 0.15%; Pai 0.15%; Hani 0.12%; Kazakh 0.10%; Li 0.10%; Tai 0.09%; other 0.54%. **Religious affiliation** (2005): nonreligious 39.2%; Chinese folk-religionist 28.7%; Christian 10.0%, of which unregistered Protestant 7.7%, registered Protestant 1.2%, unregistered Roman Catholic 0.5%, registered Roman Catholic 0.4%; Buddhist 8.4%; atheist 7.8%; traditional beliefs 4.4%; Muslim 1.5%. **Major urban agglomerations** (2007): Shanghai 14,987,000; Beijing 11,106,000;

Guangzhou 8,829,000; Shenzhen 7,581,000; Wuhan 7,243,000; Tianjin 7,180,000; Chongqing 6,461,000; Shenyang 4,787,000; Dongguan 4,528,000; Chengdu 4,123,000; Xi'an 4,009,000; Nanjing 3,679,000; Guiyang 3,662,000; Harbin 3,621,000; Changchun 3,183,000; Dalian 3,167,000; Zibo 3,061,000; Hangzhou 3,007,000; Kunming 2,931,000; Taiyuan 2,913,000; Qingdao 2,866,000; Jinan 2,798,000; Zhengzhou 2,636,000; Fuzhou 2,606,000; Changsha 2,604,000; Lanzhou 2,561,000. **Location:** eastern Asia, bordering Mongolia, Russia, North Korea, the Yellow Sea, the East China Sea, the South China Sea, Vietnam, Laos, Myanmar (Burma), India, Bhutan, Nepal, Pakistan, Afghanistan, Tajikistan, Kyrgyzstan, and Kazakhstan. **Mobility** (2004). Population residing in registered enumeration area 91.3%; population not residing in registered enumeration area for more than 6 months 7.4%; remainder 1.3%.

Vital statistics

Birth rate per 1,000 population (2006): 12.1 (world avg. 20.3). **Death rate** per 1,000 population (2006): 6.8 (world avg. 8.6). **Natural increase rate** per 1,000 population (2006): 5.3 (world avg. 11.7). **Total fertility rate** (avg. births per childbearing woman; 2005): 1.72. **Life expectancy** at birth (2005): male 70.9 years; female 74.3 years.

Social indicators

Educational attainment (2000). Percentage of population ages 15 and over having: no schooling/incomplete primary education 15.6%; completed primary 35.7%; some secondary 34.0%; complete secondary 11.1%; some postsecondary through advanced degree 3.6%. **Quality of working life.** Average workweek (1998) 40 hours. Annual rate per 100,000 workers (2006) for: death in mining, industrial, or commercial enterprises 3.33. Death toll from work accidents (2006) 112,822. **Access to services.** Percentage of population having access to electricity (2003) 97.7%. Percentage of total (urban, rural) population with safe public water supply (2002) 83.6% (94.0%, 73.0%). Sewage system (1999): total (urban, rural) households with flush apparatus 20.7% (50.0%, 4.3%); with pit latrines 69.3% (33.6%, 86.7%); with no latrine 5.3% (7.8%, 4.1%). **Social participation.** Trade union membership in total labor force (2004) 18%. Percentage of population who consider themselves religious (2005–06) 31.4%. **Social deviance.** Annual reported arrest rate per 100,000 population (2004) for: murder, n.a.; rape, n.a.; thievery 197; robbery 23. **Material well-being.** Urban households possessing (number per household; 2004): bicycles 1.4; color televisions 1.3; washing machines 1.0; refrigerators 0.9; air conditioners 0.7; cameras 0.5. Rural families possessing (number per household; 2004): bicycles 1.2; color televisions 0.8; washing machines 0.4; refrigerators 0.2; air conditioners 0.05; cameras 0.04.

National economy

Gross national income (2007): US$3,120,891,-000,000 (US$2,360 per capita). **Budget** (2004). Revenue: Y 2,639,647,000,000 (tax revenue 91.5%, of

---

1 metric ton = about 1.1 short tons;   1 kilometer = 0.6 mi (statute);   1 metric ton-km cargo = about 0.68 short ton-mi cargo;   c.i.f.: cost, insurance, and freight;   f.o.b.: free on board

which VAT 34.2%, corporate taxes 15.0%, business tax 13.6%, consumption tax 5.7%; nontax revenue 8.5%). *Expenditures:* Y 2,848,689,000,000 (economic development 27.8%, of which agriculture 8.3%; social, cultural, and educational development 26.3%; administration 19.4%; defense 7.7%; other 18.8%). **Public debt** (external, outstanding; 2006): US$85,802,000,000. **Production** (metric tons except as noted). *Agriculture and fishing* (2007): grains—rice 185,490,000, corn (maize) 151,830,-000, wheat 109,860,000, barley 3,851,000; oilseeds—soybeans 15,600,000, peanuts (groundnuts) 13,016,000, rapeseed 10,375,000, sunflower seeds 1,800,000; fruits and nuts—watermelons 63,000,000, apples 27,500,000, citrus 19,617,-100, cantaloupes 13,650,000, pears 12,500,000, bananas 7,100,000; other—sugarcane 105,651,-000, sweet potatoes 102,000,000, potatoes 72,000,000, cabbage 36,000,000, tomatoes 33,500,000, cucumbers 28,000,000, seed cotton 22,872,000, onions 20,500,000, eggplants 18,000,000, chilies and peppers 14,000,000, garlic 12,000,000, spinach 12,000,000, asparagus 6,250,000, tobacco leaves 2,395,000, tea 1,186,500, silkworm cocoons (2003) 667,000; livestock (number of live animals) 501,475,621 pigs, 197,267,883 goats, 171,961,000 sheep, 116,859,793 cattle, 22,717,000 water buffalo, 4,509,633,000 chickens, 736,912,000 ducks; fisheries production (2005) 49,467,309 (from aquaculture 66%); aquatic plants production (2005) 11,103,395 (from aquaculture 97%). *Mining and quarrying* (2005; by world rank): metal content of mine output—iron ore 138,000,000 (3), zinc 2,450,000 (1), manganese 1,100,000 (5), lead 1,000,000 (1), copper 740,000 (7), antimony 120,000 (1), tin 110,000 (1), tungsten 61,000 (1), silver 2,500 (3), gold 225 (2); metal ores—bauxite 18,000,000 (3), vanadium 17,000 (1); nonmetals—salt 44,547,000 (2), phosphate rock 9,130,000 (2), magnesite 4,700,000 (1), barite 4,200,000 (1), talc 3,000,000 (1), fluorspar 2,700,000 (1), asbestos 520,000 (2), strontium 140,000 (2). *Manufacturing* (value added in US$'000,000; 2003): electrical machinery (including telecommunications equipment) 66,521; industrial chemicals, paints, and soaps 45,727; transportation equipment 35,000; iron and steel 34,119; nonelectrical machinery (including computers) 31,395; food products 25,776; textiles 23,036; tobacco products 19,010; cement, bricks, and tiles 16,334; refined petroleum products 15,554; fabricated metal products 11,731; wearing apparel 11,073; nonferrous base metals 10,899. *Distribution of industrial production* (percentage of total value added by sector; 2004): directly state-owned and state-controlled enterprises 42.4%; private enterprises 15.1%; collectives 5.3%; other 37.2%. *Retail trade* (percentage of total sales by sector; 2004): domestically funded enterprises 81.8%, of which shareholding corporations 29.2%, limited liability corporations 23.8%, private enterprises 18.3%, state-owned enterprises 6.8%, collectives 1.0%; foreign-funded enterprises 11.1%; Hong Kong-, Macau-, or Taiwan-based enterprises 7.1%. *Energy production (consumption):* electricity (kW-hr; 2007) 3,180,560,000,000 ([2005] 2,491,258,000,000); hard coal (metric tons; 2006) 2,210,000,000 ([2005] 2,145,000,000 [including lignite]); lignite (metric tons; 2006) 110,000 (n.a.); crude petroleum (barrels; 2007) 1,367,000,000 ([2006] 2,346,-000,000); petroleum products (metric tons; 2005)

225,341,000 (248,048,000); natural gas (cu m; 2007) 68,611,000,000 ([2006] 55,600,000,000). **Population economically active** (2003): total 766,430,000; activity rate of total population 59.0% (participation rates: ages 15–64, 82.4%; female 44.6%; registered unemployed in urban areas [2005] 4.2%). Urban employed workforce (2004): 264,760,000; by sector: state enterprises 67,100,000, privately run enterprises 29,940,000, self-employment 25,210,000, limited liability corporations 14,360,000. **Selected balance of payments data.** Receipts from (US$'000,000): tourism (2006) 33,950; remittances (2007) 25,703; foreign direct investment (FDI) (2004–06 avg.) 67,501; official development assistance (2006) 1,245. Disbursements for (US$'000,000): tourism (2006) 24,322; remittances (2007) 3,025; FDI (2004–06 avg.) 11,296.

Foreign trade

Imports (2006; c.i.f.): US$791,461,000,000 (machinery and apparatus 41.4%, of which electronic integrated circuits and micro-assemblies 13.4%, computers and office machines 5.1%, telecommunications equipment and parts 4.1%; mineral fuels 11.2%, of which crude petroleum 8.4%; chemical products 11.0%; metal ore and metal scrap 5.6%; optical devices 4.5%). *Major import sources:* Japan 14.6%; South Korea 11.3%; Taiwan 11.0%; Chinese free trade zones 9.3%; US 7.5%; Germany 4.8%; Malaysia 3.0%; Australia 2.4%; Thailand 2.3%; Philippines 2.2%. **Exports** (2006; f.o.b.): US$968,-936,000,000 (machinery and apparatus 43.2%, of which computers and office machines 13.9%, electrical machinery 10.5%, telecommunications equipment and parts 8.8%; wearing apparel and accessories 9.8%; textile yarn, fabrics, and made-up articles 5.0%; chemical products 4.6%; iron and steel 3.4%). *Major export destinations:* US 21.0%; Hong Kong 16.0%; Japan 9.5%; South Korea 4.6%; Germany 4.2%; The Netherlands 3.2%; UK 2.5%; Singapore 2.4%; Taiwan 2.1%; Italy 1.6%.

Transport and communications

Transport. *Railroads* (2005): route length (2004) 74,400 km; passenger-km 662,200,000,000; metric ton-km cargo 2,195,400,000,000. *Roads* (2005): total length 1,930,544 km (paved 82%). *Vehicles* (2005): passenger cars 19,186,682; trucks 12,383,863. *Air transport* (2007): passenger-km 271,476,000,000; metric ton-km cargo 11,116,-608,000. **Communications**, in total units (units per 1,000 persons). Telephone landlines (2006): 367,810,000 (279); cellular telephone subscribers (2006): 461,080,000 (350); personal computers (2004): 52,990,000 (40); total Internet users (2007): 210,000,000 (158); broadband Internet subscribers (2007): 66,464,000 (50).

Education and health

Literacy (2000): percentage of total population ages 15 and over literate 90.9%; males literate 95.1%; females literate 86.5%. **Health** (2006): physicians 1,970,000 (1 per 668 persons); hospital beds 3,216,000 (1 per 409 persons); infant mortality rate per 1,000 live births (2005) 24.4; undernourished population (2002–04) 150,000,000 (12% of total population based on the consumption of a minimum daily requirement of 1,930 calories).

Military

Total active duty personnel (2007): 2,105,000 (army 76.0%, navy 12.1%, air force 11.9%). **Military expenditure as percentage of GDP** (2005): 2.0%; per capita expenditure US$34.

Background

The discovery of Peking man (*Homo erectus*) in 1927 dated the advent of early humans in what is now China to the Middle Pleistocene, about 900,000 to 130,000 years ago. Chinese civilization probably spread from the Huang He (Yellow River) valley, where it existed c. 3000 BC. The first dynasty for which there is definite historical material is the Shang (c. 16th century BC), which had a writing system and a calendar. The Zhou overthrew its Shang rulers in the 11th century BC and ruled until the 3rd century BC. Taoism and Confucianism were founded in this era.

A time of conflict, called the Warring States period, lasted from the 5th century BC until 221 BC, when the Qin (Ch'in) dynasty (from whose name China is derived) was established after its rulers had conquered rival states and created a unified empire. The Han dynasty was established in 206 BC and ruled until AD 220. A time of turbulence followed, and Chinese reunification was not achieved until the Sui dynasty was established in 581.

After the founding of the Song dynasty in 960, the capital was moved to the south because of northern invasions. In 1279 this dynasty was overthrown and Mongol (Yuan) domination began. During this time Marco Polo visited Kublai Khan. The Ming dynasty followed the period of Mongol rule and lasted from 1368 to 1644, cultivating antiforeign feelings to the point that China closed itself off from the rest of the world. Peoples from Manchuria overran China in 1644 and established the Qing (Manchu) dynasty. Ever-increasing incursions by Western and Japanese interests led in the 19th century to the Opium Wars, the Taiping Rebellion, and the Sino-Japanese War, all of which weakened the Manchus.

The dynasty fell in 1911, and a republic was proclaimed in 1912 by Sun Yat-sen. The power struggles of warlords weakened the republic. Under Sun's successor, Chiang Kai-shek, some national unification was achieved in the 1920s, but Chiang soon broke with the Communists, who had formed their own armies. Japan invaded northern China in 1937; its occupation lasted until 1945. The Communists gained support after the Long March (1934–35), in which Mao Zedong emerged as their leader.

Upon Japan's surrender at the end of World War II, a fierce civil war began; in 1949 the Nationalists fled to the island of Taiwan and the Communists proclaimed the People's Republic of China. The Communists undertook extensive reforms, but pragmatic policies alternated with periods of revolutionary upheaval, most notably in the Great Leap Forward and the Cultural Revolution. The anarchy, terror, and economic paralysis of the latter led, after Mao's death in 1976, to a turn to moderation under Deng Xiaoping, who undertook economic reforms and renewed China's ties to the West; the country established diplomatic ties with the US in 1979. The economy has been in transition since the late 1970s, moving from central planning and state-run industries to a mixture of state-owned and private enterprises in manufacturing and services, in the process growing dramatically and transforming Chinese society. The Tiananmen Square incident in 1989 was a challenge to an otherwise increasingly stable political environment after 1980. The death of Deng in 1997 marked the end of a political era, but power passed peacefully to Jiang Zemin. In 1997 Hong Kong reverted to Chinese rule, as did Macao in 1999.

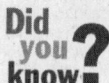 **Did you know?** Playing cards are thought to have originated in China in about the 10th century. An Indian origin has been suggested by the resemblance of symbols on some early European decks to the ring, sword, cup, and baton classically depicted in the four hands of Hindu statues. Yet another theory is that cards derived from ancient divinatory procedures used by primitive peoples.

Recent Developments

The Beijing Olympic Games in August 2008 went relatively smoothly. A policy of shifting heavy industry outside Beijing and last-minute traffic-control measures effectively reduced smog levels. Visitors found a modern capital city studded with ambitious architecture, including the Beijing National Stadium, known as the Bird's Nest. It was the location of the Games' opening ceremony, a spectacle that involved some 15,000 performers and celebrated 5,000 years of Chinese cultural achievements. Protest zones where residents could protest if they registered to receive a permit were set up. No permits were granted, however, and 58 foreigners were deported during the Games for protesting. Prior to the Games, the tour of the Olympic torch drew protests around the world in support of Tibetan and human rights.

Despite record high oil prices and the world financial crisis, China's economy continued its rapid expansion in 2008. Economic growth reached 9.0%, and China's trade surplus continued to increase at a record-setting pace. China's foreign-exchange reserves—the world's largest—grew to almost US$1.95 trillion by the end of the year—up to US$1 trillion of which was held in US treasury bills. A dramatic drop in share prices on the Shanghai Stock Exchange, however, combined with a sharp decline in real-estate transactions in major cities and slower growth in industrial output, contributed to fears that the economy would continue to slow down in 2009.

Direct talks between China and Taiwan resumed in 2008 after having been suspended for nearly a decade. Historic agreements on expansion of direct flights and trade between the two were signed in Taipei in November. The Chinese were dismayed by the Russian invasion of Georgia and Russia's diplomatic recognition of South Ossetia and Abkhazia, since these acts could create precedents for the diplomatic recognition of Tibet or Taiwan as independent countries. Chinese ties with Africa continued to expand, with bilateral trade hitting US$100 billion during the year.

Internet resources: <www.stats.gov.cn/english>.

---

1 metric ton = about 1.1 short tons;   1 kilometer = 0.6 mi (statute);   1 metric ton-km cargo = about 0.68 short ton-mi cargo;   c.i.f.: cost, insurance, and freight;   f.o.b.: free on board

Colombia

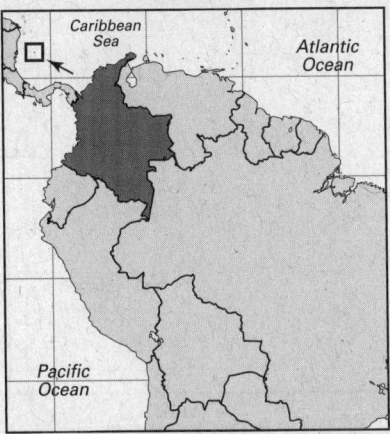

Caribbean Sea

Atlantic Ocean

Pacific Ocean

Official name: República de Colombia (Republic of Colombia). **Form of government:** unitary multiparty republic with two legislative houses (Senate [102]; House of Representatives [166]). **Head of state and government:** President Álvaro Uribe Vélez (from 2002). **Capital:** Bogotá. **Official language:** Spanish. **Official religion:** none. **Monetary unit:** 1 peso (Col$) = 100 centavos; valuation (1 Jul 2009) US$1 = Col$2,142.50.

Demography

Area: 440,762 sq mi, 1,141,568 sq km. **Population** (2008): 44,442,000. **Density** (2008): persons per sq mi 100.8, persons per sq km 38.9. **Urban** (2005): 72.7%. **Sex distribution** (2005): male 49.25%; female 50.75%. **Age breakdown** (2005): under 15, 30.3%; 15–29, 27.1%; 30–44, 21.6%; 45–59, 13.4%; 60–74, 5.6%; 75–84, 1.6%; 85 and over, 0.4%. **Ethnic composition** (2000): mestizo 47.3%; mulatto 23.0%; white 20.0%; black 6.0%; black-Amerindian 1.0%; Amerindian/other 2.7%. **Religious affiliation** (2005): Roman Catholic 92.5%; Protestant 2.8%; independent Christian 2.4%; Mormon 0.3%; Muslim 0.2%; other 1.8%. **Major cities** (2005): Bogotá 6,763,325; Medellín 2,187,356; Cali 2,039,626; Barranquilla 1,109,067; Cartagena 845,801. **Location:** northern South America, bordering the Caribbean Sea, Venezuela, Brazil, Peru, Ecuador, the Pacific Ocean, and Panama.

Vital statistics

Birth rate per 1,000 population (2006): 20.5 (world avg. 20.3). **Death rate** per 1,000 population (2006): 5.6 (world avg. 8.6). **Natural increase rate** per 1,000 population (2006): 14.9 (world avg. 11.7). **Total fertility rate** (avg. births per childbearing woman; 2006): 2.54. **Life expectancy** at birth (2006): male 68.2 years; female 76.0 years.

National economy

Budget (2003–04). *Revenue:* Col$39,951,400,-000,000 (tax revenue 92.0%; nontax revenue 8.0%). *Expenditures:* Col$53,934,600,000,000 (transfers 53.1%; debt service 19.0%). **Public debt** (external,

outstanding; 2006): US$25,764,000,000. **Population economically active** (2006): total 20,177,100; activity rate of total population 44.5% (participation rates: ages 12–55, 63.2%; female 43.0%; unemployed 12.7%). **Production** (metric tons except as noted). *Agriculture and fishing* (2007): sugarcane 40,000,000, plantains 3,600,000, rice 2,250,000 (also major producer of cut flowers; export value [2006] US$1,000,000,000); livestock (number of live animals) 26,000,000 cattle, 3,400,000 sheep, 2,500,000 horses; fisheries production (2006) 155,100 (from aquaculture 39%). *Mining and quarrying* (2005): nickel (metal content) 81,000; gold 35,785 kg; emeralds 6,746,000 carats. *Manufacturing* (value added in Col$'000,000,000; 2003): processed food products 6,471; chemical products 5,737; beverages 3,775; petroleum products 3,712 (illegal cocaine production [2004] 430 metric tons). *Energy production (consumption):* electricity (kW-hr; 2005) 50,665,000,000 (48,923,000,000); hard coal (metric tons; 2005) 59,100,000 (4,170,000); crude petroleum (barrels; 2007) 191,900,000 ([2005] 107,600,000); petroleum products (metric tons; 2005) 13,613,000 (9,438,000); natural gas (cu m; 2005) 8,229,000,000 (8,229,000,000). **Gross national income** (2007): US$149,934,000,-000 (US$3,250 per capita). **Selected balance of payments data.** Receipts from (US$'000,000): tourism (2006) 1,550; remittances (2007) 4,523; foreign direct investment (FDI) (2004–06 avg.) 6,545; official development assistance (2006) 988. Disbursements for (US$'000,000): tourism (2006) 1,329; remittances (2007) 95; FDI (2004–06 avg.) 1,967.

Foreign trade

Imports (2006): US$26,162,000,000 (chemical products 20.2%; transportation equipment 15.3%; nonelectrical machinery 11.2%; telecommunications equipment 8.6%). *Major import sources* (2006): US 26.5%; Mexico 8.8%; China 8.5%; Brazil 7.2%; Venezuela 5.7%. **Exports** (2006): US$24,391,-000,000 (crude and refined petroleum 26.0%; coal 11.9%; chemical products 7.4%; base metals 6.6%; food, beverages, and tobacco 6.5%). *Major export destinations* (2006): US 39.6%; EU 13.7%; Venezuela 11.1%; Ecuador 5.1%; Peru 2.8%.

Transport and communications

Transport. *Railroads* (1999): route length (2004) 3,304 km; passenger-km, negligible; metric ton-km cargo 473,000,000. *Roads* (2005): total length 164,257 km (paved. [2000] 23%). *Vehicles* (2005): cars 1,606,880; trucks and buses 1,079,247. *Air transport* (2007): passenger-km 9,552,000,000; metric ton-km cargo 189,804,000. **Communications,** in total units (units per 1,000 persons). Telephone landlines (2007): 7,936,000 (172); cellular telephone subscribers (2007): 33,941,000 (735); personal computers (2005): 1,892,000 (44); total Internet users (2007): 12,100,000 (262); broadband Internet subscribers (2007): 1,207,000 (28).

Education and health

Educational attainment (2005). Percentage of population ages 25 and over having: no schooling/unknown 10.2%; primary education 40.1%; secondary 34.2%; higher 15.5%. **Literacy** (2003): percentage of total population ages 15 and over literate 92.5%;

males literate 92.4%; females literate 92.6%. **Health** (2004): physicians 59,235 (1 per 714 persons); hospital beds 50,773 (1 per 833 persons); infant mortality rate per 1,000 live births (2006) 20.4; undernourished population (2002–04) 5,900,000 (13% of total population based on the consumption of a minimum daily requirement of 1,830 calories).

Military

Total active duty personnel (2007): 254,259 (army 85.3%, navy 10.9%, air force 3.8%). **Military expenditure as percentage of GDP** (2005): 3.7%; per capita expenditure US$106.

Background

The Spanish arrived in what is now Colombia c. 1500 and by 1538 had defeated the area's Chibchan-speaking Indians and made the area subject to the Viceroyalty of Peru. After 1740 authority was transferred to the newly created Viceroyalty of New Granada. Parts of Colombia threw off Spanish jurisdiction in 1810, and full independence came after Spain's defeat by Simón Bolívar in 1819. Civil war in 1840 checked development. Conflict between the Liberal and Conservative parties led to the War of a Thousand Days (1899–1903). Years of relative peace followed, but hostility erupted again in 1948; the two parties agreed in 1958 to a scheme for alternating governments. A new constitution was adopted in 1991, but democratic power remained threatened by civil unrest. Many leftist rebels and right-wing paramilitary groups funded their activities through kidnappings and narcotics trafficking.

Recent Developments

The left-wing paramilitary group the Revolutionary Armed Forces of Colombia (FARC) suffered several major setbacks in 2008. In March the Colombian military struck a rebel camp in Ecuador, killing senior leader Raúl Reyes and setting off a diplomatic skirmish with Venezuela, Nicaragua, and Ecuador. In May the group revealed that its leader and founding member, Pedro Antonio Marín, had died. In July the Colombian military rescued 15 FARC hostages, including former presidential candidate Ingrid Betancourt. A military operation in September resulted in the killing of a particularly violent FARC commander, Aicardo de Jesús Agudelo. In April 2009 Daniel Rendón Herrera, a drug lord whose organization was thought to be responsible for 3,000 murders since 2008, was captured and extradited to the US, where he was charged with conspiring to support terrorism (for his affiliation with the right-wing paramilitary group the United Self-Defense Groups of Colombia [AUC]) and to import tons of cocaine.

Internet resources: <www.turiscolombia.andes.com/colombia_eng.htm>.

Comoros

Official names: Udzima wa Komori (Comorian); Jumhuriyat al-Qamar al-Muttahidah (Arabic); Union des Comores (French) (Union of the Comoros). **Form**

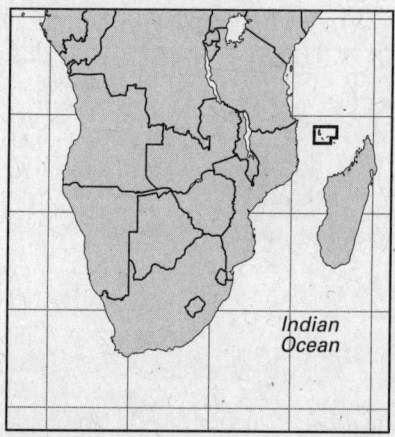

Indian
Ocean

of government: republic with one legislative house (Assembly of the Union [33]). **Head of state and government:** President Ahmed Abdallah Mohamed Sambi (from 2006). **Capital:** Moroni. **Official languages:** Comorian (Shikomor); Arabic; French. **Official religion:** Islam. **Monetary unit:** 1 Comorian franc (CF) = 100 centimes; valuation (1 Jul 2009) US$1 = CF 349.50.

Demography

Area: 719 sq mi, 1,862 sq km. **Population** (2008): 645,000. **Density** (2008): persons per sq mi 897.1, persons per sq km 346.4. **Urban** (2007): 28.0%. **Sex distribution** (2006): male 49.61%; female 50.39%. **Age breakdown** (2006): under 15, 42.7%; 15–29, 26.6%; 30–44, 17.8%; 45–59, 8.2%; 60–74, 3.9%; 75 and over, 0.8%. **Ethnic composition** (2000): Comorian (a mixture of Bantu, Arab, Malay, and Malagasy peoples) 97.1%; Makua 1.6%; French 0.4%; Arab 0.1%; other 0.8%. **Religious affiliation** (2005): Muslim (nearly all Sunni) 98.4%; other 1.6%. **Major cities** (2002): Moroni (2003) 41,557 (urban agglomeration [2003] 53,000); Mutsamudu 21,558; Domoni 13,254; Fomboni 13,053; Tsembehou 10,552. **Location:** islands in the western Indian Ocean, between Madagascar and Mozambique.

Vital statistics

Birth rate per 1,000 population (2006): 36.9 (world avg. 20.3). **Death rate** per 1,000 population (2006): 8.2 (world avg. 8.6). **Natural increase rate** per 1,000 population (2006): 28.7 (world avg. 11.7). **Total fertility rate** (avg. births per childbearing woman; 2006): 5.03. **Life expectancy** at birth (2006): male 60.0 years; female 64.7 years.

National economy

Budget (2005). *Revenue:* CF 30,509,000,000 (tax revenue 58.3%, of which taxes on international trade 31.0%, income and profit taxes 20.3%; grants 21.4%; nontax revenue 20.3%). *Expenditures:* CF 30,425,-000,000 (current expenditures 77.3%, of which edu-

---

1 metric ton = about 1.1 short tons;   1 kilometer = 0.6 mi (statute);   1 metric ton-km cargo = about 0.68 short ton-mi cargo;   c.i.f.: cost, insurance, and freight;   f.o.b.: free on board

cation 25.1%, health 15.6%; development expenditures 22.7%). **Public debt** (external, outstanding; 2004): US$301,000,000. **Production** (metric tons except as noted). *Agriculture and fishing* (2007): coconuts 77,000, bananas 65,000, cassava 58,000, vanilla 90, ylang-ylang essence (2006) 47; livestock (number of live animals) 115,000 goats, 45,000 cattle, 21,000 sheep; fisheries production (2006) 15,070 (from aquaculture, none). *Mining and quarrying:* sand, gravel, and crushed stone from coral mining for local construction. *Manufacturing:* products of small-scale industries include processed vanilla and ylang-ylang, cement, woodwork, and clothing. *Energy production (consumption):* electricity (kW-hr; 2006) 50,600,000 ([2005] 35,900,000); petroleum products (metric tons; 2005) none (29,000). **Population economically active** (2000): total 287,000; activity rate of total population 41.0% (participation rates: ages 15–64, 73.2%; female 40.4%; unemployed [2005] 13.3%). **Gross national income** (2007): US$425,000,000 (US$680 per capita). **Selected balance of payments data.** Receipts from (US$'000,000): tourism (2006) 27; remittances (2007) 12; foreign direct investment (2004–06 avg.) 1; official development assistance (2006) 30. Disbursements for (US$'000,000): tourism (2006) 11.

Foreign trade

Imports (2004; c.i.f.): CF 33,917,000,000 (food products 30.3%, of which rice 14.3%, meat 8.9%; petroleum products 20.9%; vehicles 11.5%; cement 5.1%). *Major import sources:* France 23%; South Africa 11%; UAE 7%; Kenya 7%; Mauritius 6%. **Exports** (2004; f.o.b.): CF 5,777,000,000 (cloves 49.9%; vanilla 30.8%; ylang-ylang 14.7%). *Major export destinations:* US 42%; France 18%; Singapore 16%; Turkey 5%; Germany 4%.

Transport and communications

Transport. *Railroads:* none. *Roads* (2004): total length 793 km (paved 70%). *Vehicles* (1996): passenger cars 9,100; trucks and buses 4,950. *Air transport* (2001): passengers arriving/departing Moroni 108,000. **Communications**, in total units (units per 1,000 persons). Telephone landlines (2005): 17,000 (28); cellular telephone subscribers (2007): 40,000 (48); personal computers (2004): 5,000 (6.3); total Internet users (2006): 21,000 (26).

Education and health

Educational attainment (1996). Percentage of population ages 25 and over having: no formal schooling/unknown 73.9%; primary education 11.0%; secondary 15.1%. **Literacy** (2007): percentage of total population ages 15 and over literate 57.1%; males literate 64.2%; females literate 50.1%. **Health** (2004): physicians 48 (1 per 12,417 persons); hospital beds (1995) 1,450 (1 per 342 persons); infant mortality rate per 1,000 live births (2006) 72.9; undernourished population (2002–04) 500,000 (60% of total population based on the consumption of a minimum daily requirement of 1,830 calories).

Military

Total active duty personnel (2006): the Comorian small standing army is not necessarily accepted by each of the islands; each island also has its own armed security. France provides training for military personnel. **Military expenditure as percentage of GDP** (2005): 3.5%; per capita expenditure US$21.

Background

The Comoro Islands were known to European navigators from the 16th century. In 1843 France officially took possession of Mayotte and in 1886 placed the other three islands under protection. Subordinated to Madagascar in 1912, Comoros became an overseas territory of France in 1947. In 1961 it was granted autonomy. In 1974 majorities on three of the islands voted for independence, which was granted in 1975. The following decade saw several coup attempts, which culminated in the assassination of the president in 1989. French intervention permitted multiparty elections in 1990, but the country remained in a state of chronic instability. Anjouan and Mohéli seceded from the Comoros federation in 1997. The army took control of the government in 1999. A referendum at the end of 2001 renamed the country the Union of the Comoros and granted the three main islands partially autonomous status.

Recent Developments

In March 2009 the people of Mayotte voted overwhelmingly to become a French overseas department. Once a part of Comoros when ruled by France, Mayotte had voted against independence in 1974. Comoran Pres. Ahmed Abdallah Mohamed Sambi denounced the referendum and called upon Arab leaders to repudiate it. Several protests occurred, and the US State Department issued an alert against travel to Comoros in the immediate aftermath.

Internet resources: <www.bancecom.com>.

Congo, Democratic Republic of the

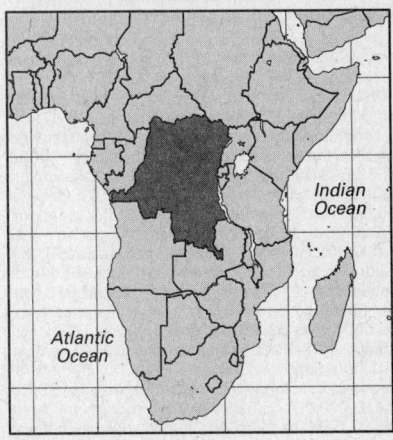

Official name: République Democratique du Congo (Democratic Republic of the Congo). **Form of government:** unitary multiparty republic with two legislative bodies (Senate [108]; National Assembly [500]). **Chief of state:** President Joseph Kabila (from 2001). **Head of government:** Prime Minister Adolphe Muzito (from 2008). **Capital:** Kinshasa. **Official languages:** French (Kongo, Lingala, Swahili, and Tshiluba are national languages). **Official religion:** none. **Monetary unit:** Congolese franc (FC) = 100 centimes; valuation (1 Jul 2009) US$1 = FC 748.18.

Demography

Area: 905,355 sq mi, 2,344,858 sq km. **Population** (2008): 66,515,000. **Density** (2008): persons per sq mi 73.5, persons per sq km 28.4. **Urban** (2005): 32.1%. **Sex distribution** (2005): male 49.48%; female 50.52%. **Age breakdown** (2005): under 15, 47.2%; 15–29, 27.1%; 30–44, 14.2%; 45–59, 7.4%; 60–74, 3.4%; 75–84, 0.6%; 85 and over, 0.1%. **Ethnic composition** (1983): Luba 18.0%; Kongo 16.1%; Mongo 13.5%; Rwanda 10.3%; Azande 6.1%; Bangi and Ngale 5.8%; Rundi 3.8%; Teke 2.7%; Boa 2.3%; Chokwe 1.8%; Lugbara 1.6%; Banda 1.4%; other 16.6%. **Religious affiliation** (2004): Roman Catholic 50%; Protestant 20%; Kimbanguist (indigenous Christian) 10%; Muslim 10%; traditional beliefs and syncretic sects 10%. **Major urban areas** (2004): Kinshasa 7,273,947; Lubumbashi 1,283,380; Mbuji-Mayi 1,213,726; Kananga 720,362; Kisangani 682,599. **Location:** central Africa, bordering the Central African Republic, The Sudan, Uganda, Rwanda, Burundi, Tanzania, Zambia, Angola, the South Atlantic Ocean, and the Republic of the Congo.

Vital statistics

Birth rate per 1,000 population (2005): 49.6 (world avg. 20.3). **Death rate** per 1,000 population (2005): 18.7 (world avg. 8.6). **Natural increase rate** per 1,000 population (2005): 30.9 (world avg. 11.7). **Total fertility rate** (avg. births per childbearing woman; 2005): 6.70. **Life expectancy** at birth (2005): male 44.3 years; female 47.0 years.

National economy

Budget (2005). *Revenue:* FC 564,900,000,000 (grants 31.1%; customs and excise taxes 25.7%; direct and indirect taxes 19.7%; petroleum royalties and taxes 17.4%). *Expenditures:* FC 655,500,000,-000 (current expenditures 65.3%, of which interest on external debt 14.8%; capital expenditures 17.4%; expenditures on demobilization and reintegration 14.8%). **Public debt** (external, outstanding; 2006): US$9,848,000,000. **Production** (metric tons except as noted). *Agriculture and fishing* (2007): cassava 15,000,000; sugarcane 1,550,000, plantains 1,200,000; livestock (number of live animals) 4,000,000 goats, 957,000 pigs, game meat 89,000 metric tons; fisheries production 222,965 (from aquaculture 1%). *Mining and quarrying* (2005): copper (metal content) 92,000; cobalt (metal content) 22,000; silver 53,553 kg; gold 4,200 kg; diamonds 30,300,000 carats. *Manufacturing* (2004): cement 402,500; flour 199,000; steel 130,000. *Energy production (consumption):* electricity (kW-hr; 2005) 7,419,000,000 (5,625,000,000); coal (metric tons; 2005) 120,000 (163,000); crude petroleum (barrels; 2005) 7,200,000 (negligible); petroleum products (metric tons; 2005) none (373,000). **Gross national income** (2007): US$8,573,000,000 (US$140 per capita). **Population economically active** (2003): total

21,718,000; activity rate of total population 40.0% (participation rates: ages 15–64, 77.1%; female 41.1%; unemployed, n.a.). **Selected balance of payments data.** Receipts from (US$'000,000): tourism (2005) 1.0; foreign direct investment (2004–06 avg.) 37; official development assistance (2005) 1,828. Disbursements for (US$'000,000): tourism (1997) 7.0.

Foreign trade

Imports (2005): US$2,465,000,000 (aid-related imports 22.9%; other imports 77.1%). *Major import sources* (2004): South Africa 18.5%; Belgium 15.6%; France 10.9%; US 6.2%; Germany 5.9%. **Exports** (2005): US$2,042,000,000 (diamonds 38.4%; crude petroleum 20.0%; cobalt [2004] 15.0%; copper [2004] 3.3%; coffee [2004] 0.9%; gold [2004] 0.7%). *Major export destinations:* Belgium 42.5%; Finland 17.8%; Zimbabwe 12.2%; US 9.2%; China 6.5%.

Transport and communications

Transport. *Railroads* (2003): length (2004) 5,138 km; passenger-km 152,930,000; metric ton-km cargo 506,010,000. *Roads* (2004): total length 153,497 km (paved 2%). *Vehicles* (1999): passenger cars 172,600; trucks and buses 34,600. *Air transport* (1999): passenger-km 263,000,000; metric ton-km cargo 39,000,000. **Communications**, in total units (units per 1,000 persons). Telephone landlines (2006): 9,700 (0.2); cellular telephone subscribers (2007): 6,592,000 (105); total Internet users (2007): 230,000 (3.7); broadband Internet subscribers (2007): 1,500 (0.02).

Education and health

Literacy (2003): percentage of total population ages 15 and over literate 65.5%; males literate 76.2%; females literate 55.1%. **Health:** physicians (2004) 5,827 (1 per 9,585 persons); infant mortality rate per 1,000 live births (2005) 116.5; undernourished population (2002–04) 39,000,000 (74% of total population based on the consumption of a minimum daily requirement of 1,830 calories).

Military

Total active duty personnel (2007): 134,484 (army 93.1%, air force 1.9%, navy 5.0%); UN peacekeepers (April 2008): 16,700 troops; 1,100 police. **Military expenditure as percentage of GDP** (2005): 2.4%; per capita expenditure US$2.

Background

Prior to European colonization, several native kingdoms had emerged in the Congo region, including the 16th-century Luba kingdom and the Kuba federation, which reached its peak in the 18th century. European development began late in the 19th century when King Léopold II of Belgium financed Henry Morton Stanley's exploration of the Congo River. The 1884–85 Berlin West Africa Conference recognized the Congo Free State with Léopold as its sovereign. The growing demand for rubber helped finance the exploitation of the Congo, but abuses against native

---

1 metric ton = about 1.1 short tons;   1 kilometer = 0.6 mi (statute);   1 metric ton-km cargo = about 0.68 short ton-mi cargo;   c.i.f.: cost, insurance, and freight;   f.o.b.: free on board

peoples outraged Western nations and forced Léopold to grant the Free State a colonial charter as the Belgian Congo in 1908. Independence was granted in 1960, and the country's name was changed to Zaire in 1971. The postindependence period was marked by unrest, culminating in a military coup that brought Gen. Mobutu Sese Seko to power in 1965. Mismanagement, corruption, and increasing violence devastated the infrastructure and economy. Mobutu was deposed in 1997 by Laurent Kabila, who restored the country's name to Democratic Republic of the Congo (DRC). Instability in neighboring countries, an influx of refugees from Rwanda, and a desire for Congo's mineral wealth led to military involvement by various African countries. Unrest continued in the early 21st century.

Recent Developments

The savage violence continued in the DRC—rebel militias from several countries remained active there. In March the UN Security Council unanimously called for the immediate and unconditional disarmament and repatriation of all Rwandan rebels in the DRC. That same month, however, Rwandan Pres. Paul Kagame accused the DRC of arming and supplying the Hutu Democratic Forces for the Liberation of Rwanda (FDLR). Starting on Christmas Eve in 2008 and continuing into 2009, Ugandan rebels of the Lord's Resistance Army massacred some 865 villagers in the northern DRC, forcing 140,000 Congolese to flee their homes. Fighters from the FDLR continued attacks on DRC soil in 2009, killing at least seven in April. The peacekeeping UN Organization Mission in the DRC (MONUC) saw its mandate extended through 2009 and its approved military component enlarged to almost 20,000 soldiers.

Internet resources: <www.bcc.cd>.

Congo, Republic of the

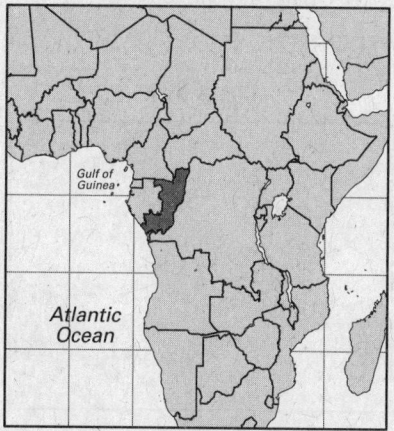

Official name: République du Congo (Republic of the Congo). **Form of government:** republic with two legislative houses (Senate [72]; National Assembly [137]). **Chief of state and government:** President Denis Sassou-Nguesso (from 1997), assisted by Prime Minister Isidore Mvouba (from 2005). **Capital:** Brazzaville. **Official language:** French (Lingala and Monokutuba are national languages). **Official religion:** none. **Monetary unit:** 1 CFA franc (CFAF) = 100 centimes; valuation (1 Jul 2009) US$1 = CFAF 462.89.

Demography

Area: 132,047 sq mi, 342,000 sq km. **Population** (2008): 3,847,000. **Density** (2008): persons per sq mi 29.1, persons per sq km 11.2. **Urban** (2007): 61.0%. **Sex distribution** (2006): male 49.68%; female 50.32%. **Age breakdown** (2006): under 15, 46.4%; 15–29, 27.1%; 30–44, 14.9%; 45–59, 7.3%; 60–74, 3.5%; 75 and over, 0.8%. **Ethnic composition** (2000): Kongo 21.2%; Yombe 11.5%; Teke 10.7%; Kougni 8.0%; Mboshi 5.4%; Ngala 4.2%; Sundi 4.0%; other 35.0%. **Religious affiliation** (2005): Roman Catholic 49%; independent Christian 13%; Protestant 11%; Muslim 2%; other (mostly traditional beliefs and nonreligious) 25%. **Major cities** (2004): Brazzaville 1,174,005; Pointe-Noire 663,359; Dolisie 106,262; Nkayi 56,686; Ouesso 24,322. **Location:** west-central Africa, bordering Cameroon, the Central African Republic, the Democratic Republic of the Congo, Angola, the South Atlantic Ocean, and Gabon.

Did you know? One of Africa's least-explored regions, the northern part of the Republic of the Congo, an area of huge swamps and nearly impenetrable forests, was traversed by foot in 1999. Dr. Michael Fay, an ecologist with the Wildlife Conservation Society, and a team of 12 others undertook a 1,200-mi (1,900-km) survey of this area as well as similar areas in neighboring Gabon. The team concluded that this wilderness is seriously threatened.

Vital statistics

Birth rate per 1,000 population (2006): 42.6 (world avg. 20.3). **Death rate** per 1,000 population (2006): 12.9 (world avg. 8.6). **Natural increase rate** per 1,000 population (2006): 29.6 (world avg. 11.7). **Total fertility rate** (avg. births per childbearing woman; 2006): 6.07. **Life expectancy** at birth (2006): male 51.7 years; female 54.0 years.

National economy

Budget (2005). *Revenue:* CFAF 1,300,100,000,000 (petroleum revenue 80.6%; nonpetroleum revenue 16.9%; grants 2.5%). *Expenditures:* CFAF 736,400,000,000 (current expenditures 77.0%, of which debt interest 20.4%, wages and salaries 17.7%; capital expenditures 23.0%). **Public debt** (external, outstanding; 2006): US$5,328,000,000. **Gross national income** (2007): US$5,797,000,000 (US$1,540 per capita). **Production** (metric tons except as noted). *Agriculture and fishing* (2007): cassava 915,000, sugarcane 550,000, oil palm fruit 90,000, cacao beans 1,000; livestock (number of live animals) 290,000 goats, 110,000 cattle, 99,000 sheep; fisheries production (2006) 59,506 (from aquaculture, negligible). *Mining and quarrying* (2006): gold 100 kg; diamonds 50,000 carats (the Republic of the Congo was a major illegal transshipment conduit for diamonds from nearby countries and was expelled from the Kimberley Process in 2004; it was readmitted in 2007). *Manufacturing* (2000): residual fuel oils 206,000; refined sugar (2001) 71,814; distillate fuel oils 62,000; gasoline 40,000; aviation gas 38,000. *Energy production (consumption):* electricity (kW-hr; 2005) 356,000,-000 (774,000,000); crude petroleum (barrels; 2005) 92,100,000 (4,140,000); petroleum products (metric tons; 2005) 430,000 (305,000); natural gas (cu m; 2005) 122,400,000 (122,400,000). **Population economically active** (2000): total 1,232,000; activity rate of total population 35.7% (participation rates: ages 15–64, 60.3%; female [1997] 43.4%; unemployed, n.a.). **Selected balance of payments data.** Receipts from (US$'000,000): tourism (2005) 34; remittances (2007) 11; foreign direct investment (2004–06 avg.) 352; official development assistance (2006) 254. Disbursements for (US$'000,000): tourism (2005) 103; remittances (2007) 45.

Foreign trade

Imports (2005): CFAF 746,400,000,000 (nonpetroleum sector 85.9%; petroleum sector 14.1%). *Major import sources* (2002): France 26%; US 11%; Italy 8%; Lebanon 6%; The Netherlands 5%. **Exports** (2005): CFAF 2,484,300,000,000 (crude petroleum 92.5%; wood products 4.6%; refined petroleum products 1.2%). *Major export destinations* (2002): Taiwan 27%; North Korea 11%; US 10%; South Korea 7%; France 7%.

Transport and communications

Transport. *Railroads* (1998): length 894 km; passenger-km 242,000,000; metric ton-km cargo 135,000,000. *Roads* (2004): total length 17,289 km (paved 5%). *Vehicles:* passenger cars (2002) 30,000; trucks and buses (1997) 15,500. *Air transport* (2002): passenger-km 27,000,000; metric ton-km cargo 3,000,000. **Communications,** in total units (units per 1,000 persons). Telephone landlines (2005): 16,000 (4); cellular telephone subscribers (2007): 1,334,000 (354); personal computers (2005): 19,000 (4.8); total Internet users (2006): 70,000 (17).

Education and health

Educational attainment (2005). Percentage of population ages 15–49 having: no formal schooling 5.6%; primary education 28.1%; lower secondary 47.2%; upper secondary/higher 19.1%. **Literacy** (2005): percentage of total population ages 15 and over literate 87.4%; males literate 92.3%; females literate 82.9%. **Health:** physicians (2000) 540 (1 per 5,745 persons); hospital beds (2001) 5,195 (1 per 623 persons); infant mortality rate per 1,000 live births (2006) 85.3; undernourished population (2002–04) 1,200,000 (33% of total population based on the consumption of a minimum daily requirement of 1,830 calories).

Military

Total active duty personnel (2007): 10,000 (army 80.0%, navy 8.0%, air force 12.0%). **Military expendi-** ture as percentage of GDP (2005): 1.4%; per capita expenditure US$22.

Background

In precolonial days the Congo area was home to several thriving kingdoms, including the Kongo, which had its beginnings in the 1st millennium AD. The slave trade began in the 15th century with the arrival of the Portuguese; it supported the local kingdoms and dominated the area until its suppression in the 19th century. The French arrived in the mid-19th century and established treaties with two of the kingdoms, placing them under French protection prior to their becoming part of the colony of French Congo. In 1910 the French possessions were renamed French Equatorial Africa, and Congo became known as Middle (Moyen) Congo. In 1946 Middle Congo became a French overseas territory and in 1958 voted to become an autonomous republic within the French Community. Full independence came two years later. The area has suffered from political instability since independence. Congo's first president was ousted in 1963. A Marxist party, the Congolese Labor Party, gained strength, and in 1968 another coup, led by Maj. Marien Ngouabi, created the People's Republic of the Congo. Ngouabi was assassinated in 1977, and a series of military rulers followed. Fighting between local militias that began in 1997 badly disrupted the economy, and though a 2003 peace agreement largely ended the conflict, sporadic violence continued.

Recent Developments

In June 2008 a program of disarmament and reintegration of the former rebels known as "Ninjas" was launched in the southern Pool region. There were an estimated 30,000 combatants from the bloody 1998–2003 rebellion eligible for the program. While security had greatly improved in the region, the presence of thousands of former rebels still bearing arms continued to create a volatile situation.

Internet resources: <www.cnsee.org>.

Costa Rica

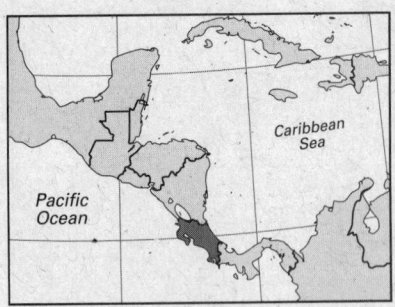

Caribbean Sea

Pacific Ocean

Official name: República de Costa Rica (Republic of Costa Rica). **Form of government:** unitary multiparty republic with one legislative house (Legislative Assembly [57]). **Head of state and government:** President Óscar Arias Sánchez (from 2006). **Capital:** San José. **Official language:** Spanish. **Official religion:** Roman Catholicism. **Monetary unit:** 1 Costa Rican colón (₡) = 100 céntimos; valuation (1 Jul 2009) US$1 = ₡571.00.

Demography

Area: 19,730 sq mi, 51,100 sq km. **Population** (2008): 4,389,000. **Density** (2008): persons per sq mi 222.5, persons per sq km 85.9. **Urban** (2003): 60.6%. **Sex distribution** (2006): male 50.76%; female 49.24%. **Age breakdown** (2005): under 15, 28.4%; 15–29, 28.1%; 30–44, 21.5%; 45–59, 13.7%; 60–74, 5.9%; 75–84, 1.8%; 85 and over, 0.6%. **Ethnic composition** (2000): white 77.0%; mestizo 17.0%; black/mulatto 3.0%; East Asian (mostly Chinese) 2.0%; Amerindian 1.0%. **Religious affiliation** (2004): Roman Catholic (practicing) 47%; Roman Catholic (nonpracticing) 25%; Evangelical Protestant 13%; nonreligious 10%; other 5%. **Major cities** (2006): San José 344,747 (urban agglomeration [2003] 1,085,000); Limón 68,215; Alajuela 49,376; San Isidro de El General 46,490; San Francisco 45,972. **Location:** Central America, bordering Nicaragua, the Caribbean Sea, Panama, and the North Pacific Ocean.

Vital statistics

Birth rate per 1,000 population (2007): 16.3 (world avg. 20.3); within marriage 40.1%; outside of marriage 59.9%. **Death rate** per 1,000 population (2007): 3.8 (world avg. 8.6). **Natural increase rate** per 1,000 population (2007): 12.5 (world avg. 11.7). **Total fertility rate** (avg. births per childbearing woman; 2006): 1.97. **Life expectancy** at birth (2006): male 77.0 years; female 81.4 years.

National economy

Budget (2004). *Revenue:* ₡1,860,988,000,000 (taxes on goods and services 38.5%; social security contributions 27.2%; income tax 14.4%). *Expenditures:* ₡1,951,392,000,000 (current expenditures 92.9%, of which wages 37.7%, transfers 25.8%, debt interest 17.2%; development expenditures 7.1%). **Public debt** (external, outstanding; 2006): US$3,669,000,000. **Gross national income** (2007): US$24,831,000,000 (US$5,560 per capita). **Production** (metric tons except as noted). *Agriculture and fishing* (2007): sugarcane 4,300,000, bananas 2,240,000, pineapples 1,225,000; livestock (number of live animals) 1,000,000 cattle, 550,000 pigs, 19,500,000 chickens; fisheries production (2006) 42,302 (from aquaculture 47%). *Mining and quarrying* (2005): limestone 920,000; gold 150 kg. *Manufacturing* (value added in US$'000,000; 2003): food products 734; beverages 188; paints, soaps, and pharmaceuticals 169. *Energy production (consumption):* electricity (kW-hr; 2005) 8,252,000,000 (8,263,000,000); coal (metric tons; 2005) none (63,000); crude petroleum (barrels; 2005) none (3,920,000); petroleum products (metric tons; 2005) 475,000 (1,948,000). **Population economically active** (2005): total 1,903,068; activity rate of total population 44.6% (participation rates: ages 12–59, 60.8%; female 36.2%; unemployed 6.6%). **Selected balance of payments data.** Receipts from (US$'000,000): tourism (2006) 1,732; remittances (2007) 650; foreign direct investment (FDI) (2004–06 avg.) 1,041; official development assistance (2006) 24. Disbursements for (US$'000,000): tourism (2006) 485; remittances (2007) 271; FDI (2004–06 avg.) 43.

Foreign trade

Imports (2005; c.i.f.): US$9,640,100,000 (machinery and apparatus 34.2%; chemical products 11.0%; mineral fuels 10.5%; plastics 7.0%; fabricated metal products 6.8%). *Major import sources:* US 40.1%; Japan 5.8%; Mexico 5.0%; Venezuela 4.9%; Ireland 4.5%. **Exports** (2005; f.o.b.): US$7,150,690,000 (machinery and apparatus 29.8%; food products 24.8%, of which bananas 6.8%, pineapples 4.6%, coffee 3.7%; professional and scientific equipment 8.1%; textiles 7.5%; chemical products 6.0%). *Major export destinations:* US 40.2%; Hong Kong 6.8%; The Netherlands 6.3%; Guatemala 4.0%; Nicaragua 3.9%.

Transport and communications

Transport. *Railroads* (2004): 278 km. *Roads* (2004): total length 35,330 km (paved 24%). *Vehicles* (2004): passenger cars 620,992; trucks and buses 220,456. *Air transport* (Lacsa [Costa Rican Airlines] only; 2005): passenger-km 2,284,000,000; metric ton-km cargo 10,351,000. **Communications,** in total units (units per 1,000 persons). Telephone landlines (2007): 1,437,000 (322); cellular telephone subscribers (2007): 1,508,000 (338); personal computers (2005): 1,000,000 (233); total Internet users (2007): 1,500,000 (336); broadband Internet subscribers (2007): 131,000 (29).

Education and health

Educational attainment (2004). Percentage of population ages 5 and over having: no formal schooling/unknown 12.8%; incomplete primary education 23.3%; complete primary 24.5%; incomplete secondary 18.2%; complete secondary 8.5%; higher 12.7%. **Literacy** (2003): percentage of total population ages 15 and over literate 96.0%; males literate 95.9%; females literate 96.1%. **Health** (2004): physicians 6,600 (1 per 644 persons); hospital beds (2003) 5,908 (1 per 714 persons); infant mortality rate per 1,000 live births (2007) 10.1; undernourished population (2002–04) 200,000 (5% of total population based on the consumption of a minimum daily requirement of 1,930 calories).

Military

Paramilitary expenditure as percentage of GDP (2005): 0.4%; per capita expenditure US$24. The army was officially abolished in 1948. Paramilitary (police) forces had 9,800 members in 2007.

Background

Christopher Columbus landed in Costa Rica in 1502 in an area inhabited by a number of small, independent Indian tribes. These peoples were not easily dominated, and it took almost 60 years for the Spanish to establish a permanent settlement. Ignored by the Spanish crown because of its lack of mineral wealth, the colony grew slowly. Coffee exports and the construction of a rail line improved its economy in the 19th century. It joined the short-lived Mexican Empire in 1821, was a member of the United Provinces of Central America (1823–38), and adopted a constitution in 1871. In 1890 Costa Ricans held what is considered to be the first free and honest election in Central America, beginning a tradition of democracy for which Costa Rica is renowned. In 1987 then president Óscar Arias Sánchez was awarded the Nobel Peace Prize. In the early 21st century, many Costa Ricans looked to increasingly free trade with the US as a solution to the country's economic woes.

Recent Developments

International relations dominated Costa Rican news in 2009. Although extremely controversial, the Central America–Dominican Republic Free Trade Agreement (CAFTA–DR) came into force between the US and Costa Rica on 1 January. In March it was announced that the country would restore diplomatic ties with Cuba. Costa Rica and El Salvador had been the only Central American states maintaining the freeze. The next month the Organisation for Economic Co-operation and Development announced that it was moving Costa Rica off its blacklist of tax havens to a "gray list" of countries that were cooperating but had not yet passed required financial transparency legislation.

Internet resources: <www.tourism.co.cr>.

Côte d'Ivoire

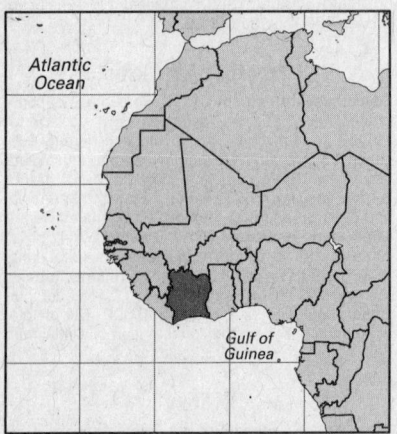

Atlantic Ocean

Gulf of Guinea

Official name: République de Côte d'Ivoire (Republic of Côte d'Ivoire). Form of government: transitional regime with one legislative house (National Assembly [225]). Chief of state and government: President Laurent Gbagbo (from 2000), assisted by Prime Minister Guillaume Soro (from 2007). Capital: Abidjan. Official language: French. Official religion: none. Monetary unit: 1 CFA franc (CFAF) = 100 centimes; valuation (1 Jul 2009) US$1 = CFAF 462.89.

Demography

Area: 123,863 sq mi, 320,803 sq km. Population (2008): 19,624,000. Density (2008): persons per sq mi 158.4, persons per sq km 61.2. Urban (2007): 48.1%. Sex distribution (2007): male 50.75%; female 49.25%. Age breakdown (2007): under 15, 41.2%; 15–29, 29.2%; 30–44, 16.5%; 45–59, 8.4%; 60–74, 3.9%; 75–84, 0.6%; 85 and over, 0.2%. Ethnolinguistic composition (1998): Akan 42.1%; Mande 26.5%; other 31.4%. Religious affiliation (2005): traditional beliefs 37%; Christian 32%, of which Roman Catholic 17%, Protestant 8%, independent Christian 7%; Muslim 28%; other 3%. Major cities (2005): Abidjan (urban agglomeration) 3,576,000; Bouaké 573,700; Daloa 215,100; Yamoussoukro (2003) 185,600; Korhogo (2003) 115,000. Location: western Africa, bordering Mali, Burkina Faso, Ghana, the Atlantic Ocean, Liberia, and Guinea.

Vital statistics

Birth rate per 1,000 population (2007): 33.3 (world avg. 20.3). Death rate per 1,000 population (2007): 11.6 (world avg. 8.6). Total fertility rate (avg. births per childbearing woman; 2007): 4.33. Life expectancy at birth (2007): male 53.3 years; female 54.5 years.

National economy

Budget (2005). Revenue: CFAF 1,566,000,000,000 (tax revenue 79.9%; nontax revenue 14.1%; grants 6.0%). Expenditures: CFAF 1,536,600,000,000 (current expenditures 78.4%; public debt interest 11.5%). Public debt (external, outstanding; 2006): US$10,830,000,000. Production (metric tons except as noted). Agriculture and fishing (2007): yams 4,900,000, cassava 2,110,000, plantains 1,590,-000,. cacao beans 1,300,000, natural rubber 128,000, fonio 9,700; livestock (number of live animals) 1,523,000 sheep, 1,500,000 cattle; fisheries production 33,461 (from aquaculture 2%). Mining and quarrying (2006): gold 1,324 kg; diamonds 420,000 carats (a UN embargo on rough diamond exports was in effect from November 2004 to November 2007). Manufacturing (value added in CFAF '000,000,000; 1997): food products 156.6, of which cocoa and chocolate 72.4; chemical products 60.2; wood products 55.9; refined petroleum products 46.0. Energy production (consumption): electricity (kW-hr; 2005) 5,578,000,000 (4,181,000,000); crude petroleum (barrels; 2007) 18,800,000 ([2005] 30,000,000); petroleum products (metric tons; 2005) 3,136,000 (974,000); natural gas (cu m; 2005) 1,661,000,000 (1,661,000,000). Population economically active (2003): total 6,544,000; activity rate of total population 37.2% (participation rates: ages 15–64, 65.5%; female 28.9%). Selected balance of payments data. Receipts from (US$'000,000): tourism (2003) 50; remittances (2007) 179; foreign direct investment (2004–06 avg.) 283; official development assistance (2006) 251. Disbursements for (US$'000,000): tourism (2001) 192; remittances (2007) 19. Gross national income (2007): US$17,543,000,000 (US$910 per capita).

---

1 metric ton = about 1.1 short tons;   1 kilometer = 0.6 mi (statute);   1 metric ton-km cargo = about 0.68 short ton-mi cargo;   c.i.f.: cost, insurance, and freight;   f.o.b.: free on board

Foreign trade

Imports (2005): CFAF 2,687,000,000,000 (machinery and transportation equipment 40.1%; crude and refined petroleum 32.3%; food products 17.0%). *Major import sources* (2004): France 24.3%; Nigeria 19.2%; UK 4.0%; China 4.0%; Italy 3.8%. **Exports** (2005): CFAF 3,950,000,000,000 (cocoa beans and products 27.5%; crude and refined petroleum 26.9%; wood products 3.8%; coffee 2.1%). *Major export destinations* (2004): US 11.6%; The Netherlands 10.3%; France 9.5%; Italy 5.5%; Belgium 4.7%.

Transport and communications

Transport. *Railroads* (1999): route length (2004) 660 km; passenger-km 93,100,000; metric ton-km cargo 537,600,000. *Roads* (2004): total length 80,000 km (paved 8%). *Vehicles*: passenger cars (2002) 114,000; trucks and buses (2001) 54,900. *Air transport* (Abidjan airport only; 2002): passenger arrivals and departures 821,400; cargo unloaded and loaded 16,699 metric tons. **Communications**, in total units (units per 1,000 persons). Telephone landlines (2006): 261,000 (14); cellular telephone subscribers (2007): 7,050,000 (366); personal computers (2004): 262,000 (16); total Internet users (2006): 300,000 (16); broadband Internet subscribers (2005): 1,200 (0.07).

Education and health

Educational attainment (1998–99). Percentage of population ages 25 and over having: no formal schooling/unknown 63.0%; primary education 19.4%; secondary 14.3%; higher 3.3%. **Literacy** (2007): percentage of total population ages 15 and over literate 55.5%; males literate 65.1%; females literate 45.5%. **Health:** physicians (2004) 2,081 (1 per 8,143 persons); hospital beds (2001) 5,981 (1 per 2,660 persons); infant mortality rate per 1,000 live births (2007) 71.6; undernourished population (2002–04) 2,200,000 (13% of total population based on the consumption of a minimum daily requirement of 1,850 calories).

Military

Total active duty personnel (2007): 17,050 (army 38.1%, navy 5.3%, air force 4.1%, presidential guard 7.9%, gendarmerie 44.6%); peacekeeping troops: UN (September 2008) 7,800, French (March 2008) 1,800; however, dismantling of the buffer zone occupied by the peacekeeping troops began in April 2007. **Military expenditure as percentage of GDP** (2005): 1.2%; per capita expenditure US$11.

Background

Europeans came to the area to trade in ivory and slaves beginning in the 15th century, and local kingdoms gave way to French influence in the 19th century. The French colony of Côte d'Ivoire was founded in 1893, and full occupation took place during 1908–18. In 1946 it became a territory in the French Union. Côte d'Ivoire achieved independence in 1960, when Félix Houphouët-Boigny was elected president. The country's first multiparty presidential elections were held in 1990. In 2002 the country began to fracture politically into north and south, and civil war ensued. A power-sharing agreement was signed in 2007.

Recent Developments

In January 2009 the UN Security Council voted to continue its peacekeeping operations in Côte d'Ivoire's "zone of confidence"—by midyear there were nearly 9,200 uniformed personnel in the force. In May 2008 more than 1,000 former members of the New Forces rebel group had participated in a disarmament ceremony in Bouaké. Public services in the north began reopening as the 2007 peace pact held. In January 2008 post office employees started to clear the five-year mail backlog, and customs officials resumed their duties in the north in May.

Internet resources: <www.ins.ci>.

Croatia

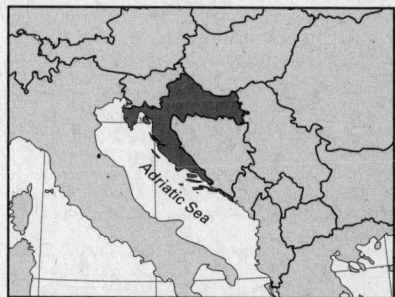

Official name: Republika Hrvatska (Republic of Croatia). **Form of government:** multiparty republic with one legislative house (Croatian Parliament [153]). **Head of state:** President Stipe Mesic (from 2000). **Head of government:** Prime Minister Jadranka Kosor (from 2009). **Capital:** Zagreb. **Official language:** Croatian. **Official religion:** none (Roman Catholicism has special status and receives financial support from the state). **Monetary unit:** 1 kuna (kn; plural kune) = 100 lipa; valuation (1 Jul 2009) US$1 = kn 5.13.

Demography

Area: 21,831 sq mi, 56,542 sq km. **Population** (2008): 4,433,000. **Density** (2008): persons per sq mi 202.9, persons per sq km 78.3. **Urban** (2005): 56.5%. **Sex distribution** (2006): male 48.17%; female 51.83%. **Age breakdown** (2004): under 15, 16.1%; 15–29, 20.2%; 30–44, 20.9%; 45–59, 20.7%; 60–74, 15.9%; 75–84, 5.3%; 85 and over, 0.9%. **Ethnic composition** (2001): Croat 89.6%; Serb 4.5%; Bosniac 0.5%; Italian 0.4%; Hungarian 0.4%; other 4.6%. **Religious affiliation** (2001): Christian 92.6%, of which Roman Catholic 87.8%, Eastern Orthodox 4.4%; Muslim 1.3%; nonreligious/atheist 5.2%; other 0.9%. **Major cities** (2001): Zagreb 691,724; Split 175,140; Rijeka 143,800; Osijek 90,411; Zadar 69,556. **Location:** southeastern Europe, bordering Slovenia, Hungary, Serbia, Montenegro, Bosnia and Herzegovina, and the Adriatic Sea.

Vital statistics

Birth rate per 1,000 population (2006): 9.5 (world avg. 20.3); within marriage 89.0%; outside of marriage 11.0%. **Death rate** per 1,000 population (2006): 11.5 (world avg. 8.6). **Natural increase rate** per 1,000 population (2006): −2.0 (world avg. 11.7). **Total fertility rate** (avg. births per childbearing woman; 2006): 1.38. **Life expectancy** at birth (2005): male 71.8 years; female 78.8 years.

National economy

Budget (2006). *Revenue:* kn 95,236,000,000 (tax revenue 61.4%, of which VAT 36.7%, excise taxes 12.1%; social security contributions 35.6%; nontax revenue 2.8%; grants 0.2%). *Expenditures:* kn 95,948,000,000 (social security and welfare 43.5%; wages and salaries 25.3%; debt interest 4.9%). **Population economically active** (2005): total 1,802,000; activity rate of total population 40.5% (participation rates: ages 15–64, 58.3%; female 45.5%; unemployed [July 2005–June 2006] 12.7%). **Production** (metric tons except as noted). *Agriculture and fishing* (2007): sugar beets 1,582,606, corn (maize) 1,424,599, wheat 950,000, sunflower seed 54,303; livestock (number of live animals) 1,489,000 pigs, 680,000 sheep, 483,000 cattle; fisheries production (2006) 52,750 (from aquaculture 28%). *Mining and quarrying* (2005): ceramic clay 200,000; ornamental stone 1,000,000 sq m. *Manufacturing* (value added in kn '000,000; 2004): food and beverages 7,112; refined petroleum products 4,005; chemical products 2,774; bricks, cement, and ceramics 2,642; fabricated metal products 2,623. *Energy production (consumption):* electricity (kW-hr; 2007) 12,540,000,000 ([2005] 17,574,000,000); coal (metric tons; 2005) none (1,140,000); crude petroleum (barrels; 2007) 6,710,000 ([2005] 35,800,-000); petroleum products (metric tons; 2005) 4,807,000 (4,478,000); natural gas (cu m; 2007) 2,713,000,000 ([2005] 2,834,000,000). **Gross national income** (2007): US$46,426,000,000 (US$10,460 per capita). **Public debt** (external, outstanding; December 2006): US$8,350,000,000. **Selected balance of payments data.** Receipts from (US$'000,000): tourism (2006) 7,990; remittances (2007) 1,788; foreign direct investment (FDI) (2004–06 avg.) 2,191; official development assistance (2006) 200. Disbursements for (US$'000,-000): tourism (2006) 737; remittances (2007) 86; FDI (2004–avg.) 267.

Foreign trade

Imports (2006; c.i.f.): US$21,503,000,000 (machinery and apparatus 20.0%; mineral fuels 15.9%; chemical products 10.8%; road vehicles and parts 9.2%). *Major import sources:* Italy 16.7%; Germany 14.5%; Russia 10.1%; Slovenia 6.3%; Austria 5.4%. **Exports** (2006; f.o.b.): US$10,377,000,000 (machinery and apparatus 15.7%; mineral fuels 15.1%; ships and boats [particularly tankers] 10.5%; chemical products 9.2%; food products 9.1%). *Major export destinations:* Italy 23.1%; Bosnia and Herzegovina 12.6%; Germany 10.3%; Slovenia 8.2%; Austria 6.0%.

Transport and communications

Transport. *Railroads* (2006): length (2004) 2,726 km; passenger-km 1,339,000,000; metric ton-km

cargo 3,183,000,000. *Roads* (2005): total length 28,472 km (paved [2003] 85%). *Vehicles* (2006): passenger cars 1,435,781; trucks and buses 174,612. *Air transport* (2007): passenger-km 1,080,000,000; metric ton-km cargo 2,220,000. **Communications,** in total units (units per 1,000 persons). Telephone landlines (2007): 1,825,000 (401); cellular telephone subscribers (2007): 5,035,000 (1,105); personal computers (2004): 842,000 (191); total Internet users (2007): 1,995,000 (438); broadband Internet subscribers (2007): 385,000 (87).

Education and health

Educational attainment (2001). Percentage of population ages 15 and over having: no schooling/unknown 3.5%; incomplete primary education 15.8%; primary 21.7%; secondary 47.1%; postsecondary and higher 11.9%. **Literacy** (2003): percentage of total population ages 15 and over literate 98.5%; males literate 99.4%; females literate 97.8%. **Health** (2005): physicians 8,216 (1 per 541 persons); hospital beds 24,000 (1 per 185 persons); infant mortality rate per 1,000 live births 5.7; undernourished population (2002–04) 300,000 (7% of total population based on the consumption of a minimum daily requirement of 2,010 calories).

Military

Total active duty personnel (2007): 17,660 (army 69.6%, navy 9.6%, air force and air defense 10.2%, headquarters staff 10.6%). **Military expenditure as percentage of GDP** (2005): 1.6%; per capita expenditure US$138.

Background

The Croats, a southern Slavic people, arrived in the area in the 7th century AD and in the 8th century came under Charlemagne's rule. They converted to Christianity soon afterward and formed a kingdom in the 10th century. Most of Croatia was taken by the Turks in 1526; the rest voted to accept Austrian rule. In 1867 it became part of Austria-Hungary, with Dalmatia and Istria ruled by Vienna and Croatia-Slavonia a Hungarian crown land. In 1918, after the defeat of Austria-Hungary in World War I, it joined other southern Slavic territories to form the Kingdom of Serbs, Croats, and Slovenes, renamed Yugoslavia in 1929. During World War II an independent state of Croatia was established by Germany and Italy, embracing Croatia-Slavonia, part of Dalmatia, and Bosnia and Herzegovina; after the war Croatia was rejoined to Yugoslavia as a people's republic. It declared its independence in 1991, sparking insurrections by Croatian Serbs, who carved out autonomous regions with Serbian-led Yugoslav army help; Croatia had taken back most of these regions by 1995. With some stability returning, Croatia's economy began to revive in the late 1990s.

Recent Developments

Croatia in 2008 continued to pursue accession negotiations with the EU, but a border dispute with

---

1 metric ton = about 1.1 short tons;   1 kilometer = 0.6 mi (statute);   1 metric ton-km cargo = about 0.68 short ton-mi cargo;   c.i.f.: cost, insurance, and freight;   f.o.b.: free on board

Slovenia led Slovenia to block Croatia's ability to begin those talks. A separate obstacle was the request by the European Commission for Croatia to reform its shipbuilding sector, to which it would be required to cease providing state subsidies upon joining the EU. Shipbuilding accounted for 12–15% of total exports and directly employed more than 11,000 workers, yet five of the six state-owned shipyards were operating at a deficit. In April 2009, however, Croatia, along with Albania, joined NATO, and Croatia was also a nonpermanent member of the UN Security Council for the 2008–09 term.

Internet resources: <www.dzs.hr/default_e.htm>.

Cuba

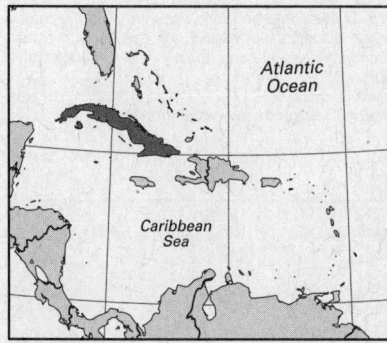

Official name: República de Cuba (Republic of Cuba). Form of government: unitary socialist republic with one legislative house (National Assembly of the People's Power [609]). Head of state and government: President Raúl Castro Ruz (from 2008). Capital: Havana. Official language: Spanish. Official religion: none. Monetary unit: 1 Cuban peso (CUP) = 100 centavos; valuation (1 Jul 2009) US$1 = 22.22 CUP.

Demography

Area: 42,804 sq mi, 110,861 sq km. Population (2008): 11,236,000. Density (2008): persons per sq mi 264.8, persons per sq km 102.3. Urban (2005): 75.5%. Sex distribution (2007): male 50.08%; female 49.92%. Age breakdown (2005): under 15, 19.2%; 15–29, 20.5%; 30–44, 27.6%; 45–59, 17.0%; 60–74, 10.8%; 75–84, 3.6%; 85 and over, 1.3%. Ethnic composition (1994): mixed 51.0%; white 37.0%; black 11.0%; other 1.0%. Religious affiliation (2005): Roman Catholic 47%; Protestant 5%; nonreligious 22%; other 26%. Major cities (2006): Havana 2,174,790; Santiago de Cuba 425,990; Camagüey 306,702; Holguín 274,805; Santa Clara 208,739; Guantánamo 208,579. Location: island southeast of Florida (US), between the North Atlantic Ocean and the Caribbean Sea.

Vital statistics

Birth rate per 1,000 population (2007): 10.0 (world avg. 20.3). Death rate per 1,000 population (2007): 7.3 (world avg. 8.6). Natural increase rate per 1,000 population (2007): 2.7 (world avg. 11.7). Total fertility rate (avg. births per childbearing woman; 2007): 1.43. Life expectancy at birth (2006): male 75.1 years; female 79.0 years.

National economy

Budget (2006). Revenue: CUP 30,012,400,000 (tax revenue 73.6%; nontax revenue 26.4%). Expenditures: CUP 31,742,400,000 (current expenditures 84.2%, of which education 14.8%, social security contributions 11.2%, health 9.7%, housing and community services 7.2%; capital expenditures 15.8%). Public debt (external, outstanding; 2004): US$12,000,000,000. Production (metric tons except as noted). Agriculture and fishing (2007): sugarcane 11,100,000, tomatoes 640,000, plantains 540,000, tobacco leaves 30,000; livestock (number of live animals) 3,750,000 cattle, 2,765,000 sheep, 1,765,000 pigs; fisheries production (2006) 54,753 (from aquaculture 50%). Mining and quarrying (2006): nickel (metal content) 75,000; cobalt (metal content) 4,300. Manufacturing (2006): cement 1,713,900; steel 257,200; cigarettes (2004) 12,800,000,000 units. Energy production (consumption): electricity (kW-hr; 2006) 16,468,500,000 ([2005] 15,638,000,000); coal (metric tons; 2005) none (13,000); crude petroleum (barrels; 2006) 18,700,000 ([2005] 30,300,000); petroleum products (metric tons; 2005) 1,954,000 (4,925,000); natural gas (cu m; 2006) 1,085,000,000 ([2005] 754,000,000). Population economically active (2004): total 4,729,386; activity rate of total population 42.1% (participation rates: ages 15 and over, 52.3%; female 36.5%; unemployed [2006] 1.9%). Gross national income (2006): US$51,504,000,000 (US$4,571 per capita). Selected balance of payments data. Receipts from (US$'000,000): tourism (2006) 2,138; remittances (2003) 1,200; foreign direct investment (2004–06 avg.) 2; official development assistance (2006) 78.

Foreign trade

Imports (2004; c.i.f.): US$5,610,000,000 (food products 18.4%, of which cereals 8.0%; machinery and apparatus 17.5%; refined petroleum products 12.8%; chemical products 9.6%; crude petroleum 9.4%). Major import sources (2006): Venezuela 23.5%; China 16.7%; Spain 9.0%; Germany 6.5%; US 5.1%. Exports (2004; f.o.b.): US$2,332,000,000 (nickel oxide 45.5%; food products 19.7%, of which raw cane sugar 11.5%; cigars 8.7%; medicine 6.0%). Major export destinations (2006): The Netherlands 28.0%; Canada 19.8%; Venezuela 10.7%; China 8.9%; Spain 5.4%.

Transport and communications

Transport. Railroads (Cuban Railways only; length of railways exclusively for the transport of sugar equals 7,742 km; 2003): length 4,226 km; (2001) passenger-km 1,766,600; metric ton-km cargo 806,900,000. Roads (2000): total length 60,856 km (paved 49%). Vehicles (1998): passenger cars 172,574; trucks and buses 185,495. Air transport (Cubana airline only; 2003): passenger-km 2,044,000,000; metric ton-km cargo 40,933,000. Communications, in total units (units per 1,000 persons). Telephone landlines (2007): 1,043,000 (93); cellular telephone subscribers (2007): 198,000 (18); personal computers (2005): 377,000 (33); total Internet users (2007): 1,310,000 (116); broadband Internet subscribers (2007): 1,900 (0.2).

Education and health

Educational attainment (2002): Percentage of population ages 25 and over having: no formal schooling 14.1%; primary education 17.2%; secondary 26.6%; vocational/technical/teacher training 32.8%; university 9.3%. **Literacy** (2004): percentage of total population ages 15 and over literate 96.9%; males literate 97.0%; females literate 96.8%. **Health** (2006): physicians 70,594 (1 per 160 persons); hospital beds (2004) 70,079 (1 per 160 persons); infant mortality rate per 1,000 live births (2007) 5.3; undernourished population (2002–04) less than 2.5% of total population.

Military

Total active duty personnel (2007): 49,000 (army 77.6%, navy 6.1%, air force 16.3%); US military forces at Naval Base Guantánamo Bay (2007) 903. **Military expenditure as percentage of GDP** (2005): 3.8%; per capita expenditure US$151.

Background

Several Indian groups, including the Ciboney, the Taino, and the Arawak, inhabited Cuba at the time of the first Spanish contact. Christopher Columbus claimed the island for Spain in 1492, and the Spanish conquest began in 1511, when the settlement of Baracoa was founded. The native Indians were eradicated over the succeeding centuries, and African slaves, from the 18th century until slavery was abolished in 1886, were imported to work the sugar plantations. Cuba revolted unsuccessfully against Spain in the Ten Years' War (1868–78); a second war of independence began in 1895. In 1898 the US entered the war; Spain relinquished its claim to Cuba, which was occupied by the US for three years before gaining its independence in 1902. The US invested heavily in the Cuban sugar industry in the first half of the 20th century, and this, combined with tourism and gambling, caused the economy to prosper. Inequalities in the distribution of wealth persisted, however, as did political corruption. In 1958–59 the communist revolutionary Fidel Castro overthrew Cuba's longtime dictator, Fulgencio Batista, and established a socialist state aligned with the Soviet Union, abolishing capitalism and nationalizing foreign-owned enterprises. Relations with the US deteriorated, reaching a low point with the 1961 Bay of Pigs invasion and the 1962 Cuban missile crisis. In 1980 about 125,000 Cubans, including many that their government officially labeled "undesirables," were shipped to the US in what became known as the "Mariel boatlift." When communism collapsed in the USSR, Cuba lost important financial backing and its economy suffered greatly. The latter gradually improved in the 1990s with the encouragement of tourism, though diplomatic relations with the US were not resumed.

Recent Developments

Fidel Castro officially resigned as president of Cuba in February 2008, thus ending his 49-year tenure as the country's leader. His younger brother and longtime minister of defense, Raúl Castro, was elevated to the presidency, and he stated that the government would embrace a limited path of economic reform. In March the government lifted a ban on buying consumer electronic goods, such as DVD players and cell phones, and dropped a stricture preventing Cubans from staying in the country's top tourist hotels, and in April it introduced a plan allowing thousands of Cubans to receive titles to their homes, eliminated salary caps, and raised pensions for the country's retirees. New US Pres. Barack Obama called for increased dialogue between the US and Cuban governments, and in April 2009, weeks after a US congressional delegation visited the island and met with Fidel, Obama signed a law easing travel restrictions to Cuba for Cuban Americans and allowing for eased remittance transfers.

Internet resources: <www.cubatravel.cu>.

Cyprus

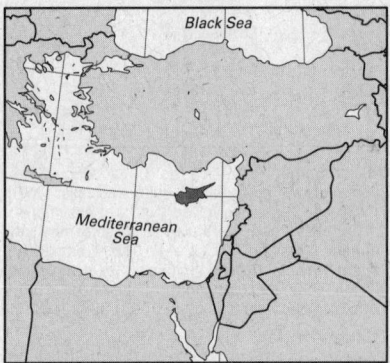

Two de facto states currently exist on the island of Cyprus: the Republic of Cyprus (ROC), predominantly Greek in character, occupying the southern two-thirds of the island, which is the original and still the internationally recognized de jure government of the whole island; and the Turkish Republic of Northern Cyprus (TRNC), proclaimed unilaterally 15 Nov 1983, on territory originally secured for the Turkish Cypriot population by the 20 Jul 1974 intervention of Turkey. Only Turkey recognizes the TRNC, and the two ethnic communities have failed to reestablish a single state. Provision of separate data below does not imply recognition of either state's claims but is necessitated by the lack of unified data.

Area: 3,572 sq mi, 9,251 sq km. **Population** (2008): 1,076,000; includes 140,000–150,000 "settlers" (mostly from Turkey) in the TRNC; excludes 3,300 British military in the Sovereign Base Areas (SBAs) in the ROC and 850 UN peacekeeping forces. **Location:**

---

1 metric ton = about 1.1 short tons;   1 kilometer = 0.6 mi (statute);   1 metric ton-km cargo = about 0.68 short ton-mi cargo;   c.i.f.: cost, insurance, and freight;   f.o.b.: free on board

the Middle East, island in the Mediterranean Sea, south of Turkey.

Republic of Cyprus

Official name: Kipriaki Dhimokratia (Greek); Kibris Cumhuriyeti (Turkish) (Republic of Cyprus). **Form of government:** unitary multiparty republic with a unicameral legislature (House of Representatives [80]). **Head of state and government:** President Dimitris Christofias (from 2008). **Capital:** Lefkosia (Nicosia). **Official languages:** Greek; Turkish. **Monetary unit:** 1 euro (€) = 100 cents; valuation (1 Jul 2009) US$1 = €0.71 (the euro replaced the Cyprus pound [£C] 1 Jan 2008, at the rate of €1 = £C 0.59).

Demography

Area: 2,276 sq mi, 5,896 sq km (includes 99 sq mi [256 sq km] of British military SBAs and 107 sq mi [278 sq km] of the UN Buffer Zone). **Population** (2008): 805,000; excludes 3,300 British military in the SBAs and 850 UN peacekeeping troops. **Age breakdown** (2005): under 15, 18.4%; 15–29, 23.9%; 30–44, 21.8%; 45–59, 19.2%; 60–74, 11.7%; 75–84, 3.9%; 85 and over, 1.1%. **Ethnic composition** (2000): Greek Cypriot 91.8%; Armenian 3.3%; Arab 2.9%, of which Lebanese 2.5%; British 1.4%; other 0.6%. **Religious affiliation** (2001): Greek Orthodox 94.8%; Roman Catholic 2.1%, of which Maronite 0.6%; Anglican 1.0%; Muslim 0.6%; other 1.5%. **Urban areas** (2004): Lefkosia (ROC only) 219,200; Limassol 172,500; Larnaca 77,000.

Vital statistics

Birth rate per 1,000 population (2006): 11.2 (world avg. 20.3). **Death rate** per 1,000 population (2006): 6.8 (world avg. 8.6). **Total fertility rate** (avg. births per childbearing woman; 2005): 1.42. **Life expectancy** at birth (2004–05): male 77.0 years; female 81.7 years.

National economy

Budget (2005). *Revenue:* £C 3,273,700,000 (excises and import duties 41.4%; income tax 22.3%; social security contributions 19.9%). *Expenditures:* £C 3,459,300,000 (current expenditures 91.3%; development expenditures 8.7%). **Gross national income** (2007): US$19,617,000,000 (US$24,940 per capita). **Production.** *Agriculture and livestock* (in '000 metric tons; 2007): potatoes 135.0, pork 50.4, grapes 45.5, chicken meat 22.0, olives 18.0. *Manufacturing* (value added in US$'000,000; 2005): food, beverages, and tobacco 281; cement, bricks, and ceramics 98; base and fabricated metals 67; paper products 56. *Energy production (consumption):* electricity (kW-hr; 2005) 4,338,000,000 (3,931,000,000). **Selected balance of payments data.** Receipts from (US$'000,000): tourism (2006) 2,240; remittances (2007) 172; foreign direct investment (FDI) (2004–06 avg.) 1,265. Disbursements for (US$'000,000): tourism (2006) 982; remittances (2007) 371; FDI (2004–06 avg.) 636.

Foreign trade

Imports (2006; c.i.f.): US$7,046,000,000 (refined petroleum products 17.2%; machinery and apparatus 16.4%; road vehicles 11.0%; food products 9.2%).

Major import sources: Greece 17.3%; Italy 11.4%; UK 8.9%; Germany 8.9%; Israel 6.2%. **Exports** (2006; f.o.b.): US$1,414,900,000 (refined petroleum products 18.2%; telecommunications equipment 9.9%; road vehicles 9.8%; vegetables and fruit 8.9%; medicine 8.6%). *Major export destinations:* UK 14.6%; Greece 13.2%; France 7.4%; Germany 4.5%.

Transport and communications

Transport. *Roads* (2004): total length 12,059 km (paved 65%). *Vehicles* (2004): cars 335,634; trucks and buses 121,024. *Air transport* (Cyprus Airways only; 2007): passenger-km 3,385,000,000; metric ton-km cargo 53,000,000. **Communications,** in total units (units per 1,000 persons). Telephone landlines (2007): 376,000 (440); cellular telephone subscribers (2007): 962,000 (1,126); personal computers (2004): 249,000 (309); total Internet users (2007): 380,000 (445); broadband Internet subscribers (2006): 81,000 (77).

Education and health

Educational attainment (2004). Percentage of population ages 20 and over having: no formal schooling/incomplete primary education 10%; complete primary 20%; secondary 45%; higher education 25%. **Health** (2004): physicians 1,965 (1 per 375 persons); hospital beds 3,075 (1 per 240 persons); infant mortality rate per 1,000 live births (2005) 4.6.

Military

Total active duty personnel (2007): 10,000 (national guard 100%); Greek troops 950. **Military expenditure as percentage of GDP** (2005): 1.4%; per capita expenditure US$241.

Turkish Republic of Northern Cyprus

Official name: Kuzey Kibris Turk Cumhuriyeti (Turkish) (Turkish Republic of Northern Cyprus). **Capital:** Lefkosa (Nicosia). **Official language:** Turkish. **Monetary unit:** new Turkish lira (YTL) = 100 new kurus; valuation (1 Jul 2009) US$1 = YTL 1.52. **Population** (2008): 271,100; includes 140,000–150,000 "settlers" (mostly from Turkey). **Urban areas** (2006): Lefkosa (TRNC only) 49,237; Magusa (Famagusta) 34,803; Girne (Kyrenia) 24,122; Guzelyurt (Morphou) 12,425. **Sex distribution** (2006): male 53.99%; female 46.01%. **Ethnic composition** (2006): Turkish Cypriot/Turkish 96.8%; other 3.2%. **Birth rate** per 1,000 population (2004): 16.0 (world avg. 21.1). **Death rate** per 1,000 population (2004): 8.0 (world avg. 8.8). **Total fertility rate** (avg. births per childbearing woman; 2004) 1.90. **Budget** (2004). *Revenue:* US$885,187,000 (indirect taxes 21.4%; direct taxes 18.8%; foreign aid 13.9%; loans 11.8%). *Expenditures:* US$885,187,000 (wages and salaries 29.7%; social transfers 22.9%; investments 10.3%; defense 6.2%). **Imports** (2004; c.i.f.): US$853,100,000 (machinery and transportation equipment 35.7%; food products 9.4%). *Major import sources:* Turkey 60.1%; UK 10.7%. **Exports** (2004; f.o.b.): US$62,000,000 (citrus fruits 32.4%; clothing 18.9%). *Major export destinations:* Turkey 46.3%; UK 21.8%. **Health** (2004): physicians 422 (1 per 573 persons); hospital beds 1,291 (1 per 186 persons); infant mortality rate per 1,000 live births 10.0.

Background

By the late Bronze Age Cyprus had been visited and settled by Mycenaeans and Achaeans, who introduced Greek culture and language, and it became a trading center. By 800 BC Phoenicians had begun to settle there. Ruled over the centuries by the Assyrian, Persian, and Ptolemaic empires, it was annexed by Rome in 58 BC. It was part of the Byzantine Empire in the 4th–12th centuries AD. Cyprus was conquered by the English king Richard I in 1191. A part of the Venetian empire from 1489, it was taken by Ottoman Turks in 1571. In 1878 the British assumed control, and Cyprus became a British crown colony in 1925. It gained independence in 1960. Conflict between Greek and Turkish Cypriots led to the establishment of a UN peacekeeping mission in 1964. In 1974, fearing a movement to unite Cyprus with Greece, Turkish soldiers occupied the northern third of the country, and Turkish Cypriots established a government, which obtained recognition only from Turkey. Conflict has continued to the present, and the UN peacekeeping mission has remained in place. The Republic of Cyprus joined the European Union in 2004 and adopted the euro as its official currency in 2008.

Recent Developments

The political situation on the divided island of Cyprus showed signs of improvement in 2008. The presidents of the two sides agreed on a single sovereignty and a single citizenship. Major negotiations continued throughout the year. The border was increasingly porous, with goods and people crossing in both directions. The two regimes still differed on foreign policy, however. Turkish Cyprus recognized Kosovo's independence—the Greek zone did not share the enthusiasm. On 1 Jan 2008 Greek Cyprus adopted the euro, and the Cyprus pound ceased to be legal tender a month later.

Internet resources: <www.visitcyprus.com>.

Czech Republic

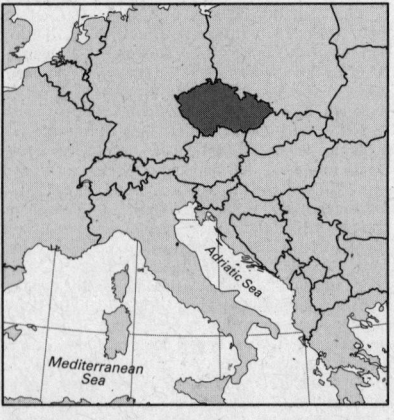

Official name: Ceska Republika (Czech Republic). **Form of government:** unitary multiparty republic with two legislative houses (Senate [81]; Chamber of Deputies [200]). **Chief of state:** President Vaclav Klaus (from 2003). **Head of government:** Prime Minister Mirek Topolanek (from 2006). **Capital:** Prague. **Official language:** Czech. **Official religion:** none. **Monetary unit:** 1 koruna (Kc) = 100 haleru; valuation (1 Jul 2009) US$1 = 18.12 Kc.

Demography

Area: 30,451 sq mi, 78,867 sq km. **Population** (2008): 10,408,000. **Density** (2008): persons per sq mi 341.8, persons per sq km 132.0. **Urban** (2003): 74.3%. **Sex distribution** (2006): male 48.83%; female 51.17%. **Age breakdown** (2004): under 15, 14.9%; 15–29, 22.1%; 30–44, 21.3%; 45–59, 22.0%; 60–74, 13.6%; 75–84, 5.2%; 85 and over, 0.9%. **Ethnic composition** (2001): Czech 90.4%; Moravian 3.7%; Slovak 1.9%; Polish 0.5%; German 0.4%; Silesian 0.1%; Rom (Gypsy) 0.1%; other 2.9%. **Religious affiliation** (2000): Christian 63.0%, of which Roman Catholic 40.4%, unaffiliated Christian 16.0%, Protestant (mostly Lutheran) 3.1%, independent Christian (mostly independent Catholic [Hussite Church of the Czech Republic]) 2.6%; atheist 5.0%; Jewish 0.1%; nonreligious 31.9%. **Major cities** (2006): Prague 1,188,126; Brno 366,680; Ostrava 309,098; Plzen 163,392; Olomouc 100,168. **Location:** central Europe, bordering Germany, Poland, Slovakia, and Austria.

Vital statistics

Birth rate per 1,000 population (2007): 11.1 (world avg. 20.3); (2007) within marriage 65.5%; outside of marriage 34.5%. **Death rate** per 1,000 population (2007): 10.2 (world avg. 8.6). **Natural increase rate** per 1,000 population (2007): 0.9 (world avg. 11.7). **Total fertility rate** (avg. births per childbearing woman; 2007): 1.44. **Life expectancy** at birth (2007): male 73.7 years; female 79.9 years.

National economy

Budget (2005). *Revenue:* Kc 1,279,628,000,000 (tax revenue 82.8%, of which social security contributions 32.5%, taxes on goods and services 26.8%, taxes on income and profits 22.4%; nontax revenue 4.5%; grants 2.5%). *Expenditures:* Kc 1,279,054,-000,000 (social security and welfare 29.1%; health 14.5%; transportation and communications 9.8%; education 9.6%). **Production** (metric tons except as noted). *Agriculture and fishing* (2007): cereals 7,065,752 (of which wheat 3,955,437, barley 1,919,712, corn [maize] 608,179), sugar beets 2,598,676, rapeseed 1,038,400; livestock (number of live animals) 2,741,300 pigs, 1,389,600 cattle; fisheries production (2006) 25,077 (from aquaculture 81%). *Mining and quarrying* (2005): kaolin 3,882,000; feldspar 472,000. *Manufacturing* (value added in Kc '000,000; 2003): base and fabricated metals 93,380; food, beverages, and tobacco products 81,440; electrical and optical equipment 70,800; transportation equipment 64,144; nonelectrical machinery and apparatus 57,837. *Energy production (consumption):* electricity (kW-hr; 2007) 88,187,000,000 ([2005] 69,944,000,000); hard coal (metric tons; 2007) 12,900,000 ([2005] 9,220,000); lignite (metric tons; 2007) 49,300,000 ([2005] 47,600,000); crude petroleum (barrels; 2005) 3,860,000 (58,300,000); petroleum products (metric tons; 2005) 5,567,000 (6,811,000); natural gas (cu m; 2007) 223,000,000 ([2005] 9,217,000,000). **Population economically active** (2005): total 5,174,000; activity rate of total population 50.6% (participation rates: ages 15–64, 70.4%; female 44.1%; unemployed [2006] 7.1%). **Public debt** (external, outstanding; 2004): US$12,020,000,000. **Gross national income** (2007): US$149,378,-000,000 (US$14,450 per capita). **Selected balance of payments data.** Receipts from (US$'000,000): tourism (2006) 5,026; remittances (2007) 1,300; foreign direct investment (FDI) (2004–06 avg.) 7,530. Disbursements for (US$'000,000): tourism (2006) 2,670; remittances (2007) 2,831; FDI (2004–06 avg.) 850.

Foreign trade

Imports (2006): Kc 2,111,100,000,000 (machinery and apparatus 31.9%; chemical products 10.2%; mineral fuels 9.0%; road vehicles and parts 8.5%). *Major import sources:* Germany 28.5%; China 6.1%; Russia 6.0%; Poland 5.6%; Slovakia 5.4%. **Exports** (2006): Kc 2,149,800,000,000 (machinery and apparatus 34.7%, of which computers, office machinery, and parts 7.8%, general industrial machinery 6.8%; motor vehicles and parts 15.7%; chemical products 5.8%; fabricated metal products 5.5%). *Major export destinations:* Germany 31.9%; Slovakia 8.4%; Poland 5.7%; France 5.5%; Austria 5.1%.

Transport and communications

Transport. *Railroads* (2004): route length 9,441 km; passenger-km (2005) 6,667,000; metric ton-km cargo (2005) 14,866,000,000. *Roads* (2004): total length 127,781 km (paved 100%). *Vehicles* (2005): passenger cars 3,958,708; trucks and buses 435,235. *Air transport* (2007): passenger-km 6,288,000,000; metric ton-km cargo 32,508,000. **Communications,** in total units (units per 1,000 persons). Telephone landlines (2006): 3,541,000 (345); cellular telephone subscribers (2007): 13,075,000 (1,284); personal computers (2004): 5,100,000 (500); total Internet users (2007): 4,400,000 (432); broadband Internet subscribers (2007): 1,625,000 (158).

Education and health

Educational attainment (2001). Percentage of population ages 15 and over having: no formal schooling 0.2%; primary education 21.6%; secondary 68.7%; higher 9.5%. **Literacy** (2001): 99.8%. **Health** (2005): physicians 36,381 (1 per 282 persons); hospital beds 65,022 (1 per 158 persons); infant mortality rate per 1,000 live births (2007) 3.1; undernourished population (2002–04) less than 2.5% of total population.

Military

Total active duty personnel (2007): 23,092 (army 73.5%, air force 26.5%). **Military expenditure as per-**centage of GDP (2005): 1.8%; per capita expenditure US$216.

Background

Until 1918 the history of what is now the Czech Republic was largely that of Bohemia. In that year the independent republic of Czechoslovakia was born through the union of Bohemia and Moravia with Slovakia. Czechoslovakia came under the domination of the Soviet Union after World War II, and from 1948 to 1989 it was ruled by a communist government. Its growing political liberalization was suppressed by a Soviet invasion in 1968. After communist rule collapsed in 1989–90, separatist sentiments emerged among the Slovaks, and in 1992 the Czechs and Slovaks agreed to break up their federated state. On 1 Jan 1993 the Czechoslovakian republic was peacefully dissolved and replaced by two new countries, the Czech Republic and Slovakia, with the region of Moravia remaining in the former. In 1999 the Czech Republic entered NATO and in 2004 the EU.

Recent Developments

The proposed radar installation in the Czech Republic, part of a planned US antimissile shield, continued to be a source of contention. Russia, which saw it as a threat, repeatedly protested against the move and vowed to station short-range missiles in its exclave of Kaliningrad in response. In April 2009 US Pres. Barack Obama traveled to Prague, where he said that the missile shield was integral to the defense of Europe against rogue states, such as Iran, but that if the threat of a missile launch from Iran were removed, there would be no need for the missile shield in Europe. This was interpreted as a message to the Russians seeking their help in ending Iran's uranium enrichment and missile projects.

Internet resources:
<www.czso.cz/eng/redakce.nsf/i/home>.

Denmark

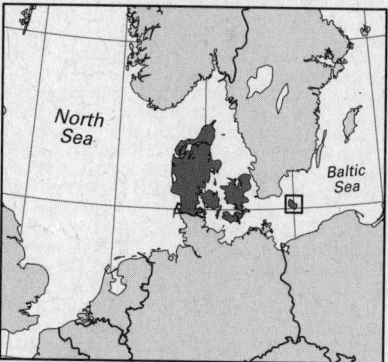

Official name: Kongeriget Danmark (Kingdom of Denmark). **Form of government:** constitutional monarchy with one legislative house (Folketing [179]). **Chief of state:** Queen Margrethe II (from 1972). **Head of government:** Prime Minister Anders Fogh Rasmussen (from 2001). **Capital:** Copenhagen.

Official language: Danish. Official religion: Evangelical Lutheran. Monetary unit: 1 Danish krone (DKK; plural kroner) = 100 øre; valuation (1 Jul 2009) US$1 = DKK 5.25.

Demography

Area: 16,640 sq mi, 43,098 sq km (excludes the Faroe Islands and Greenland). Population (2008): 5,494,000. Density (2008): persons per sq mi 330.2, persons per sq km 127.5. Urban (2004): 85.4%. Sex distribution (2007): male 49.54%; female 50.46%. Age breakdown (2006): under 15, 18.6%; 15–29, 17.3%; 30–44, 21.9%; 45–59, 20.2%; 60–74, 15.0%; 75–84, 5.1%; 85 and over, 1.9%. Ethnic composition (2006): Danish 91.9%; Turkish 0.6%; German 0.5%; Iraqi 0.4%; Swedish 0.4%; Norwegian 0.3%; Bosnian 0.3%; other 5.6%. Religious affiliation (2006): Evangelical Lutheran 83.0%; other Christian 1.3%; Muslim 3.7%; nonreligious 5.4%; atheist 1.5%; other 5.1%. Major urban areas (2007): Greater Copenhagen 1,153,615; Århus 237,551; Odense 158,163; Ålborg 121,818; Esbjerb 70,880. Location: northern Europe, bordering the North Sea, the Baltic Sea, and Germany.

Vital statistics

Birth rate per 1,000 population (2007): 11.7 (world avg. 20.3); (2005) within marriage 54.3%; outside of marriage 45.7%. Death rate per 1,000 population (2007): 10.2 (world avg. 8.6). Natural increase rate per 1,000 population (2007): 1.5 (world avg. 11.7). Total fertility rate (avg. births per childbearing woman; 2007): 1.85. Life expectancy at birth (2006–07): male 76.0 years; female 80.5 years.

National economy

Budget (2005). Revenue: DKK 882,940,000,000 (income/wealth taxes 54.4%; import/production taxes 31.0%). Expenditures: DKK 821,539,000,000 (social protection 41.9%; education 15.2%; health 13.4%; economic affairs 6.6%). National debt (December 2006): US$57,887,000,000. Population economically active (2005): total 2,876,100; activity rate of total population 53.1% (participation rates: ages 15–64, 80.2%; female 47.0%; unemployed [July 2005–June 2006] 5.0%). Production (metric tons except as noted). Agriculture and fishing (2007): wheat 4,519,200, barley 3,104,200, sugar beets 2,255,300; livestock (number of live animals) 13,599,000 pigs, 1,579,000 cattle; fisheries production (2006) 904,894 metric tons (from aquaculture 4%). Mining and quarrying (2006): sand and gravel 28,600,000 cu m; chalk 1,900,000 metric tons. Manufacturing (value of sales in DKK '000,000; 2005): food products 121,040; nonelectrical machinery and apparatus 66,050; computer and telecommunications equipment 49,078. Energy production (consumption): electricity (kW-hr; 2007) 37,394,000,000 ([2005] 37,644,000,000); coal (metric tons; 2006) none (9,436,000); crude petroleum (barrels; 2007) 111,300,000 ([2005] 57,100,000); petroleum products (metric tons; 2005) 7,495,000 (6,660,000); natural gas (cu m; 2006) 10,053,000,000 (4,918,000,000). Gross national income (2007): US$299,804,000,000 (US$54,910 per capita). Selected balance of payments data. Receipts from (US$'000,000): tourism (2006) 5,587; remittances (2007) 987; foreign direct investment (FDI) (2004–06 avg.) 3,231. Disbursements for (US$'000,000): tourism (2006) 7,428; remittances (2007) 2,933; FDI (2004–06 avg.) 4,282.

Foreign trade

Imports (2006; c.i.f.): DKK 502,587,000,000 (machinery and apparatus 25.9%; chemical products 10.8%; food products 9.2%; road vehicles 8.5%). Major import sources: Germany 21.5%; Sweden 14.3%; The Netherlands 6.2%; UK 5.8%; China 5.3%. Exports (2006; f.o.b.): DKK 535,933,000,000 (machinery and apparatus 23.3%, of which general industrial machinery 6.4%, power-generating machinery 4.5%; food products 16.1%, of which meat 5.6% [including swine meat 3.8%]; crude petroleum 9.3%; medicine and pharmaceuticals 7.3%). Major export destinations: Germany 15.5%; Sweden 13.8%; UK 8.4%; US 6.0%; Norway 5.7%.

Transport and communications

Transport. Railroads (2004): route length 2,644 km; passenger-km 6,132,000,000; metric ton-km cargo 1,976,000,000. Roads (2006): total length 72,362 km (paved 100%). Vehicles (2006): passenger cars 2,020,013; trucks and buses 508,788. Air transport (Danish share of Scandinavian Airlines System only; 2007): passenger-km 5,928,000,000; metric ton-km cargo 8,748,000. Communications, in total units (units per 1,000 persons). Telephone landlines (2007): 2,825,000 (519); cellular telephone subscribers (2007): 6,230,000 (1,145); personal computers (2004): 3,543,000 (659); total Internet users (2007): 3,500,000 (643); broadband Internet subscribers (2007): 1,977,000 (363).

Education and health

Educational attainment (2004). Percentage of population ages 25–69 having: completed lower secondary or not stated 30.3%; completed upper secondary or vocational 43.9%; undergraduate 19.6%; graduate 6.2%. Literacy: percentage of total population literate 100%. Health: physicians (2004) 19,450 (1 per 278 persons); hospital beds (2005) 20,487 (1 per 265 persons); infant mortality rate per 1,000 live births (2007) 4.0; undernourished population (2002–04) less than 2.5% of total population.

Military

Total active duty personnel (2007): 29,960 (army 47.5%, air force 12.2%, navy 12.8%, other 27.5%). Military expenditure as percentage of GDP (2005): 1.8%; per capita expenditure US$640.

Background

The Danes, a Scandinavian branch of the Teutons, settled the area c. the 6th century AD. During the Viking period the Danes expanded their territory, and by the 11th century the united Danish kingdom included parts of what are now Germany, Sweden, Eng-

1 metric ton = about 1.1 short tons;　1 kilometer = 0.6 mi (statute);　1 metric ton-km cargo = about 0.68 short ton-mi cargo;　c.i.f.: cost, insurance, and freight;　f.o.b.: free on board

land, and Norway. Scandinavia was united under Danish rule from 1397 until 1523, when Sweden became independent; a series of debilitating wars with Sweden in the 17th century resulted in the Treaty of Copenhagen (1660), which established the modern Scandinavian frontiers. Denmark gained and lost various other territories, including Norway, in the 19th and 20th centuries; it went through three constitutions between 1849 and 1915 and was occupied by Nazi Germany in 1940–45. A founding member of NATO (1949), Denmark adopted its current constitution in 1953. It became a member of the European Community in 1973 and of the EU in 1993, but it negotiated exemptions from certain EU provisions in response to some Danes' concerns regarding environmental protection and social welfare.

Recent Developments

The Muhammad cartoon scandal that sparked virulent anti-Denmark protest across the Muslim world in 2006 reemerged in February 2008. After Danish police arrested three young people—two Tunisians and a Dane of Moroccan origin—suspected of plotting to kill one of the cartoonists behind the satiric drawings, major Danish newspapers, in a show of support for freedom of speech, reprinted the infamous caricatures. This again sparked mass demonstrations by Danish Muslims and scattered protests throughout the Islamic world, culminating in June in a car bomb attack on the Danish embassy in Islamabad, Pakistan, in which six Pakistanis were killed and 30 injured. In an Internet statement, al-Qaeda took responsibility for the blast, warning that further action would ensue if Denmark failed to apologize for publishing the cartoons.

Internet resources: <www.dst.dk/HomeUK.aspx>.

Djibouti

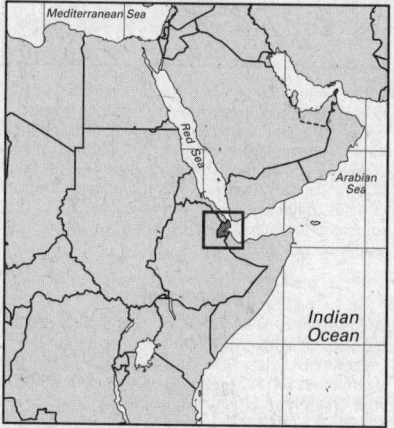

Mediterranean Sea

Red Sea

Arabian Sea

Indian Ocean

Official name: Jumhuriyah Jibuti (Arabic); République de Djibouti (French) (Republic of Djibouti). Form of government: multiparty republic with one legislative house (National Assembly [65]). Chief of state and head of government: President Ismail Omar Guelleh (from 1999), assisted by Prime Minister Dileita

Muhammad Dileita (from 2001). Capital: Djibouti. Official languages: Arabic; French. Official religion: none. Monetary unit: 1 Djibouti franc (FDJ) = 100 centimes; valuation (1 Jul 2009) US$1 = FDJ 174.26.

Demography

Area: 8,950 sq mi, 23,200 sq km. Population (2009): 864,000. Density (2009): persons per sq mi 96.5, persons per sq km 37.2. Urban (2007): 86.9%. Sex distribution (2006): male 51.19%; female 48.81%. Age breakdown (2006): under 15, 43.3%; 15–29, 28.0%; 30–44, 13.7%; 45–59, 9.2%; 60–74, 5.1%; 75 and over, 0.7%. Ethnic composition (2000): Somali 46.0%; Afar 35.4%; Arab 11.0%; mixed African and European 3.0%; French 1.6%; other/unspecified 3.0%. Religious affiliation (2000): Muslim (nearly all Sunni) 94.1%; Christian 4.5%, of which Orthodox 3.0%, Roman Catholic 1.4%; nonreligious 1.3%; other 0.1%. Major city and towns (2009): Djibouti (2007) 583,000; 'Ali Sabieh 23,000; Dikhil 16,700; Arta 11,600; Tadjourah 8,700. Location: the Horn of Africa, bordering Eritrea, the Red Sea, the Gulf of Aden, Somalia, and Ethiopia.

Vital statistics

Birth rate per 1,000 population (2006): 39.5 (world avg. 20.3). Death rate per 1,000 population (2006): 19.3 (world avg. 8.6). Natural increase rate per 1,000 population (2006): 20.2 (world avg. 11.7). Total fertility rate (avg. births per childbearing woman; 2006): 5.31. Life expectancy at birth (2006): male 41.9 years; female 44.5 years.

National economy

Budget (2005). Revenue: FDJ 46,710,000,000 (tax revenue 65.8%, of which indirect taxes 26.3%, direct taxes 24.8%, transit taxes, harbor dues and other registration fees 14.7%; nontax revenue 17.5%; grants 16.7%). Expenditures: FDJ 46,378,000,000 (current expenditures 74.7%; capital expenditures 25.3%). Public debt (external, outstanding; February 2006): US$474,000,000. Production (metric tons except as noted). Agriculture and fishing (2007): lemons and limes 1,800, dry beans 1,500, tomatoes 1,200; livestock (number of live animals) 512,000 goats, 466,000 sheep, 297,000 cattle, 69,000 camels; fisheries production (2006) 260 (from aquaculture, none). Mining and quarrying: mineral production limited to locally used construction materials such as basalt and evaporated salt (2006) 138,000. Manufacturing (2003): products of limited value include furniture, nonalcoholic beverages, meat and hides, light electromechanical goods, and mineral water. Energy production (consumption): electricity (kW-hr; 2005) 255,000,000 (255,000,000); petroleum products (metric tons; 2005) none (135,000); natural gas (cu m; 2004) none (4,380,000); geothermal, wind, and solar resources are substantial but largely undeveloped. Population economically active (2003): total 299,000; activity rate of total population 39.1% (participation rates: ages 15–64, 69.0%; female 39.5%; unemployed [2006] 60%). Gross national income (2007): US$908,000,000 (US$1,090 per capita). Selected balance of payments data. Receipts from (US$'000,000): tourism (2006) 9.2; remittances (2007) 28; foreign direct investment (2004–06 avg.) 56; official development assistance (2006) 117. Disbursements for (US$'000,000): tourism (2006) 3.5; remittances (2007) 5.

Foreign trade

Imports (1999): US$152,700,000 (food and beverages 25.0%; machinery and electric appliances 12.5%; khat 12.2%; petroleum products 10.9%; transportation equipment 10.3%). *Major import sources* (2004): Saudi Arabia 21.9%; India 18.7%; China 10.2%; Ethiopia 4.8%; France 4.7%. Exports (2001): US$10,200,000 (aircraft parts 24.5%; hides and skins of cattle, sheep, goats, and camels 20.6%; unspecified special transactions 8.8%; leather 7.8%; live animals 6.9%). *Major export destinations* (2005): Somalia 66.4%; Ethiopia 21.5%; Yemen 3.4%.

Transport and communications

Transport. *Railroads* (2006): length 100 km; passenger-km (1999) 81,000,000; metric ton-km cargo (2002) 201,000,000. *Roads* (2002): total length 2,890 km (paved 13%). *Vehicles* (2002): passenger cars 15,700; trucks and buses 3,200. *Air transport* (2005): passenger arrivals and departures 219,119; metric tons of freight loaded and unloaded 10,973. Communications, in total units (units per 1,000 persons). Telephone landlines (2005): 11,000 (23); cellular telephone subscribers (2007): 45,000 (54); personal computers (2005): 19,000 (41); total Internet users (2006): 11,000 (23); broadband Internet subscribers (2005): 40 (0.09).

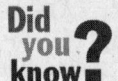

Did you know? Djibouti, virtually a city-state, is a deepwater port city and railhead bordered on three sides by a sparsely populated hot, arid landscape. In 1985 this small country won the first world cup men's team marathon.

Education and health

Literacy (2007): percentage of total population ages 15 and over literate 72.2%; males literate 81.2%; females literate 63.8%. Health: physicians (2004) 129 (1 per 3,619 persons); hospital beds (2000) 694 (1 per 621 persons); infant mortality rate per 1,000 live births (2006) 102.4; undernourished population (2002–04) 200,000 (24% of total population based on the consumption of a minimum daily requirement of 1,770 calories).

Military

Total active duty personnel (2007): 10,950 (army 73.1%, navy 1.8%, air force 2.3%, national security force 22.8%). Foreign troops: French (2007) 2,850; US and German military personnel at Camp Lemonier (2007) 2,038 and 257, respectively. Military expenditure as percentage of GDP (2004): 4.0%; per capita expenditure US$52.

Background

Settled around the 3rd century BC by the Arab ancestors of the Afars, Djibouti was later populated by So-

mali Issas. In AD 825 Islam was brought to the area by missionaries. Arabs controlled the trade in this region until the 16th century; it became the French protectorate of French Somaliland in 1888. In 1946 it became a French overseas territory, and in 1977 it gained its independence. In the late 20th century, the country received refugees from the Ethiopian-Somali war and from civil conflicts in Eritrea. In the 1990s it suffered from political unrest.

Recent Developments

Djibouti faced a tumultuous year in 2008 as it teetered on the brink of a war with Eritrea. In April Eritrea amassed troops along the Ras Doumeira border area of Djibouti; this action resulted in border skirmishes that led to the deaths of some 35 people, including about 20 Djibouti soldiers. The UN Security Council called on both sides to pull back forces and negotiate, but as of April 2009, Eritrean troops remained on the border.

Internet resources: <www.ministere-finances.dj>.

Dominica

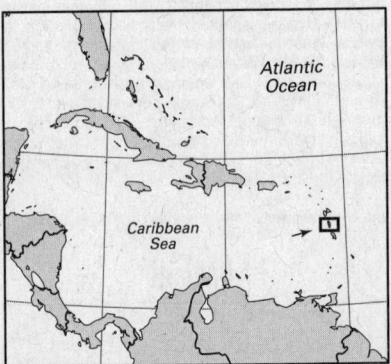

Atlantic Ocean

Caribbean Sea

Official name: Commonwealth of Dominica. **Form of government:** multiparty republic with one legislative house (House of Assembly [32]). **Chief of state:** President Nicholas Liverpool (from 2003). **Head of government:** Prime Minister Roosevelt Skerrit (from 2004). **Capital:** Roseau. **Official language:** English. **Official religion:** none. **Monetary unit:** 1 East Caribbean dollar (EC$) = 100 cents; valuation (1 Jul 2009) US$1 = EC$2.67.

Demography

Area: 290 sq mi, 750 sq km. **Population** (2008): 72,500. **Density** (2008): persons per sq mi 250.0, persons per sq km 96.7. **Urban** (2003): 72.0%. **Sex distribution** (2006): male 50.34%; female 49.66%. **Age breakdown** (2006): under 15, 26.1%; 15–29, 23.8%; 30–44, 27.4%; 45–59, 12.4%; 60–74, 7.0%; 75 and over, 3.3%. **Ethnic composition** (2000): black 88.3%; mulatto 7.3%; black-Amerindian 1.7%; British expatriates 1.0%; Indo-Pakistani 1.0%; other 0.7%. **Religious affiliation** (2001): Roman Catholic 61%;

1 metric ton = about 1.1 short tons;　1 kilometer = 0.6 mi (statute);　1 metric ton-km cargo = about 0.68 short ton-mi cargo;　c.i.f.: cost, insurance, and freight;　f.o.b.: free on board

four largest Protestant groups (including Seventh-day Adventist, Pentecostal groups, and Methodist) 28%; nonreligious 6%; other 5%. **Major towns** (2006): Roseau 16,600; Portsmouth 3,600; Marigot 2,900; Berekua 2,600; Atkinson 2,500. **Location:** island in the southern Caribbean Sea, south of Guadeloupe and north of Martinique.

Vital statistics

Birth rate per 1,000 population (2006): 15.3 (world avg. 20.3); (1991) within marriage 24.1%; outside of marriage 75.9%. **Death rate** per 1,000 population (2006): 6.7 (world avg. 8.6). **Natural increase rate** per 1,000 population (2006): 8.5 (world avg. 11.7). **Total fertility rate** (avg. births per childbearing woman; 2006): 1.94. **Life expectancy** at birth (2006): male 72.0 years; female 77.9 years.

National economy

Budget (2005–06). *Revenue:* EC$325,000,000 (tax revenue 73.7%, of which taxes on international trade and transactions 29.8%, taxes on goods and services 25.3%; grants 18.6%; nontax revenue 7.3%; development revenue 0.4%). *Expenditures:* EC$315,300,000 (current expenditures 76.2%, of which wages and salaries 33.4%, transfers 14.7%, debt interest 13.6%; development expenditures and net lending 23.8%). **Public debt** (external, outstanding; 2005): US$208,400,000. **Gross national income** (2007): US$310,000,000 (US$4,250 per capita). **Population economically active** (2001): total 27,865; activity rate of total population 40.0% (participation rates: ages 15–64, 64.7%; female 38.9%; unemployed [2002] 25%). **Production** (metric tons except as noted). *Agriculture and fishing* (2007): bananas 30,000, root crops 26,870 (of which taro 11,200, yams 8,000, yautia 4,550, sweet potatoes 1,850), grapefruit and pomelos 17,000; livestock (number of live animals) 13,500 cattle, 9,700 goats, 7,600 sheep; fisheries production (2006) 694 (from aquaculture, negligible). *Mining and quarrying:* pumice, limestone, and sand and gravel are quarried primarily for local consumption. *Manufacturing* (value of production in EC$'000; 2004): toilet and laundry soap 24,588; toothpaste 8,774; crude coconut oil (2001) 1,758; other products include fruit juices, beer, garments, bottled spring water, and cardboard boxes. *Energy production (consumption):* electricity (kW-hr; 2005) 84,000,000 (84,000,000); petroleum products (metric tons; 2005) none (37,000). **Selected balance of payments data.** Receipts from (US$'000,000): tourism (2006) 68; remittances (2007) 5; foreign direct investment (2004–06 avg.) 31; official development assistance (2006) 19. Disbursements for (US$'000,000): tourism (2006) 10.

Foreign trade

Imports (2006; c.i.f): US$166,900,000 (machinery and apparatus 17.1%; food products 15.5%; refined petroleum products 14.2%; chemical products 12.2%; road vehicles 5.9%). *Major import sources:* US 36.1%; Trinidad and Tobago 22.1%; UK 5.8%; Japan 4.0%; China 3.9%. **Exports** (2006; f.o.b.): US$41,500,000 (food products 32.8%, of which bananas 21.2%; soap 25.3%; dental/oral hygiene preparations 13.5%; stone, sand, and gravel 6.7%). *Major export destinations:* UK 18.6%; Jamaica 15.2%; Antigua and Barbuda 13.0%; France 8.2%; Trinidad and Tobago 7.5%.

Transport and communications

Transport. *Railroads:* none. *Roads* (1999): total length 780 km (paved 50%). *Vehicles* (1998): passenger cars 8,700; trucks and buses 3,400. *Air transport* (1997): passenger arrivals and departures 74,100; cargo unloaded 575 metric tons, cargo loaded 363 metric tons. **Communications,** in total units (units per 1,000 persons). Telephone landlines (2004): 21,000 (295); cellular telephone subscribers (2004): 42,000 (589); personal computers (2004): 13,000 (182); total Internet users (2005): 26,000 (372); broadband Internet subscribers (2004): 3,300 (46).

Education and health

Educational attainment (2002). Percentage of population ages 15 and over having: primary education 62%; secondary 31%; vocational through university 7%. **Literacy** (1996): percentage of total population ages 15 and over literate, 94.0%. **Health** (2004): physicians 38 (1 per 1,824 persons); hospital beds (2002) 270 (1 per 257 persons); infant mortality rate per 1,000 live births (2006) 13.7; undernourished population (2002–04) 5,000 (8% of total population based on the consumption of a minimum daily requirement of 1,930 calories).

Military

Total active duty personnel (2003): none (a 300-member police force includes a coast guard unit).

Background

At the time of the arrival of Christopher Columbus in 1493, Dominica was inhabited by the Caribs. With its steep coastal cliffs and inaccessible mountains, it was one of the last islands to be explored by Europeans, and the Caribs remained in possession until the 18th century; it was then settled by the French and ultimately taken by Britain in 1783. Subsequent hostilities between the settlers and the native inhabitants resulted in the Caribs' near extinction. Incorporated with the Leeward Islands in 1883 and with the Windward Islands in 1940, it became a member of the West Indies Federation in 1958. Dominica became independent in 1978.

Recent Developments

Dominica joined the Bolivarian Alternative for the Americas (ALBA), a group vigorously promoted by Venezuelan Pres. Hugo Chávez, in early 2008. ALBA aimed to promote more government control over the economy and integration among Latin American and Caribbean states. Besides Venezuela, ALBA's membership included Cuba, Bolivia, Honduras, Nicaragua, and Saint Vincent and the Grenadines.

Internet resources: <www.ndcdominica.dm>.

Dominican Republic

Official name: República Dominicana (Dominican Republic). **Form of government:** multiparty republic with two legislative houses (Senate [32]; Chamber of

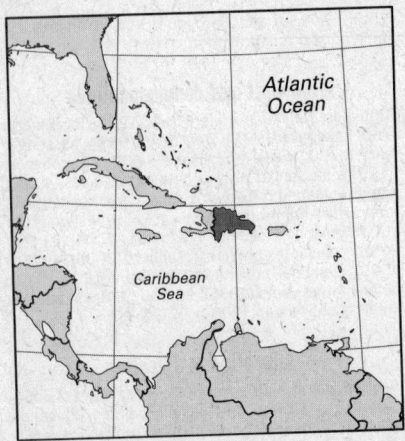

Atlantic
Ocean

Caribbean
Sea

Deputies [178]). **Head of state and government:** President Leonel Fernández Reyna (from 2004). **Capital:** Santo Domingo. **Official language:** Spanish. **Official religion:** none (Roman Catholicism is the state religion per concordat with Vatican City). **Monetary unit:** 1 Dominican peso (RD$) = 100 centavos; valuation (1 Jul 2009) US$1 = RD$35.85.

Demography

Area: 18,792 sq mi, 48,671 sq km. **Population** (2008): 9,507,000. **Density** (2008): persons per sq mi 505.9, persons per sq km 195.3. **Urban** (2005): 66.8%. **Sex distribution** (2005): male 50.18%; female 49.82%. **Age breakdown** (2002): under 15, 33.5%; 15–29, 26.6%; 30–44, 20.2%; 45–59, 11.7%; 60–74, 5.9%; 75–84, 1.6%; 85 and over, 0.5%. **Ethnic composition** (2003): mulatto 73%; white 16%; black 11%. **Religious affiliation** (2004): Roman Catholic 64.4%; other Christian 11.4%; nonreligious 22.5%; other 1.7%. **Major urban centers** (2002): Santo Domingo 1,887,586; Santiago 507,418; San Pedro de Macorís 193,713; La Romana 191,303; San Cristóbal 137,422. **Location:** eastern two-thirds of the island of Hispaniola, bordered by the North Atlantic Ocean, the Caribbean Sea, and Haiti.

Vital statistics

Birth rate per 1,000 population (2006): 23.2 (world avg. 20.3). **Death rate** per 1,000 population (2006): 5.4 (world avg. 8.6). **Total fertility rate** (avg. births per childbearing woman; 2006): 2.83. **Life expectancy** at birth (2006): male 71.0 years; female 74.5 years.

National economy

Budget (2005). *Revenue:* RD$157,585,000,000 (tax revenue 94.2%, of which taxes on goods and services 49.0%, import duties 24.0%, income tax 18.8%; non-tax revenue 5.8%). *Expenditures:* RD$161,612,-000,000 (current expenditures 75.7%; development expenditures 24.3%). **Public debt** (external, outstanding; 2006): US$6,571,000,000. **Gross national income** (2007): US$34,611,000,000 (US$3,550 per capita). **Production** (metric tons except as noted). *Agriculture and fishing* (2007): sugarcane 5,700,000, rice 710,000, bananas 552,500; livestock (number of live animals) 2,210,000 cattle, 47,500,000 chickens; fisheries production (2006) 13,894 (from aquaculture 7%). *Mining* (2006): nickel (metal content) 46,526; marble 6,000 cu m. *Manufacturing* (2005): cement 2,779,000; refined sugar 139,203; beer 4,541,000 hectoliters; rum 499,000 hectoliters. *Energy production (consumption):* electricity (kW-hr; 2005) 12,961,000,000 (12,961,000,000); coal (metric tons; 2005) none (476,000); crude petroleum (barrels; 2005) none (15,800,000); petroleum products (metric tons; 2005) 1,970,000 (5,084,000); natural gas (cu m; 2005) none (9,300,000). **Population economically active** (2004): total 3,701,804; activity rate of total population 43.1% (participation rates: ages 10 and over, 55.1%; female 38.7%; unemployed [2006] 16.2%). **Selected balance of payments data.** Receipts from (US$'000,000): tourism (2006) 3,792; remittances (2007) 3,414; foreign direct investment (2004–06 avg.) 1,038; official development assistance (2006) 53. Disbursements for (US$'000,000): tourism (2006) 333; remittances (2007) 28.

Foreign trade

Imports (2006): US$8,745,000,000 (consumer goods 50.7%, of which refined petroleum products 21.0%, food products 5.8%; capital goods 15.4%; crude petroleum 10.9%). *Major import sources* (2005): US 50.0%; Colombia 6.2%; Mexico 5.8%. **Exports** (2006): US$6,440,000,000 (reexports of free zones 70.0%, of which clothing 24.8%, electronics 10.3%, jewelry 9.8%; ferronickel 11.0%; mineral fuels 5.6%; raw sugar 1.6%). *Major export destinations* (2005): US 78.9%; The Netherlands 2.4%; Mexico 1.9%.

Transport and communications

Transport. *Railroads* (2004): route length 615 km. *Roads* (2002): total length 19,705 km (paved 51%). *Vehicles* (2005): passenger cars 690,027; trucks and buses 335,294. *Air transport:* passenger-km (1999) 4,900,000; metric ton-km cargo (2003) 200,000. **Communications,** in total units (units per 1,000 persons). Telephone landlines (2007): 907,000 (93); cellular telephone subscribers (2007): 5,513,000 (565); personal computers (2005): 206,000 (22); total Internet users (2007): 1,677,000 (172); broadband Internet subscribers (2007): 154,000 (16).

Education and health

Educational attainment (2002). Percentage of population ages 25 and older having: no formal education/unknown 4.1%; primary education 53.1%; secondary 25.9%; undergraduate 15.9%; graduate 1.0%. **Literacy** (2003): percentage of total population ages 15 and over literate 84.7%. **Health** (2005): physicians (public sector only) 12,966 (1 per 730 persons); hospital beds 9,640 (1 per 982 persons); infant mortality rate per 1,000 live births (2006) 29.0; undernourished population (2002–04) 2,500,000 (29% of total population based on the consumption of a minimum daily requirement of 1,920 calories).

1 metric ton = about 1.1 short tons;   1 kilometer = 0.6 mi (statute);   1 metric ton-km cargo = about 0.68 short ton-mi cargo;   c.i.f.: cost, insurance, and freight;   f.o.b.: free on board

Military

Total active duty personnel (2007): 49,910 (army 81.0%, navy 8.0%, air force 11.0%). Military expenditure as percentage of GDP (2005): 0.5%; per capita expenditure US$20.

Background

The Dominican Republic was originally part of the Spanish colony of Hispaniola. In 1697 the western third of the island, which later became Haiti, was ceded to France; the remainder of the island passed to France in 1795. The eastern two-thirds of the island was returned to Spain in 1809, and the colony declared its independence in 1821. Within a matter of weeks it was overrun by Haitian troops and occupied until 1844. Since then the country has been under the rule of a succession of dictators, except for short interludes of democratic government, and the US has frequently been involved in its affairs. The termination of the dictatorship of Rafael Trujillo in 1961 led to civil war in 1965 and US military intervention. The country frequently suffered from severe hurricanes, as in 1979 and 1998.

Recent Developments

The global economic downturn had a serious impact in 2008 on a country that was heavily dependent on tourism, free trade, remittances from the US, and mining. GDP growth was more than 5%—high by regional standards—but faltering. Contradictions between fiscal performance and quality of life for a large percentage of Dominicans stood out. The neglect of investment in human and physical infrastructure steadily eroded the government's popularity. A survey detailing the decline of public education in Latin America put the Dominican Republic in last place. Public outrage over endemic electrical outages resulted in widespread demonstrations and several deaths. Drug trafficking flourished in a climate of corrupt and weak institutions. Complaints about a profligate election system persisted. Despite food and fuel subsidies, inflation ran at 13%.

Internet resources: <www.bancentral.gov.do/english/index-e.asp>.

East Timor (Timor-Leste)

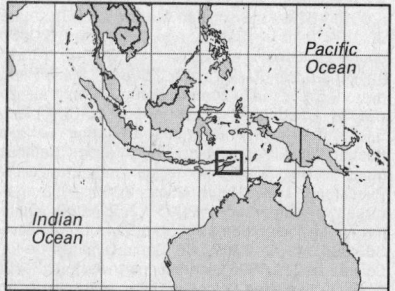

Official name: Republika Demokratika Timor Lorosa'e (Tetum); República Democrática de Timor-Leste (Portuguese) (Democratic Republic of Timor-Leste). Form of government: republic with one legislative body (National Parliament [65]). Chief of State: President José Ramos-Horta (from 2007). Head of government: Prime Minister Xanana Gusmão (from 2007). Capital: Dili. Official languages: Tetum; Portuguese. Official religion: none. Monetary unit: 1 US dollar (US$) = 100 centavos.

Demography

Area: 5,760 sq mi, 14,919 sq km. Population (2008): 1,078,000. Density (2008): persons per sq mi 187.2, persons per sq km 72.3. Urban (2005): 7.8%. Sex distribution (2004): male 50.90%; female 49.10%. Age breakdown (2004): under 15, 43.2%; 15–29, 24.7%; 30–44, 17.0%; 45–59, 9.4%; 60–74, 4.5%; 75 and over, 1.2%. Ethnic composition (1999): East Timorese 80%; other (nearly all Indonesian, and particularly West Timorese) 20%. Religious affiliation (2005): Roman Catholic 98%; Protestant 1%; Muslim 1%. Major urban areas (2004): Dili 151,026; Los Palos (Lospalos) 12,612; Same 9,966; Pante Macassar 9,754; Maliana 9,721. Location: southeast Asia, eastern end of the island of Timor plus an exclave on the western end, bordering the Timor Sea and Indonesia.

Vital statistics

Birth rate per 1,000 population (2006): 27.0 (world avg. 20.3). Death rate per 1,000 population (2006): 6.2 (world avg. 8.6). Natural increase rate per 1,000 population (2006): 20.8 (world avg. 11.7). Total fertility rate (avg. births per childbearing woman; 2006): 3.53. Life expectancy at birth (2006): male 64.0 years; female 68.7 years.

National economy

Budget (2005–06). Revenue: US$485,000,000 (oil and gas revenue 93.1%, of which taxes 74.8%, royalties 15.5%; domestic revenue 6.9%). Expenditures: US$93,000,000 (current expenditures 71.3%; capital expenditures 16.9%; previous year spending 11.8%). Production (metric tons except as noted). Agriculture and fishing (2007): corn (maize) 63,430; cassava 49,720; rice 41,386, candlenut (2001) 1,063; livestock (number of live animals) 346,000 pigs, 171,000 cattle, 110,000 buffalo; fisheries production (2006) 350 (from aquaculture, none). Mining and quarrying (2006): commercial quantities of marble are exported. Manufacturing (2001): principally the production of textiles, garments, handicrafts, bottled water, and processed coffee. Energy production (consumption): electricity (kW-hr; 2005) 300,000,-000 (300,000,000); crude petroleum (barrels; 2005) 1,130,000 (negligible); petroleum products (metric tons; 2005) 6,725,000 (57,000). Population economically active (2001): total 232,000; activity rate of total population 28% (participation rates: ages 15–64, 57%; unemployed 50%). Gross national income (2007): US$1,604,000,000 (US$1,510 per capita). Selected balance of payments data. Receipts from (US$'000,000): foreign direct investment (2004–06 avg.) 2; official development assistance (2006) 210.

Foreign trade

Imports (2005): US$101,600,000 (mineral fuels 34.6%; machinery and apparatus 13.1%; food products 11.0%; road vehicles 6.9%; iron and steel 4.7%). *Major import sources:* Indonesia 47.0%; Singapore 14.6%; Australia 13.9%; Japan 10.4%; Vietnam 4.5%. **Exports** (2005): US$8,100,000 (coffee 94.3%). *Major export destinations:* US 49.2%; Germany 20.7%; Portugal 12.0%; Australia 5.5%; Indonesia 5.0%.

Transport and communications

Transport. *Railroads:* none. *Roads* (2005): total length 5,000 km (paved 50%). *Vehicles* (1998): passenger cars 3,156; trucks and buses 7,140. **Communications,** in total units (units per 1,000 persons). Telephone landlines (1996): 6,600 (8); cellular telephone subscribers (2007): 69,000 (60); total Internet users (2004): 1,000 (1.1).

Education and health

Educational attainment (2002). Percentage of population ages 15 and over having: no formal education 54.3%; some primary education 14.4%; complete primary 6.2%; lower secondary 10.4%; upper secondary and higher 14.7%. **Literacy** (2005): percentage of total population ages 15 and over literate 49%; males literate 54%; females literate 45%. **Health:** physicians (2002) 47 (1 per 17,355 persons); hospital beds (1999) 560 (1 per 1,277 persons); infant mortality rate per 1,000 live births (2006) 45.9.

Military

Total active duty personnel (2007): 1,286 (army 97%, navy 3%); Australian peacekeeping troops (August 2008) 750. **Military expenditure as percentage of GDP** (2003): 1.3%; per capita expenditure US$5.

Background

The Portuguese first settled on the island of Timor in 1520 and were granted rule over Timor's eastern half in 1860. The Timorese political party Fretilin declared East Timor independent in 1975 after Portugal withdrew its troops. It was invaded by Indonesian forces and was incorporated as a province of Indonesia in 1976. The takeover, which resulted in thousands of East Timorese deaths during the next two decades, was disputed by the UN. In 1999 an independence referendum won overwhelmingly; civilian militias, armed by the military and led by local supporters of integration, then rampaged through the province, killing 1,000–2,000 people. The Indonesian parliament rescinded Indonesia's annexation of the territory, and East Timor was returned to its preannexation status as a non-self-governing territory, though this time under UN supervision. Preparation for independence got under way in 2001, with East Timorese voting by universal suffrage in August for a Constituent Assembly of 88 members. Independence was declared on 20 May 2002 and was followed by the swearing in of Xanana Gusmão as the first president of the country.

Recent Developments

Maj. Alfredo Reinado, leader of a band of disaffected soldiers known as "the petitioners," was said to have been responsible for the 2008 assassination attempt on Pres. José Ramos-Horta. Reinado was killed by the president's security guards during the incident; consequently, motives were hard to determine. The attack led to a security crisis that threatened East Timor's precarious grip on parliamentary democracy.

Internet resources:
<www.bancocentral.tl/en/main.asp>.

Ecuador

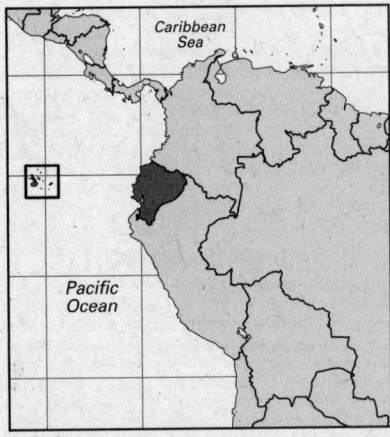

Official name: República del Ecuador (Republic of Ecuador). **Form of government:** unitary multiparty republic with one legislative house (National Assembly [124]). **Head of state and government:** President Rafael Correa Delgado (from 2007). **Capital:** Quito. **Official language:** Spanish (Quechua and Shuar are also official languages for the indigenous peoples). **Official religion:** none. **Monetary unit:** 1 US dollar (US$) = 100 centavos.

Demography

Area: 105,037 sq mi, 272,045 sq km. **Population** (2008): 13,481,000. **Density** (2008): persons per sq mi 128.3, persons per sq km 49.6. **Urban** (2005): 62.8%. **Sex distribution** (2005): male 50.15%; female 49.85%. **Age breakdown** (2005): under 15, 32.6%; 15–29, 27.4%; 30–44, 19.5%; 45–59, 12.1%; 60–74, 6.1%; 75–84, 1.8%; 85 and over, 0.5%. **Ethnic composition** (2000): mestizo 42.0%; Amerindian 40.8%; white 10.6%; black 5.0%; other 1.6%. **Religious affiliation** (2005): Roman Catholic (practicing) 35%; Roman Catholic (nonpracticing) 50%; other (significantly Evangelical Protestant) 15%. **Major cities** (2003): Guayaquil (urban agglomeration; 2005) 2,387,000; Quito (urban agglomeration; 2005) 1,514,000; Cuenca 303,994; Machala 217,266; Santo Domingo de los Colorados 211,689. **Location:** northwestern South America, bordering Colombia, Peru, and the Pacific Ocean.

---

1 metric ton = about 1.1 short tons; 1 kilometer = 0.6 mi (statute); 1 metric ton-km cargo = about 0.68 short ton-mi cargo; c.i.f.: cost, insurance, and freight; f.o.b.: free on board

Vital statistics

Birth rate per 1,000 population (2005): 22.1 (world avg. 20.3). **Death rate** per 1,000 population (2005): 5.0 (world avg. 8.6). **Total fertility rate** (avg. births per childbearing woman; 2005): 2.70. **Life expectancy** at birth (2005): male 71.7 years; female 77.6 years.

National economy

Budget (2006). *Revenue:* US$6,895,000,000 (nonpetroleum revenue 75.1%, of which VAT 32.3%, income tax 15.5%, customs duties 9.0%; petroleum export revenue 24.9%). *Expenditures:* US$7,011,-000,000 (current expenditures 76.2%; capital expenditures 23.8%). **Production** (metric tons except as noted). *Agriculture and fishing* (2007): sugarcane 7,300,000, bananas 6,130,000, oil palm fruit 2,100,000, pyrethrum and dried flowers (2004) 105; livestock (live animals) 5,050,000 cattle, 1,300,000 pigs, 1,050,000 sheep; fisheries production (2006) 527,128 (from aquaculture 15%). *Mining and quarrying* (2004): limestone 5,160,000; gold 5,300 kg. *Manufacturing* (value added in US$'000,000; 2004): refined petroleum products 1,794; food products 870; beverages 845; plastics 341; printing and publishing 233. *Energy production (consumption):* electricity (kW-hr; 2005) 13,404,000,000 (15,127,-000,000); crude petroleum. (barrels; 2007) 187,000,000 ([2006] 55,500,000); petroleum products (metric tons; 2005) 7,419,000 (7,221,000); natural gas (cu m; 2005) 756,000,000 (756,000,000). **Population economically active** (2005): total 4,225,400; activity rate of total population 47.9% (participation rates: ages 15–64, 70.6%; female 41.5%; unemployed [March 2006–February 2007] 10.1%). **Gross national income** (2007): US$41,148,000,000 (US$3,080 per capita). **Selected balance of payments data.** Receipts from (US$'000,000): tourism (2006) 490; remittances (2007) 3,080; foreign direct investment (2004–06 avg.) 1,631; official development assistance (2006) 189. Disbursements for (US$'000,000): tourism (2006) 466; remittances (2006) 62.

Foreign trade

Imports (2006): US$12,114,000,000 (mineral fuels 21.1%; machinery and apparatus 20.0%; chemical products 15.3%; road vehicles and parts 11.5%; iron and steel 6.0%). *Major import sources:* US 22.6%; Colombia 12.8%; Brazil 7.3%; China 6.8%; Chile 4.0%. **Exports** (2006): US$12,728,000,000 (crude petroleum 54.5%; bananas and plantains 9.5%; fish 5.4%; shrimp 4.6%; refined petroleum 3.9%; cut flowers 3.4%). *Major export destinations:* US 53.6%; Peru 8.2%; Colombia 5.6%; Chile 4.4%; Italy 3.4%.

Transport and communications

Transport. *Railroads* (2005): route length 965 km; passenger-km (2004) 3,000,000; metric ton-km cargo (2004) 2,000. *Roads* (2004): total length 43,197 km (paved 15%). *Vehicles* (2004): passenger cars 413,432; trucks and buses 310,009. *Air transport* (2005): passenger-km 867,100,000; metric ton-km cargo 5,400,000. **Communications,** in total units (units per 1,000 persons). Telephone landlines (2007): 1,805,000 (135); cellular telephone subscribers (2007): 10,086,000 (756); personal computers (2005): 866,000 (65); total Internet users (2006): 1,549,000 (115); broadband Internet subscribers (2007): 319,000 (24).

Education and health

Educational attainment (1995). Percentage of population ages 25 and over having: no formal schooling/incomplete primary education 18.8%; complete primary/incomplete secondary 47.2%; complete secondary 16.1%; higher 17.9%. **Literacy** (2003): total population ages 15 and over literate 92.5%; males literate 94.0%; females literate 91.0%. **Health:** physicians (2004) 21,625 (1 per 603 persons); hospital beds (2004) 21,200 (1 per 615 persons); infant mortality rate per 1,000 live births (2005) 23.0; undernourished population (2002–04) 700,000 (6% of total population based on the consumption of a minimum daily requirement of 1,820 calories).

Military

Total active duty personnel (2007): 57,100 (army 82.3%, navy 10.7%, air force 7.0%). **Military expenditure as percentage of GDP** (2005): 2.6%; per capita expenditure US$66.

Background

Ecuador was conquered by the Incas in AD 1450 and came under Spanish control in 1534. Under the Spaniards it was a part of the Viceroyalty of Peru until 1740, when it became a part of the Viceroyalty of New Granada. It gained its independence from Spain in 1822 as part of the republic of Gran Colombia, and in 1830 it became a sovereign state. A succession of authoritarian governments ruled into the mid-20th century, and economic hardship and social unrest prompted the military to take a strong role. Border disputes led to war between Peru and Ecuador in 1941; the two fought periodically until agreeing to a final demarcation in 1998. The economy, booming in the 1970s with petroleum profits, was depressed in the 1980s by reduced oil prices and earthquake damage. A new constitution was adopted in 1979. In the 1990s social unrest caused political instability and several changes of heads of state. In a controversial move to help stabilize the economy, the US dollar replaced the sucre as the national currency in 2000.

Recent Developments

Ecuadoran Pres. Rafael Correa secured popular support for sweeping political change in a referendum held in September 2008. More than 60% of those who voted approved a new constitution that entrenched programs, such as social security benefits for mothers and the self-employed, and increased presidential powers over economic and monetary policy. Strong world prices for oil, Ecuador's principal export, enabled Correa to stimulate the economy with social-spending programs that would provide seeds to farmers and building materials to would-be homeowners. Meanwhile, Correa said that the lease (scheduled to expire in November 2009) allowing the US to conduct anti-drug-trafficking surveillance flights from the Manta air base would not be renewed.

Internet resources: <www.ecuador.com>.

Egypt

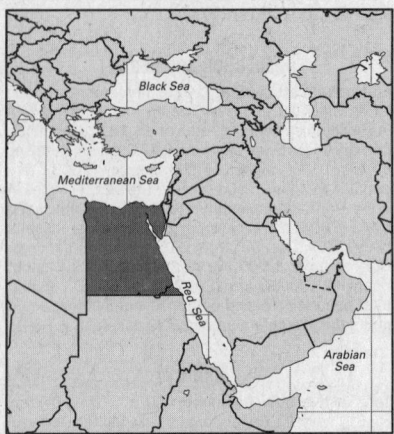

Official name: Jumhuriah Misr al-ʿArabiyah (Arab Republic of Egypt). **Form of government:** republic with two legislative houses (Shoura Assembly [264]; People's Assembly [454]). **Chief of state:** President Hosni Mubarak (from 1981). **Head of government:** Prime Minister Ahmed Nazif (from 2004). **Capital:** Cairo. **Official language:** Arabic. **Official religion:** Islam. **Monetary unit:** 1 Egyptian pound (LE) = 100 piastres; valuation (1 Jul 2009) US$1 = LE 5.60.

Demography

Area: 385,250 sq mi, 997,793 sq km. **Population** (2008): 74,805,000. **Density** (2008): persons per sq mi 194.2, persons per sq km 75.0. **Urban** (2006): 42.6%. **Sex distribution** (2006): male 51.11%; female 48.89%. **Age breakdown** (2005): under 15, 33.0%; 15–29, 28.0%; 30–44, 19.8%; 45–59, 12.3%; 60–74, 5.7%; 75 and over, 1.2%. **Ethnic composition** (2000): Egyptian Arab 84.1%; Sudanese Arab 5.5%; Arabized Berber 2.0%; Bedouin 2.0%; Rom (Gypsy) 1.6%; other 4.8%. **Religious affiliation** (2000): Muslim 84.4% (nearly all Sunni); Christian 15.1%, of which Orthodox 13.6%; nonreligious 0.5%. **Major cities** ('000; 2006): Cairo 6,759 (urban agglomeration [2005] 11,128); Alexandria 4,085; Al-Jizah 2,891; Shubra al-Khaymah 1,026; Port Said 571. **Location:** northern Africa, bordering the Mediterranean Sea, the Gaza Strip, Israel, the Red Sea, The Sudan, and Libya.

Vital statistics

Birth rate per 1,000 population (2005): 25.5 (world avg. 20.3). **Death rate** per 1,000 population (2005): 6.4 (world avg. 8.6). **Natural increase rate** per 1,000 population (2005): 19.1 (world avg. 11.7). **Total fertility rate** (avg. births per childbearing woman; 2006): 2.83. **Life expectancy** at birth (2006): male 69.2 years; female 73.6 years.

National economy

Budget (2003–04). *Revenue:* LE 116,490,000,000 (income and profits taxes 28.3%; sales taxes 19.4%; customs duties 13.0%; Suez Canal fees 4.4%; petroleum revenue 3.5%). *Expenditures:* LE 159,600,-000,000 (current expenditures 76.6%; capital expenditures 23.4%). **Population economically active** (2005): total 22,310,000; activity rate 31.3% (participation rates: ages 15–64 [2001] 46.9%; female 23.3%; unemployed [2006] 9.3%). **Production** ('000; Metric tons except as noted). *Agriculture and fishing* (2007): sugarcane 16,200, tomatoes 7,550, wheat 7,379, dates 1,130; livestock ('000; number of live animals) 5,180 sheep, 4,550 cattle, 3,950 buffalo, 120 camels; fisheries production (2006) 970,924 (from aquaculture 61%). *Mining and quarrying* (2006): gypsum 3,300; iron ore 2,600; phosphate rock 2,200; kaolin 416. *Manufacturing* (value added in US$'000,000; 2002): chemical products 2,823; food products 1,016; textiles and wearing apparel 618; bricks, cement, ceramics 466; paper products 160. *Energy production (consumption):* electricity ('000,000 kW-hr; 2005) 108,690 (107,912); coal ('000 metric tons; 2005) 33 (1,850); crude petroleum ('000 barrels; 2007) 221,000 ([2005] 237,000); petroleum products ('000 metric tons; 2005) 31,202 (30,025); natural gas ('000,000 cu m; 2006) 54,000 (37,000). **Gross national income** (2007): US$119,405,000,000 (US$1,580 per capita). **Public debt** (external, outstanding; 2006): US$28,000,000,000. **Selected balance of payments data.** Receipts from (US$'000,000): tourism (2006) 7,591; remittances (2007) 5,865; foreign direct investment (FDI) (2004–06 avg.) 5,859; official development assistance (2006) 873. Disbursements for (US$'000,-000): tourism (2006) 1,784; remittances (2007) 135; FDI (2004–06 avg.) 133.

Foreign trade

Imports (2005–06; c.i.f.): US$30,441,000,000 (crude petroleum 17.6%; machinery and apparatus 10.9%; food products 9.7%; metal products 7.3%; chemical products 6.0%). *Major import sources* (2006): free zones 14%; US 8%; Saudi Arabia 7%; China 6%; Kuwait 5%. **Exports** (2005–06; f.o.b.): US$18,455,100,000 (crude and refined petroleum 55.4%, of which crude petroleum 17.4%; finished goods 28.0%; semi-manufactured goods 6.4%; raw cotton 0.8%). *Major export destinations* (2006): free zones 12%; India 10%; Italy 9%; US 9%; Spain 8%.

Transport and communications

Transport. *Railroads* (2005): length 9,525 km; passenger-km 54,853,000,000; metric ton-km cargo 4,234,000,000. *Roads* (2004): length 92,370 km (paved 81%). *Vehicles:* passenger cars (2004) 1,960,000; trucks and buses (2002) 650,000. *Inland water* (2006): Suez Canal, number of transits 18,664; metric ton cargo 742,708,000. *Air transport* (2006): passenger-km 10,332,000,000; metric ton-km cargo 323,160,000. **Communications**, in total units (units per 1,000 persons). Telephone landlines (2007): 11,229,000 (149); cellular telephone sub-

---

1 metric ton = about 1.1 short tons;   1 kilometer = 0.6 mi (statute);   1 metric ton-km cargo = about 0.68 short ton-mi cargo;   c.i.f.: cost, insurance, and freight;   f.o.b.: free on board

scribers (2007): 30,065,000 (398); personal computers (2005): 2,800,000 (40); total Internet users (2007): 8,620,000 (114); broadband Internet subscribers (2007): 427,000 (5.8).

Education and health

Educational attainment (2006). Percentage of population ages 10 and over having: no formal schooling 42.9%; incomplete primary 19.4%; complete primary 24.9%; secondary 3.2%; higher 9.6%. **Literacy** (2001): percentage of total population ages 15 and over literate 56.1%; males literate 67.2%; females literate 44.8%. **Health** (2006): physicians 161,000 (1 per 451 persons); hospital beds (2007) 185,000 (1 per 393 persons); infant mortality rate per 1,000 live births (2005) 20.5; undernourished population (2002–04) 2,600,000 (4% of total population based on the consumption of a minimum daily requirement of 1,900 calories).

Military

Total active duty personnel (2007): 468,500 (army 72.6%, navy 3.9%, air force [including air defense] 23.5%). **Military expenditure as percentage of GDP** (2005): 2.8%; per capita expenditure US$37.

Background

Egypt is home to one of the world's oldest continuous civilizations. Upper and Lower Egypt were united c. 3000 BC, beginning a period of cultural achievement and a line of native rulers that lasted nearly 3,000 years. Egypt's ancient history is divided into the Old, Middle, and New Kingdoms, spanning 31 dynasties and lasting to 332 BC. The pyramids date from the Old Kingdom, the cult of Osiris and the refinement of sculpture from the Middle Kingdom, and the era of empire and the Exodus of the Jews from the New Kingdom. An Assyrian invasion occurred in the 7th century BC, and the Persian Achaemenids established a dynasty in 525 BC. The invasion by Alexander the Great in 332 BC inaugurated the Macedonian Ptolemaic period and the ascendancy of Alexandria. The Romans held Egypt from 30 BC to AD 395; later it was placed under the control of Constantinople. Constantine's granting of tolerance in 313 to the Christians began the development of a formal Egyptian (Coptic) church. Egypt came under Arab control in 642 and ultimately was transformed into an Arabic-speaking state, with Islam as the dominant religion. Held by the Umayyad and Abbasid dynasties, in 969 it became the center of the Fatimid dynasty. In 1250 the Mamluks established a dynasty that lasted until 1517, when Egypt fell to the Ottoman Turks. An economic decline ensued, and with it a decline in Egyptian culture. Egypt became a British protectorate in 1914 and received nominal independence in 1922, when a constitutional monarchy was established. A coup overthrew the monarchy in 1952, with Gamal Abdel Nasser taking power. Following three wars with Israel, Egypt, under Nasser's successor, Anwar el-Sadat, ultimately played a leading role in Middle East peace talks. Sadat was succeeded by Hosni Mubarak, who followed Sadat's peace initiatives and in 1982 regained Egyptian sovereignty (lost in 1967) over the Sinai Peninsula. Although Egypt took part in the coalition against Iraq during the Persian Gulf War (1991), it later made peace overtures to Iraq and other countries in the region.

Recent Developments

Egypt experienced an unprecedented surge in 2008 in the political involvement of its citizens, whose activities flouted limitations imposed since 1981 by the state of emergency. Rising food prices, unemployment, the poor quality of health services and education, and charges of nepotism and corruption were among the many grievances, and there was support for the breakout of the besieged population of Gaza into Egypt. A strike in April by textile workers marked a watershed in civil political action. An estimated 25,000 workers and thousands of irate supporters staged a preannounced strike to protest the government's failure to honor a promise for an improved compensation package.

Internet resources: <www.capmas.gov.eg>.

El Salvador

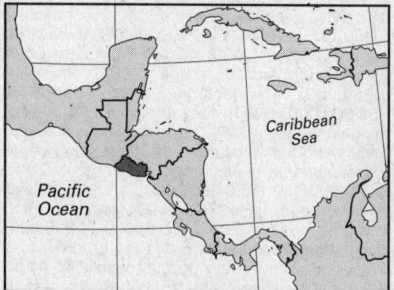

Official name: República de El Salvador (Republic of El Salvador). **Form of government:** republic with one legislative house (Legislative Assembly [84]). **Chief of state and government:** President Mauricio Funes (from 2009). **Capital:** San Salvador. **Official language:** Spanish. **Official religion:** none (Roman Catholicism, though not official, enjoys special recognition in the constitution). **Monetary unit:** 1 colón (₡) = 100 centavos; valuation (1 Jul 2009) US$1 = ₡8.58 (the US dollar [US$] has also been legal tender since 1 Jan 2001; the colón is rarely in use).

Demography

Area: 8,124 sq mi, 21,041 sq km. **Population** (2008): 5,794,000. **Density** (2008): persons per sq mi 713.2, persons per sq km 275.4. **Urban** (2007): 62.7%. **Sex distribution** (2007): male 47.34%; female 52.66%. **Age breakdown** (2007): under 15, 33.9%; 15–29, 26.9%; 30–44, 18.5%; 45–59, 11.3%; 60–74, 6.5%; 75–84, 2.1%; 85 and over, 0.8%. **Ethnic composition** (2000): mestizo 88.3%; Amerindian 9.1%, of which Pipil 4.0%; white 1.6%; other/unknown 1.0%. **Religious affiliation** (2005): Roman Catholic 71%; independent Christian 11%; Protestant 10%; Jehovah's Witness 2%; other 6%. **Major cities** (2007): San Salvador 316,090 (urban agglomeration 1,433,000); Santa Ana 245,421; Soyapango 241,403; San Miguel 218,410; Mejicanos 140,751. **Location:** Central America, bordering Guatemala, Honduras, and the North Pacific Ocean.

Vital statistics

Birth rate per 1,000 population (2005): 16.3 (world avg. 20.3); (1998) within marriage 27.2%; outside of marriage 72.8%. **Death rate** per 1,000 population (2005): 4.5 (world avg. 8.6). **Natural increase rate** per 1,000 population (2005): 11.8 (world avg. 11.7). **Total fertility rate** (avg. births per childbearing woman; 2006): 3.12. **Life expectancy** at birth (2006): male 67.9 years; female 75.3 years.

National economy

Budget (2005). *Revenue:* US$2,307,500,000 (VAT 47.8%; income tax 29.0%; import duties 7.8%; non-tax revenue 5.5%). *Expenditures:* US$2,484,-600,000 (education 18.6%; defense and public security 11.4%; public health and welfare 9.8%; public works 6.3%). **Public debt** (external, outstanding; 2006): US$5,504,000,000. **Production** (metric tons except as noted). *Agriculture and fishing* (2007): sugarcane 5,400,000, corn (maize) 836,695, sorghum 181,694; livestock (number of live animals) 1,380,112 cattle, 451,482 pigs, 96,000 horses; fisheries production (2006) 46,296 (from aquaculture 7%). *Mining and quarrying* (2004): limestone 1,161,000. *Manufacturing* (value added in US$'000,000; 2004): food products 875; textiles and wearing apparel 262; chemical products 262; refined petroleum products 234. *Energy production (consumption):* electricity (kW-hr; 2006) 5,293,000,000 (5,204,000,000); crude petroleum (barrels; 2005) none (7,280,000); petroleum products (metric tons; 2005) 1,012,000 (1,898,000). **Population economically active** (2004): total 2,710,237; activity rate of total population 40.1% (participation rates: ages 15–64, 63.2%; female 39.6%; unemployed [2005] 7.2%). **Gross national income** (2007): US$19,520,000,000 (US$2,850 per capita). **Selected balance of payments data.** Receipts from (US$'000,000): tourism (2006) 871; remittances (2007) 3,695; foreign direct investment (FDI) (2004–06 avg.) 366; official development assistance (2006) 157. Disbursements for (US$'000,000): tourism (2006) 518; remittances (2007) 29; FDI (2004–06 avg.) 38.

Foreign trade

Imports (2006; c.i.f.): US$7,627,000,000 (food, beverages, and tobacco 16.2%; imports for reexport 15.8%; machinery and apparatus 14.4%; crude petroleum 13.7%). *Major import sources:* US 40.5%; Guatemala 8.0%; Mexico 7.7%; Brazil 4.0%; Costa Rica 2.9%. **Exports** (2006; f.o.b.): US$3,513,-000,000 (reexports [mostly clothing] 45.6%; fabricated metal products 5.9%; coffee 5.4%; distilled spirits 4.5%; paper products 4.2%). *Major export destinations:* US 57.1%; Guatemala 13.0%; Honduras 8.0%; Nicaragua 4.8%; Costa Rica 3.4%.

Transport and communications

Transport. *Railroads* (2007): length 562 km. *Roads* (2002): total length 11,458 km (paved 23%). *Vehicles* (2000): passenger cars 148,000; trucks and buses 250,800. *Air transport* (TACA International Airlines only; 2005): passenger-km 8,117,465,000; metric ton-km cargo 37,883,000. **Communications,** in total units (units per 1,000 persons). Telephone landlines (2007): 1,080,000 (158); cellular telephone subscribers (2007): 6,137,000 (895); personal computers (2005): 350,000 (51); total Internet users (2006): 700,000 (100); broadband Internet subscribers (2007): 90,000 (13).

Education and health

Educational attainment (2004). Percentage of population ages 26 and over having: no formal schooling 22.0%; primary education: grades 1–3 19.1%, grades 4–6 19.9%; secondary: grades 7–9 13.9%, grades 10–12 14.6%; higher 10.5%. **Literacy** (2007): total population ages 15 and over literate 74.0%; males literate 72.7%; females literate 75.2%. **Health** (2005): physicians 8,670 (1 per 794 persons); hospital beds 4,816 (1 per 1,429 persons); infant mortality rate per 1,000 live births (2004) 10.5; undernourished population (2002–04) 700,000 (11% of total population based on the consumption of a minimum daily requirement of 1,800 calories).

Military

Total active duty personnel (2007): 15,660 (army 88.4%, navy 5.5%, air force 6.1%). **Military expenditure as percentage of GDP** (2007): 0.6%; per capita expenditure US$16.

Background

The Spanish arrived in the area in 1524 and subjugated the Pipil Indian kingdom of Cuzcatlán by 1539. The country was divided into two districts, San Salvador and Sonsonate, both attached to Guatemala. When independence came in 1821, San Salvador was incorporated into the Mexican Empire; upon its collapse in 1823, Sonsonate and San Salvador combined to form the new state of El Salvador within the United Provinces of Central America. From its founding, El Salvador experienced a high degree of political turmoil and was under military rule from 1931 to 1979, when the government was ousted in a coup. Elections held in 1982 set up a new government, and in 1983 a new constitution was adopted, but civil war continued through the 1980s. An accord in 1992 brought an uneasy truce.

Recent Developments

El Salvador enjoyed economic growth of 7.5% in 2008. Rising foreign trade and remittances from Salvadorans in the United States accounted for much of this success. Although the Central America–Dominican Republic Free Trade Agreement (CAFTA-DR) had not provided all the benefits that the government promised, it had increased trade with the US and the Dominican Republic. Separate trade agreements with Chile, Mexico, Panama, and Taiwan had further expanded Salvadoran trade, and negotiations with Caricom (Caribbean Community and Common Market), Canada, Israel, and the European Union promised additional growth. The global economic downturn, however, slowed the economy in late 2008.

Internet resources: <www.bcr.gob.sv/?lang=en>.

---

1 metric ton = about 1.1 short tons;   1 kilometer = 0.6 mi (statute);   1 metric ton-km cargo = about 0.68 short ton-mi cargo;   c.i.f.: cost, insurance, and freight;   f.o.b.: free on board

Equatorial Guinea

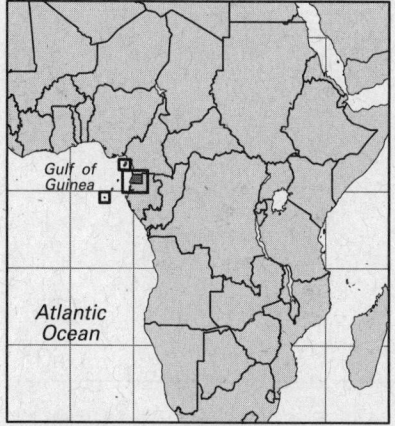

Gulf of Guinea

Atlantic Ocean

Official name: República de Guinea Ecuatorial (Spanish); République du Guinée Équatoriale (French) (Republic of Equatorial Guinea). **Form of government:** republic with one legislative house (House of People's Representatives [100]). **Chief of state:** President Teodoro Obiang Nguema Mbasogo (from 1979). **Head of government:** Prime Minister Ignacio Milam Tang (from 2008). **Capital:** Malabo. **Official languages:** Spanish; French. **Official religion:** none. **Monetary unit:** 1 CFA franc (CFAF) = 100 centimes; valuation (1 Jul 2009) US$1 = CFAF 462.89.

Demography

Area: 10,831 sq mi, 28,051 sq km. **Population** (2008): 616,000. **Density** (2008): persons per sq mi 56.9, persons per sq km 22.0. **Urban** (2006): 50.9%. **Sex distribution** (2005): male 48.82%; female 51.18%. **Age breakdown** (2005): under 15, 42.4%; 15–29, 26.2%; 30–44, 15.5%; 45–59, 9.5%; 60–74, 5.0%; 75–84, 1.2%; 85 and over, 0.2%. **Ethnic composition** (2000): Fang 56.6%; migrant laborers from Nigeria 12.5%, of which Yoruba 8.0%, Igbo 4.0%; Bubi 10.0%; Seke 2.9%; Spanish 2.8%; other 15.2%. **Religious affiliation** (2000): Roman Catholic 79.9%; Sunni Muslim 4.1%; independent Christian 3.7%; Protestant 3.2%; traditional beliefs 2.1%; nonreligious/atheist 4.9%; other 2.1%. **Major cities** (2003): Malabo 92,900; Bata 66,800; Mbini 11,600; Ebebiyin 9,100; Luba 6,800. **Location:** western Africa, the mainland portion bordering Cameroon, Gabon, and the Bight of Biafra.

Did you know? Equatorial Guinea has seen its economic condition radically change as a result of oil and gas discoveries in the past decade. Its per capita GNI, estimated at US$590 in 1998, was US$12,860 in 2007.

Vital statistics

Birth rate per 1,000 population (2005): 39.1 (world avg. 20.3). **Death rate** per 1,000 population (2005): 15.6 (world avg. 8.6). **Natural increase rate** per 1,000 population (2005): 23.5 (world avg. 11.7). **Total fertility rate** (avg. births per childbearing woman; 2005): 5.50. **Life expectancy** at birth (2005): male 49.2 years; female 51.7 years.

National economy

Budget (2005). *Revenue:* CFAF 1,528,825,000,000 (oil revenue 94.3%, of which profit sharing 32.1%, royalties 30.1%; non-oil revenue 5.6%, of which tax revenue 3.8%, nontax revenue 1.8%; grants 0.1%). *Expenditures:* CFAF 697,948,000,000 (capital expenditures 63.9%; current expenditures 22.8%; net lending 13.3%). **Public debt** (external, outstanding; 2006): US$156,800,000. **Gross national income** (2007): US$6,527,000,000 (US$12,860 per capita). **Production** (metric tons except as noted). *Agriculture and fishing* (2007): roots and tubers 105,000 (of which cassava 45,000, sweet potatoes 36,000), oil palm fruit 35,000, plantains 31,000, cacao beans 3,000; livestock (number of live animals) 37,600 sheep, 9,000 goats, 6,100 pigs; fisheries production (2006) 2,500 (from aquaculture, none). *Mining and quarrying:* gold (2006) 200 kg. *Manufacturing* (2004): methanol 1,027,300; processed timber 31,200 cu m. *Energy production (consumption):* electricity (kW-hr; 2005) 27,000,000 (27,000,000); crude petroleum (barrels; 2007) 133,000,000 ([2005] negligible); petroleum products (metric tons; 2005) none (47,000); natural gas (cu m; 2005) 1,247,000,000 (1,247,000,000). **Population economically active** (1997): total 177,000; activity rate of total population 40.0% (participation rates: ages 15–64, 74.7%; female 35.4%; unemployed [1998] 30%). **Selected balance of payments data.** Receipts from (US$'000,000): tourism (2005) 5; foreign direct investment (2004–06 avg.) 1,727; official development assistance (2006) 27.

Foreign trade

Imports (2005): CFAF 1,112,500,000,000 (for petroleum sector 55.8%; for public sector 33.0%; petroleum products 4.5%). *Major import sources* (2005): US 26.8%; Côte d'Ivoire 21.4%; Spain 13.6%; France 8.8%; UK 7.8%. **Exports** (2005): CFAF 3,764,200,-000,000 (crude petroleum 92.1%; methanol 6.9%; timber 0.7%). *Major export destinations* (2005): US 24.6%; China 21.8%; Spain 10.8%; Canada 7.3%; The Netherlands 5.2%.

Transport and communications

Transport. *Railroads:* none. *Roads* (2000): total length 2,880 km (paved 13%). *Vehicles* (2002): passenger cars 8,380; trucks and buses 6,618. **Communications,** in total units (units per 1,000 persons). Telephone landlines (2005): 10,000 (20); cellular telephone subscribers (2007): 220,000 (434); personal computers (2004): 7,000 (3.3); total Internet users (2006): 8,000 (16).

Education and health

Literacy (2006): percentage of total population ages 15 and over literate 87.0%; males literate 93.4%; females literate 80.5%. **Health:** physicians (2004) 101 (1 per 5,020 persons); hospital beds (1998) 907 (1 per 472 persons); infant mortality rate per 1,000 live births (2005) 96.5.

Military

Total active duty personnel (2007): 1,320 (army 83.3%, navy 9.1%, air force 7.6%). **Military expenditure as percentage of GDP** (2005): 0.1%; per capita expenditure US$14.

Background

The first inhabitants of the mainland region appear to have been Pygmies. The now-prominent Fang and Bubi reached the mainland region in the 17th-century Bantu migrations. Equatorial Guinea was ceded by the Portuguese to the Spanish in the late 18th century; it was frequented by slave traders, as well as by British, German, Dutch, and French merchants. Independence was declared in 1968, followed by a reign of terror and economic chaos under the dictatorial president Macías Nguema, who was overthrown by a military coup in 1979 and later executed. A new constitution was adopted in 1982, but political unrest persisted into the 21st century despite the country's oil wealth.

Recent Developments

Equatorial Guinea continued to be Africa's third largest oil producer (after Nigeria and Angola) in 2008. A pressing issue was the maritime border dispute with Gabon over the island of Mbanie in the Gulf of Guinea, where oil had been discovered. The UN appointed a Swiss legal expert to try to resolve the dispute. New attention was focused on Equatorial Guinea when British mercenary Simon Mann—who was accused of having led a coup in 2004 to topple Pres. Teodoro Obiang Nguema Mbasogo—was extradited secretly from Zimbabwe, where he had served four years in prison. Mann was put on trial in Malabo, and the proceedings were broadcast internationally. He revealed new details about the failed coup attempt, implicating the son of former British prime minister Margaret Thatcher and claiming that Spain, South Africa, and the United States knew of the plot and approved it.

Internet resources: <http://guinea-equatorial.com>.

Eritrea

Official name: State of Eritrea. **Form of government:** transitional regime with one interim legislative body (transitional National Assembly [150]). **Head of state and government:** President Isaias Afwerki (from 1993). **Capital:** Asmara. **Official language:** none. **Official religion:** none. **Monetary unit:** 1 nakfa (Nfa) = 100 cents; valuation (1 Jul 2009) US$1 = Nfa 15.04.

Demography

Area: 46,774 sq mi, 121,144 sq km. **Population** (2008): 5,028,000. **Density** (2008): persons per sq mi 128.9, persons per sq km 49.8. **Urban** (2006): 21.3%. **Sex distribution** (2006): male 49.84%; female 50.16%. **Age breakdown** (2006): under 15, 44.0%; 15–29, 27.9%; 30–44, 14.3%; 45–59, 8.2%; 60–74, 4.5%; 75 and over, 1.1%. **Ethnolinguistic composition** (2004): Tigrinya (Tigray) 50.0%; Tigré

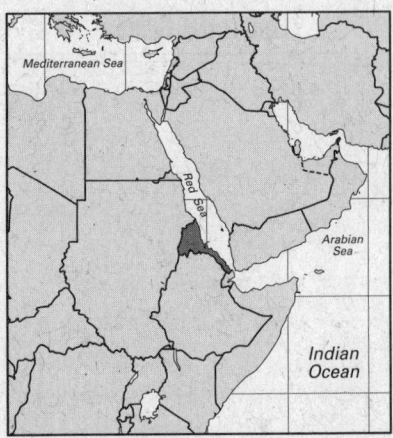

31.4%; Afar 5.0%; Saho 5.0%; Beja 2.5%; Bilen 2.1%; other 4.0%. **Religious affiliation** (2004): Muslim (virtually all Sunni) 50%; Christian 48%, of which Eritrean Orthodox 40%, Roman Catholic 5%; traditional beliefs 2%. **Major cities** (2003): Asmara 435,000; Keren 57,000; Assab 28,000; Mendefera 25,000; Massawa 25,000. **Location:** the Horn of Africa, bordering The Sudan, the Red Sea, Djibouti, and Ethiopia.

Vital statistics

Birth rate per 1,000 population (2006): 34.3 (world avg. 20.3). **Death rate** per 1,000 population (2006): 9.6 (world avg. 8.6). **Natural increase rate** per 1,000 population (2006): 24.7 (world avg. 11.7). **Total fertility rate** (avg. births per childbearing woman; 2006): 5.08. **Life expectancy** at birth (2006): male 57.4 years; female 60.7 years.

National economy

Budget (2002). *Revenue:* Nfa 3,409,800,000 (tax revenue 45.1%, of which import duties 18.1%, sales tax 10.8%, corporate tax 9.9%; grants 32.8%; nontax revenue 21.2%; extraordinary revenue 0.9%). *Expenditures:* Nfa 6,138,200,000 (defense 34.3%; health 9.6%; humanitarian assistance 7.9%; education 7.6%). **Public debt** (external, outstanding; 2006): US$781,000,000. **Gross national income** (2007): US$1,108,000,000 (US$230 per capita). **Production** (metric tons except as noted). *Agriculture and fishing* (2007): sorghum 130,000, millet 20,000, sesame seeds 19,000; livestock (number of live animals) 2,120,000 sheep, 1,960,000 cattle, 1,720,000 goats, 76,000 camels; fisheries production (2006) 8,813 (from aquaculture, none). *Mining and quarrying* (2005): granite 350,280, basalt 184,027, coral 91,348. *Manufacturing* (value added in US$'000,-000; 2004): beverages 31; tobacco products 8; furniture 7. *Energy production (consumption):* electricity (kW-hr; 2005) 289,000,000 (289,000,000); petroleum products (metric tons; 2005) none (240,000). **Population economically active** (2000): 1,451,000; activity rate of total population 40.8% (participation rates: ages 15–64, 75.4%; female 41.5%; unemployed, n.a.). **Selected balance of payments data.** Receipts from (US$'000,000): tourism (2006) 60; remittances (2003) 150; foreign direct disinvestment (2004–06 avg.) −2; official development assistance (2006) 129. Disbursements for (US$'000,000): remittances (2000) 1.

Foreign trade

Imports (2003; c.i.f.): US$432,800,000 (food and live animals 40.5%, of which cereals 25.5%; machinery and apparatus 14.8%; road vehicles 7.3%; chemical products 6.1%). *Major import sources* (2005): Italy 31.4%; US 11.9%; Belarus 5.9%; France 5.1%; Germany 4.6%. **Exports** (2003; f.o.b.): US$6,600,000 (food and live animals 36.4%, of which fresh fish 22.7%; leather products 10.6%; corals and shells 9.1%). *Major export destinations* (2005): Italy 15.1%; France 11.8%; US 9.5%; Germany 8.6%; Taiwan 7.4%.

Transport and communications

Transport, *Railroads* (2005): route length 306 km. *Roads* (2004): total length 4,000 km (paved 20%). *Vehicles* (1996): automobiles 5,940. *Air transport* (Asmara airport only; 2001): passenger arrivals 39,266, passenger departures 46,448; freight loaded 202 metric tons, freight unloaded 1,548 metric tons. **Communications,** in total units (units per 1,000 persons). Telephone landlines (2006): 38,000 (8.2); cellular telephone subscribers (2007): 70,000 (14); personal computers (2005): 35,000 (7.5); total Internet users (2007): 120,000 (24).

Education and health

Educational attainment (2002). Percentage of population ages 25 and over having: no formal education/unknown 67.6%; incomplete primary education 16.6%; complete primary 1.3%; incomplete secondary 5.8%; complete secondary 5.7%; higher 3.0%. **Literacy** (2006): total population ages 15 and over literate 61.4%; males literate 72.3%; females literate 50.7%. **Health:** physicians (2004) 215 (1 per 20,791 persons); hospital beds (2000) 3,126 (1 per 1,187 persons); infant mortality rate per 1,000 live births (2006) 46.3; undernourished population (2002–04) 3,100,000 (75% of total population based on the consumption of a minimum daily requirement of 1,730 calories).

Military

Total active duty personnel (2007): 201,750 (army 99.1%, navy 0.7%, air force 0.2%); mandate for the UN peacekeeping force along the Eritrean-Ethiopian border was terminated in July 2008. **Military expenditure as percentage of GDP** (2003): 24.1%; per capita expenditure US$49.

Background

As the site of the main ports of the Aksumite empire, Eritrea was linked to the beginnings of the Ethiopian kingdom, but it retained much of its independence until it came under Ottoman rule in the 16th century. From the 17th to the 19th centuries, control of the territory was disputed between Ethiopia, the Ottomans, the kingdom of Tigray, Egypt, and Italy; it became an Italian colony in 1890. Eritrea was used as

the base for the Italian invasions of Ethiopia (1896 and 1935–36) and in 1936 became part of Italian East Africa. It was captured by the British in 1941, federated to Ethiopia in 1952, and made a province of Ethiopia in 1962. Thirty years of guerrilla warfare by Eritrean secessionist groups ensued. A provisional Eritrean government was established in 1991, and independence came in 1993. A border war with Ethiopia that began in 1998 ended in an Ethiopian victory in 2000.

Recent Developments

Eritrea entered into another frontier dispute in 2008, this time with its neighbor Djibouti. In June soldiers of the two countries clashed along their undemarcated border, leading to more than 30 deaths. The fighting came as the UN prepared to disband a mission aimed at preserving a fragile cease-fire between Eritrea and Ethiopia. The UN, which had earlier complained that Eritrea had cut off fuel supplies to the mission (which had arrived in December 2000 to keep the peace after a deal was reached to end a two-year war in which 70,000 lives were lost), completed the pullout in July.

Internet resources: <www.shabait.com>.

Estonia

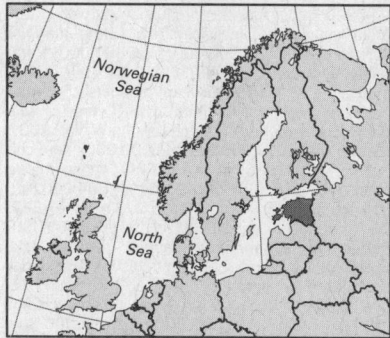

Official name: Eesti Vabariik (Republic of Estonia). **Form of government:** unitary multiparty republic with a single legislative body (Riigikogu [101]). **Chief of state:** President Toomas Hendrik Ilves (from 2006). **Head of government:** Prime Minister Andrus Ansip (from 2005). **Capital:** Tallinn. **Official language:** Estonian. **Official religion:** none. **Monetary unit:** 1 kroon (EEK; plural krooni) = 100 senti; valuation (1 Jul 2009) US$1 = EEK 11.04.

Demography

Area: 17,462 sq mi, 45,227 sq km. **Population** (2008): 1,340,000. **Density** (2008): persons per sq mi 81.9, persons per sq km 31.6. **Urban** (2005): 69.3%. **Sex distribution** (2005): male 46.06%; female 53.94%. **Age breakdown** (2005): under 15, 15.1%; 15–29, 22.7%; 30–44, 20.5%; 45–59, 20.2%; 60–74, 14.7%; 75–84, 5.7%; 85 and over, 1.1%. **Ethnic composition** (2005): Estonian 68.6%; Russian 25.7%; Ukrainian 2.1%; Belarusian 1.2%; Finnish 0.8%; other 1.6%. **Religious affiliation**

(2000): Christian 63.5%, of which unaffiliated Christian 25.6%, Protestant (mostly Lutheran) 17.2%, Orthodox 16.5%; nonreligious 25.1%; atheist 10.9%; other 0.5%. **Major cities** (2006): Tallinn 396,852; Tartu 101,965; Narva 66,712; Kohtla-Järve 45,399; Pärnu 44,074. **Location:** eastern Europe, bordering the Gulf of Finland, Russia, Latvia, the Gulf of Riga, and the Baltic Sea.

Vital statistics

Birth rate per 1,000 population (2007): 11.8 (world avg. 20.3); within marriage 41.9%; outside of marriage 58.1%. **Death rate** per 1,000 population (2007): 13.0 (world avg. 8.6). **Total fertility rate** (avg. births per childbearing woman; 2007): 1.64. **Life expectancy** at birth (2006): male 67.4 years; female 78.5 years.

National economy

Budget (2004). *Revenue:* EEK 54,836,300,000 (tax revenue 82.3%, of which social security contributions 28.3%, VAT 20.6%, income tax 17.4%, excise taxes 9.6%; nontax revenue 11.8%; grants 5.9%). *Expenditures:* EEK 52,429,100,000 (current expenditures 90.9%, of which social benefits 29.6%; capital expenditures 7.8%; other 1.3%). **Production** (metric tons except as noted). *Agriculture and fishing* (2007): barley 372,800, wheat 322,000, potatoes 173,700; livestock (number of live animals) 345,800 pigs, 244,800 cattle; fisheries production (2006) 87,193 (from aquaculture, negligible). *Mining and quarrying* (2005): oil shale 11,500,000; peat 800,000. *Manufacturing* (value added in US$'000,000; 2004): food products 163; fabricated metal products 150; wood products (excluding furniture) 138. *Energy production (consumption):* electricity (kW-hr; 2007) 12,135,000,000 ([2005] 8,394,000,000); hard coal (metric tons; 2005) none (56,000); lignite (metric tons; 2007) 16,508,000 ([2005] 14,804,000); petroleum products (metric tons; 2005) none (867,-000); natural gas (cu m; 2005) none (953,000,000). **Population economically active** (2005): total 659,600; activity rate of total population 48.8% (participation rates: ages 15–64, 69.6%; female 50.1%; unemployed [2007] 4.7%). **Gross national income** (2007): US$17,706,000,000 (US$13,200 per capita). **Selected balance of payments data.** Receipts from (US$'000,000): tourism (2006) 1,035; remittances (2007) 426; foreign direct investment (FDI) (2004–06 avg.) 1,841. Disbursements for (US$'000,000): tourism (2006) 592; remittances (2007) 96; FDI (2004–06 avg.) 667.

Foreign trade

Imports (2006; c.i.f.): EEK 165,298,500,000 (mineral fuels 16.1%; electrical machinery and apparatus 15.9%; transportation equipment 12.1%; chemical products 6.5%; textiles and wearing apparel 5.1%). *Major import sources:* Finland 18.2%; Russia 13.1%; Germany 12.4%; Sweden 9.0%; Lithuania 6.5%. **Exports** (2006; f.o.b.): EEK 119,519,700,000 (electrical machinery and apparatus 19.4%; mineral fuels 15.9%; wood and paper products 11.6%; transportation equipment 6.7%; textiles and wearing apparel 5.2%). *Major export destinations:* Finland 18.2%;

Sweden 12.3%; Latvia 8.7%; Russia 7.9%; Germany 5.0%.

Transport and communications

Transport. *Railroads* (2004): route length 958 km; passenger-km (2005) 246,951,000; metric ton-km cargo (2005) 10,629,398,000. *Roads* (2005): total length 57,016 km (paved 23%). *Vehicles* (2005): passenger cars 493,800; trucks and buses 91,400. *Air transport* (2007): passenger-km 756,000,000; metric ton-km cargo 1,044,000. **Communications,** in total units (units per 1,000 persons). Telephone landlines (2007): 496,000 (371); cellular telephone subscribers (2007): 1,982,000 (1,484); personal computers (2005): 650,000 (483); total Internet users (2007): 780,000 (584); broadband Internet subscribers (2007): 278,000 (208).

Education and health

Educational attainment (2000). Percentage of population ages 10 and over having: no formal schooling/incomplete primary education 6.7%; complete primary/lower secondary 31.6%; complete secondary 29.2%; higher vocational 17.5%; undergraduate 12.3%; advanced degree 0.4%; unknown 2.3%. **Literacy** (2003): percentage of total population literate, virtually 100%. **Health:** physicians (2003) 4,277 (1 per 316 persons); hospital beds (2004) 7,850 (1 per 172 persons); infant mortality rate per 1,000 live births (2007) 5.0; undernourished population (2002–04) less than 2.5% of total population.

Military

Total active duty personnel (2007): 4,100 (army 87.8%, navy 7.3%, air force 4.9%). **Military expenditure as a percentage of GDP** (2005): 1.7%; per capita expenditure US$152.

Background

The lands on the eastern shores of the Baltic Sea were invaded by Vikings in the 9th century AD, but the Estonians were able to withstand the assaults until the Danes took control in 1219. In 1346 the Danes sold their sovereignty to the Teutonic Order, which was then in possession of Livonia (southern Estonia and Latvia). In the mid-16th century Estonia was once again divided, with northern Estonia capitulating to Sweden and Poland gaining Livonia, which it surrendered to Sweden in 1629. Russia acquired Livonia and Estonia in 1721. Serfdom was abolished, and from 1881 Estonia underwent intensive Russification. In 1918 Estonia obtained independence from Russia, which lasted until the Soviet Union occupied the country in 1940 and forcibly incorporated it into the USSR. Germany held the region (1941–44) during World War II, but the Soviet regime was restored in 1944, after which Estonia's economy was collectivized and integrated into that of the Soviet Union. In 1991, along with other parts of the former USSR, it proclaimed its independence and subsequently held elections. Estonia continued negotiations with Russia to settle their common border, and, along with the other Baltic states, Estonia joined the EU and NATO in 2004.

---

1 metric ton = about 1.1 short tons;   1 kilometer = 0.6 mi (statute);   1 metric ton-km cargo = about 0.68 short ton-mi cargo;   c.i.f.: cost, insurance, and freight;   f.o.b.: free on board

Recent Developments

After nearly a decade of rapid growth, Estonia suffered a sharp economic downturn and the onset of a recession in 2008, further magnified by the global financial crisis late in the year. The inflation rate reached double digits, which made adoption of the euro—a key government goal—unlikely before 2011.

Internet resources: <www.vm.ee/estonia>.

Ethiopia

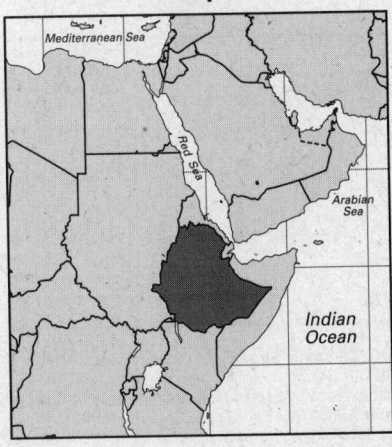

Official name: Federal Democratic Republic of Ethiopia. **Form of government:** federal republic with two legislative houses (House of the Federation [112]; House of Peoples' Representatives [547]). **Chief of state:** President Girma Wolde-Giorgis (from 2001). **Head of government:** Prime Minister Meles Zenawi (from 1995). **Capital:** Addis Ababa. **Official language:** none (Amharic is the "working" language). **Official religion:** none. **Monetary unit:** 1 birr (Br) = 100 cents; valuation (1 Jul 2009) US$1 = Br 11.22.

Demography

Area: 435,186 sq mi, 1,127,127 sq km. **Population** (2008): 78,254,000. **Density** (2008): persons per sq mi 179.8, persons per sq km 69.4. **Urban** (2007): 16.6%. **Sex distribution** (2006): male 49.88%; female 50.12%. **Age breakdown** (2006): under 15, 43.7%; 15–29, 28.1%; 30–44, 15.3%; 45–59, 8.5%; 60–74, 3.7%; 75 and over, 0.7%. **Ethnolinguistic composition** (2000) Oromo 35.8%; Amharic 31.0%; Tigrinya 6.1%; Gurage 4.9%; Sidamo 3.8%; Welaita 2.1%; Somali 1.4%; other 14.9%. **Religious affiliation** (2005): Muslim 33.7%; Ethiopian Orthodox 33.4%; Protestant 16.3%; traditional beliefs 10.4%; other 6.2%. **Major cities** (2006): Addis Ababa 2,973,000; Dire Dawa 281,750; Nazret 228,623; Gonder 194,773; Dese 169,104. **Location:** the Horn of Africa, bordering Eritrea, Djibouti, Somalia, Kenya, and The Sudan.

Vital statistics

Birth rate per 1,000 population (2006): 38.0 (world avg. 20.3). **Death rate** per 1,000 population (2006): 14.9 (world avg. 8.6). **Total fertility rate** (avg. births per childbearing woman; 2006): 5.22. **Life expectancy** at birth (2006): male 47.9 years; female 50.2 years.

National economy

Budget (2004–05). *Revenue:* Br 20,032,000,000 (tax revenue 61.2%, of which import duties 28.7%, income and profits tax 17.8%, sales tax 9.3%; grants 22.8%; nontax revenue 16.0%). *Expenditures:* Br 24,551,000,000 (current expenditures 53.1%, of which defense 11.9%, education 11.8%; capital expenditures 46.9%, of which economic development 31.6%). **Public debt** (external, outstanding; 2006): US$2,212,000,000. **Gross national income** (2007): US$17,565,000,000 (US$220 per capita). **Production** (metric tons except as noted). *Agriculture and fishing* (2007): corn (maize) 4,000,000, wheat 3,000,000, teff (2006–07) 2,437,700, maté 260,000; leading producer of beeswax, honey, cut flowers, and khat; livestock (number of live animals) 43,000,000 cattle, 23,700,000 sheep, 18,000,000 goats, 2,300,000 camels, (1998) 3,037 civets; fisheries production (2006) 9,890 (from aquaculture, negligible). *Mining and quarrying* (2006): rock salt 218,000; tantalum 70,000 kg; niobium 11,000 kg; gold 4,028 kg. *Manufacturing* (value added in US$'000,000; 2004): food products 157; beverages 118; bricks, cement, and ceramics 69. *Energy production (consumption):* electricity (kW-hr; 2005) 2,872,000,000 (2,872,000,000); crude petroleum (barrels; 2005) none (5,640,000); petroleum products (metric tons; 2005) 3,000 (1,547,000). **Population economically active** (2005): total 32,158,392; activity rate of total population 50.9% (participation rates: ages 10 and over, 78.4%; female [1999] 45.5%; unemployed 5.0%). **Selected balance of payments data.** Receipts from (US$'000,000): tourism (2006) 162; remittances (2007) 172; foreign direct investment (2004–06 avg.) 377; official development assistance (2006) 1,947. Disbursements for (US$'000,000): tourism (2006) 97; remittances (2007) 14.

Foreign trade

Imports (2006; c.i.f.): US$5,207,000,000 (machinery and apparatus 20.7%; refined petroleum products 19.5%; road vehicles 14.1%; chemical products 11.0%; food 6.7%). *Major import sources:* Saudi Arabia 17.9%; China 12.3%; Italy 7.7%; UAE 7.6%; India 5.8%. **Exports** (2006): US$1,043,000,000 (coffee and khat 40.8%; sesame seeds 15.4%; gum products, cut flowers, and foliage 12.4%; gold 6.2%; leather products 4.2%). *Major export destinations:* Germany 12.6%; China 9.7%; Japan 8.4%; Switzerland 6.4%; Saudi Arabia 6.3%.

Transport and communications

Transport. *Railroads* (2003): length 781 km; passenger-km (1998–99) 151,000,000; metric ton-km cargo (1998–99) 90,000,000. *Roads* (2006): total length 39,477 km (paved [2004] 19%). *Vehicles* (2003): passenger cars 71,311; trucks and buses 65,557. *Air transport* (2007): passenger-km 8,340,000,000; metric ton-km cargo 160,320,000. **Communications,** in total units (units per 1,000 persons). Telephone landlines (2007): 880,000 (11); cellular telephone subscribers (2007): 1,209,000 (15);

personal computers (2004): 113,000 (1.7); total Internet users (2007): 291,000 (3.5); broadband Internet subscribers (2007): 300.

Education and health

Educational attainment (2000). Percentage of population ages 15 and over having: no formal schooling 63.8%; incomplete primary education 21.6%; primary 2.6%; incomplete secondary 8.1%; secondary 2.5%; postsecondary 1.4%. **Literacy** (2007): total population ages 15 and over literate 47.5%. **Health** (2004–05): physicians 1,077 (1 per 66,236 persons); hospital beds 13,851 (1 per 5,150 persons); infant mortality rate per 1,000 live births (2006) 93.6; undernourished population (2002–04) 32,700,000 (46% of total population based on the consumption of a minimum daily requirement of 1,720 calories).

Military

Total active duty personnel (2007): 138,000 (army 97.8%, air force 2.2%); mandate for the UN peacekeeping force along the Ethiopian-Eritrean border was terminated in July 2008. **Military expenditure as percentage of GDP** (2005): 3.9%; per capita expenditure US$5.

Background

Ethiopia, the Biblical land of Cush, was inhabited from earliest antiquity and was once under ancient Egyptian rule. Ge'ez-speaking agriculturalists established the kingdom of Da'amat in the 2nd millennium BC. After 300 BC they were superseded by the kingdom of Aksum, whose King Menilek I, according to legend, was the son of King Solomon and the Queen of Sheba. Christianity was introduced in the 4th century AD and became widespread. Ethiopia's prosperous Mediterranean trade was cut off by the Muslim Arabs in the 7th and 8th centuries, and the area's interests were directed eastward. Contact with Europe resumed in the late 15th century with the arrival of the Portuguese. Modern Ethiopia began with the reign of Tewodros II, who began the consolidation of the country. In the wake of European encroachment, the coastal region was made an Italian colony in 1890, but under Emperor Menilek II the Italians were defeated and ousted in 1896. Ethiopia prospered under his rule, and his modernization programs were continued by Emperor Haile Selassie in the 1930s. In 1936 Italy again gained control of the country, and it was held as part of Italian East Africa until 1941, when it was liberated by the British. Ethiopia incorporated Eritrea in 1952. In 1974 Haile Selassie was deposed, and a Marxist government, plagued by civil wars and famine, controlled the country until 1991. In 1993 Eritrea gained its independence, but there were continuing border conflicts with it and neighboring Somalia into the 21st century.

Recent Developments

The Ethiopian economy was estimated to have grown at the vibrant rate of 11.6% in 2008, marking four straight years of double-digit growth. Most exports came from the agricultural sector, particularly coffee (exports grew by 40% in 2008), tea, spices, cereals, pulses, oilseeds, flowers, fruits, and vegetables. Whereas tourism and other aspects of the economy continued to grow in 2008, inflation and rising prices on consumer goods strained the government's ability to meet local demand. In early 2009 Ethiopia completed the withdrawal of thousands of troops in Somalia that had been supporting the Transitional Federal Government against insurgents since late 2006.

Internet resources: <www.csa.gov.et>.

Fiji

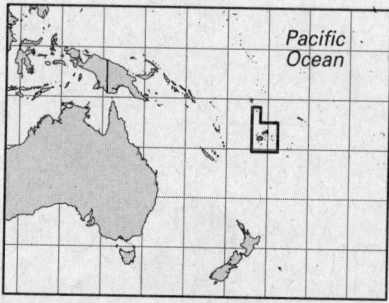

Pacific Ocean

Official name: Republic of the Fiji Islands; Matanitu Tu-Vaka-i-koya ko Viti (Fijian); Fiji Ripablik (Hindustani). **Form of government:** interim regime. **Chief of state:** President Ratu Josefa Iloilo (from 2000). **Head of government:** Prime Minister Voreque Bainimarama (from 2007). **Capital:** Suva. **Official languages:** English, Fijian, and Hindustani have equal status per constitution. **Official religion:** none. **Monetary unit:** 1 Fiji dollar (F$) = 100 cents; valuation (1 Jul 2009) US$1 = F$2.04.

Demography

Area: 7,055 sq mi, 18,272 sq km. **Population** (2008): 839,000. **Density** (2008): persons per sq mi 118.9, persons per sq km 45.9. **Urban** (2007): 50.9%. **Sex distribution** (2006): male 50.17%; female 49.83%. **Age breakdown** (2006): under 15, 31.1%; 15–29, 28.6%; 30–44, 19.7%; 45–59, 13.6%; 60–74, 6.1%; 75 and over, 0.9%. **Ethnic composition** (2007): Fijian 57.3%; Indian 37.6%; Rotuman (Polynesian) 1.2%; other 3.9%. **Religious affiliation** (2005): Protestant (mostly Methodist) 35%; Hindu 33%; independent Christian 11%; Roman Catholic 8%; Muslim 7%; other 6%. **Major urban areas** (2007): Nasinu 87,433; Suva 86,702 (urban agglomeration 241,432); Lautoka 52,867; Nausori 47,074; Nadi 43,367. **Location:** Oceania, archipelago in the South Pacific Ocean, between Hawaii (US) and New Zealand.

Vital statistics

Birth rate per 1,000 population (2006): 22.6 (world avg. 20.3). **Death rate** per 1,000 population (2006): 5.7 (world avg. 8.6). **Natural increase rate** per 1,000 population (2006): 16.9 (world avg. 11.7). **Total fer-**

---

1 metric ton = about 1.1 short tons; 1 kilometer = 0.6 mi (statute); 1 metric ton-km cargo = about 0.68 short ton-mi cargo; c.i.f.: cost, insurance, and freight; f.o.b.: free on board

tility rate (avg. births per childbearing woman; 2006): 2.73. **Life expectancy** at birth (2006): male 67.3 years; female 72.5 years.

National economy

Budget (2005). *Revenue:* F$1,218,332,000 (customs duties and port dues 59.4%; income tax 28.9%; fees and royalties 4.7%). *Expenditures:* F$1,231,556,000 (department expenditures 70.7%; public debt interest 26.3%). **Public debt** (external, outstanding; March 2008): US$262,600,000. **Production** (metric tons except as noted). *Agriculture and fishing* (2007): sugarcane 3,200,000, coconuts 140,000, taro 38,000, yaqona (kava) (2006) 2,259; livestock (number of live animals) 315,000 cattle, 4,300,000 chickens; fisheries production (2006) 47,319 (from aquaculture 1%). *Mining and quarrying* (2005): gold 3,800 kg; silver 1,500 kg. *Manufacturing* (value added in F$'000,000; 2001): food products 94.6; textiles and wearing apparel 92.4; beverages and tobacco 88.3. *Energy production (consumption):* electricity (kW-hr; 2005) 823,000,000 (823,000,000); coal (metric tons; 2005) none (12,000); petroleum products (metric tons; 2005) none (509,000). **Population economically active** (2000): total 341,700; activity rate of total population 42.2% (participation rates: ages 15–64 [1996] 60.6%; female 32.2%; unemployed [2002] 14.1%). **Gross national income** (2007): US$3,189,000,000 (US$3,800 per capita). **Selected balance of payments data.** Receipts from (US$'000,000): tourism (2006) 433; remittances (2007) 165; foreign direct investment (2004–06 avg.) 64; official development assistance (2006) 56. Disbursements for (US$'000,000): tourism (2006) 101; remittances (2007) 30.

Foreign trade

Imports (2006; c.i.f.): F$3,119,920,000 (mineral products 33.4%; machinery and apparatus 14.9%; transportation equipment 7.1%; chemical products 5.3%; textiles and wearing apparel 5.0%). *Major import sources:* Singapore 34.4%; Australia 22.4%; New Zealand 15.9%; Japan 3.6%; China 3.6%. **Exports** (2006; f.o.b.): F$1,175,206,000 (reexports 29.4%; sugar 18.3%; fish 8.3%; wearing apparel 8.1%; mineral water 7.4%). *Major export destinations:* Australia 17.4%; US 14.4%; UK 11.2%; Japan 8.1%; New Zealand 5.9%.

Transport and communications

Transport. *Railroads* (owned by the Fiji Sugar Corporation; 2003): length 597 km. *Roads* (1999): total length 3,440 km (paved 49%). *Vehicles* (2005): passenger cars 76,273; trucks and buses 42,311. *Air transport* (Air Pacific only; 2004–05): passenger-km 2,360,000,000; metric ton-km cargo 92,108,000. **Communications,** in total units (units per 1,000 persons). Telephone landlines (2007): 108,000 (130); cellular telephone subscribers (2007): 437,000 (524); personal computers (2004): 44,000 (52); total Internet users (2006): 80,000 (94); broadband Internet subscribers (2006): 8,500 (10).

Education and health

Educational attainment (1996). Percentage of population ages 25 and over having: no formal schooling 4.4%; some education 22.3%; incomplete secondary 47.7%; complete secondary 17.0%; some higher 6.7%; university degree 1.9%. **Literacy** (2003): total population ages 15 and over literate 93.7%; males literate 95.5%; females literate 91.9%. **Health** (2005): physicians 361 (1 per 2,343 persons); hospital beds 1,810 (1 per 467 persons); infant mortality rate per 1,000 live births (2006) 12.3; undernourished population (2002–04) 40,000 (5% of total population based on the consumption of a minimum daily requirement of 1,920 calories).

Military

Total active duty personnel (2007): 3,500 (army 91.4%, navy 8.6%, air force, none). **Military expenditure as percentage of GDP** (2004): 1.2%; per capita expenditure US$36.

Background

Archaeological evidence shows that the islands of Fiji were occupied in the late 2nd millennium BC. The first European sighting was by the Dutch in the 17th century; in 1774 the islands were visited by Capt. James Cook, who found a mixed Melanesian-Polynesian population with a complex society. Traders and the first missionaries arrived in 1835. In 1857 a British consul was appointed, and in 1874 Fiji was proclaimed a crown colony. It became independent as a member of the Commonwealth in 1970 and was declared a republic in 1987 following a military coup. Elections in 1992 restored civilian rule. A new constitution was approved in 1997. Coups in 2000 and 2006 created continuing political instability.

Recent Developments

A standoff between Fiji's interim government and its Pacific neighbors continued throughout 2008. The interim military leadership insisted that the objectives of the 2006 coup—the elimination of institutional corruption and the adoption of a People's Charter—should precede general elections tentatively scheduled for early 2009 and the return of an elected government. The Pacific Islands Forum, a regional organization headquartered in Fiji and of which Fiji was a founding member, suspended Fiji's membership after a deadline to publish a schedule for the election passed in May 2009.

Internet resources: <www.statsfiji.gov.fj>.

Finland

Official names: Suomen Tasavalta (Finnish); Republiken Finland (Swedish) (Republic of Finland). **Form of government:** multiparty republic with one legislative house (Parliament [200]). **Chief of state:** President Tarja Halonen (from 2000). **Head of government:** Prime Minister Matti Vanhanen (from 2003). **Capital:** Helsinki. **Official languages:** none (Finnish and Swedish are national [not official] languages). **Official religion:** none. **Monetary unit:** 1 euro (€) = 100 cents; valuation (1 Jul 2009) US$1 = €0.71.

Demography

Area (includes inland water area of 13,255 sq mi [34,331 sq km]): 130,664 sq mi; 338,417 sq km. **Population** (2008): 5,310,000. **Density** (2008): per-

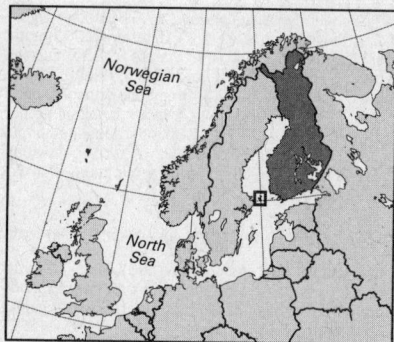

sons per sq mi 45.2, persons per sq km 17.5. **Urban** (2004): 62.1% **Sex distribution** (2006): male 48.96%; female 51.04%. **Age breakdown** (2006): under 15, 17.1%; 15–29, 18.7%; 30–44, 19.5%; 45–59, 22.3%; 60–74, 14.7%; 75–84, 5.9%; 85 and over, 1.8%. **Linguistic composition** (2006): Finnish 91.5%; Swedish 5.5%; Russian 0.8%; other 2.2%. **Religious affiliation** (2005): Evangelical Lutheran 83.1%; nonreligious 14.7%; Finnish (Greek) Orthodox 1.1%; Muslim 0.4%; other 0.7%. **Major cities** (2007): Helsinki 568,531 (urban agglomeration [2003] 1,075,000); Espoo 238,047; Tampere 207,866; Vantaa 192,522; Turku 175,286. **Location:** northern Europe, bordering Norway, Russia, the Gulf of Finland, the Baltic Sea, the Gulf of Bothnia, and Sweden.

Vital statistics

Birth rate per 1,000 population (2007): 11.1 (world avg. 20.3); within marriage 59.4%; outside of marriage 40.6%. **Death rate** per 1,000 population (2007): 9.3 (world avg. 8.6). **Natural increase rate** per 1,000 population (2007): 1.8 (world avg. 11.7). **Total fertility rate** (avg. births per childbearing woman; 2007): 1.83. **Life expectancy** at birth (2007): male 75.9 years; female 82.9 years.

National economy

Budget (2006). *Revenue:* €39,582,000,000 (VAT 33.3%; income and property taxes 32.4%; excise duties 11.7%). *Expenditures:* €39,582,000,000 (social security and health 28.6%; education 16.3%; agriculture and forestry 6.8%; defense 5.7%;). **Public debt** (2007): US$83,629,000,000. **Production** (metric tons except as noted). *Agriculture and fishing* (2007): barley 1,984,000, oats 1,222,000, wheat 797,000; livestock (number of live animals) 1,448,000 pigs, 927,000 cattle, 193,000 reindeer; fisheries production (2006) 162,341 (from aquaculture 8%). *Mining and quarrying* (2006): chromite 320,000; zinc (metal content) 66,109; gold 5,292 kg. *Manufacturing* (value added in €'000,000; 2005): electrical and optical equipment (largely telephone apparatus) 7,187; nonelectrical machinery and apparatus 3,744; chemical products 3,615. *Energy production (consumption):* electricity (kW-hr; 2007) 77,970,000,000 ([2005] 87,539,000,000); coal (metric tons; 2005) none (4,598,000); crude petroleum (barrels; 2005) none (72,100,000); petroleum products (metric tons;

2005) 11,825,000 (10,234,000); natural gas (cu m; 2005) none ([2005] 4,344,000,000). **Population economically active** (2006): total 2,648,000; activity rate of total population 50.3% (participation rates: ages 15–64 [2004] 73.8%; female [2004] 48.1%; unemployed 7.7%). **Gross national income** (2007): US$234,833,000,000 (US$44,400 per capita). **Selected balance of payments data.** Receipts from (US$'000,000): tourism (2006) 2,357; remittances (2007) 772; foreign direct investment (FDI) (2004–06 avg.) 3,739. Disbursements for (US$'000,000): tourism (2006) 3,417; remittances (2007) 391; FDI (2004–06 avg.) 1,136.

Foreign trade

Imports (2006; c.i.f.): €55,341,000,000 (machinery and apparatus 26.8%; crude petroleum 11.6%; chemical products 10.8%; road vehicles and parts 8.5%). *Major import sources* (2006): Russia 14.1%; Germany 13.9%; Sweden 9.8%; China 7.4%; UK 4.8%. **Exports** (2006; f.o.b.): €61,599,000,000 (telecommunications equipment 15.7%; paper and cardboard 13.2%; chemical products 6.1%; specialized machinery 5.7%; refined petroleum products 4.9%). *Major export destinations* (2006): Germany 11.3%; Sweden 10.5%; Russia 10.1%; UK 6.5%; US 6.5%.

Transport and communications

Transport. *Railroads* (2007): route length 5,899 km; passenger-km 3,800,000,000; metric ton-km cargo 10,400,000,000. *Roads* (2004): total length 78,168 km (paved 65%). *Vehicles* (2005): passenger cars 2,430,345; trucks and buses 363,644. *Air transport* (2007): passenger-km 15,564,000,000; metric ton-km cargo 489,672,000. **Communications,** in total units (units per 1,000 persons). Telephone landlines (2007): 1,740,000 (330); cellular telephone subscribers (2007): 6,080,000 (1,152); personal computers (2004): 2,515,000 (482); total Internet users (2007): 3,600,000 (682); broadband Internet subscribers (2007): 1,759,000 (333).

Education and health

Educational attainment (2003). Percentage of population ages 25 and over having: incomplete upper-secondary education 35.6%; complete upper secondary or vocational 35.8%; higher 28.6%. **Literacy:** virtually 100%. **Health** (2004): physicians (2007) 18,843 (1 per 281 persons); hospital beds 36,082 (1 per 145 persons); infant mortality rate per 1,000 live births 3.3; undernourished population (2002–04) less than 2.5% of total population.

Military

Total active duty personnel (2007): 29,300 (army 70.0%, navy 14.0%, air force 16.0%). **Military expenditure as percentage of GDP** (2005): 1.4%; per capita expenditure US$515.

Background

Recent archaeological discoveries have led some to suggest that human habitation in Finland dates back at least 100,000 years. Ancestors of the Sami ap-

1 metric ton = about 1.1 short tons;   1 kilometer = 0.6 mi (statute);   1 metric ton-km cargo = about 0.68 short ton-mi cargo;   c.i.f.: cost, insurance, and freight;   f.o.b.: free on board

parently were present in Finland by about 7000 BC. The ancestors of the present-day Finns came from the southern shore of the Gulf of Finland in the 1st millennium BC. The area was gradually Christianized from the 11th century. From the 12th century Sweden and Russia contested for supremacy in Finland, but by 1323 Sweden ruled most of the country. Russia was ceded part of Finnish territory in 1721; in 1808 Alexander I of Russia invaded Finland, which in 1809 was formally ceded to Russia. The subsequent period saw the growth of Finnish nationalism. Russia's losses in World War I and the Russian Revolution of 1917 set the stage for Finland's independence in 1917. It was defeated by the Soviet Union in the Russo-Finnish War (1939–40) but then sided with Nazi Germany against the Soviets during World War II and regained the territory it had lost. Facing defeat again by the advancing Soviets in 1944, it reached a peace agreement with the USSR, ceding territory and paying reparations. Finland's economy recovered after World War II. It joined the EU in 1995.

Recent Developments

Although the Finnish economy remained relatively strong, the global financial crisis negatively affected it. In 2008 unemployment dropped half a percent to 6.4% and the economy grew by 3.6%, but this was half the growth rate of the previous two years, and exports and foreign investment stagnated. Key indicators began to fall in the second half of the year, and by March 2009 unemployment had jumped to 8.3%. Former president (1994–2000) and career diplomat Martti Ahtisaari in October 2008 was awarded the Nobel Prize for Peace.

Internet resources: <www.stat.fi/index_en.html>.

France

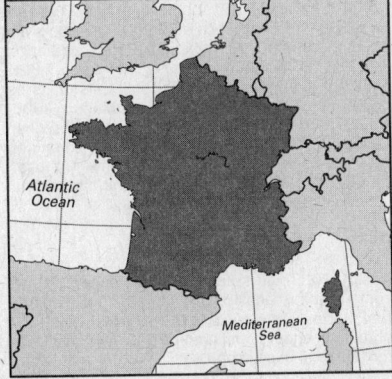

Atlantic
Ocean

Mediterranean
Sea

Official name: République Française (French Republic). **Form of government:** republic with two legislative houses (Senate [343], National Assembly [577]). **Chief of state:** President Nicolas Sarkozy (from 2007). **Head of government:** Prime Minister François Fillon (from 2007). **Capital:** Paris. **Official language:** French. **Official religion:** none. **Monetary unit:** 1 euro (€) = 100 cents; valuation (1 Jul 2009) US$1 = €0.71.

Demography

Area: 210,026 sq mi, 543,965 sq km. **Population** (2008): 62,028,000. **Density** (2008): persons per sq mi 295.3, persons per sq km 114.0. **Urban** (2003): 76.3%. **Sex distribution** (2006): male 48.60%; female 51.40%. **Age breakdown** (2005): under 15, 18.4%; 15–29, 19.1%; 30–44, 21.1%; 45–59, 20.4%; 60–74, 12.7%; 75–84, 6.3%; 85 and over, 2.0%. **Ethnic composition** (2000): French 76.9%; Algerian and Moroccan Berber 2.2%; Italian 1.9%; Portuguese 1.5%; Moroccan Arab 1.5%; Fleming 1.4%; Algerian Arab 1.3%; Basque 1.3%; Jewish 1.2%; German 1.2%; Vietnamese 1.0%; Catalan 0.5%; other 8.1%. **Religious affiliation** (2004): Roman Catholic 64.3%, of which practicing 8%; nonreligious/atheist 27%; Muslim 4.3%; Protestant 1.9%; Buddhist 1%; Jewish 0.6%; Jehovah's Witness 0.4%; Orthodox 0.2%; other 0.3%. **Major cities (urban agglomeration)** (2005): Paris 2,153,600 (9,854,000); Marseille 820,900 (1,384,000); Lyon 466,400 (1,408,000); Toulouse 435,000 (839,000); Nice 347,900 (915,000); Nantes 281,800; Strasbourg 272,700; Montpellier 244,300; Bordeaux 230,600 (794,000); Lille 225,100 (1,031,000); Rennes 209,900; Reims 184,800; Le Havre 183,900; Saint-Étienne 175,700. **Location:** western Europe, bordering the North Atlantic Ocean, Belgium, Luxembourg, Germany, Switzerland, Italy, the Mediterranean Sea, Spain, and Andorra. **Immigration:** total immigrant population (2004) 4,850,000; immigrants admitted (2002) 205,707, of which North African 30.7%, EU 20.8%, sub-Saharan African 15.2%, Asian 14.1%, other European 11.8%.

Vital statistics

Birth rate per 1,000 population (2006): 13.1 (world avg. 20.3); (2005) within marriage 52.6%; outside of marriage 47.4%. **Death rate** per 1,000 population (2006): 8.4 (world avg. 8.6). **Natural increase rate** per 1,000 population (2006): 4.7 (world avg. 11.7). **Total fertility rate** (avg. births per childbearing woman; 2006): 2.00. **Life expectancy** at birth (2006): male 77.2 years; female 84.1 years.

Social indicators

Educational attainment (2002). Percentage of population ages 25–64 having: no formal schooling through lower-secondary education 35%; upper secondary/higher vocational 41%; university 24%. **Quality of working life.** Legally worked week for full-time employees (2005) 36.0 hours. Rate of fatal injuries per 100,000 insured workers (2004) 3.7. Average days lost to labor stoppages per 1,000 workers (2004) 13. Trade union membership (2003) 1,900,000 (8% of labor force). **Access to services** (2004). Percentage of principal residences having: electricity 97.4%; indoor toilet 94.6%; indoor kitchen with sink 94.2%; hot water 60.3%; air conditioner 15.4%. **Social participation.** Population ages 16 and over participating in voluntary associations (1997) 28.0%. Percentage of population who "never" or "almost never" attend church services (2000) 60%; percentage of Roman Catholic population who attend Mass weekly (2003) 12%. **Social deviance.** Offense rate per 100,000 population (2006) for: murder 1.5, rape 16.0, other assault 269.2; theft (including burglary and housebreaking) 3,403.8. Incidence per 100,000 in general population (2001) of: homicide

0.8; suicide 16.1. **Leisure.** Members of sports federations (2004): 15,226,000, of which football (soccer) 2,147,000, tennis 1,066,000. Movie tickets sold (2005) 174,200,000. Average daily hours of television viewing for population ages 4 and over' (2005) 3.43. **Material well-being** (2004). Households possessing: automobile 81%; color television 95%; personal computer 45%; washing machine 92%; microwave 74%; dishwasher (2001) 39%.

National economy

Gross national income (2006): US$2,256,465,000,000 (US$35,725 per capita). **Budget** (2004). *Revenue:* €330,140,000,000 (VAT 47.1%; direct taxes 38.3%; other taxes 14.6%). *Expenditures:* €355,470,000,000 (current civil expenditures 86.0%; military expenditures 8.7%; development expenditures 5.3%). **Public debt** (2005): US$1,375,000,000,000. **Production** (metric tons except as noted). *Agriculture and fishing* (2007): wheat 36,840,806, sugar beets 31,242,506, corn (maize) 13,107,000, barley 9,472,000, grapes 6,500,000, potatoes 6,271,000, rapeseed 4,554,000, apples 1,800,000, triticale 1,539,000, sunflower seeds 1,376,000, tomatoes 750,000, carrots and turnips 710,000, dry peas 643,000, lettuce and chicory 471,000, oats 443,000, peaches and nectarines 401,000, cauliflower and broccoli 370,000, green peas 355,000, string beans 355,000, leeks 182,910, chicory roots 141,000, mushrooms and truffles 125,000, flax fiber and tow 95,000; livestock (number of live animals) 19,359,000 cattle, 14,736,000 pigs, 8,499,000 sheep, 161,500,000 chickens, 28,105,000 turkeys, 23,190,000 ducks; fisheries production (2005) 832,793 (from aquaculture 31%); aquatic plants production 76,678 (from aquaculture, negligible). *Mining and quarrying* (2005): gypsum 3,500,000; crude talc 340,000; kaolin 316,000; gold (2004) 1,312 kg. *Manufacturing* (value added in US$'000,000; 2003): food products 27,023; pharmaceuticals, soaps, and paints 22,675; motor vehicles, trailers, and motor vehicle parts 20,269; fabricated metal products 14,264; general purpose machinery 10,595; plastic products 8,754; medical, measuring, and testing appliances 7,551; aircraft and spacecraft 7,476; publishing 6,911; special purpose machinery 6,605; bricks, cement, and ceramics 5,922; basic chemicals 5,843; base metals 5,547, of which basic iron and steel 4,117; paper products 5,532; beverages 5,509; furniture 4,218. *Energy production (consumption):* electricity (kW-hr; 2005) 575,351,000,000 (515,055,000,000); coal (metric tons; 2007) 168,000 ([2005] 21,346,000); lignite (metric tons; 2005) negligible (36,000); crude petroleum (barrels; 2007) 7,430,000 ([2005] 627,000,000); petroleum products (metric tons; 2005) 73,322,000 (73,378,000); natural gas (cu m; 2007) 1,079,000,000 ([2005] 50,857,000,000). **Retail trade** (value of sales in €'000,000; 2004): large food stores 162,600; large nonfood stores 136,400; auto repair shops 120,400; pharmacies and stores selling orthopedic equipment 32,600; shops selling bread, pastries, or meat 31,800; small food stores and boutiques 15,300. **Population economically active** (2005): total 27,635,800; activity rate of total population 45.5% (participation rates: ages 15–64, 69.1%; female

46.4%; unemployed [April 2007] 8.2%). **Selected balance of payments data.** Receipts from (US$'000,000): tourism (2005) 42,283; remittances (2006) 12,554; foreign direct investment (FDI) (2004–06 avg.) 64,900. Disbursements for (US$'000,000): tourism (2005) 31,180; remittances (2006) 4,268; FDI (2004–06 avg.) 97,581.

Foreign trade

Imports (2006; c.i.f.): US$529,902,000,000 (machinery and apparatus 22.1%, of which electrical machinery and parts 5.4%, general industrial machinery 3.9%, office machines and computers 3.5%; mineral fuels 14.8%, of which crude petroleum 7.5%, refined petroleum products 3.5%; chemical products 12.7%, of which medicines and pharmaceuticals 3.5%; road vehicles and parts 10.2%; wearing apparel 3.5%; iron and steel 3.2%). *Major import sources:* Germany 16.3%; Italy 8.5%; Belgium 8.3%; Spain 6.9%; UK 6.1%; US 6.0%; China 5.7%; The Netherlands 4.1%; Japan 2.4%; Russia 2.4%. **Exports** (2006; f.o.b.): US$479,013,000,000 (machinery and apparatus 22.1%, of which electrical machinery and parts 6.2%, general industrial machinery 4.8%, power-generating machinery 3.7%, telecommunications equipment 3.1%; chemical products 15.7%, of which medicines and pharmaceuticals 5.1%, perfumery and cosmetics 2.3%; road vehicles and parts 12.1%; food products 6.1%; aircraft and parts 6.0%; mineral fuels 4.3%; iron and steel 3.7%; alcoholic beverages [mostly wine] 2.4%). *Major export destinations:* Germany 14.5%; Spain 9.9%; Italy 9.1%; UK 8.5%; Belgium 7.4%; US 6.9%; The Netherlands 4.1%; Switzerland 2.7%; China 2.1%; Poland 1.8%.

Transport and communications

Transport. *Railroads* (2003): route length (in operation; 2004) 29,085 km; passenger-km 53,080,000,000; metric ton-km cargo 46,840,000,000. *Roads* (2004): total length 951,220 km (paved 100%). *Vehicles* (2004): passenger cars 29,900,000; trucks and buses 6,139,000. *Air transport* (2005): passenger-km 115,116,000,000; metric ton-km cargo 5,526,000,000. **Communications,** in total units (units per 1,000 persons). Telephone landlines (2006): 33,897,000 (558); cellular telephone subscribers (2006): 51,662,000 (851); personal computers (2005): 35,000,000 (573); total Internet users (2006): 30,100,000 (496); broadband Internet subscribers (2006): 12,699,000 (208).

Health

Health (2003): physicians 203,487 (1 per 296 persons); hospital beds 457,132 (1 per 132 persons); infant mortality rate per 1,000 live births (2006) 3.7; undernourished population (2002–04) less than 2.5% of total population.

Military

Total active duty personnel (2007): 254,895 (army 52.4%, navy 17.3%, air force 24.9%, headquarters staff 2.0%, health services 3.4%). **Military expenditure as percentage of GDP** (2005): 2.5%; per capita expenditure US$871.

---

1 metric ton = about 1.1 short tons;   1 kilometer = 0.6 mi (statute);   1 metric ton-km cargo = about 0.68 short ton-mi cargo;   c.i.f.: cost, insurance, and freight;   f.o.b.: free on board

Background

Archaeological excavations in France indicate continuous settlement from Paleolithic times. About 1200 BC the Gauls migrated into the area, and in 600 BC Ionian Greeks established several settlements, including one at Marseille. Julius Caesar completed the Roman conquest of Gaul in 50 BC. During the 6th century AD, the Salian Franks ruled; by the 8th century power had passed to the Carolingians, the greatest of whom was Charlemagne. The Hundred Years' War (1337–1453) resulted in the return to France of land that had been held by the British; by the end of the 15th century, France approximated its modern boundaries. The 16th century was marked by the Wars of Religion between Protestants (Huguenots) and Roman Catholics. Henry IV's Edict of Nantes (1598) granted substantial religious toleration, but this was revoked in 1685 by Louis XIV, who helped to raise monarchical absolutism to new heights. In 1789 the French Revolution proclaimed the rights of the individual and destroyed the ancien régime. Napoleon ruled from 1799 to 1814, after which a limited monarchy was restored until 1871, when the Third Republic was created. World War I (1914–18) ravaged the northern part of France. After Nazi Germany's invasion during World War II, the collaborationist Vichy regime governed. Liberated by Allied and Free French forces in 1944, France restored parliamentary democracy under the Fourth Republic. A costly war in Indochina and rising nationalism in French colonies during the 1950s overwhelmed the Fourth Republic. The Fifth Republic was established in 1958 under Charles de Gaulle, who presided over the dissolution of most of France's overseas colonies. In 1981 François Mitterrand became France's first elected Socialist president. During the 1990s the French government, balancing right- and left-wing forces, moved toward solidifying European unity.

Recent Developments

The legislature gave the necessary 60% majority approval to constitutional reforms supported by French Pres. Nicolas Sarkozy that would give the Assembly more power, including the right to be informed within three days of any foreign military operation and the right to veto any such operation lasting more than four months. The reforms also limited the president's tenure to two five-year terms. Sarkozy pushed on with his economic reforms even as France began to feel the effects of the international credit crisis. Legislation was passed to encourage people to work more (by allowing more overtime beyond the standard 35-hour workweek) and longer (by offering incentives for older people to stay in the workforce). In March 2009 the government announced that it would provide compensation to surviving participants of France's nuclear testing from the 1960s to the 1990s. French foreign and defense policies during 2008 were marked by a further shift toward the US and NATO. The improvement in relations with Washington, begun during Sarkozy's successful 2007 trip to the US, continued as the French president kept to his tough line toward Iran and friendly tone to Israel and as a result of his decisions on NATO and Afghanistan. Sarkozy broadly endorsed a high-level military commission's recommendations in June for big troop and base cuts (with financial savings going into better equipment), more stress on intelligence, and the reintegration of French forces into NATO's military command. There was political resistance, however, and Sarkozy made France's reintegration into NATO conditional on parallel improvement in EU military cooperation. France was the only European member of NATO to send reinforcements to Afghanistan in 2008, transporting 800 additional troops.

Internet resources: <www.insee.fr/en>.

Gabon

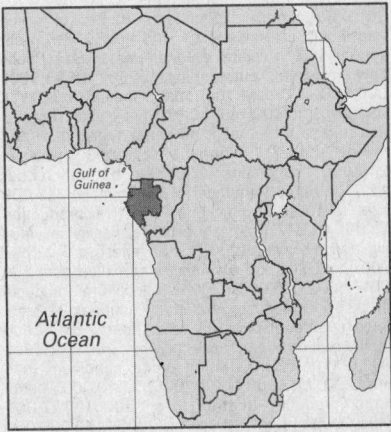

Official name: République Gabonaise (Gabonese Republic). **Form of government:** unitary multiparty republic with two legislative houses (Senate [102]; National Assembly [120]). **Chief of state:** President Rose Francine Rogombé (from 2009). **Head of government:** Prime Minister Paul Biyoghé Mba (from 2009). **Capital:** Libreville. **Official language:** French. **Official religion:** none. **Monetary unit:** 1 CFA franc (CFAF) = 100 centimes; valuation (1 Jul 2009) US$1 = CFAF 462.89.

Demography

Area: 103,347 sq mi, 267,667 sq km. **Population** (2008): 1,486,000. **Density** (2008): persons per sq mi 14.3, persons per sq km 5.6. **Urban** (2006): 85.7%. **Sex distribution** (2006): male 49.67%; female 50.33%. **Age breakdown** (2005): under 15, 40.0%; 15–29, 28.3%; 30–44, 16.1%; 45–59, 9.3%; 60–74, 4.6%; 75–84, 1.4%; 85 and over, 0.3%. **Ethnic composition** (2000): Fang 28.6%; Punu 10.2%; Nzebi 8.9%; French 6.7%; Mpongwe 4.1%; Teke 4.0%; other 37.5%. **Religious affiliation** (2005): Christian 73%, of which Roman Catholic 45%, Protestant/independent Christian 28%; Muslim 12%; traditional beliefs 10%; nonreligious 5%. **Major urban areas** (2003): Libreville 661,600; Port-Gentil 116,200; Franceville 41,300; Lambaréné 9,000. **Location:** western Africa, bordering Cameroon, the Republic of the Congo, the South Atlantic Ocean, and Equatorial Guinea.

Vital statistics

Birth rate per 1,000 population (2006): 36.2 (world avg. 20.3). **Death rate** per 1,000 population (2006):

12.3 (world avg. 8.6). **Natural increase rate** per 1,000 population (2006): 23.9 (world avg. 11.7). **Total fertility rate** (avg. births per childbearing woman; 2006): 4.74. **Life expectancy** at birth (2006): male 53.2 years; female 55.8 years.

National economy

Budget (2005). *Revenue:* CFAF 1,432,200,000,000 (oil revenues 63.3%; taxes on international trade 15.0%, of which VAT 5.6%; direct taxes 9.7%; indirect taxes 7.9%). *Expenditures:* CFAF 872,400,-000,000 (current expenditures 82.2%, of which wages and salaries 26.1%, transfers 23.8%, debt service 14.8%; capital expenditures 17.8%). **Public debt** (external, outstanding; 2006): US$3,860,-000,000. **Gross national income** (2007): US$8,876,000,000 (US$6,670 per capita). **Production** (metric tons except as noted). *Agriculture and fishing* (2007): plantains 275,000, cassava 240,000, sugarcane 220,000, natural rubber 12,000; livestock (number of live animals) 213,000 pigs, 3,100,000 chickens; fisheries production (2006) 41,647 (from aquaculture, negligible). *Mining and quarrying* (2005): manganese ore 2,859,-`000; gold 300 kg. *Manufacturing* (value added in CFAF '000,000,000; 2004): agricultural products 48.0; wood products (excluding furniture) 31.3; refined petroleum products 18.1. *Energy production (consumption):* electricity (kW-hr; 2005) 1,569,-000,000 (1,569,000,000); crude petroleum (barrels; 2007) 83,900,000 ([2005] 5,540,000); petroleum products (metric tons; 2005) 727,000 (431,000); natural gas (cu m; 2005) 126,000,000 (126,000,000). **Population economically active** (2003): total 570,000; activity rate of total population 42.5% (participation rates: ages 15–64, 74.1%; female 43.0%; unemployed 21%). **Selected balance of payments data.** Receipts from (US$'000,000): tourism (2005) 15; remittances (2007) 7; foreign direct investment (2004–06 avg.) 269; official development assistance (2006) 31. Disbursements for (US$'000,000): tourism (2004) 214; remittances (2007) 110.

Foreign trade

Imports (2006; c.i.f.): US$1,725,000,000 (machinery and apparatus 27.6%, of which general industrial machinery 8.8%; food products 13.0%; road vehicles and parts 9.9%; chemical products 9.2%). *Major import sources:* France 39.9%; Belgium 14.2%; US 7.3%; Cameroon 3.5%; Japan 3.0%. **Exports** (2006; f.o.b.): US$6,015,000,000 (crude petroleum 84.4%; rough wood 5.1%; manganese ore and concentrate 3.1%; veneer and plywood 2.0%; refined petroleum products 1.2%). *Major export destinations:* US 58.4%; China 10.6%; France 7.1%; Singapore 5.3%; Switzerland 2.6%.

Transport and communications

Transport. *Railroads* (2002): route length (2005) 814 km; passenger-km 97,500,000; metric ton-km cargo 1,553,000,000. *Roads* (2004): total length 9,170 km (paved 10%). *Vehicles* (1997): passenger cars 24,750; trucks and buses 16,490. *Air transport* (2002): passenger-km 643,000,000. **Communica-**

tions, in total units (units per 1,000 persons). Telephone landlines (2007): 27,000 (18); cellular telephone subscribers (2007): 1,169,000 (803); personal computers (2005): 45,000 (33); total Internet users (2007): 145,000 (100); broadband Internet subscribers (2007): 2,000 (1.3).

Education and health

Educational attainment (2000). Percentage of population ages 15–59 having: no formal schooling 6.2%; incomplete primary and complete primary education 32.7%; lower secondary 41.3%; upper secondary 14.2%; higher 5.6%. **Literacy** (2000): percentage of total population ages 15 and over literate 71%; males literate 80%; females literate 62%. **Health** (2003–04): physicians 270 (1 per 5,006 persons); hospital beds 4,460 (1 per 303 persons); infant mortality rate per 1,000 live births (2006) 54.5; undernourished population (2002–04) 60,000 (5% of total population based on the consumption of a minimum daily requirement of 1,850 calories).

Military

Total active duty personnel (2007): 4,700 (army 68.1%, navy 10.6%, air force 21.3%); French troops (2007) 2,260. **Military expenditure as percentage of GDP** (2005): 1.5%; per capita expenditure US$79.

Background

Artifacts dating from late Paleolithic and early Neolithic times have been found in Gabon, but it is not known when the Bantu speakers who established Gabon's ethnic composition arrived. Pygmies were probably the original inhabitants. The Fang arrived in the late 18th century and were followed by the Portuguese and by French, Dutch, and English traders. The slave trade dominated commerce in the 18th and much of the 19th century. The French then took control, and Gabon was administered (1843–86) with French West Africa. In 1886 the colony of French Congo was established to include both Gabon and the Congo; in 1910 Gabon became a separate colony within French Equatorial Africa. An overseas territory of France from 1946, it became an autonomous republic within the French Community in 1958 and declared its independence in 1960. Rule by a sole political party was established in the 1960s, but discontent with it led to riots in Libreville in 1989. Legalization of opposition parties led to new elections in 1990. The country continued to face economic difficulties despite large revenues from petroleum exports.

Recent Developments

Under the auspices of the UN, diplomats from Gabon and Equatorial Guinea met in New York City in June 2008 to negotiate a long-standing dispute over ownership of oil-rich Mbanie island. In 2009 the government planned to open up some 100,000 sq km (40,000 sq mi) of offshore territory for oil exploration.

Internet resources:
<www.legabon.org/uk/home.php>.

---

1 metric ton = about 1.1 short tons; 1 kilometer = 0.6 mi (statute); 1 metric ton-km cargo = about 0.68 short ton-mi cargo; c.i.f.: cost, insurance, and freight; f.o.b.: free on board

Gambia, The

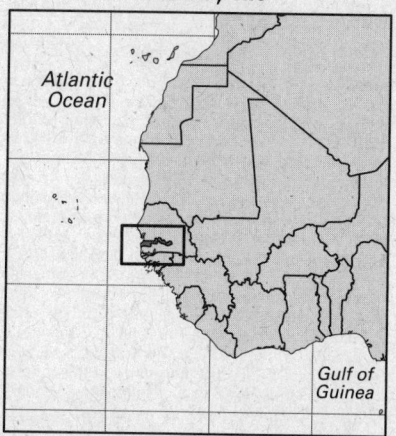

Atlantic Ocean

Gulf of Guinea

Official name: Republic of The Gambia. **Form of government:** multiparty republic with one legislative house (National Assembly [53]). **Head of state and government:** President Col. Yahya Jammeh (from 1994). **Capital:** Banjul. **Official language:** English. **Official religion:** none. **Monetary unit:** 1 dalasi (D) = 100 bututs; valuation (1 Jul 2009) US$1 = D 25.93.

Demography

Area: 4,363 sq mi, 11,300 sq km. **Population** (2008): 1,754,000. **Density** (2008): persons per sq mi 402.0, persons per sq km 155.2. **Urban** (2006): 26.2%. **Sex distribution** (2003): male 49.59%; female 50.41%. **Age breakdown** (2005): under 15, 40.1%; 15–29, 26.4%; 30–44, 17.3%; 45–59, 10.2%; 60–74, 5.0%; 75–84, 0.9%; 85 and over, 0.1%. **Ethnic composition** (2003): Malinke 42%; Fulani 18%; Wolof 16%; Diola 10%; Soninke 9%; other 5%. **Religious affiliation** (2005): Muslim 90%; Christian (mostly Roman Catholic) 9%; traditional beliefs/other 1%. **Major cities** (2004): Serekunda 225,500; Brikama 81,400; Bakau 74,700; Banjul 36,100 (Greater Banjul [2003] 523,589); Farafenni 31,600. **Location:** western Africa, bordering Senegal and the North Atlantic Ocean.

Vital statistics

Birth rate per 1,000 population (2006): 39.4 (world avg. 20.3). **Death rate** per 1,000 population (2006): 12.3 (world avg. 8.6). **Natural increase rate** per 1,000 population (2006): 27.1 (world avg. 11.7). **Total fertility rate** (avg. births per childbearing woman; 2003): 5.13. **Life expectancy** at birth (2006): male 52.3 years; female 56.0 years.

National economy

Budget (2005). *Revenue:* D 2,823,500,000 (tax revenue 80.2%, of which taxes on international trade 42.7%, corporate taxes 14.4%; nontax revenue 12.0%; grants 7.8%). *Expenditures:* D 3,961,-100,000 (current expenditures 61.1%, of which interest payments 28.6%; capital expenditures 38.9%). **Production** (metric tons except as noted). *Agriculture* *and fishing* (2007): millet 160,000, peanuts (groundnuts) 100,000, sorghum 40,000, findo (local cereal; 2005) 600; livestock (number of live animals) 334,000 cattle, 280,000 goats, 150,000 sheep; fisheries production (2006) 34,912 (from aquaculture, negligible). *Mining and quarrying:* sand, clay ([2006] 13,700), and gravel are excavated for local use. *Manufacturing* (value added in US$; 1995): food and beverages 6,000,000; textiles, wearing apparel, and footwear 750,000; wood products 550,000. *Energy production (consumption):* electricity (kW-hr; 2005) 151,000,000 (151,000,000); petroleum products (metric tons; 2005) none (102,000). **Population economically active** (2003): total 730,000; activity rate of total population 52.2% (participation rates: female 44.2%; unemployed [2004] extremely high). **Public debt** (external, outstanding; 2006): US$689,000,000. **Gross national income** (2007): US$544,000,000 (US$320 per capita). **Selected balance of payments data.** Receipts from (US$'000,-000): tourism (2006) 66; remittances (2007) 64; foreign direct investment (2004–06 avg.) 55; official development assistance (2006) 74. Disbursements for (US$'000,000): tourism (2006) 6; remittances (2007) 1.

Foreign trade

Imports (2004; c.i.f.): US$236,600,000 (food and live animals 27.3%; machinery and transportation equipment 18.1%; mineral fuels 10.1%; chemical products 7.4%). *Major import sources:* China 24.6%; Brazil 16.8%; Senegal 10.4%; UK 5.8%; The Netherlands 4.5%. **Exports** (2004; f.o.b.): US$127,000,000 (reexports 79.7%; peanuts [groundnuts] 13.3%; fruits and vegetables 4.1%). *Major export destinations:* Thailand 16.5%; UK 15.4%; France 14.0%; India 12.8%; Germany 9.1%.

Transport and communications

Transport. *Railroads:* none. *Roads* (2004): total length 3,742 km (paved 19%). *Vehicles* (2004): passenger cars 8,109; trucks and buses 2,961. *Air transport* (Yumdum International Airport at Banjul only; 2001): passenger arrivals 300,000, passenger departures 300,000; cargo loaded and unloaded 2,700 metric tons. **Communications,** in total units (units per 1,000 persons). Telephone landlines (2007): 76,000 (45); cellular telephone subscribers (2007): 796,000 (469); personal computers (2004): 23,000 (16); total Internet users (2007): 100,000 (59); broadband Internet subscribers (2005): 100 (0.06).

Education and health

Literacy (2007): percentage of total population ages 15 and over literate 44.9%; males literate 52.3%; females literate 37.8%. **Health** (2003): physicians 156 (1 per 9,769 persons); hospital beds (2000) 1,140 (1 per 1,199 persons); infant mortality rate per 1,000 live births (2006) 71.6; undernourished population (2002–04) 450,000 (29% of total population based on the consumption of a minimum daily requirement of 1,850 calories).

Military

Total active duty personnel (2007): 800 (army 100%). **Military expenditure as percentage of GDP** (2005): 0.5%; per capita expenditure US$2.

Background

Beginning about the 13th century AD, the Wolof, Malinke, and Fulani peoples settled in different parts of what is now The Gambia and established villages and then kingdoms in the region. European exploration began when the Portuguese sighted the Gambia River in 1455. Britain and France both settled in the area in the 17th century. The British Ft. James, on an island about 20 mi (32 km) from the river's mouth, was an important collection point for the slave trade. In 1783 the Treaty of Versailles reserved the Gambia River for Britain. After the British abolished slavery in 1807, they built a fort at the mouth of the river to block the continuing slave trade. In 1889 The Gambia's boundaries were agreed upon by Britain and France; the British declared a protectorate over the area in 1894. Independence was proclaimed in 1965, and The Gambia became a republic within the Commonwealth in 1970. It formed a limited confederation with Senegal in 1982 that was dissolved in 1989. During the 1990s the government was in turmoil.

Recent Developments

When rising world food and oil prices began to have a serious impact on the economy in 2008, Pres. Yahya Jammeh called on Gambians to work for food self-sufficiency. Human rights monitors continued to express concern about numerous infringements of press freedom in the country.

Internet resources: <www.gambia.gm>.

Georgia

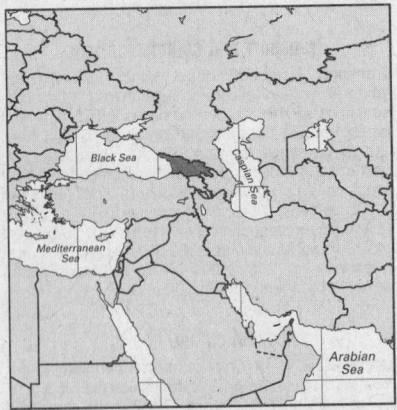

Official name: Sakartvelo (Georgia). **Form of government:** unitary multiparty republic with a single legislative body (Parliament [150]). **Head of state and government:** President Mikheil Saakashvili (from 2008), assisted by Prime Minister Nika Gilauri (from 2009). **Capital:** Tbilisi. **Official language:** Georgian (locally Abkhazian, in Abkhazia). **Official religion:** none (special recognition is given to the Georgian Or-

thodox Church). **Monetary unit:** 1 Georgian lari (GEL) = 100 tetri; valuation (1 Jul 2009) US$1 = 1.65 lari.

Demography

Area: 27,086 sq mi, 70,152 sq km. **Population** (2008): 4,360,000. **Density** (2008): persons per sq mi 196.0, persons per sq km 75.7. **Urban** (2004): 52.3%. **Sex distribution** (2005): male 47.50%; female 52.50%. **Age breakdown** (2005): under 15, 17.9%; 15–29, 24.2%; 30–44, 21.5%; 45–59, 18.9%; 60 and over, 17.5%. **Ethnic composition** (2002): Georgian 83.8%; Azerbaijani 6.5%; Armenian 5.7%; Russian 1.5%; Ossetian 0.9%; other 1.6%. **Religious affiliation** (2005): Georgian Orthodox 54.8%; Sunni Muslim 14.5%; Shiʻi Muslim 5.0%; Armenian Apostolic (Orthodox) 3.9%; Catholic 0.8%; Yazidi 0.4%; Protestant 0.4%; nonreligious 13.0%; other 7.2%. **Major cities** (2006): Tbilisi 1,103,300; Kutaisi 190,100; Batumi 122,100; Rustavi 118,200; Sokhumi (2002) 45,000. **Location:** northern Transcaucasia, bordering Russia, Azerbaijan, Armenia, Turkey, and the Black Sea.

Vital statistics

Birth rate per 1,000 population (2005): 10.7 (world avg. 20.3); within marriage 50.3%; outside of marriage 49.7%. **Death rate** per 1,000 population (2005): 9.9 (world avg. 8.6). **Natural increase rate** per 1,000 population (2005): 0.8 (world avg. 11.7). **Total fertility rate** (avg. births per childbearing woman; 2005): 1.35. **Life expectancy** at birth (2005): male 69.3 years; female 76.7 years.

National economy

Budget (2005). *Revenue:* GEL 3,257,200,000 (tax revenue 74.0%, of which VAT 30.3%, income tax 8.9%, excise tax 8.8%, corporate taxes 6.5%; nontax revenue 23.0%; grants 3.0%). *Expenditures:* GEL 3,280,800,000 (social security and welfare 19.1%; defense 12.1%; general public service 10.8%; education 8.8%; public order 8.7%). **Population economically active** (2005): total 2,023,900; activity rate of total population 44.1% (participation rates: ages 15–64, 68.4%; female 46.9%; unemployed 13.8%). **Production** (metric tons except as noted). *Agriculture and fishing* (2007): potatoes 174,500, grapes 93,000, wheat 92,300; livestock (number of live animals) 1,318,800 cattle, 509,700 pigs; fisheries production (2006) 3,075 (from aquaculture 2%). *Mining and quarrying* (2004): manganese ore 218,700. *Manufacturing* (value of production in GEL '000,000; 2005): food and beverages 799.6; base metals 205.7; cement, bricks, and ceramics 131.2. *Energy production (consumption):* electricity (kW-hr; 2005) 7,267,000,000 (8,613,000,000); coal (metric tons; 2005) 5,000 (18,000); crude petroleum (barrels; 2005) 487,000 (145,000); petroleum products (metric tons; 2005) 5,000 (653,000); natural gas (cu m; 2005) 13,000,000 (1,283,000,000). **Gross national income** (2007): US$9,337,000,000 (US$2,120 per capita). **Public debt** (external, outstanding; 2006): US$1,457,000,000. **Selected balance of payments data.** Receipts from (US$'000,000): tourism (2006) 313; remittances (2007) 705; foreign direct investment (2004–06

---

1 metric ton = about 1.1 short tons; 1 kilometer = 0.6 mi (statute); 1 metric ton-km cargo = about 0.68 short ton-mi cargo; c.i.f.: cost, insurance, and freight; f.o.b.: free on board

avg.) 675; official development assistance (2006) 361. Disbursements for (US$'000,000): tourism (2006) 167; remittances (2007) 28.

Foreign trade

Imports (2006; c.i.f.): US$3,681,230,000 (mineral fuels 17.8%; food and beverages 15.4%; motor vehicles 9.1%; nonelectrical machinery 9.1%; chemical products 8.2%). *Major import sources* (2007): Turkey 14.0%; Russia 11.1%; Ukraine 11.0%; Germany 7.4%; Azerbaijan 7.3%. **Exports** (2006; f.o.b.): US$993,054,000 (food and beverages [significantly wine] 23.3%; iron and steel 16.6%; transportation equipment 14.1%; chemical products 7.8%). *Major export destinations* (2007): Turkey 13.9%; US 12.1%; Azerbaijan 11.1%; Armenia 8.9%; Ukraine 7.6%.

Transport and communications

Transport. *Railroads* (2005): 1,559 km; passenger-km 719,500,000; metric ton-km cargo 6,127,100,-000. *Roads* (2005): 20,329 km (paved [2004] 40%). *Vehicles* (2004): passenger cars 255,200; trucks and buses 68,600. *Air transport* (2005): passenger-km 510,800,000; metric ton-km cargo 3,600,000. **Communications**, in total units (units per 1,000 persons). Telephone landlines (2006): 553,000 (119); cellular telephone subscribers (2006): 1,704,000 (368); personal computers (2004): 192,000 (42); total Internet users (2007): 360,000 (82); broadband Internet subscribers (2007): 47,000 (11).

Education and health

Educational attainment (2004). Percentage of population ages 15 and over having: no formal education/unknown 1.6%; primary education 4.1%; incomplete secondary 10.5%; secondary 48.2%; incomplete higher 12.3%; higher 23.3%. **Literacy** (2004): percentage of total population literate, virtually 100%. **Health** (2005): physicians 20,311 (1 per 226 persons); hospital beds 17,100 (1 per 268 persons); infant mortality rate per 1,000 live births 19.7; undernourished population (2002–04) 500,000 (9% of total population based on the consumption of a minimum daily requirement of 1,960 calories).

Military

Total active duty personnel (2007): 21,150 (army 84.0%, national guard 7.5%, navy 2.3%, air force 6.2%); Russian troops to be stationed in Abkhazia and South Ossetia per September 2008 official announcement: 3,800 in each. **Military expenditure as percentage of GDP** (2005): 3.5%; per capita expenditure US$51.

Background

Ancient Georgia was the site of the kingdoms of Iberia and Colchis, whose fabled wealth was known to the ancient Greeks. The area was part of the Roman Empire by 65 BC and became Christian in AD 337. For the next three centuries it was involved in the conflicts between the Byzantine and Persian empires; after 654 it was controlled by Arab caliphs, who established an emirate in Tbilisi. It was controlled by the Bagratids from the 8th to the 12th century, and the zenith of Georgia's power was reached in the reign of Queen Tamara, whose realm stretched from Azerbaijan to Circassia, forming a pan-Caucasian empire. Invasions by Mongols and Turks in the 13th and 14th centuries disintegrated the kingdom, and the fall of Constantinople (now Istanbul) to the Ottoman Turks in 1453 isolated it from Western Christendom. The next three centuries saw repeated invasions by the Armenians, Turks, and Persians. Georgia sought Russian protection in 1783, and in 1801 it was annexed to Russia. After the Russian Revolution of 1917, the area was briefly independent; in 1921 a Soviet regime was installed, and in 1936 Georgia became the Georgian SSR, a full member of the Soviet Union. In 1990 a noncommunist coalition came to power in the first free elections ever held in Soviet Georgia, and in 1991 Georgia declared independence. In the 1990s, while Pres. Eduard Shevardnadze tried to steer a middle course, internal dissension resulted in conflicts with the northwestern republic of Abkhazia and the northern republic of South Ossetia, and external distrust of Russian motives in the area grew. In 1992 Abkhazia reinstated its 1925 constitution and declared independence, which Georgia refused to recognize.

Recent Developments

Tensions between the Georgian government and the breakaway republics of Abkhazia and South Ossetia increased in 2008. Following several weeks of sporadic exchanges of gunfire between Georgian troops and rebel forces in South Ossetia, Georgian troops entered the republic on 7 August. In response, Russian tanks and troops advanced into South Ossetia on 8 August, bombed the port of Poti and several military bases, and occupied Gori. Several hundred servicemen and civilians died during the fighting, and tens of thousands were forced to flee their homes. Following the deployment of EU observers in October, Russian troops withdrew from the conflict zones. Although Georgia was not offered a NATO membership action plan in 2008, NATO exercises were held in Georgia in May 2009.

Internet resources:
<www.statistics.ge/index.php?plang=1>.

Germany

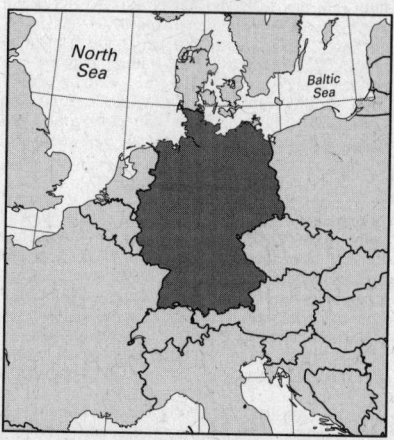

North Sea

Baltic Sea

Official name: Bundesrepublik Deutschland (Federal Republic of Germany). **Form of government:** federal multiparty republic with two legislative houses (Federal Council [69]; Federal Diet [612]). **Chief of state:** President Horst Köhler (from 2004). **Head of government:** Chancellor Angela Merkel (from 2005). **Capital:** Berlin; some ministries remain in Bonn, the previous capital of West Germany. **Official language:** German. **Official religion:** none. **Monetary unit:** 1 euro (€) = 100 cents; valuation (1 Jul 2009) US$1 = €0.71.

Demography

Area: 137,874 sq mi, 357,093 sq km. **Population (2008):** 82,143,000. **Density (2008):** persons per sq mi 595.8, persons per sq km 230.0. **Urban (2003):** 88.1%. **Major cities (urban agglomerations) (2005):** Berlin 3,395,189 (4,200,072); Hamburg 1,743,627 (2,549,339); Munich 1,259,677 (7,940,477); Cologne 983,347 (1,846,241); Frankfurt am Main 651,899 (1,915,002); Stuttgart 592,569 (2,625,690); Dortmund 588,168 (5,746,018); Essen 585,430 (5,746,018); Düsseldorf 574,514 (1,318,512); Bremen 546,852 (858,488); Hannover 515,729 (1,001,580); Leipzig 502,651 (580,050); Duisburg 501,564 (5,746,018); Nuremberg (Nürnberg) 499,237 (1,030,168). **Location:** central Europe, bordering Denmark, the Baltic Sea, Poland, the Czech Republic, Austria, Switzerland, France, Luxembourg, Belgium, The Netherlands, and the North Sea. **Sex distribution (2007):** male 48.98%; female 51.02%. **Ethnic composition** (by nationality; 2000): German 88.2%; Turkish 3.4% (including Kurdish 0.7%); Italian 1.0%; Greek 0.7%; Serb 0.6%; Russian 0.6%; Polish 0.4%; other 5.1%. **Age breakdown (2003):** under 15, 14.7%; 15–29, 17.4%; 30–44, 23.9%; 45–59, 19.3%; 60–74, 16.9%; 75–84, 6.1%; 85 and over, 1.7%. **Religious affiliation (2005):** Protestant 35.0%, of which Lutheran/Reformed churches 34%; Roman Catholic 32.5%; Sunni Muslim 4.3%; Orthodox 1.7%; New Apostolic (an independent Christian group) 0.5%; Buddhist 0.3%; Jewish 0.2%; nonreligious 18.0%; atheist 2.0%; other 5.5%. **Immigration (2003):** immigrant arrivals 601,759, from Poland 14.6%, Turkey 8.0%, Russia 5.2%, Romania 3.9%.

Vital statistics

Birth rate per 1,000 population (2007): 8.3 (world avg. 20.3); (2004) within marriage 72.0%; outside of marriage 28.0%. **Death rate** per 1,000 population (2007): 10.1 (world avg. 8.6). **Natural increase rate** per 1,000 population (2007): −1.8 (world avg. 11.7). **Total fertility rate** (avg. births per childbearing woman; 2007): 1.37. **Life expectancy** at birth (2005–07): male 76.9 years; female 82.3 years.

Social indicators

Educational attainment (2002). Percentage of population ages 25–64 having: no formal schooling through lower secondary education 17%; upper secondary/higher vocational 60%; university 23%. **Quality of working life.** Average workweek (2005) 38.2 hours. Annual rate per 100,000 workers (2005) for: injuries or accidents at work 2,835; deaths 2.4. Proportion of labor force insured for damages of income loss resulting from: injury, virtually 100%; permanent disability, virtually 100%; death, virtually 100%. Average days lost to labor stoppages per 1,000 workers (2005) 0.5. **Access to services.** Proportion of dwellings (2002) having: electricity, virtually 100%; piped water supply, virtually 100%; public fire protection, virtually 100%. **Social participation.** Trade union membership in total workforce (2003): 18%. Practicing religious population: 5% of Protestants (1994) and 15% of Roman Catholics (2003) "regularly" attend religious services. **Social deviance (2000).** Offense rate per 100,000 population for: murder and manslaughter 3.8; sexual abuse 37.0, of which rape and forcible sexual assault 11.7, child molestation 10.2; assault and battery 153.2; theft 754.2. **Leisure.** Favorite leisure activities include playing football (soccer; registered participants, 2004) 6,272,804, as well as watching television, going to the cinema, attending theatrical and musical performances, and visiting museums. **Material well-being (2005).** Households possessing: automobile 76.8%; telephone (2006) 95.2%; mobile telephone (2006) 80.6%; refrigerator 99.1%; television (2004) 95.0%; DVD player 50.1%; washing machine (2004) 95.5%; clothes dryer 39.3%; personal computer (2006) 71.6%; dishwasher 59.1%; microwave oven 67.0%; Internet access (2006) 57.9%; MP3 player 14.7%.

National economy

Budget (2004). *Revenue:* €639,220,000,000 (social security contributions 58.3%; tax revenue 37.6%, of which income tax 13.7%, taxes on goods and services 10.2%, excise taxes 10.2%; nontax revenue 2.2%; other 1.9%). *Expenditures:* €691,480,000,000 (social benefits 71.4%; grants 7.9%; debt interest 5.7%; wages and salaries 5.5%). **Total public debt (2004):** US$1,732,000,000,000. **Production** (metric tons except as noted; 2007). *Agriculture and fishing:* cereal grains 42,294,600 (of which wheat 21,366,800, barley 11,034,200), sugar beets 26,114,000, potatoes 11,604,500, rapeseed 5,320,000, grapes 1,300,000, apples 911,900, cabbages 735,500, gooseberries (2006) 40,000, hops 28,600, currants 8,800; livestock (number of live animals) 26,530,000 pigs, 12,600,800 cattle, 2,444,400 sheep, 108,000,000 chickens; fisheries production (2006) 333,216 (from aquaculture 11%). *Mining and quarrying* (metric tons; 2005): potash (potassium oxide content) 3,664,000; feldspar 500,000. *Manufacturing* (value added in US$'000,000; 2003): transportation equipment 80,003, of which motor vehicles 46,854, motor vehicle parts 20,655; nonelectrical machinery and apparatus 64,943; electrical machinery and electronics 47,403, of which electricity distribution and control apparatus 18,799; fabricated metal products 41,855; food products 31,727; paints, soaps, and pharmaceuticals 26,172; industrial chemicals 20,211; printing and publishing 19,829; professional and scientific equipment 19,045, of which medical, measuring, and testing appliances 16,737; plastic products 17,333; cement, bricks, and ceramics 10,736. *Energy production (consumption):* electricity (kW-hr; 2007) 522,779,000,000 ([2005] 615,734,000,000); hard coal (metric tons; 2007) 21,500,000 ([2005] 64,000,000); lignite (metric tons; 2007) 180,400,000 ([2005] 177,900,000); crude petroleum (barrels; 2007) 33,100,000 ([2005]

840,700,000); petroleum products (metric tons; 2005) 106,211,000 (98,378,000); natural gas (cu m; 2007) 21,832,000,000 ([2005] 101,222,-000,000). **Gross national income** (2007): US$3,197,029,000,000 (US$38,860 per capita). **Population economically active** (2005): total 41,150,000; activity rate of total population 49.9% (participation rates: ages 15–64, 73.7%; female 44.8%; unemployed [2006] 8.1%). **Selected balance of payments data.** Receipts from (US$'000,000): tourism (2006) 32,846; remittances (2007) 7,000; foreign direct investment (FDI) (2004–06 avg.) 23,180. Disbursements for (US$'000,000): tourism (2006) 74,123; remittances (2007) 12,344; FDI (2004–06 avg.) 49,923.

Foreign trade

Imports (2005; c.i.f.): €625,632,000,000 (machinery and apparatus 21.7%, of which televisions, telecommunications equipment, and electronic components 6.4%; office machinery and computers 4.6%; transportation equipment 14.2%, of which road vehicles 10.2%; chemical products 11.3%; crude petroleum and natural gas 8.3%; base metals 6.0%; food and beverages 4.5%; wearing apparel 2.6%). *Major import sources* (2006): France 8.7%; The Netherlands 8.3%; China 6.7%; US 6.6%; UK 5.9%; Italy 5.5%; Belgium 4.9%; Russia 4.1%; Austria 4.1%; Switzerland 3.4%. **Exports** (2005; f.o.b.): €786,186,000,000 (machinery and apparatus 26.5%, of which televisions, telecommunications equipment, and electronic components 4.7%; transportation equipment 22.6%, of which road vehicles 19.2%; chemical products 13.1%; base metals 5.2%; medical and precision instruments and watches and clocks 4.2%). *Major export destinations* (2006): France 9.6%; US 8.7%; UK 7.3%; Italy 6.7%; The Netherlands 6.2%; Belgium 5.5%; Austria 5.5%; Spain 4.7%; Switzerland 3.9%; Poland 3.2%.

Transport and communications

Transport. *Railroads* (2001): length 85,653 km; passenger-km (2003) 71,292,000,000; metric ton-km cargo (2004) 86,400,000,000. *Roads* (2005): total length 231,480 km (paved [2003] 100%). *Vehicles* (2006): passenger cars 46,090,300; trucks and buses 2,573,100. *Air transport* (2007): passenger-km 206,112,000,000; metric ton-km cargo 8,345,976,000. **Communications,** in total units (units per 1,000 persons). Telephone landlines (2007): 53,750,000 (651); cellular telephone subscribers (2007): 97,151,000 (1,176); personal computers (2004): 46,300,000 (561); total Internet users (2007): 42,500,000 (515); broadband Internet subscribers (2007): 19,800,000 (241).

Health

Health (2006): physicians 311,000 (1 per 265 persons); hospital beds 510,767 (1 per 161 persons); infant mortality rate per 1,000 live births 4.1; undernourished population (2002–04) less than 2.5% of total population.

Military

Total active duty personnel (2007): 245,702 (army 65.4%, navy 9.9%, air force 24.7%); German peacekeeping troops abroad (April 2006) more than 7,500;

US troops in Germany (2008) 56,200; British troops (2007) 22,000; French troops (2007) 2,800; Dutch troops (2007) 2,300. **Military expenditure as percentage of GDP** (2005): 1.4%; per capita expenditure US$462.

Background

Germanic tribes entered the region about the 2nd century BC, displacing the Celts. The Romans failed to conquer the region, which became a political entity only with the division of the Carolingian empire in the 9th century AD. The monarchy's control was weak, and power increasingly devolved upon the nobility, organized in feudal states. The monarchy was restored under Saxon rule in the 10th century, and the Holy Roman Empire, centering on Germany and northern Italy, was revived. Continuing conflict between the Holy Roman emperors and the Roman Catholic popes undermined the empire, and its dissolution was accelerated by Martin Luther's revolt in 1517, which divided Germany, and ultimately Europe, into Protestant and Roman Catholic camps, culminating in the Thirty Years' War (1618–48). Germany's population and borders were greatly reduced, and its numerous feudal princes gained virtually full sovereignty. In 1862 Otto von Bismarck came to power in Prussia and over the next decade reunited Germany in the German Empire. It was dissolved in 1918 after the German defeat in World War I. Germany was stripped of much of its territory and all of its colonies. In 1933 Adolf Hitler became chancellor and established a totalitarian state, the Third Reich, dominated by the Nazi Party. Hitler's invasion of Poland in 1939 plunged the world into World War II. Following its defeat in 1945, Germany was divided by the Allied Powers into four zones of occupation. Disagreement with the USSR over the reunification of the zones led to the creation in 1949 of the Federal Republic of Germany (West Germany) and the German Democratic Republic (East Germany). Berlin, the former capital, remained divided. West Germany became a prosperous parliamentary democracy and East Germany a one-party state under Soviet control. The East German Communist government was brought down peacefully in 1989, and Germany was reunited in 1990. After the initial euphoria over unity, the former West Germany sought to incorporate the former East Germany both politically and economically, resulting in heavy financial burdens for the wealthier western Germans. The country continued to move toward deeper political and economic integration with Western Europe through its membership in the European Union.

Recent Developments

Western countries such as the UK and the US demanded in 2008 that Berlin take on more military responsibility in international conflicts. After World War II, it was clear in the collective German mind that there would never again be a German military presence, and by 2008 young Germans found it difficult to even contemplate that military force might be a solution in any conflict. Moreover, the suggestion that Germany should provide troops, as opposed to giving financial aid or noncombatant support within the remit of a peacekeeping force, triggered immediate public disapproval. In October, after months of pressure from NATO, the Bundestag agreed to send 1,000 additional troops to Afghanistan and to extend the mission there by 14 months, but Berlin still resisted transferring German forces from the relative peace in northern Afghanistan to the war-torn south. By mid-2009 Germany had roughly 3,800 troops in the country.

Internet resources: <www.destatis.de/jetspeed/portal/cms>.

Ghana

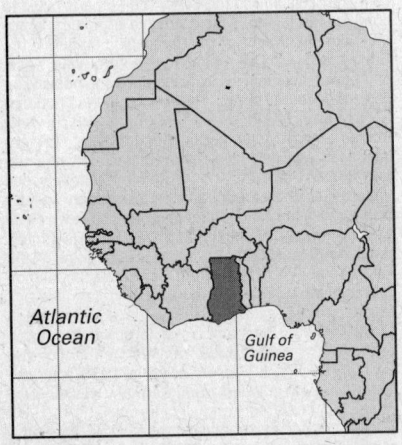

Atlantic Ocean

Gulf of Guinea

Official name: Republic of Ghana. **Form of government:** unitary multiparty republic with one legislative house (House of Parliament [230]). **Head of state and government:** President John Atta Mills (from 2009). **Capital:** Accra. **Official language:** English. **Official religion:** none. **Monetary unit:** 1 Ghana cedi (GH¢) = 100 pesewas; valuation (1 Jul 2009) US$1 = GH¢ 15,144.90 (the Ghana cedi replaced the cedi [¢] 1 Jul 2007, at the rate of 1 GH¢ = ¢10,000).

Demography

Area: 92,098 sq mi, 238,533 sq km. **Population** (2008): 23,383,000. **Density** (2008): persons per sq mi 253.9, persons per sq km 98.0. **Urban** (2006): 46.8%. **Sex distribution** (2006): male 50.05%; female 49.95%. **Age breakdown** (2006): under 15, 38.7%; 15–29, 29.0%; 30–44, 18.1%; 45–59, 8.9%; 60–74, 4.2%; 75–84 1.0%; 85 and over, 0.1%. **Ethnic composition** (2000): Akan 41.6%; Mossi 23.0%; Ewe 10.0%; Ga-Adangme 7.2%; Gurma 3.4%; Nzima 1.8%; Yoruba 1.6%; other 11.4%. **Religious affiliation** (2005): Protestant 23.7%; traditional beliefs 21.5%; Sunni Muslim 20.1%; independent Christian 15.9%; Roman Catholic 12.2%; other 6.6%. **Major cities** (2002): Accra (2003) 1,847,432; Kumasi 627,600; Tamale 269,200; Tema 237,700; Obuasi 122,600. **Location:** western Africa, bordering Burkina Faso, Togo, the Atlantic Ocean, and Côte d'Ivoire.

Vital statistics

Birth rate per 1,000 population (2006): 30.5 (world avg. 20.3). **Death rate** per 1,000 population (2006):

9.7 (world avg. 8.6). **Total fertility rate** (avg. births per childbearing woman; 2006): 3.99. **Life expectancy** at birth (2006): male 58.0 years; female 59.6 years.

National economy

Budget (2006). *Revenue:* ¢31,917,680,000,000 (tax revenue 77.2%, of which VAT 18.4%, trade tax 17.0%, petroleum tax 12.8%, income tax 9.7%; grants 19.9%; nontax revenue 2.9%). *Expenditures:* ¢38,734,730,000,000 (current expenditures 63.9%, of which transfers 14.7%, debt service 10.2%; capital expenditures 36.1%). **Public debt** (external, outstanding; March 2008): US$3,739,040,000. **Gross national income** (2007): US$13,905,000,000 (US$590 per capita). **Production** (metric tons except as noted). *Agriculture and fishing* (2007): cassava 9,650,000, yams 3,550,000, plantains 2,930,000, cacao 690,000; livestock (number of live animals) 3,704,700 goats, 3,420,000 sheep, 1,427,100 cattle; fisheries production (2006) 368,069 (from aquaculture, negligible). *Mining and quarrying* (2006): bauxite 842,000; manganese (metal content) 560,000; gold 66,205 kg; gem diamonds 780,000 carats. *Manufacturing* (value added in US$'000,000; 2003): wood products 157; chemical products 115; food products 108; refined petroleum products 55. *Energy production (consumption):* electricity (kW-hr; 2005) 6,793,000,000 (6,969,000,000); crude petroleum (barrels; 2006) none ([2005] 14,700,000); petroleum products (metric tons; 2005) 1,655,000 (1,718,000). **Population economically active** (2000): total 9,039,318; activity rate of total population 47.8% (participation rates: ages 15–64, 76.2%; female 54.1%; unemployed [2001] 20.3%). **Selected balance of payments data.** Receipts from (US$'000,000): tourism (2006) 861; remittances (2007) 105; foreign direct investment (2004–06 avg.) 240; official development assistance (2006) 1,176. Disbursements for (US$'000,000): tourism (2006) 345; remittances (2007) 6.

Foreign trade

Imports (2006; c.i.f.): US$5,329,000,000 (machinery and apparatus 19.1%; road vehicles 14.8%; crude petroleum 12.9%; food products 12.2%; chemical products 10.8%). *Major import sources:* Nigeria 9.6%; China 9.5%; UK 8.9%; US 6.6%; Belgium 5.6%. **Exports** (2006; f.o.b.): US$3,614,000,000 (cocoa 34.3%; gold 31.3%; woven cotton fabrics 6.3%; wood products [excluding furniture] 5.5%). *Major export destinations:* South Africa 25.8%; Burkina Faso 12.6%; The Netherlands 11.1%; Switzerland 6.8%; France 4.6%.

Transport and communications

Transport. *Railroads* (2002): route length (2005) 953 km; passenger-km 238,000,000; metric ton-km cargo 168,000,000. *Roads* (2003): total length 47,787 km (paved 18%). *Vehicles* (2002): passenger cars 463,000; trucks and buses 56,000. *Air transport* (Ghana Airways only [which ceased operations in July 2004]; 2003): passenger-km 906,000,000; metric ton-km cargo 16,630,000. **Communications**, in total units (units per 1,000 persons). Telephone land-

---

1 metric ton = about 1.1 short tons;   1 kilometer = 0.6 mi (statute);   1 metric ton-km cargo = about 0.68 short ton-mi cargo;   c.i.f.: cost, insurance, and freight;   f.o.b.: free on board

lines (2007): 377,000 (16); cellular telephone subscribers (2007): 7,604,000 (324); personal computers (2004): 112,000 (5.2); total Internet users (2007): 650,000 (28); broadband Internet subscribers (2007): 14,000 (0.6).

Education and health

Educational attainment (2003). Percentage of population ages 25 and over having: no formal schooling/unknown 41.8%; incomplete primary education 9.6%; primary 3.6%; incomplete secondary 35.0%; secondary 5.4%; higher 4.6%. **Literacy** (2005): percentage of total population ages 15 and over literate 77.0%; males literate 84.2%; females literate 70.0%. **Health:** physicians (2004) 3,240 (1 per 6,631 persons); hospital beds (2001) 18,448 (1 per 1,089 persons); infant mortality rate per 1,000 live births (2006) 54.9; undernourished population (2002–04) 2,300,000 (11% of total population based on the consumption of a minimum daily requirement of 1,860 calories).

Military

Total active duty personnel (2007): 13,500 (army 74.1%, navy 14.8%, air force 11.1%). **Military expenditure as percentage of GDP** (2005): 0.7%; per capita expenditure US$4.

Background

The modern state of Ghana is named after the ancient Ghana empire that flourished until the 13th century AD in the western Sudan, about 800 km (500 mi) northwest of the modern state. The Akan peoples then founded their first states in modern Ghana. Gold-seeking Mande traders arrived by the 14th century, and Hausa merchants arrived by the 16th century. During the 15th century the Mande founded the states of Dagomba and Mamprussi in the northern half of the region. The Asante, an Akan people, originated in the central forest region and formed a strongly centralized empire that was at its height in the 18th and 19th centuries. European exploration of the region began early in the 15th century, when the Portuguese landed on the Gold Coast; they later established a settlement at Elmina as headquarters for the slave trade. By the mid-18th century the Gold Coast was dominated by numerous forts controlled by Dutch, British, and Danish merchants. Britain made the Gold Coast a crown colony in 1874, and British protectorates over Asante and the northern territories were established in 1901. In 1957 the Gold Coast became the independent state of Ghana.

Recent Developments

Although Ghana in 2008 enjoyed unhampered prosperity owing to an economic boom, reigned as the world's second largest cocoa producer and Africa's second largest gold producer, and was looking forward to the start of offshore oil production in 2010, there was rising public anger over the inflation (about 17%) in the price of food and fuel imports. Additional concerns involved disputes over land rights and sporadic ethnic clashes, especially in the northern region.

Internet resources: <www.touringghana.com>.

Greece

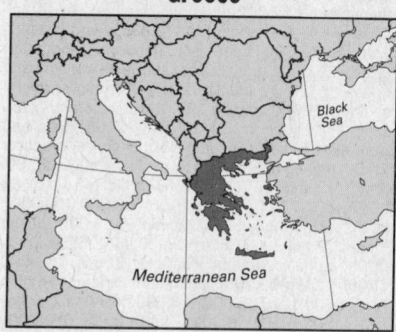

Official name: Elliniki Dhimokratia (Hellenic Republic). **Form of government:** unitary multiparty republic with one legislative house (Hellenic Parliament [300]). **Chief of state:** President Karolos Papoulias (from 2005). **Head of government:** Prime Minister Konstantinos (Kostas) Karamanlis (from 2004). **Capital:** Athens. **Official language:** Greek. **Official religion:** Eastern Orthodox. **Monetary unit:** 1 euro (€) = 100 cents; valuation (1 Jul 2009) US$1 = €0.71.

Demography

Area: 50,949 sq mi, 131,957 sq km. **Population** (2008): 11,239,000. **Density** (2008): persons per sq mi 220.6, persons per sq km 85.2. **Urban** (2005): 60.4%. **Sex distribution** (2006): male 49.51%; female 50.49%. **Age breakdown** (2006): under 15, 14.3%; 15–29, 19.3%; 30–44, 22.9%; 45–59, 19.7%; 60–74, 15.8%; 75–84, 6.6%; 85 and over, 1.4%. **Ethnic composition** (2000; unofficial source; government states there are no ethnic divisions in Greece): Greek 90.4%; Macedonian 1.8%; Albanian 1.5%; Turkish 1.4%; Pomak 0.9%; Rom (Gypsy) 0.9%; other 3.1%. **Religious affiliation** (2005): Orthodox 90%; Sunni Muslim 5%; Roman Catholic 2%; other 3%. **Major cities** (2001): Athens 745,514 (urban agglomeration 3,187,734); Thessaloniki 363,987 (urban agglomeration 800,764); Piraeus (Piraievs) 175,697; Patrai 161,114; Peristerion 137,918. **Location:** southern Europe, bordering Albania, Macedonia, Bulgaria, Turkey, and the Mediterranean Sea.

Vital statistics

Birth rate per 1,000 population (2006): 10.0 (world avg. 20.3); (2005) within marriage 94.9%; outside of marriage 5.1%. **Death rate** per 1,000 population (2006): 9.5 (world avg. 8.6). **Total fertility rate** (avg. births per childbearing woman; 2005): 1.28. **Life expectancy** at birth (2005): male 76.6 years; female 81.5 years.

National economy

Budget (2006). *Revenue:* €48,600,000,000 (tax revenue 92.2%, of which VAT 32.6%, income tax 30.4%; nontax revenue 7.8%). *Expenditures:* €50,413,-000,000 (pensions and salaries 38.8%; debt interest 18.9%; health and social insurance 17.2%; operating expenditures 17.0%). **Public debt** (consolidated, general; 2007): US$328,757,540,000. **Production** (metric tons except as noted). *Agriculture and fishing*

(2007): olives 2,600,000, corn (maize) 1,767,500, tomatoes 1,450,000; livestock (number of live animals) 8,803,350 sheep, 5,570,885 goats (in addition, 1,315,000 beehives); fisheries production (2006) 211,622 (from aquaculture 54%). *Mining and quarrying* (2006): bauxite 2,162,900; nickel (metal content) 21,670; marble 150,000 cu m. *Manufacturing* (value added in US$'000,000; 2005): food and beverages 5,300; textiles 1,950; chemical products 1,750; refined petroleum and coal derivatives 1,500. *Energy production (consumption):* electricity (kW-hr; 2007) 59,776,000,000 ([2005] 63,800,000,000); hard coal (metric tons; 2005) none (563,000); lignite (metric tons; 2007) 63,448,000 ([2005] 70,096,-000); crude petroleum (barrels; 2006) 760,000 ([2005] 137,000,000); petroleum products (metric tons; 2005) 19,768,000 (18,695,000); natural gas (cu m; 2006) 16,000,000 ([2005] 2,806,000,000). **Population economically active** (2007): total 4,917,900; activity rate of total population 44.1% (participation rates: ages 15–64 [2006] 66.9%; female 40.9%; unemployed [April 2007–March 2008] 8.1%). **Gross national income** (2007): US$331,658,-000,000 (US$29,630 per capita). **Selected balance of payments data.** Receipts from (US$'000,000): tourism (2006) 14,402; remittances (2007) 1,543; foreign direct investment (FDI) (2004–06 avg.) 2,690. Disbursements for (US$'000,000): tourism (2006) 2,997; remittances (2007) 982; FDI (2004–06 avg.) 2,216.

Foreign trade

Imports (2006; c.i.f.): US$63,739,000,000 (machinery and apparatus 14.4%; crude petroleum 13.1%; food products 8.7%; road vehicles and parts 8.5%; medicine and pharmaceuticals 5.8%). *Major import sources:* Germany 12.5%; Italy 11.6%; Russia 7.1%; France 5.9%; The Netherlands 5.2%. **Exports** (2006; f.o.b.): US$20,943,000,000 (food products 14.0%; refined petroleum products 12.4%; machinery and apparatus 10.6%; wearing apparel 7.4%; medicine 5.3%). *Major export destinations:* Germany 11.3%; Italy 11.2%; Bulgaria 6.3%; UK 6.0%; Cyprus 5.3%.

Transport and communications

Transport. *Railroads* (2006): length 2,509 km; passenger-km 1,811,000,000; metric ton-km cargo 662,000,000. *Roads* (2005): total length 34,863 km (paved 93%). *Vehicles* (2007): passenger cars 4,798,530; trucks and buses 1,283,047. *Air transport* (Aegean Airlines and Olympic Airlines only; 2007): passenger-km 10,919,000,000; metric ton-km cargo 81,000,000. **Communications,** in total units (units per 1,000 persons). Telephone landlines (2007): 6,227,000 (559); cellular telephone subscribers (2007): 11,997,000 (1,076); personal computers (2004): 1,476,000 (150); total Internet users (2007): 2,540,000 (228); broadband Internet subscribers (2007): 1,018,000 (91).

Education and health

Educational attainment (2001). Percentage of population ages 25 and over having: no formal schooling 12.7%; primary education 34.3%; lower secondary 8.5%; upper secondary 25.7%; higher 18.8%. **Liter-**

acy (2007): percentage of total population ages 15 and over literate 97.1%; males literate 98.2%; females literate 96.0%. **Health** (2006): physicians (public health institutions only) 21,038 (1 per 436 persons); hospital beds (public health institutions only) 44,307 (1 per 207 persons); infant mortality rate per 1,000 live births 3.7; undernourished population (2002–04) less than 2.5% of total population.

Military

Total active duty personnel (2007): 156,600 (army 59.7%, navy 12.8%, air force 20.1%, joint staff 7.4%); Greek troops in Cyprus (2007) 1,150. **Military expenditure as percentage of GDP** (2005): 4.1%; per capita expenditure US$833.

Background

The earliest urban society in Greece was the palace-centered Minoan civilization, which reached its height on Crete c. 2000 BC. It was succeeded by the mainland Mycenaean civilization, which arose c. 1600 BC following a wave of Indo-European invasions. About 1200 BC a second wave of invasions destroyed the Bronze Age cultures, and a dark age followed, known mostly through the epics of Homer. At the end of this time, classical Greece began to emerge (c. 750 BC) as a collection of independent city-states, including Sparta in the Peloponnese and Athens in Attica. The civilization reached its zenith after repelling the Persians at the beginning of the 5th century BC and began to decline after the civil strife of the Peloponnesian War at the century's end. In 338 BC the Greek city-states were taken over by Philip II of Macedon, and Greek culture was spread by Philip's son Alexander the Great throughout his empire. The Romans, themselves heavily influenced by Greek culture, conquered the Greek states in the 2nd century BC. After the fall of Rome, Greece remained part of the Byzantine Empire until the mid-15th century, when it became part of the expanding Ottoman Empire; it gained its independence in 1832. It was occupied by Nazi Germany during World War II. Civil war followed and lasted until 1949, when communist forces were defeated. In 1952 Greece joined NATO. A military junta ruled the country from 1967 to 1974, when democracy was restored and a referendum declared an end to the Greek monarchy. In 1981 Greece joined the European Community, the first Eastern European country to do so. Upheavals in the Balkans in the 1990s strained Greece's relations with some neighboring states, notably the former Yugoslav entity that took the name Republic of Macedonia.

Recent Developments

In January 2008 Konstantinos (Kostas) Karamanlis became the first Greek prime minister since 1959 to pay an official visit to Turkey, where both sides pledged to "open a new page" in their relations. Foreign policy was dominated, however, by the ongoing dispute with Macedonia over that country's name, and Greece vetoed Macedonia's accession to NATO after no resolution had been found. The Greek economy was hurt by the global economic crisis, with GDP growing by 6.5% but inflation reaching 4.4% and unemployment rising to 7.9%. In April 2009 a European

---

1 metric ton = about 1.1 short tons; 1 kilometer = 0.6 mi (statute); 1 metric ton-km cargo = about 0.68 short ton-mi cargo; c.i.f.: cost, insurance, and freight; f.o.b.: free on board

Commission report predicted that GDP would fall by 0.9% in 2009.

Internet resources:
<www.statistics.gr/Main_eng.asp>.

Greenland

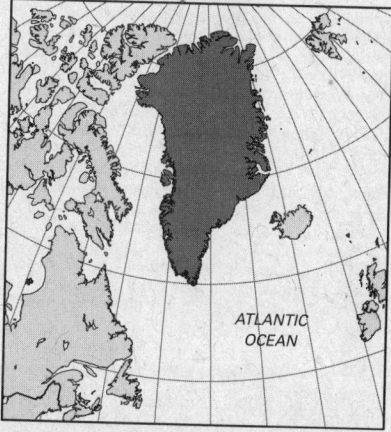

ATLANTIC OCEAN

Official name: Kalaallit Nunaat (Greenlandic) (Greenland). **Political status:** integral part of the Danish realm with one legislative house (Parliament [31]). **Chief of state:** Danish Queen Margrethe II (from 1972). **Heads of government:** High Commissioner (for Denmark) Søren Hald Møller (from 2005); Prime Minister (for Greenland) Hans Enoksen (from 2002). **Capital:** Nuuk. **Official language:** Greenlandic. **Official religion:** Evangelical Lutheran (Lutheran Church of Greenland). **Monetary unit:** 1 Danish krone (DKK; plural kroner) = 100 øre; valuation (1 Jul 2009) US$1 = DKK 5.25.

Demography

Area: 836,330 sq mi, 2,166,086 sq km. **Population** (2008): 56,700. **Density** (2008): persons per sq mi 0.36, persons per sq km 0.14. **Urban** (2005): 82.7%. **Sex distribution** (2005): male 53.04%; female 46.96%. **Age breakdown** (2006): under 15, 23.9%; 15–29, 21.1%; 30–44, 24.3%; 45–59, 19.4%; 60–74, 8.8%; 75–84, 1.7%; 85 and over, 0.8%. **Ethnic composition** (2000): Greenland Eskimo 79.1%; Danish 13.6%; other 7.3%. **Religious affiliation** (2000): Protestant 69.2%, of which Evangelical Lutheran 64.2%, Pentecostal 2.8%; other Christian 27.4%; other/nonreligious 3.4%. **Major towns** (2006): Nuuk (Godthåb) 14,719; Sisimiut (Holsteinsborg) 5,344; Ilulissat (Jakobshavn) 4,512; Qaqortoq (Julianehåb) 3,238. **Location:** island in the North Atlantic Ocean, east of northern Canada.

Vital statistics

Birth rate per 1,000 population (2006): 16.0 (world avg. 20.3); (1993) within marriage 29.2%; outside of marriage 70.8%. **Death rate** per 1,000 population (2006): 7.9 (world avg. 8.6). **Natural increase rate** per 1,000 population (2006): 8.1 (world avg. 11.7). **Total**

fertility rate (avg. births per childbearing woman; 2006): 2.40. **Life expectancy** at birth (2006): male 66.4 years; female 73.6 years.

National economy

Budget (general government; 2005). *Revenue:* DKK 8,031,552,000 (block grant from Danish government 45.4%; income tax 32.3%; import duties 6.9%). *Expenditures:* DKK 7,466,650,000 (social welfare 25.4%; education 17.9%; health 12.0%; public order 3.2%; defense 3.0%). **Tourism** (2006): number of overnight stays at hotels 245,432, of which visitors from within Greenland 104,012, from Denmark 101,387, from the US 9,536. **Production** (metric tons except as noted). *Agriculture, fishing, other marine:* locally grown broccoli, cauliflower, and cabbage were sold commercially for the first time in 2007, potatoes also were produced; fish catch (2004) 262,200 (by local boats 192,100, of which prawn 144,400, capelin 42,000, halibut 40,600, crab 6,400; by foreign boats 70,100); other marine catch (2006): whales/narwhals 606, porpoises 2,373, seals (2005) 188,068; livestock (number of live animals; 2006) 21,289 sheep, 2,318 tame reindeer, 217 horses; animal products (value of external sales in DKK '000; 2004) sealskins 23,026, polar bear skins (1998) 579 (164 polar bears were killed by trophy hunters in 2004). *Mining and quarrying* (2008): n.a. *Manufacturing:* principally handicrafts and fish processing. *Energy production (consumption):* electricity (kW-hr; 2005) 272,000,000 (272,000,000); petroleum products (metric tons; 2005) none (181,000). **Gross national income** (2006): US$1,618,000,000 (US$27,991 per capita). **Public debt** (2000): US$53,000,000. **Population economically active** (2003): total 32,119; activity rate of total population 56.5% (participation rates: ages 15–62, 83.5%; female [2002] 45.7%; unemployed [2006] 8.6%).

Foreign trade

Imports (2006): DKK 3,454,000,000 (refined petroleum products 21.8%; machinery and apparatus 16.9%; food products 16.5%; fabricated metal products 5.4%). *Major import sources:* Denmark 59.7%; Sweden 22.5%; Germany 3.0%; Norway 1.8%. **Exports** (2006): DKK 2,418,000,000 (shrimp 49.5%; halibut 21.1%; gold 6.9%; cod 5.3%; crab 2.2%; seal, whale, and shark products 1.9%). *Major export destinations:* Denmark 86.6%; Spain 7.0%; UK 1.9%; Iceland 1.6%.

Transport and communications

Transport. *Railroads:* none. *Roads* (1998): total length 150 km (paved 60%). *Vehicles* (2004): passenger cars 2,861; trucks and buses 1,531. *Air transport* (Air Greenland A/S only; 2006): passenger-km 441,422,000; metric ton-km cargo 49,485,000. **Communications,** in total units (units per 1,000 persons). Telephone landlines (2005): 24,000 (421); cellular telephone subscribers (2007): 66,000 (1,175); total Internet users (2007): 52,000 (920).

Education and health

Educational attainment (2002). Two-thirds of labor force has no formal education. **Literacy** (2001): percentage of total population ages 15 and over literate, virtually 100%. **Health:** physicians (2004) 91 (1 per

626 persons); hospital beds (2001) 406 (1 per 139 persons); infant mortality rate per 1,000 live births (2006) 15.4.

Military

Total active duty personnel. Denmark is responsible for Greenland's defense. Greenlanders are not liable for military service. US troops (2007) 138.

Background

The Inuit probably crossed to Greenland from North America, along the islands of the Canadian Arctic, from 4000 BC to AD 1000. The Norwegian Erik the Red visited Greenland in 982; his son, Leif Eriksson, introduced Christianity. Greenland came under joint Danish-Norwegian rule in the late 14th century. The original Norse settlements became extinct in the 15th century, but Greenland was recolonized by Denmark. In 1776 Denmark closed the Greenland coast to foreign trade; it was not reopened until 1950. Greenland became part of Denmark in 1953. Home rule was established in 1979. In the early 21st century, the movement for full independence gained support, as did the belief that global warming was responsible for the accelerated melting of the Greenlandic ice.

Recent Developments

In May 2008 Ilulissat, Greenland, was the site of an international summit on Arctic sovereignty attended by official representatives from Canada, Denmark, Norway, Russia, and the US. The Ilulissat Declaration, released at the end of the summit, provided a legal framework for Arctic development. In November the electorate in Greenland voted resoundingly in favor of greater autonomy from Denmark.

Internet resources: <www.stat.gl>.

Grenada

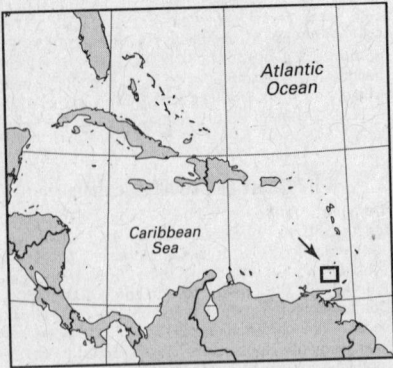

Atlantic Ocean

Caribbean Sea

Official name: Grenada. Form of government: constitutional monarchy with two legislative houses (Senate [13]; House of Representatives [15]). Chief of state: British Queen Elizabeth II (from 1952), represented by Governor-General Carlyle Glean (from 2008). Head of government: Prime Minister Tillman Thomas (from 2008). Capital: St. George's. Official language: English. Official religion: none. Monetary unit: 1 East Caribbean dollar (EC$) = 100 cents; valuation (1 Jul 2009) US$1 = EC$2.67.

Demography

Area: 133 sq mi, 344 sq km. Population (2008): 108,000. Density (2008): persons per sq mi 812.0, persons per sq km 314.0. Urban (2004): 41.5%. Sex distribution (2001): male 49.19%; female 50.81%. Age breakdown (2001): under 15, 35.1%; 15–29, 28.1%; 30–44, 17.6%; 45–59, 9.0%; 60 and over, 10.2%. Ethnic composition (2000): black 51.7%; mixed 40.0%; Indo-Pakistani 4.0%; white 0.9%; other 3.4%. Religious affiliation (2005): Roman Catholic 41%; Protestant (significantly Anglican and Seventh-day Adventist) 30%; Rastafarian 5%; nonreligious/ other 24%. Major localities (2004): St. George's 4,300 (urban agglomeration [2001] 35,559); Gouyave 3,200; Grenville 2,300; Victoria 2,100. Location: island between the Caribbean Sea and the Atlantic Ocean, north of Trinidad and Tobago.

Vital statistics

Birth rate per 1,000 population (2006): 22.1 (world avg. 20.3). Death rate per 1,000 population (2006): 6.9 (world avg. 8.6). Natural increase rate per 1,000 population (2006): 15.2 (world avg. 11.7). Total fertility rate (avg. births per childbearing woman; 2006): 2.34. Life expectancy at birth (2006): male 63.1 years; female 66.7 years.

National economy

Budget (2006). Revenue: EC$490,800,000 (tax revenue 73.3%, of which tax on international trade 43.3%, income tax 11.4%; grants 21.3%; nontax revenue 5.4%). Expenditures: EC$588,800,000 (current expenditures 53.9%, of which wages and salaries 26.2%, transfers 11.6%, debt service 4.9%; capital expenditures 46.1%). Public debt (external, outstanding; 2007): US$249,740,000. Gross national income (2007): US$505,000,000 (US$4,670 per capita). Production (metric tons except as noted). Agriculture and fishing (2007): sugarcane 7,200, coconuts 7,000, bananas 4,300, cacao 1,000; livestock (number of live animals) 13,200 sheep, 7,200 goats, 2,650 pigs; fisheries production (2006) 2,169 (from aquaculture, negligible). Mining and quarrying: excavation of limestone, sand, and gravel for local use. Manufacturing (value of production in EC$'000; 1997): wheat flour 13,390; soft drinks 9,798; beer 7,072. Energy production (consumption): electricity (kW-hr; 2005) 166,000,000 (166,000,000); petroleum products (metric tons; 2005) none (76,000). Population economically active (2004): total 37,000; activity rate of total population 35% (participation rates: ages 15–64 [1998] 78%; female [1998] 43.5%; unemployed [2002] 12.2%). Selected balance of payments data. Receipts from (US$'000,000): tourism (2006) 93; remittances (2007) 25; foreign direct investment (2004–06 avg.) 90; official development assistance (2006) 27. Disbursements for (US$'000,-000): tourism (2006) 11; remittances (2007) 2.

Foreign trade

Imports (2005): US$334,000,000 (machinery and apparatus 17.5%; food products 14.2%; chemical products 8.1%; fabricated metal products 6.9%; iron and steel 6.5%; refined petroleum 6.4%). *Major import sources:* US 37.5%; Trinidad and Tobago 21.0%; UK 5.8%; Japan 4.0%; China 3.2%. **Exports** (2005): US$27,600,000 (food products 61.2%, of which spices [nearly all nutmeg and mace] 29.7%, wheat flour 13.8%, fish 9.9%; toilet paper 8.7%). *Major export destinations:* US 21.4%; The Netherlands 14.1%; Trinidad and Tobago 10.1%; Saint Lucia 9.4%; Barbados 6.2%.

Transport and communications

Transport. *Railroads:* none. *Roads* (2000): total length 1,127 km (paved 61%). *Vehicles* (2001): passenger cars 15,800; trucks and buses 4,200. *Air transport* (Point Salines airport only; 2001): passengers 331,000; cargo 2,747 metric tons. **Communications,** in total units (units per 1,000 persons). Telephone landlines (2006): 28,000 (262); cellular telephone subscribers (2006): 46,000 (431); personal computers (2004): 16,000 (155); total Internet users (2007): 23,000 (218); broadband Internet subscribers (2006): 5,500 (52).

Education and health

Educational attainment (2001). Percentage of population ages 18 and over having: no formal schooling or unknown 7.6%; primary education 65.1%; secondary 21.7%; higher 5.6%. **Literacy** (2004): percentage of total population ages 15 and over literate 98.0%. **Health** (2003): physicians 127 (1 per 803 persons); hospital beds 330 (1 per 309 persons); infant mortality rate per 1,000 live births (2006) 14.3; undernourished population (2002–04) 7,000 (7% of total population based on the consumption of a minimum daily requirement of 1,910 calories).

Military

Total active duty personnel (2001) A 755-member police force includes an 80-member paramilitary unit and a 40-member coast guard unit.

Background

The warlike Carib Indians dominated Grenada when Christopher Columbus sighted the island in 1498 and named it Concepción; they ruled it for the next 150 years. In 1674 it became subject to the French crown and remained so until 1762, when British forces captured it. In 1833 the island's black slaves were freed. Grenada was the headquarters of the government of the British Windward Islands (1885–1958) and a member of the West Indies Federation (1958–62). It became a self-governing state in association with Britain in 1967 and gained its independence in 1974. In 1979 a left-wing government took control in a bloodless coup. Relations with its US-oriented Latin American neighbors became strained as Grenada leaned toward Cuba and the Soviet bloc. In order to counteract this trend, the US invaded the island in 1983; democratic self-government was reestablished

in 1984. Grenada's relations with Cuba, once suspended, were restored in 1997.

Recent Developments

In early 2008 a receiver was appointed to take over the operations of Grenada's Capital Bank International because of the bank's "failure" to accede to withdrawal requests by customers, raising questions about its solvency.

Internet resources: <www.grenadagrenadines.com>.

Guatemala

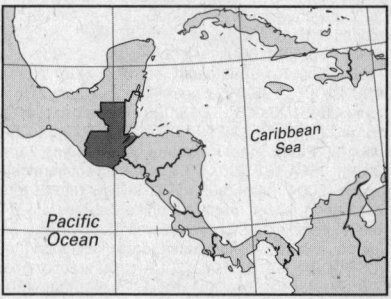

Official name: República de Guatemala (Republic of Guatemala). **Form of government:** republic with one legislative house (Congress of the Republic [158]). **Head of state and government:** President Álvaro Colom Caballeros (from 2008). **Capital:** Guatemala City. **Official language:** Spanish. **Official religion:** none. **Monetary unit:** 1 quetzal (Q) = 100 centavos; valuation (1 Jul 2009) US$1 = Q 8.02.

Demography

Area: 42,130 sq mi, 109,117 sq km. **Population** (2008): 13,002,000. **Density** (2008): persons per sq mi 308.6, persons per sq km 119.2. **Urban** (2005): 47.2%. **Sex distribution** (2006): male 49.35%; female 50.65%. **Age breakdown** (2006): under 15, 41.5%; 15–29, 28.6%; 30–44, 14.7%; 45–59, 9.6%; 60–74, 4.4%; 75–84, 1.1%; 85 and over, 0.1%. **Ethnic composition** (2000): mestizo 63.7%; Amerindian (virtually all Mayan) 33.1%; black 2.0%; white 1.0%; other 0.2%. **Religious affiliation** (2005): Roman Catholic 57%; Protestant/independent Christian 40%; traditional Mayan religions 1%; other 2%. **Major cities** (2002): Guatemala City 942,348 (urban agglomeration [2001] 3,366,000); Mixco 277,400; Villa Nueva 187,700; Quetzaltenango 106,700; Escuintla 65,400. **Location:** Central America, bordering Mexico, Belize, the Caribbean Sea, Honduras, El Salvador, and the Pacific Ocean.

Vital statistics

Birth rate per 1,000 population (2006): 29.6 (world avg. 20.3). **Death rate** per 1,000 population (2006): 5.4 (world avg. 8.6). **Natural increase rate** per 1,000 population (2006): 24.2 (world avg. 11.7). **Total fertility rate** (avg. births per childbearing woman; 2005): 4.30. **Life expectancy** at birth (2005): male 64.3 years; female 71.6 years.

National economy

Budget (2005). *Revenue:* Q 24,521,300,000 (tax revenue 95.2%, of which VAT 43.8%, income tax 24.7%; nontax revenue 4.8%). *Expenditures:* Q 28,500,-500,000 (current expenditures 66.4%; capital expenditures 33.6%). **Production** (metric tons except as noted). *Agriculture and fishing* (2007): sugarcane 18,000,000, corn (maize) 1,100,000, bananas 1,010,000, cardamom and nutmeg 19,000; livestock (number of live animals; 2007) 2,800,000 cattle, 265,000 sheep, 27,000,000 chickens; fisheries production (2006) 34,960 (from aquaculture 47%). *Mining and quarrying* (2005): gypsum 349,589; gold 740 kg; marble 3,000 cu m. *Manufacturing* (value added in Q '000,000 at prices of 1958; 2005): food products 213; beverages 98; textiles 75. *Energy production (consumption):* electricity (kW-hr; 2005) 7,550,000,-000 (7,238,000,000); coal (metric tons; 2005) none (408,000); crude petroleum (barrels; 2006) 7,340,-000 ([2005] 735,000); petroleum products (metric tons; 2005) 26,000 (3,048,000). **Gross national income** (2007): US$32,585,000,000 (US$2,440 per capita). **Public debt** (external, outstanding; April 2007): US$4,162,600,000. **Population economically active** (2004): total 5,059,800; activity rate of total population 40.5% (participation rates: ages 15–64, 64.7%; female 34.9%; unemployed [2003] 7.5%). **Selected balance of payments data.** Receipts from (US$'000,000): tourism (2006) 969; remittances (2007) 4,130; foreign direct investment (FDI) (2004–06 avg.) 245; official development assistance (2006) 487. Disbursements for (US$'000,000): tourism (2006) 494; remittances (2007) 35; FDI (2004–06 avg.) 24.

Foreign trade

Imports (2006; c.i.f.): US$9,540,000,000 (machinery and apparatus 18.5%; refined petroleum products 17.1%; chemical products 16.0%; road vehicles 10.1%). *Major import sources:* US 38.8%; Mexico 9.1%; China 4.8%; Brazil 3.9%; Panama 3.8%. **Exports** (2006; f.o.b.): US$3,198,000,000 (coffee 14.5%; raw sugar 9.3%; bananas 7.3%; crude petroleum 7.3%; toiletries and perfumery 3.9%; natural rubber 2.9%). *Major export destinations:* US 31.4%; El Salvador 15.3%; Honduras 9.7%; Mexico 5.4%; Nicaragua 4.4%.

Transport and communications

Transport. *Railroads* (2004): route length 886 km. *Roads* (2002): total length 14,044 km (paved 39%). *Vehicles* (2004): passenger cars 1,328,100; trucks and buses (2000) 53,236. *Air transport* (1999): passenger-km 341,700,000; metric ton-km cargo (2003) 200,-000. **Communications,** in total units (units per 1,000 persons). Telephone landlines (2006): 1,355,000 (105); cellular telephone subscribers (2007): 10,-150,000 (760); personal computers (2005): 262,000 (21); total Internet users (2006): 1,320,000 (102); broadband Internet subscribers (2005): 27,000 (2.1).

Education and health

Educational attainment (2002). Percentage of heads of households having: no formal schooling 33.3%; incomplete/complete primary education 46.1%; incomplete/complete secondary 15.0%; higher 5.6%. **Literacy** (2005): percentage of total population ages 15 and over literate 71.8%; males literate 79.1%; females literate 64.6%. **Health** (2003): physicians 11,700 (1 per 1,053 persons); hospital beds 6,118 (1 per 1,961 persons); infant mortality rate per 1,000 live births (2006) 30.8; undernourished population (2002–04) 2,800,000 (22% of total population based on the consumption of a minimum daily requirement of 1,760 calories).

Military

Total active duty personnel (2007): 15,500 (army 86.7%, navy 6.4%, air force 6.9%). **Military expenditure as percentage of GDP** (2005): 0.3%; per capita expenditure US$8.

Background

From simple farming villages dating to 2500 BC, the Maya of Guatemala and the Yucatán developed an impressive civilization. The civilization of the Maya declined after AD 900, and the Spanish began the subjugation of their descendants in 1523. The Central American colonies declared independence from Spain in Guatemala City in 1821, and Guatemala became part of the Mexican Empire until its collapse in 1823. In 1839 Guatemala became an independent republic under the first of a series of dictators who held power almost continuously for the next century. In 1945 a liberal-democratic coalition came to power and instituted sweeping reforms. Attempts to expropriate land belonging to American business interests prompted the US government in 1954 to sponsor an invasion. In the following years Guatemala's social revolution came to an end and most of the reforms were reversed. Chronic political instability and violence thenceforth marked Guatemalan politics; most of the 200,000 deaths that resulted were blamed on government forces. In 1991 the country abandoned its long-standing claims of sovereignty over Belize, and the two established diplomatic relations. It continued to experience violence as guerrillas sought to seize power. A peace treaty was signed in 1996, and the country started slowly to recover from its civil war.

Recent Developments

Following his inauguration on 14 Jan 2008, Guatemalan Pres. Álvaro Colom launched an ambitious program of social reform. A Council of Social Cohesion, headed by his wife, Sandra Torres de Colom, coordinated educational and economic benefits for the rural poor. By July Colom had improved access to drinking water, health care, and education, and he had initiated hydroelectric and thermal-energy projects. Guatemala opened trade with India and China and negotiated new trade agreements with the EU and Brazil. Remittances from Guatemalans abroad (mostly in the US) remained crucially important.

Internet resources:
<www.visitguatemala.com/nuevo/mainE.asp>.

---

1 metric ton = about 1.1 short tons;   1 kilometer = 0.6 mi (statute);   1 metric ton-km cargo = about 0.68 short ton-mi cargo;   c.i.f.: cost, insurance, and freight;   f.o.b.: free on board

Guinea

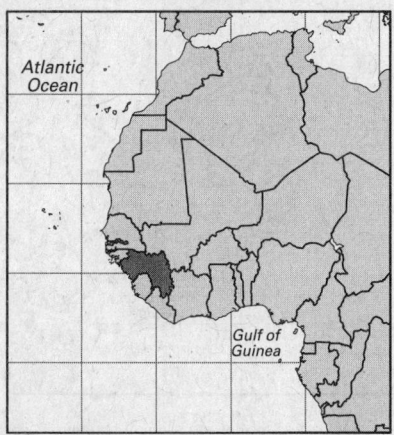

Atlantic Ocean

Gulf of Guinea

Official name: République de Guinée (Republic of Guinea). **Form of government:** military regime. **Head of state and government:** President Moussa Dadis Camara (from 2008), assisted by Prime Minister Kabiné Komara (from 2009). **Capital:** Conakry. **Official language:** French. **Official religion:** none. **Monetary unit:** 1 Guinean franc (FG) = 100 centimes; valuation (1 Jul 2009) US$1 = FG 4,892.12.

Demography

Area: 94,918 sq mi, 245,836 sq km. **Population** (2008): 9,572,000. **Density** (2008): persons per sq mi 100.8, persons per sq km 38.9. **Urban** (2007): 33.7%. **Sex distribution** (2005): male 50.00%; female 50.00%. **Age breakdown** (2005): under 15, 44.4%; 15–29, 26.5%; 30–44, 15.4%; 45–59, 8.7%; 60–74, 4.1%; 75 and over, 0.9%. **Ethnic composition** (2000): Fulani 38.3%; Malinke 25.6%; Susu 12.2%; Kpelle 5.2%; Kisi 4.8%; other 13.9%. **Religious affiliation** (2005): Muslim (nearly all Sunni) 85%; Christian 8%; traditional beliefs 7%. **Major cities** (2004): Conakry 1,851,800; Kankan 113,900; Labé (2001) 64,500; Kindia (2001) 56,000; Nzérékoré (2001) 55,000. **Location:** western Africa, bordering Guinea-Bissau, Senegal, Mali, Côte d'Ivoire, Liberia, Sierra Leone, and the North Atlantic Ocean.

Vital statistics

Birth rate per 1,000 population (2005): 42.0 (world avg. 20.3). **Death rate** per 1,000 population (2005): 15.6 (world avg. 8.6). **Natural increase rate** per 1,000 population (2005): 26.4 (world avg. 11.7). **Total fertility rate** (avg. births per childbearing woman; 2005): 5.83. **Life expectancy** at birth (2005): male 48.2 years; female 50.6 years.

National economy

Budget (2006). *Revenue:* FG 2,397,800,000,000 (current revenue 90.6%, of which mining sector revenue 28.2%, taxes on domestic production and trade 25.9%, taxes on international trade 18.2%, income tax 11.7%, nontax revenue 6.7%; grants 9.4%). *Expenditures:* FG 2,871,400,000,000 (current expenditures 76.2%, of which debt interest 18.7%, wages and salaries 15.5%; capital expenditures 23.4%; net lending and restructuring 0.4%). **Public debt** (external, outstanding; 2006): US$2,980,000,000. **Production** (metric tons except as noted). *Agriculture and fishing* (2007): rice 1,401,592, cassava 1,122,171, oil palm fruit 883,000, fonio 243,361; livestock (number of live animals) 4,180,965 cattle, 1,590,400 goats, 1,330,600 sheep; fisheries production 94,000 (from aquaculture, negligible). *Mining and quarrying* (2006): bauxite 16,956,200; gold 25,100 kg; diamonds 444,000 carats. *Manufacturing* (2006): cement 151,500; flour 54,600; paints 1,362. *Energy production (consumption):* electricity (kW-hr; 2006) 583,400,000 ([2005] 802,000,000); petroleum products (metric tons; 2005) none (384,000). **Population economically active** (2003): total 4,247,000; activity rate of total population 49.0% (participation rates: ages 15–64, 86.2%; female 46.3%; unemployed, n.a.). **Gross national income** (2007): US$3,722,000,000 (US$400 per capita). **Selected balance of payments data.** Receipts from (US$'000,000): tourism (2006) 70; remittances (2007) 42; foreign direct investment (2004–06 avg.) 103; official development assistance (2006) 164. Disbursements for (US$'000,000): tourism (2005) 28; remittances (2007) 48.

Foreign trade

Imports (2004): US$569,320,000 (machinery and apparatus 28.0%; food products 20.6%; refined petroleum products 18.9%). *Major import sources:* France 14.6%; China 9.6%; The Netherlands 6.8%; Belgium 6.0%; US 5.9%. **Exports** (2004): US$772,820,000 (bauxite 39.0%; alumina 20.3%; gold 18.9%; diamonds 6.5%; cotton 5.6%;). *Major export destinations:* South Korea 15.6%; Russia 13.1%; Spain 12.3%; Ireland 9.1%; US 7.5%.

Transport and communications

Transport. *Railroads* (2006): route length (mostly for bauxite transport) 837 km; metric ton-km cargo (1993) 710,000,000. *Roads* (2003): total length 44,348 km (paved 10%). *Vehicles* (2003): passenger cars 47,524; trucks and buses 26,467. *Air transport* (1999): passenger-km 94,000,000; metric ton-km cargo 10,000,000. **Communications,** in total units (units per 1,000 persons). Telephone landlines (2005): 26,000 (3.3); cellular telephone subscribers (2005): 189,000 (24); personal computers (2005): 45,000 (5.6); total Internet users (2006): 50,000 (5.4).

Education and health

Educational attainment (1999). Percentage of population ages 25 and over having: no formal schooling or unknown 81.4%; primary education 7.8%; secondary 6.8%; higher 4.0%. **Literacy** (2006): percentage of total population ages 15 and over literate 29.5%; males literate 42.6%; females literate 18.1%. **Health** (2004): physicians 987 (1 per 9,323 persons); hospital beds 2,990 (1 per 3,078 persons); infant mortality rate per 1,000 live births (2006) 96.0; undernourished population (2002–04) 2,000,000 (24% of total population based on the consumption of a minimum daily requirement of 1,830 calories).

Military

Total active duty personnel (2007): 9,700 (army 87.7%, navy 4.1%, air force 8.2%). Military expenditure as percentage of GDP (2005): 2.8%; per capita expenditure US$8.

Background

About AD 900 successive migrations of the Susu swept down from the desert and pushed the original inhabitants of Guinea, the Baga, to the Atlantic coast. Small kingdoms of the Susu rose in importance in the 13th century and later extended their rule to the coast. In the mid-15th century the Portuguese visited the coast and developed a slave trade. In the 16th century the Fulani established domination over the Fouta Djallon region; they ruled into the 19th century. In the early 19th century the French arrived and in 1849 proclaimed the coastal region a French protectorate. In 1895 French Guinea became part of the federation of French West Africa. In 1946 it was made an overseas territory of France, and in 1958 it achieved independence. Following a military coup in 1984, Guinea began implementing Westernized government systems. A new constitution was adopted in 1991, and the first multiparty elections were held in 1993. During the 1990s Guinea accommodated several hundred thousand war refugees from neighboring Liberia and Sierra Leone.

Recent Developments

Pres. Lansana Conté, leader of Guinea for almost 25 years, died on 22 Dec 2008. A military coup quickly followed, prompting international condemnation, including suspension from the African Union that month and from the Economic Community of West African States in January 2009. The US also suspended all nonhumanitarian aid until the resumption of civilian rule.

Internet resources: <www.stat-guinee.org>.

Guinea-Bissau

Official name: República da Guiné-Bissau (Republic of Guinea-Bissau). Form of government: republic with one legislative house (National People's Assembly [102]). Head of state and government: President Malam Bacai Sanhá (from 2009), assisted by Prime Minister Carlos Gomes Júnior (from 2009). Capital: Bissau. Official language: Portuguese. Official religion: none. Monetary unit: 1 CFA franc (CFAF) = 100 centimes; valuation (1 Jul 2009) US$1 = CFAF 462.89.

Demography

Area: 13,948 sq mi, 36,125 sq km. Population (2008): 1,503,000. Density (2008): persons per sq mi 138.4, persons per sq km 53.4. Urban (2003): 34.0%. Sex distribution (2005): male 48.53%; female 51.47%. Age breakdown (2005): under 15, 41.6%; 15–29, 28.1%; 30–44, 16.1%; 45–59, 9.4%; 60–74, 4.1%; 75 and over, 0.7%. Ethnic composition (1996): Balante 30%; Fulani 20%; Mandyako 14%;

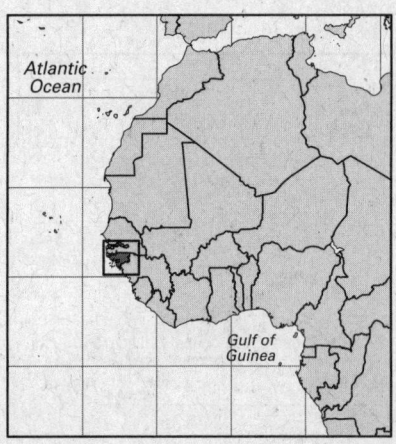

Malinke 13%; Pepel 7%; nonindigenous Cape Verdean mulatto 2%; other 14%. Religious affiliation (2005): traditional beliefs 49%; Muslim 42%; Christian and other 9%. Major cities (2004): Bissau 305,700; Bafatá 15,000; Cacheu 14,000; Gabú 10,000. Location: western Africa, bordering Senegal, Guinea, and the North Atlantic Ocean.

Vital statistics

Birth rate per 1,000 population (2005): 37.6 (world avg. 20.3). Death rate per 1,000 population (2005): 16.7 (world avg. 8.6). Natural increase rate per 1,000 population (2005): 20.9 (world avg. 11.7). Total fertility rate (avg. births per childbearing woman; 2005): 4.93. Life expectancy at birth (2005): male 44.8 years; female 48.5 years.

National economy

Budget (2005). Revenue: CFAF 41,378,000,000 (tax revenue 44.3%, of which taxes on international trade 15.5%, general sales tax 13.6%; grants 32.4%; nontax revenue 23.3%, of which fishing licenses 18.2%). Expenditures: CFAF 60,524,000,000 (current expenditures 72.7%, of which wages and salaries 35.1%, scheduled external debt interest 11.1%; capital expenditures 27.3%). Production (metric tons except as noted). Agriculture and fishing (2007): rice 88,700, cashew nuts 81,000, oil palm fruit 80,000; livestock (number of live animals) 549,800 cattle, 390,500 pigs; fisheries production (2006) 6,200 (from aquaculture, none). Mining and quarrying: extraction of construction materials only. Manufacturing (2003): processed wood 11,000; bakery products 7,900; wood products 4,400. Energy production (consumption): electricity (kW-hr; 2005) 61,000,000 (61,000,000); petroleum products (metric tons; 2005) none (88,000). Selected balance of payments data. Receipts from (US$'000,000): tourism (2005) 1.6; remittances (2006) 29; foreign direct investment (2006 avg.) 18; official development assistance (2006) 82. Disbursements for (US$'000,000): tourism (2005) 10; remittances (2006) 5. Population economically active (2003): total 643,000; activity

---

1 metric ton = about 1.1 short tons;   1 kilometer = 0.6 mi (statute);   1 metric ton-km cargo = about 0.68 short ton-mi cargo;   c.i.f.: cost, insurance, and freight;   f.o.b.: free on board

rate of total population 47.2% (participation rates [1995]: ages 11 and over, 65.5%; female 39.9%; unemployed, n.a.). **Public debt** (external, outstanding; 2006): US$695,000,000. **Gross national income** (2007): US$331,000,000 (US$200 per capita).

Foreign trade

Imports (2005; c.i.f.): US$119,100,000 (construction material 17.3%; refined petroleum products 13.3%; food 12.6%, of which rice 9.1%; transportation equipment 11.1%; machinery and apparatus 10.1%). *Major import sources:* Senegal 34.6%; Italy 20.4%; Portugal 12.7%; The Netherlands 3.0%; France 2.5%. **Exports** (2005; f.o.b.): US$100,-800,000 (cashew nuts 89.5%; cotton 1.4%; wood products 1.4%). *Major export destinations:* India 67.4%; Nigeria 19.0%; Senegal 1.5%; Portugal 1.1%.

Transport and communications

Transport. *Railroads:* none. *Roads* (2003): total length 2,755 km (paved 28%). *Vehicles* (1996): passenger cars 7,120; trucks and buses 5,640. *Air transport* (1998): passenger-km 10,000,000. **Communications**, in total units (units per 1,000 persons). Telephone landlines (2005): 4,600 (3.1); cellular telephone subscribers (2007): 296,000 (201); total Internet users (2006): 37,000 (26).

Education and health

Literacy (2003): percentage of total population ages 15 and over literate 32.2%; males literate (2001) 55.2%; females literate (2001) 24.7%. **Health:** physicians (2004) 188 (1 per 7,374 persons); hospital beds (2001) 1,448 (1 per 902 persons); infant mortality rate per 1,000 live births (2005) 107.2; undernourished population (2002–04) 600,000 (39% of total population based on the consumption of a minimum daily requirement of 1,800 calories).

Military

Total active duty personnel (2007): 9,250 (army 73.5%, navy 3.8%, air force 1.1%, paramilitary [gendarmerie] 21.6%). **Military expenditure as percentage of GNP** (2005): 4.0%; per capita expenditure US$6.

Background

More than 1,000 years ago the coast of Guinea-Bissau was occupied by iron-using agriculturists. They grew irrigated and dry rice and were also the major suppliers of marine salt to the western Sudan. At about the same time, the region came under the influence of the Mali empire and became a tributary kingdom known as Gabú. After 1546 Gabú was virtually autonomous; vestiges of the kingdom lasted until 1867. The earliest overseas contacts came in the 15th century with the Portuguese, who imported slaves from the Guinea area to the offshore Cape Verde Islands. Portuguese control of Guinea-Bissau was marginal despite claims to sovereignty there. The end of the slave trade forced the Portuguese inland in search of new profits. Their subjugation of the interior was slow and sometimes violent; it was not effectively achieved until 1915, though sporadic resistance continued until 1936.

Guerrilla warfare in the 1960s led to the country's independence in 1974, but political turmoil continued and the government was overthrown by a military coup in 1980. A new constitution was adopted in 1984, and the first multiparty elections were held in 1994. A destructive civil war in 1998 was followed by a military coup in 1999 and another in 2003.

Recent Developments

A failed coup occurred in Guinea-Bissau in 2008, and its alleged leader, the head of the country's navy, escaped by sea but was soon arrested in The Gambia. Another apparent coup attempt followed the November legislative election, with Pres. João Bernardo Vieira surviving an attack at his home by mutinous soldiers. In March 2009, however, army chief of staff and Vieira rival Gen. Tagme Na Waie was killed in a bombing, and only hours later President Vieira was shot dead, allegedly by the military.

Internet resources: <www.guineabissau-government.com/english/index-english.php>.

Guyana

Official name: Co-operative Republic of Guyana. **Form of government:** unitary multiparty republic with one legislative house (National Assembly [65]). **Head of state and government:** President Bharrat Jagdeo (from 1999). **Capital:** Georgetown. **Official language:** English. **Official religion:** none. **Monetary unit:** 1 Guyanese dollar (G$) = 100 cents; valuation (1 Jul 2009) US$1 = G$147.03.

Demography

Area: 83,012 sq mi, 214,999 sq km. **Population** (2008): 736,000. **Density** (2008): persons per sq mi 9.7, persons per sq km 3.7. **Urban** (2005): 38.5%. **Sex distribution** (2007): male 50.06%; female 49.94%. **Age breakdown** (2005): under 15, 26.5%; 15–29, 29.7%; 30–44, 23.0%; 45–59, 13.3%; 60–74, 5.6%; 75 and over, 1.9%. **Ethnic composition** (2002): East Indian 43.5%; black 30.2%; mixed race 16.7%; Amerindian 9.2%; other 0.4%. **Religious affil-**

iation (2002): Christian 57.3%, of which Protestant and independent Christian 48.2% (including Anglican 6.9%), Roman Catholic 8.0%, Jehovah's Witness 1.1%; Hindu 28.4%; Muslim 7.2%; Rastafarian 0.5%; nonreligious 4.3%; other/unknown 2.3%. **Major cities** (2002): Georgetown 134,497; Linden 29,298; New Amsterdam 17,033; Anna Regina 12,391; Corriverton 11,494. **Location:** northern South America, bordering the North Atlantic Ocean, Suriname, Brazil, and Venezuela.

Vital statistics

Birth rate per 1,000 population (2005): 18.5 (world avg. 20.3). **Death rate** per 1,000 population (2005): 8.3 (world avg. 8.6). **Natural increase rate** per 1,000 population (2005): 10.2 (world avg. 11.7). **Total fertility rate** (avg. births per childbearing woman; 2005): 2.05. **Life expectancy** at birth (2005): male 62.9 years; female 68.3 years.

National economy

Budget (2005): *Revenue:* G$69,414,800,000 (tax revenue 76.2%, of which income tax 34.2%, consumption taxes 31.0%, taxes on international trade 6.9%; nontax revenue 4.6%; grants 11.4%). *Expenditures:* G$88,861,400,000 (current expenditures 60.5%, of which wages and salaries 20.9%, transfers 13.3%, interest payments 4.9%; development expenditures 39.5%). **Production** (metric tons except as noted). *Agriculture and fishing* (2007): sugarcane 3,250,000, rice 475,000, coconuts 45,000; livestock (number of live animals) 130,000 sheep, 110,000 cattle, 21,500,000 chickens; fisheries production (2006) 54,660 (from aquaculture 1%), of which shrimp or prawns 19,860. *Mining and quarrying* (2007): bauxite 2,248,929; gold 7,412 kg; diamonds 268,945 carats. *Manufacturing* (2006): flour 37,400; margarine 2,265; rum 119,000 hectoliters. *Energy production (consumption):* electricity (kW-hr; 2005) 862,000,000 (862,000,000); petroleum products (metric tons; 2005) none (485,000). **Population economically active** (2006): total 279,100; activity rate of total population 37% (participation rates: ages 15–65, 60%; female [2002] 34.1%; unemployed [2002] 11.7%). **Gross national income** (2007): US$959,000,000 (US$1,300 per capita). **Public debt** (external, outstanding; 2007): US$718,513,000. **Selected balance of payments data.** Receipts from (US$'000,000): tourism (2006) 37; remittances (2007) 218; foreign direct investment (2004–06 avg.) 70; official development assistance (2006) 173. Disbursements for (US$'000,000): tourism (2006) 49; remittances (2007) 48.

Foreign trade

Imports (2006; c.i.f.): US$892,900,000 (refined petroleum products 29.1%; machinery and apparatus 20.4%; chemical products 10.2%; food products 10.1%). *Major import sources:* Trinidad and Tobago 33.6%; US 27.2%; China 5.1%; UK 4.5%; Netherlands Antilles 4.0%. **Exports** (2006; f.o.b.): US$567,400,000 (sugar 22.9%; gold 14.0%; rice 8.8%; sawn wood 8.0%; diamonds 6.8%). *Major export destinations:* UK 20.4%; Canada 18.0%; US 15.5%; The Netherlands 6.3%; Trinidad and Tobago 6.2%.

Transport and communications

Transport. *Railroads* (devoted entirely to the transportation of ore; 2001): 187 km. *Roads* (2000): total length 7,970 km (paved 7%). *Vehicles* (2001): passenger cars 61,300; trucks and buses 15,500. *Air transport* (2001): passenger-km 174,800,000; metric ton-km cargo 1,600,000. **Communications,** in total units (units per 1,000 persons). Telephone landlines (2005): 110,000 (146); cellular telephone subscribers (2005): 281,000 (375); personal computers (2005): 29,000 (39); total Internet users (2007): 190,000 (258); broadband Internet subscribers (2005): 2,000 (2.6).

Education and health

Educational attainment (2002). Percentage of population ages 15 and over having: no formal schooling/unknown 3.4%; primary education 26.0%; secondary 62.1%; postsecondary 3.7%; higher 4.8%. **Literacy** (2005): percentage of total population ages 15 and over literate 99.0%; males literate 99.2%; females literate 98.7%. **Health** (2005): physicians 323 (1 per 2,325 persons); hospital beds 3,267 (1 per 230 persons); infant mortality rate per 1,000 live births 33.3; undernourished population (2002–04) 60,000 (8% of total population based on the consumption of a minimum daily requirement of 1,880 calories).

Military

Total active duty personnel (2007): 1,100 (army 81.8%, navy 9.1%, air force 9.1%). **Military expenditure as percentage of GDP** (2004): 1.8%; per capita expenditure US$19.

Background

Guyana was colonized by the Dutch in the 17th century. During the Napoleonic Wars the British occupied the territory and afterward purchased the colonies of Demerara, Berbice, and Essequibo, united in 1831 as British Guiana. The slave trade was abolished in 1807, but emancipation of the 100,000 slaves in the colonies was not completed until 1838. From the 1840s East Indian and Chinese indentured servants were brought to work the plantations; by 1917 almost 240,000 East Indians had migrated to British Guiana. It was made a crown colony in 1928 and granted home rule in 1953. Political parties began to emerge, developing on racial lines as the People's Progressive Party (largely East Indian) and the People's National Congress (largely black). The PNC formed a coalition government and led the country into independence as Guyana in 1966. In 1970 Guyana became a republic within the Commonwealth; in 1980 it adopted a new constitution. Venezuela has long claimed land west of the Essequibo River, and the UN continued to arbitrate the issue in the early 21st century.

Recent Developments

Following the settlement of Guyana's maritime boundary dispute with Suriname in 2007, it was announced in May 2008 that the world's largest oil

---

1 metric ton = about 1.1 short tons;   1 kilometer = 0.6 mi (statute);   1 metric ton-km cargo = about 0.68 short ton-mi cargo;   c.i.f.: cost, insurance, and freight;   f.o.b.: free on board

company, ExxonMobil, had begun exploration work in its offshore Stabroek block.

Internet resources: <www.statisticsguyana.gov.gy>.

Haiti

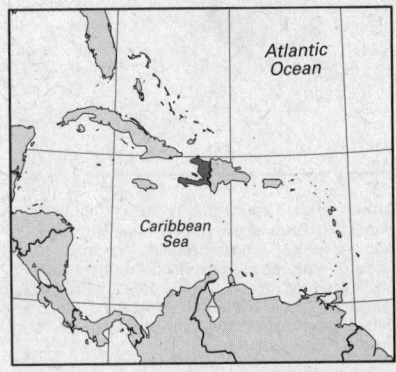

Official name: Repiblik d' Ayiti (Haitian Creole); République d'Haïti (French) (Republic of Haiti). **Form of government:** republic with two legislative houses (Senate [30, statutory number]; Chamber of Deputies [99]). **Chief of state:** President Renê Préval (from 2006). **Head of government:** Prime Minister Michèle Pierre-Louis (from 2008). **Capital:** Port-au-Prince. **Official languages:** Haitian Creole; French. **Official religions:** Roman Catholicism has special recognition per concordat with the Vatican; voodoo became officially sanctioned per governmental decree of April 2003. **Monetary unit:** 1 gourde (G) = 100 centimes; valuation (1 Jul 2009) US$1 = G 39.03.

Demography

Area: 10,695 sq mi, 27,700 sq km. **Population** (2008): 9,751,000. **Density** (2008): persons per sq mi 911.7, persons per sq km 352.0. **Urban** (2007): 40.1%. **Sex distribution** (2005): male 49.29%; female 50.71%. **Age breakdown** (2005): under 15, 42.6%; 15–29, 30.5%; 30–44, 14.2%; 45–59, 7.5%; 60–74, 4.2%; 75 and over, 1.0%. **Ethnic composition** (2000): black 94.2%; mulatto 5.4%; other 0.4%. **Religious affiliation** (2003): Roman Catholic 54.7% (about 80% of all Roman Catholics also practice voodoo); Protestant and independent Christian 28.5%, of which Baptist 15.4%, Pentecostal 7.9%; voodoo 2.1%; nonreligious 10.2%; other/unknown 4.5%. **Major cities** (2003): Port-au-Prince 703,023 (metropolitan area 1,977,036); Carrefour (1999) 336,222; Delmas (1999) 284,079; Cap-Haïtien 111,094; Gonaïves 104,825. **Location:** western third of the island of Hispaniola, bordered by the North Atlantic Ocean, the Caribbean Sea, and the Dominican Republic.

Vital statistics

Birth rate per 1,000 population (2007): 27.9 (world avg. 20.3). **Death rate** per 1,000 population (2007): 9.2 (world avg. 8.6). **Natural increase rate** per 1,000 population (2007): 18.7 (world avg. 11.7). **Total fertility rate** (avg. births per childbearing woman; 2007):

3.50. **Life expectancy** at birth (2007): male 59.1 years; female 62.8 years.

National economy

Budget (2007). *Revenue:* G 25,323,750,000 (customs duties 53.1%; sales tax 27.5%; individual taxes on income and profits 17.8%). *Expenditures:* G 29,534,070,000 (current expenditures 77.1%, of which wages and salaries 33.9%, transfers 4.2%, interest on public debt 2.3%; capital expenditures 22.9%). **Gross national income** (2007): US$5,366,000,000 (US$560 per capita). **Production** (metric tons except as noted). *Agriculture and fishing* (2007): sugarcane 1,000,000, cassava 330,000, bananas 293,000; livestock (number of live animals) 1,900,000 goats, 1,450,000 cattle, 1,000,000 pigs; fisheries production (2006) 10,000 (from aquaculture, none). *Mining and quarrying* (2006): sand 2,000,000 cu m. *Manufacturing* (value added in G '000,000 at prices of 1986–87; 2002): food and beverages 484.5; textiles, wearing apparel, and footwear 195.7; chemical and rubber products 63.8. *Energy production (consumption):* electricity (kW-hr; 2007) 241,990,000 (215,400,000 [estimate]); petroleum products (metric tons; 2005) none (527,000). **Population economically active** (2003): total 3,467,000; activity rate of total population 41.8% (participation rates: ages 15–64, 69.5%; female 41.5%; unemployed [official estimate] 32.7%). **Public debt** (external, outstanding; December 2007): US$1,478,000,000. **Selected balance of payments data.** Receipts from (US$'000,000): tourism (2006) 135; remittances (2007) 1,184; foreign direct investment (2004–06 avg.) 64; official development assistance (2006) 581. Disbursements for (US$'000,000): tourism (2006) 56; remittances (2007) 68.

Foreign trade

Imports (2006): US$1,623,600,000 (food products 21.9%; refined petroleum products 19.7%; machinery and transportation equipment 17.1%). *Major import sources* (2004): US 52.9%; Dominican Republic 6.0%; Japan 2.9%. **Exports** (2006): US$511,500,000 (reexports to US 88.4%, of which wearing apparel or accessories 87.7%; mangoes 1.8%; cacao 1.5%; essential oils 1.3%; coffee 1.0%). *Major export destinations* (2004): US 81.8%; Dominican Republic 7.2%; Canada 4.2%.

Transport and communications

Transport. *Railroads:* none. *Roads* (1999): total length 4,160 km (paved 24%). *Vehicles* (1999): passenger cars 93,000; trucks and buses 61,600. **Communications,** in total units (units per 1,000 persons). Telephone landlines (2006): 150,000 (17); cellular telephone subscribers (2007): 2,200,000 (229); personal computers (2005): 16,000 (1.9); total Internet users (2007): 1,000,000 (104).

Education and health

Educational attainment (2000). Percentage of population ages 25 and over having: no formal schooling/unknown 46.1%; incomplete primary education 28.9%; primary 5.3%; incomplete secondary 15.6%; secondary 1.8%; higher 2.3%. **Literacy** (2007): percentage of total population ages 15 and over literate 62.1%; males literate 60.1%; females literate 64.0%.

Health: physicians (1999) 1,910 (1 per 4,000 persons); hospital beds (2000) 6,431 (1 per 1,234 persons); infant mortality rate per 1,000 live births (2007) 71.0; undernourished population (2002–04) 3,800,000 (46% of total population based on the consumption of a minimum daily requirement of 1,940 calories).

Military

Total active duty personnel: The Haitian army was disbanded in 1995. The national police force had 2,000 personnel in late 2007; peacekeeping forces (July 2008): 7,105 UN troops and 1,935 UN personnel.

Background

Haiti gained its independence when the former slaves of the island rebelled against French rule in 1791–1804. The new republic encompassed the entire island of Hispaniola, but the eastern portion was restored to Spain in 1809. The island was reunited under Haitian Pres. Jean-Pierre Boyer (1818–43); after his overthrow the eastern portion revolted and formed the Dominican Republic. Haiti's government was marked by instability, with frequent coups and assassinations. It was occupied by the US in 1915–34. In 1957 the dictator François ("Papa Doc") Duvalier came to power. Despite an economic decline and civil unrest, Duvalier ruled until his death in 1971. He was succeeded by his son, Jean-Claude ("Baby Doc") Duvalier, who was forced into exile in 1986. Haiti's first free presidential elections, held in 1990, were won by Jean-Bertrand Aristide. He was deposed by a military coup in 1991, after which tens of thousands of Haitians attempted to flee to the US in small boats. The military government stepped down in 1994, and Aristide returned from exile and resumed the presidency. Economic and political instability continued to plague Haiti in the early 21st century.

Recent Developments

Skyrocketing food and fuel prices hit Haiti hard in 2008, owing to dependence on costly imports in a country where 78% of the population lived on less than US$2 a day. Resilient crime, especially urban kidnapping, and the government's inability to improve material conditions of the population dampened hopes for a brighter future. Remittances, reaching US$1.83 billion, or 30% of GDP, in 2007, were expected to stagnate or decline. A new coalition government led by Michèle Pierre-Louis, a respected educator and social activist, confronted a country ravaged by two hurricanes and two tropical storms within a 23-day period (16 August–7 September). The storms displaced hundreds of thousands of people, left 800 dead, and caused massive food deficits, thus setting back national efforts to address dependence on costly imported rice. The renewal in mid-October of the one-year mandate of the UN Stabilization Mission in Haiti (MINUSTAH) offered relief, however, particularly in view of its capabilities in disaster response and in reinforcing public safety.

Internet resources: <www.brh.net>.

Honduras

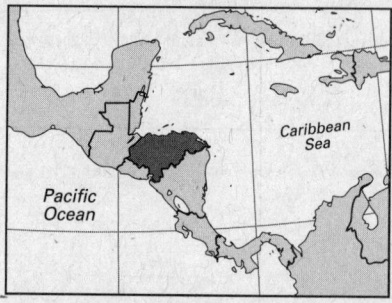

Official name: República de Honduras (Republic of Honduras). **Form of government:** multiparty republic with one legislative house (National Assembly [128]). **Head of state and government:** President Roberto Micheletti (from 2009). **Capital:** Tegucigalpa. **Official language:** Spanish. **Official religion:** none. **Monetary unit:** 1 lempira (L) = 100 centavos; valuation (1 Jul 2009) US$1 = L 18.54.

Demography

Area: 43,433 sq mi, 112,492 sq km. **Population** (2008): 7,639,000. **Density** (2008): persons per sq mi 175.9, persons per sq km 67.9. **Urban** (2006): 45.5%. **Sex distribution** (2006): male 48.47%; female 51.53%. **Age breakdown** (2005): under 15, 40.5%; 15–29, 29.2%; 30–44, 16.7%; 45–59, 8.6%; 60–74, 3.9%; 75 and over, 1.1%. **Ethnic composition** (2000): mestizo 86.6%; Amerindian 5.5%; black (including Black Carib) 4.3%; white 2.3%; other 1.3%. **Religious affiliation** (2002): Roman Catholic 63%; Evangelical Protestant 23%; other 14%. **Major cities** (2007): Tegucigalpa 944,400; San Pedro Sula 600,600; Choloma 200,400; La Ceiba 162,200; El Progreso 114,500. **Location:** Central America, bordering the Caribbean Sea, Nicaragua, the North Pacific Ocean, El Salvador, and Guatemala.

Vital statistics

Birth rate per 1,000 population (2005): 28.5 (world avg. 20.3). **Death rate** per 1,000 population (2005): 6.0 (world avg. 8.6). **Natural increase rate** per 1,000 population (2005): 22.5 (world avg. 11.7). **Total fertility rate** (avg. births per childbearing woman; 2005): 3.50. **Life expectancy** at birth (2005): male 66.5 years; female 70.7 years.

National economy

Budget (2005). *Revenue:* L 32,305,100,000 (tax revenue 82.7%; nontax revenue 5.8%; transfers 11.5%). *Expenditures:* L 37,017,900,000 (current expenditures 78.6%; capital expenditures 21.4%). **Public debt** (external, outstanding; March 2006): US$4,327,500,000. **Production** (metric tons except as noted). *Agriculture and fishing* (2007): sugarcane 5,000,000, oil palm fruit 1,250,000, bananas 910,000; livestock (number of live animals) 2,510,000 cattle, 490,000 pigs, 19,000,000 chickens; fisheries

1 metric ton = about 1.1 short tons;   1 kilometer = 0.6 mi (statute);   1 metric ton-km cargo = about 0.68 short ton-mi cargo;   c.i.f.: cost, insurance, and freight;   f.o.b.: free on board

production (2006) 46,294 (from aquaculture 64%). *Mining and quarrying* (2005): gypsum 60,000; zinc (metal content) 42,698; silver 53,617 kg; gold 3,600 kg. *Manufacturing* (value added in US$'000,000; 2005): food and beverages 542; wearing apparel 371; bricks, cement, and ceramics 94. *Energy production (consumption)*: electricity (kW-hr; 2005) 5,545,000,000 (5,604,000,000); coal (metric tons; 2005) none (32,000); petroleum products (metric tons; 2005) none (2,157,000). **Population economically active** (2005): total 2,651,300; activity rate of total population 36.5% (participation rates: ages 15 and over, 57.7%; female 32.4%; unofficially unemployed [2006] 27.9%). **Gross national income** (2007): US$11,339,000,000 (US$1,600 per capita). **Selected balance of payments data.** Receipts from (US$'000,000): tourism (2006) 488; remittances (2007) 2,675; foreign direct investment (FDI) (2004–06 avg.) 361; official development assistance (2006) 587. Disbursements for (US$'000,000): tourism (2006) 283; remittances (2007) 1; FDI (2004–06 avg.) 23.

Foreign trade

Imports (2006): US$5,417,800,000 (mineral fuels and lubricants 20.6%; food products and live animals 16.6%; machinery and electrical equipment 15.6%; chemical products 12.9%, fabricated metal products 7.6%%). *Major import sources* (2005): US 37.5%; Guatemala 9.0%; El Salvador 5.9%; Costa Rica 5.5%; Mexico 5.3%. **Exports** (2006): US$1,929,500,000 (coffee 20.9%; bananas 13.0%; shrimp 9.4%; zinc 5.8%; gold 4.1%). *Major export destinations* (2005): US 36.8%; El Salvador 10.5%; Germany 8.5%; Guatemala 7.9%; Belgium 5.4%.

Transport and communications

Transport. *Railroads* (2005): serviceable lines 253 km (most tracks are out of use). *Roads* (2005): total length 13,720 km (paved 22%). *Vehicles* (2003): passenger cars 386,468; trucks and buses 113,744. *Air transport* (1995): passenger-km 341,000,000; metric ton-km cargo 33,000,000. **Communications,** in total units (units per 1,000 persons). Telephone landlines (2006): 708,000 (97); cellular telephone subscribers (2006): 2,241,000 (306); personal computers (2005): 120,000 (17); total Internet users (2006): 337,000 (46).

Education and health

Educational attainment (1988). Percentage of population ages 10 and over having: no formal schooling 33.4%; primary education 50.1%; secondary education 13.4%; higher 3.1%. **Literacy** (2005): percentage of total population ages 15 and over literate 78.0%; males literate 77.6%; females literate 78.3%. **Health:** physicians (2001) 5,681 (1 per 1,149 persons); hospital beds (2005) 5,546 (1 per 1,292 persons); infant mortality rate per 1,000 live births (2005) 26.5; undernourished population (2002–04) 1,600,000 (23% of total population based on the consumption of a minimum daily requirement of 1,780 calories).

Military

Total active duty personnel (2007): 12,000 (army 69.2%, navy 11.7%, air force 19.1%); US troops

(2008) 406. **Military expenditure as percentage of GDP** (2005): 0.6%; per capita expenditure US$7.

Background

Early residents of Honduras were part of the Mayan civilization that flourished in the 1st millennium AD. Christopher Columbus reached Honduras in 1502, and permanent settlement followed. A major war between the Spanish and the Indians broke out in 1537, culminating in the decimation of the Indian population through disease and enslavement. After 1570 Honduras was part of the captaincy general of Guatemala until Central American independence in 1821. Part of the United Provinces of Central America, Honduras withdrew in 1838 and declared its independence. In the 20th century, under military rule, there was constant civil war and some intervention by the US. A civilian government assumed office in 1982. The military remained in the background, however, as the activity of leftist guerrillas increased.

Recent Developments

To counter rising oil prices, in 2008 Honduras joined PetroCaribe, which enabled it to receive petroleum from Venezuela at a reduced price. Tegucigalpa also negotiated agreements that would allow Hondurans to work in Canada and Spain legally.

Internet resources: <www.honduras.com>.

Hong Kong

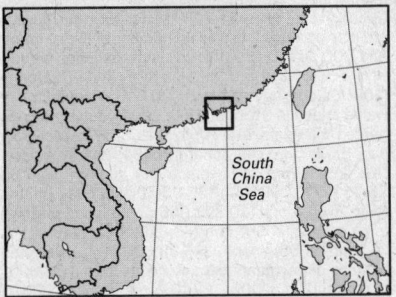

South
China
Sea

Official name: Xianggang Tebie Xingzhengqu (Chinese); Hong Kong Special Administrative Region (English). **Political status:** special administrative region of the People's Republic of China with one legislative house (Legislative Council [60]). **Chief of state:** Chinese President Hu Jintao (from 2003). **Head of government:** Chief Executive Donald Tsang (from 2005). **Official languages:** Chinese; English. **Official religion:** none. **Monetary unit:** 1 Hong Kong dollar (HK$) = 100 cents; valuation (1 Jul 2009) US$1 = HK$7.75.

Demography

Area: 426 sq mi, 1,104 sq km. **Population** (2008): 6,992,000. **Density** (2008): persons per sq mi 16,413, persons per sq km 6,333. **Urban** (2003): 100.0%. **Sex distribution** (2008): male 47.68%, female 52.32%. **Age breakdown** (2005): under 15, 14.2%; 15–29, 19.9%; 30–44, 27.0%; 45–59, 23.3%; 60–74, 10.2%; 75–84, 4.2%; 85 and over,

1.2%. **Ethnic composition** (2006): Chinese 95.0%; Filipino 1.6%; Indonesian 1.3%; assorted Caucasian 0.5%; Indian 0.3%; Nepalese 0.2%; other 1.1%. **Religious affiliation** (2002): nonreligious/non-practitioner of religion 57%; participant of religious practice 43%, of which Protestant 4.5%, Roman Catholic 3.5%, Muslim 1.5%, remainder (mostly Buddhist, Taoist, or Confucianist) 33.5%. **Major built-up areas** (2006): Kowloon 2,019,533; Victoria 981,714; Tuen Mun 488,249; Sha Tin 425,140; Tseung Kwan O 344,872. **Location:** eastern Asia, bordering China and the South China Sea.

Vital statistics

Birth rate per 1,000 population (2006): 9.6 (world avg. 20.3). **Death rate** per 1,000 population (2006): 5.4 (world avg. 8.6). **Natural increase rate** per 1,000 population (2006): 4.2 (world avg. 11.7). **Total fertility rate** (avg. births per childbearing woman; 2005): 0.97. **Life expectancy** at birth (2006): male 79.5 years; female 85.6 years.

National economy

Budget (2005–06). *Revenue:* HK$247,035,000,000 (earnings and profits taxes 45.6%; indirect taxes 20.4%; capital revenue 17.3%). *Expenditures:* HK$245,000,000,000 (education 22.0%; social welfare 13.6%; health 12.9%; police 10.1%; housing 6.2%; economic services 5.3%). **Public debt** (external, outstanding; January 2007): US$1,673,-000,000. **Gross national income** (2007): US$218,-910,000,000 (US$31,610 per capita). **Production** (metric tons except as noted). *Agriculture and fishing* (2006): vegetables 21,200, fruits 450, cut flowers are also produced; livestock (number of live animals) 381,200 pigs, 9,155,000 chickens; fisheries production 158,661 (from aquaculture 3%). *Quarrying* (2006): stone/aggregates 6,000,000. *Manufacturing* (value added in HK$'000,000; 2004): publishing and printed materials 11,270; textiles 6,067; food products 5,031; wearing apparel 4,454. *Energy production (consumption):* electricity (kW-hr; 2005) 38,451,000,000 (44,955,000,000); coal (metric tons; 2005) none (10,893,000); petroleum products (metric tons; 2005) none (3,816,000); natural gas (cu m; 2005) none (2,198,000,000). **Selected balance of payments data.** Receipts from (US$'000,-000): tourism (2006) 11,461; remittances (2007) 348; foreign direct investment (FDI) (2004–06 avg.) 36,847. Disbursements for (US$'000,000): tourism (2006) 13,974; remittances (2007) 380; FDI (2004–06 avg.) 38,792. **Population economically active** (2004): total 3,529,000; activity rate of total population 52.0% (participation rates: 15–64, 70.2%; female 44.2%; unemployed [January 2007–March 2007] 4.3%).

Foreign trade

Imports (2007; c.i.f.): HK$2,868,000,000,000 (capital goods 29.4%; consumer goods 26.6%; mineral fuels and lubricants 3.1%; foodstuffs 2.7%). *Major import sources:* China 46.4%; Japan 10.0%; Taiwan 7.2%; EU 7.2%; Singapore 6.8%. **Exports** (2007; f.o.b.): HK$2,687,500,000,000 (reexports 95.9%, of which capital goods 30.7%, consumer goods 30.3%;

domestic exports 4.1%, of which clothing accessories and apparel 1.4%). *Major export destinations:* China 48.7%; US 13.7%; EU 13.5%; Japan 4.3%.

Transport and communications

Transport. *Railroads* (2003): route length 64 km. *Roads* (2006): total length 1,984 km (paved 100%). *Vehicles* (2006): passenger cars 378,000; trucks and buses 131,000. *Air transport* (Cathay Pacific and Dragonair only; 2005): passenger-km 71,595,000,-000; metric ton-km cargo 8,026,729,000. **Communications,** in total units (units per 1,000 persons). Telephone landlines (2007): 3,875,000 (559); cellular telephone subscribers (2007): 10,550,000 (1,516); personal computers (2005): 4,172,000 (602); total Internet users (2007): 3,961,000 (572); broadband Internet subscribers (2007): 1,879,000 (271).

Education and health

Literacy (2000): percentage of total population ages 15 and over literate 93.5%; males literate 96.5%; females literate 90.2%. **Health** (2005): physicians 11,775 (1 per 588 persons) (there were an additional 4,848 practitioners of traditional Chinese medicine in Hong Kong in 2005); hospital beds 33,939 (1 per 204 persons); infant mortality rate per 1,000 live births (2006) 1.8.

Military

Total active duty personnel (2007): 7,000 troops of Chinese military (including elements of army, navy, and air force); Hong Kong residents are exempted from military service.

Background

The island of Hong Kong and adjacent islets were ceded by China to the British in 1842, and the Kowloon Peninsula and the New Territories were later leased by the British from China for 99 years (1898–1997). A joint Chinese-British declaration, signed on 19 Dec 1984, paved the way for the entire territory to be returned to China, which occurred on 1 Jul 1997.

Recent Developments

Hong Kong, whose stock market was a leading indicator of Asian financial health, was negatively affected by the global financial crisis in the second half of 2008. The economy grew only 2.5% for the year, and it contracted 2.6% in the fourth quarter compared to the same period in 2007. By April 2009 unemployment had reached 5.1%.

Internet resources:
<www.censtatd.gov.hk/home/index.jsp>.

Hungary

Official name: Magyar Köztársaság (Republic of Hungary). **Form of government:** unitary multiparty republic with one legislative house (National Assembly [386]). **Chief of state:** President László Sólyom (from

---

1 metric ton = about 1.1 short tons;   1 kilometer = 0.6 mi (statute);   1 metric ton-km cargo = about 0.68 short ton-mi cargo;   c.i.f.: cost, insurance, and freight;   f.o.b.: free on board

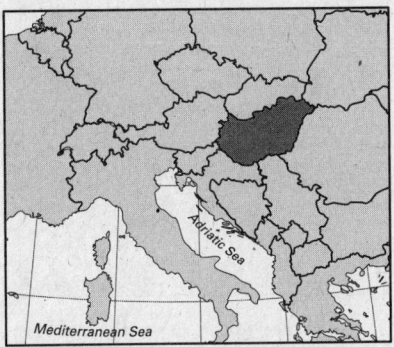

2005). **Head of government:** Prime Minister Gordon Bajnai (from 2009). **Capital:** Budapest. **Official language:** Hungarian. **Official religion:** none. **Monetary unit:** 1 forint (Ft) = 100 filler; valuation (1 Jul 2009) US$1 = Ft 189.51.

Demography

Area: 35,919 sq mi, 93,030 sq km. **Population** (2008): 10,032,000. **Density** (2008): persons per sq mi 279.3, persons per sq km 107.8. **Urban** (2004): 64.8%. **Sex distribution** (2007): male 47.48%; female 52.52%. **Age breakdown** (2005): under 15, 15.6%; 15–29, 21.3%; 30–44, 20.4%; 45–59, 21.3%; 60–74, 14.7%; 75–84, 5.6%; 85 and over, 1.1%. **Ethnic composition** (2000): Hungarian 84.4%; Rom 5.3%; Ruthenian 2.9%; German 2.4%; Romanian 1.0%; Slovak 0.9%; Jewish 0.6%; other 2.5%. **Religious affiliation** (2001): Roman Catholic 51.9%; Reformed 15.9%; Lutheran 3.0%; Greek Catholic 2.6%; Jewish 0.1%; nonreligious 14.5%; other/unknown 12.0%. **Major cities** (2007): Budapest 1,702,297; Debrecen 205,084; Miskolc 171,096; Szeged 167,039; Pécs 156,664. **Location:** central Europe, bordering Slovakia, Ukraine, Romania, Serbia, Croatia, Slovenia, and Austria.

Vital statistics

Birth rate per 1,000 population (2007): 9.7 (world avg. 20.3); (2004) within marriage 66.0%; outside of marriage 34.0%. **Death rate** per 1,000 population (2007): 13.2 (world avg. 8.6). **Total fertility rate** (avg. births per childbearing woman; 2007): 1.32. **Life expectancy** at birth (2007): male 69.2 years; female 77.3 years.

National economy

Budget (2005). *Revenue:* Ft 6,458,391,000,000 (VAT 27.6%; income tax 15.5%; corporate taxes 15.5%; excise taxes 11.4%). *Expenditures:* Ft 7,003,392,000,-000 (general administration 47.6%; public debt interest 13.1%; family benefits 7.1%; housing grant 3.3%). **Production** (metric tons except as noted). *Agriculture and fishing* (2007): corn (maize) 8,400,000, wheat 3,988,177, sugar beets 1,676,000, sunflower seeds 1,043,000, Hungarian red paprika (2006) 32,633; livestock (number of live animals) 3,987,000 pigs, 702,000 cattle, 2,708,000 geese; fisheries production (2006) 22,229 (from aquaculture 66%). *Mining and quarrying* (2005): bauxite 535,000. *Manufactur-

ing (value added in US$'000,000; 2004): electrical machinery and apparatus 2,087; motor vehicles and parts 1,988; food products 1,868. *Energy production (consumption):* electricity ('000,000 kW-hr; 2007) 32,749 ([2005] 41,983); hard coal ('000 metric tons; 2005) none (1,341); lignite ('000 metric tons; 2007) 9,813 ([2005] 10,247); crude petroleum ('000 barrels; 2007) 5,630 ([2005] 51,800); petroleum products ('000 metric tons; 2005) 6,178 (5,988); natural gas ('000,000 cu m; 2007) 2,535 ([2005] 14,628). **Selected balance of payments data.** Receipts from (US$'000,000): tourism (2006) 4,254; remittances (2007) 363; foreign direct investment (FDI) (2004–06 avg.) 6,074. Disbursements for (US$'000,000): tourism (2006) 2,126; remittances (2007) 190; FDI (2004–06 avg.) 2,154. **Population economically active** (2006): total 4,246,900; activity rate of total population 42.2% (participation rates: ages 15–64, 62.0%; female [2004] 45.7%; unemployed 7.5%). **Gross national income** (2007): US$116,303,-000,000 (US$11,570 per capita). **Public debt** (external, outstanding; 2006): US$28,017,000,000.

Foreign trade

Imports (2006; c.i.f.): Ft 16,196,000,000,000 (electrical machinery 14.9%; nonelectrical machinery 13.0%; chemical products 9.1%; mineral fuels 7.4%; road vehicles 7.3%). *Major import sources* (2006): Germany 27.4%; Russia 8.2%; Austria 6.2%; China 5.1%; France 4.7%. **Exports** (2006; f.o.b.): Ft 15,581,000,000,000 (nonelectrical machinery 16.9%, of which engines and parts 9.2%; telecommunications equipment 10.9%; electrical machinery 10.5%; road vehicles 9.5%). *Major export destinations* (2006): Germany 29.4%; Italy 5.4%; Austria 4.8%; France 4.6%; UK 4.5%.

Transport and communications

Transport. *Railroads* (2007): route length (2003) 7,898 km; passenger-km 8,751,000,000; metric ton-km cargo 9,998,000,000. *Roads* (2003): total length 159,568 km (paved 44%). *Vehicles* (2007): passenger cars 3,012,165; trucks and buses 416,045. *Air transport* (Malév Hungarian Airlines only; 2007): passenger-km 4,537,000,000; metric ton-km cargo 29,000,000. **Communications,** in total units (units per 1,000 persons). Telephone landlines (2007): 3,251,000 (324); cellular telephone subscribers (2007): 11,030,000 (1,100); personal computers (2005): 1,504,000 (149); total Internet users (2007): 4,200,000 (419); broadband Internet subscribers (2007): 1,510,000 (150).

Education and health

Educational attainment (2002). Percentage of population ages 25–64 having: no formal schooling through lower-secondary education 29%; upper secondary/higher vocational 57%; university 14%. **Health** (2004): physicians 38,877 (1 per 260 persons); hospital beds 79,610 (1 per 127 persons); infant mortality rate per 1,000 live births (2007) 5.9.

Military

Total active duty personnel (2007): 32,300 (army 74.2%, air force 23.2%, headquarters staff 2.6%). **Military expenditure as percentage of GDP** (2005): 1.5%; per capita expenditure US$158.

Background

The western part of Hungary was incorporated into the Roman Empire in 14 BC. The Magyars, a nomadic people, occupied the middle basin of the Danube River in the late 9th century AD. Stephen I, crowned in 1000, Christianized the country and organized it into a strong and independent state. Invasions by the Mongols in the 13th century and by the Ottoman Turks in the 14th century devastated the country, and by 1568 the territory of modern Hungary had been divided into three parts: Royal Hungary went to the Habsburgs; Transylvania gained autonomy in 1566 under the Turks; and the central plain remained under Turkish control until the late 17th century, when the Austrian Habsburgs took over. Hungary declared its independence from Austria in 1849, and in 1867 the dual monarchy of Austria-Hungary was established. Its defeat in World War I resulted in the dismemberment of Hungary, leaving it only those areas in which Magyars predominated. In an attempt to regain some of this lost territory, Hungary cooperated with the Germans against the Soviet Union during World War II. After the war, a pro-Soviet provisional government was established, and in 1949 the Hungarian People's Republic was formed. Opposition to this Stalinist regime broke out in 1956 but was suppressed. Nevertheless, from 1956 to 1988 communist Hungary grew to become the most tolerant of the Soviet-bloc nations of Eastern Europe. It gained its independence in 1989 and soon attracted the largest amount of direct foreign investment in east-central Europe. In 1999 it joined NATO and in 2004 the European Union.

Recent Developments

The drying up of credit markets led in the autumn of 2008 to a crisis of investor confidence and a weakening of the forint, which triggered the most serious budget crisis the country had seen since the fall of communism in 1989. Tension was high, as a key criterion for membership in the euro zone was the reduction of the country's budget deficit (3.4% of GDP in 2008). A Hungarian austerity program and the global financial meltdown combined to hold GDP growth to 0.6%, while soaring fuel and food prices pushed inflation to 6.1%.

Internet resources: <www.hungary.com>.

Iceland

Official name: Lýdhveldidh Ísland (Republic of Iceland). **Form of government:** unitary multiparty republic with one legislative house (Althingi [63]). **Chief of state:** President Ólafur Ragnar Grímsson (from 1996). **Head of government:** Prime Minister Jóhanna Sigurðardóttir (from 2009). **Capital:** Reykjavík. **Official language:** Icelandic. **Official religion:** Evangelical Lutheran. **Monetary unit:** 1 króna (ISK; plural krónur) = 100 aurar; valuation (1 Jul 2009) US$1 = ISK 125.93.

Demography

Area: 39,769 sq mi, 103,000 sq km. **Population** (2008): 315,000. **Density** (2008): persons per sq mi

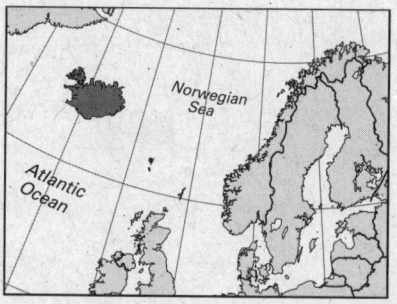

34.3, persons per sq km 13.2. **Urban** (2007): 92.6%. **Sex distribution** (2008): male 51.10%; female 48.90%. **Age breakdown** (2005): under 15, 21.8%; 15–29, 21.9%; 30–44, 21.5%; 45–59, 18.9%; 60–74, 10.2%; 75–84, 4.3%; 85 and over, 1.4%. **Ethnic composition** (2008): Icelandic 93.2%; European 5.5%, of which Polish 2.7%, Nordic 0.6%; Asian 0.8%; other 0.5%. **Religious affiliation** (2007): Evangelical Lutheran 80.7%; Roman Catholic 2.5%; other Christian 6.8%; other/not specified 10.0%. **Major cities** (2008): Reykjavík 119,000 (urban area [2005] 187,426); Kópavogur 29,795; Hafnarfjörður 25,434; Akureyri 17,390; Garðabaer 10,272. **Location:** northern Europe, island between the Greenland Sea, the Norwegian Sea, and the North Atlantic Ocean.

Vital statistics

Birth rate per 1,000 population (2007): 14.6 (world avg. 20.3); within marriage 36.2%; outside of marriage 63.8%. **Death rate** per 1,000 population (2007): 6.2 (world avg. 8.6). **Natural increase rate** per 1,000 population (2007): 8.4 (world avg. 11.7). **Total fertility rate** (avg. births per childbearing woman; 2007): 2.10. **Life expectancy** at birth (2007): male 79.4 years; female 82.9 years.

National economy

Budget (2007). *Revenue:* ISK 454,588,000,000 (tax revenue 78.4%, of which VAT 42.9%, income tax 31.5%; nontax revenue 21.6%, of which social security contributions 8.9%). *Expenditures:* ISK 403,199,-000,000 (social security and health 48.8%; education 10.6%; social affairs 9.4%; interest payment 6.9%). *Production* (metric tons except as noted). *Agriculture and fishing* (2007): potatoes 13,000, cereals 11,246, tomatoes 1,603; livestock (number of live animals) 454,812 sheep, 70,660 cattle, 41,497 mink; fisheries production (value in ISK '000,000) 80,251, of which cod 29,585, haddock 14,538, redfish 7,646, herring 5,700, saithe 4,263, capelin 4,247, blue whiting 3,022; fisheries production by tonnage 1,395,716 (from aquaculture [2006] 1%). *Mining and quarrying* (2005): diatomite 3,236. *Manufacturing* (value of sales in ISK '000,000; 2007): food and beverages (mainly preserved and processed fish) 202,606; base metals 76,581; printing and publishing 37,075. *Energy production (consumption):* electricity (kW-hr; 2006) 9,924,900,000 (9,925,-000,000); coal (metric tons; 2005) none (117,000);

---

1 metric ton = about 1.1 short tons;   1 kilometer = 0.6 mi (statute);   1 metric ton-km cargo = about 0.68 short ton-mi cargo;   c.i.f.: cost, insurance, and freight;   f.o.b.: free on board

petroleum products (metric tons; 2005) none (720,000). **Selected balance of payments data.** Receipts from (US$'000,000): tourism (2006) 439; remittances (2007) 41; foreign direct investment (FDI) (2004–06 avg.) 2,555. Disbursements for (US$'000,000): tourism (2006) 1,076; remittances (2007) 100; FDI (2004–06 avg.) 4,815. **Population economically active** (2007): total 181,500; activity rate of total population 58.5% (participation rates: ages 16–74, 83.3%; female 45.5%; unemployed [July 2007–June 2008] 2.4%). **Gross national income** (2007): US$16,826,000,000 (US$54,100 per capita). **Public debt** (December 2005): US$4,222,000,000.

Foreign trade

Imports (2006): ISK 420,545,000,000 (nonelectrical machinery 13.2%; road vehicles 10.9%; refined petroleum products 8.2%; aircraft and parts 7.5%; electrical machinery 7.3%). *Major import sources:* US 13.1%; Germany 12.4%; Norway 7.2%; Sweden 7.1%; Denmark 6.2%. **Exports** (2006): ISK 242,390,000,000 (fresh fish 33.1%; aluminum 23.5%; dried and salted fish 9.8%; aircraft and parts 6.2%; fish foodstuff for animals 4.2%). *Major export destinations:* The Netherlands 16.6%; UK 15.6%; Germany 15.0%; US 10.9%; Spain 6.4%.

Transport and communications

Transport. *Railroads:* none. *Roads* (2006): total length 13,038 km (paved 33%). *Vehicles* (2007): passenger cars 207,513; trucks and buses 33,038. *Air transport* (Icelandair only; 2007): passenger-km 4,252,000; metric ton-km cargo (2005) 121,591,000. **Communications,** in total units (units per 1,000 persons). Telephone landlines (2007): 187,000 (620); cellular telephone subscribers (2007): 348,000 (1,154); personal computers (2005): 142,000 (481); total Internet users (2007): 202,000 (672); broadband Internet subscribers (2007): 105,000 (348).

Education and health

Educational attainment (2003): Percentage of population ages 25–64 having unknown to lower secondary education 34%; upper secondary 40%; higher 26%. **Literacy:** percentage of total population literate, virtually 100%. **Health:** physicians (2006) 1,120 (1 per 270 persons); hospital beds (2002) 2,432 (1 per 118 persons); infant mortality rate per 1,000 live births (2007) 2.4; undernourished population (2002–04) less than 2.5% of total population.

Military

Total active duty personnel (2007): 130 coast guard personnel; NATO-sponsored US-manned Iceland Defense Force (2005): 1,250; US military withdrew permanently in September 2006, and NATO agreed to begin regular supervision of Icelandic airspace from July 2007. **Coast guard expenditure as percentage of GDP** (2005): 0.3%; per capita expenditure US$140.

Background

Iceland was settled by Norwegian seafarers in the 9th century and was Christianized by 1000. Its legislature, the Althing, was founded in 930, making it one of the oldest legislative assemblies in the world. Iceland united with Norway in 1262. It became an independent state of Denmark in 1918 but severed those ties to become an independent republic in 1944. Vigdís Finnbogadóttir became the world's first female elected president in 1980.

Recent Developments

Iceland's economy, in recent years one of the fastest growing in the developed world, was brought to a halt by the global financial crisis in late 2008. The government was forced to nationalize its leading banks, which held debt worth six times the Icelandic GDP, and secure some $US10 billion in loans from the IMF and donor countries, including its Nordic neighbors. In early 2009 the government collapsed as a result of the financial emergency.

Internet resources: <www.statice.is>.

India

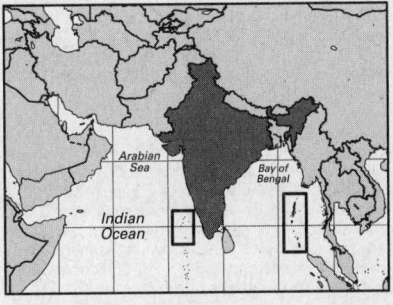

Official name: Bharat (Hindi); Republic of India (English). **Form of government:** multiparty federal republic with two legislative houses (Council of States [245], House of the People [545]). **Chief of state:** President Pratibha Patil (from 2007). **Head of government:** Prime Minister Manmohan Singh (from 2004). **Capital:** New Delhi. **Official languages:** Hindi; English. **Official religion:** none. **Monetary unit:** 1 Indian rupee (Re; plural Rs) = 100 paise; valuation (1 Jul 2009) US$1 = Rs 47.92.

Demography

Area: 1,222,559 sq mi, 3,166,414 sq km (excludes 46,660 sq mi [120,849 sq km] of territory claimed by India as part of Jammu and Kashmir but occupied by Pakistan or China). **Population** (2008): 1,147,996,000. **Density** (2008): persons per sq mi 939.0, persons per sq km 362.6. **Urban** (2004): 28.5%. **Sex distribution** (2005): male 51.57%; female 48.43%. **Age breakdown** (2005): under 15, 32.1%; 15–29, 27.1%; 30–44, 20.2%; 45–59, 12.7%; 60–74, 6.2%; 75–84, 1.4%; 85 and over, 0.3%. **Major cities (urban agglomerations)** (2006 [2007]): Mumbai (Bombay) 12,880,000 (18,978,000); Delhi 11,220,000 (15,926,000); Kolkata (Calcutta) 4,640,000 (14,787,000); Chennai (Madras) 4,350,000 (7,163,000); Bengaluru (Bangalore) 5,100,000 (6,787,000); Hyderabad

3,630,000 (6,376,000); Ahmadabad 3,770,000 (5,375,000); Pune (Poona) 3,040,000 (4,672,000); Surat 3,020,000 (3,842,000); Kanpur 2,900,000 (3,162,000); Jaipur 2,820,000 (2,917,000); New Delhi (2001) 302,363. **Location:** southern Asia, bordering Pakistan, China, Nepal, Bhutan, Myanmar (Burma), Bangladesh, and the Indian Ocean. **Linguistic composition** (2001): Hindi 41.03%; Bengali 8.11%; Telugu 7.19%; Marathi 6.99%; Tamil 5.91%; Urdu 5.01%; Gujarati 4.48%; Kannada 3.69%; Malayalam 3.21%; Oriya 3.21%; Punjabi 2.83%; Assamese 1.28%; Maithili 1.18%; Bhili/Bhilodi 0.93%; Santhali 0.63%; Kashmiri 0.54%; Nepali 0.28%; Gondi 0.26%; Sindhi 0.25%; Konkani 0.24%; Dogri 0.22%; Khandeshi 0.20%; Tulu 0.17%; Kurukh/Oraon 0.17%; Manipuri 0.14%; Bodo 0.13%; Khasi 0,11%; Mundari 0.10%; Ho 0.10%; Sanskrit 0.0013%; other 1.41%. Hindi (roughly 66%) and English (roughly 33%) are also spoken as lingua francas. **Castes/ tribes** (2001): number of Scheduled Castes (formerly referred to as "Untouchables") 166,635,700; number of Scheduled Tribes (aboriginal peoples) 84,326,240. **Religious affiliation** (2005): Hindu 72.04%; Muslim 12.26%, of which Sunni 8.06%, Shi'i 4.20%; Christian 6.81%, of which independent Christian 3.23%, Protestant 1.74%, Roman Catholic 1.62%, Orthodox 0.22%; traditional beliefs 3.83%; Sikh 1.87%; Buddhist 0.67%; Jain 0.51%; Baha'i 0.17%; Zoroastrian (Parsi) 0.02%; nonreligious 1.22%; atheist 0.17%; unknown 0.43%.

Vital statistics

Birth rate per 1,000 population (2006): 23.5 (world avg. 20.3). **Death rate** per 1,000 population (2006): 7.5 (world avg. 8.6). **Natural increase rate** per 1,000 population (2006): 16.0 (world avg. 11.7). **Total fertility rate** (avg. births per childbearing woman; 2005): 2.78. **Life expectancy** at birth (2005): male 63.6 years; female 65.2 years.

Social indicators

Educational attainment (2001). Percentage of population ages 25 and over having: no formal schooling 48.1%; incomplete primary education 9.0%; complete primary 22.1%; secondary 13.7%; higher 7.1%. **Quality of working life.** Average workweek (2006) 50 hours. Rate of fatal injuries per 100,000 employees (2004) 28. Agricultural workers in servitude to creditors (early 1990s) 10–20%. Children ages 5–14 working as child laborers (2003) 35,000,000 (14% of age group). Percentage of population living below the poverty line (2004–05) 21.7%. **Access to services** (2001). Percentage of total (urban, rural) households having access to: electricity for lighting purposes (2003) 61.5% (90.8%, 51.6%); kerosene for lighting purposes 36.9% (8.3%, 46.6%); water closets 18.0% (46.1%, 7.1%); pit latrines 11.5% (14.6%, 10.3%); no latrines 63.6% (26.3%, 78.1%); closed drainage for wastewater 12.5% (34.5%, 3.9%); open drainage for wastewater 33.9% (43.4%, 30.3%); no drainage for wastewater 53.6% (22.1%, 65.8%). Type of fuel used for cooking in households (2003): firewood 61.1% (20.0%, 74.9%); liquefied petroleum gas 20.8% (55.4%, 9.1%); cow dung 7.4%

(1.8%, 9.3%); kerosene 4.7% (13.0%, 1.9%); coal 1.5% (3.3%, 0.9%); other 4.6% (6.6%, 3.9%). Source of drinking water: hand pump or tube well 41.3% (21.3%, 48.9%); piped water 36.7% (68.7%, 24.3%); well 18.2% (7.7%, 22.2%); river, canal, spring, public tank, pond, or lake 2.7% (0.7%, 3.5%). **Social participation.** Registered trade unions (2004) 74,403. **Social deviance** (2003). Offense rate per 100,000 population for: murder 3.1; rape 1.5; dacoity (gang robbery) 0.5; theft 23.0; riots 5.4. Rate of suicide per 100,000 population (2002) 11.2. **Material well-being** (2001). Total (urban, rural) households possessing: television receivers 31.6% (64.3%, 18.9%); telephones 9.1% (23.0%, 3.8%); scooters, motorcycles, or mopeds 11.7% (24.7%, 6.7%); cars, jeeps, or vans 2.5% (5.6%, 1.3%). Households availing banking services 35.5% (49.5%, 30.1%).

National economy

Gross national income (2007): US$1,069,427,-000,000 (US$950 per capita). **Budget** (2004). *Revenue:* Rs 3,941,400,000,000 (tax revenue 80.6%, of which taxes on income and profits 35.4%, excise taxes 27.7%; nontax revenue 18.1%). *Expenditures:* Rs 5,104,800,000,000 (general public services 59.3%, of which public debt payments 24.6%; economic affairs 17.7%; defense 15.1%; housing 4.2%; education 2.2%). **Public debt** (external, outstanding; 2006): US$59,570,000,000. **Production** (in '000 metric tons except as noted). *Agriculture and fishing* (2007): sugarcane 355,520, cereals 252,121 (of which rice 141,134, wheat 74,890, corn [maize] 16,780, millet 10,610, sorghum 7,402), fruits 51,142 (of which bananas 21,766, mangoes 13,501, oranges 3,900, lemons and limes 2,060, apples 2,001, pineapples 1,308), oilseeds 45,321 (of which soybeans 9,433, rapeseed 7,097, peanuts [groundnuts] 6,600, sunflower seeds 1,420, castor beans 830, sesame 670), potatoes 26,280, pulses 14,500 (of which chickpeas 5,970, dry beans 3,000, pigeon peas 2,510), seed cotton 9,480, coconuts 9,400, eggplants 8,450, cauliflower 5,014, okra 3,497, jute 2,140, anise, badian, fennel, and coriander 1,100, tea 949, natural rubber 803, garlic 645, tobacco 555, betel 520, ginger 420; livestock (number of live animals) 177,840,000 cattle, 125,456,000 goats, 98,700,000 water buffalo, 64,269,000 sheep, 14,000,000 pigs, 632,000 camels; fisheries production (2006) 6,979 (from aquaculture 45%). *Mining and quarrying* (2005): mica 1.6 (world rank: 1); iron ore (metal content) 90,000 (world rank: 4); bauxite 11,957; chromium 3,255; barite 1,000; manganese (metal content) 640; zinc (metal content) 200; lead (metal content) 42.0; copper (metal content) 26.9; gold 3,200 kg; gem diamonds 16,000 carats. *Manufacturing* (value added in US$'000,000; 2003): refined petroleum products 5,955; iron and steel 5,834; paints, soaps, varnishes, drugs, and medicines 4,891; industrial chemicals 4,105; food products 3,467; textiles 3,432; motor vehicles and parts 3,193; nonelectrical machinery and apparatus 2,333; cements, bricks, and tiles 2,029. **Energy production** *(consumption):* electricity (kW-hr; 2007) 695,196,000,000 ([2005] 699,048,000,000); coal (metric tons; 2007) 445,448,000 ([2005] 432,271,000); lignite (metric

---

1 metric ton = about 1.1 short tons;   1 kilometer = 0.6 mi (statute);   1 metric ton-km cargo = about 0.68 short ton-mi cargo;   c.i.f.: cost, insurance, and freight;   f.o.b.: free on board

tons; 2007) 33,292,000 ([2005] 29,555,000); crude petroleum (barrels; 2007) 253,500,000 ([2005] 968,200,000); petroleum products (metric tons; 2005-06) 121,940,000 ([2005] 88,854,000); natural gas (cu m; 2007) 32,229,000,000 ([2005] 27,226,000,000). **Population economically active** (2001): total 402,234,724; activity rate of total population 39.1% (participation rates: ages 15-69, 60.2%; female 31.6%; unemployed [2005] 9.9%). **Service enterprises** (net value added in Rs '000,000,000; 1998-99): wholesale and retail trade 1,562; finance, real estate, and insurance 1,310; transport and storage 804; community, social, and personal services 763; construction 545. **Selected balance of payments data.** Receipts from (US$'000,000): tourism (2006) 8,934; remittances (2007) 27,000; foreign direct investment (FDI) (2004-06 avg.) 9,776; official development assistance (2006) 1,379. Disbursements for (US$'000,-000): tourism (2006) 7,352; remittances (2007) 1,580; FDI (2004-06 avg.) 4,783.

Foreign trade

Imports (2006): US$185,385,000,000 (crude petroleum 25.4%; nonelectrical machinery and apparatus 8.3%; gold 7.8%; organic and inorganic chemicals 4.2%; diamonds 3.9%; telecommunications equipment and parts 3.8%; refined petroleum products 3.5%; iron and steel 3.4%; copper ore and concentrates 2.8%; aircraft 2.8%). *Major import sources:* China 9.4%; Saudi Arabia 7.2%; US 6.3%; Switzerland 4.9%; UAE 4.7%; Iran 4.1%; Germany 4.1%; Nigeria 3.8%; Australia 3.8%; Kuwait 3.2%. **Exports** (2006): US$126,125,000,000 (refined petroleum products 14.5%; diamonds 8.0%; food products 7.6%; wearing apparel and accessories 7.5%; machinery and apparatus 7.5%; textile yarn, fabrics, and made-up articles 7.1%; iron and steel 5.6%; organic chemicals 4.3%; gold and silver jewelry 3.9%). *Major export destinations:* US 15.0%; UAE 9.5%; China 6.6%; Singapore 4.8%; UK 4.4%; Hong Kong 3.7%; Germany 3.1%; Italy 2.8%; Belgium 2.7%; Japan 2.3%.

Transport and communications

Transport. *Railroads* (2005-06): route length 63,000 km; passenger-km 616,000,000,000; metric ton-km cargo 440,000,000,000. *Roads* (2002): total length 3,319,644 km (paved 46%). *Vehicles* (2003): passenger cars 8,619,000; trucks and buses 4,215,000. *Air transport* (2006): passenger-km 55,524,000,000; metric ton-km .cargo 763,-536,000. **Communications,** in total units (units per 1,000 persons). Telephone landlines (2007): 39,420,000 (34); cellular telephone subscribers (2007): 233,620,000 (200); personal computers (2005): 17,000,000 (15); total Internet users (2007): 81,000,000 (69); broadband Internet subscribers (2007): 3,130,000 (2.8).

Education and health

Literacy (2003): percentage of total population ages 15 and over literate 59.5%; males literate 70.2%; females literate 48.3%. **Health:** physicians (2005) 767,500 (1 per 1,425 persons); hospital beds (2003) 963,720 (1 per 1,111 persons); infant mortality rate per 1,000 live births (2006) 57.0; undernourished population (2002-04) 209,500,000 (20%

of total population based on the consumption of a minimum daily requirement of 1,820 calories).

Military

Total active duty personnel (2007): 1,288,000 (army 85.4%, navy 4.3%, air force 10.3%); personnel in paramilitary forces 1,300,586. **Military expenditure as percentage of GDP** (2005): 2.8%; per capita expenditure US$20.

Background

Agriculture in India dates back to at least the 7th millennium BC, and an urban civilization, that of the Indus valley, was established by 2600 BC. Buddhism and Jainism arose in the 6th century BC in reaction to the caste-based society created by the Vedic religion and its successor, Hinduism. Muslim invasions began c. AD 1000, establishing the long-lived Delhi sultanate in 1206 and the Mughal dynasty in 1526. Vasco da Gama's voyage to India in 1498 initiated several centuries of commercial rivalry among the Portuguese, Dutch, English, and French. British conquests in the 18th and 19th centuries led to the rule of the British East India Co., and direct administration by the British Empire began in 1858. After Mohandas K. Gandhi helped end British rule in 1947, Jawaharlal Nehru became India's first prime minister, and he, Indira Gandhi (his daughter), and Rajiv Gandhi (his grandson) guided the nation's destiny for all but a few years until 1989. The subcontinent was partitioned into two countries—India, with a Hindu majority, and Pakistan, with a Muslim majority—in 1947. A later clash with Pakistan resulted in the creation of Bangladesh in 1971. In the 1980s and '90s, Sikhs sought to establish an independent state in Punjab, and ethnic and religious conflicts took place in other parts of the country as well. In particular, the Kashmir region in the northwest has been a source of violent conflict.

Recent Developments

In late November 2008 India was rocked by terrorist attacks in Mumbai (Bombay). Gunmen believed to be connected to Lashkar-e-Taiba, a Pakistan-based terrorist organization, attacked 10 locations across the city with grenades and automatic weapons, taking hostages in several buildings, including two luxury hotels. When the police finally gained control three days later, at least 174 people had been killed and more than 300 wounded.

Securing an unconditional waiver from the Nuclear Suppliers Group for the resumption of commerce in civil nuclear energy became the most important foreign-policy objective for India in 2008. The measure was approved in September, shortly before Prime Minister Manmohan Singh's visit to the US, where he met with US Pres. George W. Bush. A bilateral agreement with the US was signed and ratified in October, opening the doors for increased trade in nuclear and high-technology areas. India signed a bilateral agreement in September with France and a civil nuclear cooperation agreement in early December with Russia. In October India also elevated its international status by launching an unmanned spacecraft, Chandrayaan-1, that would orbit the Moon and send a probe to its surface.

Internet resources: <http://mospi.nic.in>.

Indonesia

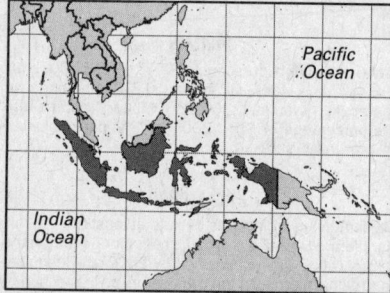

Official name: Republik Indonesia (Republic of Indonesia). **Form of government:** multiparty republic with two legislative houses (Regional Representatives Council [128]; House of Representatives [560]). **Head of state and government:** President Susilo Bambang Yudhoyono (from 2004). **Capital:** Jakarta. **Official language:** Indonesian (Bahasa Indonesia). **Official religion:** monotheism. **Monetary unit:** 1 Indonesian rupiah (Rp) = 100 sen; valuation (1 Jul 2009) US$1 = Rp 10,101.00.

Demography

Area: 718,289 sq mi, 1,860,360 sq km. **Population** (2008): 234,342,000. **Density** (2008): persons per sq mi 326.3, persons per sq km 126.0. **Urban** (2003): 45.6%. **Sex distribution** (2006): male 50.01%; female 49.99%. **Age breakdown** (2006): under 15, 29.1%; 15–29, 27.0%; 30–44, 22.2%; 45–59, 13.5%; 60–74, 6.7%; 75–84, 1.4%; 85 and over, 0.1%. **Ethnic composition** (2000): Javanese 36.4%; Sundanese 13.7%; Malay 9.4%; Madurese 7.2%; Han Chinese 4.0%; Minangkabau 3.6%; other 25.7%. **Religious affiliation** (2005): Muslim (excluding syncretists) 55.8%; Neoreligionists (syncretists) 21.2%; Christian 13.2%; Hindu 3.2%; traditional beliefs 2.6%; nonreligious 1.8%; other 2.2%. **Major municipalities** (2005): Jakarta 8,603,349; Surabaya 2,611,506; Bandung 2,288,570; Medan 2,029,797; Bekasi 1,940,308; Tangerang 1,451,595; Semarang 1,352,869; Depok 1,339,263; Palembang 1,323,169; Makasar 1,168,258. **Location:** archipelago in southeastern Asia, bordering Malaysia, the Pacific Ocean, Papua New Guinea, the Indian Ocean, and East Timor.

Vital statistics

Birth rate per 1,000 population (2006): 20.1 (world avg. 20.3). **Death rate** per 1,000 population (2006): 6.3 (world avg. 8.6). **Total fertility rate** (avg. births per childbearing woman; 2006): 2.41. **Life expectancy** at birth (2006): male 67.4 years; female 72.4 years.

National economy

Budget (2005). *Revenue:* Rp 495,444,000,000,000 (tax revenue 70.0%, of which income tax 35.4%, VAT 20.4%; nontax revenue 30.0%, of which revenue from petroleum 14.7%). *Expenditures:* Rp 509,419,000,-000,000 (current expenditures 58.5%; regional expenditures 29.5%; developmental expenditures 12.0%). **Public debt** (external, outstanding; December 2007): US$80,609,000,000. **Population economically active** (2006): total 106,388,935; activity rate of total population 46.5% (participation rates: ages 16 and over, 66.2%; unemployed 10.3%). **Production** (metric tons except as noted). *Agriculture and fishing* (2007): rice 57,048,558, sugarcane 25,200,-000, cassava 19,610,071, coconuts 17,000,000, corn (maize) 12,381,561, natural rubber 2,540,000, cloves 84,000, cinnamon 60,000; livestock (number of live animals) 14,873,516 goats, 11,365,873 cattle, 9,859,667 sheep; fisheries production (2006) 6,051,979 (from aquaculture 21%); aquatic plants production 920,466 (from aquaculture 99%). *Mining and quarrying* (2006): bauxite 1,502,000; copper (metal content) 793,000; nickel (metal content) 140,000; silver 327,557 kg; gold 164,400 kg. *Manufacturing* (value added in US$'000,000; 2003): textiles, wearing apparel, and footwear 5,011; tobacco products 4,584; transportation equipment 4,189; food products 3,970; chemical products 3,464; paper products 1,774. *Energy production (consumption):* electricity (kW-hr; 2005) 127,362,000,000 (127,362,000,000); coal (metric tons; 2007) 174,800,000 ([2005] 41,300,000); crude petroleum (barrels; 2007) 357,500,000 ([2005] 424,100,000); petroleum products (metric tons; 2005) 44,196,000 (58,025,000); natural gas (cu m; 2007) 85,200,-000,000 (37,700,000,000). **Gross national income** (2007): US$373,125,000,000 (US$1,650 per capita). **Selected balance of payments data.** Receipts from (US$'000,000): tourism (2006) 4,448; remittances (2007) 6,143; foreign direct investment (FDI) (2004–06 avg.) 5,263; official development assistance (2006) 1,404. Disbursements for (US$'000,000): tourism (2006) 3,600; remittances (2007) 2,003; FDI (2004–06 avg.) 3,297.

Foreign trade

Imports (2005–06; c.i.f.): US$65,712,154,000 (crude petroleum and natural gas 23.7%; machinery and apparatus 16.8%; chemical products 10.4%; base metals 8.8%; transportation equipment 6.5%). *Major import sources* (2006): Singapore 16.4%; China 10.9%; Japan 9.0%; US 6.7%; Saudi Arabia 5.5%. **Exports** (2005–06; f.o.b.): US$78,-740,892,000 (crude petroleum and natural gas 27.4%; rubber products 15.7%; machinery and apparatus 14.5%; textiles 10.8%; base metals 7.0%). *Major export destinations* (2006): Japan 21.6%; US 11.2%; Singapore 8.9%; China 8.3%; South Korea 7.6%.

Transport and communications

Transport. *Railroads* (2004): route length 6,458 km; passenger-km 15,077,000,000; metric ton-km cargo 4,698,000,000. *Roads* (2005): length 391,009 km (paved 55%). *Vehicles* (2005): passenger cars 5,494,034; trucks and buses 4,105,746. *Air transport* (2005): passenger-km 22,986,000,000; metric ton-km cargo (2004) 248,000,000. **Communications,** in total units (units per 1,000 persons). Telephone landlines (2007): 17,828,000 (77); cellular telephone subscribers (2007): 81,835,000 (353);

---

1 metric ton = about 1.1 short tons; 1 kilometer = 0.6 mi (statute); 1 metric ton-km cargo = about 0.68 short ton-mi cargo; c.i.f.: cost, insurance, and freight; f.o.b.: free on board

personal computers (2005): 3,285,000 (15); total Internet users (2007): 13,000,000 (56); broadband Internet subscribers (2007): 257,000 (1.1).

Education and health

Educational attainment (2002–03). Percentage of population ages 15–64 having: no schooling or incomplete primary education 19.3%; primary and some secondary 57.2%; complete secondary 19.3%; higher 4.2%. **Literacy** (2003): percentage of total population ages 15 and over literate 88.4%; males literate 92.8%; females literate 84.1%. **Health:** physicians (2003) 29,499 (1 per 7,368 persons); hospital beds (2001) 124,834 (1 per 1,697 persons); infant mortality rate per 1,000 live births (2006) 33.3; undernourished population (2002–04) 13,800,000 (6% of total population based on the consumption of a minimum daily requirement of 1,840 calories).

Military

Total active duty personnel (2007): 302,000 (army 77.2%, navy 14.9%, air force 7.9%). **Military expenditure as percentage of GDP** (2005): 1.2%; per capita expenditure US$38.

Background

Proto-Malay peoples migrated to Indonesia from mainland Asia before 1000 BC. Commercial relations were established with China in about the 5th century AD, and Hindu and Buddhist cultural influences from India began to take hold. Arab traders brought Islam to the islands in the 13th century; the religion took hold throughout the islands, except for Bali, which retained its Hindu religion and culture. European influence began in the 16th century, and the Dutch ruled Indonesia from the late 17th century until 1942, when the Japanese invaded. Independence leader Sukarno declared Indonesia's sovereignty in 1945, which the Dutch granted, with nominal union to The Netherlands, in 1949; Indonesia dissolved this union in 1954. The suppression of an alleged coup attempt in 1965 resulted in the deaths of more than 300,000 people the government claimed to be communists, and by 1968 Gen. Suharto had taken power. His government forcibly incorporated East Timor into Indonesia in 1975–76, with much loss of life; East Timor became independent in 2002. In the 1990s the country was beset by political, economic, and environmental problems, and Suharto was deposed in 1998.

Recent Developments

The falling popularity in 2008 of Indonesian Pres. Susilo Bambang Yudhoyono (commonly known as SBY) was attributed in part to the government's decision to reduce fuel subsidies by an average of almost 30%. The rising cost of these subsidies—some US$19 billion annually, or about one-fifth of total budget outlays—had become unsustainable, especially as the cost of crude oil imports spiraled upward. Though welcomed by most economists, the fuel price rises sparked public protests, some of them violent. The government sought to offset the impact of price rises on the poor by introducing a direct payment of 100,000 rupiah (about US$10) per month to low-income households. Initially criticized as financially inadequate and prone to corruption, the direct pay-

ments eventually won cautious approval from both grassroots communities and welfare groups. Despite the backlash on fuel prices, SBY's economic record remained good. The overall economy continued to grow more strongly than most others in the region, recording an annual increase of 6.4%, though inflation was relatively high, at 12.2%. Unemployment levels fell slightly, from 9.75% in early 2007 to 8.39% in mid-2008.

Internet resources: <www.bps.go.id>.

Iran

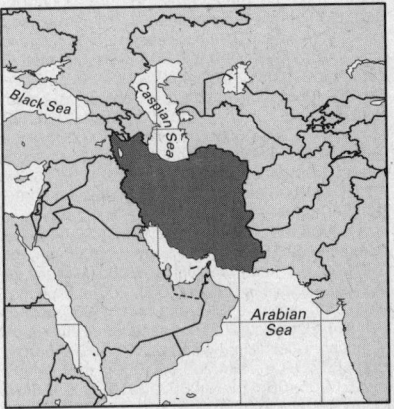

Official name: Jomhuri-ye Eslami-ye Iran (Islamic Republic of Iran). **Form of government:** unitary Islamic republic with one legislative house (Islamic Consultative Assembly [290]). **Supreme political/religious authority:** *Rahbar* (Spiritual Leader) Ayatollah Sayyed Ali Khamenei (from 1989). **Head of state and government:** President Mahmoud Ahmadinejad (from 2005). **Capital:** Tehran. **Official language:** Farsi (Persian). **Official religion:** Islam. **Monetary unit:** 1 rial (Rls) = 100 dinars; valuation (1 Jul 2009) US$1 = Rls 9,933.00.

Demography

Area (land area only): 628,874 sq mi, 1,628,777 sq km. **Population** (2008): 72,269,000. **Density** (2008): persons per sq mi 113.6, persons per sq km 43.8. **Urban** (2006): 69.4%. **Sex distribution** (2006–07): male 50.88%; female 49.12%. **Age breakdown** (2006–07): under 15, 25.1%; 15–29, 35.4%; 30–44, 20.6%; 45–59, 11.6%; 60–74, 5.4%; 75–84, 1.6%; 85 and over, 0.3%. **Ethnic composition** (2000): Persian 34.9%; Azerbaijani 15.9%; Kurdish 13.0%; Luri 7.2%; Gilaki 5.1%; Mazandarani 5.1%; Afghan 2.8%; Arab 2.5%; other 13.5%. **Religious affiliation** (2005): Muslim 98.2% (Shiʿi 86.1%, Sunni 10.1%, other 2.0%); Bahaʾi 0.5%; Christian 0.4%; Zoroastrian 0.1%; other 0.8%. **Major cities** (2007): Tehran 7,873,000; Mashhad 2,469,000; Esfahan 1,628,000; Karaj 1,423,000; Tabriz 1,240,000. **Location:** the Middle East, bordering the Caspian Sea, Turkmenistan, Afghanistan, Pakistan, the Gulf of Oman, the Persian Gulf, Iraq, Turkey, Azerbaijan, and Armenia.

Vital statistics

Birth rate per 1,000 population (2006–07): 17.8 (world avg. 20.3). **Death rate** per 1,000 population (2006–07): 5.8 (world avg. 8.6). **Total fertility rate** (avg. births per childbearing woman; 2005): 1.82. **Life expectancy** at birth (2005): male 68.6 years; female 71.4 years.

National economy

Budget (2005–06). *Revenue:* Rls 503,765,000,-000,000 (petroleum and natural gas revenue 71.8%; taxes 20.4%, of which corporate taxes 10.4%, import duties 7.1%). *Expenditures:* Rls 484,332,000,-000,000 (current expenditures 68.3%; development expenditures 24.1%). **Public debt** (external, outstanding; 2006): US$11,090,000,000. **Gross national income** (2007): US$246,544,000,000 (US$3,470 per capita). **Production** (metric tons except as noted). *Agriculture and fishing* (2007): wheat 15,000,000, sugarcane 5,700,000, sugar beets 5,300,000, dates 1,000,000; livestock (number of live animals) 52,220,000 sheep, 25,860,000 goats, 9,776,000 cattle, 146,000 camels; fisheries production (2006) 575,560 (from aquaculture 23%). *Mining and quarrying* (2004–05): iron ore (metal content) 9,000,000; chromite 223,563; copper ore (metal content) 190,000; zinc (metal content) 125,000. *Manufacturing* (value added in US$'000,000; 2005): base metals 3,032; motor vehicles and parts 2,850; refined petroleum products 2,210. *Energy production (consumption):* electricity (kW-hr; 2007) 189,356,000,-000 ([2005–06] 134,238,000,000); coal (metric tons; 2005–06) 1,898,000 ([2005] 1,810,000); crude petroleum (barrels; 2007) 1,345,100,000 ([2005] 519,600,000); petroleum products (metric tons; 2005) 76,973,000 (68,951,000); natural gas (cu m; 2006–07) 143,200,000,000 (121,200,000,-000). **Population economically active** (2006–07): total 23,469,000; activity rate of total population 33.3% (participation rates: ages 10 and over, 39.4%; female 15.5%; unemployed 12.7%). **Selected balance of payments data.** Receipts from (US$'000,-000): tourism (2006) 1,194; remittances (2007) 1,115; foreign direct investment (FDI) (2004–06 avg.) 514; official development assistance (2006) 121. Disbursements for (US$'000,000): tourism (2006) 4,597; FDI (2004–06 avg.) 302.

Foreign trade

Imports (2005–06; c.i.f.): US$40,969,000,000 (nonelectrical machinery 23.5%; base metals 13.8%; road vehicles 13.0%; chemical products 10.7%). *Major import sources:* UAE 19.7%; Germany 13.1%; France 6.8%; Italy 6.0%; China 5.5%. **Exports** (2005–06; f.o.b.): US$60,013,000,000 (crude petroleum 73.1%; chemical products 5.2%; fruits and nuts 2.2%, of which pistachios 1.4%; wool carpets 0.8%). *Major export destinations:* Japan 16.9%; China 11.9%; Turkey 5.8%; Italy 5.7%; South Korea 5.7%.

Transport and communications

Transport. *Railroads* (2006–07): route length 8,565 km; passenger-km 12,549,000,000; metric ton-km cargo 20,542,000,000. *Roads* (2006–07): length 72,611 km (paved 92%). *Vehicles* (2006–07): passenger cars 920,136; trucks and buses 184,629. *Air transport* (Iran Air only; 2005): passenger-km 7,347,795,000; metric ton-km cargo 83,396,000. **Communications,** in total units (units per 1,000 persons). Telephone landlines (2007): 23,835,000 (335); cellular telephone subscribers (2007): 29,770,000 (418); personal computers (2005): 8,694,000 (125); total Internet users (2007): 23,000,000 (323); broadband Internet subscribers (2006): 465,000 (6.7).

Education and health

Literacy (2006–07): percentage of total population ages 6 and over literate 84.6%; males literate 88.7%; females literate 80.3%. **Health** (2006–07): physicians (public sector only) 29,937 (1 per 2,355 persons); hospital beds 116,474 (1 per 605 persons); infant mortality rate per 1,000 live births (2005) 41.6; undernourished population (2002–04) 2,500,000 (4% of total population based on the consumption of a minimum daily requirement of 1,850 calories).

Military

Total active duty personnel (2007): 545,000 (revolutionary guard corps 22.9%, army 64.2%, navy 3.3%, air force 9.6%). **Military expenditure as percentage of GDP** (2005): 5.8%; per capita expenditure US$130.

Background

Habitation in Iran dates to c. 100,000 BC, but recorded history began with the Elamites c. 3000 BC. The Medes flourished from c. 728 BC but were overthrown (550 BC) by the Persians, who were in turn conquered by Alexander the Great in the 4th century BC. The Parthians created a Greek-speaking empire that lasted from 247 BC to AD 226, when control passed to the Sasanians. Arab Muslims conquered them in 640 and ruled Iran for 850 years. In 1502 the Safavids established a dynasty that lasted until 1736. The Qajars ruled from 1779, but in the 19th century the country was controlled economically by the Russian and British empires. Reza Khan seized power in a coup (1921). His son Mohammad Reza Shah Pahlavi alienated religious leaders with a program of modernization and Westernization and was overthrown in 1979; Shi'ite cleric Ruhollah Khomeini then set up a fundamentalist Islamic republic, and Western influence was suppressed. The destructive Iran-Iraq War of the 1980s ended in a stalemate. Among the most contentious of Iran's foreign policy issues at the beginning of the 21st century was the ongoing question of the development of its nuclear capabilities. Iran insisted that its nuclear pursuits were intended for peaceful purposes, but the international community, expressing deep suspicion that Iran's activities included the development of nuclear weapons, advocated efforts to suspend them.

Recent Developments

Pres. Mahmoud Ahmadinejad's alleged continuing preoccupation with obtaining nuclear weaponry was opposed by the US and the EU, which continued in 2008 to attempt to deny Iran the capability to manu-

---

1 metric ton = about 1.1 short tons;   1 kilometer = 0.6 mi (statute);   1 metric ton-km cargo = about 0.68 short ton-mi cargo;   c.i.f.: cost, insurance, and freight;   f.o.b.: free on board

facture nuclear warheads. In March the UN Security Council passed the third in a series of minor sanctions against Iran. In dialogue with Security Council members and Germany, Iran was given more incentives to dissuade it from enriching uranium; the talks, however, only gave Iran time to press ahead. After Iran tested long-range missiles in July, the Security Council warned Tehran to comply with its resolution or face further sanctions, and at the end of September the council imposed a freeze on Iran's financial assets. Meanwhile, the International Atomic Energy Agency reported that month that Iran had increased the number of uranium-enrichment centrifuges and was poised to install thousands more. In June 2009, a presidential election was held, and Ahmadinejad was declared the winner under a cloud of allegations of irregularities and cheating. Thousands protested the results—hundreds were arrested and as many as 69 killed in clashes with security forces.

Internet resources: <www.cbi.ir/default_en.aspx>.

Iraq

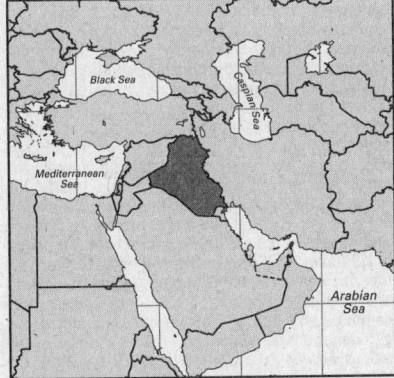

Official name: Al-Jumhuriyah al-ʻIraqiyah (Republic of Iraq). **Form of government:** multiparty republic with one legislative house (Council of Representatives [275]). **Head of state:** President Jalal Talabani (from 2005). **Head of government:** Prime Minister Nuri al-Maliki (from 2006). **Capital:** Baghdad. **Official languages:** Arabic; Kurdish. **Official religion:** Islam. **Monetary unit:** 1 Iraqi dinar (ID) = 1,000 fils; valuation (1 Jul 2009) US$1 = ID 1,167.35.

Demography

Area: 167,618 sq mi, 434,128 sq km. **Population** (2008): 29,492,000 (including about 1,400,000 Iraqi refugees in Syria, 500,000 Iraqi refugees in Jordan, and 400,000 elsewhere; nearly 2.8 million Iraqis were internally displaced in March 2008). **Density** (2008): persons per sq mi 175.9, persons per sq km 67.9. **Urban** (2007): 66.5%. **Sex distribution** (2007): male 50.35%; female 49.65%. **Age breakdown** (2007): under 15, 43.1%; 15–29, 27.9%; 30–44, 16.4%; 45–59, 8.2%; 60–74, 3.3%; 75 and over, 1.0%. **Ethnic composition** (2000): Arab 64.7%; Kurdish 23.0%; Azerbaijani 5.6%; Turkmen 1.2%; Persian 1.1%; other 4.4%. **Religious affiliation** (2000):

Shiʻi Muslim 62.0%; Sunni Muslim 34.0%; Christian (primarily Chaldean rite and Syrian rite Catholic and Nestorian) 3.2%; other (primarily Yazidi syncretist) 0.8%. **Major urban agglomerations** (2007): Baghdad 5,054,000; Mosul 1,316,000; Irbil 926,000; Al-Basrah 870,000; Karkuk (2003) 750,000. **Location:** the Middle East, bordering Turkey, Iran, the Persian Gulf, Kuwait, Saudi Arabia, Jordan, and Syria.

Vital statistics

Birth rate per 1,000 population (2005): 32.5 (world avg. 20.3). **Death rate** per 1,000 population (2005): 5.5 (world avg. 8.6). **Natural increase rate** per 1,000 population (2005): 27.0 (world avg. 11.7). **Total fertility rate** (avg. births per childbearing woman; 2005): 4.28. **Life expectancy** at birth (2005): male 67.5 years; female 70.0 years.

National economy

Budget (2006). *Revenue:* ID 61,650,000,000,000 (petroleum revenue 79.9%; grants 20.1%). *Expenditures:* ID 53,480,000,000,000 (current expenditures 79.8%; development expenditures 20.2%). **Public debt** (external, outstanding; December 2007): US$100,900,000,000. **Production** (metric tons except as noted). *Agriculture and fishing* (2007): wheat 1,700,000, tomatoes 830,000, potatoes 740,000, dates 290,000; livestock (number of live animals) 6,200,000 sheep, 1,500,000 cattle; fisheries production (2006) 74,126 (from aquaculture 20%). *Mining and quarrying* (2005): phosphate rock 1,000. *Manufacturing* (value added in US$'000,000; 1995): refined petroleum products 143; bricks, tiles, and cement 103; food products 59. *Energy production (consumption):* electricity (kW-hr; 2005) 34,000,000,000 (35,388,000,000); crude petroleum (barrels; 2007) 783,000,000 ([2005] 171,100,000); petroleum products (metric tons; 2005) 19,099,000 (21,960,000); natural gas (cu m; 2006) 1,800,000,000 ([2005] 2,580,000,000). **Population economically active** (1997): total 4,757,000; activity rate of total population 24.8% (participation rates: ages 15–59, 42.9%; female 10.5%; unemployed [2004] 28%). **Gross national income** (2006): US$55,726,000,000 (US$1,955 per capita). **Selected balance of payments data.** Receipts from (US$'000,000): tourism (2002) 45; foreign direct investment (FDI) (2004–06 avg.) 362; official development assistance (2006) 8,661. Disbursements for (US$'000,000): tourism (2002) 26; FDI (2001–05 avg.) negligible.

Foreign trade

Imports (2007): US$18,289,000,000 (private sector imports 55.7%, of which capital goods 41.8%, consumer goods 13.9%; government imports 44.3%, of which refined petroleum products 7.9%). *Major import sources* (2006): Syria 29.9%; Turkey 19.3%; US 10.8%; Jordan 4.9%; China 4.6%. **Exports** (2007): US$39,590,000,000 (crude petroleum 95.4%; refined petroleum products 4.0%). *Major export destinations* (2006): US 40.0%; Italy 13.7%; Spain 5.6%; Canada 5.5%; France 4.7%.

Transport and communications

Transport. *Railroads* (2006): route length 580 km. *Roads* (2002): total length 45,550 km (paved 84%). *Vehicles* (2001): passenger cars 754,066; trucks and buses 372,241. *Air transport:* Iraqi Airways resumed international flights in September 2004 after 14 years of being grounded by war and sanctions. **Communications,** in total units (units per 1,000 persons). Telephone landlines (2004): 1,034,000 (40); cellular telephone subscribers (2007): 14,021,000 (484); personal computers (2002): 212,000 (8.3); total Internet users (2007): 54,000 (1.9).

Education and health

Educational attainment (2004). Percentage of population ages 25 and over having: no formal schooling 28%; incomplete primary education 12%; primary 36%; secondary 9%; higher 15%. **Literacy** (2003): percentage of total population ages 15 and over literate 40.4%; males literate 55.9%; females literate 24.4%. **Health** (2003): physicians 16,594 (1 per 1,587 persons); hospital beds 34,505 (1 per 763 persons); infant mortality rate per 1,000 live births (2005) 50.3.

Military

Total active duty personnel (2008): 444,500 (army 40.6%, army support 4.4%, navy 0.3%, air force 0.3%, ministry of interior/police 53.6%, special operations 0.8%); US forces (2008) 147,400; allied coalition forces (2007) 12,400.

Background

Called Mesopotamia in Classical times, the region gave rise to the world's earliest civilizations, including those of Sumer, Akkad, and Babylon. Conquered by Alexander the Great in 330 BC, the area later became a battleground between Romans and Parthians and then between Sasanians and Byzantines. Arab Muslims conquered it in the 7th century AD and ruled until the Mongols took over in 1258. The Ottomans took control in the 16th century and ruled until 1917. The British occupied the country during World War I and created the kingdom of Iraq in 1921. The British occupied Iraq again during World War II. A king was restored following the war, but a revolution ended the monarchy in 1958. Following a series of military coups, the socialist Ba'th Party, led by Saddam Hussein, took control and established totalitarian rule in 1968. The Iran-Iraq War of the 1980s and the Persian Gulf War (precipitated by the Iraqi invasion of Kuwait in 1990) brought heavy casualties and disrupted the economy. The 1990s were dominated by economic and political turmoil. In response to increasingly willful and autocratic behavior by Saddam and the contention that Iraq was in possession of weapons of mass destruction (none were ever found), on 19 Mar 2003 air attacks on Baghdad began, and soon afterward US and British ground forces invaded southern Iraq from Kuwait; within a month most of the country was under the control of coalition forces. Saddam was taken into custody in December. In July 2003 US authorities established an Iraqi Governing Council, and a new interim constitution was agreed upon in late February 2004. Almost immediately after the occupation began, however, various forms of Iraqi opposition arose, and resistance attacks grew in frequency and violence in the years that followed.

Recent Developments

Despite acts of violence, including kidnappings and suicide bombings, the security situation improved noticeably in Baghdad and elsewhere in Iraq in 2008. The decline in violence was due in part to the "surge" of US forces starting in 2007 and to the commitment of US-backed Sunni militias—the Awakening Councils—who in 2006 had turned against al-Qaeda. In October the Shi'ite-dominated Iraqi government, eager to assert its control, took command of the Sunni Awakening Councils from the US. A shift toward national reconciliation occurred when Iraq's largest Sunni bloc, the Iraqi National Accord (INA), ended a nearly yearlong boycott and in July rejoined the cabinet—the INA had left Prime Minister Nuri al-Maliki's government in 2007 at the height of violence between Sunni and Shi'ite Arabs. The Iraqi parliament in September passed a crucial election law organizing the important provincial elections later held in January 2009, except in Kirkuk and the three provinces in the Kurdish region. Passage of the law fulfilled a major benchmark requested by the US and marked an important advance in the political sphere. Although Iraq's long-awaited oil law was stalled in the parliament at year's end, Royal Dutch Shell concluded a natural-gas agreement with the state-run Southern Oil Co. in September and set up an office in Baghdad. It was the first major international oil and gas firm to return to Iraq since the nationalization of the Iraqi oil industry in 1972. Several Arab countries (including Kuwait and Syria) sent ambassadors to Iraq, signaling an Arab thaw toward Baghdad. During the year Iraq negotiated a status-of-forces security agreement that would decide the future of US forces in Iraq. The final accord, approved in November, called for US forces to leave Iraqi towns and villages by June 2009 and for a total withdrawal of US forces from Iraq by the end of 2011. Iraqi authorities were given the right to prosecute US soldiers and defense contractors in cases of serious crimes committed off duty and off bases. A broader strategic framework agreement covered future bilateral relations between the US and Iraq. In early 2009 the UK's campaign in Iraq officially ended with a ceremony handing control of the southern city of Basra over to American forces. Limited numbers of British forces were scheduled to remain in Iraq for the immediate future, however. Controversy arose in May 2009 when it was reported that official Iraqi government statistics put the number of Iraqi civilians killed since the March 2003 invasion at more than 110,600.

Internet resources: <www.cbi.iq/index2.htm>.

Ireland

Official name: Éire (Irish); Ireland (English). **Form of government:** unitary multiparty republic with two legislative houses (Senate [60]; House of Representatives [166]). **Chief of state:** President Mary McAleese (from 1997). **Head of government:** Prime Minister Brian Cowen (from 2008). **Capital:** Dublin. **Official languages:** Irish; English. **Official religion:** none. **Monetary unit:** 1 euro (€) = 100 cents; valuation (1 Jul 2009) US$1 = €0.71.

---

1 metric ton = about 1.1 short tons;   1 kilometer = 0.6 mi (statute);   1 metric ton-km cargo = about 0.68 short ton-mi cargo;   c.i.f.: cost, insurance, and freight;   f.o.b.: free on board

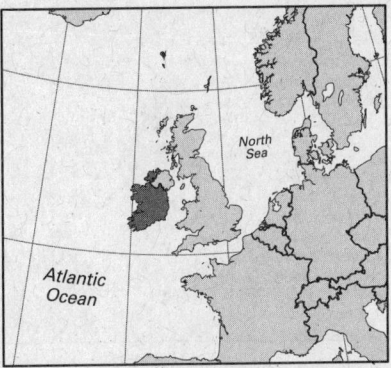

coal (metric tons; 2005) none (2,923,000); crude petroleum (barrels; 2005) none (24,200,000); petroleum products (metric tons; 2005) 3,115,000 (7,104,000); natural gas (cu m; 2007) 498,000,000 ([2005] 4,126,000,000); peat (metric tons; 2006) 4,300,000 (n.a.). **Population economically active** (2005): total 2,014,800 (in 2005 there were 243,000 foreigners in the labor force, of which 120,000 were from Poland); activity rate of total population 48.8% (participation rates: ages 15–64, 70.2%; female 42.3%; unemployed [March 2005–February 2006] 4.4%). **Selected balance of payments data.** Receipts from (US$'000,000): tourism (2006) 6,677; remittances (2007) 580; foreign direct disinvestment (2004–06 avg.) −9,643. Disbursements for (US$'000,000): tourism (2006) 6,862; remittances (2007) 2,554; foreign direct investment (2004–06 avg.) 17,913.

Demography

Area: 27,133 sq mi, 70,273 sq km. **Population** (2008): 4,467,000. **Density** (2008): persons per sq mi 164.6, persons per sq km 63.6. **Urban** (2005): 60.5%. **Sex distribution** (2006): male 50.03%; female 49.97%. **Age breakdown** (2006): under 15, 20.4%; 15–29, 23.7%; 30–44, 23.0%; 45–59, 17.6%; 60–74, 10.5%; 75–84, 3.7%; 85 and over, 1.1%. **Ethnic composition** (2000): Irish 95.0%; British 1.7%, of which English 1.4%; Ulster Irish 1.0%; US white 0.8%; other 1.5%. **Religious affiliation** (2006): Roman Catholic 86.8%; Church of Ireland (Anglican) 3.0%; other Christian 2.7%; nonreligious 4.4%; other 3.1%. **Major cities** (2006): Dublin 506,211 (urban agglomeration 1,186,159); Cork 119,418; Galway 72,414; Limerick 52,539; Waterford 45,748. **Location:** western Europe, bordering the UK (Northern Ireland), the Irish Sea, the Celtic Sea, and the North Atlantic Ocean.

Vital statistics

Birth rate per 1,000 population (2006): 15.2 (world avg. 20.3); within marriage 66.8%; outside of marriage 33.2%. **Death rate** per 1,000 population (2006): 6.5 (world avg. 8.6). **Total fertility rate** (avg. births per childbearing woman; 2006): 1.90. **Life expectancy** at birth (2005): male 75.0 years; female 80.3 years.

National economy

Budget (2005). *Revenue:* €39,849,000,000 (VAT 30.3%; income tax 28.3%; corporate taxes 13.5%). *Expenditures:* €33,496,000,000 (current expenditures 88.4%; capital expenditures 11.6%). **Total public debt** (December 2005): US$50,288,000,000. **Gross national income** (2007): US$210,168,000,000 (US$48,140 per capita). *Production* (metric tons except as noted). *Agriculture and fishing* (2007): barley 1,125,000, wheat 713,000, potatoes 399,000; livestock (number of live animals) 6,704,000 cattle, 5,522,000 sheep, 1,588,000 pigs; fisheries production (2006) 264,232 (from aquaculture 20%). *Mining and quarrying* (2007): zinc ore (metal content) 428,596; lead ore (metal content) 63,810. *Manufacturing* (gross value added in €'000,000; 2003): chemical products 15,988; food, beverages, and tobacco 9,111; electrical and optical equipment 6,677. *Energy production (consumption):* electricity (kW-hr; 2007) 27,888,000,000 ([2005] 28,072,000,000);

Foreign trade

Imports (2006; c.i.f.): €60,665,000,000 (machinery and apparatus 33.0%, of which office machines and parts 17.2%, electrical machinery 6.3%; chemical products 13.2%; transportation equipment 9.0%; mineral fuels 7.7%; food products 6.7%). *Major import sources* (2006): UK 31.9%; US 11.2%; Germany 8.2%; China 7.3%; The Netherlands 4.0%. **Exports** (2006; f.o.b.): €86,861,000,000 (organic chemicals 19.6%; medicinal and pharmaceutical products 16.4%; office machines and parts 16.2%; food products 8.1%). *Major export destinations* (2006): US 18.7%; UK 17.9%; Belgium 14.1%; Germany 8.1%; France 5.8%.

Transport and communications

Transport. *Railroads* (2004): route length 3,312 km; passenger-km 1,581,698,000; metric ton-km cargo 343,747,000. *Roads* (2003): length 96,602 km (paved 100%). *Vehicles* (2003): passenger cars 1,507,106; trucks and buses 251,130. *Air transport* (Aer Lingus only; 2007): passenger-km 14,807,000,000; metric ton-km cargo 75,400,000. **Communications,** in total units (units per 1,000 persons). Telephone landlines (2007): 2,112,000 (502); cellular telephone subscribers (2007): 4,940,000 (1,149); personal computers (2005): 2,198,000 (530); total Internet users (2007): 1,708,000 (397); broadband Internet subscribers (2007): 705,000 (163).

Education and health

Educational attainment (2005). Percentage of population ages 25–64 having: no formal schooling/unknown through primary education 19.3%; secondary 52.4%; some higher 10.4%; complete higher 17.9%. **Health:** physicians (2004) 11,141 (1 per 365 persons); hospital beds (public hospitals only; 2004) 12,377 (1 per 330 persons); infant mortality rate per 1,000 live births (2007) 2.9; undernourished population (2002–04) less than 2.5% of total population.

Military

Total active duty personnel (2007): 10,460 (army 81.3%, navy 10.5%, air force 8.2%). **Military expenditure as percentage of GDP** (2005): 0.6%; per capita expenditure US$275.

Background

Human settlement in Ireland began c. 6000 BC, and Celtic migration dates from c. 300 BC. St. Patrick is credited with Christianizing the country in the 5th century AD. Norse domination began in 795 and ended in 1014, when the Norse were defeated by Brian Boru. Gaelic Ireland's independence ended in 1171, when English King Henry II proclaimed himself overlord of the island. Beginning in the 16th century, Irish Catholic landowners fled religious persecution by the English and were replaced by English and Scottish Protestants. The United Kingdom of Great Britain and Ireland was established in 1801. The Great Famine of the 1840s led over two million people to emigrate and built momentum for Irish Home Rule. The Easter Rising (1916) was followed by civil war (1919–21) between the Catholic majority in southern Ireland, who favored complete independence, and the Protestant majority in the north, who preferred continued union with Britain. Southern Ireland was granted dominion status and became the Irish Free State in 1921, and in 1937 it adopted the name Éire and became a sovereign independent nation. Britain recognized the status of Ireland in 1949 but declared that cession of the northern six counties could not occur without the consent of the Parliament of Northern Ireland. In 1973 Ireland joined the European Economic Community (later the European Community); it is now a member of the EU. The late 20th century was dominated by sectarian hostilities. The Irish government played a pivotal role in winning public support for the Belfast Agreement (1998), which secured it a consultative role in the affairs of Northern Ireland and removed Ireland's constitutional claim to the entire island's territory.

Recent Developments

The end of a decade of growth in housing construction—the famed "Celtic Tiger"—had been flagged in 2007, but there were hopes of a "soft landing." When it came, however, the landing provided quite a shock, as the economy shrank 1.5% in 2008. In the first 11 months of 2008, average house prices fell by 8.3%, with a year-on-year drop of 9.6%. (The figures reflected only completed deals, taking no account of an excess of unsold stock.) The "live register" measure of unemployment increased from 181,449 in January 2008 to 291,363 in December, taking the annual rate to 8.6%; by April 2009 the total had reached 384,448. The rise in unemployment owed much to the drop in construction output, down by 25.2% in 2008. By the end of 2008, the government reported an €8 billion shortfall in tax receipts, due to the construction slump and slowing consumer spending.

Internet resources: <www.cso.ie>.

Israel

Official name: Medinat Yisrael (Hebrew); Dawlat Israil (Arabic) (State of Israel). **Form of government:** multiparty republic with one legislative house (Knesset [120]). **Chief of state:** President Shimon Peres (from 2007). **Head of government:** Prime Minister Benjamin Netanyahu (from 2009). **Capital:** Jerusalem is

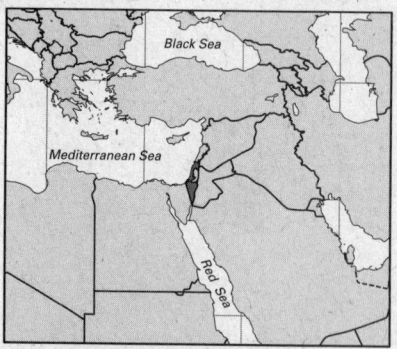

the proclaimed capital of Israel and the actual seat of government, but recognition of its status as capital by the international community has largely been withheld. **Official languages:** Hebrew; Arabic. **Official religion:** none. **Monetary unit:** 1 new (Israeli) sheqel (NIS) = 100 agorot; valuation (1 Jul 2009) US$1 = NIS 3.86.

Demography

Area: 8,357 sq mi, 21,643 sq km (excludes the West Bank and the Gaza Strip; includes the Golan Heights and East Jerusalem). **Population** (2008): 7,018,000 (excludes Jewish population of West Bank [290,-000]). **Density** (2008): persons per sq mi 839.8, persons per sq km 324.3. **Urban** (2004): 91.5%. **Sex distribution** (2005): male 49.39%; female 50.61%. **Age breakdown** (2005): under 15, 28.3%; 15–29, 24.2%; 30–44, 19.0%; 45–59, 15.6%; 60–74, 8.3%; 75–84, 3.6%; 85 and over, 1.0%. **Ethnic composition** (2005): Jewish 76.2%; Arab and other 23.8%. **Religious affiliation** (2005): Jewish 76.3%, of which "secular" 33%, "traditionally observant" 30%, Orthodox 7%, ultra-Orthodox 6%; Muslim 16.1%; Christian 2.1%; Druze 1.6%; other 3.9%. **Major cities** (2006): Jerusalem 729,100; Tel Aviv–Yafo 382,500 (metro area 3,040,400); Haifa 267,000 (metro area 996,000); Rishon LeZiyyon 221,500. **Location:** Middle East, bordering Lebanon, Syria, Jordan, the West Bank, Egypt, the Gaza Strip, and the Mediterranean Sea.

Vital statistics

Birth rate per 1,000 population (2007): 21.1 (world avg. 20.3). **Death rate** per 1,000 population (2007): 5.5 (world avg. 8.6). **Natural increase rate** per 1,000 population (2007): 15.6 (world avg. 11.7). **Total fertility rate** (avg. births per childbearing woman; 2007): 2.90. **Life expectancy** at birth (2006): male 78.5 years; female 82.2 years.

National economy

Budget (2005). *Revenue:* NIS 262,954,000,000 (tax revenue 67.3%; social contributions 15.5%; nontax revenue 13.2%; grants 4.0%). *Expenditures:* NIS 276,000,000,000 (social security and welfare 24.4%; defense 17.2%; education 15.2%; debt interest 11.2%; health 10.5%). **Public debt** (2004):

US$121,839,000,000. **Gross national income** (2007): US$157,065,000,000 (US$21,900 per capita). **Production** (metric tons except as noted). *Agriculture and fishing* (2007): potatoes 579,000, tomatoes 472,000, grapefruit and pomelos 245,000, dates 17,900; livestock (number of live animals) 455,000 sheep, 440,000 cattle; fisheries production (2006) 26,036 (from aquaculture 85%). *Mining and quarrying* (2006): phosphate rock 2,949,000; potash 2,220,000. *Manufacturing* (value added in US$'000,000; 2003): medical, measuring, and testing appliances 1,959; fabricated metal products 1,766; food products 1,661. *Energy production (consumption)*: electricity (kW-hr; 2005) 49,843,-000,000 (48,180,000,000); coal (metric tons; 2005) none (12,124,000); lignite (metric tons; 2005) 413,000 (413,000); crude petroleum (barrels; 2006) 24,500 ([2005] 68,700,000); petroleum products (metric tons; 2005) 10,953,000 (11,422,000); natural gas (cu m; 2006) 2,313,000,000 ([2005] 1,549,000,000). **Population economically active** (2004): total 2,678,500; activity rate of total population 40.8% (participation rates: ages 15 and over, 54.9%; female 49.6%; unemployed [April 2006–March 2007] 8.2%). **Selected balance of payments data.** Receipts from (US$'000,000): tourism (2006) 2,777; remittances (2007) 1,265; foreign direct investment (FDI) (2004–06 avg.) 7,044. Disbursements for (US$'000,000): tourism (2006) 2,983; remittances (2007) 2,770; FDI (2004–06 avg.) 7,291.

Foreign trade

Imports (2006; c.i.f.): US$47,834,000,000 (machinery and apparatus 20.6%; diamonds 18.9%; chemical products 11.2%; crude petroleum 10.0%; road vehicles 5.6%). *Major import sources:* US 12.4%; Belgium 8.2%; Germany 6.7%; Switzerland 5.9%; UK 5.1%. **Exports** (2006; f.o.b.): US$46,792,000,000 (worked diamonds 27.7%; machinery and apparatus 16.1%; rough diamonds 6.7%; medicine 6.4%; professional and scientific equipment 2.9%). *Major export destinations:* US 38.4%; Belgium 6.6%; Hong Kong 5.9%; Germany 3.8%; UK 3.4%.

Transport and communications

Transport. *Railroads* (2007): route length 913 km; passenger-km 1,834,000,000, metric ton-km cargo 1,716,000,000. *Roads* (2007): total length 17,870 km (paved 100%). *Vehicles* (2006): passenger cars 1,684,694; trucks and buses 367,021. *Air transport* (El Al only; 2007): passenger-km 17,712,000,000; metric ton-km cargo 897,000,000. **Communications,** in total units (units per 1,000 persons). Telephone landlines (2006): 3,005,000 (439); cellular telephone subscribers (2007): 8,902,000 (1,285); personal computers (2004): 5,037,000 (734); total Internet users (2007): 2,000,000 (289); broadband Internet subscribers (2007): 1,529,000 (222).

Education and health

Educational attainment (2004). Percentage of population ages 25 and over having: no formal schooling/unknown 3.7%; primary education 12.5%; secondary 37.9%; postsecondary, vocational, and higher 45.9%. **Literacy** (2003): percentage of total population ages 15 and over literate 95.4%; males literate 97.3%; females literate 93.6%. **Health** (2005): physicians 25,058 (1 per 266 persons); hospital beds

42,632 (1 per 157 persons); infant mortality rate per 1,000 live births (2007) 3.9; undernourished population (2002–04) less than 2.5% of total population.

Military

Total active duty personnel (2007): 176,500 (army 75.4%, navy 5.4%, air force 19.2%). **Military expenditure as percentage of GDP** (2005): 9.7%; per capita expenditure US$1,875.

Background

The record of human habitation in Israel is at least 100,000 years old. Efforts by Jews to establish a national state there began in the late 19th century. Britain supported Zionism and in 1922 assumed political responsibility for what was Palestine. Migration of Jews there during Nazi persecution led to deteriorating relations with Arabs. In 1947 the UN voted to partition the region into separate Jewish and Arab states, a decision opposed by neighboring Arab countries. The State of Israel was proclaimed in 1948, and Egypt, Transjordan, Syria, Lebanon, and Iraq immediately declared war on it. Israel won this war as well as the 1967 Six-Day War, in which it claimed the West Bank from Jordan and the Gaza Strip from Egypt. Another war with its Arab neighbors followed in 1973, but the Camp David Accords led to the signing of a peace treaty between Israel and Egypt in 1979. Israel invaded Lebanon to quell the Palestine Liberation Organization (PLO) in 1982, and in the late 1980s a Palestinian resistance movement arose in the occupied territories. Peace negotiations between Israel and the Arab states and Palestinians began in 1991. Israel and the PLO agreed in 1993 upon a five-year extension of self-government to the Palestinians of the West Bank and the Gaza Strip. Israel signed a full peace treaty with Jordan in 1994. Israeli soldiers and Lebanon's Hezbollah forces clashed in 1997. Following numerous contentious talks between Israel and Lebanon, Israeli troops abruptly withdrew from Lebanon in 2000, and negotiations between Israel and the Palestinians broke down amid violence that claimed hundreds of lives. In an effort to stem the fighting, Israel in 2005 withdrew its soldiers and settlers from parts of the West Bank and from all of the Gaza Strip, which came under Palestinian control.

Recent Developments

In September 2008 Israeli Prime Minister Ehud Olmert resigned after more than two years of intensive police investigations. Six days before his resignation, Olmert leaked details of a far-reaching peace offer made to the Palestinians. In return for peace, Israel would hand over the equivalent of 100% of the West Bank, set up a temporary joint regime for Jerusalem's holy basin, and agree to the return to Israel proper of 2,000 Palestinian refugees annually over a 10-year period. The radical group Hamas categorically rejected any peacemaking with Israel and throughout the year fired thousands of rockets and mortar shells at Israeli towns and villages bordering the Gaza Strip. In an attempt to pressure Hamas, Israel maintained a land and sea blockade, causing a degree of humanitarian suffering for which it was widely criticized. Partly out of concern that the Gaza violence might overflow into Egypt, Cairo mediated a truce that went into effect on 19 June. In December Hamas refused to renew the truce and later fired more than 70 rockets and mortar shells at civilian targets in Israel. Israel's response was harsh. On 27 December, in an initial strike that lasted just under 4 minutes, Israeli warplanes and helicopters destroyed dozens of Hamas government buildings and installations, killing about 150 people, most of them militiamen. By the end of January 2009, an estimated 1,300 Gazans, many of them civilians, had been killed.

Internet resources: <www.cbs.gov.il/engindex.htm>.

Italy

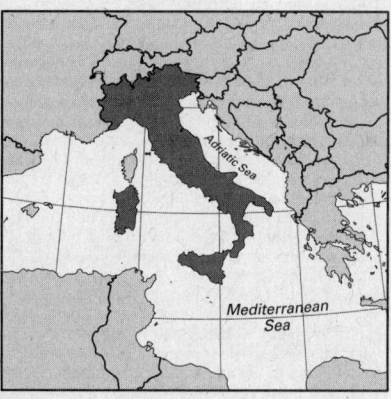

Official name: Repubblica Italiana (Italian Republic). **Form of government:** republic with two legislative houses (Senate [322]; Chamber of Deputies [630]). **Chief of state:** President Giorgio Napolitano (from 2006). **Head of government:** Prime Minister Silvio Berlusconi (from 2008). **Capital:** Rome. **Official language:** Italian. **Official religion:** none. **Monetary unit:** 1 euro (€) = 100 cents; valuation (1 Jul 2009) US$1 = €0.71.

Demography

Area: 116,346 sq mi, 301,336 sq km. **Population** (2008): 59,760,000. **Density** (2008): persons per sq mi 513.6, persons per sq km 198.3. **Urban** (2005): 67.6%. **Sex distribution** (2004): male 48.54%; female 51.46%. **Age breakdown** (2005): under 15, 14.0%; 15–29, 16.5%; 30–44, 23.8%; 45–59, 20.1%; 60–74, 16.3%; 75–84, 7.2%; 85 and over, 2.1%. **Ethnolinguistic composition** (2000): Italian 96.0%; North African Arab 0.9%; Italo-Albanian 0.8%; Albanian 0.5%; German 0.4%; Austrian 0.4%; other 1.0%. **Religious affiliation** (2005): Roman Catholic 83%, of which practicing 28%; Muslim 2%; nonreligious/atheist 14%; other 1%. **Major cities (urban agglomerations)** (2007): Rome 2,705,603 (3,339,-000); Milan 1,303,437 (2,945,000); Naples 975,139 (2,250,000); Turin 900,569 (1,652,000); Palermo 666,552 (863,000); Genoa 615,686; Bologna 373,026; Florence 365,966; Bari 325,052; Catania 301,564; Venice 268,934; Verona 260,718; Messina 245,159; Padua 210,301. **Location:** south-

ern Europe, bordering Switzerland, Austria, Slovenia, the Mediterranean Sea, and France; wholly contained within Italy are the countries of San Marino and Vatican City. **Immigration** (2006): foreign residents 4,000,000 (mostly North African but also including 500,000 Romanians).

Vital statistics

Birth rate per 1,000 population (2006): 9.5 (world avg. 20.3); (2004) within marriage 85.1%; outside of marriage 14.9%. **Death rate** per 1,000 population (2006): 9.4 (world avg. 8.6). **Natural increase rate** per 1,000 population (2006): 0.1 (world avg. 11.7). **Total fertility rate** (avg. births per childbearing woman; 2006): 1.35. **Life expectancy** at birth (2006): male 78.6 years; female 84.0 years.

Social indicators

Educational attainment (2002). Percentage of labor force ages 25 to 64 having: no formal schooling through lower secondary education 55.6%; completed upper secondary 34.0%; completed higher 10.4%. **Quality of working life.** Average workweek (2004) 39.7 hours. Annual rate per 100,000 workers (2005) for: nonfatal injury 2,848; fatal injury 5. Number of working days lost to labor stoppages per 1,000 workers (2005) 40. **Material well-being.** Rate per 100 households possessing (2006): mobile phone 82.3; personal computer 46.1; Internet access 35.6; satellite television 25.0. **Social participation.** Trade union membership in total workforce (2004) 30%. **Social deviance** (2003). Offense rate per 100,000 population for: murder 1.2; rape 4.8; theft 2,306; robbery 72.5; drug trafficking 64.7; suicide (2002) 7.0. **Access to services** (2002). Nearly 100% of dwellings have access to electricity, a safe water supply, and toilet facilities. **Leisure** (2006). Favorite leisure activities (attendance per 100 people ages 6 and over): cinema 48.9; museum/art exhibition 27.7; sporting events 27.3; discotheque 24.8; archaeological sites/monuments 21.1.

National economy

Gross national income (2007): US$1,991,284,-000,000 (US$33,540 per capita). **Budget** (2006). *Revenue:* €680,054,000,000 (current revenue 99.3%, of which indirect taxes 32.1%, direct taxes 31.4%, social security contributions 28.2%; capital revenue 0.7%). *Expenditures:* €745,558,000,000 (current expenditures 88.1%, of which social assistance benefits 39.5%, wages and salaries 21.9%, interest payments 9.1%; capital expenditures 11.9%). **Public debt** (April 2008): US$2,593,196,000,000. **Production** (metric tons except as noted). *Agriculture and fishing* (2007): corn (maize) 9,891,362, grapes 8,519,418, wheat 7,260,309, tomatoes 6,025,613, sugar beets 4,629,900, olives 3,481,379, oranges 2,293,466, apples 2,072,500, potatoes 1,837,844, peaches and nectarines 1,718,938, pears 840,516, artichokes 474,253, kiwi fruit 454,609, hazelnuts 130,743; livestock (number of live animals) 9,281,000 pigs, 8,227,000 sheep, 6,109,500 cattle, 100,000,000 chickens; fisheries production (2006) 488,519 (from aquaculture 35%). *Mining and quarrying* (2005): limestone 120,000,000; marble

1 metric ton = about 1.1 short tons;   1 kilometer = 0.6 mi (statute);   1 metric ton-km cargo = about 0.68 short ton-mi cargo;   c.i.f.: cost, insurance, and freight;   f.o.b.: free on board

5,600,000; feldspar 3,000,000; pumice 600,000. *Manufacturing* (value added in US$'000,000; 2003): nonelectrical machinery and apparatus 31,422; fabricated metal products 30,311; paints, soaps, pharmaceuticals 13,975; food products 13,203; bricks, cement, ceramics 11,749; printing and publishing 9,454; textiles 9,093; plastic products 8,473; motor vehicles and parts 7,796; wearing apparel 7,761; furniture 7,120; footwear and leather products 6,230. *Energy production (consumption):* electricity (kW-hr; 2007) 312,840,000,000 ([2005] 352,854,000,-000); coal (metric tons; 2005) 95,000 (24,248,000); crude petroleum (barrels; 2007) 39,300,000 ([2005] 687,000,000); petroleum products (metric tons; 2005) 91,405,000 (77,465,000); natural gas (cu m; 2007) 9,717,000,000 ([2005] 84,517,000,000). **Population economically active** (2005): total 24,451,400; activity rate of total population 42.1% (participation rates: ages 15–64, 62.4%; female 40.1%; unemployed [2006] 6.8%). **Selected balance of payments data.** Receipts from (US$'000,000): tourism (2006) 38,257; remittances (2007) 3,165; foreign direct investment (FDI) (2004–06 avg.) 25,315. Disbursements for (US$'000,000): tourism (2006) 23,152; remittances (2007) 11,287; FDI (2004–06 avg.) 34,373.

Foreign trade

Imports (2006; c.i.f.): US$437,397,000,000 (machinery and apparatus 16.5%; chemical products 12.4%; road vehicles and parts 10.6%; crude petroleum 9.2%; food products 6.4%; iron and steel 5.1%). *Major import sources:* Germany 16.4%; France 9.1%; China 5.2%; The Netherlands 5.1%; Belgium 4.2%; Spain 4.1%; UK 3.5%; Libya 3.1%; US 3.1%; Switzerland 3.0%. **Exports** (2006; f.o.b.): US$410,845,-000,000 (assorted manufactured goods 21.1%, of which iron and steel 4.8%, fabricated metal products 4.3%; nonelectrical machinery and apparatus 21.0%, of which general industrial machinery 9.6%, specialized machinery 6.1%; chemical products 10.5%; road vehicles and parts 7.8%; electrical machinery and apparatus 5.6%; wearing apparel and accessories 4.8%; food products 4.5%). *Major export destinations:* Germany 13.1%; France 11.6%; US 7.5%; Spain 7.2%; UK 6.0%; Switzerland 3.9%; Belgium 2.8%; Austria 2.4%; The Netherlands 2.4%; Russia 2.3%.

Transport and communications

Transport. *Railroads* (2003): length (2004) 19,319 km; passenger-km 45,221,000,000; metric ton-km cargo 22,457,000,000. *Roads* (2003): total length 484,688 km (paved 100%). *Vehicles* (2004): passenger cars 33,973,147; trucks and buses 4,108,486. *Air transport* (Alitalia and Alitalia Express only; 2006): passenger-km 39,502,000,000; metric ton-km cargo 1,473,000,000. **Communications**, in total units (units per 1,000 persons). Telephone landlines (2005): 25,049,000 (431); cellular telephone subscribers (2006): 78,571,000 (1,333); personal computers (2005): 21,486,000 (370); total Internet users (2007): 32,000,000 (539); broadband Internet subscribers (2007): 10,860,000 (183).

Education and health

Literacy (2003): percentage of total population ages 15 and over literate 98.6%; males literate 99.0%; females literate 98.3%. **Health:** physicians (2002) 353,-692 (1 per 162 persons); hospital beds (2003) 237,216 (1 per 243 persons); infant mortality rate per 1,000 live births (2004) 6.1; undernourished population (2002–04) less than 2.5% of total population.

Military

Total active duty personnel (2007): 186,049 (army 58.0%, navy 18.3%, air force 23.7%); US military forces (2008) 9,700. **Military expenditure as percentage of GDP** (2005): 1.9%; per capita expenditure US$578.

Background

The Etruscan civilization arose in the 9th century BC and was overthrown by the Romans in the 4th–3rd centuries BC. Barbarian invasions of the 4th and 5th centuries AD destroyed the Western Roman Empire. Italy's political fragmentation lasted for centuries but did not diminish its impact on European culture, notably during the Renaissance. From the 15th to the 18th century, Italian lands were ruled by France, the Holy Roman Empire, Spain, and Austria. When Napoleonic rule ended in 1815, Italy was again a grouping of independent states. The Risorgimento successfully united most of Italy, including Sicily and Sardinia, by 1861, and the unification of peninsular Italy was completed by 1870. Italy joined the Allies during World War I, but social unrest in the 1920s brought to power the Fascist movement of Benito Mussolini, and Italy allied itself with Nazi Germany in World War II. Defeated by the Allies in 1943, Italy proclaimed itself a republic in 1946. It was a charter member of NATO (1949) and of the European Community. It completed the process of setting up regional legislatures with limited autonomy in the 1970s. Since World War II it has experienced rapid changes of government but has remained socially stable. It worked with other European countries to establish the European Union.

Recent Developments

In 2008 Roberto Maroni, an official of the anti-immigration Northern League party, was named interior minister of Italy, and he swiftly produced controversial legislation intended to rein in immigration. In July Italy declared a state of emergency to limit the country's rising Roma (Gypsy) population. A plan to fingerprint all Roma in nomad camps was decried by UNICEF as a violation of the UN Convention on the Rights of the Child. New immigration and crime legislation also called for proof of income and residence for stays of more than 90 days from foreign residents in Italy. Prime Minister Silvio Berlusconi recommended the implementation of a satellite tracking system to help deter potential immigrants at their point of origin, most often from Balkan and North African seaports.

Internet resources: <www.istat.it/english>.

Jamaica

Official name: Jamaica. **Form of government:** constitutional monarchy with two legislative houses (Senate [21]; House of Representatives [60]). **Chief of state:** British Queen Elizabeth II (from 1952), represented by Governor-General Patrick Allen (from 2009). **Head**

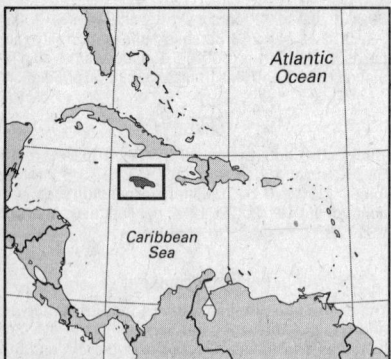

Atlantic
Ocean

Caribbean
Sea

of government: Prime Minister Bruce Golding (from 2007). **Capital:** Kingston. **Official language:** English. **Official religion:** none. **Monetary unit:** 1 Jamaican dollar (J$) = 100 cents; valuation (1 Jul 2009) US$1 = J$88.83.

Demography

Area: 4,244 sq mi, 10,991 sq km. **Population** (2008): 2,688,000. **Density** (2008): persons per sq mi 633.4, persons per sq km 244.6. **Urban** (2005): 52.2%. **Sex distribution** (2005): male 49.41%; female 50.59%. **Age breakdown** (2005): under 15, 33.7%; 15–29, 29.4%; 30–44, 17.6%; 45–59, 9.5%; 60–74, 6.7%; 75 and over, 3.1%. **Ethnic composition** (2001): black 91.6%; mixed race 6.2%; East Indian 0.9%; Chinese 0.2%; white 0.2%; other/unknown 0.9%. **Religious affiliation** (2001): Protestant 61.2%, of which Church of God 23.8%, Seventh-day Adventist 10.8%, Pentecostal 9.5%; Roman Catholic 2.6%; other Christian 1.7%; Rastafarian 0.9%; nonreligious 20.9%; other 12.7%. **Major cities** (2006): Kingston (urban agglomeration) 585,300; Spanish Town 148,800; Portmore 103,900; Montego Bay 82,700; Mandeville 47,700. **Location:** island in the Caribbean Sea, south of Cuba.

Vital statistics

Birth rate per 1,000 population (2007): 17.0 (world avg. 20.3). **Death rate** per 1,000 population (2007): 6.4 (world avg. 8.6). **Natural increase rate** per 1,000 population (2007): 10.6 (world avg. 11.7). **Total fertility rate** (avg. births per childbearing woman; 2005): 2.50. **Life expectancy** at birth (2005): male 69.2 years; female 72.7 years.

National economy

Budget (2005). *Revenue:* J$177,986,900,000 (tax revenue 88.4%, of which income tax 35.2%, taxes on goods and services 27.5%, customs duties 8.6%; nontax revenue 6.4%). *Expenditures:* J$204,513,-700,000 (public debt 42.4%; wages and salaries 30.8%; capital expenditures 8.1%). **Public debt** (external, outstanding; June 2008): US$6,456,500,000. **Production** (metric tons except as noted). *Agriculture and fishing* (2007): sugarcane 2,000,000, coconuts

170,000, yams 127,000, coffee 2,700; livestock (number of live animals) 430,000 cattle, 12,500,000 chickens; fisheries production (2006) 18,700 (from aquaculture 30%). *Mining and quarrying* (2006): bauxite 14,865,400; alumina 4,099,500; gypsum 375,000. *Manufacturing* (2005): cement 848,365,-000; animal feeds 367,600; sugar 127,001; rum [and other distilled spirits] 246,740 hectoliters. *Energy production (consumption):* electricity (kW-hr; 2005) 7,526,000,000 (7,526,000,000); coal (metric tons; 2005) none (60,000); crude petroleum (barrels; 2005) none (3,450,000); petroleum products (metric tons; 2005) 460,000 (3,120,000). **Population economically active** (2006): total 1,251,600; activity rate of total population 46.9% (participation rates: ages 14 and over, 64.6%; female 44.2%; unemployed [April 2008] 8.9%). **Gross national income** (2007): US$9,923,000,000 (US$3,710 per capita). **Selected balance of payments data.** Receipts from (US$'000,-000): tourism (2006) 1,870; remittances (2007) 2,021; foreign direct investment (FDI) (2004–06 avg.) 711; official development assistance (2006) 37. Disbursements for (US$'000,000): tourism (2006) 273; remittances (2007) 385; FDI (2004–06 avg.) 90.

Foreign trade

Imports (2006; c.i.f.): US$5,041,000,000 (crude petroleum 23.6%; machinery and apparatus 15.5%; food products 12.5%; chemical products 11.3%; road vehicles 6.1%). *Major import sources:* US 36.8%; Trinidad and Tobago 11.5%; Venezuela 10.7%; Japan 4.2%; China 4.1%. **Exports** (2006; f.o.b.): US$1,989,-000,000 (alumina 52.3%; refined petroleum products 13.5%; food products 12.0%, of which raw sugar 4.5%, coffee 1.5%; alcoholic beverages 4.2%). *Major export destinations:* US 30.4%; Canada 15.6%; China 15.1%; UK 10.3%; The Netherlands 7.0%.

Transport and communications

Transport. *Railroads* (2004): route length 201 km. *Roads* (2005): total length 21,532 km (paved 74%). *Vehicles* (2004): passenger cars 357,660; trucks and buses 128,239. *Air transport* (Air Jamaica only; 2006): passenger-km 3,907,530,000; metric ton-km cargo 20,192,000. **Communications,** in total units (units per 1,000 persons). Telephone landlines (2005): 342,000 (125); cellular telephone subscribers (2005): 2,804,000 (1,058); personal computers (2005): 179,000 (68); total Internet users (2007): 1,500,000 (553); broadband Internet subscribers (2006): 79,000 (30).

Education and health

Educational attainment (2001). Percentage of population ages 15 and over having: no formal schooling/unknown 6.7%; primary education 25.5%; secondary 55.5%; higher 12.3%, of which university 4.2%. **Literacy** (2005): percentage of total population ages 15 and over literate 88.7%; males literate 85.0%; females literate 92.3%. **Health:** physicians (2003) 2,253 (1 per 1,193 persons); hospital beds (2004) 4,882 (1 per 556 persons); infant mortality rate per 1,000 live births (2005) 19.2; undernourished population (2002–04) 250,000 (9% of total

1 metric ton = about 1.1 short tons;   1 kilometer = 0.6 mi (statute);   1 metric ton-km cargo = about 0.68 short ton-mi cargo;   c.i.f.: cost, insurance, and freight;   f.o.b.: free on board

population based on the consumption of a minimum daily requirement of 1,930 calories).

Military

Total active duty personnel (2007): 2,830 (army 88.3%, coast guard 6.7%, air force 5.0%). Military expenditure as percentage of GDP (2005): 0.6%; per capita expenditure US$20.

Background

The island of Jamaica was settled by Arawak Indians c. AD 600. It was sighted by Christopher Columbus in 1494; Spain colonized it in the early 16th century but neglected it because it lacked gold reserves. Britain gained control in 1655, and by the end of the 18th century Jamaica had become a prized colonial possession due to the volume of sugar produced by slave laborers. Slavery was abolished in the late 1830s, and the plantation system collapsed. Jamaica gained full internal self-government in 1959 and became an independent country within the British Commonwealth in 1962.

Recent Developments

Jamaica in April 2008 began soliciting proposals for the provision of 73 MW of renewable energy. Additionally, the takeover of Jamaica's five sugar factories by Brazil's Infinity Bio-Energy was confirmed in July, with the company stressing its intention to use sugar as the basis of a significant ethanol industry in the country.

Internet resources: <www.statinja.com>.

Japan

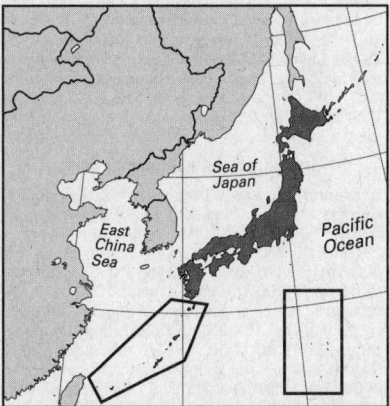

Official name: Nihon, Nippon (Japan). Form of government: constitutional monarchy with a national Diet consisting of two legislative houses (House of Councillors [242]; House of Representatives [480]). Symbol of state: Emperor Akihito (from 1989). Head of government: Prime Minister Taro Aso (from 2008). Capital: Tokyo. Official language: Japanese. Official religion: none. Monetary unit: 1 yen (¥) = 100 sen; valuation (1 Jul 2009) US$1 = ¥96.40.

Demography

Area: 145,898 sq mi, 377,873 sq km. Population (2008): 127,674,000. Density (2008): persons per sq mi 875.0, persons per sq km 337.8. Urban (2003): 65.4%. Sex distribution (2008): male 48.76%; female 51.24%. Age breakdown (2008): under 15, 13.5%; 15–29, 16.5%; 30–44, 21.1%; 45–59, 20.1%; 60–74, 18.5%; 75–84, 7.6%; 85 and over, 2.7%. Composition by nationality (2004): Japanese 98.5%; Korean 0.5%; Chinese 0.4%; Brazilian 0.2%; other 0.4%. Migration (2005). Permanent immigrants/registered aliens in Japan 2,011,555; from North and South Korea 29.8%, Taiwan, Hong Kong, Macau, and China 25.8%, Brazil 15.0%, Philippines 9.3%, Peru 2.9%, US 2.5%, other 14.7%. Japanese living abroad 1,012,547; in the US 34.7%, in China 11.3%, in Brazil 6.5%, in the UK 5.4%, in Australia 5.2%, other 36.9%. Major cities (2008): Tokyo 8,731,000; Yokohama 3,648,000; Osaka 2,651,000; Nagoya 2,246,000; Sapporo 1,898,000; Kobe 1,533,000; Kyoto 1,467,000; Fukuoka 1,437,000; Kawasaki 1,388,000; Saitama 1,210,000; Hiroshima 1,166,000; Sendai 1,031,000; Kita-Kyushu 985,000. Major metropolitan areas (2005): Tokyo 35,197,000; Osaka-Kobe 11,268,000; Nagoya 3,179,000; Fukuoka–Kita-Kyushu 2,800,000; Sapporo 2,530,000; Sendai 2,224,000; Hiroshima 2,044,000. Location: eastern Asia, island chain between the North Pacific Ocean and the Sea of Japan. Religious affiliation (2003): Shinto and related beliefs 84.2%; Buddhism and related beliefs 73.6%; Christian 1.7%; Muslim 0.1%; other 7.8%. Mobility (2007). Percentage of total population moving: within a prefecture 2.3%; between prefectures 2.0%.

Vital statistics

Birth rate per 1,000 population (2007): 8.6 (world avg. 20.3). Death rate per 1,000 population (2007): 8.8 (world avg. 8.6). Natural increase rate per 1,000 population (2007): −0.2 (world avg. 11.7). Total fertility rate (avg. births per childbearing woman; 2007): 1.34. Life expectancy at birth (2007): male 79.2 years; female 86.0 years.

Social indicators

Educational attainment (2003). Percentage of population ages 25–64 having: no formal schooling through lower-secondary education 16%; upper secondary/higher vocational 47%; university 37%. Quality of working life. Average hours worked per month (2007) 154.2. Annual rate of industrial deaths per 100,000 workers (2006) 3.0. Proportion of labor force insured for damages or income loss resulting from injury, permanent disability, and death (2005) 53.1%. Average man-days lost to labor stoppages per 1,000 workdays (2006) 1.8. Average duration of journey to work (2003) 34.2 minutes. Rate per 1,000 workers of discouraged workers (unemployed no longer seeking work; 1997) 89.4. Access to services (2004). Proportion of households having access to: safe public water supply 96.9%; public sewage system 65%. Social participation. Adult population working as volunteers at least once in the year (2006) 26.2%. Trade union membership in total workforce (2006) 15.1%. Social deviance (2005). Offense rate per 100,000 population for: homicide 1.0; robbery 3.0; larceny and theft 151.6. Rate of suicide per

100,000 population (2007) 24.1. **Material well-being** (2003–04). Households possessing: automobile 81.6%; air conditioner (2002) 87.2%; personal computer 77.5%; cellular phone 91.1%; Internet connection (2004) 86.8%.

National economy

Gross national income (2007): US$4,813,341,-000,000 (US$37,670 per capita). **Budget** (2007–08): *Revenue:* ¥83,000,000,000,000 (government bonds 30.5%; corporate taxes 20.1%; income tax 19.6%; VAT 12.8%). *Expenditures:* ¥83,000,000,-000,000 (social security 26.2%; debt service 24.3%; public works 8.1%; education and science 6.4%; national defense 5.8%). **Public debt** (July 2008): US$7,699,508,000,000. **Population economically active** (2008): total 66,620,000; activity rate of total population 52.2% (participation rates: ages 15 and over, 60.3%; female 41.7%; unemployed [August 2007–July 2008] 3.9%). **Production** (metric tons except as noted). *Agriculture and fishing* (2007): rice 10,970,000, sugar beets 4,025,000, potatoes 2,650,000, cabbages 2,390,000, sugarcane 1,275,000, dry onions 1,165,000, sweet potatoes 1,000,000, wheat 858,000, tangerines and mandarin oranges 853,000, apples 850,000, carrots 750,000, tomatoes 750,000, cucumbers 634,000, green onions 560,000, lettuce 560,000, eggplant 375,000, pears 325,000, spinach 302,000, persimmons 240,000, pumpkins 237,000, soybeans 235,000, grapes 215,000, yams 205,000, taro 195,000, strawberries 193,000, peaches 150,000, chilies 150,000, cauliflower 132,000, apricots 125,000, tea 95,000, mushrooms 67,000, ginger 42,000, chestnuts 24,000, cherries 22,000; livestock (number of live animals) 9,759,000 pigs, 4,398,000 cattle, 288,511,000 chickens; fisheries production (2005) 4,819,116, of which mackerel 811,728, anchovy 348,647, skipjack tuna 293,087, Yesso scallop 287,486 (from aquaculture 15% [including Pacific oyster 218,896, Yesso scallop 203,352]); aquatic plants 612,635 (from aquaculture [mostly seaweed] 83%); 945 whales caught]; pearls (2007) 27 metric tons. *Mining and quarrying* (2006): limestone 166,621,000; silica sand 4,593,000; dolomite 3,695,000; pyrophyllite 350,000; zinc 7,162; lead 777; silver 11,463 kg; gold 8,904 kg. *Manufacturing* (value added in US$'000,000; 2004): machinery and apparatus 250,137, of which nonelectrical machinery 108,196, electronics, televisions, and radios 104,767, electrical machinery 37,174; transportation equipment 127,800; chemical products 103,999; food products 83,185; fabricated metal products 70,485; rubber and plastic products 52,461, of which plastic products 40,150; iron and steel 38,052; printing 32,332; beverages and tobacco 25,491; cement, bricks, and ceramics 25,205; paper products 25,057; professional and scientific equipment and watches 23,569; textiles, wearing apparel, and footwear 21,776. *Energy production (consumption):* electricity (kW-hr; 2007) 1,004,620,000,000 (959,660,000,000); coal (metric tons; 2006) 1,341,000 ([2005] 174,710,-000); crude petroleum (barrels; 2007) 5,950,000 ([2005] 1,520,000,000); petroleum products (metric tons; 2005) 178,255,000 (184,128,000); natural gas (cu m; 2007) 3,358,000,000 ([2005] 84,117,-

000,000). *Composition of energy supply by source* (2002): crude oil and refined petroleum products 49.7%; coal 19.5%; natural gas 13.5%; nuclear power 11.6%; hydroelectric power 3.2%; solar power 2.4%; geothermal 0.1%. *Domestic energy demand by end use* (1998): mining and manufacturing 46.3%; residential and commercial 26.3%; transportation 25.2%; other 2.2%. **Selected balance of payments data.** Receipts from (US$'000,000): tourism (2006) 8,470; remittances (2007) 1,577; foreign direct investment (FDI) (2004–06 avg.) 1,362. Disbursements for (US$'000,000): tourism (2006) 26,876; remittances (2007) 4,037; FDI (2004–06 avg.) 42,333.

Foreign trade

Imports (2006; c.i.f.): ¥67,345,000,000,000 (mineral fuels 27.9%, of which crude petroleum 20.1%, natural gas 5.3%, coal 2.5%; machinery and apparatus 21.1%, of which heavy machinery 4.8%, office machines and computers 4.6%, electronic integrated circuits and micro-assemblies 3.7%; food products 7.4%, of which marine products 2.3%; chemical products 7.1%; metal ores and metal scrap 4.2%; wearing apparel and accessories 4.1%; nonferrous base metals [particularly aluminum and platinum-group metals] 3.1%; professional/scientific equipment 2.7%; road vehicles 2.4%). *Major import sources:* China 20.5%; US 12.0%; Saudi Arabia 6.4%; UAE 5.5%; Australia 4.8%; South Korea 4.7%; Indonesia 4.2%; unspecified Asia (probably Taiwan) 3.5%; Germany 3.2%; Thailand 2.9%. **Exports** (2006; f.o.b.): ¥75,214,000,000,000 (machinery and apparatus 39.5%, of which microcircuits and transistors 6.5%, machinery specialized for particular industries 5.9%, general industrial machinery 5.4%, telecommunications equipment 5.2%, office machines and computers 3.7%, power-generating machinery 3.7%; road vehicles 21.6%, of which passenger cars 14.6%, parts for road vehicles 4.1%; chemical products 8.9%; iron and steel 4.6%). *Major export destinations:* US 22.8%; China 14.3%; South Korea 7.8%; unspecified Asia (probably Taiwan) 6.8%; Hong Kong 5.6%; Thailand 3.5%; Germany 3.2%; Singapore 3.0%; UK 2.4%; The Netherlands 2.3%.

Transport and communications

Transport. *Railroads* (2006): length (2004) 23,577 km; passengers carried 22,243,000; passenger-km (2007) 395,908,000,000; metric ton-km cargo 23,191,000,000. *Roads* (2004): total length 1,188,-000 km (paved 80%). *Vehicles* (2008): passenger cars 57,617,000; trucks and buses 16,490,000. *Air transport* (2007): passengers carried 112,543,000; passenger-km 162,954,000,000; metric ton-km cargo 9,449,850,000. *Urban transport* (Tokyo, Nagoya, and Osaka metropolis traffic range only; 2000): passengers carried 57,719,000, of which by rail 34,020,000, by road 19,466,000, by subway 4,233,000. **Communications**, in total units (units per 1,000 persons). Telephone landlines (2007): 51,232,000 (400); cellular telephone subscribers (2007): 107,339,000 (839); personal computers (2005): 86,389,000 (675); total Internet users (2007): 88,110,000 (689); broadband Internet subscribers (2007): 28,750,000 (225). *Radio and televi-*

---

1 metric ton = about 1.1 short tons;   1 kilometer = 0.6 mi (statute);   1 metric ton-km cargo = about 0.68 short ton-mi cargo;   c.i.f.: cost, insurance, and freight;   f.o.b.: free on board

sion broadcasting (2003): total radio stations 1,612, of which commercial 723; total television stations 15,021, of which commercial 8,276. Commercial broadcasting hours (by percentage of programs): reports—radio 12.3%, television 19.8%; education—radio 2.4%, television 12.3%; culture—radio 13.3%, television 25.1%; entertainment—radio 69.3%, television 37.5%. Advertisements (daily average): radio 149, television 445.

Education and health

Literacy: percentage of total population ages 15 and over literate, virtually 100%. **Health** (2006): physicians 275,127 (1 per 464 persons); dentists 95,944 (1 per 1,332 persons); nurses and assistant nurses 1,194,129 (1 per 107 persons); pharmacists 234,-429 (1 per 545 persons); midwives (2004) 25,257 (1 per 5,059 persons); hospital beds 1,626,589 (1 per 79 persons); infant mortality rate per 1,000 live births (2007) 2.6; undernourished population (2002–04) less than 2.5% of total population.

Military

Total active duty personnel (2007): 240,400 (army 61.7%, navy 18.5%, air force 19.1%, central staff 0.7%); US troops (2008) 33,122. **Military expenditure as percentage of GDP** (2005): 1.0%; per capita expenditure US$345.

Background

Japan's history began with the accession of the legendary first emperor, Jimmu, in 660 BC. The Yamato court established the first unified Japanese state in the 4th–5th centuries AD; during this period Buddhism arrived in Japan by way of Korea. For centuries Japan borrowed heavily from Chinese culture, but it began to sever its links with the mainland by the 9th century. In 1192 Minamoto Yoritomo established Japan's first *bakufu,* or shogunate. Unification was achieved in the late 1500s under the leadership of Oda Nobunaga, Toyotomi Hideyoshi, and Tokugawa Ieyasu. During the Tokugawa shogunate, beginning in 1603, the government imposed a policy of isolation. Under the leadership of Emperor Meiji (1868–1912), it adopted a constitution (1889) and began a program of modernization and Westernization. Japanese imperialism led to war with China (1894–95) and Russia (1904–05) as well as to the annexation of Korea (1910) and Manchuria (1931). During World War II Japan attacked US forces in Hawaii and the Philippines (December 1941) and occupied European colonial possessions in South Asia. In 1945 the US dropped atomic bombs on Hiroshima and Nagasaki, and Japan surrendered to the Allied powers. US postwar occupation of Japan led to a new democratic constitution in 1947. In rebuilding Japan's ruined industrial plant, new technology was used in every major industry. A tremendous economic recovery followed, and it was able to maintain a favorable balance of trade into the 1990s.

Recent Developments

In July the International Monetary Fund (IMF) reported that the Japanese economy was showing "resilience to recent external shocks" and that "activity remained robust through the first quarter of 2008." By October, though, it was apparent that the world-wide economic slowdown that had begun in the US after the collapse of the housing bubble was hitting Japan hard. Contraction of Japan's economy in the third quarter pushed it into recession, and it shrank by nearly 1.6% for the year. In the first quarter of 2009, the Japanese economy recorded its largest annual contraction ever, 15.2% over the preceding 12 months. The rise in Japan's import bill as the country paid record-high prices for imported oil, combined with a slump in exports, was devastating. The slowdown was also a product of developments at home, where both private residential investment and public investment declined sharply. These developments fed a sharp decline in the Japanese stock markets; the Nikkei 225 Stock Average fell to a 26-year low in late October before recovering slightly at year's end. The unemployment rate moved up to 4.0% in 2008, and by April 2009 it had risen another 1.1%. In response to the slowdown, the government passed a fiscal stimulus package valued at ¥1.8 trillion (about US$18.8 billion) in October 2008. A second package, valued at ¥5 trillion (about US$52.3 billion) was announced on 30 October. The next day, the Bank of Japan announced that it was lowering interest rates from 0.5% to 0.3%, the first time the central bank had cut rates in seven years. Additional measures designed to inject public funds into banks, along with a major economic stimulus package, worked their way through the Diet in late 2008.

Japan improved its relations with China and Europe in 2008. Chinese Pres. Hu Jintao traveled to Japan in May—the first visit by a Chinese head of state since 1998. His trip—which came after several years in which visits by Japanese heads of state to the Yasukuni Shrine (where both Japanese war dead and 14 Class A war criminals were enshrined) and anti-Japanese demonstrations in China had aggravated relations between the two neighbors—marked a milestone in improving ties. Nevertheless, the two countries continued to face difficulties dealing with issues such as the Chinese tainted-food scandal, which caused problems throughout Asia and elsewhere during the year.

Internet resources: <www.stat.go.jp/english>.

Jordan

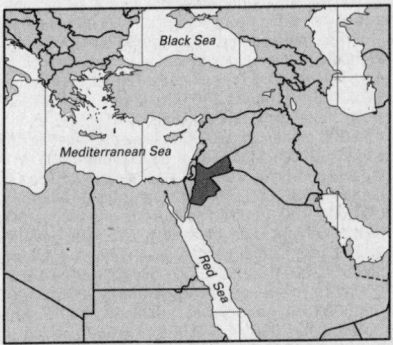

Official name: Al-Mamlakah al-Urdunniyah al-Hashimiyah (Hashemite Kingdom of Jordan). **Form of government:** constitutional monarchy with two legislative houses (Senate [55]; House of Representatives [110]). **Head of state and government:** King Abdullah II (from 1999), assisted by Prime Minister Nader Dahabi (from 2007). **Capital:** Amman. **Official language:** Arabic. **Official religion:** Islam. **Monetary unit:** 1 Jordanian dinar (JD) = 1,000 fils; valuation (1 Jul 2009) US$1 = JD 0.71.

Demography

Area: 34,277 sq mi, 88,778 sq km. **Population** (2008): 5,844,000 (includes roughly 1,900,000 registered Palestinian refugees and excludes roughly 600,000 Iraqi refugees). **Density** (2008): persons per sq mi 170.5, persons per sq km 65.8. **Urban** (2004): 78.3%. **Sex distribution** (2006): male 51.55%; female 48.45%. **Age breakdown** (2005): under 15, 37.2%; 15–29, 28.9%; 30–44, 20.7%; 45–59, 8.2%; 60–74, 4.2%; 75–84, 0.7%; 85 and over, 0.1%. **Ethnic composition** (2000): Arab 97.8%, of which Jordanian 32.4%, Palestinian 32.2%, Iraqi 14.0%, Bedouin 12.8%; Circassian 1.2%; other 1.0%. **Religious affiliation** (2005): Sunni Muslim 95%; Christian 3%; other (mostly Shi'i Muslim and Druze) 2%. **Major cities** (2004): Amman 1,036,330; Al-Zarqa 395,227; Irbid 250,645; Al-Rusayfah 227,735; Al-Quwaysimah 135,500. **Location:** the Middle East, bordering Syria, Iraq, Saudi Arabia, the Gulf of Aqaba, Israel, and the West Bank.

Vital statistics

Birth rate per 1,000 population (2006): 29.1 (world avg. 20.3). **Death rate** per 1,000 population (2006): 3.6 (world avg. 8.6). **Natural increase rate** per 1,000 population (2006): 25.5 (world avg. 11.7). **Total fertility rate** (avg. births per childbearing woman; 2005): 2.71. **Life expectancy** at birth (2003): male 70.6 years; female 72.4 years.

National economy

Budget (2004). *Revenue:* JD 2,949,800,000 (tax revenue 48.4%, of which sales tax 28.0%, customs duties 8.8%, income and profits taxes 7.4%; foreign grants 27.5%; nontax revenue 22.0%, of which licenses and fees 12.4%; repayments 2.1%). *Expenditures:* JD 3,102,100,000 (current expenditures 75.0%, of which defense 21.1%, wages and salaries 15.0%, social security and pensions 12.9%, oil subsidies 8.4%; capital expenditures 25.0%). **Public debt** (external, outstanding; 2006): US$7,143,000,000. **Production** (metric tons except as noted). *Agriculture and fishing* (2007): tomatoes 550,000, potatoes 170,000, cucumbers 140,000, olives 115,000; livestock (number of live animals) 2,100,000 sheep, 434,000 goats, 25,000,000 chickens; fisheries production (2006) 1,045 (from aquaculture 54%). *Mining and quarrying* (2005): phosphate ore 6,375,000; potash 1,830,000. *Manufacturing* (value added in US$'000,000; 2004): chemical products 347; bricks, cement, and ceramics 287; food products 232. *Energy production (consumption):* electricity (kW-hr; 2007) 12,564,000,000 ([2005] 10,388,-000,000); crude petroleum (barrels; 2005) 7,200 (33,600,000); petroleum products (metric tons; 2005) 4,197,000 (4,743,000); natural gas (cu m; 2005) 214,000,000 (1,650,000,000). **Population economically active** (2003): total 1,293,000; activity

rate of total population 23.6% (participation rates: ages 16 and over, 37.9%; female 14.9%; unemployed 14.5%). **Gross national income** (2007): US$16,282,000,000 (US$2,850 per capita). **Selected balance of payments data.** Receipts from (US$'000,000): tourism (2006) 1,642; remittances (2006) 2,934; foreign direct investment (FDI) (2004–06 avg.) 1,768; official development assistance (2006) 580. Disbursements for (US$'000,-000): tourism (2006) 625; remittances (2006) 402; FDI (2004–avg.), none.

Foreign trade

Imports (2006; c.i.f.): JD 8,116,000,000 (crude petroleum 17.7%; machinery and apparatus 14.8%; food products 12.9%; road vehicles 8.8%; chemical products 8.7%). *Major import sources:* Saudi Arabia 25.6%; China 10.4%; Germany 7.8%; US 4.7%; Egypt 4.2%. **Exports** (2006; f.o.b.): JD 3,663,000,000 (wearing apparel 24.3%; machinery and apparatus 9.2%; crude fertilizers [potash] 8.0%; medicine 5.9%; gold 5.4%;). *Major export destinations:* US 25.1%; Iraq 12.3%; India 7.7%; free zones 7.6%; Saudi Arabia 7.1%.

Transport and communications

Transport. *Railroads* (2003): length 788 km; passenger-km 2,100,000; metric ton-km cargo 348,000,-000. *Roads* (2005): total length 7,601 km (paved 100%). *Vehicles* (2005): passenger cars 429,306; trucks and buses 201,127. *Air transport* (Royal Jordanian airlines only; 2006): passenger-km 5,521,-000,000; metric ton-km cargo 210,000,000. **Communications,** in total units (units per 1,000 persons). Telephone landlines (2007): 586,000 (99); cellular telephone subscribers (2007): 4,771,000 (805); personal computers (2005): 355,000 (62); total Internet users (2007): 1,127,000 (190); broadband Internet subscribers (2007): 92,000 (16).

Did you know? Since 1986 Jordan's only seaport, Aqaba, has been the site of an ongoing archaeological excavation that is revealing the city plan of an Islamic city in existence from the mid-7th century to the early 12th century.

Education and health

Educational attainment (2004). Percentage of population ages 25 and over having: no formal schooling 18.8% (illiterate 14.0%, literate 4.8%); primary/lower secondary education 36.6%; upper secondary 19.4%; some higher 25.1%, of which advanced degree 2.1%; unknown 0.1%. **Literacy** (2005): percentage of total population ages 15 and over literate 91.1%; males literate 95.2%; females literate 87.0%. **Health:** physicians (2005) 17,569 (1 per 316 persons); hospital beds (2006) 11,049 (1 per 507 persons); infant mortality rate per 1,000 live births (2005) 24.0; undernourished population (2002–04) 300,000 (6% of total population based on the consumption of a minimum daily requirement of 1,810 calories).

---

1 metric ton = about 1.1 short tons; 1 kilometer = 0.6 mi (statute); 1 metric ton-km cargo = about 0.68 short ton-mi cargo; c.i.f.: cost, insurance, and freight; f.o.b.: free on board

Military

Total active duty personnel (2007): 100,500 (army 84.6%, navy 0.5%, air force 14.9%). **Military expenditure as percentage of GDP** (2008): 10.6%; per capita expenditure US$332.

Background

Jordan shares much of its history with Israel, since both occupy the area known historically as Palestine. Much of present-day eastern Jordan was incorporated into Israel under Kings David and Solomon c. 1000 BC. It fell to the Seleucids in 330 BC and to Muslim Arabs in the 7th century AD. The Crusaders extended the kingdom of Jerusalem east of the Jordan River in 1099. Jordan submitted to Ottoman Turkish rule during the 16th century. In 1920 the area comprising Jordan (then known as the Transjordan) was established within the British mandate of Palestine. Transjordan became an independent state in 1927, although the British mandate did not end until 1948. After hostilities with the new state of Israel ceased in 1949, Jordan annexed the West Bank of the Jordan River, administering the territory until Israel gained control of it in the Six-Day War of 1967. In 1970–71 Jordan was wracked by fighting between the government and guerrillas of the Palestine Liberation Organization (PLO), a struggle that ended in the expulsion of the PLO from Jordan. In 1988 King Hussein renounced all Jordanian claims to the West Bank in favor of the PLO. In 1994 Jordan and Israel signed a full peace agreement. Upon the death of King Hussein in 1999, his son Abdullah took over the throne.

Recent Developments

Despite mounting inflation in 2008 spurred by unbridled increases in world oil and cereal prices, which was a risk factor for social upheaval, the government seemed firmly in control of the domestic security situation as it also tried to cope with its population of 750,000 Iraqi refugees. Though subsidies were eliminated, the salaries of public- and private-sector employees were raised. The Jordanian economy grew at an estimated annual rate of 6%, but officials considered rates of unemployment and poverty high.

Internet resources:
<www.dos.gov.jo/dos_home_e/main/index.htm>.

Kazakhstan

Official name: Qazaqstan Respublikasy (Kazakh); Kazakhstan Respublika (Russian) (Republic of Kazakhstan). **Form of government:** unitary republic with a parliament consisting of two chambers (Senate [47] and Assembly [107]). **Head of state and government:** President Nursultan Nazarbayev (from 1990), assisted by Prime Minister Karim Masimov (from 2007). **Capital:** Astana. **Official languages:** Kazakh; Russian. **Official religion:** none. **Monetary unit:** 1 tenge (T) = 100 tiyn; valuation (1 Jul 2009) US$1 = T 148.27.

Demography

Area: 1,052,100 sq mi, 2,724,900 sq km. **Population** (2008): 15,655,000. **Density** (2008): persons

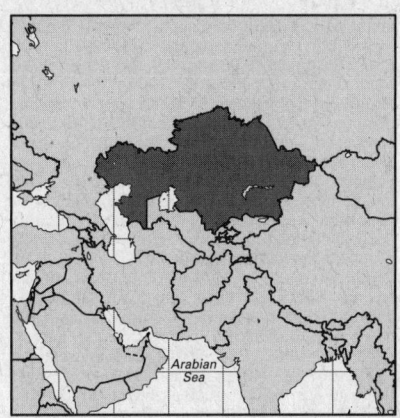

per sq mi 14.9, persons per sq km 5.7. **Urban** (2006): 57.4%. **Sex distribution** (2005): male 48.30%; female 51.70%. **Age breakdown** (2005): under 15, 23.7%; 15–29, 28.7%; 30–44, 20.7%; 45–59, 16.4%; 60–74, 7.9%; 75–84, 2.3%; 85 and over, 0.3%. **Ethnic composition** (2003): Kazakh 57.2%; Russian 27.2%; Ukrainian 3.1%; Uzbek 2.7%; German 1.6%; Tatar 1.6%; Uighur 1.5%; other 5.1%. **Religious affiliation** (2000): Muslim (mostly Sunni) 42.7%; nonreligious 29.3%; Christian 16.7%, of which Orthodox 8.6%; atheist 10.9%; other 0.4%. **Major cities** (2005): Almaty 1,247,896; Astana 550,438; Shymkent (Chimkent) 526,140; Qaraghandy (Karaganda) 446,139; Taraz 336,057. **Location:** central Asia, bordering Russia, China, Kyrgyzstan, Uzbekistan, the Aral Sea, Turkmenistan, and the Caspian Sea.

Vital statistics

Birth rate per 1,000 population (2006): 19.7 (world avg. 20.3); (2000) within marriage 76.1%, outside of marriage 23.9%. **Death rate** per 1,000 population (2006): 10.3 (world avg. 8.6). **Natural increase rate** per 1,000 population (2006): 9.4 (world avg. 11.7). **Total fertility rate** (avg. births per childbearing woman; 2005): 1.90. **Life expectancy** at birth (2006): male 60.6 years; female 72.0 years.

National economy

Budget (2004). *Revenue:* T 1,441,000,000,000 (tax revenue 90.7%, of which corporate taxes 33.8%, VAT 16.9%, social security 11.7%, petroleum taxes 10.0%; nontax revenue 9.3%). *Expenditures:* T 1,289,300,000,000 (social security 21.1%; education 14.8%; health 10.2%; public order 9.2%). **Public debt** (external, outstanding; 2006): US$2,136,-000,000. **Population economically active** (2006): total 8,028,900; activity rate of total population 52.4% (participation rates: ages 15–64 [2004] 76.6%; female [2004] 49.0%; unemployed 7.8%). **Production** (metric tons except as noted). *Agriculture and fishing* (2007): wheat 16,500,000, barley 2,600,000, potatoes 2,414,800; livestock (number of live animals) 13,046,800 sheep, 5,660,400 cattle, 2,303,500 goats; fisheries production (2006) 35,676 (from aquaculture 1%). *Mining and quarrying* (2005): iron ore 16,469,900; bauxite 4,800,000;

chromite 3,579,000; copper (metal content) 402,000; zinc (metal content) 400,000; silver 832,000 kg; gold 18,062 kg. *Manufacturing* (value of production in T '000,000; 2004): base metals 600,000; food products 356,000; coke, refined petroleum products, and nuclear fuel 134,000. *Energy production (consumption):* electricity (kW-hr; 2007) 76,145,000,000 (76,283,000,000); hard coal (metric tons; 2005) 86,600,000 (61,900,000); lignite (metric tons; 2005) 4,500,000 (4,240,000); crude petroleum (barrels; 2007) 496,600,000 (92,000,-000); petroleum products (metric tons; 2005) 11,841,000 (7,625,000); natural gas (cu m; 2006) 25,655,000,000 (31,007,000,000). **Gross national income** (2007): US$78,281,000,000 (US$5,060 per capita). **Selected balance of payments data.** Receipts from (US$'000,000): tourism (2006) 838; remittances (2007) 223; foreign direct investment (2004–06 avg.) 4,092; official development assistance (2006) 172. Disbursements for (US$'000,-000): tourism (2006) 821; remittances (2007) 4,297.

Foreign trade

Imports (2006; c.i.f.): US$23,663,000,000 (machinery and apparatus 27.7%; road vehicles 10.9%; crude petroleum 10.1%; chemical products 8.6%; iron and steel 8.3%). *Major import sources:* Russia 38.3%; China 8.1%; Germany 7.6%; Italy 6.0%; US 4.7%. **Exports** (2006; f.o.b.): US$38,244,-000,000 (crude petroleum 61.7%; nonferrous metals 10.4%, of which refined copper 6.2%; iron and steel 5.5%; metal ore and metal scrap 5.0%). *Major export destinations:* Italy 18.0%; Switzerland 17.6%; Russia 9.8%; China 9.4%; France 8.8%.

Transport and communications

Transport. *Railroads* (2006): route length (2004) 13,700 km; passenger-km 12,705,000,000; metric ton-km cargo 191,000,000,000. *Roads* (2004): total length 90,018 km (paved 93%). *Vehicles* (2005): passenger cars 1,405,325; trucks and buses 347,236. *Air transport* (2006): passenger-km 3,716,-000,000; metric ton-km cargo (2003) 94,000,000. **Communications,** in total units (units per 1,000 persons). Telephone landlines (2007): 3,237,000 (210); cellular telephone subscribers (2007): 12,588,000 (816); total Internet users (2007): 1,901,000 (128); broadband Internet subscribers (2007): 381,000 (25).

Education and health

Educational attainment (1999). Percentage of population ages 25 and over having: no formal schooling/some primary education 9.1%; primary 23.1%; secondary/some postsecondary 57.8%; higher 10.0%. **Literacy** (2003): percentage of total population ages 15 and over literate, virtually 100%. **Health** (2006): physicians 57,500 (1 per 266 persons); hospital beds 119,000 (1 per 129 persons); infant mortality rate per 1,000 live births 13.9; undernourished population (2002–04) 900,000 (6% of total population based on the consumption of a minimum daily requirement of 1,950 calories).

Military

Total active duty personnel (2007): 49,000 (army 61.2%, navy 6.1%, air force 24.5%, Ministry of Defense staff 8.2%). **Military expenditure as percentage of GDP** (2005): 1.1%; per capita expenditure US$39.

Background

Named for its earliest inhabitants, the Kazakhs, the area came under Mongol rule in the 13th century. The Kazakhs consolidated a nomadic empire in the 15th–16th centuries. Under Russian rule by the mid-19th century, it became part of the Kirgiz Autonomous Republic formed by the Soviets in 1920, and in 1925 its name was changed to the Kazakh Autonomous Soviet Socialist Republic. Kazakhstan obtained its independence in 1991, and during the 1990s it attempted to stabilize its economy.

Recent Developments

The political leadership in Kazakhstan spent 2008 seeking to prove its worthiness to head the Organization for Security and Co-operation in Europe in 2010 and pledged to meet certain requirements in the areas of political reform. Kazakhstan showed less willingness to meet international standards in the sphere of human rights protection. The government was sharply criticized by the international human rights community for handing Uzbek asylum seekers over to Uzbek security services on what were widely believed to be trumped-up charges.

Internet resources: <www.eng.stat.kz>.

Kenya

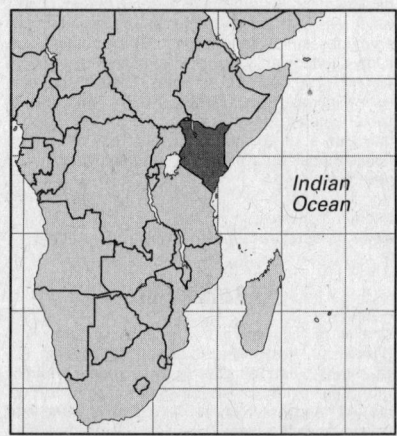

Indian Ocean

Official name: Jamhuri ya Kenya (Swahili); Republic of Kenya (English). **Form of government:** unitary multiparty republic with one legislative house (National Assembly [224]). **Head of state and government:** President Mwai Kibaki (from 2002), assisted by Prime Minister Raila Odinga (from 2008). **Capital:**

1 metric ton = about 1.1 short tons;   1 kilometer = 0.6 mi (statute);   1 metric ton-km cargo = about 0.68 short ton-mi cargo;   c.i.f.: cost, insurance, and freight;   f.o.b.: free on board

Nairobi. **Official languages:** Swahili; English. **Official religion:** none. **Monetary unit:** 1 Kenya shilling (K Sh) = 100 cents; valuation (1 Jul 2009) US$1 = K Sh 75.95.

Demography

Area: 224,961 sq mi, 582,646 sq km. **Population** (2008): 37,954,000. **Density** (2008): persons per sq mi 168.7, persons per sq km 65.1. **Urban** (2005): 20.7%. **Sex distribution** (2006): male 48.90%; female 51.10%. **Age breakdown** (2006): under 15, 43.1%; 15–29, 30.2%; 30–44, 15.2%; 45–59, 7.0%; 60–74, 3.5%; 75 and over, 1.0%. **Ethnic composition** (2004): Kikuyu 21%; Luhya 14%; Luo 13%; Kalenjin 11%; Kamba 11%; Gusii 6%; Meru 5%; other 19%. **Religious affiliation** (2006): Protestant and independent Christian 66%; Roman Catholic 23%; Muslim 8%; nonreligious 2%; traditional beliefs 1%. **Major cities** (2006): Nairobi 2,864,700; Mombasa 823,500; Nakuru 266,500; Eldoret 227,800; Kisumu 220,000. **Location:** eastern Africa, bordering Ethiopia, Somalia, the Indian Ocean, Tanzania, Uganda, and The Sudan.

Vital statistics

Birth rate per 1,000 population (2005): 40.1 (world avg. 20.3). **Death rate** per 1,000 population (2005): 14.7 (world avg. 8.6). **Natural increase rate** per 1,000 population (2005): 25.5 (world avg. 11.7). **Total fertility rate** (avg. births per childbearing woman; 2005): 4.96. **Life expectancy** at birth (2006): male 54.3 years; female 59.1 years.

National economy

Budget (2004–05). *Revenue:* K Sh 304,705,-000,000 (tax revenue 79.7%, of which income and profit taxes 32.6%, VAT 24.9%, excise tax 14.5%; nontax revenue 15.4%; grants 4.9%). *Expenditures:* K Sh 303,705,000,000 (recurrent expenditures 85.0%, of which wages and salaries 34.3%, interest payments 10.0%; development expenditures 15.0%). **Production** (metric tons except as noted). *Agriculture and fishing* (2007): sugarcane 4,950,000, corn (maize) 3,240,000, cassava 850,000, largest supplier to EU of cut flowers (25% of total market in 2002); livestock (number of live animals) 12,500,-000 cattle, 9,300,000 sheep; fisheries production (2006) 159,696 (from aquaculture, negligible). *Mining and quarrying* (2004): soda ash 355,380; fluorite 108,000; salt 22,000. *Manufacturing* (value added in US$'000,000; 2002): food products 400; textiles and wearing apparel 245; chemical products 142. *Energy production (consumption):* electricity (kW-hr; 2005) 6,003,000,000 (5,994,000,000); coal (metric tons; 2005) none (108,000); crude petroleum (barrels; 2005) none (13,003,000); petroleum products (metric tons; 2005) 1,586,000 (3,013,000). **Population economically active** (2001): total 12,952,000; activity rate of total population 42.1% (participation rates [1998–99]: ages 15–64, 73.6%; female [1997] 46.1%; unemployed 14.6%). **Gross national income** (2007): US$25,559,-000,000 (US$680 per capita). **Public debt** (external, outstanding; 2006): US$5,807,000,000. **Selected balance of payments data.** Receipts from (US$'000,-000): tourism (2006) 688; remittances (2007) 1,300; foreign direct investment (2004–06 avg.) 39; official development assistance (2007) 943. Dis-bursements for (US$'000,000): tourism (2006) 178; remittances (2007) 25.

Foreign trade

Imports (2006; c.i.f.): K Sh 526,870,000,000 (machinery and transportation equipment 30.7%; crude and refined petroleum products 23.9%; chemical products 13.7%; food and live animals 5.2%). *Major import sources* (2006): UAE 14.7%; India 7.1%; UK 6.5%; South Africa 6.4%; Japan 5.6%. **Exports** (2006; f.o.b.): K Sh 267,900,000,000 (soda ash 35.6%; food products 22.4%, of which tea 17.3%, coffee 3.6%; cut flowers 15.7%; refined petroleum products 2.7%). *Major export destinations* (2006): Uganda 10.4%; UK 10.1%; The Netherlands 7.3%; Tanzania 6.8%; US 6.6%.

Transport and communications

Transport. *Railroads* (2000): route length 2,700 km; passenger-km 302,000,000; metric ton-km cargo 1,557,000,000. *Roads* (2000): total length 63,942 km (paved 12%). *Vehicles* (2000): passenger cars 244,836; trucks and buses 96,726. *Air transport* (Kenya Airways only, 2004): passenger-km 5,283,000,000; metric ton-km cargo 193,430,000. **Communications,** in total units (units per 1,000 persons). Telephone landlines (2007): 265,000 (7); cellular telephone subscribers (2007): 11,440,000 (301); personal computers (2004): 330,000 (9.5); total Internet users (2007): 3,000,000 (79); broadband Internet subscribers (2006): 18,000 (0.5).

Education and health

Educational attainment (1998–99). Percentage of population ages 6 and over having: no formal schooling/unknown 20.2%; primary education 59.0%; secondary 19.7%; university 1.1%. **Literacy** (2002): percentage of total population ages 15 and over literate 84.3%; males literate 90.0%; females literate 78.5%. **Health:** physicians (2007) 6,271 (1 per 5,886 persons); hospital beds (2004) 65,971 (1 per 485 persons); infant mortality rate per 1,000 live births (2005) 61.5; undernourished population (2002–04) 9,900,000 (31% of total population based on the consumption of a minimum daily requirement of 1,840 calories).

Military

Total active duty personnel (2008): 24,120 (army 82.9%, navy 6.7%, air force 10.4%). **Military expenditure as percentage of GDP** (2008): 2.1%; per capita expenditure US$17.

Background

The coastal region of East Africa was dominated by Arabs until it was seized by the Portuguese in the 16th century. The Masai people held sway in the north and moved into central Kenya in the 18th century, while the Kikuyu expanded from their home region in south-central Kenya. The interior was explored by European missionaries in the 19th century. After the British took control, Kenya was established as a British protectorate (1890) and a crown colony (1920). The Mau Mau rebellion of the 1950s was directed against European colonialism. In 1963 the country became fully independent, and a year later a republican government under Jomo Kenyatta was elected. In 1992 Kenyan Pres. Daniel arap Moi allowed the country's first multiparty elections in three decades, though the balloting was marred by violence and fraud. Political turmoil occurred over the following years.

Recent Developments

Fighting between Kalenjin ethnic groups, who claimed traditional ownership of the land, and Kikuyu tenant farmers, who had settled in the area that was occupied by white farmers prior to independence, became politicized and violent in 2008 after the disputed presidential election in December 2007. Candidate Raila Odinga accused the government of having rigged the election when incumbent Mwai Kibaki was sworn in as president before an official result was announced. Violence by Odinga's supporters in the west was countered by Kikuyu attacks on western ethnic-group settlers. More than 1,000 people were killed, and 300,000–600,000 people were displaced. In February an outline agreement to create the new post of prime minister was signed, with Kibaki remaining president and Odinga named prime minister.

Internet resources: <www.cbs.go.ke>.

Kiribati

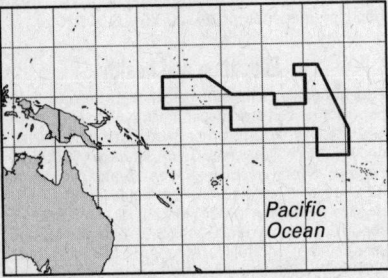

Pacific Ocean

Official name: Republic of Kiribati. **Form of government:** unitary republic with a unicameral legislature (House of Assembly [46]). **Head of state and government:** President Anote Tong (from 2003). **Capital:** Bairiki, on Tarawa Atoll. **Official language:** English. **Official religion:** none. **Monetary unit:** 1 Australian dollar ($A) = 100 cents; valuation (1 Jul 2009) US$1 = $A 1.24.

Demography

Area: 312.9 sq mi, 810.5 sq km. **Population** (2008): 97,200. **Density** (2008): persons per sq mi 347.1, persons per sq km 133.9. **Urban** (2005): 47.5%. **Sex distribution** (2007): male 49.64%; female 50.36%. **Age breakdown** (2007): under 15, 38.2%; 15–29, 27.7%; 30–44, 18.0%; 45–59, 10.7%; 60–74, 4.5%; 75 and over, 0.9%. **Ethnic composition** (2000): Micronesian 98.8%; Polynesian 0.7%; European 0.2%; other 0.3%. **Religious affiliation** (2005): Roman Catholic 55.3%; Kiribati Protestant (Congregational)

35.7%; Mormon 3.1%; Baha'i 2.2%; other/nonreligious 3.7%. **Major villages** (2005): Betio 12,509; Bikenibeu 6,170; Teaoraereke 3,939; Bairiki 2,766. **Location:** Oceania, islands in the western Pacific Ocean, south of the Hawaiian Islands (US).

Vital statistics

Birth rate per 1,000 population (2007): 30.5 (world avg. 20.3). **Death rate** per 1,000 population (2007): 8.1 (world avg. 8.6). **Natural increase rate** per 1,000 population (2007): 22.4 (world avg. 11.7). **Total fertility rate** (avg. births per childbearing woman; 2007): 4.12. **Life expectancy** at birth (2007): male 59.4 years; female 65.7 years.

National economy

Budget (2005). *Revenue:* $A 182,369,000 (nontax revenue 35.7%; tax revenue 16.7%; grants 47.6%). *Expenditures:* $A 78,560,000 (education 25.3%; health 16.7%; economic services 15.6%; defense 7.3%). *Production* (metric tons except as noted). *Agriculture and fishing* (2007): coconuts 110,000, roots and tubers 8,200 (of which taro 2,200), bananas 5,800; livestock (number of live animals) 12,600 pigs, 480,000 chickens; fisheries production (2006) 31,010 (from aquaculture, negligible); aquatic plants (all seaweed) production 3,900 (from aquaculture 100%). *Mining and quarrying:* none. *Manufacturing:* copra (6,194 metric tons produced in 2005), processed fish, wearing apparel, and handicrafts. *Energy production (consumption):* electricity (kW-hr; 2005) 10,000,000 (10,000,000); petroleum products (metric tons; 2005) none (8,000). **Selected balance of payments data.** Receipts from (US$'000,000): tourism (2001) 3.2; remittances (2007) 7; foreign direct investment (2004–06 avg.) 11; official development assistance (2006) –45. Disbursements for (US$'000,000): tourism (1999) 2.0. **Population economically active** (2005): total 36,969; activity rate of total population 38.8% (participation rates: ages 16 and over, 63.4%; female 45.9%; unemployed 6.1%). **Gross national income** (2007): US$120,000,000 (US$1,170 per capita). **Public debt** (external, outstanding; 2002): US$3,900,000.

Foreign trade

Imports (2005): $A 96,900,000 (food products 29.6%, of which rice 10.7%; refined petroleum products 16.8%; machinery and apparatus 14.6%, of which starting equipment and generators 6.2%; road vehicles 5.7%). *Major import sources:* Australia 35.5%; Fiji 20.9%; Japan 17.0%; New Zealand 5.4%; other Asia (probably Taiwan) 5.0%. **Exports** (2003): $A 4,470,000 (domestic exports 82.2%, of which copra 47.3%, shark fins 10.5%, seaweed 8.6%, aquarium fish 7.2%, trepang 5.7%; reexports 17.8%). *Major export destinations* (2005): free zones 34%; Australia 22%; Fiji 17%; other Asia (probably Taiwan) 14%; Hong Kong 8%.

Transport and communications

Transport. *Roads* (1999): total length 670 km (paved [1996] 5%). *Vehicles* (registered vehicles in South

1 metric ton = about 1.1 short tons;   1 kilometer = 0.6 mi (statute);   1 metric ton-km cargo = about 0.68 short ton-mi cargo;   c.i.f.: cost, insurance, and freight;   f.o.b.: free on board

Tarawa only; 2004): passenger cars 610; trucks and buses 808. *Air transport* (1998): passenger-km 11,000,000; metric ton-km cargo 2,000,000 (Air Kiribati international service ended in 2004). **Communications**, in total units (units per 1,000 persons). Telephone landlines (2006): 4,000 (43); cellular telephone subscribers (2007): 700 (7.5); personal computers (2005): 1,000 (11); total Internet users (2007): 2,000 (21).

Education and health

Educational attainment (2005). Percentage of population ages 5 and over having: no schooling/unknown 9.2%; primary education 40.3%; secondary 47.6%; higher 2.9%. **Literacy** (2001): percentage of total population ages 15 and over literate 94.0%; males literate 93.0%; females literate 95.0%. **Health:** physicians (2006) 30 (1 per 3,120 persons); hospital beds (2005) 140 (1 per 681 persons); infant mortality rate per 1,000 live births (2007) 45.9; undernourished population (2002–04) 5,000 (7% of total population based on the consumption of a minimum daily requirement of 1,810 calories).

Military

Total active duty personnel (2008): none; defense assistance is provided by Australia and New Zealand.

Background

The islands were settled by Austronesian-speaking peoples before the 1st century AD. In 1765 the British discovered the island of Nikunau; the first permanent European settlers arrived in 1837. In 1916 the Gilbert and Ellice islands and Banaba became a crown colony of Britain; they were later joined by the Phoenix and Line islands. The Ellice Islands declared independence (as Tuvalu) in 1978, and in 1979 the remaining islands became the nation of Kiribati.

Recent Developments

In 2008 Kiribati confronted serious challenges to its future from accelerating climate change and rising sea levels, which some analysts predicted could leave the low-lying island country uninhabitable by the end of the century. However, the same sea was thought to contain mineral wealth, and Kiribati was seeking recognition of a huge submerged continental shelf area beyond the country's 370-km (200-nautical-mile) exclusive economic zone.

Internet resources: <www.spc.int/prism/Country/KI/Stats>.

Korea, North

Official name: Choson Minjujuui In'min Konghwaguk (Democratic People's Republic of Korea). **Form of government:** unitary single-party republic with one legislative house (Supreme People's Assembly [687]). **Head of state and government:** Chairman of the National Defense Commission Kim Jong Il (from 1998). **Capital:** P'yongyang. **Official language:** Korean. **Official religion:** none. **Monetary unit:** 1 North Korean won (W) = 100 chon; valuation (1 Jul 2009) US$1 = 140.00 won.

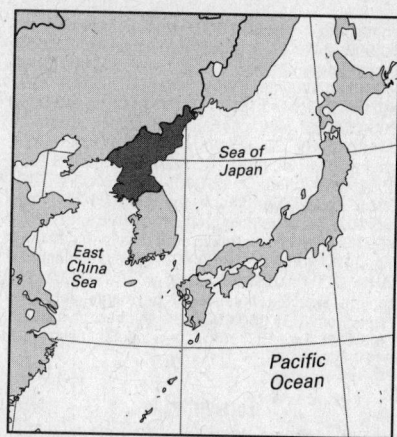

Demography

Area: 47,399 sq mi, 122,762 sq km. **Population** (2008): 23,867,000. **Density** (2008): persons per sq mi 503.5, persons per sq km 194.4. **Urban** (2005): 61.6%. **Sex distribution** (2005): male 48.49%; female 51.51%. **Age breakdown** (2005): under 15, 24.2%; 15–29, 22.8%; 30–44, 25.5%; 45–59, 15.0%; 60–74, 10.5%; 75 and over, 2.0%. **Ethnic composition** (1999): Korean 99.8%; Chinese 0.2%. **Religious affiliation** (2005): mostly nonreligious/atheist; autonomous religious activities almost nonexistent. **Major cities** (2005): P'yongyang (urban agglomeration) 3,351,000; Namp'o (urban agglomeration) 1,102,000; Hamhung (urban agglomeration) 804,000; Ch'ongjin (1993) 582,480; Kaesong (1993) 334,433. **Location:** eastern Asia, bordering China, Russia, the Sea of Japan (East Sea), the Republic of Korea, and the Yellow Sea.

Vital statistics

Birth rate per 1,000 population (2005): 16.1 (world avg. 20.3). **Death rate** per 1,000 population (2005): 7.1 (world avg. 8.6). **Natural increase rate** per 1,000 population (2005): 9.0 (world avg. 11.7). **Total fertility rate** (avg. births per childbearing woman; 2005): 2.15. **Life expectancy** at birth (2005): male 68.7 years; female 74.2 years.

National economy

Budget (1999). *Revenue:* W 19,801,000,000 (turnover tax and profits from state enterprises). *Expenditures:* W 20,018,200,000 (1994; national economy 67.8%; social and cultural affairs 19.0%; defense 11.6%). **Population economically active** (2003): total 10,708,000; activity rate of total population 48.1% (participation rates: ages 15–64, 67.4%; female 39.4%; unemployed [2000] 24.1%). **Production** (metric tons except as noted). *Agriculture and fishing* (2007): rice 2,165,000, potatoes 1,900,000, corn (maize) 1,645,000, cabbages 700,000; livestock (number of live animals) 3,300,000 pigs, 2,760,000 goats, 576,000 cattle; fisheries production (2006) 268,700 (from aquaculture 24%). *Mining and quarrying* (2007): iron ore (metal content) 1,400,000; magnesite 1,000,000;

phosphate rock 300,000; zinc (metal content) 70,000; sulfur 42,000; lead (metal content) 13,000; copper (metal content) 12,000; silver 20; gold 2,000 kg. *Manufacturing* (2006): cement 6,155,000; steel semimanufactures (1994) 2,700,000; coke 2,000,-000. *Energy production (consumption):* electricity (kW-hr; 2005) 22,913,000,000 (22,913,000,000); hard coal (metric tons; 2005) 24,060,000 (23,935,-000); lignite (metric tons; 2005) 7,746,000 (7,746,-000); crude petroleum (barrels; 2005) none (3,500,000); petroleum products (metric tons; 2005) 459,000 (916,000). **Public debt** (external, outstanding; 2000): US$12,500,000,000. **Gross national income** (2007): US$26,700,000,000 (US$1,152 per capita). **Selected balance of payments data.** Receipts from (US$'000,000): foreign direct investment (2004–06 avg.) 127; official development assistance (2006) 55.

Foreign trade

Imports (2005): US$2,718,472,000 ([excluding trade with South Korea; 2002] food, beverages, and other agricultural products 19.3%; mineral fuels and lubricants 15.5%; machinery and apparatus 15.4%; textiles and wearing apparel 10.4%). *Major import sources:* China 39.8%; South Korea 26.3%; Russia 8.2%; Thailand 7.6%; Singapore 2.7%. **Exports** (2005): US$1,338,281,000 ([excluding trade with South Korea; 2002] live animals and agricultural products 39.3%; textiles and wearing apparel 16.7%; machinery and apparatus 11.6%; mineral fuels and lubricants 9.5%). *Major export destinations:* China 37.3%; South Korea 25.4%; Japan 9.8%; Thailand 9.3%; Russia 0.6%.

Transport and communications

Transport. *Railroads* (2007): length 5,242 km. *Roads* (2007): total length 25,621 km (paved [2004] 12%). *Vehicles* (1990): passenger cars 248,000. *Air transport* (2004): passenger-km (2002) 35,000,000; metric ton-km cargo 2,000,000. **Communications,** in total units (units per 1,000 persons). Telephone landlines (2004): 980,000 (44); a ban on cellular phones, which was imposed in 2004, was lifted in 2008, and service began in December 2008; in 2005 an estimated 20,000 North Koreans had access to black market Chinese cellular phones.

Education and health

Educational attainment (1987–88). Percentage of population ages 16 and over having attended or graduated from postsecondary-level school 13.7%. **Literacy** (1997): percentage of total population literate 95%. **Health:** physicians (2003) 74,597 (1 per 299 persons); hospital beds (2002) 292,340 (1 per 76 persons); infant mortality rate per 1,000 live births (2005) 24.0; undernourished population (2002–04) 7,600,000 (33% of total population based on the consumption of a minimum daily requirement of 1,900 calories).

Military

Total active duty personnel (2008): 1,106,000 (army 85.9%, navy 4.2%, air force 9.9%). **Military expendi-**

ture as percentage of GNP (2004): 8.1%; per capita expenditure US$80.

Background

According to tradition, the ancient kingdom of Choson was established in the northern part of the Korean peninsula, probably by peoples from northern China, in the 3rd millennium BC and was conquered by China in 108 BC. The kingdom was ruled by the Yi dynasty from 1392 to 1910. That year Korea was formally annexed by Japan. It was freed from Japanese control in 1945, at which time the USSR occupied the area north of latitude 38° N and the US occupied the area south of it. The Democratic People's Republic of Korea was established as a communist state in 1948. North Korea launched an invasion of South Korea in 1950, initiating the Korean War, which ended with an armistice in 1953. Under Kim Il-sung, North Korea became one of the most harshly regimented societies in the world, with a state-owned economy that failed to produce adequate food. In the late 1990s, under Kim Il-sung's successor, Kim Jong Il, the country endured a serious famine; as many as one million Koreans may have died. In October 2006 North Korea conducted an underground nuclear test.

Recent Developments

Ongoing international negotiations to rid North Korea of nuclear weapons and related programs made no progress. In April 2009 North Korea controversially test-fired a long-range missile, and after receiving international condemnation, it announced that it was pulling out of disarmament talks and restarting its nuclear facilities, including those aimed at producing plutonium. On 25 May the country conducted its second nuclear test, an underground explosion roughly equal in strength to those that destroyed Hiroshima and Nagasaki in World War II. The next day it test-fired two more missiles. South Korea responded to the nuclear test by joining the Proliferation Security Initiative, a US-led effort involving 94 nations' navies that intercepted and searched ships around the world suspected of carrying weapons of mass destruction. North Korea, in turn, pointedly refused to guarantee the safety of any US or South Korean ships in the vicinity of its waters. It also declared that it was no longer bound by the terms of the cease-fire that had effectively ended the Korean War more than 50 years earlier.

Internet resources: <www.kcna.co.jp/index-e.htm>.

Korea, South

Official name: Taehan Min'guk (Republic of Korea). **Form of government:** unitary multiparty republic with one legislative house (National Assembly [299]). **Head of state and government:** President Lee Myung Bak (from 2008), assisted by Prime Minister Han Seung Soo (from 2008). **Capital:** Seoul. **Official language:** Korean. **Official religion:** none. **Monetary unit:** 1 South Korean won (W) = 100 chon; valuation (1 Jul 2009) US$1 = W 1,260.11.

1 metric ton = about 1.1 short tons; 1 kilometer = 0.6 mi (statute); 1 metric ton-km cargo = about 0.68 short ton-mi cargo; c.i.f.: cost, insurance, and freight; f.o.b.: free on board

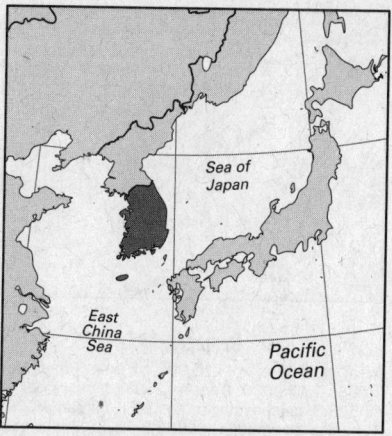

Demography

Area: 38,486 sq mi, 99,678 sq km. **Population** (2008): 50,187,000. **Density** (2008): persons per sq mi 1,304.2, persons per sq km 503.5. **Urban** (2005): 81.5%. **Sex distribution** (2005): male 49.97%; female 50.03%. **Age breakdown** (2005): under 15, 18.6%; 15–29, 22.5%; 30–44, 26.0%; 45–59, 19.2%; 60–74, 10.7%; 75–84, 2.5%; 85 and over, 0.5%. **Ethnic composition** (2000): Korean 97.7%; Japanese 2.0%; US white 0.1%; Han Chinese 0.1%; other 0.1%. **Religious affiliation** (2005): Christian 43%, of which Protestant 17%, independent Christian 16%, Roman Catholic 9%; traditional beliefs 15%; Buddhist 14%; New Religionist 14%; Confucianist 10%; other 4%. **Major cities** (2007): Seoul 10,421,782; Pusan 3,615,101; Inch'on 2,710,540; Taegu 2,512,670; Taejon 1,487,836. **Location:** eastern Asia, bordering the Democratic People's Republic of Korea, the Sea of Japan (East Sea), and the Yellow Sea.

Vital statistics

Birth rate per 1,000 population (2007): 10.1 (world avg. 20.3). **Death rate** per 1,000 population (2007): 5.0 (world avg. 8.6). **Total fertility rate** (avg. births per childbearing woman; 2007): 1.26. **Life expectancy** at birth (2005): male 75.1 years; female 81.9 years.

National economy

Budget (2005). *Revenue:* W 191,447,000,000,000 (current revenue 99.3%, of which tax revenue 79.6%, nontax revenue 19.7%; capital revenue 0.7%). *Expenditures:* W 184,922,000,000,000 (current expenditures 86.7%; capital expenditures 13.3%). **Production** (metric tons except as noted). *Agriculture and fishing* (2007): rice 5,959,500, cabbages 3,000,000, tangerines, mandarins, and satsumas 615,000; livestock (number of live animals) 9,850,000 pigs, 2,580,000 cattle, 121,000,000 chickens; fisheries production (2006) 2,263,497 (from aquaculture 23%); aquatic plants production (2006) 779,349 (from aquaculture 98%). *Mining and quarrying* (2006): feldspar 427,378, iron ore (metal content) 155,000. *Manufacturing* (value added in US$'000,000; 2005): electrical machinery and apparatus 79,423, of which televisions, radios, telecommunica-

tions equipment, and electronic parts 57,865; transportation equipment 42,071, of which automobiles 18,026, automobile parts 12,962, ships and boats 9,191; chemical products 25,157; nonelectrical machinery 23,009; iron and steel 19,714. *Energy production (consumption):* electricity (kW-hr; 2007) 403,129,000,000 ([2005] 389,390,000,000); coal (metric tons; 2007) 2,915,000 ([2005] 79,410,000); lignite (metric tons; 2005) none (2,862,000); crude petroleum (barrels; 2005) 396,000 (842,000,000); petroleum products (metric tons; 2005) 93,880,000 (59,802,000); natural gas (cu m; 2006) 453,000,000 (32,281,000,000). **Gross national income** (2007): US$955,802,000,000 (US$19,690 per capita). **Public debt** (2005): US$240,000,000,000. **Population economically active** (2005): total 23,743,000; activity rate of total population 49.3% (participation rates: ages 15–64, 66.4%; female 41.5%; unemployed [July 2007] 3.2%). **Selected balance of payments data.** Receipts from (US$'000,000): tourism (2006) 5,322; remittances (2007) 1,128; foreign direct investment (FDI) (2004–06 avg.) 6,993. Disbursements for (US$'000,000): tourism (2006) 18,241; remittances (2007) 4,070; FDI (2004–06 avg.) 5,362.

Foreign trade

Imports (2006; c.i.f.): US$309,379,000,000 (mineral fuels 28.0%, of which crude petroleum 18.1%; machinery and apparatus 27.1%, of which heavy machinery 8.6%, electronic microcircuits 7.0%; chemical products 8.9%). *Major import sources:* Japan 16.8%; China 15.7%; US 10.9%; Saudi Arabia 6.6%; UAE 4.2%. **Exports** (2006; f.o.b.): US$325,457,000,000 (road vehicles 13.0%; telecommunications equipment 10.4%; electronic microcircuits 7.8%; organic chemicals and plastic products 7.5%; heavy machinery 7.3%). *Major export destinations:* China 21.3%; US 13.3%; Japan 8.2%; Hong Kong 5.8%; Germany 3.1%.

Transport and communications

Transport. *Railroads* (2005): length (2001) 6,819 km; passenger-km 31,004,200,000; metric ton-km cargo 9,336,000,000. *Roads* (2005): total length 102,293 km (paved 77%). *Vehicles* (2005): passenger cars 11,122,199; trucks and buses 4,274,513. *Air transport* (2006): passenger-km 74,184,000,000; metric ton-km cargo 9,486,060,000. **Communications,** in total units (units per 1,000 persons). Telephone landlines (2007): 23,905,000 (496); cellular telephone subscribers (2007): 43,498,000 (902); personal computers (2005): 25,685,000 (532); total Internet users (2007): 35,590,000 (738); broadband Internet subscribers (2007): 14,198,000 (293).

Education and health

Educational attainment (2002). Percentage of population ages 25–64 having: no formal schooling through lower secondary education 29%; upper secondary/higher vocational 45%; university 26%. **Literacy** (2001): percentage of total population ages 15 and over literate 97.9%; males literate 99.2%; females literate 96.6%. **Health** (2005): physicians 85,369 (1 per 564 persons); hospital beds (2004) 353,289 (1 per 136 persons); infant mortality rate per 1,000 live births (2007) 3.5; undernourished population (2002–04) less than 2.5% of total population.

Military

Total active duty personnel (2007): 687,000 (army 81.5%, navy 9.2%, air force 9.3%); US military forces (2008) 26,339. **Military expenditure as percentage of GDP** (2005): 2.6%; per capita expenditure US$430.

Background

Civilization in the Korean peninsula dates to the 3rd millennium BC. The Republic of Korea was established in 1948 in the southern portion of the Korean peninsula. In 1950 North Korean troops invaded South Korea, precipitating the Korean War. UN forces sided with South Korea, while Chinese troops backed North Korea in the war, which ended with an armistice in 1953. The devastated country was rebuilt with US aid, and South Korea prospered in the postwar era, developing a strong export-oriented economy. It experienced an economic downturn in the mid-1990s that affected many Asian economies. Efforts at reconciliation between North and South Korea, including the first-ever summit between their leaders (2000) and reunions of families from both countries, were accompanied by periods of continuing tension.

Recent Developments

South Korea, a country heavily dependent on foreign trade and investment, was hit hard by the global economic downturn in 2008. The stock market plummeted nearly 40% for the year, while at one point the local currency lost half of its value against the US dollar. Korea also experienced a trade deficit for the first time since 1997. Amazingly, the unemployment rate remained low (3.3% in December), and economic growth was positive for the year, but Pres. Lee Myung-bak warned that the economy could shrink in 2009. Fortunately, the crisis did lead to something that two successive nuclear standoffs with North Korea had failed to accomplish: the first-ever summit between South Korea, China, and Japan, which took place on 13 December. China and Japan agreed to provide South Korea with a badly needed foreign-currency swap, and the three countries agreed to make their gathering an annual occurrence.

Internet resources:
<www.nso.go.kr/eng2006/emain/index.html>.

Kosovo

Official name: Republika e Kosovës (Albanian); Republika Kosovo (Serbian) (Republic of Kosovo). **Form of government:** multiparty transitional republic with one legislative house (Assembly of Kosovo [120]). **Chief of state:** President Fatmir Sejdiu (from 2008; final authority rests with UN Interim Administrator Lamberto Zannier [from 2008]). **Head of government:** Prime Minister Hashim Thaçi (from 2008). **Capital:** Pristina. **Official languages:** Albanian; Serbian. **Official religion:** none. **Monetary unit:** 1 euro (€) = 100 cents; valuation (1 Jul 2009) US$1 = €0.71 (Kosovo uses the euro as its official currency, even though it is not a member of the EU).

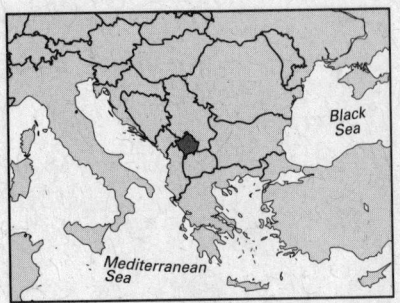

Demography

Area: 4,212 sq mi, 10,908 sq km. **Population** (2008): 2,143,000. **Density** (2008): persons per sq mi 508.8, persons per sq km 196.5. **Urban** (2006): 37%. **Sex distribution** (2006): male 50.9%; female 49.1%. **Age breakdown** (2003): under 15, 32.2%; 15–59, 58.7%; 60 and over, 9.1%. **Ethnic composition** (2008): Albanian 92.0%; Serb 5.3%; other 2.7%. **Religious affiliation** (2006): Muslim 91%; Orthodox 5.5%; Roman Catholic 3%; Protestant 0.5%. **Major cities** (2003): Pristina 165,844; Prizren 107,614; Ferizaj 71,758; Mitrovicë 68,929; Gjakovë 68,645. **Location:** southeastern Europe, bordering Serbia, Macedonia, Albania, and Montenegro.

Vital statistics

Birth rate per 1,000 population (2007): 15.6 (world avg. 20.3); within marriage 55.0%; outside of marriage 41.5%; unknown 3.5%. **Death rate** per 1,000 population (2007): 3.1 (world avg. 8.6). **Natural increase rate** per 1,000 population (2007): 12.5 (world avg. 11.7). **Total fertility rate** (avg. births per childbearing woman; 2003): 3.0. **Life expectancy** at birth (2004): male 69.8 years; female 71.4 years.

National economy

Budget (2007–08). *Revenue:* €2,148,400,000 (tax revenue 79.7%, of which border taxes [including customs duties and VAT] 59.8%, domestic taxes [mostly income and corporate taxes] 19.9%; nontax revenue 20.3%). *Expenditures:* €1,523,000,000 (current expenditures 81.1%, of which wages and salaries 32.8%, transfers 27.8%; capital expenditures 18.9%). **Production** (metric tons except as noted). *Agriculture and fishing* (2006): wheat 239,464, corn (maize) 138,248, potatoes 71,245; livestock (number of live animals) 381,995 cattle, 100,814 sheep, 2,337,081 chickens. *Manufacturing* (2006): cement, bricks, and tiles for reconstruction of housing; food products; and beverages. *Energy production (consumption):* electricity (kW-hr; 2007–08) 4,192,–650,000 (2,710,462,000); lignite (metric tons; 2007–08) 6,787,305 (n.a.). **Gross national income** (at current market prices; 2005): US$3,364,000,000 (US$1,640 per capita). **Population economically active** (2007): total 633,000; activity rate of total population 30% (participation rates: ages 15–64, 47%; female 28%; unemployed [June 2008] 15.7%). **Selected balance of payments data.** Receipts from

---

1 metric ton = about 1.1 short tons;   1 kilometer = 0.6 mi (statute);   1 metric ton-km cargo = about 0.68 short ton-mi cargo;   c.i.f.: cost, insurance, and freight;   f.o.b.: free on board

(US$'000,000): tourism (2006) 32; remittances (2006) 586; foreign direct investment (2004–06 avg.) 505. Disbursements for (US$'000,000): tourism (2006) 78; remittances (2006) 126.

Foreign trade

Imports (2007; c.i.f.): €1,575,600,000 (food and live animals 24.4%; mineral fuels 20.2%; machinery and apparatus 12.5%; iron and steel [all forms] 9.2%; chemical products 7.5%). *Major import sources:* Macedonia 15.0%; Serbia 14.1%; Germany 9.1%; China 6.6%; Turkey 6.4%. **Exports** (2007; f.o.b.): €165,100,000 (iron and steel [all forms] 44.9%; mineral fuels 16.5%; machinery and apparatus 12.9%; food and live animals 10.7%). *Major export destinations:* Albania 11.5%; Serbia 10.2%; Germany 9.4%; Macedonia 9.3%; Switzerland 7.5%.

Transport and communications

Transport. *Railroads* (2007): route length 430 km. *Roads* (2007): total length 1,924 km (paved 87%). *Air transport* (Pristina airport only; 2007–08): passenger arrivals 542,781; passenger departures 1,061,353. **Communications,** in total units (units per 1,000 persons). Telephone landlines (2006): 135,000 (65); cellular telephone subscribers (2006): 540,000 (259); total Internet users (2006): 50,000 (24); broadband Internet subscribers (2005): 4,700 (2.3).

Education and health

Educational attainment (2003). Percentage of population ages 25–49 having: no formal schooling 3.5%; incomplete/complete primary education 46.0%; incomplete/complete secondary 45.0%; higher 5.5%. **Literacy** (2004): percentage of total population ages 15 and over literate 94.1%; males literate 97.3%; females literate 91.3%. **Health** (2006): physicians 1,534 (1 per 1,368 persons); hospital beds (2005) 5,308 (1 per 387 persons); infant mortality rate per 1,000 live births (2007) 11.1.

Military

Total active duty personnel (2008): NATO-led Kosovo Force 15,900.

Background

The Kingdom of the Serbs, Croats, and Slovenes was created after the collapse of Austria-Hungary at the end of World War I. The country signed treaties with Czechoslovakia and Romania in 1920–21, marking the beginning of the Little Entente. In 1929 an absolute monarchy was established, the country's name was changed to Yugoslavia, and it was divided into regions without regard to ethnic boundaries. Axis powers invaded Yugoslavia in 1941, and German, Italian, Hungarian, and Bulgarian troops occupied it for the rest of World War II. In 1945 the Socialist Federal Republic of Yugoslavia was established; it included the republics of Bosnia and Herzegovina, Croatia, Macedonia, Montenegro, Serbia, and Slovenia. Its independent form of communism under Josip Broz Tito's leadership provoked the USSR. Internal ethnic tensions flared up in the 1980s, causing the country's ultimate collapse. In 1991–92 independence was declared by Croatia, Slovenia, Macedonia, and Bosnia and Herzegovina; the new Federal Republic of Yugoslavia (containing roughly 45% of the population and 40% of the area of its predecessor) was proclaimed by Serbia and Montenegro. Still fueled by long-standing ethnic tensions, hostilities continued into the 1990s. Despite the approval of the Dayton Peace Agreement (1995), sporadic fighting continued and was followed in 1998–99 by Serbian repression and expulsion of ethnic populations in the province of Kosovo. In September–October 2000, the battered nation of Yugoslavia ended the autocratic rule of Pres. Slobodan Milosevic. In April 2001 he was arrested and in June extradited to The Hague to stand trial for war crimes, genocide, and crimes against humanity committed during the fighting in Kosovo. In February 2003 both houses of the Yugoslav federal legislature voted to accept a new state charter and change the name of the country from Yugoslavia to Serbia and Montenegro. Henceforth, defense, international political and economic relations, and human rights matters would be handled centrally, while all other functions would be run from the republican capitals, Belgrade and Podgorica, respectively. The move was seen as an acknowledgment that Serbia and Montenegro had little in common, and a provision was included for both states to vote on independence after three years; Serbia declared its independence in June 2006, shortly after Montenegro severed its federal union with Serbia. From 1999 an autonomous region administered by the UN, Kosovo declared its independence from Serbia on 17 Feb 2008. That December the UN transferred most of its powers of oversight to the EU.

Recent Developments

On 17 Feb 2008, Kosovo formally declared its independence from Serbia. Though calm endured in much of the country, tension centered on the ethnically divided northern town of Mitrovica, where Serbia's influence on Kosovo's Serbs remained significant and violence broke out. Organized crime and a thriving black market continued to be concerns, along with an unemployment rate of more than 40% and a per capita income that remained among the lowest in Europe. By year's end 53 countries (including all of the neighboring states except Serbia) recognized Kosovo's independence.

Internet resources: <www.ks-gov.net/esk/eng>.

Kuwait

Official name: Dawlat al-Kuwayt (State of Kuwait). **Form of government:** constitutional monarchy with one legislative body (National Assembly [50]). **Head of state and government:** Emir Sheikh Sabah al-Ahmad al-Jabir al-Sabah (from 2006), assisted by Prime Minister Sheikh Nassar Muhammad al-Ahmad al-Sabah (from 2006). **Capital:** Kuwait (city). **Official language:** Arabic. **Official religion:** Islam. **Monetary unit:** 1 Kuwaiti dinar (KD) = 1,000 fils; valuation (1 Jul 2009) US$1 = KD 0.29.

Demography

Area: 6,880 sq mi, 17,818 sq km. **Population** (2008): 3,530,000. **Density** (2008): persons per sq mi 513.1, persons per sq km 198.1. **Urban** (2005): 98.3%. **Sex distribution** (2005): male 62.69%; female 37.31%. **Age breakdown** (2005): under 15, 24.3%; 15–29,

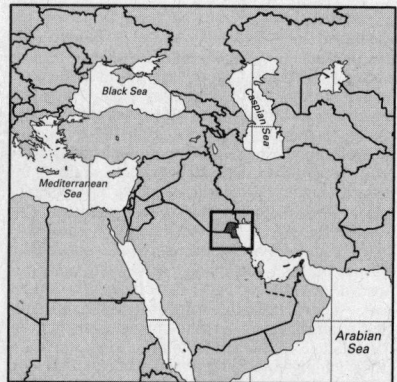

26.8%; 30–44, 34.2%; 45–59, 11.6%; 60–74, 2.7%; 75–84, 0.3%; 85 and over, 0.1%. **Ethnic composition** (2005): Arab 57%, of which Kuwaiti 35%; Bedouin 4%; non-Arab (primarily Asian) 39%. **Religious affiliation** (2005): Muslim 74%, of which Sunni 59%, Shi'i 15%; Christian 13%, of which Roman Catholic 9%; Hindu 10%; Buddhist 3%. **Major cities** (2005): Qalib al-Shuyukh 179,264; Al-Salimiyah 145,328; Hawalli 106,992; Kuwait (city) 32,403 (urban agglomeration 1,810,000). **Location:** the Middle East, bordering Iraq, the Persian Gulf, and Saudi Arabia.

Vital statistics

Birth rate per 1,000 population (2006): 17.1 (world avg. 20.3). **Death rate** per 1,000 population (2006): 1.7 (world avg. 8.6). **Natural increase rate** per 1,000 population (2006): 15.4 (world avg. 11.7). **Total fertility rate** (avg. births per childbearing woman; 2004): 3.00. **Life expectancy** at birth (2004): male 75.9 years; female 77.9 years.

National economy

Budget (2004–05). *Revenue:* KD 12,346,700,000 (oil revenue 93.8%). *Expenditures:* KD 6,315,200,-000 (defense 20.9%; transfers 18.5%; public utilities 14.0%; education 8.0%; health 5.6%. **Public debt** (external, outstanding; 2004): US$668,000,000. **Gross national income** (2007): US$122,780,-000,000 (US$43,063 per capita). **Production** (metric tons except as noted). *Agriculture and fishing* (2007): tomatoes 55,500, cucumbers and gherkins 35,000, potatoes 23,500, dates 14,500; livestock (number of live animals) 900,000 sheep, 160,000 goats, 28,000 cattle, 5,000 camels; fisheries production (2006) 6,203 (from aquaculture 9%). *Mining and quarrying* (2006): sulfur 650,000; lime 50,000. *Manufacturing* (value added in US$'000,000; 2004): refined petroleum products 2,701; chemical products 533; fabricated metal products 319. *Energy production (consumption):* electricity (kW-hr; 2005) 43,734,000,000 (43,734,000,000); crude petroleum (barrels; 2007) 899,400,000 ([2005] 330,000,000); petroleum products (metric tons; 2005) 36,930,000 (14,060,000); natural gas (cu m; 2005) 13,298,000,000 (13,298,000,000). **Popula-**tion economically active (2004): total 1,634,315, of which Kuwaiti 18.3%, non-Kuwaiti 81.7%; activity rate of total population 59.4% (participation rates: ages 15 and over, 76.4%; female [2002] 25.7%; unemployed 2.2%). **Selected balance of payments data.** Receipts from (US$'000,000): tourism (2006) 205; foreign direct investment (FDI) (2004–06 avg.) 128. Disbursements for (US$'000,000): tourism (2006) 5,253; remittances (2007) 3,021; FDI (2004–06 avg.) 5,187.

Foreign trade

Imports (2006): KD 4,629,000,000 (industrial requirements 31.0%; capital goods [both machinery and transportation equipment] 24.2%; durable consumer goods 11.1%; food and beverages 10.0%). *Major import sources:* US 11.9%; Germany 11.2%; Saudi Arabia 8.0%; Japan 7.6%; China 7.0%. **Exports** (2006): KD 17,015,000,000 (crude petroleum 67.3%; refined petroleum products 23.2%; liquefied petroleum gas 4.5%; ethylene products 2.0%). *Major export destinations* (2005): Japan 20%; South Korea 15%; US 12%; Taiwan 11%; Singapore 10%.

Transport and communications

Transport. *Railroads:* none. *Roads* (2004): total length 5,720 km (paved [1999] 81%). *Vehicles* (2004): passenger cars 848,590; trucks and buses 172,219. *Air transport* (2006): passenger-km 6,948,000,000; metric ton-km cargo 260,052,000. **Communications,** in total units (units per 1,000 persons). Telephone landlines (2005): 510,000 (190); cellular telephone subscribers (2007): 2,774,000 (973); personal computers (2005): 600,000 (223); total Internet users (2007): 900,000 (316); broadband Internet subscribers (2005): 25,000 (8.1).

Education and health

Educational attainment (2005). Percentage of population ages 10 and over having: no formal schooling 44.1% (illiterate 6.2%, literate 37.9%); primary education 12.7%; lower secondary 20.8%; upper secondary 11.7%; some higher 4.1%; completed undergraduate 6.6%. **Literacy** (2005): percentage of total population ages 15 and over literate 84.4%; males literate 85.7%; females literate 82.8%. **Health** (2006): physicians 4,775 (1 per 646 persons); hospital beds 5,760 (1 per 535 persons); infant mortality rate per 1,000 live births 8.6; undernourished population (2002–04) 120,000 (5% of total population based on the consumption of a minimum daily requirement of 1,980 calories).

Military

Total active duty personnel (2007): 15,500 (army 71.0%, navy 12.9%, air force 16.1%); US troops for Iraqi support (2007) 10,000–20,000. **Military expenditure as percentage of GDP** (2005): 4.8%; per capita expenditure US$1,370.

Background

Faylakah Island, in Kuwait Bay, had a civilization dating back to the 3rd millennium BC that flourished

---

1 metric ton = about 1.1 short tons;   1 kilometer = 0.6 mi (statute);   1 metric ton-km cargo = about 0.68 short ton-mi cargo;   c.i.f.: cost, insurance, and freight;   f.o.b.: free on board

until 1200 BC. Greek colonists resettled the island in the 4th century BC. Abd Rahim of the Sabah dynasty became sheikh in 1756, the first of a family that continues to rule Kuwait. In 1899, to thwart German and Ottoman influences, Kuwait gave Britain control of its foreign affairs. Following the outbreak of war in 1914, Britain established a protectorate there. In 1961, after Kuwait became independent, Iraq laid claim to it. British troops defended Kuwait, the Arab League recognized its independence, and Iraq dropped its claim. Iraqi forces invaded and occupied Kuwait in 1990, and a US-led military coalition drove them out in 1991. The destruction of many of Kuwait's oil wells complicated reconstruction efforts.

Recent Developments

Declining economic conditions in Kuwait for foreign workers, who made up two-thirds of the population, led them in July 2008 to strike. Disturbances continued for three days, resulting in clashes with the security force and the deportation of hundreds of workers (mainly Bengalis). In an attempt to address the problem, the government announced plans to raise the workers' minimum wage, revise work contracts, and improve living conditions. Kuwaiti nationals also protested the rise in food and commodity prices. In response the government twice increased the salaries of Kuwaitis working in the public sector by 170 Kuwaiti dinars (about US$643). Relations between Kuwait and Iraq saw a noticeable improvement during the year. In July Kuwait announced the appointment of an ambassador in Baghdad, the first since Iraq's 1990 invasion.

Internet resources: <www.cbk.gov.kw>.

Kyrgyzstan

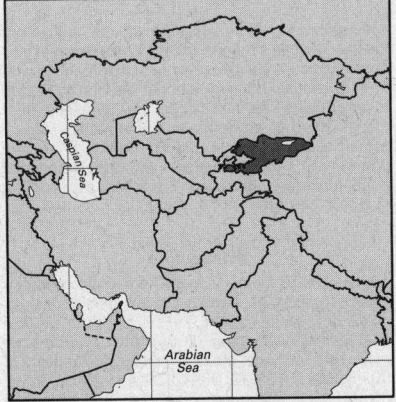

Official name: Kyrgyz Respublikasy (Kyrgyz); Respublika Kirgizstan (Russian) (Kyrgyz Republic). Form of government: unitary multiparty republic with one legislative house (Supreme Council [90]). Head of state and government: President Kurmanbek Bakiyev (from 2005), assisted by Prime Minister Igor Chudinov (from 2007). Capital: Bishkek. Official languages: Kyrgyz; Russian. Official religion: none. Mon-

etary unit: 1 som (KGS) = 100 tyiyn; valuation (1 Jul 2009) US$1 = KGS 43.26.

Demography

Area: 77,182 sq mi, 199,900 sq km. Population (2008): 5,281,000. Density (2008): persons per sq mi 68.4, persons per sq km 26.4. Urban (2007): 34.7%. Sex distribution (2005): male 49.03%; female 50.97%. Age breakdown (2005): under 15, 31.5%; 15–29, 29.8%; 30–44, 18.8%; 45–59, 12.0%; 60–74, 5.7%; 75–84, 1.9%; 85 and over, 0.3%. Ethnic composition (2005): Kyrgyz 67.4%; Uzbek 14.2%; Russian 10.3%; Hui 1.1%; Uighur 1.0%; other 6.0%. Religious affiliation (2000): Muslim (mostly Sunni) 60.8%; Christian 10.4%, of which Russian Orthodox 7.7%; nonreligious 21.6%; atheist 6.3%; other 0.9%. Major cities (1999): Bishkek 750,327; Osh 208,520; Jalal-Abad 70,401; Karakol 64,322; Tokmok 59,409. Location: central Asia, bordering Kazakhstan, China, Tajikistan, and Uzbekistan.

Vital statistics

Birth rate per 1,000 population (2007): 23.5 (world avg. 20.3); (1994) within marriage 83.2%; outside of marriage 16.8%. Death rate per 1,000 population (2007): 7.3 (world avg. 8.6). Natural increase rate per 1,000 population (2007): 16.2 (world avg. 11.7). Total fertility rate (avg. births per childbearing woman; 2005): 2.69. Life expectancy at birth (2007): male 63.6 years; female 72.2 years.

National economy

Budget (2005). Revenue: KGS 20,368,100,000 (tax revenue 80.3%, of which VAT 34.8%, income tax 8.6%, profit tax 6.3%; nontax revenue 17.7%; grants 2.0%). Expenditures: KGS 20,143,700,000 (administration, defense, and police 30.5%; education 24.4%; social security 14.2%; health 11.3%). Public debt (external, outstanding; 2006): US$1,860,000,000. Population economically active (2005): total 2,260,600; activity rate of total population 43.4% (participation rates: ages 15–64 [2002] 68.7%; female 42.9%; unemployed 8.1%). Production (metric tons except as noted). Agriculture and fishing (2007): potatoes 1,373,800, wheat 708,900, corn (maize) 460,700; livestock (number of live animals) 3,198,000 sheep, 1,117,000 cattle, 350,600 horses; fisheries production (2006) 27 (from aquaculture 74%). Mining and quarrying (2005): mercury 200; antimony 10; gold 16,700 kg. Manufacturing (value of production in KGS '000,000; 2004): base and fabricated metals 24,330; food and tobacco products 6,811; cement, bricks, and ceramics 3,574. Energy production (consumption): electricity (kW-hr; 2005) 16,415,000,000 (13,731,000,000); coal (metric tons; 2005) 49,000 (887,000); lignite (metric tons; 2005) 286,000 (452,000); crude petroleum (barrels; 2005) 542,000 (579,000); petroleum products (metric tons; 2005) 76,000 (561,000); natural gas (cu m; 2005) 25,000,000 (736,000,000). Gross national income (2007): US$3,099,000,000 (US$590 per capita). Selected balance of payments data. Receipts from (US$'000,000): tourism (2006) 167; remittances (2007) 715; foreign direct investment (FDI) (2004–06 avg.) 113; official development assistance (2006) 311. Disbursements for (US$'000,-

000): tourism (2006) 92; remittances (2007) 218; FDI (2004–06 avg.) 15.

Foreign trade

Imports (2006; c.i.f.): US$1,718,200,000 (refined petroleum products 25.1%; machinery and apparatus 16.2%; chemical products 10.4%; road vehicles 6.0%). *Major import sources* (2006): Russia 38.0%; China 14.4%; Kazakhstan 11.6%; US 5.7%; Uzbekistan 3.8%. **Exports** (2006; f.o.b.): US$794,100,000 (gold 25.9%; refined petroleum products 15.2%; machinery and apparatus 6.4%; fruit and vegetables 4.6%; cotton 4.6%;). *Major export destinations* (2006): Switzerland 26.2%; Kazakhstan 20.5%; Russia 19.4%; Afghanistan 9.4%; China 4.8%.

Transport and communications

Transport. *Railroads* (2004): length (2000) 424 km; passenger-km 45,300,000; metric ton-km cargo 714,900,000. *Roads* (2000): total length 18,500 km (paved 91%). *Vehicles* (2005): passenger cars 201,430. *Air transport* (2007): passenger-km 456,000,000; metric ton-km cargo 1,200,000. **Communications,** in total units (units per 1,000 persons). Telephone landlines (2007): 482,000 (91); cellular telephone subscribers (2007): 2,152,000 (405); personal computers (2005): 100,000 (19); total Internet users (2007): 750,000 (141); broadband Internet subscribers (2007): 2,900 (0.5).

Education and health

Educational attainment (1999). Percentage of population ages 15 and over having: primary education 6.3%; some secondary 18.3%; completed secondary 50.0%; some postsecondary 14.9%; higher 10.5%. **Literacy** (2003): percentage of total population ages 15 and over literate 98.7%; males literate 99.3%; females literate 98.1%. **Health:** physicians (2004) 13,996 (1 per 363 persons); hospital beds (2004) 26,040 (1 per 195 persons); infant mortality rate per 1,000 live births (2007) 30.6; undernourished population (2002–04) 200,000 (4% of total population based on the consumption of a minimum daily requirement of 1,930 calories).

Military

Total active duty personnel (2007): 10,900 (army 78.0%, air force 22.0%); Russian troops (2007) 500. **Military expenditure as percentage of GDP** (2005): 3.1%; per capita expenditure US$15.

Background

The Kyrgyz, a nomadic people of Central Asia, settled in the Tian Shan region in ancient times. They were conquered by Genghis Khan's son Jochi in 1207. The area became part of the Qing empire of China in the mid-18th century. The region came under Russian control in the 19th century, and its rebellion against Russia in 1916 resulted in a long period of brutal repression. Kirgiziya became an autonomous province of the USSR in 1924 and was made the Kirghiz Soviet Socialist Republic in 1936. Kyrgyzstan gained independence in 1991. It subsequently struggled with

creating a democratic process and with establishing a stable economy.

Recent Developments

Despite large amounts of international assistance to the development of its economy, Kyrgyzstan continued in 2008 to flounder both politically and economically. According to the country's national bank, by the beginning of 2009 more than US$1 billion had been poured into Kyrgyzstan in the form of foreign investment and grants. Increasing numbers of Kyrgyz citizens were searching for work abroad, and in early 2008 the National Migration Agency reported that 250,000 Kyrgyz were employed in Russia—a figure that did not include the number working in Kazakhstan and other neighboring countries. The World Bank noted that remittances from labor migrants made up 37% of Kyrgyzstan's GDP.

Internet resources: <www.nbkr.kg/web/ interfeis.builder_frame?language=ENG>.

Laos

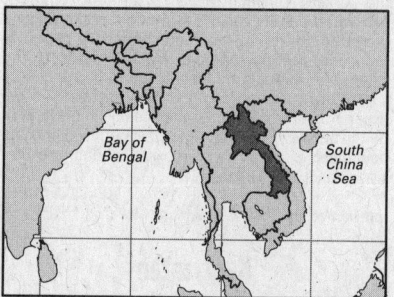

Official name: Sathalanalat Paxathipatai Paxaxon Lao (Lao People's Democratic Republic). **Form of government:** unitary single-party people's republic with one legislative house (National Assembly [115]). **Chief of state:** President Choummaly Sayasone (from 2006). **Head of government:** Prime Minister Bouasone Bouphavanh (from 2006). **Capital:** Vientiane (Viangchan). **Official language:** Lao. **Official religion:** none. **Monetary unit:** 1 kip (KN) = 100 at; valuation (1 Jul 2009) US$1 = KN 8,337.20.

Demography

Area: 91,429 sq mi, 236,800 sq km. **Population** (2008): 5,963,000. **Density** (2008): persons per sq mi 65.2, persons per sq km 25.2. **Urban** (2005): 27.1%. **Sex distribution** (2005): male 49.81%; female 50.19%. **Age breakdown** (2005): under 15, 39.4%; 15–29, 28.3%; 30–44, 17.0%; 45–59, 9.5%; 60–74, 4.4%; 75 and over, 1.4%. **Ethnic composition** (2005): Lao 54.6%; Khmou 10.9%; Hmong 8.0%; Tai 3.8%; Phu Tai (Phouthay) 3.3%; Lue 2.2%; Katang 2.1%; Makong 2.1%; other 13.0%. **Religious affiliation** (2005): traditional beliefs 49%; Buddhist 43%; Christian 2%; nonreligious/other 6%. **Major cities** (2003): Vientiane 194,200 (urban agglomeration

---

1 metric ton = about 1.1 short tons;   1 kilometer = 0.6 mi (statute);   1 metric ton-km cargo = about 0.68 short ton-mi cargo;   c.i.f.: cost, insurance, and freight;   f.o.b.: free on board

[2005] 702,000); Savannakhét 58,200; Pakxé 50,100; Xam Nua 40,700; Muang Khammouan 27,300. **Location:** southeastern Asia, bordering China, Vietnam, Cambodia, Thailand, and Myanmar (Burma).

Vital statistics

Birth rate per 1,000 population (2005): 34.7 (world avg. 20.3). **Death rate** per 1,000 population (2005): 9.8 (world avg. 8.6). **Natural increase rate** per 1,000 population (2005): 24.9 (world avg. 11.7). **Total fertility rate** (avg. births per childbearing woman; 2005): 4.77. **Life expectancy** at birth (2005): male 53.1 years; female 57.2 years.

National economy

Budget (2005–06). *Revenue:* KN 4,962,000,-000,000 (tax revenue 73.4%, of which sales tax 17.9%, excise tax 16.1%; grants 14.0%; nontax revenue 12.6%). *Expenditures:* KN 6,205,000,000,000 (current expenditures 50.3%; capital expenditures 49.7%, of which foreign-financed expenditure 26.9%). **Public debt** (external, outstanding; 2006): US$2,191,000,000. **Population economically active** (2005): total 2,778,000; activity rate of total population 66.6% (participation rates: ages 15–64, 81.3%; female 50.2%; unofficially unemployed [2004] 7.0%). **Production** (metric tons except as noted). *Agriculture and fishing* (2007): rice 2,870,000, corn (maize) 450,000, sugarcane 220,000, natural rubber (hectares; 2006) 11,778; livestock (number of live animals) 2,260,000 pigs, 1,337,000 cattle, 1,120,000 water buffalo; fisheries production (2006) 107,800 (from aquaculture 72%). *Mining and quarrying* (2007): gypsum 775,000; limestone 750,000; copper (metal content) 99,040; tin (metal content) 450; gold 4,161 kg. *Manufacturing* (value added in US$'000,000; 1999): food products 22; wearing apparel 14; tobacco products 8. *Energy production (consumption):* electricity (kW-hr; 2005) 3,513,000,000 (733,000,000); coal (metric tons; 2005) 300,000 (300,000); petroleum products (metric tons; 2005) none (126,000). **Gross national income** (2007): US$3,413,000,000 (US$580 per capita). **Selected balance of payments data.** Receipts from (US$'000,000): tourism (2006) 173; remittances (2007) 1.0; foreign direct investment (2004–06 avg.) 77; official development assistance (2006) 364. Disbursements for (US$'000,000): tourism (2001) 0.1; remittances (2007) 1.0.

Foreign trade

Imports (2006; c.i.f.): US$1,384,000,000 (capital goods 52.6%; crude petroleum 14.5%; materials for wearing apparel assembly 7.1%). *Major import sources* (2005): Thailand 67%; China 9%; Vietnam 6%; Singapore 3%; Japan 2%. **Exports** (2006; f.o.b.): US$996,000,000 (copper 41.1%; timber 15.9%; wearing apparel 13.3%; gold 11.7%; electricity 10.8%). *Major export destinations* (2005): Thailand 29%; Vietnam 12%; France 6%; Germany 5%; China 3%.

Transport and communications

Transport. *Railroads:* none. *Roads* (2004): total length 24,000 km (paved 16%). *Vehicles* (1996): passenger cars 16,320; trucks and buses 4,200. *Air*

transport (2004): passenger-km 216,300,000; metric ton-km cargo 2,000,000. **Communications**, in total units (units per 1,000 persons). Telephone landlines (2007): 95,000 (16); cellular telephone subscribers (2007): 1,478,000 (252); personal computers (2005): 100,000 (17); total Internet users (2007): 100,000 (17); broadband Internet subscribers (2007): 3,600 (0.6).

Education and health

Educational attainment (2005). Percentage of population ages 25 and over having: no formal schooling 32.8%; incomplete primary education 21.6%; complete primary 18.2%; lower secondary 11.4%; upper secondary 6.2%; higher 9.8%. **Literacy** (2005): percentage of total population ages 15 and over literate 72.7%; males literate 82.5%; females literate 63.2%. **Health** (2005): physicians 5,000 (1 per 1,129 persons); hospital beds 6,736 (1 per 838 persons); infant mortality rate per 1,000 live births 85.2; undernourished population (2002–04) 1,100,000 (19% of total population based on the consumption of a minimum daily requirement of 1,730 calories).

Military

Total active duty personnel (2007): 29,100 (army 88.0%, air force 12.0%). **Military expenditure as percentage of GDP** (2004): 0.4%; per capita expenditure US$2.

Background

The Lao people migrated into Laos from southern China after the 8th century AD, displacing indigenous tribes. In the 14th century Fa Ngum founded the first Laotian state, Lan Xang. Except for a period of rule by Burma (1574–1637), the Lan Xang kingdom ruled Laos until 1713, when it split into three kingdoms. France gained control of the region in 1893. In 1945 Japan seized it and declared Laos independent. The area reverted to French rule after World War II. The Geneva Conference of 1954 unified and granted independence to Laos. Communist forces took control in 1975, establishing the Lao People's Democratic Republic. Laos held its first election in 1989 and promulgated a new constitution in 1991. Although its economy was adversely affected by the mid-1990s Asian monetary crises, it realized a longtime goal in 1997 when it joined the Association of Southeast Asian Nations.

Recent Developments

In exchange for a 50-year concession of thousands of acres of wetlands north of the capital, a Chinese-led joint venture agreed in 2008 to build a sports complex on the outskirts of Vientiane in preparation for the 2009 Southeast Asian Games. This agreement was received very poorly by the population living in the capital. Land concessions had emerged as a serious and complex issue over the past few years in Laos—they often covered village lands, owing to poorly defined and enforced regulations governing land rights. The most controversial aspect of land concessions concerned the lease of vast areas of cultivable land to foreign investors for the commercial production of crops (notably rubber and cassava).

Internet resources: <www.visit-laos.com>.

Latvia

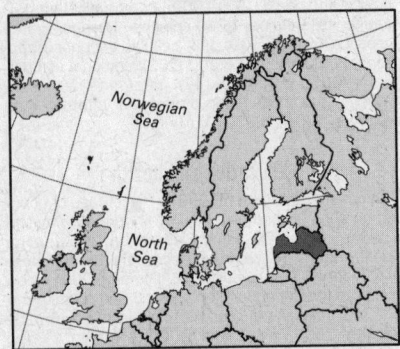

Official name: Latvijas Republika (Republic of Latvia). **Form of government:** unitary multiparty republic with a single legislative body (Parliament, or Saeima [100]). **Chief of state:** President Valdis Zatlers (from 2007). **Head of government:** Prime Minister Valdis Dombrovskis (from 2009). **Capital:** Riga. **Official language:** Latvian. **Official religion:** none. **Monetary unit:** 1 lats (Ls; plural lati) = 100 santimi; valuation (1 Jul 2009) US$1 = 0.50 Ls.

Demography

Area: 24,938 sq mi, 64,589 sq km. **Population** (2008): 2,266,000. **Density** (2008): persons per sq mi 90.9, persons per sq km 35.1. **Urban** (2007): 67.9%. **Sex distribution** (2007): male 46.10%; female 53.90%. **Age breakdown** (2007): under 15, 13.7%; 15–29, 22.8%; 30–44, 20.9%; 45–59, 20.5%; 60–74, 15.0%; 75–89, 6.8%; 90 and over, 0.3%. **Ethnic composition** (2007): Latvian 59.2%; Russian 28.0%; Belarusian 3.7%; Ukrainian 2.5%; Polish 2.4%; Lithuanian 1.3%; other 2.9%. **Religious affiliation** (2005): Orthodox 29%, of which Russian 16%; Roman Catholic 19%; Lutheran 14%; nonreligious 26%; atheist/other 12%. **Major cities** (2007): Riga 717,371; Daugavpils 105,958; Liepaja 85,050; Jelgava 65,635; Jurmala 55,580. **Location:** eastern Europe, bordering Estonia, Russia, Belarus, Lithuania, and the Baltic Sea.

Vital statistics

Birth rate per 1,000 population (2007): 10.2 (world avg. 20.3); within marriage 57.0%; outside of marriage 43.0%. **Death rate** per 1,000 population (2007): 14.5 (world avg. 8.6). **Natural increase rate** per 1,000 population (2007): −3.3 (world avg. 11.7). **Total fertility rate** (avg. births per childbearing woman; 2007): 1.41. **Life expectancy** at birth (2007): male 65.8 years; female 76.5 years.

National economy

Budget (2006). *Revenue:* Ls 4,213,000,000 (tax revenue 56.4%, of which VAT 22.3%, income tax 16.0%, corporate taxes 6.0%; nontax revenue 43.6%, of which social security contributions 23.2%). *Expenditures:* Ls 4,237,100,000 (social security and welfare

25.9%; education 14.6%; health 10.3%; police 6.7%; defense 4.2%). **Public debt** (external, outstanding; March 2007): US$1,224,000,000. **Production** (metric tons except as noted). *Agriculture and fishing* (2007): wheat 807,300, potatoes 642,000, barley 363,200; livestock (number of live animals) 416,800 pigs, 377,100 cattle; fisheries production 153,800 (from aquaculture, negligible). *Mining and quarrying* (2006): peat 1,000,000; limestone 468,100. *Manufacturing* (value added in Ls '000,000; 2006): food products 262.4; wood products (excluding furniture) 231.6; printing and publishing 85.3. *Energy production (consumption):* electricity (kW-hr; 2007–08) 4,803,000,000 (7,658,000,000); coal (metric tons; 2007–08) none (174,000); petroleum products (metric tons; 2007–08) none (1,531,000); natural gas (cu m; 2007–08) none (1,652,000,000). **Gross national income** (2007): US$22,595,000,000 (US$9,930 per capita). **Population economically active** (2007): total 1,191,100; activity rate of total population 52.2% (participation rates: ages 15–64, 72.9%; female 48.5%; unemployed [April 2007–March 2008] 5.9%). **Selected balance of payments data.** Receipts from (US$'000,000): tourism (2006) 480; remittances (2007) 552; foreign direct investment (FDI) (2004–06 avg.) 998. Disbursements for (US$'000,000): tourism (2006) 704; remittances (2007) 45; FDI (2004–06 avg.) 125.

Foreign trade

Imports (2007; c.i.f.): Ls 7,782,131,000 (machinery and apparatus 20.8%; transportation equipment 14.6%; mineral fuels 11.5%; iron and steel [all forms] 9.6%; food products 9.1%). *Major import sources:* Germany 15.2%; Lithuania 13.9%; Russia 8.4%; Estonia 8.1%; Poland 7.0%. **Exports** (2007; f.o.b.): Ls 3,299,000,000 (wood products 22.5%; iron and steel [all forms] 14.6%; food products 14.1%; machinery and apparatus 11.0%; chemical products 7.4%). *Major export destinations:* Lithuania 15.8%; Estonia 14.4%; Russia 9.6%; Germany 8.7%; Sweden 7.7%.

Transport and communications

Transport. *Railroads* (2007): length 2,265 km; passenger-km 983,000,000; metric ton-km cargo 18,313,000,000. *Roads* (2007): total length 51,600 km (paved 39%). *Vehicles* (2007): passenger cars 904,900; trucks and buses 140,200. *Air transport* (2007): passenger-km 2,766,000,000; metric ton-km cargo 13,000,000. **Communications,** in total units (units per 1,000 persons). Telephone landlines (2007): 644,000 (283); cellular telephone subscribers (2007): 2,217,000 (974); personal computers (2005): 566,000 (245); total Internet users (2007): 1,177,000 (517); broadband Internet subscribers (2007): 146,000 (64).

Education and health

Educational attainment (2007). Percentage of population ages 15–74 having: none/unknown through complete primary education 26.1%; secondary 25.5%; vocational 30.1%; higher 18.3%. **Literacy** (2003): percentage of total population ages 15 and over literate, virtually 100%. **Health** (2007): physicians 8,014 (1 per 283 persons); hospital beds

1 metric ton = about 1.1 short tons;   1 kilometer = 0.6 mi (statute);   1 metric ton-km cargo = about 0.68 short ton-mi cargo;   c.i.f.: cost, insurance, and freight;   f.o.b.: free on board

17,497 (1 per 130 persons); infant mortality rate per 1,000 live births (2007) 8.7; undernourished population (2002–04) 70,000 (3% of total population based on the consumption of a minimum daily requirement of 1,960 calories).

Military

Total active duty personnel (2007): 5,696 (army 26.8%, navy 10.6%, air force 8.4%, headquarters/administrative 54.2%). **Military expenditure as percentage of GDP** (2005): 1.7%; per capita expenditure US$119.

Background

Latvia was settled by the Balts in ancient times. It was conquered by the Vikings in the 9th century and later dominated by its German-speaking neighbors, who Christianized the people in the 12th–13th centuries. By 1230 German rule was established. From the mid-16th to the early 18th century, the region was split between Poland and Sweden, but by the end of the 18th century all of Latvia had been annexed by Russia. Latvia declared its independence after the Russian Revolution of 1917, but in 1940 the Soviet Red Army invaded. Held by Nazi Germany in 1941–44, the country was recaptured by the Soviets and incorporated into the Soviet Union. Latvia gained its independence in 1991 with the breakup of the Soviet Union; subsequently it sought to build ties with Western Europe (becoming a member of both the EU and NATO in 2004).

Recent Developments

In 2008 Latvia's economy, which had enjoyed growth of 10.3% in 2007, was affected by the international financial crises and contracted to a trickle. Inflation hit 16.5%, the cost of natural gas and electricity rose 30–40%, and earlier promises to raise pensions and the salaries of medical personnel and the police had to be broken. In the realm of foreign affairs, Latvia deplored Russia's invasion of Georgia; Riga increased its assistance to that country and supported the EU's peace-fostering efforts there. Nonetheless, Riga focused on forging specific bilateral agreements with Russia and also discussed energy and trade with Kazakhstan, Uzbekistan, and Turkmenistan.

Internet resources:
<www.csb.lv/avidus.cfm?lng=en>.

Lebanon

Official name: Al-Jumhuriyah al-Lubnaniyah (Lebanese Republic). **Form of government:** unitary multiparty republic with one legislative house (National Assembly [128]). **Chief of state:** President Michel Suleiman (from 2008). **Head of government:** Prime Minister Fouad Siniora (from 2005). **Capital:** Beirut. **Official language:** Arabic. **Official religion:** none. **Monetary unit:** 1 Lebanese pound (LBP) = 100 piastres; valuation (1 Jul 2009) US$1 = LBP 1,503.00.

Demography

Area: 4,016 sq mi, 10,400 sq km. **Population** (2008): 4,142,000 (includes about 415,000 regis-

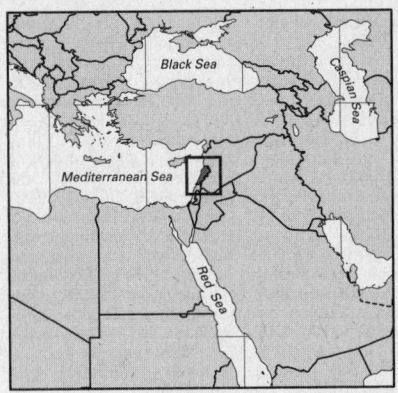

tered Palestinian refugees). **Density** (2008): persons per sq mi 1,031, persons per sq km 398.3. **Urban** (2005): 86.6%. **Sex distribution** (2005): male 48.99%; female 51.01%. **Age breakdown** (2005): under 15, 28.6%; 15–29, 26.2%; 30–44, 21.2%; 45–59, 13.7%; 60–74, 7.9%; 75–84, 2.1%; 85 and over, 0.3%. **Ethnic composition** (2000): Arab 84.5%, of which Lebanese 71.2%, Palestinian 12.1%; Armenian 6.8%; Kurdish 6.1%; other 2.6%. **Religious affiliation** (1995): Muslim 55.3%, of which Shiʻi 34.0%, Sunni 21.3%; Christian 37.6%, of which Catholic 25.1% (Maronite 19.0%, Greek Catholic or Melchite 4.6%), Orthodox 11.7% (Greek Orthodox 6.0%, Armenian Apostolic 5.2%), Protestant 0.5%; Druze 7.1%. **Major cities** (2003): Beirut (urban agglomeration; 2005) 1,777,000; Tripoli 212,900; Sidon 149,000; Tyre (Sur) 117,100; Al-Nabatiyah 89,400. **Location:** the Middle East, bordering Syria, Israel, and the Mediterranean Sea.

Vital statistics

Birth rate per 1,000 population (2007): 19.7 (world avg. 20.3). **Death rate** per 1,000 population (2007): 5.1 (world avg. 8.6). **Natural increase rate** per 1,000 population (2007): 14.6 (world avg. 11.7). **Total fertility rate** (avg. births per childbearing woman; 2005): 1.92. **Life expectancy** at birth (2005): male 70.2 years; female 75.2 years.

National economy

Budget (2005). *Revenue:* LBP 6,984,200,000,000 (tax revenue 69.7%, of which VAT 24.2%, customs and excise revenues 18.1%; nontax revenue 30.3%). *Expenditures:* LBP 7,802,200,000,000 (general expenditures 54.7%; interest expenditures 45.3%, of which foreign debt 25.7%). **Public debt** (external, outstanding; July 2008): US$21,495,000,000. **Gross**

national income (2007): US$23,651,000,000 (US$5,770 per capita). **Production** (metric tons except as noted). *Agriculture and fishing* (2007): potatoes 490,000, tomatoes 255,000, oranges 195,000, olives 83,000, almonds 27,000; livestock (number of live animals) 495,000 goats, 340,000 sheep, 77,000 cattle; fisheries production (2006) 4,614 (from aquaculture 17%). *Mining and quarrying* (2006): gypsum 30,000; lime 14,000; salt 3,500. *Manufacturing* (value added in US$'000,000; 1998): food products 345; cement, bricks, and ceramics 212; wood products 188, of which furniture (including metal furniture) 135. *Energy production (consumption):* electricity (kW-hr; 2007) 9,072,000,000 (10,590,000,000); coal (metric tons; 2004) none (200,000); petroleum products (metric tons; 2005) none (4,797,000). **Population economically active** (2004): total 1,170,800; activity rate of total population 30% (participation rates: ages 15–64 [1997] 49.2%; female 21.2%; unemployed 8.2%). **Selected balance of payments data.** Receipts from (US$'000,000): tourism (2006) 5,015; remittances (2007) 5,769; foreign direct investment (FDI) (2004–06 avg.) 2,513; official development assistance (2006) 707. Disbursements for (US$'000,000): tourism (2006) 3,006; remittances (2007) 2,845; FDI (2004–06 avg.) 135.

Foreign trade

Imports (2005; c.i.f.): US$9,339,900,000 (mineral products 23.8%; electrical equipment 11.4%; food and live animals 10.3%; chemical products 8.8%; transportation equipment 8.7%). *Major import sources:* Italy 10.4%; France 8.4%; China 7.9%; Germany 7.0%; US 5.9%. **Exports** (2005): US$1,879,800,000 (electrical equipment 16.7%; base metals 14.7%; precious metal jewelry and stones [significantly gold and pearls] 11.9%; food and live animals 10.7%; chemical products 8.7%). *Major export destinations:* Syria 10.0%; Iraq 9.5%; UAE 8.2%; Saudi Arabia 7.4%; Switzerland 6.7%.

Transport and communications

Transport. *Railroads* (2004): length 401 km. *Roads* (2004): total length 7,300 km (paved 85%). *Vehicles* (2001): passenger cars 1,370,897; trucks and buses 102,394. *Air transport* (Middle East Airlines only; 2007): passenger-km 2,225,000,000; metric ton-km cargo 34,000,000. **Communications,** in total units (units per 1,000 persons). Telephone landlines (2006): 681,000 (178); cellular telephone subscribers (2007): 1,260,000 (307); personal computers (2005): 409,000 (102); total Internet users (2006): 950,000 (248); broadband Internet subscribers (2006): 170,000 (44).

Education and health

Educational attainment (2004). Percentage of population ages 4 and over having: no formal education/unknown 13.7%; incomplete primary education 3.2%; primary 54.2%; secondary/vocational 15.5%; upper vocational 1.7%; higher 11.7%. **Literacy** (2005): percentage of total population ages 15 and over literate 88.3%; males literate 93.6%; females literate 83.4%. **Health** (2004): physicians 10,304 (1

per 364 persons); hospital beds (2006) 9,786 (1 per 414 persons); infant mortality rate per 1,000 live births (2005) 24.5; undernourished population (2002–04) 120,000 (3% of total population based on the consumption of a minimum daily requirement of 1,920 calories).

Military

Total active duty personnel (2007): 56,000 (army 96.3%, navy 2.0%, air force 1.7%); UN peacekeeping troops (June 2007): 13,300; Syrian troops ended a 29-year presence in April 2005. **Military expenditure as percentage of GDP** (2005): 4.5%; per capita expenditure US$280.

Background

Much of present-day Lebanon corresponds to ancient Phoenicia, which was settled c. 3000 BC. In the 6th century AD, Christians fleeing Syrian persecution settled in what is now northern Lebanon and founded the Maronite Church. Arab tribesmen settled in southern Lebanon and by the 11th century had founded the Druze faith. Lebanon was later ruled by the Mamluks. In 1516 the Ottoman Turks seized control; the Turks ended the local rule of the Druze Shihab princes in 1842. After the massacre of Maronites by Druze in 1860, France forced the Ottomans to form an autonomous province for the Christian area, known as Mount Lebanon. Following World War I, it was administered by the French military, but by 1946 it was fully independent. After the Arab-Israeli War of 1948–49, Palestinian refugees settled in southern Lebanon. In 1970 the Palestine Liberation Organization (PLO) moved its headquarters there and began raids into northern Israel. Political and religious divisions and a growing Palestinian "state within a state" fueled a descent into civil war. In 1976 Syria intervened on behalf of the Christians, and in 1982 Israeli forces attempted to drive Palestinian fighters out of southern Lebanon. Israeli troops had withdrawn from all but a narrow buffer zone in the south by 1985; thereafter, guerrillas from the Lebanese Shi'ite militia Hezbollah clashed with the Israelis regularly, including open warfare in 2006. Israeli soldiers completely withdrew from Lebanon in 2000, and Syrian forces disengaged from the country in 2005.

Recent Developments

In May 2008, following an 18-month political standoff between various Lebanese factions and a brush with civil war between the Sunnis and the Shi'ites two weeks earlier, Gen. Michel Suleiman was elected president in Lebanon. The election was made possible by the Qatari-brokered Doha Agreement, which entailed important concessions on the part of the pro-Saudi, pro-Western, Sunni-dominated government whereby the majority consented to turn a blind eye toward Hezbollah arms stockpiles and agreed to give veto power in the cabinet to the organization. They also gave the Christian opposition, through a reenactment of the 1960 electoral law, the political strength to elect their own representatives without the need to enlist the votes of Muslims. The security situation remained unstable, especially in the north of the country. A visit in August by President Suleiman

---

1 metric ton = about 1.1 short tons;   1 kilometer = 0.6 mi (statute);   1 metric ton-km cargo = about 0.68 short ton-mi cargo;   c.i.f.: cost, insurance, and freight;   f.o.b.: free on board

to Damascus resulted in an agreement to establish diplomatic relations between the two countries. Suleiman also visited the UN and Washington DC, but he was disappointed that Washington did not agree to rearm the Lebanese army with technologically advanced weapons that would counter the technology of Hezbollah.

Internet resources: <www.cas.gov.lb>.

Lesotho

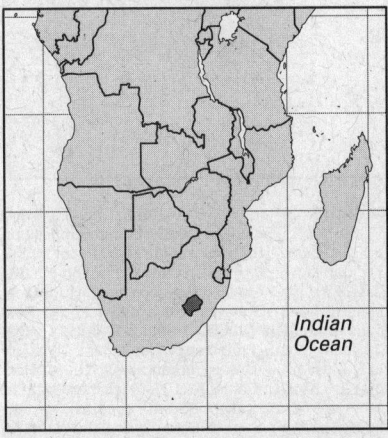

Indian Ocean

Official name: Musa oa Lesotho (Sotho); Kingdom of Lesotho (English). **Form of government:** constitutional monarchy with two legislative houses (Senate [33]; National Assembly [120]). **Chief of state:** King Letsie III (from 1996). **Head of government:** Prime Minister Bethuel Pakalitha Mosisili (from 1998). **Capital:** Maseru. **Official languages:** Sotho; English. **Official religion:** Christianity. **Monetary unit:** 1 loti (plural maloti [M]) = 100 licente; valuation (1 Jul 2009) US$1 = M 7.76 (the South African rand is also accepted as legal tender).

Demography

Area: 11,720 sq mi, 30,355 sq km. **Population** (2008): 2,020,000. **Density** (2008): persons per sq mi 172.4, persons per sq km 66.5. **Urban** (2007): 24.8%. **Sex distribution** (2006): male 48.69%; female 51.31%. **Age breakdown** (2001): under 15, 35.8%; 15–29, 31.2%; 30–44, 14.7%; 45–59, 10.0%; 60–74, 6.0%; 75 and over, 2.1%; unknown 0.2%. **Ethnic composition** (2000): Sotho 80.3%; Zulu 14.4%; other 5.3%. **Religious affiliation** (2000): Christian 91.0%, of which Roman Catholic 37.5%, unaffiliated Christian 23.9%, Protestant (mostly Reformed and Anglican) 17.7%, independent Christian 11.8%; traditional beliefs 7.7%; other 1.3%. **Major urban centers** (2004): Maseru 178,300; Maputsoe 36,200; Mafeteng 36,000; Teyateyaneng 23,700; Hlotse 23,400. **Location:** southern Africa, surrounded by South Africa.

Vital statistics

Birth rate per 1,000 population (2006): 25.1 (world avg. 20.3). **Death rate** per 1,000 population (2006):

22.7 (world avg. 8.6). **Natural increase rate** per 1,000 population (2006): 2.4 (world avg. 11.7). **Total fertility rate** (avg. births per childbearing woman; 2006): 3.28. **Life expectancy** at birth (2006): male 40.4 years; female 39.1 years.

National economy

Budget (2006–07). *Revenue:* M 6,479,200,000 (tax revenue 89.3%, of which customs receipts 60.9%, income and profit tax 15.0%, sales tax 11.0%; nontax revenue 9.3%; grants 1.4%). *Expenditures:* M 4,909,100,000 (education and community services 26.8%; health and social security 14.0%; public order 11.9%; defense 5.4%; interest payments 2.0%). **Public debt** (external, outstanding; 2006): US$633,-000,000. **Production** (metric tons except as noted). *Agriculture and fishing* (2007): potatoes 96,000, corn (maize) 50,800, sorghum 11,200; livestock (number of live animals) 1,025,000 sheep, 715,000 goats, 695,000 cattle; fisheries production (2006) 47 (from aquaculture 4%). *Mining and quarrying* (2006): diamonds 37,000 carats. *Manufacturing* (value of manufactured exports; US$'000,000; 2002): wearing apparel and accessories 233.7; footwear 23.9; television receivers 13.8. *Energy production (consumption):* electricity (kW-hr; 2004) 250,000,000 (244,500,000); petroleum products (metric tons; 2003) none (100,000). **Population economically active** (2003): total 640,000; activity rate of total population 35.5% (participation rates: ages 15–64, 60.8%; female 45.0%; unemployed [2005] 50%). **Gross national income** (2007): US$2,007,000,000 (US$1,000 per capita). **Selected balance of payments data.** Receipts from (US$'000,000): tourism (2006) 28; remittances (2007) 371; foreign direct investment (2004–06 avg.) 56; official development assistance (2006) 72. Disbursements for (US$'000,000): tourism (2006) 19; remittances (2007) 11.

Foreign trade

Imports (2006; c.i.f.): US$1,278,000,000 (assorted manufactured goods 40%; food products 24%; chemical products 13%; machinery and transportation equipment 13%). *Major import sources* (2004): other Africa 73%; Asian countries 24%. **Exports** (2004–05; f.o.b.): US$633,000,000 (wearing apparel, accessories, and textiles 69%, of which woven clothing for males 42%, knitted or crocheted clothing 9%, footwear 7%; beverages 4%; rawhides and skins 4%). *Major export destinations* (2006): Western Hemisphere (mostly US) 61%; other Africa 25%; Europe 13%.

Transport and communications

Transport. *Railroads* (2001): length 12.6 km. *Roads* (2000): total length 5,940 km (paved 18%). *Vehicles* (1996): passenger cars 12,610; trucks and buses 25,000. **Communications,** in total units (units per 1,000 persons). Telephone landlines (2005): 48,000 (24); cellular telephone subscribers (2007): 456,000 (227); personal computers (2005): 1,000 (0.5); total Internet users (2007): 70,000 (35); broadband Internet subscribers (2005): 50 (0.02).

Education and health

Educational attainment (2001). Percentage of population ages 25 and over having: no formal education

22%; incomplete primary 40%; complete primary 17%; secondary and higher 21%. **Literacy** (2007): percentage of total population ages 15 and over literate 86.5%; males literate 77.1%; females literate 95.6%. **Health** (2003): physicians 140 (1 per 16,298 persons); hospital beds 1,025 (1 per 2,226 persons); infant mortality rate per 1,000 live births (2006) 81.3; undernourished population (2002–04) 250,000 (13% of total population based on the consumption of a minimum daily requirement of 1,850 calories).

Military

Total active duty personnel (2007): 2,000 (army 100%). **Military expenditure as percentage of GDP** (2005): 2.3%; per capita expenditure US$17.

Background

Bantu-speaking farmers created a number of chiefdoms in the area in the 16th century. The most powerful organized the Basotho in 1824 and obtained British protection in 1843 as tension between the Basotho and the South African Boers increased. The area became a British territory in 1868 and was annexed to the Cape Colony in 1871. The colony's effort to disarm the Basotho resulted in revolt in 1880, and four years later it separated from the colony and became a British High Commission Territory. In 1966 it gained independence. A new constitution (1993) ended seven years of military rule. At the beginning of the 21st century, Lesotho suffered from a deteriorating economy and one of the world's highest HIV/AIDS infection rates.

Recent Developments

Although Lesotho's 2008 crops were better than those of previous years, some 352,000 people required food or financial assistance—the World Food Programme helped provide free meals for some 80,000 schoolchildren. The country's HIV prevalence rate was 23.2%, one of the world's highest; life expectancy fell to only 35 years; and more than 100,000 children had been orphaned by AIDS.

Internet resources: <www.bos.gov.ls>.

Liberia

Official name: Republic of Liberia. **Form of government:** multiparty republic with two legislative bodies (Senate [30]; House of Representatives [64]). **Head of state and government:** President Ellen Johnson-Sirleaf (from 2006). **Capital:** Monrovia. **Official language:** English. **Official religion:** none. **Monetary unit:** 1 Liberian dollar (L$) = 100 cents; valuation (1 Jul 2009) US$1 = L$70.00.

Demography

Area: 37,466 sq mi, 97,036 sq km. **Population** (2008): 3,543,000. **Density** (2008): persons per sq mi 93.9, persons per sq km 36.2. **Urban** (2006): 59.0%. **Sex distribution** (2007): male 49.75%; female 50.25%. **Age breakdown** (2007): under 15,

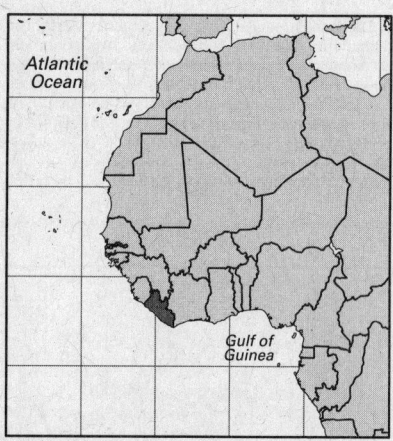

43.6%; 15–29, 27.7%; 30–44, 15.2%; 45–59, 8.9%; 60–74, 4.0%; 75 and over, 0.6%. **Ethnic composition** (2000): Kpelle 18.9%; Bassa 13.1%; Grebo 10.3%; Gio (Dan) 7.4%; Kru 6.9%; Mano 6.1%; Loma 5.3%; Kissi 3.8%; Krahn 3.7%; Americo-Liberians (descendants of freed US slaves) 2.4%; other 22.1%. **Religious affiliation** (2005): traditional beliefs 40%; Christian (mostly Protestant/independent Christian) 40%; Muslim 20%. **Major urban areas** (2008): Monrovia 1,010,970; Ganta 41,106; Buchanan 34,270; Gbarnga 34,046; Kakata 33,945. **Location:** western Africa, bordering Guinea, Côte d'Ivoire, the North Atlantic Ocean, and Sierra Leone.

Vital statistics

Birth rate per 1,000 population (2007): 43.8 (world avg. 20.3). **Death rate** per 1,000 population (2007): 22.2 (world avg. 8.6). **Natural increase rate** per 1,000 population (2007): 21.6 (world avg. 11.7). **Total fertility rate** (avg. births per childbearing woman; 2007): 5.94. **Life expectancy** at birth (2007): male 38.9 years; female 41.9 years.

National economy

Budget (2007). *Revenue:* L$10,222,400,000 (customs and excise duties 44.3%; direct taxes 32.1%; indirect taxes 12.6%; maritime revenue 7.6%). *Expenditures:* L$9,498,000,000 (general administration 41.5%; social and community services 19.8%; economic services 6.9%). **Public debt** (external, outstanding; 2006): US$1,115,000,000. **Population economically active** (2003): total 1,182,000; activity rate 36.7% (participation rates: ages 15–64, 70.0%; female 39.8%; unemployed [2007] 80%). **Production** (metric tons except as noted). *Agriculture and fishing* (2007): cassava 550,000, sugarcane 265,000, oil palm fruit 183,000, natural rubber 100,000, cacao beans 3,000; livestock (number of live animals) 261,600 goats, 230,340 sheep, 173,000 pigs; fisheries production (2006) 10,424 (from aquaculture, none). *Mining and quarrying* (2007): diamonds 21,699 carats (UN sanctions on exports of rough diamonds from 2001 ended in April 2007); gold 284 kg. *Manufacturing* (value of sales in L$'000; 2007): cement 1,308,767; beer 1,023,734; carbonated beverages 429,776. *International maritime licensing* (registration fees earned; 2007): more than US$12,000,000. *Energy production (consumption):* electricity (kW-hr; 2005) 335,000,000 (335,000,-000); petroleum products (metric tons; 2005) negligible (148,000). **Gross national income** (2007): US$554,000,000 (US$150 per capita). **Selected balance of payments data.** Receipts from (US$'000,-000): remittances (2007) 685; foreign direct disinvestment (2004–06 avg.) −108; official development assistance (2006) 269. Disbursements for (US$'000,000): remittances (2006) 639; foreign direct investment (2004–06 avg.) 362.

Foreign trade

Imports (2007): US$499,000,000 (refined petroleum products 25.1%; food products 24.4%, of which rice 13.1%; machinery and transportation equipment 18.1%; assorted manufactures 12.8%). *Major import sources* (2005): South Korea 38%; Japan 21%; Singapore 14%; Croatia 5%; China 3%. **Exports** (2007): US$184,000,000 (rubber 92.8%; gold 2.4%; diamonds 1.2%). *Major export destinations* (2005): Belgium 42%; Spain 12%; US 9%; Malaysia 6%; Thailand 5%.

Transport and communications

Transport. *Railroads* (2007): route length 78 km. *Roads* (2003): total length 10,600 km (paved 6%). *Vehicles* (2002): passenger cars 17,100; trucks and buses 12,800. **Communications,** in total units (units per 1,000 persons). Telephone landlines (2007): 2,000 (0.5); cellular telephone subscribers (2007): 563,000 (150); total Internet users (2007): 20,000 (5.3).

Education and health

Literacy (2007): percentage of total population ages 15 and over literate 55.5%; males literate 60.2%; females literate 50.9%. **Health:** physicians (2004) 103 (1 per 27,255 persons); hospital beds (2001) 2,751 (1 per 1,003 persons); infant mortality rate per 1,000 live births (2007) 149.7; undernourished population (2002–04) 1,700,000 (50% of total population based on the consumption of a minimum daily requirement of 1,820 calories).

Military

Total active duty personnel (2007): 2,400; UN peacekeeping troops (May 2008): 13,934. **Military expenditure as percentage of GDP** (2003): 11%; per capita expenditure US$16.

Background

Africa's oldest republic, Liberia was established as a home for freed American slaves under the American Colonization Society, which founded a colony at Cape Mesurado in 1821. Joseph Jenkins Roberts, Liberia's first nonwhite governor, proclaimed Liberian independence in 1847. In 1980 a coup led by Samuel K. Doe marked the end of the Americo-Liberians' long political dominance over the descendants of indigenous Africans. A destructive civil war consumed the 1990s. A National Transitional Government, supported by UN peacekeeping troops, was established in 2003. Presidential elections were held in 2005, and Ellen Johnson Sirleaf was declared the winner, the first woman to be elected head of state in Africa.

Recent Developments

In January 2008 the Truth and Reconciliation Commission, established to investigate war crimes committed during Liberia's civil war, began proceedings. Modeled on South Africa's postapartheid body, the seven-member commission heard testimony from people around the country, including gruesome accounts of child-soldier recruitment, severed limbs, and rape. Former rebel commander Milton Blahyi (also known as General Butt-Naked) testified about having taken part in human sacrifices. Meanwhile, international attention turned to the war crimes trials of former president Gen. Charles Taylor in The Hague and his son Charles (Chuckie) Taylor, Jr., in the US. In October Chuckie was convicted of charges of torture and related war crimes. He was sentenced in January 2009 to 97 years in prison.

Internet resources: <www.cbl.org.lr>.

Libya

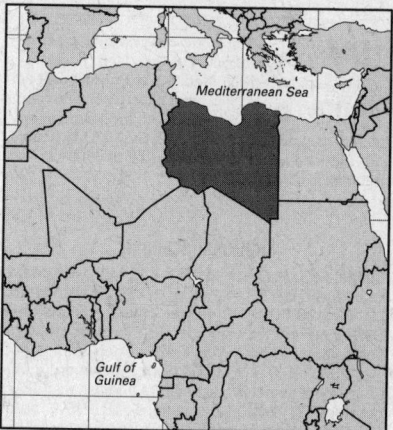

Official name: Al-Jamahiriyah al-ʿArabiyah al-Libiyah al-Shaʿbiyah al-Ishtirakiyah al-ʿUzma (Great Socialist People's Libyan Arab Jamahiriya). **Form of government:** authoritarian state with one policy-making body (General People's Congress [468]). **Chief of state:** Muammar al-Qaddafi (de facto; from 1969); Secretary of the General People's Congress Mubarak Abdallah al-Shamikh (de jure; from 2009). **Head of government:** Secretary of the General People's Committee (Prime Minister) Al-Baghdadi Ali al-Mahmudi (from 2006). **Capital:** Tripoli. **Official language:** Arabic. **Official religion:** Islam. **Monetary unit:** 1 Libyan dinar (LD) = 1,000 dirhams; valuation (1 Jul 2009) US$1 = LD 1.22.

Demography

Area: 679,362 sq mi, 1,759,540 sq km. **Population** (2008): 5,871,000. **Density** (2008): persons per sq mi 8.6, persons per sq km 3.3. **Urban** (2005): 84.8%. **Sex distribution** (2006): male 51.93%; female 48.07%. **Age breakdown** (2005): under 15, 30.1%; 15–29, 32.2%; 30–44, 19.8%; 45–59, 11.4%; 60–74, 5.3%; 75–84, 1.0%; 85 and over, 0.2%. **Ethnic composition** (2000): Arab 87.1%, of which Libyan 57.2%, Bedouin 13.8%, Egyptian 7.7%, Sudanese 3.5%, Tunisian 2.9%; Amazigh (Berber) 6.8%, of which Arabized 4.2%; other 6.1%. **Religious affiliation** (2000): Muslim (nearly all Sunni) 96.1%; Orthodox 1.9%; Roman Catholic 0.8%; other 1.2%. **Major cities** (2005): Tripoli (Tarabulus) 911,643 (urban agglomeration 2,098,000); Banghazi 685,367 (urban agglomeration 1,114,000); Misratah (2003) 121,669. **Location:** northern Africa, bordering the Mediterranean Sea, Egypt, The Sudan, Chad, Niger, Algeria, and Tunisia.

Vital statistics

Birth rate per 1,000 population (2005): 26.8 (world avg. 20.3). **Death rate** per 1,000 population (2005): 3.5 (world avg. 8.6). **Natural increase rate** per 1,000 population (2005): 23.3 (world avg. 11.7). **Total fertility rate** (avg. births per childbearing woman; 2005): 3.34. **Life expectancy** at birth (2005): male 74.3 years; female 78.8 years.

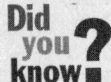 **Did you know?** The world's largest civil engineering scheme, called the "Great Man-Made River Project," will tap Libya's vast underground reserves of water beneath the southern deserts and deliver it via a series of 4-m (14-ft) pipes to cities and agricultural areas as far as 1500 km (900 mi) away.

National economy

Budget (2007). *Revenue:* LD 54,114,000,000 (petroleum revenues 89.9%; other 10.1%). *Expenditures:* LD 31,018,000,000 (development expenditures 59.7%; current expenditures 40.3%, of which wages and salaries 23.5%). **Public debt** (external, outstanding; 2005): US$3,900,000,000. **Production** (metric tons except as noted). *Agriculture and fishing* (2007): potatoes 196,000, dry onions 181,000, dates 175,000, olives 165,000; livestock (number of live animals) 4,500,000 sheep, 1,265,000 goats, 130,-000 cattle, 47,000 camels; fisheries production (2006) 40,827 (from aquaculture 1%). *Mining and quarrying* (2006): lime 250,000; gypsum 175,000; salt 40,000. *Manufacturing* (value of production in LD '000,000; 1996): base metals 212; electrical equipment 208; petrochemicals 175. *Energy production (consumption):* electricity (kW-hr; 2005) 22,500,000,000 (22,500,000,000); coal (metric tons; 2002) none (4,000); crude petroleum (barrels; 2007) 653,800,000 ([2005] 129,000,000); petroleum products (metric tons; 2007) 16,300,000 (8,607,000); natural gas (cu m; 2005) 11,700,-000,000 (6,441,000,000). **Population economically active** (2003): total 2,137,000; activity rate of total population 37.9% (participation rates: ages 15 to 64, 56.7%; female 24.7%; unemployed [2004] 30.0%).

Gross national income (2007): US$55,473,000,000 (US$9,010 per capita). **Selected balance of payments data.** Receipts from (US$'000,000): tourism (2006) 190; remittances (2007) 16; foreign direct investment (2004–06 avg.) 1,043; official development assistance (2006) 37. Disbursements for (US$'000,000): tourism (2006) 668; remittances (2007) 945.

Foreign trade

Imports (2004): US$8,768,000,000 (machinery and transportation equipment 48.0%; food and live animals 14.1%; chemical products 4.0%). *Major import sources* (2006): Europe 58.7%, of which Italy 9.9%, Germany 8.5%, UK 3.7%; Arab countries 11.3%; Japan 5.7%. **Exports** (2004): US$20,600,000,000 (hydrocarbons [mostly crude petroleum] 95.7%). *Major export destinations* (2006): Europe 82.3%, of which Italy 42.5%, Germany 9.8%, Spain 8.5%, France 4.8%; Asian countries 5.4%.

Transport and communications

Transport. *Railroads:* none. *Roads* (2000): total length 83,200 km (paved 57%). *Vehicles* (2005): passenger cars 1,356,987; trucks and buses 145,935. *Air transport* (2003): passenger-km 825,000,000; metric ton-km cargo (2001) 259,000. **Communications,** in total units (units per 1,000 persons). Telephone landlines (2006): 483,000 (81); cellular telephone subscribers (2007): 4,500,000 (731); personal computers (2005): 130,000 (21); total Internet users (2005): 232,000 (40).

Education and health

Literacy (2007): percentage of total population ages 15 and over literate 85.4%; males literate 94.1%; females literate 76.0%. **Health:** physicians (2004) 7,405 (1 per 775 persons); hospital beds (2002) 21,400 (1 per 256 persons); infant mortality rate per 1,000 live births (2005) 24.6; undernourished population (2002–04) less than 2.5% of total population.

Military

Total active duty personnel (2007): 76,000 (army 59.2%, navy 10.5%, air force 30.3%). **Military expenditure as percentage of GDP** (2005): 2.0%; per capita expenditure US$128.

Background

Greeks and Phoenicians settled the area in the 7th century BC. It was conquered by Rome in the 1st century BC and by Arabs in the 7th century AD. In the 16th century the Ottoman Turks combined Libya's three regions under one regency in Tripoli. In 1911 Italy claimed control of Libya, and by the outbreak of World War II, 150,000 Italians lived there. It became an independent state in 1951. The discovery of oil in 1959 brought wealth to Libya. A decade later a group of army officers led by Muammar al-Qaddafi deposed the king and made the country an Islamic republic. Under Qaddafi's rule it supported the Palestinian Liberation Organization and terrorist groups, bringing protests from many countries, particularly the US. In-

---

1 metric ton = about 1.1 short tons;   1 kilometer = 0.6 mi (statute);   1 metric ton-km cargo = about 0.68 short ton-mi cargo;   c.i.f.: cost, insurance, and freight;   f.o.b.: free on board

termittent warfare with Chad during the 1970s and '80s ended with Chad's defeat of Libya in 1987. International relations in the 1990s were dominated by the consequences of the 1988 bombing of an American airliner over Lockerbie, Scotland; the US accused Libyan nationalists of the deed and imposed a trade embargo on Libya, endorsed by the UN in 1992. This sanction was lifted in 2003.

Recent Developments

Five years of fence mending between Libya and Western countries culminated in a visit to Tripoli in September 2008 by US Secretary of State Condoleezza Rice—the first direct contact by a high-ranking US official since 1957. Rice's trip marked a major thaw in relations and paved the way for trade and investment by American corporations, particularly in the energy sector. Although in October Libya completed the compensation payments to the families of the victims of the Lockerbie tragedy, the moneys due to the families of the victims of the 1986 Berlin disco bombing, for which Libya also took responsibility, remained unpaid. The US Congress blocked the establishment of formal diplomatic relations until this had been settled. During his August visit to Libya, Italian Prime Minister Silvio Berlusconi offered a formal apology for Italy's years of colonial rule (1911–43) as well as US$5 billion in compensation. In return Italy expected to receive favorable concessions in the energy sector and cooperation in combating illegal boat immigrants who sailed from Libyan territorial waters. In another sign of international acceptance, Libyan leader Muammar al-Qaddafi assumed the chairmanship of the African Union in February 2009.

Internet resources: <www.cbl.gov.ly/en>.

Liechtenstein

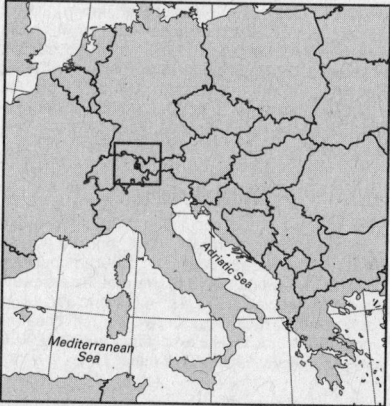

Official name: Fürstentum Liechtenstein (Principality of Liechtenstein). **Form of government:** constitutional monarchy with one legislative house (Diet [25]). **Chief of state:** Prince Hans Adam II (from 1989). **Head of government:** Prime Minister Klaus Tschütscher (from 2009). **Capital:** Vaduz. **Official language:** German. **Official religion:** none. **Monetary unit:** 1 Swiss franc (CHF) = 100 centimes; valuation (1 Jul 2009) US$1 = CHF 1.07.

Demography

Area: 62.0 sq mi, 160.5 sq km. **Population** (2008): 35,500. **Density** (2008): persons per sq mi 572.6, persons per sq km 221.2. **Urban** (2005): 14.3%. **Sex distribution** (2006): male 49.31%; female 50.69%. **Age breakdown** (2006): under 15, 17.0%; 15–29, 18.7%; 30–44, 24.4%; 45–59, 22.3%; 60–74, 12.5%; 75–84, 3.8%; 85 and over, 1.3%. **Ethnic composition** (2006): Liechtensteiner 66.1%; Swiss 10.3%; Austrian 5.8%; Italian 3.4%; German 3.4%; other 11.0%. **Religious affiliation** (2002): Christian 83.9%, of which Roman Catholic 76.0%, Protestant 7.0%, Orthodox 0.8%, Muslim 4.1%; nonreligious/other 12.0%. **Major cities** (2007): Schaan 5,690; Vaduz 5,109; Triesen 4,713; Balzers 4,509; Eschen 4,137. **Location:** central Europe, between Austria and Switzerland.

Vital statistics

Birth rate per 1,000 population (2007): 10.0 (world avg. 20.3); within marriage 82.9%; outside of marriage 17.1%. **Death rate** per 1,000 population (2007): 6.4 (world avg. 8.6). **Natural increase rate** per 1,000 population (2007): 3.6 (world avg. 11.7). **Total fertility rate** (avg. births per childbearing woman; 2006): 1.42. **Life expectancy** at birth (2006): male 78.9 years; female 83.1 years.

National economy

Budget (2004). *Revenue:* CHF 1,068,400,000 (current revenue 72.0%, of which taxes and duties 55.4%, investment income 10.9%; capital revenue 28.0%). *Expenditures:* CHF 1,048,500,000 (current expenditures 74.5%, of which financial affairs 21.7%, social welfare 17.3%, education 12.3%; capital expenditures 25.5%). **Public debt:** none. **Tourism** (2007): 59,603 tourist arrivals. **Population economically active** (2005): total 15,667; activity rate of total population 44.8% (participation rates: ages 15 and over, 54.3%; female [2003] 41.4%; unemployed [2006] 3.3%). **Production** (metric tons except as noted). *Agriculture and fishing* (2006): grapes 200; significantly market gardening, other crops include cereals and apples; livestock (number of live animals) 6,000 cattle, 3,000 pigs, 3,000 sheep. *Manufacturing* (2007): small-scale precision manufacturing includes optical lenses, electron microscopes, electronic equipment, and high-vacuum pumps. *Energy production (consumption):* electricity (kW-hr; 2007) 72,273,000 (379,013,000); coal (metric tons; 2004) none ([2003] 13); petroleum products (metric tons; 2004) none (50,000).

Foreign trade

Imports (2007; excludes trade with and transshipments through Switzerland, with which Liechtenstein has had a customs union since 1923): CHF 2,416,000,000 (base and fabricated metals 36.8%; machinery and electronics 31.9%; mineral fuels and chemical products 15.2%; glass products, ceramics, and textiles 8.5%). *Major import sources:* Germany 40.2%; Austria 36.9%; Italy 5.2%; US 1.8%; France 1.8%. **Exports** (2007; excludes trade with and transshipments through Switzerland, with which Liechtenstein has had a customs union since 1923): CHF 4,182,000,000 (machinery and electronics 34.0%; fabricated metal products and precision tools 33.2%; transportation equipment 8.6%; glass and ceramic products [including lead crystal and specialized dental products] and textiles 7.3%). *Major export destinations:* Germany 20.0%; US 14.3%; Austria 11.5%; France 9.9%; Italy 6.3%.

Transport and communications

Transport. *Railroads* (2006): length 18.5 km. *Roads* (2007): total length 380 km (paved 100%). *Vehicles* (2007): passenger cars 24,368; trucks and buses 7,532. *Air transport:* the nearest scheduled airport service is through Zürich, Switzerland. **Communications,** in total units (units per 1,000 persons). Telephone landlines (2006): 20,000 (575); cellular telephone subscribers (2006): 29,000 (820); total Internet users (2006): 22,000 (627); broadband Internet subscribers (2006): 10,000 (285).

Education and health

Educational attainment (2000). Percentage of population ages 25 and over having: incomplete compulsory education (schooling to age 16) 3.0%; complete compulsory 22.9%; lower vocational 44.5%; higher vocational, teacher training 13.8%; university 6.6%; unknown 9.2%. **Literacy:** percentage of total population literate, virtually 100%. **Health:** physicians (2005) 79 (1 per 441 persons); hospital beds (1997) 108 (1 per 288 persons); infant mortality rate per 1,000 live births (2006) 5.5.

Military

Total active duty personnel: none. Liechtenstein has had no standing army since 1868; defense is the responsibility of Switzerland.

Background

The Rhine plain was occupied for centuries by two independent lordships of the Holy Roman Empire, Vaduz and Schellenberg. The principality of Liechtenstein, consisting of these two lordships, was founded in 1719 and remained part of the Holy Roman Empire. It was included in the German Confederation (1815–66). In 1866 it became independent, recognizing Vaduz and Schellenberg as unique regions forming separate electoral districts. An almost 60-year ruling coalition dissolved in 1997, and the prince won the passage of constitutional reforms in 2003 that greatly strengthened royal power.

Recent Developments

Liechtenstein found itself in trouble for its banking practices in 2008. A former clerk at LGT, the bank owned by the Liechtenstein royal family, had offered Germany's Federal Intelligence Service a CD-ROM with data on German clients who held secret accounts at the Liechtenstein bank as part of a cross-border tax-evasion scheme.

Internet resources: <www.liechtenstein.li/en>.

Lithuania

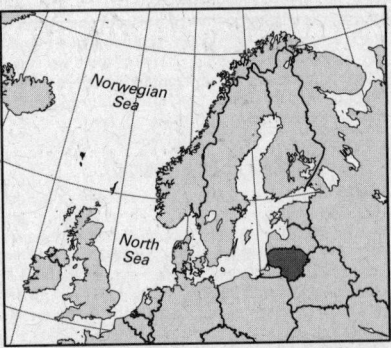

Official name: Lietuvos Respublika (Republic of Lithuania). **Form of government:** unitary multiparty republic with a single legislative body (Seimas [141]). **Head of state:** President Dalia Grybauskaite (from 2009). **Head of government:** Prime Minister Andrius Kubilius (from 2008). **Capital:** Vilnius. **Official language:** Lithuanian. **Official religion:** none. **Monetary unit:** 1 litas (LTL; plural litai) = 100 centai; valuation (1 Jul 2009) US$1 = LTL 2.45.

Demography

Area: 25,212 sq mi, 65,300 sq km. **Population** (2008): 3,358,000. **Density** (2008): persons per sq mi 133.2, persons per sq km 51.4. **Urban** (2006): 66.8%. **Sex distribution** (2006): male 46.59%; female 53.41%. **Age breakdown** (2005): under 15, 16.7%; 15–29, 22.1%; 30–44, 22.4%; 45–59, 18.2%; 60–74, 14.2%; 75–84, 5.3%; 85 and over, 1.1%. **Ethnic composition** (2001): Lithuanian 83.5%; Polish 6.7%; Russian 6.3%; Belarusian 1.2%; Ukrainian 0.7%; other 1.6%. **Religious affiliation** (2001): Roman Catholic 79.0%; Orthodox 4.8%, of which Old Believers 0.8%; Protestant 1.0%; nonreligious 9.5%; unknown 5.7%. **Major cities** (2007): Vilnius 544,206; Kaunas 355,586; Klaipeda 184,657; Siauliai 127,059; Panevezys 113,653. **Location:** eastern Europe, bordering Latvia, Belarus, Poland, Russia, and the Baltic Sea.

Vital statistics

Birth rate per 1,000 population (2007): 9.5 (world avg. 20.3); within marriage 70.8%; outside of marriage 29.2%. **Death rate** per 1,000 population (2007): 13.5 (world avg. 8.6). **Natural increase rate** per 1,000 population (2007): −4.0 (world avg. 11.7). **Total fertility rate** (avg. births per childbearing woman; 2006): 1.31. **Life expectancy** at birth (2006): male 65.3 years; female 77.1 years.

National economy

Budget (2004). *Revenue:* LTL 17,960,900,000 (tax revenue 59.2%, of which VAT 36.4%, income tax 22.2%; social security contributions 32.0%). *Expenditures:* LTL 17,817,400,000 (social security and welfare 40.4%; wages and salaries 18.3%; grants

1 metric ton = about 1.1 short tons;   1 kilometer = 0.6 mi (statute);   1 metric ton-km cargo = about 0.68 short ton-mi cargo;   c.i.f.: cost, insurance, and freight;   f.o.b.: free on board

and subsidies 17.3%; interest on debt 3.4%). **Gross national income** (2007): US$33,472,000,000 (US$9,920 per capita). **Production** (metric tons except as noted). *Agriculture and fishing* (2007): wheat 1,390,700, barley 1,013,700, sugar beets 799,900; livestock (number of live animals) 1,127,100 pigs, 838,800 cattle; fisheries production (2006) 156,772 (from aquaculture, negligible). *Mining and quarrying* (2005): limestone 1,242,200; peat 535,000; sulfur 74,277. *Manufacturing* (value added in LTL '000,000; 2005): food and beverages 2,569; refined petroleum products 2,077; textiles 1,395. *Energy production (consumption):* electricity (kW-hr; 2005) 14,784,000,000 (11,818,000,000); coal (metric tons; 2005) none (284,000); crude petroleum (barrels; 2005) 1,570,000 (68,037,000); petroleum products (metric tons; 2005) 8,870,000 (2,308,000); natural gas (cu m; 2005) none (2,952,000,000). **Public debt** (external, outstanding; March 2006): US$3,156,000,000. **Population economically active** (2007): total 1,603,100; activity rate of total population 47.6% (participation rates: ages 15–64, 67.9%; female 49.3%; registered unemployed 4.3%). **Selected balance of payments data.** Receipts from (US$'000,000): tourism (2006) 1,038; remittances (2007) 994; foreign direct investment (FDI) (2004–06 avg.) 1,206. Disbursements for (US$'000,000): tourism (2006) 909; remittances (2007) 426; FDI (2004–06 avg.) 294.

Foreign trade

Imports (2006; c.i.f.): LTL 53,357,000,000 (machinery and apparatus 23.4%; crude petroleum 18.3%; motor vehicles 11.8%; chemical products 11.5%). *Major import sources:* Russia 24.2%; Germany 14.9%; Poland 9.5%; Latvia 4.8%; The Netherlands 3.7%. **Exports** (2006; f.o.b.): LTL 38,900,000,000 (refined petroleum products 21.6%; machinery and apparatus 12.4%; food products 11.7%; chemical products 9.1%; motor vehicles and parts 7.7%). *Major export destinations:* Russia 12.8%; Latvia 11.1%; Germany 8.6%; Estonia 6.5%; Poland 6.1%.

Transport and communications

Transport. *Railroads* (2007): length 2,180 km; passenger-km 408,710,000; metric ton-km cargo 14,372,677,000. *Roads* (2007): total length 80,715 km (paved 88%). *Vehicles* (2007): passenger cars 1,587,903; trucks and buses 140,995. *Air transport* (2007): passenger-km 1,521,700,000; metric ton-km cargo 5,777,000. **Communications,** in total units (units per 1,000 persons). Telephone landlines (2007): 799,000 (236); cellular telephone subscribers (2007): 4,912,000 (1,449); personal computers (2005): 616,000 (180); total Internet users (2007): 1,333,000 (393); broadband Internet subscribers (2007): 508,000 (150).

Education and health

Educational attainment (2005). Percentage of population ages 15 and over having: no schooling through complete primary education 14.7%; lower secondary 18.0%; higher secondary 28.2%; vocational/technical 19.3%; higher 19.8%. **Literacy** (2003): percentage of total population ages 15 and over literate, virtually 100%. **Health** (2006): physicians 13,510 (1 per 251 persons); hospital beds

27,114 (1 per 125 persons); infant mortality rate per 1,000 live births (2007) 5.9; undernourished population (2002–04) less than 2.5% of total population.

Military

Total active duty personnel (2007): 13,850 (army 90.3%, navy 3.2%, air force 6.5%). **Military expenditure as percentage of GDP** (2005): 1.2%; per capita expenditure US$90.

Background

Lithuanian tribes united in the mid-13th century to oppose the Teutonic knights. Gediminas, one of the grand dukes, expanded Lithuania into an empire that dominated much of Eastern Europe in the 14th through 16th centuries. In 1386 the Lithuanian grand duke became the king of Poland, and the two countries remained closely associated until Lithuania was acquired by Russia in the Third Partition of Poland in 1795. Occupied by Germany during World War I, it declared its independence in 1918. In 1940 the Soviet Red Army gained control of Lithuania. Germany occupied it again in 1941–44, but the USSR regained control in 1944. With the breakup of the USSR, Lithuania became independent in 1991. It signed a border treaty with Russia in 1997, and it joined the European Union and NATO in 2004.

Recent Developments

Lithuania supported Georgia following the August 2008 incursion into that country by Russian troops. Pres. Valdas Adamkus traveled to Tbilisi—together with the leaders of Estonia, Latvia, and Poland—and in a joint declaration demanded the withdrawal of the Russian troops and suggested that the NATO Membership Action Plan be offered to Georgia. In 2009 Vilnius was named one of two European Capitals of Culture, and Lithuania celebrated the 1,000th anniversary of its name.

Internet resources: <www.stat.gov.lt/en>.

Luxembourg

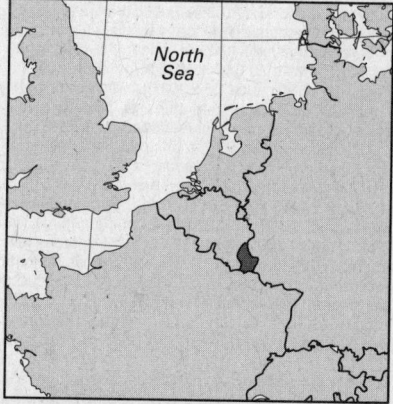

Official name: Groussherzogtum Lëtzebuerg (Luxembourgian); Grand-Duché de Luxembourg (French); Grossherzogtum Luxemburg (German) (Grand Duchy of Luxembourg). Form of government: constitutional monarchy with one legislative body (Chamber of Deputies [60]). Chief of state: Grand Duke Henri (from 2000). Head of government: Prime Minister Jean-Claude Juncker (from 1995). Capital: Luxembourg. Official language: none (Luxembourgian is the national language, French is used for most official purposes, and German is the lingua franca). Official religion: none. Monetary unit: 1 euro (€) = 100 cents; valuation (1 Jul 2009) US$1 = €0.71.

Demography

Area: 999 sq mi, 2,586 sq km. Population (2008): 488,000. Density (2008): persons per sq mi 488.5, persons per sq km 188.7. Urban (2005): 82.8%. Sex distribution (2007): male 49.52%; female 50.48%. Age breakdown (2007): under 15, 18.2%; 15–29, 18.6%; 30–44, 24.1%; 45–59, 20.4%; 60–74, 12.1%; 75–84, 5.2%; 85 and over, 1.4%. Ethnic composition (nationality; 2007): Luxembourger 57.4%; Portuguese 15.8%; French 5.5%; Italian 3.9%; Belgian 3.4%; German 2.4%; other 11.6%. Religious affiliation (2005): Roman Catholic (including nonpracticing) 90%; Protestant 3%; Muslim 2%; Orthodox 1%; other 4%. Major cities (2007): Luxembourg 85,467; Esch-sur-Alzette 29,515; Differdange 20,443; Dudelange 18,052; Pétange 15,151. Location: western Europe, bordering Belgium, Germany, and France.

Vital statistics

Birth rate per 1,000 population (2007): 11.3 (world avg. 20.3); (2006) within marriage 71.2%; outside of marriage 28.8%. Death rate per 1,000 population (2007): 8.0 (world avg. 8.6). Natural increase rate per 1,000 population (2007): 3.3 (world avg. 11.7). Total fertility rate (avg. births per childbearing woman; 2005): 1.70. Life expectancy at birth (2005): male 76.2 years; female 82.3 years.

National economy

Budget (2004). Revenue: €6,392,568,500 (indirect taxes 48.6%; direct taxes 46.2%). Expenditures: €6,476,725,500 (current expenditure 89.7%; development expenditure 10.3%). Public debt (2007): negligible. Production (metric tons except as noted). Agriculture and fishing (2007): wheat 70,400, barley 44,600, triticale 20,600; livestock (number of live animals) 191,500 cattle, 96,920 pigs; Mining and quarrying (2006): limited quantities of limestone and slate. Manufacturing (value added in €'000,000; 2007): base metals 589; fabricated metal products 490; cement, bricks, and ceramics 317. Energy production (consumption): electricity (kW-hr; 2006) 4,333,500,000 ([2005] 6,140,000,000); coal (metric tons; 2005) none (111,000); petroleum products (metric tons; 2005) none (2,586,000); natural gas (cu m; 2007) none (1,403,300,000). Gross national income (2007): US$36,420,000,000 (US$75,880 per capita). Population economically active (2007): total 213,200; activity rate of total population 44.8% (participation rates: ages 15–64, 66.1%; female 44.5%; unemployed [September 2007–August 2008] 4.3%). Selected balance of payments data. Receipts from (US$'000,000): tourism (2006) 3,626; remittances (2007) 1,565; foreign direct investment (FDI) (2004–06 avg.) 14,126. Disbursements for (US$'000,000): tourism (2006) 3,136; remittances (2007) 9,279; FDI (2004–06 avg.) 6,130.

Foreign trade

Imports (2006; c.i.f.): US$19,640,000,000 (machinery and apparatus 15.3%; motor vehicles 11.5%; chemical products 9.4%; refined petroleum products 9.3%; iron and steel 7.1%). Major import sources: Belgium 34.0%; Germany 25.7%; France 11.5%; The Netherlands 5.7%; US 3.1%. Exports (2006; f.o.b.): US$14,183,000,000 (iron and steel 23.3%; machinery and apparatus 17.9%; chemical products 6.3%; motor vehicles and parts 5.9%; nonferrous metals [particularly aluminum] 5.9%). Major export destinations: Germany 24.6%; France 16.7%; Belgium 12.3%; Italy 5.5%; The Netherlands 5.0%.

Transport and communications

Transport. Railroads (2007): route length, 275 km; passenger-km 316,000,000; metric ton-km cargo 293,000,000. Roads (2007): total length 2,894 km (paved 100%). Vehicles (2007): passenger cars 321,520; trucks and buses 28,498. Air transport (Luxair only; 2007): passenger-km 1,211,000,000; metric ton-km cargo, negligible. Communications, in total units (units per 1,000 persons). Telephone landlines (2007): 248,000 (532); cellular telephone subscribers (2007): 604,000 (1,295); personal computers (2005): 290,000 (634); total Internet users (2007): 345,000 (740); broadband Internet subscribers (2007): 113,000 (242).

Education and health

Educational attainment (2003). Percentage of population ages 25–64 having: no formal schooling through primary education 19%; lower secondary 10%; upper secondary/higher vocational 56%; higher 15%. Literacy (2007): percentage of total population literate, virtually 100%. Health: physicians (2005) 1,675 (1 per 273 persons); hospital beds (2004) 3,045 (1 per 149 persons); infant mortality rate per 1,000 live births (2007) 1.8; undernourished population (2002–04) less than 2.5% of total population.

Military

Total active duty personnel (2007): 900 (army 100%). Military expenditure as percentage of GDP (2005): 0.8%; per capita expenditure US$584.

Background

At the time of Roman conquest (57–50 BC), Luxembourg was inhabited by a Belgic tribe. After AD 400, Germanic tribes invaded the region. Made a duchy in 1354, it was ceded to the house of Burgundy in 1443 and to the Habsburgs in 1477. In the mid-16th century it became part of the Spanish Netherlands. It was made a grand duchy in 1815. After an upris-

1 metric ton = about 1.1 short tons;   1 kilometer = 0.6 mi (statute);   1 metric ton-km cargo = about 0.68 short ton-mi cargo;   c.i.f.: cost, insurance, and freight;   f.o.b.: free on board

ing in 1830, its western portion became part of Belgium, while the remainder was held by The Netherlands. In 1867 the European powers guaranteed the neutrality and independence of Luxembourg. In the late 19th century it exploited its extensive iron-ore deposits. It was invaded and occupied by Germany in both world wars. It abandoned its neutrality by joining NATO in 1949; it had joined the Benelux Economic Union in 1944. A member of the European Union, its economy has continued to expand. On 7 Oct 2000, Grand Duke Jean abdicated power in favor of his son, Crown Prince Henri, after 36 years on the throne.

Recent Developments

Luxembourg's economy continued to provide an extraordinarily high standard of living in 2008, with a GDP per capita ranked second in the world. However, the meltdown in the world's financial markets was expected to affect even Luxembourg's economy in 2009, as experts predicted a contraction of 4.8%.

Internet resources: <www.ont.lu>.

Macedonia

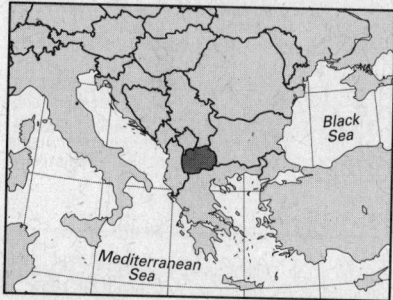

Official name: Republika Makedonija (Macedonian); Republika e Maqedonisë (Albanian) (Republic of Macedonia [member of the UN under the name The Former Yugoslav Republic of Macedonia]). **Form of government:** unitary multiparty republic with a unicameral legislature (Assembly [120]). **Head of state:** President Branko Crvenkovski (from 2004). **Head of government:** Prime Minister Nikola Gruevski (from 2006). **Capital:** Skopje. **Official languages:** Macedonian; Albanian. **Official religion:** none. **Monetary unit:** 1 denar (MKD) = 100 deni; valuation (1 Jul 2009) US$1 = 43.39 MKD.

Demography

Area: 9,928 sq mi, 25,713 sq km. **Population** (2008): 2,039,000. **Density** (2008): persons per sq mi 205.4, persons per sq km 79.3. **Urban** (2005): 68.9%. **Sex distribution** (2005): male 49.95%; female 50.05%. **Age breakdown** (2005): under 15, 20.5%; 15–29, 23.8%; 30–44, 21.8%; 45–59, 18.8%; 60–74, 11.5%; 75–84, 3.2%; 85 and over, 0.4%. **Ethnic composition** (2002): Macedonian 64.2%; Albanian 25.2%; Turkish 3.9%; Rom (Gypsy) 2.7%; Serbian 1.8%; Bosniac 0.8%; other 1.4%. **Religious affiliation** (2005): Orthodox 65%; Sunni Muslim

32%; Roman Catholic 1%; other (mostly Protestant) 2%. **Major municipalities** (2002): Skopje (city; 2004) 506,926; Kumanovo 103,025; Bitola 86,408; Prilep 73,351; Tetovo 70,841. **Location:** southeastern Europe, bordering Kosovo, Serbia, Bulgaria, Greece, and Albania.

Vital statistics

Birth rate per 1,000 population (2006): 11.2 (world avg. 20.3); within marriage 87.5%; outside of marriage 12.5%. **Death rate** per 1,000 population (2006): 9.1 (world avg. 8.6). **Natural increase rate** per 1,000 population (2006): 2.1 (world avg. 11.7). **Total fertility rate** (avg. births per childbearing woman; 2005): 1.57. **Life expectancy** at birth (2005): male 71.3 years; female 76.4 years.

National economy

Budget (2005). *Revenue:* MKD 92,805,000,000 (tax revenue 90.8%, of which social contributions 30.8%, VAT 29.2%, excise taxes 12.7%, income and profit tax 11.8%, import duties 5.7%; nontax revenue 9.2%). *Expenditures:* MKD 92,228,000,000 (transfers 55.0%; wages and salaries 24.0%). **Production** (metric tons except as noted). *Agriculture and fishing* (2007): grapes 225,000, potatoes 192,500, wheat 157,400; livestock (number of live animals) 817,500 sheep, 253,800 cattle; fisheries production 735 (from aquaculture 88%). *Mining and quarrying* (2006): copper (metal content) 33,591; zinc (metal content) 21,700; lead (metal content) 15,600. *Manufacturing* (value added in US$'000,000; 2006): food and beverages 297; cement, bricks, and glass products 177; iron and steel (including ferronickel) 103. *Energy production (consumption):* electricity (kW-hr; 2005) 6,942,000,000 (8,541,000,000); coal (metric tons; 2005) none (3,000); lignite (metric tons; 2005) 6,881,000 (7,470,000); crude petroleum (barrels; 2005) none (6,940,000); petroleum products (metric tons; 2005) 921,000 (848,000); natural gas (cu m; 2005) none (77,000,000). **Population economically active** (2006): total 891,679; activity rate of total population 55.1% (participation rates: ages 15–64, 61.4%; female 39.5%; unemployed 36.0%). **Gross national income** (2007): US$7,052,000,000 (US$3,460 per capita). **Public debt** (external, outstanding; 2006): US$1,498,000,000. **Selected balance of payments data.** Receipts from (US$'000,-000): tourism (2006) 129; remittances (2007) 267; foreign direct investment (2004–06 avg.) 203; official development assistance (2006) 200. Disbursements for (US$'000,000): tourism (2006) 71; remittances (2007) 18.

Did you know? In Plutarch's classic history of Alexander the Great, he claims that the famous Macedonian general was tutored as a youth by none other than Aristotle.

Foreign trade

Imports (2006; c.i.f.): US$3,763,000,000 (crude petroleum 14.3%; machinery and apparatus 12.2%; iron and steel 9.9%; food products 9.8%; chemical products 9.7%). *Major import sources:* Russia 15.1%;

Germany 9.8%; Greece 8.5%; Serbia 7.5%; Bulgaria 6.6%. **Exports** (2006; f.o.b.): US$2,401,000,000 (iron and steel 27.8%, of which flat-rolled products 9.1%, ferronickel 8.4%; clothing and accessories 21.2%, of which female outerwear 11.9%; refined petroleum products 8.4%; food products 8.0%; tobacco [all forms] 4.7%). *Major export destinations:* Serbia 23.2%; Germany 15.6%; Greece 15.0%; Italy 9.9%; Bulgaria 5.4%.

Transport and communications

Transport. *Railroads* (2005): length (2004) 699 km; passenger-km 94,000,000; metric ton-km cargo 531,000,000. *Roads* (2000): length 12,522 km (paved 58%). *Vehicles* (2002): passenger cars 307,581; trucks and buses 33,002. *Air transport* (Macedonian Airlines only; 2005): passenger-km 266,000,000; metric ton-km cargo 111,000. **Communications,** in total units (units per 1,000 persons). Telephone landlines (2007): 464,000 (227); cellular telephone subscribers (2007): 1,518,000 (744); personal computers (2005): 451,000 (221); total Internet users (2007): 685,000 (336); broadband Internet subscribers (2007): 45,000 (22).

Education and health

Educational attainment (2002). Percentage of population ages 15 and over having: less than full primary education 18.1%; primary 35.0%; secondary 36.9%; postsecondary and higher 10.0%. **Literacy** (2003): percentage of total population ages 10 and over literate 96.1%; males literate 98.2%; females literate 94.1%. **Health:** physicians (2001) 4,459 (1 per 452 persons); hospital beds (2002) 9,757 (1 per 207 persons); infant mortality rate per 1,000 live births (2006) 8.9; undernourished population (2002–04) 100,000 (5% of total population based on the consumption of a minimum daily requirement of 1,980 calories).

Military

Total active duty personnel (2007): 10,890 (army 89.6%, air force 10.4%). **Military expenditure as percentage of GDP** (2005): 2.2%; per capita expenditure US$62.

Background

Macedonia has been inhabited since before 7000 BC. Part of it was incorporated into a Roman province in AD 29. It was settled by Slavic tribes by the mid-6th century AD. Seized by the Bulgarians in 1185, it was ruled by the Ottoman Empire from 1371 to 1912. The north and center of the region were annexed by Serbia in 1913 and in 1918 became part of what was later known as Yugoslavia. When Yugoslavia was partitioned by the Axis powers in 1941, Yugoslav Macedonia was occupied principally by Bulgaria. Macedonia again became part of Yugoslavia in 1946. After Croatia and Slovenia seceded from Yugoslavia, fear of Serbian dominance drove Macedonia to declare its independence in 1991. Because of Greek objections over using the name of an ancient Greek province, it entered the UN in 1993 as "The Former Yugoslav Republic of Macedonia."

Recent Developments

Macedonia's bid to join NATO was vetoed in April 2008 by Greece during the alliance's summit meeting in Bucharest, Romania. Prior to the summit, a round of intense UN-mediated talks between Skopje and Athens over Macedonia's name had failed to produce any results. Though talks continued throughout 2008, both sides stuck to their previous positions. Macedonia's GDP grew 4.8% in 2008, but inflation rose to 8.4% and unemployment stood at 34.5%.

Internet resources:
<www.stat.gov.mk/english/glavna_eng.asp>.

Madagascar

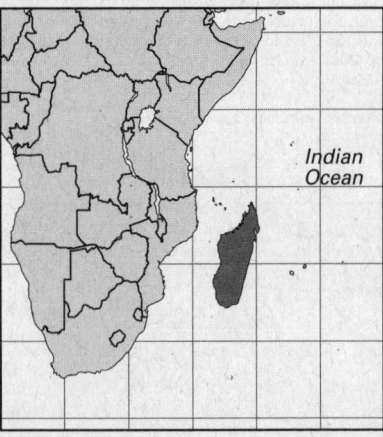

Official name: Repoblikan'i Madagasikara (Malagasy); République de Madagascar (French) (Republic of Madagascar). **Form of government:** transitional regime with two legislative houses (Senate [33]; National Assembly [127]; both suspended from March 2007). **Heads of state and government:** President of High Authority of Transition Andry Rajoelina (from 2009), assisted by Prime Minister Monja Roindefo (from 2009). **Capital:** Antananarivo. **Official languages:** French; English (Malagasy is the national language). **Official religion:** none. **Monetary unit:** 1 ariary (MGA) = 100 iraimbilanja; valuation (1 Jul 2009) US$1 = MGA 1,889.10.

Demography

Area: 226,662 sq mi, 587,051 sq km. **Population** (2008): 20,215,000. **Density** (2008): persons per sq mi 89.2, persons per sq km 34.4. **Urban** (2006): 27.3%. **Sex distribution** (2005): male 49.72%; female 50.28%. **Age breakdown** (2006): under 15, 44.1%; 15–29, 27.1%; 30–44, 15.7%; 45–59, 8.4%; 60–74, 3.7%; 75–84, 0.9%; 85 and over, 0.1%. **Ethnic composition** (2000): Malagasy 95.9%, of which Merina 24.0%, Betsi-misaraka 13.4%, Betsileo 11.3%, Tsimihety 7.0%, Sakalava 5.9%, Makua 1.1%; French 0.6%; Comorian 0.5%; Reunionese

1 metric ton = about 1.1 short tons;   1 kilometer = 0.6 mi (statute);   1 metric ton-km cargo = about 0.68 short ton-mi cargo;   c.i.f.: cost, insurance, and freight;   f.o.b.: free on board

0.4%; other 1.5%. **Religious affiliation** (2005): traditional beliefs 42%; Protestant (significantly Lutheran) 27%; Roman Catholic 20%; Sunni Muslim 2%; other 9%. **Major cities** (2001): Antananarivo 1,403,449; Toamasina 179,045; Antsirabe 160,356; Fianarantsoa 144,225; Mahajanga 135,660. **Location:** island in the Indian Ocean, east of Mozambique.

Vital statistics

Birth rate per 1,000 population (2006): 38.8 (world avg. 20.3). **Death rate** per 1,000 population (2006): 8.7 (world avg. 8.6). **Natural increase rate** per 1,000 population (2006): 30.1 (world avg. 11.7). **Total fertility rate** (avg. births per childbearing woman; 2006): 5.29. **Life expectancy** at birth (2006): male 59.9 years; female 63.7 years.

National economy

Budget (2004). *Revenue:* MGA 1,653,000,000,000 (tax revenue 53.7%, of which import duties 26.9%, VAT 10.5%; grants 40.6%; nontax revenue 5.7%). *Expenditures:* MGA 2,045,000,000,000 (current expenditures 50.2%; capital expenditures 49.8%). **Public debt** (external, outstanding; 2006): US$1,236,000,000. **Production** (metric tons except as noted). *Agriculture and fishing* (2007): rice 3,596,000, sugarcane 2,700,000, cassava 2,400,-000, vanilla 2,600; livestock (number of live animals) 9,600,000 cattle, 1,610,000 pigs, 3,000,000 geese; fisheries production (2006) 145,630 (from aquaculture 8%). *Mining and quarrying* (2006): chromite ore 100,000; graphite 15,000; sapphires 4,700 kg; rubies 920 kg; gold 5 kg (illegally smuggled, 2,000 kg). *Manufacturing* (value in US$'000,-000; 2004): beverages 107; wearing apparel 57; fabricated metal products 35. *Energy production (consumption):* electricity (kW-hr; 2005) 1,035,-000,000 (1,035,000,000); coal (metric tons; 2005) none (10,000); crude petroleum (barrels; 2005) none (3,504,000); petroleum products (metric tons; 2005) 325,000 (736,000). **Population economically active** (2005): total 9,844,100; activity rate of total population 52.8% (participation rates: ages 15–64, 88.1%; female 49.6%; unemployed 2.8%). **Selected balance of payments data.** Receipts from (US$'000,000): tourism (2006) 237; remittances (2007) 11; foreign direct investment (2004–06 avg.) 137; official development assistance (2006) 754. Disbursements for (US$'000,000): tourism (2006) 86; remittances (2007) 21. **Gross national income** (2007): US$6,331,000,000 (US$320 per capita).

Foreign trade

Imports (2006; c.i.f.): US$1,760,300,000 (refined petroleum products 17.7%; machinery and apparatus 12.8%; food products 11.4%, of which cereals 4.3%; fabrics 9.3%; chemical products 8.6%). *Major import sources:* China 17.8%; Bahrain 16.4%; France 13.2%; South Africa 5.7%; US 3.6%. **Exports** (2006; f.o.b.): US$1,008,200,000 (food and spices 32.4%, of which shrimp 12.0%, vanilla 4.7%, fish 4.4%, cloves 2.7%; wearing apparel and accessories 25.0%; refined petroleum products 7.9%; precious and semiprecious stones 2.6%). *Major export destinations:* France 39.5%; US 15.0%; Germany 6.0%; Italy 4.2%; UK 3.0%.

Transport and communications

Transport. *Railroads* (2000): route length (2003) 901 km; passenger-km 24,471,000; metric ton-km cargo 27,200,000. *Roads* (2000): total length 49,827 km (paved 12%). *Vehicles* (1998): passenger cars 64,000; trucks and buses 9,100. *Air transport* (2007): passenger-km 1,248,000,000; metric ton-km cargo (2006) 18,768,000. **Communications,** in total units (units per 1,000 persons). Telephone landlines (2007): 134,000 (6.8); cellular telephone subscribers (2007): 2,218,000 (113); personal computers (2005): 102,000 (5.5); total Internet users (2006): 110,000 (5.8).

Education and health

Educational attainment (2003–04). Percentage of population ages 25–59 (male) and 25–49 (female) having: no formal schooling 20.4%; incomplete primary education 33.6%; complete primary 13.2%; incomplete secondary 23.0%; complete secondary 6.4%; higher 3.4%. **Literacy** (2006): percentage of total population ages 15 and over literate 70.7%; males literate 76.5%; females literate 65.3%. **Health** (2004): physicians 1,861 (1 per 9,998 persons); hospital beds 9,303 (1 per 2,000 persons); infant mortality rate per 1,000 live births (2006) 58.5; undernourished population (2002–04) 6,600,000 (38% of total population based on the consumption of a minimum daily requirement of 1,800 calories).

Military

Total active duty personnel (2007): 13,500 (army 92.6%, navy 3.7%, air force 3.7%). **Military expenditure as percentage of GDP** (2005): 1.1%; per capita expenditure US$3.

Background

Indonesians migrated to Madagascar about AD 700. The first European to visit the island was Portuguese navigator Diogo Dias in 1500. Trade in arms and slaves allowed the development of Malagasy kingdoms at the beginning of the 17th century. The Merina kingdom became dominant in the 18th century and in 1868 signed a treaty granting France control over the northwestern coast. In 1895 French troops took the island, and Madagascar became a French overseas territory in 1946. As the Malagasy Republic, it gained independence in 1960. It severed ties with France in the 1970s. A new constitution was adopted in 1992, and the country was named the Republic of Madagascar. The country has since been both politically and economically unstable.

Recent Developments

Though the cyclones that hit the northern part of Madagascar in early 2008 did not do as much damage as those the previous year, hundreds of thousands of people were left without homes, much of the harvest in the areas affected was destroyed, and the steep rise in food and fuel prices in 2008 brought further hardship to many—the UN estimated in 2009 that nearly 3.4 million people required humanitarian assistance.

Internet resources: <www.wildmadagascar.org>.

Malawi

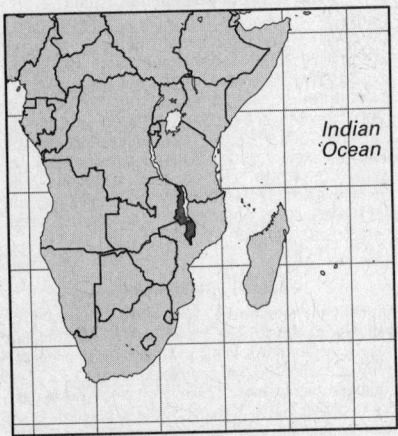

Indian Ocean

Official name: Republic of Malawi. **Form of government:** multiparty republic with one legislative house (National Assembly [193]). **Head of state and government:** President Bingu wa Mutharika (from 2004). **Capital:** Lilongwe. **Official language:** none. **Official religion:** none. **Monetary unit:** 1 Malawian kwacha (MK) = 100 tambala; valuation (1 Jul 2009) US$1 = MK 138.19.

Demography

Area: 45,747 sq mi, 118,484 sq km. **Population** (2008): 13,932,000. **Density** (2008): persons per sq mi 382.7, persons per sq km 147.8. **Urban** (2007): 18.2%. **Sex distribution** (2008): male 48.72%; female 51.28%. **Age breakdown** (2007): under 15, 46.1%; 15–29, 29.3%; 30–44, 13.1%; 45–59, 7.3%; 60–74, 3.5%; 75 and over, 0.7%. **Ethnic composition** (2000): Chewa 34.7%; Maravi 12.2%; Ngoni 9.0%; Yao 7.9%; Tumbuka 7.9%; Lomwe 7.7%; Ngonde 3.5%; other 17.1%. **Religious affiliation** (2005): Protestant and independent Christian 55%; Roman Catholic 20%; Muslim 20%; traditional beliefs 3%; other 2%. **Major cities** (2008): Lilongwe 669,021; Blantyre 661,444; Mzuzu 128,432; Zomba 87,366; Kasungu 42,351. **Location:** southeastern Africa, bordering Tanzania, Mozambique, and Zambia.

Vital statistics

Birth rate per 1,000 population (2007): 42.1 (world avg. 20.3). **Death rate** per 1,000 population (2007): 18.2 (world avg. 8.6). **Natural increase rate** per 1,000 population (2007): 23.9 (world avg. 11.7). **Total fertility rate** (avg. births per childbearing woman; 2007): 5.74. **Life expectancy** at birth (2007): male 43.4 years; female 42.6 years.

National economy

Budget (2005). *Revenue:* MK 103,298,600,000 (tax revenue 52.9%, of which VAT 16.7%, income tax 11.7%; grants 38.7%; nontax revenue 8.4%). *Expen-* ditures: MK 110,943,700,000 (current expenditures 76.3%; capital expenditures 21.0%; other 2.7%). **Production** (metric tons except as noted). *Agriculture and fishing* (2007): corn (maize) 3,444,700, sugarcane 2,500,000, cassava 2,150,000, seed cotton 42,000; livestock (number of live animals) 1,900,000 goats, 752,000 cattle, 458,000 pigs; fisheries production (2006) 72,787 (from aquaculture 2%). *Mining and quarrying* (2006): limestone 34,226; gemstones (including rubies and sapphires) 2,171 kg. *Manufacturing* (value added in US$'000,000; 2001): food products 62; beverages 28; chemical products 11. *Energy production (consumption):* electricity (kW-hr; 2005) 1,273,000,000 (1,265,000,000); coal (metric tons; 2006) 48,000 ([2005] 52,000); petroleum products (metric tons; 2005) none (261,000). **Population economically active** (2003): total 5,707,000; activity rate of total population 46.3% (participation rates: ages 15–64, 88.0%; female 49.7%; unemployed, n.a.). **Gross national income** (2007): US$3,506,-000,000 (US$250 per capita). **Public debt** (external, outstanding; March 2008): US$556,920,000. **Selected balance of payments data.** Receipts from (US$'000,000): tourism (2006) 24; remittances (2007) 1.0; foreign direct investment (2004–06 avg.) 26; official development assistance (2006) 669. Disbursements for (US$'000,000): tourism (2006) 65; remittances (2007) 1.0.

Foreign trade

Imports (2006): MK 164,468,000,000 (chemical products 18.6%, of which fertilizers 6.1%; motor vehicles 15.7%; machinery and apparatus 13.0%; refined petroleum products 10.8%; cereals 5.2%). *Major import sources:* South Africa 35.9%; Mozambique 12.5%; UAE 6.0%; UK 5.8%; India 4.1%. **Exports** (2006): MK 90,911,000,000 (tobacco 61.4%; tea 7.4%; wearing apparel and accessories 6.1%; raw sugar 5.7%; cotton 2.2%). *Major export destinations:* South Africa 22.2%; UK 13.2%; Germany 10.5%; US 8.2%; Egypt 5.1%.

Transport and communications

Transport. *Railroads:* route length (2006) 797 km; passenger-km (2004) 29,523,000; metric ton-km cargo (2007) 18,438,000. *Roads* (2003): total length 15,451 km (paved 45%). *Vehicles* (2001): passenger cars 22,500; trucks and buses 57,600. *Air transport* (Air Malawi only; 2005): passenger-km 201,000,000; metric ton-km cargo 1,364,000. **Communications,** in total units (units per 1,000 persons). Telephone landlines (2007): 175,000 (13); cellular telephone subscribers (2007): 1,051,000 (76); personal computers (2006): 25,000 (1.9); total Internet users (2007): 140,000 (10); broadband Internet subscribers (2007): 1,600 (0.1).

Education and health

Educational attainment (2004). Percentage of population ages 25 and over having: no formal education/unknown 33.5%; incomplete primary education 24.2%; complete primary 27.9%; secondary and university 14.4%. **Literacy** (2007): percentage of total population ages 15 and over literate 65.9%; males literate 78.1%; females literate 53.9%. **Health:** physi-

---

1 metric ton = about 1.1 short tons;   1 kilometer = 0.6 mi (statute);   1 metric ton-km cargo = about 0.68 short ton-mi cargo;   c.i.f.: cost, insurance, and freight;   f.o.b.: free on board

cians (2004) 266 (1 per 46,644 persons); hospital beds (1998) 14,087 (1 per 735 persons); infant mortality rate per 1,000 live births (2007) 92.1; undernourished population (2002–04) 4,200,000 (35% of total population based on the consumption of a minimum daily requirement of 1,790 calories).

Military

Total active duty personnel (2007): 5,300 (army 100%). Military expenditure as percentage of GDP (2005): 0.7%; per capita expenditure US$1.

Background

Inhabited since at least 8000 BC, the region was settled by Bantu-speaking peoples between the 1st and the 4th century AD. About 1480 they founded the Maravi Confederacy, which encompassed most of central and southern Malawi. In northern Malawi the Ngonde people established a kingdom about 1600. The slave trade flourished during the 18th–19th centuries. Britain established colonial authority in 1891, and the area became known as Nyasaland in 1907. The colonies of Northern and Southern Rhodesia and Nyasaland formed (1951–53) a federation, which was dissolved in 1963. The next year Malawi achieved independence. In 1966 it became a republic, with Hastings Banda as president. In 1971 Banda was designated president for life, and he ruled until he was defeated in multiparty elections in 1994. A new constitution was adopted in 1995.

Recent Developments

Heavy rains and floods destroyed homes and crops in Malawi in 2008 and aroused fears of food shortages. The government's assurances that there were adequate reserves from previous years failed to silence criticisms of the export in 2007 of 300,000 metric tons of corn (maize) to Zimbabwe. The food-shortage fears, however, eventually proved unfounded. The government's distribution of subsidized seed and fertilizers was so effective that it even became possible to again export some of the surplus grain.

Internet resources: <www.nso.malawi.net>.

Malaysia

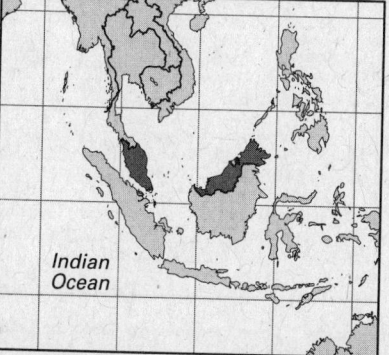

Indian Ocean

Official name: Malaysia. **Form of government:** federal constitutional monarchy with two legislative houses (Senate [70]; House of Representatives [222]). **Chief of state:** Yang di-Pertuan Agong (Paramount Ruler) Tuanku Mizan Zainal Abidin ibni al-Marhum Sultan Mahmud (from 2006). **Head of government:** Prime Minister Datuk Seri Najib Tun Razak (from 2009). **Capital:** transferring from Kuala Lumpur to Putrajaya between 1999 and 2012. **Official language:** Malay. **Official religion:** Islam. **Monetary unit:** 1 ringgit, or Malaysian dollar (RM) = 100 sen; valuation (1 Jul 2009) US$1 = RM 3.52.

Demography

Area: 127,366 sq mi, 329,876 sq km. **Population** (2008): 27,027,000. **Density** (2008): persons per sq mi 212.2, persons per sq km 81.9. **Urban** (2006): 68.3%. **Sex distribution** (2005): male 50.75%; female 49.25%. **Age breakdown** (2005): under 15, 32.4%; 15–29, 26.2%; 30–44, 20.6%; 45–59, 13.8%; 60–74, 5.6%; 75–84, 1.2%; 85 and over, 0.2%. **Ethnic composition** (2005): indigenous 61.5%, of which Malay 50.5%; Chinese 23.5%; Indian 7.0%; other citizen 1.2%; noncitizen 6.8%. **Religious affiliation** (2000): Muslim 60.4%; Buddhist 19.2%; Christian 9.1%; Hindu 6.3%; Chinese folk religionist 2.6%; animist 0.8%; other 1.6%. **Major cities** (2006): Kuala Lumpur 1,482,400; Subang Jaya 954,300; Klang 936,700; Johor Bahru 838,900; Ipoh 692,200; Putrajaya 55,000. **Location:** southeastern Asia, on the Malay Peninsula and the northern third of the island of Borneo, bordering Thailand, the South China Sea, Brunei, and Indonesia.

Vital statistics

Birth rate per 1,000 population (2007): 17.6 (world avg. 20.3). **Death rate** per 1,000 population (2007): 4.4 (world avg. 8.6). **Total fertility rate** (avg. births per childbearing woman; 2007): 2.60. **Life expectancy** at birth (2007): male 71.9 years; female 76.4 years.

National economy

Budget (2007). *Revenue:* RM 139,885,000,000 (tax revenue 68.0%, of which corporate taxes 23.0%, taxes on petroleum 14.6%; nontax revenue 32.0%). *Expenditures:* RM 163,648,000,000 (current expenditures 75.2%; development expenditures 24.8%). **Population economically active** (2007): total 10,889,500; activity rate of total population 41.0% (participation rates: ages 15–64 [2000] 65.5%; female 36.1%; unemployed [June 2008] 3.5%). **Production** (metric tons except as noted). *Agriculture and fishing* (2007): oil palm fruit 77,700,000, rice 2,231,000, natural rubber 1,270,000, pepper 19,000; livestock (number of live animals) 2,290,000 pigs, 138,000 buffalo; fisheries production (2006) 1,464,652 (from aquaculture 11%). *Mining and quarrying* (2006): iron ore 667,082; tin (metal content) 2,398; gold 3,497 kg. *Manufacturing* (value added in RM '000,000; 2005): electrical machinery and electronics 31,238; petroleum and coal products 16,058; chemical products 15,056. *Energy production (consumption):* electricity (kW-hr; 2006) 100,831,000,000 ([2005] 85,068,000,000); coal (metric tons; 2006) 901,801 ([2005] 11,380,000); crude petroleum (barrels; 2007–08) 251,370,000

([2005] 190,200,000); petroleum products (metric tons; 2005) 20,475,000 (23,937,000); natural gas (cu m; 2007–08) 69,000,000,000 ([2005] 61,780,-000,000). **Gross national income** (2007): US$173,-705,000,000 (US$6,540 per capita). **Public debt** (external, outstanding; 2006): US$21,899,000,000. **Selected balance of payments data.** Receipts from (US$'000,000): tourism (2006) 10,427; remittances (2007) 1,700; foreign direct investment (FDI) (2004–06 avg.) 4,883; official development assistance (2006) 240. Disbursements for (US$'000,-000): tourism (2006) 4,020; remittances (2007) 6,385; FDI (2004–06 avg.) 3,691.

Foreign trade

Imports (2006; c.i.f.): RM 481,000,000,000 (microcircuits and transistors 23.9%; crude petroleum 8.3%; office machinery and computers 7.8%; chemical products 7.8%; base metals 6.8%). *Major import sources:* Japan 13.2%; US 12.5%; China 12.1%; Singapore 11.7%; Thailand 5.5%. **Exports** (2006; f.o.b.): RM 589,367,000,000 (office machinery and computers 17.4%; microcircuits and transistors 15.9%; crude petroleum 8.9%; telecommunications equipment 5.7%; natural gas 4.8%; palm oil 3.2%). *Major export destinations:* US 18.8%; Singapore 15.4%; Japan 8.9%; China 7.2%; Thailand 5.3%.

Transport and communications

Transport. *Railroads* (2007): route length (2006) 1,890 km; passenger-km 1,315,900,000; metric ton-km cargo 1,354,900,000. *Roads* (2004): total length 77,695 km (paved 76%). *Vehicles* (2004): passenger cars 5,987,421; trucks and buses 827,215. *Air transport* (2007): passenger-km 40,096,000,000; metric ton-km cargo 2,621,500,000. **Communications,** in total units (units per 1,000 persons). Telephone landlines (2007): 4,350,000 (164); cellular telephone subscribers (2007): 23,347,000 (879); personal computers (2005): 5,600,000 (218); total Internet users (2007): 15,868,000 (597); broadband Internet subscribers (2007): 1,369,000 (52).

Education and health

Educational attainment (2002). Percentage of population ages 25–64 having: no formal schooling/unknown 8.4%; primary education 28.7%; lower secondary 20.7%; upper secondary 31.1%; higher 11.1%. **Literacy** (2007): percentage of total population ages 15 and over literate 91.9%; males literate 94.2%; females literate 89.6%. **Health** (2006): physicians 21,937 (1 per 1,214 persons); hospital beds 50,262 (1 per 530 persons); infant mortality rate per 1,000 live births (2007) 6.7; undernourished population (2002–04) 600,000 (3% of total population based on the consumption of a minimum daily requirement of 1,850 calories).

Military

Total active duty personnel (2007): 109,000 (army 73.4%, navy 12.8%, air force 13.8%). **Military expenditure as percentage of GDP** (2005): 2.4%; per capita expenditure US$119.

Background

Malaya has been inhabited for 6,000–8,000 years, and small kingdoms existed in the 2nd–3rd centuries AD, when adventurers from India first arrived. Sumatran exiles founded the city-state of Malacca about 1400, and it flourished as a trading and Islamic religious center until its capture by the Portuguese in 1511. Malacca passed to the Dutch in 1641. The British founded a settlement on Singapore Island in 1819, and by 1867 they had established the Straits Settlements, including Malacca, Singapore, and Penang. During the late 19th century the Chinese began to migrate to Malaya. Japan invaded in 1941. Opposition to British rule led to the creation of the United Malays National Organization (UNMO) in 1946, and in 1948 the peninsula was federated with Penang. Malaya gained independence in 1957, and the Federation of Malaysia was established in 1963. Its economy expanded greatly from the late 1970s, but it suffered from the economic slump that struck the area in the mid-1990s.

Recent Developments

Malaysia's economy continued its strong expansion for the most part in 2008, with GDP growth of 6.7% during the first half of the year and 4.6% overall. The country benefited from surging fuel prices, with the value of its palm-oil and crude-petroleum exports increasing by more than 50%. The global financial crisis at the end of the year was sobering, however. Unemployment grew slightly, to 3.7%. Inflation, already on the rise, soared to 8.5% in July, the highest level in 27 years. Analysts attributed the spike to a 40% reduction in government fuel subsidies in June. Rubber exports fell more than 10%, total external public debt rose by US$11.2 billion, and the ringgit fell 4.5% against the US dollar. Analysts warned that the impact of a string of collapses of US financial institutions on the country's crucial Asian export markets could be severe.

Internet resources: <www.bnm.gov.my>.

Maldives

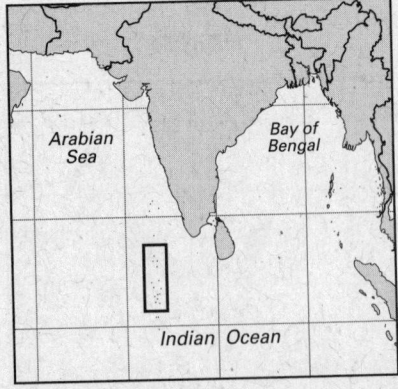

Arabian Sea

Bay of Bengal

Indian Ocean

---

1 metric ton = about 1.1 short tons;   1 kilometer = 0.6 mi (statute);   1 metric ton-km cargo = about 0.68 short ton-mi cargo;   c.i.f.: cost, insurance, and freight;   f.o.b.: free on board

Official name: Dhivehi Raajjeyge Jumhooriyyaa (Republic of Maldives). **Form of government:** multiparty republic with one legislative house (People's Majlis [77]). **Head of state and government:** President Mohamed Nasheed (from 2008). **Capital:** Male. **Official language:** Dhivehi. **Official religion:** Islam. **Monetary unit:** 1 rufiyaa (Rf) = 100 laari; valuation (1 Jul 2009) US$1 = Rf 12.62.

Demography

Area: 115 sq mi, 298 sq km. **Population** (2008): 386,000 (including foreign workers). **Density** (2008): persons per sq mi 8,559, persons per sq km 3,305. **Urban** (2006): 34.7%. **Sex distribution** (2006): male 50.66%; female 49.34%. **Age breakdown** (2006): under 15, 31.1%; 15–29, 33.2%; 30–44, 18.3%; 45–59, 9.2%; 60–74, 5.2%; 75–84, 1.1%; 85 and over, 0.2%; unknown 1.7%. **Ethnic composition** (2000): Maldivian 98.5%; Sinhalese 0.7%; other 0.8%. **Religious affiliation:** Sunni Muslim, virtually 100%. **Major islets** (2006): Male (capital island) 103,693; Hithadhoo 9,465; Fuvammulah 7,636; Kulhudhuffushi 6,998; Thinadhoo 4,442. **Location:** islands in the Indian Ocean, south of India.

Vital statistics

Birth rate per 1,000 population (2006): 19.5 (world avg. 20.3). **Death rate** per 1,000 population (2006): 3.6 (world avg. 8.6). **Natural increase rate** per 1,000 population (2006): 15.9 (world avg. 11.7). **Total fertility rate** (avg. births per childbearing woman; 2005): 2.72. **Life expectancy** at birth (2005): male 71.7 years; female 72.7 years.

National economy

Budget (2006). *Revenue:* Rf 6,548,800,000 (nontax revenue 41.3%, of which resort lease rent 19.2%; tax revenue 32.2%, of which import duties 23.2%; grants 25.9%; other 0.6%). *Expenditures:* Rf 8,644,700,000 (community programs 25.7%; economic services 18.0%; general administration 17.6%; education 13.6%). **Public debt** (external, outstanding; 2007): US$523,700,000. **Production** (metric tons except as noted). *Agriculture and fishing* (2007): bananas 11,000, coconuts 2,625, nuts 2,100; fisheries production (2006) 184,158, of which skipjack tuna 138,458, yellowfin tuna 21,772 (from aquaculture, none). *Mining and quarrying:* coral for construction materials. *Manufacturing:* major industries include boat building and repairing, coir yarn and mat weaving, coconut and fish processing, lacquerwork, garment manufacturing, and handicrafts. *Energy production (consumption):* electricity (kW-hr; 2005) 160,000,000 (160,000,000); petroleum products (metric tons; 2005) none (233,000). **Selected balance of payments data.** Receipts from (US$'000,000): tourism (2006) 434; remittances (2007) 2; foreign direct investment (2004–06 avg.) 13; official development assistance (2006) 39. Disbursements for (US$'000,000): tourism (2006) 78; remittances (2007) 84. **Population economically active** (2006): total 128,836; activity rate of total population 43.1% (participation rates: ages 15–64, 65.8%; female 41.3%; unemployed 14.4%). **Gross national income** (2007): US$977,000,000 (US$3,200 per capita).

Foreign trade

Imports (2007; c.i.f.): US$1,096,300,000 (consumer goods 33.6%, of which food products 16.0%; refined petroleum products 18.5%; goods for construction 15.7%; transportation equipment 7.2%). *Major import sources:* Singapore 22.5%; UAE 19.1%; India 11.5%; Malaysia 8.5%; Sri Lanka 6.9%. **Exports** (2007; f.o.b.): US$228,000,000 (reexports [mostly jet fuel] 52.7%; fish 46.0%, of which skipjack tuna 18.4%, yellowfin tuna 15.5%, canned fish 4.7%). *Major export destinations:* Thailand 40.9%; Sri Lanka 14.9%; UK 11.4%; France 7.3%; Japan 4.5%.

Transport and communications

Transport. *Railroads:* none. *Vehicles:* passenger cars (2007) 3,393; trucks and buses (2005) 1,573. *Air transport* (Male airport only; 2005): passenger arrivals 773,845, passenger departures 761,922; cargo unloaded 17,336 metric tons, cargo loaded 10,923 metric tons. **Communications,** in total units (units per 1,000 persons). Telephone landlines (2007): 33,000 (109); cellular telephone subscribers (2007): 318,000 (1,040); personal computers (2005): 45,000 (152); total Internet users (2007): 33,000 (108); broadband Internet subscribers (2007): 7,500 (25).

Education and health

Educational attainment (2000). Percentage of population ages 25 and over with university education 0.4%. **Literacy** (2006): percentage of total population ages 15 and over literate 93.5%; males literate 92.5%; females literate 94.5%. **Health** (2005): physicians 380 (1 per 775 persons); hospital beds 765 (1 per 384 persons); infant mortality rate per 1,000 live births 12.1; undernourished population (2002–04) 30,000 (10% of total population based on the consumption of a minimum daily requirement of 1,840 calories).

Military

Total active duty personnel (2006): the national security service (paramilitary police force) includes an air element and coast guard. **Military expenditure as percentage of GDP** (2005): 5.5%; per capita expenditure US$169.

Background

The archipelago was settled in the 5th century BC by Buddhists from Sri Lanka and southern India, and Islam was adopted there in 1153. The Portuguese held sway in Male in 1558–73. The islands were a sultanate under the Dutch rulers of Ceylon (now Sri Lanka) during the 17th century. After the British gained control of Ceylon in 1796, the area became a British protectorate, a status formalized in 1887. The islands won full independence from Britain in 1965, and in 1968 a republic was founded. The Maldives joined the Commonwealth in 1982.

Recent Developments

The adoption in 2008 of a democratic constitution marked the beginning of a remarkable political change in Maldives, which on 8 October held multiparty elections for the first time in its history. Observers from the UN, the Commonwealth of Nations, and the EU monitored the balloting, in which voter turnout was registered at about 86%. A runoff poll was won by Mohamed Nasheed, ending Pres. Maumoon Abdul Gayoom's 30-year rule. The constitution also fixed a maximum of two five-year terms for candidates seeking election to the presidency, strengthened the People's Majlis (parliament), and ensured the independence of the judiciary.

Internet resources: <www.visitmaldives.com>.

Mali

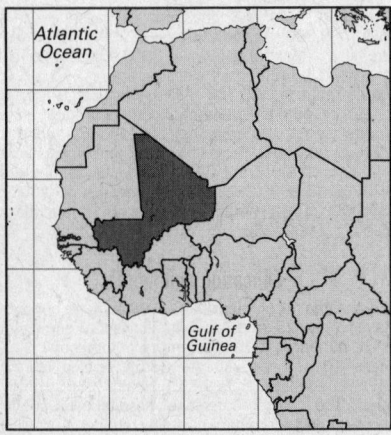

Official name: République du Mali (Republic of Mali). **Form of government:** multiparty republic with one legislative house (National Assembly [147]). **Chief of state:** President Amadou Toumani Touré (from 2002). **Head of government:** Prime Minister Modibo Sidibé (from 2007). **Capital:** Bamako. **Official language:** French. **Official religion:** none. **Monetary unit:** 1 CFA franc (CFAF) = 100 centimes; valuation (1 Jul 2009) US$1 = CFAF 462.89.

Demography

Area: 482,077 sq mi, 1,248,574 sq km. **Population** (2008): 12,324,000. **Density** (2008): persons per sq mi 25.6, persons per sq km 9.9. **Urban** (2005): 30.5%. **Sex distribution** (2006): male 49.67%; female 50.33%. **Age breakdown** (2006): under 15, 48.1%; 15–29, 27.7%; 30–44, 12.9%; 45–59, 6.4%; 60–74, 4.1%; 75–84, 0.7%; 85 and over, 0.1%. **Ethnic composition** (2000): Bambara 30.6%; Senufo 10.5%; Fula Macina (Niafunke) 9.6%; Soninke 7.4%; Tuareg 7.0%; Maninka 6.6%; Songhai 6.3%; Dogon 4.3%; Bobo 3.5%; other 14.2%. **Religious affiliation** (2005): Muslim (nearly all Sunni) 90%; Christian (mostly Roman Catholic) 5%; traditional beliefs/non-religious 5%. **Major cities** (1998): Bamako (urban agglomeration; 2007) 1,494,000; Sikasso 113,803; Ségou 90,898; Mopti 79,840; Koutiala 74,153. **Location:** western Africa, bordering Algeria, Niger, Burkina Faso, Côte d'Ivoire, Guinea, Senegal, and Mauritania.

Vital statistics

Birth rate per 1,000 population (2006): 49.9 (world avg. 20.3). **Death rate** per 1,000 population (2006): 16.9 (world avg. 8.6). **Natural increase rate** per 1,000 population (2006): 33.0 (world avg. 11.7). **Total fertility rate** (avg. births per childbearing woman; 2006): 7.42. **Life expectancy** at birth (2006): male 47.2 years; female 51.0 years.

National economy

Budget (2006). *Revenue:* CFAF 694,300,000,000 (tax revenue 66.1%; grants 23.4%; nontax revenue 4.3%). *Expenditures:* CFAF 795,100,000,000 (current expenditures 56.8%; capital expenditures 43.2%). **Public debt** (external, outstanding; 2006): US$1,411,000,000. **Selected balance of payments data.** Receipts from (US$'000,000): tourism (2006) 167; remittances (2007) 212; foreign direct investment (2004–06 avg.) 170; official development assistance (2006) 825. Disbursements for (US$'000,-000): tourism (2005) 77; remittances (2007) 57. **Population economically active** (2004): total 2,598,200; activity rate of total population 23% (participation rates: ages 15–64, 51.1%; female 42.5%; officially unemployed 8.8%). **Production** (metric tons except as noted). *Agriculture and fishing* (2007): millet 1,074,440, rice 955,300, sorghum 907,966, seed cotton 414,965; livestock (number of live animals) 13,010,000 goats, 8,595,000 sheep, 7,917,000 cattle, 476,000 camels; fisheries production 101,000 (from aquaculture 1%). *Mining and quarrying* (2007): gold 52,800 kg. *Manufacturing* (2002): raw sugar (2005) 35,000; cement 18,125; soft drinks 197,700 hectoliters. *Energy production (consumption):* electricity (kW-hr; 2005) 459,000,000 (459,000,000); petroleum products (metric tons; 2005) none (184,000). **Gross national income** (2007): US$6,136,000,000 (US$500 per capita).

Foreign trade

Imports (2007): CFAF 842,700,000,000 (machinery and apparatus 30.3%; refined petroleum products 28.9%; food products 19.7%). *Major import sources* (2004): France 15.9%; Senegal 12.2%; Côte d'Ivoire 9.4%; Togo 8.5%; Benin 7.4%. **Exports** (2007): CFAF 705,600,000,000 (gold 73.0%; raw cotton and cotton products 15.2%; livestock 4.3%). *Major export destinations* (2004): South Africa 30.9%; Switzerland 20.4%; Senegal 6.3%; China 4.7%; Côte d'Ivoire 4.7%.

Transport and communications

Transport. *Railroads* (2002): route length (2004) 729 km; passenger-km 196,000,000; metric ton-km cargo 188,000,000. *Roads* (2004): total length 18,709 km (paved 18%). *Vehicles* (2001): passenger cars 18,900; trucks and buses 31,700. **Communications,** in total units (units per 1,000 persons). Telephone landlines (2007): 85,000 (7.1); cellular telephone subscribers (2007): 2,483,000 (207);

---

1 metric ton = about 1.1 short tons;   1 kilometer = 0.6 mi (statute);   1 metric ton-km cargo = about 0.68 short ton-mi cargo;   c.i.f.: cost, insurance, and freight;   f.o.b.: free on board

personal computers (2005): 45,000 (4.1); total Internet users (2007): 100,000 (8.3); broadband Internet subscribers (2007): 3,200 (0.3).

Education and health

Educational attainment (2001). Percentage of population ages 25 and over having: no formal schooling/unknown 82.1%; incomplete primary education 7.7%; complete primary 2.0%; secondary 6.5%; higher 1.7%. **Literacy** (2005): percentage of total population ages 15 and over literate 29.5%; males literate 40.0%; females literate 19.4%. **Health: physicians** (2004) 1,053 (1 per 10,566 persons); **hospital beds** (2001) 1,664 (1 per 6,203 persons); **infant mortality rate** per 1,000 live births (2006) 107.5; **undernourished population** (2002–04) 3,800,000 (29% of total population based on the consumption of a minimum daily requirement of 1,800 calories).

Military

Total active duty personnel (2007): 7,350 (army 100%). **Military expenditure as percentage of GDP** (2005): 2.3%; per capita expenditure US$10.

Background

Inhabited since prehistoric times, the region was situated on a caravan route across the Sahara. In the 12th century, the Malinke empire of Mali was founded on the Upper and Middle Niger. In the 15th century, the Songhai empire in the Timbuktu-Gao region gained control. In 1591 Morocco invaded the area, and Timbuktu remained under the Moors for two centuries. In the mid-19th century, the French conquered the area, which became a part of French West Africa known as the French Sudan. In 1946 it became an overseas territory of the French Union. It was proclaimed the Sudanese Republic in 1958, briefly joined with Senegal (1959–60) to form the Mali Federation, and became the Republic of Mali in 1960. The government was overthrown by military coups in 1968 and 1991. Democratic multiparty elections have been held every five years since 1992.

Recent Developments

Efforts to resolve the Tuareg rebellion in the deserts of northern Mali continued. In March 2008, Tuaregs led by Ibrahim Ag Bahanga released the last hostages captured in August 2007. In February 2009 it was announced that fighters for Ag Bahanga, who reportedly had fled Mali, were the only Tuareg group who had not rejoined peace talks.

Internet resources: <www.malitourisme.com>.

Malta

Official name: Repubblika ta' Malta (Maltese); Republic of Malta (English). **Form of government:** unitary multiparty republic with one legislative house (Kamra tad-Deputati, or House of Representatives [65]). **Chief of state:** President Eddie Fenech Adami (from 2004). **Head of government:** Prime Minister Lawrence Gonzi (from 2004). **Capital:** Valletta. **Official languages:** Maltese; English. **Official religion:** Roman Catholicism. **Monetary unit:** 1 euro (€) = 100

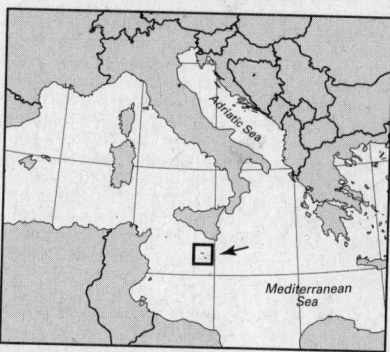

cents; valuation (1 Jul 2009) US$1 = €0.71 (the euro replaced the Maltese lira [Lm] 1 Jan 2008, at the rate of €1 = Lm 0.43).

Demography

Area: 121.9 sq mi, 315.6 sq km. **Population** (2008): 412,000. **Density** (2008): persons per sq mi 3,380, persons per sq km 1,305. **Urban** (2005): 95.3%. **Sex distribution** (2007): male 49.75%; female 50.25%. **Age breakdown** (2007): under 15, 16.2%; 15–29, 21.6%; 30–44, 19.7%; 45–59, 21.9%; 60–74, 14.6%; 75–84, 4.7%; 85 and over, 1.3%. **Ethnic composition** (2005): Maltese 97.0%; other European 2.3%, of which British 1.2%; other 0.7%. **Religious affiliation** (2004): Roman Catholic 95%, of which practicing 63%; other Christian 0.5%; Muslim 0.7%; nonreligious/atheist 2%; other 1.8%. **Major localities** (2007): Birkirkara 22,241; Mosta 19,018; Qormi 16,625; Zabbar 14,849; Valletta 6,319 (urban agglomeration 81,204). **Location:** islands in the Mediterranean Sea, south of Sicily (Italy).

Vital statistics

Birth rate per 1,000 population (2007): 9.5 (world avg. 20.3); within marriage 75.1%; outside of marriage 24.9%. **Death rate** per 1,000 population (2007): 7.6 (world avg. 8.6). **Natural increase rate** per 1,000 population (2007): 1.9 (world avg. 11.7). **Total fertility rate** (avg. births per childbearing woman; 2007): 1.37. **Life expectancy** at birth (2005): male 77.7 years; female 81.4 years.

National economy

Budget (2005). *Revenue:* Lm 1,032,046,000 (social security 21.5%; income tax 19.0%; grants and loans 17.1%; VAT 16.3%). *Expenditures:* Lm 985,552,000 (recurrent expenditures 76.7%, of which social security 22.4%, education 5.2%; capital expenditures 13.3%; public debt service 9.0%). **Public debt** (December 2007): US$4,053,000,000. **Production** (metric tons except where noted): *Agriculture and fishing* (2007): potatoes 25,000, tomatoes 16,600, wheat 9,200; livestock (number of live animals) 73,683 pigs, 19,233 cattle, 1,100,000 chickens; fisheries production (2006) 3,537 (from aquaculture 32%). *Mining and quarrying* (2006): limestone 1,200,000 cu m; small quantities of salt. *Manufacturing* (value added in US$'000,000; 2004): telecommunications equipment and electronics 171; food products 78; printing and publishing 59. *Energy production (consumption):*

electricity (kW-hr; 2005) 2,240,000,000 (2,240,-000,000); petroleum products (metric tons; 2005) none (831,000). **Population economically active** (2006): total 164,400; activity rate of total population 40.5% (participation rates: ages 15–64, 59.1%; female 32.1%; unemployed [March 2007] 6.8%). **Gross national income** (2007): US$7,200,000,000 (US$17,600 per capita). **Selected balance of payments data.** Receipts from (US$'000,000): tourism (2006) 770; remittances (2007) 40; foreign direct investment (2004–06 avg.) 914. Disbursements for (US$'000,000): tourism (2006) 321; remittances (2007) 51; foreign direct disinvestment (2004–06 avg.) –8.

Foreign trade

Imports (2006; c.i.f.): US$4,260,000,000 (machinery and apparatus 39.5%, of which electronic integrated circuits and micro-assemblies 22.9%; food products 9.7%; refined petroleum products 8.7%; chemical products 8.6%). *Major import sources:* Italy 28.3%; UK 10.0%; France 9.5%; Germany 7.7%; Singapore 6.3%. **Exports** (2006; f.o.b.): US$2,780,-000,000 (machinery and apparatus 59.9%, of which semiconductor devices 47.3%; food products 5.5%; medicine 4.6%; printed matter 3.7%; professional and scientific equipment 3.6%). *Major export destinations:* France 15.0%; Germany 12.8%; Singapore 12.7%; US 12.5%; UK 9.4%.

Transport and communications

Transport. *Railroads:* none. *Roads* (2004): total length 2,254 km (paved 88%). *Vehicles* (2005): passenger cars 207,055; trucks and buses 45,054. *Air transport* (Air Malta only; 2006): passenger-km 2,376,000,000; metric ton-km cargo 11,000,000. **Communications,** in total units (units per 1,000 persons). Telephone landlines (2007): 198,000 (484); cellular telephone subscribers (2007): 372,000 (908); personal computers (2005): 67,000 (166); total Internet users (2007): 158,000 (386); broadband Internet subscribers (2007): 61,000 (150).

Education and health

Educational attainment (2005). Percentage of population ages 15 and over having: no formal schooling 2.4%; special education for disabled 0.3%; primary education 25.9%; secondary 45.3%; some postsecondary 16.5%; undergraduate or professional qualification 7.2%; graduate 2.4%. **Literacy** (2005): percentage of total population ages 10 and over literate 92.8%; males literate 91.7%; females literate 93.9%. **Health:** physicians (2006) 1,320 (1 per 308 persons); hospital beds (2002) 1,932 (1 per 205 persons); infant mortality rate per 1,000 live births (2005) 6.0; undernourished population (2002–04) less than 2.5% of total population.

Military

Total active duty personnel (2008): 1,954 (armed forces includes air and marine elements); Italian troops (2008) 49. **Military expenditure as percentage of GDP** (2007): 0.6%; per capita expenditure US$107.

Background

Inhabited as early as 3800 BC, Malta was ruled by the Carthaginians from the 6th century BC until it came under Roman control in 218 BC. In AD 60 the apostle Paul converted the inhabitants to Christianity. It was under Byzantine rule until the Arabs seized control in 870. In 1091 the Normans defeated the Arabs, and Malta was ruled by feudal lords until it came under the Knights of Malta in 1530. Napoleon seized control in 1798; the British took it in 1800 and returned it to the Knights in 1802. The Maltese protested and acknowledged the British as sovereign, an arrangement ratified in 1814. It became self-governing in 1921 but reverted to a colonial regime in 1936. Malta was severely bombed by Germany and Italy during World War II, and in 1942 it received the George Cross, Britain's highest civilian decoration. In 1964 it gained independence within the Commonwealth and in 1974 became a republic. In 2004 it joined the EU, and it adopted the euro as its official currency in 2008.

Recent Developments

On 1 Jan 2008, after three years of working to get the economy back on track, Malta joined the euro zone, replacing the Maltese lira, which had been in existence since May 1972. Illegal immigration was on the increase throughout the year, as Frontex, the EU's border security agency, did not achieve the positive results anticipated.

Internet resources: <www.nso.gov.mt/>.

Marshall Islands

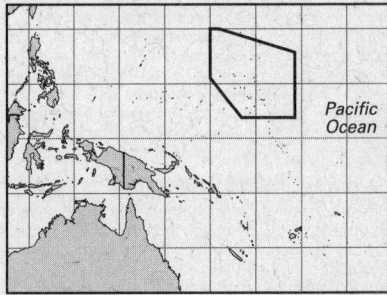

Pacific Ocean

Official name: Majol (Marshallese); Republic of the Marshall Islands (English). **Form of government:** unitary republic with one legislative house (Nitijela [33]). **Head of state and government:** President Litokwa Tomeing (from 2008). **Capital:** Majuro (Rita). **Official languages:** Marshallese (Kajin-Majol); English. **Official religion:** none. **Monetary unit:** 1 US dollar (US$) = 100 cents.

Demography

Area: 70.05 sq mi, 181.43 sq km. **Population** (2008): 53,200. **Density** (2008): persons per sq mi

---

1 metric ton = about 1.1 short tons;   1 kilometer = 0.6 mi (statute);   1 metric ton-km cargo = about 0.68 short ton-mi cargo;   c.i.f.: cost, insurance, and freight;   f.o.b.: free on board

759.5, persons per sq km 293.2. **Urban** (2005): 66.1%. **Sex distribution** (2006): male 51.02%; female 48.98%. **Age breakdown** (2006): under 15, 38.1%; 15–29, 30.8%; 30–44, 16.5%; 45–59, 10.3%; 60–74, 3.4%; 75–84, 0.8%; 85 and over, 0.1%. **Ethnic composition** (nationality; 2000): Marshallese 88.5%; US white 6.5%; other Pacific Islander and East Asian 5.0%. **Religious affiliation** (1999): Protestant 85.0%, of which United Church of Christ 54.8%, Assemblies of God 25.8%; Roman Catholic 8.4%; Mormon 2.1%; nonreligious 1.5%; other/unknown 3.0%. **Major towns** (1999): Majuro (2004) 20,800; Ebeye 9,345; Laura 2,256; Ajeltake 1,170; Enewetak 823. **Location:** Oceania, group of atolls and reefs in the North Pacific Ocean, halfway between Hawaii (US) and Papua New Guinea.

Vital statistics

Birth rate per 1,000 population (2006): 33.0 (world avg. 20.3). **Death rate** per 1,000 population (2006): 4.7 (world avg. 8.6). **Natural increase rate** per 1,000 population (2006): 28.3 (world avg. 11.7). **Total fertility rate** (avg. births per childbearing woman; 2006): 3.84. **Life expectancy** at birth (2006): male 68.3 years; female 72.3 years.

National economy

Budget (2005). *Revenue:* US$83,900,000 (US government grants 63.9%; tax revenue 26.4%, of which income tax 11.7%, import duties 9.3%; nontax revenue 9.7%). *Expenditures:* US$86,900,000 (current expenditures 80.2%; capital expenditures 19.8%). **Public debt** (external, outstanding; 2006–07): US$98,700,000. **Production** (metric tons except as noted). *Agriculture and fishing* (2002–03): copra (2007) 5,491, breadfruit 4,536, coconuts 885, pandanus 114; livestock (number of live animals) 12,900 pigs, 86,000 chickens; fisheries production (2006) 42,019, of which skipjack tuna 37,661 (from aquaculture, none). *Mining and quarrying:* for local construction only. *Manufacturing* (2005): copra 5,194; coconut oil and processed (chilled or frozen) fish are important products; the manufacture of handicrafts and personal items (clothing, mats, boats, etc.) is also significant. *Energy production (consumption):* electricity (kW-hr; 2005) 81,000,000 (81,000,000). **Population economically active** (1999): total 14,677; activity rate of total population 28.9% (participation rates: ages 15–64, 52.1%; unemployed [2007] 30.9%). **Gross national income** (2007): US$204,-000,000 (US$3,070 per capita). **Selected balance of payments data.** Receipts from (US$'000,000): tourism (2004–05) 5.5; remittances (2005) 0.4; foreign direct investment (FDI) (2004–06 avg.) 279; official development assistance (2006) 55. Disbursements for (US$'000,000): FDI (2004–06 avg.) 13.

Foreign trade

Imports (2000): US$68,200,000 (mineral fuels and lubricants 43.6%; machinery and transportation equipment 16.9%; food, beverages, and tobacco 10.9%). *Major import sources* (2005): US 47.1%; Guam 13.5%; Australia 8.5%; Japan 7.9%; Philippines 5.9%. **Exports** (2005): US$16,400,000 (reexports of diesel fuel 80.9%; crude coconut oil 15.4%). *Major export destinations* (2005): mostly the US.

Transport and communications

Transport. *Roads* (2002): only Majuro and Kwajalein have paved roads (64.5 km). *Vehicles* (2004): passenger cars 1,694; trucks and buses 602. *Air transport* (Air Marshall Islands only; 2006): passenger-km 31,236,000; metric ton-km cargo 348,000. **Communications,** in total units (units per 1,000 persons). Telephone landlines (2004): 4,500 (82); cellular telephone subscribers (2004): 600 (12); personal computers (2004): 5,000 (92); total Internet users (2006): 2,200 (36).

Education and health

Educational attainment (2006). Percentage of population ages 25 and over having: no formal schooling 2.1%; elementary education 28.0%; secondary 55.8%; some higher 7.9%; undergraduate degree 5.1%; advanced degree 1.1%. **Literacy** (2000): percentage of total population ages 15 and over literate 92.0%; males literate 92.0%; females literate 92.0%. **Health** (2004): physicians 33 (1 per 1,744 persons); hospital beds 140 (1 per 411 persons); infant mortality rate per 1,000 live births (2006) 28.3.

Military

Total active duty personnel: none. The US provides for the defense of the Republic of the Marshall Islands under the 1984 and 2003 compacts of free association; the US Army's premier ballistic missile test site is at Kwajalein.

Background

The islands were sighted in 1529 by the Spanish navigator Álvaro Saavedra. Germany purchased them from Spain in 1899, and Japan seized them in 1914. During World War II the US took Kwajalein and Enewetak, and the Marshall Islands were made part of a UN trust territory under US jurisdiction in 1947. Bikini and Enewetak atolls served as testing grounds for US nuclear weapons from 1946 to 1958. The country became an internally self-governing republic in 1979. In 1986 it became fully self-governing when it entered into a Compact of Free Association with the US, which was renewed in 2003.

Recent Developments

Economic growth in the Marshall Islands hovered around 1% in 2008. Debt was roughly 75% of the GDP, and a number of loans were coming due. Meanwhile, nearly US$10 million in taxes remained uncollected, and there was little investment in the private sector.

Internet resources: <www.visitmarshallislands.com>.

Mauritania

Official name: Al-Jumhuriyah al-Islamiyah al-Muritaniyah (Islamic Republic of Mauritania). **Form of government:** transitional regime with two legislative houses (Senate [56]; National Assembly [95]). **Head of state and government:** President Mohamed Ould Abdel Aziz (from 2009), assisted by Prime Minister Moulaye Ould Mohamed Laghdaf (from 2008). **Capital:**

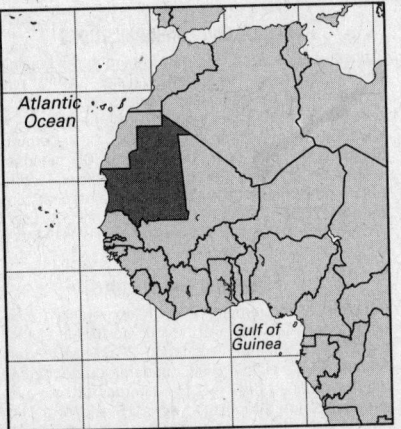

Atlantic
Ocean

Gulf of
Guinea

Nouakchott. **Official language:** Arabic (Arabic, Fulani, Soninke, and Wolof are national languages). **Official religion:** Islam. **Monetary unit:** 1 ouguiya (UM) = 5 khoums; valuation (1 Jul 2009) US$1 = UM 259.48.

Demography

Area: 398,000 sq mi, 1,030,700 sq km. **Population** (2008): 3,204,000. **Density** (2008): persons per sq mi 8.1, persons per sq km 3.1. **Urban** (2006): 65.5%. **Sex distribution** (2006): male 49.50%; female 50.50%. **Age breakdown** (2006): under 15, 45.6%; 15–29, 27.2%; 30–44, 15.6%; 45–59, 8.0%; 60–74, 3.1%; 75 and over, 0.5%. **Ethnic composition** (2003): black African-Arab-Berber (Black Moor) 40%; Arab-Berber (White Moor) 30%; black African (mostly Wolof, Tukulor, Soninke, and Fulani) 30%. **Religious affiliation** (2000): Sunni Muslim 99.1%; traditional beliefs 0.5%; Christian 0.3%; other 0.1%. **Major cities** (2005): Nouakchott 743,500; Nouadhibou 94,700; Rosso (2000) 48,922; Boghe (2000) 37,531; Adel Bagrou (2000) 36,007. **Location:** northern Africa, bordering Western Sahara, Algeria, Mali, Senegal, and the North Atlantic Ocean.

Vital statistics

Birth rate per 1,000 population (2006): 41.0 (world avg. 20.3). **Death rate** per 1,000 population (2006): 12.2 (world avg. 8.6). **Total fertility rate** (avg. births per childbearing woman; 2006): 5.86. **Life expectancy** at birth (2006): male 50.9 years; female 55.4 years.

National economy

Budget (2005). *Revenue:* UM 131,300,000,000 (tax revenue 57.9%, of which VAT 20.3%, corporate taxes 17.0%, import taxes 8.2%; nontax revenue 34.3%, of which fishing royalties 26.9%; grants 7.8%). *Expenditures:* UM 166,100,000,000 (current expenditures 76.2%, of which goods and services 36.5%, wages and salaries 13.5%, defense 10.7%; capital expenditures 23.8%). **Public debt** (external, outstanding;

2007): US$1,751,000,000. **Production** (metric tons except as noted). *Agriculture and fishing* (2007): rice 77,000, sorghum 58,000, dates 22,000; livestock (number of live animals) 8,850,000 sheep, 5,600,000 goats, 1,692,000 cattle, 1,600,000 camels; fisheries production (2006) 571,496, of which octopuses 15,589 (from aquaculture, none). *Mining and quarrying* (gross weight; 2006–07): iron ore 11,439,000; gypsum (2005) 39,000; copper 5,000. *Manufacturing* (value added in US$'000,000; 1997): food, beverages, and tobacco products 5.2; machinery, transportation equipment, and fabricated metal products 3.8; bricks, tiles, and cement 1.6. *Energy production (consumption):* electricity (kW-hr; 2006–07) 404,000,000 (290,000,000); coal (metric tons; 2004) none (7,000); crude petroleum (barrels; 2006–07) 9,600,000 ([2004] 8,830,000); petroleum products (metric tons; 2006–07) none (431,000). **Selected balance of payments data.** Receipts from (US$'000,000): tourism (2005) 11; remittances (2007) 2; foreign direct investment (2004–06 avg.) 418; official development assistance (2006) 188. Disbursements for (US$'000,000): tourism (1999) 55. **Population economically active** (2006): total 1,238,000; activity rate of total population 39.2% (participation rates: ages 16 and over, 68.8%; female 40.4%; unemployed [2005] 32.5%). **Gross national income** (2007): US$2,636,000,000 (US$840 per capita).

Did you know? The Atlantic Ocean off Mauritania has historically been among the richest fisheries in the world for both pelagic (open sea) and demersal (seafloor) species. Since gaining its independence in 1960, Mauritania has derived a significant proportion of national revenue from regulating the fishing fleets of Japan, China, the EU, and others. A lack of enforcement of these regulations by 2002 led to a dramatic fall in overall species catch because of overfishing (particularly for octopus), as well as a damaged marine environment.

Foreign trade

Imports (2007): US$1,198,800,000 (imports for extractive industries 28.3%; refined petroleum products 23.1%). *Major import sources* (2006): France 11.9%; China 8.2%; US 6.8%; Belgium 6.7%; Italy 5.9%. **Exports** (2007): US$1,342,500,000 (iron ore 39.7%; crude petroleum 23.1%; fish 15.3%). *Major export destinations* (2006): China 26.3%; Italy 11.8%; France 10.2%; Belgium 6.8%; Spain 6.7%.

Transport and communications

Transport. *Railroads* (2000): route length (2005) 697 km; passenger-km, negligible; metric ton-km cargo 7,766,000,000. *Roads* (2005): total length 9,144 km (paved 30%). *Vehicles* (2001): passenger cars 12,200; trucks and buses 18,200. **Communications,** in total units (units per 1,000 persons). Telephone landlines (2006): 34,000 (11); cellular telephone subscribers (2007): 1,300,000 (416); personal computers (2005): 42,000 (14); total Internet users

1 metric ton = about 1.1 short tons;   1 kilometer = 0.6 mi (statute);   1 metric ton-km cargo = about 0.68 short ton-mi cargo;   c.i.f.: cost, insurance, and freight;   f.o.b.: free on board

(2006): 100,000ₘ (33); broadband Internet sub-scribers (2006): 700 (0.2).

Education and health

Educational attainment (2000). Percentage of population ages 6 and over having: no formal schooling 43.9% (illiterate 41.4%, literate 2.5%); Islamic schooling 18.4%; primary education 23.2%; lower secondary 5.3%; upper secondary 4.6%; higher technical 0.4%; higher 1.7%. **Literacy** (2007): percentage of total population ages 15 and over literate 43.6%; males literate 53.2%; females literate 34.3%. **Health** (2006): physicians (2005) 477 (1 per 6,212 persons); hospital beds 1,826 (1 per 1,667 persons); infant mortality rate per 1,000 live births 69.5; undernourished population (2002–04) 300,000 (10% of total population based on the consumption of a minimum daily requirement of 1,840 calories).

Military

Total active duty personnel (2008): 15,870 (army 94.5%, navy 3.9%, air force 1.6%). **Military expenditure as percentage of GDP** (2007): 0.5%; per capita expenditure US$6.

Background

Inhabited in ancient times by Sanhadja Berbers, in the 11th and 12th centuries Mauritania was the center of the Berber Almoravid movement, which imposed Islam. Arab tribes arrived in the 15th century and formed powerful confederations; the Portuguese also arrived then. France gained control of the coast in 1817 and in 1903 made the territory a protectorate. In 1904 it was added to French West Africa, and later it became a colony. In 1960 Mauritania achieved independence. Its first president was ousted in a 1978 military coup. After a series of military rulers, in 1991 a new constitution was adopted, and multiparty elections were held in 1992. The country faced continued economic hardship and political unrest, including coups, in the late 20th and early 21st centuries.

Recent Developments

Mauritania's brief experiment with democracy ended in August 2008, when a military coup toppled Pres. Sidi Mohamed Ould Cheikh Abdallahi, the country's first democratically elected president since independence in 1960. The coup immediately elicited international condemnation, the freezing of aid from major donors, suspension from the African Union, and in early 2009, the severing of ties with the EU.

Internet resources: <www.ons.mr>.

Mauritius

Official name: Republic of Mauritius. **Form of government:** republic with one legislative house (National Assembly [70]). **Chief of state:** President Sir Anerood Jugnauth (from 2003). **Head of government:** Prime Minister Navin Ramgoolam (from 2005). **Capital:** Port Louis. **Official language:** English. **Official religion:** none. **Monetary unit:** 1 Mauritian rupee (Mau Re; plural Mau Rs) = 100 cents; valuation (1 Jul 2009) US$1 = Mau Rs 31.79.

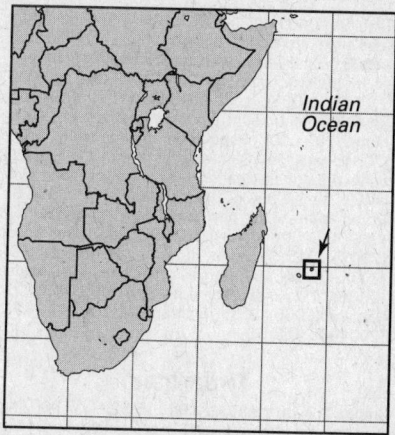

Demography

Area: 788 sq mi, 2,040 sq km. **Population** (2008): 1,269,000. **Density** (2008): persons per sq mi 1,610, persons per sq km 622.1. **Urban** (2006): 42.1%. **Sex distribution** (2007): male 49.42%; female 50.58%. **Age breakdown** (2006): under 15, 23.9%; 15–29, 24.9%; 30–44, 23.4%; 45–59, 18.0%; 60–74, 7.2%; 75–84, 2.1%; 85 and over, 0.5%. **Ethnic composition** (2000): Indo-Pakistani 67.0%; Creole (mixed Caucasian, Indo-Pakistani, and African) 27.4%; Chinese 3.0%; other 2.6%. **Religious affiliation** (2000): Hindu 49.6%; Christian 32.2%, of which Roman Catholic 23.6%; Muslim 16.6%; Buddhist 0.4%; other 1.2%. **Major municipalities** (2007): Port Louis 148,939; Beau Bassin–Rose Hill 109,701; Vacoas-Phoenix 106,865; Curepipe 83,754; Quatre Bornes 80,780. **Location:** island in the Indian Ocean, east of Madagascar.

Vital statistics

Birth rate per 1,000 population (2007): 13.5 (world avg. 20.3). **Death rate** per 1,000 population (2007): 6.7 (world avg. 8.6). **Natural increase rate** per 1,000 population (2007): 6.8 (world avg. 11.7). **Total fertility rate** (avg. births per childbearing woman; 2006): 1.73. **Life expectancy** at birth (2007): male 69.1 years; female 75.8 years.

National economy

Budget (2005–06). *Revenue:* Mau Rs 39,220,-000,000 (tax revenue 90.2%, of which taxes on goods and services 47.8%, taxes on trade 18.3%, corporate taxes 12.0%; nontax revenue and grants 9.8%). *Expenditures:* Mau Rs 48,875,000,000 (social security 21.1%; interest on debt 15.0%; education 14.0%; police and defense 8.8%; health 8.6%). **Public debt** (external, outstanding; 2006): US$585,-000,000. **Gross national income** (2007): US$6,878,-000,000 (US$5,450 per capita). **Production** (metric tons except as noted). *Agriculture and fishing* (2007): sugarcane 4,400,000, potatoes 13,000, bananas 10,500; livestock (number of live animals) 28,500 cattle, 10,000,000 chickens; fisheries production (2006) 8,784 (from aquaculture 5%). *Mining* (2005): marine salt 7,900. *Manufacturing* (value added in

Mau Rs '000,000; 2005): wearing apparel 8,823; food products 6,220; beverages and tobacco products 3,053. *Energy production (consumption):* electricity (kW-hr; 2007) 2,465,000,000 ([2005] 2,271,000,000); coal (metric tons; 2005) none (364,000); petroleum products (metric tons; 2005) none (796,000). **Population economically active** (2004): total 549,600; activity rate of total population 44.5% (participation rates: ages 15 and over, 59.2%; female 35.0%; unemployed [2006] 8.9%). **Selected balance of payments data.** Receipts from (US$'000,000): tourism (2006) 1,005; remittances (2007) 215; foreign direct investment (FDI) (2004–06 avg.) 54; official development assistance (2006) 19. Disbursements for (US$'000,000): tourism (2006) 327; remittances (2007) 13; FDI (2004–06 avg.) 30.

Foreign trade

Imports (2006; c.i.f.): Mau Rs 115,522,000,000 (machinery and apparatus 21.0%, of which telecommunications equipment 8.5%; food products 15.0%, of which fish 5.2%; refined petroleum products 14.7%; aircraft and parts 6.2%; fabrics and yarn 6.1%). *Major import sources:* France 14.3%; India 13.6%; China 8.6%; South Africa 7.3%; Germany 4.0%. **Exports** (2006; f.o.b.): Mau Rs 68,927,000,000 (wearing apparel and accessories 35.5%; food products 29.2%, of which raw sugar 16.2%, tuna 7.2%; telecommunications equipment 12.3%). *Major export destinations:* UK 32.4%; France 15.1%; UAE 11.4%; US 8.3%; Madagascar 4.8%.

Transport and communications

Transport. *Railroads:* none. *Roads* (2005): total length 2,020 km (paved 98%). *Vehicles* (2005): passenger cars 84,818; trucks and buses 38,596. *Air transport* (Air Mauritius only; 2005): passenger-km 6,274,000,000; metric ton-km cargo 211,716,000. **Communications,** in total units (units per 1,000 persons). Telephone landlines (2006): 357,000 (285); cellular telephone subscribers (2007): 936,000 (742); personal computers (2005): 210,000 (169); total Internet users (2007): 340,000 (270); broadband Internet subscribers (2006): 22,000 (17).

Education and health

Educational attainment (2000). Percentage of population ages 25 and over having: no formal education/unknown 12.8%; primary 44.1%; lower secondary 23.2%; upper secondary/some higher 17.3%; complete higher 2.6%. **Literacy** (2000): percentage of total population ages 12 and over literate 85.1%; males literate 88.7%; females literate 81.6%. **Health** (2007): physicians 1,444 (1 per 873 persons); hospital beds 3,756 (1 per 336 persons); infant mortality rate per 1,000 live births (2006) 14.1; undernourished population (2002–04) 60,000 (5% of total population based on the consumption of a minimum daily requirement of 1,910 calories).

Military

Total active duty personnel (2007): none; a 2,000-person paramilitary force includes a 500-person

coast guard unit. **Paramilitary expenditure as percentage of GDP** (2005): 0.2%; per capita expenditure US$9.

Background

The island was visited by the Portuguese in the early 16th century. The Dutch took possession in 1598 and made attempts to settle it (1638–58 and 1664–1710) before abandoning it to pirates. The French East India Company occupied Mauritius in 1721 and administered it until the French government took over in 1767. Sugar production allowed the colony to prosper. The British captured the island in 1810 and were granted formal control in 1814. In the late 19th century, competition from beet sugar and the opening of the Suez Canal caused an economic decline. After World War II, Mauritius adopted political and economic reforms, and in 1968 it became an independent state within the Commonwealth. In 1992 it became a republic. It experienced political unrest during the 1990s.

Recent Developments

In a bid to strengthen trade ties with China, the Mauritian government in 2008 agreed to a US$730 million project, the country's largest foreign direct investment, to build a trade-development zone that would house several Chinese businesses. Mauritius's two main economic sectors, sugarcane and textiles, had suffered downturns since the lifting in 2005 of trade preferences, and officials hoped the deal would result in making the country a center for regional economic development.

Internet resources: <www.mauritius.net>.

Mexico

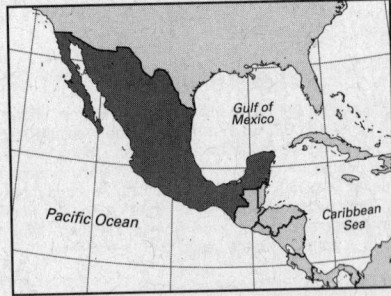

Official name: Estados Unidos Mexicanos (United Mexican States). **Form of government:** federal republic with two legislative houses (Senate [128]; Chamber of Deputies [500]). **Head of state and government:** President Felipe Calderón Hinojosa (from 2006). **Capital:** Mexico City. **Official language:** Spanish. **Official religion:** none. **Monetary unit:** 1 Mexican peso (Mex$) = 100 centavos; valuation (1 Jul 2009) US$1 = Mex$13.10.

---

1 metric ton = about 1.1 short tons;   1 kilometer = 0.6 mi (statute);   1 metric ton-km cargo = about 0.68 short ton-mi cargo;   c.i.f.: cost, insurance, and freight;   f.o.b.: free on board

Demography

Area: 758,450 sq mi, 1,964,375 sq km. **Population** (2008): 106,683,000. **Density** (2008): persons per sq mi 140.7, persons per sq km 54.3. **Urban** (2005): 76.0%. **Sex distribution** (2005): male 48.66%; female 51.34%. **Age breakdown** (2005): under 15, 30.7%; 15–29, 26.3%; 30–44, 20.4%; 45–59, 11.8%; 60–74, 5.9%; 75–84, 1.7%; 85 and over, 0.5%; unknown 2.7%. **Ethnic composition** (2000): mestizo 64.3%; Amerindian 18.0%, of which detribalized 10.5%; Mexican white 15.0%; Arab 1.0%; Mexican black 0.5%; Spanish 0.3%; US white 0.2%; other 0.7%. **Religious affiliation** (2000): Christian 96.3%, of which Roman Catholic 87.0%, Protestant 3.2%, independent Christian 2.7%, unaffiliated Christian 1.4%, other Christian (mostly Mormon and Jehovah's Witness) 2.0%; Muslim 0.3%; nonreligious 3.1%; other 0.3%. **Major cities (urban agglomerations)** (2005 [2007]): Mexico City 8,463,906 (19,028,000); Ecatepec 1,687,549; Guadalajara 1,600,894 (4,198,000); Puebla 1,399,519 (2,195,000); Juárez 1,301,452 (1,343,000); Tijuana 1,286,187 (1,553,000); León 1,137,465 (1,488,000); Ciudad Netzahualcóyotl 1,136,300; Monterrey 1,133,070 (3,712,000); Zapopan 1,026,492; Naucalpan 792,226; Chihuahua 748,518 (841,000); Mérida 734,153 (1,017,000); Guadelupe 691,434; San Luis Potosí 685,934 (1,050,000); Tlalnepantla 674,417; Aguascalientes 663,671 (927,000); Mexicali 653,046 (935,000); Hermosillo 641,791; Saltillo 633,667 (802,000); Acapulco 616,394; Morelia 608,049; Culiacán 605,304 (837,000); Querétaro 596,450 (1,032,-000); Torreon 548,723 (1,201,000); Toluca 467,712 (1,584,000). **Location:** southern North America, bordering the US, the Gulf of Mexico, the Caribbean Sea, Belize, Guatemala, and the North Pacific Ocean. **Migration.** Legal Mexican immigrants entering the US (2004) 173,664; total number of illegal Mexican immigrants in US (2006) roughly 6,600,000.

Vital statistics

Birth rate per 1,000 population (2007): 18.6 (world avg. 20.3). **Death rate** per 1,000 population (2007): 4.8 (world avg. 8.6). **Natural increase rate** per 1,000 population (2007): 13.8 (world avg. 11.7). **Total fertility rate** (avg. births per childbearing woman; 2007): 2.10. **Life expectancy** at birth (2006): male 72.4 years; female 77.2 years.

Social indicators

Educational attainment (2005). Percentage of population ages 15 and over having: no formal schooling/unknown 10.9%; incomplete primary education 14.3%; complete primary 17.6%; secondary 25.2%; vocational/professional 31.3%; advanced university (master's or doctorate degree) 0.7%. **Access to services** (2005). Proportion of dwellings having: electricity 96.6%; piped water supply 87.8%; piped sewage 84.8%. **Material well-being.** Percentage of households possessing (2005): television 91.0%; refrigerator 79.0%; washing machine 62.7%; computer 19.6%. **Quality of working life.** Average workweek (2004) 43.5 hours. Annual rate per 100,000 insured workers for (2004): injury 2,922; death 11. Labor stoppages (2001): 35, involving 23,234 workers. **Social participation.** Trade union membership in total workforce (2000): formal sector only, less than 20%; both formal and informal sectors, 17%. Practicing religious population (1995–97): percentage of adult population attending church services at least once per week 46%. **Social deviance** (2006). Formally registered offense rate per 100,000 population for: murder 6.1; property damage 14.9; rape 4.5; battery 31.5; robbery 67.1; illegal narcotics possession 15.6; fraud 4.5; breaking and entering 2.7. Incidence per 100,000 in general population of: alcoholism (2000) 7.6; suicide (2006) 3.4.

National economy

Gross national income (2007): US$878,020,-000,000 (US$8,340 per capita). **Budget** (2007). *Revenue:* Mex$2,485,600,000,000 (tax revenue 40.3%, of which income tax 21.2%; nontax revenue 28.6%; revenue from PEMEX state oil company 15.0%; revenue from other state-owned organizations or companies 16.1%). *Expenditures:* Mex$2,483,000,000,000 (current expenditures 59.4%; capital expenditures 16.9%; extra-budgetary expenditures 23.7%). **Public debt** (external, outstanding; 2006): US$96,304,-000,000. **Production** (metric tons except as noted). *Agriculture and fishing* (2007): sugarcane 50,680,000, corn (maize) 22,500,000, sorghum 5,500,000, oranges 4,160,000, wheat 3,000,000, tomatoes 2,900,000, bananas 2,200,000, guavas and mangoes 2,050,000, lemons and limes 1,880,000, chilies and green peppers 1,690,000, potatoes 1,530,000, dry beans 1,390,000, dry onions 1,200,000, avocados 1,140,000, papayas 800,000, blue agave (2006) 778,000, string beans 755,000, pineapples 635,000, grapefruit and pomelos 390,000, coffee (green) 320,000, nuts 165,000, green onions and shallots 150,000; livestock (number of live animals) 29,000,000 cattle, 15,500,000 pigs, 8,900,000 goats, 7,500,000 sheep, 6,350,000 horses, 290,000,000 chickens; fisheries production (2006) 1,458,642 (from aquaculture 11%); aquatic plants production (2006) 27,000 (from aquaculture, none). *Mining and quarrying* (2005): fluorite 876,000 (world rank: 2); bismuth (metal content) 970 (world rank: 2); silver (metal content) 2,894,161 kg (world rank: 2); celestite 110,833 (world rank: 3); lead (metal content) 134,388 (world rank: 5); cadmium (metal content) 1,627 (world rank: 5); gypsum 6,251,969 (world rank: 6); zinc (metal content) 476,307 (world rank: 6); iron ore (metal content) 7,012,000; sulfur 1,590,000; copper (metal content) 429,042; gold 30,356 kg. *Manufacturing* (value added in US$'000,000; 2005): food and beverages 29,000; motor vehicles and parts 20,800; chemical products 13,100; bricks, cement, and ceramics 7,600; base metals 7,350; fabricated metal products 4,900; nonelectrical machinery and apparatus 4,150; textiles 4,050; rubber and plastic products 3,800; electrical machinery and apparatus 3,550; radio, television, and communications equipment 3,450; paper products 2,800; printing and publishing 2,800; computers and office machinery 2,700; refined petroleum products, coke, and nuclear fuel 2,550. *Energy production (consumption):* electricity (kW-hr; 2005) 234,895,-000,000 (233,691,000,000,000); coal (metric tons; 2005) 1,790,000 (1,830,000); lignite (metric tons; 2005) 8,960,000 (15,100,000); crude petroleum (barrels; 2007) 1,160,000,000 ([2005] 530,000,-000); petroleum products (metric tons; 2005) 66,952,000 (74,614,000); natural gas (cu m; 2007) 66,081,000,000 ([2005] 52,701,000,000). **Population economically active** (2006): total 43,575,500; activity rate of total population 41.6% (participation rates: ages 15–64, 63.0%; female 37.1%; unemployed 3.2%). **Selected balance of payments data.** Receipts from (US$'000,000): tourism (2007) 12,901, of which border shoppers only 2,648; remittances (2007) 23,979; foreign direct investment (FDI) (2004–06 avg.) 20,390; official development assistance (2006) 247. Disbursements for (US$'000,000): tourism (2007) 8,378, of which border shoppers only 4,089; FDI (2004–06 avg.) 5,555.

Foreign trade

Imports (2006): US$256,130,000,000 (non-maquiladora sector 65.8%, of which imports for the automotive industry 10.9%, special machinery for industries 9.8%, imports for extractive industries 8.2%, electrical and electronic equipment 6.3%, imports for the chemical industry 5.6%; maquiladora sector 34.2%, of which electrical machinery and electronics 15.5%). *Major import sources:* US 50.9%; China 9.5%; Japan 6.0%; South Korea 4.2%; Germany 3.7%; Canada 2.9%; Brazil 2.2%; Taiwan 1.9%; Malaysia 1.7%; Italy 1.6%. **Exports** (2006): US$249,997,000,-000 (non-maquiladora sector 55.3%, of which motor vehicles and parts 15.1%, crude petroleum 13.9%, special machinery for industries 3.1%, electrical machinery and electronics 2.5%, food, beverages, and tobacco products 2.4%; maquiladora sector 44.7%, of which electrical machinery and electronics 20.1%, exports of the automotive industry 6.1%, professional and scientific equipment 2.6%). *Major export destinations:* US 84.7%; Canada 2.1%; Spain 1.3%; Germany 1.2%; Colombia 0.9%; Venezuela 0.7%; China 0.7%.

Transport and communications

Transport. *Railroads* (2006): route length 26,662 km; passenger-km 73,000,000; metric ton-km cargo 55,113,000,000. *Roads* (2005): total length 355,796 km (paved 34%). *Vehicles* (2004): passenger cars 14,713,085; trucks and buses 7,158,105. *Air transport* (2005): passenger-km 27,864,000,-000; metric ton-km cargo 177,048,000. **Communications,** in total units (units per 1,000 persons). Telephone landlines (2007): 19,754,000 (187); cellular telephone subscribers (2007): 68,254,000 (645); personal computers (2005): 14,000,000 (131); total Internet users (2007): 22,812,000 (216); broadband Internet subscribers (2007): 4,549,000 (43).

Education and health

Literacy (2005): percentage of total population ages 15 and over literate (2005) 91.6%; males literate 93.2%; females literate 90.2%. **Health** (2005): physicians 134,157 (1 per 777 persons); hospital beds 76,420 (1 per 1,364 persons); infant mortality rate per 1,000 live births (2006) 16.2; undernourished population (2002–04) 5,300,000 (5% of total population based on the consumption of a minimum daily requirement of 1,900 calories).

Military

Total active duty personnel (2007): 248,700 (army 71.6%, navy 18.6%, marines 5.1%, air force 4.7%). **Military expenditure as percentage of GDP** (2005): 0.4%; per capita expenditure US$29.

Background

Inhabited for more than 20,000 years, Mexico produced great civilizations in AD 100–900, including the Olmec, Toltec, Mayan, and Aztec. The Aztec were conquered in 1521 by Spanish explorer Hernán Cortés, who established Mexico City on the site of the Aztec capital, Tenochtitlán. Francisco de Montejo conquered the remnants of Mayan civilization in the mid-16th century, and Mexico became part of the Viceroyalty of New Spain. In 1821 rebels negotiated a status quo independence from Spain, and in 1823 a new congress declared Mexico a republic. In 1845 the US voted to annex Texas, initiating the Mexican-American War. Under the Treaty of Guadalupe Hidalgo in 1848, Mexico ceded a vast territory in what is now the western and southwestern US. The Mexican government endured several rebellions and civil wars in the late 19th and early 20th centuries. During World War II it declared war on the Axis powers (1942), and in the postwar era it was a founding member of the UN (1945) and the Organization of American States (1948). In 1993 it ratified the North American Free Trade Agreement. The election of Vicente Fox to the presidency in 2000 ended 71 years of rule by the Institutional Revolutionary Party.

Recent Developments

The most serious challenge confronting Mexico was an increasingly violent struggle against drug traffickers. Since assuming office in 2006, Pres. Felipe Calderón had dispatched approximately 40,000 army troops and federal police officers to different Mexican states in a high-visibility offensive against drug cartels. During 2008 the government arrested several prominent traffickers and maintained its policy of extraditing cartel leaders to the US. These advances, however, came at a very high price for Mexico. As shipping cocaine, marijuana, and other drugs into the US became more difficult, traffickers began selling a higher proportion of their products in Mexico, where addiction levels rose steadily. Fragmented cartels waged war against each other for control over lucrative smuggling routes, and they increasingly turned their formidable firepower (derived in large part from sophisticated armaments smuggled from the US) against army and police personnel. In a particularly gruesome turn, they frequently beheaded their victims. The violence claimed victims ranging from rival cartel members to senior federal police commanders and law-enforcement personnel to innocent bystanders. Furthermore, the overall incidence of drug-related violence was on the rise, with more than 6,500 deaths in 2008. Mexico-US relations during the year focused heavily on the challenges posed by illegal drug trafficking and undocumented migration. The Mexican government objected to US congressional amendments that conditioned proposed aid on the Mexican military's human rights record, and it insisted that the US government do more to control the flow of illegal firearms into Mexico. Following lengthy bilateral negotiations, in June 2008 the US Congress finally approved revised legislation that provided a US$400 million aid package to Mexico during the first year of a three-year technical assistance program known as the Mérida Initiative.

Internet resources: <www.visitmexico.com>.

1 metric ton = about 1.1 short tons;   1 kilometer = 0.6 mi (statute);   1 metric ton-km cargo = about 0.68 short ton-mi cargo;   c.i.f.: cost, insurance, and freight;   f.o.b.: free on board

Micronesia, Federated States of

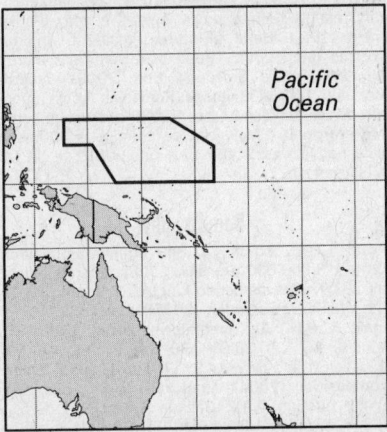

Pacific Ocean

Official name: Federated States of Micronesia. **Form of government:** federal nonparty republic in free association with the US with one legislative house (Congress [14]). **Head of state and government:** President Emanuel Mori (from 2007). **Capital:** Palikir. **Official language:** none. **Official religion:** none. **Monetary unit:** 1 US dollar (US$) = 100 cents.

Demography

Area: 270.8 sq mi, 701.4 sq km. **Population (2008):** 110,000. **Density (2008):** persons per sq mi 406.2, persons per sq km 156.8. **Urban (2007):** 22.0%. **Sex distribution (2007):** male 50.37%; female 49.63%. **Age breakdown (2005);** under 15, 37.1%; 15–29, 29.6%; 30–44, 17.2%; 45–59, 11.7%; 60–74, 3.5%; 75 and over, 0.9%. **Ethnic composition (2000):** Chuukese/Mortlockese 33.6%; Pohnpeian 24.9%; Yapese 10.6%; Kosraean 5.2%; US white 4.5%; Asian 1.3%; other 19.9%. **Religious affiliation (2005):** Roman Catholic 50%; Protestant 47%; other 3%. **Major towns (2000):** Weno 13,802; Palikir 6,444; Nett 6,158; Kolonia 5,681; Colonia 3,216. **Location:** Oceania, island group in the North Pacific Ocean, northeast of New Guinea.

Did you know? Pohnpei, the largest island in Micronesia, has over 767 varieties of plant and flora species, 111 of which are not found anywhere else in the world. Many of these unique plants are found in the upland forest regions of the island where rainfall can average over 400 in annually.

Vital statistics

Birth rate per 1,000 population (2007): 25.5 (world avg. 20.3); (2003) within marriage 78.9%; outside of marriage 21.1%. **Death rate** per 1,000 population (2007): 5.5 (world avg. 8.6). **Natural increase rate** per 1,000 population (2007): 20.0 (world avg. 11.7). **Total fertility rate** (avg. births per childbearing woman; 2007): 4.00. **Life expectancy** at birth (2007): male 67.4 years; female 68.0 years.

National economy

Budget (2005–06). *Revenue:* US$140,000,000 (external grants 60.9%; tax revenue 21.2%; nontax revenue 17.9%, of which fishing access revenue [foreign licenses and transshipment fees] 9.5%). *Expenditures:* US$153,000,000 (current expenditures 95.7%; capital expenditures 4.3%). **Public debt** (external, outstanding; 2005): US$60,800,000. **Population economically active (2000):** total 37,414; activity rate of total population 35.0% (participation rates: ages 15–64, 60.7%; female 42.9%; unemployed 22.0%). **Production** (metric tons except as noted). *Agriculture and fishing* (2007): coconuts 41,000, cassava 12,000, sweet potatoes 3,200, betel nuts (2005) 228; livestock (number of live animals) 33,000 pigs, 14,000 cattle; fisheries production (2006) 11,630, of which significantly skipjack tuna (from aquaculture, none). *Mining and quarrying:* quarrying of sand and aggregate for local construction only. *Manufacturing:* n.a.; however, copra and coconut oil, traditionally important products, are being displaced by garment production; the manufacture of handicrafts and personal items (clothing, mats, boats, etc.) by individuals is also important. *Energy production (consumption):* electricity (kW-hr; 2005) 74,400,000 (n.a.). **Gross national income** (2007): US$274,000,000 (US$2,470 per capita). **Selected balance of payments data.** Receipts from (US$'000,000): tourism (2005) 17; remittances (2005) 6.0; official development assistance (2006) 108. Disbursements for (US$'000,000): tourism (2005) 5.7.

Foreign trade

Imports (2006; c.i.f.): US$137,993,000 (food and beverages 32.1%; mineral fuels 22.4%; machinery and apparatus 10.6%; transportation equipment 6.0%; chemical products 5.9%). *Major import sources* (2006): US 39.7%; Japan 8.8%; South Korea 5.8%; Singapore 4.6%; Philippines 4.4%. **Exports** (2005; f.o.b.): US$12,984,000 (deep-sea products [nearly all fish] 89.9%; reef fish 4.0%; betel nuts 3.1%; kava [*sakau*] 1.0%). *Major export destinations* (2004): Japan 21.4%; US 20.9%; Guam 3.4%; Northern Mariana Islands 1.0%.

Transport and communications

Transport. *Railroads:* none. *Roads* (2000): total length 240 km (paved 18%). *Vehicles* (2004): passenger cars 4,601; trucks and buses 3,770. *Air transport* (Continental Micronesia only; 2006): passenger-km 4,762,000,000; metric ton-km cargo 102,000,000. **Communications,** in total units (units per 1,000 persons). Telephone landlines (2007): 8,700 (78); cellular telephone subscribers (2007): 27,000 (247); personal computers (2005): 6,000 (55); total Internet users (2007): 15,000 (135).

Education and health

Educational attainment (2000). Percentage of population ages 25 and over having: no formal schooling/unknown 13.4%; primary education 37.0%; some secondary 18.3%; secondary 12.9%; some college 18.4%. **Literacy (2000):** percentage of total population ages 10 and over literate 92.4%; males literate 92.9%; females literate 91.9%. **Health:** physicians (2005) 62 (1 per 1,774 persons); hospital beds (2006) 365 (1 per 301 persons); infant mortality rate per 1,000 live births (2007) 37.5.

Military

Total active duty personnel: none. External security is provided by the US.

Background

The islands of Micronesia were probably settled by people from eastern Melanesia some 3,500 years ago. Europeans first landed on the islands in the 16th century. Spain took control of the islands in 1886 and then sold them to Germany in 1899. The islands came under Japanese rule after World War I. They were captured by US forces during World War II, and in 1947 they became a UN trust territory administered by the US. The group of islands centered on the Caroline Islands became an internally self-governing federation in 1979. In 1986 the Federated States of Micronesia (FSM) entered into a Compact of Free Association with the US, which was amended in 2003. In the early 21st century, Micronesia found itself threatened by rising water levels.

Recent Developments

The economy of the FSM contracted by an estimated 3.5% in 2008. Meanwhile, external debt equaled 25.1% of GDP. The FSM remained highly dependent on US government transfers provided under the amended Compact of Free Association, which represented 65% of the FSM's revenue, and on payments by the US to the FSM Trust Fund, which would eventually replace compact income.

Internet resources: <www.spc.int/prism/country/fm/stats>.

Moldova

Black Sea

Mediterranean Sea

Official name: Republica Moldova (Republic of Moldova). **Form of government:** unitary parliamentary republic with a single legislative body (Parliament [101]). **Head of state:** President Vladimir Voronin (from 2001). **Head of government:** Prime Minister Zinaida Greceanii (from 2008). **Capital:** Chisinau. **Official language:** Romanian (constitutionally designated as Moldovan). **Official religion:** none. **Monetary unit:** 1 Moldovan leu (plural lei) = 100 bani; valuation (1 Jul 2009) free rate, US$1 = 11.02 Moldovan lei.

Demography

Area: 13,067 sq mi, 33,843 sq km. **Population** (2008): 3,760,000. **Density** (2008): persons per sq mi 287.7, persons per sq km 111.1. **Urban** (2007): 41.3%. **Sex distribution** (2007): male 48.06%; female 51.94%. **Age breakdown** (2004): under 15, 19.1%; 15–29, 26.3%; 30–44, 20.9%; 45–59, 19.1%; 60 and over, 14.3%; unknown 0.3%. **Ethnic composition** (2004): Moldovan 75.8%; Ukrainian 8.4%; Russian 5.9%; Gagauz 4.4%; Rom (Gypsy) 2.2%; Bulgarian 1.9%; other 1.4%. **Religious affiliation** (2005): Moldovan Orthodox 31.8%; Bessarabian Orthodox 16.1%; Russian Orthodox 15.4%; Sunni Muslim 5.5%; Protestant 1.7%; Jewish 0.6%; nonreligious 19.9%; other 9.0%. **Major cities** (2007): Chisinau 630,300; Tiraspol 155,000; Balti 122,200; Bender (Tighina) 95,000; Rabnita (Rybnitsa) 52,000. **Location:** eastern Europe, bordering Ukraine and Romania.

Vital statistics

Birth rate per 1,000 population (2007): 10.6 (world avg. 20.3); within marriage 77.3%; outside of marriage 22.7%. **Death rate** per 1,000 population (2007): 12.0 (world avg. 8.6). **Total fertility rate** (avg. births per childbearing woman; 2006): 1.22. **Life expectancy** at birth (2006): male 64.6 years; female 72.2 years.

National economy

Budget (2004). *Revenue:* 11,324,000,000 Moldovan lei (tax revenue 84.3%, of which VAT 30.3%, social fund contributions 22.0%; nontax and extra budgetary revenue 14.6%; grants 1.1%). *Expenditures:* 11,092,000,000 Moldovan lei (current expenditures 95.5%, of which social fund expenditures 25.0%, education 15.2%, interest payments 5.5%; capital expenditures 4.5%). **Production** (metric tons except as noted). *Agriculture and fishing* (2007): sugar beets 612,000, grapes 598,000, wheat 402,000; livestock (number of live animals) 835,077 sheep, 531,818 pigs, 299,105 cattle; fisheries production (2006) 5,082 (from aquaculture 88%). *Mining and quarrying* (2005): gypsum 110,000. *Manufacturing* (value of production in '000,000 Moldovan lei; 2004): alcoholic beverages 4,013, of which wine 3,098; food products 3,461; cement, bricks, and ceramics 1,273. *Energy production (consumption):* electricity (kW-hr; 2005) 3,865,000,000 (7,006,000,000); coal (metric tons; 2005) none (167,000); petroleum products (metric tons; 2005) 4,000 (621,000); natural gas (cu m; 2005) none (2,924,000,000). **Population economically active**

1 metric ton = about 1.1 short tons;   1 kilometer = 0.6 mi (statute);   1 metric ton-km cargo = about 0.68 short ton-mi cargo;   c.i.f.: cost, insurance, and freight;   f.o.b.: free on board

(2005): total 1,422,300; activity rate of total de facto population 39.5% (participation rates: ages 15–64, 53.2%; female 51.5%; unemployed [2006] 7.4%). **Gross national income** (2007): US$4,323,000,000 (US$1,260 per capita). **Public debt** (external, outstanding; end of 2006): US$718,000,000. **Selected balance of payments data.** Receipts from (US$'000,000): tourism (2006) 112; remittances (2007) 1,498; foreign direct investment (2004–06 avg.) 190; official development assistance (2006) 228. Disbursements for (US$'000,000): tourism (2006) 187; remittances (2007) 87.

Foreign trade

Imports (2006; c.i.f.): US$2,693,000,000 (machinery and apparatus 13.8%; refined petroleum products 12.6%; chemical products 11.9%; natural gas 8.1%; food products 7.4%). *Major import sources:* Ukraine 19.2%; Russia 15.5%; Romania 12.8%; Germany 7.9%; Italy 7.3%. **Exports** (2006; f.o.b.): US$1,051,000,000 (food products 19.8%, of which cereals 4.3%, walnuts 3.6%; wearing apparel and accessories 19.1%; wine and grape must 15.4%; machinery and apparatus 5.2%). *Major export destinations:* Russia 17.3%; Romania 14.8%; Ukraine 12.2%; Italy 11.1%; Belarus 7.0%.

Transport and communications

Transport. *Railroads* (2007): length 1,154 km; passenger-km 468,000,000; metric ton-km cargo 3,120,000,000. *Roads* (2007): total length 9,337 km (paved 94%). *Vehicles* (2003): passenger cars 252,490; trucks and buses 77,534. *Air transport* (2007): passenger-km 550,000,000; metric ton-km cargo 1,300,000. **Communications**, in total units (units per 1,000 persons). Telephone landlines (2007): 1,080,000 (285); cellular telephone subscribers (2007): 1,883,000 (496); personal computers (2005): 348,000 (83); total Internet users (2007): 700,000 (185); broadband Internet subscribers (2007): 47,000 (12).

Education and health

Literacy (2003): percentage of total population ages 15 and over literate 99.1%. **Health** (2006): physicians 12,674 (1 per 283 persons); hospital beds 22,471 (1 per 160 persons); infant mortality rate per 1,000 live births (2007) 11.3; undernourished population (2002–04) 450,000 (11% of total population based on the consumption of a minimum daily requirement of 1,970 calories).

Military

Total active duty personnel (2008): 6,000 (army 85.8%, air force 14.2%); opposition forces (excluding Russian troops) in Transdniestria (2008) 7,500; Russian troops in Transdniestria (2008) 1,500. **Military expenditure as percentage of GDP** (2008): 0.4%; per capita expenditure US$7.

Background

Moldova, once part of the principality of Moldavia, was founded by the Vlachs in the 14th century. In the mid-16th century it was under Ottoman rule.

In 1774 it came under Russian control and lost portions of its territory. In 1859 it joined with the principality of Walachia to form the state of Romania, and in 1918 some of the territory it had ceded earlier also joined Romania. Romania was compelled to cede some of the Moldavian area to Russia in 1940, and that area combined with what Russia already controlled to become the Moldavian SSR. In 1991 Moldavia declared independence from the Soviet Union. It adopted the Romanian spelling of Moldova after having legitimized the use of the Roman rather than the Cyrillic alphabet in 1989. It was admitted to the UN in 1992.

Recent Developments

Moldovan Pres. Vladimir Voronin met in January 2008 with his Russian counterpart, Vladimir Putin, and in August with Putin's successor, Dmitry Medvedev. The future of the breakaway territory of Transdniestria dominated the talks. In a referendum held in 2006, 97% of Transdniestrian residents had expressed a desire to join the Russian Federation, but the Russian preference was for a reunified Moldova in which the breakaway region would enjoy substantial autonomy and be able to influence the central government. In April, for the first time since 2001, Voronin met with Igor Smirnov (the leader of the Transdniestrian regime), with whom he agreed to launch confidence-building measures designed to lead eventually to reunification.

Internet resources:
<www.statistica.md/index.php?l=en>.

Monaco

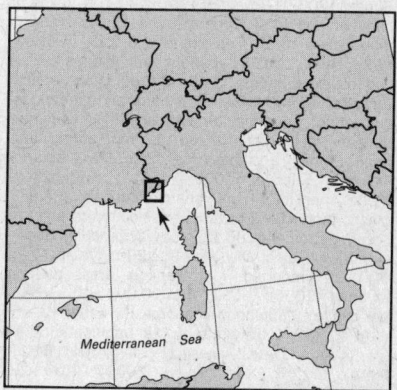

Official name: Principauté de Monaco (Principality of Monaco). **Form of government:** constitutional monarchy with one legislative body (National Council [24]). **Chief of state:** Prince Albert II (from 2005). **Head of government:** Minister of State Jean-Paul Proust (from 2005). **Capital:** no separate area is distinguished as such. **Official language:** French. **Official religion:** Roman Catholicism. **Monetary unit:** 1 euro (€) = 100 centimes; valuation (1 Jul 2009) US$1 = €0.71 (Monaco uses the euro as its official currency, even though it is not a member of the EU).

Demography

Area: 0.76 sq mi, 1.97 sq km. **Population (2008):** 34,300. **Density (2008):** persons per sq mi 43,974, persons per sq km 16,980. **Urban (2008):** urban 100%. **Sex distribution (2008):** male 47.94%; female 52.06%. **Age breakdown (2008):** under 15, 12.8%; 15–29, 12.7%; 30–44, 19.2%; 45–59, 21.8%; 60–74, 19.1%; 75–84, 7.9%; 85 and over, 4.2%; unknown 2.3%. **Ethnic composition (2007):** French 47%; Italian 16%; Monegasque 16%; other 21%. **Religious affiliation (2000):** Christian 93.2%, of which Roman Catholic 89.3%; Jewish 1.7%; nonreligious and other 5.1%. **Location:** western Europe, bordering the Mediterranean Sea and France.

Vital statistics

Birth rate per 1,000 population (2006): 26.8 (world avg. 20.3); (2005) within marriage 61.4%, outside of marriage 38.6%. **Death rate** per 1,000 population (2006): 16.3 (world avg. 8.6). **Natural increase rate** per 1,000 population (2006): 10.5 (world avg. 11.7). **Total fertility rate** (avg. births per childbearing woman; 2005): 1.70. **Life expectancy** at birth (2005): male 74.7 years; female 83.6 years.

 Monaco is the second smallest country in the world and the smallest country in the United Nations. Its area covers only two square kilometers.

National economy

Budget (2007). *Revenue:* €845,600,700 (taxes on commerce 47.4%; property taxes 12.9%; state-run monopolies 10.0%; customs duties 3.1%). *Expenditures:* €843,119,681 (current expenditures 65.1%; capital expenditures 34.9%). **Production.** *Agriculture and fishing:* some horticulture and greenhouse cultivation; no agriculture as such; fisheries production (metric tons; 2006) 1 (from aquaculture, none). *Mining and quarrying:* none. *Manufacturing* (value of sales in €'000; 2007): chemicals, cosmetics, perfumery, and pharmaceuticals 364,077; plastic products 266,366; light electronics and precision instruments 86,113. *Energy production (consumption):* electricity (kW-hr; 2001) n.a. (475,-000,000 [imported from France]). **Gross national income (2006):** US$1,165,000,000 (US$35,725 per capita). **Population economically active (2005):** total 40,289; activity rate of total population 58.4% (participation rates: ages 17–64 [2000] 61.1%; female 41.4%; unemployed [2000] 3.6%). **Selected balance of payments data.** Tourism (2007): 2,773 hotel rooms, 327,985 overnight visitors.

Foreign trade

Imports (2007; excludes trade with France, with which Monaco has participated in a customs union since 1963): €850,202,845 (nonelectrical machinery and apparatus 40.2%; pharmaceuticals, perfumes, clothing, and publishing 19.2%; rubber and plastic products, glass, construction materials, organic chemicals, and paper products 15.7%; food products 7.4%; motor vehicles and parts 7.0%). *Major import sources:* China 34.9%; Italy 18.6%; Japan 8.5%; UK 7.1%; Belgium 5.3%. **Exports** (2007; excludes trade with France, with which Monaco has participated in a customs union since 1963): €834,108,-693 (rubber and plastic products, glass, construction materials, organic chemicals, and paper products 39.9%; motor vehicles and parts 12.7%; pharmaceuticals, perfumes, clothing, and publishing 12.2%; nonelectrical machinery and apparatus 12.1%; food products 9.6%). *Major export destinations:* Germany 10.7%; Italy 8.4%; Spain 7.9%; UK 6.6%; Lithuania 5.2%.

Transport and communications

Transport. *Railroads* (2001): length 1.7 km; passengers 2,171,100; cargo 3,357 tons. *Roads* (2001): total length 50 km (paved 100%). *Vehicles* (1997): passenger cars 21,120; trucks and buses 2,770. *Air transport:* fixed-wing service is provided at Nice, France; helicopter service is available at Fontvieille. **Communications,** in total units (units per 1,000 persons). Telephone landlines (2005): 34,000 (1,019); cellular telephone subscribers (2005): 17,000 (510); total Internet users (2006): 20,000 (593); broadband Internet subscribers (2005): 9,400 (282).

Education and health

Educational attainment (2000). Percentage of population ages 17 and over having: primary/lower secondary education 24.7%; upper secondary 27.6%; vocational 12.7%; university 35.0%. **Literacy:** percentage of total population literate, virtually 100%. **Health** (2002): physicians 156 (1 per 207 persons); hospital beds 521 (1 per 62 persons); infant mortality rate per 1,000 live births (2005) 5.4.

Military

Total active duty personnel: none. Defense responsibility lies with France according to the terms of the Versailles Treaty of 1919.

Background

Inhabited since prehistoric times, Monaco was known to the Phoenicians, Greeks, Carthaginians, and Romans. In 1191 the Genoese took possession of it; in 1297 the reign of the Grimaldi family began. The Grimaldis allied themselves with France except for the period 1524–1641, when they were under the protection of Spain. France annexed Monaco in 1793, and it remained under French control until the fall of Napoleon, when the Grimaldis returned. In 1815 it was put under the protection of Sardinia. A treaty in 1861 called for the sale of the towns of Menton and Roquebrune to France and the establishment of Monaco's independence. It joined the UN in 1993. In 1997 the 700-year rule of the Grimaldis, then under Prince Rainier III, was celebrated. Although not a member of the EU, Monaco adopted the euro as its currency in 2002.

1 metric ton = about 1.1 short tons;   1 kilometer = 0.6 mi (statute);   1 metric ton-km cargo = about 0.68 short ton-mi cargo;   c.i.f.: cost, insurance, and freight;   f.o.b.: free on board

Recent Developments

Monaco's land-reclamation project, which would increase the principality's area by approximately 10 ha (about 25 ac), was put on hold in December 2008 because of environmental concerns and the financial climate.

Internet resources: < www.monte-carlo.mc>.

Mongolia

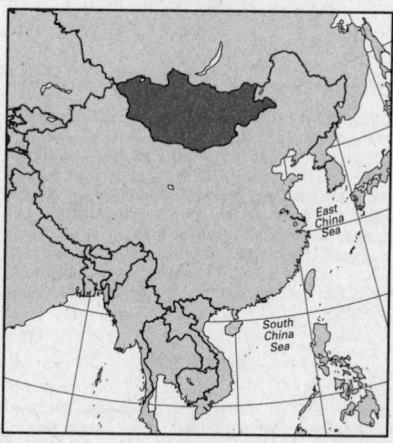

Official name: Mongol Uls (Mongolia). **Form of government:** unitary multiparty republic with one legislative house (State Great Hural [76]). **Chief of state:** President Tsakhiagiyn Elbegdorj (from 2009). **Head of government:** Prime Minister Sanj Bayar (from 2007). **Capital:** Ulaanbaatar (Ulan Bator). **Official language:** Khalkha Mongolian. **Official religion:** none. **Monetary unit:** 1 tugrik (Tug) = 100 mongo; valuation (1 Jul 2009) US$1 = Tug 1,435.49.

Demography

Area: 603,930 sq mi, 1,564,160 sq km. **Population** (2008): 2,652,000. **Density** (2008): persons per sq mi 4.4, persons per sq km 1.7. **Urban** (2006): 60.9%. **Sex distribution** (2004): male 49.60%; female 50.40%. **Age breakdown** (2005): under 15, 28.9%; 15–29, 32.3%; 30–44, 22.6%; 45–59, 10.3%; 60–74, 4.5%; 75–84, 1.1%; 85 and over, 0.3%. **Ethnic composition** (2000): Khalkha Mongol 81.5%; Kazakh 4.3%; Dorbed Mongol 2.8%; Bayad 2.1%; Buryat Mongol 1.7%; Dariganga Mongol 1.3%; Zakhchin 1.3%; Tuvan (Uriankhai) 1.1%; other 3.9%. **Religious affiliation** (2005): traditional beliefs (shamanism) 32%; Buddhist (Lamaism) 23%; Muslim 5%; Christian 1%; nonreligious 30%; atheist/other 9%. **Major cities** (2007): Ulaanbaatar (Ulan Bator) 1,031,200; Erdenet 74,300; Darhan 72,400; Choybalsan (2000) 41,714; Ulaangom (2000) 26,319. **Location:** north-central Asia, bordering Russia and China.

Vital statistics

Birth rate per 1,000 population (2007): 21.2 (world avg. 20.3); (2001) within marriage 82.2%; outside of marriage 17.8%. **Death rate** per 1,000 population (2007): 5.9 (world avg. 8.6). **Natural increase rate** per 1,000 population (2007): 15.3 (world avg. 11.7). **Total fertility rate** (avg. births per childbearing woman; 2005): 1.97. **Life expectancy** at birth (2004): male 61.6 years; female 67.8 years.

National economy

Budget (2006). *Revenue:* Tug 1,360,400,000,000 (tax revenue 83.0%, of which income tax 35.0%, taxes on goods and services 25.9%; nontax revenue 16.6%; other 0.4%). *Expenditures:* Tug 1,237,000,000,000 (economic services 26.1%; social security 20.8%; general administration 19.6%; education 15.6%). **Population economically active** (2004): total 986,100; activity rate of total population 39.3% (participation rates: ages 16–59, 63.7%; female 51.0%; unemployed [2006] 3.2%). **Production** (metric tons except as noted). *Agriculture and fishing* (2007): hay 930,405, potatoes 114,490, wheat 109,560; livestock (number of live animals) 15,451,700 goats, 14,815,100 sheep, 2,167,900 cattle, 2,114,800 horses, 253,500 camels; fisheries production (2006) 289 (from aquaculture, none). *Mining and quarrying* (2006): fluorspar 393,000; copper (metal content) 129,693; molybdenum (metal content) 1,404; gold 22,561 kg. *Manufacturing* (value of production in Tug '000,000; 2006): textiles 93,475; base metals 74,879; food products 71,428. *Energy production (consumption):* electricity (kW-hr; 2005) 3,419,000,000 (3,575,000,000); coal (metric tons; 2005) 1,225,000 (1,225,000); lignite (metric tons; 2005) 6,292,000 (4,176,000); crude petroleum (barrels; 2005) 201,000 (n.a.); petroleum products (metric tons; 2005) none (545,000). **Gross national income** (2007): US$3,362,000,000 (US$1,290 per capita). **Public debt** (external; 2006): US$1,361,000,000. **Selected balance of payments data.** Receipts from (US$'000,000): tourism (2006) 225; remittances (2007) 194; foreign direct investment (2004–06 avg.) 147; official development assistance (2006) 203. Disbursements for (US$'000,000): tourism (2006) 188; remittances (2007) 77.

Foreign trade

Imports (2006; c.i.f.): US$1,489,200,000 (mineral fuels 30.0%; machinery and apparatus 18.2%; food and agricultural products 12.4%; transportation equipment 10.3%). *Major import sources:* Russia 36.6%; China 27.5%; Japan 6.8%; South Korea 5.6%; Kazakhstan 3.5%. **Exports** (2006; f.o.b.): US$1,528,800,000 (copper concentrate 42.7%; gold 18.1%; refined copper 7.2%; combed goat down 5.3%; raw [greasy] cashmere 4.2%, molybdenum 3.2%). *Major export destinations:* China 68.1%; Canada 11.2%; US 7.8%; Russia 2.9%; UK 2.5%.

Transport and communications

Transport. *Railroads* (2006): route length 1,810 km; passenger-km 1,287,000,000; metric ton-km cargo 10,513,000,000. *Roads* (2002): total length 49,250 km (paved 4%). *Vehicles* (2006): passenger cars 95,115; trucks and buses 41,234. *Air transport* (2006): passenger-km 835,800,000; metric ton-km cargo 86,400,000. **Communications,** in total units

(units per 1,000 persons). Telephone landlines (2005): 156,000 (59); cellular telephone subscribers (2005): 557,000 (211); personal computers (2005): 340,000 (133); total Internet users (2007): 320,000 (123); broadband Internet subscribers (2007): 7,400 (2.8).

Education and health

Educational attainment (2000). Percentage of population ages 10 and over having: no formal education 11.6%; primary education 23.5%; secondary 46.1%; vocational secondary 11.2%; higher 7.6%. **Literacy** (2004): percentage of total population ages 15 and over literate 97.8%; males literate 98.0%; females literate 97.5%. **Health** (2004): physicians 6,590 (1 per 384 persons); hospital beds 18,400 (1 per 138 persons); infant mortality rate per 1,000 live births (2006) 19.8; undernourished population (2002–04) 700,000 (27% of total population based on the consumption of a minimum daily requirement of 1,870 calories).

Military

Total active duty personnel (2007): 8,600 (army 87.2%, air force 9.3%, unspecified 3.5%). **Military expenditure as percentage of GDP** (2005): 1.6%; per capita expenditure US$12.

Background

In Neolithic times Mongolia was inhabited by small groups of nomads. During the 3rd century BC it became the center of the Xiongnu empire. Turkic-speaking peoples held sway in the 4th–10th centuries AD. In the early 13th century Genghis Khan united the Mongol tribes and conquered central Asia. His successor, Ogodei, conquered the Chin dynasty of China in 1234. Kublai Khan established the Yuan, or Mongol, dynasty in China in 1279. After the 14th century the Ming dynasty of China confined the Mongols to their homeland in the steppes; later they became part of the Chinese Ch'ing dynasty. Inner Mongolia was incorporated into China in 1644. After the fall of the Ch'ing dynasty in 1911, Mongol princes declared Mongolia's independence from China, and in 1921 Russian forces helped drive off the Chinese. The Mongolian People's Republic was established in 1924 and recognized by China in 1946. The nation adopted a new constitution in 1992 and shortened its name to Mongolia.

Recent Developments

Despite the fall in the world prices of some metal commodities, Mongolia's outlook for 2009 was positive. The Finance Ministry in October 2008 projected economic growth topping 14% and unemployment under 3%. A leading producer of copper, silver, gold, and uranium, among other metals, Mongolia in March 2009 announced the completion of a survey indicating large uranium reserves in the Dornod project area in the northeast of the country. Production there was to begin in the next three years.

Internet resources:
<www.nso.mn/v2/index2.php>.

Montenegro

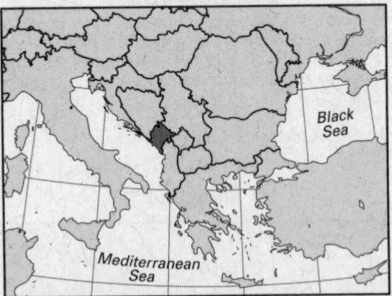

Official name: Crna Gora (Montenegro). **Form of government:** multiparty republic with one legislative house (Parliament [81]). **Chief of state:** President Filip Vujanovic (from 2003). **Head of government:** Prime Minister Milo Djukanovic (from 2008). **Capital:** Podgorica; Cetinje is the old royal capital. **Official language:** Montenegrin. **Official religion:** none. **Monetary unit:** 1 euro (€) = 100 cents; valuation (1 Jul 2009) US$1 = €0.71 (Montenegro uses the euro as its official currency, even though it is not a member of the EU).

Demography

Area: 5,333 sq mi, 13,812 sq km. **Population** (2008): 626,000. **Density** (2008): persons per sq mi 117.4, persons per sq km 45.3. **Urban** (2005): 52.2%. **Sex distribution** (2006): male 49.28%; female 50.72%. **Age breakdown** (2005): under 15, 19.6%; 15–29, 23.6%; 30–44, 19.8%; 45–59, 19.1%; 60–74, 12.8%; 75–84, 4.3%; 85 and over, 0.8%. **Ethnic composition** (2003): Montenegrin 43.2%; Serb 32.0%; Bosniac/Muslim 11.8%; Albanian 5.0%; undeclared 4.0%; other 4.0%. **Religious affiliation** (2003): Orthodox 70%; Muslim 21%; Roman Catholic 4%; other 5%. **Major cities** (2006): Podgorica 174,000; Niksic 75,000; Bijelo Polje 50,000; Bar 41,000; Berane 35,000. **Location:** southeastern Europe, bordering Bosnia and Herzegovina, Serbia, Kosovo, Albania, the Mediterranean Sea, and Croatia.

Vital statistics

Birth rate per 1,000 population (2007): 12.6 (world avg. 20.3); (2005) within marriage 79.1%, outside of marriage 20.9%. **Death rate** per 1,000 population (2007): 9.6 (world avg. 8.6). **Natural increase rate** per 1,000 population (2007): 3.0 (world avg. 11.7). **Total fertility rate** (avg. births per childbearing woman; 2006): 1.64. **Life expectancy** at birth (2004): male 71 years; female 75 years.

National economy

Budget (2006). *Revenue:* €582,258,287 (tax revenue 85.8%, of which VAT 44.5%, income tax 12.5%, excise tax 12.4%; nontax revenue 14.2%). *Expenditures:* €579,780,129 (wages and salaries

---

1 metric ton = about 1.1 short tons;   1 kilometer = 0.6 mi (statute);   1 metric ton-km cargo = about 0.68 short ton-mi cargo;   c.i.f.: cost, insurance, and freight;   f.o.b.: free on board

27.4%; transfers 20.7%; debt service 20.0%). **Public debt** (external, outstanding; January 2008): US$680,259,100. **Production** (metric tons except as noted). *Agriculture and fishing* (2007): potatoes 130,000, grapes 41,000, tomatoes 22,000; livestock (number of live animals) 249,281 sheep, 114,922 cattle, 13,294 pigs; fisheries production (2006) 911 (from aquaculture 1%). *Mining and quarrying* (2007): bauxite 667,053. *Manufacturing* (gross value added in €'000; 2004): base and fabricated metals (mostly aluminum) 58,718; food, beverages, and tobacco products 56,846; paper products, publishing, and printing 6,647. *Energy production* (*consumption*): electricity (kW-hr; 2007) 2,144,000,000 ([2005] 19,000,000); coal (metric tons; 2006) 10,000 ([2005] 66,900); lignite (metric tons; 2007) 1,195,500 ([2005] 1,230,000); crude petroleum (barrels; 2004) n.a. (164,000). **Population economically active** (2007): total 269,500; activity rate of total population 43.2% (participation rates: ages 15 and over, 52.9%; female 43.0%; unemployed [September 2007–August 2008] 15.8%). **Gross national income** (2007): US$3,109,000,000 (US$5,180 per capita). **Selected balance of payments data.** Receipts from (US$'000,000): tourism (2006) 340; remittances (2006) 100; foreign direct investment (FDI) (2004–06 avg.) 391; official development assistance (2006) 96. Disbursements for (US$'000,-000): FDI (2004–06 avg.) 14.

Foreign trade

Imports (2007; c.i.f.): €2,134,377,900 (mineral fuels 11.6%; motor vehicles 11.4%; nonelectrical machinery and apparatus 9.0%; electrical machinery and apparatus 8.8%; base and fabricated metals 7.1%). *Major import sources:* Serbia 29.9%; Germany 10.0%; Italy 9.8%; Croatia 3.9%; Greece 3.5%. **Exports** (2007; f.o.b.): €599,020,700,000 (aluminum products 47.0%; base metals 11.9%; beverages and tobacco 8.9%; mineral fuels 8.1%). *Major export destinations:* Serbia 28.3%; Italy 27.4%; Greece 12.3%; Hungary 11.1%; Bosnia and Herzegovina 5.1%.

Transport and communications

Transport. *Railroads* (2007): length (2006) 250 km; passenger-km 110,000,000; metric ton-km cargo 184,957,000. *Roads* (2006): total length 7,368 km (paved 64%). *Vehicles* (2006): passenger cars 152,581. *Air transport* (2007): passengers 1,024,491; freight 1,320 metric tons. **Communications,** in total units (units per 1,000 persons). Telephone landlines (2006): 353,000 (589); cellular telephone subscribers (2006): 644,000 (1,073); personal computers (2004): 389,000 (359); total Internet users (2007): 280,000 (468); broadband Internet subscribers (2006): 26,000 (42).

Education and health

Educational attainment (2005). Percentage of population ages 15 and over having: no formal education 3.2%; incomplete primary 6.8%; complete primary 22.5%; secondary 55.0%; higher 12.5%. **Literacy** (2003): percentage of total population ages 20 and over literate 97.3%; males literate 99.2%; females literate 95.5%. **Health** (2006): physicians 1,274 (1 per

490 persons); hospital beds 4,043 (1 per 154 persons); infant mortality rate per 1,000 live births (2007) 7.4.

Military

Total active duty personnel (2007): 5,800 (army 43.1%, navy 56.9%).

Background

The Kingdom of the Serbs, Croats, and Slovenes was created after the collapse of Austria-Hungary at the end of World War I. The country signed treaties with Czechoslovakia and Romania in 1920–21, marking the beginning of the Little Entente. In 1929 an absolute monarchy was established, the country's name was changed to Yugoslavia, and it was divided into regions without regard to ethnic boundaries. Axis powers invaded Yugoslavia in 1941, and German, Italian, Hungarian, and Bulgarian troops occupied it for the rest of World War II. In 1945 the Socialist Federal Republic of Yugoslavia was established; it included the republics of Bosnia and Herzegovina, Croatia, Macedonia, Montenegro, Serbia, and Slovenia. Its independent form of communism under Josip Broz Tito's leadership provoked the USSR. Internal ethnic tensions flared up in the 1980s, causing the country's ultimate collapse. In 1991–92 independence was declared by Croatia, Slovenia, Macedonia, and Bosnia and Herzegovina; the new Federal Republic of Yugoslavia (containing roughly 45% of the population and 40% of the area of its predecessor) was proclaimed by Serbia and Montenegro. Still fueled by long-standing ethnic tensions, hostilities continued into the 1990s. Despite the approval of the Dayton Peace Agreement (1995), sporadic fighting continued and was followed in 1998–99 by Serbian repression and expulsion of ethnic populations in the province of Kosovo. In September–October 2000, the battered nation of Yugoslavia ended the autocratic rule of Pres. Slobodan Milosevic. In April 2001 he was arrested and in June extradited to The Hague to stand trial for war crimes, genocide, and crimes against humanity committed during the fighting in Kosovo. In February 2003 both houses of the Yugoslav federal legislature voted to accept a new state charter and change the name of the country from Yugoslavia to Serbia and Montenegro. Henceforth, defense, international political and economic relations, and human rights matters would be handled centrally, while all other functions would be run from the republican capitals, Belgrade and Podgorica, respectively. A provision was included for both states to vote on independence after three years, and in June 2006 Montenegro's parliament declared the republic's independence, severing some 88 years of union with Serbia.

Recent Developments

Montenegro's marked economic improvement continued to attract foreign investors in 2008, especially for tourism and construction projects. The World Travel and Tourism Council ranked Montenegro as a top tourism destination, with growth estimated at 10% annually through 2016, and 1,188,116 tourists visited the country in 2008 compared with 1,133,432 in 2007. The central bank estimated that per capita foreign direct investment was US$2,200, among the highest in Europe. The GDP growth was 18.9%; inflation fell from 7.7% in 2007 to 7.2%; and the unemployment rate dropped from 16.5% to 14.4%. In April 2008 Montenegro concluded a World Trade Organization agreement with the EU and attended a major NATO conference in Bucharest, Romania. In October Montenegro recognized Kosovo's independence. Western observers regarded the action as a snub to Serbia, Montenegro's traditional ally. Montenegro formally applied for EU membership on 15 December.

Internet resources:
<www.monstat.cg.yu/EngPrva.htm>.

Morocco

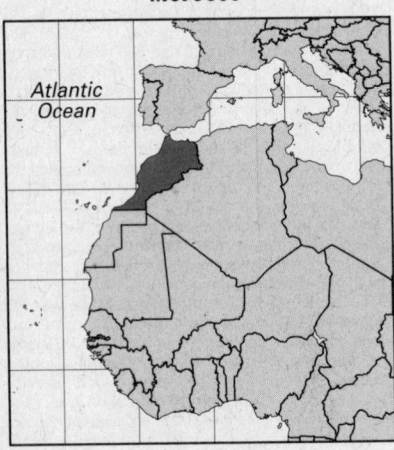

Atlantic
Ocean

Official name: Al-Mamlakah al-Maghribiyah (Kingdom of Morocco). **Form of government:** constitutional monarchy with two legislative houses (House of Councillors [270]; House of Representatives [325]). **Chief of state and head of government:** King Muhammad VI (from 1999), assisted by Prime Minister Abbas El Fassi (from 2007). **Capital:** Rabat. **Official language:** Arabic. **Official religion:** Islam. **Monetary unit:** 1 Moroccan dirham (DH) = 100 santimat; valuation (1 Jul 2009) US$1 = DH 7.94.

Demography

Area: 274,461 sq mi, 710,850 sq km (includes Western Sahara). **Population** (2008): 32,103,000 (includes Western Sahara). **Density** (2008): persons per sq mi 117.0, persons per sq km 45.2 (includes Western Sahara). **Urban** (2006): 56.0%. **Sex distribution** (2006): male 49.51%; female 50.49%. **Age breakdown** (2006): under 15, 29.8%; 15–29, 29.2%; 30–44, 20.3%; 45–59, 12.7%; 60–74, 5.9%; 75 and over, 2.1%. **Ethnic composition** (2000): Amazigh (Berber) 45%, of which Arabized 24%; Arab 44%; Moors originally from Mauritania 10%; other 1%. **Religious affiliation** (2004): Mus-

lim more than 99% (including Sunni 97%; Shi'i 2%); other less than 1%. **Major urban agglomerations** (2007): Casablanca 3,181,000; Fès 1,002,000; Marrakech 872,000; Salé (2004) 760,186; Tangier (2004) 669,685. **Location:** northern Africa, bordering the Mediterranean Sea, the Spanish exclaves of Ceuta and Melilla, Algeria, Mauritania, and the North Atlantic Ocean.

Vital statistics

Birth rate per 1,000 population (2005): 22.3 (world avg. 20.3). **Death rate** per 1,000 population (2005): 5.6 (world avg. 8.6). **Total fertility rate** (avg. births per childbearing woman; 2005): 2.73. **Life expectancy** at birth (2005): male 68.4 years; female 73.1 years.

National economy

Budget. Revenue (2007): DH 167,904,000,000 (VAT 29.6%; corporate taxes 18.1%; income tax 16.5%; nontax revenue 8.8%). Expenditures (2007): DH 168,959,000,000 (current expenditures 78.5%; capital expenditures 16.3%). **Public debt** (external, outstanding; 2006): US$14,108,000,000. **Population economically active** (2006): total 10,990,000; activity rate of total population 36.0% (participation rates: ages 15 and over, 51.3%; female [2005] 27.5%; unemployed 9.7%). **Production** (metric tons except as noted). Agriculture and fishing (2007): sugar beets 3,000,000, wheat 1,583,000, potatoes 1,450,000, olives 657,000; livestock (number of live animals) 17,250,000 sheep, 2,700,000 cattle, 140,000,000 chickens; fisheries production (2006) 866,083 (roughly 60% of Morocco's fisheries production comes from Atlantic waters off Western Sahara) (from aquaculture, negligible). Mining and quarrying (2006): phosphate rock 28,000,000; barite 612,800; zinc (metal content) 72,600; lead (metal content) 45,000; cobalt (metal content) 1,100; silver 245,700 kg. Manufacturing (value added in US$'000,000; 2004): food products 1,130; wearing apparel 733; tobacco products 595. Energy production (consumption): electricity (kW-hr; 2007) 19,116,000,000 ([2005] 20,057,-000,000); coal (metric tons; 2005) none (6,750,-000);. crude petroleum (barrels; 2007) 81,000 ([2005] 51,500,000); petroleum products (metric tons; 2005) 5,815,000 (7,481,000); natural gas (cu m; 2007) 61,000,000 ([2005] 460,000,000). **Selected balance of payments data.** Receipts from (US$'000,000): tourism (2006) 5,984; remittances (2007) 5,700; foreign direct investment (FDI) (2004–06 avg.) 2,305; official development assistance (2006) 1,046. Disbursements for (US$'000,000): tourism (2006) 703; remittances (2007) 41; FDI (2004–06 avg.) 225. **Gross national income** (2007): US$69,352,000,000 (US$2,250 per capita).

Foreign trade

Imports (2006; c.i.f.): DH 204,934,000,000 (mineral fuels 21.6%, of which crude petroleum 12.3%; machinery and apparatus 19.6%; chemical products 9.7%; food products 7.0%; fabrics 6.1%). Major import sources: France 16.5%; Spain 11.6%;

---

1 metric ton = about 1.1 short tons;   1 kilometer = 0.6 mi (statute);   1 metric ton-km cargo = about 0.68 short ton-mi cargo;   c.i.f.: cost, insurance, and freight;   f.o.b.: free on board

Saudi Arabia 6.8%; Italy 6.4%; China 5.4%. **Exports** (2006; f.o.b.): DH 110,219,000,000 (wearing apparel and accessories 25.8%; fish, shrimp, and octopuses 9.3%; inorganic chemicals 8.2%; vegetables and fruit 6.8%; equipment for distributing electricity 6.7%; additionally, cannabis is an important illegal export; Morocco was the world's largest producer in 2005). *Major export destinations:* France 28.4%; Spain 20.8%; UK 6.0%; Italy 4.9%; India 4.3%.

Transport and communications

Transport. *Railroads* (2004): route length 1,907 km; passenger-km 2,645,000,000; metric ton-km cargo 5,563,000,000. *Roads* (2004): total length 56,987 km (paved 61%). *Vehicles:* passenger cars (2002) 1,326,108; trucks and buses (2000) 415,700. *Air transport* (Royal Air Maroc only; 2006): passenger-km 8,643,000,000; metric ton-km cargo 72,000,-000. **Communications,** in total units (units per 1,000 persons). Telephone landlines (2007): 2,394,000 (75); cellular telephone subscribers (2007): 20,029,-000 (632); personal computers (2005): 740,000 (24); total Internet users (2007): 7,300,000 (230); broadband Internet subscribers (2007): 477,000 (15).

Education and health

Educational attainment (2004). Percentage of population ages 10 and over having: no formal schooling through incomplete primary education 45.5%; complete primary 40.8%; secondary 8.7%; higher 5.0%. **Literacy** (2005): percentage of total population ages 16 and over literate 53.5%; males literate 65.5%; females literate 41.5%. **Health** (2004): physicians 16,775 (1 per 1,778 persons); hospital beds (public hospitals only) 26,136 (1 per 1,141 persons); infant mortality rate per 1,000 live births (2005) 41.6; undernourished population (2002–04) 1,800,000 (6% of total population based on the consumption of a minimum daily requirement of 1,870 calories).

Military

Total active duty personnel (2007): 195,800 (army 89.4%, navy 4.0%, air force 6.6%). **Military expenditure as percentage of GDP** (2005): 4.5%; per capita expenditure US$77.

Background

The Berbers entered Morocco near the end of the 2nd millennium BC. Phoenicians established trading posts along the Mediterranean during the 12th century BC, and Carthage had settlements along the Atlantic in the 5th century BC. After the fall of Carthage, Morocco became a loyal ally of Rome, and in AD 42 it was annexed by Rome as part of the province of Mauretania. It was invaded by Muslims in the 7th century. Beginning in the mid-11th century, the Almoravids, Almohads, and Marinids ruled successively. After the fall of the Marinids in the mid-15th century, the Sa'dis ruled for a century beginning in 1550. The French fought Morocco over the Algerian boundary in the 1840s, and the Spanish seized part of Moroccan territory in 1859. It was a French protectorate from 1912 until its independence in 1956. In the mid-1970s it reasserted claim to the Western Sahara,

and in 1976 Spanish troops withdrew from the region, leaving behind the Algerian-supported Saharan guerrillas of the Polisario movement. Relations with Mauritania and Algeria deteriorated, and fighting over the region continued. Attempts at mediation have repeatedly been made by the international community.

Recent Developments

Negotiations in 2008 between Morocco and the Polisario Front over the disputed region of the Western Sahara did not yield a solution. Though King Muhammad VI supported French Pres. Nicolas Sarkozy's initiative for the establishment of a Union for the Mediterranean, he did not attend the inaugural conference in July in Paris, irritated over French overtures to Algeria (where Polisario camps housed Saharawi refugees). In March 2009 Morocco severed diplomatic ties to Iran over alleged meddling in Morocco's religious affairs.

Internet resources:
<www.visitmorocco.com/index.php/eng>.

Mozambique

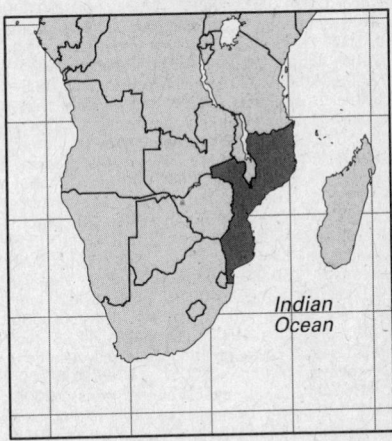

Indian Ocean

Official name: República de Moçambique (Republic of Mozambique). **Form of government:** multiparty republic with a single legislative house (Assembly of the Republic [250]). **Head of state and government:** President Armando Guebuza (from 2005). **Capital:** Maputo. **Official language:** Portuguese. **Official religion:** none. **Monetary unit:** 1 (new) metical (MTn; plural meticais) = 100 centavos; valuation (1 Jul 2009) US$1 = MTn 26.52 (the [new] metical replaced the [old] metical [MT] 1 Jul 2006, at the rate of 1 MTn = MT 1,000).

Demography

Area: 308,642 sq mi, 799,379 sq km. **Population** (2008): 21,285,000. **Density** (2008): persons per sq mi 69.0, persons per sq km 26.6. **Urban** (2007): 36.2%. **Sex distribution** (2007): male 47.67%; female 52.33%. **Age breakdown** (2005):

under 15, 43.1%; 15–29, 26.8%; 30–44, 16.5%; 45–59, 9.0%; 60–74, 3.9%; 75 and over, 0.7%. **Ethnic composition** (2000): Makuana 15.3%; Makua 14.5%; Tsonga 8.6%; Sena 8.0%; Lomwe 7.1%; Tswa 5.7%; Chwabo 5.5%; other 35.3%. **Religious affiliation** (2005): traditional beliefs 46%; Christian 37%, of which Roman Catholic 19%, Protestant 11%; Muslim 9%; other 8%. **Major cities** (2007): Maputo 1,094,315 (urban agglomeration 1,766,823); Matola 672,508; Nampula 477,900; Beira 431,583; Chimoio 237,278. **Location:** southern Africa, bordering Tanzania, the Indian Ocean, South Africa, Swaziland, Zimbabwe, Zambia, and Malawi.

Vital statistics

Birth rate per 1,000 population (2006): 39.0 (world avg. 20.3). **Death rate** per 1,000 population (2006): 20.7 (world avg. 8.6). **Natural increase rate** per 1,000 population (2006): 18.3 (world avg. 11.7). **Total fertility rate** (avg. births per childbearing woman; 2006): 5.35. **Life expectancy** at birth (2006): male 41.2 years; female 40.4 years.

National economy

Budget (2004). *Revenue:* MT 26,891,000,000,000 (tax revenue 58.0%, of which VAT 23.9%, income tax 9.0%, taxes on international trade 8.5%; grants 37.4%; nontax revenue 4.6%). *Expenditures:* MT 32,602,000,000,000 (current expenditures 58.3%; capital expenditures 38.5%; net lending 3.2%). **Public debt** (external, outstanding; 2006): US$2,511,000,000. **Production** (metric tons except as noted). *Agriculture and fishing* (2007): cassava 7,350,000, sugarcane 2,650,000, corn (maize) 1,579,400; livestock (number of live animals) 1,330,000 cattle, 393,000 goats, 28,500,000 chickens; fisheries production (2006) 43,710 (from aquaculture 3%). *Mining and quarrying* (2006): limestone 750,000; bauxite 12,000; tantalite 240,000 kg; garnet 4,400 kg; gold 68 kg. *Manufacturing* (value added in MT '000,000,000; 2003): aluminum 19,067; beverages 4,773; food products 2,577. *Energy production (consumption):* electricity (kW-hr; 2005) 13,289,000,000 (10,866,000,000); coal (metric tons; 2005) 41,000 (26,000); petroleum products (metric tons; 2005) none (478,000); natural gas (cu m; 2005) 2,256,000,000 (73,191,000). **Population economically active** (2003): total 8,981,000; activity rate 47.1% (participation rates: ages 15–64, 84.4%; female 53.8%; unemployed, n.a.). **Gross national income** (2007): US$6,787,000,000 (US$320 per capita). **Selected balance of payments data.** Receipts from (US$'000,000): tourism (2006) 140; remittances (2007) 80; foreign direct investment (2004–06 avg.) 169; official development assistance (2006) 1,611. Disbursements for (US$'000,000): tourism (2006) 179; remittances (2007) 26.

Foreign trade

Imports (2006): US$2,869,000,000 (machinery and apparatus 14.5%; refined petroleum products 13.1%; food products 11.4%, of which cereals 6.7%; motor vehicles 9.4%). *Major import sources:* South Africa 37.4%; The Netherlands 15.8%; India 4.6%; UAE 4.2%; US 3.5%. **Exports** (2006): US$2,381,000,000 (aluminum 58.9%; food products 10.2%, of which shrimp 3.6%; electricity 7.5%; natural gas 4.6%; tobacco 4.6%). *Major export destinations:* The Netherlands 59.7%; South Africa 14.1%; Zimbabwe 3.2%; Switzerland 2.2%.

Transport and communications

Transport. *Railroads* (2003): route length (2002) 3,123 km; passenger-km 167,000,000; metric ton-km cargo 1,362,000,000. *Roads* (2000): total length 30,400 km (paved 19%). *Vehicles* (2001): passenger cars 81,600; trucks and buses 76,000. *Air transport* (LAM [Linhas Aéreas de Moçambique] only; 2007): passenger-km 440,000,000; metric ton-km cargo 6,000,000. **Communications,** in total units (units per 1,000 persons). Telephone landlines (2006): 67,000 (3.3); cellular telephone subscribers (2007): 3,300,000 (154); personal computers (2005): 283,000 (14); total Internet users (2007): 200,000 (9.3).

Education and health

Educational attainment (1997). Percentage of population ages 15 and over having: no formal schooling/unknown 79.0%; primary education 18.4%; secondary 2.0%; technical 0.4%; higher 0.2%. **Literacy** (2007): percentage of total population ages 15 and over literate 53.0%; males literate 67.9%; females literate 38.6%. **Health:** physicians (2003) 635 (1 per 30,525 persons); hospital beds (2003) 16,493 (1 per 1,175 persons); infant mortality rate per 1,000 live births (2006) 112.1; undernourished population (2002–04) 8,300,000 (44% of total population based on the consumption of a minimum daily requirement of 1,890 calories).

Military

Total active duty personnel (2008): 11,200 (army 89.3%, navy 1.8%, air force 8.9%). **Military expenditure as percentage of GDP** (2007): 0.7%; per capita expenditure US$3.

Background

Mozambique was settled by Bantu peoples about the 3rd century AD. Arab traders occupied the coastal region from the 14th century, and the Portuguese controlled the area from the early 16th century. The slave trade later became an important part of the economy. In the late 19th century private trading companies began to administer parts of the inland areas. It became an overseas province of Portugal in 1951. After years of war beginning in the 1960s, the country was granted independence in 1975. It was wracked by civil war in the 1970s and '80s. In 1990 a new constitution was promulgated, and a peace treaty was signed with the rebels in 1992. The first multiparty elections were held two years later.

1 metric ton = about 1.1 short tons; 1 kilometer = 0.6 mi (statute); 1 metric ton-km cargo = about 0.68 short ton-mi cargo; c.i.f.: cost, insurance, and freight; f.o.b.: free on board

Recent Developments

Following the unexpected return in May 2008 of some 26,000 Mozambicans from South Africa, a state of emergency was called. The local population in South Africa had turned on foreign workers, who, they believed, were taking jobs from South African nationals. Buildings were burned and immigrants driven from their homes, and at least 56 people, most of them Mozambicans, were killed.

Internet resources: <www.moztour.com>.

Myanmar (Burma)

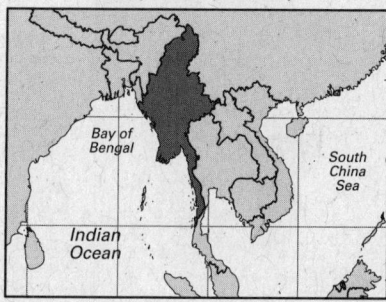

Official name: Pyidaungzu Myanma Naingngandaw (Union of Myanmar). **Form of government:** military regime. **Head of state and government:** Chairman of the State Peace and Development Council Gen. Than Shwe (from 1997), assisted by Prime Minister Thein Sein (from 2007). **Capital:** Naypyidaw (Nay Pyi Taw). **Official language:** Burmese. **Official religion:** none. **Monetary unit:** 1 Myanmar kyat (K) = 100 pyas; valuation (1 Jul 2009) US$1 = K 6.31.

Did you know? Myanmar was one of the first areas in Southeast Asia to receive Buddhism, and by the 11th century it had become the center of the Theravada branch. Almost 90% of the population practices Buddhism.

Demography

Area: 261,228 sq mi, 676,577 sq km. **Population** (2008): 47,758,000. **Density** (2008): persons per sq mi 182.8, persons per sq km 70.6. **Urban** (2005): 30.6%. **Sex distribution** (2006): male 49.48%; female 50.52%. **Age breakdown** (2006): under 15, 26.5%; 15–29, 29.2%; 30–44, 23.1%; 45–59, 13.5%; 60–74, 6.1%; 75–84, 1.4%; 85 and over, 0.2%. **Ethnic composition** (2000): Burman 55.9%; Karen 9.5%; Shan 6.5%; Han Chinese 2.5%; Mon 2.3%; Yangbye 2.2%; Kachin 1.5%; other 19.6%. **Religious affiliation** (2005): Buddhist 74%; Protestant 6%; Muslim 3%; Hindu 2%; traditional beliefs 11%; other 4%. **Major urban agglomerations** (2007): Yangon (Rangoon) 4,088,000; Mandalay 961,000;

Naypyidaw (Nay Pyi Taw) 930,000; Mawlamyine (Moulmein; city, 2004) 405,800; Pathein (Bassein; city, 2004) 215,600. **Location:** southeastern Asia, bordering China, Laos, Thailand, the Andaman Sea, the Bay of Bengal, Bangladesh, and India.

Vital statistics

Birth rate per 1,000 population (2006): 17.7 (world avg. 20.3). **Death rate** per 1,000 population (2006): 9.4 (world avg. 8.6). **Total fertility rate** (avg. births per childbearing woman; 2006): 1.98. **Life expectancy** at birth (2006): male 59.9 years; female 64.4 years.

National economy

Budget (2002–03). *Revenue:* K 279,377,000,000 (nontax revenue 59.6%; tax revenue 40.3%, of which taxes on goods and services 22.1%, income tax 16.3%; foreign grants 0.1%). *Expenditures:* K 353,389,000,000 (economic affairs 31.4%; public services 23.4%; defense 21.5%; education 14.6%). **Public debt** (external, outstanding; 2006): US$5,234,000,000. **Production** (metric tons except as noted). *Agriculture and fishing* (2007): rice 32,610,000, sugarcane 7,450,000, sesame seeds 600,000, pigeon peas 540,000, sunflower seeds 365,000, chickpeas 225,000; livestock (number of live animals) 12,500,000 cattle, 6,300,000 pigs, 94,500,000 chickens; fisheries production (2006) 2,581,780 (from aquaculture 22%). *Mining and quarrying* (2006): copper (metal content; 2005) 34,500; jade 20,647,000 kg; rubies 1,685,000 carats; spinel 908,000 carats; sapphires 423,000 carats. *Manufacturing* (value added in US$'000,-000; 2003): tobacco products (2002) 1,320; non-electrical machinery and apparatus 728; transportation equipment 483. *Energy production (consumption):* electricity (kW-hr; 2005) 6,015,-000,000 (6,015,000,000); coal (metric tons; 2005) 993,000 (124,000); lignite (metric tons; 2005) 367,000 (72,000); crude petroleum (barrels; 2006) 7,675,000 ([2005] 5,153,000); petroleum products (metric tons; 2005) 645,000 (1,844,000); natural gas (cu m; 2006) 12,502,000,000 ([2005] 2,526,000,000). **Selected balance of payments data.** Receipts from (US$'000,000): tourism (2006) 46; remittances (2007) 125; foreign direct investment (2004–06 avg.) 210; official development assistance (2006) 147. Disbursements for (US$'000,000): tourism (2006) 37; remittances (2007) 32. **Population economically active** (2003): total 26,361,000; activity rate of total population 53.3% (participation rates: ages 15–64, 78.7%; female 44.9%; unemployed [2006] 10.2%).

Foreign trade

Imports (2006–07; c.i.f.): K 16,835,000,000 (mineral fuels 24.8%; nonelectrical machinery and transportation equipment 15.9%; base and fabricated metals 7.0%; synthetic fabrics 6.5%). *Major import sources:* Singapore 36.5%; China 24.4%; Thailand 10.3%; India 5.3%; Japan 4.9%. **Exports** (2006–07; f.o.b.): K 30,026,000,000 (natural gas 42.6%; pulses [mostly beans] 11.1%; hardwood 10.0%, of which teak 6.0%; garments 5.3%). *Major export destinations:* Thailand 48.9%; India 13.7%; Hong Kong 8.2%; China 7.9%; Singapore 3.5%.

Transport and communications

Transport. *Railroads* (2006): route length (2004) 3,955 km; passenger-km 5,263,000,000; metric ton-km cargo 829,000,000. *Roads* (1999): total length 27,966 km (paved 11%). *Vehicles* (2006): passenger cars 203,441; trucks and buses 74,037. *Air transport* (2006): passenger-km 124,697,000; metric ton-km cargo 245,000,000. **Communications,** in total units (units per 1,000 persons). Telephone landlines (2005): 504,000 (9.3); cellular telephone subscribers (2006): 214,000 (4.2); personal computers (2005): 400,000 (8.6); total Internet users (2007): 40,000 (0.8); broadband Internet subscribers (2007): 1,500.

Education and health

Literacy (2003): percentage of total population ages 15 and over literate 89.7%; males literate 93.7%; females literate 86.2%. **Health** (2004–05): physicians 17,564 (1 per 2,660 persons); hospital beds 34,654 (1 per 1,350 persons); infant mortality rate per 1,000 live births (2006) 52.3; undernourished population (2002–04) 2,400,000 (5% of total population based on the consumption of a minimum daily requirement of 1,820 calories).

Military

Total active duty personnel (2007): 513,250 (army 73.1%, navy 3.1%, air force 2.9%, paramilitary [people's militia and people's police] 20.9%). **Military expenditure as percentage of GDP** (2004): 7.6%.

Background

Myanmar, until 1989 known as Burma, has long been inhabited, with the Mon and Pyu states dominant between the 1st century BC and the 9th century AD. It was united in the 11th century under a Burmese dynasty that was overthrown by the Mongols in the 13th century. The Portuguese, Dutch, and English traded there in the 16th–17th centuries. The modern Burmese state was founded in the 18th century. It fell to the British in 1885 and became a province of India. It was occupied by Japan in World War II and became independent in 1948. A military coup took power in 1962 and nationalized major economic sectors. Civilian unrest in the 1980s led to antigovernment rioting. In 1990 opposition parties won in national elections, but the army remained in control. Trying to negotiate for a freer government amid the unrest, Aung San Suu Kyi, the National League for Democracy leader, was awarded the Nobel Peace Prize in 1991. She spent extended periods of the 1990s and 2000s under house arrest.

Recent Developments

Tragedy struck in early May 2008 when Cyclone Nargis swept across Myanmar's Irrawaddy delta, leaving more than 138,000 dead or missing and causing more than US$4 billion in damages. The economy remained weak, with real GDP growth estimated at 0.9% and inflation at 27.7%, owing partly to the surge in food prices in the wake of the cyclone. On the positive side, export revenues were buoyant at US$3.5 billion, largely as a result of exports of oil, natural gas, and gems.

Internet resources:
<www.myanmar-tourism.com>.

Namibia

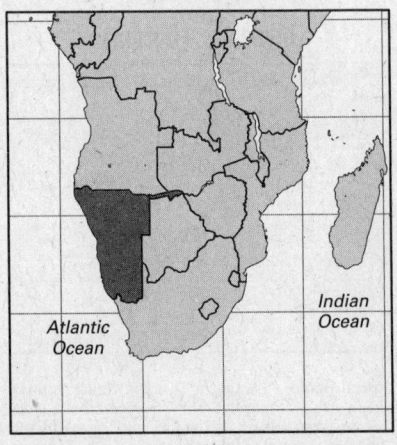

Atlantic Ocean   *Indian Ocean*

Official name: Republic of Namibia. **Form of government:** republic with two legislative houses (National Council [26]; National Assembly [78]). **Head of state and government:** President Hifikepunye Pohamba (from 2005). **Capital:** Windhoek. **Official language:** English. **Official religion:** none. **Monetary unit:** 1 Namibian dollar (N$) = 100 cents; valuation (1 Jul 2009) US$1 = N$7.63.

Demography

Area: 318,193 sq mi, 824,116 sq km. **Population** (2008): 2,089,000. **Density** (2008): persons per sq mi 6.6, persons per sq km 2.5. **Urban** (2007): 36.3%. **Sex distribution** (2006): male 50.13%; female 49.87%. **Age breakdown** (2006): under 15, 38.2%; 15–29, 31.3%; 30–44, 15.6%; 45–59, 9.2%; 60–74, 4.5%; 75 and over, 1.2%. **Ethnic composition** (2000): Ovambo 34.4%; mixed race (black/white) 14.5%; Kavango 9.1%; Afrikaner 8.1%; San (Bushmen) and Bergdama 7.0%; Herero 5.5%; Nama 4.4%; Kwambi 3.7%; German 2.8%; other 10.5%. **Religious affiliation** (2000): Protestant (mostly Lutheran) 49.3%; Roman Catholic 17.7%; unaffiliated Christian 14.1%; independent Christian 10.8%; traditional beliefs 6.0%; other 2.1%. **Major urban localities** (2006): Windhoek 277,300; Rundu 62,300; Walvis Bay 54,900; Oshakati 34,900; Swakopmund 26,700. **Location:** southwestern Africa, bordering Angola, Zambia,

Botswana, South Africa, and the South Atlantic Ocean.

Vital statistics

Birth rate per 1,000 population (2006): 24.3 (world avg. 20.3). **Death rate** per 1,000 population (2006): 18.9 (world avg. 8.6). **Natural increase rate** per 1,000 population (2006): 5.4 (world avg. 11.7). **Total fertility rate** (avg. births per childbearing woman; 2006): 3.06. **Life expectancy** at birth (2006): male 44.5 years; female 42.3 years.

National economy

Budget (2006–07). *Revenue:* N$16,209,000,000 (tax revenue 90.0%, of which customs duties and excises 39.9%, income tax 28.9%, VAT 19.7%; non-tax revenue and grants 10.0%). *Expenditures:* N$15,287,800,000 (current expenditures 82.0%, of which wages and salaries 40.2%; capital expenditures 18.0%). **Production** (metric tons except as noted). *Agriculture and fishing* (2007): millet 58,000, corn (maize) 40,000, wheat 10,000; livestock (number of live animals) 2,700,000 sheep, 2,500,000 cattle, 2,000,000 goats; fisheries production (2006) 509,445 (from aquaculture, negligible). *Mining and quarrying* (2006): fluorspar 132,249; zinc (metal content) 100,000; lead (metal content) 11,830; copper (metal content) 6,262; uranium oxide 3,617; amethyst 40,000 kg; silver 31,307 kg; gold 2,790 kg; gem diamonds 2,356,000 carats. *Manufacturing* (value added in N$'000,000; 2006): food products 2,633 (of which processed fish 620, processed meat 101); other manufactures (including fur products [from Karakul sheep], textiles, carved wood products, and refined metals) 2,962. *Energy production (consumption):* electricity (kW-hr; 2004) 1,397,000,000 (2,819,-000,000). **Selected balance of payments data.** Receipts from (US$'000,000): tourism (2006) 381; remittances (2007) 17; foreign direct investment (2004–06 avg.) 300; official development assistance (2006) 145. Disbursements for (US$'000,000): tourism (2006) 118; remittances (2007) 20; foreign direct disinvestment (2004–06 avg.) –16. **Population economically active** (2006): total 656,000; activity rate of total population 32.0% (participation rates: ages 16 and over, 54.0%; female 43.4%; officially unemployed 5.3%). **Public debt** (external, outstanding; 2006–07): US$2,526,000,000. **Gross national income** (2007): US$6,970,000,000 (US$3,360 per capita).

Foreign trade

Imports (2006): N$21,719,000,000 (refined petroleum products 18.3%; transportation equipment 16.0%; chemical, rubber, and plastic products 12.1%; food, beverages, and tobacco 11.5%; machinery and apparatus 9.8%). *Major import sources* (2004): South Africa 85.4%; UK 2.6%; Germany 1.9%; China 1.2%; Zimbabwe 0.8%. **Exports** (2006): N$20,605,000,000 (diamonds 33.0%; fish 18.2%; other minerals [mainly gold, zinc, copper, lead, and silver] 12.4%; refined zinc 12.2%; meat preparations [mostly beef] 7.8%). *Major export destinations* (2004): South Africa 27.8%; UK 14.9%; Angola 13.8%; US 11.0%; Spain 9.6%.

Transport and communications

Transport. *Railroads:* route length (2006) 2,382 km; passenger-km (1995–96) 48,300,000; metric ton-km (2003–04) 1,247,400. *Roads* (2004): total length 42,237 km (paved 13%). *Vehicles* (2002): passenger cars 82,580; trucks and buses 81,002. *Air transport* (Air Namibia only; 2006): passenger-km 1,588,466,000; metric ton-km cargo (2005) 60,429,000. **Communications,** in total units (units per 1,000 persons). Telephone landlines (2007): 138,000 (67); cellular telephone subscribers (2007): 800,000 (386); personal computers (2004): 220,000 (109); total Internet users (2007): 101,000 (49); broadband Internet subscribers (2007): 300.

Education and health

Educational attainment (2000). Percentage of population ages 25 and over having: no formal schooling/unknown 26.5%; incomplete primary education 25.5%; complete primary 8.0%; incomplete secondary 24.9%; complete secondary 11.4%; higher 3.7%. **Literacy** (2007): percentage of total population ages 15 and over literate 86.6%; males literate 86.5%; females literate 86.7%. **Health:** physicians (2004) 598 (1 per 3,201 persons); hospital beds (public sector only; 2004–05) 6,811 (1 per 283 persons); infant mortality rate per 1,000 live births (2006) 48.1; undernourished population (2002–04) 450,000 (24% of total population based on the consumption of a minimum daily requirement of 1,830 calories).

Military

Total active duty personnel (2007): 9,200 (army 97.8%, navy 2.2%). **Military expenditure as percentage of GDP** (2005): 3.2%; per capita expenditure US$92.

Background

Long inhabited by indigenous peoples, Namibia was explored by the Portuguese in the late 15th century. In 1884 it was annexed by Germany as German South West Africa. It was captured in World War I by South Africa, which received it as a mandate from the League of Nations in 1920 and refused to give it up after World War II. A UN resolution in 1966 ending the mandate was challenged by South Africa in the 1970s and '80s. Through long negotiations involving many factions and interests, Namibia achieved independence in 1990.

Recent Developments

A strike at TransNamib in 2008 crippled road and rail transport before the Labour Court ordered the striking workers to return to work. In April 2008 a 16th-century Portuguese trading ship that had lain undisturbed for hundreds of years on Namibia's "Skeleton Coast" was unearthed in mining operations. Although negatively affected by the global economic crisis, Namibia saw its inflation rate drop to a 19-month low in June 2009.

Internet resources:
<www.npc.gov.na/cbs/index.htm>.

Nauru

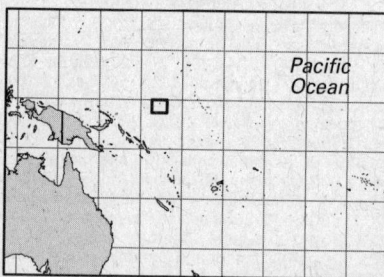

Pacific Ocean

Official name: Naoero (Republic of Nauru). **Form of government:** republic with one legislative house (Parliament [18]). **Head of state and government:** President Marcus Stephen (from 2007). **Capital:** government offices are located in Yaren district. **Official language:** none (Nauruan is the national language; English is the language of business and government). **Official religion:** none. **Monetary unit:** 1 Nauruan dollar ($N) = 1 Australian dollar ($A) = 100 Nauruan and Australian cents; valuation (1 Jul 2009) US$1 = $A 1.24.

Demography

Area: 8.2 sq mi, 21.2 sq km. **Population (2008):** 10,200. **Density (2008):** persons per sq mi 1,244, persons per sq km 481.1. **Urban (2006):** urban 100%. **Sex distribution (2005):** male 50.11%; female 49.89%. **Age breakdown (2005):** under 15, 37.5%; 15–29, 29.5%; 30–44, 17.8%; 45–59, 11.8%; 60–74, 3.1%; 75 and over, 0.3%. **Ethnic composition (2006):** Nauruan 95.8%; Kiribertese (Gilbertese) 1.5%; Asian 1.4%; other Pacific Islander 0.3%; other/unknown 1.0%. **Religious affiliation (2005):** Protestant 49%, of which Congregational 29%; Roman Catholic 24%; Chinese folk-religionist 10%; other 17%. **Major cities:** none; population of Yaren urban area (2007) 4,616. **Location:** Oceania, island in the western Pacific Ocean, near the equator east of Papua New Guinea.

Vital statistics

Birth rate per 1,000 population (2005): 25.1 (world avg. 20.3). **Death rate** per 1,000 population (2005): 6.8 (world avg. 8.6). **Natural increase rate** per 1,000 population (2005): 18.3 (world avg. 11.7). **Total fertility rate** (avg. births per childbearing woman; 2005): 3.19. **Life expectancy** at birth (2005): male 59.2 years; female 66.5 years.

National economy

Budget (2006). *Revenue:* $A 20,905,000 (grants 46.4%; property income 36.7%; sales of goods and services 10.4%). *Expenditures:* $A 25,935,000. **Total public and private external debt (2006):** US$249,000,000. **Gross national income** (at current market prices; 2007): US$32,240,000 (US$3,176

per capita). **Production** (metric tons except as noted). *Agriculture and fishing* (2007): coconuts 1,800, vegetables 500 (tropical fruit, coffee, almonds, figs, and pandanus are also cultivated); livestock (number of live animals) 2,900 pigs, 5,000 chickens; fisheries production (2006) 39 (from aquaculture, none). *Mining and quarrying* (2007): phosphate rock (gross weight including basic slag and guano) 45,000 (phosphate extraction, the backbone of the Nauruan economy, halted in 2003 but resumed in 2006; expect phosphate extraction for the next 5 years [on the surface] to 20 years [from the subsurface] using processing refurbishments). *Manufacturing:* none; virtually all consumer manufactures are imported. *Energy production (consumption):* electricity (kW-hr; 2005) 32,000,000 (32,000,000); petroleum products (metric tons; 2005) none (46,000). **Population economically active (2002):** 3,280; activity rate of total population 32.6% (participation rates: ages 16 and over, 76.7%; female 45.5%; unemployed 22.7%). **Selected balance of payments data.** Receipts from (US$'000,000): foreign direct investment (2004–06 avg.) 1.0; official development assistance (2006) 17.

Foreign trade

Imports (2005–06): $A 32,300,000 (mostly personal material needs). *Major import sources (2005):* South Korea 48%; Australia 36%; US 6%; Germany 5%. **Exports (2005–06):** $A 1,500,000 (phosphate, virtually 100% [coral gravel, a by-product of phosphate extraction, was exported in 2008]). *Major export destinations (2005):* South Korea 30%; Canada 24%.

Transport and communications

Transport. *Railroads* (2001): length 5 km. *Roads* (2004): total length 40 km (paved 73%). *Air transport* (2001): passenger-km 287,000,000; metric ton-km cargo 29,000,000. **Communications,** in total units (units per 1,000 persons). Telephone landlines (2003): 1,600 (160); cellular telephone subscribers (2003): 1,300 (130).

Education and health

Educational attainment (2002). Percentage of population ages 6 and over having: primary education 4.9%; secondary 88.5%; higher 3.3%; unknown 3.3%. **Literacy (2004):** percentage of total population ages 15 and over literate 97%. **Health (2004):** physicians 5 (1 per 2,012 persons); hospital beds 60 (1 per 168 persons); infant mortality rate per 1,000 live births (2005) 10.0.

Military

Total active duty personnel (2007): none. Nauru does not have any military establishment. The defense is assured by Australia, but no formal agreement exists.

Background

Nauru was inhabited by Pacific islanders when British explorers arrived in 1798. Annexed by Ger-

1 metric ton = about 1.1 short tons;   *1 kilometer = 0.6 mi (statute);*   *1 metric ton-km cargo = about 0.68 short ton-mi cargo;*   *c.i.f.: cost, insurance, and freight;*   *f.o.b.: free on board*

many in 1888, in 1919 it was placed under a joint mandate of Britain, Australia, and New Zealand. During World War II it was occupied by the Japanese. Made a UN trust territory under Australian administration in 1947, it gained independence in 1968 and became a member of the Commonwealth and the UN in 1999. Nauru once had the world's largest concentration of phosphate and became wealthy from mining and processing it. The deposits have been severely depleted, however, and the economy has been converting to fishing activities.

Recent Developments

In early 2008 a group of Sri Lankan refugees left Nauru for Australia, the last asylum seekers to be detained at Australia's controversial offshore immigration-processing center. Nauru's economy was badly affected by Australia's decision to close the establishment. In July, however, Australia agreed to provide US$27 million in development assistance. Nauru also was once again making money from phosphate mining, as the global food crisis had tripled the price of fertilizer.

Internet resources:
<www.spc.int/prism/country/nr/stats>.

Nepal

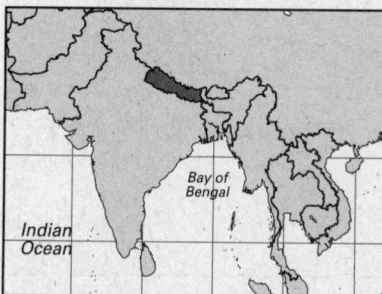

Official name: Sanghiya Loktantrik Ganatantra Nepal (Federal Democratic Republic of Nepal). **Form of government:** multiparty republic with interim legislature (Constituent Assembly [601]). **Chief of state:** President Ram Baran Yadav (from 2008). **Head of government:** Prime Minister Madhav Kumar Nepal (from 2009). **Capital:** Kathmandu. **Official language:** Nepali. **Official religion:** none. **Monetary unit:** 1 Nepalese rupee (NR; plural NRs) = 100 paisa; valuation (1 Jul 2009) US$1 = NRs 75.00.

Demography

Area: 56,827 sq mi, 147,181 sq km. **Population** (2008): 28,757,000. **Density** (2008): persons per sq mi 506.0, persons per sq km 195.4. **Urban** (2006): 16.7%. **Sex distribution** (2007): male 50.10%; female 49.90%. **Age breakdown** (2005): under 15, 39.0%; 15–29, 27.9%; 30–44, 17.2%; 45–59, 10.2%; 60–74, 4.7%; 75–84, 0.9%; 85 and over, 0.1%. **Ethnic composition** (2000):

Nepalese 55.8%; Maithili 10.8%; Bhojpuri 7.9%; Tharu 4.4%; Tamang 3.6%; Newar 3.0%; Awadhi 2.7%; Magar 2.5%; Gurkha 1.7%; other 7.6%. **Religious affiliation** (2001): Hindu 80.6%; Buddhist 10.7%; Muslim 4.2%; Kirat (local traditional belief) 3.6%; Christian 0.5%; other 0.4%. **Major cities** (2001): Kathmandu 671,846; Biratnagar 166,674; Lalitpur 162,991; Pokhara 156,312; Birganj 112,484. **Location:** south-central Asia, bordering China and India.

Mt. Everest, the tallest mountain on Earth at 8,850 m (29,035 feet), is located between Nepal and China on Nepal's northern border.

Vital statistics

Birth rate per 1,000 population (2007): 29.2 (world avg. 20.3). **Death rate** per 1,000 population (2007): 8.5 (world avg. 8.6). **Natural increase rate** per 1,000 population (2007): 20.7 (world avg. 11.7). **Total fertility rate** (avg. births per childbearing woman; 2007): 3.10. **Life expectancy** at birth (2007): male 63.3 years; female 64.1 years.

National economy

Budget (2006–07). *Revenue:* NRs 87,712,100,000 (tax revenue 81.1%, of which VAT 29.8%, customs duties 19.0%, corporate taxes 13.2%; nontax revenue 18.9%). *Expenditures:* NRs 125,323,600,000 (current expenditures 59.1%; capital expenditures 25.8%). **Public debt** (external, outstanding; July 2007): US$3,263,200,000. **Production** (metric tons except as noted). *Agriculture and fishing* (2007): rice 3,680,839, sugarcane 2,599,789, potatoes 1,943,246, ginger 158,905, mustard seed 141,000; livestock (number of live animals) 7,847,624 goats, 7,044,279 cattle, 4,366,813 buffalo; fisheries production (2006) 45,425 (from aquaculture 56%). *Mining and quarrying* (2006): limestone 402,130; marble 28,110 sq m; talc 6,648. *Manufacturing* (value added in US$'000,000; 2002): food products 83; textiles and wearing apparel 73; tobacco products 55. *Energy production (consumption):* electricity (kW-hr; 2005–06) 2,777,400,000 (2,066,400,000); coal (metric tons; 2006) 11,963 ([2005] 309,000); petroleum products (metric tons; 2005) none (704,000). **Gross national income** (2007): US$9,660,000,000 (US$340 per capita). **Population economically active** (2003): total 9,981,000; activity rate of total population 38.3% (participation rates: ages 15–64, 66.3%; female 41.0%; unofficially unemployed [2004] 42%). **Selected balance of payments data.** Receipts from (US$'000,000): tourism (2006) 128; remittances (2007) 1,734; foreign direct disinvestment (2004–06 avg.) −2.0; official development assistance (2006) 514. Disbursements for (US$'000,000): tourism (2006) 185; remittances (2007) 79.

Foreign trade

Imports (2006–07; c.i.f.): NRs 191,709,000,000 (basic manufactures [including fabrics, yarns, and made-up articles] 24.8%; mineral fuels [mostly refined petroleum products] 19.0%; machinery and transportation equipment 18.6%; chemical products 13.5%). *Major import sources* (2006): India 48%; China 13%; UAE 12%; Saudi Arabia 5%; Kuwait 4%. **Exports** (2006–07; f.o.b.): NRs 60,796,000,000 (ready-made garments 9.8%; woolen carpets 9.2%; vegetable ghee 6.8%; thread 6.7%; zinc sheets 5.9; jute goods 4.5%). *Major export destinations* (2006): India 58%; US 14%; Germany 6%; UK 3%; France 2%.

Transport and communications

Transport. *Railroads* (2006): route length 59 km; passengers carried (2002) 1,600,000; freight handled 22,000 metric tons. *Roads* (2006): total length 17,433 km (paved 29%). *Vehicles* (2006): passenger cars 83,369; trucks and buses 49,700. *Air transport:* passenger-km (2003) 652,000,000; metric ton-km cargo (2005) 7,000,000. **Communications,** in total units (units per 1,000 persons). Telephone landlines (2007): 766,000 (27); cellular telephone subscribers (2006): 1,157,000 (42); personal computers (2005): 132,000 (4.9); total Internet users (2007): 337,000 (12); broadband Internet subscribers (2007): 14,000 (0.5).

Education and health

Educational attainment (2005–06). Percentage of population having: unknown through literacy 15.4%; primary education 22.0%; secondary 44.0%; higher 18.6%. **Literacy** (2003–04): percentage of total population ages 15 and over literate 48.0%; males literate 64.5%; females literate 33.8%. **Health** (2006): physicians (public health system only) 1,259 (1 per 21,737 persons); hospital beds 9,881 (1 per 2,801 persons); infant mortality rate per 1,000 live births (2007) 48.0; undernourished population (2002–04) 4,400,000 (17% of total population based on the consumption of a minimum daily requirement of 1,810 calories).

Military

Total active duty personnel (2007): 69,000 (army 100%). **Military expenditure as percentage of GDP** (2005): 2.1%; per capita expenditure US$6.

Background

Nepal developed under early Buddhist influence, and dynastic rule dates from about the 4th century AD. It was formed into a single kingdom in 1769 and fought border wars with China, Tibet, and British India in the 18th–19th centuries. Its independence was recognized by Britain in 1923. A new constitution in 1990 restricted royal authority and accepted a democratically elected parliamentary government. The Communist Party of Nepal (Maoist) began an armed insurgency in 1996. Nepal signed trade agreements with India in 1997. On 1 Jun 2001, King Birendra, the queen, and seven other members of the royal family were fatally shot by Crown Prince Dipendra, who then

turned the gun on himself. After a historic vote by a constituent assembly in 2008, the monarchy was abolished and Nepal became a multiparty republic.

Recent Developments

The Maoists emerged as the largest single party after Nepal's election for its new Constituent Assembly (CA) in April 2008. At its first meeting, the CA dissolved the 240-year-old monarchy. Pushpa Kamal Dahal of the Maoists—popularly known as Prachanda—was elected prime minister, and the CA elected Ram Baran Yadav the first president of Nepal. Prachanda resigned in May 2009, however, after Yadav reversed the government's firing of the army chief, who had refused to integrate former Maoist rebels into the military. Violent protests continued in mid-2009.

Internet resources: <www.welcomenepal.com>.

Netherlands, The

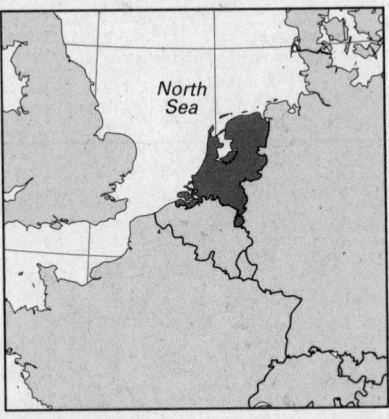

North Sea

Official name: Koninkrijk der Nederlanden (Kingdom of The Netherlands). **Form of government:** constitutional monarchy with a parliament (States General) comprising two legislative houses (Senate [75]; House of Representatives [150]). **Chief of state:** Queen Beatrix (from 1980). **Head of government:** Prime Minister Jan Peter Balkenende (from 2002). **Capital:** Amsterdam. **Seat of government:** The Hague. **Official language:** Dutch. **Official religion:** none. **Monetary unit:** 1 euro (€) = 100 cents; valuation (1 Jul 2009) US$1 = €0.71.

Demography

Area: 16,034 sq mi, 41,528 sq km. **Population** (2008): 16,433,000. **Density** (2008): persons per sq mi 1,260, persons per sq km 486.4. **Urban** (2005): 80.2%. **Sex distribution** (2006): male 49.45%; female 50.55%. **Age breakdown** (2005):

---

1 metric ton = about 1.1 short tons;   1 kilometer = 0.6 mi (statute);   1 metric ton-km cargo = about 0.68 short ton-mi cargo;   c.i.f.: cost, insurance, and freight;   f.o.b.: free on board

under 15, 18.3%; 15–29, 18.1%; 30–44, 23.0%; 45–59, 21.3%; 60–74, 12.9%; 75–84, 4.9%; 85 and over, 1.5%. **Ethnic composition** (by place of origin [including 2nd generation]; 2005): Netherlander 80.7%; Indonesian 2.4%; Turkish 2.2%; Surinamese 2.0%; Moroccan 2.0%; other 10.7%. **Religious affiliation** (2004): Roman Catholic 30%; Reformed/Lutheran tradition 20%; Muslim 6%; nonreligious/atheist 40%; other 4%. **Major urban agglomerations** (2007): Amsterdam 1,482,287; Rotterdam 1,169,800; The Hague 997,323; Utrecht 592,463; Haarlem 407,521. **Location:** northwestern Europe, bordering the North Sea, Germany, and Belgium.

Vital statistics

Birth rate per 1,000 population (2007): 11.1 (world avg. 20.3); within marriage 60.5%; outside of marriage 39.5%. **Death rate** per 1,000 population (2007): 8.1 (world avg. 8.6). **Total fertility rate** (avg. births per childbearing woman; 2007): 1.72. **Life expectancy** at birth (2006): male 77.6 years; female 81.9 years.

National economy

Budget (2007). *Revenue:* €261,628,000,000 (social security contributions 31.3%; indirect taxes 28.3%; direct taxes 26.0%; nontax revenue 7.3%). *Expenditures:* €259,526,000,000 (current expenditures 92.3%, of which social security and welfare 45.3%; development expenditures 7.7%). **National debt** (2006): US$322,400,000,000. **Production** (metric tons except as noted). *Agriculture and fishing* (2007): potatoes 7,200,000, sugar beets 5,400,000, wheat 990,000, flowering bulbs and tubers 80,000 acres (32,400 hectares), of which tulips 27,200 acres (11,000 hectares), cut flowers/plants under glass 10,900 acres (4,400 hectares); livestock (number of live animals) 11,663,000 pigs, 3,763,000 cattle, 1,369,000 sheep; fisheries production (2006) 479,280 (from aquaculture 9%). *Manufacturing* (value added in €'000,000; 2002): food, beverages, and tobacco 12,936; chemical products 7,542; printing and publishing 5,743. *Energy production (consumption):* electricity (kW-hr; 2005) 96,366,000,000 (95,556,-000,000); coal (metric tons; 2005) negligible (13,009,000); crude petroleum (barrels; 2005) 10,578,000 (385,133,000); petroleum products (metric tons; 2005) 64,640,000 (27,433,000); natural gas (cu m; 2005) 82,707,000,000 (51,924,-000,000). **Gross national income** (2007): US$750,-526,000,000 (US$45,820 per capita). **Population economically active** (2005): total 8,308,000; activity rate of total population 51% (participation rates: ages 15–64, 75.1%; female 45.1%; unemployed [April 2005–March 2006] 6.3%). **Selected balance of payments data.** Receipts from (US$'000,000): tourism (2006) 11,381; remittances (2007) 3,004; foreign direct investment (FDI) (2004–06 avg.) 15,983. Disbursements for (US$'000,000): tourism (2006) 17,087; remittances (2007) 7,650; FDI (2004–06 avg.) 64,063.

Foreign trade

Imports (2006; c.i.f.): €264,236,000,000 (machinery and apparatus 28.5%, of which office machinery and computers 12.5%; mineral fuels 17.8%, of which

crude petroleum 8.7%; chemical products 12.6%; food products 7.0%). *Major import sources:* Germany 18.1%; Belgium 10.3%; US 8.8%; China 8.7%; UK 6.2%. **Exports** (2006; f.o.b.): €295,094,000,000 (machinery and apparatus 26.7%, of which office machinery and computers 11.0%; chemical products 17.0%; food products 10.5%; refined petroleum products 8.6%). *Major export destinations:* Germany 24.2%; Belgium 11.9%; UK 8.6%; France 8.2%; US 5.4%.

Transport and communications

Transport. *Railroads* (2006): length 2,797 km; passenger-km (2004) 14,097,000,000; metric ton-km cargo (2001) 4,293,000,000. *Roads* (2006): total length 134,981 km (paved 90%). *Vehicles* (2006): passenger cars 7,230,178; trucks and buses 1,064,846. *Air transport* (2007): passenger-km 75,012,000,000; metric ton-km cargo 4,735,500,-000. **Communications**, in total units (units per 1,000 persons). Telephone landlines (2007): 7,334,000 (447); cellular telephone subscribers (2005): 15,834,000 (971); personal computers (2005): 12,060,000 (740); total Internet users (2007): 15,000,000 (914); broadband Internet subscribers (2007): 5,507,000 (336).

Education and health

Educational attainment (2004). Percentage of population ages 15–64 having: primary education 9.5%; lower secondary 9.6%; upper secondary 10.7%; vocational 44.0%; higher 25.4%, of which university 9.2%; unknown 0.8%. **Health:** physicians (2003) 50,854 (1 per 319 persons); hospital beds (2003) 81,125 (1 per 200 persons); infant mortality rate per 1,000 live births (2007) 4.1; undernourished population (2002–04) less than 2.5% of total population.

Military

Total active duty personnel (2007): 45,608 (army 40.0%, navy 22.8%, air force 22.2%, military constabulary 15.0%). **Military expenditure as percentage of GDP** (2005): 1.5%; per capita expenditure US$523.

Background

Celtic and Germanic tribes inhabited the Netherlands at the time of the Roman conquest. Under the Romans, trade and industry flourished, but by the mid-3rd century AD Roman power had waned, eroded by resurgent German tribes and the encroachment of the sea. A Germanic invasion (406–07) ended Roman control. The Merovingian dynasty followed the Romans but was supplanted in the 7th century by the Carolingian dynasty, which converted the area to Christianity. After Charlemagne's death in 814, the area was increasingly the target of Viking attacks. It became part of the kingdom of Lotharingia, which established an Imperial Church. In the 12th–14th centuries dike building occurred on a large scale. The dukes of Burgundy gained control in the late 14th century. By the early 16th century the Low Countries were ruled by the Spanish Habsburgs. In 1581 the seven northern provinces, led by Calvinists, declared their independence from Spain, and in 1648, following the Thirty Years' War, Spain recognized Dutch independence. The 17th century was the golden age of Dutch civilization. The Dutch East India Company secured Asian colonies, and the country's standard of living soared. In the 18th century the region was conquered by the French and became the Kingdom of Holland under Napoleon (1806). It remained neutral in World War I and declared neutrality in World War II but was occupied by Germany. It joined NATO in 1949, was a founding member of what is now the European Community, and is part of the EU.

Recent Developments

The Dutch parliament voted in July 2008 to extend the Dutch contribution to the NATO training mission in Iraq, to maintain troops in the EU's force in Bosnia and Herzegovina, and to continue its activities in Afghanistan through 2010. The economy of The Netherlands was stable in 2008, though its strongly international orientation made it vulnerable to the worldwide turbulence in the autumn. Unemployment was low at 3.8%, GDP grew by 2.1%, and the national pension and social security systems remained healthy, though public debt increased by €87 billion (US$123 billion). In light of the aging population and high standards for social services, the government offered financial incentives to individuals who would continue to work after age 62 and to employers who would hire seniors, the long-term unemployed, or those who were disabled. The Netherlands saw its first three-month decrease in the prices of homes in 18 years; the sales volume also dropped dramatically. In response to the international crisis in the banking and financial markets, the government set aside €200 billion (US$272 billion) in guarantees for interbank lending.

Internet resources:
<www.cbs.nl/en-GB/menu/home>.

New Zealand

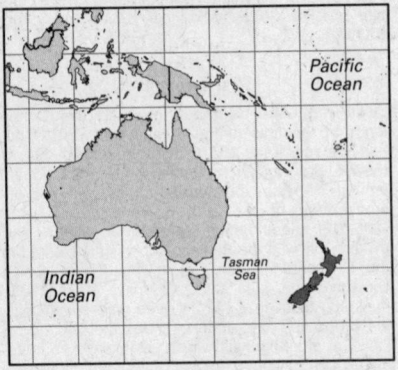

Official name: New Zealand (English); Aotearoa (Maori). **Form of government:** constitutional monar-

chy with one legislative house (House of Representatives [120]). **Chief of state:** British Queen Elizabeth II (from 1952), represented by Governor-General Anand Satyanand (from 2006). **Head of government:** Prime Minister John Key (from 2008). **Capital:** Wellington. **Official languages:** English; Maori. **Official religion:** none. **Monetary unit:** 1 New Zealand dollar (NZ$) = 100 cents; valuation (1 Jul 2009) US$1 = NZ$ 1.55.

Demography

Area: 104,515 sq mi, 270,692 sq km. **Population** (2008): 4,268,000. **Density** (2008): persons per sq mi 40.8, persons per sq km 15.8. **Urban** (2007): 86.0%. **Sex distribution** (2006): male 48.96%; female 51.04%. **Age breakdown** (2006): under 15, 21.1%; 15–29, 20.8%; 30–44, 21.8%; 45–59, 19.5%; 60–74, 11.2%; 75 and over, 5.6%. **Ethnic composition** (2006): European 67.6%, of which New Zealand European 59.1%; Maori (local Polynesian) 14.6%; Asian 9.2%, of which Chinese 3.7%; other Pacific peoples (mostly other Polynesian) 6.9%; other 1.7%. **Religious affiliation** (2006): Christian 51.1%, of which Anglican 13.3%, Roman Catholic 12.2%, Presbyterian 9.2%, Methodist 2.9%, Maori (indigenous) Christian 1.6%; Hindu 1.6%; Buddhist 1.3%; Muslim 1.0%; nonreligious 31.1%; other 13.9%. **Major urban agglomerations** (2008): Auckland 1,313,200; Christchurch 382,200; Wellington 381,900; Hamilton 197,300; Napier 122,600. **Location:** Oceania, islands between the South Pacific Ocean and the Tasman Sea, southeast of Australia.

Vital statistics

Birth rate per 1,000 population (2007): 15.4 (world avg. 20.3); within marriage 52.8%; outside of marriage 47.2%. **Death rate** per 1,000 population (2007): 6.8 (world avg. 8.6). **Total fertility rate** (avg. births per childbearing woman; 2007): 2.17. **Life expectancy** at birth (2004–06): male 77.9 years; female 81.9 years.

National economy

Budget (2004–05). *Revenue:* NZ$51,489,000,000 (tax revenue 91.8%, of which income tax 45.7%, taxes on goods and services 26.7%; nontax revenue 8.0%; grants 0.2%). *Expenditures:* NZ$44,099,000,000 (social protection 35.0%; health 20.0%; education 17.9%; defense 3.0%). **Production** (metric tons except as noted). *Agriculture and fishing* (2007): potatoes 505,000, barley 400,000, apples 380,000, kiwifruit 315,000, grapes 190,000; livestock (number of live animals) 40,000,000 sheep, 9,650,000 cattle; fisheries production (2006) 578,230 (from aquaculture 19%); aquatic plants 225 (from aquaculture, none). *Mining. and quarrying* (2006): limestone/marl 5,032,000; silver 27,221 kg; gold 10,618 kg. *Manufacturing* (value added in US$'000,000; 2005): food products 4,175; fabricated metal products 1,350; printing and publishing 1,250. *Energy production (consumption):* electricity (kW-hr; 2007–08) 42,728,000,000 ([2006] 37,390,000,000); coal (metric tons; 2007–08) 2,178,000 ([2005]

1 metric ton = about 1.1 short tons;   1 kilometer = 0.6 mi (statute);   1 metric ton-km cargo = about 0.68 short ton-mi cargo;   c.i.f.: cost, insurance, and freight;   f.o.b.: free on board

173,000); lignite (metric tons; 2007–08) 2,855,000 ([2005] 4,038,000); crude petroleum (barrels; 2007–08) 20,607,500 ([2005] 33,537,-500); petroleum products (metric tons; 2007–08) 5,187,000 ([2005] 6,266,000); natural gas (cu m; 2007–08) 4,290,200,000 ([2006] 3,700,000,000). **Population economically active** (2007): total 2,235,400; activity rate of total population 52.8% (participation rates: ages 15–64, 76.9%; female 46.3%; unemployed [July 2007–June 2008] 3.6%). **Gross national income** (2007): US$121,708,-000,000 (US$28,780 per capita). **Public debt** (external, outstanding; 2007): n.a. **Selected balance of payments data.** Receipts from (US$'000,000): tourism (2006) 4,563; remittances (2007) 650; foreign direct investment (2004–06 avg.) 4,183. Disbursements for (US$'000,000): tourism (2006) 2,526; remittances (2007) 1,207; foreign direct disinvestment (2004–06 avg.) −287.

Foreign trade

Imports (2006): NZ$40,774,000,000 (machinery and apparatus 21.4%; mineral fuels 14.9%; motor vehicles 11.7%; aircraft 4.2%; plastics 3.8%). *Major import sources:* Australia 20.1%; China 12.2%; US 12.1%; Japan 9.1%; Germany 4.4%. **Exports** (2006): NZ$34,619,000,000 (dairy products 20.6%; beef and sheep meat 12.1%; wood and paper [all forms] 9.4%; machinery and apparatus 8.6%; aluminum 4.3%). *Major export destinations:* Australia 20.5%; US 13.1%; Japan 10.3%; China 5.4%; UK 4.9%.

Transport and communications

Transport. *Railroads* (2006): route length 4,128 km; metric ton-km cargo (1999–2000) 4,040,-000,000. *Roads* (2005): total length 93,148 km (paved 64%). *Vehicles* (2007): passenger cars 2,775,717; trucks and buses 558,412. *Air transport* (Air New Zealand only; 2007): passenger-km 28,423,000,000; metric ton-km cargo 906,000,-000. **Communications,** in total units (units per 1,000 persons). Telephone landlines (2007): 1,747,000 (418); cellular telephone subscribers (2007): 4,251,000 (1,017); personal computers (2005): 2,077,000 (507); total Internet users (2007): 2,260,000 (541); broadband Internet subscribers (2007): 709,000 (170).

Education and health

Educational attainment (2007). Percentage of population ages 15 and over having: no formal schooling through incomplete primary education 26.8%; complete primary 9.0%; vocational 29.8%; secondary 15.0%; higher 19.4%. **Literacy:** percentage of total population literate, virtually 100%. **Health:** physicians (2006) 9,547 (1 per 434 persons); hospital beds (2002) 23,825 (1 per 165 persons); infant mortality rate per 1,000 live births (2007) 5.0; undernourished population (2002–04) less than 2.5% of total population.

Military

Total active duty personnel (2007): 9,051 (army 50.6%, navy 22.5%, air force 26.9%). **Military expenditure as percentage of GDP** (2005): 1.0%; per capita expenditure US$269.

Background

Polynesian occupation of New Zealand dates to about AD 1000. First sighted by Dutch explorer Abel Janszoon Tasman in 1642, the main islands were charted by Capt. James Cook in 1769. Named a British crown colony in 1840, the area was the scene of warfare between colonists and native Maori through the 1860s. In 1907 the colony became the Dominion of New Zealand. It administered Western Samoa during 1919–62 and participated in both world wars. New Zealand took a strong stand against nuclear proliferation, since the mid-1980s banning nuclear-powered ships or those carrying nuclear weapons from its waters. There has been a revival of traditional Maori culture and art, and Maori social and economic activism have been central to political developments in the country since the late 20th century.

Recent Developments

After nine years in office, the Labour-led government of Prime Minister Helen Clark was defeated in elections held in New Zealand in November 2008, ceding power to an administration led by National Party leader John Key. Key initiated a 100-day action plan that included tax cuts; a line-by-line review of departmental spending; enhancement of the country's infrastructure; and a transitional relief package for those individuals worst hit by job losses. In April New Zealand became the first Organisation for Economic Co-operation and Development member country to conclude a comprehensive free-trade agreement with China, in a deal calculated to boost New Zealand's annual exports to China by up to NZ$400 million (about US$300 million). Under the terms of the agreement, New Zealand would concede tariff-free access to China for 96% of its products by 2019.

Internet resources: <www.stats.govt.nz>.

Nicaragua

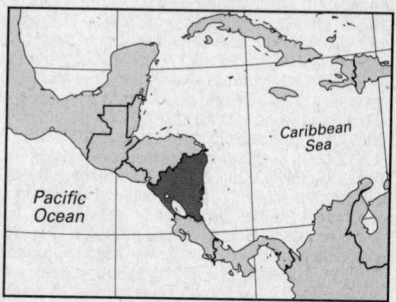

Official name: República de Nicaragua (Republic of Nicaragua). **Form of government:** unitary multiparty republic with one legislative house (National Assembly [92]). **Head of state and government:** President Daniel Ortega (from 2007). **Capital:** Managua. **Official language:** Spanish. **Official religion:** none. **Monetary unit:** 1 córdoba (CUS$) = 100 centavos; valuation (1 Jul 2009) US$1 = CUS$19.41.

Demography

Area: 50,337 sq mi, 130,373 sq km; land area alone equals 46,464 sq mi, 120,340 sq km. **Population** (2008): 5,667,000. **Density** (2008): persons per sq mi 122.0, persons per sq km 47.1. **Urban** (2005): 55.9%. **Sex distribution** (2006): male 49.67%; female 50.33%. **Age breakdown** (2005): under 15, 37.6%; 15–29, 29.9%; 30–44, 17.1%; 45–59, 9.3%; 60–74, 4.3%; 75–84, 1.3%; 85 and over, 0.5%. **Ethnic composition** (2000): mestizo (Spanish/Indian) 63.1%; white 14.0%; black 8.0%; multiple ethnicities 5.0%; other 9.9%. **Religious affiliation** (2005): Roman Catholic 58.5%; Protestant/independent Christian 23.2%, of which Evangelical 21.6%, Moravian 1.6%; nonreligious 15.7%; other 2.6%. **Major urban agglomerations** (2005): Managua 908,892; León 139,433; Chinandega 95,614; Masaya 92,598; Estelí 90,294. **Location:** Central America, bordering Honduras, the Caribbean Sea, Costa Rica, and the North Pacific Ocean.

Vital statistics

Birth rate per 1,000 population (2006): 22.4 (world avg. 20.3). **Death rate** per 1,000 population (2006): 3.0 (world avg. 8.6). **Natural increase rate** per 1,000 population (2006): 19.4 (world avg. 11.7). **Total fertility rate** (avg. births per childbearing woman; 2005): 2.94. **Life expectancy** at birth (2005): male 68.3 years; female 74.4 years.

National economy

Budget (2004). *Revenue:* CUS$12,250,700,000 (tax revenue 96.3%, of which sales tax 38.2%, import duties 27.8%, tax on income and profits 25.9%; nontax revenue 3.7%). *Expenditures:* CUS$16,697,-800,000 (current expenditures 58.4%; development expenditures 41.6%). **Production** (metric tons except as noted). *Agriculture and fishing* (2007): sugarcane 4,875,000, corn (maize) 569,948, rice 302,697; livestock (number of live animals) 3,600,000 cattle, 268,000 horses; fisheries production (2006) 44,500, of which lobster 3,726 (from aquaculture 25%). *Mining and quarrying* (2004–05): gold 123,600 troy oz. *Manufacturing* (value added in CUS$'000,000 at prices of 1994; 2003): food products 1,917; textiles and wearing apparel 969; beverages 713. *Energy production (consumption):* electricity (kW-hr; 2005) 2,866,000,000 (2,883,-000,000); crude petroleum (barrels; 2005) none (5,512,000); petroleum products (metric tons; 2005) 711,000 (1,234,000). **Population economically active** (2006): total 2,204,300; activity rate of total population 39.9% (participation rates: ages 10 and over [2005] 55.0%; female [2005] 35.2%; officially unemployed 5.2%). **Gross national income** (2007): US$5,519,000,000 (US$980 per capita). **Public debt** (external, outstanding; 2006): US$3,425,000,000. **Selected balance of payments data.** Receipts from (US$'000,000): tourism (2006) 231; remittances (2007) 990; foreign direct investment (FDI) (2004–06 avg.) 258; official development assistance (2006) 733. Disbursements for (US$'000,000): tourism (2006) 97; FDI (2004–06 avg.) 6.

Foreign trade

Imports (2006): US$2,741,000,000 (chemical products 16.7%; machinery and apparatus 15.6%; crude petroleum 13.2%; refined petroleum products 10.8%; food products 9.7%). *Major import sources:* US 22.8%; Mexico 14.8%; China 7.6%; Venezuela 6.8%; Costa Rica 5.4%. **Exports** (2006): US$759,000,000 (coffee 26.4%; bovine meat 10.3%; crustaceans 9.3%; gold 7.7%; raw sugar 6.6%). *Major export destinations:* US 46.5%; Mexico 6.2%; Canada 6.0%; Spain 4.5%; Honduras 4.4%.

Transport and communications

Transport. *Railroads* (private rail service only; 2004): length 6 km. *Roads* (2004): total length 18,669 km (paved [2002] 11%). *Vehicles* (2004): passenger cars 94,998; trucks and buses 152,813. *Air transport* (2000): passenger-km 72,200,000; metric ton-km cargo (2003) 200,000. **Communications,** in total units (units per 1,000 persons). Telephone landlines (2006): 248,000 (44); cellular telephone subscribers (2007): 2,123,000 (379); personal computers (2005): 220,000 (43); total Internet users (2006): 155,000 (28); broadband Internet subscribers (2006): 19,000 (3.6).

Education and health

Educational attainment (2005). Percentage of population ages 10 and over having: no formal schooling/unknown 20.5%; 1–3 years 16.6%; 4–6 years 27.0%; 7–9 years 16.1%; 10–12 years 10.5%; vocational 2.3%; incomplete university 2.6%; complete university 4.4%. **Literacy** (2005): percentage of total population ages 15 and over literate 78.0%; males literate 78.1%; females literate 77.9%. **Health** (2003): physicians 2,076 (1 per 2,538 persons); hospital beds 5,030 (1 per 1,047 persons); infant mortality rate per 1,000 live births (2005) 26.4; undernourished population (2002–04) 1,500,000 (27% of total population based on the consumption of a minimum daily requirement of 1,820 calories).

Military

Total active duty personnel (2007): 14,000 (army 85.7%, navy 5.7%, air force 8.6%). **Military expenditure as percentage of GDP** (2005): 0.7%; per capita expenditure US$6.

Background

Nicaragua has been inhabited for thousands of years, most notably by the Maya. Christopher Columbus arrived in 1502, and Spanish explorers discovered Lake Nicaragua soon thereafter. Nicaragua was governed by Spain until 1821, when it declared its independence. It was part of Mexico and then the United Provinces of Central America until 1838, when full independence was achieved. The US intervened in political affairs by maintaining troops there in 1912–33. Ruled by the dictatorial Somoza dynasty from 1936 to 1979, it was taken over by the Sandinistas after a popular

---

1 metric ton = about 1.1 short tons;   1 kilometer = 0.6 mi (statute);   1 metric ton-km cargo = about 0.68 short ton-mi cargo;   c.i.f.: cost, insurance, and freight;   f.o.b.: free on board

revolt. They were opposed by armed insurgents, the US-backed contras, from 1981. The Sandinista government nationalized several sectors of the economy. They lost the national elections in 1990, but Sandinista leader Daniel Ortega returned to power after winning the presidential election of 2006.

Recent Developments

Nicaragua claimed US$520 million in Venezuelan aid in 2008; however, this remained off the official budget and without state oversight. The central bank of Nicaragua worked to increase foreign reserves and to return to more orthodox monetary policies aimed at controlling inflation. Nonetheless, high food and oil prices dampened economic growth while raising inflation. The government responded by increasing the minimum wage by 18%. Exports grew strongly due to rising coffee prices and expansion in the US market, and Nicaragua remained committed to the Central America–Dominican Republic Free Trade Agreement (CAFTA-DR). It sought to reduce its dependence on oil by bringing wind turbines online and by signing an agreement with Brazil to build a 160-MW hydroelectric plant.

Internet resources: <www.intur.gob.ni>.

Niger

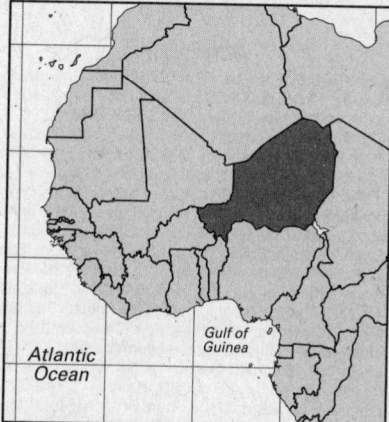

Official name: République du Niger (Republic of Niger). **Form of government:** multiparty republic with one legislative house (National Assembly [113]). **Head of state and government:** President Mamadou Tandja (from 1999), assisted by Prime Minister Seyni Oumarou (from 2007). **Capital:** Niamey. **Official language:** French. **Official religion:** none. **Monetary unit:** 1 CFA franc (CFAF) = 100 centimes; valuation (1 Jul 2009) US$1 = CFAF 462.89.

Demography

Area: 459,286 sq mi, 1,189,546 sq km. **Population** (2008): 14,731,000. **Density** (2008): persons per sq mi 32.1, persons per sq km 12.4. **Urban** (2006): 16.6%. **Sex distribution** (2005): male 50.69%; female 49.31%. **Age breakdown** (2005): under 15, 47.9%; 15–29, 24.1%; 30–44, 14.7%; 45–59, 8.5%; 60–74, 3.6%; 75–84, 0.9%; 85 and over, 0.3%. **Ethnolinguistic composition** (2001): Hausa 55.4%; Zarma-Songhai-Dendi 21.0%; Tuareg 9.3%; Fulani (Peul) 8.5%; Kanuri 4.7%; other 1.1%. **Religious affiliation** (2005): Muslim 90%, of which Sunni 85%, Shi'i 5%; traditional beliefs 9%; other 1%. **Major cities** (2001): Niamey 707,951 (urban agglomeration [2007] 915,000); Zinder 170,575; Maradi 148,017; Agadez 78,289; Tahoua 73,002. **Location:** western Africa, bordering Algeria, Libya, Chad, Nigeria, Benin, Burkina Faso, and Mali.

Vital statistics

Birth rate per 1,000 population (2006): 50.7 (world avg. 20.3). **Death rate** per 1,000 population (2006): 20.9 (world avg. 8.6). **Natural increase rate** per 1,000 population (2006): 29.8 (world avg. 11.7). **Total fertility rate** (avg. births per childbearing woman; 2006): 7.46. **Life expectancy** at birth (2006): male 43.8 years; female 43.7 years.

National economy

Budget (2007). *Revenue:* CFAF 427,600,000,000 (tax revenue 54.5%; external aid and grants 27.7%; nontax revenue 16.7%). *Expenditures:* CFAF 446,500,000,000 (current expenditures 53.6%; capital expenditures 46.4%). **Public debt** (external, outstanding; 2006): US$703,000,000. **Selected balance of payments data.** Receipts from (US$'000,000): tourism (2006) 35; remittances (2007) 66; foreign direct investment (2004–06 avg.) 23; official development assistance (2006) 401. Disbursements for (US$'000,000): tourism (2006) 31; remittances (2007) 29. **Gross national income** (2007): US$3,992,000,000 (US$280 per capita). **Production** (metric tons except as noted). *Agriculture and fishing* (2007): millet 2,781,928, cowpeas 1,001,139, sorghum 975,223, sesame seed 35,000; livestock (number of live animals) 7,400,000 goats, 4,750,000 sheep, 2,360,000 cattle, 430,000 camels; fisheries production (2006) 29,875 (from aquaculture, negligible). *Mining and quarrying* (2007): uranium 3,154; gold (2006) 2,615 kg. *Manufacturing* (value added in CFAF '000,000; 2002): textiles 1,876; food products 1,695; soaps and other chemical products 1,302. *Energy production (consumption):* electricity (kW-hr; 2005) 250,000,000 (470,000,000); coal (metric tons; 2006) 176,320 ([2005] 182,000); petroleum products (metric tons; 2005) none (179,000). **Population economically active** (2006): total 6,139,000; activity rate of total population 42.6% (participation rates: ages 15 and over, 83.5%; female 41.9%; unemployed, n.a.).

Foreign trade

Imports (2006): CFAF 391,300,000,000 (machinery and apparatus 41.4%; refined petroleum products 20.6%). *Major import sources* (2005): France 15.8%; Côte d'Ivoire 9.1%; Nigeria 5.5%; China 5.5%; US 5.4%. **Exports** (2006): CFAF 265,600,000,000 (uranium 30.0%; livestock [significantly cattle] 13.4%; gold 9.4%; cowpeas 7.2%; onions are another important food export). *Major export destinations* (2005): France 30.9%; Switzerland 18.6%; Nigeria 14.3%; Japan 11.8%; Ghana 3.9%.

Transport and communications

Transport. *Railroads:* none. *Roads* (2005): total length 18,423 km (paved 21%). *Vehicles* (2005): passenger cars 21,360. *Air transport* (Niamey airport only; 2005): passenger arrivals 50,002, passenger departures 59,824; cargo unloaded 3,085 metric tons, cargo loaded 140 metric tons. **Communications,** in total units (units per 1,000 persons). Telephone landlines (2005): 24,000 (1.9); cellular telephone subscribers (2007): 900,000 (63); personal computers (2005): 10,000 (0.8); total Internet users (2006): 40,000 (3.1); broadband Internet subscribers (2005): 200 (0.02).

Education and health

Educational attainment (Niamey only; 2006). Percentage of population ages 25 and over having: no formal schooling/unknown 86.2%; incomplete primary education 6.9%; complete primary 1.0%; incomplete secondary 3.7%; complete secondary 0.4%; higher 0.9%. **Literacy** (2006): percentage of total population ages 15 and over literate 28.7%; males literate 42.9%; females literate 15.1%. **Health** (2005): physicians 452 (1 per 27,599 persons); hospital beds 1,865 (1 per 6,689 persons); infant mortality rate per 1,000 live births (2006) 118.2; undernourished population (2002–04) 3,900,000 (32% of total population based on the consumption of a minimum daily requirement of 1,800 calories).

Military

Total active duty personnel (2007): 5,300 (army 98.1%, air force 1.9%). **Military expenditure as percentage of GDP** (2006): 1.1%; per capita expenditure US$2.

Background

In the territory of Niger, there is evidence of Neolithic culture, and several kingdoms existed there before the colonialists arrived. First explored by Europeans in the late 18th century, it became a French colony in 1922. It became an overseas territory of France in 1946 and gained independence in 1960. The first multiparty elections were held in 1993.

Recent Developments

The Tuareg rebellion in northern Niger escalated during 2008. In January members of the Movement of Nigerians for Justice killed 7 policemen in Tanout and kidnapped 11 others, including the mayor, and confrontations continued throughout the year. In April 2009, however, it was announced that the two sides had agreed to peace at Libyan-brokered talks.

Internet resources: <www.niger-tourisme.com/accueil_gb.php>.

Nigeria

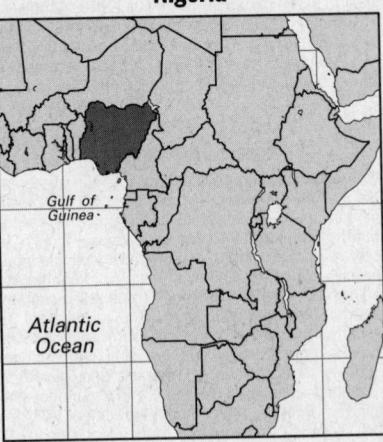

Official name: Federal Republic of Nigeria. **Form of government:** federal republic with two legislative bodies (Senate [109]; House of Representatives [360]). **Head of state and government:** President Umaru Musa Yar'Adua (from 2007). **Capital:** Abuja. **Official language:** English. **Official religion:** none. **Monetary unit:** 1 naira (N) = 100 kobo; valuation (1 Jul 2009) US$1 = N147.43.

Demography

Area: 356,669 sq mi, 923,768 sq km. **Population** (2008): 146,255,000. **Density** (2008): persons per sq mi 410.1, persons per sq km 158.3. **Urban** (2007): 47.7%. **Sex distribution** (2006): male 50.80%; female 49.20%. **Age breakdown** (2005): under 15, 44.4%; 15–29, 27.7%; 30–44, 15.0%; 45–59, 8.3%; 60–74, 3.8%; 75–84, 0.7%; 85 and over, 0.1%. **Ethnic composition** (2000): Yoruba 17.5%; Hausa 17.2%; Igbo (Ibo) 13.3%; Fulani 10.7%; Ibibio 4.1%; Kanuri 3.6%; Egba 2.9%; Tiv 2.6%; Igbira 1.1%; Nupe 1.0%; Edo 1.0%; Ijo 0.8%; detribalized 0.9%; other 23.3%. **Religious affiliation** (2003): Muslim 50.5%; Christian 48.2%, of which Protestant 15.0%, Roman Catholic 13.7%, other (mostly independent Christian) 19.5%; other 1.3%. **Major urban agglomerations** (2007): Lagos 9,466,000; Kano 3,140,000; Ibadan 2,628,000; Abuja 1,576,000; Kaduna 1,442,000. **Location:** western Africa, bordering Niger, Chad, Cameroon, the Atlantic Ocean, and Benin.

Vital statistics

Birth rate per 1,000 population (2007): 39.9 (world avg. 20.3). **Death rate** per 1,000 population (2007): 16.8 (world avg. 8.6). **Total fertility rate** (avg. births per childbearing woman; 2007): 5.30. **Life expectancy** at birth (2007): male 46.4 years; female 47.3 years.

National economy

Budget (2007). *Revenue:* N5,715,600,000,000 (petroleum and gas revenue 78.1%, of which crude pe-

---

1 metric ton = about 1.1 short tons;   *1 kilometer = 0.6 mi (statute);*   *1 metric ton-km cargo = about 0.68 short ton-mi cargo;*   *c.i.f.: cost, insurance, and freight;*   *f.o.b.: free on board*

troleum export proceeds 32.4%, petroleum profits tax 26.3%, crude petroleum sales to domestic refineries 19.2%; nonpetroleum revenue 21.9%). *Expenditures:* N2,450,900,000,000 (current expenditures 64.8%, of which wages and salaries 35.4%, debt service 8.7%; capital expenditures 31.0%). **Public debt** (external, outstanding; January 2008): US$3,629,000,000. **Production** (metric tons except as noted). *Agriculture and fishing* (2007): cassava 45,750,000, yams 37,150,000, sorghum 10,500,000, sugarcane 10,290,000, oil palm fruit 8,500,000, corn (maize) 7,800,000, millet 7,700,000, taro 5,485,000, rice 4,677,400, peanuts (groundnuts) 3,835,600, sweet potatoes 3,490,000, cowpeas 3,150,000, plantains 2,800,000, cashews 660,000, cocoa beans 500,000, ginger 138,000, sesame seeds 100,000; livestock (number of live animals) 28,583,000 goats, 23,993,500 sheep, 16,258,560 cattle; fisheries production 711,500 (from aquaculture 11%). *Mining and quarrying* (2006): limestone 15,300,000; marble 200,000. *Manufacturing* (value added in N'000,000; 2006): refined petroleum products 40,740; cement 20,291; other unspecified (particularly food, beverages, and textiles) 432,335. *Energy production (consumption):* electricity (kW-hr; 2005) 20,468,000,000 (20,468,000,000); coal (metric tons; 2006) 10,000 ([2005] 8,000); crude petroleum (barrels; 2007–08) 767,080,000 ([2005] 75,388,000); petroleum products (metric tons; 2005) 4,190,000 ([2007] 6,954,000); natural gas (cu m; 2007) 57,753,700,000 (39,374,800,000). **Gross national income** (2007): US$137,091,000 (US$930 per capita). **Population economically active** (2003): total 45,165,000; activity rate of total population 35.9% (participation rates: ages 15–64, 65.9%; female 35.1%; officially unemployed [2007] 14.6%). **Selected balance of payments data.** Receipts from (US$'000,000): tourism (2006) 21; remittances (2007) 3,329; foreign direct investment (FDI) (2004–06 avg.) 3,658; official development assistance (2006) 11,434. Disbursements for (US$'000,000): tourism (2006) 1,664; remittances (2007) 18; FDI (2004–06 avg.) 230.

Foreign trade

Imports (2007): N4,687,982,160,000 (basic manufactures 32.8%; chemical products 24.2%; machinery and transportation equipment 22.6%; food and live animals 6.2%). *Major import sources* (nonpetroleum imports only [78.7% of all imports]): US 29.6%; Japan 22.9%; China 13.0%; India 9.5%; France 8.3%. **Exports** (2007): N8,126,000,510,000 (crude petroleum 89.9%; natural gas 8.0%; skins 0.5%; cocoa [all forms] 0.4%). *Major export destinations* (petroleum exports only): US 39.5%; India 7.6%; Spain 5.2%; Italy 4.2%; France 4.2%.

Transport and communications

Transport. *Railroads* (2005): length (2006) 3,505 km; passenger-km 75,170,000; metric ton-km cargo 18,027,000. *Roads* (2005): total length 34,403 km (paved 64%). *Vehicles* (2004): passenger cars 2,176,000. *Air transport* (2006): passenger-km (Virgin Nigeria Airways only) 969,900,000; metric ton-km cargo (2005) 10,000,000. **Communications**, in total units (units per 1,000 persons). Telephone landlines (2007): 1,580,000 (11); cellular telephone

subscribers (2007): 40,396,000 (273); personal computers (2006): 1,200,000 (8.9); total Internet users (2007): 10,000,000 (68); broadband Internet subscribers (2005): 500.

Education and health

Educational attainment (2003). Percentage of population ages 25 and over having: no formal schooling/unknown 50.4%; primary education 20.4%; secondary 20.1%; higher 9.1%. **Literacy** (2007): percentage of total population ages 15 and over literate 73.1%; males literate 79.4%; females literate 67.0%. **Health** (2005): physicians 42,563 (1 per 3,234 persons); hospital beds 85,523 (1 per 1,609 persons); infant mortality rate per 1,000 live births (2007) 109.0; undernourished population (2002–04) 11,400,000 (9% of total population based on the consumption of a minimum daily requirement of 1,830 calories).

Military

Total active duty personnel (2007): 80,000 (army 77.5%, navy 10.0%, air force 12.5%). **Military expenditure as percentage of GDP** (2005): 0.7%; per capita expenditure US$5.

Background

Inhabited for thousands of years, Nigeria was the center of the Nok culture from 500 BC to AD 200 and of several precolonial empires, including the state of Kanem-Bornu and the Songhai, Hausa, and Fulani kingdoms. Visited in the 15th century by Europeans, it became a center for the slave trade. The area began to come under British control in 1861; by 1903 British rule was total. Nigeria gained independence in 1960 and became a republic in 1963. Ethnic strife soon led to military coups, and military groups ruled the country from 1966 to 1979 and from 1983 to 1999. A civil war between the central government and the former Eastern Region—which seceded and called itself Biafra—began in 1967 and ended in 1970 with Biafra's surrender after widespread starvation and civilian deaths. In 1991 the capital was moved from Lagos to Abuja. The government's execution of environmental activist Ken Saro-Wiwa in 1995 led to international sanctions, and civilian rule was finally reestablished in 1999. Ethnic conflicts continued in the early 21st century, as did violent protests over oil production in the Niger delta. Friction also increased between Muslims and Christians after some of the northern and central states adopted Islamic law.

Did you know? Nigeria is Africa's most populous country and a land of extreme diversity, with at least 250 different ethnic groups and more than 500 spoken languages.

Recent Developments

In 2008 Nigeria's economy was severely affected by the global financial crisis. The price of crude oil, the country's major export, underwent wild fluctuations—beginning the year at US$95, peaking at US$147 in July, and then plunging below US$40 at the end of the year. Nigeria's prospects had looked hopeful midyear to realize its Vision 2020 (plans for the economy to rank in the top 20 in the world and first in Africa by 2020)—the average growth rate was about 7%, external reserves amounted to some US$63 billion, and the non-oil sector showed strong performance. By mid-October, however, the government had depleted US$14.6 billion in windfall oil profits. Violence in the Niger delta surged to new levels, pushing the region to the verge of anarchy and resulting in the loss of billions of dollars in oil revenue. A volatile mix of armed militias, unemployed youths, corrupt police and military officers, and intransigent oil companies competed for a share in oil profits. In June and September, the Movement for the Emancipation of the Niger Delta spearheaded sophisticated armed operations against the oil companies and the federal army, which forced Royal Dutch Shell to suspend production temporarily, and attacks on and kidnappings of foreign oil workers continued in 2009. Rather than address the socioeconomic roots of unrest, the government's Joint Task Force launched military attacks on rebel camps and arrested hundreds of suspected militants.

Internet resources:
<http://nigerianstat.gov.ng/index.php>.

Norway

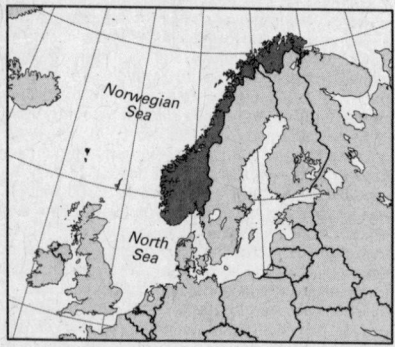

Norwegian Sea

North Sea

Official name: Kongeriket Norge (Kingdom of Norway). **Form of government:** constitutional monarchy with one legislative house (Parliament [169]). **Chief of state:** Norwegian King Harald V (from 1991). **Head of government:** Prime Minister Jens Stoltenberg (from 2005). **Capital:** Oslo. **Official language:** Norwegian. **Official religion:** Evangelical Lutheran. **Monetary unit:** 1 Norwegian krone (NOK; plural kroner) = 100 øre; valuation (1 Jul 2009) US$1 = NOK 6.32.

Demography

Area: 148,726 sq mi, 385,199 sq km. **Population** (2008): 4,762,000. **Density** (2008): persons per sq mi 37.5, persons per sq km 14.5. **Urban** (2005): 77.4%. **Sex distribution** (2007): male 49.81%; female 50.19%. **Age breakdown** (2007): under 15, 19.2%; 15–29, 18.9%; 30–44, 21.8%; 45–59, 19.6%; 60–74, 13.0%; 75–84, 5.3%; 85 and over, 2.2%. **Ethnic composition** (2000): Norwegian 93.8%; Vietnamese 2.4%; Swedish 0.5%; Punjabi 0.4%; Urdu 0.3%; US white 0.3%; Lapp 0.3%; other 2.0%. **Religious affiliation** (2003): Evangelical Lutheran 85.7%; other Christian 4.5%; Muslim 1.8%; other/nonreligious 8.0%. **Major cities** (2007): Oslo 560,484 (urban agglomeration 856,915); Bergen 247,746; Trondheim 165,191; Stavanger 119,586; Baerum 108,144. **Location:** northern Europe, bordering the Barents Sea, Russia, Finland, Sweden, the North Sea, and the Norwegian Sea.

Vital statistics

Birth rate per 1,000 population (2007): 12.4 (world avg. 20.3); within marriage 45.5%; outside of marriage 54.5%. **Death rate** per 1,000 population (2007): 8.9 (world avg. 8.6). **Natural increase rate** per 1,000 population (2007): 3.5 (world avg. 11.7). **Total fertility rate** (avg. births per childbearing woman; 2007): 1.90. **Life expectancy** at birth (2007): male 78.2 years; female 82.7 years.

National economy

Budget (2005). *Revenue:* NOK 1,066,860,000,000 (income tax 41.1%; social security 16.2%; VAT 14.8%). *Expenditures:* NOK 763,318,000,000 (social security and welfare 40.5%; health 17.2%; education 14.0%; general public service 9.7%). **Production** (metric tons except as noted). *Agriculture and fishing* (2007): barley 580,000, wheat 380,000, potatoes 380,000; livestock (number of live animals) 2,400,000 sheep, 930,000 cattle; fisheries production 2,964,293 (from aquaculture 24%); aquatic plants production 145,429 (from aquaculture, none). *Mining and quarrying* (2006): ilmenite concentrate 850,000, iron ore (metal content) 400,000, cobalt (refined metal) 4,927. *Manufacturing* (value added in US$'000,000; 2004): food products 3,382; chemical products 2,238; ships and oil platforms 2,224. *Energy production (consumption):* electricity (kW-hr; 2005) 138,108,-000,000 (126,065,000,000); coal (metric tons; 2005) 1,471,000 (795,000); crude petroleum (barrels; 2005) 986,700,000 (130,990,000); petroleum products (metric tons; 2005) 20,340,000 (10,435,000); natural gas (cu m; 2005) 88,041,-000,000 (5,923,000,000). **Selected balance of payments data.** Receipts from (US$'000,000): tourism (2006) 3,613; remittances (2007) 613; foreign direct investment (FDI) (2004–06 avg.) 4,947. Disbursements for (US$'000,000): tourism (2006) 11,586; remittances (2007) 3,791; FDI (2004–06 avg.) 12,230. **Population economically active** (2006): total 2,446,000; activity rate of total population ·52.5% (participation rates: ages 15–64, 80.8%; female 47.1%; unemployed 3.4%). **Gross national income** (2007): US$360,036,000,000 (US$76,450 per capita). **Public debt** (2003): US$79,880,000,000.

---

1 metric ton = about 1.1 short tons; 1 kilometer = 0.6 mi (statute); 1 metric ton-km cargo = about 0.68 short ton-mi cargo; c.i.f.: cost, insurance, and freight; f.o.b.: free on board

Foreign trade

Imports (2006; c.i.f.): NOK 411,624,000,000 (machinery and apparatus 25.5%, of which nonelectrical machinery and apparatus 11.8%; base and fabricated metals 10.7%; motor vehicles 10.2%; chemical products 9.1%; metal ore and metal scrap 5.3%). *Major import sources:* Sweden 15.0%; Germany 13.5%; Denmark 6.9%; UK 6.4%; China 5.7%. **Exports** (2006; f.o.b.): NOK 780,009,000,000 (crude petroleum 42.5%; natural gas 18.0%; machinery and apparatus 5.8%; refined petroleum products 4.6%; aluminum 4.2%). *Major export destinations:* UK 26.0%; Germany 11.8%; The Netherlands 10.1%; France 8.1%; Sweden 6.1%.

Transport and communications

Transport. *Railroads* (2006): route length 4,087 km; passenger-km 2,827,000,000; metric ton-km cargo (2001) 3,351,000,000. *Roads* (2006): total length 92,946 km (paved [2002] 78%). *Vehicles:* passenger cars (2007) 2,153,730; trucks and buses (2005) 431,257. *Air transport* (SAS [Norwegian part], Braathens, Norwegian, and Widerøe only; 2004): passenger-km 13,229,000,000; metric ton-km cargo 177,522,000. **Communications,** in total units (units per 1,000 persons). Telephone landlines (2007): 1,988,000 (423); cellular telephone subscribers (2007): 5,192,000 (1,105); personal computers (2004): 2,630,000 (578); total Internet users (2007): 3,800,000 (809); broadband Internet subscribers (2007): 1,436,000 (305).

Education and health

Educational attainment (2007). Percentage of population ages 16 and over having: primary and lower secondary education 29.6%; higher secondary 41.3%; higher 24.8%; unknown 4.3%. **Literacy** (2000): percentage of total population literate, virtually 100%. **Health** (2006): physicians 15,443 (1 per 302 persons); hospital beds 16,303 (1 per 286 persons); infant mortality rate per 1,000 live births (2007) 3.1; undernourished population (2002–04) less than 2.5% of total population.

Military

Total active duty personnel (2007): 15,800 (army 42.4%, navy 25.9%, air force 31.7%). **Military expenditure as percentage of GDP** (2005): 1.7%; per capita expenditure US$1,058.

Background

Several principalities were united into the kingdom of Norway in the 11th century. From 1380 it had the same king as Denmark until it was ceded to Sweden in 1814. The union with Sweden was dissolved in 1905, and Norway's economy grew rapidly. The country remained neutral during World War I, although its shipping industry played a vital role in the conflict. It declared its neutrality in World War II but was invaded and occupied by German troops. Norway is a member of NATO but turned down membership in the EU in 1994. Its economy grew consistently during the 1990s.

Recent Developments

Norway's economy remained strong in 2008 despite turbulence in the global financial market. Oil prices reached new heights in the summer before retreating in the autumn, and exports of fish and industrial products continued to expand. GDP growth was 2.0%, and employment grew by 3.2%. However, inflation reached 3.5% during the year and manufacturing fell 4.0%. During the global financial crisis that began in September, the Government Pension Fund experienced big losses in its investments in international financial instruments. Economists proclaimed that such a large fund with long-term investments could handle short-term losses.

Internet resources: <www.ssb.no/english>.

Oman

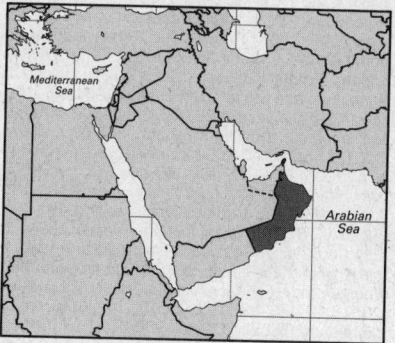

Official name: Saltanat ʿUman (Sultanate of Oman). **Form of government:** monarchy with two advisory bodies (State Council [70]; Consultative Council [84]). **Head of state and government:** Sultan (from 1970) and Prime Minister (from 1972) Qabus ibn Saʿid. **Capital:** Muscat. **Official language:** Arabic. **Official religion:** Islam. **Monetary unit:** 1 Omani rial (RO) = 1,000 baiza; valuation (1 Jul 2009) US$1 = RO 0.38.

Demography

Area: 119,500 sq mi, 309,500 sq km. **Population** (2008): 2,651,000. **Density** (2008): persons per sq mi 22.2, persons per sq km 8.6. **Urban** (2005): 71.5%. **Sex distribution** (2007): male 59.13%; female 40.87%. **Age breakdown** (2007): under 15, 28.8%; 15–29, 34.2%; 30–44, 24.9%; 45–59, 9.1%; 60–74, 2.5%; 75 and over, 0.5%. **Ethnic composition** (2000): Omani Arab 48.1%; Indo-Pakistani 31.7%, of which Balochi 15.0%, Bengali 4.4%, Tamil 2.5%; other Arab 7.2%; Persian 2.8%; Zanzibari (blacks originally from Zanzibar) 2.5%; other 7.7%. **Religious affiliation** (2005): Muslim 89%, of which Ibadiyah 75%, Sunni 8%, Shiʿi 6%; Hindu 5%; Christian 5%; other 1%. **Major cities** (populations of districts; 2007): Al-Sib 268,259; Matrah 203,159; Bawshar 193,778; Salalah 185,780; Muscat 28,987 (urban agglomeration 620,000). **Location:** the Middle East, bordering the Gulf of Oman, the Arabian Sea, Yemen, Saudi Arabia, and the UAE; the Ruʿus al-Jibal exclave occupies the northern tip of the Musandam Peninsula and borders the UAE, the Persian Gulf, and the Strait of Hormuz.

Vital statistics

Birth rate per 1,000 population (2007): 25.0 (world avg. 20.3). **Death rate** per 1,000 population (2007): 3.1 (world avg. 8.6). **Natural increase rate** per 1,000 population (2007): 21.9 (world avg. 11.7). **Total fertility rate** (avg. births per childbearing woman; 2005): 5.84. **Life expectancy** at birth (2007): male 70.4 years; female 73.6 years.

National economy

Budget (2006). *Revenue:* RO 5,027,200,000 (oil revenue 64.2%; natural gas revenue 12.2%; tax revenue 7.2%). *Expenditures:* RO 4,936,100,000 (current expenditures 71.5%, of which defense 31.4%, education 11.3%, social security and welfare 6.8%; capital expenditures 24.3%). **Public debt** (external, outstanding; 2006): US$819,000,000. **Gross national income** (2007): US$38,325,000,000 (US$14,768 per capita). **Production** (metric tons except as noted). *Agriculture and fishing* (2007): dates 260,000, tomatoes 41,000, bananas 26,000; livestock (number of live animals) 1,600,000 goats, 360,000 sheep, 310,000 cattle, 120,000 camels; fisheries production (2006) 154,078 (from aquaculture, negligible). *Mining and quarrying* (2007): limestone 4,438,000; marble 964,100; chromite (gross weight) 407,700; gypsum 187,200. *Manufacturing* (value added in US$'000,000; 2004): petroleum products 1,168; cement, bricks, and ceramics 232; food products 152. *Energy production (consumption):* electricity (kW-hr; 2007) 14,443,000,000 (11,191,000,000); crude petroleum (barrels; 2007) 259,000,000 ([2005] 32,000,000); petroleum products (metric tons; 2005) 3,987,000 (3,562,000); natural gas (cu m; 2005) 18,968,000,000 (8,368,000,000). **Population economically active** (2003): total 736,624; activity rate of total population 31.5% (participation rates: female 15.4%; unemployed [2004] 15%). **Selected balance of payments data.** Receipts from (US$'000,000): tourism (2006) 538; remittances (2007) 43; foreign direct investment (FDI) (2004–06 avg.) 694; official development assistance (2006) 35. Disbursements for (US$'000,000): tourism (2006) 686; remittances (2007) 2,788; FDI (2004–06 avg.) 204.

Foreign trade

Imports (2007; c.i.f.): RO 6,144,000,000 (motor vehicles and parts 24.1%; nonelectrical machinery and apparatus 17.8%; food and live animals 8.3%; iron and steel 8.2%; chemical products 6.4%). *Major import sources:* UAE 26.5%; Japan 15.8%; India 6.5%; US 5.8%; Germany 5.3%. **Exports** (2007; f.o.b.): RO 9,494,000,000 (domestic exports 89.4%, of which crude petroleum 58.5%, liquefied natural gas 12.4%, refined petroleum products 4.9%; reexports 10.6%, of which motor vehicles and parts 8.3%). *Major export destinations* (2005): China 28%; South Korea 25%; Thailand 16%; UAE 9%; Iran 5%.

Transport and communications

Transport. *Railroads:* none. *Roads* (2004): total length 40,116 km (paved 37%). *Vehicles* (2003): passenger cars 324,085; trucks and buses 116,438. *Air transport* (Oman Air only; 2006): passenger-km 1,749,000,000; metric ton-km cargo 11,000,000. **Communications,** in total units (units per 1,000 persons). Telephone landlines (2007): 268,000 (103); cellular telephone subscribers (2007): 2,500,000 (963); personal computers (2005): 130,000 (51); total Internet users (2007): 340,000 (131); broadband Internet subscribers (2007): 19,000 (7.3).

Education and health

Educational attainment (2003). Percentage of population ages 10 and over having: no formal schooling 38.2% (illiterate 15.9%, literate 22.3%); primary education 35.3%; secondary 17.0%; higher technical 3.3%; higher undergraduate 5.2%; higher graduate 0.7%; other 0.3%. **Literacy** (2003): percentage of total population ages 15 and over literate 75.8%; males literate 83.0%; females literate 67.2%. **Health** (2007): physicians 4,909 (1 per 529 persons); hospital beds 5,403 (1 per 480 persons); infant mortality rate per 1,000 live births 10.1.

Military

Total active duty personnel (2007): 42,600 (army 58.7%, navy 9.9%, air force 11.7%, royal household/foreign troops 19.7%). **Military expenditure as percentage of GDP** (2005): 11.9%; per capita expenditure US$1,516.

Background

Oman has been inhabited for at least 10,000 years. Arabs began migrating there in the 9th century BC. Tribal warfare was endemic until the conversion to Islam in the 7th century AD. It was ruled by Ibadi imams until 1154, when a royal dynasty was established. The Portuguese controlled the coastal areas from about 1507 to 1650, when they were expelled. The Al Bu Sa'id dynasty, founded in the mid-18th century, still rules Oman. Oil was discovered in 1964. In 1970 the sultan was deposed by his son, who began a policy of modernization, and under him the country joined the Arab League and the UN. In the Persian Gulf War, Oman cooperated with the allied forces against Iraq. In the 1990s it continued to expand its foreign relations.

Recent Developments

Petroleum prices remained crucial to Oman's economy, which grew 6% in 2008, allowing continued expansion of the sultanate's burgeoning tourism and transportation sectors. Three new airports were opened, and *Vogue* magazine declared Oman the top travel destination for 2008. Meanwhile, the port of Salalah gained the distinction of being the only port between Europe and Singapore that could handle the world's largest container vessels.

Internet resources: <www.mone.gov.om/index.asp>.

1 metric ton = about 1.1 short tons;   1 kilometer = 0.6 mi (statute);   1 metric ton-km cargo = about 0.68 short ton-mi cargo;   c.i.f.: cost, insurance, and freight;   f.o.b.: free on board

Pakistan

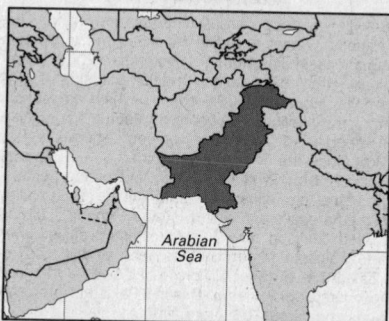

Arabian
Sea

Official name: Islamic Republic of Pakistan. **Form of government:** federal republic with two legislative houses (Senate [100]; National Assembly [342]). **Chief of state and government:** President Asif Ali Zardari (from 2008), assisted by Prime Minister Yousaf Raza Gilani (from 2008). **Capital:** Islamabad. **Official language:** none (Urdu is the national language). **Official religion:** Islam. **Monetary unit:** 1 Pakistan rupee (PKR) = 100 paisa; valuation (1 Jul 2009) US$1 = PKR 81.10.

Demography

Area and density data exclude the 33,125-sq-mi (85,793-sq-km) area of Pakistani-administered Jammu and Kashmir (comprising both Azad Kashmir [AK] and the Northern Areas [NA]); population and density data exclude Afghan refugees and the 2008 populations of AK (3,799,000) and the NA (996,000). **Area:** 307,374 sq mi, 796,096 sq km. **Population** (2008): 161,910,000. **Density** (2008): persons per sq mi 526.8, persons per sq km 203.4. **Urban** (2007): 36.0%. **Sex distribution** (2007): male 51.89%; female 48.11%. **Age breakdown** (2005): under 15, 37.2%; 15–29, 29.9%; 30–44, 16.8%; 45–59, 10.2%; 60–74, 4.7%; 75–84, 1.0%; 85 and over, 0.2%. **Ethnic composition** (2000): Punjabi 52.6%; Pashtun 13.2%; Sindhi 11.7%; Urdu-speaking *muhajir* 7.5%; Balochi 4.3%; other 10.7%. **Religious affiliation** (2000): Muslim 96.1% (mostly Sunni, with Shi'i constituting about 17% of total population); Christian 2.5%; Hindu 1.2%; others (including Ahmadiyah) 0.2%. **Major urban agglomerations** (2007): Karachi 12,130,000; Lahore 6,577,000; Faisalabad 2,617,-000; Rawalpindi 1,858,000; Multan 1,522,000; Gujranwala 1,513,000; Hyderabad 1,459,000; Peshawar 1,303,000. **Location:** southern Asia, bordering China, India, the Arabian Sea, Iran, and Afghanistan.

Vital statistics

Birth rate per 1,000 population (2007): 25.5 (world avg. 20.3). **Death rate** per 1,000 population (2007): 7.9 (world avg. 8.6). **Total fertility rate** (avg. births per childbearing woman; 2007): 3.13. **Life expectancy** at birth (2007): male 64.3 years; female 64.4 years.

National economy

Budget (2007–08). *Revenue:* PKR 1,368,139,-000,000 (tax revenue 75.3%, of which corporate profits 28.4%, sales tax 27.4%, customs 11.3%; nontax revenue 24.7%). *Expenditures:* PKR 1,353,660,000,000 (general public service 47.4%; defense 20.3%; economic affairs 5.8%). **Production** (metric tons except as noted). *Agriculture and fishing* (2007): sugarcane 54,752,000, wheat 23,520,-000, rice 8,300,000, sunflower seeds 560,000; livestock (number of live animals) 53,800,000 goats, 29,600,000 cattle, 27,300,000 buffalo, 900,000 camels; fisheries production (2007–08) 640,000 (from aquaculture [2006] 20%). *Mining and quarrying* (2007–08): limestone 30,825,000; gypsum 682,000; kaolin (2006) 38,000. *Manufacturing* (value of production in PKR '000,000,000; 2000–01): textiles 321; food products 189; refined petroleum products and coke 94. *Energy production (consumption):* electricity (kW-hr; 2007–08) 109,021,000,000 ([2006–07] 72,712,000,000); coal (metric tons; 2007–08) 3,482,000 ([2006–07] 7,894,000); crude petroleum (barrels; 2007–08) 25,610,000 ([2005] 89,000,000); petroleum products (metric tons; 2005) 10,189,000 ([2006–07] 16,847,000); natural gas (cu m; 2007–08) 40,981,000,000 ([2006–07] 34,601,000,000). **Population economically active** (2007): total 50,331,000; activity rate of total population 31.8% (participation rates: ages 15–64, 53.7%; female 20.7%; officially unemployed 5.3%). **Gross national income** (2007): US$141,009,000,000 (US$870 per capita). **Public debt** (external, outstanding; June 2008): US$40,243,000,000. **Selected balance of payments data.** Receipts from (US$'000,000): tourism (2006) 255; remittances (2007–08 avg.) 6,449; foreign direct investment (FDI) (2004–08 avg.) 4,420; official development assistance (2006) 2,147. Disbursements for (US$'000,000): tourism (2006) 1,545; remittances (2007) 3.0; FDI (2004–06 avg.) 69.

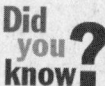

Did you know? The mountainous northern region of Pakistan is home to the world's highest road, the Karakoram Highway, which extends for about 800 km (500 mi) from Kashgar, China, to Islamabad, Pakistan.

Foreign trade

Imports (2007–08): US$35,417,333,000 (refined petroleum products 17.4%; machinery and apparatus 16.2%; chemical products 14.4%; crude petroleum 12.2%; food products 10.0%). *Major import sources:* UAE 14.5%; Saudi Arabia 10.2%; China 8.6%; Kuwait 6.9%; Singapore 4.8%. **Exports** (2007–08): US$20,122,394,000 (textiles 49.8%, of which woven cotton fabric 11.5%, knitwear 10.5%, bedding 6.9%, ready-made garments 5.5%, cotton yarn 5.3%; rice 5.6%; refined petroleum products 3.7%). *Major export destinations:* US 18.6%; UAE 8.6%; UK 5.3%; Afghanistan 5.1%; Germany 4.1%.

Transport and communications

Transport. *Railroads* (2007): length (2005–06) 11,515 km; passenger-km 25,821,000,000; metric ton-km cargo 5,876,000,000. *Roads* (2007–08): total length 264,853 km (paved 67%). *Vehicles* (2006): passenger cars 1,418,790; trucks and buses 352,172. *Air transport* (Pakistan International Airlines only; 2007–08): passenger-km 12,772,-500,000; metric ton-km cargo 325,700,000. **Communications,** in total units (units per 1,000 persons). Telephone landlines (2007): 4,940,000 (30); cellular telephone subscribers (2007): 78,853,000 (481); personal computers (2005): 803,000 (5.2); total Internet users (2007): 17,500,000 (107); broadband Internet subscribers (2007): 129,000 (0.8).

Education and health

Literacy (2006–07): percentage of total population ages 15 and over literate 52%; males literate 65%; females literate 38%. **Health:** physicians (2007) 127,859 (1 per 1,280 persons); hospital beds (2006) 103,285 (1 per 1,585 persons); infant mortality rate per 1,000 live births (2007) 68.0; undernourished population (2002–04) 37,500,000 (24% of total population based on the consumption of a minimum daily requirement of 1,770 calories).

Military

Total active duty personnel (2008): 617,000 (army 89.1%, navy 3.6%, air force 7.3%). **Military expenditure as percentage of GDP** (2008): 2.8%; per capita expenditure US$21.

Background

Pakistan has been inhabited since about 3500 BC. From the 3rd century BC to the 2nd century AD, it was part of the Mauryan and Kushan kingdoms. The first Muslim conquests were in the 8th century AD. The British East India Company subdued the reigning Mughal dynasty in 1757. During the period of British colonial rule, what is now Pakistan was part of India. When the British withdrew in 1947, the new state of Pakistan came into existence by act of the British Parliament. Kashmir remained a disputed territory between Pakistan and India, resulting in full-scale war in 1965 and continued military clashes. Civil war between East Pakistan and West Pakistan resulted in independence for the former, which became Bangladesh, in 1971. Many Afghan refugees migrated to Pakistan during the Soviet-Afghan war in the 1980s. Pakistan elected Benazir Bhutto prime minister in 1988; she was the first woman to head a modern Islamic state. She was ousted in 1990 on charges of corruption and incompetence. During the 1990s border flare-ups with India continued, and Pakistan conducted tests of nuclear weapons. Pakistan's political landscape changed dramatically after the terrorist attacks of September 11. It was quickly determined that they had been staged by the Muslim militant organization al-Qaeda, which was operating out of Afghanistan with the support of the Taliban regime, with which Pakistan had diplomatic relations. As the US prepared to move militarily against both organizations, Pakistan chose to provide support to the US-led coalition.

Recent Developments

Suicide bombings, assassinations, and military operations against terrorists remained the top preoccupations in Pakistan. In September 2008 Islamabad cited 88 suicide attacks, causing 1,188 deaths, since mid-2007—twice as high as the toll from the previous five years. In February a suicide bomber killed the army's surgeon general, and in November the former commander of the Special Services Group was murdered. Government negotiators and pro-Taliban militants in the Swat valley signed a peace agreement in May. Fighting involving US-led coalition forces in Afghanistan spilled over into Pakistan throughout the year, and it was revealed that US Special Forces had been authorized to operate in Pakistan. Despite Pakistani protestations, numerous US drone attacks claimed an increasing number of al-Qaeda and Taliban operatives. Militants were not subdued, however. Islamabad's Marriott Hotel was demolished by a truck bomb in September, killing at least 54. In late November Pakistan-based terrorists struck multiple targets in Mumbai (Bombay), killing at least 174. In March 2009 an ambush of the Sri Lankan cricket team in Lahore left six policemen and two bystanders dead. In response, the International Cricket Council stripped Pakistan of its hosting duties for the 2011 Cricket World Cup. Throughout the first half of 2009, Pakistani forces battled militants in the tribal areas near the border with Afghanistan, and the peace accord in the Swat valley was effectively abandoned.

Internet resources: <www.statpak.gov.pk>.

Palau

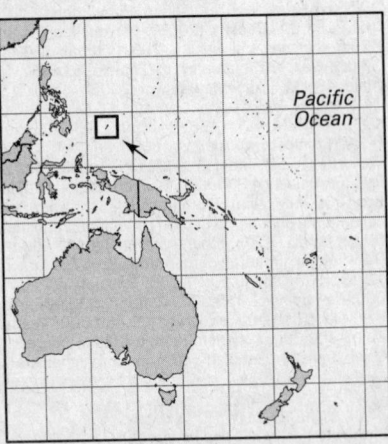

Official name: Beluu er a Belau (Palauan); Republic of Palau (English). **Form of government:** republic with two legislative houses (Senate [13]; House of Delegates [16]). **Head of state and government:** President Johnson Toribiong (from 2009). **Capital:** Melekeok. **Official languages:** Palauan; English.

---

1 metric ton = about 1.1 short tons;   1 kilometer = 0.6 mi (statute);   1 metric ton-km cargo = about 0.68 short ton-mi cargo;   c.i.f.: cost, insurance, and freight;   f.o.b.: free on board

Official religion: none. **Monetary unit:** 1 US dollar (US$) = 100 cents.

Demography

Area: 188 sq mi, 488 sq km. **Population** (2008): 20,300. **Density** (2008): persons per sq mi 108.0, persons per sq km 41.6. **Urban** (2005): 70.0%. **Sex distribution** (2006): male 53.72%; female 46.28%. **Age breakdown** (2006): under 15, 23.4%; 15–29, 21.6%; 30–44, 28.4%; 45–59, 18.3%; 60–74, 5.9%; 75 and over, 2.4%. **Ethnic composition** (2005): Palauan 65.2%; Asian 30.3%, of which Filipino 21.6%, Vietnamese 2.3%; other Micronesian 3.1%; white 1.1%; other 0.3%. **Religious affiliation** (2005): Roman Catholic 51.0%; Protestant 26.7%; Modekngei (marginal Christian sect) 8.9%; other Christian 1.8%; other 11.6%. **Major towns** (2005): Koror 10,743; Meyuns 1,153. **Location:** Oceania, island group in the North Pacific Ocean, east of the Philippines.

Vital statistics

Birth rate per 1,000 population (2006): 12.9 (world avg. 20.3). **Death rate** per 1,000 population (2006): 7.2 (world avg. 8.6). **Natural increase rate** per 1,000 population (2006): 5.7 (world avg. 11.7). **Total fertility rate** (avg. births per childbearing woman; 2005): 1.80. **Life expectancy** at birth (2005): male 68.0 years; female 72.0 years.

National economy

Budget (2005–06). *Revenue:* US$83,671,000 (grants from the US 53.7%; tax revenue 34.9%; nontax revenue 7.9%; trust fund revenue 3.5%). *Expenditures:* US$87,586,000 (current expenditures 74.1%; capital expenditures 25.9%). **Public debt** (gross external debt; 2006–07): US$22,857,000. **Production** (metric tons except as noted). *Agriculture and fishing* (value of sales in US$; 2001): cabbages 116,948, cucumbers 44,009, green onions 23,043; livestock (number of live animals; 2001) 702 pigs, 21,189 poultry; fisheries production (2006) 972 (from aquaculture 1%). *Manufacturing:* includes handicrafts and small items. *Energy production (consumption):* electricity (kW-hr; 2005) 128,000,000 ([2006] 114,000,000); petroleum products (metric tons; 2005) none (37,000). **Selected balance of payments data.** Receipts from (US$'000,000): tourism (2006) 90; foreign direct investment (FDI) (2004–06 avg.) 3; official development assistance (2006) 37. Disbursements for (US$'000,000): tourism (2006) 1.4. **Population economically active** (2005): total 10,203; activity rate of total population 51.3% (participation rates: ages 16 and over, 69.1%; female 39.1%; unemployed 4.2%). **Gross national income** (2007): US$167,000,000 (US$8,210 per capita).

Foreign trade

Imports (2006–07): US$91,287,000 (mineral fuels and lubricants 37.5%; machinery and transportation equipment 17.6%; beverages and tobacco products 14.9%; food and live animals 9.4%; chemical products 8.7%). *Major import sources* (2006–07): US 33.2%; Singapore 24.8%; Guam 11.2%; Japan 9.6%; Philippines 7.6%. **Exports** (2006–07): US$10,081,000 (mostly high-grade tuna and garments).

Major export destinations (2003): Japan 86.7%; Vietnam 5.9%; Zambia 4.6%.

Transport and communications

Transport. *Railroads:* none. *Roads* (2004): total length 61 km (paved 59%). *Vehicles* (2004): passenger cars and trucks 7,247. *Air transport* (2003): passenger arrivals 80,017, passenger departures 78,608. **Communications,** in total units (units per 1,000 persons). Telephone landlines (2006): 8,000 (399); cellular telephone subscribers (2006): 8,300 (414); total Internet users (2003): 3,200 (156).

Education and health

Educational attainment (2005). Percentage of population ages 25 and over having: no formal schooling 1.9%; incomplete primary education 9.0%; complete primary 3.9%; incomplete secondary 14.9%; complete secondary 42.2%; some postsecondary 10.0%; vocational 4.1%; higher 14.0%. **Literacy** (2005): percentage of total population ages 15 and over literate, virtually 100%. **Health** (2004): physicians 21 (1 per 942 persons); hospital beds 135 (1 per 147 persons); infant mortality rate per 1,000 live births (2006) 7.7.

Military

Total active duty personnel: none. The US is responsible for the external security of Palau, as specified in the Compact of Free Association of 1 Oct 1994.

Background

Palau's inhabitants began arriving 3,000 years ago in successive waves from the Indonesian and Philippine archipelagos and from Polynesia. The islands had been under nominal Spanish ownership for more than three centuries when they were sold to Germany in 1899. They were seized by Japan in 1914 and taken by Allied forces in 1944 during World War II. Palau became part of the UN Trust Territory of the Pacific Islands in 1947 and became a sovereign state in 1994; the US provides economic assistance and maintains a military presence in the islands.

Recent Developments

Palau's economy, already damaged by the world financial turmoil, was further injured in May 2008 when Far Eastern Air Transport stopped flying to Palau from Taiwan, Palau's largest source of tourist income.

Internet resources: <www.palaugov.net/stats>.

Panama

Official name: República de Panamá (Republic of Panama). **Form of government:** multiparty republic with one legislative house (National Assembly [71]). **Head of state and government:** President Ricardo Martinelli (from 2009). **Capital:** Panama City. **Official language:** Spanish. **Official religion:** none. **Monetary unit:** 1 balboa (B) = 100 centésimos; valuation (1 Jul 2009) US$1 = B 0.98.

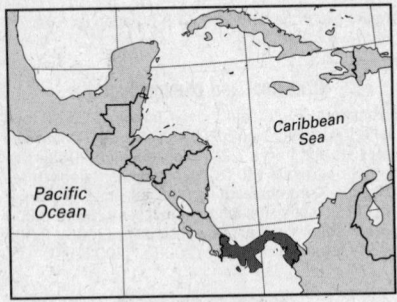

hr; 2005) 5,850,000,000 (5,799,000,000); crude petroleum, none (negligible); petroleum products (metric tons; 2005) negligible (1,782,000). **Selected balance of payments data.** Receipts from (US$'000,000): tourism (2006) 960; remittances (2007) 173; foreign direct investment (FDI) (2004–06 avg.) 1,530; official development assistance (2006) 30. Disbursements for (US$'000,000): tourism (2006) 271; remittances (2007) 151; FDI (2004–06 avg.) 1,492. **Population economically active** (2006): total 1,332,059; activity rate of total population 39.8% (participation rates: ages 15–64, 66.9%; female 37.1%; unemployed 9.1%). **Gross national income** (2007): US$18,423,000,000 (US$5,510 per capita). **Public debt** (external, outstanding; 2006): US$7,774,000,000.

Demography

Area: 29,024 sq mi, 75,173 sq km. **Population** (2008): 3,310,000. **Density** (2008): persons per sq mi 114.0, persons per sq km 44.0. **Urban** (2005): 70.8%. **Sex distribution** (2005): male 50.54%; female 49.46%. **Age breakdown** (2005): under 15, 30.5%; 15–29, 26.3%; 30–44, 21.4%; 45–59, 12.8%; 60–74, 6.6%; 75 and over, 2.4%. **Ethnic composition** (2000): mestizo 58.1%; black and mulatto 14.0%; white 8.6%; Amerindian 6.7%; Asian 5.5%; other 7.1%. **Religious affiliation** (2000): Roman Catholic 70.6%; Protestant/independent Christian 14.0%; Muslim 4.4%; Baha'i 1.2%; Buddhist 0.8%; traditional beliefs 0.7%; nonreligious 2.5%; other 5.8%. **Major cities** (2000): Panama City 415,964 (urban agglomeration [2005] 1,216,000; San Miguelito 293,745; David 77,734; Arraiján 63,753. **Location:** Central America, bordering the Caribbean Sea, Colombia, the North Pacific Ocean, and Costa Rica.

Vital statistics

Birth rate per 1,000 population (2007): 20.2 (world avg. 20.3); (2006) within marriage 17.3%; outside of marriage 82.7%. **Death rate** per 1,000 population (2007): 4.4 (world avg. 8.6). **Natural increase rate** per 1,000 population (2007): 15.8 (world avg. 11.7). **Total fertility rate** (avg. births per childbearing woman; 2006): 2.40. **Life expectancy** at birth (2005): male 72.7 years; female 77.9 years.

National economy

Budget (2004). *Revenue:* B 2,042,000,000 (tax revenue 59.2%, of which income tax 23.9%, taxes on domestic transactions 20.9%; other current revenue 39.9%, of which revenue from Panama Canal 9.0%). *Expenditures:* B 2,810,000,000 (current expenditures 83.8%, of which wages and salaries 27.2%, transfers 26.3%, debt service 21.1%; development expenditures 16.2%). **Production** (metric tons except as noted). *Agriculture and fishing* (2005): sugarcane 1,800,000, bananas 440,000, rice 280,000; livestock (number of live animals) 1,650,000 cattle, 300,000 pigs, 190,000 horses; fisheries production (2006) 235,569 (from aquaculture 4%). *Mining and quarrying* (2005): limestone 270,000. *Manufacturing* (value added in B '000,000; 2004): food products 410; beverages 167; cement, bricks, and ceramics 70. *Energy production (consumption):* electricity (kW-

Foreign trade

Imports (2006; c.i.f.): US$4,828,000,000 (machinery and apparatus 18.3%; refined petroleum products 15.9%; motor vehicles 10.8%; food products 9.6%; iron and steel 4.7%). *Major import sources:* US 27.0%; free zones 15.6%; Netherlands Antilles 10.1%; Costa Rica 5.1%; Japan 4.7%. **Exports** (2006; f.o.b.): US$1,086,000,000 (food and live animals 77.0%, of which fish 25.9% [including tuna 8.0%, salmon 5.5%], melons and papayas 15.3%, bananas 10.1%, crustaceans 5.7%). *Major export destinations:* US 39.0%; Spain 7.7%; The Netherlands 6.3%; Sweden 5.2%.

Transport and communications

Transport. *Railroads* (2002): route length (2005) 355 km; passenger-km (data for Panama Canal Railway, which reopened in 2001, and National Railway of Chiriquí only) 35,693,000,000; metric ton-km cargo (data for Panama Canal Railway only) 20,665,-000,000. *Roads* (2005): total length 11,984 km (paved 72%). *Vehicles* (2005): passenger cars 269,704; trucks and buses 78,699. *Panama Canal traffic* (2006–07): oceangoing transits 13,223; cargo 211,572,000 metric tons. *Air transport* (COPA only; 2007): passenger-km 7,944,000,000; metric ton-km cargo (2005) 37,226,000. **Communications,** in total units (units per 1,000 persons). Telephone landlines (2007): 492,000 (147); cellular telephone subscribers (2007): 2,392,000 (715); personal computers (2005): 147,000 (47); total Internet users (2007): 525,000 (157); broadband Internet subscribers (2007): 35,000 (10).

Education and health

Educational attainment (2000). Percentage of population ages 25 and over having: no formal schooling/unknown 13.8%; primary 36.4%; secondary 33.9%; undergraduate 14.4%; graduate 1.5%. **Literacy** (2005): percentage of total population ages 15 and over literate 93.0%; males 93.6%; females 92.4%. **Health** (2004): physicians 4,321 (1 per 715 persons); hospital beds 7,564 (1 per 408 persons); infant mortality rate per 1,000 live births (2007) 14.7; undernourished population (2002–04) 700,000 (23% of total population based on the consumption of a minimum daily requirement of 1,830 calories).

1 metric ton = about 1.1 short tons; 1 kilometer = 0.6 mi (statute); 1 metric ton-km cargo = about 0.68 short ton-mi cargo; c.i.f.: cost, insurance, and freight; f.o.b.: free on board

Military

Total active duty personnel (2007): none (military was abolished in 1990; a 12,000-member paramilitary includes air and maritime units). **Paramilitary expenditure as percentage of GDP** (2005): 1.1%; per capita expenditure US$50.

Background

Panama was inhabited by Native Americans when the Spanish arrived in 1501. The first successful Spanish settlement was founded by Vasco Núñez de Balboa in 1510. Panama was part of the Viceroyalty of New Granada until it declared its independence from Spain in 1821 to join the Gran Colombia union. In 1903 it revolted and was recognized by the US, to which it ceded the Canal Zone. The completed Panama Canal was opened in 1914; its jurisdiction reverted from the US to Panama in 1999. An invasion by US troops in 1989 overthrew the de facto ruler, Gen. Manuel Noriega. In 2007 a project to expand the canal began.

Recent Developments

Panama's economy, benefiting from a continued boom in the construction sector, grew at an annual rate of 9.2% in 2008, and unemployment dropped to 5.8%. In the previous three years, the economy had experienced growth ranging from 7.2% to 11.5% and unemployment had been as high as 10.3%. The rate of growth was expected to slow in 2009 as a result of the global financial crisis. Meanwhile, the US$5.2 billion expansion of the Panama Canal remained on schedule.

Internet resources:
<www.visitpanama.com/?id=&lang=en>.

Papua New Guinea

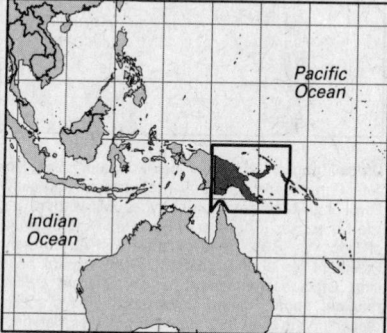

Pacific
Ocean

Indian
Ocean

Official names: Independent State of Papua New Guinea (English); Gau Hedinarai ai Papua–Matamata Guinea (Hiri Motu); Papua–Niugini (Tok Pisin). **Form of government:** constitutional monarchy with one legislative house (National Parliament [109]). **Chief of state:** British Queen Elizabeth II (from 1952), represented by Governor-General Sir Paulias Matane (from 2004). **Head of government:** Prime Minister Sir Michael Somare (from 2002). **Capital:** Port Moresby. **Official languages:** English; Hiri Motu; Tok Pisin. **Official religion:** none. **Monetary unit:** 1 kina (K) = 100 toea; valuation (1 Jul 2009) US$1 = K 2.57.

Demography

Area: 178,704 sq mi; 462,840 sq km. **Population** (2008): 6,474,000. **Density** (2008): persons per sq mi 36.2, persons per sq km 14.0. **Urban** (2005): 13.4%. **Sex distribution** (2005): male 50.79%; female 49.21%. **Age breakdown** (2005): under 15, 40.6%; 15–29, 27.3%; 30–44, 18.9%; 45–59, 9.3%; 60–74, 3.3%; 75–84, 0.5%; 85 and over, 0.1%. **Ethnic composition** (1983): New Guinea Papuan 84.0%; New Guinea Melanesian 15.0%; other 1.0%. **Religious affiliation** (2005): Protestant and independent Christian 44%; Roman Catholic 22%; traditional beliefs 34%. **Major cities** (2006): Port Moresby 289,900; Lae 75,600; Arawa 40,300; Mount Hagen 34,900; Popondetta 30,400. **Location:** Oceania, group of islands, including the eastern half of the island of New Guinea, in the South Pacific Ocean near the Equator, bordering Indonesia and to the north of Australia.

Vital statistics

Birth rate per 1,000 population (2005): 31.8 (world avg. 20.3). **Death rate** per 1,000 population (2005): 9.8 (world avg. 8.6). **Natural increase rate** per 1,000 population (2005): 22.0 (world avg. 11.7). **Total fertility rate** (avg. births per childbearing woman; 2005): 4.05. **Life expectancy** at birth (2005): male 54.3 years; female 60.2 years.

National economy

Budget (2007). *Revenue:* K 7,167,000,000 (tax revenue 79.4%, of which taxes on minerals and petroleum 33.6%, indirect taxes 18.2%, income tax 13.9%; grants 14.1%; nontax revenue 6.5%). *Expenditures:* K 6,845,000,000 (current expenditures 52.2%, of which transfers to provincial governments 10.9%, interest payments 5.4%; development expenditures 47.8%). **Public debt** (external, outstanding; June 2008): US$1,101,000,000. **Production** (metric tons except as noted). *Agriculture and fishing* (2007): oil palm fruit 1,400,000, bananas 870,000, coconuts 677,000, cacao 50,300, natural rubber 4,700; livestock (number of live animals) 1,800,000 pigs; fisheries production (2006) 274,680 (from aquaculture, negligible). *Mining and quarrying* (2007): copper (metal content) 169,184; gold 65,000 kg; silver 51,300 kg. *Manufacturing* (value of exports in US$'000; 2005): forest products 153,000; palm oil 126,100; coconut oil 30,200. *Energy production (consumption):* electricity (kW-hr; 2005) 3,500,-000,000 (3,500,000,000); coal (metric tons; 2004) none (1,000); crude petroleum (barrels; 2005) 15,837,000 (3,124,000); petroleum products (metric tons; 2005) 420,000 (1,386,000); natural gas (cu m; 2005) 128,135,000 (128,135,000). **Population economically active** (2000): total 2,413,357; activity rate of total population 46.5% (participation rates: ages 15–64, 73.2%; female 47.9%; unemployed, n.a.). **Gross national income** (2007): US$5,400,-000,000 (US$850 per capita). **Selected balance of payments data.** Receipts from (US$'000,000): tourism (2005) 3.6; remittances (2007) 13; foreign direct investment (FDI) (2004–06 avg.) 31; official development assistance (2006) 279. Disbursements for (US$'000,000): tourism (2005) 56; remittances (2007) 135; FDI (2004–06 avg.) 2.

Foreign trade

Imports (2003): K 4,628,000,000 (nonelectrical machinery 18.5%; food products 14.8%, of which cereals 7.3%; refined petroleum products 12.9%; transportation equipment 8.8%; chemical products 8.4%). *Major import sources* (2007): Australia 41.9%; US 19.6%; Singapore 15.1%; Japan 4.3%; China 3.0%. **Exports** (2007): K 13,847,000,000 (copper 30.1%; gold 26.5%; crude petroleum 21.5%; palm oil 4.9%; logs 4.1%). *Major export destinations* (2007): Australia 40.4%; Japan 16.9%; Germany 8.3%; Philippines 7.7%; China 3.4%.

Transport and communications

Transport. *Railroads:* none. *Roads* (2000): total length 19,600 km (paved 4%). *Vehicles* (2002): passenger cars 24,900; trucks and buses 87,800. *Air transport:* passenger-km (Air Niugini only; 2006) 748,000,000; metric ton-km cargo 22,000,000. **Communications,** in total units (units per 1,000 persons). Telephone landlines (2007): 60,000 (9.5); cellular telephone subscribers (2007): 300,000 (47); personal computers (2005): 391,000 (64); total Internet users (2006): 110,000 (18).

Education and health

Educational attainment (1990). Percentage of population ages 25 and over having: no formal schooling 82.6%; some primary education 8.2%; completed primary 5.0%; some secondary 4.2%. **Literacy** (2003): percentage of total population ages 15 and over literate 57.3%; males literate 63.4%; females literate 50.9%. **Health** (2005): physicians 750 (1 per 7,849 persons); hospital beds (2000) 14,516 (1 per 371 persons); infant mortality rate per 1,000 live births 63.0.

Military

Total active duty personnel (2008): 3,100 (army 80.6%, maritime element [coastal patrol] 12.9%, air force 6.5%). **Military expenditure as percentage of GDP** (2008): 0.6%; per capita expenditure US$7.

Did you know? Papua New Guinea's 96-km (60-mi) Kokoda Trail across the Owen Stanley Range to the northeast of Port Moresby was the site of an epic World War II struggle (in 1942) between invading Japanese forces and Australian troops.

Background

Papua New Guinea (PNG) has been inhabited since prehistoric times. The Portuguese sighted the coast of New Guinea in 1512. The first colony was founded in 1793 by the British. In 1828 the Dutch claimed the western half as part of the Dutch East Indies. In 1884 Britain annexed the southeastern part and Germany took over the northeastern sector. The British part became the Territory of Papua in 1906 and passed to Australia, which also governed the German sector after World War I. After World War II, Australia governed both sectors as the Territory of Papua and New Guinea. Dutch New Guinea was annexed to Indonesia in 1969. Papua New Guinea achieved independence in 1975 and joined the British Commonwealth. It moved to resolve its war with independence fighters on the island of Bougainville in the 1990s. The decadelong war ended when final terms for peace were negotiated on 1 Jun 2001; Bougainville became an autonomous region in 2005.

Recent Developments

An agreement between the PNG government and a consortium including ExxonMobil was signed in 2008, launching a US$11 billion liquefied natural gas (LNG) deal. Thought to be PNG's largest investment project, it would create 5,000 jobs in the construction phase and add 15% to the country's GDP.

Internet resources: <www.nso.gov.pg>.

Paraguay

Official name: República del Paraguay (Spanish); Tetã Paraguáype (Guaraní) (Republic of Paraguay). **Form of government:** multiparty republic with two legislative houses (Chamber of Senators [45]; Chamber of Deputies [80]). **Head of state and government:** President Fernando Lugo (from 2008). **Capital:** Asunción. **Official languages:** Spanish; Guaraní. **Official religion:** none (Roman Catholicism enjoys special recognition in the 1992 constitution). **Monetary unit:** 1 guaraní (₲; plural guaraníes) = 100 céntimos; valuation (1 Jul 2009) US$1 = ₲ 4,966.70.

Demography

Area: 157,048 sq mi, 406,752 sq km. **Population** (2008): 6,238,000. **Density** (2008): persons per sq mi 39.7, persons per sq km 15.3. **Urban** (2006):

---

1 metric ton = about 1.1 short tons;   1 kilometer = 0.6 mi (statute);   1 metric ton-km cargo = about 0.68 short ton-mi cargo;   c.i.f.: cost, insurance, and freight;   f.o.b.: free on board

57.1%. **Sex distribution** (2006): male 50.57%; female 49.43%. **Age breakdown** (2006): under 15, 35.4%; 15–29, 28.8%; 30–44, 17.4%; 45–59, 11.4%; 60–74, 5.2%; 75 and over, 1.8%. **Ethnic composition** (2000): mixed (white/Amerindian) 85.6%; white 9.3%, of which German 4.4%, Latin American 3.4%; Amerindian 1.8%; other 3.3%. **Religious affiliation** (2002): Roman Catholic 89.6%; Protestant (including all Evangelicals) 6.2%; other Christian 1.1%; nonreligious/atheist 1.1%; traditional beliefs 0.6%; other/unknown 1.4%. **Major urban areas** (2002): Asunción (2006) 519,361 (urban agglomeration [2007] 1,870,000); Ciudad del Este 222,274; San Lorenzo 204,356; Luque 170,986; Capiatá 154,274. **Location:** central South America, bordering Brazil, Argentina, and Bolivia.

Vital statistics

Birth rate per 1,000 population (2005): 25.8 (world avg. 20.3). **Death rate** per 1,000 population (2005): 5.7 (world avg. 8.6). **Natural increase rate** per 1,000 population (2005): 20.1 (world avg. 11.7). **Total fertility rate** (avg. births per childbearing woman; 2005): 3.30. **Life expectancy** at birth (2005): male 69.2 years; female 73.4 years.

National economy

Budget (2006–07): *Revenue:* ₲10,174,723,000,-000 (tax revenue 65.2%, of which VAT 28.5%, income tax 10.9%, taxes on international trade 8.5%; nontax revenue [including grants] 34.8%). *Expenditures:* ₲9,682,282,000,000 (current expenditures 77.3%, of which wages and salaries 42.9%; capital expenditures 22.7%). **Public debt** (external, outstanding; December 2007): US$2,197,000,000. **Population economically active** (2006): total 2,735,646; activity rate of total population 46.0% (participation rates: ages 15–64 [2002] 61.4%; female 38.5%; unemployed 11.1%). **Production** (metric tons except as noted). *Agriculture and fishing* (2007): cassava 5,100,000, soybeans 3,900,000, sugarcane 3,400,000, maté 87,500; livestock (number of live animals; 2007) 10,000,000 cattle, 1,600,000 pigs, 17,000,000 chickens; fisheries production (2006) 22,100 (from aquaculture 10%). *Mining and quarrying* (2006): dimension stone 70,000; kaolin 66,000. *Manufacturing* (value added in US$'000,000; 2002): food products 253; chemical products 77; beverages 67. *Energy production (consumption):* electricity (kW-hr; 2005) 51,156,000,000 (Paraguay is the world's second largest net exporter of electricity) (7,375,-000,000); crude petroleum (barrels; 2005) none (249,000); petroleum products (metric tons; 2005) 33,000 (1,157,000). **Gross national income** (2007): US$10,225,000,000 (US$1,670 per capita). **Selected balance of payments data.** Receipts from (US$'000,000): tourism (2006) 91; remittances (2007) 450; foreign direct investment (FDI) (2004–06 avg.) 89; official development assistance (2006) 56. Disbursements for (US$'000,000): tourism (2006) 91; FDI (2004–06 avg.) 9.

Foreign trade

Imports (2006): US$5,254,271,000 (machinery and apparatus 35.9%; mineral fuels 13.2%; transportation equipment 11.5%; chemical products 6.3%; food, beverages, and tobacco products 6.1%). *Major import sources:* China 27.0%; Brazil 20.0%; Argentina

13.6%; Japan 8.3%; US 6.4%. **Exports** (2006): US$1,906,367,000 (excludes electricity exports; contracted value of electricity sold to Brazil [2006] US$210,000,000) (soybeans 23.0%; meat 22.3%; cereals 11.4%; flour 7.5%; vegetable oils 6.2%). *Major export destinations:* Uruguay 22.0%; Brazil 17.2%; Russia 11.9%; Argentina 8.8%; Chile 6.9%.

Transport and communications

Transport. *Railroads* (2006): operational route length 36 km. *Roads* (1999): total length 29,500 km (paved 51%). *Vehicles* (2005): passenger cars 360,070; trucks 81,207. *Air transport* (Transportes Aéreos del Mercosur only; 2005): passenger-km 501,000,000; metric ton-km cargo, none. **Communications,** in total units (units per 1,000 persons). Telephone landlines (2007): 454,000 (74); cellular telephone subscribers (2007): 4,330,000 (707); personal computers (2005): 460,000 (78); total Internet users (2007): 280,000 (46); broadband Internet subscribers (2007): 49,000 (8).

Education and health

Educational attainment (2003). Percentage of population ages 15 and over having: no formal schooling 4.1%; incomplete primary education 30.2%; complete primary 30.8%; secondary 26.9%; higher 8.0%. **Literacy** (2005): percentage of total population ages 15 and over literate 94.9%; males literate 95.9%; females literate 93.9%. **Health** (2005): physicians 5,517 (1 per 873 persons); hospital beds 5,843 (1 per 1,010 persons); infant mortality rate per 1,000 live births 33.8; undernourished population (2002–04) 900,000 (15% of total population based on the consumption of a minimum daily requirement of 1,850 calories).

Military

Total active duty personnel (2007): 10,650 (army 71.4%, navy 18.3%, air force 10.3%). **Military expenditure as percentage of GDP** (2005): 0.7%; per capita expenditure US$9.

Background

Seminomadic tribes speaking Guaraní were in Paraguay long before it was settled by Spain in the 16th and 17th centuries. Paraguay was part of the Viceroyalty of the Río de la Plata until it became independent in 1811. It suffered from dictatorial governments in the 19th century and from the 1865 war with Brazil, Argentina, and Uruguay. The Chaco War with Bolivia over disputed territory was settled primarily in Paraguay's favor by the peace treaty of 1938. Military governments, including that of Alfredo Stroessner, predominated in the mid-20th century until the election of a civilian president, Juan Carlos Wasmosy, in 1993. Paraguay suffered political unrest and a financial crisis beginning in the 1990s and continuing into the 21st century.

Recent Developments

Former Roman Catholic bishop Fernando Lugo won a stunning victory in Paraguay's presidential election in April 2008, putting an end to the Colorado Party's 61-year hold on power. Lugo faced massive challenges in a country in which Colorado Party functionaries still occupied nearly all posts in the judicial and administrative systems—and in which 1% of the population controlled more than three-fourths of the arable land, while 42% of the population lived in poverty. Peasant groups staged dozens of land invasions, particularly of soybean producers because of concerns over their use of toxic pesticides. By promising that it would redistribute some 8 million ha (20 million ac) allegedly seized by former dictator Alfredo Stroessner (1954–89) and handed out to his cronies, Lugo's administration persuaded most peasant leaders to halt the invasions.

Internet resources: <www.paraguay.com>.

Peru

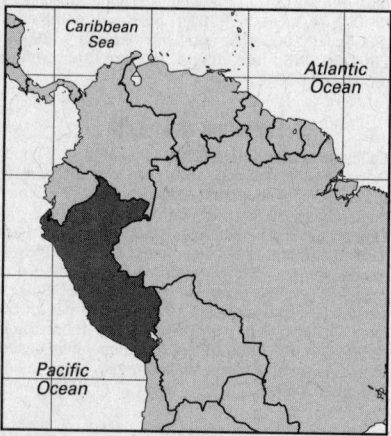

Official name: República del Perú (Spanish) (Republic of Peru). Form of government: unitary multiparty republic with one legislative house (Congress [120]). Head of state and government: President Alan García (from 2006), assisted by Prime Minister Yehude Simon (from 2008). Capital: Lima. Official languages: Spanish; Quechua; Aymara. Official religion: none. Monetary unit: 1 nuevo sol (S/.) = 100 céntimos; valuation (1 Jul 2009) US$1 = S/. 3.01.

Demography

Area: 496,218 sq mi, 1,285,198 sq km. Population (2008): 28,534,000. Density (2008): persons per sq mi 57.5, persons per sq km 22.2. Urban (2007): 75.9%. Sex distribution (2007): male 49.68%; female 50.32%. Age breakdown (2007): under 15, 30.5%; 15–29, 27.5%; 30–44, 20.4%; 45–59, 12.5%; 60–74, 6.4%; 75–84, 2.0%; 85 and over, 0.7%. Ethnic composition (2000): Quechua 47.0%; mestizo 31.9%; white 12.0%; Aymara 5.4%; Japanese 0.5%; other 3.2%. Religious affiliation (2005): Roman Catholic 85%, of which practicing weekly 15%; Protestant 7%; independent Christian 4%; other 4%. Major cities (2007): Lima (urban agglomeration) 8,472,935; Arequipa 749,291; Trujillo 682,834; Chiclayo 524,442; Piura 377,496. Location: western

South America, bordering Ecuador, Colombia, Brazil, Bolivia, Chile, and the South Pacific Ocean.

Vital statistics

Birth rate per 1,000 population (2007): 20.2 (world avg. 20.3). Death rate per 1,000 population (2007): 6.2 (world avg. 8.6). Total fertility rate (avg. births per childbearing woman; 2007): 2.46. Life expectancy at birth (2007): male 68.3 years; female 72.0 years.

National economy

Budget (2005). Revenue: S/. 41,432,000,000 (tax revenue 85.8%, of which VAT 44.6%, corporate taxes 14.8%; nontax revenue 14.2%). Expenditures: S/. 43,534,000,000 (current expenditures 77.1%, of which transfers 30.1%; debt service 11.7%; capital expenditures 11.2%). Production (metric tons except as noted). Agriculture and fishing (2007): sugarcane 8,246,406, potatoes 3,388,147, rice 2,455,809, quinoa 34,000 (in 2007 Peru was the world's second largest producer of coca, with 116,800 metric tons produced); livestock (number of live animals) 15,000,000 sheep, 5,300,000 cattle, (2005) 4,500,000 llamas and alpacas; fisheries production (2006) 7,045,884 (from aquaculture, negligible). Mining and quarrying (metal content; 2006): iron ore 4,785,000; zinc 1,201,786; copper 1,049,933; lead 313,322; molybdenum 17,209; silver 3,471. Manufacturing (value in S/. '000; 2005): food products 11,854; textiles and wearing apparel 5,310; chemical products 4,212. Energy production (consumption): electricity (kW-hr; 2005) 25,660,000,000 (25,660,000,000); coal (metric tons; 2005) 43,000 (1,075,000); crude petroleum (barrels; 2005) 28,828,000 (59,710,000); petroleum products (metric tons; 2005) 9,010,000 (6,598,000); natural gas (cu m; 2005) 1,965,000,000 (1,965,000,000). Selected balance of payments data. Receipts from (US$'000,000): tourism (2006) 1,381; remittances (2007) 2,100; foreign direct investment (FDI) (2004–06 avg.) 2,548; official development assistance (2006) 468. Disbursements for (US$'000,000): tourism (2006) 760; remittances (2007) 133; FDI (2004–06 avg.) 220. Population economically active (2002): total 12,892,000; activity rate of total population 48.2% (participation rates: ages 15–64, 72.6%; female 42.0%; urban unemployed [2005] 9.6%). Gross national income (2007): US$96,241,000,000 (US$3,450 per capita). Public debt (external, outstanding; 2006): US$21,825,000,000.

Foreign trade

Imports (2006; c.i.f.): US$15,312,000,000 (machinery and apparatus 24.5%; chemical products 15.2%; crude petroleum 14.3%; food products 8.2%; base and fabricated metals 8.2%). Major import sources: US 16.4%; Brazil 10.4%; China 10.3%; Ecuador 7.1%; Colombia 6.2%. Exports (2006): US$23,765,000,000 (ores and concentrates 26.7%, of which copper 12.1%, zinc 7.4%, molybdenum 3.6%; gold 16.8%; food products 13.8%, of which fish meal 5.0%; refined copper 12.9%; crude petroleum 7.9%). Major export destinations: US 24.0%; China 9.5%; Switzerland 7.1%; Canada 6.8%; Chile 6.0%.

1 metric ton = about 1.1 short tons;   1 kilometer = 0.6 mi (statute);   1 metric ton-km cargo = about 0.68 short ton-mi cargo;   c.i.f.: cost, insurance, and freight;   f.o.b.: free on board

Transport and communications

Transport. *Railroads* (2002): length (2005) 3,462 km; passenger-km 98,000,000; metric ton-km cargo 1,008,000,000. *Roads* (2004): total length 78,829 km (paved 14%). *Vehicles* (2004): passenger cars 824,613; trucks and buses 462,803. *Air transport* (2007): passenger-km 4,440,000,000; metric ton-km cargo 117,072,000. **Communications**, in total units (units per 1,000 persons). Telephone landlines (2007): 2,673,000 (96); cellular telephone subscribers (2007): 15,417,000 (553); personal computers (2005): 2,800,000 (103); total Internet users (2007): 7,636,000 (274); broadband Internet subscribers (2007): 570,000 (20).

Education and health

Educational attainment (2005). Percentage of population ages 15 and over. having: no formal schooling 11.8%; less than complete primary education 24.3%; complete primary 11.5%; incomplete secondary 15.3%; complete secondary 19.0%; higher 18.1%. **Literacy** (2005): percentage of total population ages 15 and over literate 91.6%; males literate 95.6%; females literate 87.7%. **Health** (2004): physicians 41,266 (1 per 651 persons); hospital beds (2005) 42,159 (1 per 647 persons); infant mortality rate per 1,000 live births (2007) 30.5; undernourished population (2002–04) 3,300,000 (12% of total population based on the consumption of a minimum daily requirement of 1,820 calories).

Military

Total active duty personnel (2007): 114,000 (army 64.9%, navy 20.2%, air force 14.9%). **Military expenditure as percentage of GDP** (2005): 1.4%; per capita expenditure US$39.

Background

Peru was the center of the Inca empire, which was established about 1230 with its capital at Cuzco. In 1533 it was conquered by Francisco Pizarro, and it was dominated by Spain for almost 300 years as the Viceroyalty of Peru. It declared its independence in 1821, and freedom was achieved in 1824. Peru was defeated in the War of the Pacific with Chile (1879–83). A boundary dispute with Ecuador erupted into war in 1941 and gave Peru control over a larger part of the Amazon basin; further disputes ensued until the border was demarcated again in 1998. The government was overthrown by a military junta in 1968, and civilian rule was restored in 1980. The government of Alberto Fujimori dissolved the legislature in 1992 and promulgated a new constitution the following year. It later successfully combated the Sendero Luminoso (Shining Path) and Tupac Amarú rebel movements. Fujimori won a second term in 1995 and a controversial third term in 2000, but he left office and the country late that year amid allegations of corruption.

Recent Developments

The year 2008 saw Peru's economy advance strongly, growing 9.8%, with significant increases across the board in mining, agriculture, construction, manufacturing, and the entire service sector. A no-table sign of overall economic well-being emerged when Peru's debt was moved up to investment grade status by international brokerage houses Standard & Poor's and Fitch Ratings. However, while some parts of the country were booming (notably Lima and along the coast), many residents of southern and highland Peru, where many of the country's indigenous peoples lived, continued to see themselves as left out. Work in the informal sector often provided only part-time employment, poor wages, and no benefits, and many Peruvians were also alarmed at the emergence of inflation that rekindled memories of the late 1980s and its 7,600% hyperinflation. In January 2009 US Pres. George W. Bush signed a controversial free-trade agreement with Peru, though detractors argued that Peru had not enacted key environmental and labor-rights legislation.

Internet resources: <www.peru.info/perueng.asp>.

Philippines

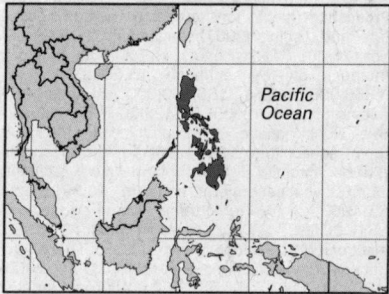

Official name: Republika ng Pilipinas (Filipino); Republic of the Philippines (English). **Form of government:** unitary republic with two legislative houses (Senate [24]; House of Representatives [240]). **Chief of state and head of government:** President Gloria Macapagal-Arroyo (from 2001). **Capital:** Manila; other government offices and ministries are located in Quezon City. **Official languages:** Filipino; English. **Official religion:** none. **Monetary unit:** 1 Philippine piso (P) = 100 sentimos; valuation (1 Jul 2009) US$1 = P 47.98.

Demography

Area: 122,121 sq mi, 316,294 sq km. **Population** (2008): 90,227,000. **Density** (2008): persons per sq mi 779.0, persons per sq km 300.8. **Urban** (2007): 64.0%. **Sex distribution** (2005): male 50.35%; female 49.65%. **Age breakdown** (2005): under 15, 35.1%; 15–29, 28.8%; 30–44, 19.0%; 45–59, 11.0%; 60–74, 5.0%; 75–84, 1.0%; 85 and over, 0.1%. **Ethnic composition** (2000): Tagalog 20.9%; Visayan (Cebu) 19.0%; Ilocano 11.1%; Hiligaynon (Visaya) 9.4%; Waray-Waray (Binisaya) 4.7%; Central Bikol (Naga) 4.6%; Filipino mestizo 3.5%; Pampango 3.1%; other 23.7%. **Religious affiliation** (2005): Roman Catholic 64.9%; independent Christian 17.7%; Muslim 5.1%; Protestant 5.0%; traditional beliefs 2.2%; other 5.1%. **Major cities** (2007): Quezon City 2,679,450; Manila 1,660,714 (National Capital Region 11,553,427); Caloocan

1,378,856; Davao 1,363,337; Cebu City 798,809. **Location:** southeastern Asia, archipelago between the Philippine Sea and the South China Sea, east of Vietnam.

Vital statistics

Birth rate per 1,000 population (2005): 24.1 (world avg. 20.3). **Death rate** per 1,000 population (2005): 5.6 (world avg. 8.6). **Total fertility rate** (avg. births per childbearing woman; 2005): 3.41. **Life expectancy** at birth (2005): male 67.0 years; female 72.9 years.

National economy

Budget (2005). *Revenue:* P 757,945,000,000 (income tax 47.1%; taxes on international trade 19.6%; general sales tax 16.1%; nontax revenues 11.8%). *Expenditures:* P 899,990,000,000 (debt service 33.5%; local government allotments 16.8%; education and culture 15.1%; transportation and communications 6.1%). **Public debt** (external, outstanding; September 2007): US$37,082,000,000. **Production** (metric tons except as noted). *Agriculture and fishing* (2007): sugarcane 25,300,000, rice 16,000,000, coconuts 15,580,000; livestock (number of live animals) 13,250,000 pigs, 3,365,000 buffalo, 136,000,000 chickens; fisheries production (2006) 2,942,000 (from aquaculture 21%); aquatic plants production 1,469,000 (from aquaculture 100%). *Mining and quarrying* (2005): chromite 36,070; nickel (metal content) 22,560; copper (metal content) 16,320; gold 37,490 kg. *Manufacturing* (value added in US$'000,000; 2003): petroleum products 1,980; electronics 1,696; food products 1,338. *Energy production (consumption):* electricity (kW-hr; 2005) 56,549,000,000 (56,549,000,000); coal (metric tons; 2005) 178,000 (3,566,000); lignite (metric tons; 2005) 2,986,000 (6,254,000); crude petroleum (barrels; 2005) 211,000 (79,500,000); petroleum products (metric tons; 2005) 9,909,000 (13,573,000); natural gas (cu m; 2005) 3,269,000,-000 (3,269,000,000). **Selected balance of payments data.** Receipts from (US$'000,000): tourism (2006) 3,501; remittances (2007) 17,217; foreign direct investment (FDI) (2004–06 avg.) 1,629. Disbursements for (US$'000,000): tourism (2006) 1,232; remittances (2007) 20; FDI (2004–06 avg.) 290. **Gross national income** (2007): US$142,623,-000,000 (US$1,620 per capita). **Population economically active** (2007): total 36,434,000; activity rate of total population 41% (participation rates: ages 15 and over, 63.6%; female [2006] 39.4%; unemployed [April 2007–March 2008] 7.2%).

Foreign trade

Imports (2006; c.i.f.): US$54,078,000,000 (electronics 33.6%; crude petroleum 14.1%; chemical products 7.4%; parts for office machines and computers 6.6%; food products 5.9%). *Major import sources:* US 16.2%; Japan 14.2%; Singapore 8.4%; Taiwan 7.9%; China 7.2%. **Exports** (2006; f.o.b.): US$47,410,000,000 (microcircuits and transistors 35.8%; computers, office machinery, and parts 17.2%; wearing apparel and accessories 5.5%; food products 3.8%). *Major export*

destinations: US 18.3%; Japan 16.7%; The Netherlands 10.1%; China 9.8%; Hong Kong 7.8%.

Transport and communications

Transport. *Railroads* (2004): route length 897 km; passenger-km 83,400,000; metric ton-km cargo (2000) 660,000,000. *Roads* (2003): total length 200,037 km (paved 10%). *Vehicles* (2006): passenger cars 767,000; trucks and buses 240,000. *Air transport* (Philippines Airlines only; 2006): passenger-km 13,513,000,000; metric ton-km cargo 257,000,000. **Communications**, in total units (units per 1,000 persons). Telephone landlines (2006): 3,633,000 (43); cellular telephone subscribers (2007): 51,795,000 (586); personal computers (2005): 4,521,000 (54); total Internet users (2007): 5,300,000 (60); broadband Internet subscribers (2007): 968,000 (11).

Education and health

Educational attainment (2000). Percentage of population ages 25 and over having: no formal schooling/unknown 6.1%; primary education 38.5%; incomplete secondary 12.5%; complete secondary 17.2%; technical 5.9%; incomplete undergraduate 11.8%; complete undergraduate 7.3%; graduate 0.7%. **Literacy** (2003): percentage of total population ages 15 and over literate 92.6%. **Health:** physicians (2005) 98,210 (1 per 865 persons); hospital beds (2006) 106,316 (1 per 815 persons); infant mortality rate per 1,000 live births (2007) 21.9; undernourished population (2002–04) 14,600,000 (18% of total population based on the consumption of a minimum daily requirement of 1,810 calories).

Military

Total active duty personnel (2007): 106,000 (army 62.3%, navy 22.6%, air force 15.1%). **Military expenditure as percentage of GDP** (2005): 0.9%; per capita expenditure US$10.

Background

Waves of diverse immigrants from the Asian mainland occupied the Philippines in ancient times. Ferdinand Magellan arrived in 1521. The islands were colonized by the Spanish, who retained control until the islands were ceded to the US in 1898 following the Spanish-American War. The Commonwealth of the Philippines was established in 1935 to prepare the country for political and economic independence, which was delayed by World War II and the Japanese invasion. The islands were liberated by US forces during 1944–45, and the Republic of the Philippines was proclaimed in 1946, with a government patterned on that of the US. In 1965 Ferdinand Marcos was elected president. He declared martial law in 1972, and it lasted until 1981. After 20 years of dictatorial rule, he was driven from power in 1986. Corazon Aquino became president and instituted democratic rule. The government has tried to come to terms with Muslim independence fighters in the south by establishing the Muslim Mindanao autonomous region in Mindanao and nearby islands, but violent conflict continued into the 21st century.

1 metric ton = about 1.1 short tons; 1 kilometer = 0.6 mi (statute); 1 metric ton-km cargo = about 0.68 short ton-mi cargo; c.i.f.: cost, insurance, and freight; f.o.b.: free on board

Recent Developments

An attempt to end decades of conflict in the southern Philippines collapsed in August 2008, and this led to intensified fighting between government forces and Muslim insurgents who sought to strengthen an autonomous Islamic state. In July the government had reached an agreement with the Moro Islamic Liberation Front (MILF), which provided for an expanded homeland with greater autonomy for some four million Muslims on the southern island of Mindanao. In August, however, officials from the Roman Catholic areas of Mindanao obtained a Supreme Court order temporarily blocking the formal signing of the agreement. MILF guerrillas angrily reacted to the order by launching attacks on government forces and villages in Mindanao, and that month the government canceled the agreement. The resumed fighting in Mindanao caused nearly 100 deaths, and some 500,000 people fled their homes. The MILF said that it would take its case to the UN as well as to the Organization of the Islamic Conference. Meanwhile, both the MILF and the government indicated that they would resume observing a cease-fire they had signed in 2003, but violent clashes continued throughout 2009.

Internet resources: <www.nscb.gov.ph>.

Poland

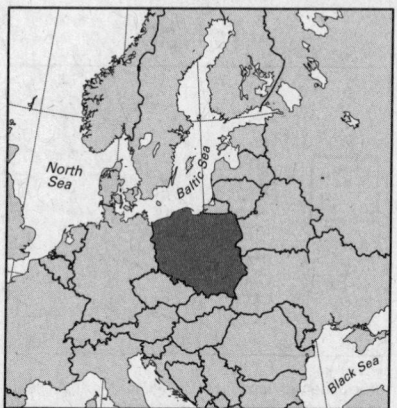

North Sea

Baltic Sea

Black Sea

Official name: Rzeczpospolita Polska (Republic of Poland). **Form of government:** unitary multiparty republic with two legislative houses (Senate [100]; Sejm [460]). **Chief of state:** President Lech Kaczynski (from 2005). **Head of government:** Prime Minister Donald Tusk (from 2007). **Capital:** Warsaw. **Official languages:** Polish. **Official religion:** none (Roman Catholicism has special recognition per 1997 concordat with Vatican City). **Monetary unit:** 1 zloty (Zl) = 100 groszy; valuation (1 Jul 2009) US$1 = Zl 3.07.

Demography

Area: 120,726 sq mi, 312,679 sq km. **Population** (2008): 38,111,000. **Density** (2008): persons per sq mi 315.7, persons per sq km 121.9. **Urban** (2008): 61.1%. **Sex distribution** (2008): male 48.32%; female 51.68%. **Age breakdown** (2008): under 16, 17.0%; 16–29, 22.6%; 30–44, 20.3%; 45–59, 22.3%; 60–74, 11.9%; 75–84, 4.9%; 85 and over, 1.0%. **Ethnic composition** (2000): Polish 90.0%; Ukrainian 4.0%; German 4.0%; Belarusian 0.5%; Kashubian 0.4%; other 1.1%. **Religious affiliation** (2006): Roman Catholic 88.8%; other Catholic 0.3%; Polish Orthodox 1.3%; Protestant 0.4%; Jehovah's Witness 0.3%; other (mostly nonreligious) 8.9%. **Major cities** (2007): Warsaw 1,706,624; Krakow 756,583; Lodz 753,192; Wroclaw 632,930; Poznan 560,932. **Location:** central Europe, bordering the Baltic Sea, the Russian exclave of Kaliningrad, Lithuania, Belarus, Ukraine, Slovakia, Czech Republic, and Germany.

Vital statistics

Birth rate per 1,000 population (2007): 10.2 (world avg. 20.3); (2006) within marriage 81.1%; outside of marriage 18.9%. **Death rate** per 1,000 population (2007): 9.9 (world avg. 8.6). **Natural increase rate** per 1,000 population (2007): 0.3 (world avg. 11.7). **Total fertility rate** (avg. births per childbearing woman; 2007): 1.31. **Life expectancy** at birth (2007): male 71.0 years; female 79.7 years.

National economy

Budget (2007). *Revenue:* Zl 236,367,500,000 (VAT 40.8%; excise tax 20.7%; income tax 15.0%; corporate taxes 10.4%). *Expenditures:* Zl 252,323,-900,000 (social security and welfare 21.5%; transfers 14.6%; public debt 10.9%; wages and salaries 10.7%). **Gross national income** (2007): US$374,-633,000,000 (US$9,840 per capita). **Production** (metric tons except as noted). *Agriculture and fishing* (2007): potatoes 11,221,100, sugar beets 11,057,-800, wheat 8,378,600, triticale 4,201,600; livestock (number of live animals) 18,128,510 pigs, 5,696,200 cattle (in addition, 1,450,000 beehives); fisheries production (2006) 180,265 (from aquaculture 20%). *Mining and quarrying* (2006): sulfur (2007–08) 860,200; copper ore (metal content) 570,000; silver (metal content) 1,300. *Manufacturing* (value of sales in Zl'000,000; 2007): food products 153,080; transportation equipment 93,977; fabricated metal products 61,857. *Energy production (consumption):* electricity ('000,000 kW-hr; 2007–08) 158,162 ([2006] 135,333); coal ('000 metric tons; 2007–08) 84,998 ([2006] 86,130); lignite ('000 metric tons; 2007–08) 58,189 ([2006] 60,801); crude petroleum (barrels; 2007) 5,311,000 ([2006] 148,730,900); petroleum products (metric tons; 2007–08) 27,680,000 ([2006] 21,354,000); natural gas (cu m; 2007–08) 5,506,000,000 ([2006] 16,521,000,000). **Public debt** (external, outstanding; January 2008): US$49,742,000,000. **Population economically active** (2007): total 16,860,000; activity rate of total population 44.2% (participation rates: ages 15–64, 63.2%; female 45.2%; unemployed [October 2007–September 2008] 10.3%). **Selected balance of payments data.** Receipts from (US$'000,000): tourism (2006) 7,239; remittances (2007) 10,671; foreign direct investment (FDI) (2004–06 avg.) 12,138. Disbursements for (US$'000,000): tourism (2006) 5,760; remittances (2007) 1,279; FDI (2004–06 avg.) 2,694.

Foreign trade

Imports (2007; c.i.f.): Zl 456,828,439,700 (chemical products 13.0%; electrical equipment 12.9%; base and fabricated metals 12.3%; machinery and apparatus 11.7%; transportation equipment 11.0%). *Major import sources:* Germany 24.1%; Russia 8.7%; China 7.1%; Italy 6.9%; France 5.1%. **Exports** (2007; f.o.b.): Zl 386,555,639,200 (transportation equipment 16.4%; electrical equipment 13.6%; base and fabricated metals 12.7%; machinery and apparatus 10.9%; food products 8.1%). *Major export destinations:* Germany 25.9%; Italy 6.6%; France 6.1%; UK 5.9%; Czech Republic 5.5%.

Transport and communications

Transport (2007). *Railroads:* length 20,107 km; passenger-km 19,859,000,000; metric ton-km cargo 54,253,000,000. *Roads* (public roads only): total length 383,100 km (paved 68%). *Vehicles:* passenger cars 14,588,700; trucks and buses 2,608,100. *Air transport:* passenger-km 11,291,000,000; metric ton-km cargo 98,000,000. **Communications,** in total units (units per 1,000 persons). Telephone landlines (2007): 10,243,000 (269); cellular telephone subscribers (2007): 41,510,000 (1,089); personal computers (2004): 7,362,000 (191); total Internet users (2007): 16,000,000 (420); broadband Internet subscribers (2006): 2,911,000 (76).

Education and health

Educational attainment (2006). Percentage of population ages 13 and over having: no formal schooling/incomplete primary education 2.5%; complete primary 20.9%; lower secondary/vocational 28.2%; upper secondary and postsecondary 33.1%; university 15.3%. **Literacy** (2003): percentage of total population literate, virtually 100%. **Health** (2006): physicians 77,479 (1 per 492 persons); hospital beds 234,691 (1 per 163 persons); infant mortality rate per 1,000 live births (2007) 5.9; undernourished population (2002–04) less than 2.5% of total population.

Military

Total active duty personnel (2007): 127,266 (army 62.1%, navy 9.1%, air force 22.4%, centrally controlled staff 6.4%). **Military expenditure as percentages of GDP** (2005): 1.9%; per capita expenditure US$154.

Background

Established as a kingdom in 922 under Mieszko I, Poland united with Lithuania in 1386 under the Jagiellon dynasty (1386–1572) to become the dominant power in east-central Europe. In 1466 it wrested western and eastern Prussia from the Teutonic Order, and its lands eventually stretched to the Black Sea. Wars with Sweden and Russia in the late 17th century led to the loss of considerable territory. In 1697 the electors of Saxony became kings of Poland, virtually ending Polish independence. In the late 18th century, Poland was divided among Prussia, Russia, and Austria. After 1815 the former Polish lands came under Russian domination, and from 1863 Poland

was a Russian province. After World War I, an independent Poland was established by the Allies. The invasion of Poland in 1939 by the USSR and Germany precipitated World War II, during which the Nazis sought to purge its culture and its large Jewish population. Reoccupied by Soviet forces in 1945, it was controlled by a Soviet-dominated government from 1947. In the 1980s the Solidarity labor movement led by Lech Walesa achieved major political reforms, and free elections were held in 1989. An economic austerity program instituted in 1990 sped the transition to a market economy. Poland became a member of NATO in 1999 and the EU in 2004.

Recent Developments

The war between Georgia and Russia in August 2008 inspired Pres. Lech Kaczynski to take a strong anti-Russian stand. On 12 August he and the presidents of Estonia, Latvia, Lithuania, and Ukraine flew to Tbilisi to express support for Georgia. Also in August, after 18 months of tough negotiations and influenced strongly by the developments in Georgia, Poland signed an agreement with the US to host antiballistic interceptor missiles as part of the proposed US global missile defense system. Although the agreement remained to be ratified by the Polish parliament and signed into law by the president, the move angered Russia, who saw it as a threat and promised to aim missiles at Poland if the system was installed.

Internet resources: <www.stat.gov.pl/english>.

Portugal

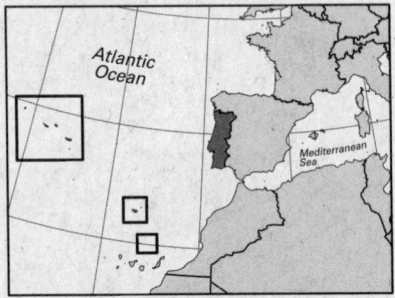

Atlantic Ocean

Mediterranean Sea

Official name: República Portuguesa (Portuguese Republic). **Form of government:** republic with one legislative house (Assembly of the Republic [230]). **Chief of state:** President Aníbal Cavaco Silva (from 2006). **Head of government:** Prime Minister José Sócrates (from 2005). **Capital:** Lisbon. **Official language:** Portuguese. **Official religion:** none. **Monetary unit:** 1 euro (€) = 100 cents; valuation (1 Jul 2009) US$1 = €0.71.

Demography

Area: 35,556 sq mi, 92,090 sq km. **Population** (2008): 10,649,000. **Density** (2008): persons per sq mi 299.5, persons per sq km 115.6. **Urban** (2005): 57.6%. **Sex distribution** (2005): male 48.40%; female 51.60%. **Age breakdown** (2005): under 15, 15.7%; 15–29, 20.4%; 30–44, 22.6%; 45–59, 19.2%; 60–74, 14.8%; 75–84, 5.9%; 85 and over, 1.4%. **Ethnic composition** (2000): Portuguese 91.9%; mixed-race people from Angola, Mozambique, and Cape Verde 1.6%; Brazilian 1.4%; Marrano 1.2%; other European 1.2%; Han Chinese 0.9%; other 1.8%. **Religious affiliation** (2000): Christian 92.4%, of which Roman Catholic 87.4%, independent Christian 2.7%, Protestant 1.3%, other Christian 1.0%; nonreligious/atheist 6.5%; Buddhist 0.6%; other 0.5%. **Major cities** (2001): Lisbon 564,657 (urban agglomeration [2005] 2,761,000); Porto 263,131 (urban agglomeration [2005] 1,309,000); Braga 164,192; Coimbra 148,443; Funchal 103,961. **Location:** southwestern Europe, bordering Spain and the North Atlantic Ocean.

Vital statistics

Birth rate per 1,000 population (2007): 9.7 (world avg. 20.3); within marriage 66.4%; outside of marriage 33.6%. **Death rate** per 1,000 population (2007): 9.8 (world avg. 8.6). **Natural increase rate** per 1,000 population (2007): −0.1 (world avg. 11.7). **Total fertility rate** (avg. births per childbearing woman; 2007): 1.30. **Life expectancy** at birth (2007): male 75.2 years; female 81.6 years.

National economy

Budget (2004). *Revenue:* €59,636,000,000 (social contributions 30.9%; indirect taxes 28.4%; direct taxes 21.0%). *Expenditures:* €63,511,000,000 (current expenditures 90.0%; development expenditures 10.0%). **Public debt** (2007): US$158,000,000,000. **Production** (metric tons except as noted). *Agriculture and fishing* (2007): grapes 1,050,000, tomatoes 1,000,000, corn (maize) 646,500, cork (2008) 165,000; livestock (number of live animals) 3,549,000 sheep, 2,295,450 pigs, 1,407,270 cattle; fisheries production (2006) 235,853 (from aquaculture 3%). *Mining and quarrying* (2006): marble (2005) 752,000; kaolin (2005) 164,072; copper (metal content) 78,660; tungsten (metal content) 780. *Manufacturing* (value added in US$'000,000; 2003): food products 2,148; cement, tiles, and ceramics 1,611; fabricated metal products 1,536. *Energy production (consumption):* electricity (kW-hr; 2005) 46,575,000,000 (53,399,000,000); coal (metric tons; 2005) none (5,476,000); crude petroleum (barrels; 2005) none (96,324,000); petroleum products (metric tons; 2005) 11,682,000 (12,600,000); natural gas (cu m; 2005) none (4,471,000,000). **Population economically active** (2006): total 5,587,300; activity rate of total population 52.5% (participation rates: ages 15–64, 73.9%; female 46.6%; unemployed 7.7%). **Gross national income** (2007): US$201,079,000,000 (US$18,950 per capita). **Selected balance of payments data.** Receipts from (US$'000,000): tourism (2006) 8,388; remittances (2007) 3,750; foreign direct investment (FDI) (2004–06 avg.) 4,554. Disbursements for (US$'000,000): tourism (2006) 3,298; remittances (2007) 1,386; FDI (2004–06 avg.) 4,477.

Foreign trade

Imports (2006; c.i.f.): €53,162,000,000 (machinery and apparatus 18.7%; chemical products 10.9%; motor vehicles 10.3%; crude petroleum 9.5%; food products 9.3%). *Major import sources:* Spain 28.9%; Germany 13.1%; France 8.1%; Italy 5.6%; The Netherlands 4.4%. **Exports** (2006; f.o.b.): €34,561,000,000 (machinery, apparatus, and electronics 18.6%; motor vehicles and parts 12.5%; base and fabricated metals 7.4%; wearing apparel and accessories 6.8%; chemical products 6.5%). *Major export destinations:* Spain 26.5%; Germany 12.8%; France 12.0%; UK 6.6%; US 6.1%.

Transport and communications

Transport. *Railroads* (2004): length 2,836 km; passenger-km 3,217,000,000; metric ton-km cargo 2,588,000,000. *Roads* (2004): total length 78,470 km (paved 86%). *Vehicles* (2003): passenger cars 4,918,310; trucks and buses 372,179. *Air transport* (Continental Portugal only; 2007): passenger-km 20,592,000,000; metric ton-km cargo 321,396,000. **Communications,** in total units (units per 1,000 persons). Telephone landlines (2007): 4,139,000 (390); cellular telephone subscribers (2007): 13,413,000 (1,263); personal computers (2005): 1,406,000 (133); total Internet users (2007): 3,549,000 (334); broadband Internet subscribers (2007): 1,608,000 (151).

Education and health

Educational attainment (2002). Percentage of population ages 25–64 having: no formal schooling through complete primary education 67%; complete lower secondary 13%; complete upper secondary 11%; higher 9%. **Literacy** (2002): percentage of total population ages 15 and over literate 92.5%; males literate 95.2%; females literate 90.3%. **Health:** physicians (2007) 37,904 (1 per 280 persons); hospital beds (2006) 36,563 (1 per 290 persons); infant mortality rate per 1,000 live births (2007) 3.4; undernourished population (2002–04) less than 2.5% of total population.

Military

Total active duty personnel (2008): 42,910 (army 62.2%, navy 21.2%, air force 16.6%); US troops (2008) 792. **Military expenditure as percentage of GDP** (2007): 1.5%; per capita expenditure US$319.

Background

Celtic peoples settled the Iberian Peninsula in the 1st millennium BC. They were conquered about 140 BC by the Romans, who ruled until the 5th century AD, when the area was invaded by Germanic tribes. A Muslim invasion in 711 left only the northern part of Portugal in Christian hands. In 1139 it became the kingdom of Portugal and expanded as it reconquered the Muslim-held sectors. The boundaries of modern continental Portugal were completed in 1270 under King Afonso III. In the 15th and 16th centuries, exploration took Portuguese navigators to Africa, India, Indonesia, China, the Middle East, and South America, where colonies were established. António de Oliveira Salazar ruled Portugal as a dictator in the mid-20th century; he died in office in 1970, and his successor was ousted in a coup in 1974. A new constitution was adopted in 1976 (revised 1982), and civilian rule resumed. The government returned Macau, its last overseas territory, to Chinese rule in 1999. Portugal was a charter member of NATO and is a member of the EU.

Recent Developments

Against the backdrop of the global financial crisis, the Portuguese economy stalled in 2008. While exports remained robust, they were outpaced by import growth, and consumer confidence dwindled, resulting in stagnating GDP growth. Since Portugal's housing market had long been more stable than that of neighboring Spain, there was little backlash from that segment; however, unemployment was essentially steady at 7.6% and inflation ran at 2.6% on an annualized basis, driven by the higher prices of fuel and food. Prime Minister José Sócrates signed a series of trade agreements with Venezuela, which pledged to send crude oil to Portugal in exchange for finished goods. The stock prices of Galp Energia, Portugal's only oil refiner, soared after the Brazil-based consortium in which it held a 10% stake made a series of potentially huge crude oil discoveries off the Brazilian coast. The Portuguese government also launched one of the world's first wave-powered generators in the waters off northern Portugal.

Internet resources: <www.ine.pt/index_eng.htm>.

Puerto Rico

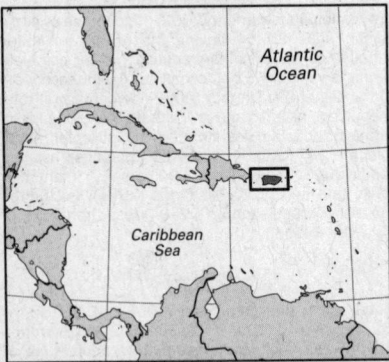

Atlantic Ocean

Caribbean Sea

Official name: Estado Libre Asociado de Puerto Rico (Spanish); Commonwealth of Puerto Rico (English). **Political status:** self-governing commonwealth in association with the US, with two legislative houses (Senate [27]; House of Representatives [51]). **Chief of state:** US President Barack Obama (from 2009). **Head of government:** Governor Luis Fortuño (from 2009). **Capital:** San Juan. **Official languages:** Spanish; English. **Monetary unit:** 1 US dollar (US$) = 100 cents.

Demography

Area: 3,515 sq mi, 9,104 sq km. **Population** (2008): 3,958,000. **Density** (2008): persons per sq mi 1,126, persons per sq km 434.8. **Urban** (2005): 97.6%. **Sex distribution** (2007): male 48.00%; female 52.00%. **Age breakdown** (2007): under 15, 20.9%; 15–29, 22.0%; 30–44, 20.3%; 45–59, 18.5%; 60–74, 12.6%; 75 and over, 5.7%. **Ethnic**

composition (2000): local white 72.1%; black 15.0%; mulatto 10.0%; US white 2.2%; other 0.7%. **Religious affiliation** (2000): Roman Catholic 74%; Protestant 13%; independent Christian 6%; Jehovah's Witness 2%; nonreligious/atheist 2%; Spiritist 1%; other 2%. **Major metropolitan areas** (2006): San Juan 2,590,824; Aguadilla 333,408; Ponce 263,799; San Germán 144,595; Yauco 123,441. **Location:** island in the Caribbean Sea, east of Cuba.

Vital statistics

Birth rate per 1,000 population (2007): 12.7 (world avg. 20.3). **Death rate** per 1,000 population (2007): 7.8 (world avg. 8.6). **Total fertility rate** (avg. births per childbearing woman; 2007): 1.76. **Life expectancy** at birth (2007): male 74.5 years; female 82.6 years.

National economy

Budget. *Revenue* (2005–06): US$14,155,000,000 (tax revenue 58.0%, of which income tax 43.7%; excise taxes 14.2%; federal grants 32.9%). *Expenditures* (2005–06): US$15,957,000,000 (education 25.7%; public housing and welfare 19.6%; general government services 15.6%; public safety 13.2%). **Public debt** (December 2007): US$42,818,000,000. **Production** (in metric tons except as noted). *Agriculture and fishing* (2007): plantains 80,000, bananas 53,500, oranges 19,500; livestock (number of live animals) 380,000 cattle, 50,000 pigs, 13,000,000 chickens; fisheries production (2006) 2,308 (from aquaculture 12%). *Mining and quarrying* (2005): crushed stone 7,830,000. *Manufacturing* (value added in US$'000,000; 2004): chemical products (nearly all drugs and medicine) 20,276; nonelectrical machinery and apparatus 3,271; professional and scientific equipment 3,211. *Energy production (consumption):* electricity (kW-hr; 2006) 24,900,000,000 ([2007–08] 19,602,000,000); crude petroleum (barrels; 2005) none (70,800,000); petroleum products (metric tons; 2002) 3,001,000 (6,610,000); natural gas (cu m; 2005) none (694,000,000). **Gross national income** (2007): US$60,107,000,000 (US$15,062 per capita). **Population economically active** (2005): total 1,410,000; activity rate of total population 36.0% (participation rates: ages 16–64, 56.1%; female 43.7%; unemployed [September 2007–August 2008] 11.0%. **Selected balance of payments data.** Receipts from (US$'000,000): tourism (2006) 3,369; foreign direct investment (2004–06 avg.) 26. Disbursements for (US$'000,000): tourism (2006) 1,205.

Foreign trade

Imports (2006–07): US$45,266,000,000 (imports for pharmaceutical industry 36.4%; petroleum and coal products 9.2%; base chemicals 9.2%; computers, electronics, and electrical equipment 8.8%; food products 5.4%). *Major import sources* (2006): US 55.0%; Ireland 23.7%; Japan 5.4%. **Exports** (2006–07): US$60,011,000,000 (pharmaceuticals and medicine 60.9%; computers, office machinery, and parts 6.7%; food products 6.3%). *Major export destinations* (2006): US 90.3%; UK 1.6%; The Netherlands 1.4%.

1 metric ton = about 1.1 short tons;   1 kilometer = 0.6 mi (statute);   1 metric ton-km cargo = about 0.68 short ton-mi cargo;   c.i.f.: cost, insurance, and freight;   f.o.b.: free on board

Transport and communications

Transport. *Railroads* (privately owned railway for sugarcane transport only; 2004): length 96 km. *Roads* (2005): total length 25,735 km (paved 95%). *Vehicles* (2006): passenger cars 2,341,820; trucks and buses 104,344. *Air transport* (2006): passenger arrivals and departures 11,450,700; cargo loaded and unloaded 352,396 metric tons. **Communications**, in total units (units per 1,000 persons). Telephone landlines (2005): 1,038,000 (262); cellular telephone subscribers (2005): 3,354,000 (848); personal computers (2005): 33,000 (8.3); total Internet users (2007): 1,000,000 (254); broadband Internet subscribers (2006): 118,000 (30).

Education and health

Educational attainment (2000). Percentage of population ages 25 and over having: no formal schooling to lower secondary education 25.4%; some upper secondary to some higher 56.3%; undergraduate or graduate degree 18.3%. **Literacy** (2002): percentage of total population ages 15 and over literate 94.1%. **Health:** physicians (2001) 7,623 (1 per 504 persons); hospital beds (2002) 12,351 (1 per 312 persons); infant mortality rate per 1,000 live births (2007) 8.8.

Military

Total active duty personnel (US troops; 2008): 191 (the US naval base at Ceiba was closed in March 2004); Puerto Rican paramilitary forces (national guard; 2007): 11,000.

Background

Puerto Rico was inhabited by Arawak Indians when it was settled by the Spanish in the early 16th century. It remained largely undeveloped economically until the late 18th century. After 1830 it gradually developed a plantation economy based on the export crops of sugarcane, coffee, and tobacco. The independence movement began in the late 19th century, and Spain ceded the island to the US in 1898, after the Spanish-American War. In 1917 Puerto Ricans were granted US citizenship, and in 1952 the island became a commonwealth with autonomy in internal affairs. The question of Puerto Rican statehood has been a political issue, with commonwealth status approved by voters in 1967, 1993, and 1998.

Recent Developments

Former Puerto Rican governor Aníbal Acevedo Vilá was acquitted in March 2009 of nine counts of corruption. The charges included collecting illegal donations to pay off campaign debts and using campaign money for personal expenses.

Internet resources: <www.gotopuertorico.com>.

Qatar

Official name: Dawlat Qatar (State of Qatar). **Form of government:** constitutional emirate with one advisory body (Advisory Council [35]). **Head of state and government:** Emir Sheikh Hamad ibn Khalifa

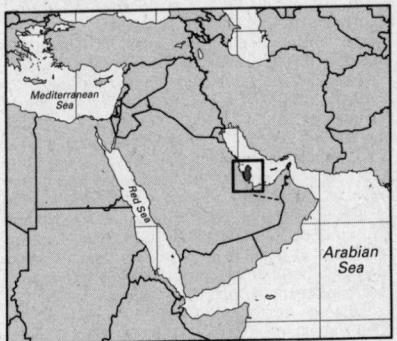

al-Thani (from 1995), assisted by Prime Minister Sheikh Hamad ibn Jassim ibn Jabr al-Thani (from 2007). **Capital:** Doha. **Official language:** Arabic. **Official religion:** Islam. **Monetary unit:** 1 riyal (QR) = 100 dirhams; valuation (1 Jul 2009) US$1 = QR 3.64.

Demography

Area: 4,184 sq mi, 10,836 sq km. **Population** (2008): 1,448,000. **Density** (2008): persons per sq mi 346.1, persons per sq km 133.6. **Urban** (2005): 95.4%. **Sex distribution** (2007): male 75.60%; female 24.40%. **Age breakdown** (2005): under 15, 21.8%; 15–29, 25.5%; 30–44, 33.7%; 45–59, 16.3%; 60–74, 2.4%; 75 and over, 0.3%. **Ethnic composition** (2000): Arab 52.5%, of which Palestinian 13.4%, Qatari 13.3%, Lebanese 10.4%, Syrian 9.4%; Persian 16.5%; Indo-Pakistani 15.2%; black African 9.5%; other 6.3%. **Religious affiliation** (2000): Muslim 83%, of which Sunni 73%, Shiʿi 10%; Christian 10%, of which Roman Catholic 6%; Hindu 3%; Buddhist 2%; nonreligious 2%. **Major cities** (2004): Doha 339,847; Al-Rayyan 258,193; Al-Wakrah 26,993; Umm Salal Muhammad 25,413; Al-Khawr 18,036. **Location:** the Middle East, bordering the Persian Gulf and Saudi Arabia.

Vital statistics

Birth rate per 1,000 population (2007): 12.8 (world avg. 20.3). **Death rate** per 1,000 population (2007): 1.4 (world avg. 8.6). **Natural increase rate** per 1,000 population (2007): 11.4 (world avg. 11.7). **Total fertility rate** (avg. births per childbearing woman; 2005): 2.80. **Life expectancy** at birth (2005): male 74.4 years; female 75.8 years.

National economy

Budget (2005–06). *Revenue:* QR 64,984,000,000 (oil and natural gas revenue 67.1%; investment income 21.9%). *Expenditures:* QR 50,833,000,000 (current expenditures 64.4%; capital expenditures 35.6%). **Production** (metric tons except as noted). *Agriculture and fishing* (2007): dates 21,000, tomatoes 5,400, barley 5,000; livestock (number of live animals) 160,000 goats, 120,000 sheep, 14,000 camels; fisheries production (2006) 16,412 (from aquaculture, negligible). *Mining and quarrying* (2006): limestone 1,100,000; gypsum, sand and gravel, and clay are also produced. *Manufacturing* (value added in QR '000,000; 2005): refined petroleum products 4,502; chemical products 2,168; base metals 1,959. *Energy production (consumption):* electricity (kW-hr; 2005) 14,396,000,000 (14,396,-000,000); crude petroleum (barrels; 2006) 272,-600,000 ([2005] 40,121,000); petroleum products (metric tons; 2005) 7,046,000 (2,564,000); natural gas (cu m; 2005) 45,764,000,000 (16,074,000,-000). **Population economically active** (2004): total 444,133; activity rate of total population 59.7% (participation rates: ages 15 and over, 77.1%; female 15.1%; unemployed 1.5%). **Gross national income** (2007): US$61,194,000,000 (US$72,795 per capita). **Selected balance of payments data.** Receipts from (US$'000,000): tourism (2006) 374; foreign direct investment (FDI) (2004–06 avg.) 1,379. Disbursements for (US$'000,000): tourism (2006) 3,993; remittances (2006–07) 5,000; FDI (2004–06 avg.) 308.

Foreign trade

Imports (2006; c.i.f.): US$16,440,000,000 (nonelectrical machinery and apparatus 23.5%; iron and steel 13.7%; electrical machinery and apparatus 8.6%; motor vehicles 6.8%; chemical products 5.1%). *Major import sources:* Japan 12.0%; US 9.9%; Germany 9.3%; Italy 9.3%; UAE 6.0%. **Exports** (2006; f.o.b.): US$34,051,000,000 (crude petroleum 46.9%; liquefied natural gas 34.8%; refined petroleum products 4.6%; liquefied propane and butane 3.4%; polyethylene 3.3%). *Major export destinations:* Japan 41.5%; South Korea 13.9%; Singapore 9.5%; India 4.9%; UAE 4.3%.

Transport and communications

Transport. *Railroads:* none. *Roads* (2000): total length 1,230 km (paved 90%). *Vehicles* (2004): passenger cars 265,609; trucks and buses 114,115. *Air transport* (Qatar Airways only; 2007): passenger-km 32,329,000,000; metric ton-km cargo 1,328,000,-000. **Communications,** in total units (units per 1,000 persons). Telephone landlines (2007): 237,000 (282); cellular telephone subscribers (2007): 1,264,-000 (1,504); personal computers (2005): 145,000 (182); total Internet users (2007): 351,000 (418); broadband Internet subscribers (2007): 70,000 (83).

Education and health

Educational attainment (2004). Percentage of population ages 10 and over having: no formal education/unknown 34.9%, of which illiterate 10.2%; primary 13.0%; preparatory (lower secondary) 16.2%; secondary 20.0%; postsecondary 15.9%. **Literacy** (2004): percentage of total population ages 15 and over literate 89.0%; males literate 89.1%; females literate 88.6%. **Health** (2007): physicians (public sector only) 1,775 (1 per 691 persons); hospital beds (public sector only) 1,651 (1 per 743 persons); infant mortality rate per 1,000 live births 7.5.

Military

Total active duty personnel (2007): 11,800 (army 72.0%, navy 15.3%, air force 12.7%); US troops (2007) 512. **Military expenditure as percentage of GDP** (2005): 6.2%; per capita expenditure US$2,751.

Background

Qatar was partly controlled by Bahrain in the 18th and 19th centuries and was part of the Ottoman Empire until World War I. In 1916 it became a British protectorate. Oil was discovered in 1939, and the country rapidly modernized. Qatar declared independence in 1971, when the British protectorate ended. In 1991 it served as a base for air strikes against Iraq in the Persian Gulf War.

Recent Developments

Qatar's economy, which already boasted one of the world's highest per capita incomes, continued to soar in 2008 as a result of increased hydrocarbon production and heightened revenues from energy exports. The country remained the world's largest producer of gas-to-liquids fuels and increasingly invested substantial surplus revenues in foreign financial institutions. The rapid economic expansion was accompanied by a dramatic rise in inflation, however, resulting partly from significantly higher costs for imported skilled labor and the scarcity of construction materials.

Internet resources: <www.qsa.gov.qa>.

Romania

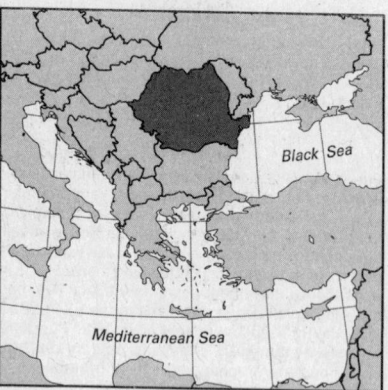

Official name: Romania. **Form of government:** unitary republic with two legislative houses (Senate [137]; Chamber of Deputies [334]). **Chief of state:** President Traian Basescu (from 2004). **Head of government:** Prime Minister Emil Boc (from 2008). **Capital:** Bucharest. **Official language:** Romanian. **Official religion:** none. **Monetary unit:** 1 Romanian (new) leu (RON; plural lei) = 100 bani; valuation (1 Jul 2009) US$1 = 2.96 (new) lei (the [new] leu replaced the [old] leu [ROL] 1 Jul 2005, at the rate of 1 RON = 10,000 ROL).

Demography

Area: 92,043 sq mi, 238,391 sq km. **Population** (2008): 21,508,000. **Density** (2008): persons per sq mi 233.7, persons per sq km 90.2. **Urban** (2007):

55.3%. **Sex distribution** (2007): male 48.84%; female 51.16%. **Age breakdown** (2005): under 15, 15.7%; 15–29, 23.8%; 30–44, 21.5%; 45–59, 19.7%; 60–74, 13.8%; 75–84, 4.8%; 85 and over, 0.7%. **Ethnic composition** (2002): Romanian 89.5%; Hungarian 6.6%; Rom (Gypsy) 2.5%; Ukrainian 0.3%; German 0.3%; other 0.8%. **Religious affiliation** (2002): Romanian Orthodox 86.7%; Protestant 6.3%; Roman Catholic 4.7%; Greek Catholic 0.9%; Muslim 0.3%; other 1.1%. **Major cities** (2007): Bucharest 1,931,838; Iasi 315,214; Cluj-Napoca 310,243; Timisoara 307,347; Constanta 304,279. **Location:** southeastern Europe, bordering Ukraine, Moldova, the Black Sea, Bulgaria, Serbia, and Hungary.

Vital statistics

Birth rate per 1,000 population (2007): 10.0 (world avg. 20.3); within marriage 73.3%; outside of marriage 26.7%. **Death rate** per 1,000 population (2007): 11.7 (world avg. 8.6). **Total fertility rate** (avg. births per childbearing woman; 2007): 1.29. **Life expectancy** at birth (2007): male 69.2 years; female 76.1 years.

National economy

Budget (in ROL '000,000,000,000; 2004). *Revenue:* 322.0 (VAT 35.0%; excise tax 24.7%; tax on profits 20.0%; nontax revenue 5.8%). *Expenditures:* 340.7 (economic affairs 26.7%; social assistance 14.0%; police 11.9%; defense 10.5%; interest payments 7.7%). **Public debt** (external, outstanding; 2006): US$14,204,000,000. **Population economically active** (2006): total 10,041,600; activity rate of total population 46.5% (participation rates: ages 15–64, 63.7%; female 45.0%; unemployed [2007] 6.4%). **Production** (metric tons except as noted). *Agriculture and fishing* (2007): corn (maize) 3,686,502, potatoes 3,498,443, wheat 2,866,234; livestock (number of live animals) 7,678,000 sheep, 6,815,000 pigs, 2,934,000 cattle; fisheries production (2006) 14,752 (from aquaculture 55%). *Mining and quarrying* (2006): copper (metal content) 12,200; zinc (metal content) 9,574; lead (metal content) 7,500. *Manufacturing* (value added in US$'000,000; 2004): wearing apparel 1,015; iron and steel 883; food products 782. *Energy production (consumption):* electricity (kW-hr; 2006) 61,829,000,000 ([2005] 56,510,-000,000); coal (metric tons; 2005) negligible (3,041,000); lignite (metric tons; 2006) 32,400,000 ([2005] 32,961,000); crude petroleum (barrels; 2006) 35,900,000 ([2005] 104,108,000); petroleum products (metric tons; 2005) 13,531,000 (8,808,000); natural gas (cu m; 2006) 10,231,-000,000 ([2005] 16,275,000,000). **Gross national income** (2007): US$132,502,000,000 (US$6,150 per capita). **Selected balance of payments data.** Receipts from (US$'000,000): tourism (2006) 1,308; remittances (2007) 8,533; foreign direct investment (FDI) (2004–06 avg.) 8,131. Disbursements for (US$'000,000): tourism (2006) 1,310; remittances (2007) 351; FDI (2004–06 avg.) 26.

Foreign trade

Imports (2006): US$51,106,000,000 (mineral fuels 13.5%, of which crude petroleum 7.7%; nonelectrical machinery and apparatus 11.1%; motor vehicles 10.6%; chemical products 10.6%; base and fabricated metals 9.7%). *Major import sources:* Germany 15.2%; Italy 14.6%; Russia 7.9%; France 6.5%; Turkey 5.0%. **Exports** (2006): US$32,336,000,000 (wearing apparel and accessories 13.7%; base and fabricated metals 12.6%; refined petroleum products 8.9%; nonelectrical machinery and apparatus 8.0%; motor vehicles and parts 6.2%). *Major export destinations:* Italy 18.1%; Germany 15.7%; Turkey 7.7%; France 7.5%; Hungary 4.9%.

Transport and communications

Transport. *Railroads* (2007): route length (2003) 11,053 km; passenger-km 7,476,000,000; metric ton-km cargo 16,000,000,000. *Roads* (public roads only; 2004): length 79,454 km (paved 26%). *Vehicles* (2007): cars 3,541,000; trucks and buses 519,000. *Air transport* (2007): passenger-km 3,696,000,000; metric ton-km cargo 5,688,000. **Communications,** in total units (units per 1,000 persons). Telephone landlines (2007): 4,300,000 (201); cellular telephone subscribers (2007): 22,875,000 (1,067); personal computers (2005): 2,800,000 (129); total Internet users (2007): 12,000,000 (560); broadband Internet subscribers (2007): 2,132,000 (99).

Education and health

Educational attainment (2002). Percentage of population ages 10 and over having: no formal schooling 5.5%; primary education 20.1%; lower secondary 27.6%; upper secondary/vocational 36.7%; higher vocational 3.0%; university 7.1%. **Literacy** (2004): percentage of total population ages 15 and over literate 97.3%; males literate 98.4%; females literate 96.3%. **Health** (2007): physicians 47,531 (1 per 453 persons); hospital beds 138,010 (1 per 156 persons); infant mortality rate per 1,000 live births 12.0; undernourished population (2002–04) less than 2.5% of total population.

Military

Total active duty personnel (2007): 74,267 (army 56.8%, navy 10.9%, air force 14.1%, other 18.2%). **Military expenditure as percentage of GDP** (2005): 2.0%; per capita expenditure US$90.

Background

Romania was formed in 1862 by the unification of the principalities Moldavia and Walachia, which had once been part of the ancient country of Dacia. During World War I, Romania sided with the Allies and doubled its territory in 1918 with the addition of Transylvania, Bukovina, and Bessarabia. Allied with Germany in World War II, it was occupied by Soviet troops in 1944 and became a satellite country of the USSR in 1948. During the 1960s Romania's foreign policy was frequently independent of the Soviet Union's. The communist regime of Nicolae Ceausescu was overthrown in 1989, and free elections were held in 1990. In 2004 it joined NATO, and in 2007 it became a member of the EU.

Recent Developments

In August 2008 the European Commission complained that the refusal of Romanian authorities to combat high-level corruption was the main problem affecting the country's relations with the rest of the EU, but the commission declined to impose sanctions on Romania for failing to bring its justice procedures into line with those of established EU members. The government reported that in the second quarter Romania recorded a 9.3% growth rate year-on-year; it was the highest pace in the 27-member EU. Growth for the entire year was 7.1%. Much of this was derived from foreign investment in the property sector, however, and did not boost long-term employment, and the International Monetary Fund projected in May 2009 that GDP would contract an alarming 4.1% over the course of the year.

Internet resources:
<www.insse.ro/cms/rw/pages/index.en.do>.

Russia

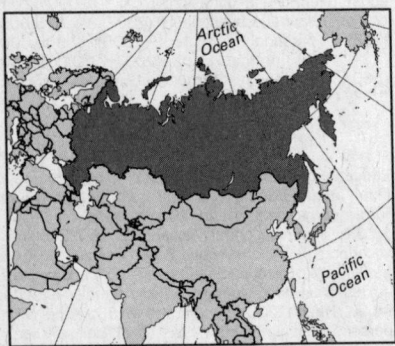

Official name: Rossiyskaya Federatsiya (Russian Federation). **Form of government:** federal multiparty republic with a bicameral legislative body (Federal Assembly comprising the Federation Council [178] and the State Duma [450]). **Head of state:** President Dmitry Medvedev (from 2008). **Head of government:** Prime Minister Vladimir Putin (from 2008). **Capital:** Moscow. **Official language:** Russian. **Official religion:** none. **Monetary unit:** 1 ruble (RUB) = 100 kopecks; valuation (1 Jul 2009) market rate, US$1 = RUB 30.92.

Demography

Area: 6,592,800 sq mi, 17,075,400 sq km. **Population** (2008): 141,841,000. **Density** (2008): persons per sq mi 21.5, persons per sq km 8.3. **Urban** (2007): 73.0%. **Sex distribution** (2007): male 46.22%; female 53.78%. **Age breakdown** (2007): under 15, 14.6%; 15–29, 23.9%; 30–44, 21.3%; 45–59, 22.8%; 60–74, 11.9%; 75–84, 4.7%; 85 and over, 0.8%. **Ethnic composition** (2002): Russian 79.82%; Tatar 3.83%; Ukrainian 2.03%; Bashkir 1.15%; Chuvash 1.13%; Chechen 0.94%; Armenian 0.78%; Mordvin 0.58%; Belarusian 0.56%; Avar 0.52%; Kazakh 0.45%; Udmurt 0.44%; Azerbaijani 0.43%; Mari 0.42%; German 0.41%; Kabardinian 0.36%; Ossetian 0.35%; Dargin 0.35%; Buryat 0.31%; Sakha 0.31%; other 4.83%. **Religious affiliation** (2005): Christian 58.4%, of which Russian Orthodox 53.1%,

Roman Catholic 1.0%, Ukrainian Orthodox 0.9%, Protestant 0.9%; Muslim 8.2%; traditional beliefs 0.8%; Jewish 0.6%; nonreligious 25.8%; atheist 5.0%; other 1.2%. **Major cities** (2006): Moscow 10,425,075; St. Petersburg 4,580,620; Novosibirsk 1,397,015; Yekaterinburg 1,308,441; Nizhny Novgorod 1,283,553; Samara 1,143,346; Omsk 1,138,822; Kazan 1,112,673; Chelyabinsk 1,092,-958; Rostov-na-Donu 1,054,865; Ufa 1,029,616. **Location:** eastern Europe and northern Asia, bordering the Arctic Ocean, the North Pacific Ocean, North Korea, China, Mongolia, Kazakhstan, the Caspian Sea, Azerbaijan, Georgia, the Black Sea, Ukraine, Belarus, Latvia, Estonia, Finland, and Norway; the exclave of Kaliningrad on the Baltic Sea borders Lithuania and Poland. **Migration** (2006): immigrants 186,380; emigrants 54,061. Refugees (2008): 159,500; from Afghanistan 84,500, Georgia 45,000.

Vital statistics

Birth rate per 1,000 population (2007): 11.1 (world avg. 20.3); (2005) within marriage 70.0%; outside of marriage 30.0%. **Death rate** per 1,000 population (2007): 14.5 (world avg. 8.6). **Natural increase rate** per 1,000 population (2007): −3.4 (world avg. 11.7). **Total fertility rate** (avg. births per childbearing woman; 2007): 1.39. **Life expectancy** at birth (2005): male 60.4 years; female 73.2 years.

Social indicators

Educational attainment (2002). Percentage of population ages 15 and over having: no formal schooling 2.1%; primary education 7.7%; some secondary 18.1%; complete secondary/basic vocational 53.0%; incomplete higher 3.1%; complete higher 16.0%, of which advanced degrees 0.3%. **Quality of working life** (2006). Average workweek (2004) 40 hours. Annual rate per 100,000 workers of: injury or accident 290; industrial illness 16.0; death 11.8. Average working days lost to labor strikes per 1,000 employees 0.2. **Social participation.** Trade union membership in total workforce (2003) 45%. **Social deviance.** Offense rate per 100,000 population (2007) for: murder and attempted murder 15.6; rape and attempted rape 4.9; serious injury 33.3; burglary 207.6; drug abuse 162.6; robbery 31.9; theft 1,102.7. Incidence per 100,000 population of suicide (2007) 29.0.

National economy

Public debt (external, outstanding; March 2008): US$35,200,000,000. **Budget** (2007). *Revenue:* RUB 7,443,000,000,000 (VAT 30.0%; taxes on natural resources 15.0%; corporate taxes 8.5%; income tax 5.2%). *Expenditures:* RUB 6,531,400,000,000 (transfers 29.7%; social and cultural services 14.1%; defense 12.8%; national economy 11.2%; public security 10.3%). **Gross national income** (2007): US$1,071,000,000,000 (US$7,560 per capita). **Production** (metric tons except as noted). *Agriculture and fishing* (2007): wheat 49,389,860, potatoes 36,784,200, sugar beets 29,000,000, barley 15,663,110 (world's leading producer), sunflower seeds 5,656,500 (world's leading producer), oats 5,407,000 (world's leading producer), corn (maize) 3,953,240, rye 3,910,290 (world's leading producer),

---

1 metric ton = about 1.1 short tons;   1 kilometer = 0.6 mi (statute);   1 metric ton-km cargo = about 0.68 short ton-mi cargo;   c.i.f.: cost, insurance, and freight;   f.o.b.: free on board

tomatoes 2,393,000, apples 2,211,000, carrots and turnips 1,900,000, dry onions 1,770,000, currants 600,000 (world's leading producer), raspberries (2005) 175,000 (world's leading producer), sour cherries 153,000 (world's leading producer); livestock (number of live animals) 21,466,000 cattle, 17,508,000 sheep, 15,793,000 pigs; fisheries production (2006) 3,389,651 (from aquaculture 3%); aquatic plants production (2006) 66,372 (from aquaculture 1%). *Mining and quarrying* (2006): nickel (metal content) 320,000 (world rank: 1); platinum-group metals 138,300 (world rank: 2), of which palladium 96,800 (world rank: 1); mica 100,000 (world rank: 2); gem diamonds 23,400,000 carats (world rank: 2); vanadium (metal content) 15,100 (world rank: 3); industrial diamonds 15,000,000 carats (world rank: 3); iron ore (metal content) 59,100,000 (world rank: 5); cobalt (metal content) 5,100 (world rank: 5); copper ore (metal content) 725,000 (world rank: 6); molybdenum (metal content) 3,100 (world rank: 6); gold 159,340 kg (world rank: 7). *Manufacturing* (value added in US$'000,000; 2005): refined petroleum products 28,950; food products 12,942; iron and steel 11,904; nonferrous base metals 9,981; base chemicals 8,524; cement, bricks, and ceramics 4,892; beverages 4,532; general purpose machinery 4,075; motor vehicles 3,423; fabricated metal products 2,831; special purpose machinery 2,802; rubber products 2,313; paints, soaps, and pharmaceuticals 2,155; professional and scientific equipment 2,151; paper products 1,982; publishing 1,733; wood products (excluding furniture) 1,730. *Energy production (consumption):* electricity (kW-hr; 2007) 1,015,872,-000,000 ([2005] 940,734,000,000); coal (metric tons; 2007) 242,100,000 ([2005] 141,440,000); lignite (metric tons; 2007) 72,200,000 ([2005] 73,-200,000); crude petroleum (barrels; 2007) 3,568,-000,000 ([2005] 1,444,000,000); petroleum products (metric tons; 2005) 186,292,000 (92,877,000); natural gas (cu m; 2007) 654,000,000,000 ([2005] 470,000,000,000). **Population economically active** (2006): total 74,146,000; activity rate of total population 52.0% (participation rates: ages 15–64, 73.0%; female 49.4%; unemployed [October 2007] 6.1%). **Selected balance of payments data.** Receipts from (US$'000,000): tourism (2006) 7,628; remittances (2007) 4,100; foreign direct investment (FDI) (2004–06 avg.) 18,981. Disbursements for (US$'000,000): tourism (2006) 18,235; remittances (2007) 17,716; FDI (2004–06 avg.) 14,841.

Foreign trade

Imports (2006; c.i.f.): US$137,728,000,000 (machinery and apparatus 27.6%, of which telecommunications equipment and television receivers 6.3%, general industrial machinery 6.2%, machinery specialized for particular industries 5.4%, electrical machinery, electronics, and parts 5.3%; motor vehicles and parts 13.4%; chemical products 12.2%, of which pharmaceuticals and medicine 4.6%; food products 11.9%; base and fabricated metals 6.9%, of which iron and steel 3.6%). *Major import sources:* Germany 13.4%; China 9.4%; Ukraine 6.7%; Japan 5.7%; Belarus 5.0%; South Korea 4.9%; US 4.7%; France 4.3%; Italy 4.2%; Finland 2.9%. **Exports** (2006; f.o.b.): US$301,551,000,000 (crude petroleum 32.1%; refined petroleum products 14.7%; natural gas 14.2%; nonferrous base metals 6.2%, of which aluminum 2.5%, nickel 2.0%, copper 1.5%; iron and steel 5.7%; chemical products 3.8%, of which fertilizers 1.4%;

machinery and apparatus 2.4%; coal and coke 1.5%; food products 1.2%). *Major export destinations:* The Netherlands 11.9%; Italy 8.3%; Germany 8.1%; China 5.2%; Ukraine 5.0%; Turkey 4.7%; Belarus 4.3%; Switzerland 4.0%; Poland 3.8%; UK 3.4%.

Transport and communications

Transport. *Railroads* (2005): length (2007) 85,000 km; passenger-km 171,600,000,000; metric ton-km cargo 1,858,000,000,000. *Roads* (2007): total length 854,000 km (paved 85%). *Vehicles* (2002): passenger cars 22,342,000; trucks and buses (2000) 5,040,700. *Air transport* (2006–07): passenger-km 97,510,000,000; metric ton-km cargo 2,980,000,000. **Communications**, in total units (units per 1,000 persons). Telephone landlines (2006): 43,900,000 (308); cellular telephone subscribers (2007): 170,000,000 (1,196); personal computers (2005): 17,400,000 (121); total Internet users (2007): 30,000,000 (211); broadband Internet subscribers (2006): 2,900,000 (20).

Health

Health (2006): physicians 690,000 (1 per 206 persons); hospital beds 1,575,000 (1 per 90 persons); infant mortality rate per 1,000 live births (2007) 9.2; undernourished population (2002–04) 3,900,000 (3% of total population based on the consumption of a minimum daily requirement of 1,980 calories).

Military

Total active duty personnel (2007): 1,027,000 (army 38.5%, navy 13.8%, air force 15.6%, strategic deterrent forces 7.8%, command and support 24.3%). **Military expenditure as percentage of GDP** (2005): 4.1%; per capita expenditure US$217.

Background

The region between the Dniester and Volga rivers was inhabited from ancient times by various peoples, including the Slavs. The area was overrun from the 8th century BC to the 6th century AD by successive nomadic peoples, including the Sythians, Sarmatians, Goths, Huns, and Avars. Kievan Rus, a confederation of principalities ruled from Kiev, emerged c. the 10th century. It lost supremacy in the 11th and 12th centuries to independent principalities, including Novgorod and Vladimir. Novgorod ascended in the north and was the only Russian principality to escape the domination of the Mongol Golden Horde in the 13th century. In the 14th–15th centuries the princes of Moscow gradually overthrew the Mongols. Under Ivan IV, Russia began to expand. The Romanov dynasty arose in 1613. Expansion continued under Peter I (the Great) and Catherine II (the Great). The area was invaded by Napoleon in 1812; after his defeat, Russia received most of the grand duchy of Warsaw (1815). Russia annexed Georgia, Armenia, and other Caucasian territories in the 19th century. The Russian southward advance against the Ottoman Empire was of key importance to Europe. Russia was defeated in the Crimean War. It sold Alaska to the US in 1867. Russia's defeat in the Russo-Japanese War led to an unsuccessful uprising in 1905. In World War I it fought against the Central Powers.

The Russian Revolution that overthrew the czarist regime in 1917 marked the beginning of a government of soviets (councils). The Bolsheviks brought the main part of the former empire under communist control and organized it as the Russian Soviet Federated Socialist Republic (RSFSR; coextensive with present-day Russia). The RSFSR joined other soviet republics in 1922 to form the Union of Soviet Socialist Republics (USSR). Although it fought with the Allies in World War II, after the war tensions with the West led to the decades-long Cold War. Upon the dissolution of the USSR in 1991, the RSFSR was renamed Russia and became the leading member of the Commonwealth of Independent States. It adopted a new constitution in 1993. During the 1990s and into the 21st century, it struggled on several fronts, beset with economic difficulties, political corruption, and independence movements. Vladimir Putin was elected president in 2000, with economic reform, governmental reorganization, cutbacks in the military, and rooting out corruption and favoritism as his chief goals.

Recent Developments

On 2 Mar 2008, Dmitry Medvedev was elected Russia's president, the handpicked successor of the outgoing president, Vladimir Putin, who was, after two consecutive terms in office, obliged by the constitution to stand down. As soon as he was sworn in, Medvedev named Putin, a hugely popular figure credited with rescuing Russia from the virtual economic disintegration of the 1990s, prime minister. It soon became clear that Putin retained the dominant role in the government.

Tensions over Russia's demand for *droit de regard* in former Soviet territory culminated in August in five days of armed conflict with neighboring Georgia. Moscow's relations with Tbilisi had been fraught since the collapse of the USSR, the flashpoint being Russia's support for Georgia's secessionist provinces, Abkhazia and South Ossetia. Tensions erupted when on 7 August the Georgian military launched a ground and air attack against the South Ossetian capital. Russia, which had peacekeepers stationed in the region, sent additional armed forces into South Ossetia and launched bombing raids against Georgia. The Russians went on to eject the Georgian forces from South Ossetia and occupy one-third of the territory of Georgia proper. The conflict caused substantial loss of civilian life and displaced more than 100,000 people. Moscow protested that it had been compelled to act in order to protect the lives of its peacekeepers and of those residents of South Ossetia with Russian citizenship. The EU brokered a cease-fire on 12 August. Although Medvedev announced on 26 August Russia's formal recognition of both South Ossetia and Abkhazia as independent states, Russia failed to persuade any other country—with the sole exception of Nicaragua—to recognize the breakaway provinces. In October, following the conflict, Moscow withdrew most of its forces, though Russian troops remained in Abkhazia and South Ossetia. In April 2009 Moscow officially suspended its military operations in the breakaway republic of Chechnya, declaring victory over the separatists. The 10-year campaign had left more than 20,000 dead.

Internet resources: <www.gks.ru/wps/portal/english>.

Rwanda

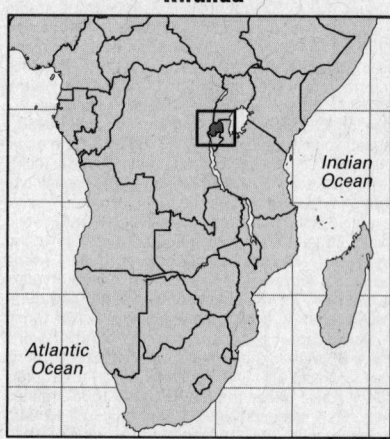

Indian Ocean

Atlantic Ocean

Official name: Republika y'u Rwanda (Rwanda); République Rwandaise (French); Republic of Rwanda (English). **Form of government:** multiparty republic with two legislative bodies (Senate [26]; Chamber of Deputies [80]). **Head of state and government:** President Maj. Gen. Paul Kagame (from 2000), assisted by Prime Minister Bernard Makuza (from 2000). **Capital:** Kigali. **Official languages:** Rwanda; French; English. **Official religion:** none. **Monetary unit:** 1 Rwandan franc (RF); valuation (1 Jul 2009) US$1 = RF 557.69.

Demography

Area: 10,185 sq mi, 26,379 sq km. **Population** (2008): 10,009,000. **Density** (2008): persons per sq mi 1,024, persons per sq km 395.4. **Urban** (2007): 17.6%. **Sex distribution** (2007): male 49.75%; female 50.25%. **Age breakdown** (2007): under 15, 41.9%; 15–29, 30.8%; 30–44, 15.5%; 45–59, 8.1%; 60–74, 2.9%; 75 and over, 0.8%. **Ethnic composition** (2002): Hutu 85%; Tutsi 14%; Twa 1%. **Religious affiliation** (2005): Roman Catholic 44%; Protestant 25%; Muslim 13%; other 18%. **Major cities** (2002): Kigali (2003) 656,153; Gitarama 84,669; Butare 77,449; Ruhengeri 71,511; Gisenyi 67,766. **Location:** east-central Africa, bordering Uganda, Tanzania, Burundi, and the Democratic Republic of the Congo.

Vital statistics

Birth rate per 1,000 population (2007): 40.2 (world avg. 20.3). **Death rate** per 1,000 population (2007): 14.9 (world avg. 8.6). **Natural increase rate** per 1,000 population (2007): 25.3 (world avg. 11.7). **Total fertility rate** (avg. births per childbearing woman; 2007): 5.37. **Life expectancy** at birth (2007): male 47.9 years; female 50.2 years.

National economy

Budget (2007). *Revenue:* RF 472,300,000,000 (grants 46.6%; taxes on goods and services 25.6%;

income tax 18.2%; import and export duties 6.6%; nontax revenue 3.0%). *Expenditures:* RF 491,400,-000,000 (current expenditures 63.7%, of which wages and salaries 10.7%, defense 6.5%; capital expenditures 36.3%). **Public debt** (external, outstanding; 2007): US$503,200,000. **Production** (metric tons except as noted). *Agriculture and fishing* (2007): plantains 2,580,000, potatoes 1,200,000, sweet potatoes 940,000, pyrethrum 15; livestock (number of live animals) 1,300,000 goats, 950,000 cattle, 470,000 sheep; fisheries production (2006) 8,200 (from aquaculture 5%). *Mining and quarrying* (2006): cassiterite (tin content) 700; tungsten (wolframite content) 400; niobium 88,000 kg; tantalum 62,000 kg. *Manufacturing* (value added in RF '000,000; 2007): food, beverages, and tobacco products 63,000; cement, bricks, and ceramics 10,000; chemical products 6,000. *Energy production (consumption):* electricity (kW-hr; 2007–08) 170,800,-000 ([2005] 245,000,000); petroleum products (metric tons; 2005) none (180,000); natural gas (cu m; 2005) 589,400 (589,400). **Population economically active** (2002): total 3,418,047; activity rate of total population 42.0% (participation rates: ages 6 and over, 52.1%; female 55.2%; officially unemployed [2006] 1.0%). **Gross national income** (2007): US$3,072,000,000 (US$320 per capita). **Selected balance of payments data.** Receipts from (US$'000,-000): tourism (2004) 44; remittances (2007) 51; foreign direct investment (FDI) (2004–06 avg.) 11; official development assistance (2006) 585. Disbursements for (US$'000,000): tourism (2004) 31; remittances (2007) 68; FDI (2004–06 avg.) negligible.

Foreign trade

Imports (2006): US$582,000,000 (intermediate goods 25.1%; machinery and apparatus 21.8%; mineral fuels 19.8%; food products 8.2%). *Major import sources* (2003): Kenya 28.4%; Belgium 12.2%; Uganda 7.7%; UAE 7.6%; Tanzania 5.6%. **Exports** (2006): US$142,700,000 (coffee 37.9%; tea 22.5%; cassiterite [major ore of tin] 11.1%; tungsten 7.8%; columbite/tantalite 6.7%). *Major export destinations* (2003): Kenya 40.9%; Uganda 26.6%; Tanzania 7.9%; UK 6.2%; Democratic Republic of the Congo 4.2%.

Transport and communications

Transport. *Railroads:* none. *Roads* (2004): total length 14,008 km (paved 19%). *Vehicles* (vehicles registered since 2003 only; 2006): passenger cars 12,269; trucks 15,093. *Air transport* (Kigali airport only; 2006): passengers embarked and disembarked 180,000; cargo loaded and unloaded (2000) 4,300 metric tons. **Communications,** in total units (units per 1,000 persons). Telephone landlines (2007): 23,000 (2.4); cellular telephone subscribers (2007): 635,000 (65); personal computers (2006): 19,000 (2.2); total Internet users (2006): 100,000 (11); broadband Internet subscribers (2007): 700 (0.1).

Education and health

Educational attainment (2005). Percentage of population ages 15–49 having: no formal education/unknown 21.4%; primary education 68.2%; secondary 9.6%; higher 0.8%. **Literacy** (2007): percentage of total population ages 15 and over literate 74.7%;

males literate 79.3%; females literate 70.2%. **Health:** physicians (2005) 450 (1 per 19,054 persons); hospital beds (2007) 14,246 (1 per 588 persons); infant mortality rate per 1,000 live births (2007) 85.3; undernourished population (2002–04) 2,800,000 (33% of total population based on the consumption of a minimum daily requirement of 1,750 calories).

Military

Total active duty personnel (2007): 33,000 (army 97.0%, air force 3.0%). **Military expenditure as percentage of GDP** (2005): 2.9%; per capita expenditure US$7.

Background

Originally inhabited by the Twa, a Pygmy people, Rwanda became home to the Hutu, who were well established there when the Tutsi appeared in the 14th century. The Tutsi conquered the Hutu and in the 15th century founded a kingdom near Kigali. The Belgians occupied Rwanda in 1916, and the League of Nations created Ruanda-Urundi as a Belgian mandate in 1923. The Tutsi retained their dominance until shortly before Rwanda reached independence in 1962, when the Hutu took control of the government and stripped the Tutsi of much of their land. Many Tutsi fled Rwanda, and the Hutu dominated the country's political system, waging sporadic civil wars until mid-1994, when the death of the country's leader in a plane crash—apparently shot down—led to massive violence. The Tutsi-led Rwandan Patriotic Front took over the country by force after the massacre of almost one million Tutsi and Tutsi sympathizers by the Hutu. A transitional government was replaced in 2003 following the country's first multiparty elections.

Recent Developments

On 18 Dec 2008, the International Criminal Tribunal for Rwanda, whose mandate was extended through 2009, issued its first convictions for the organization of the 1994 genocide. Former army colonel Théoneste Bagosora and two codefendants were sentenced to life imprisonment for having masterminded the killings. The local *gacacas* ("traditional courts"), which had been convened in 2002 to help alleviate the backlog of cases involving the genocide, continued their work. By March 2009 some 1.5 million cases had gone before these courts, and they were expected to close in 2010.

Internet resources: <www.rwandatourism.com>.

Saint Kitts and Nevis

Official name: Federation of Saint Kitts and Nevis. **Form of government:** federated constitutional monarchy with one legislative house (National Assembly [15]). **Chief of state:** British Queen Elizabeth II (from 1952), represented by Governor-General Sir Cuthbert Sebastian (from 1996). **Head of government:** Prime Minister Denzil Douglas (from 1995). **Capital:** Basseterre. **Official language:** English. **Official religion:** none. **Monetary unit:** 1 Eastern Caribbean dollar (EC$) = 100 cents; valuation (1 Jul 2009) US$1 = EC$2.67.

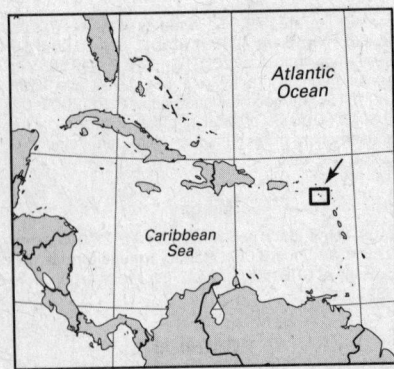

Atlantic Ocean

Caribbean Sea

Demography

Area: 104.0 sq mi, 269.4 sq km. **Population** (2008): 51,300. **Density** (2008): persons per sq mi 493.3, persons per sq km 190.4. **Urban** (2005): 33%. **Sex distribution** (2001): male 49.70%; female 50.30%. **Age breakdown** (2000): under 15, 30.7%; 15–29, 26.5%; 30–44, 21.1%; 45–59, 10.8%; 60–74, 6.1%; 75–84, 2.9%; 85 and over, 1.9%. **Ethnic composition** (2000): black 90.4%; mulatto 5.0%; Indo-Pakistani 3.0%; white 1.0%; other/unspecified 0.6%. **Religious affiliation** (2005): Protestant 75%, of which Anglican 24%, Methodist 23%; Roman Catholic 11%; other 14%. **Major towns** (2006): Basseterre 12,900; Charlestown 1,500; St. Paul's 1,200. **Location:** islands in the Caribbean Sea, between the US Virgin Islands and Antigua and Barbuda.

Vital statistics

Birth rate per 1,000 population (2005): 18.1 (world avg. 20.3). **Death rate** per 1,000 population (2005): 8.5 (world avg. 8.6). **Natural increase rate** per 1,000 population (2005): 9.6 (world avg. 11.7). **Total fertility rate** (avg. births per childbearing woman; 2005): 2.33. **Life expectancy** at birth (2005): male 69.3 years; female 75.2 years.

National economy

Budget (2006). *Revenue:* EC$524,600,000 (tax revenue 71.3%, of which taxes on international trade 33.6%, taxes on domestic goods and services 17.3%, corporate taxes 12.7%; nontax revenue 22.4%). *Expenditures:* EC$551,200,000 (current expenditures 86.0%, of which interest payments 19.1%; development expenditures 14.0%). **Production** (metric tons except as noted). *Agriculture and fishing* (2007): sugarcane (2005) 100,000 (sugarcane production ended in July 2005), coconuts 1,000, pineapples (2006) 55; livestock (number of live animals) 16,000 goats, 12,600 sheep, 4,850 cattle; fisheries production (2006) 450 (from aquaculture, negligible). *Mining and quarrying:* excavation of sand and crushed stone for local use. *Manufacturing* (2003): raw sugar 22,000; carbonated beverages (2002) 32,000 hectoliters; beer (2002) 20,000 hectoliters; other manufactures include electronic components, garments, and cement. *Energy production (consumption):* elec-

tricity (kW-hr; 2005) 133,000,000 (133,000,000); petroleum products (metric tons; 2005) none (44,000). **Gross national income** (2007): US$470,-000,000 (US$9,630 per capita). **Public debt** (external, outstanding; 2007): US$272,000,000. **Population economically active** (1995): total 18,170; activity rate of total population 41.7% (participation rates [1991]: ages 15–64, 70.5%; female 44.4%; unemployed [2006] 5.1%). **Selected balance of payments data.** Receipts from (US$'000,000): tourism (2006) 116; remittances (2007) 4; foreign direct investment (2004–06 avg.) 120; official development assistance (2006) 5.2. Disbursements for (US$'000,-000): tourism (2006) 12; remittances (2007) 3.

Foreign trade

Imports (2006): US$249,500,000 (machinery and apparatus 23.1%, of which electrical machinery and parts 10.6%; food products 15.5%; base and fabricated metals 9.2%; refined petroleum products 6.6%; motor vehicles 6.5%). *Major import sources:* US 58.3%; Trinidad and Tobago 12.5%; UK 5.3%; Japan 4.3%; Canada 2.6%. **Exports** (2006): US$39,700,000 (electrical switches 43.8%; telecommunications equipment and parts 25.4%; generators 9.8%; beverages [water and beer] 5.5%). *Major export destinations:* US 89.3%; UK 2.3%; Trinidad and Tobago 1.5%.

Transport and communications

Transport. *Railroads* (2003): length 58 km. *Roads* (2002): total length 383 km (paved [2001] 44%). *Vehicles* (2002): passenger cars 6,900; trucks and buses 2,500. *Air transport* (Saint Kitts airport only; 2001): passenger arrivals 135,237, passenger departures 134,937; cargo handled 1,802. **Communications**, in total units (units per 1,000 persons). Telephone landlines (2004): 25,000 (513); cellular telephone subscribers (2004): 10,000 (205); personal computers (2004): 11,000 (226); total Internet users (2002): 10,000 (214); broadband Internet subscribers (2002): 500 (11).

Education and health

Educational attainment (1991). Percentage of population ages 25 and over having: no formal schooling/unknown 6.8%; primary education 45.9%; secondary 38.4%; higher 8.9%. **Literacy** (2004): percentage of total population ages 15 and over literate 97.8%. **Health** (2005): physicians 62 (1 per 796 persons); hospital beds 247 (1 per 200 persons); infant mortality rate per 1,000 live births 14.5; undernourished population (2002–04) 5,000 (10% of total population based on the consumption of a minimum daily requirement of 1,910 calories).

Military

Total active duty personnel: the defense force includes coast guard and police units.

Background

Saint Kitts became the first British colony in the West Indies in 1623. Anglo-French rivalry grew in the

17th century and lasted more than a century. In 1783, by the Treaty of Versailles, the islands became wholly British possessions. They were united with Anguilla from 1882 to 1980 but became an independent federation within the British Commonwealth in 1983.

Recent Developments

Saint Kitts and Nevis was actively pursuing nontraditional energy sources in 2008, and a company called West Indies Power launched a drilling program in Nevis to access geothermal energy. The company's planned five wells were forecast to fulfill all of Nevis's power requirements.

Internet resources: <www.stkittsnevishta.org>.

Saint Lucia

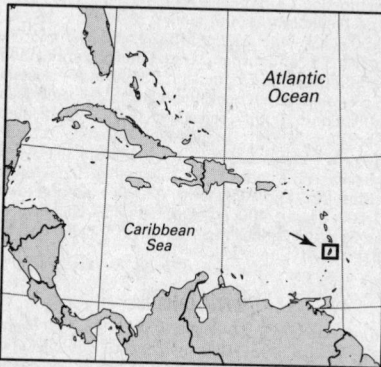

Official name: Saint Lucia. **Form of government:** constitutional monarchy with two legislative houses (Senate [11]; House of Assembly [17]). **Chief of state:** British Queen Elizabeth II (from 1952), represented by Governor-General Dame Pearlette Louisy (from 1997). **Head of government:** Prime Minister Stephenson King (from 2007). **Capital:** Castries. **Official language:** English. **Official religion:** none. **Monetary unit:** 1 Eastern Caribbean dollar (EC$) = 100 cents; valuation (1 Jul 2009) US$1 = EC$2.67.

Demography

Area: 238 sq mi, 617 sq km. **Population** (2008): 171,000. **Density** (2008): persons per sq mi 718.5, persons per sq km 277.1. **Urban** (2005): 28.0%. **Sex distribution** (2005): male 48.91%; female 51.09%. **Age breakdown** (2005): under 15, 28.4%; 15–29, 28.4%; 30–44, 21.5%; 45–59, 12.3%; 60–74, 6.5%; 75 and over, 2.9%. **Ethnic composition** (2000): black 50%; mulatto 44%; East Indian 3%; white 1%; other 2%. **Religious affiliation** (2001): Roman Catholic 67.5%; Protestant 22.0%, of which Seventh-day Adventist 8.4%, Pentecostal 5.6%, Rastafarian 2.1%; nonreligious 4.5%; other/unknown 3.9%. **Major towns** (2006): Castries 65,000; Vieux Fort 4,600; Micoud 3,400; Soufrière 2,900; Dennery 2,900. **Location:** island between the Caribbean Sea and North Atlantic Ocean, north of Saint Vincent and the Grenadines.

Vital statistics

Birth rate per 1,000 population (2005): 15.1 (world avg. 20.3); within marriage 15.0%; outside of marriage 85.0%. **Death rate** per 1,000 population (2005): 7.2 (world avg. 8.6). **Natural increase rate** per 1,000 population (2005): 7.9 (world avg. 11.7). **Total fertility rate** (avg. births per childbearing woman; 2005): 2.21. **Life expectancy** at birth (2005): male 70.0 years; female 77.4 years.

National economy

Budget (2005). *Revenue:* EC$575,700,000 (tax revenue 93.9%, of which taxes, duties, and service charges on imports 47.7%, taxes on domestic goods and services 15.5%, corporate taxes 10.5%; nontax revenue 6.1%). *Expenditures:* EC$663,200,000 (current expenditures 74.9%, of which interest payments 10.6%; development expenditures 25.1%). **Public debt** (external, outstanding; 2007–08): US$397,500,000. **Production** (metric tons except as noted). *Agriculture and fishing* (2007): bananas 34,000, coconuts 14,000, plantains 750, pepper 260; livestock (number of live animals) 15,000 pigs, 12,500 sheep, 12,500 cattle; fisheries production (2006) 1,496, of which tuna 410 (from aquaculture, negligible). *Mining and quarrying:* excavation of sand for local construction and pumice. *Manufacturing* (value of production in EC$'000; 2007): food, beverages (significantly alcoholic beverages), and tobacco products 81,005; electrical products 31,489; paper products and cardboard boxes 21,253. *Energy production (consumption):* electricity (kW-hr; 2005) 310,000,000 (310,000,000); petroleum products (metric tons; 2005) none (121,000). **Population economically active** (2004): total 80,600; activity rate of total population 49.7% (participation rates: ages 15 and over, 68.6%; female [2000] 47.2%; unemployed [2006] 15.7%). **Gross national income** (2007): US$929,000,000 (US$5,530 per capita). **Selected balance of payments data.** Receipts from (US$'000,000): tourism (2006) 347; remittances (2007) 3; foreign direct investment (2004–06 avg.) 94; official development assistance (2006) 18. Disbursements for (US$'000,000): tourism (2006) 43; remittances (2007) 1.

Foreign trade

Imports (2006; c.i.f.): US$592,300,000 (food products 15.9%; machinery and apparatus 15.3%; motor vehicles 10.2%; chemical products 6.9%; base and fabricated metals 6.2%; refined petroleum products 5.7%). *Major import sources* (2006): US 39.2%; Trinidad and Tobago 16.8%; UK 6.9%; Japan 6.3%; Barbados 4.4%. **Exports** (2005; f.o.b.): US$64,200,000 (bananas 24.1%; beer 16.2%; refined petroleum products 15.4%; nonelectrical machinery and apparatus 6.7%; paperboard cartons 5.1%). *Major export destinations* (2005): UK 26.0%; Trinidad and Tobago 22.4%; US 14.0%; Barbados 10.1%; Grenada 5.1%.

Transport and communications

Transport. *Railroads:* none. *Roads* (1999): total length 1,210 km (paved 5%). *Vehicles* (2001): passenger cars 22,453; trucks and buses 8,972. *Air transport* (Castries and Vieux Fort airports only; 2001): passenger arrivals and departures 679,000;

cargo unloaded and loaded 3,500 metric tons. **Communications,** in total units (units per 1,000 persons). Telephone landlines (2002): 51,000 (336); cellular telephone subscribers (2005): 106,000 (657); personal computers (2004): 26,000 (173); total Internet users (2004): 55,000 (339).

Education and health

Educational attainment (2004). Percentage of population ages 15 and over having: no formal schooling/unknown 9.8%; incomplete primary education 7.4%; complete primary 45.0%; secondary 28.6%; higher vocational 6.2%; university 3.0%. **Literacy** (2004): percentage of total population literate 94.8%. **Health** (2005): physicians 83 (1 per 1,983 persons); hospital beds 477 (1 per 345 persons); infant mortality rate per 1,000 live births 18.9; undernourished population (2002–04) 8,000 (5% of total population based on the consumption of a minimum daily requirement of 1,900 calories).

Military

Total active duty personnel (2006): a 300-member police force includes a specially trained paramilitary unit and a coast guard unit.

Background

Caribs replaced early Arawak inhabitants on the island c. AD 800–1300. Settled by the French in 1650, it was ceded to Great Britain in 1814 and became one of the Windward Islands in 1871. It became fully independent as Saint Lucia in 1979. The economy is based on agriculture and tourism.

Recent Developments

It was announced in March 2008 that the government had accepted a Cuban proposal that Saint Lucia become the hub for the transit of Cuban-made goods to the eastern Caribbean. Transportation between the two countries would be upgraded, and Air Cubana would convert some of its older aircraft to cargo planes in support of the venture.

Internet resources: <www.stats.gov.lc>.

Saint Vincent and the Grenadines

Official name: Saint Vincent and the Grenadines. **Form of government:** constitutional monarchy with one legislative house (House of Assembly [22]). **Chief of state:** British Queen Elizabeth II (from 1952), represented by Governor-General Sir Frederick Ballantyne (from 2002). **Head of government:** Prime Minister Ralph Gonsalves (from 2001). **Capital:** Kingstown. **Official language:** English. **Official religion:** none. **Monetary unit:** 1 Eastern Caribbean dollar (EC$) = 100 cents; valuation (1 Jul 2009) US$1 = EC$2.67.

Demography

Area: 150.3 sq mi, 389.3 sq km. **Population** (2008): 106,000. **Density** (2008): persons per sq mi 705.3,

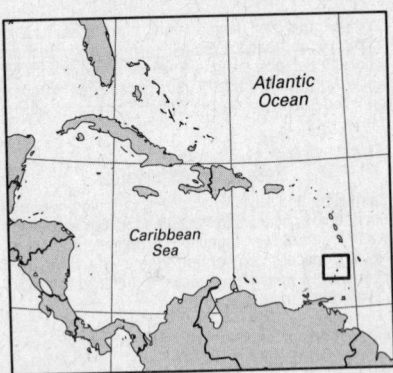

persons per sq km 272.3. **Urban** (2006): 46.3%. **Sex distribution** (2005): male 50.85%; female 49.15%. **Age breakdown** (2005): under 15, 27.1%; 15–29, 30.0%; 30–44, 22.1%; 45–59, 12.1%; 60–74, 5.8%; 75 and over, 2.9%. **Ethnic composition** (1999): black 65.5%; mulatto 23.5%; Indo-Pakistani 5.5%; white 3.5%; black-Amerindian 2.0%. **Religious affiliation** (2000): Protestant 47.0%; unaffiliated Christian 20.3%; independent Christian 11.7%; Roman Catholic 8.8%; Hindu 3.4%; Spiritist 1.8%; Muslim 1.5%; nonreligious 2.3%; other 3.2%. **Major cities** (2006): Kingstown 18,200; Georgetown 1,700; Byera 1,400; Port Elizabeth 850. **Location:** islands in the Caribbean Sea, north of Trinidad and Tobago.

Vital statistics

Birth rate per 1,000 population (2006): 20.0 (world avg. 20.3); (2003) within marriage 15.6%; outside of marriage 84.4%. **Death rate** per 1,000 population (2006): 6.7 (world avg. 8.6). **Natural increase rate** per 1,000 population (2006): 13.3 (world avg. 11.7). **Total fertility rate** (avg. births per childbearing woman; 2006): 2.20. **Life expectancy** at birth (2006): male 69.0 years; female 74.6 years.

National economy

Budget (2006). *Revenue:* EC$399,240,000 (tax revenue 90.6%, of which taxes on international trade and transactions 40.6%, income tax 12.4%, corporate taxes 10.9%, stamp duty 9.6%; nontax revenue 9.4%). *Expenditures:* EC$456,740,000 (current expenditures 77.8%, of which wages and salaries 37.5%; development expenditures 22.2%). **Public debt** (external, outstanding; 2005): US$248,300,-000. **Production** (metric tons except as noted). *Agriculture and fishing* (2007): bananas 51,000, sugarcane 20,000, plantains 3,600; soursops, papayas, and eddoes and dasheens (varieties of taro roots) are also grown; livestock (number of live animals) 12,000 sheep, 9,150 pigs, 7,200 goats; fisheries production 2,745 (from aquaculture, none). *Mining and quarrying:* sand and gravel for local use. *Manufacturing* (value added in EC$'000,000; 2000): beverages and tobacco products 17.4; food products 15.6; paper products and publishing 3.6; textiles, wearing apparel, and footwear 3.3. *Energy produc-*

tion (consumption): electricity (kW-hr; 2005) 124,000,000 (124,000,000); petroleum products (metric tons; 2005) none (62,000). **Selected balance of payments data.** Receipts from (US$'000,-000): tourism (2006) 113; remittances (2006) 5.0; foreign direct investment (FDI) (2004–06 avg.) 64; official development assistance (2006) 4.7. Disbursements for (US$'000,000): tourism (2005) 14; remittances (2006) 2.0; FDI (2001–05 avg.) negligible. **Gross national income** (2007): US$507,-000,000 (US$4,210 per capita). **Population economically active** (2006): total 58,000; activity rate of total population 48.3% (participation rates: ages 15–64, 75.3%; female 41.4%; unemployed [2004] 12.0%).

Foreign trade

Imports (2006): US$271,300,000 (machinery and apparatus 17.4%; food products 17.1%; refined petroleum products 13.0%; base and fabricated metals 8.6%; chemical products 8.0%). *Major import sources:* US 32.7%; Trinidad and Tobago 25.9%; UK 7.1%; Japan 3.9%; Canada 3.6%. **Exports** (2006): US$38,100,000 (food products 72.4%, of which bananas 29.4%, wheat flour 13.1%; roots and tubers 10.8%; rice 10.0%; base and fabricated metals 6.6%; aerated water 3.9%). *Major export destinations:* UK 25.5%; Trinidad and Tobago 14.7%; Barbados 13.9%; Saint Lucia 12.1%; Antigua and Barbuda 7.9%.

Transport and communications

Transport. *Railroads:* none. *Roads* (2004): total length 829 km (paved 70%). *Vehicles* (2003): passenger cars 12,196; trucks and buses 4,447. *Air transport* (2003): passenger arrivals 133,769; passenger departures 137,899. **Communications,** in total units (units per 1,000 persons). Telephone landlines (2007): 23,000 (190); cellular telephone subscribers (2007): 111,000 (918); personal computers (2005): 16,000 (152); total Internet users (2007): 57,000 (473); broadband Internet subscribers (2007): 8,000 (75).

Education and health

Educational attainment (2001). Percentage of employed population having: no formal schooling/unknown 1.7%; primary education 55.6%; secondary 27.3%; higher vocational 15.1%; university 0.3%. **Literacy** (2004): percentage of total population ages 15 and over literate 88.1%. **Health** (2005): physicians 72 (1 per 1,458 persons); hospital beds 472 (1 per 222 persons); infant mortality rate per 1,000 live births 15.7; undernourished population (2002–04) 10,000 (10% of total population based on the consumption of a minimum daily requirement of 1,900 calories).

Military

Total active duty personnel (2007): no regular military forces; the paramilitary includes coast guard and police units.

Background

The French and the British contested for control of Saint Vincent and the Grenadines until 1763, when it was ceded to England by the Treaty of Paris. The original inhabitants, the Caribs, recognized British sovereignty but revolted in 1795. Most of the Caribs were deported; many who remained were killed in volcanic eruptions in 1812 and 1902. In 1969 Saint Vincent and the Grenadines became a self-governing state in association with the United Kingdom, and in 1979 it achieved full independence.

Recent Developments

The prime minister in May 2008 condemned those who portrayed Venezuelan Pres. Hugo Chávez as a "monster," shortly after the arrival from Venezuela of millions of dollars' worth of construction equipment for the country's new international airport.

Internet resources: <www.svgtourism.com>.

Samoa

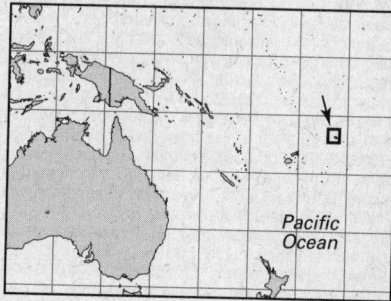

Pacific Ocean

Official name: Malo Sa'oloto Tuto'atasi o Samoa (Samoan); Independent State of Samoa (English). **Form of government:** mix of parliamentary democracy and constitutional monarchy with one legislative house (Legislative Assembly [49]). **Chief of state:** Head of State Tuiatua Tupua Tamasese Efi (from 2007). **Head of government:** Prime Minister Tuila'epa Sa'ilele Malielegaoi (from 1998). **Capital:** Apia. **Official languages:** Samoan; English. **Official religion:** none. **Monetary unit:** 1 tala (SAT) = 100 sene; valuation (1 Jul 2009) US$1 = SAT 2.62.

Demography

Area: 1,093 sq mi, 2,831 sq km. **Population** (2008): 180,000. **Density** (2008): persons per sq mi 164.7, persons per sq km 63.6. **Urban** (2007): 23.0%. **Sex distribution** (2006): male 51.88%; female 48.12%. **Age breakdown** (2001): under 15, 40.7%; 15–29, 25.5%; 30–44, 17.8%; 45–59, 9.3%; 60–74, 5.0%; 75–84, 1.3%; 85 and over, 0.2%; unknown 0.2%. **Ethnic composition** (2000): Samoan (Polynesian) 88.1%; Euronesian (European and Polynesian) 10.1%; European and US white 1.2%; other 0.6%. **Religious affiliation** (2001): Congregational 34.8%; Roman Catholic 19.6%; Methodist 15.0%; Mormon 12.7%; Assemblies of God 6.6%; other Christian 9.6%; other/unknown 1.7%. **Major towns** (2006): Apia 37,237 (urban agglomeration 60,702); Vaitele 6,294; Faleasi'u 3,548; Vailele 3,174; Le'auva'a 3,015. **Location:** Oceania, group of islands in the South Pacific Ocean, about halfway between Hawaii (US) and New Zealand.

Vital statistics

Birth rate per 1,000 population (2005): 27.1 (world avg. 20.3). **Death rate** per 1,000 population (2005): 5.6 (world avg. 8.6). **Natural increase rate** per 1,000 population (2005): 21.5 (world avg. 11.7). **Total fertility rate** (avg. births per childbearing woman; 2005): 4.17. **Life expectancy** at birth (2005): male 67.8 years; female 74.2 years.

National economy

Budget (2005–06). *Revenue:* SAT 387,200,000 (tax revenue 70.5%, of which VAT 28.0%, excise taxes 17.8%, income tax 12.2%; grants 18.6%; nontax revenue 10.9%). *Expenditures:* SAT 391,700,000 (current expenditures 72.0%, of which general services 22.9%, economic services 14.4%, education 14.1%, health 12.1%; development expenditures 22.0%). **Production** (metric tons except as noted). *Agriculture and fishing* (2007): coconuts 146,000, bananas 23,000, taro 17,600, noni (fruit known locally as *nonu;* also known as Indian mulberry), n.a.; livestock (number of live animals) 202,000 pigs, 29,000 cattle; fisheries production 3,340 (from aquaculture, negligible). *Manufacturing* (value of manufactured exports in SAT '000; 2006–07): beer 3,520; noni juice 3,130; coconut cream 2,130. *Energy production (consumption):* electricity (kW-hr; 2006) 113,-000,000 (90,000,000); petroleum products (metric tons; 2005) none (49,000). **Population economically active** (2003): total 64,000; activity rate of total population 35% (participation rates: ages 15–64, 63%; female 32%; unemployed, n.a.). **Public debt** (external, outstanding; March 2008): US$192,000,000. **Gross national income** (2007): US$454,000,000 (US$2,430 per capita). **Selected balance of payments data.** Receipts from (US$'000,000): tourism (2007–08) 110; remittances (2007–08) 122; foreign direct disinvestment (2004–06 avg.) −1; official development assistance (2006) 47. Disbursements for (US$'000,000): tourism (2006) 6; remittances (2007) 2; foreign direct investment (2004–06 avg.) 1.

Foreign trade

Imports (2007): SAT 593,000,000 (refined petroleum products 20.6%; products for government 5.1%; unspecified 74.3%). *Major import sources* (2005–06): New Zealand 29.3%; Australia 18.8%; US 10.6%; Fiji 7.0%; China 5.3%. **Exports** (2007): SAT 36,000,000 (fresh fish 55.3%; noni juice 10.6%; beer 8.6%; coconut cream 6.5%; noni fruit 1.9%). *Major export destinations* (2005–06): American Samoa 49.1%; US 32.6%; New Zealand 9.4%; Australia 3.4%; Japan 3.1%.

Transport and communications

Transport. *Railroads:* none. *Roads* (2001): total length 2,337 km (paved 14%). *Vehicles* (2005): passenger cars 4,638; trucks and buses 4,894. *Air transport* (Polynesian Airlines only; 2004): passenger-km 326,090,000; metric ton-km cargo 2,709,000. **Communications,** in total units (units per 1,000 persons). Telephone landlines (2005): 19,000 (106); cellular telephone subscribers (2007): 86,000 (479); personal computers (2005): 4,000 (22); total Internet users (2006): 8,000 (45); broadband Internet subscribers (2005): 100 (0.5).

Education and health

Educational attainment (2002). Percentage of population ages 25 and over having: no formal schooling 1.8%; primary education 32.4%; secondary 55.4%; higher 10.4%. **Literacy** (2003): percentage of total population ages 16 and over literate 99.7%. **Health** (2005): physicians 50 (1 per 3,570 persons); hospital beds 229 (1 per 780 persons); infant mortality rate per 1,000 live births 27.7; undernourished population (2002–04) 7,000 (4% of total population based on the consumption of a minimum daily requirement of 1,870 calories).

Military

Total active duty personnel: none; informal defense ties exist with New Zealand.

Background

Polynesians inhabited the islands of the Samoan archipelago for thousands of years before they were visited by Europeans in the 18th century. Control of the islands was contested by the US, Britain, and Germany until 1899, when they were divided between the US and Germany. In 1914 Western Samoa was occupied by New Zealand, which received it as a League of Nations mandate in 1920. After World War II, it became a UN trust territory administered by New Zealand, and it achieved independence in 1962. In 1997 the word Western was dropped from the country's name.

Recent Developments

Samoa's economic growth slowed to 3% in 2008 as the country confronted higher fuel and food prices. Food security again became a national issue, with politicians urging Samoans to increase production of traditional staples to counter growing dependence on imported foodstuffs. Banks were encouraged to lend to the primary sector to increase local food production.

Internet resources: <www.visitsamoa.ws>.

San Marino

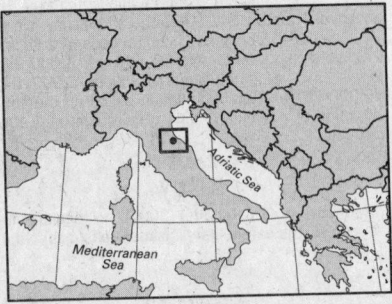

1 metric ton = about 1.1 short tons;   1 kilometer = 0.6 mi (statute);   1 metric ton-km cargo = about 0.68 short ton-mi cargo;   c.i.f.: cost, insurance, and freight;   f.o.b.: free on board

Official name: Repubblica di San Marino (Republic of San Marino). Form of government: unitary multiparty republic with one legislative house (Great and General Council [60]). Heads of state and government: two captains-regent who serve six-month terms beginning in April and October. Capital: San Marino. Official language: Italian. Official religion: none. Monetary unit: 1 euro (€) = 100 cents; valuation (1 Jul 2009) US$1 = €0.71 (San Marino uses the euro as its official currency, even though it is not a member of the EU).

Demography

Area: 23.63 sq mi, 61.20 sq km. Population (2008): 31,000. Density (2008): persons per sq mi 1,312, persons per sq km 506.5. Urban (2005): 96%. Sex distribution (2008): male 49.08%; female 50.92%. Age breakdown (2004): under 15, 15.3%; 15–29, 16.1%; 30–44, 27.3%; 45–59, 19.6%; 60–74, 14.1%; 75–84, 6.0%; 85 and over, 1.6%. Ethnic composition (2006): Sammarinesi 87.0%; Italian 11.4%; other 1.6%. Religious affiliation (2000): Roman Catholic 88.7%; other Christian 3.5%; nonreligious 5.1%; other 2.7%. Major municipalities (2008): Serravalle 10,051; Borgo Maggiore 6,198; San Marino 4,376. Location: southern Europe, surrounded by Italy.

Vital statistics

Birth rate per 1,000 population (2006): 9.9 (world avg. 20.3); (2005) within marriage 90.1%; outside of marriage 9.9%. Death rate per 1,000 population (2006): 7.4 (world avg. 8.6). Natural increase rate per 1,000 population (2007): 2.5 (world avg. 11.7). Total fertility rate (avg. births per childbearing woman; 2005): 1.11. Life expectancy at birth (2007): male 79.6 years; female 85.3 years.

National economy

Budget (2005). Revenue: €504,800,000 (VAT 23.6%; social contributions 21.3%; income tax 20.2%). Expenditures: €433,100,000 (wages and salaries 35.4%; social benefits 30.5%). Public debt (2003): US$52,900,000. Tourism: number of visitor arrivals (2007–08) 2,166,066. Population economically active (2007): total 22,056; activity rate of total population 72.3% (participation rates: ages 15–64 [2002] 72.1%; female 41.9%; unemployed 2.6%). Production. Agriculture and fishing: small amounts of wheat, grapes, and barley; livestock (number of live animals; 2005) 991 cattle, 91 sheep, 32 pigs. Quarrying: building stone is an important export product. Manufacturing (2005): processed meats 283,674 kg, of which beef 270,616 kg, veal 8,549 kg, pork 3,615 kg; cheese 56,610 kg; butter 8,110 kg; other major products include electrical appliances, musical instruments, printing ink, paint, cosmetics, furniture, floor tiles, gold and silver jewelry, clothing, and postage stamps. Energy production (consumption): all electrical power is imported via electrical grid from Italy (kW-hr; consumption [2006] 230,070,000); coal, none (n.a.); petroleum products, none (n.a.); natural gas (cu m; 2006) none (54,888,000). Gross national income (2007): US$1,493,000,000 (US$48,285 per capita).

Foreign trade

Imports (2005): US$2,582,000,000 (manufactured goods of all kinds, petroleum products, natural gas, electricity, and gold). Major import source (2004): sig-
nificantly Italy (a customs union with Italy has existed since 1862). Exports (2005): US$2,531,000,000 (goods include electronics, postage stamps, leather products, ceramics, wine, wood products, and building stone). Major export destination (2004): Italy 90% (a customs union with Italy has existed since 1862).

Transport and communications

Transport. Railroads: none (nearest rail terminal is at Rimini, Italy, 27 km northeast). Roads (2001): total length 252 km. Vehicles (2007): passenger cars 34,025; trucks and buses 5,084. Air transport: a heliport provides passenger and cargo service between San Marino and Rimini, Italy, during the summer months. Communications, in total units (units per 1,000 persons). Telephone landlines (2006): 21,000 (696); cellular telephone subscribers (2006): 17,000 (576); personal computers (2003): 23,000 (819); total Internet users (2006): 15,000 (510); broadband Internet subscribers (2006): 1,500 (50).

Education and health

Educational attainment (2007). Percentage of population ages 15 and over having: basic literacy or primary education 55.3%; secondary or vocational 34.5%; higher degree 10.2%. Literacy (2001): percentage of total population ages 15 and over literate 98.7%; males literate 98.9%; females literate 98.4%. Health (2002): physicians 117 (1 per 230 persons); hospital beds 134 (1 per 191 persons); infant mortality rate per 1,000 live births (2004) 3.4.

Military

Total active duty personnel (2007): defense is the responsibility of Italy; a small voluntary military force performs ceremonial duties and provides limited assistance to police.

Background

According to tradition, San Marino was founded in the early 4th century AD by St. Marinus. By the 12th century it had developed into a commune and remained independent despite challenges from neighboring rulers, including the Malatesta family in nearby Rimini, Italy. San Marino survived the Renaissance as a relic of the self-governing Italian city-state and remained an independent republic after the unification of Italy in 1861. It is one of the smallest republics in the world, and it may be the oldest one in Europe.

Recent Developments

San Marino continued to enjoy economic growth in 2008. GNP increased by 5.2%, an extraordinary result, considering the sluggish economy of European countries in general. San Marino's robust economic performance translated into high levels of remuneration and solid employment rates, with fewer than 300 workers reported unemployed.

Internet resources: <www.upeceds.sm/eng>.

São Tomé and Príncipe

Official name: República Democrática de São Tomé e Príncipe (Democratic Republic of São Tomé and

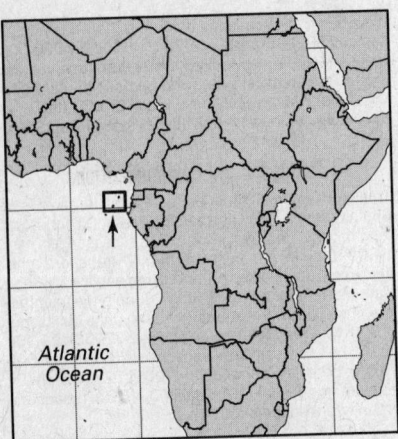

Atlantic Ocean

Príncipe). **Form of government:** multiparty republic with one legislative house (National Assembly [55]). **Chief of state:** President Fradique de Menezes (from 2003). **Head of government:** Prime Minister Joaquim Rafael Branco (from 2008). **Capital:** São Tomé. **Official language:** Portuguese. **Official religion:** none. **Monetary unit:** 1 dobra (Db) = 100 cêntimos; valuation (1 Jul 2009) US$1 = Db 15,233.00.

Demography

Area: 386 sq mi, 1,001 sq km. **Population** (2008): 160,000. **Density** (2008): persons per sq mi 414.5, persons per sq km 159.8. **Urban** (2007): 59.9%. **Sex distribution** (2006): male 48.63%, female 51.37%. **Age breakdown** (2006): under 15, 41.2%; 15–29, 30.8%; 30–44, 14.6%; 45–59, 7.8%; 60–74, 4.1%; 75 and over, 1.5%. **Ethnic composition** (2000): black-white admixture 79.5%; Fang 10.0%; Angolar (descendants of former Angolan slaves) 7.6%; Portuguese 1.9%; other 1.0%. **Religious affiliation** (2005): Roman Catholic 80%; Protestant 15%; Muslim 3%; other 2%. **Major urban agglomerations** (2001): São Tomé 49,957; Neves 6,635; Santana 6,228; Trindade 6,049; Santo António 1,010. **Location:** islands in the Gulf of Guinea, straddling the Equator west of Gabon.

Vital statistics

Birth rate per 1,000 population (2006): 33.4 (world avg. 20.3). **Death rate** per 1,000 population (2006): 7.3 (world avg. 8.6). **Natural increase rate** per 1,000 population (2006): 26.1 (world avg. 11.7). **Total fertility rate** (avg. births per childbearing woman; 2005): 5.71. **Life expectancy** at birth (2006): male 63.5 years; female 68.5 years.

National economy

Budget (2005). *Revenue:* Db 972,100,000,000 (petroleum exploration bonuses 57.8%; grants 18.9%; tax revenue 18.9%, of which consumption taxes 7.1%; nontax revenue 4.4%). *Expenditures:* Db 545,500,000,000 (current expenditures 58.7%;

capital expenditures 35.5%). **Public debt** (external, outstanding; 2005): US$293,700,000. **Production** (metric tons except as noted). *Agriculture and fishing* (2007): oil palm fruit 40,000, coconuts 28,000, taro 27,000; livestock (number of live animals) 5,000 goats, 4,600 cattle, 2,800 sheep; fisheries production (2006) 4,000 (from aquaculture, none). *Mining and quarrying:* some quarrying to support local construction industry. *Manufacturing* (value in Db; 1995): beer 880,000; wearing apparel 679,000; lumber 369,000. *Energy production (consumption):* electricity (kW-hr; 2005) 19,000,000 (19,000,000); petroleum products (metric tons; 2005) none (33,000). **Population economically active** (2006): total 53,266; activity rate of total population 35.1% (participation rates: ages 10 and over (2001) 43.7%; female 41.6%; unemployed 30%). **Gross national income** (2007): US$138,000,000 (US$870 per capita). **Selected balance of payments data.** Receipts from (US$'000,000): tourism (2005) 14; remittances (2007) 2; foreign direct disinvestment (2004–06 avg.) −1; official development assistance (2006) 22. Disbursements for (US$'000,000): tourism (2002) 0.6; remittances (2007) 1.

Foreign trade

Imports (2006): US$70,853,000 (food and beverages 30.1%; refined petroleum products 20.4%; machinery and apparatus 13.5%; construction materials 8.7%; transportation equipment 8.2%). *Major import sources:* Portugal 63.6%; Angola 18.3%; Belgium 4.6%; Gabon 3.5%. **Exports** (2006): US$3,820,000 (cocoa beans 64.9%; coffee 24.2%). *Major export destinations:* Portugal 33.3%; The Netherlands 27.1%; Belgium 14.3%; France 8.9%; US 5.3%.

Transport and communications

Transport. *Railroads:* none. *Roads* (2000): total length 320 km (paved 68%). *Vehicles* (1996): passenger cars 4,040; trucks and buses 1,540. *Air transport* (2001): passenger-km 7,000,000. **Communications,** in total units (units per 1,000 persons). Telephone landlines (2007): 7,700 (49); cellular telephone subscribers (2007): 30,000 (191); personal computers (2005): 6,000 (38); total Internet users (2007): 23,000 (146); broadband Internet subscribers (2007): 2,500 (16).

Did you know?

Cocoa has been the chief export of São Tomé and Príncipe since the late 19th century. Prior to independence in 1975, the cocoa plantations (*roças*) were worked by indentured laborers (slavery was officially abolished in 1875) recruited by Portuguese plantation managers. Some of the distinctive colonial buildings on the *roças* are now tourist attractions.

Education and health

Educational attainment (2001). Percentage of population ages 25 and over having: no formal school-

---

1 metric ton = about 1.1 short tons;   1 kilometer = 0.6 mi (statute);   1 metric ton-km cargo = about 0.68 short ton-mi cargo;   c.i.f.: cost, insurance, and freight;   f.o.b.: free on board

ing/unknown 22.9%; primary education 41.4%; lower secondary 25.0%; upper secondary/vocational 8.8%; higher 1.9%. **Literacy** (2006): percentage of total population ages 15 and over literate 85%; males literate 92%; females literate 78%. **Health:** physicians (2006) 58 (1 per 2,621 persons); hospital beds (1991) 532 (1 per 211 persons); infant mortality rate per 1,000 live births (2006) 43.9; undernourished population (2002–04) 15,000 (10% of total population based on the consumption of a minimum daily requirement of 1,770 calories).

Military

Total active duty personnel (2005): 460 (army and coast guard 65.2%; presidential guard 34.8%). **Military expenditure as percentage of GDP** (2005): 1.2%; per capita expenditure US$4.

Background

First visited by European navigators in the 1470s, the islands of São Tomé and Príncipe were colonized by the Portuguese in the 16th century and were used in the trade and transshipment of slaves. Sugarcane and cacao were the main cash crops. The islands became an overseas province of Portugal in 1951 and achieved independence in 1975. Príncipe became autonomous in 1995. During recent decades the country's economy has been heavily dependent on international assistance.

Recent Developments

New hope for political stability arose in São Tomé and Príncipe in February 2008 when Patrice Trovoada became the new prime minister. Only three months later, however, the new coalition government lost a parliamentary vote of confidence after Trovoada was accused of corruption. Portugal, the country's main donor, responded by postponing its debt pardon, approved in 2007.

Internet resources: <www.saotome.st>.

Saudi Arabia

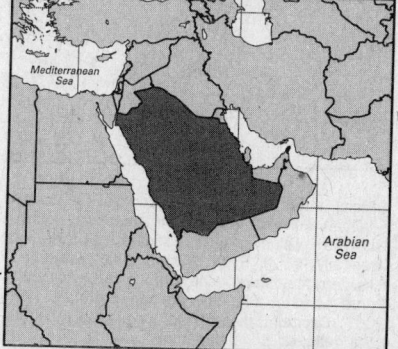

Official name: Al-Mamlakah al-ʿArabiyah al-Suʿudiyah (Kingdom of Saudi Arabia). **Form of government:** monarchy (assisted by the Consultative Council consisting of 150 appointed members). **Head of state**

and government: King Abdullah (from 2005). **Capital:** Riyadh. **Official language:** Arabic. **Official religion:** Islam. **Monetary unit:** 1 Saudi riyal (SR) = 100 halala; valuation (1 Jul 2009) US$1 = SR 3.75.

Demography

Area: 830,000 sq mi, 2,149,690 sq km. **Population** (2008): 24,780,000. **Density** (2008): persons per sq mi 29.9, persons per sq km 11.5. **Urban** (2005): 81.0%. **Sex distribution** (2007): male 55.24%; female 44.76%. **Age breakdown** (2007): under 15, 32.6%; 15–29, 27.5%; 30–44, 25.2%; 45–59, 10.5%; 60–74, 3.3%; 75 and over, 0.9%. **Ethnic composition** (2005): Saudi Arab 74%; expatriates 26%, of which Indian 5%, Bangladeshi 3.5%, Pakistani 3.5%, Filipino 3%, Egyptian 3%, Palestinian 1%, other 7%. **Religious affiliation** (2000): Muslim 94%, of which Sunni 84%, Shiʿi 10%; Christian 3.5%, of which Roman Catholic 3%; Hindu 1%; nonreligious/other 1.5%. **Major urban agglomerations** (2007): Riyadh 4,465,000; Jiddah 3,012,000; Mecca 1,385,000; Medina 1,010,000; Al-Dammam 822,000. **Location:** the Middle East, bordering Iraq, Kuwait, the Persian Gulf, Qatar, the UAE, Oman, Yemen, the Red Sea, the Gulf of Aqaba, and Jordan.

Vital statistics

Birth rate per 1,000 population (2007): 24.5 (world avg. 20.3). **Death rate** per 1,000 population (2007): 3.9 (world avg. 8.6). **Total fertility rate** (avg. births per childbearing woman; 2007): 3.17. **Life expectancy** at birth (2006): male 73.7 years; female 77.8 years.

National economy

Budget (2007). *Revenue:* SR 642,800,000,000 (oil revenues 87.5%). *Expenditures:* SR 466,248,000,000 (current expenditures 74.5%; capital expenditures 25.5%). **National debt** (public only; end of 2007): US$71,200,000,000. *Production* (metric tons except as noted). *Agriculture and fishing* (2007): wheat 2,700,000, dates 970,000, potatoes 570,000; livestock (number of live animals) 7,000,000 sheep, 2,200,000 goats, 372,000 cattle, 260,000 camels; fisheries production (2006) 81,057 (from aquaculture 19%). *Mining and quarrying* (2007): gypsum 537,537; silver 8,230 kg; gold 4,048 kg. *Manufacturing* (value added in US$'000,000; 1998): industrial chemicals 3,349; refined petroleum products 1,806; cement, bricks, and tiles 1,505. *Energy production (consumption):* electricity (kW-hr; 2006) 156,119,000,000 ([2007] 169,302,800,000); crude petroleum (barrels; 2007–08) 3,291,300,000 (69,390,000); petroleum products (metric tons; 2005) 115,372,000 (63,272,000); natural gas (cu m; 2006) 75,853,300,000 ([2005] 71,237,600,000). **Population economically active** (2007): total 8,229,654, of which 4,029,955 Saudi workers and 4,199,699 foreign nationals; activity rate of total population 34.0% (participation rates: ages 15–64, 51.8%; female 15.4%; unemployed 5.6%). **Gross national income** (2007): US$373,490,000,000 (US$15,440 per capita). **Selected balance of payments data.** Receipts from (US$'000,000): tourism (2007) 5,230; foreign direct investment (FDI) (2004–06 avg.) 10,777; official development assistance (2006) 25. Disbursements for (US$'000,000): tourism (2007) 4,883; remittances (2007) 15,611; FDI (2004–06 avg.) 882.

Foreign trade

Imports (2007; c.i.f.): SR 338,088,000,000 (machinery and apparatus 29.5%; transportation equipment 17.6%; base and fabricated metals 15.0%; food and live animals 13.3%; chemical products 11.8%). *Major import sources:* US 13.6%; China 9.7%; Germany 8.9%; Japan 8.7%; Italy 4.5%. **Exports** (2007; f.o.b.): SR 877,457,000,000 (crude petroleum 75.8%; refined petroleum products 12.2%; other mineral fuels [mostly natural gas] 6.2%). *Major export destinations* (2006): Japan 16.5%; US 15.1%; South Korea 9.2%; China 6.3%; India 6.1%.

Transport and communications

Transport. *Railroads* (2007): route length (2006) 1,392 km; passenger-km 343,000,000; metric ton-km cargo 1,257,000,000. *Roads* (2007): total length 178,946 km (paved 100%). *Vehicles* (2001): passenger cars 4,452,793; trucks and buses 4,110,271. *Air transport* (Saudi Arabian Airlines only; 2007): passenger-km 26,904,000,000; metric ton-km cargo 1,238,000,000. **Communications,** in total units (units per 1,000 persons). Telephone landlines (2007): 3,996,000 (162); cellular telephone subscribers (2007): 23,381,000 (1,147); personal computers (2005): 8,184,000 (354); total Internet users (2007): 6,200,000 (251); broadband Internet subscribers (2007): 600,000 (24).

Education and health

Educational attainment (2007). Percentage of Saudi ([2000] non-Saudi) population ages 10 and over who: are illiterate 13.7% (12.1%); are literate/have primary education 34.0% (40.6%); have some/completed secondary 42.1% (36.0%); have at least begun university 10.2% (11.3%). **Literacy** (2005): percentage of total population ages 15 and over literate 80.4%; males literate 85.8%; females literate 73.3%. **Health** (2006): physicians 45,589 (1 per 520 persons); hospital beds 54,724 (1 per 433 persons); infant mortality rate per 1,000 live births (2007) 17.9; undernourished population (2002–04) 1,000,000 (4% of total population based on the consumption of a minimum daily requirement of 1,860 calories).

Military

Total active duty personnel (2007): 114,500 (army 65.5%, navy 13.5%, air force 17.5%, air defense forces 3.5%); US troops (2008) 287. **Military expenditure as percentage of GDP** (2008): 8.6%; per capita expenditure US$1,540.

Background

Saudi Arabia is the historical home of Islam, founded by Muhammad in Medina in 622. During medieval times, local and foreign rulers fought for control of the Arabian Peninsula; in 1517 the Ottomans prevailed. In the 18th–19th centuries Islamic leaders supporting religious reform struggled to regain Saudi territory, all of which was restored by 1904. The British held Saudi lands as a protectorate from 1915 to 1927; then they acknowledged the sovereignty of the Kingdom of the Hejaz and Najd. The two kingdoms were unified as the Kingdom of Saudi Arabia in 1932. Since World War II, it has supported the Palestinian cause in the Middle East and maintained close ties with the US.

Recent Developments

Saudi Arabia's King Abdullah made international headlines in July 2008 when he convened a three-day interfaith conference in Madrid that was attended by more than 200 religious and political leaders from around the world. The conference, which marked the first time that a Saudi ruler had invited Jewish clerics to participate in a religious meeting, was aimed at developing mutual understanding and tolerance between the followers of different faiths. King Abdullah attended a second interfaith meeting in November in New York City. On the economic front, Saudi Arabia continued to enjoy ample revenues from the sale of crude oil. A joint-exploration venture between Royal Dutch Shell and the state-owned oil company Saudi Aramco in the Rubʻ al-Khali desert reportedly yielded a new natural gas discovery in August. Also in August, Riyadh announced that nonresident foreign investors would be allowed to buy shares of Saudi stocks through licensed Saudi intermediaries; this move was perceived as a major step toward opening up the Saudi stock market completely.

Internet resources: <www.planning.gov.sa>.

Senegal

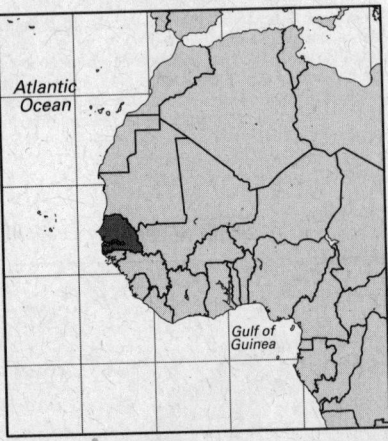

Official name: République du Sénégal (Republic of Senegal). **Form of government:** multiparty republic with two legislative houses (Senate [100]; National Assembly [150]). **Head of state and government:** President Abdoulaye Wade (from 2000), assisted by Prime Minister Cheikh Hadjibou Soumaré (from 2007). **Capital:** Dakar. **Official language:** French. **Official religion:** none. **Monetary unit:** 1 CFA franc (CFAF) = 100 centimes; valuation (1 Jul 2009) US$1 = CFAF 462.89.

1 metric ton = about 1.1 short tons;   1 kilometer = 0.6 mi (statute);   1 metric ton-km cargo = about 0.68 short ton-mi cargo;   c.i.f.: cost, insurance, and freight;   f.o.b.: free on board

Demography

Area: 75,955 sq mi, 197,021 sq km. **Population** (2008): 12,688,000. **Density** (2008): persons per sq mi 166.8, persons per sq km 64.4. **Urban** (2007): 42.1%. **Sex distribution** (2006): male 49.99%; female 50.01%. **Age breakdown** (2006): under 15, 42.2%; 15–29, 28.4%; 30–44, 16.0%; 45–59, 8.7%; 60–74, 3.9%; 75–84, 0.7%; 85 and over, 0.1%. **Ethnic composition** (2000): Wolof 34.6%; Peul (Fulani) and Tukulor 27.1%; Serer 12.0%; Malinke (Mandingo) 9.7%; other 16.6%. **Religious affiliation** (2005): Muslim 94%, of which Shi'i 5%; Christian (mostly Roman Catholic) 4%; other 2%. **Major cities** (2007): Dakar 2,243,400; Touba 529,200; Thiès 263,500; Kaolack 186,000; Mbour 181,800. **Location:** western Africa, bordering Mauritania, Mali, Guinea, Guinea-Bissau, the North Atlantic Ocean, and The Gambia.

Vital statistics

Birth rate per 1,000 population (2006): 38.3 (world avg. 20.3). **Death rate** per 1,000 population (2006): 11.2 (world avg. 8.6). **Natural increase rate** per 1,000 population (2006): 27.1 (world avg. 11.7). **Total fertility rate** (avg. births per childbearing woman; 2006): 5.13. **Life expectancy** at birth (2006): male 55.0 years; female 57.7 years.

National economy

Budget (2005). *Revenue:* CFAF 955,800,000,000 (tax revenue 89.0%, of which taxes on domestic goods and services 28.7%, income tax 21.4%, taxes on imports 19.7%; grants 7.9%; nontax revenue 3.1%). *Expenditures:* CFAF 1,084,400,000,000 (current expenditures 58.0%, of which public debt interest payments 4.3%; development expenditures 42.0%). **Public debt** (external, outstanding; 2006): US$1,712,000,000. **Production** (metric tons except as noted). *Agriculture and fishing* (2007): sugarcane 836,000, peanuts (groundnuts) 427,093, millet 362,825; livestock (number of live animals) 5,131,-300 sheep, 4,382,900 goats, 3,180,900 cattle, 521,160 horses; fisheries production (2006) 377,-885 (from aquaculture, negligible). *Mining and quarrying* (2006): calcium phosphate 584,000. *Manufacturing* (value added in US$'000,000; 2002): food products 108; industrial chemicals 70; cement, bricks, and ceramics 31. *Energy production (consumption):* electricity (kW-hr; 2005) 2,595,000,000 (2,595,000,000); crude petroleum (barrels; 2005) none (6,641,000); petroleum products (metric tons; 2005) 883,000 (1,220,000); natural gas (cu m; 2005) 16,145,000 (16,145,000). **Population economically active** (2003): total 4,383,000; activity rate of total population 39.4% (participation rates: ages 15–64, 71.5%; female 42.0%; unemployed [2005] 40%). **Selected balance of payments data.** Receipts from (US$'000,000): tourism (2005) 242; remittances (2007) 874; foreign direct investment (2004–06 avg.) 60; official development assistance (2006) 825. Disbursements for (US$'000,000): tourism (2005) 65; remittances (2007) 77. **Gross national income** (2007): US$10,170,000,000 (US$820 per capita).

Foreign trade

Imports (2006; c.i.f.): US$3,671,000,000 (mineral fuels 25.9%, of which refined petroleum products 18.4%; food products 19.0%, of which cereals 8.8%; chemical products 9.4%; nonelectrical machinery and apparatus 9.0%). *Major import sources:* France 24.4%; UK 6.0%; China 4.3%; Thailand 4.0%; Spain 3.8%. **Exports** (2006; f.o.b.): US$1,492,000,000 (food products 27.8%, of which fish 10.7%, crustaceans and mollusks 6.9%; refined petroleum products 24.3%; portland cement 5.3%; phosphoric acid [and related products] 5.2%). *Major export destinations:* Mali 20.2%; bunkers and ships' stores 16.2%; France 7.6%; The Gambia 5.6%; India 5.3%.

Transport and communications

Transport. *Railroads* (2004): route length (2005) 906 km; passenger-km 122,000,000; metric ton-km cargo 358,000,000. *Roads* (2003): total length 13,576 km (paved 29%). *Vehicles* (2004): passenger cars 147,000; trucks and buses 46,000. *Air transport* (Air Sénégal International only; 2006): passenger-km 937,000,000; metric ton-km cargo, none. **Communications,** in total units (units per 1,000 persons). Telephone landlines (2007): 269,000 (22); cellular telephone subscribers (2007): 4,123,000 (333); personal computers (2005): 250,000 (21); total Internet users (2007): 820,000 (66); broadband Internet subscribers (2007): 38,000 (3).

Education and health

Educational attainment (2005). Percentage of population ages 25 and over having: no formal schooling/unknown 70.0%; incomplete primary education 13.0%; complete primary 3.7%; incomplete secondary 9.5%; complete secondary 1.4%; higher 2.4%. **Literacy** (2007): percentage of total population ages 15 and over literate 44.0%; males literate 53.4%; females literate 34.9%. **Health:** physicians (2005) 693 (1 per 17,115 persons); hospital beds (1998) 3,582 (1 per 2,500 persons); infant mortality rate per 1,000 live births (2006) 61.4; undernourished population (2002–04) 2,100,000 (20% of total population based on the consumption of a minimum daily requirement of 1,850 calories).

Military

Total active duty personnel (2007): 13,620 (army 87.4%, navy 7.0%, air force 5.6%); French troops (2007) 841. **Military expenditure as percentage of GDP** (2005): 1.5%; per capita expenditure US$11.

Background

Links between the peoples of Senegal and North Africa were established in the 10th century AD. Islam was introduced in the 11th century, though animism retained a hold on the country into the 19th century. The Portuguese explored the coast in 1445, and in 1638 the French established a trading post—the Europeans exported slaves, ivory, and gold from Senegal. The French gained control over the coast in the early 19th century, checking the expansion of the Tukulor empire; in 1895 Senegal became part of French West Africa. Its inhabitants were made French citizens in 1946, and it became an overseas territory of France. It became an autonomous republic in 1958 and was federated with Mali in 1959–60. It became an independent state in 1960. In 1982 it entered a confederation with The Gambia, called Senegambia, which was dissolved in 1989. Separatists fighting in the south since the early 1980s signed a peace accord with the government in 2004.

Recent Developments

Poor rains and escalating global food prices resulted in high levels of malnutrition in Senegal in 2008, and approximately two million faced food shortages. Pres. Abdoulaye Wade attacked the Food and Agriculture Organization's policy of retaining 20% of the private donations destined for African countries facing a food crisis.

Internet resources: <www.senegal-tourism.com>.

Serbia

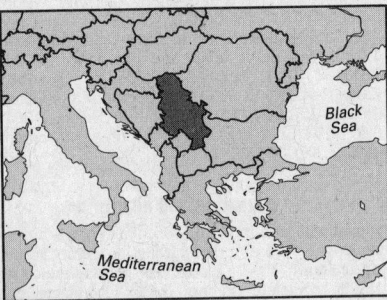

Black Sea

Mediterranean Sea

Many of these statistics include Kosovo, which declared its independence in February 2008. **Official name:** Republika Srbija (Republic of Serbia). **Form of government:** republic with National Assembly (250). **Chief of state:** President Boris Tadic (from 2004). **Head of government:** Prime Minister Mirko Cvetkovic (from 2008). **Capital:** Belgrade. **Official language:** Serbian. **Official religion:** none. **Monetary unit:** 1 Serbian dinar (CSD) = 100 paras; valuation (1 Jul 2009) US$1 = 66.22 CSD.

Demography

Area: 29,922 sq mi, 77,498 sq km. **Population** (2008): 7,352,000. **Density** (2008): persons per sq mi 245.7, persons per sq km 94.9. **Urban** (2002): 56.4%. **Sex distribution** (2007): male 48.62%; female 51.38%. **Age breakdown** (2002): under 15, 15.7%; 15–29, 20.2%; 30–44, 19.9%; 45–59, 21.1%; 60–74, 17.2%; 75–84, 4.7%; 85 and over, 0.6%; unknown 0.6%. **Ethnic composition** (2002): Serb 82.9%; Hungarian 3.9%; Bosniac 1.8%; Rom (Gypsy) 1.4%; Yugoslav 1.1%; Croat 0.9%; Montenegrin 0.9%; other 7.1%. **Religious affiliation** (2002): Orthodox 85.0%; Roman Catholic 5.5%; Muslim 3.2%; Protestant 1.1%; other/unknown 5.2%. **Major cities** (2002): Belgrade 1,120,092; Novi Sad 191,405; Nis 173,724; Kragujevac 146,373; Subotica 99,981. **Location:** southeastern Europe, bordering Romania, Bulgaria, Macedonia, Kosovo, Montenegro, Bosnia and Herzegovina, Croatia, and Hungary.

Vital statistics

Birth rate per 1,000 population (2007): 9.2 (world avg. 20.3); within marriage 77.7%; outside of marriage 22.3%. **Death rate** per 1,000 population (2007): 13.9 (world avg. 8.6). **Total fertility rate** (avg. births per childbearing woman; 2007): 1.40. **Life expectancy** at birth (2007): male 70.7 years; female 76.2 years.

National economy

Budget (2006). *Revenue:* CSD 867,500,000,000 (social security contributions 26.7%; VAT 26.0%; income tax 13.7%; excises tax 10.0%). *Expenditures:* CSD 898,400,000,000 (current expenditures 89.9%; capital expenditures 8.9%). **Population economically active** (2007): total 3,241,200; activity rate of total population 42.9% (participation rates: ages 15–64, 63.4%; female 43.4%; unemployed 18.1%). **Production** (metric tons except as noted). *Agriculture and fishing* (including Kosovo; 2007): corn (maize) 3,904,825, sugar beets 3,206,380, wheat 1,863,811, sunflower seeds 294,502; livestock (number of live animals) 3,998,927 pigs, 1,106,000 cattle; fisheries production (2006) 7,463 (from aquaculture 65%). *Mining and quarrying* (including Kosovo; 2006): copper (metal content) 28,000; zinc (metal content) 2,100. *Manufacturing* (value added in CSD '000,000 in constant prices of 2002; 2006): food and beverages 52,302; chemical products 23,813; cement, bricks, and ceramics 11,532. *Energy production (consumption):* electricity (kW-hr; 2007) 35,360,000,000 ([2006] 26,253,000,000); coal (including Kosovo; metric tons; 2006) 65,000 ([also including Montenegro; 2005] 161,000); lignite (metric tons; 2007) 37,005,000 ([including Kosovo and Montenegro; 2005] 40,449,000); crude petroleum (including Kosovo; barrels; 2006) 4,790,000 ([also including Montenegro; 2005] 29,900,000); petroleum products (including Kosovo and Montenegro; metric tons; 2005) 3,242,000 (3,244,000); natural gas (cu m; 2007) 271,000,000 ([including Kosovo and Montenegro; 2005] 2,308,000,000). **Gross national income** (2007): US$34,969,000,000 (US$4,730 per capita). **Public debt** (external, outstanding; September 2008): US$8,559,000,000. **Selected balance of payments data.** Receipts from (US$'000,000): tourism (2006) 398; remittances (including Montenegro; 2007) 4,910; foreign direct investment (including Montenegro; 2004–06 avg.) 2,358; official development assistance (including Montenegro; 2006) 1,586. Disbursements for (US$'000,000): tourism (2006) 322.

Foreign trade

Imports (2006): US$13,172,000,000 (mineral fuels 19.7%; machinery and apparatus 18.1%; chemical products 14.2%; base metals 7.9%; motor vehicles 7.2%). *Major import sources:* Russia 16.3%; Germany 9.5%; unspecified EU 9.2%; Italy 8.3%; China 5.9%. **Exports** (2006): US$6,428,000,000 (food products 16.6%; iron and steel 13.6%; nonferrous metals 9.5%, of which copper 6.4%; machinery and apparatus 9.1%; wearing apparel and accessories 5.0%).

1 metric ton = about 1.1 short tons;   1 kilometer = 0.6 mi (statute);   1 metric ton-km cargo = about 0.68 short ton-mi cargo;   c.i.f.: cost, insurance, and freight;   f.o.b.: free on board

Major export destinations: Italy 14.4%; Bosnia and Herzegovina 11.7%; Germany 9.9%; Montenegro 9.6%; Russia 4.8%.

Transport and communications

Transport. *Railroads* (2006): route length (2004) 3,809 km; passenger-km 684,000,000; metric ton-km cargo 4,232,000,000. *Roads* (2006): total length 38,616 km (paved 62%). *Vehicles* (2005): passenger cars 1,497,418; trucks and buses 257,642. *Air transport* (2006): passenger-km 1,252,000,000; metric ton-km cargo 5,470,000. **Communications,** in total units (units per 1,000 persons). Telephone landlines (2007): 2,993,000 (315); cellular telephone subscribers (2007): 8,453,000 (890); personal computers (2005): 446,000 (55); total Internet users (2007): 1,500,000 (158); broadband Internet subscribers (2007): 326,000 (34).

Education and health

Educational attainment (2002). Percentage of population ages 15 and over having: no formal schooling/unknown 7.8%; incomplete primary education 16.2%; complete primary 23.9%; secondary 41.1%; higher 11.0%. **Health** (2006): physicians 20,157 (1 per 368 persons); hospital beds 43,115 (1 per 172 persons); infant mortality rate per 1,000 live births (2007) 7.1; undernourished population (including Kosovo and Montenegro; 2002–04) 900,000 (9% of total population based on the consumption of a minimum daily requirement of 2,000 calories).

Military

Total active duty personnel (2007): 24,257 (army 46.1%, air force/air defense 17.1%, training/ministry of defense 36.8%). **Military expenditure as percentage of GDP** (2006) 2.3%; per capita expenditure US$99.

Background

The Kingdom of the Serbs, Croats, and Slovenes was created after the collapse of Austria-Hungary at the end of World War I. The country signed treaties with Czechoslovakia and Romania in 1920–21, marking the beginning of the Little Entente. In 1929 an absolute monarchy was established, the country's name was changed to Yugoslavia, and it was divided into regions without regard to ethnic boundaries. Axis powers invaded Yugoslavia in 1941, and German, Italian, Hungarian, and Bulgarian troops occupied it for the rest of World War II. In 1945 the Socialist Federal Republic of Yugoslavia was established; it included the republics of Bosnia and Herzegovina, Croatia, Macedonia, Montenegro, Serbia, and Slovenia. Its independent form of communism under Josip Broz Tito's leadership provoked the USSR. Internal ethnic tensions flared up in the 1980s, causing the country's ultimate collapse. In 1991–92 independence was declared by Croatia, Slovenia, Macedonia, and Bosnia and Herzegovina; the new Federal Republic of Yugoslavia (containing roughly 45% of the population and 40% of the area of its predecessor) was proclaimed by Serbia and Montenegro. Fueled by long-standing ethnic tensions, hostilities continued into the 1990s. Despite the approval of the Dayton Peace Agreement (1995), sporadic fighting continued and was followed in 1998–99 by Serbian repression and expulsion of ethnic populations in the province of Kosovo. In September–October 2000, the battered nation of Yugoslavia ended the autocratic rule of Pres. Slobodan Milosevic. In April 2001 he was arrested and in June extradited to The Hague to stand trial for war crimes, genocide, and crimes against humanity committed during the fighting in Kosovo. In February 2003 the government accepted a new state charter and changed the name of the country from Yugoslavia to Serbia and Montenegro. Henceforth, defense, international political and economic relations, and human rights matters would be handled centrally, while all other functions would be run from the republican capitals, Belgrade and Podgorica, respectively. A provision was included for both states to vote on independence after three years; Serbia declared its independence in June 2006, shortly after Montenegro severed its federal union with Serbia. In 2008 Kosovo formally seceded, but Serbia refused to recognize it as an independent country.

Recent Developments

On 17 Feb 2008 the southern province of Kosovo formally declared its independence from Serbia. By year's end 53 countries had recognized Kosovo. Serbia, meanwhile, supported Serbs in northern Kosovo who challenged the new Kosovar government. At the same time, Serbia made increased efforts toward European integration. The Serbian parliament ratified the Stability and Association Agreement, a required step toward consideration for European Union membership. The country also cooperated with the International Criminal Tribunal for the Former Yugoslavia (ICTY); in July Serbian authorities arrested Radovan Karadzic, the former leader of the Bosnian Serb Republic whom the ICTY had indicted in 1995 for war crimes. Prime Minister Mirko Cvetkovic noted that Serbia had extradited 44 out of 46 suspected war criminals sought by the ICTY and pledged to apprehend Bosnian Serb Gen. Ratko Mladic and Goran Hadzic, former leader of Croatia's Krajina Serbs.

Internet resources:
<http://webrzs.statserb.sr.gov.yu/axd/en>.

Seychelles

Official name: Repiblik Sesel (Creole); République des Seychelles (French); Republic of Seychelles (English). **Form of government:** multiparty republic with one legislative house (National Assembly [34]). **Head of state and government:** President James Michel (from 2004). **Capital:** Victoria. **Official languages:** none (Creole, English, and French are national languages). **Official religion:** none. **Monetary unit:** 1 Seychelles rupee (SR) = 100 cents; valuation (1 Jul 2009) US$1 = SR 13.59.

Demography

Area: 176 sq mi, 455 sq km. **Population** (2008): 85,500. **Density** (2008): persons per sq mi 486.6, persons per sq km 187.9. **Urban** (2005): 53%. **Sex distribution** (2008): male 51.75%; female 48.25%. **Age breakdown** (2006): under 15, 23.8%; 15–29, 26.4%; 30–44, 24.4%; 45–59, 15.1%; 60–74, 7.0%; 75 and over, 3.3%. **Ethnic composition** (2000): Sey-

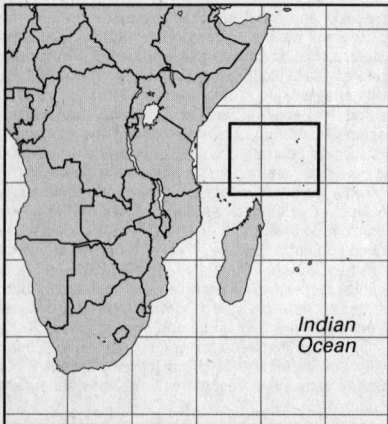

Indian
Ocean

chellois Creole (mixture of Asian, African, and European) 93.2%; British 3.0%; French 1.8%; Chinese 0.5%; Indian 0.3%; other unspecified 1.2%. **Religious affiliation** (2002): Roman Catholic 82.3%; Anglican 6.4%; other Christian 4.5%; Hindu 2.1%; Muslim 1.1%; other 2.1%; unknown 1.5%. **Major towns** (2004): Victoria 23,200; Anse Royale 3,800. **Location:** group of islands in the Indian Ocean, northeast of Madagascar.

Vital statistics

Birth rate per 1,000 population (2007): 17.6 (world avg. 20.3); (2007) within marriage 20.8%; outside of marriage 79.2%. **Death rate** per 1,000 population (2007): 7.4 (world avg. 8.6). **Natural increase rate** per 1,000 population (2007): 10.2 (world avg. 11.7). **Total fertility rate** (avg. births per childbearing woman; 2006): 2.11. **Life expectancy** at birth (2006): male 68.9 years; female 75.7 years.

National economy

Budget (2006). *Revenue:* SR 2,476,000,000 (current revenue 97.1%, of which dividends and interest 14.0%, income and business tax 12.0%, indirect taxes on services 9.5%, trades tax 9.1%, indirect taxes on locally manufactured goods 8.8%). *Expenditures:* SR 2,302,000,000 (current expenditures 82.5%, of which public debt interest charges 17.6%, education 8.6%, health 8.4%; development expenditures 17.5%). **Public debt** (2006): US$1,035,-000,000. **Gross national income** (2007): US$762,-000,000 (US$8,960 per capita). **Production** (metric tons except as noted). *Agriculture and fishing* (2007): coconuts 3,200, bananas 2,000, cinnamon 315; livestock (number of live animals) 18,700 pigs, 5,200 goats, 575,000 chickens; fisheries production (2006) 93,327 (from aquaculture 1%). *Mining and quarrying* (2006): granite 93,000. *Manufacturing* (2006): canned tuna 40,222; fish meal 14,821; copra 253. *Energy production (consumption):* electricity (kW-hr; 2006) 251,000,000 ([2005] 220,-000,000); petroleum products (metric tons; 2005) none (189,000). **Population economically active**

(2002): total 43,859; activity rate of total population 53.6% (participation rates: ages 15–64, 80.1%; female [1997] 47.6%; unemployed [2006] 2.6%). **Selected balance of payments data.** Receipts from (US$'000,000): tourism (2006) 228; remittances (2007) 15; foreign direct investment (FDI) (2004–06 avg.) 90; official development assistance (2006) 14. Disbursements for (US$'000,000): tourism (2006) 36; remittances (2007) 17; FDI (2004–06 avg.) 8.

Foreign trade

Imports (2007; c.i.f.): SR 5,728,000,000 (mineral fuels 25.1%; machinery and apparatus 22.4%; food products 19.5%, of which marine products 11.9%; transportation equipment 4.1%; iron and steel 3.4%). *Major import sources:* Saudi Arabia 24.8%; Germany 9.5%; Singapore 8.5%; France 7.8%; Spain 6.6%. **Exports** (2007; f.o.b.): SR 2,435,000,000 (domestic exports 55.3%, of which canned tuna 50.6%, fish meal 1.2%, medicine and medical appliances 1.2%; reexports 44.7%, of which petroleum products to ships and aircraft 43.1%). *Major export destinations* (domestic exports only): UK 40.1%; France 34.7%; Italy 10.0%; Germany 3.2%.

Transport and communications

Transport. *Railroads:* none. *Roads* (2006): total length 502 km (paved 96%). *Vehicles* (2006): passenger cars 7,070; trucks and buses 2,796. *Air transport* (Air Seychelles only; 2006–07): passenger-km 1,593,000,000; metric ton-km cargo 31,000,000. **Communications,** in total units (units per 1,000 persons). Telephone landlines (2007): 23,000 (262); cellular telephone subscribers (2007): 77,000 (892); personal computers (2005): 16,000 (193); total Internet users (2007): 32,000 (370); broadband Internet subscribers (2007): 3,000 (36).

Education and health

Educational attainment (2003). Percentage of population ages 12 and over having: primary education or less 23.2%; secondary 73.4%; higher 3.4%. **Literacy** (2006): percentage of total population ages 15 and over literate 91.8%; males literate 91.4%; females literate 92.3%. **Health** (2006): physicians 83 (1 per 1,019 persons); hospital beds 417 (1 per 203 persons); infant mortality rate per 1,000 live births (2007) 10.7; undernourished population (2002–04) 7,000 (9% of total population based on the consumption of a minimum daily requirement of 1,810 calories).

Military

Total active duty personnel (2007): 200 (army 100%). **Military expenditure as percentage of GDP** (2005): 1.8%; per capita expenditure US$157.

Background

The first recorded landing on the uninhabited Seychelles was made in 1609 by an expedition of the British East India Co. The archipelago was claimed

---

1 metric ton = about 1.1 short tons;   1 kilometer = 0.6 mi (statute);   1 metric ton-km cargo = about 0.68 short ton-mi cargo;   c.i.f.: cost, insurance, and freight;   f.o.b.: free on board

by the French in 1756 and surrendered to the British in 1810. Seychelles became a British crown colony in 1903 and a republic within the Commonwealth in 1976. A one-party socialist state since 1979, Seychelles began moving toward democracy in the 1990s; it adopted a new constitution in 1993.

Recent Developments

As a result of the global food crisis and a spike in oil and commodities prices, the Seychelles government in 2008 entered into a debt-restructuring program with the aim of alleviating the US$800 million debt burden, which was one of the highest in the world.

Internet resources: <www.nsb.gov.sc>.

Sierra Leone

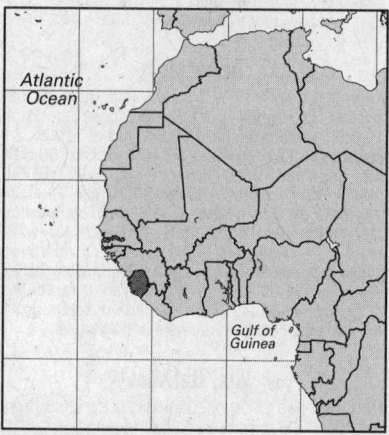

Atlantic Ocean

Gulf of Guinea

Official name: Republic of Sierra Leone. **Form of government:** republic with one legislative body (Parliament [124]). **Head of state and government:** President Ernest Bai Koroma (from 2007). **Capital:** Freetown. **Official language:** English. **Official religion:** none. **Monetary unit:** 1 leone (Le) = 100 cents; valuation (1 Jul 2009) US$1 = Le 3,255.13.

Demography

Area: 27,699 sq mi, 71,740 sq km. **Population** (2008): 5,969,000. **Density** (2008): persons per sq mi 215.5, persons per sq km 83.2. **Urban** (2005): 40.7%. **Sex distribution** (2005): male 49.23%; female 50.77%. **Age breakdown** (2005): under 15, 42.8%; 15–29, 26.1%; 30–44, 16.0%; 45–59, 9.6%; 60–74, 4.7%; 75–84, 0.7%; 85 and over, 0.1%. **Ethnic composition** (2000): Mende 26.0%; Temne 24.6%; Limba 7.1%; Kuranko 5.5%; Kono 4.2%; Fulani 3.8%; Bullom-Sherbro 3.5%; other 25.3%. **Religious affiliation** (2005): Muslim 65%; Christian 25%; traditional beliefs/other 10%. **Major cities** (2004): Freetown 772,873; Bo 149,957; Kenema 128,402; Makeni 82,840; Koidu 80,025. **Location:** western Africa, bordering Guinea, Liberia, and the North Atlantic Ocean.

Vital statistics

Birth rate per 1,000 population (2005): 46.5 (world avg. 20.3). **Death rate** per 1,000 population (2005): 22.8 (world avg. 8.6). **Natural increase rate** per 1,000 population (2005): 23.7 (world avg. 11.7). **Total fertility rate** (avg. births per childbearing woman; 2005): 6.49. **Life expectancy** at birth (2005): male 40.1 years; female 43.5 years.

National economy

Budget (2007). *Revenue:* Le 1,179,000,000,000 (grants 42.7%; import duties 21.8%; corporate taxes 7.7%; income tax 7.1%; excise duties on petroleum products 6.6%). *Expenditures:* Le 1,222,000,000,-000 (current expenditures 63.4%; capital expenditures 36.6%). **Gross national income** (2007): US$1,537,000,000 (US$260 per capita). **Production** (metric tons except as noted). *Agriculture and fishing* (2007): rice 650,000, cassava 370,000, oil palm fruit 195,000, cacao beans 12,000; livestock (number of live animals) 300,000 cattle, 7,500,000 chickens; fisheries production (2006) 148,146 (from aquaculture, negligible). *Mining and quarrying* (2007): bauxite 1,169,000; rutile 82,810; ilmenite 15,750; diamonds 603,700 carats; gold 212 kg. *Manufacturing* (2006): soap 467,360; cement 234,-440; paint 142,730 gallons. *Energy production (consumption):* electricity (kW-hr; 2005) 102,000,000 (102,000,000); crude petroleum (barrels; 2005) none (1,960,000); petroleum products (metric tons; 2005) 178,000 (228,000). **Public debt** (external, outstanding; 2006): US$1,323,000,000. **Population economically active** (2003–04): total 2,005,900; activity rate of total population 40.0% (participation rates: ages 15–64,. 68.2%; female 53.6%; unofficially unemployed [2007] 65%). **Selected balance of payments data.** Receipts from (US$'000,000): tourism (2006) 23; remittances (2007) 38; foreign direct investment (2004–06 avg.) 54; official development assistance (2006) 364. Disbursements for (US$'000,000): tourism (2006) 12; remittances (2007) 35.

Foreign trade

Imports (2007; c.i.f.): Le 1,333,189,000,000 (mineral fuels 37.7%; machinery and transportation equipment 16.8%; food products 15.2%, of which rice 5.4%; manufactured goods 11.6%). *Major import sources* (2005): Germany 19%; Côte d'Ivoire 11%; UK 8%; US 7%; China 6%. **Exports** (2007; f.o.b.): Le 733,407,000,000 (diamonds 57.8%; rutile 15.5%; bauxite 13.3%; cacao 4.6%; gold 1.2%). *Major export destinations* (2007): Belgium 49.5%; US 20.6%; The Netherlands 4.6%; Canada 4.0%.

Transport and communications

Transport. *Railroads* (Marampa Mineral Railway only [there are no passenger railways]; 2002): length 84 km. *Roads* (2002): total length 11,300 km (paved 8%). *Vehicles* (2005): passenger cars 7,700; trucks and buses 7,700. *Air transport* (2004): passenger-km 85,000,000; metric ton-km cargo 8,000,000. **Communications,** in total units (units per 1,000 persons). Telephone landlines (2002): 24,000 (4.8); cellular telephone subscribers (2007): 776,000 (132); personal computers (1999): 100; total Internet users (2007): 13,000 (2.2).

Education and health

Educational attainment (2004): percentage of total population having: no formal schooling 62.2%; primary education 24.6%; lower secondary 6.4%; upper secondary 4.2%; vocational 2.0%; higher 0.6%. **Literacy** (2004): percentage of total population ages 10 and over literate 39%; males literate 49%; females literate 29%. **Health:** physicians (2004) 168 (1 per 32,083 persons); hospital beds (2001) 2,770 (1 per 1,698 persons); infant mortality rate per 1,000 live births (2005) 163.0; undernourished population (2002–04) 2,500,000 (51% of total population based on the consumption of a minimum daily requirement of 1,820 calories).

Military

Total active duty personnel (2007): 10,500 (army 98%, navy 2%, air force, none). **Military expenditure as percentage of GDP** (2005): 1.0%; per capita expenditure US$2.

Background

The earliest inhabitants of Sierra Leone were probably the Buloms; the Mende and Temne peoples arrived in the 15th century. The coastal region was visited by the Portuguese in the 15th century, and by 1495 there was a Portuguese fort on the site of modern Freetown. European ships visited the coast regularly to trade for slaves and ivory, and the English built trading posts on offshore islands in the 17th century. British abolitionists and philanthropists founded Freetown in 1787 as a private venture for freed and runaway slaves. In 1808 the coastal settlement became a British colony. The region became a British protectorate in 1896. It achieved independence in 1961 and became a republic in 1971. It was marked by political and economic turmoil in the late 20th century as successive military regimes tried to assume power. UN peacekeeping forces were stationed there but were ineffectual in preventing bloodletting and atrocities until 2002, when a formal cease-fire was signed.

Recent Developments

The environment in Sierra Leone remained grim in 2008. More than 70% of the country's population lived below the poverty line; the UN ranked the country as the second least developed in the world; and an estimated two-thirds of its youth were unemployed. The country had the world's highest rates of child and maternal mortality: one-quarter of the children died before their fifth birthday, and a woman's risk of dying during pregnancy or childbirth was one in eight.

Internet resources: <www.statistics.sl>.

Singapore

Official name: Xinjiapo Gongheguo (Mandarin Chinese); Republik Singapura (Malay); Cingkappur Kudiyarasu (Tamil); Republic of Singapore (English). **Form of government:** unitary multiparty republic with one leg-

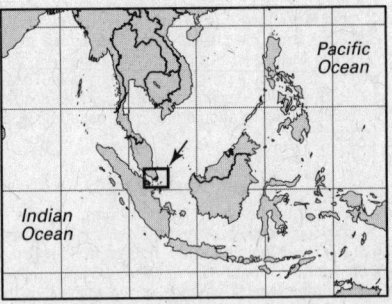

islative house (Parliament [94]). **Head of state:** President Sellapan Rama (S.R.) Nathan (from 1999). **Head of state government:** Prime Minister Lee Hsien Loong (from 2004). **Capital:** Singapore. **Official languages:** Mandarin Chinese; Malay; Tamil; English. **Official religion:** none. **Monetary unit:** 1 Singapore dollar (S$) = 100 cents; valuation (1 Jul 2009) US$1 = S$1.44.

Demography

Area: 273.0 sq mi, 707.1 sq km. **Population** (2008): 4,839,000. **Density** (2008): persons per sq mi 17,725, persons per sq km 6,843. **Urban:** 100%. **Sex distribution** (2007): male 49.48%; female 50.52%. **Age breakdown** (2007): under 15, 18.9%; 15–29, 20.2%; 30–44, 25.8%; 45–59, 22.7%; 60–74, 9.1%; 75–84, 2.6%; 85 and over, 0.7%. **Ethnic composition** (2007): Chinese 74.8%; Malay 13.5%; Indian 9.0%; other 2.7%. **Religious affiliation** (2000): Buddhist/Taoist/Chinese folk-religionist 51.0%; Muslim 14.9%; Christian 14.6%; Hindu 4.0%; traditional beliefs 0.6%; nonreligious 14.9%. **Location:** southeastern Asia, islands between Malaysia and Indonesia.

Vital statistics

Birth rate per 1,000 population (2007): 10.3 (world avg. 20.3). **Death rate** per 1,000 population (2007): 4.5 (world avg. 8.6). **Natural increase rate** per 1,000 population (2007): 5.8 (world avg. 11.7). **Total fertility rate** (avg. births per childbearing woman; 2007): 1.29. **Life expectancy** at birth (2007): male 78.2 years; female 82.9 years.

National economy

Budget (2006). *Revenue:* S$31,072,000,000 (income tax 48.1%; goods and services tax 12.7%; fees and charges 6.8%). *Expenditures:* S$29,875,000,-000 (security and external relations 42.8%; education 21.3%; transportation 6.8%; health 6.2%). **Public debt** (2006): US$122,000,000,000. **Production** (metric tons except as noted). *Agriculture and fishing* (2007): orchids (15% of the world market) and other ornamental plants are cultivated for export; livestock (number of live animals) 260,000 pigs, 2,700,000 chickens; fisheries production 11,676 (from aquaculture 73%) (aquarium fish farming is also an important economic pursuit; Singapore produces 30% of the world's ornamental fish). *Manufacturing* (value added in S$'000,000; 2005): pharmaceuticals 8,204; semiconductors 7,636; computer-related electronics 7,218; professional and scientific equipment 6,203; refined petroleum products and petrochemicals 4,826; other electronics 3,066. *Energy production (consumption):* electricity (kW-hr; 2005) 38,213,000,000 (34,761,000,000); crude petroleum (barrels; 2005) none (400,365,000); petroleum products (metric tons; 2005) 38,894,000 (8,141,-000); natural gas (cu m; 2005) none (7,076,000,-000). **Gross national income** (2007): US$148,992,-000,000 (US$32,470 per capita). **Population economically active** (2006): total 1,880,800; activity rate of total population 52.1% (participation rates: ages 15–64, 71.3%; female 42.5%; unemployed 3.6%). **Selected balance of payments data.** Receipts from (US$'000,000): tourism (2006) 7,069; foreign direct investment (FDI) (2004–06 avg.) 19,680. Disbursements for (US$'000,000): tourism (2006) 10,384; FDI (2004–06 avg.) 7,245.

Foreign trade

Imports (2006; c.i.f.): S$379,277,000,000 (electrical machinery and electronics 26.2%; refined petroleum products 10.1%; nonelectrical machinery and apparatus 9.1%; crude petroleum 8.6%; office machinery and computers 8.1%; telecommunications equipment 6.8%). *Major import sources* (2007): Malaysia 13.1%; US 12.3%; China 12.1%; Japan 8.2%; Taiwan 5.9%. **Exports** (2006; f.o.b.): S$431,-864,000,000 (machinery and apparatus 55.5%, of which electronic integrated circuits and micro-assemblies 20.9%, office machinery and computers 11.8%, nonelectrical machinery and apparatus 6.8%; refined petroleum products 12.5%; organic chemicals 4.8%). *Major export destinations* (2007): Malaysia 12.9%; Hong Kong 10.5%; Indonesia 9.8%; China 9.7%; US 8.8%.

Transport and communications

Transport. *Railroads* (2006): length 39 km. *Roads* (2005): total length 3,234 km (paved [2004] 99%). *Vehicles* (2007): passenger cars 517,041; trucks and buses 165,509. *Air transport* (2007): passenger-km 93,684,000,000; metric ton-km cargo 7,956,000,-000. **Communications,** in total units (units per 1,000 persons). Telephone landlines (2007): 1,859,000 (419); cellular telephone subscribers (2007): 5,619,000 (1,267); personal computers (2005): 2,960,000 (682); total Internet users (2007): 3,105,000 (700); broadband Internet subscribers (2007): 881,000 (193).

Education and health

Educational attainment (nonstudent population only; 2005). Percentage of population ages 15 and over having: no schooling 16.4%; primary education 22.0%; lower secondary 21.3%; upper secondary 15.1%; technical 8.2%; university 17.0%. **Literacy** (2007): percentage of total population literate 95.7%. **Health** (2007): physicians 7,384 (1 per 618 persons); hospital beds 11,580 (1 per 394 persons); infant mortality rate per 1,000 live births 2.1.

Military

Total active duty personnel (2007): 72,500 (army 69.0%, navy 12.4%, air force 18.6%). **Military expenditure as percentage of GDP** (2005): 4.7%; per capita expenditure US$1,274.

Background

Long inhabited by fishermen and pirates, Singapore was an outpost of the Sumatran empire of Srivijaya until the 14th century, when it passed to Java and then to Siam. It became part of the Malacca empire in the 15th century. In the 16th century the Portuguese controlled the area, followed by the Dutch. In 1819 Singapore was ceded to the British East India Co., becoming part of the Straits Settlements and the center of British colonial activity in Southeast Asia. The Japanese occupied the islands in 1942–45. In 1946 it became a crown colony. It achieved full internal self-government in 1959, became a part of Malaysia in 1963, and gained independence in 1965. It is influential in the affairs of the Association of Southeast Asian Nations and has become a regional economic powerhouse. The country's dominant voice in politics for 30 years after independence was Lee Kuan Yew.

Recent Developments

Inflation surged in 2008 to almost 7%, a 25-year high. As the prices of basic foodstuffs such as rice and cooking oil escalated sharply, some hoarding began to take place. By the end of the year, however, recession had replaced inflation as the biggest worry. Singapore became the first country in Southeast Asia to record a technical recession (defined as two fiscal quarters of contraction) in 2008; its extremely open and trade-dependent economy made it vulnerable to economic slumps in the United States and Europe.

Internet resources: <www.singstat.gov.sg>.

Slovakia

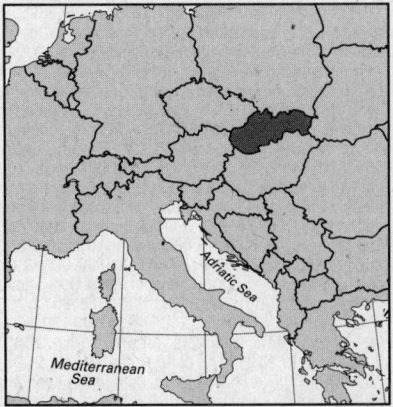

Official name: Slovenska Republika (Slovak Republic). **Form of government:** unitary multiparty republic with one legislative house (National Council [150]). **Chief of state:** President Ivan Gasparovic (from 2004). **Head of government:** Prime Minister Robert Fico (from 2006). **Capital:** Bratislava. **Official language:** Slovak. **Official religion:** none. **Monetary unit:** 1 euro (€) = 100 cents; valuation (1 Jul 2009) US$1 = €0.71 (the euro replaced the Slovak koruna [Sk] 1 Jan 2009, at the rate of €1 = Sk 30.126).

Demography

Area: 18,932 sq mi, 49,034 sq km. **Population** (2008): 5,401,000. **Density** (2008): persons per sq mi 285.3, persons per sq km 110.1. **Urban** (2006): 55.4%. **Sex distribution** (2005): male 48.54%; female 51.46%. **Age breakdown** (2007): under 15, 16.4%; 15–29, 24.4%; 30–44, 21.9%; 45–59, 21.0%; 60–74, 11.3%; 75–84, 4.2%; 85 and over, 0.8%. **Ethnic composition** (2001): Slovak 85.8%; Hungarian 9.7%; Rom (Gypsy) 1.7%; Czech 0.8%; Ruthenian and Ukrainian 0.7%; other 1.3%. **Religious affiliation** (2001): Roman Catholic 68.9%; Protestant 9.2%, of which Lutheran 6.9%, Reformed Christian 2.0%; Greek Catholic 4.1%; Eastern Orthodox 0.9%; nonreligious 13.0%; other/unknown 3.9%. **Major cities** (2005): Bratislava 417,653; Kosice 222,492; Presov 91,621; Zilina 85,425; Nitra 85,172. **Location:** central Europe, bordering Poland, Ukraine, Hungary, Austria, and the Czech Republic.

Vital statistics

Birth rate per 1,000 population (2007): 9.9 (world avg. 20.3); (2004) within marriage 75.2%; outside of marriage 24.8%. **Death rate** per 1,000 population (2007): 10.0 (world avg. 8.6). **Natural increase rate** per 1,000 population (2007): −0.1 (world avg. 11.7). **Total fertility rate** (avg. births per childbearing woman; 2005): 1.25. **Life expectancy** at birth (2006): male 70.4 years; female 78.2 years.

National economy

Budget (2006). *Revenue:* Sk 573,650,000,000 (tax revenue 49.5%, of which taxes on goods and services 31.9%; social security contributions 35.0%; nontax revenue 14.3%; grants 1.2%). *Expenditures:* Sk 634,860,000,000 (social protection 29.0%; health 16.9%; general administration 16.6%; economic affairs 13.4%; education 9.9%). **Production** (metric tons except as noted). *Agriculture and fishing* (2007): wheat 1,440,637, sugar beets 855,343, barley 695,042, sunflower seeds 135,376; livestock (number of live animals) 1,104,830 pigs, 507,820 cattle; fisheries production (2006) 2,981 (from aquaculture 42%). *Mining and quarrying* (2006): magnesite 555,710; kaolin 30,000; barite 25,000. *Manufacturing* (value added in US$'000,000; 2006): fabricated metal products 1,200; nonelectrical machinery and apparatus 1,165; motor vehicles and parts 1,000. *Energy production (consumption):* electricity (kW-hr; 2007) 28,063,000,000 ([2005] 28,190,000,000); coal (metric tons; 2005) none (4,983,000); lignite (metric tons; 2007) 2,113,000 ([2005] 3,307,000); crude petroleum (barrels; 2005) 210,000 (39,900,000); petroleum products (metric tons; 2005) 5,269,000 (3,122,000); natural gas (cu m; 2005) 151,000,000 (7,014,000,000). **Population economically active** (2006): total 2,654,800; activity rate of total population 49.2% (participation rates: ages 15–64, 68.9%; female 45.8%; unemployed [2007] 8.4%). **Public debt** (external, outstanding; 2006): US$4,508,000,000. **Gross national income** (2007): US$63,324,000,000 (US$11,730 per capita). **Selected balance of payments data.** Receipts from (US$'000,000): tourism (2006) 1,513; remittances (2007) 424; foreign direct investment (FDI)

(2004–06 avg.) 3,101. Disbursements for (US$'000,000): tourism (2006) 1,055; remittances (2007) 16; FDI (2004–06 avg.) 168.

Foreign trade

Imports (2006): US$44,383,000,000 (machinery and apparatus 26.3%; mineral fuels 13.6%; motor vehicles and parts 12.1%; base and fabricated metals 9.7%; chemical products 8.9%). *Major import sources:* Germany 20.4%; Czech Republic 12.0%; Russia 11.5%; Italy 4.6%; Hungary 4.6%. **Exports** (2006): US$41,719,000,000 (machinery and apparatus 27.5%, of which color television receivers 7.6%; motor vehicles and parts 20.5%, of which passenger cars 15.3%; base and fabricated metals 14.4%, of which iron and steel 8.5%; refined petroleum products 5.2%). *Major export destinations:* Germany 23.5%; Czech Republic 13.7%; Italy 6.5%; Poland 6.2%; Austria 6.0%.

Transport and communications

Transport. *Railroads* (2005): length (2006) 3,658 km; passenger-km 2,181,000,000; metric ton-km cargo 9,463,000,000. *Roads* (2004): total length 43,000 km (paved 87%). *Vehicles* (2006): passenger cars 1,334,000; trucks and buses 182,000. *Air transport* (SkyEurope and Slovak airlines only; 2006): passenger-km 2,596,207,000; metric ton-km cargo 29,000. **Communications,** in total units (units per 1,000 persons). Telephone landlines (2007): 1,151,000 (213); cellular telephone subscribers (2007): 6,068,000 (1,124); personal computers (2005): 1,929,000 (358); total Internet users (2007): 2,350,000 (435); broadband Internet subscribers (2007): 444,000 (82).

Education and health

Educational attainment (2002). Percentage of population ages 25–64 having: primary education 1%; complete lower secondary 13%; complete upper secondary 75%; higher 11%. **Literacy** (2007): percentage of total population ages 15 and over literate, virtually 100%. **Health** (2005): physicians 20,158 (1 per 267 persons); hospital beds 48,622 (1 per 111 persons); infant mortality rate per 1,000 live births 6.4; undernourished population (2002–04) 400,000 (7% of total population based on the consumption of a minimum daily requirement of 2,030 calories).

Military

Total active duty personnel (2007): 17,129 (army 42.8%, air force 25.0%, headquarters staff 15.3%, support/training 16.9%). **Military expenditure as percentage of GDP** (2005): 1.7%; per capita expenditure US$153.

Background

Slovakia was inhabited in the first centuries AD by Illyrian, Celtic, and Germanic tribes. Slovaks settled there around the 6th century. It became part of Great Moravia in the 9th century but was conquered by the Magyars c. 907. It remained in the kingdom of Hungary until the end of World War I, when the Slovaks

---

1 metric ton = about 1.1 short tons;   1 kilometer = 0.6 mi (statute);   1 metric ton-km cargo = about 0.68 short ton-mi cargo;   c.i.f.: cost, insurance, and freight;   f.o.b.: free on board

joined the Czechs to form the new state of Czechoslovakia in 1918. Slovakia was nominally independent under German protection in 1939–45. After the expulsion of the Germans, Slovakia joined a reconstituted Czechoslovakia, which came under Soviet domination in 1948. In 1969 a partnership between the Czechs and the Slovaks established the Slovak Socialist Republic. The fall of the communist regime in 1989 led to a revival of interest in autonomy, and Slovakia became an independent nation in 1993. It joined both NATO and the EU in 2004.

Recent Developments

The most important development for Slovakia was its entry into the euro zone on 1 Jan 2009. Despite skepticism over Slovak inflation prospects, European Union authorities backed the move, and the final conversion rate was set at 30.126 koruny per euro, a much stronger rate than was originally expected. Although many Slovaks also feared that euro adoption could negatively affect inflation, the accession was a source of pride. Slovakia was the second EU state in the former communist bloc—after Slovenia—to be admitted to the euro zone. The Slovak economy continued to hold up well after the international financial crisis struck; GDP growth for 2008 was 9.5%.

Internet resources: <http://portal.statistics.sk/showdoc.do?docid=359>.

Slovenia

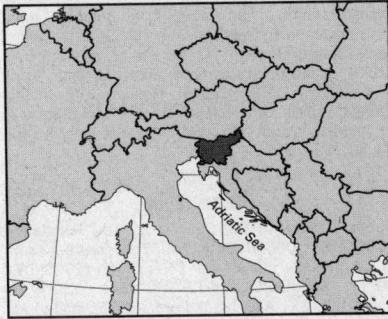

Official name: Republika Slovenija (Republic of Slovenia). **Form of government:** unitary multiparty republic with two legislative houses (National Council [40]; National Assembly [90]). **Head of state:** President Danilo Turk (from 2007). **Head of government:** Prime Minister Borut Pahor (from 2008). **Capital:** Ljubljana. **Official language:** Slovene. **Official religion:** none. **Monetary unit:** 1 euro (€) = 100 cents; valuation (1 Jul 2009) US$1 = €0.71 (the euro replaced the tolar [SIT] 1 Jan 2007, at the rate of €1 = SIT 239.64).

Demography

Area: 7,827 sq mi, 20,273 sq km. **Population** (2008): 2,029,000. **Density** (2008): persons per sq mi 259.2, persons per sq km 100.1. **Urban** (2005): 51.0%. **Sex distribution** (2008): male 49.64%; female 50.36%. **Age breakdown** (2007): under 15, 13.9%; 15–29, 20.0%; 30–44, 22.6%; 45–59, 22.4%; 60–74, 14.1%; 75–84, 5.7%; 85 and over,

1.3%. **Ethnic composition** (2002): Slovene 91.2%; Serb 2.2%; Croat 2.0%; Bosniac 1.8%; other 2.8%. **Religious affiliation** (2002): Roman Catholic 57.8%, Muslim 2.4%, Orthodox 2.3%, Protestant 0.8%, nonreligious/atheist 10.2%, other/unknown 26.5%. **Major municipalities** (2007): Ljubljana 267,760; Maribor 111,340; Kranj 53,872; Koper 50,708; Celje 49,501. **Location:** southeastern Europe, bordering Austria, Hungary, Croatia, the Adriatic Sea, and Italy.

Vital statistics

Birth rate per 1,000 population (2007): 9.8 (world avg. 20.3); within marriage 49.2%; outside of marriage 50.8%. **Death rate** per 1,000 population (2007): 9.2 (world avg. 8.6). **Natural increase rate** per 1,000 population (2007): 0.6 (world avg. 11.7). **Total fertility rate** (avg. births per childbearing woman; 2007): 1.38. **Life expectancy** at birth (2007): male 75.0 years; female 82.3 years.

National economy

Budget (2007). *Revenue:* €13,658,091,000 (tax revenue 59.7%, of which taxes on goods and services 32.9%, income tax 13.2%; social security contributions 33.7%; nontax revenue 5.2%; other [including grants] 1.4%). *Expenditures:* €13,092,376,000 (current expenditures 88.8%, of which social protection 46.9%, wages and salaries 21.5%; capital expenditures 11.2%). **Public debt** (2007): US$10,875,000,000. **Production** (metric tons except as noted). *Agriculture and fishing* (2007): corn (maize) 308,259, sugar beets 260,000, wheat 133,339, hops 2,157; livestock (number of live animals) 575,120 pigs, 451,293 cattle (in addition, 212,000 beehives); fisheries production 1,967 (from aquaculture 54%). *Mining and quarrying* (2007): sand and gravel 11,008,600; salt (2005) 125,000. *Manufacturing* (value added in €'000,000; 2007): chemical products 971; fabricated metal products 961; nonelectrical machinery and apparatus 776. *Energy production (consumption):* electricity (kW-hr; 2007) 14,044,000,000 (13,337,000,000); hard coal (metric tons; 2005) none (49,000); lignite (metric tons; 2007) 4,562,000 (5,197,000); crude petroleum (barrels; 2007) 2,199 (negligible); petroleum products (metric tons; 2007) none (2,296,000); natural gas (cu m; 2007) 3,400,000 (1,124,000,000). **Gross national income** (2007): US$42,306,000,000 (US$20,960 per capita). **Population economically active** (2007): total 1,041,600; activity rate of total population 51.8% (participation rates: ages 15–64, 71.7%; female 46.0%; unemployed [April 2007–March 2008] 7.4%). **Selected balance of payments data.** Receipts from (US$'000,000): tourism (2006) 1,797; remittances (2007) 300; foreign direct investment (FDI) (2004–06 avg.) 562. Disbursements for (US$'000,000): tourism (2006) 974; remittances (2007) 207; FDI (2004–06 avg.) 620.

Foreign trade

Imports (2007; c.i.f.): €21,487,000,000 (base and fabricated metals 14.1%; motor vehicles 13.2%; chemical products 12.1%; nonelectrical machinery and apparatus 10.6%; mineral fuels 9.4%). *Major import sources:* Germany 19.4%; Italy 18.3%; Austria 12.5%; France 5.4%; Croatia 4.0%. **Exports** (2007; f.o.b.): €19,385,000,000 (motor vehicles and parts

15.9%; base and fabricated metals 13.6%; nonelectrical machinery and apparatus 12.5%; electrical machinery and electronics 9.6%; medicine and pharmaceuticals 7.2%). *Major export destinations:* Germany 18.9%; Italy 13.2%; Croatia 8.1%; Austria 7.8%; France 6.5%.

Transport and communications

Transport. *Railroads* (2007): length 1,228 km; passenger-km 812,000,000; metric ton-km cargo 3,603,000,000. *Roads* (2006): total length 38,562 km (paved 100%). *Vehicles* (2007): passenger cars 1,014,122; trucks and buses 79,898. *Air transport* (2007): passenger-km 1,186,000,000; metric ton-km cargo 3,724,000. **Communications,** in total units (units per 1,000 persons). Telephone landlines (2007): 857,000 (428); cellular telephone subscribers (2007): 1,928,000 (964); personal computers (2005): 808,000 (404); total Internet users (2007): 992,000 (496); broadband Internet subscribers (2007): 345,000 (172).

Education and health

Educational attainment (2006). Percentage of population ages 15 and over having: no formal schooling through complete primary education 27.7%; secondary 6.0%; vocational 55.1%; some higher 2.9%; undergraduate 7.1%; advanced degree 1.2%. **Literacy** (2007): percentage of total population literate, virtually 100%. **Health** (2007): physicians 4,441 (1 per 453 persons); hospital beds 9,414 (1 per 214 persons); infant mortality rate per 1,000 live births 2.8; undernourished population (2002–04) 60,000 (3% of total population based on the consumption of a minimum daily requirement of 1,990 calories).

Military

Total active duty personnel (2007): 5,973 (army 100%). **Military expenditure as percentage of GNI** (2005): 1.5%; per capita expenditure US$257.

Background

The Slovenes settled the region in the 6th century AD. In the 8th century it was incorporated into the Frankish empire of Charlemagne, and in the 10th century it came under Germany as part of the Holy Roman Empire. Except for 1809–14, when Napoleon ruled the area, most of the lands belonged to Austria until the formation of the Kingdom of Serbs, Croats, and Slovenes in 1918. It became a constituent republic of Yugoslavia in 1946. In 1990 Slovenia held the first contested multiparty elections in Yugoslavia since before World War II. In 1991 it seceded from Yugoslavia. Subsequently it sought to privatize the economy and build ties with Western Europe, joining both the EU and NATO in 2004.

Recent Developments

Slovenia presided over the Council of the European Union (EU) during the first half of 2008; it was the first postcommunist country to do so. During its tenure Slovenia led efforts to ratify the Lisbon Treaty, which would streamline the workings of the EU; to renew the Lisbon Strategy, an EU economic development plan; and to establish the Ljubljana Process, which would accelerate cooperation between European research institutions. The global financial crisis dominated economic news, with the Slovenian stock-exchange index SBI 20 plunging about 67% during the year.

Internet resources: <www.stat.si/eng/index.asp>.

Solomon Islands

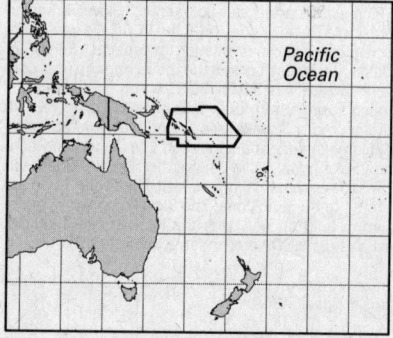

Pacific Ocean

Official name: Solomon Islands. **Form of government:** constitutional monarchy with one legislative house (National Parliament [50]). **Chief of state:** British Queen Elizabeth II (from 1952), represented by Governor-General Sir Nathaniel Waena (from 2004). **Head of government:** Prime Minister Derek Sikua (from 2007). **Capital:** Honiara. **Official language:** English. **Official religion:** none. **Monetary unit:** 1 Solomon Islands dollar (SI$) = 100 cents; valuation (1 Jul 2009) US$1 = SI$6.97.

Demography

Area: 10,954 sq mi, 28,370 sq km. **Population** (2008): 517,000. **Density** (2008): persons per sq mi 47.2, persons per sq km 18.2. **Urban** (2005–06): 16.0%. **Sex distribution** (2006): male 51.53%; female 48.47%. **Age breakdown** (2006): under 15, 40.0%; 15–29, 28.7%; 30–44, 17.9%; 45–59, 8.5%; 60–74, 3.9%; 75 and over, 1.0%. **Ethnic composition** (2002): Melanesian 93.0%; Polynesian 4.0%; Micronesian 1.5%; other 1.5%. **Religious affiliation** (2005): Protestant 70%, of which Anglican 32%, Adventist 10%; Roman Catholic 18%; traditional beliefs 5%; other 7%. **Major towns** (2004): Honiara 57,600; Gizo 6,200; Auki 4,700; Buala 2,900. **Location:** Oceania, island group in the South Pacific Ocean, east of Papua New Guinea.

Vital statistics

Birth rate per 1,000 population (2006): 30.0 (world avg. 20.3). **Death rate** per 1,000 population (2006): 3.9 (world avg. 8.6). **Natural increase rate** per 1,000 population (2006): 26.1 (world avg. 11.7). **Total fertility rate** (avg. births per childbearing woman; 2006):

---

1 metric ton = about 1.1 short tons;   1 kilometer = 0.6 mi (statute);   1 metric ton-km cargo = about 0.68 short ton-mi cargo;   c.i.f.: cost, insurance, and freight;   f.o.b.: free on board

3.78. **Life expectancy** at birth (2006): male 70.4 years; female 75.5 years.

National economy

Budget (2006). *Revenue:* SI$946,200,000 (tax revenue 73.0%, of which VAT 17.9%, logging duties 13.6%, import duties 9.3%, corporate taxes 8.2%; nontax revenue 13.9%; grants 13.1%). *Expenditures:* SI$911,100,000 (current expenditures 90.5%, of which wages and salaries 27.3%, debt service 13.9%; capital expenditures 9.5%). **Public debt** (external, outstanding; 2007): US$147,300,000. **Gross national income** (2007): US$363,000,000 (US$730 per capita). **Population economically active** (2006): total 201,000; activity rate of total population 41.0% (participation rates: ages 15 and over 68.8%; female 38.3%; unemployed [2003] 15.2%). **Production** (metric tons except as noted). *Agriculture and fishing* (2007): coconuts 276,000, oil palm fruit 155,000, sweet potatoes 86,000; livestock (number of live animals) 54,000 pigs, 13,600 cattle, 235,000 chickens; fisheries production (2006) 39,336 (from aquaculture, negligible); aquatic plants production (2006) 120 (from aquaculture 100%). *Mining and quarrying* (2005): gold 10 kg. *Manufacturing* (2006): coconut oil 59,000, vegetable oils and fats (2002) 50,000, copra 21,214. *Energy production (consumption):* electricity (kW-hr; 2006) 68,000,000 (55,000,000); petroleum products (metric tons; 2005) none (57,000). **Selected balance of payments data.** Receipts from (US$'000,000): tourism (2006) 2; remittances (2007) 20; foreign direct investment (2004–06 avg.) 15; official development assistance (2006) 205. Disbursements for (US$'000,000): tourism (2006) 8; remittances (2007) 3.

Foreign trade

Imports (2006; c.i.f.): US$250,613,000 (machinery and transportation equipment 24.7%; petroleum [all forms] 21.7%; food products 14.1%; construction materials 10.0%; chemical products 5.2%). *Major import sources:* Australia 25.3%; Singapore 23.4%; Japan 7.8%; New Zealand 5.0%; Fiji 4.2%. **Exports** (2007; f.o.b.): US$156,008,000 (logs 63.7%; palm oil 8.6%; frozen fish 7.2%; cacao beans 5.8%; copra 3.7%). *Major export destinations* (2006): China 45.7%; South Korea 14.0%; Japan 8.5%; Thailand 4.4%; Philippines 4.0%.

Transport and communications

Transport. *Railroads:* none. *Roads* (2007): total length 1,500 km (paved 2.7%). *Vehicles* (1993): passenger cars 2,052; trucks and buses 2,574. *Air transport* (Solomon Airlines only; 2006): passenger-km 74,870,000; metric ton-km cargo 648,000. **Communications,** in total units (units per 1,000 persons). Telephone landlines (2005): 7,400 (16); cellular telephone subscribers (2007): 11,000 (22); personal computers (2005): 22,000 (47); total Internet users (2006): 8,000 (17); broadband Internet subscribers (2007): 1,000 (2).

Education and health

Educational attainment (2005–06). Percentage of population ages 15 and over having: no schooling/unknown 15.6%; primary education 46.7%; sec-

ondary 32.8%; vocational 4.0%; higher 0.9%. **Literacy** (2004): percentage of total population ages 15 and over literate 76.6%. **Health** (2005): physicians 89 (1 per 5,293 persons); hospital beds 691 (1 per 682 persons); infant mortality rate per 1,000 live births (2006) 20.6; undernourished population (2002–04) 90,000 (21% of total population based on the consumption of a minimum daily requirement of 1,780 calories).

Military

Total active duty personnel (2007): none; 200–300 military troops and police in an Australian-led multinational regional intervention force (from mid-2003) maintain civil and political order.

Background

The Solomon Islands were settled c. 2000 BC by Austronesian people. Visited by the Spanish in 1568, the islands were subsequently explored by the Dutch, the French, and the British. They came under British protection in 1893. During World War II, the Japanese invasion of 1942 ignited three years of the most bitter fighting in the Pacific, particularly on Guadalcanal. The protectorate became self-governing in 1976 and fully independent in 1978. In the late 20th and early 21st centuries, ethnic tensions led to political instability; a multinational force led by Australia helped restore order.

Recent Developments

The Regional Assistance Mission to Solomon Islands (RAMSI) continued to guarantee the country's security in 2009. Fifteen neighboring nations contributed to RAMSI's police force, while four, led by Australia and New Zealand, contributed troops. RAMSI also provided technical assistance to rebuild Solomon Islands' governance structures, civil service, and economy, all of which were proceeding well.

Internet resources: <www.spc.int/prism/country/sb/stats>.

Somalia

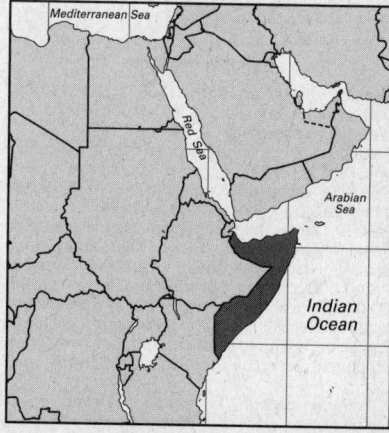

Proclamation of the "Republic of Somaliland" in May 1991 on territory corresponding to the former British Somaliland had not received international recognition as of early 2009. This entity represents about a quarter of Somalia's territory. **Official name:** Soomaaliya (Somali); Al-Sumal (Arabic) (Somalia). **Form of government:** transitional regime (the "new transitional government" from October 2004 lacked effective control in mid-2009) with one legislative body (Transitional Federal Assembly [550]). At present Somalia is divided into three autonomous regions: Somaliland in the northwest, Puntland in the northeast, and Somalia in the south. **Head of state and government:** President Sheikh Sharif Sheikh Ahmed (from 2009), assisted by Prime Minister Omar Abdirashid Ali Sharmarke (from 2009). **Capital:** Mogadishu. **Official languages:** Somali; Arabic. **Official religion:** Islam. **Monetary unit:** 1 Somali shilling (So.Sh.) = 100 cents; valuation (1 Jul 2009) US$1 = So.Sh. 1,372.74 (in early 2008 the black-market value was about 34,000 So.Sh. = US$1).

Demography

Area: 246,201 sq mi, 637,657 sq km. **Population** (2008): 8,956,000. **Density** (2008): persons per sq mi 36.4, persons per sq km 14.0. **Urban** (2006): 36.5%. **Sex distribution** (2005): male 49.60%; female 50.40%. **Age breakdown** (2005): under 15, 44.1%; 15–29, 27.1%; 30–44, 16.1%; 45–59, 8.5%; 60–74, 3.5%; 75–84, 0.6%; 85 and over, 0.1%. **Ethnic composition** (2000): Somali 92.4%; Arab 2.2%; Afar 1.3%; other 4.1%. **Religious affiliation** (2005): Muslim (nearly all Sunni) 99%; other 1%. **Major cities** (2008): Mogadishu (2007) 1,100,000; Hargeysa 436,232; Burao 151,451; Belet Weyne 108,125; Boosaaso 108,016. **Location:** the Horn of Africa, bordering Djibouti, the Gulf of Aden, the Indian Ocean, Kenya, and Ethiopia.

Vital statistics

Birth rate per 1,000 population (2005): 45.6 (world avg. 20.3). **Death rate** per 1,000 population (2005): 17.0 (world avg. 8.6). **Natural increase rate** per 1,000 population (2005): 28.6 (world avg. 11.7). **Total fertility rate** (avg. births per childbearing woman; 2005): 6.84. **Life expectancy** at birth (2005): male 46.4 years; female 49.9 years.

National economy

Budget: n.a.; UN assistance (2007): US$175,000,-000, of which food aid US$50,000,000. **Public debt** (external, outstanding; 2006): US$1,923,000,000. **Production** (metric tons except as noted). *Agriculture and fishing* (2007): milk 2,166,000 (from camels 870,000, sheep 468,000, cows 435,000), sugarcane 215,000, corn (maize) 99,000, cassava 82,000; other tree/bush products include khat, frankincense, and myrrh; livestock (number of live animals) 13,100,000 sheep, 12,700,000 goats, 7,000,000 camels; fisheries production (2006) 30,000 (from aquaculture, none). *Mining and quarrying* (2006): small quantities of gemstones (including garnet and opal) and salt. *Manufacturing:* small manufacturers produce textiles, handicrafts, and

processed meat. *Energy production (consumption):* electricity (kW-hr; 2005) 290,000,000 (290,000,-000); crude petroleum (barrels; 2005) none (388,000); petroleum products (metric tons; 2005) 30,000 (169,000). **Population economically active** (2001–02): total 3,906,000; activity rate of total population 52.6% (participation rates: ages 15–64, 56.4%; unemployed 47.4%). **Gross national income** (2007): US$2,450,000,000 (US$282 per capita). **Selected balance of payments data.** Receipts from (US$'000,000): remittances (2007) 1,000; foreign direct investment (2004–06 avg.) 38; official development assistance (2006) 392.

Foreign trade

Imports (2005): US$671,000,000 (agricultural products 37.9%, of which cereals and cereal products 15.8%, sugar 10.3%; unspecified 62.1%). *Major import sources:* Djibouti 30%; Kenya 14%; India 8%; Brazil 7%; Oman 5%. **Exports** (2005): US$249,-000,000 (goats 11.8%; cattle 9.0%; sheep 6.4%; unspecified 72.8%). *Major export destinations:* UAE 48%; Yemen 21%; Oman 6%; India 4%; Saudi Arabia 3%.

Transport and communications

Transport. *Railroads:* none. *Roads* (2003): total length 22,000 km (paved 12%). *Air transport* (four Somaliland airports only; 2003): passenger arrivals 50,096, passenger departures 41,979; cargo unloaded 3,817 metric tons, cargo loaded 152 metric tons. **Communications,** in total units (units per 1,000 persons). Telephone landlines (2007): 100,000 (11); cellular telephone subscribers (2007): 600,000 (69); personal computers (2005): 75,000 (9.1); total Internet users (2007): 98,000 (11).

Education and health

Literacy (2002): percentage of total population ages 15 and over literate 19.2%; males literate 25.1%; females literate 13.1%. **Health** (2006): physicians 34 (1 per 250,000 persons); infant mortality rate per 1,000 live births (2005) 121.8.

Military

Total active duty personnel: no national army from 1991; African Union peacekeeping troops from Uganda and Burundi (December 2008) 3,000 (of planned 8,000).

Background

Muslim Arabs and Persians first established trading posts along the coasts of Somalia in the 7th–10th centuries. By the 10th century Somali nomads occupied the area inland from the Gulf of Aden, and the south and west were inhabited by various groups of pastoral Oromo peoples. Intensive European exploration began after the British occupation of Aden in 1839, and in the late 19th century Britain and Italy set up protectorates in the region. During World War II the Italians invaded British Somaliland (1940); a year later British troops retook the area, and Britain administered the region until 1950,

---

1 metric ton = about 1.1 short tons;　1 kilometer = 0.6 mi (statute);　1 metric ton-km cargo = about 0.68 short ton-mi cargo;　c.i.f.: cost, insurance, and freight;　f.o.b.: free on board

when Italian Somaliland became a UN trust territory. In 1960 it was united with the former British Somaliland, and the two became the independent Republic of Somalia. Since then it has suffered political and civil strife, including military dictatorship, civil war, drought, and famine. No effective central government has existed since the early 1990s. In 1991 a proclamation of a Republic of Somaliland, on territory corresponding to the former British Somaliland, was issued by a breakaway group, but it did not receive international recognition. A multinational force intervened from 1992 to 1994 in an unsuccessful attempt to stabilize the region. The country remained in turmoil.

Recent Developments

Somalia continued to be wracked by violence and anarchy. An African Union peacekeeping force, composed of 2,600 troops from Uganda and Burundi, continued to operate in Somalia, but that force had been unable to stop the fighting and was limited to providing VIP escorts and guarding the presidential residence, airport, and seaport in Mogadishu, the country's capital. Ethiopian troops who had entered the country in late 2006 began their withdrawal from Somalia in early 2009. In March 2008 it was reported that many refugee families were surviving on less than one meal a day. Food prices in Somalia were soaring, partly due to the emerging global food crisis and partly because the country, which was heavily dependent on agriculture, was in the midst of a severe three-year drought.

Internet resources: <www.unsomalia.net>.

South Africa

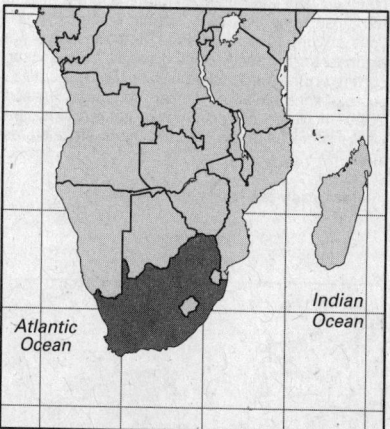

Official name: Republic of South Africa. **Form of government:** multiparty republic with two legislative houses (National Council of Provinces [90]; National Assembly [400]). **Head of state and government:** President Jacob Zuma (from 2009). **Capitals** (de facto): Pretoria/Tshwane (executive); Bloemfontein/Mangaung (judicial); Cape Town (legislative). **Official languages:** Afrikaans; English; Ndebele; Pedi; Sotho; Swazi; Tsonga; Tswana; Venda; Xhosa; Zulu.

Official religion: none. **Monetary unit:** 1 rand (R) = 100 cents; valuation (1 Jul 2009) US$1 = R 7.72.

Demography

Area: 471,359 sq mi, 1,220,813 sq km. **Population** (2008): 48,783,000. **Density** (2008): persons per sq mi 103.5, persons per sq km 40.0. **Urban** (2005): 59.28%. **Sex distribution** (2007): male 49.24%; female 50.76%. **Age breakdown** (2007): under 15, 31.9%; 15–29, 29.2%; 30–44, 19.3%; 45–59, 11.7%; 60–74, 6.3%; 75 and over, 1.6%. **Ethnic composition** (2001): black 78.4%, of which Zulu 23.8%, Xhosa 17.6%, Pedi 9.4%, Tswana 8.2%, Sotho 7.9%, Tsonga 4.4%, Swazi 2.7%, other black 4.4%; white 9.6%; mixed white/black 8.9%; Asian 2.5%; other 0.6%. **Religious affiliation** (2005): independent Christian 37.1%, of which Zion Christian 9.5%; Protestant 26.1%; traditional beliefs 8.9%; Roman Catholic 6.7%; Muslim 2.5%; Hindu 2.4%; nonreligious 3.0%; other/unknown 13.3%. **Major urban agglomerations** (2005): Johannesburg 3,288,000; Cape Town 3,103,000; Ekurhuleni (East Rand) 3,043,000; eThekwini (Durban) 2,643,000; Tshwane (name of larger municipality including Pretoria) 1,282,000. **Location:** southern Africa, bordering Namibia, Botswana, Zimbabwe, Mozambique, Swaziland, and the Indian and South Atlantic oceans; wholly contained within South Africa is the country of Lesotho.

Vital statistics

Birth rate per 1,000 population (2005): 18.5 (world avg. 20.3). **Death rate** per 1,000 population (2005): 21.3 (world avg. 8.6). **Total fertility rate** (avg. births per childbearing woman; 2007): 2.69. **Life expectancy** at birth (2008): male 50.3 years; female 53.9 years.

National economy

Budget (2005–06). *Revenue:* R 411,085,100,000 (income tax 30.6%; VAT 28.0%; corporate taxes 23.5%). *Expenditures:* R 417,819,200,000 (transfer to provinces 36.0%; debt payments 12.7%; police and prisons 9.0%; defense 5.4%). **Production** (in metric tons except as noted). *Agriculture and fishing* (2007): sugarcane 20,500,000, corn (maize) 7,338,738, potatoes 1,900,000, grapes 1,600,000; livestock (number of live animals) 25,000,000 sheep, 13,500,000 cattle; fisheries production (2006) 620,740 (from aquaculture, negligible); aquatic plants production (2006) 9,600 (from aquaculture 31%). *Mining and quarrying* (value of sales in R '000,000,000; 2007): platinum-group metals 79.9; coal 43.1; gold 39.0; iron ore 13.4; rough diamond production 15,249,000 carats. *Manufacturing* (value of sales in R '000,000; 2005): food and beverages 153,496; transportation equipment 137,870; chemical products 81,240. *Energy production (consumption)* (data include Botswana, Lesotho, Namibia, and Swaziland): electricity (kW-hr; 2005) 248,075,000,000 (248,975,000,000); coal (metric tons; 2005) 246,313,000 (176,736,000); crude petroleum (barrels; 2005) 10,576,000 (166,670,000); petroleum products (metric tons; 2005) 26,263,000 (20,104,000); natural gas (cu m; 2005) 2,126,000,000 (4,331,000,000) **Population economically active** (2005): total 16,788,000; activity rate of total population 35.8% (participation rates: ages 15–64,

56.5%; female 45.7%; unemployed 26.7%). **Gross national income** (2007): US$274,009,000,000 (US$5,760 per capita). **Public debt** (external, outstanding; 2006): US$13,940,000,000. **Selected balance of payments data.** Receipts from (US$'000,-000): tourism (2006) 7,876; remittances (2007) 834; foreign direct investment (FDI) (2004–06 avg.) 2,242; official development assistance (2006) 718. Disbursements for (US$'000,000): tourism (2006) 3,384; remittances (2007) 1,186; FDI (2004–06 avg.) 2,985.

Foreign trade

Imports (2006): US$69,185,000,000 (machinery and apparatus 26.5%; crude petroleum 13.9%; motor vehicles 9.6%; chemical products 8.9%). *Major import sources:* Germany 12.5%; China 10.0%; US 7.6%; Japan 6.5%; Saudi Arabia 5.3%. **Exports** (2006): US$53,170,000,000 (excluding gold export earnings estimated at US$5,400,000,000) (platinum-group metals 15.3%; iron and steel 10.8%; motor vehicles 9.0%; metal ores 7.4%; coal 6.0%; diamonds 4.6%). *Major export destinations:* Japan 11.9%; US 11.5%; UK 8.8%; Germany 7.5%; The Netherlands 5.2%.

Transport and communications

Transport. *Railroads* (2001): route length (2005) 20,872 km; passenger-km 3,930,000,000; metric ton-km cargo 106,786,000,000. *Roads* (2002): length 362,099 km (paved 20%). *Vehicles* (2005): passenger cars 4,574,972; trucks and buses 2,112,601. *Air transport* (2007): passenger-km 27,576,000,000; metric ton-km cargo 935,600,000. **Communications,** in total units (units per 1,000 persons). Telephone landlines (2007): 4,642,000 (96); cellular telephone subscribers (2007): 42,300,000 (871); personal computers (2005): 3,966,000 (85); total Internet users (2007): 3,966,000 (82); broadband Internet subscribers (2007): 378,000 (7.8).

Education and health

Educational attainment (2006). Percentage of population ages 20 and over having: no formal schooling 10.4%; some primary education 21.1%; complete primary/some secondary 34.0%; complete secondary 24.9%; higher 9.1%. **Literacy** (2007): percentage of total population ages 15 and over literate 87.8%. **Health:** physicians (2006) 33,220 (1 per 1,427 persons); hospital beds (2004) 153,465 (1 per 303 persons); infant mortality rate per 1,000 live births (2007) 45.2; undernourished population (2002–04) less than 2.5% of total population.

Military

Total active duty personnel (2007): 62,334 (army 66.3%, navy 9.3%, air force 14.7%, military health service 9.7%). **Military expenditure as percentage of GDP** (2005): 1.5%; per capita expenditure US$76.

Background

San and Khoikhoi peoples roamed southern Africa as hunters and gatherers in the Stone Age, and the latter had developed a pastoralist culture by the time of European contact. By the 14th century, Bantu-speaking peoples had settled in the area and developed gold and copper mining and an active East African trade. In 1652 the Dutch established a colony at the Cape of Good Hope; the Dutch settlers became known as Boers and later as Afrikaners, after their Afrikaans language. In 1795 British forces captured the Cape, and in the 1830s, to escape British rule, Dutch settlers began the Great Trek northward and established the independent Boer republics of the Orange Free State and the South African Republic (later the Transvaal region), which the British annexed as colonies by 1902 as a result of the 30-month-long Boer War. In 1910 the British colonies of Cape Colony, Transvaal, Natal, and Orange River were unified into the new Union of South Africa. It became independent and withdrew from the Commonwealth in 1961. Throughout the 20th century South African politics were dominated by the issue of maintaining white supremacy over the country's black majority, and in 1948 apartheid was formally instituted. Faced by increasing worldwide condemnation, it began dismantling the apartheid laws in 1990. In free elections in 1994, Nelson Mandela became the country's first black president. The country also rejoined the Commonwealth in 1994. A permanent nonracial constitution was promulgated in 1997.

Recent Developments

South Africa continued to struggle with "two centers of power" in 2008 following the election of Jacob Zuma as president of the African National Congress (ANC), replacing South African Pres. Thabo Mbeki. In September the Natal High Court significantly upheld Zuma's claims that there had been political interference from the presidency in the prosecuting of a case against Zuma on allegations of corruption and fraud. The atmosphere was highly charged, and violent disputes between supporters of Zuma and those of Mbeki affected all aspects of the new South African democracy. In April 2009, however, the case was thrown out, and weeks later Zuma was selected South Africa's president.

Internet resources: <www.statssa.gov.za>.

Spain

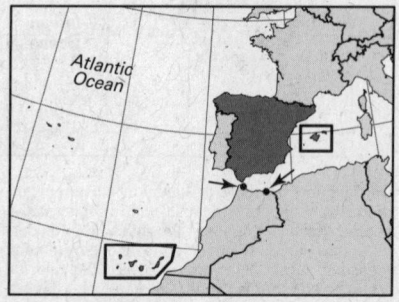

Official name: Reino de España (Kingdom of Spain). **Form of government:** constitutional monarchy with two legislative houses (Senate [259]; Congress of Deputies [350]). **Chief of state:** King Juan Carlos I (from 1975). **Head of government:** Prime Minister José Luis Rodríguez Zapatero (from 2004). **Capital:** Madrid. **Official language:** Castilian Spanish (per constitution, Euskera [Basque], Catalan, Galician, and all other Spanish languages are also official in their autonomous communities). **Official religion:** none. **Monetary unit:** 1 euro (€) = 100 cents; valuation (1 Jul 2009) US$1 = €0.71.

Demography

Area: 195,364 sq mi, 505,990 sq km. **Population** (2008): 45,661,000. **Density** (2008): persons per sq mi 233.7, persons per sq km 90.2. **Urban** (2005): 76.7%. **Sex distribution** (2008): male 49.38%; female 50.62%. **Age breakdown** (2008): under 15, 14.7%; 15–29, 18.9%; 30–44, 25.4%; 45–59, 19.2%; 60–74, 13.4%; 75–84, 6.3%; 85 and over, 2.1%. **Ethnic composition** (2000): Spanish 44.9%; Catalonian 28.0%; Galician 8.2%; Basque 5.5%; Aragonese 5.0%; Rom (Gypsy) 2.0%; other 6.4% (foreign residents [2007]: 4.5 million, of which Moroccan 13%, Romanian 12%, Ecuadorian 9%). **Religious affiliation** (2006): Roman Catholic 77%, of which practicing weekly 19%; Muslim 2.5%; Protestant 1%; other (mostly nonreligious) 19.5%. **Major cities** (2007): Madrid 3,132,463 (urban agglomeration 5,764,000); Barcelona 1,595,110 (urban agglomeration 5,057,000); Valencia 797,654; Sevilla 699,145; Zaragoza 654,390. **Location:** southwestern Europe, bordering France, Andorra, the Mediterranean Sea, Gibraltar, the Atlantic Ocean, and Portugal; the North African exclaves of Ceuta and Melilla border Morocco.

Vital statistics

Birth rate per 1,000 population (2007): 10.8 (world avg. 20.3); (2006) within marriage 71.6%; outside of marriage 28.4%. **Death rate** per 1,000 population (2007): 8.5 (world avg. 8.6). **Total fertility rate** (avg. births per childbearing woman; 2007): 1.37. **Life expectancy** at birth (2007): male 77.3 years; female 83.8 years.

National economy

Budget (2007). *Revenue:* €147,545,000,000 (direct taxes 56.9%; indirect taxes 34.4%; transfers 3.9%). *Expenditures:* €188,417,000,000 (current expenditures 63.8%, of which wages and salaries 12.6%; debt service 8.5%; capital expenditures 10.2%, of which transfers 4.9%). **Public debt** (2007): US$520,918,000,000. **Gross national income** (2007): US$1,321,756,000,000 (US$29,450 per capita). **Production** (metric tons except as noted). *Agriculture and fishing* (2007): barley 11,684,000, wheat 6,376,900, grapes 6,013,000, olives 5,787,600, almonds 201,100, garlic 142,400; livestock (number of live animals) 26,034,000 pigs, 21,847,050 sheep, 6,456,350 cattle (in addition, 2,500,000 beehives); fisheries production (2006) 1,242,802 (from aquaculture 24%). *Mining and quarrying* (2005): slate 1,200,000; sepiolite 800,000; fluorspar 133,495; gold 5,500 kg. *Manufacturing* (value added in US$'000,000; 2004): food products 15,786; fabricated metal products 15,717; transportation equipment 14,508. *Energy production*

(consumption): electricity (kW-hr; 2007–08) 303,-278,000,000 (279,709,000,000); coal (metric tons; 2007) 10,995,000 (36,281,000); lignite (metric tons; 2007) 6,016,000 (6,016,000); crude petroleum (barrels; 2007–08) 1,133,400 (453,309,900); petroleum products (metric tons; 2007–08) 55,886,-000 ([2005] 60,628,000); natural gas (cu m; 2007–08) 15,447,500 (39,414,926,000). **Population economically active** (2007): total 22,189,900; activity rate of total population 49.7% (participation rates: ages 16–64, 72.6%; female 42.3%; unemployed [October 2007–September 2008] 10.0%). **Selected balance of payments data.** Receipts from (US$'000,000): tourism (2007–08) 62,905; remittances (2007) 10,633; foreign direct investment (FDI) (2004–06 avg.) 23,266. Disbursements for (US$'000,000): tourism (2007–08) 21,277; remittances (2007) 14,721; FDI (2004–06 avg.) 64,013.

Foreign trade

Imports (2006; c.i.f.): €263,024,000,000 (machinery and apparatus 19.7%; mineral fuels 15.7%; motor vehicles and parts 14.6%; chemical products 11.0%; base and fabricated metals 7.6%). *Major import sources* (2007): Germany 15.2%; France 12.2%; Italy 8.7%; China 6.7%; UK 4.7%. **Exports** (2006; f.o.b.): €170,628,000,000 (motor vehicles and parts 20.7%; machinery and apparatus 15.2%; food products 10.9%, of which fruits and vegetables 5.8%; base and fabricated metals 8.9%). *Major export destinations* (2007): France 18.6%; Germany 10.8%; Portugal 8.6%; Italy 8.5%; UK 7.5%.

Transport and communications

Transport. *Railroads* (2007–08): route length (2006) 15,212 km; passenger-km 22,794,600,000; metric ton-km cargo 10,839,100,000. *Roads* (2006): length 681,224 km (paved 100%). *Vehicles* (2007): cars 21,440,700; trucks, vans, and buses 5,273,000. *Air transport* (2007–08): passenger-km 81,252,000,-000; metric ton-km cargo 1,169,204,000. **Communications,** in total units (units per 1,000 persons). Telephone landlines (2007): 20,328,000 (459); cellular telephone subscribers (2007): 48,813,000 (1,102); personal computers (2005): 12,000,000 (269); total Internet users (2007): 20,097,000 (454); broadband Internet subscribers (2007): 8,070,000 (182).

Education and health

Educational attainment (2007). Percentage of population ages 16 and over having: no formal schooling through incomplete primary education 11.6%; complete primary 20.9%; secondary 44.4%; undergraduate degree 14.2%; graduate degree 8.9%. **Literacy** (2003): percentage of total population ages 15 and over literate 97.9%; males literate 98.7%; females literate 97.2%. **Health** (2007): physicians 208,098 (1 per 218 persons); hospital beds 160,292 (1 per 283 persons); infant mortality rate per 1,000 live births (2007) 3.7; undernourished population (2002–04) less than 2.5% of total population.

Military

Total active duty personnel (2007): 149,150 (army 64.1%, navy 15.6%, air force 14.0%, other 6.3%). **Mil-**

itary expenditure as percentage of GDP (2005): 1.1%; per capita expenditure US$268.

Background

Remains of Stone Age populations dating back some 35,000 years have been found in Spain. Celtic peoples arrived in the 9th century BC, followed by the Romans, who dominated Spain from c. 200 BC until the Visigoth invasion in the early 5th century. In the early 8th century most of the peninsula fell to Muslims (Moors) from North Africa and remained under their control until it was gradually reconquered by the Christian kingdoms of Castile, Aragon, and Portugal. Spain was reunited in 1479 following the marriage of Ferdinand II (of Aragon) and Isabella I (of Castile). The last Muslim kingdom, Granada, was reconquered in 1492, and around this time Spain also established a colonial empire in the Americas. In 1516 the throne passed to the Habsburgs, whose rule ended in 1700 when Philip V became the first Bourbon king of Spain. His ascendancy caused the War of the Spanish Succession, which resulted in the loss of numerous European possessions and sparked revolution in most of Spain's American colonies. Spain lost its remaining overseas possessions to the US in the Spanish-American War (1898). It became a republic in 1931. The Spanish Civil War (1936–39) ended in victory for the Nationalists under Gen. Francisco Franco, who ruled as dictator until his death in 1975. His successor as head of state, King Juan Carlos I, restored the monarchy; a new constitution in 1978 established a parliamentary monarchy. Spain joined NATO in 1982 and the European Community in 1986. In the late 20th and early 21st centuries, Basque separatists continued to resort to violence as they pressed for independence, but it was Islamic militants who were responsible for the 11 Mar 2004 bombings in Madrid that killed 191 people—the worst terrorist incident in Europe since World War II.

Recent Developments

Almost exactly four years after the terrorist attacks on Madrid that helped to bring the Socialist Workers' Party to power in 2004, Spanish Prime Minister José Luis Rodríguez Zapatero won a second term in the general elections held on 9 Mar 2008. The Socialists and the opposition Popular Party found common ground in the fight against the Basque separatist organization Euskadi Ta Askatasuna (ETA). The government's resolve to defeat ETA was strengthened following the end of the organization's 14-month cease-fire in June 2007. In February two political parties associated with ETA were suspended (followed later by their illegalization) and thereby prevented from standing in the March general elections, which resulted in the first non-nationalist local government in the Basque region in nearly 30 years. French police detained the alleged top leader of ETA in May, the organization's alleged military chief in November, and, just weeks later, the man reported to have succeeded as military chief. In 2009 the trend continued, as French authorities arrested the alleged ETA leader and military chief in April.

Internet resources: <www.ine.es/welcoing.htm>.

Sri Lanka

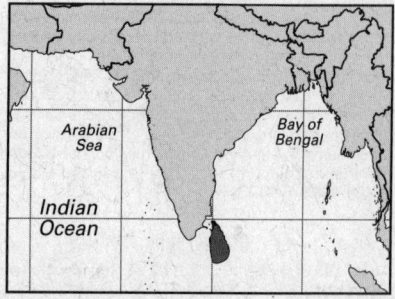

Official name: Sri Lanka Prajatantrika Samajavadi Janarajaya (Sinhala); Ilangai Jananayaka Socialisa Kudiarasu (Tamil) (Democratic Socialist Republic of Sri Lanka). **Form of government:** unitary multiparty republic with one legislative house (Parliament [225]). **Head of state and government:** President Mahinda Rajapakse (from 2005), assisted by Prime Minister Ratnasiri Wickremanayake (from 2005). **Capitals:** Colombo (executive and judicial); Sri Jayewardenepura Kotte (Colombo suburb; legislative). **Official languages:** Sinhala; Tamil. **Official religion:** none. **Monetary unit:** 1 Sri Lankan rupee (LKR) = 100 cents; valuation (1 Jul 2009) US$1 = LKR 114.85.

Demography

Area: 25,332 sq mi, 65,610 sq km. **Population** (2008): 19,394,000. **Density** (2008): persons per sq mi 765.6, persons per sq km 295.6. **Urban** (2005): 15.1%. **Sex distribution** (2005): male 49.42%; female 50.58%. **Age breakdown** (2005): under 15, 24.1%; 15–29, 26.6%; 30–44, 21.4%; 45–59, 18.1%; 60–74, 7.4%; 75–84, 1.9%; 85 and over, 0.5%. **Ethnic composition** (2000): Sinhalese 72.4%; Tamil 17.8%; Sri Lankan Moor 7.4%; other 2.4%. **Religious affiliation** (2005): Buddhist 70%; Hindu 15%; Christian (mostly Roman Catholic) 8%; Muslim (nearly all Sunni) 7%. **Major cities** (2004): Colombo 669,700 (greater Colombo 2,490,300); Dehiwala–Mount Lavinia 218,800; Moratuwa 184,800; Jaffna 172,300; Negombo 127,200. **Location:** island in the Indian Ocean, southeast of India.

Vital statistics

Birth rate per 1,000 population (2006): 18.7 (world avg. 20.3). **Death rate** per 1,000 population (2006): 5.8 (world avg. 8.6). **Total fertility rate** (avg. births per childbearing woman; 2005): 2.11. **Life expectancy** at birth (2005): male 72.5 years; female 76.5 years.

National economy

Budget (2005). *Revenue:* LKR 584,783,000,000 (tax revenue 57.6%, of which VAT 23.7%, excises 13.2%; domestic borrowings 21.2%; foreign loans and grants 13.8%; nontax revenue 7.4%). *Expenditures:* LKR 584,783,000,000 (interest payments 20.5%; welfare

15.9%; education 10.9%; defense 10.5%; tsunami expenditures 4.1%). **Public debt** (external, outstanding; 2006): US$10,140,000,000. **Selected balance of payments data.** Receipts from (US$'000,000): tourism (2006) 410; remittances (2007) 2,700; foreign direct investment (2004–06 avg.) 328; official development assistance (2006) 796. Disbursements for (US$'000,000): tourism (2006) 373; remittances (2007) 283. **Production** (metric tons except as noted). *Agriculture and fishing* (2007): rice 3,131,000, coconuts 954,000, sugarcane 785,510, natural rubber 117,600, peppercorns 19,390, cinnamon 13,360; livestock (number of live animals) 1,222,990 cattle, 318,920 buffalo; fisheries production (2006) 234,346 (from aquaculture 2%). *Mining and quarrying* (2006): kaolin 9,500; graphite 3,200; sapphires 790,000 carats. *Manufacturing* (value added in LKR '000,000; 2007): food, beverages, and tobacco 282,843; textiles and wearing apparel 131,522; rubber and plastic products 45,753. *Energy production (consumption):* electricity (kW-hr; 2005) 8,769,000,000 (8,769,000,000); coal (metric tons; 2005) none (95,000); crude petroleum (barrels; 2005) none (14,500,000); petroleum products (metric tons; 2005) 1,824,000 (3,405,000). **Gross national income** (2007): US$30,785,000,000 (US$1,540 per capita). **Population economically active** (2006): total 7,602,000; activity rate 38.2% (participation rates: ages 15–59 [2000] 60.6%; female 36.3%; unemployed 6.5%).

Foreign trade

Imports (2007; c.i.f.): LKR 1,251,135,000,000 (cotton yarn and textiles 14.4%; machinery and apparatus 13.9%; refined petroleum products 13.0%; crude petroleum 9.1%; food and beverages 7.3%). *Major import sources:* India 22.3%; Singapore 9.6%; China 7.9%; Iran 7.2%; Hong Kong 6.2%. **Exports** (2007; f.o.b.): LKR 856,808,000,000 (garments 40.6%; tea 13.3%, of which black 11.5%; gemstones 5.7%, of which diamonds 4.5%; rubber tires 4.5%; coconut products 1.8%; fish 1.6%; rubber 1.4%; cinnamon 1.0%). *Major export destinations:* US 24.5%; UK 12.7%; India 6.4%; Germany 5.5%; Belgium 5.0%.

Transport and communications

Transport. *Railroads* (2004): route length 1,449 km; passenger-km 4,684,000,000; metric ton-km cargo 134,000,000. *Roads* (2003): total length 97,286 km (paved 81%). *Vehicles* (2004): passenger cars 293,747; trucks and buses 453,610. *Air transport* (2007): passenger-km 9,768,000,000; metric ton-km cargo 345,720,000. **Communications,** in total units (units per 1,000 persons). Telephone landlines (2007): 2,742,000 (142); cellular telephone subscribers (2007): 7,984,000 (414); personal computers (2005): 734,000 (35); total Internet users (2007): 772,000 (40); broadband Internet subscribers (2007): 63,000 (3.3).

Education and health

Literacy (2003–04): percentage of total population ages 5 and over literate 93.0%; males literate 94.9%; females literate 91.3%. **Health** (2004): physicians 8,749 (1 per 2,351 persons); hospital beds 60,328 (1 per 341 persons); infant mortality rate per 1,000 live births (2003) 11.2; undernourished population (2002–04) 4,200,000 (22% of total population

based on the consumption of a minimum daily requirement of 1,860 calories).

Military

Total active duty personnel (2007): 150,900 (army 78.1%, navy 9.9%, air force 12.0%). **Military expenditure as percentage of GDP** (2005): 2.6%; per capita expenditure US$30.

Background

The Sinhalese people of Sri Lanka (Ceylon) probably originated with the blending of aboriginal inhabitants and migrating Indo-Aryans from India c. the 5th century BC. The Tamils were later immigrants from Dravidian India, migrating over a period from the early centuries AD to c. 1200. Buddhism was introduced during the 3rd century BC. As Buddhism spread, the Sinhalese kingdom extended its political control over Ceylon but lost it to invaders from southern India in the 10th century AD. Between 1200 and 1505 Sinhalese power gravitated to southwestern Ceylon, while a southern Indian dynasty seized power in the north and established the Tamil kingdom in the 14th century. Foreign invasions from India, China, and Malaya occurred in the 13th–15th centuries. In 1505 the Portuguese arrived, and by 1619 they controlled most of the island. The Sinhalese enlisted the Dutch to help oust the Portuguese and eventually came under the control of the Dutch East India Co., which relinquished power in 1796 to the British. In 1802 Ceylon became a crown colony, gaining independence in 1948. It became the Republic of Sri Lanka in 1972 and took its current name in 1978. Civil strife between Tamil and Sinhalese groups has beset the country in recent years, with the Tamils demanding a separate autonomous state in northern Sri Lanka.

Did you know? Adam's Peak (Sri Pada), a modest-sized mountain in southern Sri Lanka, has a long history as a sacred monument. Early inhabitants of the island (the Veddas) were the first known to worship it as a religious place. Present-day Buddhists, Christians, Hindus, and Muslims in Sri Lanka, for various reasons, have Adam's Peak as a centerpiece in their religious histories.

Recent Developments

Sri Lanka's civil war, which began in 1983 and had claimed between 80,000 and 100,000 lives, appeared to end in May 2009. By late spring, the Liberation Tigers of Tamil Eelam (LTTE), a terrorist organization in the eyes of the US and the EU, were surrounded, along with hundreds of thousands of civilians. The government estimated that 1,000 civilians a day lost their lives in fighting from late April until 18 May, the day that LTTE leader Vellupillai Prabhakaran, his naval commander, and his intelligence chief were killed in battle. Pres. Mahinda Rajapaksa officially declared victory in parliament on 19 May and assured the world that the Tamil minority in Sri Lanka would be embraced.

Internet resources: <www.statistics.gov.lk>.

The Sudan

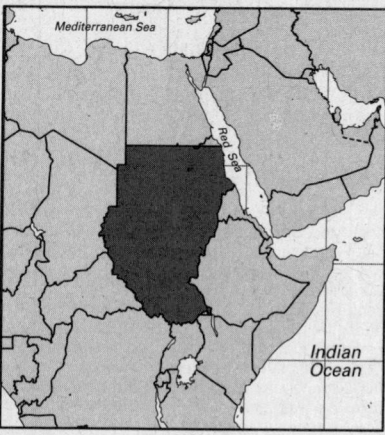

Official name: Jumhuriyat al-Sudan (Republic of the Sudan). **Form of government:** military-backed interim regime with two legislative houses (Council of States [50]; National Assembly [450]). **Head of state and government:** President Omar Hassan Ahmad al-Bashir (from 1989). **Capitals:** Khartoum (executive); Omdurman (legislative). **Official language:** Arabic; English has been designated the "principal" language in southern Sudan. **Official religion:** Islamic law and custom are sources of national law per 1998 constitution. **Monetary unit:** 1 Sudanese pound (SDG); valuation (1 Jul 2009) US$1 = SDG 2.38 (the Sudanese pound replaced the Sudanese dinar [SDD] 10 Jan 2007, at the rate of 1 SDG = 100 SDD).

Demography

Area: 967,499 sq mi, 2,505,810 sq km. **Population** (2008): 39,445,000. **Density** (2008): persons per sq mi 40.8, persons per sq km 15.7. **Urban** (2006): 37.6%. **Sex distribution** (2006): male 50.69%; female 49.31%. **Age breakdown** (2006): under 15, 42.1%; 15–29, 28.4%; 30–44, 16.9%; 45–59, 8.4%; 60–74, 3.6%; 75–84, 0.5%; 85 and over, 0.1%. **Ethnic composition** (2003): black 52%; Arab 39%; Beja 6%; foreigners 2%; other 1%. **Religious affiliation** (2005): Sunni Muslim 68.4%; traditional beliefs 10.8%; Roman Catholic 9.5%; Protestant 8.8%, of which Anglican 5.4%; other 2.5%. **Major cities** (1993): Omdurman 1,271,403; Khartoum 947,483 (urban agglomeration [2008] 8,000,000); Khartoum North 700,887; Port Sudan 308,195; Kassala 234,622. **Location:** northeastern Africa, bordering Egypt, the Red Sea, Eritrea, Ethiopia, Kenya, Uganda, the Democratic Republic of the Congo, the Central African Republic, Chad, and Libya.

Vital statistics

Birth rate per 1,000 population (2006): 35.3 (world avg. 20.3). **Death rate** per 1,000 population (2006):

15.2 (world avg. 8.6). **Total fertility rate** (avg. births per childbearing woman; 2006): 4.79. **Life expectancy** at birth (2006): male 47.1 years; female 48.8 years.

National economy

Budget (2007). *Revenue:* SDG 18,555,000,000 (nontax revenue 66.1%, of which government receipts for crude petroleum 58.7%; tax revenue 31.1%, of which taxes on international trade 11.8%, VAT 7.2%). *Expenditures:* SDG 21,414,000,000 (federal government 65.6%; transfers to: northern states 18.7%, southern Sudan 15.7%). **Public debt** (external, outstanding; 2006): US$11,609,000,-000. **Gross national income** (2007): US$37,031,-000,000 (US$960 per capita). **Production** (metric tons except as noted). *Agriculture and fishing* (2007): sugarcane 7,500,000, sorghum 5,048,000, millet 792,000, sesame seeds 260,000, gum arabic (2005–06) 11,600; livestock (number of live animals) 49,000,000 sheep, 42,000,000 goats, 39,500,000 cattle, 3,700,000 camels; fisheries production (2006) 64,600 (from aquaculture 2%). *Mining and quarrying* (2006): marble 11,470 cu m; gold 3,246 kg. *Manufacturing* (2006): diesel 1,817,000; flour 1,200,000; benzene 1,139,000. *Energy production (consumption):* electricity (kW-hr; 2006) 4,521,000,000 (3,458,000,000); crude petroleum (barrels; 2007) 176,700,000 ([2006] 34,300,000); petroleum products (metric tons; 2006) 3,912,000 (3,623,000). **Population economically active** (2006): total 11,504,000; activity rate of total population 30.5% (participation rates: ages 15–64, 52.0%; female 30.3%; unemployed, n.a.). **Selected balance of payments data.** Receipts from (US$'000,000): tourism (2006) 126; remittances (2007) 1,156; foreign direct investment (2004–06 avg.) 2,452; official development assistance (2006) 2,058. Disbursements for (US$'000,000): tourism (2006) 1,403; remittances (2007) 2.

Foreign trade

Imports (2007; c.i.f.): US$8,775,000,000 (machinery and apparatus 36.4%; manufactured goods 22.1%; transportation equipment 16.7%; food products 8.4%, of which wheat and wheat flour 4.1%). *Major import sources:* China 27.8%; EU 12.5%; African countries 8.5%; Saudi Arabia 7.5%; India 6.2%. **Exports** (2007; f.o.b.): US$8,879,000,000 (crude petroleum 90.7%; refined petroleum products 4.1%; sesame seeds 1.0%; livestock [mainly sheep and camels] 0.9%; cotton 0.8%; gold 0.7%; gum arabic 0.6%). *Major export destinations:* China 82.0%; Japan 8.5%; UAE 2.5%; Saudi Arabia 1.1%; The Netherlands 1.1%.

Transport and communications

Transport. *Railroads* (2006): route length 4,578 km; passenger-km 49,000,000; metric ton-km cargo 893,000,000. *Roads* (2000): total length 11,900 km (paved 36%). *Vehicles* (2002): passenger cars 47,300; trucks and buses 62,500. *Air transport* (2004): passenger-km 758,000,000; metric ton-km cargo 100,000,000. **Communications,** in total units (units per 1,000 persons). Telephone landlines

(2007): 345,000 (8.9); cellular telephone subscribers (2007): 7,464,000 (194); total Internet users (2007): 1,500,000 (39); broadband Internet subscribers (2006): 3,500 (0.09).

Education and health

Literacy (2003): percentage of total population ages 15 and over literate 60.9%; males literate 71.6%; females literate 50.4%. **Health** (2006): physicians 8,799 (1 per 4,384 persons); hospital beds 26,577 (1 per 1,451 persons); infant mortality rate per 1,000 live births 96.8; undernourished population (2002–04) 8,700,000 (26% of total population based on the consumption of a minimum daily requirement of 1,840 calories).

Military

Total active duty personnel (2007): 109,300 (army 96.1%, navy 1.2%, air force 2.7%); foreign troops (September 2008): UN peacekeeping force in southern Sudan 8,700; African Union/UN hybrid peacekeeping force in Darfur 8,300. **Military expenditure as percentage of GDP** (2005): 1.8%; per capita expenditure US$13.

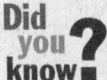

Did you know? The Sudan is geographically the largest country on the African continent. At just under 1,000,000 square miles in area, the massive country encompasses a range of climes, from the Sahara, the world's largest desert, in the north, to the fertile valley of the Nile, the world's longest river.

Background

From the end of the 4th millennium BC, Nubia (now the northern Sudan) periodically came under Egyptian rule, and it was part of the kingdom of Cush from the 11th century BC to the 4th century AD. Christian missionaries converted the Sudan's three principal kingdoms during the 6th century AD; these black Christian kingdoms coexisted with their Muslim Arab neighbors in Egypt for centuries, until the influx of Arab immigrants brought about their collapse in the 13th–15th centuries. Egypt had conquered all of the Sudan by 1874 and encouraged British interference in the region; this aroused Muslim opposition and led to the revolt of al-Mahdi, who captured Khartoum in 1885 and established a Muslim theocracy in the Sudan that lasted until 1898, when Mahdist forces were defeated by the British. The British ruled the country, generally in partnership with Egypt, until The Sudan achieved independence in 1956. Since then the country has fluctuated between ineffective parliamentary government and unstable military rule. The non-Muslim population of the south began rebellion against the Muslim-controlled government of the north in the early 1980s, leading to famines and the displacement of millions of people. Meanwhile, fighting broke out in 2003 between non-Arab Muslims in the Darfur region of western Sudan and government-backed Arab militias known as Janjaweed; tens of thousands of people were killed and hundreds of thousands more were displaced.

Recent Developments

Raids by government aircraft and militia ground forces on suspected rebel bases—as well as on camps for displaced persons and even on AU and UN peacekeeping troops—continued in The Sudan. In June 2008 the International Criminal Court declared the Sudanese government responsible for the situation in Darfur, and on 4 Mar 2009 an arrest warrant was issued for Pres. Omar al-Bashir for crimes against humanity in the war-torn province. While international attention was largely focused on Darfur, events in the border region between northern and southern Sudan proved an equally serious threat to the country's stability. In particular, armed northern nomads began to prevent southerners displaced during the civil war from returning to their homes in the border area. This was interpreted as a northern plot to distort a census scheduled for April in order to enhance the north's claims to the oil-rich border region. At the south's insistence, the census was postponed, but meetings between representatives of northern and southern Sudan to find a solution to the conflict proved unavailing.

Internet resources: <http://cbs.gov.sd>.

Suriname

Official name: Republiek Suriname (Republic of Suriname). **Form of government:** multiparty republic with one legislative house (National Assembly [51]). **Head of state and government:** President Ronald Venetiaan (from 2000). **Capital:** Paramaribo. **Official language:** Dutch. **Official religion:** none. **Monetary unit:** 1 Surinamese dollar (SRD) = 100 cents; valuation (1 Jul 2009) US$1 = SRD 2.70.

Demography

Area: 63,251 sq mi, 163,820 sq km. **Population** (2008): 516,000. **Density** (2008): persons per sq mi 8.2, persons per sq km 3.1. **Urban** (2005): 73.9%. **Sex distribution** (2006): male 49.71%; female 50.29%. **Age breakdown** (2006): under 15, 28.5%; 15–29, 26.8%; 30–44, 24.3%; 45–59, 12.0%;

60–74, 6.2%; 75 and over, 2.2%. **Ethnic composition** (2004): Indo-Pakistani ("Hindustani") 27.4%; Suriname Creole ("Afro-Surinamese") 17.7%; Maroon (descendants of runaway slaves living in the interior) 14.7%; Javanese ("Indonesian") 14.6%; mixed race 12.5%; Amerindian 1.5%; other/unknown 11.6%. **Religious affiliation** (2004): Christian (mostly Roman Catholic and Moravian) 40.7%; Hindu 19.9%; Muslim 13.5%; nonreligious 4.4%; traditional beliefs 3.3%; other 2.5%; unknown 15.7%. **Major city/towns** (2004): Paramaribo 242,946; Lelydorp (1996–97) 15,600; Nieuw Nickerie 13,842; Mungo (Moengo; 1996–97) 6,800; Nieuw Amsterdam 5,489. **Location:** northern South America, bordering the North Atlantic Ocean, French Guiana, Brazil, and Guyana.

Vital statistics

Birth rate per 1,000 population (2006): 17.6 (world avg. 20.3). **Death rate** per 1,000 population (2006): 5.5 (world avg. 8.6). **Natural increase rate** per 1,000 population (2006): 12.1 (world avg. 11.7). **Total fertility rate** (avg. births per childbearing woman; 2006): 2.05. **Life expectancy** at birth (2006): male 70.3 years; female 75.8 years.

National economy

Budget (2007). *Revenue:* SRD 2,002,000,000 (tax revenue 79.1%, of which corporate taxes 22.0%, taxes on international trade 21.5%, income tax 15.4%; nontax revenue 16.0%; grants 4.9%). *Expenditures:* SRD 1,806,500,000 (current expenditures 87.5%, of which wages and salaries 37.6%, transfers 12.0%, debt interest 5.2%; capital expenditures 12.5%). **Production** (metric tons except as noted). *Agriculture and fishing* (2007): rice 195,000, sugarcane 120,000, bananas 44,000; livestock (number of live animals) 137,000 cattle, 24,500 pigs, 3,800,000 chickens; fisheries production (2006) 30,801 (from aquaculture 1%). *Mining and quarrying* (2007): bauxite 5,331,000; alumina 2,152,000; gold (2005) 10,619 kg (recorded production; unrecorded production may be as high as 30,000 kg). *Manufacturing* (value of production at factor cost in SRG; 1993): food products 992,000,000; beverages 558,000,000; tobacco 369,000,000. *Energy production (consumption):* electricity (kW-hr; 2005) 1,571,000,000 (1,571,000,000); crude petroleum (barrels; 2006) 4,800,000 ([2005] 3,378,000); petroleum products (metric tons; 2005) 390,000 (609,000). **Population economically active** (2004): total 173,130; activity rate of total population 35.1% (participation rates: ages 15–64, 56.0%; female 36.7%; unemployed 9.5%). **Gross national income** (2007): US$2,166,000,000 (US$4,730 per capita). **Public debt** (external, outstanding; 2007): US$161,100,000. **Selected balance of payments data.** Receipts from (US$'000,000): tourism (2006) 95; remittances (2007) 140; foreign direct investment (2004–06 avg.) 336; official development assistance (2006) 64. Disbursements for (US$'000,-000): tourism (2006) 18; remittances (2007) 65.

Foreign trade

Imports (2005): US$1,099,900,000 (machinery and transportation equipment 26.8%; mineral fuels

15.6%; food products 9.1%; chemical products 6.9%). *Major import sources* (2007): US 31.7%; The Netherlands 20.4%; Trinidad and Tobago 17.9%; China 5.5%; Japan 3.6%. **Exports** (2005): US$929,100,000 (alumina 48.1%; gold 36.4%; shrimp and fish 6.1%; crude petroleum 5.8%; rice 1.5%). *Major export destinations* (2007): Canada 23.0%; Norway 14.4%; US 12.1%; Trinidad and Tobago 7.2%; France 5.4%.

Transport and communications

Transport. *Railroads* (2003): there are no public railways operating in Suriname; 83 km of private railroad were operational in 2003. *Roads* (2003): total length 4,304 km (paved 26%). *Vehicles* (2004): passenger cars 76,466; trucks and buses 29,946. *Air transport* (2005): passenger-km 1,745,800,000; metric ton-km cargo 27,100,000. **Communications**, in total units (units per 1,000 persons). Telephone landlines (2006): 82,000 (162); cellular telephone subscribers (2006): 320,000 (634); personal computers (2001): 20,000 (45); total Internet users (2007): 44,000 (96); broadband Internet subscribers (2006): 2,700 (5.3).

Education and health

Literacy (2004): percentage of total population ages 15 and over literate 89.6%; males literate 92.0%; females literate 87.2%. **Health:** physicians (2001) 236 (1 per 2,000 persons); hospital beds (2005) 1,797 (1 per 278 persons); infant mortality rate per 1,000 live births (2006) 20.8; undernourished population (2002–04) 40,000 (8% of total population based on the consumption of a minimum daily requirement of 1,910 calories).

Military

Total active duty personnel (2007): 1,840 (army 76.1%, navy 13.0%, air force 10.9%). **Military expenditure as percentage of GDP** (2005): 1.6%; per capita expenditure US$43.

Background

Suriname was inhabited by various native peoples prior to European settlement. Spanish explorers claimed it in 1593, but the Dutch began to settle there in 1602, followed by the English in 1651. It was ceded to the Dutch in 1667, and in 1682 the Dutch West India Co. introduced coffee and sugarcane plantations and African slaves to cultivate them. Slavery was abolished in 1863, and indentured servants were brought from China, Java, and India to work the plantations, adding to the population mix. Except for brief interludes of British rule (1799–1802, 1804–15), it remained a Dutch colony. It gained internal autonomy in 1954 and independence in 1975. A military coup in 1980 ended civilian control until the electorate approved a new constitution in 1987. Military control resumed after a coup in 1990. Elections were held in 1991, followed by a resumption of democratic government.

Recent Developments

Although GDP growth figures were lowered as the worldwide financial crisis unfolded at the end of

---

1 metric ton = about 1.1 short tons;   1 kilometer = 0.6 mi (statute);   1 metric ton-km cargo = about 0.68 short ton-mi cargo;   c.i.f.: cost, insurance, and freight;   f.o.b.: free on board

2008, Suriname's economy enjoyed a modestly successful year. The external debt ratio was the third lowest in the Caribbean area. Production from onshore oil fields reached the level of domestic consumption. Agriculture, with the exception of the troubled rice industry, also performed well.

Internet resources:
<www.surinametourism.com>.

Swaziland

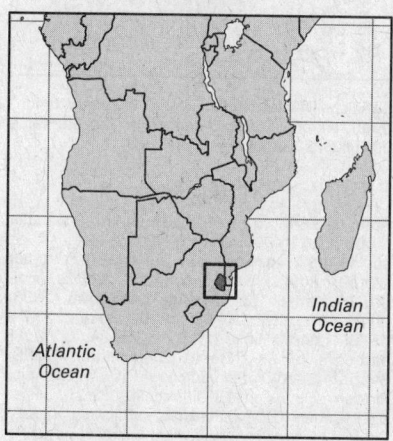

Atlantic Ocean

Indian Ocean

Official name: Umbuso weSwatini (Swati); Kingdom of Swaziland (English). **Form of government:** constitutional monarchy with two legislative houses (Senate [30]; House of Assembly [65]). **Head of state and government:** King Mswati III (from 1986), assisted by Prime Minister Barnabas Sibusiso Dlamini (from 2008). **Capitals:** Mbabane (administrative and judicial); Lozitha and Ludzidzini (royal); Lobamba (legislative). **Official languages:** Swati (Swazi); English. **Official religion:** none. **Monetary unit:** 1 lilangeni (plural emalangeni [E]) = 100 cents; valuation (1 Jul 2009) US$1 = E 7.80.

Demography

Area: 6,704 sq mi, 17,364 sq km. **Population** (2008): 1,018,000. **Density** (2008): persons per sq mi 151.8, persons per sq km 58.6. **Urban** (2007): 22.1%. **Sex distribution** (2007): male 47.27%; female 52.73%. **Age breakdown** (2007): under 15, 40.3%; 15–29, 33.9%; 30–44, 12.9%; 45–59, 7.6%; 60–74, 4.1%; 75 and over, 1.2%. **Ethnic composition** (2000): Swazi 82.3%; Zulu 9.6%; Tsonga 2.3%; Afrikaner 1.4%; mixed (black-white) 1.0%; other 3.4%. **Religious affiliation** (2006): Protestant 35%; syncretistic Christianity/traditional beliefs 30%; Roman Catholic 25%; Muslim 1%; other (including Baha'i and Mormon) 9%. **Major towns** (2006): Manzini (urban agglomeration) 115,200; Mbabane 78,700; Lobamba 11,000; Big Bend 10,400; Malkerns 10,000. **Location:** southern Africa, bordering South Africa and Mozambique.

Vital statistics

Birth rate per 1,000 population (2007): 27.0 (world avg. 20.3). **Death rate** per 1,000 population (2007): 30.4 (world avg. 8.6). **Natural increase rate** per 1,000 population (2007): −3.4 (world avg. 11.7). **Total fertility rate** (avg. births per childbearing woman; 2007): 3.43. **Life expectancy** at birth (2007): male 31.8 years; female 32.6 years.

National economy

Budget (2007–08). *Revenue:* E 8,341,100,000 (receipts from Customs Union of Southern Africa 59.8%; income tax 13.5%; sales taxes 8.7%). *Expenditures:* E 6,992,900,000 (education 24.1%; police and defense 18.2%; general administration 16.9%; transportation and communications 9.6%; health 8.9%). **Gross national income** (2007): US$2,951,000,000 (US$2,580 per capita). **Population economically active** (2006): total 337,200; activity rate of total population 32.8% (unemployed 30%). **Public debt** (external; March 2008): US$403,100,000. **Production** (metric tons except as noted). *Agriculture and fishing* (2007): sugarcane 5,000,000, corn (maize) 68,000, grapefruit and pomelos 37,000; livestock (number of live animals) 585,000 cattle, 276,000 goats, 3,200,000 chickens; fisheries production (2006) 70 (from aquaculture, negligible). *Mining and quarrying* (2007): ferrovanadium (2006) 491; crushed stone 207,535 cu m. *Manufacturing* (value of exports in US$'000; 2007): wearing apparel and accessories (2002) 173,500; sugar 159,821; unbleached wood pulp 97,099. *Energy production (consumption):* electricity (kW-hr; 2007) 134,200,000 (1,151,900,000); coal (metric tons; 2007) 241,200 ([2003] 372,000); petroleum products, none (n.a.). **Selected balance of payments data.** Receipts from (US$'000,000): tourism (2006) 74; remittances (2007) 99; foreign direct investment (2004–06 avg.) 19; official development assistance (2006) 35. Disbursements for (US$'000,000): tourism (2006) 48; remittances (2007) 17; foreign direct disinvestment (2004–06 avg.) −8.0.

Foreign trade

Imports (2005; c.i.f.): US$1,654,000,000 (food products 15.1%; chemical products 13.5%; machinery and apparatus 13.0%; refined petroleum products 10.2%; motor vehicles and parts 7.6%). *Major import sources:* South Africa 88.3%; unspecified Asia (probably Taiwan) 2.8%; China 2.3%. **Exports** (2005): US$1,570,000,000 (essential oils 38.4%; food products 16.2%, of which raw sugar 8.8%; wearing apparel and accessories 12.0%; pulp and waste paper 4.0%). *Major export destinations:* South Africa 74.6%; US 7.5%; Mozambique 5.4%.

Transport and communications

Transport. *Railroads* (2006): route length 301 km; metric ton-km cargo (2004) 710,000,000. *Roads* (2002): total length 3,594 km (paved 30%). *Vehicles* (2003): passenger cars 44,113; trucks and buses 47,761. *Air transport* (2000): passenger-km 68,000,000; metric ton-km cargo 6,000,000. **Communications**, in total units (units per 1,000 persons). Telephone landlines (2006): 44,000 (43); cellular telephone subscribers (2007): 380,000 (333); personal computers (2006): 42,000 (37); total Internet users (2006): 42,000 (41).

Education and health

Literacy (2007): percentage of total population ages 15 and over literate 84.0%; males literate 84.7%; females literate 83.4%. **Health** (2004): physicians 171 (1 per 6,047 persons); hospital beds (2000) 1,570 (1 per 665 persons); infant mortality rate per 1,000 live births (2007) 70.7; undernourished population (2002–04) 250,000 (22% of total population based on the consumption of a minimum daily requirement of 1,840 calories).

Military

Total active duty personnel (2006): 3,000. **Military expenditure as percentage of GDP** (2004): 1.8%; per capita expenditure US$39.

Background

Stone tools and rock paintings indicate prehistoric habitation in the region, but it was not settled until the Bantu-speaking Swazi people migrated there in the 18th century. The British gained control in the 19th century after the Swazi king sought their aid against the Zulus. Following the South African War, the British governor of Transvaal administered Swaziland; his powers were transferred to the British high commissioner in 1906. In 1949 the British rejected the Union of South Africa's request to control Swaziland. The country gained limited self-government in 1963 and achieved independence in 1968. In the 1970s new constitutions were framed based on the supreme authority of the king. During the 1990s forces demanding democracy arose, but the kingdom remained in place. In 2005 a new constitution was signed that contained a bill of rights, but it retained the ban on political parties. Swaziland has one of the highest rates of HIV infection in the world.

Recent Developments

Poverty, hunger, unemployment, the HIV/AIDS epidemic, and political uncertainty remained the major challenges in Swaziland in 2008. The cost of living was high, and energy and food prices increased over the previous year. Swaziland's per capita GPD was US$2,903, and almost 70% of the population was living below the poverty line. The rate of HIV/AIDS infection was reported to be 26% among Swazi adults ages 15–49 and 19% overall.

Internet resources:
<www.welcometoswaziland.com>.

Sweden

Official name: Konungariket Sverige (Kingdom of Sweden). **Form of government:** constitutional monarchy with one legislative house (Parliament [349]). **Chief of state:** King Carl XVI Gustaf (from 1973). **Head of government:** Prime Minister Fredrik Reinfeldt (from 2006). **Capital:** Stockholm. **Official language:**

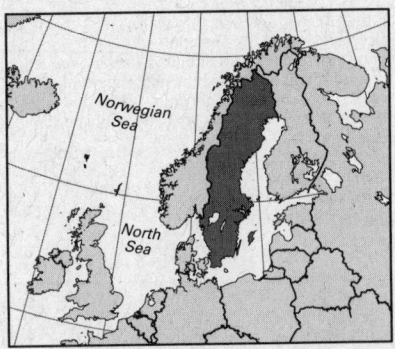

Swedish. **Official religion:** none. **Monetary unit:** 1 Swedish krona (SEK; plural kronor) = 100 ore; valuation (1 Jul 2009) US$1 = SEK 7.56.

Demography

Area: 173,860 sq mi, 450,295 sq km. **Population** (2008): 9,214,000. **Density** (2008) persons per sq mi 58.2, persons per sq km 22.5. **Urban** (2005): 84.4%. **Sex distribution** (2007): male 49.70%; female 50.30%. **Age breakdown** (2006): under 15, 17.0%; 15–29, 18.8%; 30–44, 20.7%; 45–59, 19.5%; 60–74, 15.2%; 75–84, 6.2%; 85 and over, 2.6%. **Ethnic composition** (2005): Swedish 83.8%; other European 10.1%, of which Finnish 2.9%, pre-1991 Yugoslav 2.2%; Asian 4.1%; other 2.0%. **Religious affiliation** (2005): Church of Sweden (including nonpracticing) 77%; other Protestant 4.5%; Muslim 4%; Roman Catholic 1.5%; Orthodox 1%; other 12%. **Major cities** (2007): Stockholm 795,163; Göteborg 493,502; Malmö 280,801; Uppsala 187,541; Linköping 140,367. **Location:** northern Europe, bordering Finland, the Gulf of Bothnia, the Baltic Sea, and Norway.

Vital statistics

Birth rate per 1,000 population (2007): 11.7 (world avg. 20.3); (2007) within marriage 45.3%; outside of marriage 54.7%. **Death rate** per 1,000 population (2007): 10.0 (world avg. 8.6). **Total fertility rate** (avg. births per childbearing woman; 2007): 1.88. **Life expectancy** at birth (2007): male 78.9 years; female 83.0 years.

National economy

Budget (2005). *Revenue:* SEK 718,249,000,000 (taxes on goods and services 45.6%; social security fees 37.9%; income/profits/capital gains taxes 9.5%). *Expenditures:* SEK 750,965,000,000 (social insurance 40.0%; defense 5.9%; education 5.9%; health 5.1%). **Public debt** (September 2007): US$175,055,000,000. **Production** (metric tons except as noted). *Agriculture and fishing* (2007): wheat 2,254,700, sugar beets 2,000,000, barley 1,439,000; livestock (number of live animals) 1,694,570 pigs, 1,560,670 cattle, 505,466 sheep, (2004) 250,500 reindeer; fisheries production (2006)

1 metric ton = about 1.1 short tons;   1 kilometer = 0.6 mi (statute);   1 metric ton-km cargo = about 0.68 short ton-mi cargo;   c.i.f.: cost, insurance, and freight;   f.o.b.: free on board

276,800 (from aquaculture 3%). *Mining and quarrying* (metal content; 2006): iron ore 16,000,000; zinc 208,551; copper 86,700; silver 292,000 kg. *Manufacturing* (value added in SEK '000,000 at constant prices of 2000; 2005): electrical machinery, telecommunications equipment, and electronics 108,909; motor vehicles and parts 65,211; chemical products 62,320; nonelectrical machinery and apparatus 61,004; paper products 44,198. *Energy production (consumption):* electricity (kW-hr; 2005) 154,981,-000,000 (147,587,000,000); coal (metric tons; 2005) none (3,070,000); crude petroleum (barrels; 2005) none (146,700,000); petroleum products (metric tons; 2005) 17,620,000 (11,442,000); natural gas (cu m; 2005) none (1,005,000,000). **Gross national income** (2007): US$421,342,000,000 (US$46,060 per capita). **Population economically active** (2006): total 4,586,000; activity rate of total population 50.5% (participation rates: ages 16–64, 78.7%; female 47.6%; unemployed [October 2008] 5.7%). **Selected balance of payments data.** Receipts from (US$'000,000): tourism (2006) 9,133; remittances (2007) 336; foreign direct investment (FDI) (2004–06 avg.) 16,288. Disbursements for (US$'000,000): tourism (2006) 11,543; remittances (2007) 589; FDI (2004–06 avg.) 24,298.

Foreign trade

Imports (2006; c.i.f.): SEK 908,300,000,000 (motor vehicles 10.9%; crude and refined petroleum 10.8%; nonelectrical machinery and apparatus 10.1%; office machinery and telecommunications equipment 9.9%; base metals 6.8%). *Major import sources:* Germany 17.9%; Denmark 9.4%; Norway 8.7%; The Netherlands 6.3%; UK 6.2%. **Exports** (2006; f.o.b.): SEK 1,067,600,000,000 (nonelectrical machinery and apparatus 14.4%; motor vehicles 13.6%; telecommunications equipment 8.5%; paper products 6.8%; medicines and pharmaceuticals 6.0%). *Major export destinations:* Germany 9.9%; US 9.4%; Norway 9.3%; UK 7.2%; Denmark 7.0%.

Transport and communications

Transport. *Railroads* (2004): length 11,050 km; (2005) passenger-km 8,922,000,000; metric ton-km cargo 21,675,000,000. *Roads* (2005): total length 425,383 km (paved 31%). *Vehicles* (2005): passenger cars 4,154,000; trucks and buses 474,000. *Air transport* (includes SAS international and domestic traffic applicable to Sweden only; 2007): passenger-km 4,896,000,000; metric ton-km cargo 2,580,000. **Communications,** in total units (units per 1,000 persons). Telephone landlines (2007): 5,506,000 (604); cellular telephone subscribers (2007): 10,371,000 (1,137); personal computers (2005): 7,548,000 (836); total Internet users (2007): 7,000,000 (768); broadband Internet subscribers (2007): 3,280,000 (360).

Education and health

Educational attainment (2005). Percentage of population ages 15–74 having: incomplete or complete primary education 24.1%; incomplete or complete secondary 50.4%; incomplete or complete higher 23.9%; unknown 1.6%. **Health** (2005): physicians 27,600 (1 per 327 persons); hospital beds 26,540 (1 per 340 persons); infant mortality rate per 1,000 live births (2007) 2.5; undernourished population (2002–04) less than 2.5% of total population.

Military

Total active duty personnel (2007): 24,000 (army 42.5%, navy 32.9%, air force 24.6%). **Military expenditure as percentage of GDP** (2005): 1.5%; per capita expenditure US$612.

Background

The first inhabitants of Sweden were apparently hunters who crossed the land bridge from Europe c. 9000 BC. During the Viking era (9th–10th centuries) the Swedes controlled river trade in eastern Europe between the Baltic Sea and the Black Sea and also raided western European lands. Sweden was loosely united and Christianized in the 11th–12th centuries. It conquered the Finns in the 12th century and in the 14th united with Norway and Denmark under a single monarchy. It broke away in 1523 under Gustav I Vasa. In the 17th century it emerged as a great European power in the Baltic region, but its dominance declined after its defeat in the Second Northern War (1700–21). Sweden became a constitutional monarchy in 1809 and united with Norway in 1814; it acknowledged Norwegian independence in 1905. It maintained its neutrality during both world wars. It was a charter member of the UN but abstained from membership in the European Union until 1995 and in NATO altogether. A new constitution drafted in 1975 reduced the monarch's role to that of ceremonial head of state. By the early 21st century, Sweden had emerged as a European center of telecommunications and information technology.

Recent Developments

In 2008 Sweden's economy worsened in line with the global financial downturn. The decline could be seen in a sharply lower stock market, falling housing prices, diminishing pension funds, rising unemployment, and a weakening currency. In 2008 GDP grew only 1%, with the central bank assuming zero growth for 2009. Unemployment in Sweden reached 6%, the Swedish stock market plunged some 40%, and housing prices fell 10–20%, depending on location and price.

Internet resources:
<www.scb.se/default____2154.aspx>.

Switzerland

Official name: Confédération Suisse (French); Schweizerische Eidgenossenschaft (German); Confederazione Svizzera (Italian); Confederaziun Svizra (Romansh) (Swiss Confederation). **Form of government:** federal state with two legislative houses (Council of States [46]; National Council [200]). **Head of state and government:** President Hans-Rudolf Merz (from 2009). **Capitals:** Bern (administrative); Lausanne (judicial). **Official languages:** French; German; Italian; Romansh (locally). **Official religion:** none. **Monetary unit:** 1 Swiss franc (CHF) = 100 centimes; valuation (1 Jul 2009) US$1 = CHF 1.07.

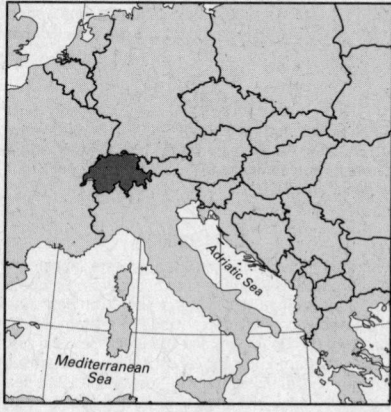

Demography

Area: 15,940 sq mi, 41,284 sq km. **Population** (2008): 7,617,000. **Density** (2008): persons per sq mi 477.9, persons per sq km 184.5. **Urban** (2005): 75.2%. **Sex distribution** (2007): male 49.08%; female 50.92%. **Age breakdown** (2007): under 15, 15.5%; 15–29, 18.3%; 30–44, 23.0%; 45–59, 20.9%; 60–74, 14.4%; 75–84, 5.7%; 85 and over, 2.2%. **National composition** (2007): Swiss 78.9%; Italian 3.8%; German 2.7%; Serb or Montenegrin 2.5%; Portuguese 2.4%; Turkish 1.0%; other 8.7%. **Religious affiliation** (2000): Roman Catholic 41.8%; Protestant 33.0%; Muslim 4.3%; Orthodox 1.8%; Jewish 0.2%; other Christian 2.7%; nonreligious 11.1%; other 0.8%; unknown 4.3%. **Major urban agglomerations** (2006): Zürich 1,111,909; Geneva 497,386; Basel 486,952; Bern 344,724; Lausanne 313,074. **Location:** central Europe, bordering Germany, Austria, Liechtenstein, Italy, and France.

Vital statistics

Birth rate per 1,000 population (2007): 9.9 (world avg. 20.3); within marriage 83.8%; outside of marriage 16.2%. **Death rate** per 1,000 population (2007): 8.0 (world avg. 8.6). **Total fertility rate** (avg. births per childbearing woman; 2007): 1.45. **Life expectancy** at birth (2007): male 79.4 years; female 84.2 years.

National economy

Budget (2007). *Revenue:* CHF 165,097,000,000 (tax revenue 59.1%, of which taxes on income and wealth 39.6%; nontax revenue 22.2%; social security obligations 18.7%). *Expenditures:* CHF 170,738,000,000 (social security 19.0%; social welfare 16.2%; education 16.2%; health 11.3%; transportation 8.4%). **Production** (metric tons except as noted). *Agriculture and fishing* (2007): sugar beets 1,584,000, wheat 562,200, potatoes 490,000; livestock (number of live animals) 1,650,000 pigs, 1,565,000 cattle; fisheries production (2006) 2,636 (from aquaculture 46%). *Mining* (2006): salt 560,000 (polished diamond exports [2006] US$661,000,000). *Manufacturing* (value added in CHF '000,000; 2006): chemi-

cal products and refined petroleum products 18,260; professional and scientific equipment and watches 13,488; nonelectrical machinery and apparatus 12,804; fabricated metal products 8,564; food, beverages, and tobacco 8,325. *Energy production (consumption):* electricity (kW-hr; 2007) 65,918,000,000 ([2005] 65,962,000,000); coal (metric tons; 2005) none (183,000); crude petroleum (barrels; 2005) none (35,000,000); petroleum products (metric tons; 2005) 4,756,000 (10,702,000); natural gas (cu m; 2005) none (3,318,000,000). **Population economically active** (2006): total 4,220,000 (foreign workers account for roughly 26% of the economically active population); activity rate of total population 55.8% (participation rates: ages 15–64, 81.2%; female 45.7%; unemployed [May 2007–April 2008] 2.6%). **Gross national income** (2007): US$452,121,-000,000 (US$59,880 per capita). **Public debt** (December 2006): US$188,701,000,000. **Selected balance of payments data.** Receipts from (US$'000,-000): tourism (2006) 10,640; remittances (2007) 2,077; foreign direct investment (FDI) (2004–06 avg.) 8,398. Disbursements for (US$'000,000): tourism (2006) 9,919; remittances (2007) 15,422; FDI (2004–06 avg.) 54,029.

Foreign trade

Imports (2006; c.i.f.): CHF 177,287,000,000 (machinery and apparatus 18.8%; medicine and pharmaceuticals 10.5%; base and fabricated metals [excluding gold] 10.2%; mineral fuels 7.9%; motor vehicles 6.5%). *Major import sources* (2007): Germany 31.5%; Italy 10.4%; France 9.0%; US 4.8%; The Netherlands 4.4%. **Exports** (2006; f.o.b.): CHF 185,382,000,000 (medicine and pharmaceuticals 21.1%; nonelectrical machinery and apparatus 15.1%; watches 6.9%; organic chemicals 6.8%). *Major export destinations* (2007): Germany 20.8%; US 9.3%; Italy 8.9%; France 8.4%; UK 4.8%.

Transport and communications

Transport. *Railroads* (2005): length 5,062 km; passenger-km 16,144,000,000; metric ton-km cargo 10,149,000,000. *Roads* (2006): total length 71,353 km. *Vehicles* (2007): passenger cars 3,955,787; trucks and buses 324,153. *Air transport* (2006): passenger-km 22,788,000,000; metric ton-km cargo 1,039,032,000. **Communications**, in total units (units per 1,000 persons). Telephone landlines (2007): 5,000,000 (662); cellular telephone subscribers (2007): 8,096,000 (1,072); personal computers (2005): 6,430,000 (857); total Internet users (2007): 4,610,000 (611); broadband Internet subscribers (2007): 2,400,000 (318).

Education and health

Educational attainment (2006). Percentage of resident Swiss and resident alien population ages 25–64 having: compulsory education 17.9%; secondary 52.2%; higher 29.9%. **Health:** physicians (2005) 28,251 (1 per 263 persons); hospital beds (2006) 40,347 (1 per 185 persons); infant mortality rate per 1,000 live births (2007) 3.9; undernourished population (2002–04) less than 2.5% of total population.

1 metric ton = about 1.1 short tons;   1 kilometer = 0.6 mi (statute);   1 metric ton-km cargo = about 0.68 short ton-mi cargo;   c.i.f.: cost, insurance, and freight;   f.o.b.: free on board

Military

Total active duty personnel (2007): 22,600. Military expenditure as percentage of GDP (2005): 1.0%; per capita expenditure US$464.

Background

The original inhabitants of Switzerland were the Helvetians, who were conquered by the Romans in the 1st century BC. Germanic tribes penetrated the region from the 3rd to the 6th century AD, and Muslim and Magyar raiders ventured in during the 10th century. It came under the Holy Roman Empire in the 11th century. In 1291 three cantons formed an anti-Habsburg league that became the nucleus of the Swiss Confederation. It was a center of the Reformation, which divided the confederation and led to a period of political and religious conflict. The French organized Switzerland as the Helvetic Republic in 1798. In 1815 the Congress of Vienna recognized Swiss independence and guaranteed its neutrality. A new federal state was formed in 1848 with Bern as the capital. It remained neutral in both world wars and thereafter. With the formation of the EU, Switzerland took steps toward provisional association with the European economic area, and it joined the UN in 2002.

 **Did you know?** Although Switzerland has officially been neutral since 1815, it is the famed Swiss Guards who have guarded the lives of the popes in the Vatican City for over 500 years.

Recent Developments

The legendary stability of the Swiss banking system was shaken in 2008 when the government had to intervene in October with a package of nearly US$60 billion to rescue the country's biggest bank, UBS AG. Both UBS and the second largest bank, Credit Suisse, were hard hit by bad loans originating in the United States, and UBS Chairman Marcel Ospel resigned in April after the bank reported a first-quarter net loss of 12 billion Swiss francs (about US$12 billion). In February 2009 the bank announced that it would lift the veil on the famous Swiss banking secrecy by agreeing to provide the names of American account holders suspected of being tax evaders. The bank also admitted to conspiring to defraud the US Internal Revenue Service and agreed to pay a fine of US$780 million. With a high rate of gross national savings—more than one-third of GDP—non-EU member Switzerland looked set to weather the global economic turmoil better than many European neighbors.

Internet resources:
<www.bfs.admin.ch/bfs/portal/en/index.html>.

Syria

Official name: Al-Jumhuriyah al-'Arabiyah al-Suriyah (Syrian Arab Republic). **Form of government:** unitary multiparty republic with one legislative house (People's Assembly [250]). **Head of state and government:** President Bashar al-Assad (from 2000).

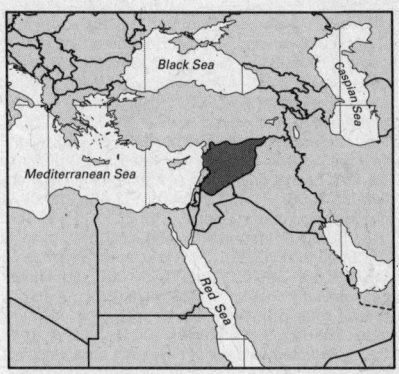

Capital: Damascus. **Official language:** Arabic. **Official religion:** none (Islam is the required religion of the head of state and is the basis of the legal system). **Monetary unit:** 1 Syrian pound (S.P) = 100 piastres; valuation (1 Jul 2009) US$1 = S.P 45.05.

Demography

Area: 71,498 sq mi, 185,180 sq km. **Population** (2008): 19,639,000. **Density** (2008): persons per sq mi 274.7, persons per sq km 106.1. **Urban** (2005): 50.6%. **Sex distribution** (2007): male 51.11%; female 48.89%. **Age breakdown** (2006): under 15, 37.0%; 15–29, 31.1%; 30–44, 18.7%; 45–59, 8.4%; 60–74, 3.7%; 75 and over, 1.1%. **Ethnic composition** (2000): Syrian Arab 74.9%; Bedouin Arab 7.4%; Kurdish 7.3%; Palestinian Arab 3.9%; Armenian 2.7%; other 3.8%. **Religious affiliation** (2000): Muslim 86%, of which Sunni 74%, 'Alawite (Shi'i) 11%; Christian 8%, of which Orthodox 5%, Roman Catholic 2%; Druze 3%; nonreligious/atheist 3%. **Major cities** (2004): Aleppo 1,975,200; Damascus 1,614,500; Homs (Hims) 800,400; Latakia 468,700; Hamah 366,800. **Location:** the Middle East, bordering Turkey, Iraq, Jordan, Israel, Lebanon, and the Mediterranean Sea.

Vital statistics

Birth rate per 1,000 population (2006): 27.8 (world avg. 20.3). **Death rate** per 1,000 population (2006): 4.8 (world avg. 8.6). **Total fertility rate** (avg. births per childbearing woman; 2006): 3.40. **Life expectancy** at birth (2006): male 69.0 years; female 71.7 years.

National economy

Budget (2005). *Revenue:* S.P 377,100,000,000 (petroleum royalties and taxes 33.2%; nonpetroleum nontax revenues 27.0%; nonpetroleum tax on income and profits 13.5%; taxes on international trade 6.7%). *Expenditures:* S.P 436,500,000,000 (current expenditures 61.4%; capital expenditures 38.6%). **Public debt** (external, outstanding; 2006): US$5,576,000,000. **Gross national income** (2007): US$34,993,000,000 (US$1,760 per capita). **Production** (metric tons except as noted). *Agriculture and fishing* (2007): wheat 4,500,000, sugar beets 1,150,000, seed cotton 1,100,000, almonds

132,000; livestock (number of live animals) 21,000,000 sheep, 1,350,000 goats, 1,150,000 cattle; fisheries production (2006) 17,166 (from aquaculture 52%). *Mining and quarrying* (2006): phosphate rock 3,664,000; gypsum 443,800. *Manufacturing* (value added in S.P '000,000; 2002): food, beverages, and tobacco 23,788; textiles and wearing apparel 20,344; fabricated metal products 15,462. *Energy production (consumption):* electricity (kW-hr; 2006) 37,453,000,000 (37,453,000,000); crude petroleum (barrels; 2006) 147,825,000 (83,950,000); petroleum products (metric tons; 2005) 10,246,000 (11,005,000); natural gas (cu m; 2006) 8,500,000,000 (5,100,000,000). **Population economically active** (2006): total 7,880,000; activity rate of total population 40.4% (participation rates: ages 15–64, 66.8%; female 30.9%; unemployed 8.5%). **Selected balance of payments data.** Receipts from (US$'000,000): tourism (2006) 2,025; remittances (2007) 824; foreign direct investment (FDI) (2004–06 avg.) 458; official development assistance (2006) 27. Disbursements for (US$'000,000): tourism (2006) 540; remittances (2007) 235; FDI (2004–06 avg.) 55.

Foreign trade

Imports (2006; c.i.f.): US$11,488,000,000 (refined petroleum products 24.4%; food products 10.7%; motor vehicles 8.6%; iron and steel 8.3%; nonelectrical machinery and apparatus 7.3%). *Major import sources:* Russia 10.2%; China 6.5%; Ukraine 5.3%; Egypt 5.2%; Saudi Arabia 5.1%. **Exports** (2006; f.o.b.): US$10,919,000,000 (crude petroleum 33.6%; food and live animals 14.9%; wearing apparel and accessories 7.9%; textile yarn, fabrics, and made-up articles 7.5%; refined petroleum products 6.7%). *Major export destinations:* Italy 19.6%; France 8.8%; Saudi Arabia 8.7%; Iraq 6.4%; UK 4.3%.

Transport and communications

Transport. *Railroads* (2006): route length 2,711 km; passenger-km 658,605,000; metric ton-km cargo 2,458,088,000. *Roads* (2006): total length 51,967 km (paved 75%). *Vehicles* (2006): passenger cars 358,032; trucks and buses 527,177. *Air transport* (SyrianAir only; 2006): passenger-km 2,340,000,-000; metric ton-km cargo 16,000,000. **Communications,** in total units (units per 1,000 persons). Telephone landlines (2007): 3,452,000 (173); cellular telephone subscribers (2007): 6,700,000 (336); personal computers (2005): 800,000 (44); total Internet users (2007): 3,470,000 (174); broadband Internet subscribers (2007): 7,000 (0.3).

Education and health

Educational attainment (2003–04). Percentage of population having: no formal education 24.2% (illiterate 14.3%, literate 9.9%); primary education 45.8%; secondary 22.5%; incomplete higher 3.9%; higher 3.6%. **Literacy** (2005): percentage of total population ages 15 and over literate 78.4%; males literate 90.6%; females literate 66.1%. **Health** (2006): physicians 27,636 (1 per 671 persons); hospital beds 27,443 (1 per 676 persons); infant mortality rate per 1,000 live births (2006) 28.6; undernourished population (2002–04) 600,000 (4% of total population based on the consumption of a minimum daily requirement of 1,840 calories).

Military

Total active duty personnel (2007): 292,600 (army 73.5%, navy 2.6%, air force 10.3%, air defense 13.6%); UN peacekeeping troops in Golan Heights (September 2008) 1,043. **Military expenditure as percentage of GDP** (2005): 7.2%; per capita expenditure US$80.

Background

Syria has been inhabited for several thousand years. From the 3rd millennium BC it was under the control variously of Sumerians, Akkadians, Amorites, Egyptians, Hittites, Assyrians, and Babylonians. In the 6th century BC it became part of the Persian Achaemenian dynasty, which fell to Alexander the Great in 330 BC. Seleucid rulers governed it from 301 BC to c. 164 BC; Parthians and Nabataean Arabs then divided the region. It flourished as a Roman province (64 BC–AD 300) and as part of the Byzantine Empire (300–634) until Muslims invaded and established control. It came under the Ottoman Empire in 1516, which held it, except for brief rules by Egypt, until the British invaded in World War I. After the war it became a French mandate; it achieved independence in 1945. It united with Egypt in the United Arab Republic (1958–61). During the Six-Day War (1967), it lost the Golan Heights to Israel. Syrian troops frequently clashed with Israeli troops in Lebanon during the 1980s and '90s. Hafez al-Assad's long and harsh regime (1971–2000) was marked also by antagonism toward Syria's neighbors Turkey and Iraq.

Recent Developments

Violence spread in Syria in 2008. A car bombing in Damascus in February killed 'Imad Mughniyyah, a commander in the military wing of the Lebanese Islamic extremist organization Hezbollah. In March a crowd celebrating the Kurdish New Year skirmished with police, resulting in three deaths. In July ethnic violence erupted among inmates at Saidnaya prison outside the capital, and two dozen prisoners were killed when guards stormed the cell blocks. One of Syria's most powerful military officers, Gen. Muhammad Sulaiman, was assassinated in August. His ties to both Pres. Bashar al-Assad and Hezbollah, his purported rivalry with Gen. 'Asif Shawkat, and intimations of an aborted coup d'état precipitated a variety of rumors surrounding his death. Equally puzzling was a September car bomb that killed more than a dozen people at the crossroads leading to the mausoleum of Sayyidah Zainab south of the capital. Because the explosion took place outside the headquarters of one of the security services, some speculated that it was an attack on a senior commander there. Others linked the bombing to the Shi'ite pilgrims, particularly from Iran, who frequented the district.

Internet resources:
<www.syriatourism.org/index.php?newlang=eng>.

---

1 metric ton = about 1.1 short tons; 1 kilometer = 0.6 mi (statute); 1 metric ton-km cargo = about 0.68 short ton-mi cargo; c.i.f.: cost, insurance, and freight; f.o.b.: free on board

Taiwan

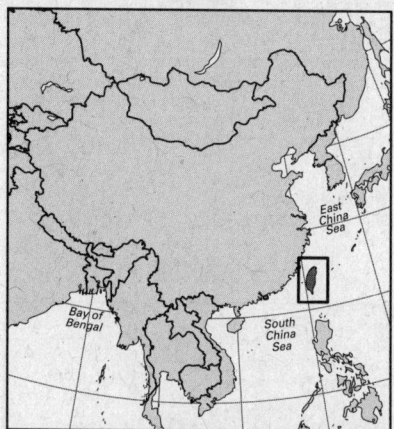

Official name: Chung-hua Min-kuo (Republic of China) Form of government: multiparty republic with one legislative body (Legislative Yuan [113]). Chief of state: President Ma Ying-jeou (from 2008). Head of government: Premier Liu Chao-shiuan (from 2008). Administrative center: Taipei. Official language: Mandarin Chinese. Official religion: none. Monetary unit: 1 New Taiwan dollar (NT$) = 100 cents; valuation (1 Jul 2009) US$1 = NT$32.69.

Demography

Area: 13,972 sq mi, 36,188 sq km. Population (2008): 22,996,000. Density (2008): persons per sq mi 1,646, persons per sq km 635. Urban (2005): 81%. Sex distribution (2007): male 50.57%; female 49.43%. Age breakdown (2007): under 15, 17.6%; 15–29, 23.2%; 30–44, 24.4%; 45–59, 21.2%; 60–74, 9.3%; 75–84, 3.5%; 85 and over, 0.8%. Ethnic composition (2003): Taiwanese 84%; mainland Chinese 14%; indigenous tribal peoples 2%, of which Ami 0.6%. Religious affiliation (2002): Buddhism 23.8%; Taoism 19.7%; Christian 4.5%, of which Protestant 2.6%, Roman Catholic 1.3%; I-kuan Tao 3.7% (syncretistic religion); Muslim 0.6%; other (mostly Chinese folk-religionist or nonreligious) 47.7%. Major cities (urban agglomerations) (2007): Taipei 2,629,269 (6,698,319); Kao-hsiung 1,520,-555 (2,767,655); T'ai-chung 1,055,898 (2,218,527); T'ao-yuan 391,822 (1,905,973); T'ai-nan 764,658 (1,255,450). Location: island between the East China Sea, the Philippine Sea, and the South China Sea, north of the Philippines and southeast of mainland China.

Vital statistics

Birth rate per 1,000 population (2007): 8.9 (world avg. 20.3); within marriage 95.6%; outside of marriage 4.4%. Death rate per 1,000 population (2007): 6.2 (world avg. 8.6). Natural increase rate per 1,000 population (2007): 2.7 (world avg. 11.7). Total fertility rate (avg. births per childbearing woman; 2007): 1.10. Life expectancy at birth (2007): male 75.1 years; female 81.9 years.

National economy

Budget (2006). Revenue: NT$2,172,436,000,000 (tax revenue 71.7%; income from public enterprises 14.3%). Expenditures: NT$2,261,958,000,000 (education, science, and culture 21.6%; economic development 17.0%; general administration 15.3%; social welfare 13.6%; defense 10.5%). Population economically active (2006): total 10,522,000; activity rate of total population 46.3% (participation rates: ages 15–64, 57.9%; female 42.4%; unemployed [2007] 3.9%). Production (metric tons except as noted). Agriculture and fishing (2007): rice 1,363,458, pineapples 476,811, bamboo shoots 291,709, betel nuts 134,497, tea 17,502; livestock (number of live animals; 2006) 7,068,621 pigs, 134,793 cattle; fisheries production 1,498,-197 (from aquaculture 22%). Mining and quarrying (2006): marble 25,493,000. Manufacturing (value added in NT$'000,000,000; 2006): electronic parts and components 610; base metals 288; base chemicals 230; refined petroleum products and coal products 206; computers, telecommunications, video electronics 191; nonelectrical machinery and apparatus 164. Energy production (consumption): electricity (kW-hr; 2005) 210,300,000,000 (201,580,000,000); coal (metric tons; 2006) none (66,000,000); crude petroleum (barrels; 2007) 292,000 ([2006] 347,000,000); natural gas (cu m; 2007) 396,000,000 (11,298,000,000). Gross national income (2007): US$393,200,000,000 (US$17,169 per capita). Selected balance of payments data. Receipts from (US$'000,000): tourism (2006) 5,136; remittances (2006) 355; foreign direct investment (FDI) (2004–06 avg.) 3,649. Disbursements for (US$'000,000): tourism (2006) 8,746; remittances (2006) 1,370; FDI (2004–06 avg.) 6,857.

Foreign trade

Imports (2007; c.i.f.): US$219,252,000,000 (mineral fuels 20.9%; electronics 16.6%; base and fabricated metals 12.1%; chemical products 11.3%). Major import sources: Japan 21.0%; US 12.1%; China 11.3%; South Korea 6.9%; Saudi Arabia 4.5%. Exports (2007; f.o.b.): US$246,677,000,000 (machinery and electronic goods 47.8%; base and fabricated metals 11.3%; precision instruments, watches, and musical instruments 8.1%; plastics and rubber products 7.7%). Major export destinations: China 21.0%; Hong Kong 15.4%; US 13.0%; Japan 6.5%; Singapore 4.3%.

Transport and communications

Transport. Railroads (Taiwan Railway Administration only; 2006): route length 1,118 km; passenger-km (2007) 15,769,000,000, metric ton-km cargo (2007) 890,000,000. Roads (2006): total length 39,286 km (paved, n.a.). Vehicles (2007): passenger cars 5,713,000; trucks and buses 1,003,000. Air transport (China Airlines, EVA, and Far Eastern Air only; 2006): passenger-km 59,108,000,000; metric ton-km cargo 11,470,000,000. Communications, in total units (units per 1,000 persons). Telephone landlines (2007): 14,313,000 (625); cellular telephone subscribers (2007): 24,302,000 (1,061); personal computers (2005): 13,098,000 (575); total Internet users (2007): 14,760,000 (644); broadband Internet subscribers (2007): 4,794,000 (209).

Education and health

Educational attainment (2003). Percentage of population ages 15 and over having: no formal schooling 4.6%; primary education 19.8%; vocational 23.7%; secondary 26.8%; some college 12.0%; higher 13.1%. **Literacy** (2006): percentage of population ages 15 and over literate 97.5%. **Health** (2007): physicians 35,849 (excludes 4,862 doctors of Chinese medicine) (1 per 639 persons); hospital beds 150,628 (1 per 152 persons); infant mortality rate per 1,000 live births (2007) 4.7.

Military

Total active duty personnel (2007): 290,000 (army 69.0%, navy 15.5%, air force 15.5%). **Military expenditure as percentage of GDP** (2005): 2.2%; per capita expenditure US$324.

Background

Known to the Chinese as early as the 7th century, Taiwan was widely settled by them early in the 17th century. In 1646 the Dutch seized control of the island, only to be ousted in 1661 by a large influx of Chinese refugees from the Ming dynasty. Taiwan fell to the Manchus in 1683 and was not open to Europeans again until 1858. In 1895 it was ceded to Japan following the Sino-Japanese War. A Japanese military center in World War II, it was frequently bombed by US planes. After Japan's defeat it was returned to China, which was then governed by the Nationalists. When the Communists took over mainland China in 1949, the Nationalist government fled to Taiwan and made it their seat of government, with Gen. Chiang Kai-shek as president. In 1954 he and the US signed a mutual defense treaty, and Taiwan received US support for almost three decades, developing its economy in spectacular fashion. It was recognized by many noncommunist countries as the representative of all China until 1971, when it was replaced in the UN by the People's Republic of China. Martial law was lifted in Taiwan in 1987 and travel restrictions with mainland China in 1988. In 1989 opposition parties were legalized. The relationship with the mainland became increasingly close in the 1990s.

Recent Developments

In January 2008 the Kuomintang (KMT), or Nationalist Party, and its allies won 86 seats in Taiwan's 113-seat legislature, and the KMT's Ma Ying-jeou easily won in the presidential election held in March. Ma moved quickly to mend relations with China. A June agreement allowed regular charter flights across the Taiwan Strait. Further agreements on the expansion of direct flights and trade between Taiwan and China were signed in November, and in March 2009 the first direct passenger cruise between the two countries took place. In August 2008 the administration changed the official name of the national postal service back to its original name, Chunghwa ("Chinese") Post. Chiang Kai-shek Memorial Hall in Taipei was reopened, and the official system of romanization was switched from one developed in Taiwan to Hanyu pinyin, the standard used in China. The new administration also declared a unilateral truce in the decades-long struggle between Taipei and Beijing over diplomatic recognition of Taiwan by other countries. In return for not seeking new diplomatic allies, Taipei hoped that Beijing would allow the island republic to maintain as allies the 19 countries that already recognized it. Moreover, Taipei abandoned its annual bid for admission to the UN after 15 successive failures.

Internet resources:
<http://eng.dgbas.gov.tw/mp.asp?mp=2>.

Tajikistan

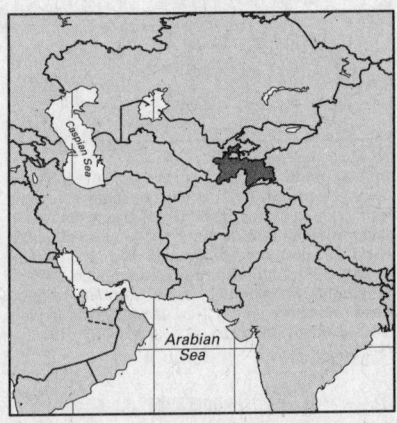

Official name: Jumhurii Tojikiston (Republic of Tajikistan). **Form of government:** republic with two legislative houses (National Assembly [34]; Assembly of Representatives [63]). **Chief of state:** President Imomalii Rakhmon (from 1994). **Head of government:** Prime Minister Akil Akilov (from 1999). **Capital:** Dushanbe. **Official language:** Tajik (Tojik). **Official religion:** none. **Monetary unit:** 1 somoni (TJS) = 100 dirams; valuation (1 Jul 2009) US$1 = TJS 4.40.

Demography

Area: 55,300 sq mi, 143,100 sq km **Population** (2008): 6,839,000 (includes at least 1,000,000 Tajik workers abroad [particularly in Russia]). **Density** (2008): persons per sq mi 123.7, persons per sq km 47.8. **Urban** (2007): 26.3%. **Sex distribution** (2007): male 49.74%; female 50.26%. **Age breakdown** (2007): under 15, 35.0%; 15–29, 31.5%; 30–44, 18.8%; 45–59, 9.7%; 60–74, 3.8%; 75 and over, 1.2%. **Ethnic composition** (2000): Tajik 80.0%; Uzbek 15.3%; Russian 1.1%; Tatar 0.3%; other 3.3%. **Religious affiliation** (2005): Sunni Muslim 78%; Shi'i Muslim 6%; nonreligious 12%; other (mostly Christian) 4%. **Major cities** (2006): Dushanbe 660,900; Khujand 154,700; Kulyab 91,900; Kurgan-Tyube 69,900; Ura-Tyube 59,200. **Location:** central Asia, bordering Kyrgyzstan, China, Afghanistan, and Uzbekistan.

1 metric ton = about 1.1 short tons; 1 kilometer = 0.6 mi (statute); 1 metric ton-km cargo = about 0.68 short ton-mi cargo; c.i.f.: cost, insurance, and freight; f.o.b.: free on board

Vital statistics

Birth rate per 1,000 population (2007): 27.3 (world avg. 20.3); (1994) within marriage 90.8%; outside of marriage 9.2%. **Death rate** per 1,000 population (2007): 7.0 (world avg. 8.6). **Natural increase rate** per 1,000 population (2007): 20.0 (world avg. 11.7). **Total fertility rate** (avg. births per childbearing woman; 2007): 3.09. **Life expectancy** at birth (2007): male 61.6 years; female 67.8 years.

National economy

Budget (2006). *Revenue:* TJS 1,566,000,000 (tax revenue 87.7%, of which taxes on goods and services 46.5%, customs duties 16.1%, payroll tax 11.0%, income tax 10.0%; nontax revenue 9.8%; grants 2.3%). *Expenditures:* TJS 1,944,000,000 (education 17.3%; defense 12.3%; social security and welfare 12.2%; general administrative services 9.5%; health 5.5%). **Public debt** (external, outstanding; 2006): US$982,000,000. **Production** (metric tons except as noted). *Agriculture and fishing* (2007): potatoes 659,900, wheat 612,000, raw seed cotton 419,700; livestock (number of live animals) 1,922,000 sheep, 1,418,000 cattle, 1,250,000 goats, 42,000 camels; fisheries production (2006) 210 (from aquaculture 12%). *Mining and quarrying* (2005): antimony (metal content) 2,000; silver 5,000 kg; gold 3,000 kg. *Manufacturing* (value of production in TJS '000,000 at constant prices of 1998; 2007): nonferrous metals (nearly all aluminum) 585,103; food products 301,156; textiles 209,375. *Energy production (consumption):* electricity (kW-hr; 2007–08) 16,294,200,000 ([2007] 17,600,000,000); coal (metric tons; 2007) 165,000 ([2005] 91,000); lignite (metric tons; 2005) 15,000 (15,000); crude petroleum (barrels; 2007) 190,600 ([2005] 124,600); petroleum products (metric tons; 2005) none (1,377,000); natural gas (cu m; 2007) 15,000,000 (689,000,000). **Population economically active** (2007): total 2,201,000; activity rate of total population 30.5% (participation rates: ages 15–62 [male], 15–57 [female] 51.7%; female [1996] 46.5%; officially unemployed 2.3%). **Gross national income** (2007): US$3,103,-000,000 (US$460 per capita). **Selected balance of payments data.** Receipts from (US$'000,000): tourism (2004) 1.0; remittances (2007) 1,250; foreign direct investment (FDI) (2004–06 avg.) 237; official development assistance (2006) 240. Disbursements for (US$'000,000): tourism (2004) 3.0; remittances (2007) 395; FDI (2004–06 avg.) negligible.

Foreign trade

Imports (2007; c.i.f.): US$2,547,000,000 (refined petroleum products 10.8%; grain and flour 5.3%; electricity 2.6%; natural gas 2.6%). *Major import sources:* Russia 19.8%; China 19.4%; Kazakhstan 8.8%; Uzbekistan 8.3%; Azerbaijan 6.5%. **Exports** (2007; f.o.b.): US$1,468,000,000 (cotton fiber 9.4%; electricity 4.1%). *Major export destinations:* Norway 10.4%; Turkey 8.9%; Italy 6.8%; Iran 6.8%; Russia 5.8%.

Transport and communications

Transport. *Railroads* (2003): length (2006) 482 km; passenger-km 50,000,000; metric ton-km cargo 1,087,000,000. *Roads* (2000): total length 27,767 km (paved [1996] 83%). *Air transport* (Tajikistan Airlines only; 2005): passenger-km 1,030,000,000; metric ton-km cargo 7,031,000. **Communications,** in total units (units per 1,000 persons). Telephone landlines (2005): 280,000 (43); cellular telephone subscribers (2005): 265,000 (40); total Internet users (2005): 20,000 (3.1); broadband Internet subscribers (2003): 10,000 (1.6).

Education and health

Literacy (2007): percentage of total population ages 15 and over literate, virtually 100%. **Health** (2007): physicians 13,400 (1 per 510 persons); hospital beds 38,800 (1 per 176 persons); infant mortality rate per 1,000 live births (2007) 43.6; undernourished population (2002–04) 3,500,000 (56% of total population based on the consumption of a minimum daily requirement of 1,910 calories).

Military

Total active duty personnel (2008): 8,800 (army 83%, air force 17%); Russian troops (2008) 5,500. **Military expenditure as percentage of GDP** (2007): 2.4%; per capita expenditure US$13.

Background

Settled by the Persians c. the 6th century BC, Tajikistan was part of the empires of the Persians and of Alexander the Great and his successors. In the 7th–8th centuries AD it was conquered by the Arabs, who introduced Islam. The Uzbeks controlled the region in the 15th–18th centuries. In the 1860s Russia took over much of Tajikistan. In 1924 it became an autonomous republic under the administration of the Uzbek Soviet Socialist Republic, and it gained republic status in 1929. It achieved independence with the collapse of the Soviet Union in 1991. Civil war raged through much of the 1990s between government forces and an opposition of mostly Islamic forces. Peace was achieved in 1997.

Recent Developments

In 2008 Tajikistan experienced its most severe winter in 44 years, with estimated damage to the country's economy of at least US$1 billion. The economic growth rate was halved, as most of the country's industries lacked power and were closed temporarily. The price of bread and cooking oil doubled, and many families were forced to choose between food and fuel. The number of labor migrants, believed to exceed one-seventh of the population, increased as the domestic situation worsened, and Dushanbe appealed to Russia to raise from 600,000 to 800,000 the official quota for the number of Tajiks allowed to work in Russia.

Internet resources:
<www.stat.tj/english/database.htm>.

Tanzania

Official name: Jamhuri ya Muungano wa Tanzania (Swahili); United Republic of Tanzania (English). **Form of government:** unitary multiparty republic with one

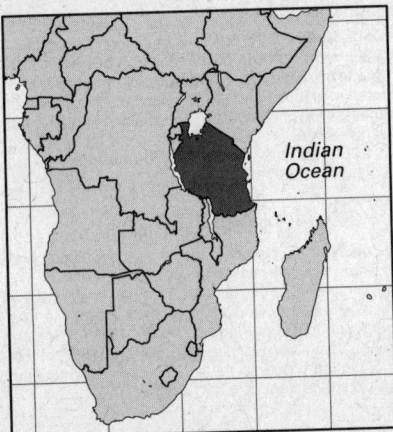

Indian
Ocean

27.6%, income tax 19.4%; nontax revenue 5.7%; grants 25.8%). *Expenditures:* TZS 4,474,680,-900,000 (current expenditures 70.1%, of which interest payments on debt 4.8%; capital expenditures 29.9%). **Gross national income** (2007): US$16,287,-000,000 (US$400 per capita). **Public debt** (external, outstanding; 2006): US$2,929,000,000. **Production** (metric tons except as noted). *Agriculture and fishing* (2007): cassava 6,600,000, corn (maize) 3,400,000, rice 1,240,000, cloves 9,900; livestock (number of live animals) 18,000,000 cattle, 12,550,000 goats, 3,550,000 sheep; fisheries production (2006) 341,120 (from aquaculture, negligible); aquatic plants production (2006) 320 (from aquaculture 100%). *Mining and quarrying* (2006): gold 47,000 kg; garnets 5,900 kg; tanzanites 3,400 kg; rubies 2,700 kg; diamonds 272,200 carats. *Manufacturing* (2005): cement 1,281,000; wheat flour 347,296; sugar 202,200; konyagi (a Tanzanian liquor) 41,050 hectoliters. *Energy production (consumption):* electricity (kW-hr; 2005) 3,036,000,000 (3,172,000,-000); coal (metric tons; 2005) 75,000 (75,000); petroleum products (metric tons; 2005) none (1,149,000). **Population economically active** (2002): total 14,841,000; activity rate of total population 43.1% (participation rates: ages 10 and over, 64.9%; female 48.0%; officially unemployed 3.7%). **Selected balance of payments data.** Receipts from (US$'000,000): tourism (2006) 914; remittances (2007) 15; foreign direct investment (2004–06 avg.) 385; official development assistance (2006) 1,825. Disbursements for (US$'000,000): tourism (2006) 534; remittances (2007) 30.

legislative house (National Assembly [323]). **Head of state and government:** President Jakaya Kikwete (from 2005). **Capital:** Dar es Salaam (Dodoma is the capital designate). **Official languages:** Swahili; English. **Official religion:** none. **Monetary unit:** 1 Tanzania shilling (TZS) = 100 cents; valuation (1 Jul 2009) US$1 = TZS 1,295.17.

Demography

Area: 364,901 sq mi, 945,090 sq km. **Population** (2008): 40,213,000. **Density** (2008): persons per sq mi 110.2, persons per sq km 42.5. **Urban** (2006): 38.5%. **Sex distribution** (2006): male 49.46%; female 50.54%. **Age breakdown** (2006): under 15, 44.3%; 15–29, 29.1%; 30–44, 14.6%; 45–59, 7.6%; 60–74, 3.6%; 75–84, 0.7%; 85 and over, 0.1%. **Ethnolinguistic composition** (2000): 130 different Bantu tribes 95%, of which Sukuma 9.5%, Hehe and Bena 4.5%, Gogo 4.4%, Haya 4.2%, Nyamwezi 3.6%, Makonde 3.3%, Chagga 3.0%, Ha 2.9%; other 5%. **Religious affiliation** (2005): Muslim 35%, of which Sunni 30%, Shi'i 5%; Christian 35%; other (significantly traditional beliefs) 30%; Zanzibar only is 99% Muslim. **Major urban areas** (2002): Dar es Salaam 2,339,910; Arusha 270,485; Mbeya 232,596; Mwanza 209,806; Morogoro 209,058. **Location:** eastern Africa, bordering Kenya, the Indian Ocean, Mozambique, Malawi, Zambia, the Democratic Republic of the Congo, Burundi, Rwanda, and Uganda.

Vital statistics

Birth rate per 1,000 population (2007): 41.6 (world avg. 20.3). **Death rate** per 1,000 population (2007): 14.9 (world avg. 8.6). **Total fertility rate** (avg. births per childbearing woman; 2006): 4.93. **Life expectancy** at birth (2006): male 48.5 years; female 50.9 years.

National economy

Budget (2006–07). *Revenue:* TZS 3,691,247,-900,000 (tax revenue 68.5%, of which excise tax

Foreign trade

Imports (2006): TZS 5,558,000,000,000 (refined petroleum products 23.7%; nonelectrical machinery and apparatus 12.0%; chemical products 11.5%; motor vehicles 9.9%; food products 6.5%). *Major import sources:* South Africa 12.3%; UAE 11.3%; Bahrain 9.2%; China 7.0%; Saudi Arabia 5.7%. **Exports** (2006): TZS 2,116,000,000,000 (gold 34.9%; other metal ores [including copper and silver] 11.0%; fish 10.2%; tobacco 6.2%; vegetables and fruit 4.7%). *Major export destinations:* Switzerland 21.7%; South Africa 14.3%; China 8.9%; Germany 6.7%; The Netherlands 6.0%.

Transport and communications

Transport. *Railroads* (2001): length 3,690 km; passenger-km (2003) 1,305,000,000; metric ton-km cargo (2003) 4,461,000,000. *Roads* (2007): length 78,892 km (paved 6%). *Vehicles:* passenger cars (2000) 36,000; trucks and buses (1999) 98,800. *Air transport* (2007): passenger-km 228,000,000; metric ton-km (2006) 1,704,000. **Communications,** in total units (units per 1,000 persons). Telephone landlines (2007): 237,000 (5.8); cellular telephone subscribers (2007): 8,252,000 (204); personal computers (2005): 356,000 (9.3); total Internet users (2007): 400,000 (9.9).

Education and health

Educational attainment (2002). Percentage of population ages 25 and over having: no formal school-

1 metric ton = about 1.1 short tons; 1 kilometer = 0.6 mi (statute); 1 metric ton-km cargo = about 0.68 short ton-mi cargo; c.i.f.: cost, insurance, and freight; f.o.b.: free on board

ing/unknown 49.6%; primary education 44.0%; secondary 5.5%; postsecondary 0.9%. **Literacy** (2006): percentage of total population ages 15 and over literate 69.4%; males literate 77.5%; females literate 62.2%. **Health** (2002): physicians 822 (1 per 42,085 persons); hospital beds 36,853 (1 per 939 persons); infant mortality rate per 1,000 live births (2006) 73.0; undernourished population (2002–04) 16,400,000 (44% of total population based on the consumption of a minimum daily requirement of 1,810 calories).

Military

Total active duty personnel (2007): 27,000 (army 85.2%, navy 3.7%, air force 11.1%). **Military expenditure as percentage of GDP** (2005): 1.1%; per capita expenditure US$4.

Background

Inhabited from the 1st millennium BC, Tanzania was occupied by Arab and Indian traders and Bantu-speaking peoples by the 10th century AD. The Portuguese gained control of the coastline in the late 15th century, but they were driven out by the Arabs of Oman and Zanzibar in the late 18th century. German colonists entered the area in the 1880s, and in 1891 the Germans declared the region a protectorate as German East Africa. In World War I, Britain captured the German holdings, which became a British mandate (1920) under the name Tanganyika. Britain retained control of the region after World War II when it became a UN trust territory (1947). Tanganyika gained independence in 1961 and became a republic in 1962. In 1964 it united with Zanzibar under the name Tanzania.

Did you know? It is believed that *Homo erectus* used wood for fire at least 750,000 years ago. The oldest evidence of the use of wood for construction, found at the Kalambo Falls site in Tanzania, dates from some 60,000 years ago. Fossils at another site, on the eastern Serengeti Plain, show evidence of hominid habitation in Tanzania dating as far back as 1.75 million years.

Recent Developments

The cost of living rose markedly in Tanzania in 2008 because of increased food and fuel prices. It was welcome news early in the year, therefore, when the Tanzanian National Microfinance Bank launched a US$6.1 million scheme to train poor farmers and ease access to fertilizers and seed. The awareness of endemic corruption in official circles and of the divisive potential of oil and natural gas exploitation forced the governments of both mainland Tanzania and Zanzibar to give serious consideration to methods by which they might share equitably the profits from offshore exploration. The announcement in October of the expansion of drilling for gas in Mnazi Bay promised even richer returns and more potential conflicts.

Internet resources: <www.nbs.go.tz>.

Thailand

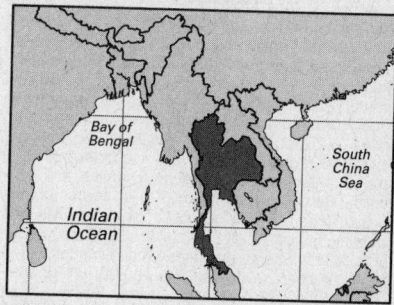

Official name: Ratcha Anachak Thai (Kingdom of Thailand). **Form of government:** constitutional monarchy with two legislative houses (Senate [150]; House of Representatives [480]). **Chief of state:** King Bhumibol Adulyadej (from 1946). **Head of government:** Prime Minister Abhisit Vejjajiva (from 2008). **Capital:** Bangkok. **Official language:** Thai. **Official religion:** none. **Monetary unit:** 1 baht (THB) = 100 satang; valuation (1 Jul 2009) US$1 = THB 34.08.

Demography

Area: 198,117 sq mi, 513,120 sq km. **Population** (2008): 64,316,000. **Density** (2008): persons per sq mi 324.6, persons per sq km 125.3. **Urban** (2006): 29.9%. **Sex distribution** (2006): male 49.35%; female 50.65%. **Age breakdown** (2006): under 15, 20.9%; 15–29, 23.6%; 30–44, 25.6%; 45–59, 17.3%; 60–74, 7.8%; 75–84, 2.0%; 85 and over, 0.5%; unknown/not citizen 2.3%. **Ethnic composition** (2000): Tai peoples 81.4%, of which Thai (Siamese) 34.9%; Lao 26.5%; Han Chinese 10.6%; Malay 3.7%; Khmer 1.9%; other 2.4%. **Religious affiliation** (2005): Buddhist 83%; Muslim (nearly all Sunni) 9%; traditional beliefs 2.5%; nonreligious 2%; other (significantly Christian) 3.5%. **Major cities** (2000): Bangkok (2007) 6,704,000; Samut Prakan 378,741; Nonthaburi 291,555; Udon Thani 222,425; Nakhon Ratchasima 204,641. **Location:** southeastern Asia, bordering Laos, Cambodia, the Gulf of Thailand, Malaysia, and Myanmar (Burma).

Vital statistics

Birth rate per 1,000 population (2006): 13.9 (world avg. 20.3). **Death rate** per 1,000 population (2006): 7.0 (world avg. 8.6). **Natural increase rate** per 1,000 population (2006): 6.9 (world avg. 11.7). **Total fertility rate** (avg. births per childbearing woman; 2005): 1.84. **Life expectancy** at birth (2006): male 69.9 years; female 74.7 years.

National economy

Budget (2007). *Revenue:* THB 1,703,700,000,000 (tax revenue 87.9%, of which VAT 25.5%, corporate taxes 22.6%, excise tax 16.9%, income tax 11.3%; nontax revenue 12.1%). *Expenditures:* THB 1,575,000,000,000 (current expenditures 78.7%; capital expenditures 21.3%). **Public debt** (external, outstanding; 2006): US$11,914,000,000. **Production** (metric tons except as noted). *Agriculture and fishing* (2007): sugarcane 64,365,682, rice 27,879,000, cassava 26,411,233, oil palm fruit 7,642,598, natural rubber 3,121,883; livestock (number of live animals) 8,381,122 pigs, 6,480,876 cattle, 209,105,000 chickens; fisheries production 4,162,096 (from aquaculture 33%). *Mining and quarrying* (2006): gypsum 8,355,000; feldspar 1,068,000; dolomite 899,512; zinc [metal content] 32,100; gemstones (significantly rubies and sapphires) 81,000 carats; gold 3,500 kg. *Manufacturing* (value added in US$'000,000; 2000): textiles and wearing apparel 1,905; electronics 1,817; food products 1,311. *Energy production (consumption):* electricity (kW-hr; 2007) 142,538,000,000 (138,609,-000,000); coal (metric tons; 2005) none (6,703,000); lignite (metric tons; 2006) 19,056,000 ([2005] 21,046,000); crude petroleum (barrels; 2007) 39,000,000 (250,000,000); petroleum products (metric tons; 2005) 43,347,000 (39,345,-000); natural gas (cu m; 2007) 26,254,000,000 ([2005] 29,066,000,000). **Population economically active** (2006): total 36,867,200; activity rate of total population 56.4% (participation rates: ages 15–59, 78.5%; female 46.0%; unemployed [2007] 1.4%). **Gross national income** (2007): US$217,-348,000,000 (US$3,400 per capita). **Selected balance of payments data.** Receipts from (US$'000,-000): tourism (2006) 12,432; remittances (2007) 1,635; foreign direct investment (FDI) (2004–06 avg.) 8,190. Disbursements for (US$'000,000): tourism (2006) 4,632; FDI (2004–06 avg.) 473.

Foreign trade

Imports (2007; c.i.f.): THB 4,872,000,000,000 (mineral fuels 18.4%, of which crude petroleum 13.9%; base and fabricated metals 12.4%; electronic parts 11.3%; electrical machinery and apparatus 9.0%; nonelectrical machinery and apparatus 7.0%). *Major import sources:* Japan 20.3%; China 11.6%; US 6.8%; Malaysia 6.2%; UAE 4.9%. **Exports** (2007; f.o.b.): THB 5,255,000,000,000 (integrated circuits 12.8%; computer equipment 10.3%; motor vehicles and parts 8.4%; agricultural products 7.8%; electrical machinery and apparatus 7.5%). *Major export destinations:* US 12.6%; Japan 11.9%; China 9.7%; Singapore 6.2%; Hong Kong 5.7%.

Transport and communications

Transport. *Railroads* (2006): route length 4,044 km; passenger-km 8,824,000,000; metric ton-km cargo 3,508,000,000. *Roads* (2004): total length 57,403 km (paved 99%). *Vehicles* (2006): passenger cars 3,312,941; trucks and buses 4,568,895. *Air transport* (Thai and Bangkok airways only; 2006): passenger-km 56,891,000,000; metric ton-km cargo 2,107,000,000. **Communications**, in total units (units per 1,000 persons). Telephone landlines (2007): 7,024,000 (110); cellular telephone subscribers (2007): 51,377,000 (804); personal computers (2005): 4,408,000 (70); total Internet users (2007): 13,416,000 (210); broadband Internet subscribers (2007): 913,000 (14).

Education and health

Educational attainment (2007). Percentage of employed population having: no formal schooling/unknown 5.4%; incomplete primary education 32.4%; complete primary 21.2%; lower secondary 29.6%; upper secondary/higher 11.4%. **Literacy** (2007): percentage of total population ages 15 and over literate 94.1%; males literate 95.9%; females literate 92.6%. **Health:** physicians (2004) 18,918 (1 per 3,307 persons); hospital beds (2005) 134,016 (1 per 470 persons); infant mortality rate per 1,000 live births (2005) 11.3; undernourished population (2002–04) 13,800,000 (22% of total population based on the consumption of a minimum daily requirement of 1,870 calories).

Military

Total active duty personnel (2007): 306,600 (army 62.0%, navy 23.0%, air force 15.0%). **Military expenditure as percentage of GDP** (2005): 1.1%; per capita expenditure US$31.

Background

The region of Thailand has been occupied continuously for 20,000 years. It was part of the Mon and Khmer kingdoms from the 9th century AD. Thai-speaking peoples emigrated from China c. the 10th century. During the 13th century two Thai states emerged: the Sukhothai kingdom, founded c. 1220 after a successful revolt against the Khmer, and Chiang Mai, founded in 1296 after the defeat of the Mon. In 1350 the Thai kingdom of Ayutthaya succeeded Sukhothai. The Burmese were its most powerful rivals, occupying it briefly in the 16th century and destroying the kingdom in 1767. The Chakri dynasty came to power in 1782, moving the capital to Bangkok and extending the empire along the Malay Peninsula and into Laos and Cambodia. The country was named Siam in 1856. Though Western influence increased during the 19th century, Siam's rulers avoided colonization by granting concessions to European countries; it was the only Southeast Asian nation able to do so. In 1917 it entered World War I on the side of the Allies. It became a constitutional monarchy following a military coup in 1932 and was officially renamed Thailand in 1939. It was occupied by Japan in World War II. It participated in the Korean War as a UN forces member and was allied with South Vietnam in the Vietnam War. Along with other Southeast Asian nations, it suffered from the 1990s regional financial crisis.

Recent Developments

Prime Minister Samak Sundaravej faced criticism in June 2008 when his government endorsed Cambodia's bid to have the temple of Preah Vihear—a source of long-standing land disputes between the two countries—listed as a UNESCO World Heritage site. This conflict led to a troop build-up on each side that continued in 2009—in April, 3 Thai soldiers were killed and 10 arrested during an exchange of

1 metric ton = about 1.1 short tons;   1 kilometer = 0.6 mi (statute);   1 metric ton-km cargo = about 0.68 short ton-mi cargo;   c.i.f.: cost, insurance, and freight;   f.o.b.: free on board

gunfire. Ih addition, Samak faced a defamation charge, and against this backdrop, he was found guilty by the Constitutional Court of having illegally accepted payment for appearing on a television cooking show and was ordered to step down in September 2008. In December the parliament elected as prime minister Abhisit Vejjajiva, while supporters of former prime minister Thaksin Shinawatra disrupted the scheduled opening of parliament. These protests continued in 2009, and clashes with the army claimed hundreds of injuries and at least two deaths in April.

Internet resources: <web.nso.go.th/index.htm>.

Togo

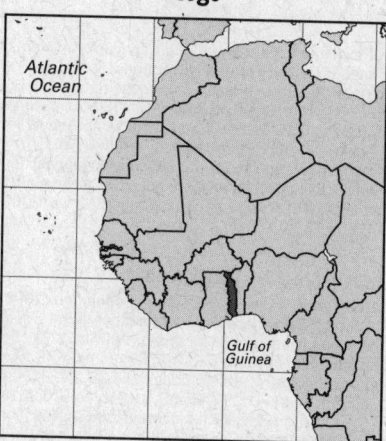

Official name: République Togolaise (Togolese Republic). **Form of government:** multiparty republic with one legislative body (National Assembly [81]). **Head of state and government:** President Faure Gnassingbé (from 2005), assisted by Prime Minister Gilbert Houngbo (from 2008). **Capital:** Lomé. **Official language:** French. **Official religion:** none. **Monetary unit:** 1 CFA franc (CFAF) = 100 centimes; valuation (1 Jul 2009) US$1 = CFAF 462.89.

Demography

Area: 21,925 sq mi, 56,785 sq km. **Population** (2008): 6,762,000. **Density** (2008): persons per sq mi 308.4, persons per sq km 119.1. **Urban** (2007): 41.4%. **Sex distribution** (2005): male 49.07%; female 50.93%. **Age breakdown** (2005): under 15, 42.3%; 15–29, 29.9%; 30–44, 15.6%; 45–59, 8.0%; 60–74, 3.5%; 75 and over, 0.7%. **Ethnic composition** (2000): Ewe 22.2%; Kabre 13.4%; Wachi 10.0%; Mina 5.6%; Kotokoli 5.6%; Bimoba 5.2%; Losso 4.0%; Gurma 3.4%; Lamba 3.2%; Adja 3.0%; other 24.4%. **Religious affiliation** (2004): Christian 47.2%, of which Roman Catholic 27.8%, Protestant 9.5%, independent and other Christian 9.9%; traditional beliefs 33.0%; Muslim 13.7%; nonreligious 4.9%; other 1.2%. **Major cities** (2005): Lomé 921,000 (urban agglomeration 1,337,000); Sokodé 106,300; Kara 100,400; Atakpamé 72,700; Kpalimé 71,400. **Location:** western Africa, bordering Burkina Faso, Benin, the Atlantic Ocean, and Ghana.

Vital statistics

Birth rate per 1,000 population (2005): 37.2 (world avg. 20.3). **Death rate** per 1,000 population (2005): 10.0 (world avg. 8.6). **Total fertility rate** (avg. births per childbearing woman; 2005): 5.01. **Life expectancy** at birth (2005): male 55.0 years; female 59.1 years.

National economy

Budget (2005). *Revenue:* CFAF 175,600,000,000 (tax revenue 87.0%, of which taxes on international trade 41.5%; nontax revenue 7.0%; grants 6.0%). *Expenditures:* CFAF 168,400,000,000 (current expenditures 80.0%; capital expenditures 20.0%). **Production** (metric tons except as noted). *Agriculture and fishing* (2007): cassava 770,000, yams 630,000, corn (maize) 500,000; livestock (number of live animals) 1,950,100 sheep, 1,499,000 goats; fisheries production (2006) 27,899 (from aquaculture 11%). *Mining and quarrying* (2006): limestone 2,400,000; phosphate rock 1,650,000; diamonds 28,200 carats. *Manufacturing* (value added in CFAF '000,000; 2006): food, beverages, and tobacco products 33,800; bricks, cement, and ceramics 19,300; base and fabricated metals 10,800. *Energy production (consumption):* electricity (kW-hr; 2005) 187,000,000 (673,000,000); petroleum products (metric tons; 2005) none (308,000). **Population economically active** (2003): total 2,295,000; activity rate of total population 38.9% (participation rates: ages 16 and over, 70.2%; female 37.0%; unemployed [2004] 32%). **Gross national income** (2007): US$2,383,000,000 (US$360 per capita). **Public debt** (external, outstanding; 2006): US$1,565,000,000. **Selected balance of payments data.** Receipts from (US$'000,000): tourism (2006) 10; remittances (2007) 193; foreign direct investment (2004–06 avg.) 64; official development assistance (2006) 79. Disbursements for (US$'000,000): tourism (2006) 3; remittances (2007) 35.

Foreign trade

Imports (2005; c.i.f.): US$592,600,000 (refined petroleum products 28.5%; food products 10.5%, of which cereals 5.5%; machinery and apparatus 10.1%; iron and steel 6.9%; cement clinker 6.3%). *Major import sources:* France 17.6%; China 13.2%; Côte d'Ivoire 6.5%; Italy 4.5%; The Netherlands 3.9%. **Exports** (2005; f.o.b.): US$359,900,000 (food products 17.4%, of which cocoa 5.6%; cement clinker 16.3%; portland cement 11.1%; crude fertilizer 9.7%; iron and steel 9.0%). *Major export destinations:* Ghana 20.3%; Burkina Faso 18.4%; Benin 11.6%; Mali 7.4%; India 5.9%.

Transport and communications

Transport. *Railroads* (2001): route length (2004) 568 km; passenger-km 44,000,000; metric ton-km cargo 440,000,000. *Roads* (2001): total length 7,500 km (paved 24%). *Vehicles* (2002): passenger cars 51,400; trucks and buses 24,500. *Air transport:* passenger-km (2001) 130,000,000; metric ton-km cargo (2003) 7,000,000. **Communications,** in total units

(units per 1,000 persons). Telephone landlines (2006): 82,000 (13); cellular telephone subscribers (2007): 1,190,000 (181); personal computers (2005): 185,000 (34); total Internet users (2006): 320,000 (51).

Education and health

Educational attainment (1998). Percentage of population ages 25 and over having: no formal schooling/unknown 57.2%; primary education 24.5%; secondary and higher 18.3%. **Literacy** (2007): percentage of total population ages 15 and over literate 65.8%; males literate 79.1%; females literate 52.8%. **Health:** physicians (2004) 225 (1 per 23,357 persons); hospital beds (2002) 4,991 (1 per 997 persons); infant mortality rate per 1,000 live births (2005) 62.2; undernourished population (2002–04) 1,200,000 (24% of total population based on the consumption of a minimum daily requirement of 1,830 calories).

Military

Total active duty personnel (2007): 8,550 (army 94.7%, navy 2.3%, air force 3.0%). **Military expenditure as percentage of GDP** (2005): 1.5%; per capita expenditure US$5.

Background

Until 1884 what is now Togo was an intermediate zone between the black African military states of Asante and Dahomey, and its various ethnic groups lived in general isolation from each other. In 1884 it became part of the Togoland German protectorate, which was occupied by British and French forces in 1914. In 1922 the League of Nations assigned eastern Togoland to France and the western portion to Britain. In 1946 the British and French governments placed the territories under UN trusteeship. Ten years later British Togoland was incorporated into the Gold Coast, and French Togoland became an autonomous republic within the French Union. Togo gained independence in 1960. It suspended its constitution in 1967–80. A multiparty constitution was approved in 1992, but the political situation remained unstable.

Recent Developments

Togo returned to favor among international donors in 2008. The African Development Bank, France, Germany, the EU, and the World Bank granted substantial sums for economic and social projects. In August UN and African Union representatives remarked on the human rights improvements Togo had made over the previous few years—though they observed that much more needed to be done—and in October the European commissioner for development and humanitarian aid, Louis Michel, congratulated the government for the progress it had made over the previous three years, calling Togo an example for the rest of Africa.

Internet resources: <www.togo-tourisme.com/index-eng.php>.

Tonga

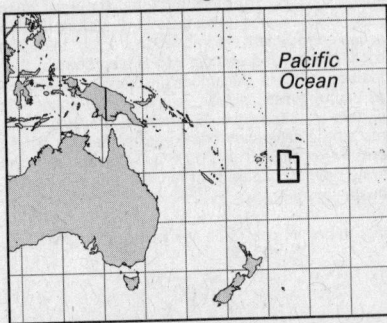

Pacific Ocean

Official name: Fakatu'i 'o Tonga (Tongan); Kingdom of Tonga (English). **Form of government:** constitutional monarchy with one legislative house (Legislative Assembly [34]). **Chief of state:** King Siaosi (George) Tupou V (from 2006). **Head of government:** Prime Minister of the Privy Council Feleti Sevele (from 2006). **Capital:** Nuku'alofa. **Official languages:** Tongan; English. **Official religion:** none. **Monetary unit:** 1 pa'anga (T$) = 100 seniti; valuation (1 Jul 2009) US$1 = T$2.04.

Demography

Area: 289.5 sq mi, 749.9 sq km. **Population** (2008): 103,000. **Density** (2008): persons per sq mi 370.4, persons per sq km 143.0. **Urban** (2006): 23.2%. **Sex distribution** (2006): male 50.76%; female 49.24%. **Age breakdown** (2006): under 15, 38.2%; 15–29, 26.3%; 30–44, 17.2%; 45–59, 10.1%; 60–74, 6.1%; 75 and over, 2.1%. **Ethnic composition** (2006): Tongan 96.6%; mixed (Tongan/other) 1.6%; white 0.6%; Chinese 0.4%; other 0.8%. **Religious affiliation** (2006): Protestant 64.9%, of which Methodist-related denominations 55.9%; Mormon 16.8%; Roman Catholic 15.6%; Baha'i 0.7%; unknown 1.4%; other 0.6%. **Major towns** (2006): Nuku'alofa 23,658 (Greater Nuku'alofa 34,311); Neiafu 4,123; Haveloloto 3,405; Tofoa-Koloua 3,213; Pangai-Hihifo 2,523. **Location:** Oceania, archipelago in the South Pacific Ocean between Hawaii (US) and New Zealand.

Vital statistics

Birth rate per 1,000 population (2007): 25.0 (world avg. 20.3). **Death rate** per 1,000 population (2007): 5.7 (world avg. 8.6). **Natural increase rate** per 1,000 population (2007): 19.3 (world avg. 11.7). **Total fertility rate** (avg. births per childbearing woman; 2006): 3.30. **Life expectancy** at birth (2007): male 72.2 years; female 74.2 years.

National economy

Budget (2005–06). *Revenue:* T$172,446,000 (tax revenue 72.9%; grants 15.1%; nontax revenue 12.0%). *Expenditures:* T$166,031,000 (current expenditures 93.0%; development expenditures 7.0%). **Public debt** (external, outstanding; 2006): US$84,000,000. **Gross national income** (2007):

1 metric ton = about 1.1 short tons;　1 kilometer = 0.6 mi (statute);　1 metric ton-km cargo = about 0.68 short ton-mi cargo;　c.i.f.: cost, insurance, and freight;　f.o.b.: free on board

US$233,000,000 (US$2,320 per capita). **Production** (metric tons except as noted). *Agriculture and fishing* (2007): coconuts 58,500, pumpkins, squash, and gourds 21,000, cassava 9,700; livestock (number of live animals) 81,200 pigs, 12,600 goats, 11,500 horses; fisheries production (2006) 2,505 (from aquaculture, negligible); aquatic plants production (2006) 356 (from aquaculture, negligible). *Mining and quarrying:* coral and sand for local use. *Manufacturing* (value of production in T$'000; 2005): food and beverages 19,722; bricks, cement, and ceramics 4,109; chemical products 2,044. *Energy production (consumption):* electricity (kW-hr; 2007) 46,000,000 (42,000,000); petroleum products (metric tons; 2005) none (38,000). **Population economically active** (2003): total 36,450; activity rate of total population 34.1% (participation rates: ages 15–64 [1996] 60.4%; female 41.9%; unemployed 5.2%). **Selected balance of payments data.** Receipts from (US$'000,000): tourism (2006–07) 13; remittances (2007) 77; foreign direct investment (2004–06 avg.) 11; official development assistance (2006) 21. Disbursements for (US$'000,000): tourism (2006) 8; remittances (2007) 12.

Foreign trade

Imports (2006–07): T$245,200,000 (food and beverages 31.4%; refined petroleum products 29.5%; machinery and transportation equipment 14.2%). *Major import sources:* New Zealand 33.5%; Fiji 27.3%; Australia 13.8%; US 10.3%. **Exports** (2006–07): T$20,900,000 (fish 40.2%; squash 26.8%; root crops 13.9%; kava 6.7%). *Major export destinations:* Japan 35.2%; New Zealand 20.2%; US 12.2%; Australia 6.1%.

Transport and communications

Transport. *Railroads:* none. *Roads* (2000): total length 680 km (paved 27%). *Vehicles* (2004): passenger cars 7,705; trucks and buses 5,297. *Air transport* (2002): passenger-km 14,000,000; metric ton-km cargo 1,000,000. **Communications,** in total units (units per 1,000 persons). Telephone landlines (2007): 21,000 (210); cellular telephone subscribers (2007): 47,000 (464); personal computers (2005): 5,000 (50); total Internet users (2007): 8,400 (84); broadband Internet subscribers (2007): 800 (7.8).

Education and health

Educational attainment (2006). Percentage of population ages 25 and over having: no formal schooling/unknown 1.8%; primary education 29.5%; lower secondary 46.7%; upper secondary 11.0%; higher 11.0%, of which university 3.6%. **Literacy** (2006): percentage of total population literate 99%. **Health** (2004): physicians 41 (1 per 2,447 persons); hospital beds 296 (1 per 332 persons); infant mortality rate per 1,000 live births (2006) 20.0.

Military

Total active duty personnel (2007): 450-member force includes air and coast guard elements. Tonga has defense cooperation agreements with both Australia and New Zealand. **Military expenditure as percentage of GDP** (2004): 1.0%; per capita expenditure US$23.

Background

Tonga was inhabited at least 3,000 years ago by people of the Lapita culture. The Tongans developed a stratified social system headed by a paramount ruler whose dominion by the 13th century extended as far as the Hawaiian Islands. The Dutch visited the islands in the 17th century; in 1773 Capt. James Cook arrived and named the archipelago the Friendly Islands. The modern kingdom was established during the reign (1845–93) of King George Tupou I. It became a British protectorate in 1900. This was dissolved in 1970 when Tonga, the only ancient kingdom surviving from the pre-European period in Polynesia, achieved complete independence within the Commonwealth.

Recent Developments

The rebuilding of Tonga's capital, destroyed in November 2006 during antigovernment riots, continued in 2008. Tensions ebbed during the August coronation of King Siaosi (George) Tupou V when the king pledged to surrender many of his royal powers, accept a reduced role in the state, and divest himself of business interests that he had acquired when state trading operations were privatized and that had been a source of contention.

Internet resources:
<www.spc.int/prism/country/to/stats>.

Trinidad and Tobago

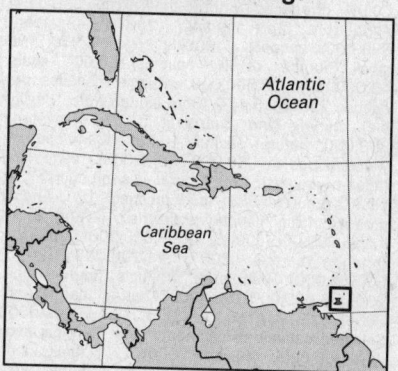

Official name: Republic of Trinidad and Tobago. **Form of government:** multiparty republic with two legislative houses (Senate [31]; House of Representatives [41]). **Chief of state:** President George Maxwell Richards (from 2003). **Head of government:** Prime Minister Patrick Manning (from 2001). **Capital:** Port of Spain. **Official language:** English. **Official religion:** none. **Monetary unit:** 1 Trinidad and Tobago dollar (TT$) = 100 cents; valuation (1 Jul 2009) US$1 = TT$6.18.

Demography

Area: 1,990 sq mi, 5,155 sq km. **Population** (2008): 1,305,000. **Density** (2008): persons per sq mi 655.8, persons per sq km 253.2. **Urban** (2005): 12.2%. **Sex distribution** (2005): male 49.17%; female 50.83%. **Age breakdown** (2005): under 15, 22.3%; 15–29, 30.2%; 30–44, 22.6%; 45–59, 15.4%; 60–74, 7.0%; 75–84, 2.0%; 85 and over, 0.5%. **Ethnic composition** (2000): black 39.2%; East Indian 38.6%; mixed 16.3%; Chinese 1.6%; white 1.0%; other/unknown 3.3%. **Religious affiliation** (2005): Roman Catholic 29%; Hindu 24%; Protestant 19%; independent and other Christian 7%; Muslim 7%; nonreligious 2%; other/unknown 12%. **Major cities/built-up areas** (2006): Chaguanas 73,100; San Juan 57,100; San Fernando 56,600; Port of Spain 49,800 (greater Port of Spain [2004] 264,000); Arima 35,600. **Location**: islands northeast of Venezuela, between the North Atlantic Ocean and the Caribbean Sea.

Vital statistics

Birth rate per 1,000 population (2006): 13.7 (world avg. 20.3). **Death rate** per 1,000 population (2006): 7.7 (world avg. 8.6). **Natural increase rate** per 1,000 population (2006): 6.0 (world avg. 11.7). **Total fertility rate** (avg. births per childbearing woman; 2005): 1.63. **Life expectancy** at birth (2005): male 67.3 years; female 71.4 years.

National economy

Budget (2006–07). *Revenue:* TT$40,064,000,000 (taxes on petroleum and natural gas corporations 40.5%; VAT 12.1%; nonoil corporate taxes 12.0%; nontax revenue 6.7%; import duties 5.0%). *Expenditures:* TT$37,766,000,000 (current expenditures 79.4%; development expenditures and net lending 20.6%). *Production* (metric tons except as noted). *Agriculture and fishing* (2007): sugarcane 358,000, bananas 7,000, oranges 5,250; livestock (number of live animals) 60,000 goats, 45,000 pigs, 28,500,000 chickens; fisheries production (2006) 8,444 (from aquaculture, negligible). *Mining and quarrying* (2006): limestone 850,000; natural asphalt 16,200. *Manufacturing* (value added in US$'000,000; 2003): refined petroleum products and natural gas products 732; base chemicals 515; food products 129. *Energy production (consumption):* electricity (kW-hr; 2006) 7,110,000,000 ([2005] 7,058,000,000); crude petroleum (barrels; 2007) 44,200,000 ([2005] 60,500,000); petroleum products (metric tons; 2005) 8,080,000 (887,000); natural gas (cu m; 2006) 37,973,000,000 ([2005] 13,086,000,000). **Selected balance of payments data.** Receipts from (US$'000,000): tourism (2006) 177; remittances (2007) 92; foreign direct investment (FDI) (2004–06 avg.) 909. Disbursements for (US$'000,000): tourism (2006) 82; FDI (2004–06 avg.) 245. **Gross national income** (2007): US$18,795,000,000 (US$14,100 per capita). **Population economically active** (2005): total 623,700; activity rate of total population 48.2% (participation rates: ages 15–64, 70.1%; female 41.9%; unemployed [2007] 5.5%). **Public debt** (external, outstanding; 2007): US$1,265,000,000.

Foreign trade

Imports (2006; c.i.f.): US$6,477,700,000 (crude petroleum 33.1%; nonelectrical machinery and ap-

paratus 11.5%; chemical products 8.1%; base and fabricated metals 7.5%). *Major import sources:* US 27.6%; Brazil 13.9%; Republic of the Congo 6.0%; Colombia 5.9%; Nigeria 5.9%. **Exports** (2006; f.o.b.): US$14,018,700,000 (liquefied natural gas 31.2%; refined petroleum products 27.3%; crude petroleum 15.0%; ammonia 6.4%; methanol 6.3%). *Major export destinations:* US 58.1%; Jamaica 5.8%; Spain 5.3%; Barbados 3.3%; France 3.2%.

Transport and communications

Transport. *Railroads:* none. *Roads* (2000): total length 8,320 km (paved 51%). *Vehicles* (2005): passenger cars 320,000; trucks and buses 71,000. *Air transport* (BWIA only; 2005): passenger-km 3,101,000,000; metric ton-km cargo 47,883,000. **Communications,** in total units (units per 1,000 persons). Telephone landlines (2007): 324,000 (249); cellular telephone subscribers (2007): 1,008,000 (773); personal computers (2005): 129,000 (100); total Internet users (2007): 431,000 (331); broadband Internet subscribers (2007): 16,000 (12).

Education and health

Educational attainment (2000). Percentage of population ages 15 and over having: no formal schooling/unknown 8.0%; primary education 35.4%; secondary 52.0%; university 4.6%. **Literacy** (2002): percentage of total population ages 15 and over literate 98.5%; males literate 99.0%; females literate 97.9%. **Health** (2006): physicians 1,592 (1 per 815 persons); hospital beds 3,556 (1 per 365 persons); infant mortality rate per 1,000 live births (2005) 13.8; undernourished population (2002–04) 130,000 (10% of total population based on the consumption of a minimum daily requirement of 1,950 calories).

Military

Total active duty personnel (2007): 2,700 (army 74.1%, coast guard 25.9%). **Military expenditure as percentage of GNP** (2005): 0.2%; per capita expenditure US$25.

Background

When Christopher Columbus visited Trinidad in 1498, it was inhabited by the Arawak Indians; Caribs inhabited Tobago. The islands were settled by the Spanish in the 16th century. In the 17th and 18th centuries African slaves were imported for plantation labor to replace the original Indian population, which had been worked to death by the Spanish. Trinidad was surrendered to the British in 1797. The British attempted to settle Tobago in 1721, but the French captured the island in 1781 and transformed it into a sugar-producing colony; the British acquired it in 1802. After slavery ended in the islands in 1834–38, immigrants from India were brought in to work the plantations. The islands of Trinidad and Tobago were administratively combined in 1889. Granted limited self-government in 1925, the islands became an independent state within the

---

1 metric ton = about 1.1 short tons; 1 kilometer = 0.6 mi (statute); 1 metric ton-km cargo = about 0.68 short ton-mi cargo; c.i.f.: cost, insurance, and freight; f.o.b.: free on board

Commonwealth in 1962 and a republic in 1976. Political unrest was followed in 1990 by an attempted Muslim fundamentalist coup against the government.

Recent Developments

Trinidad and Tobago's success in discovering offshore natural gas was again evident in 2008 when 17 billion–37 billion cu m (600 billion–1.3 trillion cu ft) of new reserves were identified north of Tobago. The economy of the country, the world's fifth-largest exporter of liquefied natural gas and the leading source for the US, grew 3.5%, the 17th straight year of growth.

Internet resources: <www.cso.gov.tt>.

Tunisia

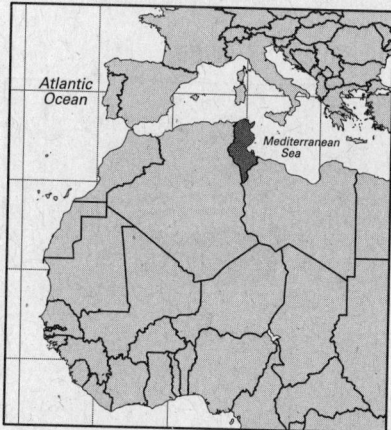

Official name: Al-Jumhuriyah al-Tunisiyah (Tunisian Republic). **Form of government:** multiparty republic with two legislative houses (Chamber of Councilors [126]; Chamber of Deputies [189]). **Chief of state:** President Zine al-Abidine Ben Ali (from 1987). **Head of government:** Prime Minister Mohamed Ghannouchi (from 1999). **Capital:** Tunis. **Official language:** Arabic. **Official religion:** Islam. **Monetary unit:** 1 dinar (TND) = 1,000 millimes; valuation (1 Jul 2009) US$1 = TND 1.33.

Demography

Area: 63,170 sq mi, 163,610 sq km. **Population** (2008): 10,325,000. **Density** (2008): persons per sq mi 163.4, persons per sq km 63.1. **Urban** (2007): 66.1%. **Sex distribution** (2007): male 50.30%; female 49.70%. **Age breakdown** (2005): under 15, 25.9%; 15–29, 30.1%; 30–44, 22.1%; 45–59, 13.2%; 60–74, 6.6%; 75–84, 1.8%; 85 and over, 0.3%. **Ethnic composition** (2000): Tunisian Arab 67.2%; Bedouin Arab 26.6%; Algerian Arab 2.4%; Amazigh (Berber) 1.4%; other 2.4%. **Religious affiliation** (2005): Muslim 99%, of which Sunni 97%; other 1%. **Major cities** (2004): Tunis (2007) 745,000; Safaqis 265,131; Al-Arianah 240,749; Susah 173,047; Ettadhamen 118,487. **Location:** northern Africa, bordering the Mediterranean Sea, Libya, and Algeria.

Vital statistics

Birth rate per 1,000 population (2007): 17.4 (world avg. 20.3). **Death rate** per 1,000 population (2007): 5.5 (world avg. 8.6). **Total fertility rate** (avg. births per childbearing woman; 2007): 2.03. **Life expectancy** at birth (2007): male 72.4 years; female 76.3 years.

National economy

Budget (2007). *Revenue:* TND 13,880,700,000 (tax revenue 68.6%, of which VAT 19.2%, income tax 9.8%; grants and loans 17.5%; nontax revenue 13.9%). *Expenditures:* TND 15,089,000,000 (social services 40.9%; debt service 26.0%; economic services 17.4%). **Production** (metric tons except as noted). *Agriculture and fishing* (2007): wheat 1,442,800, tomatoes 1,000,000, olives 900,000; livestock (live animals) 7,618,350 sheep, 1,550,650 goats, 710,130 cattle, 230,000 camels; fisheries production 105,100 (from aquaculture [2006] 2%). *Mining and quarrying* (2007–08): phosphate rock 7,659,300; iron ore 178,100. *Manufacturing* (value added in TND '000,000; 2007): textiles, leather, and wearing apparel 2,574; electrical machinery and apparatus 1,868; crude and refined petroleum (2005) 1,478. *Energy production (consumption):* electricity (kW-hr; 2007–08) 13,485,-700,000 (11,612,500,000); coal (metric tons; 2002) none (1,000); crude petroleum (barrels; 2007–08) 31,415,000 ([2005] 13,740,000); petroleum products (metric tons; 2007–08) 1,742,700 (3,844,000); natural gas (cu m; 2007–08) 2,038,700,000 (4,063,400,000). **Gross national income** (2007): US$32,820,000,000 (US$3,200 per capita). **Public debt** (external, outstanding; 2007): US$10,380,000,000. **Population economically active** (2007): total 3,593,200; activity rate of total population 35.1% (participation rates: ages 15 and over 46.8%; female 25.3%; unemployed 14.1%). **Selected balance of payments data.** Receipts from (US$'000,000): tourism (2007) 2,401; remittances (2007) 1,669; foreign direct investment (FDI) (2004–06 avg.) 1,578; official development assistance (2006) 432. Disbursements for (US$'000,-000): tourism (2006) 410; remittances (2007) 16; FDI (2004–06 avg.) 17.

Foreign trade

Imports (2007; c.i.f.): TND 24,438,700,000 (machinery and apparatus 42.7%; food products 10.7%; chemical products 9.3%; fabric 8.5%; refined petroleum products 7.9%). *Major import sources:* France 21.4%; Italy 19.3%; Germany 7.9%; Spain 4.7%; Russia 4.1%. **Exports** (2007; f.o.b.): TND 19,409,-600,000 (machinery and apparatus 27.1%; wearing apparel 17.8%; crude petroleum 13.6%; food products 9.7%; phosphate products [mostly fertilizers] 6.5%). *Major export destinations:* France 32.1%; Italy 23.3%; Germany 8.2%; Spain 5.2%; Libya 4.6%.

Transport and communications

Transport. *Railroads* (2007–08): route length (2006) 2,153 km; passenger-km 1,491,400,000; metric ton-km cargo 2,158,500,000. *Roads* (2004): total length 19,232 km (paved 66%). *Vehicles* (2004): passenger cars 825,990; trucks and buses 119,064. *Air transport* (Tunis Air only; 2007): passenger-km 3,035,000,000; metric ton-km cargo 17,000,000. **Communications**, in total units (units per 1,000 persons). Telephone landlines (2007): 1,273,000 (123); cellular telephone subscribers (2007): 7,842,000 (759); personal computers (2005): 568,000 (56); total Internet users (2007): 1,722,000 (167); broadband Internet subscribers (2007): 114,000 (11).

Education and health

Educational attainment (2005). Percentage of population ages 10 and over having: no formal schooling 22.0%; primary education 36.5%; secondary 33.1%; higher 8.4%. **Literacy** (2007): percentage of total population ages 10 and over literate 77.9%; males literate 87.0%; females literate 68.7%. **Health** (2007): physicians 10,554 (1 per 969 persons); hospital beds 17,998 (1 per 568 persons); infant mortality rate per 1,000 live births 18.5; undernourished population (2002–04) less than 2.5% of total population.

Military

Total active duty personnel (2007): 35,800 (army 75.4%, navy 13.4%, air force 11.2%). **Military expenditure as percentage of GDP** (2005): 1.6%; per capita expenditure US$29.

Background

From the 12th century BC the Phoenicians had a series of trading posts on the northern African coast. By the 6th century BC the Carthaginian kingdom encompassed most of present-day Tunisia. The Romans ruled from 146 BC until the Muslim Arab invasions in the mid-7th century AD. The area was fought over, won, and lost by many, including the Abbasids, the Almohads, the Spanish, and the Ottoman Turks, who finally conquered it in 1574 and held it until the late 19th century. For a time it maintained autonomy as the French, the British, and the Italians contended for the region. In 1881 Tunisia became a French protectorate. In World War II, US and British forces captured it (1943) to end a brief German occupation. In 1956 France granted it full independence; Habib Bourguiba assumed power and remained in office until 1987.

Recent Developments

Tunisia's economy was estimated to have grown by more than 5% in 2008, while carrying a budget deficit of almost 4% of GDP, largely because of the global economic downturn. The European Union provided 82% of Tunisia's imports and absorbed 74% of its exports. Increased imported energy and food costs took year-on-year inflation to over 5%. The value of energy imports doubled in the first half of the year, and Tunisia imported more than 600,000 tons of soft wheat. As a result, the trade deficit rose by more than 7%, to US$4.25 billion. Increased domestic prices caused riots in June in Redayef and in nearby Gafsa, where unemployment reached 30%.

Security continued to be a concern, though less acute than elsewhere in North Africa. Of the 30 individuals arrested on charges of having threatened attacks on foreign embassies after clashes with security forces in December 2006 and January 2007, 2 were sentenced to death, but one sentence was commuted upon appeal in February 2008; the other 28 received lengthy prison sentences. Fourteen members of the Soldiers of Assad Ibn al-Fourat had been killed in the clashes with police. In late February 2008, two Austrian tourists traveling in southern Tunisia were kidnapped by an Islamic militant group as a protest against Western support of Israel. They were taken to Mali, where their captors first demanded the release of prisoners held in Tunisia and Algeria but later demanded a ransom. The tourists eventually were freed in November, and tourism continued to be an important economic engine in Tunisia.

Internet resources: <www.tourismtunisia.com>.

Turkey

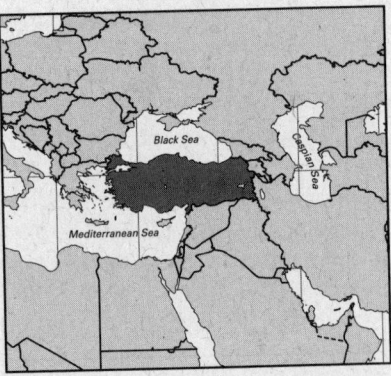

Official name: Turkiye Cumhuriyeti (Republic of Turkey). **Form of government:** multiparty republic with one legislative house (Grand National Assembly of Turkey [550]). **Chief of state:** President Abdullah Gul (from 2007). **Head of government:** Prime Minister Recep Tayyip Erdogan (from 2003). **Capital:** Ankara. **Official language:** Turkish. **Official religion:** none. **Monetary unit:** 1 new Turkish lira (YTL) = 100 kurus; valuation (1 Jul 2009) US$1 = YTL 1.52.

Demography

Area: 302,535 sq mi, 783,562 sq km. **Population** (2008): 71,002,000. **Density** (2008): persons per sq mi 234.7, persons per sq km 90.6. **Urban** (2007): 70.5%. **Sex distribution** (2007): male 50.12%, female 49.88%. **Age breakdown** (2005): under 15, 28.3%; 15–29, 27.7%; 30–44, 22.4%; 45–59, 13.4%; 60–74, 6.5%; 75–84, 1.5%; 85 and over, 0.2%. **Ethnic composition** (2000): Turkish 65.1%; Kurdish 18.9%; Crimean Tatar 7.2%; Arab 1.8%; Azerbaijani 1.0%; Yoruk 1.0%; other 5.0%. **Religious**

affiliation (2005): Muslim 97.5%, of which Sunni 82.5%, Shi'i (mostly nonorthodox Alevi) 15.0%; non-religious 2.0%; other (mostly Christian) 0.5%. **Major cities** (2007): Istanbul 10,757,327; Ankara 3,763,591; Izmir 2,606,294; Bursa 1,431,172; Adana 1,366,027; Gaziantep 1,175,042. **Location:** southwestern Asia and southeastern Europe, bordering the Black Sea, Georgia, Armenia, Azerbaijan, Iran, Iraq, Syria, the Mediterranean Sea, Greece, and Bulgaria.

Vital statistics

Birth rate per 1,000 population (2007): 19.4 (world avg. 20.3). **Death rate** per 1,000 population (2007): 6.6 (world avg. 8.6). **Total fertility rate** (avg. births per childbearing woman; 2007): 2.17. **Life expectancy** at birth (2007): male 69.3 years; female 74.2 years.

National economy

Budget (2005). *Revenue:* YTL 134,819,231,000 (tax revenue 79.3%, of which income tax 22.5%; nontax revenue 17.2%; grants and other revenue 3.5%). *Expenditures:* YTL 141,020,860,000 (finances 51.8%; education 10.5%; labor and social security 10.2%; defense 7.2%). **Production** (in '000 metric tons except as noted). *Agriculture and fishing* (2007): wheat 17,678, sugar beets 14,800, tomatoes 9,920, barley 7,423, potatoes 4,281, grapes 3,923, corn (maize) 3,875, seed cotton 2,500, apples 2,266, cucumbers and gherkins 1,876; livestock (number of live animals) 25,400,000 sheep, 10,871,364 cattle, 344,820,000 chickens, (2004) 230,037 angora goats; fisheries production (2006) 662 (from aquaculture 20%). *Mining and quarrying* (2006): magnesite 2,088; refined borates 1,021; chromite 458; copper ore (metal content) 46; marble 1,200,000 cu m. *Manufacturing* (value added in US$'000,000; 2005): food products 8,800; telecommunications equipment and electronics 7,450; chemical products 7,400; base metals 7,000; motor vehicles and parts 6,500; textiles 6,100. *Energy production (consumption):* electricity (kW-hr; 2005) 161,955,000,000 (160,793,000,000); coal (metric tons; 2005) 2,170,000 (19,421,000); lignite (metric tons; 2005) 56,170,000 (57,315,000); crude petroleum (barrels; 2006) 15,900,000 ([2005] 189,500,-000); petroleum products (metric tons; 2005) 21,775,000 (24,474,000); natural gas (cu m; 2005) 923,000,000 (27,172,000,000). **Population economically active** (2006): total 24,775,000; activity rate of total population 34.2% (participation rates: ages 15–64, 51.1%; female 26.1%; unemployed [May 2006–April 2007] 9.7%). **Gross national income** (2007): US$592,850,000,000 (US$8,020 per capita). **Public debt** (external, outstanding; June 2007): US$65,310,000,000. **Selected balance of payments data.** Receipts from (US$'000,000): tourism (2006) 21,503; remittances (2007) 1,200; foreign direct investment (FDI) (2004–06 avg.) 10,935; official development assistance (2006) 570. Disbursements for (US$'000,000): tourism (2006) 2,743; remittances (2007) 107; FDI (2004–06 avg.) 957.

Foreign trade

Imports (2007; c.i.f.): US$170,057,000,000 (machinery and apparatus 21.1%; mineral fuels 20.6%; base and fabricated metals 15.2%; transportation equipment 8.5%). *Major import sources:* Russia 13.8%; Germany 10.3%; China 7.8%; Italy 5.9%; US 4.8%. **Exports** (2007; f.o.b.): US$107,213,000,000 (textiles and wearing apparel 21.4%; transportation equipment 17.0%; machinery and apparatus 15.1%; base and fabricated metals 14.6%; vegetables, fruits, and nuts 4.1%). *Major export destinations:* Germany 11.2%; UK 8.1%; Italy 7.0%; France 5.6%; Russia 4.4%.

Transport and communications

Transport. *Railroads* (2006): length 8,697 km; passenger-km 5,277,000; metric ton-km cargo 9,676,000,000. *Roads* (2005): total length 426,914 km (paved [2004] 45%). *Vehicles* (2007): passenger cars 6,472,156; trucks and buses 3,181,390. *Air transport* (Atlasjet, Turkish, Pegasus, and Sun Express airlines only; 2006): passenger-km 37,512,-000,000; metric ton-km cargo 391,831,000. **Communications**, in total units (units per 1,000 persons). Telephone landlines (2007): 18,413,000 (246); cellular telephone subscribers (2007): 61,976,000 (828); personal computers (2005) 4,073,000 (57); total Internet users (2007): 21,141,000 (282); broadband Internet subscribers (2007): 4,554,000 (61).

Did you know? In 1928, the replacement of the Arabic script by the Latin alphabet was a reform of truly revolutionary proportions in Turkey. This action set Turkey on the path to achieving one of the highest literacy rates in the Middle East. Mustafa Kemal (later called Atatürk) went into the countryside, and with chalk and a blackboard he demonstrated the new alphabet to the Turkish people and explained how the letters should be pronounced.

Education and health

Educational attainment (2003). Percentage of population ages 25–64 having: no formal schooling through primary education 64%; lower secondary 10%; upper secondary/higher vocational 17%; university 9%. **Literacy** (2006): percentage of total population ages 15 and over literate 88.1%; males literate 96.0%; females literate 80.4%. **Health:** physicians (2004) 104,226 (1 per 683 persons); hospital beds (2006) 180,767 (1 per 404 persons); infant mortality rate per 1,000 live births (2007) 21.7; undernourished population (2002–04) 2,100,000 (3% of total population based on the consumption of a minimum daily requirement of 1,970 calories).

Military

Total active duty personnel (2007): 510,600 (army 78.7%, navy 9.5%, air force 11.8%); US troops in Turkey (2008) 1,570. **Military expenditure as percentage of GDP** (2005): 2.8%; per capita expenditure US$143.

Background

Turkey's early history corresponds to that of Asia Minor, the Byzantine Empire, and the Ottoman Empire. Byzantine rule emerged when Constantine the Great made Constantinople (now Istanbul) his capital. The Ottoman Empire, begun in the 12th century, dominated for more than 600 years; it ended in 1918 after the Young Turk revolt. Under the leadership of Mustafa Kemal Ataturk, a republic was proclaimed in 1923, and the caliphate was abolished in 1924. Turkey remained neutral throughout most of World War II, siding with the Allies in 1945. It has since alternated between civil and military governments and has had several conflicts with Greece over Cyprus. The early 21st century saw political and civic turmoil between fundamentalist Muslims and secularists and ongoing violent conflict with Kurdish separatists.

Recent Developments

Turkey's ruling conservative Justice and Development Party (AKP), led by Prime Minister Recep Tayyip Erdogan, was threatened with closure in 2008, less than a year after it had won a second term in office. In March the Constitutional Court agreed to hear a petition by Turkey's chief prosecutor, who alleged that the AKP had become a "focus of activity against the secular order" and asked that the party be closed down and that its leading members be banned from politics for five years. Although the court accepted the charge in July, it failed to muster the majority needed for the ban. The Kurdish nationalist separatists of the Kurdistan Workers' Party (PKK) persistently attacked security personnel and engaged in other terrorist activities from northern Iraq. The army launched an incursion into the area in February and claimed to have killed some 250 militants, while in April 2009 the Turkish air force bombed PKK bases there. Explosions blamed on the PKK killed 17 in Istanbul in July 2008; 15 soldiers perished at a border post in October; and in April 2009, 10 soldiers died in two attacks.

Internet resources:
<www.tourismturkey.org>.

Turkmenistan

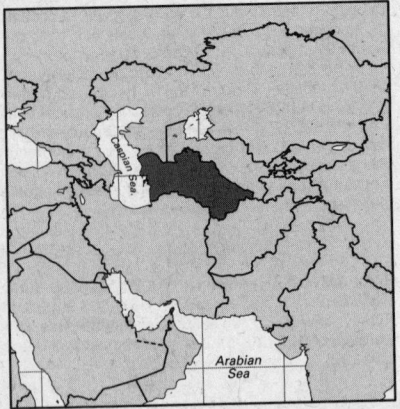

Official name: Turkmenistan. **Form of government:** unitary single-party republic with one legislative body (Mejlis, or Assembly [125]). **Head of state and government:** President Gurbanguly Berdymukhammedov (from 2006). **Capital:** Ashgabat. **Official language:** Turkmen. **Official religion:** none. **Monetary unit:** 1 (new) manat (TMT) = 100 tennesi; valuation (1 Jul 2009) US$1 = TMT 2.85 (the [new] manat replaced the [old] manat 1 Jan 2009, at the rate of [new] TMT 1 = [old] TMM 5,000).

Demography

Area: 188,500 sq mi, 488,100 sq km. **Population (2008):** 5,180,000. **Density (2008):** persons per sq mi 27.5, persons per sq km 10.6. **Urban (2005):** 47.3%. **Sex distribution (2005):** male 49.24%; female 50.76%. **Age breakdown (2005):** under 15, 31.8%; 15–29, 30.0%; 30–44, 20.6%; 45–59, 11.4%; 60–74, 4.6%; 75–84, 1.4%; 85 and over, 0.2%. **Ethnic composition (2000):** Turkmen 79.2%; Uzbek 9.0%; Russian 3.0%; Kazakh 2.5%; Tatar 1.1%; other 5.2%. **Religious affiliation (2000):** Muslim (mostly Sunni) 87.2%; Russian Orthodox 1.7%; nonreligious 9.0%; other 2.1%. **Major cities (1999):** Ashgabat (2007) 744,000; Turkmenabat 203,000; Dasoguz 165,000; Mary 123,000; Balkanabat 108,000. **Location:** central Asia, bordering Kazakhstan, Uzbekistan, Afghanistan, Iran, and the Caspian Sea.

Vital statistics

Birth rate per 1,000 population (2006): 25.6 (world avg. 20.3); (1998) within marriage 96.2%; outside of marriage 3.8%. **Death rate** per 1,000 population (2006): 6.3 (world avg. 8.6). **Natural increase rate** per 1,000 population (2006): 19.3 (world avg. 11.7). **Total fertility rate** (avg. births per childbearing woman; 2006): 3.19. **Life expectancy** at birth (2006): male 64.9 years; female 71.3 years.

National economy

Budget (2006). *Revenue:* TMM 22,474,000,-000,000 (tax revenue 93.8%; nontax revenue 6.2%). *Expenditures:* TMM 16,631,000,000,000 (current expenditures 94.2%; development expenditures 5.8%). **Public debt** (external, outstanding; 2006): US$725,000,000. **Production** (metric tons except as noted). *Agriculture and fishing* (2007): wheat 2,700,000, seed cotton 946,000, tomatoes 256,000; livestock (number of live animals) 15,500,000 sheep, 1,948,000 cattle; fisheries production (2006) 15,016 (from aquaculture, negligible). *Mining and quarrying* (2005): iodine 270,000, salt 215,000, gypsum 100,000. *Manufacturing* (2004): distillate fuel (gas-diesel oil) 2,511,000; residual fuel oils 1,745,000; motor spirits (gasoline) 1,265,000. *Energy production (consumption):* electricity (kW-hr; 2005) 12,820,000,000 (9,902,000,-000); crude petroleum (barrels; 2007) 65,700,000 (40,200,000); petroleum products (metric tons; 2005) 6,466,000 (3,533,000); natural gas (cu m; 2006) 62,000,000,000 ([2005] 14,619,000,000). **Population economically active** (2006): total 2,181,000; activity rate of total population 44.5%

(participation rates: ages 15–64, 68.5%; female 46.9%; unofficially unemployed, n.a.). **Gross national income** (2007): US$6,820,000,000 (US$1,374 per capita). **Selected balance of payments data.** Receipts from (US$'000,000): foreign direct investment (2004–06 avg.) 501; official development assistance (2006) 26.

Foreign trade

Imports (2003; c.i.f.): US$2,450,000,000 (machinery and transportation equipment 45.9%; basic manufactures 19.9%; chemical products 11.1%; food products 5.3%). *Major import sources* (2007): UAE 15%; Turkey 11%; China 10%; Ukraine 9%; Russia 8%. **Exports** (2003; f.o.b.): US$3,720,000,000 (natural gas 49.7%; petrochemicals 18.3%; crude petroleum 8.9%; cotton fiber 3.2%; cotton yarn 2.2%). *Major export destinations* (2007): Ukraine 49%; Iran 18%; Azerbaijan 5%; Turkey 5%.

Transport and communications

Transport. *Railroads* (2006): length 2,980 km; passenger-km (1999) 701,000,000; metric ton-km cargo (2002) 7,476,000,000. *Roads* (2001): total length 22,000 km (paved 82%). *Vehicles* (1995): passenger cars 220,000; trucks and buses 58,200. *Air transport* (Turkmenistan Airlines only; 2005): passenger-km 1,913,000,000; metric ton-km cargo 25,997,000. **Communications,** in total units (units per 1,000 persons). Telephone landlines (2005): 398,000 (81); cellular telephone subscribers (2006): 217,000 (43); personal computers (2005): 348,000 (72); total Internet users (2007): 70,000 (14).

Education and health

Educational attainment (2000). Percentage of population ages 25 and over having: no formal schooling/unknown 3.2%; incomplete primary to complete standard secondary education 60.1%; vocational secondary 23.5%; higher 13.2%. **Literacy** (2007): percentage of total population ages 15 and over literate, virtually 100%. **Health:** physicians (2004) 12,722 (1 per 381 persons); hospital beds (2002) 23,524 (1 per 199 persons); infant mortality rate per 1,000 live births (2006) 55.2; undernourished population (2002–04) 300,000 (7% of total population based on the consumption of a minimum daily requirement of 1,930 calories).

Military

Total active duty personnel (2008): 22,000 (army 84.1%, navy 2.3%, air force 13.6%). **Military expenditure as percentage of GDP** (2007): 1.7%; per capita expenditure US$44.

Background

The earliest traces of human settlement in central Asia, dating back to Paleolithic times, have been found in Turkmenistan. The nomadic, tribal Turkmen probably entered the area in the 11th century AD. They were conquered by the Russians in the early 1880s, and the region became part of Russian Turkistan. It was organized as the Turkmen So-

viet Socialist Republic in 1924 and became a constituent republic of the USSR in 1925. The country gained full independence from the USSR in 1991 under the name Turkmenistan. From 1990 to 2006 the country was ruled by the ever more autocratic and mercurial strongman Saparmurad Niyazov.

Recent Developments

The process of reform in Turkmenistan proceeded unevenly in 2008. Turkmenistan's isolation from the international community weakened, and travel abroad for many Turkmen became easier. The influence of the security services on everyday life, however, continued to be overwhelming. One reform that proved to be unpopular was the introduction in February of free gasoline (water, electricity, and natural gas were already supplied free of cost). Whereas car owners were entitled to a certain amount of free fuel per month, they paid a steep price if additional fuel was needed. Turkmenistan's huge natural gas resources continued to generate worldwide interest in the country. Russia's energy giant Gazprom promised in July to buy increasing amounts of Turkmen gas at world market prices, the US urged Turkmenistan to diversify its gas-export routes, and a gas pipeline to China was under construction. American firms interested in the development of Turkmenistan's energy sector lobbied the government.

Internet resources:
<www.turkmenistanembassy.org>.

Tuvalu

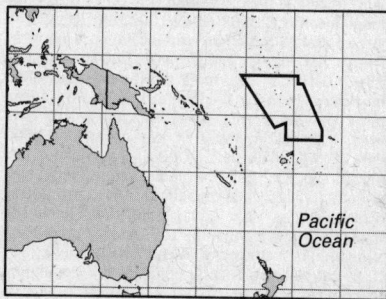

Pacific Ocean

Official name: Tuvalu. **Form of government:** constitutional monarchy with one legislative house (Parliament [15]). **Chief of state:** British Queen Elizabeth II (from 1952), represented by Governor-General Filoimea Telito (from 2005). **Head of government:** Prime Minister Apisai Ielemia (from 2006). **Capital:** government offices are at Vaiaku, on Funafuti atoll. **Official language:** none. **Official religion:** none. **Monetary units:** 1 Tuvaluan dollar ($T) = 1 Australian dollar ($A) = 100 Tuvaluan and Australian cents; valuation (1 Jul 2009) US$1 = $A 1.24.

Demography

Area: 9.90 sq mi, 25.63 sq km. **Population** (2008): 9,700. **Density** (2008): persons per sq mi 979.8, persons per sq km 378.5. **Urban** (2004): 55.2%. **Sex distribution (2007): male 48.84%; female 51.16%. **Age breakdown** (2007): under 15, 29.7%; 15–29, 27.9%; 30–44, 20.0%; 45–59, 14.9%; 60–74, 5.7%; 75 and over, 1.8%. **Ethnic composition** (2004–05): Tuvaluan (Polynesian) 95.1%; mixed (Tuvaluan/other) 3.4%; I-Kiribati 1.1%; other 0.4%. **Religious affiliation** (2002): Christian 97.0%, of which Church of Tuvalu (Congregational) 91.0%, Seventh-day Adventist 2.0%, Roman Catholic 1.0%; Baha'i 1.9%; other 1.1%. **Major locality** (2002): Fongafale islet of Funafuti atoll 4,492. **Location:** Oceania, group of islands in the South Pacific Ocean, east of Papua New Guinea.

Vital statistics

Birth rate per 1,000 population (2007): 22.4 (world avg. 20.3); (2005) within marriage 92.7%; outside of marriage 7.3%. **Death rate** per 1,000 population (2007): 7.0 (world avg. 8.6). **Natural increase rate** per 1,000 population (2007): 15.4 (world avg. 11.7). **Total fertility rate** (avg. births per childbearing woman; 2007): 2.96. **Life expectancy** at birth (2007): male 66.4 years; female 71.0 years.

National economy

Budget (2007). *Revenue:* $A 19,126,000 (tax revenue 33.1%; nontax revenue [including remittances from phosphate miners in Nauru and seafarers on German ships, rentals of fishing resources to Japan, Taiwan, and the US, and the leasing of the country's Internet domain "tv"] 48.1%; grants 18.8%). *Expenditures:* $A 23,682,000 (current expenditures 91.6%; development expenditures 8.4%). **Public debt** (external; 2002): US$5,000,000. **Gross national income** (2006): US$26,000,000 (US$2,441 per capita). **Production** (metric tons except as noted). *Agriculture and fishing* (2007): coconuts 1,700, bananas 280, roots and tubers 150, other agricultural products include breadfruit, *pulaka* (taro), pandanus fruit, sweet potatoes, and pawpaws; livestock (number of live animals) 13,600 pigs, 45,000 chickens, 15,000 ducks; fisheries production (2006) 2,201 (from aquaculture, negligible). *Manufacturing* (value added in $A '000; 2002): local cigarettes 755; cottage industries (including handicrafts and garments) 158. *Energy production (consumption):* electricity (kW-hr; 2006) n.a. (4,235,-100); petroleum products, none (none). **Population economically active** (2004): total 4,302; activity rate of total population 44.8% (participation rates: ages 15 and over [2002] 58.2%; female [2002] 43.4%; unemployed 16.3%). **Selected balance of payments data.** Receipts from (US$'000,000): tourism (1998) 0.2; remittances (2006) 3.0; foreign direct investment (FDI) (2004–06 avg.) none; official development assistance (2006) 15. Disbursements for (US$'000,000): FDI (2004–06 avg.) negligible.

Foreign trade

Imports (2007; c.i.f.): $A 18,386,120 (food products [including live animals] 30.2%; mineral fuels 16.1%, of which diesel fuel 9.1%; telecommunications equipment 4.4%; wearing apparel 4.1%; base and fabri-

cated metals 3.9%). *Major import sources:* Australia 24.9%; Fiji 24.6%; Singapore 13.5%; New Zealand 11.3%; China 7.7%. **Exports** (2007; f.o.b.): $A 109,413 ([2005] precision instruments 18.6%; machinery and apparatus 17.4%; base and fabricated metals 15.4%; wood products 12.5%; transportation equipment 11.6%). *Major export destinations:* Fiji 93.1%; El Salvador 4.6%; New Zealand 2.2%; UK 0.1%.

Transport and communications

Transport. *Railroads:* none. *Roads* (2002): total length 8 km (paved 100%). *Vehicles* (2007): passenger cars 15; trucks and buses 2. **Communications,** in total units (units per 1,000 persons). Telephone landlines (2006): 900 (85); cellular telephone subscribers (2006): 1,300 (124); total Internet users (2006): 1,700 (162).

Education and health

Educational attainment (2004–05). Percentage of population ages 15 and over having: no formal education/unknown 8.8%; primary education 52.4%; secondary 29.8%; higher 9.0%. **Literacy** (2004): percentage of total population literate 95%. **Health:** physicians (2003) 4 (1 per 2,393 persons); hospital beds (2001) 56 (1 per 170 persons); infant mortality rate per 1,000 live births (2007) 19.5.

Military

Total active duty personnel (2007): none; Tuvalu has nonformal security arrangements with Australia and New Zealand.

Background

The original Polynesian settlers of Tuvalu probably came mainly from Samoa or Tonga. The islands were sighted by the Spanish in the 16th century. Europeans settled there in the 19th century and intermarried with Tuvaluans. During this period Peruvian slave traders, known as "blackbirders," decimated the population. In 1856 the US claimed the four southern islands for guano mining. Missionaries from Europe arrived in 1865 and rapidly converted the islanders to Christianity. In 1892 Tuvalu joined the British Gilbert Islands, a protectorate that became the Gilbert and Ellice Islands Colony in 1916. Tuvaluans voted in 1974 for separation from the Gilberts (now Kiribati), whose people are Micronesian. Tuvalu gained independence in 1978, and in 1979 the US relinquished its claims. Elections were held in 1981, and a revised constitution was adopted in 1986. In recent decades, the government has tried to find overseas job opportunities for its citizens.

Recent Developments

Tuvalu faced continuing threats in 2008 from rising sea levels, which were beginning to contaminate its freshwater aquifers, and from accelerating coastal degradation. Talks continued with Australia and New Zealand concerning the taking in of Tuvaluans when

---

1 metric ton = about 1.1 short tons;   1 kilometer = 0.6 mi (statute);   1 metric ton-km cargo = about 0.68 short ton-mi cargo;   c.i.f.: cost, insurance, and freight;   f.o.b.: free on board

their islands eventually become uninhabitable. Tuvalu became the 11th signatory to ratify the Pacific Island Countries Trade Agreement, and a new biweekly air service from Funafuti to Fiji opened the possibility of expanding tourism.

Internet resources: <www.spc.int/prism/country/tv/stats>.

Uganda

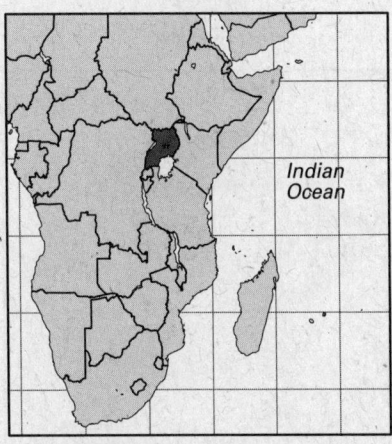

Indian Ocean

Official name: Republic of Uganda. **Form of government:** multiparty republic with one legislative house (Parliament [333]). **Head of state and government:** President Yoweri Museveni (from 1986), assisted by Prime Minister Apolo Nsibambi (from 1999). **Capital:** Kampala. **Official language:** English; Swahili. **Official religion:** none. **Monetary unit:** 1 Ugandan shilling (UGX) = 100 cents; valuation (1 Jul 2009) US$1 = UGX 2,055.00.

Demography

Area: 93,263 sq mi, 241,551 sq km. **Population** (2008): 29,166,000. **Density** (2008): persons per sq mi 382.4, persons per sq km 147.6. **Urban** (2007): 12.6%. **Sex distribution** (2006): male 50.08%; female 49.92%. **Age breakdown** (2006): under 15, 50.3%; 15–29, 27.7%; 30–44, 12.9%; 45–59, 5.7%; 60–74, 2.7%; 75–84, 0.6%; 85 and over, 0.1%. **Ethnolinguistic composition** (2002): Ganda 17.3%; Nkole 9.8%; Soga 8.6%; Kiga 7.0%; Teso 6.6%; Lango 6.2%; Acholi 4.8%; Gisu 4.7%. **Religious affiliation** (2002): Christian 85.3%, of which Roman Catholic 41.9%, Anglican 35.9%, Pentecostal 4.6%, Seventh-day Adventist 1.5%; Muslim 12.1%; traditional beliefs 1.0%; nonreligious 0.9%; other 0.7%. **Major cities** (2002): Kampala (urban agglomeration) 1,208,544; Gulu 119,430; Lira 80,879; Jinja 71,213; Mbale 71,130. **Location:** eastern Africa, bordering The Sudan, Kenya, Tanzania, Rwanda, and the Democratic Republic of the Congo.

Vital statistics

Birth rate per 1,000 population (2006): 48.1 (world avg. 20.3). **Death rate** per 1,000 population (2006): 13.0 (world avg. 8.6). **Natural increase rate** per 1,000 population (2006): 35.1 (world avg. 11.7). **Total fertility rate** (avg. births per childbearing woman; 2006): 6.88. **Life expectancy** at birth (2006): male 50.2 years; female 51.9 years.

National economy

Budget (2006–07). *Revenue:* UGX 3,574,000,-000,000 (tax revenue 63.3%, of which VAT and sales tax 21.7%, petroleum taxes 10.1%, income tax 6.9%; grants 25.4%; nontax revenue 11.3%). *Expenditures:* UGX 4,031,900,000,000 (current expenditures 60.6%, of which public administration 14.7%, defense 9.3%; public order 4.6%; capital expenditures 39.4%). **Production** (metric tons except as noted). *Agriculture and fishing* (2007): plantains 9,231,000, cassava 4,456,000, sweet potatoes 2,602,000, sesame 168,000, pigeon peas 89,000, cowpeas 75,000; livestock (number of live animals) 8,275,020 goats, 7,182,293 cattle, 2,000,000 pigs; fisheries production (2006) 399,491 (from aquaculture 8%). *Mining and quarrying* (2006): cobalt 689; columbite-tantalite 275 kg. *Manufacturing* (2005): cement 692,709; sugar 182,906; soap 127,589. *Energy production (consumption):* electricity (kW-hr; 2005) 1,835,000,000 (1,670,000,000); petroleum products (metric tons; 2005) none (647,000). **Gross national income** (2007): US$10,469,000,000 (US$340 per capita). **Population economically active** (2002–03): total 9,773,000; activity rate of total population 37.7% (participation rates [2001]: ages 15–64, 78.9%; female 35.2%; officially unemployed 3.5%). **Public debt** (external, outstanding; 2006): US$1,107,000,000. **Selected balance of payments data.** Receipts from (US$'000,000): tourism (2006) 355; remittances (2007) 849; foreign direct investment (2004–06 avg.) 262; official development assistance (2006) 1,551. Disbursements for (US$'000,000): tourism (2006) 137; remittances (2007) 364.

Foreign trade

Imports (2006; c.i.f.): US$2,557,300,000 (refined petroleum products 20.2%; machinery and apparatus 17.2%; chemical products 13.2%; food products 9.1%, of which cereals 6.1%; motor vehicles 8.5%). *Major import sources:* Kenya 15.7%; UAE 12.7%; India 8.2%; Japan 6.8%; South Africa 6.1%. **Exports** (2006; f.o.b.): US$962,200,000 (food and beverages 49.2%, of which coffee 19.5%, fresh fish 14.4%, black tea 5.2%; gold 12.7%; telecommunications equipment 5.7%). *Major export destinations:* UAE 19.4%; The Sudan 9.5%; Kenya 9.1%; The Netherlands 6.4%; Switzerland 4.7%.

Transport and communications

Transport. *Railroads* (2005): route length 1,244 km; metric ton-km cargo 185,559,000. *Roads* (2003): total length 70,746 km (paved 23%). *Vehicles* (2005): passenger cars 65,472; trucks and buses 100,323. *Air transport:* passenger-km (2003) 237,000,000; metric ton-km cargo (2004) 27,000,000. **Communications,** in total units (units per 1,000 persons). Telephone landlines (2007): 162,000 (5.3); cellular telephone subscribers (2007): 4,195,000 (136); personal computers

(2005): 300,000 (10); total Internet users (2006): 750,000 (25); broadband Internet subscribers (2007): 1,900 (0.1).

Education and health

Educational attainment (2002). Percentage of population ages 25 and over having: no formal schooling 34.4%; incomplete primary education 36.0%; complete primary 11.1%; incomplete secondary 12.0%; complete secondary (some higher) 1.8%; complete higher (including vocational) 4.7%. **Literacy** (2007): percentage of total population ages 15 and over literate 73.2%; males literate 81.7%; females literate 64.8%. **Health** (2004): physicians 2,209 (1 per 11,947 persons); hospital beds 26,772 (1 per 986 persons); infant mortality rate per 1,000 live births (2006) 68.5; undernourished population (2002–04) 4,800,000 (19% of total population based on the consumption of a minimum daily requirement of 1,770 calories).

Military

Total active duty personnel (2007): 45,000 (army 100%). **Military expenditure as percentage of GDP** (2005): 2.3%; per capita expenditure US$7.

Background

By the 19th century the region around Uganda comprised several separate kingdoms inhabited by various peoples, including Bantu- and Nilotic-speaking tribes. Arab traders reached the area in the 1840s. The native kingdom of Buganda was visited by the first European explorers in 1862. Protestant and Roman Catholic missionaries arrived in the 1870s, and the development of religious factions led to persecution and civil strife. In 1894 Buganda was formally proclaimed a British protectorate. As Uganda, it gained its independence in 1962, and in 1967 it adopted a republican constitution. The civilian government was overthrown in 1971 and replaced by a military regime under Idi Amin. His invasion of Tanzania in late 1978 resulted in the collapse of his regime. In 1985 the civilian government was again deposed by the military, which in turn was overthrown in 1986. A constituent assembly enacted a new constitution in 1995.

Recent Developments

Any prospect of an end to the civil war in Uganda waged by the Lord's Resistance Army (LRA) —responsible for thousands of deaths and the displacement of an estimated two million Ugandans—appeared as elusive as ever. Discussions between representatives of the government and the LRA recommenced on 31 Jan 2008 in Juba, Sudan, but soon afterward an LRA spokesman said that its leader, Joseph Kony, would sign no final agreement until the charges of war crimes and crimes against humanity brought against him by the International Criminal Court had been withdrawn. LRA fighters were increasingly forced into the Central African Republic and the Democratic Republic of the Congo

(DRC), where in December 2008 they massacred an estimated 300 villagers. Forces from southern Sudan, the DRC, and Uganda launched combined attacks against the LRA, and despite failing to capture Kony, they captured Col. Thomas Kwoyelo, the LRA's field operations commander, in March 2009. Meanwhile, Uganda continued in 2009 to provide soldiers for the 4,300-strong African Union peacekeeping force in Somalia.

Internet resources: <www.ubos.org>.

Ukraine

Official name: Ukrayina (Ukraine). **Form of government:** unitary multiparty republic with a single legislative body (Parliament [450]). **Head of state:** President Viktor Yushchenko (from 2005). **Head of government:** Prime Minister Yuliya Tymoshenko (from 2007). **Capital:** Kiev (Kyiv). **Official language:** Ukrainian. **Official religion:** none. **Monetary unit:** 1 hryvnya (UAH) = 100 kopiykas; valuation (1 Jul 2009) US$1 = UAH 7.62.

Demography

Area: 233,062 sq mi, 603,628 sq km. **Population** (2008): 46,222,000. **Density** (2008): persons per sq mi 198.3, persons per sq km 76.6. **Urban** (2008): 68.3%. **Sex distribution** (2005): male 45.97%; female 54.03%. **Age breakdown** (2006): under 15, 14.3%; 15–29, 23.0%; 30–44, 21.1%; 45–59, 21.2%; 60–74, 14.1%; 75–84, 5.5%; 85 and over, 0.8%. **Ethnic composition** (2001): Ukrainian 77.8%; Russian 17.3%; Belarusian 0.6%; Moldovan 0.5%; Crimean Tatar 0.5%; other 3.3%. **Religious affiliation** (2004): Ukrainian Orthodox, of which "Kiev patriarchy" 19%, "no particular patriarchy" 16%, "Moscow patriarchy" 9%; Ukrainian Autocephalous Orthodox 2%; Ukrainian Catholic 6%; Protestant 2%; Latin Catholic 2%; Muslim 1%; Jewish 0.5%; nonreligious/atheist/other 42.5%. **Major cities** (2005): Kiev (Kyiv) 2,718,000; Kharkiv 1,461,000; Dnipropetrovsk 1,039,000; Odessa (Odesa) 1,001,000; Donetsk 999,975. **Location:**

---

1 metric ton = about 1.1 short tons; 1 kilometer = 0.6 mi (statute); 1 metric ton-km cargo = about 0.68 short ton-mi cargo; c.i.f.: cost, insurance, and freight; f.o.b.: free on board

eastern Europe, bordering Belarus, Russia, the Black Sea, Romania, Moldova, Hungary, Slovakia, and Poland.

Did you know? The Pripet Marshes, a 104,000-sq-mi (270,000-sq-km) waterlogged region in southern Belarus and northwestern Ukraine, is Europe's largest swamp.

Vital statistics

Birth rate per 1,000 population (2007): 10.2 (world avg. 20.3); within marriage 78.6%; outside of marriage 21.4%. **Death rate** per 1,000 population (2007): 16.4 (world avg. 8.6). **Total fertility rate** (avg. births per childbearing woman; 2006): 1.30. **Life expectancy** at birth (2006): male 62.4 years; female 74.1 years.

National economy

Budget (2007). *Revenue:* UAH 165,942,000,000 (tax revenue 70.3%, of which VAT 35.8%, corporate taxes 20.5%, excise tax 6.3%; nontax revenue 25.4%). *Expenditures:* UAH 174,236,000,000 (social security 16.8%; education and health 13.4%; transportation and communications 6.7%; energy and construction 4.7%; agriculture 4.6%). **Production** (metric tons except as noted). *Agriculture and fishing* (2007): potatoes 19,102,300, sugar beets 16,978,000, wheat 13,800,000, sunflower seeds 4,173,700, sour cherries 126,000; livestock (number of live animals) 8,055,000 pigs, 6,175,400 cattle, 145,600,000 chickens; fisheries production (2006) 242,764 (from aquaculture 2%). *Mining and quarrying* (2005): iron ore (2007) 77,952,000; manganese (metal content) 770,000; ilmenite concentrate 370,000. *Manufacturing* (value of sales in UAH '000,000,000; 2007): base and fabricated metals 157.5; food, beverages, and tobacco products 110.0; coke and refined petroleum products 52.5. *Energy production (consumption):* electricity (kW-hr; 2007) 195,230,000,000 ([2005] 177,702,-000,000); coal (metric tons; 2007) 58,742,000 ([2005] 64,013,000); crude petroleum (barrels; 2007) 31,700,000 ([2005] 132,600,000); petroleum products (metric tons; 2005) 17,558,000 (11,957,000); natural gas (cu m; 2007) 20,200,-000,000 ([2005] 80,428,000,000). **Population economically active** (2005): total 22,280,800; activity rate of total population 47% (participation rates [2003]: ages 15–64, 65.8%; female 48.9%; unemployed [2007] 6.9%). **Gross national income** (2007): US$118,445,000,000 (US$2,550 per capita). **Public debt** (external; April 2008): US$15,100,000,000. **Selected balance of payments data.** Receipts from (US$'000,000): tourism (2006) 3,485; remittances (2007) 1,170; foreign direct investment (2004–06 avg.) 4,909; official development assistance (2006) 484. Disbursements for (US$'000,000): tourism (2006) 2,834; remittances (2007) 42.

Foreign trade

Imports (2006; c.i.f.): US$45,022,000,000 (machinery and apparatus 17.7%; crude petroleum 15.2%;

chemical products 12.1%; natural gas 10.6%; motor vehicles and parts 10.5%). *Major import sources:* Russia 30.6%; Germany 9.5%; Turkmenistan 7.8%; China 5.1%; Poland 4.7%. **Exports** (2006; f.o.b.): US$38,368,000,000 (iron and steel 38.5%, of which ingots 11.4%; machinery and apparatus 8.8%; crude petroleum 5.0%; cereals 3.9%; metal ore and scrap 3.9%). *Major export destinations:* Russia 22.5%; Italy 6.5%; Turkey 6.2%; Poland 3.5%; Germany 3.3%.

Transport and communications

Transport. *Railroads* (2007): length 21,852 km; passenger-km 52,400,000,000; metric ton-km cargo 223,400,000,000. *Roads* (2007): total length 169,422 km (paved 98%). *Vehicles:* passenger cars (2005) 5,538,972; trucks and buses 490,495. *Air transport* (2006): passenger-km 4,393,000,000; metric ton-km cargo 40,692,000,000. **Communications**, in total units (units per 1,000 persons). Telephone landlines (2007): 12,859,000 (277); cellular telephone subscribers (2007): 55,240,000 (1,188); total Internet users (2007): 10,000,000 (215); broadband Internet subscribers (2007): 800,000 (17).

Education and health

Educational attainment (2001). Percentage of population ages 25 and over having: no formal schooling 0.7%; incomplete primary education 2.8%; complete primary/incomplete secondary 22.7%; complete secondary 35.9%; incomplete higher 21.7%; complete higher 16.2%. **Literacy** (2004): percentage of total population literate, virtually 100%. **Health** (2006): physicians 225,000 (1 per 208 persons); hospital beds 444,000 (1 per 105 persons); infant mortality rate per 1,000 live births (2007) 11.0; undernourished population (2002–04) less than 2.5% of total population.

Military

Total active duty personnel (2007): 129,925 (army 54.5%, air force/air defense 34.8%, navy 10.7%); Russian naval forces at Sevastopol (2007) 13,000. **Military expenditure as percentage of GDP** (2005): 2.4%; per capita expenditure US$42.

Background

The area around Ukraine was invaded and occupied in the 1st millennium BC by the Cimmerians, Scythians, and Sarmatians and in the 1st millennium AD by the Goths, Huns, Bulgars, Avars, Khazars, and Magyars. Slavic tribes settled there after the 4th century. Kiev was the chief town of Kievan Rus. The Mongol conquest in the mid-13th century decisively ended Kievan power. Ruled by Lithuania in the 14th century and Poland in the 16th century, it fell to Russian rule in the 18th century. The Ukrainian National Republic, established in 1917, declared its independence from Soviet Russia in 1918 but was reconquered in 1919; it was made the Ukrainian Soviet Socialist Republic of the USSR in 1922. The northwestern region was held by Poland from 1919 to 1939. Ukraine suffered a severe famine in 1932–33 under Soviet leader Joseph Stalin; over five million Ukrainians died of starvation. Overrun by Axis armies in 1941 in World War II, it was further devastated before being retaken by the Soviets in 1944. It was the site of the 1986 accident in Chernobyl, at a Soviet-built nuclear power plant. Ukraine declared independence in 1991. The turmoil it experienced in the 1990s as it attempted to implement economic and political reforms culminated in the disputed presidential election of 2004; mass protests over the results came to be known as the Orange Revolution.

Recent Developments

There was a divided response in Ukraine to the war that broke out between Georgia and Russia in August 2008. Whereas Pres. Viktor Yushchenko condemned Russia's presence in Georgia and reportedly authorized military aid to Georgia, Prime Minister Yuliya Tymoshenko took a neutral position and met with Russian Pres. Dmitry Medvedev in Moscow in October. At the NATO summit in Bucharest, Romania, in April, membership for Ukraine was supported by US Pres. George W. Bush but rejected by Germany, France, and the UK. Moreover, Russia warned that Ukrainian entry into NATO would seriously strain relations, already tense, between the two countries. The Russian natural-gas monopoly Gazprom demanded that Ukraine repay debts totaling US$2 billion for gas imports, and after talks between the countries failed, Russia cut off gas supplies to Ukraine in January 2009. The worldwide financial crisis had a devastating impact on Ukraine. In November 2008 the economy shrank by more than 14%, and the metallurgical industry, which had accounted for almost 30% of GDP, suffered a 50% drop in production. Unemployment rose to almost 7% and inflation reached 22%. Much of the initial tranche of a US$16.5 billion loan from the International Monetary Fund (IMF) was used to stabilize the national currency. In April 2009 the IMF predicted that Ukraine's economy would contract by 8% in 2009.

Internet resources: <www.ukrstat.gov.ua>.

United Arab Emirates

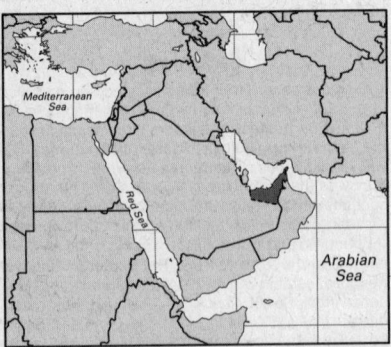

Official name: Al-Imarat al-ʻArabiyah al-Muttahidah (United Arab Emirates). **Form of government:** federation of seven emirates with one advisory body (Federal National Council [40]). **Chief of state:** President Sheikh Khalifah ibn Zayid al-Nahyan (from 2004). **Head of government:** Prime Minister Sheikh Muhammad ibn Rashid al-Maktum (from 2006). **Capital:** Abu Dhabi. **Official language:** Arabic. **Official religion:** Islam. **Monetary unit:** 1 UAE dirham (AED) = 100 fils; valuation (1 Jul 2009) US$1 = AED 3.67.

Demography

Area: 32,280 sq mi, 83,600 sq km. **Population** (2008): 4,660,000. **Density** (2008): persons per sq mi 144.4, persons per sq km 55.7. **Urban** (2006): 82.5%. **Sex distribution** (2007): male 68.65%; female 31.35%. **Age breakdown** (2007): under 15, 20.6%; 15–29, 29.2%; 30–44, 37.0%; 45–59, 11.4%; 60–74, 1.6%; 75 and over, 0.2%. **Ethnic composition** (2000): Arab 48.1%, of which UAE Arab 12.2%, UAE Bedouin 9.4%, Egyptian Arab 6.2%, Omani Arab 4.1%, Saudi Arab 4.0%; South Asian 35.7%, of which Pashtun 7.1%, Balochi 7.1%, Malayali 7.1%; Persian 5.0%; Filipino 3.4%; white 2.4%; other 5.4%. **Religious affiliation** (2005): Muslim 62% (mostly Sunni); Hindu 21%; Christian 9%; Buddhist 4%; other 4%. **Major cities** (2007): Dubai 1,225,137; Abu Dhabi 633,136; Sharjah 584,286; Al-ʻAyn 444,331; ʻAjman 250,808. **Location:** the Middle East, bordering the Persian Gulf, the Gulf of Oman, Oman, and Saudi Arabia.

Vital statistics

Birth rate per 1,000 population (2007): 16.1 (world avg. 20.3). **Death rate** per 1,000 population (2007): 2.2 (world avg. 8.6). **Natural increase rate** per 1,000 population (2007): 13.9 (world avg. 11.7). **Total fertility rate** (avg. births per childbearing woman; 2007): 2.43. **Life expectancy** at birth (2007): male 73.2 years; female 78.3 years.

National economy

Budget (2007). *Revenue:* AED 228,750,000,000 (royalties on hydrocarbons 77.1%; tax revenue 6.0%). *Expenditures:* AED 159,726,000,000 (current expenditures 76.0%; loans, net equity, and foreign grants 13.2%; development expenditures 10.8%). **Gross national income** (2007): US$204,556,000,000 (US$46,030 per capita). **Public debt** (2005): US$20,000,000,000. **Production** (metric tons except as noted). *Agriculture and fishing* (2007): dates 755,000, tomatoes 215,000, eggplants 22,000; livestock (number of live animals) 1,570,000 goats, 615,000 sheep, 260,000 camels; fisheries production (2006) 87,570 (from aquaculture 1%). *Mining and quarrying* (2006): gypsum 130,000; lime 60,000. *Manufacturing* (value added in AED '000,000; 2002): chemical products (including refined petroleum products) 18,467; textiles and wearing apparel 4,281; fabricated metal products and machinery 3,695. *Energy production (consumption):* electricity (kW-hr; 2007) 76,532,000,000 (74,717,000,000); crude petro-

1 metric ton = about 1.1 short tons;   1 kilometer = 0.6 mi (statute);   1 metric ton-km cargo = about 0.68 short ton-mi cargo;   c.i.f.: cost, insurance, and freight;   f.o.b.: free on board

leum (barrels; 2007–08) 852,511,000 ([2005] 153,000,000); petroleum products (metric tons; 2005) 20,931,000 (10,051,000); natural gas (cu 222222 **Population economically active** (2005): total 2,559,668; activity rate of total population 54.6% (participation rates: ages 15–64, 78.1%; female 13.5%; unemployed 3.1%). **Selected balance of payments data.** Receipts from (US$'000,000): tourism (2006) 4,972; foreign direct investment (FDI) (2006 est.) 9,763. Disbursements for (US$'000,000): tourism (2006) 8,827; FDI (2006 est.) 2,758.

Foreign trade

Imports (2006): AED 316,280,000,000 (emirate imports 78.7%; free zone imports 21.3%). *Major import sources:* US 11.4%; China 11.0%; India 9.8%; Germany 6.2%; Japan 5.8%. **Exports** (2006): AED 523,350,000,000 (crude petroleum 40.8%; reexports 32.3%; free zone exports 14.4%; natural gas 5.0%; nonpetroleum emirate-produced exports 4.1%; refined petroleum products 3.4%). *Major export destinations:* Japan 25.9%; South Korea 10.3%; Thailand 5.9%; India 4.5%; Iran 3.6%.

Transport and communications

Transport. *Railroads:* none. *Roads* (2008): total length, n.a. (paved roads only, 4,080 km). *Vehicles* (2007): passenger cars 1,279,098; trucks and buses 48,205. *Air transport* (2007): passenger-km 90,530,000,000; metric ton-km cargo 5,497,149,-000. **Communications,** in total units (units per 1,000 persons). Telephone landlines (2007): 1,386,000 (316); cellular telephone subscribers (2007): 7,732,000 (1,765); personal computers (2005): 850,000 (208); total Internet users (2007): 2,260,000 (516); broadband Internet subscribers (2007): 380,000 (87).

Education and health

Educational attainment (2005). Percentage of population ages 10 and over having: no formal schooling 23.3% (illiterate/unknown 9.4%, literate 13.9%); primary education 14.6%; incomplete/complete secondary 43.7%; postsecondary 4.0%; undergraduate 12.8%; graduate 1.6%. **Literacy** (2007): percentage of total population ages 10 and over literate 90.4%; males literate 90.9%; females literate 89.2%. **Health** (2005): physicians 7,289 (1 per 643 persons); hospital beds 7,891 (1 per 594 persons); infant mortality rate per 1,000 live births (2007) 13.5; undernourished population (2002–04) less than 2.5% of total population.

Military

Total active duty personnel (2007): 51,000 (army 86.3%, navy 4.9%, air force 8.8%). **Military expenditure as percentage of GDP** (2005): 2.0%; per capita expenditure US$546.

Background

The Persian Gulf was the location of important trading centers as early as Sumerian times. Its people converted to Islam in Muhammad's lifetime. The Portuguese entered the region in the early 16th century, and the British East India Company arrived about 100 years later. In 1820 the British exacted a peace treaty with local rulers along the coast of the eastern Arabian Peninsula. The area formerly called the Pirate Coast became known as the Trucial Coast. In 1892 the rulers agreed to restrict foreign relations to Britain. Though the British administered the region from 1853, they never assumed sovereignty; each state maintained full internal control. The states formed the Trucial States Council in 1960. In 1971 the sheikhs terminated defense treaties with Britain and established the six-member federation. Ras al-Khaymah joined it in 1972. The United Arab Emirates (UAE) aided coalition forces against Iraq in the Persian Gulf War (1990–91).

Recent Developments

The UAE's economic growth, based largely on oil and tourism revenue, slowed to an estimated 6.6% in 2008. The stock market declined, but panic was averted by an injection of US$6.8 billion into local banks. Economic turmoil notwithstanding, a US$7 billion loan to Iraq was forgiven in its entirety in an effort to build international confidence in the Iraqi government, and the Emirati envoy to the UN pledged an "unlimited financial contribution" to ease the suffering of the Palestinians.

Internet resources: <www.economy.ae>.

United Kingdom

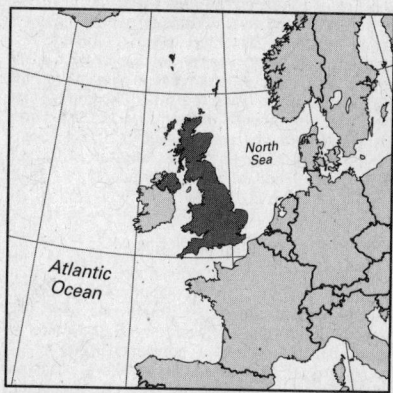

Official name: United Kingdom of Great Britain and Northern Ireland. **Form of government:** constitutional monarchy with two legislative houses (House of Lords [732]; House of Commons [646]). **Chief of state:** British Queen Elizabeth II (from 1952). **Head of government:** Prime Minister Gordon Brown (from 2007). **Capital:** London. **Official languages:** English (also Scots Gaelic in Scotland and Welsh in Wales). **Official religion:** Churches of England and Scotland "established" (protected by the state but not "official") in their respective countries; no established church in Northern Ireland or Wales. **Monetary unit:** 1 pound sterling (£) = 100 new pence; valuation (1 Jul 2009) US$1 = £0.61.

Demography

Area: 93,851 sq mi, 243,073 sq km (England 50,302 sq mi, 130,281 sq km; Wales 8,005 sq mi, 20,732 sq km; Scotland 30,087 sq mi, 77,925 sq km; Northern Ireland 5,457 sq mi, 14,135 sq km). **Population** (2008): 61,446,000. **Density** (2008): persons per sq mi 654.7, persons per sq km 252.8. **Urban** (2005): 89.7% **Age breakdown** (2006): under 15, 17.7%; 15–29, 19.3%; 30–44, 22.3%; 45–59, 19.4%; 60–74, 13.6%; 75–84, 5.6%; 85 and over, 2.1%. **Ethnic composition** (2005): white 87.8%, of which British 83.4%; Asian 4.9%, of which Indian 1.8%, Pakistani 1.4%, Bangladeshi 0.6%, *Chinese 0.4%; black 2.2%, of which from Africa 1.1%, from the Caribbean 1.0%; mixed race 1.0%; other 1.2%; unknown 2.9%. **Religious affiliation** (2001): Christian 71.8%, of which Anglican-identified 29%, other Protestant-identified (significantly Presbyterian) 14%, Roman Catholic-identified 10%; Muslim 2.8%; Hindu 1.0%; Sikh 0.6%; Jewish 0.5%; nonreligious 15.0%; other 0.5%; unknown 7.8%. **Sex distribution** (2006): male 49.01%; female 50.99%. **Major cities (urban agglomerations)** (2006 [2007]): London 7,512,000 (8,567,000); Birmingham 1,007,000 (2,285,000); Manchester 452,000 (2,230,000); Leeds 750,000 (1,529,000); Glasgow 581,000 (1,160,000); Newcastle 271,000 (882,000); Liverpool 436,000 (811,000); Sheffield 526,000; Bradford 493,000; Edinburgh 464,000; Bristol 411,000; Wakefield 321,000; Cardiff 318,000; Coventry 307,000; Sunderland 291,000; Doncaster 290,000; Leicester 290,000; Nottingham 286,000; Belfast 267,000. **Location:** western Europe, bordering the North Sea, the English Channel, the Celtic Sea, the Irish Sea, and Ireland. **Mobility** (2001). Population living in the same residence as 2000, 88.6%; different residence, same country/region (of the UK) 8.6%; different residence, different country/region (of the UK) 2.1%; from outside the UK 0.7%. **Immigration** (2004): permanent residents 518,000; from Bangladesh, India, and Sri Lanka 10.6%, South Africa 5.6%, Australia 5.0%, Pakistan 4.1%, US 2.7%, New Zealand 1.5%, Canada 1.0%, other 69.5% (of which EU 20.8%).

Vital statistics

Birth rate per 1,000 population (2007): 12.6 (world avg. 20.3); (2006) within marriage 56.3%; outside of marriage 43.7%. **Death rate** per 1,000 population (2007): 9.4 (world avg. 8.6). **Natural increase rate** per 1,000 population (2007): 3.2 (world avg. 11.7). **Total fertility rate** (avg. births per childbearing woman; 2006): 1.85. **Life expectancy** at birth (2007): male 77.6 years; female 81.7 years.

Social indicators

Educational attainment (2003). Percentage of population ages 25–64 having: up to lower secondary education only 16%; upper secondary 56%; higher 28%, of which at least some university 19%. **Quality of working life.** Average full-time workweek (hours; 2006): male 38.9; female 34.0. Annual rate per 100,000 workers for (2006–07): injury or accident 1,113; death 1.0. Proportion of labor force (employed persons) insured for damages or income loss resulting from (2004): injury 100%; permanent disability 100%; death 100%. Average days lost to labor stoppages per 1,000 employee workdays (2007) 38. **Social participation.** Population ages 16 and over participating in voluntary work (Great Britain [England, Scotland, and Wales] only; 2001) 39%. Trade union membership in total workforce (2004) 25%. Percentage of population attending weekly church services (2001) 8%. **Social deviance** (England and Wales only; 2005–06). Offense rate per 100,000 population for: theft and handling stolen goods 3,342; criminal damage 1,961; violence against a person 1,754; burglary 1,068; fraud and forgery 386; drug offenses 295; robbery 163; sex offenses 103. **Material well-being** (2005–06). Households possessing: automobile 74%, of which two cars 23%, three cars 5%; refrigerator/freezer 97%; washing machine 95%; central heating 94%; digital, cable, or satellite television receiver 65%; Internet connection 55%; dishwasher 35%.

National economy

Budget (2005–06). *Revenue:* £485,400,000,000 (income tax 26.9%; production and import taxes 24.9%; social security contributions 17.6%). *Expenditures:* £500,700,000,000 (social protection 34.2%; health 17.7%; education 13.9%; defense 6.1%; public order 6.0%). **Public debt** (December 2007): US$1,068,000,000,000. **Gross national income** (2007): US$2,608,513,000,000 (US$42,740 per capita). **Production** (metric tons except as noted). *Agriculture and fishing* (2007): wheat 13,362,000, sugar beets 6,500,000, potatoes 5,635,000, barley 5,149,000, rapeseed 2,108,-000, carrots 859,300, mushrooms and truffles 72,000; livestock (number of live animals) 33,582,000 sheep, 9,987,570 cattle, 157,265,-000 chickens; fisheries production (2006) 795,671 (from aquaculture 22%). *Mining and quarrying* (2006): sand and gravel 95,000,000; rock salt 2,000,000; china clay (kaolin) 1,900,000; slate 900,000; potash 700,000. *Manufacturing* (value added in US$'000,000; 2006): chemical products 42,400; food and beverages 39,100; nonelectrical machinery and apparatus 26,000; printing and publishing 24,800; fabricated metal products 23,900; motor vehicles and parts 19,400; rubber and plastic products 13,300; bricks, cement, and ceramics 11,800; telecommunications equipment 11,800. *Energy production (consumption):* electricity (kW-hr; 2007) 356,954,000,000 ([2005] 408,845,000,000); coal (metric tons; 2007) 17,031,000 ([2005] 61,800,000); crude petroleum (barrels; 2007) 580,000,000 ([2005] 607,000,-000); petroleum products (metric tons; 2005) 81,644,000 (68,397,000); natural gas (cu m; 2006) 80,000,000,000 ([2005] 111,948,000,000). **Population economically active** (2006): total 30,613,000; activity rate of total population 50.6% (participation rates: ages 16 and over, 60.1%; female 45.9%; unemployed [2007] 5.4%). **Selected balance of payments data.** Receipts from (US$'000,000): tourism (2006) 33,888; remittances (2007) 8,124; foreign direct investment

---

1 metric ton = about 1.1 short tons;　1 kilometer = 0.6 mi (statute);　1 metric ton-km cargo = about 0.68 short ton-mi cargo;　c.i.f.: cost, insurance, and freight;　f.o.b.: free on board

(FDI) (2004–06 avg.) 129,733. Disbursements for (US$'000,000): tourism (2006) 63,319; remittances (2007) 4,850; FDI (2004–06 avg.) 84,728.

Foreign trade

Imports (2006; c.i.f.): US$606,428,000,000 (machinery and apparatus 23.6%, of which industrial and power-generating machinery 7.0%, telecommunications equipment and televisions 6.9%, computers and office machinery 4.8%; motor vehicles and parts 10.2%; chemical products 9.6%; mineral fuels 8.9%, of which crude petroleum 7.3%; food products 6.2%; base and fabricated metals 5.3%; wearing apparel and accessories 3.7%). *Major import sources:* Germany 12.1%; unspecified Europe 8.7%; US 8.0%; France 6.6%; The Netherlands 6.2%; China 6.1%; Norway 4.4%; Belgium 4.3%; Italy 3.8%; Spain 3.2%. **Exports** (2006; f.o.b.): US$444,439,000,000 (machinery and apparatus 34.7%, of which telecommunications equipment 11.5%, industrial machinery 6.3%, power-generating machinery 5.7%, electrical machinery and electronics 4.8%, office machinery and computers 4.7%; chemical products 14.4%, of which medicine and pharmaceuticals 5.7%; mineral fuels 9.7%, of which crude petroleum 8.7%; motor vehicles and parts 8.0%; base and fabricated metals 6.0%; food products 2.8%; whiskey 1.0%). *Major export destinations:* US 13.2%; France 11.9%; Germany 11.1%; Ireland 7.1%; The Netherlands 6.8%; Belgium 5.4%; Spain 5.1%; Italy 3.9%; Sweden 2.1%; Switzerland 1.8%.

Transport and communications

Transport. *Railroads* (2005–06): length (2005) 17,156 km; passenger-km (Great Britain only) 43,211,000,000; metric ton-km cargo (Great Britain only) 22,000,000,000. *Roads* (Great Britain only; 2005): total length 388,008 km (paved 100%). *Vehicles* (2004): passenger cars 27,765,100; trucks and buses 3,522,424. *Air transport* (2006): passenger-km 231,515,000,000; metric ton-km cargo 6,215,000,000. **Communications,** in total units (units per 1,000 persons). Telephone landlines (2007): 33,682,000 (552); cellular telephone subscribers (2007): 71,993,000 (1,179); personal computers (2005): 45,659,000 (765); total Internet users (2007): 40,200,000 (658); broadband Internet subscribers (2007): 15,529,000 (254).

Education and health

Literacy (2006): percentage of total population literate, about 99%. **Health** (2007): physicians (England and Scotland only) 143,220 (1 per 393 persons [England and Scotland only]); hospital beds (2005) 226,300 (1 per 266 persons); infant mortality rate per 1,000 live births (2008) 4.7; undernourished population (2002–04) less than 2.5% of total population.

Military

Total active duty personnel (2008): 160,280 (army 59.7%, navy 19.3%, air force 21.0%); UK troops deployed abroad (2008) 41,700; US troops in the UK (2008) 9,600. **Military expenditure as percentage of GDP** (2008): 2.3%; per capita expenditure US$972.

Background

The early pre-Roman inhabitants of Britain were Celtic-speaking peoples, including the Brythonic people of Wales, the Picts of Scotland, and the Britons of Britain. Celts also settled in Ireland c. 500 BC. Julius Caesar invaded and took control of the area in 55–54 BC. The Roman province of Britannia endured until the 5th century AD and included present-day England and Wales. Germanic tribes, including Angles, Saxons, and Jutes, invaded Britain in the 5th century. The invasions had little effect on the Celtic peoples of Wales and Scotland. Christianity began to flourish in the 6th century. During the 8th–9th centuries, Vikings, particularly Danes, raided the coasts of Britain. In the late 9th century Alfred the Great repelled a Danish invasion, which helped bring about the unification of England under Athelstan. The Scots attained dominance in Scotland, which was finally unified under Malcolm II (1005–34).

William of Normandy took England in 1066. The Norman kings established a strong central government and feudal state. The French language of the Norman rulers eventually merged with the Anglo-Saxon of the common people to form the English language. From the 11th century, Scotland came under the influence of the English throne. Henry II conquered Ireland in the late 12th century. His sons Richard I and John had conflicts with the clergy and nobles, and eventually John was forced to grant the nobles concessions in the Magna Carta (1215). The concept of community of the realm developed during the 13th century, providing the foundation for parliamentary government. During the reign of Edward I, statute law developed to supplement English common law, and the first Parliament was convened. In 1314 Robert the Bruce won independence for Scotland.

The Tudors became the ruling family of England following the Wars of the Roses (1455–85). Henry VIII established the Church of England and made Wales part of his realm. The reign of Elizabeth I began a period of colonial expansion; 1588 brought the defeat of the Spanish Armada. In 1603 James VI of Scotland ascended to the English throne, becoming James I, and established a personal union of the two kingdoms.

The English Civil Wars erupted in 1642 between Royalists and Parliamentarians, ending in the execution of Charles I (1649). After 11 years of Puritan rule under Oliver Cromwell and his son (1649–60), the monarchy was restored with Charles II. In 1707 England and Scotland assented to the Act of Union, forming the kingdom of Great Britain. The Hanoverians ascended to the English throne in 1714, when George Louis, elector of Hanover, became George I of Great Britain. During the reign of George III, Great Britain's American colonies won independence (1783). This was followed by a period of war with revolutionary France and later with the empire of Napoleon (1789–1815). In 1801 legislation united Great Britain with Ireland to create the United Kingdom of Great Britain and Ireland. Britain was the birthplace of the Industrial Revolution in the late 18th century, and it remained the world's foremost economic power until the late 19th century. During the reign of Queen Victoria, Britain's colonial expansion reached its zenith, though the older dominions, including Canada and Australia, were granted independence (1867 and 1901, respectively).

The UK entered World War I allied with France and Russia in 1914. Following the war, revolutionary disorder erupted in Ireland, and in 1921 the Irish Free State was granted dominion status. The six counties of Ulster, however, remained in the UK as Northern Ireland. The UK entered World War II in 1939. Following the war the Irish Free State became the Irish Republic and left the Commonwealth. India gained independence from the UK in 1947. Throughout the postwar period and into the 1970s, the UK continued to grant independence to its overseas colonies and dependencies. With UN forces, it participated in the Korean War (1950–53). In 1956 it intervened militarily in Egypt during the Suez Crisis. It joined the European Economic Community, a forerunner of the European Union, in 1973. In 1982 it defeated Argentina in the Falkland Islands War. As a result of continuing social strife in Northern Ireland, it joined with Ireland in several peace initiatives, which eventually resulted in an agreement to establish an assembly in Northern Ireland. In 1997 referenda approved in Scotland and Wales devolved power to both countries, though both remained part of the UK. In 1991 the UK joined an international coalition to reverse Iraq's conquest of Kuwait. In 2003 the UK and the US attacked Iraq and overthrew the government of Saddam Hussein. Terrorist bombings in London on 7 Jul 2005 killed more than 50 people.

Recent Developments

The United Kingdom's economy suffered from the global financial crisis in 2008. The GDP, which had grown in each quarter for 16 years, began to contract in the second half of the year. Unemployment reached 6.0%, house prices fell by almost 20% from their 2007 peak, and the main index of share prices was down 31%. A number of well-known companies went out of business, most notably Woolworths, whose 800 general stores had for decades formed the heart of many high streets. As house prices fell and worries about bad debts grew, it became almost impossible to borrow the full price of a home; demands for down payments of 20% or more became common. Even more serious, banks almost completely stopped lending to each other; the wholesale market in loans virtually dried up. In October Prime Minister Gordon Brown announced that the government would buy preference shares in Britain's banks worth up to £50 billion (about US$87 billion) and would provide £200 billion (about US$350 billion) in short-term loans to revive interbank lending and £250 billion (about US$438 billion) to guarantee bank debts. A second plan, worth a further £200 billion (about US$300 billion) was unveiled in early 2009.

The mission of all but about 300 British troops based in southern Iraq to train and advise Iraq's police and armed forces came to an official close in a ceremony handing over Basra to American forces in March 2009. Since the invasion in 2003, 179 British soldiers had died in Iraq, including those killed in accidents and by "friendly fire." The UK also retained some 8,000 troops in Afghanistan, mainly in Helmand province and the capital. By June 2009 the number of fatalities among British troops in Afghanistan since 2001 had reached 166.

In June 2008 Ian Paisley stepped down as Northern Ireland's first minister and leader of the Democratic Unionist Party (since its founding in 1971). In September the International Monitoring Council declared that the Army Council of the Provisional Irish Republican Army (IRA) was "no longer operational." The council had directed the IRA's terrorist campaign against British rule for three decades until the Good Friday Agreement in 1998. In March 2009, however, two British soldiers were shot dead in an attack in Northern Ireland committed by a splinter group, the Real IRA. They were the first British soldiers killed in Northern Ireland in 12 years.

Internet resources: <www.visitbritain.com>.

United States

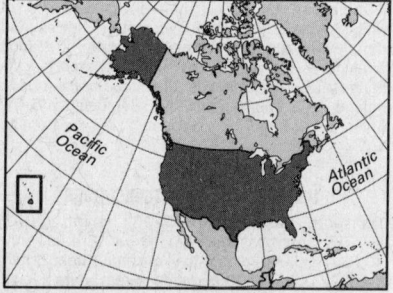

Official name: United States of America. Form of government: federal republic with two legislative houses (Senate [100]; House of Representatives [435, excluding 5 nonvoting delegates from the District of Columbia, the US Virgin Islands, American Samoa, the Northern Mariana Islands, and Guam and a nonvoting resident commissioner from Puerto Rico]). Head of state and government: President Barack Obama (from 2009). Capital: Washington DC. Official language: none. Official religion: none. Monetary unit: 1 US dollar (US$) = 100 cents.

Demography

Area: 3,676,486 sq mi, 9,522,055 sq km; inland water area equals 78,797 sq mi (204,083 sq km), and Great Lakes water area equals 60,251 sq mi (156,049 sq km). Population (2008): 305,146,000. Density (2008): persons per sq mi 86.3, persons per sq km 33.3. Urban (2005): 80.8%. Sex distribution (2005): male 49.26%; female 50.74%. Age breakdown (2005): under 15, 20.5%; 15–29, 20.9%; 30–44, 21.6%; 45–59, 20.2%; 60–74, 10.7%; 75–84, 4.4%; 85 and over, 1.7%. Population by race and Hispanic origin (2006): non-Hispanic white 66.4%; Hispanic 14.8%; non-Hispanic black 12.8%; Asian and Pacific Islander 4.6%; American Indian and Eskimo 1.0%; other 0.4%. **Religious affiliation** (2005): Christian 83.3%, of which independent Christian 23.2%, Roman Catholic 19.6%, Protestant (including Anglican) 18.9%, unaffiliated Christian 16.5%, Orthodox 1.8%, other Christian (primarily Mormon and Jehovah's Witness) 3.3%; Jewish 1.9%; Muslim 1.6%; Buddhist 0.9%; New Religionists 0.5%; Hindu 0.4%; traditional beliefs 0.4%; Baha'i 0.3%; Sikh 0.1%; nonreligious 9.8%; atheist 0.5%; other 0.3%. **Mobility** (2005). Reported gross percentage of population living in the same residence as in 2004: 86%; different residence, same county 8%; different county, same state 3%; different state 3%; moved from abroad 1%. **Place of birth** (2005): native-born 255,999,000 (87.9%); foreign-born 35,157,000 (12.1%), of which (2004) Mexico 10,011,000, the Philippines 1,222,000, China and Hong Kong 1,067,000, India 1,007,000, Cuba 952,000, Vietnam 863,000, El Salvador 765,000, South Korea 701,000. **Location:** North America, bordering Canada, the North Atlantic Ocean, the Gulf of Mexico, Mexico, and the North Pacific Ocean; the outlying state of Alaska nearly touches eastern Russia and borders the Arctic Ocean, Canada, and the North Pacific Ocean; Hawaii is an island group in the North Pacific Ocean. **Immigration** (2006–07): permanent immigrants admitted 1,052,415; from Mexico 14.1%, China 7.3%, Philippines 6.9%, India 6.2%, Vietnam 2.7%, Dominican Republic 2.7%, South Korea 2.1%, El Salvador 2.0%, Jamaica 1.8%, Guatemala 1.7%, Peru 1.7%, Canada 1.5%, UK 1.4%, other 39.0%. Refugees (2005) 380,000. Asylum seekers (end of 2000) 386,330.

Vital statistics

Birth rate per 1,000 population (2007): 14.3 (world avg. 20.3); (2006) within marriage 64.2%; outside of marriage 35.8%. **Death rate** per 1,000 population (2007): 8.0 (world avg. 8.6). **Natural increase rate** per 1,000 population (2007): 6.3 (world avg. 11.7). **Total fertility rate** (avg. births per childbearing woman; 2007): 2.09. **Life expectancy** at birth (2004): male 75.2 years, of which white male 75.7 years, black male 69.8 years; female 80.4 years, of which white female 80.8 years, black female 76.5 years.

Social indicators

Educational attainment (2006). Percentage of population ages 25 and over having: unknown/primary and incomplete secondary education 14.6%; secondary 31.7%; some postsecondary 25.7%; 4-year higher degree 18.3%; advanced degree 9.7%. Number of earned degrees (2005): associate's degree 697,000; bachelor's degree 1,439,000; master's degree 575,000; doctoral degree 53,000; first-professional degrees (in fields such as medicine, theology, and law) 87,000. **Quality of working life** (2005). Average workweek (2007) 41.3 hours. Annual death rate per 100,000 workers (2006): 3.9; leading causes of occupational deaths: transportation incidents 42%, falls 14%, assaults/violent acts 13%, struck by object 10%. Annual occupational injury rate per 100,000 workers 4.6. Average duration of journey to work (2006) 25.0 minutes (private automobile 86.7%, of which drive alone 76.0%, carpool 10.7%; take public transportation 4.8%; walk

2.5%; work at home 4.0%; other 2.0%). Rate per 1,000 employed workers of discouraged workers (unemployed no longer seeking work) 3.1. **Access to services** (2005). Proportion of occupied dwellings having access to: electricity 100%; safe public water supply 100%; public sewage collection 79.8%; septic tanks 20.2%. **Social participation** (2006). Population ages 16 and over volunteering for an organization 26.7%; median annual hours 52. Trade union membership in total workforce 12.0%. **Social deviance** (2007). Offense rate per 100,000 population for: murder 5.6; rape 30.0; robbery 147.6; aggravated assault 283.8; motor-vehicle theft 363.3; burglary and housebreaking 722.5; larceny-theft 2,177.8; drug-abuse violation (2005) 560.1; drunkenness (2003) 149.1. Estimated drug and substance users (current users in population ages 12 and over; 2005): cigarettes 24.9%; binge alcohol (drinking 5 or more drinks on the same occasion on at least one day in the past 30 days per survey population) 22.7%; marijuana and hashish 6.0%. Rate per 100,000 population of suicide (2005) 10.7. **Leisure** (2006). Favorite leisure activities (percentage of total population ages 18 and over that undertook activity at least once in the previous year): dining out 48.6%; entertaining friends or relatives at home 40.2%; reading books 38.7%; barbecuing 33.9%; going to the beach 22.9%. **Material well-being** (2005). Occupied dwellings with householder possessing: automobiles, trucks, or vans 91.5%, 1 car with or without trucks or vans 47.5%, 2 cars 23.9%, only trucks and vans 12.7%, no cars, trucks, or vans 8.5%, 3 or more cars 7.4%; telephone 97.1%; television receiver 98.2%; video 90.2%; washing machine 82.0%; clothes dryer 79.1%; air conditioner 89.5%; cable television 67.5%; personal computer (2003) 61.8%; Internet connection (2003) 54.6%; broadband Internet (2003) 19.9%. **Recreational expenditures** (2003): US$660,700,000,000 (television and radio receivers, computers, and video equipment 18.4%; golfing, bowling, and other participatory activities 13.5%; sports supplies 10.3%; nondurable toys and sports equipment 9.1%; books and maps 5.8%).

National economy

Budget (2007). *Revenue:* US$2,415,900,000,000 (income tax 45.4%; social-insurance taxes and contributions 36.6%; corporate taxes 10.8%; excise taxes 3.1%). *Expenditures:* US$2,700,700,000,000 (social security and medicare 36.3%; defense 17.3%; health 10.2%; interest on debt 9.0%). **Total outstanding national debt** (November 2008): US$10,681,135,920,000, of which debt held by the public US$6,434,879,220,000, intragovernment holdings US$4,246,256,700,000. **Gross national income** (2007): US$13,886,472,000,000 (US$46,-040 per capita). **Production.** *Agriculture and fishing* (value of production in US$'000,000 except as noted; 2007): corn (maize) 52,090, soybeans 26,752, wheat 13,669, alfalfa hay 8,972, cotton 5,197, grapes 3,381, potatoes 3,198, lettuce 2,751, apples 2,398, almonds 2,325, rice 2,274, tomatoes 2,179, oranges 2,111, sorghum 1,951, strawberries 1,746, sugar beets (2006) 1,526, tobacco 1,310, cottonseed 1,061, mushrooms 956, sugarcane (2006) 897, barley 852, onions 840, broccoli 764, peanuts (groundnuts) 763, cherries 651, carrots 614, sunflowers 607, blueberries 589, peppers 588, walnuts (2006) 564, pistachios 549, peaches 499, watermelons 476, cabbage 413, lemons 403, pecans 376, sweet potatoes 374, pears 346, cantaloupe 313; livestock (number of live animals) 97,003,000 cattle, 61,860,000 pigs, 9,500,000 horses, 6,165,000 sheep, 2,050,-000,000 chickens; fisheries production (2006) 5,324,933 metric tons (from aquaculture 9%); aquatic plants production (2006) 6,238 (from aquaculture, none). *Metals mining* (metal content in metric tons unless otherwise noted; 2007): molybdenum 59,400 (world rank: 1); beryllium 100 (world rank: 1); copper 1,190,000 (world rank: 3); lead 430,000 (world rank: 3); zinc 740,000 (world rank: 4); gold 240,000 kg (world rank: 4); palladium 13,500 kg (world rank: 4); platinum 3,400 kg (world rank: 5); iron 52,000,000 (world rank: 7); silver 1,220,000 kg (world rank: 7). *Nonmetals mining* (metric tons; 2007): diatomite 830,000 (world rank: 1); bromine 235,000 (world rank: 1); boron (2006) 1,150,000 (world rank: 2); perlite 444,000 (world rank: 2); kyanite 90,000 (world rank: 2); vermiculite 100,000 (world rank: 3); barite 540,000 (world rank: 4); feldspar 760,000 (world rank: 6); silicon 156,000 (world rank: 6). *Quarrying* (metric tons; 2007): gypsum 22,000,000 (world rank: 1); salt 43,800,000 (world rank: 2); phosphate rock 29,700,000 (world rank: 2); lime 20,200,000 (world rank: 2). *Manufacturing* (value added in US$'000,000; 2005): chemical products 328,440, of which pharmaceuticals and medicine 124,586; transportation equipment 254,665, of which motor vehicle parts 81,600, motor vehicles 78,772, aerospace products and parts 71,221; food products 235,673; electronic products 226,319, of which navigational, measuring, medical, and scientific equipment 68,730, computers and related components 36,407, communications equipment 32,413; fabricated metal products 154,928; nonelectrical machinery and apparatus 142,488; crude petroleum and coal 117,541; plastic and rubber products 96,348; beverages and tobacco products 80,716; base metals 77,179; paper products 75,889; cement, bricks, and ceramics 64,545; printing and publishing 58,930; general electrical equipment 54,318; furniture 46,801; wood products 44,763; textiles 32,395. *Construction* (completed; 2006): private US$937,047,000,000, of which residential US$641,332,000,000, nonresidential US$295,-715,000,000; public US$255,191,000,000. *Energy production (consumption):* electricity (kW-hr; 2005) 4,286,357,000,000 (4,311,081,000,000); coal (metric tons; 2005) 531,822,000 (514,818,000); lignite (metric tons; 2005) 506,769,000 (514,903,-000); crude petroleum (barrels; 2005) 1,882,000,-000 (5,786,000,000); petroleum products (metric tons; 2005) 816,677,000 (847,867,000); natural gas (cu m; 2005) 519,875,000,000 (623,534,-000,000). Domestic production of energy by source (2005): coal 33.3%, natural gas 27.2%, crude petroleum 15.7%, nuclear power 11.8%, renewable energy 8.8%, other 3.2%. Energy consumption by source (2006): crude petroleum and refined petroleum products 40.3%, natural gas 22.4%, coal 22.5%, nuclear electric power 8.2%, hydroelectric and thermal 2.9%, other renewable energy 3.7%; by end use: industrial 32.3%, residential and commercial 39.2%, transportation 28.5%. **Population** eco-

nomically active (November 2008): total (civilian population only) 154,616,000; activity rate of total population 50.7% (participation rates [2004]: ages 16–64, 74.0%; female [2007] 46.5%; unemployed 6.7%). **Selected balance of payments data.** Receipts from (US$'000,000): tourism (2006) 106,736; remittances (2007) 2,962; foreign direct investment (FDI) (2004–06 avg.) 137,415. Disbursements for (US$'000,000): tourism (2006) 76,807; remittances (2007) 43,680; FDI (2004–06 avg.) 148,948. Number of foreign visitors (2007) 56,716,277 (17,735,000 from Canada, 15,-089,000 from Mexico, 11,406,000 from Europe); number of nationals traveling abroad (2007) 64,052,000 (19,453,000 to Mexico, 13,371,000 to Canada, 12,304,000 to Europe).

Foreign trade

Imports (2007): US$1,953,698,800,000 (crude and refined petroleum 16.5%; motor vehicles and parts 10.8%; chemical products 8.0%; telecommunications equipment 6.6%; electrical machinery and apparatus 5.8%; computers and office equipment 5.2%; wearing apparel 4.2%; industrial machinery 3.3%; food and beverages 3.1%). *Major import sources:* China 16.5%; Canada 16.0%; Mexico 10.8%; Japan 7.4%; Germany 4.8%; UK 2.9%; South Korea 2.4%; France 2.1%; Venezuela 2.0%; Taiwan 2.0%; Saudi Arabia 1.8%; Italy 1.8%; Malaysia 1.7%; Nigeria 1.7%; Ireland 1.6%. **Exports** (2007): US$1,162,708,300,000 (chemical products 13.6%; electrical machinery and apparatus 9.0%; motor vehicles and parts 8.8%; other transportation equipment 7.0%; agricultural commodities 5.9%; power-generating machinery 4.6%; general industrial machinery 4.5%; specialized industrial machinery 4.4%; scientific and precision equipment 4.1%; computers and office equipment 4.0%; mineral fuels 3.6%; telecommunications equipment 3.3%). *Major export destinations:* Canada 21.4%; Mexico 11.7%; China 5.6%; Japan 5.4%; UK 4.3%; Germany 4.3%; South Korea 3.0%; The Netherlands 2.8%; France 2.4%; Taiwan 2.3%; Singapore 2.3%; Belgium 2.2%; Brazil 2.1%; Hong Kong 1.7%; Australia 1.7%.

Transport and communications

Transport. *Railroads* (2004): route length 156,300 km, of which Amtrak operates 35,610 km; passenger-km 41,574,000,000; metric ton-km cargo (2006) 2,835,000,000,000. *Roads* (2006): total length 6,487,956 km (paved 65%). *Vehicles* (2006): passenger cars 135,399,945; trucks and buses 108,765,741. *Merchant marine* (2006): vessels (1,000 gross tons and over) 625; total deadweight tonnage 10,172,000. *Navigable channels* (2004): 41,843 km. *Oil pipeline length* (2005) 210,824 km; *gas pipeline length* (2004) 2,353,300 km. *Air transport* (2007): passenger-km 1,334,-199,200,000; metric ton-km cargo 43,104,-300,000. *Certified route passenger/cargo air carriers* (2005): 80; operating revenue (US$'000,000; 2007) 173,104; operating expenses (US$'000,000; 2007) 163,894. **Communications,** in total units (units per 1,000 persons). Telephone landlines (2007): 163,170,000 (534); cellular telephone sub-

---

1 metric ton = about 1.1 short tons;   1 kilometer = 0.6 mi (statute);   1 metric ton-km cargo = about 0.68 short ton-mi cargo;   c.i.f.: cost, insurance, and freight;   f.o.b.: free on board

scribers (2007): 255,396,000 (835); personal computers (2005): 223,810,000 (755); total Internet users (2007): 220,000,000 (719); broadband Internet subscribers (2007): 73,207,000 (239).

Education and health

Literacy (2003): percentage of total population ages 16 and over "illiterate" (able to perform no more than the most simple literacy skills) 14% (or 30,000,000 people); "basically literate" (able to perform simple and everyday literacy activities) 29% (or 63,000,000 people); "intermediately and proficiently literate" (able to perform moderately challenging to complex literacy activities) 57% (or 123,000,000 people). An additional 6,500,000 people were not interviewed for this 2003 survey because they did not speak English or had cognitive or mental disabilities. **Food** (2005): daily per capita caloric intake 3,754 (vegetable products 72.2%, animal products 27.8%); 143% of FAO recommended minimum requirement. Per capita consumption of major food groups (kilograms annually; 2005): milk 256.4; fresh vegetables 125.5; cereal products 177.2; fresh fruits 122.7; red meat 62.7; potatoes 54.7; poultry products 55.8; fats and oil 31.6; sugar 30.2; fish and shellfish 23.4; undernourished population (2002–04) less than 2.5% of total population. **Health** (2005): doctors of medicine 902,100 (1 per 329 persons), of which office-based practice 563,200 (male 72.8%; female 27.2%) (including specialties in internal medicine 17.1%, general and family practice 10.3%, pediatrics 8.2%, obstetrics and gynecology 4.7%, psychiatry 4.6%, anesthesiology 4.5%, general surgery 4.2%, emergency medicine 3.2%, diagnostic radiology 2.7%, orthopedic surgery 2.7%, cardiovascular diseases 2.5%, pathology 2.2%, ophthalmology 2.1%); doctors of osteopathy 56,500; nurses (2004) 2,421,000 (1 per 824 persons); dentists (2004) 167,000 (1 per 1,760 persons); hospital beds 947,000 (1 per 314 persons), of which nonfederal 95.1% (community hospitals 84.7%, psychiatric 8.7%, long-term general and special 1.6%), federal 4.9%; infant mortality rate per 1,000 live births (2007) 6.4.

Military

Total active duty personnel (2007): 1,498,157 (army 39.6%, navy 22.8%, air force 22.4%, marines 12.5%, coast guard 2.7%). **Total reserve duty personnel** (2007): national guard 458,030 (army 76.7%, air force 23.3%); ready reserves 1,082,718 (army 62.4%, navy 11.9%, air force 16.5%, marines 8.5%, coast guard 0.7%). **Total special operations forces** (2007): active 31,496; reserve 11,247. **Military expenditure as percentage of GDP** (2007): 4.5%; per capita expenditure US$2,060. **Foreign military sales to the world** (2007): US$19,119,-454,000, of which to Australia 16.0%, to Turkey 10.6%, to Saudi Arabia 9.0%, to UAE 8.6%, to Iraq 7.4%, to Canada 6.8%.

Background

The territory that is now the United States was originally inhabited for several thousand years by numerous American Indian peoples who had probably emigrated from Asia. European exploration and settlement from the 16th century began displacement of the Indians. The first permanent European settlement, by the Spanish, was at St. Augustine FL in 1565; the British settled Jamestown VA (1607), Plymouth MA (1620), Maryland (1632), and Pennsylvania (1681). They took New York, New Jersey, and Delaware from the Dutch in 1664, a year after the Carolinas had been granted to British noblemen. The British defeat of the French in 1763 ensured British political control over the 13 colonies.

Political unrest caused by British colonial policy culminated in the American Revolution (1775–83) and the Declaration of Independence (1776). The US was first organized under the Articles of Confederation (1781) and then finally under the Constitution (1787) as a federal republic. Boundaries extended west to the Mississippi River, excluding Spanish Florida. Land acquired from France by the Louisiana Purchase (1803) nearly doubled the country's territory. The US fought the War of 1812 with the British and acquired Florida from Spain in 1819. In 1830 it legalized removal of American Indians to lands west of the Mississippi River. Settlement expanded to the West Coast in the mid-19th century, especially after the discovery of gold in California in 1848. Victory in the Mexican-American War (1846–48) brought the territory of seven more future states (including California and Texas) into US hands. The northwestern boundary was established by treaty with Great Britain in 1846. The US acquired southern Arizona by the Gadsden Purchase (1853). It suffered disunity during the conflict between the slavery-based plantation economy in the South and the free industrial and agricultural economy in the North, culminating in the American Civil War (1861–65) and the abolition of slavery under the 13th Amendment.

After Reconstruction (1865–77), the US experienced rapid growth, urbanization, industrial development, and European immigration. In 1877 it authorized allotment of Indian reservation land to individual tribesmen, resulting in widespread loss of land to whites. By the beginning of the 20th century, it had acquired outlying territories, including Alaska, the Midway Islands, the Hawaiian Islands, the Philippines, Puerto Rico, Guam, Wake Island, American Samoa, the Panama Canal Zone, and part of the Virgin Islands. The US participated in World War I during 1917–18. It granted suffrage to women in 1920 and citizenship to American Indians in 1924. The stock market crash of 1929 led to the Great Depression. The US entered World War II after the Japanese bombing of Pearl Harbor (7 Dec 1941). The explosion of the first atomic bomb (6 Aug 1945), on Hiroshima, Japan, brought about the end of the war and sent the US apart as a military power. After the war the US was involved in the reconstruction of Europe and Japan and embroiled in a rivalry with the Soviet Union that became known as the Cold War. It participated in the Korean War (1950–53). In 1952 it granted autonomous commonwealth status to Puerto Rico.

Racial segregation in schools was declared unconstitutional in 1954. Alaska and Hawaii were made states in 1959, bringing the total to 50. In 1964 Congress passed the Civil Rights Act and authorized full-scale intervention in the Vietnam War. The mid- to late 1960s were marked by widespread civil disorder, including race riots and antiwar demonstrations. The US accomplished the first manned lunar landing in 1969. All US troops were withdrawn from Vietnam by 1973. With the dissolution of the Soviet Union in 1991, the US assumed the status of sole world superpower. The US led a coalition of forces against Iraq in the Persian Gulf War (1990–91). Administration of the Panama Canal was turned over to Panama in 1999. After the September 11 attacks on the US in 2001 destroyed the World Trade Center and part of the Pentagon, the US attacked Afghanistan's Taliban government for harboring and refusing to extradite the mastermind of the terrorist acts, Osama bin Laden. In 2003 the US attacked Iraq, with British support, and overthrew the government of Saddam Hussein.

Did you know? It is a common misperception that John F. Kennedy was the youngest US president. Kennedy was the youngest elected president, at age 43, but Theodore Roosevelt, at age 42, was the youngest to be inaugurated, following the assassination of President McKinley.

Recent Developments

Waning confidence in the value of securitized home mortgages and derivatives finally caught up with the US economy, prompting a disastrous chain reaction that eventually infected financial markets worldwide. The mortgages were packaged together and sold in bundles, backed by intricate and highly leveraged financial contracts designed by Wall Street lawyers outside government regulatory oversight. When cracks appeared it created a domino effect that spread across the financial system, from housing to mortgage lending, to investment banks, to securities firms, and beyond. In July 2008 Pres. George W. Bush signed a bill designed to strengthen mortgage lenders by guaranteeing up to US$300 billion in new fixed-rate mortgages. The measure was ineffectual, however, and in September the dam broke. The government essentially nationalized both Fannie Mae and Freddie Mac, which together owned or guaranteed half of the country's US$12 trillion mortgage market. Merrill Lynch, the country's largest brokerage house, was sold to Bank of America under duress. Investment bank Lehman Brothers filed for bankruptcy, and federal regulators said that the firm owned so many toxic assets that a bailout attempt would be futile. The Federal Reserve (Fed) offered US$105 billion to shore up money funds and also pumped US$85 billion into insurance giant American International Group (AIG), which had provided backing for mortgage instruments. Washington Mutual, the country's largest thrift institution, was seized as insolvent and sold for a fraction of its former value. A US$700 billion rescue bill—the Troubled Asset Relief Program (TARP)—was approved by Congress on 3 October. It allowed federal authorities to purchase assets of failing banks and eased rules requiring strict valuation of distressed securities. The week of 6–10 October, however, proved to be the worst one on Wall Street in at least 75 years, with the Dow Jones Industrial Average (DJIA) down 18%. Under pressure to prevent a complete financial collapse, that month the Fed made more than US$2.5 trillion in emergency loans to businesses and lowered interest rates. In November, as confidence continued to erode, plans to buy troubled assets under TARP were abandoned. A plan was launched to recapitalize financial firms, mostly by purchasing preferred shares of banks. The Fed also pledged another US$800 billion to shore up distressed mortgages. Those actions, in addition to similar moves by European and Asian governments, appeared to stabilize investor confidence. The stock market hit bottom for the year on 20 November, with the DJIA settling at just over half of its record level of a year earlier. The federal deficit for the fiscal year that ended 30 September almost tripled, to US$454.8 billion, and analysts predicted that it would top US$1 trillion in 2009. Investors lost an estimated US$7.3 trillion in value from the decline in the 5,000 largest stocks alone, and the median home resale price dropped 13% while an estimated 1 in 10 homeowners was in financial distress. Unemployment started the year at a modest 5% but stood at 7.2% in December and had risen to nearly 9.5% in mid-2009. In February 2009 Pres. Barack Obama, historically elected the previous November, signed a US$787 billion stimulus plan. By the middle of 2009, two of the Big Three automakers, Chrysler and General Motors, had entered bankruptcy protection after having received billions of dollars in aid.

More than five years after leading the invasion that toppled Saddam Hussein, the US signed a status-of-forces agreement with Iraq that called for the removal of allied troops from Iraqi cities by mid-2009 and the complete withdrawal of US combat troops by the end of 2011. The agreement also gave Iraqi authorities criminal jurisdiction over off-duty US troops who committed crimes while away from their bases. In March 2008 the Iraqi government deployed 30,000 Iraqi troops to Basra in a successful thrust to depose the Mahdi Army, a radical Shi'ite militia that had long controlled the port city. Iraqi troops later occupied Sadr City, a Shi'ite section of Baghdad, without significant resistance. In September Anbar province, once the cradle of the Sunni insurgency against the government, was turned over to full Iraqi control. The military progress in Iraq was offset by renewed violence in Afghanistan, as militant groups, including the Taliban and al-Qaeda, challenged NATO forces. In tacit recognition of the threat, US Army Gen. David Petraeus, architect of the Iraq "surge" strategy, was elevated in October to head the US Central Command, effectively taking control of allied military strategy in the war on terrorism. No progress was made in relations with North Korea. As a show of good faith, President Bush removed Pyongyang from an international blacklist as a state sponsor of terrorism in October 2008. In May 2009, however, less than two months after controversially test-firing a long-range missile, North Korea conducted its second nuclear-weapon explosion, worsening the already tense environment between the two countries.

Internet resources: <www.fedstats.gov>.

---

1 metric ton = about 1.1 short tons;   1 kilometer = 0.6 mi (statute);   1 metric ton-km cargo = about 0.68 short ton-mi cargo;   c.i.f.: cost, insurance, and freight;   f.o.b.: free on board

Uruguay

Atlantic
Ocean

Official name: República Oriental del Uruguay (Oriental Republic of Uruguay). **Form of government:** republic with two legislative houses (Senate [31]; Chamber of Representatives [99]). **Head of state and government:** President Tabaré Ramón Vázquez Rosas (from 2005). **Capital:** Montevideo. **Official language:** Spanish. **Official religion:** none. **Monetary unit:** 1 Uruguayan peso (UYU) = 100 centésimos; valuation (1 Jul 2009) US$1 = UYU 22.74.

Demography

Area: 68,679 sq mi, 177,879 sq km. **Population** (2008): 3,350,000. **Density** (2008): persons per sq mi 48.8, persons per sq km 18.8. **Urban** (2007): 93.7%. **Sex distribution** (2007): male 48.30%; female 51.70%. **Age breakdown** (2007): under 15, 23.4%; 15–29, 22.8%; 30–44, 19.6%; 45–59, 16.5%; 60–74, 11.5%; 75–84, 4.7%; 85 and over, 1.5%. **Ethnic composition** (2006): white (mostly Spanish, Italian, or mixed Spanish-Italian) 87.4%; black/part-black 8.4%; Amerindian/part-Amerindian 3.0%; other/unknown 1.2%. **Religious affiliation** (2004): Roman Catholic 54%; Protestant 11%; Mormon 3%; Jewish 0.8%; nonreligious/atheist 26%; other 5.2%. **Major cities** (2004): Montevideo 1,269,552; Salto 99,072; Paysandú 73,272; Las Piedras 69,222; Rivera 64,426. **Location:** southern South America, bordering Brazil, the South Atlantic Ocean, and Argentina.

Vital statistics

Birth rate per 1,000 population (2007): 14.7 (world avg. 20.3); (2002) within marriage 42.9%; outside of marriage 57.1%. **Death rate** per 1,000 population (2007): 9.4 (world avg. 8.6). **Total fertility rate** (avg. births per childbearing woman; 2007): 2.02. **Life expectancy** at birth (2007): male 72.3 years; female 79.6 years.

National economy

Budget (2006). *Revenue:* UYU 111,321,000,000 (taxes on goods and services 59.1%; corporate taxes

12.3%; property taxes 7.1%; nontax revenue 6.7%). *Expenditures:* UYU 117,225,000,000 (social security and welfare 27.6%; government transfers including debt servicing 20.7%; public administration 13.9%; education 12.3%). **Production** (metric tons except as noted). *Agriculture and fishing* (2007): rice 1,200,000, soybeans 800,000, wheat 620,000, sunflower seeds 60,000; livestock (number of live animals) 12,000,000 cattle, 11,000,000 sheep; fisheries production (2006) 134,140 (from aquaculture, negligible). *Mining and quarrying* (2005): limestone 1,185,000; clays 64,450; gold 3,151 kg. *Manufacturing* (value added in UYU '000,000; 2005): food and beverages 17,390; refined petroleum products 5,945; textiles, hides, and leather goods 4,633. *Energy production (consumption):* electricity (kW-hr; 2005) 7,684,000,000 (8,428,000,000); coal (metric tons; 2005) none (1,000); crude petroleum (barrels; 2005) none (15,700,000); petroleum products (metric tons; 2005) 2,020,000 (1,532,000); natural gas (cu m; 2005) none (105,000,000). **Population economically active** (2006): total 1,580,400; activity rate of total population 47.7% (participation rates: ages 14–64, 72.7%; female 43.5%; unemployed [2007] 9.2%). **Gross national income** (2007): US$21,186,000,000 (US$6,380 per capita). **Public debt** (external, outstanding; 2006): US$7,211,-000,000. **Selected balance of payments data.** Receipts from (US$'000,000): tourism (2006) 597; remittances (2007) 97; foreign direct investment (FDI) (2004–06 avg.) 851; official development assistance (2006) 21. Disbursements for (US$'000,000): tourism (2006) 213; remittances (2007) 4; FDI (2004–06 avg.) 17.

Foreign trade

Imports (2006; c.i.f.): US$4,775,000,000 (crude and refined petroleum 27.5%; machinery and apparatus 16.0%; chemical products 12.7%; food, beverages, and tobacco products 8.7%; transportation equipment 7.4%). *Major import sources:* Argentina 22.6%; Brazil 22.6%; Venezuela 12.6%; China 7.3%; US 6.8%. **Exports** (2006; f.o.b.): US$3,952,000,000 (beef 23.7%; hides and leather goods 8.6%; dairy products, eggs, and honey 6.9%; textiles and wearing apparel 6.8%; rice 5.5%). *Major export destinations:* Brazil 14.7%; US 13.2%; Argentina 7.6%; Russia 5.7%; Germany 4.2%.

Transport and communications

Transport. *Railroads* (2006): route length 2,073 km; passenger-km (2004) 11,000,000; metric ton-km cargo (2005) 331,000,000. *Roads* (2007): length 16,398 km (paved 22%). *Vehicles* (2005): passenger cars 523,866; trucks and buses 84,354. *Air transport* (PLUNA only; 2006): passenger-km 1,096,000,000; metric ton-km cargo, none. **Communications,** in total units (units per 1,000 persons). Telephone landlines (2007): 965,000 (289); cellular telephone subscribers (2007): 3,004,000 (899); personal computers (2005): 450,000 (135); total Internet users (2007): 968,000 (290); broadband Internet subscribers (2007): 165,000 (49).

Education and health

Educational attainment (2006). Percentage of population ages 25 and over having: no formal schooling 1.9%; incomplete primary education 15.1%; complete primary 25.8%; incomplete secondary 20.8%; complete secondary 17.6%; incomplete higher 7.2%; complete higher 11.6%. **Literacy** (2003): percentage of total population ages 15 and over literate 98.0%; males literate 97.6%; females literate 98.4%. **Health:** physicians (2006) 13,603 (1 per 245 persons); hospital beds (2003) 6,661 (1 per 499 persons); infant mortality rate per 1,000 live births (2006) 10.5; undernourished population (2002–04) less than 2.5% of total population.

Military

Total active duty personnel (2007): 25,400 (army 66.1%, navy and coast guard 22.1%, air force 11.8%). **Military expenditure as percentage of GDP** (2005): 1.3%; per capita expenditure US$67.

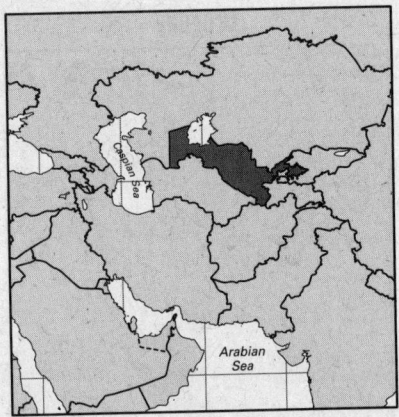

Background

The Spanish navigator Juan Díaz de Solís sailed into the Río de la Plata in 1516. The Portuguese established Colonia in 1680. Subsequently, the Spanish established Montevideo in 1726, driving the Portuguese from their settlement; 50 years later Uruguay became part of the Viceroyalty of the Río de la Plata. It gained independence from Spain in 1811. The Portuguese regained it in 1821, incorporating it into Brazil as a province. A revolt against Brazil in 1825 led to its being recognized as an independent state in 1828. It battled Paraguay in 1865–70. For much of World War II, Uruguay remained neutral. The presidential office was abolished in 1951 but restored in 1966. A military coup occurred in 1973, but the country returned to civilian rule in 1985. The 1990s brought a general upturn in the economy, largely the result of reform measures and membership in Mercosul, the Southern Common Market, from 1991.

Recent Developments

Uruguay experienced a year of positive economic results in 2008, with GDP growth of about 18.4%. Inflation remained under double digits, running at 9.2%, and unemployment dropped to 6.8%. In the second half of the year, however, the global economic crisis began to affect the country, with the Uruguayan peso falling from 19 to 24 against the US dollar and significant layoffs occurring in the meatpacking and textile industries. Nevertheless, Pres. Tabaré Vázquez vowed to bring down the retailer inflation rate to the promised 3–7% threshold (the figure had risen to 8.1% in the first 11 months of the year) and to guard against food price speculation or monopolization of food.

Internet resources: <www.turismo.gub.uy>.

Uzbekistan

Official name: Uzbekiston Respublikasi (Republic of Uzbekistan). **Form of government:** republic with two legislative bodies (Senate [100]; Legislative Chamber [120]). **Chief of state and government:** President Islam Karimov (from 1990), assisted by Prime Minister Shavkat Mirziyayev (from 2003). **Capital:** Tashkent (Toshkent). **Official language:** Uzbek. **Official religion:** none. **Monetary unit:** sum (UZS; plural sumy); valuation (1 Jul 2009) US$1 = UZS 1,462.36.

Demography

Area: 172,700 sq mi, 447,400 sq km. **Population** (2008): 27,345,000. **Density** (2008): persons per sq mi 158.3, persons per sq km 61.1. **Urban** (2006): 35.9%. **Sex distribution** (2006): male 49.56%; female 50.44%. **Age breakdown** (2006): under 15, 32.9%; 15–29, 30.3%; 30–44, 19.6%; 45–59, 11.2%; 60–74, 4.3%; 75 and over, 1.7%. **Ethnic composition** (2000): Uzbek 78.3%; Tajik 4.7%; Kazakh 4.1%; Tatar 3.3%; Russian 2.5%; Karakalpak 2.1%; other 5.0%. **Religious affiliation** (2000): Muslim (mostly Sunni) 76.2%; Russian Orthodox 0.8%; Jewish 0.2%; nonreligious 18.1%; other 4.7%. **Major cities** (2007): Tashkent (Toshkent) 1,959,190; Namangan 446,237; Andijon 321,622; Samarkand 312,863; Bukhara 249,037. **Location:** central Asia, bordering Kazakhstan, Kyrgyzstan, Tajikistan, Afghanistan, and Turkmenistan.

Vital statistics

Birth rate per 1,000 population (2007): 22.4 (world avg. 20.3). **Death rate** per 1,000 population (2007): 5.2 (world avg. 8.6). **Total fertility rate** (avg. births per childbearing woman; 2006): 2.91. **Life expectancy** at birth (2006): male 61.2 years; female 68.1 years.

National economy

Budget (2006). *Revenue:* UZS 6,406,000,000,000 (taxes on income and profits 20.2%; VAT 17.3%; taxes on property and resources 12.2%; excise taxes 10.2%). *Expenditures:* UZS 6,331,000,-000,000 (health and education 34.4%; social se-

---

1 metric ton = about 1.1 short tons;   1 kilometer = 0.6 mi (statute);   1 metric ton-km cargo = about 0.68 short ton-mi cargo;   c.i.f.: cost, insurance, and freight;   f.o.b.: free on board

curity 27.0%; national economy 9.0%; centralized investments 8.1%). **Public debt** (external, outstanding; 2006): US$3,343,000,000. **Production** (metric tons except as noted). *Agriculture and fishing* (2007): wheat 5,900,000, seed cotton 3,300,000, tomatoes 1,327,000, raw silk 487; livestock (number of live animals) 10,450,000 sheep, 7,042,500 cattle, 1,974,300 goats, 16,500 camels; fisheries production (2006) 7,200 (from aquaculture 53%). *Mining and quarrying* (2005): copper (metal content) 100,000; uranium (metal content) 2,300; gold 90,000 kg. *Manufacturing* (value of production in UZS '000,000,000; 2006): nonferrous metals 2,705; mineral fuels 2,487; machinery and metalworking products 1,986. *Energy production (consumption):* electricity (kW-hr; 2007) 48,950,-000,000 ([2006] 47,000,000,000); lignite (metric tons; 2005) 3,003,000 (2,930,000); crude petroleum (barrels; 2006) 39,465,000 ([2005] 25,729,-000); petroleum products (metric tons; 2005) 5,062,000 (4,821,000); natural gas (cu m; 2006) 62,500,000,000 (48,400,000,000). **Population economically active** (2004): total 9,945,500; activity rate of total population 38.7% (participation rates [2001]: ages 16–59 [male], 16–54 [female] 70.4%; female 44.0%; officially unemployed [2007] 0.8%). **Gross national income** (2007): US$19,721,000,000 (US$730 per capita). **Selected balance of payments data.** Receipts from (US$'000,000): tourism (2006) 43; remittances (2003) 600; foreign direct investment (2004–06 avg.) 146; official development assistance (2006) 149.

Foreign trade

Imports (2006; c.i.f.): US$4,395,900,000 (machinery and metalworking products 40.3%; chemical products 15.0%; base metals 10.4%; food products 8.1%). *Major import sources:* Russia 27.8%; South Korea 15.2%; China 10.4%; Kazakhstan 7.3%; Germany 7.1%. **Exports** (2006; f.o.b.): US$6,389,800,000 (cotton fiber 17.2%; energy products [including natural gas and crude petroleum] 13.1%; base metals 12.9%; machinery and apparatus 10.1%; gold, n.a.; uranium, n.a. *Major export destinations:* Russia 23.7%; Poland 11.7%; China 10.4%; Turkey 7.7%; Kazakhstan 5.9%.

Transport and communications

Transport. *Railroads* (2007): length (2006) 3,950 km; passenger-km 2,400,000,000; metric ton-km cargo 21,600,000,000. *Roads* (2005): total length 84,400 km (paved 85%). *Vehicles* (1994): passenger cars 865,300; buses 14,500. *Air transport* (2007): passenger-km 5,400,000,000; metric ton-km cargo 76,600,000. **Communications**, in total units (units per 1,000 persons). Telephone landlines (2005): 1,794,000 (67); cellular telephone subscribers (2005): 720,000 (27); total Internet users (2007): 1,200,000 (44); broadband Internet subscribers (2005): 8,300 (0.3).

Education and health

Educational attainment (2002). Percentage of population ages 25 and over having: no formal education/unknown 2.5%; incomplete primary education

9.0%; primary 7.3%; secondary 66.0%; higher 15.2%. **Literacy** (2003): percentage of total population ages 15 and over literate, virtually 100%. **Health** (2005): physicians 70,159 (1 per 371 persons); hospital beds 135,143 (1 per 193 persons); infant mortality rate per 1,000 live births (2006) 70.0; undernourished population (2002–04) 6,500,000 (25% of total population based on the consumption of a minimum daily requirement of 1,930 calories).

Military

Total active duty personnel (2007): 67,000 (army 74.6%, air force 25.4%); German troops 163. **Military expenditure as percentage of GDP** (2005): 0.4%; per capita expenditure US$2.

Background

Genghis Khan's grandson Shibaqan received the territory of Uzbekistan as his inheritance in the 13th century AD. His Mongols ruled over nearly 100 mainly Turkic tribes, who would eventually intermarry with the Mongols to form the Uzbeks and other Turkic peoples of central Asia. In the early 16th century, a federation of Mongol-Uzbeks invaded and occupied settled regions, including an area called Transoxania that would become the Uzbeks' permanent homeland. By the early 19th century the region was dominated by the khanates of Khiva, Bukhara, and Quqon, all of which eventually succumbed to Russian domination. The Uzbek Soviet Socialist Republic was created in 1924. In June 1990 Uzbekistan became the first Central Asian republic to declare sovereignty. It achieved full independence from the USSR in 1991. During the 1990s its economy was considered the strongest in Central Asia, though its political system was deemed harsh.

Recent Developments

In 2008 Uzbekistan continued to maintain good relations with Russia. In March the Uzbek Senate ratified Uzbekistan's return to the Collective Security Treaty Organization. During Russian Prime Minister Vladimir Putin's visit to Tashkent in September, an economic cooperation pact was signed. Included in the accord was an agreement on the construction of a new pipeline for the export of Uzbek natural gas to Russia. Relations were less smooth with Tajikistan. Much of the Central Asian region was affected by the extremely cold weather in January and February; Uzbek authorities, however, refused to honor an agreement to deliver electricity to Tajikistan, which was far more severely affected than was Uzbekistan, on the grounds that the power was needed at home. In August Uzbekistan accused Kyrgyzstan of having violated a water-sharing agreement by holding back water that was needed for irrigation of Uzbek farms. Agreements between the five Central Asian states in October raised hopes in the region that a solution might soon be found to intraregional power and water-use problems.

Internet resources:
<www.stat.uz/STAT/index.php?lng=1>.

Vanuatu

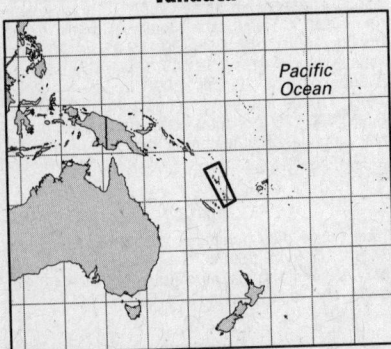

Pacific Ocean

Official name: Ripablik blong Vanuatu (Bislama); République de Vanuatu (French); Republic of Vanuatu (English). **Form of government:** republic with a single legislative house (Parliament [52]). **Chief of state:** President Maxime Carlot Korman (from 2009). **Head of government:** Prime Minister Edward Natapei (from 2008). **Capital:** Port-Vila. **Official languages:** Bislama; French; English. **Official religion:** none. **Monetary unit:** vatu (Vt); valuation (1 Jul 2009) US$1 = Vt 102.00.

Demography

Area: 4,707 sq mi, 12,190 sq km. **Population** (2008): 233,000. **Density** (2008): persons per sq mi 49.5, persons per sq km 19.1. **Urban** (2005): 23.5%. **Sex distribution** (2003): male 51.40%; female 48.60%. **Age breakdown** (1999): under 15, 42.2%; 15–29, 26.9%; 30–44, 17.0%; 45–59, 8.8%; 60–74, 3.7%; 75 and over, 1.4%. **Ethnic composition** (1999): Ni-Vanuatu (Melanesian) 98.7%; European and other Pacific Islanders 1.3%. **Religious affiliation** (2005): Protestant 70%, of which Presbyterian 32%, Anglican 13%, Adventist 11%; Roman Catholic 13%; traditional beliefs (significantly John Frum cargo cult) 5%; other 12%. **Major towns** (2006): Port-Vila 37,100; Luganville 13,900; Norsup 3,000; Isangel 1,500. **Location:** Oceania, island group between the South Pacific Ocean and the Coral Sea.

Vital statistics

Birth rate per 1,000 population (2005): 23.1 (world avg. 20.3). **Death rate** per 1,000 population (2005): 7.9 (world avg. 8.6). **Natural increase rate** per 1,000 population (2005): 15.2 (world avg. 11.7). **Total fertility rate** (avg. births per childbearing woman; 2005): 2.77. **Life expectancy** at birth (2005): male 61.0 years; female 64.1 years.

National economy

Budget (2007). *Revenue:* Vt 11,764,000,000 (tax revenue 83.5%; nontax revenue 10.2%; foreign grants 6.3%). *Expenditures:* Vt 11,860,000,000 (wages and salaries 55.0%; goods and services 27.1%; transfers 9.1%; interest payments 3.3%). **Public debt** (external, outstanding; 2004): US$71,900,000. **Production** (metric tons except as noted). *Agriculture and fishing* (2007): coconuts 322,000, copra 21,644, bananas 14,500, kava (2004) 825; livestock (number of live animals) 174,137 cattle, 88,694 pigs, 8,792 goats; fisheries production (2006) 88,189 (from aquaculture, negligible). *Mining and quarrying:* small quantities of coral-reef limestone, crushed stone, sand, and gravel. *Manufacturing* (value added in Vt '000,000; 1995): food, beverages, and tobacco 645; wood products 423; fabricated metal products 377. *Energy production (consumption):* electricity (kW-hr; 2005) 45,000,000 (45,000,000); petroleum products (metric tons; 2005) none (29,000). **Population economically active** (1999): total 76,370; activity rate of total population 40.9% (participation rates: ages 15–64, 75.1%; female 44.9%; unemployed [2000] 1.7%). **Gross national income** (2007): US$417,000,000 (US$1,840 per capita). **Selected balance of payments data.** Receipts from (US$'000,000): tourism (2006) 92; remittances (2007) 11; foreign direct investment (FDI) (2004–06 avg.) 31; official development assistance (2006) 49. Disbursements for (US$'000,000): tourism (2006) 9; remittances (2007) 18; FDI (2004–06 avg.) 1.

Foreign trade

Imports (2006; c.i.f.): Vt 17,645,000,000 (machinery and transportation equipment 25.9%; food and live animals 18.3%; mineral fuels 11.9%; chemical products 9.6%). *Major import sources* (2007): Australia 31.3%; New Zealand 16.8%; Singapore 12.5%; Fiji 9.1%; Japan 4.5%. **Exports** (2006; f.o.b.): Vt 5,130,000,000 (domestic exports 71.2%, of which kava 13.6%, beef 9.1%, copra 6.3%, timber 6.0%, cocoa 5.4%; reexports 28.8%). *Major export destinations* (domestic exports only; 2007): EU 23.1%; New Caledonia 13.3%; Japan 7.3%; Australia 4.3%; New Zealand 3.9%.

Transport and communications

Transport. *Railroads:* none. *Roads* (2000): total length 1,070 km (paved 24%). *Vehicles* (2001): passenger cars 2,600; trucks and buses 4,400. *Air transport* (Air Vanuatu only; 2005): passenger-km 220,861,000; metric ton-km cargo 1,647,000. **Communications,** in total units (units per 1,000 persons). Telephone landlines (2007): 8,800 (39); cellular telephone subscribers (2007): 26,000 (115); personal computers (2005): 3,000 (14); total Internet users (2007): 17,000 (75); broadband Internet subscribers (2004): 20 (0.1).

Education and health

Educational attainment (1999). Percentage of population ages 15 and over having: no formal schooling 18.0%; incomplete primary education 20.6%; completed primary 35.5%; some secondary 12.2%; completed secondary 8.5%; higher 5.2%, of which university 1.3%. **Literacy** (2007): percentage of total population ages 15 and over literate 74%.

---

1 metric ton = about 1.1 short tons; 1 kilometer = 0.6 mi (statute); 1 metric ton-km cargo = about 0.68 short ton-mi cargo; c.i.f.: cost, insurance, and freight; f.o.b.: free on board

Health (2004): physicians 29 (1 per 7,138 persons); hospital beds (2003) 397 (1 per 511 persons); infant mortality rate per 1,000 live births (2005) 55.2; undernourished population (2002–04) 20,000 (11% of total population based on the consumption of a minimum daily requirement of 1,790 calories).

Military

Total active duty personnel (2008): none; Australia and New Zealand assist paramilitary forces through defense assistance programs.

Background

The islands of Vanuatu were inhabited for at least 3,000 years by Melanesian peoples before being discovered in 1606 by the Portuguese. They were rediscovered by French navigator Louis-Antoine de Bougainville in 1768 and then explored by English mariner Capt. James Cook in 1774 and named the New Hebrides. Sandalwood merchants and European missionaries arrived in the mid-19th century; they were followed by British and French cotton planters. Control of the islands was sought by both the French and British, who agreed in 1906 to form a condominium government. During World War II a major Allied naval base was on Espíritu Santo; the island group escaped Japanese invasion. The New Hebrides became the independent Republic of Vanuatu in 1980. Much of the nation's housing was ravaged by a hurricane in 1987.

Recent Developments

Vanuatu's economy grew by 5.7% in 2008, but growth was slower in inaccessible rural areas, with continuing expansion of squatter settlements. Despite the problems, tourism revenues rose by 8.5%, and low-cost regional airlines opened markets in Australia and New Zealand, which saw airline arrivals increase by 19%. Vanuatu sent its first 200 overseas seasonal workers to labor in New Zealand's horticulture industry, and the country was invited to participate in a parallel temporary-worker scheme to be set up in Australia. Remittances from these seasonal workers were expected to broaden the sources of Vanuatu's national income.

Internet resources: <www.vanuatutourism.com>.

Vatican City State

Official name: State of the Vatican City (Holy See). **Form of government:** ecclesiastical. **Chief of state:** Pope Benedict XVI (from 2005). **Head of government:** Secretary of State Tarcisio Cardinal Bertone (from 2006). **Capital:** Vatican City. **Languages:** Italian; Latin. **Religion:** Roman Catholic. **Monetary unit:** 1 euro (€) = 100 cents; valuation (1 Jul 2009) US$1 = €0.71.

Demography

Area: 0.17 sq mi, 0.44 sq km. **Population** (2008): 930. **Density** (2008): persons per sq mi 5,471, persons per sq km 2,114. **Location:** southern Europe, within the commune of Rome, Italy. **Annual**

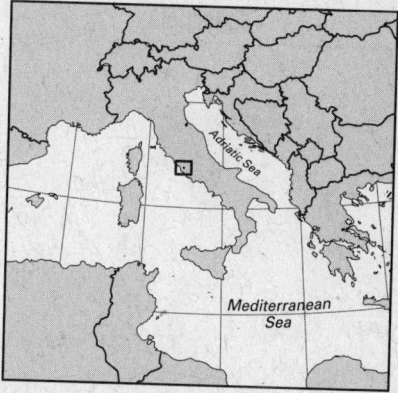

Adriatic Sea

Mediterranean Sea

budget: US$209,000,000. **Industries:** banking and finance; printing; production of a small amount of mosaics and uniforms; tourism.

Background

Vatican City, the independent papal state, is the smallest independent state in the world. Its medieval and Renaissance walls form its boundaries except on the southeast, at St. Peter's Square. Within the walls is a miniature nation, with its own diplomatic missions, newspaper, post office, radio station, banking system, army of more than 100 Swiss Guards, and publishing house. Extraterritoriality of the state extends to Castel Gandolfo, summer home of the Pope, and to several churches and palaces in Rome proper. Its independent sovereignty was recognized in the Lateran Treaty of 1929. The pope has absolute executive, legislative, and judicial powers within the city. He appoints the members of the Vatican's government organs, which are separate from those of the Holy See. The state's many imposing buildings include St. Peter's Basilica, the Vatican Palace, and the Vatican Museums. Frescoes by Michelangelo and Pinturicchio (in the Sistine Chapel) and Raphael's Stanze are also there. The Vatican Library contains a priceless collection of manuscripts from the pre-Christian and Christian eras.

Recent Developments

As part of the Vatican's diplomatic outreach, Pope Benedict XVI met visitors from many countries in 2008. One was Iraqi Prime Minister Nuri al-Maliki, who in turn invited the pontiff to Iraq. In early November the Vatican hosted an unprecedented summit with Muslim representatives from several countries and branches of Islam. In April Benedict made his first trip to the US as pope. Changes in the Roman Catholic liturgy for the Good Friday celebration prompted members of the Jewish faith to also express the wish to intensify dialogue. Benedict visited Israel and the West Bank in May 2009 (only the second papal visit ever to Israel) and publicly supported the creation of a Palestinian state.

Internet resources:
<www.vatican.va/phome_en.htm>.

Venezuela

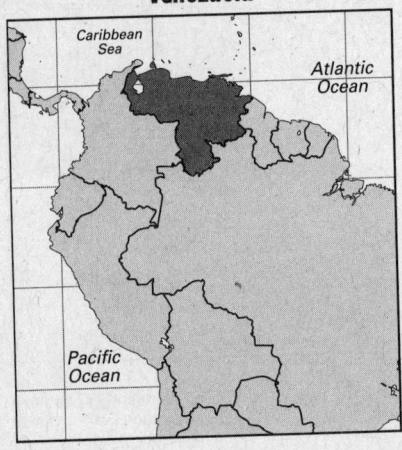

Official name: República Bolivariana de Venezuela (Bolivarian Republic of Venezuela). **Form of government:** federal multiparty republic with a unicameral legislature (National Assembly [167]). **Head of state and government:** President Hugo Chávez Frias (from 2002). **Capital:** Caracas. **Official language:** Spanish (31 indigenous Indian languages were made official in May 2002). **Official religion:** none. **Monetary unit:** 1 bolívar fuerte (VEF) = 100 céntimos; valuation (1 Jul 2009) US$1 = VEF 2.15 (the bolívar fuerte replaced the bolívar [VEB] 1 Jan 2008, at the rate of 1 VEF = VEB 1,000).

Demography

Area: 353,841 sq mi, 916,445 sq km. **Population (2008):** 27,884,000. **Density (2008):** persons per sq mi 78.8, persons per sq km 30.4. **Urban (2005):** 93.4%. **Sex distribution (2007):** male 50.19%; female 49.81%. **Age breakdown (2006):** under 15, 32.1%; 15–29, 26.9%; 30–44, 20.5%; 45–59, 13.2%; 60–74, 5.5%; 75–84, 1.5%; 85 and over, 0.3%. **Ethnic composition (2000):** mestizo 63.7%; local white 20.0%; local black 10.0%; other white 3.3%; Amerindian 1.3%; other 1.7%. **Religious affiliation (2005):** Roman Catholic 84.5%; Protestant 4.0%; nonreligious/other 11.5%. **Major cities (urban agglomerations) (2001 [2007]):** Caracas 1,836,286 (2,985,000); Maracaibo 1,571,885 (2,072,000); Valencia 1,199,510 (1,770,000); Barquisimeto 862,519 (1,116,000); Ciudad Guayana 635,978. **Location:** northern South America, bordering the Caribbean Sea, the North Atlantic Ocean, Guyana, Brazil, and Colombia.

Vital statistics

Birth rate per 1,000 population (2007): 21.5 (world avg. 20.3). **Death rate** per 1,000 population (2007): 5.1 (world avg. 8.6). **Total fertility rate** (avg. births per childbearing woman; 2007): 2.58. **Life ex-**
pectancy at birth (2007): male 70.7 years; female 76.6 years.

National economy

Budget (2006). *Revenue:* VEB 117,326,000,000,-000 (petroleum income 52.9%, of which royalties 37.5%, taxes 13.0%; nonpetroleum income 47.1%, of which VAT 22.4%). *Expenditures:* VEB 117,255,-000,000,000 (current expenditures 75.0%; development expenditures 22.8%; other 2.2%). **Public debt** (external, outstanding; 2006): US$27,180,-000,000. **Production** (metric tons except as noted). *Agriculture and fishing* (2007): sugarcane 9,300,000, corn (maize) 2,104,000, rice 800,000; livestock (number of live animals) 16,700,000 cattle, 120,000,000 chickens; fisheries production (2006) 482,210 (from aquaculture 5%). *Mining and quarrying* (2006): iron ore (metal content) 15,200,000; bauxite 5,928,000; phosphate rock 400,000; gold 12,400 kg; gem diamonds 45,000 carats. *Manufacturing* (value added in VEB '000,000,000; 2004): food products 8,122; iron and steel 3,022; refined petroleum products 2,890. *Energy production (consumption):* electricity (kW-hr; 2005) 101,544,000,000 (101,544,000,-000); coal (metric tons; 2005) 7,195,000 (52,000); crude petroleum (barrels; 2007) 888,000,000 ([2005] 384,000,000); petroleum products (metric tons; 2005) 60,084,000 (25,901,000); natural gas (cu m; 2005) 24,320,000,000 (24,320,000,000). **Selected balance of payments data.** Receipts from (US$'000,000): tourism (2006) 768; remittances (2007) 136; foreign direct investment (FDI) (2004–06 avg.) 1,174; official development assistance (2006) 58. Disbursements for (US$'000,-000): tourism (2006) 1,229; remittances (2007) 598; FDI (2004–06 avg.) 1,297. **Gross national income** (2007): US$201,146,000,000 (US$7,320 per capita). **Population economically active (2006):** total 12,379,700; activity rate of total population 45.9% (participation rates: ages 15–64, 68.7%; female 38.6%; unemployed [July 2006–June 2007] 9.4%).

Foreign trade

Imports (2006): US$30,559,000,000 (machinery and apparatus 26.6%; motor vehicles 12.1%; chemical products 11.0%, food products 5.9%). *Major import sources:* US 30.6%; Colombia 10.2%; Brazil 10.1%; Mexico 5.9%; China 4.9%. **Exports** (2006): US$61,385,000,000 (crude petroleum 91.6%; iron and steel 2.8%; aluminum 1.7%; organic chemicals 0.6%). *Major export destinations:* US 46.2%; Netherlands Antilles 13.5%; China 3.2%.

Transport and communications

Transport. *Railroads* (2005): route length 768 km; metric ton-km cargo (2004) 22,000,000. *Roads* (2004): total length 96,200 km (paved 34%). *Vehicles* (2004): passenger cars 2,466,000; trucks and buses 677,000. *Air transport* (2005): passenger-km 2,578,700,000; metric ton-km cargo (2004) 2,100,000. **Communications,** in total units (units per 1,000 persons). Telephone landlines (2007): 5,082,000

---

1 metric ton = about 1.1 short tons;   1 kilometer = 0.6 mi (statute);   1 metric ton-km cargo = about 0.68 short ton-mi cargo;   c.i.f.: cost, insurance, and freight;   f.o.b.: free on board

(184); cellular telephone subscribers (2007): 23,820,000 (861); personal computers (2005): 2,475,000 (98); total Internet users (2007): 5,720,000 (207); broadband Internet subscribers (2007): 858,000 (31).

Education and health

Educational attainment (2003). Percentage of head-of-household population having: no formal schooling 10.2%; primary education or less 38.5%; some secondary 36.9%; completed secondary/higher 14.4%. **Literacy** (2003): percentage of total population literate 93.0%. **Health** (2003): physicians 35,756 (1 per 722 persons); hospital beds 74,866 (1 per 345 persons); infant mortality rate per 1,000 live births (2006) 23.0; undernourished population (2002–04) 4,700,000 (18% of total population based on the consumption of a minimum daily requirement of 1,850 calories).

Military

Total active duty personnel (2008): 115,000 (army 54.8%, navy 15.2%, air force 10.0%, national guard 20.0%). **Military expenditure as percentage of GDP** (2007): 1.2%; per capita expenditure US$101.

Background

In 1498 Christopher Columbus sighted Venezuela; in 1499 the navigators Alonso de Ojeda, Amerigo Vespucci, and Juan de la Cosa traced the coast. A Spanish missionary established the first European settlement at Cumaná c. 1520. In 1718 it was included in the Viceroyalty of New Granada and was made a captaincy general in 1731. Venezuelan Creoles led by Francisco de Miranda and Simón Bolívar spearheaded the South American independence movement, and though Venezuela declared independence from Spain in 1811, that status was not assured until 1821. Military dictators generally ruled the country from 1830 until the overthrow of Marcos Pérez Jiménez in 1958. A new constitution adopted in 1961 marked the beginning of democracy. As a founding member of OPEC, it enjoyed relative economic prosperity from oil production during the 1970s, and its economy has remained dependent on the world petroleum market. The leftist president Hugo Chávez promulgated a new constitution in 1999, and he was reelected in 2002; a period of great political and economic tumult ensued.

Recent Developments

In November 2008 Pres. Hugo Chávez called for a popular referendum that would amend the constitution to allow for the removal of presidential term limits. Voters had narrowly rejected a similar proposal in December 2007, but in February 2009 the referendum passed, clearing the way for Chávez to run for a third term in 2012. The country continued to develop close ties with Russia, from whom Venezuela had purchased more than US$4 billion in arms, including aircraft and attack submarines, since 2005. In December 2008 the countries engaged in joint naval exercises, marking the first time that Russian ships

had acted openly in the Caribbean since the Cold War. In September Venezuela had controversially hosted two Russian bombers, and in March 2009 Chávez stated that Russian bombers continued to be welcome in his country. Venezuelan maneuvering was an important consideration in US Pres. George W. Bush's decision to reestablish the US Navy's Fourth Fleet (oriented in the Caribbean and Latin America) in April 2008.

Internet resources: <www.venezuelatuya.com/index-eng.htm>.

Vietnam

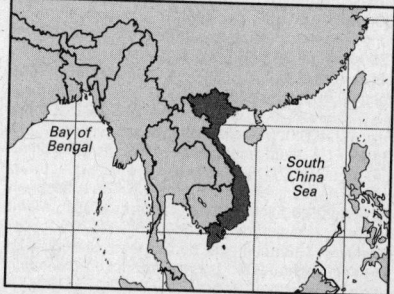

Official name: Cong Hoa Xa Hoi Chu Nghia Viet Nam (Socialist Republic of Vietnam). **Form of government:** socialist republic with one legislative house (National Assembly [493]). **Head of state:** President Nguyen Minh Triet (from 2006). **Head of government:** Prime Minister Nguyen Tan Dung (from 2006). **Capital:** Hanoi. **Official language:** Vietnamese. **Official religion:** none. **Monetary unit:** 1 dong (VND) = 10 hao = 100 xu; valuation (1 Jul 2009) US$1 = VND 17,802.00.

Demography

Area: 127,882 sq mi, 331,212 sq km. **Population** (2008): 88,537,000. **Density** (2008): persons per sq mi 692.3, persons per sq km 267.3. **Urban** (2005): 27.0%. **Sex distribution** (2007): male 49.15%; female 50.85%. **Age breakdown** (2005): under 15, 27.9%; 15–29, 30.1%; 30–44, 22.2%; 45–59, 12.1%; 60–74, 5.4%; 75–84, 1.9%; 85 and over, 0.4%. **Ethnic composition** (1999): Vietnamese 86.2%; Tho (Tay) 1.9%; Montagnards 1.7%; Thai 1.7%; Muong 1.5%; Khmer 1.4%; Nung 1.1%; Miao (Hmong) 1.0%; Dao 0.8%; other 2.7%. **Religious affiliation** (2005): Buddhist 48%; New-Religionist (mostly Cao Dai and Hoa Hao) 11%; traditional beliefs 10%; Roman Catholic 7%; Protestant 1%; nonreligious/atheist 20%; other 3%. **Major cities (urban agglomerations)** (2004 [2005]): Ho Chi Minh City 3,452,100 (5,065,000); Hanoi 1,420,400 (4,164,000); Haiphong 591,100 (1,873,000); Da Nang 459,400. **Location:** southeastern Asia, bordering China, the Gulf of Tonkin, the South China Sea, the Gulf of Thailand, Cambodia, and Laos.

Vital statistics

Birth rate per 1,000 population (2005): 17.1 (world avg. 20.3). **Death rate** per 1,000 population (2005):

6.2 (world avg. 8.6). **Total fertility rate** (avg. births per childbearing woman; 2005): 1.94. **Life expectancy** at birth (2005): male 67.8 years; female 73.6 years.

National economy

Budget (2007). *Revenue:* VND 281,900,000,000,-000 (tax revenue 82.1%, of which corporate taxes 35.1%, VAT 28.0%; nontax revenues 16.8%; grants 1.1%). *Expenditures:* VND 360,100,000,000,000 (current expenditures 61.5%, of which social services 27.0%; capital expenditures 27.6%; off-budget investment expenditures 10.9%). **Public debt** (external, outstanding; 2006): US$17,518,000,000. **Gross national income** (2007): US$67,236,-000,000 (US$790 per capita). **Production** (metric tons except as noted). *Agriculture and fishing* (2007): rice 35,566,800, sugarcane 16,000,000, cassava 8,900,000, black pepper 82,000, cinnamon 9,500; livestock (number of live animals) 26,500,000 pigs, 6,840,000 cattle, 2,921,100 buffalo, 62,800,000 ducks; fisheries production (2006) 3,617,627 (from aquaculture 46%); aquatic plants production (2006) 30,000 (from aquaculture 100%). *Mining and quarrying* (2006): phosphate rock 1,220,000; tin (metal content) 3,500. *Manufacturing* (value added in US$'000,000; 2000): food products 736; cement, bricks, and pottery 418; wearing apparel 376. *Energy production (consumption):* electricity (kW-hr; 2005) 53,463,000,000 (53,463,000,000); coal (metric tons; 2005) 32,400,000 (14,900,000); crude petroleum (barrels; 2005) 131,725,000 (negligible); petroleum products (metric tons; 2005) 343,000,000 (11,-811,000); natural gas (cu m; 2005) 6,342,000,000 (6,342,000,000). **Population economically active** (2004): total 43,242,000; activity rate of total population 52.9% (participation rates: ages 15–64, 77.7%; female 49.0%; unemployed [2006] 4.8%). **Selected balance of payments data.** Receipts from (US$'000,000): tourism (2006) 3,200; remittances (2007) 5,500; foreign direct investment (FDI) (2004–06 avg.) 1,982; official development assistance (2006) 1,846. Disbursements for (US$'000,-000): FDI (2005–06 avg.) 68.

Foreign trade

Imports (2005; c.i.f.): US$36,761,000,000 (machinery and apparatus [including aircraft] 20.7%; chemical products 14.4%; refined petroleum products 13.7%; textile yarn, fabrics, and made-up articles 9.3%; iron and steel 8.7%). *Major import sources* (2006): China 16.5%; Singapore 14.0%; Taiwan 10.7%; Japan 10.5%; South Korea 8.6%. **Exports** (2005; f.o.b.): US$32,447,000,000 (crude petroleum 22.7%; garments 14.4%; footwear 9.5%; marine products 8.5%; electrical machinery and apparatus 4.5%). *Major export destinations* (2006): US 19.7%; Japan 13.1%; Australia 9.2%; China 7.6%; Singapore 4.1%.

Transport and communications

Transport. *Railroads* (2005): route length 2,600 km; passenger-km 4,580,000,000; metric ton-km cargo 2,948,400,000. *Roads* (2004): total length 137,359 km (paved 44%). *Vehicles* (2003): passenger cars, trucks, and buses 600,000. *Air transport* (2005–06): passenger-km 11,787,000,000; metric ton-km cargo 251,100,000. **Communications,** in total units (units per 1,000 persons). Telephone landlines (2007): 28,529,000 (327); cellular telephone subscribers (2007): 23,730,000 (272); personal computers (2005): 1,174,000 (14); total Internet users (2007): 17,872,000 (205); broadband Internet subscribers (2007): 1,294,000 (15).

Education and health

Educational attainment (1999). Percentage of population ages 18 and over having: no formal education 9.0%; primary education 29.2%; lower secondary 32.5%; upper secondary 24.9%; incomplete/complete higher 4.3%; advanced degree 0.1%. **Literacy** (2003): percentage of total population ages 15 and over literate 94.0%; males literate 95.8%; females literate 92.3%. **Health** (2007): physicians 54,798 (1 per 1,594 persons); hospital beds 210,800 (1 per 415 persons); infant mortality rate per 1,000 live births (2005) 26.0; undernourished population (2002–04) 13,000,000 (16% of total population based on the consumption of a minimum daily requirement of 1,840 calories).

Military

Total active duty personnel (2007): 455,000 (army 90.5%, navy 2.9%, air force 6.6%). **Military expenditure as percentage of GDP** (2005): 6.0%; per capita expenditure US$38.

Vietnam is perhaps best known for its wars of rebellion and unification in the latter half of the 20th century, yet perhaps even more important to the national psyche are the 2,000 years of struggle against recurrent invasions from the north.

Background

A distinct Vietnamese group began to emerge c. 200 BC in the independent kingdom of Nam Viet, which was annexed to China in the 1st century BC. The Vietnamese were under continuous Chinese control until the 10th century AD. The southern region was gradually overrun by Vietnamese from the north in the late 15th century. The area was divided into two parts in the early 17th century, with the northern part known as Tonkin and the southern part as Cochin China. In 1802 the northern and southern parts of Vietnam were unified under a single dynasty. Following several years of attempted French colonial expansion in the region, the French captured Saigon in 1859 and later the rest of the area, controlling it until World War II. The Japanese occupied Vietnam in 1940–45 and declared it independent at the end of World War II, a move the French opposed. The French and Vietnamese

1 metric ton = about 1.1 short tons;   1 kilometer = 0.6 mi (statute);   1 metric ton-km cargo = about 0.68 short ton-mi cargo;   c.i.f.: cost, insurance, and freight;   f.o.b.: free on board

fought the First Indochina War until French forces with US financial backing were defeated at Dien Bien Phu in 1954; evacuation of French troops ensued. Following an international conference at Geneva, Vietnam was partitioned along the 17th parallel, with the northern part under Ho Chi Minh and the southern part under Bao Dai; the partition was to be temporary, but the reunification elections scheduled for 1956 were never held. Bao Dai declared the independence of South Vietnam (Republic of Vietnam), while the Communists established North Vietnam (Democratic Republic of Vietnam). The activities of North Vietnamese guerrillas and pro-communist rebels in South Vietnam led to US intervention and the Vietnam War. A cease-fire agreement was signed in 1973, and US troops were withdrawn. The civil war soon resumed, and in 1975 North Vietnam invaded South Vietnam and the South Vietnamese government collapsed. In 1976 the two Vietnams were united as the Socialist Republic of Vietnam. From the mid-1980s the government enacted a series of economic reforms and began to open up to Asian and Western nations. In 1995 the US officially normalized relations with Vietnam.

Recent Developments

Inflation began to rise in Vietnam in February 2008, reaching a high of 28.3% in August, and by year's end Vietnam's economy had begun to feel the impact of the global financial crisis. Accelerated inflation resulted in more than 500 strikes in the first half of the year by workers who could not subsist on their wages. Vietnam's top leaders—party Secretary-General Nong Duc Manh, Pres. Nguyen Minh Triet, and Prime Minister Nguyen Tan Dung—visited Beijing in 2008. On 31 December, just hours before the midnight deadline, Vietnam and China settled the demarcation boundary for a long-disputed border area. A maritime dispute was still pending, but in March 2009 both countries reiterated their intention to resolve this peacefully, and an encrypted hotline was established between the two capitals.

Internet resources:
<www.gso.gov.vn/default_en.aspx>.

Yemen

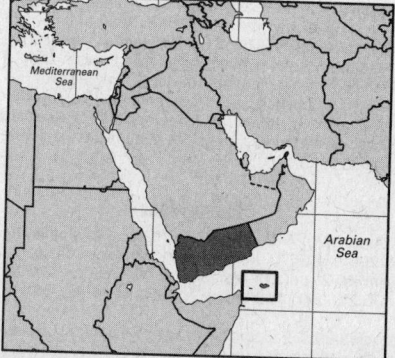

Official name: Al-Jumhuriyah al-Yamaniyah (Republic of Yemen). **Form of government:** multiparty republic with two legislative houses (Consultative Council [111]; House of Representatives [301]). **Head of state:** President Major General 'Ali 'Abdallah Salih (from 1990). **Head of government:** Prime Minister Ali Muhammad Mujawar (from 2007). **Capital:** Sanaa. **Official language:** Arabic. **Official religion:** Islam. **Monetary unit:** 1 Yemeni rial (YR) = 100 fils; valuation (1 Jul · 2009): US$1 = YR 199.75.

Demography

Area: 203,891 sq mi, 528,076 sq km. **Population** (2008): 23,013,000. **Density** (2008): persons per sq mi 112.9, persons per sq km 43.6. **Urban** (2006): 28.6%. **Sex distribution** (2007): male 50.84%; female 49.16%. **Age breakdown** (2007): under 15, 46.3%; 15–29, 29.0%; 30–44, 13.2%; 45–59, 7.5%; 60–74, 3.1%; 75 and over, 0.9%. **Ethnic composition** (2000): Arab 92.8%; Somali 3.7%; black 1.1%; Indo-Pakistani 1.0%; other 1.4%. **Religious affiliation** (2005): Muslim, nearly 100%, of which Sunni 58%, Shi'i 42%. **Major cities** (2004): Sanaa (2007) 2,006,619; Aden 588,938; Ta'izz 466,968; Al-Hudaydah 409,994; Ibb 212,992. **Location:** the Middle East, bordering Saudi Arabia, Oman, the Arabian Sea, the Gulf of Aden, and the Red Sea.

Vital statistics

Birth rate per 1,000 population (2007): 42.7 (world avg. 20.3). **Death rate** per 1,000 population (2007): 8.1 (world avg. 8.6). **Natural increase rate** per 1,000 population (2007): 34.6 (world avg. 11.7). **Total fertility rate** (avg. births per childbearing woman; 2007): 6.49. **Life expectancy** at birth (2007): male 60.6 years; female 64.5 years.

National economy

Budget (2007). *Revenue:* YR 1,406,400,000,000 (petroleum revenue 69.1%; tax revenue 21.9%; non-tax revenue and grants 9.0%). *Expenditures:* YR 1,748,300,000,000 (transfers and subsidies 29.7%; wages and salaries 27.9%; interest on debt 5.7%). **Population economically active** (2005–06): total 4,944,763; activity rate of total population 24.3% (participation rates: ages 15 and over, 44.4%; female 12.0%; unemployed 16.1%). **Production** (metric tons except as noted). *Agriculture and fishing* (2007): sorghum 429,972, potatoes 231,432, tomatoes 212,000, khat 147,444 (khat's agricultural and nonagricultural contribution to total GDP is about 10%; khat cultivation employs nearly 15% of the labor force); livestock (number of live animals) 8,420,000 sheep, 8,220,000 goats, 1,480,000 cattle, 500,000 asses, 361,000 camels; fisheries production (2006) 250,000 (from aquaculture, none). *Mining and quarrying* (2007): gypsum 44,000. *Manufacturing* (value added in YR '000,000; 2006): food and beverages 121,761; cement, bricks, and ceramics 34,294; tobacco products 26,556. *Energy production (consumption):* electricity (kW-hr; 2007) 5,243,000,000 (4,094,-000,000); crude petroleum (barrels; 2007) 117,029,000 ([2005] 31,000,000); petroleum products (metric tons; 2005) 3,115,000 (4,975,000); natural gas (cu m; 2007) 25,000,000,000 (virtually all natural gas was flared or reinjected for field pressure maintenance). **Gross national income** (2007): US$19,421,000,000 (US$870 per capita). **Public debt** (external, outstanding; January 2008): US$5,818,700,000. **Selected balance of payments data.** Receipts from (US$'000,000): tourism (2006) 181; remittances (2006) 1,283; foreign direct disinvestment (2004–06 avg.) −181; official development assistance (2006) 284. Disbursements for (US$'000,000): tourism (2006) 162; remittances (2007) 120; foreign direct investment (2004–06 avg.) 28.

Foreign trade

Imports (2006; c.i.f.): YR 1,043,119,407,000 (crude and refined petroleum 24.8%; food and live animals 19.2%; machinery and apparatus 13.7%; base and fabricated metals 10.2%; transportation equipment 9.7%). *Major import sources:* UAE 22.0%; Saudi Arabia 9.7%; Switzerland 9.1%; China 7.3%; Kuwait 6.7%. **Exports** (2006; f.o.b.): YR 1,316,197,658,000 (crude and refined petroleum 91.7%; food and live animals 3.9%, of which fish 2.0%; machinery and apparatus 1.3%; transportation equipment 1.0%). *Major export destinations:* India 24.0%; China 22.5%; Thailand 14.4%; UK 5.9%; US 5.7%.

Transport and communications

Transport. *Railroads:* none. *Roads* (2007): total length 71,300 km (paved 9%). *Vehicles* (2004): passenger cars 522,437; trucks and buses 506,766. *Air transport* (2005): passenger-km (2003) 1,956,000,000; metric ton-km cargo 67,000,000. **Communications,** in total units (units per 1,000 persons). Telephone landlines (2007): 968,000 (44); cellular telephone subscribers (2007): 4,283,000 (193); personal computers (2005): 300,000 (14); total Internet users (2007): 320,000 (14).

Education and health

Educational attainment (2004). Percentage of population ages 10 and over having: no formal schooling 46.0%; reading and writing ability 31.5%; primary education 12.0%; secondary 7.2%; higher 3.3%. **Literacy** (2005): percentage of total population ages 15 and over literate 53.0%; males literate 74.7%; females literate 52.4%. **Health** (2007): physicians 6,024 (1 per 3,690 persons); hospital beds 14,970 (1 per 1,485 persons); infant mortality rate per 1,000 live births 57.9; undernourished population (2002–04) 7,600,000 (38% of total population based on the consumption of a minimum daily requirement of 1,770 calories).

Military

Total active duty personnel (2007): 66,700 (army 90.0%, navy 2.5%, air force 7.5%). **Military expenditure as percentage of GDP** (2005): 7.0%; per capita expenditure US$50.

Background

Yemen was the home of ancient Minaean, Sabaean, and Himyarite kingdoms. The Romans invaded the region in the 1st century AD. In the 6th century it was conquered by Ethiopians and Persians. Following conversion to Islam in the 7th century, it was ruled nominally under a caliphate. The Egyptian Ayyubid dynasty ruled there from 1173 to 1229, after which the region passed to the Rasulids. From 1517 through 1918, the Ottoman Empire maintained varying degrees of control, especially in the northwestern section. A boundary agreement was reached in 1934 between the northwestern imam-controlled territory, which subsequently became the Yemen Arab Republic (North Yemen), and the southeastern British-controlled territory, which subsequently became the People's Democratic Republic of Yemen (South Yemen). Relations between the two Yemens remained tense and were marked by conflict throughout the 1970s and 1980s. Reaching an accord, the two officially united as the Republic of Yemen in 1990. Its 1993 elections were the first free, multiparty general elections held in the Arabian Peninsula, and they were the first in which women participated. In 1994, after a two-month civil war, a new constitution was approved.

Recent Developments

In 2008 Yemen continued its open-door policy for tens of thousands of Somali refugees fleeing poverty and war, a policy that put a strain on the country's meager resources. Many refugees died during treacherous journeys across the Gulf of Aden. The UN High Commissioner for Refugees recommended a global initiative to address the problem of Somali and other African refugees in Yemen. During the year media attention was brought to the Yemeni practice of child marriage when three Yemeni child brides—one only eight years old—came forward to accuse their fathers of having forced them to marry against their wills and to seek divorces in the Yemeni courts.

Internet resources: <www.yementourism.com>.

Zambia

Official name: Republic of Zambia. **Form of government:** multiparty republic with one legislative house (National Assembly [158]). **Head of state and government:** President Rupiah Banda (from 2008). **Capital:** Lusaka. **Official language:** English. **Official religion:** none (however, in 1996 Zambia was declared a Christian nation per the preamble of a constitutional amendment). **Monetary unit:** 1 Zambian kwacha (K) = 100 ngwee; valuation (1 Jul 2009) US$1 = K 5,170.00.

Demography

Area: 290,585 sq mi, 752,612 sq km. **Population** (2008): 11,670,000. **Density** (2008): persons per sq mi 40.2, persons per sq km 15.5. **Urban** (2007): 35.2%. **Sex distribution** (2005): male 49.75%; fe-

1 metric ton = about 1.1 short tons;   1 kilometer = 0.6 mi (statute);   1 metric ton-km cargo = about 0.68 short ton-mi cargo;   c.i.f.: cost, insurance, and freight;   f.o.b.: free on board

20 Jan 2009, Washington DC: New Pres. Barack Obama and wife Michelle wave as they walk toward the White House following his inauguration at the US Capitol before an audience estimated as larger than 1 million people. Obama, then 47, made history as the first African American elected president. The former US senator from Illinois, a Democrat who defeated Republican John McCain in the 2008 election, was born to

Plate 2   WORLD EVENTS

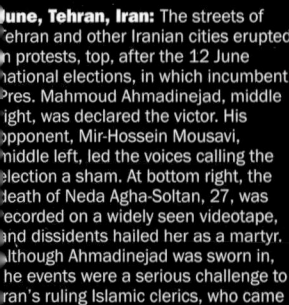

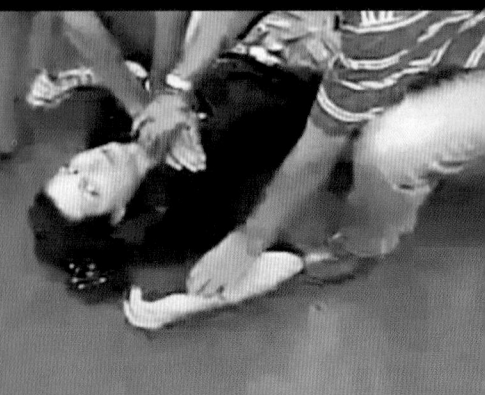

June, Tehran, Iran: The streets of Tehran and other Iranian cities erupted in protests, top, after the 12 June national elections, in which incumbent Pres. Mahmoud Ahmadinejad, middle right, was declared the victor. His opponent, Mir-Hossein Mousavi, middle left, led the voices calling the election a sham. At bottom right, the death of Neda Agha-Soltan, 27, was recorded on a widely seen videotape, and dissidents hailed her as a martyr. Although Ahmadinejad was sworn in, the events were a serious challenge to Iran's ruling Islamic clerics, who came to power in the revolution of 1979.

29 Apr 2009, Baghdad, Iraq: Civilians study the remains of one of two vehicles used in a car-bombing attack that killed 51 people at a market in Sadr City, Baghdad's Shi'ite enclave. The number of such attacks declined in 2009, as stability returned to most of Iraq's cities, and US troops handed over more responsibility for security to Iraqi troops. A new timeline ordered by President Obama calls for almost all US troops to leave the nation by the end of 2010.

7 Jun Baghdad, Iraq: Top US general Ray Odierno gives a buzz cut to TV comic Stephen Colbert, who broadcast his satirical show from Iraq for a week, delighting American troops.

29 Jun 2009 Iraq: As the US began to transfer full authority for Iraq's security to that nation's troops, Iraqi soldiers celebrated in Ramadi, above, while US troops cheered in Basra, right.

Plate 4 **WORLD EVENTS**

3 Jul 2009, Helmand province, Afghanistan: US Marines take up positions in the war-torn southwestern province. Even as the Obama administration accelerated the timetable for US troop withdrawal from Iraq, the president heeded the recommendation of military and security advisers and deployed 17,000 more US troops to Afghanistan, where resurgent Taliban forces had been gaining sway over more territory.

27 May 2009, Lahore, Pakistan: Citizens carry the coffin of a police officer who died in a car bombing that killed 30 people and injured some 250 more in the capital city of the Punjab. The bombers targeted police and intelligence service buildings. The nuclear-armed Islamic nation was rocked by turmoil in 2009, but on 5 Aug a US drone killed Baitullah Mehsud, the leader of Pakistan's largest insurgent group.

Aug 2009, Burbank CA: American journalists Laura Ling, left, and Euna Lee, right, were reunited with their families following their release from North Korea, where they were convicted in June of being spies and sentenced to 12 years of hard labor. Following secret negotiations between the US and the isolated Asian country, former president Bill Clinton flew to Pyongyang, where he met with leader Kim Jong Il and secured their release. The two are employees of a TV company headed by former vice president Al Gore.

Mar 2009, West Bank: A worker toils at a building site where new Israeli settlements are being erected in the West Bank, a Palestinian area controlled by Israel since 1967. In a May meeting at the White House, President Obama informed Israel's new prime minister, Benjamin Netanyahu, that the US opposes the

Plate 6   **UNITED STATES**

Spring 2009, Washington DC:
New president and first lady
Barack and Michelle Obama
brought charisma and energy to
the White House, as well as a
young family. Daughters Malia,
11, top left, and Sasha, 8, right,
were the youngest children to
live in the White House since the
Kennedy Administration. Above,
the First Family walks new puppy
Bo, a Portuguese water dog,
on 14 April.

Michelle Obama, 45, proved
an active First Lady who started
a White House garden, left, held
glittering cultural evenings at the
White House, and inspired young
people around the world.

**3 Apr 2009, Strasbourg,
France:** The Obamas pose with
French Pres. Nicolas Sarkozy and
wife Carla Bruni during a NATO
summit meeting. Obama was
popular around the world, and
multiple opinion polls showed an
upsurge in foreign respect for the
US after his inauguration. The
president reached out to the
Muslim world with major
speeches to Turkey's parliament
in Ankara and to Egyptian
academics at Cairo University—
though some critics said his
conciliatory appeals amounted

Joe Biden: The Obama administration includes many veteran Democratic figures, some fresh faces, and a few Republicans. Vice Pres. Joe Biden, a longtime US senator from Delaware, was given a large portfolio that emphasized foreign affairs.

Hillary Clinton: Obama enlisted the former first lady, his chief rival for his party's 2008 nomination, to serve as his secretary of state.

Rahm Emanuel: The outspoken Illinois congressman became Obama's chief of staff.

Eric Holder: The superior court judge became the first African American US attorney general.

Robert Gates: George W. Bush's secretary of defense remained in office at Obama's request.

Timothy Geithner: He left the Federal Reserve and took a hot seat as secretary of the treasury amid an economic crisis.

Steven Chu: Obama asked the physicist and academic, a Nobel Prize winner for his work on lasers, to serve as secretary of energy and promote a greener America.

Plate 8   UNITED STATES

15 Jan 2009, New York NY: The world cheered a superb act of heroism when veteran airline pilot Chesley Sullenberger, top left, ditched his US Airways Airbus A320 jet in the Hudson River after both of its engines failed shortly after takeoff from La Guardia Airport. As passengers huddled on the wings of the sinking plane, Capt. Sullenberger walked the length of the craft twice to make sure that all had exited. A speedy response by boats plying New York Harbor ensured that all 155 passengers and crew survived.

11 Apr 2009, Mombasa, Kenya: The freighter *Maersk Alabama* reaches port without its American captain, Richard Phillips, who was being held by Somali pirates hundreds of miles offshore. After the pirates took control of the freighter, Phillips offered himself as a hostage. The pirates released the ship but held Phillips aboard a small boat, awaiting ransom. On 12 April, three US Navy SEAL snipers killed the three pirates on the boat. At top right, Phillips and daughter Mariah cheer his return to the US.

Sarah Palin: In a hastily called press conference on 3 July, the governor of Alaska, who was the GOP vice presidential candidate in 2008, declared she would resign as governor within weeks, 17 months before her term was to end.

Arnold Schwarzenegger: California's Republican governor battled with state legislators of both parties for months over the details of a budget package that would address the Golden State's estimated US$26 billion deficit. On 24 July legislators approved a plan that aims to cut US$15 billion in state spending, primarily on education.

Mark Sanford: South Carolina's governor, a Republican and father of four boys, surprised constituents in June after his staff said he was hiking the Appalachian Trail alone over Father's Day weekend—but he was later found to have traveled to Argentina to visit a single woman he described in a confessional press conference as his "soul mate."

Sonia Sotomayor: Pres. Obama nominated the federal appeals court judge to fill the US Supreme Court position vacated by retiring justice David Souter. On 6 Aug 2009, the Senate confirmed the nomination, 68 to 31. She will be the third woman and the first Hispanic to take a seat on the court

Plate 10   BUSINESS & SOCIETY

17 Feb 2009, Washington DC: Taking office amid a severe economic crisis, the president pushed a US$787 billion stimulus package, left, through Congress. Critics denounced the plan's deficit spending and held "tea parties" in protest, top right.

30 Jul 2009, Washington DC: After noted black professor Henry Louis Gates, Jr. was arrested at his home in Cambridge MA by white policeman Sgt. James Crowley, Pres. Obama said the police had acted "stupidly." All parties later met for beer at the White House, joined by V.P. Joe Biden.

29 Jun 2009, New York NY: Wall Street investment adviser Bernard (Bernie) Madoff, left, pleaded guilty to 11 counts of fraud and was sentenced to 150 years in jail. Federal prosecutors accused him of having run a Ponzi scheme that bilked investors of an estimated US$65 billion.

1 May 2009, Iowa City IA: As Americans remained divided on the issue of gay marriage, partners Lawrence Miskel, left, and Ryan Parker, right, exchange vows after Iowa's Supreme Court ruled such unions legal in April. Same-sex marriages are now legal in 6 US states, not legal in 44, and are not recognized at the federal level.

11 May 2009, Mexico City, Mexico: A schoolboy wears a face mask to guard against infection from swine flu. The virus, formally called the H1N1 virus, is believed to have originated in Mexico. It traveled quickly around the world in May, leading World Health Organization scientists to label it a pandemic by June, though in most cases the flu's symptoms were mild and it was not deadly. While strong preventive measures helped control the influenza in the spring, health officials warned that a stronger form of the virus might strike in the fall.

19 Jul 2009, Jupiter: The world's amateur astronomers cheered when Australian sky-watching enthusiast Anthony Wesley became the first to report an unusual spot on the surface of Jupiter. Scientists later declared the disturbance was most likely caused when a comet collided with the giant gas planet, and they estimated the comet was as small as 1 km in diameter.

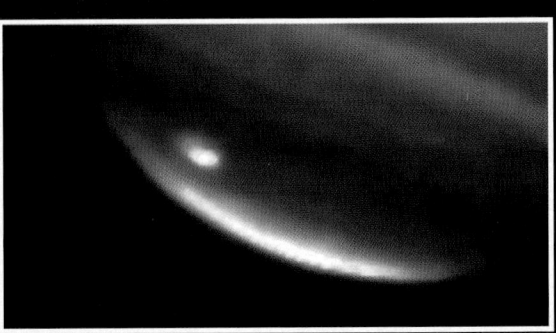

13 May 2009, Tübingen, Germany: Scientists announced the 2008 discovery of a 35,000- to 40,000-year-old carved figure of a human female, below, in Hohle Fels, Germany.

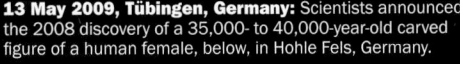

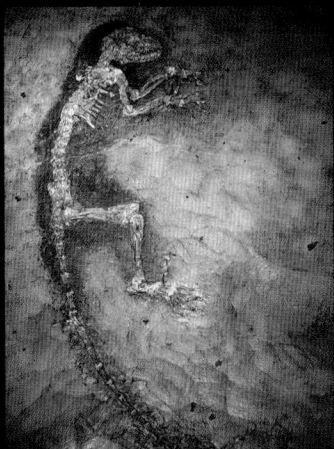

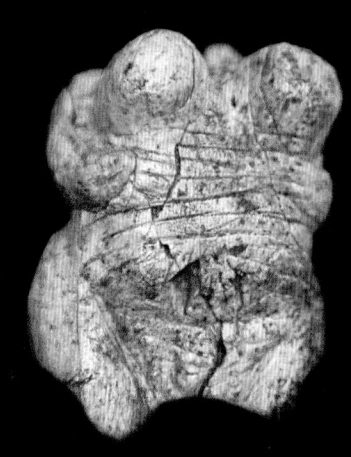

19 May 2009, New York NY: Scientists unveiled a 47-million-year-old fossilized primate, above. The early primate was first unearthed in Germany in 1983.

Plate 12 | Sport

![Golf photo]

19 Jul 2009, Ayrshire, Scotland: Veteran American golfer Tom Watson, right, thrilled fans by holding the lead in Britain's Open Championship until the 72nd hole, when the 59-year-old, a five-time Open champion, failed to make par, forcing him into a play-off with American Stewart Cink, 36. Cink won the play-off.

4–5 Jul 2009, Wimbledon, England: Swiss tennis pro Roger Federer beat American Andy Roddick to win the Wimbledon tournament in a marathon final match, taking the fifth set 16–14. It was Federer's 15th major championship, breaking his tie with Pete Sampras as holder of the most major titles. American Serena Williams beat older sister Venus to win the Wimbledon women's championship for the third time.

4 Jun 2009, Orlando FL: Kobe Bryant affirmed his status as the NBA's best player by leading the Los Angeles Lakers to a 4–1 victory over the Orlando Magic in the NBA finals. Bryant was named MVP of the series.

1 Feb 2009, Tampa FL: The Pittsburgh Steelers defeated the Arizona Cardinals 27–23 in Super Bowl XLIII, thanks to a last-minute, game-winning catch by Santonio Holmes, top right.

2 May 2009, Louisville KY: In a riveting race, long shot Mine That Bird and jockey Calvin Borel accelerated from last place to win the 135th Kentucky Derby by nearly seven lengths.

11 Jul 2009, Andorra: American cycling legend Lance Armstrong, left, a seven-time winner of the Tour de France, returned to the grinding contest at age 37, after a three-year layoff. His chief rival was Astana teammate Alberto Contador, right, a Spaniard and the 2007 Tour winner. Above, the two duel in the eighth stage of the event. Contador, 26, took a late lead and won the Tour. Armstrong finished third.

Plate 14   ARTS, ENTERTAINMENT, & LEISURE

29 May 2009, Los Angeles CA: Pixar Films, a unit of the Walt Disney Co., continued its string of box-office successes in computer-generated animated films with *Up*, which had grossed US$358 million worldwide by 1 August.

20 Nov 2009, Los Angeles CA: The second film based on the hit Twilight series of novels is expected to accelerate the craze for tales of modern-day vampires.

Jun 2009, New York NY: The British import *Billy Elliot: The Musical,* the story of a young male dancer based on a 2000 film, swept Broadway's Tony Awards, garnering honors in 10 categories.

1 Apr 2009, London, England: Unassuming Scottish singer Susan Boyle's delivery of a song from *Les Misérables* on the TV show *Britain's Got Talent* thrilled viewers and became a YouTube sensation.

Walter Cronkite: The veteran CBS anchorman, who reported many of the seminal events of the second half of the 20th century and was often called the most trusted man in the US, died on 17 July at 92.

John Updike: The acclaimed writer's novels, stories, poems, and critical essays chronicled American manners, marriages, and mores. He died at 76 on 27 January.

Corazon Aquino: The widow of murdered Filipino dissident Benigno Aquino went on to lead the stirring "people power" revolution of 1986 that overthrew the Philippines' corrupt Marcos regime. She died on 1 August at 76.

Ed McMahon: The affable second banana to TV legend Johnny Carson leveraged his success on NBC's *Tonight Show* to become a popular TV host and pitchman. He died at age 86 on 23 June.

Farrah Fawcett: The Texas-born TV star became a pop-culture icon in the 1970s as one of *Charlie's Angels* and via a racy swimsuit poster. She later earned respect as a serious actress and for her long struggle with anal cancer. She died on 25 June at 62.

Robert McNamara: Serving as US secretary of defense in two 1960s administrations, he helped direct the failed US intervention in Vietnam. In later years he expressed strong regret for his policies. He died at age 93 on 6 July.

Plate 16   OBITUARIES

Michael Jackson: The death of the pop superstar from cardiac arrest at only 50 on 25 Jun 2009 shocked the world. Jackson's career had suffered in the past 15 years, following allegations of child molestation, substance abuse, and weird personal behavior, but in death, fans recalled his brilliance as a songwriter, electrifying dancer, and video star.

While police investigated the death as possibly due to prescription drug abuse, on 7 July a lavish memorial service was held in the Staples Center in Los Angeles, right.

Edward Kennedy: The long-serving Massachusetts senator succumbed to brain cancer on 25 Aug 2009 at 77. The brother of Pres. John F. Kennedy and Sen. Robert F. Kennedy—whose personal life was stormy at times—was an outspoken liberal who nevertheless earned respect for his bipartisanship and was often called the "Lion of the Senate." At left, Kennedy is shown with then-candidate Barack Obama at a campaign rally in Washington DC on 28 Jan 2008.

Older sister Eunice Kennedy Shriver, founder of the Special Olympics, preceded her brother in death by two weeks. She was 88.

Afghanistan   Albania   Algeria   Andorra*

Angola   Antigua & Barbuda   Argentina   Armenia

Australia   Austria*   Azerbaijan   The Bahamas

Bahrain   Bangladesh   Barbados   Belarus

Belgium   Belize   Benin   Bhutan   Bolivia*

Bosnia & Herzegovina   Botswana   Brazil   Brunei

Bulgaria   Burkina Faso   Burundi   Cambodia

Cameroon   Canada   Cape Verde   Central African Republic

Chad   Chile   China   Colombia   Comoros

Civil flags are shown except where marked thus (*); in these cases, government flags are shown in order to illustrate emblems. Both styles are official national flags.

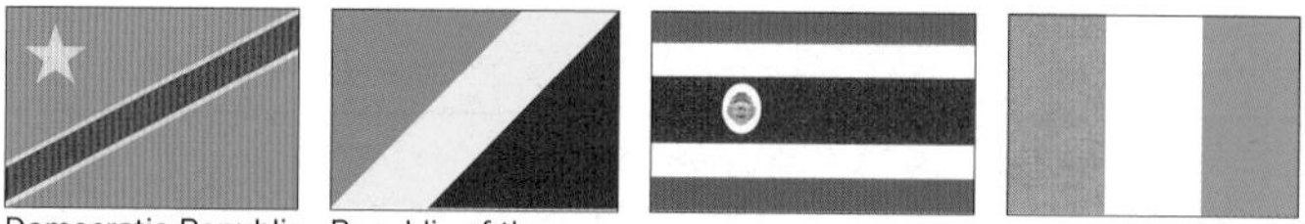

Plate 18

FLAGS OF THE WORLD

Democratic Republic of the Congo

Republic of the Congo

Costa Rica*

Côte d'Ivoire

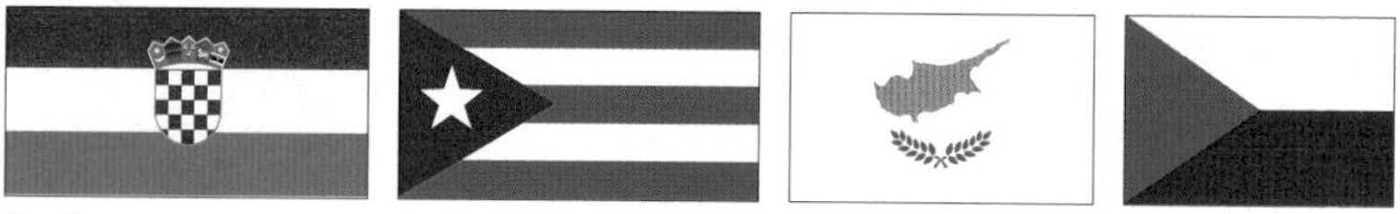

Croatia

Cuba

Cyprus

Czech Republic

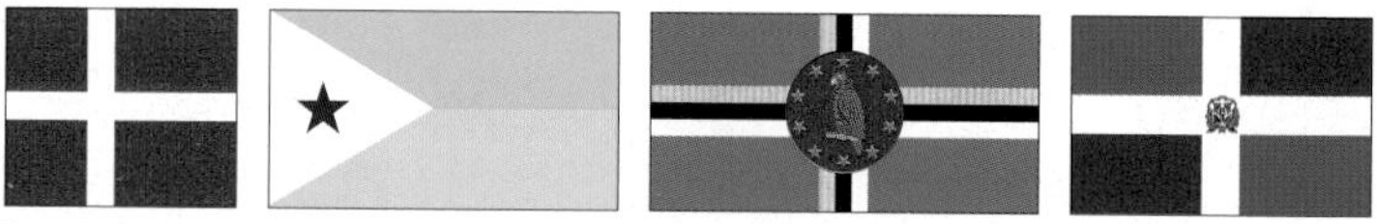

Denmark

Djibouti

Dominica

Dominican Republic*

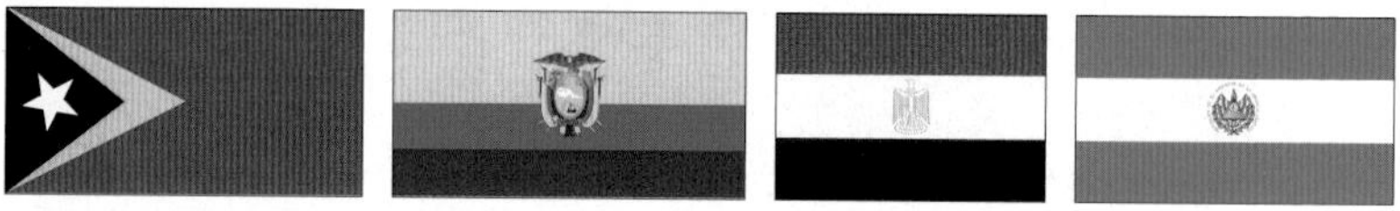

East Timor (Timor-Leste)

Ecuador*

Egypt

El Salvador

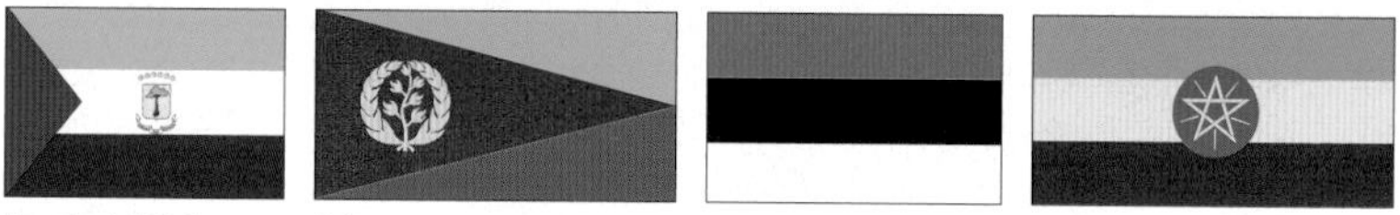

Equatorial Guinea

Eritrea

Estonia

Ethiopia

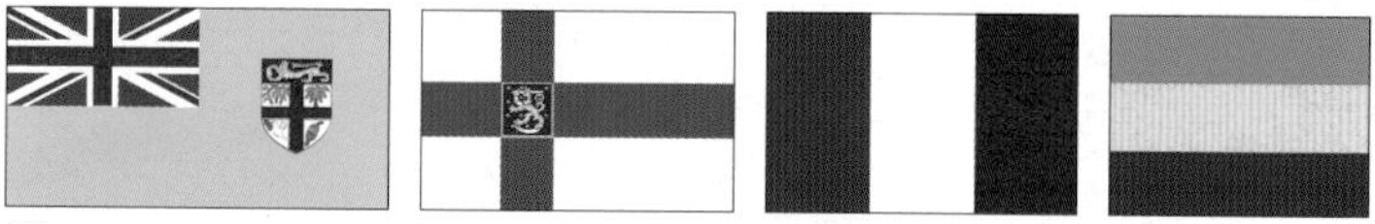

Fiji

Finland*

France

Gabon

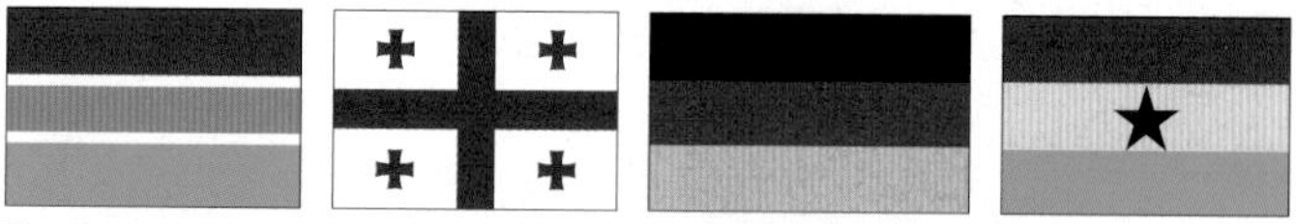

The Gambia

Georgia

Germany

Ghana

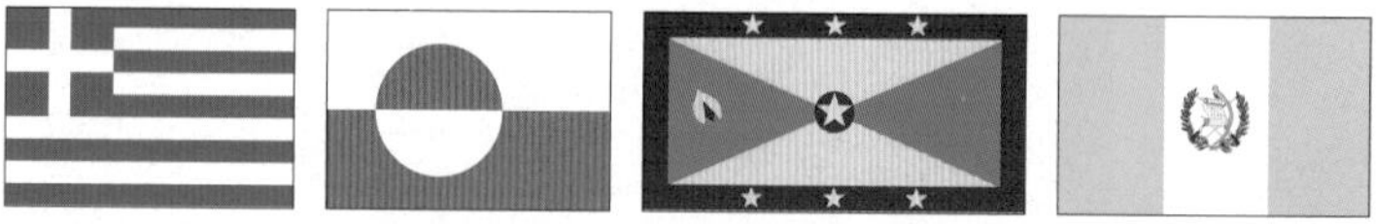

Greece

Greenland

Grenada

Guatemala*

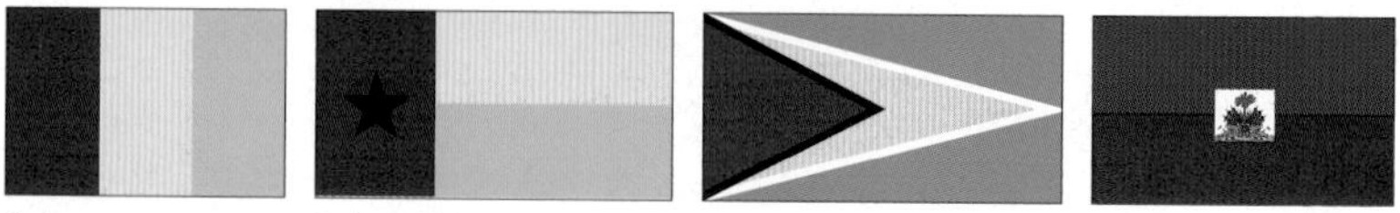

Guinea

Guinea-Bissau

Guyana

Haiti*

Civil flags are shown except where marked thus (*); in these cases, government flags are shown in order to illustrate emblems. Both styles are official national flags.

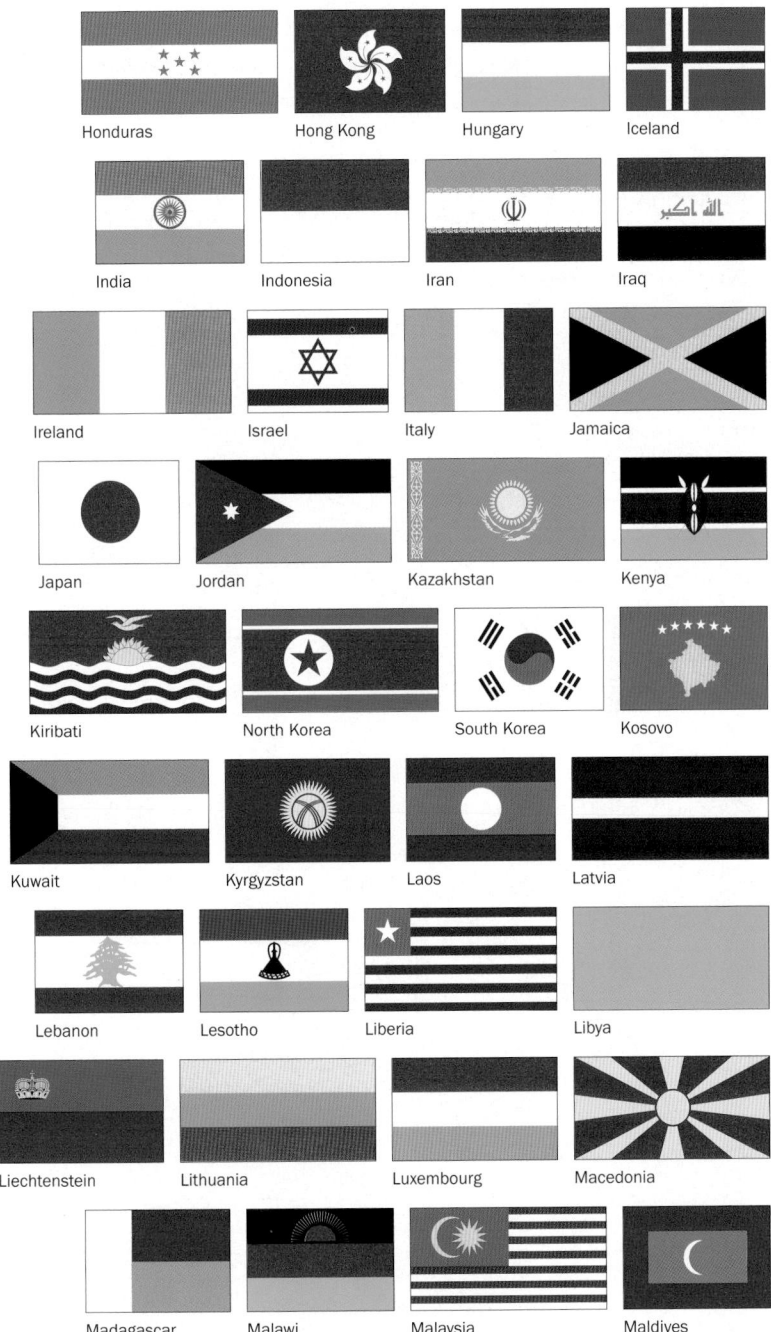

Honduras   Hong Kong   Hungary   Iceland

India   Indonesia   Iran   Iraq

Ireland   Israel   Italy   Jamaica

Japan   Jordan   Kazakhstan   Kenya

Kiribati   North Korea   South Korea   Kosovo

Kuwait   Kyrgyzstan   Laos   Latvia

Lebanon   Lesotho   Liberia   Libya

Liechtenstein   Lithuania   Luxembourg   Macedonia

Madagascar   Malawi   Malaysia   Maldives

Civil flags are shown except where marked thus (*); in these cases, government flags are shown in order to illustrate emblems. Both styles are official national flags.

Plate 20

FLAGS OF THE WORLD

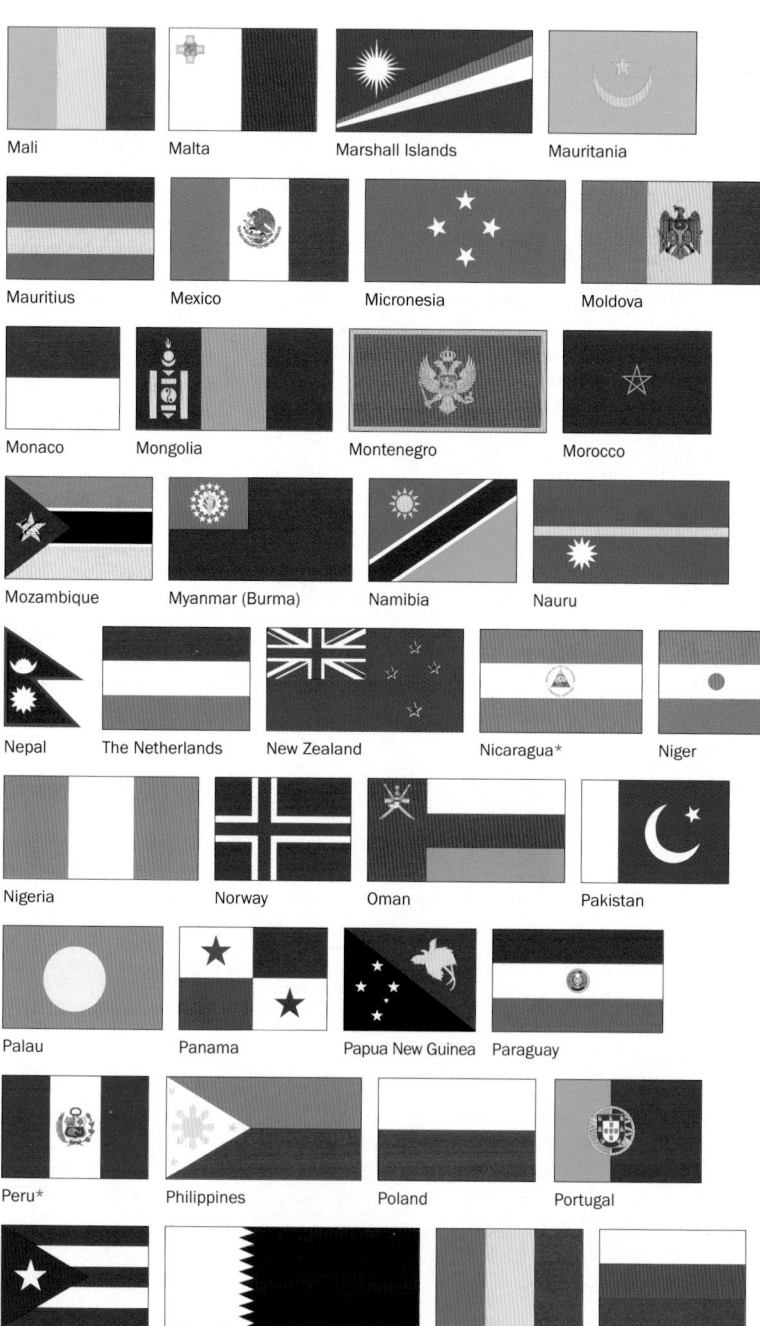

Mali Malta Marshall Islands Mauritania

Mauritius Mexico Micronesia Moldova

Monaco Mongolia Montenegro Morocco

Mozambique Myanmar (Burma) Namibia Nauru

Nepal The Netherlands New Zealand Nicaragua* Niger

Nigeria Norway Oman Pakistan

Palau Panama Papua New Guinea Paraguay

Peru* Philippines Poland Portugal

Puerto Rico Qatar Romania Russia

Civil flags are shown except where marked thus (*); in these cases, government flags are shown in order to illustrate emblems. Both styles are official national flags.

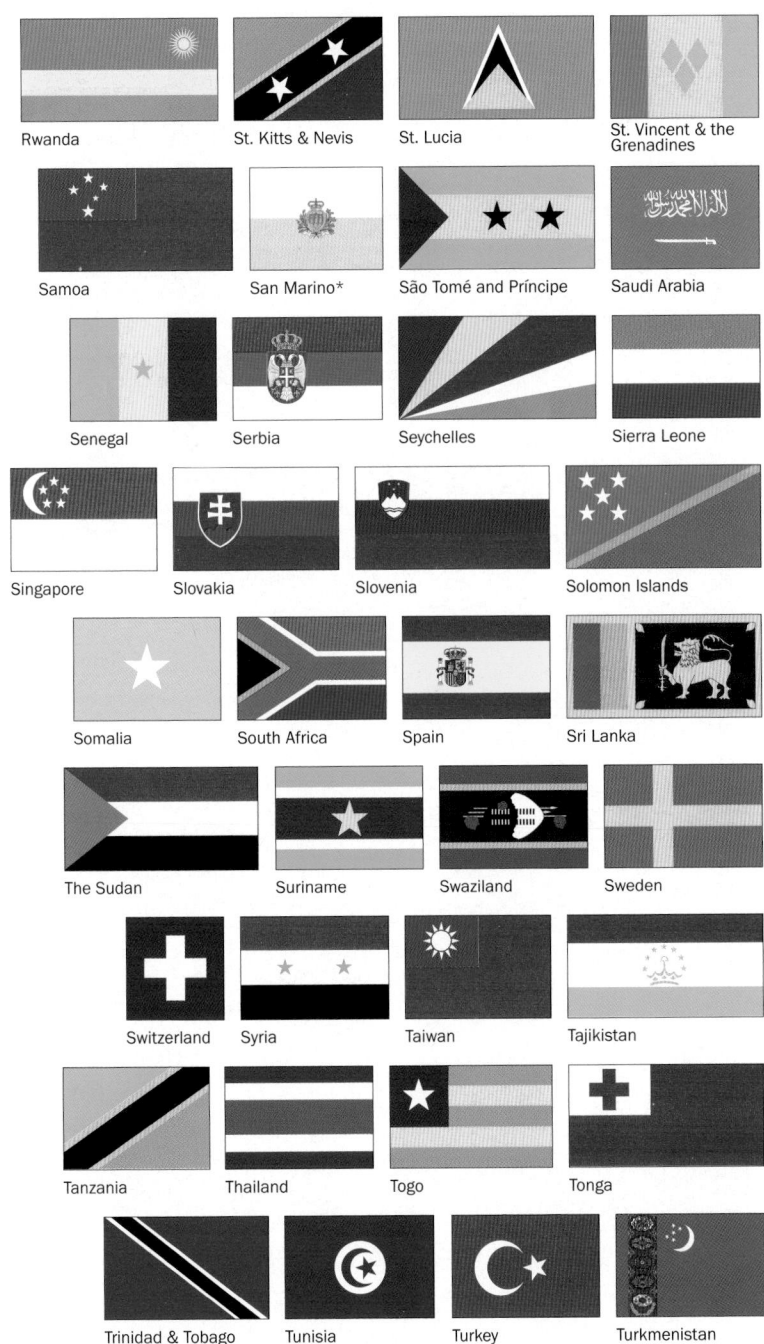

Rwanda

St. Kitts & Nevis

St. Lucia

St. Vincent & the Grenadines

Samoa

San Marino*

São Tomé and Príncipe

Saudi Arabia

Senegal

Serbia

Seychelles

Sierra Leone

Singapore

Slovakia

Slovenia

Solomon Islands

Somalia

South Africa

Spain

Sri Lanka

The Sudan

Suriname

Swaziland

Sweden

Switzerland

Syria

Taiwan

Tajikistan

Tanzania

Thailand

Togo

Tonga

Trinidad & Tobago

Tunisia

Turkey

Turkmenistan

Civil flags are shown except where marked thus (*); in these cases, government flags are shown in order to illustrate emblems. Both styles are official national flags.

Plate 22   FLAGS OF THE WORLD

Tuvalu

Uganda

Ukraine

United Arab Emirates

United Kingdom

United States

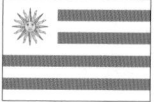

Uruguay

Uzbekistan

Vanuatu

Vatican City

Venezuela*

Vietnam

Yemen

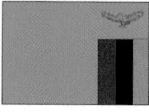

Zambia

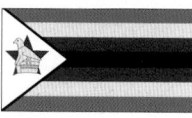

Zimbabwe

Civil flags are shown except where marked thus (*); in these cases, government flags are shown in order to illustrate emblems. Both styles are official national flags.

World Religions

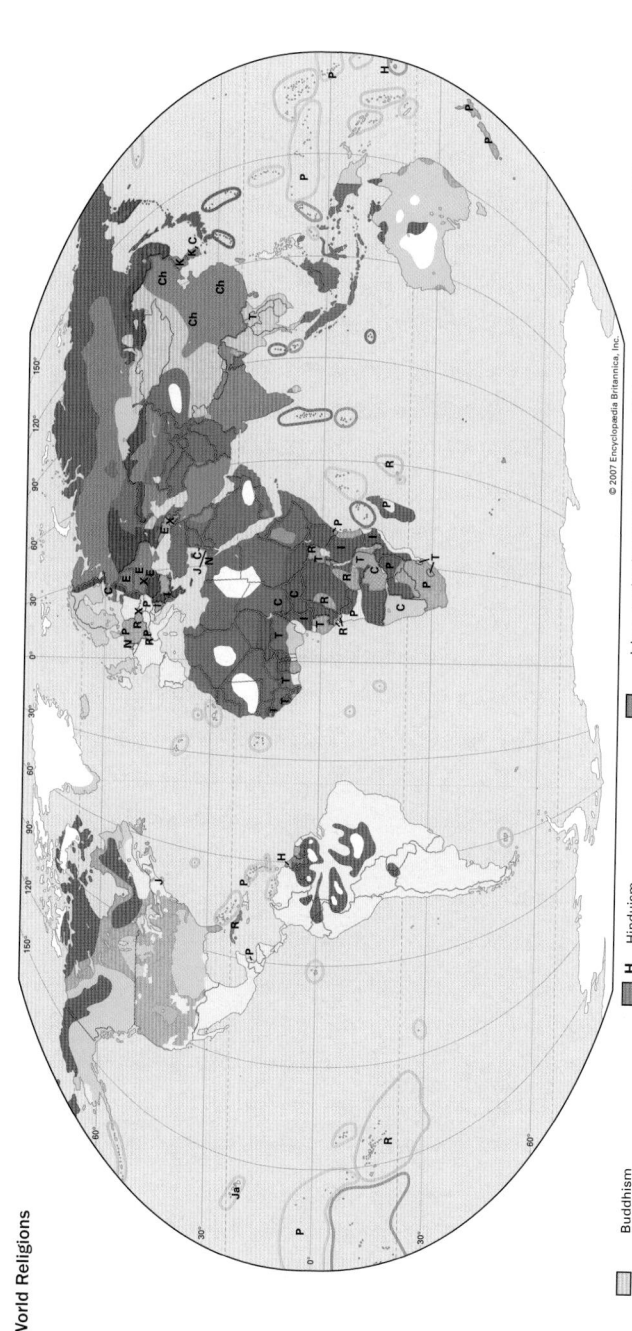

Buddhism

Ch Chinese religions[1]

C Christianity, undifferentiated by branch[2]

E Eastern Orthodoxy[3]

Hinduism

N Independent churches of Eastern Christianity[4]

T Indigenous (tribal) religions

I Islam, predominantly Sunni

Islam, predominantly Shi'ite

Ja Japanese religions[1]

J Judaism

K Korean religions[1]

Mormonism

Sikhism

P Protestantism

R Roman Catholicism

X Nonreligious

No dominant religion

Uninhabited

© 2007 Encyclopædia Britannica, Inc.

Note:
The majority of the inhabitants in each of the areas colored on the map share the religious tradition indicated. Letter symbols show religious traditions shared by at least 25 percent of the inhabitants within areas no smaller than 1,000 square miles. Therefore minority religions of city dwellers have generally not been represented.

Footnotes:
[1] In certain eastern Asian areas, many of the people have plural religious affiliations. Religions in China and Korea include Buddhism, Taoism, Confucianism, and folk cults. The Japanese religions include Shinto and Buddhism.
[2] Chiefly mingled Protestantism and Roman Catholicism, neither predominant.
[3] Including Greek and Russian Orthodox Christianity.
[4] Including Armenian, Coptic, Ethiopian, East and West Syrian.

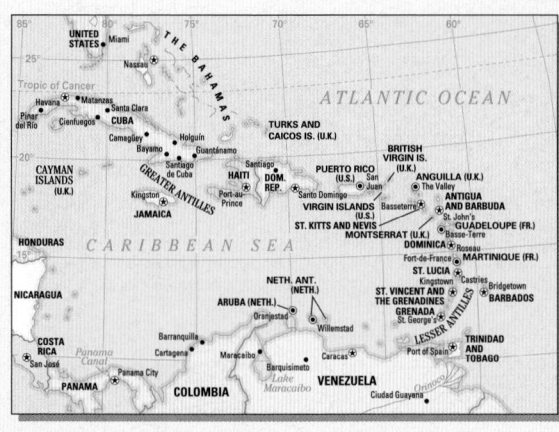
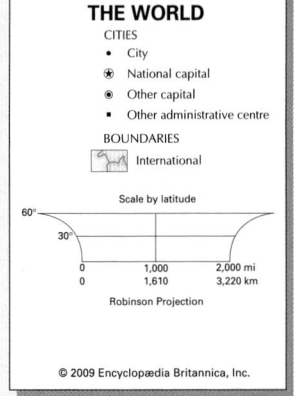

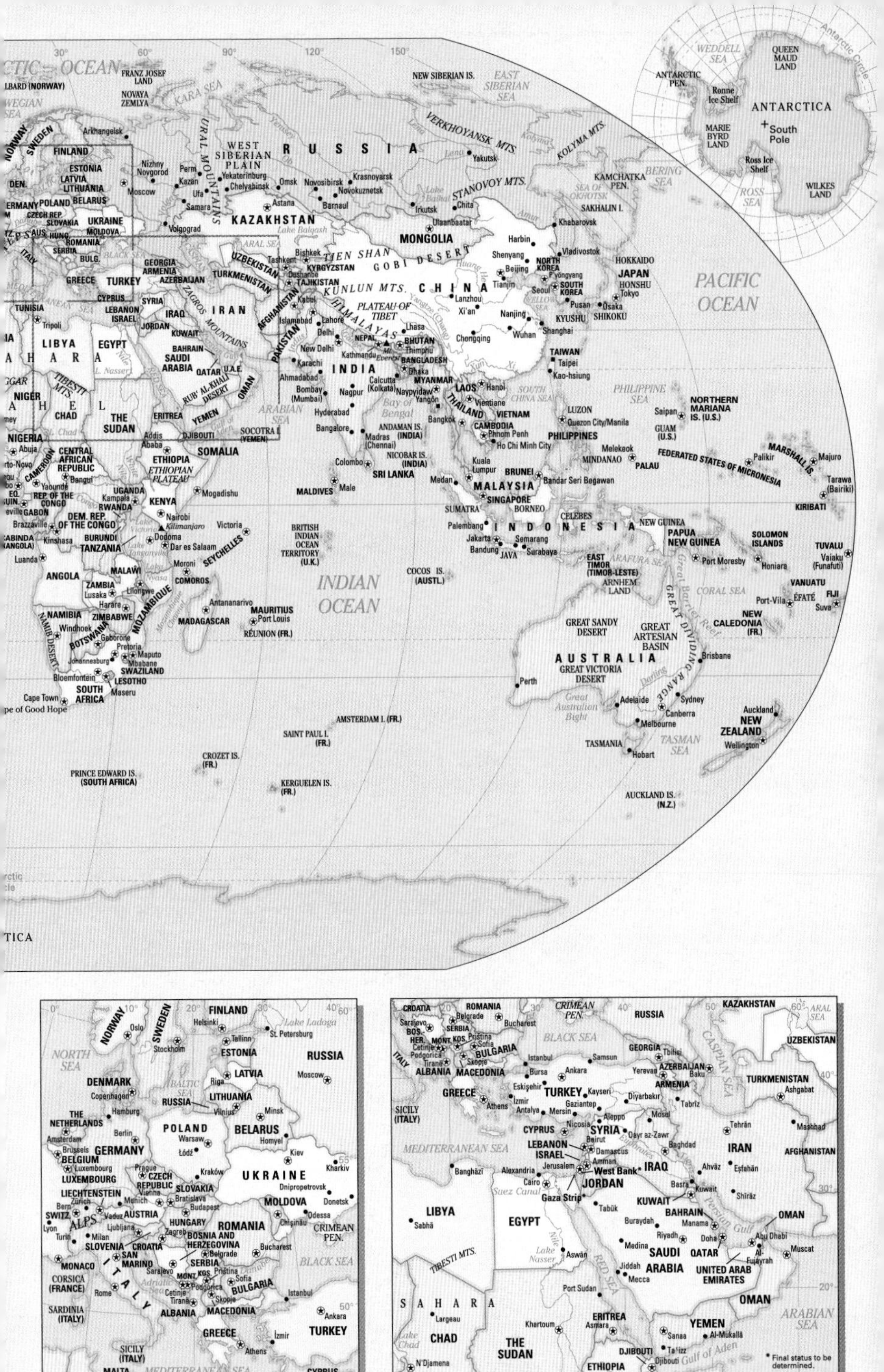

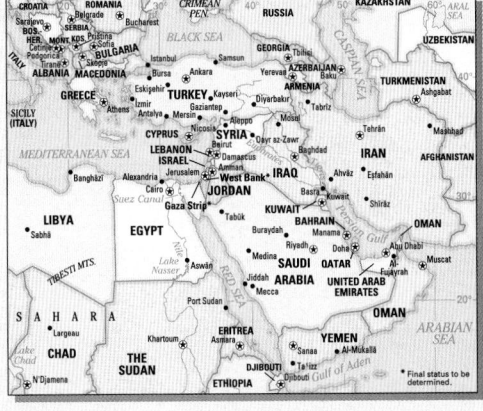

Plate 26

WORLD MAPS

Africa

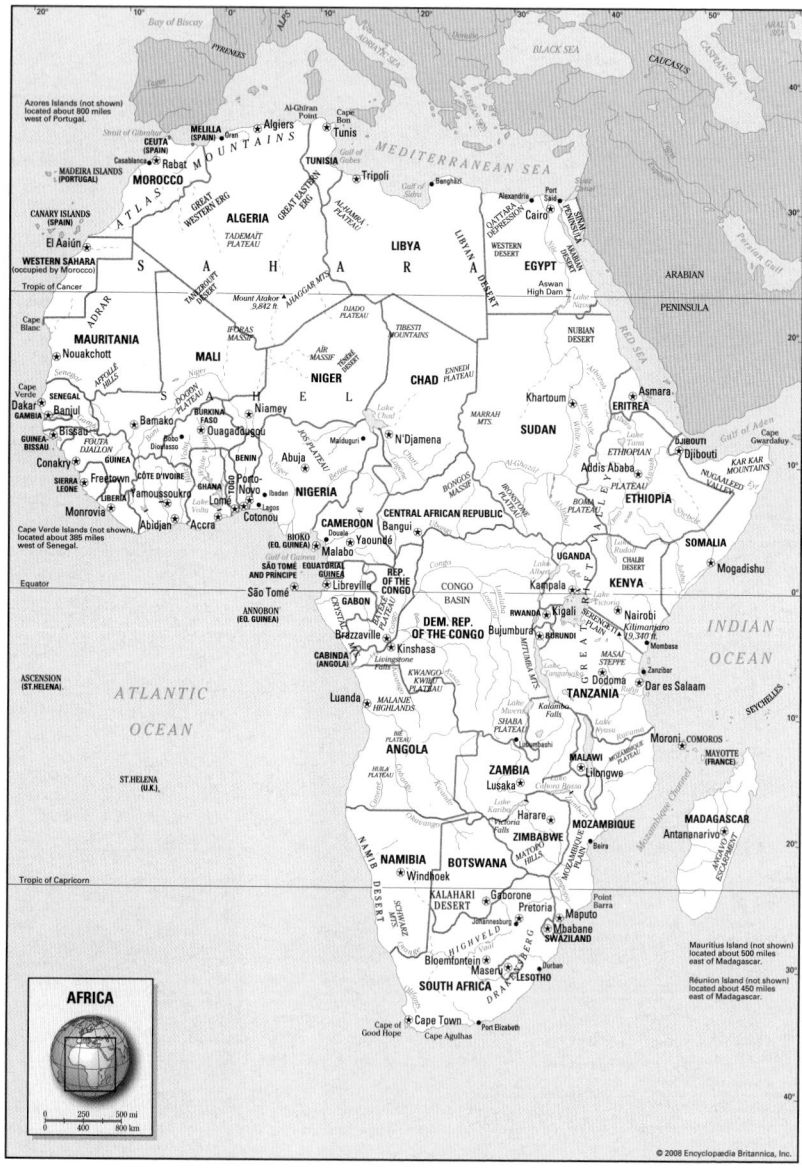

Asia

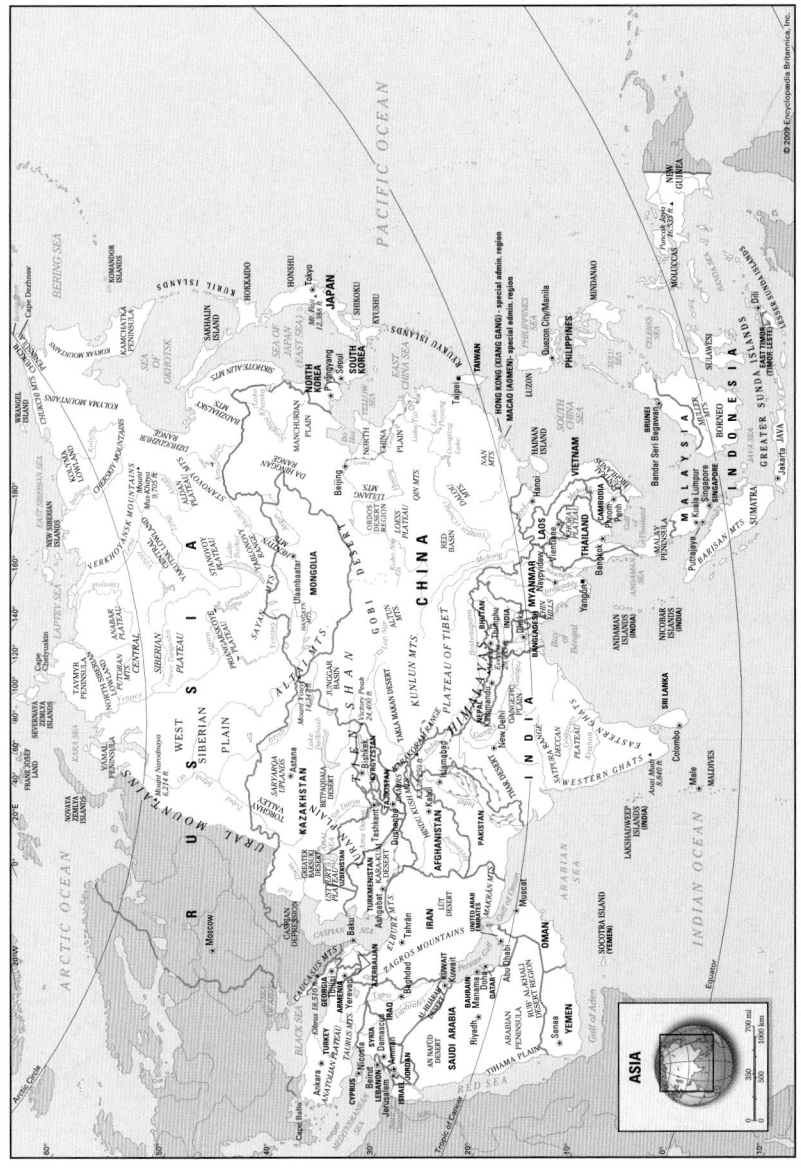

Plate 28   WORLD MAPS

Europe

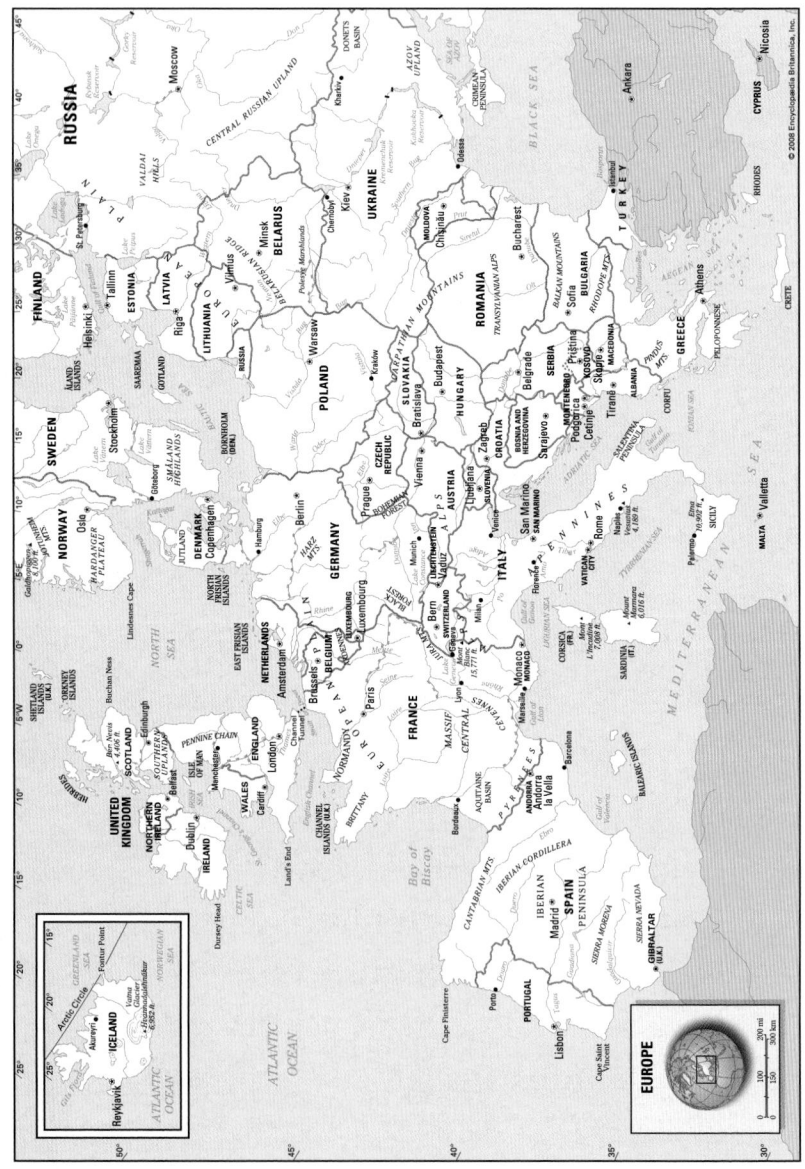

© 2008 Encyclopædia Britannica, Inc.

EUROPE

North America

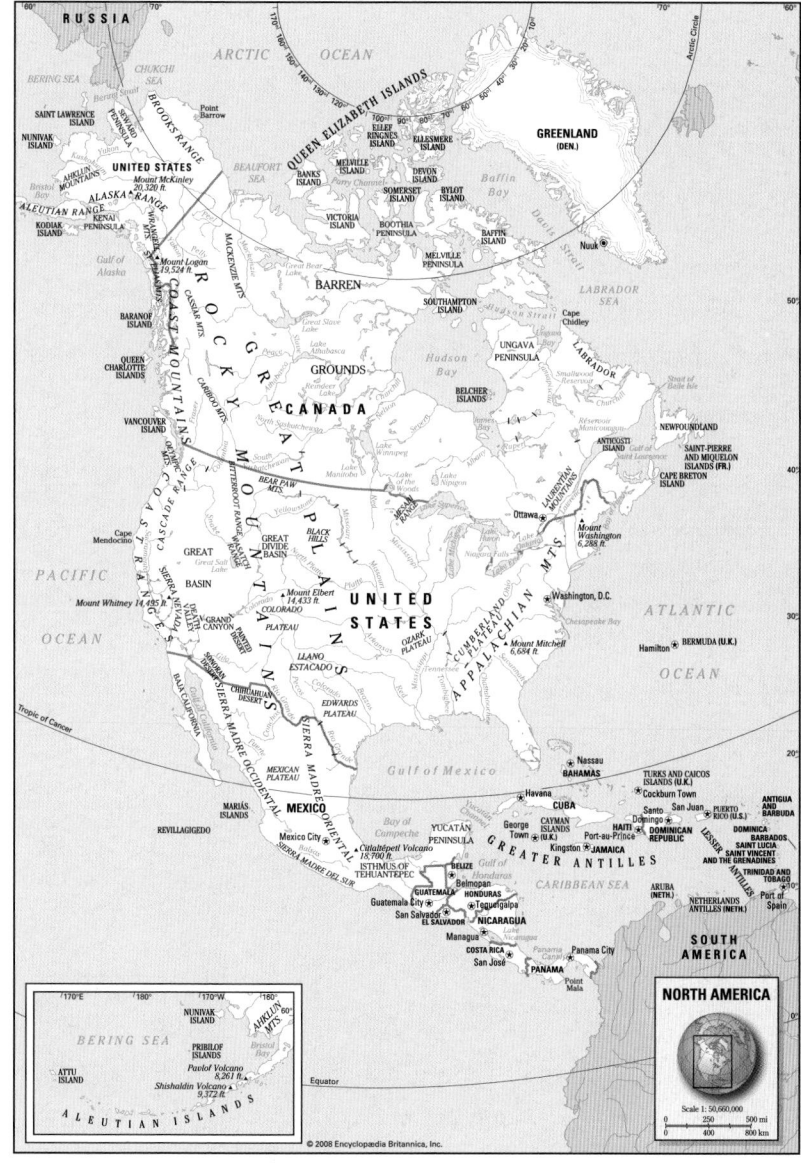

© 2008 Encyclopædia Britannica, Inc.

Plate 30   WORLD MAPS

South America

CARIBBEAN SEA

Point Gallinas
Gulf of Venezuela
Gulf of Paria

Bolívar Peak
18,947 ft.

SEGOVIA HIGHLANDS
CORDILLERA DE MÉRIDA
Caracas
Barima Point

LLANOS
IMATACA MTS.
VENEZUELA
Mount Roraima 9,219 ft.
Georgetown
Paramaribo
Cayenne

CORDILLERA OCCIDENTAL
CORDILLERA CENTRAL
CORDILLERA ORIENTAL
Bogotá
Angel Falls
SIERRA PACARAIMA
SURINAME
FRENCH GUIANA (FR.)

ATLANTIC OCEAN

10°

Duida 8,652 ft.
GUIANA
GUYANA
TUMUC-HUMAC MTS.
Cabo Norte

COLOMBIA
Neblina Peak 9,886 ft.
HIGHLANDS

Equator 0°

Chimborazo Volcano 20,561 ft.
Quito

Balbina Reservoir

Cape São Roque

ECUADOR
A M A Z O N

Cape Branco

B A S I N

Tucuruí Dam
Tucuruí Reservoir

SERRA DO CACHIMBO
SERRA DOS CARAJÁS

Sobradinho Reservoir

Huascarán 22,205 ft.
Tingo Pass
PERU
Lima

SERRA DOS PARECIS
NORTE HILLS
B R A Z I L I A N   H I G H L A N D S
BRAZIL
MESTRE UPLANDS
Paulo Afonso Falls

10°

CHINCHA ISLANDS

MOXOS PLAINS
CORDILLERA OCCIDENTAL
CORDILLERA ORIENTAL
BOLIVIA
La Paz
Chacani 19,931 ft.

Galapagos Islands, Ecuador (not shown), located about 550 miles west of Ecuador.

PLANALTO DE MATO GROSSO
Brasília

Nevado Sajama 21,391 ft.
Mount Illimani 21,201 ft.
Sucre
LLANOS DE CHIQUITOS

PANTANAL
Ilha Solteira Reservoir

SERRA DO ESPINHAÇO

PACIFIC OCEAN

Sucre

20°

GRAN
CHACO CENTRAL
PARAGUAY
Asunción

Furnas Reservoir
Três Marias Reservoir
Pico da Bandeira 9,495 ft.
Pão de Açúcar 1,296 ft.

Llullaillaco Volcano 22,057 ft.
PUNA DE ATACAMA

ATACAMA DESERT

CHACO
CHACO AUSTRAL

Itaipu Reservoir
Iguaçu Falls
SERRA DA MANTIQUEIRA

Tropic of Capricorn

Bonete 22,546 ft.

PAMPEAN SIERRAS

SERRA DE CÓRDOBA
Champaquí 7,350 ft.

Lagoa dos Patos

SERRA DO MAR

URUGUAY
GRANDE RANGE

Lagoa Mirim

30°

Mount Aconcagua 22,834 ft.
Valparaíso
Santiago
Bermejo Pass

JUAN FERNÁNDEZ ISLANDS (CHILE)

Buenos Aires
Montevideo

P A M P A S

CHILE
Domuyo Volcano 15,446 ft.
ARGENTINA

SIERRA DEL TANDIL
Point Sur del Cabo San Antonio

ATLANTIC OCEAN

Mount Tronador 11,660 ft.
CHILOÉ ISLAND

San Matías Gulf
Blanca Bay

40°

Cape Tres Puntas
San Jorge Gulf

Gulf of Penas

FALKLAND ISLANDS (ISLAS MALVINAS)
(Administered by U.K., claimed by Argentina)
Stanley

Fitz Roy 11,073 ft.
Grande Lake

TIERRA DEL FUEGO
ISLA DE LOS ESTADOS

SOUTH AMERICA

Mount Darwin 7,997 ft.
DIEGO RAMÍREZ ISLANDS
Cape Horn
Drake Passage

SOUTH GEORGIA (U.K.)

0   200   400 mi
0   300   600 km

50°

© 2008 Encyclopædia Britannica, Inc.

80° 70° 60° 50° 40°

Australia

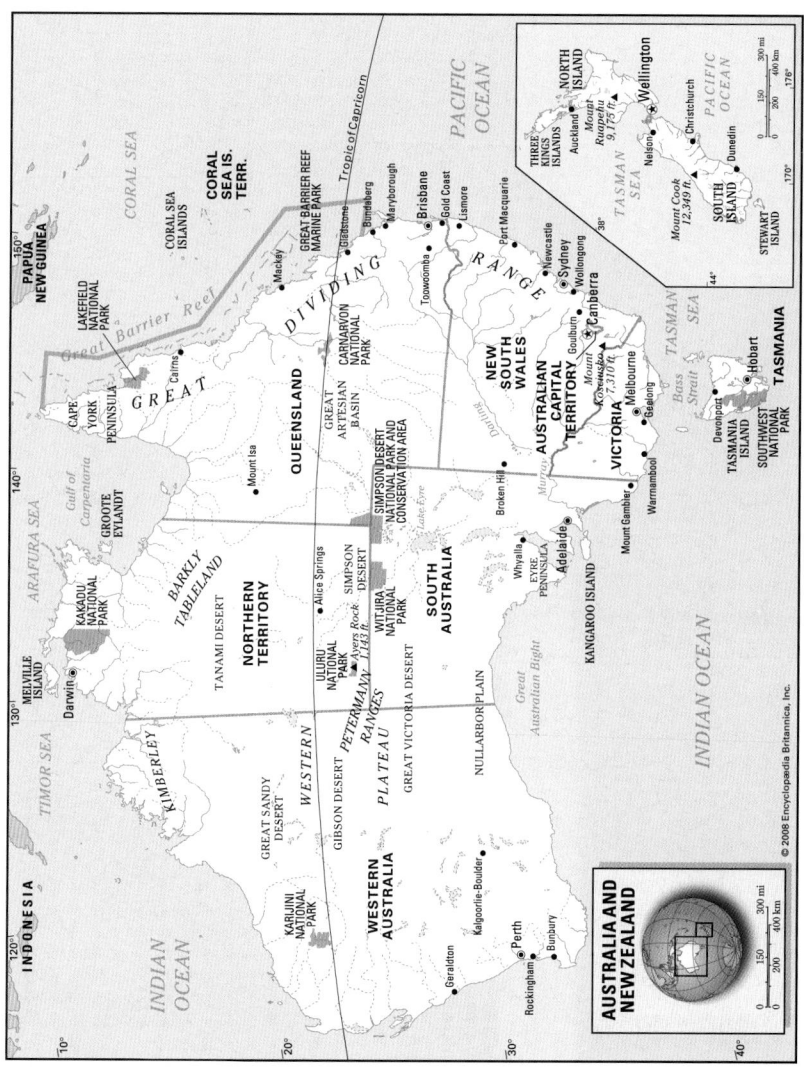

Plate 32   **WORLD MAPS**

Oceania/Pacific Islands

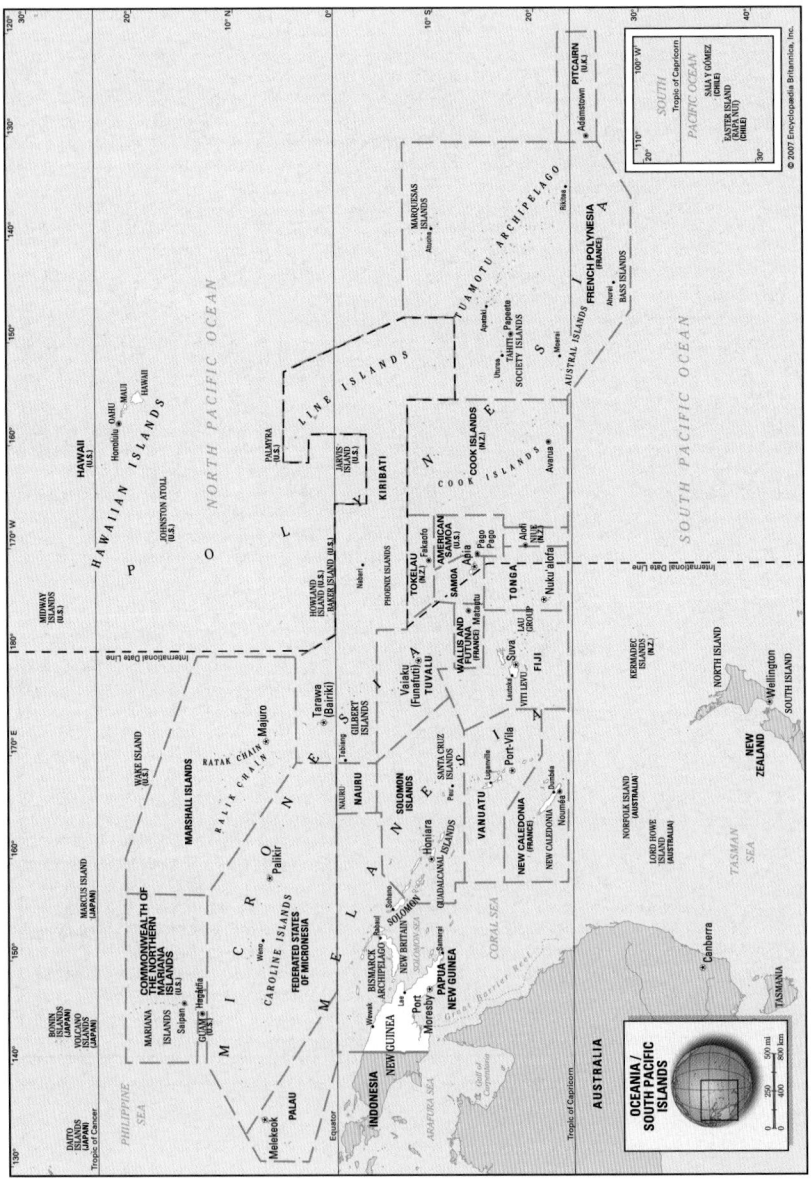

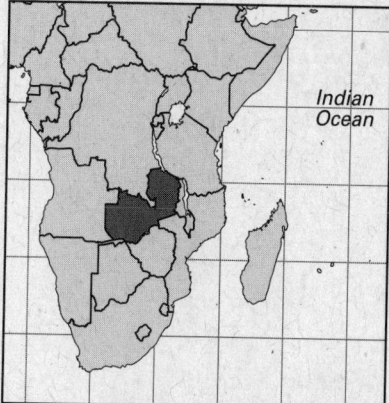

Indian Ocean

Energy production (consumption): electricity (kW-hr; 2005) 8,938,000,000 (8,695,000,000); coal (metric tons; 2005) 244,000 (161,000); crude petroleum (barrels; 2005) none (4,266,000); petroleum products (metric tons; 2005) 525,000 (553,000). **Selected balance of payments data.** Receipts from (US$'000,000): tourism (2006) 110; remittances (2007) 59; foreign direct investment (2004–06 avg.) 365; official development assistance (2006) 1,425. Disbursements for (US$'000,000): tourism (2006) 53; remittances (2007) 124. **Population economically active** (2000): total 3,165,200; activity rate of total population 32.0% (participation rates: ages 12–64, 55.8%; female 41.3%; unemployed 12.7%). **Gross national income** (2007): US$9,479,000,000 (US$800 per capita). **Public debt** (external, outstanding; 2006): US$1,003,000,000.

Did you know? Zambia is home to 19 national parks and 33 game management areas that contribute to the protection of its biodiversity. Cookson's wildebeest, the red lechwa, and Thornicroft's giraffe are among the rare and endangered species enjoying protection in Zambia.

male 50.25%. **Age breakdown** (2005): under 15, 46.2%; 15–29, 30.6%; 30–44, 13.4%; 45–59, 6.1%; 60–74, 3.0%; 75–84, 0.6%; 85 and over, 0.1%. **Ethnic composition** (2000): Bemba 21.5%; Tonga 11.3%; Lozi 5.2%; Nsenga 5.1%; Tumbuka 4.3%; Ngoni 3.8%; Chewa 2.9%; other 45.9%. **Religious affiliation** (2000): Christian 82.4%, of which Roman Catholic 29.7%, Protestant (including Anglican) 28.2%, independent Christian 15.2%, unaffiliated Christian 5.5%; traditional beliefs 14.3%; Baha'i 1.8%; Muslim 1.1%; other 0.4%. **Major cities** (2000): Lusaka 1,084,703 (urban agglomeration [2005] 1,260,000); Ndola 374,757; Kitwe 363,734; Kabwe 176,758; Chingola 147,448. **Location:** southern Africa, bordering Tanzania, Malawi, Mozambique, Zimbabwe, Botswana, Namibia, Angola, and the Democratic Republic of the Congo.

Vital statistics

Birth rate per 1,000 population (2006): 41.0 (world avg. 20.3). **Death rate** per 1,000 population (2006): 21.8 (world avg. 8.6). **Natural increase rate** per 1,000 population (2006): 19.2 (world avg. 11.7). **Total fertility rate** (avg. births per childbearing woman; 2006): 5.39. **Life expectancy** at birth (2006): male 38.0 years; female 38.2 years.

National economy

Budget (2006). *Revenue:* K 16,635,000,000,000 (grants 60.2%; tax revenue 38.4%, of which income tax 18.0%, VAT 10.9%; nontax revenue 1.4%). *Expenditures:* K 9,248,000,000,000 (current expenditures 77.1%; capital expenditures 20.3%; other 2.6%). **Production** (metric tons except as noted). *Agriculture and fishing* (2007): sugarcane 2,500,000, corn (maize) 1,366,158, cassava 940,000, sunflower seeds 8,200, cut flowers (value of sales; 2000) US$21,000,000; livestock (number of live animals) 2,610,000 cattle, 1,275,000 goats, 340,000 pigs; fisheries production (2006) 70,125 (from aquaculture 7%). *Mining and quarrying* (2006): copper (metal content) 514,000; cobalt (metal content) 8,000; amethyst 1,200,000 kg; emeralds 2,600 kg. *Manufacturing* (2005): cement 435,000; refined copper 399,000; vegetable oils (2001) 11,800; refined cobalt 5,422.

Foreign trade

Imports (2006; c.i.f.): US$3,074,000,000 (machinery and apparatus 29.7%, of which industrial machinery and equipment 19.5%; chemical products 14.6%; crude petroleum 13.6%; motor vehicles 10.0%). *Major import sources:* South Africa 47.0%; UAE 10.4%; Zimbabwe 5.7%; Norway 4.0%; UK 3.7%. **Exports** (2006; f.o.b.): US$3,770,000,000 (refined copper 67.9%; copper ore and concentrate 11.2%; cobalt 3.8%; food products 3.8%). *Major export destinations:* Switzerland 39.8%; South Africa 11.0%; Thailand 7.7%; China 6.8%; Egypt 4.2%.

Transport and communications

Transport. *Railroads* (1998): length (2006) 2,157 km; passenger-km 586,000,000; metric ton-km cargo 702,000,000. *Roads* (2001): total length 91,440 km (paved 22%). *Vehicles* (1996): passenger cars 157,000; trucks and buses 81,000. *Air transport* (Zambian Airways Limited only; 2006): passenger-km 56,609,000; metric ton-km cargo, none. **Communications,** in total units (units per 1,000 persons). Telephone landlines (2007): 92,000 (7.7); cellular telephone subscribers (2007): 2,639,000 (221); personal computers (2005): 131,000 (11); total Internet users (2007): 500,000 (42); broadband Internet subscribers (2006): 2,300 (0.2).

Education and health

Educational attainment (2001–02). Percentage of population ages 15 and over having: no formal schooling/unknown 14.7%; some primary education 33.4%; completed primary 19.7%; some secondary 22.0%; completed secondary 5.9%; higher 4.3%. **Literacy** (2007): percentage of total population ages 15 and over literate 83.5%; males literate 88.5%; females literate 78.6%. **Health:** physicians (2004) 1,264 (1 per 8,672 persons); hospital beds (2004) 21,924 (1 per 500 persons); infant mortality rate per 1,000 live births (2006) 100.5; undernourished population (2002–04) 5,000,000 (46% of total population based on the consumption of a minimum daily requirement of 1,820 calories).

Military

Total active duty personnel (2008): 15,100 (army 89.4%; navy, none; air force 10.6%). **Military expenditure as percentage of GDP** (2007): 2.2%; per capita expenditure US$20.

Background

Archaeological evidence suggests that early humans roamed present-day Zambia one to two million years ago. Ancestors of the modern Tonga tribe reached the region early in the 2nd millennium BC, but other modern peoples from Congo and Angola reached the country only in the 17th and 18th centuries. Portuguese trading missions were established early in the 18th century. Emissaries of Cecil Rhodes and the British South Africa Co. concluded treaties with most of the Zambian chiefs during the 1890s. The company administered the region known as Northern Rhodesia until 1924, when it became a British protectorate. It was part of the Central African Federation of Rhodesia and Nyasaland in 1953–63. In 1964 Northern Rhodesia became the independent republic of Zambia. A constitutional amendment was passed in 1990 allowing opposition parties; the following years were filled with political tension.

Recent Developments

Economic growth remained impressive in the early part of 2008, but inflation soared later as a result of the high cost of food and fuel. Heavy floods at the beginning of the year increased food shortages, damaging between 60% and 80% of the country's food crops and prompting a ban on the export of corn (maize). Moreover, there was concern that the country relied disproportionately on foreign earnings from copper exports. Meanwhile, the vast majority of Zambians remained poor, and jobs were scarce. The government attempted to help poorer farmers by supplying subsidized seed and fertilizer, but the country's poor infrastructure made marketing crops difficult.

Internet resources: <www.zamstats.gov.zm>.

Zimbabwe

Official name: Republic of Zimbabwe. **Form of government:** multiparty republic with two legislative houses (Senate [93]; House of Assembly [210]). **Chiefs of state and government:** President Robert Mugabe (from 1987), assisted by Prime Minister Morgan Tsvangirai (from 2009). **Capital:** Harare. **Official**

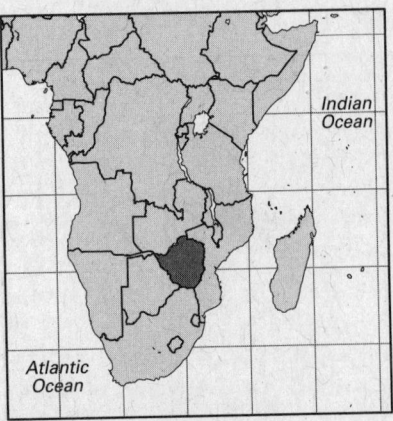

language: English. **Official religion:** none. **Monetary unit:** 1 (redenominated) Zimbabwean dollar (Z$) = 100 cents; valuation (1 Jul 2009) US$1 = Z$37,410,030.00 (the [redenominated] dollar replaced the [third, second, and old] dollar 1 Aug 2008, at the rate of [redenominated] Z$1 = [old] Z$12,000,000,000,000,000; previous redenominations of the dollar occurred on 1 Aug 2006 and 6 Sep 2007; on 10 Sep 2008 the black-market value was about [redenominated] Z$2,000 = US$1).

Demography

Area: 150,872 sq mi, 390,757 sq km. **Population** (2008): 11,350,000 (includes 3,000,000 Zimbabweans living outside of the country, many of whom are in South Africa). **Density** (2008): persons per sq mi 75.2, persons per sq km 29.0. **Urban** (2007): 36.7%. **Sex distribution** (2005): male 49.95%; female 50.05%. **Age breakdown** (2005): under 15, 37.6%; 15–29, 35.2%; 30–44, 14.5%; 45–59, 7.7%; 60–74, 3.8%; 75 and over, 1.2%. **Ethnic composition** (2003): Shona 71%; Ndebele 16%; other African 11%; white 1%; mixed race/Asian 1%. **Religious affiliation** (2005): African independent Christian 38%; traditional beliefs 25%; Protestant 14%; Roman Catholic 8%; Muslim 1%; other (mostly unaffiliated Christian) 14%. **Major cities** (2002): Harare 1,444,534; Bulawayo 676,787; Chitungwiza 321,782; Mutare 170,106; Gweru 141,260. **Location:** southern Africa, bordering Mozambique, South Africa, Botswana, Namibia, and Zambia.

Vital statistics

Birth rate per 1,000 population (2007): 31.8 (world avg. 20.3). **Death rate** per 1,000 population (2007): 18.3 (world avg. 8.6). **Total fertility rate** (avg. births per childbearing woman; 2007): 3.74. **Life expectancy** at birth (2007): male 43.9 years; female 41.9 years.

National economy

Budget (2004). *Revenue:* (old) Z$8,071,700,000,000 (tax revenue 96.2%, of which income tax

1 metric ton = about 1.1 short tons;　1 kilometer = 0.6 mi (statute);　1 metric ton-km cargo = about 0.68 short ton-mi cargo;　c.i.f.: cost, insurance, and freight;　f.o.b.: free on board

50.5%, sales tax 29.4%, customs duties 11.5%; non-tax revenue 3.8%). *Expenditures:* (old) Z$9,630,900,000,000 (current expenditures 87.3%, of which goods and services 52.1%, transfer payments 21.7%, interest payments 13.5%; development expenditures 12.7%). **Population economically active** (2003): total 5,542,000; activity rate of total population 43.1% (participation rates: ages 15–64, 74.0%; female 44.0%; unemployed [2006] 70%). **Production** (metric tons except as noted). *Agriculture and fishing* (2007): sugarcane 3,600,000, corn (maize) 952,600, seed cotton 235,000; livestock (number of live animals) 5,400,000 cattle, 3,000,000 goats, 630,000 pigs; fisheries production (2006) 15,450 (from aquaculture 16%). *Mining and quarrying* (2006): chromite 700,001; asbestos 97,000; nickel (metal content) 8,825; cobalt (metal content) 26; gold 11,354 kg; platinum-group metals (palladium, platinum, rhodium, ruthenium, and iridium) 9,894 kg; diamonds 1,046,000 carats. *Manufacturing* (value added in US$'000,000; 1998): beverages 171; food products 148; textiles 99. *Energy production (consumption):* electricity (kW-hr; 2005) 10,269,000,000 (13,246,000,000); coal (metric tons; 2005) 3,622,-000 (3,699,000); petroleum products (metric tons; 2005) none (648,000). **Public debt** (external, outstanding; 2006): US$3,452,000,000. **Gross national income** (2007): US$2,112,000,000 (US$158 per capita). **Selected balance of payments data.** Receipts from (US$'000,000): tourism (2006) 338; remittances (2005) 500–1,300; foreign direct investment (2004–06 avg.) 51; official development assistance (2006) 280. Disbursements for (US$'000,-000): tourism (1998) 131.

Foreign trade

Imports (2005; c.i.f.): US$2,072,000,000 (copper [all forms] 28.2%; machinery and apparatus 10.4%; electricity 9.0%; chemical products 7.0%; refined petroleum products 5.7%). *Major import sources:* Zambia 40.9%; South Africa 15.0%; Mozambique 9.9%; Botswana 5.0%; Kuwait 4.0%. **Exports** (2005; f.o.b.): US$1,393,000,000 (nickel [all forms] 16.4%; raw tobacco and cigarettes 15.8%; gold 14.9%; iron and steel 13.5%; food products 9.8%). *Major export destinations:* South Africa 41.5%; US 6.9%; Switzerland 6.4%; Zambia 5.6%; UK 5.3%.

Transport and communications

Transport. *Railroads* (2004): route length 3,077 km; (1998) passenger-km 408,223,000; metric ton-km cargo 1,377,000. *Roads* (2002): total length 97,267 km (paved 19%). *Vehicles* (2002): passenger cars 570,866; trucks and buses 84,456. *Air transport* (Air Zimbabwe only; 2006): passenger-km 671,185,000; metric ton-km cargo 8,547,000. **Communications,** in total units (units per 1,000 persons). Telephone landlines (2007): 345,000 (26); cellular telephone subscribers (2007): 1,226,000 (92); personal computers (2005): 850,000 (71); total Internet users (2007): 1,351,000 (101); broadband Internet subscribers (2007): 15,000 (1.1).

Education and health

Educational attainment (1992). Percentage of population ages 25 and over having: no formal schooling 22.3%; primary education 54.3%; secondary 13.1%; higher 3.4%. **Literacy** (2007): percentage of total population ages 15 and over literate 92.8%; males literate 95.8%; females literate 89.9%. **Health:** physicians (2004) 2,086 (1 per 5,792 persons); hospital beds (1996) 22,975 (1 per 501 persons); infant mortality rate per 1,000 live births (2007) 35.8; undernourished population (2002–04) 6,000,000 (47% of total population based on the consumption of a minimum daily requirement of 1,840 calories).

Military

Total active duty personnel (2008): 29,000 (army 86.2%, air force 13.8%). **Military expenditure as percentage of GDP** (2005): 2.3%; per capita expenditure US$11.

Background

Remains of Stone Age cultures dating back 500,000 years have been found in the Zimbabwe area. The first Bantu-speaking peoples reached it during the 5th–10th centuries AD, driving the San (Bushmen) inhabitants into the desert. A second migration of Bantu speakers began c. 1830. During this period the British and the Afrikaners moved up from the south, and the area came under the administration of the British South Africa Co. in 1889–1923. Called Southern Rhodesia (1911–64), it became a self-governing British colony in 1923. The colony united in 1953 with Nyasaland (Malawi) and Northern Rhodesia (Zambia) to form the Central African Federation of Rhodesia and Nyasaland. The federation dissolved in 1963, and Southern Rhodesia reverted to its former colonial status; beginning in 1964 it called itself Rhodesia. In 1965 it issued a unilateral declaration of independence considered illegal by the British government, which led to economic sanctions against it. The country proclaimed itself a republic in 1970. In 1979 it instituted limited majority rule and changed its name to Zimbabwe Rhodesia. It was granted independence by Britain in 1980 and became Zimbabwe. Robert Mugabe, Zimbabwe's first prime minister, became president in 1987. Although a multiparty system was established in 1990, Mugabe's rule became more and more autocratic.

Recent Developments

After a lengthy delay, Morgan Tsvangirai was reported to have tallied 48% of the vote in the presidential election held in Zimbabwe in March 2008. Incumbent Pres. Robert Mugabe of the Zimbabwe African National Union–Patriotic Front (ZANU–PF) received 43%. Because neither candidate garnered the constitutionally required minimum of 50% plus one vote, a runoff election was scheduled. Violent intimidation of Tsvangirai supporters by police and ZANU–PF members began immediately, causing Tsvangirai to withdraw from the contest and take refuge in the Dutch embassy. The election went ahead, however, and Mugabe was sworn in as president in June. South African Pres. Thabo Mbeki attempted to reconcile the opposing factions. In September the parties signed a power-sharing agreement, and on 11 Feb 2009, Tsvangirai was inaugurated to the newly reinstated post of prime minister, leading to hope among millions for stability and peace.

Internet resources: <www.gta.gov.zw>.

Antarctica

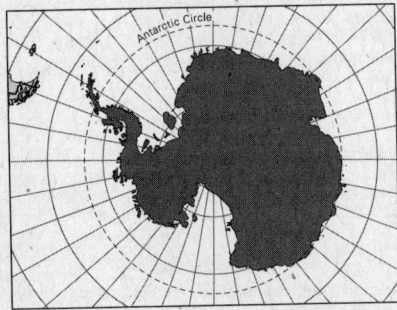

Background

The Russian F.G. von Bellingshausen, the Englishman Edward Bransfield, and the American Nathaniel Palmer all claimed first sightings of the continent in 1820. The period from the 1760s to c. 1900 was dominated by the exploration of Antarctic and subantarctic seas. In the early 20th century, the "heroic era" of Antarctic exploration, Robert Scott and, later, Ernest Shackleton made expeditions deep into the interior. Roald Amundsen reached the South Pole in December 1911, and Scott followed in 1912. The first half of the 20th century was also Antarctica's colonial period. Seven nations claimed sectors of the continent, while many other nations carried out explorations. In 1957–58, 12 nations established over 50 stations on the continent for cooperative study. In 1961 the Antarctic Treaty, which reserved Antarctica for free and nonpolitical scientific study, was enacted. A 1991 agreement imposed a 50-year ban on mineral exploitation.

Recent Developments

During the 2008–09 austral summer, about 44,500 tourists traveled to Antarctica by ship, with about three-fourths of them landing in the Antarctic Treaty area. In December 2008 the passenger ship MV Ushuaia ran aground at the entrance of Wilhelmina Bay with 82 passengers and 40 crew on board. Although the passengers were not in immediate danger, they were evacuated the next day by the Chilean naval vessel Aquiles. In February 2008 a 400-sq-km (155-sq-mi) section of ice broke away from the Wilkins Ice Shelf on the west coast of the Antarctic Peninsula in a sudden collapse, and in the spring of 2009 an ice bridge that had been preventing the remaining ice shelf from breaking away from the peninsula collapsed; serious fears that the ice shelf would disappear persisted.

Internet resources: <www.antarctica.org>.

Arctic Regions

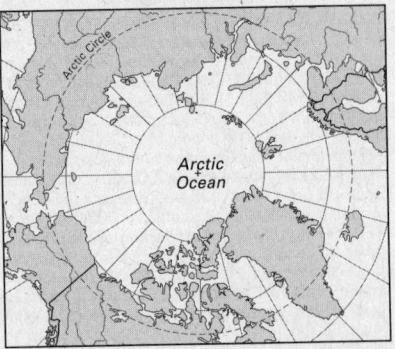

The Arctic regions may be defined in physical terms (astronomical [north of the Arctic Circle], climatic [above the 10 °C (50 °F) July isotherm], or vegetational [above the northern limit of the tree line]) or in human terms (the territory inhabited by the circumpolar cultures—Inuit [Eskimo] and Aleut in North America and Russia, Sami [Lapp] in northern Scandinavia and Russia, and 29 other peoples of the Russian North, Siberia, and East Asia). The region includes portions of Canada, the United States, Russia, Finland, Sweden, Norway, Iceland, and Greenland (part of Denmark). The Arctic Ocean, 14.09 million sq km (5.44 million sq mi) in area, constitutes about two-thirds of the region. The land area consists of permanent ice cap, tundra, or taiga. The population of peoples belonging to the circumpolar cultures (2008 estimate) is about 535,000 (Aleuts [in Russia and Alaska], more than 4,000; Athabascans [North America], 40,000; Inuits [or Eskimos, in Russian Chukhotka, North America, and Greenland], 155,000; Sami [Northern Europe], 85,000; and 41 indigenous peoples of the Russian North, totaling about 250,000). International organizations concerned with the Arctic include the Arctic Council, the Inuit Circumpolar Council, and the Indigenous Peoples' Secretariat. In 2008 the amount of summer sea ice hit its second lowest level on record, 34% below the long-term average from 1979 to 2000, and the Greenland Ice Sheet, the largest ice mass in the Northern Hemisphere, lost 222 cu km (53 cu mi), an increase of 70% in melt over previous years. Released in July, the US Geological Survey's four-year study on Arctic oil and gas reserves stated that the "extensive Arctic continental shelves may constitute the geographically largest unexplored prospective area for petroleum remaining on Earth." Overall, the Arctic was estimated to hold 22–23% of the world's oil and gas, about 13% of global oil reserves, and 30% of global gas reserves. For the first time, both the Northwest Passage in North America and the Northern Sea Route in Eurasia opened concurrently, and it was thus possible to circumnavigate the Arctic Ocean.

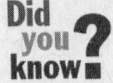

Did you know Throughout most of the Arctic, the cold is so intense that the ground is permanently frozen except for a shallow zone called the active layer, which thaws during the brief summer.

---

1 metric ton = about 1.1 short tons;   1 kilometer = 0.6 mi (statute);   1 metric ton-km cargo = about 0.68 short ton-mi cargo;   c.i.f.: cost, insurance, and freight;   f.o.b.: free on board

Membership in International Organizations

African Union (AU)
Founded: 1963. Members: 52 countries of Africa (all except Morocco), Western Sahara (Guinea was suspended in December 2008; Madagascar was suspended in March 2009).
Web site: <www.africa-union.org>.

Asia-Pacific Economic Cooperation (APEC)
Founded: 1989. Members: Australia, Brunei, Canada, Chile, China, Hong Kong, Indonesia, Japan, Republic of Korea, Malaysia, Mexico, New Zealand, Papua New Guinea, Peru, Philippines, Russia, Singapore, Taiwan, Thailand, US, Vietnam.
Web site: <www.apec.org>.

Association of Southeast Asian Nations (ASEAN)
Founded: 1967. Members: Brunei, Cambodia, Indonesia, Laos, Malaysia, Myanmar (Burma), Philippines, Singapore, Thailand, Vietnam.
Web site: <www.aseansec.org>.

Caribbean Community (Caricom)
Founded: 1973. Members: Antigua and Barbuda, The Bahamas, Barbados, Belize, Dominica, Grenada, Guyana, Haiti, Jamaica, Montserrat, Saint Kitts and Nevis, Saint Lucia, Saint Vincent and the Grenadines, Suriname, Trinidad and Tobago; associate members Anguilla, Bermuda, British Virgin Islands, Cayman Islands, Turks and Caicos Islands.
Web site: <www.caricom.org>.

Commonwealth (also called Commonwealth of Nations)
Founded: 1931. Members: United Kingdom and 52 other countries, all of which were once under British rule or administratively connected to another member country (Fiji was suspended in December 2006; Nauru is a Member in Arrears).
Web site: <www.thecommonwealth.org>.

Commonwealth of Independent States (CIS)
Founded: 1991. Members: Armenia, Azerbaijan, Belarus, Kazakhstan, Kyrgyzstan, Moldova, Russia, Tajikistan, Turkmenistan, Ukraine, Uzbekistan.
Web site: <www.cisstat.com>.

Community of Portuguese Language Countries (CPLP)
Founded: 1996. Members: Angola, Brazil, Cape Verde, East Timor (Timor-Leste), Guinea-Bissau, Mozambique, Portugal, São Tomé and Príncipe; observer states Equatorial Guinea, Mauritius, Senegal.
Web site: <www.cplp.org>.

Council of Europe
Founded: 1949. Members: 47 European and former Soviet countries; observer states Canada, Japan, Mexico, US, Vatican City.
Web site: <www.coe.int>.

Economic Community of West African States (ECOWAS)
Founded: 1975. Members: Benin, Burkina Faso, Cape Verde, Côte d'Ivoire, The Gambia, Ghana, Guinea, Guinea-Bissau, Liberia, Mali, Niger, Nigeria, Senegal, Sierra Leone, Togo (Guinea was suspended in January 2009).
Web site: <www.ecowas.int>.

European Union (EU)
Founded: 1950. Members: Austria, Belgium, Bulgaria, Cyprus, Czech Republic, Denmark, Estonia, Finland, France, Germany, Greece, Hungary, Ireland, Italy, Latvia, Lithuania, Luxembourg, Malta, The Netherlands, Poland, Portugal, Romania, Slovakia, Slovenia, Spain, Sweden, UK.
Web site: <http://europa.eu>.

Group of Eight (G8)
Founded: 1975. Members: Canada, France, Germany, Italy, Japan, Russia, UK, US.
Web site: <www.g8.utoronto.ca>.

Gulf Cooperation Council (GCC)
Founded: 1981. Members: Bahrain, Kuwait, Oman, Qatar, Saudi Arabia, UAE.
Web site: <www.gccsg.org/eng/index.php>.

League of Arab States (LAS; also called Arab League)
Founded: 1945. Members: Algeria, Bahrain, Comoros, Djibouti, Egypt, Iraq, Jordan, Kuwait, Lebanon, Libya, Mauritania, Morocco, Oman, Palestinian Authority, Qatar, Saudi Arabia, Somalia, The Sudan, Syria, Tunisia, UAE, Yemen; observer states Eritrea, Venezuela.
Web site: <www.arableagueonline.org/las/index_en.jsp>.

North Atlantic Treaty Organization (NATO)
Founded: 1949. Members: Albania, Belgium, Bulgaria, Canada, Croatia, Czech Republic, Denmark, Estonia, France, Germany, Greece, Hungary, Iceland, Italy, Latvia, Lithuania, Luxembourg, The Netherlands, Norway, Poland, Portugal, Romania, Slovakia, Slovenia, Spain, Turkey, UK, US.
Web site: <www.nato.int>.

Organisation for Economic Co-operation and Development (OECD)
Founded: 1961. Members: Australia, Austria, Belgium, Canada, Czech Republic, Denmark, Finland, France, Germany, Greece, Hungary, Iceland, Ireland, Italy, Japan, Republic of Korea, Luxembourg, Mexico, The Netherlands, New Zealand, Norway, Poland, Portugal, Slovakia, Spain, Sweden, Switzerland, Turkey, UK, US.
Web site: <www.oecd.org>.

Organization for Security and Co-operation in Europe (OSCE)
Founded: 1972. Members: 54 countries of Europe and Central Asia, plus Canada and the US.
Web site: <www.osce.org>.

Organization of American States (OAS)
Founded: 1948. Members: all 35 independent countries of the Western Hemisphere (Honduras was suspended in July 2009); 63 permanent observer states (including the EU).
Web site: <www.oas.org>.

Organization of the Petroleum Exporting Countries (OPEC)
Founded: 1960. Members: Algeria, Angola, Ecuador, Iran, Iraq, Kuwait, Libya, Nigeria, Qatar, Saudi Arabia, UAE, Venezuela.
Web site: <www.opec.org>.

Organization of the Islamic Conference (OIC)
Founded: 1969. **Members:** 56 Islamic countries (mainly in Africa and Asia), Palestinian Authority; observer states Bosnia and Herzegovina, Central African Republic, Russia, Thailand, Turkish Republic of Northern Cyprus.
Web site: <www.oic-oci.org>.

Secretariat of the Pacific Community (SPC)
Founded: 1947. **Members:** American Samoa, Australia, Cook Islands, Federated States of Micronesia, Fiji, France, French Polynesia, Guam, Kiribati, Marshall Islands, Nauru, New Caledonia, New Zealand, Niue, Northern Mariana Islands, Palau, Papua New Guinea, Pitcairn Islands, Samoa, Solomon Islands, Tokelau, Tonga, Tuvalu, US, Vanuatu, Wallis and Futuna.
Web site: <www.spc.int>.

Union of South American Nations (UNASUR/UNASUL)
Founded: 2004. **Members:** Argentina, Bolivia, Brazil, Chile, Colombia, Ecuador, Guyana, Paraguay, Peru, Suriname, Uruguay, Venezuela.
Web site: <www.comunidadandina.org>.

Southern African Development Community (SADC)
Founded: 1979. **Members:** Angola, Botswana, Democratic Republic of the Congo, Lesotho, Madagascar, Malawi, Mauritius, Mozambique, Namibia, Seychelles, South Africa, Swaziland, Tanzania, Zambia, Zimbabwe (Madagascar was suspended in March 2009).
Web site: <www.sadc.int>.

World Trade Organization (WTO)
Founded: 1995. **Members:** 153 member countries worldwide; 30 observer states as of July 2008.
Web site: <www.wto.org>.

United Nations Membership by Date of Admission

COUNTRY	DATE OF ADMISSION	COUNTRY	DATE OF ADMISSION	COUNTRY	DATE OF ADMISSION
Argentina	24 Oct 1945	Ecuador	21 Dec 1945	Gabon	20 Sep 1960
Belarus	24 Oct 1945	Iraq	21 Dec 1945	Madagascar	20 Sep 1960
Brazil	24 Oct 1945	Belgium	27 Dec 1945	Niger	20 Sep 1960
Chile	24 Oct 1945	Afghanistan	19 Nov 1946	Somalia	20 Sep 1960
China[1]	24 Oct 1945	Iceland	19 Nov 1946	Togo	20 Sep 1960
Cuba	24 Oct 1945	Sweden	19 Nov 1946	Mali	28 Sep 1960
Denmark	24 Oct 1945	Thailand	16 Dec 1946	Senegal	28 Sep 1960
Dominican Rep.	24 Oct 1945	Pakistan	30 Sep 1947	Nigeria	7 Oct 1960
Egypt	24 Oct 1945	Yemen	30 Sep 1947	Sierra Leone	27 Sep 1961
El Salvador	24 Oct 1945	Myanmar	19 Apr 1948	Mauritania	27 Oct 1961
France	24 Oct 1945	Israel	11 May 1949	Mongolia	27 Oct 1961
Haiti	24 Oct 1945	Indonesia	28 Sep 1950	Tanzania	14 Dec 1961
Iran	24 Oct 1945	Albania	14 Dec 1955	Burundi	18 Sep 1962
Lebanon	24 Oct 1945	Austria	14 Dec 1955	Jamaica	18 Sep 1962
Luxembourg	24 Oct 1945	Bulgaria	14 Dec 1955	Rwanda	18 Sep 1962
New Zealand	24 Oct 1945	Cambodia	14 Dec 1955	Trinidad and Tobago	18 Sep 1962
Nicaragua	24 Oct 1945	Finland	14 Dec 1955	Algeria	8 Oct 1962
Paraguay	24 Oct 1945	Hungary	14 Dec 1955	Uganda	25 Oct 1962
Philippines	24 Oct 1945	Ireland	14 Dec 1955	Kuwait	14 May 1963
Poland	24 Oct 1945	Italy	14 Dec 1955	Kenya	16 Dec 1963
USSR (later Russia)	24 Oct 1945	Jersey	14 Dec 1955	Malawi	1 Dec 1964
Saudi Arabia	24 Oct 1945	Jordan	14 Dec 1955	Malta	1 Dec 1964
Syria	24 Oct 1945	Laos	14 Dec 1955	Zambia	1 Dec 1964
Turkey	24 Oct 1945	Libya	14 Dec 1955	The Gambia	21 Sep 1965
Ukraine	24 Oct 1945	Nepal	14 Dec 1955	Maldives	21 Sep 1965
UK	24 Oct 1945	Portugal	14 Dec 1955	Singapore	21 Sep 1965
US	24 Oct 1945	Romania	14 Dec 1955	Guyana	20 Sep 1966
Greece	25 Oct 1945	Spain	14 Dec 1955	Lesotho	17 Oct 1966
India	30 Oct 1945	Sri Lanka	14 Dec 1955	Botswana	17 Oct 1966
Peru	31 Oct 1945	Morocco	12 Nov 1956	Barbados	9 Dec 1966
Australia	1 Nov 1945	The Sudan	12 Nov 1956	Mauritius	24 Apr 1968
Costa Rica	2 Nov 1945	Tunisia	12 Nov 1956	Swaziland	24 Sep 1968
Liberia	2 Nov 1945	Japan	18 Dec 1956	Equatorial Guinea	12 Nov 1968
Colombia	5 Nov 1945	Ghana	8 Mar 1957	Fiji	13 Oct 1970
Mexico	7 Nov 1945	Malaysia	17 Sep 1957	Bahrain	21 Sep 1971
South Africa	7 Nov 1945	Guinea	12 Dec 1958	Bhutan	21 Sep 1971
Canada	9 Nov 1945	Benin	20 Sep 1960	Qatar	21 Sep 1971
Ethiopia	13 Nov 1945	Burkina Faso	20 Sep 1960	Oman	7 Oct 1971
Panama	13 Nov 1945	Cameroon	20 Sep 1960	United Arab Emirates	9 Dec 1971
Bolivia	14 Nov 1945	Central African Rep.	20 Sep 1960	The Bahamas	18 Sep 1973
Venezuela	15 Nov 1945	Chad	20 Sep 1960	Germany	18 Sep 1973
Guatemala	21 Nov 1945	Dem. Rep. of the Congo	20 Sep 1960	Bangladesh	17 Sep 1974
Norway	27 Nov 1945			Grenada	17 Sep 1974
The Netherlands	10 Dec 1945	Rep. of the Congo	20 Sep 1960	Guinea-Bissau	17 Sep 1974
Honduras	17 Dec 1945	Côte d'Ivoire	20 Sep 1960	Cape Verde	16 Sep 1975
Uruguay	18 Dec 1945	Cyprus	20 Sep 1960	Mozambique	16 Sep 1975

United Nations Membership by Date of Admission (continued)

COUNTRY	DATE OF ADMISSION	COUNTRY	DATE OF ADMISSION	COUNTRY	DATE OF ADMISSION
São Tomé and Príncipe	16 Sep 1975	Brunei	21 Sep 1984	Bosnia and Herzegovina	22 May 1992
Papua New Guinea	10 Oct 1975	Namibia	23 Apr 1990	Croatia	22 May 1992
Comoros	12 Nov 1975	Liechtenstein	18 Sep 1990	Slovenia	22 May 1992
Suriname	4 Dec 1975	Estonia	17 Sep 1991	Georgia	31 Jul 1992
Seychelles	21 Sep 1976	Dem. People's Republic of Korea	17 Sep 1991	Czech Republic	19 Jan 1993
Angola	1 Dec 1976	Republic of Korea	17 Sep 1991	Slovakia	19 Jan 1993
Samoa	15 Dec 1976	Latvia	17 Sep 1991	Macedonia[2]	8 Apr 1993
Djibouti	20 Sep 1977	Lithuania	17 Sep 1991	Eritrea	28 May 1993
Vietnam	20 Sep 1977	Marshall Islands	17 Sep 1991	Monaco	28 May 1993
Solomon Islands	19 Sep 1978	Federated States of Micronesia	17 Sep 1991	Andorra	28 Jul 1993
Dominica	18 Dec 1978	Armenia	2 Mar 1992	Palau	15 Dec 1994
St. Lucia	18 Sep 1979	Azerbaijan	2 Mar 1992	Kiribati	14 Sep 1999
Zimbabwe	25 Aug 1980	Kazakhstan	2 Mar 1992	Nauru	14 Sep 1999
St. Vincent and the Grenadines	16 Sep 1980	Kyrgyzstan	2 Mar 1992	Tonga	14 Sep 1999
Vanuatu	15 Sep 1981	Moldova	2 Mar 1992	Tuvalu	5 Sep 2000
Belize	25 Sep 1981	San Marino	2 Mar 1992	Serbia	1 Nov 2000
Antigua and Barbuda	11 Nov 1981	Tajikistan	2 Mar 1992	Switzerland	10 Sep 2002
St. Kitts and Nevis	23 Sep 1983	Turkmenistan	2 Mar 1992	East Timor (Timor-Leste)	27 Sep 2002
		Uzbekistan	2 Mar 1992	Montenegro	28 Jun 2006

[1]The Republic of China (Taiwan) held the seat until 25 Oct 1971, when UN Res. 2758 gave the membership and a seat on the Security Council to the People's Republic of China. [2]Macedonia is known in the UN as The Former Yugoslav Republic of Macedonia.

Secretaries-General of the United Nations

The UN General Assembly appoints the Secretary-General to a five-year term on the recommendation of the 15-member Security Council; permanent members of the Security Council have veto power over nominees. The Secretary-General balances diverse and sometimes conflicting duties in the various roles of diplomat, advocate, administrator, and civil servant. The Secretary-General has a broad mandate, being able to marshal resources and advocacy on issues as various as peace efforts around the globe and disease prevention and treatment. *Internet resource:* <www.un.org>.

SECRETARY GENERAL	TERM	COMMENTS
Sir Gladwyn Jebb (acting) (UK)	1945–1946	
Trygve Lie (Norway)	1946–1952	resigned in November 1952
Dag Hammarskjöld (Sweden)	1953–1961	died in September 1961
U Thant (Burma, now Myanmar)	1962–1971	acting Secretary-General November 1961; elected 1962
Kurt Waldheim (Austria)	1972–1981	China vetoed a third term
Javier Pérez de Cuéllar (Peru)	1982–1991	
Boutros Boutros-Ghali (Egypt)	1992–1996	US vetoed a second term
Kofi Annan (Ghana)	1997–2006	
Ban Ki-moon (Republic of Korea)	2007–	

International Criminal Court

The International Criminal Court (ICC) was established by the Rome Statute of the International Criminal Court on 17 Jul 1998. The statute that created the ICC went into force on 1 Jul 2002; the court was fully operational as of July 2003. As of 29 Jun 2009, the ICC has 109 member countries.

President
Song Sang-Hyun (Republic of Korea)

First Vice President
Fatoumata Dembele Diarra (Mali)

Second Vice President
Hans-Peter Kaul (Germany)

Chief Prosecutor
Luis Moreno-Ocampo (Argentina)

Judges
List A—elected as experts in criminal law and procedure
Joyce Aluoch (Kenya)
Bruno Cotte (France)
Fatoumata Dembele Diarra (Mali)
Adrian Fulford (United Kingdom)
Daniel David Ntanda Nsereko (Uganda)
Elizabeth Odio Benito (Costa Rica)
Song Sang-Hyun (Republic of Korea)
Sylvia Steiner (Brazil)
Cuno Tarfusser (Italy)

International Criminal Court (continued)

Judges—List A (continued)
Ekaterina Trendafilova (Bulgaria)
Christine Van den Wyngaert (Belgium)

*List B—elected as experts in international law and
human rights law*
René Blattmann (Bolivia)
Hans-Peter Kaul (Germany)
Philippe Kirsch (Canada)

Judges—List B (continued)
Erkki Kourula (Finland)
Akua Kuenyehia (Ghana)
Sanji Mmasenono Monageng (Botswana)
Anita Usacka (Latvia)

Registrar
Silvana Arbia (Italy)

Rulers and Regimes

Europe

Roman Emperors

Overlapping reigns denote corulers. Diocletian (284–305) laid the foundation for the Byzantine Empire in the East when he appointed Maximian (286–305) to rule over the Western portion of the empire. Rome thus remained a unified state but was divided administratively. Theodosius I (379–395) was the last emperor to rule over a unified Roman Empire. When he died, Rome split into Eastern and Western empires. For a complete list of the Eastern emperors after the fall of Rome, see "Byzantine Empire."

REIGN	BYNAME	FULL NAME
27 BC–AD 14	Augustus	Caesar Augustus
14–37	Tiberius	Tiberius Caesar Augustus
37–41	Caligula	Gaius Caesar Augustus Germanicus
41–54	Claudius	Tiberius Claudius Caesar Augustus Germanicus
54–68	Nero	Nero Claudius Caesar Augustus Germanicus
68–69	Galba	Servius Galba Caesar Augustus
69	Otho	Marcus Otho Caesar Augustus
69	Vitellius	Aulus Vitellius Germanicus
69–79	Vespasian	Caesar Vespasianus Augustus
79–81	Titus	Titus Vespasianus Augustus
81–96	Domitian	Caesar Domitianus Augustus
96–98	Nerva	Nerva Caesar Augustus
98–117	Trajan	Caesar Nerva Traianus Augustus
117–138	Hadrian	Caesar Traianus Hadrianus Augustus
138–161	Antoninus Pius	Caesar Titus Aelius Hadrianus Antoninus Augustus Pius
161–180	Marcus Aurelius	Marcus Aurelius Antoninus
161–169	Lucius Verus	Lucius Aurelius Verus
177–192	Commodus	Lucius Aelius Aurelius Commodus
193	Pertinax	Publius Helvius Pertinax
193	Didius Julianus	Marcus Didius Severus Julianus
193–211	Septimius Severus	Lucius Septimius Severus Pertinax
198–217	Caracalla	Marcus Aurelius Severus Antoninus
209–212	Geta	Publius Septimius Geta
217–218	Macrinus	Marcus Opellius Severus Macrinus
218–222	Elagabalus	Sacerdos dei invicti solis Elagabali Marcus Aurelius Antoninus
222–235	Alexander Severus	Marcus Aurelius Severus Alexander
235–238	Maximin	Gaius Julius Verus Maximinus
238	Gordian I	Marcus Antonius Gordianus Sempronianus Romanus Africanus
238	Gordian II	Marcus Antonius Gordianus Sempronianus Romanus Africanus
238	Maximus	Marcus Clodius Pupienus Maximus
238	Balbinus	Decius Caelius Calvinus Balbinus
238–244	Gordian III	Marcus Antonius Gordianus
244–249	Philip	
249–251	Decius	Galus Messius Quintus Trianus Decius
251	Hostilian	Gaius Valens Hostilianus Messius Quintus
251–253	Gallus	Gaius Vibius Trebonianus Gallus
253	Aemilian	Marcus Aemilius Aemilianus
253–260	Valerian	Publius Licinius Valerianus
253–268	Gallienus	Publius Licinius Egnatius Gallienus
268–270	Claudius II Gothicus	Marcus Aurelius Valerius Claudius
269–270	Quintillus	Marcus Aurelius Claudius Quintillus
270–275	Aurelian	Lucius Domitius Aurelianus
275–276	Tacitus	Marcus Claudius Tacitus

Roman Emperors (continued)

REIGN	BYNAME	FULL NAME
276	Florian	Marcus Annius Florianus
276–282	Probus	Marcus Aurelius Probus
282–283	Carus	Marcus Aurelius Carus
283–285	Carinus	Marcus Aurelius Carinus
283–284	Numerian	Marcus Aurelius Numerius Numerianus
284–305[1]	Diocletian	Gaius Aurelius Valerius Diocletianus
286–305[2]	Maximian	Marcus Aurelius Valerius Maximianus Heraclius
305–311[1]	Galerius	Gaius Galerius Valerius Maximianus
305–306[2]	Constantius I Chlorus	Flavius Valerius Constantius
306–307[2]	Severus	Flavius Valerius Severus
306–312[2]	Maxentius	Marcus Aurelius Valerius Maxentius
308–324[1]	Licinius	Valerius Licinianus Licinius
312–337[2]	Constantine I	Flavius Valerius Constantinus
337–340[2]	Constantine II	Flavius Claudius [or Julius] Constantinus
337–350[2]	Constans I	Flavius Julius Constans
337–361[2]	Constantius II	Flavius Julius [or Valerius] Constantius
350–353[2]	Magnentius	Flavius Magnus Magnentius
361–363[2]	Julian	Flavius Claudius Julianus
363–364[2]	Jovian	Flavius Jovianus
364–375[2]	Valentinian I	Flavius Valentinianus
364–378[1]	Valens	Flavius Valens
365–366[1]	Procopius	
375–383[2]	Gratian	Flavius Gratianus Augustus
375–392[2]	Valentinian II	Flavius Valentinianus
379–395[2]	Theodosius I	Flavius Theodosius
395–408[1]	Arcadius	Flavius Arcadius
395–423[2]	Honorius	Flavius Honorius
408–450[1]	Theodosius II	
421[2]	Constantius III	
425–455[2]	Valentinian III	Flavius Placidius Valentinianus
450–457[1]	Marcian	Marcianus
455[2]	Petronius Maximus	Flavius Ancius Petronius Maximus
455–456[2]	Avitus	Flavius Maccilius Eparchus Avitus
457–474[1]	Leo I	Leo Thrax Magnus
457–461[2]	Majorian	Julius Valerius Majorianus
461–467[2]	Libius Severus	Libius Severianus Severus
467–472[2]	Anthemius	Procopius Anthemius
472[2]	Olybrius	Anicius Olybrius
473–474[2]	Glycerius	
474–475[2]	Julius Nepos	
474[1]	Leo II	
474–491[1]	Zeno	
475–476[2]	Romulus Augustulus	Flavius Momyllus Romulus Augustulus

[1]Ruled in the East only.   [2]Ruled in the West only.

Sovereigns of Britain

SOVEREIGN	DYNASTY OR HOUSE	REIGN
Kings of Wessex (West Saxons)		
Egbert	Saxon	802–839
Aethelwulf (Ethelwulf)	Saxon	839–856/858
Aethelbald (Ethelbald)	Saxon	855/856–860
Aethelberht (Ethelbert)	Saxon	860–865/866
Aethelred I (Ethelred)	Saxon	865/866–871
Alfred the Great	Saxon	871–899
Edward the Elder	Saxon	899–924
Sovereigns of England		
Athelstan[1]	Saxon	925–939
Edmund I	Saxon	939–946
Eadred (Edred)	Saxon	946–955
Eadwig (Edwy)	Saxon	955–959
Edgar	Saxon	959–975
Edward the Martyr	Saxon	975–978
Ethelred II the Unready (Aethelred)	Saxon	978–1013

SOVEREIGN	DYNASTY OR HOUSE	REIGN
Sovereigns of England (continued)		
Sweyn Forkbeard	Danish	1013–14
Ethelred II the Unready (restored)	Saxon	1014–16
Edmund II Ironside	Saxon	1016
Canute	Danish	1016–35
Harold I Harefoot	Danish	1035–40
Hardecanute	Danish	1040–42
Edward the Confessor	Saxon	1042–66
Harold II	Saxon	1066
William I the Conqueror	Norman	1066–87
William II	Norman	1087–1100
Henry I	Norman	1100–35
Stephen	Blois	1135–54
Henry II	Plantagenet	1154–89
Richard I	Plantagenet	1189–99

Sovereigns of Britain (continued)

SOVEREIGN	DYNASTY OR HOUSE	REIGN
Sovereigns of England (continued)		
John	Plantagenet	1199–1216
Henry III	Plantagenet	1216–72
Edward I	Plantagenet	1272–1307
Edward II	Plantagenet	1307–27
Edward III	Plantagenet	1327–77
Richard II	Plantagenet	1377–99
Henry IV	Plantagenet: Lancaster	1399–1413
Henry V	Plantagenet: Lancaster	1413–22
Henry VI	Plantagenet: Lancaster	1422–61
Edward IV	Plantagenet: York	1461–70
Henry VI (restored)	Plantagenet: Lancaster	1470–71
Edward IV (restored)	Plantagenet: York	1471–83
Edward V	Plantagenet: York	1483
Richard III	Plantagenet: York	1483–85
Henry VII	Tudor	1483–1509
Henry VIII	Tudor	1509–47
Edward VI	Tudor	1547–53
Mary I	Tudor	1553–58
Elizabeth I	Tudor	1558–1603

SOVEREIGN	DYNASTY OR HOUSE	REIGN
Sovereigns of Great Britain and the United Kingdom[2, 3]		
James I (VI of Scotland)[2]	Stuart	1603–25
Charles I	Stuart	1625–49
Commonwealth		
Oliver Cromwell, Lord Protector		1653–58
Richard Cromwell, Lord Protector		1658–59
Sovereigns of Great Britain and the United Kingdom (restored)		
Charles II	Stuart	1660–85
James II	Stuart	1685–88
William III and Mary II[4]	Orange/ Stuart	1689–1702
Anne	Stuart	1702–14
George I	Hanover	1714–27
George II	Hanover	1727–60
George III[3]	Hanover	1760–1820
George IV[5]	Hanover	1820–30
William IV	Hanover	1830–37
Victoria	Hanover	1837–1901
Edward VII	Saxe-Coburg-Gotha	1901–10
George V[6]	Windsor	1910–36
Edward VIII[7]	Windsor	1936
George VI	Windsor	1936–52
Elizabeth II	Windsor	1952–

[1]Athelstan was king of Wessex and the first king of all England.   [2]James VI of Scotland became also James I of England in 1603. Upon accession to the English throne he styled himself "King of Great Britain" and was so proclaimed. Legally, however, he and his successors held separate English and Scottish kingships until the Act of Union of 1707, when the two kingdoms were united as the Kingdom of Great Britain.   [3]The United Kingdom was formed on 1 Jan 1801, with the union of Great Britain and Ireland. After 1801 George III was styled "King of the United Kingdom of Great Britain and Ireland."   [4]William and Mary, as husband and wife, reigned jointly until Mary's death in 1694. William then reigned alone until his own death in 1702.   [5]George IV was regent from 5 Feb 1811.   [6]In 1917, during World War I, George V changed the name of his house from Saxe-Coburg-Gotha to Windsor.   [7]Edward VIII succeeded upon the death of his father, George V, on 20 Jan 1936, but abdicated on 11 Dec 1936, before coronation.

British Prime Ministers

The origin of the term prime minister and the question of to whom it should originally be applied have long been issues of scholarly and political debate. Although the term was used as early as the reign of Queen Anne (1702–14), it acquired wider currency during the reign of George II (1727–60), when it began to be used as a term of reproach toward Robert Walpole. The title prime minister did not become official until 1905, to refer to the leader of a government.

Before the development of the Conservative and Liberal parties in the mid-19th century, parties in Britain were, for the most part, simply alliances of prominent groups or aristocratic families. The designations Whig and Tory tend often to be approximate. In all cases, the party designation is that of the prime minister; he or she might lead a coalition government, as did David Lloyd George and Winston Churchill (in his first term).

PRIME MINISTER	PARTY	TERM
Robert Walpole	Whig	1721–42
Spencer Compton	Whig	1742–43
Henry Pelham	Whig	1743–54
Thomas Pelham-Holles	Whig	1754–56
William Cavendish	Whig	1756–57
Thomas Pelham-Holles	Whig	1757–62
John Stuart		1762–63
George Grenville		1763–65
Charles Watson Wentworth	Whig	1765–66
William Pitt		1766–68
Augustus Henry Fitzroy		1768–70

PRIME MINISTER	PARTY	TERM
Frederick North		1770–82
Charles Watson Wentworth	Whig	1782
William Petty-Fitzmaurice		1782–83
William Henry Cavendish-Bentinck	Whig	1783
William Pitt	Tory	1783–1801
Henry Addington	Tory	1801–04
William Pitt	Tory	1804–06
William Wyndham Grenville		1806–07

British Prime Ministers (continued)

PRIME MINISTER	PARTY	TERM	PRIME MINISTER	PARTY	TERM
William Henry Cavendish-Bentinck	Whig	1807–09	Archibald Philip Primrose	Liberal	1894–95
Spencer Perceval	Tory	1809–12	Robert Cecil	Conservative	1895–1902
Robert Banks Jenkinson	Tory	1812–27	Arthur James Balfour	Conservative	1902–05
George Canning	Tory	1827	Henry Campbell-Bannerman	Liberal	1905–08
Frederick John Robinson	Tory	1827–28	H.H. Asquith	Liberal	1908–16
Arthur Wellesley	Tory	1828–30	David Lloyd George	Liberal	1916–22
Charles Grey	Whig	1830–34	Bonar Law	Conservative	1922–23
William Lamb	Whig	1834	Stanley Baldwin	Conservative	1923–24
Arthur Wellesley	Tory	1834	Ramsay Macdonald	Labour	1924
Robert Peel	Tory	1834–35	Stanley Baldwin	Conservative	1924–29
William Lamb	Whig	1835–41	Ramsay Macdonald	Labour	1929–35
Robert Peel	Conservative	1841–46	Stanley Baldwin	Conservative	1935–37
John Russell	Whig-Liberal	1846–52	Neville Chamberlain	Conservative	1937–40
Edward Geoffrey Stanley	Conservative	1852	Winston Churchill	Conservative	1940–45
George Hamilton-Gordon		1852–55	Clement Attlee	Labour	1945–51
Henry John Temple	Liberal	1855–58	Winston Churchill	Conservative	1951–55
Edward Geoffrey Stanley	Conservative	1858–59	Anthony Eden	Conservative	1955–57
Henry John Temple	Liberal	1859–65	Harold Macmillan	Conservative	1957–63
John Russell	Liberal	1865–66	Alec Douglas-Home	Conservative	1963–64
Edward Geoffrey Stanley	Conservative	1866–68	Harold Wilson	Labour	1964–70
Benjamin Disraeli	Conservative	1868	Edward Heath	Conservative	1970–74
William Ewart Gladstone	Liberal	1868–74	Harold Wilson	Labour	1974–76
Benjamin Disraeli	Conservative	1874–80	James Callaghan	Labour	1976–79
William Ewart Gladstone	Liberal	1880–85	Margaret Thatcher	Conservative	1979–90
Robert Cecil	Conservative	1885–86	John Major	Conservative	1990–97
William Ewart Gladstone	Liberal	1886	Tony Blair	Labour	1997–2007
Robert Cecil	Conservative	1886–92	Gordon Brown	Labour	2007–
William Ewart Gladstone	Liberal	1892–94			

Rulers of France

RULER	REIGN	RULER	REIGN
Carolingian dynasty		**Capetian dynasty (continued)**	
Pippin III the Short	751–768	Louis VI	1108–37
Charles I (Charlemagne, Kingdom of the Franks)	768–814	Louis VII	1137–80
		Philip II (Philippe)	1180–1223
Louis I (Kingdom of the Franks)	814–840	Louis VIII	1223–26
civil war	840–843	Louis IX (Saint Louis)	1226–70
Charles II (Kingdom of the West Franks)	843–877	Philip III (Philippe)	1270–85
Louis II (Kingdom of the West Franks)	877–879	Philip IV (Philippe)	1285–1314
Louis III (Kingdom of the West Franks)	879–882	Louis X	1314–16
Carloman (Kingdom of the West Franks)	879–884	John I (Jean)	1316
Charles (III) (Charles III, Holy Roman Empire)	884–887	Philip V (Philippe)	1316–22
		Charles IV	1322–28
Robertian (Capetian) dynasty		**Valois dynasty**	
Eudes	888–898	Philip VI (Philippe)	1328–50
		John II (Jean)	1350–64
Carolingian dynasty		Charles V	1364–80
Charles III	893/898–923	Charles VI	1380–1422
		Charles VII	1422–61
Robertian (Capetian) dynasty		Louis XI	1461–83
Robert I	922–923	Charles VIII	1483–98
Rudolf (Raoul, or Rodolphe)	923–936		
		Valois dynasty (Orléans branch)	
Carolingian dynasty		Louis XII	1498–1515
Louis IV	936–954		
Lothair (Lothaire)	954–986	**Valois dynasty (Angoulême branch)**	
Louis V	986–987	Francis I (François)	1515–47
		Henry II (Henri)	1547–59
Capetian dynasty		Francis II (François)	1559–60
Hugh Capet (Hugues Capet)	987–996	Charles IX	1560–74
Robert II	996–1031	Henry III (Henri)	1574–89
Henry I (Henri)	1031–60		
Philip I (Philippe)	1060–1108		

Rulers of France (continued)

RULER	REIGN
House of Bourbon	
Henry IV (Henri)	1589–1610
Louis XIII	1610–43
Louis XIV	1643–1715
Louis XV	1715–74
Louis XVI	1774–92
Louis (XVII)	1793–95
First Republic	
National Convention	1792–95
Directorate	1795–99
Consulate (Napoléon Bonaparte)	1799–1804
First Empire (emperors)	
Napoleon I (Napoléon Bonaparte)	1804–14, 1815
Napoleon (II)	1815
House of Bourbon	
Louis XVIII	1814–24
Charles X	1824–30
House of Orléans	
Louis-Philippe	1830–48
Second Republic (president)	
Louis-Napoléon Bonaparte	1848–52
Second Empire (emperor)	
Napoleon III (Louis-Napoléon Bonaparte)	1852–70

RULER	REIGN
Third Republic (presidents)	
Adolphe Thiers	1871–73
Marie-Edmé-Patrice-Maurice	1873–79
Jules Grévy	1879–87
Sadi Carnot	1887–94
Jean Casimir-Périer	1894–95
Félix Faure	1895–99
Émile Loubet	1899–1906
Armand Fallières	1906–13
Raymond Poincaré	1913–20
Paul Deschanel	1920
Alexandre Millerand	1920–24
Gaston Doumergue	1924–31
Paul Doumer	1931–32
Albert Lebrun	1932–40
French State (État Français, or Vichy France)	
Philippe Pétain	1940–44
Provisional government	1944–47
Fourth Republic (presidents)	
Vincent Auriol	1947–54
René Coty	1954–59
Fifth Republic (presidents)	
Charles de Gaulle	1959–69
Georges Pompidou	1969–74
Valéry Giscard d'Estaing	1974–81
François Mitterrand	1981–95
Jacques Chirac	1995–2007
Nicolas Sarkozy	2007–

Rulers of Germany

On 25 Jul 1806 the Confederation of the Rhine was founded, with Karl Theodor von Dalberg as prince primate (1806–13). After the dissolution of the Rhine Confederation, there was no true central power until 1815, when the German Confederation was founded. In 1867 the governing structure became the North German Confederation, and in 1871 the German Reich. For rulers of Germany before the Confederation of the Rhine, see Holy Roman Emperors.

RULER	REIGN OR TERM
Emperors	
Hohenzollern dynasty	
Wilhelm I	1871–88
Friedrich III	1888
Wilhelm II	1888–1918
Presidents	
Richard Müller	1918
Robert Leinert	1918–19
Wilhelm Pfannkuch	1919
Eduard David	1919
Friedrich Ebert	1919–25
Paul von Hindenburg	1925–34
Adolf Hitler (Führer)	1934–45
Karl Dönitz	1945
Chancellors	
Otto Fürst von Bismarck	1871–90
Leo Graf von Caprivi	1890–94
Chlodwig Fürst zu Hohenlohe-Schillingsfürst	1894–1900
Bernhard Graf Fürst von Bülow	1900–09
Theobald von Bethmann Hollweg	1909–17
Georg Michaelis	1917

RULER	REIGN OR TERM
Chancellors (continued)	
Georg Graf von Hertling	1917–18
Maximilian Prinz von Baden	1918
Friedrich Ebert	1918
Philipp Scheidemann	1919
Gustav Bauer	1919–20
Wolfgang Kapp (in rebellion)	1920
Hermann Müller	1920
Konstantin Fehrenbach	1920–21
Joseph Wirth	1921–22
Wilhelm Cuno	1922–23
Gustav Stresemann	1923
Wilhelm Marx	1923–24
Hans Luther	1925–26
Wilhelm Marx	1926–28
Hermann Müller	1928–30
Heinrich Brüning	1930–32
Franz von Papen	1932
Kurt von Schleicher	1932–33
Adolf Hitler	1933–45
Joseph Goebbels	1945
Lutz Graf Schwerin von Krosigk (chairman of interim government)	1945

Rulers of Germany (continued)

Allied occupation   1945-49

German Democratic Republic (East Germany)[1]

Presidents		Chairmen of the Council of State (continued)	
Wilhelm Pieck	1949-60	Erich Honecker	1976-89
		Egon Krenz	1989
Chairmen of the Council of State		Sabine Bergmann-Pohl	1990
Walter Ulbricht	1960-73		
Willi Stoph	1973-76		

Federal Republic of Germany (West Germany)[1]

Presidents		Chancellors	
Theodor Heuss	1949-59	Konrad Adenauer	1949-63
Heinrich Lübke	1959-69	Ludwig Erhard	1963-66
Gustav Heinemann	1969-74	Kurt Georg Kiesinger	1966-69
Walter Scheel	1974-79	Willy Brandt	1969-74
Karl Carstens	1979-84	Helmut Schmidt	1974-82
Richard von Weizsäcker	1984-94	Helmut Kohl	1982-98
Roman Herzog	1994-99	Gerhard Schröder	1998-2005
Johannes Rau	1999-2004	Angela Merkel	2005-
Horst Köhler	2004-		

[1]After World War II, Germany was split into four occupational zones, governed by the French, British, American, and Soviet powers. The Western zones were merged and, on 23 May 1949, became the independent Federal Republic of Germany. On 7 October of the same year, the Soviet zone was proclaimed the German Democratic Republic. On 3 Oct 1990, the latter was incorporated into the Federal Republic of Germany.

Holy Roman Emperors

The Holy Roman Empire encompassed a varying complex of lands in Western and Central Europe. Ruled over by Frankish and then German kings, the empire officially dissolved on 6 Aug 1806, when Francis II resigned his title.

EMPEROR	REIGN	EMPEROR	REIGN
Carolingian dynasty		**Salian dynasty (continued)**	
Charlemagne (Charles I)	800-814	Henry IV	1056-1106
Louis I	814-840	Rival claimants:	
Civil War	840-843	Rudolf	1077-80
Lothair I	843-855	Hermann	1081-93
Louis II	855-875	Conrad	1093-1101
Charles II	875-877	Henry V	1105/06-25
Interregnum	877-881		
Charles III	881-887	**House of Supplinburg**	
interregnum	887-891	Lothair II	1125-37
House of Spoleto		**House of Hohenstaufen**	
Guy	891-894	Conrad III	1138-52
Lambert	894-898	Frederick I (Barbarossa)	1152-90
		Henry VI	1190-97
Carolingian dynasty		Philip	1198-1208
Arnulf	896-899		
Louis III	901-905	**Welf dynasty**	
		Otto IV	1198-1214
House of Franconia			
Conrad I	911-918	**House of Hohenstaufen**	
		Frederick II	1215-50
Carolingian dynasty		Rival claimants:	
Bérengar	915-924	Henry (VII)	1220-35
		Henry Raspe	1246-47
House of Saxony (Liudolfings)		William of Holland	1247-56
Henry I	919-936	Conrad IV	1250-54
Otto I	936-973	*Great Interregnum*	1254-73
Otto II	973-983	Richard	1257-72
Otto III	983-1002	Alfonso (Alfonso X of Castile)	1257-75
Henry II	1002-24		
		House of Habsburg	
Salian dynasty		Rudolf I	1273-91
Conrad II	1024-39		
Henry III	1039-56		

Holy Roman Emperors (continued)

EMPEROR	REIGN
House of Nassau	
Adolf	1292–98
House of Habsburg	
Albert I	1298–1308
House of Luxembourg	
Henry VII	1308–13
House of Habsburg	
Frederick (III)	1314–26
House of Wittelsbach	
Louis IV	1314–46
House of Luxembourg	
Charles IV	1346–78
Wenceslas	1378–1400
House of Wittelsbach	
Rupert	1400–10
House of Luxembourg	
Jobst	1410–11
Sigismund	1410–37

EMPEROR	REIGN
House of Habsburg	
Albert II	1438–39
Frederick III	1440–93
Maximilian I	1493–1519
Charles V	1519–56
Ferdinand I	1556–64
Maximilian II	1564–76
Rudolf II	1576–1612
Matthias	1612–19
Ferdinand II	1619–37
Ferdinand III	1637–57
Leopold I	1658–1705
Joseph I	1705–11
Charles VI	1711–40
House of Wittelsbach	
Charles VII	1742–45
House of Habsburg	
Francis I	1745–65
Joseph II	1765–90
Leopold II	1790–92
Francis II	1792–1806

Rulers of Russia[1]

RULER	REIGN
Princes and Grand Princes of Moscow (Muscovy): Danilovich dynasty[2]	
Daniel (son of Alexander Nevsky)	c. 1276–1303
Yury	1303–25
Ivan I	1325–40
Semyon (Simeon)	1340–53
Ivan II	1353–59
Dmitry Donskoy	1359–89
Vasily I	1389–1425
Vasily II	1425–62
Ivan III	1462–1505
Vasily III	1505–33
Ivan IV	1533–47
Tsars of Russia: Danilovich dynasty	
Ivan IV	1547–84
Fyodor I	1584–98
Tsars of Russia: Time of Troubles	
Boris Godunov	1598–1605
Fyodor II	1605
False Dmitry	1605–06
Vasily (IV)	1606–10
Interregnum	1610–12
Tsars and Empresses of Russia and the Russian Empire: Romanov dynasty[3]	
Michael III	1613–45
Alexis	1645–76
Fyodor III	1676–82
Peter I (Ivan V coruler 1682–96)	1682–1725
Catherine I	1725–27

RULER	REIGN
Tsars and Empresses of Russia and the Russian Empire: Romanov dynasty[3] (continued)	
Peter II	1727–30
Anna	1730–40
Ivan VI	1740–41
Elizabeth	1741–61 (O.S.)
Peter III[4]	1761–62 (O.S.)
Catherine II	1762–96
Paul	1796–1801
Alexander I	1801–25
Nicholas I	1825–55
Alexander II	1855–81
Alexander III	1881–94
Nicholas II	1894–1917
Provisional government	1917
Chairmen (or First Secretaries) of the Communist Party of the Soviet Union	
Vladimir Lenin	1917–24
Joseph Stalin	1924–53
Georgy Malenkov	1953
Nikita Khrushchev	1953–64
Leonid Brezhnev	1964–82
Yury Andropov	1982–84
Konstantin Chernenko	1984–85
Mikhail Gorbachev	1985–91
Presidents of Russia	
Boris Yeltsin	1990–99
Vladimir Putin	2000–08
Dmitry Medvedev	2008–

[1]This table includes leaders of Muscovy, Russia, the Russian Empire, and the Soviet Union.   [2]The Danilovich dynasty is a late branch of the Rurik dynasty, named after its progenitor, Daniel.   [3]On 22 Oct (Old Style) 1721, Peter I the Great took the title of "emperor." However, despite the official titling, conventional usage took an odd

Rulers of Russia[1] (continued)

turn. Every male sovereign continued usually to be called tsar, but every female sovereign was conventionally called empress. [4]*The direct line of the Romanov dynasty came to an end in 1761 with the death of Elizabeth, daughter of Peter I, but subsequent rulers of the "Holstein-Gottorp dynasty" (the first, Peter III, was son of Charles Frederick, duke of Holstein-Gottorp, and Anna, daughter of Peter I) took the family name of Romanov.*

Middle East

Byzantine Emperors

The Byzantine Empire comprised what was previously the eastern half of the Roman Empire. It survived for nearly 1,000 years after the western half had crumbled into various feudal kingdoms; it finally fell to Ottoman Turkish onslaughts in 1453. For emperors of the Eastern Roman Empire (at Constantinople) before the fall of Rome, see "Roman Emperors."

EMPEROR	REIGN
Zeno	474–491
Anastasius I	491–518
Justin I	518–527
Justinian I	527–565
Justin II	565–578
Tiberius II Constantine	578–582
Maurice Tiberius	582–602
Phocas	602–610
Heraclius	610–641
Heraclius Constantine	641
Heraclonas (or Heraclius)	641
Constans II (Constantine Pogonatus)	641–668
Constantine IV	668–685
Justinian II Rhinotmetus	685–695
Leontius	695–698
Tiberius III	698–705
Justinian II Rhinotmetus (restored)	705–711
Philippicus	711–713
Anastasius II	713–715
Theodosius III	715–717
Leo III	717–741
Constantine V Copronymus	741–775
Leo IV	775–780
Constantine VI	780–797
Irene (empress)	797–802
Nicephorus I	802–811
Stauracius	811
Michael I Rhangabe	811–813
Leo V	813–820
Michael II Balbus	820–829
Theophilus	829–842
Michael III	842–867
Basil I	867–886
Leo VI	886–912
Alexander	912–913
Constantine VII Porphyrogenitus	913–959
Romanus I Lecapenus	920–944
Romanus II	959–963
Nicephorus II Phocas	963–969
John I Tzimisces	969–976
Basil II Bulgaroctonus	976–1025
Constantine VIII	1025–28
Romanus III Argyrus	1028–34
Michael IV	1034–41
Michael V Calaphates	1041–42
Zoe (empress)	1042–56
Constantine IX Monomachus	1042–55

EMPEROR	REIGN
Theodora (empress)	1055–56
Michael VI Stratioticus	1056–57
Isaac I Comnenus	1057–59
Constantine X Ducas	1059–67
Romanus IV Diogenes	1067–71
Michael VII Ducas	1071–78
Nicephorus III Botaniates	1078–81
Alexius I Comnenus	1081–1118
John II Comnenus	1118–43
Manuel I Comnenus	1143–80
Alexius II Comnenus	1180–83
Andronicus I Comnenus	1183–85
Isaac II Angelus	1185–95
Alexius III Angelus	1195–1203
Isaac II Angelus (restored) and Alexius IV Angelus (joint ruler)	1203–04
Alexius V Ducas Murtzuphlus	1204
Latin emperors	
Baldwin I	1204–06
Henry	1206–16
Peter	1217
Yolande (empress)	1217–19
Robert	1221–28
Baldwin II	1228–61
John	1231–37
Nicaean emperors	
Constantine (XI) Lascaris	1204–05?
Theodore I Lascaris	1205?–22
John III Ducas Vatatzes	1222–54
Theodore II Lascaris	1254–58
John IV Lascaris	1258–61
Greek emperors restored	
Michael VIII Palaeologus	1261–82
Andronicus II Palaeologus	1282–1328
Andronicus III Palaeologus	1328–41
John V Palaeologus	1341–76
John VI Cantacuzenus	1347–54
Andronicus IV Palaeologus	1376–79
John V Palaeologus (restored)	1379–90
John VII Palaeologus	1390
John V Palaeologus (restored)	1390–91
Manuel II Palaeologus	1391–1425
John VIII Palaeologus	1421–48
Constantine XI Palaeologus	1449–53

Caliphs

When Muhammad died on 8 Jun 632, Abu Bakr, his father-in-law, succeeded to his political and administrative functions. He and his three immediate successors are known as the "perfect" or "rightly guided" caliphs. After them, the title was borne by the 14 Umayyad caliphs of Damascus (from 661–750) and subsequently by the 38 'Abbasid caliphs of Baghdad (both are named after their clans of origin). The empire of the caliphate grew rapidly through conquest during its first two centuries to include most of southwestern Asia, North Africa, and Spain. 'Abbasid power ended in 945,

when the Buyids took Baghdad under their rule. They retained the 'Abbasid caliphs as figureheads; other dynasties in Central Asia and the Ganges River basin acknowledged the 'Abbasid caliphs as spiritual leaders. The Fatimids, however, proclaimed a new caliphate in 920 in their capital of al-Mahdiyah in Tunisia; it lasted until 1171, by which time opposition within the sect caused it to disintegrate. 'Abbasid authority was partially restored in the 12th century, but the caliphate ceased to exist with the Mongol destruction of Baghdad in 1258. Some principal caliphs are listed below.

CALIPH	REIGN
"Perfect" caliphs	
Abu Bakr	632–634
'Umar I	634–644
'Uthman ibn 'Affan	644–656
'Ali	656–661
Umayyad caliphs (Damascus)	
Mu'awiyah I	661–680
'Abd al-Malik	685–705
al-Walid	705–715
Hisham	724–743
Marwan II	744–750
'Abbasid caliphs (Baghdad)	
al-Saffah	749–754
Harun al-Rashid	786–809
al-Mamun	813–833

CALIPH	REIGN
Fatimid caliphs (al-Mahdiyah)	
al-Mahdi	909–934
al-Qaim	934–946
al-Mansur	946–953
al-Mu'izz	953–975
al-Hakim	996–1021
al-Mustansir	1036–94
al-Musta'li	1094–1101
'Abbasid caliph (Baghdad)	
al-Nasir	1180–1225

Sultans of the Ottoman Empire

One of the most powerful states in the world during the 15th and 16th centuries, the Ottoman empire was created by Turkish tribes in Anatolia and spanned more than 600 years. It came to an end in 1922, when it was replaced by the Turkish Republic and various successor states in southeastern Europe and the Middle East. At its height

the empire included most of southeastern Europe, the Middle East as far east as Iraq, North Africa as far west as Algeria, and most of the Arabian Peninsula. The term Ottoman is a dynastic appellation derived from Osman (Arabic: 'Uthman), the nomadic Turkmen chief who founded both the dynasty and the empire.

SULTAN	REIGN
Osman I	c. 1300–1324
Orhan	1324–1360
Murad I	1360–1389
Bayezid I	1389–1402
Mehmed I	1413–1421
Murad II	1421–1444
Mehmed II	1444–1446
Murad II (second reign)	1446–1451
Mehmed II (second reign)	1451–1481
Bayezid II	1481–1512
Selim I	1512–1520
Suleyman I	1520–1566
Selim II	1566–1574
Murad III	1574–1595
Mehmed III	1595–1603
Ahmed I	1603–1617
Mustafa I	1617–1618
Osman II	1618–1622
Mustafa I (second reign)	1622–1623
Murad IV	1623–1640

SULTAN	REIGN
Ibrahim	1640–1648
Mehmed IV	1648–1687
Suleyman II	1687–1691
Ahmed II	1691–1695
Mustafa II	1695–1703
Ahmed III	1703–1730
Mahmud I	1730–1754
Osman III	1754–1757
Mustafa III	1757–1774
Abdulhamid I	1774–1789
Selim III	1789–1807
Mustafa IV	1807–1808
Mahmud II	1808–1839
Abdulmecid I	1839–1861
Abdulaziz	1861–1876
Murad V	1876
Abdulhamid II	1876–1909
Mehmed V	1909–1918
Mehmed VI	1918–1922

Persian Dynasties

Dates given are approximate and may overlap.

DYNASTY/KINGDOM	PERIOD	DYNASTY/KINGDOM	PERIOD
Median	728–550 BC	Seljuqs	1038–1157
Achaemenian	559–330 BC	Mongols[4]	1220–1335
Hellenistic period of Alexander		Timurids and Ottoman Turks	1380–1501
and the Seleucids[1]	330 BC–247 BC	Safavid	1502–1736
Parthian period (Arsacid dynasty)[2]	247 BC–AD 224	Afghan interlude	1723–36
Sasanian	224–651	Nader Shah	1736–47
Arab invasion and the advent of		Zand	1750–79
Islam	640–829	Qajars	1794–1925
Iranian intermezzo[3]	821–1055	Pahlavi	1925–79

[1]Dates from the death of Darius III, the last Achaemenian king, and the invasion of Alexander the Great.
[2]Dates from the year in which the Parnian chief Arsaces first battled the Seleucids. [3]Includes the Tahirid, Samanid, Ghaznavids, and Buyid dynasties. [4]Mainly the Il-Khanid dynasty (1256–1353).

Asia

Indian Dynasties

Dates given are approximations.

DYNASTY	LOCATION	DATES	DYNASTY	LOCATION	DATES
Nanda	Ganges Valley	400 BC	Pala	Bengal	800–1100
Maurya	India, barring the	400–200 BC	Pratihara	western India and	900–1100
	area south of			upper Ganges Valley	
	Mysore (Karnataka)		Rastrakuta	western and central	800–1100
Indo-Greeks	northern India	200–100 BC		Deccan	
Sunga	Ganges Valley and	200–100 BC	Cola	Tamil Nadu	900–1300
	parts of central		Candella	Bundelkhand	1000–1200
	India		Cauhan	Rajasthan	1000–1200
Satavahana	northern Deccan	100 BC–AD 300	Caulukya	Gujarat	1000–1300
Saka	western India	100 BC–AD 400	Paramara	western and central	1000–1100
Kusana	northern India and	AD 100–300		India	
	Central Asia		Later Calukya	western and central	1000–1200
Gupta	northern India	400–600		Deccan	
Harsa	northern India	700	Hoysala	central and southern	1200–1400
Pallava	Tamil Nadu	400–900		Deccan	
Calukya	western and central	600–800	Yadava	northern Deccan	1200–1300
	Deccan		Pandya	Tamil Nadu	1300–1400

Japanese Historical Periods and Rulers

PERIOD	DATES	PERIOD	DATES
Asuka	552–710	Muromachi (or Ashikaga)	1338–1573
Nara	710–784	Azuchi-Momoyama	1574–1600
Heian	794–1185	Edo (or Tokugawa)	1603–1867
Kamakura	1192–1333	Meiji	1868–1912

Reign dates for the first 28 sovereigns (Jimmu through Senka) are taken from the *Nihon shoki* ("Chronicles of Japan"). The first 14 sovereigns are considered legendary, and while the next 14 are known to have existed, their exact reign dates have not been verified historically. When the year of actual accession and year of formal coronation are different, the latter is placed in parentheses after the former. If the two events took place in the same year, no special notation is used. If only the coronation year is known, it is placed in parentheses.

EMPEROR	REIGN	EMPEROR	REIGN
Jimmu	(660)–585 BC	Kogen	(214)–158 BC
Suizei	(581)–549 BC	Kaika	158–98 BC
Annei	549–511 BC	Sujin	(97)–30 BC
Itoku	(510)–477 BC	Suinin	(29 BC)–AD 70
Kosho	(475)–393 BC	Keiko	(71)–130
Koan	(392)–291 BC	Seimu	(131)–190
Korei	(290)–215 BC	Chuai	(192)–200

Japanese Historical Periods and Rulers (continued)

EMPEROR	REIGN	EMPEROR	REIGN
Jingu Kogo (regent)	201–269	Toba	1107–23
Ojin	(270)–310	Sutoku	1123–41
Nintoku	(313)–399	Konoe	1141–55
Richu	(400)–405	Go-Shirakawa	1155–58
Hanzei	(406)–410	Nijo	1158–65
Ingyo	(412)–453	Rokujo	1165–68
Anko	453–456	Takakura	1168–80
Yuryaku	456–479	Antoku	1180–85[1]
Seinei	(480)–484	Go-Toba	1183 (1184)–98
Kenzo	(485)–487	Tsuchimikado	1198–1210
Ninken	(488)–498	Juntoku	1210 (1211)–21
Buretsu	498–506	Chukyo	1221
Keitai	(507)–531	Goshirakawa	1221 (1222)–32
Ankan	531 (534)–535	Shijo	1232 (1233)–42
Senka	535–539	Go-Saga	1242–46
Kimmei	539–571	Go-Fukakusa	1246–59/60
Bidatsu	(572)–585	Kameyama	1259/60–74
Yomei	585–587	Gouda	1274–87
Sushun	587–592	Fushimi	1287 (1288)–98
Suiko (empress regnant)	593–628	Go-Fushimi	1298–1301
Jomei	(629)–641	Go-Nijo	1301–08
Kogyoku (empress regnant)	(642)–645	Hanazono	1308–18
Kotoku	645–654	Go-Daigo	1318–39
Saimei (empress regnant:	(655)–661	Go-Murakami	1339–68
Kogyoku rethroned)		Chokei	1368–83
Tenji	661 (668)–672	Go-Kameyama	1383–92
Kobun	672		
Temmu	672 (673)–686	**The Northern court**[2]	
Jito (empress regnant)	686 (690)–697	Kogon	1331 (1332)–33
Mommu	697–707	Komyo	1336 (1337/38)–48
Gemmei (empress regnant)	707–715	Suko	1348 (1349/50)–51
Gensho (empress regnant)	715–724	Go-Kogon	1351 (1353/54)–71
Shomu	724–749	Go-Enyu	1371 (1374/75)–82
Koken (empress regnant)	749–758	Go-Komatsu	1382–92
Junnin	758–764	Go-Komatsu	1392–1412
Shotoku (empress regnant:	764 (765)–770	Shoko	1412 (1414)–28
Koken rethroned)		Go-Hanazono	1428 (1429/30)–64
Konin	770–781	Go-Tsuchimikado	1464 (1465/66)–1500
Kammu	781–806	Go-Kashiwabara	1500 (1521)–26
Heizei	806–809	Go-Nara	1526 (1536)–57
Saga	809–823	Ogimachi	1557 (1560)–86
Junna	823–833	Go-Yozei	1586 (1587)–1611
Nimmyo	833–850	Go-Mizunoo	1611–29
Montoku	850–858	Meisho (empress regnant)	1629 (1630)–43
Seiwa	858–876	Go-Komyo	1643–54
Yozei	876 (877)–884	Go-Sai	1654/55 (1656)–63
Koko	884–887	Reigen	1663–87
Uda	887–897	Higashiyama	1687–1709
Daigo	897–930	Nakamikado	1709 (1710)–35
Suzaku	930–946	Sakuramachi	1735–47
Murakami	946–967	Momozono	1747–62
Reizei	967–969	Go-Sakuramachi (empress regnant)	1762 (1763)–71
En'yu	969–984	Go-Momozono	1771–79
Kazan	984–986	Kokaku	1780–1817
Ichijo	986–1011	Ninko	1817–46
Sanjo	1011–16	Komei	1846 (1847)–66
Go-Ichijo	1016–36	Meiji (personal name:	1867 (1868)–1912
Go-Suzaku	1036–45	Mutsuhito; era name: Meiji)	
Go-Reizei	1045–68	Taisho (personal name:	1912 (1915)–26
Go-Sanjo	1068–72	Yoshihito; era name: Taisho)	
Shirakawa	1072–86	Hirohito (era name: Showa)	1926 (1928)–1989
Horikawa	1086–1107	Akihito (era name: Heisei)	1989 (1990)–

[1]Antoku's reign overlaps that of Go-Toba. Go-Toba was placed on the throne by the Minamoto clan after the rival Taira clan had fled Kyoto with Antoku.   [2]From 1336 until 1392 Japan witnessed the spectacle of two contending Imperial courts—the Southern court of Go-Daigo and his descendants, whose sphere of influence was restricted to the immediate vicinity of the Yoshino Mountains, and the Northern court of Kogon and his descendants, which was under the domination of the Ashikaga family.

Chinese Dynasties

Dates given for early dynasties are approximate and may overlap.

DYNASTY	ALTERNATE NAME	DATES	DYNASTY	ALTERNATE NAME	DATES
Hsia[1]	Xia	c. 2205–1766 BC	Six Dynasties[2] (continued)		
Shang		c. 1760–1030 BC	Southern Qi		479–502
Western Zhou	Chou	c. 1050–771 BC	Southern Liang		502–57
Eastern Zhou	Chou	c. 771–255 BC	Southern Chen		557–89
Qin	Ch'in	221–206 BC	Sui		581–618
Han		206 BC–AD 220	T'ang	Tang	618–907
Western Jin	Chin	265–317	Five Dynasties[3]	Ten Kingdoms[3]	907–960
Eastern Jin[2]	Chin	317–420	Sung	Song	960–1279
Six Dynasties[2]		220–589	Yüan	Yuan, Mongol	1206–1368
Wu		222–80	Ming		1368–1644
Eastern Jin[2]		317–420	Ch'ing	Qing, Manchu	1644–1911/12
Liusong		420–79			

[1]*The Hsia Dynasty is mentioned in legends but is of undetermined historicity.* [2]*Between the fall of the Han and the establishment of the Sui, China was divided into two societies, northern and southern. The Six Dynasties had their capital at Nanjing in the south. The Eastern Jin is considered one of these six dynasties and so is listed twice.* [3]*Period of time between the fall of the T'ang dynasty and the founding of the Sung dynasty, when five would-be dynasties followed one another in quick succession in North China. The era is also known as the period of the Ten Kingdoms because 10 regimes dominated separate regions of South China during the same period.*

Leaders of the People's Republic of China Since 1949

Chinese Communist Party leaders

NAME	TITLE	DATES
Mao Zedong	CCP chairman	1949–1976
Hua Guofeng	CCP chairman	1976–1981
Hu Yaobang	CCP chairman; after September 1982, general secretary of the CCP	1981–1987
Zhao Ziyang	CCP general secretary	1987–1989
Jiang Zemin	CCP general secretary	1989–2002
Hu Jintao	CCP general secretary	2002–

premiers

NAME	DATES
Zhou Enlai	1949–1976
Hua Guofeng	1976–1980
Zhao Ziyang	1980–1987
Li Peng	1987–1998
Zhu Rongji	1998–2003
Wen Jiabao	2003–

Note: although he held no top party or state position, Deng Xiaoping was de facto leader of China from 1977 to 1997.

Dalai Lamas

The Dalai Lama is the head of the dominant Dge-lugs-pa (Yellow Hat) order of Tibetan Buddhists and, until 1959, was both spiritual and temporal ruler of Tibet. In accordance with the belief in reincarnate lamas, which began to develop in the 14th century, the successors of the first Dalai Lama were considered his rebirths and came to be regarded as physical manifestations of the compassionate bodhisattva ("buddha-to-be"), Avalokitesvara.

DALAI LAMA	NAME	LIVED	DALAI LAMA	NAME	LIVED
first	Dge-'dun-grub-pa	1391–1475	eighth	'Jam-dpal-rgya-mtsho	1758–1804
second	Dge-'dun-rgya-mtsho	1475–1542	ninth	Lung-rtogs-rgya-mtsho	1806–1815[1]
third	Bsod-nams-rgya-mtsho	1543–1588	tenth	Tshul-khrims-rgya-mtsho	1816–1837[1]
fourth	Yon-tan-rgya-mtsho	1589–1617	eleventh	Mkhas-grub-rgya-mtsho	1838–1856[1]
fifth	Ngag-dbang-rgya-mtsho	1617–1682	twelfth	'Phrin-las-rgya-mtsho	1856–1875[1]
sixth	Tshangs-dbyangs-rgya-mtsho	1683–1706	thirteenth	Thub-bstan-rgya-mtsho	1875–1933[2]
seventh	Bskal-bzang-rgya-mtsho	1708–1757	fourteenth	Bstan-'dzin-rgya-mtsho	1935–[3]

[1]*Dalai Lamas 9–12 all died young, and the country was ruled by regencies.* [2]*Reigned as head of a sovereign state from 1912.* [3]*Ruled from exile in Dharmsala, India, from 1960.*

Did you know? One of Africa's least-explored regions, the northern part of the Republic of the Congo, an area of huge swamps and nearly impenetrable forests, was traversed by foot in 1999. Dr. Michael Fay, an ecologist with the Wildlife Conservation Society, and a team of 12 others undertook a 1,200-mi (1,900-km) survey of this area as well as similar areas in neighboring Gabon. The team concluded that this wilderness is seriously threatened.

The Americas

Pre-Columbian Civilizations

Various aboriginal American Indian cultures evolved in Meso-America (part of Mexico and Central America) and the Andean region (western South America) prior to Spanish exploration and conquest in the 16th century. These pre-Columbian civilizations were extraordinary developments in human society and culture, characterized by kingdoms and empires, great monuments and cities, and refinements in the arts, metallurgy, and writing. Dates given below are approximations.

CULTURE	LOCATION	DATES
Meso-American civilizations		
Olmec	Gulf coast of southern Mexico	1150 BC–800 BC
Zapotec	Oaxaca, particularly Monte Albán	500 BC–AD 900
Totonac	east-central Mexico	500 BC–AD 900
Teotihuacán	Teotihuacán, in the Valley of Mexico	AD 400–600
Maya	southern Mexico and Guatemala	250–900
Toltec	central Mexico	900–1200
Aztec	central and southern Mexico	1400–early 1500s
Andean civilizations		
Nazca	southern coast of Peru	200 BC–AD 600
Recuay	northern highlands of Peru	200 BC–AD 600
Tiwanaku	Lake Titicaca, Bolivia	200 BC–AD 1000
Moche (Mochica)	northern coast of Peru	AD 1–700
Inca	Pacific coast of South America	1100–1532

Africa

Historic Sub-Saharan African States

STATE	LOCATION IN PRESENT-DAY COUNTRIES	FLOURISHED
Aksumite kingdom	Ethiopia, Sudan	1st–10th centuries
Asante empire	Ghana	18th–19th centuries
Basuto kingdom	Lesotho	19th century
Benin kingdom	Nigeria	12th–19th centuries
kingdom of Buganda	Uganda	14th–20th centuries
kingdom of Bunyoro	Uganda	15th–19th centuries
kingdom of Burundi	Burundi	17th–20th centuries
kingdom of Dahomey	Benin	17th–19th centuries
Darfur	Sudan	17th–19th centuries
kingdom of Dongola	Sudan	7th–14th centuries
Fulani empire	Cameroon, Niger, Nigeria	19th–20th centuries
Ghana empire	Mali, Mauritania	4th–13th centuries
Hausa states	Nigeria	14th–19th centuries
Kanem-Bornu	Nigeria, Chad, Cameroon, Niger, Libya	9th–19th centuries
Kongo kingdom	Angola, Dem. Rep. of Congo	14th–17th centuries
Kuba kingdom	Dem. Rep. of Congo	17th–19th centuries
kingdom of Kush	Egypt, Sudan	c. 850 BC–c. AD 325
Luba empire	Dem Rep. of Congo	16th–19th centuries
Lunda empire	Dem. Rep. of Congo, Angola, Zambia	17th–19th centuries
Mali empire	Mali, Mauritania, Senegal, Gambia, Guinea-Bissau	13th–16th centuries
Ndongo kingdom	Angola	14th–17th centuries
kingdom of Nubia	Egypt, Sudan	4th–7th centuries
Oyo empire	Nigeria	16th–19th centuries
Rozwi empire	Zimbabwe, Botswana	17th–19th centuries
Shewa empire	Ethiopia	15th–19th centuries
Songhai empire	Nigeria, Niger	6th–17th centuries
Tukulor empire	Mali	19th century
Wolof empire	Senegal	14th–19th centuries
Zeng empire	Somalia, Kenya, Tanzania, Mozambique	10th–16th centuries
Zulu kingdom	South Africa	19th century

Populations

Largest Urban Agglomerations

Agglomerations include a central city and associated neighboring communities.
Source: <www.citypopulation.de>.

RANK	AGGLOMERATION	COUNTRY	POPULATION (JANUARY 2009)	RANK	AGGLOMERATION	COUNTRY	POPULATION (JANUARY 2009)
1	Tokyo	Japan	33,800,000	16	Cairo	Egypt	14,800,000
2	Seoul	Rep. of Korea	23,900,000	17	Buenos Aires	Argentina	13,800,000
3	Mexico City	Mexico	22,900,000	18	Moscow	Russia	13,500,000
4	Delhi	India	22,400,000	19	Beijing	China	13,200,000
5	Mumbai (Bombay)	India	22,300,000	20	Dhaka	Bangladesh	13,100,000
6	New York City	US	21,900,000	21	Istanbul	Turkey	12,500,000
7	São Paulo	Brazil	21,000,000		Rio de Janeiro	Brazil	12,500,000
8	Manila	Philippines	19,200,000		Tehran	Iran	12,500,000
9	Los Angeles	US	18,000,000	24	London	UK	12,300,000
10	Shanghai	China	17,900,000	25	Lagos	Nigeria	11,400,000
11	Osaka	Japan	16,700,000	26	Paris	France	10,000,000
12	Kolkata (Calcutta)	India	16,000,000	27	Chicago	US	9,850,000
13	Karachi	Pakistan	15,700,000	28	Shenzhen	China	9,400,000
14	Guangzhou	China	15,300,000	29	Wuhan	China	9,000,000
15	Jakarta	Indonesia	15,100,000	30	Lima	Peru	8,850,000

Migration of Foreigners into Selected Countries

Percentages of foreign-born populations in selected Organisation for Economic Co-operation and Development countries. N/A means not available. Source: <www.oecd.org>.

COUNTRY	FOREIGN-BORN AS % OF TOTAL POPULATION 2000	2006	COUNTRY	FOREIGN-BORN AS % OF TOTAL POPULATION 2000	2006
Luxembourg[1]	37.3	41.6	The Netherlands	10.1	10.6
Australia	23.0	24.1	UK	7.9	10.1
Switzerland	21.9	24.1	Norway	6.8	8.7
New Zealand	17.2	21.2	France	7.4	8.3
Canada	18.1	19.8	Germany[1]	8.9	8.2
Ireland	8.7	14.4	Denmark	5.8	6.6
Austria	10.5	14.1	Portugal	5.1	6.1
US	11.0	13.0	Slovakia	N/A	5.6
Sweden	11.3	12.9	Czech Republic	4.2	5.5
Belgium	10.3	12.5	Greece[1]	2.9	5.3
Spain	4.9	11.9	Italy[1]	2.4	5.0

[1]Foreign population.

Persons of Concern Worldwide

The Office of the UN High Commissioner for Refugees (UNHCR) attempts to ease the plight of various "persons of concern," including refugees and asylum seekers. Sources: UNHCR, 2008 Global Trends: Refugees, Asylum-seekers, Returnees, Internally Displaced and Stateless Persons; Internal Displacement Monitoring Centre.

Persons of Concern to UNHCR by Region and Category (estimates as of 1 Jan 2009)

REGION	REFUGEES	ASYLUM SEEKERS	RETURNED REFUGEES	INTERNALLY DISPLACED PERSONS (IDPs)[1]	STATELESS AND OTHER	TOTAL[2]
Asia and Oceania	6,527,205	176,752	306,310	4,617,979	—	12,017,539
Africa	2,769,100	236,933	294,505	6,343,016	—	10,676,348
Europe	539,452	41,320	3,046	444,410	—	1,134,433
Northern America	2,238	1,816	—	—	—	4,054
Latin America and the Caribbean	446,950	114,209	33	3,000,000	—	3,561,192
total[2]	10,478,621	827,323	603,943	14,405,405	6,572,167	34,415,751

Persons of Concern Worldwide (continued)

Total Number of Refugees (estimates as of 1 January of each year)

YEAR	REFUGEES	YEAR	REFUGEES
2000	11,625,700	2005	9,236,500
2001	12,062,500	2006	8,394,400
2002	12,029,900	2007	9,877,700
2003	10,389,600	2008	11,390,670
2004	9,671,800	2009	10,478,621

Origin of Major Refugee Populations[3] (estimates as of 1 Jan 2009)

COUNTRY OF ORIGIN	TOTAL	COUNTRY OF ORIGIN	TOTAL
Afghanistan	2,833,128	Democratic Republic of the Congo	367,995
Iraq	1,903,519	Vietnam	328,183
Colombia	373,532	Burundi	281,592
Somalia	561,154	Turkey	214,378
The Sudan	419,248	Eritrea	186,398

Host Country of Major Refugee Populations (estimates as of 1 Jan 2009)

COUNTRY OF ASYLUM	TOTAL	COUNTRY OF ASYLUM	TOTAL
Pakistan	1,780,935	Chad	330,510
Syria	1,105,698	Tanzania	321,909
Iran	980,109	Kenya	320,605
Germany	582,735	China	300,967
Jordan	500,413	United Kingdom	292,097

Internally Displaced Persons (estimates as of 1 Dec 2008)

COUNTRY	TOTAL	COUNTRY	TOTAL
The Sudan	4,900,000	Philippines	308,000+
Iraq	2,840,000	Kenya	300,000–600,000
Colombia	2,650,000–4,360,000	Georgia	252,000–279,000
Democratic Republic of the Congo	1,400,000	Afghanistan	235,000+
		Serbia	226,000
Somalia	1,300,000	Ethiopia	200,000–300,000
Turkey	954,000–1,201,000	Cyprus	200,000–202,500
Uganda	869,000	Israel	200,000
Côte d'Ivoire	621,000+	Chad	180,000
Azerbaijan	573,000–603,000	Peru	150,000
Zimbabwe	570,000–1,000,000	Bosnia and Herzegovina	125,000
India	500,000+	Central African Republic	108,000
Sri Lanka	485,000	Burundi	100,000
Pakistan	480,000+	Lebanon	90,000–390,000
Myanmar (Burma)	451,000+	Indonesia	70,000–120,000
Syria	433,000	Bangladesh	60,000–500,000

[1]Data include only those IDPs to whom UNHCR extends protection and/or assistance. [2]Includes unlisted returned IDPs and various unclassified persons. [3]A separate mandate of the UN Relief and Works Agency for Palestine Refugees in the Near East (UNRWA) covers more than 4,600,000 Palestinans. Palestinian refugees outside of the UNRWA mandate numbered 340,016 in 2009.

Language

Most Widely Spoken Languages

Listing the languages spoken by more than 1% of humankind, this table enumerates speakers of each tongue as a primary or secondary language. Figures based on data from Linguasphere 2000.

LANGUAGE	NUMBER OF SPEAKERS (MILLIONS)	% OF WORLD POPULATION (APPROXIMATE)	LANGUAGE FAMILY
English	1,000	16	Indo-European (Germanic)
Mandarin	1,000	16	Sino-Tibetan (Chinese)
Hindi/Urdu[1]	900	15	Indo-European (Indo-Aryan)
Spanish	450	7	Indo-European (Romance)

Most Widely Spoken Languages (continued)

LANGUAGE	NUMBER OF SPEAKERS (MILLIONS)	% OF WORLD POPULATION (APPROXIMATE)	LANGUAGE FAMILY
Russian/Belarusian	320	5	Indo-European (Slavic)
Arabic	250	4	Afro-Asiatic (Semitic)
Bengali/Sylhetti	250	4	Indo-European (Indo-Aryan)
Malay/Indonesian	200	3	Austronesian (Malayo-Polynesian)
Portuguese	200	3	Indo-European (Romance)
Japanese	130	2	isolated language
French	125	2	Indo-European (Romance)
German	125	2	Indo-European (Germanic)
Thai/Lao	90	1	Tai
Punjabi	85	1	Indo-European (Indo-Aryan)
Wu	85	1	Sino-Tibetan (Chinese)
Javanese	80	1	Austronesian (Malayo-Polynesian)
Marathi	80	1	Indo-European (Indo-Aryan)
Turkish/Azeri/Turkmen	80	1	Altaic (Turkic)
Korean	75	1	isolated language
Vietnamese	75	1	Mon-Khmer (Vietic)

[1]*Although Hindi and Urdu use different writing systems, these languages are branches of Hindustani and are orally mutually intelligible.*

English Neologisms

New entries from Merriam-Webster's Collegiate Dictionary, 11th ed. (2009). The date in parentheses is the date of the word's earliest recorded use in English. Italics are used to signify new definitions of established words.

acai *n* (1868): a small dark purple fleshy berrylike fruit of a tall slender palm (*Euterpe oleracea*) of tropical Central and South America that is often used in beverages

carbon footprint *n* (1999): the negative impact that something (as a person or business) has on the environment; *specifically*: the amount of carbon emitted by something during a given period

cardioprotective *adj* (1984): serving to protect the heart

earmark *n* (15th century): *a provision in Congressional legislation that allocates a specified amount of money for a specific project, program, or organization*

fan fiction *n* (1944): stories involving popular fictional characters that are written by fans and often posted on the Internet

flash mob *n* (1987): a group of people summoned (as by e-mail or text message) to a designated location at a specified time to perform an indicated action before dispersing

frenemy *n* (1977): one who pretends to be a friend but is actually an enemy

goji *n* (2003): the dark red mildly tart berry of a thorny chiefly Asian shrub (*Lycium barbarum*) that is typically dried and used in beverages

green-collar *adj* (1990): of, relating to, or involving actions for protecting the natural environment

haram *adj* (1979): forbidden by Islamic law

locavore *n* (2005): one who eats foods grown locally whenever possible

memory foam *n* (1987): a dense polyurethane foam that becomes more pliable when in contact with heat

missalette *n* (1973): a shortened form of a missal published periodically for congregational use

naproxen *n* (1971): an analgesic and antipyretic NSAID $C_{14}H_{14}O_3$ often used in the form of its sodium salt

neuroprotective *adj* (1987): serving to protect neurons from injury or degeneration

pharmacogenetics *n* (1960): the study of how genetic differences among individuals cause varied responses to a drug

physiatry *n* (1947): physical medicine and rehabilitation

reggaeton *n* (2002): popular music of Puerto Rican origin that combines rap with Caribbean rhythms

shawarma *n* (1953): a sandwich especially of sliced lamb or chicken, vegetables, and often tahini wrapped in pita bread

sock puppet *n* (1959): *a false online identity used for deceptive purposes*

staycation *n* (2005): a vacation spent at home or nearby

vlog *n* (2002): a blog that contains video material

waterboarding *n* (2004): an interrogation technique in which water is forced into a detainee's mouth and nose so as to induce the sensation of drowning

webisode *n* (1996): an episode especially of a TV show that may or may not have been telecast but can be viewed at a Web site

zip line *n* (1984): a cable suspended above an incline to which a pulley and harness are attached for a rider

Scholarship

National Libraries of the World

The national libraries listed below are generally open to the public. National libraries are usually the primary repository for a nation's printed works. Sources: "National Libraries of the World: An Address List," IFLA Publications; *International Dictionary of Library Histories*, 2001, Fitzroy Dearborn Publishers.

LIBRARY	LOCATION	YEAR FOUNDED[1]	SPECIAL COLLECTIONS, ARCHIVES, PAPERS
Biblioteca Nacional de España	Madrid, Spain	1836	manuscripts, Miguel de Cervantes
Biblioteca Nacional de México	Mexico City	1867	Jesuit works, early Mexican printing
Biblioteca Nacional de Portugal	Lisbon	1796	Luís de Camões, Desiderius Erasmus
Biblioteca Nacional de Venezuela	Caracas	1833	politics and diplomacy, Simón Bolívar
Biblioteca Nazionale Centrale di Firenze	Florence, Italy	1861	Reformation, Galileo Galilei
Biblioteca Nazionale Centrale di Roma	Rome, Italy	1876	Jesuit collections, Gabriele D'Annunzio
Biblioteka Narodowa	Warsaw, Poland	1928	engravings, music
Bibliotheca Alexandrina	Alexandria, Egypt	2002[2]	ancient manuscripts, Egyptian heritage
Bibliothèque Nationale de France	Paris	1461	Denis Diderot, Jean-Paul Sartre
British Library	London	1973[3]	Charles Dickens, George B. Shaw
Deutsche Nationalbibliothek Frankfurt am Main	Germany	2006	bibliographies, exile literature (1933–45)
Deutsche Nationalbibliothek Leipzig	Germany	2006	socialism, Anne-Frank-Shoah-Bibliothek
Fundação Biblioteca Nacional	Rio de Janeiro, Brazil	1810	botany, Latin American music
Jewish National and University Library	Jerusalem, Israel	1892	world Jewish history, Albert Einstein
Koninklijke Bibliotheek	The Hague, Netherlands	1798	Hugo Grotius, Constantijn Huygens
Library and Archives Canada	Ottawa	2004	hockey, portraits of Canadians
Library of Congress	Washington DC	1800	Americana, folk music, early motion pictures
National Agricultural Library	Beltsville MD	1962	research reports
National Diet Library[4]	Tokyo, Japan	1948	Japanese culture, Allied occupation
National Library of Australia	Canberra	1960	Asian and Pacific area
National Library of China[5]	Beijing	1909	art, early communism
National Library of Education	Washington DC	1994	research reports
National Library of Greece[6]	Athens	1866[7]	incunabula
National Library of India	Kolkata (Calcutta)	1903	rare journals of vernacular languages
National Library of Ireland	Dublin	1877	biography, Gaelic manuscripts
National Library of Medicine	Bethesda MD	1956	history of medicine
National Library of New Zealand[8]	Wellington	1965	European exploration, missionary activity
National Library of Pakistan	Islamabad	1993	manuscripts, censuses
National Library of Russia[9]	St. Petersburg	1795	rare books, Russian history
National Library of Scotland	Edinburgh	1925	mountaineering, witchcraft
National Library of South Africa	Pretoria; Cape Town	1999	Africana, cookery
National Library of Sweden[10]	Stockholm	1661	Scandinavian cartography and manuscripts
National Library of Wales	Aberystwyth	1907	publications of overseas Welsh settlements

[1]*In present institutional form.* [2]*Originally founded in the 3rd century BC.* [3]*Originally founded in 1753 as the British Museum Library.* [4]*Kokuritsu Kokkai Toshokan.* [5]*Zhongguo Guojia Tushuguan.* [6]*Ethnike Bibliotheke tes Hellados.* [7]*Originally founded in 1832 as the Public Library.* [8]*Te Puna Matauranga o Aotearoa.* [9]*Rossyskaya Natsionalnaya Biblioteka.* [10]*Kungliga Biblioteket.*

World Education Profile

This table provides comparative data about the education systems in selected countries. Definitions as well as information gathering and reporting methods vary widely from country to country, so the statistics presented here are not always exactly comparable.

Compulsory education = the number of years of education and ages of pupils required by the system; **enrollment ratio** for primary and secondary education = the actual number of children attending primary school or secondary school as a percentage of all children in the primary school or secondary school age group as defined by the country (number may exceed 100%); **enrollment ratio** for higher education = the total enrollment in higher education, regardless of age, as a percentage of all persons of school-leaving age to five years thereafter; **student/teacher ratio** = the number of pupils or students per teacher at each level; **expenditure** = the total public expenditure on education as a percentage of GDP in 2007.

Sources: *Encyclopædia Britannica World Data*, 2009; UNESCO Institute for Statistics.

World Education Profile (continued)

| COUNTRY | YEAR | % LITERACY RATE OF THOSE 15 AND OLDER | | | COMPULSORY EDUCATION | | ENROLLMENT RATIO (2007) | | | STUDENT/TEACHER RATIO (2004) | | | EXPEN-DITURE |
		TOTAL	M	F	# YEARS	AGES	PRI.	SEC.	HIGHER	PRI.	SEC.	HIGHER	
Africa													
Egypt	2007	72.0	83.6	60.7	9	6–14	105	88[1]	35[2]	21.4[3]	13.7[3]	—	3.8
Senegal	2007	42.6	53.1	32.3	6	7–12	84	26	7	43.2	26.4	24.6[2]	4.8[4]
South Africa	2007	88.0	88.9	87.2	9	7–15	103	97	15[4]	33.8[3]	29.6[3]	16.7[3]	5.4
Asia													
China	2007	93.3	96.5	90.0	9	6–14	112	77	23	20.0	18.6	15.5	1.9[5]
India	2007	66.0	76.9	54.5	9	6–14	112	55[4]	12	41.3	32.0	26.4	3.2[2]
Indonesia	2007	91.4	94.9	88.0	9	7–15	117	73	17	20.3[3]	14.2[3]	14.7[3]	3.5
Iran	2007	84.7	90.0	79.4	8	6–13	121	81[2]	31	22.6	24.2	—	5.5
Israel	2003	95.4	97.3	93.6	11	5–15	111	92	60	12.0	6.2[2]	—	6.2[4]
Japan	2007	100	100	100	10	6–15	100	101	58	17.3[2]	14.5[2]	17.8[2]	3.5[4]
Turkey	2007	88.7	96.2	81.2	9	6–14	96	80	36	26.9[6]	20.7[6]	25.7[4]	4.0[1]
Europe													
France	1995	98.8	98.9	98.7	11	6–16	110	113	56	10.9[4]	10.3[4]	25.4[4]	5.6[4]
Germany	1998	100	100	100	13	6–18	104	100	51[3]	35.3[4]	23.5[4]	12.1[4]	4.4[4]
Italy	2007	98.9	99.1	98.6	9	6–14	105	101	68	10.8[3]	14.5[3]	21.9[3]	4.8[4]
Russia	2007	99.5	99.7	99.4	10	6–15	96	84	75	—	—	17.9[6]	3.9[4]
United Kingdom	2006	100	100	100	12	5–16	104	97	59	21.3[4]	16.0[4]	19.7[3]	5.5[2]
Latin America													
Argentina	2007	97.6	97.6	97.7	10	5–14	114[4]	84[4]	67[4]	15.2[7]	18.7[7]	10.2[7]	4.5[4]
Brazil	2007	90.5	90.1	90.9	8	7–14	130	100	30	21.5[3]	18.6[3]	19.6[3]	5.1[4]
Cuba	2007	99.8	99.8	99.8	9	6–14	102[8]	92[8]	122[8]	10.6[6]	10.1[6]	14.6[6]	13.3
Mexico	2007	92.4	94.4	90.6	10	6–15	114	89	27	24.3[9]	16.0[9]	9.9[9]	5.5[4]
Northern America													
Canada	2005	100	100	100	11	6–16	99[4]	102[4]	62[1]	17.4[9]	18.4	19.8[1]	4.9[2]
United States	1998	95.5	95.7	95.3	12	6–17	99	94	82	—	—	13.5[4]	5.7[4]
Oceania													
Australia	2006	100	100	100	11	5–15	107	149	75	16.0[4]	12.1[4]	10.6[4]	5.2[4]

[1] 2004 data. [2] 2005 data. [3] 2003 data. [4] 2006 data. [5] 1999 data. [6] 2007 data. [7] 2001 data. [8] 2008 data. [9] 2002 data.

Religion

Chronological List of Popes

According to Roman Catholic doctrine, the pope is the successor of **St. Peter**, who was head of the Apostles. The pope thus is seen to have full and supreme power of jurisdiction over the universal church in matters of faith and morals, as well as in church discipline and government. Until the 4th century, the popes were usually known only as bishops of Rome. From 1309–77, the popes' seat was at Avignon, France. In the table, **antipopes**, who opposed the legitimately elected bishop of Rome and endeavored to secure the papal throne, are listed in italics. The elections of several antipopes are greatly obscured by incomplete or biased records, and at times even their contemporaries could not decide who was the true pope. It is impossible, therefore, to establish an absolutely definitive list of antipopes.

POPE	REIGN	POPE	REIGN	POPE	REIGN
Peter	?–c. 64	Eleutherius	c. 175–189	Dionysius	259–268
Linus	c. 67–76/79	Victor I	c. 189–199	Felix I	269–274
Anacletus	76–88 or 79–91	Zephyrinus	c. 199–217	Eutychian	275–283
Clement I	88–97 or 92–101	Calixtus I (Callistus)	217?–222	Gaius	283–296
		Hippolytus	217, 218–235	Marcellinus	291/296–304
Evaristus	c. 97–c. 107	Urban I	222–230	Marcellus I	308–309
Alexander I	105–115 or 109–119	Pontian	230–235	Eusebius	309/310
		Anterus	235–236	Miltiades (Melchiades)	311–314
Sixtus I	c. 115–c. 125	Fabian	236–250	Sylvester I	314–335
Telesphorus	c. 125–c. 136	Cornelius	251–253	Mark	336
Hyginus	c. 136–c. 140	*Novatian*	. 251	Julius I	337–352
Pius I	c. 140–155	Lucius I	253–254	Liberius	352–366
Anicetus	c. 155–c. 166	Stephen I	254–257	*Felix (II)*	355–358
Soter	c. 166–c. 175	Sixtus II	257–258	Damasus I	366–384

Chronological List of Popes (continued)

POPE	REIGN	POPE	REIGN	POPE	REIGN
Ursinus	366–367	Adrian I	772–795	Benedict IX	1047–48
Siricius	384–399	Leo III	795–816	(3rd time)	
Anastasius I	399–401	Stephen IV (or V)[2]	816–817	Damasus II	1048
Innocent I	401–417	Paschal I	817–824	Leo IX	1049–54
Zosimus	417–418	Eugenius II	824–827	Victor II	1055–57
Boniface I	418–422	Valentine	827	Stephen IX (or X)[2]	1057–58
Eulalius	418–419	Gregory IV	827–844	*Benedict X*	1058–59
Celestine I	422–432	*John*	844	Nicholas II	1059–61
Sixtus III	432–440	Sergius II	844–847	Alexander II	1061–73
Leo I	440–461	Leo IV	847–855	*Honorius (II)*	1061–72
Hilary	461–468	Benedict III	855–858	Gregory VII	1073–85
Simplicius	468–483	*Anastasius*	855	*Clement (III)*	1080–1100
Felix III (or II)[1]	483–492	*(Anastasius*		Victor III	1086–87
Gelasius I	492–496	*the Librarian)*		Urban II	1088–99
Anastasius II	496–498	Nicholas I	858–867	Paschal II	1099–1118
Symmachus	498–514	Adrian II	867–872	*Theodoric*	1100–02
Laurentius	498, 501–	John VIII	872–882	*Albert (Aleric)*	1102
	c. 505/507	Marinus I	882–884	*Sylvester (IV)*	1105–11
Hormisdas	514–523	Adrian III	884–885	Gelasius II	1118–19
John I	523–526	Stephen V (or VI)[2]	885–891	*Gregory (VIII)*	1118–21
Felix IV (or III)[1]	526–530	Formosus	891–896	Calixtus II	1119–24
Dioscorus	530	Boniface VI	896	(Callistus)	
Boniface II	530–532	Stephen VI (or VII)[2]	896	Honorius II	1124–30
John II	533–535	Romanus	897	*Celestine (II)*	1124
Agapetus I	535–536	Theodore II	897	Innocent II	1130–43
Silverius	536–537	John IX	898–900	*Anacletus (II)*	1130–38
Vigilius	537–555	Benedict IV	900	*Victor (IV)*	1138
Pelagius I	556–561	Leo V	903	Celestine II	1143–44
John III	561–574	*Christopher*	903–904	Lucius II	1144–45
Benedict I	575–579	Sergius III	904–911	Eugenius III	1145–53
Pelagius II	579–590	Anastasius III	911–913	Anastasius IV	1153–54
Gregory I	590–604	Lando	913–914	Adrian IV	1154–59
Sabinian	604–606	John X	914–928	Alexander III	1159–81
Boniface III	604	Leo VI	928	*Victor (IV)*	1159–64
Boniface IV	608–615	Stephen VII (or VIII)[2]	929–931	*Paschal (III)*	1164–68
Deusdedit	615–618	John XI	931–935	*Calixtus (III)*	1168–78
(Adeodatus I)		Leo VII	936–939	*Innocent (III)*	1179–80
Boniface V	619–625	Stephen VIII (or IX)[2]	939–942	Lucius III	1181–85
Honorius I	625–638	Marinus II	942–946	Urban III	1185–87
Severinus	640	Agapetus II	946–955	Gregory VIII	1187
John IV	640–642	John XII	955–964	Clement III	1187–91
Theodore I	642–649	Leo VIII[3]	963–965	Celestine III	1191–98
Martin I	649–655	Benedict V[3]	964–966?	Innocent III	1198–1216
Eugenius I	654–657	John XIII	965–972	Honorius III	1216–27
Vitalian	657–672	Benedict VI	973–974	Gregory IX	1227–41
Adeodatus II	672–676	*Boniface VII*	974	Celestine IV	1241
Donus	676–678	*(1st time)*		Innocent IV	1243–54
Agatho	678–681	Benedict VII	974–983	Alexander IV	1254–61
Leo II	682–683	John XIV	983–984	Urban IV	1261–64
Benedict II	684–685	*Boniface VII*	984–985	Clement IV	1265–68
John V	685–686	*(2nd time)*		Gregory X	1271–76
Conon	686–687	John XV (or XVI)[4]	985–996	Innocent V	1276
Sergius I	687–701	Gregory V	996–999	Adrian V	1276
Theodore	687	*John XVI (or XVII)*[4]	997–998	John XXI[4]	1276–77
Paschal	687	Sylvester II	999–1003	Nicholas III	1277–80
John VI	701–705	John XVII (or XVIII)[4]	1003	Martin IV[5]	1281–85
John VII	705–707	John XVIII (or XIX)[4]	1004–09	Honorius IV	1285–87
Sisinnius	708	Sergius IV	1009–12	Nicholas IV	1288–92
Constantine	708–715	*Gregory (VI)*	1012	Celestine V	1294
Gregory II	715–731	Benedict VIII	1012–24	Boniface VIII	1294–1303
Gregory III	731–741	John XIX (or XX)[4]	1024–32	Benedict XI	1303–04
Zacharias (Zachary)	741–752	Benedict IX	1032–44	Clement V (at	1305–14
Stephen (II)[2]	752	*(1st time)*		Avignon from	
Stephen II (or III)[2]	752–757	Sylvester III	1045	1309)	
Paul I	757–767	Benedict IX	1045	John XXII[4]	1316–34
Constantine (II)	767–768	*(2nd time)*		(at Avignon)	
Philip	768	Gregory VI	1045–46	*Nicholas (V)*	1328–30
Stephen III (or IV)[2]	768–772	Clement II	1046–47	*(at Rome)*	

Chronological List of Popes (continued)

POPE	REIGN	POPE	REIGN	POPE	REIGN
Benedict XII (at Avignon)	1334–42	Calixtus III (Callistus)	1455–58	Alexander VII	1655–67
Clement VI (at Avignon)	1342–52	Pius II	1458–64	Clement IX	1667–69
		Paul II	1464–71	Clement X	1670–76
Innocent VI (at Avignon)	1352–62	Sixtus IV	1471–84	Innocent XI	1676–89
		Innocent VIII	1484–92	Alexander VIII	1689–91
Urban V (at Avignon)	1362–70	Alexander VI	1492–1503	Innocent XII	1691–1700
		Pius III	1503	Clement XI	1700–21
Gregory XI (at Avignon, then Rome from 1377)	1370–78	Julius II	1503–13	Innocent XIII	1721–24
		Leo X	1513–21	Benedict XIII	1724–30
		Adrian VI	1522–23	Clement XII	1730–40
Urban VI	1378–89	Clement VII	1523–34	Benedict XIV	1740–58
Clement (VII) (at Avignon)	1378–94	Paul III	1534–49	Clement XIII	1758–69
		Julius III	1550–55	Clement XIV	1769–74
Boniface IX	1389–1404	Marcellus II	1555	Pius VI	1775–99
Benedict (XIII) (at Avignon)	1394–1423	Paul IV	1555–59	Pius VII	1800–23
		Pius IV	1559–65	Leo XII	1823–29
Innocent VII	1404–06	Pius V	1566–72	Pius VIII	1829–30
Gregory XII	1406–15	Gregory XIII	1572–85	Gregory XVI	1831–46
Alexander (V) (at Bologna)	1409–10	Sixtus V	1585–90	Pius IX	1846–78
		Urban VII	1590	Leo XIII	1878–1903
John (XXIII) (at Bologna)	1410–15	Gregory XIV	1590–91	Pius X	1903–14
		Innocent IX	1591	Benedict XV	1914–22
Martin V[5]	1417–31	Clement VIII	1592–1605	Pius XI	1922–39
Clement (VIII)	1423–29	Leo XI	1605	Pius XII	1939–58
Eugenius IV	1431–47	Paul V	1605–21	John XXIII	1958–63
Felix (V) (Amadeus VIII of Savoy)	1439–49	Gregory XV	1621–23	Paul VI	1963–78
		Urban VIII	1623–44	John Paul I	1978
Nicholas V	1447–55	Innocent X	1644–55	John Paul II	1978–2005
				Benedict XVI	2005–

[1]The higher number is used if Felix (II), who reigned from 355 to 358 and is ordinarily classed as an antipope, is counted as a pope. [2]Though elected on 23 Mar 752, Stephen (II) died two days later before he could be consecrated and thus is ordinarily not counted. The issue has made the numbering of subsequent Stephens somewhat irregular. [3]Either Leo VIII or Benedict V may be considered an antipope. [4]A confusion in the numbering of popes named John after John XIV (reigned 983–984) resulted because some 11th-century historians mistakenly believed that there had been a pope named John between antipope Boniface VII and the true John XV (reigned 985–996). Therefore they mistakenly numbered the real popes John XV to XIX as John XVI to XX. These popes have since customarily been renumbered XV to XIX, but John XXI and John XXII continue to bear numbers that they themselves formally adopted on the assumption that there had indeed been 20 Johns before them. In current numbering there thus exists no pope by the name of John XX. [5]In the 13th century the papal chancery misread the names of the two popes Marinus as Martin, and as a result of this error Simon de Brie in 1281 assumed the name of Pope Martin IV instead of Martin II. The enumeration has not been corrected, and thus there exist no Martin II and Martin III.

World Religions

At the beginning of the 21st century, one-third of the world's population is Christian, one-fifth is Muslim, one-eighth is Hindu, and one-eighth is nonreligious. Most people living in Europe and the Americas are Christian, while the vast majority of Muslims and Hindus are found in Asia. The plurality of Christians are Roman Catholics, of Muslims are Sunnis, and of Hindus are Vaishnavites. Africa hosts slightly more Christians than Muslims, with much of the rest of the population listed as ethnic religionists, which describes followers of local, tribal, animistic, or shamanistic religions.

In addition to the adherents of the predominant world religions (Christianity, Islam, Hinduism), there are small but noticeable percentages of Chinese folk religionists, Buddhists, other ethnic religionists, atheists, and new religionists. Among adherents of the remaining distinct religions, Sikhs, Spiritists, Jews, Baha'is, Confucianists, Jains, Shintoists, Taoists, and Zoroastrians each make up less than one-half of one percent of religious adherents.

Christianity

Christianity traces its origins to the 1st century AD and to Jesus of Nazareth, whom it affirms to be the chosen one (Christ) of God. Geographically the most widely diffused of all faiths, it has a constituency of more than two billion people. Its largest groups are the Roman Catholic Church, the Eastern Orthodox churches, and the Protestant churches; in addition, there are several independent churches of Eastern Christianity as well as numerous sects throughout the world.

Christianity's sacred scripture is the Bible, particularly the New Testament. Its principal tenets are that Jesus is the son of God (the second figure of the Holy Trinity), that God's love for the world is the essential component of his being, and that Jesus died to redeem humankind.

Christianity was originally a movement of Jews who accepted Jesus as the Messiah, but the movement

(continued on page 511)

The 2009 Annual Megacensus of Religions

David B. Barrett, Todd M. Johnson, and Peter F. Crossing

Each year since 1750, churches and religions around the world have generated increasing volumes of new statistical data. Much of this information is uncovered in decennial governmental censuses; half the countries of the world have long asked their populations to state their religions, if any, and they still do today. The other major source of data each year consists of the decentralized censuses undertaken by many religious headquarters. Each year almost all Christian denominations ask and answer statistical questions on major religious subjects. A third annual source is

Worldwide Adherents of All Religions, mid-2009

	AFRICA	ASIA	EUROPE	LATIN AMERICA
Christians	483,376,000	345,188,000	585,357,000	542,293,000
Affiliated	459,515,000	340,984,000	560,519,000	536,509,000
Roman Catholics	164,242,000	136,507,000	275,506,000	473,684,000
Protestants	133,740,000	85,944,000	67,754,000	56,039,000
Independents	96,500,000	138,905,000	10,534,000	41,282,000
Orthodox	47,284,000	15,737,000	201,276,000	1,040,000
Anglicans	49,466,000	853,000	26,260,000	883,000
Marginal Christians	3,520,000	3,108,000	4,165,000	11,083,000
Doubly affiliated	−35,237,000	−40,070,000	−24,976,000	−47,502,000
Unaffiliated	23,861,000	4,204,000	24,838,000	5,784,000
Muslims	408,001,150	1,006,329,000	40,836,000	1,836,000
Hindus	2,848,000	928,531,000	996,000	777,000
Buddhists	287,000	456,709,000	1,820,000	783,000
Chinese folk religionists	68,800	453,052,000	409,000	188,000
Ethnoreligionists	105,478,000	146,271,000	1,150,000	3,685,000
New religionists	129,000	60,126,000	374,000	1,794,000
Sikhs	69,500	22,932,000	502,000	6,500
Jews	130,000	5,865,000	1,847,000	930,000
Spiritists	3,600	0	144,000	13,477,000
Daoists	0	8,833,000	0	0
Baha'is	2,124,000	3,492,000	142,000	923,000
Confucianists	19,800	6,359,000	18,400	490
Jains	90,300	5,458,000	18,700	1,300
Shintoists	0	2,713,000	0	7,900
Zoroastrians	850	152,000	5,700	0
Other religionists	85,000	225,000	275,000	120,000
Nonreligious (agnostics)	6,041,000	491,203,000	81,450,000	16,900,810
Atheists	611,000	117,487,000	15,503,200	2,867,000
Total population	**1,009,363,000**	**4,120,925,000**	**730,848,000**	**586,590,000**

Regions. These follow current UN demographic terminology, which now divides the world into the six major areas shown above. See United Nations, *World Population Prospects: The 2006 Revision* (New York: UN, 2007), with populations of all continents, regions, and countries covering the period 1950–2050, with 100 variables for every country each year. Note that "Asia" includes the former Soviet Central Asian states, and "Europe" includes all of Russia eastward to the Pacific.

Change rate. This column documents the annual change in 2009 (calculated as an average annual change from 2005 to 2010) in worldwide religious and nonreligious adherents. Note that in 2009 the annual growth of world populations was 1.17%, or a net increase of 78,362,400 adherents.

Countries. The last column enumerates sovereign and nonsovereign countries in which each religion or religious grouping has a numerically significant and organized following.

Adherents. As defined in the 1948 Universal Declaration of Human Rights, a person's religion is what he or she professes, confesses, or states that it is. Totals are enumerated for each of the world's 239 countries following the methodology of the *World Christian Encyclopedia*, 2nd ed. (2001), and *World Christian Trends* (2001), using recent censuses, polls, surveys, reports, Web sites, literature, and other data. See the World Christian Database <www.worldchristiandatabase.org> for more detail. Religions (including nonreligious and atheists) are ranked in order of worldwide size in mid-2009.

Total population. UN medium variant figures for mid-2009, as given in *World Population Prospects: The 2006 Revision.*

Alphabetical listing of religions

Atheists. Persons professing atheism, skepticism, disbelief, or irreligion, including the militantly antireligious (opposed to all religion). In recent years a flurry of books have outlined the Western philosophical and scientific basis for atheism. Ironically, the vast majority of atheists today are found in Asia (primarily Chinese communists).

Buddhists. 56% Mahayana, 38% Theravada (Hinayana), 6% Tantrayana (Lamaism).

Chinese folk religionists. Followers of a unique complex of beliefs and practices that may include universism (yin/yang cosmology with dualities earth/heaven, evil/good, darkness/light), ancestor cult, Confucian ethics, divination, festivals, folk religion, goddess worship, household gods, local deities, mediums, metaphysics, monasteries, neo-Confucianism, popular religion, sacrifices, shamans, spirit writing, and Daoist and Buddhist elements.

the total of 27,000 new books on the religious situation in each single country, as well as some 9,000 printed annual yearbooks or official handbooks. Together, these three major sources of data constitute a massive annual megacensus, though decentralized and uncoordinated. The two tables below combine all these data on religious affiliation. The first table summarizes worldwide adherents by religion. The second goes into more detail for the United States of America. This year there are two new publications both supporting and mapping the data below. First, the Atlas of Global Christianity (Edinburgh University Press, 2009) puts Christian data in the context of 1910–2010. Second, the World Religion Database (www.worldreligiondatabase.org) offers sources and analysis of global religious dynamics.

Detail may not add to total given because of rounding.

NORTHERN AMERICA	OCEANIA	WORLD	%	CHANGE RATE (%)	NUMBER OF COUNTRIES
280,659,000	27,619,000	2,264,492,000	33.2	1.26	239
225,155,000	23,288,000	2,145,970,000	31.4	1.29	239
83,845,000	8,820,000	1,142,604,000	16.7	1.12	236
61,315,000	8,177,000	412,969,000	6.0	1.50	233
72,820,000	1,238,000	361,279,000	5.3	2.16	222
7,101,000	917,000	273,335,000	4.0	0.38	137
2,866,000	5,032,000	85,360,000	1.3	1.61	164
11,708,000	659,000	34,243,000	0.5	1.90	217
−14,500,000	−1,555,000	−163,840,000	−2.4	1.29	173
55,504,000	4,331,000	118,522,000	1.7	0.82	232
5,647,000	563,000	1,523,212,150	22.3	1.79	213
1,788,000	520,000	935,460,000	13.7	1.39	127
3,614,000	608,000	463,821,000	6.8	1.05	141
755,000	107,000	454,579,800	6.7	0.82	96
1,572,000	345,000	258,501,000	3.8	1.12	145
1,655,000	103,000	64,181,000	0.9	0.40	117
663,000	49,700	24,222,700	0.4	1.52	53
5,668,000	109,000	14,549,000	0.2	0.60	138
178,000	7,400	13,810,000	0.2	1.20	56
12,300	4,400	8,849,700	0.1	1.88	6
518,000	106,000	7,305,000	0.1	1.92	222
0	49,200	6,446,890	0.1	0.22	15
97,500	3,200	5,669,000	0.1	−0.04	19
61,900	0	2,782,800	0.0	1.42	8
20,700	2,400	181,650	0.0	−0.33	25
690,000	12,000	1,407,000	0.0	1.31	79
39,867,600	4,444,700	639,907,110	9.4	−0.13	238
1,878,000	431,000	138,777,200	2.0	−0.07	221
345,345,000	35,084,000	6,828,155,000	100	1.17	239

Christians. Followers of Jesus Christ, enumerated here under **Affiliated**—those affiliated with Christian churches (church members, with names written on church rolls, usually total number of baptized persons including children baptized, dedicated, or undedicated), the total in 2009 being 2,145,970,000, shown above divided among the six standardized ecclesiastical megablocs and with (negative and italicized) figures for those **Doubly affiliated** persons (all who are baptized members of two denominations)—and **Unaffiliated,** who are persons professing or confessing in censuses or polls to be Christians though not so affiliated. **Independents.** This term here denotes members of Christian churches and networks that regard themselves as postdenominationalist and neoapostolic and thus independent of historical, mainstream, organized, institutionalized, confessional, denominationalist Christianity. **Marginal Christians.** Members of denominations who define themselves as Christians but who are on the margins of organized mainstream Christianity (e.g., Unitarians, Mormons, Jehovah's Witnesses, Christian Scientists, and Religious Scientists).

Confucianists. Non-Chinese followers of Confucius and Confucianism, mostly Koreans in Korea.

Ethnoreligionists. Followers of local, tribal, animistic, or shamanistic religions, with members restricted to one ethnic group.

Hindus. 68% Vaishnavites, 27% Shaivites, 2% neo-Hindus and reform Hindus.

Jews. Adherents of Judaism. For detailed data on "core" Jewish population, see the annual "World Jewish Populations" article in the American Jewish Committee's American Jewish Year Book.

Muslims. 84% Sunnis, 14% Shi'ites, 2% other schools.

New religionists. Followers of Asian 20th-century new religions, New Religious Movements, radical new crisis religions, and non-Christian syncretistic mass religions.

Nonreligious (agnostics). Persons professing no religion, nonbelievers, agnostics, freethinkers, uninterested, or dereligionized secularists indifferent to all religion but not militantly so.

Other religionists. Including a handful of religions, quasi-religions, pseudoreligions, parareligions, religious or mystic systems, and religious and semireligious brotherhoods of numerous varieties.

Religious Adherents in the United States of America, 1900–2005

For categories not described below, see notes to Worldwide Adherents of All Religions, pp. 508–09.

	1900	%	MID-1970	%	MID-1990	%
Christians	73,260,000	96.4	190,520,000	90.7	218,720,600	85.4
Affiliated	54,425,000	71.6	152,754,000	72.7	176,030,000	68.7
Independents	5,850,000	7.7	34,702,000	16.5	66,900,000	26.1
Roman Catholics	10,775,000	14.2	48,305,000	23.0	56,500,000	22.1
Protestants	35,000,000	46.1	58,568,000	27.9	60,216,000	23.5
Marginal Christians	800,000	1.1	6,114,000	2.9	8,940,000	3.5
Orthodox	400,000	0.5	4,395,000	2.1	5,150,000	2.0
Anglicans	1,600,000	2.1	3,196,000	1.5	2,450,000	1.0
Doubly affiliated	0	0.0	−2,526,000	−1.2	−24,126,000	−9.4
Evangelicals	32,068,000	42.2	35,117,000	16.7	38,400,000	15.0
evangelicals	11,000,000	14.5	45,500,000	21.7	90,656,000	35.4
Unaffiliated	18,835,000	24.8	37,766,000	18.0	42,690,600	16.7
Jews	1,500,000	2.0	6,700,000	3.2	5,535,000	2.2
Muslims	10,000	0.0	800,000	0.4	3,500,000	1.4
Black Muslims	0	0.0	200,000	0.1	1,250,000	0.5
Buddhists	30,000	0.0	200,000	0.1	1,880,000	0.7
New religionists	10,000	0.0	560,000	0.3	1,155,000	0.5
Ethnoreligionists	100,000	0.1	70,000	0.0	780,000	0.3
Hindus	1,000	0.0	100,000	0.0	750,000	0.3
Baha'is	2,800	0.0	138,000	0.1	600,000	0.2
Sikhs	0	0.0	10,000	0.0	160,000	0.1
Spiritists	0	0.0	0	0.0	120,000	0.0
Chinese folk religionists	70,000	0.1	90,000	0.0	76,000	0.0
Shintoists	0	0.0	3,000	0.0	5,000	0.0
Zoroastrians	0	0.0	0	0.0	50,000	0.0
Daoists	0	0.0	0	0.0	14,400	0.0
Jains	0	0.0	0	0.0	10,000	0.0
Other religionists	10,200	0.0	450,000	0.2	530,000	0.2
Nonreligious (agnostics)	1,000,000	1.3	10,270,000	4.9	21,442,000	8.4
Atheists	1,000	0.0	200,000	0.1	770,000	0.3
US population	**75,995,000**	**100**	**210,111,000**	**100**	**256,098,000**	**100**

Methodology. This table extracts and analyzes a microcosm of the world religion table. It depicts the United States, the country with the largest number of adherents to Christianity, the world's largest religion. Statistics at five points in time from 1900 to 2005 are presented. Each religion's **Annual Change** for 2000–05 is also analyzed by **Natural** increase (births minus deaths, plus immigrants minus emigrants) per year and **Conversion** increase (new converts minus new defectors) per year, which together constitute the **Total** increase per year. **Rate** increase is then computed as a percentage per year.

Structure. Vertically the table lists 30 major religious categories. The major categories (including nonreligious) in the US are listed, with the largest (Christians) first. Indented names of groups in the adherents column on the far left are subcategories of the groups above them and are also counted in these unindented totals, so they should not be added twice into the column total. Figures in italics draw adherents from all categories of Christians above and so cannot be added together with them. Figures for Christians are built upon detailed head counts by churches, often to the last digit, and the totals are then rounded to the nearest 1,000. Because of rounding, the corresponding percentage figures may sometimes not total exactly 100%. Religions are ranked in order of size in 2005.

Christians. All persons who profess publicly to follow Jesus Christ as God and Savior. This category is subdivided into **Affiliated** Christians (church members) and **Unaffiliated** (nominal) Christians (professing Christians not affiliated with any church). See also the note on Christians to the world religion table. The first six lines under "Affiliated" Christians are ranked by size in 2005 of each of the 6 megablocs (Anglican, Independent, Marginal Christian, Orthodox, Protestant, and Roman Catholic).

Evangelicals/evangelicals. These two designations—italicized and enumerated separately here—cut across all of the six Christian traditions or ecclesiastical blocs listed above and should be considered separately from them. The **Evangelicals** (capital *E*) are mainly Protestant churches, agencies, and individuals who call themselves by this term (for example, members of the National Association of Evangelicals); they usually emphasize 5 or more of 7, 9, or 21 fundamental doctrines (salvation by faith, personal acceptance, verbal inspiration of Scripture, depravity of man, Virgin Birth, miracles of Christ, atonement, evangelism, Second Advent, et al.). The **evangelicals** (lowercase *e*) are Christians of evangelical conviction from all traditions who are committed to the evangel (gospel) and involved in personal witness and mission in the world.

Jews. Core Jewish population relating to Judaism, excluding Jewish persons professing a different religion.

Other categories. Definitions are as given under the world religion table.

MID-2000	%	MID-2005	%	NATURAL	CONVERSION	TOTAL	RATE (%)
				ANNUAL CHANGE, 2000–05			
235,965,500	82.8	246,202,200	82.1	2,483,300	-436,000	2,047,300	0.85
190,404,000	66.8	198,617,000	66.2	2,003,800	-361,200	1,642,600	0.85
65,153,000	22.9	68,286,000	22.8	685,700	-59,100	626,600	0.94
62,970,000	22.1	67,902,000	22.6	662,700	323,700	986,400	1.52
57,544,000	20.2	57,105,000	19.0	605,600	-693,400	-87,800	-0.15
10,085,000	3.5	10,677,000	3.6	106,100	12,300	118,400	1.15
5,516,000	1.9	5,868,000	2.0	58,000	12,400	70,400	1.24
2,300,000	0.8	2,248,000	0.7	24,200	-34,600	-10,400	-0.46
-13,164,000	-4.6	-13,469,000	-4.5	-138,500	77,500	-61,000	0.46
39,780,000	14.0	40,463,000	13.5	418,600	-282,000	136,600	0.34
95,900,000	33.7	100,669,000	33.6	1,009,200	-55,400	953,800	0.98
45,561,500	16.0	47,585,200	15.9	479,500	-74,800	404,700	0.87
5,385,000	1.9	5,302,000	1.8	56,700	-73,300	-16,600	-0.31
4,319,000	1.5	4,745,000	1.6	45,500	39,700	85,200	1.90
1,650,000	0.6	1,850,000	0.6	17,400	22,600	40,000	2.31
2,527,000	0.9	2,824,000	0.9	26,600	32,800	59,400	2.25
1,401,000	0.5	1,495,000	0.5	14,700	4,100	18,800	1.31
1,334,000	0.5	1,423,000	0.5	14,000	3,800	17,800	1.30
1,238,000	0.4	1,338,000	0.4	13,000	7,000	20,000	1.57
403,000	0.1	457,000	0.2	4,200	6,600	10,800	2.55
239,000	0.1	270,000	0.1	2,500	3,700	6,200	2.47
180,000	0.1	190,000	0.1	1,900	100	2,000	1.09
80,300	0.0	86,700	0.0	800	500	1,300	1.55
74,100	0.0	79,500	0.0	800	300	1,100	1.42
57,500	0.0	60,600	0.0	600	0	600	1.06
16,200	0.0	17,000	0.0	200	0	200	0.97
11,400	0.0	12,000	0.0	100	0	100	1.03
580,000	0.2	600,000	0.2	6,100	-2,100	4,000	0.68
29,889,000	10.5	33,569,000	11.2	314,500	421,500	736,000	2.35
1,157,000	0.4	1,175,000	0.4	12,200	-8,600	3,600	0.31
284,857,000	100	299,846,000	100	2,998,000	0	2,998,000	1.03

Did you know? The first sale of a military airplane was made on 8 Feb 1908, when Orville and Wilbur Wright contracted to supply one Wright Model A flyer to the US Army Signal Corps, plus a US$5,000 bonus should it exceed the speed requirement of 40 miles (65 km) per hour. The next year the plane completed its trial flights and met the condition for the bonus.

World Religions (continued)

(continued from page 507)
quickly became predominantly Gentile. Nearly all Christian churches have an ordained clergy, who lead group worship services and are viewed as intermediaries between the laity and the divine in some churches. Most Christian churches administer at least two sacraments: baptism and the Lord's Supper.

Islam

Islam is a religion that originated in the Middle East and was promulgated by the Prophet Muhammad in Arabia in the 7th century AD. The Arabic term *islam*, literally "surrender," illuminates the fundamental religious idea of Islam—that the believer (called a Muslim, from the active particle of *islam*) accepts "surrender to the will of Allah" (Arabic: "God"). Allah's will is made known through the sacred scriptures, the Qur'an, which Allah revealed to his messenger, Muhammad. In Islam, Muhammad is considered the last of a series of prophets (including Adam, Noah, Jesus, and others), and his message simultaneously consummates and abrogates the "revelations" attributed to earlier prophets.

The religious obligations of all Muslims are summed up in the Five Pillars of Islam. The fundamental concept in Islam is the Shari'ah, or Law, which embraces the total way of life commanded by God. Observant Muslims pray five times a day and join in community worship on Fridays at the mosque, where worship is led by an imam. Every believer is required to make a pilgrimage to Mecca, the holiest city, at least once in a lifetime, barring poverty or physical incapacity. The month of Ramadan is set aside for fasting. Jihad, considered a sixth pillar by some sects, is not accepted by most of the Islamic community as a call to wage physical war against unbelievers.

Divisions occurred early in Islam, brought about by disputes over the succession to the caliphate, resulting in various sects (Sunnis, Shi'ites, Isma'ilis, Sufis). From the 19th century, the concept of the Islamic community inspired Muslim peoples to cast off Western colonial rule, and in the late 20th century fundamentalist movements toppled a number of secular Middle Eastern governments. A movement of African American Muslims emerged in the 20th century in the US.

Hinduism

Hinduism is the oldest of the world's major religions, dating back more than 3,000 years, though its pres-

World Religions (continued)

ent forms are of more recent origin. It evolved from Vedism, the religion of the Indo-European peoples who settled in India at the end of the 2nd millennium BC. The vast majority of the world's Hindus live in India, though significant minorities may be found in Pakistan and Sri Lanka, and smaller numbers live in Myanmar (Burma), South Africa, Trinidad, Europe, and the US.

Though the various Hindu sects each rely on their own set of scriptures, they all revere the ancient Vedas, which were brought to India by Aryan invaders after 1200 BC. The philosophical Vedic texts called the Upanishads explore the search for knowledge that will allow mankind to escape the cycle of reincarnation. Fundamental to Hinduism is the belief in a cosmic principle of ultimate reality, called brahman, and its identity with the individual soul, or atman. All creatures go through a cycle of rebirth, or samsara, which can be broken only by spiritual self-realization, after which liberation, or moksha, is attained. The principle of karma determines a being's status within the cycle of rebirth.

The greatest Hindu deities are Brahma, Vishnu, and Shiva. The major sources of classical mythology are the Mahabharata (which includes the Bhagavadgita, the most important religious text of Hinduism), the Ramayana, and the Puranas. The hierarchical social structure of the caste system is important in Hinduism; it is supported by the principle of dharma. During the 20th century Hinduism was blended with Indian nationalism to become a potent political force.

Other major religions
Buddhism, a religion concentrated in Asia with some representation in North America, was founded by the Buddha (Siddhartha Gautama, or Gotama) in northeast India in the 5th century BC. By adhering to the Buddha's teachings, the believer can alleviate suffering through an understanding of the transitory nature of existence, in the hopes of achieving enlightenment. Distinct from Buddhism, **Shinto** is the indigenous religion of Japan and has no founder, sacred scriptures, or fixed dogmas. Also based in Asia,

Chinese folk religions worship local deities and teach ancestor worship and divination. They also adhere to Confucian ethics, though statistically only non-Chinese (mostly Korean) followers of Confucius, a Chinese philosopher of the 6th century BC, are categorized as followers of **Confucianism.** Confucianism is not an organized religion as much as it is a political and social ideology. Also in the Confucian tradition, adherents of **Daoism** seek the correct path of human conduct and an understanding of the Absolute Dao.

Zoroastrianism is an ancient pre-Islamic religion of Iran that survives there and in India. It was founded by the Iranian prophet Zoroaster in the 6th century BC and has both monotheistic and dualistic features. Also founded in Iran is the **Baha'i** faith, created as a universal religion in the mid-19th century AD for the worship of Baha' Ullah and his forerunner, the Bab; it has no priesthood or formal sacraments and is chiefly concerned with social ethics.

Jainism was founded in India in the 6th century BC by Vardhamana, or Mahavira, a monastic reformer in the Vedic, or early Hindu, tradition. Jainism emphasizes a path to spiritual purity and enlightenment through a disciplined mode of life founded upon the tradition of ahimsa, nonviolence to all living creatures.

Sikhism is a monotheistic religion founded in the late 15th century AD in India, historically associated with the Punjab region, though it includes representation in Europe and North America.

Judaism, like Christianity and Islam, is monotheistic and maintains the manifestation of God in human events, particularly through Moses in the Torah at Mount Sinai in the 13th century BC. Jews, who come together in both religious and ethnic communities, have worldwide representation, with the greatest concentration in North America and the Middle East.

New Religious Movements and non-Christian syncretistic mass religions also have significant followings.

Terrorism
International Terrorist Organizations

"Terrorism" is a subjective term. The list of organizations included here is that of the US Department of State, issued on 7 Jul 2009. The list is updated periodically. Translations and acronyms of organizations' names are given in bold parenthetically; names and acronyms by which organizations are also known follow and are not in bold.

Abu Nidal Organization (ANO) (Fatah Revolutionary Council, Arab Revolutionary Brigades, Black September, Revolutionary Organization of Socialist Muslims)
    founded in 1974 as a splinter group from the Palestinian Liberation Organization (PLO); led by Sabri al-Banna
    country or region of operation: Middle East, primarily Iraq and Lebanon; has also operated in Asia and Europe
    primary goals: elimination of Israel, establishment of a Palestinian state
Abu Sayyaf Group (ASG)
    founded in the early 1990s as a splinter group from Moro National Liberation Front by Abdurajak Abubakar Janjalani; mainly made up of semiautonomous factions
    country or region of operation: Philippines, Malaysia
    primary goals: establishment of an independent Islamic state in the southern Philippines
Ansar al-Islam (Partisans of Islam)
    founded in 2001 as an offshoot of the Islamic Movement in Iraqi Kurdistan by Najmeddin Faraj Ahmed
    country or region of operation: Iraq
    primary goals: establishment of an Islamic state in the Kurdish areas of northern Iraq

International Terrorist Organizations (continued)

al-Aqsa Martyrs Brigades
founded in 2000 as an offshoot of Fatah; diffuse cell-based leadership structure
country or region of operation: Gaza Strip, West Bank, Israel
primary goals: establishment of a Palestinian state with Jerusalem as its capital

Armed Islamic Group (GIA)
founded in 1992; leadership uncertain; fewer than 50 active members thought to be at large
country or region of operation: Algeria
primary goals: replacement of secular Algerian government with an Islamic state

Asbat al-Ansar
founded in the late 1980s; led by Abou Mahjan, aka Abdel Karim al-Saadi
country or region of operation: Lebanon
primary goals: replacement of secular Lebanese government with an Islamic state

AUM Shinrikyo (AUM Supreme Truth, Aleph)
founded in 1987 by Shoko Asahara; led by Fumihiro Joyu
country or region of operation: Japan
primary goals: takeover of Japan and the world

Basque Fatherland and Liberty (Euzkadi Ta Askatasuna, ETA)
founded in 1959; allegedly led by Jurdan Martitegi Lizaso (arrested in April 2009)
country or region of operation: Basque autonomous regions of northern Spain and southwestern France
primary goals: establishment of an independent Basque state based on Marxism

Communist Party of the Philippines/New People's Army (CPP/NPA)
founded in 1969 as a Maoist movement; led from exile by José María Sisón
country or region of operation: Philippines
primary goals: overthrow of the Philippine government

Continuity Irish Republican Army (CIRA)
founded in 1994 as a splinter group of Irish Republican Army (IRA) after the latter declared its first cease-fire
country or region of operation: Northern Ireland, Republic of Ireland
primary goals: removal of British forces from Northern Ireland

Hamas (Islamic Resistance Movement)
founded in 1987 by Sheikh Ahmed Yasin as an offshoot of Muslim Brotherhood; led by Khalid Mesha
country or region of operation: Gaza Strip, West Bank, Israel; also present throughout the Middle East
primary goals: elimination of Israel, establishment of an Islamic Palestinian state

Harakat ul-Jihad-i-Islami/Bangladesh (HUJI-B)
founded in the 1990s; affiliated with al-Qaeda
country or region of operation: Bangladesh
primary goals: establishment of Bangladesh as an Islamic state

Harakat ul-Mujahidin (HUM) (Movement of Holy Warriors)
founded in the mid-1980s or early 1990s; led by Farooq Kashmiri
country or region of operation: the Kashmir region of Pakistan and India
primary goals: establishment of Kashmir as part of an Islamic state

Hezbollah (Party of God) (Islamic Jihad, Revolutionary Justice Organization, Organization of the Oppressed on Earth, Islamic Jihad for the Liberation of Palestine)
founded in 1982; spiritual leader Sheikh Muhammad Hussein Fadlallah
country or region of operation: Lebanon; also has cells worldwide
primary goals: establishment of Islamic rule in Lebanon, elimination of Israel, liberation of occupied Arab lands

Islamic Jihad Group (IJG)
founded in 2004; offshoot of Islamic Movement of Uzbekistan (IMU)
country or region of operation: Central Asia
primary goals: replacement of the secular Uzbek government with an Islamic state

Islamic Movement of Uzbekistan (IMU)
founded in 1996; led by Tohir Yoldashev
country or region of operation: primarily Uzbekistan, Tajikistan, Kyrgyzstan, Afghanistan, Iran, and Pakistan
primary goals: replacement of the secular Uzbek government with an Islamic state

Jaish-e-Mohammed (Army of Muhammad)
founded in 2000 as a spin-off from Harakat ul-Mujahidin; led by Maulana Masood Azhar
country or region of operation: South Asia, primarily Pakistan and India
primary goals: establishment of Pakistani control over India-administered Kashmir

al-Jama'ah al-Islamiyah (Islamic Group, IG)
founded in the late 1970s; loosely organized in two factions led by Mustafa Hamza (currently in custody in Egypt) and Rifai Taha Musa; spiritual leader Sheikh Umar Abd al-Rahman
country or region of operation: Egypt; also operates in several countries worldwide
primary goals: replacement of Egyptian government with an Islamic state

Jemaah Islamiyah (JI)
founded in the mid-1990s as a successor to Darul Islam; led by Abu Bakar Baasyir
country or region of operation: Southeast Asia, particularly Indonesia, Singapore, and Malaysia
primary goals: establishment of a pan-Islamic state in Southeast Asia

International Terrorist Organizations (continued)

al-Jihad (Egyptian Islamic Jihad, Jihad Group, Islamic Jihad)
   founded in the late 1970s by Ayman al-Zawahiri; merged with al-Qaeda in 2001
   country or region of operation: Egypt, Yemen, Afghanistan, Pakistan, Lebanon, Great Britain
   primary goals: replacement of Egyptian government with an Islamic state, attacks on US and Israeli interests

Kahane Chai (Kach)
   founded in 1971 by Meir Kahane; Kahane Chai founded as follow-up group after Meir's assassination in 1990
   country or region of operation: Israel, West Bank
   primary goals: expansion of Israel, removal of Palestinians

Kata'ib Hizballah (KH) (Hezbollah Brigades)
   founded in 2007
   country or region of operation: Iraq
   primary goals: expulsion of American and allied forces from Iraq

Kongra-Gel (KGK) (formerly Kurdistan Workers' Party, PKK, KADEK)
   founded in 1974; led by Abdullah Ocalan (imprisoned since 1999)
   country or region of operation: Turkey; also operates in Europe and the Middle East
   primary goals: establishment of independent Kurdish state

Lashkar-e-Taiba (LT, Army of the Righteous)
   founded in 1990; led by Abdul Wahid Kashmiri
   country or region of operation: South Asia, primarily Pakistan and India
   primary goals: establishment of Pakistani control over India-administered Kashmir

Lashkar I Jhangvi
   founded in 1996; decentralized leadership structure
   country or region of operation: Pakistan
   primary goals: replacement of the Pakistani government with an Islamic state

Liberation Tigers of Tamil Eelam (LTTE)
   founded in 1976; led by Velupillai Prabhakaran (until his death in May 2009)
   country or region of operation: Sri Lanka
   primary goals: establishment of an independent Tamil state

Libyan Islamic Fighting Group (LIFG)
   founded in 1995 among Libyans who had fought against Soviet forces in Afghanistan; led by Anas Sebai
   country or region of operation: Libya, various Middle Eastern and European countries
   primary goals: overthrow of the government of Libyan leader Muammar al-Qaddafi

Moroccan Islamic Combatant Group (GICM)
   founded in the 1990s as an offshoot of the Moroccan organization Shabiba Islamiya (Islamic Youth)
   country or region of operation: Afghanistan, Belgium, Denmark, Egypt, France, Morocco, Spain, Turkey, UK
   primary goals: creation of an Islamic state in Morocco

Mojahedin-e Khalq Organization (MEK)
   founded in the 1960s; led by Maryam and Masud Rajavi
   country or region of operation: Iran, Iraq
   primary goals: establishment of a secular government in Iran

National Liberation Army (ELN)
   founded in 1965; led by Nicolas Rodríguez Bautista
   country or region of operation: Colombia
   primary goals: replacement of the ruling Colombian government with a Marxist state

Palestine Liberation Front (PLF)
   founded in the mid-1970s as splinter group from PFLP–GC
   country or region of operation: Israel, Iraq
   primary goals: elimination of Israel, establishment of a Palestinian state

Palestinian Islamic Jihad (PIJ)
   founded in the 1970s; most active faction led by Ramadan Shallah
   country or region of operation: primarily Israel, West Bank, Gaza Strip, Lebanon, and Syria
   primary goals: elimination of Israel, establishment of an Islamic Palestinian state

Popular Front for the Liberation of Palestine (PFLP)
   founded in 1967 by George Habash; led by Ahmed Sadat (imprisoned by Israel since 2006)
   country or region of operation: Syria, Lebanon, Israel, West Bank, Gaza Strip
   primary goals: revitalization of the PLO, opposition to peace negotiations with Israel

Popular Front for the Liberation of Palestine–General Command (PFLP–GC)
   founded in 1968 as splinter group from PFLP; led by Ahmad Jibril
   country or region of operation: Syria, Lebanon, Israel, West Bank, Gaza Strip
   primary goals: opposition to the PLO and to peace negotiations with Israel

al-Qaeda
   founded in the late 1980s; established and led by Osama bin Laden
   country or region of operation: worldwide
   primary goals: establishment of worldwide Islamic rule, overthrow of non-Islamic governments, expulsion of
   Western influences from Muslim states, killing of US citizens

al-Qaeda Organization in the Islamic Maghreb (formerly Salafist Group for Call and Combat, GSPC)
   founded in 1996 as a splinter of the Armed Islamic Group; led by Abou Mossaab Abdelouadoud
   country or region of operation: primarily Algeria, with significant activity elsewhere in North Africa and in Europe
   primary goals: replacement of the Algerian government with an Islamic state

International Terrorist Organizations (continued)

Real IRA (True IRA)
   founded in 1998 as a splinter group of the Irish Republican Army (IRA); led by Michael ("Mickey") McKevitt (imprisoned since 2001)
   country or region of operation: Northern Ireland; also elsewhere in Great Britain and in Ireland
   primary goals: removal of British forces from Northern Ireland, unification of Ireland

Revolutionary Armed Forces of Colombia (FARC)
   founded in 1964 as the military branch of the Colombian Communist Party; governed by a group led by Alfonso Cano and including Jorge Briceño and five others
   country or region of operation: Colombia; also some operations in Venezuela, Ecuador, and Panama
   primary goals: replacement of the ruling Colombian government with a Marxist state

Revolutionary Nuclei (Revolutionary Cells)
   founded in 1995 as an offshoot of or successor to Revolutionary People's Struggle (ELA)
   country or region of operation: Greece, primarily Athens
   primary goals: elimination of US military bases in Greece, opposition to capitalism and NATO/EU membership

Revolutionary Organization 17 November
   founded in 1975; allegedly led by Alexandros Giotopoulos (imprisoned in Greece since 2002)
   country or region of operation: Greece, primarily Athens
   primary goals: elimination of US military bases in Greece, removal of Turkish forces from Cyprus, opposition to capitalism and NATO/EU membership

Revolutionary People's Liberation Party/Front (DHKP/C) (Devrimci Sol, Revolutionary Left, Dev Sol)
   founded in 1978 as a splinter group from Turkish People's Liberation Party/Front
   country or region of operation: Turkey, primarily Istanbul
   primary goals: promotion of Marxism, opposition to US and NATO

al-Shabaab
   founded in 2006 by fighters from the recently ousted Islamic Courts Union
   country or region of operation: Somalia
   primary goals: ejection of foreign troops from Somalia, reestablishment of an Islamic government in the country

Shining Path (Sendero Luminoso, SL)
   founded in the late 1960s by Abimael Guzman; led by Macario Ala
   country or region of operation: Peru, primarily rural areas
   primary goals: replacement of the Peruvian government with a communist state

Tanzim Qaidat al-Jihad fi Bilad al-Rafidayn (QJBR, al-Qaeda in Iraq) (formerly Jamaat al-Tawhid waal-Jihad, JTJ, al-Zarqawi Network)
   founded in April 2004 by Abu Musab al-Zarqawi shortly after the commencement of Operation Iraqi Freedom (OIF); adopted current name in October 2004 after merging with Osama bin Laden's al-Qaeda
   country or region of operation: Iraq
   primary goals: expulsion of OIF coalition from Iraq, establishment of Islamic state in Iraq

United Self-Defense Forces of Colombia (Autodefensas Unidas de Colombia, AUC)
   founded in 1997 as an umbrella organization of paramilitary groups
   country or region of operation: Colombia
   primary goals: opposition to and defense against leftist guerrilla groups

Military Affairs

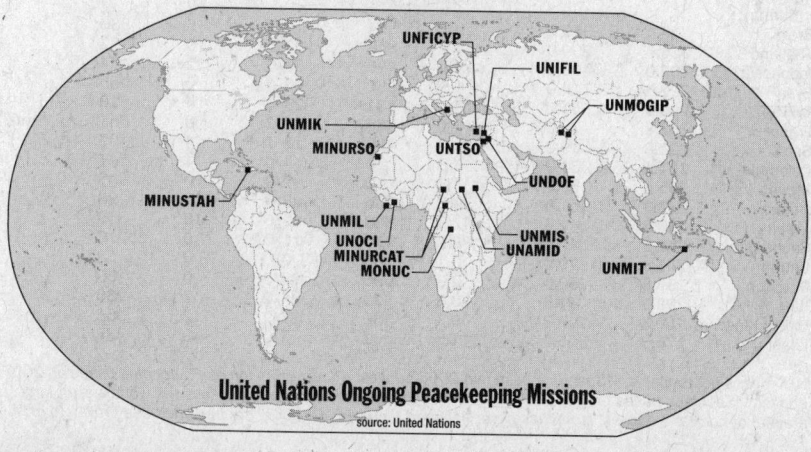

United Nations Ongoing Peacekeeping Missions

source: United Nations

United Nations Ongoing Peacekeeping Missions (continued)

MINURCAT United Nations Mission in the Central African Republic and Chad—since September 2007 (3,043)

MINURSO United Nations Mission for the Referendum in Western Sahara—since April 1991 (229)

MINUSTAH United Nations Stabilization Mission in Haiti—since June 2004 (9,055[1])

MONUC United Nations Organization Mission in the Democratic Republic of the Congo—since November 1999 (18,381)

UNAMID African Union/United Nations Hybrid Operation in Darfur—since July 2007 (16,402)

UNDOF United Nations Disengagement Observer Force (in the Golan Heights)—since May 1974 (1,045)

UNFICYP United Nations Peacekeeping Force in Cyprus—since March 1964 (926)

UNIFIL United Nations Interim Force in Lebanon—since March 1978 (12,158)

UNMIK United Nations Interim Administration Mission in Kosovo—since June 1999 (14)

UNMIL United Nations Mission in Liberia—since September 2003 (11,374[1])

UNMIS United Nations Mission in Sudan—since March 2005 (9,891)

UNMIT United Nations Integrated Mission in Timor-Leste—since August 2006 (1,518)

UNMOGIP United Nations Military Observer Group in India and Pakistan—since January 1949 (40)

UNOCI United Nations Operation in Côte d'Ivoire—since April 2004 (9,048)

UNTSO United Nations Truce Supervision Organization (in the Middle East)—since May 1948 (149)

Parenthetical figures indicate military personnel as of 31 May 2009. Civilian forces, including police officers, are not included in this table. [1]Data are as of 31 Mar 2009.

Nations with Largest Armed Forces

The top 30 countries in terms of active-personnel military strength are included. Personnel numbers are in thousands ('000) and reflect November 2008 data; spending totals are from 2008 budgets except where noted. Source: The International Institute of Strategic Studies, The Military Balance 2009.

COUNTRY	MILITARY PERSONNEL ACTIVE	MILITARY PERSONNEL RESERVES	DEFENSE SPENDING (US$ BILLIONS)	MAIN BATTLE TANKS	MAJOR WARSHIPS/ CARRIERS	SUB- MARINES	COMBAT AIRCRAFT	STRATEGIC NUCLEAR WEAPONS
China	2,185.0	800.0	61.1	8,810+	78/0	62	1,943	yes
United States	1,539.6	979.4	693.0	8,023+	107/11	71	4,293	yes
India	1,281.2	1,155.0	25.3	4,065	47/1	16	632	yes
D.P.R. Korea	1,106.0	4,700.0	2.3[1]	4,060+	8/0	63	620	yes
Russia	1,027.0	20,000.0	36.4	24,471	103/1	136	2,364	yes
Rep. of Korea	687.0	4,500.0	28.6	2,390	47/0	12	499	
Pakistan	617.0	304.0[2]	3.6	2,461+	6/0	8	399	yes
Iran	523.0	350.0	7.5[3]	1,693+	6/0	3	319	
Turkey	510.6	378.7	8.8	4,205	23/0	14	435	
Iraq	577.1	0.0	N/A	149+	0/0	0	0	
Egypt	468.5	479.0	4.6[3]	3,505	11/0	4	458	
Vietnam	455.0	5,000.0	3.7[3]	1,935	11/0	2	219	
Myanmar (Burma)	406.0	107.3[2]	7.0[3]	255	3/0	0	125	
Brazil	326.4	1,340.0	20.2	354	16/1	5	336	
Thailand	306.6	200.0	4.2	848	20/1	0	182	
Indonesia	302.0	400.0	3.1	405	29/0	2	94	
Syria	292.6	314.0	1.5[3]	4,950	2/0	0	555	
Taiwan	290.0	1,657.0	10.5	1,831+	26/0	4	510	
France	352.8	70.3	41.1	665	32/2	9	351	yes
Spain	221.8	319.0	11.0	420	12/1	4	197	
Colombia	267.2	61.9	8.3	0	4/0	4	117	
Mexico	255.5	39.9	3.8	0	7/0	0	85	
Germany	244.3	161.8	39.9	2,035	18/0	12	298	
Japan	230.3	41.8	47.3	880	52/0	16	350	
Saudi Arabia	221.5	15.5[2]	38.2	910	11/0	0	276	
Eritrea	201.8	120.0	0.1[4]	150	0/0	0	18	
Morocco	195.8	150.0	2.8	696	3/0	0	89	
Italy	293.0	41.9	20.8	320	24/2	7	266	
United Kingdom	160.3	199.3	59.7	386	27/2	13	356	yes
Israel	176.5	565.0	11.6[3]	3,501	3/0	3	435	[5]

N/A means not available. [1]Spending based on 2006 budget. [2]Paramilitary forces. [3]Spending based on 2007 budget. [4]Spending based on 2005 budget. [5]Although believed by many to possess the world's sixth largest arsenal of nuclear weapons, Israel has never declared a nuclear capability nor has one been proven to exist.

United States

The Great Recession: America Becomes Thrift Nation

by Nancy Gibbs, TIME

Sometimes we change because we want to: lose weight, go vegan, find God, get sober. But sometimes we change because we have no choice, and since this violates our manifest destiny to do as we please, it may take a while before we notice that those are often the changes we need to make most. Americans ran a good long road test of the premise that more is better: we built houses that could hold all our stuff but were too big to heat; we bought cars that could ferry a soccer team but were too big to park; we thought we were embracing the simple life by squeezing in a yoga class between working and shopping and took an extra job to pay for it all.

Now we're stripping down and starting over. In April 2009, a platoon of TIME reporters and pollsters fanned out across the country to measure—anecdotally and empirically—what's changed in the way we set our priorities and spend our money since the Great Recession began. Most people think the pain will be lasting and the effects permanent: TIME's survey of Americans found only 12% expected economic recovery to begin within six months, half believed it would be another year or two, and 14% believed we were at the start of a long-term decline.

Our institutions watch for economic vital signs. But maybe, for individuals, the sickness is what came before—the hallucination that debt would never need to be repaid, that values only rise, that bubbles never burst. When the markets collapsed in 2008, that fever broke. In our assumptions and attitudes and expectations, the recovery is already well under way. Talk to people not just about how they feel but about how they're living now, and you hear more resolve than regret. Nearly half say their economic status declined in 2009, and 57% now think the American Dream is harder to achieve.

And yet pain and promise are a package deal; even after all this, fully 56% believe that America's best days are ahead. It would be nice if it took something short of a heart attack to get us to work out, eat better, and spend more time with our kids. But in the end, where we wind up matters more than how we got there.

Unlike any other downturn since the 1930s, this one has affected everyone, either the fact of it or the fear of it. Even when prosperity returns, 61% predict, they'll continue to spend less than they did before. Among people earning less than US$50,000 a year—roughly half of US households—34% have not gone to the doctor because of the cost, 31% have been out of work at some point, and 13% have been hungry. At the same time, 4 in 10 people earning more than US$100,000 say they are buying more store brands, 36% are using coupons more, and 39% have postponed or canceled a vacation to save money. Forty percent of people at all income levels say they feel anxious, 32% have trouble sleeping, and 20% are depressed. Forty-three percent are watching the news even more than before the down-turn, taking the medicine even if it tastes bad because skipping it could be risky.

The calculus of life suddenly offers new equations. Insurance agents see clients raising their deductibles to lower premiums or skipping collision coverage for older cars so that they bear more of the risks themselves. Twenty-seven percent have raided their retirement or college savings to pay the bills. Violent crime may not be up, but fear of it is: 40% of people say that since the downturn began, they are more worried about their personal safety.

For all the reflexive analogies, this is not the 1930s. And yet we're channeling our grandparents, who were taught, like a mantra, to use it up, wear it out, make it do, do without. Now, if you can make it, you don't have to buy it: just replace the lawn with a vegetable garden, eat your fill, and then store whatever is left. Sales of canning and freezing supplies rose 15% during the first three months of the year compared with the same period last year. Cough- and cold-remedy sales are down 9% because you can make your own chicken soup; vitamin sales are up, maybe because you hope you won't need to. Common sense is back in style, meaning we're less willing to buy what we can have for free: bottled-water sales have dropped 10%. The 137-year-old Los Angeles public-library system set record highs in circulation and visitors. And film and camera sales have plunged 33% in 2009, because who would want this winter in their album?

There's a natural longing to find the upside in the downturn. A college-admissions officer, watching families reassess their means and ends, suggests that maybe the insane competitiveness will recede. The yoga instructor says living more simply relaxes us, as if the entire country needs to slow its breathing. The discount shoppers view their task as a scavenger hunt and take a certain pride in finding the bargain, cutting the deal; 23% of us are haggling more, a profitable contact sport.

No one wishes for hardship. But as we pick through the economic rubble, we may find that our riches have buried our treasures. Money does not buy happiness; Scripture asserts this, research confirms it. Multiple opinion polls show that once individuals reach the median level of income, roughly US$50,000 a year, wealth and contentment go their separate ways, and studies find that a millionaire is no more likely to be happy than someone earning one-twentieth as much. Now a third of people polled say they are spending more time with family and friends, and nearly four times as many people say their relations with their kids have improved during this crisis than say they have gotten worse.

A consumer culture invites us to want more than we can ever have; a culture of thrift invites us to be grateful for whatever we can get. So we pass the time by tending our gardens and patching our safety nets and debating whether, years from now, this season will be remembered more for what we lost, or for all that we found.

United States History

United States Chronology

1492 Christopher Columbus, sailing under the Spanish flag, arrives in the Americas, 12 October.

1513 Ponce de León of Spain lands in Florida and gives that region its name.

1534 France sends Jacques Cartier to find a route to the Far East; he explores along the St. Lawrence River, and France lays claim to part of North America.

1541 Hernando de Soto of Spain sights the Mississippi River near the location of present-day Memphis.

1565 St. Augustine, the oldest permanent settlement in the US, is founded by Spaniards.

1587 A party under John White lands at Roanoke Island (now in North Carolina); when White returns three years later, the entire settlement has disappeared.

1607 The English make the first permanent settlement in the New World at Jamestown; Virginia becomes the first of the 13 English colonies.

1619 The first representative assembly in America, the House of Burgesses, meets in Virginia.

1620 Pilgrims from the ship *Mayflower* found a settlement at Plymouth.

1649 The Act Concerning Religion passed by Maryland's legislature is the first law of religious toleration in the English colonies.

1682 The Sieur de La Salle explores the lower Mississippi valley and claims the entire region for France.

1733 Georgia, the 13th and last of the English colonies in America, is founded.

1754 The French and Indian War between France and England begins in America.

1763 The Treaty of Paris ends the French and Indian War; Florida is ceded to Britain.

1765 The Quartering Act and the Stamp Act anger Americans; nine colonies are represented at the Stamp Act Congress.

1770 British troops fire on a crowd, killing five people in the so-called Boston Massacre.

1773 The Boston Tea Party, the first action in a chain leading to war with Britain, takes place.

1774 The First Continental Congress meets at Philadelphia and protests the five Intolerable Acts.

1775 The battles of Lexington and Concord and Bunker Hill occur; the Second Continental Congress meets.

1776 The Declaration of Independence is adopted.

1778-79 Gen. George Rogers Clark leads a victorious expedition into the Northwest Territory.

1781 George Washington accepts the surrender of Charles Cornwallis at Yorktown VA; the Articles of Confederation become the government of the US.

1783 A treaty of peace with Great Britain is signed at Paris, formally ending the Revolutionary War.

1786-87 Shays's Rebellion in Massachusetts shows weaknesses of the Confederation government.

1787 The Northwest Territory is organized by Congress; a convention meets to draft a new constitution.

1788 The US Constitution is ratified by the necessary nine states to ensure adoption.

1789 The new US government goes into effect; Washington is inaugurated president; the first Congress meets in New York City.

1791 The Bill of Rights is added to the Constitution; Vermont is the first new state admitted to the Union.

1793 Eli Whitney invents the cotton gin, which leads to large-scale cotton growing in the South.

1800 The national capital is moved from Philadelphia to Washington DC.

1803 Louisiana is purchased from France; the Supreme Court makes its *Marbury* v. *Madison* decision, establishing judicial review; Congress halts the importation of slaves into the US after 1807.

1804-06 Meriwether Lewis and William Clark blaze an overland trail to the Pacific and return.

1807 Robert Fulton's steamboat makes a successful journey from New York City to Albany NY.

1812-14 The US maintains its independence in a conflict with Britain, the War of 1812.

1820 The Missouri Compromise settles the problem of slavery in new states for the next 30 years.

1823 The Monroe Doctrine warns European nations that the US will protect the Americas.

1825 The Erie Canal, from the Hudson River to the Great Lakes, becomes a great water highway to the Middle West.

1829 The inauguration of Pres. Andrew Jackson introduces the era of Jacksonian Democracy.

1836 Texas wins its independence from Mexico.

1843 The first migration begins on the Oregon Trail.

1845 Texas is annexed and admitted as a state.

1846 The Oregon boundary dispute is settled with Britain; the Mexican War begins.

1847 Brigham Young leads a party of Mormons into the Salt Lake valley, Utah.

1848 The Mexican War ends; the US gains possession of the California and New Mexico regions.

1849 The gold rush to California begins.

1850 The Compromise of 1850 admits California as a free state, postponing war between the North and South.

1853 The Gadsden Purchase adds 117,935 sq km (45,535 sq mi) to what is now the southwestern US.

1854 The Republican Party is organized in opposition to slavery.

1857 The Dred Scott decision of the Supreme Court declares that the Missouri Compromise is illegal.

1860 Abraham Lincoln is elected president; South Carolina secedes from the Union.

1861 The Confederate States of America is formed; the Civil War begins; telegraph links New York City with San Francisco.

1862 Gen. Ulysses S. Grant launches a Union attack in the West; the Confederate invasion of Maryland is halted at Antietam; the Homestead Act grants 160 acres to each settler.

1863 Federal forces win decisive battles at Gettysburg PA, Vicksburg MS, and Chattanooga TN; the Emancipation Proclamation is delivered.

1864 Gen. William Tecumseh Sherman captures Atlanta and marches across Georgia.

1865 Gen. Robert E. Lee surrenders to Grant at Appomattox (VA) Court House, ending the Civil War; Lincoln is assassinated.

1867 Reconstruction acts impose military rule on the South; Alaska is purchased from Russia.

1869 The first transcontinental railroad is completed as two lines meet at Promontory UT.

1876 The telephone is invented; the Centennial Exposition in Philadelphia celebrates the 100th birthday of the US.

1877 The withdrawal of the last federal troops from the South ends the Reconstruction period.

1879 The first practical electric light is invented by Thomas A. Edison.

1884–85 The first skyscraper, the Home Insurance Building, is erected in Chicago.

1886 The American Federation of Labor (AFL) is organized; its first president is Samuel Gompers.

1887 The Interstate Commerce Act is adopted to control railroads that cross state lines.

1889–90 The first pan-American conference is held in Washington DC.

1890 The Sherman Anti-Trust Act is passed in an effort to curb the growth of monopolies.

1896 Henry Ford's first car is driven on the streets of Detroit.

1898 The US wins the Spanish-American War and gains the Philippines, Puerto Rico, and Guam.

1903 The air age begins with the successful airplane flight by the Wright brothers.

1906 The Federal Food and Drug Act is passed to protect the public from impure food and drugs.

1913 Federal income tax is authorized by the 16th Amendment.

1914 The Panama Canal is opened under the control of the US; World War I breaks out in Europe; Pres. Woodrow Wilson appeals for neutrality in the US.

1915 A German submarine sinks the British ship *Lusitania* with the loss of 124 American lives; a telephone line is established coast-to-coast.

1917 The US declares war against Germany.

1918 Pres. Wilson proposes "Fourteen Points" as the basis for peace; Americans fight at Château-Thierry, Belleau Wood, Saint-Mihiel, and Argonne Forest in France; an armistice ends the war.

1918–19 Pres. Wilson attends the Paris Peace Conference of victorious nations.

1919 The US Senate rejects the League of Nations; prohibition is established by the 18th Amendment.

1920 The right to vote is given to women by the 19th Amendment.

1921 National immigration quotas are introduced.

1921–22 The Washington Conference restricts warship construction among the chief naval powers.

1924 The army plane *Chicago* makes the first flight around the world.

1927 Charles A. Lindbergh makes the first nonstop solo flight across the Atlantic.

1928 The Kellogg-Briand Pact outlaws war.

1929 The stock market reaches a new high and then crashes; the panic marks the beginning of the Great Depression; millions of workers are unemployed.

1932 Franklin Delano Roosevelt is elected president.

1933 The New Deal is launched; the gold standard is suspended; the National Recovery Act is passed; bank deposits are insured; the Tennessee Valley Authority is organized; the 21st Amendment repeals prohibition.

1934 Congress tightens control over securities, passes the first Reciprocal Trade Agreement Act, and launches the federal housing program.

1935 The National Labor Relations (Wagner) Act guarantees collective bargaining to labor; the Congress of Industrial Organizations (CIO) is founded; the Social Security Act is passed.

1936 The Boulder Dam (now Hoover Dam) is completed across the Colorado River.

1938 The Fair Labor Standards Act provides a federal yardstick for wages and hours of workers.

1939 Germany invades Poland, beginning World War II; the US declares neutrality.

1940 The US begins a huge rearmament program; the first peacetime draft takes effect; Roosevelt de-

fies tradition and accepts the presidential nomination for a third term.

1941 The Japanese attack on Pearl Harbor, Hawaii, brings the US into World War II.

1942 Americans launch a counteroffensive in the Pacific; the Allies invade North Africa.

1943 The invasion of Italy is the Allies' first landing on the European continent.

1944 The Allies launch the greatest sea-to-land assault in history in the invasion of France; the GI Bill of Rights is passed.

1945 Germany surrenders, 8 May; the US drops atomic bombs on Japan at Hiroshima, 6 August, and Nagasaki, 9 August; Japan surrenders, 2 September; the Cold War begins between the US and the Soviet Union.

1946 The Philippines is granted independence by the US; the Atomic Energy Commission is created.

1947 The Truman Doctrine, offering aid to counter communism in Greece and Turkey, is declared; the Department of Defense consolidates the army, navy, and air force.

1948 The European Recovery Program is enacted.

1949 The Fair Deal program of social reform is announced; the US and its allies force the Soviet Union to lift the Berlin blockade; the North Atlantic Treaty Organization (NATO) is founded.

1950 The US and several other members of the UN send military forces to the aid of the Republic of Korea; bitter war develops.

1951 A two-term limit is put on the presidency by ratification of the 22nd Amendment.

1952 The US and its allies end the occupation of West Germany; the election of Dwight D. Eisenhower ends 20 years of Democratic governance.

1953 The Korean War ends; the Department of Health, Education, and Welfare becomes the 10th cabinet post.

1954 Racial segregation of public schools is declared illegal by the Supreme Court.

1955 The two largest labor organizations merge into one group—the AFL-CIO; the Salk poliomyelitis vaccine is proved successful.

1956 Legislation is passed providing funding for the US Interstate Highway System.

1957 The Eisenhower Doctrine to strengthen the US position in the Middle East is adopted.

1958 The first US artificial Earth satellite is launched; the US joins the International Atomic Energy Agency.

1959 Alaska becomes the 49th state, Hawaii the 50th.

1960 A US spy plane is downed over the Soviet Union.

1961 The CIA is involved in an unsuccessful invasion of Cuba at the Bay of Pigs; Alan Shepard becomes the first American to make spaceflight; American troops are sent to defend West Berlin.

1962 The Cuban missile crisis erupts; the Soviets remove missiles from Cuba at the urging of the US.

1963 The March on Washington for Jobs and Freedom takes place; Pres. John F. Kennedy is assassinated in Dallas TX; a nuclear test-ban treaty is signed.

1964 The landmark Civil Rights Act is passed.

1965 US combat forces fight in Vietnam; the Medicare Act is signed; the Department of Housing and Urban Development becomes the 11th cabinet post.

1966 The Department of Transportation becomes the 12th cabinet post.

1967 The 25th Amendment to the Constitution provides for presidential succession.

1968 The assassinations of Martin Luther King, Jr., and Robert F. Kennedy provoke riots.

1969 US astronauts land on the Moon.

1970 Four students at Kent State University in Ohio are killed by National Guard soldiers during anti-Vietnam War protests.

1971 The 26th Amendment to the Constitution gives 18-year-olds the right to vote in all elections.

1972 Pres. Richard M. Nixon visits China and the Soviet Union.

1973 The US withdraws its troops from Vietnam; gas prices go up as OPEC raises the price of petroleum 400%.

1974 The Watergate Scandal and the threat of impeachment force Nixon to resign.

1977 The Department of Energy becomes a new cabinet post; a treaty is signed to return the Panama Canal to Panama by the year 2000.

1978 Pres. Jimmy Carter hosts the Camp David talks between Israel's Menachem Begin and Egypt's Anwar el-Sadat.

1979 The second Strategic Arms Limitation Talks (SALT II) treaty is signed by the US and the Soviet Union; militants seize 66 American hostages in a takeover of the US embassy in Iran.

1980 The Department of Health, Education, and Welfare is separated into the Department of Health and Human Services and the Department of Education.

1981 Pres. Ronald Reagan is wounded in an assassination attempt; Sandra Day O'Connor is appointed the first woman Supreme Court justice.

1983 Reagan announces the Star Wars missile-defense program; the US invades Grenada.

1985 A summit between Reagan and Soviet leader Mikhail Gorbachev is held in Geneva, Switzerland.

1986 The space shuttle *Challenger* explodes shortly after liftoff; the US bombs targets in Libya; the Iran-Contra Affair is revealed.

1987 The Iran-Contra hearings are held; the stock market collapses; Reagan and Gorbachev sign the Intermediate-Range Nuclear Forces (INF) Treaty.

1988 The Department of Veterans Affairs is approved as a cabinet post.

1989 The *Exxon Valdez* supertanker spills 10 million gallons of crude oil off the Alaskan coast; the US invades Panama; the Berlin Wall ceases to divide the two Germanys, signaling the end of the Cold War.

1990 US troops are sent to Saudi Arabia in response to Iraq's invasion of Kuwait.

1991 An air and ground war leads to the Iraqi surrender and withdrawal from Kuwait; the Soviet Union comes apart.

1992 Riots erupt in Los Angeles after white policemen accused of beating African American Rodney King are acquitted; the North American Free Trade Agreement (NAFTA) is signed by the US, Canada, and Mexico.

1993 Janet Reno becomes the first woman attorney general; the World Trade Center in New York City is bombed.

1995 Timothy McVeigh detonates a bomb in a terrorist attack on the Alfred P. Murrah Federal Building in Oklahoma City, killing 168 people.

1998 Pres. Bill Clinton is impeached for perjury and obstruction of justice; he is acquitted by the Senate the following year.

2000 The results of the presidential election are challenged by Vice Pres. Al Gore; the US Supreme Court overrules the Florida Supreme Court's order for a statewide manual recount of ballots; George W. Bush wins the presidency.

2001 On 11 September, two hijacked airplanes demolish the World Trade Center in New York City, another crashes into the Pentagon outside Washington DC, and a fourth crashes in the southern Pennsylvania countryside; Pres. Bush calls for a global "war on terror", and sends US troops into Afghanistan, eventually displacing the Taliban regime.

2002 Republicans take control of both houses of Congress, holding both the legislative and executive branches of government for the first time since 1952.

2003 The US launches a war to depose the Saddam Hussein regime in Iraq and takes control of the country after just weeks of fighting; Congress passes a US$350 billion tax cut.

2004 Scandal erupts with the publication of photos of prisoner abuse at Abu Ghraib prison in Iraq; the independent 9/11 Commission finds no credible evidence of a connection between Iraq and al-Qaeda's attacks of 11 Sep 2001; Bush is reelected president.

2005 Hurricane Katrina strikes the Gulf Coast, destroying much of New Orleans and killing more than 1,500 people.

2006 Conservative lawyer John G. Roberts, Jr., is appointed to the Supreme Court as chief justice; Al Gore's film, *An Inconvenient Truth*, which will win an Academy Award in 2007, warns of the danger of global warming to the environment; Democrats gain control of both houses of Congress.

2007 In an effort to quell a persistent insurrection against the US-backed government of Iraq, Pres. Bush orders a "surge" of 20,000 additional US troops.

2008 A crisis in the subprime mortgage industry, leading to foreclosures and falling home values, together with record-high prices of petroleum, pushes the US economy to the brink of recession; US troop deaths in Iraq top 4,100 by July, while deaths in Afghanistan reach 475.

2009 In a historic ceremony on 20 January, Barack Obama is sworn in as the first African American president of the United States; two of the Big Three automobile manufacturers—Chrysler and General Motors—declare bankruptcy; American troops meet the 30 June deadline to withdraw from Iraqi cities under an agreement that calls for all American forces to leave Iraq by the end of 2011.

Important Documents in US History

Mayflower Compact

On 21 Nov 1620 (11 November, Old Style), 41 male passengers on the Mayflower signed the following compact prior to their landing at Plymouth (now Massachusetts). The compact resulted from the fear that some members of the company might leave the group and settle on their own. The Mayflower Compact bound the signers into a body politic for the purpose of forming a government and pledged them to abide by any laws and regulations that would later by established. The document was not a constitution but rather an adaptation of the usual church covenant to a civil situation. It became the foundation of Plymouth's government.

In the name of God, Amen.

We whose names are underwritten, the loyal subjects of our dread sovereign Lord, King James, by the grace of God, of Great Britain, France and Ireland king, defender of the faith, etc., having undertaken, for the glory of God, and advancement of the Christian faith, and honor of our king and country, a voyage to plant the first colony in the Northern parts of Virginia, do by these presents solemnly and mutually in the presence of God, and one of another, covenant and combine ourselves together into a civil body politic, for our better ordering and preservation and furtherance of the ends aforesaid; and by virtue hereof to enact, constitute, and frame such just and equal laws, ordinances, acts, constitutions, and offices, from time to time, as shall be thought most meet and convenient for the general good of the colony, unto which we promise all due submission and obedience.

In witness whereof we have hereunder subscribed our names at Cape-Cod the 11 of November, in the year of the reign of our sovereign lord, King James, of England, France, and Ireland the eighteenth, and of Scotland the fifty-fourth. Anno Domine 1620.

Declaration of Independence

On 4 Jul 1776 the Continental Congress officially adopted the Declaration of Independence. Two days before, the Congress had "unanimously" voted (with New York abstaining) to be free and independent from Britain. The Declaration of Independence was written largely by Thomas Jefferson. After modifications by the Congress, the document was prepared and voted upon. New York delegates voted to accept it on 15 July, and on 19 July the Congress ordered the document to be engrossed as "The Unanimous Declaration of the Thirteen United States of America." It was accordingly put on parchment, and members of the Congress present on 2 August affixed their signatures to this parchment copy on that day, and others later. The last signer was Thomas McKean of Delaware, whose name was not placed on the document before 1777.

The Unanimous Declaration of the Thirteen United States of America

When in the Course of human events, it becomes necessary for one people to dissolve the political bands which have connected them with another, and to assume among the powers of the earth, the separate and equal station to which the Laws of Nature and of Nature's God entitle them, a decent respect to the opinions of mankind requires that they should declare the causes which impel them to the separation.—We hold these truths to be self-evident, that all men are created equal, that they are endowed by their Creator with certain unalienable Rights, that among these are Life, Liberty and the pursuit of Happiness.—That to secure these rights, Governments are instituted among Men, deriving their just powers from the consent of the governed,—That whenever any Form of Government becomes destructive of these ends, it is the Right of the People to alter or to abolish it, and to institute new Government, laying its foundation on such principles and organizing its powers in such form, as to them shall seem most likely to effect their Safety and Happiness.

Prudence, indeed, will dictate that Governments long established should not be changed for light and transient causes; and accordingly all experience hath shown, that mankind are more disposed to suffer, while evils are sufferable, than to right themselves by abolishing the forms to which they are accustomed. But when a long train of abuses and usurpations, pursuing invariably the same Object evinces a design to reduce them under absolute Despotism, it is their right, it is their duty, to throw off such Government, and to provide new Guards for their future security.— Such has been the patient sufferance of these Colonies; and such is now the necessity which constrains them to alter their former Systems of Government. The history of the present King of Great Britain is a history of repeated injuries and usurpations, all having in direct object the establishment of an absolute Tyranny over these States.

To prove this, let Facts be submitted to a candid world.—He has refused his Assent to Laws, the most wholesome and necessary for the public good.—He has forbidden his Governors to pass Laws of immediate and pressing importance, unless suspended in their operation till his Assent should be obtained; and when so suspended, he has utterly neglected to attend to them.—He has refused to pass other Laws for the accommodation of large districts of people, unless those people would relinquish the right of Representation in the Legislature, a right inestimable to them and formidable to tyrants only.—He has called together legislative bodies at places unusual, uncomfortable, and distant from the depository of their public Records, for the sole purpose of fatiguing them into compliance with his measures.—He has dissolved Representative Houses repeatedly, for opposing with manly firmness his invasions on the rights of the people.—He has refused for a long time, after such dissolutions, to cause others to be elected; whereby the Legislative powers, incapable of Annihilation, have returned to the People at large for their exercise; the State remaining in the mean time exposed to all the dangers of invasion from without, and convulsions within.—He has endeavoured to prevent the population of these States; for that purpose obstructing the Laws for Naturalization of Foreigners; refusing to pass others to encourage their migration hither, and raising the conditions of new Appropriations of Lands.—He has obstructed the Administration of Justice, by refusing his Assent to Laws for establishing Judiciary powers.—He has made judges dependent on his Will alone, for the tenure of their offices, and the amount and payment of their salaries.—He has erected a multitude of New Offices, and sent hither swarms of Officers to harrass our people, and eat out their substance.—He has kept among us, in times of peace, Standing Armies, without the Consent of our legislatures.—He has affected to render the Military independent of and superior to the Civil power.—He has combined with others to subject us to a jurisdiction foreign to our constitution, and unacknowledged by our laws; giving his Assent to their Acts of pretended Legislation:—For quartering large bodies of armed troops among us:—For protecting them, by a mock Trial, from punishment for any Murders which they should commit on the Inhabitants of these States:—For cutting off our Trade with all parts of the world:—For imposing Taxes on us without our Consent:—For depriving us in many cases, of the benefits of Trial by Jury:—For transporting us beyond Seas to be tried for pretended offences:—For abolishing the free System of English Laws in a neighbouring Province, establishing therein an Arbitrary government, and enlarging its Boundaries so as to render it at once an example and fit instrument for introducing the same absolute rule into these Colonies:—For taking away our Charters, abolishing our most valuable Laws, and altering fundamentally the Forms of our Governments:—For suspending our own Legislatures, and declaring themselves invested with power to legislate for us in all cases whatsoever.—He has abdicated Government here, by declaring us out of his Protection and waging War against us.—He has plundered our seas, ravaged our Coasts, burnt our towns, and destroyed the lives of our people.—He is at this time transporting large Armies of foreign Mercenaries to compleat the works of death, desolation and tyranny, already begun with circumstances of Cruelty & perfidy scarcely paralleled in the most barbarous ages, and totally unworthy the Head of a civilized nation.—He has constrained our fellow Citizens taken Captive on the high Seas to bear Arms against their Country, to become the executioners of their friends and Brethren, or to fall themselves by their Hands.—He has excited domestic insurrections amongst us, and has endeavoured to bring on the inhabitants of our frontiers, the merciless Indian Savages, whose known rule of warfare, is an undistinguished destruction of all ages, sexes and conditions. In every stage of these Oppressions We have Petitioned for Redress in the most humble terms: Our repeated Petitions have been answered only by repeated injury. A Prince, whose character is thus marked by every act which may define a Tyrant, is unfit to be the ruler of a free people. Nor have We been wanting in attentions to our Brittish brethren. We have warned them from time to time of attempts by their legislature to extend an unwarrantable jurisdiction over us. We have reminded them of the circumstances of our emigration and settlement here. We have appealed to their native justice and magnanimity, and we have conjured them by the ties of our common kindred to disavow these usurpations, which, would inevitably interrupt our connections and correspondence. They too have been deaf to the voice of justice and of consanguinity. We must, therefore, acquiesce in the necessity, which denounces our Separation, and hold them, as we hold the rest of mankind. Enemies in War, in Peace Friends.—

We, therefore, the Representatives of the United States of America, in General Congress, Assembled, appealing to the Supreme Judge of the world for the rectitude of our intentions, do, in the Name, and by Authority of the good People of these Colonies, solemnly publish and declare, That these United Colonies are, and of Right ought to be Free and Independent States; that they are Absolved from all Allegiance to the British Crown, and that all political connection between them and the State of Great Britain, is and ought to be totally dissolved; and that as Free and Independent States, they have full Power to levy War, conclude Peace, contract Alliances, establish Commerce, and to do all other Acts and Things which Independent States may of right do.—And for the support of this Declaration, with a firm reliance on the protection of Divine Providence, we mutually pledge to each other our Lives, our Fortunes and our sacred Honor.

Signers of the Declaration of Independence

Connecticut
Samuel Huntington
Roger Sherman
William Williams
Oliver Wolcott

Delaware
Thomas McKean
George Read
Caesar Rodney

Georgia
Button Gwinnett
Lyman Hall
George Walton

Maryland
Charles Carroll
Samuel Chase
William Paca
Thomas Stone

Massachusetts
John Adams
Samuel Adams
Elbridge Gerry
John Hancock
Robert Treat Paine

New Hampshire
Josiah Bartlett
Matthew Thornton
William Whipple

New Jersey
Abraham Clark
John Hart
Francis Hopkinson
Richard Stockton
John Witherspoon

New York
William Floyd
Francis Lewis
Philip Livingston
Lewis Morris

North Carolina
Joseph Hewes
William Hooper
John Penn

Pennsylvania
George Clymer
Benjamin Franklin
Robert Morris
John Morton
George Ross
Benjamin Rush
James Smith
George Taylor
James Wilson

Rhode Island
William Ellery
Stephen Hopkins

South Carolina
Thomas Heyward, Jr.
Thomas Lynch, Jr.
Arthur Middleton
Edward Rutledge

Virginia
Carter Braxton
Thomas Jefferson
Benjamin Harrison
Francis Lightfoot Lee
Richard Henry Lee
Thomas Nelson, Jr.
George Wythe

Did you know? Thomas Jefferson was the first governor of a US state—Virginia—to go on to serve as president of the United States (1801–09). Sixteen governors since have been elected president, including 4 of the last 6 executives. William Henry Harrison and Andrew Jackson served as territorial governors of Indiana (1800–12) and Florida (1821) prior to their elections to the presidency.

The Constitution of the United States

The Constitution was written during the summer of 1787 in Philadelphia by 55 delegates to a Constitutional Convention that was called ostensibly to amend the Articles of Confederation. It was submitted for ratification to the 13 states on 28 Sep 1787. In June 1788, after the Constitution had been ratified by nine states (as required by Article VII), Congress set 4 Mar 1789 as the date for the new government to commence proceedings.

Preamble

We the People of the United States, in Order to form a more perfect Union, establish Justice, insure domestic Tranquility, provide for common defence, promote the general Welfare, and secure the Blessings of Liberty to ourselves and our Posterity, do ordain and establish this Constitution for the United States of America.

Article I

Section 1—

All legislative Powers herein granted shall be vested in a Congress of the United States, which shall consist of a Senate and House of Representatives.

Section 2—

The House of Representatives shall be composed of Members chosen every second Year by the People of the several States, and the Electors in each State shall have the Qualifications requisite for Electors of the most numerous Branch of the State Legislature.

No Person shall be a Representative who shall not have attained to the Age of twenty five Years, and been seven Years a Citizen of the United States, and who shall not, when elected, be an Inhabitant of that State in which he shall be chosen.

Representatives and direct Taxes shall be apportioned among the several States which may be included within this Union, according to their respective Numbers, which shall be determined by adding to the whole Number of free Persons, including those bound to Service for a Term of Years, and excluding Indians not taxed, three fifths of all other Persons. The actual Enumeration shall be made within three Years after the first Meeting of the Congress of the United States, and within every subsequent Term of ten Years, in such Manner as they shall by Law direct. The Number of Representatives shall not exceed one for every thirty Thousand, but each State shall have at Least one Representative; and until such enumeration shall be made, the State of New Hampshire shall be entitled to chuse three, Massachusetts eight, Rhode-Island and Providence Plantations one, Connecticut five, New-York six, New Jersey four, Pennsylvania eight, Delaware one, Maryland six, Virginia ten, North Carolina five, South Carolina five, and Georgia three.

When vacancies happen in the Representation from any State, the Executive Authority thereof shall issue Writs of Election to fill such Vacancies.

The House of Representatives shall chuse their speaker and other Officers; and shall have the sole Power of Impeachment.

Section 3—

The Senate of the United States shall be composed of two Senators from each State, chosen by the Legislature thereof for six Years; and each Senator shall have one Vote.

Immediately after they shall be assembled in Consequence of the first Election, they shall be divided as equally as may be into three Classes. The Seats of the Senators of the first Class shall be vacated at the Expiration of the second Year, of the second Class at the Expiration of the fourth Year, and of the third Class at the Expiration of the sixth Year, so that one third may be chosen every second Year; and if Vacancies happen by Resignation, or otherwise, during the Recess of the Legislature of any State, the Executive thereof may make temporary Appointments until the next Meeting of the Legislature, which shall then fill such Vacancies.

No Person shall be a Senator who shall not have attained to the Age of thirty Years, and been nine Years a Citizen of the United States, and who shall not, when elected, be an Inhabitant of that State for which he shall be chosen.

The Vice President of the United States shall be President of the Senate, but shall have no Vote, unless they be equally divided.

The Senate shall chuse their other Officers, and also a President pro tempore, in the Absence of the Vice President, or when he shall exercise the Office of President of the United States.

The Senate shall have the sole Power to try all Impeachments. When sitting for that Purpose, they shall be on Oath or Affirmation. When the President of the United States is tried, the Chief Justice shall preside: And no Person shall be convicted without the concurrence of two thirds of the Members present. Judgment in Cases of Impeachment shaLl not extend further than to removal from Office, and disqualification to hold and enjoy any Office of honor, Trust or Profit under the United States: but the Party convicted shall nevertheless be liable and subject to Indictment, Trial, Judgment and Punishment, according to law.

Section 4—

The Times, Places and Manner of holding Elections for Senators and Representatives, shall be prescribed in each State by the Legislature thereof; but the Congress may at any time by Law make or alter such Regulations, except as to the Places of chusing Senators.

The Congress shall assemble at least once in every Year, and such Meeting shall be on the first Monday in December, unless they shall by Law appoint a different Day.

Section 5—

Each House shall be the Judge of the Elections, Returns and Qualifications of its own Members, and a Majority of each shall constitute a Quorum to do business; but a smaller Number may adjourn from day to day, and may be authorized to compel the Attendance of absent Members, in such Manner, and under such Penalties as each House may provide.

Each House may determine the Rules of its Proceedings, punish its Members for disorderly Behaviour, and, with the Concurrence of two thirds, expel a Member.

Each House shall keep a journal of its Proceedings, and from time to time publish the same, excepting such Parts as may in their Judgment require Secrecy; and the yeas and Nays of the Members of either House on any question shall, at the Desire of one fifth of those Present, be entered on the journal.

Neither House, during the Session of Congress, shall, without the Consent of the other, adjourn for more than three days, nor to any other place than that in which the two Houses shall be sitting.

Section 6—

The Senators and Representatives shall receive a Compensation for their Services, to be ascertained by Law, and paid out of the Treasury of the United States. They shall in all Cases, except Treason, Felony and Breach of the Peace, be privileged from Arrest during their Attendance at the Session of their respective Houses, and in going to and returning from the same; and for any Speech or Debate in either House, they shall not be questioned in any other Place.

No Senator or Representative shall, during the Time for which he was elected, be appointed to any civil Office under the Authority of the United States, which shall have been created, or the Emoluments whereof shall have been encreased during such time; and no Person holding any Office under the United States, shall be a Member of either House during his Continuance in Office.

Section 7—

All Bills for raising Revenue shall originate in the House of Representatives; but the Senate may propose or concur with Amendments as on other Bills.

Every Bill which shall have passed the House of Representatives and the Senate, shall, before it become a Law, be presented to the President of the United States; If he approve he shall sign it, but if not he shall return it, with his Objections to that House in which it shall have originated, who shall enter the Objections at large on their Journal, and proceed to reconsider it. If after such Reconsideration two thirds of that House shall agree to pass the Bill, it shall be sent, together with the Objections, to the other House, by which it shall likewise be reconsidered, and if approved by two thirds of that House, it shall become a Law. But in all such Cases the Votes of both Houses shall be determined by yeas and Nays, and the Names of the Persons voting for and against the Bill shall be entered on the Journal of each House respectively. If any Bill shall not be returned by the President within ten Days (Sundays excepted) after it shall have been presented to him, the Same shall be a Law, in like Manner as if he had signed it, unless the Congress by their Adjournment prevent its Return, in which Case it shall not be a Law.

Every Order, Resolution, or Vote to which the Concurrence of the Senate and House of Representatives may be necessary (except on a question of Adjournment) shall be presented to the President of the United States; and before the Same shall take Effect, shall be approved by him, or being disapproved by him, shall be repassed by two thirds of the Senate and House of Representatives, according to the Rules and Limitations prescribed in the Case of a Bill.

Section 8—

The Congress shall have Power To lay and collect Taxes, Duties, Imposts and Excises, to pay the Debts and provide for the common Defence and general Welfare of the United States; but all Duties, Imposts and Excises shall be uniform throughout the United States;

To borrow Money on the credit of the United States;

To regulate Commerce with foreign Nations, and among the several States, and with the Indian Tribes;

To establish an uniform Rule of Naturalization, and uniform Laws on the subject of Bankruptcies throughout the United States;

To coin Money, regulate the Value thereof, and of foreign Coin, and fix the Standard of Weights and Measures;

To provide for the Punishment of counterfeiting the Securities and current Coin of the United States;

To establish Post Offices and post Roads;

To promote the Progress of Science and useful Arts, by securing for limited Times to Authors and Inventors the exclusive Right to their respective Writings and Discoveries;

To constitute Tribunals inferior to the supreme Court;

To define and punish Piracies and Felonies committed on the high Seas, and Offences against the Law of Nations;

To declare War, grant Letters of Marque and Reprisal, and make rules concerning Captures on Land and Water;

To raise and support Armies, but no Appropriation of Money to that Use shall be for a longer Term than two Years;

To provide and maintain a Navy;

To make Rules for the Government and Regulation of the land and naval Forces;

To provide for calling forth the Militia to execute the Laws of the Union, suppress Insurrections and repel Invasions;

To provide for organizing, arming, and disciplining, the Militia, and for governing such Part of them as may be employed in the Service of the United States, reserving to the States respectively, the Appointment of the Officers, and the Authority of training the Militia according to the discipline prescribed by Congress;

To exercise exclusive Legislation in all Cases whatsoever, over such District (not exceeding ten Miles square) as may, by Cession of particular States, and the Acceptance of Congress, become the Seat of the Government of the United States, and to exercise like Authority over all Places purchased by the Consent of the Legislature of the State in which the Same shall be for the Erection of Forts, Magazines, Arsenals, dock-Yards, and other needful Buildings; — And

To make all Laws which shall be necessary and proper for carying into Execution the foregoing Powers, and all other Powers vested by this Constitution in the Government of the United States, or in any Department or Officer thereof.

Section 9—

The Migration or Importation of such Persons as any of the States now existing shall think proper to admit, shall not be prohibited by the Congress prior to the Year one thousand eight hundred and eight, but a Tax or duty may be imposed on such Importation, not exceeding ten dollars for each Person.

The Privilege of the Writ of Habeas Corpus shall not be suspended, unless when in Cases of Rebellion or Invasion the public Safety may require it.

No Bill of Attainder or ex post facto Law shall be passed.

No Capitation, or other direct, Tax shall be laid, unless in Proportion to the Census or Enumeration herein before directed to be taken.

No Tax or Duty shall be laid on Articles exported from any State.

No Preference shall be given by any Regulation of Commerce or Revenue to the Ports of one State over those of another; nor shall Vessels bound to, or from, one State, be obliged to enter, clear or pay Duties in another.

No money shall be drawn from the Treasury, but in Consequence of Appropriations made by Law; and a regular Statement and Account of the Receipts and Expenditures of all public Money shall be published from time to time.

No Title of Nobility shall be granted by the United States: And no Person holding any Office of Profit or Trust under them, shall, without the Consent of the Congress, accept of any present, Emolument, Office, or Title, of any kind whatever, from any King, Prince, or foreign State.

Section 10—

No State shall enter into any Treaty, Alliance, or Confederation; grant Letters of Marque and Reprisal; coin Money; emit Bills of Credit; make any Thing but gold and silver Coin a Tender in Payment of Debts; pass any Bill of Attainder, ex post facto Law, or Law impairing the Obligation of Contracts, or grant any Title of Nobility.

No State shall, without the Consent of the Congress, lay any Imposts or Duties on Imports or Exports, except what may be absolutely necessary for executing it's inspection Laws: and the net Produce of all Duties and Imposts, laid by any State on Imports or Exports, shall be for the Use of the Treasury of the United States; and all such Laws shall be subject to the Revision and Controul of the Congress.

No State shall, without the Consent of Congress, lay any Duty of Tonnage, keep Troops, or Ships of War in time of Peace, enter into any Agreement or Compact with another State, or with a foreign Power, or engage in War, unless actually invaded, or in such imminent Danger as will not admit of delay.

Article II
Section 1—

The executive Power shall be vested in a President of the United States of America. He shall hold his Office during the Term of four Years, and, together with the Vice President, chosen for the same Term, be elected, as follows

Each State shall appoint, in such Manner as the Legislature thereof may direct, a Number of Electors, equal to the whole Number of Senators and Representatives to which the State may be entitled in the Congress: but no Senator or Representative, or Person holding an Office of Trust or Profit under the United States, shall be appointed an Elector.

The Electors shall meet in their respective States, and vote by Ballot for two Persons, of whom one at least shall not be an Inhabitant of the same State with themselves. And they shall make a List of all the Persons voted for, and of the Number of Votes for each; which List they shall sign and certify, and transmit sealed to the Seat of the Government of the United States, directed to the President of the Senate. The President of the Senate shall, in the Presence of the Senate and House of Representatives, open all the Certificates, and the Votes shall then be counted. The Person having the greatest Number of Votes shall be the President, if such Number be a Majority of the whole Number of Electors appointed; and if there be more than one who have such Majority, and have an equal Number of Votes, then the House of Representatives shall immediately chuse by Ballot one of them for President: and if no Person have a Majority, then from the five highest on the List the said House shall in like Manner chuse the President. But in chusing the President, the Votes shall be taken by States, the Representation from each State having one Vote; A quorum for this Purpose shall consist of a Member or Members from two thirds of the States, and a Majority of all the States shall be necessary to a Choice. In every Case, after the Choice of the President, the Person having the greatest Number of Votes of the Electors shall be the Vice President. But if there should remain two or more who have equal Votes, the Senate shall chuse from them by Ballot the Vice President.

The Congress may determine the Time of chusing the Electors, and the Day on which they shall give their Votes; which Day shall be the same throughout the United States.

No Person except a natural born Citizen, or a Citizen of the United States, at the time of the Adoption of this Constitution, shall be eligible to the Office of President; neither shall any Person be eligible to that Office who shall not have attained to the Age of thirty five Years, and been fourteen Years a Resident within the United States.

In Case of the Removal of the President from Office, or of his Death, Resignation, or Inability to discharge the Powers and Duties of the said Office, the Same shall devolve on the Vice President, and the Congress may by Law provide for the Case of Removal, Death, Resignation or Inability, both of the President and Vice President, declaring what Officer shall then act as President, and such Officer shall act accordingly, until the Disability be removed, or a President shall be elected.

The President shall, at stated Times, receive for his Services, a Compensation, which shall neither be encreased nor diminished during the Period for which he shall have been elected, and he shall not receive within that Period any other Emolument from the United States, or any of them.

Before he enter on the Execution of his Office, he shall take the following Oath or Affirmation: "I do solemnly swear (or affirm) that I will faithfully execute the Office of President of the United States, and will to the best of my Ability, preserve, protect and defend the Constitution of the United States."

Section 2—

The President shall be Commander in Chief of the Army and Navy of the United States, and of the Militia of the several States, when called into the actual Service of the United States; he may require the Opinion, in writing, of the principal Officer in each of the executive Departments, upon any Subject relating to the Duties of their respective Offices, and he shall have Power to grant Reprieves and Pardons for Offences against the United States, except in Cases of Impeachment.

He shall have Power, by and with the Advice and Consent of the Senate, to make Treaties, provided two thirds of the Senators present concur; and he shall nominate, and by and with the Advice and Consent of the Senate, shall appoint Ambassadors, other public Ministers and Consuls, Judges of the supreme Court, and all other Officers of the United States, whose Appointments are not herein otherwise provided for, and which shall be established by Law: but the Congress may by Law vest the Appointment of such inferior Officers, as they think proper, in the President alone, in the Courts of Law, or in the Heads of Departments.

The President shall have Power to fill up all Vacancies that may happen during the Recess of the Senate, by granting Commissions which shall expire at the End of their next Session.

Section 3—

He shall from time to time give to the Congress Information of the State of the Union, and recommend to their Consideration such Measures as he shall judge necessary and expedient; he may, on extraordinary Occasions, convene both Houses, or either of them, and in Case of Disagreement between them, with Respect to the Time of Adjournment, he may adjourn them to such Time as he shall think proper; he shall receive Ambassadors and other public Ministers; he shall take Care that the Laws be faithfully executed, and shall Commission all the Officers of the United States.

Section 4—

The President, Vice President and all civil Officers of the United States, shall be removed from Office on Impeachment for, and Conviction of, Treason, Bribery, or other High Crimes and Misdemeanors.

Article III

Section 1—

The judicial Power of the United States, shall be vested in one supreme Court, and in such inferior Courts as the Congress may from time to time ordain and establish. The Judges, both of the supreme and inferior Courts, shall hold their Offices during good Behaviour, and shall, at stated Times, receive for their Services, a Compensation, which shall not be diminished during their Continuance in Office.

Section 2—

The judicial Power shall extend to all Cases, in Law and Equity, arising under this Constitution, the Laws of the United States, and Treaties made, or which shall be made, under their Authority; — to all Cases affecting Ambassadors, other public Ministers and Consuls; — to all Cases of admiralty and maritime jurisdiction; — to Controversies to which the United States shall be a Party; — to Controversies between two or more States;-between a State and Citizens of another State; — between Citizens of different States; — between Citizens of the same State claiming Lands under Grants of different States, and between a State, or the Citizens thereof, and foreign States, Citizens or Subjects.

In all Cases affecting Ambassadors, other public Ministers and Consuls, and those in which a State shall be Party, the supreme Court shall have original Jurisdiction. In all the other Cases before mentioned, the supreme Court shall have appellate Jurisdiction, both as to Law and Fact, with such Exceptions, and under such Regulations as the Congress shall make.

The Trial of all Crimes, except in Cases of Impeachment, shall be by Jury; and such Trial shall be held in the State where the said Crimes shall have been committed; but when not committed within any State, the Trial shall be at such Place or Places as the Congress may by Law have directed.

Section 3—

Treason against the United States, shall consist only in levying War against them, or in adhering to their Enemies, giving them Aid and Comfort. No Person shall be convicted of Treason unless on the Testimony of two Witnesses to the same overt Act, or on Confession in open Court.

The Congress shall have Power to declare the Punishment of Treason, but no Attainder of Treason shall work Corruption of Blood, or Forfeiture except during the Life of the Person attainted.

Article IV

Section 1—

Full Faith and Credit shall be given in each State to the public Acts, Records, and judicial Proceedings of every other State. And the Congress may by general Laws prescribe the Manner in which such Acts, Records and Proceedings shall be proved, and the Effect thereof.

Section 2—

The Citizens of each State shall be entitled to all Privileges and Immunities of Citizens in the several States.

A person charged in any State with Treason, Felony, or other Crime, who shall flee from justice, and be found in another State, shall on Demand of the executive Authority of the State from which he fled, be delivered up, to be removed to the State having Jurisdiction of the Crime.

No Person held to Service or Labour in one State, under the Laws thereof, escaping into another, shall in Consequence of any Law or Regulation therein, be discharged from such Service or Labour, but shall be delivered upon on Claim of the Party to whom such Service or Labour may be due.

Section 3—

New States may be admitted by the Congress into this Union; but no new State shall be formed or erected within the Jurisdiction of any other State; nor any State be formed by the Junction of two or more States, or Parts of States, without the Consent of the Legislatures of the States concerned as well as of the Congress.

The Congress shall have Power to dispose of and make all needful Rules and Regulations respecting the Territory or other Property belonging to the United States; and nothing in this Constitution shall be so construed as to Prejudice any Claims of the United States, or of any particular State.

Section 4—

The United States shall guarantee to every State in this Union a Republican Form of Government, and shall protect each of them against Invasion; and on Application of the Legislature, or of the Executive (when the Legislature cannot be convened) against domestic Violence.

Article V

The Congress, whenever two thirds of both Houses shall deem it necessary, shall propose Amendments to this Constitution, or, on the Application of the Legislatures of two thirds of the several States, shall call a Convention for proposing Amendments, which, in either Case, shall be valid to all Intents and Purposes, as Part of this Constitution, when ratified by the Legislatures of three fourths of the several States, or by Conventions in three fourths thereof, as the one or the other Mode of Ratification may be proposed by the Congress; Provided that no Amendment which may be made prior to the Year One thousand eight hundred and eight shall in any Manner affect the first and fourth Clauses in the Ninth Section of the first

Article; and that no State, without its Consent, shall be deprived of its equal Suffrage in the Senate.

Article VI

All Debts contracted and Engagements entered into, before the Adoption of this Constitution, shall be as valid against the United States under this Constitution, as under the Confederation.

This Constitution, and the Laws of the United States which shall be made in Pursuance thereof; and all Treaties made, or which shall be made, under the Authority of the United States, shall be the supreme Law of the Land; and the Judges in every State shall be bound thereby, any Thing in the Constitution or Laws of any State to the Contrary notwithstanding.

The Senators and Representatives before mentioned, and the Members of the several State Legislatures, and all executive and judicial Officers, both of the United States and of the several States, shall be bound by Oath or Affirmation, to support this Constitution; but no religious Test shall ever be required as a Qualification to any Office or public Trust under the United States.

Article VII

The Ratification of the Conventions of nine States, shall be sufficient for the Establishment of this Constitution between the States so ratifying the Same.

Done in Convention by the Unanimous Consent of the States present the Seventeenth Day of September in the Year of our Lord one thousand seven hundred and Eighty seven and of the Independence of the United States of America the Twelfth IN WITNESS whereof We have hereunto subscribed our Names,

G⁰ Washington—
Presid. *and deputy from Virginia*

New Hampshire
John Langdon
Nicholas Gilman

Massachusetts
Nathaniel Gorham
Rufus King

Connecticut
Wm. Saml. Johnson
Roger Sherman

New York
Alexander Hamilton

New Jersey
Wil: Livingston
David Brearley
Wm. Paterson
Jona: Dayton

Pennsylvania
B. Franklin
Thomas Mifflin
Robᵗ Morris
Geo. Clymer
Thos. FitzSimons
Jared Ingersoll
James Wilson
Gouv Morris

Delaware
Geo: Read
Gunning Bedford jun
John Dickinson
Richard Bassett
Jaco: Broom

Maryland
James McHenry
Dan of Sᵗ Thos. Jenifer
Danˡ Carroll

Virginia
John Blair—
James Madison Jr.

North Carolina
Wm. Blount
Rich'd Dobbs Spaight
Hu Williamson

South Carolina
J. Rutledge
Charles Cotesworth Pinckney
Charles Pinckney
Pierce Butler

Georgia
William Few
Abr Baldwin

Attest:
William Jackson, *Secretary*

[*Rhode Island and the Providence Plantations*
Rhode Island did not send delegates to the Constitutional Convention.]

Bill of Rights

The first 10 amendments to the Constitution were adopted as a single unit on 15 Dec 1791. Together, they constitute a collection of mutually reinforcing guarantees of individual rights and of limitations on federal and state governments.

Amendment I

Congress shall make no law respecting an establishment of religion, or prohibiting the free exercise thereof; or abridging the freedom of speech, or of the press; or the right of the people peaceably to assemble, and to petition the Government for a redress of grievances.

Amendment II

A well regulated Militia, being necessary to the security of a free State, the right of the people to keep and bear Arms, shall not be infringed.

Amendment III

No Soldier shall, in time of peace be quartered in any house, without the consent of the Owner, nor in time of war, but in a manner to be prescribed by law.

Amendment IV

The right of the People to be secure in their persons, houses, papers, and effects, against unreasonable searches and seizures, shall not be violated, and no Warrants shall issue, but upon probable cause, supported by Oath or affirmation, and particularly describing the place to be searched, and the persons or things to be seized.

Amendment V

No person shall be held to answer for a capital, or otherwise infamous crime, unless on a presentment or indictment of a Grand Jury, except in cases arising in the land or naval forces, or in the Militia, when in actual service in time of War or public danger; nor shall any person be subject for the same offence to be twice put in jeopardy of life or limb; nor shall be compelled in any criminal case to be a witness against himself, nor be deprived of life, liberty, or property, without due process of law; nor shall private property be taken for public use, without just compensation.

Amendment VI

In all criminal prosecutions, the accused shall enjoy the right to a speedy and public trial, by an impartial jury of the State and district wherein the crime shall have been committed, which district shall have been previously ascertained by law, and to be informed of the nature and cause of the accusation; to be confronted with the witnesses against him; to have compulsory process for obtaining witnesses in his favor, and to have Assistance of Counsel for his defence.

Amendment VII

In Suits at common law, where the value in controversy shall exceed twenty dollars, the right of trial by jury shall be preserved, and no fact tried by a jury, shall be otherwise re-examined in any Court of the United States, than according to the rules of the common law.

Amendment VIII

Excessive bail shall not be required, nor excessive fines imposed, nor cruel and unusual punishments inflicted.

Amendment IX

The enumeration in the Constitution, of certain rights, shall not be construed to deny or disparage others retained by the people.

Amendment X

The powers not delegated to the United States by the Constitution, nor prohibited by it to the States, are reserved to the States respectively, or to the people.

Further Amendments

Amendment XI
(ratified 7 Feb 1795)

The Judicial power of the United States shall not be construed to extend to any suit in law or equity, commenced or prosecuted against one of the United States by Citizens of another State, or by Citizens or Subjects of any Foreign State.

Amendment XII
(ratified 15 Jun 1804)

The Electors shall meet in their respective states and vote by ballot for President and Vice-President, one of whom, at least, shall not be an inhabitant of the same state with themselves; they shall name in their ballots the person voted for as President, and in distinct ballots the person voted for as Vice-President, and they shall make distinct lists of all persons voted for as President, and of all persons voted for as Vice-President, and of the number of votes for each, which lists they shall sign and certify, and transmit sealed to the seat of the government of the United States, directed to the President of the Senate; — The President of the Senate shall, in the presence of the Senate and House of Representatives, open all the certificates and the votes shall then be counted; — The person having the greatest number of votes for President, shall be the President, if such number be a majority of the whole number of Electors appointed; and if no person have such majority, then from the persons having the highest numbers not exceeding three on the list of those voted for as President, the House of Representatives shall choose immediately, by ballot, the President. But in choosing the President, the votes shall be taken by states, the representation from each state having one vote; a quorum for this purpose shall consist of a member or members from two-thirds of the states, and a majority of all the states shall be necessary to a choice. And if the House of Representatives shall not choose a President whenever the right of choice shall devolve upon then, before the fourth day of March next following, then the Vice-President shall act as President, as in the case of the death or other constitutional disability of the President. — The person having the greatest number of votes as Vice-President, shall be the Vice-President, if such number be a majority of the whole number of Electors appointed, and if no person have a majority, then from the two highest numbers on the list, the Senate shall choose the Vice-President; a quorum for the purpose shall consist of two-thirds of the whole number of Senators, and a majority of the whole number shall be necessary to a choice. But no person constitutionally ineligible to the office of President shall be eligible to that of Vice-President of the United States.

Amendment XIII
(ratified 6 Dec 1865)

Section 1—
Neither slavery nor involuntary servitude, except as a punishment for crime whereof the party shall have been duly convicted, shall exist within the United States, or any place subject to their jurisdiction.

Section 2—
Congress shall have power to enforce this article by appropriate legislation.

Amendment XIV
(ratified 9 Jul 1868)

Section 1—
All persons born or naturalized in the United States, and subject to the jurisdiction thereof, are citizens of the United States and of the State wherein they reside. No State shall make or enforce any law which shall abridge the privileges or immunities of citizens of the United States; nor shall any State deprive any person of life, liberty, or property, without due process of law; nor deny to any person within its jurisdiction the equal protection of the laws.

Section 2—

Representatives shall be apportioned among the several States according to their respective numbers, counting the whole number of persons in each State, excluding Indians not taxed. But when the right to vote at any election for the choice of electors for President and Vice President of the United States, Representatives in Congress, the Executive and Judicial officers of a State, or the members of the Legislature thereof, is denied to any of the male inhabitants of such State, being twenty-one years of age, and citizens of the United States, or in any way abridged, except for participation in rebellion, or other crime, the basis of representation therein shall be reduced in the proportion which the number of such male citizens shall bear to the whole number of male citizens twenty-one years of age in such State.

Section 3—

No person shall be a Senator or Representative in Congress, or elector of President and Vice President, or hold any office, civil or military, under the United States, or under any State, who, having previously taken an oath, as a member of Congress, or as an officer of the United States, or as a member of any State legislature, or as an executive or judicial officer of any State, to support the Constitution of the United States, shall have engaged in insurrection or rebellion against the same, or given aid or comfort to the enemies thereof. But Congress may by a vote of two-thirds of each House, remove such disability.

Section 4—

The validity of the public debt of the United States, authorized by law, including debts incurred for payment of pensions and bounties for services in suppressing insurrection or rebellion, shall not be questioned. But neither the United States nor any State shall assume or pay any debt or obligation incurred in aid of insurrection or rebellion against the United States, or any claim for the loss or emancipation of any slave; but all such debts, obligations and claims shall be held illegal and void.

Section 5—

The Congress shall have power to enforce, by appropriate legislation, the provisions of this article.

Amendment XV
(ratified 8 Feb 1870)

Section 1—

The right of citizens of the United States to vote shall not be denied or abridged by the United States or by any State on account of race, color, or previous condition of servitude.

Section 2—

The Congress shall have power to enforce this article by appropriate legislation.

Amendment XVI
(ratified 3 Feb 1913)

The Congress shall have power to lay and collect taxes on incomes, from whatever source derived, without apportionment among the several States, and without regard to any census or enumeration.

Amendment XVII
(ratified 13 Feb 1913)

The Senate of the United States shall be composed of two Senators from each State, elected by the people thereof for six years; and each Senator shall have one vote. The electors in each State shall have the qualifications requisite for electors of the most numerous branch of the State legislatures.

When vacancies happen in the representation of any State in the Senate, the executive authority of such State shall issue writs of election to fill such vacancies: Provided, That the legislature of any State may empower the executive thereof to make temporary appointments until the people fill the vacancies by election as the legislature may direct.

This amendment shall not be so construed as to affect the election or term of any Senator chosen before it becomes valid as part of the Constitution.

Amendment XVIII
(ratified 16 Jan 1919; repealed 5 Dec 1933 by Amendment XXI)

Section 1—

After one year from the ratification of this article the manufacture, sale, or transportation of intoxicating liquors within, the importation thereof into, or the exportation thereof from the United States and all territory subject to the jurisdiction thereof for beverage purposes is hereby prohibited.

Section 2—

The Congress and the several States shall have concurrent power to enforce this article by appropriate legislation.

Section 3—

This article shall be inoperative unless it shall have been ratified as an amendment to the Constitution by the legislatures of the several States as provided in the Constitution, within seven years from the date of the submission hereof to the States by the Congress.

Amendment XIX
(ratified 18 Aug 1920)

The right of citizens of the United States to vote shall not be denied or abridged by the United States or by any State on account of sex.

Congress shall have power to enforce this article by appropriate legislation.

Amendment XX
(ratified 23 Jan 1933)

Section 1—

The terms of the President and Vice President shall end at noon on the 20th day of January, and the terms of Senators and Representatives at noon on the 3d day of January, of the years in which such terms would have ended if this article had not been ratified; and the terms of their successors shall then begin.

Section 2—

The Congress shall assemble at least once in every year, and such meeting shall begin at noon on the 3d day of January, unless they shall by law appoint a different day.

Section 3—

If, at the time fixed for the beginning of the term of the President, the President elect shall have died, the Vice President elect shall become President. If a President shall not have been chosen before the time fixed for the beginning of his term, or if the President elect shall have failed to qualify, then the Vice President elect shall act as President until a President shall have qualified; and the Congress may by law provide for the case wherein neither a President elect nor a Vice President elect shall have qualified, declaring who shall then act as President, or the manner in which one who is to act shall be selected, and such person shall act accordingly until a President or Vice President shall have qualified.

Section 4—
The Congress may by law provide for the case of the death of any of the persons from whom the House of Representatives may choose a President whenever the right of choice shall have devolved upon them, and for the case of the death of any of the persons from whom the Senate may choose a Vice President whenever the right of choice shall have devolved upon them.

Section 5—
Sections 1 and 2 shall take effect on the 15th day of October following the ratification of this article.

Section 6—
This article shall be inoperative unless it shall have been ratified as an amendment to the Constitution by the legislatures of three-fourths of the several States within seven years from the date of its submission.

Amendment XXI
(ratified 5 Dec 1933)

Section 1—
The eighteenth article of amendment to the Constitution of the United States is hereby repealed.

Section 2—
The transportation or importation into any State, Territory, or possession of the United States for delivery or use therein of intoxicating liquors, in violation of the laws thereof, is hereby prohibited.

Section 3—
This article shall be inoperative unless it shall have been ratified as an amendment to the Constitution by conventions in the several States, as provided in the Constitution, within seven years from the date of the submission hereof to the States by the Congress.

Amendment XXII
(ratified 27 Feb 1951)

Section 1—
No person shall be elected to the office of the President more than twice, and no person who has held the office of President, or acted as President, for more than two years of a term to which some other person was elected President shall be elected to the office of the President more than once. But this Article shall not apply to any person holding the office of President when this Article was proposed by the Congress, and shall not prevent any person who may be holding the office of President, or acting as President, during the term within which this Article becomes operative from holding the office of President or acting as President during the remainder of such term.

Section 2—
This Article shall be inoperative unless it shall have been ratified as an amendment to the Constitution by the legislatures of three-fourths of the several States within seven years from the date of its submission to the States by the Congress.

Amendment XXIII
(ratified 29 Mar 1961)

Section 1—
The District constituting the seat of Government of the United States shall appoint in such manner as the Congress may direct:
A number of electors of President and Vice President equal to the whole number of Senators and Representatives in Congress to which the District would be entitled if it were a State, but in no event more than the least populous State; they shall be in addition to those appointed by the States, but they shall be considered, for the purposes of the election of President and Vice President, to be electors appointed by a State; and they shall meet in the District and perform such duties as provided by the twelfth article of amendment.

Section 2—
The Congress shall have power to enforce this article by appropriate legislation.

Amendment XXIV
(ratified 23 Jan 1964)

Section 1—
The right of citizens of the United States to vote in any primary or other election for President or Vice President, for electors for President or Vice President, or for Senator or Representative in Congress, shall not be denied or abridged by the United States or any State by reason of failure to pay any poll tax or other tax.

Section 2—
The Congress shall have power to enforce this article by appropriate legislation.

Amendment XXV
(ratified 23 Jan 1967)

Section 1—
In case of the removal of the President from office or of his death or resignation, the Vice President shall become President.

Section 2—
Whenever there is a vacancy in the office of the Vice President, the President shall nominate a Vice President who shall take office upon confirmation by a majority vote of both Houses of Congress.

Section 3—
Whenever the President transmits to the President pro tempore of the Senate and the Speaker of the House of Representatives his written declaration that he is unable to discharge the powers and duties of his office, and until he transmits to them a written declaration to the contrary, such powers and duties shall be discharged by the Vice President as Acting President.

Section 4—
Whenever the Vice president and a majority of either the principal officers of the executive departments or of such other body as Congress may by law provide, transmit to the President pro tempore of the Senate and the Speaker of the House of Representatives their written declaration that the President is unable to discharge the powers and duties of his office, the Vice President shall immediately assume the powers and duties of the office as Acting President.

Thereafter, when the President transmits to the President pro tempore of the Senate and the Speaker of the House of Representatives his written declaration that no inability exists, he shall resume the powers and duties of his office unless the Vice President and a majority of either the principal officers of the executive department or of such other body as Congress may by law provide, transmit within four days to the President pro tempore of the Senate and the Speaker of the House of Representatives their written declaration that the President is unable to discharge the powers and duties of his office. Thereupon Congress shall decide the issue, assembling within forty-eight hours for that purpose if not in session. If the Congress, within twenty-one days after receipt of the latter written declaration, or, if Congress is not in session, within twenty-one days after Congress is required to assemble, determines by two-thirds vote of both Houses that the President is unable to discharge the powers and duties of his office, the Vice President shall continue to discharge the same as Acting President; otherwise, the President shall resume the powers and duties of his office.

Amendment XXVI
(ratified 1 Jul 1971)

Section 1—
The right of citizens of the United States, who are eighteen years of age or older, to vote shall not be denied or abridged by the United States or by any State on account of age.

Section 2—
The Congress shall have power to enforce this article by appropriate legislation.

Amendment XXVII
(ratified 7 May 1992)

No law, varying the compensation for the services of the Senators and Representatives, shall take effect, until an election of representatives shall have intervened.

Confederate States and Secession Dates

In the months following Abraham Lincoln's election as president in 1860, seven states of the Deep South held conventions and approved secession, thus precipitating the Civil War. After the attack on Fort Sumter SC on 12 Apr 1861, Virginia, Arkansas, North Carolina, and Tennessee also seceded (Tennessee was the only state to hold a popular referendum without a convention on secession). The Confederacy operated as a separate government, with Jefferson Davis as president and Alexander H. Stephens as vice president. Its principal goals were the preservation of states' rights and the institution of slavery. Although it enjoyed a series of military victories in the first two years of fighting, the surrender at Appomattox VA by Gen. Robert E. Lee on 9 Apr 1865 signaled its dissolution.

STATE	DATE	STATE	DATE	STATE	DATE
South Carolina	20 Dec 1860	Georgia	19 Jan 1861	Arkansas	6 May 1861
Mississippi	9 Jan 1861	Louisiana	26 Jan 1861	North Carolina	20 May 1861
Florida	10 Jan 1861	Texas	1 Feb 1861	Tennessee	8 Jun 1861
Alabama	11 Jan 1861	Virginia	17 Apr 1861		

Emancipation Proclamation

The Emancipation Proclamation was issued by Pres. Abraham Lincoln and freed the slaves of the Confederate states in rebellion against the Union. After the Battle of Antietam (17 Sep 1862), Lincoln issued his proclamation calling on the revolted states to return to their allegiance before the next year, otherwise their slaves would be declared free men. No state returned, and the threatened declaration was issued on 1 Jan 1863.

By the President of the United States of America:

A Proclamation.

Whereas, on the twenty-second day of September, in the year of our Lord one thousand eight hundred and sixty-two, a proclamation was issued by the President of the United States, containing, among other things, the following, to wit:

"That on the first day of January, in the year of our Lord one thousand eight hundred and sixty-three, all persons held as slaves within any State or designated part of a State, the people whereof shall then be in rebellion against the United States, shall be then, thenceforward, and forever free; and the Executive Government of the United States, including the military and naval authority thereof, will recognize and maintain the freedom of such persons, and will do no act or acts to repress such persons, or any of them, in any efforts they may make for their actual freedom.

"That the Executive will, on the first day of January aforesaid, by proclamation, designate the States and parts of States, if any, in which the people thereof, respectively, shall then be in rebellion against the United States; and the fact that any State, or the people thereof, shall on that day be, in good faith, represented in the Congress of the United States by members chosen thereto at elections wherein a majority of the qualified voters of such State shall have participated, shall, in the absence of strong countervailing testimony, be deemed conclusive evidence that such State, and the people thereof, are not then in rebellion against the United States."

Now, therefore I, Abraham Lincoln, President of the United States, by virtue of the power in me vested as Commander-in-Chief, of the Army and Navy of the

United States in time of actual armed rebellion against the authority and government of the United States, and as a fit and necessary war measure for suppressing said rebellion, do, on this first day of January, in the year of our Lord one thousand eight hundred and sixty-three, and in accordance with my purpose so to do publicly proclaimed for the full period of one hundred days, from the day first above mentioned, order and designate as the States and parts of States wherein the people thereof respectively, are this day in rebellion against the United States, the following, to wit:

Arkansas, Texas, Louisiana, (except the Parishes of St. Bernard, Plaquemines, Jefferson, St. John, St. Charles, St. James Ascension, Assumption, Terrebonne, Lafourche, St. Mary, St. Martin, and Orleans, including the City of New Orleans) Mississippi, Alabama, Florida, Georgia, South Carolina, North Carolina, and Virginia, (except the forty-eight counties designated as West Virginia, and also the counties of Berkley, Accomac, Northampton, Elizabeth City, York, Princess Ann, and Norfolk, including the cities of Norfolk and Portsmouth[]), and which excepted parts, are for the present, left precisely as if this proclamation were not issued.

And by virtue of the power, and for the purpose aforesaid, I do order and declare that all persons held as slaves within said designated States, and parts of States, are, and henceforward shall be free; and that the Executive government of the United States, including the military and naval authorities thereof, will recognize and maintain the freedom of said persons.

And I hereby enjoin upon the people so declared to be free to abstain from all violence, unless in necessary self-defence; and I recommend to them that, in all cases when allowed, they labor faithfully for reasonable wages.

And I further declare and make known, that such persons of suitable condition, will be received into the armed service of the United States to garrison forts, positions, stations, and other places, and to man vessels of all sorts in said service.

And upon this act, sincerely believed to be an act of justice, warranted by the Constitution, upon military necessity, I invoke the considerate judgment of mankind, and the gracious favor of Almighty God.

In witness whereof, I have hereunto set my hand and caused the seal of the United States to be affixed.

Done at the City of Washington, this first day of January, in the year of our Lord one thousand eight hundred and sixty three, and of the Independence of the United States of America the eighty-seventh.

By the President: Abraham Lincoln.
William H. Seward, Secretary of State.

Gettysburg Address

On 19 Nov 1863, Pres. Abraham Lincoln delivered this speech at the consecration of the National Cemetery at Gettysburg PA, the site of one of the most decisive battles of the American Civil War.

Four score and seven years ago our fathers brought forth on this continent a new nation, conceived in Liberty, and dedicated to the proposition that all men are created equal. Now we are engaged in a great civil war, testing whether that nation or any nation so conceived and so dedicated, can long endure. We are met on a great battle-field of that war. We have come to dedicate a portion of that field, as a final resting place for those who here gave their lives that that nation might live. It is altogether fitting and proper that we should do this. But, in a larger sense, we can not dedicate—we can not consecrate—we can not hallow—this ground. The brave men, living and dead, who struggled here, have consecrated it, far above our poor power to add or detract. The world will little note, nor long remember what we say here, but it can never forget what they did here. It is for us the living, rather, to be dedicated here to the unfinished work which they who fought here have thus far so nobly advanced. It is rather for us to be here dedicated to the great task remaining before us—that from these honored dead we take increased devotion to that cause for which they gave the last full measure of devotion—that we here highly resolve that these dead shall not have died in vain—that this nation, under God, shall have a new birth of freedom—and that government of the people, by the people, for the people, shall not perish from the earth.

United States Government

The Presidency at a Glance

	PRESIDENT	POLITICAL PARTY	TIME IN OFFICE	VICE PRESIDENT
1	George Washington	Federalist	1789–1797	John Adams
2	John Adams	Federalist	1797–1801	Thomas Jefferson
3	Thomas Jefferson	Jeffersonian Republican	1801–1809	Aaron Burr George Clinton
4	James Madison	Jeffersonian Republican	1809–1817	George Clinton Elbridge Gerry
5	James Monroe	Jeffersonian Republican	1817–1825	Daniel D. Tompkins
6	John Quincy Adams	National Republican	1825–1829	John C. Calhoun

The Presidency at a Glance (continued)

7	Andrew Jackson	Democratic	1829–1837	John C. Calhoun Martin Van Buren
8	Martin Van Buren	Democratic	1837–1841	Richard M. Johnson
9	William Henry Harrison*	Whig	4 Mar–4 Apr 1841	John Tyler
10	John Tyler	Whig	1841–1845	none
11	James K. Polk	Democratic	1845–1849	George Mifflin Dallas
12	Zachary Taylor*	Whig	1849–1850	Millard Fillmore
13	Millard Fillmore	Whig	1850–1853	none
14	Franklin Pierce	Democratic	1853–1857	William Rufus de Vane King
15	James Buchanan	Democratic	1857–1861	John C. Breckinridge
16	Abraham Lincoln*†	Republican	1861–1865	Hannibal Hamlin Andrew Johnson
17	Andrew Johnson	Democratic (Union)	1865–1869	none
18	Ulysses S. Grant	Republican	1869–1877	Schuyler Colfax Henry Wilson
19	Rutherford B. Hayes	Republican	1877–1881	William A. Wheeler
20	James A. Garfield*†	Republican	4 Mar–19 Sep 1881	Chester A. Arthur
21	Chester A. Arthur	Republican	1881–1885	none
22	Grover Cleveland	Democratic	1885–1889	Thomas A. Hendricks
23	Benjamin Harrison	Republican	1889–1893	Levi Parons Morton
24	Grover Cleveland	Democratic	1893–1897	Adlai E. Stevenson
25	William McKinley*†	Republican	1897–1901	Garret A. Hobart Theodore Roosevelt
26	Theodore Roosevelt	Republican	1901–1909	Charles Warren Fairbanks
27	William Howard Taft	Republican	1909–1913	James Schoolcraft Sherman
28	Woodrow Wilson	Democratic	1913–1921	Thomas R. Marshall
29	Warren G. Harding*	Republican	1921–1923	Calvin Coolidge
30	Calvin Coolidge	Republican	1923–1929	Charles G. Dawes
31	Herbert Hoover	Republican	1929–1933	Charles Curtis
32	Franklin D. Roosevelt*	Democratic	1933–1945	John Nance Garner Henry A. Wallace Harry S. Truman
33	Harry S. Truman	Democratic	1945–1953	Alben W. Barkley
34	Dwight D. Eisenhower	Republican	1953–1961	Richard M. Nixon
35	John F. Kennedy*†	Democratic	1961–1963	Lyndon B. Johnson
36	Lyndon B. Johnson	Democratic	1963–1969	Hubert H. Humphrey
37	Richard M. Nixon**	Republican	1969–1974	Spiro T. Agnew Gerald R. Ford
38	Gerald R. Ford	Republican	1974–1977	Nelson A. Rockefeller
39	Jimmy Carter	Democratic	1977–1981	Walter F. Mondale
40	Ronald Reagan	Republican	1981–1989	George H.W. Bush
41	George H.W. Bush	Republican	1989–1993	Dan Quayle
42	Bill Clinton	Democratic	1993–2001	Albert Gore
43	George W. Bush	Republican	2001–2009	Richard B. Cheney
44	Barack Obama	Democratic	2009–	Joe Biden

*Died in office.   **Resigned from office.   †Assassinated.

Presidential Biographies

George Washington (22 Feb [11 Feb, Old Style] 1732, Westmoreland county VA–14 Dec 1799, Mount Vernon, in Fairfax county VA), American Revolutionary commander-in-chief (1775–83) and first president of the US (1789–97). Born into a wealthy family, he inherited his brother's estate at Mount Vernon, including 18 slaves whose ranks grew by 49 by 1760. In the French and Indian War he was commissioned a colonel and sent to the Ohio Territory, and later he became commander of all Virginia forces, entrusted with defending the western frontier (1755–58). He resigned to manage his estate and in 1759 married Martha Dandridge Custis (1731–1802), a widow. He served in the House of Burgesses (1759–74), where he supported the colonists' cause, and in the Continental Congress (1774–75). In 1775 he was elected to command the Continental Army. In the ensuing American Revolution, he proved a brilliant commander and stalwart leader despite several defeats. With the war effectively ended by the capture of Yorktown (1781), he resigned his commission and returned to Mount Vernon. He was a delegate to and presiding officer of the Constitutional Convention (1787) and helped secure ratification of the Constitution in Virginia. When the state electors met to select the first president (1789), Washington was the unanimous choice. He formed a cabinet to balance sectional and political differences but was committed to a strong central government.

Elected to a second term, he followed a middle course between the political factions that became the Federalist Party and Democratic Party. He proclaimed a policy of neutrality in the war between Britain and France (1793) and sent troops to suppress the Whiskey Rebellion (1794). He declined to serve a third term, setting a 144-year precedent, and retired in 1797. Known as the "father of his country," he is regarded as one of the greatest figures in US history.

John Adams (30 Oct [19 Oct, Old Style] 1735, Braintree [now in Quincy] MA—4 Jul 1826, Quincy MA), first vice president (1789–97) and second president (1797–1801) of the US. He practiced law in Boston and in 1764 married Abigail Smith. Active in the American independence movement, he was elected to the Massachusetts legislature and served as a delegate to the Continental Congress (1774–78), where he was appointed to a committee with Thomas Jefferson and others to draft the Declaration of Independence. He served as a diplomat in France, The Netherlands, and England (1778–88). In the first US presidential election, he received the second largest number of votes and became vice president under George Washington. Adams's term as president was marked by controversy over his signing the Alien and Sedition Acts in 1798 and by his alliance with the conservative Federalist Party. In 1800 he was defeated for reelection by Thomas Jefferson and retired to live a secluded life in Massachusetts. In 1812 he began an illuminating correspondence with Jefferson. Both men died on 4 Jul 1826, the Declaration's 50th anniversary. Pres. John Quincy Adams was his son.

Thomas Jefferson (13 Apr [2 Apr, Old Style] 1743, Shadwell VA—4 Jul 1826, Monticello VA), third president of the US (1801–9). He was a planter and lawyer from 1767, as well as a slaveholder. While a member of the House of Burgesses (1769–75), he initiated the Committee of Correspondence (1773) with Richard Henry Lee and Patrick Henry. In 1774 he wrote the influential *Summary View of the Rights of British America*, stating that the British Parliament had no authority to legislate for the colonies. A delegate to the Second Continental Congress, he was appointed to the committee to draft the Declaration of Independence and became its primary author. He was elected governor of Virginia (1779–81) but was unable to organize effective opposition when British forces invaded the colony (1780–81). Again a member of the Continental Congress (1783–85), he proposed territorial provisions later incorporated in the Northwest Ordinances. He became minister to France (1785–89), and George Washington made him secretary of state (1790–93). He soon became embroiled in conflict with Alexander Hamilton over their opposing interpretations of the Constitution. This led to the rise of factions and political parties, with Jefferson representing the Democratic-Republicans. He served as vice president (1797–1801) but opposed the Alien and Sedition Acts enacted under Pres. John Adams. In 1801 he became president after an electoral-vote tie with Aaron Burr was settled by the House of Representatives. Jefferson oversaw the Louisiana Purchase and authorized the Lewis and Clark Expedition. He sought to avoid involvement in the Napoleonic Wars by signing the Embargo Act. He retired to his plantation, Monticello, where he pursued his many interests in science, philosophy, and architecture, and in 1819 he

founded and designed the University of Virginia. In January 2000, the Thomas Jefferson Memorial Foundation accepted the conclusion, supported by DNA evidence, that Jefferson had fathered at least one, and perhaps as many as six, children with Sally Hemings, one of his house slaves.

James Madison (16 Mar [5 Mar, Old Style] 1751, Port Conway VA—28 Jun 1836, Montpelier VA), fourth president of the US (1809–17). At the Constitutional Convention (1787), his active participation and his careful notes on the debates earned him the title "father of the Constitution." To promote ratification, he collaborated with Alexander Hamilton and John Jay on the Federalist papers. In the House of Representatives (1789–97), he sponsored the Bill of Rights, was a leading Jeffersonian Republican, and split with Hamilton over funding state war debts. He was appointed secretary of state (1801–09) by Thomas Jefferson, with whom he developed US foreign policy. Elected president in 1808, he was occupied by the trade and shipping embargo problems caused by France and Britain that led to the War of 1812. He was reelected in 1812; his second term was marked principally by the war, during which he reinvigorated the Army. He retired to his Virginia estate, Montpelier, with his wife, Dolley (1768–1849), whose political acumen he had long prized. He served as rector of the University of Virginia until his death (1826–36).

James Monroe (28 Apr 1758, Westmoreland county VA—4 Jul 1831, New York NY), fifth president of the US (1817–25). He fought in the American Revolution and studied law under Thomas Jefferson. He became minister to France (1794–96), where he misled the French about US politics and was recalled. He served as governor of Virginia (1799–1802). President Jefferson sent him to France to help negotiate the Louisiana Purchase (1803), then named him minister to Britain (1803–07). He returned to Virginia and became governor (1811), but he resigned to become US secretary of state (1811–17) and secretary of war (1814–15). He served two terms as president, presiding in a period that became known as the Era of Good Feelings. He oversaw the First Seminole War (1817–18) and the acquisition of the Floridas (1819–21) and signed the Missouri Compromise (1820). With Secretary of State John Quincy Adams, he developed the principles of US foreign policy later called the Monroe Doctrine.

John Quincy Adams (11 Jul 1767, Braintree [now in Quincy] MA—23 Feb 1848, Washington DC), sixth president of the US (1825–29). He was the eldest son of Pres. John Adams and Abigail. He accompanied his father to Europe on diplomatic missions (1778–80) and was later appointed minister to The Netherlands (1794) and Prussia (1797). In 1801 he returned to Massachusetts and served in the Senate (1803–8). Resuming his diplomatic service, he became minister to Russia (1809–11) and Britain (1815–17). Appointed secretary of state (1817–24), he was instrumental in acquiring Florida from Spain and in drafting the Monroe Doctrine. He was one of three candidates in the 1824 presidential election, in which none received a majority of the electoral votes, though Andrew Jackson received a plurality. The decision went to the House of Representatives, where Adams received crucial support from Henry Clay and the electoral votes necessary to elect him president. He appointed Clay secretary of state, which further angered Jackson. Adams's presidency was unsuccessful; when he ran for reelection, Jackson defeated him. In 1830 he was elected to the House of Representatives, where he served until his death. He was outspoken in his opposition to slavery and in 1839 proposed a constitutional amendment forbidding slavery in any new state admitted to the Union. In 1841 he successfully defended the slaves in the *Amistad* mutiny case.

Andrew Jackson (15 Mar 1767, Waxhaws region, South Carolina—8 Jun 1845, the Hermitage, near Nashville TN), seventh president of the US (1829–37). He fought briefly in the American Revolution near his frontier home, where his family was killed. He studied law and in 1788 was appointed prosecuting attorney for western North Carolina. When the region became the state of Tennessee, he was elected to the House of Representatives (1796–97) and Senate (1797–98). He served on the state supreme court (1798–1804) and in 1802 was elected major general of the Tennessee militia. When the War of 1812 began, he offered the US the services of his 50,000-volunteer militia. He was sent to fight the Creek Indians in Mississippi Territory. After a lengthy battle (1813–14), he defeated them at the Battle of Horseshoe Bend. After capturing Pensacola FL from the British-allied Spanish, he marched overland to engage the British in Louisiana. A decisive victory at the Battle of New Orleans made him a national hero, dubbed "Old Hickory" by the press. After US acquisition of Florida, he was named governor of the territory (1821). In 1828 Jackson defeated Adams after a fierce campaign and became the first president elected from west of the Appalachian Mountains. He replaced many federal officeholders with his supporters, a process that became known as the spoils system. He pursued a policy of moving Native Americans westward with the Indian Removal Acts. During his tenure a strong Democratic Party developed that led to a vigorous two-party system.

Martin Van Buren (5 Dec 1782, Kinderhook NY—24 Jul 1862, Kinderhook NY), eighth president of the US (1837–41). He practiced law in the NY state senate (1812–20) and as state attorney general (1816–19). He was elected to the US Senate (1821–28), where he supported states' rights and opposed a strong central government. After John Quincy Adams became president, Van Buren joined with Andrew Jackson and others to form a group that later became the Democratic Party. He was elected governor of New York (1828) but resigned to become US secretary of state (1829–31). He was nominated for vice president at the first Democratic Party convention (1832) and served under Jackson (1833–37). As Jackson's chosen successor, he defeated William H. Harrison to win the 1836 election. His presidency was marked by an economic depression, the Maine-Canada border dispute, the Second Seminole War in Florida, and debate over the annexation of Texas. He was defeated in his bid for reelection and failed to win the Democratic nomination in 1844 because of his antislavery views. In 1848 he was nominated for president by the Free Soil Party but failed to win the election and retired.

William Henry Harrison (9 Feb 1773, Charles City county VA—4 Apr 1841, Washington DC), ninth president of the US (1841). Born into a political family, he enlisted in the army at 18 and served under Anthony Wayne at the Battle of Fallen Timbers. In 1798 he became secretary of the Northwest Territories and in 1800 governor of the new Indiana Territory. In response to pressure from white settlers, he negotiated treaties with the Native Americans that ceded millions of acres of land to the US. When the chief Tecumseh organized an uprising in 1811, Harrison led a US force to defeat the Indians at the Battle of Tippecanoe, a victory that largely established his reputation in the public mind. In the War of 1812 he was made a brigadier general and defeated the British and their Indian allies at the Battle of the Thames in Ontario. He served in the House of Representatives (1816–19) and Senate (1825–28). As the Whig party candidate in the 1836 presidential election, he lost narrowly. In 1840 he and his running mate, John Tyler, won election with a slogan emphasizing Harrison's frontier triumph: "Tippecanoe and Tyler too!" The 68-year-old Harrison delivered his inaugural speech without a hat or overcoat in a cold drizzle, contracted pneumonia, and died one month later, the first president to die in office.

John Tyler (29 Mar 1790, Charles City county VA—18 Jan 1862, Richmond VA), 10th president of the US (1841–45). He practiced law before serving as governor of Virginia (1825–27). In the House of Representatives (1817–21) and Senate (1827–36), he was a states-rights supporter. Though a slaveholder, he sought to prohibit the slave trade in the District of Columbia, provided Maryland and Virginia concurred. He resigned from the Senate rather than acquiesce to state instructions to change his vote on a censure of Pres. Andrew Jackson. After breaking with the Democratic Party, he was nominated by the Whig Party for vice president under William Henry Harrison. They won the 1840 election, carefully avoiding the issues and stressing party loyalty and the slogan "Tippecanoe and Tyler too!" Harrison died a month after taking office, and Tyler became the first to attain the presidency "by accident." He vetoed a national bank bill supported by the Whigs, and all but one member of the cabinet resigned, leaving him without party support. Nonetheless, he reorganized the navy, settled the second of the Seminole Wars in Florida, and oversaw the annexation of Texas. Committed to states' rights but opposed to secession, he organized the Washington Peace Conference (1861) to resolve sectional differences.

James Knox Polk (2 Nov 1795, Mecklenburg county NC—15 Jun 1849, Nashville TN), 11th president of the US (1845–49). He became a lawyer in Tennessee and a friend and supporter of Andrew Jackson, who helped Polk win election to the House of Representatives (1825–39). He left the House to become governor of Tennessee (1839–41). At the deadlocked 1844 Democratic convention Polk was nominated as the compromise candidate; he is considered the first dark-horse presidential candidate. A proponent of western expansion, he campaigned with the slogan "Fifty-four Forty or Fight," to bring a solution to the Oregon Question. Elected at 49, the youngest president to that time, he successfully concluded the Oregon border dispute with Britain (1846) and secured passage of the Walker Tariff Act (1846), which lowered import duties and helped foreign trade. He led the prosecution of the Mexican-American War, which resulted in large territorial gains but reopened the debate over the extension of slavery. His administration established the US Naval Academy and the Smithsonian Institution, oversaw revision of the treasury system, and proclaimed the validity of the Monroe Doctrine. He died three months after leaving office.

Zachary Taylor (24 Nov 1784, Montebello VA–9 Jul 1850, Washington DC), 12th president of the US (1849–50). Born in Virginia, he grew up on the Kentucky frontier. He fought in the War of 1812, the Black Hawk War (1832), and the Second Seminole War in Florida (1835–42), earning the nickname "Old Rough-and-Ready" for his indifference to hardship. Sent to Texas in anticipation of war with Mexico, he defeated the Mexican invaders at the Battles of Palo Alto and Resaca de la Palma (1846). After the Mexican-American War formally began, he captured Monterrey and granted the Mexican army an eight-week armistice. Displeased, Pres. James Polk moved Taylor's best troops to serve under Winfield Scott in the invasion of Veracruz. Taylor ignored orders to remain in Monterrey and marched south to defeat a large Mexican force at the Battle of Buena Vista (1847). He became a national hero and won the presidency as the Whig candidate (1848). His brief term was marked by a controversy over the new territories that produced the Compromise of 1850. He died, probably of cholera, after only 16 months in office.

Millard Fillmore (7 Jan 1800, Locke Township NY–8 Mar 1874, Buffalo NY), 13th president of the US (1850–53). Born into poverty, he became an indentured apprentice at 15. Initially identified with the Anti-Masonic Party (1828–34), he followed his political mentor, Thurlow Weed, to the Whigs and was soon a leader of the party's northern wing. He served in the House of Representatives (1833–35, 1837–43), where he became a follower of Henry Clay. In 1848 the Whigs nominated Fillmore as vice president, and he was elected with Zachary Taylor. He became president on Taylor's death in 1850. Though he abhorred slavery, he supported the Compromise of 1850 and insisted on federal enforcement of the Fugitive Slave Act. His stand, which alienated the North, led to his defeat by Winfield Scott at the Whigs' nominating convention in 1852 and effectively led to the death of the party. In 1853 he sent Matthew Perry with a US fleet to Japan, forcing its isolationist government to enter into trade and diplomatic relations. He was nominated for president by the third-party Know-Nothing Party in 1856, but he was defeated by Democrat James Buchanan.

Franklin Pierce (23 Nov 1804, Hillsboro NH–8 Oct 1869, Concord NH), 14th president of the US (1853–57). He served in the House of Representatives (1833–37) and Senate (1837–42) and briefly fought in the Mexican-American War. At the deadlocked Democratic convention of 1852, he was nominated as the compromise candidate; though largely unknown nationally, he unexpectedly trounced Winfield Scott in the general election. For the sake of harmony and business prosperity, he was inclined to oppose antislavery agitation so as to placate Southern opinion. He promoted US territorial expansion, resulting in the diplomatic controversy of the Ostend Manifesto, which urged the seizure of Cuba from Spain. He encouraged plans for a transcontinental railroad and approved the Gadsden Purchase. To promote northwestern migration and conciliate sectional demands, he approved the Kansas-Nebraska Act but was unable to settle the resultant problems. Defeated for renomination by James Buchanan in 1856, he retired from politics.

James Buchanan (23 Apr 1791, near Mercersburg PA–1 Jun 1868, near Lancaster PA), 15th president of the US (1857–61). He served in the House of Representatives (1821–31), as minister to Russia (1832–34), and in the Senate (1834–45). He was secretary of state in James Polk's cabinet (1845–49). As minister to Britain (1853–56), he helped draft the Ostend Manifesto. In 1856 he secured the Democratic nomination and election as president, defeating John C. Fremont. He equivocated on the question of Kansas's status as a slaveholding state, and the ensuing split within his party allowed Abraham Lincoln to win the election of 1860. He denounced the secession of South Carolina following the election and sent reinforcements to Fort Sumter, but he failed to respond further to the mounting crisis.

Abraham Lincoln (12 Feb 1809, near Hodgenville KY–15 Apr 1865, Washington DC), 16th president of the US (1861–65). Born in a Kentucky log cabin, he moved to Indiana in 1816 and to Illinois in 1830. He worked as a storekeeper, rail-splitter, postmaster, and surveyor and then enlisted as a volunteer in the Black Hawk War and became a captain. Though largely self-taught, he practiced law in Springfield IL and served in the state legislature (1834–40). He was elected as a Whig to the House of Representatives (1847–49). He later became one of the state's most successful lawyers, noted for his shrewdness and honesty (earning him the nickname "Honest Abe"). In 1856 he joined the Republican Party, which nominated him as its candidate in the 1858 Senate election. In a series of seven debates with Stephen A. Douglas (the Lincoln-Douglas Debates), he argued against the extension of slavery into the territories, though not against slavery itself. Although morally opposed to slavery, he was not an abolitionist. During the campaign, he attempted to rebut Douglas's charge that he was a dangerous radical by reassuring audiences that he did not favor political equality for blacks. Despite his loss in the election, the debates brought him national attention. He again ran against Douglas in the 1860 presidential election, which he won by a large margin. But the South opposed his position on slavery in the territories, and before his inauguration seven Southern states had seceeded from the Union. The ensuing American Civil War completely consumed Lincoln's administration. He excelled as a wartime leader, combining statecraft and overall command of the armies with what some have called military genius. However, his abrogation of some civil liberties, especially the writ of habeas corpus, and the closing of several newspapers by his generals disturbed both Democrats and Republicans. To unite the North and influence foreign opinion, he issued the Emancipation Proclamation (1863); his Gettysburg Address (1863) further ennobled the war's purpose. His platform for reelection in 1864 included passage of the 13th Amendment outlawing slavery (ratified 1865), and he easily defeated George B. McClellan. At his second inaugural, with victory in sight, he spoke of moderation in reconstructing the South and building a harmonious Union. On 14 April, five days after the war ended, he was shot by John Wilkes Booth and soon after died.

Andrew Johnson (29 Dec 1808, Raleigh NC–31 Jul 1875, near Carter Station TN), 17th president of the US (1865–69). Born in North Carolina and reared in Tennessee, he organized a working-man's party and was elected to the state legislature (1835–43). He served in the House of Representatives (1843–53) and as governor of Tennessee (1853–57). Elected to the Senate (1857–62), he opposed antislavery agitation, but in 1860 he opposed Southern secession, even after Tennessee seceded in 1861, and during the Civil War he was the only Southern senator who refused to join the Confederacy. In 1862 he was appointed military governor of Tennessee, then under Union control. In 1864 he ran for vice president with Pres. Abraham Lincoln; he assumed the presidency after Lincoln's assassination. During Reconstruction he favored a moderate policy that readmitted former Confederate states to the Union with few provisions for reform or civil rights for freedmen. In 1867 the Radical Republicans in Congress passed civil rights legislation and established the Freedmen's Bureau. His veto angered Congress, which passed the Tenure of Office Act requiring congressional approval for the removal of any civil officers. In 1868, in defiance of the act, Johnson dismissed secretary of war Edwin M. Stanton, an ally of the Radicals, and the House responded by impeaching the president for the first time in US history. In the subsequent Senate trial, the charges proved weak and the necessary two-thirds vote needed for conviction failed by one vote. Johnson remained in office until 1869, but his effectiveness had ended. He returned to Tennessee, where he won reelection to the Senate shortly before he died.

Ulysses S. Grant (Hiram Ulysses Grant; 27 Apr 1822, Point Pleasant OH–23 Jul 1885, Mount McGregor NY), 18th president of the US (1869–77). He served in the Mexican-American War under Zachary Taylor. Allegations that he became a drunkard after the war, though never proved, would affect his reputation. When the Civil War began (1861), he was appointed brigadier general; his 1862 attack on Ft. Donelson in Tennessee produced the first major Union victory. He drove off a Confederate attack at Shiloh but was criticized for heavy Union losses. He devised the campaign to take the stronghold of Vicksburg MS in 1863, cutting the Confederacy in half from east to west. Following his victory at the Battle of Chattanooga in 1864, he was appointed commander of the Union army. While William T. Sherman made his famous march across Georgia, Grant attacked Robert E. Lee's forces in Virginia, bringing the war to an end in 1865. His successful Republican presidential campaign made him, at 46, the youngest man yet elected president. His two terms were marred by administrative inaction and political scandal involving members of his cabinet, including the Crédit Mobilier scandal and the Whiskey Ring operation. He supported amnesty for Confederate leaders and protection for black civil rights. His veto of a bill to increase the amount of legal tender (1874) diminished the currency crisis in the next 25 years. His memoirs were published by his friend Mark Twain.

Rutherford Birchard Hayes (4 Oct 1822, Delaware OH–17 Jan 1893, Fremont OH), 19th president of the US (1877–81). After fighting in the Union army, he served in the House of Representatives (1865–67). As governor of Ohio (1868–72, 1875–76), he advocated a sound currency backed by gold. In 1876 he won the Republican nomination for president. His opponent, Samuel Tilden, won a larger popular vote, but Hayes's managers contested the electoral-vote returns in four states, and a special

Electoral Commission awarded the election to Hayes. As part of a secret compromise reached with Southerners, he withdrew the remaining federal troops from the South, ending Reconstruction, and promised not to interfere with elections there, ensuring the return of white Democratic supremacy. At the request of state governors, he used federal troops against strikers in the railroad strikes of 1877. He declined to run for a second term.

James Abram Garfield (19 Nov 1831, near Orange [in Cuyahoga county] OH–19 Sep 1881, Elberon [now in Long Branch] NJ), 20th president of the US (1881). In the Civil War he led the 42nd Ohio Volunteers and fought at Shiloh and Chickamauga. He resigned as a major general to serve in the House of Representatives (1863–80). A Radical Republican during Reconstruction, he was the House Republican leader from 1876 to 1880, when he was elected to the Senate. At the 1880 Republican nominating convention, the delegates supporting Ulysses S. Grant and James Blaine became deadlocked. On the 36th ballot, Garfield was nominated as a compromise presidential candidate, with Chester Arthur as vice president, and he won by a narrow margin. His term was brief—less than 150 days. On 2 July he was shot at Washington's railroad station by Charles J. Guiteau, an Arthur supporter. He died on 19 September after 11 weeks of public debate over the ambiguous constitutional conditions for presidential succession (later clarified by the 20th and 25th Amendments).

Chester Alan Arthur (5 Oct 1829, North Fairfield VT–18 Nov 1886, New York NY), 21st president of the US (1881–85). Active in New York City Republican politics, he was appointed customs collector for the port of New York (1871–78), an office long known for its employment of the spoils system. He conducted the business of the office with integrity but continued to pad its payroll with loyalists of Sen. Roscoe Conkling. At the Republican National Convention in 1880, Arthur was the compromise choice for vice president on the ticket with James Garfield, and he became president upon Garfield's assassination. As president, Arthur displayed unexpected independence by vetoing measures that rewarded political patronage and signing the Pendleton Act, which created a civil-service system based on merit. He also recommended the appropriations for rebuilding the navy toward the strength it later achieved in the Spanish-American War (1898), but he failed to win his party's nomination for a second term.

(Stephen) Grover Cleveland (18 Mar 1837, Caldwell NJ–24 Jun 1908, Princeton NJ), 22nd and 24th president of the US (1885–89, 1893–97). As mayor of Buffalo NY (1881–82), he was known as a foe of corruption. As governor of New York (1883–85), he earned the hostility of Tammany Hall with his independence, but in 1884 he won the Democratic nomination for president and the election. The first Democratic president since 1856, he supported civil-service reform and opposed high protective tariffs, which became an issue in the 1888 election, when he was narrowly defeated by Benjamin Harrison. In 1892 he was reelected by a huge popular plurality. In 1893 he attributed the US's severe economic depression to the Sherman Silver Purchase Act of 1890 and strongly urged Congress to repeal the act. By 1896, however, supporters of the Free Silver Movement controlled the

Democratic Party, which nominated William Jennings Bryan instead of Cleveland for president.

Benjamin Harrison (20 Aug 1833, North Bend OH– 13 Mar 1901, Indianapolis IN), 23rd president of the US (1889–93). The grandson of Pres. William H. Harrison, he served in the Union army in the Civil War, rising to brigadier general. He served a term in the Senate (1881–87) and, even though he lost reelection, was nominated for president by the Republicans. He went on to defeat the incumbent, Grover Cleveland, who lost despite winning more of the popular vote. As president, his domestic policy was marked by passage of the Sherman Antitrust Act, and his foreign policy expanded US influence abroad. His administration oversaw the conference that led to the establishment of the Pan-American Union, resisted pressure to abandon US interests in the Samoa Islands (1889), and negotiated a treaty with Britain in the Bering Sea Dispute (1891). He was defeated for reelection by Cleveland in 1892. In 1898–99 he was the leading counsel for Venezuela in its boundary dispute with Britain.

William McKinley (29 Jan 1843, Niles OH–14 Sep 1901, Buffalo NY), 25th president of the US (1897–1901). He served in the Civil War as an aide to Col. Rutherford B. Hayes, who later encouraged his political career. He was elected to the House of Representatives (1877–91), where he sponsored the McKinley Tariff of 1890, and he served as elected governor of Ohio (1892–96). In 1896 he won the Republican presidential nomination and the general election, defeating William Jennings Bryan. He was soon embroiled in events in Cuba and responses to the sinking of the USS *Maine*, which led to the Spanish-American War. At the war's end, he advocated US dependency status for the Philippines, Puerto Rico, and other former Spanish territories. He again defeated Bryan by a large majority in 1900. In Buffalo NY on 6 Sep 1901, he was fatally shot by an anarchist, Leon Czolgosz.

Theodore Roosevelt (27 Oct 1858, New York NY–6 Jan 1919, Oyster Bay NY), 26th president of the US (1901–09). He was elected to the New York legislature in 1882, where he became a Republican leader opposed to the Democratic political machine, and he went on to serve on the US Civil Service Commission (1889–95) and as head of New York City's board of police commissioners (1895–97). A supporter of William McKinley, he served as assistant secretary of the navy (1897–98). When the Spanish-American War was declared, he resigned to organize a cavalry unit, the Rough Riders. He returned to New York a hero and was elected governor in 1899. As the Republican vice-presidential nominee, he took office when McKinley was reelected, and he became president on McKinley's assassination in 1901. One of his early initiatives was to urge enforcement of the Sherman Antitrust Act against business monopolies. He won election in his own right in 1904, and at his urging, Congress regulated railroad rates and passed the Pure Food and Drug Act and Meat Inspection Act (both 1906) to provide new consumer protections. He set aside national forests, parks, and mineral, oil, and coal lands for conservation. For mediating an end to the Russo-Japanese War, he received the 1906 Nobel Peace Prize. He secured a treaty with Panama for construction of a trans-isthmus canal. Declining to seek reelection, he secured the nomination for William H. Taft. He tried to win the Republican presidential nomination

in 1912; when he was rejected, he organized the Bull Moose Party and ran on a policy of New Nationalism, but he failed to win the election.

William Howard Taft (15 Sep 1857, Cincinnati OH–8 Mar 1930, Washington DC), 27th president of the US (1909–13). He served as US solicitor general (1890–92) and as US appellate judge (1892–1900). He was appointed head of the Philippine Commission to set up a civilian government in the islands and was its first civilian governor (1901–04). He served as US secretary of war (1904–08) under Pres. Theodore Roosevelt, who supported Taft's nomination for president in 1908. He won the election but became allied with the conservative Republicans, causing a rift with party progressives. He was again the nominee in 1912, but the split with Roosevelt and the Bull Moose Party resulted in the electoral victory of Woodrow Wilson. Taft later was a supporter of the League of Nations. As chief justice of the Supreme Court (1921–30), he secured passage of the Judges Act of 1925, which gave the Court wider discretion in accepting cases.

(Thomas) Woodrow Wilson (28 Dec 1856, Staunton VA–3 Feb 1924, Washington DC), 28th president of the US (1913–21). He taught political science at Princeton University (1890–1902) and was its president (1902–10). With the support of progressives, he was elected governor of New Jersey. His reform measures attracted national attention, and he became the Democratic presidential nominee in 1912. His campaign emphasized the progressive measures of his New Freedom policy, and he defeated Theodore Roosevelt and William H. Taft to win the presidency. As president, he approved legislation that created the Federal Reserve System, established the Federal Trade Commission, and strengthened labor unions. In foreign affairs he promoted self-government for the Philippines and sought to contain the Mexican civil war. He maintained US neutrality in World War I, offering to mediate a settlement and initiate peace negotiations. Campaigning on the theme that he had "kept us out of war," he was narrowly reelected in 1916, defeating Charles Evans Hughes. Germany's continued submarine attacks on unarmed passenger ships caused Wilson to ask for a declaration of war in April 1917. In a continuing effort to negotiate a peace agreement, he led the US delegation to the Paris Peace Conference, where he attempted to stand on his original principles but was forced to compromise by the demands of various countries. The Treaty of Versailles faced opposition in the Senate from the Republican majority. In search of popular support for the treaty and its League of Nations, Wilson began a cross-country speaking tour, but he collapsed and returned to Washington DC, where a stroke left him partially paralyzed. He rejected any attempts to compromise his version of the League of Nations and as a result eventually urged his Senate followers to vote against ratification of the treaty, which was defeated in 1920. He was awarded the 1919 Nobel Peace Prize for his work on the League of Nations.

Warren Gamaliel Harding (2 Nov 1865, Caledonia [now Blooming Grove] OH–2 Aug 1923, San Francisco CA), 29th president of the US (1921–23). He served successively as Ohio state senator (1899–1902), lieutenant governor (1903–04), and US senator (1915–21), supporting conservative policies. At the deadlocked 1920 Republican presidential convention, he was chosen as the compromise candidate. Pledging a "return to normalcy" after World War I, he defeated James Cox with over 60% of the popular vote, the largest margin to that time. On his recommendation Congress established a budget system for the federal government, passed a high protective tariff, revised wartime taxes, and restricted immigration. His ill-advised cabinet and patronage appointments led to the Teapot Dome Scandal and characterized his administration as corrupt. While in Alaska he received word of the corruption about to be exposed and headed back. He arrived in San Francisco exhausted, reportedly suffering from food poisoning and other ills, and died there under unclear circumstances, to be succeeded by his vice president, Calvin Coolidge.

(John) Calvin Coolidge (4 Jul 1872, Plymouth VT—5 Jan 1933, Northampton MA), 30th president of the US (1923–29). He served as lieutenant governor of Massachusetts before being elected governor in 1918. He gained national attention by calling out the state guard during the Boston police strike in 1919. At the 1920 Republican convention, "Silent Cal" was nominated for vice president on Warren G. Harding's winning ticket. When Harding died in office in 1923, Coolidge became president. He restored confidence in an administration discredited by scandals and won the presidential election in 1924, defeating Robert La Follette. His presidency was marked by apparent prosperity. Congress maintained a high protective tariff and instituted tax reductions that favored capital. Coolidge declined to run for a second full term. His conservative policies of domestic and international inaction have come to symbolize the era between World War I and the Great Depression.

Herbert Hoover (10 Aug 1874, West Branch IA—20 Oct 1964, New York NY), 31st president of the US (1929–33). He headed Allied relief operations in England and Belgium prior to World War I, at which time he was appointed national food administrator (1917–19) and instituted programs that furnished food to famine-stricken areas of Europe. Appointed secretary of commerce (1921–27), he oversaw commissions to build Boulder (later Hoover) Dam and the St. Lawrence Seaway. In 1928, as the Republican presidential candidate, he soundly defeated Alfred E. Smith. His hopes for a "New Day" program were quickly overwhelmed by the Great Depression. As a believer in individual freedom, he vetoed bills to create a federal unemployment agency and to fund public-works projects, instead favoring private charity. In 1932 he finally allowed relief to farmers through the Reconstruction Finance Corp., but he was overwhelmingly defeated in 1932 by Franklin Roosevelt.

Franklin Delano Roosevelt (30 Jan 1882, Hyde Park NY—12 Apr 1945, Warm Springs GA), 32nd president of the US (1933–45). He was attracted to politics as an admirer of his cousin Pres. Theodore Roosevelt and became active in the Democratic Party. In 1905 he married distant cousin Eleanor Roosevelt, who would become a valued adviser in future years. He served as assistant secretary of the navy (1913–20). In 1920 he was nominated for vice president. The next year he was stricken with polio; though unable to walk, he remained active in politics. As governor of New York (1929–33), he set up the first state relief agency in the US. In 1932 he won the Democratic presidential nomination and

easily defeated Pres. Herbert Hoover. In his inaugural address to a nation of more than 13 million unemployed, he pronounced that "the only thing we have to fear is fear itself." Congress passed most of the changes he sought in his New Deal program in the first hundred days of his term. He was overwhelmingly reelected in 1936 over Alf Landon. By the late 1930s economic recovery had slowed, but Roosevelt was more concerned with the growing threat of war. In 1940 he was reelected to an unprecedented third term, defeating Wendell Willkie. He maintained US neutrality toward the war in Europe but approved the principle of lend-lease and in 1941 met with Winston Churchill to draft the Atlantic Charter. With US entry into World War II, he mobilized industry for military production and formed an alliance with Britain and the Soviet Union; he met with Churchill and Joseph Stalin to form war policy at Tehran (1943) and Yalta (1945). Despite declining health, he won reelection for a fourth term against Thomas Dewey (1944) but served only briefly before his death.

Harry S. Truman (8 May 1884, Lamar MO—26 Dec 1972, Kansas City MO), 33rd president of the US (1945–53). He served with distinction in World War I, and he later entered Democratic Party politics in Missouri. His reputation for honesty and good management gained him bipartisan support. In the Senate (1935–45), he led a committee that exposed fraud in defense production. In 1944 he was chosen to replace the incumbent Henry Wallace as vice-presidential nominee and was elected with Pres. Franklin Roosevelt. After only 82 days as vice president, he became president on Roosevelt's death (April 1945). He quickly made final arrangements for the San Francisco charter-writing meeting of the UN; helped arrange Germany's unconditional surrender on 8 May, which ended World War II in Europe; and in July attended the Potsdam Conference. The Pacific war ended officially on 2 September, after he ordered atomic bombs dropped on Hiroshima and Nagasaki; his justification was a report that 500,000 US troops would be lost in a conventional invasion of Japan. He announced the Truman Doctrine to aid Greece and Turkey (1947), established the Central Intelligence Agency, and pressed for passage of the Marshall Plan to aid European countries. In 1948 he defeated Thomas Dewey to gain reelection. He hewed to a foreign policy of containment to restrict the Soviet Union's sphere of influence and initiated the Berlin airlift and the NATO pact of 1949. In the Korean War he sent troops under Gen. Douglas MacArthur to head the United Nations forces. Though he was often criticized during his presidency, Truman's reputation grew steadily in later years.

Dwight David Eisenhower (14 Oct 1890, Denison TX—28 Mar 1969, Washington DC), 34th president of the US (1953–61). He graduated from West Point (1915) and then served in the Panama Canal Zone (1922–24) and in the Philippines under Douglas MacArthur (1935–39). In World War II, Gen. George Marshall chose him to command US forces in Europe (1942). After planning the invasions of North Africa, Sicily, and Italy, he was appointed supreme commander of Allied forces (1943). He planned the Normandy campaign (1944) and the conduct of the war in Europe until the German surrender (1945). He was promoted to five-star general (1944) and was named army chief of staff in 1945 and supreme commander of NATO in 1951. Both

Democrats and Republicans courted Eisenhower as a presidential candidate; in 1952, as the Republican candidate, he defeated Adlai Stevenson with the largest popular vote up to that time. He defeated Stevenson again in 1956 in an even larger landslide. His achievements included efforts to contain communism with the Eisenhower Doctrine. He sent federal troops to Little Rock AR to enforce integration of a city high school (1957). When the Soviet Union launched Sputnik 1 (1957), he was criticized for having failed to develop the US space program and responded by creating NASA (1958). In his last weeks in office the US broke diplomatic relations with Cuba.

John Fitzgerald Kennedy (29 May 1917, Brookline MA—22 Nov 1963, Dallas TX), 35th president of the US (1961–63). He joined the navy in World War II, where he earned medals for heroism. Elected to the House of Representatives (1947–53) and the Senate (1953–60), he supported social legislation and became increasingly committed to civil rights legislation. In 1960 he won the Democratic nomination for president; after a vigorous campaign, managed by his brother Robert F. Kennedy, he narrowly defeated Richard Nixon. He was the youngest person and the first Roman Catholic elected president. In his inaugural address he called on Americans to "ask not what your country can do for you, ask what you can do for your country." He proposed tax-reform and civil rights legislation but received little congressional support. He established the Peace Corps and the Alliance for Progress. His foreign policy began with the abortive Bay of Pigs invasion (1961), which emboldened the Soviet Union to move missiles to Cuba, sparking the Cuban missile crisis. In 1963 he successfully concluded the Nuclear Test-Ban Treaty. In November 1963 he was assassinated by a sniper, allegedly Lee Harvey Oswald, while riding in a motorcade in Dallas. The killing is considered the most notorious political murder of the 20th century. Kennedy's youth, energy, and charming family brought him world adulation and sparked the idealism of a generation, for whom the Kennedy White House became known as "Camelot."

Lyndon Baines Johnson (27 Aug 1908, Gillespie county TX—22 Jan 1973, San Antonio TX), 36th president of the US (1963–69). He won a seat in the House of Representatives (1937–49) as the New Deal was under conservative attack. His loyalty impressed Pres. Franklin Roosevelt, who made Johnson a protégé. He won election to the Senate in 1949 in a vicious campaign that saw fraud on both sides. As Democratic whip (1951–55) and majority leader (1955–61), he developed a talent for consensus building among dissident factions with methods both tactful and ruthless. He was largely responsible for passage of the civil rights bills of 1957 and 1960, the first in the 20th century. In 1960 he was elected vice president; he became president after the assassination of John F. Kennedy. In his first few months in office he won from Congress passage of a huge quantity of important civil rights, tax-reduction, antipoverty, and conservation legislation. He defeated Barry Goldwater in the 1964 election by the largest popular majority to that time and announced his Great Society program, which never came to fruition because of the escalation of US involvement in the Vietnam War, beginning with the Gulf of Tonkin Resolution. His approval ratings diminished markedly and led to his decision not to seek reelection in 1968.

Richard Milhous Nixon (9 Jan 1913, Yorba Linda CA—22 Apr 1994, New York NY), 37th president of the US (1969–74). After serving in World War II, he was elected to the House of Representatives in 1947, employing harsh campaign tactics, and to the Senate in 1951, again following a bitter campaign. He won the vice presidency in 1952 on a ticket with Dwight D. Eisenhower; they were reelected easily in 1956. As presidential candidate in 1960, he lost narrowly to John F. Kennedy. He reentered politics by running for president in 1968, and he defeated Hubert H. Humphrey with his "Southern strategy" of seeking votes from Southern and Western conservatives in both parties. As president, he began to gradually withdraw US military forces in an effort to end the Vietnam War while ordering the secret bombing of North Vietnamese military centers in Laos and Cambodia, which drew widespread protest. Economic problems included the largest US budget to date, and in 1971 Nixon established unprecedented peacetime controls on wages and prices. He won reelection in 1972 with a landslide victory over George McGovern. Assisted by Henry A. Kissinger, he concluded the Vietnam War. He reopened communications with China and made a state visit there. On his visit to the Soviet Union, the first by a US president, he signed the bilateral Strategic Arms Limitation Talks (SALT) agreements. The Watergate Scandal overshadowed his second term; his complicity in efforts to cover up his involvement and the likelihood of impeachment led to his becoming, in August 1974, the first president to resign from office.

Gerald Rudolph Ford, Jr. (Leslie Lynch King, Jr.; 14 Jul 1913, Omaha NE—26 Dec 2006, Rancho Mirage CA), 38th president of the US (1974–77). He served in the House of Representatives (1948–73), becoming minority leader in 1965. After Spiro Agnew resigned as vice president in 1973, Richard Nixon nominated Ford to fill the vacant post. When the Watergate Scandal forced Nixon's departure, Ford became the first president who had not been elected to either the vice presidency or the presidency. A month later he pardoned Nixon; to counter widespread outrage, he voluntarily appeared before a House subcommittee to explain his action. His administration gradually lowered the high inflation rate it inherited. Ford's relations with the Democratic-controlled Congress were typified by his more than 50 vetoes, of which more than 40 were sustained. In the final days of the Vietnam War in 1975, he ordered an airlift of 237,000 anticommunist Vietnamese refugees, most of whom came to the US. Reaction against Watergate contributed to his defeat by James Earl Carter, Jr., in 1976.

James Earl Carter, Jr. (1 Oct 1924, Plains GA), 39th president of the US (1977–81). As governor (1971–75) he opened Georgia's government offices to blacks and women and introduced stricter budgeting procedures for state agencies. In 1976, though lacking a national political base or major backing, he won the Democratic nomination and the presidency, defeating the sitting president, Gerald Ford. As president, Carter helped negotiate a peace treaty between Egypt and Israel, signed a treaty with Panama to make the Panama Canal a neutral zone after 1999, and established full diplomatic relations with China. In 1979–80 the Iran hostage crisis became a major political liability. He responded forcefully to the USSR's invasion of

Afghanistan in 1979, embargoing the shipment of US grain to that country and leading a boycott of the 1980 Summer Olympics in Moscow. Hampered by high inflation and a recession engineered to tame it, he lost his bid for reelection to Ronald Reagan. He subsequently became involved in international diplomatic negotiations and helped oversee elections in countries with insecure democratic traditions. Carter was awarded the Nobel Peace Prize in 2002.

Ronald Wilson Reagan (6 Feb 1911, Tampico IL–5 Jun 2004, Bel Air CA), 40th president of the US (1981–89). In his career as a Hollywood movie actor, he had roles in 50 films and was twice president of the Screen Actors Guild (1947–52, 1959–60). Having gradually changed his political affiliation from liberal Democrat to conservative Republican, he served as governor of California (1967–75). In 1980 he defeated incumbent Pres. Jimmy Carter to become president. Shortly after taking office, he was wounded in an assassination attempt. Reagan adopted supply-side economics to promote rapid economic growth and reduce the federal deficit. Congress approved most of his proposals in 1981, which succeeded in lowering inflation but doubled the national debt by 1986. He began the largest peacetime military buildup in US history and in 1983 proposed construction of the Strategic Defense Initiative to place antimissile technology in space. His foreign policy decisions included signing the Intermediate-Range Nuclear Forces (INF) Treaty to restrict intermediate-range nuclear weapons and invading Grenada. In 1984 Reagan defeated Walter Mondale in a landslide for reelection. Details of his administration's involvement in the Iran-Contra Affair emerged in 1986 and significantly weakened his popularity and authority. Though his intellectual capacity for governing was often disparaged (and in 1994 he revealed that he had Alzheimer disease), his artful communication skills enabled him to pursue numerous conservative policies with conspicuous success.

George Herbert Walker Bush (12 Jun 1924, Milton MA), 41st president of the US (1989–93). He served in World War II, graduated from Yale University, and started an oil business in Texas. He served in the House of Representatives (1966–70) as a Republican. He then served as ambassador to the UN (1971–72), chief liaison to China (1974–76), and head of the CIA (1976–77). In 1980 he ran for president but lost the nomination to Ronald Reagan. Bush served as vice president with Reagan (1981–89), whom he succeeded as president, defeating Michael Dukakis. He made no dramatic departures from Reagan's policies. In 1989 he ordered a brief military invasion of Panama, which toppled that country's leader, Gen. Manuel Noriega. He helped impose a UN-approved embargo against Iraq in 1990 to force its withdrawal from Kuwait. When Iraq refused, he authorized a US-led air offensive that began the Persian Gulf War. Despite general approval of his foreign policy, an economic recession led to his defeat by Bill Clinton in 1992. His son George W. Bush was elected president in 2000 and reelected in 2004.

William Jefferson Clinton (William Jefferson Blythe III; 19 Aug 1946, Hope AR), 42nd president of the US (1993–2001). He served as state attorney general (1977–79) and served several terms as governor (1979–81, 1983–92), during which he reformed Arkansas's educational system and encouraged the growth of industry through favorable tax policies. He won the Democratic presidential nomination in 1992, after withstanding charges of personal impropriety, and defeated the incumbent, George H.W. Bush. As president he obtained approval of the North American Free Trade Agreement (NAFTA) in 1993. He and his wife, Hillary Rodham Clinton, strongly advocated their plan to overhaul the US health care system, but Congress rejected it. He committed US forces to a peacekeeping initiative in Bosnia and Herzegovina. In 1994 the Democrats lost control of Congress for the first time since 1954. Clinton defeated Robert Dole to win reelection in 1996. He faced renewed charges of personal impropriety, this time involving Monica Lewinsky, and as a result, in 1998 he became the second president in history to be impeached. Charged with perjury and obstruction of justice, he was acquitted at his Senate trial in 1999. His two terms saw sustained economic growth and successive budget surpluses, the first in three decades.

George Walker Bush (6 Jul 1946, New Haven CT), 43rd president of the US (2001–09). The eldest child of Pres. George H.W. Bush, he served as governor of Texas (1995–2000). Despite losing the national popular vote to Vice President Al Gore by more than 500,000 votes in 2000, he gained the electoral college and the presidency when a Supreme Court ruling ended a recount of ballots in Florida. His response to the terrorist attacks on 11 Sep 2001 gave shape to his administration. The invasion of Iraq by US-led forces in March 2003 was followed by a problematic occupation during which a burgeoning insurgency threatened Iraqi efforts to stabilize a democratically elected government. Bush won reelection in 2004. The loss of Republican control of Congress in elections in November 2006 limited his power to steer legislation to passage at the end of his time in the White House.

Barack Hussein Obama II (4 Aug 1961, Honolulu HI), 44th president of the US (from 2009). He graduated from Columbia University (1983) and magna cum laude from Harvard Law School (1991), where he was the first African American to serve as president of the *Harvard Law Review*. He served as a community organizer on Chicago's largely impoverished Far South Side and lectured in constitutional law at the University of Chicago. He was elected (1996) to the Illinois Senate as a member of the Democratic Party. In 2004 he was elected to the US Senate, the third African American to be elected to that body since the end of Reconstruction. He quickly became a major national political figure. In 2008 Obama won an upset victory in the Democratic primary over US senator and former first lady Hillary Clinton to become the Democratic presidential nominee. He easily defeated Republican candidate John McCain to become the first African American president, capturing nearly 53 percent of the popular vote and 365 electoral votes. Not only did he hold all the states that John Kerry had won in the 2004 election, but he also captured a number of states (e.g., Colorado, Florida, Nevada, Ohio, and Virginia) that the Republicans had carried in the previous two presidential elections. He is the author of two books, the memoir *Dreams from My Father* (1995) and *The Audacity of Hope* (2006), a mainstream polemic on his vision for the United States.

Presidents' Spouses and Children

Maiden names of the presidents' wives appear in small capital letters.

DATE OF MARRIAGE	PRESIDENTS, SPOUSES, AND CHILDREN
	George Washington
6 Jan 1759	**Martha DANDRIDGE Custis** (2 Jun 1731–22 May 1802)
	no children
	John Adams
25 Oct 1764	**Abigail SMITH** (22 Nov 1744–28 Oct 1818)
	▸ Abigail Amelia Adams (1765–1813), ▸ John Quincy Adams (1767–1848), ▸ Susanna Adams (1768–70), ▸ Charles Adams (1770–1800), ▸ Thomas Boylston Adams (1772–1832)
	Thomas Jefferson
1 Jan 1772	**Martha WAYLES Skelton** (30 Oct 1748–6 Sep 1782)
	▸ Martha Washington Jefferson (1772–1836), ▸ Jane Randolph Jefferson (1774–75), ▸ infant son (1777), ▸ Mary Jefferson (1778–1804), ▸ Lucy Elizabeth Jefferson (1780–81), ▸ Lucy Elizabeth Jefferson (1782–84)
	James Madison
15 Sep 1794	**Dolley PAYNE Todd** (20 May 1768–12 Jul 1849)
	no children
	James Monroe
16 Feb 1786	**Elizabeth KORTRIGHT** (30 Jun 1768–23 Sep 1830)
	▸ Eliza Kortright Monroe (1786–1835), ▸ James Spence Monroe (1799–1800), ▸ Maria Hester Monroe (1803–50)
	John Quincy Adams
26 Jul 1797	**Louisa Catherine JOHNSON** (12 Feb 1775–15 May 1852)
	▸ George Washington Adams (1801–29), ▸ John Adams (1803–34), ▸ Charles Francis Adams (1807–86), ▸ Louisa Catherine Adams (1811–12)
	Andrew Jackson
Aug 1791	**Rachel DONELSON Robards** (15? Jun 1767–22 Dec 1828)
	no children
	Martin Van Buren
21 Feb 1807	**Hannah HOES** (8 Mar 1783–5 Feb 1819)
	▸ Abraham Van Buren (1807–73), ▸ John Van Buren (1810–66), ▸ Martin Van Buren (1812–55), ▸ Smith Thompson Van Buren (1817–76)
	William Henry Harrison
25 Nov 1795	**Anna Tuthill SYMMES** (25 Jul 1775–25 Feb 1864)
	▸ Elizabeth Bassett Harrison (1796–1846), ▸ John Cleves Symmes Harrison (1798–1830), ▸ Lucy Singleton Harrison (1800–26), ▸ William Henry Harrison (1802–38), ▸ John Scott Harrison (1804–78), ▸ Benjamin Harrison (1806–40), ▸ Mary Symmes Harrison (1809–42), ▸ Carter Bassett Harrison (1811–39), ▸ Anna Tuthill Harrison (1813–65), ▸ James Findlay Harrison (1814–17)
	John Tyler
29 Mar 1813	**Letitia CHRISTIAN** (12 Nov 1790–10 Sep 1842)
	▸ Mary Tyler (1815–48), ▸ Robert Tyler (1816–77), ▸ John Tyler (1819–96), ▸ Letitia Tyler (1821–1907), ▸ Elizabeth Tyler (1823–50), ▸ Anne Contesse Tyler (1825), ▸ Alice Tyler (1827–54), ▸ Tazewell Tyler (1830–74)
26 Jun 1844	**Julia GARDINER** (4 May 1820–10 Jul 1889)
	▸ David Gardiner Tyler (1846–1927), ▸ John Alexander Tyler (1848–83), ▸ Julia Gardiner Tyler (1849?–71), ▸ Lachlan Tyler (1851–1902), ▸ Lyon Gardiner Tyler (1853–1935), ▸ Robert Fitzwalter Tyler (1856–1927), ▸ Pearl Tyler (1860–1947)
	James K. Polk
1 Jan 1824	**Sarah CHILDRESS** (4 Sep 1803–14 Aug 1891)
	no children
	Zachary Taylor
21 Jun 1810	**Margaret Mackall SMITH** (21 Sep 1788–14 Aug 1852)
	▸ Anne Margaret Mackall Taylor (1811–75), ▸ Sarah Knox Taylor (1814–35), ▸ Octavia Pannel Taylor (1816–20), ▸ Margaret Smith Taylor (1819–20), ▸ Mary Elizabeth Taylor (1824–1909), ▸ Richard Taylor (1826–79)

Presidents' Spouses and Children (continued)

DATE OF MARRIAGE	PRESIDENTS, SPOUSES, AND CHILDREN

Millard Fillmore

5 Feb 1826   **Abigail Powers** (13 Mar 1798–30 Mar 1853)
▸ Millard Powers Fillmore (1828–89), ▸ Mary Abigail Fillmore (1832–54)

10 Feb 1858   **Caroline Carmichael McIntosh** (21 Oct 1813–11 Aug 1881)
no children

Franklin Pierce

10 Nov 1834   **Jane Means Appleton** (12 Mar 1806–2 Dec 1863)
▸ Franklin Pierce (1836), ▸ Frank Robert Pierce (1839–43), ▸ Benjamin Pierce (1841–53)

James Buchanan
never married

Abraham Lincoln

4 Nov 1842   **Mary Ann Todd** (13 Dec 1818–16 Jul 1882)
▸ Robert Todd Lincoln (1843–1926), ▸ Edward Baker Lincoln (1846–50), ▸ William Wallace Lincoln (1850–62), ▸ Thomas Lincoln (1853–71)

Andrew Johnson

17 May 1827   **Eliza McCardle** (4 Oct 1810–15 Jan 1876)
▸ Martha Johnson (1828–1901), ▸ Charles Johnson (1830–63), ▸ Mary Johnson (1832–83), ▸ Robert Johnson (1834–69), ▸ Andrew Johnson (1852–79)

Ulysses S. Grant

22 Aug 1848   **Julia Boggs Dent** (26 Jan 1826–14 Dec 1902)
▸ Frederick Dent Grant (1850–1912), ▸ Ulysses Simpson Grant (1852–1929), ▸ Ellen Wrenshall Grant (1855–1922), ▸ Jesse Root Grant (1858–1934)

Rutherford B. Hayes

30 Dec 1852   **Lucy Ware Webb** (28 Aug 1831–25 Jun 1889)
▸ Birchard Austin Hayes (1853–1926), ▸ James Webb Cook Hayes (1856–1934), ▸ Rutherford Platt Hayes (1858–1927), ▸ Joseph Thompson Hayes (1861–63), ▸ George Crook Hayes (1864–66), ▸ Frances Hayes (1867–1950), ▸ Scott Russell Hayes (1871–1923), ▸ Manning Force Hayes (1873–74)

James A. Garfield

11 Nov 1858   **Lucretia Rudolph** (19 Apr 1832–13 Mar 1918)
▸ Eliza Arabella Garfield (1860–63), ▸ Harry Augustus Garfield (1863–1942), ▸ James Rudolph Garfield (1865–1950), ▸ Mary Garfield (1867–1947), ▸ Irvin McDowell Garfield (1870–1951), ▸ Abram Garfield (1872–1958), ▸ Edward Garfield (1874–76)

Chester A. Arthur

25 Oct 1859   **Ellen Lewis Herndon** (30 Aug 1837–12 Jan 1880)
▸ William Lewis Herndon Arthur (1860–63), ▸ Chester Alan Arthur (1864–1937), ▸ Ellen Herndon Arthur (1871–1915)

Grover Cleveland

2 Jun 1886   **Frances Folsom** (21 Jul 1864–29 Oct 1947)
▸ Ruth Cleveland (1891–1904), ▸ Esther Cleveland (1893–1980), ▸ Marion Cleveland (1895–1977), ▸ Richard Folsom Cleveland (1897–1974), ▸ Francis Grover Cleveland (1903–95)

Benjamin Harrison

20 Oct 1853   **Caroline Lavinia Scott** (1 Oct 1832–25 Oct 1892)
▸ Russell Benjamin Harrison (1854–1936), ▸ Mary Scott Harrison (1858–1930)

6 Apr 1896   **Mary Scott Lord Dimmick** (30 Apr 1858–5 Jan 1948)
▸ Elizabeth Harrison (1897–1955)

William McKinley

25 Jan 1871   **Ida Saxton** (8 Jun 1847–26 May 1907)
▸ Katherine McKinley (1871–75), ▸ Ida McKinley (1873)

Presidents' Spouses and Children (continued)

DATE OF MARRIAGE	PRESIDENTS, SPOUSES, AND CHILDREN

Theodore Roosevelt

27 Oct 1880   **Alice Hathaway LEE** (29 Jul 1861–14 Feb 1884)
▸ Alice Lee Roosevelt (1884–1980)

2 Dec 1886   **Edith Kermit CAROW** (6 Aug 1861–30 Sep 1948)
▸ Theodore Roosevelt (1887–1944), ▸ Kermit Roosevelt (1889–1943), ▸ Ethel Carow Roosevelt (1891–1977), ▸ Archibald Bulloch Roosevelt (1894–1979), ▸ Quentin Roosevelt (1897–1918)

William Howard Taft

19 Jun 1886   **Helen HERRON** (2 Jun 1861–22 May 1943)
▸ Robert Alphonso Taft (1889–1953), ▸ Helen Herron Taft (1891–1987), ▸ Charles Phelps Taft (1897–1983)

Woodrow Wilson

24 Jun 1885   **Ellen Louise AXSON** (15 May 1860–6 Aug 1914)
▸ Margaret Woodrow Wilson (1886–1944), ▸ Jessie Woodrow Wilson (1887–1933), ▸ Eleanor Randolph Wilson (1889–1967)

18 Dec 1915   **Edith BOLLING Galt** (15 Oct 1872–28 Dec 1961)
no children

Warren G. Harding

8 Jul 1891   **Florence Mabel KLING DeWolfe** (15 Aug 1860–21 Nov 1924)
no children

Calvin Coolidge

4 Oct 1905   **Grace Anna GOODHUE** (3 Jan 1879–8 Jul 1957)
▸ John Coolidge (1906–2000), ▸ Calvin Coolidge (1908–24)

Herbert Hoover

10 Feb 1899   **Lou HENRY** (29 Mar 1874–7 Jan 1944)
▸ Herbert Clark Hoover (1903–69), ▸ Allan Henry Hoover (1907–93)

Franklin D. Roosevelt

17 Mar 1905   **Anna Eleanor (Eleanor) ROOSEVELT** (11 Oct 1884–7 Nov 1962)
▸ Anna Eleanor Roosevelt (1906–75), ▸ James Roosevelt (1907–91), ▸ Franklin Delano Roosevelt (1909), ▸ Elliott Roosevelt (1910–90), ▸ Franklin Delano Roosevelt (1914–88), ▸ John Aspinwall Roosevelt (1916–81)

Harry S. Truman

28 Jun 1919   **Elizabeth Virginia (Bess) WALLACE** (13 Feb 1885–18 Oct 1982)
▸ Mary Margaret Truman (1924–2008)

Dwight D. Eisenhower

1 Jul 1916   **Mamie Geneva DOUD** (14 Nov 1896–1 Nov 1979)
▸ Doud Dwight Eisenhower (1917–21), ▸ John Sheldon Doud Eisenhower (1922–   )

John F. Kennedy

12 Sep 1953   **Jacqueline Lee BOUVIER** (28 Jul 1929–19 May 1994)
▸ Caroline Bouvier Kennedy (1957–   ), ▸ John Fitzgerald Kennedy (1960–99), ▸ Patrick Bouvier Kennedy (1963)

Lyndon B. Johnson

17 Nov 1934   **Claudia Alta (Lady Bird) TAYLOR** (22 Dec 1912–11 Jul 2007)
▸ Lynda Bird Johnson (1944–   ), ▸ Lucy Baines Johnson (1947–   )

Richard M. Nixon

21 Jun 1940   **Thelma Catherine (Pat) RYAN** (16 Mar 1912–22 Jun 1993)
▸ Patricia Nixon (1946–   ), ▸ Julie Nixon (1948–   )

Gerald R. Ford

15 Oct 1948   **Elizabeth Ann (Betty) BLOOMER Warren** (8 Apr 1918–   )
▸ Michael Gerald Ford (1950–   ), ▸ John Gardner Ford (1952–   ), ▸ Steven Meigs Ford (1956–   ), ▸ Susan Elizabeth Ford (1957–   )

Jimmy Carter

7 Jul 1946   **Eleanor Rosalynn (Rosalynn) SMITH** (18 Aug 1927–   )
▸ John William Carter (1947–   ), ▸ James Earl Carter (1950–   ), ▸ Donnel Jeffrey Carter (1952–   ), ▸ Amy Lynn Carter (1967–   )

Presidents' Spouses and Children (continued)

DATE OF MARRIAGE	PRESIDENTS, SPOUSES, AND CHILDREN
	Ronald Reagan
24 Jan 1940	**Jane Wyman (née Sarah Jane MAYFIELD [FULKS])** (4 Jan 1914–10 Sep 2007)
	▸ Maureen Elizabeth Reagan (1941–2001), ▸ Michael Edward Reagan (1945–), ▸ Christine Reagan (1947)
4 Mar 1952	**Nancy Davis (née Anne Frances ROBBINS)** (6 Jul 1921–)
	▸ Patricia Ann Reagan (1952–), ▸ Ronald Prescott Reagan (1958–)
	George H.W. Bush
6 Jan 1945	**Barbara PIERCE** (8 Jun 1925–)
	▸ George Walker Bush (1946–), ▸ Pauline Robinson Bush (1949–53), ▸ John Ellis Bush (1953–), ▸ Neil Mallon Bush (1955–), ▸ Marvin Pierce Bush (1956–), ▸ Dorothy Walker Bush (1959–)
	Bill Clinton
11 Oct 1975	**Hillary Diane RODHAM** (26 Oct 1947–)
	▸ Chelsea Victoria Clinton (1980–)
	George W. Bush
5 Nov 1977	**Laura Lane WELCH** (4 Nov 1946–)
	▸ Barbara Pierce Bush (1981–), ▸ Jenna Welch Bush (1981–)
	Barack Obama
18 Oct 1992	**Michelle LaVaughn ROBINSON** (17 Jan 1964–)
	▸ Malia Ann Obama (1998–), ▸ Natasha Obama (2001–)

Did you know?

Whitcomb L. Judson invented the zipper in the early 1900s; it was further refined by Swedish inventor Gideon Sundback in his 1917 patent, and it was first called a "zipper" when the B.F. Goodrich company began using the device in its rubber boots and galoshes. Most zippers have the letters "YKK" on them, which stands for the Yoshida Kogyo Kabushililaisha corporation of Japan, the world's leading zipper manufacturer.

US Presidential Cabinets

The cabinet is composed of the heads of executive departments chosen by the president with the consent of the Senate. Cabinet officials do not hold seats in Congress and are not regulated by the US Constitution, which makes no mention of such a body. The existence of the cabinet is a matter of custom dating back to George Washington, who consulted regularly with his department heads as a group. Original dates of service are given for officials appointed midterm and for newly created posts. Interim officials are not listed. Presidencies and new positions are indicated in bold.

George Washington

30 APR 1789–3 MARCH 1793 (TERM 1)

State	Thomas Jefferson
Treasury	Alexander Hamilton
War	Henry Knox
Attorney General	Edmund Randolph

4 MAR 1793–3 MAR 1797 (TERM 2)

State	Thomas Jefferson; Edmund Randolph (2 Jan 1794); Timothy Pickering (20 Aug 1795)
Treasury	Alexander Hamilton; Oliver Wolcott, Jr. (2 Feb 1795)
War	Henry Knox; Timothy Pickering (2 Jan 1795); James McHenry (6 Feb 1796)
Attorney General	Edmund Randolph; William Bradford (29 Jan 1794); Charles Lee (10 Dec 1795)

John Adams

4 MAR 1797–3 MAR 1801

State	Timothy Pickering; John Marshall (6 Jun 1800)
Treasury	Oliver Wolcott, Jr.; Samuel Dexter (1 Jan 1801)
War	James McHenry; Samuel Dexter (12 Jun 1800)
Navy	Benjamin Stoddert (18 Jun 1798)
Attorney General	Charles Lee

US Presidential Cabinets (continued)

Thomas Jefferson

4 MAR 1801–3 MAR 1805 (TERM 1)

State	James Madison
Treasury	Samuel Dexter; Albert Gallatin (14 May 1801)
War	Henry Dearborn
Navy	Benjamin Stoddert; Robert Smith (27 Jul 1801)
Attorney General	Levi Lincoln

4 MAR 1805–3 MAR 1809 (TERM 2)

State	James Madison
Treasury	Albert Gallatin
War	Henry Dearborn
Navy	Robert Smith
Attorney General	John Breckenridge; Caesar Augustus Rodney (20 Jan 1807)

James Madison

4 MAR 1809–3 MAR 1813 (TERM 1)

State	Robert Smith
Treasury	Albert Gallatin
War	John Smith; William Eustis (8 Apr 1809); John Armstrong (5 Feb 1813)
Navy	Robert Smith; Paul Hamilton (15 May 1809); William Jones (19 Jan 1813)
Attorney General	Caesar Augustus Rodney; William Pinkney (6 Jan 1812)

4 MAR 1813–3 MAR 1817 (TERM 2)

State	James Monroe
Treasury	Albert Gallatin; George Washington Campbell (9 Feb 1814); Alexander James Dallas (14 Oct 1814); William Harris Crawford (22 Oct 1816)
War	John Armstrong; James Monroe (1 Oct 1814); William Harris Crawford (8 Aug 1815)
Navy	William Jones; Benjamin Williams Crowninshield (16 Jan 1815)
Attorney General	William Pinkney; Richard Rush (11 Feb 1814)

James Monroe

4 MAR 1817–3 MAR 1821 (TERM 1)

State	John Quincy Adams
Treasury	William Harris Crawford
War	John C. Calhoun
Navy	Benjamin Williams Crowninshield; Smith Thompson (1 Jan 1819)
Attorney General	Richard Rush; William Wirt (15 Nov 1817)

4 MAR 1821–3 MAR 1825 (TERM 2)

State	John Quincy Adams
Treasury	William Harris Crawford
War	John C. Calhoun
Navy	Smith Thompson; Samuel Lewis Southard (16 Sep 1823)
Attorney General	William Wirt

John Quincy Adams

4 MAR 1825–3 MAR 1829

State	Henry Clay
Treasury	Richard Rush
War	James Barbour; Peter Buell Porter (21 Jun 1828)
Navy	Samuel Lewis Southard
Attorney General	William Wirt

Andrew Jackson

4 MAR 1829–3 MAR 1833 (TERM 1)

State	Martin Van Buren; Edward Livingston (24 May 1831)
Treasury	Samuel Delucenna Ingham; Louis McLane (8 Aug 1831)
War	John Henry Eaton; Lewis Cass (8 Aug 1831)
Navy	John Branch; Levi Woodbury (23 May 1831)
Attorney General	John Macpherson Berrien; Roger Brooke Taney (20 Jul 1831)

US Presidential Cabinets (continued)

Andrew Jackson (continued)

4 MAR 1833–3 MAR 1837 (TERM 2)

State	Edward Livingston; Louis McLane (29 May 1833); John Forsyth (1 Jul 1834)
Treasury	Louis McLane; William John Duane (1 Jun 1833); Roger Brooke Taney (23 Sep 1833); Levi Woodbury (1 Jul 1834)
War	Lewis Cass
Navy	Levi Woodbury; Mahlon Dickerson (30 Jun 1834)
Attorney General	Roger Brooke Taney; Benjamin Franklin Butler (18 Nov 1833)

Martin Van Buren

4 MAR 1837–3 MAR 1841

State	John Forsyth
Treasury	Levi Woodbury
War	Joel Roberts Poinsett
Navy	Mahlon Dickerson; James Kirke Paulding (1 Jul 1838)
Attorney General	Benjamin Franklin Butler; Felix Grundy (1 Sep 1838); Henry Dilworth Gilpin (11 Jan 1840)

William Henry Harrison

4 MAR 1841–4 APR 1841

State	Daniel Webster
Treasury	Thomas Ewing
War	John Bell
Navy	George Edmund Badger
Attorney General	John Jordan Crittenden

John Tyler

6 APR 1841–3 MAR 1845

State	Daniel Webster; Abel Parker Upshur (24 Jul 1843); John C. Calhoun (1 Apr 1844)
Treasury	Thomas Ewing; Walter Forward (13 Sep 1841); John Canfield Spencer (8 Mar 1843); George Mortimer Bibb (4 Jul 1844)
War	John Bell; John Canfield Spencer (12 Oct 1841); James Madison Porter (8 Mar 1843); William Wilkins (20 Feb 1844)
Navy	George Edmund Badger; Abel Parker Upshur (11 Oct 1841); David Henshaw (24 Jul 1843); Thomas Walker Gilmer (19 Feb 1844); John Young Mason (26 Mar 1844)
Attorney General	John Jordan Crittenden; Hugh Swinton Legaré (20 Sep 1841); John Nelson (1 Jul 1843)

James K. Polk

4 MAR 1845–3 MAR 1849

State	James Buchanan
Treasury	Robert James Walker
War	William Learned Marcy
Navy	George Bancroft; John Young Mason (9 Sep 1846)
Attorney General	John Young Mason; Nathan Clifford (17 Oct 1846); Isaac Toucey (29 Jun 1848)

Zachary Taylor

4 MAR 1849–9 JUL 1850

State	John Middleton Clayton
Treasury	William Morris Meredith
War	George Washington Crawford
Navy	William Ballard Preston
Attorney General	Reverdy Johnson
Interior	Thomas Ewing (8 Mar 1849)

Millard Fillmore

10 JUL 1850–3 MAR 1853

State	Daniel Webster; Edward Everett (6 Nov 1852)
Treasury	Thomas Corwin
War	George Washington Crawford; Charles Magill Conrad (15 Aug 1850)
Navy	William Alexander Graham; John Pendleton Kennedy (26 Jul 1852)
Attorney General	Reverdy Johnson; John Jordan Crittenden (14 Aug 1850)
Interior	Thomas Ewing; Thomas McKean Thompson McKennan (15 Aug 1850); Alexander Hugh Holmes Stuart (16 Sep 1850)

US Presidential Cabinets (continued)

Franklin Pierce

4 MAR 1853–3 MAR 1857

State	William Learned Marcy
Treasury	James Guthrie
War	Jefferson Davis
Navy	James Cochran Dobbin
Attorney General	Caleb Cushing
Interior	Robert McClelland

James Buchanan

4 MAR 1857–3 MAR 1861

State	Lewis Cass; Jeremiah Sullivan Black (17 Dec 1860)
Treasury	Howell Cobb; Philip Francis Thomas (12 Dec 1860); John Adams Dix (15 Jan 1861)
War	John Buchanan Floyd
Navy	Isaac Toucey
Attorney General	Jeremiah Sullivan Black; Edwin McMasters Stanton (22 Dec 1860)
Interior	Jacob Thompson

Abraham Lincoln

4 MAR 1861–3 MAR 1865 (TERM 1)

State	William Henry Seward
Treasury	Salmon Portland Chase; William Pitt Fessenden (5 Jul 1864)
War	Simon Cameron; Edwin McMasters Stanton (20 Jun 1862)
Navy	Gideon Welles
Attorney General	Edward Bates; James Speed (5 Dec 1864)
Interior	Caleb Blood Smith; John Palmer Usher (8 Jan 1863)

4 MAR 1865–15 APR 1865 (TERM 2)

State	William Henry Seward
Treasury	Hugh McCulloch
War	Edwin McMasters Stanton
Navy	Gideon Welles
Attorney General	James Speed
Interior	John Palmer Usher

Andrew Johnson

15 APR 1865–3 MAR 1869

State	William Henry Seward
Treasury	Hugh McCulloch
War	Edwin McMasters Stanton; John McAllister Schofield (1 Jun 1868)
Navy	Gideon Welles
Attorney General	James Speed; Henry Stanbery (23 Jul 1866); William Maxwell Evarts (20 Jul 1868)
Interior	John Palmer Usher; James Harlan (15 May 1865); Orville Hickman Browning (1 Sep 1866)

Ulysses S. Grant

4 MAR 1869–3 MAR 1873 (TERM 1)

State	Elihu Benjamin Washburne; Hamilton Fish (17 Mar 1869)
Treasury	George Sewall Boutwell
War	John Aaron Rawlins; William Tecumseh Sherman (11 Sep 1869); William Worth Belknap (1 Nov 1869)
Navy	Adolph Edward Borie; George Maxwell Robeson (25 Jun 1869)
Attorney General	Ebenezer Rockwood Hoar; Amos Tappan Akerman (8 Jul 1870); George Henry Williams (10 Jan 1872)
Interior	Jacob Dolson Cox; Columbus Delano (1 Nov 1870)

4 MAR 1873–3 MAR 1877 (TERM 2)

State	Hamilton Fish
Treasury	William Adams Richardson; Benjamin Helm Bristow (4 Jun 1874); Lot Myrick Morrill (7 Jul 1876)
War	William Worth Belknap; Alphonso Taft (11 Mar 1876); James Donald Cameron (1 Jun 1876)
Navy	George Maxwell Robeson
Attorney General	George Henry Williams; Edward Pierrepont (15 May 1875); Alphonso Taft (1 Jun 1876)
Interior	Columbus Delano; Zachariah Chandler (19 Oct 1875)

US Presidential Cabinets (continued)

Rutherford B. Hayes

4 MAR 1877–3 MAR 1881

State	William Maxwell Evarts
Treasury	John Sherman
War	George Washington McCrary; Alexander Ramsey (12 Dec 1879)
Navy	Richard Wigginton Thompson; Nathan Goff, Jr. (6 Jan 1881)
Attorney General	Charles Devens
Interior	Carl Schurz

James A. Garfield

4 MAR 1881–19 SEP 1881

State	James Gillespie Blaine
Treasury	William Windom
War	Robert Todd Lincoln
Attorney General	(Isaac) Wayne MacVeagh
Navy	William Henry Hunt
Interior	Samuel Jordan Kirkwood

Chester A. Arthur

20 SEP 1881–3 MAR 1885

State	James Gillespie Blaine; Frederick Theodore Frelinghuysen (19 Dec 1881)
Treasury	William Windom; Charles James Folger (14 Nov 1881); Walter Quintin Gresham (24 Sep 1884); Hugh McCulloch (31 Oct 1884)
War	Robert Todd Lincoln
Navy	William Henry Hunt; William Eaton Chandler (17 Apr 1882)
Attorney General	(Isaac) Wayne MacVeagh; Benjamin Harris Brewster (3 Jan 1882)
Interior	Samuel Jordan Kirkwood; Henry Moore Teller (17 Apr 1882)

Grover Cleveland

4 MAR 1885–3 MAR 1889

State	Thomas Francis Bayard
Treasury	Daniel Manning; Charles Stebbins Fairchild (1 Apr 1887)
War	William Crowninshield Endicott
Navy	William Collins Whitney
Attorney General	Augustus Hill Garland
Interior	Lucius Quintus Cincinnatus Lamar; William Freeman Vilas (16 Jan 1888)
Agriculture	Norman Jay Colman (13 Feb 1889)

Benjamin Harrison

4 MAR 1889–3 MAR 1893

State	James Gillespie Blaine; John Watson Foster (29 Jun 1892)
Treasury	William Windom; Charles Foster (24 Feb 1891)
War	Redfield Proctor; Stephen Benton Elkins (24 Dec 1891)
Navy	Benjamin Franklin Tracy
Attorney General	William Henry Harrison Miller
Interior	John Willock Noble
Agriculture	Jeremiah McLain Rusk

Grover Cleveland

4 MAR 1893–3 MAR 1897

State	Walter Quintin Gresham; Richard Olney (10 Jun 1895)
Treasury	John Griffin Carlisle
War	Daniel Scott Lamont
Navy	Hilary Abner Herbert
Attorney General	Richard Olney; Judson Harmon (11 Jun 1895)
Interior	Hoke Smith; David Rowland Francis (4 Sep 1896)
Agriculture	Julius Sterling Morton

William McKinley

4 MAR 1897–3 MAR 1901 (TERM 1)

State	John Sherman; William Rufus Day (28 Apr 1898); John Hay (30 Sep 1898)
Treasury	Lyman Judson
War	Russell Alexander Alger; Elihu Root (1 Aug 1899)
Navy	John Davis Long
Attorney General	Joseph McKenna; John William Griggs (1 Feb 1898)
Interior	Cornelius Newton Bliss; Ethan Allen Hitchcock (20 Feb 1899)
Agriculture	James Wilson

US Presidential Cabinets (continued)

William McKinley (continued)

4 MAR 1901–14 SEP 1901 (TERM 2)

State	John Hay
Treasury	Lyman Judson Gage
War	Elihu Root
Navy	John Davis Long
Attorney General	John William Griggs; Philander Chase Knox (10 Apr 1901)
Interior	Ethan Allen Hitchcock
Agriculture	James Wilson

Theodore Roosevelt

14 SEP 1901–3 MAR 1905 (TERM 1)

State	John Hay
Treasury	Lyman Judson Gage; Leslie Mortier Shaw (1 Feb 1902)
War	Elihu Root; William Howard Taft (1 Feb 1904)
Navy	John Davis Long; William Henry Moody (1 May 1902); Paul Morton (1 Jul 1904)
Attorney General	Philander Chase Knox; William Henry Moody (1 Jul 1904)
Interior	Ethan Allen Hitchcock
Agriculture	James Wilson
Commerce and Labor	George Bruce Cortelyou (16 Feb 1903); Victor Howard Metcalf (1 Jul 1904)

4 MAR 1905–3 MAR 1909 (TERM 2)

State	John Hay; Elihu Root (19 Jul 1905); Robert Bacon (27 Jan 1909)
Treasury	Leslie Mortier Shaw; George Bruce Cortelyou (4 Mar 1907)
War	William Howard Taft; Luke Edward Wright (1 Jul 1908)
Navy	Paul Morton; Charles Joseph Bonaparte (1 Jul 1905); Victor Howard Metcalf (17 Dec 1906); Truman Handy Newberry (1 Dec 1908)
Attorney General	William Henry Moody; Charles Joseph Bonaparte (17 Dec 1906)
Interior	Ethan Allen Hitchcock; James Rudolph Garfield (4 Mar 1907)
Agriculture	James Wilson
Commerce and Labor	Victor Howard Metcalf; Oscar Solomon Straus (17 Dec 1906)

William Howard Taft

4 MAR 1909–3 MAR 1913

State	Philander Chase Knox
Treasury	Franklin MacVeagh
War	Jacob McGavock Dickinson; Henry Lewis Stimson (22 May 1911)
Navy	George von Lengerke Meyer
Attorney General	George Woodward Wickersham
Interior	Richard Achilles Ballinger; Walter Lowrie Fisher (7 Mar 1911)
Agriculture	James Wilson
Commerce and Labor	Charles Nagel

Woodrow Wilson

4 MAR 1913–3 MAR 1917 (TERM 1)

State	William Jennings Bryan; Robert Lansing (23 Jun 1915)
Treasury	William Gibbs McAdoo
War	Lindley Miller Garrison; Newton Diehl Baker (9 Mar 1916)
Navy	Josephus Daniels
Attorney General	James Clark McReynolds; Thomas Watt Gregory (3 Sep 1914)
Interior	Franklin Knight Lane
Agriculture	David Franklin Houston
Commerce	William Cox Redfield
Labor	William Bauchop Wilson

4 MAR 1917–3 MAR 1921 (TERM 2)

State	Robert Lansing; Bainbridge Colby (23 Mar 1920)
Treasury	William Gibbs McAdoo; Carter Glass (16 Dec 1918); David Franklin Houston (2 Feb 1920)
War	Newton Diehl Baker
Navy	Josephus Daniels
Attorney General	Thomas Watt Gregory; Alexander Mitchell Palmer (5 Mar 1919)
Interior	Franklin Knight Lane; John Barton Payne (13 Mar 1920)
Agriculture	David Franklin Houston; Edwin Thomas Meredith (2 Feb 1920)
Commerce	William Cox Redfield; Joshua Willis Alexander (16 Dec 1919)
Labor	William Bauchop Wilson

US Presidential Cabinets (continued)

Warren G. Harding

4 MAR 1921–2 AUG 1923

State	Charles Evans Hughes
Treasury	Andrew William Mellon
War	John Wingate Weeks
Navy	Edwin Denby
Attorney General	Harry Micajah Daugherty
Interior	Albert Bacon Fall; Hubert Work (5 Mar 1923)
Agriculture	Henry Cantwell Wallace
Commerce	Herbert Hoover
Labor	James John Davis

Calvin Coolidge

3 AUG 1923–3 MAR 1925 (TERM 1)

State	Charles Evans Hughes
Treasury	Andrew William Mellon
War	John Wingate Weeks
Navy	Edwin Denby; Curtis Dwight Wilbur (18 Mar 1924)
Attorney General	Harry Micajah Daugherty; Harlan Fiske Stone (9 Apr 1924)
Interior	Hubert Work
Agriculture	Henry Cantwell Wallace; Howard Mason Gore (21 Nov 1924)
Commerce	Herbert Hoover
Labor	James John Davis

4 MAR 1925–3 MAR 1929 (TERM 2)

State	Frank Billings Kellogg
Treasury	Andrew William Mellon
War	John Wingate Weeks; Dwight Filley Davis (14 Oct 1925)
Navy	Curtis Dwight Wilbur
Attorney General	John Garibaldi Sargent
Interior	Hubert Work; Roy Owen West (21 Jan 1929)
Agriculture	William Marion Jardine
Commerce	Herbert Hoover; William Fairfield Whiting (11 Dec 1928)
Labor	James John Davis

Herbert Hoover

4 MAR 1929–3 MAR 1933

State	Henry Lewis Stimson
Treasury	Andrew William Mellon; Ogden Livingston Mills (13 Feb 1932)
War	James William Good; Patrick Jay Hurley (9 Dec 1929)
Navy	Charles Francis Adams
Attorney General	William De Witt Mitchell
Interior	Ray Lyman Wilbur
Agriculture	Arthur Mastick Hyde
Commerce	Robert Patterson Lamont; Roy Dikeman Chapin (14 Dec 1932)
Labor	James John Davis; William Nuckles Doak (9 Dec 1930)

Franklin D. Roosevelt

4 MAR 1933–20 JAN 1937 (TERM 1)

State	Cordell Hull
Treasury	William Hartman Woodin; Henry Morgenthau, Jr. (8 Jan 1934)
War	George Henry Dern
Navy	Claude Augustus Swanson
Attorney General	Homer Stille Cummings
Interior	Harold LeClaire Ickes
Agriculture	Henry Agard Wallace
Commerce	Daniel Calhoun Roper
Labor	Frances Perkins

20 JAN 1937–20 JAN 1941 (TERM 2)

State	Cordell Hull
Treasury	Henry Morgenthau, Jr.
War	Harry Hines Woodring; Henry Lewis Stimson (10 Jul 1940)
Attorney General	Homer Stille Cummings; Frank Murphy (17 Jan 1939); Robert Houghwout Jackson (18 Jan 1940)
Navy	Claude Augustus Swanson; Charles Edison (11 Jan 1940); Frank Knox (10 Jul 1940)
Interior	Harold LeClaire Ickes
Agriculture	Henry Agard Wallace; Claude Raymond Wickard (5 Sep 1940)

US Presidential Cabinets (continued)

Franklin D. Roosevelt (continued)

20 JAN 1937–20 JAN 1941 (TERM 2) (CONTINUED)

Commerce	Daniel Calhoun Roper; Harry Lloyd Hopkins (23 Jan 1939); Jesse Holman Jones (19 Sep 1940)
Labor	Frances Perkins

20 JAN 1941–20 JAN 1945 (TERM 3)

State	Cordell Hull; Edward Reilly Stettinius (1 Dec 1944)
Treasury	Henry Morgenthau, Jr.
War	Henry Lewis Stimson
Navy	Frank Knox; James Vincent Forrestal (18 May 1944)
Attorney General	Robert Houghwout Jackson; Francis Biddle (5 Sep 1941)
Interior	Harold LeClaire Ickes
Agriculture	Claude Raymond Wickard
Commerce	Jesse Holman Jones
Labor	Frances Perkins

20 JAN 1945–12 APR 1945 (TERM 4)

State	Edward Reilly Stettinius
Treasury	Henry Morgenthau, Jr.
War	Henry Lewis Stimson
Navy	James Vincent Forrestal
Attorney General	Francis Biddle
Interior	Harold LeClaire Ickes
Agriculture	Claude Raymond Wickard
Commerce	Jesse Holman Jones; Henry Agard Wallace (2 Mar 1945)
Labor	Frances Perkins

Harry S. Truman

12 APR 1945–20 JAN 1949 (TERM 1)

State	Edward Reilly Stettinius; James Francis Byrnes (3 Jul 1945); George Catlett Marshall (21 Jan 1947)
Treasury	Henry Morgenthau, Jr.; Frederick Moore (23 Jul 1945); John Wesley Snyder (25 Jun 1946)
War	Henry Lewis Stimson; Robert Porter Patterson (27 Sep 1945); Kenneth Claiborne Royall (25 Jul 1947–17 Sep 1947)
Defense	James Vincent Forrestal (17 Sep 1947)
Navy	James Vincent Forrestal (–17 Sep 1947)
Attorney General	Francis Biddle; Thomas Campbell Clark (1 Jul 1945)
Interior	Harold LeClaire Ickes; Julius Albert Krug (18 Mar 1946)
Agriculture	Claude Raymond Wickard; Clinton Presba Anderson (30 Jun 1945); Charles Franklin Brannan (2 Jun 1948)
Commerce	Henry Agard Wallace; William Averell Harriman (28 Jan 1947); Charles Sawyer (6 May 1948)
Labor	Frances Perkins; Lewis Baxter Schwellenbach (1 Jul 1945)

20 JAN 1949–20 JAN 1953 (TERM 2)

State	Dean Gooderham Acheson
Treasury	John Wesley Snyder
Defense	James Vincent Forrestal; Louis Arthur Johnson (28 Mar 1949); George Catlett Marshall (21 Sep 1950); Robert Abercrombie Lovett (17 Sep 1951)
Attorney General	Thomas Campbell Clark; James Howard McGrath (24 Aug 1949)
Interior	Julius Albert Krug; Oscar Littleton Chapman (19 Jan 1950)
Agriculture	Charles Franklin Brannan
Commerce	Charles Sawyer
Labor	Maurice Joseph Tobin

Dwight D. Eisenhower

20 JAN 1953–20 JAN 1957 (TERM 1)

State	John Foster Dulles
Treasury	George Magoffin Humphrey
Defense	Charles Erwin Wilson
Attorney General	Herbert Brownell
Interior	Douglas McKay; Frederick Andrew Seaton (8 Jun 1956)
Agriculture	Ezra Taft Benson
Commerce	Sinclair Weeks
Labor	Martin Patrick Durkin; James Paul Mitchell (9 Oct 1953)
Health, Education, and Welfare	Oveta Culp Hobby (11 Apr 1953); Marion Bayard Folson (1 Aug 1955)

US Presidential Cabinets (continued)

Dwight D. Eisenhower (continued)

20 JAN 1957–20 JAN 1961 (TERM 2)

State	John Foster Dulles; Christian Archibald Herter (22 Apr 1959)
Treasury	George Magoffin Humphrey; Robert Bernard Anderson (29 Jul 1957)
Defense	Charles Erwin Wilson; Neil Hosler McElroy (9 Oct 1957); Thomas Sovereign Gates, Jr. (2 Dec 1959)
Attorney General	Herbert Brownell, Jr.; William Pierce Rogers (27 Jan 1958)
Interior	Frederick Andrew Seaton
Agriculture	Ezra Taft Benson
Commerce	Sinclair Weeks; Frederick Henry Mueller (10 Aug 1959)
Labor	James Paul Mitchell
Health, Education, and Welfare	Marion Bayard Folsom; Arthur Sherwood Flemming (1 Aug 1958)

John F. Kennedy

20 JAN 1961–22 NOV 1963

State	David Dean Rusk
Treasury	C. Douglas Dillon
Defense	Robert S. McNamara
Attorney General	Robert F. Kennedy
Interior	Stewart L. Udall
Agriculture	Orville Lothrop Freeman
Commerce	Luther H. Hodges
Labor	Arthur J. Goldberg; W. Willard Wirtz (25 Sep 1962)
Health, Education, and Welfare	Abraham Ribicoff; Anthony J. Celebrezze (31 Jul 1962)

Lyndon B. Johnson

22 NOV 1963–20 JAN 1965 (TERM 1)

State	David Dean Rusk
Treasury	C. Douglas Dillon
Defense	Robert S. McNamara
Attorney General	Robert F. Kennedy
Interior	Stewart L. Udall
Agriculture	Orville Lothrop Freeman
Commerce	Luther H. Hodges
Labor	W. Willard Wirtz
Health, Education, and Welfare	Anthony J. Celebrezze

20 JAN 1965–20 JAN 1969 (TERM 2)

State	David Dean Rusk
Treasury	C. Douglas Dillon; Henry H. Fowler (1 Apr 1965); Joseph W. Barr (21 Dec 1968)
Defense	Robert S. McNamara; Clark M. Clifford (1 Mar 1968)
Attorney General	Nicholas Katzenbach; Ramsey Clark (10 Mar 1967)
Interior	Stewart L. Udall
Agriculture	Orville Lothrop Freeman
Commerce	John T. Connor; Alexander B. Trowbridge (14 Jun 1967); C.R. Smith (6 Mar 1968)
Labor	W. Willard Wirtz
Health, Education, and Welfare	Anthony J. Celebrezze; John W. Gardner (18 Aug 1965); Wilbur J. Cohen (9 May 1968)
Housing and Urban Development	Robert C. Weaver (18 Jan 1966); Robert C. Wood (7 Jan 1969)
Transportation	Alan Stephenson Boyd (16 Jan 1967)

Richard M. Nixon

20 JAN 1969–20 JAN 1973 (TERM 1)

State	William Pierce Rogers
Treasury	David M. Kennedy; John B. Connally (11 Feb 1971); George P. Shultz (12 Jun 1972)
Defense	Melvin R. Laird
Attorney General	John N. Mitchell; Richard G. Kleindienst (12 Jun 1972)
Interior	Walter Hickel; Rogers C.B. Morton (29 Jan 1971)
Agriculture	Clifford Morris Hardin; Earl Lauer Butz (2 Dec 1971)
Commerce	Maurice H. Stans; Peter G. Peterson (21 Feb 1972)
Labor	George P. Shultz; James D. Hodgson (2 Jul 1970)
Health, Education, and Welfare	Robert H. Finch; Elliot L. Richardson (24 Jun 1970)
Housing and Urban Development	George W. Romney
Transportation	John Anthony Volpe

US Presidential Cabinets (continued)

Richard M. Nixon (continued)

20 JAN 1973–9 AUG 1974 (TERM 2)

State	William Pierce Rogers; Henry Alfred Kissinger (22 Sep 1973)
Treasury	George P. Shultz; William E. Simon (8 May 1974)
Defense	Elliot L. Richardson; James R. Schlesinger (2 Jul 1973)
Attorney General	Richard G. Kleindienst; Elliot L. Richardson (25 May 1973); William B. Saxbe (4 Jan 1974)
Interior	Rogers C.B. Morton
Agriculture	Earl Lauer Butz
Commerce	Frederick B. Dent
Labor	Peter J. Brennan
Health, Education, and Welfare	Caspar W. Weinberger
Housing and Urban Development	James T. Lynn
Transportation	Claude Stout Brinegar

Gerald R. Ford

9 AUG 1974–20 JAN 1977

State	Henry Alfred Kissinger
Treasury	William E. Simon
Defense	James R. Schlesinger; Donald H. Rumsfeld (20 Nov 1975)
Attorney General	William B. Saxbe; Edward H. Levi (7 Feb 1975)
Interior	Rogers C.B. Morton; Stanley K. Hathaway (13 Jun 1975); Thomas S. Kleppe (17 Oct 1975)
Agriculture	Earl Lauer Butz; John Albert Knebel (4 Nov 1976)
Commerce	Frederick B. Dent; Rogers C.B. Morton (1 May 1975); Elliot L. Richardson (2 Feb 1976)
Labor	Peter J. Brennan; John T. Dunlop (18 Mar 1975); W.J. Usery, Jr. (10 Feb 1976)
Health, Education, and Welfare	Caspar W. Weinberger; David Mathews (8 Aug 1975)
Housing and Urban Development	James T. Lynn; Carla A. Hills (10 Mar 1975)
Transportation	Claude Stout Brinegar; William Thaddeus Coleman, Jr. (7 Mar 1975)

Jimmy Carter

20 JAN 1977–20 JAN 1981

State	Cyrus Roberts Vance; Edmund Sixtus Muskie (8 May 1980)
Treasury	W. Michael Blumenthal; G. William Miller (6 Aug 1979)
Defense	Harold Brown
Attorney General	Griffin B. Bell; Benjamin R. Civiletti (16 Aug 1979)
Interior	Cecil D. Andrus
Agriculture	Robert Selmer Bergland
Commerce	Juanita M. Kreps; Philip M. Klutznick (9 Jan 1980)
Labor	Ray Marshall
Health, Education, and Welfare	Joseph A. Califano, Jr.; Patricia Roberts Harris (3 Aug 1979–4 May 1980)
Health and Human Services	Patricia Roberts Harris (4 May 1980)
Housing and Urban Development	Patricia Roberts Harris; Moon Landrieu (24 Sep 1979)
Transportation	Brockman Adams; Neil Edward Goldschmidt (24 Sep 1979)
Energy	James R. Schlesinger (1 Oct 1977); Charles W. Duncan, Jr. (24 Aug 1979)
Education	Shirley M. Hufstedler (6 Dec 1979)

Ronald Reagan

20 JAN 1981–20 JAN 1985 (TERM 1)

State	Alexander Meigs Haig, Jr.; George P. Shultz (16 Jul 1982)
Treasury	Donald T. Regan
Defense	Caspar W. Weinberger
Attorney General	William French Smith
Interior	James G. Watt; William P. Clark (21 Nov 1983)
Agriculture	John Rusling Block
Commerce	Malcolm Baldrige
Labor	Raymond J. Donovan
Health and Human Services	Richard S. Schweiker; Margaret M. Heckler (9 Mar 1983)
Housing and Urban Development	Samuel R. Pierce, Jr.
Transportation	Andrew Lindsay Lewis, Jr.; Elizabeth Hanford Dole (7 Feb 1983)
Energy	James B. Edwards; Donald Paul Hodel (8 Dec 1982)
Education	Terrel H. Bell

20 JAN 1985–20 JAN 1989 (TERM 2)

State	George P. Shultz
Treasury	James A. Baker III; Nicholas F. Brady (18 Aug 1988)

US Presidential Cabinets (continued)

Ronald Reagan (continued)

20 JAN 1985–20 JAN 1989 (TERM 2) (CONTINUED)

Defense	Caspar W. Weinberger; Frank C. Carlucci (21 Nov 1987)
Attorney General	William French Smith; Edwin Meese III (25 Feb 1985); Richard Thornburgh (11 Aug 1988)
Interior	Donald Paul Hodel
Agriculture	John Rusling Block; Richard Edmund Lyng (7 Mar 1986)
Commerce	Malcolm Baldrige; C. William Verity (19 Oct 1987)
Labor	Raymond J. Donovan; William E. Brock (29 Apr 1985); Ann Dore McLaughlin (17 Dec 1987)
Health and Human Services	Margaret M. Heckler; Otis R. Bowen (13 Dec 1985)
Housing and Urban Development	Samuel R. Pierce, Jr.
Transportation	Elizabeth Hanford Dole; James Horace Burnley IV (3 Dec 1987)
Energy	John S. Herrington
Education	William J. Bennett; Lauro F. Cavazos, Jr. (20 Sep 1988)

George H.W. Bush

20 JAN 1989–20 JAN 1993

State	James A. Baker III; Lawrence Sidney Eagleburger (8 Dec 1992)
Treasury	Nicholas F. Brady
Defense	Richard B. Cheney
Attorney General	Richard Thornburgh; William Barr (20 Nov 1991)
Interior	Manuel Lujan, Jr.
Agriculture	Clayton Keith Yeutter; Edward Rell Madigan (7 Mar 1991)
Commerce	Robert A. Mosbacher; Barbara H. Franklin (27 Feb 1992)
Labor	Elizabeth Hanford Dole; Lynn Morley Martin (7 Feb 1991)
Health and Human Services	Louis W. Sullivan
Housing and Urban Development	Jack F. Kemp
Transportation	Samuel Knox Skinner; Andrew Hill Card, Jr. (22 Jan 1992)
Energy	James D. Watkins
Education	Lauro F. Cavazos, Jr.; Lamar Alexander (14 Mar 1991)
Veterans Affairs	Edward J. Derwinski (15 Mar 1989)

Bill Clinton

20 JAN 1993–20 JAN 1997 (TERM 1)

State	Warren Minor Christopher
Treasury	Lloyd M. Bentsen; Robert E. Rubin (10 Jan 1995)
Defense	Les Aspin; William J. Perry (3 Feb 1994)
Attorney General	Janet Reno
Interior	Bruce Babbitt
Agriculture	Alphonso Michael Espy; Daniel Robert Glickman (30 Mar 1995)
Commerce	Ronald H. Brown; Mickey Kantor (12 Apr 1996)
Labor	Robert B. Reich
Health and Human Services	Donna E. Shalala
Housing and Urban Development	Henry G. Cisneros
Transportation	Federico Fabian Peña
Energy	Hazel R. O'Leary
Education	Richard W. Riley
Veterans Affairs	Jesse Brown

20 JAN 1997–20 JAN 2001 (TERM 2)

State	Madeleine Korbel Albright
Treasury	Robert E. Rubin; Lawrence H. Summers (2 Jul 1999)
Defense	William S. Cohen
Attorney General	Janet Reno
Interior	Bruce Babbitt
Agriculture	Daniel Robert Glickman
Commerce	William M. Daley; Norman Y. Mineta (21 Jul 2000)
Labor	Alexis Herman
Health and Human Services	Donna E. Shalala
Housing and Urban Development	Andrew M. Cuomo
Transportation	Rodney Earl Slater
Energy	Federico Fabian Peña; Bill Richardson (18 Aug 1998)
Education	Richard W. Riley
Veterans Affairs	Togo D. West, Jr.

US Presidential Cabinets (continued)

George W. Bush

20 JAN 2001–20 JAN 2005 (TERM 1)

State	Colin L. Powell
Treasury	Paul H. O'Neill; John W. Snow (3 Feb 2003)
Defense	Donald H. Rumsfeld
Attorney General	John Ashcroft
Interior	Gale A. Norton
Agriculture	Ann M. Veneman
Commerce	Donald L. Evans
Labor	Elaine L. Chao
Health and Human Services	Tommy G. Thompson
Housing and Urban Development	Mel Martinez; Alphonso Jackson (1 Apr 2004)
Transportation	Norman Y. Mineta
Energy	Spencer Abraham
Education	Rod Paige
Veterans Affairs	Anthony J. Principi
Homeland Security	Tom Ridge (8 Oct 2001)

20 JAN 2005–20 JAN 2009 (TERM 2)

State	Condoleezza Rice
Treasury	John W. Snow; Henry M. Paulson, Jr. (10 Jul 2006)
Defense	Donald Rumsfeld; Robert M. Gates (18 Dec 2006)
Attorney General	Alberto R. Gonzales; Michael Mukasey (9 Nov 2007)
Interior	Gale A. Norton; Dirk Kempthorne (26 May 2006)
Agriculture	Mike Johanns; Ed Schafer (28 Jan 2008)
Commerce	Carlos M. Gutierrez
Labor	Elaine L. Chao
Health and Human Services	Michael O. Leavitt
Housing and Urban Development	Alphonso Jackson; Steve Preston (5 Jun 2008)
Transportation	Norman Y. Mineta; Mary E. Peters (30 Sep 2006)
Energy	Samuel W. Bodman
Education	Margaret Spellings
Veterans Affairs	R. James Nicholson; James B. Peake (20 Dec 2007)
Homeland Security	Michael Chertoff

Barack Obama

20 JAN 2009–

		WEB SITE
State	Hillary Clinton	<www.state.gov>
Treasury	Tim Geithner	<www.ustreas.gov>
Defense	Robert M. Gates	<www.defenselink.mil>
Attorney General	Eric Holder	<www.usdoj.gov>
Interior	Ken Salazar	<www.doi.gov>
Agriculture	Tom Vilsack	<www.usda.gov>
Commerce	Gary Locke	<www.commerce.gov>
Labor	Hilda Solis	<www.dol.gov>
Health and Human Services	Kathleen Sebelius	<www.hhs.gov>
Housing and Urban Development	Shaun Donovan	<www.hud.gov>
Transportation	Ray LaHood	<www.dot.gov>
Energy	Steven Chu	<www.energy.gov>
Education	Arne Duncan	<www.ed.gov>
Veterans Affairs	Eric Shinseki	<www.va.gov>
Homeland Security	Janet Napolitano	<www.dhs.gov>

Additionally, the White House lists the following as cabinet-rank members: Vice President Joe Biden, Chief of Staff Rahm Emanuel, Environmental Protection Agency Administrator Lisa P. Jackson, US Trade Representative Ron Kirk, Office of Management and Budget Director Peter Orszag, Council of Economic Advisers Chair Christina Romer, and United States Ambassador to the United Nations Susan Rice.

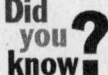

Did you know? Joseph Valachi, who turned informer in 1962, was the first member ever to describe the history, membership, and inner workings of the national crime syndicate popularly called the Mafia, which Valachi termed La Cosa Nostra ("Our Thing"). Attorney General Robert Kennedy called Valachi's testimony the "biggest single intelligence breakthrough yet in combating organized crime and racketeering in the United States."

Supreme Court

Justices of the Supreme Court of the United States

Listed under presidents who made appointments (bold). Chief justices' names appear in italics.

NAME	TERM OF SERVICE[1]
George Washington	
John Jay	1789–95
James Wilson	1789–98
John Rutledge	1790–91
William Cushing	1790–1810
John Blair	1790–96
James Iredell	1790–99
Thomas Johnson	1792–93
William Paterson	1793–1806
John Rutledge[2]	1795
Samuel Chase	1796–1811
Oliver Ellsworth	1796–1800
John Adams	
Bushrod Washington	1799–1829
Alfred Moore	1800–04
John Marshall	1801–35
Thomas Jefferson	
William Johnson	1804–34
Brockholst Livingston	1807–23
Thomas Todd	1807–26
James Madison	
Gabriel Duvall	1811–35
Joseph Story	1812–45
James Monroe	
Smith Thompson	1823–43
John Quincy Adams	
Robert Trimble	1826–28
Andrew Jackson	
John McLean	1830–61
Henry Baldwin	1830–44
James M. Wayne	1835–67
Roger Brooke Taney	1836–64
Philip P. Barbour	1836–41
Martin Van Buren	
John Catron	1837–65
John McKinley	1838–52
Peter V. Daniel	1842–60
John Tyler	
Samuel Nelson	1845–72
James K. Polk	
Levi Woodbury	1845–51
Robert C. Grier	1846–70
Millard Fillmore	
Benjamin R. Curtis	1851–57
Franklin Pierce	
John Archibald Campbell	1853–61
James Buchanan	
Nathan Clifford	1858–81
Abraham Lincoln	
Noah H. Swayne	1862–81
Samuel Freeman Miller	1862–90
David Davis	1862–77
Stephen Johnson Field	1863–97
Salmon P. Chase	1864–73

NAME	TERM OF SERVICE[1]
Ulysses S. Grant	
William Strong	1870–80
Joseph P. Bradley	1870–92
Ward Hunt	1873–82
Morrison Remick Waite	1874–88
Rutherford B. Hayes	
John Marshall Harlan	1877–1911
William B. Woods	1881–87
James A. Garfield	
Stanley Matthews	1881–89
Chester A. Arthur	
Horace Gray	1882–1902
Samuel Blatchford	1882–93
Grover Cleveland	
Lucius Q.C. Lamar	1888–93
Melville Weston Fuller	1888–1910
Benjamin Harrison	
David J. Brewer	1890–1910
Henry B. Brown	1891–1906
George Shiras, Jr.	1892–1903
Howell E. Jackson	1893–95
Grover Cleveland	
Edward Douglass White	1894–1910
Rufus Wheeler Peckham	1896–1909
William McKinley	
Joseph McKenna	1898–1925
Theodore Roosevelt	
Oliver Wendell Holmes	1902–32
William R. Day	1903–22
William H. Moody	1906–10
William Howard Taft	
Horace H. Lurton	1910–14
Charles Evans Hughes	1910–16
Willis Van Devanter	1911–37
Joseph R. Lamar	1911–16
Edward Douglass White	1910–21
Mahlon Pitney	1912–22
Woodrow Wilson	
James C. McReynolds	1914–41
Louis Brandeis	1916–39
John H. Clarke	1916–22
Warren G. Harding	
William Howard Taft	1921–30
George Sutherland	1922–38
Pierce Butler	1923–39
Edward T. Sanford	1923–30
Calvin Coolidge	
Harlan Fiske Stone	1925–41
Herbert Hoover	
Charles Evans Hughes	1930–41
Owen Roberts	1930–45
Benjamin N. Cardozo	1932–38

NAME	TERM OF SERVICE[1]
Franklin D. Roosevelt	
Hugo L. Black	1937–71
Stanley F. Reed	1938–57
Felix Frankfurter	1939–62
William O. Douglas	1939–75
Frank Murphy	1940–49
Harlan Fiske Stone	1941–46
James F. Byrnes	1941–42
Robert H. Jackson	1941–54
Wiley B. Rutledge	1943–49
Harry S. Truman	
Harold H. Burton	1945–58
Fred M. Vinson	1946–53
Tom C. Clark	1949–67
Sherman Minton	1949–56
Dwight D. Eisenhower	
Earl Warren	1953–69
John Marshall Harlan	1955–71
William J. Brennan, Jr.	1956–90
Charles E. Whittaker	1957–62
Potter Stewart	1958–81
John F. Kennedy	
Byron R. White	1962–93
Arthur J. Goldberg	1962–65
Lyndon B. Johnson	
Abe Fortas	1965–69
Thurgood Marshall	1967–91
Richard M. Nixon	
Warren E. Burger	1969–86
Harry A. Blackmun	1970–94
Lewis F. Powell, Jr.	1972–87
William H. Rehnquist	1972–86
Gerald Ford	
John Paul Stevens	1975–
Ronald Reagan	
Sandra Day O'Connor	1981–2006
William H. Rehnquist	1986–2005
Antonin Scalia	1986–
Anthony M. Kennedy	1988–
George H.W. Bush	
David H. Souter	1990–2009
Clarence Thomas	1991–
Bill Clinton	
Ruth Bader Ginsburg	1993–
Stephen G. Breyer	1994–
George W. Bush	
John G. Roberts	2005–
Samuel Anthony Alito, Jr.	2006–
Barack Obama	
Sonia Sotomayor	2009–

[1]*The year the justice took the judicial oath is here used as the beginning date of service, for until that oath is taken the justice is not vested with the prerogatives of the office. Justices, however, receive their commissions ("letters patent") before taking their oaths—in some instances, in the preceding year.* [2]*John Rutledge was acting chief justice; the US Senate refused to confirm him.*

Milestones of US Supreme Court Jurisprudence

Information includes cases' short names, citation, year of release, and a short description of the Supreme Court's findings and importance for US law.

Marbury v. *Madison*, 5 U.S. 137 (1803): the first instance in which the high court declared an act of Congress (the Judiciary Act of 1789, which in part authorized the court to compel action by the executive branch) to be unconstitutional, thus establishing the doctrine of judicial review.

Martin v. *Hunter's Lessee*, 14 U.S. 304 (1816): asserted the US Supreme Court's power of appellate review of state Supreme Court decisions.

Dred Scott v. *Sandford*, 60 U.S. 393 (1857): ruled that blacks, free or enslaved, were not citizens under the Constitution, and further determined that only states, and not Congress or territorial governments, had the power to prohibit slavery, thus overturning the Missouri Compromise of 1820 and legalizing slavery in all US territories.

Plessy v. *Ferguson*, 163 U.S. 537 (1896): permitted racial segregation in "separate but equal" public facilities.

Lochner v. *New York*, 198 U.S. 45 (1905): found that a state labor law limiting the number of hours in the work week violated due process because the "right of contract between the employer and employees" is protected under the Fourteenth Amendment.

Standard Oil Co. of New Jersey et al. v. *United States*, 221 U.S. 1 (1911): ruled that the activities of the Standard Oil Company of New Jersey, a holding company that through its subsidiaries controlled most of the US petroleum industry, constituted an undue restraint of trade and ordered the company's dissolution under the Sherman Antitrust Act.

Schenck v. *United States*, 249 U.S. 47 (1919): found, in the case of an American socialist convicted of espionage for distributing antidraft leaflets during wartime, that First Amendment freedom of expression is limited when there exists a "clear and present danger that [the speech] will bring about the substantive evils that Congress has a right to prevent."

Brown v. *Board of Education of Topeka*, 349 U.S. 294 (1954): ruled that racial segregation in public schools violated the Fourteenth Amendment, overturning the doctrine of "separate but equal" facilities reached in *Plessy* v. *Ferguson*.

Mapp v. *Ohio*, 367 U.S. 643 (1961): found that the Fourth Amendment prohibition of unreasonable search and seizure, and the inadmissibility of evidence obtained in violation of it, applied to state as well as to federal government.

Gideon v. *Wainwright*, 372 U.S. 335 (1963): declared that the Sixth Amendment right to counsel applies to defendants in state as well as federal courts.

New York Times Co. v. *Sullivan*, 376 U.S. 254 (1964): protected the press from the prospects of large damage awards in libel cases by requiring that "actual malice" be demonstrated; public officials who sue for damages must prove that a falsehood had been issued with knowledge that it was false or in reckless disregard of whether it was false or not.

Heart of Atlanta Motel v. *United States*, 379 U.S. 241; *Katzenbach* v. *McClung*, 379 U.S. 294 (1964): upheld Title II of the Civil Rights Act of 1964 (which prohibits segregation or discrimination in places of public accommodation involved in interstate commerce) in the cases of an Atlanta motel and a Birmingham AL restaurant, both of which discriminated against blacks. The court ruled that both engaged in transactions affecting interstate commerce, and thus were within the purview of congressional regulation, and that the Civil Rights Act itself was constitutional.

Griswold v. *Connecticut*, 381 U.S. 479 (1965): ruled that a state law prohibiting the use of contraceptives (including providing information, advice, or prescriptions for them) violated "the right of marital privacy" implied within the Bill of Rights.

Miranda v. *Arizona*, 384 U.S. 436 (1966): ruled that the prosecution may not use statements made by a person in police custody unless minimum procedural safeguards were followed and established guidelines to guarantee arrested persons' Fifth Amendment right not to be compelled to incriminate themselves. These guidelines included informing arrestees prior to questioning that they have the right to remain silent, that anything they say may be used against them as evidence, and that they have the right to the counsel of an attorney.

Loving v. *Virginia*, 388 U.S. 1 (1967): declared that antimiscegenation laws (prohibitions of interracial marriage) have no legitimate purpose outside of racial discrimination and thus violate the Fourteenth Amendment.

New York Times Co. v. *United States*, 403 U.S. 713 (1971): in what was known as the "Pentagon Papers" case, the court vacated a US Justice Department injunction that restrained the *New York Times* and *Washington Post* from publishing excerpts of a top-secret report on the Vietnam War, ruling that such prior restraint of the press was subject to a "heavy burden of...justification," which the government failed to meet.

Roe v. *Wade*, 410 U.S. 113 (1973): held that overly restrictive state regulation of abortion is unconstitutional. In balancing the "compelling state interest[s]" in protecting the health of pregnant women and the potential life of fetuses, the court ruled that regulation of abortion could begin no sooner than about the end of the first trimester, with increasing regulation permissible in the second and third trimesters; the state's interest in protecting the fetus was found to increase with the fetus's "capability for meaningful life outside the mother's womb."

Gregg v. *Georgia*, 428 U.S. 153; *Proffitt* v. *Florida*, 428 U.S. 242; *Jurek* v. *Texas*, 428 U.S. 262 (1976): ruled that the death penalty, in and of itself, does not violate the Eighth Amendment if applied under certain guidelines in first-degree murder cases.

Cruzan by Cruzan v. *Director, Missouri Department of Health*, 497 U.S. 261 (1990): found that, in the absence of "clear and convincing evidence" of a person's desire to refuse medical treatment or not to live on life support, a state could require that such treatment continue. When such evidence exists, however, a patient's wishes must be respected.

Planned Parenthood of Southeastern Pennsylvania v. *Casey*, 505 U.S. 833 (1992): softened the ruling in *Roe* v. *Wade* by finding that some state regulation of abortion prior to fetal viability, including a 24-hour waiting period, mandatory counseling, and a parental-consent requirement for minors, is permissible as long as the regulations do not place an "undue burden" on the woman.

Romer v. Evans, 517 U.S. 620 (1996): invalidated a Colorado referendum passed by popular vote that prohibited conferral of protected status on the basis of sexual orientation; the court ruled that the referendum was overbroad, bore little relationship to legimate state interests, and violated the Fourteenth Amendment of the US Constitution.

Oncale v. Sundowner Offshore Services, Inc., et al., 523 U.S. 75 (1998): found that Title VII's prohibition of workplace sexual discrimination applied equally in cases when the harasser and victim are of the same sex.

Boy Scouts of America v. Dale, 530 U.S. 640 (2000): ruled that the Boy Scouts, because it is a private organization, was within its rights when it dismissed a scoutmaster expressly because of his avowed homosexuality. The court reasoned that a state statute banning discrimination on the basis of sexual orientation in places of public accommodation was outweighed by the Scouts' First Amendment right to freedom of association.

Stenberg v. Carhart, 530 U.S. 914 (2000): ruled that a state law criminalizing the performance of dilation and extraction—or "partial-birth"—abortions violated the Constitution (following the same reasoning as in *Roe v. Wade*) because it allowed no consideration of the health of the woman in choosing the procedure.

Bush v. Gore, 531 U.S. 98 (2000): stopped the manual recounts, then under way in certain Florida counties at the demand of Al Gore, of disputed ballots from the November 2000 presidential election on the grounds that inconsistent vote-counting standards among the several counties involved amounted to a violation of the Fourteenth Amendment's equal protection clause. Because George W. Bush at the time led Al Gore in the number of officially recognized Florida votes, the decision meant that he would win the state and thus the general election, despite having lost the popular vote.

Atkins v. Virginia, 536 U.S. 304 (2002): ruled that the death penalty, when applied to mentally retarded individuals, constitutes a "cruel and unusual punishment" prohibited by the Eighth Amendment.

Lockyer v. Andrade, 538 U.S. 63; Ewing v. California, 538 U.S. 11 (2003): upheld a "three-strikes" law that imposes long prison sentences for a third offense, even nonviolent crimes.

State Farm Mutual Auto Insurance Co. v. Campbell, 538 U.S. 408 (2003): placed limits on "irrational and arbitrary" punitive damages and established new guidelines that generally bar consideration of a defendant's wealth or conduct outside the state's borders and lower the ratio of punitive to compensatory damages.

United States v. American Library Association, 539 U.S. 194 (2003): upheld the Children's Internet Protection Act, which conditions access to federal grants and subsidies upon the installation of antipornography filters on all Internet-connected computers.

Georgia v. Ashcroft, 539 U.S. 461 (2003): ruled that race-sensitive redistricting could consider more general minority influence in the political process when drawing particular district lines rather than addressing only the actual number of minority voters present.

Lawrence v. Texas, 539 U.S. 558 (2003): explicitly overruling *Bowers v. Hardwick*, 478 U.S. 186 (1986), the court declared that gay men and lesbians are "entitled to respect for their private lives" under the due process clause of the Fourteenth Amendment and rendered unconstitutional state statutes outlawing sex between adults of the same gender.

Blakely v. Washington, 542 U.S. 296 (2004): held that the Washington state system permitting judges to make independent findings that increase a convicted defendant's sentence beyond the ordinary range for the crime violated the Sixth Amendment guarantee of a right to trial by jury and to a higher standard of proof.

Cheney v. US District Court, 542 U.S. 367 (2004): sent the Sierra Club and Judicial Watch back to the lower court in a dispute over the level of executive privilege the vice president's energy-policy task force exercised in the face of discovery orders. The court held that "[s]pecial considerations control when the Executive's interests in maintaining its autonomy and safeguarding its communications' confidentiality are implicated."

Hamdi v. Rumsfeld, 542 U.S. 507; Rasul v. Bush, 542 U.S. 466 (2004): ruled that while Congress may empower the executive branch to detain even US citizens as enemy combatants, any enemy combatant in US custody may challenge detention as illegal in federal court with the assistance of counsel. The court declared that "a state of war is not a blank check for the president when it comes to the rights of the nation's citizens."

United States v. Booker and **United States v. Fanfan, 543 U.S. 220 (2005):** ruled that mandatory federal sentencing guidelines violated defendants' Sixth Amendment right to jury trials because they require judges to make decisions affecting prison time.

Roper v. Simmons, 543 U.S. 551 (2005): held that the execution of a felon who had committed a capital crime while a juvenile violates the Eighth Amendment prohibition of cruel and unusual punishment, noting that "the State cannot extinguish [the juvenile defendant's] life and his potential to attain a mature understanding of his own humanity."

Kelo v. City of New London, 545 U.S. 469 (2005): found that governmental entities may exercise the power of eminent domain over private property and cede the property to private developers to promote economic growth, so long as a carefully formulated plan to provide significant benefits to the community provides a rational basis for the taking.

Gonzales v. Oregon, 546 U.S. 243 (2006): ruled that an Oregon law permitting physicians to provide lethal drugs to terminally ill patients did not violate the Controlled Substances Act.

Hamdan v. Rumsfeld, 548 U.S. 557 (2006): ruled that the government's special military commissions were not lawful courts. The commissions were to have tried some of the prisoners who had been captured in the "global war on terror."

Gonzales v. Carhart, 550 U.S. 124 (2007): held that a federal law banning "partial-birth" abortion was not unconstitutional.

Parents Involved in Community Schools v. Seattle School District No. 1, 551 U.S. 701 (2007): held that using a student's race in determining the availability of a spot at a desired school, even for the purpose of preventing resegregation, violated the 14th Amendment.

Hein v. Freedom from Religion Foundation, 551 U.S. 587 (2007): ruled that taxpayers had no standing to challenge the use of federal money to support the Office of Faith-Based and Community Initiatives, despite questions about the separation of church and state.

District of Columbia v. Heller, 554 U.S. ___ (2008): ruled that citizens have the right to bear arms without the need to be in service to a militia. This decision struck down a Washington DC handgun ban and threatened scores of other such bans nationwide.

Boumediene v. Bush, 553 U.S. ___ (2008): ruled that foreign prisoners held at Guantánamo Bay, Cuba, have the right to challenge their detention in US courts.

District Attorney's Office for the Third Judicial District v. Osborne, 557 U.S. ___ (2009): ruled that persons convicted of crimes do not have the constitutionally protected right to order advanced post-conviction DNA testing of evidence, even in the face of technological advances that may prove the innocence of the convicted person.

Ricci v. DeStefano, 557 U.S. ___ (2009): held that Title VII of the Civil Rights Act of 1964 prohibiting intentional acts of employment discrimination based on, among other factors, race, was violated by a ruling giving employment to minority candidates who had scored lower on employment tests than had white candidates.

United States Congress

Parties: Democratic (D); Republican (R); Independent (I).

Senate, 111th Congress

*Party totals: **Democrats:** 58; **Republicans:** 40; **Independents:** 2.*

According to Article I, Section 3 of the US Constitution, a US senator must be at least 30 years old, must reside in the state he or she represents at the time of the election, and must have been a citizen of the United States for at least nine years. Voters elect two senators from each state; terms are for six years and begin on 3 January. Each current senator's annual salary is US$174,000. The majority and minority leaders and the president pro tempore receive US$193,400 per year.

Senate leadership

president:	Joe Biden
president pro tempore:	Robert C. Byrd
majority leader:	Harry Reid
minority leader:	Mitch McConnell
asst. majority leader (majority whip):	Dick Durbin
asst. minority leader (minority whip):	Jon Kyl

US Senate Web site: <www.senate.gov>.

STATE	NAME (PARTY)	SERVICE BEGAN	TERM ENDS
Alabama	Richard Shelby (R)	1987	2011
	Jeff Sessions (R)	1997	2015
Alaska	Lisa Murkowski (R)	2002	2011
	Mark Begich (D)	2009	2015
Arizona	John McCain (R)	1987	2011
	Jon Kyl (R)	1995	2013
Arkansas	Blanche Lincoln (D)	1999	2011
	Mark Pryor (D)	2003	2015
California	Dianne Feinstein (D)	1992[1]	2013
	Barbara Boxer (D)	1993	2011
Colorado	Mark Udall (D)	2009	2015
	Michael F. Bennet (D)	2009[2]	2011
Connecticut	Chris Dodd (D)	1981	2011
	Joe Lieberman (ID)	1989	2013
Delaware	Tom Carper (D)	2001	2013
	Ted Kaufman (D)	2009[3]	2011
Florida	Bill Nelson (D)	2001	2013
	George LeMieux (R)	2009[4]	2011
Georgia	Saxby Chambliss (R)	2003	2015
	Johnny Isakson (R)	2005	2011
Hawaii	Daniel K. Inouye (D)	1963	2011
	Daniel Kahikina Akaka (D)	1990[5]	2013
Idaho	Mike Crapo (R)	1999	2011
	James E. Risch (R)	2009	2015
Illinois	Dick Durbin (D)	1997	2015
	Roland W. Burris (D)	2009[6]	2011
Indiana	Richard G. Lugar (R)	1977	2013
	Evan Bayh (D)	1999	2011
Iowa	Chuck Grassley (R)	1981	2011
	Tom Harkin (D)	1985	2015
Kansas	Sam Brownback (R)	1996[7]	2011
	Pat Roberts (R)	1997	2015
Kentucky	Mitch McConnell (R)	1985	2015
	Jim Bunning (R)	1999	2011
Louisiana	Mary L. Landrieu (D)	1997	2015
	David Vitter (R)	2005	2011
Maine	Olympia J. Snowe (R)	1995	2013
	Susan Collins (R)	1997	2015
Maryland	Barbara Mikulski (D)	1987	2011
	Benjamin L. Cardin (D)	2007	2013

Senate, 111th Congress (continued)

STATE	NAME (PARTY)	SERVICE BEGAN	TERM ENDS
Massachusetts	John Kerry (D)	1985	2015
	vacant[8]		
Michigan	Carl Levin (D)	1979	2015
	Debbie Stabenow (D)	2001	2013
Minnesota	Amy Klobuchar (D)	2007	2013
	Al Franken (D)	2009	2015
Mississippi	Thad Cochran (R)	1979	2015
	Roger Wicker (R)	2007[9]	2015
Missouri	Kit Bond (R)	1987	2011
	Claire McCaskill (D)	2007	2013
Montana	Max Baucus (D)	1979	2015
	Jon Tester (D)	2007	2013
Nebraska	Ben Nelson (D)	2001	2013
	Mike Johanns (R)	2009	2015
Nevada	Harry Reid (D)	1987	2011
	John Ensign (R)	2001	2013
New Hampshire	Judd Gregg (R)	1993	2011
	Jeanne Shaheen (D)	2009	2015
New Jersey	Frank R. Lautenberg (D)	2003	2015
	Robert Menendez (D)	2006[10]	2013
New Mexico	Jeff Bingaman (D)	1983	2013
	Tom Udall (D)	2009	2015
New York	Charles E. Schumer (D)	1999	2011
	Kirsten Gillibrand (D)	2009[11]	2011
North Carolina	Richard Burr (R)	2005	2011
	Kay Hagan (D)	2009	2015
North Dakota	Kent Conrad (D)	1987	2013
	Byron L. Dorgan (D)	1993	2011
Ohio	George V. Voinovich (R)	1999	2011
	Sherrod Brown (D)	2007	2013
Oklahoma	James M. Inhofe (R)	1994[12]	2015
	Tom Coburn (R)	2005	2011
Oregon	Ron Wyden (D)	1996[13]	2011
	Jeff Merkley (D)	2009	2015
Pennsylvania	Arlen Specter (D)	1981	2011
	Robert P. Casey (D)	2007	2013
Rhode Island	Jack Reed (D)	1997	2015
	Sheldon Whitehouse (D)	2007	2013
South Carolina	Lindsey Graham (R)	2003	2015
	Jim DeMint (R)	2005	2011
South Dakota	Tim Johnson (D)	1997	2015
	John Thune (R)	2005	2011
Tennessee	Lamar Alexander (R)	2003	2015
	Bob Corker (R)	2007	2013
Texas	Kay Bailey Hutchison (R)	1993[14]	2013
	John Cornyn (R)	2002	2015
Utah	Orrin G. Hatch (R)	1977	2013
	Bob Bennett (R)	1993	2011
Vermont	Patrick Leahy (D)	1975	2011
	Bernie Sanders (I)	2007	2013
Virginia	Jim Webb (D)	2007	2013
	Mark R. Warner (D)	2009	2015
Washington	Patty Murray (D)	1993	2011
	Maria Cantwell (D)	2001	2013
West Virginia	Robert C. Byrd (D)	1959	2013
	Jay Rockefeller (D)	1985	2015
Wisconsin	Herb Kohl (D)	1989	2013
	Russ Feingold (D)	1993	2011
Wyoming	Mike Enzi (R)	1997	2015
	John Barrasso (R)	2007[15]	2015

[1]*Dianne Feinstein was elected in November 1992 to complete the term of Pete Wilson, who resigned in 1991 to become California's governor.* [2]*Michael F. Bennet was appointed in January 2009 to complete the term of Ken Salazar, who resigned to become secretary of the interior.* [3]*Ted Kaufman was appointed in January 2009 to replace Joe Biden, who resigned to become vice president.* [4]*George LeMieux was appointed in September 2009 to complete the term of Mel Martinez, who resigned.* [5]*Daniel Kahikina Akaka was appointed in April 1990 after winning a special election to fill the vacancy caused by the death of Spark M. Matsunaga.* [6]*Roland W. Burris was appointed in December 2008 and took office in January 2009 to complete the term of Barack Obama, who*

Senate, 111th Congress (continued)

resigned to become president. [7]Sam Brownback was elected in November 1996 to complete the term of Bob Dole, who resigned to campaign for the presidency. [8]At press time the seat made vacant by the death of Edward M. Kennedy had not been filled. [9]Roger Wicker was appointed in December 2007 to fill the vacancy caused by the resignation of Trent Lott. [10]Robert Menendez was appointed in January 2006 to fill the vacancy caused by the resignation of Jon S. Corzine. [11]Kirsten Gillibrand was appointed in January 2009 to replace Hillary Rodham Clinton, who resigned to become secretary of state. [12]James M. Inhofe was elected in November 1994 to complete the term of David Boren, who resigned to become president of the University of Oklahoma. [13]Ron Wyden was elected in January 1996 to complete the term of Bob Packwood, who resigned in 1995. [14]Kay Bailey Hutchison was elected in June 1993 to complete the term of Lloyd Bentsen, Jr., who resigned to become secretary of the treasury. [15]John Barrasso was appointed in June 2007 to fill the vacancy caused by the death of Craig Thomas.

Senate Standing Committees

COMMITTEE	CHAIRMAN (PARTY–STATE)	RANKING MINORITY MEMBER (PARTY–STATE)	NUMBER OF MEMBERS MAJORITY	NUMBER OF MEMBERS MINORITY	NUMBER OF SUBCOMMITTEES
Agriculture, Nutrition, and Forestry	Tom Harkin (D-IA)	Saxby Chambliss (R-GA)	12	8	5
Appropriations	Daniel K. Inouye (D-HI)	Thad Cochran (R-MS)	18	12	12
Armed Services	Carl Levin (D-MI)	John McCain (R-AZ)	15	11	6
Banking, Housing, and Urban Affairs	Chris Dodd (D-CT)	Richard Shelby (R-AL)	13	10	5
Budget	Kent Conrad (D-ND)	Judd Gregg (R-NH)	13[1]	10	none
Commerce, Science, and Transportation	Jay Rockefeller (D-WV)	Kay Bailey Hutchison (R-TX)	14	11	7
Energy and Natural Resources	Jeff Bingaman (D-NM)	Lisa Murkowski (R-AK)	13[1]	10	4
Environment and Public Works	Barbara Boxer (D-CA)	James M. Imhofe (R-OK)	12[1]	7	7
Finance	Max Baucus (D-MT)	Chuck Grassley (R-IA)	13	10	5
Foreign Relations	John Kerry (D-MA)	Richard G. Lugar (R-IN)	11	7	7
Health, Education, Labor, and Pensions	vacant	Mike Enzi (R-WY)	11[1]	10	3
Homeland Security and Governmental Affairs	Joe Lieberman (ID-CT)	Susan Collins (R-ME)	10	6	3
Judiciary	Patrick Leahy (D-VT)	Jeff Sessions (R-AL)	12	7	7
Rules and Administration	Charles E. Schumer (D-NY)	Bob Bennett (R-UT)	11	8	none
Small Business and Entrepreneurship	Mary L. Landrieu (D-LA)	Olympia J. Snowe (R-ME)	11	8	none
Veterans' Affairs	Daniel Kahikina Akaka (D-HI)	Richard Burr (R-NC)	10[1]	5	none

[1]Bernie Sanders is an Independent but caucuses with the Democratic Party.

Senate Special, Select, and Other Committees

COMMITTEE	CHAIRMAN (PARTY–STATE)	RANKING MINORITY MEMBER (PARTY–STATE)	NUMBER OF MEMBERS MAJORITY	NUMBER OF MEMBERS MINORITY
Special Committee on Aging	Herb Kohl (D-WI)	vacant	12	6
Select Committee on Ethics	Barbara Boxer (D-CA)	Johnny Isakson (R-GA)	3	3
Committee on Indian Affairs	Byron L. Dorgan (D-ND)	John Barrasso (R-WY)	8	6
Select Committee on Intelligence	Dianne Feinstein (D-CA)	Kit Bond (R-MO)	8	7

House of Representatives, 111th Congress

Party totals: **Democrats** 256; **Republicans** 178.

According to Article I, Section 2 of the US Constitution, a US representative must be at least 25 years old, must reside in the state he or she represents at the time of the election, and must have been a citizen of the United States for at least seven years. Each state is entitled to at least one representative, with additional seats apportioned based on population. Each congressperson originally represented 30,000 people; the range in 2008 was from 525,394 (Rhode Island) to 967,440 (Montana) persons per representative. Terms are for two years and begin on 3 January (unless otherwise noted). The current representative's salary is US$174,000 per year. The majority and minority leaders receive US$193,400 per year; the speaker of the House receives US$223,500 per year.

American Samoa, the District of Columbia, Guam, the Northern Mariana Islands, and the Virgin Islands

House of Representatives, 111th Congress (continued)

elect delegates; Puerto Rico elects a resident commissioner. Their formal duties are the same, but the resident commissioner serves a four-year term. They may participate in debate and serve on committees but are not permitted to vote.

Numbers preceding the names refer to districts. Certain states gained (+) or lost (−) districts by reapportionment since the 107th Congress.

House leadership

speaker of the House:	Nancy Pelosi
majority leader:	Steny H. Hoyer
minority leader:	John A. Boehner
majority whip:	James E. Clyburn
minority whip:	Eric Cantor

US House Web site: <www.house.gov>.

STATE	REPRESENTATIVES	SERVICE BEGAN
Alabama	1. Jo Bonner (R)	Jan 2003
	2. Bobby Bright (D)	Jan 2009
	3. Mike Rogers (R)	Jan 2003
	4. Robert B. Aderholt (R)	Jan 1997
	5. Parker Griffith (D)	Jan 2009
	6. Spencer Bachus (R)	Jan 1993
	7. Artur Davis (D)	Jan 2003
Alaska	Don Young (R)	Mar 1973
Arizona (+2)	1. Ann Kirkpatrick (D)	Jan 2009
	2. Trent Franks (R)	Jan 2003
	3. John B. Shadegg (R)	Jan 1995
	4. Ed Pastor (D)	Sep 1991
	5. Harry E. Mitchell (D)	Jan 2007
	6. Jeff Flake (R)	Jan 2001
	7. Raúl M. Grijalva (D)	Jan 2003
	8. Gabrielle Giffords (D)	Jan 2007
Arkansas	1. Marion Berry (D)	Jan 1997
	2. Vic Snyder (D)	Jan 1997
	3. John Boozman (R)[1]	Nov 2001
	4. Mike Ross (D)	Jan 2001
California (+1)	1. Mike Thompson (D)	Jan 1999
	2. Wally Herger (R)	Jan 1987
	3. Daniel E. Lungren (R)	Jan 2005
	4. Tom McClintock (R)	Jan 2009
	5. Doris O. Matsui (D)[2]	Mar 2005
	6. Lynn C. Woolsey (D)	Jan 1993
	7. George Miller (D)	Jan 1975
	8. Nancy Pelosi (D)	Jun 1987
	9. Barbara Lee (D)	Apr 1998
	10. vacant[3]	
	11. Jerry McNerney (D)	Jan 2007
	12. Jackie Speier (D)[4]	Apr 2008
	13. Fortney ("Pete") Stark (D)	Jan 1973
	14. Anna G. Eshoo (D)	Jan 1993
	15. Michael M. Honda (D)	Jan 2001
	16. Zoe Lofgren (D)	Jan 1995
	17. Sam Farr (D)	Jun 1993
	18. Dennis A. Cardoza (D)	Jan 2003
	19. George Radanovich (R)	Jan 1995
	20. Jim Costa (D)	Jan 2005
	21. Devin Nunes (R)	Jan 2003
	22. Kevin McCarthy (R)	Jan 2007
	23. Lois Capps (D)	Mar 1998
	24. Elton Gallegly (R)	Jan 1987
	25. Howard P. ("Buck") McKeon (R)	Jan 1993
	26. David Dreier (R)	Jan 1981
	27. Brad Sherman (D)	Jan 1997
	28. Howard L. Berman (D)	Jan 1983
	29. Adam B. Schiff (D)	Jan 2001
	30. Henry A. Waxman (D)	Jan 1975
	31. Xavier Becerra (D)	Jan 1993
	32. Judy Chu (D)[5]	Jul 2009
	33. Diane E. Watson (D)[6]	Jun 2001
	34. Lucille Roybal-Allard (D)	Jan 1993

STATE	REPRESENTATIVES	SERVICE BEGAN
California (cont.)	35. Maxine Waters (D)	Jan 1991
	36. Jane Harman (D)[7]	Jan 1993
	37. Laura Richardson (D)[8]	Sep 2007
	38. Grace F. Napolitano (D)	Jan 1999
	39. Linda T. Sánchez (D)	Jan 2003
	40. Edward R. Royce (R)	Jan 1993
	41. Jerry Lewis (R)	Jan 1979
	42. Gary G. Miller (R)	Jan 1999
	43. Joe Baca (D)	Nov 1999
	44. Ken Calvert (R)	Jan 1993
	45. Mary Bono Mack (R)	Apr 1998
	46. Dana Rohrabacher (R)	Jan 1989
	47. Loretta Sanchez (D)	Jan 1997
	48. John Campbell (R)[9]	Dec 2005
	49. Darrell E. Issa (R)	Jan 2001
	50. Brian P. Bilbray (R)[10]	Jan 1995
	51. Bob Filner (D)	Jan 1993
	52. Duncan Hunter (R)	Jan 2009
	53. Susan A. Davis (D)	Jan 2001
Colorado (+1)	1. Diana DeGette (D)	Jan 1997
	2. Jared Polis (D)	Jan 2009
	3. John T. Salazar (D)	Jan 2005
	4. Betsy Markey (D)	Jan 2009
	5. Doug Lamborn (R)	Jan 2007
	6. Mike Coffman (R)	Jan 2009
	7. Ed Perlmutter (D)	Jan 2007
Connecticut (−1)	1. John B. Larson (D)	Jan 1999
	2. Joe Courtney (D)	Jan 2007
	3. Rosa L. DeLauro (D)	Jan 1991
	4. James A. Himes (D)	Jan 2009
	5. Christopher S. Murphy (D)	Jan 2007
Delaware	Michael N. Castle (R)	Jan 1993
Florida (+2)	1. Jeff Miller (R)[11]	Oct 2001
	2. Allen Boyd (D)	Jan 1997
	3. Corrine Brown (D)	Jan 1993
	4. Ander Crenshaw (R)	Jan 2001
	5. Ginny Brown-Waite (R)	Jan 2003
	6. Cliff Stearns (R)	Jan 1989
	7. John L. Mica (R)	Jan 1993
	8. Alan Grayson (D)	Jan 2009
	9. Gus M. Bilirakis (R)	Jan 2007
	10. C.W. Bill Young (R)	Jan 1971
	11. Kathy Castor (D)	Jan 2007
	12. Adam H. Putnam (R)	Jan 2001
	13. Vern Buchanan (R)	Jan 2007
	14. Connie Mack (R)	Jan 2005
	15. Bill Posey (R)	Jan 2009
	16. Thomas J. Rooney (R)	Jan 2009
	17. Kendrick B. Meek (D)	Jan 2003
	18. Ileana Ros-Lehtinen (R)	Aug 1989
	19. Robert Wexler (D)	Jan 1997
	20. Debbie Wasserman Schultz (D)	Jan 2005
	21. Lincoln Diaz-Balart (R)	Jan 1993
	22. Ron Klein (D)	Jan 2007

House of Representatives, 111th Congress (continued)

STATE	REPRESENTATIVES	SERVICE BEGAN
Florida (cont.)	23. Alcee L. Hastings (D)	Jan 1993
	24. Suzanne M. Kosmas (D)	Jan 2009
	25. Mario Diaz-Balart (R)	Jan 2003
Georgia (+2)	1. Jack Kingston (R)	Jan 1993
	2. Sanford D. Bishop, Jr. (D)	Jan 1993
	3. Lynn A. Westmoreland (R)	Jan 2005
	4. Henry C. ("Hank") Johnson, Jr. (D)	Jan 2007
	5. John Lewis (D)	Jan 1987
	6. Tom Price (R)	Feb 2005
	7. John Linder (R)	Jan 1993
	8. Jim Marshall (D)	Jan 2003
	9. Nathan Deal (R)	Jan 1993
	10. Paul C. Broun (R)[12]	Jul 2007
	11. Phil Gingrey (R)	Jan 2003
	12. John Barrow (D)	Jan 2005
	13. David Scott (D)	Jan 2003
Hawaii	1. Neil Abercrombie (D)[13]	Sep 1986
	2. Mazie K. Hirono (D)	Jan 2007
Idaho	1. Walt Minnick (D)	Jan 2009
	2. Michael K. Simpson (R)	Jan 1999
Illinois (−1)	1. Bobby L. Rush (D)	Jan 1993
	2. Jesse L. Jackson, Jr. (D)	Dec 1995
	3. Daniel Lipinski (D)	Jan 2005
	4. Luis V. Gutierrez (D)	Jan 1993
	5. Mike Quigley (D)[14]	Apr 2009
	6. Peter J. Roskam (R)	Jan 2007
	7. Danny K. Davis (D)	Jan 1997
	8. Melissa L. Bean (D)	Jan 2005
	9. Janice D. Schakowsky (D)	Jan 1999
	10. Mark Steven Kirk (R)	Jan 2001
	11. Deborah L. Halvorson (D)	Jan 2009
	12. Jerry F. Costello (D)	Aug 1988
	13. Judy Biggert (R)	Jan 1999
	14. Bill Foster (D)[15]	Mar 2008
	15. Timothy V. Johnson (R)	Jan 2001
	16. Donald A. Manzullo (R)	Jan 1993
	17. Phil Hare (D)	Jan 2007
	18. Aaron Schock (R)	Jan 2009
	19. John Shimkus (R)	Jan 1997
Indiana (−1)	1. Peter J. Visclosky (D)	Jan 1985
	2. Joe Donnelly (D)	Jan 2007
	3. Mark E. Souder (R)	Jan 1995
	4. Steve Buyer (R)	Jan 1993
	5. Dan Burton (R)	Jan 1983
	6. Mike Pence (R)	Jan 2001
	7. André Carson (D)[16]	Mar 2008
	8. Brad Ellsworth (D)	Jan 2007
	9. Baron P. Hill (D)[17]	Jan 1999
Iowa	1. Bruce L. Braley (D)	Jan 2007
	2. David Loebsack (D)	Jan 2007
	3. Leonard L. Boswell (D)	Jan 1997
	4. Tom Latham (R)	Jan 1995
	5. Steve King (R)	Jan 2003
Kansas	1. Jerry Moran (R)	Jan 1997
	2. Lynn Jenkins (R)	Jan 2009
	3. Dennis Moore (D)	Jan 1999
	4. Todd Tiahrt (R)	Jan 1995
Kentucky	1. Ed Whitfield (R)	Jan 1995
	2. Brett Guthrie (R)	Jan 2009

STATE	REPRESENTATIVES	SERVICE BEGAN
Kentucky (cont.)	3. John A. Yarmuth (D)	Jan 2007
	4. Geoff Davis (R)	Jan 2005
	5. Harold Rogers (R)	Jan 1981
	6. Ben Chandler (D)[18]	Feb 2004
Louisiana	1. Steve Scalise (R)[19]	May 2008
	2. Anh ("Joseph") Cao (R)	Jan 2009
	3. Charlie Melancon (D)	Jan 2005
	4. John Fleming (R)	Jan 2009
	5. Rodney Alexander (R)	Jan 2003
	6. Bill Cassidy (R)	Jan 2009
	7. Charles W. Boustany, Jr. (R)	Jan 2005
Maine	1. Chellie Pingree (D)	Jan 2009
	2. Michael H. Michaud (D)	Jan 2003
Maryland	1. Frank M. Kratovil, Jr. (D)	Jan 2009
	2. C.A. ("Dutch") Ruppersberger (D)	Jan 2003
	3. John P. Sarbanes (D)	Jan 2007
	4. Donna F. Edwards (D)[20]	Jun 2008
	5. Steny H. Hoyer (D)	May 1981
	6. Roscoe G. Bartlett (R)	Jan 1993
	7. Elijah E. Cummings (D)	Apr 1996
	8. Chris Van Hollen (D)	Jan 2003
Massa-chusetts	1. John W. Olver (D)	Jun 1991
	2. Richard E. Neal (D)	Jan 1989
	3. James P. McGovern (D)	Jan 1997
	4. Barney Frank (D)	Jan 1981
	5. Niki Tsongas (D)[21]	Oct 2007
	6. John F. Tierney (D)	Jan 1997
	7. Edward J. Markey (D)	Nov 1976
	8. Michael E. Capuano (D)	Jan 1999
	9. Stephen F. Lynch (D)[22]	Oct 2001
	10. Bill Delahunt (D)	Jan 1997
Michigan (−1)	1. Bart Stupak (D)	Jan 1993
	2. Peter Hoekstra (R)	Jan 1993
	3. Vernon J. Ehlers (R)	Dec 1993
	4. Dave Camp (R)	Jan 1991
	5. Dale E. Kildee (D)	Jan 1977
	6. Fred Upton (R)	Jan 1987
	7. Mark H. Schauer (D)	Jan 2009
	8. Mike Rogers (R)	Jan 2001
	9. Gary C. Peters (D)	Jan 2009
	10. Candice S. Miller (R)	Jan 2003
	11. Thaddeus G. McCotter (R)	Jan 2003
	12. Sander M. Levin (D)	Jan 1983
	13. Carolyn C. Kilpatrick (D)	Jan 1997
	14. John Conyers, Jr. (D)	Jan 1965
	15. John D. Dingell (D)	Dec 1955
Minnesota	1. Timothy J. Walz (D)	Jan 2007
	2. John Kline (R)	Jan 2003
	3. Erik Paulsen (R)	Jan 2009
	4. Betty McCollum (D)	Jan 2001
	5. Keith Ellison (D)	Jan 2007
	6. Michele Bachmann (R)	Jan 2007
	7. Collin C. Peterson (D)	Jan 1991
	8. James L. Oberstar (D)	Jan 1975
Mississippi (−1)	1. Travis W. Childers (D)[23]	May 2008
	2. Bennie G. Thompson (D)	Apr 1993

House of Representatives, 111th Congress (continued)

STATE	REPRESENTATIVES	SERVICE BEGAN
Mississippi (cont.)	3. Gregg Harper (R)	Jan 2009
	4. Gene Taylor (D)	Oct 1989
Missouri	1. William Lacy Clay (D)	Jan 2001
	2. W. Todd Akin (R)	Jan 2001
	3. Russ Carnahan (D)	Jan 2005
	4. Ike Skelton (D)	Jan 1977
	5. Emanuel Cleaver (D)	Jan 2005
	6. Sam Graves (R)	Jan 2001
	7. Roy Blunt (R)	Jan 1997
	8. Jo Ann Emerson (R)	Nov 1996
	9. Blaine Luetkemeyer (R)	Jan 2009
Montana	Denny Rehberg (R)	Jan 2001
Nebraska	1. Jeff Fortenberry (R)	Jan 2005
	2. Lee Terry (R)	Jan 1999
	3. Adrian Smith (R)	Jan 2007
Nevada (+1)	1. Shelley Berkley (D)	Jan 1999
	2. Dean Heller (R)	Jan 2007
	3. Dina Titus (D)	Jan 2009
New Hampshire	1. Carol Shea-Porter (D)	Jan 2007
	2. Paul W. Hodes (D)	Jan 2007
New Jersey	1. Robert E. Andrews (D)	Nov 1990
	2. Frank A. LoBiondo (R)	Jan 1995
	3. John H. Adler (D)	Jan 2009
	4. Christopher H. Smith (R)	Jan 1981
	5. Scott Garrett (R)	Jan 2003
	6. Frank Pallone, Jr. (D)	Nov 1988
	7. Leonard Lance (R)	Jan 2009
	8. Bill Pascrell, Jr. (D)	Jan 1997
	9. Steven R. Rothman (D)	Jan 1997
	10. Donald M. Payne (D)	Jan 1989
	11. Rodney P. Freling-huysen (R)	Jan 1995
	12. Rush D. Holt (D)	Jan 1999
	13. Albio Sires (D)[24]	Nov 2006
New Mexico	1. Martin Heinrich (D)	Jan 2009
	2. Harry Teague (D)	Jan 2009
	3. Ben Ray Luján (D)	Jan 2009
New York (−2)	1. Timothy H. Bishop (D)	Jan 2003
	2. Steve Israel (D)	Jan 2001
	3. Peter T. King (R)	Jan 1993
	4. Carolyn McCarthy (D)	Jan 1997
	5. Gary L. Ackerman (D)	Mar 1983
	6. Gregory W. Meeks (D)	Feb 1998
	7. Joseph Crowley (D)	Jan 1999
	8. Jerrold Nadler (D)	Nov 1992
	9. Anthony D. Weiner (D)	Jan 1999
	10. Edolphus Towns (D)	Jan 1983
	11. Yvette D. Clarke (D)	Jan 2007
	12. Nydia M. Velázquez (D)	Jan 1993
	13. Michael E. McMahon (D)	Jan 2009
	14. Carolyn B. Maloney (D)	Jan 1993
	15. Charles B. Rangel (D)	Jan 1971
	16. José E. Serrano (D)	Mar 1990
	17. Eliot L. Engel (D)	Jan 1989
	18. Nita M. Lowey (D)	Jan 1989
	19. John J. Hall (D)	Jan 2007
	20. Scott Murphy (D)[25]	Apr 2009
	21. Paul Tonko (D)	Jan 2009
	22. Maurice D. Hinchey (D)	Jan 1993

STATE	REPRESENTATIVES	SERVICE BEGAN
New York (cont.)	23. John M. McHugh (R)	Jan 1993
	24. Michael A. Arcuri (D)	Jan 2007
	25. Daniel B. Maffei (D)	Jan 2009
	26. Christopher John Lee (R)	Jan 2009
	27. Brian Higgins (D)	Jan 2005
	28. Louise McIntosh Slaughter (D)	Jan 1987
	29. Eric J.J. Massa (D)	Jan 2009
North Carolina (+1)	1. G.K. Butterfield (D)[26]	Jul 2004
	2. Bob Etheridge (D)	Jan 1997
	3. Walter B. Jones (R)	Jan 1995
	4. David E. Price (D)	Jan 1997
	5. Virginia Foxx (R)	Jan 2005
	6. Howard Coble (R)	Jan 1985
	7. Mike McIntyre (D)	Jan 1997
	8. Larry Kissell (D)	Jan 2009
	9. Sue Wilkins Myrick (R)	Jan 1995
	10. Patrick T. McHenry (R)	Jan 2005
	11. Heath Shuler (D)	Jan 2007
	12. Melvin L. Watt (D)	Jan 1993
	13. Brad Miller (D)	Jan 2003
North Dakota	Earl Pomeroy (D)	Jan 1993
Ohio (−1)	1. Steve Driehaus (D)	Jan 2009
	2. Jean Schmidt (R)	Sep 2005
	3. Michael R. Turner (R)	Jan 2003
	4. Jim Jordan (R)	Jan 2007
	5. Robert E. Latta (R)[27]	Dec 2007
	6. Charles A. Wilson (D)	Jan 2007
	7. Steve Austria (R)	Jan 2009
	8. John A. Boehner (R)	Jan 1991
	9. Marcy Kaptur (D)	Jan 1983
	10. Dennis J. Kucinich (D)	Jan 1997
	11. Marcia L. Fudge (D)[28]	Nov 2008
	12. Patrick J. Tiberi (R)	Jan 2001
	13. Betty Sutton (D)	Jan 2007
	14. Steven C. LaTourette (R)	Jan 1995
	15. Mary Jo Kilroy (D)	Jan 2009
	16. John A. Boccieri (D)	Jan 2009
	17. Tim Ryan (D)	Jan 2003
	18. Zachary T. Space (D)	Jan 2007
Oklahoma (−1)	1. John Sullivan (R)[29]	Feb 2002
	2. Dan Boren (D)	Jan 2005
	3. Frank D. Lucas (R)	May 1994
	4. Tom Cole (R)	Jan 2003
	5. Mary Fallin (R)	Jan 2007
Oregon	1. David Wu (D)	Jan 1999
	2. Greg Walden (R)	Jan 1999
	3. Earl Blumenauer (D)	May 1996
	4. Peter A. DeFazio (D)	Jan 1987
	5. Kurt Schrader (D)	Jan 2009
Penn-sylvania (−2)	1. Robert A. Brady (D)	May 1998
	2. Chaka Fattah (D)	Jan 1995
	3. Kathleen A. Dahlkemper (D)	Jan 2009
	4. Jason Altmire (D)	Jan 2007
	5. Glenn Thompson (R)	Jan 2009
	6. Jim Gerlach (R)	Jan 2003
	7. Joe Sestak (D)	Jan 2007
	8. Patrick J. Murphy (D)	Jan 2007
	9. Bill Shuster (R)	May 2001

House of Representatives, 111th Congress (continued)

STATE	REPRESENTATIVES	SERVICE BEGAN	STATE	REPRESENTATIVES	SERVICE BEGAN
Penn-sylvania (cont.)	10. Christopher P. Carney (D)	Jan 2007	Texas (cont.)	22. Pete Olson (R)	Jan 2009
	11. Paul E. Kanjorski (D)	Jan 1985		23. Ciro D. Rodriguez (D)[34]	Apr 1997
	12. John P. Murtha (D)	Feb 1974		24. Kenny Marchant (R)	Jan 2005
	13. Allyson Y. Schwartz (D)	Jan 2005		25. Lloyd Doggett (D)	Jan 2005
	14. Michael F. Doyle (D)	Jan 1995		26. Michael C. Burgess (R)	Jan 2003
	15. Charles W. Dent (R)	Jan 2005		27. Solomon P. Ortiz (D)	Jan 1983
	16. Joseph R. Pitts (R)	Jan 1997		28. Henry Cuellar (D)	Jan 2005
	17. Tim Holden (D)	Jan 1993		29. Gene Green (D)	Jan 1993
	18. Tim Murphy (R)	Jan 2003		30. Eddie Bernice Johnson (D)	Jan 1993
	19. Todd Russell Platts (R)	Jan 2001		31. John R. Carter (R)	Jan 2003
				32. Pete Sessions (R)	Jan 1997
Rhode Island	1. Patrick J. Kennedy (D)	Jan 1995			
	2. James R. Langevin (D)	Jan 2001	Utah	1. Rob Bishop (R)	Jan 2003
				2. Jim Matheson (D)	Jan 2001
South Carolina	1. Henry E. Brown, Jr. (R)	Jan 2001		3. Jason Chaffetz (R)	Jan 2009
	2. Joe Wilson (R)[30]	Dec 2001			
	3. J. Gresham Barrett (R)	Jan 2003	Vermont	Peter Welch (D)	Jan 2007
	4. Bob Inglis (R)	Jan 2005			
	5. John M. Spratt, Jr. (D)	Jan 1983	Virginia	1. Robert J. Wittman (R)[35]	Dec 2007
	6. James E. Clyburn (D)	Jan 1993		2. Glenn C. Nye (D)	Jan 2009
				3. Robert C. ("Bobby") Scott (D)	Jan 1993
South Dakota	Stephanie Herseth Sandlin (D)[31]	Jun 2004		4. J. Randy Forbes (R)[36]	Jun 2001
				5. Thomas S.P. Perriello (D)	Jan 2009
Tennessee	1. David P. Roe (R)	Jan 2009		6. Bob Goodlatte (R)	Jan 1993
	2. John J. Duncan, Jr. (R)	Nov 1988		7. Eric Cantor (R)	Jan 2001
	3. Zach Wamp (R)	Jan 1995		8. James P. Moran (D)	Jan 1991
	4. Lincoln Davis (D)	Jan 2003		9. Rick Boucher (D)	Jan 1983
	5. Jim Cooper (D)[32]	Jan 1983		10. Frank R. Wolf (R)	Jan 1981
	6. Bart Gordon (D)	Jan 1985		11. Gerald E. Connolly (D)	Jan 2009
	7. Marsha Blackburn (R)	Jan 2003			
	8. John S. Tanner (D)	Jan 1989	Washington	1. Jay Inslee (D)[37]	Jan 1993
	9. Steve Cohen (D)	Jan 2007		2. Rick Larsen (D)	Jan 2001
				3. Brian Baird (D)	Jan 1999
Texas (+2)	1. Louie Gohmert (R)	Jan 2005		4. Doc Hastings (R)	Jan 1995
	2. Ted Poe (R)	Jan 2005		5. Cathy McMorris Rodgers (R)	Jan 2005
	3. Sam Johnson (R)	May 1991		6. Norman D. Dicks (D)	Jan 1977
	4. Ralph M. Hall (R)	Jan 1981		7. Jim McDermott (D)	Jan 1989
	5. Jeb Hensarling (R)	Jan 2003		8. David G. Reichert (R)	Jan 2005
	6. Joe Barton (R)	Jan 1985		9. Adam Smith (D)	Jan 1997
	7. John Abney Culberson (R)	Jan 2001			
	8. Kevin Brady (R)	Jan 1997	West Virginia	1. Alan B. Mollohan (D)	Jan 1983
	9. Al Green (D)	Jan 2005		2. Shelley Moore Capito (R)	Jan 2001
	10. Michael T. McCaul (R)	Jan 2005		3. Nick J. Rahall II (D)	Jan 1977
	11. K. Michael Conaway (R)	Jan 2005			
	12. Kay Granger (R)	Jan 1997	Wisconsin (−1)	1. Paul Ryan (R)	Jan 1999
	13. Mac Thornberry (R)	Jan 1995		2. Tammy Baldwin (D)	Jan 1999
	14. Ron Paul (R)	Jan 1997		3. Ron Kind (D)	Jan 1997
	15. Rubén Hinojosa (D)	Jan 1997		4. Gwen Moore (D)	Jan 2005
	16. Silvestre Reyes (D)	Jan 1997		5. F. James Sensen-brenner, Jr. (R)	Jan 1979
	17. Chet Edwards (D)	Jan 2005		6. Thomas E. Petri (R)	Apr 1979
	18. Sheila Jackson-Lee (D)	Jan 1995		7. David R. Obey (D)	Apr 1969
	19. Randy Neugebauer (R)[33]	Jun 2003		8. Steve Kagen (D)	Jan 2007
	20. Charles A. Gonzalez (D)	Jan 1999	Wyoming	Cynthia M. Lummis (R)	Jan 2009
	21. Lamar Smith (R)	Jan 1987			

JURISDICTION	REPRESENTATIVES	SERVICE BEGAN
American Samoa	(Delegate) Eni F.H. Faleomavaega (D)	Jan 1989
District of Columbia	(Delegate) Eleanor Holmes Norton (D)	Jan 1991
Guam	(Delegate) Madeleine Z. Bordallo (D)	Jan 2003
Northern Mariana Islands	(Delegate) Gregorio Kilili Camacho Sablan (D)	Jan 2009
Puerto Rico	(Resident Commissioner) Pedro R. Pierluisi (New Progressive)	Jan 2009
US Virgin Islands	(Delegate) Donna M. Christensen (D)	Jan 1997

House of Representatives, 111th Congress (continued)

[1]John Boozman was elected 20 Nov 2001 following the resignation of Asa Hutchinson. [2]Doris O. Matsui was elected 8 Mar 2005 following the death of Robert T. Matsui. [3]Vacant following the resignation of Ellen O. Tauscher, 26 Jun 2009. [4]Jackie Speier was elected 8 Apr 2008 following the death of Tom Lantos. [5]Judy Chu was elected 14 Jul 2009 following the resignation of Hilda L. Solis. [6]Diane E. Watson was elected 5 Jun 2001 following the death of Julian C. Dixon. [7]Jane Harman did not serve 3 Jan 1999–3 Jan 2001. [8]Laura Richardson was elected 21 Aug 2007 following the death of Juanita Millender-McDonald. [9]John Campbell was elected 6 Dec 2005 following the resignation of Christopher Cox. [10]Brian P. Bilbray did not serve 3 Jan 2001–6 Jun 2005. He was elected 6 Jun 2005 following the resignation of Randall ("Duke") Cunningham. [11]Jeff Miller was elected 16 Oct 2001 following the resignation of Joe Scarborough. [12]Paul C. Broun was elected 17 Jul 2007 following the death of Charlie Norwood. [13]Neil Abercrombie did not serve 3 Jan 1987–3 Jan 1991. [14]Mike Quigley was elected 7 Apr 2009 following the resignation of Rahm Emanuel. [15]Bill Foster was elected 8 Mar 2008 following the resignation of J. Dennis Hastert. [16]André Carson was elected 11 Mar 2008 following the death of Julia Carson. [17]Baron P. Hill did not serve 3 Jan 2005–3 Jan 2007. [18]Ben Chandler was elected 17 Feb 2004 following the resignation of Ernie Fletcher. [19]Steve Scalise was elected 3 May 2008 following the resignation of Bobby Jindal. [20]Donna F. Edwards was elected 17 Jun 2007 following the resignation of Albert Russell Wynn. [21]Niki Tsongas was elected 16 Oct 2007 following the resignation of Martin T. Meehan. [22]Stephen F. Lynch was elected 16 Oct 2001 following the death of John Joseph Moakley. [23]Travis W. Childers was elected 13 May 2008 following the resignation of Roger F. Wicker. [24]Albio Sires was elected 7 Nov 2006 following the resignation of Robert Menendez. [25]Scott Murphy was elected 31 Mar 2009 following the resignation of Kirsten E. Gillibrand. [26]G.K. Butterfield was elected 20 Jul 2004 following the resignation of Frank Ballance. [27]Robert E. Latta was elected 11 Dec 2007 following the death of Paul E. Gillmor. [28]Marcia L. Fudge was elected 18 Nov 2008 following the death of Stephanie Tubbs Jones. [29]John Sullivan was elected 8 Jan 2002 following the resignation of Steve Largent. [30]Joe Wilson was elected 18 Dec 2001 following the death of Floyd Spence. [31]Stephanie Herseth Sandlin was elected 1 Jun 2004 following the resignation of William Janklow. [32]Jim Cooper did not serve 3 Jan 1995–3 Jan 2003. [33]Randy Neugebauer was elected 3 Jun 2003 following the resignation of Larry Combest. [34]Ciro D. Rodriguez took office 12 Apr 1997 following the death of Frank Tejada. He did not serve 3 Jan 2005–3 Jan 2007. [35]Robert J. Wittman was elected 11 Dec 2007 following the death of Jo Ann Davis. [36]J. Randy Forbes was elected 19 Jun 2001 following the death of Norman Sisisky. [37]Jay Inslee did not serve 3 Jan 1995–3 Jan 1999.

House of Representatives Standing and Select Committees

COMMITTEE	CHAIRMAN (PARTY-STATE)	RANKING MINORITY MEMBER (PARTY-STATE)	NUMBER OF MEMBERS MAJORITY	MINORITY	NUMBER OF SUBCOMMITTEES
Agriculture	Collin C. Peterson (D-MN)	Frank D. Lucas (R-OK)	28	18	6
Appropriations	David R. Obey (D-WI)	Jerry Lewis (R-CA)	37	23	12
Armed Services	Ike Skelton (D-MO)	John M. McHugh (R-NY)	37	25	7
Budget	John M. Spratt, Jr. (D-SC)	Paul Ryan (R-WI)	24	15	none
Education and Labor	George Miller (D-CA)	Howard P. "Buck" McKeon (R-CA)	29	19	5
Energy and Commerce	Henry A. Waxman (D-CA)	Joe Barton (R-TX)	36	23	5
Financial Services	Barney Frank (D-MA)	Spencer Bachus (R-AL)	42	29	6
Foreign Affairs	Howard L. Berman (D-CA)	Ileana Ros-Lehtinen (R-FL)	28	19	7
Homeland Security	Bennie G. Thompson (D-MS)	Peter T. King (R-NY)	20	13	6
House Administration	Robert A. Brady (D-PA)	Daniel E. Lungren (R-CA)	6	3	2
Judiciary	John Conyers, Jr. (D-MI)	Lamar S. Smith (R-TX)	24	16	5
Natural Resources	Nick J. Rahall II (D-WV)	Doc Hastings (R-WA)	29	20	5
Oversight and Government Reform	Edolphus Towns (D-NY)	Darrell E. Issa (R-CA)	24	16	5
Rules	Louise McIntosh Slaughter (D-NY)	David Dreier (R-CA)	9	4	2
Science and Technology	Bart Gordon (D-TN)	Ralph M. Hall (R-TX)	26	17	5
Small Business	Nydia M. Velázquez (D-NY)	Sam Graves (R-MO)	17	12	5
Standards of Official Conduct	Zoe Lofgren (D-CA)	Jo Bonner (R-AL)	5	5	none
Transportation and Infrastructure	James L. Oberstar (D-MN)	John L. Mica (R-FL)	45	30	6
Veterans' Affairs	Bob Filner (D-CA)	Steve Buyer (R-IN)	18	11	4
Ways and Means	Charles B. Rangel (D-NY)	Dave Camp (R-MI)	26	15	6
Permanent Select Committee on Intelligence	Silvestre Reyes (D-TX)	Peter Hoekstra (R-MI)	13	9	4
Select Committee on Energy Independence and Global Warming	Edward J. Markey (D-MA)	F. James Sensenbrenner, Jr. (R-WI)	9	6	none

Joint Committees of Congress

The joint committees of Congress include members from both the Senate and the House of Representatives. They function as overseeing entities but do not have the power to approve appropriations or legislation. Chairmanship of the Joint Economic Committee is determined by seniority and alternates between the Senate and the House every Congress. The Joint Committee on the Library of Congress is evenly made up of members from the House

Administration Committee and the Senate Rules and Administration Committee. Chairmanship and vice-chairmanship of the Joint Committee on Printing alternate between the House and the Senate every Congress. The Joint Committee on Taxation is composed of five members from the Senate Committee on Finance and five members from the House Committee on Ways and Means (three majority and two minority members from each).

COMMITTEE	CHAIRMAN (PARTY-STATE)	VICE-CHAIRMAN (PARTY-STATE)	NUMBER OF MEMBERS MAJORITY	MINORITY
Economic	Rep. Carolyn B. Maloney (D-NY)	Sen. Charles E. Schumer (D-NY)	12	8
Library	Rep. Robert A. Brady (D-PA)	Sen. Charles E. Schumer (D-NY)	5	4
Printing	Rep. Robert A. Brady (D-PA)	Sen. Charles E. Schumer (D-NY)	6	4
Taxation	Rep. Charles B. Rangel (D-NY)	Sen. Max Baucus (D-MT)	6	4

Did you know? Henri Matisse's painting *Le Bateau* (*The Boat*) was accidentally hung upside down in New York's Museum of Modern Art for 47 days in 1961. During that time 116,000 visitors saw it, but it wasn't until stockbroker Genevieve Habert called the *New York Times* about the mistake that the director of exhibitions was notified and the work was rehung properly.

Electoral Votes by State

Each state receives one electoral vote for each of its representatives and one for each of its two senators, ensuring at least three votes for each state, as the Constitution guarantees at least one representative

regardless of population. Allocations are based on the 2000 census and are applicable for subsequent elections.

Total: 538; Majority needed to elect president and vice president: 270

STATE	NUMBER OF VOTES	STATE	NUMBER OF VOTES	STATE	NUMBER OF VOTES
Alabama	9	Kentucky	8	North Dakota	3
Alaska	3	Louisiana	9	Ohio	20
Arizona	10	Maine	4	Oklahoma	7
Arkansas	6	Maryland	10	Oregon	7
California	55	Massachusetts	12	Pennsylvania	21
Colorado	9	Michigan	17	Rhode Island	4
Connecticut	7	Minnesota	10	South Carolina	8
Delaware	3	Mississippi	6	South Dakota	3
District of Columbia	3	Missouri	11	Tennessee	11
Florida	27	Montana	3	Texas	34
Georgia	15	Nebraska	5	Utah	5
Hawaii	4	Nevada	5	Vermont	3
Idaho	4	New Hampshire	4	Virginia	13
Illinois	21	New Jersey	15	Washington	11
Indiana	11	New Mexico	5	West Virginia	5
Iowa	7	New York	31	Wisconsin	10
Kansas	6	North Carolina	15	Wyoming	3

Congressional Apportionment

The US Constitution requires a decennial census to determine the apportionment of representatives for each state in the House of Representatives.

STATE	REPRESENTATIVES	STATE	REPRESENTATIVES	STATE	REPRESENTATIVES
Alabama	7	Georgia	13	Maine	2
Alaska	1	Hawaii	2	Maryland	8
Arizona	8	Idaho	2	Massachusetts	10
Arkansas	4	Illinois	19	Michigan	15
California	53	Indiana	9	Minnesota	8
Colorado	7	Iowa	5	Mississippi	4
Connecticut	5	Kansas	4	Missouri	9
Delaware	1	Kentucky	6	Montana	1
Florida	25	Louisiana	7	Nebraska	3

Congressional Apportionment (continued)

STATE	REPRESENTATIVES	STATE	REPRESENTATIVES	STATE	REPRESENTATIVES
Nevada	3	Oklahoma	5	Utah	3
New Hampshire	2	Oregon	5	Vermont	1
New Jersey	13	Pennsylvania	19	Virginia	11
New Mexico	3	Rhode Island	2	Washington	9
New York	29	South Carolina	6	West Virginia	3
North Carolina	13	South Dakota	1	Wisconsin	8
North Dakota	1	Tennessee	9	Wyoming	1
Ohio	18	Texas	32	Total	435

Military Affairs

US Military Leadership

President, Commander in Chief:	Barack Obama (20 Jan 2009)
Secretary of Defense:	Robert M. Gates (18 Dec 2006)
Chairman, Joint Chiefs of Staff:	Adm. Mike Mullen (1 Oct 2007)
Vice Chairman, Joint Chiefs of Staff:	Gen. James E. Cartwright (31 Aug 2007)

RANK/POSITION	NAME (DATE ASSUMED POST)
Army	
Chief of Staff	Gen. George W. Casey, Jr. (10 Apr 2007)
Vice Chief of Staff	Gen. Peter W. Chiarelli (4 Aug 2008)
Sergeant Major	Kenneth O. Preston (15 Jan 2004)
Sec. of the Army	Pete Geren (16 Jul 2007)
Under Sec. of the Army	vacant
Navy	
Chief of Naval Operations	Adm. Gary Roughead (29 Sep 2007)
Vice Chief of Naval Operations	Adm. Patrick M. Walsh (April 2007)
Master Chief Petty Officer	Rick D. West (12 Dec 2008)
Sec. of the Navy	Ray Mabus (19 May 2009)
Under Sec. of the Navy	Robert O. Work (19 May 2009)

RANK/POSITION	NAME (DATE ASSUMED POST)
Air Force	
Chief of Staff	Gen. Norton A. Schwartz (12 Aug 2008)
Vice Chief of Staff	Gen. William M. Fraser III (2 Oct 2008)
Chief Master Sgt.	James A. Roy (30 Jun 2009)
Sec. of the Air Force	Michael B. Donley (2 Oct 2008)
Under Sec. of the Air Force	vacant
Marine Corps	
Commandant	Gen. James T. Conway (13 Nov 2006)
Asst. Commandant	Gen. James F. Amos (2 Jul 2008)
Sergeant Major	Carlton W. Kent (25 Apr 2007)
Coast Guard	
Commandant	Adm. Thad W. Allen (25 May 2006)
Vice Commandant	Vice Adm. Vivien S. Crea (5 Jun 2006)
Chief of Staff	Vice Adm. Clifford I. Pearson (June 2008)
Master Chief Petty Officer	Charles W. Bowen (14 Jun 2006)

Unified Combatant Commands

The Unified Combatant Commands provide operational control of US combat forces and are organized geographically to a significant extent. Unified Commanders receive orders through the chairman of the Joint Chiefs of Staff. Although the number of commands may vary, each command must be composed of forces from at least two of the armed services. Information is current as of June 2009.

COMMAND	HEADQUARTERS	COMMANDER
US European Command	Stuttgart-Vaihingen, Germany	Adm. James G. Stavridis, USN
US Pacific Command	Camp H.M. Smith, Hawaii	Adm. Timothy J. Keating, USN
US Joint Forces Command	Norfolk VA	Gen. James N. Mattis, USMC
US Southern Command	Doral FL	Gen. Douglas M. Fraser, USAF
US Central Command	MacDill Air Force Base, Florida	Gen. David Petraeus, USA
US Northern Command	Peterson Air Force Base, Colorado	Gen. Victor E. Renuart, Jr., USAF
US Special Operations Command	MacDill Air Force Base, Florida	Adm. Eric T. Olson, USN
US Transportation Command	Scott Air Force Base, Illinois	Gen. Duncan J. McNabb, USAF
US Strategic Command	Offutt Air Force Base, Nebraska	Gen. Kevin P. Chilton, USAF
US Africa Command	Stuttgart-Möhringen, Germany	Gen. William E. Ward, USA

North Atlantic Treaty Organization (NATO) International Commands

The NATO military command structure comprises two main strategic commands, Allied Command Operations (ACO) and Allied Command Transformation (ACT, which works closely with the US Joint Forces Command). Their subordinate centers, also listed, change as their security measures evolve.

ALLIED COMMAND OPERATIONS (ACO)
Headquarters: Casteau, Belgium
Supreme Allied Commander, Europe (SACEUR):
  Adm. James G. Stavridis, USN (2 Jul 2009–)

SUBORDINATE OPERATIONAL COMMANDS
Allied Joint Force Command (JFC) Brunssum,
  JFC Headquarters: Brunssum, Netherlands
Commander in Chief: Gen. Egon Ramms (Army,
  Germany) (26 Jan 2007–)

Allied Joint Force Command (JFC) Naples,
  JFC Headquarters: Naples, Italy
Commander in Chief: Adm. Mark Fitzgerald (USN)
  (30 Nov 2007–)

Allied Joint Command (JC) Lisbon,
  JC Headquarters: Oeiras, Portugal
Commander in Chief: Vice Adm. Bruce W. Clingan
  (USN) (14 Aug 2008–)

ALLIED COMMAND TRANSFORMATION (ACT)
Headquarters: Norfolk VA
Supreme Allied Commander, Transformation (SACT):
  Gen. James N. Mattis (USMC) (9 Nov 2007–)

SUBORDINATE CENTERS AND SCHOOLS
Joint Analysis and Lessons Learned Centre (JALLC),
  Monsanto, Portugal
Joint Force Training Centre (JFTC), Bydgoszcz, Poland
Joint Warfare Centre (JWC), Stavanger, Norway
NATO Communications and Information Systems
  School (NCISS), Latina, Italy
NATO Defense College (NDC), Rome, Italy
NATO School, Oberammergau, Germany
NATO Undersea Research Centre (NURC), La Spezia,
  Italy

Chairmen of the Joint Chiefs of Staff

The 1949 amendments to the National Security Act of 1947 created the position of chairman of the Joint Chiefs of Staff, the principal military adviser to the president, the secretary of defense, and the National Security Council. The president appoints the chairman for a two-year term with the advice and consent of the Senate. In 1986 the chairman's eligibility for service increased from two to three reappointments (there is no limit on reappointment during wartime). The Joint Chiefs of Staff consist of the chairman, a vice chairman, the chief of staff of the Army, the chief of staff of the Air Force, the chief of naval operations, and the commandant of the Marine Corps. Acting chairmen are not included in this table.

NAME	MILITARY BRANCH	DATES OF SERVICE
Gen. of the Army Omar N. Bradley	US Army	16 Aug 1949–14 Aug 1953
Adm. Arthur W. Radford	US Navy	15 Aug 1953–14 Aug 1957
Gen. Nathan F. Twining	US Air Force	15 Aug 1957–30 Sep 1960
Gen. Lyman L. Lemnitzer	US Army	1 Oct 1960–30 Sep 1962
Gen. Maxwell D. Taylor	US Army	1 Oct 1962–1 Jul 1964
Gen. Earle G. Wheeler	US Army	3 Jul 1964–1 Jul 1970
Adm. Thomas H. Moorer	US Navy	2 Jul 1970–30 Jun 1974
Gen. George S. Brown	US Air Force	1 Jul 1974–20 Jun 1978
Gen. David C. Jones	US Air Force	21 Jun 1978–17 Jun 1982
Gen. John W. Vessey, Jr.	US Army	18 Jun 1982–30 Sep 1985
Adm. William J. Crowe, Jr.	US Navy	1 Oct 1985–30 Sep 1989
Gen. Colin L. Powell	US Army	1 Oct 1989–30 Sep 1993
Gen. John M. Shalikashvili	US Army	25 Oct 1993–30 Sep 1997
Gen. Harry Shelton	US Army	1 Oct 1997–30 Sep 2001
Gen. Richard B. Myers	US Air Force	1 Oct 2001–29 Sep 2005
Gen. Peter Pace	US Marine Corps	30 Sep 2005–30 Sep 2007
Adm. Mike Mullen	US Navy	1 Oct 2007–

Worldwide Deployment of the US Military

Deployments of active duty military personnel as of 1 Jan 2009. Regional totals include countries and areas not shown in the table. Source: US Department of Defense.

COUNTRY/REGIONAL AREA	TOTAL	ARMY	NAVY	MARINE CORPS	AIR FORCE
US and territories[1]					
contiguous US	910,788	428,206	111,033	119,262	252,287
Alaska	20,468	12,696	46	19	7,707

Worldwide Deployment of the US Military (continued)

COUNTRY/REGIONAL AREA	TOTAL	ARMY	NAVY	MARINE CORPS	AIR FORCE
US and territories (continued)					
Hawaii	37,094	21,858	5,342	5,298	4,596
Guam	3,133	42	1,194	11	1,886
Puerto Rico	191	94	48	23	26
transients	58,407	9,546	9,629	34,799	4,433
afloat	88,549	0	88,549	0	0
total ashore and afloat	**1,118,638**	**472,443**	**215,841**	**159,416**	**270,938**
Europe					
Belgium	1,256	667	98	23	468
Germany[1]	54,974	39,794	263	317	14,600
Greece	358	10	279	12	57
Greenland	138	0	0	0	138
Italy[1]	9,160	2,900	2,263	52	3,945
The Netherlands	541	258	23	13	247
Portugal	778	26	29	7	716
Serbia and Kosovo	1,120	1,100	0	20	0
Spain	1,230	93	685	141	311
Turkey	1,559	62	8	14	1,475
United Kingdom[1]	9,357	338	387	79	8,553
afloat	692	0	692	0	0
total ashore and afloat	**81,582**	**45,337**	**4,759**	**847**	**30,639**
East Asia and Pacific					
Australia	142	29	29	26	58
Japan[1]	34,039	2,538	3,785	15,100	12,616
Republic of Korea[1]	24,655	16,507	242	112	7,794
Philippines	116	13	5	88	10
Singapore	126	8	88	16	14
Thailand	105	37	8	34	26
afloat	7,387	0	7,387	0	0
total ashore and afloat	**66,750**	**19,186**	**11,561**	**15,464**	**20,539**
Africa, Near East, and South Asia					
Iraq (Operation Iraqi Freedom)[2]	178,300	116,000	19,700	21,900	20,700
Afghanistan (Operation Enduring Freedom)[2]	31,400	22,600	1,200	1,500	6,100
Bahrain	1,467	18	1,283	142	24
Diego Garcia	249	0	214	0	35
Djibouti	1,349	356	434	382	177
Egypt	276	214	6	23	33
Qatar	425	195	6	43	181
Saudi Arabia	276	143	29	26	78
afloat	420	0	420	0	0
total ashore and afloat (excluding Iraq and Afghanistan)	**5,094**	**1,048**	**2,438**	**917**	**691**
Western Hemisphere					
Canada	128	7	31	7	83
Cuba (Guantánamo Bay)	953	309	508	136	0
Honduras	418	224	2	6	186
total ashore and afloat	**2,039**	**714**	**635**	**341**	**349**
all foreign countries (excluding Iraq and Afghanistan)					
ashore	268,920	70,122	101,172	39,486	58,140
afloat	14,669	0	14,669	0	0
total ashore and afloat	**283,589**	**70,122**	**115,841**	**39,486**	**58,140**
worldwide (excluding Iraq and Afghanistan)					
ashore	1,299,009	542,565	228,464	198,902	329,078
afloat	103,218	0	103,218	0	0
total ashore and afloat	**1,402,227**	**542,565**	**331,682**	**198,902**	**329,078**

[1]Includes service members deployed to Operation Iraqi Freedom and Operation Enduring Freedom.   [2]Includes deployed Reserve/National Guard.

Number of Living Veterans[1]

Source: Statistical Abstract of the US: 2009.

AGE IN YEARS	KOREAN CONFLICT	VIETNAM ERA	GULF WAR[2]	TOTAL WARTIME[3,4]	TOTAL PEACETIME	TOTAL VETERANS[4]
under 35	—	—	1,894,000	1,894,000	6,000	1,900,000
35–39	—	—	1,064,000	1,064,000	196,000	1,259,000
40–44	—	—	727,000	727,000	851,000	1,578,000
45–49	—	23,000	535,000	556,000	1,320,000	1,876,000
50–54	—	883,000	364,000	1,155,000	796,000	1,950,000
55–59	—	2453,000	237,000	2,540,000	179,000	2,718,000
60–64	—	2,981,000	105,000	3,003,000	230,000	3,233,000
65 and over	2,961,000	1,545,000	41,000	6,802,000	2,500,000	9,302,000
female, total	71,000	258,000	795,000	1,226,000	555,000	1,780,000
total[5]	2,961,000	7,884,000	4,966,000	17,739,000	6,077,000	23,816,000

[1]As of 30 Sep 2007. Includes those living outside of the US. Estimated. [2]Service from 2 Aug 1990 to the present. [3]Veterans who served in more than one wartime period are counted only once. [4]Includes an estimated 2,912,000 veterans of World War II, all 65 or over, of which 137,000 are female. [5]Detail may not add to total given because of rounding.

US Casualties of War

Data prior to World War I are based on incomplete records. Casualty data exclude personnel captured or missing in action. N/A means not available. Sources: US Department of Defense and US Coast Guard.

WAR	SERVICE BRANCH	NUMBER OF COMBATANTS	WOUNDED[1]	BATTLE DEATHS	OTHER DEATHS	TOTAL DEATHS
Revolutionary War	Army	N/A	6,004	4,044	N/A	N/A
(1775–83)	Navy	N/A	114	342	N/A	N/A
	Marines	N/A	70	49	N/A	N/A
	total	184,000–250,000[2]	6,188	4,435	20,000[2]	24,435
War of 1812	Army	N/A	4,000	1,950	N/A	N/A
(1812–15)	Navy	N/A	439	265	N/A	N/A
	Marines	N/A	66	45	N/A	N/A
	Coast Guard	100	N/A	0	N/A	N/A
	total	286,830	4,505[3]	2,260	N/A	N/A
Indian Wars (about 1817–98)	total	106,000[2]	N/A	1,000[2]	N/A	N/A
Mexican-American War	Army	N/A	4,102	1,721	11,550	13,271
(1846–48)	Navy	N/A	3	1	N/A	N/A
	Marines	N/A	47	11	N/A	N/A
	Coast Guard	71	N/A	N/A	N/A	N/A
	total	78,789	4,152[3]	1,733[3]	N/A	N/A
Civil War (1861–65)	Army	2,128,948	280,040	138,154	221,374	359,528
Union	Navy	N/A	1,710	2,112	2,411	4,523
	Marines	84,415	131	148	312	460
	Coast Guard	219	N/A	1	N/A	N/A
	total	N/A	281,881[3]	140,415	224,097[3]	364,512[3]
Confederate[4]	total	600,000–1,500,000[2]	137,000[2]	74,524	124,000[2]	198,524
Spanish-American War	Army	280,564	1,594	369	2,061	2,430
(1898)	Navy	22,875	47	10	N/A	N/A
	Marines	3,321	21	6	N/A	N/A
	Coast Guard	660	N/A	0	N/A	0
	total[5]	307,420	1,662[3]	385	2,061[3]	N/A
World War I	Army[5]	4,057,101	193,663	50,510	55,868	106,378
(1917–18)	Navy	599,051	819	431	6,856	7,287
	Marines	78,839	9,520	2,461	390	2,851
	Coast Guard	8,835	N/A	111	81	192
	total	4,743,826	204,002[3]	53,513	63,195	116,708
World War II	Army[5]	11,260,000	565,861	234,874	83,400	318,274
(1941–46)	Navy	4,183,466	37,778	36,950	25,664	62,614
	Marines	669,100	68,207	19,733	4,778	24,511
	Coast Guard	241,093	N/A	574	1,343	1,917
	total	16,353,659	671,846[3]	292,131	115,185	407,316
Korean War	Army	2,834,000	77,596	27,731	2,125	29,856
(1950–53)	Navy	1,177,000	1,576	506	154	660
	Marines	424,000	23,744	4,266	242	4,508

US Casualties of War (continued)

WAR	SERVICE BRANCH	NUMBER OF COMBATANTS	CASUALTIES			
			WOUNDED[1]	BATTLE DEATHS	OTHER DEATHS	TOTAL DEATHS
Korean War (1950–53) (cont.)	Air Force	1,285,000	368	1,238	314	1,552
	Coast Guard	8,500[6]	0	0	0	0
	total	5,764,143	103,284	33,741	2,835	36,576
Vietnam War (1964–73)	Army	4,368,000	96,802	30,952	7,261	38,213
	Navy	1,842,000	. 4,178	1,628	934	2,562
	Marines	794,000	51,392	13,091	1,749	14,840
	Air Force	1,740,000	931	1,744	841	2,585
	Coast Guard	8,000	7	7	N/A	7
	total	8,752,000	153,363[7]	47,422	10,785[3]	58,207
Persian Gulf War[8] (1990–91)	Army	338,636	354	98	126	224
	Navy	152,419	12[9]	5[9]	50[9]	55[9]
	Marines	97,878	92	24	44	68
	Air Force	76,543	9	20	15	35
	Coast Guard	400	N/A	N/A	N/A	N/A
	total	665,876	467	147	235	382
War on Terrorism[10] (2001–)	Army	N/A	2,600	385	161	546
	Navy[9]	N/A	54	29	17	46
	Marines	N/A	406	49	34	83
	Air Force	N/A	102	19	20	39
	Coast Guard	N/A	N/A	N/A	N/A	N/A
	total	N/A	3,162	482	232	714
Iraq War[11] (2003–)	Army	N/A	21,759	2,508	635	3,143
	Navy[9]	N/A	631	65	36	101
	Marines	N/A	8,622	850	169	1,019
	Air Force	N/A	418	28	21	49
	Coast Guard	N/A	N/A	N/A	N/A	N/A
other[12]	total	N/A	31,430	3,451	861	4,312

[1]Data in this column account for the total number of wounds, except for Marine Corps data for World War II, the Spanish-American War, and earlier wars, which represent the number of combatants wounded. [2]Estimate. [3]Excluding unavailable data from one or more service branches. [4]US service members only. [5]Includes air service. [6]Number eligible for Korean Service Medal. [7]Excludes 150,332 wounded who did not require hospital care. [8]Data for military personnel serving in the theater of operation. [9]Includes Coast Guard. [10]Operation Enduring Freedom; data for 7 Oct 2001–4 Jul 2009. [11]Operation Iraqi Freedom; data for 19 Mar 2003–4 Jul 2009. [12]US casualties of other recent military operations: in Grenada (1983) 119 wounded, 19 battle deaths; in Panama (1989) 324 wounded, 23 battle deaths; in Somalia (1992–94) 153 wounded, 43 battle deaths.

Leading Department of Defense Contractors

Top 40 Department of Defense contractors listed according to net value of prime contract awards, fiscal year 2007. Source: <www.fpds.gov>.

RANK	CONTRACTOR	AMOUNT (US$)
1	Lockheed Martin	28,544,756,640
2	Boeing	22,995,150,080
3	Northrop Grumman	15,349,895,946
4	General Dynamics	13,657,725,914
5	Raytheon	11,067,001,370
6	BAE Systems	9,735,891,823
7	L-3 Communications Holdings	6,029,594,189
8	United Technologies	5,321,219,671
9	KBR[1]	4,825,829,496
10	Science Applications International	3,600,291,896
11	Humana	3,403,619,620
12	MacAndrews & Forbes Holdings	3,360,972,194
13	General Electric	2,480,293,969
14	Oshkosh Truck	2,343,938,264
15	Computer Sciences	2,290,958,632
16	Health Net	2,224,967,117
17	ITT	2,204,059,768
18	Royal Dutch Shell	2,118,387,545
19	TriWest Healthcare Alliance	2,110,825,320
20	Textron	2,059,843,214
21	Electronic Data Systems	1,935,642,660
22	Bell Boeing Joint Project Office	1,901,454,598
23	Agility	1,805,282,231
24	DRS Technologies	1,772,582,604
25	URS	1,579,786,638
26	Booz Allen Hamilton	1,566,129,263
27	Honeywell International	1,514,040,515
28	Harris	1,508,788,143
29	AmerisourceBergen	1,455,008,752
30	Federal Express Charter Program Team Arrangement	1,345,887,845
31	Bechtel Group	1,341,254,838
32	Cerberus Capital Management	1,284,713,543
33	International Military and Government	1,166,805,361
34	Rockwell Collins	1,149,150,763
35	Force Protection	1,139,559,711
36	CACI International	1,131,446,219

Leading Department of Defense Contractors (continued)

RANK	CONTRACTOR	AMOUNT (US$)	RANK	CONTRACTOR	AMOUNT (US$)
37	Evergreen International Airlines	1,105,610,723	39	Valero Energy	1,027,333,706
38	EDO	1,089,774,596	40	Alliant Techsystems	992,969,478

[1]Until April 2007 KBR was a subsidiary of Halliburton.

CIA Directors

The National Security Act of 26 Jul 1947 established the Central Intelligence Agency (CIA) on 18 Sep 1947. The director coordinates the nation's intelligence activities and informs the president on issues of national security. Acting directors are not included in this table.

NAME	DATES OF SERVICE
Rear Adm. Sidney W. Souers, USNR	23 Jan 1946–9 Jun 1946
Lt. Gen. Hoyt S. Vandenberg, USA	10 Jun 1946–30 Apr 1947
Rear Adm. Roscoe H. Hillenkoetter, USN	1 May 1947–6 Oct 1950
Gen. Walter Bedell Smith, USA	7 Oct 1950–9 Feb 1953
Allen W. Dulles	26 Feb 1953–28 Nov 1961
John A. McCone	29 Nov 1961–27 Apr 1965
Vice Adm. William F. Raborn, Jr., USN	28 Apr 1965–29 Jun 1966
Richard M. Helms	30 Jun 1966–1 Feb 1973
James R. Schlesinger	2 Feb 1973–2 Jul 1973

NAME	DATES OF SERVICE
William E. Colby	4 Sep 1973–29 Jan 1976
George H.W. Bush	30 Jan 1976–20 Jan 1977
Adm. Stansfield Turner, USN	9 Mar 1977–20 Jan 1981
William J. Casey	28 Jan 1981–29 Jan 1987
William H. Webster	26 May 1987–31 Aug 1991
Robert M. Gates	6 Nov 1991–20 Jan 1993
R. James Woolsey	5 Feb 1993–10 Jan 1995
John M. Deutch	10 May 1995–15 Dec 1996
George J. Tenet	11 Jul 1997–11 Jul 2004
Porter J. Goss	24 Sep 2004–26 May 2006
Gen. Michael V. Hayden, USAF	30 May 2006–12 Feb 2009
Leon E. Panetta	13 Feb 2009–

National Security Council (NSC)

The National Security Act of 1947 established the NSC to advise the president on issues relating to national security.

chair	Barack Obama (president)
members	Joe Biden (vice president)
	Hillary Clinton (secretary of state)
	Robert M. Gates (secretary of defense)
	Steven Chu (secretary of energy)
	Tim Geithner (secretary of the treasury)
	Eric Holder (attorney general)
	Janet Napolitano (secretary of homeland security)
	Susan Rice (US ambassador to the United Nations)
	Rahm Emanuel (chief of staff to the president)
	James L. Jones (assistant to the president for national security affairs)
military adviser	Mike Mullen (chairman of the Joint Chiefs of Staff)
intelligence adviser	Dennis C. Blair (director of national intelligence)
additional participants[1]	Gregory B. Craig (counsel to the president)
	Thomas E. Donilon (deputy assistant to the president for national security affairs)

In 1953 Pres. Dwight D. Eisenhower established the office of assistant to the president for national security affairs (commonly referred to as the national security advisor). Holders of this office are listed below.

NAME	DATES OF SERVICE
Robert Cutler	23 Mar 1953–1 Apr 1955
Dillon Anderson	2 Apr 1955–1 Sep 1956
Robert Cutler	7 Jan 1957–23 Jun 1958
Gordon Gray	24 Jun 1958–13 Jan 1961
McGeorge Bundy	20 Jan 1961–28 Feb 1966
Walt W. Rostow	1 Apr 1966–1 Dec 1968
Henry A. Kissinger	2 Dec 1968–2 Nov 1975[2]
Brent Scowcroft	3 Nov 1975–19 Jan 1977
Zbigniew Brzezinski	20 Jan 1977–20 Jan 1981
Richard V. Allen	21 Jan 1981–4 Jan 1982
William P. Clark	4 Jan 1982–16 Oct 1983

NAME	DATES OF SERVICE
Robert C. McFarlane	17 Oct 1983–3 Dec 1985
John M. Poindexter	4 Dec 1985–25 Nov 1986
Frank C. Carlucci	2 Dec 1986–22 Nov 1987
Colin L. Powell	23 Nov 1987–19 Jan 1989
Brent Scowcroft	20 Jan 1989–19 Jan 1993
W. Anthony Lake	20 Jan 1993–13 Mar 1997
Samuel R. Berger	14 Mar 1997–20 Jan 2001
Condoleezza Rice	22 Jan 2001–25 Jan 2005
Stephen Hadley	26 Jan 2005–19 Jan 2009
James L. Jones	20 Jan 2009–

[1]Regular attendees are the secretary of commerce, the US trade representative, the assistant to the president for economic policy, the chair of the Council of Economic Advisers, and the assistant to the president for homeland security and counterterrorism. [2]Henry A. Kissinger served concurrently as secretary of state from 21 Sep 1973.

United States Population

US Population by Race, Sex, Median Age, and Residence

Numbers are in thousands ('000) except for the median age figures and the residency percentages.
N/A means not available. Source: US Census Bureau.

YEAR	RACE WHITE	RACE BLACK	RACE OTHER[1]	SEX MALE	SEX FEMALE	MEDIAN AGE	RESIDENCE[2] URBAN (%)	RESIDENCE[2] RURAL (%)
1790	3,172	757	N/A	N/A	N/A	N/A	5.1	94.9
1800	4,306	1,002	N/A	N/A	N/A	N/A	6.1	93.9
1810	5,862	1,378	N/A	N/A	N/A	N/A	7.3	92.7
1820	7,867	1,772	N/A	4,897	4,742	16.7	7.2	92.8
1830	10,537	2,329	N/A	6,532	6,334	17.2	8.8	91.2
1840	14,196	2,874	N/A	8,689	8,381	17.8	10.8	89.2
1850	19,553	3,639	N/A	11,838	11,354	18.9	15.4	84.6
1860	26,923	4,442	79	16,085	15,358	19.4	19.8	80.2
1870	34,337	5,392	89	19,494	19,065	20.2	25.7	74.3
1880	43,403	6,581	172	25,519	24,637	20.9	28.2	71.8
1890	55,101	7,489	358	32,237	30,711	22.0	35.1	64.9
1900	66,809	8,834	351	38,816	37,178	22.9	39.6	60.4
1910	81,732	9,828	413	47,332	44,640	24.1	45.6	54.4
1920	94,821	10,463	427	53,900	51,810	25.3	51.2	48.8
1930	110,287	11,891	597	62,137	60,638	26.4	56.1	43.9
1940	118,215	12,866	589	66,062	65,608	29.0	56.5	43.5
1950	134,942	15,042	713	74,833	75,864	30.2	64.0	36.0
1960	158,832	18,872	1,620	88,331	90,992	29.5	69.9	30.1
1970	178,098	22,581	2,557	98,926	104,309	28.0	73.6	26.3
1980	194,713	26,683	5,150	110,053	116,493	30.0	73.7	26.3
1990	199,686	29,986	9,233	121,271	127,494	32.8	78.0	22.0
2000	211,461	34,658	13,118	138,054	143,368	35.3	79.0	21.0
2008	242,639	39,059	22,362	149,925	154,135	36.8	N/A	N/A

[1]*"Other" refers to Asians, Native Hawaiians, other Pacific Islanders, American Indians, Alaska Natives, and those belonging to two or more races. Data for Alaska and Hawaii are not included until 1960, the first census after they became states in 1959.* [2]*The census definitions for urban and rural areas have changed through the decades.*

US Population by Race and Hispanic Origin

Census 2000 was the first US census in which individuals could report themselves as being of more than one race. For the comparison between these census results and the 2008 data, this table uses the 2000 census information that was revised in April 2000. Hispanic or Latino people may be of any race.

Source: US Census Bureau.

RACE	2000 CENSUS NUMBER[1]	%[1]	2008 NUMBER[1]	%[1]	% DIFFERENCE 2000/2008[1]
white	228,107,000	81.1	242,639,242	79.8	+6.4
black or African American	35,705,000	12.7	39,058,834	12.8	+9.4
American Indian or Alaska Native	2,664,000	0.9	3,083,434	1.0	+15.7
Asian	10,589,000	3.8	13,549,064	4.5	+28.0
Native Hawaiian or other Pacific Islander	463,000	0.2	562,121	0.2	+21.4
two or more races	3,898,000	1.4	5,167,029	1.7	+32.6
total population	281,425,000	100.0	304,059,724	100.0	+8.0

HISPANIC OR LATINO POPULATION	2000 CENSUS NUMBER[1]	%[1]	2008 NUMBER[1]	%[1]	% DIFFERENCE 2000/2008[1]
Hispanic or Latino (of any race)	35,306,000	12.5	46,943,613	15.4	+33.0
not Hispanic or Latino	246,118,000	87.5	257,116,111	84.6	+4.5
total population	281,425,000	100.0	304,059,724	100.0	+8.0

[1]*Detail may not add to total given because of rounding.*

State Populations, 1790–2008

Resident population of the states and the District of Columbia. Numbers are in thousands ('000)[1].
Source: US Census Bureau.

STATE	1790	1800	1810	1820	1830	1840	1850	1860	1870	1880	1890	1900
AL		1	9	128	310	591	772	964	997	1,263	1,513	1,829
AK										33	32	64
AZ									10	40	88	123
AR			1	14	30	98	210	435	484	803	1,128	1,312
CA							93	380	560	865	1,213	1,485
CO								34	40	194	413	540
CT	238	251	262	275	298	310	371	460	537	623	746	908
DE	59	64	73	73	77	78	92	112	125	147	168	185
DC		8	15	23	30	34	52	75	132	178	230	279
FL					35	54	87	140	188	269	391	529
GA	83	163	252	341	517	691	906	1,057	1,184	1,542	1,837	2,216
HI												154
ID									15	33	89	162
IL			12	55	157	476	851	1,712	2,540	3,078	3,826	4,822
IN		6	25	147	343	686	988	1,350	1,681	1,978	2,192	2,516
IA						43	192	675	1,194	1,625	1,912	2,232
KS								107	364	996	1,428	1,470
KY	74	221	407	564	688	780	982	1,156	1,321	1,649	1,859	2,147
LA			77	153	216	352	518	708	727	940	1,119	1,382
ME	97	152	229	298	399	502	583	628	627	649	661	694
MD	320	342	381	407	447	470	583	687	781	935	1,042	1,188
MA	379	423	472	523	610	738	995	1,231	1,457	1,783	2,239	2,805
MI			5	9	32	212	398	749	1,184	1,637	2,094	2,421
MN							6	172	440	781	1,310	1,751
MS		8	31	75	137	376	607	791	828	1,132	1,290	1,551
MO			20	67	140	384	682	1,182	1,721	2,168	2,679	3,107
MT									21	39	143	243
NE								29	123	452	1,063	1,066
NV								7	42	62	47	42
NH	142	184	214	244	269	285	318	326	318	347	377	412
NJ	184	211	246	278	321	373	490	672	906	1,131	1,445	1,884
NM							62	94	92	120	160	195
NY	340	589	959	1,373	1,919	2,429	3,097	3,881	4,383	5,083	6,003	7,269
NC	394	478	556	639	738	753	869	993	1,071	1,400	1,618	1,894
ND								5	2	37	191	319
OH		45	231	581	938	1,519	1,980	2,340	2,665	3,198	3,672	4,158
OK											259	790
OR							12	52	91	175	318	414
PA	434	602	810	1,049	1,348	1,724	2,312	2,906	3,522	4,283	5,258	6,302
RI	69	69	77	83	97	109	148	175	217	277	346	429
SC	249	346	415	503	581	594	669	704	706	996	1,151	1,340
SD									12	98	349	402
TN	36	106	262	423	682	829	1,003	1,110	1,259	1,542	1,768	2,021
TX							213	604	819	1,592	2,236	3,049
UT							11	40	87	144	211	277
VT	85	154	218	236	281	292	314	315	331	332	332	344
VA	692	808	878	938	1,044	1,025	1,119	1,220	1,225	1,513	1,656	1,854
WA							1	12	24	75	357	518
WV	56	79	105	137	177	225	302	377	442	618	763	959
WI						31	305	776	1,055	1,315	1,693	2,069
WY									9	21	63	93
US total[2]	3,929	5,308	7,240	9,638	12,866	17,069	23,192	31,443	39,818[3]	50,156	62,948	75,995

[1]Detail may not add to total given because of rounding. [2]Data for Alaska and Hawaii are not included until 1960,

State Populations, 1790–2008 (continued)

1910	1920	1930	1940	1950	1960	1970	1980	1990	2000	2008 EST.
2,138	2,348	2,646	2,833	3,062	3,267	3,444	3,894	4,040	4,452	4,662
64	55	59	73	129	226	300	402	550	627	686
204	334	436	499	750	1,302	1,771	2,718	3,665	5,167	6,500
1,574	1,752	1,854	1,949	1,910	1,786	1,923	2,286	2,351	2,678	2,855
2,378	3,427	5,677	6,907	10,586	15,717	19,953	23,668	29,811	33,999	36,757
799	940	1,036	1,123	1,325	1,754	2,207	2,890	3,294	4,328	4,939
1,115	1,381	1,607	1,709	2,007	2,535	3,032	3,108	3,287	3,412	3,501
202	223	238	267	318	446	548	594	666	786	873
331	438	487	663	802	764	757	638	607	572	592
753	968	1,468	1,897	2,771	4,952	6,789	9,746	12,938	16,047	18,328
2,609	2,896	2,909	3,124	3,445	3,943	4,590	5,463	6,478	8,230	9,686
192	256	368	423	500	633	769	965	1,108	1,211	1,288
326	432	445	525	589	667	713	944	1,007	1,299	1,524
5,639	6,485	7,631	7,897	8,712	10,081	11,114	11,427	11,431	12,438	12,902
2,701	2,930	3,239	3,428	3,934	4,662	5,194	5,490	5,544	6,091	6,377
2,225	2,404	2,471	2,538	2,621	2,758	2,824	2,914	2,777	2,928	3,003
1,691	1,769	1,881	1,801	1,905	2,179	2,247	2,364	2,478	2,693	2,802
2,290	2,417	2,615	2,846	2,945	3,038	3,219	3,661	3,687	4,049	4,269
1,656	1,799	2,102	2,364	2,684	3,257	3,641	4,206	4,222	4,469	4,411
742	768	797	847	914	969	992	1,125	1,228	1,277	1,316
1,295	1,450	1,632	1,821	2,343	3,101	3,922	4,217	4,781	5,310	5,634
3,366	3,852	4,250	4,317	4,691	5,149	5,689	5,737	6,016	6,363	6,498
2,810	3,668	4,842	5,256	6,372	7,823	8,875	9,262	9,295	9,955	10,003
2,076	2,387	2,564	2,792	2,982	3,414	3,805	4,076	4,376	4,934	5,220
1,797	1,791	2,010	2,184	2,179	2,178	2,217	2,521	2,575	2,848	2,939
3,293	3,404	3,629	3,785	3,955	4,320	4,677	4,917	5,117	5,606	5,912
376	549	538	559	591	675	694	787	799	903	967
1,192	1,296	1,378	1,316	1,326	1,411	1,483	1,570	1,578	1,713	1,783
82	77	91	110	160	285	489	800	1,202	2,018	2,600
431	443	465	492	533	607	738	921	1,109	1,240	1,316
2,537	3,156	4,041	4,160	4,835	6,067	7,168	7,365	7,748	8,431	8,683
327	360	423	532	681	951	1,016	1,303	1,515	1,821	1,984
9,114	10,385	12,588	13,479	14,830	16,782	18,237	17,558	17,991	18,998	19,490
2,206	2,559	3,170	3,572	4,062	4,556	5,082	5,882	6,632	8,079	9,222
577	647	681	642	620	632	618	653	639	641	641
4,767	5,759	6,647	6,908	7,947	9,706	10,652	10,798	10,847	11,364	11,486
1,657	2,028	2,396	2,336	2,233	2,328	2,559	3,025	3,146	3,454	3,642
673	783	954	1,090	1,521	1,769	2,091	2,633	2,842	3,431	3,790
7,665	8,720	9,631	9,900	10,498	11,319	11,794	11,864	11,883	12,285	12,448
543	604	687	713	792	859	947	947	1,003	1,051	1,051
1,515	1,684	1,739	1,900	2,117	2,383	2,591	3,122	3,486	4,023	4,480
584	637	693	643	653	681	666	691	696	756	804
2,185	2,338	2,617	2,916	3,292	3,567	3,924	4,591	4,877	5,703	6,215
3,897	4,663	5,825	6,415	7,711	9,580	11,197	14,229	16,986	20,946	24,327
373	449	508	550	689	891	1,059	1,461	1,723	2,244	2,736
356	352	360	359	378	390	444	511	563	610	621
2,062	2,309	2,422	2,678	3,319	3,967	4,648	5,347	6,189	7,104	7,769
1,142	1,357	1,563	1,736	2,379	2,853	3,409	4,132	4,867	5,911	6,549
1,221	1,464	1,729	1,902	2,006	1,860	1,744	1,950	1,793	1,807	1,814
2,334	2,632	2,939	3,138	3,435	3,952	4,418	4,706	4,892	5,374	5,628
146	194	226	251	291	330	332	470	454	494	533
91,972	105,711	122,775	131,669	150,697	179,323	203,302[3]	226,546[3]	248,791[3]	282,172[3]	304,060

the first census after they became states in 1959. [3]Figures were revised by the Census Bureau after the census.

Population of US Territories

Total midyear population. Source: US Census Bureau.

YEAR	PUERTO RICO	GUAM	VIRGIN ISLANDS	AMERICAN SAMOA	NORTHERN MARIANA ISLANDS
1960	2,358,000	66,900	32,500	20,000	8,861
1965	2,596,774	74,100	43,500	24,600	10,465
1970	2,721,754	86,470	63,476	27,267	12,359
1975	2,935,124	102,110	94,484	29,640	14,938
1980	3,209,648	106,869	99,636	32,418	16,890
1985	3,382,106	120,615	100,760	38,633	21,386
1990	3,536,910	134,125	103,963	47,199	44,037
1995	3,683,103	144,190	107,817	53,906	57,229
2000	3,814,413	155,324	108,639	57,771	69,706
2005	3,910,707	168,614	109,600	62,399	70,636
2009	3,966,213	178,430	109,825	65,628	51,484

Foreign-Born Population in the US, 1850–2007

The foreign-born population consists of persons born outside the United States to parents who were not US citizens. Populations of Alaska and Hawaii were included starting in 1960. In 1850 and 1860 data, the entire slave population was considered native-born.

Source: *Statistical Abstract of the United States: 2009.*

YEAR	POPULATION TOTAL	FOREIGN-BORN	% OF TOTAL	YEAR	POPULATION TOTAL	FOREIGN-BORN	% OF TOTAL
1850	23,191,876	2,244,602	9.7	1940	131,669,275	11,594,896	8.8
1860	31,443,321	4,138,697	13.2	1950	150,216,110	10,347,395	6.9
1870	38,558,371	5,567,229	14.4	1960	179,325,671	9,738,091	5.4
1880	50,155,783	6,679,943	13.3	1970	203,210,158	9,619,302	4.7
1890	62,622,250	9,249,547	14.8	1980	226,545,805	14,079,906	6.2
1900	75,994,575	10,341,276	13.6	1990	248,709,873	19,767,316	7.9
1910	91,972,266	13,515,886	14.7	2000	281,421,906	31,107,889	11.1
1920	105,710,620	13,920,692	13.2	2006[1]	293,834,000	35,659,000	12.1
1930	122,775,046	14,204,149	11.6	2007[1]	296,824,000	37,279,000	12.6

[1] As of March.

Total Immigrants Admitted to the US, 1901–2008

Numbers shown include only immigrant aliens admitted for permanent residence and are for fiscal years. Currently the fiscal year begins 1 October and ends 30 September. Prior to 1976, the fiscal year began 1 July and ended 30 June.

Source: *Yearbook of Immigration Statistics, 2008.*

YEAR	NUMBER	YEAR	NUMBER	YEAR	NUMBER	YEAR	NUMBER
1901	487,918	1911	878,587	1921	805,228	1931	97,139
1902	648,743	1912	838,172	1922	309,556	1932	35,576
1903	857,046	1913	1,197,892	1923	522,919	1933	23,068
1904	812,870	1914	1,218,480	1924	706,896	1934	29,470
1905	1,026,499	1915	326,700	1925	294,314	1935	34,956
1906	1,100,735	1916	298,826	1926	304,488	1936	36,329
1907	1,285,349	1917	295,403	1927	335,175	1937	50,244
1908	782,870	1918	110,618	1928	307,255	1938	67,895
1909	751,786	1919	141,132	1929	279,678	1939	82,998
1910	1,041,570	1920	430,001	1930	241,700	1940	70,756
totals 1901–10	8,795,386	1911–20	5,735,811	1921–30	4,107,209	1931–40	528,431
1941	51,776	1951	205,717	1961	271,344	1971	370,478
1942	28,781	1952	265,520	1962	283,763	1972	384,685
1943	23,725	1953	170,434	1963	306,260	1973	398,515
1944	28,551	1954	208,177	1964	292,248	1974	393,919
1945	38,119	1955	237,790	1965	296,697	1975	385,378
1946	108,721	1956	321,625	1966	323,040	1976[1]	499,093
1947	147,292	1957	326,867	1967	361,972	1977	458,755
1948	170,570	1958	253,265	1968	454,448	1978	589,810
1949	188,317	1959	260,686	1969	358,579	1979	394,244
1950	249,187	1960	265,398	1970	373,326	1980	524,295
totals 1941–50	1,035,039	1951–60	2,515,479	1961–70	3,321,677	1971–80	4,399,172

Total Immigrants Admitted to the US, 1901–2008 (continued)

YEAR	NUMBER	YEAR	NUMBER	YEAR	NUMBER
1981	595,014	1991	1,826,595	2001	1,058,902
1982	533,624	1992	973,445	2002	1,059,356
1983	550,052	1993	903,916	2003	703,542
1984	541,811	1994	803,993	2004	957,883
1985	568,149	1995	720,177	2005	1,122,257
1986	600,027	1996	915,560	2006	1,266,129
1987	599,889	1997	797,847	2007	1,052,415
1988	641,346	1998	653,206	2008	1,107,126
1989	1,090,172	1999	644,787		
1990	1,535,872	2000	841,002		
totals 1981–90	7,255,956	1991–2000	9,080,528	2001–08	8,327,610

totals 1901–2008: 55,102,298

[1]Includes the 15 months from 1 Jul 1975 through 30 Sep 1976.

Immigrants Admitted to the US by State of Residence and Country of Birth

Fiscal year 2008. Korea used to designate both North and South Korea.
Source: <www.dhs.gov>.

STATE OF RESIDENCE	TOTAL IMMIGRANTS	TOP FIVE COUNTRIES OF BIRTH (NUMBER OF IMMIGRANTS)
Alabama	3,877	Mexico (590), China (300), India (299), Korea (236), Guatemala (204)
Alaska	1,534	Philippines (451), Mexico (99), China (90), Thailand (80), Korea (62)
Arizona	20,638	Mexico (10,557), Philippines (745), China (627), India (611), Vietnam (471)
Arkansas	2,997	Mexico (1,267), El Salvador (203), China (163), Philippines (135), India (130)
California	238,444	Mexico (73,648), Philippines (22,423), China (21,925), India (14,112), Vietnam (11,086)
Colorado	12,741	Mexico (4,219), China (637), Ethiopia (561), Vietnam (472), India (393)
Connecticut	12,190	Jamaica (939), India (896), China (782), Haiti (500), Colombia (494)
Delaware	2,295	Mexico (249), India (244), China (138), Haiti (130), Philippines (96)
District of Columbia	2,652	Ethiopia (432), El Salvador (263), China (84), Nigeria (83), United Kingdom (82)
Florida	133,445	Cuba (40,946), Haiti (14,682), Colombia (13,481), Venezuela (6,050), Jamaica (5,307)
Georgia	27,769	Mexico (4,002), India (2,085), China (1,170), Colombia (1,072), Korea (1,063), Vietnam (1,063)
Hawaii	6,572	Philippines (3,513), China (795), Japan (465), Korea (266), Vietnam (210)
Idaho	2,766	Mexico (1,122), Uzbekistan (192), China (149), Philippines (94), Russia (94)
Illinois	42,723	Mexico (11,389), India (4,114), Poland (2,746), Philippines (2,365), China (2,313)
Indiana	8,028	Mexico (1,577), China (649), India (628), Philippines (319), Nigeria (237)
Iowa	3,696	Mexico (1,015), Vietnam (252), China (199), The Sudan (195), India (183)
Kansas	5,344	Mexico (1,877), Vietnam (421), India (305), China (259), Philippines (214)
Kentucky	5,315	Cuba (909), Mexico (395), China (260), India (260), Somalia (210)
Louisiana	4,011	Vietnam (428), Mexico (396), India (256), China (240), Honduras (229)
Maine	1,617	Somalia (346), Kenya (166), Canada (93), China (84), The Sudan (69)
Maryland	27,062	Nigeria (1,692), India (1,642), China (1,626), El Salvador (1,595), Ethiopia (1,420)
Massachusetts	30,369	China (2,771), Dominican Republic (2,434), Brazil (2,065), Haiti (1,944), India (1,787)
Michigan	17,947	India (1,741), Mexico (1,391), Iraq (1,348), China (1,047), Albania (781)
Minnesota	15,832	Somalia (3,372), Ethiopia (1,199), Liberia (1,025), Mexico (857), Thailand (651)
Mississippi	1,679	Mexico (290), India (201), China (121), Philippines (118), Vietnam (110)
Missouri	7,078	Mexico (802), China (578), India (433), Philippines (366), Vietnam (336)

Immigrants Admitted to the US by Country of Birth and State of Residence (continued)

STATE OF RESIDENCE	TOTAL IMMIGRANTS	TOP FIVE COUNTRIES OF BIRTH (NUMBER OF IMMIGRANTS)
Montana	543	Philippines (65), Canada (62), Mexico (59), China (45), United Kingdom (21)
Nebraska	3,668	Mexico (1,194), The Sudan (257), Vietnam (169), Guatemala (161), Somalia (161)
Nevada	11,768	Mexico (3,690), Philippines (1,660), Cuba (952), China (743), El Salvador (433)
New Hampshire	2,466	China (159), India (133), Dominican Republic (124), Canada (123), Philippines (95)
New Jersey	53,997	India (8,083), Dominican Republic (4,159), Colombia (2,752), China (2,631), Philippines (2,347)
New Mexico	3,509	Mexico (2,013), Cuba (155), China (130), Philippines (126), India (79)
New York	143,679	China (23,981), Dominican Republic (15,563), Jamaica (6,615), Bangladesh (5,744), India (5,561)
North Carolina	15,174	Mexico (2,178), Vietnam (1,046), India (1,002), China (789), Colombia (573)
North Dakota	662	Somalia (89), China (56), Canada (46), The Sudan (40), Philippines (33)
Ohio	14,595	Somalia (1,303), India (1,169), China (1,038), Mexico (575), Ghana (497)
Oklahoma	4,306	Mexico (1,519), Vietnam (278), China (242), India (242), Philippines (163)
Oregon	9,028	Mexico (2,152), China (734), Vietnam (667), Ukraine (466), India (413)
Pennsylvania	23,646	India (2,272), China (2,124), Dominican Republic (1,184), Liberia (1,181), Mexico (997)
Rhode Island	3,735	Dominican Republic (768), Guatemala (316), Cape Verde (305), Liberia (261), Colombia (198)
South Carolina	4,241	Mexico (570), India (324), China (276), Colombia (247), Philippines (203)
South Dakota	773	Ethiopia (105), The Sudan (59), Mexico (58), Philippines (46), Guatemala (42)
Tennessee	8,348	Mexico (1,090), India (709), Egypt (622), China (499), Somalia (470)
Texas	89,811	Mexico (41,060), India (4,811), Vietnam (3,534), China (3,131), Philippines (2,567)
Utah	6,087	Mexico (1,710), Peru (251), China (238), Vietnam (237), Philippines (201)
Vermont	771	Uzbekistan (57), Canada (56), India (51), Somalia (48), United Kingdom (47)
Virginia	30,257	India (2,561), El Salvador (1,810), Korea (1,416), China (1,345), Pakistan (1,329)
Washington	23,170	Mexico (3,023), India (1,813), China (1,758), Philippines (1,623), Vietnam (1,570)
West Virginia	798	China (73), Philippines (62), India (44), Mexico (39), Pakistan (31), United Kingdom (31)
Wisconsin	7,306	Mexico (1,521), Thailand (594), India (516), China (398), Laos (361)
Wyoming	458	Mexico (122), Canada (33), China (33), Philippines (24), India (20)

Americans 65 and Older, 1900–2009

Data for Hawaii and Alaska are included after 1950. Source: US Census Bureau.

CENSUS YEAR	NUMBER OF PEOPLE 65 AND OLDER	% OF TOTAL POPULATION	CENSUS YEAR	NUMBER OF PEOPLE 65 AND OLDER	% OF TOTAL POPULATION
1900	3,080,498	4.1	1960	16,559,580	9.2
1910	3,949,524	4.3	1970	20,065,502	9.8
1920	4,933,215	4.7	1980	25,549,427	11.3
1930	6,633,805	5.4	1990	31,241,831	12.6
1940	9,019,314	6.8	2000	34,991,753	12.4
1950	12,269,537	8.1	2009	39,472,928	12.8

Poverty Level by State, 1980–2007

Source: US Census Bureau. Detail may not add to total given because of rounding.

STATE	% OF PEOPLE IN POVERTY			NUMBER OF PEOPLE IN POVERTY ('000)		
	1980	1990	2007	1980	1990	2007
Alabama	21.2	19.2	14.5	810	779	662
Alaska	9.6	11.4	7.6	36	57	51

Poverty Level by State, 1980–2007 (continued)

STATE	% OF PEOPLE IN POVERTY			NUMBER OF PEOPLE IN POVERTY ('000)		
	1980	1990	2007	1980	1990	2007
Arizona	12.8	13.7	14.3	354	484	912
Arkansas	21.5	19.6	13.8	484	472	387
California	11.0	13.9	12.7	2,619	4,128	4,589
Colorado	8.6	13.7	9.8	247	461	478
Connecticut	8.3	6.0	8.9	255	196	309
Delaware	11.8	6.9	9.3	68	48	80
District of Columbia	20.9	21.1	17.9	131	120	104
Florida	16.7	14.4	12.5	1,692	1,896	2,250
Georgia	13.9	15.8	13.6	727	1,001	1,294
Hawaii	8.5	11.0	7.4	81	121	94
Idaho	14.7	14.9	9.9	138	157	149
Illinois	12.3	13.7	10.0	1,386	1,606	1,262
Indiana	11.8	13.0	11.8	645	714	740
Iowa	10.8	10.4	8.9	311	289	264
Kansas	9.4	10.3	11.7	215	259	319
Kentucky	19.3	17.3	15.5	701	628	653
Louisiana	20.3	23.6	16.1	868	952	673
Maine	14.6	13.1	10.8	158	162	142
Maryland	9.5	9.9	8.8	389	468	491
Massachusetts	9.5	10.7	11.2	542	626	707
Michigan	12.9	14.3	10.8	1,194	1,315	1,076
Minnesota	8.7	12.0	9.3	342	524	482
Mississippi	24.3	25.7	22.6	591	684	655
Missouri	13.0	13.4	12.8	625	700	742
Montana	13.2	16.3	13.0	102	134	122
Nebraska	13.0	10.3	9.9	199	167	174
Nevada	8.3	9.8	9.7	70	119	250
New Hampshire	7.0	6.3	5.8	63	68	76
New Jersey	9.0	9.2	8.7	659	711	742
New Mexico	20.6	20.9	14.0	268	319	271
New York	13.8	14.3	14.5	2,391	2,571	2,757
North Carolina	15.0	13.0	15.5	877	829	1,423
North Dakota	15.5	13.7	9.3	99	87	57
Ohio	9.8	11.5	12.8	1,046	1,256	1,446
Oklahoma	13.9	15.6	13.4	406	481	476
Oregon	11.5	9.2	12.8	309	267	481
Pennsylvania	9.8	11.0	10.4	1,142	1,328	1,273
Rhode Island	10.7	7.5	9.5	97	71	99
South Carolina	16.8	16.2	14.1	534	548	617
South Dakota	18.8	13.3	9.4	127	93	74
Tennessee	19.6	16.9	14.8	884	833	906
Texas	15.7	15.9	16.5	2,247	2,684	3,903
Utah	10.0	8.2	9.6	148	143	255
Vermont	12.0	10.9	10.0	62	61	61
Virginia	12.4	11.1	8.6	647	705	664
Washington	12.7	8.9	10.2	538	434	661
West Virginia	15.2	18.1	14.8	297	328	265
Wisconsin	8.5	9.3	11.0	403	448	601
Wyoming	10.4	11.0	10.8	49	51	56
all US	13.0	13.5	12.5	29,272	33,585	37,726

Did you know? Ouroboros was the emblematic serpent of ancient Egypt and Greece, represented with its tail in its mouth as continually devouring itself and being reborn. It represented the eternal cycle of destruction and re-creation. In the 19th century, a vision of Ouroboros gave the German chemist Friedrich August Kekule von Stradonitz the idea of linked carbon atoms forming the benzene ring.

States and Other Areas of the United States

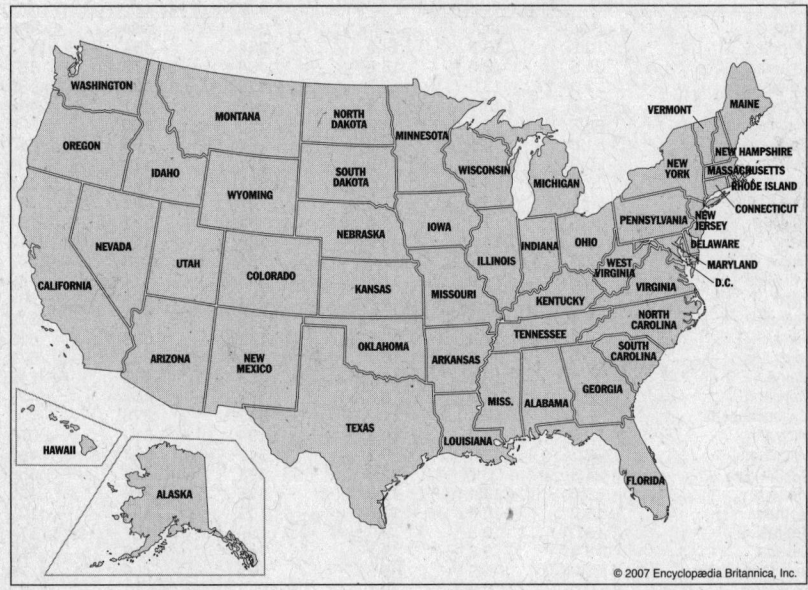

© 2007 Encyclopædia Britannica, Inc.

Alabama

Name: Alabama, from the Choctaw language, meaning "thicket clearers." **Nickname:** Heart of Dixie. **Capital:** Montgomery. **Rank:** population: 23rd; area: 30th. **Motto:** "Audemus jura nostra defendere" ("We dare defend our rights"). **Song:** "Alabama," words by Julia S. Tutwiler and music by Edna Gockel Gussen. **Amphibian:** Red Hills salamander. **Bird:** yellowhammer. **Fish:** largemouth bass (freshwater); tarpon (saltwater). **Flower:** camellia. **Fossil:** *Basilosaurus cetoides.* **Gemstone:** star blue quartz. **Insect:** monarch butterfly. **Mineral:** hematite. **Reptile:** Alabama red-bellied turtle. **Rock:** marble. **Tree:** southern longleaf pine.

Natural features

Land area: 51,700 sq mi, 133,902 sq km. **Mountain ranges:** Appalachian, Raccoon, Lookout. **Highest point:** Cheaha Mountain, 734 m (2,407 ft). **Largest lake:** Lake Guntersville. **Major rivers:** Mobile, Alabama, Tombigbee, Tennessee, Chattahoochee. **Natural regions:** the Appalachian Plateaus, extending across the north-central region; Interior Low Plateaus, far north; Valley and Ridge Province and small portion of the Piedmont Province, covering the east; Coastal Plain, covering the southern half of the state. **Land use:** forest, 64.4%; agricultural, 7.5%; pasture, 0.2%; other, 27.9%.

People

Population (2007): 4,627,851; persons per sq mi 89.5, persons per sq km 34.6. **Vital statistics** (2006; per 1,000 population): birth rate, 13.7; death rate, 10.2; marriage rate, 8.6; divorce rate, 4.8. **Major cities** (2007): Birmingham 229,800; Montgomery 204,086; Mobile 191,411; Huntsville 171,327; Tuscaloosa 88,722.

Government

Statehood: entered the Union on 14 Dec 1819 as the 22nd state. **State constitution:** adopted 1901. **Representation in US Congress:** 2 senators; 7 representatives. **Electoral college:** 9 votes. **Political divisions:** 67 counties.

Economy

Employment (2007): services 29.7%; government 15.7%; trade 14.8%; finance, insurance, real estate 13.2%; manufacturing 11.7%. **Production** (2007): finance, insurance, real estate 21.3%; manufacturing 17.3%; government 15.5%; services 15.2%; trade 13.8%. **Chief agricultural products:** *Crops:* cotton, corn (maize), soybeans, peanuts (groundnuts), potatoes, sweet potatoes, peaches, pecans, winter wheat, hay. *Livestock:* cattle and calves, poultry, hogs. *Fish catch:* red snapper, catfish, shrimp, crab, mussels, oysters. **Chief manufactured products:** food products; textiles; wearing apparel; wood products; mobile homes; paper products; refined petroleum products; plastics and rubber products; base metals.

Internet resources: <www.alabama.travel/>; <www.alabama.gov>.

Alaska

Name: Alaska, from the Aleut word *Alyeska,* meaning "great land." **Nickname:** The Last Frontier. **Capital:** Juneau. **Rank:** population: 47th; area: 1st. **Motto:** "North to the future." **Song:** "Alaska's Flag," words by

Marie Drake and music by Elinor Dusenbury. **Bird:** willow ptarmigan. **Fish:** giant king salmon. **Flower:** forget-me-not. **Fossil:** *Mammuthus primigenius* (woolly mammoth). **Gemstone:** jade. **Insect:** four-spot skimmer dragonfly. **Mammal:** moose. **Marine mammal:** bowhead whale. **Mineral:** gold. **Tree:** sitka spruce.

Natural features

Land area: 589,194 sq mi, 1,526,005 sq km. **Mountain ranges:** Wrangell, Chugach, Alaska, Brooks, Aleutian, Boundary. **Highest point:** Mt. McKinley (Denali), 6,194 m (20,320 ft). **Largest lake:** Iliamna Lake. **Major rivers:** Yukon, Porcupine, Tanana, Koyukuk, Noataks. **Natural regions:** panhandle, a narrow strip of land that includes portions of the Coast Mountains; coastal archipelago and the Gulf of Alaska islands; the Alaska Peninsula and Aleutian island chain that separates the North Pacific from the Bering Sea; the Alaska Range, extending across the south-central region; the Interior Plateau, including the basin of the Yukon River, the central plains and tablelands of the interior, the Seward Peninsula to the west, and the Brooks Range, sometimes called the North Slope, to the north; the Arctic Coastal Plain, a treeless region of tundra lying at the northernmost edge of the state; tundra-covered islands of the Bering Sea. **Land use:** forest, 24.1%; pasture, 0.0%; other, 75.9%.

People

Population (2007): 683,478; persons per sq mi 1.2, person per sq km 0.4. **Vital statistics** (2006; per 1,000 population): birth rate, 16.4; death rate, 5.0; marriage rate, 7.8; divorce rate, 4.4. **Major cities** (2007): Anchorage 279,671; Fairbanks 34,540; Juneau 30,690; College 13,600; Sitka 8,874.

Government

Statehood: entered the Union on 3 Jan 1959 as the 49th state. **State constitution:** adopted 1956. **Representation in US Congress:** 2 senators; 1 representative. **Electoral college:** 3 votes. **Political divisions:** 16 boroughs.

Economy

Employment (2007): services 28.9%; government 23.6%; trade 12.1%; transportation, public utilities 7.5%; finance, insurance, real estate 12.3%. **Production** (2007): mining 31.0%; government 17.5%; finance, insurance, real estate 13.9%; transportation, public utilities 13.0%; services 11.8%. **Chief agricultural products:** *Crops:* hay, milk, potatoes, timber. *Livestock:* cattle and calves, pigs. *Fish catch:* salmon, herring, groundfish, shellfish, crab, shrimp. **Chief manufactured products:** processed fish and seafood (fresh, frozen, canned, and cured); wood products; paper products; transportation products.

Internet resources: <www.travelalaska.com>; <www.alaska.gov>.

Arizona

Name: Arizona, from *arizonac,* derived from two Papago Indian words meaning "place of the young spring." **Nickname:** Grand Canyon State. **Capital:** Phoenix. **Rank:** population: 16th; area: 6th. **Motto:** "Ditat Deus" ("God enriches"). **Song:** "Arizona March Song," words by Margaret Rowe Clifford and music by Maurice Blumenthal. **Amphibian:** Arizona treefrog. **Bird:** cactus wren. **Fish:** Arizona trout. **Flower:** saguaro blossom. **Fossil:** petrified wood. **Gemstone:** turquoise. **Mammal:** ringtail. **Reptile:** Arizona ridgenose rattlesnake. **Tree:** palo verde.

Natural features

Land area: 113,999 sq mi, 295,256 sq km. **Mountain ranges:** Black, Gila Bend, Chuska, Hualapai, San Francisco, White. **Highest point:** Humphreys Peak, 3,851 m (12,633 ft). **Largest lake:** Lake Roosevelt. **Major rivers:** Colorado, Little Colorado, Verde, Salt, Gila. **Natural regions:** the Colorado Plateaus, northeast third of the state, include the Grand Canyon and the Painted Desert; the Basin and Range Province, south, east, central, and northwest, includes the Sonoran Desert in the southwest corner and part of the Great Basin Desert to the northwest. **Land use:** pasture, 44.2%; forest, 5.7%; agricultural, 1.3%; other, 48.8%.

People

Population (2007): 6,338,755; persons per sq mi 55.6, persons per sq km 21.5. **Vital statistics** (2006; per 1,000 population): birth rate, 16.6; death rate, 7.5; marriage rate, 6.3; divorce rate, 3.9. **Major cities** (2007): Phoenix 1,552,259; Tucson 525,529; Mesa 452,933; Glendale 253,152; Chandler 246,399; Scottsdale 235,677; Gilbert 207,550; Tempe 174,091.

Government

Statehood: entered the Union on 14 Feb 1912 as the 48th state. **State constitution:** adopted 1911. **Representation in US Congress:** 2 senators; 8 representatives. **Electoral college:** 10 votes. **Political divisions:** 15 counties.

Economy

Employment (2007): services 33.0%; finance, insurance, real estate 19.3%; trade 15.2%; government 12.7%; construction 8.1%. **Production** (2007): finance, insurance, real estate 31.2%; services 18.7%; trade 13.8%; government 12.1%; manufacturing 7.9%. **Chief agricultural products:** *Crops:* cotton and cottonseed, wheat, sorghum, hay, barley, corn (maize), potatoes, grapes, apples, dairy products. *Livestock:* cattle and calves, hogs and pigs, sheep and lambs, angora goats. **Chief manufactured products:** semiconductors; telecommunications equipment; electrical equipment; transportation equipment; soap products; nonferrous metal products.

Internet resources: <www.arizonaguide.com>; <www.az.gov>.

Did you know? Tombstone AZ was ironically named by Ed Schieffelin, who discovered silver there after being told that all he would find would be his tombstone.

For details about state governments, see pages 608–613; for energy data, see pages 627–628.

Arkansas

Name: Arkansas, from an unknown Native American word describing the Quapaw tribe (also known as the Arkansaw), meaning "people who live downstream." **Nickname:** Natural State. **Capital:** Little Rock. **Rank:** population: 32nd; area: 27th. **Motto:** "Regnat populus" ("The people rule"). **Songs:** "Arkansas," words and music by Wayland Holyfield; "Oh, Arkansas," words and music by by Terry Rose and Gary Klaff. **Bird:** mockingbird. **Flower:** apple blossom. **Gemstone:** diamond. **Insect:** honeybee. **Mammal:** white-tailed deer. **Mineral:** quartz crystal. **Rock:** bauxite. **Tree:** pine tree.

Natural features

Land area: 53,178 sq mi, 137,730 sq km. **Mountain ranges:** Ozark, Ouachita. **Highest point:** Mt. Magazine, 839 m (2,753 ft). **Largest lake:** Lake Chicot. **Major rivers:** Arkansas, Red, Ouachita, White. **Natural regions:** the Ozark Plateaus, including the Boston Mountains, north and northwest regions; the Ouachita Province, including the Arkansas valley and the Ouachita Mountains, central region; the Coastal Plain, extends from southwest to northeast. **Land use:** forest, 44.1%; agricultural, 22.1%; pasture, 0.1%; other, 33.7%.

People

Population (2007): 2,834,797; persons per sq mi 53.3, persons per sq km 20.6. **Vital statistics** (2006; per 1,000 population): birth rate, 14.6; death rate, 9.9; marriage rate, 12.2; divorce rate, 5.7. **Major cities** (2007): Little Rock 187,452; Fort Smith 84,375; Fayetteville 72,208; Springdale 66,881; Jonesboro 63,190.

Government

Statehood: entered the Union on 15 Jun 1836 as the 25th state. **State constitution:** adopted 1874. **Representation in US Congress:** 2 senators; 4 representatives. **Electoral college:** 6 votes. **Political divisions:** 75 counties.

Economy

Employment (2007): services 28.9%; government 14.4%; trade 13.8%; manufacturing 12.2%; finance, insurance, real estate 12.1%. **Production** (2007): finance, insurance, real estate 19.1%; manufacturing 17.8%; services 15.3%; trade 13.9%; government 13.5%. **Chief agricultural products:** *Crops:* corn (maize), cotton, soybeans, wheat, apples, blueberries, grapes, peaches, pecans, strawberries. *Livestock:* cattle and calves, hogs and pigs, poultry. *Fish catch:* catfish. **Chief manufactured products:** food products; lumber and paper products; refined petroleum products; chemical products; plastic and rubber products; base metals; fabricated metal products; machinery and apparatus; transportation equipment.

Internet resources: <www.arkansas.com>; <www.arkansas.gov>.

California

Name: California, from unknown origins. **Nickname:** Golden State. **Capital:** Sacramento. **Rank:** population: 1st; area: 3rd. **Motto:** "Eureka" ("I have found it"). **Song:** "I Love You, California," words by F.B. Silverwood and music by A.F. Frankenstein. **Bird:** California quail. **Fish:** golden trout (freshwater); garibaldi (saltwater). **Flower:** California poppy. **Fossil:** saber-tooth cat. **Gemstone:** benitoite. **Insect:** California dogface butterfly. **Mammal:** California grizzly bear. **Marine mammal:** California gray whale. **Mineral:** gold. **Reptile:** desert tortoise. **Rock:** serpentine. **Tree:** California redwood.

Natural features

Land area: 158,633 sq mi, 410,858 sq km. **Mountain ranges:** Coast, Sierra Nevada, Cascade, Santa Lucia, Klamath, Tehachapi, San Gabriel, San Bernardino. **Highest point:** Mt. Whitney, 4,418 m (14,494 ft). **Largest lake:** Lake Tahoe. **Major rivers:** Colorado, Sacramento, Pit, San Joaquin. **Natural regions:** Basin and Range Province, northeast corner, also eastern border with Arizona and southern Nevada; Cascade-Sierra Mountains, running from north to south along the east-central region; Pacific Border Province, west, including the Coast Ranges to the west, the Klamath Mountains to the north, the Los Angeles Ranges to the south, and the California Trough (commonly referred to as the Central Valley) to the east; Lower Californian Province, southwestern tip. **Land use:** pasture, 17.5%; forest, 13.7%; agricultural, 9.3%; other, 59.5%.

People

Population (2007): 36,553,215; persons per sq mi 230.4, persons per sq km 89.0. **Vital statistics** (2006; per 1,000 population): birth rate, 15.4; death rate, 6.5; marriage rate, 6.0; divorce rate (2001), 6.6. **Major cities** (2007): Los Angeles 3,834,340; San Diego 1,266,731; San Jose 939,899; San Francisco 764,976; Fresno 470,508; Long Beach 466,520; Sacramento 460,242; Oakland 401,489.

Government

Statehood: entered the Union on 9 Sep 1850 as the 31st state. **State constitution:** adopted 1879. **Representation in US Congress:** 2 senators; 53 representatives. **Electoral college:** 55 votes. **Political divisions:** 58 counties.

Economy

Employment (2007): services 32.0%; finance, insurance, real estate 19.8%; trade 14.0%; government 12.8%; manufacturing 7.3%. **Production** (2007): finance, insurance, real estate 33.5%; services 16.1%; trade 12.7%; government 11.3%; transportation, public utilities 10.3%. **Chief agricultural products:** *Crops:* wheat, oats, rice, apples, apricots, cherries, grapes, olives, peaches, pears, strawberries, onions, lima beans, artichokes, broccoli, snap beans, dairy products, eggs. *Livestock:* cattle and calves, sheep and lambs. *Fish catch:* bonito, halibut, mackerel, groundfish, rockfish (Pacific red snapper), sablefish (black cod), soles and sand dabs, sardines, white sea bass, shark, swordfish, tuna, crab, California spiny lobster, Pacific Ocean shrimp, prawns, squid. **Chief manufactured products:** food products; soft drinks; beer and wine; textiles; wearing apparel; lumber and wood products; paper products; printing; refined petroleum products; asphalt;

chemical products; plastic and rubber products; glass products; construction materials; base metals; fabricated metal products; machinery and apparatus; telecommunications equipment; semiconductors and computers; electronics; transportation equipment; furniture; medical equipment; sporting goods.

Internet resources: <www.visitcalifornia.com>; <www.ca.gov>.

Colorado

Name: Colorado, from a Spanish word meaning "red." **Nickname:** Centennial State. **Capital:** Denver. **Rank:** population: 22nd; area: 8th. **Motto:** "Nil sine numine" ("Nothing without Providence"). **Songs:** "Where the Columbines Grow," words and music by A.J. Flynn; "Rocky Mountain High," words and music by John Denver. **Bird:** lark bunting. **Fish:** greenback cutthroat trout. **Flower:** white and lavender columbine. **Fossil:** stegosaurus. **Gemstone:** aquamarine. **Insect:** Colorado hairstreak butterfly. **Mammal:** Rocky Mountain bighorn sheep. **Tree:** Colorado blue spruce.

Natural features

Land area: 104,094 sq mi, 269,602 sq km. **Mountain ranges:** Rocky, Front, Medicine Bow, Park, Rabbit Ears, San Juan, Sangre de Cristo, Sawatch. **Highest point:** Mt. Elbert, 4,399 m (14,433 ft). **Largest lakes:** Blue Mesa Reservoir (man-made); Grand Lake (natural). **Major rivers:** Colorado, Arkansas, South Platte, Rio Grande. **Natural regions:** the Great Plains Province, eastern half of state, includes the High Plains to the east, Colorado Piedmont to the west, and Raton Section to the south; Southern Rocky Mountains, running down the middle of the state; Middle Rocky Mountains and Wyoming Basin, northwest corner; Colorado Plateaus, western and southwestern border, include the Uinta Basin to the north, the Canyon Lands in the middle, and the Navajo Section to the south. **Land use:** pasture, 37.2%; agricultural, 12.5%; forest, 4.9%; other, 45.4%.

People

Population (2007): 4,861,515; persons per sq mi 46.7, persons per sq km 18.0. **Vital statistics** (2006; per 1,000 population): birth rate, 14.9; death rate, 6.2; marriage rate, 7.6; divorce rate, 4.4. **Major cities** (2007): Denver 588,349; Colorado Springs 376,427; Aurora 311,794; Lakewood 140,305; Fort Collins 133,899.

Government

Statehood: entered the Union on 1 Aug 1876 as the 38th state. **State constitution:** adopted 1876. **Representation in US Congress:** 2 senators; 7 representatives. **Electoral college:** 9 votes. **Political divisions:** 64 counties.

Economy

Employment (2007): services 31.5%; finance, insurance, real estate 20.2%; trade 13.7%; government

13.2%; construction 7.9%. **Production** (2007): finance, insurance, real estate 29.8%; services 16.7%; transportation, public utilities 12.8%; government 11.9%; trade 11.7%. **Chief agricultural products:** *Crops:* millet, corn (maize), potatoes, onions, sugar beets, sunflowers, wheat, dairy products, eggs, greenhouse products. *Livestock:* cattle and calves, hogs and pigs, sheep and lambs. **Chief manufactured products:** meat products; beverages; printing; semiconductors; computer and electronic products.

Internet resources: <www.colorado.com>; <www.colorado.gov>.

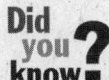 **Did you know?** Colorado's Rocky Mountains, which make up part of the North American Cordillera stretching more than 3,000 miles from Alaska to Mexico, contain some of the highest peaks in North America. The most impressive of these, perhaps, are the "Fourteeners," which is the name that mountain climbers give to the peaks that top 14,000 feet. In the state of Colorado, there are more than 50 "Fourteeners."

Connecticut

Name: Connecticut, from the Mohegan word *Quinnehtukqut,* meaning "long river place" or "beside the long tidal river." **Nickname:** Constitution State. **Capital:** Hartford. **Rank:** population: 29th; area: 48th. **Motto:** "Qui transtulit sustinet" ("He who transplanted still sustains"). **Song:** "Yankee Doodle," words and music from folk tradition. **Bird:** robin. **Flower:** mountain laurel. **Fossil:** *Eubrontes giganteus.* **Insect:** praying mantis. **Mammal:** sperm whale. **Mineral:** garnet. **Shellfish:** eastern oyster. **Tree:** white oak.

Natural features

Land area: 5,006 sq mi, 12,965 sq km. **Mountain range:** Berkshire Hills. **Highest point:** Mt. Frissell, 725 m (2,380 ft). **Largest lake:** Candlewood Lake. **Major rivers:** Connecticut, Housatonic, Thames. **Natural regions:** the New England Province covers the state, divided into the Western Upland, Central Lowland (Connecticut Valley), and Eastern Upland. **Land use:** forest, 53.4%; agricultural, 5.4%; other, 41.2%.

People

Population (2007): 3,502,309; persons per sq mi 700.0, persons per sq km 270.1. **Vital statistics** (2006; per 1,000 population): birth rate, 11.9; death rate, 8.4; marriage rate, 5.0; divorce rate, 2.8. **Major cities** (2007): Bridgeport 136,695; Hartford 124,563; New Haven 123,932; Stamford 118,475; Waterbury 107,174.

Government

Statehood: entered the Union on 9 Jan 1788 as the 5th state. **State constitution:** adopted 1965. **Representation in US Congress:** 2 senators; 5 representatives. **Electoral college:** 7 votes. **Political divisions:** 8 counties.

For details about state governments, see pages 608–613; for energy data, see pages 627–628.

Economy

Employment (2007): services 33.8%; finance, insurance, real estate 20.1%; trade 13.9%; government 12.0%; manufacturing 8.9%. **Production** (2007): finance, insurance, real estate 40.5%; services 16.3%; manufacturing 12.7%; trade 10.6%; government 9.0%. **Chief agricultural products:** *Crops:* corn (maize), silage, hay, tobacco, apples, pears, dairy products, eggs. *Livestock:* poultry, cattle and calves, sheep and lambs, horses. *Fish catch:* lobster, clams, oysters, shad. **Chief manufactured products:** printing; pharmaceutical products; soap and cleaning products; plastic products; fabricated metal products; machinery and apparatus; telecommunications equipment; electronics; aerospace products; aircraft engines.

Internet resources: <www.ctvisit.com>; <www.ct.gov>.

Delaware

Name: Delaware, from Delaware River and Bay; named in turn for Sir Thomas West, Baron De La Warr. **Nickname:** First State. **Capital:** Dover. **Rank:** population: 45th; area: 49th. **Motto:** "Liberty and independence." **Song:** "Our Delaware," words by George B. Hynson and music by Will M.S. Brown. **Bird:** Blue Hen chicken. **Fish:** weakfish. **Flower:** peach blossom. **Insect:** ladybug. **Mineral:** sillimanite. **Tree:** American holly.

Natural features

Land area: 2,026 sq mi, 5,247 sq km. **Highest point:** Ebright Azimuth, 137 m (448 ft). **Largest lake:** Red Mill Pond. **Major rivers:** Delaware, Nanticoke, Pocomoke. **Natural regions:** the Piedmont Province, including the Piedmont Upland, covers the northernmost tip of the state; the remainder consists of the Coastal Plain. **Land use:** agricultural, 29.8%; forest, 22.2%; other, 48.0%.

People

Population (2007): 864,764; persons per sq mi 426.8, persons per sq km 164.8. **Vital statistics** (2006; per 1,000 population): birth rate, 14.0; death rate, 8.4; marriage rate, 6.0; divorce rate, 4.5. **Major cities** (2007): Wilmington 72,868; Dover 35,811; Newark 29,992; Pike Creek 22,000; Bear 18,600.

Government

Statehood: entered the Union on 7 Dec 1787 as the 1st state. **State constitution:** adopted 1897. **Representation in US Congress:** 2 senators; 1 representative. **Electoral college:** 3 votes. **Political divisions:** 3 counties.

Economy

Employment (2007): services 31.6%; finance, insurance, real estate 21.9%; trade 14.8%; government 12.9%; construction 7.2%. **Production** (2007): finance, insurance, real estate 54.7%; services 12.1%; government 8.8%; trade 7.7%; manufacturing 7.3%. **Chief agricultural products:** *Crops:* corn (maize), soybeans, wheat, barley, peas, dairy products. *Livestock:* poultry, cattle and calves, hogs. *Fish catch:* crustaceans, crab, clams. **Chief manufactured products:** chemical products; food products; paper products; rubber and plastics products; fabricated metal products; printing.

Internet resources: <www.visitdelaware.com>; <www.delaware.gov>.

District of Columbia

Name: District of Columbia, named in honor of Christopher Columbus. **Motto:** "Justitia omnibus" ("Justice for all"). **Bird:** woodthrush. **Flower:** American Beauty rose. **Tree:** scarlet oak.

Natural features

Land area: 68 sq mi, 176 sq km. **Major river:** Potomac.

People

Population (2007): 588,292; persons per sq mi 8,651.4, persons per sq km 3,342.6. **Vital statistics:** (2006; per 1,000 population): birth rate, 14.7; death rate, 9.2; marriage rate, 3.9; divorce rate, 2.1.

Government

Representation in US Congress: 1 congressional delegate. **Political divisions:** 8 wards.

Economy

Employment: services 37.0%; government 30.6%; finance, insurance, real estate 21.4%; transportation, public utilities 4.2%; trade 3.4%. **Production:** finance, insurance, real estate 37.1%; government 32.5%; services 19.3%; transportation, public utilities 7.6%; trade 2.2%; construction 1.1%. **Chief manufactured products:** printing and publishing products.

Internet resources: <www.washington.org>; <www.dc.gov>.

Florida

Name: Florida, in honor of Pascua Florida ("feast of the flowers"), Spain's Easter celebration. **Nickname:** Sunshine State. **Capital:** Tallahassee. **Rank:** population: 4th; area: 24th. **Motto:** "In God we trust." **Song:** "Old Folks at Home" ("Swanee River"), words and music by Stephen Foster. **Bird:** mockingbird. **Butterfly:** zebra longwing. **Fish:** sailfish (saltwater); largemouth bass (freshwater). **Flower:** orange blossom. **Gemstone:** moonstone. **Animal:** Florida panther. **Marine mammal:** manatee. **Saltwater mammal:** porpoise. **Reptile:** alligator. **Rock:** agatized coral. **Tree:** sabal palm.

Natural features

Land area: 58,599 sq mi, 151,771 sq km. **Highest point:** Britton Hill 105 m (345 ft). **Largest lake:** Lake Okeechobee. **Major rivers:** Kissimmee, Suwannee, St. Johns, Caloosahatchee, Indian. **Natural regions:** Western Highlands, a region at the westernmost end of the panhandle; Marianna Lowlands, east of the Western Highlands; Tallahassee Hills, covering the northern border with Georgia; Central Highlands, extending down the middle two-thirds of the peninsula;

Coastal Lowlands, curving along the eastern, southern, and western coasts of the peninsula; the Everglades, far southern quarter of the peninsula. **Land use:** forest, 33.9%; agricultural, 7.7%; pasture, 7.2%; other, 51.2%.

People

Population (2007): 18,251,243; persons per sq mi 311.5, persons per sq km 120.3. **Vital statistics** (2006; per 1,000 population): birth rate, 13.1; death rate, 9.4; marriage rate, 8.6; divorce rate, 4.9. **Major cities** (2007): Jacksonville 805,605; Miami 409,719; Tampa 336,823; St. Petersburg 246,407; Orlando 227,907; Hialeah 212,217; Fort Lauderdale 183,606; Tallahassee 168,979.

Government

Statehood: entered the Union on 3 Mar 1845 as the 27th state. **State constitution:** adopted 1968. **Representation in US Congress:** 2 senators; 25 representatives. **Electoral college:** 27 votes. **Political divisions:** 67 counties.

Economy

Employment (2007): services 36.7%; finance, insurance, real estate 18.4%; trade 15.1%; government 11.3%; construction 7.7%. **Production** (2007): finance, insurance, real estate 32.2%; services 21.2%; trade 14.2%; government 11.6%; transportation, public utilities 8.7%. **Chief agricultural products:** *Crops:* citrus fruit, cotton, peanuts (groundnuts), soybeans, sugarcane, tobacco, honey, dairy products, eggs, nursery plants and flowers. *Livestock:* cattle and calves, poultry, hogs and pigs. *Fish catch:* catfish, crab, shrimp, oysters. **Chief manufactured products:** food products; soft drinks; wearing apparel; paper products; pesticides and fertilizers; agricultural chemicals; plastic products; construction materials; fabricated metal products; machinery and apparatus; telecommunications equipment; semiconductors; electronics; aerospace products; airplane engines; ships and boats; medical and surgical equipment.

Internet resources: <www.flausa.com>; <www.myflorida.com>.

Georgia

Name: Georgia, named for George II, king of England at the time the colony of Georgia was founded. **Nicknames:** Empire State of the South; Peach State. **Capital:** Atlanta. **Rank:** population: 9th; area: 23rd. **Mottoes:** "Wisdom, justice, and moderation"; "Agriculture and commerce, 1776." **Song:** "Georgia on My Mind," words by Stuart Gorrell and music by Hoagy Carmichael. **Bird:** brown thrasher. **Fish:** largemouth bass. **Flower:** Cherokee rose. **Fossil:** shark tooth. **Gemstone:** quartz. **Insect:** honeybee. **Marine mammal:** right whale. **Mineral:** staurolite. **Reptile:** gopher tortoise. **Tree:** live oak.

Natural features

Land area: 58,922 sq mi, 152,607 sq km. **Mountain range:** Blue Ridge. **Highest point:** Brasstown Bald, 1,458 m (4,784 ft). **Largest lake:** Lanier. **Major**

rivers: Chattahoochee, Flint, Apalachicola, Ocmulgee, Oconee. **Natural regions:** Blue Ridge Province, north-central edge; Valley and Ridge Province, northwest corner; Piedmont Province, northern half of state; Coastal Plain, southern half of state, divided into the Sea Island Section (southeast) and the East Gulf Coastal Plain (southwest). **Land use:** forest, 58.0%; agricultural, 11.0%; other, 31.0%.

People

Population (2007): 9,544,750; persons per sq mi 162.0, persons per sq km 62.5. **Vital statistics** (2006; per 1,000 population): birth rate, 15.9; death rate, 7.2; marriage rate, 7.1; divorce rate (2001), 3.8. **Major cities** (2007): Atlanta 519,145; Augusta 192,142; Columbus 187,046; Savannah 130,331; Athens 112,760.

Government

Statehood: entered the Union on 2 Jan 1788 as the 4th state. **State constitution:** adopted 1982. **Representation in US Congress:** 2 senators; 13 representatives. **Electoral college:** 15 votes. **Political divisions:** 159 counties.

Economy

Employment (2007): services 31.5%; finance, insurance, real estate 16.1%; trade 14.9%; government 14.1%; manufacturing 8.1%. **Production** (2007): finance, insurance, real estate 26.7%; services 15.9%; trade 14.3%; government 13.1%; transportation, public utilities 13.1%. **Chief agricultural products:** *Crops:* peanuts (groundnuts), pecans, cotton and cottonseed, tobacco, peaches, apples, blueberries, grapes, honey, dairy products. *Livestock:* poultry, pigs, cattle and calves. *Fish catch:* catfish, trout. **Chief manufactured products:** food products; soft drinks; textiles; wood products; paper products; chemical products; transportation equipment.

Internet resources: <www.georgia.org>; <www.georgia.gov>.

Hawaii

Name: Hawaii, from the Polynesian Hawaiki, the name for the ancestral home of Polynesians. **Nickname:** Aloha State. **Capital:** Honolulu. **Rank:** population: 42nd; area: 47th. **Motto:** "Ua mau ke ea o ka aina i ka pono" ("The life of the land is perpetuated in righteousness"). **Song:** "Hawai'i Pono'i" ("Our Hawaii"), words by King David Kalakaua and music by Henry Berger. **Bird:** nene, or Hawaiian goose. **Fish:** rectangular triggerfish. **Flower:** yellow hibiscus. **Gemstone:** black coral. **Marine mammal:** humpback whale. **Tree:** candlenut.

Natural features

Land area: 6,461 sq mi, 16,734 sq km; the eight largest islands: *Hawaii:* 4,028 sq mi, 10,433 sq km; *Maui:* 728 sq mi, 1,886 sq km; *Oahu:* 607 sq mi, 1,574 sq km; *Kauai:* 552 sq mi, 1,430 sq km; *Molokai:* 280 sq mi, 725 sq km; *Lanai:* 140 sq mi,

363 sq km; *Niihau:* 72 sq mi, 186 sq km; *Kahoolawe:* 45 sq mi, 117 sq km. **Mountain ranges:** Koolau, Waianae (both Oahu). **Highest point:** Mauna Kea (Hawaii), 4,205 m (13,796 ft). **Major rivers:** Wailuku (Hawaii); Waimea, Hanalei (Kauai). **Natural regions:** The eight major islands at the eastern end of the 1,500-mile-long chain of islands are, from west to east, Niihau, Kauai, Oahu, Molokai, Lanai, Kahoolawe, Maui, and Hawaii; each island contains regions of mountains, deeps, ridges, and wide beaches; active volcanoes are found on the island of Hawaii. **Land use:** forest, 28.9%; pasture, 23.4%; agricultural, 7.1%; other, 40.6%.

People

Population (2007): Total, 1,283,388; persons per sq 198.6 mi, persons per sq km 76.7. **Vital statistics** (2006; per 1,000 population): birth rate, 14.8; death rate, 7.4; marriage rate, 22.4; divorce rate (2001), 3.8. **Major cities** (2000): Honolulu (2007) 375,571; Hilo 40,759; Kailua 36,513; Kaneohe 34,970; Waipahu 33,108.

Government

Statehood: entered the Union on 21 Aug 1959 as the 50th state. **State constitution:** adopted 1950. **Representation in US Congress:** 2 senators; 2 representatives. **Electoral college:** 4 votes. **Political divisions:** 4 counties.

Economy

Employment (2007): services 37.0%; government 20.2%; finance, insurance, real estate 14.3%; trade 13.0%; construction 5.9%. **Production** (2007): finance, insurance, real estate 27.4%; services 23.1%; government, 22.9%; trade 10.4%; transportation, public utilities 8.1%. **Chief agricultural products:** *Crops:* pineapples, sugarcane, cut flowers, macadamia nuts, coffee, dairy products, eggs. *Livestock:* cattle and calves. *Fish catch:* fish, shellfish. **Chief manufactured products:** food products, including processed sugar, canned pineapple, and preserved fruits and vegetables; wearing apparel; textiles; printing and publishing.

Internet resources: <www.gohawaii.com>; <www.hawaiitourismauthority.org>.

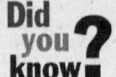 **Did you know?** Any island not named as part of a specific county in Hawaii is considered part of the city of Honolulu, making this the city with the longest borders in the entire world. Containing all of the islands in the Hawaiian and Pacific Islands National Wildlife Refuge, Honolulu officially stretches more than 1,300 miles.

Idaho

Name: Idaho, from a Shoshone phrase meaning "gem of the mountains." **Nickname:** Gem State. **Capital:** Boise. **Rank:** population: 39th; area: 14th. **Motto:** "Esto perpetua" ("It is forever"). **Song:** "Here We Have Idaho," words by McKinley Helm and Albert J. Tompkins and music by Sallie Hume

Douglas. **Bird:** mountain bluebird. **Fish:** cutthroat trout. **Flower:** syringa. **Fossil:** Hagerman horse fossil (*Equus simplicidens*). **Gemstone:** star garnet. **Horse:** Appaloosa. **Insect:** monarch butterfly. **Tree:** western white pine.

Natural features

Land area: 83,570 sq mi, 216,445 sq km. **Mountain ranges:** Northern Rocky, Middle Rocky, Sawtooth, Pioneer, Continental Divide, Beaverhead, Clearwater, Bitterroot, Salmon River, Lost River, Lemhi. **Highest point:** Borah Peak, 3,859 m (12,662 ft). **Largest lake:** Lake Pend Oreille. **Major rivers:** Snake, Salmon. **Natural regions:** Northern Rocky Mountains, covering most of the northern half of the state; Columbia Plateau, extending across the south-central and southwestern regions; Great Basin region of the Basin and Range Province, southeast; Middle Rocky Mountains, extreme southeastern tip. **Land use:** pasture, 12.0%; agricultural, 10.2%; forest, 7.5%; other, 70.3%.

People

Population (2007): 1,499,402; persons per sq mi 17.9, persons per sq km 6.9. **Vital statistics** (2006; per 1,000 population): birth rate, 16.5; death rate, 7.2; marriage rate, 10.1; divorce rate, 5.1. **Major cities** (2007): Boise 202,832; Nampa 79,249; Meridian 64,642; Pocatello 54,572; Idaho Falls 53,279.

Government

Statehood: entered the Union on 3 Jul 1890 as the 43rd state. **State constitution:** adopted 1889. **Representation in US Congress:** 2 senators; 2 representatives. **Electoral college:** 4 votes. **Political divisions:** 44 counties.

Economy

Employment (2007): services 29.1%; finance, insurance, real estate 15.4%; trade 15.0%; government 13.4%; construction 9.1%. **Production** (2007): finance, insurance, real estate 26.4%; services 16.4%; trade 14.0%; government 13.5%; manufacturing 10.3%. **Chief agricultural products:** *Crops:* potatoes, timber, sugar beets, alfalfa, Kentucky bluegrass seed, hops, onions, peas, honey, dairy products. *Livestock:* cattle and calves, sheep and lambs. *Fish catch:* trout. **Chief manufactured products:** food products; lumber and wood products; paper products; printing; chemical products; plastics and rubber products; cement, bricks, and ceramics; fabricated metal products; machinery and apparatus; computers and electronics.

Internet resources: <www.visitidaho.org>; <www.idaho.gov>.

Illinois

Name: Illinois, from a Native American word meaning "tribe of superior men." **Nickname:** Prairie State. **Capital:** Springfield. **Rank:** population: 5th; area: 25th. **Motto:** "State sovereignty, national union." **Slogan:** Land of Lincoln. **Song:** "Illinois," words by Charles H. Chamberlain and music by Archibald

Johnston. **Bird:** cardinal. **Fish:** bluegill. **Flower:** violet. **Fossil:** Tully monster. **Insect:** monarch butterfly. **Mammal:** white-tailed deer. **Mineral:** fluorite. **Tree:** white oak.

Natural features

Land area: 57,915 sq mi, 149,999 sq km. **Highest point:** Charles Mound, 376 m (1,235 ft). **Largest lake:** Carlyle Lake. **Major rivers:** Mississippi, Ohio, Wabash. **Natural regions:** Central Lowland, a region of sloping hills and broad, shallow river valleys covering almost the entire state; Ozark Plateaus, extreme southwest; Interior Low Plateaus and Coastal Plain, extreme southeastern tip. **Land use:** agricultural, 66.5%; forest, 11.0%; other, 22.5%.

People

Population (2007): 12,852,548; persons per sq mi 221.9, persons per sq km 85.7. **Vital statistics** (2006; per 1,000 population): birth rate, 14.1; death rate, 8.0; marriage rate, 6.1; divorce rate, 2.5. **Major cities** (2007): Chicago 2,836,658; Aurora 170,855; Rockford 156,596; Joliet 144,316; Naperville 142,479.

Government

Statehood: entered the Union on 3 Dec 1818 as the 21st state. **State constitution:** adopted 1970. **Representation in US Congress:** 2 senators; 20 representatives. **Electoral college:** 21 votes. **Political divisions:** 102 counties.

Economy

Employment (2007): services 33.4%; finance, insurance, real estate 17.9%; trade 14.5%; government 11.8%; manufacturing 9.2%. **Production** (2007): finance, insurance, real estate 33.3%; services 16.9%; trade 12.7%; manufacturing 12.6%; transportation, public utilities 9.9%. **Chief agricultural products:** *Crops:* corn (maize), soybeans, wheat, oats, sorghum, apples, peaches, snap beans, sweet corn, potatoes, cabbage, dairy products, eggs. *Livestock:* pigs, cattle and calves, horses, poultry. **Chief manufactured products:** food products; beverages; textiles; leather goods; wearing apparel; wood products; paper products; printing; refined petroleum and coal products; asphalt; chemical products; plastics and rubber products; cement, bricks, and ceramics; base metals; fabricated metal products; machinery and apparatus; computers and electronics; transportation equipment.

Internet resources: <www.enjoyillinois.com>; <www.illinois.gov>.

Indiana

Name: Indiana, generally thought to mean "land of the Indians." **Nickname:** Hoosier State. **Capital:** Indianapolis. **Rank:** population: 15th; area: 38th. **Motto:** "The crossroads of America." **Song:** "On the Banks of the Wabash, Far Away," words and music by Paul Dresser. **Bird:** cardinal. **Flower:** peony. **Rock:** limestone. **Tree:** tulip tree (yellow poplar).

Natural features

Land area: 36,418 sq mi, 94,322 sq km. **Highest point:** Hoosier Hill, 383 m (1,257 ft). **Largest lake:** Lake Monroe. **Major rivers:** Wabash, Ohio. **Natural regions:** Central Lowland comprises most of the state and includes the Eastern Lake Section to the north and the Till Plains in the center; Interior Low Plateaus, including the Highland Rim Section, cover the southern quarter of the state. **Land use:** agricultural, 57.5%; forest, 16.5%; other, 26.0%.

People

Population (2007): 6,345,289; persons per sq mi 174.2, persons per sq km 67.3. **Vital statistics** (2006; per 1,000 population): birth rate, 14.0; death rate, 8.8; marriage rate, 8.1; divorce rate, N/A. **Major cities** (2007): Indianapolis 795,458; Fort Wayne 251,247; Evansville 116,253; South Bend 104,069; Gary 96,429.

Government

Statehood: entered the Union on 11 Dec 1816 as the 19th state. **State constitution:** adopted 1851. **Representation in US Congress:** 2 senators; 10 representatives. **Electoral college:** 11 votes. **Political divisions:** 92 counties.

Economy

Employment (2007): services 32.1%; manufacturing 15.1%; trade 14.7%; government 12.0%; finance, insurance, real estate 11.9%. **Production** (2007): manufacturing 25.4%; finance, insurance, real estate 20.5%; services 17.4%; trade 12.1%; government 9.9%. **Chief agricultural products:** *Crops:* corn (maize), soybeans, wheat, popcorn, tobacco, peppermint, spearmint, blueberries, apples, eggs. *Livestock:* pigs, cattle and calves, poultry. **Chief manufactured products:** base metals; fabricated metal products; motor vehicle parts; machinery and apparatus; food products; dairy products; soft drinks; wood products; paper products; mobile homes.

Internet resources: <www.visitindiana.net>; <www.in.gov>.

Iowa

Name: Iowa, named for the Iowa (or Ioway) Indians who once inhabited the area. **Nickname:** Hawkeye State. **Capital:** Des Moines. **Rank:** population: 30th; area: 26th. **Motto:** "Our liberties we prize and our rights we will maintain." **Song:** "The Song of Iowa," words by S.H.M. Byers, to the tune of "O Tannenbaum." **Bird:** eastern goldfinch. **Flower:** wild rose. **Rock:** geode. **Tree:** oak.

Natural features

Land area: 56,271 sq mi, 145,741 sq km. **Highest point:** Hawkeye Point, 509 m (1,670 ft). **Largest lake:** Spirit Lake. **Major rivers:** Des Moines, Mississippi, Missouri, Big Sioux. **Natural regions:** overall, Central Lowland, including the Western Lake Section, north and central regions; Dissected Till Plains, south; Wisconsin

Driftless Section, northeast corner. **Land use:** agricultural, 70.8%; forest, 6.4%; other, 22.8%.

People

Population (2007): 2,988,046; persons per sq mi 53.1, persons per sq km 20.5. **Vital statistics** (2006; per 1,000 population): birth rate, 13.6; death rate, 9.2; marriage rate, 6.7; divorce rate, 2.7. **Major cities** (2007): Des Moines 196,998; Cedar Rapids 126,396; Davenport 98,975; Sioux City 82,684; Iowa City 67,062.

Government

Statehood: entered the Union on 28 Dec 1846 as the 29th state. **State constitution:** adopted 1857. **Representation in US Congress:** 2 senators; 5 representatives. **Electoral college:** 7 votes. **Political divisions:** 99 counties.

Economy

Employment (2007): services 30.1%; trade 15.1%; government 13.0%; finance, insurance, real estate 12.5%; manufacturing 11.6%. **Production** (2007): finance, insurance, real estate 23.1%; manufacturing 20.2%; services 14.7%; trade 11.6%; government 11.6%. **Chief agricultural products:** *Crops:* corn (maize), soybeans, oats, milk, eggs, butter, honey, popcorn, sorghum. *Livestock:* poultry, hogs and pigs, beef cattle, sheep and lambs. **Chief manufactured products:** food products; dairy products; pesticides, fertilizers, and other agricultural chemicals; farm machinery; construction machinery; motor vehicle parts.

Internet resources: <www.traveliowa.com>; <www. iowa.gov>.

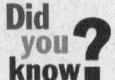 **Did you know?** The geodetic center of North America, the center point from which all maps of the continent base their coordinates and borders, was located in 1901 on Meade's Ranch in north-central Kansas. Some 40 miles north, near the town of Lebanon KS, lies the geographic center of the 48 coterminous US states.

Kansas

Name: Kansas, from the Sioux word *kansa* ("people of the south wind") for the Native Americans who lived in the region. **Nickname:** Sunflower State. **Capital:** Topeka. **Rank:** population: 33rd; area: 15th. **Motto:** "Ad astra per aspera" ("To the stars through difficulties"). **Song:** "Home on the Range," words by Brewster Higley and music by Dan Kelly. **Amphibian:** barred tiger salamander. **Bird:** western meadowlark. **Flower:** wild native sunflower. **Insect:** honeybee. **Mammal:** American buffalo. **Reptile:** ornate box turtle. **Tree:** cottonwood.

Natural features

Land area: 82,277 sq mi, 213,096 sq km. **Highest point:** Mt. Sunflower, 1,231 m (4,039 ft). **Largest lake:** Milford Lake. **Major rivers:** Kansas, Arkansas,

Big Blue, Republican, Solomon. **Natural regions:** the Great Plains Province, covering the western half of the state, consists of the High Plains to the west and the Plains Border to the east; the Central Lowland covers the eastern half of the state and consists of the Dissected Till Plains to the north and the Osage Plains to the south. **Land use:** agricultural, 50.3%; pasture, 30.1%; forest, 2.9%; other, 16.7%.

People

Population (2007): 2,775,997; persons per sq mi 33.7, persons per sq km 13.0. **Vital statistics** (2006; per 1,000 population): birth rate, 14.8; death rate, 8.9; marriage rate, 6.8; divorce rate, 3.3. **Major cities** (2007): Wichita 361,420; Overland Park 169,403; Kansas City 142,320; Topeka 122,642; Olathe 118,034.

Government

Statehood: entered the Union on 29 Jan 1861 as the 34th state. **State constitution:** adopted 1859. **Representation in US Congress:** 2 senators; 4 representatives. **Electoral college:** 6 votes. **Political divisions:** 105 counties.

Economy

Employment (2007): services 29.1%; government 16.0%; trade 14.1%; finance, insurance, real estate 13.2%; manufacturing 10.4%. **Production** (2007): finance, insurance, real estate 20.8%; services 15.6%; manufacturing 15.1%; government 14.3%; trade 12.8%. **Chief agricultural products:** *Crops:* wheat, corn (maize), sorghum, soybeans, sunflower seed and oil, apples, peaches, pecans. *Livestock:* beef cattle, dairy cattle, hogs, sheep and lambs, horses and other equines. **Chief manufactured products:** food products; printing; refined petroleum products; soap and cleaning products; plastic products; aerospace products and parts; aircraft.

Internet resources: <www.travelks.com>; <www. kansas.gov>.

Kentucky

Name: Kentucky, possibly from the Iroquois word for "prairie." **Nickname:** Bluegrass State. **Capital:** Frankfort. **Rank:** population: 26th; area: 37th. **Motto:** "United we stand, divided we fall." **Song:** "My Old Kentucky Home," words and music by Stephen Foster. **Bird:** cardinal. **Butterfly:** viceroy butterfly. **Fish:** Kentucky bass. **Flower:** goldenrod. **Horse:** Thoroughbred. **Tree:** tulip poplar. **Wild animal:** gray squirrel.

Natural features

Land area: 40,409 sq mi, 104,659 sq km. **Mountain ranges:** Cumberland, Pine. **Highest point:** Black Mountain, 1,263 m (4,145 ft). **Largest lake:** Kentucky Lake. **Major rivers:** Mississippi, Ohio, Big Sandy, Licking, Kentucky. **Natural regions:** Appalachian Plateaus cover the eastern third of the state; Interior Low Plateaus, including the Highland Rim Section and the Lexington Plain, cover the remainder, with the exception of the Coastal Plain, which covers the extreme southwestern tip. **Land use:** forest, 40.6%; agricultural, 21.2%; other, 38.2%.

People

Population (2007): 4,241,474; persons per sq mi 105.0, persons per sq km 40.5. **Vital statistics** (2006; per 1,000 population): birth rate, 13.9; death rate, 9.5; marriage rate, 8.8; divorce rate, 5.1. **Major cities** (2007): Louisville 557,789; Lexington 279,044; Owensboro 55,398; Bowling Green 54,244; Covington 43,062.

Government

Statehood: entered the Union on 1 Jun 1792 as the 15th state. **State constitution:** adopted 1891. **Representation in US Congress:** 2 senators; 6 representatives. **Electoral college:** 8 votes. **Political divisions:** 120 counties.

Economy

Employment (2007): services 30.1%; government 14.9%; trade 14.4%; finance, insurance, real estate 11.8%; manufacturing 10.8%. **Production** (2007): finance, insurance, real estate 18.9%; manufacturing 18.9%; services 16.3%; government 15.1%; trade 12.9%. **Chief agricultural products:** Crops: tobacco, soybeans, corn (maize), wheat, hay, sorghum, eggs, dairy products. Livestock: racing and show horses, beef cattle, dairy cattle, hogs, poultry, sheep and lambs. **Chief manufactured products:** food products; meatpacking; beverages; tobacco; wearing apparel; paper products; printing; chemical products; resin and synthetic rubber products; plastic products; iron and steel; aluminum; fabricated metal products; machinery; appliances; motor vehicles.

Internet resources: <www.kentuckytourism.com>; <www.kentucky.gov>.

Louisiana

Name: Louisiana, named for Louis XIV, king of France. **Nickname:** Pelican State. **Capital:** Baton Rouge. **Rank:** population: 25th; area: 31st. **Motto:** "Union, justice, and confidence." **Songs:** "Give Me Louisiana," words and music by Doralice Fontane; "You Are My Sunshine," words and music by Jimmy H. Davis and Charles Mitchell. **Amphibian:** green tree frog. **Bird:** brown pelican. **Crustacean:** crawfish. **Fish:** white perch (freshwater); spotted sea trout, or speckled trout (saltwater). **Flower:** magnolia. **Fossil:** petrified palmwood. **Gemstone:** agate. **Insect:** honeybee. **Mammal:** black bear. **Reptile:** alligator. **Tree:** bald cypress.

Natural features

Land area: 47,716 sq mi, 123,584 sq km. **Highest point:** Driskill Mountain, 163 m (535 ft). **Largest lake:** Lake Pontchartrain. **Major rivers:** Mississippi, Red, Sabine. **Natural regions:** the entire state consists of the Coastal Plain and is divided into the West Gulf Coastal Plain to the west, the Mis-

sissippi Alluvial Plain to the northeast, and the East Gulf Coastal Plain in the southeast. **Land use:** forest, 42.5%; agricultural, 17.3%; pasture, 0.9%; other, 39.3%.

People

Population (2007): 4,293,204; persons per sq mi 90.0, persons per sq km 34.7. **Vital statistics** (2006; per 1,000 population): birth rate, 14.8; death rate, 9.3; marriage rate (2001), 8.1; divorce rate, N/A. **Major cities** (2007): New Orleans 239,124; Baton Rouge 227,071; Shreveport 199,569; Metairie 130,000; Lafayette 113,544.

Government

Statehood: entered the Union on 30 Apr 1812 as the 18th state. **State constitution:** adopted 1974. **Representation in US Congress:** 2 senators; 5 representatives. **Electoral college:** 9 votes. **Political divisions:** 64 parishes.

Economy

Employment (2007): services 32.2%; government 15.6%; trade 14.2%; finance, insurance, real estate 13.1%; construction 8.3%. **Production** (2007): manufacturing 23.0%; finance, insurance, real estate 15.4%; mining 14.4%; services 13.9%; trade 10.2%. **Chief agricultural products:** Crops: soybeans, cotton, sorghum, sugarcane, rice, wheat, sweet potatoes, pecans, strawberries, peaches. Livestock: cattle and calves, chickens, hogs. Fish catch: catfish, crawfish, shrimp, oysters. **Chief manufactured products:** industrial chemicals; agricultural chemicals; plastics; refined petroleum products; cane sugar products; paper products; fabricated metal products; wood products; telecommunications equipment; ships, boats, and nautical equipment.

Internet resources: <www.louisianatravel.com>; <www.louisiana.gov>.

Maine

Name: Maine, possibly named for the former French province of Maine, or used to distinguish the mainland portion of the territory from offshore islands. **Nickname:** Pine Tree State. **Capital:** Augusta. **Rank:** population: 40th; area: 39th. **Motto:** "Dirigo" ("I direct"). **Song:** "State of Maine Song," words and music by Roger Vinton Snow. **Bird:** chickadee. **Fish:** landlocked salmon. **Flower:** white pine cone and tassel. **Fossil:** Pertica quadrifaria. **Gemstone:** tourmaline. **Insect:** honeybee. **Mammal:** moose. **Tree:** white pine.

Natural features

Land area: 33,126 sq mi, 85,796 sq km. **Mountain ranges:** Appalachian, Longfellow. **Highest point:** Mt. Katahdin, 1,606 m (5,268 ft). **Largest lake:** Moosehead Lake. **Major rivers:** Saco, Androscoggin, Kennebec, Penobscot, St. John's. **Natural regions:** entire state is part of the larger New England Province, subdivided into the White Moun-

For details about state governments, see pages 608–613; for energy data, see pages 627–628.

tain section (southwest), Seaboard Lowland Section (southeast coastline), and New England Upland Section (north and central regions). **Land use:** forest, 84.0%; agricultural, 1.8%; other 14.2%.

People

Population (2007): 1,317,207; persons per sq mi 39.8, persons per sq km 15.4. **Vital statistics** (2006; per 1,000 population): birth rate, 10.7; death rate, 9.3; marriage rate, 7.4; divorce rate, 3.6. **Major cities** (2007): Portland 62,825; Lewiston 35,234; Bangor 31,853; South Portland 23,748; Auburn 23,203.

Government

Statehood: entered the Union on 15 Mar 1820 as the 23rd state. **State constitution:** adopted 1819. **Representation in US Congress:** 2 senators; 2 representatives. **Electoral college:** 4 votes. **Political divisions:** 16 counties.

Economy

Employment (2007): services 34.3%; trade 16.0%; government 13.5%; finance, insurance, real estate 13.2%; construction 7.7%. **Production** (2007): finance, insurance, real estate 26.0%; services 20.8%; government 14.3%; trade 14.2%; manufacturing 11.0%. **Chief agricultural products:** *Crops:* potatoes, blueberries, apples, cranberries, oats, honey, corn (maize), dairy products, eggs. *Livestock:* poultry, cattle and calves, sheep and lambs. *Fish catch:* salmon, rainbow trout, lobster, shrimp, crab, clams, haddock, cod, mackerel. **Chief manufactured products:** paper products; leather products; lumber and wood products; food products; semiconductors; wearing apparel; printing and publishing; plastic products; ships and boats.

Internet resources: <www.visitmaine.com>; <www.maine.gov>.

Maryland

Name: Maryland, in honor of Henrietta Maria, queen of England at the time the colony of Maryland was founded. **Nickname:** Old Line State. **Capital:** Annapolis. **Rank:** population: 19th; area: 42nd. **Motto:** "Fatti maschii, parole femine" ("Manly deeds, womanly words"). **Song:** "Maryland, My Maryland," words by James Ryder Randall, to the tune of "O Tannenbaum." **Bird:** Baltimore oriole. **Crustacean:** Maryland blue crab. **Dinosaur:** *Astrodon johnstoni.* **Fish:** rockfish (striped bass). **Flower:** black-eyed Susan. **Insect:** Baltimore checkerspot. **Reptile:** diamondback terrapin. **Tree:** white oak.

Natural features

Land area: 10,454 sq mi, 27,076 sq km. **Mountain ranges:** Allegheny, Appalachian. **Highest point:** Backbone Mountain, 1,024 m (3,360 ft). **Largest lake:** Deep Creek Lake. **Major rivers:** Potomac, Patuxent, Susquehanna. **Natural regions:** Coastal Plain, eastern half of the state, includes the Embayed Section near the southwest corner of the peninsula; Piedmont Province, central, includes the Piedmont Upland to the north and

the Piedmont Lowlands to the west; Blue Ridge Province, northwest; Valley and Ridge Province, part of western neck; Appalachian Plateau, extreme western neck. **Land use:** forest, 30.1%; agricultural, 19.3%; other, 50.6%.

People

Population (2007): 5,618,344; persons per sq mi 537.4, persons per sq km 207.5. **Vital statistics** (2006; per 1,000 population): birth rate, 13.8; death rate, 7.8; marriage rate, 6.5; divorce rate, 3.0. **Major cities** (2007): Baltimore 637,455; Columbia (2006) 94,700; Silver Spring 73,000; Frederick 59,220; Rockville 58,706.

Government

Statehood: entered the Union on 28 Apr 1788 as the 7th state. **State constitution:** adopted 1867. **Representation in US Congress:** 2 senators; 8 representatives. **Electoral college:** 10 votes. **Political divisions:** 23 counties.

Economy

Employment (2007): services 33.7%; finance, insurance, real estate 19.5%; government 15.8%; trade 13.7%; construction 7.6%. **Production** (2007): finance, insurance, real estate 33.9%; services 17.6%; government 17.4%; trade 11.0%; transportation, public utilities 8.9%. **Chief agricultural products:** *Crops:* corn (maize), soybeans, wheat, potatoes, tobacco, dairy products, eggs. *Livestock:* cattle and calves, pigs, poultry. *Fish catch:* hybrid striped bass, catfish, tilapia, trout, oysters, blue crab, other crustaceans, oysters, mollusks. **Chief manufactured products:** base metals; food products; transportation equipment, including motor vehicles and ships and boats; chemical products; plastics and rubber products; fabricated metal products; machinery and apparatus; computers and electronics.

Internet resources: <www.mdisfun.org>; <www.maryland.gov>.

Massachusetts

Name: Massachusetts, named for the Massachusett tribe of Native Americans who lived in the Great Blue Hill region south of Boston; the word *Massachusett* means "at or about the great hill." **Nickname:** Bay State. **Capital:** Boston. **Rank:** population: 14th; area: 45th. **Motto:** "Ense petit placidam sub libertate quietem" ("By the sword we seek peace, but peace only under liberty"). **Song:** "All Hail to Massachusetts," words and music by Arthur J. Marsh. **Bird:** black-capped chickadee. **Fish:** cod. **Flower:** mayflower. **Fossil:** theropod dinosaur tracks. **Gemstone:** rhodonite. **Insect:** ladybug. **Marine mammal:** right whale. **Mineral:** babingtonite. **Rock:** Roxbury puddingstone. **Tree:** American elm.

Natural features

Land area: 8,263 sq mi, 21,401 sq km. **Mountain ranges:** Berkshire Mountains, Hoosac Range, Taconic Range. **Highest point:** Mt. Greylock, 1,064 m (3,491 ft). **Largest lake:** Webster Lake. **Major rivers:** Connecticut, Charles, Merrimack,

Housatonic, Taunton. **Natural regions:** the New England Province, comprising most of the state, subdivided into the Taconic Section along the west, the New England Upland Section in the central region, and the Seaboard Lowland Section, covering the eastern third of the state; Coastal Plain, comprising the peninsula region. **Land use:** forest, 49.9%; agricultural, 4.7%; other, 45.4%.

People

Population (2007): 6,449,755; persons per sq mi 780.6, persons per sq km 301.4. **Vital statistics** (2006; per 1,000 population): birth rate, 12.1; death rate, 8.3; marriage rate, 6.0; divorce rate, 2.3. **Major cities** (2007): Boston 599,351; Worcester 173,966; Springfield 149,938; Lowell 103,512; Cambridge 101,388.

Government

Statehood: entered the Union on 6 Feb 1788 as the 6th state. **State constitution:** adopted 1780. **Representation in US Congress:** 2 senators; 10 representatives. **Electoral college:** 12 votes. **Political divisions:** 14 counties.

Economy

Employment (2007): services 37.2%; finance, insurance, real estate 20.2%; trade 13.4%; government 10.6%; manufacturing 7.3%. **Production** (2007): finance, insurance, real estate 37.9%; services 20.2%; trade 10.8%; manufacturing 9.9%; government 8.8%. **Chief agricultural products:** *Crops:* tobacco, cranberries, potatoes, sweet corn, dairy products, eggs. *Livestock:* cattle and calves, poultry. *Fish catch:* lobster, crab, mollusks, oysters, quahogs, soft-shelled clams, scallops. **Chief manufactured products:** food products; dairy products; soft drinks; textiles; paper products; printing; pharmaceuticals; plastic products; cement, bricks, and ceramics; fabricated metal products.

Internet resources: <www.mass-vacation.com>; <www.mass.gov>.

Michigan

Name: Michigan, from the Native American word *michi-gama,* meaning "great, or large, lake." **Nicknames:** Wolverine State; Great Lake State. **Capital:** Lansing. **Rank:** population: 8th; area: 11th. **Motto:** "Si quaeris peninsulam amoenam, circumspice" ("If you seek a pleasant peninsula, look around you"). **Song:** "Michigan, My Michigan," words by Giles Kavanagh and music by H.J. O'Reilly Clint. **Bird:** robin. **Fish:** brook trout. **Flower:** apple blossom. **Gemstone:** chlorastrolite. **Mammal:** white-tailed deer (game mammal). **Reptile:** painted turtle. **Rock:** Petoskey stone. **Tree:** white pine.

Natural features

Land area: 96,716 sq mi, 250,493 sq km. **Highest point:** Mt. Arvon, 603 m (1,979 ft). **Largest lake:** Houghton Lake. **Major rivers:** Montreal, Brule, Menominee, St. Clair. **Natural regions:** the Central

Lowland, Eastern Lake Section, covers all of Lower Michigan and part of the Upper Peninsula region; the western half of the Upper Peninsula consists of Superior Upland, as do two small areas at the eastern end. **Land use:** forest, 44.7%; agricultural, 21.7%; other, 33.6%.

People

Population (2007): 10,071,822; persons per sq mi 104.1, persons per sq km 40.2. **Vital statistics** (2006; per 1,000 population): birth rate, 12.6; death rate, 8.5; marriage rate, 5.9; divorce rate, 3.5. **Major cities** (2007): Detroit 916,952; Grand Rapids 193,627; Warren 134,223; Sterling Heights 127,349; Ann Arbor 115,092.

Government

Statehood: entered the Union on 26 Jan 1837 as the 26th state. **State constitution:** adopted 1963. **Representation in US Congress:** 2 senators; 15 representatives. **Electoral college:** 17 votes. **Political divisions:** 83 counties.

Economy

Employment (2007): services 34.2%; finance, insurance, real estate 15.5%; trade 14.6%; government 12.3%; manufacturing 11.8%. **Production** (2007): finance, insurance, real estate 28.1%; services 18.0%; manufacturing 16.9%; trade 12.7%; government 11.3%. **Chief agricultural products:** *Crops:* apples, asparagus, blueberries, cherries, flowers, grapes and wine, honey, maple syrup, mint, plums. *Livestock:* beef cattle, dairy cattle, pigs, poultry, sheep and lambs. *Fish catch:* rainbow, brook, and brown trout, yellow perch, catfish. **Chief manufactured products:** motor vehicles; plastic products; pharmaceuticals; soaps; milled grain and dry cereals; agricultural machinery; furniture; dairy products; printing; electrical equipment.

Internet resources: <www.michigan.org>; <www.michigan.gov>.

Minnesota

Name: Minnesota, from a Dakota word meaning "sky-tinted water." **Nickname:** North Star State. **Capital:** St. Paul. **Rank:** population: 21st; area: 12th. **Motto:** "L'Étoile du nord" ("The star of the north"). **Song:** "Hail! Minnesota," first verse and music by Truman E. Rickard, second verse by Arthur E. Upson. **Bird:** common loon. **Fish:** walleye pike. **Flower:** pink and white lady slipper. **Gemstone:** Lake Superior agate. **Insect:** monarch butterfly. **Tree:** Norway pine.

Natural features

Land area: 86,939 sq mi, 225,171 sq km. **Mountain ranges:** Mesabi, Vermillion, Cuyuna. **Highest point:** Eagle Mountain, 701 m (2,301 ft). **Largest lake:** Red Lake. **Major rivers:** Minnesota, St. Croix, Mississippi. **Natural regions:** Superior Upland, northeast corner; Central Lowland, covering most of the state; Western Lake Section, center; Dissected Till Plains, extreme southwest corner and south-central edge; Wisconsin Driftless Section, extreme southeast. **Land use:** agricultural, 39.1%; forest, 30.3%; other, 30.6%.

People

Population (2007): 5,197,621; persons per sq mi 59.8, persons per sq km 23.1. **Vital statistics** (2006; per 1,000 population): birth rate, 14.2; death rate, 7.2; marriage rate, 6.0; divorce rate (2004), 2.8. **Major cities** (2007): Minneapolis 377,392; St. Paul 277,251; Rochester 99,121; Duluth 84,397; Bloomington 81,446.

Government

Statehood: entered the Union on 11 May 1858 as the 32nd state. **State constitution:** adopted 1857. **Representation in US Congress:** 2 senators; 8 representatives. **Electoral college:** 10 votes. **Political divisions:** 87 counties.

Economy

Employment (2007): services 32.9%; finance, insurance, real estate 16.5%; trade 14.7%; government 11.8%; manufacturing 10.0%. **Production** (2007): finance, insurance, real estate 31.8%; services 17.0%; manufacturing 13.3%; trade 12.7%; government 10.3%. **Chief agricultural products:** *Crops:* corn (maize), green peas, onions, apples, spring wheat, barley, potatoes, sugar beets, flaxseed, dairy products. *Livestock:* pigs, cattle and calves, poultry, sheep and lambs. **Chief manufactured products:** food products; malt beverages and other alcoholic products; dairy products; machinery and apparatus; computers and office machinery; electronics and electrical equipment; precision instruments; printing and publishing; information technology; lumber and wood products.

Internet resources: <www.exploreminnesota.com>; <www.state.mn.us>.

Did you know? The original name of Saint Paul, the capital of the state of Minnesota, was Pig's Eye Landing. Named after Pierre ("Pig's Eye") Parrant, a French-Canadian tavern owner who in 1838 made the first official land claim on the area, the community that was to become Minnesota's second largest city did not receive its current name until 1841.

Mississippi

Name: Mississippi, from a Native American word meaning "great waters" or "father of waters." **Nickname:** Magnolia State. **Capital:** Jackson. **Rank:** population: 31st; area: 32nd. **Motto:** "Virtute et armis" ("By valor and arms"). **Song:** "Go, Mississippi," words and music by Houston Davis. **Bird:** mockingbird. **Fish:** largemouth bass. **Flower:** magnolia. **Fossil:** prehistoric whale. **Insect:** honeybee. **Mammal:** white-tailed deer. **Marine mammal:** bottle-nosed dolphin (porpoise). **Rock:** petrified wood. **Tree:** magnolia tree.

Natural features

Land area: 47,692 sq mi, 123,522 sq km. **Highest point:** Woodall Mountain, 246 m (806 ft). **Major rivers:** Mississippi, Pearl, Big Black, Yazoo, Tombigbee. **Natural regions:** the entire state consists of the Coastal Plain, subdivided into the Mississippi Alluvial Plain, in the west, and the East Gulf Coastal Plain, comprising the central and eastern regions. **Land use:** forest, 54.9%; agricultural, 16.3%; other, 28.8%.

People

Population (2007): 2,918,785; persons per sq mi 61.2, persons per sq km 23.6. **Vital statistics** (2006; per 1,000 population): birth rate, 15.8; death rate, 9.8; marriage rate, 5.8; divorce rate, 4.7. **Major cities** (2007): Jackson 175,710; Gulfport 66,271; Hattiesburg 50,233; Biloxi 44,292; Southaven 42,567.

Government

Statehood: entered the Union on 10 Dec 1817 as the 20th state. **State constitution:** adopted 1890. **Representation in US Congress:** 2 senators; 5 representatives. **Electoral college:** 6 votes. **Political divisions:** 82 counties.

Economy

Employment (2007): services 29.5%; government 17.8%; trade 13.9%; manufacturing 11.1%; finance, insurance, real estate 10.6%. **Production** (2007): services 17.4%; finance, insurance, real estate 17.3%; government 17.2%; manufacturing 15.6%; trade 13.6%. **Chief agricultural products:** *Crops:* cotton, soybeans, rice, wheat, corn (maize), greenhouse and nursery plants, sweet potatoes, pecans. *Livestock:* cattle and calves. *Fish catch:* catfish, pearls, shrimp, oysters, crustaceans. **Chief manufactured products:** food products; transportation equipment; wearing apparel; textiles; electrical equipment; rubber products.

Internet resources: <www.visitmississippi.org>; <www.mississippi.gov>.

Missouri

Name: Missouri, named for a Native American tribe that lived in the region; the name means "town of the large canoes." **Nickname:** Show Me State. **Capital:** Jefferson City. **Rank:** population: 18th; area: 20th. **Motto:** "Salus populi suprema lex esto" ("The welfare of the people shall be the supreme law"). **Song:** "Missouri Waltz," words by J.R. Shannon and music by John Valentine Eppel. **Aquatic animal:** paddlefish. **Bird:** bluebird. **Fish:** channel catfish. **Flower:** white hawthorn blossom. **Fossil:** crinoid. **Insect:** honeybee. **Mammal:** Missouri mule. **Mineral:** galena. **Rock:** mozarkite. **Tree:** flowering dogwood.

Natural features

Land area: 69,704 sq mi, 180,533 sq km. **Mountain ranges:** Ozark Plateau, St. Francois. **Highest point:** Taum Sauk Mountain, 540 m (1,772 ft). **Largest lake:** Truman Lake. **Major rivers:** Missouri, Mississippi, Des Plaines. **Natural regions:** Central Lowland, northwestern, subdivided into the Dissected Till Plains to the north and the Osage Plains to the west; Ozark Plateaus, including the Springfield-Salem Plateaus, southeast; Coastal Plain, including the Mississippi Alluvial Plain, extreme southeastern tip. **Land use:** agricultural, 30.7%; forest, 28.1%; pasture, 0.2%; other, 41.0%.

People

Population (2007): 5,878,415; persons per sq mi 84.3, persons per sq km 32.6. **Vital statistics** (2006; per 1,000 population): birth rate, 13.9; death rate, 9.4; marriage rate, 7.0; divorce rate, 3.9. **Major cities** (2007): Kansas City 450,375; St. Louis 350,759; Springfield 154,777; Independence 110,704; Columbia 99,174.

Government

Statehood: entered the Union on 10 Aug 1821 as the 24th state. **State constitution:** adopted 1945. **Representation in US Congress:** 2 senators; 9 representatives. **Electoral college:** 11 votes. **Political divisions:** 114 counties.

Economy

Employment (2007): services 32.1%; finance, insurance, real estate 15.5%; trade 14.6%; government 13.3%; manufacturing 8.5%. **Production** (2007): finance, insurance, real estate 25.8%; services 18.8%; trade 13.4%; manufacturing 13.3%; government 12.1%. **Chief agricultural products:** *Crops:* soybeans, corn (maize), cotton, rice, sorghum, wheat, dairy products. *Livestock:* cattle and calves, pigs, sheep and lambs, poultry. **Chief manufactured products:** industrial machinery; transportation equipment; food products; malt beverages and other alcoholic products; soft drinks; soaps and detergents; agricultural chemicals; pharmaceuticals; printing and publishing; base metals.

Internet resources: <www.visitmo.com>; <www.missouri.gov>.

Montana

Name: Montana, from the Spanish word *montaña* ("mountain," or "mountainous region"). **Nickname:** Treasure State. **Capital:** Helena. **Rank:** population: 44th; area: 4th. **Motto:** "Oro y plata" ("Gold and silver"). **Song:** "Montana," words by Charles C. Cohan and music by Joseph E. Howard. **Bird:** western meadowlark. **Fish:** cutthroat trout. **Flower:** bitterroot. **Fossil:** *Maiasaura*. **Gemstones:** agate; sapphire. **Mammal:** grizzly bear. **Tree:** ponderosa pine.

Natural features

Land area: 147,042 sq mi, 380,837 sq km. **Mountain ranges:** Rocky, Grand Teton. **Highest point:** Granite Peak, 3,901 m (12,799 ft). **Largest lake:** Flathead Lake. **Major rivers:** Kootenai, Clark Fork, Flathead, Missouri, Yellowstone. **Natural regions:** Northern Rocky Mountains, western two-fifths of the state; Middle Rocky Mountains, small area along the south-central border; Missouri Plateau region of the Great Plains Province, eastern three-fifths of the state. **Land use:** pasture, 39.0%; agricultural, 15.4%; forest, 5.7%; other, 39.9%.

People

Population (2007): 957,861; persons per sq mi 6.5, persons per sq km 2.5. **Vital statistics** (2006; per 1,000 population): birth rate, 13.2; death rate, 9.0; marriage rate, 7.1; divorce rate, 3.6. **Major cities** (2007): Billings 101,876; Missoula 67,165; Great Falls 58,827; Bozeman 37,981; Butte–Silver Bow 31,967.

Government

Statehood: entered the Union on 8 Nov 1889 as the 41st state. **State constitution:** adopted 1972. **Representation in US Congress:** 2 senators; 1 representative. **Electoral college:** 3 votes. **Political divisions:** 56 counties.

Economy

Employment (2007): services 32.8%; trade 14.9%; government 14.4%; finance, insurance, real estate 13.4%; construction 8.5%. **Production** (2007): finance, insurance, real estate 20.8%; services 18.8%; government 15.6%; trade 12.3%; transportation, public utilities 11.5%. **Chief agricultural products:** *Crops:* wheat, safflowers, sunflowers, mustard, sugar beets, grapes, garlic, potatoes, honey, cherries. *Livestock:* beef cattle, dairy cattle, sheep and lambs, poultry, horses, llamas. **Chief manufactured products:** food products; lumber and wood products; fabricated metal products; refined petroleum products; chemical products; cement, bricks, and ceramics; machinery and apparatus.

Internet resources: <www.visitmt.com>; <www.mt.gov>.

Nebraska

Name: Nebraska, from a Native American word meaning "flat water," a reference to the Platte River. **Nickname:** Cornhusker State. **Capital:** Lincoln, **Rank:** population: 38th; area: 16th. **Motto:** "Equality before the law." **Song:** "Beautiful Nebraska," words by Jim Fras and Guy Gage Miller and music by Jim Fras. **Bird:** western meadowlark. **Fish:** channel catfish. **Flower:** goldenrod. **Fossil:** mammoth. **Gemstone:** blue agate. **Insect:** honeybee. **Mammal:** white-tailed deer. **Rock:** prairie agate. **Tree:** cottonwood.

Natural features

Land area: 77,353 sq mi, 200,343 sq km. **Highest point:** Panorama Point 1,653 m (5,424 ft). **Largest lake:** Lake McConaughy. **Major rivers:** Missouri, Platte, Elkhorn, Loup, Republican. **Natural regions:** Great Plains Province, western three-quarters of the state; Missouri Plateau, at the northern corners; High Plains, central and north central; Plains Border, southern border; Central Lowland, including the Dissected Till Plains, eastern quarter of the state. **Land use:** pasture, 46.6%; agricultural, 39.5%; forest, 1.6%; other, 12.3%.

For details about state governments, see pages 608–613; for energy data, see pages 627–628.

People

Population (2007): 1,774,571; persons per sq mi 22.9, persons per sq km 8.9. **Vital statistics** (2006; per 1,000 population): birth rate, 15.1; death rate, 8.4; marriage rate, 6.8; divorce rate, 3.5. **Major cities** (2007): Omaha 424,482; Lincoln 248,744; Bellevue 48,391; Grand Island 44,802; Kearney 30,129.

Government

Statehood: entered the Union on 1 Mar 1867 as the 37th state. **State constitution:** adopted 1875. **Representation in US Congress:** 2 senators; 3 representatives. **Electoral college:** 5 votes. **Political divisions:** 93 counties.

Economy

Employment (2007): services 30.1%; trade 14.7%; finance, insurance, real estate 14.5%; government 13.9%; manufacturing 8.4%. **Production** (2007): finance, insurance, real estate 23.8%; services 15.1%; government 13.7%; trade 11.5%; manufacturing 11.3%. **Chief agricultural products:** *Crops:* corn (maize), soybeans, wheat, sorghum, dry beans, sugar beets. *Livestock:* beef cattle, dairy cattle, pigs, sheep and lambs, poultry. **Chief manufactured products:** food products, including canned and frozen fruits and vegetables, flour, cereal, grain products, and livestock feeds; beverages; dairy products; transportation equipment; printing and publishing; plastics and rubber goods; fabricated metal products; base metals.

Internet resources: <www.visitnebraska.org>; <www.nebraska.gov>.

Nevada

Name: Nevada, from the Spanish *nevada* ("snow-clad"), a reference to the high mountain scenery of the Sierra Nevada on the southwestern border with California. **Nicknames:** Sagebrush State; Silver State. **Capital:** Carson City. **Rank:** population: 35th; area: 7th. **Motto:** "All for our country." **Song:** "Home Means Nevada," words and music by Bertha Raffeto. **Bird:** mountain bluebird. **Fish:** Lahontan cutthroat trout. **Flower:** sagebrush. **Fossil:** ichthyosaur. **Gemstones:** fire opal; turquoise. **Mammal:** desert bighorn sheep. **Metal:** silver. **Reptile:** desert tortoise. **Rock:** sandstone. **Trees:** single-leaf piñon; bristlecone pine.

Natural features

Land area: 110,561 sq mi, 286,352 sq km. **Mountain ranges:** Snake, Schell Creek, Monitor, Toiyabe, Shoshone, Humboldt, Santa Rosa. **Highest point:** Boundary Peak, 4,006 m (13,143 ft). **Largest lakes:** Pyramid Lake (natural); Lake Mead (man-made). **Major rivers:** Humboldt, Truckee, Carson, Walker, Muddy. **Natural regions:** the Basin and Range Province covers all of the state, except for the southwestern corner, which consists of the Cascade-Sierra Mountains, and the northeastern corner, which comprises part of the Columbia Plateau. **Land use:** pasture, 11.7%; agricultural, 0.9%; forest, 0.4%; other, 87.0%.

People

Population (2007): 2,565,382; persons per sq mi 23.2, persons per sq km 9.0. **Vital statistics** (2006; per 1,000 population): birth rate, 16.1; death rate, 7.4; marriage rate, 52.9; divorce rate, 6.7, **Major cities** (2007) Las Vegas 558,880; Henderson 249,386; Reno 214,853; North Las Vegas 212,114; Sunrise Manor 191,966; Paradise 185,935; Spring Valley 176,815; Enterprise 143,917.

Government

Statehood: entered the Union on 31 Oct 1864 as the 36th state. **State constitution:** adopted 1864. **Representation in US Congress:** 2 senators; 3 representatives. **Electoral college:** 5 votes. **Political divisions:** 16 counties; 1 independent city.

Economy

Employment (2007): services 39.7%; finance, insurance, real estate 18.3%; trade 13.0%; government 10.1%; construction 9.4%. **Production** (2007): finance, insurance, real estate 30.2%; services 26.9%; trade 11.8%; government 10.1%; construction 8.1%. **Chief agricultural products:** *Crops:* wheat, corn (maize), potatoes, rye, alfalfa, barley, dairy products. *Livestock:* cattle and calves, horses, sheep and lambs, hogs, poultry. **Chief manufactured products:** food products, including candy and frozen desserts; dairy products; soft drinks; paper products; chemical products; plastics; construction materials; machinery and apparatus; printing and publishing.

Internet resources: <travelnevada.com>; <www.nevada.gov>.

New Hampshire

Name: New Hampshire, named for Hampshire, England, by Captain John Mason. **Nickname:** Granite State. **Capital:** Concord. **Rank:** population: 41st; area: 44th. **Motto:** "Live free or die." **Songs:** "Old New Hampshire," words by John F. Holmes and music by Maurice Hoffmann; "New Hampshire, My New Hampshire," words by Julius Richelson and music by Walter P. Smith. **Amphibian:** red-spotted newt. **Bird:** purple finch. **Fish:** brook trout (freshwater); striped bass (saltwater). **Flower:** purple lilac. **Gemstone:** smoky quartz. **Insect:** ladybug. **Mammal:** white-tailed deer. **Mineral:** beryl. **Rock:** granite. **Tree:** white birch.

Natural features

Land area: 9,282 sq mi, 24,040 sq km. **Mountain ranges:** White, Ossipee, Sandwich, Presidential. **Highest point:** Mt. Washington, 1,917 m (6,288 ft). **Largest lake:** Lake Winnipesaukee. **Major rivers:** Merrimack, Salmon Falls, Connecticut, Saco, Piscataqua. **Natural regions:** the New England Province covers the entire state and is subdivided into the White Mountain Section in the northern third, the New England Upland Section in the south-central region, and the Seaboard Lowland Section in the southeast corner. **Land use:** forest, 65.6%; agricultural, 2.1%; other, 32.3%.

People

Population (2007): 1,315,828; persons per sq mi 141.8, persons per sq km 54.7. **Vital statistics** (2006; per 1,000 population): birth rate, 10.9; death rate, 7.6; marriage rate, 7.1; divorce rate, 4.0. **Major cities** (2007): Manchester 108,874; Nashua 86,837; Concord 42,392; Rochester 30,527; Dover 28,775.

Government

Statehood: entered the Union on 21 Jun 1788 as the 9th state. **State constitution:** adopted 1784. **Representation in US Congress:** 2 senators; 2 representatives. **Electoral college:** 4 votes. **Political divisions:** 10 counties.

Economy

Employment (2007): services 33.4%; trade 17.6%; finance, insurance, real estate 15.8%; government 11.1%; manufacturing 9.7%. **Production** (2007): finance, insurance, real estate 30.7%; services 20.4%; trade 14.0%; manufacturing 11.1%; government 9.4%. **Chief agricultural products:** *Crops:* apples, honey, ornamental horticulture, Christmas trees, dairy products, eggs, maple syrup. *Livestock:* horses, dairy cattle, sheep and lambs. **Chief manufactured products:** machinery and apparatus; computers and software; electrical equipment; semiconductors; food products; medical, surgical, and precision instruments; fabricated metal products; plastics and rubber products; printing and publishing; paper products.

Internet resources: <www.visitnh.gov>; <www.nh.gov>.

New Jersey

Name: New Jersey, named for the island of Jersey in the English Channel. **Nickname:** Garden State. **Capital:** Trenton. **Rank:** population: 11th; area: 46th. **Motto:** "Liberty and prosperity." **Bird:** eastern goldfinch. **Fish:** brook trout. **Flower:** violet. **Fossil:** *Hadrosaurus foulkii*. **Insect:** honeybee. **Mammal:** horse. **Tree:** red oak.

Natural features

Land area: 7,813 sq mi, 20,236 sq km. **Mountain range:** Appalachian. **Highest point:** Kittatinny Mountain, 550 m (1,803 ft). **Largest lake:** Lake Hopatcong. **Major rivers:** Delaware, Hudson, Passaic, Hackensack, Raritan. **Natural regions:** the Valley and Ridge Province, Middle Section, northwest corner; the New England Province, consisting of the New England Upland Section, east of the Valley and Ridge area; the Piedmont Province, including the Piedmont Lowlands, extending from the northeast corner to part of the border with Pennsylvania; the Coastal Plain, Embayed Section, southern half of the state. **Land use:** forest, 30.8%; agricultural, 10.1%; other, 59.1%.

People

Population (2007): 8,685,920; persons per sq mi 1,111.7, persons per sq km 429.2. **Vital statistics** (2006; per 1,000 population): birth rate, 13.2; death rate, 8.1; marriage rate, 4.9; divorce rate, 3.0. **Major cities** (2007): Newark 280,135; Jersey City 242,389; Paterson 146,545; Elizabeth 124,862; Edison 99,884.

Government

Statehood: entered the Union on 18 Dec 1787 as the 3rd state. **State constitution:** adopted 1947. **Representation in US Congress:** 2 senators; 13 representatives. **Electoral college:** 15 votes. **Political divisions:** 21 counties.

Economy

Employment (2007): services 32.5%; finance, insurance, real estate 20.3%; trade 15.8%; government 12.8%; transportation, public utilities 10.2%. **Production** (2007): finance, insurance, real estate 36.2%; services 16.7%; trade 14.1%; government 10.3%; manufacturing 8.8%. **Chief agricultural products:** *Crops:* cranberries, blueberries, peaches, asparagus, bell peppers, spinach, sweet corn, escarole and endive, eggplants, nursery and greenhouse products. *Livestock:* horses, cattle, poultry. *Fish catch:* bluefish, tilefish, flounder, hake, shellfish. **Chief manufactured products:** chemical products, including pharmaceuticals; electronics and electrical equipment; telecommunications equipment; semiconductors; industrial equipment; refined petroleum products; fabricated metal products; cement, bricks, and ceramics; food products.

Internet resources: <www.newjersey.gov>; <www.state.nj.us/travel>.

New Mexico

Name: New Mexico, named for the country of Mexico. **Nickname:** Land of Enchantment. **Capital:** Santa Fe. **Rank:** population: 36th; area: 5th. **Motto:** "Crescit eundo" ("It grows as it goes"). **Songs:** "O, Fair New Mexico," words and music by Elizabeth Garrett; "Así es Nuevo Mexico," words and music by Amadeo Lucero. **Bird:** roadrunner. **Fish:** New Mexico cutthroat trout. **Flower:** yucca. **Fossil:** coelophysis. **Gemstone:** turquoise. **Insect:** tarantula hawk wasp. **Tree:** piñon pine.

Natural features

Land area: 121,590 sq mi, 314,917 sq km. **Mountain ranges:** Rocky, Sangre de Cristo. **Highest point:** Wheeler Peak, 4,011 m (13,161 ft). **Largest lake:** Elephant Butte Reservoir. **Major rivers:** Rio Grande, Pecos, Canadian, San Juan, Gila. **Natural regions:** Great Plains Province, eastern third of the state, subdivided into the Raton Section to the north, the High Plains along the eastern edge, and the Pecos Valley to the west; Southern Rocky Mountains, north-central region; Colorado Plateau, northwest corner, including the Navajo Section and Datil Section; Basin and Range Province, central region and southwest corner, with the Sacramento Section to the east and the Mexican Highland to the south. **Land use:** pasture, 51.3%; forest, 7.0%; agricultural, 2.0%; other, 39.7%.

For details about state governments, see pages 608–613; for energy data, see pages 627–628.

People

Population (2007): 1,969,915; persons per sq mi 16.2, persons per sq km 6.3. **Vital statistics** (2006; per 1,000 population): birth rate, 15.3; death rate, 7.8; marriage rate, 6.9; divorce rate, 4.3. **Major cities** (2007): Albuquerque 518,271; Las Cruces 89,722; Rio Rancho 75,978; Santa Fe 73,199; Roswell 45,569.

Government

Statehood: entered the Union on 6 Jan 1912 as the 47th state. **State constitution:** adopted 1911. **Representation in US Congress:** 2 senators; 3 representatives. **Electoral college:** 5 votes. **Political divisions:** 33 counties.

Economy

Employment (2007): services 32.3%; government 18.8%; finance, insurance, real estate 14.5%; trade 13.6%; construction 7.4%. **Production** (2007): finance, insurance, real estate 22.2%; government 17.0%; services 15.6%; mining 14.2%; trade 10.1%. **Chief agricultural products:** *Crops:* pecans, apples, potatoes, onions, chilies, peanuts (groundnuts), sorghum, corn (maize), wheat, eggs. *Livestock:* dairy cattle, beef cattle, poultry, sheep and lambs. **Chief manufactured products:** electronics; semiconductors; printing and publishing; food products.

Internet resources: <www.newmexico.org>; <www.newmexico.gov>.

New York

Name: New York, named in honor of the English duke of York. **Nickname:** Empire State. **Capital:** Albany. **Rank:** population: 3rd; area: 28th. **Motto:** "Excelsior" ("Ever upward"). **Song:** "I Love New York," words and music by Steve Karmen. **Bird:** bluebird. **Fish:** brook trout. **Flower:** rose. **Fossil:** *Eurypterus remipes.* **Gemstone:** garnet. **Mammal:** beaver. **Tree:** sugar maple.

Natural features

Land area: 53,097 sq mi, 137,521 sq km. **Mountain ranges:** Adirondack, Catskill, Shawangunk, Taconic. **Highest point:** Mt. Marcy, 1,629 m (5,344 ft). **Largest lake:** Oneida Lake. **Major rivers:** Hudson, Mohawk, Genesee, Oswego, Delaware. **Natural regions:** Central Lowland, Eastern Lake Section, extends along the northern coast of Lake Ontario; St. Lawrence Valley, Northern Section, extends along the northern border with Canada; Adirondack Province, northeast; Appalachian Plateaus, including the Mohawks, Southern New York, and Catskill Sections, extend along the southern border with Pennsylvania and up halfway through the state; Valley and Ridge Province, southeastern edge bordering Connecticut and Massachusetts; Coastal Plain, Embayed Section, covers the islands of Manhattan and Long Island. **Land use:** forest, 56.1%; agricultural, 17.1%; other, 26.8%.

People

Population (2007): 19,297,729; persons per sq mi 363.4, persons per sq km 140.3. **Vital statistics** (2006; per 1,000 population): birth rate, 13.0; death rate, 7.7; marriage rate, 6.6; divorce rate, 2.9. **Major**

cities (2007): New York 8,274,527; Buffalo 272,632; Rochester 206,759; Yonkers 199,244; Syracuse 139,079.

Government

Statehood: entered the Union on 26 Jul 1788 as the 11th state. **State constitution:** adopted 1894. **Representation in US Congress:** 2 senators; 29 representatives. **Electoral college:** 31 votes. **Political divisions:** 62 counties.

Economy

Employment (2007): services 36.0%; finance, insurance, real estate 20.0%; government 13.7%; trade 13.3%; transportation, public utilities 6.1%. **Production** (2007): finance, insurance, real estate 43.3%; services 16.6%; transportation, public utilities 11.2%; government 10.0%; trade 9.8%. **Chief agricultural products:** *Crops:* apples, cabbage, corn (maize), potatoes, onions, grapes, snap beans, cherries, strawberries, maple syrup, horticultural products, milk, other dairy products, eggs. *Livestock:* cattle and calves, chickens. **Chief manufactured products:** food products; chemical products; wearing apparel; base metals; machinery and apparatus; computers and software; scientific and measuring instruments; transportation equipment; electronics and electrical equipment; printing and publishing; biotechnology products.

Internet resources: <www.iloveny.com>; <www.ny.gov>.

North Carolina

Name: North Carolina, named in honor of Charles I of England. **Nickname:** Old North State. **Capital:** Raleigh. **Rank:** population: 10th; area: 29th. **Motto:** "Esse quam videri" ("To be rather than to seem"). **Song:** "The Old North State," words by William Gaston, to the tune of a traditional German melody. **Bird:** cardinal. **Fish:** channel bass. **Flower:** dogwood. **Gemstone:** emerald. **Insect:** honeybee. **Mammal:** gray squirrel. **Reptile:** eastern box turtle. **Rock:** granite. **Tree:** pine.

Natural features

Land area: 52,671 sq mi, 136,417 sq km. **Mountain ranges:** Appalachian, Great Smoky, Blue Ridge. **Highest point:** Mt. Mitchell, 2,037 m (6,684 ft). **Largest lake:** Lake Mattamuskeet. **Major rivers:** Roanoke, Yadkin, Pee Dee. **Natural regions:** Valley and Ridge Province, far western edge; Piedmont Province, consisting of the Piedmont Upland, extending in a southwest to northeast direction through the center of the state; Coastal Plain, eastern third, divided into the Sea Island Section to the south and the Embayed Section to the north. **Land use:** forest, 45.9%; agricultural, 16.4%; other, 37.7%.

People

Population (2007): 9,061,032; persons per sq mi 172.0, persons per sq km 66.4. **Vital statistics** (2006; per 1,000 population): birth rate, 14.4; death rate, 8.4; marriage rate, 6.2; divorce rate, 4.1. **Major cities** (2007): Charlotte 671,588; Raleigh 375,806;

Greensboro 247,183; Durham 217,847; Winston-Salem 215,348; Fayetteville 171,853; Cary 121,796; High Point 100,432.

Government

Statehood: entered the Union on 21 Nov 1789 as the 12th state. **State constitution:** adopted 1970. **Representation in US Congress:** 2 senators, 13 representatives. **Electoral college:** 15 votes. **Political divisions:** 100 counties.

Economy

Employment (2007): services 31.6%; government 15.2%; finance, insurance, real estate 14.5%; trade 14.2%; manufacturing 10.3%. **Production** (2007): finance, insurance, real estate 29.1%; manufacturing 18.6%; services 14.6%; government 12.9%; trade 11.6%. **Chief agricultural products:** *Crops:* tobacco, peanuts (groundnuts), apples, blueberries, grapes, peaches, pecans, strawberries, sweet potatoes, Christmas trees. *Livestock:* cattle and calves, chickens, pigs, horses. *Fish catch:* catfish, trout. **Chief manufactured products:** textiles; cotton and synthetic fibers, yarns, and threads; cigarettes and tobacco products; chemical products; electronics and electrical equipment; furniture; lumber; paper products; food products.

Internet resources: <www.visitnc.com>; <www.northcarolina.gov>.

North Dakota

Name: North Dakota, from the Dakota division of the Sioux, the Native American tribe that inhabited the plains before the arrival of Europeans; *dakota* is the Sioux word for "friend." **Nickname:** Peace Garden State. **Capital:** Bismarck. **Rank:** population: 48th; area: 18th. **Motto:** "Liberty and union now and forever, one and inseparable." **Song:** "North Dakota Hymn," words by James W. Foley and music by C.S. Putnam. **Bird:** western meadowlark. **Fish:** northern pike. **Flower:** wild prairie rose. **Fossil:** Teredo petrified wood. **Tree:** American elm.

Natural features

Land area: 70,700 sq mi, 183,112 sq km. **Highest point:** White Butte, 1,069 m (3,506 ft). **Largest lake:** Devils Lake. **Major rivers:** Red, Souris, Missouri, Little Missouri, James. **Natural regions:** Central Lowland covers eastern half of the state, with the Western Lake Section lying in the east-central region; Great Plains Province covers western half of the state, including sections of the Missouri Plateau to the north and south. **Land use:** agricultural, 53.6%; pasture, 24.5%; forest, 1.0%; other, 20.9%.

People

Population (2007): 639,715; persons per sq mi 9.0, persons per sq km 3.5. **Vital statistics** (2006; per 1,000 population): birth rate, 13.6; death rate, 9.2; marriage rate, 6.8; divorce rate, 2.6. **Major cities** (2007) Fargo 92,660; Bismarck 59,503; Grand Forks 51,740; Minot 35,281; West Fargo 23,081.

Government

Statehood: entered the Union on 2 Nov 1889 as the 39th state. **State constitution:** adopted 1889. **Representation in US Congress:** 2 senators; 1 representative. **Electoral college:** 3 votes. **Political divisions:** 53 counties.

Economy

Employment (2007): services 29.7%; government 16.7%; trade 15.6%; finance, insurance, real estate 11.5%; agriculture, forestry, fishing 8.3%. **Production** (2007): finance, insurance, real estate 18.3%; services 15.8%; government 15.0%; trade 14.3%; transportation, public utilities 11.3%. **Chief agricultural products:** *Crops:* spring wheat, durum wheat, flaxseed, canola, dry beans, sunflowers, barley, honey, potatoes, dairy products. *Livestock:* cattle and calves, sheep and lambs, pigs. **Chief manufactured products:** food products; wood products; refined petroleum products; transportation equipment; machinery and apparatus.

Internet resources: <www.ndtourism.com>; <www.nd.gov>.

Did you know? A 12-foot-tall bronze statue of Sakakawea (Sacagawea), the Shoshone woman who traveled thousands of miles providing indispensable aid to the famous Lewis and Clark Expedition (1804–06), stands on the grounds of the North Dakota Heritage Center in Bismarck.

Ohio

Name: Ohio, from an Iroquois word meaning "great river." **Nickname:** Buckeye State. **Capital:** Columbus. **Rank:** population: 7th; area: 34th. **Motto:** "With God, all things are possible." **Song:** "Beautiful Ohio," words by Ballard MacDonald and music by Mary Earl. **Bird:** cardinal. **Flower:** red carnation. **Fossil:** *Trilobite isotelus.* **Gemstone:** flint. **Insect:** ladybug. **Mammal:** white-tailed deer. **Reptile:** black racer snake. **Tree:** Ohio buckeye.

Natural features

Land area: 44,825 sq mi, 116,096 sq km. **Highest point:** Campbell Hill, 472 m (1,549 ft). **Largest lake:** Grand Lake St. Marys. **Major rivers:** Ohio, Maumee, Cuyahoga, Miami, Scioto. **Natural regions:** the Appalachian Plateau, eastern half of the state, includes the Southern New York Section to the north and the Kanawha Section to the east; the Central Lowlands, western half of the state, includes the Eastern Lake Section in the northwest corner, the Till Plains in the central region, and the Lexington Plain in the southwest. **Land use:** agricultural, 42.5%; forest, 27.3%; other, 30.2%.

People

Population (2007): 11,466,917; persons per sq mi 255.8, persons per sq km 98.8. **Vital statistics** (2006; per 1,000 population): birth rate, 13.1; death rate, 9.3; marriage rate, 6.4; divorce rate, 3.6. **Major cities** (2007): Columbus 747,755; Cleveland 438,042; Cincinnati 332,458; Toledo 295,029; Akron 207,934; Dayton 155,461.

Government

Statehood: entered the Union on 1 Mar 1803 as the 17th state. **State constitution:** adopted 1851. **Representation in US Congress:** 2 senators; 18 representatives. **Electoral college:** 20 votes. **Political divisions:** 88 counties.

Economy

Employment (2007): services 33.7%; finance, insurance, real estate 14.8%; trade 14.7%; government 12.3%; manufacturing 11.7%. **Production** (2007): finance, insurance, real estate 27.6%; manufacturing 18.2%; services 17.3%; trade 12.6%; government 11.1%. **Chief agricultural products:** *Crops:* corn (maize), soybeans, grapes, apples, tobacco, winter wheat, dairy products, eggs, greenhouse and nursery products. *Livestock:* cattle and calves, hogs, poultry, goats. **Chief manufactured products:** machinery and apparatus; nonelectrical machinery; food products; transportation equipment; fabricated metal products; base metals; chemical products; rubber products.

Internet resources: <consumer.discoverohio.com>; <www.ohio.gov>.

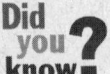

Did you know? Cambridge, Ohio's own John Glenn is famous for having been the first American astronaut to orbit Earth and later for serving four terms as a US Senator from Ohio. Less known is the fact that in late 1998 Glenn returned to space on the space shuttle *Discovery*, at 77 becoming the oldest person ever to travel in space.

Oklahoma

Name: Oklahoma, from two Choctaw words: *okla,* meaning "people," and *humma,* meaning "red." **Nickname:** Sooner State. **Capital:** Oklahoma City. **Rank:** population: 28th; area: 19th. **Motto:** "Labor omnia vincit" ("Labor conquers all things"). **Song:** "Oklahoma," words by Oscar Hammerstein and music by Richard Rodgers. **Bird:** scissor-tailed flycatcher. **Fish:** white, or sand, bass. **Flower:** mistletoe. **Insect:** honeybee. **Mammal:** bison. **Reptile:** collared lizard (also known as the mountain boomer). **Rock:** rose rock. **Tree:** redbud.

Natural features

Land area: 69,898 sq mi, 181,035 sq km. **Mountain ranges:** Ouachita, Arbuckle, Wichita, Sandstone Hills. **Highest point:** Black Mesa, 1,516 m (4,973 ft). **Largest lake:** Lake Eufaula. **Major rivers:** Arkansas, Red, Canadian. **Natural regions:** Great Plains Province, panhandle region, includes the High Plains to the west and the Plains Border to the east; Central Lowland, covering most of the state, includes the Osage Plains in the central region; West Gulf Coastal Plain, southeastern corner; Oua-

chita Province, east-central region, includes the Arkansas Valley in the center and the Ouachita Mountains to the south; Ozark Plateaus, northeast corner, include the Boston Mountains and Springfield-Salem Plateaus. **Land use:** pasture, 31.6%; agricultural, 20.1%; forest, 16.5%; other, 31.8%.

People

Population (2007): 3,617,316; persons per sq mi 51.8, persons per sq km 20.0. **Vital statistics** (2006; per 1,000 population): birth rate, 15.1; death rate, 9.9; marriage rate, 7.3; divorce rate, 5.3. **Major cities** (2007): Oklahoma City 547,274; Tulsa 384,037; Norman 106,707; Lawton 91,568; Broken Arrow 90,714.

Government

Statehood: entered the Union on 16 Nov 1907 as the 46th state. **State constitution:** adopted 1907. **Representation in US Congress:** 2 senators; 5 representatives. **Electoral college:** 7 votes. **Political divisions:** 77 counties.

Economy

Employment (2007): services 30.5%; government 16.7%; trade 13.4%; finance, insurance, real estate 12.8%; manufacturing 7.3%. **Production** (2007): finance, insurance, real estate 18.3%; government 15.7%; services 15.3%; mining 14.0%; trade 11.4%. **Chief agricultural products:** *Crops:* wheat, sorghum, soybeans, cotton, dairy products. *Livestock:* cattle and calves, poultry, hogs and pigs. **Chief manufactured products:** electronics and electrical equipment; telecommunications equipment; transportation equipment; food products; refined petroleum products.

Internet resources: <www.travelok.com>; <www.ok.gov>.

Oregon

Name: Oregon, of uncertain origin. **Nickname:** Beaver State. **Capital:** Salem. **Rank:** population: 27th; area: 10th. **Motto:** "Alis volat propiis" ("She flies with her own wings"). **Song:** "Oregon, My Oregon," words by J.A. Buchanan and music by Henry B. Murtagh. **Bird:** western meadowlark. **Fish:** chinook salmon. **Flower:** Oregon grape. **Gemstone:** Oregon sunstone. **Insect:** Oregon swallowtail. **Mammal:** beaver. **Rock:** thunder egg. **Tree:** Douglas fir.

Natural features

Land area: 97,047 sq mi, 251,351 sq km. **Mountain ranges:** Coast, Klamath, Cascade, Blue, Wallowa. **Highest point:** Mt. Hood, 3,425 m (11,239 ft). **Largest lake:** Upper Klamath Lake. **Major rivers:** Snake, Owyhee, Columbia, Coquille. **Natural regions:** northern Rocky Mountains, northeastern corner, include the Blue Mountain Section; Columbia Plateaus, north and north-central region, include the Walla Walla Plateau in the central region, Harney Section to the south, and Payette Section to the southeast; Basin and Range Province, south-central border, includes the Great Basin; Cascade Sierra Mountains, west central region, include the Middle and Southern Cascades; Pacific

Border Province, western coast, includes the Klamath Mountains to the south, the Oregon Coast Range in the center and north, and the Puget Trough to the east. **Land use:** forest, 20.5%; pasture, 15.1%; agricultural, 6.0%; other, 58.4%.

People

Population (2007): 3,747,455; persons per sq mi 38.6, persons per sq km 14.9. **Vital statistics** (2006; per 1,000 population): birth rate, 13.2; death rate, 8.5; marriage rate, 7.3; divorce rate, 3.9. **Major cities** (2007): Portland 550,396; Salem 151,913; Eugene 149,004; Gresham 99,721; Hillsboro 91,436.

Government

Statehood: entered the Union on 14 Feb 1859 as the 33rd state. **State constitution:** adopted 1857. **Representation in US Congress:** 2 senators; 5 representatives. **Electoral college:** 7 votes. **Political divisions:** 36 counties.

Economy

Employment (2007): services 32.6%; trade 14.9%; finance, insurance, real estate 14.5%; government 12.5%; manufacturing 9.4%. **Production** (2007): finance, insurance, real estate 25.0%; manufacturing 19.1%; services 16.5%; trade 12.2%; government 12.2%. **Chief agricultural products:** *Crops:* horticultural and nursery products, Christmas trees, pears, cherries, apples, hazelnuts, potatoes, mint, hops, sugar beets. *Livestock:* cattle and calves, horses, mink, poultry, sheep and lambs. *Fish catch:* tuna, salmon, shellfish, crab, shrimp. **Chief manufactured products:** lumber and wood products; food products; aircraft and spacecraft; semiconductors; computers.

Internet resources: <www.traveloregon.com>; <www.oregon.gov>.

Pennsylvania

Name: Pennsylvania, named for Adm. Sir William Penn, father of the territory's founder, William Penn, and also including the Latin term *sylvania* ("woodlands"). **Nickname:** Keystone State. **Capital:** Harrisburg. **Rank:** population: 6th; area: 33rd. **Motto:** "Virtue, liberty, and independence". **Song:** "Pennsylvania," words and music by Eddie Khoury and Ronnie Bonner. **Bird:** ruffled grouse. **Fish:** brook trout. **Flower:** mountain laurel. **Fossil:** *Phacops rana*. **Insect:** firefly. **Mammal:** white-tailed deer. **Tree:** hemlock.

Natural features

Land area: 46,056 sq mi, 119,284 sq km. **Mountain ranges:** Appalachian, Allegheny. **Highest point:** Mt. Davis, 979 m (3,213 ft). **Largest lake:** Raystown Lake. **Major rivers:** Delaware, Lehigh, Schuylkill, Susquehanna, Ohio. **Natural regions:** Central Lowland, Eastern Lake Section, extreme northwestern edge; Appalachian Plateaus, including the Southern New York, Allegheny Mountain, and Kanawha sections, western

half of state; Valley and Ridge Province, central region, including portions of the Appalachian Mountains; Piedmont Province, comprising the Piedmont Lowlands and Upland, southeast corner; Coastal Plain, extreme southeast edge; New England Province, New England Upland Section, east-central border. **Land use:** forest, 53.9%; agricultural, 17.7%; other, 28.4%.

People

Population (2007): 12,432,792; persons per sq mi 269.9, persons per sq km 104.2. **Vital statistics** (2006; per 1,000 population): birth rate, 12.0; death rate, 10.1; marriage rate, 5.5; divorce rate, 2.2. **Major cities** (2007): Philadelphia 1,449,634; Pittsburgh 311,218; Allentown 107,117; Erie 103,650; Reading 80,769.

Government

Statehood: entered the Union on 12 Dec 1787 as the 2nd state. **State constitution:** adopted 1968. **Representation in US Congress:** 2 senators, 19 representatives. **Electoral college:** 21 votes. **Political divisions:** 67 counties.

Economy

Employment (2007): services 35.6%; finance, insurance, real estate 16.0%; trade 14.7%; government 11.1%; manufacturing 9.4%. **Production** (2007): finance, insurance, real estate 28.8%; services 19.7%; manufacturing 14.2%; trade 12.2%; transportation, public utilities 10.1%. **Chief agricultural products:** *Crops:* mushrooms, apples, tobacco, grapes, peaches, cut flowers, dairy products. *Livestock:* cattle and calves, poultry, pigs, horses. **Chief manufactured products:** electronics; telecommunications systems; semiconductors; chemical products; food products; base metals; machinery and apparatus; transportation equipment; paper products.

Internet resources: <www.visitpa.com>; <www.pa.gov>.

Rhode Island

Name: Rhode Island, from the Greek island of Rhodes. **Nicknames:** Little Rhody; Ocean State. **Capital:** Providence. **Rank:** population: 43rd; area: 50th. **Motto:** "Hope". **Song:** "Rhode Island's It for Me," words by Charlie Hall and music by Maria Day. **Bird:** Rhode Island Red chicken. **Flower:** violet. **Mineral:** bowenite. **Rock:** cumberlandite.

Natural features

Land area: 1,223 sq mi, 3,168 sq km. **Highest point:** Jerimoth Hill, 247 m (812 ft). **Largest lake:** Scituate Reservoir. **Major rivers:** Blackstone, Pawtuxet, Pawcatuck. **Natural regions:** the entire state is part of the New England Province, subdivided into the New England Upland (western two-thirds) and the Seaboard Lowland (eastern third). **Land use:** forest, 45.9%; agricultural, 2.5%; other, 51.6%.

For details about state governments, see pages 608–613; for energy data, see pages 627–628.

People

Population (2007): 1,057,832; persons per sq mi 864.9, persons per sq km 333.9. **Vital statistics** (2006; per 1,000 population): birth rate, 11.6; death rate, 9.1; marriage rate, 6.5; divorce rate, 2.9. **Major cities** (2007): Providence 172,459; Warwick 85,097; Cranston 80,463; Pawtucket 72,342; East Providence 48,779.

Government

Statehood: entered the Union on 29 May 1790 as the 13th state. **State constitution:** adopted 1986. **Representation in US Congress:** 2 senators; 2 representatives. **Electoral college:** 4 votes. **Political divisions:** 5 counties.

Economy

Employment (2007): services 38.8%; finance, insurance, real estate 16.7%; trade 13.1%; government 12.2%; manufacturing 8.6%. **Production** (2007): finance, insurance, real estate 34.8%; services 20.0%; government 12.4%; trade 11.4%; manufacturing 9.6%. **Chief agricultural products:** Crops: apples, peaches, dairy products, eggs, potatoes. Livestock: poultry, cattle and calves, sheep and lambs. Fish catch: shellfish. **Chief manufactured products:** jewelry; silverware; textiles; fabricated metal products; electrical equipment; machinery and apparatus; surgical instruments; plastics.

Internet resources: <www.visitrhodeisland.com>; <www.ri.gov>.

South Carolina

Name: South Carolina, named in honor of Charles I of England. **Nickname:** Palmetto State. **Capital:** Columbia. **Rank:** population: 24th; area: 40th. **Mottoes:** "Animis opibusque parati" ("Prepared in mind and resources"); *Dum Spiro Spero* (While I Breathe, I Hope). **Songs:** "Carolina," words by Henry Timrod and music by Anne Custis Burgess; "South Carolina on My Mind," words and music by Hank Martin and Buzz Arledge. **Amphibian:** spotted salamander. **Bird:** Carolina wren. **Fish:** striped bass. **Flower:** Carolina jessamine. **Gemstone:** amethyst. **Insect:** Carolina mantid. **Mammal:** white-tailed deer. **Reptile:** loggerhead turtle. **Rock:** blue granite. **Tree:** palmetto.

Natural features

Land area: 31,118 sq mi, 80,595 sq km. **Mountain range:** Blue Ridge. **Highest point:** Sassafras Mountain, 1,085 m (3,560 ft). **Largest lake:** Lake Marion. **Major rivers:** Pee Dee, Savannah, Ashley, Combahee, Edisto. **Natural regions:** Coastal Plain covers the eastern two-thirds of the state and includes the Sea Island Section in the central region; Piedmont Province extends across the central and western region and includes the Piedmont Upland; Blue Ridge Province covers the far northwestern corner and includes the Southern Section. **Land use:** forest, 56.0%; agricultural, 11.9%; other, 32.1%.

People

Population (2007): 4,407,709; persons per sq mi 141.6, persons per sq km 54.7. **Vital statistics**

(2006; per 1,000 population): birth rate, 14.4; death rate, 9.0; marriage rate, 7.6; divorce rate, 3.0. **Major cities** (2007): Columbia 124,818; Charleston 110,015; North Charleston 91,421; Rock Hill 64,858; Mount Pleasant 64,707.

Government

Statehood: entered the Union on 23 May 1788 as the 8th state. **State constitution:** adopted 1895. **Representation in US Congress:** 2 senators; 6 representatives. **Electoral college:** 8 votes. **Political divisions:** 46 counties.

Economy

Employment (2007): services 31.5%; government 15.7%; trade 14.8%; finance, insurance, real estate 13.8%; manufacturing 10.3%. **Production** (2007): finance, insurance, real estate 21.6%; services 17.2%; government 16.6%; manufacturing 16.0%; trade 14.0%. **Chief agricultural products:** Crops: tobacco, cotton, barley, peanuts (groundnuts), peaches, apples, pecans, sweet potatoes, snap beans, dairy products. Livestock: cattle and calves, chickens, pigs. Fish catch: marine fish, oysters, clams, shrimp. **Chief manufactured products:** chemical products, including pharmaceuticals and fertilizers; textiles; wearing apparel; machinery and apparatus; plastics and rubber products; paper and paperboard; electronics and electrical equipment; transportation equipment; lumber.

Internet resources: <www.discoversouthcarolina.com>; <www.sc.gov>.

South Dakota

Name: South Dakota, from the Dakota division of the Sioux, the Native American tribe that inhabited the plains before the arrival of Europeans; *dakota* is the Sioux word for "friend." **Nickname:** Mount Rushmore State. **Capital:** Pierre. **Rank:** population: 46th; area: 17th. **Motto:** "Under God the people rule." **Song:** "Hail! South Dakota," words and music by Deecort Hammitt. **Bird:** Chinese ring-necked pheasant. **Fish:** walleye. **Flower:** pasque. **Fossil:** triceratops. **Gemstone:** Fairburn agate. **Insect:** honeybee. **Mammal:** coyote. **Mineral:** rose quartz. **Tree:** Black Hills spruce.

Natural features

Land area: 77,117 sq mi, 199,732 sq km. **Mountain range:** Black Hills. **Highest point:** Harney Peak, 2,207 m (7,242 ft). **Largest lake:** Lake Thompson. **Major rivers:** Big Sioux, Vermillion, James, Grand, Moreau. **Natural regions:** the Central Lowland, eastern third of the state, includes the Dissected Till Plains along the eastern edge and the Western Lake Section at the center; the Great Plains Province, western two-thirds of the state; the Black Hills, far west; the High Plains, southern border; the Missouri Plateau, west. **Land use:** pasture, 44.7%; agricultural, 34.6%; forest, 1.0%; other, 19.7%.

People

Population (2007): 796,214; persons per sq mi 10.3, persons per sq km 4.0. **Vital statistics** (2006; per 1,000 population): birth rate, 15.2; death rate,

9.1; marriage rate, 8.0; divorce rate, 3.2. **Major cities** (2007): Sioux Falls 151,505; Rapid City 63,997; Aberdeen 24,410; Watertown 20,530; Brookings 19,463.

Government

Statehood: entered the Union on 2 Nov 1889 as the 40th state. **State constitution:** adopted 1889. **Representation in US Congress:** 2 senators; 1 representative. **Electoral college:** 3 votes. **Political divisions:** 66 counties.

Economy

Employment (2007): services 31.4%; trade 15.4%; government 14.3%; finance, insurance, real estate 12.8%; manufacturing 7.8%. **Production** (2007): finance, insurance, real estate 30.2%; services 16.9%; trade 12.6%; government 12.3% manufacturing 9.8%. **Chief agricultural products:** *Crops:* corn (maize), wheat, sunflowers, dairy products, eggs, flaxseed, barley, rye. *Livestock:* cattle and calves, pigs, sheep and lambs. **Chief manufactured products:** machinery and apparatus; office machinery; computers; food products; electronics; printing and publishing; lumber; fabricated metal products; medical instruments; jewelry.

Internet resources: <www.travelsd.com>; <www.sd.gov>.

Did you know? The state of Tennessee was once called Franklin. Settlers from the east moved into the area in 1768, and by 1777 the territory had become Washington County, a part of North Carolina. In 1784 some of the settlers declared themselves independent of North Carolina and formed the State of Franklin, adopting their own constitution.

Tennessee

Name: Tennessee, from Cherokee village name. **Nickname:** Volunteer State. **Capital:** Nashville. **Rank:** population: 17th; area: 35th. **Motto:** "Agriculture and commerce." **Songs:** "My Homeland, Tennessee," words by Nell Grayson Taylor and music by Roy Lamont Smith; "When It's Iris Time in Tennessee," words and music by Willa Mae Waid; "The Tennessee Waltz," words and music by Redd Stewart and Pee Wee King; "Rocky Top," words and music by Boudleaux and Felice Bryant; "The Pride of Tennessee," words and music by Fred Congdon, Thomas Vaughn, and Carol Elliot. **Amphibian:** cave salamander. **Bird:** mockingbird. **Fish:** largemouth bass; channel catfish. **Flower:** iris. **Gemstone:** river pearl. **Insects:** firefly; ladybug. **Mammal:** raccoon. **Reptile:** box turtle. **Rocks:** limestone; agate. **Tree:** tulip poplar.

Natural features

Land area: 42,143 sq mi, 109,150 sq km. **Mountain ranges:** Unaka, Great Smoky. **Highest point:** Clingmans Dome, 2,025 m (6,643 ft). **Largest lake:** Reelfoot. **Major rivers:** Tennessee, Cumberland, Mississippi. **Natural regions:** Blue Ridge Province, eastern border; Valley and Ridge Province, extending from southwest to northeast; Appalachian Plateau, central,

running from south to north, includes the Cumberland Plateau Section in the center and the Cumberland Mountain Section at the northern end; Interior Low Plateau, west central, includes the Nashville Basin and Highland Rim Section. **Land use:** forest, 44.3%; agricultural, 17.6%; other, 38.1%.

People

Population (2007): 6,156,719; persons per sq mi 146.1, persons per sq km 56.4. **Vital statistics** (2006; per 1,000 population): birth rate, 14.0; death rate, 9.4; marriage rate, 10.5; divorce rate, 4.3. **Major cities** (2007): Memphis 674,028; Nashville 590,807; Knoxville 183,546; Chattanooga 169,884; Clarksville 119,284.

Government

Statehood: entered the Union on 1 Jun 1796 as the 16th state. **State constitution:** adopted 1870. **Representation in US Congress:** 2 senators; 9 representatives. **Electoral college:** 11 votes. **Political divisions:** 95 counties.

Economy

Employment (2007): services 32.7%; trade 15.1%; finance, insurance, real estate 13.6%; government 12.0%; manufacturing 10.5%. **Production** (2007): finance, insurance, real estate 22.4%; services 21.2%; manufacturing 16.1%; trade 15.3%; government 11.0%. **Chief agricultural products:** *Crops:* cotton, tobacco, peaches, apples, tomatoes, snap beans, honey, dairy products, wheat, sorghum. *Livestock:* cattle and calves, poultry, hogs, sheep and lambs. *Fish catch:* catfish, trout. **Chief manufactured products:** transportation equipment, including motor vehicles, aircraft parts, and boats; chemical products; printing and publishing; electronics; lumber; paper products; wearing apparel; surgical instruments and supplies.

Internet resources: <www.tnvacation.com>; <www.tn.gov>.

Texas

Name: Texas, from the Caddo Indian word *teysha*, or *tejas*, which means "hello friend." **Nickname:** Lone Star State. **Capital:** Austin. **Rank:** population: 2nd; area: 2nd. **Motto:** "Friendship." **Song:** "Texas, Our Texas," words and music by William J. Marsh and Gladys Yoakum Wright. **Bird:** mockingbird. **Fish:** Guadalupe bass. **Flower:** bluebonnet. **Fossil:** pleurocoelus. **Gemstone:** Texas blue topaz. **Insect:** monarch butterfly. **Mammal:** Mexican free-tailed bat (flying); longhorn (large); armadillo (small). **Reptile:** horned lizard. **Rock:** petrified palmwood. **Tree:** pecan.

Natural features

Land area: 266,853 sq mi, 691,146 sq km. **Mountain ranges:** Rocky, Guadalupe. **Highest point:** Guadalupe Peak, 2,667 m (8,749 ft). **Largest lake:** Caddo Lake. **Major rivers:** Red, Trinity, Brazos, Colorado, Rio Grande. **Natural regions:** Coastal Plain, southern and eastern regions, includes the West

For details about state governments, see pages 608–613; for energy data, see pages 627–628.

Gulf Coastal Plain near the east-central coast; Central Lowland, north central, includes the Osage Plains; Great Plains Province, extending from the panhandle across most of central and western Texas, includes the Edwards Plateau to the south, Pecos Valley to the west, High Plains to the north, and Central Texas Section; Basin and Range Province, extreme western region, comprises the Mexican Highland to the south and the Sacramento Section to the north. **Land use:** pasture, 56.2%; agricultural, 14.9%; forest, 6.2%; other, 22.7%.

People

Population (2007): 23,904,380; persons per sq mi 89.6, persons per sq km 34.6. **Vital statistics** (2006; per 1,000 population): birth rate, 17.0; death rate, 6.7; marriage rate, 7.5; divorce rate, 3.3. **Major cities** (2007): Houston 2,208,180; San Antonio 1,328,984; Dallas 1,240,499; Austin 743,074; Fort Worth 681,818; El Paso 606,913; Arlington 371,038; Corpus Christi 285,507.

Government

Statehood: entered the Union on 29 Dec 1845 as the 28th state. **State constitution:** adopted 1876. **Representation in US Congress:** 2 senators; 32 representatives. **Electoral college:** 34 votes. **Political divisions:** 254 counties.

Economy

Employment (2007): services 31.1%; finance, insurance, real estate 16.3%; trade 14.6%; government 13.3%; construction 7.2%. **Production** (2007): finance, insurance, real estate 22.7%; services 14.5%; manufacturing 13.4%; trade 12.5%; transportation, public utilities 11.2%. **Chief agricultural products:** *Crops:* cotton, apples, greenhouse and nursery products, corn (maize), sorghum, wheat, dairy products, eggs, rice. *Livestock:* cattle and calves, pigs, chickens. *Fish catch:* shrimp. **Chief manufactured products:** refined petroleum products; food products; computers; electronics; chemical products; plastics; wearing apparel; wood products; paper products; nonelectrical machinery; fabricated metal products; transportation equipment, including aerospace products and parts, aircraft parts, and motor vehicle parts.

Internet resources: <www.traveltex.com>; <www.texas.gov>.

Utah

Name: Utah, named for the Ute tribe; the word *ute* means "people of the mountains." **Nickname:** Beehive State. **Capital:** Salt Lake City. **Rank:** population: 34th; area: 13th. **Motto:** "Industry." **Song:** "Utah, This Is the Place," words by Sam and Gary Francis and music by Gary Francis. **Bird:** California seagull. **Fish:** Bonneville cutthroat trout. **Flower:** sego lily. **Fossil:** allosaurus. **Gemstone:** topaz. **Insect:** honeybee. **Mammal:** Rocky Mountain elk. **Mineral:** copper. **Rock:** coal. **Tree:** blue spruce.

Natural features

Land area: 84,899 sq mi, 219,887 sq km. **Mountain ranges:** Uinta, Wasatch, Rocky. **Highest point:** Kings

Peak, 4,123 m (13,528 ft). **Largest lake:** Great Salt Lake. **Major rivers:** Colorado, Green, Sevier. **Natural regions:** Basin and Range Province, western half of the state, includes the Great Salt Lake Desert and Bonneville Salt Flats to the north and the Great Basin to the south; Middle Rocky Mountains, northeast; Colorado Plateaus, east-central and southeast regions, include the Grand Canyon Section to the south, the High Plateaus of Utah and Canyon Lands in the center, the Navajo Section in the extreme southeast corner, and the Uinta Basin to the north. **Land use:** pasture, 19.6%; forest, 3.5%; agricultural, 3.1%; other, 73.8%.

People

Population (2007): 2,645,330; persons per sq mi 31.2, persons per sq km 12.0. **Vital statistics** (2006; per 1,000 population): birth rate, 21.0; death rate, 5.4; marriage rate, 9.2; divorce rate, 3.8. **Major cities** (2007): Salt Lake City 180,651; West Valley City 122,374; Provo 117,592; West Jordan 102,445; Sandy 96,074.

Government

Statehood: entered the Union on 4 Jan 1896 as the 45th state. **State constitution:** adopted 1895. **Representation in US Congress:** 2 senators; 3 representatives. **Electoral college:** 5 votes. **Political divisions:** 29 counties.

Economy

Employment (2007): services 29.4%; finance, insurance, real estate 18.3%; trade 14.5%; government 13.4%; construction 8.4%. **Production** (2007): finance, insurance, real estate 28.7%; services 15.8%; government 13.1%; trade 12.7%; manufacturing 11.3%. **Chief agricultural products:** *Crops:* peaches, cherries, onions, dairy products. *Livestock:* cattle and calves, sheep and lambs, mink, poultry. *Fish catch:* trout. **Chief manufactured products:** machinery and apparatus; computers; office machinery; transportation equipment, including aerospace products, missile parts, and motor vehicle parts; surgical tools and electromedical equipment; food products.

Internet resources: <www.utah.com>; <www.utah.gov>.

Vermont

Name: Vermont, from the French *vert mont,* meaning "green mountain." **Nickname:** Green Mountain State. **Capital:** Montpelier. **Rank:** population: 49th; area: 43rd. **Motto:** "Freedom and unity." **Song:** "These Green Mountains," words and music by Diane Martin. **Bird:** hermit thrush. **Flower:** red clover. **Insect:** honeybee. **Mammal:** Morgan horse. **Tree:** sugar maple.

Natural features

Land area: 9,615 sq mi, 24,903 sq km. **Mountain ranges:** Green, Appalachian, Hoosac, Taconic. **Highest point:** Mt. Mansfield, 1,339 m (4,393 ft). **Largest lake:** Lake Champlain. **Major rivers:** Lamoille, Winooski, Otter Creek, Poultney, White. **Nat-**

ural regions: the New England Province, eastern two-thirds of the state, includes the Taconic Section to the south, the Green Mountain Section in the center, the New England Upland Section along the east-central edge, and the White Mountain Section in the far northeast corner; the St. Lawrence Valley, western edge of the state, includes the Champlain Valley in the central portion; the Valley and Ridge Province, small section along the west-central edge, includes the Hudson Valley. **Land use:** forest, 67.1%; agricultural, 9.5%; other, 23.4%.

People

Population (2007): 621,254; persons per sq mi 64.6, persons per sq km 24.9. **Vital statistics** (2006; per 1,000 population): birth rate, 10.4; death rate, 8.1; marriage rate, 8.7; divorce rate, 3.5. **Major cities** (2007): Burlington 38,531; South Burlington 17,445; Rutland 16,826; Montpelier 7,806.

Government

Statehood: entered the Union on 4 Mar 1791 as the 14th state. **State constitution:** adopted 1793. **Representation in US Congress:** 2 senators; 1 representative. **Electoral college:** 3 votes. **Political divisions:** 14 counties.

Economy

Employment (2007): services 35.9%; trade 14.4%; government 13.2%; finance, insurance, real estate 12.3%; manufacturing 9.1%. **Production** (2007): finance, insurance, real estate 24.2%; services 21.8%; government 13.7%; trade 13.0%; manufacturing 11.5%. **Chief agricultural products:** *Crops:* apples, honey, greenhouse and nursery products, Christmas trees, maple syrup, dairy products, eggs. *Livestock:* cattle and calves, chickens, turkeys, sheep and lambs, horses. **Chief manufactured products:** electronics and electrical equipment; fabricated metal products; nonelectrical machinery; paper products; printing and publishing; food products; transportation equipment; lumber and wood products.

Internet resources: <www.travel-vermont.com>; <www.vermont.gov>.

Did you know? Hampton Roads, Virginia, witnessed a battle on 9 Mar 1862 between USS *Monitor* and CSS *Virginia* (formerly USS *Merrimack*). The battle, which ended in a draw, featured the first combat between two iron-armored ships and ushered in the age of modern naval warfare.

Virginia

Name: Virginia, named in honor of Elizabeth I of England, known as the Virgin Queen. **Nickname:** Old Dominion. **Capital:** Richmond. **Rank:** population: 12th; area: 36th. **Motto:** "Sic semper tyrannis" ("Thus ever to tyrants"). **Song:** "Carry Me Back to Old Virginia," words and music by James B. Bland. **Bird:** cardinal. **Fish:** brook trout. **Flower:**

dogwood. **Fossil:** *Chesapecten jeffersonius*. **Insect:** tiger swallowtail butterfly. **Tree:** dogwood.

Natural features

Land area: 40,600 sq mi, 105,154 sq km. **Mountain ranges:** Blue Ridge, Appalachian. **Highest point:** Mt. Rogers, 1,746 m (5,729 ft). **Largest lake:** Smith Mountain Lake. **Major rivers:** Potomac, Shenandoah, James, Roanoke. **Natural regions:** Coastal Plain, eastern region below the Potomac River; Piedmont Province, extending from the south-central border up to the border with Maryland, includes the Piedmont Upland and Piedmont lowlands; Blue Ridge Province, west of the Piedmont Province; Valley and Ridge region, covering most of western Virginia, includes the Shenandoah Valley and Allegheny, Shenandoah, and Appalachian mountains; Appalachian Plateau, extreme western tip of the state, includes the Cumberland Mountain and Kanawha sections. **Land use:** forest, 48.7%; agricultural, 10.6%; other, 40.7%.

People

Population (2007): 7,712,091; persons per sq mi 190.0, persons per sq km 73.3. **Vital statistics** (2006; per 1,000 population): birth rate, 14.1; death rate, 7.5; marriage rate, 8.0; divorce rate, 4.1. **Major cities** (2007): Virginia Beach 434,743; Norfolk 235,747; Chesapeake 219,154; Arlington 204,568; Richmond 200,123; Newport News 179,153; Hampton 146,439; Alexandria 140,024.

Government

Statehood: entered the Union on 26 Jun 1788 as the 10th state. **State constitution:** adopted 1970. **Representation in US Congress:** 2 senators; 11 representatives. **Electoral college:** 13 votes. **Political divisions:** 95 counties.

Economy

Employment (2007): services 29.7%; finance, insurance, real estate 19.5%; government 17.5%; trade 13.3%; construction 7.2%. **Production** (2007): finance, insurance, real estate 34.0%; government 18.0%; services 14.4%; trade 10.1%; transportation, public utilities 9.4%. **Chief agricultural products:** *Crops:* tobacco, soybeans, peanuts (groundnuts), cotton, apples, tomatoes, wheat, potatoes, honey. *Livestock:* chickens, turkeys, pigs, cattle and calves, sheep and lambs. *Fish catch:* clams, softshell and blue crabs, oysters, trout, catfish, hybrid striped bass. **Chief manufactured products:** electronics and electrical equipment; paper products; tobacco products; plastics and rubber products; chemical products; food products; printing and publishing.

Internet resources: <www.virginia.org>; <www.virginia.gov>.

Washington

Name: Washington, named in honor of George Washington. **Nickname:** Evergreen State. **Capital:** Olympia. **Rank:** population: 13th; area: 21st. **Motto:** "Alki" ("By and by"). **Song:** "Washington My

---

For details about state governments, see pages 608–613; for energy data, see pages 627–628.

Home," words and music by Helen Davis. **Bird:** willow goldfinch. **Fish:** steelhead trout. **Flower:** coast rhododendron. **Fossil:** Columbian mammoth. **Gemstone:** petrified wood. **Insect:** green darner dragonfly. **Tree:** western hemlock.

Natural features

Land area: 68,097 sq mi, 176,370 sq km. **Mountain ranges:** Olympic, Cascade, Blue. **Highest point:** Mt. Rainier, 4,392 m (14,410 ft). **Largest lake:** Moses Lake. **Major rivers:** Columbia, Pend Oreille, Snake, Yakima. **Natural regions:** Pacific Border Province, western quarter of the state, includes the Olympic Mountains to the west and the Puget Trough to the east; Cascade-Sierra Mountains, running north to south down center of state, include the Northern and Middle Cascades; Northern Rocky Mountains, northeast corner; Columbia Plateaus, eastern, central, and southern regions, include the Walla Walla Plateau in the center and the Blue Mountain Section in the southeast corner. **Land use:** forest, 28.9%; agricultural, 14.7%; pasture, 13.3%; other, 43.1%.

People

Population (2007): 6,468,424; persons per sq mi 95.0, persons per sq km 36.7. **Vital statistics** (2006; per 1,000 population): birth rate, 13.6; death rate, 7.2; marriage rate, 6.4; divorce rate, 3.8. **Major cities** (2007): Seattle 594,210; Spokane 200,975; Tacoma 196,520; Vancouver 161,436; Bellevue 121,347.

Government

Statehood: entered the Union on 11 Nov 1889 as the 42nd state. **State constitution:** adopted 1889. **Representation in US Congress:** 2 senators; 9 representatives. **Electoral college:** 11 votes. **Political divisions:** 39 counties.

Economy

Employment (2007): services 30.1%; finance, insurance, real estate 16.2%; government 15.4%; trade 14.1%; manufacturing 7.9%. **Production** (2007): finance, insurance, real estate 27.5%; services 15.9%; government 13.7%; trade 13.2%; transportation, public utilities 12.8%. **Chief agricultural products:** *Crops:* apples, peaches, pears, cherries, grapes, apricots, raspberries, asparagus, sweet corn, mint. *Livestock:* cattle and calves, chickens, turkeys, horses. *Fish catch:* oysters, clams, mussels, crab, shrimp, geoduck, sea cucumbers, salmon. **Chief manufactured products:** aerospace equipment; food products; forest products; advanced medical and technology products; aluminum products.

Internet resources: <www.experiencewa.com>; <www.wa.gov>.

West Virginia

Name: West Virginia, named in honor of Elizabeth I of England, known as the Virgin Queen. **Nickname:** Mountain State. **Capital:** Charleston. **Rank:** population: 37th; area: 41st. **Motto:** "Montani semper liberi" ("Mountaineers are always free"). **Songs:** "This Is My West Virginia," words and music by Iris Bell; "West Virginia, My Home Sweet Home," words and music by Julian G. Hearne, Jr.; "The West Virginia Hills," words by Ellen King and music by H.E. Engle. **Bird:** cardinal. **Fish:** brook trout. **Flower:** rhododendron. **Gemstone:** West Virginia fossil coral. **Insect:** monarch butterfly. **Mammal:** black bear. **Tree:** sugar maple.

Natural features

Land area: 24,230 sq mi, 62,755 sq km. **Mountain ranges:** Appalachian, Allegheny. **Highest point:** Spruce Knob, 1,482 m (4,863 ft). **Largest lake:** Summersville Lake. **Major rivers:** Ohio, Big Sandy, Guyandotte, Great Kanawha, Little Kanawha. **Natural regions:** the Valley and Ridge Province, eastern edge of the state, includes portions of the Shenandoah Mountains; the remainder of the state consists of the Appalachian Plateaus and includes the Kanawha Section to the south, and the Allegheny Mountains in the northeast. **Land use:** forest, 68.1%; agricultural, 5.3%; other, 26.6%.

People

Population (2007): 1,812,035; persons per sq mi 74.8, persons per sq km 28.9. **Vital statistics** (2006; per 1,000 population): birth rate, 11.5; death rate, 11.4; marriage rate, 7.3; divorce rate, 4.7. **Major cities** (2007): Charleston 50,478; Huntington 48,982; Parkersburg 31,617; Morgantown 29,361; Wheeling 29,101.

Government

Statehood: entered the Union on 20 Jun 1863 as the 35th state. **State constitution:** adopted 1872. **Representation in US Congress:** 2 senators; 3 representatives. **Electoral college:** 5 votes. **Political divisions:** 55 counties.

Economy

Employment (2007): services 33.1%; government 16.5%; trade 15.3%; finance, insurance, real estate 10.6%; manufacturing 6.7%. **Production** (2007): finance, insurance, real estate 17.9%; services 17.9%; government 17.6%; trade 12.6%; transportation, public utilities 11.3%. **Chief agricultural products:** *Crops:* apples, tobacco, peaches, dairy products. *Livestock:* cattle and calves, sheep and lambs, poultry. **Chief manufactured products:** chemical products; automobile parts; base metals; fabricated metal products; glassware; computer software; wood products; electrical equipment; machinery and apparatus.

Internet resources: <www.escape2wv.com>; <www.wv.gov>.

Wisconsin

Name: Wisconsin, an anglicized version of a French rendering of a Native American name said to mean "the place where we live." **Nickname:** Badger State. **Capital:** Madison. **Rank:** population: 20th; area: 22nd. **Motto:** "Forward." **Song:** "On, Wisconsin," words and music by William T. Purdy. **Bird:** robin. **Fish:** muskellunge (muskie). **Flower:** wood violet. **Fossil:** trilobite. **Insect:** honeybee. **Mammal:** badger. **Mineral:** galena. **Rock:** red granite. **Tree:** sugar maple.

Natural features

Land area: 65,498 sq mi, 169,639 sq km. **Mountain ranges:** Baraboo, Rib, Gogebic. **Highest point:** Timms Hill, 595 m (1,952 ft). **Largest lake:** Lake Winnebago. **Major rivers:** Wisconsin, St. Croix, Rock, Mississippi, Namekagon. **Natural regions:** Superior Upland, northern half of the state, divided into highland and lowland sections; Central Lowland, southern half of the state, divided into the Wisconsin Driftless Section to the west and the Eastern Lake Section to the east, with a section of the Till Plains occupying a small area at the southern border. **Land use:** forest, 40.4%; agricultural, 28.7%; other, 30.9%.

People

Population (2007): 5,601,640; persons per sq mi 85.5, persons per sq km 33.0. **Vital statistics** (2006; per 1,000 population): birth rate, 13.0; death rate, 8.3; marriage rate, 5.8; divorce rate, 2.9. **Major cities** (2007): Milwaukee 602,191; Madison 228,775; Green Bay 100,781; Kenosha 96,265; Racine 78,805.

Government

Statehood: entered the Union on 29 May 1848 as the 30th state. **State constitution:** adopted 1848. **Representation in US Congress:** 2 senators; 8 representatives. **Electoral college:** 10 votes. **Political divisions:** 72 counties.

Economy

Employment (2007): services 31.3%; trade 14.9%; manufacturing 14.4%; finance, insurance, real estate 13.3%; government 11.8%. **Production** (2007): finance, insurance, real estate 25.5%; manufacturing 20.6%; services 16.9%; trade 12.0%; government 10.9%. **Chief agricultural products:** Crops: dairy products, corn (maize), honey, maple syrup, potatoes, strawberries, cherries, cranberries, Christmas trees, mint oil. Livestock: cattle and calves, hogs, mink. Fish catch: bass, trout, pike. **Chief manufactured products:** food products; beer; machinery and apparatus; paper products; fabricated metal products; transportation equipment; household appliances.

Internet resources: <www.travelwisconsin.com>; <www.wisconsin.gov>.

Wyoming

Name: Wyoming, from a Delaware Indian word meaning "mountains and valleys alternating." **Nicknames:** Equality State; Cowboy State. **Capital:** Cheyenne. **Rank:** population: 50th; area: 9th. **Motto:** "Equal rights." **Song:** "Wyoming," words by Charles E. Winter and music by George E. Knapp. **Bird:** meadowlark. **Fish:** cutthroat trout. **Flower:** In-

dian paintbrush. **Fossil:** Knightia. **Gemstone:** jade. **Mammal:** bison. **Reptile:** horned toad. **Tree:** plains cottonwood.

Natural features

Land area: 97,813 sq mi, 253,335 sq km. **Mountain ranges:** Rocky, Big Horn, Grand Teton, Wind River, Continental Divide, Sierra Madre, Washakie. **Highest point:** Gannett Peak, 4,207 m (13,804 ft). **Largest lake:** Yellowstone Lake. **Major rivers:** Snake, Colorado, Green, Columbia. **Natural regions:** Great Plains Province, eastern third of the state, includes the Black Hills in the northeast corner, the High Plains in the southwest corner, and the Missouri Plateau in the center; Wyoming Basin, central and southern regions; Southern Rocky Mountains, southern border; Middle Rocky Mountains, northwest third of the state, also cover a small area on the southern border; Northern Rocky Mountains, extreme northwestern tip of the state. **Land use:** pasture, 44.0%; agricultural, 3.5%; forest, 1.5%; other, 51.0%.

People

Population (2007): 522,830; persons per sq mi 5.3, persons per sq km 2.1. **Vital statistics** (2006; per 1,000 population): birth rate, 14.9; death rate, 8.4; marriage rate, 9.8; divorce rate, 5.4. **Major cities** (2007): Cheyenne 55,641; Casper 53,003; Laramie 27,241; Gillette 25,031; Rock Springs 19,659.

Government

Statehood: entered the Union on 10 Jul 1890 as the 44th state. **State constitution:** adopted 1889. **Representation in US Congress:** 2 senators; 1 representative. **Electoral college:** 3 votes. **Political divisions:** 23 counties.

Economy

Employment (2007): services 26.8%; government 17.9%; trade 13.2%; finance, insurance, real estate 12.2%; construction 9.4%. **Production** (2007): mining 30.6%; government 13.3%; finance, insurance, real estate 13.1%; transportation, public utilities 12.4%; services 11.0%. **Chief agricultural products:** Crops: wheat, barley, sugar beets, corn (maize). Livestock: cattle and calves, sheep and lambs. **Chief manufactured products:** refined petroleum products; lumber and wood products; food products; fabricated metal products.

Internet resources: <www.wyomingtourism.org>; <www.wyoming.gov>.

Did you know? Wyoming is the home of Shoshone National Forest, the oldest national forest in the United States (declared in 1891). Yellowstone National Park, the oldest national park in the world and one of the largest, was established by Congress in 1872 and also lies mostly within the boundaries of Wyoming.

For details about state governments, see pages 608–613; for energy data, see pages 627–628.

State Government

Governors of US States and Territories

Governors of New Hampshire and Vermont serve two-year terms; all others serve four-year terms. Parties: Democratic (D); Republican (R); New Progressive (NP); Covenant (C). Sources: National Governors Association; Council of State Governments.

STATE	GOVERNOR	IN OFFICE SINCE	PRESENT TERM EXPIRES
Alabama	Bob Riley (R)	January 2003	January 2011
Alaska	Sean R. Parnell (R)[1]	July 2009	December 2010*
Arizona	Jan Brewer (R)[2]	January 2009	January 2011*
Arkansas	Mike Beebe (D)	January 2007	January 2011*
California	Arnold Schwarzenegger (R)[3]	November 2003	January 2011
Colorado	Bill Ritter (D)	January 2007	January 2011*
Connecticut	M. Jodi Rell (R)[4]	July 2004	January 2011*
Delaware	Jack Markell (D)	January 2009	January 2013*
Florida	Charlie Crist (R)	January 2007	January 2011*
Georgia	Sonny Perdue (R)	January 2003	January 2011
Hawaii	Linda Lingle (R)	December 2002	December 2010
Idaho	C.L. "Butch" Otter (R)	January 2007	January 2011*
Illinois	Pat Quinn (D)[5]	January 2009	January 2011*
Indiana	Mitch Daniels (R)	January 2005	January 2013
Iowa	Chet Culver (D)	January 2007	January 2011*
Kansas	Mark Parkinson (D)[6]	April 2009	January 2011*
Kentucky	Steve Beshear (D)	December 2007	December 2011*
Louisiana	Bobby Jindal (R)	January 2008	January 2012*
Maine	John E. Baldacci (D)	January 2003	January 2011
Maryland	Martin O'Malley (D)	January 2007	January 2011*
Massachusetts	Deval Patrick (D)	January 2007	January 2011*
Michigan	Jennifer Granholm (D)	January 2003	January 2011
Minnesota	Tim Pawlenty (R)	January 2003	January 2011*
Mississippi	Haley Barbour (R)	January 2004	January 2012
Missouri	Jay Nixon (D)	January 2009	January 2013*
Montana	Brian Schweitzer (D)	January 2005	January 2013
Nebraska	Dave Heineman (R)[7]	January 2005	January 2011*
Nevada	Jim Gibbons (R)	January 2007	January 2011*
New Hampshire	John Lynch (D)	January 2005	January 2011*
New Jersey	Jon Corzine (D)	January 2006	January 2010*
New Mexico	Bill Richardson (D)	January 2003	January 2011
New York	David A. Paterson (D)[8]	March 2008	January 2011*
North Carolina	Beverly Perdue (D)	January 2009	January 2013*
North Dakota	John Hoeven (R)	December 2000	December 2012*
Ohio	Ted Strickland (D)	January 2007	January 2011*
Oklahoma	Brad Henry (D)	January 2003	January 2011
Oregon	Ted Kulongoski (D)	January 2003	January 2011
Pennsylvania	Edward G. Rendell (D)	January 2003	January 2011
Rhode Island	Don Carcieri (R)	January 2003	January 2011
South Carolina	Mark Sanford (R)	January 2003	January 2011
South Dakota	Mike Rounds (R)	January 2003	January 2011
Tennessee	Phil Bredesen (D)	January 2003	January 2011
Texas	Rick Perry (R)[9]	December 2000	January 2011*
Utah	Jon M. Huntsman, Jr. (R)	January 2005	January 2013*
Vermont	Jim Douglas (R)	January 2003	January 2011*
Virginia	Tim Kaine (D)	January 2006	January 2010
Washington	Chris Gregoire (D)	January 2005	January 2013*
West Virginia	Joe Manchin III (D)	January 2005	January 2013
Wisconsin	Jim Doyle (D)	January 2003	January 2011*
Wyoming	Dave Freudenthal (D)	January 2003	January 2011

TERRITORY	GOVERNOR	IN OFFICE SINCE	PRESENT TERM EXPIRES
American Samoa	Togiola T.A. Tulafono (D)[10]	April 2003	January 2013
Guam	Felix Perez Camacho (R)	January 2003	January 2011
Northern Mariana Islands	Benígno Fitial (C)	January 2006	January 2010*
Puerto Rico	Luis G. Fortuño (R) (NP)	January 2009	January 2013*
Virgin Islands	John deJongh, Jr. (D)	January 2007	January 2011*

Governors of US States and Territories (continued)

*Present governor is eligible for reelection. [1]Lieut. Gov. Sean R. Parnell became governor on 26 Jul 2009 following Sarah Palin's resignation. [2]Secretary of State Jan Brewer became governor on 21 Jan 2009 following Janet Napolitano's appointment to the office of US secretary of homeland security. [3]Arnold Schwarzenegger was elected in October 2003 following the recall of former governor Gray Davis. Gov. Schwarzenegger was elected to a full term in November 2006. [4]Lieut. Gov. M. Jodi Rell became governor on 1 Jul 2004 following John G. Rowland's resignation. Gov. Rell was elected to a full term in November 2006. [5]Lieut. Gov. Patrick Quinn became governor on 29 Jan 2009 following Rod Blagojevich's removal from office. [6]Lieut. Gov. Mark Parkinson became governor on 28 Apr 2009 following Kathleen Sebelius's appointment to the office of US secretary of health and human services. [7]Lieut. Gov. Dave Heineman became governor on 21 Jan 2005 following Mike Johanns's appointment to the office of US secretary of agriculture. Gov. Heineman was elected to a full term in November 2006. [8]Lieut. Gov. David A. Paterson became governor in March 2008 following Eliot Spitzer's resignation. [9]Lieut. Gov. Rick Perry became governor in December 2000 following George W. Bush's election as president of the United States. Gov. Perry was elected to a full term in November 2002. [10]Lieut. Gov. Togiola T.A. Tulafono became governor in April 2003 following the death of Gov. Tauese Sunia. Gov. Tulafono was elected to a full term in November 2004.

State Officers and Legislatures

Sources: Web sites of the individual states; The Book of the States, vol. 41; and the CSG State Directory, published by the Council of State Governments. Legislature figures are as of February 2009. N/A means not available.

STATE/OFFICE	OFFICEHOLDER	PAY[1]
Alabama		
Governor	Bob Riley (R)	US$112,895
Lieut. Gov.	Jim Folsom, Jr. (D)	US$61,714
Sec. of State	Beth Chapman (R)	US$79,580
Atty. Gen.	Troy King (R)	US$161,794
Treasurer	Kay Ivey (R)	US$79,580
Legislature		
Senate	Dem: 19; Rep: 13; vacant: 3	
House	Dem: 62; Rep: 43	
Alaska		
Governor	Sean R. Parnell	US$125,000
Lieut. Gov.	vacant	US$100,000
Sec. of State[2]		
Atty. Gen.	Daniel S. Sullivan	US$122,640
Treasurer[3]	Jerry Burnett (Deputy Treasury Commissioner)	US$119,868
Legislature		
Senate	Dem: 10; Rep: 10	
House	Dem: 18; Rep: 22	
Arizona		
Governor	Jan Brewer (R)	US$95,000
Lieut. Gov.[4]		
Sec. of State	Ken Bennett (R)	US$70,000
Atty. Gen.	Terry Goddard (D)	US$90,000
Treasurer	Dean Martin (R)	US$70,000
Legislature		
Senate	Dem: 12; Rep: 18	
House	Dem: 24; Rep: 36	
Arkansas		
Governor	Mike Beebe (D)	US$87,352
Lieut. Gov.	Bill Halter (D)	US$42,219
Sec. of State	Charlie Daniels (D)	US$54,594
Atty. Gen.	Dustin McDaniel (D)	US$72,794
Treasurer	Martha A. Shoffner (D)	US$54,594
General Assembly		
Senate	Dem: 27; Rep: 8	
House	Dem: 71; Rep: 28; Green: 1	
California		
Governor	Arnold Schwarzenegger (R)	US$212,179
Lieut. Gov.	John Garamendi (D)	US$159,134
Sec. of State	Debra Bowen (D)	US$159,134

STATE/OFFICE	OFFICEHOLDER	PAY[1]
California (continued)		
Atty. Gen.	Edmund G. Brown, Jr. (D)	US$184,301
Treasurer	Bill Lockyer (D)	US$169,743
Legislature		
Senate	Dem: 25; Rep: 14; vacant: 1	
Assembly	Dem: 51; Rep: 29	
Colorado		
Governor	Bill Ritter (D)	US$90,000
Lieut. Gov.	Barbara O'Brien (D)	US$68,500
Sec. of State	Bernie Buescher (D)	US$68,500
Atty. Gen.	John W. Suthers (R)	US$80,000
Treasurer	Cary Kennedy (D)	US$68,500
General Assembly		
Senate	Dem: 21; Rep: 14	
House	Dem: 38; Rep: 27	
Connecticut		
Governor	M. Jodi Rell (R)	US$150,000
Lieut. Gov.	Michael C. Fedele (R)	US$110,000
Sec. of State	Susan Bysiewicz (D)	US$110,000
Atty. Gen.	Richard Blumenthal (D)	US$110,000
Treasurer	Denise L. Nappier (D)	US$110,000
General Assembly		
Senate	Dem: 24; Rep: 12	
House	Dem: 114; Rep: 36; vacant: 1	
Delaware		
Governor	Jack Markell (D)	US$171,000
Lieut. Gov.	Matthew Denn (D)	US$76,250
Sec. of State	Jeffrey Bullock (D)	US$123,850
Atty. Gen.	Joseph Biden III (D)	US$140,950
Treasurer	Velda Jones-Potter (D)	US$110,050
General Assembly		
Senate	Dem: 16; Rep: 5	
House	Dem: 24; Rep: 17	
Florida		
Governor	Charlie Crist (R)	US$132,932
Lieut. Gov.	Jeffrey D. Kottkamp (R)	US$127,399
Sec. of State	Kurt Browning (R)	US$120,000
Atty. Gen.	Bill McCollum (R)	US$131,604
Treasurer[3]	Alex Sink (Chief Financial Officer)	US$131,604
Legislature		
Senate	Dem: 14; Rep: 26	
House	Dem: 44; Rep: 76	

State Officers and Legislatures (continued)

STATE/OFFICE	OFFICEHOLDER	PAY[1]
Georgia		
Governor	Sonny Perdue (R)	US$139,339
Lieut. Gov.	Casey Cagle (R)	US$91,609
Sec. of State	Karen Handel (R)	US$123,636
Atty. Gen.	Thurbert E. Baker (D)	US$137,791
Treasurer[3]	W. Daniel Ebersole	US$130,927
	(Dir., Office of Treasury and Fiscal Services)	
General Assembly		
Senate	Dem: 22; Rep: 34	
House	Dem: 73; Rep: 107	
Hawaii		
Governor	Linda Lingle (R)	US$123,480
Lieut. Gov.	James R. Aiona, Jr. (R)	US$120,444
Sec. of State[2]		
Atty. Gen.	Mark J. Bennett (R)	US$120,444
Treasurer[3]	Georgina K. Kawamura	US$114,708
	(Director of Finance)	
Legislature		
Senate	Dem: 23; Rep: 2	
House	Dem: 45; Rep: 6	
Idaho		
Governor	C.L. "Butch" Otter (R)	US$108,727
Lieut. Gov.	Brad Little (R)	US$28,655
Sec. of State	Ben Ysursa (R)	US$88,374
Atty. Gen.	Lawrence Wasden (R)	US$98,105
Treasurer	Ron G. Crane (R)	US$88,374
Legislature		
Senate	Dem: 7; Rep: 28	
House	Dem: 18; Rep: 52	
Illinois		
Governor	Pat Quinn (D)	US$177,500
Lieut. Gov.	vacant	US$135,700
Sec. of State	Jesse White (D)	US$156,600
Atty. Gen.	Lisa Madigan (D)	US$156,600
Treasurer	Alexi Giannoulias (D)	US$130,800
General Assembly		
Senate	Dem: 37; Rep: 22	
House	Dem: 70; Rep: 48	
Indiana		
Governor	Mitch Daniels (R)	US$95,000
Lieut. Gov.	Becky Skillman (R)	US$79,172
Sec. of State	Todd Rokita (R)	US$68,772
Atty. Gen.	Greg Zoeller (R)	US$100,000
Treasurer	Richard E. Mourdock (R)	US$68,772
General Assembly		
Senate	Dem: 17; Rep: 33	
House	Dem: 52; Rep: 48	
Iowa		
Governor	Chet Culver (D)	US$130,000
Lieut. Gov.	Patty Judge (D)	US$103,212
Sec. of State	Michael A. Mauro (D)	US$103,212
Atty. Gen.	Tom Miller (D)	US$123,669
Treasurer	Michael L. Fitzgerald (D)	US$103,212
General Assembly		
Senate	Dem: 32; Rep: 18	
House	Dem: 56; Rep: 44	
Kansas		
Governor	Mark Parkinson (D)	US$110,707
Lieut. Gov.	vacant	US$31,313
Sec. of State	Ron Thornburgh (R)	US$86,003

STATE/OFFICE	OFFICEHOLDER	PAY[1]
Kansas (continued)		
Atty. Gen.	Stephen Six (D)	US$98,901
Treasurer	Dennis McKinney	US$82,563
Legislature		
Senate	Dem: 9; Rep: 31	
House	Dem: 49; Rep: 76	
Kentucky		
Governor	Steve Beshear (D)	US$142,498
Lieut. Gov.	Daniel Mongiardo (D)	US$105,840
Sec. of State	Trey Grayson (R)	US$105,840
Atty. Gen.	Jack Conway (D)	US$105,840
Treasurer	Todd Hollenbach (D)	US$105,840
General Assembly		
Senate	Dem: 15; Rep: 21; Ind.: 1; vacant: 1	
House	Dem: 65; Rep: 35	
Louisiana		
Governor	Bobby Jindal (R)	US$130,000
Lieut. Gov.	Mitch Landrieu (D)	US$115,000
Sec. of State	Jay Dardenne (R)	US$115,000
Atty. Gen.	James D. Caldwell (D)	US$115,000
Treasurer	John Kennedy (D)	US$115,000
Legislature		
Senate	Dem: 22 Rep: 15; vacant: 2	
House	Dem: 51; Rep: 50; Ind: 3; vacant: 1	
Maine		
Governor	John E. Baldacci (D)	US$70,000
Lieut. Gov.[5]		
Sec. of State	Matthew Dunlap (D)	US$83,844
Atty. Gen.	Janet T. Mills (D)	US$92,248
Treasurer	David G. Lemoine (D)	US$83,844
Legislature		
Senate	Dem: 20; Rep: 15	
House	Dem: 95; Rep: 55; unenrolled: 1	
Maryland		
Governor	Martin O'Malley (D)	US$150,000
Lieut. Gov.	Anthony G. Brown (D)	US$125,000
Sec. of State	John McDonough (D)	US$87,500
Atty. Gen.	Douglas F. Gansler (D)	US$125,000
Treasurer	Nancy K. Kopp (D)	US$125,000
General Assembly		
Senate	Dem: 33; Rep: 14	
House	Dem: 104; Rep: 36; Ind.: 1	
Massachusetts		
Governor	Deval Patrick (D)	US$140,535
Lieut. Gov.	Timothy Murray (D)	US$124,920
Sec. of State	William F. Galvin (D)	US$130,916
Atty. Gen.	Martha Coakley (D)	US$133,644
Treasurer	Timothy Cahill (D)	US$130,916
General Court (legislature)		
Senate	Dem: 35; Rep: 5	
House	Dem: 142; Rep: 16; Ind.: 1; vacant: 1	
Michigan		
Governor	Jennifer Granholm (D)	US$177,000
Lieut. Gov.	John D. Cherry, Jr. (D)	US$123,900
Sec. of State	Terri Lynn Land (R)	US$124,900
Atty. Gen.	Mike Cox (R)	US$124,900
Treasurer	Robert J. Kleine	US$174,204
Legislature		
Senate	Dem: 16; Rep: 21; vacant: 1	
House	Dem: 67; Rep: 43	

State Officers and Legislatures (continued)

STATE/OFFICE	OFFICEHOLDER	PAY[1]
Minnesota		
Governor	Tim Pawlenty (R)	US$120,303
Lieut. Gov.	Carol Molnau (R)	US$78,197
Sec. of State	Mark Ritchie (D)	US$90,227
Atty. Gen.	Lori Swanson (D)	US$114,288
Treasurer[3]	Tom J. Hanson	US$108,388
	° (Commissioner of Finance)	
Legislature		
Senate	Dem: 46; Rep: 21	
House	Dem: 87; Rep: 47	
Mississippi		
Governor	Haley Barbour (R)	US$122,160
Lieut. Gov.	Phil Bryant (R)	US$60,000
Sec. of State	C. Delbert Hosemann, Jr. (R)	US$90,000
Atty. Gen.	Jim Hood (D)	US$108,960
Treasurer	Tate Reeves (R)	US$90,000
Legislature		
Senate	Dem: 27; Rep: 25	
House	Dem: 74; Rep: 48	
Missouri		
Governor	Jay Nixon (D)	US$133,821
Lieut. Gov.	Peter Kinder (R)	US$86,484
Sec. of State	Robin Carnahan (D)	US$107,746
Atty. Gen.	Chris Koster (D)	US$116,437
Treasurer	Clint Zweifel (D)	US$107,746
General Assembly		
Senate	Dem: 11; Rep: 23	
House	Dem: 74; Rep: 89	
Montana		
Governor	Brian Schweitzer (D)	US$100,121
Lieut. Gov.	John Bohlinger (R)	US$79,007
Sec. of State	Lind McCulloch (D)	US$79,129
Atty. Gen.	Steve Bullock (D)	US$89,602
Treasurer[3]	Janet Kelly (Dir., Dept. of Administration)	US$96,967
Legislature		
Senate	Dem: 23; Rep: 27	
House	Dem: 50; Rep: 50	
Nebraska		
Governor	Dave Heineman (R)	US$105,000
Lieut. Gov.	Rick Sheehy (R)	US$75,000
Sec. of State	John A. Gale (R)	US$85,000
Atty. Gen.	Jon Bruning (R)	US$95,000
Treasurer	Shane Osborn (R)	US$85,000
Legislature (unicameral)	49 nonpartisan members	
Nevada		
Governor	Jim Gibbons (R)	US$141,000
Lieut. Gov.	Brian K. Krolicki (R)	US$60,000
Sec. of State	Ross Miller (D)	US$87,982
Atty. Gen.	Catherine Cortez Masto (D)	US$133,000
Treasurer	Kate Marshall (D)	US$97,000
Legislature		
Senate	Dem: 12; Rep: 9	
Assembly	Dem: 28; Rep: 14	
New Hampshire		
Governor	John Lynch (D)	US$113,834
Lieut. Gov.[5]		
Sec. of State	William Gardner (D)	US$104,364
Atty. Gen.	Kelly Ayotte (R)	US$110,114

STATE/OFFICE	OFFICEHOLDER	PAY[1]
New Hampshire (continued)		
Treasurer	Catherine Provencher	US$104,364
General Court (legislature)		
Senate	Dem: 14; Rep: 10	
House	Dem: 224; Rep: 175; vacant: 1	
New Jersey		
Governor	Jon Corzine (D)	US$175,000
Lieut. Gov.[5]		
Sec. of State	Nina Mitchell Wells (D)	US$141,000
Atty. Gen.	Anne Milgram (D)	US$141,000
Treasurer	R. David Rousseau	US$141,000
Legislature		
Senate	Dem: 23; Rep: 16; vacant: 1	
General Assembly	Dem: 48; Rep: 32	
New Mexico		
Governor	Bill Richardson (D)	US$110,000
Lieut. Gov.	Diane Denish (D)	US$85,000
Sec. of State	Mary Herrera (D)	US$85,000
Atty. Gen.	Gary K. King (D)	US$95,000
Treasurer	James B. Lewis (D)	US$85,000
Legislature		
Senate	Dem: 27; Rep: 15	
House	Dem: 45; Rep: 25	
New York		
Governor	David A. Paterson (D)	US$179,000
Lieut. Gov.	Richard Ravitch (D)	US$151,500
Sec. of State	Lorraine Cortés-Vázquez (D)	US$120,800
Atty. Gen.	Andrew M. Cuomo (D)	US$151,500
Treasurer	Aida Brewer	US$127,000
Legislature		
Senate	Dem: 32; Rep: 30	
Assembly	Dem: 108; Rep: 41; Ind.: 1	
North Carolina		
Governor	Beverly Perdue (D)	US$139,590
Lieut. Gov.	Walter Dalton (D)	US$123,198
Sec. of State	Elaine F. Marshall (D)	US$123,198
Atty. Gen.	Roy Cooper (D)	US$123,198
Treasurer	Jane Cowell (D)	US$123,198
General Assembly		
Senate	Dem: 30; Rep: 20	
House	Dem: 68; Rep: 52	
North Dakota		
Governor	John Hoeven (R)	US$100,030
Lieut. Gov.	Jack Dalrymple (R)	US$77,655
Sec. of State	Alvin A. Jaeger (R)	US$79,572
Atty. Gen.	Wayne Stenehjem (R)	US$87,351
Treasurer	Kelly Schmidt (R)	US$75,146
Legislative Assembly		
Senate	Dem: 21; Rep: 26	
House	Dem: 36; Rep: 58	
Ohio		
Governor	Ted Strickland (D)	US$144,269
Lieut. Gov.	Lee Fisher (D)	US$142,501
Sec. of State	Jennifer Brunner (D)	US$109,554
Atty. Gen.	Richard Cordray (D)	US$109,554
Treasurer	Kevin L. Boyce	US$109,554
General Assembly		
Senate	Dem: 12; Rep: 21	
House	Dem: 53; Rep: 46	

State Officers and Legislatures (continued)

STATE/OFFICE	OFFICEHOLDER	PAY[1]
Oklahoma		
Governor	Brad Henry (D)	US$147,000
Lieut. Gov.	Jari Askins (D)	US$114,713
Sec. of State	M. Susan Savage (D)	US$94,500
Atty. Gen.	W.A. Drew Edmondson (D)	US$132,850
Treasurer	Scott Meacham (D)	US$114,713
Legislature		
Senate	Dem: 22; Rep: 26	
House	Dem: 40; Rep: 61	
Oregon		
Governor	Ted Kulongoski (D)	US$93,600
Lieut. Gov.[4]		
Sec. of State	Kate Brown (D)	US$72,000
Atty. Gen.	John R. Kroger (D)	US$77,200
Treasurer	Ben Westlund (D)	US$72,000
Legislative Assembly		
Senate	Dem: 18; Rep: 12	
House	Dem: 36; Rep: 24	
Pennsylvania		
Governor	Edward G. Rendell (D)	US$174,914
Lieut. Gov.	Joseph B. Scarnati (R)	US$146,926
Sec. of State	Pedro A. Cortés (D)	US$125,939
Atty. Gen.	Tom Corbett (R)	US$145,529
Treasurer	Robert McCord (D)	US$145,529
General Assembly		
Senate	Dem: 21; Rep: 29	
House	Dem: 104; Rep: 99	
Rhode Island		
Governor	Don Carcieri (R)	US$117,817
Lieut. Gov.	Elizabeth H. Roberts (D)	US$99,214
Sec. of State	A. Ralph Mollis (D)	US$99,214
Atty. Gen.	Patrick C. Lynch (D)	US$105,416
Treasurer	Frank T. Caprio (D)	US$99,214
General Assembly		
Senate	Dem: 33; Rep: 4; Ind.: 1	
House	Dem: 69; Rep: 6	
South Carolina		
Governor	Mark Sanford (R)	US$106,078
Lieut. Gov.	André Bauer (R)	US$46,545
Sec. of State	Mark Hammond (R)	US$92,007
Atty. Gen.	Henry McMaster (R)	US$92,007
Treasurer	Converse Chellis (R)	US$92,007
General Assembly		
Senate	Dem: 19; Rep: 27	
House	Dem: 52; Rep: 71; vacant: 1	
South Dakota		
Governor	Mike Rounds (R)	US$115,331
Lieut. Gov.	Dennis Daugaard (R)	US$17,699
Sec. of State	Chris Nelson (R)	US$78,363
Atty. Gen.	Larry Long (R)	US$97,928
Treasurer	Vernon L. Larson (R)	US$78,363
Legislature		
Senate	Dem: 14; Rep: 21	
House	Dem: 24; Rep: 46	
Tennessee		
Governor	Phil Bredesen (D)	US$164,292
Lieut. Gov.[6]	Ron Ramsey (R)	US$57,027
Sec. of State	Tre Hargett (R)	US$180,000
Atty. Gen.	Robert E. Cooper, Jr. (D)	US$159,288
Treasurer	David H. Lillard, Jr.	US$180,000

STATE/OFFICE	OFFICEHOLDER	PAY[1]
Tennessee (continued)		
General Assembly		
Senate	Dem: 14; Rep: 19	
House	Dem: 49; Rep: 50	
Texas		
Governor	Rick Perry (R)	US$150,000
Lieut. Gov.	David Dewhurst (R)	US$7,200
Sec. of State	Esperanza Andrade	US$125,880
Atty. Gen.	Greg Abbott (R)	US$150,000
Treasurer[3]	Susan Combs (R) (Comptroller)	US$150,000
Legislature		
Senate	Dem: 12; Rep: 19	
House	Dem: 74; Rep: 76	
Utah		
Governor	Jon M. Huntsman, Jr. (R)	US$109,900
Lieut. Gov.	Gary R. Herbert (R)	US$104,405
Sec. of State[2]		
Atty. Gen.	Mark Shurtleff (R)	US$104,405
Treasurer	Richard K. Ellis (R)	US$104,405
Legislature		
Senate	Dem: 8; Rep: 21	
House	Dem: 22; Rep: 53	
Vermont		
Governor	Jim Douglas (R)	US$142,542
Lieut. Gov.	Brian Dubie (R)	US$60,507
Sec. of State	Deborah L. Markowitz (D)	US$90,376
Atty. Gen.	William H. Sorrell (D)	US$108,202
Treasurer	Jeb Spaulding (D)	US$90,376
General Assembly		
Senate	Dem: 23; Rep: 7	
House	Dem: 95; Rep: 48; Ind: 2; Progressive: 5	
Virginia		
Governor	Tim Kaine (D)	US$175,000
Lieut. Gov.	Bill Bolling (R)	US$36,321
Sec. of State	Katherine K. Hanley (D)	US$152,793
Atty. Gen.	Bill Mims (R)	US$150,000
Treasurer	Manju Ganeriwala	US$146,943
General Assembly		
Senate	Dem: 21; Rep: 19	
House	Dem: 45; Rep: 53; Ind: 2	
Washington		
Governor	Chris Gregoire (D)	US$166,891
Lieut. Gov.	Brad Owen (D)	US$93,948
Sec. of State	Sam Reed (R)	US$116,950
Atty. Gen.	Rob McKenna (R)	US$151,718
Treasurer	James L. McIntire (D)	US$116,950
Legislature		
Senate	Dem: 31; Rep: 18	
House	Dem: 61; Rep: 36; vacant: 1	
West Virginia		
Governor	Joe Manchin III (D)	US$95,000
Lieut. Gov.[7]	Earl Ray Tomblin (D)	N/A
Sec. of State	Natalie Tennant (D)	US$70,000
Atty. Gen.	Darrell V. McGraw, Jr. (D)	US$85,000
Treasurer	John D. Perdue (D)	US$75,000
Legislature		
Senate	Dem: 26; Rep: 8	
House	Dem: 71; Rep: 29	

State Officers and Legislatures (continued)

STATE/OFFICE	OFFICEHOLDER	PAY[1]	STATE/OFFICE	OFFICEHOLDER	PAY[1]
Wisconsin			**Wyoming**		
Governor	Jim Doyle (D)	US$137,092	Governor	Dave Freudenthal (D)	US$105,000
Lieut. Gov.	Barbara Lawton (D)	US$72,394	Lieut. Gov.[4]		
Sec. of State	Douglas La Follette (D)	US$65,079	Sec. of State	Max Maxfield (R)	US$92,000
Atty. Gen.	J.B. Van Hollen (R)	US$133,033	Atty. Gen.	Bruce A. Salzburg (D)	US$137,150
Treasurer	Dawn Marie Sass (D)	US$65,079	Treasurer	Joseph B. Meyer (R)	US$92,000
Legislature			Legislature		
Senate	Dem: 18; Rep: 15		Senate	Dem: 7; Rep: 23	
Assembly	Dem: 52; Rep: 46; Ind.: 1		House	Dem: 19; Rep: 41	

[1]The salary rates are from March 2009.   [2]The lieutenant governor serves as secretary of state.   [3]No official state treasurer; the official in charge of the general treasury performs duties.   [4]The secretary of state assumes duties of lieutenant governor.   [5]No official lieutenant governor; the president of the Senate succeeds the governor.   [6]In Tennessee the speaker of the Senate and the lieutenant governor are one and the same.   [7]In West Virginia the president of the Senate and the lieutenant governor are one and the same.

Cities of the United States

US Urban Growth, 1850–2008

Source: US Census Bureau.

RANK	CITY	1850	1900	1950	1990	2000	2008
1	New York NY[1]	515,547	3,437,202	7,891,957	7,322,564	8,008,278	8,363,710
2	Los Angeles CA	1,610	102,479	1,970,358	3,485,398	3,694,820	3,833,995
3	Chicago IL	29,963	1,698,575	3,620,962	2,783,726	2,896,016	2,853,114
4	Houston TX	2,396	44,633	596,163	1,630,553	1,953,631	2,242,193
5	Phoenix AZ		5,544	106,818	983,403	1,321,045	1,567,924
6	Philadelphia PA[1]	121,376	1,293,697	2,071,605	1,585,577	1,517,550	1,447,395
7	San Antonio TX	3,488	53,321	408,442	935,933	1,144,646	1,351,305
8	Dallas TX		42,638	434,462	1,006,877	1,188,580	1,279,910
9	San Diego CA		17,700	334,387	1,110,549	1,223,400	1,279,329
10	San Jose CA		21,500	95,280	782,248	894,943	948,279
11	Detroit MI	21,019	285,704	1,849,568	1,027,974	951,270	912,062
12	San Francisco CA[1]	34,776	342,782	775,357	723,959	776,733	808,976
13	Jacksonville FL	1,045	28,429	204,517	635,230	735,617	807,815
14	Indianapolis IN[1]	8,091	169,164	427,173	731,726[2]	781,870[2]	798,382[2]
15	Austin TX	629	22,258	132,459	465,622	656,562	757,688
16	Columbus OH	17,882	125,560	375,901	632,910	711,470	754,885
17	Fort Worth TX		26,688	278,778	447,619	534,694	703,073
18	Charlotte NC	1,065	18,091	134,042	395,934	540,828	687,456
19	Memphis TN	8,841	102,320	396,000	610,337	650,100	669,651
20	Baltimore MD	169,054	508,957	949,708	736,014	651,154	636,919
21	El Paso TX		15,906	130,485	515,342	563,662	613,190
22	Boston MA	136,881	560,892	801,444	574,283	589,141	609,023
23	Milwaukee WI	20,061	285,315	637,392	628,088	596,974	604,477
24	Denver CO[1]		133,859	415,786	467,610	554,636	598,707
25	Seattle WA		80,671	467,591	516,259	563,374	598,541

[1]Cities with boundaries contiguous with their respective counties (year consolidated): New York (1683), Philadelphia (1854), San Francisco (1856), Indianapolis (Marion county) (1970), and Denver (1902).   [2]Figure represents the "balance," or the population of the consolidated city minus any semi-incorporated places located within the consolidated city.

Fifteen Fastest-Growing Cities in the US

Based on a population of 100,000 or more. Source: US Census Bureau.

CITY	POPULATION		CHANGE (%)
	1 APR 2000	1 JUL 2008	
McKinney TX	54,427	121,211	+122.7
Gilbert AZ	114,701	216,449	+88.7
North Las Vegas NV	115,531	217,253	+88.0
Port St. Lucie FL	88,883	154,353	+73.7
Victorville CA	64,058	110,318	+72.2

Fifteen Fastest-Growing Cities in the US (continued)

CITY	1 APR 2000	1 JUL 2008	CHANGE (%)
Round Rock TX	61,594	104,446	+69.6
Elk Grove CA	81,103	133,033	+64.0
Cape Coral FL	102,468	156,835	+53.1
Miramar FL	72,739	108,484	+49.1
Peoria AZ	108,917	157,960	+45.0
Murfreesboro TN	70,340	101,753	+44.7
Denton TX	82,616	119,454	+44.6
Irvine CA	144,145	207,500	+44.0
Henderson NV	175,273	252,064	+43.8
Roseville CA	79,961	112,660	+40.9

Fifteen Cities with the Greatest Population Losses in the US

Based on a population of 100,000 or more. Source: US Census Bureau.

CITY	POPULATION 1 APR 2000	1 JUL 2008	CHANGE (%)	CITY	POPULATION 1 APR 2000	1 JUL 2008	CHANGE (%)
New Orleans LA	484,674	311,853	−35.7	Rochester NY	219,774	206,886	−5.9
Flint MI	124,943	112,900	−9.6	Syracuse NY	146,464	138,068	−5.7
Cleveland OH	477,472	433,748	−9.2	Jackson MS	184,260	173,861	−5.6
Buffalo NY	292,648	270,919	−7.4	Birmingham AL	242,452	228,798	−5.6
Pittsburgh PA	334,563	310,037	−7.3	Philadelphia PA	1,517,550	1,447,395	−4.6
Dayton OH	166,210	154,200	−7.2	Lansing MI	119,371	113,968	−4.5
Hialeah FL	226,440	210,542	−7.0	Akron OH	217,106	207,510	−4.4
Toledo OH	313,782	293,201	−6.6				

Racial Makeup of the Fifteen Largest US Cities

Information is given in percent of the total population. The Hispanic or Latino category is listed for comparative purposes even though Hispanic or Latino people may be of any race; thus, the rows of racial percentages will not add up to 100 if the Hispanic or Latino entries are included. Data are preliminary.

Source: US Census Bureau, *American Community Survey*, 2007 Data Profiles.

CITY	WHITE	BLACK OR AFRICAN AMERICAN	AMERICAN INDIAN AND ALASKA NATIVE	ASIAN	NATIVE HAWAIIAN AND OTHER PACIFIC ISLANDER	SOME OTHER RACE	TWO OR MORE RACES	HISPANIC OR LATINO	TOTAL POPULATION
New York NY	43.7	25.2	0.3	11.8	0.1	16.9	2.1	27.4	8,274,527
Los Angeles CA	49.6	10.0	0.5	10.4	0.2	26.3	3.1	48.4	3,806,003
Chicago IL	37.0	34.9	0.2	4.9	—	21.3	1.7	28.2	2,737,996
Houston TX	52.6	24.5	0.4	5.4	0.1	16.0	1.0	41.1	2,046,792
Phoenix AZ	75.0	5.3	1.9	2.7	0.1	13.4	1.6	42.7	1,513,777
Philadelphia PA	42.8	43.5	0.2	5.5	—	6.0	1.9	10.7	1,449,634
San Antonio TX	63.5	6.9	0.7	2.1	0.1	24.5	2.3	60.7	1,284,332
San Diego CA	67.3	6.7	0.5	14.9	0.3	6.6	3.8	27.4	1,276,740
Dallas TX	56.4	23.2	0.5	2.6	0.1	16.1	1.1	43.4	1,240,044
San Jose CA	51.1	3.0	0.6	30.0	0.5	11.3	3.5	32.7	922,389
Jacksonville FL	62.6	30.3	0.2	3.3	0.1	1.7	1.8	6.1	808,526
Detroit MI	10.7	82.7	0.2	1.2	—	3.8	1.4	6.5	808,327
Indianapolis IN	66.4	25.5	0.2	1.7	0.1	3.9	2.2	7.2	793,010
San Francisco CA	54.9	6.7	0.4	31.4	0.4	3.4	2.9	14.0	764,976
Austin TX	62.9	8.1	0.6	5.7	0.1	20.3	2.2	34.8	749,659

— Less than 0.05 percent.
Detail may not add to total given because of rounding.

Area and Zip Codes Web Sites

US telephone area codes and postal codes change frequently to accommodate telecommunications user patterns and expansions and shifts in patterns of business and residential development. Check local listings to determine whether to dial "1" before dialing outside of the area code or to dial the area code as well as the telephone number when dialing within the area code.

Area codes: <www.nanpa.com>.
Zip codes: <http://zip4.usps.com/zip4/welcome.jsp>.

Law and Crime

State Crime Rates, 2000–07

Crimes reported to the police per 100,000 population.

STATE	2000 TOTAL	2001[1] TOTAL	2002 TOTAL	2003 TOTAL	2004 TOTAL	2005 TOTAL	2006 TOTAL	2007 TOTAL
AL	4,546	4,319	4,465	4,475	4,452	4,324	4,361	4,420
AK	4,249	4,236	4,310	4,360	4,018	4,244	4,293	4,041
AZ	5,830	6,077	6,386	6,147	5,845	5,351	5,129	4,897
AR	4,115	4,134	4,158	4,088	4,512	4,585	4,519	4,483
CA	3,740	3,903	3,944	4,006	3,971	3,849	3,703	3,556
CO	3,983	4,219	4,348	4,299	4,293	4,436	3,843	3,354
CT	3,233	3,118	2,997	2,984	2,913	2,833	2,785	2,656
DE	4,478[2]	4,053	3,939	4,090	3,732	3,744	4,099	4,059
DC[3]	7,277	7,710	8,022	7,489	6,230	6,206	6,162	6,328
FL	5,695	5,570	5,421	5,188	4,891	4,716	4,698	4,812
GA	4,751	4,646	4,507	4,715	4,722	4,621	4,360	4,394
HI	5,199	5,386	6,044	5,547	5,047	5,048	4,512	4,498
ID	3,186	3,133	3,173	3,175	3,039	2,955	2,666	2,486
IL[4]	4,286	4,098	4,016	3,844	3,729	3,632	3,561	3,469
IN	3,752	3,831	3,750	3,708	3,723	3,780	3,817	3,730
IA	3,234	3,301	3,448	3,254	3,176	3,125	3,086	2,910
KS	4,409[4]	4,321	4,087	4,408	4,349	4,174	4,175	4,131
KY	2,960[4]	2,938[4]	2,903[4]	2,759[4]	2,783	2,797	2,808	2,813
LA	5,423	5,338	5,098	4,948	5,049	4,278	4,691	4,806
ME	2,620	2,688	2,656	2,559	2,514	2,525	2,634	2,547
MD	4,816	4,867	4,747	4,503	4,341	4,247	4,159	4,073
MA	3,026	3,099	3,094	3,036	2,919	2,821	2,838	2,823
MI	4,110	4,082	3,874	3,790	3,548	3,643	3,775	3,602
MN	3,488	3,584	3,535	3,376	3,309	3,381	3,391	3,325
MS	4,004	4,185	4,159	4,031	3,774	3,539	3,507	3,492
MO	4,528	4,776	4,602	4,575	4,395	4,453	4,372	4,243
MT	3,533[4]	3,689	3,513	3,461	3,230	3,424	2,941	3,053
NE	4,096	4,330	4,257	4,046	3,830	3,710	3,623	3,464
NV	4,269	4,266	4,498	4,903	4,823	4,848	4,830	4,528
NH	2,433	2,322	2,220	2,203	2,207	1,928	2,013	2,029
NJ	3,161	3,225	3,024	2,914	2,785	2,688	2,643	2,542
NM	5,519	5,324	5,078	4,756	4,885	4,851	4,580	4,390
NY	3,100	2,925	2,804	2,715	2,641	2,554	2,488	2,393
NC	4,919	4,938	4,721	4,725	4,608	4,543	4,596	4,554
ND	2,288	2,418	2,406	2,190	1,996	2,076	2,128	2,032
OH	4,042	4,178	4,107	3,984	4,015	4,014	4,029	3,798
OK	4,559	4,607	4,743	4,818	4,743	4,551	4,102	4,026
OR	4,845	5,044	4,868	5,061	4,929	4,687	3,952	3,814
PA	2,995	2,961	2,841	2,828	2,826	2,842	2,883	2,778
RI	3,476	3,685	3,589	3,281	3,131	2,970	2,814	2,850
SC	5,221	4,753	5,297	5,328	5,289	5,101	5,008	5,060
SD	2,320	2,332	2,279	2,177	2,106	1,952	1,791	1,822
TN	4,890	5,153	5,019	5,080	5,002	5,028	4,888	4,842
TX	4,956	5,153	5,190	5,153	5,035	4,862	4,598	4,632
UT	4,476	4,243	4,452	4,505	4,322	4,096	3,741	3,735
VT	2,987	2,769	2,530	2,343	2,420	2,400	2,441	2,447
VA	3,028	3,178	3,140	3,000	2,953	2,921	2,760	2,736
WA	5,106	5,152	5,107	5,102	5,193	5,239	4,826	4,364
WV	2,603	2,560	2,515	2,594	2,777	2,898	2,901	2,800
WI	3,209	3,321	3,253	3,101	2,873	2,902	3,102	3,129
WY	3,298	3,518	3,581	3,578	3,564	3,385	3,220	3,105
US	4,125	4,161	4,119	4,067	3,983	3,899	3,808	3,730

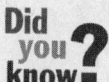

Did you know? Rudolph the Red-Nosed Reindeer made his debut as part of a promotional campaign for Chicago's Montgomery Ward department stores in 1939. The song "Rudolph the Red-Nosed Reindeer," based on a poem written by Montgomery Ward ad copywriter Robert L. May, did not become popular until Gene Autry's hit recording 10 years later. Rudolph's name was originally proposed to be Rollo or Reginald.

State Crime Rates, 2000–07 (continued)

2007 CRIME RATES IN DETAIL

	VIOLENT CRIME RATES					PROPERTY CRIME RATES			
STATE	MURDER[5]	FORCIBLE RAPE	AGGRAVATED ASSAULT	ROBBERY	TOTAL	BURGLARY	LARCENY/ THEFT	MOTOR VEHICLE THEFT	TOTAL
AL	8.9	33.4	246	160	448	980	2,685	308	3,972
AK	6.4	77.4	492	85.3	661	539	2,487	354	3,380
AZ	7.4	29.3	294	152	483	912	2,738	763	4,414
AR	6.7	44.7	371	107	529	1,131	2,574	247	3,953
CA	6.2	24.7	299	193	523	648	1,784	600	3,033
CO	3.1	41.1	233	71.0	348	591	2,069	345	3,006
CT	3.0	18.8	131	103	256	433	1,705	262	2,400
DE	4.3	38.9	449	197	689	733	2,369	268	3,370
DC[3]	30.8	32.6	627	724	1,414	667	2,955	1,292	4,914
FL	6.6	33.7	473	209	723	996	2,689	404	4,089
GA	7.5	22.8	281	182	493	950	2,505	446	3,901
HI	1.7	25.4	160	86.1	273	709	2,993	523	4,225
ID	3.3	38.5	182	15.5	239	465	1,633	149	2,247
IL[4]	5.9	31.9	316	180	533	588	2,085	264	2,936
IN	5.6	27.5	176	124	334	739	2,349	308	3,397
IA	1.2	30.3	219	43.9	295	567	1,885	164	2,616
KS	3.9	44.3	332	72.6	453	730	2,640	309	3,679
KY	4.8	32.6	162	95.9	295	653	1,661	205	2,518
LA	14.2	32.4	541	142	730	1,039	2,684	354	4,076
ME	1.6	29.7	60.2	26.5	118	507	1,826	95.6	2,429
MD	9.8	21.0	375	236	642	660	2,266	505	3,432
MA	2.9	25.3	295	109	432	553	1,606	232	2,392
MI	6.7	45.5	351	133	536	749	1,898	419	3,066
MN	2.2	36.0	159	91.8	289	571	2,225	241	3,037
MS	7.1	35.6	150	98.2	291	958	1,990	253	3,201
MO	6.5	29.2	347	122	505	739	2,595	405	3,738
MT	1.5	30.3	236	19.9	288	316	2,266	183	2,765
NE	3.8	29.7	207	62.4	302	510	2,359	293	3,161
NV	7.5	42.7	430	270	751	968	1,939	871	3,778
NH	1.1	25.3	78.0	32.8	137	379	1,414	98.7	1,892
NJ	4.4	12.1	168	145	329	432	1,529	253	2,213
NM	8.2	52.4	486	118	664	964	2,308	454	3,726
NY	4.2	15.2	234	161	414	336	1,497	145	1,979
NC	6.5	26.3	284	150	466	1,201	2,578	309	4,087
ND	1.9	32.4	97.2	10.9	142	338	1,408	143	1,890
OH	4.5	38.8	141	159	343	859	2,302	295	3,455
OK	6.1	43.1	357	93.2	500	943	2,211	372	3,526
OR	1.9	33.5	176	76.4	288	609	2,529	388	3,526
PA	5.8	27.7	226	157	417	451	1,698	213	2,361
RI	1.8	24.2	130	71.0	227	495	1,823	305	2,623
SC	8.0	39.5	597	144	788	1,026	2,860	386	4,272
SD	2.1	38.7	114	14.1	169	299	1,261	92.3	1,652
TN	6.4	35.3	533	179	753	1,002	2,734	352	4,089
TX	5.9	35.3	307	162	511	955	2,773	393	4,121
UT	2.2	34.3	145	53.7	235	588	2,580	333	3,500
VT	1.9	19.8	89.7	12.9	124	500	1,720	103	2,323
VA	5.3	22.6	143	99.2	270	411	1,873	182	2,466
WA	2.7	40.6	196	93.6	333	815	2,634	582	4,031
WV	3.5	20.4	204	47.0	275	597	1,736	193	2,525
WI	3.3	21.8	168	97.7	291	497	2,101	240	2,838
WY	3.1	30.6	190	16.1	239	449	2,265	152	2,866
Total US	5.6	30.0	284	148	467	723	2,178	363	3,264

[1]This table does not include the murder and nonnegligent homicides that occurred because of the terrorist attacks of 11 Sep 2001. [2]Forcible rape count estimated. [3]Includes reported offenses at the National Zoo and, from 2002, offenses reported by the Metro Transit Police. [4]Data are estimated or incomplete. [5]Includes nonnegligent manslaughter.

Source: US Bureau of Justice Statistics, <http://bjsdata.ojp.usdoj.gov/dataonline>.

Crime in the US, 1985–2007

This table presents the number of crimes reported in the seven categories that, with arson, are known as Part I crimes and are used by the Federal Bureau of Investigation to assess trends in criminality in the country.

Source: Federal Bureau of Investigation.

| | | VIOLENT CRIME | | | PROPERTY CRIME | | |
| | | FORCIBLE | | AGGRA-VATED | | LARCENY/ | MOTOR VEHICLE |
YEAR	MURDER[1]	RAPE	ROBBERY	ASSAULT	BURGLARY	THEFT	THEFT
1985	18,976	87,671	497,874	723,246	3,073,348	6,926,380	1,102,862
1986	20,613	91,459	542,775	834,322	3,241,410	7,257,153	1,224,137
1987	20,096	91,111	517,704	855,088	3,236,184	7,499,851	1,288,674
1988	20,675	92,486	542,968	910,092	3,218,077	7,705,872	1,432,916
1989	21,500	94,504	578,326	951,707	3,168,170	7,872,442	1,564,800
1990	23,438	102,555	639,271	1,054,863	3,073,909	7,945,670	1,635,907
1991	24,703	106,593	687,732	1,092,739	3,157,150	8,142,228	1,661,738
1992	23,760	109,062	672,478	1,126,974	2,979,884	7,915,199	1,610,834
1993	24,526	106,014	659,870	1,135,607	2,834,808	7,820,909	1,563,060
1994	23,326	102,216	618,949	1,113,179	2,712,774	7,879,812	1,539,287
1995	21,606	97,470	580,509	1,099,207	2,593,784	7,997,710	1,472,441
1996	19,645	96,252	535,594	1,037,049	2,506,400	7,904,685	1,394,238
1997	18,208	96,153	498,534	1,023,201	2,460,526	7,743,760	1,354,189
1998	16,974	93,144	447,186	976,583	2,332,735	7,376,311	1,242,781
1999	15,522	89,411	409,371	911,740	2,100,739	6,955,520	1,152,075
2000	15,586	90,178	408,016	911,706	2,050,992	6,971,590	1,160,002
2001	16,037	90,863	423,557	909,023	2,116,531	7,092,267	1,228,391
2002	16,204	95,136	420,637	894,348	2,151,875	7,052,922	1,246,096
2003	16,528	93,883	414,235	859,030	2,154,834	7,026,802	1,261,226
2004	16,148	95,089	401,470	847,381	2,144,446	6,937,089	1,237,851
2005	16,692	93,934	417,122	862,947	2,154,126	6,776,807	1,235,226
2006	17,034	92,455	447,403	860,853	2,183,746	6,607,013	1,192,809
2007	16,929	90,427	445,125	855,856	2,179,140	6,568,572	1,095,769

Crime trends: percent change in number of offenses[2]

| | | VIOLENT CRIME | | | PROPERTY CRIME | | |
YEARS COMPARED	MURDER[1]	FORCIBLE RAPE	ROBBERY	AGGRA-VATED ASSAULT	BURGLARY	LARCENY/ THEFT	MOTOR VEHICLE THEFT
2007/2006	−0.6	−2.5	−0.5	−0.6	−0.2	−0.6	−8.1
2007/2003	+2.4	−3.7	+7.5	−0.4	+1.1	−6.5	−13.1
2007/1998	−0.3	−2.9	−0.5	−12.4	−6.6	−11.0	−11.8

[1]Includes the crime of nonnegligent manslaughter.   [2]A minus sign indicates a decrease in crime; a plus sign indicates an increase.

US Cities with Most and Fewest Violent Crimes

This table ranks cities with populations greater than 100,000 by the number of violent crimes reported during 2008.
Source: Federal Bureau of Investigation, *Preliminary Annual Uniform Crime Report, January to December 2008.*

CITIES	VIOLENT CRIMES[1]	MURDER	FORCIBLE RAPE	ROBBERY	AGGRAVATED ASSAULT	BURGLARY	LARCENY/ THEFT	CAR THEFT
Most Violent Crimes								
New York NY	48,430	523	890	22,186	24,831	19,867	117,682	12,440
Los Angeles CA	26,553	384	949	13,422	11,798	19,726	58,472	22,623
Houston TX	24,779	294	750	10,603	13,132	26,947	68,598	15,214
Philadelphia PA	20,771	331	1,038	9,618	9,784	12,845	40,681	9,058
Detroit MI	17,428	306	330	6,115	10,677	17,818	18,836	16,441
Las Vegas NV	13,324	120	729	4,932	7,543	14,902	26,856	11,402
Memphis TN	12,927	137	362	4,786	7,642	15,871	32,533	5,413
Dallas TX	11,420	170	499	6,466	4,285	21,149	42,402	12,208
Phoenix AZ	10,465	167	481	4,825	4,992	18,783	48,685	15,221
Baltimore MD	10,080	234	137	4,026	5,683	7,832	17,230	5,508
Fewest Violent Crimes								
Murrieta CA	89	1	12	25	51	448	897	166
Cary NC	107	3	12	47	45	503	1,761	78
Surprise AZ	115	0	8	45	62	594	1,753	208
Round Rock TX	129	0	20	30	79	396	2,213	80

US Cities with Most and Fewest Violent Crimes (continued)

CITIES	VIOLENT CRIMES[1]	MURDER	FORCIBLE RAPE	ROBBERY	AGGRAVATED ASSAULT	BURGLARY	LARCENY/ THEFT	CAR THEFT
Fewest Violent Crimes (continued)								
Irvine CA	129	1	18	54	56	452	2,556	203
Amherst NY	141	0	2	45	94	206	1,819	57
Thousand Oaks CA	148	2	16	37	93	308	1,367	94
Norman OK	167	2	44	55	66	727	2,435	200
Bellevue WA	168	0	33	72	63	687	3,327	275
Provo UT	182	1	37	21	123	449	2,353	138

[1]*Data for overall incidents of violent crimes are composites of data for murder, forcible rape, robbery, and aggravated assault. Data are not available for Chicago IL or Naperville IL, on the list for most and fewest violent crimes, respectively, in recent years.*

Total Arrests in the US

Estimates for the year 2007. Source: Federal Bureau of Investigation, Crime in the United States, 2007.

TYPE OF CRIME	NUMBER OF ARRESTS
violent crime	
aggravated assault	433,945
robbery	126,715
forcible rape	23,307
murder and nonnegligent manslaughter	13,480
violent crime total	**597,447**
property crime	
larceny/theft	1,172,762
burglary	303,853
motor vehicle theft	118,231
arson	15,242
property crime total	**1,610,088**
other crime types	
drug abuse violations	1,841,182
driving under the influence	1,427,494
other assaults	1,305,693
disorderly conduct	709,105
liquor laws	633,654

TYPE OF CRIME	NUMBER OF ARRESTS
other crime types (continued)	
drunkenness	589,402
vandalism	291,575
fraud	252,873
weapons (carrying, possessing, etc.)	188,891
curfew and loitering law violations	143,002
offenses against the family and children	122,812
stolen property (buying, receiving, possessing)	122,061
runaways	108,879
forgery and counterfeiting	103,448
sex offenses (except forcible rape and prostitution)	83,979
prostitution and commercialized vice	77,607
vagrancy	33,666
embezzlement	22,381
gambling	12,161
suspicion (not included in total)	2,176
all other offenses (except traffic)	3,931,965
total arrests	**14,209,365**

US State and Federal Prison Population

Source: US Bureau of Justice Statistics.

STATE	NUMBER OF PRISONERS				% CHANGE (31 DEC 2006 TO 31 DEC 2007)
	31 DEC 1980	31 DEC 1990	31 DEC 2006	31 DEC 2007	
Alabama	6,543	15,665	28,241	29,412	+4.1
Alaska[1]	822	2,622	5,069	5,167	+1.9
Arizona[2]	4,372	14,261	35,801	37,746	+5.4
Arkansas	2,911	7,322	13,729	14,314	+4.3
California	24,569	97,309	175,512	174,282	−0.7
Colorado	2,629	7,671	22,481	22,841	+1.6
Connecticut[1]	4,308	10,500	20,566	20,924	+1.7
Delaware[1]	1,474	3,471	7,186	7,276	+1.3
Florida	20,735	44,387	92,969	98,219	+5.6
Georgia[2]	12,178	22,411	52,792	54,256	+2.8
Hawaii[1]	985	2,533	5,967	5,978	+0.2
Idaho	817	1,961	7,124	7,319	+2.7
Illinois	11,899	27,516	45,106	45,215	+0.2
Indiana	6,683	12,736	26,091	27,132	+4.0
Iowa[2]	2,481	3,967	8,838	8,732	−1.2
Kansas	2,494	5,775	8,816	8,696	−1.4
Kentucky	3,588	9,023	20,000	22,457	+12.3
Louisiana	8,889	18,599	37,012	37,540	+1.4
Maine	814	1,523	2,120	2,222	+4.8

US State and Federal Prison Population (continued)

STATE	NUMBER OF PRISONERS				% CHANGE (31 DEC 2006 TO 31 DEC 2007)
	31 DEC 1980	31 DEC 1990	31 DEC 2006	31 DEC 2007	
Maryland	7,731	17,848	22,945	23,433	+2.1
Massachusetts	3,185	8,345	11,032	11,436	+3.7
Michigan	15,124	34,267	51,577	50,233	-2.6
Minnesota	2,001	3,176	9,108	9,468	+4.0
Mississippi	3,902	8,375	21,068	22,431	+6.5
Missouri	5,726	14,943	30,167	29,857	-1.0
Montana	739	1,425	3,563	3,462	-2.8
Nebraska	1,446	2,403	4,407	4,505	+2.2
Nevada	1,839	5,322	12,901	13,400	+3.9
New Hampshire	326	1,342	2,805	2,943	+4.9
New Jersey	5,884	21,128	27,371	26,827	-2.0
New Mexico	1,279	3,187	6,639	6,466	-2.6
New York	21,815	54,895	63,315	62,623	-1.1
North Carolina	15,513	18,411	37,460	37,970	+1.4
North Dakota	253	483	1,363	1,416	+3.9
Ohio	13,489	31,822	49,166	50,731	+3.2
Oklahoma	4,796	12,285	26,243	25,849	-1.5
Oregon	3,177	6,492	13,707	13,948	+1.8
Pennsylvania	8,171	22,290	44,397	45,969	+3.5
Rhode Island[1]	813	2,392	3,996	4,018	+0.6
South Carolina	7,862	17,319	23,616	24,239	+2.6
South Dakota	635	1,341	3,359	3,311	-1.4
Tennessee	7,022	10,388	25,745	26,267	+2.0
Texas	29,892	50,042	172,116	171,790	-0.2
Utah	932	2,496	6,433	6,509	+1.2
Vermont[1]	480	1,049	2,215	2,145	-3.2
Virginia	8,920	17,593	36,688	38,069	+3.8
Washington	4,399	7,995	17,561	17,772	+1.2
West Virginia	1,257	1,565	5,733	6,056	+5.6
Wisconsin	3,980	7,465	23,415	23,743	+1.4
Wyoming	534	1,110	2,114	2,084	-1.4
state	305,458	708,393	1,377,645	1,398,698	+1.5
federal[3]	24,363	65,526	193,046	199,618	+3.4
US total	**329,821**	**773,919**	**1,570,691**	**1,598,316**	**+1.8**

[1]Jails and prisons are part of an integrated system. Data include total jail and prison populations.   [2]Population figures are based on custody counts.   [3]As of the end of 2001, when the transfer of responsibility for sentenced felons from the District of Columbia to the Federal Bureau of Prisons was completed, the District of Columbia no longer operates a prison system, and its prisoners are from that date forward included in federal data only.

Directors of the Federal Bureau of Investigation (FBI)

The FBI evolved from an unnamed force appointed by Attorney General Charles J. Bonaparte on 26 Jul 1908. It is the unit of the Department of Justice responsible for investigating foreign intelligence and terrorist activities and violations of federal criminal law. The president appoints the director of the FBI with confirmation from the Senate. Since J. Edgar Hoover's tenure, a director's term may not exceed 10 years. Acting directors are not included in this table.

NAME	DATES OF SERVICE
Stanley Finch	26 Jul 1908–30 Apr 1912
Alexander Bruce Bielaski	30 Apr 1912–10 Feb 1919
William J. Flynn	1 Jul 1919–21 Aug 1921
William J. Burns	22 Aug 1921–14 Jun 1924
J. Edgar Hoover	10 Dec 1924–2 May 1972

NAME	DATES OF SERVICE
Clarence M. Kelley	9 Jul 1973–15 Feb 1978
William H. Webster	23 Feb 1978–25 May 1987
William S. Sessions	2 Nov 1987–19 Jul 1993
Louis J. Freeh	1 Sep 1993–25 Jun 2001
Robert S. Mueller, III	4 Sep 2001–

Society

Average Family Size, 1950–2007

Source: US Census Bureau.

YEAR	NUMBER OF FAMILIES ('000)	PEOPLE PER FAMILY (AVERAGE)	YEAR	NUMBER OF FAMILIES ('000)	PEOPLE PER FAMILY (AVERAGE)	YEAR	NUMBER OF FAMILIES ('000)	PEOPLE PER FAMILY (AVERAGE)
1950	39,303	3.54	1970	51,586	3.58	1990	66,090	3.17
1955	41,951	3.59	1975	55,712	3.42	1995	69,305	3.19
1960	45,111	3.67	1980	59,550	3.29	2000	72,025	3.17
1965	47,956	3.70	1985	62,706	3.23	2007	78,425	3.13

US Population by Age, 2009

Numbers are in thousands ('000). Source: US Census Bureau. Detail may not add to total given because of rounding.

AGE	POPULATION NUMBER	(%)	AGE	POPULATION NUMBER	(%)
under 5 years	20,925,316	6.8	55 to 64 years	34,942,327	11.4
5 to 9 years	20,633,038	6.7	65 to 74 years	20,886,622	6.8
10 to 14 years	20,386,477	6.6	75 years and over	18,586,306	6.0
15 to 19 years	21,946,106	7.1	total population	307,212,123	100
20 to 24 years	21,386,250	7.0			
25 to 34 years	41,250,463	13.4	under 20 years	83,890,937	27.3
35 to 44 years	41,714,326	13.6	20 years and over	223,321,186	72.7
45 to 54 years	44,554,892	14.5	65 years and over	39,472,928	12.8

Living Arrangements of Children Under 18 in the US, 2007

Numbers in thousands ('000). Hispanics may be of any race. Detail may not add to total given because of rounding. Source: US Census Bureau.

LIVING IN HOUSEHOLD WITH	RACE/ETHNICITY ALL RACES	WHITE	BLACK	HISPANIC
both parents	52,138	43,179	4,467	10,564
mother only	16,667	9,727	5,678	3,703
father only	2,360	1,799	407	317
neither parent	2,581	1,518	769	544
total	73,746	56,223	11,310	15,113

Children Under 18 Living Below the Poverty Level, 1984–2007

Numbers are in thousands ('000). Hispanics may be of any race. N/A means not available. Source: US Census Bureau. For the definition of the poverty level, see <www.census.gov/hhes/www/poverty/povdef.html>.

	% OF CHILDREN BELOW THE POVERTY LEVEL					NUMBER OF CHILDREN BELOW THE POVERTY LEVEL				
YEAR	ALL[1]	WHITE[2]	BLACK	ASIAN/ PACIFIC ISLANDER	HISPANIC	ALL[1]	WHITE[2]	BLACK	ASIAN/ PACIFIC ISLANDER	HISPANIC
1984	21.5	13.7	46.6	N/A	39.2	13,420	6,156	4,413	N/A	2,376
1985	20.7	12.8	43.6	N/A	40.3	13,010	5,745	4,157	N/A	2,606
1986	20.5	13.0	43.1	N/A	37.7	12,876	5,789	4,148	N/A	2,507
1987	20.3	11.8	45.1	23.5	39.3	12,843	5,230	4,385	455	2,670
1988	19.5	11.0	43.5	24.1	37.6	12,455	4,888	4,296	474	2,631
1989	19.6	11.5	43.7	19.8	36.2	12,590	5,110	4,375	392	2,603
1990	20.6	12.3	44.8	17.6	38.4	13,431	5,532	4,550	374	2,865
1991	21.8	13.1	45.9	17.5	40.4	14,341	5,918	4,755	360	3,094
1992	22.3	13.2	46.6	16.4	40.0	15,294	6,017	5,106	363	3,637
1993	22.7	13.6	46.1	18.2	40.9	15,727	6,255	5,125	375	3,873
1994	21.8	12.5	43.8	18.3	41.5	15,289	5,823	4,906	318	4,075
1995	20.8	11.2	41.9	19.5	40.0	14,665	5,115	4,761	564	4,080
1996	20.5	11.1	39.9	19.5	40.3	14,463	5,072	4,519	571	4,237
1997	19.9	11.4	37.2	20.3	36.8	14,113	5,204	4,225	628	3,972
1998	18.9	10.6	36.7	18.0	34.4	13,467	4,822	4,151	564	3,837

Children Under 18 Living Below the Poverty Level, 1984–2007 (continued)

| | % OF CHILDREN BELOW THE POVERTY LEVEL | | | | | NUMBER OF CHILDREN BELOW THE POVERTY LEVEL | | | | |
| | | | | ASIAN/ PACIFIC | | | | | ASIAN/ PACIFIC | |
YEAR	ALL[1]	WHITE[2]	BLACK	ISLANDER	HISPANIC	ALL[1]	WHITE[2]	BLACK	ISLANDER	HISPANIC
1999	16.9	9.4	33.2	11.9	30.3	12,280	4,155	3,813	381	3,693
2000	16.2	9.1	31.2	12.7	28.4	11,587	4,018	3,581	420	3,522
2001	16.3	9.5	30.2	11.5	28.0	11,733	4,194	3,492	369	3,570
2002	16.7	9.4	32.3	12.2	28.6	12,133	4,090	3,645	351	3,782
2003	17.6	9.8	34.1	12.7	29.7	12,866	4,233	3,877	377	4,077
2004	17.8	10.5	33.7	10.1	28.9	13,041	4,519	3,788	305	4,098
2005	17.6	10.0	34.5	11.0	28.3	12,896	4,254	3,841	333	4,143
2006	17.4	10.0	33.4	12.5	26.9	12,827	4,208	3,777	391	4,072
2007	18.0	10.1	34.5	12.5	28.6	13,324	4,255	3,904	396	4,482

[1]Includes other and unclassified. [2]Excludes Hispanic population.

US Adoptions of Foreign-Born Children

Adoptions of foreign children by US citizens are tracked by the number of immigrant visas issued to orphans entering the US. Source: US Department of State.

TOP 10 COUNTRIES OF ORIGIN	ADOPTIONS FISCAL YEAR		TOP 10 COUNTRIES OF ORIGIN	ADOPTIONS FISCAL YEAR		TOTAL FOREIGN ADOPTIONS	
	2007	2008		2007	2008	FISCAL YEAR	ADOPTIONS
1 Guatemala	4,728	4,123	6 Vietnam	828	751	2003	21,616
2 China	5,453	3,909	7 Ukraine	606	457	2004	22,884
3 Russia	2,310	1,861	8 Kazakhstan	540	380	2005	22,728
4 Ethiopia	1,255	1,725	9 India	416	307	2006	20,679
5 Rep. of Korea	939	1,065	10 Colombia	310	306	2007	19,613
						2008	17,438

US Nursing Home Population

The data in these tables were gathered through interviews conducted for the most recent National Nursing Home Survey (2004) and through the publication *Health, United States, 2008*. Only those residents who described themselves as being of one race are included. Data on residents under the age of 65 are not available. Detail may not add to total given because of rounding.

Source: US National Center for Health Statistics.

| AGE AT INTERVIEW | TOTAL RESIDENTS | % | GENDER (2004) | | | | |
			MALE	%	FEMALE	%	
65–74	174,100	13.2	75,400	22.4	98,800	10.1	
75–84	468,900	35.6	140,800	41.8	328,000	33.5	
85 and older	674,200	51.2	120,600	35.8	553,600	56.5	
total	1,317,200	100.0	336,800	100.0	980,400	100.0	

| | RACE (2004) | | | | |
	WHITE	%	BLACK	%	
65–74	134,200	11.7	34,500	23.7	
75–84	406,000	35.3	54,600	37.6	
85 and older	608,600	53.0	56,300	38.7	
total	1,148,800	100.0	145,400	100.0	

| | RESIDENT LOCATION (1999) | | | | | | | |
	NORTHWEST	%	MIDWEST	%	SOUTH	%	WEST	%
65–74	46,400	12.1	58,900	11.8	63,400	11.9	26,100	12.1
75–84	118,500	30.9	153,200	30.8	179,100	33.7	66,800	31.1
85 and older	184,300	48.1	241,100	48.4	237,700	44.7	94,000	43.7
total	383,400	100.0	498,200	100.0	531,500	100.0	215,200	100.0

| | RESIDENT LOCATION (2007) | | | | | | | |
	NORTHEAST	%	MIDWEST	%	SOUTH	%	WEST	%
TOTAL RESIDENTS	334,069	23.4	413,435	29.0	483,487	33.9	193,833	13.6

Marital Status of Population by Sex, 1950–2007

The data in this table are taken from surveys of individuals 18 or over conducted by the US Census Bureau and exclude members of the armed forces except those living off post or with their families on post. Data exclude Alaska and Hawaii prior to 1960. Detail may not add to total given because of rounding.
Source: US Census Bureau.

	TOTAL						
	1950	1960	1970	1980	1990	2000	2007
Total individuals surveyed in hundred thousands ('000,000)	111.7	125.5	132.5	159.5	181.8	201.8	222.6
Percentage of individuals never married	22.8	22.0	16.2	20.3	22.2	23.9	25.2
Percentage of individuals married	67.0	67.3	71.7	65.5	61.9	59.5	58.3
Percentage of individuals widowed	8.3	8.4	8.9	8.0	7.6	6.8	6.2
Percentage of individuals divorced	1.9	2.3	3.2	6.2	8.3	9.8	10.2
Percentage of males never married	26.2	25.3	18.9	23.8	25.8	27.0	28.7
Percentage of males married	68.0	69.1	75.3	68.4	64.3	61.5	59.9
Percentage of males widowed	4.2	3.7	3.3	2.6	2.7	2.7	2.5
Percentage of males divorced	1.7	1.9	2.5	5.2	7.2	8.8	8.9
Percentage of females never married	11.1	12.3	13.7	17.1	18.9	21.1	22.0
Percentage of females married	37.6	42.6	68.5	63.0	59.7	57.6	56.7
Percentage of females widowed	7.0	8.3	13.9	12.8	12.1	10.5	9.8
Percentage of females divorced	1.2	1.7	3.9	7.1	9.3	10.8	11.5

Unmarried-Couple Households in the US

Data based on Current Population Survey or American Community Survey except for census years of 1960 and 1970. 2006 data shown separately. Numbers in thousands ('000). Source: US Census Bureau.

YEAR	TOTAL US HOUSEHOLDS	UNMARRIED-COUPLE HOUSEHOLDS (OPPOSITE SEX)	% OF TOTAL HOUSEHOLDS	NO CHILDREN UNDER 15	WITH CHILDREN UNDER 15
1960 census	52,799	439	0.8	242	197
1970 census	63,401	523	0.8	327	196
1980	80,776	1,589	2.0	1,159	431
1985	86,789	1,983	2.3	1,380	603
1990	93,347	2,856	3.1	1,966	891
1995	98,990	3,668	3.7	2,349	1,319
2000	104,705	4,736	4.5	3,061	1,675

UNMARRIED-COUPLE HOUSEHOLDS	2006
male householder/female partner	2,706
male householder/male partner	417
female householder/female partner	363
female householder/male partner	2,532
unmarried-couple households	6,017
total households	111,617

Did you know? The only royal palace located in the United States sits on more than 11 acres in Honolulu HI. The Iolani Palace, built in 1882, was the official residence of the last two monarchs of the Kingdom of Hawaii, King Kalakaua (1874–91) and his sister, Queen Liliuokalani (1891–95), the kingdom's last monarch and the only queen in its history. The residence, the name of which comes from *io*, Hawaiian for "hawk," and *lani*, meaning "royal" or "heavenly," was outfitted lavishly with modern conveniences, including indoor plumbing, electric lighting, and telephones. After the annexation of Hawaii, the palace served for a time as the legislative seat, and it now houses a museum.

United States Education

Educational Attainment by Gender and Race

For persons ages 25 years old and older. Percentage rates for 1960, 1970, and 1980 are based on sample data from the decennial censuses. Rates for 1990, 2000, and 2007 are based on the Current Population Survey. N/A means not available. Source: US Census Bureau.

Percentage who had graduated from high school[1]

YEAR	ALL RACES[2]		WHITE		BLACK		ASIAN/PACIFIC ISLANDER		HISPANIC[3]	
	MALE	FEMALE	MALE	FEMALE	MALE	FEMALE	MALE	FEMALE	MALE	FEMALE
1960	39.5	42.5	41.6	44.7	18.2	21.8	N/A	N/A	N/A	N/A
1970	51.9	52.8	54.0	55.0	30.1	32.5	N/A	N/A	37.9	34.2
1980	67.3	65.8	69.6	68.1	50.8	51.5	N/A	N/A	67.3	65.8
1990	77.7	77.5	79.1	79.0	65.8	66.5	84.0	77.2	50.3	51.3
2000	84.2	84.0	84.8	85.0	78.7	78.3	88.2	83.4	56.6	57.5
2007	85.0	86.4	85.3	87.1	81.9	82.6	89.8	85.9	58.2	62.5

Percentage who had graduated from college[4]

YEAR	ALL RACES[2]		WHITE		BLACK		ASIAN/PACIFIC ISLANDER		HISPANIC[3]	
	MALE	FEMALE	MALE	FEMALE	MALE	FEMALE	MALE	FEMALE	MALE	FEMALE
1960	9.7	5.8	10.3	6.0	2.8	3.3	N/A	N/A	N/A	N/A
1970	13.5	8.1	14.4	8.4	4.2	4.6	N/A	N/A	7.8	4.3
1980	20.1	12.8	21.3	13.3	8.4	8.3	N/A	N/A	9.4	6.0
1990	24.4	18.4	25.3	19.0	11.9	10.8	44.9	35.4	9.8	8.7
2000	27.8	23.6	28.5	23.9	16.3	16.7	47.6	40.7	10.7	10.6
2007	29.5	28.0	29.9	28.3	18.0	19.0	55.2	49.3	11.8	13.7

[1]Through 1990, finished four years or more of high school. [2]Includes races not shown separately in the table. [3]Hispanics may be of any race. [4]Through 1990, finished four years or more of college.

National Spelling Bee

A spelling bee is a contest or game in which players attempt to spell correctly and aloud words assigned them by an impartial judge. Competition may be individual, with players eliminated when they misspell a word and the last remaining player being the winner, or between teams, the winner being the team with the most players remaining at the close of the contest. The spelling bee is an old custom that was revived in schools in the United States in the late 19th century and enjoyed a great vogue there and in Great Britain. In the US, local, regional, and national competitions continue to be held annually. The US National Spelling Bee was begun by the Louisville Courier-Journal newspaper in 1925, and it was taken over by Scripps Howard, Inc., in 1941. To qualify, spellers must meet 12 requirements, including that they have neither reached their 16th birthday nor passed beyond the eighth grade.

National Spelling Bee Web site: <www.spellingbee.com>.

YEAR	CHAMPION	WINNING WORD	YEAR	CHAMPION	WINNING WORD
1925	Frank Neuhauser	gladiolus	1938	Marian Richardson	pronunciation
1926	Pauline Bell	cerise	1939	Elizabeth Ann Rice	canonical
1927	Dean Lucas	abrogate	1940	Laurel Kuykendall	therapy[1]
1928	Betty Robinson	knack	1941	Louis Edward Sissman	chrysanthemum
1929	Virginia Hogan	luxuriance	1942	Richard Earnhart	sacrilegious
1930	Helen Jensen	albumen	1943–45	not held	
1931	Ward Randall	foulard	1946	John McKinney	semaphore
1932	Dorothy Greenwald	knack[1]	1947	Mattie Lou Pollard	chlorophyll
1933	Alma Roach	torsion	1948	Jean Chappelear	psychiatry
1934	Sarah Wilson	brethren	1949	Kim Calvin	onerous
1935	Clara Mohler	intelligible	1950	Diana Reynard;	meticulosity[1]
1936	Jean Trowbridge	eczema		Colquitt Dean (tied)	
1937	Waneeta Beckley	promiscuous	1951	Irving Belz	insouciant

National Spelling Bee (continued)

YEAR	CHAMPION	WINNING WORD	YEAR	CHAMPION	WINNING WORD
1952	Doris Ann Hall	vignette	1980	Jacques Bailly	elucubrate
1953	Elizabeth Hess	soubrette	1981	Paige Pipkin	sarcophagus
1954	William Cashore	transept	1982	Molly Dieveney	psoriasis
1955	Sandra Sloss	crustaceology	1983	Blake Giddens	Purim
1956	Melody Sachko	condominium	1984	Daniel Greenblatt	luge
1957	Sandra Owen;	schappe[2]	1985	Balu Natarajan	milieu
	Dana Bennett (tied)		1986	Jon Pennington	odontalgia
1958	Jolitta Schlehuber	syllepsis	1987	Stephanie Petit	staphylococci
1959	Joel Montgomery	catamaran	1988	Rageshree Ramachandran	elegiacal
1960	Henry Feldman	eudaemonic	1989	Scott Isaacs	spoliator
1961	John Capehart	smaragdine	1990	Amy Marie Dimak	fibranne
1962	Nettie Crawford;	esquamulose[2]	1991	Joanne Lagatta	antipyretic
	Michael Day (tied)		1992	Amanda Goad	lyceum
1963	Glen Van Slyke III	equipage	1993	Geoff Hooper	kamikaze
1964	William Kerek	sycophant	1994	Ned G. Andrews	antediluvian
1965	Michael Kerpan, Jr.	eczema	1995	Justin Tyler Carroll	xanthosis
1966	Robert A. Wake	ratoon	1996	Wendy Guey	vivisepulture
1967	Jennifer Reinke	chihuahua	1997	Rebecca Sealfon	euonym
1968	Robert L. Walters	abalone	1998	Jody-Anne Maxwell	chiaroscurist
1969	Susan Yoachum	interlocutory	1999	Nupur Lala	logorrhea
1970	Libby Childress	croissant	2000	George Abraham Thampy	demarche
1971	Jonathan Knisely	shalloon	2001	Sean Conley	succedaneum
1972	Robin Kral	macerate	2002	Pratyush Buddiga	prospicience
1973	Barrie Trinkle	vouchsafe	2003	Sai R. Gunturi	pococurante
1974	Julie Ann Junkin	hydrophyte	2004	David Tidmarsh	autochthonous
1975	Hugh Tosteson	incisor	2005	Anurag Kashyap	appoggiatura
1976	Tim Kneale	narcolepsy	2006	Kerry Close	Ursprache
1977	John Paola	cambist	2007	Evan M. O'Dorney	serrefine
1978	Peg McCarthy	deification	2008	Sameer Mishra	guerdon
1979	Katie Kerwin	maculature	2009	Kavya Shivashankar	Laodicean

[1]*It has not been independently verified that this was the winning, or final, word.*   [2]*Neither winning contestant spelled the winning word correctly, and the contest was declared a draw.*

Business

The Future of Work

by David von Drehle and Anne Fisher, TIME

Ten years ago, Facebook didn't exist. Ten years before that, we didn't have the Web. So who knows what jobs will be born a decade from now? Though unemployment in 2009 was at a 25-year high, work will eventually return. But it won't look the same. No one is going to pay you just to show up. We will see a more flexible, more freelance, more collaborative, and far less secure work world. It will be run by a generation with new values—Generation X. But one seemingly old-fashioned form of work—manufacturing—won't be going away. Ten years from now, Americans will still be making stuff. Indeed, the death of American manufacturing has been greatly exaggerated. According to UN statistics, the US remains by far the world's largest manufacturer, producing nearly twice as much value as No. 2 China. Since 1990, US manufacturing output has grown by nearly US$800 billion—an amount larger than the entire manufacturing economy of Germany, a global powerhouse.

But growth does not mean jobs. While sales soared (at least until the recession), manufacturing employment sank. Using constantly improving technology to make more-valuable goods, American workers doubled their productivity in less than a generation—which, paradoxically, rendered millions of them obsolete. This new manufacturing workforce can be seen in the gleaming and antiseptic room in southern California where Edwards Lifesciences produces artificial-heart valves. You could say the small group of workers at the Edwards plant, most of them Asian women, are seamstresses. Unlike the thousands of US textile workers whose jobs have migrated to low-wage countries, however, these highly skilled women occupy a niche in which US firms are dominant and growing. Each replacement valve requires 8 to 12 hours of meticulous hand-sewing—some 1,800 stitches so tiny that the work is done under a microscope. Up to a year of training goes into preparing a new hire to join the operation.

Highly skilled workers creating high-value products in high-stakes industries—that's the sweet spot for manufacturing workers in coming years. After an initial surge of enthusiasm for shipping jobs of all kinds to low-wage countries, many US companies are making a distinction between exportable jobs and jobs that should stay home. Edwards, for example, has moved its rote assembly work—building electronic monitoring machines—to such lower-wage and -tax locales as Puerto Rico. But when quality is a matter of life or death and production processes involve trade secrets worth billions, the US wins, says the company's head of global operations, Corinne Lyle. "We like to keep close tabs on our processes." Recent corner-cutting scandals in China—lead-paint-tainted children's toys, melamine-laced milk—have underlined the advantages of manufacturing at home. A botched toy is one thing; a botched batch of heparin or a faulty aircraft component is quite another. According to Clemson (SC) University's Aleda Roth, who studies quality control in global supply chains, the successful companies of coming years will be the ones that make product safety—not just price—a "big factor in their decisions about where to locate jobs."

Innovative companies will also stay home thanks to America's superior network of universities and its relatively stringent intellectual-property laws. Consider, for instance, the secretive and successful South Carolina textile maker Milliken & Co. While the rest of the region's low-tech, backward-looking textile industry was fading away, Milliken pushed ahead, investing heavily in research and becoming a hive of new patents.

US manufacturing will also be buoyed by a third source of power: the American consumer. Even in our current battered condition, the US is the world's most prosperous marketplace. As global economic activity rebounds, so will energy prices. The cost of shipping foreign-made goods to the US market will begin to offset overseas wage advantages. We saw that in 2008 when oil prices zoomed toward US$200 per barrel. Thus, even if fewer cars are built by America's wounded automakers, there will still be plenty of car factories in the US. They will be owned by Japanese and Chinese and Korean and German and Italian firms, but they will employ American workers. It just makes sense to build the cars near the people you expect to buy them.

The Gen X managers who will be holding all this together will need to be adept at a few things that earlier generations, with their more-hierarchical management styles and relative geographical insularity, never really had to learn. One of those is collaborative decision making that might involve team members scattered around the world, from Beijing to Barcelona to Boston, whom the nominal leader of a given project may never have met in person. "By 2019, every leader will have to be culturally dexterous on a global scale," says Janet Reid, managing partner at Global Lead, a consulting firm that advises companies like PepsiCo and Procter & Gamble.

Superannuated boomers won't vanish from the workplace altogether: people in their 60s and 70s—because of either need or desire—will be among the 40% of the US workforce that will rent out its skills. "Boomers will be working part-time as coaches, strategists, and consultants," predicts Joanne Sujansky, a coauthor of the 2009 book *Keeping the Millennials*. "By 2019, there will be many more of those opportunities than there are now because boomers will need the income and companies will need their expertise." Says Reid, "We'll see an increase in job-sharing at very senior levels. You might have two boomers who share the job of chief financial officer, for instance, which lets them keep working and also have some leisure time."

Raised on images of Carnegie and Ford, we rue the loss of once smoky, now silent megaplants but are blind to the small and midsize companies replacing them. Ultimately, what's endangered is not US manufacturing. It is our deeply ingrained cultural image of the factory and its workers.

US Economy

Denominations of US Currency

PAPER MONEY

VALUE	PORTRAIT ON FRONT	DESIGN ON BACK	WHEN CIRCULATED
$1	George Washington	Great Seal of US	1929–
$2	Thomas Jefferson	Monticello	1929–75
$2	Thomas Jefferson	John Trumbull's *Signing of the Declaration of Independence*	1976–
$5[1]	Abraham Lincoln	Lincoln Memorial	2000–
$10[1]	Alexander Hamilton	US Treasury	2000–
$20[1]	Andrew Jackson	White House	1998–
$50[1]	Ulysses S. Grant	US Capitol	1997–
$100[1]	Benjamin Franklin	Independence Hall	1996–
$500	William McKinley	ornate figure of value	1929–69
$1,000	Grover Cleveland	ornate figure of value	1929–69
$5,000	James Madison	ornate figure of value	1929–69
$10,000	Salmon P. Chase	ornate figure of value	1929–69
$100,000[2]	Woodrow Wilson	ornate figure of value	—

[1]*Earlier versions issued starting in 1929 had same subjects as current version.*   [2]*Never issued to public.*

COINS

VALUE	PORTRAIT ON FRONT	DESIGN ON BACK	WHEN CIRCULATED
1¢	Abraham Lincoln	"one cent" and wheat	1909–58
1¢	Abraham Lincoln	Lincoln Memorial	1959–2008
1¢	Abraham Lincoln	scenes from Lincoln's life	2009
5¢	Thomas Jefferson	Monticello	1938–2003; 2006–
5¢	Thomas Jefferson	"Westward Journey" designs	2004–05
10¢	Franklin D. Roosevelt	torch	1946–
25¢	George Washington	eagle	1932–74; 1977–98
25¢ (bicentennial)	George Washington	colonial drummer	1975–76
25¢	George Washington	50 state designs	1999–2008
25¢	George Washington	Washington DC, US territories designs	2009
50¢	John F. Kennedy	presidential seal	1964–74; 1977–
50¢ (bicentennial)	John F. Kennedy	Independence Hall	1975–76
$1	Dwight D. Eisenhower	eagle	1971–74; 1977–78
$1 (bicentennial)	Dwight D. Eisenhower	Liberty Bell and Moon	1975–76
$1	Susan B. Anthony	eagle	1979–80; 1999
$1	Sacagawea	eagle	2000–06
$1	Sacagawea	Native American farmer	2009
$1	presidential portraits	Statue of Liberty	2007–16

50 STATE QUARTERS PROGRAM

STATE	WHEN ISSUED	STATE	WHEN ISSUED	STATE	WHEN ISSUED
Alabama	2003	Louisiana	2002	Ohio	2002
Alaska	2008	Maine	2003	Oklahoma	2008
Arizona	2008	Maryland	2000	Oregon	2005
Arkansas	2003	Massachusetts	2000	Pennsylvania	1999
California	2005	Michigan	2004	Rhode Island	2001
Colorado	2006	Minnesota	2005	South Carolina	2000
Connecticut	1999	Mississippi	2002	South Dakota	2006
Delaware	1999	Missouri	2003	Tennessee	2002
Florida	2004	Montana	2007	Texas	2004
Georgia	1999	Nebraska	2006	Utah	2007
Hawaii	2008	Nevada	2006	Vermont	2001
Idaho	2007	New Hampshire	2000	Virginia	2000
Illinois	2003	New Jersey	1999	Washington	2007
Indiana	2002	New Mexico	2008	West Virginia	2005
Iowa	2004	New York	2001	Wisconsin	2004
Kansas	2005	North Carolina	2001	Wyoming	2007
Kentucky	2001	North Dakota	2006		

PRESIDENTIAL $1 COINS PROGRAM

2007	George Washington, John Adams, Thomas Jefferson, James Madison
2008	James Monroe, John Quincy Adams, Andrew Jackson, Martin Van Buren
2009	William Henry Harrison, John Tyler, James K. Polk, Zachary Taylor
2010	Millard Fillmore, Franklin Pierce, James Buchanan, Abraham Lincoln

US Currency and Coins in Circulation

*Currency and coins outstanding and currency in circulation by denomination,
31 Dec 2008. Source: Treasury Bulletin, March 2009.*

	TOTAL CURRENCY AND COINS	CURRENCY	COINS[1]
amounts in circulation	$ 889,885,178,367	$ 853,647,642,706	$36,237,535,661
amounts held by:			
US Treasury	268,121,155	7,181,372	260,939,783
Federal Reserve Banks	171,370,083,161	169,681,830,702	1,688,252,459
total amounts outstanding	1,061,523,382,683	1,023,336,654,780	38,186,727,903

DENOMINATION	TOTAL CURRENCY IN CIRCULATION	FEDERAL RESERVE NOTES[2]	US NOTES	CURRENCY NO LONGER ISSUED
$1	$ 9,476,926,931	$ 9,333,994,305	$ 143,503	$142,789,123
$2	1,664,966,010	1,532,830,864	132,122,518	12,628
$5	11,029,794,255	10,894,067,815	108,798,010	26,928,430
$10	16,287,189,690	16,266,182,690	6,300	21,000,700
$20	125,119,302,520	125,099,191,900	3,840	20,106,780
$50	64,727,257,900	64,715,752,450	500	11,504,950
$100	625,028,920,800	625,005,840,700	1,073,000	22,007,100
$500	142,317,000	142,107,500	5,500	204,000
$1,000	165,667,000	165,415,000	5,000	247,000
$5,000	1,780,000	1,710,000	—	70,000
$10,000	3,520,000	3,360,000	—	160,000
fractional notes[3]	600	—	90	510
total currency	853,647,642,706	853,160,453,224	242,158,261	245,031,221

[1]*Excludes coins sold to collectors at premium prices.* [2]*Issued on or after 1 Jul 1929.* [3]*Represents value of certain partial denominations not presented for redemption.*

Energy
Energy Consumption by Source
*Figures represent '000,000,000,000 BTU for the year 2007.
Source: US Energy Information Administration, <www.eia.doe.gov>.*

	PETROLEUM	NATURAL GAS	COAL	HYDRO-ELECTRIC POWER[1, 2]	NUCLEAR ELECTRIC POWER[1]	TOTAL[1]
Alabama	626	431	888	72	333	2,141
Alaska	324	372	13	12	0	754
Arizona	595	402	439	67	251	1,531
Arkansas	387	228	275	15	159	1,145
California	3,946	2,440	66	334	477	8,420
Colorado	525	516	389	18	0	1,428
Connecticut	397	184	40	5	173	849
Delaware	136	50	64	0	0	301
District of Columbia	23	34	1	0	0	176
Florida	1,984	950	721	2	328	4,610
Georgia	1,100	454	935	26	334	3,146
Hawaii	306	3	19	1	0	332
Idaho	166	84	10	112	0	515
Illinois	1,418	979	1,090	2	982	3,946
Indiana	878	548	1,575	5	0	2,862
Iowa	442	262	464	9	53	1,207
Kansas	425	292	396	[3]	98	1,051
Kentucky	747	236	1,020	26	0	1,971
Louisiana	1,600	1,423	250	7	175	3,803
Maine	236	48	7	42	0	458
Maryland	557	209	328	21	144	1,452
Massachusetts	685	417	120	15	61	1,479
Michigan	987	848	800	15	303	2,998
Minnesota	706	397	366	6	138	1,822
Mississippi	471	375	185	0	109	1,216
Missouri	759	278	802	2	106	1,913
Montana	211	75	203	101	0	429
Nebraska	235	146	217	9	94	659

Energy Consumption by Source (continued)

	PETROLEUM	NATURAL GAS	COAL	HYDRO-ELECTRIC POWER[1,2]	NUCLEAR ELECTRIC POWER[1]	TOTAL[1]
Nevada	293	264	83	20	0	767
New Hampshire	170	65	45	15	98	313
New Jersey	1,373	641	112	[3]	340	2,605
New Mexico	285	240	296	2	0	683
New York	1,633	1,219	258	271	441	3,940
North Carolina	971	245	828	38	417	2,659
North Dakota	143	63	420	15	0	411
Ohio	1,357	836	1,462	6	176	3,893
Oklahoma	578	691	373	6	0	1,603
Oregon	385	258	45	375	0	1,112
Pennsylvania	1,456	782	1,491	28	786	3,933
Rhode Island	92	91	[3]	[3]	0	216
South Carolina	577	180	444	18	530	1,708
South Dakota	121	54	33	34	0	272
Tennessee	827	230	672	77	258	2,313
Texas	5,887	3,641	1,609	7	431	11,744
Utah	306	232	391	7	0	786
Vermont	88	9	[3]	15	53	164
Virginia	1,017	333	458	13	288	2,545
Washington	847	280	96	813	97	2,054
West Virginia	289	123	983	16	0	829
Wisconsin	620	404	465	17	128	1,819
Wyoming	176	118	495	8	0	481
total[4]	40,358	23,678	22,740	2,869	8,214	99,521

[1]Data for 2006.   [2]Data do not include results from pumped-storage hydroelectricity.   [3]Negligible.   [4]Detail may not add to total given because of rounding and the inclusion of energy that has not been allocated to a state.

Travel and Tourism

Passports, Visas, and Immunizations

With certain exceptions, a **passport** (also called a passport book) is required by law for all US citizens, including infants, to travel outside the United States and its territories. The exceptions of travel without passport to Mexico, Canada, Bermuda, and countries in the Caribbean were eliminated in 2007 by implementation of the Western Hemisphere Travel Initiative. A wallet-sized **passport card** was created as a more convenient, less expensive alternative to the passport book for reentry into the US from those formerly exempt areas (it is valid only for reentry from those areas). A new passport card costs US$45 for persons ages 16 and older and US$35 for those under 16; the renewal fee is US$20. Passports can be applied for at 9,000 passport acceptance facilities nationwide, including most government facilities. State Department passport agencies accept applications only by appointment, usually from those in need of expedited service (two weeks or less). Passport agencies are located in Aurora CO, Boston MA, Chicago IL, Detroit MI, Honolulu HI, Houston TX, Los Angeles CA, Miami FL, Minneapolis MN, New Orleans LA, New York NY, Norwalk CT, Philadelphia PA, San Francisco CA, Seattle WA, and Washington DC. Everyone must apply in person for his or her first passport; those issued to persons ages 16 and older may be renewed by mail if the person's expiring passport is undamaged and in his or her possession and was issued no more than 15 years previously. Applicants should submit the appropriate paperwork several months in advance of planned travel to allow for processing. New passport fees total US$100 for persons ages 16 and older (US$75 application fee, US$25 execution fee) and US$85 for those under 16 (US$60 application fee, US$25 execution fee); expedited service is an additional US$60. Renewal fees are US$75 for all ages. Passports are mailed to applicants in about six weeks or about two weeks for rush service. The status of a passport application may be checked online at <http://travel.state.gov/passport/get/status/status_2567.html> or by contacting the National Passport Information Center at 1-877-487-2778 (toll-free; automated information; representatives available weekdays 8 AM to 10 PM ET, except federal holidays).

Applying in person for a passport requires submission of an application form; proof of US citizenship, such as a certified birth certificate; proof of identity, such as a driver's license; two identical recent 2×2-inch photographs; a social security number; and all applicable fees. Options for proving identity or citizenship are listed on the State Department Web site. A passport is valid for 10 years, or 5 years if issued to a person age 15 or younger. Renewing by mail requires submission of an application form, the most recent passport, two identical photographs, and applicable fees. Frequent travelers may request a passport with extra pages. A passport that is lost or stolen in a foreign country must immediately be reported to local police and the nearest US embassy or consulate to allow for the citizen's reentry into the US. Replacing a lost or stolen passport requires completion of a form reporting the loss or theft and an application for a new passport, as well as the usual documentation, photographs, and fees.

Passports, Visas, and Immunizations (continued)

Visas. A visa is usually a stamp placed on a US passport by a foreign country's officials allowing the passport owner to visit that country. It is the traveler's responsibility to check visa regulations and obtain visas where necessary before traveling to a foreign country. Visas may be acquired from the embassy or consulate of the intended destination and can be applied for by mail. Processing fees vary among countries.

Immunizations. Under regulations adopted by the World Health Organization, some countries require International Certificates of Vaccination against yellow fever. Other immunizations, such as those for tetanus and polio, should also be up-to-date. Preventive measures for malaria are recommended for some destinations. There are no immunization requirements for returning to the United States. Many countries require HIV/AIDS testing for work, study, or residence permits or for long-term stays.

For passport information, forms, and office locations, access the State Department Web site at <http://travel.state.gov/passport>. Entry requirements for foreign countries, including necessity of visas, immunizations, and HIV testing, are available at <http://travel.state.gov/travel/cis_pa_tw/cis/cis_1765.html>. Additional information on required or recommended health care measures can be obtained from the Centers for Disease Control and Prevention (CDC) at <www.cdc.gov/travel> or by calling 1-877-FYI-TRIP; also helpful are local health departments and the Government Printing Office publication *Health Information for International Travel,* available at the CDC Web site.

Travelers to and from the US

Data for 2002 showed that overseas travel to the US dropped significantly during 2002, primarily as a response to the terrorist attacks of 11 Sep 2001. Since then, however, travel has rebounded at varying levels. Data for 2008 for all US resident travel to specific overseas countries are not available, but data for air travel to the various regions, as well as to Mexico and Canada, are presented below. Source: US Department of Commerce, International Trade Administration, Office of Travel and Tourism Industries.

TOP COUNTRIES OF ORIGIN FOR VISITORS TO THE US (2008)		% CHANGE FROM 2007
UK	4,564,895	+1.5
Japan	3,249,578	−8.0
Germany	1,782,299	+16.9
France	1,243,942	+24.7
Italy	779,463	+22.9
Brazil	769,232	+20.3
Republic of Korea	759,394	−5.8
Australia	689,927	+3.0
Spain	658,333	+27.5
China[1]	632,317	+17.1
total overseas	**25,341,451**	**+6.1**
Canada	18,925,264	+6.6
Mexico	13,763,000	−3.9
total worldwide	**58,029,715**	**+3.7**

REGIONAL DESTINATION OF US AIR TRAVELERS ABROAD (2008)		% CHANGE FROM 2007
Europe	12,420,662	−6.3
Caribbean	5,634,789	+0.1
Asia	5,487,373	−1.7
Central America	2,566,229	+1.0
South America	2,535,245	+3.4
Middle East	852,368	+45.7
Oceania	764,399	−6.9
Africa	317,343	+54.7
total overseas	**30,578,408**	**−1.6**
Mexico	5,866,545	+1.8
Canada	3,581,759	−5.2
total worldwide	**40,026,712**	**−1.4**

TOP 10 STATES AND CITIES VISITED BY OVERSEAS VISITORS (2008)[2]

STATE	VISITORS/ IN THOUSANDS ('000)	% CHANGE FROM 2007	CITY	VISITORS/ IN THOUSANDS ('000)	% CHANGE FROM 2007
New York	8,413	+6.4	New York NY	8,211	+7.4
California	5,296	+2.1	Los Angeles CA	2,788	+5.1
Florida	5,246	+12.0	San Francisco CA	2,610	+15.0
Nevada	2,103	+18.9	Miami FL	2,585	+10.4
Hawaii	1,825	−2.1	Orlando FL	2,433	+18.4
Illinois	1,419	+21.2	Las Vegas NV	2,027	+17.8
Massachusetts	1,267	+8.2	Oahu/Honolulu HI	1,495	−3.7
Guam[3]	1,191	+8.4	Washington DC	1,470	+23.0
Texas	1,090	+8.7	Chicago IL	1,368	+19.3
New Jersey	1,039	+8.7	Boston MA	1,115	+3.7

[1]Data for China include Hong Kong. [2]Excludes Canadian and Mexican visitors to the US. [3]Guam is a US territory. If Guam were excluded, Pennsylvania would rank 10th on the list with about 1,014,000 overseas visitors.

Customs Exemptions

Upon returning to the US from a foreign country, travelers must pay duty on items acquired outside the US. If the value of the items is greater than the allowable exemption, duty must be paid on the excess amount. The general exemption is US$800 per person, but it can also be US$200 or US$1,600 in certain situations. Exemptions apply if the items are in the traveler's possession, are for the traveler's own use, and are declared to US Customs. The traveler must also have been out of the country for at least 48 hours (unless returning from Mexico or the US Virgin Islands) and must not have used any part of the exemption within the past 30 days; if one or both of these requirements does not apply, the allowable exemption drops to US$200 per person and includes additional restrictions. The general exemption of US$800 includes no more than 200 previously exported cigarettes, 100 cigars, and no more than one liter of alcoholic beverages. Cuban tobacco products are prohibited unless purchased in Cuba on authorized travel. Family members may combine their total exemptions in a joint declaration. The US$800 exemption also applies to travelers returning from any of 28 countries and dependencies in the Caribbean Basin or Andean Region but may include two liters of alcoholic beverages, as long as one of the liters was produced in one of these. The 28 countries and dependencies are Antigua and Barbuda, Aruba, The Bahamas, Barbados, Belize, Bolivia, the British Virgin Islands, Colombia, Costa Rica, Dominica, the Dominican Republic, Ecuador, El Salvador, Grenada, Guatemala, Guyana, Haiti, Honduras, Jamaica, Montserrat, the Netherlands Antilles, Nicaragua, Panama, Peru, Saint Kitts and Nevis, Saint Lucia, Saint Vincent and the Grenadines, and Trinidad and Tobago. A US$1,600 exemption applies to travelers returning from a trip that included the US Virgin Islands, American Samoa, or Guam and includes 1,000 cigarettes and five liters of alcoholic beverages; of this amount, 800 cigarettes and one liter of alcohol must be from one of the US islands. The US$1,600 exemption also applies to multi-country travel (such as a cruise) to a US possession and any of the 28 Caribbean Basin and Andean Region countries and dependencies, as long as no more than US$800 worth of goods was purchased in those locations.

Gifts valued at US$100 or less (US$200 or less for gifts sent from American Samoa, Guam, or the US Virgin Islands) may be sent to the US without duty as long as no single person receives more than this value within a single day. Alcoholic beverages may not be sent by mail; tobacco and alcohol-based perfumes worth more than US$5 are not included in the exemption. Travelers may ship goods home for personal use without duty if the value of the goods is US$200 or less and no single person receives more than this value within a single day. This personal exemption increases to US$1,600 for goods purchased and shipped from American Samoa, Guam, or the US Virgin Islands.

Customs information is available from the Customs and Border Protection Web site at <www.cbp.gov/xp/cgov/travel>.

US State Department Travel Warnings

The State Department issues Travel Warnings when it is believed best for Americans to avoid certain countries in the interest of safety. It also releases Travel Alerts of more short-term hazards, such as terrorist threats or political coups, that may endanger American travelers; these include an expiration date when the announcement need no longer be heeded. The department also makes available Consular Information Sheets for all countries, which may discuss safety conditions not severe enough to require a travel warning. Current information can be found at <http://travel.state.gov>.

Travel Warnings were in effect on 2 Jul 2009 for the following countries: Afghanistan, Algeria, Burundi, the Central African Republic, Chad, Colombia, the Democratic Republic of the Congo, Côte d'Ivoire, Eritrea, Georgia, Haiti, Iran, Iraq, Israel (including the West Bank and the Gaza Strip), Kenya, Lebanon, Madagascar, Mali, Nepal, Nigeria, Pakistan, the Philippines, Saudi Arabia, Somalia, Sri Lanka, The Sudan, Syria, Uzbekistan, and Yemen.

Travel Alerts in effect on the same day and set to expire on various dates from July through December 2009 included advisories for China, Gabon, Guinea-Bissau, Honduras, and Mexico and a general notice alerting US citizens to the dangers of hurricane season in the Atlantic and Pacific oceans, the Caribbean Sea, and the Gulf of Mexico. A worldwide caution on the continuing threat of terrorist acts and violence against Americans was also in effect.

Employment

US Employment by Gender and Occupation

Detail may not add to total given because of rounding. Source: US Bureau of Labor Statistics.

OCCUPATION	WORKERS 16 YEARS AND OLDER (NUMBERS IN '000)					
	TOTAL		MEN		WOMEN	
	2007	2008	2007	2008	2007	2008
management, professional, and related occupations	51,788	52,761	25,593	25,948	26,195	26,813
management, business, and financial-operations occupations	21,577	22,059	12,375	12,647	9,203	9,412
management occupations	15,486	15,852	9,686	9,925	5,800	5,926
business and financial-operations occupations	6,207	6,091	2,688	2,721	3,403	3,486

US Employment by Gender and Occupation (continued)

OCCUPATION	WORKERS 16 YEARS AND OLDER (NUMBERS IN '000)					
	TOTAL		MEN		WOMEN	
	2007	2008	2007	2008	2007	2008
management, professional, and related occupations (cont.)						
professional and related occupations	30,210	30,702	13,218	13,301	16,992	17,401
computer and mathematical occupations	3,441	3,676	2,560	2,765	881	911
architecture and engineering occupations	2,932	2,931	2,511	2,536	421	395
life, physical, and social-science occupations	1,382	1,307	792	704	591	603
community and social-services occupations	2,265	2,293	890	909	1,375	1,383
legal occupations	1,668	1,671	809	803	858	867
education, training, and library occupations	8,485	8,605	2,267	2,234	6,218	6,371
arts, design, entertainment, sports, and media occupations	2,789	2,820	1,476	1,471	1,313	1,349
health-care-practitioner and technical occupations	7,248	7,399	1,913	1,878	5,335	5,521
service occupations	24,137	24,451	10,337	10,471	13,800	13,980
health-care-support occupations	3,138	3,212	338	359	2,800	2,853
protective-service occupations	3,071	3,047	2,380	2,352	691	695
food-preparation and serving-related occupations	7,699	7,824	3,354	3,443	4,345	4,381
building- and grounds-cleaning and maintenance occupations	5,469	5,445	3,280	3,254	2,189	2,192
personal-care and service occupations	4,760	4,923	986	1,064	3,774	3,859
sales and office occupations	36,212	35,544	13,264	13,067	22,948	22,477
sales and related occupations	16,698	16,295	8,424	8,221	8,275	8,073
office and administrative-support occupations	19,513	19,249	4,840	4,845	14,673	14,404
natural-resources, construction, and maintenance occupations	15,740	14,806	15,078	14,181	662	626
farming, fishing, and forestry occupations	960	988	759	780	201	208
construction and extraction occupations	9,535	8,667	9,276	8,448	258	219
installation, maintenance, and repair occupations	5,245	5,152	5,043	4,953	202	199
production, transportation, and material-moving occupations	18,171	17,800	13,983	13,820	4,188	3,980
production occupations	9,395	8,973	6,563	6,313	2,832	2,661
transportation and material-moving occupations	8,776	8,827	7,420	7,507	1,355	1,319
total	146,047	145,362	78,254	77,486	67,792	67,876

US Federal Minimum Wage Rates, 1953–2009

The table shows the actual minimum wage for the year in question and the value of that minimum wage adjusted for inflation in the year 2009. Source: US Bureau of Labor Statistics.

	minimum wage			minimum wage			minimum wage	
YEAR	US DOLLARS	2009 DOLLARS	YEAR	US DOLLARS	2009 DOLLARS	YEAR	US DOLLARS	2009 DOLLARS
1953	0.75	5.99	1958	1.00	7.38	1963	1.25	8.71
1954	0.75	5.95	1959	1.00	7.33	1964	1.25	8.60
1955	0.75	5.97	1960	1.00	7.20	1965	1.25	8.46
1956	1.00	7.84	1961	1.15	8.20	1966	1.25	8.23
1957	1.00	7.59	1962	1.15	8.12	1967	1.40	8.94

US Federal Minimum Wage Rates, 1953–2009 (continued)

	minimum wage			minimum wage			minimum wage	
YEAR	US DOLLARS	2009 DOLLARS	YEAR	US DOLLARS	2009 DOLLARS	YEAR	US DOLLARS	2009 DOLLARS
1968	1.60	9.80	1982	3.35	7.40	1996	4.75	6.46
1969	1.60	9.30	1983	3.35	7.17	1997	5.15	6.84
1970	1.60	8.79	1984	3.35	6.88	1998	5.15	6.74
1971	1.60	8.42	1985	3.35	6.64	1999	5.15	6.59
1972	1.60	8.16	1986	3.35	6.52	2000	5.15	6.38
1973	1.60	7.68	1987	3.35	6.29	2001	5.15	6.20
1974	2.00	8.65	1988	3.35	6.04	2002	5.15	6.10
1975	2.10	8.32	1989	3.35	5.76	2003	5.15	5.97
1976	2.30	8.62	1990	3.80	6.20	2004	5.15	5.81
1977	2.30	8.09	1991	4.25	6.65	2005	5.15	5.62
1978	2.65	8.67	1992	4.25	6.46	2006	5.15	5.45
1979	2.90	8.52	1993	4.25	6.27	2007	5.85	6.02
1980	3.10	8.02	1994	4.25	6.12	2008	6.55	6.49
1981	3.35	7.86	1995	4.25	5.95	2009	7.25	7.25

US Workers Earning the Minimum Wage

This table refers to wage and salary workers who were paid hourly rates in 2008, excluding the incorporated self-employed. The prevailing federal minimum wage was US$5.85/hour until 24 Jul 2008 and US$6.55 thereafter. Workers earning less than minimum wage may have been working in jobs that are exempted from the minimum-wage provision of the Fair Labor Standards Act. Numbers are in thousands ('000).

Source: US Bureau of Labor Statistics.

WORKER CHARACTERISTICS	TOTAL NUMBER OF WORKERS	BELOW MINIMUM WAGE	AT MINIMUM WAGE	TOTAL NUMBER OF WORKERS AT OR BELOW MINIMUM WAGE	
				NUMBER	%
age					
16–24 years	15,680	961	161	1,122	7.2
25 years and over	59,626	979	125	1,104	1.9
total (16 years and over)	75,305	1,940	286	2,226	3.0
men					
16–24 years	7,978	326	58	384	4.8
25 years and over	29,356	313	32	345	1.2
16 years and over	37,334	638	90	728	2.0
women					
16–24 years	7,701	635	103	738	9.6
25 years and over	30,270	666	93	759	2.5
16 years and over	37,972	1,302	196	1,497	3.9
race and Hispanic or Latino ethnicity[1]					
white (16 years and over)	60,464	1,568	215	1,783	2.9
black (16 years and over)	9,866	259	49	308	3.1
Asian (16 years and over)	2,844	58	11	69	2.4
Hispanic or Latino (16 years and over)	13,070	285	39	324	2.5
full- and part-time workers[2]					
full-time	56,837	778	95	873	1.5
part-time	18,334	1,162	191	1,353	7.4

[1]Hispanics may be of any race and are also included in white, black, and Asian population groups. For this reason, data within this category do not add up to total. [2]Full- and part-time workers are distinguished by the number of hours worked. These data do not add up to total because of a small number of multiple jobholders whose status on the principal job is unknown.

Did you know? The Michelin guides were initiated by André Michelin, whose aim was to promote tourism by car and thus to support his tire company. His first *Red Guide* (1900) listed French towns of interest that were large enough to contain hotels and garages. It included the prototypical rating symbols for which Michelin became famous. A select number of restaurants that provide "cooking worth a special journey" are indicated by the presence of three stars.

Median Income by Educational and Social Variables

This table refers to persons who worked full-time throughout the year and are 15 years old and older as of March of the following year. Median income dollar amounts are not adjusted for inflation. N/A means not available. Source: US Census Bureau.

	median income (US$) males				median income (US$) females			
	1980	1990	2000	2007	1980	1990	2000	2007
full-time workers	19,173	28,979	38,891	46,224	11,591	20,591	29,123	36,167
educational level[1]								
less than 9th grade	N/A	10,319	14,131	16,625	N/A	6,268	8,546	10,539
9th to 12th grade (no diploma)	N/A	14,736	18,915	20,643	N/A	7,055	10,063	11,982
high school graduate	N/A	21,546	27,480	31,337	N/A	10,818	15,153	18,162
some college (no degree)	N/A	26,591	33,319	37,447	N/A	13,963	20,166	23,532
associate degree	N/A	29,358	38,026	43,006	N/A	17,364	23,124	27,668
bachelor's degree	N/A	36,067	49,080	56,826	N/A	20,967	30,418	36,167
master's degree	N/A	43,125	59,732	71,097	N/A	29,747	40,619	48,077
professional degree	N/A	63,741	83,701	100,000	N/A	34,064	46,084	61,875
doctoral degree	N/A	51,845	71,271	86,171	N/A	37,242	51,460	61,554
race and origin[2,3]								
white	13,328	21,170	29,797	35,141	4,947	10,317	16,079	21,069
white (non-Hispanic)	13,681	21,958	31,508	37,373	4,980	10,581	16,665	21,687
black	8,009	12,868	21,343	25,822	4,580	8,328	15,881	19,752
Hispanic origin	9,659	13,470	19,498	24,451	4,405	7,532	12,248	16,748
age[2]								
15 to 24 years	4,597	6,319	9,546	11,209	3,124	4,902	7,360	8,959
25 to 34 years	15,580	21,393	30,254	32,875	6,973	12,589	21,049	25,884
35 to 44 years	20,037	29,773	37,922	45,018	6,465	14,504	22,077	27,702
45 to 54 years	19,974	31,007	41,039	45,849	6,403	14,230	23,732	29,453
55 to 64 years	15,914	24,804	34,189	42,129	4,926	9,400	16,920	25,262
65 years and over	7,339	14,183	19,411	24,323	4,226	8,044	11,023	14,021
all workers over age 14	12,530	20,293	28,343	33,196	4,920	10,070	16,063	20,922

[1]The income figures for the various educational levels are for workers 25 years old and over. Before 1991, the level of education categories used by the US Census Bureau differed from the categories presented in this table. Because of this, the 1980 figures for the median income by educational level are not completely comparable with the figures for later years. The figures presented in the 1990 column for educational levels are actually for 1991, the first year the educational categories listed in this table were used by the US Census Bureau. [2]The figures presented in the 1980 column for race and origin and age pertain to civilian workers only. [3]Hispanic people may be of any race.

The 20 US Metropolitan Areas with the Highest Average Annual Per Capita Incomes

Personal income is income received from all sources, including wages and salaries, property rental, transfers, and interest and dividends. Source: US Bureau of Economic Analysis.

METROPOLITAN AREA	ANNUAL INCOME (US$) 2006	2007	INCOME CHANGE (%)	METROPOLITAN AREA	ANNUAL INCOME (US$) 2006	2007	INCOME CHANGE (%)
Bridgeport, CT[1]	74,281	80,192	8.0	Midland, TX	48,644	52,294	7.5
Naples, FL[2]	57,446	61,788	7.6	Napa, CA	47,491	50,817	7.0
San Francisco, CA[3]	57,747	61,337	6.2	Seattle-Tacoma-Bellevue, WA	45,369	48,499	6.9
San Jose, CA[4]	55,020	58,716	6.7	Bradenton-Sarasota-Venice, FL	46,486	48,498	4.3
Sebastian, FL[5]	54,045	58,144	7.6	Barnstable, MA	45,445	48,468	6.7
Washington, DC, VA, MD, WV[6]	51,868	54,211	4.5	Santa Cruz–Watsonville, CA	45,194	47,923	6.0
Boston, MA, NH[7]	50,542	53,763	6.4	Hartford, CT[9]	44,835	47,641	6.3
New York, NY, NJ, PA[8]	49,789	53,423	7.3	Casper, WY	44,152	47,354	7.3
Boulder, CO	49,628	52,438	5.7	Reno-Sparks, NV	44,337	46,734	5.4
Trenton-Ewing, NJ	49,847	52,388	5.1	Minneapolis, MN, WI[10]	44,237	46,458	5.0

[1]Includes Stamford and Norwalk. [2]Includes Marco Island. [3]Includes Oakland and Fremont. [4]Includes Sunnyvale and Santa Clara. [5]Includes Vero Beach. [6]Includes Arlington and Alexandria. [7]Includes Cambridge and Quincy. [8]Includes Long Island. [9]Includes West Hartford and East Hartford. [10]Includes St. Paul and Bloomington.

US Civilian Federal Employment

Source: Statistical Abstract of the United States: 2009.

AGENCIES	1970	1980	1990	2000	2007
legislative branch	29,939	39,710	37,495	31,157	29,573
judicial branch	6,879	15,178	23,605	32,186	32,921
executive branch	2,829,495	2,820,978	3,067,167	2,644,758	2,632,435
Executive Office of the President	997	1,886	1,731	1,658	1,719
executive departments	1,772,363	1,716,970	2,065,542	1,592,200	1,696,893
State	40,042	23,497	25,288	27,983	34,657
Treasury	90,683	124,663	158,655	143,508	111,577
Defense	1,169,173	960,116	1,034,152	676,268	673,722
Justice	40,075	56,327	83,932	125,970	106,946
Interior	71,671	77,357	77,679	73,818	70,256
Agriculture	114,309	129,139	122,594	104,466	99,629
Commerce	36,124	48,563	69,920	47,652	40,163
Labor	10,928	23,400	17,727	16,040	15,855
Health and Human Services	110,186	155,662	123,959	62,605	61,217
Housing and Urban Development	15,046	16,964	13,596	10,319	9,718
Transportation	66,970	72,361	67,364	63,598	53,536
Energy	7,156	21,557	17,731	15,692	14,696
Education	0	7,364	4,771	4,734	4,146
Veterans Affairs	169,241	228,285	248,174	219,547	245,537
Homeland Security	0	0	0	0	155,397
independent agencies[1,2]	1,056,135	1,102,122	999,894	1,050,900	933,833
Board of Governors of the Federal Reserve System	N/A	N/A	1,525	2,372	1,874
Environmental Protection Agency	0	14,715	17,123	18,036	19,153
Equal Employment Opportunity Commission	797	3,515	2,880	2,780	2,191
Federal Communications Commission	N/A	N/A	1,778	1,965	1,827
Federal Deposit Insurance Corporation	2,462	3,520	17,641	6,958	4,573
Federal Trade Commission	N/A	N/A	988	1,019	1,094
General Services Administration[3]	37,661	37,654	20,277	14,334	12,099
National Aeronautics and Space Administration	30,674	23,714	24,872	18,819	19,378
National Archives and Records Administration	N/A	N/A	3,120	2,702	2,973
National Labor Relations Board	N/A	N/A	2,263	2,054	1,772
National Science Foundation	N/A	N/A	1,318	1,247	1,356
Nuclear Regulatory Commission	0	3,283	3,353	2,858	3,609
Office of Personnel Management	5,513	8,280	6,636	3,780	5,291
Peace Corps	N/A	N/A	1,178	1,065	1,077
Railroad Retirement Board	N/A	N/A	1,772	1,176	990
Securities and Exchange Commission	N/A	N/A	2,302	2,955	3,534
Small Business Administration	4,397	5,804	5,128	4,150	4,234
Smithsonian Institution	2,547	4,403	5,092	5,065	5,008
Social Security Administration	N/A	N/A	N/A	64,474	62,769
Tennessee Valley Authority	23,785	51,714	28,392	13,145	12,293
US Information Agency	10,156	8,138	8,555	2,436	2,046
US International Development Cooperation Agency	14,493	6,152	4,698	2,552	2,761
US Postal Service	721,183	660,014	816,886	860,726	753,254
total, all agencies[1]	2,866,313	2,875,866	3,128,267	2,708,101	2,694,929

N/A means not available. [1]Includes other agencies not shown separately. [2]The Defense Intelligence Agency was excluded as of November 1984 and the National Imagery and Mapping Agency as of October 1996. Entries for 1990, 2000, and 2007 exclude the Central Intelligence Agency and the National Security Agency. [3]Entries for 1970 and 1980 include the National Archives and Records Administration, which became an independent agency in 1985.

Strikes and Lockouts in the US

Strikes and lockouts are referred to as work stoppages by the Bureau of Labor Statistics. This table covers work stoppages since 1951 involving 1,000 workers or more. The number of workers and stoppages are for stoppages begun during that year. The number of days of work lost pertains to all strikes or lockouts in effect during the year, whether they began in that year or not. Percentage of working time pertains to all workers except those employed in private households, forestry, or fisheries. A minus sign (−) indicates a percentage less than 0.005.

Source: US Bureau of Labor Statistics.

Strikes and Lockouts in the US (continued)

YEAR	strikes and lockouts NUMBER	WORKERS INVOLVED ('000)	work time lost DAYS LOST ('000)	% OF WORKING TIME	YEAR	strikes and lockouts NUMBER	WORKERS INVOLVED ('000)	work time lost DAYS LOST ('000)	% OF WORKING TIME
1951	415	1,462	15,070	0.12	1980	187	795	20,844	0.09
1952	470	2,746	48,820	0.38	1981	145	729	16,908	0.07
1953	437	1,623	18,130	0.14	1982	96	656	9,061	0.04
1954	265	1,075	16,630	0.13	1983	81	909	17,461	0.08
1955	363	2,055	21,180	0.16	1984	62	376	8,499	0.04
1956	287	1,370	26,840	0.20	1985	54	324	7,079	0.03
1957	279	887	10,340	0.07	1986	69	533	11,861	0.05
1958	332	1,587	17,900	0.13	1987	46	174	4,481	0.02
1959	245	1,381	60,850	0.43	1988	40	118	4,381	0.02
1960	222	896	13,260	0.09	1989	51	452	16,996	0.07
1961	195	1,031	10,140	0.07	1990	44	185	5,926	0.02
1962	211	793	11,760	0.08	1991	40	392	4,584	0.02
1963	181	512	10,020	0.07	1992	35	364	3,989	0.01
1964	246	1,183	16,220	0.11	1993	35	182	3,981	0.01
1965	268	999	15,140	0.10	1994	45	322	5,021	0.02
1966	321	1,300	16,000	0.10	1995	31	192	5,771	0.02
1967	381	2,192	31,320	0.18	1996	37	273	4,889	0.02
1968	392	1,855	35,367	0.20	1997	29	339	4,497	0.01
1969	412	1,576	29,397	0.16	1998	34	387	5,116	0.02
1970	381	2,468	52,761	0.29	1999	17	73	1,996	0.01
1971	298	2,516	35,538	0.19	2000	39	394	20,419	0.06
1972	250	975	16,764	0.09	2001	29	99	1,151	–
1973	317	1,400	16,260	0.08	2002	19	46	660	–
1974	424	1,796	31,809	0.16	2003	14	129	4,091	0.01
1975	235	965	17,563	0.09	2004	17	171	3,344	0.01
1976	231	1,519	23,962	0.12	2005	22	100	1,736	0.01
1977	298	1,212	21,258	0.10	2006	20	70	2,688	0.01
1978	219	1,006	23,774	0.11	2007	21	189	1,265	–
1979	235	1,021	20,409	0.09	2008	15	72	1,954	0.01

US Trade Union Membership

Numbers are in thousands ('000). N/A means not available. Source: US Bureau of Labor Statistics.

YEAR	NUMBER OF UNION MEMBERS	% OF TOTAL LABOR FORCE	YEAR	NUMBER OF UNION MEMBERS	% OF TOTAL LABOR FORCE	YEAR	NUMBER OF UNION MEMBERS	% OF TOTAL LABOR FORCE
1900[1]	791	N/A	1940	8,717	26.9	1980	20,095	23.0
1905	1,918	N/A	1945	14,322	35.5	1985	16,996	18.0
1910	2,116	N/A	1950	14,300[3]	31.5	1990	16,740	16.1
1915	2,560	N/A	1955	16,802	33.2	1995	16,360	14.9
1920	5,034	N/A	1960	17,049	31.4	2000	16,258	13.5
1925	3,566	N/A	1965	17,299	28.4	2005	15,685	12.5
1930[2]	3,401	11.6	1970	19,381	27.4	2007	15,670	12.1
1935	3,584	13.2	1977[4]	19,335	23.8	2008	16,098	12.4

[1]Data from 1900 to 1925 include Canadian members whose union headquarters were in the US.   [2]Agricultural workers were not included as part of the total labor force for the years from 1930 to 1970.   [3]Rounded to nearest hundred thousand.   [4]Data for 1975 are not available. Data for 1977 on include only employed union members.

US Unemployment Rates

Unemployment rates of the civilian labor force ages 16 years and older. Source: US Bureau of Labor Statistics.

YEAR	UNEMPLOYMENT RATE (%)	YEAR	UNEMPLOYMENT RATE (%)	YEAR	UNEMPLOYMENT RATE (%)	YEAR	UNEMPLOYMENT RATE (%)
1949	5.9	1955	4.4	1961	6.7	1967	3.8
1950	5.3	1956	4.1	1962	5.5	1968	3.6
1951	3.3	1957	4.3	1963	5.7	1969	3.5
1952	3.0	1958	6.8	1964	5.2	1970	4.9
1953	2.9	1959	5.5	1965	4.5	1971	5.9
1954	5.5	1960	5.5	1966	3.8	1972	5.6

US Unemployment Rates (continued)

YEAR	UNEMPLOYMENT RATE (%)	YEAR	UNEMPLOYMENT RATE (%)	YEAR	UNEMPLOYMENT RATE (%)	YEAR	UNEMPLOYMENT RATE (%)
1973	4.9	1982	9.7	1991	6.8	2000	4.0
1974	5.6	1983	9.6	1992	7.5	2001	4.7
1975	8.5	1984	7.5	1993	6.9	2002	5.8
1976	7.7	1985	7.2	1994	6.1	2003	6.0
1977	7.1	1986	7.0	1995	5.6	2004	5.5
1978	6.1	1987	6.2	1996	5.4	2005	5.1
1979	5.8	1988	5.5	1997	4.9	2006	4.6
1980	7.1	1989	5.3	1998	4.5	2007	4.6
1981	7.6	1990	5.6	1999	4.2	2008	5.8

Social Characteristics of the Unemployed in the US

Unemployment as a % of the civilian labor force. N/A means not available. Source: US Bureau of Labor Statistics.

SOCIAL CHARACTERISTICS	UNEMPLOYMENT RATES BY YEAR (%)									
	1975	1980	1985	1990	1995	2000	2005	2006	2007	2008
age (both sexes)										
16 and over[1]	19.9	17.8	18.6	15.5	17.3	13.1	5.1	4.6	4.6	5.8
25-54[2]	6.0	5.1	5.6	4.4	4.3	3.0	4.1	3.8	3.7	4.8
sex (16 years and older)[3]										
men	6.8	5.9	6.2	5.0	4.8	3.3	5.1	4.6	4.7	6.1
women	8.0	6.4	6.6	4.9	4.9	3.6	5.1	4.6	4.5	5.4
race/ethnicity										
white	7.8	6.3	6.2	4.8	4.9	3.5	4.4	4.0	4.1	5.2
black	14.8	14.3	15.1	11.4	10.4	7.6	10.0	8.9	8.3	10.1
Hispanic[4]	12.2	10.1	10.5	8.2	9.3	5.7	6.0	5.2	5.6	7.6
family										
women maintaining families	10.0	9.2	10.4	8.3	8.0	5.9	7.8	N/A	N/A	N/A
married men, spouse present	5.1	4.2	4.3	3.4	3.3	2.0	2.8	2.4	2.5	N/A
overall unemployment	8.5	7.1	7.2	5.6	5.6	4.0	5.1	4.6	4.6	5.8

[1]Data for ages 16–19 until 2005. [2]Data for ages 25 and older until 2005. [3]Data for ages 20 years and older until 2005. [4]Hispanics may be of any race and are included in both the white and black racial categories in this table.

US Work-Related Fatalities by Cause

Totals for major categories may include some subcategories not listed in the table. Detail may not add to total given because of rounding. Source: US Bureau of Labor Statistics.

CAUSE OF FATALITY	2001-05 NUMBER (AVG.)	2007 NUMBER	2007 (%)
transportation incidents	2,451	2,351	41.6
highway	1,394	1,414	25.0
collision between vehicles, mobile equipment	686	687	12.1
moving in same direction	151	164	2.9
moving in opposite directions, oncoming	254	281	5.0
moving in intersection	137	125	2.2
vehicle struck stationary object or equipment	337	368	6.5
noncollision	335	308	5.4
jackknifed or overturned—no collision	274	271	4.8
nonhighway (farm, industrial premises)	335	296	5.2
overturned	175	166	2.9
worker struck by a vehicle	369	345	6.1
railway accident	60	49	0.9
water vehicle accident	82	71	1.3
aircraft accident	206	174	3.1

US Work-Related Fatalities by Cause (continued)

CAUSE OF FATALITY	2001–05 NUMBER (AVG.)	2007 NUMBER	(%)
assaults and violent acts	850	864	15.3
homicides	602	628	11.1
shooting	465	503	8.9
stabbing	60	45	0.8
self-inflicted injury	207	196	3.5
contact with objects and equipment	952	920	16.3
struck by object	560	504	8.9
struck by falling object	345	328	5.8
struck by flying object	50	58	1.0
caught in or compressed by equipment or objects	256	296	5.2
caught in running equipment or machinery	128	140	2.5
caught in or crushed in collapsing materials	118	108	1.9
falls	763	847	15.0
fall to lower level	669	746	13.2
fall from ladder	125	135	2.4
fall from roof	154	163	2.9
fall from scaffold, staging	87	89	1.6
fall on same level	73	81	1.4
exposure to harmful substances or environments	498	497	8.8
contact with electric current	265	212	3.7
contact with overhead power lines	118	94	1.7
contact with temperature extremes	44	40	0.7
exposure to caustic, noxious, or allergenic substances	114	161	2.8
inhalation of substance	56	64	1.1
oxygen deficiency	74	82	1.4
drowning, submersion	54	62	1.1
fires and explosions	174	152	2.7
total	5,704	5,657	100

Consumer Prices

US Consumer Price Index, 1914–2008

This table presents the annual change in the Consumer Price Index (CPI) since 1914. The CPI is used as an indicator of price changes in the goods and services purchased by US consumers. The information provided is based on the purchases of a specific group of urban consumers who serve as a sample population representing more than 80% of the total US population. Each annual CPI is compared with the average index level of 100, which is a base number that represents the average price level for the 36-month period covering the years 1982, 1983, and 1984. A minus sign indicates a decrease.

Source: US Bureau of Labor Statistics.

YEAR	ANNUAL CPI	% ANNUAL CHANGE IN CPI	YEAR	ANNUAL CPI	% ANNUAL CHANGE IN CPI	YEAR	ANNUAL CPI	ANNUAL CHANGE IN CPI
1914	10.0		1929	17.1	0.0	1944	17.6	1.7
1915	10.1	1.0	1930	16.7	−2.3	1945	18.0	2.3
1916	10.9	7.9	1931	15.2	−9.0	1946	19.5	8.3
1917	12.8	17.4	1932	13.7	−9.9	1947	22.3	14.4
1918	15.1	18.0	1933	13.0	−5.1	1948	24.1	8.1
1919	17.3	14.6	1934	13.4	3.1	1949	23.8	−1.2
1920	20.0	15.6	1935	13.7	2.2	1950	24.1	1.3
1921	17.9	−10.5	1936	13.9	1.5	1951	26.0	7.9
1922	16.8	−6.1	1937	14.4	3.6	1952	26.5	1.9
1923	17.1	1.8	1939	13.9	−1.4	1953	26.7	0.8
1924	17.1	0.0	1938	14.1	−2.1	1954	26.9	0.7
1925	17.5	2.3	1940	14.0	0.7	1955	26.8	−0.4
1926	17.7	1.1	1941	14.7	5.0	1956	27.2	1.5
1927	17.4	−1.7	1942	16.3	10.9	1957	28.1	3.3
1928	17.1	−1.7	1943	17.3	6.1	1958	28.9	2.8

US Consumer Price Index, 1914–2008 (continued)

YEAR	ANNUAL CPI	% ANNUAL CHANGE IN CPI	YEAR	ANNUAL CPI	% ANNUAL CHANGE IN CPI	YEAR	ANNUAL CPI	% ANNUAL CHANGE IN CPI
1959	29.1	0.7	1976	56.9	5.8	1993	144.5	3.0
1960	29.6	1.7	1977	60.6	6.5	1994	148.2	2.6
1961	29.9	1.0	1978	65.2	7.6	1995	152.4	2.8
1962	30.2	1.0	1979	72.6	11.3	1996	156.9	3.0
1963	30.6	1.3	1980	82.4	13.5	1997	160.5	2.3
1964	31.0	1.3	1981	90.9	10.3	1998	163.0	1.6
1965	31.5	1.6	1982	96.5	6.2	1999	166.6	2.2
1966	32.4	2.9	1983	99.6	3.2	2000	172.2	3.4
1967	33.4	3.1	1984	103.9	4.3	2001	177.1	2.8
1968	34.8	4.2	1985	107.6	3.6	2002	179.9	1.6
1969	36.7	5.5	1986	109.6	1.9	2003	184.0	2.3
1970	38.8	5.7	1987	113.6	3.6	2004	188.9	2.7
1971	40.5	4.4	1988	118.3	4.1	2005	195.3	3.4
1972	41.8	3.2	1989	124.0	4.8	2006	201.6	3.0
1973	44.4	6.2	1990	130.7	5.4	2007	207.3	2.8
1974	49.3	11.0	1991	136.2	4.2	2008	215.3	3.8
1975	53.8	9.1	1992	140.3	3.0			

US Consumer Price Indexes by Item Group, 1975–2008

The information provided is based on the purchases of a specific group of urban consumers who serve as a sample population representing more than 80% of the total US population. Each annual CPI is compared with the average index level of 100, which is a base number that represents the average price level for the 36-month period covering the years 1982, 1983, and 1984. A minus sign indicates a decrease.

Source: US Bureau of Labor Statistics.

ITEM GROUP	CONSUMER PRICE INDEX								
	1975	1980	1985	1990	1995	2000	2005	2007	2008
all items	53.8	82.4	107.6	130.7	152.4	172.2	195.3	207.3	215.3
commodities	58.2	86.0	105.4	122.8	136.4	149.2	160.2	167.5	174.8
energy	42.1	86.0	101.6	102.1	105.2	124.6	177.1	207.7	236.7
food	59.8	86.8	105.6	132.4	148.4	167.8	190.7	202.9	214.1
shelter	48.8	81.0	109.8	140.0	165.7	193.4	224.4	240.6	246.7
transportation	50.1	83.1	106.4	120.5	139.1	153.3	173.9	184.7	195.5
medical care	47.5	74.9	113.5	162.8	220.5	260.8	323.2	351.1	364.1
apparel	72.5	90.9	105.0	124.1	132.0	129.6	119.5	119.0	118.9

ITEM GROUP	% CHANGE IN CPI[1]								
	1975	1980	1985	1990	1995	2000	2005	2007	2008
all items	9.1	13.5	3.6	5.4	2.8	3.4	3.4	2.8	3.8
commodities	8.8	12.3	2.1	5.2	1.9	3.3	3.6	2.1	4.3
energy	10.5	30.9	0.7	8.3	0.6	16.9	17.0	5.5	13.9
food	8.5	8.6	2.3	5.8	2.8	2.3	2.4	4.0	5.5
shelter	9.9	17.6	5.6	5.4	3.2	3.3	2.6	3.7	2.5
transportation	9.4	17.9	2.6	5.6	3.6	6.2	6.6	2.1	5.9
medical care	12.0	11.0	6.3	9.0	4.5	4.1	4.2	4.4	3.7
apparel	4.5	7.1	2.8	4.6	-1.0	-1.3	-0.7	-0.4	-0.1

[1]Annual percent change from the preceding year.

US Budget

US Public Debt

In order to fund governmental operations, the Department of the Treasury borrows money by selling Treasury bills, US savings bonds, and other securities to the public. The money borrowed by the Treasury is referred to as the public debt. A broader measure of the federal debt is known as the gross federal debt. It consists of the public debt plus money borrowed by federal agencies. The GDP is the gross domestic product.

Source: US Office of Management and Budget.

US Public Debt (continued)

END OF FISCAL YEAR	PUBLIC DEBT (IN US$ MILLIONS)	% OF GDP	GROSS FEDERAL DEBT (IN US$ MILLIONS)	% OF GDP	END OF FISCAL YEAR	PUBLIC DEBT (IN US$ MILLIONS)	% OF GDP	GROSS FEDERAL DEBT (IN US$ MILLIONS)	% OF GDP
1940	42,772	44.2	50,696	52.4	1990	2,411,558	42.0	3,206,290	55.9
1950	219,023	80.1	256,853	93.9	2000	3,409,804	35.1	5,628,700	58.0
1960	236,840	45.6	290,525	56.0	2006	4,828,973	37.0	8,451,351	64.7
1970	283,198	28.0	380,921	37.6	2007	5,049,306	36.7	9,007,653	65.5
1980	711,923	26.1	909,041	33.3	2008	5,808,692	40.0	10,024,725	69.1

US Governmental Spending, 1800–2008

Entries for the years prior to 1933 are based on the administrative budget concept rather than on the unified budget concept. For a discussion of the unified budget concept and related topics, see <www.fms.treas.gov/bulletin/b2008-2ffotxt.doc>. The figures are in thousands ('000). A minus sign indicates a deficit.

Source: US Office of Management and Budget.

YEAR[1]	FEDERAL INCOME	FEDERAL SPENDING	SURPLUS OR DEFICIT	YEAR[1]	FEDERAL INCOME	FEDERAL SPENDING	SURPLUS OR DEFICIT
1800	10,849	10,786	63	1848	35,736	45,377	−9,641
1801	12,935	9,395	3,541	1849	31,208	45,052	−13,844
1802	14,996	7,862	7,134	1850	43,603	39,543	4,060
1803	11,064	7,852	3,212	1851	52,559	47,709	4,850
1804	11,826	8,719	3,107	1852	49,847	44,195	5,652
1805	13,561	10,506	3,054	1853	61,587	48,184	13,403
1806	15,560	9,804	5,756	1854	73,800	58,045	15,755
1807	16,398	8,354	8,044	1855	65,351	59,743	5,608
1808	17,061	9,932	7,128	1856	74,057	69,571	4,486
1809	7,773	10,281	−2,507	1857	68,965	67,796	1,170
1810	9,384	8,157	1,228	1858	46,655	74,185	−27,530
1811	14,424	8,058	6,365	1859	53,486	69,071	−15,585
1812	9,801	20,281	−10,480	1860	56,065	63,131	−7,066
1813	14,340	31,682	−17,341	1861	41,510	66,547	−25,037
1814	11,182	34,721	−23,539	1862	51,987	474,762	−422,774
1815	15,729	32,708	−16,979	1863	112,697	714,741	−602,043
1816	47,678	30,587	17,091	1864	264,627	865,323	−600,696
1817	33,099	21,844	11,255	1865	333,715	1,297,555	−963,841
1818	21,585	19,825	1,760	1866	558,033	520,809	37,223
1819	24,603	21,464	3,140	1867	490,634	357,543	133,091
1820	17,881	18,261	−380	1868	405,638	377,340	28,298
1821	14,573	15,811	−1,237	1869	370,944	322,865	48,078
1822	20,232	15,000	5,232	1870	411,255	309,654	101,602
1823	20,541	14,707	5,834	1871	383,324	292,177	91,147
1824	19,381	20,327	−945	1872	374,107	277,518	96,589
1825	21,841	15,857	5,984	1873	333,738	290,345	43,393
1826	25,260	17,036	8,225	1874	304,979	302,634	2,345
1827	22,966	16,139	6,827	1875	288,000	274,623	13,377
1828	24,764	16,395	8,369	1876	294,096	265,101	28,995
1829	24,828	15,203	9,624	1877	281,406	241,334	40,072
1830	24,844	15,143	9,701	1878	257,764	236,964	20,800
1831	28,527	15,248	13,279	1879	273,827	266,948	6,879
1832	31,866	17,289	14,577	1880	333,527	267,643	65,884
1833	33,948	23,018	10,931	1881	360,782	260,713	100,069
1834	21,792	18,628	3,164	1882	403,525	257,981	145,544
1835	35,430	17,573	17,857	1883	398,288	265,408	132,879
1836	50,827	30,868	19,959	1884	348,520	244,126	104,394
1837	24,954	37,243	−12,289	1885	323,691	260,227	63,464
1838	26,303	33,865	−7,562	1886	336,440	242,483	93,957
1839	31,483	26,899	4,584	1887	371,403	267,932	103,471
1840	19,480	24,318	−4,837	1888	379,266	267,925	111,341
1841	16,860	26,566	−9,706	1889	387,050	299,289	87,761
1842	19,976	25,206	−5,230	1890	403,081	318,041	85,040
1843	8,303	11,858	−3,555	1891	392,612	365,774	26,839
1844	29,321	22,338	6,984	1892	354,938	345,023	9,914
1845	29,970	22,937	7,033	1893	385,820	383,478	2,342
1846	29,700	27,767	1,933	1894	306,355	367,525	−61,170
1847	26,496	57,281	−30,786	1895	324,729	356,195	−31,466

US Governmental Spending, 1800–2008 (continued)

YEAR[1]	FEDERAL INCOME	FEDERAL SPENDING	SURPLUS OR DEFICIT	YEAR[1]	FEDERAL INCOME	FEDERAL SPENDING	SURPLUS OR DEFICIT
1896	338,142	352,179	-14,037	1953	69,608,000	76,101,000	-6,493,000
1897	347,722	365,774	-18,052	1954	69,701,000	70,855,000	-1,154,000
1898	405,321	443,369	-38,047	1955	65,451,000	68,444,000	-2,993,000
1899	515,961	605,072	-89,112	1956	74,587,000	70,640,000	3,947,000
1900	567,241	520,861	46,380	1957	79,990,000	76,578,000	3,412,000
1901	587,685	524,617	63,068	1958	79,636,000	82,405,000	-2,769,000
1902	562,478	485,234	77,244	1959	79,249,000	92,098,000	-12,849,000
1903	561,881	517,006	44,875	1960	92,492,000	92,191,000	301,000
1904	541,087	583,660	-42,573	1961	94,388,000	97,723,000	-3,335,000
1905	544,275	567,279	-23,004	1962	99,676,000	106,821,000	-7,146,000
1906	594,984	570,202	24,782	1963	106,560,000	111,316,000	-4,756,000
1907	665,860	579,129	86,732	1964	112,613,000	118,528,000	-5,915,000
1908	601,862	659,196	-57,334	1965	116,817,000	118,228,000	-1,411,000
1909	604,320	693,744	-89,423	1966	130,835,000	134,532,000	-3,698,000
1910	675,512	693,617	-18,105	1967	148,822,000	157,464,000	-8,643,000
1911	701,833	691,202	10,631	1968	152,973,000	178,134,000	-25,161,000
1912	692,609	689,881	2,728	1969	186,882,000	183,640,000	3,242,000
1913	714,463	714,864	-401	1970	192,807,000	195,649,000	-2,842,000
1914	725,117	725,525	-408	1971	187,139,000	210,172,000	-23,033,000
1915	683,417	746,093	-62,676	1972	207,309,000	230,681,000	-23,373,000
1916	761,445	712,967	48,478	1973	230,799,000	245,707,000	-14,908,000
1917	1,100,500	1,953,857	-853,357	1974	263,224,000	269,359,000	-6,135,000
1918	3,645,240	12,677,359	-9,032,120	1975	279,090,000	332,332,000	-53,242,000
1919	5,130,042	18,492,665	-13,362,623	1976	298,060,000	371,792,000	-73,732,000
1920	6,648,898	6,357,677	291,222	TQ	81,232,000	95,975,000	-14,744,000
1921	5,570,790	5,061,785	509,005	1977	355,559,000	409,218,000	-53,659,000
1922	4,025,901	3,289,404	736,496	1978	399,561,000	458,746,000	-59,185,000
1923	3,852,795	3,140,287	712,508	1979	463,302,000	504,028,000	-40,726,000
1924	3,871,214	2,907,847	963,367	1980	517,112,000	590,941,000	-73,830,000
1925	3,640,805	2,923,762	717,043	1981	599,272,000	678,241,000	-78,968,000
1926	3,795,108	2,929,964	865,144	1982	617,766,000	745,743,000	-127,977,000
1927	4,012,794	2,857,429	1,155,365	1983	600,562,000	808,364,000	-207,802,000
1928	3,900,329	2,961,245	939,083	1984	666,486,000	851,853,000	-185,367,000
1929	3,861,589	3,127,199	734,391	1985	734,088,000	946,396,000	-212,308,000
1930	4,057,884	3,320,211	737,673	1986	769,215,000	990,430,000	-221,215,000
1931	3,115,557	3,577,434	-461,877	1987	854,353,000	1,004,082,000	-149,728,000
1932	1,923,892	4,659,182	-2,735,290	1988	909,303,000	1,064,455,000	-155,152,000
1933	1,996,844	4,598,496	-2,601,652	1989	991,190,000	1,143,646,000	-152,456,000
1934	2,955,000	6,541,000	-3,586,000	1990	1,031,969,000	1,253,165,000	-221,195,000
1935	3,609,000	6,412,000	-2,803,000	1991	1,055,041,000	1,324,369,000	-269,328,000
1936	3,923,000	8,228,000	-4,304,000	1992	1,091,279,000	1,381,655,000	-290,376,000
1937	5,387,000	7,580,000	-2,193,000	1993	1,154,401,000	1,409,489,000	-255,087,000
1938	6,751,000	6,840,000	-89,000	1994	1,258,627,000	1,461,877,000	-203,250,000
1939	6,295,000	9,141,000	-2,846,000	1995	1,351,830,000	1,515,802,000	-163,972,000
1940	6,548,000	9,468,000	-2,920,000	1996	1,453,062,000	1,560,535,000	-107,473,000
1941	8,712,000	13,653,000	-4,941,000	1997	1,579,292,000	1,601,250,000	-21,958,000
1942	14,634,000	35,137,000	-20,503,000	1998	1,721,798,000	1,652,585,000	69,213,000
1943	24,001,000	78,555,000	-54,554,000	1999	1,827,454,000	1,701,891,000	125,563,000
1944	43,747,000	91,304,000	-47,557,000	2000	2,025,218,000	1,788,773,000	236,445,000
1945	45,159,000	92,712,000	-47,553,000	2001	1,991,194,000	1,863,770,000	127,424,000
1946	39,296,000	55,232,000	-15,936,000	2002	1,853,173,000	2,010,970,000	-157,797,000
1947	38,514,000	34,496,000	4,018,000	2003	1,782,342,000	2,157,637,000	-375,295,000
1948	41,560,000	29,764,000	11,796,000	2004	1,880,071,000	2,292,215,000	-412,144,000
1949	39,415,000	38,835,000	580,000	2005	2,153,859,000	2,472,205,000	-318,346,000
1950	39,443,000	42,562,000	-3,119,000	2006	2,407,254,000	2,655,435,000	-248,181,000
1951	51,616,000	45,514,000	6,102,000	2007	2,540,096,000	2,784,267,000	-244,176,000
1952	66,167,000	67,686,000	-1,519,000	2008	2,662,474,000	2,901,861,000	-239,387,000

[1]The fiscal year ended on 31 December for the budgets from 1800 to 1842. It ended on 30 June for the budgets from 1844 through 1976 and on 30 September from fiscal year 1977. The budget figures for 1843 are for the period from 1 January to 30 June. The third quarter of 1976 was budgeted separately because of the change in the fiscal year calendar. It is referred to as the Transition Quarter (TQ).

Annual National Average Terms on Conventional Single-Family Mortgages, 1980–2007

Source: Federal Housing Finance Board Monthly Interest Rate Survey.

YEAR	CONTRACT INTEREST RATE (%)	INITIAL FEES AND CHARGES (%)	EFFECTIVE INTEREST RATE (%)	TERM TO MATURITY (YEARS)	MORTGAGE AMOUNT (US$'000)	PURCHASE PRICE (US$'000)	LOAN-TO-PRICE RATIO (%)
1980	12.46	1.97	12.84	27.2	51.7	73.4	72.9
1981	14.39	2.39	14.91	26.4	53.7	76.3	73.1
1982	14.73	2.65	15.31	25.6	55.0	78.4	72.9
1983	12.26	2.39	12.73	26.0	59.9	83.1	74.5
1984	11.99	2.57	12.48	26.8	64.5	86.6	77.0
1985	11.17	2.51	11.64	25.9	70.2	96.1	75.8
1986	9.79	2.21	10.18	25.6	79.3	110.6	74.1
1987	8.95	2.08	9.30	26.8	89.1	121.8	75.2
1988	8.98	1.96	9.30	27.7	97.4	131.6	76.0
1989	9.81	1.87	10.13	27.7	104.5	142.8	74.8
1990	9.74	1.79	10.05	27.0	104.0	142.6	74.7
1991	9.07	1.58	9.34	26.5	106.3	146.7	74.4
1992	7.83	1.58	8.11	25.4	108.7	146.4	76.6
1993	6.93	1.20	7.13	25.5	107.0	143.1	77.2
1994	7.31	1.10	7.49	27.1	109.9	142.0	79.9
1995	7.69	0.97	7.85	27.4	110.4	142.8	79.9
1996	7.58	0.97	7.74	26.9	118.7	155.1	79.0
1997	7.52	0.98	7.68	27.5	126.6	164.5	79.4
1998	6.97	0.85	7.10	27.8	131.8	173.4	78.9
1999	7.14	0.74	7.25	28.2	139.3	184.2	78.5
2000	7.86	0.67	7.96	28.7	148.3	198.9	77.8
2001	6.94	0.53	7.03	27.6	155.7	215.5	76.2
2002	6.44	0.46	6.51	27.3	163.4	231.2	75.1
2003	5.67	0.37	5.73	26.8	167.9	243.4	73.5
2004	5.68	0.40	5.74	27.9	185.5	262.0	74.9
2005	5.85	0.38	5.90	28.5	211.9	299.8	74.7
2006	6.52	0.41	6.58	29.0	222.3	306.4	76.5
2007	6.43	0.48	6.50	29.3	224.5	300.4	79.4

US Bankruptcy Filings

This table shows the number of business and nonbusiness (consumer) bankruptcy filings in the US since 1980. Bankruptcy is intended to give debtors a fresh start in managing their resources by cancelling many of their debts through a court order called a "discharge." It is also meant to give creditors a fair share of the money that the debtors can afford to pay back.

Businesses may file for bankruptcy under chapter 11 of the Internal Revenue Code. Chapter 11 offers protection from creditor demands to a business in debt so that its officers and managers have time to reorganize in order to fulfill obligations to creditors. In some instances, creditors may receive dollar-for-dollar what the business owes them, plus interest. In others, the creditor may only receive pennies on the owed dollar.

Individuals may file for bankruptcy under either chapter 7 of the Internal Revenue Code (under which debtors may liquidate assets with the supervision of a trustee in order to receive a nearly immediate discharge of debts) or chapter 13 (under which the debtor enters into a payment plan to repay debt out of future earnings over a three-to-five-year period, with the oversight of a trustee).

Source: American Bankruptcy Institute.

YEAR	TOTAL FILINGS	BUSINESS FILINGS	CONSUMER FILINGS	CONSUMER FILINGS AS A PERCENTAGE OF TOTAL FILINGS
1980	331,264	43,694	287,570	86.81%
1985	412,510	71,277	341,233	82.72%
1990	782,960	64,853	718,107	91.72%
1995	926,601	51,959	874,642	94.39%
2000	1,253,444	35,472	1,217,972	97.17%
2001	1,492,129	40,099	1,452,030	97.31%
2002	1,577,651	38,540	1,539,111	97.56%
2003	1,660,245	35,037	1,625,208	97.89%
2004	1,597,462	34,317	1,563,145	97.85%
2005	2,078,415	39,201	2,039,214	98.11%
2006	617,660	19,695	597,965	96.81%
2007	850,912	28,322	822,590	96.67%
2008	1,117,771	43,546	1,074,225	96.10%

US Taxes

US Federal Taxation Structure

This table shows the range of income taxes for various types of households in each tax bracket. In 2009 the standard deductions for most filers were US$5,700 for those submitting returns under status "single" and status "married filing separately," US$8,350 for those filing under status "head of household," and US$11,400 for those submitting returns under status "married filing jointly" or "qualifying widow(er) with dependent child." Source: US Department of the Treasury, Internal Revenue Service.

Single — Schedule X

IF TAXABLE INCOME IS OVER	BUT NOT OVER	THEN THE TAX IS	PLUS	OF THE AMOUNT OVER
US$0	US$8,350	—	10%	US$0
US$8,350	US$33,950	US$835.00	15%	US$8,350
US$33,950	US$82,250	US$4,675.00	25%	US$33,950
US$82,250	US$171,550	US$16,750.00	28%	US$82,250
US$171,550	US$372,950	US$41,754.00	33%	US$171,550
US$372,950	—	US$108,216.00	35%	US$372,950

Married Filing Jointly or Qualifying Widow(er) — Schedule Y-1

IF TAXABLE INCOME IS OVER	BUT NOT OVER	THEN THE TAX IS	PLUS	OF THE AMOUNT OVER
US$0	US$16,700	—	10%	US$0
US$16,700	US$67,900	US$1,670.00	15%	US$16,700
US$67,900	US$137,050	US$9,350.00	25%	US$67,900
US$137,050	US$208,850	US$26,637.50	28%	US$137,050
US$208,850	US$372,950	US$46,741.50	33%	US$208,850
US$372,950	—	US$100,894.50	35%	US$372,950

Married Filing Separately — Schedule Y-2

IF TAXABLE INCOME IS OVER	BUT NOT OVER	THEN THE TAX IS	PLUS	OF THE AMOUNT OVER
US$0	US$8,350	—	10%	US$0
US$8,350	US$33,950	US$835.00	15%	US$8,350
US$33,950	US$68,525	US$4,675.00	25%	US$33,950
US$68,525	US$104,425	US$13,318.75	28%	US$68,525
US$104,425	US$186,475	US$23,370.75	33%	US$104,425
US$186,475	—	US$50,447.25	35%	US$186,475

Head of Household — Schedule Z

IF TAXABLE INCOME IS OVER	BUT NOT OVER	THEN THE TAX IS	PLUS	OF THE AMOUNT OVER
US$0	US$11,950	—	10%	US$0
US$11,950	US$45,500	US$1,195.00	15%	US$11,950
US$45,500	US$117,450	US$6,227.50	25%	US$45,500
US$117,450	US$190,200	US$24,215.00	28%	US$117,450
US$190,200	US$372,950	US$44,585.00	33%	US$190,200
US$372,950	—	US$104,892.50	35%	US$372,950

Individual Income Taxes by US State

This table shows tax rates as of 15 May 2009 and income brackets as of 1 Jan 2009 for tax year 2009. Tax rates are given in percentages; income brackets and personal exemptions are given in US$. Source: Tax Foundation, <www.taxfoundation.org/taxdata>.

STATE	TAX RATES LOW	TAX RATES HIGH	NUMBER OF BRACKETS	INCOME BRACKETS[1] LOW	INCOME BRACKETS[1] HIGH	PERSONAL EXEMPTIONS SINGLE	PERSONAL EXEMPTIONS JOINT	PERSONAL EXEMPTIONS DEPENDENTS	FEDERAL TAX DEDUCTIBLE
AL[2]	2.0	5.0	3	500	3,000	1,500	3,000	300	yes
AK	no state income tax								
AZ	2.59	4.54	5	10,000	150,000	2,100	4,200	2,100	
AR[2]	1.0[3]	7.0[3]	6	3,800[3,4]	31,700[3,4]	23[5]	46[5]	23[5]	
CA	1.25	10.55	7	7,168[4]	1,000,000[4]	99[4,5]	198[4,5]	309[4,5]	
CO	4.63		1	——flat rate——		——none——			
CT	3.0	5.0	2	10,000	10,000	13,500[6]	26,000[6]	0	

Individual Income Taxes by US State (continued)

STATE	TAX RATES LOW	HIGH	NUMBER OF BRACKETS	INCOME BRACKETS[1] LOW	HIGH	PERSONAL EXEMPTIONS SINGLE	JOINT	DEPENDENTS	FEDERAL TAX DEDUCTIBLE
DE[2]	2.2	5.95	6	2,000	60,000	110[5]	220[5]	110[5]	
DC	4.0	8.5	3	10,000	40,000	1,750	3,500	1,750	
FL	no state income tax								
GA	1.0	6.0	6	750	7,000	2,700	5,400	3,000	
HI	1.4	11.0	12	2,400	200,000	1,040	2,080	1,040	
ID	1.6	7.8	8	1,237[4]	24,736[4]	3,500[7,8]	7,000[7,8]	3,500[7,8]	
IL	3.0		1	—flat rate—		2,000	4,000	2,000	
IN[2]	3.4		1	—flat rate—		1,000	2,000	2,500[9]	
IA[2]	0.36	8.98	9	1,379[4]	62,055[4]	40[5]	80[5]	40[5]	yes
KS	3.5	6.45	3	15,000	30,000	2,250	4,500	2,250	
KY[2]	2.0	6.0	6	3,000	75,000	20[5]	40[5]	20[5]	
LA	2.0	6.0	3	12,500	50,000	4,500[10]	9,000[10]	1,000	yes
ME	2.0	8.5	4	4,850[4]	19,450[4]	2,850	5,700	2,850	
MD[2]	2.0	6.25	8	1,000	1,000,000	3,200	6,400	3,200	
MA	5.3	12.0[11]	1	—flat rate—		4,400	8,800	1,000	
MI[2]	4.35		1	—flat rate—		3,500[7]	7,000[7]	3,500[7,12]	
MN	5.35	7.85	3	21,800[4]	71,590[4]	3,500[7]	7,000[7]	3,500[7]	
MS	3.0	5.0	3	5,000	10,000	6,000	12,000	1,500	
MO[2]	1.5	6.0	10	1,000	9,000	2,100	4,200	1,200	yes[13]
MT	1.0	6.9	7	2,600[4]	15,600[4]	2,140[4]	4,280[4]	2,140[4]	yes[14]
NE	2.56	6.84	4	2,400	27,000	106[5]	212[5]	106[5]	
NV	no state income tax								
NH	state income tax is limited to dividends and interest income only								
NJ[2]	1.4	8.97	6	20,000	500,000	1,000	2,000	1,500	
NM	1.7	4.9	4	5,500	16,000	3,500[7]	7,000[7]	3,500[7]	
NY[2]	4.0	6.85	5	8,000	20,000	—none—		1,000	
NC	6.0	7.75	3	12,750	60,000	15	15	15	
ND	1.84	4.86	5	33,950	372,950	3,500[7]	7,000[7]	3,500[7]	
OH[2]	0.587	5.925	9	5,000	200,000	1,450[4,8]	2,900[4,8]	1,450[4,8]	
OK	0.5	5.5	7	1,000	8,700	1,000	2,000	1,000	
OR[2]	5.0	9.0	3	3,050[4]	7,600[4]	169[4,5]	338[4,5]	169[4,5]	yes[16]
PA[2]	3.07		1	—flat rate—		—none—			
RI	3.75[17]	9.9[17]	5	32,550[4,17]	357,700[4,17]	3,500[7]	7,000[7]	3,500[7]	
SC	0.0	7.0	6	2,670[4]	13,350[4]	3,500[7]	7,000[7]	3,500[7]	
SD	no state income tax								
TN	state income tax is limited to dividends and interest income only								
TX	no state income tax								
UT	5.0		1	—flat rate—		2,625[18]	5,250[18]	2,625[18]	
VT	3.6	9.5	5	32,550[4]	357,700[4]	3,500[7]	7,000[7]	3,500[7]	
VA	2.0	5.75	4	3,000	17,000	930	1,860	930	
WA	no state income tax								
WV	3.0	6.5	5	10,000	60,000	2,000	4,000	2,000	
WI	4.6	6.75	4	9,700[4]	145,460[4]	700	1,400	700	
WY	no state income tax								

[1]Applies to single taxpayers and married people filing separately. Some states increase bracket widths for joint filers.   [2]Local (county- or city-level) rates are excluded.   [3]Rates apply to regular tax table. A special tax table is available for low-income taxpayers that reduces their tax payments.   [4]Values adjusted for inflation each year. Release dates for tax-bracket inflation adjustments vary by state and may fall after the end of the tax year in question. The brackets listed are for tax year 2008.   [5]Tax credit.   [6]Maximum exemption. Value decreases as income increases. There is a US$1,000 reduction in the exemption for every US$1,000 of adjusted gross income over US$27,000.   [7]Exemption tied to federal tax system. Federal exemptions are indexed for inflation.   [8]Taxpayers receive a US$20 tax credit per exemption in addition to the normal exemption amount.   [9]US$2,500 exemption is for each dependent child. If the dependent is not the taxpayer's child, the exemption is US$1,000.   [10]Combined standard deduction and personal exemption.   [11]The 12% rate applies to short-term capital gains, long- and short-term capital gains on collectibles, and pre-1996 installment sales classified as capital gain income for Massachusetts purposes. Taxpayers have the choice of paying an optional higher rate of 5.85%.   [12]Additional US$600 exemption per dependent under 18 years old.   [13]Federal tax deduction limited to US$5,000 or US$10,000.   [14]Available only if itemizing deductions.   [15]Federal taxable income (adjusted gross income minus all deductions and exemptions) is the starting point for determining state taxable income. For tax year 2008, single filers with income less than US$60,000 (US$100,000 for married filing jointly) were required to add US$1,000

Individual Income Taxes by US State (continued)

to their taxable income. Filers with income over the applicable threshold were required to add US$1,500 to their taxable income.   [16]Deduction limited to no more than US$5,600.   [17]Taxpayers may also calculate tax under a flat tax system and pay the lesser of the liability. The flat tax applies to all types of income with no exemptions or deductions and treats capital income as wages. The flat tax rate is 6.5 percent for 2009.   [18]Three-quarters of the federal exemption.

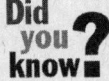

Many insects are sensitive to small variations in temperature. Insects placed on a surface that is warmer at one end and cooler at the other often congregate in a narrow band of temperature. Mosquitoes fly readily to a warm, odorless, inanimate surface as if it were that of a warm-blooded creature. Bees, in the brood season, accurately regulate temperature in the hive between 95 and 97 degrees Fahrenheit by behavior such as beating wings to circulate air.

Arts, Entertainment, & Leisure

The Culture Crunch: Arts and the Recession

by Richard Lacayo, TIME

On their first date, Barack and Michelle Obama went to the Art Institute of Chicago. Back then it was possible for them to go to a museum without attracting much attention. But when Michelle paid a visit to another museum on 18 May 2009, people took note. The first lady traveled to New York City to inaugurate the newly refurbished American Wing of the Metropolitan Museum of Art. Later she moved across town to the city's other Met—the Metropolitan Opera House—to celebrate the opening night of the American Ballet Theatre and speak to the glamorously packed house about the importance of the arts to "our future as an innovative country."

As a moment of social and cultural pageantry, the visit was a hit. But it carried an anxious subtext. The Great Recession has struck museums and performing-arts groups with a vengeance. No one expects the federal government to bail them out. But the people who run these organizations—and the people who care about them—were eager to see a sign that the White House knows just how bad things have gotten for them.

And how bad is that? You could start with the Metropolitan Museum. The nation's largest and wealthiest art museum is in no danger of disappearing. But having watched its mighty endowment shrink last year from US$2.9 billion to US$2.1 billion, its administrators decided a few months ago to cut staff 10%.

The Met is not alone. Endowments have shrunk everywhere, and sizable budget cuts have been the rule at museums in Atlanta, Baltimore, Denver, Detroit, Indianapolis, Los Angeles, Philadelphia, and San Diego. In February 2009 the 35-year-old Las Vegas Art Museum simply gave up and shut its doors for good.

In the world of performing arts, the news has been just as bleak. All around the country, orchestras, opera houses, theater troupes, and dance companies are cutting salaries, jobs, and programs. A few have simply collapsed. The Hartford-based Connecticut Opera closed this year after 67 seasons. So did the 58-year-old Baltimore Opera Company. The problem is that these groups have been hit in all three of their main revenue streams. For many of them, audiences are down sharply, because in a recession a theater ticket or concert seat can seem like an indulgence. Meanwhile, with corporate profits tanking and charitable endowments badly deflated, donations and underwriting have also been drying up. And as state and local governments contend with huge deficits, arts spending has been a major casualty. In Michigan, where the struggling Detroit Institute of Arts recently laid off 20% of its staff, the 2010 budget proposed by Gov. Jennifer Granholm would cut arts funding to exactly nothing.

Finding ways to tweak the revenue stream is not as simple as raising prices. For instance, for most museums that charge admission, fees at the door account for less than 10% of annual income, so hiking ticket prices doesn't do much to close a budget gap. And because many museums benefit from taxpayer support, any attempt to charge more can turn into a battle over the right of the public to have affordable access to a place it subsidizes.

Help from the Top? The Obama administration's stimulus package included US$50 million for the National Endowment for the Arts (NEA). And in May the president nominated a firecracker, the Broadway producer Rocco Landesman, to be the NEA's next chairman. But at the same time, arts groups are worried about what they see as a serious threat to their donor base: the White House proposal to reduce by as much as 20% the tax deduction that higher-income families can take for charitable contributions.

So back to the private sector, which, after all, has been the lifeblood of American arts since the 19th century. But how to operate there at such a treacherous time is a puzzle for a lot of arts groups. This is why Michael Kaiser, president of the John F. Kennedy Center for the Performing Arts in Washington DC and an expert at rescuing imperiled institutions, established Arts in Crisis, a free consulting service for arts groups on the verge of a nervous breakdown.

Kaiser's message to all of the groups is to resist the temptation to cut their programming and their profile. When times are bad, he argues, it's crucial to make yourself interesting and vital and to let everybody know you're there. "Organizations that are cutting performances and marketing are going to be the losers," he warns. He also cautions them against reaching for the most familiar programming—Beethoven's *Fifth*! *The Nutcracker*! *Grease*!—in the hope of drawing guaranteed crowds.

One of the shell-shocked organizations that went to Kaiser for advice was the Beck Center for the Arts, a theater and arts-education group near Cleveland. In January ticket sales and donor money "fell off a cliff," says Lucinda Einhouse, the Beck Center's president. In April she traveled to Washington to meet with Kaiser. She went home and instituted some, if not all, of his gospel. Marketing will be maintained. But the theater will mount fewer shows next year, and some will be tried-and-true chestnuts like *Fiddler on the Roof* and *Peter Pan*.

Will it work? "It's too soon to tell," she says. "But after we had that sharp decline, we did an urgent appeal to the community, and we got more than 800 contributions in one month—over US$152,000. They came with all of these notes from people about how much they cared about the Beck Center. It really made a statement that especially in troubling times, it's important to people to have the release and escape of the arts and an opportunity to dream." For now, at least, the biggest dream of all may be a balanced budget.

Motion Pictures

Academy Awards (Oscars), 2008

The Academy of Motion Picture Arts and Sciences was formed in 1927 and first awarded the Academy Awards of Merit in May 1929. The honored categories have varied over the years, but best picture, actor, actress, and director have been awarded since the beginning. Awards for supporting actor and actress were added for the films of 1936 and best foreign-language film for 1947. The ceremony is generally held in the early part of the year following the release of films under consideration; the latest Oscars were awarded 22 Feb 2009 in Los Angeles. Award: gold-plated statuette of a man with a sword.

Academy of Motion Picture Arts and Sciences Web site: <www.oscars.org>.

CATEGORY	WINNER
Motion picture of the year	*Slumdog Millionaire* (UK; Christian Colson, producer)
Director	Danny Boyle (*Slumdog Millionaire,* UK)
Actor	Sean Penn (*Milk,* US)
Actress	Kate Winslet (*The Reader,* US/Germany)
Supporting actor	Heath Ledger (*The Dark Knight,* US/UK)
Supporting actress	Penélope Cruz (*Vicky Cristina Barcelona,* Spain/US)
Foreign-language film	*Okuribito (Departures)* (Japan; Yojiro Takita, director)
Animated feature	*WALL•E* (US; Andrew Stanton, director)
Animated short	*La Maison et petits cubes* (Japan; Kunio Kato, director)
Live-action short	*Spielzeugland (Toyland)* (Germany; Jochen Alexander Freydank, director)
Documentary feature	*Man on Wire* (UK/US; James Marsh, director)
Documentary short	*Smile Pinki* (US; Megan Mylan, director)
Cinematography	Anthony Dod Mantle (*Slumdog Millionaire,* UK)
Art direction	Donald Graham Burt, art direction; Victor J. Zolfo, set decoration (*The Curious Case of Benjamin Button,* US)
Film editing	Chris Dickens (*Slumdog Millionaire,* UK)
Costume design	Michael O'Connor (*The Duchess,* UK/Italy/France)
Makeup	Greg Cannom (*The Curious Case of Benjamin Button,* US)
Original score	A.R. Rahman (*Slumdog Millionaire,* UK)
Original song	"Jai Ho," A.R. Rahman and Gulzar (*Slumdog Millionaire,* UK)
Sound mixing	Ian Tapp, Richard Pryke, and Resul Pookutty (*Slumdog Millionaire,* UK)
Sound editing	Richard King (*The Dark Knight,* US/UK)
Visual effects	Eric Barba, Steve Preeg, Burt Dalton, and Craig Barron (*The Curious Case of Benjamin Button,* US)
Adapted screenplay	Simon Beaufoy (*Slumdog Millionaire,* UK)
Original screenplay	Dustin Lance Black (*Milk,* US)

Academy Awards (Oscars), 1928–2008

BEST PICTURE

- 1928 *Wings*
- 1929 *The Broadway Melody*
- 1930 *All Quiet on the Western Front*
- 1931 *Cimarron*
- 1932 *Grand Hotel*
- 1933 *Cavalcade*
- 1934 *It Happened One Night*
- 1935 *Mutiny on the Bounty*
- 1936 *The Great Ziegfeld*
- 1937 *The Life of Emile Zola*
- 1938 *You Can't Take It with You*
- 1939 *Gone with the Wind*
- 1940 *Rebecca*
- 1941 *How Green Was My Valley*
- 1942 *Mrs. Miniver*
- 1943 *Casablanca*
- 1944 *Going My Way*
- 1945 *The Lost Weekend*
- 1946 *The Best Years of Our Lives*
- 1947 *Gentleman's Agreement*
- 1948 *Hamlet*
- 1949 *All the King's Men*
- 1950 *All About Eve*
- 1951 *An American in Paris*

BEST PICTURE (CONTINUED)

- 1952 *The Greatest Show on Earth*
- 1953 *From Here to Eternity*
- 1954 *On the Waterfront*
- 1955 *Marty*
- 1956 *Around the World in 80 Days*
- 1957 *The Bridge on the River Kwai*
- 1958 *Gigi*
- 1959 *Ben-Hur*
- 1960 *The Apartment*
- 1961 *West Side Story*
- 1962 *Lawrence of Arabia*
- 1963 *Tom Jones*
- 1964 *My Fair Lady*
- 1965 *The Sound of Music*
- 1966 *A Man for All Seasons*
- 1967 *In the Heat of the Night*
- 1968 *Oliver!*
- 1969 *Midnight Cowboy*
- 1970 *Patton*
- 1971 *The French Connection*
- 1972 *The Godfather*
- 1973 *The Sting*

BEST PICTURE (CONTINUED)

- 1974 *The Godfather Part II*
- 1975 *One Flew Over the Cuckoo's Nest*
- 1976 *Rocky*
- 1977 *Annie Hall*
- 1978 *The Deer Hunter*
- 1979 *Kramer vs. Kramer*
- 1980 *Ordinary People*
- 1981 *Chariots of Fire*
- 1982 *Gandhi*
- 1983 *Terms of Endearment*
- 1984 *Amadeus*
- 1985 *Out of Africa*
- 1986 *Platoon*
- 1987 *The Last Emperor*
- 1988 *Rain Man*
- 1989 *Driving Miss Daisy*
- 1990 *Dances with Wolves*
- 1991 *The Silence of the Lambs*
- 1992 *Unforgiven*
- 1993 *Schindler's List*
- 1994 *Forrest Gump*
- 1995 *Braveheart*
- 1996 *The English Patient*
- 1997 *Titanic*

Academy Awards (Oscars), 1928–2008 (continued)

BEST PICTURE (CONTINUED)
1998 Shakespeare in Love
1999 American Beauty
2000 Gladiator
2001 A Beautiful Mind

BEST PICTURE (CONTINUED)
2002 Chicago
2003 The Lord of the Rings:
      The Return of the King
2004 Million Dollar Baby

BEST PICTURE (CONTINUED)
2005 Crash
2006 The Departed
2007 No Country for Old Men
2008 Slumdog Millionaire

BEST ACTOR
1928 Emil Jannings (The Last Command; The Way of All Flesh)
1929 Warner Baxter (In Old Arizona)
1930 George Arliss (Disraeli)
1931 Lionel Barrymore (A Free Soul)
1932 Wallace Beery (The Champ); Fredric March (Dr. Jekyll and Mr. Hyde) (tied)
1933 Charles Laughton (The Private Life of Henry VIII)
1934 Clark Gable (It Happened One Night)
1935 Victor McLaglen (The Informer)
1936 Paul Muni (The Story of Louis Pasteur)
1937 Spencer Tracy (Captains Courageous)
1938 Spencer Tracy (Boys Town)
1939 Robert Donat (Goodbye, Mr. Chips)
1940 James Stewart (The Philadelphia Story)
1941 Gary Cooper (Sergeant York)
1942 James Cagney (Yankee Doodle Dandy)
1943 Paul Lukas (Watch on the Rhine)
1944 Bing Crosby (Going My Way)
1945 Ray Milland (The Lost Weekend)
1946 Fredric March (The Best Years of Our Lives)
1947 Ronald Colman (A Double Life)
1948 Laurence Olivier (Hamlet)
1949 Broderick Crawford (All the King's Men)
1950 José Ferrer (Cyrano de Bergerac)
1951 Humphrey Bogart (The African Queen)
1952 Gary Cooper (High Noon)
1953 William Holden (Stalag 17)
1954 Marlon Brando (On the Waterfront)
1955 Ernest Borgnine (Marty)
1956 Yul Brynner (The King and I)
1957 Alec Guinness (The Bridge on the River Kwai)
1958 David Niven (Separate Tables)
1959 Charlton Heston (Ben-Hur)
1960 Burt Lancaster (Elmer Gantry)
1961 Maximilian Schell (Judgment at Nuremberg)
1962 Gregory Peck (To Kill a Mockingbird)
1963 Sidney Poitier (Lilies of the Field)
1964 Rex Harrison (My Fair Lady)
1965 Lee Marvin (Cat Ballou)
1966 Paul Scofield (A Man for All Seasons)
1967 Rod Steiger (In the Heat of the Night)
1968 Cliff Robertson (Charly)
1969 John Wayne (True Grit)
1970 George C. Scott (Patton) (declined)
1971 Gene Hackman (The French Connection)
1972 Marlon Brando (The Godfather) (declined)
1973 Jack Lemmon (Save the Tiger)
1974 Art Carney (Harry and Tonto)
1975 Jack Nicholson (One Flew Over the Cuckoo's Nest)
1976 Peter Finch (Network)[1]
1977 Richard Dreyfuss (The Goodbye Girl)
1978 Jon Voight (Coming Home)
1979 Dustin Hoffman (Kramer vs. Kramer)
1980 Robert De Niro (Raging Bull)
1981 Henry Fonda (On Golden Pond)
1982 Ben Kingsley (Gandhi)
1983 Robert Duvall (Tender Mercies)
1984 F. Murray Abraham (Amadeus)
1985 William Hurt (Kiss of the Spider Woman)

BEST ACTOR (CONTINUED)
1986 Paul Newman (The Color of Money)
1987 Michael Douglas (Wall Street)
1988 Dustin Hoffman (Rain Man)
1989 Daniel Day-Lewis (My Left Foot)
1990 Jeremy Irons (Reversal of Fortune)
1991 Anthony Hopkins (The Silence of the Lambs)
1992 Al Pacino (Scent of a Woman)
1993 Tom Hanks (Philadelphia)
1994 Tom Hanks (Forrest Gump)
1995 Nicolas Cage (Leaving Las Vegas)
1996 Geoffrey Rush (Shine)
1997 Jack Nicholson (As Good as It Gets)
1998 Roberto Benigni (Life Is Beautiful)
1999 Kevin Spacey (American Beauty)
2000 Russell Crowe (Gladiator)
2001 Denzel Washington (Training Day)
2002 Adrien Brody (The Pianist)
2003 Sean Penn (Mystic River)
2004 Jamie Foxx (Ray)
2005 Philip Seymour Hoffman (Capote)
2006 Forest Whitaker (The Last King of Scotland)
2007 Daniel Day-Lewis (There Will Be Blood)
2008 Sean Penn (Milk)

BEST ACTRESS
1928 Janet Gaynor (7th Heaven; Street Angel; Sunrise)
1929 Mary Pickford (Coquette)
1930 Norma Shearer (The Divorcee)
1931 Marie Dressler (Min and Bill)
1932 Helen Hayes (The Sin of Madelon Claudet)
1933 Katharine Hepburn (Morning Glory)
1934 Claudette Colbert (It Happened One Night)
1935 Bette Davis (Dangerous)
1936 Luise Rainer (The Great Ziegfeld)
1937 Luise Rainer (The Good Earth)
1938 Bette Davis (Jezebel)
1939 Vivien Leigh (Gone with the Wind)
1940 Ginger Rogers (Kitty Foyle)
1941 Joan Fontaine (Suspicion)
1942 Greer Garson (Mrs. Miniver)
1943 Jennifer Jones (The Song of Bernadette)
1944 Ingrid Bergman (Gaslight)
1945 Joan Crawford (Mildred Pierce)
1946 Olivia de Havilland (To Each His Own)
1947 Loretta Young (The Farmer's Daughter)
1948 Jane Wyman (Johnny Belinda)
1949 Olivia de Havilland (The Heiress)
1950 Judy Holliday (Born Yesterday)
1951 Vivien Leigh (A Streetcar Named Desire)
1952 Shirley Booth (Come Back, Little Sheba)
1953 Audrey Hepburn (Roman Holiday)
1954 Grace Kelly (The Country Girl)
1955 Anna Magnani (The Rose Tattoo)
1956 Ingrid Bergman (Anastasia)
1957 Joanne Woodward (The Three Faces of Eve)
1958 Susan Hayward (I Want to Live!)
1959 Simone Signoret (Room at the Top)
1960 Elizabeth Taylor (Butterfield 8)
1961 Sophia Loren (Two Women)
1962 Anne Bancroft (The Miracle Worker)
1963 Patricia Neal (Hud)

Academy Awards (Oscars), 1928–2008 (continued)

BEST ACTRESS (CONTINUED)

1964 Julie Andrews (*Mary Poppins*)
1965 Julie Christie (*Darling*)
1966 Elizabeth Taylor (*Who's Afraid of Virginia Woolf?*)
1967 Katharine Hepburn (*Guess Who's Coming to Dinner*)
1968 Katharine Hepburn (*The Lion in Winter*); Barbra Streisand (*Funny Girl*) (tied)
1969 Maggie Smith (*The Prime of Miss Jean Brodie*)
1970 Glenda Jackson (*Women in Love*)
1971 Jane Fonda (*Klute*)
1972 Liza Minnelli (*Cabaret*)
1973 Glenda Jackson (*A Touch of Class*)
1974 Ellen Burstyn (*Alice Doesn't Live Here Anymore*)
1975 Louise Fletcher (*One Flew Over the Cuckoo's Nest*)
1976 Faye Dunaway (*Network*)
1977 Diane Keaton (*Annie Hall*)
1978 Jane Fonda (*Coming Home*)
1979 Sally Field (*Norma Rae*)
1980 Sissy Spacek (*Coal Miner's Daughter*)
1981 Katharine Hepburn (*On Golden Pond*)
1982 Meryl Streep (*Sophie's Choice*)
1983 Shirley MacLaine (*Terms of Endearment*)
1984 Sally Field (*Places in the Heart*)
1985 Geraldine Page (*The Trip to Bountiful*)
1986 Marlee Matlin (*Children of a Lesser God*)
1987 Cher (*Moonstruck*)
1988 Jodie Foster (*The Accused*)
1989 Jessica Tandy (*Driving Miss Daisy*)
1990 Kathy Bates (*Misery*)
1991 Jodie Foster (*The Silence of the Lambs*)
1992 Emma Thompson (*Howards End*)
1993 Holly Hunter (*The Piano*)
1994 Jessica Lange (*Blue Sky*)
1995 Susan Sarandon (*Dead Man Walking*)
1996 Frances McDormand (*Fargo*)
1997 Helen Hunt (*As Good as It Gets*)
1998 Gwyneth Paltrow (*Shakespeare in Love*)
1999 Hilary Swank (*Boys Don't Cry*)
2000 Julia Roberts (*Erin Brockovich*)
2001 Halle Berry (*Monster's Ball*)
2002 Nicole Kidman (*The Hours*)
2003 Charlize Theron (*Monster*)
2004 Hilary Swank (*Million Dollar Baby*)
2005 Reese Witherspoon (*Walk the Line*)
2006 Helen Mirren (*The Queen*)
2007 Marion Cotillard (*La Vie en rose*)
2008 Kate Winslet (*The Reader*)

BEST SUPPORTING ACTOR

1936 Walter Brennan (*Come and Get It*)
1937 Joseph Schildkraut (*The Life of Emile Zola*)
1938 Walter Brennan (*Kentucky*)
1939 Thomas Mitchell (*Stagecoach*)
1940 Walter Brennan (*The Westerner*)
1941 Donald Crisp (*How Green Was My Valley*)
1942 Van Heflin (*Johnny Eager*)
1943 Charles Coburn (*The More the Merrier*)
1944 Barry Fitzgerald (*Going My Way*)
1945 James Dunn (*A Tree Grows in Brooklyn*)
1946 Harold Russell (*The Best Years of Our Lives*)
1947 Edmund Gwenn (*Miracle on 34th Street*)
1948 Walter Huston (*The Treasure of the Sierra Madre*)
1949 Dean Jagger (*Twelve O'Clock High*)
1950 George Sanders (*All About Eve*)

BEST SUPPORTING ACTOR (CONTINUED)

1951 Karl Malden (*A Streetcar Named Desire*)
1952 Anthony Quinn (*Viva Zapata!*)
1953 Frank Sinatra (*From Here to Eternity*)
1954 Edmond O'Brien (*The Barefoot Contessa*)
1955 Jack Lemmon (*Mister Roberts*)
1956 Anthony Quinn (*Lust for Life*)
1957 Red Buttons (*Sayonara*)
1958 Burl Ives (*The Big Country*)
1959 Hugh Griffith (*Ben-Hur*)
1960 Peter Ustinov (*Spartacus*)
1961 George Chakiris (*West Side Story*)
1962 Ed Begley (*Sweet Bird of Youth*)
1963 Melvyn Douglas (*Hud*)
1964 Peter Ustinov (*Topkapi*)
1965 Martin Balsam (*A Thousand Clowns*)
1966 Walter Matthau (*The Fortune Cookie*)
1967 George Kennedy (*Cool Hand Luke*)
1968 Jack Albertson (*The Subject Was Roses*)
1969 Gig Young (*They Shoot Horses, Don't They?*)
1970 John Mills (*Ryan's Daughter*)
1971 Ben Johnson (*The Last Picture Show*)
1972 Joel Grey (*Cabaret*)
1973 John Houseman (*The Paper Chase*)
1974 Robert De Niro (*The Godfather Part II*)
1975 George Burns (*The Sunshine Boys*)
1976 Jason Robards (*All the President's Men*)
1977 Jason Robards (*Julia*)
1978 Christopher Walken (*The Deer Hunter*)
1979 Melvyn Douglas (*Being There*)
1980 Timothy Hutton (*Ordinary People*)
1981 John Gielgud (*Arthur*)
1982 Louis Gossett, Jr. (*An Officer and a Gentleman*)
1983 Jack Nicholson (*Terms of Endearment*)
1984 Haing S. Ngor (*The Killing Fields*)
1985 Don Ameche (*Cocoon*)
1986 Michael Caine (*Hannah and Her Sisters*)
1987 Sean Connery (*The Untouchables*)
1988 Kevin Kline (*A Fish Called Wanda*)
1989 Denzel Washington (*Glory*)
1990 Joe Pesci (*Goodfellas*)
1991 Jack Palance (*City Slickers*)
1992 Gene Hackman (*Unforgiven*)
1993 Tommy Lee Jones (*The Fugitive*)
1994 Martin Landau (*Ed Wood*)
1995 Kevin Spacey (*The Usual Suspects*)
1996 Cuba Gooding, Jr. (*Jerry Maguire*)
1997 Robin Williams (*Good Will Hunting*)
1998 James Coburn (*Affliction*)
1999 Michael Caine (*The Cider House Rules*)
2000 Benicio Del Toro (*Traffic*)
2001 Jim Broadbent (*Iris*)
2002 Chris Cooper (*Adaptation*)
2003 Tim Robbins (*Mystic River*)
2004 Morgan Freeman (*Million Dollar Baby*)
2005 George Clooney (*Syriana*)
2006 Alan Arkin (*Little Miss Sunshine*)
2007 Javier Bardem (*No Country for Old Men*)
2008 Heath Ledger (*The Dark Knight*)[1]

BEST SUPPORTING ACTRESS

1936 Gale Sondergaard (*Anthony Adverse*)
1937 Alice Brady (*In Old Chicago*)
1938 Fay Bainter (*Jezebel*)
1939 Hattie McDaniel (*Gone with the Wind*)
1940 Jane Darwell (*The Grapes of Wrath*)
1941 Mary Astor (*The Great Lie*)
1942 Teresa Wright (*Mrs. Miniver*)

Academy Awards (Oscars), 1928–2008 (continued)

BEST SUPPORTING ACTRESS (CONTINUED)

1943 Katina Paxinou (*For Whom the Bell Tolls*)
1944 Ethel Barrymore (*None but the Lonely Heart*)
1945 Anne Revere (*National Velvet*)
1946 Anne Baxter (*The Razor's Edge*)
1947 Celeste Holm (*Gentleman's Agreement*)
1948 Claire Trevor (*Key Largo*)
1949 Mercedes McCambridge (*All the King's Men*)
1950 Josephine Hull (*Harvey*)
1951 Kim Hunter (*A Streetcar Named Desire*)
1952 Gloria Grahame (*The Bad and the Beautiful*)
1953 Donna Reed (*From Here to Eternity*)
1954 Eva Marie Saint (*On the Waterfront*)
1955 Jo Van Fleet (*East of Eden*)
1956 Dorothy Malone (*Written on the Wind*)
1957 Miyoshi Umeki (*Sayonara*)
1958 Wendy Hiller (*Separate Tables*)
1959 Shelley Winters (*The Diary of Anne Frank*)
1960 Shirley Jones (*Elmer Gantry*)
1961 Rita Moreno (*West Side Story*)
1962 Patty Duke (*The Miracle Worker*)
1963 Margaret Rutherford (*The V.I.P.s*)
1964 Lila Kedrova (*Zorba the Greek*)
1965 Shelley Winters (*A Patch of Blue*)
1966 Sandy Dennis (*Who's Afraid of Virginia Woolf?*)
1967 Estelle Parsons (*Bonnie and Clyde*)
1968 Ruth Gordon (*Rosemary's Baby*)
1969 Goldie Hawn (*Cactus Flower*)
1970 Helen Hayes (*Airport*)
1971 Cloris Leachman (*The Last Picture Show*)
1972 Eileen Heckart (*Butterflies Are Free*)
1973 Tatum O'Neal (*Paper Moon*)
1974 Ingrid Bergman (*Murder on the Orient Express*)
1975 Lee Grant (*Shampoo*)
1976 Beatrice Straight (*Network*)
1977 Vanessa Redgrave (*Julia*)
1978 Maggie Smith (*California Suite*)
1979 Meryl Streep (*Kramer vs. Kramer*)
1980 Mary Steenburgen (*Melvin and Howard*)
1981 Maureen Stapleton (*Reds*)
1982 Jessica Lange (*Tootsie*)
1983 Linda Hunt (*The Year of Living Dangerously*)
1984 Peggy Ashcroft (*A Passage to India*)
1985 Anjelica Huston (*Prizzi's Honor*)
1986 Dianne Wiest (*Hannah and Her Sisters*)
1987 Olympia Dukakis (*Moonstruck*)
1988 Geena Davis (*The Accidental Tourist*)
1989 Brenda Fricker (*My Left Foot*)
1990 Whoopi Goldberg (*Ghost*)
1991 Mercedes Ruehl (*The Fisher King*)
1992 Marisa Tomei (*My Cousin Vinny*)
1993 Anna Paquin (*The Piano*)
1994 Dianne Wiest (*Bullets over Broadway*)
1995 Mira Sorvino (*Mighty Aphrodite*)
1996 Juliette Binoche (*The English Patient*)
1997 Kim Basinger (*L.A. Confidential*)
1998 Judi Dench (*Shakespeare in Love*)
1999 Angelina Jolie (*Girl, Interrupted*)
2000 Marcia Gay Harden (*Pollock*)
2001 Jennifer Connelly (*A Beautiful Mind*)
2002 Catherine Zeta-Jones (*Chicago*)
2003 Renée Zellweger (*Cold Mountain*)
2004 Cate Blanchett (*The Aviator*)
2005 Rachel Weisz (*The Constant Gardener*)
2006 Jennifer Hudson (*Dreamgirls*)
2007 Tilda Swinton (*Michael Clayton*)
2008 Penélope Cruz (*Vicky Cristina Barcelona*)

FOREIGN LANGUAGE FILM (AMERICAN TITLES)

1947 *Shoe-Shine*
1948 *Monsieur Vincent*
1949 *The Bicycle Thief*
1950 *The Walls of Malapaga*
1951 *Rashomon*
1952 *Forbidden Games*
1953 not awarded
1954 *Gate of Hell*
1955 *Samurai, the Legend of Musashi*
1956 *La Strada*
1957 *The Nights of Cabiria*
1958 *My Uncle*
1959 *Black Orpheus*
1960 *The Virgin Spring*
1961 *Through a Glass Darkly*
1962 *Sundays and Cybele*
1963 *Federico Fellini's 8½*
1964 *Yesterday, Today, and Tomorrow*
1965 *The Shop on Main Street*
1966 *A Man and a Woman*
1967 *Closely Watched Trains*
1968 *War and Peace*
1969 *Z*
1970 *Investigation of a Citizen Above Suspicion*
1971 *The Garden of the Finzi-Continis*
1972 *The Discreet Charm of the Bourgeoisie*
1973 *Day for Night*
1974 *Amarcord*
1975 *Dersu Uzala*
1976 *Black and White in Color*
1977 *Madame Rosa*
1978 *Get Out Your Handkerchiefs*
1979 *The Tin Drum*
1980 *Moscow Does Not Believe in Tears*
1981 *Mephisto*
1982 *To Begin Again*
1983 *Fanny & Alexander*
1984 *Dangerous Moves*
1985 *The Official Story*
1986 *The Assault*
1987 *Babette's Feast*
1988 *Pelle the Conqueror*
1989 *Cinema Paradiso*
1990 *Journey of Hope*
1991 *Mediterraneo*
1992 *Indochine*
1993 *Belle Epoque*
1994 *Burnt by the Sun*
1995 *Antonia's Line*
1996 *Kolya*
1997 *Character*
1998 *Life Is Beautiful*
1999 *All About My Mother*
2000 *Crouching Tiger, Hidden Dragon*
2001 *No Man's Land*
2002 *Nowhere in Africa*
2003 *The Barbarian Invasions*
2004 *The Sea Inside*
2005 *Tsotsi*
2006 *The Lives of Others*
2007 *The Counterfeiters*
2008 *Departures*

DIRECTING

1928 Lewis Milestone (*Two Arabian Knights*); Frank Borzage (*7th Heaven*)
1929 Frank Lloyd (*The Divine Lady*)

Academy Awards (Oscars), 1928–2008 (continued)

DIRECTING (CONTINUED)

1930 Lewis Milestone (*All Quiet on the Western Front*)
1931 Norman Taurog (*Skippy*)
1932 Frank Borzage (*Bad Girl*)
1933 Frank Lloyd (*Cavalcade*)
1934 Frank Capra (*It Happened One Night*)
1935 John Ford (*The Informer*)
1936 Frank Capra (*Mr. Deeds Goes to Town*)
1937 Leo McCarey (*The Awful Truth*)
1938 Frank Capra (*You Can't Take It with You*)
1939 Victor Fleming (*Gone with the Wind*)
1940 John Ford (*The Grapes of Wrath*)
1941 John Ford (*How Green Was My Valley*)
1942 William Wyler (*Mrs. Miniver*)
1943 Michael Curtiz (*Casablanca*)
1944 Leo McCarey (*Going My Way*)
1945 Billy Wilder (*The Lost Weekend*)
1946 William Wyler (*The Best Years of Our Lives*)
1947 Elia Kazan (*Gentleman's Agreement*)
1948 John Huston (*The Treasure of the Sierra Madre*)
1949 Joseph L. Mankiewicz (*A Letter to Three Wives*)
1950 Joseph L. Mankiewicz (*All About Eve*)
1951 George Stevens (*A Place in the Sun*)
1952 John Ford (*The Quiet Man*)
1953 Fred Zinnemann (*From Here to Eternity*)
1954 Elia Kazan (*On the Waterfront*)
1955 Delbert Mann (*Marty*)
1956 George Stevens (*Giant*)
1957 David Lean (*The Bridge on the River Kwai*)
1958 Vincente Minnelli (*Gigi*)
1959 William Wyler (*Ben-Hur*)
1960 Billy Wilder (*The Apartment*)
1961 Robert Wise, Jerome Robbins (*West Side Story*)
1962 David Lean (*Lawrence of Arabia*)
1963 Tony Richardson (*Tom Jones*)
1964 George Cukor (*My Fair Lady*)
1965 Robert Wise (*The Sound of Music*)
1966 Fred Zinnemann (*A Man for All Seasons*)
1967 Mike Nichols (*The Graduate*)
1968 Carol Reed (*Oliver!*)
1969 John Schlesinger (*Midnight Cowboy*)
1970 Franklin J. Schaffner (*Patton*)
1971 William Friedkin (*The French Connection*)
1972 Bob Fosse (*Cabaret*)
1973 George Roy Hill (*The Sting*)
1974 Francis Ford Coppola (*The Godfather Part II*)
1975 Milos Forman (*One Flew Over the Cuckoo's Nest*)
1976 John G. Avildsen (*Rocky*)
1977 Woody Allen (*Annie Hall*)
1978 Michael Cimino (*The Deer Hunter*)
1979 Robert Benton (*Kramer vs. Kramer*)
1980 Robert Redford (*Ordinary People*)
1981 Warren Beatty (*Reds*)
1982 Richard Attenborough (*Gandhi*)
1983 James L. Brooks (*Terms of Endearment*)
1984 Milos Forman (*Amadeus*)
1985 Sydney Pollack (*Out of Africa*)
1986 Oliver Stone (*Platoon*)
1987 Bernardo Bertolucci (*The Last Emperor*)
1988 Barry Levinson (*Rain Man*)
1989 Oliver Stone (*Born on the Fourth of July*)
1990 Kevin Costner (*Dances with Wolves*)
1991 Jonathan Demme (*The Silence of the Lambs*)
1992 Clint Eastwood (*Unforgiven*)

DIRECTING (CONTINUED)

1993 Steven Spielberg (*Schindler's List*)
1994 Robert Zemeckis (*Forrest Gump*)
1995 Mel Gibson (*Braveheart*)
1996 Anthony Minghella (*The English Patient*)
1997 James Cameron (*Titanic*)
1998 Steven Spielberg (*Saving Private Ryan*)
1999 Sam Mendes (*American Beauty*)
2000 Steven Soderbergh (*Traffic*)
2001 Ron Howard (*A Beautiful Mind*)
2002 Roman Polanski (*The Pianist*)
2003 Peter Jackson (*The Lord of the Rings: The Return of the King*)
2004 Clint Eastwood (*Million Dollar Baby*)
2005 Ang Lee (*Brokeback Mountain*)
2006 Martin Scorsese (*The Departed*)
2007 Joel Coen, Ethan Coen (*No Country for Old Men*)
2008 Danny Boyle (*Slumdog Millionaire*)

ADAPTED SCREENPLAY[2]

1928 Benjamin Glazer (*7th Heaven*)
1929 Hans Kraly (*The Patriot*)
1930 no award given
1931 Howard Estabrook (*Cimarron*)
1932 Edwin Burke (*Bad Girl*)
1933 Victor Heerman, Sarah Y. Mason (*Little Women*)
1934 Robert Riskin (*It Happened One Night*)
1935 Dudley Nichols (*The Informer*)[3] (declined)
1936 Pierre Collings, Sheridan Gibney (*The Story of Louis Pasteur*)[3]
1937 Norman Reilly Raine, Heinz Herald, Geza Herczeg (*The Life of Emile Zola*)[3]
1938 George Bernard Shaw, W.P. Lipscomb, Cecil Lewis, Ian Dalrymple (*Pygmalion*)[3]
1939 Sidney Howard (*Gone with the Wind*)[1,3]
1940 Donald Ogden Stewart (*The Philadelphia Story*)[3]
1941 Sidney Buchman, Seton I. Miller (*Here Comes Mr. Jordan*)[3]
1942 George Froeschel, James Hilton, Claudine West, Arthur Wimperis (*Mrs. Miniver*)[3]
1943 Julius J. Epstein, Philip G. Epstein, Howard Koch (*Casablanca*)[3]
1944 Frank Butler, Frank Cavett (*Going My Way*)[3]
1945 Charles Brackett, Billy Wilder (*The Lost Weekend*)[3]
1946 Robert E. Sherwood (*The Best Years of Our Lives*)[3]
1947 George Seaton (*Miracle on 34th Street*)[3]
1948 John Huston (*The Treasure of the Sierra Madre*)[3]
1949 Joseph L. Mankiewicz (*A Letter to Three Wives*)[3]
1950 Joseph L. Mankiewicz (*All About Eve*)[3]
1951 Michael Wilson, Harry Brown (*A Place in the Sun*)[3]
1952 Charles Schnee (*The Bad and the Beautiful*)[3]
1953 Daniel Taradash (*From Here to Eternity*)[3]
1954 George Seaton (*The Country Girl*)[3]
1955 Paddy Chayefsky (*Marty*)[3]
1956 James Poe, John Farrow, S.J. Perelman (*Around the World in 80 Days*)
1957 Michael Wilson[4], Carl Foreman[4] (Pierre Boulle, *The Bridge on the River Kwai*)
1958 Alan Jay Lerner (*Gigi*)
1959 Neil Paterson (*Room at the Top*)
1960 Richard Brooks (*Elmer Gantry*)
1961 Abby Mann (*Judgment at Nuremberg*)

Academy Awards (Oscars), 1928–2008 (continued)

ADAPTED SCREENPLAY[2] (CONTINUED)

1962 Horton Foote (*To Kill a Mockingbird*)
1963 John Osborne (*Tom Jones*)
1964 Edward Anhalt (*Becket*)
1965 Robert Bolt (*Doctor Zhivago*)
1966 Robert Bolt (*A Man for All Seasons*)
1967 Stirling Silliphant (*In the Heat of the Night*)
1968 James Goldman (*The Lion in Winter*)
1969 Waldo Salt (*Midnight Cowboy*)
1970 Ring Lardner, Jr. (*M*A*S*H*)
1971 Ernest Tidyman (*The French Connection*)
1972 Mario Puzo, Francis Ford Coppola (*The Godfather*)
1973 William Peter Blatty (*The Exorcist*)
1974 Francis Ford Coppola, Mario Puzo (*The Godfather Part II*)
1975 Lawrence Hauben, Bo Goldman (*One Flew Over the Cuckoo's Nest*)
1976 William Goldman (*All the President's Men*)
1977 Alvin Sargent (*Julia*)
1978 Oliver Stone (*Midnight Express*)
1979 Robert Benton (*Kramer vs. Kramer*)
1980 Alvin Sargent (*Ordinary People*)
1981 Ernest Thompson (*On Golden Pond*)
1982 Costa-Gavras, Donald Stewart (*Missing*)
1983 James L. Brooks (*Terms of Endearment*)
1984 Peter Shaffer (*Amadeus*)
1985 Kurt Luedtke (*Out of Africa*)
1986 Ruth Prawer Jhabvala (*A Room with a View*)
1987 Mark Peploe, Bernardo Bertolucci (*The Last Emperor*)
1988 Christopher Hampton (*Dangerous Liaisons*)
1989 Alfred Uhry (*Driving Miss Daisy*)
1990 Michael Blake (*Dances with Wolves*)
1991 Ted Tally (*The Silence of the Lambs*)
1992 Ruth Prawer Jhabvala (*Howards End*)
1993 Steven Zaillian (*Schindler's List*)
1994 Eric Roth (*Forrest Gump*)
1995 Emma Thompson (*Sense and Sensibility*)
1996 Billy Bob Thornton (*Sling Blade*)
1997 Brian Helgeland, Curtis Hanson (*L.A. Confidential*)
1998 Bill Condon (*Gods and Monsters*)
1999 John Irving (*The Cider House Rules*)
2000 Stephen Gaghan (*Traffic*)
2001 Akiva Goldsman (*A Beautiful Mind*)
2002 Ronald Harwood (*The Pianist*)
2003 Fran Walsh, Philippa Boyens, Peter Jackson (*The Lord of the Rings: The Return of the King*)
2004 Alexander Payne, Jim Taylor (*Sideways*)
2005 Larry McMurtry, Diana Ossana (*Brokeback Mountain*)
2006 William Monahan (*The Departed*)
2007 Joel Coen, Ethan Coen (*No Country for Old Men*)
2008 Simon Beaufoy (*Slumdog Millionaire*)

ORIGINAL SCREENPLAY[2]

1928 Ben Hecht (*Underworld*)[5]; Joseph Farnham (*The Fair Co-Ed; Laugh, Clown, Laugh; Telling the World*)[6]
1929 *no award given*
1930 Frances Marion (*The Big House*)
1931 John Monk Saunders (*The Dawn Patrol*)[5]
1932 Frances Marion (*The Champ*)[5]
1933 Robert Lord (*One Way Passage*)[5]
1934 Arthur Caesar (*Manhattan Melodrama*)[5]
1935 Ben Hecht, Charles MacArthur (*The Scoundrel*)[5]

ORIGINAL SCREENPLAY[2] (CONTINUED)

1936 Pierre Collings, Sheridan Gibney (*The Story of Louis Pasteur*)[5]
1937 William A. Wellman, Robert Carson (*A Star Is Born*)[5]
1938 Eleanore Griffin, Dore Schary (*Boys Town*)[5]
1939 Lewis R. Foster (*Mr. Smith Goes to Washington*)[5]
1940 Benjamin Glazer, John S. Toldy (*Arise, My Love*)[5]; Preston Sturges (*The Great McGinty*)[7]
1941 Harry Segall (*Here Comes Mr. Jordan*)[5]; Herman J. Mankiewicz, Orson Welles (*Citizen Kane*)[7]
1942 Emeric Pressburger (*Forty-Ninth Parallel*)[5]; Michael Kanin, Ring Lardner, Jr. (*Woman of the Year*)[7]
1943 William Saroyan (*The Human Comedy*)[5]; Norman Krasna (*Princess O'Rourke*)[7]
1944 Leo McCarey (*Going My Way*)[5]; Lamar Trotti (*Wilson*)[7]
1945 Charles G. Booth (*The House on 92nd Street*)[5]; Richard Schweizer (*Marie-Louise*)[7]
1946 Clemence Dane (*Vacation from Marriage*)[5]; Muriel Box, Sydney Box (*The Seventh Veil*)[7]
1947 Valentine Davies (*Miracle on 34th Street*)[5]; Sidney Sheldon (*The Bachelor and the Bobby-Soxer*)[7]
1948 Richard Schweizer, David Wechsler (*The Search*)[5]
1949 Douglas Morrow (*The Stratton Story*)[5]; Robert Pirosh (*Battleground*)[7]
1950 Edna Anhalt, Edward Anhalt (*Panic in the Streets*)[5]; Charles Brackett, Billy Wilder, D.M. Marshman, Jr. (*Sunset Blvd.*)[7]
1951 Paul Dehn, James Bernard (*Seven Days to Noon*)[5]; Alan Jay Lerner (*An American in Paris*)[7]
1952 Fredric M. Frank, Theodore St. John, Frank Cavett (*The Greatest Show on Earth*)[5]; T.E.B. Clarke (*The Lavender Hill Mob*)[7]
1953 Dalton Trumbo[4] (Ian McLellan Hunter, *Roman Holiday*)[5]; Charles Brackett, Walter Reisch, Richard L. Breen (*Titanic*)[7]
1954 Philip Yordan (*Broken Lance*)[5]; Budd Schulberg (*On the Waterfront*)[7]
1955 Daniel Fuchs (*Love Me or Leave Me*)[5]; William Ludwig, Sonya Levien (*Interrupted Melody*)[7]
1956 Dalton Trumbo[4] (as Robert Rich, *The Brave One*)[5]; Albert Lamorisse (*The Red Balloon*)[7]
1957 George Wells (*Designing Woman*)
1958 Nedrick Young[4] (as Nathan E. Douglas), Harold Jacob Smith (*The Defiant Ones*)
1959 Russell Rouse, Clarence Greene, Stanley Shapiro, Maurice Richlin (*Pillow Talk*)
1960 Billy Wilder, I.A.L. Diamond (*The Apartment*)
1961 William Inge (*Splendor in the Grass*)
1962 Ennio de Concini, Alfredo Giannetti, Pietro Germi (*Divorce—Italian Style*)
1963 James R. Webb (*How the West Was Won*)
1964 S.H. Barnett, Peter Stone, Frank Tarloff (*Father Goose*)
1965 Frederic Raphael (*Darling*)
1966 Claude Lelouch, Pierre Uytterhoeven (*A Man and a Woman*)
1967 William Rose (*Guess Who's Coming to Dinner*)
1968 Mel Brooks (*The Producers*)
1969 William Goldman (*Butch Cassidy and the Sundance Kid*)

Academy Awards (Oscars), 1928–2008 (continued)

ORIGINAL SCREENPLAY[2] (CONTINUED)

1970 Francis Ford Coppola, Edmund H. North (*Patton*)
1971 Paddy Chayefsky (*The Hospital*)
1972 Jeremy Larner (*The Candidate*)
1973 David S. Ward (*The Sting*)
1974 Robert Towne (*Chinatown*)
1975 Frank Pierson (*Dog Day Afternoon*)
1976 Paddy Chayefsky (*Network*)
1977 Woody Allen, Marshall Brickman (*Annie Hall*)
1978 Nancy Dowd, Waldo Salt, Robert C. Jones (*Coming Home*)
1979 Steve Tesich (*Breaking Away*)
1980 Bo Goldman (*Melvin and Howard*)
1981 Colin Welland (*Chariots of Fire*)
1982 John Briley (*Gandhi*)
1983 Horton Foote (*Tender Mercies*)
1984 Robert Benton (*Places in the Heart*)
1985 Earl W. Wallace, William Kelley, Pamela Wallace (*Witness*)
1986 Woody Allen (*Hannah and Her Sisters*)
1987 John Patrick Shanley (*Moonstruck*)
1988 Ronald Bass, Barry Morrow (*Rain Man*)
1989 Tom Schulman (*Dead Poets Society*)
1990 Bruce Joel Rubin (*Ghost*)
1991 Callie Khouri (*Thelma & Louise*)
1992 Neil Jordan (*The Crying Game*)
1993 Jane Campion (*The Piano*)
1994 Quentin Tarantino, Roger Avary (*Pulp Fiction*)
1995 Christopher McQuarrie (*The Usual Suspects*)
1996 Joel Coen, Ethan Coen (*Fargo*)
1997 Ben Affleck, Matt Damon (*Good Will Hunting*)
1998 Marc Norman, Tom Stoppard (*Shakespeare in Love*)
1999 Alan Ball (*American Beauty*)
2000 Cameron Crowe (*Almost Famous*)
2001 Julian Fellowes (*Gosford Park*)
2002 Pedro Almodóvar (*Talk to Her*)
2003 Sofia Coppola (*Lost in Translation*)
2004 Charlie Kaufman (*Eternal Sunshine of the Spotless Mind*)
2005 Paul Haggis, Bobby Moresco (*Crash*)
2006 Michael Arndt (*Little Miss Sunshine*)
2007 Diablo Cody (*Juno*)
2008 Dustin Lance Black (*Milk*)

CINEMATOGRAPHY

1928 Charles Rosher, Karl Struss (*Sunrise*)
1929 Clyde De Vinna (*White Shadows in the South Seas*)
1930 Joseph T. Rucker, Willard Van Der Veer (*With Byrd at the South Pole*)
1931 Floyd Crosby (*Tabu*)
1932 Lee Garmes (*Shanghai Express*)
1933 Charles Bryant Lang, Jr. (*A Farewell to Arms*)
1934 Victor Milner (*Cleopatra*)
1935 Hal Mohr (*A Midsummer Night's Dream*)
1936 Gaetano Gaudio (*Anthony Adverse*)
1937 Karl Freund (*The Good Earth*)
1938 Joseph Ruttenberg (*The Great Waltz*)
1939 Gregg Toland (*Wuthering Heights*)[8]; Ernest Haller, Ray Rennahan (*Gone with the Wind*)[9]
1940 George Barnes (*Rebecca*)[8]; Georges Perinal (*The Thief of Bagdad*)[9]
1941 Arthur Miller (*How Green Was My Valley*)[8]; Ernest Palmer, Ray Rennahan (*Blood and Sand*)[9]
1942 Joseph Ruttenberg (*Mrs. Miniver*)[8]; Leon Shamroy (*The Black Swan*)[9]

CINEMATOGRAPHY (CONTINUED)

1943 Arthur Miller (*The Song of Bernadette*)[8]; Hal Mohr, W. Howard Greene (*The Phantom of the Opera*)[9]
1944 Joseph LaShelle (*Laura*)[8]; Leon Shamroy (*Wilson*)[9]
1945 Harry Stradling (*The Picture of Dorian Gray*)[8]; Leon Shamroy (*Leave Her to Heaven*)[9]
1946 Arthur Miller (*Anna and the King of Siam*)[8]; Charles Rosher, Leonard Smith, Arthur Arling (*The Yearling*)[9]
1947 Guy Green (*Great Expectations*)[8]; Jack Cardiff (*Black Narcissus*)[9]
1948 William Daniels (*The Naked City*)[8]; Joseph Valentine, William V. Skall, Winton Hoch (*Joan of Arc*)[9]
1949 Paul C. Vogel (*Battleground*)[8]; Winton Hoch (*She Wore a Yellow Ribbon*)[9]
1950 Robert Krasker (*The Third Man*)[8]; Robert Surtees (*King Solomon's Mines*)[9]
1951 William C. Mellor (*A Place in the Sun*)[8]; Alfred Gilks, John Alton (*An American in Paris*)[9]
1952 Robert Surtees (*The Bad and the Beautiful*)[8]; Winton C. Hoch, Archie Stout (*The Quiet Man*)[9]
1953 Burnett Guffey (*From Here to Eternity*)[8]; Loyal Griggs (*Shane*)[9]
1954 Boris Kaufman (*On the Waterfront*)[8]; Milton Krasner (*Three Coins in the Fountain*)[9]
1955 James Wong Howe (*The Rose Tattoo*)[8]; Robert Burks (*To Catch a Thief*)[9]
1956 Joseph Ruttenberg (*Somebody Up There Likes Me*)[8]; Lionel Lindon (*Around the World in 80 Days*)[9]
1957 Jack Hildyard (*The Bridge on the River Kwai*)
1958 Sam Leavitt (*The Defiant Ones*)[8]; Joseph Ruttenberg (*Gigi*)[9]
1959 William C. Mellor (*The Diary of Anne Frank*)[8]; Robert L. Surtees (*Ben-Hur*)[9]
1960 Freddie Francis (*Sons and Lovers*)[8]; Russell Metty (*Spartacus*)[9]
1961 Eugen Shuftan (*The Hustler*)[8]; Daniel L. Fapp (*West Side Story*)[9]
1962 Jean Bourgoin, Walter Wottitz (*The Longest Day*)[8]; Fred A. Young (*Lawrence of Arabia*)[9]
1963 James Wong Howe (*Hud*)[8]; Leon Shamroy (*Cleopatra*)[9]
1964 Walter Lassally (*Zorba the Greek*)[8]; Harry Stradling (*My Fair Lady*)[9]
1965 Ernest Laszlo (*Ship of Fools*)[8]; Freddie Young (*Doctor Zhivago*)[9]
1966 Haskell Wexler (*Who's Afraid of Virginia Woolf?*)[8]; Ted Moore (*A Man for All Seasons*)[9]
1967 Burnett Guffey (*Bonnie and Clyde*)
1968 Pasqualino De Santis (*Romeo and Juliet*)
1969 Conrad Hall (*Butch Cassidy and the Sundance Kid*)
1970 Freddie Young (*Ryan's Daughter*)
1971 Oswald Morris (*Fiddler on the Roof*)
1972 Geoffrey Unsworth (*Cabaret*)
1973 Sven Nykvist (*Cries and Whispers*)
1974 Fred Koenekamp, Joseph Biroc (*The Towering Inferno*)
1975 John Alcott (*Barry Lyndon*)
1976 Haskell Wexler (*Bound for Glory*)
1977 Vilmos Zsigmond (*Close Encounters of the Third Kind*)
1978 Nestor Almendros (*Days of Heaven*)
1979 Vittorio Storaro (*Apocalypse Now*)
1980 Geoffrey Unsworth[1], Ghislain Cloquet (*Tess*)

Academy Awards (Oscars), 1928–2008 (continued)

CINEMATOGRAPHY (CONTINUED)

1981 Vittorio Storaro (*Reds*)
1982 Billy Williams, Ronnie Taylor (*Gandhi*)
1983 Sven Nykvist (*Fanny & Alexander*)
1984 Chris Menges (*The Killing Fields*)
1985 David Watkin (*Out of Africa*)
1986 Chris Menges (*The Mission*)
1987 Vittorio Storaro (*The Last Emperor*)
1988 Peter Biziou (*Mississippi Burning*)
1989 Freddie Francis (*Glory*)
1990 Dean Semler (*Dances with Wolves*)
1991 Robert Richardson (*JFK*)
1992 Philippe Rousselot (*A River Runs Through It*)
1993 Janusz Kaminski (*Schindler's List*)
1994 John Toll (*Legends of the Fall*)
1995 John Toll (*Braveheart*)
1996 John Seale (*The English Patient*)
1997 Russell Carpenter (*Titanic*)
1998 Janusz Kaminski (*Saving Private Ryan*)
1999 Conrad L. Hall (*American Beauty*)
2000 Peter Pau (*Crouching Tiger, Hidden Dragon*)
2001 Andrew Lesnie (*The Lord of the Rings: The Fellowship of the Ring*)
2002 Conrad L. Hall (*Road to Perdition*)[1]
2003 Russell Boyd (*Master and Commander: The Far Side of the World*)
2004 Robert Richardson (*The Aviator*)
2005 Dion Beebe (*Memoirs of a Geisha*)
2006 Guillermo Navarro (*Pan's Labyrinth*)
2007 Robert Elswit (*There Will Be Blood*)
2008 Anthony Dod Mantle (*Slumdog Millionaire*)

VISUAL EFFECTS[10]

1939 Fred Sersen (*The Rains Came*)
1940 Lawrence Butler (*The Thief of Bagdad*)
1941 Farciot Edouart, Gordon Jennings (*I Wanted Wings*)
1942 Farciot Edouart, Gordon Jennings, William L. Pereira (*Reap the Wild Wind*)
1943 Fred Sersen (*Crash Dive*)
1944 A. Arnold Gillespie, Donald Jahraus, Warren Newcombe (*Thirty Seconds Over Tokyo*)
1945 John P. Fulton (*Wonder Man*)
1946 Thomas Howard (*Blithe Spirit*)
1947 A. Arnold Gillespie, Warren Newcombe (*Green Dolphin Street*)
1948 Paul Eagler, J. McMillan Johnson, Russell Shearman, Clarence Slifer (*Portrait of Jennie*)
1949 *Mighty Joe Young*
1950 *Destination Moon*
1951 *When Worlds Collide*
1952 *Plymouth Adventure*
1953 *The War of the Worlds*
1954 *20,000 Leagues Under the Sea*
1955 *The Bridges at Toko-Ri*
1956 John Fulton (*The Ten Commandments*)
1957 [10]
1958 Tom Howard (*tom thumb*)
1959 A. Arnold Gillespie, Robert MacDonald (*Ben-Hur*)
1960 Gene Warren, Tim Baar (*The Time Machine*)
1961 Bill Warrington (*The Guns of Navarone*)
1962 Robert MacDonald (*The Longest Day*)
1963 Emil Kosa, Jr. (*Cleopatra*)
1964 Peter Ellenshaw, Hamilton Luske, Eustace Lycett (*Mary Poppins*)
1965 John Stears (*Thunderball*)
1966 Art Cruickshank (*Fantastic Voyage*)
1967 L.B. Abbott (*Doctor Dolittle*)

VISUAL EFFECTS[10] (CONTINUED)

1968 Stanley Kubrick (*2001: A Space Odyssey*)
1969 Robbie Robertson (*Marooned*)
1970 A.D. Flowers, L.B. Abbott (*Tora! Tora! Tora!*)
1971 Alan Maley, Eustace Lycett, Danny Lee (*Bedknobs and Broomsticks*)
1972 L.B. Abbott, A.D. Flowers (*The Poseidon Adventure*)
1974 Frank Brendel, Glen Robinson, Albert Whitlock (*Earthquake*)
1975 Albert Whitlock, Glen Robinson (*The Hindenburg*)
1976 Carlo Rambaldi, Glen Robinson, Frank Van der Veer (*King Kong*); L.B. Abbott, Glen Robinson, Matthew Yuricich (*Logan's Run*)
1977 John Stears, John Dykstra, Richard Edlund, Grant McCune, Robert Blalack (*Star Wars*)
1978 Les Bowie[1], Colin Chilvers, Denys Coop, Roy Field, Derek Meddings, Zoran Perisic (*Superman*)
1979 H.R. Giger, Carlo Rambaldi, Brian Johnson, Nick Allder, Denys Ayling (*Alien*)
1980 Brian Johnson, Richard Edlund, Dennis Muren, Bruce Nicholson (*The Empire Strikes Back*)
1981 Richard Edlund, Kit West, Bruce Nicholson, Joe Johnston (*Raiders of the Lost Ark*)
1982 Carlo Rambaldi, Dennis Muren, Kenneth F. Smith (*E.T.: The Extra-Terrestrial*)
1983 Richard Edlund, Dennis Muren, Ken Ralston, Phil Tippet (*Return of the Jedi*)
1984 Dennis Muren, Michael McAlister, Lorne Peterson, George Gibbs (*Indiana Jones and the Temple of Doom*)
1985 Ken Ralston, Ralph McQuarrie, Scott Farrar, David Berry (*Cocoon*)
1986 Robert Skotak, Stan Winston, John Richardson, Suzanne Benson (*Aliens*)
1987 Dennis Muren, William George, Harley Jessup, Kenneth Smith (*Innerspace*)
1988 Ken Ralston, Richard Williams, Edward Jones, George Gibbs (*Who Framed Roger Rabbit*)
1989 John Bruno, Dennis Muren, Hoyt Yeatman, Dennis Skotak (*The Abyss*)
1990 Eric Brevig, Rob Bottin, Tim McGovern, Alex Funke (*Total Recall*)
1991 Robert Skotak (*Terminator 2: Judgment Day*)
1992 Ken Ralston, Doug Chiang, Doug Smythe, Tom Woodruff, Jr. (*Death Becomes Her*)
1993 Dennis Muren, Stan Winston, Phil Tippett, Michael Lantieri (*Jurassic Park*)
1994 Ken Ralston, George Murphy, Stephen Rosenbaum, Allen Hall (*Forrest Gump*)
1995 Scott E. Anderson, Charles Gibson, Neal Scanlan, John Cox (*Babe*)
1996 Volker Engel, Douglas Smith, Clay Pinney, Joseph Viskocil (*Independence Day*)
1997 Robert Legato, Mark Lasoff, Thomas L. Fisher, Michael Kanfer (*Titanic*)
1998 Joel Hynek, Nicholas Brooks, Stuart Robertson, Kevin Mack (*What Dreams May Come*)
1999 John Gaeta, Janek Sirrs, Steve Courtley, Jon Thum (*The Matrix*)
2000 John Nelson, Neil Corbould, Tim Burke, Rob Harvey (*Gladiator*)
2001 Jim Rygiel, Randall William Cook, Richard Taylor, Mark Stetson (*The Lord of the Rings: The Fellowship of the Ring*)

Academy Awards (Oscars), 1928–2008 (continued)

VISUAL EFFECTS[10] (CONTINUED)

2002　Jim Rygiel, Joe Letteri, Randall William Cook, Alex Funke (*The Lord of the Rings: The Two Towers*)

2003　Jim Rygiel, Joe Letteri, Randall William Cook, Alex Funke (*The Lord of the Rings: The Return of the King*)

2004　John Dykstra, Scott Stokdyk, Anthony LaMolinara, John Frazier (*Spider-Man 2*)

2005　Joe Letteri, Brian Van't Hul, Christian Rivers, Richard Taylor (*King Kong*)

2006　John Knoll, Hal Hickel, Charles Gibson, Allen Hall (*Pirates of the Caribbean: Dead Man's Chest*)

2007　Michael Fink, Bill Westenhofer, Ben Morris, Trevor Wood (*The Golden Compass*)

2008　Eric Barba, Steve Preeg, Burt Dalton, Craig Barron (*The Curious Case of Benjamin Button*)

MAKEUP

1981　Rick Baker (*An American Werewolf in London*)
1982　Sarah Monzani, Michele Burke (*Quest for Fire*)
1983　no award given
1984　Paul LeBlanc, Dick Smith (*Amadeus*)
1985　Michael Westmore, Zoltan Elek (*Mask*)
1986　Chris Walas, Stephan Dupuis (*The Fly*)
1987　Rick Baker (*Harry and the Hendersons*)
1988　Ve Neill, Steve La Porte, Robert Short (*Beetlejuice*)
1989　Manlio Rocchetti, Lynn Barber, Kevin Haney (*Driving Miss Daisy*)
1990　John Caglione, Jr., Doug Drexler (*Dick Tracy*)
1991　Stan Winston, Jeff Dawn (*Terminator 2: Judgment Day*)
1992　Greg Cannom, Michele Burke, Matthew W. Mungle (*Bram Stoker's Dracula*)
1993　Greg Cannom, Ve Neill, Yolanda Toussieng (*Mrs. Doubtfire*).
1994　Rick Baker, Ve Neill, Yolanda Toussieng (*Ed Wood*)
1995　Peter Frampton, Paul Pattison, Lois Burwell (*Braveheart*)
1996　Rick Baker, David LeRoy Anderson (*The Nutty Professor*)
1997　Rick Baker, David LeRoy Anderson (*Men in Black*)
1998　Jenny Shircore (*Elizabeth*)
1999　Christine Blundell, Trefor Proud (*Topsy-Turvy*)
2000　Rick Baker, Gail Ryan (*Dr. Seuss' How the Grinch Stole Christmas*)
2001　Peter Owen, Richard Taylor (*The Lord of the Rings: The Fellowship of the Ring*)
2002　John Jackson, Beatrice Alba (*Frida*)
2003　Richard Taylor, Peter King (*The Lord of the Rings: The Return of the King*)
2004　Valli O'Reilly, Bill Corso (*Lemony Snicket's A Series of Unfortunate Events*)
2005　Howard Berger, Tami Lane (*The Chronicles of Narnia: The Lion, the Witch, and the Wardrobe*)
2006　David Martí, Montse Ribé (*Pan's Labyrinth*)
2007　Didier Lavergne, Jan Archibald (*La Vie en rose*)
2008　Greg Cannom (*The Curious Case of Benjamin Button*)

ORIGINAL SCORE

1938　Erich Wolfgang Korngold (*The Adventures of Robin Hood*)
1939　Herbert Stothart (*The Wizard of Oz*)

ORIGINAL SCORE (CONTINUED)

1940　Leigh Harline, Paul J. Smith, Ned Washington (*Pinocchio*)
1941　Bernard Herrmann (*All That Money Can Buy*)
1942　Max Steiner (*Now, Voyager*)
1943　Alfred Newman (*The Song of Bernadette*)
1944　Max Steiner (*Since You Went Away*)
1945　Miklós Rózsa (*Spellbound*)
1946　Hugo Friedhofer (*The Best Years of Our Lives*)
1947　Miklós Rózsa (*A Double Life*)
1948　Brian Easdale (*The Red Shoes*)
1949　Aaron Copland (*The Heiress*)
1950　Franz Waxman (*Sunset Blvd.*)
1951　Franz Waxman (*A Place in the Sun*)
1952　Dimitri Tiomkin (*High Noon*)
1953　Bronislau Kaper (*Lili*)
1954　Dimitri Tiomkin (*The High and Mighty*)
1955　Alfred Newman (*Love Is a Many-Splendored Thing*)
1956　Victor Young (*Around the World in 80 Days*)[1]
1957　Malcolm Arnold (*The Bridge on the River Kwai*)[11]
1958　Dimitri Tiomkin (*The Old Man and The Sea*)
1959　Miklós Rózsa (*Ben-Hur*)
1960　Ernest Gold (*Exodus*)
1961　Henry Mancini (*Breakfast at Tiffany's*)
1962　Maurice Jarre (*Lawrence of Arabia*)
1963　John Addison (*Tom Jones*)
1964　Richard M. Sherman, Robert B. Sherman (*Mary Poppins*)
1965　Maurice Jarre (*Doctor Zhivago*)
1966　John Barry (*Born Free*)
1967　Elmer Bernstein (*Thoroughly Modern Millie*)
1968　John Barry (*The Lion in Winter*)[12]; John Green (*Oliver!*)[13]
1969　Burt Bacharach (*Butch Cassidy and the Sundance Kid*)[12]; Lennie Hayton, Lionel Newman (*Hello, Dolly!*)[13]
1970　Francis Lai (*Love Story*); The Beatles (*Let It Be*)[14]
1971　Michel Legrand (*Summer of '42*)
1972　Charles Chaplin, Raymond Rasch[1], Larry Russell[1] (*Limelight*)
1973　Marvin Hamlisch (*The Way We Were*)
1974　Nino Rota, Carmine Coppola (*The Godfather Part II*)
1975　John Williams (*Jaws*)
1976　Jerry Goldsmith (*The Omen*)
1977　John Williams (*Star Wars*)
1978　Giorgio Moroder (*Midnight Express*)
1979　Georges Delerue (*A Little Romance*)
1980　Michael Gore (*Fame*)
1981　Vangelis (*Chariots of Fire*)
1982　John Williams (*E.T.: The Extra-Terrestrial*); Henry Mancini, Leslie Bricusse (*Victor/Victoria*)[14]
1983　Bill Conti (*The Right Stuff*); Michel Legrand, Alan Bergman, Marilyn Bergman (*Yentl*)[14]
1984　Maurice Jarre (*A Passage to India*); Prince (*Purple Rain*)[14]
1985　John Barry (*Out of Africa*)
1986　Herbie Hancock (*'Round Midnight*)
1987　Ryuichi Sakamoto, David Byrne, Cong Su (*The Last Emperor*).
1988　Dave Grusin (*The Milagro Beanfield War*)
1989　Alan Menken (*The Little Mermaid*)
1990　John Barry (*Dances with Wolves*)
1991　Alan Menken (*Beauty and the Beast*)
1992　Alan Menken (*Aladdin*)

Academy Awards (Oscars), 1928–2008 (continued)

ORIGINAL SCORE (CONTINUED)

1993 John Williams (*Schindler's List*)
1994 Hans Zimmer (*The Lion King*)
1995 Luis Enrique Bacalov (*Il Postino*)[12]; Alan Menken, Stephen Schwartz (*Pocahontas*)[15]
1996 Gabriel Yared (*The English Patient*)[12]; Rachel Portman (*Emma*)[15]
1997 James Horner (*Titanic*)[12]; Anne Dudley (*The Full Monty*)[15]
1998 Nicola Piovani (*Life Is Beautiful*)[12]; Stephen Warbeck (*Shakespeare in Love*)[15]
1999 John Corigliano (*The Red Violin*)
2000 Tan Dun (*Crouching Tiger, Hidden Dragon*)
2001 Howard Shore (*The Lord of the Rings: The Fellowship of the Ring*)
2002 Elliot Goldenthal (*Frida*)
2003 Howard Shore (*The Lord of the Rings: The Return of the King*)
2004 Jan A.P. Kaczmarek (*Finding Neverland*)
2005 Gustavo Santaolalla (*Brokeback Mountain*)
2006 Gustavo Santaolalla (*Babel*)
2007 Dario Marianelli (*Atonement*)
2008 A.R. Rahman (*Slumdog Millionaire*)

ORIGINAL SONG

1934 Con Conrad, Herb Magidson, "The Continental" (*The Gay Divorcee*)
1935 Harry Warren, Al Dubin, "Lullaby of Broadway" (*Gold Diggers of 1935*)
1936 Jerome Kern, Dorothy Fields, "The Way You Look Tonight" (*Swing Time*)
1937 Harry Owens, "Sweet Leilani" (*Waikiki Wedding*)
1938 Ralph Rainger, Leo Robin, "Thanks for the Memory" (*The Big Broadcast of 1938*)
1939 Harold Arlen, E.Y. Harburg, "Over the Rainbow" (*The Wizard of Oz*)
1940 Leigh Harline, Ned Washington, "When You Wish Upon a Star" (*Pinocchio*)
1941 Jerome Kern, Oscar Hammerstein II, "The Last Time I Saw Paris" (*Lady Be Good*)
1942 Irving Berlin, "White Christmas" (*Holiday Inn*)
1943 Harry Warren, Mack Gordon, "You'll Never Know" (*Hello, Frisco, Hello*)
1944 James Van Heusen, Johnny Burke, "Swinging on a Star" (*Going My Way*)
1945 Richard Rodgers, Oscar Hammerstein II, "It Might As Well Be Spring" (*State Fair*)
1946 Harry Warren, Johnny Mercer, "On the Atchison, Topeka, and the Santa Fe" (*The Harvey Girls*)
1947 Allie Wrubel, Ray Gilbert, "Zip-a-dee-doo-dah" (*Song of the South*)
1948 Jay Livingston, Ray Evans, "Buttons and Bows" (*The Paleface*)
1949 Frank Loesser, "Baby, It's Cold Outside" (*Neptune's Daughter*)
1950 Ray Evans, Jay Livingston, "Mona Lisa" (*Captain Carey, U.S.A.*)
1951 Hoagy Carmichael, Johnny Mercer, "In The Cool, Cool, Cool of the Evening" (*Here Comes the Groom*)
1952 Dimitri Tiomkin, Ned Washington, "High Noon (Do Not Forsake Me, Oh My Darlin')" (*High Noon*)
1953 Sammy Fain, Paul Francis Webster, "Secret Love" (*Calamity Jane*)

ORIGINAL SONG (CONTINUED)

1954 Jule Styne, Sammy Cahn, "Three Coins in the Fountain" (*Three Coins in the Fountain*)
1955 Sammy Fain, Paul Francis Webster, "Love Is a Many-Splendored Thing" (*Love Is a Many-Splendored Thing*)
1956 Jay Livingston, Ray Evans, "Whatever Will Be, Will Be (Que Sera, Sera)" (*The Man Who Knew Too Much*)
1957 James Van Heusen, Sammy Cahn, "All the Way" (*The Joker Is Wild*)
1958 Frederick Loewe, Alan Jay Lerner, "Gigi" (*Gigi*)
1959 James Van Heusen, Sammy Cahn, "High Hopes" (*A Hole in the Head*)
1960 Manos Hadjidakis, "Never on Sunday" (*Never on Sunday*)
1961 Henry Mancini, Johnny Mercer, "Moon River" (*Breakfast at Tiffany's*)
1962 Henry Mancini, Johnny Mercer, "Days of Wine and Roses" (*Days of Wine and Roses*)
1963 James Van Heusen, Sammy Cahn, "Call Me Irresponsible" (*Papa's Delicate Condition*)
1964 Richard M. Sherman, Robert B. Sherman, "Chim Chim Cher-ee" (*Mary Poppins*)
1965 Johnny Mandel, Paul Francis Webster, "The Shadow of Your Smile" (*The Sandpiper*)
1966 John Barry, Don Black, "Born Free" (*Born Free*)
1967 Leslie Bricusse, "Talk to the Animals" (*Doctor Dolittle*)
1968 Michel Legrand, Alan Bergman, Marilyn Bergman, "The Windmills of Your Mind" (*The Thomas Crown Affair*)
1969 Burt Bacharach, Hal David, "Raindrops Keep Fallin' On My Head" (*Butch Cassidy and the Sundance Kid*)
1970 Fred Karlin, Robb Royer (as Robb Wilson), James Griffin (as Arthur James), "For All We Know" (*Lovers and Other Strangers*)
1971 Isaac Hayes, "Theme from *Shaft*" (*Shaft*)
1972 Al Kasha, Joel Hirschhorn, "The Morning After" (*The Poseidon Adventure*)
1973 Marvin Hamlisch, Alan Bergman, Marilyn Bergman, "The Way We Were" (*The Way We Were*)
1974 Al Kasha, Joel Hirschhorn, "We May Never Love Like This Again" (*The Towering Inferno*)
1975 Keith Carradine, "I'm Easy" (*Nashville*)
1976 Barbra Streisand, Paul Williams, "Evergreen (Love Theme from *A Star Is Born*)" (*A Star Is Born*)
1977 Joseph Brooks, "You Light Up My Life" (*You Light Up My Life*)
1978 Paul Jabara, "Last Dance" (*Thank God It's Friday*)
1979 David Shire, Norman Gimbel, "It Goes Like It Goes" (*Norma Rae*)
1980 Michael Gore, Dean Pitchford, "Fame" (*Fame*)
1981 Burt Bacharach, Carole Bayer Sager, Christopher Cross, Peter Allen, "Arthur's Theme (Best That You Can Do)" (*Arthur*)
1982 Jack Nitzsche, Buffy Sainte-Marie, Will Jennings, "Up Where We Belong" (*An Officer and a Gentleman*)
1983 Giorgio Moroder, Keith Forsey, Irene Cara, "Flashdance...What a Feeling" (*Flashdance*)

Academy Awards (Oscars), 1928–2008 (continued)

ORIGINAL SONG (CONTINUED)

1984 Stevie Wonder, "I Just Called To Say I Love You" (*The Woman in Red*)

1985 Lionel Richie, "Say You, Say Me" (*White Nights*)

1986 Giorgio Moroder, Tom Whitlock, "Take My Breath Away" (*Top Gun*)

1987 Franke Previte, John DeNicola, Donald Markowitz, "(I've Had) The Time of My Life" (*Dirty Dancing*)

1988 Carly Simon, "Let the River Run" (*Working Girl*)

1989 Alan Menken, Howard Ashman, "Under the Sea" (*The Little Mermaid*)

1990 Stephen Sondheim, "Sooner or Later (I Always Get My Man)" (*Dick Tracy*)

1991 Alan Menken, Howard Ashman[1], "Beauty and the Beast" (*Beauty and the Beast*)

1992 Alan Menken, Tim Rice, "A Whole New World" (*Aladdin*)

1993 Bruce Springsteen, "Streets of Philadelphia" (*Philadelphia*)

1994 Elton John, Tim Rice, "Can You Feel the Love Tonight" (*The Lion King*)

1995 Alan Menken, Stephen Schwartz, "Colors of the Wind" (*Pocahontas*)

1996 Andrew Lloyd Webber, Tim Rice, "You Must Love Me" (*Evita*)

ORIGINAL SONG (CONTINUED)

1997 James Horner, Will Jennings, "My Heart Will Go On" (*Titanic*)

1998 Stephen Schwartz, "When You Believe" (*The Prince of Egypt*)

1999 Phil Collins, "You'll Be in My Heart" (*Tarzan*)

2000 Bob Dylan, "Things Have Changed" (*Wonder Boys*)

2001 Randy Newman, "If I Didn't Have You" (*Monsters, Inc.*)

2002 Eminem, Jeff Bass, Luis Resto, "Lose Yourself" (*8 Mile*)

2003 Fran Walsh, Howard Shore, Annie Lennox, "Into the West" (*The Lord of the Rings: The Return of the King*)

2004 Jorge Drexler, "Al otro lado del río" (*The Motorcycle Diaries*)

2005 Jordan Houston, Cedric Coleman, Paul Beauregard, "It's Hard Out Here for a Pimp" (*Hustle & Flow*)

2006 Melissa Etheridge, "I Need To Wake Up" (*An Inconvenient Truth*)

2007 Glen Hansard, Marketa Irglova, "Falling Slowly" (*Once*)

2008 A.R. Rahman, Gulzar, "Jai Ho" (*Slumdog Millionaire*)

[1]*Posthumously.* [2]*The current screenplay categories were adopted for the 1957 awards. Until then, various separate writing awards were given for silent-film title writing, screenplay, story and screenplay, and motion picture story.* [3]*Screenplay (for script only).* [4]*Actual winner was blacklisted at the time of the award and the honored work was attributed to another name or person; pseudonym or nominal winner is listed in parentheses.* [5]*Motion picture story (for narrative only; also called original story).* [6]*Title writing.* [7]*Story and screenplay (for narrative and script; also called original screenplay).* [8]*Black and white.* [9]*Color.* [10]*Until 1963, both visual and sound effects were honored as special effects. Only those recipients honored for visual effects are listed here. In 1957 only a sound-effects engineer was honored.* [11]*Scoring.* [12]*Drama or not a musical.* [13]*Musical.* [14]*Song score.* [15]*Musical or comedy.*

Golden Globe Awards, 2008

The Hollywood Foreign Press Association, a group of film critics for publications outside the US, began awarding prizes for outstanding American motion pictures and acting in 1944 and created the Golden Globe Awards in 1945. Over the years the prizes have expanded from recognizing only motion pictures and acting to include directing, screenwriting, film music

scoring, foreign-language films, and television, as well as a number of other categories of achievement. The television network on which each winning series appears is given in parentheses. Prize: globe encircled by a strip of motion picture film, in gold.

Golden Globes/Hollywood Foreign Press Association Web site: <www.goldenglobes.org>.

Film

Drama	*Slumdog Millionaire* (UK; director, Danny Boyle)
Musical/comedy	*Vicky Cristina Barcelona* (Spain/US; director, Woody Allen)
Director	Danny Boyle (*Slumdog Millionaire*, UK)
Actress, drama	Kate Winslet (*Revolutionary Road*, US/UK)
Actor, drama	Mickey Rourke (*The Wrestler*, US/France)
Actress, musical/comedy	Sally Hawkins (*Happy-Go-Lucky*, UK)
Actor, musical/comedy	Colin Farrell (*In Bruges*, UK/US)
Animated feature film	*WALL•E* (US; director, Andrew Stanton)
Foreign-language film	*Vals im Bashir* (*Waltz with Bashir*) (Israel/Germany/France/US; director, Ari Folman)
Supporting actress	Kate Winslet (*The Reader*, US/Germany)
Supporting actor	Heath Ledger (*The Dark Knight*, US/UK)
Screenplay	Simon Beaufoy (*Slumdog Millionaire*, UK)
Original score	A.R. Rahman (*Slumdog Millionaire*, UK)
Original song	"The Wrestler" (*The Wrestler*, US/France); music and lyrics, Bruce Springsteen

Golden Globe Awards, 2008 (continued)

Television

Drama series	Mad Men (AMC)
Actress, drama series	Anna Paquin (True Blood)
Actor, drama series	Gabriel Byrne (In Treatment)
Musical/comedy series	30 Rock (NBC)
Actress, musical/comedy series	Tina Fey (30 Rock)
Actor, musical/comedy series	Alec Baldwin (30 Rock)
Miniseries/movie made for TV	John Adams (HBO)
Actress, miniseries/movie made for TV	Laura Linney (John Adams)
Actor, miniseries/movie made for TV	Paul Giamatti (John Adams)
Supporting actress, series/miniseries/movie	Laura Dern (Recount)
Supporting actor, series/miniseries/movie	Tom Wilkinson (John Adams)

Sundance Film Festival, 2009

Founded as the Utah/US Film Festival in Salt Lake City in 1978, the exhibition has traditionally focused on documentary and dramatic works from outside the Hollywood mainstream. It came under the auspices of actor Robert Redford's Sundance Institute in 1985 and is held every January in Park City UT.

Sundance Institute Web site: <www.sundance.org>.

Grand Jury Prize, drama	Push: Based on the Novel by Sapphire (US; director, Lee Daniels)
Grand Jury Prize, documentary	We Live in Public (US; director, Ondi Timoner)
World Cinema Jury Prize, drama	La Nana (The Maid) (Chile; director, Sebastián Silva)
World Cinema Jury Prize, documentary	Rough Aunties (UK; director, Kim Longinotto)
Audience Award, drama	Push: Based on the Novel by Sapphire (US; director, Lee Daniels)
Audience Award, documentary	The Cove (US; director, Louie Psihoyos)
World Cinema Audience Award, drama	An Education (UK; director, Lone Scherfig)
World Cinema Audience Award, documentary	Afghan Star (US/Afghanistan; director, Havana Marking)
Directing Award, drama	Cary Fukunaga (Sin Nombre, Mexico/US)
Directing Award, documentary	Natalia Almada (El General [The General], Mexico/US)
World Cinema Directing Award, drama	Oliver Hirschbiegel (Five Minutes of Heaven, UK)
World Cinema Directing Award, documentary	Havana Marking (Afghan Star, US/Afghanistan)
Editing Award, documentary	Karen Schmeer (Sergio, US)
World Cinema Editing Award, documentary	Janus Billeskov Jansen and Thomas Papapetros (Burma VJ: reporter i et lukket land [Burma VJ: Reporting from a Closed Country], Denmark)
Cinematography Award, drama	Adriano Goldman (Sin Nombre, Mexico/US)
Cinematography Award, documentary	Robert Richman (The September Issue, US)
World Cinema Cinematography Award, drama	John de Borman (An Education, UK)
World Cinema Cinematography Award, documentary	John Maringouin (Big River Man, US)
Waldo Salt Screenwriting Award	Nicholas Jasenovec and Charlyne Yi (Paper Heart, US)
World Cinema Screenwriting Award	Guy Hibbert (Five Minutes of Heaven, UK)
Special Jury Prize, drama (for acting)	Mo'Nique (Push: Based on the Novel by Sapphire, US)
Special Jury Prize, drama (for the spirit of independence)	Lynn Shelton (Humpday, US)
Special Jury Prize, documentary	Good Hair (US; director, Jeff Stilson)
World Cinema Special Jury Prize, drama (for originality)	Louise-Michel (France; directors, Gustave de Kervern and Benoît Delépine)
World Cinema Special Jury Prize, documentary	Tibet in Song (US; director, Ngawang Choephel)
Jury Prize, short filmmaking	Short Term 12 (US; director, Destin Cretton)
International Jury Prize, short filmmaking	Lögner (Lies) (Sweden; director, Jonas Odell)
Sundance/NHK International Filmmakers Award	Ciencias Morales (Moral Sciences) (Argentina; director, Diego Lerman); The Girl (US; director, David Riker); Speed Girl (Japan; director, Qurata Kenji); Evolution (France; director, Lucile Hadzihalilovic)
Alfred P. Sloan Prize	Adam (US; director, Max Mayer)

Toronto International Film Festival, 2008

Founded in 1976, the Toronto International Film Festival is one of North America's best-attended exhibitions and a frequent forum for the premieres of major feature films. The festival, held in September, awards seven prizes, three of which are for Canadian films.

Toronto International Film Festival Web site: <www.tiff.net>.

Toronto International Film Festival, 2008 (continued)

Canadian feature film	*Lost Song* (director, Rodrigue Jean)
Canadian first feature	*Before Tomorrow* (directors, Marie-Hélène Cousineau and Madeline Piujuq Ivalu)
Canadian short	*Block B* (director, Chris Chan Fui Chong)
FIPRESCI Prize for Discovery	*Lymelife* (US; director, Derick Martini)
FIPRESCI Prize for Special Presentations	*Disgrace* (Australia/South Africa; director, Steve Jacobs)
People's Choice Award	*Slumdog Millionaire* (UK; director, Danny Boyle)
Discovery Award	*Hunger* (UK/Ireland; director, Steve McQueen)

Cannes International Film Festival, 2009

Established in 1946, the Cannes Festival is among the best-known and most influential film exhibitions in the world. An eight-member feature-film jury and a four-member short-film and Cinéfondation jury give awards to the best film (Palme d'Or) and other outstanding films (special jury prizes) in their respective categories. The Grand Prix goes to the feature film judged the most original, and the feature jury also chooses the winners of the performance, direction, and screenplay awards. The Caméra d'Or, for best first film, is awarded by a jury comprising film industry professionals and members of the moviegoing public. The Cinéfondation awards are for works of one hour or less by film-school students.

Cannes Festival Web site: <www.festival-cannes.fr>.

feature films ▸ **Palme d'Or:** *Das weisse Band* (*The White Ribbon*) (Austria/France/Germany/Italy; director, Michael Haneke); ▸ **Grand Prix:** *Un Prophète* (*A Prophet*) (France/Italy; director, Jacques Audiard); ▸ **best actress:** Charlotte Gainsbourg (*Antichrist*, Denmark/Germany/France/Sweden/Italy/Poland); ▸ **best actor:** Christoph Waltz (*Inglourious Basterds*, US/Germany); ▸ **best director:** Brillante Mendoza (*Kinatay* [*The Execution of P*], Philippines/France); ▸ **best screenplay:** Mei Feng (*Chung feng chen zui de ye wan* [*Spring Fever*], China/Hong Kong/France); ▸ **jury prize:** *Fish Tank* (UK; director, Andrea Arnold); *Bakjwi* (*Thirst*) (South Korea; director, Park Chan-wook); ▸ **Caméra d'Or:** *Samson and Delilah* (Australia; director, Warwick Thornton)

short films ▸ **Palme d'Or:** *Arena* (Portugal; director, João Salaviza)

Cinéfondation ▸ **1st prize:** *Baba* (Czech Republic; director, Zuzana Kirchnerova-Spidlova); ▸ **2nd prize:** *Goodbye* (China; director, Song Fang); ▸ **3rd prize:** *Diploma* (Israel; director, Yaelle Kayam); *Nammae Ui Jip* (*Don't Step Out of the House*) (South Korea; director, Jo Sung-hee)

Berlin International Film Festival, 2009

The Berlin International Film Festival (Internationale Filmfestspiele Berlin), held annually since its founding in West Berlin in 1951, comprises some 20 separate competitions and juries emphasizing aspects of both worldwide and German cinema, each with their own prizes. The International Jury, made up of film-industry figures from across the globe, selects the winners of the Golden and Silver Bears, the festival's top awards.

Berlin International Film Festival Web site: <www.berlinale.de>.

Golden Bear	*La teta asustada* (*The Milk of Sorrow*) (Spain/Peru; director, Claudia Llosa)
Jury Grand Prix (Silver Bear)	*Alle anderen* (*Everyone Else*) (Germany; director, Maren Ade); *Gigante* (Uruguay/Argentina/Germany/Spain; director, Adrián Biniez)
Silver Bear, director	Asghar Farhadi (*Darbareye Elly* [*About Elly*], Iran)
Silver Bear, actress	Birgit Minichmayr (*Alle anderen* [*Everyone Else*], Germany)
Silver Bear, actor	Sotigui Kouyate (*London River*, UK/France/Algeria)
Silver Bear, script	Oren Moverman and Alessandro Camon (*The Messenger*, US)
Silver Bear, artistic contribution	Gábor Erdély and Tamás Székely (sound design) (*Katalin Varga*, Romania/UK/Hungary)
Alfred Bauer Prize (for a work of particular innovation)	*Gigante* (Uruguay/Argentina/Germany/Spain; director, Adrián Biniez); *Tatarak* (*Sweet Rush*) (Poland; director, Andrzej Wajda)
Ecumenical Jury prizes	Competition: *Lille soldat* (*Little Soldier*) (Denmark; director, Annette K. Olesen); Panorama: *Welcome* (France; director, Philippe Lioret); Forum: *Treeless Mountain* (US/South Korea; director, So Yong Kim)
FIPRESCI prizes	Competition: *La teta asustada* (*The Milk of Sorrow*) (Spain/Peru; director, Claudia Llosa); Panorama: *Nord* (*North*) (Norway; director, Rune Denstad Langlo); Forum: *Ai no mukidashi* (*Love Exposure*) (Japan; director, Sion Sono)
Best First Feature Award	*Gigante* (Uruguay/Argentina/Germany/Spain; director, Adrián Biniez)

Worldwide Top-Grossing Films (Actual US Dollars)

As of 25 Aug 2009. Includes reissues. Source: <www.boxofficemojo.com>.

1	Titanic	1997
2	The Lord of the Rings: The Return of the King	2003
3	Pirates of the Caribbean: Dead Man's Chest	2006
4	The Dark Knight	2008
5	Harry Potter and the Sorcerer's Stone	2001
6	Pirates of the Caribbean: At World's End	2007
7	Harry Potter and the Order of the Phoenix	2007
8	The Lord of the Rings: The Two Towers	2002
9	Star Wars: Episode I—The Phantom Menace	1999
10	Shrek 2	2004
11	Jurassic Park	1993
12	Harry Potter and the Goblet of Fire	2005
13	Spider-Man 3	2007
14	Harry Potter and the Half-Blood Prince	2009
15	Harry Potter and the Chamber of Secrets	2002
16	The Lord of the Rings: The Fellowship of the Ring	2001
17	Finding Nemo	2003
18	Star Wars: Episode III—Revenge of the Sith	2005
19	Transformers: Revenge of the Fallen	2009
20	Spider-Man	2002

US Top-Grossing Films (Constant US Dollars, Estimated)

Admissions—the number of tickets sold to a movie—tell a different story from the raw dollars earned. While recent films have made hundreds of millions of dollars, only 2 of the top 10 films in terms of attendance were released after 1980. Includes reissues. Source: <www.boxofficemojo.com>.

		ADMISSIONS	2009 US DOLLARS	ACTUAL US DOLLARS
1	Gone with the Wind (1939)	202,044,600	1,450,680,400	198,676,459
2	Star Wars (1977)	178,119,600	1,278,898,700	460,998,007
3	The Sound of Music (1965)	142,415,400	1,022,542,400	158,671,368
4	E.T.: The Extra-Terrestrial (1982)	141,854,300	1,018,514,100	435,110,554
5	The Ten Commandments (1956)	131,000,000	940,580,000	65,500,000
6	Titanic (1997)	128,345,900	921,523,500	600,788,188
7	Jaws (1975)	128,078,800	919,605,900	260,000,000
8	Doctor Zhivago (1965)	124,135,500	891,292,600	111,721,910
9	The Exorcist (1973)	110,568,700	793,883,100	232,671,011
10	Snow White and the Seven Dwarfs (1937)	109,000,000	782,620,000	184,925,486

US Top-Grossing Film Openings

As of 25 Aug 2009. Table lists the largest box-office receipts over the first three days of theatrical release in the United States. Source: <www.boxofficemojo.com>.

		ACTUAL US DOLLARS			ACTUAL US DOLLARS
1	The Dark Knight (2008)	158,411,483	11	Harry Potter and the Goblet of Fire (2005)	102,685,961
2	Spider-Man 3 (2007)	151,116,516	12	Indiana Jones and the Kingdom of the Crystal Skull (2008)	100,137,835
3	Pirates of the Caribbean: Dead Man's Chest (2006)	135,634,554	13	Iron Man (2008)	98,618,668
4	Shrek the Third (2007)	121,629,270	14	Harry Potter and the Prisoner of Azkaban (2004)	93,687,367
5	Spider-Man (2002)	114,844,116	15	The Matrix Reloaded (2003)	91,774,413
6	Pirates of the Caribbean: At World's End (2007)	114,732,820	16	Harry Potter and the Sorcerer's Stone (2001)	90,294,621
7	Transformers: Revenge of the Fallen (2009)	108,966,307	17	Harry Potter and the Chamber of Secrets (2002)	88,357,488
8	Star Wars: Episode III—Revenge of the Sith (2005)	108,435,841	18	Spider-Man 2 (2004)	88,156,227
9	Shrek 2 (2004)	108,037,878	19	X2: X-Men United (2003)	85,558,731
10	X-Men: The Last Stand (2006)	102,750,665	20	X-Men Origins: Wolverine (2009)	85,058,003

Top US DVD Rentals and Sales, 2008

Source: Video Business. Web site: <www.videobusiness.com>.

	RENTALS	SALES
1	I Am Legend	The Dark Knight
2	The Bucket List	Iron Man
3	3:10 to Yuma	Alvin and the Chipmunks
4	No Country for Old Men	I Am Legend
5	Juno	Kung Fu Panda
6	National Treasure 2: Book of Secrets	Wall•E

Top US DVD Rentals and Sales, 2008 (continued)

RENTALS		SALES
7	American Gangster	National Treasure 2: Book of Secrets
8	Good Luck Chuck	Indiana Jones and the Kingdom of the Crystal Skull
9	Fool's Gold	Enchanted
10	27 Dresses	Bee Movie
11	The Game Plan	Mamma Mia!
12	21	Juno
13	Iron Man	American Gangster
14	Jumper	Hancock
15	Michael Clayton	Sex and the City
16	The Brave One	The Game Plan
17	Dan in Real Life	The Chronicles of Narnia: Prince Caspian
18	Baby Mama	Horton Hears a Who!
19	Gone Baby Gone	27 Dresses
20	P.S. I Love You	Tinker Bell

Television

Emmy Awards, 2008

The Academy of Television Arts and Sciences was founded in 1946 and gave out its first awards for excellence in television, named the Emmys after the nickname of an early television camera part, for the 1948 season. That first year six awards were presented. In the ensuing decades the categories have evolved to include separate prime-time, daytime, and regional Emmy Awards. The latest Emmys were awarded 21 Sep 2008 in Los Angeles. Award: statuette of a winged woman holding an atom.

Emmy Awards Web site:
<http://www.emmys.tv/awards>.

Comedy: *30 Rock* (NBC)
Lead actor, comedy: Alec Baldwin, *30 Rock* (NBC)
Lead actress, comedy: Tina Fey, *30 Rock* (NBC)
Supporting actor, comedy: Jeremy Piven, *Entourage* (HBO)
Supporting actress, comedy: Jean Smart, *Samantha Who?* (ABC)
Drama: *Mad Men* (AMC)
Lead actor, drama: Bryan Cranston, *Breaking Bad* (AMC)
Lead actress, drama: Glenn Close, *Damages* (FX)

Supporting actor, drama: Zeljko Ivanek, *Damages* (FX)
Supporting actress, drama: Dianne Wiest, *In Treatment* (HBO)
Miniseries: *John Adams* (HBO)
Lead actor, miniseries or movie: Paul Giamatti, *John Adams* (HBO)
Lead actress, miniseries or movie: Laura Linney, *John Adams* (HBO)
Variety/music/comedy: *The Daily Show with Jon Stewart* (Comedy Central)
Nonfiction: *American Masters* (PBS); *This American Life* (Showtime)

Emmy Awards, 1949–2008[1]

1949
Most popular program: *Pantomime Quiz*, KTLA
TV film: *Your Show Time: The Necklace*

1950
Live show: *The Ed Wynn Show*, KTTV
Kinescope show: *The Texaco Star Theater*, KNBH (NBC)
TV film: *The Life of Riley*, KNBH
Public service/cultural/educational: *Crusade in Europe*, KECA-TV/KTTV (ABC)
Children's: *Time for Beany*, KTLA

1951
Variety: *The Alan Young Show*, KTTV (CBS)
Drama: *Pulitzer Prize Playhouse*, KECA-TV (ABC)
Game/audience participation: *Truth or Consequences*, KTTV (CBS)
Children's: *Time for Beany*, KTLA

1951 (continued)
Educational: *KFI-TV University*, KFI-TV
Cultural: *Campus Chorus and Orchestra*, KTSL

1952
Variety: *Your Show of Shows* (NBC)
Comedy: *The Red Skelton Show* (NBC)
Drama: *Studio One* (CBS)

1953
Variety: *Your Show of Shows* (NBC)
Comedy: *I Love Lucy* (CBS)
Drama: *Robert Montgomery Presents* (NBC)
Mystery/action/adventure: *Dragnet* (NBC)
Public affairs: *See It Now* (CBS)
Audience participation/quiz/panel: *What's My Line?* (CBS)
Children's: *Time for Beany* (syndicated)

Emmy Awards, 1949–2008[1] (continued)

1954
Variety: *Omnibus* (CBS)
Comedy: *I Love Lucy* (CBS)
Drama: *The U.S. Steel Hour* (ABC)
Mystery/action/adventure: *Dragnet* (NBC)
Public affairs: *Victory at Sea* (NBC)
Audience participation/quiz/panel: *This Is Your Life* (NBC); *What's My Line?* (CBS)
Children's: *Kukla, Fran, and Ollie* (NBC)

1955
Variety: *Disneyland* (ABC)
Comedy: *Make Room for Daddy* (ABC)
Drama: *The U.S. Steel Hour* (ABC)
Mystery/intrigue: *Dragnet* (NBC)
Western/adventure: *Stories of the Century* (syndicated)
Cultural/religious/educational: *Omnibus* (CBS)
Audience participation/quiz/panel: *This Is Your Life* (NBC)
Children's: *Lassie* (CBS)

1956
Variety: *The Ed Sullivan Show* (CBS)
Comedy: *The Phil Silvers Show: You'll Never Get Rich* (CBS)
Drama: *Producers' Showcase* (NBC)
Action/adventure: *Disneyland* (ABC)
Music: *Your Hit Parade* (NBC)
Documentary: *Omnibus* (CBS)
Audience participation: *The $64,000 Question* (CBS)
Children's: *Lassie* (CBS)

1957
Series (½ hr. or less): *The Phil Silvers Show: You'll Never Get Rich* (CBS)
Series (1 hr. or more): *Caesar's Hour* (NBC)
New series: *Playhouse 90* (CBS)

1958
Musical/variety/audience participation/quiz: *The Dinah Shore Chevy Show* (NBC)
Comedy: *The Phil Silvers Show: You'll Never Get Rich* (CBS)
Drama, continuing: *Gunsmoke* (CBS)
Drama, anthology: *Playhouse 90* (CBS)
New series: *The Seven Lively Arts* (CBS)
Public service: *Omnibus* (ABC/NBC)

1959
Musical/variety: *The Dinah Shore Chevy Show* (NBC)
Comedy: *The Jack Benny Show* (CBS)
Drama (<1 hr.): *Alcoa-Goodyear Playhouse* (NBC)
Drama (1 hr.+): *Playhouse 90* (CBS)
Western: *Maverick* (ABC)
News reporting: *The Huntley-Brinkley Report* (NBC)
Public service: *Omnibus* (NBC)
Panel/quiz/audience participation: *What's My Line?* (CBS)

1960
Variety: *The Fabulous Fifties* (CBS)
Humor: *Art Carney Special* (NBC)
Drama: *Playhouse 90* (CBS)
News: *The Huntley-Brinkley Report* (NBC)
Public affairs/education: *The Twentieth Century* (CBS)
Children's: *Huckleberry Hound* (syndicated)

1961
Variety: *Astaire Time* (NBC)
Humor: *The Jack Benny Show* (CBS)
Drama: *Hallmark Hall of Fame: Macbeth* (NBC)
News: *The Huntley-Brinkley Report* (NBC)
Public affairs/education: *The Twentieth Century* (CBS)
Children's: "Aaron Copland's Birthday Party," *Young People's Concert* (CBS)
Program of the year: *Hallmark Hall of Fame: Macbeth* (NBC)

1962
Variety: *The Garry Moore Show* (CBS)
Humor: *The Bob Newhart Show* (NBC)
Drama: *The Defenders* (CBS)
News: *The Huntley-Brinkley Report* (NBC)
Educational/public affairs: *David Brinkley's Journal* (NBC)
Children's: *New York Philharmonic Young People's Concerts with Leonard Bernstein* (CBS)
Program of the year: *Hallmark Hall of Fame: Victoria Regina* (NBC)

1963
Variety: *The Andy Williams Show* (NBC)
Humor: *The Dick Van Dyke Show* (CBS)
Drama: *The Defenders* (CBS)
News: *The Huntley-Brinkley Report* (NBC)
Commentary/public affairs: *David Brinkley's Journal* (NBC)
Documentary: *The Tunnel* (NBC)
Panel/quiz/aud. particip.: *The G.E. College Bowl* (CBS)
Children's: *Walt Disney's Wonderful World of Color* (NBC)
Program of the year: *The Tunnel* (NBC)

1964
Variety: *The Danny Kaye Show* (CBS)
Comedy: *The Dick Van Dyke Show* (CBS)
Drama: *The Defenders* (CBS)
News reports: *The Huntley-Brinkley Report* (NBC)
Commentary/public affairs: "Cuba—Part I: The Bay of Pigs" and "Cuba—Part II: The Missile Crisis," *NBC White Paper* (NBC)
Documentary: *The Making of the President 1960* (ABC)
Children's: *Discovery '63–'64* (ABC)
Program of the year: *The Making of the President 1960* (ABC)

1965
Entertainment: *The Dick Van Dyke Show* (CBS); *Hallmark Hall of Fame: The Magnificent Yankee* (NBC); *My Name Is Barbra* (CBS); "What Is Sonata Form?," *New York Philharmonic Young People's Concerts with Leonard Bernstein* (CBS)
News/docu./info./sports: "I, Leonardo da Vinci," *Saga of Western Man* (ABC); *The Louvre* (NBC)

1966
Variety: *The Andy Williams Show* (NBC)
Comedy: *The Dick Van Dyke Show* (CBS)
Drama: *The Fugitive* (ABC)

1967
Variety: *The Andy Williams Show* (NBC)
Comedy: *The Monkees* (NBC)
Drama: *Mission: Impossible* (CBS)

Emmy Awards, 1949–2008[1] (continued)

1968
Musical/variety: *Rowan and Martin's Laugh-In* (NBC)
Comedy: *Get Smart* (NBC)
Drama: *Mission: Impossible* (CBS)

1969
Variety/musical: *Rowan and Martin's Laugh-In* (NBC)
Comedy: *Get Smart* (NBC)
Drama: *NET Playhouse* (NET)

1970
Variety/musical: *The David Frost Show* (syndicated)
Comedy: *My World and Welcome to It* (NBC)
Drama: *Marcus Welby, M.D.* (ABC)

1971
Comedy: *All in the Family* (CBS)
Drama: *The Bold Ones: The Senator* (NBC)
Variety, musical: *The Flip Wilson Show* (NBC)
Variety, talk: *The David Frost Show* (syndicated)
New series: *All in the Family* (CBS)

1972
Comedy: *All in the Family* (CBS)
Drama: *Masterpiece Theatre: Elizabeth R* (PBS)
Variety, musical: *The Carol Burnett Show* (CBS)
Variety, talk: *The Dick Cavett Show* (ABC)
New series: *Masterpiece Theatre: Elizabeth R* (PBS)

1973
Comedy: *All in the Family* (CBS)
Drama (continuing): *The Waltons* (CBS)
Drama/comedy (limited): *Masterpiece Theatre: Tom Brown's Schooldays* (PBS)
Variety, musical: *The Julie Andrews Hour* (ABC)
New series: *America* (NBC)

1974
Comedy: *M*A*S*H* (CBS)
Drama: *Masterpiece Theatre: Upstairs, Downstairs* (PBS)
Limited series: *Columbo* (NBC)
Music/variety: *The Carol Burnett Show* (CBS)

1975
Comedy: *The Mary Tyler Moore Show* (CBS)
Drama: *Masterpiece Theatre: Upstairs, Downstairs* (PBS)
Limited series: *Benjamin Franklin* (CBS)
Comedy-variety/music: *The Carol Burnett Show* (CBS)

1976
Comedy: *The Mary Tyler Moore Show* (CBS)
Drama: *Police Story* (NBC)
Limited series: *Masterpiece Theatre: Upstairs, Downstairs* (PBS)
Comedy-variety/music: *NBC's Saturday Night* (NBC)

1977
Comedy: *The Mary Tyler Moore Show* (CBS)
Drama: *Masterpiece Theatre: Upstairs, Downstairs* (PBS)
Limited series: *Roots* (ABC)
Comedy-variety/music: *Van Dyke and Company* (NBC)

1978
Comedy: *All in the Family* (CBS)
Drama: *The Rockford Files* (NBC)

1978 (continued)
Limited series: *Holocaust* (NBC)
Comedy-variety/music: *The Muppet Show* (syndicated)
Informational: *The Body Human* (CBS)

1979
Comedy: *Taxi* (ABC)
Drama: *Lou Grant* (CBS)
Limited series: *Roots: The Next Generations* (ABC)

1980
Comedy: *Taxi* (ABC)
Drama: *Lou Grant* (CBS)
Limited series: *Edward & Mrs. Simpson* (syndicated)

1981
Comedy: *Taxi* (ABC)
Drama: *Hill Street Blues* (NBC)
Limited series: *Shogun* (NBC)
Informational: *Steve Allen's Meeting of Minds* (PBS)

1982
Comedy: *Barney Miller* (ABC)
Drama: *Hill Street Blues* (NBC)
Limited series: *Marco Polo* (NBC)
Informational: *Creativity with Bill Moyers* (PBS)

1983
Comedy: *Cheers* (NBC)
Drama: *Hill Street Blues* (NBC)
Limited series: *Nicholas Nickleby* (syndicated)
Informational: *The Barbara Walters Specials* (ABC)

1984
Comedy: *Cheers* (NBC)
Drama: *Hill Street Blues* (NBC)
Limited series: *American Playhouse: Concealed Enemies* (PBS)
Informational: *A Walk Through the 20th Century with Bill Moyers* (PBS)

1985
Comedy: *The Cosby Show* (NBC)
Drama: *Cagney & Lacey* (CBS)
Limited series: *Masterpiece Theatre: The Jewel in the Crown* (PBS)
Informational: *The Living Planet: A Portrait of the Earth* (PBS)

1986
Comedy: *The Golden Girls* (NBC)
Drama: *Cagney & Lacey* (CBS)
Miniseries: *Peter the Great* (NBC)
Informational: *Great Performances: Laurence Olivier—A Life* (PBS); *Planet Earth* (PBS)

1987
Comedy: *The Golden Girls* (NBC)
Drama: *L.A. Law* (NBC)
Miniseries: *A Year in the Life* (NBC)
Informational: *Smithsonian World* (PBS); *American Masters: Unknown Chaplin* (PBS)

1988
Comedy: *The Wonder Years* (ABC)
Drama: *thirtysomething* (ABC)

Emmy Awards, 1949–2008[1] (continued)

1988 (continued)
Miniseries: *The Murder of Mary Phagan* (NBC)
Informational: *American Masters: Buster Keaton: A Hard Act To Follow* (PBS); *Nature* (PBS)

1989
Comedy: *Cheers* (NBC)
Drama: *L.A. Law* (NBC)
Miniseries: *War and Remembrance* (ABC)
Informational: *Nature* (PBS)

1990
Comedy: *Murphy Brown* (CBS)
Drama: *L.A. Law* (NBC)
Miniseries: *Drug Wars: The Camarena Story* (NBC)
Variety/music/comedy: *In Living Color* (Fox)
Informational: *Smithsonian World* (PBS)

1991
Comedy: *Cheers* (NBC)
Drama: *L.A. Law* (NBC)
Miniseries: *Separate but Equal* (ABC)
Informational: *The Civil War* (PBS)

1992
Comedy: *Murphy Brown* (CBS)
Drama: *Northern Exposure* (CBS)
Miniseries: *A Woman Named Jackie* (NBC)
Variety/music/comedy: *The Tonight Show Starring Johnny Carson* (NBC)
Informational: *MGM: When the Lion Roars* (TNT)

1993
Comedy: *Seinfeld* (NBC)
Drama: *Picket Fences* (CBS)
Miniseries: *Prime Suspect 2* (PBS)
Variety/music/comedy: *Saturday Night Live* (NBC)
Informational: *Healing and the Mind with Bill Moyers* (PBS)

1994
Comedy: *Frasier* (NBC)
Drama: *Picket Fences* (CBS)
Miniseries: *Prime Suspect 3* (PBS)
Variety/music/comedy: *Late Show with David Letterman* (CBS)
Informational: *Later with Bob Costas* (NBC)

1995
Comedy: *Frasier* (NBC)
Drama: *NYPD Blue* (ABC)
Miniseries: *Joseph* (TNT)
Variety/music/comedy: *The Tonight Show with Jay Leno* (NBC)
Informational: *Baseball* (PBS); *TV Nation* (NBC)

1996
Comedy: *Frasier* (NBC)
Drama: *ER* (NBC)
Miniseries: *Gulliver's Travels* (NBC)
Variety/music/comedy: *Dennis Miller Live* (HBO)
Informational: *Lost Civilizations* (NBC)

1997
Comedy: *Frasier* (NBC)
Drama: *Law & Order* (NBC)
Miniseries: *Prime Suspect 5: Errors of Judgment* (PBS)

1997 (continued)
Variety/music/comedy: *Tracey Takes On...* (HBO)
Informational: *Biography* (A&E); *The Great War and the Shaping of the 20th Century* (PBS)

1998
Comedy: *Frasier* (NBC)
Drama: *The Practice* (ABC)
Miniseries: *From the Earth to the Moon* (HBO)
Variety/music/comedy: *Late Show with David Letterman* (CBS)
Nonfiction: *The American Experience* (PBS)

1999
Comedy: *Ally McBeal* (Fox)
Drama: *The Practice* (ABC)
Miniseries: *Horatio Hornblower: The Even Chance* (A&E)
Variety/music/comedy: *Late Show with David Letterman* (CBS)
Nonfiction: *The American Experience* (PBS); *American Masters* (PBS)

2000
Comedy: *Will & Grace* (NBC)
Drama: *The West Wing* (NBC)
Miniseries: *The Corner* (HBO)
Variety/music/comedy: *Late Show with David Letterman* (CBS)
Nonfiction: *American Masters* (PBS)

2001
Comedy: *Sex and the City* (HBO)
Drama: *The West Wing* (NBC)
Miniseries: *Anne Frank* (ABC)
Variety/music/comedy: *Late Show with David Letterman* (CBS)
Nonfiction: *American Masters* (PBS)

2002
Comedy: *Friends* (NBC)
Drama: *The West Wing* (NBC)
Miniseries: *Band of Brothers* (HBO)
Variety/music/comedy: *Late Show with David Letterman* (CBS)
Nonfiction: *Biography* (A&E)

2003
Comedy: *Everybody Loves Raymond* (CBS)
Drama: *The West Wing* (NBC)
Miniseries: *Steven Spielberg Presents Taken* (Sci Fi)
Variety/music/comedy: *The Daily Show with Jon Stewart* (Comedy Central)
Nonfiction: *American Masters* (PBS)

2004
Comedy: *Arrested Development* (Fox)
Drama: *The Sopranos* (HBO)
Miniseries: *Angels in America* (HBO)
Variety/music/comedy: *The Daily Show with Jon Stewart* (Comedy Central)
Nonfiction: *American Masters* (PBS)

2005
Comedy: *Everybody Loves Raymond* (CBS)
Drama: *Lost* (ABC)
Miniseries: *Masterpiece Theatre: The Lost Prince* (PBS)

Emmy Awards, 1949–2008[1] (continued)

2005 (continued)
Variety/music/comedy: *The Daily Show with Jon Stewart* (Comedy Central)
Nonfiction: *Broadway: The American Musical* (PBS)

2006
Comedy: *The Office* (NBC)
Drama: *24* (Fox)
Miniseries: *Elizabeth I* (HBO)
Variety/music/comedy: *The Daily Show with Jon Stewart* (Comedy Central)
Nonfiction: *10 Days That Unexpectedly Changed America* (The History Channel)

2007
Comedy: *30 Rock* (NBC)
Drama: *The Sopranos* (HBO)
Miniseries: *Broken Trail* (AMC)
Variety/music/comedy: *The Daily Show with Jon Stewart* (Comedy Central)
Nonfiction: *Planet Earth* (Discovery Channel)

2008
Comedy: *30 Rock* (NBC)
Drama: *Mad Men* (AMC)
Miniseries: *John Adams* (HBO)
Variety/music/comedy: *The Daily Show with Jon Stewart* (Comedy Central)
Nonfiction: *American Masters* (PBS); *This American Life* (Showtime)

[1]*From 1949 to 1958, awards were given for programs broadcast the previous year only; awards since have been given for programs broadcast in part of the previous year and in part of the year named.*

Theater

Tony Awards, 2009

The American Theatre Wing (ATW), established in 1939, created the Tony Awards, named for former ATW director Antoinette Perry, in 1947 to recognize distinguished achievement in the theater arts as presented on Broadway; since 1967 they have been presented in conjunction with the Broadway League (formerly the League of American Theatres and Producers), a trade association. Nominees are selected each May from among the year's new or newly revived Broadway shows; a body of some 750 current and former theater professionals, critics, and agents votes for the winners. The awards are presented in New York City in June. Prize: silver medallion, set in a base, depicting on one face the masks of tragedy and comedy and on the other the profile of Antoinette Perry.

Tony Awards Web site: <www.tonyawards.com>.

▸ **musical:** *Billy Elliot: The Musical* (book and lyrics, Lee Hall; music, Elton John); ▸ **play:** *God of Carnage* (playwright, Yasmina Reza); ▸ **revival of a musical:** *Hair* (book, Gerome Ragni and James Rado; music, Galt MacDermot; lyrics, Gerome Ragni and James Rado); ▸ **revival of a play:** *The Norman Conquests* (playwright, Alan Ayckbourn); ▸ **book, musical:** *Billy Elliot: The Musical*; ▸ **score:** Tom Kitt (music) and Brian Yorkey (lyrics) (*Next to Normal*); ▸ **leading actress, musical:** Alice Ripley (*Next to Normal*); ▸ **leading actor, musical:** David Alvarez, Trent Kowalik, and Kiril Kulish (*Billy Elliot: The Musical*); ▸ **leading actress, play:** Marcia Gay Harden (*God of Carnage*); ▸ **leading actor, play:** Geoffrey Rush (*Exit the King*); ▸ **featured actress, musical:** Karen Olivo (*West Side Story*); ▸ **featured actor, musical:** Gregory Jbara (*Billy Elliot: The Musical*); ▸ **featured actress, play:** Angela Lansbury (*Blithe Spirit*); ▸ **featured actor, play:** Roger Robinson (*Joe Turner's Come and Gone*); ▸ **direction, musical:** Stephen Daldry (*Billy Elliot: The Musical*); ▸ **direction, play:** Matthew Warchus (*God of Carnage*); ▸ **costume design, musical:** Tim Hatley (*Shrek the Musical*); ▸ **costume design, play:** Anthony Ward (*Mary Stuart*); ▸ **lighting design, musical:** Rick Fisher (*Billy Elliot: The Musical*); ▸ **lighting design, play:** Brian MacDevitt (*Joe Turner's Come and Gone*); ▸ **scenic design, musical:** Ian MacNeil (*Billy Elliot: The Musical*); ▸ **scenic design, play:** Derek McLane (*33 Variations*); ▸ **sound design, musical:** Paul Arditti (*Billy Elliot: The Musical*); ▸ **sound design, play:** Gregory Clarke (*Equus*); ▸ **orchestrations:** Martin Koch (*Billy Elliot: The Musical*); Michael Starobin and Tom Kitt (*Next to Normal*) (tied); ▸ **choreography:** Peter Darling (*Billy Elliot: The Musical*); ▸ **regional theater award:** Signature Theatre, Arlington VA; ▸ **lifetime achievement:** Jerry Herman.

Tony Awards, 1947–2009

YEAR	BEST MUSICAL	BEST PLAY
1947	*not awarded*	*All My Sons* (Arthur Miller)[1]
1948	*not awarded*	*Mister Roberts* (Thomas Heggen and Joshua Logan)
1949	*Kiss Me, Kate* (book, Bella Spewack and Samuel Spewack; music and lyrics, Cole Porter)	*Death of a Salesman* (Arthur Miller)
1950	*South Pacific* (book, Oscar Hammerstein II and Joshua Logan; music, Richard Rodgers; lyrics, Oscar Hammerstein II)	*The Cocktail Party* (T.S. Eliot)
1951	*Guys and Dolls* (book, Jo Swerling and Abe Burrows; music and lyrics, Frank Loesser)	*The Rose Tattoo* (Tennessee Williams)
1952	*The King and I* (book and lyrics, Oscar Hammerstein II; music, Richard Rodgers)	*The Fourposter* (Jan de Hartog)

Tony Awards, 1947–2009 (continued)

YEAR	BEST MUSICAL	BEST PLAY
1953	*Wonderful Town* (book, Joseph Fields and Jerome Chodorov; music, Leonard Bernstein; lyrics, Betty Comden and Adolph Green)	*The Crucible* (Arthur Miller)
1954	*Kismet* (book, Charles Lederer and Luther Davis; music, Alexander Borodin; adaptation and lyrics, Robert Wright and George Forrest)	*The Teahouse of the August Moon* (John Patrick)
1955	*The Pajama Game* (book, George Abbott and Richard Bissell; music and lyrics, Richard Adler and Jerry Ross)	*The Desperate Hours* (Joseph Hayes)
1956	*Damn Yankees* (book, George Abbott and Douglass Wallop; music and lyrics, Richard Adler and Jerry Ross)	*The Diary of Anne Frank* (Frances Goodrich and Albert Hackett)
1957	*My Fair Lady* (book and lyrics, Alan Jay Lerner; music, Frederick Loewe)	*Long Day's Journey into Night* (Eugene O'Neill)
1958	*The Music Man* (book, Meredith Willson and Franklin Lacey; music and lyrics, Meredith Willson)	*Sunrise at Campobello* (Dore Schary)
1959	*Redhead* (book, Herbert Fields, Dorothy Fields, Sidney Sheldon, and David Shaw; music, Albert Hague; lyrics, Dorothy Fields)	*J.B.* (Archibald MacLeish)
1960	*The Sound of Music* (book, Howard Lindsay and Russel Crouse; music, Richard Rodgers; lyrics, Oscar Hammerstein II); *Fiorello!* (book, Jerome Weidman and George Abbott; music, Jerry Brock; lyrics, Sheldon Harnick) (tied)	*The Miracle Worker* (William Gibson)
1961	*Bye Bye Birdie* (book, Michael Stewart; music, Charles Strouse; lyrics, Lee Adams)	*Beckett* (Jean Anouilh, translated by Lucienne Hill)
1962	*How To Succeed in Business Without Really Trying* (book, Abe Burrows, Jack Weinstock, and Willie Gilbert; music and lyrics, Frank Loesser)	*A Man for All Seasons* (Robert Bolt)
1963	*A Funny Thing Happened on the Way to the Forum* (book, Burt Shevelove and Larry Gelbart; music and lyrics, Stephen Sondheim)	*Who's Afraid of Virginia Woolf?* (Edward Albee)
1964	*Hello, Dolly!* (book, Michael Stewart; music and lyrics, Jerry Herman)	*Luther* (John Osborne)
1965	*Fiddler on the Roof* (book, Joseph Stein; music, Jerry Bock; lyrics, Sheldon Harnick)	*The Subject Was Roses* (Frank Gilroy)
1966	*Man of La Mancha* (book, Dale Wasserman; music, Mitch Leigh; lyrics, Joe Darion)	*Marat/Sade* (Peter Weiss, translated by Geoffrey Skelton)
1967	*Cabaret* (book, Joe Masteroff; music, John Kander; lyrics, Fred Ebb)	*The Homecoming* (Harold Pinter)
1968	*Hallelujah, Baby!* (book, Arthur Laurents; music, Jule Styne; lyrics, Betty Comden and Adolph Green)	*Rosencrantz and Guildenstern Are Dead* (Tom Stoppard)
1969	*1776* (book, Peter Stone; music and lyrics, Sherman Edwards)	*The Great White Hope* (Howard Sackler)
1970	*Applause* (book, Betty Comden and Adolph Green; music, Charles Strouse; lyrics, Lee Adams)	*Borstal Boy* (Frank McMahon)
1971	*Company* (book, George Furth; music and lyrics, Stephen Sondheim)	*Sleuth* (Anthony Shaffer)
1972	*Two Gentlemen of Verona* (book, John Guare and Mel Shapiro; music, Galt MacDermot; lyrics, John Guare)	*Sticks and Bones* (David Rabe)
1973	*A Little Night Music* (book, Hugh Wheeler; music and lyrics, Stephen Sondheim)	*That Championship Season* (Jason Miller)
1974	*Raisin* (book, Robert Nemiroff and Charlotte Zaltzberg; music, Judd Woldin; lyrics, Robert Brittan)	*The River Niger* (Joseph A. Walker)
1975	*The Wiz* (book, William F. Brown; music and lyrics, Charlie Smalls)	*Equus* (Peter Shaffer)
1976	*A Chorus Line* (book, James Kirkwood and Nicholas Dante; music, Marvin Hamlisch; lyrics, Edward Kleban)	*Travesties* (Tom Stoppard)
1977	*Annie* (book, Thomas Meehan; music, Charles Strouse; lyrics, Martin Charnin)	*The Shadow Box* (Michael Christofer)
1978	*Ain't Misbehavin'* (book, Murray Horwitz and Richard Maltby, Jr.; music, Fats Waller; lyrics, Fats Waller and many others)	*Da* (Hugh Leonard)
1979	*Sweeney Todd* (book, Hugh Wheeler; music and lyrics, Stephen Sondheim)	*The Elephant Man* (Bernard Pomerance)
1980	*Evita* (book and lyrics, Tim Rice; music, Andrew Lloyd Webber)	*Children of a Lesser God* (Mark Medoff)
1981	*42nd Street* (book, Michael Stewart and Mark Bramble; music, Harry Warren; lyrics, Al Dubin)	*Amadeus* (Peter Shaffer)
1982	*Nine* (book, Arthur Kopit; music and lyrics, Maury Yeston)	*The Life and Adventures of Nicholas Nickleby* (David Edgar)
1983	*Cats* (book and lyrics, T.S. Eliot; music, Andrew Lloyd Webber)	*Torch Song Trilogy* (Harvey Fierstein)
1984	*La Cage aux folles* (book, Harvey Fierstein; music and lyrics, Jerry Herman)	*The Real Thing* (Tom Stoppard)
1985	*Big River* (book, William Hauptman; music and lyrics, Roger Miller)	*Biloxi Blues* (Neil Simon)
1986	*The Mystery of Edwin Drood* (book, music, and lyrics, Rupert Holmes)	*I'm Not Rappaport* (Herb Gardner)
1987	*Les Misérables* (book, Alain Boublil and Claude-Michel Schönberg; music, Claude-Michel Schönberg; lyrics, Herbert Kretzmer and Alain Boublil)	*Fences* (August Wilson)

Tony Awards, 1947–2009 (continued)

YEAR	BEST MUSICAL	BEST PLAY
1988	*The Phantom of the Opera* (book, Richard Stilgoe and Andrew Lloyd Webber; music, Andrew Lloyd Webber; lyrics, Charles Hart and Richard Stilgoe)	*M. Butterfly* (David Henry Hwang)
1989	*Jerome Robbins' Broadway* (compilation)	*The Heidi Chronicles* (Wendy Wasserstein)
1990	*City of Angels* (book, Larry Gelbart; music, Cy Coleman; lyrics, David Zippel)	*The Grapes of Wrath* (Frank Galati)
1991	*The Will Rogers Follies* (book, Peter Stone; music, Cy Coleman; lyrics, Betty Comden and Adolph Green)	*Lost in Yonkers* (Neil Simon)
1992	*Crazy for You* (book, Ken Ludwig; music and lyrics, George Gershwin and Ira Gershwin)	*Dancing at Lughnasa* (Brian Friel)
1993	*Kiss of the Spider Woman* (book, Terrence McNally; music, John Kander; lyrics, Fred Ebb)	*Angels in America: Millennium Approaches* (Tony Kushner)
1994	*Passion* (book, James Lapine; music and lyrics, Stephen Sondheim)	*Angels in America: Perestroika* (Tony Kushner)
1995	*Sunset Boulevard* (book and lyrics, Don Black and Christopher Hampton; music, Andrew Lloyd Webber)	*Love! Valour! Compassion!* (Terrence McNally)
1996	*Rent* (book, music, and lyrics, Jonathan Larson)	*Master Class* (Terrence McNally)
1997	*Titanic* (book, Peter Stone; music and lyrics, Maury Yeston)	*The Last Night of Ballyhoo* (Alfred Uhry)
1998	*The Lion King* (book, Roger Allers and Irene Mecchi; music and lyrics, Elton John, Tim Rice, and others)	*Art* (Yasmina Reza)
1999	*Fosse* (compilation)	*Side Man* (Warren Leight)
2000	*Contact* (book, John Weidman; music and lyrics, various artists)	*Copenhagen* (Michael Frayn)
2001	*The Producers* (book, Mel Brooks and Thomas Meehan; music and lyrics, Mel Brooks)	*Proof* (David Auburn)
2002	*Thoroughly Modern Millie* (book, Richard Morris and Dick Scanlan; music, Jeanine Tesori; lyrics, Dick Scanlan)	*The Goat, or Who Is Sylvia?* (Edward Albee)
2003	*Hairspray* (book, Mark O'Donnell and Thomas Meehan; music, Marc Shaiman; lyrics, Scott Wittman and Marc Shaiman)	*Take Me Out* (Richard Greenberg)
2004	*Avenue Q* (book, Jeff Whitty; music and lyrics, Robert Lopez and Jeff Marx)	*I Am My Own Wife* (Doug Wright)
2005	*Monty Python's Spamalot* (book, Eric Idle; music and lyrics, John Du Prez and Eric Idle)	*Doubt* (John Patrick Shanley)
2006	*Jersey Boys* (book, Marshall Brickman and Rick Elice; music, Bob Gaudio; lyrics, Bob Crewe)	*The History Boys* (Alan Bennett)
2007	*Spring Awakening* (book and lyrics, Steven Sater; music, Duncan Sheik)	*The Coast of Utopia* (Tom Stoppard)
2008	*In the Heights* (book, Quiara Alegría Hudes; music and lyrics, Lin-Manuel Miranda)	*August: Osage County* (Tracy Letts)
2009	*Billy Elliot: The Musical* (book and lyrics, Lee Hall; music, Elton John)	*God of Carnage* (Yasmina Reza)

[1]Awarded to playwright for Best Author.

Longest-Running Broadway Shows

As of 4 Aug 2009. Source: *Internet Broadway Database*, <www.ibdb.com>.

	SHOW	RUN	PERFORMANCES		SHOW	RUN	PERFORMANCES
1	The Phantom of the Opera	1988–	8,947	6	Beauty and the Beast	1994–2007	5,461
2	Cats	1982–2000	7,485	7	Chicago (revival)	1996–	5,276
3	Les Misérables	1987–2003	6,680	8	Rent	1996–2008	5,123
4	A Chorus Line	1975–90	6,137	9	The Lion King	1997–	4,861
5	Oh! Calcutta! (revival)	1976–89	5,959	10	Miss Saigon	1991–2001	4,092

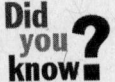

Did you know? Ava Gardner, who transformed herself from tomboyish farm girl into one of the most beautiful women in screen history, was given a screen test by MGM studios in 1941. In it, her lack of refinement was painfully evident and her thick southern drawl rendered much of what she said unintelligible. Upon seeing the test, studio chief Louis B. Mayer declared, "She can't act. She can't talk. She's terrific. Sign her."

Encyclopædia Britannica's 20 Notable US Theater Companies

COMPANY	LOCATION	ARTISTIC DIRECTOR (2009)
The Acting Company	New York NY	Margot Harley[1]
Actors Theatre of Louisville	Louisville KY	Marc Masterson
Alley Theatre	Houston TX	Gregory Boyd
American Conservatory Theater	San Francisco CA	Carey Perloff
American Repertory Theatre	Cambridge MA	Diane Paulus
Arena Stage	Washington DC	Molly Smith
Center Theatre Group	Los Angeles CA	Michael Ritchie
Chicago Shakespeare Theater	Chicago IL	Barbara Gaines
El Teatro Campesino	San Juan Bautista CA	Luis Valdez
Folger Theatre	Washington DC	Janet Alexander Griffin[2]
Goodman Theatre	Chicago IL	Robert Falls
Guthrie Theater	Minneapolis MN	Joe Dowling[3]
La Jolla Playhouse	La Jolla CA	Christopher Ashley
Long Wharf Theatre	New Haven CT	Gordon Edelstein
Oregon Shakespeare Festival	Ashland OR	Bill Rauch
Pasadena Playhouse	Pasadena CA	Sheldon Epps
The Public Theater	New York NY	Oskar Eustis
Seattle Repertory Theatre	Seattle WA	Jerry Manning[1]
Steppenwolf Theatre Company	Chicago IL	Martha Lavey
Yale Repertory Theatre	New Haven CT	James Bundy

[1]Producing artistic director. [2]Artistic producer. [3]Director.

Music

Grammy Awards, 2008

The National Academy of Recording Arts and Sciences was established in 1957 as a professional organization for musicians, producers, technicians, and executives in the US recording industry. The Grammys, first awarded in 1958, recognize excellence in the recording industry without regard to record sales or chart position. Nominees and winners are selected by the Academy's individual members according to the members' areas of expertise. In addition to the four general categories (record, album, and song of the year and best new artist) for which all members are eligible to vote, for 2008 there were 110 categories in 31 fields, of which Academy members were permitted to vote in no more than 8 fields. Prizes for works released 1 Oct 2007–30 Sep 2008 were awarded in Los Angeles on 8 Feb 2009. Prize: gold miniature phonograph.

Grammy Award Web site: <www.grammy.com>.

category: winner (performer in parentheses for songwriting/production awards)

▸ **record (single) of the year:** "Please Read the Letter," Robert Plant and Alison Krauss; ▸ **album of the year:** *Raising Sand,* Robert Plant and Alison Krauss; ▸ **song of the year:** "Viva la Vida," Guy Berryman, Jonny Buckland, Will Champion, and Chris Martin, songwriters (Coldplay); ▸ **new artist:** Adele; ▸ **pop vocal performance, female:** "Chasing Pavements," Adele; ▸ **pop vocal performance, male:** "Say," John Mayer; ▸ **pop vocal performance, duo/group:** "Viva la Vida," Coldplay; ▸ **pop vocal album:** *Rockferry,* Duffy; ▸ **pop vocal album, traditional:** *Still Unforgettable,* Natalie Cole; ▸ **rock vocal performance, solo:** "Gravity," John Mayer; ▸ **rock vocal performance, duo/group:** "Sex on Fire," Kings of Leon; ▸ **hard rock performance:** "Wax Simulacra," The Mars Volta; ▸ **metal performance:** "My Apocalypse," Metallica; ▸ **rock song:** "Girls in Their Summer Clothes," Bruce Springsteen, songwriter (Bruce Springsteen); ▸ **rock album:** *Viva la Vida or Death and All His Friends,* Coldplay; ▸ **alternative music album:** *In Rainbows,* Radiohead; ▸ **R&B vocal performance, female:** "Superwoman," Alicia Keys; ▸ **R&B vocal performance, male:** "Miss Independent," Ne-Yo; ▸ **R&B vocal performance, duo/group:** "Stay with Me (by the Sea)," Al Green featuring John Legend; ▸ **R&B song:** "Miss Independent," Mikkel S. Eriksen, T.E. Hermansen, and S. Smith, songwriters (Ne-Yo); ▸ **R&B album:** *Jennifer Hudson,* Jennifer Hudson; ▸ **R&B album, contemporary:** *Growing Pains,* Mary J. Blige; ▸ **rap performance, solo:** "A Milli," Lil Wayne; ▸ **rap performance, duo/group:** "Swagga Like Us," Jay-Z and T.I. featuring Kanye West and Lil Wayne; ▸ **rap song:** "Lollipop," D. Carter, S. Garrett, D. Harrison, J. Scheffer, and R. Zamor, songwriters (Lil Wayne featuring Static Major); ▸ **rap album:** *Tha Carter III,* Lil Wayne; ▸ **country vocal performance, female:** "Last Name," Carrie Underwood; ▸ **country vocal performance, male:** "Letter to Me," Brad Paisley; ▸ **country vocal performance, duo/group:** "Stay," Sugarland; ▸ **country song:** "Stay," Jennifer Nettles, songwriter (Sugarland); ▸ **country album:** *Troubadour,* George Strait; ▸ **bluegrass album:** *Honoring the Fathers of Bluegrass: Tribute to 1946 and 1947,* Ricky Skaggs and Kentucky Thunder; ▸ **new age album:** *Peace Time,* Jack DeJohnette; ▸ **jazz album, contemporary:** *Randy in Brasil,* Randy Brecker; ▸ **jazz vocal album:** *Loverly,* Cassandra Wilson; ▸ **jazz instrumental solo:** Terence Blanchard ("Be-Bop"); ▸ **jazz instrumental album:** *The New Crystal Silence,* Chick Corea and Gary Burton; ▸ **jazz album, large ensemble:** *Monday Night Live at the Village Vanguard,* The Vanguard Jazz Orchestra;

Grammy Awards, 2008 (continued)

▸ **jazz album, Latin:** *Song for Chico,* Arturo O'Farrill and the Afro-Latin Jazz Orchestra; ▸ **gospel song:** "Help Me Believe," Kirk Franklin, songwriter (Kirk Franklin); ▸ **gospel album, rock/rap:** *Alive and Transported,* tobyMac; ▸ **gospel album, pop/contemporary:** *Thy Kingdom Come,* CeCe Winans; ▸ **gospel album, Southern/country/bluegrass:** *Lovin' Life,* Gaither Vocal Band; ▸ **gospel album, traditional:** *Down in New Orleans,* The Blind Boys of Alabama; ▸ **gospel album, contemporary R&B:** *The Fight of My Life,* Kirk Franklin; ▸ **Latin album, pop:** *La vida...es un ratico,* Juanes; ▸ **Latin album, rock/alternative:** *45,* Jaguares; ▸ **Latin album, urban:** *Los Extraterrestres,* Wisin y Yandel ▸ **Latin album, tropical:** *Señor Bachata,* José Feliciano ▸ **regional Mexican album:** *Amor, dolor, y lágrimas: música ranchera,* Mariachi los Camperos de Nati Cano; *Canciones de amor,* Mariachi Divas (tied); ▸ **Tejano album:** *¡Viva la revolucion!,* Ruben Ramos and the Mexican Revolution; ▸ **blues album, traditional:** *One Kind Favor,* B.B. King; ▸ **blues album, contemporary:** *City That Care Forgot,* Dr. John and the Lower 911; ▸ **folk album, traditional:** *At 89,* Pete Seeger; ▸ **folk album, contemporary/Americana:** *Raising Sand,* Robert Plant and Alison Krauss; ▸ **Native American music album:** *Come to Me Great Mystery: Native American Healing Songs,* various artists; ▸ **Hawaiian music album:** *'Ikena,* Tia Carrere and Daniel Ho; ▸ **reggae album:** *Jah Is Real,* Burning Spear; ▸ **world music album, traditional:** *Ilembe: Honoring Shaka Zulu,* Ladysmith Black Mambazo; ▸ **world music album, contemporary:** *Global Drum Project,* Mickey Hart, Zakir Hussain, Sikiru Adepoju, and Giovanni Hidalgo; ▸ **polka album:** *Let the Whole World Sing,* Jimmy Sturr and His Orchestra; ▸ **spoken word album:** *An Inconvenient Truth,* Beau Bridges, Cynthia Nixon, and Blair Underwood; ▸ **comedy album:** *It's Bad for Ya,* George Carlin; ▸ **producer, nonclassical:** Rick Rubin; ▸ **producer, classical:** David Frost; ▸ **classical album:** *Rise and Fall of the City of Mahagonny,* James Conlon, conductor; Fred Vogler, producer (Los Angeles Opera Orchestra); ▸ **orchestral performance:** *Symphony No. 4,* Chicago Symphony Orchestra; Bernard Haitink, conductor; ▸ **opera recording:** *Rise and Fall of the City of Mahagonny,* James Conlon, conductor; Anthony Dean Griffey, Patti LuPone, and Audra McDonald, soloists; Fred Vogler, producer (Donnie Ray Albert, John Easterlin, Steven Humes, Mel Ulrich, and Robert Wörle; Los Angeles Opera Orchestra; Los Angeles Opera Chorus); ▸ **chamber music performance:** *String Quartets Nos. 1 and 5,* Pacifica Quartet; ▸ **classical vocal performance:** *Mr. Tambourine Man: Seven Poems of Bob Dylan,* Hila Plitmann, soloist; ▸ **contemporary classical composition:** *Mr. Tambourine Man: Seven Poems of Bob Dylan,* John Corigliano, composer; ▸ **short-form music video:** "Pork and Beans," Weezer; Mathew Cullen, director; Bernard Rahill, producer

Grammy Awards, 1958—2008

The year denotes the period (from the fall of the previous year to the fall of the year named) for which the winning work or artist was recognized; the prizes are generally awarded during the following year.

YEAR	RECORD (SINGLE) OF THE YEAR	ALBUM OF THE YEAR	BEST NEW ARTIST
1958	"Nel blu dipinto di blu (Volare)," Domenico Modugno	*The Music from Peter Gunn,* Henry Mancini	not awarded
1959	"Mack the Knife," Bobby Darin	*Come Dance with Me,* Frank Sinatra	Bobby Darin
1960	"The Theme from *A Summer Place,*" Percy Faith	*The Button-Down Mind of Bob Newhart,* Bob Newhart	Bob Newhart
1961	"Moon River," Henry Mancini	*Judy at Carnegie Hall,* Judy Garland	Peter Nero
1962	"I Left My Heart in San Francisco," Tony Bennett	*The First Family,* Vaughn Meader	Robert Goulet
1963	"The Days of Wine and Roses," Henry Mancini	*The Barbra Streisand Album,* Barbra Streisand	Ward Swingle (The Swingle Singers)
1964	"The Girl from Ipanema," Stan Getz and Astrud Gilberto	*Getz/Gilberto,* Stan Getz and João Gilberto	The Beatles
1965	"A Taste of Honey," Herb Alpert	*September of My Years,* Frank Sinatra	Tom Jones
1966	"Strangers in the Night," Frank Sinatra	*A Man and His Music,* Frank Sinatra	not awarded
1967	"Up, Up, and Away," The 5th Dimension	*Sgt. Pepper's Lonely Hearts Club Band,* The Beatles	Bobbie Gentry
1968	"Mrs. Robinson," Simon & Garfunkel	*By the Time I Get to Phoenix,* Glen Campbell	José Feliciano
1969	"Aquarius/Let the Sunshine In," The 5th Dimension	*Blood, Sweat & Tears,* Blood, Sweat & Tears	Crosby, Stills & Nash
1970	"Bridge over Troubled Water," Simon & Garfunkel	*Bridge over Troubled Water,* Simon & Garfunkel	The Carpenters
1971	"It's Too Late," Carole King	*Tapestry,* Carole King	Carly Simon
1972	"The First Time Ever I Saw Your Face," Roberta Flack	*The Concert for Bangla Desh,* George Harrison and Friends	America
1973	"Killing Me Softly with His Song," Roberta Flack	*Innervisions,* Stevie Wonder	Bette Midler
1974	"I Honestly Love You," Olivia Newton-John	*Fulfillingness' First Finale,* Stevie Wonder	Marvin Hamlisch
1975	"Love Will Keep Us Together," Captain & Tennille	*Still Crazy After All These Years,* Paul Simon	Natalie Cole

Grammy Awards, 1958–2008 (continued)

YEAR	RECORD (SINGLE) OF THE YEAR	ALBUM OF THE YEAR	BEST NEW ARTIST
1976	"This Masquerade," George Benson	*Songs in the Key of Life*, Stevie Wonder	Starland Vocal Band
1977	"Hotel California," The Eagles	*Rumours*, Fleetwood Mac	Debby Boone
1978	"Just the Way You Are," Billy Joel	*Saturday Night Fever*, The Bee Gees	A Taste of Honey
1979	"What a Fool Believes," The Doobie Brothers	*52nd Steet*, Billy Joel	Rickie Lee Jones
1980	"Sailing," Christopher Cross	*Christopher Cross*, Christopher Cross	Christopher Cross
1981	"Bette Davis Eyes," Kim Carnes	*Double Fantasy*, John Lennon and Yoko Ono	Sheena Easton
1982	"Rosanna," Toto	*Toto IV*, Toto	Men at Work
1983	"Beat It," Michael Jackson	*Thriller*, Michael Jackson	Culture Club
1984	"What's Love Got To Do with It," Tina Turner	*Can't Slow Down*, Lionel Richie	Cyndi Lauper
1985	"We Are the World," USA for Africa	*No Jacket Required*, Phil Collins	Sade
1986	"Higher Love," Steve Winwood	*Graceland*, Paul Simon	Bruce Hornsby and the Range
1987	"Graceland," Paul Simon	*The Joshua Tree*, U2	Jody Watley
1988	"Don't Worry, Be Happy," Bobby McFerrin	*Faith*, George Michael	Tracy Chapman
1989	"Wind Beneath My Wings," Bette Midler	*Nick of Time*, Bonnie Raitt	Milli Vanilli (revoked)
1990	"Another Day in Paradise," Phil Collins	*Back on the Block*, Quincy Jones	Mariah Carey
1991	"Unforgettable," Natalie Cole with Nat King Cole	*Unforgettable: With Love*, Natalie Cole	Marc Cohn
1992	"Tears in Heaven," Eric Clapton	*Unplugged*, Eric Clapton	Arrested Development
1993	"I Will Always Love You," Whitney Houston	*The Bodyguard*, Whitney Houston	Toni Braxton
1994	"All I Wanna Do," Sheryl Crow	*MTV Unplugged*, Tony Bennett	Sheryl Crow
1995	"Kiss from a Rose," Seal	*Jagged Little Pill*, Alanis Morissette	Hootie and the Blowfish
1996	"Change the World," Eric Clapton	*Falling into You*, Celine Dion	LeAnn Rimes
1997	"Sunny Came Home," Shawn Colvin	*Time Out of Mind*, Bob Dylan	Paula Cole
1998	"My Heart Will Go On," Celine Dion	*The Miseducation of Lauryn Hill*, Lauryn Hill	Lauryn Hill
1999	"Smooth," Santana featuring Rob Thomas	*Supernatural*, Santana	Christina Aguilera
2000	"Beautiful Day," U2	*Two Against Nature*, Steely Dan	Shelby Lynne
2001	"Walk On," U2	*O Brother, Where Art Thou?*, various artists	Alicia Keys
2002	"Don't Know Why," Norah Jones	*Come Away with Me*, Norah Jones	Norah Jones
2003	"Clocks," Coldplay	*Speakerboxxx/The Love Below*, OutKast	Evanescence
2004	"Here We Go Again," Ray Charles and Norah Jones	*Genius Loves Company*, Ray Charles and various artists	Maroon 5
2005	"Boulevard of Broken Dreams," Green Day	*How To Dismantle an Atomic Bomb*, U2	John Legend
2006	"Not Ready To Make Nice," Dixie Chicks	*Taking the Long Way*, Dixie Chicks	Carrie Underwood
2007	"Rehab," Amy Winehouse	*River: The Joni Letters*, Herbie Hancock	Amy Winehouse
2008	"Please Read the Letter," Robert Plant and Alison Krauss	*Raising Sand*, Robert Plant and Alison Krauss	Adele

Eurovision Song Contest

The European Broadcasting Union (EBU), an association of television and radio companies from Europe and the Mediterranean, began the Eurovision Song Contest in 1956. Each EBU member country, along with several provisional participants, can nominate one original song per year, with a maximum length of three minutes. The winner is selected based on votes from fans and juries in each participating country. Prize: crystal microphone.
Eurovision Song Contest Web site: <www.eurovision.tv>.

YEAR	SONG, SONGWRITER(S) (PERFORMER, COUNTRY)
1956	"Refrain," Émile Gardaz, Géo Voumard (Lys Assia, Switzerland)
1957	"Net als toen," Willy van Hemert, Guus Jansen (Corry Brokken, The Netherlands)
1958	"Dors mon amour," Pierre Delanoë, Hubert Giraud (André Claveau, France)
1959	"Een beetje," Willy van Hemert, Dick Schallies (Teddy Scholten, The Netherlands)

Eurovision Song Contest (continued)

YEAR	SONG, SONGWRITER(S) (PERFORMER, COUNTRY)
1960	"Tom Pillibi," Pierre Cour, André Popp (Jacqueline Boyer, France)
1961	"Nous les amoureux," Jacques Datin, Maurice Vidalin (Jean-Claude Pascal, Luxembourg)
1962	"Un Premier amour," Rolande Valade, Claude Henri Vic (Isabelle Aubret, France)
1963	"Dansevise," Sejr Volmer-Sørensen, Otto Francker (Grethe and Jørgen Ingmann, Denmark)
1964	"Non ho l'étà," Nicola Salerno (Gigliola Cinquetti, Italy)
1965	"Poupée de cire, poupée de son," Serge Gainsbourg (France Gall, Luxembourg)
1966	"Merci chérie," Udo Jürgens, Thomas Hörbiger (Udo Jürgens, Austria)
1967	"Puppet on a String," Bill Martin, Phil Coulter (Sandie Shaw, United Kingdom)
1968	"La, la, la," Ramón Arcusa, Manuel de la Calva (Massiel, Spain)
1969	"Vivo cantando," Aniano Alcalde, Maria José de Cerato (Salomé, Spain); "Boom Bang-a-Bang," Peter Warne, Alan Moorhouse (Lulu, United Kingdom); "De troubadour," Lenny Kuhr, David Hartsena (Lenny Kuhr, The Netherlands); "Un Jour, un enfant," Eddy Marnay, Emile Stern (Frida Boccara, France) (four-way tie)
1970	"All Kinds of Everything," Derry Lindsay, Jackie Smith (Dana, Ireland)
1971	"Un Banc, un arbre, une rue," Yves Dessca, Jean-Pierre Bourtayre (Séverine, Monaco)
1972	"Après toi," Klaus Munro, Yves Dessca, Mario Panas (Vicky Leandros, Luxembourg)
1973	"Tu te reconnaîtras," Vline Buggy, Claude Morgan (Anne-Marie David, Luxembourg)
1974	"Waterloo," Stikkan Anderson, Benny Andersson, Björn Ulvaeus (ABBA, Sweden)
1975	"Ding-a-Dong," Will Luikinga, Eddy Ouwens, Dick Bakker (Teach-In, The Netherlands)
1976	"Save Your Kisses for Me," Tony Hiller, Lee Sheriden, Martin Lee (Brotherhood of Man, United Kingdom)
1977	"L'Oiseau et l'enfant," José Gracy, Jean-Paul Cara (Marie Myriam, France)
1978	"A-Ba-Ni-Bi," ehud Manor, Nurit Hirsh (Izhar COhen and the Alphabeta, Israel)
1979	"Hallelujah," Shimrit Orr, Kobi Oshrat (Gali Atari and Milk and Honey, Israel)
1980	"What's Another Year," Shay Healy (Johnny Logan, Ireland)
1981	"Making Your Mind Up," Andy Hill, John Danter (Bucks Fizz, United Kingdom)
1982	"Ein bisschen Frieden," Bernd Meinunger, Ralph Siegel (Nicole, West Germany)
1983	"Si la vie est cadeau," Alain Garcia, Jean-Pierre Millers (Corinne Hermès, Luxembourg)
1984	"Diggi-loo diggi-ley," Britt Lindeborg, Torgny Söderberg (Herrey's, Sweden)
1985	"La det swinge," Rolf Løvland (Bobbysocks, Norway)
1986	"J'aime la vie," Marino Atria, Jean-Pierre Furnémont, Angelo Crisci (Sandra Kim, Belgium)
1987	"Hold Me Now," Sean Sherrard (Johnny Logan, Ireland)
1988	"Ne partez pas sans moi," Nella Martinetti, Atilla Sereftug (Céline Dion, Switzerland)
1989	"Rock Me," Stevo Cvikich, Rajko Dujmich (Riva, Yugoslavia)
1990	"Insieme: 1992," Toto Cutugno (Toto Cutugno, Italy)
1991	"Fångad av en stormvind," Stephan Berg (Carola, Sweden)
1992	"Why Me," Sean Sherrard (Linda Martin, Ireland)
1993	"In Your Eyes," Jimmy Walsh (Niamh Kavanagh, Ireland)
1994	"Rock 'n' Roll Kids," Brendan Graham (Paul Harrington and Charlie McGettigan, Ireland)
1995	"Nocturne," Petter Skavlan, Rolf Løvland (Secret Garden, Norway)
1996	"The Voice," Brendan Graham (Eimear Quinn, Ireland)
1997	"Love Shine a Light," Kimberley Rew (Katrina and the Waves, United Kingdom)
1998	"Diva," Yoav Ginay (Dana International, Israel)
1999	"Take Me to Your Heaven," Gert Lengstrand (Charlotte Nilsson, Sweden)
2000	"Fly on the Wings of Love," Jørgen Olsen (Olsen Brothers, Denmark)
2001	"Everybody," Maian-Anna Kärmas, Ivar Must (Tanel Padar, Dave Benton, and 2XL, Estonia)
2002	"I Wanna," Marija Naumova, Marats Samauskis (Marie N, Latvia)
2003	"Every Way That I Can," Demir Demirkan, Sertab Erener (Sertab Erener, Turkey)
2004	"Wild Dances," Ruslana Lyzhichko, Aleksandr Ksenofontov (Ruslana, Ukraine)
2005	"My Number One," Christos Dantis, Natalia Germanou (Helena Paparizou, Greece)
2006	"Hard Rock Hallelujah," LORDI (LORDI, Finland)
2007	"Molitva," Sasa Milosevic Mare (Marija Serifovic, Serbia)
2008	"Believe," Dima Bilan, Jim Beanz (Dima Bilan, Russia)
2009	"Fairytale," Alexander Rybak (Alexander Rybak, Norway)

Brit Awards, 2009

The British Phonographic Industry, a trade association of record companies, established the Brit Awards in 1977 to recognize pop acts from Great Britain and abroad. Prize: statuette. **Web site:** *<www.brits.co.uk>.*

BRITISH CATEGORIES
Male solo artist: Paul Weller
Female solo artist: Duffy
Group: Elbow
MasterCard Album: Duffy, *Rockferry*
Breakthrough act: Duffy
Single: Girls Aloud, "The Promise"
Live act: Iron Maiden

INTERNATIONAL CATEGORIES
Male solo artist: Kanye West
Female solo artist: Katy Perry
Group: Kings of Leon
Album: Kings of Leon, *Only by the Night*

ADDITIONAL CATEGORIES
Outstanding contribution: Pet Shop Boys
Critics' choice: Florence and the Machine

Country Music Association Awards, 2008

The Country Music Association, founded in 1958 as a trade organization for the country and western music industry, began its annual awards ceremony in 1967 and made it the first nationally televised music awards show the following year. Ceremonies are held in November. Prize: hand-blown crystal statuette. **Country Music Association Awards Web site:** <www.cmaawards.com>.

▸ **entertainer of the year:** Kenny Chesney; ▸ **female vocalist of the year:** Carrie Underwood; ▸ **male vocalist of the year:** Brad Paisley; ▸ **new artist of the year:** Lady Antebellum; ▸ **vocal duo of the year:** Sugarland; ▸ **vocal group of the year:** Rascal Flatts; ▸ **album of the year:** Troubadour, George Strait; Tony Brown and George Strait, producers; ▸ **song of the year:** "Stay" (Jennifer Nettles), Jennifer Nettles, songwriter; ▸ **single of the year:** "I Saw God Today," George Strait; Tony Brown and George Strait, producers; ▸ **music video of the year:** "Waitin' on a Woman," Brad Paisley featuring Andy Griffith; Jim Shea and Peter Tilden, directors; ▸ **musical event of the year:** "Gone Gone Gone," Robert Plant and Alison Krauss; ▸ **musician of the year:** Mac McAnally (guitar)

All-Time Best-Selling Albums in the United States

As of July 2009. Album sales are given only to the nearest million units, and in the case of a tie albums are listed alphabetically. Source: Recording Industry Association of America (RIAA), <www.riaa.com>.

	ALBUM	ARTIST	YEAR		ALBUM	ARTIST	YEAR
1	Their Greatest Hits (1971–1975)	Eagles	1976	27	...Baby One More Time	Britney Spears	1999
2	Thriller	Michael Jackson	1982		Backstreet Boys	Backstreet Boys	1997
3	untitled ("Led Zeppelin IV")	Led Zeppelin	1971		Bat out of Hell	Meat Loaf	1977
	The Wall	Pink Floyd	1979		Metallica	Metallica	1991
5	Back in Black	AC/DC	1980		Ropin' the Wind	Garth Brooks	1991
6	Double Live	Garth Brooks	1998		Simon & Garfunkel's Greatest Hits	Simon & Garfunkel	1972
	Greatest Hits, Volume I & Volume II	Billy Joel	1985	33	Greatest Hits 1974–1978	Steve Miller Band	1978
8	Come On Over	Shania Twain	1997		Live/1975–85	Bruce Springsteen & the E Street Band	1986
9	The Beatles ("The White Album")	The Beatles	1968		Millennium	Backstreet Boys	1999
	Rumours	Fleetwood Mac	1977		Purple Rain (soundtrack)	Prince and the Revolution	1984
11	Appetite for Destruction	Guns N' Roses	1987		Ten	Pearl Jam	1991
12	The Bodyguard (soundtrack)	Whitney Houston and various artists	1992		Whitney Houston	Whitney Houston	1985
	Boston	Boston	1976	39	Abbey Road	The Beatles	1969
	No Fences	Garth Brooks	1990		Breathless	Kenny G	1992
15	Cracked Rear View	Hootie & the Blowfish	1994		Forrest Gump (soundtrack)	various artists	1994
	Greatest Hits	Elton John	1974		Hot Rocks 1964–1971	The Rolling Stones	1972
	Hotel California	Eagles	1976		Hysteria	Def Leppard	1987
	Jagged Little Pill	Alanis Morissette	1995		Kenny Rogers' Greatest Hits	Kenny Rogers	1980
	1967–70	The Beatles	1973		Led Zeppelin II	Led Zeppelin	1969
	Physical Graffiti	Led Zeppelin	1975		No Jacket Required	Phil Collins	1985
21	Born in the U.S.A.	Bruce Springsteen	1984		Pieces of You	Jewel	1995
	Dark Side of the Moon	Pink Floyd	1973		Slippery When Wet	Bon Jovi	1986
	Greatest Hits 1962–66	The Beatles	1973		II	Boyz II Men	1994
	Saturday Night Fever (soundtrack)	The Bee Gees and various artists	1977		Wide Open Spaces	Dixie Chicks	1998
					The Woman in Me	Shania Twain	1995
	Supernatural	Santana	1999		Yourself or Someone Like You	Matchbox 20	1996

Rock and Roll Hall of Fame

Music-industry professionals established the Rock and Roll Hall of Fame Foundation in 1983 in order to "recognize the contributions of those who have had a significant impact on the evolution, development, and perpetuation of rock and roll." Performers are eligible for induction 25 years after the release of their first record. The foundation's nominating committee compiles an annual list of eligible artists and distributes this list to about 1,000 rock experts throughout the world. Those performers receiving the highest number of votes, as well as at least 50% of the vote, are inducted. Special committees select inductees in other categories. Inductees for 2009 appear in **bold-face**.

Rock and Roll Hall of Fame and Museum Web site: <www.rockhall.com>.

Rock and Roll Hall of Fame (continued)

NAME (YEAR OF INDUCTION)

AC/DC (2003)
Paul Ackerman[1] (1995)
Aerosmith (2001)
The Allman Brothers Band (1995)
Herb Alpert and Jerry Moss[2] (2006)
The Animals (1994)
Louis Armstrong[3] (1990)
Chet Atkins[4] (2002)
LaVern Baker (1991)
Hank Ballard (1990)
The Band (1994)
Dave Bartholomew[1] (1991)
Frank Barsalona[2] (2005)
Ralph Bass[1] (1991)
The Beach Boys (1988)
The Beatles (1988)
Jeff Beck (2009)
The Bee Gees (1997)
Benny Benjamin[4] (2003)
Chuck Berry (1986)
Bill Black[4] (2009)
Black Sabbath (2006)
Chris Blackwell[1] (2001)
Hal Blaine[4] (2000)
Bobby "Blue" Bland (1992)
Blondie (2006)
Booker T. and the MG's (1992)
David Bowie (1996)
Charles Brown[3] (1999)
James Brown (1986)
Ruth Brown (1993)
Jackson Browne (2004)
Buffalo Springfield (1997)
Solomon Burke (2001)
James Burton[4] (2001)
The Byrds (1991)
Johnny Cash (1992)
Ray Charles (1986)
Leonard Chess[1] (1987)
Charlie Christian[3] (1990)
Eric Clapton (2000)
Dick Clark[1] (1993)
The Clash (2003)
The Coasters (1987)
Eddie Cochran (1987)
Leonard Cohen (2008)
Nat King Cole[3] (2000)
Sam Cooke (1986)
Elvis Costello and the Attractions (2003)
Floyd Cramer[4] (2003)
Cream (1993)
Creedence Clearwater Revival (1993)
Crosby, Stills & Nash (1997)
Bobby Darin (1990)
The Dave Clark Five (2008)
Clive Davis[1] (2000)
Miles Davis (2006)
The Dells (2004)
Bo Diddley (1987)
Dion (1989)
Willie Dixon[3] (1994)
Fats Domino (1986)
Tom Donahue[1] (1996)
The Doors (1993)
Steve Douglas[4] (2003)

NAME (YEAR OF INDUCTION)

The Drifters (1988)
Bob Dylan (1988)
Eagles (1998)
Earth, Wind & Fire (2000)
Duane Eddy (1994)
Ahmet Ertegun[1] (1987)
Nesuhi Ertegun[2] (1991)
The Everly Brothers (1986)
Leo Fender[1] (1992)
The Flamingos (2001)
Fleetwood Mac (1998)
D.J. Fontana[4] (2009)
The Four Seasons (1990)
The Four Tops (1990)
Aretha Franklin (1987)
Alan Freed[1] (1986)
Milt Gabler[1] (1993)
Kenny Gamble and Leon Huff[1] (2008)
Marvin Gaye (1987)
Gerry Goffin and Carole King[1] (1990)
Berry Gordy, Jr.[1] (1988)
Bill Graham[1] (1992)
Grandmaster Flash and the Furious Five (2007)
Grateful Dead (1994)
Al Green (1995)
Woody Guthrie[3] (1988)
Buddy Guy (2005)
Bill Haley (1987)
John Hammond[2] (1986)
George Harrison (2004)
Isaac Hayes (2002)
The Jimi Hendrix Experience (1992)
Billie Holiday[3] (2000)
Holland, Dozier, and Holland[1] (1990)
Buddy Holly (1986)
John Lee Hooker (1991)
Howlin' Wolf[3] (1991)
The Impressions (1991)
The Ink Spots[3] (1989)
The Isley Brothers (1992)
Mahalia Jackson[3] (1997)
Michael Jackson (2001)
Wanda Jackson[3] (2009)
The Jackson 5 (1997)
James Jamerson[4] (2000)
Elmore James[3] (1992)
Etta James (1993)
Jefferson Airplane (1996)
Billy Joel (1999)
Elton John (1994)
Little Willie John (1996)
Johnnie Johnson[4] (2001)
Robert Johnson[3] (1986)
Janis Joplin (1995)
Louis Jordan[3] (1987)
B.B. King (1987)
King Curtis[4] (2000)
The Kinks (1990)
Gladys Knight and the Pips (1996)
Leadbelly[3] (1988)
Led Zeppelin (1995)
Brenda Lee (2002)

NAME (YEAR OF INDUCTION)

Jerry Leiber and Mike Stoller[1] (1987)
John Lennon (1994)
Jerry Lee Lewis (1986)
Little Anthony and the Imperials (2009)
Little Richard (1986)
Little Walter (2008)
The Lovin' Spoonful (2000)
Frankie Lymon and the Teenagers (1993)
Lynyrd Skynyrd (2006)
Madonna (2008)
The Mamas and the Papas (1998)
Bob Marley (1994)
Martha and the Vandellas (1995)
George Martin[1] (1999)
Curtis Mayfield (1999)
Paul McCartney (1999)
Clyde McPhatter (1987)
John Mellencamp (2008)
Metallica (2009)
Joni Mitchell (1997)
Bill Monroe[3] (1997)
The Moonglows (2000)
Scotty Moore[4] (2000)
Van Morrison (1993)
Jelly Roll Morton[3] (1998)
Syd Nathan[1] (1997)
Ricky Nelson (1987)
The O'Jays (2005)
Spooner Oldham[4] (2009)
Roy Orbison (1987)
The Orioles[3] (1995)
Mo Ostin[1] (2003)
Johnny Otis[1] (1994)
Earl Palmer[4] (2000)
Parliament-Funkadelic (1997)
Les Paul[3] (1988)
Carl Perkins (1987)
Tom Petty and the Heartbreakers (2002)
Sam Phillips[1] (1986)
Wilson Pickett (1991)
Pink Floyd (1996)
Gene Pitney (2002)
The Platters (1990)
The Police (2003)
Doc Pomus[1] (1992)
Elvis Presley (1986)
The Pretenders (2005)
Lloyd Price (1998)
Prince (2004)
Professor Longhair[3] (1992)
Queen (2001)
Ma Rainey[3] (1990)
Bonnie Raitt (2000)
The Ramones (2002)
Otis Redding (1989)
Jimmy Reed (1991)
R.E.M. (2007)
The Righteous Brothers (2003)
Smokey Robinson (1987)
Jimmie Rodgers[3] (1986)
The Rolling Stones (1989)
The Ronettes (2007)
Run-D.M.C. (2009)

Rock and Roll Hall of Fame (continued)

NAME (YEAR OF INDUCTION)
Sam and Dave (1992)
Santana (1998)
Pete Seeger[3] (1996)
Bob Seger (2004)
The Sex Pistols (2006)
Del Shannon (1999)
The Shirelles (1996)
Paul Simon (2001)
Simon & Garfunkel (1990)
Percy Sledge (2005)
Sly and the Family Stone (1993)
Bessie Smith[3] (1989)
Patti Smith (2007)
The Soul Stirrers[3] (1989)
Phil Spector[1] (1989)
Dusty Springfield (1999)
Bruce Springsteen (1999)
The Staple Singers (1999)

NAME (YEAR OF INDUCTION)
Steely Dan (2001)
Seymour Stein[2] (2005)
Jim Stewart[1] (2002)
Rod Stewart (1994)
The Supremes (1988)
Talking Heads (2002)
James Taylor (2000)
The Temptations (1989)
Allen Toussaint[1] (1998)
Traffic (2004)
Big Joe Turner (1987)
Ike and Tina Turner (1991)
U2 (2005)
Ritchie Valens (2001)
Van Halen (2007)
The Velvet Underground (1996)
The Ventures (2008)
Gene Vincent (1998)

NAME (YEAR OF INDUCTION)
T-Bone Walker[3] (1987)
Dinah Washington[3] (1993)
Muddy Waters (1987)
Jann S. Wenner[2] (2004)
Jerry Wexler[1] (1987)
The Who (1990)
Hank Williams[3] (1987)
Bob Wills and His Texas Playboys[3] (1999)
Jackie Wilson (1987)
Bobby Womack (2009)
Stevie Wonder (1989)
Jimmy Yancey[3] (1986)
The Yardbirds (1992)
Neil Young (1995)
The (Young) Rascals (1997)
Frank Zappa (1995)
ZZ Top (2004)

[1]Ahmet Ertegun Award (nonperformers).   [2]Lifetime Achievement.   [3]Early Influences.   [4]Sidemen.

Encyclopædia Britannica's 20 World-Class Orchestras

ORCHESTRA	LOCATION	FOUNDED	MUSIC DIRECTOR OR CONDUCTOR (2009)
Berlin Philharmoniker	Berlin, Germany	1882	Simon Rattle
Boston Symphony Orchestra	Boston MA	1881	James Levine
Chicago Symphony Orchestra	Chicago IL	1891	Bernard Haitink[1]
Gewandhausorchester	Leipzig, Germany	1743	Riccardo Chailly
Israel Philharmonic Orchestra	Tel Aviv, Israel	1936	Zubin Mehta
Koninklijk Concertgebouworkest	Amsterdam, Netherlands	1888	Mariss Jansons
London Philharmonic Orchestra	London, England	1932	Vladimir Jurowski
London Symphony Orchestra	London, England	1904	Valery Gergiev
Los Angeles Philharmonic	Los Angeles CA	1919	Gustavo Dudamel
New York Philharmonic	New York NY	1842	Alan Gilbert
NHK Symphony Orchestra	Tokyo, Japan	1926	Vladimir Ashkenazy
Orchestre National de France	Paris, France	1934	Daniele Gatti
Orchestre Symphonique de Montréal	Montreal, QC, Canada	1934	Kent Nagano
Oslo-Filharmonien	Oslo, Norway	1919	Jukka-Pekka Saraste
Philadelphia Orchestra	Philadelphia PA	1900	Charles Dutoit[2]
Philharmonia Orchestra	London, England	1945	Esa-Pekka Salonen
Pittsburgh Symphony Orchestra	Pittsburgh PA	1896	Manfred Honeck
Saint Louis Symphony Orchestra	St. Louis MO	1880	David Robertson
San Francisco Symphony	San Francisco CA	1911	Michael Tilson Thomas
Wiener Philharmoniker	Vienna, Austria	1842	guest conductors

[1]Principal conductor. Riccardo Muti will assume the musical directorship of the Chicago Symphony Orchestra in September 2010. [2]Chief conductor and artistic adviser. The search for a music director is ongoing in 2009.

Encyclopædia Britannica's Top 20 Opera Companies

COMPANY	LOCATION	FOUNDED	GENERAL OR ARTISTIC DIRECTOR (2009)
Arena di Verona[1]	Verona, Italy	1913	Gianni Tangucci
Bayerische Staatsoper	Munich, Germany	1653	Nikolaus Bachler
Bolshoi Opera	Moscow, Russia	1776	Makvala Kasrashvili
Canadian Opera Company	Toronto, ON, Canada	1950	Alexander Neef
Los Angeles Opera	Los Angeles CA	1986	Plácido Domingo
Lyric Opera of Chicago	Chicago IL	1954	William Mason
Magyar Állami Operaház	Budapest, Hungary	1884	Lajos Vass

Encyclopædia Britannica's Top 20 Opera Companies (continued)

COMPANY	LOCATION	FOUNDED	GENERAL OR ARTISTIC DIRECTOR (2009)
Mariinsky Opera Company	St. Petersburg, Russia	1783	Valery Gergiev
Metropolitan Opera	New York NY	1883	Peter Gelb
Opera Australia	Sydney, NSW, and Melbourne, VIC, Australia	1956	Lyndon Terracini
Opéra National de Paris	Paris, France	1669	Gerard Mortier
Royal Opera	London, England	1732	Elaine Padmore[2]
Staatsoper Unter den Linden	Berlin, Germany	1742	Daniel Barenboim
Teatro alla Scala (La Scala)	Milan, Italy	1778	Stéphane Lissner
Teatro dell'Opera di Roma	Rome, Italy	1880	Mauro Trombetta
Teatro di San Carlo	Naples, Italy	1737	[3]
Teatro Massimo	Palermo, Italy	1897	Lorenzo Mariani
Théâtre du Châtelet	Paris, France	1862	Jean-Luc Choplin
Washington National Opera	Washington DC	1956	Plácido Domingo
Wiener Staatsoper	Vienna, Austria	1869	Ioan Holender

[1]*The Arena di Verona was built in the 1st century AD; it has been primarily an opera venue since 1913.* [2]*Director of opera.* [3]*The Teatro di San Carlo had no general or artistic director at press time.*

Arts and Letters Awards

Pulitzer Prizes

The Pulitzer Prizes are awarded annually by Columbia University, New York City, based on recommendations from the Pulitzer Prize Board, for works published or produced in the previous calendar year (for music, works must be performed or released between 16 January of the previous year and 15 January of the award year). The prizes, originally endowed by newspaper editor Joseph Pulitzer, were first awarded in 1917. There are currently 21 prizes presented. Most prizes include a US$10,000 cash award; the exception is the prize for public service in journalism, which is a gold medal.
Pulitzer Prize Web site: <www.pulitzer.org>.

Journalism, 2009

CATEGORY AND DESCRIPTION	WINNER	PUBLICATION	SUBJECT
Public Service: awarded to a newspaper for notable public service	Alexandra Berzon and staff	*Las Vegas Sun*	investigation into the high death rate of construction workers on the Vegas Strip
Breaking News Reporting: awarded for local reporting of breaking news	staff	*New York Times*	coverage of the sex scandal involving then New York governor Eliot Spitzer
Investigative Reporting: awarded to an individual or team for an investigative article or series	David Barstow	*New York Times*	exposure of the ties of some retired generals working as news analysts to the Pentagon and defense companies
Explanatory Reporting: awarded for clarification of a difficult subject through clear communication of in-depth knowledge	Bettina Boxall and Julie Cart	*Los Angeles Times*	examination of the various ways to combat the threat of forest fires in the western US
Local Reporting: awarded for consistent, intelligent coverage of a particular topic	staff (notably Jim Schaefer and M.L. Elrick)	*Detroit Free Press*	reports on the sexual relationship between Detroit's mayor, Kwame Kilpatrick, and a staffer
	Ryan Gabrielson and Paul Giblin	*East Valley Tribune* (Mesa AZ)	study of a local sheriff's focus on illegal immigration over traditional public-safety issues
National Reporting: awarded for coverage of national news	staff	*St. Petersburg (FL) Times*	"PolitiFact," a fact-checking feature for claims made during the presidential election
International Reporting: awarded for coverage of international news	staff	*New York Times*	coverage of America's military and political challenges in Pakistan and Afghanistan
Feature Writing	Lane DeGregory	*St. Petersburg (FL) Times*	portrait of an abused child's adoption by a loving family

Journalism, 2009 (continued)

CATEGORY AND DESCRIPTION	WINNER	PUBLICATION	SUBJECT
Commentary	Eugene Robinson	Washington Post	columns that celebrate the election of the first African American US president
Criticism	Holland Cotter	New York Times	art criticism
Editorial Writing: awarded for ability to sway public opinion through solid reasoning, clear style, and "moral purpose"	Mark Mahoney	Post-Star (Glens Falls NY)	editorials on the danger of secrecy in local government
Editorial Cartooning: awarded for a cartoon or group of cartoons displaying creativity, superior drawing, and editorial effectiveness	Steve Breen	San Diego Union-Tribune	
Breaking News Photography: awarded for color or black-and-white photographs of breaking news, individually or as a group	Patrick Farrell	Miami Herald	depiction of the devastation wrought by Hurricane Ike and other deadly storms in Haiti
Feature Photography: awarded for color or black-and-white feature photographs, individually or as a group	Damon Winter	New York Times	photographic chronicle of the presidential campaign of Barack Obama

Letters, Drama, and Music

Fiction
Awarded for a work of fiction, preferably about American life, by an American author.

YEAR	TITLE	AUTHOR	YEAR	TITLE	AUTHOR
1917	no award		1947	All the King's Men	Robert Penn Warren
1918	His Family	Ernest Poole			
1919	The Magnificent Ambersons	Booth Tarkington	1948	Tales of the South Pacific	James A. Michener
1920	no award		1949	Guard of Honor	James Gould Cozzens
1921	The Age of Innocence	Edith Wharton			
1922	Alice Adams	Booth Tarkington	1950	The Way West	A.B. Guthrie, Jr.
1923	One of Ours	Willa Cather	1951	The Town	Conrad Richter
1924	The Able McLaughlins	Margaret Wilson	1952	The Caine Mutiny	Herman Wouk
1925	So Big	Edna Ferber	1953	The Old Man and the Sea	Ernest Hemingway
1926	Arrowsmith	Sinclair Lewis (declined)	1954	no award	
1927	Early Autumn	Louis Bromfield	1955	A Fable	William Faulkner
1928	The Bridge of San Luis Rey	Thornton Wilder	1956	Andersonville	MacKinlay Kantor
1929	Scarlet Sister Mary	Julia Peterkin	1957	no award	
1930	Laughing Boy	Oliver Lafarge	1958	A Death in the Family[1]	James Agee
1931	Years of Grace	Margaret Ayer Barnes	1959	The Travels of Jaimie McPheeters	Robert Lewis Taylor
1932	The Good Earth	Pearl S. Buck	1960	Advise and Consent	Allen Drury
1933	The Store	T.S. Stribling	1961	To Kill a Mockingbird	Harper Lee
1934	Lamb in His Bosom	Caroline Miller	1962	The Edge of Sadness	Edwin O'Connor
1935	Now in November	Josephine Winslow Johnson	1963	The Reivers	William Faulkner
			1964	no award	
1936	Honey in the Horn	Harold L. Davis	1965	The Keepers of the House	Shirley Ann Grau
1937	Gone with the Wind	Margaret Mitchell			
1938	The Late George Apley	John Phillips Marquand	1966	Collected Stories	Katherine Anne Porter
1939	The Yearling	Marjorie Kinnan Rawlings	1967	The Fixer	Bernard Malamud
			1968	The Confessions of Nat Turner	William Styron
1940	The Grapes of Wrath	John Steinbeck	1969	House Made of Dawn	N. Scott Momaday
1941	no award		1970	Collected Stories	Jean Stafford
1942	In This Our Life	Ellen Glasgow	1971	no award	
1943	Dragon's Teeth	Upton Sinclair	1972	Angle of Repose	Wallace Stegner
1944	Journey in the Dark	Martin Flavin	1973	The Optimist's Daughter	Eudora Welty
1945	A Bell for Adano	John Hersey	1974	no award	
1946	no award				

Letters, Drama, and Music (continued)

Fiction (continued)

YEAR	TITLE	AUTHOR	YEAR	TITLE	AUTHOR
1975	The Killer Angels	Michael Shaara	1994	The Shipping News	E. Annie Proulx
1976	Humboldt's Gift	Saul Bellow	1995	The Stone Diaries	Carol Shields
1977	no award		1996	Independence Day	Richard Ford
1978	Elbow Room	James Alan McPherson	1997	Martin Dressler: The Tale of an American Dreamer	Steven Millhauser
1979	The Stories of John Cheever	John Cheever	1998	American Pastoral	Philip Roth
1980	The Executioner's Song	Norman Mailer	1999	The Hours	Michael Cunningham
1981	A Confederacy of Dunces[1]	John Kennedy Toole	2000	Interpreter of Maladies	Jhumpa Lahiri
1982	Rabbit Is Rich	John Updike	2001	The Amazing Adventures of Kavalier and Clay	Michael Chabon
1983	The Color Purple	Alice Walker	2002	Empire Falls	Richard Russo
1984	Ironweed	William Kennedy	2003	Middlesex	Jeffrey Eugenides
1985	Foreign Affairs	Alison Lurie	2004	The Known World	Edward P. Jones
1986	Lonesome Dove	Larry McMurtry	2005	Gilead	Marilynne Robinson
1987	A Summons to Memphis	Peter Taylor	2006	March	Geraldine Brooks
1988	Beloved	Toni Morrison	2007	The Road	Cormac McCarthy
1989	Breathing Lessons	Anne Tyler	2008	The Brief Wondrous Life of Oscar Wao	Junot Díaz
1990	The Mambo Kings Play Songs of Love	Oscar Hijuelos	2009	Olive Kitteridge	Elizabeth Strout
1991	Rabbit at Rest	John Updike			
1992	A Thousand Acres	Jane Smiley			
1993	A Good Scent from a Strange Mountain	Robert Olen Butler			

[1]Work published and prize awarded posthumously.

Drama
Awarded for a play, preferably about American life, by an American author.

YEAR	TITLE	AUTHOR	YEAR	TITLE	AUTHOR
1917	no award		1946	State of the Union	Russel Crouse and Howard Lindsay
1918	Why Marry?	Jesse Lynch Williams	1947	no award	
1919	no award		1948	A Streetcar Named Desire	Tennessee Williams
1920	Beyond the Horizon	Eugene O'Neill	1949	Death of a Salesman	Arthur Miller
1921	Miss Lulu Bett	Zona Gale	1950	South Pacific	Richard Rodgers, Oscar Hammerstein II, and Joshua Logan
1922	Anna Christie	Eugene O'Neill			
1923	Icebound	Owen Davis			
1924	Hell-Bent fer Heaven	Hatcher Hughes			
1925	They Knew What They Wanted	Sidney Howard	1951	no award	
1926	Craig's Wife	George Kelly	1952	The Shrike	Joseph Kramm
1927	In Abraham's Bosom	Paul Green	1953	Picnic	William Inge
1928	Strange Interlude	Eugene O'Neill	1954	The Teahouse of the August Moon	John Patrick
1929	Street Scene	Elmer L. Rice			
1930	The Green Pastures	Marc Connelly	1955	Cat on a Hot Tin Roof	Tennessee Williams
1931	Alison's House	Susan Glaspell			
1932	Of Thee I Sing	George S. Kaufman, Morrie Ryskind, and Ira Gershwin	1956	The Diary of Anne Frank	Albert Hackett and Frances Goodrich
			1957	Long Day's Journey into Night[1]	Eugene O'Neill
1933	Both Your Houses	Maxwell Anderson	1958	Look Homeward, Angel	Ketti Frings
1934	Men in White	Sidney Kingsley	1959	J.B.	Archibald MacLeish
1935	The Old Maid	Zoe Akins			
1936	Idiot's Delight	Robert E. Sherwood	1960	Fiorello!	Jerome Weidman, George Abbott, Jerry Bock, and Sheldon Harnick
1937	You Can't Take It with You	Moss Hart and George S. Kaufman			
1938	Our Town	Thornton Wilder			
1939	Abe Lincoln in Illinois	Robert E. Sherwood			
1940	The Time of Your Life	William Saroyan	1961	All the Way Home	Tad Mosel
1941	There Shall Be No Night	Robert E. Sherwood	1962	How To Succeed in Business Without Really Trying	Frank Loesser and Abe Burrows
1942	no award				
1943	The Skin of Our Teeth	Thornton Wilder			
1944	no award		1963	no award	
1945	Harvey	Mary Chase	1964	no award	

Letters, Drama, and Music (continued)

<u>Drama</u> (continued)

YEAR	TITLE	AUTHOR
1965	*The Subject Was Roses*	Frank D. Gilroy
1966	no award	
1967	*A Delicate Balance*	Edward Albee
1968	no award	
1969	*The Great White Hope*	Howard Sackler
1970	*No Place To Be Somebody*	Charles Gordone
1971	*The Effect of Gamma Rays on Man-in-the-Moon Marigolds*	Paul Zindel
1972	no award	
1973	*That Championship Season*	Jason Miller
1974	no award	
1975	*Seascape*	Edward Albee
1976	*A Chorus Line*	Michael Bennett, James Kirkwood, Nicholas Dante, Marvin Hamlisch, and Edward Kleban
1977	*The Shadow Box*	Michael Cristofer
1978	*The Gin Game*	Donald L. Coburn
1979	*Buried Child*	Sam Shepard
1980	*Talley's Folly*	Lanford Wilson
1981	*Crimes of the Heart*	Beth Henley
1982	*A Soldier's Play*	Charles Fuller
1983	*'Night, Mother*	Marsha Norman
1984	*Glengarry Glen Ross*	David Mamet
1985	*Sunday in the Park with George*	Stephen Sondheim and James Lapine

YEAR	TITLE	AUTHOR
1986	no award	
1987	*Fences*	August Wilson
1988	*Driving Miss Daisy*	Alfred Uhry
1989	*The Heidi Chronicles*	Wendy Wasserstein
1990	*The Piano Lesson*	August Wilson
1991	*Lost in Yonkers*	Neil Simon
1992	*The Kentucky Cycle*	Robert Schenkkan
1993	*Angels in America: Millennium Approaches*	Tony Kushner
1994	*Three Tall Women*	Edward Albee
1995	*The Young Man from Atlanta*	Horton Foote
1996	*Rent*[1]	Jonathan Larson
1997	no award	
1998	*How I Learned To Drive*	Paula Vogel
1999	*Wit*	Margaret Edson
2000	*Dinner with Friends*	Donald Margulies
2001	*Proof*	David Auburn
2002	*Topdog/Underdog*	Suzan-Lori Parks
2003	*Anna in the Tropics*	Nilo Cruz
2004	*I Am My Own Wife*	Doug Wright
2005	*Doubt: A Parable*	John Patrick Shanley
2006	no award	
2007	*Rabbit Hole*	David Lindsay-Abaire
2008	*August: Osage County*	Tracy Letts
2009	*Ruined*	Lynn Nottage

[1]Awarded posthumously

History

Awarded for a work on the subject of American history.

YEAR	TITLE	AUTHOR
1917	*With Americans of Past and Present Days*	J.J. Jusserand
1918	*A History of the Civil War, 1861–1865*	James Ford Rhodes
1919	no award	
1920	*The War with Mexico,* 2 vols.	Justin H. Smith
1921	*The Victory at Sea*	William Sowden Sims and Burton Jesse Hendrick
1922	*The Founding of New England*	James Truslow Adams
1923	*The Supreme Court in United States History*	Charles Warren
1924	*The American Revolution: A Constitutional Interpretation*	Charles Howard McIlwain
1925	*History of the American Frontier*	Frederic L. Paxson
1926	*A History of the United States*	Edward Channing
1927	*Pinckney's Treaty*	Samuel Flagg Bemis
1928	*Main Currents in American Thought,* 2 vols.	Vernon Louis Parrington

YEAR	TITLE	AUTHOR
1929	*The Organization and Administration of the Union Army, 1861–1865*	Fred Albert Shannon
1930	*The War of Independence*	Claude H. Van Tyne
1931	*The Coming of the War, 1914*	Bernadotte E. Schmitt
1932	*My Experiences in the World War*	John J. Pershing
1933	*The Significance of Sections in American History*[1]	Frederick J. Turner
1934	*The People's Choice*	Herbert Agar
1935	*The Colonial Period of American History*	Charles McLean Andrews
1936	*A Constitutional History of the United States*	Andrew C. McLaughlin
1937	*The Flowering of New England, 1815–1865*	Van Wyck Brooks
1938	*The Road to Reunion, 1865–1900*	Paul Herman Buck
1939	*A History of American Magazines*	Frank Luther Mott
1940	*Abraham Lincoln: The War Years*	Carl Sandburg

Letters, Drama, and Music (continued)

History (continued)

YEAR	TITLE	AUTHOR
1941	The Atlantic Migration, 1607–1860	Marcus Lee Hansen
1942	Reveille in Washington, 1860–1865	Margaret Leech
1943	Paul Revere and the World He Lived In	Esther Forbes
1944	The Growth of American Thought	Merle Curti
1945	Unfinished Business	Stephen Bonsal
1946	The Age of Jackson	Arthur M. Schlesinger, Jr.
1947	Scientists Against Time	James Phinney Baxter III
1948	Across the Wide Missouri	Bernard De Voto
1949	The Disruption of American Democracy	Roy Franklin Nichols
1950	Art and Life in America	Oliver W. Larkin
1951	The Old Northwest: Pioneer Period, 1815–1840	R. Carlyle Buley
1952	The Uprooted	Oscar Handlin
1953	The Era of Good Feelings	George Dangerfield
1954	A Stillness at Appomattox	Bruce Catton
1955	Great River: The Rio Grande in North American History	Paul Horgan
1956	The Age of Reform	Richard Hofstadter
1957	Russia Leaves the War: Soviet-American Relations, 1917–1920	George F. Kennan
1958	Banks and Politics in America	Bray Hammond
1959	The Republican Era: 1869–1901	Leonard D. White and Jean Schneider
1960	In the Days of McKinley	Margaret Leech
1961	Between War and Peace: The Potsdam Conference	Herbert Feis
1962	The Triumphant Empire: Thunder-Clouds Gather in the West, 1763–1766	Lawrence H. Gipson
1963	Washington, Village and Capital, 1800–1878	Constance McLaughlin Green
1964	Puritan Village: The Formation of a New England Town	Sumner Chilton Powell
1965	The Greenback Era	Irwin Unger
1966	The Life of the Mind in America[1]	Perry Miller
1967	Exploration and Empire: The Explorer and the Scientist in the Winning of the American West	William H. Goetzmann
1968	The Ideological Origins of the American Revolution	Bernard Bailyn
1969	Origins of the Fifth Amendment	Leonard W. Levy

YEAR	TITLE	AUTHOR
1970	Present at the Creation: My Years in the State Department	Dean Acheson
1971	Roosevelt: The Soldier of Freedom	James MacGregor Burns
1972	Neither Black nor White	Carl N. Degler
1973	People of Paradox: An Inquiry Concerning the Origins of American Civilization	Michael Kammen
1974	The Americans: The Democratic Experience	Daniel J. Boorstin
1975	Jefferson and His Time, vols. 1–5	Dumas Malone
1976	Lamy of Santa Fe	Paul Horgan
1977	The Impending Crisis, 1841–1867[2]	David M. Potter and Don E. Fehrenbacher
1978	The Visible Hand: The Managerial Revolution in American Business	Alfred D. Chandler, Jr.
1979	The Dred Scott Case	Don E. Fehrenbacher
1980	Been in the Storm So Long	Leon F. Litwack
1981	American Education: The National Experience, 1783–1876	Lawrence A. Cremin
1982	Mary Chesnut's Civil War	C. Vann Woodward[3]
1983	The Transformation of Virginia, 1740–1790	Rhys L. Isaac
1984	no award	
1985	Prophets of Regulation	Thomas K. McCraw
1986	The Heavens and the Earth: A Political History of the Space Age	Walter A. McDougall
1987	Voyagers to the West: A Passage in the Peopling of America on the Eve of the Revolution	Bernard Bailyn
1988	The Launching of Modern American Science, 1846–1876	Robert V. Bruce
1989	Battle Cry of Freedom: The Civil War Era	James M. McPherson
	Parting the Waters: America in the King Years, 1954–1963	Taylor Branch
1990	In Our Image: America's Empire in the Philippines	Stanley Karnow
1991	A Midwife's Tale	Laurel Thatcher Ulrich
1992	The Fate of Liberty: Abraham Lincoln and Civil Liberties	Mark E. Neely, Jr.
1993	The Radicalism of the American Revolution	Gordon S. Wood
1994	no award	
1995	No Ordinary Time: Franklin and Eleanor Roosevelt: The Home Front in World War II	Doris Kearns Goodwin

Letters, Drama, and Music (continued)

History (continued)

YEAR	TITLE	AUTHOR
1996	William Cooper's Town: Power and Persuasion on the Frontier of the Early American Republic	Alan Taylor
1997	Original Meanings: Politics and Ideas in the Making of the Constitution	Jack N. Rakove
1998	Summer for the Gods: The Scopes Trial and America's Continuing Debate over Science and Religion	Edward J. Larson
1999	Gotham: A History of New York City to 1898	Edwin G. Burrows and Mike Wallace
2000	Freedom from Fear: The American People in Depression and War, 1929–1945	David M. Kennedy
2001	Founding Brothers: The Revolutionary Generation	Joseph J. Ellis
2002	The Metaphysical Club: A Story of Ideas in America	Louis Menand
2003	An Army at Dawn: The War in North Africa, 1942–1943	Rick Atkinson
2004	A Nation Under Our Feet: Black Political Struggles in the Rural South from Slavery to the Great Migration	Steven Hahn
2005	Washington's Crossing	David Hackett Fischer
2006	Polio: An American Story	David M. Oshinsky
2007	The Race Beat: The Press, the Civil Rights Struggle, and the Awakening of a Nation	Gene Roberts and Hank Klibanoff
2008	What Hath God Wrought: The Transformation of America, 1815–1848	Daniel Walker Howe
2009	The Hemingses of Monticello: An American Family	Annette Gordon-Reed

[1]Awarded posthumously.   [2]Potter died before completing the work; Fehrenbacher wrote the final chapters and edited it.   [3]Editor.

Biography or Autobiography
Awarded for a biography or autobiography by an American author.

YEAR	TITLE	AUTHOR
1917	Julia Ward Howe	Laura Elizabeth Howe Richards and Maude Howe Elliott; assisted by Florence Howe Hall
1918	Benjamin Franklin, Self-Revealed	William Cabell Bruce
1919	The Education of Henry Adams[1]	Henry Adams
1920	The Life of John Marshall, 4 vols.	Albert J. Beveridge
1921	The Americanization of Edward Bok	Edward Bok
1922	A Daughter of the Middle Border	Hamlin Garland
1923	The Life and Letters of Walter H. Page	Burton J. Hendrick
1924	From Immigrant to Inventor	Michael Idvorsky Pupin
1925	Barrett Wendell and His Letters	M.A. De Wolfe Howe
1926	The Life of Sir William Osler, 2 vols.	Harvey Cushing
1927	Whitman	Emory Holloway
1928	The American Orchestra and Theodore Thomas	Charles Edward Russell
1929	The Training of an American: The Earlier Life and Letters of Walter H. Page	Burton J. Hendrick
1930	The Raven	Marquis James
1931	Charles W. Eliot	Henry James
1932	Theodore Roosevelt	Henry F. Pringle
1933	Grover Cleveland	Allan Nevins
1934	John Hay	Tyler Dennett
1935	R.E. Lee	Douglas S. Freeman
1936	The Thought and Character of William James	Ralph Barton Perry
1937	Hamilton Fish	Allan Nevins
1938	Andrew Jackson, 2 vols.	Marquis James
	Pedlar's Progress	Odell Shepard
1939	Benjamin Franklin	Carl Van Doren
1940	Woodrow Wilson, Life and Letters, vols. 7 and 8	Ray Stannard Baker
1941	Jonathan Edward	Ola Elizabeth Winslow
1942	Crusader in Crinoline	Forrest Wilson
1943	Admiral of the Ocean Sea	Samuel Eliot Morison
1944	The American Leonardo: The Life of Samuel F.B. Morse	Carleton Mabee
1945	George Bancroft: Brahmin Rebel	Russell Blaine Nye
1946	Son of the Wilderness	Linnie Marsh Wolfe
1947	The Autobiography of William Allen White	William Allen White
1948	Forgotten First Citizen: John Bigelow	Margaret Clapp

Letters, Drama, and Music (continued)

Biography or Autobiography (continued)

YEAR	TITLE	AUTHOR
1949	Roosevelt and Hopkins	Robert E. Sherwood
1950	John Quincy Adams and the Foundations of American Foreign Policy	Samuel Flagg Bemis
1951	John C. Calhoun: American Portrait	Margaret Louise Coit
1952	Charles Evans Hughes	Merlo J. Pusey
1953	Edmund Pendleton, 1721–1803	David J. Mays
1954	The Spirit of St. Louis	Charles A. Lindbergh
1955	The Taft Story	William S. White
1956	Benjamin Henry Latrobe	Talbot Faulkner Hamlin
1957	Profiles in Courage	John F. Kennedy
1958	George Washington, 7 vols.[2]	Douglas Southall Freeman, John Alexander Carroll, and Mary Wells Ashworth
1959	Woodrow Wilson, American Prophet	Arthur Walworth
1960	John Paul Jones	Samuel Eliot Morison
1961	Charles Sumner and the Coming of the Civil War	David Herbert Donald
1962	no award	
1963	Henry James	Leon Edel
1964	John Keats	Walter Jackson Bate
1965	Henry Adams, 3 vols.	Ernest Samuels
1966	A Thousand Days	Arthur M. Schlesinger, Jr.
1967	Mr. Clemens and Mark Twain	Justin Kaplan
1968	Memoirs	George E. Kennan
1969	The Man from New York: John Quinn and His Friends	Benjamin Lawrence Reid
1970	Huey Long	T. Harry Williams
1971	Robert Frost: The Years of Triumph, 1915–1938	Lawrance Thompson
1972	Eleanor and Franklin	Joseph P. Lash
1973	Luce and His Empire	W.A. Swanberg
1974	O'Neill, Son and Artist	Louis Sheaffer
1975	The Power Broker: Robert Moses and the Fall of New York	Robert A. Caro
1976	Edith Wharton: A Biography	R.W.B. Lewis
1977	A Prince of Our Disorder: The Life of T.E. Lawrence	John E. Mack
1978	Samuel Johnson	Walter Jackson Bate
1979	Days of Sorrow and Pain: Leo Baeck and the Berlin Jews	Leonard Baker

YEAR	TITLE	AUTHOR
1980	The Rise of Theodore Roosevelt	Edmund Morris
1981	Peter the Great: His Life and World	Robert K. Massie
1982	Grant: A Biography	William McFeely
1983	Growing Up	Russell Baker
1984	Booker T. Washington: The Wizard of Tuskegee, 1901–1915	Louis R. Harlan
1985	The Life and Times of Cotton Mather	Kenneth Silverman
1986	Louise Bogan: A Portrait	Elizabeth Frank
1987	Bearing the Cross: Martin Luther King, Jr., and the Southern Christian Leadership Conference	David J. Garrow
1988	Look Homeward: A Life of Thomas Wolfe	David Herbert Donald
1989	Oscar Wilde[1]	Richard Ellmann
1990	Machiavelli in Hell	Sebastian de Grazia
1991	Jackson Pollock	Steven Naifeh and Gregory White Smith
1992	Fortunate Son: The Healing of a Vietnam Vet	Lewis B. Puller, Jr.
1993	Truman	David McCullough
1994	W.E.B. Du Bois: Biography of a Race, 1868–1919	David Levering Lewis
1995	Harriet Beecher Stowe: A Life	Joan D. Hedrick
1996	God: A Biography	Jack Miles
1997	Angela's Ashes: A Memoir	Frank McCourt
1998	Personal History	Katharine Graham
1999	Lindbergh	A. Scott Berg
2000	Vera (Mrs. Vladimir Nabokov)	Stacy Schiff
2001	W.E.B. Du Bois: The Fight for Equality and the American Century, 1919–1963	David Levering Lewis
2002	John Adams	David McCullough
2003	Master of the Senate	Robert A. Caro
2004	Khrushchev: The Man and His Era	William Taubman
2005	De Kooning: An American Master	Mark Stevens and Annalyn Swan
2006	American Prometheus: The Triumph and Tragedy	Kai Bird and Martin J. Sherwin
2007	The Most Famous Man in America: The Biography of Henry Ward Beecher	Debby Applegate
2008	Eden's Outcasts: The Story of Louisa May Alcott and Her Father	John Matteson
2009	American Lion: Andrew Jackson in the White House	Jon Meacham

[1]Awarded posthumously.   [2]Freeman died in 1953 after completing vols. 1–6; Carroll and Ashworth continued his work with vol. 7.

Letters, Drama, and Music (continued)

Poetry

Awarded for a collection of original verse by an American author.

YEAR	TITLE	AUTHOR
1922	Collected Poems	Edwin Arlington Robinson
1923	The Ballad of the Harp-Weaver; A Few Figs from Thistles; eight sonnets in American Poetry, 1922: A Miscellany	Edna St. Vincent Millay
1924	New Hampshire: A Poem with Notes and Grace Notes	Robert Frost
1925	The Man Who Died Twice	Edwin Arlington Robinson
1926	What's O'Clock[1]	Amy Lowell
1927	Fiddler's Farewell	Leonora Speyer
1928	Tristram	Edwin Arlington Robinson
1929	John Brown's Body	Stephen Vincent Benét
1930	Selected Poems	Conrad Aiken
1931	Collected Poems	Robert Frost
1932	The Flowering Stone	George Dillon
1933	Conquistador	Archibald MacLeish
1934	Collected Verse	Robert Hillyer
1935	Bright Ambush	Audrey Wurdemann
1936	Strange Holiness	Robert P. Tristram Coffin
1937	A Further Range	Robert Frost
1938	Cold Morning Sky	Marya Zaturenska
1939	Selected Poems	John Gould Fletcher
1940	Collected Poems	Mark Van Doren
1941	Sunderland Capture	Leonard Bacon
1942	The Dust Which Is God	William Rose Benét
1943	A Witness Tree	Robert Frost
1944	Western Star[1]	Stephen Vincent Benét
1945	V-Letter and Other Poems	Karl Shapiro
1946	no award	
1947	Lord Weary's Castle	Robert Lowell
1948	The Age of Anxiety	W.H. Auden
1949	Terror and Decorum	Peter Viereck
1950	Annie Allen	Gwendolyn Brooks
1951	Complete Poems	Carl Sandburg
1952	Collected Poems	Marianne Moore
1953	Collected Poems, 1917–1952	Archibald MacLeish
1954	The Waking	Theodore Roethke
1955	Collected Poems	Wallace Stevens
1956	Poems: North & South—A Cold Spring	Elizabeth Bishop
1957	Things of This World	Richard Wilbur
1958	Promises: Poems 1954–1956	Robert Penn Warren
1959	Selected Poems, 1928–1958	Stanley Kunitz
1960	Heart's Needle	W.D. Snodgrass
1961	Times Three: Selected Verse from Three Decades	Phyllis McGinley

YEAR	TITLE	AUTHOR
1962	Poems	Alan Dugan
1963	Pictures from Breughel[1]	William Carlos Williams
1964	At the End of the Open Road	Louis Simpson
1965	77 Dream Songs	John Berryman
1966	Selected Poems	Richard Eberhart
1967	Live or Die	Anne Sexton
1968	The Hard Hours	Anthony Hecht
1969	Of Being Numerous	George Oppen
1970	Untitled Subjects	Richard Howard
1971	The Carrier of Ladders	W.S. Merwin
1972	Collected Poems	James Wright
1973	Up Country	Maxine Kumin
1974	The Dolphin	Robert Lowell
1975	Turtle Island	Gary Snyder
1976	Self-Portrait in a Convex Mirror	John Ashbery
1977	Divine Comedies	James Merrill
1978	Collected Poems	Howard Nemerov
1979	Now and Then	Robert Penn Warren
1980	Selected Poems	Donald Justice
1981	The Morning of the Poem	James Schuyler
1982	The Collected Poems[2]	Sylvia Plath
1983	Selected Poems	Galway Kinnell
1984	American Primitive	Mary Oliver
1985	Yin	Carolyn Kizer
1986	The Flying Change	Henry Taylor
1987	Thomas and Beulah	Rita Dove
1988	Partial Accounts: New and Selected Poems	William Meredith
1989	New and Collected Poems	Richard Wilbur
1990	The World Doesn't End	Charles Simic
1991	Near Changes	Mona Van Duyn
1992	Selected Poems	James Tate
1993	The Wild Iris	Louise Glück
1994	Neon Vernacular: New and Selected Poems	Yusef Komunyakaa
1995	The Simple Truth	Philip Levine
1996	The Dream of the Unified Field	Jorie Graham
1997	Alive Together: New and Selected Poems	Lisel Mueller
1998	Black Zodiac	Charles Wright
1999	Blizzard of One	Mark Strand
2000	Repair	C.K. Williams
2001	Different Hours	Stephen Dunn
2002	Practical Gods	Carl Dennis
2003	Moy Sand and Gravel	Paul Muldoon
2004	Walking to Martha's Vineyard	Franz Wright
2005	Delights & Shadows	Ted Kooser
2006	Late Wife	Claudia Emerson
2007	Native Guard	Natasha Trethewey
2008	Time and Materials	Robert Hass
	Failure	Philip Schultz
2009	The Shadow of Sirius	W.S. Merwin

[1]Awarded posthumously.   [2]Work published and prize awarded posthumously.

Letters, Drama, and Music (continued)

General Nonfiction
Awarded for a work of nonfiction, ineligible for any other category, by an American author.

YEAR	TITLE	AUTHOR
1962	The Making of the President, 1960	Theodore H. White
1963	The Guns of August	Barbara W. Tuchman
1964	Anti-intellectualism in American Life	Richard Hofstadter
1965	O Strange New World	Howard Mumford Jones
1966	Wandering Through Winter	Edwin Way Teale
1967	The Problem of Slavery in Western Culture	David Brion Davis
1968	Rousseau and Revolution: A History of Civilization in France, England, and Germany from 1756 and in the Remainder of Europe from 1715 to 1789	Will and Ariel Durant
1969	The Armies of the Night	Norman Mailer
	So Human an Animal	Rene Jules Dubos
1970	Gandhi's Truth	Erik H. Erikson
1971	The Rising Sun	John Toland
1972	Stilwell and the American Experience in China, 1911–1945	Barbara W. Tuchman
1973	Fire in the Lake: The Vietnamese and the Americans in Vietnam	Frances Fitzgerald
	Children of Crisis, vols. 2 and 3	Robert Coles
1974	The Denial of Death[1]	Ernest Becker
1975	Pilgrim at Tinker Creek	Annie Dillard
1976	Why Survive?: Being Old in America	Robert N. Butler
1977	Beautiful Swimmers	William W. Warner
1978	The Dragons of Eden	Carl Sagan
1979	On Human Nature	Edward O. Wilson
1980	Gödel, Escher, Bach: An Eternal Golden Braid	Douglas R. Hofstadter
1981	Fin-de-Siècle Vienna: Politics and Culture	Carl E. Schorske
1982	The Soul of a New Machine	Tracy Kidder
1983	Is There No Place on Earth for Me?	Susan Sheehan
1984	The Social Transformation of American Medicine	Paul Starr
1985	The Good War: An Oral History of World War Two	Studs Terkel
1986	Common Ground: A Turbulent Decade in the Lives of Three American Families	J. Anthony Lukas
	Move Your Shadow: South Africa, Black and White	Joseph Lelyveld
1987	Arab and Jew: Wounded Spirits in a Promised Land	David K. Shipler
1988	The Making of the Atomic Bomb	Richard Rhodes

YEAR	TITLE	AUTHOR
1989	A Bright Shining Lie: John Paul Vann and America in Vietnam	Neil Sheehan
1990	And Their Children After Them	Dale Maharidge and Michael Williamson
1991	The Ants	Bert Holldobler and Edward O. Wilson
1992	The Prize: The Epic Quest for Oil, Money, and Power	Daniel Yergin
1993	Lincoln at Gettysburg: The Words That Remade America	Garry Wills
1994	Lenin's Tomb: The Last Days of the Soviet Empire	David Remnick
1995	The Beak of the Finch: A Story of Evolution in Our Time	Jonathan Weiner
1996	The Haunted Land: Facing Europe's Ghosts After Communism	Tina Rosenberg
1997	Ashes to Ashes: America's Hundred-Year Cigarette War, the Public Health, and the Unabashed Triumph of Philip Morris	Richard Kluger
1998	Guns, Germs, and Steel: The Fates of Human Societies	Jared Diamond
1999	Annals of the Former World	John McPhee
2000	Embracing Defeat: Japan in the Wake of World War II	John W. Dower
2001	Hirohito and the Making of Modern Japan	Herbert P. Bix
2002	Carry Me Home: Birmingham, Alabama, the Climactic Battle of the Civil Rights Revolution	Diane McWhorter
2003	"A Problem from Hell": America and the Age of Genocide	Samantha Power
2004	Gulag: A History	Anne Applebaum
2005	Ghost Wars	Steve Coll
2006	Imperial Reckoning: The Untold Story of Britain's Gulag in Kenya	Caroline Elkins
2007	The Looming Tower: Al-Qaeda and the Road to 9/11	Lawrence Wright
2008	The Years of Extermination: Nazi Germany and the Jews, 1939–1945	Saul Friedländer
2009	Slavery by Another Name:The Re-Enslavement of Black Americans from the Civil War to World War II	Douglas A. Blackmon

[1] Awarded posthumously.

Letters, Drama, and Music (continued)

<u>Music</u>
Awarded for a musical piece of "significant dimension" composed by an American and first performed or recorded in the United States between 16 January of the previous year and 15 January of the year of the award.

YEAR	TITLE	COMPOSER	YEAR	TITLE	COMPOSER
1943	Secular Cantata No. 2: A Free Song	William Schuman	1981	no award	
			1982	Concerto for Orchestra	Roger Sessions
1944	Symphony No. 4, Opus 34	Howard Hanson	1983	Symphony No. 1 (Three Movements for Orchestra)	Ellen Taaffe Zwilich
1945	Appalachian Spring	Aaron Copland			
1946	The Canticle of the Sun	Leo Sowerby	1984	"Canti del sole" for Tenor and Orchestra	Bernard Rands
1947	Symphony No. 3	Charles Ives			
1948	Symphony No. 3	Walter Piston	1985	Symphony RiverRun	Stephen Albert
1949	music for the film Louisiana Story	Virgil Thomson	1986	Wind Quintet IV	George Perle
			1987	The Flight into Egypt	John Harbison
1950	The Consul	Gian Carlo Menotti	1988	12 New Etudes for Piano	William Bolcom
1951	Giants in the Earth	Douglas S. Moore			
1952	Symphony Concertante	Gail Kubik	1989	Whispers out of Time	Roger Reynolds
1953	no award		1990	"Duplicates": A Concerto for Two Pianos and Orchestra	Mel Powell
1954	Concerto for Two Pianos and Orchestra	Quincy Porter			
1955	The Saint of Bleecker Street	Gian Carlo Menotti	1991	Symphony	Shulamit Ran
			1992	The Face of the Night, the Heart of the Dark	Wayne Peterson
1956	Symphony No. 3	Ernst Toch			
1957	Meditation on Ecclesiastics	Norman Dello Joio	1993	Trombone Concerto	Christopher Rouse
1958	Vanessa	Samuel Barber			
1959	Concerto for Piano and Orchestra	John LaMontaine	1994	Of Reminiscences and Reflections	Gunther Schuller
1960	Second String Quartet	Elliott Carter	1995	Stringmusic	Morton Gould
1961	Symphony No. 7	Walter Piston	1996	Lilacs, for Voice and Orchestra	George Walker
1962	The Crucible	Robert Ward			
1963	Piano Concerto No. 1	Samuel Barber	1997	Blood on the Fields	Wynton Marsalis
1964	no award		1998	String Quartet No. 2 (Musica Instrumentalis)	Aaron Jay Kernis
1965	no award				
1966	Variations for Orchestra	Leslie Bassett			
1967	Quartet No. 3	Leon Kirchner	1999	Concerto for Flute, Strings, and Percussion	Melinda Wagner
1968	Echoes of Time and the River	George Crumb			
1969	String Quartet No. 3	Karel Husa	2000	Life Is a Dream, Opera in Three Acts: Act II, Concert Version	Lewis Spratlan
1970	Time's Encomium	Charles Wuorinen			
1971	Synchronisms No. 6 for Piano and Electronic Sound	Mario Davidovsky	2001	Symphony No. 2 for String Orchestra	John Corigliano
			2002	Ice Field	Henry Brant
1972	Windows	Jacob Druckman	2003	On the Transmigration of Souls	John Adams
1973	String Quartet No. 3	Elliott Carter			
1974	Notturno	Donald Martino	2004	Tempest Fantasy	Paul Moravec
1975	From the Diary of Virginia Woolf	Dominick Argento	2005	Second Concerto for Orchestra	Steven Stucky
1976	Air Music	Ned Rorem	2006	Piano Concerto: "Chiavi in mano"	Yehudi Wyner
1977	Visions of Terror and Wonder	Richard Wernick			
1978	Deja Vu for Percussion Quartet and Orchestra	Michael Colgrass	2007	Sound Grammar	Ornette Coleman
			2008	The Little Match Girl Passion	David Lang
1979	Aftertones of Infinity	Joseph Schwantner			
1980	In Memory of a Summer Day	David Del Tredici	2009	Double Sextet	Steve Reich

<u>Special Awards and Citations</u>[1]

YEAR	RECIPIENT	FOR	YEAR	RECIPIENT	FOR
1992	Art Spiegelman	his graphic novel Maus	1999	Duke Ellington[2]	centennial commemoration of his birth, celebrating his life's work in music
1996	Herb Caen	his contributions as a voice of San Francisco			
1998	George Gershwin[2]	centennial commemoration of his birth, celebrating his life's work in music	2006	Edmund S. Morgan	his life's work as an American historian
				Thelonious Monk[2]	his contributions to jazz

Letters, Drama, and Music (continued)

Special Awards and Citations[1] (continued)

YEAR	RECIPIENT	FOR	YEAR	RECIPIENT	FOR
2007	Ray Bradbury	his contributions to science fiction and fantasy	2008	Bob Dylan	his profound influence on pop culture and American music
	John Coltrane[2]	his contributions to jazz			

[1]For the past 20 years.   [2]Awarded posthumously.

It has been speculated that when King James I of England hired 54 of the best writers and scholars in the country for a new English version of the Bible in 1611, William Shakespeare might have been among them. Although there is no conclusive evidence for the Bard's participation in the project, it is nevertheless intriguing that the 46th word of the 46th Psalm is "shake," and the 46th word from the end of the Psalm is "spear." Shakespeare, who was fond of cryptograms, was 46 years old at the time.

National Book Awards

In 1950 a consortium of publishing groups established the National Book Awards. The goals were to bring exceptional books written by Americans to the public's attention and to encourage reading. The number of award categories has varied from the inaugural 3 to as many as 28 in 1980. Today, the awards recognize achievements in four genres: fiction, nonfiction, poetry, and young people's literature. A five-member judging panel chooses a winner for each genre. Award: US$10,000 cash and a bronze sculpture.

Fiction

YEAR	TITLE	AUTHOR
1950	The Man with the Golden Arm	Nelson Algren
1951	The Collected Stories of William Faulkner	William Faulkner
1952	From Here to Eternity	James Jones
1953	Invisible Man	Ralph Ellison
1954	The Adventures of Augie March	Saul Bellow
1955	A Fable	William Faulkner
1956	Ten North Frederick	John O'Hara
1957	The Field of Vision	Wright Morris
1958	The Wapshot Chronicle	John Cheever
1959	The Magic Barrel	Bernard Malamud
1960	Goodbye, Columbus	Philip Roth
1961	The Waters of Kronos	Conrad Richter
1962	The Moviegoer	Walker Percy
1963	Morte d'Urban	J.F. Powers
1964	The Centaur	John Updike
1965	Herzog	Saul Bellow
1966	The Collected Stories of Katherine Anne Porter	Katherine Anne Porter
1967	The Fixer	Bernard Malamud
1968	The Eighth Day	Thornton Wilder
1969	Steps	Jerzy Kosinski
1970	Them	Joyce Carol Oates
1971	Mr. Sammler's Planet	Saul Bellow
1972	The Complete Stories	Flannery O'Connor
1973	Augustus	John Williams
	Chimera	John Barth
1974	A Crown of Feathers and Other Stories	Isaac Bashevis Singer
	Gravity's Rainbow	Thomas Pynchon
1975	Dog Soldiers: A Novel	Robert Stone
	The Hair of Harold Roux	Thomas Williams
1976	J.R.	William Gaddis

Fiction (continued)

YEAR	TITLE	AUTHOR
1977	The Spectator Bird	Wallace Stegner
1978	Blood Tie	Mary Lee Settle
1979	Going After Cacciato	Tim O'Brien
1980	Sophie's Choice[1]	William Styron
1981	Plains Song[1]	Wright Morris
1982	Rabbit Is Rich[1]	John Updike
1983	The Color Purple[1]	Alice Walker
1984	Victory over Japan: A Book of Stories	Ellen Gilchrist
1985	White Noise	Don DeLillo
1986	World's Fair	E.L. Doctorow
1987	Paco's Story	Larry Heinemann
1988	Paris Trout	Pete Dexter
1989	Spartina	John Casey
1990	Middle Passage	Charles Johnson
1991	Mating	Norman Rush
1992	All the Pretty Horses	Cormac McCarthy
1993	The Shipping News	E. Annie Proulx
1994	A Frolic of His Own	William Gaddis
1995	Sabbath's Theater	Philip Roth
1996	Ship Fever	Andrea Barrett
1997	Cold Mountain	Charles Frazier
1998	Charming Billy	Alice McDermott
1999	Waiting	Ha Jin
2000	In America	Susan Sontag
2001	The Corrections	Jonathan Franzen
2002	Three Junes	Julia Glass
2003	The Great Fire	Shirley Hazzard
2004	The News from Paraguay	Lily Tuck
2005	Europe Central	William T. Vollmann
2006	The Echo Maker	Richard Powers
2007	Tree of Smoke	Denis Johnson
2008	Shadow Country	Peter Matthiessen

Nonfiction

YEAR	TITLE	AUTHOR
1950	The Life of Ralph Waldo Emerson	Ralph L. Rusk
1951	Herman Melville	Newton Arvin
1952	The Sea Around Us	Rachel Carson
1953	The Course of Empire	Bernard A. De Voto
1954	A Stillness at Appomattox	Bruce Catton

National Book Awards (continued)

Nonfiction (continued)

YEAR	TITLE	AUTHOR
1955	The Measure of Man: On Freedom, Human Values, Survival, and the Modern Temper	Joseph Wood Krutch
1956	American in Italy	Herbert Kubly
1957	Russia Leaves the War	George F. Kennan
1958	The Lion and the Throne: The Life and Times of Sir Edward Coke (1552–1634)	Catherine Drinker Bowen
1959	Mistress to an Age: A Life of Madame de Staël	J. Christopher Herold
1960	James Joyce	Richard Ellmann
1961	The Rise and Fall of the Third Reich: A History of Nazi Germany	William L. Shirer
1962	The City in History: Its Origins, Its Transformations, and Its Prospects	Lewis Mumford
1963	Henry James, Vol. II: The Conquest of London (1870–1881); Vol. III: The Middle Years (1882–1895)	Leon Edel
1964	The Rise of the West: A History of the Human Community[2]	William H. McNeill
1965	The Life of Lenin[2]	Louis Fischer
1966	A Thousand Days: John F. Kennedy in the White House[2]	Arthur M. Schlesinger, Jr.
1967	The Enlightenment: An Interpretation, Vol. I[2]	Peter Gay
1968	Memoirs: 1925–1950[2]	George F. Kennan
1969	White over Black: American Attitudes Toward the Negro, 1550–1812[2]	Winthrop D. Jordan
1970	Huey Long[2]	T. Harry Williams
1971	Roosevelt: The Soldier of Freedom[2]	James MacGregor Burns
1972	Eleanor and Franklin: The Story of Their Relationship, Based on Eleanor Roosevelt's Private Papers[3]	Joseph P. Lash
1973	George Washington, Vol. IV: Anguish and Farewell, 1793–1799[3]	James Thomas Flexner
1974	Macaulay: The Shaping of the Historian[4]	John Clive
1975	The Life of Emily Dickinson[3]	Richard B. Sewall
1976	The Problem of Slavery in the Age of Revolution, 1770–1823[2]	David Brion Davis
1977	Norman Thomas: The Last Idealist[5]	W.A. Swanberg
1978	Samuel Johnson[5]	W. Jackson Bate
1979	Robert Kennedy and His Times[5]	Arthur M. Schlesinger, Jr.
1980	The Right Stuff[6]	Tom Wolfe
1981	China Men[6]	Maxine Hong Kingston
1982	The Soul of a New Machine[6]	Tracy Kidder
1983	China: Alive in the Bitter Sea[6]	Fox Butterfield
1984	Andrew Jackson and the Course of American Democracy, 1833–1845	Robert V. Remini
1985	Common Ground: A Turbulent Decade in the Lives of Three American Families	J. Anthony Lukas
1986	Arctic Dreams	Barry Lopez
1987	The Making of the Atomic Bomb	Richard Rhodes
1988	A Bright Shining Lie: John Paul Vann and America in Vietnam	Neil Sheehan
1989	From Beirut to Jerusalem	Thomas L. Friedman
1990	The House of Morgan: An American Banking Dynasty and the Rise of Modern Finance	Ron Chernow
1991	Freedom	Orlando Patterson
1992	Becoming a Man: Half a Life Story	Paul Monette
1993	United States: Essays, 1952–1992	Gore Vidal
1994	How We Die: Reflections on Life's Final Chapter	Sherwin B. Nuland
1995	The Haunted Land: Facing Europe's Ghosts After Communism	Tina Rosenberg
1996	An American Requiem: God, My Father, and the War That Came Between Us	James Carroll
1997	American Sphinx: The Character of Thomas Jefferson	Joseph J. Ellis
1998	Slaves in the Family	Edward Ball
1999	Embracing Defeat: Japan in the Wake of World War II	John W. Dower
2000	In the Heart of the Sea: The Tragedy of the Whaleship Essex	Nathaniel Philbrick
2001	The Noonday Demon: An Atlas of Depression	Andrew Solomon
2002	Master of the Senate: The Years of Lyndon Johnson	Robert A. Caro
2003	Waiting for Snow in Havana	Carlos Eire
2004	Arc of Justice: A Saga of Race, Civil Rights, and Murder in the Jazz Age	Kevin Boyle
2005	The Year of Magical Thinking	Joan Didion
2006	The Worst Hard Time: The Untold Story of Those Who Survived the Great American Dust Bowl	Timothy Egan
2007	Legacy of Ashes: The History of the CIA	Tim Weiner
2008	The Hemingses of Monticello: An American Family	Annette Gordon-Reed

Poetry

YEAR	TITLE	AUTHOR
1950	Paterson: Book III and Selected Poems	William Carlos Williams
1951	The Auroras of Autumn	Wallace Stevens
1952	Collected Poems	Marianne Moore
1953	Collected Poems, 1917–1952	Archibald MacLeish
1954	Collected Poems	Conrad Aiken

National Book Awards (continued)

Poetry (continued)

YEAR	TITLE	AUTHOR
1955	The Collected Poems of Wallace Stevens	Wallace Stevens
1956	The Shield of Achilles	W.H. Auden
1957	Things of This World: Poems	Richard Wilbur
1958	Promises: Poems, 1954–1956	Robert Penn Warren
1959	Words for the Wind: The Collected Verse of Theodore Roethke	Theodore Roethke
1960	Life Studies	Robert Lowell
1961	The Woman at the Washington Zoo	Randall Jarrell
1962	Poems	Alan Dugan
1963	Traveling Through the Dark	William Stafford
1964	Selected Poems	John Crowe Ransom
1965	The Far Field	Theodore Roethke
1966	Buckdancer's Choice: Poems	James Dickey
1967	Nights and Days	James Merrill
1968	The Light Around the Body: Poems	Robert Bly
1969	His Toy, His Dream, His Rest: 308 Dream Songs	John Berryman
1970	The Complete Poems	Elizabeth Bishop
1971	To See, To Take: Poems	Mona Van Duyn
1972	The Collected Poems of Frank O'Hara	Frank O'Hara
	Selected Poems	Howard Moss
1973	Collected Poems, 1951–1971	A.R. Ammons
1974	Diving into the Wreck: Poems, 1971–1972	Adrienne Rich
	The Fall of America: Poems of These States	Allen Ginsberg
1975	Presentation Piece	Marilyn Hacker
1976	Self-Portrait in a Convex Mirror: Poems	John Ashbery
1977	Collected Poems, 1930–1976	Richard Eberhart
1978	The Collected Poems of Howard Nemerov	Howard Nemerov
1979	Mirabell: Books of Number	James Merrill
1980	Ashes: Poems New & Old	Philip Levine
1981	The Need to Hold Still	Lisel Mueller
1982	Life Supports: New and Collected Poems	William Bronk
1983	Country Music: Selected Early Poems	Charles Wright
1984	Selected Poems	Galway Kinnell
1985	Yin	Carolyn Kizer
1986	The Flying Change	Henry Taylor
1987	Thomas and Beulah	Rita Dove
1988	Partial Accounts: New and Selected Poems	William Meredith
1989	New and Collected Poems	Richard Wilbur
1990	The World Doesn't End	Charles Simic
1991	What Work Is: Poems	Philip Levine
1992	New and Selected Poems	Mary Oliver
1993	Garbage	A.R. Ammons
1994	Worshipful Company of Fletchers: Poems	James Tate
1995	Passing Through: The Later Poems, New and Selected	Stanley Kunitz
1996	Scrambled Eggs & Whiskey: Poems, 1991–1995	Hayden Carruth
1997	Effort at Speech: New and Selected Poems	William Meredith
1998	This Time: New and Selected Poems	Gerald Stern
1999	Vice: New and Selected Poems	Ai
2000	Blessing the Boats: New and Selected Poems, 1988–2000	Lucille Clifton
2001	Poems Seven: New and Complete Poetry	Alan Dugan
2002	In the Next Galaxy	Ruth Stone
2003	The Singing	C.K. Williams
2004	Door in the Mountain: New and Collected Poems, 1965–2003	Jean Valentine
2005	Migration: New and Selected Poems	W.S. Merwin
2006	Splay Anthem	Nathaniel Mackey
2007	Time and Materials	Robert Hass
2008	Fire to Fire: New and Collected Poems	Mark Doty

Young People's Literature

YEAR	TITLE	AUTHOR
1969	Journey from Peppermint Street	Meindert De Jong
1970	A Day of Pleasure: Stories of a Boy Growing Up in Warsaw[7]	Isaac Bashevis Singer
1971	The Marvelous Misadventures of Sebastian[7]	Lloyd Alexander
1972	The Slightly Irregular Fire Engine; or, The Hithering Thithering Djinn[7]	Donald Barthelme
1973	The Farthest Shore[7]	Ursula Le Guin
1974	The Court of the Stone Children[7]	Eleanor Cameron
1975	M.C. Higgins, the Great[7]	Virginia Hamilton
1976	Bert Breen's Barn	Walter D. Edmonds

National Book Awards (continued)

Young People's Literature (continued)

YEAR	TITLE	AUTHOR
1977	The Master Puppeteer	Katherine Paterson
1978	The View from the Oak: The Private Worlds of Other Creatures	Judith and Herbert Kohl
1979	The Great Gilly Hopkins	Katherine Paterson
1980	A Gathering of Days: A New England Girl's Journal, 1830–32[8]	Joan W. Blos
1981	The Night Swimmers[9]	Betsy Byars
1982	Westmark[9]	Lloyd Alexander
1983	Homesick: My Own Story[9]	Jean Fritz
1996	Parrot in the Oven: Mi Vida	Victor Martinez
1997	Dancing on the Edge	Han Nolan
1998	Holes	Louis Sachar
1999	When Zachary Beaver Came to Town	Kimberly Willis Holt
2000	Homeless Bird	Gloria Whelan
2001	True Believer	Virginia Euwer Wolff
2002	The House of the Scorpion	Nancy Farmer
2003	The Canning Season	Polly Horvath
2004	The Godless	Pete Hautman
2005	The Penderwicks	Jeanne Birdsall
2006	The Astonishing Life of Octavian Nothing, Traitor to the Nation, Vol. 1: The Pox Party	M.T. Anderson
2007	The Absolutely True Diary of a Part-Time Indian	Sherman Alexie
2008	What I Saw and How I Lied	Judy Blundell

[1]Fiction (Hardcover). [2]History and Biography (Nonfiction). [3]Biography. [4]History. [5]Biography and Autobiography. [6]General Nonfiction (Hardcover). [7]Children's Books. [8]Children's Books (Hardcover). [9]Children's Books, Fiction (Hardcover).

Newbery Medal

The American Library Association (ALA) began awarding the John Newbery Medal in 1922 to the author of the most distinguished American children's book of the previous year, as judged by the ALA's Children's Librarians' Section (now called the Association for Library Service to Children). Established at the suggestion of Frederic G. Melcher of the R.R. Bowker Publishing Company, the award is named for John Newbery, the 18th-century English publisher who was among the first to publish books exclusively for children. Prize: inscribed bronze medal.

ALA Newbery Medal Web site:
<www.ala.org/alsc/newbery.html>.

YEAR	TITLE	AUTHOR
1922	The Story of Mankind	Hendrik Willem van Loon
1923	The Voyages of Doctor Dolittle	Hugh Lofting
1924	The Dark Frigate	Charles Hawes
1925	Tales from Silver Lands	Charles Finger
1926	Shen of the Sea	Arthur Bowie Chrisman
1927	Smoky, the Cowhorse	Will James
1928	Gay Neck, the Story of a Pigeon	Dhan Gopal Mukerji
1929	The Trumpeter of Krakow	Eric P. Kelly
1930	Hitty, Her First Hundred Years	Rachel Field
1931	The Cat Who Went to Heaven	Elizabeth Coatsworth
1932	Waterless Mountain	Laura Adams Armer
1933	Young Fu of the Upper Yangtze	Elizabeth Lewis
1934	Invincible Louisa: The Story of the Author of Little Women	Cornelia Meigs
1935	Dobry	Monica Shannon
1936	Caddie Woodlawn	Carol Ryrie Brink
1937	Roller Skates	Ruth Sawyer
1938	The White Stag	Kate Seredy
1939	Thimble Summer	Elizabeth Enright
1940	Daniel Boone	James Daugherty
1941	Call It Courage	Armstrong Sperry
1942	The Matchlock Gun	Walter Edmonds
1943	Adam of the Road	Elizabeth Janet Gray
1944	Johnny Tremain	Esther Forbes
1945	Rabbit Hill	Robert Lawson
1946	Strawberry Girl	Lois Lenski
1947	Miss Hickory	Carolyn Sherwin Bailey
1948	The Twenty-One Balloons	William Pène du Bois
1949	King of the Wind	Marguerite Henry
1950	The Door in the Wall	Marguerite de Angeli
1951	Amos Fortune, Free Man	Elizabeth Yates
1952	Ginger Pye	Eleanor Estes
1953	Secret of the Andes	Ann Nolan Clark
1954	...And Now Miguel	Joseph Krumgold
1955	The Wheel on the School	Meindert De Jong
1956	Carry On, Mr. Bowditch	Jean Lee Latham
1957	Miracles on Maple Hill	Virginia Sorenson
1958	Rifles for Watie	Harold Keith
1959	The Witch of Blackbird Pond	Elizabeth George Speare
1960	Onion John	Joseph Krumgold
1961	Island of the Blue Dolphins	Scott O'Dell
1962	The Bronze Bow	Elizabeth George Speare

Newbery Medal (continued)

YEAR	TITLE	AUTHOR
1963	A Wrinkle in Time	Madeleine L'Engle
1964	It's Like This, Cat	Emily Neville
1965	Shadow of a Bull	Maia Wojciechowska
1966	I, Juan de Pareja	Elizabeth Borton de Treviño
1967	Up a Road Slowly	Irene Hunt
1968	From the Mixed-Up Files of Mrs. Basil E. Frankweiler	E.L. Konigsburg
1969	The High King	Lloyd Alexander
1970	Sounder	William H. Armstrong
1971	Summer of the Swans	Betsy Byars
1972	Mrs. Frisby and the Rats of NIMH	Robert C. O'Brien
1973	Julie of the Wolves	Jean Craighead George
1974	The Slave Dancer	Paula Fox
1975	M.C. Higgins, the Great	Virginia Hamilton
1976	The Grey King	Susan Cooper
1977	Roll of Thunder, Hear My Cry	Mildred D. Taylor
1978	Bridge to Terabithia	Katherine Paterson
1979	The Westing Game	Ellen Raskin
1980	A Gathering of Days: A New England Girl's Journal, 1830–1832	Joan W. Blos
1981	Jacob Have I Loved	Katherine Paterson
1982	A Visit to William Blake's Inn: Poems for Innocent and Experienced Travelers	Nancy Willard
1983	Dicey's Song	Cynthia Voigt
1984	Dear Mr. Henshaw	Beverly Cleary
1985	The Hero and the Crown	Robin McKinley
1986	Sarah, Plain and Tall	Patricia MacLachlan

YEAR	TITLE	AUTHOR
1987	The Whipping Boy	Sid Fleischman
1988	Lincoln: A Photo-biography	Russell Freedman
1989	Joyful Noise: Poems for Two Voices	Paul Fleischman
1990	Number the Stars	Lois Lowry
1991	Maniac Magee	Jerry Spinelli
1992	Shiloh	Phyllis Reynolds Naylor
1993	Missing May	Cynthia Rylant
1994	The Giver	Lois Lowry
1995	Walk Two Moons	Sharon Creech
1996	The Midwife's Apprentice	Karen Cushman
1997	The View from Saturday	E.L. Konigsburg
1998	Out of the Dust	Karen Hesse
1999	Holes	Louis Sachar
2000	Bud, Not Buddy	Christopher Paul Curtis
2001	A Year Down Yonder	Richard Peck
2002	A Single Shard	Linda Sue Park
2003	Crispin: The Cross of Lead	Avi
2004	The Tale of Despereaux: Being the Story of a Mouse, a Princess, Some Soup, and a Spool of Thread	Kate DiCamillo
2005	Kira-Kira	Cynthia Kadohata
2006	Criss Cross	Lynne Rae Perkins
2007	The Higher Power of Lucky	Susan Patron
2008	Good Masters! Sweet Ladies! Voices from a Medieval Village	Laura Amy Schlitz
2009	The Graveyard Book	Neil Gaiman

Caldecott Medal

The American Library Association (ALA) awards the Caldecott Medal annually to "the artist of the most distinguished American picture book for children." It was established by the ALA in 1938 on the suggestion of Frederic G. Melcher, chairman of the board of the R.R. Bowker Publishing Company, and named for the 19th-century English illustrator Randolph Caldecott. If the author/reteller/translator/editor is someone other than the illustrator, that person's name appears in parentheses after that of the illustrator. Prize: inscribed bronze medal.

Web site: <www.ala.org/alsc/caldecott.html>.

YEAR	TITLE	ILLUSTRATOR
1938	Animals of the Bible: A Picture Book	Dorothy P. Lathrop (Helen Dean Fish)
1939	Mei Li	Thomas Handforth
1940	Abraham Lincoln	Ingri and Edgar Parin d'Aulaire
1941	They Were Strong and Good	Robert Lawson
1942	Make Way for Ducklings	Robert McCloskey
1943	The Little House	Virginia Lee Burton
1944	Many Moons	Louis Slobodkin (James Thurber)
1945	Prayer for a Child	Elizabeth Orton Jones (Rachel Field)
1946	The Rooster Crows	Maud and Miska Petersham
1947	The Little Island	Leonard Weisgard (Golden MacDonald, pseud. [Margaret Wise Brown])
1948	White Snow, Bright Snow	Roger Duvoisin (Alvin Tresselt)
1949	The Big Snow	Berta and Elmer Hader
1950	Song of the Swallows	Leo Politi
1951	The Egg Tree	Katherine Milhous
1952	Finders Keepers	Nicolas, pseud. (Nicholas Mordvinoff) (Will, pseud. [William Lipkind])
1953	The Biggest Bear	Lynd Ward

Caldecott Medal (continued)

YEAR	TITLE	ILLUSTRATOR
1954	Madeline's Rescue	Ludwig Bemelmans
1955	Cinderella, or the Little Glass Slipper	Marcia Brown (translated from Charles Perrault by Marcia Brown)
1956	Frog Went A-Courtin'	Feodor Rojankovsky (John Langstaff)
1957	A Tree Is Nice	Marc Simont (Janice Udry)
1958	Time of Wonder	Robert McCloskey
1959	Chanticleer and the Fox	Barbara Cooney (adapted from Chaucer's The Canterbury Tales by Barbara Cooney)
1960	Nine Days to Christmas	Marie Hall Ets (Marie Hall Ets and Aurora Labastida)
1961	Baboushka and the Three Kings	Nicolas Sidjakov (Ruth Robbins)
1962	Once a Mouse	Marcia Brown
1963	The Snowy Day	Ezra Jack Keats
1964	Where the Wild Things Are	Maurice Sendak
1965	May I Bring a Friend?	Beni Montresor (Beatrice Schenk de Regniers)
1966	Always Room for One More	Nonny Hogrogian (Sorche Nic Leodhas, pseud. [Leclair Alger])
1967	Sam, Bangs & Moonshine	Evaline Ness
1968	Drummer Hoff	Ed Emberley (Barbara Emberley)
1969	The Fool of the World and the Flying Ship	Uri Shulevitz (Arthur Ransome)
1970	Sylvester and the Magic Pebble	William Steig
1971	A Story, a Story	Gail E. Haley
1972	One Fine Day	Nonny Hogrogian
1973	The Funny Little Woman	Blair Lent (Arlene Mosel)
1974	Duffy and the Devil	Margot Zemach (Harve Zemach)
1975	Arrow to the Sun	Gerald McDermott
1976	Why Mosquitoes Buzz in People's Ears	Leo and Diane Dillon (Verna Aardema)
1977	Ashanti to Zulu: African Traditions	Leo and Diane Dillon (Margaret Musgrove)
1978	Noah's Ark	Peter Spier
1979	The Girl Who Loved Wild Horses	Paul Goble
1980	Ox-Cart Man	Barbara Cooney (Donald Hall)
1981	Fables	Arnold Lobel
1982	Jumanji	Chris Van Allsburg
1983	Shadow	Marcia Brown (translated from Blaise Cendrars by Marcia Brown)
1984	The Glorious Flight: Across the Channel with Louis Blériot	Alice and Martin Provensen
1985	Saint George and the Dragon	Trina Schart Hyman (Margaret Hodges)
1986	The Polar Express	Chris Van Allsburg
1987	Hey, Al	Richard Egielski (Arthur Yorinks)
1988	Owl Moon	John Schoenherr (Jane Yolen)
1989	Song and Dance Man	Stephen Gammell (Karen Ackerman)
1990	Lon Po Po: A Red-Riding Hood Story from China	Ed Young
1991	Black and White	David Macaulay
1992	Tuesday	David Wiesner
1993	Mirette on the High Wire	Emily Arnold McCully
1994	Grandfather's Journey	Allen Say (Walter Lorraine)
1995	Smoky Night	David Diaz (Eve Bunting)
1996	Officer Buckle and Gloria	Peggy Rathmann
1997	Golem	David Wisniewski
1998	Rapunzel	Paul O. Zelinsky
1999	Snowflake Bentley	Mary Azarian (Jacqueline Briggs Martin)
2000	Joseph Had a Little Overcoat	Simms Taback
2001	So You Want To Be President?	David Small (Judith St. George)
2002	The Three Pigs	David Wiesner
2003	My Friend Rabbit	Eric Rohmann
2004	The Man Who Walked Between the Towers	Mordicai Gerstein
2005	Kitten's First Full Moon	Kevin Henkes
2006	The Hello, Goodbye Window	Chris Raschka (Norton Juster)
2007	Flotsam	David Wiesner
2008	The Invention of Hugo Cabret	Brian Selznick
2009	The House in the Night	Beth Krommes (Susan Marie Swanson)

Coretta Scott King Award

Established in 1970, the Coretta Scott King Award honors outstanding African American authors and illustrators of books for young people. The books, which may be fiction or nonfiction, must be original works that portray some aspect of the black experience. In 1982 the award came under the aegis of the American Li-

Coretta Scott King Award (continued)

brary Association. Only authors were eligible for the award until 1974, and no illustrator awards were given in 1975–1977 and 1985. Prize: citation, honorarium, and encyclopedia set.

Coretta Scott King Award Web site: <www.ala.org/ala/emiert/corettascottking bookaward/corettascott.htm>.

1970	Lillie Patterson, *Martin Luther King, Jr.: Man of Peace*
1971	Charlemae Rollins, *Black Troubador: Langston Hughes*
1972	Elton C. Fax, *17 Black Artists*
1973	*I Never Had It Made: The Autobiography of Jackie Robinson*, as told to Alfred Duckett
1974	author: Sharon Bell Mathis, *Ray Charles;* illustrator: George Ford, *Ray Charles*
1975	author: Dorothy Robinson, *The Legend of Africana*
1976	author: Pearl Bailey, *Duey's Tale*
1977	author: James Haskins, *The Story of Stevie Wonder*
1978	author: Eloise Greenfield, *Africa Dream;* illustrator: Carole Byard, *Africa Dream*
1979	author: Ossie Davis, *Escape to Freedom;* illustrator: Tom Feelings, *Something on My Mind*
1980	author: Walter Dean Myers, *The Young Landlords;* illustrator: Carole Byard, *Corn-rows*
1981	author: Sidney Poitier, *This Life;* illustrator: Ashley Bryan, *Beat the Story Drum, Pum-Pum*
1982	author: Mildred D. Taylor, *Let the Circle Be Unbroken;* illustrator: John Steptoe, *Mother Crocodile*
1983	author: Virginia Hamilton, *Sweet Whispers, Brother Rush;* illustrator: Peter Mugabane, *Black Child*
1984	author: Lucille Clifton, *Everett Anderson's Goodbye;* illustrator: Pat Cummings, *My Mama Needs Me*
1985	author: Walter Dean Myers, *Motown and Didi*
1986	author: Virginia Hamilton, *The People Could Fly: American Black Folktales;* illustrator: Jerry Pinkney, *The Patchwork Quilt*
1987	author: Mildred Pitts Walter, *Justin and the Best Biscuits in the World;* illustrator: Jerry Pinkney, *Half a Moon and One Whole Star*
1988	author: Mildred D. Taylor, *The Friendship;* illustrator: John Steptoe, *Mufaro's Beautiful Daughters: An African Tale*
1989	author: Walter Dean Myers, *Fallen Angels;* illustrator: Jerry Pinkney, *Mirandy and Brother Wind*
1990	authors: Patricia C. and Frederick L. McKissack, *A Long Hard Journey: The Story of the Pullman Porter;* illustrator: Jan Spivey Gilchrist, *Nathaniel Talking*
1991	author: Mildred D. Taylor, *The Road to Memphis;* illustrators: Leo and Diane Dillon, *Aida*
1992	author: Walter Dean Myers, *Now Is Your Time: The African American Struggle for Freedom;* illustrator: Faith Ringgold, *Tar Beach*
1993	author: Patricia C. McKissack, *Dark Thirty: Southern Tales of the Supernatural;* illustrator: Kathleen Atkins Wilson, *The Origin of Life on Earth: An African Creation Myth*
1994	author: Angela Johnson, *Toning the Sweep;* illustrator: Tom Feelings, *Soul Looks Back in Wonder*
1995	authors: Patricia C. and Frederick L. McKissack, *Christmas in the Big House, Christmas in the Quarters;* illustrator: James Ransome, *The Creation*
1996	author: Virginia Hamilton, *Her Stories;* illustrator: Tom Feelings, *The Middle Passage: White Ships/Black Cargo*
1997	author: Walter Dean Myers, *Slam;* illustrator: Jerry Pinkney, *Minty: A Story of Young Harriet Tubman*
1998	author: Sharon M. Draper, *Forged by Fire;* illustrator: Javaka Steptoe, *In Daddy's Arms I Am Tall: African Americans Celebrating Fathers*
1999	author: Angela Johnson, *Heaven;* illustrator: Michele Wood, *i see the rhythm*
2000	author: Christopher Paul Curtis, *Bud, Not Buddy;* illustrator: Brian Pinkney, *In the Time of Drums*
2001	author: Jacqueline Woodson, *Miracle's Boys;* illustrator: Bryan Collier, *Uptown*
2002	author: Mildred D. Taylor, *The Land;* illustrator: Jerry Pinkney, *Goin' Someplace Special*
2003	author: Nikki Grimes, *Bronx Masquerade;* illustrator: E.B. Lewis, *Talkin' About Bessie: The Story of Aviator Elizabeth Coleman*
2004	author: Angela Johnson, *The First Part Last;* illustrator: Ashley Bryan, *Beautiful Blackbird*
2005	author: Toni Morrison, *Remember: The Journey to School Integration;* illustrator: Kadir Nelson, *Ellington Was Not a Street*
2006	author: Julius Lester, *Day of Tears: A Novel in Dialogue;* illustrator: Bryan Collier, *Rosa*
2007	author: Sharon Draper, *Copper Sun;* illustrator: Kadir Nelson, *Moses: When Harriet Tubman Led Her People to Freedom*
2008	author: Christopher Paul Curtis, *Elijah of Buxton;* illustrator: Ashley Bryan, *Let It Shine*
2009	author: Kadir Nelson, *We Are the Ship: The Story of Negro League Baseball;* illustrator: Floyd Cooper, *The Blacker the Berry*

The Man Booker Prize

Awarded to the best full-length novel of the year written by a citizen of the Commonwealth or the Republic of Ireland and published in the UK between 1 October and 30 September. Prize: £50,000 (about US$82,800); each short-listed author re-

ceives £1,000 (about US$1,650). In 1993 Salman Rushdie was awarded the Booker of Bookers, a special award to mark 25 years of the Booker Prize, for *Midnight's Children*. In 2008 the Best of Bookers prize, to mark 40 years, was also won by Salman

The Man Booker Prize (continued)

Rushdie's *Midnight's Children*. In 2005 the Man Booker International Prize was created, to be awarded biennially to a living writer for outstanding lifetime achievement. Prize: £60,000 (about US$99,400). Albanian novelist Ismail Kadare won the first Man Booker International Prize in 2005. Nigerian author Chinua Achebe won the second in 2007. Canadian short-story writer Alice Munro was awarded the third in 2009.

Web site: <www.themanbookerprize.com>.

YEAR	TITLE	AUTHOR
1969	Something to Answer For	P.H. Newby
1970	The Elected Member	Bernice Rubens
1971	In a Free State	V.S. Naipaul
1972	G.	John Berger
1973	The Siege of Krishnapur	J.G. Farrell
1974	The Conservationist	Nadine Gordimer
1974	Holiday	Stanley Middleton
1975	Heat and Dust	Ruth Prawer Jhabvala
1976	Saville	David Storey
1977	Staying On	Paul Scott
1978	The Sea, The Sea	Iris Murdoch
1979	Offshore	Penelope Fitzgerald
1980	Rites of Passage	William Golding
1981	Midnight's Children	Salman Rushdie
1982	Schindler's Ark	Thomas Keneally
1983	Life and Times of Michael K	J.M. Coetzee
1984	Hotel du Lac	Anita Brookner
1985	The Bone People	Keri Hulme
1986	The Old Devils	Kingsley Amis
1987	Moon Tiger	Penelope Lively
1988	Oscar and Lucinda	Peter Carey
1989	The Remains of the Day	Kazuo Ishiguro
1990	Possession	A.S. Byatt
1991	The Famished Road	Ben Okri
1992	The English Patient	Michael Ondaatje
1992	Sacred Hunger	Barry Unsworth
1993	Paddy Clarke Ha Ha Ha	Roddy Doyle
1994	How Late It Was, How Late	James Kelman
1995	The Ghost Road	Pat Barker
1996	Last Orders	Graham Swift
1997	The God of Small Things	Arundhati Roy
1998	Amsterdam	Ian McEwan
1999	Disgrace	J.M. Coetzee
2000	The Blind Assassin	Margaret Atwood
2001	True History of the Kelly Gang	Peter Carey
2002	Life of Pi	Yann Martel
2003	Vernon God Little	DBC Pierre
2004	The Line of Beauty	Alan Hollinghurst
2005	The Sea	John Banville
2006	The Inheritance of Loss	Kiran Desai
2007	The Gathering	Anne Enright
2008	The White Tiger	Aravind Adiga

The Costa Book Awards

The Whitbread Book Awards were inaugurated in 1971, and in 2006 Britain's Costa chain of coffee shops took over the prize. Since 1985, awards have been given in five categories: Novel, First Novel, Biography, Poetry, and Children's. From these a panel of judges chooses one overall winner—the Costa Book of the Year. The total prize fund is £50,000 (about US$82,000): each of the category award winners receives £5,000 (about US$8,200), and the Book of the Year winner receives an additional £25,000 (about US$41,000).

This list includes Novel award winners from 1971 to 1984 and Book of the Year winners from 1985 to 2008.

Costa Book Awards Web site: <www.costabookawards.com>.

YEAR	TITLE	AUTHOR
1971	The Destiny Waltz	Gerda Charles
1972	The Bird of Night	Susan Hill
1973	The Chip-Chip Gatherers	Shiva Naipaul
1974	The Sacred and Profane Love Machine	Iris Murdoch
1975	Docherty	William McIlvanney
1976	The Children of Dynmouth	William Trevor
1977	Injury Time	Beryl Bainbridge
1978	Picture Palace	Paul Theroux
1979	The Old Jest	Jennifer Johnston
1980	How Far Can You Go?	David Lodge
1981	Silver's City	Maurice Leitch
1982	Young Shoulders	John Wain
1983	Fools of Fortune	William Trevor
1984	Kruger's Alp	Christopher Hope
1985	Elegies	Douglas Dunn
1986	An Artist of the Floating World	Kazuo Ishiguro
1987	Under the Eye of the Clock	Christopher Nolan
1988	The Comforts of Madness	Paul Sayer
1989	Coleridge: Early Visions	Richard Holmes
1990	Hopeful Monsters	Nicholas Mosley
1991	A Life of Picasso	John Richardson
1992	Swing Hammer Swing!	Jeff Torrington
1993	Theory of War	Joan Brady
1994	Felicia's Journey	William Trevor
1995	Behind the Scenes at the Museum	Kate Atkinson
1996	The Spirit Level	Seamus Heaney
1997	Tales from Ovid	Ted Hughes
1998	Birthday Letters	Ted Hughes
1999	Beowulf	Seamus Heaney
2000	English Passengers	Matthew Kneale
2001	The Amber Spyglass	Philip Pullman
2002	Samuel Pepys: The Unequalled Self	Claire Tomalin
2003	The Curious Incident of the Dog in the Night-Time	Mark Haddon
2004	Small Island	Andrea Levy
2005	Matisse: The Master	Hilary Spurling
2006	The Tenderness of Wolves	Stef Penney
2007	Day	A.L. Kennedy
2008	The Secret Scripture	Sebastian Barry

The Orange Broadband Prize

Awarded to a work of published fiction written in English by a woman and published in the United Kingdom or Ireland. Prize: £30,000 (about US$49,200) and a bronze figurine called the "Bessie."
Orange Broadband Prize Web site: <www.orangeprize.co.uk>.

YEAR	TITLE	AUTHOR
1996	A Spell of Winter	Helen Dunmore
1997	Fugitive Pieces	Anne Michaels
1998	Larry's Party	Carol Shields
1999	A Crime in the Neighbourhood	Suzanne Berne
2000	When I Lived in Modern Times	Linda Grant
2001	The Idea of Perfection	Kate Grenville
2002	Bel Canto	Ann Patchett
2003	Property	Valerie Martin
2004	Small Island	Andrea Levy
2005	We Need To Talk About Kevin	Lionel Shriver
2006	On Beauty	Zadie Smith
2007	Half of a Yellow Sun	Chimamanda Ngozi Adichie
2008	The Road Home	Rose Tremain
2009	Home	Marilynne Robinson

Prix Goncourt

The Prix de l'Académie Goncourt was first awarded in 1903 from the estate of the brothers and French literary figures Edmond Huot de Goncourt (1822–1896) and Jules Huot de Goncourt (1830–1870) for a work of contemporary prose in French. Additional prizes have been awarded for such categories as best work of poetry, best first novel, and best biography. Prize: €10 (about US$14).

YEAR	TITLE	AUTHOR
1903	Force ennemie	John-Antoine Nau
1904	La Maternelle	Léon Frapié
1905	Les Civilisés	Claude Farrère
1906	Dingley, l'illustre écrivain	Jérôme and Jean Tharaud
1907	Terres lorraines	Emile Moselly
1908	Ecrit sur l'eau	Francis de Miomandre
1909	En France	Marius-Ary Leblond
1910	De Goupil à Margot	Louis Pergaud
1911	Monsieur des Lourdines	Alphonse de Chateaubriant
1912	Les Filles de la pluie	André Savignon
1913	Le Peuple de la mer	Marc Elder
1914	L'Appel du sol	Adrien Bertrand
1915	Gaspard	René Benjamin
1916	Le Feu	Henri Barbusse
1917	La Flamme au poing	Henri Malherbe
1918	Civilisation	Georges Duhamel
1919	A l'ombre des jeunes filles en fleur	Marcel Proust
1920	Nene	Ernest Pérochon
1921	Batouala	René Maran
1922	Le Vitriol de la lune; Le Martyre de l'obèse	Henri Béraud
1923	Rabevel; ou, le mal des ardents	Lucien Fabre
1924	Le Chèvrefeuille; Le Purgatoire; Le Chapitre treize d'Athénée	Thierry Sandre
1925	Raboliot	Maurice Genevoix
1926	Le Supplice de Phèdre	Henry Deberly
1927	Jérôme, 60° latitude nord	Maurice Bedel
1928	Un Homme se penche sur son passé	Maurice Constantin-Weyer
1929	L'Ordre	Marcel Arland
1930	Malaisie	Henri Fauconnier
1931	Mal d'amour	Jean Fayard
1932	Les Loups	Guy Mazeline
1933	La Condition humaine	André Malraux
1934	Capitaine Conan	Roger Vercel
1935	Sang et lumières	Joseph Peyré
1936	L'Empreinte de Dieu	Maxence van der Meersch
1937	Faux passeports	Charles Plisnier
1938	L'Araigne	Henri Troyat
1939	Les Enfants gâtés	Philippe Hériat
1940	Les Grandes Vacances	Francis Ambrière
1941	Vent de Mars	Henri Pourrat
1942	Pareil à des enfants	Bernard Marc
1943	Passage de l'homme	Marius Grout
1944	Le Premier Accroc coûte 200 francs	Elsa Triolet
1945	Mon village à l'heure allemande	Jean-Louis Bory
1946	Histoire d'un fait divers	Jean-Jacques Gautier
1947	Les Forêts de la nuit	Jean-Louis Curtis
1948	Les Grandes Familles	Maurice Druon
1949	Week-end à Zuydcoote	Robert Merle
1950	Les Jeux sauvages	Paul Colin
1951	Le Rivage des Syrtes	Julien Gracq (declined)
1952	Léon Morin, prêtre	Béatrice Beck
1953	Les Bêtes; Le Temps des morts	Pierre Gascar
1954	Mandarins	Simone de Beauvoir
1955	Les Eaux mêlées	Roger Ikor
1956	Les Racines du ciel	Romain Gary
1957	La Loi	Roger Vailland
1958	Saint Germain; ou, la négociation	Francis Walder
1959	Le Dernier des justes	André Schwartz-Bart
1960	Dieu est né en exil	Vintila Horia
1961	La Pitié de Dieu	Jean Cau
1962	Les Bagages de sable	Anna Langfus
1963	Quand la mer se retire	Armand Lanoux
1964	L'État sauvage	Georges Conchon
1965	L'Adoration	Jacques Borel
1966	Oublier Palerme	Edmonde Charles-Roux
1967	La Marge	André Pieyre de Mandiargues
1968	Les Fruits de l'hiver	Bernard Clavel
1969	Creezy	Félicien Marceau
1970	Le Roi des Aulnes	Michel Tournier
1971	Les Bêtises	Jacques Laurent
1972	L'Épervier de Maheux	Jean Carrière
1973	L'Ogre	Jacques Chessex

Prix Goncourt (continued)

YEAR	TITLE	AUTHOR	YEAR	TITLE	AUTHOR
1974	La Dentellière	Pascal Lainé	1993	La Rocher de Tanios	Amin Maalouf
1975	La Vie devant soi	Emile Ajar (declined)	1994	Un Aller simple	Didier van Cauwelaert
1976	Les Flamboyants	Patrick Grainville			
1977	John l'enfer	Didier Decoin	1995	Le Testament français	Andreï Makine
1978	Rue des boutiques obscures	Patrick Modiano			
			1996	Le Chasseur zéro	Pascale Roze
1979	Pélagie-la-charrette	Antonine Maillet	1997	La Bataille	Patrick Rambaud
1980	Le Jardin d'acclimatation	Yves Navarre	1998	Confidence pour confidence	Paule Constant
1981	Anne Marie	Lucien Bodard			
1982	Dans la main de l'ange	Dominique Fernandez	1999	Je m'en vais	Jean Echenoz
			2000	Ingrid Caven	Jean-Jacques Schuhl
1983	Les Égarés	Frédérick Tristan	2001	Rouge Brésil	Jean-Christophe Rufin
1984	L'Amant	Marguerite Duras			
1985	Les Noces barbares	Yann Queffélec	2002	Les Ombres errantes	Pascal Quignard
1986	Valet de nuit	Michel Host	2003	La Maîtresse de Brecht	Jacques-Pierre Amette
1987	La Nuit sacrée	Tahar Ben Jelloun			
1988	L'Exposition coloniale	Erik Orsenna	2004	Le Soleil des Scorta	Laurent Gaudé
1989	Un Grand Pas vers le Bon Dieu	Jean Vautrin	2005	Trois jours chez ma mère	François Weyergans
1990	Les Champs d'honneur	Jean Rouaud	2006	Les Bienveillantes	Jonathan Littell
			2007	Alabama Song	Gilles Leroy
1991	Les Filles du calvaire	Pierre Combescot	2008	Syngué sabour: pierre de patience	Atiq Rahimi
1992	Texaco	Patrick Chamoiseau			

T.S. Eliot Prize

Great Britain's Poetry Book Society awards the T.S. Eliot Prize to the best new collection of poetry published in the UK or the Republic of Ireland during the preceding year. The prize is £15,000 (about US$24,600).

YEAR	WORK	AUTHOR	COUNTRY
1993	First Language	Ciaran Carson	Ireland
1994	The Annals of Chile	Paul Muldoon	United Kingdom
1995	My Alexandria	Mark Doty	United States
1996	Subhuman Redneck Poems	Les Murray	Australia
1997	God's Gift to Women	Don Paterson	United Kingdom
1998	Birthday Letters	Ted Hughes	United Kingdom
1999	Billy's Rain	Hugo Williams	United Kingdom
2000	The Weather in Japan	Michael Longley	United Kingdom
2001	The Beauty of the Husband	Anne Carson	Canada
2002	Dart	Alice Oswald	United Kingdom
2003	Landing Light	Don Paterson	United Kingdom
2004	Reel	George Szirtes	United Kingdom
2005	Rapture	Carol Ann Duffy	United Kingdom
2006	District and Circle	Seamus Heaney	Ireland
2007	The Drowned Book	Sean O'Brien	United Kingdom
2008	Nigh-No-Place	Jen Hadfield	United Kingdom

The Bollingen Prize in Poetry

The Bollingen Prize in Poetry is awarded biennially to the American poet whose work represents the highest achievement in the field of American poetry during the preceding two-year period. The committee considers published work, particularly work published during that preceding two-year period. Former winners of the US$100,000 prize are not eligible. Web site: <http://beinecke.library.yale.edu/bollingen>.

YEAR	POET	YEAR	POET	YEAR	POET
1948	Ezra Pound	1957	E.E. Cummings	1971	Richard Wilbur
1949	Wallace Stevens	1958	Theodore Roethke		Mona Van Duyn
1950	John Crowe Ransom	1959	Delmore Schwartz	1973	James Merrill
1951	Marianne Moore	1960	Yvor Winters	1975	A.R. Ammons
1952	Archibald MacLeish	1961	Richard Eberhart	1977	David Ignatow
	William Carlos Williams		John Hall Wheelock	1979	W.S. Merwin
1953	W.H. Auden	1963	Robert Frost	1981	May Swenson
1954	Léonie Adams	1965	Horace Gregory		Howard Nemerov
	Louise Bogan	1967	Robert Penn Warren	1983	Anthony Hecht
1955	Conrad Aiken	1969	John Berryman		John Hollander
1956	Allen Tate		Karl Shapiro		

The Bollingen Prize in Poetry (continued)

YEAR	POET	YEAR	POET	YEAR	POET
1985	John Ashbery	1993	Mark Strand	2005	Jay Wright
	Fred Chappell	1995	Kenneth Koch	2007	Frank Bidart
1987	Stanley Kunitz	1997	Gary Snyder	2009	Allen Grossman
1989	Edgar Bowers	1999	Robert Creeley		
1991	Laura Riding Jackson	2001	Louise Glück		
	Donald Justice	2003	Adrienne Rich		

Pritzker Architecture Prize

The Pritzker Architecture Prize, awarded by the Hyatt Foundation since 1979, is given to an outstanding living architect for built work. Prize: US$100,000 and a bronze medallion. Web site: <www.pritzkerprize.com>.

YEAR	NAME	COUNTRY	YEAR	NAME	COUNTRY
1979	Philip Johnson	United States	1995	Tadao Ando	Japan
1980	Luis Barragán	Mexico	1996	Rafael Moneo	Spain
1981	James Stirling	Great Britain	1997	Sverre Fehn	Norway
1982	Kevin Roche	United States	1998	Renzo Piano	Italy
1983	I.M. Pei	United States	1999	Norman Foster	Great Britain
1984	Richard Meier	United States	2000	Rem Koolhaas	The Netherlands
1985	Hans Hollein	Austria	2001	Jacques Herzog	Switzerland
1986	Gottfried Böhm	West Germany		Pierre de Meuron	Switzerland
1987	Kenzo Tange	Japan	2002	Glenn Murcutt	Australia
1988	Gordon Bunshaft	United States	2003	Jørn Utzon	Denmark
	Oscar Niemeyer	Brazil	2004	Zaha Hadid	Great Britain
1989	Frank O. Gehry	United States	2005	Thom Mayne	United States
1990	Aldo Rossi	Italy	2006	Paulo Mendes da Rocha	Brazil
1991	Robert Venturi	United States	2007	Richard Rogers	Great Britain
1992	Alvaro Siza	Portugal	2008	Jean Nouvel	France
1993	Fumihiko Maki	Japan	2009	Peter Zumthor	Switzerland
1994	Christian de Portzamparc	France			

Sport

Sport Coverage

The tables that follow contain information about the top contests of all the major sports that are international in character, as well as some professional and amateur sports that attract a huge national following—such as baseball in the United States and cricket in the United Kingdom, Australia, India, and the other Test match countries. In many sports the Olympic Games held every four years constitute the world championships; they are included in the listings below. In some cases circumstances such as marriage or divorce have changed the name of a winning athlete. The following tables give the name by which the athlete was known for the given year, resulting in instances in which the athlete may appear under two or more names in the same table. Similarly, if the citizenship of an athlete or name of the athlete's country changes, the tables reflect the accurate name for each given year.

Sporting Codes for Countries
Codes of the International Olympic Committee (IOC)

Code	Country	Code	Country	Code	Country
AFG	Afghanistan	CUB	Cuba	KEN	Kenya
AHO	Netherlands Antilles	CYP	Cyprus	KGZ	Kyrgyzstan
ALB	Albania	CZE	Czech Republic	KIR	Kiribati
ALG	Algeria	DEN	Denmark	KOR	Korea, Republic of
AND	Andorra	DJI	Djibouti		(South Korea)
ANG	Angola	DMA	Dominica	KSA	Saudi Arabia
ANT	Antigua and Barbuda	DOM	Dominican Republic	KUW	Kuwait
ARG	Argentina	ECU	Ecuador	LAO	Laos
ARM	Armenia	EGY	Egypt	LAT	Latvia
ARU	Aruba	ERI	Eritrea	LBA	Libya
ASA	American Samoa	ESA	El Salvador	LBR	Liberia
AUS	Australia	ESP	Spain	LCA	Saint Lucia
AUT	Austria	EST	Estonia	LES	Lesotho
AZE	Azerbaijan	ETH	Ethiopia	LIB	Lebanon
BAH	Bahamas, The	FIJ	Fiji	LIE	Liechtenstein
BAN	Bangladesh	FIN	Finland	LTU	Lithuania
BAR	Barbados	FRA	France	LUX	Luxembourg
BDI	Burundi	FSM	Micronesia, Fed. States of	MAD	Madagascar
BEL	Belgium	GAB	Gabon	MAR	Morocco
BEN	Benin	GAM	Gambia, The	MAS	Malaysia
BER	Bermuda	GBR	Great Britain	MAW	Malawi
BHU	Bhutan	GBS	Guinea-Bissau	MDA	Moldova
BIH	Bosnia and Herzegovina	GEO	Georgia	MDV	Maldives
BIZ	Belize	GEQ	Equatorial Guinea	MEX	Mexico
BLR	Belarus	GER	Germany	MGL	Mongolia
BOL	Bolivia	GHA	Ghana	MHL	Marshall Islands
BOT	Botswana	GRE	Greece	MKD	Macedonia[1]
BRA	Brazil	GRN	Grenada	MLI	Mali
BRN	Bahrain	GUA	Guatemala	MLT	Malta
BRU	Brunei	GUI	Guinea	MNE	Montenegro
BUL	Bulgaria	GUM	Guam	MON	Monaco
BUR	Burkina Faso	GUY	Guyana	MOZ	Mozambique
CAF	Central African Republic	HAI	Haiti	MRI	Mauritius
CAM	Cambodia	HKG	Hong Kong	MTN	Mauritania
CAN	Canada	HON	Honduras	MYA	Myanmar (Burma)
CAY	Cayman Islands	HUN	Hungary	NAM	Namibia
CGO	Congo, Republic of the	INA	Indonesia	NCA	Nicaragua
CHA	Chad	IND	India	NED	Netherlands, The
CHI	Chile	IRI	Iran	NEP	Nepal
CHN	China	IRL	Ireland	NGR	Nigeria
CIV	Côte d'Ivoire	IRQ	Iraq	NIG	Niger
CMR	Cameroon	ISL	Iceland	NOR	Norway
COD	Congo, Democratic	ISR	Israel	NRU	Nauru
	Republic of the	ISV	US Virgin Islands	NZL	New Zealand
COK	Cook Islands	ITA	Italy	OMA	Oman
COL	Colombia	IVB	British Virgin Islands	PAK	Pakistan
COM	Comoros	JAM	Jamaica	PAN	Panama
CPV	Cape Verde	JOR	Jordan	PAR	Paraguay
CRC	Costa Rica	JPN	Japan	PER	Peru
CRO	Croatia	KAZ	Kazakhstan	PHI	Philippines

Sporting Codes for Countries (continued)
Codes of the International Olympic Committee (IOC) (continued)

PLE	Palestine	SLO	Slovenia	TOG	Togo
PLW	Palau	SMR	San Marino	TPE	Taiwan
PNG	Papua New Guinea	SOL	Solomon Islands	TRI	Trinidad and Tobago
POL	Poland	SOM	Somalia	TUN	Tunisia
POR	Portugal	SRB	Serbia	TUR	Turkey
PRK	Korea, Democratic	SRI	Sri Lanka	TUV	Tuvalu
	People's Republic of	STP	São Tomé and Príncipe	UAE	United Arab Emirates
	(North Korea)	SUD	Sudan, The	UGA	Uganda
PUR	Puerto Rico	SUI	Switzerland	UKR	Ukraine
QAT	Qatar	SUR	Suriname	URU	Uruguay
ROU	Romania	SVK	Slovakia	USA	United States
RSA	South Africa	SWE	Sweden	UZB	Uzbekistan
RUS	Russia	SWZ	Swaziland	VAN	Vanuatu
RWA	Rwanda	SYR	Syria	VEN	Venezuela
SAM	Samoa	TAN	Tanzania	VIE	Vietnam
SEN	Senegal	TGA	Tonga	VIN	Saint Vincent and
SEY	Seychelles	THA	Thailand		the Grenadines
SIN	Singapore	TJK	Tajikistan	YEM	Yemen
SKN	Saint Kitts and Nevis	TKM	Turkmenistan	ZAM	Zambia
SLE	Sierra Leone	TLS	East Timor (Timor-Leste)	ZIM	Zimbabwe

Historical and Other Country Codes

ENG	England	GGY	Guernsey	TCH	Czechoslovakia
FRG	Germany, Federal Republic	IMN	Isle of Man	UNT	Unified Team[2]
	of (East Germany)	JEY	Jersey	URS	USSR
GDR	German Democratic	NIR	Northern Ireland	WAL	Wales
	Republic (West	SCO	Scotland	YUG	Yugoslavia
	Germany)				

[1]Macedonia is known by the IOC as the Former Yugoslav Republic of Macedonia. [2]The Unified Team consisted of athletes from the Commonwealth of Independent States plus Georgia.

The Olympic Games

By the 6th century BC several sporting festivals had achieved cultural importance in the Greek world. The most prominent among them were the Olympic Games at the city of Olympia, first recorded in 776 BC and held at four-year intervals thereafter. Those games, comprising many of the sports now included in the Summer Games, were abolished in AD 393 by the Roman emperor Theodosius I, probably because of their pagan associations.

In 1887 the 24-year-old French aristocrat and educator Pierre, baron de Coubertin, conceived the idea of reviving the Olympic Games and spent seven years gathering support for his plan. At a international congress in 1894, his plan was accepted and the International Olympic Committee (IOC) was founded. The first modern Olympic Games were held in Athens in April 1896, with some 300 representatives from 13 nations competing. The revival led to the formation of international amateur sports organizations and national Olympic committees throughout the world.

The IOC is responsible for maintaining the regular celebration of the games, seeing that the games are carried out in a spirit of peace and intercultural communication, and promoting amateur sport throughout the world. IOC members may not accept from the government of their country, or from any other entity, instructions that compromise their independence.

The Olympic Games have come to be regarded as the world's foremost sports competition. Before the 1970s the Games were officially limited to amateurs, but since that time many events have been opened to professional athletes. In 1924 the Winter Games were created, and in 1986 the IOC voted to alternate the Winter and Summer Games every two years, beginning in 1994.

The games were canceled during the two world wars (1916, 1940, and 1944) and have frequently served as venues for the expression of political dissent. China refused to participate in the Summer Games from 1956 until 1984 because of Taiwan's participation; 26 nations boycotted the games in 1976 over the participation of New Zealand, some of whose athletes had competed in apartheid-era South Africa; the United States and some 60 other countries boycotted the 1980 games in Moscow to protest the Soviet invasion of Afghanistan, and the Communist bloc and Cuba in turn boycotted the 1984 Los Angeles games.

In light of the IOC's declared independence from political and financial interests, in 1998 the world was shocked by allegations of widespread corruption within the committee. Several committee members, it was found, had accepted bribes to approve the bid of Salt Lake City UT as the site for the 2002 Winter Games. Impropriety was also alleged for several previous bid committees. The IOC responded by expelling six members and in 1999 announced a number of wide-ranging reforms.

IOC Web site: <www.olympic.org>.

Sites of the Modern Olympic Games

Summer Games

YEAR	LOCATION	YEAR	LOCATION	YEAR	LOCATION
1896	Athens, Greece	1940–44	*not held*	1984	Los Angeles CA
1900	Paris, France	1948	London, England	1988	Seoul, Republic of
1904	St. Louis MO	1952	Helsinki, Finland		Korea
1908	London, England	1956	Melbourne, VIC,	1992	Barcelona, Spain
1912	Stockholm, Sweden		Australia	1996	Atlanta GA
1916	*not held*	1960	Rome, Italy	2000	Sydney, NSW, Australia
1920	Antwerp, Belgium	1964	Tokyo, Japan	2004	Athens, Greece
1924	Paris, France	1968	Mexico City, Mexico	2008	Beijing, China
1928	Amsterdam, Netherlands	1972	Munich, West Germany	2012	*scheduled to be held 27*
1932	Los Angeles CA	1976	Montreal, QC, Canada		*July–12 August,*
1936	Berlin, Germany	1980	Moscow, USSR		*London, England*

Winter Games

YEAR	LOCATION	YEAR	LOCATION	YEAR	LOCATION
1924	Chamonix, France	1960	Squaw Valley CA	1994	Lillehammer, Norway
1928	St. Moritz, Switzerland	1964	Innsbruck, Austria	1998	Nagano, Japan
1932	Lake Placid NY	1968	Grenoble, France	2002	Salt Lake City UT
1936	Garmisch-Partenkirchen,	1972	Sapporo, Japan	2006	Turin, Italy
	Germany	1976	Innsbruck, Austria	2010	*scheduled to be held*
1940–44	*not held*	1980	Lake Placid NY		*12–28 February,*
1948	St. Moritz, Switzerland	1984	Sarajevo, Yugoslavia		*Vancouver, BC, Canada*
1952	Oslo, Norway	1988	Calgary, AB, Canada	2014	*scheduled to be held*
1956	Cortina d'Ampezzo, Italy	1992	Albertville, France		*7–23 February, Sochi,*
					Russia

Summer Olympic Games

Gold-medal winners in all summer events since 1896. Note: East and West Germany fielded a joint all-Germany team in 1956, 1960, and 1964, abbreviated here as GER.

Archery

MEN'S INDIVIDUAL
1972 John Williams (USA)
1976 Darrell Pace (USA)
1980 Tomi Poikolainen (FIN)
1984 Darrell Pace (USA)
1988 Jay Barrs (USA)
1992 Sebastien Flute (FRA)
1996 Justin Huish (USA)
2000 Simon Fairweather (AUS)
2004 Marco Galiazzo (ITA)
2008 Viktor Ruban (UKR)

AU CORDON DORE (50 METERS)
1900 Henri Herouin (FRA)

AU CORDON DORE (33 METERS)
1900 Hubert van Innis (BEL)

AU CHAPELET (50 METERS)
1900 Eugène Mougin (FRA)

SUR LA PERCHE A LA HERSE
1900 Emmanuel Foulon (FRA)

AU CHAPELET (33 METERS)
1900 Hubert van Innis (BEL)

SUR LA PERCHE A LA PYRAMIDE
1900 Émile Grumiaux (FRA)

Archery (continued)

DOUBLE AMERICAN ROUND
1904 George Philip Bryant (USA)

(DOUBLE) YORK ROUND
1904 George Philip Bryant (USA)
1908 William Dod (GBR)

CONTINENTAL STYLE
1908 Eugène G. Grizot (FRA)

FIXED BIRD TARGET (SMALL)
1920 Edmond van Moer (BEL)

FIXED BIRD TARGET (LARGE)
1920 Édouard Cloetens (BEL)

MOVING BIRD TARGET (28 METERS)
1920 Hubert van Innis (BEL)

MOVING BIRD TARGET (33 METERS)
1920 Hubert van Innis (BEL)

MOVING BIRD TARGET (50 METERS)
1920 Julien Brulé (FRA)

WOMEN'S INDIVIDUAL
1972 Doreen Wilber (USA)
1976 Luann Ryon (USA)
1980 Ketevan Losaberidze (URS)
1984 Seo Hyang Soon (KOR)
1988 Kim Soo Nyung (KOR)

Summer Olympic Games (continued)

Archery (continued)

WOMEN'S INDIVIDUAL (CONTINUED)
1992 Cho Youn Jeong (KOR)
1996 Kim Kyung-Wook (KOR)
2000 Yun Mi-Jin (KOR)
2004 Park Sung Hyun (KOR)
2008 Zhang Juan Juan (CHN)

DOUBLE COLUMBIA ROUND
1904 Matilda Scott Howell (USA)

(DOUBLE) NATIONAL ROUND
1904 Matilda Scott Howell (USA)
1908 Sybil Fenton "Queenie" Newall (GBR)

MEN'S TEAM
1904 United States
1988 Republic of Korea
1992 Spain
1996 United States
2000 Republic of Korea
2004 Republic of Korea
2008 Republic of Korea

WOMEN'S TEAM
1904 United States
1988 Republic of Korea
1992 Republic of Korea
1996 Republic of Korea
2000 Republic of Korea
2004 Republic of Korea
2008 Republic of Korea

FIXED TARGET (2 EVENTS)
1920 Belgium

MOVING TARGET (28 METERS)
1920 The Netherlands

MOVING TARGET (33 METERS)
1920 Belgium

MOVING TARGET (50 METERS)
1920 Belgium

Association Football (Soccer)[1]

MEN
1900 Great Britain
1904 Canada
1908 Great Britain
1912 Great Britain
1920 Belgium
1924 Uruguay
1928 Uruguay
1936 Italy
1948 Sweden
1952 Hungary
1956 USSR
1960 Yugoslavia
1964 Hungary
1968 Hungary
1972 Poland
1976 East Germany
1980 Czechoslovakia
1984 France
1988 USSR
1992 Spain
1996 Nigeria
2000 Cameroon

Association Football (Soccer)[1] (continued)

MEN (CONTINUED)
2004 Argentina
2008 Argentina

WOMEN
1996 United States
2000 Norway
2004 United States
2008 United States

Athletics (Track and Field) (men)

60 METERS		SEC
1900	Alvin Kraenzlein (USA)	7
1904	Archie Hahn (USA)	·7

100 METERS		SEC
1896	Thomas Burke (USA)	12.0
1900	Francis Jarvis (USA)	11.0
1904	Archie Hahn (USA)	11.0
1908	Reginald Walker (RSA)	10.8
1912	Ralph Craig (USA)	10.8
1920	Charles Paddock (USA)	10.8
1924	Harold Abrahams (GBR)	10.6
1928	Percy Williams (CAN)	10.8
1932	Eddie Tolan (USA)	10.3
1936	Jesse Owens (USA)	10.3
1948	Harrison Dillard (USA)	10.3
1952	Lindy Remigino (USA)	10.4
1956	Robert Morrow (USA)	10.5
1960	Armin Hary (GER)	10.2
1964	Robert Hayes (USA)	10.0
1968	James Hines (USA)	9.9
1972	Valery Borzov (URS)	10.14
1976	Hasely Crawford (TRI)	10.06
1980	Allan Wells (GBR)	10.25
1984	Carl Lewis (USA)	9.99
1988	Carl Lewis (USA)[2]	9.92
1992	Linford Christie (GBR)	9.96
1996	Donovan Bailey (CAN)	9.84
2000	Maurice Greene (USA)	9.87
2004	Justin Gatlin (USA)	9.85
2008	Usain Bolt (JAM)	9.69

200 METERS		SEC
1900	Walter Tewksbury (USA)	22.2
1904	Archie Hahn (USA)	21.6
1908	Robert Kerr (CAN)	22.6
1912	Ralph Craig (USA)	21.7
1920	Allen Woodring (USA)	22.0
1924	Jackson Scholz (USA)	21.6
1928	Percy Williams (CAN)	21.8
1932	Eddie Tolan (USA)	21.2
1936	Jesse Owens (USA)	20.7
1948	Melvin Patton (USA)	21.1
1952	Andy Stanfield (USA)	20.7
1956	Robert Morrow (USA)	20.6
1960	Livio Berruti (ITA)	20.5
1964	Henry Carr (USA)	20.3
1968	Tommie Smith (USA)	19.8
1972	Valery Borzov (URS)	20.00
1976	Donald Quarrie (JAM)	20.23
1980	Pietro Mennea (ITA)	20.19
1984	Carl Lewis (USA)	19.80
1988	Joe DeLoach (USA)	19.75
1992	Mike Marsh (USA)	20.01
1996	Michael Johnson (USA)	19.32
2000	Konstantinos Kenteris (GRE)	20.09

Summer Olympic Games (continued)

Athletics (Track and Field) (men) (continued)

200 METERS (CONTINUED)

		SEC
2004	Shawn Crawford (USA)	19.79
2008	Usain Bolt (JAM)	19.30

400 METERS

		SEC
1896	Thomas Burke (USA)	54.2
1900	Maxwell Long (USA)	49.4
1904	Harry Hillman (USA)	49.2
1908	Wyndham Halswelle (GBR)	50.0
1912	Charles Reidpath (USA)	48.2
1920	Bevil Rudd (RSA)	49.6
1924	Eric Liddell (GBR)	47.6
1928	Raymond Barbuti (USA)	47.8
1932	William Carr (USA)	46.2
1936	Archie Williams (USA)	46.5
1948	Arthur Wint (JAM)	46.2
1952	Vincent George Rhoden (JAM)	45.9
1956	Charles Jenkins (USA)	46.7
1960	Otis Davis (USA)	44.9
1964	Michael Larrabee (USA)	45.1
1968	Lee Evans (USA)	43.8
1972	Vincent Matthews (USA)	44.66
1976	Alberto Juantorena (CUB)	44.26
1980	Viktor Markin (URS)	44.60
1984	Alonzo Babers (USA)	44.27
1988	Steven Lewis (USA)	43.87
1992	Quincy Watts (USA)	43.50
1996	Michael Johnson (USA)	43.49
2000	Michael Johnson (USA)	43.84
2004	Jeremy Wariner (USA)	44.00
2008	LaShawn Merritt (USA)	43.75

800 METERS

		MIN:SEC
1896	Edwin Flack (AUS)	2:11.0
1900	Alfred Tysoe (GBR)	2:01.2
1904	James Lightbody (USA)	1:56.0
1908	Melvin Sheppard (USA)	1:52.8
1912	James Edward Meredith (USA)	1:51.9
1920	Albert Hill (GBR)	1:53.4
1924	Douglas Lowe (GBR)	1:52.4
1928	Douglas Lowe (GBR)	1:51.8
1932	Thomas Hampson (GBR)	1:49.7
1936	John Woodruff (USA)	1:52.9
1948	Malvin Whitfield (USA)	1:49.2
1952	Malvin Whitfield (USA)	1:49.2
1956	Thomas Courtney (USA)	1:47.7
1960	Peter Snell (NZL)	1:46.3
1964	Peter Snell (NZL)	1:45.1
1968	Ralph Doubell (AUS)	1:44.3
1972	David Wottle (USA)	1:45.9
1976	Alberto Juantorena (CUB)	1:43.50
1980	Steven Ovett (GBR)	1:45.40
1984	Joaquim Cruz (BRA)	1:43.00
1988	Paul Ereng (KEN)	1:43.45
1992	William Tanui (KEN)	1:43.66
1996	Vebjoern Rodal (NOR)	1:42.58
2000	Nils Schumann (GER)	1:45.08
2004	Yury Borzakovsky (RUS)	1:44.45
2008	Wilfred Bungei (KEN)	1:44.65

1,500 METERS

		MIN:SEC
1896	Edwin Flack (AUS)	4:33.2
1900	Charles Bennett (GBR)	4:06.2
1904	James Lightbody (USA)	4:05.4
1908	Melvin Sheppard (USA)	4:03.4
1912	Arnold Jackson (GBR)	3:56.8
1920	Albert Hill (GBR)	4:01.8
1924	Paavo Nurmi (FIN)	3:53.6

Athletics (Track and Field) (men) (continued)

1,500 METERS (CONTINUED)

		MIN:SEC
1928	Harry Larva (FIN)	3:53.2
1932	Luigi Beccali (ITA)	3:51.2
1936	John Lovelock (NZL)	3:47.8
1948	Henry Eriksson (SWE)	3:49.8
1952	Joseph Barthel (LUX)	3:45.1
1956	Ronald Delany (IRL)	3:41.2
1960	Herbert Elliott (AUS)	3:35.6
1964	Peter Snell (NZL)	3:38.1
1968	Hezekiah Kipchoge Keino (KEN)	3:34.9
1972	Pekka Vasala (FIN)	3:36.3
1976	John Walker (NZL)	3:39.17
1980	Sebastian Coe (GBR)	3:38.40
1984	Sebastian Coe (GBR)	3:32.53
1988	Peter Rono (KEN)	3:35.96
1992	Fermin Cacho Ruiz (ESP)	3:40.12
1996	Noureddine Morceli (ALG)	3:35.78
2000	Noah Ngeny (KEN)	3:32.07
2004	Hicham El Guerrouj (MAR)	3:34.18
2008	Rashid Ramzi (BRN)	3:32.94

5,000 METERS

		MIN:SEC
1912	Hannes Kolehmainen (FIN)	14:36.6
1920	Joseph Guillemot (FRA)	14:55.6
1924	Paavo Nurmi (FIN)	14:31.2
1928	Vilho Ritola (FIN)	14:38.0
1932	Lauri Lehtinen (FIN)	14:30.0
1936	Gunnar Höckert (FIN)	14:22.2
1948	Gaston Reiff (BEL)	14:17.6
1952	Emil Zatopek (TCH)	14:06.6
1956	Vladimir Kuts (URS)	13:39.6
1960	Murray Halberg (NZL)	13:43.4
1964	Robert Keyser Schul (USA)	13:48.8
1968	Mohamed Gammoudi (TUN)	14:05.0
1972	Lasse Viren (FIN)	13:26.4
1976	Lasse Viren (FIN)	13:24.76
1980	Miruts Yifter (ETH)	13:21.00
1984	Said Aouita (MAR)	13:05.59
1988	John Ngugi (KEN)	13:11.70
1992	Dieter Baumann (GER)	13:12.52
1996	Venuste Niyongabo (BDI)	13:07.97
2000	Millon Wolde (ETH)	13:35.49
2004	Hicham El Guerrouj (MAR)	13:14.39
2008	Kenenisa Bekele (ETH)	12:57.82

5 MILES

		MIN:SEC
1908	Emil Voigt (GBR)	25:11.2

10,000 METERS

		MIN:SEC
1912	Hannes Kolehmainen (FIN)	31:20.8
1920	Paavo Nurmi (FIN)	31:45.8
1924	Vilho Ritola (FIN)	30:23.2
1928	Paavo Nurmi (FIN)	30:18.8
1932	Janusz Kusocinski (POL)	30:11.4
1936	Ilmari Salminen (FIN)	30:15.4
1948	Emil Zatopek (TCH)	29:59.6
1952	Emil Zatopek (TCH)	29:17.0
1956	Vladimir Kuts (URS)	28:45.6
1960	Pyotr Bolotnikov (URS)	28:32.2
1964	William Mills (USA)	28:24.4
1968	Nabiba Temu (KEN)	29:27.4
1972	Lasse Viren (FIN)	27:38.4
1976	Lasse Viren (FIN)	27:40.38
1980	Miruts Yifter (ETH)	27:42.70
1984	Alberto Cova (ITA)	27:47.54
1988	Brahim Boutaib (MAR)	27:21.46
1992	Khalid Skah (MAR)	27:46.70
1996	Haile Gebrselassie (ETH)	27:07.34

Summer Olympic Games (continued)

Athletics (Track and Field) (men) (continued)

10,000 METERS (CONTINUED)		MIN:SEC
2000	Haile Gebrselassie (ETH)	27:18.20
2004	Kenenisa Bekele (ETH)	27:05.10
2008	Kenenisa Bekele (ETH)	27:01.17

MARATHON		HR:MIN:SEC
1896	Spiridon Louis (GRE)	2:58:50.0
1900	Michel Theato (FRA)	2:59:45.0
1904	Thomas Hicks (USA)	3:28:53.0
1908	John Hayes (USA)	2:55:18.4
1912	Kenneth McArthur (RSA)	2:36:54.8
1920	Hannes Kolehmainen (FIN)	2:32:35.8
1924	Albin Stenroos (FIN)	2:41:22.6
1928	Boughèra El Ouafi (FRA)	2:32:57.0
1932	Juan Carlos Zabala (ARG)	2:31:36.0
1936	Kitei Son (JPN)	2:29:19.2
1948	Delfo Cabrera (ARG)	2:34:51.6
1952	Emil Zatopek (TCH)	2:23:03.2
1956	Alain Mimoun-O-Kacha (FRA)	2:25:00.0
1960	Abebe Bikila (ETH)	2:15:16.2
1964	Abebe Bikila (ETH)	2:12:11.2
1968	Mamo Wolde (ETH)	2:20:26.4
1972	Frank Shorter (USA)	2:12:19.8
1976	Waldemar Cierpinski (GDR)	2:09:55.0
1980	Waldemar Cierpinski (GDR)	2:11:03.0
1984	Carlos Lopes (POR)	2:09:21.0
1988	Gelindo Bordin (ITA)	2:10:32.0
1992	Hwang Young-Cho (KOR)	2:13:23.0
1996	Josia Thugwane (RSA)	2:12:36.0
2000	Gezahgne Abera (ETH)	2:10:11.0
2004	Stefano Baldini (ITA)	2:10:55.0
2008	Samuel Kamau Wansiru (KEN)	2:06:32.0

110-METER HURDLES		SEC
1896[3]	Thomas Curtis (USA)	17.6
1900	Alvin Kraenzlein (USA)	15.4
1904	Frederick Schule (USA)	16.0
1908	Forrest Smithson (USA)	15.0
1912	Frederick Kelly (USA)	15.1
1920	Earl Thomson (CAN)	14.8
1924	Daniel Kinsey (USA)	15.0
1928	Sydney Atkinson (RSA)	14.8
1932	George Saling (USA)	14.6
1936	Forrest Towns (USA)	14.2
1948	William Porter (USA)	13.9
1952	Harrison Dillard (USA)	13.7
1956	Lee Calhoun (USA)	13.5
1960	Lee Calhoun (USA)	13.8
1964	Hayes Wendell Jones (USA)	13.6
1968	Willie Davenport (USA)	13.3
1972	Rodney Milburn (USA)	13.24
1976	Guy Drut (FRA)	13.30
1980	Thomas Munkelt (GDR)	13.39
1984	Roger Kingdom (USA)	13.20
1988	Roger Kingdom (USA)	12.98
1992	Mark McKoy (CAN)	13.12
1996	Allen Johnson (USA)	12.95
2000	Anier Garcia (CUB)	13.00
2004	Liu Xiang (CHN)	12.91
2008	Dayron Robles (CUB)	12.93

200-METER HURDLES		SEC
1900	Alvin Kraenzlein (USA)	25.4
1904	Harry Hillman (USA)	24.6

400-METER HURDLES		SEC
1900	Walter Tewksbury (USA)	57.6
1904[4]	Harry Hillman (USA)	53.0

Athletics (Track and Field) (men) (continued)

400-METER HURDLES (CONTINUED)		SEC
1908	Charles Bacon (USA)	55.0
1920	Frank Loomis (USA)	54.0
1924	Frederick Morgan Taylor (USA)	52.6
1928	David George Burghley (GBR)	53.4
1932	Robert Tisdall (IRL)	51.7
1936	Glenn Hardin (USA)	52.4
1948	Roy Cochran (USA)	51.1
1952	Charles Moore (USA)	50.8
1956	Glenn Davis (USA)	50.1
1960	Glenn Davis (USA)	49.3
1964	Warren Cawley (USA)	49.6
1968	David Hemery (GBR)	48.1
1972	John Akii-Bua (UGA)	47.82
1976	Edwin Moses (USA)	47.64
1980	Volker Beck (GDR)	48.70
1984	Edwin Moses (USA)	47.75
1988	Andre Phillips (USA)	47.19
1992	Kevin Young (USA)	46.78
1996	Derrick Adkins (USA)	47.54
2000	Angelo Taylor (USA)	47.50
2004	Felix Sánchez (DOM)	47.63
2008	Angelo Taylor (USA)	47.25

2,500-METER STEEPLECHASE		MIN:SEC
1900	George Orton (USA)	7:34.4

2,590-METER STEEPLECHASE		MIN:SEC
1904	James Lightbody (USA)	7:39.6

3,000-METER STEEPLECHASE		MIN:SEC
1920	Percy Hodge (GBR)	10:00.4
1924	Vilho Ritola (FIN)	9:33.6
1928	Toivo Loukola (FIN)	9:21.8
1932	Volmari Iso-Hollo (FIN)	10:33.4[5]
1936	Volmari Iso-Hollo (FIN)	9:03.8
1948	Thore Sjöstrand (SWE)	9:04.6
1952	Horace Ashenfelter (USA)	8:45.4
1956	Christopher Brasher (GBR)	8:41.2
1960	Zdislaw Krzyszkowiak (POL)	8:34.2
1964	Gaston Roelants (BEL)	8:30.8
1968	Amos Biwott (KEN)	8:51.0
1972	Kipchoge Keino (KEN)	8:23.6
1976	Anders Gärderud (SWE)	8:08.02
1980	Bronislaw Malinowski (POL)	8:09.70
1984	Julius Korir (KEN)	8:11.80
1988	Julius Kariuki (KEN)	8:05.51
1992	Mathew Birir (KEN)	8:08.84
1996	Joseph Keter (KEN)	8:07.12
2000	Reuben Kosgei (KEN)	8:21.43
2004	Ezekiel Kemboi (KEN)	8:05.81
2008	Brimin Kiprop Kipruto (KEN)	8:10.34

3,200-METER STEEPLECHASE		MIN:SEC
1908	Arthur Russell (GBR)	10:47.8

3,000 METERS (TEAM) (TEAM/INDIVIDUAL WINNER)		MIN:SEC
1912	United States/Tell Berna	8:44.6
1920	United States/Horace Brown	8:45.4
1924	Finland/Paavo Nurmi	8:32

3 MILES (TEAM) (TEAM/INDIVIDUAL WINNER)		MIN:SEC
1908	Great Britain/Joseph Deakin	14:39.6

5,000 METERS (TEAM) (TEAM/INDIVIDUAL WINNER)		MIN:SEC
1900	Great Britain–Australia/Charles Bennett	15:20

Summer Olympic Games (continued)

Athletics (Track and Field) (men) (continued)

4 MILES (TEAM) (TEAM/INDIVIDUAL WINNER)	MIN:SEC
1904	United States/Arthur Newton	21:17.8

4 × 100-METER RELAY	SEC
1912	Great Britain	42.4
1920	United States	42.2
1924	United States	41.0
1928	United States	41.0
1932	United States	40.0
1936	United States	39.8
1948	United States	40.6
1952	United States	40.1
1956	United States	39.5
1960	Germany	39.5
1964	United States	39.0
1968	United States	38.2
1972	United States	38.19
1976	United States	38.33
1980	USSR	38.26
1984	United States	37.83
1988	USSR	38.19
1992	United States	37.40
1996	Canada	37.69
2000	winner stripped; undecided by press time	
2004	Great Britain	38.07
2008	Jamaica	37.10

4 × 400-METER RELAY	MIN:SEC
1912	United States	3:16.6
1920	Great Britain	3:22.2
1924	United States	3:16.0
1928	United States	3:14.2
1932	United States	3:08.2
1936	Great Britain	3:09.0
1948	United States	3:10.4
1952	Jamaica	3:03.9
1956	United States	3:04.8
1960	United States	3:02.2
1964	United States	3:00.7
1968	United States	2:56.1
1972	Kenya	2:59.8
1976	United States	2:58.65
1980	USSR	3:01.08
1984	United States	2:57.91
1988	United States	2:56.16
1992	United States	2:55.74
1996	United States	2:55.99
2000	winner stripped; undecided by press time	
2004	United States	2:55.91
2008	United States	2:55.39

1,600-METER RELAY (200 × 200 × 400 × 800 METERS)	MIN:SEC
1908	United States	3:29.4

8,000-METER CROSS-COUNTRY	MIN:SEC
1920	Paavo Nurmi (FIN)	27:15

10,000-METER CROSS-COUNTRY	MIN:SEC
1924	Paavo Nurmi (FIN)	32:54.8

12,000-METER CROSS-COUNTRY	MIN:SEC
1912	Hannes Kolehmainen (FIN)	45:11.6

3,000-METER WALK	MIN:SEC
1920	Ugo Frigerio (ITA)	13:14.2

Athletics (Track and Field) (men) (continued)

3,500-METER WALK	MIN:SEC
1908	George Larner (GBR)	14:55

10,000-METER WALK	MIN:SEC
1912	George Goulding (CAN)	46:28.4
1920	Ugo Frigerio (ITA)	48:06.2
1924	Ugo Frigerio (ITA)	47:49.0
1948	John Mikaelsson (SWE)	45:13.2
1952	John Mikaelsson (SWE)	45:02.8

10-MILE WALK	HR:MIN:SEC
1908	George Larner (GBR)	1:15:57.4

20,000-METER WALK	HR:MIN:SEC
1956	Leonid Spirin (URS)	1:31:27.4
1960	Vladimir Golubnichy (URS)	1:34:07.2
1964	Kenneth Matthews (GBR)	1:29:34.0
1968	Vladimir Golubnichy (URS)	1:33:58.4
1972	Peter Frenkel (GDR)	1:26:42.6
1976	Daniel Bautista (MEX)	1:24:40.6
1980	Maurizio Damilano (ITA)	1:23:35.5
1984	Ernesto Canto (MEX)	1:23:13.0
1988	Jozef Pribilinec (TCH)	1:19:57.0
1992	Daniel Plaza Montero (ESP)	1:21:45.0
1996	Jefferson Pérez (ECU)	1:20:07.0
2000	Robert Korzeniowski (POL)	1:18:59.0
2004	Ivano Brugnetti (ITA)	1:19:40.0
2008	Valery Borchin (RUS)	1:19:01.0

50,000-METER WALK	HR:MIN:SEC
1932	Thomas Green (GBR)	4:50:10.0
1936	Harold Whitlock (GBR)	4:30:41.4
1948	John Ljunggren (SWE)	4:41:52.0
1952	Giuseppe Dordoni (ITA)	4:28:07.8
1956	Norman Read (NZL)	4:30:42.8
1960	Donald Thompson (GBR)	4:25:30.0
1964	Abdon Pamich (ITA)	4:11:12.4
1968	Christophe Höhne (GDR)	4:20:13.6
1972	Bernd Kannenberg (FRG)	3:56:11.6
1980	Hartwig Gauder (GDR)	3:49:24.0
1984	Raúl Gonzáles (MEX)	3:47:26.0
1988	Vyacheslav Ivanenko (URS)	3:38:29.0
1992	Andrey Perlov (UNT)	3:50:13.0
1996	Robert Korzeniowski (POL)	3:43:03.0
2000	Robert Korzeniowski (POL)	3:42:22.0
2004	Robert Korzeniowski (POL)	3:38:46.0
2008	Alex Schwazer (ITA)	3:37:09.0

HIGH JUMP	METERS
1896	Ellery Clark (USA)	1.81
1900	Irving Baxter (USA)	1.90
1904	Samuel Jones (USA)	1.80
1908	Harry Porter (USA)	1.90
1912	Alma Richards (USA)	1.93
1920	Richmond Landon (USA)	1.93
1924	Harold Osborn (USA)	1.98
1928	Robert King (USA)	1.94
1932	Duncan McNaughton (CAN)	1.97
1936	Cornelius Johnson (USA)	2.03
1948	John Winter (AUS)	1.98
1952	Walter Davis (USA)	2.04
1956	Charles Dumas (USA)	2.12
1960	Robert Shavlakadze (URS)	2.16
1964	Valery Brumel (URS)	2.18
1968	Richard Fosbury (USA)	2.24
1972	Yury Tarmak (URS)	2.23
1976	Jacek Wszola (POL)	2.25
1980	Gerd Wessig (GDR)	2.36

Summer Olympic Games (continued)

Athletics (Track and Field) (men) (continued)

HIGH JUMP (CONTINUED)

		METERS
1984	Dietmar Mögenburg (FRG)	2.35
1988	Gennady Avdeyenko (URS)	2.38
1992	Javier Sotomayor (CUB)	2.34
1996	Charles Austin (USA)	2.39
2000	Sergey Klyugin (RUS)	2.35
2004	Stefan Holm (SWE)	2.36
2008	Andrey Silnov (RUS)	2.36

STANDING HIGH JUMP

		METERS
1900	Ray Ewry (USA)	1.65
1904	Ray Ewry (USA)	1.60
1908	Ray Ewry (USA)	1.57
1912	Platt Adams (USA)	1.63

POLE VAULT

		METERS
1896	William Welles Hoyt (USA)	3.30
1900	Irving Baxter (USA)	3.30
1904	Charles Dvorak (USA)	3.50
1908	Edward Cooke (USA); Alfred Gilbert (USA) (tied)	3.71
1912	Harry Babcock (USA)	3.95
1920	Frank Foss (USA)	4.09
1924	Lee Barnes (USA)	3.95
1928	Sabin Carr (USA)	4.20
1932	William Miller (USA)	4.31
1936	Earle Meadows (USA)	4.35
1948	Owen Guinn Smith (USA)	4.30
1952	Robert Richards (USA)	4.55
1956	Robert Richards (USA)	4.56
1960	Donald Bragg (USA)	4.70
1964	Fred Hansen (USA)	5.10
1968	Robert Seagren (USA)	5.40
1972	Wolfgang Nordwig (GDR)	5.50
1976	Tadeusz Slusarski (POL)	5.50
1980	Wladyslaw Kozakiewicz (POL)	5.78
1984	Pierre Quinon (FRA)	5.75
1988	Sergey Bubka (URS)	5.90
1992	Maksim Tarasov (UNT)	5.80
1996	Jean Galfione (FRA)	5.92
2000	Nick Hysong (USA)	5.90
2004	Timothy Mack (USA)	5.95
2008	Steve Hooker (AUS)	5.96

LONG JUMP

		METERS
1896	Ellery Clark (USA)	6.35
1900	Alvin Kraenzlein (USA)	7.18
1904	Meyer Prinstein (USA)	7.34
1908	Francis Irons (USA)	7.48
1912	Albert Gutterson (USA)	7.60
1920	William Pettersson (SWE)	7.15
1924	William de Hart-Hubbard (USA)	7.44
1928	Edward Hamm (USA)	7.73
1932	Edward Gordon (USA)	7.64
1936	Jesse Owens (USA)	8.06
1948	Willie Steele (USA)	7.82
1952	Jerome Biffle (USA)	7.57
1956	Gregory Bell (USA)	7.83
1960	Ralph Boston (USA)	8.12
1964	Lynn Davies (GBR)	8.07
1968	Robert Beamon (USA)	8.90
1972	Randy Williams (USA)	8.24
1976	Arnie Robinson (USA)	8.35
1980	Lutz Dombrowski (GDR)	8.54
1984	Carl Lewis (USA)	8.54
1988	Carl Lewis (USA)	8.72
1992	Carl Lewis (USA)	8.67
1996	Carl Lewis (USA)	8.50

Athletics (Track and Field) (men) (continued)

LONG JUMP (CONTINUED)

		METERS
2000	Ivan Pedroso (CUB)	8.55
2004	Dwight Phillips (USA)	8.59
2008	Irving Jahir Saladino Aranda (PAN)	8.34

STANDING LONG JUMP

		METERS
1900	Ray Ewry (USA)	3.21
1904	Ray Ewry (USA)	3.47
1908	Ray Ewry (USA)	3.33
1912	Constantinos Tsiklitiras (GRE)	3.37

TRIPLE JUMP

		METERS
1896	James Connolly (USA)	13.71
1900	Myer Prinstein (USA)	14.47
1904	Myer Prinstein (USA)	14.35
1908	Timothy Ahearne (GBR)	14.91
1912	Gustaf Lindblom (SWE)	14.76
1920	Vilho Tuulos (FIN)	14.50
1924	Anthony Winter (AUS)	15.53
1928	Mikio Oda (JPN)	15.21
1932	Chuhei Nambu (JPN)	15.72
1936	Naoto Tajima (JPN)	16.00
1948	Arne Åhman (SWE)	15.40
1952	Adhemar Ferreira da Silva (BRA)	16.22
1956	Adhemar Ferreira da Silva (BRA)	16.35
1960	Josef Szmidt (POL)	16.81
1964	Josef Szmidt (POL)	16.85
1968	Viktor Saneyev (URS)	17.39
1972	Viktor Saneyev (URS)	17.35
1976	Viktor Saneyev (URS)	17.29
1980	Jaak Uudmae (URS)	17.35
1984	Al Joyner (USA)	17.26
1988	Khristo Markov (BUL)	17.61
1992	Michael Conley (USA)	17.63
1996	Kenny Harrison (USA)	18.09
2000	Jonathan Edwards (GBR)	17.71
2004	Christian Olsson (SWE)	17.79
2008	Nelson Évora (POR)	17.67

STANDING TRIPLE JUMP

		METERS
1900	Ray Ewry (USA)	10.58
1904	Ray Ewry (USA)	10.54

SHOT PUT

		METERS
1896	Robert Garrett (USA)	11.22
1900	Richard Sheldon (USA)	14.10
1904	Ralph Rose (USA)	14.81
1908	Ralph Rose (USA)	14.21
1912	Patrick McDonald (USA)	15.34
1920	Frans Pörhölä (FIN)	14.81
1924	Lemuel Clarence Houser (USA)	14.99
1928	John Kuck (USA)	15.87
1932	Leo Sexton (USA)	16.00
1936	Hans Woellke (GER)	16.20
1948	Wilbur Thompson (USA)	17.12
1952	William Parry O'Brien (USA)	17.41
1956	William Parry O'Brien (USA)	18.57
1960	William Nieder (USA)	19.68
1964	Dallas Long (USA)	20.33
1968	Randy Matson (USA)	20.54
1972	Wladislaw Komar (POL)	21.18
1976	Udo Beyer (GDR)	21.05
1980	Vladimir Kiselyov (URS)	21.35
1984	Alessandro Andrei (ITA)	21.26
1988	Ulf Timmermann (GDR)	22.47
1992	Michael Stulce (USA)	21.70
1996	Randy Barnes (USA)	21.62
2000	Arsi Harju (FIN)	21.29

Summer Olympic Games (continued)

Athletics (Track and Field) (men) (continued)

SHOT PUT (CONTINUED)

		METERS
2004	Yury Bilonog (UKR)	21.16
2008	Tomasz Majewski (POL)	21.51

SHOT PUT (TWO HANDS)

		METERS
1912	Ralph Rose (USA)	27.7

DISCUS THROW

		METERS
1896	Robert Garrett (USA)	29.15
1900	Rezso Bauer (HUN)	36.04
1904	Martin Sheridan (USA)	39.28
1908	Martin Sheridan (USA)	40.89
1912	Armas Taipale (FIN)	45.21
1920	Elmer Niklander (FIN)	44.68
1924	Lemuel Clarence Houser (USA)	46.15
1928	Lemuel Clarence Houser (USA)	47.32
1932	John Anderson (USA)	49.49
1936	Kenneth Carpenter (USA)	50.48
1948	Adolfo Consolini (ITA)	52.78
1952	Sim Iness (USA)	55.03
1956	Alfred Oerter (USA)	56.36
1960	Alfred Oerter (USA)	59.18
1964	Alfred Oerter (USA)	61.00
1968	Alfred Oerter (USA)	64.78
1972	Ludvig Danek (TCH)	64.40
1976	Mac Wilkins (USA)	67.50
1980	Viktor Rashchupkin (URS)	66.64
1984	Rolf Danneberg (FRG)	66.60
1988	Jürgen Schult (GDR)	68.82
1992	Romas Ubartas (LTU)	65.12
1996	Lars Riedel (GER)	69.40
2000	Virgilijus Alekna (LTU)	69.30
2004	Virgilijus Alekna (LTU)[2]	69.89
2008	Gerd Kanter (EST)	68.82

DISCUS (GREEK STYLE)

		METERS
1908	Martin Sheridan (USA)	37.99

DISCUS (TWO HANDS)

		METERS
1912	Armas Taipale (FIN)	82.86

HAMMER THROW

		METERS
1900	John Flanagan (USA)	49.73
1904	John Flanagan (USA)	51.23
1908	John Flanagan (USA)	51.92
1912	Matthew McGrath (USA)	54.74
1920	Patrick Ryan (USA)	52.87
1924	Frederick Tootell (USA)	53.30
1928	Patrick O'Callaghan (IRL)	51.39
1932	Patrick O'Callaghan (IRL)	53.92
1936	Karl Hein (GER)	56.49
1948	Imre Nemeth (HUN)	56.07
1952	Jozsef Csermak (HUN)	60.34
1956	Harold Connolly (USA)	63.19
1960	Vasily Rudenkov (URS)	67.10
1964	Romuald Klim (URS)	69.74
1968	Gyula Zsivotzky (HUN)	73.36
1972	Anatoly Bondarchuk (URS)	75.50
1976	Yury Sedykh (URS)	77.52
1980	Yury Sedykh (URS)	81.80
1984	Juha Tiainen (FIN)	78.08
1988	Sergey Litvinov (URS)	84.80
1992	Andrey Abduvaliyev (UNT)	82.53
1996	Balazs Kiss (HUN)	81.24
2000	Szymon Ziolkowski (POL)	80.02
2004	Koji Murofushi (JPN)[2]	82.91
2008	Primoz Kozmus (SLO)	82.02

Athletics (Track and Field) (men) (continued)

JAVELIN THROW

		METERS
1908	Eric Lemming (SWE)	54.83
1912	Eric Lemming (SWE)	60.64
1920	Jonni Myyrä (FIN)	65.78
1924	Jonni Myyrä (FIN)	62.96
1928	Erik Lundkvist (SWE)	66.60
1932	Matti Järvinen (FIN)	72.71
1936	Gerhard Stöck (GER)	71.84
1948	Kai Rautavaara (FIN)	69.77
1952	Cy Young (USA)	73.78
1956	Egil Danielson (NOR)	85.71
1960	Viktor Tsybulenko (URS)	84.64
1964	Pauli Nevala (FIN)	82.66
1968	Janis Lusis (URS)	90.10
1972	Klaus Wolfermann (FRG)	90.48
1976	Miklos Nemeth (HUN)	94.58
1980	Dainis Kula (URS)	91.20
1984	Arto Härkönen (FIN)	86.76
1988	Tapio Korjus (FIN)	84.28
1992	Jan Zelezny (TCH)	89.66
1996	Jan Zelezny (CZE)	88.16
2000	Jan Zelezny (CZE)	90.17
2004	Andreas Thorkildsen (NOR)	86.50
2008	Andreas Thorkildsen (NOR)	90.57

JAVELIN (FREESTYLE)

		METERS
1908	Eric Lemming (SWE)	54.45

JAVELIN (TWO HANDS)

		METERS
1912	Juho Saaristo (FIN)	109.42

56-LB WEIGHT THROW

		METERS
1904	Étienne Desmarteau (CAN)	10.46
1920	Patrick McDonald (USA)	11.26

TUG-OF-WAR

1900	Sweden-Denmark
1904	United States
1908	Great Britain
1912	Sweden
1920	Great Britain

TRIATHLON (LONG JUMP/SHOT PUT/100 YARDS)

1904	Max Emmerich (USA)

PENTATHLON

1912	Jim Thorpe (USA)[6]; Ferdinand Bie (NOR) (cowinners)
1920	Eero Lehtonen (FIN)
1924	Eero Lehtonen (FIN)

DECATHLON

1904	Thomas Kiely (IRL)
1912	Jim Thorpe (USA)[6]; Hugo Wieslander (SWE) (cowinners)
1920	Helge Lövland (NOR)
1924	Harold Osborn (USA)
1928	Paavo Yrjölä (FIN)
1932	James Bausch (USA)
1936	Glenn Morris (USA)
1948	Robert Mathias (USA)
1952	Robert Mathias (USA)
1956	Milton Campbell (USA)
1960	Rafer Johnson (USA)
1964	Willi Holdorf (GER)
1968	William Toomey (USA)
1972	Nikolay Avilov (URS)
1976	Bruce Jenner (USA)

Summer Olympic Games (continued)

Athletics (Track and Field) (men) (continued)

DECATHLON (CONTINUED)

1980	Daley Thompson (GBR)	
1984	Daley Thompson (GBR)	
1988	Christian Schenk (GDR)	
1992	Robert Zmelik (TCH)	
1996	Dan O'Brien (USA)	
2000	Erki Nool (EST)	
2004	Roman Sebrle (CZE)	
2008	Bryan Clay (USA)	

Athletics (Track and Field) (women)

100 METERS — SEC

1928	Elizabeth Robinson (USA)	12.2
1932	Stanislawa Walasiewicz (POL)	11.9
1936	Helen Stephens (USA)	11.5
1948	Francina Blankers-Koen (NED)	11.9
1952	Marjorie Jackson (AUS)	11.5
1956	Elizabeth Cuthbert (AUS)	11.5
1960	Wilma Rudolph (USA)	11.0
1964	Wyomia Tyus (USA)	11.4
1968	Wyomia Tyus (USA)	11.0
1972	Renate Stecher (GDR)	11.07
1976	Annegret Richter (FRG)	11.08
1980	Lyudmila Kondratyeva (URS)	11.06
1984	Evelyn Ashford (USA)	10.97
1988	Florence Griffith Joyner (USA)	10.54
1992	Gail Devers (USA)	10.82
1996	Gail Devers (USA)	10.94
2000	winner stripped; undecided by press time	
2004	Yuliya Nesterenko (BLR)	10.93
2008	Shelly-Ann Fraser (JAM)	10.78

200 METERS — SEC

1948	Francina Blankers-Koen (NED)	24.4
1952	Marjorie Jackson (AUS)	23.7
1956	Elizabeth Cuthbert (AUS)	23.4
1960	Wilma Rudolph (USA)	24.0
1964	Edith Marie McGuire (USA)	23.0
1968	Irena Szewinska (POL)	22.5
1972	Renate Stecher (GDR)	22.40
1976	Bärbel Eckert (GDR)	22.37
1980	Bärbel Eckert-Wöckel (GDR)	22.03
1984	Valerie Brisco-Hooks (USA)	21.81
1988	Florence Griffith Joyner (USA)	21.34
1992	Gwen Torrence (USA)	21.81
1996	Marie-Jose Perec (FRA)	22.12
2000	winner stripped; undecided by press time	
2004	Veronica Campbell (JAM)	22.05
2008	Veronica Campbell-Brown (JAM)	21.74

400 METERS — SEC

1964	Elizabeth Cuthbert (AUS)	52.0
1968	Colette Besson (FRA)	52.0
1972	Monika Zehrt (GDR)	51.08
1976	Irena Szewinska (POL)	49.29
1980	Marita Koch (GDR)	48.88
1984	Valerie Brisco-Hooks (USA)	48.83
1988	Olga Bryzgina (URS)	48.65
1992	Marie-Jose Perec (FRA)	48.83
1996	Marie-Jose Perec (FRA)	48.25
2000	Cathy Freeman (AUS)	49.11
2004	Tonique Williams-Darling (BAH)	49.41
2008	Christine Ohuruogu (GBR)	49.62

800 METERS — MIN:SEC

1928	Lina Radke-Batschauer (GER)	2:16.8
1960	Lyudmila Lysenko-Shevtsova (URS)	2:04.3
1964	Ann Packer (GBR)	2:01.1

Athletics (Track and Field) (women) (continued)

800 METERS (CONTINUED) — MIN:SEC

1968	Madeline Manning (USA)	2:00.9
1972	Hildegard Falck (FRG)	1:58.6
1976	Tatyana Kazankina (URS)	1:54.94
1980	Nadezhda Olizarenko (URS)	1:53.50
1984	Doina Melinte (ROM)	1:57.60
1988	Sigrun Wodars (GDR)	1:56.10
1992	Ellen van Langen (NED)	1:55.54
1996	Svetlana Masterkova (RUS)	1:57.73
2000	Maria Mutola (MOZ)	1:56.15
2004	Kelly Holmes (GBR)	1:56.38
2008	Pamela Jelimo (KEN)	1:54.87

1,500 METERS — MIN:SEC

1972	Lyudmila Bragina (URS)	4:01.4
1976	Tatyana Kazankina (URS)	4:05.48
1980	Tatyana Kazankina (URS)	3:56.56
1984	Gabriella Dorio (ITA)	4:03.25
1988	Paula Ivan (ROM)	3:53.96
1992	Hassiba Boulmerka (ALG)	3:55.30
1996	Svetlana Masterkova (RUS)	4:00.83
2000	Nouria Merah-Benida (ALG)	4:05.10
2004	Kelly Holmes (GBR)	3:57.90
2008	Nancy Jebet Langat (KEN)	4:00.23

3,000 METERS — MIN:SEC

1984	Maricica Puica (ROM)	8:35.96
1988	Tatyana Samolenko (URS)	8:26.53
1992	Yelena Romanova (UNT)	8:46.04

3,000-METER STEEPLECHASE — MIN:SEC

2008	Gulnara Samitova-Galkina (RUS)	8:58.81

5,000 METERS — MIN:SEC

1996	Wang Jungxia (CHN)	14:59.88
2000	Gabriela Szabo (ROM)	14:40.79
2004	Meseret Defar (ETH)	14:45.65
2008	Tirunesh Dibaba (ETH)	15:41.40

10,000 METERS — MIN:SEC

1988	Olga Bondarenko (URS)	31:05.21
1992	Derartu Tulu (ETH)	31:06.02
1996	Fernanda Ribeiro (POR)	31:01.63
2000	Derartu Tulu (ETH)	30:17.49
2004	Xing Huina (CHN)	30:24.36
2008	Tirunesh Dibaba (ETH)	29:54.66

MARATHON — HR:MIN:SEC

1984	Joan Benoit (USA)	2:24:52
1988	Rosa Mota (POR)	2:25:40
1992	Valentina Yegorova (UNT)	2:32:41
1996	Fatuma Roba (ETH)	2:26:05
2000	Naoko Takahashi (JPN)	2:23:14
2004	Mizuki Noguchi (JPN)	2:26:20
2008	Constantina Tomescu (ROM)	2:26:44

100-METER HURDLES[7] — SEC

1932	Mildred "Babe" Didrikson (USA)	11.7
1936	Trebisonda Valla (ITA)	11.7
1948	Francina Blankers-Koen (NED)	11.2
1952	Shirley Strickland de La Hunty (AUS)	10.9
1956	Shirley Strickland de La Hunty (AUS)	10.7
1960	Irina Press (URS)	10.8
1964	Karin Balzer (GER)	10.5
1968	Maureen Caird (AUS)	10.3
1972	Annelie Ehrhardt (GDR)	12.59
1976	Johanna Schaller (GDR)	12.77
1980	Vera Komisova (URS)	12.56

Summer Olympic Games (continued)

Athletics (Track and Field) (women) (continued)

100-METER HURDLES[7] (CONT.)

		SEC
1984	Benita Fitzgerald-Brown (USA)	12.84
1988	Iordanka Donkova (BUL)	12.38
1992	Paraskevi Patoulidou (GRE)	12.64
1996	Ludmila Engquist (SWE)	12.58
2000	Olga Shishigina (KAZ)	12.65
2004	Joanna Hayes (USA)	12.37
2008	Dawn Harper (USA)	12.54

400-METER HURDLES

		SEC
1984	Nawal el Moutawakel (MAR)	54.61
1988	Debra Flintoff-King (AUS)	53.17
1992	Sally Gunnell (GBR)	53.23
1996	Deon Hemmings (JAM)	52.82
2000	Irina Privalova (RUS)	53.02
2004	Fani Halkia (GRE)	52.82
2008	Melaine Walker (JAM)	52.64

4 × 100-METER RELAY

		SEC
1928	Canada	48.4
1932	United States	47.0
1936	United States	46.9
1948	The Netherlands	47.5
1952	United States	45.9
1956	Australia	44.5
1960	United States	44.5
1964	Poland	43.6
1968	United States	42.8
1972	West Germany	42.81
1976	East Germany	42.55
1980	East Germany	41.60
1984	United States	41.65
1988	United States	41.98
1992	United States	42.11
1996	United States	41.95
2000	The Bahamas	41.95
2004	Jamaica	41.73
2008	Russia	42.31

4 × 400-METER RELAY

		MIN:SEC
1972	East Germany	3:23.0
1976	East Germany	3:19.23
1980	USSR	3:20.2
1984	United States	3:18.29
1988	USSR	3:15.18
1992	Unified Team	3:20.20
1996	United States	3:20.91
2000	winner stripped; undecided by press time	
2004	United States	3:19.01
2008	United States	3:18.54

10,000-METER WALK

		MIN:SEC
1992	Chen Yueling (CHN)	44:32
1996	Yelena Nikolayeva (RUS)	41:49

20,000-METER WALK

		HR:MIN:SEC
2000	Wang Liping (CHN)	1:29:05
2004	Athanasia Tsoumeleka (GRE)	1:29:12
2008	Olga Kaniskina (RUS)	1:26:31

HIGH JUMP

		METERS
1928	Ethel Catherwood (CAN)	1.59
1932	Jean Shiley (USA)	1.66
1936	Ibolya Csak (HUN)	1.60
1948	Alice Coachman (USA)	1.68
1952	Esther Brand (RSA)	1.67
1956	Mildred Louise McDaniel (USA)	1.76
1960	Iolanda Balas (ROM)	1.85

Athletics (Track and Field) (women) (continued)

HIGH JUMP (CONTINUED)

		METERS
1964	Iolanda Balas (ROM)	1.90
1968	Miloslava Rezkova (TCH)	1.82
1972	Ulrike Meyfarth (FRG)	1.92
1976	Rosemarie Ackermann (GDR)	1.93
1980	Sara Simeoni (ITA)	1.97
1984	Ulrike Meyfarth (FRG)	2.02
1988	Louise Ritter (USA)	2.03
1992	Heike Henkel (GER)	2.02
1996	Stefka Kostadinova (BUL)	2.05
2000	Yelena Yelesina (RUS)	2.01
2004	Yelena Slesarenko (RUS)	2.06
2008	Tia Hellebaut (BEL)	2.05

POLE VAULT

		METERS
2000	Stacy Dragila (USA)	4.60
2004	Yelena Isinbayeva (RUS)	4.91
2008	Yelena Isinbayeva (RUS)	5.05

LONG JUMP

		METERS
1948	Olga Gyarmati (HUN)	5.69
1952	Yvette Williams (NZL)	6.24
1956	Elzbieta Krzesinska (POL)	6.35
1960	Vera Krepkina (URS)	6.37
1964	Mary Rand (GBR)	6.76
1968	Viorica Viscopoleanu (ROM)	6.82
1972	Heidemarie Rosendahl (FRG)	6.78
1976	Angela Voigt (GDR)	6.72
1980	Tatyana Kolpakova (URS)	7.06
1984	Anisoara Stanciu (ROM)	6.96
1988	Jackie Joyner-Kersee (USA)	7.40
1992	Heike Drechsler (GER)	7.14
1996	Chioma Ajunwa (NGR)	7.12
2000	Heike Drechsler (GER)	6.99
2004	Tatyana Lebedeva (RUS)	7.07
2008	Maurren Higa Maggi (BRA)	7.04

TRIPLE JUMP

		METERS
1996	Inessa Kravets (UKR)	15.33
2000	Tereza Marinova (BUL)	15.20
2004	Françoise Mbango Etone (CMR)	15.30
2008	Françoise Mbango Etone (CMR)	15.39

SHOT PUT

		METERS
1948	Micheline Ostermeyer (FRA)	13.75
1952	Galina Zybina (URS)	15.28
1956	Tamara Tyshkevich (URS)	16.59
1960	Tamara Press (URS)	17.32
1964	Tamara Press (URS)	18.14
1968	Margitta Gummel (GDR)	19.61
1972	Nadezhda Chizhova (URS)	21.03
1976	Ivanka Khristova (BUL)	21.16
1980	Ilona Slupianek (GDR)	22.41
1984	Claudia Losch (FRG)	20.48
1988	Natalya Lisovskaya (URS)	22.24
1992	Svetlana Krivalyova (UNT)	21.06
1996	Astrid Kumbernuss (GER)	20.56
2000	Yanina Korolchik (BLR)	20.56
2004	Yumileidi Cumba (CUB)[2]	19.59
2008	Valerie Vili (NZL)	20.56

DISCUS THROW

		METERS
1928	Halina Konopacka (POL)	39.62
1932	Lillian Copeland (USA)	40.58
1936	Gisela Mauermayer (GER)	47.63
1948	Micheline Ostermeyer (FRA)	41.92
1952	Nina Romashkova (URS)	51.42
1956	Olga Fikotova (TCH)	53.69

Summer Olympic Games (continued)

Athletics (Track and Field) (women) (continued)

DISCUS THROW (CONTINUED) — **METERS**

Year	Athlete	Meters
1960	Nina Ponomaryova-Romashkova (URS)	55.10
1964	Tamara Press (URS)	57.27
1968	Lia Manoliu (ROM)	58.28
1972	Faina Melnik (URS)	66.62
1976	Evelin Schlaak (GDR)	69.00
1980	Evelin Schlaak Jahl (GDR)	69.96
1984	Ria Stalman (NED)	65.36
1988	Martina Hellmann (GDR)	72.30
1992	Maritza Marten (CUB)	70.06
1996	Ilke Wyludda (GER)	69.66
2000	Ellina Zvereva (BLR)	68.40
2004	Natalya Sadova (RUS)	67.02
2008	Stephanie Brown Trafton (USA)	64.74

HAMMER THROW — **METERS**

Year	Athlete	Meters
2000	Kamila Skolimowska (POL)	71.16
2004	Olga Kuzenkova (RUS)	75.02
2008	Aksana Miankova (BLR)	76.34

JAVELIN THROW — **METERS**

Year	Athlete	Meters
1932	Mildred "Babe" Didrikson (USA)	43.68
1936	Tilly Fleischer (GER)	45.18
1948	Hermine Bauma (AUT)	45.57
1952	Dana Zatopkova (TCH)	50.47
1956	Inese Jaunzeme (URS)	53.86
1960	Elvira Ozolina (URS)	55.98
1964	Mihaela Penes (ROM)	60.54
1968	Angela Nemeth (HUN)	60.36
1972	Ruth Fuchs (GDR)	63.88
1976	Ruth Fuchs (GDR)	65.94
1980	María Colón (CUB)	68.40
1984	Tessa Sanderson (GBR)	69.56
1988	Petra Felke (GDR)	74.68
1992	Silke Renk (GER)	68.34
1996	Heli Rantanen (FIN)	67.94
2000	Trine Hattestad (NOR)	68.91
2004	Osleidys Menéndez (CUB)	71.53
2008	Barbora Spotakova (CZE)	71.42

HEPTATHLON[8]

1964	Irina Press (URS)
1968	Ingrid Becker (FRG)
1972	Mary Peters (GBR)
1976	Siegrun Siegl (GDR)
1980	Nadezhda Tkachenko (URS)
1984	Glynis Nunn (AUS)
1988	Jackie Joyner-Kersee (USA)
1992	Jackie Joyner-Kersee (USA)
1996	Ghada Shouaa (SYR)
2000	Denise Lewis (GBR)
2004	Carolina Klüft (SWE)
2008	Nataliya Dobrynska (UKR)

Badminton

MEN'S SINGLES

1992	Allan Budi Kusuma (INA)
1996	Poul-Erik Hoyer-Larsen (DEN)
2000	Ji Xinpeng (CHN)
2004	Taufik Hidayat (INA)
2008	Lin Dan (CHN)

MEN'S DOUBLES

1992	Republic of Korea
1996	Indonesia
2000	Indonesia
2004	Republic of Korea
2008	Indonesia

Badminton (continued)

WOMEN'S SINGLES

1992	Susi Susanti (INA)
1996	Bang Soo-Hyun (KOR)
2000	Gong Zhichao (CHN)
2004	Zhang Ning (CHN)
2008	Zhang Ning (CHN)

WOMEN'S DOUBLES

1992	Republic of Korea
1996	China
2000	China
2004	China
2008	China

MIXED DOUBLES

1996	Republic of Korea
2000	China
2004	China
2008	Republic of Korea

Baseball

1992	Cuba
1996	Cuba
2000	United States
2004	Cuba
2008	Republic of Korea

Basketball

MEN

1936	United States
1948	United States
1952	United States
1956	United States
1960	United States
1964	United States
1968	United States
1972	USSR
1976	United States
1980	Yugoslavia
1984	United States
1988	USSR
1992	United States
1996	United States
2000	United States
2004	Argentina
2008	United States

WOMEN

1976	USSR
1980	USSR
1984	United States
1988	United States
1992	Unified Team
1996	United States
2000	United States
2004	United States
2008	United States

Boxing[9]

48 KG (105.6 LB)

1968	Francisco Rodríguez (VEN)
1972	Gyorgy Gedo (HUN)
1976	Jorge Hernández (CUB)
1980	Shamil Sabyrov (URS)
1984	Paul Gonzales (USA)
1988	Ivailo Khristov (BUL)
1992	Rogelio Marcelo (CUB)
1996	Daniel Petrov Bojilov (BUL)

Summer Olympic Games (continued)

Boxing[9] (continued)

48 KG (105.6 LB) (CONTINUED)
2000	Brahim Asloum (FRA)
2004	Yan Bhartelemy Varela (CUB)
2008	Zou Shiming (CHN)

51 KG (112 LB)
1904	George Finnegan (USA)
1920	Frank di Genaro (USA)
1924	Fidel La Barba (USA)
1928	Antal Kocsis (HUN)
1932	Istvan Enekes (HUN)
1936	Willi Kaiser (GER)
1948	Pascual Pérez (ARG)
1952	Nate Brooks (USA)
1956	Terence Spinks (GBR)
1960	Gyula Torok (HUN)
1964	Fernando Atzori (ITA)
1968	Ricardo Delgado (MEX)
1972	Georgi Kostadinov (BUL)
1976	Leo Randolph (USA)
1980	Petar Lesov (BUL)
1984	Steven McCrory (USA)
1988	Kim Kwang Sun (KOR)
1992	Chol Choi Su (PRK)
1996	Maikro Romero (CUB)
2000	Wijan Ponlid (THA)
2004	Yuriorkis Gamboa Toledano (CUB)
2008	Somjit Jongjohor (THA)

54 KG (118.8 LB)
1904	Oliver Kirk (USA)
1908	Henry Thomas (GBR)
1920	Clarence Walker (RSA)
1924	William Smith (RSA)
1928	Vittorio Tamagnini (ITA)
1932	Horace Gwynne (CAN)
1936	Ulderico Sergo (ITA)
1948	Tibor Csik (HUN)
1952	Pentti Hämäläinen (FIN)
1956	Wolfgang Behrendt (GER)
1960	Oleg Grigoryev (URS)
1964	Takao Sakurai (JPN)
1968	Valery Sokolov (URS)
1972	Orlando Martínez (CUB)
1976	Gu Yong Jo (PRK)
1980	Juan Hernández (CUB)
1984	Maurizio Stecca (ITA)
1988	Kennedy McKinney (USA)
1992	Joel Casamayor (CUB)
1996	Istvan Kovacs (HUN)
2000	Guillermo Rigondeaux Ortiz (CUB)
2004	Guillermo Rigondeaux Ortiz (CUB)
2008	Badar-Uugan Enkhbat (MGL)

57 KG (125.4 LB)
1904	Oliver Kirk (USA)
1908	Richard Gunn (GBR)
1920	Paul Fritsch (FRA)
1924	John Fields (USA)
1928	Lambertus van Kleveren (NED)
1932	Carmelo Robledo (ARG)
1936	Oscar Casanovas (ARG)
1948	Ernesto Formenti (ITA)
1952	Jan Zachara (TCH)
1956	Vladimir Safronov (URS)
1960	Francesco Musso (ITA)
1964	Stanislav Stepashkin (URS)
1968	Antonio Roldan (MEX)

Boxing[9] (continued)

57 KG (125.4 LB) (CONTINUED)
1972	Boris Kuznetsov (URS)
1976	Angel Herrera (CUB)
1980	Rudi Fink (GDR)
1984	Meldrick Taylor (USA)
1988	Giovanni Parisi (ITA)
1992	Andreas Tews (GER)
1996	Somluck Kamsing (THA)
2000	Bekzat Sattarkhanov (KAZ)
2004	Aleksey Tishchenko (RUS)
2008	Vasyl Lomachenko (UKR)

60 KG (132 LB)
1904	Harry Spanger (USA)
1908	Frederick Grace (GBR)
1920	Samuel Mosberg (USA)
1924	Hans Nielsen (DEN)
1928	Carlo Orlandi (ITA)
1932	Lawrence Stevens (RSA)
1936	Imre Harangi (HUN)
1948	Gerald Dreyer (RSA)
1952	Aureliano Bolognesi (ITA)
1956	Richard McTaggart (GBR)
1960	Kazimierz Pazdzior (POL)
1964	Jozef Grudzien (POL)
1968	Ronnie Harris (USA)
1972	Jan Szczepanski (POL)
1976	Howard Davis (USA)
1980	Angel Herrera (CUB)
1984	Pernell Whitaker (USA)
1988	Andreas Zuelow (GDR)
1992	Oscar De La Hoya (USA)
1996	Hocine Soltani (ALG)
2000	Mario Kindelan (CUB)
2004	Mario César Kindelan Mesa (CUB)
2008	Aleksey Tishchenko (RUS)

64 KG (140.8 LB)
1952	Charles Adkins (USA)
1956	Vladimir Engibaryan (URS)
1960	Bohumil Nemecek (TCH)
1964	Jerzy Kulej (POL)
1968	Jerzy Kulej (POL)
1972	Ray Seales (USA)
1976	Ray Leonard (USA)
1980	Patrizio Oliva (ITA)
1984	Jerry Page (USA)
1988	Vyacheslav Yanovsky (URS)
1992	Héctor Vinent (CUB)
1996	Héctor Vinent (CUB)
2000	Mahamadkadyz Abdullayev (UZB)
2004	Manus Boonjumnong (THA)
2008	Félix Díaz (DOM)

69 KG (151.8 LB)
1904	Albert Young (USA)
1920	Julius Schneider (CAN)
1924	Jean Delarge (BEL)
1928	Edward Morgan (NZL)
1932	Edward Flynn (USA)
1936	Sten Suvio (FIN)
1948	Julius Torma (TCH)
1952	Zygmunt Chychla (POL)
1956	Nicolae Linca (ROM)
1960	Giovanni Benvenuti (ITA)
1964	Marian Kasprzyk (POL)
1968	Manfred Wolke (GDR)
1972	Emilio Correa (CUB)

Summer Olympic Games (continued)

Boxing[9] (continued)

69 KG (151.8 LB) (CONTINUED)

1976	Jochen Bachfeld (GDR)
1980	Andres Aldama (CUB)
1984	Mark Breland (USA)
1988	Robert Wangila (KEN)
1992	Michael Carruth (IRL)
1996	Oleg Saytov (RUS)
2000	Oleg Saytov (RUS)
2004	Bakhtiyar Artayev (KAZ)
2008	Bakhyt Sarsekbayev (KAZ)

71 KG (156.2 LB)

1952	Laszlo Papp (HUN)
1956	Laszlo Papp (HUN)
1960	Wilbert McClure (USA)
1964	Boris Lagutin (URS)
1968	Boris Lagutin (URS)
1972	Dieter Kottysch (FRG)
1976	Jerzy Rybicki (POL)
1980	Armando Martínez (CUB)
1984	Frank Tate (USA)
1988	Park Si Hun (KOR)
1992	Juan Lemus (CUB)
1996	David Reid (USA)
2000	Yermakhan Ibraimov (KAZ)

75 KG (165 LB)

1904	Charles Mayer (USA)
1908	John Douglas (GBR)
1920	Harry Mallin (GBR)
1924	Harry Mallin (GBR)
1928	Piero Toscani (ITA)
1932	Carmen Barth (USA)
1936	Jean Despeaux (FRA)
1948	Laszlo Papp (HUN)
1952	Floyd Patterson (USA)
1956	Gennady Shatkov (URS)
1960	Edward Crook (USA)
1964	Valery Popenchenko (URS)
1968	Christopher Finnegan (GBR)
1972	Vyatcheslav Lemeshev (URS)
1976	Michael Spinks (USA)
1980	Jose Gómez (CUB)
1984	Shin Joon Sup (KOR)
1988	Henry Maske (GDR)
1992	Ariel Hernández (CUB)
1996	Ariel Hernández (CUB)
2000	Jorge Gutiérrez (CUB)
2004	Gaydarbek Gaydarbekov (RUS)
2008	James Degale (GBR)

81 KG (178.2 LB)

1920	Edward Eagan (USA)
1924	Harry Mitchell (GBR)
1928	Viktor Avendano (ARG)
1932	David Carstens (RSA)
1936	Roger Michelot (FRA)
1948	George Hunter (RSA)
1952	Norvel Lee (USA)
1956	James Boyd (USA)
1960	Cassius Clay (USA)
1964	Cosimo Pinto (ITA)
1968	Dan Poznyak (URS)
1972	Mate Parlov (YUG)
1976	Leon Spinks (USA)
1980	Slobodan Kacar (YUG)
1984	Anton Josipovic (YUG)
1988	Andrew Maynard (USA)

Boxing[9] (continued)

81 KG (178.2 LB) (CONTINUED)

1992	Torsten May (GER)
1996	Vasily Zhirov (KAZ)
2000	Aleksandr Lebzyak (RUS)
2004	Andre Ward (USA)
2008	Zhang Xiaoping (CHN)

91 KG (200.2 LB)

1904	Samuel Berger (USA)
1908	Albert Oldman (GBR)
1920	Ronald Rawson (GBR)
1924	Otto Von Porat (NOR)
1928	Arturo Rodriguez (ARG)
1932	Alberto Santiago Lovell (ARG)
1936	Herbert Runge (GER)
1948	Rafael Iglesias (ARG)
1952	Edward Sanders (USA)
1956	Peter Rademacher (USA)
1960	Franco de Piccoli (ITA)
1964	Joseph Frazier (USA)
1968	George Foreman (USA)
1972	Teofilo Stevenson (CUB)
1976	Teofilo Stevenson (CUB)
1980	Teofilo Stevenson (CUB)
1984	Henry Tillman (USA)
1988	Ray Mercer (USA)
1992	Félix Savon (CUB)
1996	Félix Savon (CUB)
2000	Félix Savon (CUB)
2004	Odlanier Solis Fonte (CUB)
2008	Rakhim Chakhkiyev (RUS)

OVER 91 KG (200.2 LB)

1984	Tyrell Biggs (USA)
1988	Lennox Lewis (CAN)
1992	Roberto Balado (CUB)
1996	Vladimir Klichko (UKR)
2000	Audley Harrison (GBR)
2004	Aleksandr Povetkin (RUS)
2008	Roberto Cammarelle (ITA)

Canoeing (men)

KAYAK SINGLES (500 METERS)		MIN:SEC
1976	Vasile Diba (ROM)	1:46.41
1980	Vladimir Parfenovich (URS)	1:43.43
1984	Ian Ferguson (NZL)	1:47.84
1988	Zsolt Gyulay (HUN)	1:44.82
1992	Mikko Kolehmainen (FIN)	1:40.34
1996	Antonio Rossi (ITA)	1:37.423
2000	Knut Holmann (NOR)	1:57.847
2004	Adam van Koeverden (CAN)	1:37.919
2008	Ken Wallace (AUS)	1:37.252

KAYAK PAIRS (500 METERS)		MIN:SEC
1976	East Germany	1:35.87
1980	USSR	1:32.38
1984	New Zealand	1:34.21
1988	New Zealand	1:33.98
1992	Germany	1:29.84
1996	Germany	1:28.697
2000	Hungary	1:47.050
2004	Germany	1:27.040
2008	Spain	1:28.736

KAYAK SINGLES (1,000 METERS)		MIN:SEC
1936	Gregor Hradetzky (AUT)	4:22.90
1948	Gert Fredriksson (SWE)	4:33.20
1952	Gert Fredriksson (SWE)	4:07.90

Summer Olympic Games (continued)

Canoeing (men) (continued)

KAYAK SINGLES (1,000 METERS) (CONTINUED)

Year	Athlete	MIN:SEC
1956	Gert Fredriksson (SWE)	4:12.80
1960	Erik Hansen (DEN)	3:53.00
1964	Rolf Peterson (SWE)	3:57.13
1968	Mihaly Hesz (HUN)	4:03.58
1972	Aleksandr Shaparenko (URS)	3:48.06
1976	Rüdiger Helm (GDR)	3:48.20
1980	Rüdiger Helm (GDR)	3:48.77
1984	Alan Thompson (NZL)	3:45.73
1988	Gregory Barton (USA)	3:55.27
1992	Clint Robinson (AUS)	3:37.26
1996	Knut Holmann (NOR)	3:25.785
2000	Knut Holmann (NOR)	3:33.269
2004	Eirik Veraas Larsen (NOR)	3:25.897
2008	Tim Brabants (GBR)	3:26.323

KAYAK PAIRS (1,000 METERS)

Year	Country	MIN:SEC
1936	Austria	4:03.80
1948	Sweden	4:07.30
1952	Finland	3:51.10
1956	Germany	3:49.60
1960	Sweden	3:34.70
1964	Sweden	3:38.54
1968	USSR	3:37.54
1972	USSR	3:31.23
1976	USSR	3:29.01
1980	USSR	3:26.72
1984	Canada	3:24.22
1988	United States	3:32.42
1992	Germany	3:16.10
1996	Italy	3:09.190
2000	Italy	3:14.461
2004	Sweden	3:18.420
2008	Germany	3:11.809

KAYAK FOURS (1,000 METERS)

Year	Country	MIN:SEC
1964	USSR	3:14.67
1968	Norway	3:14.38
1972	USSR	3:14.02
1976	USSR	3:08.69
1980	East Germany	3:13.76
1984	New Zealand	3:02.28
1988	Hungary	3:00.20
1992	Germany	2:54.18
1996	Germany	2:51.528
2000	Hungary	2:55.188
2004	Hungary	2:56.919
2008	Belarus	2:55.714

KAYAK SINGLES (10,000 METERS)

Year	Athlete	MIN:SEC
1936	Ernst Krebs (GER)	46:01.6
1948	Gert Fredriksson (SWE)	50:47.7
1952	Thorvald Strömberg (FIN)	47:22.8
1956	Gert Fredriksson (SWE)	47:43.4

KAYAK PAIRS (10,000 METERS)

Year	Country	MIN:SEC
1936	Germany	41:45.0
1948	Sweden	46:09.4
1952	Finland	44:21.3
1956	Hungary	43:37.0

COLLAPSIBLE KAYAK SINGLES (10,000 METERS)

Year	Athlete	MIN:SEC
1936	Gregor Hradetzky (AUT)	50:01.2

COLLAPSIBLE KAYAK PAIRS (10,000 METERS)

Year	Country	MIN:SEC
1936	Sweden	45:48.9

Canoeing (men) (continued)

KAYAK SINGLES RELAY (1,500 METERS)

Year	Country	MIN:SEC
1960	Germany	7:39.43

SLALOM KAYAK SINGLES

1972	Siegbert Horn (GDR)
1992	Pierpaolo Ferrazzi (ITA)
1996	Oliver Fix (GER)
2000	Thomas Schmidt (GER)
2004	Benoit Peschier (FRA)
2008	Alexander Grimm (GER)

CANADIAN SINGLES (500 METERS)

Year	Athlete	MIN:SEC
1976	Aleksandr Rogov (URS)	1:59.23
1980	Sergey Postrekin (URS)	1:53.37
1984	Larry Cain (CAN)	1:57.01
1988	Olaf Heukrodt (GDR)	1:56.42
1992	Nikolay Bukhalov (BUL)	1:51.15
1996	Martin Doktor (CZE)	1:49.934
2000	Gyorgy Kolonics (HUN)	2:24.813
2004	Andreas Dittmer (GER)	1:46.383
2008	Maksim Opalev (RUS)	1:47.140

CANADIAN PAIRS (500 METERS)

Year	Country	MIN:SEC
1976	USSR	1:45.81
1980	Hungary	1:43.39
1984	Yugoslavia	1:43.67
1988	USSR	1:41.77
1992	Unified Team	1:41.54
1996	Hungary	1:40.420
2000	Hungary	1:51.284
2004	China	1:40.278
2008	China	1:41.025

CANADIAN SINGLES (1,000 METERS)

Year	Athlete	MIN:SEC
1936	Francis Amyot (CAN)	5:32.10
1948	Josef Holecek (TCH)	5:42.00
1952	Josef Holecek (TCH)	4:56.30
1956	Leon Rottman (ROM)	5:05.30
1960	Janos Parti (HUN)	4:33.03
1964	Jürgen Eschert (GER)	4:35.14
1968	Tibor Tatai (HUN)	4:36.14
1972	Ivan Patzaichin (ROM)	4:08.94
1976	Matija Ljubek (YUG)	4:09.51
1980	Lyubomir Lyubenov (BUL)	4:12.38
1984	Ulrich Eicke (FRG)	4:06.32
1988	Ivans Klementyev (URS)	4:12.78
1992	Nikolay Bukhalov (BUL)	4:05.92
1996	Martin Doktor (CZE)	3:54.418
2000	Andreas Dittmer (GER)	3:54.379
2004	David Cal (ESP)	3:46.201
2008	Attila Sándor Vajda (HUN)	3:50.467

CANADIAN PAIRS (1,000 METERS)

Year	Country	MIN:SEC
1936	Czechoslovakia	4:50.10
1948	Czechoslovakia	5:07.10
1952	Denmark	4:38.30
1956	Romania	4:47.40
1960	USSR	4:17.04
1964	USSR	4:04.65
1968	Romania	4:07.18
1972	USSR	3:52.60
1976	USSR	3:52.76
1980	Romania	3:47.65
1984	Romania	3:40.60
1988	USSR	3:48.36
1992	Germany	3:37.42
1996	Germany	3:31.870
2000	Romania	3:37.355

Summer Olympic Games (continued)

Canoeing (men) (continued)

CANADIAN PAIRS (1,000 METERS) (CONTINUED)

		MIN:SEC
2004	Germany	3:41.802
2008	Belarus	3:36.365

CANADIAN SINGLES (10,000 METERS)

		MIN:SEC
1948	Frantisek Capek (TCH)	62:05.2
1952	Frank Havens (USA)	57:41.1
1956	Leon Rottman (ROM)	56:41.0

CANADIAN PAIRS (10,000 METERS)

		MIN:SEC
1936	Czechoslovakia	50:35.5
1948	United States	55:55.4
1952	France	54:08.3
1956	USSR	54:02.4

SLALOM CANADIAN SINGLES

1972	Reinhard Eiben (GDR)
1992	Lukas Pollert (TCH)
1996	Michal Martikan (SVK)
2000	Tony Estanguet (FRA)
2004	Tony Estanguet (FRA)
2008	Michal Martikan (SVK)

SLALOM CANADIAN PAIRS

1972	East Germany
1992	United States
1996	France
2000	Slovakia
2004	Slovakia
2008	Slovakia

Canoeing (women)

KAYAK SINGLES (500 METERS)

		MIN:SEC
1948	Karen Hoff (DEN)	2:31.90
1952	Sylvi Saimo (FIN)	2:18.40
1956	Yelizaveta Dementyeva (URS)	2:18.90
1960	Antonina Seredina (URS)	2:08.08
1964	Lyudmila Khvedosyuk (URS)	2:12.87
1968	Lyudmila Pinayeva-Khvedosyuk (URS)	2:11.09
1972	Yuliya Ryabchinskaya (URS)	2:03.17
1976	Carola Zirzow (GDR)	2:01.05
1980	Birgit Fischer (GDR)	1:57.96
1984	Agneta Andersson (SWE)	1:58.72
1988	Vanya Gecheva (BUL)	1:55.19
1992	Birgit Fischer Schmidt (GER)	1:51.60
1996	Rita Koban (HUN)	1:47.655
2000	Josefa Idem Guerrini (ITA)	2:13.848
2004	Natasa Janics (HUN)	1:47.741
2008	Inna Osypenko-Radomska (UKR)	1:50.673

KAYAK PAIRS (500 METERS)

		MIN:SEC
1960	USSR	1:54.76
1964	Germany	1:56.95
1968	West Germany	1:56.44
1972	USSR	1:53.50
1976	USSR	1:51.15
1980	East Germany	1:43.88
1984	Sweden	1:45.25
1988	East Germany	1:43.46
1992	Germany	1:40.29
1996	Sweden	1:39.329
2000	Germany	1:56.996
2004	Hungary	1:38.101
2008	Hungary	1:41.308

KAYAK FOURS (500 METERS)

		MIN:SEC
1984	Romania	1:38.34
1988	East Germany	1:40.78

KAYAK FOURS (500 METERS) (CONTINUED)

		MIN:SEC
1992	Hungary	1:38.32
1996	Germany	1:31.077
2000	Germany	1:34.532
2004	Germany	1:34.340
2008	Germany	1:32.231

SLALOM KAYAK SINGLES

1972	Angelika Bahmann (GDR)
1992	Elisabeth Micheler (GER)
1996	Stepanka Hilgertova (CZE)
2000	Stepanka Hilgertova (CZE)
2004	Elena Kaliska (SVK)
2008	Elena Kaliska (SVK)

Cricket

1900	Great Britain

Croquet

SINGLES (ONE BALL)

1900	Aumoitte (FRA)

SINGLES (TWO BALLS)

1900	Waydelick (FRA)

DOUBLES

1900	France

Cycling (men)

1,000-METER INDIVIDUAL SPRINT

1896[10]	Paul Masson (FRA)
1900[10]	Georges Taillandier (FRA)
1920	Mauritius Peeters (NED)
1924	Lucien Michard (FRA)
1928	Roger Beaufrand (FRA)
1932	Jacobus Van Egmond (NED)
1936	Toni Merkens (GER)
1948	Mario Ghella (ITA)
1952	Enzo Sacchi (ITA)
1956	Michel Rousseau (FRA)
1960	Sante Gaiardoni (ITA)
1964	Giovanni Pettenella (ITA)
1968	Daniel Morelon (FRA)
1972	Daniel Morelon (FRA)
1976	Anton Tkac (TCH)
1980	Lutz Hesslich (GDR)
1984	Mark Gorski (USA)
1988	Lutz Hesslich (GDR)
1992	Jens Fiedler (GER)
1996	Jens Fiedler (GER)
2000	Marty Nothstein (USA)
2004	Ryan Bayley (AUS)
2008	Chris Hoy (GBR)

1,000-METER TIME TRIAL

		MIN:SEC
1896[11]	Paul Masson (FRA)	24.0
1928	Willy Falck-Hansen (DEN)	1:14.4
1932	Edgar Gray (AUS)	1:13.0
1936	Arie van Vliet (NED)	1:12.0
1948	Jacques Dupont (FRA)	1:13.5
1952	Russell Mockridge (AUS)	1:11.1
1956	Leandro Faggin (ITA)	1:09.8
1960	Sante Gaiardoni (ITA)	1:07.27
1964	Patrick Sercu (BEL)	1:09.59
1968	Pierre Trentin (FRA)	1:03.91
1972	Niels Fredborg (DEN)	1:06.44
1976	Klaus-Jürgen Grünke (GDR)	1:05.927
1980	Lothar Thoms (GDR)	1:02.955

Summer Olympic Games (continued)

Cycling (men) (continued)

1,000-METER TIME TRIAL (CONTINUED)	MIN:SEC
1984 Fredy Schmidtke (FRG)	1:06.104
1988 Aleksandr Kirichenko (URS)	1:04.499
1992 José Moreno (ESP)	1:03.342
1996 Florian Rousseau (FRA)	1:02.712
2000 Jason Queally (GBR)	1:01.609
2004 Chris Hoy (GBR)	1:00.711

1,500-METER TEAM PURSUIT
1900 United States

2,000 METERS
1904 Marcus Hurley (USA)

2,000-METER TANDEM
1908 France
1920 Great Britain
1924 France
1928 The Netherlands
1932 France
1936 Germany
1948 Italy
1952 Australia
1956 Australia
1960 Italy
1964 Italy
1968 France
1972 USSR

INDIVIDUAL PURSUIT
1964 Jiri Daler (TCH)
1968 Daniel Rebillard (FRA)
1972 Knut Knudsen (NOR)
1976 Gregor Braun (FRG)
1980 Robert Dill-Bondi (SUI)
1984 Steve Hegg (USA)
1988 Gintautas Umaras (URS)
1992 Christopher Boardman (GBR)
1996 Andrea Collinelli (ITA)
2000 Robert Bartko (GER)
2004 Bradley Wiggins (GBR)
2008 Bradley Wiggins (GBR)

TEAM PURSUIT
1908 Great Britain
1920 Italy
1924 Italy
1928 Italy
1932 Italy
1936 France
1948 France
1952 Italy
1956 Italy
1960 Italy
1964 Germany
1968 Denmark
1972 West Germany
1976 West Germany
1980 USSR
1984 Australia
1988 USSR
1992 Germany
1996 France
2000 Germany
2004 Australia
2008 Great Britain

Cycling (men) (continued)

5,000 METERS	MIN:SEC
1908 Benjamin Jones (GBR)	8:36.2

10,000 METERS	MIN:SEC
1896 Paul Masson (FRA)	17:54.2

20,000 METERS	MIN:SEC
1908 Charles Kingsbury (GBR)	34:13.6

50,000 METERS	HR:MIN:SEC
1920 Henry George (BEL)	1:16:43.2
1924 Jacobus Willems (NED)	1:18:24.0

100,000 METERS	HR:MIN:SEC
1896 Léon Flameng (FRA)	3:08:19.2
1908 Charles Bartlett (GBR)	2:41:48.6

ONE-QUARTER MILE (440 YARDS)	SEC
1904 Marcus Hurley (USA)	31.8

ONE-THIRD MILE (586⅔ YARDS)	SEC
1904 Marcus Hurley (USA)	43.8

ONE-LAP TIME TRIAL (660 YARDS)	SEC
1908 Victor Johnson (GBR)	51.2

ONE-HALF MILE (880 YARDS)	MIN:SEC
1904 Marcus Hurley (USA)	1:09.0

1 MILE	MIN:SEC
1904 Marcus Hurley (USA)	2:41.6

1-MILE 1-FURLONG (1,980-YARD) TEAM PURSUIT
1908 Great Britain

2 MILES	MIN:SEC
1904 Burton Downing (USA)	4:58.0

5 MILES	MIN:SEC
1904 Charles Schlee (USA)	13:08.2

25 MILES
1904 Burton Downing (USA)

12 HOURS
1896 Adolf Schmal (AUT)

INDIVIDUAL POINTS RACE
1984 Roger Ilegems (BEL)
1988 Dan Frost (DEN)
1992 Giovanni Lombardi (ITA)
1996 Silvio Martinello (ITA)
2000 Juan Llaneras (ESP)
2004 Mikhail Ignatyev (RUS)
2008 Joan Llaneras (ESP)

KEIRIN	SEC
2000 Florian Rousseau (FRA)	11.020
2004 Ryan Bayley (AUS)	10.601
2008 Chris Hoy (GBR)	10.450

MADISON
2000 Australia
2004 Australia
2008 Argentina

Summer Olympic Games (continued)

Cycling (men) (continued)

TEAM SPRINT		SEC
2000	France	44.233
2004	Germany	43.980
2008	Great Britain	43.128

ROAD RACE (INDIVIDUAL)[12]		HR:MIN:SEC
1896	Aristidis Konstantinidis (GRE)	3:22:31.0
1912	Rudolph Lewis (RSA)	10:42:39.0
1920	Harry Stenqvist (SWE)	4:40:01.8
1924	Armand Blanchonnet (FRA)	6:20:48.0
1928	Henry Hansen (DEN)	4:47:18.0
1932	Attilio Pavesi (ITA)	2:28:05.6
1936	Robert Charpentier (FRA)	2:33:05.0
1948	Jose Beyaert (FRA)	5:18:12.6
1952	Andre Noyelle (BEL)	5:06:03.4
1956	Ercole Baldini (ITA)	5:21:17.0
1960	Viktor Kapitonov (URS)	4:20:37.0
1964	Mario Zanin (ITA)	4:39:51.63
1968	Pierfranco Vianelli (ITA)	4:41:25.24
1972	Hennie Kuiper (NED)	4:14:37.0
1976	Bernt Johansson (SWE)	4:46:52.0
1980	Sergey Sukhoruchenkov (URS)	4:48:28.90
1984	Alexei Grewal (USA)	4:59:57.0
1988	Olaf Ludwig (GDR)	4:32:22.0
1992	Fabio Casartelli (ITA)	4:35:21.0
1996	Pascal Richard (SUI)	4:53:56.0
2000	Jan Ullrich (GER)	5:29:08.0
2004	Paolo Bettini (ITA)	5:41:44.0
2008	Samuel Sánchez (ESP)	6:23:49.0

ROAD RACE (TEAM)		HR:MIN:SEC
1912	Sweden	44:35:33.6
1920	France	19:16:43.2
1924	France	19:30:14
1928	Denmark	15:09:14
1932	Italy	7:27:15.2
1936	France	7:39:16.2
1948	Belgium	15:58:17.4
1952	Belgium	15:20:46.6
1956	France	5:21:17

ROAD TIME TRIAL (INDIVIDUAL)		HR:MIN:SEC
1996	Miguel Indurain (ESP)	1:04:05
2000	Vyacheslav Yekimov (RUS)	57:40.42
2004	Tyler Hamilton (USA)	57.31.74
2008	Fabian Cancellara (SUI)	1:02:11.43

ROAD TIME TRIAL (TEAM)		HR:MIN:SEC
1960	Italy	2:14:33.53
1964	The Netherlands	2:26:31.19
1968	The Netherlands	2:07:49.06
1972	USSR	2:11:17.8
1976	USSR	2:08:53
1980	USSR	2:01:21.7
1984	Italy	1:58:28
1988	East Germany	1:57:47.7
1992	Germany	2:01:39

MOUNTAIN BIKE		HR:MIN:SEC
1996	Bart Jan Brentjens (NED)	2:17:38
2000	Miguel Martinez (FRA)	2:09:2.50
2004	Julien Absalon (FRA)	2:15:02
2008	Julien Absalon (FRA)	1:55:59

MOTOCROSS/BMX		MIN:SEC
2008	Maris Strombergs (LAT)	36.190

Cycling (women)

500-METER TIME TRIAL		SEC
2000	Felicia Ballanger (FRA)	34.140
2004	Anna Meares (AUS)	53.016

1,000-METER INDIVIDUAL SPRINT
1988	Erika Salumae (URS)	
1992	Erika Salumae (EST)	
1996	Felicia Ballanger (FRA)	
2000	Felicia Ballanger (FRA)	
2004	Lori-Ann Muenzer (CAN)	
2008	Victoria Pendleton (GBR)	

INDIVIDUAL PURSUIT
1992	Petra Rossner (GER)
1996	Antonella Bellutti (ITA)
2000	Leontien Zijlaard–van Moorsel (NED)
2004	Sarah Ulmer (NZL)
2008	Rebecca Romero (GBR)

INDIVIDUAL POINTS RACE
1996	Nathalie Lancien (FRA)
2000	Antonella Bellutti (ITA)
2004	Olga Slyusareva (RUS)
2008	Marianne Vos (NED)

ROAD RACE (INDIVIDUAL)		HR:MIN:SEC
1984	Connie Carpenter-Phinney (USA)	2:11:14.0
1988	Monique Knol (NED)	2:00:52.0
1992	Kathryn Watt (AUS)	2:04:42.0
1996	Jeannie Longo-Ciprelli (FRA)	2:36:13.0
2000	Leontien Zijlaard–van Moorsel (NED)	3:06:31
2004	Sara Carrigan (AUS)	3:24:24
2008	Nicole Cooke (GBR)	3:32:24

ROAD TIME TRIAL (INDIVIDUAL)		MIN:SEC
1996	Zulfiya Zabirova (RUS)	36:40
2000	Leontien Zijlaard–van Moorsel (NED)	42:00.781
2004	Leontien Zijlaard–van Moorsel (NED)	31:11.53
2008	Kristin Armstrong (USA)	34:51.72

MOUNTAIN BIKE		HR:MIN:SEC
1996	Paola Pezzo (ITA)	1:50:51
2000	Paola Pezzo (ITA)	1:49:24.38
2004	Gunn-Rita Dahle (NOR)	1:56:51
2008	Sabine Spitz (GER)	1:45:11

MOTOCROSS/BMX		MIN:SEC
2008	Anne-Caroline Chausson (FRA)	35.976

Diving (men)

3-METER SPRINGBOARD DIVING
1908	Albert Zürner (GER)
1912	Paul Günther (GER)
1920	Louis Kuehn (USA)
1924	Albert White (USA)
1928	Peter Desjardins (USA)
1932	Michael Galitzen (USA)
1936	Richard Degener (USA)
1948	Bruce Harlan (USA)
1952	David Browning (USA)
1956	Robert Clotworthy (USA)
1960	Gary Tobian (USA)
1964	Kenneth Sitzberger (USA)
1968	Bernie Wrightson (USA)
1972	Vladimir Vasin (URS)

Summer Olympic Games (continued)

Diving (men) (continued)

3-METER SPRINGBOARD DIVING (CONTINUED)

1976	Philip Boggs (USA)
1980	Aleksandr Portnov (URS)
1984	Gregory Louganis (USA)
1988	Gregory Louganis (USA)
1992	Mark Edward Lenzi (USA)
1996	Xiong Ni (CHN)
2000	Xiong Ni (CHN)
2004	Peng Bo (CHN)
2008	He Chong (CHN)

10-METER PLATFORM (HIGH) DIVING

1904	George Sheldon (USA)
1908	Hjalmar Johansson (SWE)
1912	Erik Adlerz (SWE)
1920	Clarence Pinkston (USA)
1924	Albert White (USA)
1928	Peter Desjardins (USA)
1932	Harold Smith (USA)
1936	Marshall Wayne (USA)
1948	Samuel Lee (USA)
1952	Samuel Lee (USA)
1956	Joaquin Capilla Perez (MEX)
1960	Robert Webster (USA)
1964	Robert Webster (USA)
1968	Klaus DiBiasi (ITA)
1972	Klaus DiBiasi (ITA)
1976	Klaus DiBiasi (ITA)
1980	Falk Hoffman (GDR)
1984	Gregory Louganis (USA)
1988	Gregory Louganis (USA)
1992	Sun Shuwei (CHN)
1996	Dmitry Sautin (RUS)
2000	Tian Liang (CHN)
2004	Hu Jia (CHN)
2008	Matt Mitcham (AUS)

3-METER SYNCHRONIZED SPRINGBOARD DIVING

2000	China
2004	Greece
2008	China

10-METER SYNCHRONIZED PLATFORM (HIGH) DIVING

2000	Russia
2004	China
2008	China

PLUNGE FOR DISTANCE

1904	William Paul Dickey (USA)

PLAIN HIGH DIVING

1912	Erik Adlerz (SWE)
1920	Arvid Wallman (SWE)
1924	Richmond Eve (AUS)

Diving (women)

3-METER SPRINGBOARD DIVING

1920	Aileen Riggin (USA)
1924	Elizabeth Becker-Pinkton (USA)
1928	Helen Meany (USA)
1932	Georgia Coleman (USA)
1936	Marjorie Gestring (USA)
1948	Victoria Draves (USA)
1952	Patricia McCormick (USA)
1956	Patricia McCormick (USA)
1960	Ingrid Krämer-Engel-Gulbin (GER)
1964	Ingrid Krämer-Engel-Gulbin (GER)
1968	Sue Gossick (USA)

Diving (women) (continued)

3-METER SPRINGBOARD DIVING (CONTINUED)

1972	Micki King (USA)
1976	Jennifer Chandler (USA)
1980	Irina Kalinina (URS)
1984	Sylvie Bernier (CAN)
1988	Gao Min (CHN)
1992	Gao Min (CHN)
1996	Fu Mingxia (CHN)
2000	Fu Mingxia (CHN)
2004	Guo Jingjing (CHN)
2008	Guo Jingjing (CHN)

10-METER PLATFORM (HIGH) DIVING

1912	Greta Johansson (SWE)
1920	Stefani Fryland Clausen (DEN)
1924	Caroline Smith (USA)
1928	Elizabeth Anna Becker-Pinkston (USA)
1932	Dorothy Poynton (USA)
1936	Dorothy Poynton-Hill (USA)
1948	Victoria Draves (USA)
1952	Patricia McCormick (USA)
1956	Patricia McCormick (USA)
1960	Ingrid Krämer-Engel-Gulbin (GER)
1964	Lesley Leigh Bush (USA)
1968	Milena Duchkova (TCH)
1972	Ulrika Knape (SWE)
1976	Yelena Vaytsekhovskaya (URS)
1980	Martina Jäschke (GDR)
1984	Zhou Ji-Hong (CHN)
1988	Xu Yan-Mei (CHN)
1992	Fu Mingxia (CHN)
1996	Fu Mingxia (CHN)
2000	Laura Wilkinson (USA)
2004	Chantelle Newbery (AUS)
2008	Chen Ruolin (CHN)

3-METER SYNCHRONIZED SPRINGBOARD DIVING

2000	Russia
2004	China
2008	China

10-METER SYNCHRONIZED PLATFORM (HIGH) DIVING

2000	China
2004	China
2008	China

Equestrian Sports

GRAND PRIX (DRESSAGE) INDIVIDUAL		MOUNT
1912	Carl Bonde (SWE)	Emperor
1920	Janne Lundblad (SWE)	Uno
1924	Ernst Linder (SWE)	Piccolomini
1928	Carl Friedrich Freiherr von Langen-Parow (GER)	Draufgänger
1932	Xavier Lesage (FRA)	Taine
1936	Heinz Pollay (GER)	Kronos
1948	Hans Moser (SUI)	Hummer
1952	Henri St. Cyr (SWE)	Master Rufus
1956	Henri St. Cyr (SWE)	Juli
1960	Sergey Filatov (URS)	Absent
1964	Henri Chammartin (SUI)	Woermann
1968	Ivan Kizimov (URS)	Ikhor
1972	Liselott Linsenhoff (FRG)	Piaff
1976	Christine Stückelberger (SUI)	Granat
1980	Elisabeth Theurer (AUT)	Mon Cherie
1984	Reiner Klimke (FRG)	Ahlerich
1988	Nicole Uphoff (FRG)	Rembrandt 24
1992	Nicole Uphoff (GER)	Rembrandt 24
1996	Isabell Werth (GER)	Gigolo

Summer Olympic Games (continued)

Equestrian Sports (continued)

GRAND PRIX (DRESSAGE) INDIVIDUAL (CONTINUED)   MOUNT

2000	Anky van Grunsven (NED)	Bonfire
2004	Anky van Grunsven (NED)	Salinero
2008	Anky van Grunsven (NED)	Keltec Salinero

GRAND PRIX (DRESSAGE) TEAM

1928	Germany
1932	France
1936	Germany
1948	France
1952	Sweden
1956	Sweden
1964	Germany
1968	West Germany
1972	USSR
1976	West Germany
1980	USSR
1984	West Germany
1988	West Germany
1992	Germany
1996	Germany
2000	Germany
2004	Germany
2008	Germany

GRAND PRIX (JUMPING) INDIVIDUAL   MOUNT

1900	Aimé Haegeman (BEL)	Benton II
1912	Jean Cariou (FRA)	Mignon
1920	Tommaso Lequio di Assaba (ITA)	Trebecco
1924	Alphonse Gemuseus (SUI)	Lucette
1928	Frantisek Ventura (TCH)	Eliot
1932	Takeichi Nishi (JPN)	Uranus
1936	Kurt Hasse (GER)	Tora
1948	Humberto Mariles Cortés (MEX)	Arete
1952	Pierre Jonquères d'Oriola (FRA)	Ali Baba
1956	Hans-Günter Winkler (GER)	Halla
1960	Raimondo d'Inzeo (ITA)	Posillipo
1964	Pierre Jonquères d'Oriola (FRA)	Lutteur
1968	William Steinkraus (USA)	Snowbound
1972	Graziano Mancinelli (ITA)	Ambassador
1976	Alwin Schockemöhle (FRG)	Warwick Rex
1980	Jan Kowalczyk (POL)	Artemor
1984	Joe Fargis (USA)	Touch of Class
1988	Pierre Durand (FRA)	Jappeloup
1992	Ludger Beerbaum (GER)	Classic Touch
1996	Ulrich Kirchhoff (GER)	Jus des Pommes
2000	Jeroen Dubbeldam (NED)	Sjiem
2004	Rodrigo Pessoa (BRA)[2]	Baloubet du Rouet[2]
2008	Eric Lamaze (CAN)	Hickstead

GRAND PRIX (JUMPING) TEAM

1912	Sweden
1920	Sweden
1924	Sweden
1928	Spain
1936	Germany
1948	Mexico
1952	Great Britain
1956	Germany
1960	Germany
1964	Germany
1968	Canada
1972	West Germany
1976	France
1980	USSR
1984	United States
1988	West Germany
1992	The Netherlands

Equestrian Sports (continued)

GRAND PRIX (JUMPING) TEAM

1996	Germany
2000	Germany
2004	United States[2]
2008	United States

THREE-DAY EVENT (INDIVIDUAL)   MOUNT

1912	Axel Nordlander (SWE)	Lady Artist
1920	Helmer Mörner (SWE)	Germania
1924	Adolph van der Voort van Zijp (NED)	Silver Piece
1928	Charles Pahud de Mortanges (NED)	Marcroix
1932	Charles Pahud de Mortanges (NED)	Marcroix
1936	Ludwig Stubbendorff (GER)	Nurmi
1948	Bernard Chevallier (FRA)	Aiglonne
1952	Hans von Blixen-Finecke, Jr. (SWE)	Jubal
1956	Petrus Kastenman (SWE)	Iluster
1960	Lawrence Morgan (AUS)	Salad Days
1964	Mauro Checcoli (ITA)	Surbean
1968	Jean-Jacques Goyon (FRA)	Pitou
1972	Richard Meade (GBR)	Laurieston
1976	Edmund Coffin (USA)	Bally-Cor
1980	Federico Euro Roman (ITA)	Rossinan
1984	Mark Todd (NZL)	Charisma
1988	Mark Todd (NZL)	Charisma
1992	Matthew Ryan (AUS)	Kibah Tic Toc
1996	Robert Blyth Tait (NZL)	Ready Teddy
2000	David O'Connor (USA)	Custom Made
2004	Leslie Law (GBR)	Shear L'Eau
2008	Hinrich Romeike (GER)	Marius

THREE-DAY EVENT (TEAM)

1912	Sweden
1920	Sweden
1924	The Netherlands
1928	The Netherlands
1932	United States
1936	Germany
1948	United States
1952	Sweden
1956	Great Britain
1960	Australia
1964	Italy
1968	Great Britain
1972	Great Britain
1976	United States
1980	USSR
1984	United States
1988	West Germany
1992	Australia
1996	Australia
2000	Australia
2004	France
2008	Germany

HIGH JUMP   MOUNT

1900	Dominique Maximien Gardéres (FRA); Gian Giorgio Trissino (ITA) (tied)	Canela; Oreste

LONG JUMP   MOUNT

1900	Constant van Langhendonck (BEL)	Extra Dry

FIGURE RIDING (INDIVIDUAL)

1920	T. Bouckaert (BEL)

FIGURE RIDING (TEAM)

1920	Belgium

Summer Olympic Games (continued)

Fencing (men)

FOIL (INDIVIDUAL)
1896	Eugène-Henri Gravelotte (FRA)
1900	Émile Coste (FRA)
1904	Ramón Fonst (CUB)
1912	Nedo Nadi (ITA)
1920	Nedo Nadi (ITA)
1924	Roger Ducret (FRA)
1928	Lucien Gaudin (FRA)
1932	Gustavo Marzi (ITA)
1936	Giulio Gaudini (ITA)
1948	Jehan Buhan (FRA)
1952	Christian d'Oriola (FRA)
1956	Christian d'Oriola (FRA)
1960	Viktor Zhdanovich (URS)
1964	Egon Franke (POL)
1968	Ion Drimba (ROM)
1972	Witold Woyda (POL)
1976	Fabio dal Zotto (ITA)
1980	Vladimir Smirnov (URS)
1984	Mauro Numa (ITA)
1988	Stefano Cerioni (ITA)
1992	Philippe Omnes (FRA)
1996	Alessandro Puccini (ITA)
2000	Kim Young Ho (KOR)
2004	Brice Guyart (FRA)
2008	Benjamin Philip Kleibrink (GER)

FOIL (TEAM)
1904	Cuba
1920	Italy
1924	France
1928	Italy
1932	France
1936	Italy
1948	France
1952	France
1956	Italy
1960	USSR
1964	USSR
1968	France
1972	Poland
1976	West Germany
1980	France
1984	Italy
1988	USSR
1992	Germany
1996	Russia
2000	France
2004	Italy

INDIVIDUAL FOIL, PROFESSIONAL (MASTERS)
1896	Leon Pyrgos (GRE)
1900	Lucien Mérignac (FRA)

INDIVIDUAL FOIL, JUNIOR
1904	Arthur Fox (USA)

EPEE (INDIVIDUAL)
1900	Ramón Fonst (CUB)
1904	Ramón Fonst (CUB)
1908	Gaston Alibert (FRA)
1912	Paul Anspach (BEL)
1920	Armand Massard (FRA)
1924	Charles Delporte (BEL)
1928	Lucien Gaudin (FRA)
1932	Giancarlo Cornaggia-Medici (ITA)
1936	Franco Riccardi (ITA)
1948	Luigi Cantone (ITA)

Fencing (men) (continued)

EPEE (INDIVIDUAL) (CONTINUED)
1952	Edoardo Mangiarotti (ITA)
1956	Carlo Pavesi (ITA)
1960	Giuseppe Delfino (ITA)
1964	Grigory Kriss (URS)
1968	Gyoso Kulcsar (HUN)
1972	Csaba Fenyvesi (HUN)
1976	Alexander Pusch (FRG)
1980	Johan Harmenberg (SWE)
1984	Philippe Boisse (FRA)
1988	Arnd Schmitt (FRG)
1992	Eric Srecki (FRA)
1996	Aleksandr Beketov (RUS)
2000	Pavel Kolobkov (RUS)
2004	Marcel Fischer (SUI)
2008	Matteo Tagliariol (ITA)

EPEE (TEAM)
1908	France
1912	Belgium
1920	Italy
1924	France
1928	Italy
1932	France
1936	Italy
1948	France
1952	Italy
1956	Italy
1960	Italy
1964	Hungary
1968	Hungary
1972	Hungary
1976	Sweden
1980	France
1984	West Germany
1988	France
1992	Germany
1996	Italy
2000	Italy
2004	France
2008	France

INDIVIDUAL EPEE, PROFESSIONAL (MASTERS)
1900	Albert Ayat (FRA)

INDIVIDUAL EPEE, OPEN (AMATEUR AND MASTERS)
1900	Albert Ayat (FRA)

SABRE (INDIVIDUAL)
1896	Ioannis Georgiadis (GRE)
1900	Georges de la Falaise (FRA)
1904	Manuel Díaz (CUB)
1908	Jeno Fuchs (HUN)
1912	Jeno Fuchs (HUN)
1920	Nedo Nadi (ITA)
1924	Sandor Posta (HUN)
1928	Odon Vitez Tersztyanszky (HUN)
1932	Gyorgy Piller (HUN)
1936	Endre Kabos (HUN)
1948	Aladar Gerevich (HUN)
1952	Pal Kovacs (HUN)
1956	Rudolph Karpati (HUN)
1960	Rudolph Karpati (HUN)
1964	Tibor Pezsa (HUN)
1968	Jerzy Pawlowski (POL)
1972	Viktor Sidyak (URS)
1976	Viktor Krovopuskov (URS)
1980	Viktor Krovopuskov (URS)

Summer Olympic Games (continued)

Fencing (men) (continued)

SABRE (INDIVIDUAL) (CONTINUED)
1984 Jean-François Lamour (FRA)
1988 Jean-François Lamour (FRA)
1992 Bence Szabo (HUN)
1996 Stanislav Pozdnyakov (RUS)
2000 Mihai Claudiu Covaliu (ROM)
2004 Aldo Montano (ITA)
2008 Zhong Man (CHN)

SABRE (TEAM)
1908 Hungary
1912 Hungary
1920 Italy
1924 Italy
1928 Hungary
1932 Hungary
1936 Hungary
1948 Hungary
1952 Hungary
1956 Hungary
1960 Hungary
1964 USSR
1968 USSR
1972 Italy
1976 USSR
1980 USSR
1984 Italy
1988 Hungary
1992 Unified Team
1996 Russia
2000 Russia
2004 France
2008 France

INDIVIDUAL SABRE, PROFESSIONAL (MASTERS)
1900 Antonio Conte (ITA)

SINGLE STICK
1904 Albertson Van Zo Post (CUB)

Fencing (women)

FOIL (INDIVIDUAL)
1924 Ellen Osiier (DEN)
1928 Helene Mayer (GER)
1932 Ellen Preis (AUT)
1936 Ilona Schacherer-Elek (HUN)
1948 Ilona Elek (HUN)
1952 Irene Camber (ITA)
1956 Gillian Sheen (GBR)
1960 Adelheid Schmid (GER)
1964 Ildiko Ujlaki-Rejto (HUN)
1968 Yelena Novikova (URS)
1972 Antonella Ragno Lonzi (ITA)
1976 Ildiko Schwarczenberger (HUN)
1980 Pascale Trinquet (FRA)
1984 Jujie Luan (CHN)
1988 Anja Fichtel (FRG)
1992 Giovanna Trillini (ITA)
1996 Laura Gabriela Badea (ROM)
2000 Valentina Vezzali (ITA)
2004 Valentina Vezzali (ITA)
2008 Valentina Vezzali (ITA)

FOIL (TEAM)
1960 USSR
1964 Hungary
1968 USSR
1972 USSR

Fencing (women) (continued)

FOIL (TEAM) (CONTINUED)
1976 USSR
1980 France
1984 West Germany
1988 West Germany
1992 Italy
1996 Italy
2000 Italy
2008 Russia

EPEE (INDIVIDUAL)
1996 Laura Flessel (FRA)
2000 Timea Nagy (HUN)
2004 Timea Nagy (HUN)
2008 Britta Heidemann (GER)

EPEE (TEAM)
1996 France
2000 Russia
2004 Russia

SABRE (INDIVIDUAL)
2004 Mariel Zagunis (USA)
2008 Mariel Zagunis (USA)

SABRE (TEAM)
2008 Ukraine

Field Hockey

MEN
1908 Great Britain
1920 Great Britain
1928 India
1932 India
1936 India
1948 India
1952 India
1956 India
1960 Pakistan
1964 India
1968 Pakistan
1972 West Germany
1976 New Zealand
1980 India
1984 Pakistan
1988 Great Britain
1992 Germany
1996 The Netherlands
2000 The Netherlands
2004 Australia
2008 Germany

WOMEN
1980 Zimbabwe
1984 The Netherlands
1988 Australia
1992 Spain
1996 Australia
2000 Australia
2004 Germany
2008 The Netherlands

Golf

MEN, INDIVIDUAL
1900 Charles Sands (USA)
1904 George Lyon (CAN)

Summer Olympic Games (continued)

Golf (continued)

MEN, TEAM

1904　United States

WOMEN

1900　Margaret Abbott (USA)

Gymnastics (men)

COMBINED, OR ALL-AROUND (INDIVIDUAL)

1900	Gustave Sandras (FRA)
1904	Julius Lenhardt (USA)
1908	G. Alberto Braglia (ITA)
1912	G. Alberto Braglia (ITA)
1920	Giorgio Zampori (ITA)
1924	Leon Stukelj (YUG)
1928	Georges Miez (SUI)
1932	Romeo Neri (ITA)
1936	Karl-Alfred Schwarzmann (GER)
1948	Veikko Huhtanen (FIN)
1952	Viktor Chukarin (URS)
1956	Viktor Chukarin (URS)
1960	Boris Shakhlin (URS)
1964	Yukio Endo (JPN)
1968	Sawao Kato (JPN)
1972	Sawao Kato (JPN)
1976	Nikolay Andrianov (URS)
1980	Aleksandr Dityatin (URS)
1984	Koji Gushiken (JPN)
1988	Vladimir Artyomov (URS)
1992	Vitaly Shcherbo (UNT)
1996	Li Xiaosahuang (CHN)
2000	Aleksey Nemov (RUS)
2004	Paul Hamm (USA)
2008	Yang Wei (CHN)

COMBINED, OR ALL-AROUND (TEAM)

1920	Italy
1924	Italy
1928	Switzerland
1932	Italy
1936	Germany
1948	Finland
1952	USSR
1956	USSR
1960	Japan
1964	Japan
1968	Japan
1972	Japan
1976	Japan
1980	USSR
1984	United States
1988	USSR
1992	Unified Team
1996	Russia
2000	China
2004	Japan
2008	China

FLOOR EXERCISE

1932	Istvan Pelle (HUN)
1936	Georges Miez (SUI)
1948	Ferenc Pataki (HUN)
1952	William Thoresson (SWE)
1956	Valentin Muratov (URS)
1960	Nobuyuki Aihara (JPN)
1964	Franco Menichelli (ITA)
1968	Sawao Kato (JPN)
1972	Nikolay Andrianov (URS)
1976	Nikolay Andrianov (URS)

Gymnastics (men) (continued)

FLOOR EXERCISE (CONTINUED)

1980	Roland Brückner (GDR)
1984	Li Ning (CHN)
1988	Sergey Kharikov (URS)
1992	Li Xiaosahuang (CHN)
1996	Ioannis Melissanidis (GRE)
2000	Igors Vihrovs (LAT)
2004	Kyle Shewfelt (CAN)
2008	Zou Kai (CHN)

HORIZONTAL BAR

1896	Hermann Weingärtner (GER)
1904	Anton Heida (USA); Edward Henning (USA) (tied)
1924	Leon Stukelj (YUG)
1928	Georges Miez (SUI)
1932	Dallas Bixler (USA)
1936	Aleksanteri Saarvala (FIN)
1948	Josef Stalder (SUI)
1952	Jack Günthard (SUI)
1956	Takashi Ono (JPN)
1960	Takashi Ono (JPN)
1964	Boris Shakhlin (URS)
1968	Mikhail Voronin (URS); Akinori Nakayama (JPN) (tied)
1972	Mitsuo Tsukahara (JPN)
1976	Mitsuo Tsukahara (JPN)
1980	Stoyan Delchev (BUL)
1984	Shinji Morisue (JPN)
1988	Vladimir Artyomov (URS); Valery Lyukin (URS) (tied)
1992	Trent Dimas (USA)
1996	Andreas Wecker (GER)
2000	Aleksey Nemov (RUS)
2004	Igor Cassina (ITA)
2008	Zou Kai (CHN)

PARALLEL BARS

1896	Alfred Flatow (GER)
1904	George Eyser (USA)
1924	August Güttinger (SUI)
1928	Ladislav Vacha (TCH)
1932	Romeo Neri (ITA)
1936	Konrad Frey (GER)
1948	Michael Reusch (SUI)
1952	Hans Eugster (SUI)
1956	Viktor Chukarin (URS)
1960	Boris Shakhlin (URS)
1964	Yukio Endo (JPN)
1968	Akinori Nakayama (JPN)
1972	Sawao Kato (JPN)
1976	Sawao Kato (JPN)
1980	Aleksandr Tkachyov (URS)
1984	Bart Conner (USA)
1988	Vladimir Artyomov (URS)
1992	Vitaly Shcherbo (UNT)
1996	Rustam Sharipov (UKR)
2000	Li Xiaopeng (CHN)
2004	Valery Goncharov (UKR)
2008	Li Xiaopeng (CHN)

SIDE, OR POMMEL, HORSE

1896	Louis Zutter (SUI)
1904	Anton Heida (USA)
1924	Josef Wilhelm (SUI)
1928	Hermann Hänggi (SUI)
1932	Istvan Pelle (HUN)
1936	Konrad Frey (GER)

Summer Olympic Games (continued)

Gymnastics (men) (continued)

SIDE, OR POMMEL, HORSE (CONTINUED)

1948 Paavo Aaltonen (FIN); Veikko Huhtanen (FIN); Heikki Savolainen (FIN) (tied)
1952 Viktor Chukarin (URS)
1956 Boris Shakhlin (URS)
1960 Boris Shakhlin (URS); Eugen Ekman (FIN) (tied)
1964 Miroslav Cerar (YUG)
1968 Miroslav Cerar (YUG)
1972 Viktor Klimenko (URS)
1976 Zoltan Magyar (HUN)
1980 Zoltan Magyar (HUN)
1984 Li Ning (CHN); Peter Vidmar (USA) (tied)
1988 Lyubomir Geraskov (BUL); Zsolt Borkai (HUN); Dmitry Bilozerchev (URS) (tied)
1992 Vitaly Shcherbo (UNT); Pae Gil-su (PRK) (tied)
1996 Li Donghua (SUI)
2000 Marius Urzica (ROM)
2004 Teng Haibin (CHN)
2008 Xiao Qin (CHN)

LONG, OR VAULTING, HORSE

1896 Karl Schuhmann (GER)
1904 Anton Heida (USA); George Eyser (USA) (tied)
1924 Frank Kriz (USA)
1928 Eugen Mack (SUI)
1932 Savino Guglielmetti (ITA)
1936 Karl-Alfred Schnorzmann (GER)
1948 Paavo Johannes Aaltonen (FIN)
1952 Viktor Chukarin (URS)
1956 Valentin Muratov (URS); Helmut Bantz (GER) (tied)
1960 Takashi Ono (JPN); Boris Shakhlin (URS) (tied)
1964 Haruhiro Yamashita (JPN)
1968 Mikhail Voronin (URS)
1972 Klaus Köste (GDR)
1976 Nikolay Andrianov (URS)
1980 Nikolay Andrianov (URS)
1984 Lou Yun (CHN)
1988 Lou Yun (CHN)
1992 Vitaly Shcherbo (UNT)
1996 Aleksey Nemov (RUS)
2000 Gervasio Deferr (ESP)
2004 Gervasio Deferr (ESP)
2008 Leszek Blanik (POL)

RINGS

1896 Ioannis Mitropoulos (GRE)
1904 Hermann Glass (USA)
1924 Francesco Martino (ITA)
1928 Leon Stukelj (YUG)
1932 George Gulack (USA)
1936 Alois Hudec (TCH)
1948 Karl Frei (SUI)
1952 Grant Shaginyan (URS)
1956 Albert Azaryan (URS)
1960 Albert Azaryan (URS)
1964 Takuji Hayata (JPN)
1968 Akinori Nakayama (JPN)
1972 Akinori Nakayama (JPN)
1976 Nikolay Andrianov (URS)
1980 Aleksandr Dityatin (URS)
1984 Li Ning (CHN); Koji Gushiken (JPN) (tied)
1988 Holger Behrendt (GDR); Dmitry Bilozerchev (URS) (tied)
1992 Vitaly Shcherbo (UNT)
1996 Yury Chechi (ITA)

Gymnastics (men) (continued)

RINGS (CONTINUED)

2000 Szilveszter Csollany (HUN)
2004 Dimosthenis Tampakos (GRE)
2008 Chen Yibing (CHN)

TRAMPOLINE

2000 Aleksandr Moskalenko (RUS)
2004 Yury Nikitin (UKR)
2008 Lu Chunlong (CHN)

ROPE CLIMBING

1896 Nicolaos Andriakopoulos (GRE)
1904 George Eyser (USA)
1924 Bedrich Supcik (TCH)
1932 Raymond Bass (USA)

SWEDISH EXERCISES (TEAM)

1912 Sweden
1920 Sweden

OPTIONAL EXERCISES (TEAM)

1912 Norway
1920 Denmark
1932 United States

PARALLEL BARS (TEAM)

1896 Germany

HORIZONTAL BARS (TEAM)

1896 Germany

CLUB SWINGING

1904 Edward Hennig (USA)
1932 George Roth (USA)

TUMBLING

1932 Rowland Wolfe (USA)

COMBINED COMPETITION (7 APPARATUS)

1904 Anton Heida (USA)

COMBINED COMPETITION (9 EVENTS)

1904 Adolf Spinnler (SUI)

PRESCRIBED APPARATUS (TEAM)

1904 United States
1908 Sweden
1912 Italy
1952 Sweden
1956 Hungary

MASS EXERCISES (TEAM)

1952 Finland

SIDE HORSE (VAULTS)

1924 Albert Séguin (FRA)

Gymnastics (women)

COMBINED, OR ALL-AROUND (INDIVIDUAL)

1952 Mariya Gorokhovskaya (URS)
1956 Larisa Latynina (URS)
1960 Larisa Latynina (URS)
1964 Vera Caslavska (TCH)
1968 Vera Caslavska (TCH)
1972 Lyudmila Turishcheva (URS)
1976 Nadia Comaneci (ROM)
1980 Yelena Davydova (URS)
1984 Mary Lou Retton (USA)

Summer Olympic Games (continued)

Gymnastics (women) (continued)

COMBINED, OR ALL-AROUND (INDIVIDUAL) (CONTINUED)
1988 Yelena Shushunova (URS)
1992 Tatyana Gutsu (UNT)
1996 Liliya Podkopayeva (UKR)
2000 Simona Amanar (ROM)[2]
2004 Carly Patterson (USA)
2008 Nastia Liukin (USA)

COMBINED, OR ALL-AROUND (TEAM)
1928 The Netherlands
1936 Germany
1948 Czechoslovakia
1952 USSR
1956 USSR
1960 USSR
1964 USSR
1968 USSR
1972 USSR
1976 USSR
1980 USSR
1984 Romania
1988 USSR
1992 Unified Team
1996 United States
2000 Romania
2004 Romania
2008 China

BALANCE BEAM
1952 Nina Bocharova (URS)
1956 Agnes Keleti (HUN)
1960 Eva Bosakova (TCH)
1964 Vera Caslavska (TCH)
1968 Natalya Kuchinskaya (URS)
1972 Olga Korbut (URS)
1976 Nadia Comaneci (ROM)
1980 Nadia Comaneci (ROM)
1984 Ecaterina Szabo (ROM); Simona Pauca (ROM) (tied)
1988 Daniela Silivas (ROM)
1992 Tatyana Lysenko (UNT)
1996 Shannon Miller (USA)
2000 Liu Xuan (CHN)
2004 Catalina Ponor (ROM)
2008 Shawn Johnson (USA)

UNEVEN PARALLEL BARS
1952 Margit Korondi (HUN)
1956 Agnes Keleti (HUN)
1960 Polina Astakhova (URS)
1964 Polina Astakhova (URS)
1968 Vera Caslavska (TCH)
1972 Karin Janz (GDR)
1976 Nadia Comaneci (ROM)
1980 Maxi Gnauck (GDR)
1984 Julianne McNamara (USA); Ma Yanhong (CHN) (tied)
1988 Daniela Silivas (ROM)
1992 Li Lu (CHN)
1996 Svetlana Khorkina (RUS)
2000 Svetlana Khorkina (RUS)
2004 Emilie Lepennec (FRA)
2008 He Kexin (CHN)

VAULT
1952 Yekaterina Kalinchuk (URS)
1956 Larisa Latynina (URS)
1960 Margarita Nikolayeva (URS)

Gymnastics (women) (continued)

VAULT (CONTINUED)
1964 Vera Caslavska (TCH)
1968 Vera Caslavska (TCH)
1972 Karin Janz (GDR)
1976 Nelli Kim (URS)
1980 Natalya Shaposhnikova (URS)
1984 Ecaterina Szabo (ROM)
1988 Svetlana Boginskaya (URS)
1992 Henrietta Onodi (HUN); Lavinia Milosovici (ROM) (tied)
1996 Simona Amanar (ROM)
2000 Yelena Zamolodchikova (RUS)
2004 Monica Rosu (ROM)
2008 Hong Un Jong (PRK)

FLOOR EXERCISE
1952 Agnes Keleti (HUN)
1956 Larisa Latynina (URS); Agnes Keleti (HUN) (tied)
1960 Larisa Latynina (URS)
1964 Larisa Latynina (URS)
1968 Vera Caslavska (TCH); Larissa Petrik (URS) (tied)
1972 Olga Korbut (URS)
1976 Nelli Kim (URS)
1980 Nadia Comaneci (ROM); Nelli Kim (URS) (tied)
1984 Ecaterina Szabo (ROM)
1988 Daniela Silivas (ROM)
1992 Lavinia Milosovici (ROM)
1996 Liliya Podkopayeva (UKR)
2000 Yelena Zamolodchikova (RUS)
2004 Catalina Ponor (ROM)
2008 Sandra Izbasa (ROM)

RHYTHMIC GYMNASTICS (INDIVIDUAL)
1984 Lori Fung (CAN)
1988 Marina Lobatch (URS)
1992 Aleksandra Timoshenko (UNT)
1996 Yekaterina Serebryanskaya (UKR)
2000 Yuliya Barsukova (RUS)
2004 Alina Kabayeva (RUS)
2008 Yevgeniya Kanayeva (RUS)

RHYTHMIC GYMNASTICS (TEAM)
1996 Spain
2000 Russia
2004 Russia
2008 Russia

TRAMPOLINE
2000 Irina Karavayeva (RUS)
2004 Anna Dogonadze (GER)
2008 He Wenna (CHN)

HAND APPARATUS (TEAM)
1952 Sweden
1956 Hungary

Handball (team)

MEN
1936[13] Germany
1972 Yugoslavia
1976 USSR
1980 East Germany
1984 Yugoslavia
1988 USSR
1992 Unified Team

Summer Olympic Games (continued)

Handball (team) (continued)

MEN (CONTINUED)

1996 Croatia
2000 Russia
2004 Croatia
2008 France

WOMEN

1976 USSR
1980 USSR
1984 Yugoslavia
1988 Republic of Korea
1992 Republic of Korea
1996 Denmark
2000 Denmark
2004 Denmark
2008 Norway

JEU DE PAUME (ROYAL TENNIS)

1908 Jay Gould (USA)

Judo (men)[14]

60 KG (132 LB)

1964 Takehide Nakatani (JPN)
1972 Takao Kawaguchi (JPN)
1976 Héctor Rodríguez (CUB)
1980 Thierry Rey (FRA)
1984 Shinji Hosokawa (JPN)
1988 Kim Jae-Yup (KOR)
1992 Nazim Guseynov (UNT)
1996 Tadahiro Nomura (JPN)
2000 Tadahiro Nomura (JPN)
2004 Tadahiro Nomura (JPN)
2008 Choi Min Ho (KOR)

66 KG (145.2 LB)

1980 Nikolay Solodukhin (URS)
1984 Yoshiyuki Matsuoka (JPN)
1988 Lee Kyung Ken (KOR)
1992 Rogerio Sampaio Cardoso (BRA)
1996 Udo Quellmalz (GER)
2000 Huseyin Ozkan (TUR)
2004 Masato Uchishiba (JPN)
2008 Masato Uchishiba (JPN)

73 KG (160.6 LB)

1972 Takao Kawaguchi (JPN)
1976 Héctor Rodríguez Torres (CUB)
1980 Ezio Gamba (ITA)
1984 Ahn Byeong Keun (KOR)
1988 Marc Alexandre (FRA)
1992 Toshihiko Koga (JPN)
1996 Kenzo Nakamura (JPN)
2000 Giuseppe Maddaloni (ITA)
2004 Lee Won Hee (KOR)
2008 Elnur Mammadli (AZE)

81 KG (178.2 LB)

1972 Toyojazu Nomura (JPN)
1976 Vladimir Nevzorov (URS)
1980 Shota Khabareli (URS)
1984 Frank Wieneke (FRG)
1988 Waldemar Legien (POL)
1992 Hidehiko Yoshida (JPN)
1996 Djamel Bouras (FRA)
2000 Makoto Takimoto (JPN)
2004 Ilias Iliadis (GRE)
2008 Ole Bischof (GER)

Judo (men)[14] (continued)

90 KG (198 LB)

1964 Isao Okano (JPN)
1972 Shinobu Sekine (JPN)
1976 Isamu Sonoda (JPN)
1980 Jürg Röthlisberger (SUI)
1984 Peter Seisenbacher (AUT)
1988 Peter Seisenbacher (AUT)
1992 Waldemar Legien (POL)
1996 Jeon Ki-Young (KOR)
2000 Mark Huizinga (NED)
2004 Zurab Zviadauri (GEO)
2008 Irakli Tsirekidze (GEO)

100 KG (220 LB)

1972 Shota Chochoshvili (URS)
1976 Kazuhiro Ninomiya (JPN)
1980 Robert van de Walle (BEL)
1984 Ha Young Zoo (KOR)
1988 Aurelio Miguel (BRA)
1992 Antal Kovacs (HUN)
1996 Pawel Nastula (POL)
2000 Kosei Inoue (JPN)
2004 Ihar Makarau (BLR)
2008 Tuvshinbayar Naidan (MGL)

OVER 100 KG (220+ LB)

1964 Isao Inokuma (JPN)
1972 Willem Ruska (NED)
1976 Sergey Novikov (URS)
1980 Angelo Parisi (FRA)
1984 Hitoshi Saito (JPN)
1988 Hitoshi Saito (JPN)
1992 David Khakhaleishvili (UNT)
1996 David Douillet (FRA)
2000 David Douillet (FRA)
2004 Keiji Suzuki (JPN)
2008 Satoshi Ishii (JPN)

OPEN (NO WEIGHT LIMIT)

1964 Antonius Johannes Geesink (NED)
1972 Willem Ruska (NED)
1976 Haruki Uemura (JPN)
1980 Dietmar Lorenz (GDR)
1984 Yasuhiro Yamashita (JPN)

Judo (women)[15]

48 KG (105.6 LB)

1992 Cecile Nowak (FRA)
1996 Kye Sun-Hi (PRK)
2000 Ryoko Tamura (JPN)
2004 Ryoko Tani (JPN)
2008 Alina Alexandra Dumitru (ROM)

52 KG (114.4 LB)

1992 Almudena Muñoz Martínez (ESP)
1996 Marie-Claire Restoux (FRA)
2000 Legna Verdecia (CUB)
2004 Xian Dongmei (CHN)
2008 Xian Dongmei (CHN)

57 KG (125.4 LB)

1992 Miriam Blasco Soto (ESP)
1996 Driulis González Morales (CUB)
2000 Isabel Fernández (ESP)
2004 Yvonne Bönisch (GER)
2008 Giulia Quintavalle (ITA)

Summer Olympic Games (continued)

Judo (women)[15] (continued)

63 KG (138.6 LB)

1992	Catherine Fleury-Vachon (FRA)
1996	Yuko Emoto (JPN)
2000	Severine Vandenhende (FRA)
2004	Ayumi Tanimoto (JPN)
2008	Ayumi Tanimoto (JPN)

70 KG (154 LB)

1992	Odalis Reve Jiménez (CUB)
1996	Cho Min-Sun (KOR)
2000	Sibelis Veranes (CUB)
2004	Masae Ueno (JPN)
2008	Masae Ueno (JPN)

78 KG (171.6 LB)

1992	Kim Mi-Jung (KOR)
1996	Ulla Werbrouck (BEL)
2000	Tang Lin (CHN)
2004	Noriko Anno (JPN)
2008	Yang Xiuli (CHN)

OVER 78 KG (171.6+ LB)

1992	Zhuang Xiaoyan (CHN)
1996	Sun Fuming (CHN)
2000	Yuan Hua (CHN)
2004	Maki Tsukada (JPN)
2008	Tong Wen (CHN)

Lacrosse

1904	Canada
1908	Canada

Modern Pentathlon

INDIVIDUAL (MEN)

1912	Gösta Lilliehöök (SWE)
1920	Gustaf Dyrssen (SWE)
1924	Bo Lindman (SWE)
1928	Sven Thofelt (SWE)
1932	Johan Oxenstierna (SWE)
1936	Gotthardt Handrick (GER)
1948	William Grut (SWE)
1952	Lars-Goran Hall (SWE)
1956	Lars-Goran Hall (SWE)
1960	Ferenc Nemeth (HUN)
1964	Ferenc Torok (HUN)
1968	Björn Ferm (SWE)
1972	Andras Balczo (HUN)
1976	Janusz Pyciak-Peciak (POL)
1980	Anatoly Starostin (URS)
1984	Daniele Masala (ITA)
1988	Janos Martinek (HUN)
1992	Arkadiusz Skrzypaszek (POL)
1996	Aleksandr Parygin (KAZ)
2000	Dmitry Svatkovsky (RUS)
2004	Andrey Moiseyev (RUS)
2008	Andrey Moiseyev (RUS)

INDIVIDUAL (WOMEN)

2000	Stephanie Cook (GBR)
2004	Zsuzsanna Voros (HUN)
2008	Lena Schöneborn (GER)

TEAM (MEN)

1952	Hungary
1956	USSR
1960	Hungary
1964	USSR
1968	Hungary

Modern Pentathlon (continued)

TEAM (MEN) (CONTINUED)

1972	USSR
1976	Great Britain
1980	USSR
1984	Italy
1988	Hungary
1992	Poland

Motorboat Racing

OPEN CLASS, 40 NAUTICAL MILES — BOAT

1908	Émile Thubron (FRA)	Camille

8-METER CLASS, 40 NAUTICAL MILES

1908	Thomas Thornycroft, Bernard Redwood (GBR)	Cyrinus

UNDER 60-FOOT CLASS, 40 NAUTICAL MILES

1908	Thomas Thornycroft, Bernard Redwood (GBR)	Cyrinus

Polo

1900	Great Britain–United States
1908	Great Britain
1920	Great Britain
1924	Argentina
1936	Argentina

Rackets

SINGLES

1908	Evan Noel (GBR)

DOUBLES

1908	Vane Pennell, John Jacob Astor (GBR)

Roque

1904	Charles Jacobus (USA)

Rowing (men)[16]

SINGLE SCULLS — MIN:SEC

1900	Henri Barrelet (FRA)	7:35.6
1904	Frank Greer (USA)	10:08.5
1908	Harry Blackstaffe (GBR)	9:26.0
1912	William Kinnear (GBR)	7:47.6
1920	John Kelly, Sr. (USA)	7:35.0
1924	Jack Beresford (GBR)	7:49.2
1928	Henry Pearce (AUS)	7:11.0
1932	Henry Pearce (AUS)	7:44.4
1936	Gustav Schäfer (GER)	8:21.5
1948	Mervyn Wood (AUS)	7:24.4
1952	Yury Tyukalov (URS)	8:12.8
1956	Vyacheslav Ivanov (URS)	8:02.5
1960	Vyacheslav Ivanov (URS)	7:13.96
1964	Vyacheslav Ivanov (URS)	8:22.51
1968	Henri-Jan Wienese (NED)	7:47.80
1972	Yury Malyshev (URS)	7:10.12
1976	Pertti Karppinen (FIN)	7:29.03
1980	Pertti Karppinen (FIN)	7:09.61
1984	Pertti Karppinen (FIN)	7:00.24
1988	Thomas Lange (GDR)	6:49.86
1992	Thomas Lange (GER)	6:51.40
1996	Xeno Mueller (SUI)	6:44.85
2000	Robert Waddell (NZL)	6:48.90
2004	Olaf Tufte (NOR)	6:49.30
2008	Olaf Tufte (NOR)	6:59.83

Summer Olympic Games (continued)

Rowing (men)[16] (continued)

DOUBLE SCULLS

		MIN:SEC
1904	United States	10:03.2
1920	United States	7:09.0
1924	United States	6:34.0
1928	United States	6:41.4
1932	United States	7:17.4
1936	Great Britain	7:20.8
1948	Great Britain	6:51.3
1952	Argentina	7:32.2
1956	USSR	7:24.0
1960	Czechoslovakia	6:47.50
1964	USSR	7:10.66
1968	USSR	6:51.82
1972	USSR	7:01.77
1976	Norway	7:13.20
1980	East Germany	6:24.33
1984	United States	6:36.87
1988	The Netherlands	6:21.13
1992	Australia	6:17.32
1996	Italy	6:16.98
2000	Slovenia	6:16.63
2004	France	6:29.00
2008	Australia	6:27.77

FOUR SCULLS

		MIN:SEC
1976	East Germany	6:18.65
1980	East Germany	5:49.81
1984	West Germany	5:57.55
1988	Italy	5:53.37
1992	Germany	5:45.17
1996	Germany	5:56.93
2000	Italy	5:45.56
2004	Russia	5:56.85
2008	Poland	5:41.33

LIGHTWEIGHT DOUBLE SCULLS

		MIN:SEC
1996	Switzerland	6:23.47
2000	Poland	6:21.75
2004	Poland	6:20.93
2008	Great Britain	6:10.99

PAIRS (WITHOUT COXSWAIN)

		MIN:SEC
1904	United States	10:57.0
1908	Great Britain	9:41.0
1924	The Netherlands	8:19.4
1928	Germany	7:06.4
1932	Great Britain	8:00.0
1936	Germany	8:16.1
1948	Great Britain	7:21.1
1952	United States	8:20.7
1956	United States	7:55.4
1960	USSR	7:02.01
1964	Canada	7:32.94
1968	East Germany	7:26.56
1972	East Germany	6:53.16
1976	East Germany	7:23.31
1980	East Germany	6:48.01
1984	Romania	6:45.39
1988	Great Britain	6:36.84
1992	Great Britain	6:27.72
1996	Great Britain	6:20.09
2000	France	6:32.97
2004	Australia	6:30.76
2008	Australia	6:37.44

PAIRS (WITH COXSWAIN)

		MIN:SEC
1900	The Netherlands–France	7:34.2
1920	Italy	7:56.0

Rowing (men)[16] (continued)

PAIRS (WITH COXSWAIN) (CONTINUED)

		MIN:SEC
1924	Switzerland	8:39.0
1928	Switzerland	7:42.6
1932	United States	8:25.8
1936	Germany	8:36.9
1948	Denmark	8:00.5
1952	France	8:28.6
1956	United States	8:26.1
1960	Germany	7:29.14
1964	United States	8:21.23
1968	Italy	8:04.81
1972	East Germany	7:17.25
1976	East Germany	7:58.99
1980	East Germany	7:02.54
1984	Italy	7:05.99
1988	Italy	6:58.79
1992	Great Britain	6:49.83

LIGHTWEIGHT FOURS (WITHOUT COXSWAIN)

		MIN:SEC
1996	Denmark	6:09.58
2000	France	6:01.68
2004	Denmark	6:01.39
2008	Denmark	5:47.76

FOURS (WITHOUT COXSWAIN)

		MIN:SEC
1900	France	7:11.0
1904	United States	9:53.8
1908	Great Britain	8:34.0
1920	Great Britain	7:08.6
1928	Great Britain	6:36.0
1932	Great Britain	6:58.2
1936	Germany	7:01.8
1948	Italy	6:39.0
1952	Yugoslavia	7:16.0
1956	Canada	7:08.8
1960	United States	6:26.26
1964	Denmark	6:59.30
1968	East Germany	6:39.18
1972	East Germany	6:24.27
1976	East Germany	6:37.42
1980	East Germany	6:08.17
1984	New Zealand	6:03.48
1988	East Germany	6:03.11
1992	Australia	5:55.04
1996	Australia	6:06.37
2000	Great Britain	5:56.24
2004	Great Britain	6:06.98
2008	Great Britain	6:06.57

FOURS (WITH COXSWAIN)

		MIN:SEC
1900	Germany	5:59.0
1912	Germany	6:59.4
1920	Switzerland	6:54.0
1924	Switzerland	7:18.4
1928	Italy	6:47.8
1932	Germany	7:19.0
1936	Germany	7:16.2
1948	United States	6:50.3
1952	Czechoslovakia	7:33.4
1956	Italy	7:19.4
1960	Germany	6:39.12
1964	Germany	7:00.44
1968	New Zealand	6:45.62
1972	West Germany	6:31.85
1976	USSR	6:40.22
1980	East Germany	6:14.51
1984	Great Britain	6:18.64

Summer Olympic Games (continued)

Rowing (men)[16] (continued)

FOURS (WITH COXSWAIN) (CONTINUED)		MIN:SEC
1988	East Germany	6:10.74
1992	Romania	5:59.37

FOURS, INRIGGERS (WITH COXSWAIN)		MIN:SEC
1912	Denmark	7:47.0

EIGHTS (WITH COXSWAIN)		MIN:SEC
1900	United States	6:09.8
1904	United States	7:50.0
1908	Great Britain	7:52.0
1912	Great Britain	6:15.0
1920	United States	6:02.6
1924	United States	6:33.4
1928	United States	6:03.2
1932	United States	6:37.6
1936	United States	6:25.4
1948	United States	5:56.7
1952	United States	6:25.9
1956	United States	6:35.2
1960	Germany	5:57.18
1964	United States	6:18.23
1968	West Germany	6:07.00
1972	New Zealand	6:08.94
1976	East Germany	5:58.29
1980	East Germany	5:49.05
1984	Canada	5:41.32
1988	West Germany	5:46.05
1992	Canada	5:29.53
1996	The Netherlands	5:42.74
2000	Great Britain	5:33.08
2004	United States	5:42.48
2008	Canada	5:23.89

Rowing (women)[17]

SINGLE SCULLS		MIN:SEC
1976	Christine Scheiblich (GDR)	4:05.56
1980	Sanda Toma (ROM)	3:40.69
1984	Valeria Racila (ROM)	3:40.68
1988	Jutta Behrendt (GDR)	7:47.19
1992	Elisabeta Lipa (ROM)	7:25.54
1996	Yekaterina Khodotovich (BLR)	7:32.21
2000	Yekaterina Khodotovich Karsten (BLR)	7:28.14
2004	Katrin Rutschow-Stomporowski (GER)	7:18.12
2008	Rumyana Neykova (BUL)	7:22.34

DOUBLE SCULLS		MIN:SEC
1976	Bulgaria	3:44.36
1980	USSR	3:16.27
1984	Romania	3:26.75
1988	East Germany	7:00.48
1992	Germany	6:49.00
1996	Canada	6:56.84
2000	Germany	6:55.44
2004	New Zealand	7:01.79
2008	New Zealand	7:07.32

LIGHTWEIGHT DOUBLE SCULLS		MIN:SEC
1996	Romania	7:12.78
2000	Romania	7:02.64
2004	Romania	6:56.05
2008	The Netherlands	6:54.74

Rowing (women)[17] (continued)

FOUR SCULLS		MIN:SEC
1976	East Germany	3:29.99
1980	East Germany	3:15.32
1984	Romania	3:14.11
1988	East Germany	6:21.06
1992	Germany	6:20.18
1996	Germany	6:27.44
2000	Germany	6:19.58
2004	Germany	6:29.29
2008	China	6:16.06

PAIRS (WITHOUT COXSWAIN)		MIN:SEC
1976	Bulgaria	4:01.22
1980	East Germany	3:30.49
1984	Romania	3:32.60
1988	Romania	7:28.13
1992	Canada	7:06.22
1996	Australia	7:01.39
2000	Romania	7:11.00
2004	Romania	7:06.55
2008	Romania	7:20.60

FOURS (WITH COXSWAIN)		MIN:SEC
1976	East Germany	3:45.08
1980	East Germany	3:19.27
1984	Romania	3:19.3
1988	East Germany	6:56.0
1992[18]	Canada	6:30.85

EIGHTS (WITH COXSWAIN)		MIN:SEC
1976	East Germany	3:33.32
1980	East Germany	3:03.32
1984	United States	2:59.80
1988	East Germany	6:15.17
1992	Canada	6:02.62
1996	Romania	6:19.73
2000	Romania	6:06.44
2004	Romania	6:17.70
2008	United States	6:05.34

Rugby Football

1900	France
1908	Australia
1920	United States
1924	United States

Sailing (Yachting)

BOARDSAILING (WINDGLIDER/DIVISION II) (OPEN)

1984	Stephan van den Berg (NED)
1988	Anthony Bruce Kendall (NZL)

BOARDSAILING (RS:X[19]) (MEN)

1992	Franck David (FRA)
1996	Nikolaos Kaklamanakis (GRE)
2000	Christoph Sieber (AUT)
2004	Gal Fridman (ISR)
2008	Tom Ashley (NZL)

BOARDSAILING (RS:X[19]) (WOMEN)

1992	Barbara Anne Kendall (NZL)
1996	Lee Lai Shan (HKG)
2000	Alessandra Sensini (ITA)

Summer Olympic Games (continued)

Sailing (Yachting) (continued)

BOARDSAILING (RS:X[19]) (WOMEN) (CONTINUED)
2004	Faustine Merret (FRA)
2008	Yin Jian (CHN)

SINGLE-HANDED DINGHY (LASER RADIAL) (WOMEN)
1992	Linda Andersen (NOR)
1996	Kristine Roug (DEN)
2000	Shirley Anne Robertson (GBR)
2004	Siren Sundby (NOR)
2008	Anna Tunnicliffe (USA)

SINGLE-HANDED DINGHY (LASER) (MEN[20])
1996	Robert Scheidt (BRA)
2000	Ben Ainslie (GBR)
2004	Robert Scheidt (BRA)
2008	Paul Goodison (GBR)

SINGLE-HANDED DINGHY (FINN[21]) (OPEN[22])
1924	Léon Huybrechts (BEL)
1928	Sven Thorell (SWE)
1932	Jacques Lebrun (FRA)
1936	Daniel Kagchelland (NED)
1948	Paul Elvström (DEN)
1952	Paul Elvström (DEN)
1956	Paul Elvström (DEN)
1960	Paul Elvström (DEN)
1964	Wilhelm Kuhweide (GER)
1968	Valentin Mankin (URS)
1972	Serge Maury (FRA)
1976	Jochen Schümann (GDR)
1980	Esko Rechardt (FIN)
1984	Russell Coutts (NZL)
1988	José Luis Doreste (ESP)
1992	José van der Ploeg (ESP)
1996	Mateusz Kusznierewicz (POL)
2000	Iain Percy (GBR)
2004	Ben Ainslie (GBR)
2008	Ben Ainslie (GBR)

DOUBLE-HANDED DINGHY (470) (MEN)
1976	West Germany
1980	Brazil
1984	Spain
1988	France
1992	Spain
1996	Ukraine
2000	Australia
2004	United States
2008	Australia

DOUBLE-HANDED DINGHY (470) (WOMEN)
1988	United States
1992	Spain
1996	Spain
2000	Australia
2004	Greece
2008	Australia

YNGLING (WOMEN)
2004	Great Britain
2008	Great Britain

HIGH-PERFORMANCE DINGHY (49ER) (OPEN)
2000	Finland
2004	Spain
2008	Denmark

Sailing (Yachting) (continued)

MULTIHULL (TORNADO) (OPEN)
1976	Great Britain
1980	Brazil
1984	New Zealand
1988	France
1992	France
1996	Spain
2000	Austria
2004	Austria
2008	Spain

FLEET/MATCH RACE KEELBOAT (SOLING) (OPEN)
1972	United States
1976	Denmark
1980	Denmark
1984	United States
1988	East Germany
1992	Denmark
1996	Germany
2000	Denmark

TWO-PERSON KEELBOAT (STAR) (MEN[23])
1932	United States
1936	Germany
1948	United States
1952	Italy
1956	United States
1960	USSR
1964	The Bahamas
1968	United States
1972	Australia
1980	USSR
1984	United States
1988	Great Britain
1992	United States
1996	Brazil
2000	United States
2004	Brazil
2008	Great Britain

40-METER CLASS
1920	Sweden

30-METER CLASS
1920	Sweden

12-METER CLASS
1920 (old)	Norway
1920 (new)	Norway

OVER-10-METER CLASS
1900	France
1908	Great Britain
1912	Norway

10-METER CLASS
1900	Germany
1912	Sweden
1920 (old)	Norway
1920 (new)	Norway

8-METER CLASS
1900	Great Britain
1908	Great Britain
1912	Norway
1920 (old)	Norway
1920 (new)	Norway
1924	Norway

Summer Olympic Games (continued)

Sailing (Yachting) (continued)

8-METER CLASS (CONTINUED)
1928 France
1932 United States
1936 Italy

7-METER CLASS
1908 Great Britain
1920 (old)   Great Britain

6.5-METER CLASS
1920 (new) The Netherlands

6-METER CLASS
1900 Switzerland
1908 Great Britain
1912 France
1920 (old) Belgium
1920 (new) Norway
1924 Norway
1928 Norway
1932 Sweden
1936 Great Britain
1948 United States
1952 United States

5.5-METER CLASS
1952 United States
1956 Sweden
1960 United States
1964 Australia
1968 Sweden

18-FOOT CENTERBOARD BOAT
1920 Great Britain

12-FOOT CENTERBOARD BOAT
1920 The Netherlands
1924 Belgium

12-FOOT DINGHY
1928 Sweden

MONOTYPE CLASS
1932 France

MONOTYPE CLASS "NURNBERG"
1936 The Netherlands

SWALLOW
1948 Great Britain

FIREFLY
1948 Denmark

SHARPIE
1956 New Zealand

DRAGON
1948 Norway
1952 Norway
1956 Sweden
1960 Greece
1964 Denmark
1968 United States
1972 Australia

Sailing (Yachting) (continued)

TEMPEST
1972 USSR
1976 Sweden

FLYING DUTCHMAN
1960 Norway
1964 New Zealand
1968 Great Britain
1972 Great Britain
1976 West Germany
1980 Spain
1984 United States
1988 Denmark
1992 Spain

Shooting (men)

individual
TRAP (CLAY PIGEON)[24]
1900 Roger de Barbarin (FRA)
1908 Walter Ewing (CAN)
1912 James Graham (USA)
1920 Mark Arie (USA)
1924 Gyula Halasy (HUN)
1952 George Généreux (CAN)
1956 Galliano Rossini (ITA)
1960 Ion Dumitrescu (ROM)
1964 Ennio Mattarelli (ITA)
1968 John Braithwaite (GBR)
1972 Angelo Scalzone (ITA)
1976 Donald Haldeman (USA)
1980 Luciano Giovannetti (ITA)
1984 Luciano Giovannetti (ITA)
1988 Donald Monakov (URS)
1992 Petr Hrdlicka (TCH)
1996 Michael Constantine Diamond (AUS)
2000 Michael Constantine Diamond (AUS)
2004 Aleksey Alipov (RUS)
2008 David Kostelecky (CZE)

DOUBLE TRAP
1996 Russell Andrew Mark (AUS)
2000 Richard Faulds (GBR)
2004 Ahmed Almaktoum (UAE)
2008 Walton Eller (USA)

SKEET[25]
1968 Yevgeny Petrov (URS)
1972 Konrad Wirnhier (FRG)
1976 Josef Panacek (TCH)
1980 Hans Kjeld Rasmussen (DEN)
1984 Matthew Dryke (USA)
1988 Axel Wegner (GDR)
1992 Zhang Shan (CHN)
1996 Ennio Falco (ITA)
2000 Mykola Milchev (UKR)
2004 Andrea Benelli (ITA)
2008 Vincent Hancock (USA)

FREE PISTOL
1896 Sumner Paine (USA)
1900 Karl Konrad Röderer (SUI)
1912 Alfred Lane (USA)
1920 Carl Frederick (USA)
1936 Torsten Ullmann (SWE)
1948 Edwin Vásquez Cam (PER)
1952 Huelet Benner (USA)
1956 Pentti Tapio Linnosvuo (FIN)
1960 Aleksey Gushchin (URS)

Summer Olympic Games (continued)

Shooting (men) (continued)
individual (continued)

FREE PISTOL (CONTINUED)
1964	Väinö Johannes Markkanen (FIN)
1968	Grigory Kosykh (URS)
1976	Uwe Potteck (GDR)
1980	Aleksandr Melentev (URS)
1984	Xu Haifeng (CHN)
1988	Sorin Babii (ROM)
1992	Konstantin Lukachik (UNT)
1996	Boris Kokorev (RUS)
2000	Tanyu Kiryakov (BUL)
2004	Mikhail Nestruyev (RUS)
2008	Jin Jong Oh (KOR)

RAPID-FIRE PISTOL
1896	Joannis Phrangudis (GRE)
1900	Maurice Larrouy (FRA)
1908	Paul van Asbrock (BEL)
1912	Alfred Lane (USA)
1920	Guilherme Paraense (BRA)
1924	Henry Bailey (USA)
1932	Renzo Morigi (ITA)
1936	Cornelius van Oyen (GER)
1948	Karoly Takacs (HUN)
1952	Karoly Takacs (HUN)
1956	Stefan Petrescu (ROM)
1960	William McMillan (USA)
1964	Pentti Tapio Linnosvuo (FIN)
1968	Jozef Zapedzki (POL)
1972	Jozef Zapedzki (POL)
1976	Norbert Klaar (GDR)
1980	Corneliu Ion (ROM)
1984	Takeo Kamachi (JPN)
1988	Afanasy Kuzmin (URS)
1992	Ralf Schumann (GER)
1996	Ralf Schumann (GER)
2000	Sergey Alifirenko (RUS)
2004	Ralf Schumann (GER)
2008	Oleksandr Petriv (UKR)

SMALL-BORE RIFLE (PRONE)
1908	Arthur Ashton Carnell (GBR)
1912	Frederick Hird (USA)
1920	Lawrence Nuesslein (USA)
1924	Pierre Coquelin de Lisle (FRA)
1932	Bertil Rönnmark (SWE)
1936	Willy Røgeberg (NOR)
1948	Arthur Cook (USA)
1952	Iosif Sarbu (ROM)
1956	Gerald Ouellette (CAN)
1960	Peter Kohnke (GER)
1964	Laszlo Hammerl (HUN)
1968	Jan Kurka (TCH)
1972	Ho Jun Li (PRK)
1976	Karlheinz Smieszek (FRG)
1980	Karoly Varga (HUN)
1984	Edward Etzel (USA)
1988	Miroslav Varga (TCH)
1992	Lee Eun Chul (KOR)
1996	Christian Klees (GER)
2000	Jonas Edman (SWE)
2004	Matthew Emmons (USA)
2008	Artur Ayvazian (UKR)

SMALL-BORE RIFLE (3 POSITIONS)
1952	Erling Kongshaug (NOR)
1956	Anatoly Bogdanov (URS)
1960	Viktor Shamburkin (URS)

Shooting (men) (continued)
individual (continued)

SMALL-BORE RIFLE (3 POSITIONS) (CONTINUED)
1964	Lones Wesley Wigger (USA)
1968	Bernd Klingner (FRG)
1972	John Writer (USA)
1976	Lanny Bassham (USA)
1980	Viktor Vlasov (URS)
1984	Malcolm Cooper (GBR)
1988	Malcolm Cooper (GBR)
1992	Gratchia Petikian (UNT)
1996	Jean-Pierre Amat (FRA)
2000	Rajmond Debevec (SLO)
2004	Jia Zhanbo (CHN)
2008	Qiu Jian (CHN)

10-METER RUNNING (GAME) TARGET
1900	Louis Debray (FRA)
1972	Yakov Zheleznyak (URS)
1976	Aleksandr Gazov (URS)
1980	Igor Sokolov (URS)
1984	Li Yuwei (CHN)
1988	Tor Heiestad (NOR)
1992	Michael Jakosits (GER)
1996	Yang Ling (CHN)
2000	Yang Ling (CHN)
2004	Manfred Kurzer (GER)

AIR RIFLE
1984	Philippe Heberle (FRA)
1988	Goran Maksimovic (YUG)
1992	Yury Fedkin (UNT)
1996	Artyom Khadzhibekov (RUS)
2000	Cai Yalin (CHN)
2004	Zhu Quinan (CHN)
2008	Abhinav Bindra (IND)

AIR PISTOL
1988	Tanyu Kiryakov (BUL)
1992	Wang Yifu (CHN)
1996	Roberto di Donna (ITA)
2000	Franck Dumoulin (FRA)
2004	Wang Yifu (CHN)
2008	Pang Wei (CHN)

FREE RIFLE (300 METERS, 3 POSITIONS)
1908	Albert Helgerud (NOR)
1912	Paul René Colas (FRA)
1920	Morris Fisher (USA)
1924	Morris Fisher (USA)
1948	Emil Grünig (SUI)
1952	Anatoly Bogdanov (URS)
1956	Vasily Borisov (URS)
1960	Hubert Hammerer (AUT)
1964	Gary Lee Anderson (USA)
1968	Gary Lee Anderson (USA)
1972	Lones Wesley Wigger (USA)

ARMY RIFLE (300 METERS, 3 POSITIONS)
1896	Georgios Orphanidis (GRE)
1900	Emil Kellenberger (SUI)
1912	Sandor Prokop (HUN)

ARMY RIFLE (200 METERS)
1896	Pantelis Karasevdas (GRE)

FREE RIFLE (1,000 YARDS PRONE)
1908	Joshua Millner (GBR)

Summer Olympic Games (continued)

Shooting (men) (continued)

individual (continued)

FULL-BORE RIFLE (300 METERS STANDING)
1900   Lars Madsen (DEN)

FULL-BORE RIFLE (300 METERS KNEELING)
1900   Konrad Staeheli (SUI)

FULL-BORE RIFLE (300 METERS PRONE)
1900   Achille Paroche (FRA)

FULL-BORE RIFLE (300 METERS)
1900   Emil Kellenberger (SUI)

RIFLE (300 METERS, 2 POSITIONS)
1920   Morris Fisher (USA)

RIFLE (300 METERS STANDING)
1920   Carl Osburn (USA)

RIFLE (300 METERS PRONE)
1920   Otto Olsen (NOR)

RIFLE (600 METERS PRONE)
1920   Hugo Johansson (SWE)

6-MILLIMETER SMALL GUN (OPEN REAR SIGHT)
1900   C. Grosett (FRA)

SMALL-BORE RIFLE (VANISHING TARGET)
1908   William Styles (GBR)
1912   Wilhelm Carlberg (SWE)

SMALL-BORE RIFLE (MOVING TARGET)
1908   John Francis Fleming (GBR)

RUNNING DEER (100 METERS SINGLE SHOT)
1908   Oscar Swahn (SWE)
1912   Alfred Swahn (SWE)
1920   Otto Olsen (NOR)
1924   John Boles (USA)

RUNNING DEER (100 METERS DOUBLE SHOT)
1908   Walter Winans (USA)
1912   Ake Lundeberg (SWE)
1920   Ole Andreas Lilloe-Olsen (NOR)
1924   Ole Andreas Lilloe-Olsen (NOR)

RUNNING DEER (100 METERS SINGLE AND DOUBLE SHOT)
1952   John Larsen (NOR)
1956   Vitaly Romanenko (URS)

LIVE PIGEON
1900   Léon de Lunden (BEL)

GAME SHOOTING
1900   Donald Mackintosh (AUS)

MILITARY REVOLVER (25 METERS)
1896   John Paine (USA)

REVOLVER AND PISTOL
1900   Paul van Asbrock (BEL)
1908   Paul van Asbrock (BEL)
1912   Alfred Lane (USA)

Shooting (men) (continued)

individual (continued)

DUELING PISTOL
1912   Alfred Lane (USA)

team

FREE RIFLE (300 METERS)
1908   Norway
1912   Sweden

ARMY RIFLE (300 METERS)
1900   Norway

ARMY RIFLE (ALL-AROUND)
1900   United States
1908   United States
1912   United States

FULL-BORE RIFLE (300 METERS)
1900   Switzerland

SMALL-BORE RIFLE
1900   Great Britain
1908   Great Britain
1920   United States
1924   France

SMALL-BORE RIFLE (VANISHING TARGET)
1912   Sweden

RIFLE (600 METERS PRONE)
1920   United States

RIFLE (300 METERS, 2 POSITIONS)
1920   United States

RIFLE (300 METERS STANDING)
1920   Denmark

RIFLE (300 METERS PRONE)
1920   United States

RIFLE (ALL-AROUND)
1920   United States
1924   United States

RUNNING DEER (SINGLE SHOT)
1908   Sweden
1912   Sweden
1920   Norway
1924   Norway

RUNNING DEER (DOUBLE SHOT)
1920   Norway
1924   Great Britain

CLAY PIGEON
1900   Great Britain
1908   Great Britain
1912   United States
1920   United States
1924   United States

REVOLVER
1900   Switzerland

Summer Olympic Games (continued)

Shooting (men) (continued)
team (continued)

PISTOL
1920	United States
1924	United States

REVOLVER AND PISTOL
1900	United States
1908	United States
1912	United States
1920	United States

DUELING PISTOL
1912	Sweden

Shooting (women)

TRAP (CLAY PIGEON)
2000	Daina Gudzineviciute (LTU)
2004	Suzanne Balogh (AUS)
2008	Satu Mäkelä-Nummela (FIN)

DOUBLE TRAP
1996	Kimberly Rhode (USA)
2000	Pia Hansen (SWE)
2004	Kimberly Rhode (USA)

SKEET
2000	Zemfira Meftakhetdinova (AZE)
2004	Diana Igaly (HUN)
2008	Chiara Cainero (ITA)

PISTOL
1984	Linda Thom (CAN)
1988	Nino Salukvadze (URS)
1992	Marina Logvinenko (UNT)
1996	Li Duihong (CHN)
2000	Mariya Zdravkova Grozdeva (BUL)
2004	Mariya Zdravkova Grozdeva (BUL)
2008	Chen Ying (CHN)

SMALL-BORE RIFLE (3 POSITIONS)
1984	Wu Xiao-Xuan (CHN)
1988	Silvia Sperber (FRG)
1992	Launi Meili (USA)
1996	Aleksandra Ivosev (YUG)
2000	Renata Mauer (POL)
2004	Lyubov Galkina (RUS)
2008	Du Li (CHN)

AIR RIFLE
1984	Pat Spurgin (USA)
1988	Irina Chilova (URS)
1992	Yeo Kab Soon (KOR)
1996	Renata Mauer (POL)
2000	Nancy Johnson (USA)
2004	Du Li (CHN)
2008	Katerina Emmons (CZE)

AIR PISTOL
1988	Jasna Sekaric (YUG)
1992	Marina Logvinenko (UNT)
1996	Olga Klochneva (RUS)
2000	Tao Luna (CHN)
2004	Olena Kostevych (UKR)
2008	Guo Wenjun (CHN)

Softball
1996	United States
2000	United States

Softball (continued)
2004	United States
2008	Japan

Swimming (men)

50-METER FREESTYLE		SEC
1988	Matt Biondi (USA)	22.14
1992	Aleksandr Popov (UNT)	21.91
1996	Aleksandr Popov (RUS)	22.13
2000	Anthony Ervin (USA); Gary Hall, Jr. (USA) (tied)	21.98
2004	Gary Hall, Jr. (USA)	21.93
2008	César Cielo Filho (BRA)	21.30

100-METER FREESTYLE		MIN:SEC
1896	Alfred Hajos (HUN)	1:22.2
1904[26]	Zoltan Halmay (HUN)	1:02.8
1908	Charles Daniels (USA)	1:05.6
1912	Duke Paoa Kahanamoku (USA)	1:03.4
1920	Duke Paoa Kahanamoku (USA)	1:00.4
1924	Johnny Weissmuller (USA)	59.0
1928	Johnny Weissmuller (USA)	58.6
1932	Yasuji Miyazaki (JPN)	58.2
1936	Ferenc Csik (HUN)	57.6
1948	Walter Ris (USA)	57.3
1952	Clark Scholes (USA)	57.4
1956	Jon Henricks (AUS)	55.4
1960	John Devitt (AUS)	55.2
1964	Donald Schollander (USA)	53.4
1968	Michael Wenden (AUS)	52.2
1972	Mark Spitz (USA)	51.22
1976	Jim Montgomery (USA)	49.99
1980	Jörg Wöithe (GDR)	50.40
1984	Ambrose Gaines (USA)	49.80
1988	Matt Biondi (USA)	48.63
1992	Aleksandr Popov (UNT)	49.02
1996	Aleksandr Popov (RUS)	48.74
2000	Pieter van den Hoogenband (NED)	48.30
2004	Pieter van den Hoogenband (NED)	48.17
2008	Alain Bernard (FRA)	47.21

100 METER FREESTYLE FOR SAILORS		MIN:SEC
1896	Ioannis Malokinis (GRE)	2:20.4

200-METER FREESTYLE		MIN:SEC
1900	Fred Lane (AUS)	2:25.2
1904[27]	Charles Daniels (USA)	2:44.2
1968	Michael Wenden (AUS)	1:55.2
1972	Mark Spitz (USA)	1:52.78
1976	Bruce Furniss (USA)	1:50.29
1980	Sergey Koplyakov (URS)	1:49.81
1984	Michael Gross (FRG)	1:47.44
1988	Duncan Armstrong (AUS)	1:47.25
1992	Yevgeny Sadovy (UNT)	1:46.70
1996	Danyon Loader (NZL)	1:47.63
2000	Pieter van den Hoogenband (NED)	1:45.35
2004	Ian Thorpe (AUS)	1:44.71
2008	Michael Phelps (USA)	1:42.96

400-METER FREESTYLE		MIN:SEC
1896[28]	Paul Neumann (AUT)	8:12.6
1904[29]	Charles Daniels (USA)	6:16.2
1908	Henry Taylor (GBR)	5:36.8
1912	George Hodgson (CAN)	5:24.4
1920	Norman Ross (USA)	5:26.8
1924	Johnny Weissmuller (USA)	5:04.2
1928	Victoriano Zorilla (ARG)	5:01.6
1932	Clarence Crabbe (USA)	4:48.4
1936	Jack Medica (USA)	4:44.5

Summer Olympic Games (continued)

Swimming (men) (continued)

400-METER FREESTYLE (CONTINUED)

Year	Name	MIN:SEC
1948	William Smith (USA)	4:41.0
1952	Jean Boiteux (FRA)	4:30.7
1956	Murray Rose (AUS)	4:27.3
1960	Murray Rose (AUS)	4:18.3
1964	Donald Schollander (USA)	4:12.2
1968	Michael Burton (USA)	4:09.0
1972	Bradford Cooper (AUS)[2]	4:00.27
1976	Brian Goodell (USA)	3:51.93
1980	Vladimir Salnikov (URS)	3:51.31
1984	George DiCarlo (USA)	3:51.23
1988	Uwe Dassler (GDR)	3:46.95
1992	Yevgeny Sadovy (UNT)	3:45.00
1996	Danyon Loader (NZL)	3:47.97
2000	Ian Thorpe (AUS)	3:40.59
2004	Ian Thorpe (AUS)	3:43.10
2008	Park Tae Hwan (KOR)	3:41.86

1,500-METER FREESTYLE

Year	Name	MIN:SEC
1896[30]	Alfred Hajos (HUN)	18:22.2
1900[31]	Johnny Arthur Jarvis (GBR)	13:40.2
1904[32]	Emil Rausch (GER)	27:18.2
1908	Henry Taylor (GBR)	22:48.4
1912	George Hodgson (CAN)	22:00.0
1920	Norman Ross (USA)	22:23.2
1924	Andrew Charlton (AUS)	20:06.6
1928	Arne Borg (SWE)	19:51.8
1932	Kusuo Kitamura (JPN)	19:12.4
1936	Noburu Terada (JPN)	19:13.7
1948	James McLane (USA)	19:18.5
1952	Ford Konno (USA)	18:30:0
1956	Murray Rose (AUS)	17:58.9
1960	John Konrads (AUS)	17:19.6
1964	Robert Windle (AUS)	17:01.7
1968	Michael Burton (USA)	16:38.9
1972	Michael Burton (USA)	15:52.58
1976	Brian Goodell (USA)	15:02.40
1980	Vladimir Salnikov (URS)	14:58.27
1984	Michael O'Brien (USA)	15:05.20
1988	Vladimir Salnikov (URS)	15:00.40
1992	Kieren Perkins (AUS)	14:43.48
1996	Kieren Perkins (AUS)	14:56.40
2000	Grant Hackett (AUS)	14:48.33
2004	Grant Hackett (AUS)	14:43.40
2008	Oussama Mellouli (TUN)	14:40.84

4,000-METER FREESTYLE

Year	Name	MIN:SEC
1900	Johnny Arthur Jarvis (GBR)	58:24

880-YARD FREESTYLE

Year	Name	MIN:SEC
1904	Emil Rausch (GER)	13:11.4

1-MILE FREESTYLE

Year	Name	MIN:SEC
1904	Emil Rausch (GER)	27:18.2

100-METER BUTTERFLY

Year	Name	SEC
1968	Douglas Russell (USA)	55.9
1972	Mark Spitz (USA)	54.27
1976	Matt Vogel (USA)	54.35
1980	Pär Arvidsson (SWE)	54.92
1984	Michael Gross (FRG)	53.08
1988	Anthony Nesty (SUR)	53.00
1992	Pablo Morales (USA)	53.32
1996	Denis Pankratov (RUS)	52.27
2000	Lars Frölander (SWE)	52.00
2004	Michael Phelps (USA)	51.25
2008	Michael Phelps (USA)	50.58

Swimming (men) (continued)

200-METER BUTTERFLY

Year	Name	MIN
1956	William Yorzyk (USA)	2:19.3
1960	Michael Troy (USA)	2:12.8
1964	Kevin Berry (AUS)	2:06.6
1968	Carl Robie (USA)	2:08.7
1972	Mark Spitz (USA)	2:00.70
1976	Mike Bruner (USA)	1:59.23
1980	Sergey Fesenko (URS)	1:59.76
1984	Jonathan Sieben (AUS)	1:57.04
1988	Michael Gross (FRG)	1:56.94
1992	Mel Stewart (USA)	1:56.26
1996	Denis Pankratov (RUS)	1:56.51
2000	Tom Malchow (USA)	1:55.35
2004	Michael Phelps (USA)	1:54.04
2008	Michael Phelps (USA)	1:52.03

100-METER BACKSTROKE

Year	Name	MIN:SEC
1904[33]	Walter Brack (GER)	1:16.8
1908	Arno Bieberstein (GER)	1:24.6
1912	Harry Hebner (USA)	1:21.2
1920	Warren Paoa Kealoha (USA)	1:15.2
1924	Warren Paoa Kealoha (USA)	1:13.2
1928	George Kojac (USA)	1:08.2
1932	Masaji Kiyokawa (JPN)	1:08.6
1936	Adolph Kiefer (USA)	1:05.9
1948	Allen Stack (USA)	1:06.4
1952	Yoshinobu Oyakawa (JPN)	1:05.4
1956	David Theile (AUS)	1:02.2
1960	David Theile (AUS)	1:01.9
1968	Roland Matthes (GDR)	58.7
1972	Roland Matthes (GDR)	56.58
1976	John Naber (USA)	55.49
1980	Bengt Baron (SWE)	56.53
1984	Richard Carey (USA)	55.79
1988	Daichi Suzuki (JPN)	55.05
1992	Mark Tewksbury (CAN)	53.98
1996	Jeff Rouse (USA)	54.10
2000	Lenny Krayzelburg (USA)	53.72
2004	Aaron Peirsol (USA)	54.06
2008	Aaron Peirsol (USA)	52.54

200-METER BACKSTROKE

Year	Name	MIN:SEC
1900	Ernst Hoppenberg (GER)	2:47.0
1964	Jed Graef (USA)	2:10.3
1968	Roland Matthes (GDR)	2:09.6
1972	Roland Matthes (GDR)	2:02.82
1976	John Naber (USA)	1:59.19
1980	Sandor Wladar (HUN)	2:01.93
1984	Richard Carey (USA)	2:00.23
1988	Igor Polyansky (URS)	1:59.37
1992	Martin López-Zubero (ESP)	1:58.47
1996	Brad Bridgewater (USA)	1:58.54
2000	Lenny Krayzelburg (USA)	1:56.76
2004	Aaron Peirsol (USA)	1:54.95
2008	Ryan Lochte (USA)	1:53.94

100-METER BREASTSTROKE

Year	Name	MIN:SEC
1968	Donald McKenzie (USA)	1:07.7
1972	Nobutaka Tagushi (JPN)	1:04.94
1976	John Hencken (USA)	1:03.11
1980	Duncan Goodhew (GBR)	1:03.34
1984	Steve Lundquist (USA)	1:01.65
1988	Adrian Moorhouse (GBR)	1:02.04
1992	Nelson Diebel (USA)	1:01.50
1996	Frederick Deburghgraeve (BEL)	1:00.65
2000	Domenico Fioravanti (ITA)	1:00.46
2004	Kosuke Kitajima (JPN)	1:00.08
2008	Kosuke Kitajima (JPN)	0:58.91

Summer Olympic Games (continued)

Swimming (men) (continued)

200-METER BREASTSTROKE

		MIN:SEC
1908	Frederick Holman (GBR)	3:09.2
1912	Walter Bathe (GER)	3:01.8
1920	Hakan Malmroth (SWE)	3:04.4
1924	Robert Skelton (USA)	2:56.6
1928	Yoshiyuki Tsuruta (JPN)	2:48.8
1932	Yoshiyuki Tsuruta (JPN)	2:45.4
1936	Tetsuo Hamuro (JPN)	2:42.5
1948	Joseph Verdeur (USA)	2:39.3
1952	John Davies (AUS)	2:34.4
1956	Masaru Furukawa (JPN)	2:34.7
1960	William Mulliken (USA)	2:37.4
1964	Ian O'Brien (AUS)	2:27.8
1968	Felipe Muñoz (MEX)	2:28.7
1972	John Hencken (USA)	2:21.55
1976	David Wilkie (GBR)	2:15.11
1980	Robertas Zulpa (URS)	2:15.85
1984	Victor Davis (CAN)	2:13.34
1988	Jozsef Szabo (HUN)	2:13.52
1992	Mike Barrowman (USA)	2:10.16
1996	Norbert Rozsa (HUN)	2:12.57
2000	Domenico Fioravanti (ITA)	2:10.87
2004	Kosuke Kitajima (JPN)	2:09.44
2008	Kosuke Kitajima (JPN)	2:07.64

400-METER BREASTSTROKE

		MIN:SEC
1904[34]	Georg Zacharias (GER)	7:23.6
1912	Walter Bathe (GER)	6:29.6
1920	Hakan Malmroth (SWE)	6:31.8

200-YARD RELAY

		MIN:SEC
1904	United States	2:04.6

200-METER INDIVIDUAL MEDLEY

		MIN:SEC
1968	Charles Hickcox (USA)	2:12.0
1972	Gunnar Larsson (SWE)	2:07.17
1984	Alex Baumann (CAN)	2:01.42
1988	Tamas Darnyi (HUN)	2:00.17
1992	Tamas Darnyi (HUN)	2:00.76
1996	Attila Czene (HUN)	1:59.91
2000	Massimiliano Rosolino (ITA)	1:58.98
2004	Michael Phelps (USA)	1:57.14
2008	Michael Phelps (USA)	1:54.23

400-METER INDIVIDUAL MEDLEY

		MIN:SEC
1964	Richard William Roth (USA)	4:45.4
1968	Charles Hickcox (USA)	4:48.4
1972	Gunnar Larsson (SWE)	4:31.98
1976	Rod Strachan (USA)	4:23.68
1980	Aleksandr Sidorenko (URS)	4:22.89
1984	Alex Baumann (CAN)	4:17.41
1988	Tamas Darnyi (HUN)	4:14.75
1992	Tamas Darnyi (HUN)	4:14.23
1996	Tom Dolan (USA)	4:14.90
2000	Tom Dolan (USA)	4:11.76
2004	Michael Phelps (USA)	4:08.26
2008	Michael Phelps (USA)	4:03.84

4 × 100-METER MEDLEY RELAY

		MIN:SEC
1960	United States	4:05.4
1964	United States	3:58.4
1968	United States	3:54.9
1972	United States	3:48.16
1976	United States	3:42.22
1980	Australia	3:45.70
1984	United States	3:39.30
1988	United States	3:36.93
1992	United States	3:36.93

Swimming (men) (continued)

4 × 100-METER MEDLEY RELAY (CONTINUED)

		MIN:SEC
1996	United States	3:34.84
2000	United States	3:33.73
2004	United States	3:30.68
2008	United States	3:29.34

4 × 100-METER FREESTYLE RELAY

		MIN:SEC
1964	United States	3:33.2
1968	United States	3:31.7
1972	United States	3:26.42
1984	United States	3:19.03
1988	United States	3:16.53
1992	United States	3:16.74
1996	United States	3:15.41
2000	Australia	3:13.67
2004	South Africa	3:13.17
2008	United States	3:08.24

4 × 200-METER FREESTYLE RELAY

		MIN:SEC
1908	Great Britain	10:55.6
1912	Australia	10:11.2
1920	United States	10:04.4
1924	United States	9:53.4
1928	United States	9:36.2
1932	Japan	8:58.4
1936	Japan	8:51.5
1948	United States	8:46.0
1952	United States	8:31.1
1956	Australia	8:23.6
1960	United States	8:10.2
1964	United States	7:52.1
1968	United States	7:52.3
1972	United States	7:35.78
1976	United States	7:23.22
1980	USSR	7:23.50
1984	United States	7:15.69
1988	United States	7:12.51
1992	Unified Team	7:11.95
1996	United States	7:14.84
2000	Australia	7:07.05
2004	United States	7:07.33
2008	United States	6:58.56

60-METER UNDERWATER

		MIN:SEC (UNDERWATER)
1900	Charles de Vendeville (FRA)	1:08.4

200-METER OBSTACLE

		MIN:SEC
1900	Frederick Lane (AUS)	2:38.4

10-KM OPEN-WATER MARATHON

		HR:MIN:SEC
2008	Maarten van der Weijden (NED)	1:51:51.6

Swimming (women)

50-METER FREESTYLE

		SEC
1988	Kristin Otto (GDR)	25.49
1992	Yang Wenyi (CHN)	24.79
1996	Amy Van Dyken (USA)	24.87
2000	Inge de Bruijn (NED)	24.32
2004	Inge de Bruijn (NED)	24.58
2008	Britta Steffen (GER)	24.06

100-METER FREESTYLE

		MIN:SEC
1912	Fanny Durack (AUS)	1:22.2
1920	Ethelda Bleibtrey (USA)	1:13.6
1924	Ethel Lackie (USA)	1:12.4
1928	Albina Osipowich (USA)	1:11.0
1932	Helene Madison (USA)	1:06.8
1936	Hendrika Mastenbroek (NED)	1:05.9

Summer Olympic Games (continued)

Swimming (women) (continued)

100-METER FREESTYLE (CONTINUED)

		MIN:SEC
1948	Greta Andersen (DEN)	1:06.3
1952	Katalin Szoke (HUN)	1:06.8
1956	Dawn Fraser (AUS)	1:02.0
1960	Dawn Fraser (AUS)	1:01.2
1964	Dawn Fraser (AUS)	59.5
1968	Jan Henne (USA)	1:00.0
1972	Sandra Neilson (USA)	58.59
1976	Kornelia Ender (GDR)	55.65
1980	Barbara Krause (GDR)	54.79
1984	Carrie Steinseifer (USA); Nancy Hogshead (USA) (tied)	55.92
1988	Kristin Otto (GDR)	54.93
1992	Zhuang Yong (CHN)	54.64
1996	Le Jingyi (CHN)	54.50
2000	Inge de Bruijn (NED)	53.83
2004	Jodie Henry (AUS)	53.84
2008	Britta Steffen (GER)	53.12

200-METER FREESTYLE

		MIN:SEC
1968	Debbie Meyer (USA)	2:10.5
1972	Shane Gould (AUS)	2:03.56
1976	Kornelia Ender (GDR)	1:59.26
1980	Barbara Krause (GDR)	1:58.33
1984	Mary Wayte (USA)	1:59.23
1988	Heike Friedrich (GDR)	1:57.65
1992	Nicole Haislett (USA)	1:57.90
1996	Claudia Poll (CRC)	1:58.16
2000	Susie O'Neill (AUS)	1:58.24
2004	Camelia Potec (ROM)	1:58.03
2008	Federica Pellegrini (ITA)	1:54.82

400-METER FREESTYLE

		MIN:SEC
1920[35]	Ethelda Bleibtrey (USA)	4:34.0
1924	Martha Norelius (USA)	6:02.2
1928	Martha Norelius (USA)	5:42.8
1932	Helene Madison (USA)	5:28.5
1936	Hendrika Mastenbroek (NED)	5:26.4
1948	Ann Curtis (USA)	5:17.8
1952	Valeria Gyenge (HUN)	5:12.1
1956	Lorraine Crapp (AUS)	4:54.6
1960	Susan Christina von Saltza (USA)	4:50.6
1964	Virginia Duenkel (USA)	4:43.3
1968	Debbie Meyer (USA)	4:31.8
1972	Shane Gould (AUS)	4:19.04
1976	Petra Thümer (GDR)	4:09.89
1980	Ines Diers (GDR)	4:08.76
1984	Tiffany Cohen (USA)	4:07.10
1988	Janet Evans (USA)	4:03.85
1992	Dagmar Hase (GER)	4:07.18
1996	Michelle Smith (IRL)	4:07.25
2000	Brooke Bennett (USA)	4:05.80
2004	Laure Manaudou (FRA)	4:05.34
2008	Rebecca Adlington (GBR)	4:03.22

800-METER FREESTYLE

		MIN:SEC
1968	Debbie Meyer (USA)	9:24.0
1972	Keena Rothhammer (USA)	8:53.68
1976	Petra Thümer (GDR)	8:37.14
1980	Michelle Ford (AUS)	8:28.90
1984	Tiffany Cohen (USA)	8:24.95
1988	Janet Evans (USA)	8:20.20
1992	Janet Evans (USA)	8:25.52
1996	Brooke Bennett (USA)	8:27.89
2000	Brooke Bennett (USA)	8:19.67
2004	Ai Shibata (JPN)	8:24.54
2008	Rebecca Adlington (GBR)	8:14.10

Swimming (women) (continued)

100-METER BUTTERFLY

		MIN:SEC
1956	Shelley Mann (USA)	1:11.0
1960	Carolyn Schuler (USA)	1:09.5
1964	Sharon Stouder (USA)	1:04.7
1968	Lynette McClements (AUS)	1:05.5
1972	Mayumi Aoki (JPN)	1:03.34
1976	Kornelia Ender (GDR)	1:00.13
1980	Caren Metschuck (GDR)	1:00.42
1984	Mary Meagher (USA)	59.26
1988	Kristin Otto (GDR)	59.00
1992	Qian Hong (CHN)	58.62
1996	Amy Van Dyken (USA)	59.13
2000	Inge de Bruijn (NED)	56.61
2004	Petria Thomas (AUS)	57.72
2008	Lisbeth Lenton Trickett (AUS)	56.73

200-METER BUTTERFLY

		MIN:SEC
1968	Aagje Kok (NED)	2:24.7
1972	Karen Moe (USA)	2:15.57
1976	Andrea Pollack (GDR)	2:11.41
1980	Ines Geissler (GDR)	2:10.44
1984	Mary Meagher (USA)	2:06.90
1988	Kathleen Nord (GDR)	2:09.51
1992	Summer Sanders (USA)	2:08.67
1996	Susie O'Neill (AUS)	2:07.76
2000	Misty Hyman (USA)	2:05.88
2004	Otylia Jedrzejczak (POL)	2:06.05
2008	Liu Zige (CHN)	2:04.18

100-METER BACKSTROKE

		MIN:SEC
1924	Sybil Bauer (USA)	1:23.2
1928	Maria Braun (NED)	1:22.0
1932	Eleanor Holm (USA)	1:19.4
1936	Dina Senff (NED)	1:18.9
1948	Karen-Margrete Harup (DEN)	1:14.4
1952	Joan Harrison (RSA)	1:14.3
1956	Judith Grinham (GBR)	1:12.9
1960	Lynn Burke (USA)	1:09.3
1964	Cathy Ferguson (USA)	1:07.7
1968	Kaye Hall (USA)	1:06.2
1972	Melissa Belote (USA)	1:05.78
1976	Urike Richter (GDR)	1:01.83
1980	Rica Reinisch (GDR)	1:00.86
1984	Theresa Andrews (USA)	1:02.55
1988	Kristin Otto (GDR)	1:00.89
1992	Krisztina Egerszegi (HUN)	1:00.68
1996	Beth Botsford (USA)	1:01.19
2000	Diana Mocanu (ROM)	1:00.21
2004	Natalie Coughlin (USA)	1:00.37
2008	Natalie Coughlin (USA)	0:58.96

200-METER BACKSTROKE

		MIN:SEC
1968	Pokey Watson (USA)	2:24.8
1972	Melissa Belote (USA)	2:19.19
1976	Ulrike Richter (GDR)	2:13.43
1980	Rica Reinisch (GDR)	2:11.77
1984	Jolanda De Rover (NED)	2:12.38
1988	Krisztina Egerszegi (HUN)	2:09.29
1992	Krisztina Egerszegi (HUN)	2:07.06
1996	Krisztina Egerszegi (HUN)	2:07.83
2000	Diana Mocanu (ROM)	2:08.16
2004	Kirsty Coventry (ZIM)	2:09.19
2008	Kirsty Coventry (ZIM)	2:05.24

100-METER BREASTSTROKE

		MIN:SEC
1968	Djurdjica Bjedov (YUG)	1:15.8
1972	Cathy Carr (USA)	1:13.58
1976	Hannelore Anke (GDR)	1:11.16

Summer Olympic Games (continued)

Swimming (women) (continued)

100-METER BREASTSTROKE (CONTINUED)	MIN:SEC
1980	Ute Geveniger (GDR)	1:10.22
1984	Petra van Staveren (NED)	1:09.88
1988	Tanya Dangalakova (BUL)	1:07.95
1992	Yelena Rudkovskaya (UNT)	1:08.00
1996	Penelope Heyns (RSA)	1:07.73
2000	Megan Quann (USA)	1:07.05
2004	Luo Xuejuan (CHN)	1:06.64
2008	Leisel Jones (AUS)	1:05.17

200-METER BREASTSTROKE	MIN:SEC
1924	Lucy Morton (GBR)	3:33.2
1928	Hilde Schrader (GER)	3:12.6
1932	Claire Dennis (AUS)	3:06.3
1936	Hideko Maehata (JPN)	3:03.6
1948	Petronella van Vliet (NED)	2:57.2
1952	Eva Szekely (HUN)	2:51.7
1956	Ursula Happe (GER)	2:53.1
1960	Anita Lonsbrough (GBR)	2:49.5
1964	Galina Prozumenshchikova-Stepanova (URS)	2:46.4
1968	Sharon Wichman (USA)	2:44.4
1972	Beverley Whitfield (AUS)	2:41.71
1976	Marina Koshevaya (URS)	2:33.35
1980	Lina Kachushite (URS)	2:29.54
1984	Anne Ottenbrite (CAN)	2:30.38
1988	Silke Hörner (GDR)	2:26.71
1992	Kyoko Iwasaki (JPN)	2:26.65
1996	Penelope Heyns (RSA)	2:25.41
2000	Agnes Kovacs (HUN)	2:24.35
2004	Amanda Beard (USA)	2:23.37
2008	Rebecca Soni (USA)	2:20.22

200-METER INDIVIDUAL MEDLEY	MIN:SEC
1968	Claudia Kolb (USA)	2:24.7
1972	Shane Gould (AUS)	2:23.07
1984	Tracy Caulkins (USA)	2:12.64
1988	Daniela Hunger (GDR)	2:12.59
1992	Li Lin (CHN)	2:11.65
1996	Michelle Smith (IRL)	2:13.93
2000	Yana Klochkova (UKR)	2:10.68
2004	Yana Klochkova (UKR)	2:11.14
2008	Stephanie Rice (AUS)	2:08.45

400-METER INDIVIDUAL MEDLEY	MIN:SEC
1964	Donna De Varona (USA)	5:18.7
1968	Claudia Kolb (USA)	5:08.5
1972	Gail Neall (AUS)	5:02.97
1976	Ulrike Tauber (GDR)	4:42.77
1980	Petra Schneider (GDR)	4:36.29
1984	Tracy Caulkins (USA)	4:39.24
1988	Janet Evans (USA)	4:37.76
1992	Krisztina Egerszegi (HUN)	4:36.54
1996	Michelle Smith (IRL)	4:39.18
2000	Yana Klochkova (UKR)	4:33.59
2004	Yana Klochkova (UKR)	4:34.83
2008	Stephanie Rice (AUS)	4:29.45

4 × 100-METER MEDLEY RELAY	MIN:SEC
1960	United States	4:41.1
1964	United States	4:33.9
1968	United States	4:28.3
1972	United States	4:20.75
1976	East Germany	4:07.95
1980	East Germany	4:06.67
1984	United States	4:08.34
1988	East Germany	4:03.74
1992	United States	4:02.54

Swimming (women) (continued)

4 × 100-METER MEDLEY RELAY (CONTINUED)	MIN:SEC
1996	United States	4:02.88
2000	United States	3:58.30
2004	Australia	3:57.32
2008	Australia	3:52.69

4 × 100-METER FREESTYLE RELAY	MIN:SEC
1912	Great Britain	5:52.8
1920	United States	5:11.6
1924	United States	4:58.8
1928	United States	4:47.6
1932	United States	4:38.0
1936	The Netherlands	4:36.0
1948	United States	4:29.2
1952	Hungary	4:24.4
1956	Australia	4:17.1
1960	United States	4:08.9
1964	United States	4:03.8
1968	United States	4:02.5
1972	United States	3:55.19
1976	United States	3:44.82
1980	East Germany	3:42.71
1984	United States	3:43.43
1988	East Germany	3:40.63
1992	United States	3:39.46
1996	United States	3:39.29
2000	United States	3:36.61
2004	Australia	3:35.94
2008	The Netherlands	3:33.76

4 × 200-METER FREESTYLE RELAY	MIN:SEC
1996	United States	7:59.87
2000	United States	7:57.80
2004	United States	7:53.42
2008	Australia	7:44.31

10-KM OPEN-WATER MARATHON	HR:MIN:SEC
2008	Larisa Ilchenko (RUS)	1:59:27.7

Synchronized Swimming

INDIVIDUAL
1984 Tracie Ruiz (USA)
1988 Carolyn Waldo (CAN)
1992 Kristen Babb-Sprague (USA);
      Sylvie Fréchette (CAN)[36]

DUET
1984 United States
1988 Canada
1992 United States
2000 Russia
2004 Russia
2008 Russia

TEAM
1996 United States
2000 Russia
2004 Russia
2008 Russia

Table Tennis (men)

SINGLES
1988 Yoo Nam Kyu (KOR)
1992 Jan-Ove Waldner (SWE)
1996 Liu Guoliang (CHN)
2000 Kong Linghui (CHN)
2004 Ryu Seung Min (KOR)
2008 Ma Lin (CHN)

Summer Olympic Games (continued)

Table Tennis (men) (continued)

TEAM
1988	China
1992	China
1996	China
2000	China
2004	China
2008	China

Table Tennis (women)

SINGLES
1988	Chen Jing (CHN)
1992	Deng Yaping (CHN)
1996	Deng Yaping (CHN)
2000	Wang Nan (CHN)
2004	Zhang Yining (CHN)
2008	Zhang Yining (CHN)

TEAM
1988	Republic of Korea
1992	China
1996	China
2000	China
2004	China
2008	China

Taekwondo (men)

58 KG (127.6 LB)
2000	Michail Mouroutsos (GRE)
2004	Chu Mu Yen (TPE)
2008	Guillermo Pérez (MEX)

68 KG (149.6 LB)
2000	Steven Lopez (USA)
2004	Hadi Saei Bonehkohal (IRI)
2008	Son Tae Jin (KOR)

80 KG (176 LB)
2000	Angel Valodia Matos (CUB)
2004	Steven Lopez (USA)
2008	Hadi Saei (IRI)

OVER 80 KG (176+ LB)
2000	Kim Kyong-Hun (KOR)
2004	Moon Sung Dae (KOR)
2008	Cha Dong Min (KOR)

Taekwondo (women)

49 KG (107.8 LB)
2000	Lauren Burns (AUS)
2004	Chen Shih Hsin (TPE)
2008	Wu Jingyu (CHN)

57 KG (125.4 LB)
2000	Jung Jae-Eun (KOR)
2004	Jang Ji Won (KOR)
2008	Lim Su Jeong (KOR)

67 KG (147.4 LB)
2000	Lee Sun-Hee (KOR)
2004	Luo Wei (CHN)
2008	Hwang Kyung Seon (KOR)

OVER 67 KG (147.4+ LB)
2000	Chen Zhong (CHN)
2004	Chen Zhong (CHN)
2008	María del Rosario Espinoza (MEX)

Tennis (men)

SINGLES
1896	John Pius Boland (GBR)
1900	Laurie Doherty (GBR)
1904	Beals Wright (USA)
1908	Josiah Ritchie (GBR)
1912	Charles Winslow (RSA)
1920	Louis Raymond (RSA)
1924	Vincent Richards (USA)
1988	Miloslav Mecir (TCH)
1992	Marc Rosset (SUI)
1996	Andre Agassi (USA)
2000	Yevgeny Kafelnikov (RUS)
2004	Nicolas Massu (CHI)
2008	Rafael Nadal (ESP)

DOUBLES
1896	John Pius Boland (GBR), Friedrich Thraun (GER)
1900	Laurie Doherty, Reggie Doherty (GBR)
1904	Edgar Leonard, Beals Wright (USA)
1908	George Hillyard, Reggie Doherty (GBR)
1912	Harold Kitson, Charles Winslow (RSA)
1920	Oswald Noel Turnbull, Max Woosnam (GBR)
1924	Frank Hunter, Vinnie Richards (USA)
1988	Kenneth Flach, Robert Seguso (USA)
1992	Boris Becker, Michael Stich (GER)
1996	Todd Woodbridge, Mark Woodforde (AUS)
2000	Sebastien Lareau, Daniel Nestor (CAN)
2004	Fernando Gonzalez, Nicolas Massu (CHI)
2008	Roger Federer, Stanislas Wawrinka (SUI)

MIXED DOUBLES
1900	Charlotte Cooper, Reggie Doherty (GBR)
1912	Dora Köring, Heinrich Schomburgk (GER)
1920	Suzanne Lenglen, Max Décugis (FRA)
1924	Hazel Wightman, R. Norris Williams (USA)

Tennis (women)

SINGLES
1900	Charlotte Cooper (GBR)
1908	Dorothea Lambert Chambers (GBR)
1912	Marguerite Broquedis (FRA)
1920	Suzanne Lenglen (FRA)
1924	Helen Wills Moody (USA)
1988	Steffi Graf (FRG)
1992	Jennifer Capriati (USA)
1996	Lindsay Davenport (USA)
2000	Venus Williams (USA)
2004	Justine Henin-Hardenne (BEL)
2008	Yelena Dementyeva (RUS)

DOUBLES
1920	Winifred McNair, Kathleen McKane (GBR)
1924	Helen Wills Moody, Hazel Wightman (USA)
1988	Zina Garrison, Pam Shriver (USA)
1992	Gigi Fernández, Mary Joe Fernández (USA)
1996	Gigi Fernández, Mary Joe Fernández (USA)
2000	Serena Williams, Venus Williams (USA)
2004	Li Ting, Sun Tian Tian (CHN)
2008	Serena Williams, Venus Williams (USA)

Tennis—Covered Courts (Indoor Tennis)

MEN'S SINGLES
1908	Arthur Gore (GBR)
1912	André Gobert (FRA)

Summer Olympic Games (continued)

Tennis—Covered Courts (Indoor Tennis) (continued)

MEN'S DOUBLES
1908 Arthur Gore, Herbert Roper Barrett (GBR)
1912 Maurice Germot, André Gobert (FRA)

WOMEN'S SINGLES
1908 Gladys Eastlake-Smith (GBR)
1912 Edith Hannam (GBR)

MIXED DOUBLES
1912 Edith Hannam, Charles Dixon (GBR)

Triathlon (swim/bike/run) (men)
2000 Simon Whitfield (CAN)
2004 Hamish Carter (NZL)
2008 Jan Frodeno (GER)

Triathlon (swim/bike/run) (women)
2000 Brigitte McMahon (SUI)
2004 Kate Allen (AUT)
2008 Emma Snowsill (AUS)

Volleyball (men)

INDOOR
1964 USSR
1968 USSR
1972 Japan
1976 Poland
1980 USSR
1984 United States
1988 United States
1992 Brazil
1996 The Netherlands
2000 Yugoslavia
2004 Brazil
2008 United States

BEACH
1996 United States
2000 United States
2004 Brazil
2008 United States

Volleyball (women)

INDOOR
1964 Japan
1968 USSR
1972 USSR
1976 Japan
1980 USSR
1984 China
1988 USSR
1992 Cuba
1996 Cuba
2000 Cuba
2004 China
2008 Brazil

BEACH
1996 Brazil
2000 Australia
2004 United States
2008 United States

Water Polo (men)
1900 Great Britain
1904 United States
1908 Great Britain
1912 Great Britain

Water Polo (men) (continued)
1920 Great Britain
1924 France
1928 Germany
1932 Hungary
1936 Hungary
1948 Italy
1952 Hungary
1956 Hungary
1960 Italy
1964 Hungary
1968 Yugoslavia
1972 USSR
1976 Hungary
1980 USSR
1984 Yugoslavia
1988 Yugoslavia
1992 Italy
1996 Spain
2000 Hungary
2004 Hungary
2008 Hungary

Water Polo (women)
2000 Australia
2004 Italy
2008 The Netherlands

Weight Lifting (men)[37, 38]

56 KG (123.2 LB)
		KG
1972	Zygmunt Smalcerz (POL)	337.5
1976	Aleksandr Voronin (URS)	242.5
1980	Kanybek Osmanaliyev (URS)	245.0
1984	Zeng Guoqiang (CHN)	235.0
1988	Sevdalin Marinov (BUL)	270.0
1992	Ivan Ivanov (BUL)	265.0
1996	Halil Mutlu (TUR)	287.5
2000	Halil Mutlu (TUR)	305.0
2004	Halil Mutlu (TUR)	295.0
2008	Long Qingquan (CHN)	292.0

62 KG (136.4 LB)
		KG
1948	Joseph de Pietro (USA)	307.5
1952	Ivan Udodov (URS)	315.0
1956	Charles Vinci (USA)	342.5
1960	Charles Vinci (USA)	345.0
1964	Aleksey Vakhonin (URS)	357.5
1968	Mohammad Nassiri (IRI)	367.5
1972	Imre Foldi (HUN)	377.5
1976	Norair Nurikian (BUL)	262.5
1980	Daniel Núñez (CUB)	275.0
1984	Wu Shude (CHN)	267.5
1988	Oksen Mirzoyan (URS)[2]	292.5
1992	Chun Byung Kwan (KOR)	287.5
1996	Tang Ningsheng (CHN)	307.5
2000	Nikolay Pechalov (CRO)	325.0
2004	Shi Zhiyong (CHN)	325.0
2008	Zhang Xiangxiang (CHN)	319.0

69 KG (151.8 LB)
		KG
1920	Frans de Haes (BEL)	220.0
1924	Pierino Gabetti (ITA)	402.5[39]
1928	Franz Andrysek (AUT)	287.5
1932	Raymond Suvigny (FRA)	287.5
1936	Anthony Terlazzo (USA)	312.5
1948	Mahmoud Fayad (EGY)	332.5
1952	Rafael Chimishkyan (URS)	337.5
1956	Isaac Berger (USA)	352.5
1960	Yevgeny Minayev (URS)	372.5

Summer Olympic Games (continued)

Weight Lifting (men)[37, 38] (continued)

69 KG (151.8 LB) (CONTINUED)

Year	Athlete	KG
1964	Yoshinobu Miyake (JPN)	397.5
1968	Yoshinobu Miyake (JPN)	392.5
1972	Norair Nurikian (BUL)	402.5
1976	Nikolay Kolesnikov (URS)	285.0
1980	Viktor Mazin (URS)	290.0
1984	Chen Weiqiang (CHN)	282.5
1988	Naim Suleymanoglu (TUR)	342.5
1992	Naim Suleymanoglu (TUR)	320.0
1996	Naim Suleymanoglu (TUR)	335.0
2000	Galabin Boevski (BUL)	357.5
2004	Zhang Guozheng (CHN)	347.5
2008	Liao Hui (CHN)	348.0

70 KG (154 LB)

Year	Athlete	KG
1920	Alfred Neyland (EST)	257.5
1924	Edmond Décottignies (FRA)	440.0[39]
1928	Kurt Helbig (GER); Hans Haas (AUT) (tied)	322.5
1932	René Duverger (FRA)	325.0
1936	Mohamed Ahmed Mesbah (EGY); Robert Fein (AUT) (tied)	342.5
1948	Ibrahim Shams (EGY)	360.0
1952	Tommy Kono (USA)	362.5
1956	Igor Rybak (URS)	380.0
1960	Viktor Bushuyev (URS)	397.5
1964	Waldemar Baszanowski (POL)	432.5
1968	Waldemar Baszanowski (POL)	437.5
1972	Mukharbi Kirzhinov (URS)	460.0
1976	Pyotr Korol (URS)[2]	305.0
1980	Yanko Rusev (BUL)	342.5
1984	Yao Jingyuan (CHN)	320.0
1988	Joachim Kunz (GDR)[2]	340.0
1992	Israil Militosyan (UNT)	337.5
1996	Zhan Xugang (CHN)	357.5

77 KG (169.4 LB)

Year	Athlete	KG
1920	Henri Gance (FRA)	245.0
1924	Carlo Galimberti (ITA)	492.5[39]
1928	François Roger (FRA)	335.0
1932	Rudolf Ismayr (GER)	345.0
1936	Khadr el Thouni (EGY)	387.5
1948	Frank Spellman (USA)	390.0
1952	Peter George (USA)	400.0
1956	Fyodor Bogdanovsky (URS)	420.0
1960	Aleksandr Kurynov (URS)	437.5
1964	Hans Zdrazila (TCH)	445.0
1968	Viktor Kurentsov (URS)	475.0
1972	Iordan Bikov (BUL)	485.0
1976	Iordan Mitkov (BUL)	335.0
1980	Asen Zlatev (BUL)	360.0
1984	Karl-Heinz Radschinsky (FRG)	340.0
1988	Borislav Gidikov (BUL)	375.0
1992	Fyodor Kassapu (UNT)	357.5
1996	Pablo Lara (CUB)	367.5
2000	Zhan Xugang (CHN)	367.5
2004	Taner Sagir (TUR)	375.0
2008	Sa Jae Hyouk (KOR)	366.0

85 KG (187 LB)

Year	Athlete	KG
1920	Ernest Cadine (FRA)	290.0
1924	Charles Rigoulot (FRA)	502.5[39]
1928	El Sayed Nosseir (EGY)	355.0
1932	Louis Hostin (FRA)	365.0
1936	Louis Hostin (FRA)	372.5
1948	Stanley Stanczyk (USA)	417.5
1952	Trofim Lomakin (URS)	417.5
1956	Tommy Kono (USA)	447.5

Weight Lifting (men)[37, 38] (continued)

85 KG (187 LB) (CONTINUED)

Year	Athlete	KG
1960	Ireneusz Palinski (POL)	442.5
1964	Rudolph Plyukfelder (URS)	475.0
1968	Boris Selitsky (URS)	485.0
1972	Leif Jenssen (NOR)	507.5
1976	Valery Shary (URS)	365.0
1980	Yury Vardanyan (URS)	400.0
1984	Petre Becheru (ROM)	355.0
1988	Israil Arsamakov (URS)	377.5
1992	Pyrros Dimas (GRE)	370.0
1996	Pyrros Dimas (GRE)	392.5
2000	Pyrros Dimas (GRE)	390.0
2004	George Asanidze (GEO)	382.5
2008	Lu Yong (CHN)	394.0

94 KG (206.8 LB)

Year	Athlete	KG
1952	Norbert Schemansky (USA)	445.0
1956	Arkady Vorobyev (URS)	462.5
1960	Arkady Vorobyev (URS)	472.5
1964	Vladimir Golovanov (URS)	487.5
1968	Kaarlo Kangasniemi (FIN)	517.5
1972	Andon Nikolov (BUL)	525.0
1976	David Rigert (URS)	382.5
1980	Peter Baczako (HUN)	377.5
1984	Nicu Vlad (ROM)	392.5
1988	Anatoly Khrapaty (URS)	412.5
1992	Kakhi Kakhiashvili (UNT)	412.5
1996	Aleksey Petrov (RUS)	402.5
2000	Akakios Kakhiashvilis (GRE)	405.0
2004	Milen Dobrev (BUL)	407.5
2008	Ilya Ilin (KAZ)	406.0

99 KG (217.8 LB)

Year	Athlete	KG
1980	Ota Zaremba (TCH)	395.0
1984	Rolf Milser (FRG)	385.0
1988	Pavel Kuznetsov (URS)	425.0
1992	Viktor Tregubov (UNT)	410.0
1996	Akakios Kakhiashvilis (GRE)	420.0

105 KG (231 LB)

Year	Athlete	KG
1972	Jan Talts (URS)	580.0
1976	Yury Zaytsev (URS)[2]	385.0
1980	Leonid Taranenko (URS)	422.5
1984	Norberto Oberburger (ITA)	390.0
1988	Yury Zakharevitch (URS)	455.0
1992	Ronny Weller (GER)	432.5
1996	Timur Taymazov (UKR)	430.0
2000	Hossein Tavakoli (IRI)	425.0
2004	Dmitry Berestov (RUS)	425.0
2008	Andrei Aramnau (BLR)	436.0

OVER 105 KG (231+ LB)

Year	Athlete	KG
1920	Filippo Bottino (ITA)	265.5
1924	Giuseppe Tonani (ITA)	517.5[39]
1928	Josef Strassberger (GER)	372.5
1932	Jaroslav Skobla (TCH)	380.0
1936	Josef Manger (GER)	410.0
1948	John Davis (USA)	452.5
1952	John Davis (USA)	460.0
1956	Paul Anderson (USA)	500.0
1960	Yury Vlasov (URS)	537.5
1964	Leonid Zhabotinsky (URS)	572.5
1968	Leonid Zhabotinsky (URS)	572.5
1972	Vasily Alekseyev (URS)	640.0
1976	Vasily Alekseyev (URS)	440.0
1980	Sultan Rakhmanov (URS)	440.0
1984	Dinko Lukin (AUS)	412.5
1988	Aleksandr Kurlovich (URS)	462.5

Summer Olympic Games (continued)

Weight Lifting (men)[37, 38] (continued)

OVER 105 KG (231+ LB) (CONTINUED)	KG
1992 Aleksandr Kurlovich (UNT)	450.0
1996 Andrey Chemerkin (RUS)	457.5
2000 Hossein Reza Zadeh (IRI)	472.5
2004 Hossein Reza Zadeh (IRI)	472.5
2008 Matthias Steiner (GER)	461.0

ONE-HAND LIFT (UNLIMITED CLASS)	KG
1896 Launceston Elliot (GBR)	71.0

TWO-HAND LIFT (UNLIMITED CLASS)	KG
1896 Viggo Jensen (DEN)	111.5
1904 Perikles Kakousis (GRE)	111.7

ALL-AROUND DUMBBELLS (UNLIMITED CLASS)
1904 Oscar Osthoff (USA)

Weight Lifting (women)

48 KG (105.6 LB)	KG
2000 Tara Nott (USA)[2]	185.0
2004 Nurcan Taylan (TUR)	210.0
2008 Chen Xiexia (CHN)	212.0

53 KG (116.6 LB)	KG
2000 Yang Xia (CHN)	225.0
2004 Udomporn Polsak (THA)	222.5
2008 Prapawadee Jaroenrattanatarakoon (THA)	221.0

58 KG (127.6 LB)	KG
2000 Soraya Jiménez Mendívil (MEX)	222.5
2004 Chen Yanqing (CHN)	237.5
2008 Chen Yanqing (CHN)	244.0

63 KG (138.6 LB)	KG
2000 Chen Xiaomin (CHN)	242.5
2004 Natalya Skakun (UKR)	242.5
2008 Pak Hyon Suk (PRK)	241.0

69 KG (151.8 LB)	KG
2000 Lin Weining (CHN)	242.5
2004 Liu Chunhong (CHN)	275.0
2008 Liu Chunhong (CHN)	286.0

75 KG (165 LB)	KG
2000 Maria Isabel Urrutia (COL)	245.0
2004 Pawina Thongsuk (THA)	272.5
2008 Cao Lei (CHN)	282.0

OVER 75 KG (165+ LB)	KG
2000 Ding Meiyuan (CHN)	300.0
2004 Tang Gonghong (CHN)	305.0
2008 Jang Mi Ran (KOR)	326.0

Wrestling—Freestyle (men)[37]

48 KG (105.6 LB)
1904 Robert Curry (USA)
1972 Roman Dmitriyev (URS)
1976 Khassan Issaev (BUL)
1980 Claudio Pollio (ITA)
1984 Robert Weaver (USA)
1988 Takashi Kobayashi (JPN)
1992 Kim Il (PRK)
1996 Kim Il (PRK)

Wrestling—Freestyle (men)[37] (continued)

55 KG (121 LB)
1904 George Mehnert (USA)
1948 Lennart Viitala (FIN)
1952 Hasan Gemici (TUR)
1956 Mirian Tsalkalamanidze (URS)
1960 Ahmet Bilek (TUR)
1964 Yoshikatsu Yoshida (JPN)
1968 Shigeo Nakata (JPN)
1972 Kiyomi Kato (JPN)
1976 Yuji Takada (JPN)
1980 Anatoly Beloglazov (URS)
1984 Saban Trstena (YUG)
1988 Mitsuru Sato (JPN)
1992 Li Hak-son (PRK)
1996 Valentin Iordanov (BUL)
2000 Namig Amdullayev (AZE)
2004 Mavlet Batirov (RUS)
2008 Henry Cejudo (USA)

60 KG (132 LB)
1904 Isidor "Jack" Niflot (USA)
1908 George Mehnert (USA)
1924 Kustaa Pihlajamäki (FIN)
1928 Kaarlo Maakinen (FIN)
1932 Robert Pearce (USA)
1936 Odon Zombory (HUN)
1948 Nasuh Akar (TUR)
1952 Shohachi Ishii (JPN)
1956 Mustafa Dagistanli (TUR)
1960 Terence McCann (USA)
1964 Yojiro Uetake (JPN)
1968 Yojiro Uetake (JPN)
1972 Hideaki Yanagida (JPN)
1976 Vladimir Yumin (URS)
1980 Sergey Beloglazov (URS)
1984 Hideaki Tomiyama (JPN)
1988 Sergey Beloglazov (URS)
1992 Alejandro Puerto Diaz (CUB)
1996 Kendall Cross (USA)
2000 Alireza Dabir (IRI)
2004 Yandro Miguel Quintana (CUB)
2008 Mavlet Batirov (RUS)

63 KG (138.6 LB)
1904 Benjamin Bradshaw (USA)
1908 George Dole (USA)
1920 Charles Ackerly (USA)
1924 Robin Reed (USA)
1928 Allie Morrison (USA)
1932 Hermanni Pihlajamäki (FIN)
1936 Kustaa Pihlajamäki (FIN)
1948 Gazanfer Bilge (TUR)
1952 Bayram Sit (TUR)
1956 Shozo Sasahara (JPN)
1960 Mustafa Dagistanli (TUR)
1964 Osamu Watanabe (JPN)
1968 Masaaki Kaneko (JPN)
1972 Zagalav Abdulbekov (URS)
1976 Yang Jung Mo (KOR)
1980 Magomedgasan Abushev (URS)
1984 Randy Lewis (USA)
1988 John Smith (USA)
1992 John Smith (USA)
1996 Tom Brands (USA)
2000 Murad Umakhanov (RUS)

Summer Olympic Games (continued)

Wrestling—Freestyle (men)[37] (continued)

66 KG (145.2 LB)
1904	Otto Roehm (USA)
1908	George de Relwyskow (GBR)
1920	Kaarlo "Kalle" Anttila (FIN)
1924	Russell Vis (USA)
1928	Osvald Käpp (EST)
1932	Charles Pacome (FRA)
1936	Karoly Karpati (HUN)
1948	Celal Atik (TUR)
1952	Olle Anderberg (SWE)
1956	Emamali Habibi (IRI)
1960	Shelby Wilson (USA)
1964	Enio Valchev Dimov (BUL)
1968	Abdollah Movahed (IRI)
1972	Dan Gable (USA)
1976	Pavel Pinigin (URS)
1980	Saipulla Absaidov (URS)
1984	You In Tak (KOR)
1988	Arsen Fadzayev (URS)
1992	Arsen Fadzayev (UNT)
1996	Vadim Bogiyev (RUS)
2000	Daniel Igali (CAN)
2004	Elbrus Tedeyev (UKR)
2008	Ramazan Sahin (TUR)

74 KG (162.8 LB)
1904	Charles Eriksen (USA)
1924	Hermann Gehri (SUI)
1928	Arvo Haavisto (FIN)
1932	Jack van Bebber (USA)
1936	Frank Lewis (USA)
1948	Yasar Dogu (TUR)
1952	William Smith (USA)
1956	Mitsuo Ikeda (JPN)
1960	Douglas Blubaugh (USA)
1964	Ismail Ogan (TUR)
1968	Mahmut Atalay (TUR)
1972	Wayne Wells (USA)
1976	Jiichiro Date (JPN)
1980	Valentin Raychev (BUL)
1984	David Schultz (USA)
1988	Kenneth Monday (USA)
1992	Park Jang Soon (KOR)
1996	Buvaysa Saytiyev (RUS)
2000	Brandon Slay (USA)[2]
2004	Buvaysa Saytiyev (RUS)
2008	Buvaysa Saytiyev (RUS)

84 KG (184.8 LB)
1908	Stanley Bacon (GBR)
1920	Eino Leino (FIN)
1924	Fritz Haggmann (SUI)
1928	Ernst Kyburz (SUI)
1932	Ivar Johansson (SWE)
1936	Émile Poilvé (FRA)
1948	Glen Brand (USA)
1952	David Tsimakurdze (URS)
1956	Nikola Stanchev (BUL)
1960	Hasan Gungor (TUR)
1964	Prodan Stoyanov Gardchev (BUL)
1968	Boris Gurevich (URS)
1972	Levan Tediashvili (URS)
1976	John Peterson (USA)
1980	Ismail Abilov (BUL)
1984	Mark Schultz (USA)
1988	Han Myung Woo (KOR)
1992	Kevin Jackson (USA)
1996	Khadshimurad Magomedov (RUS)

Wrestling—Freestyle (men)[37] (continued)

84 KG (184.8 LB) (CONTINUED)
2000	Adam Saytev (RUS)
2004	Cael Sanderson (USA)
2008	Revazi Mindorashvili (GEO)

90 KG (198.5 LB)
1920	Anders Larsson (SWE)
1924	John Franklin Spellman (USA)
1928	Thure Sjöstedt (SWE)
1932	Peter Mehringer (USA)
1936	Knut Fridell (SWE)
1948	Henry Wittenberg (USA)
1952	Bror Wiking Palm (SWE)
1956	Gholam-Reza Takhti (IRI)
1960	Ismet Atli (TUR)
1964	Aleksandr Medved (URS)
1968	Ahmet Ayuk (TUR)
1972	Ben Peterson (USA)
1976	Levan Tediashvili (URS)
1980	Sanasar Oganesyan (URS)
1984	Ed Banach (USA)
1988	Macharbek Khadartsev (URS)
1992	Macharbek Khadartsev (UNT)
1996	Rasul Khadem Azghadi (IRI)

96 KG (211.2 LB)
1896	Karl Schumann (GER)
1904	Bernhuff Hansen (USA)
1908	George O'Kelly (GBR)
1920	Robert Rothe (SUI)
1924	Harry Steele (USA)
1928	Johan Richthoff (SWE)
1932	Johan Richthoff (SWE)
1936	Kristjan Palusalu (EST)
1948	Gyula Bobis (HUN)
1952	Arsen Mekokishvili (URS)
1956	Hamit Kaplan (TUR)
1960	Wilfried Dietrich (GER)
1964	Aleksandr Ivanitsky (URS)
1968	Aleksandr Medved (URS)
1972	Ivan Yarygin (URS)
1976	Ivan Yarygin (URS)
1980	Ilya Mate (URS)
1984	Lou Banach (USA)
1988	Vasile Puscasu (ROM)
1992	Leri Khabelov (UNT)
1996	Kurt Angle (USA)
2000	Sagid Murtasaliyev (RUS)
2004	Khajimurat Gatsalov (RUS)
2008	Shirvani Muradov (RUS)

120 KG (264 LB)
1972	Aleksandr Medved (URS)
1976	Soslan Andiyev (URS)
1980	Soslan Andiyev (URS)
1984	Bruce Baumgartner (USA)
1988	David Gobedishvili (URS)
1992	Bruce Baumgartner (USA)
1996	Mahmut Demir (TUR)
2000	David Musulbes (RUS)
2004	Artur Taymazov (UZB)
2008	Artur Taymazov (UZB)

Wrestling—Freestyle (women)

48 KG (105.6 LB)
2004	Irini Merleni (UKR)
2008	Carol Huynh (CAN)

Summer Olympic Games (continued)

Wrestling—Freestyle (women) (continued)

55 KG (121 LB)
2004 Saori Yoshida (JPN)
2008 Saori Yoshida (JPN)

63 KG (138.6 LB)
2004 Kaori Icho (JPN)
2008 Kaori Icho (JPN)

72 KG (158 LB)
2004 Wang Xu (CHN)
2008 Wang Jiao (CHN)

Wrestling—Greco-Roman[37]

48 KG (105.6 LB)
1972 Gheorghe Berceanu (ROM)
1976 Aleksey Shumakov (URS)
1980 Zhaksylyk Ushkempirov (URS)
1984 Vincenzo Maenza (ITA)
1988 Vincenzo Maenza (ITA)
1992 Oleg Kucherenko (UNT)
1996 Sim Kwon-Ho (KOR)

55 KG (121 LB)
1948 Pietro Lombardi (ITA)
1952 Boris Gurevich (URS)
1956 Nikolay Solovyev (URS)
1960 Dumitru Pirvulescu (ROM)
1964 Tsutomu Hanahara (JPN)
1968 Petar Kirov (BUL)
1972 Petar Kirov (BUL)
1976 Vitaly Konstantinov (URS)
1980 Vakhtang Blagidze (URS)
1984 Atsuji Miyahara (JPN)
1988 Jon Ronningen (NOR)
1992 Jon Ronningen (NOR)
1996 Armen Nazaryan (ARM)
2000 Sim Kwon-Ho (KOR)
2004 Istvan Majoros (HUN)
2008 Nazyr Mankiyev (RUS)

60 KG (132 LB)
1924 Eduard Pütsep (EST)
1928 Kurt Leucht (GER)
1932 Jakob Brendel (GER)
1936 Marton Lorincz (HUN)
1948 Kurt Pettersen (SWE)
1952 Imre Hodos (HUN)
1956 Konstantin Vyrupayev (URS)
1960 Oleg Karavayev (URS)
1964 Masamitsu Ichiguchi (JPN)
1968 Janos Varga (HUN)
1972 Rustem Kazakov (URS)
1976 Pertti Ukkola (FIN)
1980 Shamil Serikov (URS)
1984 Pasquale Passarelli (FRG)
1988 Andras Sike (HUN)
1992 An Han Bong (KOR)
1996 Yury Melnichenko (KAZ)
2000 Armen Nazarian (BUL)
2004 Jung Ji Hyun (KOR)
2008 Islam-Beka Albiyev (RUS)

63 KG (138.6 LB)
1912 Kaarlo Koskelo (FIN)
1920 Oskar Friman (FIN)
1924 Kalle Anttila (FIN)
1928 Voldemar Väli (EST)
1932 Giovanni Gozzi (ITA)

Wrestling—Greco-Roman[37] (continued)

63 KG (138.6 LB) (CONTINUED)
1936 Yasar Erkan (TUR)
1948 Mehmet Oktav (TUR)
1952 Yakov Punkin (URS)
1956 Rauno Leonard Mäkinen (FIN)
1960 Muzahir Sille (TUR)
1964 Imre Polyak (HUN)
1968 Roman Rurua (URS)
1972 Georgi Markov (BUL)
1976 Kazimierz Lipien (POL)
1980 Stilianos Migiakis (GRE)
1984 Kim Weon Kee (KOR)
1988 Kamandar Madzhidov (URS)
1992 Akif Pirim (TUR)
1996 Wlodzimierz Zawadzki (POL)
2000 Varteres Samurgashev (RUS)

66 KG (145.2 LB)
1908 Enrico Porro (ITA)
1912 Eemil Väre (FIN)
1920 Eemil Väre (FIN)
1924 Oskar Friman (FIN)
1928 Lajos Keresztes (HUN)
1932 Erik Malmberg (SWE)
1936 Lauri Koskela (FIN)
1948 Karl Freij (SWE)
1952 Shazam Safin (URS)
1956 Kyösti Emil Lehtonen (FIN)
1960 Avtandil Koridze (URS)
1964 Kazim Ayvaz (TUR)
1968 Munji Mumemura (JPN)
1972 Shamil Khisamutdinov (URS)
1976 Suren Nalbandyan (URS)
1980 Stefan Rusu (ROM)
1984 Vlado Lisjak (YUG)
1988 Levon Dzhulfalakyan (URS)
1992 Attila Repka (HUN)
1996 Ryszard Wolny (POL)
2000 Filiberto Ascuy Aguilera (CUB)
2004 Farid Mansurov (AZE)
2008 Steeve Guénot (FRA)

74 KG (162.8 LB)
1932 Ivar Johansson (SWE)
1936 Rudolf Svedberg (SWE)
1948 Erik Gösta Andersson (SWE)
1952 Miklos Szilvasi (HUN)
1956 Mithat Bayrak (TUR)
1960 Mithat Bayrak (TUR)
1964 Anatoly Kolesov (URS)
1968 Rudolf Vesper (GDR)
1972 Viteslav Macha (TCH)
1976 Anatoly Bykov (URS)
1980 Ferenc Kocsis (HUN)
1984 Jouko Salomaki (FIN)
1988 Kim Young Nam (KOR)
1992 Mnatsakan Iskandaryan (UNT)
1996 Filiberto Ascuy Aguilera (CUB)
2000 Murat Kardanov (URS)
2004 Aleksandr Dokturishvili (UZB)
2008 Manuchar Kvirkelia (GEO)

84 KG (184.8 LB)
1908 Frithiof Martenson (SWE)
1912 Claes Johansson (SWE)
1920 Carl Westergren (SWE)
1924 Edward Westerlund (FIN)
1928 Väinö Kokkinen (FIN)

Summer Olympic Games (continued)

Wrestling—Greco-Roman[37] (continued)

84 KG (184.8 LB) (CONTINUED)

1932	Väinö Kokkinen (FIN)
1936	Ivar Johansson (SWE)
1948	Axel Grönberg (SWE)
1952	Axel Grönberg (SWE)
1956	Givi Kartoziya (URS)
1960	Dimitar Dobrev (BUL)
1964	Branislav Simic (YUG)
1968	Lothar Metz (GDR)
1972	Csaba Hegedus (HUN)
1976	Momir Petkovic (YUG)
1980	Gennady Korban (URS)
1984	Ion Draica (ROM)
1988	Mikhail Mamiashvili (URS)
1992	Peter Farkas (HUN)
1996	Hamza Yerlikaya (TUR)
2000	Hamza Yerlikaya (TUR)
2004	Aleksey Mishin (RUS)
2008	Andrea Minguzzi (ITA)

90 KG (198.5 LB)

1908	Verner Weckman (FIN)
1912	Anders Ahlgren (SWE)
1920	Claes Johansson (SWE)
1924	Carl Westergren (SWE)
1928	Ibrahim Moustafa (EGY)
1932	Rudolf Svensson (SWE)
1936	Axel Cadier (SWE)
1948	Karl-Erik Nilsson (SWE)
1952	Kelpo Olavi Gröndahl (FIN)
1956	Valentin Nikolayev (URS)
1960	Tevfik Kis (TUR)
1964	Boyan Radev (BUL)
1968	Boyan Radev (BUL)
1972	Valery Rezantsev (URS)
1976	Valery Rezantsev (URS)
1980	Norbert Nottny (HUN)
1984	Steven Fraser (USA)
1988	Atanas Komchev (BUL)

Wrestling—Greco-Roman[37] (continued)

90 KG (198.5 LB) (CONTINUED)

1992	Maik Bullmann (GER)
1996	Vyacheslav Oleynyk (UKR)

96 KG (211.2 LB)

1896	Karl Schumann (GER)
1908	Richard Weisz (HUN)
1912	Yrjö Saarela (FIN)
1920	Adolf Lindfors (FIN)
1924	Henri Deglane (FRA)
1928	Rudolf Svensson (SWE)
1932	Carl Westergren (SWE)
1936	Kristjan Palusalu (EST)
1948	Ahmet Kirecci (TUR)
1952	Johannes Kotkas (URS)
1956	Anatoly Parfenov (URS)
1960	Ivan Bogdan (URS)
1964	Istvan Kozma (HUN)
1968	Istvan Kozma (HUN)
1972	Nicolae Martinescu (ROM)
1976	Nikolay Balboshin (URS)
1980	Georgi Raikov-Petkov (BUL)
1984	Vasile Andrei (ROM)
1988	Andrzej Wronski (POL)
1992	Héctor Milian (CUB)
1996	Andrzej Wronski (POL)
2000	Mikael Ljungberg (SWE)
2004	Karam Ibrahim (EGY)
2008	Aslanbek Khushtov (RUS)

120 KG (264 LB)

1972	Anatoly Roshchin (URS)
1976	Aleksandr Kolchinsky (URS)
1980	Aleksandr Kolchinsky (URS)
1984	Jeffrey Blatnick (USA)
1988	Aleksandr Karelin (URS)
1992	Aleksandr Karelin (UNT)
1996	Aleksandr Karelin (RUS)
2000	Rulon Gardner (USA)
2004	Khasan Baroyev (RUS)
2008	Mijain López (CUB)

[1]The competitions in 1900 and 1904 are said to be unofficial.   [2]Winner after disqualification of top finisher for drug use.   [3]100-meter event.   [4]Hurdles were 2' 6" high, not 3'.   [5]An extra lap of 460 meters was run in error.   [6]Jim Thorpe was stripped of his gold medals in 1913 when it was discovered he had briefly competed as a professional athlete; in 1982 his gold medals were restored, and he was declared "cowinner" of the events.   [7]80 meters from 1932 to 1968.   [8]Pentathlon from 1964 to 1980.   [9]Weight classifications have been revised numerous times.   [10]2,000-meter event.   [11]333.3-meter event.   [12]Distance has varied from 87 to 320 km.   [13]Held outdoors.   [14]Weight classifications were changed in 1980 and 1996.   [15]Weight classifications were changed in 2000.   [16]The distances in men's rowing events have varied from time to time. In 1904 it was 2 miles; in 1908, 1.5 miles; from 1912 to 1936, 2,000 meters; in 1948, 1 mile 350 yards; and since 1952, 2,000 meters (1 mile 427 yards).   [17]The distance in women's rowing events was 1,000 meters until 1988, at which time it became 2,000 meters.   [18]Without coxswain.   [19]From 2004.   [20]Open from 1996 to 2004.   [21]From 1952.   [22]Men-only from 1924 to 2004.   [23]Open from 1932 to 2004.   [24]Open from 1968 to 1992.   [25]Open from 1968 to 1992.   [26]100 yards.   [27]220 yards.   [28]500 meters.   [29]440 yards.   [30]1,200 meters.   [31]1,000 meters.   [32]1 mile.   [33]100 yards.   [34]440 yards.   [35]300 meters.   [36]Fréchette's gold medal awarded in 1993 on basis of error in scoring.   [37]Weight classifications have been revised numerous times, most recently after the 1996 Games.   [38]In 1976 the press lift was removed, weights given thereafter being the total for the clean and jerk and the snatch.   [39]Total of five lifts.

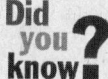

Did you know? Kano Jigoro (1860–1938) combined the knowledge of the old jujitsu schools of the Japanese samurai with the sporting ideology of the "muscular Christianity" movement and in 1882 founded his Kodokan School of judo (from the Chinese *jou-tao*, or *roudao*, meaning "gentle way"), the beginning of the sport in its modern form. By the 1960s judo associations had been established in most countries and affiliated to the International Judo Federation, which is headquartered in Budapest, Hungary.

Winter Olympic Games

Gold medalists in all winter events since 1908; separate Winter Games were not held until 1924.
Note: East and West Germany fielded a joint all-Germany team in 1956, 1960, and 1964,
abbreviated here as GER.

Biathlon (men)

10 KM   MIN:SEC
1980	Frank Ullrich (GDR)	32:10.69
1984	Eirik Kvalfoss (NOR)	30:53.8
1988	Frank-Peter Rötsch (GDR)	25:08.1
1992	Mark Kirchner (GER)	26:02.3
1994	Sergey Chepikov (RUS)	28:07.0
1998	Ole Einar Bjørndalen (NOR)	27:16.2
2002	Ole Einar Bjørndalen (NOR)	24:51.3
2006	Sven Fischer (GER)	26:11.6

12.5-KM PURSUIT   MIN:SEC
2002	Ole Einar Bjørndalen (NOR)	32:34.6
2006	Vincent Defrasne (FRA)	35:20.2

15-KM MASS START   MIN:SEC
2006	Michael Greis (GER)	47:20.0

20 KM   HR:MIN:SEC
1960	Klas Lestander (SWE)	1:33:21.6
1964	Vladimir Melanin (URS)	1:20:26.8
1968	Magnar Solberg (NOR)	1:13:45.9
1972	Magnar Solberg (NOR)	1:15:55.50
1976	Nikolay Kruglov (URS)	1:14:12.26
1980	Anatoly Alyabyev (URS)	1:08:16.31
1984	Peter Angerer (FRG)	1:11:52.70
1988	Frank-Peter Rötsch (GDR)	56:33.3
1992	Yevgeny Redkin (UNT)	57:34.4
1994	Sergey Tarasov (RUS)	57:25.3
1998	Halvard Hanevold (NOR)	56:16.4
2002	Ole Einar Bjørndalen (NOR)	51:03.3
2006	Michael Greis (GER)	54:23.0

4 × 7.5-KM RELAY   HR:MIN:SEC
1968	USSR	2:13:02.4
1972	USSR	1:51:44.92
1976	USSR	1:57:55.64
1980	USSR	1:34:03.27
1984	USSR	1:38:51.70
1988	USSR	1:22:30.00
1992	Germany	1:24:43.5
1994	Germany	1:30:22.1
1998	Germany	1:19:43.3
2002	Norway	1:23:42.3
2006	Germany	1:21:51.5

MILITARY SKI PATROL
1924	Switzerland
1928	Norway
1936	Italy
1948	Switzerland

DISTANCE SHOOTING
1936	Georg Edenhauser (AUT)

ICE SHOOTING (TEAM)
1936	Austria

TARGET SHOOTING
1936	Ignaz Reiterer (AUT)

Biathlon (women)

7.5 KM   MIN:SEC
1992	Anfisa Restsova (UNT)	24:29.2
1994	Myriam Bédard (CAN)	26:08.8

Biathlon (women) (continued)

7.5 KM (CONTINUED)   MIN:SEC
1998	Galina Kukleva (RUS)	23:08.0
2002	Kati Wilhelm (GER)	20:41.4
2006	Florence Baverel-Robert (FRA)	22:31.4

10-KM PURSUIT   MIN:SEC
2002	Olga Pyleva (RUS)	31:07.7
2006	Kati Wilhelm (GER)	36:43.6

12.5-KM MASS START   MIN:SEC
2006	Anna Carin Olofsson (SWE)	40:36.5

15 KM   MIN:SEC
1992	Antje Misersky (GER)	51:47.2
1994	Myriam Bédard (CAN)	52:06.6
1998	Ekaterina Dafovska (BUL)	54:52.0
2002	Andrea Henkel (GER)	47:29.1
2006	Svetlana Ishmuratova (RUS)	49:24.1

4 × 6-KM RELAY[1]   HR:MIN:SEC
1992	France	1:15:55.6
1994	Russia	1:47:19.5
1998	Germany	1:40:13.6
2002	Germany	1:27:55.0
2006	Russia	1:16:12.5

Bobsled

TWO-MAN BOBSLED   MIN:SEC
1932	United States	8:14.74
1936	United States	5:29.29
1948	Switzerland	5:29.2
1952	West Germany	5:24.54
1956	Italy	5:30.14
1964	Great Britain	4:21.90
1968	Italy	4:41.54
1972	West Germany	4:57.07
1976	East Germany	3:44.42
1980	Switzerland	4:09.36
1984	East Germany	3:25.56
1988	USSR	3:53.48
1992	Switzerland	4:03.26
1994	Switzerland	3:30.81
1998	Canada; Italy (tied)	3:37.24
2002	Germany	3:10.11
2006	Germany	3:43.38

FOUR-MAN BOBSLED   MIN:SEC
1924	Switzerland	5:45.54
1928[2]	United States	3:20.5
1932	United States	7:53.68
1936	Switzerland	5:19.85
1948	United States	5:20.1
1952	West Germany	5:07.84
1956	Switzerland	5:10.44
1964	Canada	4:14.46
1968	Italy	2:17.39
1972	Switzerland	4:43.07
1976	East Germany	3:40.43
1980	East Germany	3:59.92
1984	East Germany	3:20.22
1988	Switzerland	3:47.51
1992	Austria	3:53.90
1994	Germany	3:27.78
1998	Germany	2:39.41

Winter Olympic Games (continued)

Bobsled (continued)

FOUR-MAN BOBSLED (CONTINUED)

		MIN:SEC
2002	Germany	3:07.51
2006	Germany	3:40.42

TWO-WOMAN BOBSLED

		MIN:SEC
2002	United States	1:37.76
2006	Germany	3:49.98

Curling

MEN
1924	Great Britain
1998	Switzerland
2002	Norway
2006	Canada

WOMEN
1998	Canada
2002	Great Britain
2006	Sweden

Figure Skating

MEN'S SINGLES
1908	Ulrich Salchow (SWE)
1920	Gillis Gräfström (SWE)
1924	Gillis Gräfström (SWE)
1928	Gillis Gräfström (SWE)
1932	Karl Schäfer (AUT)
1936	Karl Schäfer (AUT)
1948	Richard Button (USA)
1952	Richard Button (USA)
1956	Hayes Alan Jenkins (USA)
1960	David Jenkins (USA)
1964	Manfred Schnelldorfer (GER)
1968	Wolfgang Schwarz (AUT)
1972	Ondrej Nepela (TCH)
1976	John Curry (GBR)
1980	Robin Cousins (GBR)
1984	Scott Hamilton (USA)
1988	Brian Boitano (USA)
1992	Viktor Petrenko (UNT)
1994	Aleksey Urmanov (RUS)
1998	Ilia Kulik (RUS)
2002	Aleksey Yagudin (RUS)
2006	Yevgeny Plushchenko (RUS)

WOMEN'S SINGLES
1908	Madge Syers (GBR)
1920	Magda Julin-Mauroy (SWE)
1924	Herma Planck-Szabo (AUT)
1928	Sonja Henie (NOR)
1932	Sonja Henie (NOR)
1936	Sonja Henie (NOR)
1948	Barbara Ann Scott (CAN)
1952	Jeannette Altwegg (GBR)
1956	Tenley Albright (USA)
1964	Sjoukje Dijkstra (NED)
1968	Peggy Fleming (USA)
1972	Beatrix Schuba (AUT)
1976	Dorothy Hamill (USA)
1980	Annett Potzsch (GDR)
1984	Katarina Witt (GDR)
1988	Katarina Witt (GDR)
1992	Kristi Yamaguchi (USA)
1994	Oksana Bayul (UKR)
1998	Tara Lipinski (USA)
2002	Sarah Hughes (USA)
2006	Shizuka Arakawa (JPN)

Figure Skating (continued)

PAIRS
1908	Anna Hübler, Heinrich Burger (GER)
1920	Ludoviga Jakobsson-Eilers, Walter Jakobsson (FIN)
1924	Helene Engelmann, Alfred Berger (AUT)
1928	Andrée Joly, Pierre Brunet (FRA)
1932	Andrée Brunet-Joly, Pierre Brunet (FRA)
1936	Maxi Herber, Ernst Baier (GER)
1948	Micheline Lannoy, Pierre Baugniet (BEL)
1952	Ria Falk, Paul Falk (FRG)
1956	Elisabeth Schwarz, Kurt Oppelt (AUT)
1960	Barbara Wagner, Robert Paul (CAN)
1964	Lyudmila Belousova, Oleg Protopopov (URS)
1968	Lyudmila Belousova, Oleg Protopopov (URS)
1972	Irina Rodnina, Aleksey Ulanov (URS)
1976	Irina Rodnina, Aleksandr Zaytsev (URS)
1980	Irina Rodnina, Aleksandr Zaytsev (URS)
1984	Yelena Valova, Oleg Vasilyev (URS)
1988	Yekaterina Gordeyeva, Sergey Grinkov (URS)
1992	Natalya Mishkutyonok, Artur Dmitriyev (UNT)
1994	Yekaterina Gordeyeva, Sergey Grinkov (RUS)
1998	Oksana Kazakova, Artur Dmitriyev (RUS)
2002	Yelena Berezhnaya, Anton Sikharulidze (RUS); Jamie Sale, David Pelletier (CAN) (shared)
2006	Tatyana Totmyanina, Maksim Marinin (RUS)

ICE DANCING
1976	Lyudmila Pakhomova, Aleksandr Gorshkov (URS)
1980	Natalya Linichuk, Gennady Karponosov (URS)
1984	Jayne Torvill, Christopher Dean (GBR)
1988	Natalya Bestemyanova, Andrey Bukin (URS)
1992	Marina Klimova, Sergey Ponomarenko (UNT)
1994	Oksana Grishchuk, Yevgeny Platov (RUS)
1998	Oksana Grishchuk, Yevgeny Platov (RUS)
2002	Marina Anissina, Gwendal Peizerat (FRA)
2006	Tatyana Navka, Roman Kostomarov (RUS)

Ice Hockey

MEN
1920	Canada
1924	Canada
1928	Canada
1932	Canada
1936	Great Britain
1948	Canada
1952	Canada
1956	USSR
1960	United States
1964	USSR
1968	USSR
1972	USSR
1976	USSR
1980	United States
1984	USSR
1988	USSR
1992	Unified Team
1994	Sweden
1998	Czech Republic
2002	Canada
2006	Sweden

WOMEN
1998	United States
2002	Canada
2006	Canada

Winter Olympic Games (continued)

Luge

MEN'S SINGLES

		MIN:SEC
1964	Thomas Köhler (GER)	3:26.77
1968	Manfred Schmid (AUT)	2:52.48
1972	Wolfgang Schneidel (GDR)	3:27.58
1976	Detlef Guenther (GDR)	3:27.688
1980	Bernhard Glass (GDR)	2:54.796
1984	Paul Hildgartner (ITA)	3:04.258
1988	Jens Müller (GDR)	3:05.548
1992	Georg Hackl (GER)	3:02.363
1994	Georg Hackl (GER)	3:21.571
1998	Georg Hackl (GER)	3:18.436
2002	Armin Zöggeler (ITA)	2:57.941
2006	Armin Zöggeler (ITA)	3:26.088

MEN'S DOUBLES

		MIN:SEC
1964	Austria	1:41.62
1968	East Germany	1:35.85
1972	Italy; East Germany (tied)	1:28.35
1976	East Germany	1:25.604
1980	East Germany	1:19.331
1984	West Germany	1:23.620
1988	East Germany	1:31.940
1992	Germany	1:32.053
1994	Italy	1:36.720
1998	Germany	1:41.105
2002	Germany	1:26.082
2006	Austria	1:34.497

WOMEN'S SINGLES

		MIN:SEC
1964	Ortrun Enderlein (GER)	3:24.67
1968	Erica Lechner (ITA)	2:29.37
1972	Anna-Maria Müller (GDR)	2:59.18
1976	Margit Schumann (GDR)	2:50.621
1980	Vera Zozulya (URS)	2:36.537
1984	Steffi Martin (GDR)	2:46.570
1988	Steffi Walter-Martin (GDR)	3:03.973
1992	Doris Neuner (AUT)	3:06.696
1994	Gerda Weissensteiner (ITA)	3:15.517
1998	Silke Kraushaar (GER)	3:23.779
2002	Sylke Otto (GER)	2:52.464
2006	Sylke Otto (GER)	3:07.979

Skeleton

MEN

		MIN:SEC
1928	Jennison Heaton (USA)	3:01.8
1948	Nino Bibbia (ITA)	5:23.2
2002	Jim Shea (USA)	1:41.96
2006	Duff Gibson (CAN)	1:55.88

WOMEN

		MIN:SEC
2002	Tristan Gale (USA)	1:45.11
2006	Maya Pedersen (SUI)	1:59.83

Alpine Skiing (men)

DOWNHILL

		MIN:SEC
1948	Henri Oreiller (FRA)	2:55.0
1952	Zeno Colò (ITA)	2:30.8
1956	Toni Sailer (AUT)	2:52.2
1960	Jean Vuarnet (FRA)	2:06.0
1964	Egon Zimmermann (AUT)	2:18.16
1968	Jean-Claude Killy (FRA)	1:59.85
1972	Bernhard Russi (SUI)	1:51.43
1976	Franz Klammer (AUT)	1:45.73
1980	Leonhard Stock (AUT)	1:45.50
1984	Bill Johnson (USA)	1:45.59
1988	Pirmin Zurbriggen (SUI)	1:59.63
1992	Patrick Ortlieb (AUT)	1:50.37
1994	Tommy Moe (USA)	1:45.75

Alpine Skiing (men) (continued)

DOWNHILL (CONTINUED)

		MIN:SEC
1998	Jean-Luc Cretier (FRA)	1:50.11
2002	Fritz Strobl (AUT)	1:39.13
2006	Antoine Dénériaz (FRA)	1:48.80

SLALOM

		MIN:SEC
1948	Edy Reinalter (SUI)	2:10.3
1952	Othmar Schneider (AUT)	2:00.0
1956	Toni Sailer (AUT)	3:14.7
1960	Ernst Hinterseer (AUT)	2:08.9
1964	Josef Stiegler (AUT)	2:21.13
1968	Jean-Claude Killy (FRA)	1:39.73
1972	Francisco Ochoa (ESP)	1:49.27
1976	Piero Gros (ITA)	2:03.29
1980	Ingemar Stenmark (SWE)	1:44.26
1984	Phil Mahre (USA)	1:39.41
1988	Alberto Tomba (ITA)	1:39.47
1992	Finn Christian Jagge (NOR)	1:44.39
1994	Thomas Stangassinger (AUT)	2:02.02
1998	Hans Petter Buraas (NOR)	1:49.31
2002	Jean-Pierre Vidal (FRA)	1:41.06
2006	Benjamin Raich (AUT)	1:43.14

GIANT SLALOM

		MIN:SEC
1952	Stein Eriksen (NOR)	2:25.0
1956	Toni Sailer (AUT)	3:00.1
1960	Roger Staub (SUI)	1:48.3
1964	François Bonlieu (FRA)	1:46.71
1968	Jean-Claude Killy (FRA)	3:29.28
1972	Gustavo Thöni (ITA)	3:09.62
1976	Heini Hemmi (SUI)	3:26.97
1980	Ingemar Stenmark (SWE)	2:40.74
1984	Max Julen (SUI)	2:41.18
1988	Alberto Tomba (ITA)	2:06.37
1992	Alberto Tomba (ITA)	2:06.98
1994	Markus Wasmeier (GER)	2:52.46
1998	Hermann Maier (AUT)	2:38.51
2002	Stephan Eberharter (AUT)	2:23.28
2006	Benjamin Raich (AUT)	2:35.00

SUPERGIANT SLALOM

		MIN:SEC
1988	Franck Piccard (FRA)	1:39.66
1992	Kjetil André Aamodt (NOR)	1:13.04
1994	Markus Wasmeier (GER)	1:32.53
1998	Hermann Maier (AUT)	1:34.82
2002	Kjetil André Aamodt (NOR)	1:21.58
2006	Kjetil André Aamodt (NOR)	1:30.65

ALPINE COMBINED

		MIN:SEC
1936	Franz Pfnür (GER)	
1948	Henri Oreiller (FRA)	
1972	Gustavo Thöni (ITA)	
1976	Gustavo Thöni (ITA)	
1988	Hubert Strolz (AUT)	
1992	Josef Polig (ITA)	
1994	Lasse Kjus (NOR)	3:17.53[3]
1998	Mario Reiter (AUT)	3:08.06
2002	Kjetil André Aamodt (NOR)	3:17.56
2006	Ted Ligety (USA)	3:09.35

Alpine Skiing (women)

DOWNHILL

		MIN:SEC
1948	Hedy Schlunegger (SUI)	2:28.3
1952	Trude Jochom-Beiser (AUT)	1:47.1
1956	Madeleine Berthod (SUI)	1:40.7
1960	Heidi Beibl (GER)	1:37.6
1964	Christl Haas (AUT)	1:55.39
1968	Olga Pall (AUT)	1:40.87

Winter Olympic Games (continued)

Alpine Skiing (women) (continued)

DOWNHILL (CONTINUED)

		MIN:SEC
1972	Marie-Thérèse Nadig (SUI)	1:36.68
1976	Rosi Mittermaier (FRG)	1:46.16
1980	Annemarie Moser-Pröll (AUT)	1:37.52
1984	Michael Figini (SUI)	1:13.36
1988	Marina Kiehl (FRG)	1:25.86
1992	Kerrin Lee-Gartner (CAN)	1:52.55
1994	Katja Seizinger (GER)	1:35.93
1998	Katja Seizinger (GER)	1:28.29
2002	Carole Montillet (FRA)	1:39.56
2006	Michaela Dorfmeister (AUT)	1:56.49

SLALOM

		MIN:SEC
1948	Gretchen Fraser (USA)	1:57.2
1952	Andrea Lawrence-Mead (USA)	2:10.6
1956	Renée Colliard (SUI)	1:52.3
1960	Anne Heggtveit (CAN)	1:49.6
1964	Christine Goitschel (FRA)	1:29.86
1968	Marielle Goitschel (FRA)	1:59.85
1972	Barbara Cochran (USA)	1:31.24
1976	Rosi Mittermaier (FRG)	1:30.54
1980	Hanni Wenzel (LIE)	1:25.09
1984	Paoletta Magoni (ITA)	1:36.47
1988	Vreni Schneider (SUI)	1:36.69
1992	Petra Kronberger (AUT)	1:32.68
1994	Vreni Schneider (SUI)	1:56.01
1998	Hilde Gerg (GER)	1:32.40
2002	Janica Kostelic (CRO)	1:46.10
2006	Anja Pärson (SWE)	1:29.04

GIANT SLALOM

		MIN:SEC
1952	Andrea Lawrence-Mead (USA)	2:06.8
1956	Ossi Reichert (GER)	1:56.5
1960	Yvonne Rüegg (SUI)	1:39.9
1964	Marielle Goitschel (FRA)	1:52.24
1968	Nancy Greene (CAN)	1:51.97
1972	Marie-Thérèse Nadig (SUI)	1:29.90
1976	Kathy Kreiner (CAN)	1:29.13
1980	Hanni Wenzel (LIE)	2:41.66
1984	Debbie Armstrong (USA)	2:20.98
1988	Vreni Schneider (SUI)	2:06.49
1992	Pernilla Wiberg (SWE)	2:12.74
1994	Deborah Compagnoni (ITA)	2:30.97
1998	Deborah Compagnoni (ITA)	2:50.59
2002	Janica Kostelic (CRO)	2:30.01
2006	Julia Mancuso (USA)	2:09.19

SUPERGIANT SLALOM

		MIN:SEC
1988	Sigrid Wolf (AUT)	1:19.03
1992	Deborah Compagnoni (ITA)	1:21.22
1994	Diann Roffe-Steinrotter (USA)	1:22.15
1998	Picabo Street (USA)	1:18.02
2002	Daniela Ceccarelli (ITA)	1:13.59
2006	Michaela Dorfmeister (AUT)	1:32.47

ALPINE COMBINED

		MIN:SEC
1936	Chrislt Cranz (GER)	
1948	Trude Beiser (AUT)	
1972	Annemarie Pröll (AUT)	
1976	Rosi Mittermaier (FRG)	
1988	Anita Wachter (AUT)	
1992	Petra Kronberger (AUT)	
1994	Pernilla Wiberg (SWE)	3:05.16[3]
1998	Katja Seizinger (GER)	2:40.74
2002	Janica Kostelic (CRO)	2:43.28
2006	Janica Kostelic (CRO)	2:51.08

Freestyle Skiing

MEN'S MOGULS

1992	Edgar Grospiron (FRA)
1994	Jean-Luc Brassard (CAN)
1998	Jonny Moseley (USA)
2002	Janne Lahtela (FIN)
2006	Dale Begg-Smith (AUS)[6]

MEN'S AERIALS

1994	Andreas Schönbächler (SUI)
1998	Eric Bergoust (USA)
2002	Ales Valenta (CZE)
2006	Han Xiaopeng (CHN)

WOMEN'S MOGULS

1992	Donna Weinbrecht (USA)
1994	Stine Lise Hattestad (NOR)
1998	Tae Satoya (JPN)
2002	Kari Traa (NOR)
2006	Jennifer Heil (CAN)

WOMEN'S AERIALS

1994	Lina Cheryazova (UZB)
1998	Nikki Stone (USA)
2002	Alisa Camplin (AUS)
2006	Evelyne Leu (SUI)

Nordic Skiing (men)

1.5-KM CROSS-COUNTRY SPRINT

		MIN:SEC
2002	Tor Arne Hetland (NOR)	2:56.9
2006	Björn Lind (SWE)	2:26.5

TEAM SPRINT

		MIN:SEC
2006	Sweden	17:02.9

10-KM CROSS-COUNTRY

		MIN:SEC
1992	Vegard Ulvang (NOR)	27:36.0
1994	Bjørn Daehlie (NOR)	24:20.1
1998	Bjørn Daehlie (NOR)	27:24.5

15-KM CROSS-COUNTRY[4]

		HR:MIN:SEC
1924	Thorleif Haug (NOR)	1:14:31.0
1928	Johan Grøttumsbråten (NOR)	1:37:01.0
1932	Sven Utterström (SWE)	1:23:07.0
1936	Erik-August Larsson (SWE)	1:14:38.0
1948	Martin Lundström (SWE)	1:13:50.0
1952	Hallgeir Brenden (NOR)	1:01:34.0
1956	Hallgeir Brenden (NOR)	49:39.0
1960	Hakkon Brúsveen (NOR)	51:55.5
1964	Eero Mäntyranta (FIN)	50:54.1
1968	Harald Grönningen (NOR)	47:54.2
1972	Sven-Ake Lundbäck (SWE)	45:28.24
1976	Nikolay Bazhukov (URS)	43:58.47
1980	Thomas Wassberg (SWE)	41:57.63
1984	Gunde Svan (SWE)	41:25.60
1988	Mikhail Devyatyarov (URS)	41:18.9
1998	Thomas Alsgaard (NOR)	39:13.7
2002	Andrus Veerpalu (EST)	37:07.4
2006	Andrus Veerpalu (EST)	38:01.3

COMBINED PURSUIT[5]

		HR:MIN:SEC
1992	Bjørn Daehlie (NOR)	1:05:37.9
1994	Bjørn Daehlie (NOR)	1:00:08.8
1998	Thomas Alsgaard (NOR)	1:07:01.7
2002	Thomas Alsgaard (NOR); Frode Estil (NOR) (tied)[6]	49:48.9
2006	Yevgeny Dementyev (RUS)	1:17:00.8

Winter Olympic Games (continued)

Nordic Skiing (men) (continued)

30-KM CROSS-COUNTRY

		HR:MIN:SEC
1956	Veikko Hakulinen (FIN)	1:44:06.0
1960	Sixten Jernberg (SWE)	1:51:03.9
1964	Eero Mäntyranta (FIN)	1:30:50.7
1968	Franco Nones (ITA)	1:35:39.2
1972	Vyacheslav Vedenin (URS)	1:36:31.15
1976	Sergey Savelyev (URS)	1:30:29.38
1980	Nikolay Zimyatov (URS)	1:27:02.80
1984	Nikolay Zimyatov (URS)	1:28:56.30
1988	Aleksey Prokourorov (URS)	1:24:26.3
1992	Vegard Ulvang (NOR)	1:22:27.8
1994	Thomas Alsgaard (NOR)	1:12:26.4
1998	Mika Myllylä (FIN)	1:33:56.0
2002	Christian Hoffmann (AUT)[6]	1:11:31.0

50-KM CROSS-COUNTRY

		HR:MIN:SEC
1924	Thorleif Haug (NOR)	3:44:32.0
1928	Per Erik Hedlund (SWE)	4:52:03.3
1932	Veli Saarinen (FIN)	4:28:00.0
1936	Elis Viklund (SWE)	3:30:11.0
1948	Nils Karlsson (SWE)	3:47:48.0
1952	Veikko Hakulinen (FIN)	3:33:33.0
1956	Sixten Jernberg (SWE)	2:50:27.0
1960	Kalevi Hämäläinen (FIN)	2:59:06.3
1964	Sixten Jernberg (SWE)	2:43:52.6
1968	Olle Ellefsäter (NOR)	2:28:45.8
1972	Pål Tyldum (NOR)	2:43:14.75
1976	Ivar Formo (NOR)	2:37:30.05
1980	Nikolay Zimyatov (URS)	2:27:24.60
1984	Thomas Wassberg (SWE)	2:15:55.80
1988	Gunde Svan (SWE)	2:04:30.9
1992	Bjørn Daehlie (NOR)	2:03:41.5
1994	Vladimir Smirnov (KAZ)	2:07:20.3
1998	Bjørn Daehlie (NOR)	2:05:08.2
2002	Mikhail Ivanov (RUS)[6]	2:06:20.8
2006	Giorgio Di Centa (ITA)	2:06:11.8

4 × 10-KM RELAY

		HR:MIN:SEC
1936	Finland	2:41:33.0
1948	Sweden	2:32:08.0
1952	Finland	2:20:16.0
1956	USSR	2:15:30.0
1960	Finland	2:18:45.6
1964	Sweden	2:18:34.6
1968	Norway	2:08:33.5
1972	USSR	2:04:47.94
1976	Finland	2:07:59.72
1980	USSR	1:57:03.46
1984	Sweden	1:55:06.30
1988	Sweden	1:43:58.6
1992	Norway	1:39:26.0
1994	Italy	1:41:15.0
1998	Norway	1:40:55.7
2002	Norway	1:32:45.5
2006	Italy	1:43:45.7

SKI JUMPING (70 METERS)[7]

1924	Jacob Tullin Thams (NOR)
1928	Alf Andersen (NOR)
1932	Birger Ruud (NOR)
1936	Birger Ruud (NOR)
1948	Petter Hugsted (NOR)
1952	Arnfinn Bergmann (NOR)
1956	Antti Hyvärinen (FIN)
1960	Helmut Recknagel (GER)
1964	Veikko Kankkonen (FIN)
1968	Jiri Raska (TCH)
1972	Yukio Kasaya (JPN)

Nordic Skiing (men) (continued)

SKI JUMPING (70 METERS)[7] (CONTINUED)

1976	Hans-Georg Aschenbach (GDR)
1980	Toni Innauer (AUT)
1984	Jens Weissflog (GDR)
1988	Matti Nykänen (FIN)

SKI JUMPING (95 METERS)[7]

1964	Toralf Engan (NOR)
1968	Vladimir Belousov (URS)
1972	Wojciech Fortuna (POL)
1976	Karl Schnabl (AUT)
1980	Jens Tormanen (FIN)
1984	Matti Nykänen (FIN)
1988	Matti Nykänen (FIN)
1992	Ernst Vettori (AUT)
1994	Espen Bredesen (NOR)
1998	Jani Soininen (FIN)
2002	Simon Ammann (SUI)
2006	Lars Bystøl (NOR)

SKI JUMPING (125 METERS)[7]

1992	Toni Nieminen (FIN)
1994	Jens Weissflog (GER)
1998	Kazuyoshi Funaki (JPN)
2002	Simon Ammann (SUI)
2006	Thomas Morgenstern (AUT)

NORDIC COMBINED SPRINT (7.5 KM)

2002	Samppa Lajunen (FIN)
2006	Felix Gottwald (AUT)

NORDIC COMBINED (15 KM)

1924	Thorleif Haug (NOR)
1928	Johan Grøttumsbråten (NOR)
1932	Johan Grøttumsbråten (NOR)
1936	Oddbjörn Hagen (NOR)
1948	Heikki Hasu (FIN)
1952	Simon Slåttvik (NOR)
1956	Sverre Stenersen (NOR)
1960	Georg Thoma (GER)
1964	Tormod Knutsen (NOR)
1968	Franz Keller (FRG)
1972	Ulrich Wehling (GDR)
1976	Ulrich Wehling (GDR)
1980	Ulrich Wehling (GDR)
1984	Tom Sandberg (NOR)
1988	Hippolyt Kempf (SUI)
1992	Fabrice Guy (FRA)
1994	Fred Börre Lundberg (NOR)
1998	Bjarte Engen Vik (NOR)
2002	Samppa Lajunen (FIN)
2006	Georg Hettich (GER)

TEAM SKI JUMPING (125 METERS)[8]

1988	Finland
1992	Finland
1994	Germany
1998	Japan
2002	Germany
2006	Austria

NORDIC COMBINED TEAM RELAY

1988	West Germany
1992	Japan
1994	Japan
1998	Norway
2002	Finland
2006	Austria

Winter Olympic Games (continued)

Nordic Skiing (women)

1.5-KM CROSS-COUNTRY SPRINT		MIN:SEC
2002	Yuliya Chepalova (RUS)	3:10.6
2006	Chandra Crawford (CAN)	2:12.3

TEAM SPRINT		MIN:SEC
2006	Sweden	16:36.9

5-KM CROSS-COUNTRY		MIN:SEC
1964	Klavdiya Boyarskikh (URS)	17:50.5
1968	Toini Gustafsson (SWE)	16:45.2
1972	Galina Kulakova (URS)	17:00.50
1976	Helena Takalo (FIN)	15:48.69
1980	Raisa Smetanina (URS)	15:06.92
1984	Marja-Liisa Hämäläinen (FIN)	17:04.00
1988	Marjo Matikainen (FIN)	15:04.00
1992	Marjut Lukkarinen (FIN)	14:13.8
1994	Lyubov Yegorova (RUS)	14:08.8
1998	Larisa Lazutina (RUS)	17:39.9

10-KM CROSS-COUNTRY		MIN:SEC
1952	Lydia Wideman (FIN)	41:40.0
1956	Lyubov Kozyreva (URS)	38:11.0
1960	Mariya Gusakova (URS)	39:46.6
1964	Klavdiya Boyarskikh (URS)	40:24.3
1968	Toini Gustafsson (SWE)	36:46.5
1972	Galina Kulakova (URS)	34:17.82
1976	Raisa Smetanina (URS)	30:13.41
1980	Barbara Petzold (GDR)	30:31.54
1984	Marja-Liisa Hämäläinen (FIN)	31:44.20
1988	Vida Ventsene (URS)	30:08.30
1998	Larisa Lazutina (RUS)	46:06.9
2002	Bente Skari (NOR)	28:05.6
2006	Kristina Smigun (EST)	27:51.4

COMBINED PURSUIT[9]		MIN:SEC
1992	Lyubov Yegorova (UNT)	40:08.4
1994	Lyubov Yegorova (RUS)	41:38.1
1998	Larisa Lazutina (RUS)	46:06.9
2002	Beckie Scott (CAN)[6]	25.09:9
2006	Kristina Smigun (EST)	42:48.7

15-KM CROSS-COUNTRY		MIN:SEC
1992	Lyubov Yegorova (UNT)	42:20.8
1994	Manuela Di Centa (ITA)	39:44.5
1998	Olga Danilova (RUS)	46:55.40
2002	Stefania Belmondo (ITA)	39:54.4

20-KM CROSS-COUNTRY		HR:MIN:SEC
1984	Marja-Liisa Hämäläinen (FIN)	1:01:45.0
1988	Tamara Tikhonova (URS)	55:53.6

30-KM CROSS-COUNTRY		HR:MIN:SEC
1992	Stefania Belmondo (ITA)	1:22:30.1
1994	Manuela Di Centa (ITA)	1:25:41.6
1998	Yuliya Chepalova (RUS)	1:22:01.5
2002	Gabriella Paruzzi (ITA)[6]	1:30:57.1
2006	Katerina Neumannova (CZE)	1:22:25.4

4 × 5-KM RELAY		HR:MIN:SEC
2002	Germany	49:30.6
2006	Russia	54:47.7

Sled-dog Race
1932	Emile St. Goddard (CAN)	

Snowboarding (men)

GIANT SLALOM	
1998	Ross Rebagliati (CAN)
2002	Philipp Schoch (SUI)
2006	Philipp Schoch (SUI)

HALFPIPE	
1998	Gian Simmen (SUI)
2002	Ross Powers (USA)
2006	Shaun White (USA)

SNOWBOARDCROSS	
2006	Seth Wescott (USA)

Snowboarding (women)

GIANT SLALOM	
1998	Karine Ruby (FRA)
2002	Isabelle Blanc (FRA)
2006	Daniela Meuli (SUI)

HALFPIPE	
1998	Nicola Thost (GER)
2002	Kelly Clark (USA)
2006	Hannah Teter (USA)

SNOWBOARDCROSS	
2006	Tanja Frieden (SUI)

Speed Skating (men)

4 × 5-KM RELAY[10]		HR:MIN:SEC
1956	Finland	1:09:01.0
1960	Sweden	1:04:21.4
1964	USSR	59:20.2
1968	Norway	57:30.0
1972	USSR	48:46.15
1976	USSR	1:07:49.75
1980	East Germany	1:02:11.10
1984	Norway	1:06:49.70
1988	USSR	59:51.10
1992	Unified Team	59:34.8
1994	Russia	57:12.5

500 METERS		SEC
1924	Charles Jewtraw (USA)	44.0
1928	Clas Thunberg (FIN);	43.4
	Bernt Evensen (NOR) (tied)	
1932	John Shea (USA)	43.4
1936	Ivar Ballangrud (NOR)	43.4
1948	Finn Helgesen (NOR)	43.1
1952	Kenneth Henry (USA)	43.2
1956	Yevgeny Grishin (URS)	40.2
1960	Yevgeny Grishin (URS)	40.2
1964	Richard McDermott (USA)	40.1
1968	Erhard Keller (FRG)	40.3
1972	Erhard Keller (FRG)	39.44
1976	Yevgeny Kulikov (URS)	39.17
1980	Eric Heiden (USA)	38.03
1984	Sergey Fokichev (URS)	38.19
1988	Uwe-Jens Mey (GDR)	36.45
1992	Uwe-Jens Mey (GER)	37.14
1994	Aleksandr Golubyov (RUS)	36.33
1998	Hiroyasu Shimizu (JPN)	71.35[11]
2002	Casey Fitzrandolph (USA)	69.23[11]
2006	Joey Cheek (USA)	69.76[11]

1,000 METERS		MIN:SEC
1976	Peter Mueller (USA)	1:19.32
1980	Eric Heiden (USA)	1:15.18

Winter Olympic Games (continued)

Speed Skating (men) (continued)

1,000 METERS (CONTINUED)

		MIN:SEC
1984	Gaetan Boucher (CAN)	1:15.80
1988	Nikolay Gulyayev (URS)	1:13.03
1992	Olaf Zinke (GER)	1:14.85
1994	Dan Jansen (USA)	1:12.43
1998	Ids Postma (NED)	1:10.71
2002	Gerard van Velde (NED)	1:07.18
2006	Shani Davis (USA)	1:08.89

1,500 METERS

		MIN:SEC
1924	Clas Thunberg (FIN)	2:20.8
1928	Clas Thunberg (FIN)	2:21.1
1932	John Shea (USA)	2:57.5
1936	Charles Mathisen (NOR)	2:19.2
1948	Sverre Farstad (NOR)	2:17.6
1952	Hjalmar Andersen (NOR)	2:20.4
1956	Yury Mikhaylov (URS); Yevgeny Grishin (URS) (tied)	2:08.6
1960	Yevegeny Grishin (URS); Roald Aas (NOR) (tied)	2:10.4
1964	Ants Antson (URS)	2:10.3
1968	Cornelis Verkerk (NED)	2:03.4
1972	Ard Schenk (NED)	2:02.96
1976	Jan Egil Storholt (NOR)	1:59.38
1980	Eric Heiden (USA)	1:55.44
1984	Gaetan Boucher (CAN)	1:58.36
1988	André Hoffmann (GDR)	1:52.06
1992	Johann Olav Koss (NOR)	1:54.81
1994	Johann Olav Koss (NOR)	1:51.29
1998	Ådne Søndrål (NOR)	1:47.87
2002	Derek Parra (USA)	1:43.95
2006	Enrico Fabris (ITA)	1:45.97

5,000 METERS

		MIN:SEC
1924	Clas Thunberg (FIN)	8:39.0
1928	Ivar Ballangrud (NOR)	8:50.5
1932	Irving Jaffee (USA)	9:40.8
1936	Ivar Ballangrud (NOR)	8:19.6
1948	Reidar Liaklev (NOR)	8:29.4
1952	Hjalmar Andersen (NOR)	8:10.6
1956	Boris Shilkov (URS)	7:48.7
1960	Viktor Kosichkin (URS)	7:51.3
1964	Knut Johannesen (NOR)	7:38.4
1968	Fred Anton Maier (NOR)	7:22.4
1972	Ard Schenk (NED)	7:23.61
1976	Sten Stensen (NOR)	7:24.48
1980	Eric Heiden (USA)	7:02.29
1984	Thomas Gustafson (SWE)	7:12.28
1988	Thomas Gustafson (SWE)	6:44.63
1992	Geir Karlstad (NOR)	6:59.97
1994	Johann Olav Koss (NOR)	6:34.96
1998	Gianni Romme (NED)	6:22.20
2002	Jochem Uytdehaage (NED)	6:14.66
2006	Chad Hedrick (USA)	6:14.68

10,000 METERS

		MIN:SEC
1924	Julius Skutnabb (FIN)	18:04.8
1932	Irving Jaffee (USA)	19:13.6
1936	Ivar Ballangrud (NOR)	17:24.3
1948	Ake Seyffarth (SWE)	17:26.3
1952	Hjalmar Andersen (NOR)	16:45.8
1956	Sigvard Ericsson (SWE)	16:35.9
1960	Knut Johannesen (NOR)	15:46.6
1964	Jonny Nilsson (SWE)	15:50.1
1968	Johnny Höglin (SWE)	15:23.6
1972	Ard Schenk (NED)	15:01.35
1976	Piet Kleine (NED)	14:50.59
1980	Eric Heiden (USA)	14:28.13

Speed Skating (men) (continued)

10,000 METERS (CONTINUED)

		MIN:SEC
1984	Igor Malkov (URS)	14:39.90
1988	Thomas Gustafson (SWE)	13:48.20
1992	Bart Veldkamp (NED)	14:12.12
1994	Johann Olav Koss (NOR)	13:30.55
1998	Gianni Romme (NED)	13:15.33
2002	Jochem Uytdehaage (NED)	12:58.92
2006	Bob de Jong (NED)	13:01.57

COMBINED SPEED SKATING

1924	Clas Thunberg (FIN)

TEAM PURSUIT

		MIN:SEC
2006	Italy	3:44.46

Speed Skating (women)

500 METERS

		SEC
1960	Helga Haase (GER)	45.9
1964	Lidiya Skoblikova (URS)	45.0
1972	Anne Henning (USA)	43.33
1976	Sheila Young (USA)	42.76
1980	Karin Enke (GDR)	41.78
1984	Christa Rothenburger (GDR)	41.02
1988	Bonnie Blair (USA)	39.10
1992	Bonnie Blair (USA)	40.33
1994	Bonnie Blair (USA)	39.25
1998	Catriona LeMay Doan (CAN)	76.60[11]
2002	Catriona LeMay Doan (CAN)	74.75[11]
2006	Svetlana Zhurova (RUS)	76.57[11]

1,000 METERS

		MIN:SEC
1960	Klara Guseva (URS)	1:34.1
1964	Lidiya Skoblikova (URS)	1:32.6
1968	Carolina Geijssen (NED)	1:32.6
1972	Monika Pflug (FRG)	1:31.40
1976	Tatyana Averina (URS)	1:28.43
1980	Natalya Petruseva (URS)	1:24.10
1984	Karin Enke (GDR)	1:21.61
1988	Christa Rothenburger (GDR)	1:17.65
1992	Bonnie Blair (USA)	1:21.90
1994	Bonnie Blair (USA)	1:18.74
1998	Marianne Timmer (NED)	1:16.51
2002	Chris Witty (USA)	1:13.83
2006	Marianne Timmer (NED)	1:16.05

1,500 METERS

		MIN:SEC
1960	Lidiya Skoblikova (URS)	2:25.2
1964	Lidiya Skoblikova (URS)	2:22.6
1968	Kaija Mustonen (FIN)	2:22.4
1972	Dianne Holum (USA)	2:20.85
1976	Galina Stepanskaya (URS)	2:16.58
1980	Annie Borckink (NED)	2:10.95
1984	Karin Enke (GDR)	2:03.42
1988	Yvonne van Gennip (NED)	2:00.68
1992	Jacqueline Börner (GER)	2:05.87
1994	Emese Hunyady (AUT)	2:02.19
1998	Marianne Timmer (NED)	1:57.58
2002	Anni Friesinger (GER)	1:54.02
2006	Cindy Klassen (CAN)	1:55.27

3,000 METERS

		MIN:SEC
1960	Lidiya Skoblikova (URS)	5:14.3
1964	Lidiya Skoblikova (URS)	5:14.9
1968	Johanna Schut (NED)	4:56.2
1972	Christina Baas-Kaiser (NED)	4:52.14
1976	Tatyana Averina (URS)	4:45.19
1980	Björg Eva Jensen (NOR)	4:32.13
1984	Andrea Schöne (GDR)	4:24.79

Winter Olympic Games (continued)

Speed Skating (women) (continued)

3,000 METERS (CONTINUED)   MIN:SEC

		MIN:SEC
1988	Yvonne van Gennip (NED)	4:11.94
1992	Gunda Niemann (GER)	4:19.90
1994	Svetlana Bazhanova (RUS)	4:17.43
1998	Gunda Niemann-Stirnemann (GER)	4:07.29
2002	Claudia Pechstein (GER)	3:57.70
2006	Ireen Wüst (NED)	4:02.43

5,000 METERS

		MIN:SEC
1988	Yvonne van Gennip (NED)	7:14.13
1992	Gunda Niemann (GER)	7:31.57
1994	Claudia Pechstein (GER)	7:14.37
1998	Claudia Pechstein (GER)	6:59.61
2002	Claudia Pechstein (GER)	6:46.91
2006	Clara Hughes (CAN)	6:59.07

TEAM PURSUIT

		MIN:SEC
2006	Germany	3:01.25

Short-Track Speed Skating (men)

500 METERS

		SEC
1994	Chae Ji-Hoon (KOR)	43.45
1998	Takafumi Nishitani (JPN)	42.862
2002	Marc Gagnon (CAN)	41.802
2006	Apolo Anton Ohno (USA)	41.935

1,000 METERS

		MIN:SEC
1992	Kim Ki-Hoon (KOR)	1:30.76
1994	Kim Ki-Hoon (KOR)	1:34.57
1998	Kim Dong Sung (KOR)	1:32.428
2002	Steven Bradbury (AUS)	1:29.109
2006	Ahn Hyun Soo (KOR)	1:26.739

1,500 METERS

		MIN:SEC
2002	Apolo Anton Ohno (USA)	2:18.541
2006	Ahn Hyun Soo (KOR)	2:25.341

Short-Track Speed Skating (men) (continued)

5,000-METER RELAY

		MIN:SEC
1992	Republic of Korea	7:14.02
1994	Italy	7:11.74
1998	Canada	7:06.075
2002	Canada	6:51.579
2006	Republic of Korea	6:43.376

Short-Track Speed Skating (women)

500 METERS

		SEC
1992	Cathy Turner (USA)	47.04
1994	Cathy Turner (USA)	45.98
1998	Annie Perreault (CAN)	46.568
2002	Yang Yang (A) (CHN)	44.187
2006	Wang Meng (CHN)	44.345

1,000 METERS

		MIN:SEC
1994	Chun Lee-Kyung (KOR)	1:36.87
1998	Chun Lee-Kyung (KOR)	1:42.776
2002	Yang Yang (A) (CHN)	1:36.391
2006	Jin Sun Yu (KOR)	1:32.859

1,500 METERS

		MIN:SEC
2002	Ko Gi-Hyun (KOR)	2:31.581
2006	Jin Sun Yu (KOR)	2:23.494

3,000-METER RELAY

		MIN:SEC
1992	Canada	4:36.62
1994	Republic of Korea	4:26.64
1998	Republic of Korea	4:16.260
2002	Republic of Korea	4:12.793
2006	Republic of Korea	4:17.040

Winter Pentathlon[12]

1948	Gustav Lindh (SWE)

[1]In 1992 the relay was 3 × 7.5 km; from 1994 to 2002 it was 4 × 7.5 km.   [2]Five men.   [3]Competition scored on points until 1994.   [4]From 1924 to 1952, the event was 18 km.   [5]Results of a 10- or 15-km classical leg determine the starting order of a 10- or 15-km freestyle leg, the first finisher of which is the overall winner; each leg was 15 km in the 2006 Games.   [6]Winner after disqualification of top finisher for drug use.   [7]From 1924 to 1960 the jumping was held on one 70-meter hill. In 1964 there were two events, one on a 70-meter and the other on an 80-meter hill; from 1968 to 1988 there were 70-meter and 90-meter events; from 1992 to 2002 there were 90-meter and 120-meter events; and in 2006 there were 95-meter and 125-meter events.   [8]In 1988 the event was 90 meters; from 1992 to 2002 it was 120 meters.   [9]Results of a 5- or 7.5-km classical leg determine the starting order of a 5-, 7.5-, or 10-km freestyle leg, the first finisher of which is the overall winner; each leg was 7.5 km in the 2006 Games.   [10]From 1956 to 1972 the relay was 3 × 5 km.   [11]Combined time for two runs.   [12]Included elements of cross-country skiing, downhill skiing, shooting, fencing, and horse riding.

XXIX Summer Olympic Games (2008)

The XXIX Summer Games were held in Beijing, China, 8–24 Aug 2008. Since the games, several athletes have been stripped of medals for having failed drug tests. New medalists are shown in this table.

EVENT	GOLD MEDALIST	PERFORMANCE	SILVER MEDALIST	BRONZE MEDALIST
Archery				
Men's individual	Viktor Ruban (UKR)	113–112	Park Kyung Mo (KOR)	Bair Badenov (RUS)
Men's team	South Korea	227–225	Italy	China
Women's individual	Zhang Juan Juan (CHN)	110–109	Park Sung Hyun (KOR)	Yun Ok Hee (KOR)
Women's team	South Korea	224–215	China	France
Badminton				
Men's singles	Lin Dan (CHN)	21–12, 21–8	Chong Wei Lee (MAS)	Chen Lin (CHN)
Men's doubles	Indonesia	12–21, 21–11, 21–16	China	South Korea
Women's singles	Zhang Ning (CHN)	21–12, 10–21, 21–18	Xia Xingfang (CHN)	Maria Kristin Yulianti (INA)

XXIX Summer Olympic Games (2008) (continued)

EVENT	GOLD MEDALIST	PERFORMANCE	SILVER MEDALIST	BRONZE MEDALIST
Badminton (continued)				
Women's doubles	China	21–15, 21–13	South Korea	China
Mixed doubles	South Korea	21–11, 21–17	Indonesia	China
Baseball				
	South Korea	3–2	Cuba	United States
Basketball				
Men	United States	118–107	Spain	Argentina
Women	United States	92–65	Australia	Russia
Boxing[1]				
48 kg (105.6 lb)	Zou Shiming (CHN)		Serdamba Purevdorj (MGL)	Paddy Barnes (IRL); Yampier Hernández (CUB)
51 kg (112.2 lb)	Somjit Jongjohor (THA)		Andris Laffita Hernández (CUB)	Vincenzo Picardi (ITA); Georgy Balakshin (RUS)
54 kg (118.8 lb)	Badar-Uugan Enkhbat (MGL)		Yankiel León Alarcón (CUB)	Veaceslav Gojan (MDA); Bruno Julie (MRI)
57 kg (125.4 lb)	Vasyl Lomachenko (UKR)		Khedafi Djelkhir (FRA)	Yakup Kilic (TUR); Shahin Imranov (AZE)
60 kg (132 lb)	Aleksey Tishchenko (RUS)		Daouda Sow (FRA)	Hrachik Javakhyan (ARM); Yordenis Ugás (CUB)
64 kg (140.8)	Félix Díaz (DOM)		Manus Boonjumnong (THA)	Alexis Vastine (FRA); Roniel Iglesias Sotolongo (CUB)
69 kg (151.8 lb)	Bakhyt Sarsekbayev (KAZ)		Carlos Banteaux Suárez (CUB)	Kim Jung Joo (KOR); Hanati Silamu (CHN)
75 kg (165 lb)	James Degale (GBR)		Emilio Correa Bayeaux (CUB)	Darren John Sutherland (IRL); Vijender Kumar (IND)
81 kg (178.2 lb)	Zhang Xiaoping (CHN)		Kenny Egan (IRL)	Yerekbulan Shynaliyev (KAZ); Tony Jeffries (GBR)
91 kg (200.2 lb)	Rakhim Chakhkiyev (RUS)		Clemente Russo (ITA)	Osmay Acosta Duarte (CUB); Deontay Wilder (USA)
91+ kg (200.2+ lb)	Roberto Cammarelle (ITA)		Zhang Zhilei (CHN)	David Price (GBR); Vyacheslav Glazkov (UKR)
Canoeing				
Men				
500-m kayak singles	Ken Wallace (AUS)	1 min 37.252 sec	Adam van Koeverden (CAN)	Tim Brabants (GBR)
1,000-m kayak singles	Tim Brabants (GBR)	3 min 26.323 sec	Eirik Verås Larsen (NOR)	Ken Wallace (AUS)
500-m kayak pairs	Spain	1 min 28.736 sec	Germany	Belarus
1,000-m kayak pairs	Germany	3 min 11.809 sec	Denmark	Italy
1,000-m kayak fours	Belarus	2 min 55.714 sec	Slovakia	Germany
Slalom kayak singles	Alexander Grimm (GER)	171.70 pt	Fabien Lefèvre (FRA)	Benjamin Boukpeti (TOG)
500-m Canadian singles	Maksim Opalev (RUS)	1 min 47.140 sec	David Cal (ESP)	Iurii Cheban (UKR)
1,000-m Canadian singles	Attila Sándor Vajda (HUN)	3 min 50.467 sec	David Cal (ESP)	Thomas Hall (CAN)
500-m Canadian pairs	China	1 min 41.025 sec	Russia	Germany
1,000-m Canadian pairs	Belarus	3 min 36.365 sec	Germany	Hungary
Slalom Canadian singles	Michal Martikan (SVK)	176.65 pt	David Florence (GBR)	Robin Bell (AUS)
Slalom Canadian pairs	Slovakia	190.82 pt	Czech Republic	Russia

XXIX Summer Olympic Games (2008) (continued)

EVENT	GOLD MEDALIST	PERFORMANCE	SILVER MEDALIST	BRONZE MEDALIST
Canoeing (continued)				
Women				
500-m kayak singles	Inna Osypenko-Radomska (UKR)	1 min 50.673 sec	Josefa Idem (ITA)	Katrin Wagner-Augustin (GER)
500-m kayak pairs	Hungary	1 min 41.308 sec	Poland	France
500-m kayak fours	Germany	1 min 32.231 sec	Hungary	Australia
Slalom kayak singles	Elena Kaliska (SVK)	192.64 pt	Jacqueline Lawrence (AUS)	Violetta Oblinger Peters (AUT)
Cycling				
Men				
Road race	Samuel Sánchez (ESP)	6 hr 23 min 49 sec	Davide Rebellin (ITA)	Fabian Cancellara (SUI)
Individual road time trial	Fabian Cancellara (SUI)	1 hr 2 min 11.43 sec	Gustav Larsson (SWE)	Levi Leipheimer (USA)
Individual pursuit	Bradley Wiggins (GBR)	4 min 16.977 sec	Hayden Roulston (NZL)	Steven Burke (GBR)
Team pursuit	Great Britain	3 min 53.314 sec[2]	Denmark	New Zealand
Individual sprint	Chris Hoy (GBR)		Jason Kenny (GBR)	Mickaël Bourgain (FRA)
Team sprint	Great Britain	43.128 sec	France	Germany
Individual points race	Joan Llaneras (ESP)	60 pt	Roger Kluge (GER)	Chris Newton (GBR)
Madison	Argentina		Spain	Russia
Keirin	Chris Hoy (GBR)	·	Ross Edgar (GBR)	Kiyofumi Nagai (JPN)
Mountain bike	Julien Absalon (FRA)	1 hr 55 min 59 sec	Jean-Christophe Péraud (FRA)	Nino Schurter (SUI)
Motocross/BMX	Maris Strombergs (LAT)	36.190 sec	Mike Day (USA)	Donny Robinson (USA)
Women				
Road race	Nicole Cooke (GBR)	3 hr 32 min 24 sec	Emma Johansson (SWE)	Tatiana Guderzo (ITA)
Individual road time trial	Kristin Armstrong (USA)	34 min 51.72 sec	Emma Pooley (GBR)	Karin Thürig (SUI)
Individual pursuit	Rebecca Romero (GBR)	3 min 28.321 sec	Wendy Houvenaghel (GBR)	Lesya Kalitovska (UKR)
Individual sprint	Victoria Pendleton (GBR)		Anna Meares (AUS)	Guo Shuang (CHN)
Individual points race	Marianne Vos (NED)	30 pt	Yoanka González (CUB)	Leire Olaberria (ESP)
Mountain bike	Sabine Spitz (GER)	1 hr 45 min 11 sec	Maja Wloszczowska (POL)	Irina Kalentiyeva (RUS)
Motocross/BMX	Anne-Caroline Chausson (FRA)	35.976 sec	Laëtitia Le Corguillé (FRA)	Jill Kintner (USA)
Diving				
Men				
3-m springboard	He Chong (CHN)	572.90 pt	Alexandre Despatie (CAN)	Qin Kai (CHN)
10-m platform	Matt Mitcham (AUS)	537.95 pt	Zhou Luxin (CHN)	Gleb Galperin (RUS)
3-m synchronized springboard	China	469.08 pt	Russia	Ukraine
10-m synchronized platform	China	468.18 pt	Germany	Russia
Women				
3-m springboard	Guo Jingjing (CHN)	415.35 pt	Yuliya Pakhalina (RUS)	Wu Minxia (CHN)
10-m platform	Chen Ruolin (CHN)	447.70 pt	Émilie Heymans (CAN)	Wang Xin (CHN)
3-m synchronized springboard	China	343.50 pt	Russia	Germany
10-m synchronized platform	China	363.54 pt	Australia	Mexico
Equestrian				
Individual 3-day event	Hinrich Romeike (GER)		Gina Miles (USA)	Kristina Cook (GBR)
Team 3-day event	Germany		Australia	Great Britain
Individual dressage	Anky van Grunsven (NED)		Isabell Werth (GER)	Heike Kemmer (GER)
Team dressage	Germany		Netherlands	Denmark
Individual jumping	Eric Lamaze (CAN)		Rolf-Göran Bengtsson (SWE)	Beezie Madden (USA)
Team jumping	United States		Canada	Switzerland

XXIX Summer Olympic Games (2008) (continued)

EVENT	GOLD MEDALIST	PERFORMANCE	SILVER MEDALIST	BRONZE MEDALIST
Fencing				
Men				
Individual foil	Benjamin Philip Kleibrink (GER)		Yuki Ota (JPN)	Salvatore Sanzo (ITA)
Individual épée	Matteo Tagliariol (ITA)		Fabrice Jeannet (FRA)	José Luis Abajo (ESP)
Team épée	France		Poland	Italy
Individual sabre	Zhong Man (CHN)		Nicolas Lopez (FRA)	Mihai Cavaliu (ROM)
Team sabre	France		United States	Italy
Women				
Individual foil	Valentina Vezzali (ITA)		Nam Hyun Hee (KOR)	Margherita Granbassi (ITA)
Team foil	Russia		United States	Italy
Individual épée	Britta Heidemann (GER)		Ana Maria Branza (ROM)	Ildikó Mincza-Nébald (HUN)
Individual sabre	Mariel Zagunis (USA)		Sada Jacobson (USA)	Becca Ward (USA)
Team sabre	Ukraine		China	United States
Field Hockey				
Men	Germany	1–0	Spain	Australia
Women	The Netherlands	2–0	China	Argentina
Gymnastics				
Men				
Team	China	286.125 pt	Japan	United States
All-around	Yang Wei (CHN)	94.575 pt	Kohei Uchimura (JPN)	Benoît Caranobe (FRA)
Floor exercise	Zou Kai (CHN)	16.050 pt	Gervasio Deferr (ESP)	Anton Golotsutskov (RUS)
Vault	Leszek Blanik (POL)	16.537 pt	Thomas Bouhail (FRA)	Anton Golotsutskov (RUS)
Pommel horse	Xiao Qin (CHN)	15.875 pt	Filip Ude (CRO)	Louis Smith (GBR)
Rings	Chen Yibing (CHN)	16.600 pt	Yang Wei (CHN)	Oleksandr Vorobiov (UKR)
Parallel bars	Li Xiaopeng (CHN)	16.450 pt	Yoo Won Chul (KOR)	Anton Fokin (UZB)
Horizontal bar	Zou Kai (CHN)	16.200 pt	Jonathan Horton (USA)	Fabian Hambüchen (GER)
Trampoline	Lu Chunlong (CHN)	41.00 pt	Jason Burnett (CAN)	Dong Dong (CHN)
Women				
Team	China	188.900 pt	United States	Romania
All-around	Nastia Liukin (USA)	63.325 pt	Shawn Johnson (USA)	Yang Yilin (CHN)
Floor exercise	Sandra Izbasa (ROM)	15.650 pt	Shawn Johnson (USA)	Nastia Liukin (USA)
Vault	Hong Un Jong (PRK)	15.650 pt	Oksana Chusovitina (GER)	Cheng Fei (CHN)
Uneven bars	He Kexin (CHN)	16.725 pt	Nastia Liukin (USA)	Yang Yilin (CHN)
Balance beam	Shawn Johnson (USA)	16.225 pt	Nastia Liukin (USA)	Cheng Fei (CHN)
Trampoline	He Wenna (CHN)	37.80 pt	Karen Cockburn (CAN)	Ekaterina Khilko (UZB)
Individual rhythmic	Yevgeniya Kanayeva (RUS)	75.500 pt	Inna Zhukova (BLR)	Anna Bessonova (UKR)
Team rhythmic	Russia	35.550 pt	China	Belarus
Handball (Team)				
Men	France	15–10, 13–13	Iceland	Spain
Women	Norway	18–13, 16–14	Russia	South Korea
Judo[1]				
Men				
60 kg (132 lb)	Choi Min Ho (KOR)		Ludwig Paischer (AUT)	Rishod Sobirov (UZB); Ruben Houkes (NED)
66 kg (145.2 lb)	Masato Uchishiba (JPN)		Benjamin Darbelet (FRA)	Yordanis Arencibia (CUB); Pak Chol Min (PRK)
73 kg (160.6 lb)	Elnur Mammadli (AZE)		Wang Ki Chun (KOR)	Rasul Boqiev (TJK); Leandro Guilheiro (BRA)

XXIX Summer Olympic Games (2008) (continued)

EVENT	GOLD MEDALIST	PERFORMANCE	SILVER MEDALIST	BRONZE MEDALIST
Judo[1] (continued)				
Men (continued)				
81 kg (178.2 lb)	Ole Bischof (GER)		Kim Jae Bum (KOR)	Tiago Camilo (BRA); Roman Gontiuk (UKR)
90 kg (198 lb)	Irakli Tsirekidze (GEO)		Amar Benikhlef (ALG)	Hesham Mesbah (EGY); Sergei Aschwanden (SUI)
100 kg (220 lb)	Tuvshinbayar Naidan (MGL)		Askhat Zhitkeyev (KAZ)	Movlud Miraliyev (AZE); Henk Grol (NED)
100+ kg (220+ lb)	Satoshi Ishii (JPN)		Abdullo Tangriev (UZB)	Oscar Brayson (CUB); Teddy Riner (FRA)
Women				
48 kg (105.6 lb)	Alina Alexandra Dumitru (ROM)		Yanet Bermoy (CUB)	Paula Belén Pareto (ARG); Ryoko Tani (JPN)
52 kg (114.4 lb)	Xian Dongmei (CHN)		An Kum Ae (PRK)	Soraya Haddad (ALG); Misato Nakamura (JPN)
57 kg (125.4 lb)	Giulia Quintavalle (ITA)		Deborah Gravenstijn (NED)	Ketleyn Quadros (BRA); Xu Yan (CHN)
63 kg (138.6 lb)	Ayumi Tanimoto (JPN)		Lucie Décosse (FRA)	Elisabeth Willeboordse (NED); Won Ok Im (PRK)
70 kg (154 lb)	Masae Ueno (JPN)		Anaysí Hernández (CUB)	Ronda Rousey (USA); Edith Bosch (NED)
78 kg (171.6 lb)	Yang Xiuli (CHN)		Yalennis Castillo (CUB)	Jeong Gyeong Mi (KOR); Stéphanie Possamaï (FRA)
78+ kg (171.6 lb)	Tong Wen (CHN)		Maki Tsukada (JPN)	Lucija Polavder (SLO); Idalys Ortiz (CUB)
Modern Pentathlon				
Men	Andrey Moiseyev (RUS)		Edvinas Krungolcas (LTU)	Andrejus Zadneprovskis (LTU)
Women	Lena Schöneborn (GER)		Heather Fell (GBR)	Victoria Tereshuk (UKR)
Rowing				
Men				
Single sculls	Olaf Tufte (NOR)	6 min 59.83 sec	Ondrej Synek (CZE)	Mahe Drysdale (NZL)
Double sculls	Australia	6 min 27.77 sec	Estonia	Great Britain
Quadruple sculls	Poland	5 min 41.33 sec	Italy	France
Coxless pairs (oars)	Australia	6 min 37.44 sec	Canada	New Zealand
Coxless fours (oars)	Great Britain	6 min 06.57 sec	Australia	France
Eights	Canada	5 min 23.89 sec	Great Britain	United States
Lightweight double sculls	Great Britain	6 min 10.99 sec	Greece	Denmark
Lightweight fours	Denmark	5 min 47.76 sec	Poland	Canada
Women				
Single sculls	Rumyana Neykova (BUL)	7 min 22.34 sec	Michelle Guerette (USA)	Yekaterina Karsten (BLR)
Double sculls	New Zealand	7 min 07.32 sec	Germany	Great Britain
Quadruple sculls	China	6 min 16.06 sec	Great Britain	Germany
Coxless pairs (oars)	Romania	7 min 20.60 sec	China	Belarus
Eights	United States	6 min 05.34 sec	The Netherlands	Romania
Lightweight double sculls	The Netherlands	6 min 54.74 sec	Finland	Canada
Sailing				
Men's 470	Australia		Great Britain	France
Women's 470	Australia		The Netherlands	Brazil
Men's RS:X	Tom Ashley (NZL)		Julien Bontemps (FRA)	Shahar Zubari (ISR)
Women's RS:X	Yin Jian (CHN)		Alessandra Sensini (ITA)	Bryony Shaw (GBR)

XXIX Summer Olympic Games (2008) (continued)

EVENT	GOLD MEDALIST	PERFORMANCE	SILVER MEDALIST	BRONZE MEDALIST
Sailing (continued)				
Open Finn	Ben Ainslie (GBR)		Zach Railey (USA)	Guillaume Florent (FRA)
Women's Yngling	Great Britain		The Netherlands	Greece
Open 49er	Denmark		Spain	Germany
Men's Laser	Paul Goodison (GBR)		Vasilij Zbogar (SLO)	Diego Romero (ITA)
Women's Laser Radial	Anna Tunnicliffe (USA)		Gintare Volungeviciute (LTU)	Xu Lijia (CHN)
Men's Star	Great Britain		Brazil	Sweden
Open Tornado	Spain		Australia	Argentina
Shooting				
Men				
Rapid-fire pistol	Oleksandr Petriv (UKR)	780.2 pt^3	Ralf Schumann (GER)	Christian Reitz (GER)
Free pistol	Jin Jong Oh (KOR)	660.4 pt	Tan Zongliang (CHN)	Vladimir Isakov (RUS)
Air pistol	Pang Wei (CHN)	688.2 pt	Jin Jong Oh (KOR)	Jason Turner (USA)
Small-bore (sport) rifle, 3 positions	Qiu Jian (CHN)	1272.5 pt	Jury Sukhorukov (UKR)	Rajmond Debevec (SLO)
Small-bore (sport) rifle, prone	Artur Ayvazian (UKR)	702.7 pt	Matthew Emmons (USA)	Warren Potent (AUS)
Air rifle	Abhinav Bindra (IND)	700.5 pt	Zhu Qinan (CHN)	Henri Häkkinen (FIN)
Trap	David Kostelecky (CZE)	146.0 pt^3	Giovanni Pellielo (ITA)	Aleksey Alipov (RUS)
Double trap	Walton Eller (USA)	190.0 pt^3	Francesco D'Aniello (ITA)	Hu Binyuan (CHN)
Skeet	Vincent Hancock (USA)	145.0 pt^3	Tore Brovold (NOR)	Anthony Terras (FRA)
Women				
Pistol	Chen Ying (CHN)	793.4 pt^3	Gundegmaa Otryad (MGL)	Munkhbayar Dorj-suren (GER)
Air pistol	Guo Wenjun (CHN)	492.3 pt^3	Natalya Paderina (RUS)	Nino Salukvadze (GEO)
Small-bore (sport) rifle, 3 positions	Du Li (CHN)	690.3 pt^3	Katerina Emmons (CZE)	Eglis Yaima Cruz (CUB)
Air rifle	Katerina Emmons (CZE)	503.5 pt^3	Lyubov Galkina (RUS)	Snjezana Pejcic (CRO)
Trap	Satu Mäkelä-Nummela (FIN)	91.0 pt^3	Zuzana Stefecekova (SVK)	Corey Cogdell (USA)
Skeet	Chiara Cainero (ITA)	93.0 pt^3	Kimberly Rhode (USA)	Christina Brinker (GER)
Soccer (Association Football)				
Men	Argentina	1–0	Nigeria	Brazil
Women	United States	1–0	Brazil	Germany
Softball				
	Japan	3–1	United States	Australia
Swimming				
Men				
50-m freestyle	César Cielo Filho (BRA)	21.30 sec^3	Amaury Leveaux (FRA)	Alain Bernard (FRA)
100-m freestyle	Alain Bernard (FRA)	47.21 sec	Eamon Sullivan (AUS)	César Cielo Filho (BRA); Jason Lezak (USA) (tied)
200-m freestyle	Michael Phelps (USA)	1 min 42.96 sec^2	Park Tae Hwan (KOR)	Peter Vanderkaay (USA)
400-m freestyle	Park Tae Hwan (KOR)	3 min 41.86 sec	Zhang Lin (CHN)	Larsen Jensen (USA)
1,500-m freestyle	Oussama Mellouli (TUN)	14 min 40.84 sec	Grant Hackett (AUS)	Ryan Cochrane (CAN)
100-m backstroke	Aaron Peirsol (USA)	52.54 sec^2	Matt Grevers (USA)	Hayden Stoeckel (AUS); Arkady Vyatchanin (RUS) (tied)
200-m backstroke	Ryan Lochte (USA)	1 min 53.94 sec^2	Aaron Peirsol (USA)	Arkady Vyatchanin (RUS)
100-m breaststroke	Kosuke Kitajima (JPN)	58.91 sec^2	Alexander Dale Oen (NOR)	Hugues Duboscq (FRA)
200-m breaststroke	Kosuke Kitajima (JPN)	2 min 07.64 sec^3	Brenton Rickard (AUS)	Hugues Duboscq (FRA)
100-m butterfly	Michael Phelps (USA)	50.58 sec^3	Milorad Cavic (SRB)	Andrew Lauterstein (AUS)

XXIX Summer Olympic Games (2008) (continued)

EVENT	GOLD MEDALIST	PERFORMANCE	SILVER MEDALIST	BRONZE MEDALIST
Swimming (continued)				
Men (continued)				
200-m butterfly	Michael Phelps (USA)	1 min 52.03 sec[2]	László Cseh (HUN)	Takeshi Matsuda (JPN)
200-m individual medley	Michael Phelps (USA)	1 min 54.23 sec[2]	László Cseh (HUN)	Ryan Lochte (USA)
400-m individual medley	Michael Phelps (USA)	4 min 03.84 sec[2]	László Cseh (HUN)	Ryan Lochte (USA)
10-km open-water marathon	Maarten van der Weijden (NED)	1 hr 51 min 51.60 sec	David Davies (GBR)	Thomas Lurz (GER)
4 x 100-m freestyle relay	United States	3 min 08.24 sec[2]	France	Australia
4 x 200-m freestyle relay	United States	6 min 58.56 sec[2]	Russia	Australia
4 x 100-m medley relay	United States	3 min 29.34 sec[2]	Australia	Japan
Women				
50-m freestyle	Britta Steffen (GER)	24.06 sec[3]	Dara Torres (USA	Cate Campbell (AUS)
100-m freestyle	Britta Steffen (GER)	53.12 sec[3]	Lisbeth Lenton Trickett (AUS)	Natalie Coughlin (USA)
200-m freestyle	Federica Pellegrini (ITA)	1 min 54.82 sec[2]	Sara Isakovic (SLO)	Pang Jiaying (CHN)
400-m freestyle	Rebecca Adlington (GBR)	4 min 03.22 sec	Katie Hoff (USA)	Joanne Jackson (GBR)
800-m freestyle	Rebecca Adlington (GBR)	8 min 14.10 sec[2]	Alessia Filippi (ITA)	Lotte Friis (DEN)
100-m backstroke	Natalie Coughlin (USA)	58.96 sec	Kirsty Coventry (ZIM)	Margaret Hoelzer (USA)
200-m backstroke	Kirsty Coventry (ZIM)	2 min 05.24 sec[2]	Margaret Hoelzer (USA)	Reiko Nakamura (JPN)
100-m breaststroke	Leisel Jones (AUS)	1 min 05.17 sec[3]	Rebecca Soni (USA)	Mirna Jukic (AUT)
200-m breaststroke	Rebecca Soni (USA)	2 min 20.22 sec[2]	Leisel Jones (AUS)	Sara Nordenstam (NOR)
100-m butterfly	Lisbeth Lenton Trickett (AUS)	56.73 sec	Christine Magnuson (USA)	Jessicah Schipper (AUS)
200-m butterfly	Liu Zige (CHN)	2 min 04.18 sec[2]	Jiao Liuyang (CHN)	Jessicah Schipper (AUS)
200-m individual medley	Stephanie Rice (AUS)	2 min 08.45 sec[2]	Kirsty Coventry (ZIM)	Natalie Coughlin (USA)
400-m individual medley	Stephanie Rice (AUS)	4 min 29.45 sec[2]	Kirsty Coventry (ZIM)	Katie Hoff (USA)
10-km open-water marathon	Larisa Ilchenko (RUS)	1 hr 59 min 27.70 sec	Keri-Anne Payne (GBR)	Cassandra Patten (GBR)
4 x 100-m freestyle relay	The Netherlands	3 min 33.76 sec[3]	United States	Australia
4 x 200-m freestyle relay	Australia	7 min 44.31 sec[2]	China	United States
4 x 100-m medley relay	Australia	3 min 52.69 sec[2]	United States	China
Synchronized Swimming				
Duet	Russia	99.251 pt	Spain	Japan
Team	Russia	99.500 pt	Spain	China
Table Tennis				
Men's singles	Ma Lin (CHN)	11–9, 11–9, 6–11, 11–7, 11–9	Wang Hao (CHN)	Wang Liqin (CHN)
Men's team	China	3–0	Germany	South Korea
Women's singles	Zhang Yining (CHN)	8–11, 13–11, 11–8, 11–8, 11–3	Wang Nan (CHN)	Guo Yue (CHN)
Women's team	China	3–0	Singapore	South Korea
Taekwondo[1]				
Men				
58 kg (127.6 lb)	Guillermo Pérez (MEX)		Yulis Gabriel Mercedes (DOM)	Chu Mu-yen (TPE); Ro-hullah Nikpai (AFG)
68 kg (149.6 lb)	Son Tae Jin (KOR)		Mark Lopez (USA)	Sung Yu-chi (TPE); Servet Tazegul (TUR)

XXIX Summer Olympic Games (2008) (continued)

EVENT	GOLD MEDALIST	PERFORMANCE	SILVER MEDALIST	BRONZE MEDALIST
Taekwondo[1] (continued)				
Men (continued)				
80 kg (176 lb)	Hadi Saei (IRI)		Mauro Sarmiento (ITA)	Steven Lopez (USA); Zhu Guo (CHN)
80+ kg (176+ lb)	Cha Dong Min (KOR)		Alexandros Nikolaidis (GRE)	Arman Chilmanov (KAZ); Chika Yagazie Chukwumerije (NGR)
Women				
49 kg (107.8 lb)	Wu Jingyu (CHN)		Buttree Puedpong (THA)	Dalia Contreras Rivero (VEN); Daynellis Montejo (CUB)
57 kg (125.4 lb)	Lim Su Jeong (KOR)		Azize Tanrikulu (TUR)	Diana Lopez (USA); Martina Zubcic (CRO)
67 kg (147.4 lb)	Hwang Kyung Seon (KOR)		Karine Sergerie (CAN)	Gwladys Patience Epangue (FRA); Sandra Saric (CRO)
67+ kg (147.4+ lb)	María del Rosario Espinoza (MEX)		Nina Solheim (NOR)	Natalia Falavigna (BRA); Sarah Stevenson (GBR)
Tennis				
Men's singles	Rafael Nadal (ESP)	6–3, 7–6, 6–3	Fernando González (CHI)	Novak Djokovic (SRB)
Men's doubles	Switzerland	6–3, 6–4, 6–7, 6–3	Sweden	United States
Women's singles	Yelena Dementyeva (RUS)	3–6, 7–5, 6–3	Dinara Safina (RUS)	Vera Zvonareva (RUS)
Women's doubles	United States	6–2, 6–0	Spain	China
Track and Field (Athletics)				
Men				
100 m	Usain Bolt (JAM)	9.69 sec[2]	Richard Thompson (TRI)	Walter Dix (USA)
200 m	Usain Bolt (JAM)	19.30 sec[2]	Shawn Crawford (USA)	Walter Dix (USA)
400 m	LaShawn Merritt (USA)	43.75 sec	Jeremy Wariner (USA)	David Neville (USA)
4 x 100-m relay	Jamaica	37.10 sec[2]	Trinidad and Tobago	Japan
4 x 400-m relay	United States	2 min 55.39 sec[3]	The Bahamas	Russia
800 m	Wilfred Bungei (KEN)	1 min 44.65 sec	Ismail Ahmed Ismail (SUD)	Alfred Kirwa Yego (KEN)
1,500 m	Rashid Ramzi (BRN)	3 min 32.94 sec	Asbel Kipruto Kiprop (KEN)	Nicholas Willis (NZL)
5,000 m	Kenenisa Bekele (ETH)	12 min 57.82 sec[3]	Eliud Kipchoge (KEN)	Edwin Cheruiyot Soi (KEN)
10,000 m	Kenenisa Bekele (ETH)	27 min 01.17 sec[3]	Sileshi Sihine (ETH)	Micah Kogo (KEN)
Marathon	Samuel Kamau Wansiru (KEN)	2 hr 06 min 32 sec[3]	Jaouad Gharib (MAR)	Tsegay Kedebe (ETH)
110-m hurdles	Dayron Robles (CUB)	12.93 sec	David Payne (USA)	David Oliver (USA)
400-m hurdles	Angelo Taylor (USA)	47.25 sec	Kerron Clement (USA)	Bershawn Jackson (USA)
3,000-m steeplechase	Brimin Kiprop Kipruto (KEN)	8 min 10.34 sec	Mahiedine Mekhissi-Benabbad (FRA)	Richard Kipkemboi Mateelong (KEN)
20,000-m walk	Valery Borchin (RUS)	1 hour 19 min 01 sec	Jefferson Pérez (ECU)	Jared Tallent (AUS)
50,000-m walk	Alex Schwazer (ITA)	3 hr 37 min 09 sec[3]	Jared Tallent (AUS)	Denis Nizhegorodov (RUS)
High jump	Andrey Silnov (RUS)	2.36 m	Germaine Mason (GBR)	Yaroslav Rybakov (RUS)
Long jump	Irving Jahir Saladino Aranda (PAN)	8.34 m	Khotso Mokoena (RSA)	Ibrahim Camejo (CUB)
Triple jump	Nelson Évora (POR)	17.67 m	Phillips Idowu (GBR)	Leevan Sands (BAH)
Pole vault	Steve Hooker (AUS)	5.96 m[3]	Yevgeny Lukyanenko (RUS)	Denys Yurchenko (UKR)
Shot put	Tomasz Majewski (POL)	21.51 m	Christian Cantwell (USA)	Andrei Mikhnevich (BLR)
Discus throw	Gerd Kanter (EST)	68.82 m	Piotr Malachowski (POL)	Virgilijus Alekna (LTU)
Javelin throw	Andreas Thorkildsen (NOR)	90.57 m[3]	Ainars Kovals (LAT)	Tero Pitkämäki (FIN)
Hammer throw	Primoz Kozmus (SLO)	82.02 m	Krisztian Pars (HUN)	Koji Murofushi (JPN)
Decathlon	Bryan Clay (USA)	8,791 pt	Andrei Krauchanka (BLR)	Leonel Suárez (CUB)

XXIX Summer Olympic Games (2008) (continued)

EVENT	GOLD MEDALIST	PERFORMANCE	SILVER MEDALIST	BRONZE MEDALIST
Track and Field (Athletics) (continued)				
Women				
100 m	Shelly-Ann Fraser (JAM)	10.78 sec	Sherone Simpson (JAM); Kerron Stewart (JAM) (tied)	
200 m	Veronica Campbell-Brown (JAM)	21.74 sec	Allyson Felix (USA)	Kerron Stewart (JAM)
400 m	Christine Ohuruogu (GBR)	49.62 sec	Shericka Williams (JAM)	Sanya Richards (USA)
4 x 100-m relay	Russia	42.31 sec	Belgium	Nigeria
4 x 400-m relay	United States	3 min 18.54 sec	Russia	Jamaica
800 m	Pamela Jelimo (KEN)	1 min 54.87 sec	Janeth Jepkosgei Busienei (KEN)	Hasna Benhassi (MAR)
1,500 m	Nancy Jebet Langat (KEN)	4 min 00.23 sec	Iryna Lishchynska (UKR)	Nataliya Tobias (UKR)
5,000 m	Tirunesh Dibaba (ETH)	15 min 41.40 sec	Elvan Abeylegesse (TUR)	Meseret Defar (ETH)
10,000 m	Tirunesh Dibaba (ETH)	29 min 54.66 sec[3]	Elvan Abeylegesse (TUR)	Shalane Flanagan (USA)
Marathon	Constantina Tomescu (ROM)	2 hr 26 min 44 sec	Catherine Ndereba (KEN)	Zhou Chunxiu (CHN)
100-m hurdles	Dawn Harper (USA)	12.54 sec	Sally McLellan (AUS)	Priscilla Lopes-Schliep (CAN)
400-m hurdles	Melaine Walker (JAM)	52.64 sec[3]	Sheena Tosta (USA)	Tasha Danvers (GBR)
3,000-m steeplechase	Gulnara Samitova-Galkina (RUS)	8 min 58.81 sec[2]	Eunice Jepkorir (ETH)	Yekaterina Volkova (RUS)
20-km walk	Olga Kaniskina (RUS)	1 hr 26 min 31 sec[3]	Kjersti Tysse Plätzer (NOR)	Elisa Rigaudo (ITA)
High jump	Tia Hellebaut (BEL)	2.05 m	Blanka Vlasic (CRO)	Anna Chicherova (RUS)
Long jump	Maurren Higa Maggi (BRA)	7.04 m	Tatyana Lebedeva (RUS)	Blessing Okagbare (NGR)
Triple jump	Françoise Mbango Etone (CMR)	15.39 m[3]	Tatyana Lebedeva (RUS)	Hrysopiyi Devetzi (GRE)
Pole vault	Yelena Isinbayeva (RUS)	5.05 m[2]	Jennifer Stuczynski (USA)	Svetlana Feofanova (RUS)
Shot put	Valerie Vili (NZL)	20.56 m	Natallia Mikhnevich (BLR)	Nadzeya Ostapchuk (BLR)
Discus throw	Stephanie Brown Trafton (USA)	64.74 m	Yarelys Barrios (CUB)	Olena Antonova (UKR)
Javelin throw	Barbora Spotakova (CZE)	71.42 m	Mariya Abakumova (RUS)	Christina Obergfoll (GER)
Hammer throw	Aksana Miankova (BLR)	76.34 m[3]	Yipsi Moreno (CUB)	Zhang Wenxiu (CHN)
Heptathlon	Nataliya Dobrynska (UKR)	6,733 pt	Hyleas Fountain (USA)	Tatyana Chernova (RUS)

Triathlon

Men	Jan Frodeno (GER)	1 hr 48 min 53.28 sec	Simon Whitfield (CAN)	Bevan Docherty (NZL)
Women	Emma Snowsill (AUS)	1 hr 58 min 27.66 sec	Vanessa Fernandes (POR)	Emma Moffatt (AUS)

Volleyball

Men's indoor	United States	20-25, 25-22, 25-21, 25-23, 25-23	Brazil	Russia
Women's indoor	Brazil	25-15, 18-25, 25-13, 25-21	United States	China
Men's beach	United States	23-21, 17-21, 15-4	Brazil	Brazil
Women's beach	United States	21-18, 21-18	China	China

Water Polo

Men	Hungary	14-10	United States	Serbia
Women	The Netherlands	9-8	United States	Australia

Weight Lifting
Men

56 kg (123.2 lb)	Long Qingquan (CHN)	292.0	Hoang Anh Tuan (VIE)	Eko Yuli Irawan (INA)
62 kg (136.4 lb)	Zhang Xiangxiang (CHN)	319.0 kg	Diego Salazar (COL)	Triyatno (INA)
69 kg (151.8 lb)	Liao Hui (CHN)	348.0 kg	Vencelas Dabaya-Tientcheu (FRA)	Tigran Gevorg Martirosyan (ARM)
77 kg (169.4 lb)	Sa Jae Hyouk (KOR)	366.0 kg	Li Hongli (CHN)	Gevorg Davtyan (ARM)
85 kg (187 lb)	Lu Yong (CHN)	394.0 kg	Andrei Rybakou (BLR)	Tigran Varban Martirosyan (ARM)

XXIX Summer Olympic Games (2008) (continued)

EVENT	GOLD MEDALIST	PERFORMANCE	SILVER MEDALIST	BRONZE MEDALIST
Weight Lifting (continued)				
Men (continued)				
94 kg (206.8 lb)	Ilya Ilin (KAZ)	406.0 kg	Szymon Kolecki (POL)	Khadzhimurat Akkayev (RUS)
105 kg (231 lb)	Andrei Aramnau (BLR)	436.0 kg[2]	Dmitry Klokov (RUS)	Dmitry Lapikov (RUS)
105+ kg (231+ lb)	Matthias Steiner (GER)	461.0 kg	Yevgeny Chigishev (RUS)	Viktors Scerbatihs (LAT)
Women				
48 kg (105.6 lb)	Chen Xiexia (CHN)	212.0 kg[3]	Sibel Ozkan (TUR)	Chen Wei-ling (TPE)
53 kg (116.6 lb)	Prapawadee Jaroenrattanatarakoon (THA)	221.0 kg	Yoon Jinhee (KOR)	Nastassia Novikava (BLR)
58 kg (127.6 lb)	Chen Yanqing (CHN)	244.0 kg[3]	Marina Shainova (RUS)	O Jong Ae (PRK)
63 kg (138.6 lb)	Pak Hyon Suk (PRK)	241.0 kg	Irina Nekrassova (KAZ)	Lu Ying-chi (TPE)
69 kg (151.8 lb)	Liu Chunhong (CHN)	286.0 kg[2]	Oksana Slivenko (RUS)	Natalya Davydova (UKR)
75 kg (165 lb)	Cao Lei (CHN)	282.0 kg[3]	Alla Vazhenina (KAZ)	Nadezda Yevstyukhina (RUS)
75+ kg (165 lb)	Jang Mi Ran (KOR)	326.0 kg[2]	Olha Korobka (UKR)	Mariya Grabovetskaya (KAZ)
Wrestling[1]				
Freestyle				
Men				
55 kg (121 lb)	Henry Cejudo (USA)		Tomohiro Matsunaga (JPN)	Besik Kudukhov (RUS); Radoslav Velikov (BUL)
60 kg (132 lb)	Mavlet Batirov (RUS)		Vasyl Fedoryshyn (UKR)	Seyedmorad Mohammadi (IRI); Kenichi Yumoto (JPN)
66 kg (145.2 lb)	Ramazan Sahin (TUR)		Andriy Stadnik (UKR)	Sushil Kumar (IND); Otar Tushishvili (GEO)
74 kg (162.8 lb)	Buvaysasa Saytiyev (RUS)		Soslan Tigiev (UZB)	Murad Gaidarov (BLR); Kiril Terziev (BUL)
84 kg (184.8 lb)	Revazi Mindorashvili (GEO)		Yusup Abdusalomov (TJK)	Taras Danko (UKR); Georgy Ketoyev (RUS)
96 kg (211.2 lb)	Shirvani Muradov (RUS)		Taimuraz Tigiyev (KAZ)	Khetag Gazyumov (AZE); George Gogshelidze (GEO)
120+ kg (264 lb)	Artur Taymazov (UZB)		Bakhtiyar Akhmedov (RUS)	David Musulbes (SVK); Marid Mutalimov (KAZ)
Women				
48 kg (105.6 lb)	Carol Huynh (CAN)		Chiharu Icho (JPN)	Irini Merleni (UKR); Mariya Stadnik (AZE)
55 kg (121 lb)	Saori Yoshida (JPN)		Xu Li (CHN)	Jackeline Rentería (COL); Tonya Verbeek (CAN)
63 kg (138.6 lb)	Kaori Icho (JPN)		Alena Kartashova (RUS)	Randi Miller (USA); Yelena Shalygina (KAZ)
72 kg (158.4 lb)	Wang Jiao (CHN)		Stanka Zlateva (BUL)	Kyoko Hamaguchi (JPN); Agnieszka Wieszczek (POL)
Greco-Roman				
55 kg (121 lb)	Nazyr Mankiyev (RUS)		Rovshan Bayramov (AZE)	Roman Amoyan (ARM); Park Eun Chul (KOR)
60 kg (132 lb)	Islam-Beka Albiyev (RUS)		Vitaliy Rahimov (AZE)	Nurbakyt Tengizbayev (KAZ); Ruslan Tiumenbaev (KGZ)
66 kg (145.2 lb)	Steeve Guénot (FRA)		Kanatbek Begaliev (KGZ)	Mikhail Siamonau (BLR); Armen Vardanyan (UKR)
74 kg (162.8 lb)	Manuchar Kvirkelia (GEO)		Chang Yongxiang (CHN)	Christophe Guénot (FRA); Yavor Yanakiev (BUL)

XXIX Summer Olympic Games (2008) (continued)

EVENT	GOLD MEDALIST	SILVER MEDALIST	BRONZE MEDALIST
Wrestling[1] (continued)			
Greco-Roman (continued)			
84 kg (184.8 lb)	Andrea Minguzzo (ITA)	Zoltán Fodor (HUN)	Nazmi Avluca (TUR)
96 kg (211.2 lb)	Aslanbek Khushtov (RUS)	Mirko Englich (GER)	Asset Mambetov (KAZ); Adam Wheeler (USA)
120 kg (264 lb)	Mijain López (CUB)	Khasan Baroyev (RUS)	Mindaugas Mizgaitis (LTU); Yuri Patrikeev (ARM)

[1]*Two bronze medals awarded in each weight division.*   [2]*World record.*   [3]*Olympic record.*

XX Winter Olympic Games (2006)

The XX Winter Games were held in Turin, Italy, 10–26 Feb 2006. Since the games, several athletes have been stripped of medals for having failed drug tests. New medalists are shown in this table.

EVENT	GOLD MEDALIST	PERFORMANCE	SILVER MEDALIST	BRONZE MEDALIST
Alpine Skiing				
Men				
Downhill	Antoine Dénériaz (FRA)	1 min 48.80 sec	Michael Walchhofer (AUT)	Bruno Kernen (SUI)
Slalom	Benjamin Raich (AUT)	1 min 43.14 sec	Reinfried Herbst (AUT)	Rainier Schönfelder (AUT)
Giant slalom	Benjamin Raich (AUT)	2 min 35.00 sec	Joël Chenal (FRA)	Hermann Maier (AUT)
Supergiant slalom	Kjetil André Aamodt (NOR)	1 min 30.65 sec	Hermann Maier (AUT)	Ambrosi Hoffmann (SUI)
Alpine combined	Ted Ligety (USA)	3 min 09.35 sec	Ivica Kostelic (CRO)	Rainier Schönfelder (AUT)
Women				
Downhill	Michaela Dorfmeister (AUT)	1 min 56.49 sec	Martina Schild (SUI)	Anja Pärson (SWE)
Slalom	Anja Pärson (SWE)	1 min 29.04 sec	Nicole Hosp (AUT)	Marlies Schild (AUT)
Giant slalom	Julia Mancuso (USA)	2 min 09.19 sec	Tanja Poutiainen (FIN)	Anna Ottosson (SWE)
Supergiant slalom	Michaela Dorfmeister (AUT)	1 min 32.47 sec	Janica Kostelic (CRO)	Alexandra Meissnitzer (AUT)
Alpine combined	Janica Kostelic (CRO)	2 min 51.08 sec	Marlies Schild (AUT)	Anja Pärson (SWE)
Nordic Skiing				
Men				
1.5-km sprint	Björn Lind (SWE)	2 min 26.5 sec	Roddy Darragon (FRA)	Thobias Fredriksson (SWE)
Team sprint	Thobias Fredriksson, Björn Lind (SWE)	17 min 02.9 sec	Jens Arne Svartedal, Tor Arne Hetland (NOR)	Ivan Alypov, Vasily Rochev (RUS)
15-km classical	Andrus Veerpalu (EST)	38 min 01.3 sec	Lukas Bauer (CZE)	Tobias Angerer (GER)
30-km pursuit	Yevgeny Dementyev (RUS)	1 hr 17 min 0.8 sec	Frode Estil (NOR)	Pietro Piller Cottrer (ITA)
50-km freestyle, mass start	Giorgio Di Centa (ITA)	2 hr 6 min 11.8 sec	Yevgeny Dementyev (RUS)	Mikhail Botwinov (AUT)
4 x 10-km relay	Italy	1 hr 43 min 45.7 sec	Germany	Sweden
95-m ski jump	Lars Bystøl (NOR)	266.5 pt	Matti Hautamäki (FIN)	Roar Ljøkelsøy (NOR)
125-m ski jump	Thomas Morgenstern (AUT)	276.9 pt	Andreas Kofler (AUT)	Lars Bystøl (NOR)
125-m team ski jump	Austria	984.0 pt	Finland	Norway
Nordic combined sprint (7.5 km)	Felix Gottwald (AUT)	17 min 35.0 sec	Magnus Moan (NOR)	Georg Hettich (GER)
Nordic combined (15 km)	Georg Hettich (GER)	39 min 44.6 sec	Felix Gottwald (AUT)	Magnus Moan (NOR)
Nordic combined team relay	Austria	49 min 42.6 sec	Germany	Finland
Women				
1.5-km sprint	Chandra Crawford (CAN)	2 min 12.3 sec	Claudia Künzel (GER)	Alena Sidko (RUS)
Team sprint	Anna Dahlberg, Lina Andersson (SWE)	16 min 36.9 sec	Sara Renner, Beckie Scott (CAN)	Aino Kaisa Saarinen, Virpi Kuitunen (FIN)

XX Winter Olympic Games (2006) (continued)

EVENT	GOLD MEDALIST	PERFORMANCE	SILVER MEDALIST	BRONZE MEDALIST
Nordic Skiing (continued)				
Women (continued)				
10-km classical	Kristina Smigun (EST)	27 min 51.4 sec	Marit Bjørgen (NOR)	Hilde G. Pedersen (NOR)
15-km pursuit	Kristina Smigun (EST)	42 min 48.7 sec	Katerina Neumannova (CZE)	Yevgeniya Medvedeva-Abruzova (RUS)
30-km freestyle, mass start	Katerina Neumannova (CZE)	1 hr 22 min 25.4 sec	Yuliya Chepalova (RUS)	Justyna Kowalczyk (POL)
4 x 5-km relay	Russia	54 min 47.7 sec	Germany	Italy
Biathlon				
Men				
10 km	Sven Fischer (GER)	26 min 11.6 sec	Halvard Hanevold (NOR)	Frode Andresen (NOR)
12.5-km pursuit	Vincent Defrasne (FRA)	35 min 20.2 sec	Ole Einar Bjørndalen (NOR)	Sven Fischer (GER)
20 km	Michael Greis (GER)	54 min 23.0 sec	Ole Einar Bjørndalen (NOR)	Halvard Hanevold (NOR)
4 x 7.5-km relay	Germany	1 hr 21 min 51.5 sec	Russia	France
15-km mass start	Michael Greis (GER)	47 min 20.0 sec	Tomasz Sikora (POL)	Ole Einar Bjørndalen (NOR)
Women				
7.5 km	Florence Baverel-Robert (FRA)	22 min 31.4 sec	Anna Carin Olofsson (SWE)	Liliya Yefremova (UKR)
10-km pursuit	Kali Wilhelm (GER)	36 min 43.6 sec	Martina Glagow (GER)	Albina Akhatova (RUS)
15 km	Svetlana Ishmuratova (RUS)	49 min 24.1 sec	Martina Glagow (GER)	Albina Akhatova (RUS)
4 x 6-km relay	Russia	1 hr 16 min 12.5 sec	Germany	France
12.5-km mass start	Anna Carin Olofsson (SWE)	40 min 36.5 sec	Kati Wilhelm (GER)	Uschi Disl (GER)
Freestyle Skiing				
Men				
Moguls	Dale Begg-Smith (AUS)	26.77 pt	Mikko Rönkainen (FIN)	Toby Dawson (USA)
Aerials	Han Xiaopeng (CHN)	250.77 pt	Dmitry Dashinsky (BLR)	Vladimir Lebedev (RUS)
Women				
Moguls	Jennifer Heil (CAN)	26.50 pt	Kari Traa (NOR)	Sandra Laoura (FRA)
Aerials	Evelyne Leu (SUI)	202.55 pt	Li Nina (CHN)	Alisa Camplin (AUS)
Snowboarding				
Men				
Giant slalom	Philipp Schoch (SUI)		Simon Schoch (SUI)	Siegfried Grabner (AUT)
Halfpipe	Shaun White (USA)	46.8 pt	Danny Kass (USA)	Markku Koski (FIN)
Snowboardcross	Seth Wescott (USA)		Radoslav Zidek (SVK)	Paul-Henri Delerue (FRA)
Women				
Giant slalom	Daniela Meuli (SUI)		Amelie Kober (GER)	Doris Günther (AUT)
Halfpipe	Hannah Teter (USA)	46.4 pt	Gretchen Bleiler (USA)	Kjersti Buaas (NOR)
Snowboardcross	Tanja Frieden (SUI)		Lindsey Jacobellis (USA)	Dominique Maltais (CAN)
Figure Skating				
Men	Yevgeny Plushchenko (RUS)	167.67 pt	Jeffrey Buttle (CAN)	Evan Lysacek (USA)
Women	Shizuka Arakawa (JPN)	191.34 pt	Sasha Cohen (USA)	Irina Slutskaya (RUS)

XX Winter Olympic Games (2006) (continued)

EVENT	GOLD MEDALIST	PERFORMANCE	SILVER MEDALIST	BRONZE MEDALIST
Figure Skating (continued)				
Pairs	Tatyana Totmyanina, Maksim Marinin (RUS)	135.84 pt	Zhang Dan, Zang Hao (CHN)	Shen Xue, Zhao Hongbo (CHN)
Ice dancing	Tatyana Navka, Roman Kostomarov (RUS)	200.64 pt	Tanith Belbin, Benjamin Agosto (USA)	Yelena Grushina, Ruslan Goncharov (RUS)
Speed Skating				
Men				
500 m	Joey Cheek (USA)	69.76 sec[1]	Dmitry Dorofeyev (RUS)	Lee Kang Seok (KOR)
1,000 m	Shani Davis (USA)	1 min 08.89 sec	Joey Cheek (USA)	Erben Wennemars (NED)
1,500 m	Enrico Fabris (ITA)	1 min 45.97 sec	Shani Davis (USA)	Chad Hedrick (USA)
5,000 m	Chad Hedrick (USA)	6 min 14.68 sec	Sven Kramer (NED)	Enrico Fabris (ITA)
10,000 m	Bob de Jong (NED)	13 min 01.57 sec	Chad Hedrick (USA)	Carl Verheijen (NED)
Team pursuit	Italy	3 min 44.46 sec	Canada	The Netherlands
Women				
500 m	Svetlana Zhurova (RUS)	76.57 sec[1]	Wang Manli (CHN)	Ren Hui (CHN)
1,000 m	Marianne Timmer (NED)	1 min 16.05 sec	Cindy Klassen (CAN)	Anni Friesinger (GER)
1,500 m	Cindy Klassen (CAN)	1 min 55.27 sec	Kristina Groves (CAN)	Ireen Wüst (NED)
3,000 m	Ireen Wüst (NED)	4 min 02.43 sec	Renate Groenewold (NED)	Cindy Klassen (CAN)
5,000 m	Clara Hughes (CAN)	6 min 59.07 sec	Claudia Pechstein (GER)	Cindy Klassen (CAN)
Team pursuit	Germany	3 min 01.25 sec	Canada	Russia
Short-Track Speed Skating				
Men				
500 m	Apolo Anton Ohno (USA)	41.935 sec	François-Louis Tremblay (FRA)	Ahn Hyun Soo (KOR)
1,000 m	Ahn Hyun Soo (KOR)	1 min 26.739 sec[2]	Lee Ho Suk (KOR)	Apolo Anton Ohno (USA)
1,500 m	Ahn Hyun Soo (KOR)	2 min 25.351 sec	Lee Ho Suk (KOR)	Li Jiajun (CHN)
5,000-m relay	Republic of Korea	6 min 43.376 sec[2]	Canada	United States
Women				
500 m	Wang Meng (CHN)	44.345 sec	Evgeniya Radanova (BUL)	Anouk Leblanc-Boucher (CAN)
1,000 m	Jin Sun Yu (KOR)	1 min 32.859 sec	Wang Meng (CHN)	Yang Yang (A) (CHN)
1,500 m	Jin Sun Yu (KOR)	2 min 23.494 sec	Choi Eun Kyung (KOR)	Wang Meng (CHN)
3,000-m relay	Republic of Korea	4 min 17.040 sec	Canada	Italy
Ice Hockey				
Men	Sweden	6-2-0	Finland	Czech Republic
Women	Canada	5-0-0	Sweden	United States
Curling				
Men	Canada	8-3-0	Finland	United States
Women	Sweden	9-2-0	Switzerland	Canada
Bobsled				
Two-man	André Lange, Kevin Kuske (GER 1)	3 min 43.38 sec	Pierre Lueders, Lascelles Brown (CAN 1)	Martin Annen, Beat Hefti (SUI 1)
Four-man	André Lange, Rene Hoppe, Kevin Kuske, Martin Putze (GER 1)	3 min 40.42 sec	Aleksandr Zoubkov, Filipp Yegorov, Aleksey Seliverstov, Aleksey Voyevoda (RUS 1)	Martin Annen, Thomas Lamparter, Beat Hefti, Cedric Grand (SUI 1)

XX Winter Olympic Games (2006) (continued)

EVENT	GOLD MEDALIST	PERFORMANCE	SILVER MEDALIST	BRONZE MEDALIST
Bobsled (continued)				
Two-woman	Sandra Kiriasis, Anja Schneiderheinze (GER 1)	3 min 49.98 sec	Shauna Rohbock, Valerie Fleming (USA 1)	Gerda Weissensteiner, Jennifer Isacco (ITA 1)
Luge				
Men's singles	Armin Zöggeler (ITA)	3 min 26.088 sec	Albert Demchenko (RUS)	Martins Rubenis (LAT)
Men's doubles	Andreas Linger, Wolfgang Linger (AUT)	1 min 34.497 sec	Andre Florschütz, Torsten Wustlich (GER)	Gerhard Planken-steiner, Oswald Haselrieder
Women's singles	Sylke Otto (GER)	3 min 07.979 sec	Sylke Kraushaar (GER)	Tatjana Hüfner (GER)
Skeleton				
Men	Duff Gibson (CAN)	1 min 55.88 sec	Jeff Pain (CAN)	Gregor Stähli (SUI)
Women	Maya Pedersen (SUI)	1 min 59.83 sec	Shelley Rudman (GBR)	Mellisa Holllings-worth-Richards (CAN)

[1]Time is combined total of two heats.   [2]Olympic record.

Special Olympics

The Special Olympics is an international program to provide individuals who have intellectual disabilities and are eight years of age or older with year-round sports training and athletic competition in a variety of Olympic-type summer and winter sports. Inaugurated in 1968, the Special Olympics was officially recognized by the International Olympic Committee on 15 Feb 1988. **International headquarters** are in Washington DC.

In June 1963, with support from the Joseph P. Kennedy, Jr., Foundation, **Eunice Kennedy Shriver** (sister of Pres. John F. Kennedy) started a summer day camp at her home in Rockville MD for children with mental retardation. Between 1963 and 1968, the Kennedy Foundation promoted the creation of dozens of similar camps in the United States and Canada. Special awards were developed for physical achievements, and by 1968 Shriver had persuaded the Chicago Park District to join with the Kennedy Foundation in sponsoring a "Special Olympics," held at Soldier Field on 20 July. About 1,000 athletes from 26 US states and Canada participated. The games were such a success that, in December, Special Olympics, Inc. (now **Special Olympics International**), was founded, with chapters in the United States, Canada, and France. The first International Winter Special Olympics Games were held 5–11 Feb 1977 (in Steamboat Springs CO). The number of participating countries proliferated so that by 2009 there were chapters in nearly 200 countries. More than 30,000 meets and tournaments are held worldwide each year, culminating in the Special Olympics World Games every two years, alternating between winter and summer sports and each lasting for eight or nine days.

Special Olympics Web site: <www.specialolympics.org>.

Automobile Racing

Of the various types of automobile races, the closed-circuit, or speedway, course was developed largely in the United States. The Indianapolis 500—now the premier Indy car event—was first run in 1911. A low-slung, fenderless (open-wheel) car—called an Indy car—is essential for this race; its suspension (i.e., its ability to hold the track) is as important to a car's performance as its turbocharged engine. Often the chassis manufacturer is different from the engine manufacturer, resulting in cars identified, for example, as a Brabham/Repco. In such cases the chassis maker is listed first, and the chassis maker receives any money or awards that the car may win.

Indy car racing began in 1909, when the American Automobile Association (AAA) began sponsoring a 24-race championship series, including three races at the newly opened Indianapolis Motor Speedway (IMS). In 1956 the AAA gave up its involvement with auto racing, and the United States Auto Club (**USAC**) was orga-

nized as the sport's governing body. In 1978 two race-car owners broke away from USAC to form a new organization, Championship Auto Racing Teams, Inc. (**CART**), which sponsored its own series of races. In 1980 CART and USAC joined to form the Championship Racing League, which dissolved after five races. In 1994 the IMS announced a new Indy Racing League (**IRL**) to oversee the Indianapolis 500 beginning in 1996 and a new series of IRL races (leading to an annual drivers' championship separate from those sponsored by CART.

The standard cars used for Grand Prix road (i.e., closed-highway) racing are known as Formula One (or F-1) cars because they are built according to an evolving formula that was established after World War I by the Fédération Internationale de l'Automobile (**FIA**). Like the Indy car, the Formula One racer is open-wheeled and low-slung, but the F-1 is slightly smaller and more maneuverable.

Automobile Racing (continued)

There are approximately 18 Grand Prix events held worldwide throughout the year. Drivers compete for the **World Championship of Drivers** (inaugurated in 1950), receiving a total number of points based on their placement in each of the official Grand Prix events.

Many Grand Prix drivers participate in various endurance races, the most famous of which is the **Le Mans Grand Prix d'Endurance**, held on the 13.4-km (8.3-mi) Sarthe circuit, Le Mans, France.

Another type of popular racing event is the rally, which was established in 1907. More than 35 such competitions, raced over a specified route on public roads, take place yearly throughout the world. The classic occasion for rally racing is the **Rallye Automobile Monte-Carlo**, now started in various European cities with Monaco as its terminal point.

Stock-car racing, which began in the United States in the first half of the 20th century, involves the racing of commercial cars that have been altered to increase their speed and maneuverability. The National Association for Stock Car Auto Racing (**NASCAR**) was founded in 1947, and until 2004 it awarded the Winston Cup to the driver who had earned the greatest number of points in a series of official NASCAR Winston Cup events over the stock-car racing season. In 2004 the competition was renamed the Nextel Cup, and from 2008 it is known as the Sprint Cup. The **Daytona 500** is the premiere stock-car event.

Related Web sites: Champ Car: <www.champcarworldseries.com>; USAC: <www.usacracing.com>; IRL: <www.indycar.com>; FIA: <www.fia.com>; Automobile Club de Monaco <www.acm.mc>; NASCAR: <www.nascar.com>.

Formula One Grand Prix Race Results, 2008–09

The season for the Formula One Grand Prix circuit is March–November.

RACE	DATE	LOCALE	WINNER (COUNTRY)	TIME (HR:MIN:SEC)
European Grand Prix	24 Aug 2008	Valencia, Spain	Felipe Massa (BRA)	1:35:32.339
Belgian Grand Prix	7 Sep 2008	Spa-Francorchamps	Felipe Massa (BRA)	1:22:59.394
Italian Grand Prix	14 Sep 2008	Monza	Sebastian Vettel (GER)	1:26:47.494
Singapore Grand Prix	28 Sep 2008	Singapore	Fernando Alonso (ESP)	1:57:16:304
Japanese Grand Prix	12 Oct 2008	Oyama	Fernando Alonso (ESP)	1:30:21.892
Chinese Grand Prix	19 Oct 2008	Shanghai	Lewis Hamilton (GBR)	1:31:57.403
Brazilian Grand Prix	2 Nov 2008	São Paulo	Felipe Massa (BRA)	1:34:11.435
Australian Grand Prix	29 Mar 2009	Melbourne	Jenson Button (GBR)	1:34:15.784
Malaysian Grand Prix	5 Apr 2009	Kuala Lumpur	Jenson Button (GBR)	55:30.522
Chinese Grand Prix	19 Apr 2009	Shanghai	Sebastian Vettel (GER)	1:57:43.485
Bahrain Grand Prix	26 Apr 2009	Sakhir	Jenson Button (GBR)	1:31:48.182
Spanish Grand Prix	10 May 2009	Montmeló	Jenson Button (GBR)	1:37:19.202
Monaco Grand Prix	24 May 2009	Monte-Carlo	Jenson Button (GBR)	1:40:44.282
Turkish Grand Prix	7 Jun 2009	Istanbul	Jenson Button (GBR)	1:26:24.848
British Grand Prix	21 Jun 2009	Silverstone	Sebastian Vettel (GER)	1:22:49.328
German Grand Prix	12 Jul 2009	Nürburgring	Mark Webber (AUS)	1:36:43.310
Hungarian Grand Prix	26 Jul 2009	Budapest	Lewis Hamilton (GBR)	1:38:23.876

Indianapolis 500

There was no competition in 1917–18 and 1942–45. Won by an American racer except as indicated.

YEAR	WINNER	AVG. SPEED (MPH)	YEAR	WINNER	AVG. SPEED (MPH)	YEAR	WINNER	AVG. SPEED (MPH)
1911	Ray Harroun	74.602	1929	Ray Keech	97.585	1950[3]	Johnnie Parsons	124.002
1912	Joe Dawson	78.719	1930	Billy Arnold	100.448	1951	Lee Wallard	126.244
1913	Jules Goux (FRA)	75.933	1931	Louis Schneider	96.629	1952	Troy Ruttman	128.922
1914	René Thomas (FRA)	82.474	1932	Fred Frame	104.144	1953	Bill Vukovich	128.740
			1933	Louie Meyer	104.162	1954	Bill Vukovich	130.840
1915	Ralph DePalma	89.840	1934	Bill Cummings	104.863	1955	Robert Sweikert	128.209
1916[1]	Dario Resta (FRA)	84.001	1935	Kelly Petillo	106.240	1956	Pat Flaherty	128.490
1919	Howdy Wilcox	88.050	1936	Louie Meyer	109.069	1957	Sam Hanks	135.601
1920	Gaston Chevrolet	88.618	1937	Wilbur Shaw	113.580	1958	Jimmy Bryan	133.791
1921	Tommy Milton	89.621	1938	Floyd Roberts	117.200	1959	Rodger Ward	135.857
1922	Jimmy Murphy	94.484	1939	Wilbur Shaw	115.035	1960	Jim Rathmann	138.767
1923	Tommy Milton	90.954	1940	Wilbur Shaw	114.277	1961	A.J. Foyt, Jr.	139.131
1924[2]	L.L. Corum, Joe Boyer	98.234	1941[2]	Floyd Davis, Mauri Rose	115.117	1962	Rodger Ward	140.293
						1963	Parnelli Jones	143.137
1925	Peter DePaolo	101.127	1946	George Robson	114.820	1964	A.J. Foyt, Jr.	147.350
1926[3]	Frank Lockhart	95.904	1947	Mauri Rose	116.338	1965	Jim Clark (GBR)	150.686
1927	George Souders	97.545	1948	Mauri Rose	119.814	1966	Graham Hill (GBR)	144.317
1928	Louie Meyer	99.482	1949	Bill Holland	121.327	1967	A.J. Foyt, Jr.	151.207

Indianapolis 500 (continued)

YEAR	WINNER	AVG. SPEED (MPH)	YEAR	WINNER	AVG. SPEED (MPH)	YEAR	WINNER	AVG. SPEED (MPH)
1968	Bobby Unser	152.882	1983	Tom Sneva	162.117	1998	Eddie Cheever, Jr.	145.155
1969	Mario Andretti	156.867	1984	Rick Mears	163.612	1999	Kenny Bräck (SWE)	153.176
1970	Al Unser	155.749	1985	Danny Sullivan	152.982			
1971	Al Unser	157.735	1986	Bobby Rahal	170.722	2000	Juan Montoya (COL)	167.607
1972	Mark Donohue	162.962	1987	Al Unser	162.175			
1973[3]	Gordon Johncock	159.036	1988	Rick Mears	144.809	2001	Helio Castro-neves (BRA)	153.601
			1989	Emerson Fitti-paldi (BRA)	167.581	2002	Helio Castro-neves (BRA)	166.499
1974	Johnny Rutherford	158.589	1990	Arie Luyendyk (NED)	185.984	2003	Gil de Ferran (BRA)	156.291
1975[3]	Bobby Unser	149.213						
1976[3]	Johnny Rutherford	148.725	1991	Rick Mears	176.457	2004[3]	Buddy Rice	138.518
			1992	Al Unser, Jr.	134.479	2005	Dan Wheldon (GBR)	157.603
1977	A.J. Foyt, Jr.	161.331	1993	Emerson Fitti-paldi (BRA)	157.207			
1978	Al Unser	161.363				2006	Sam Hornish, Jr.	157.085
1979	Rick Mears	158.899	1994	Al Unser, Jr.	160.872	2007	Dario Franchitti (GBR)	151.774
1980	Johnny Rutherford	142.862	1995	Jacques Ville-neuve (CAN)	153.616	2008	Scott Dixon (NZL)	143.567
1981	Bobby Unser	139.084	1996	Buddy Lazier	147.956	2009	Helio Castro-neves (BRA)	150.318
1982	Gordon Johncock	162.029	1997	Arie Luyendyk (NED)	145.827			

[1]Scheduled 300-mile race.   [2]First driver named started the race but was replaced during the race by the second driver named.   [3]Race stopped because of rain (in 1926 after 400 miles, in 1950 after 345 miles, in 1973 after 332.5 miles, in 1975 after 435 miles, in 1976 after 255 miles, and in 2004 after 450 miles).

NASCAR Sprint Cup Champions

YEAR	WINNER	YEAR	WINNER	YEAR	WINNER	YEAR	WINNER
1949	Red Byron	1964	Richard Petty	1979	Richard Petty	1994	Dale Earnhardt
1950	Bill Rexford	1965	Ned Jarrett	1980	Dale Earnhardt	1995	Jeff Gordon
1951	Herb Thomas	1966	David Pearson	1981	Darrell Waltrip	1996	Terry Labonte
1952	Tim Flock	1967	Richard Petty	1982	Darrell Waltrip	1997	Jeff Gordon
1953	Herb Thomas	1968	David Pearson	1983	Bobby Allison	1998	Jeff Gordon
1954	Lee Petty	1969	David Pearson	1984	Terry Labonte	1999	Dale Jarrett
1955	Tim Flock	1970	Bobby Isaac	1985	Darrell Waltrip	2000	Bobby Labonte
1956	Buck Baker	1971	Richard Petty	1986	Dale Earnhardt	2001	Jeff Gordon
1957	Buck Baker	1972	Richard Petty	1987	Dale Earnhardt	2002	Tony Stewart
1958	Lee Petty	1973	Benny Parsons	1988	Bill Elliott	2003	Matt Kenseth
1959	Lee Petty	1974	Richard Petty	1989	Rusty Wallace	2004	Kurt Busch
1960	Rex White	1975	Richard Petty	1990	Dale Earnhardt	2005	Tony Stewart
1961	Ned Jarrett	1976	Cale Yarborough	1991	Dale Earnhardt	2006	Jimmie Johnson
1962	Joe Weatherly	1977	Cale Yarborough	1992	Alan Kulwicki	2007	Jimmie Johnson
1963	Joe Weatherly	1978	Cale Yarborough	1993	Dale Earnhardt	2008	Jimmie Johnson

Baseball

The sport of baseball—given its definitive form in the United States in the late 19th century—is popular throughout the world, though until 2006 it was organized internationally only for **Little League** players (children ages 5–18). Little League Baseball was founded in Pennsylvania in 1939. The first Little League World Series was in 1947, and the first Little League outside the US was organized in British Columbia in 1951. Baseball is especially popular in Japan and Latin America; it is also one of the national sports of the US.

On a **professional** level, the premier event of baseball in the US is the **World Series** of **Major League Baseball**, in which the first team to win four games wins the Series. In fact, the Series is not contested on an international level, but rather it is played between the leading team of the **National League** (NL; formed 1876) and the leading team of the **American League** (AL; formed 1900 and including, from 1977, one Canadian team). In 2006 the inaugural World Baseball Classic, a competition featuring national teams, was held in Japan, Puerto Rico, and the US. The team from Japan beat Cuba's team in the finals. The second competition, held in 2009, also was won by Japan, this time defeating Korea.

Professional baseball began in Japan in 1936. Teams are organized into two leagues of six teams each. The seven-game **Japan Series**, first played in 1950, is contested between the leading team of the Central League (CL) and the leading team of the Pacific League (PL). The modern **Caribbean Series** began in 1970 with the winning team from each league in the Dominican Republic, Mexico, Puerto Rico, and Venezuela.

Related Web sites:
Major League Baseball: <http://mlb.mlb.com/index.jsp>; Little League: <www.littleleague.org>.

Major League Baseball Final Standings, 2008

American League

East Division

CLUB	WON	LOST	GAMES BACK
Tampa Bay[1]	97	65	—
Boston[1]	95	67	2
New York	89	73	8
Toronto	86	76	11
Baltimore	68	93	28½

Central Division

CLUB	WON	LOST	GAMES BACK
Chicago[1]	89	74	—
Minnesota	88	75	1
Cleveland	81	81	7½
Kansas City	75	87	13½
Detroit	74	88	14½

West Division

CLUB	WON	LOST	GAMES BACK
Los Angeles[1]	100	62	—
Texas	79	83	21
Oakland	75	86	24½
Seattle	61	101	39

National League

East Division

CLUB	WON	LOST	GAMES BACK
Philadelphia[1]	92	70	—
New York	89	73	3
Florida	84	77	7½
Atlanta	72	90	20
Washington	59	102	32½

Central Division

CLUB	WON	LOST	GAMES BACK
Chicago[1]	97	64	—
Milwaukee[1]	90	72	7½
Houston	86	75	11
St. Louis	86	76	11½
Cincinnati	74	88	23½
Pittsburgh	67	95	30½

West Division

CLUB	WON	LOST	GAMES BACK
Los Angeles[1]	84	78	—
Arizona	82	80	2
Colorado	74	88	10
San Francisco	72	90	12
San Diego	63	99	21

[1]Gained play-off berth.

Did you know? It took 56 years for a player to break the Major League Baseball record of 2,130 consecutive games set by the New York Yankees' Lou Gehrig when he played his last baseball game in 1939. Cal Ripkin of the Baltimore Orioles did so on 6 Sep 1995, and ended his streak after having played in his 2,632nd consecutive game on 19 Sep 1998.

World Series

YEAR	WINNER	RUNNER-UP	RESULTS
1903	Boston Americans (AL)	Pittsburgh Pirates (NL)	5–3
1904	not held		
1905	New York Giants (NL)	Philadelphia Athletics (AL)	4–1
1906	Chicago White Sox (AL)	Chicago Cubs (NL)	4–2
1907	Chicago Cubs (NL)	Detroit Tigers (AL)	4–0[1]
1908	Chicago Cubs (NL)	Detroit Tigers (AL)	4–1
1909	Pittsburgh Pirates (NL)	Detroit Tigers (AL)	4–3
1910	Philadelphia Athletics (AL)	Chicago Cubs (NL)	4–1
1911	Philadelphia Athletics (AL)	New York Giants (NL)	4–2
1912	Boston Red Sox (AL)	New York Giants (NL)	4–3[1]
1913	Philadelphia Athletics (AL)	New York Giants (NL)	4–1
1914	Boston Braves (NL)	Philadelphia Athletics (AL)	4–0
1915	Boston Red Sox (AL)	Philadelphia Phillies (NL)	4–1
1916	Boston Red Sox (AL)	Brooklyn Robins (NL)	4–1
1917	Chicago White Sox (AL)	New York Giants (NL)	4–2
1918	Boston Red Sox (AL)	Chicago Cubs (NL)	4–2
1919	Cincinnati Reds (NL)	Chicago White Sox (AL)	5–3
1920	Cleveland Indians (AL)	Brooklyn Robins (NL)	5–2
1921	New York Giants (NL)	New York Yankees (AL)	5–3
1922	New York Giants (NL)	New York Yankees (AL)	4–0[1]
1923	New York Yankees (AL)	New York Giants (NL)	4–2
1924	Washington Senators (AL)	New York Giants (NL)	4–3
1925	Pittsburgh Pirates (NL)	Washington Senators (AL)	4–3
1926	St. Louis Cardinals (NL)	New York Yankees (AL)	4–3
1927	New York Yankees (AL)	Pittsburgh Pirates (NL)	4–0
1928	New York Yankees (AL)	St. Louis Cardinals (NL)	4–0
1929	Philadelphia Athletics (AL)	Chicago Cubs (NL)	4–1
1930	Philadelphia Athletics (AL)	St. Louis Cardinals (NL)	4–2
1931	St. Louis Cardinals (NL)	Philadelphia Athletics (AL)	4–3
1932	New York Yankees (AL)	Chicago Cubs (NL)	4–0
1933	New York Giants (NL)	Washington Senators (AL)	4–1
1934	St. Louis Cardinals (NL)	Detroit Tigers (AL)	4–3
1935	Detroit Tigers (AL)	Chicago Cubs (NL)	4–2
1936	New York Yankees (AL)	New York Giants (NL)	4–2
1937	New York Yankees (AL)	New York Giants (NL)	4–1

World Series (continued)

YEAR	WINNER	RUNNER-UP	RESULTS
1938	New York Yankees (AL)	Chicago Cubs (NL)	4–0
1939	New York Yankees (AL)	Cincinnati Reds (NL)	4–0
1940	Cincinnati Reds (NL)	Detroit Tigers (AL)	4–3
1941	New York Yankees (AL)	Brooklyn Dodgers (NL)	4–1
1942	St. Louis Cardinals (NL)	New York Yankees (AL)	4–1
1943	New York Yankees (AL)	St. Louis Cardinals (NL)	4–1
1944	St. Louis Cardinals (NL)	St. Louis Browns (AL)	4–2
1945	Detroit Tigers (AL)	Chicago Cubs (NL)	4–3
1946	St. Louis Cardinals (NL)	Boston Red Sox (AL)	4–3
1947	New York Yankees (AL)	Brooklyn Dodgers (NL)	4–3
1948	Cleveland Indians (AL)	Boston Braves (NL)	4–2
1949	New York Yankees (AL)	Brooklyn Dodgers (NL)	4–1
1950	New York Yankees (AL)	Philadelphia Phillies (NL)	4–0
1951	New York Yankees (AL)	New York Giants (NL)	4–2
1952	New York Yankees (AL)	Brooklyn Dodgers (NL)	4–3
1953	New York Yankees (AL)	Brooklyn Dodgers (NL)	4–2
1954	New York Giants (NL)	Cleveland Indians (AL)	4–0
1955	Brooklyn Dodgers (NL)	New York Yankees (AL)	4–3
1956	New York Yankees (AL)	Brooklyn Dodgers (NL)	4–3
1957	Milwaukee Braves (NL)	New York Yankees (AL)	4–3
1958	New York Yankees (AL)	Milwaukee Braves (NL)	4–3
1959	Los Angeles Dodgers (NL)	Chicago White Sox (AL)	4–2
1960	Pittsburgh Pirates (NL)	New York Yankees (AL)	4–3
1961	New York Yankees (AL)	Cincinnati Reds (NL)	4–1
1962	New York Yankees (AL)	San Francisco Giants (NL)	4–3
1963	Los Angeles Dodgers (NL)	New York Yankees (AL)	4–0
1964	St. Louis Cardinals (NL)	New York Yankees (AL)	4–3
1965	Los Angeles Dodgers (NL)	Minnesota Twins (AL)	4–3
1966	Baltimore Orioles (AL)	Los Angeles Dodgers (NL)	4–0
1967	St. Louis Cardinals (NL)	Boston Red Sox (AL)	4–3
1968	Detroit Tigers (AL)	St. Louis Cardinals (NL)	4–3
1969	New York Mets (NL)	Baltimore Orioles (AL)	4–1
1970	Baltimore Orioles (AL)	Cincinnati Reds (NL)	4–1
1971	Pittsburgh Pirates (NL)	Baltimore Orioles (AL)	4–3
1972	Oakland Athletics (AL)	Cincinnati Reds (NL)	4–3
1973	Oakland Athletics (AL)	New York Mets (NL)	4–3
1974	Oakland Athletics (AL)	Los Angeles Dodgers (NL)	4–1
1975	Cincinnati Reds (NL)	Boston Red Sox (AL)	4–3
1976	Cincinnati Reds (NL)	New York Yankees (AL)	4–0
1977	New York Yankees (AL)	Los Angeles Dodgers (NL)	4–2
1978	New York Yankees (AL)	Los Angeles Dodgers (NL)	4–2
1979	Pittsburgh Pirates (NL)	Baltimore Orioles (AL)	4–3
1980	Philadelphia Phillies (NL)	Kansas City Royals (AL)	4–2
1981	Los Angeles Dodgers (NL)	New York Yankees (AL)	4–2
1982	St. Louis Cardinals (NL)	Milwaukee Brewers (AL)	4–3
1983	Baltimore Orioles (AL)	Philadelphia Phillies (NL)	4–1
1984	Detroit Tigers (AL)	San Diego Padres (NL)	4–1
1985	Kansas City Royals (AL)	St. Louis Cardinals (NL)	4–3
1986	New York Mets (NL)	Boston Red Sox (AL)	4–3
1987	Minnesota Twins (AL)	St. Louis Cardinals (NL)	4–3
1988	Los Angeles Dodgers (NL)	Oakland Athletics (AL)	4–1
1989	Oakland Athletics (AL)	San Francisco Giants (NL)	4–0
1990	Cincinnati Reds (NL)	Oakland Athletics (AL)	4–0
1991	Minnesota Twins (AL)	Atlanta Braves (NL)	4–3
1992	Toronto Blue Jays (AL)	Atlanta Braves (NL)	4–2
1993	Toronto Blue Jays (AL)	Philadelphia Phillies (NL)	4–2
1994	not held		
1995	Atlanta Braves (NL)	Cleveland Indians (AL)	4–2
1996	New York Yankees (AL)	Atlanta Braves (NL)	4–2
1997	Florida Marlins (NL)	Cleveland Indians (AL)	4–3
1998	New York Yankees (AL)	San Diego Padres (NL)	4–0
1999	New York Yankees (AL)	Atlanta Braves (NL)	4–0
2000	New York Yankees (AL)	New York Mets (NL)	4–1
2001	Arizona Diamondbacks (NL)	New York Yankees (AL)	4–3
2002	Anaheim Angels (AL)	San Francisco Giants (NL)	4–3
2003	Florida Marlins (NL)	New York Yankees (AL)	4–2
2004	Boston Red Sox (AL)	St. Louis Cardinals (NL)	4–0
2005	Chicago White Sox (AL)	Houston Astros (NL)	4–0

World Series (continued)

YEAR	WINNER	RUNNER-UP	RESULTS
2006	St. Louis Cardinals (NL)	Detroit Tigers (AL)	4-1
2007	Boston Red Sox (AL)	Colorado Rockies (NL)	4-0
2008	Philadelphia Phillies (NL)	Tampa Bay Rays (AL)	4-1

[1]Plus one tied game.

Major League Baseball All-Time Records[1]

Research courtesy of Baseball Almanac, <www.baseball-almanac.com>.

	PLAYERS/TEAMS	NUMBER	SEASON/DATE
Individual career records			
Games played	Pete Rose	3,562	1963-86
Consecutive games played	Cal Ripken, Jr.	2,632	1982-98
Batting average[2]	Ty Cobb	.366	1905-28
Hits	Pete Rose	4,256	1963-86
Doubles	Tris Speaker	792	1907-28
Triples	Sam Crawford	309	1899-17
Home runs	Barry Bonds	762	1986-2007
Runs	Rickey Henderson	2,295	1979-2003
Runs batted in	Hank Aaron	2,297	1954-76
Walks (batting)	Barry Bonds	2,558	1986-2007
Stolen bases	Rickey Henderson	1,406	1979-2003
Wins (pitching)	Cy Young	511	1890-1911
Earned run average[3]	Ed Walsh	1.82	1904-17
Strikeouts (pitching)	Nolan Ryan	5,714	1966-93
Saves	Trevor Hoffman[4]	554	1993-2008
No-hitters	Nolan Ryan	7	1966-93
Shutouts	Walter Johnson	110	1907-27
Wins (managing)	Connie Mack	3,731	1894-96; 1901-50
Individual season records			
Batting average[5]	Hugh Duffy	.440	1894
Hits	Ichiro Suzuki[4]	262	2004
Doubles	Earl Webb	67	1931
Triples	Chief Wilson	36	1912
Home runs	Barry Bonds	73	2001
Runs	Billy Hamilton	192	1894
Runs batted in	Hack Wilson	191	1930
Walks (batting)	Barry Bonds	232	2004
Stolen bases	Hugh Nicol	138	1887
Wins	Charley Radbourn	59	1884
Earned run average[6]	Tim Keefe	0.86	1880
Strikeouts (pitching)	Matt Kilroy	513	1886
No-hitters	4 players hold record	2	
Saves	Francisco Rodriguez[4]	62	2008
Shutouts	George Bradley; Grover Alexander	16	1876; 1916
Individual game records[7]			
Hits	Wilbert Robinson; Rennie Stennett	7	10 Jun 1892; 16 Sep 1975
Doubles	50 players hold record	4	
Triples	George Strief; Bill Joyce	4	25 Jun 1885; 18 May 1897
Home runs	15 players hold record	4	
Runs	Guy Hecker	7	15 Aug 1886
Runs batted in	Jim Bottomley; Mark Whiten	12	16 Sep 1924; 7 Sep 1993
Walks (batting)	Walt Wilmot; Jimmie Foxx	6	22 Aug 1891; 16 Jun 1938
Stolen bases	George Gore; Billy Hamilton	7	25 Jun 1881; 31 Aug 1894
Strikeouts (pitching)	Roger Clemens (twice); Kerry Wood[4]	20	29 Apr 1986 and 18 Sep 1996; 6 May 1998
Team season records			
World Series titles	New York Yankees	26	
Consecutive World Series titles	New York Yankees	5	1949-53
Games won	Chicago Cubs; Seattle Mariners	116	1906; 2001
Highest winning percentage	St. Louis Maroons	.832 (94-19)	1884
Batting average	Philadelphia Phillies	.349	1894

Major League Baseball All-Time Records[1] (continued)

	PLAYERS/TEAMS	NUMBER	SEASON/DATE
Team season records (continued)			
Doubles	Texas Rangers	376	2008
Triples	Baltimore Orioles	153	1894
Home runs	Seattle Mariners	264	1997
Runs	Boston Beaneaters	1,220	1894
Runs batted in	Boston Beaneaters	1,043	1894
Walks (batting)	Boston Red Sox	835	1949
Stolen bases	Philadelphia Athletics	638	1887
Game records			
Highest combined score	Chicago Cubs versus Philadelphia Phillies	49 (26–23)	25 Aug 1922
Longest nine-inning game	New York Yankees versus Boston Red Sox	4 hr 45 min	18 Aug 2006
Longest extra-inning game (time)	Chicago White Sox versus Milwaukee Brewers	8 hr 6 min	9 May 1984
Longest extra-inning game (innings)	Brooklyn Dodgers versus Boston Braves	26 innings	1 May 1920

[1]Through the end of the 2008 season.   [2]Minimum of 1,000 games played and 1,000 at-bats.   [3]Minimum of 2,000 innings pitched.   [4]Active in 2009.   [5]Minimum of 3.1 plate appearances per game played.   [6]Minimum of one inning pitched per game played.   [7]Nine-inning games only.

Caribbean Series

Held since 1949. Table shows results for the past 20 years.

YEAR	WINNER	COUNTRY	YEAR	WINNER	COUNTRY
1990	Escogido Lions	DOM	2000	Santurce Crabbers	PUR
1991	Licey Tigers	DOM	2001	Cibao Eagles	DOM
1992	Mayagüez Indians	PUR	2002	Culiacán Tomato Growers	MEX
1993	Santurce Crabbers	PUR	2003	Cibao Eagles	DOM
1994	Licey Tigers	DOM	2004	Licey Tigers	DOM
1995	San Juan Senators	PUR	2005	Mazatlán Deer	MEX
1996	Culiacán Tomato Growers	MEX	2006	Caracas Lions	VEN
1997	Northern Eagles	DOM	2007	Cibao Eagles	DOM
1998	Northern Eagles	DOM	2008	Licey Tigers	DOM
1999	Licey Tigers	DOM	2009	Aragua Tigers	VEN

Japan Series

Held since 1950. Table shows results for the past 10 years.

YEAR	WINNER	RUNNER-UP	RESULTS
1999	Fukuoka Daiei Hawks (PL)	Chunichi Dragons (CL)	4–1
2000	Tokyo Yomiuri Giants (CL)	Fukuoka Daiei Hawks (PL)	4–2
2001	Yakult Swallows (CL)	Osaka Kintetsu Buffaloes (PL)	4–1
2002	Yomiuri Giants (CL)	Seibu Lions (PL)	4–0
2003	Fukuoka Daiei Hawks (PL)	Hanshin Tigers (CL)	4–3
2004	Seibu Lions (PL)	Chunichi Dragons (CL)	4–3
2005	Chiba Lotte Marines (PL)	Hanshin Tigers (CL)	4–0
2006	Hokkaido Nippon Ham Fighters (PL)	Chunichi Dragons (CL)	4–1
2007	Chunichi Dragons (CL)	Hokkaido Nippon Ham Fighters (PL)	4–1
2008	Saitama Seibu Lions (PL)	Yomiuri Giants (CL)	4–3

Little League World Series

The Little League World Series, first called the National Little League Tournament, was established in 1947. Table shows results for past 10 years.

YEAR	WINNING TEAM/HOME	RUNNER-UP	SCORE
2000	Sierra Maestra/Maracaibo (VEN)	Bellaire/Bellaire TX	3–2
2001	Kitasuna/Tokyo (JPN)	Apopka National/Apopka FL	2–1
2002	Valley Sports American/Louisville KY	Sendai Higashi/Sendai (JPN)	1–0
2003	Musashi-Fuchu/Tokyo (JPN)	East Boynton Beach/Boynton Beach FL	10–1
2004	Pabao/Willemstad (AHO)	Conejo Valley/Thousand Oaks CA	5–2
2005	West Oahu/Ewa Beach HI	Pabao/Willemstad (AHO)	7–6

Little League World Series (continued)

YEAR	WINNING TEAM/HOME	RUNNER-UP	SCORE
2006	Columbus Northern/Columbus GA	Kawaguchi/Kawaguchi City (JPN)	2–1
2007	Warner Robins American/Warner Robins GA	Tokyo Kitasuna/Tokyo (JPN)	3–2
2008	Waipio/Waipahu HI	Matamoros/Matamoros (MEX)	12–3
2009	Parkview/Chula Vista CA	Kuei-Shan/Taoyuan (TPE)	6–3

Basketball

American professional basketball is directed by the **National Basketball Association** (NBA; formed 1949). The NBA is divided into the Eastern and Western conferences (EC and WC; until 1970 the Eastern and Western divisions [ED and WD]), the top-ranking teams of which compete yearly for the championship. The NBA began the **Women's National Basketball Association** (WNBA), which is also divided into an Eastern and a Western Conference (EC and WC), in 1997.

Since the inclusion of basketball as an **Olympic sport** in 1936, the winners of the Olympic tournament have been considered by many to be the world champions. The **Fédération Internationale de Basketball** (FIBA; founded 1932) instituted world championships in 1950 for men and in 1953 for women. (Women's basketball was not admitted to the Olympics until 1976.) Amateur basketball in the United States is most closely followed at the **collegiate** level, where the most important event of the season is the **National Collegiate Athletic Association (NCAA) Championship**. The NCAA tournament was first contested in 1939 (by men's teams only). Women's college basketball was first played on a national level in 1972, under the auspices of the Association for Intercollegiate Athletics for Women (AIAW), which gave way in 1982 to the NCAA's first tournament for women.

Related Web sites: NBA: <www.nba.com>; WNBA: <www.wnba.com>; FIBA: <www.fiba.com>; NCAA: <www.ncaa.org>.

National Basketball Association Final Standings, 2008–09

EASTERN CONFERENCE

Atlantic Division

TEAM	WON	LOST	GAMES BACK
Boston[1]	62	20	—
Philadelphia[1]	41	41	21
New Jersey	34	48	28
Toronto	33	49	29
New York	32	50	30

Central Division

TEAM	WON	LOST	GAMES BACK
Cleveland[1]	66	16	—
Chicago[1]	41	41	25
Detroit[1]	39	43	27
Indiana	36	46	30
Milwaukee	34	48	32

Southeast Division

TEAM	WON	LOST	GAMES BACK
Orlando[1]	59	23	—
Atlanta[1]	47	35	12
Miami[1]	43	39	16
Charlotte	35	47	24
Washington	19	63	40

WESTERN CONFERENCE

Northwest Division

TEAM	WON	LOST	GAMES BACK
Denver[1]	54	28	—
Portland[1]	54	28	—
Utah[1]	48	34	6
Minnesota	24	58	30
Oklahoma City	23	59	31

Pacific Division

TEAM	WON	LOST	GAMES BACK
L.A. Lakers[1]	65	17	—
Phoenix	46	36	19
Golden State	29	53	36
L.A. Clippers	19	63	46
Sacramento	17	65	48

Southwest Division

TEAM	WON	LOST	GAMES BACK
San Antonio[1]	54	28	—
Houston[1]	53	29	1
Dallas[1]	50	32	4
New Orleans[1]	49	33	5
Memphis	24	58	30

[1]Gained play-off berth.

National Basketball Association Championship

SEASON	WINNER	RUNNER-UP	RESULTS
1949–50	Minneapolis Lakers (CD)[1]	Syracuse Nationals (ED)	4–2
1950–51	Rochester Royals (WD)	New York Knickerbockers (ED)	4–3
1951–52	Minneapolis Lakers (WD)	New York Knickerbockers (ED)	4–3
1952–53	Minneapolis Lakers (WD)	New York Knickerbockers (ED)	4–1
1953–54	Minneapolis Lakers (WD)	Syracuse Nationals (ED)	4–3
1954–55	Syracuse Nationals (ED)	Fort Wayne Pistons (WD)	4–3
1955–56	Philadelphia Warriors (ED)	Fort Wayne Pistons (WD)	4–1
1956–57	Boston Celtics (ED)	St. Louis Hawks (WD)	4–3
1957–58	St. Louis Hawks (WD)	Boston Celtics (ED)	4–2
1958–59	Boston Celtics (ED)	Minneapolis Lakers (WD)	4–0
1959–60	Boston Celtics (ED)	St. Louis Hawks (WD)	4–3

National Basketball Association Championship (continued)

SEASON	WINNER	RUNNER-UP	RESULTS
1960–61	Boston Celtics (ED)	St. Louis Hawks (WD)	4–1
1961–62	Boston Celtics (ED)	Los Angeles Lakers (WD)	4–3
1962–63	Boston Celtics (ED)	Los Angeles Lakers (WD)	4–2
1963–64	Boston Celtics (ED)	San Francisco Warriors (WD)	4–1
1964–65	Boston Celtics (ED)	Los Angeles Lakers (WD)	4–1
1965–66	Boston Celtics (ED)	Los Angeles Lakers (WD)	4–3
1966–67	Philadelphia 76ers (ED)	San Francisco Warriors (WD)	4–2
1967–68	Boston Celtics (ED)	Los Angeles Lakers (WD)	4–2
1968–69	Boston Celtics (ED)	Los Angeles Lakers (WD)	4–3
1969–70	New York Knickerbockers (EC)	Los Angeles Lakers (WC)	4–3
1970–71	Milwaukee Bucks (WC)	Baltimore Bullets (EC)	4–0
1971–72	Los Angeles Lakers (WC)	New York Knickerbockers (EC)	4–1
1972–73	New York Knickerbockers (EC)	Los Angeles Lakers (WC)	4–1
1973–74	Boston Celtics (EC)	Milwaukee Bucks (WC)	4–3
1974–75	Golden State Warriors (WC)	Washington Bullets (EC)	4–0
1975–76	Boston Celtics (EC)	Phoenix Suns (WC)	4–2
1976–77	Portland Trail Blazers (WC)	Philadelphia 76ers (EC)	4–2
1977–78	Washington Bullets (EC)	Seattle SuperSonics (WC)	4–3
1978–79	Seattle SuperSonics (WC)	Washington Bullets (EC)	4–1
1979–80	Los Angeles Lakers (WC)	Philadelphia 76ers (EC)	4–2
1980–81	Boston Celtics (EC)	Houston Rockets (WC)	4–2
1981–82	Los Angeles Lakers (WC)	Philadelphia 76ers (EC)	4–2
1982–83	Philadelphia 76ers (EC)	Los Angeles Lakers (WC)	4–0
1983–84	Boston Celtics (EC)	Los Angeles Lakers (WC)	4–3
1984–85	Los Angeles Lakers (WC)	Boston Celtics (EC)	4–2
1985–86	Boston Celtics (EC)	Houston Rockets (WC)	4–2
1986–87	Los Angeles Lakers (WC)	Boston Celtics (EC)	4–2
1987–88	Los Angeles Lakers (WC)	Detroit Pistons (EC)	4–3
1988–89	Detroit Pistons (EC)	Los Angeles Lakers (WC)	4–0
1989–90	Detroit Pistons (EC)	Portland Trail Blazers (WC)	4–1
1990–91	Chicago Bulls (EC)	Los Angeles Lakers (WC)	4–1
1991–92	Chicago Bulls (EC)	Portland Trail Blazers (WC)	4–2
1992–93	Chicago Bulls (EC)	Phoenix Suns (WC)	4–2
1993–94	Houston Rockets (WC)	New York Knickerbockers (EC)	4–3
1994–95	Houston Rockets (WC)	Orlando Magic (EC)	4–0
1995–96	Chicago Bulls (EC)	Seattle SuperSonics (WC)	4–2
1996–97	Chicago Bulls (EC)	Utah Jazz (WC)	4–2
1997–98	Chicago Bulls (EC)	Utah Jazz (WC)	4–2
1998–99	San Antonio Spurs (WC)	New York Knickerbockers (EC)	4–1
1999–2000	Los Angeles Lakers (WC)	Indiana Pacers (EC)	4–2
2000–01	Los Angeles Lakers (WC)	Philadelphia 76ers (EC)	4–1
2001–02	Los Angeles Lakers (WC)	New Jersey Nets (EC)	4–0
2002–03	San Antonio Spurs (WC)	New Jersey Nets (EC)	4–2
2003–04	Detroit Pistons (EC)	Los Angeles Lakers (WC)	4–1
2004–05	San Antonio Spurs (WC)	Detroit Pistons (EC)	4–3
2005–06	Miami Heat (EC)	Dallas Mavericks (WC)	4–2
2006–07	San Antonio Spurs (WC)	Cleveland Cavaliers (EC)	4–0
2007–08	Boston Celtics (EC)	Los Angeles Lakers (WC)	4–2
2008–09	Los Angeles Lakers (WC)	Orlando Magic (EC)	4–1

[1]In its inaugural season, the NBA had a third division, the Central Division (CD).

National Basketball Association All-Time Records[1]

	PLAYERS/TEAMS	NUMBER	SEASON/DATE
Individual career records			
Games played	Robert Parish	1,611	1976–77—1996–97
Points scored	Kareem Abdul-Jabbar	38,387	1969–70—1988–89
Most games, 50 or more points	Wilt Chamberlain	118	1959–60—1972–73
Most consecutive games, 10 or more points	Michael Jordan	866	25 Mar 1986–26 Dec 2001
Field goals attempted	Kareem Abdul-Jabbar	28,307	1969–70—1988–89
Field goals made	Kareem Abdul-Jabbar	15,837	1969–70—1988–89
Field-goal percentage[2]	Artis Gilmore	.599	1976–77—1987–88
Three-point field goals attempted	Reggie Miller	6,486	1987–88—2004–05
Three-point field goals made	Reggie Miller	2,560	1987–88—2004–05
Three-point field-goal percentage[3]	Steve Kerr	.454	1988–89—2002–03

National Basketball Association All-Time Records[1] (continued)

	PLAYERS/TEAMS	NUMBER	SEASON/DATE
Individual career records (continued)			
Free throws attempted	Karl Malone	13,188	1985–86–2003–04
Free throws made	Karl Malone	9,787	1985–86–2003–04
Free-throw percentage[4]	Mark Price	.904	1986–87–1997–98
Assists	John Stockton	15,806	1984–85–2002–03
Rebounds	Wilt Chamberlain	23,924	1959–60–1972–73
Steals[5]	John Stockton	3,265	1984–85–2002–03
Blocked shots[5]	Hakeem Olajuwon	3,830	1984–85–2001–02
Personal fouls	Kareem Abdul-Jabbar	4,657	1969–70–1988–89
Wins (coaching)	Lenny Wilkens	1,332	1969–70–2004–05, except 1972–1974
Individual season records			
Points scored	Wilt Chamberlain	4,029	1961–62
Field goals attempted	Wilt Chamberlain	3,159	1961–62
Field goals made	Wilt Chamberlain	1,597	1961–62
Field-goal percentage	Wilt Chamberlain	.727	1972–73
Three-point field goals attempted	George McCloud	678	1995–96
Three-point field goals made	Ray Allen	269	2005–06
Three-point field-goal percentage	Steve Kerr	.524	1994–95
Free throws attempted	Wilt Chamberlain	1,363	1961–62
Free throws made	Jerry West	840	1965–66
Free-throw percentage	José Calderón	.981	2008–09
Assists	John Stockton	1,164	1990–91
Rebounds	Wilt Chamberlain	2,149	1960–61
Steals[5]	Alvin Robertson	301	1985–86
Blocked shots[5]	Mark Eaton	456	1984–85
Personal fouls	Darryl Dawkins	386	1983–84
Individual game records			
Points scored	Wilt Chamberlain	100	2 Mar 1962
Field goals attempted	Wilt Chamberlain	63	2 Mar 1962
Field goals made	Wilt Chamberlain	36	2 Mar 1962
Three-point field goals attempted	Damon Stoudamire	21	15 Apr 2005
Three-point field goals made	Kobe Bryant; Donyell Marshall	12	7 Jan 2003; 13 Mar 2005
Free throws attempted	Wilt Chamberlain	34	22 Feb 1962
Free throws made	Wilt Chamberlain; Adrian Dantley	28	2 Mar 1962; 4 Jan 1984
Assists	Scott Skiles	30	30 Dec 1990
Rebounds	Wilt Chamberlain	55	24 Nov 1960
Steals[5]	Larry Kenon; Kendall Gill	11	26 Dec 1976; 3 Apr 1999
Blocked shots[5]	Elmore Smith	17	28 Oct 1973
Team records			
Highest winning percentage (season)	Chicago Bulls	.878 (72–10)	1995–96
Consecutive games won	Los Angeles Lakers	33	5 Nov 1971– 7 Jan 1972
Championships	Boston Celtics	17	
Consecutive championships	Boston Celtics	8	1959–66
Game records			
Highest combined score	Detroit Pistons versus Denver Nuggets	370 (186–184)	13 Dec 1983
Longest game (overtime periods)	Indianapolis Olympians versus Rochester Royals	6	6 Jan 1951

[1]Through the end of the 2008–09 season.   [2]Minimum 2,000 made.   [3]Minimum 250 made.   [4]Minimum 1,200 made.   [5]Since 1973–74; before that season steals and blocked shots were not officially recorded by the NBA.

Women's National Basketball Association Championship

SEASON	WINNER	RUNNER-UP	RESULTS
1997	Houston Comets (EC)	New York Liberty (EC)	1–0
1998	Houston Comets (WC)	Phoenix Mercury (WC)	2–1
1999	Houston Comets (WC)	New York Liberty (EC)	2–1
2000	Houston Comets (WC)	New York Liberty (EC)	2–0

Women's National Basketball Association Championship (continued)

SEASON	WINNER	RUNNER-UP	RESULTS
2001	Los Angeles Sparks (WC)	Charlotte Sting (EC)	2-0
2002	Los Angeles Sparks (WC)	New York Liberty (EC)	2-0
2003	Detroit Shock (EC)	Los Angeles Sparks (WC)	2-1
2004	Seattle Storm (WC)	Connecticut Sun (EC)	2-1
2005	Sacramento Monarchs (WC)	Connecticut Sun (EC)	3-1
2006	Detroit Shock (EC)	Sacramento Monarchs (WC)	3-2
2007	Phoenix Mercury (WC)	Detroit Shock (EC)	3-2
2008	Detroit Shock (EC)	San Antonio Silver Stars (WC)	3-0

National Collegiate Athletic Association Basketball Championship—Men[1]

YEAR	WINNER	RUNNER-UP	SCORE	YEAR	WINNER	RUNNER-UP	SCORE
1939	Oregon	Ohio State	46-43	1974	North Carolina State	Marquette	76-64
1940	Indiana	Kansas	60-42				
1941	Wisconsin	Washington State	39-34	1975	UCLA	Kentucky	92-85
1942	Stanford	Dartmouth	53-38	1976	Indiana	Michigan	86-68
1943	Wyoming	Georgetown	46-34	1977	Marquette	North Carolina	67-59
1944	Utah	Dartmouth	42-40	1978	Kentucky	Duke	94-88
1945	Oklahoma A&M	New York	49-45	1979	Michigan State	Indiana State	75-64
1946	Oklahoma A&M	North Carolina	43-40	1980	Louisville	UCLA	59-54
1947	Holy Cross (MA)	Oklahoma	58-47	1981	Indiana	North Carolina	63-50
1948	Kentucky	Baylor	58-42	1982	North Carolina	Georgetown	63-62
1949	Kentucky	Oklahoma State	46-36	1983	North Carolina State	Houston	54-52
1950	City College of New York	Bradley	71-68	1984	Georgetown	Houston	84-75
1951	Kentucky	Kansas State	68-58	1985	Villanova	Georgetown	66-64
1952	Kansas	St. John's (NY)	80-63	1986	Louisville	Duke	72-69
1953	Indiana	Kansas	69-68	1987	Indiana	Syracuse	74-73
1954	La Salle	Bradley	92-76	1988	Kansas	Oklahoma	83-79
1955	San Francisco	La Salle	77-63	1989	Michigan	Seton Hall	80-79
1956	San Francisco	Iowa	83-71	1990	Nevada (Las Vegas)	Duke	103-73
1957	North Carolina	Kansas	54-53	1991	Duke	Kansas	72-65
1958	Kentucky	Seattle	84-72	1992	Duke	Michigan	71-51
1959	California (Berkeley)	West Virginia	71-70	1993	North Carolina	Michigan	77-71
				1994	Arkansas	Duke	76-72
1960	Ohio State	California (Berkeley)	75-55	1995	UCLA	Arkansas	89-78
				1996	Kentucky	Syracuse	76-67
1961	Cincinnati	Ohio State	70-65	1997	Arizona	Kentucky	84-79
1962	Cincinnati	Ohio State	71-59	1998	Kentucky	Utah	78-69
1963	Loyola (IL)	Cincinnati	60-58	1999	Connecticut	Duke	77-74
1964	UCLA	Duke	98-83	2000	Michigan State	Florida	89-76
1965	UCLA	Michigan	91-80	2001	Duke	Arizona	82-72
1966	Texas Western	Kentucky	72-65	2002	Maryland	Indiana	64-52
1967	UCLA	Dayton	79-64	2003	Syracuse	Kansas	81-78
1968	UCLA	North Carolina	78-55	2004	Connecticut	Georgia Tech	82-73
1969	UCLA	Purdue	92-72	2005	North Carolina	Illinois	75-70
1970	UCLA	Jacksonville	80-69	2006	Florida	UCLA	73-57
1971	UCLA	Villanova	68-62	2007	Florida	Ohio State	84-75
1972	UCLA	Florida State	81-76	2008	Kansas	Memphis[2]	75-68
1973	UCLA	Memphis State	87-66	2009	North Carolina	Michigan State	89-72

[1]University Division 1957-73, Division I from 1974. [2]Stripped of this result in 2009 for NCAA rules violations.

National Collegiate Athletic Association Basketball Championship—Women[1]

YEAR	WINNER	RUNNER-UP	SCORE	YEAR	WINNER	RUNNER-UP	SCORE
1982	Louisiana Tech	Cheyney State	76-62	1992	Stanford	Western Kentucky	78-62
1983	Southern California	Louisiana Tech	69-67	1993	Texas Tech	Ohio State	84-82
1984	Southern California	Tennessee	72-61	1994	North Carolina	Louisiana Tech	60-59
1985	Old Dominion	Georgia	70-65	1995	Connecticut	Tennessee	70-64
1986	Texas	Southern California	97-81	1996	Tennessee	Georgia	83-65
1987	Tennessee	Louisiana Tech	67-44	1997	Tennessee	Old Dominion	68-59
1988	Louisiana Tech	Auburn	56-54	1998	Tennessee	Louisiana Tech	93-75
1989	Tennessee	Auburn	76-60	1999	Purdue	Duke	62-45
1990	Stanford	Auburn	88-81	2000	Connecticut	Tennessee	71-52
1991	Tennessee	Virginia	70-67	2001	Notre Dame	Purdue	68-66

National Collegiate Athletic Association Basketball Championship—Women[1] (cont.)

YEAR	WINNER	RUNNER-UP	SCORE	YEAR	WINNER	RUNNER-UP	SCORE
2002	Connecticut	Oklahoma	82-70	2006	Maryland	Duke	78-75
2003	Connecticut	Tennessee	73-68	2007	Tennessee	Rutgers	59-46
2004	Connecticut	Tennessee	70-61	2008	Tennessee	Stanford	64-48
2005	Baylor	Michigan State	84-62	2009	Connecticut	Louisville	76-54

[1]Division I.

FIBA World Championship—Men

YEAR	WINNER	RUNNER-UP	YEAR	WINNER	RUNNER-UP
1936[1]	United States	Canada	1978	Yugoslavia	USSR
1948[1]	United States	France	1980[1]	Yugoslavia	Italy
1950	Argentina	United States	1982	USSR	United States
1952[1]	United States	USSR	1984[1]	United States	Spain
1954	United States	Brazil	1986	United States	USSR
1956[1]	United States	USSR	1988[1]	USSR	Yugoslavia
1959	Brazil[2]	United States	1990	Yugoslavia	USSR
1960[1]	United States	USSR	1992[1]	United States	Croatia
1963	Brazil	Yugoslavia	1994	United States	Russia
1964[1]	United States	USSR	1996[1]	United States	Yugoslavia
1967	USSR	Yugoslavia	1998	Yugoslavia	Russia
1968[1]	United States	Yugoslavia	2000[1]	United States	France
1970	Yugoslavia	Brazil	2002	Yugoslavia	Argentina
1972[1]	USSR	United States	2004[1]	Argentina	Italy
1974	USSR	Yugoslavia	2006	Spain	Greece
1976[1]	United States	Yugoslavia	2008[1]	United States	Spain

[1]Olympic championships, recognized in this table as world championships (though not by FIBA). [2]Won by default.

FIBA World Championship—Women

YEAR	WINNER	RUNNER-UP	YEAR	WINNER	RUNNER-UP
1953	United States	Chile	1986	United States	USSR
1957	United States	USSR	1988[1]	United States	Yugoslavia
1959	USSR	Bulgaria	1990	United States	Yugoslavia
1964	USSR	Czechoslovakia	1992[1]	Unified Team	China
1967	USSR	Rep. of Korea	1994	Brazil	China
1971	USSR	Czechoslovakia	1996[1]	United States	Brazil
1975	USSR	Japan	1998	United States	Russia
1976[1]	USSR	United States	2000[1]	United States	Australia
1979	United States	Rep. of Korea	2002	United States	Russia
1980[1]	USSR	Bulgaria	2004[1]	United States	Australia
1983	USSR	United States	2006	Australia	Russia
1984[1]	United States	Rep. of Korea	2008[1]	United States	Australia

[1]Olympic championships, recognized in this table as world championships (though not by FIBA).

Bowling

The world governing body for bowling is the **Fédération Internationale des Quilleurs (FIQ)**. Since 1954 it has sponsored world bowling championships.

In the **United States,** men's bowling is governed by the **American Bowling Congress (ABC)**, which was founded in 1895 but became a constituent of the **United States Bowling Congress (USBC)** in 2004. In 1901 the first national championship was organized; in 1961 the yearly competition was split into two divisions—regular (for those with a combined average score of 851 or higher) and classic (for professionals). The classic division was discontinued in 1980. The **Women's International Bowling Congress (WIBC)** was organized in 1916 and sponsored an annual women's championship until 2004, when organizational mergers created the USBC. Competition takes place between teams, doubles, and singles. The all-events category is won by the individual who has the best score of nine games—three team, three doubles, and three singles scores. The **Professional Bowlers Association (PBA)** was established in 1958. One of its major tournaments is the annual **Tournament of Champions**.

Related Web sites: FIQ: <www.fiq.org>; USBC: <www.bowl.com>; PBA: <www.pba.com>.

Professional Bowlers Association Tournament of Champions

Held since 1960. Table shows results for the past 20 years.

YEAR	CHAMPION	YEAR	CHAMPION	YEAR	CHAMPION
1989	Del Ballard, Jr.	1996	Dave D'Entremont	2003–04	Patrick Healey, Jr.
1990	Dave Ferraro	1997	John Gant	2004–05	Steve Jaros
1991	David Ozio	1998	Bryan Goebel	2005–06	Chris Barnes
1992	Marc McDowell	1999	Jason Couch	2006–07	Tommy Jones
1993	George Branham III	2000	Jason Couch	2007–08	Michael Haugen, Jr.
1994	Norm Duke	2001–02	*not held*	2008–09	Patrick Allen
1995	Mike Aulby	2002–03	Jason Couch		

United States Bowling Congress Bowling Championships—Regular Division

Held since 1901. Table shows results for the past 20 years.

YEAR	SINGLES	SCORE	ALL-EVENTS	SCORE
1990	Robert Hochrein	791	Mike Neumann	2,168
1991	Ed Deines	826	Tom Howery	2,216
1992	Gary Blatchford; Bob Youker, Jr. (tied)	801	Mike Tucker	2,158
1993	Dan Bock	798	Jeff Nimke	2,254
1994	John Weltzien	810	Thomas Holt	2,190
1995	Matt Surina	826	Jeff Kwiatkowski	2,191
1996	Don Scudder, Jr.	823	Scott Kurtz	2,224
1997	John Socha	847	Jeff Richgels	2,241
1998	John Gaines	814	Chris Barnes	2,151
1999	Dan Winter	825	Thomas Jones	2,158
2000	Garran Hein	811	Roy Daniels	2,181
2001	Nicholas Hoagland	798	D.J. Archer	2,219
2002	Mark Millsap	823	Stephen A. Hardy	2,279
2003	Ron Bahr	837	Steve Kloempken	2,215
2004[1]	John Janawicz	858	John Janawicz	2,224
2005	David Adam	791	Scott Craddock	2,131
2006	Wendy Macpherson	812	Dave A. Mitchell	2,189
2007	Frederick Aki	814	Mike Rose, Jr.	2,198
2008	Bryan Young	832	Jay Futrell	2,183
2009	Bo Goergen	862	Ron Vokes	2,321

[1]Table shows American Bowling Congress winners through 2004 and USBC winners thereafter.

United States Bowling Congress Women's Bowling Championships—Classic Division

Held since 1916. Table shows results for the past 20 years.

YEAR	SINGLES	SCORE	ALL-EVENTS	SCORE
1990	Paula Carter; Dana Miller-Mackie (tied)	705	Carol Norman	1,984
1991	Debbie Kuhn	773	Debbie Kuhn	2,036
1992	Patty Ann	680	Mitsuko Tokimoto	1,928
1993	Karen Collura; Kari Murph (tied)	747	Anne Marie Duggan	1,990
1994	Vicki Fifield	716	Wendy Macpherson-Papanos	1,940
1995	Beth Owen	749	Beth Owen	1,983
1996	Cindy Berlanga	723	Lorrie Nichols	1,985
1997	Jan Schmidt	765	Kendra Cameron	2,039
1998	Nellie Glandon	714	Liz Johnson	1,989
1999	Nikki Gianulias	746	Hidemi Mizobuchi	2,065
2000	Cathy Krasner	729	Carolyn Dorin-Ballard	2,147
2001	Lisa Wagner	756	Jonquay Armon	2,044
2002	Theresa Smith	752	Cara Honeychurch	2,150
2003	Michelle Feldman	764	Michelle Feldman	2,048
2004[1]	Sharon Smith	754	Kim Adler	2,133
2005	Leanne Barrette	774	Leanne Barrette	2,231
2006	Karen Stroud	771	Karen Stroud	2,159
2007	Tiffany Stanbrough	745	Wendy Macpherson	2,161
2008	Corrine Ham	736	Liz Johnson	2,113
2009	Michelle Feldman	816	Robin Romeo	2,172

[1]Table shows Women's International Bowling Congress winners through 2004 and USBC winners thereafter.

Cricket

Cricket is one of the **national sports** of England, and consequently it is played in nearly all the countries with which England has been associated. The world governing body is the **International Cricket Council** (ICC; founded as the Imperial Cricket Conference in 1909). The most important international cricket matches are the **Test matches**, which have been played since 1877. The Test-playing countries are England, Australia, South Africa (banned from international competition between about 1970 and 1992), West Indies (representing Barbados, Guyana, Jamaica, Trinidad and Tobago, and the Leeward and Windward islands), New Zealand, India, Pakistan, Sri Lanka, Zimbabwe (since 1992), and Bangladesh (since 2000).

The Test table is designed to be read from left to right across the columns. This will indicate, for example, that in Test match play against England, South Africa has won 26 games, has had 50 drawn matches, and has lost 54 games.

The **World Cup** is a quadrennial series of one-day, limited-overs competitions. It was first held in 1975.

International Cricket Council Web site: <www.icc-cricket.com>.

All-Time First-Class Test Cricket Standings (as of 30 Sep 2008)

	England			Australia			South Africa			West Indies			New Zealand		
	WINS	DRAWS	LOSSES	W	D	L	W	D	L	W	D	L	W	D	L
England v.	—	—	—	97	88	131	55	51	28	41	45*	52	45	41	8
Australia v.	131	88	97	—	—	—	44	18	15	50	23†	32	22	16	7
South Africa v.	28	51	55	15	18	44	—	—	—	14	5	3	20	11	4
West Indies v.	52	45*	41	32	23†	50	3	5	14	—	—	—	10	16*	9
New Zealand v.	8	41	45	7	16	22	4	11	20	9	16*	10	—	—	—
India v.	18	45	34	16	22†	34	5	7	11	11	41	30	14	22*	9
Pakistan v.	12	36	19‡	11	17	24	3	3	7	15	15	14	21	18	6
Sri Lanka v.	6	7	8	1	6	13	4	5	8	6	3	3	5	10	9
Zimbabwe v.	0	3	3	0	0	3	0	1	6	0	2	4	0	6	7
Bangladesh v.	0	0	4	0	0	4	0	0	6	0	1	3	0	0	6

	India			Pakistan			Sri Lanka			Zimbabwe			Bangladesh		
	WINS	DRAWS	LOSSES	W	D	L	W	D	L	W	D	L	W	D	L
England v.	34	45	18	19‡	36	12	8	7	6	3	3	0	4	0	0
Australia v.	34	22†	16	24	17	11	13	6	1	3	0	0	4	0	0
South Africa v.	11	7	5	7	3	3	8	5	4	6	1	0	6	0	0
West Indies v.	30	41	11	14	15	15	3	3	6	4	2	0	3	1	0
New Zealand v.	9	22*	14	6	18	21	9	10	5	7	6	0	6	0	0
India v.	—	—	—	9	38	12	11	13	5	7	2	2	4	1	0
Pakistan v.	12	38	9	—	—	—	15	10*	7	8	5*	2	6	0	0
Sri Lanka v.	5	13	11	7	10*	15	—	—	—	10	5	0	10	0	0
Zimbabwe v.	2	2	7	2	5*	8	0	5	10	—	—	—	4	3	1
Bangladesh v.	0	1	4	0	0	6	0	0	10	1	3	4	—	—	—

*Including one match abandoned.   †Including one tie.   ‡Including one forfeit.

Cycling

By all accounts, the greatest cycling event of all is the annual **Tour de France** road race (founded 1903). It is raced in several stages over a distance usually exceeding 3,500 km (2,175 mi). From 1911 to 1929 distances exceeded 5,300 km (3,290 mi). A Tour de France for women was first held in 1984, over an 18-stage course of 991 km (616 mi). In addition to this and a great number of other road races held yearly, there are yearly **road racing world championships**.

Track racing championships are also held. The oldest events of track racing are the **sprint** (in which only the last part of the race can actually be considered sprinting) and the **pursuit** (both a team and an individual event in which contestants start the race on opposite sides of the track and attempt to catch each other). **Mountain bike racing** and **cyclo-cross**, a cross-country bicycle race that requires cyclists to carry their bikes over parts of the course, developed in the latter part of the 20th century. World championships were established for these sports in 1997.

International Cycling Union (Union Cycliste Internationale—UCI) Web site: <www.uci.ch>.

Cycling Champions, 2008—09

In the case of multiday events, the concluding date is given.

EVENT	WINNER (COUNTRY)	DATE
world champions—mountain bikes		**22 Jun 2008**
men		
Cross-country	Christoph Sauser (SUI)	
Downhill	Gee Atherton (GBR)	
women		
Cross-country	Margarita Fullana Riera (ESP)	
Downhill	Rachel Atherton (GBR)	
world champions—road		**28 Sep 2008**
men		
Individual road race	Alessandro Ballan (ITA)	
Individual time trial	Bert Grabsch (GER)	
women		
Individual road race	Nicole Cook (GBR)	
Individual time trial	Amber Neben (USA)	
world champions—cyclo-cross		**1 Feb 2009**
Men	Niels Albert (BEL)	
Women	Marianne Vos (NED)	
world champions—track		**29 Mar 2009**
men		
Individual pursuit	Taylor Phinney (USA)	
Individual sprint	Grégory Baugé (FRA)	
1-km time trial	Stefan Nimke (GER)	
Points	Cameron Meyer (AUS)	
Team pursuit	Denmark	
Team sprint	France	
Keirin	Maximilian Levy (GER)	
Madison	Michael Mørkøv, Alex Rasmussen (DEN)	
Scratch	Morgan Kneisky (FRA)	
Omnium	Leigh Howard (AUS)	
women		
Individual pursuit	Alison Shanks (NZL)	
Individual sprint	Victoria Pendleton (GBR)	
500-m time trial	Simona Krupeckaite (LTU)	
Points	Giorgia Bronzini (ITA)	
Team pursuit	Great Britain	
Team sprint	Australia	
Keirin	Guo Shuang (CHN)	
Scratch	Yumari González (CUB)	
Omnium	Josephine Tomic (AUS)	
major elite road-race winners		
San Sebastian Classic (Clasica Ciclista San Sebastian)	Alejandro Valverde (ESP)	2 Aug 2008
Vattenfall Cyclassics	Robbie McEwen (AUS)	7 Sep 2008
Tour of Spain (Vuelta a España)	Alberto Contador (ESP)	21 Sep 2008
Paris–Tours	Philippe Gilbert (BEL)	12 Oct 2008
Tour of Lombardy (Giro di Lombardia)	Damiano Cunego (ITA)	18 Oct 2008
Paris–Nice	Luis León Sánchez (ESP)	15 Mar 2009
Tirreno–Adriatico	Michele Scarponi (ITA)	17 Mar 2009
Milan–San Remo	Mark Cavendish (GBR)	21 Mar 2009
Tour of Flanders (Ronde van Vlaanderen)	Stijn Devolder (BEL)	5 Apr 2009
Ghent–Wevelgem	Edvald Boasson Hagen (NOR)	8 Apr 2009
Paris–Roubaix	Tom Boonen (BEL)	12 Apr 2009
Amstel Gold	Sergei Ivanov (RUS)	19 Apr 2009
La Flèche Wallonne	Davide Rebellin (ITA)	22 Apr 2009
Liège–Bastogne–Liège	Andy Schleck (LUX)	26 Apr 2009
Tour of Romandie (Tour de Romandie)	Roman Kreuziger (CZE)	3 May 2009
Tour of Italy (Giro d'Italia)	Denis Menchov (RUS)	31 May 2009
Critérium du Dauphiné Libéré	Alejandro Valverde (ESP)	14 Jun 2009
Tour of Switzerland (Tour de Suisse)	Fabian Cancellara (SUI)	21 Jun 2009
Tour de France	Alberto Contador (ESP)	26 Jul 2009

Tour de France

YEAR	WINNER (COUNTRY)	LENGTH OF ROUTE (KM)	YEAR	WINNER (COUNTRY)	LENGTH OF ROUTE (KM)
1903	Maurice Garin (FRA)	2,428	1961	Jacques Anquetil (FRA)	4,397
1904	Henri Cornet (FRA)	2,388	1962	Jacques Anquetil (FRA)	4,274
1905	Louis Trousselier (FRA)	2,975	1963	Jacques Anquetil (FRA)	4,137
1906	René Pottier (FRA)	4,637	1964	Jacques Anquetil (FRA)	4,504
1907	Lucien Petit-Breton (FRA)	4,488	1965	Felice Gimondi (ITA)	4,183
1908	Lucien Petit-Breton (FRA)	4,487	1966	Lucien Aimar (FRA)	4,303
1909	François Faber (LUX)	4,507	1967	Roger Pingeon (FRA)	4,780
1910	Octave Lapize (FRA)	4,474	1968	Jan Janssen (NED)	4,662
1911	Gustave Garrigou (FRA)	5,344	1969	Eddy Merckx (BEL)	4,110
1912	Odile Defraye (BEL)	5,319	1970	Eddy Merckx (BEL)	4,366
1913	Philippe Thys (BEL)	5,387	1971	Eddy Merckx (BEL)	3,689
1914	Philippe Thys (BEL)	5,405	1972	Eddy Merckx (BEL)	3,846
1915–18	not held		1973	Luis Ocaña (ESP)	4,140
1919	Firmin Lambot (BEL)	5,560	1974	Eddy Merckx (BEL)	4,098
1920	Philippe Thys (BEL)	5,519	1975	Bernard Thévenet (FRA)	4,000
1921	Léon Scieur (BEL)	5,484	1976	Lucien Van Impe (BEL)	4,050
1922	Firmin Lambot (BEL)	5,375	1977	Bernard Thévenet (FRA)	4,098
1923	Henri Pélissier (FRA)	5,386	1978	Bernard Hinault (FRA)	3,920
1924	Ottavio Bottecchia (ITA)	5,425	1979	Bernard Hinault (FRA)	3,719
1925	Ottavio Bottecchia (ITA)	5,430	1980	Joop Zoetemelk (NED)	3,948
1926	Lucien Buysse (BEL)	5,745	1981	Bernard Hinault (FRA)	3,765
1927	Nicolas Frantz (LUX)	5,341	1982	Bernard Hinault (FRA)	3,489
1928	Nicolas Frantz (LUX)	5,377	1983	Laurent Fignon (FRA)	3,568
1929	Maurice De Waele (BEL)	5,286	1984	Laurent Fignon (FRA)	3,880
1930	André Leducq (FRA)	4,818	1985	Bernard Hinault (FRA)	4,100
1931	Antonin Magne (FRA)	5,095	1986	Greg LeMond (USA)	4,091
1932	André Leducq (FRA)	4,520	1987	Stephen Roche (IRL)	4,100
1933	Georges Speicher (FRA)	4,395	1988	Pedro Delgado (ESP)	3,300
1934	Antonin Magne (FRA)	4,363	1989	Greg LeMond (USA)	3,215
1935	Romain Maes (BEL)	4,338	1990	Greg LeMond (USA)	3,399
1936	Romain Maes (BEL)	4,442	1991	Miguel Indurain (ESP)	3,935
1937	Roger Lapébie (FRA)	4,415	1992	Miguel Indurain (ESP)	3,983
1938	Gino Bartali (ITA)	4,694	1993	Miguel Indurain (ESP)	3,700
1939	Sylvere Maes (BEL)	4,224	1994	Miguel Indurain (ESP)	3,978
1940–46	not held		1995	Miguel Indurain (ESP)	3,635
1947	Jean Robic (FRA)	4,640	1996	no winner[1]	3,764
1948	Gino Bartali (ITA)	4,922	1997	Jan Ullrich (GER)	3,944
1949	Fausto Coppi (ITA)	4,808	1998	Marco Pantani (ITA)	3,831
1950	Ferdi Kubler (SUI)	4,775	1999	Lance Armstrong (USA)	3,687
1951	Hugo Koblet (SUI)	4,697	2000	Lance Armstrong (USA)	3,663
1952	Fausto Coppi (ITA)	4,807	2001	Lance Armstrong (USA)	3,454
1953	Louison Bobet (FRA)	4,479	2002	Lance Armstrong (USA)	3,272
1954	Louison Bobet (FRA)	4,469	2003	Lance Armstrong (USA)	3,428
1955	Louison Bobet (FRA)	4,855	2004	Lance Armstrong (USA)	3,391
1956	Roger Walkowiak (FRA)	4,496	2005	Lance Armstrong (USA)	3,608
1957	Jacques Anquetil (FRA)	4,686	2006	Óscar Pereiro (ESP)[2]	3,657
1958	Charly Gaul (LUX)	4,319	2007	Alberto Contador (ESP)	3,550
1959	Federico Bahamontes (ESP)	4,355	2008	Carlos Sastre (ESP)	3,554
1960	Gastone Nencini (ITA)	4,173	2009	Alberto Contador (ESP)	3,445

[1] The victory for Bjarne Riis (DEN) was invalidated after he admitted to having used illegal performance-enhancing drugs. [2] Floyd Landis (USA) was stripped of the title after he was found to have had illegal performance-enhancing drugs in his system. His last appeal against the ruling was rejected in June 2008.

Football

Many types of games are known as football, among them association football (also called soccer), gridiron football (also called American football and known in the United States as, simply, football), Canadian football (also called rugby football), Australian rules football (also called footy), and rugby union and rugby league football (also known as rugby, or rugger). Each of these games is unique, though some—such as US football and Canadian football—bear more than a little resemblance, and each has its own distinct following.

American football—professional. The National Football League (NFL) championship play-offs were organized in 1933. The American Football League (founded 1959) was a rival organization until 1970, when it merged with the NFL. The resulting

Football (continued)

reorganization added a few new teams (1976) and divided the reconstituted NFL into two conferences, the American Football Conference and the National Football Conference. (There have been several expansions since.) The play-off winner in each conference becomes that conference's representative in the Super Bowl, the final game of the professional football season.

American football—college. Historically the national champion of college football has been informally selected by two rival opinion polls—one based on a survey of collegiate football coaches (currently conducted by USA Today) and the other on a survey of sportswriters (conducted by the Associated Press [AP]). The AP sportswriters' poll began in 1936. The coaches' poll was begun in 1950 by the United Press (now United Press International [UPI]). Where polls designated different teams, both are listed. Desire for a clear-cut national champion led to the creation of the Bowl Championship Series (BCS) in 1999. The BCS uses a formula involving team records, strength of schedule, and rankings to determine the top two teams, who then meet in a national championship game. The site of the game annually shifts between the four major bowls—Fiesta, Orange, Rose, and Sugar. The first of the bowl games, the Rose Bowl, had its inaugural game in 1902 during the 12th annual Tournament of Roses festival in Pasadena CA. In 1935 the Sugar Bowl (played in New Orleans LA) and the Orange Bowl (played in Miami FL) were inaugurated. The Fiesta Bowl (played in Phoenix AZ) began play in 1971.

Canadian football—professional. The rules and organization of professional football in Canada have evolved gradually for well over 100 years based on the Canadian Rugby Union (formed in 1891). Until 1936 the game included intercollegiate teams. In 1958 the Canadian Football League was formed, dividing into two conferences, Eastern and Western. In 1981 these were renamed divisions. The two teams that win the division championships meet for the championship of the League, the Grey Cup (instituted in 1909). The intercollegiate teams withdrew from the Grey Cup competition in 1936, but the league did not become strictly professional until the mid-1950s.

Australian football—professional. Australian rules football, originally called Melbourne rules football, emerged in the state of Victoria in the late 1850s as a sporting alternative during the southern winter, when cricket was not played. The Victorian Football Association (formed in 1877) was supplanted by the Victorian Football League (formed in 1896), which was renamed the Australian Football League (AFL) in 1990 after two teams from outside Victoria were admitted in 1987. Currently, the eight AFL teams with the best records at the end of a 22-week season qualify for the play-offs. The first premiership Grand Final was played in 1886.

Association football. The game of association football is governed by the Fédération Internationale de Football Association (FIFA; founded 1904). The quadrennial FIFA World Cup (organized as the World Cup in 1930) was the first official internationally contested association football match. The popularity of the World Cup and, even earlier, the Copa América (1916) in South America led to the development of several regional cup competitions, including the European Champion Clubs' Cup (1955; discontinued after the 1992–93 season and superseded by the UEFA Champions League), the Asian Cup (1956), the African Cup of Nations (1957), and the Libertadores de América Cup (1960). Competition for the FIFA Women's World Cup began in 1991. The Major League Soccer Cup in the US was launched in 1996.

Rugby union football. Rugby union football was open to amateurs only until 1995. The Six Nations Championship was first played in 1882 (as the Four Nations) and is now contested by England, Scotland, Wales, Ireland, France (since 1910), and Italy (since 2000). The international Test matches further include South Africa, New Zealand, and Australia. The International Amateur Rugby Fedperation (FIRA; now FIRA-AER) oversees rugby in 37 other (i.e., non-Test) countries. The chief international competition between rugby union clubs in the Southern Hemisphere is the tri-nation Super 14 (Super 10 from 1993 to 1995 and Super 12 from 1996 to 2005). Teams from Australia (four), South Africa (five), and New Zealand (five) play in a round-robin tournament; the four teams with the best records qualify for the semifinals. The World Cup, sponsored by the International Rugby Board (founded 1886), was inaugurated in 1987. The competition is held every four years.

Rugby league football. Rugby League World Cup competition began in 1954 between professionals from Australia, France, Great Britain, and New Zealand. In 1975–77 it was known as the International Championship. Competition was discontinued after 1977 but revived during the 1980s. The match has been held irregularly every few years.

Related Web sites: National Football League (NFL): <www.nfl.com>; Canadian Football League (CFL): <www.cfl.ca>; Australian Football League (AFL): <www.afl.com.au>; Fédération Internationale de Football Association (FIFA): <www.fifa.com>; Union of European Football Associations (UEFA): <www.uefa.com>; Major League Soccer (MLS): <www.mlsnet.com>; International Rugby Board (rugby union): <www.irb.com>; Rugby League International Federation: <www.rlif.org>; Super 14: <www.super14.com>.

National Football League Final Standings, 2008—09

American Football Conference

East Division

TEAM	WON	LOST	TIED
Miami[1]	11	5	0
New England	11	5	0
New York Jets	9	7	0
Buffalo	7	9	0

South Division

TEAM	WON	LOST	TIED
Tennessee[1]	13	3	0
Indianapolis[1]	12	4	0
Houston	8	8	0
Jacksonville	5	11	0

National Football League Final Standings, 2008–09 (continued)

American Football Conference (continued)

North Division				West Division			
TEAM	WON	LOST	TIED	TEAM	WON	LOST	TIED
Pittsburgh[1]	12	4	0	San Diego[1]	8	8	0
Baltimore[1]	11	5	0	Denver	8	8	0
Cincinnati	4	11	1	Oakland	5	11	0
Cleveland	4	12	0	Kansas City	2	14	0

National Football Conference

East Division				South Division			
TEAM	WON	LOST	TIED	TEAM	WON	LOST	TIED
New York Giants[1]	12	4	0	Carolina[1]	12	4	0
Philadelphia[1]	9	6	1	Atlanta	11	5	0
Dallas	9	7	0	Tampa Bay	9	7	0
Washington	8	8	0	New Orleans	8	8	0

North Division				West Division			
TEAM	WON	LOST	TIED	TEAM	WON	LOST	TIED
Minnesota[1]	10	6	0	Arizona[1]	9	7	0
Chicago	9	7	0	San Francisco	7	9	0
Green Bay	6	10	0	Seattle	4	12	0
Detroit	0	16	0	St. Louis	2	14	0

[1]Gained play-off berth.

Super Bowl

NFL-AFL championship 1966–70; NFL championship from 1970–71 season.

	SEASON	WINNER	RUNNER-UP	SCORE
I	1966–67	Green Bay Packers (NFL)	Kansas City Chiefs (AFL)	35–10
II	1967–68	Green Bay Packers (NFL)	Oakland Raiders (AFL)	33–14
III	1968–69	New York Jets (AFL)	Baltimore Colts (NFL)	16–7
IV	1969–70	Kansas City Chiefs (AFL)	Minnesota Vikings (NFL)	23–7
V	1970–71	Baltimore Colts (AFC)	Dallas Cowboys (NFC)	16–13
VI	1971–72	Dallas Cowboys (NFC)	Miami Dolphins (AFC)	24–3
VII	1972–73	Miami Dolphins (AFC)	Washington Redskins (NFC)	14–7
VIII	1973–74	Miami Dolphins (AFC)	Minnesota Vikings (NFC)	24–7
IX	1974–75	Pittsburgh Steelers (AFC)	Minnesota Vikings (NFC)	16–6
X	1975–76	Pittsburgh Steelers (AFC)	Dallas Cowboys (NFC)	21–17
XI	1976–77	Oakland Raiders (AFC)	Minnesota Vikings (NFC)	32–14
XII	1977–78	Dallas Cowboys (NFC)	Denver Broncos (AFC)	27–10
XIII	1978–79	Pittsburgh Steelers (AFC)	Dallas Cowboys (NFC)	35–31
XIV	1979–80	Pittsburgh Steelers (AFC)	Los Angeles Rams (NFC)	31–19
XV	1980–81	Oakland Raiders (AFC)	Philadelphia Eagles (NFC)	27–10
XVI	1981–82	San Francisco 49ers (NFC)	Cincinnati Bengals (AFC)	26–21
XVII	1982–83	Washington Redskins (NFC)	Miami Dolphins (AFC)	27–17
XVIII	1983–84	Los Angeles Raiders (AFC)	Washington Redskins (NFC)	38–9
XIX	1984–85	San Francisco 49ers (NFC)	Miami Dolphins (AFC)	38–16
XX	1985–86	Chicago Bears (NFC)	New England Patriots (AFC)	46–10
XXI	1986–87	New York Giants (NFC)	Denver Broncos (AFC)	39–20
XXII	1987–88	Washington Redskins (NFC)	Denver Broncos (AFC)	42–10
XXIII	1988–89	San Francisco 49ers (NFC)	Cincinnati Bengals (AFC)	20–16
XXIV	1989–90	San Francisco 49ers (NFC)	Denver Broncos (AFC)	55–10
XXV	1990–91	New York Giants (NFC)	Buffalo Bills (AFC)	20–19
XXVI	1991–92	Washington Redskins (NFC)	Buffalo Bills (AFC)	37–24
XXVII	1992–93	Dallas Cowboys (NFC)	Buffalo Bills (AFC)	52–17
XXVIII	1993–94	Dallas Cowboys (NFC)	Buffalo Bills (AFC)	30–13
XXIX	1994–95	San Francisco 49ers (NFC)	San Diego Chargers (AFC)	49–26
XXX	1995–96	Dallas Cowboys (NFC)	Pittsburgh Steelers (AFC)	27–17
XXXI	1996–97	Green Bay Packers (NFC)	New England Patriots (AFC)	35–21
XXXII	1997–98	Denver Broncos (AFC)	Green Bay Packers (NFC)	31–24
XXXIII	1998–99	Denver Broncos (AFC)	Atlanta Falcons (NFC)	34–19
XXXIV	1999–2000	St. Louis Rams (NFC)	Tennessee Titans (AFC)	23–16
XXXV	2000–01	Baltimore Ravens (AFC)	New York Giants (NFC)	34–7
XXXVI	2001–02	New England Patriots (AFC)	St. Louis Rams (NFC)	20–17
XXXVII	2002–03	Tampa Bay Buccaneers (NFC)	Oakland Raiders (AFC)	48–21

Super Bowl (continued)

	SEASON	WINNER	RUNNER-UP	SCORE
XXXVIII	2003–04	New England Patriots (AFC)	Carolina Panthers (NFC)	32–29
XXXIX	2004–05	New England Patriots (AFC)	Philadelphia Eagles (NFC)	24–21
XL	2005–06	Pittsburgh Steelers (AFC)	Seattle Seahawks (NFC)	21–10
XLI	2006–07	Indianapolis Colts (AFC)	Chicago Bears (NFC)	29–17
XLII	2007–08	New York Giants (NFC)	New England Patriots (AFC)	17–14
XLIII	2008–09	Pittsburgh Steelers (AFC)	Arizona Cardinals (NFC)	27–23

American Professional Football All-Time Records[1]

	PLAYERS/TEAMS	NUMBER	SEASON/DATE
Individual career records			
Total games	Morten Andersen	382	1982–2007, except 2005
Total points	Morten Andersen	2,544	1982–2007, except 2005
Touchdowns, total	Jerry Rice	208	1985–2004
Touchdowns, passing	Brett Favre	464	1991–2008
Touchdowns, receiving	Jerry Rice	197	1985–2004
Touchdowns, rushing	Emmitt Smith	164	1990–2004
Field goals made	Morten Andersen	565	1982–2007, except 2005
Extra points made (kicked)	George Blanda	943	1949–75, except 1959
Passing yardage	Brett Favre	65,127	1991–2008
Passing completions	Brett Favre	5,720	1991–2008
Receiving yardage	Jerry Rice	22,895	1985–2004
Rushing yardage	Emmitt Smith	18,355	1990–2004
Interceptions (defense)	Paul Krause	81	1964–79
Sacks (defense)[2]	Bruce Smith	200	1985–2003
Coaching, total wins	Don Shula	328	1963–95
Individual season records			
Total points	LaDainian Tomlinson	186	2006
Touchdowns, total	LaDainian Tomlinson	31	2006
Touchdowns, passing	Tom Brady	50	2007
Touchdowns, receiving	Randy Moss	23	2007
Touchdowns, rushing	LaDainian Tomlinson	28	2006
Field goals made	Neil Rackers	40	2005
Extra points made (kicked)	Stephen Gostkowski	74	2007
Passing yardage	Dan Marino	5,084	1984
Receiving yardage	Jerry Rice	1,848	1995
Rushing yardage	Eric Dickerson	2,105	1984
Interceptions (defense)	Dick Lane	14	1952
Sacks (defense)[2]	Michael Strahan	22.5	2001
Individual game records			
Total points	Ernie Nevers	40	28 Nov 1929
Touchdowns, total	Ernie Nevers; Dub Jones; Gale Sayers	6	28 Nov 1929; 25 Nov 1951; 12 Dec 1965
Touchdowns, passing	Sid Luckman; Adrian Burk; George Blanda; Y.A. Tittle; Joe Kapp	7	14 Nov 1943; 17 Oct 1954; 19 Nov 1961; 28 Oct 1962; 28 Sep 1969
Touchdowns, receiving	Bob Shaw; Kellen Winslow; Jerry Rice	5	2 Oct 1950; 22 Nov 1981; 14 Oct 1990
Touchdowns, rushing	Ernie Nevers	6	28 Nov 1929
Field goals made	Rob Bironas	8	21 Oct 2007
Longest field goal	Tom Dempsey; Jason Elam	63 yd	8 Nov 1970; 25 Oct 1998
Extra points made (kicked)	Pat Harder; Bob Waterfield; Charlie Gogolak	9	17 Oct 1948; 22 Oct 1950; 27 Nov 1966
Passing yardage	Norm Van Brocklin	554	28 Sep 1951

American Professional Football All-Time Records[1] (continued)

	PLAYERS/TEAMS	NUMBER	SEASON/DATE
Individual game records (continued)			
Receiving yardage	Willie Anderson	336	11 Nov 1989 (overtime)
Rushing yardage	Adrian Peterson	296	4 Nov 2007
Longest run from scrimmage	Tony Dorsett	99 yd	3 Jan 1983
Interceptions (defense)	*18 players hold record*	4	
Sacks (defense)[2]	Derrick Thomas	7	11 Nov 1990
Team season records			
League championships (including Super Bowls)	Green Bay Packers	12	
Super Bowl titles	Pittsburgh Steelers	6	
Consecutive Super Bowl titles	*7 teams hold record*	2	
Perfect regular season	New England Patriots;	16 wins	2007
	Miami Dolphins;	14 wins	1972
	Chicago Bears;	13 wins	1934
	Chicago Bears	11 wins	1942
Total points scored	New England Patriots	589	2007
Touchdowns, total	New England Patriots	75	2007
Touchdowns, passing	Indianapolis Colts	51	2004
Touchdowns, rushing	Green Bay Packers	36	1962
Field goals made	Arizona Cardinals	43	2005
Passing yardage	St. Louis Rams	5,232	2000
Rushing yardage	New England Patriots	3,165	1978
Game records			
Highest total score	Washington Redskins versus New York Giants	113 (72–41)	27 Nov 1966
Longest game	Miami Dolphins versus Kansas City Chiefs	82:40 (two overtimes)	25 Dec 1971

[1]*Includes National Football League from 1920 through the 2008–09 season and American Football League from 1960 to 1969.* [2]*Since 1982; before that year sacks were not officially recorded by the NFL.*

National Collegiate Athletic Association Football National Title[1]

SEASON	CHAMPION	SEASON	CHAMPION	SEASON	CHAMPION
1924–25	Notre Dame	1954–55	Ohio State (AP); UCLA (UP)	1978–79	Alabama (AP); Southern California (UPI)
1925–26	Dartmouth				
1926–27	Stanford	1955–56	Oklahoma	1979–80	Alabama
1927–28	Illinois	1956–57	Oklahoma	1980–81	Georgia
1928–29	Southern California	1957–58	Auburn (AP); Ohio State (UP)	1981–82	Clemson
1929–30	Notre Dame			1982–83	Penn State
1930–31	Notre Dame	1958–59	Louisiana State	1983–84	Miami (FL)
1931–32	Southern California	1959–60	Syracuse	1984–85	Brigham Young
1932–33	Michigan	1960–61	Minnesota	1985–86	Oklahoma
1933–34	Michigan	1961–62	Alabama	1986–87	Penn State
1934–35	Minnesota	1962–63	Southern California	1987–88	Miami (FL)
1935–36	Southern Methodist	1963–64	Texas	1988–89	Notre Dame
1936–37	Minnesota	1964–65	Alabama	1989–90	Miami (FL)
1937–38	Pittsburgh	1965–66	Alabama (AP); Michigan State (UPI)	1990–91	Colorado (AP); Georgia Tech (UPI)
1938–39	Texas Christian				
1939–40	Texas A&M	1966–67	Notre Dame	1991–92	Miami (FL) (AP); Washington (UPI)
1940–41	Minnesota	1967–68	Southern California		
1941–42	Minnesota	1968–69	Ohio State	1992–93	Alabama
1942–43	Ohio State	1969–70	Texas	1993–94	Florida State
1943–44	Notre Dame	1970–71	Nebraska (AP); Texas (UPI)	1994–95	Nebraska
1944–45	Army			1995–96	Nebraska
1945–46	Army	1971–72	Nebraska	1996–97	Florida
1946–47	Notre Dame	1972–73	Southern California	1997–98	Michigan (AP); Nebraska (*USA Today*/ESPN)
1947–48	Notre Dame	1973–74	Notre Dame (AP); Alabama (UPI)		
1948–49	Michigan				
1949–50	Notre Dame	1974–75	Oklahoma (AP); Southern California (UPI)	1998–99	Tennessee
1950–51	Oklahoma			1999–2000	Florida State
1951–52	Tennessee	1975–76	Oklahoma	2000–01	Oklahoma
1952–53	Michigan State	1976–77	Pittsburgh	2001–02	Miami (FL)
1953–54	Maryland	1977–78	Notre Dame	2002–03	Ohio State

National Collegiate Athletic Association Football National Title[1] (continued)

SEASON	CHAMPION	SEASON	CHAMPION	SEASON	CHAMPION
2003–04	Louisiana State (BCS); Southern California (AP)	2004–05	Southern California	2007–08	Louisiana State
		2005–06	Texas	2008–09	Florida
		2006–07	Florida		

[1]University Division 1956–73; Division I 1973–78; Division I-A 1978–2006; Football Bowl Subdivision from 2006.

Rose Bowl

SEASON	WINNER	RUNNER-UP	SCORE	SEASON	WINNER	RUNNER-UP	SCORE
1901–02	Michigan	Stanford	49–0	1963–64	Illinois	Washington	17–7
1915–16	Washington State	Brown	14–0	1964–65	Michigan	Oregon State	34–7
				1965–66	UCLA	Michigan State	14–12
1916–17	Oregon	Pennsylvania	14–0				
1917–18	Mare Island[1]	Camp Lewis[2]	19–7	1966–67	Purdue	Southern California	14–13
1918–19	Great Lakes[3]	Mare Island[1]	17–0				
1919–20	Harvard	Oregon	7–6	1967–68	Southern California	Indiana	14–3
1920–21	California	Ohio State	28–0	1968–69	Ohio State	Southern California	27–16
1921–22	California	Washington and Jefferson	0–0	1969–70	Southern California	Michigan	10–3
1922–23	Southern California	Penn State	14–3	1970–71	Stanford	Ohio State	27–17
1923–24	Washington	Navy	14–14	1971–72	Stanford	Michigan	13–12
1924–25	Notre Dame	Stanford	27–10	1972–73	Southern California	Ohio State	42–17
1925–26	Alabama	Washington	20–19	1973–74	Ohio State	Southern California	42–21
1926–27	Alabama	Stanford	7–7				
1927–28	Stanford	Pittsburgh	7–6	1974–75	Southern California	Ohio State	18–17
1928–29	Georgia Tech	California	8–7	1975–76	UCLA	Ohio State	23–10
1929–30	Southern California	Pittsburgh	47–14	1976–77	Southern California	Michigan	14–6
1930–31	Alabama	Washington State	24–0	1977–78	Washington	Michigan	27–20
				1978–79	Southern California	Michigan	17–10
1931–32	Southern California	Tulane	21–12	1979–80	Southern California	Ohio State	17–16
1932–33	Southern California	Pittsburgh	35–0	1980–81	Michigan	Washington	23–6
1933–34	Columbia	Stanford	7–0	1981–82	Washington	Iowa	28–0
1934–35	Alabama	Stanford	29–13	1982–83	UCLA	Michigan	24–14
1935–36	Stanford	Southern Methodist	7–0	1983–84	UCLA	Illinois	45–9
				1984–85	Southern California	Ohio State	20–17
1936–37	Pittsburgh	Washington	21–0	1985–86	UCLA	Iowa	45–28
1937–38	California	Alabama	13–0	1986–87	Arizona State	Michigan	22–15
1938–39	Southern California	Duke	7–3	1987–88	Michigan State	Southern California	20–17
1939–40	Southern California	Tennessee	14–0				
1940–41	Stanford	Nebraska	21–13	1988–89	Michigan	Southern California	22–14
1941–42	Oregon State	Duke	20–16				
1942–43	Georgia	UCLA	9–0	1989–90	Southern California	Michigan	17–10
1943–44	Southern California	Washington	29–0	1990–91	Washington	Iowa	46–34
1944–45	Southern California	Tennessee	25–0	1991–92	Washington	Michigan	34–14
1945–46	Alabama	Southern California	34–14	1992–93	Michigan	Washington	38–31
				1993–94	Wisconsin	UCLA	21–16
1946–47	Illinois	UCLA	45–14	1994–95	Penn State	Oregon	38–20
1947–48	Michigan	Southern California	49–0	1995–96	Southern California	Northwestern	41–32
				1996–97	Ohio State	Arizona State	20–17
1948–49	Northwestern	California	20–14	1997–98	Michigan	Washington State	21–16
1949–50	Ohio State	California	17–14				
1950–51	Michigan	California	14–6	1998–99	Wisconsin	UCLA	38–31
1951–52	Illinois	Stanford	40–7	1999–2000	Wisconsin	Stanford	17–9
1952–53	Southern California	Wisconsin	7–0	2000–01	Washington	Purdue	34–24
1953–54	Michigan State	UCLA	28–20	2001–02	Miami (FL)	Nebraska	37–14
1954–55	Ohio State	Southern California	20–7	2002–03	Oklahoma	Washington State	34–14
1955–56	Michigan State	UCLA	17–14	2003–04	Southern California	Michigan	28–14
1956–57	Iowa	Oregon State	35–19	2004–05	Texas	Michigan	38–37
1957–58	Ohio State	Oregon	10–7	2005–06	Texas	Southern California	41–38
1958–59	Iowa	California	38–12				
1959–60	Washington	Wisconsin	44–8	2006–07	Southern California	Michigan	32–18
1960–61	Washington	Minnesota	17–7	2007–08	Southern California	Illinois	49–17
1961–62	Minnesota	UCLA	21–3	2008–09	Southern California	Penn State	38–24
1962–63	Southern California	Wisconsin	42–37				

[1]US Marine Corps team. [2]US Army team. [3]US Navy team.

Orange Bowl

SEASON	WINNER	RUNNER-UP	SCORE	SEASON	WINNER	RUNNER-UP	SCORE
1934-35	Bucknell	Miami (FL)	26-0	1972-73	Nebraska	Notre Dame	40-6
1935-36	Catholic	Mississippi	20-19	1973-74	Penn State	Louisiana State	16-9
1936-37	Duquesne	Mississippi State	13-12	1974-75	Notre Dame	Alabama	13-11
1937-38	Auburn	Michigan State	6-0	1975-76	Oklahoma	Michigan	14-6
1938-39	Tennessee	Oklahoma	17-0	1976-77	Ohio State	Colorado	27-10
1939-40	Georgia Tech	Missouri	21-7	1977-78	Arkansas	Oklahoma	31-6
1940-41	Mississippi State	Georgetown	14-7	1978-79	Oklahoma	Nebraska	31-24
1941-42	Georgia	Texas Christian	40-26	1979-80	Oklahoma	Florida State	24-7
1942-43	Alabama	Boston College	37-21	1980-81	Oklahoma	Florida State	18-17
1943-44	Louisiana State	Texas A&M	19-14	1981-82	Clemson	Nebraska	22-15
1944-45	Tulsa	Georgia Tech	26-12	1982-83	Nebraska	Louisiana State	21-20
1945-46	Miami (FL)	Holy Cross	13-6	1983-84	Miami (FL)	Nebraska	31-30
1946-47	Rice	Tennessee	8-0	1984-85	Washington	Oklahoma	28-17
1947-48	Georgia Tech	Kansas	20-14	1985-86	Oklahoma	Penn State	25-10
1948-49	Texas	Georgia	41-28	1986-87	Oklahoma	Arkansas	42-8
1949-50	Santa Clara	Kentucky	21-13	1987-88	Miami (FL)	Oklahoma	20-14
1950-51	Clemson	Miami (FL)	15-14	1988-89	Miami (FL)	Nebraska	23-3
1951-52	Georgia Tech	Baylor	17-14	1989-90	Notre Dame	Colorado	21-6
1952-53	Alabama	Syracuse	61-6	1990-91	Colorado	Notre Dame	10-9
1953-54	Oklahoma	Maryland	7-0	1991-92	Miami (FL)	Nebraska	22-0
1954-55	Duke	Nebraska	34-7	1992-93	Florida State	Nebraska	27-14
1955-56	Oklahoma	Maryland	20-6	1993-94	Florida State	Nebraska	18-16
1956-57	Colorado	Clemson	27-21	1994-95	Nebraska	Miami	24-17
1957-58	Oklahoma	Duke	48-21	1995-96	Florida State	Notre Dame	31-26
1958-59	Oklahoma	Syracuse	21-6	1996-97	Nebraska	Virginia Tech	41-21
1959-60	Georgia	Missouri	14-0	1997-98	Nebraska	Tennessee	42-17
1960-61	Missouri	Navy	21-14	1998-99	Florida	Syracuse	31-10
1961-62	Louisiana State	Colorado	25-7	1999-2000	Michigan	Alabama	35-34
1962-63	Alabama	Oklahoma	17-0	2000-01	Oklahoma	Florida State	13-2
1963-64	Nebraska	Auburn	13-7	2001-02	Florida	Maryland	56-23
1964-65	Texas	Alabama	21-17	2002-03	Southern California	Iowa	38-17
1965-66	Alabama	Nebraska	39-28	2003-04	Miami (FL)	Florida State	16-14
1966-67	Florida	Georgia Tech	27-12	2004-05	Southern California	Oklahoma	55-19
1967-68	Oklahoma	Tennessee	26-24	2005-06	Penn State	Florida State	26-23
1968-69	Penn State	Kansas	15-14	2006-07	Louisville	Wake Forest	24-13
1969-70	Penn State	Missouri	10-3	2007-08	Kansas	Virginia Tech	24-21
1970-71	Nebraska	Louisiana State	17-12	2008-09	Virginia Tech	Cincinnati	20-7
1971-72	Nebraska	Alabama	38-6				

Sugar Bowl

SEASON	WINNER	RUNNER-UP	SCORE	SEASON	WINNER	RUNNER-UP	SCORE
1934-35	Tulane	Temple	20-14	1958-59	Louisiana State	Clemson	7-0
1935-36	Texas Christian	Louisiana State	3-2	1959-60	Mississippi	Louisiana State	21-0
1936-37	Santa Clara	Louisiana State	21-14	1960-61	Mississippi	Rice	14-6
1937-38	Santa Clara	Louisiana State	6-0	1961-62	Alabama	Arkansas	10-3
1938-39	Texas Christian	Carnegie Tech	15-7	1962-63	Mississippi	Arkansas	17-13
1939-40	Texas A&M	Tulane	14-13	1963-64	Alabama	Mississippi	12-7
1940-41	Boston College	Tennessee	19-13	1964-65	Louisiana State	Syracuse	13-10
1941-42	Fordham	Missouri	2-0				
1942-43	Tennessee	Tulsa	14-7	1965-66	Missouri	Florida	20-18
1943-44	Georgia Tech	Tulsa	20-18	1966-67	Alabama	Nebraska	34-7
1944-45	Duke	Alabama	29-26	1967-68	Louisiana State	Wyoming	20-13
1945-46	Oklahoma A&M	St. Mary's (CA)	33-13				
1946-47	Georgia	North Carolina	20-10	1968-69	Arkansas	Georgia	16-2
1947-48	Texas	Alabama	27-7	1969-70	Mississippi	Arkansas	27-22
1948-49	Oklahoma	North Carolina	14-6	1970-71	Tennessee	Air Force	34-13
1949-50	Oklahoma	Louisiana State	35-0	1971-72	Oklahoma	Auburn	40-22
1950-51	Kentucky	Oklahoma	13-7	1972-73	Oklahoma	Penn State	14-0
1951-52	Maryland	Tennessee	28-13	1973-74	Notre Dame	Alabama	24-23
1952-53	Georgia Tech	Mississippi	24-7	1974-75	Nebraska	Florida	13-10
1953-54	Georgia Tech	West Virginia	42-19	1975-76	Alabama	Penn State	13-6
1954-55	Navy	Mississippi	21-0	1976-77	Pittsburgh	Georgia	27-3
1955-56	Georgia Tech	Pittsburgh	7-0	1977-78	Alabama	Ohio State	35-6
1956-57	Baylor	Tennessee	13-7	1978-79	Alabama	Penn State	14-7
1957-58	Mississippi	Texas	39-7	1979-80	Alabama	Arkansas	24-9

Sugar Bowl (continued)

SEASON	WINNER	RUNNER-UP	SCORE	SEASON	WINNER	RUNNER-UP	SCORE
1980–81	Georgia	Notre Dame	17–10	1996–97	Florida	Florida State	52–20
1981–82	Pittsburgh	Georgia	24–20	1997–98	Florida State	Ohio State	31–14
1982–83	Penn State	Georgia	27–23	1998–99	Ohio State	Texas A&M	24–14
1983–84	Auburn	Michigan	9–7	1999–2000	Florida State	Virginia Tech	46–29
1984–85	Nebraska	Louisiana State	28–10	2000–01	Miami (FL)	Florida	37–20
1985–86	Tennessee	Miami (FL)	35–7	2001–02	Louisiana State	Illinois	47–34
1986–87	Nebraska	Louisiana State	30–15				
1987–88	Auburn	Syracuse	16–16	2002–03	Georgia	Florida State	26–13
1988–89	Florida State	Auburn	13–7	2003–04	Louisiana State	Oklahoma	21–14
1989–90	Miami (FL)	Alabama	33–25				
1990–91	Tennessee	Virginia	23–22	2004–05	Auburn	Virginia Tech	16–13
1991–92	Notre Dame	Florida	39–28	2005–06	West Virginia	Georgia	38–35
1992–93	Alabama	Miami (FL)	34–13	2006–07	Louisiana State	Notre Dame	41–14
1993–94	Florida	West Virginia	41–7				
1994–95	Florida State	Florida	23–17	2007–08	Georgia	Hawaii	41–10
1995–96	Virginia Tech	Texas	28–10	2008–09	Utah	Alabama	31–17

Fiesta Bowl

SEASON	WINNER	RUNNER-UP	SCORE	SEASON	WINNER	RUNNER-UP	SCORE
1971–72	Arizona State	Florida State	45–38	1990–91	Louisville	Alabama	34–7
1972–73	Arizona State	Missouri	49–35	1991–92	Penn State	Tennessee	42–17
1973–74	Arizona State	Pittsburgh	28–7	1992–93	Syracuse	Colorado	26–22
1974–75	Oklahoma State	Brigham Young	16–6	1993–94	Arizona	Miami (FL)	29–0
1975–76	Arizona State	Nebraska	17–14	1994–95	Colorado	Notre Dame	41–24
1976–77	Oklahoma	Wyoming	41–7	1995–96	Nebraska	Florida	62–24
1977–78	Penn State	Arizona State	42–30	1996–97	Penn State	Texas	38–15
1978–79	Arkansas	UCLA	10–10	1997–98	Kansas State	Syracuse	35–18
1979–80	Pittsburgh	Arizona	16–10	1998–99	Tennessee	Florida State	23–16
1980–81	Penn State	Ohio State	31–19	1999–2000	Nebraska	Tennessee	31–21
1981–82	Penn State	Southern California	26–10	2000–01	Oregon State	Notre Dame	41–9
				2001–02	Oregon	Colorado	38–16
1982–83	Arizona State	Oklahoma	32–21	2002–03	Ohio State	Miami (FL)	31–24
1983–84	Ohio State	Pittsburgh	28–23	2003–04	Ohio State	Kansas State	35–28
1984–85	UCLA	Miami (FL)	39–37	2004–05	Utah	Pittsburgh	35–7
1985–86	Michigan	Nebraska	27–23	2005–06	Ohio State	Notre Dame	34–20
1986–87	Penn State	Miami (FL)	14–10	2006–07	Boise State	Oklahoma	43–42
1987–88	Florida State	Nebraska	31–28	2007–08	West Virginia	Oklahoma	48–28
1988–89	Notre Dame	West Virginia	34–21	2008–09	Texas	Ohio State	24–21
1989–90	Florida State	Nebraska	41–17				

Heisman Trophy

The Heisman Trophy is named for John Heisman, former director of the Downtown Athletic Club in New York City. The trophy goes to the most outstanding college football player at the end of the football season each year.

Web site: <www.heisman.com>.

YEAR	WINNER	COLLEGE	POSITION	YEAR	WINNER	COLLEGE	POSITION
1935	Jay Berwanger	Chicago	HB	1953	John Lattner	Notre Dame	HB
1936	Larry Kelley	Yale	E	1954	Alan Ameche	Wisconsin	FB
1937	Clint Frank	Yale	HB	1955	Howard Cassady	Ohio State	HB
1938	Davey O'Brien	Texas Christian	QB	1956	Paul Hornung	Notre Dame	QB
1939	Nile Kinnick	Iowa	HB	1957	John David Crow	Texas A&M	HB
1940	Tom Harmon	Michigan	HB	1958	Pete Dawkins	Army	HB
1941	Bruce Smith	Minnesota	HB	1959	Billy Cannon	Louisiana State	HB
1942	Frank Sinkwich	Georgia	HB	1960	Joe Bellino	Navy	HB
1943	Angelo Bertelli	Notre Dame	QB	1961	Ernie Davis	Syracuse	HB
1944	Les Horvath	Ohio State	QB	1962	Terry Baker	Oregon State	QB
1945	Felix Blanchard	Army	FB	1963	Roger Staubach	Navy	QB
1946	Glenn Davis	Army	HB	1964	John Huarte	Notre Dame	QB
1947	John Lujack	Notre Dame	QB	1965	Mike Garrett	Southern California	HB
1948	Doak Walker	Southern Methodist	HB	1966	Steve Spurrier	Florida	QB
1949	Leon Hart	Notre Dame	E	1967	Gary Beban	UCLA	QB
1950	Vic Janowicz	Ohio State	HB	1968	O.J. Simpson	Southern California	HB
1951	Dick Kazmaier	Princeton	HB	1969	Steve Owens	Oklahoma	HB
1952	Billy Vessels	Oklahoma	HB	1970	Jim Plunkett	Stanford	QB

Heisman Trophy (continued)

YEAR	WINNER	COLLEGE	POSITION	YEAR	WINNER	COLLEGE	POSITION
1971	Pat Sullivan	Auburn	QB	1990	Ty Detmer	Brigham Young	QB
1972	Johnny Rodgers	Nebraska	RB	1991	Desmond Howard	Michigan	WR
1973	John Cappelletti	Penn State	HB	1992	Gino Torretta	Miami	QB
1974	Archie Griffin	Ohio State	HB	1993	Charlie Ward	Florida State	QB
1975	Archie Griffin	Ohio State	HB	1994	Rashaan Salaam	Colorado	TB
1976	Tony Dorsett	Pittsburgh	HB	1995	Eddie George	Ohio State	RB
1977	Earl Campbell	Texas	HB	1996	Danny Wuerffel	Florida	QB
1978	Billy Sims	Oklahoma	HB	1997	Charles Woodson	Michigan	DB
1979	Charles White	Southern California	HB	1998	Ricky Williams	Texas	RB
1980	George Rogers	South Carolina	HB	1999	Ron Dayne	Wisconsin	RB
1981	Marcus Allen	Southern California	HB	2000	Chris Weinke	Florida State	QB
1982	Herschel Walker	Georgia	HB	2001	Eric Crouch	Nebraska	QB
1983	Mike Rozier	Nebraska	HB	2002	Carson Palmer	Southern California	QB
1984	Doug Flutie	Boston College	QB	2003	Jason White	Oklahoma	QB
1985	Bo Jackson	Auburn	HB	2004	Matt Leinart	Southern California	QB
1986	Vinny Testaverde	Miami (FL)	QB	2005	Reggie Bush	Southern California	RB
1987	Tim Brown	Notre Dame	WR	2006	Troy Smith	Ohio State	QB
1988	Barry Sanders	Oklahoma State	RB	2007	Tim Tebow	Florida	QB
1989	Andre Ware	Houston	QB	2008	Sam Bradford	Oklahoma	QB

Canadian Football League Grey Cup

Held since 1909. Table shows results for the past 20 years.

YEAR	WINNER	RUNNER-UP	SCORE
1989	Saskatchewan Roughriders (WD)	Hamilton Tiger-Cats (ED)	43–40
1990	Winnipeg Blue Bombers (ED)	Edmonton Eskimos (WD)	50–11
1991	Toronto Argonauts (ED)	Calgary Stampeders (WD)	36–21
1992	Calgary Stampeders (WD)	Winnipeg Blue Bombers (ED)	24–10
1993	Edmonton Eskimos (WD)	Winnipeg Blue Bombers (ED)	33–23
1994	British Columbia Lions (WD)	Baltimore Stallions (ED)	26–23
1995[1]	Baltimore Stallions (SD)	Calgary Stampeders (ND)	37–20
1996	Toronto Argonauts (ED)	Edmonton Eskimos (WD)	43–37
1997	Toronto Argonauts (ED)	Saskatchewan Roughriders (WD)	47–23
1998	Calgary Stampeders (WD)	Hamilton Tiger-Cats (ED)	26–24
1999	Hamilton Tiger-Cats (ED)	Calgary Stampeders (WD)	32–21
2000	British Columbia Lions (WD)	Montreal Alouettes (ED)	28–26
2001	Calgary Stampeders (WD)	Winnipeg Blue Bombers (ED)	27–19
2002	Montreal Alouettes (ED)	Edmonton Eskimos (WD)	25–16
2003	Edmonton Eskimos (WD)	Montreal Alouettes (ED)	34–22
2004	Toronto Argonauts (ED)	British Columbia Lions (WD)	27–19
2005	Edmonton Eskimos (WD)	Montreal Alouettes (ED)	38–35
2006	British Columbia Lions (WD)	Montreal Alouettes (ED)	25–14
2007	Saskatchewan Roughriders (WD)	Winnipeg Blue Bombers (ED)	23–19
2008	Calgary Stampeders (WD)	Montreal Alouettes (ED)	22–14

[1]In 1995 only, the divisions were reconfigured and renamed Northern and Southern in response to the inclusion of American teams in the CFL (1993–96).

Australian Football League Final Standings, 2008[1]

Teams that qualified for play-offs only.

TEAM	WON	LOST	TIED	POINTS	TEAM	WON	LOST	TIED	POINTS
Geelong Cats	21	1	0	84	Sydney Swans	12	9	1	50
Hawthorn Hawks	17	5	0	68	North Melbourne Kangaroos	12	9	1	50
Western Bulldogs	15	6	1	62	Collingwood Magpies	12	10	0	48
St. Kilda Saints	13	9	0	52					
Adelaide Crows	13	9	0	52					

[1]The Hawthorn Hawks were the 2008 champions.

Rugby World Cup

YEAR	WINNER	RUNNER-UP	SCORE	YEAR	WINNER	RUNNER-UP	SCORE
1987	New Zealand	France	29–9	1999	Australia	France	35–12
1991	Australia	England	12–6	2003	England	Australia	20–17
1995	South Africa	New Zealand	15–12	2007	South Africa	England	15–6

Rugby League World Cup

YEAR	WINNER	RUNNER-UP	SCORE	YEAR	WINNER	RUNNER-UP	SCORE
1954	Great Britain	France	16–12	1977[3]	Australia	Great Britain	13–12
1957	Australia	Great Britain	[1]	1988	Australia	New Zealand	25–12
1960	Great Britain	Australia	[1]	1992	Australia	Great Britain	10–6
1968	Australia	France	20–2	1995	Australia	England	16–8
1970	Australia	Great Britain	12–7	2000	Australia	New Zealand	40–12
1972	Great Britain	Australia	10–10[2]	2008	New Zealand	Australia	34–20
1975[3]	Australia	England	[1]				

[1]Tournament played without a grand final match; winner determined by match points.   [2]Great Britain won on match points.   [3]Called International Championship from 1975 to 1977.

Super 14 Rugby Final Standings, 2009[1]

Super 12 until 2006. Four points are awarded for a win and two for a draw; one bonus point is given for a loss by seven points or fewer and one for a team that scores four or more tries.

TEAM (COUNTRY)	POINTS	W	L	D	BONUS	TEAM (COUNTRY)	POINTS	W	L	D	BONUS
Bulls (RSA)	46	10	3	0	6	Western Force (AUS)	36	6	6	1	10
Chiefs (NZL)	45	9	4	0	9	Blues (NZL)	32	5	8	0	12
Hurricanes (NZL)	44	9	4	0	8	Stormers (RSA)	27	5	8	0	7
Crusaders (NZL)	41	8	4	1	7	Highlanders (NZL)	26	4	8	0	10
New South Wales Waratahs (AUS)	41	9	4	0	5	Lions (RSA)	25	4	9	0	9
						Queensland Reds (AUS)	19	3	10	0	7
Sharks (RSA)	38	8	5	0	6	Central Cheetahs (RSA)	12	2	11	0	4
Brumbies (AUS)	38	8	5	0	6						

[1]The Bulls were the 2009 champions.

Six Nations Championship

Held since 1883; Five Nations in 1947–99. Round-robin tournament, usually ending in April.

YEAR	WINNER	YEAR	WINNER	YEAR	WINNER
1947	England; Wales[1]	1968	France[2]	1989	France
1948	Ireland[2,3]	1969	Wales[3]	1990	Scotland[2,3]
1949	Ireland[3]	1970	France; Wales[1]	1991	England[2,3]
1950	Wales[2,3]	1971	Wales[2,3]	1992	England[2,3]
1951	Ireland	1972	not completed	1993	France
1952	Wales[2,3]	1973	quintuple tie	1994	Wales
1953	England	1974	Ireland	1995	England[2,3]
1954	England[3]; France; Wales[1]	1975	Wales	1996	England[3]
1955	France; Wales[1]	1976	Wales[2,3]	1997	France[2,5]
1956	Wales	1977	France[2,4]	1998	France[2,5]
1957	England[2,3]	1978	Wales[2,3]	1999	Scotland
1958	England	1979	Wales[3]	2000	England
1959	France	1980	England[2,3]	2001	England
1960	England[3]; France[1]	1981	France[2]	2002	France[2,5]
1961	France	1982	Ireland[3]	2003	England[2,3]
1962	France	1983	France; Ireland[1]	2004	France[2,6]
1963	England	1984	Scotland[2,3]	2005	Wales[2,3]
1964	Scotland; Wales[1]	1985	Ireland[3]	2006	France[6]
1965	Wales[3]	1986	France; Scotland[1]	2007	France[6]
1966	Wales	1987	France[2]	2008	Wales[2,3]
1967	France	1988	France; Wales[1,3]	2009	Ireland[2,3]

[1]Tied.   [2]Grand Slam winner (defeats all other competitors).   [3]Triple Crown winner (Home Nation [England, Ireland, Scotland, Wales] that defeats all three other Home Nations).   [4]Triple Crown won by Wales.   [5]Triple Crown won by England.   [6]Triple Crown won by Ireland.

FIFA World Cup——Men

YEAR	WINNER	RUNNER-UP	SCORE	YEAR	WINNER	RUNNER-UP	SCORE
1930	Uruguay	Argentina	4–2	1958	Brazil	Sweden	5–2
1934	Italy	Czechoslovakia	2–1	1962	Brazil	Czechoslovakia	3–1
1938	Italy	Hungary	4–2	1966	England	West Germany	4–2
1950	Uruguay	Brazil	2–1	1970	Brazil	Italy	4–1
1954	West Germany	Hungary	3–2	1974	West Germany	The Netherlands	2–1

FIFA World Cup—Men (continued)

YEAR	WINNER	RUNNER-UP	SCORE	YEAR	WINNER	RUNNER-UP	SCORE
1978	Argentina	The Netherlands	3-1	1994	Brazil	Italy	0-0 (3-2[1])
1982	Italy	West Germany	3-1	1998	France	Brazil	3-0
1986	Argentina	West Germany	3-2	2002	Brazil	Germany	2-0
1990	West Germany	Argentina	1-0	2006	Italy	France	1-1 (5-3[1])

[1]Won in a penalty kick shoot-out.

FIFA World Cup—Women

YEAR	WINNER	RUNNER-UP	SCORE	YEAR	WINNER	RUNNER-UP	SCORE
1991	United States	Norway	2-1	2003	Germany	Sweden	2-1
1995	Norway	Germany	2-0	2007	Germany	Brazil	2-0
1999	United States	China	0-0 (5-4[1])				

[1]Won in a penalty kick shoot-out.

UEFA Champions League

Held since 1955 and known until 1992–93 as the European Champion Clubs' Cup; played on a knockout basis until 1992–93 and as a combination of group and knockout rounds since then.
Table shows results for the past 20 years.

SEASON	WINNER (COUNTRY)	RUNNER-UP (COUNTRY)	SCORE
1989-90	AC Milan (ITA)	SL Benfica (POR)	1-0
1990-91	FK Crvena Zvezda Beograd (YUG)	Olympique de Marseille (FRA)	0-0 (5-3[1])
1991-92	FC Barcelona (ESP)	Sampdoria UC (ITA)	1-0
1992-93	Olympique de Marseille (FRA)	AC Milan (ITA)	1-0
1993-94	AC Milan (ITA)	FC Barcelona (ESP)	4-0
1994-95	AFC Ajax (NED)	AC Milan (ITA)	1-0
1995-96	Juventus FC (ITA)	AFC Ajax (NED)	1-1 (4-2[1])
1996-97	BV Borussia Dortmund (GER)	Juventus FC (ITA)	3-1
1997-98	Real Madrid CF (ESP)	Juventus FC (ITA)	1-0
1998-99	Manchester United (ENG)	FC Bayern München (GER)	2-1
1999-2000	Real Madrid CF (ESP)	Valencia CF (ESP)	3-0
2000-01	FC Bayern München (GER)	Valencia CF (ESP)	1-1 (5-4[1])
2001-02	Real Madrid CF (ESP)	Bayer 04 Leverkusen (GER)	2-1
2002-03	AC Milan (ITA)	Juventus FC (ITA)	0-0 (3-2[1])
2003-04	FC Porto (POR)	AS Monaco (FRA)	3-0
2004-05	Liverpool FC (ENG)	AC Milan (ITA)	3-3 (3-2[1])
2005-06	FC Barcelona (ESP)	Arsenal FC (ENG)	2-1
2006-07	AC Milan (ITA)	Liverpool FC (ENG)	2-1
2007-08	Manchester United (ENG)	Chelsea FC (ENG)	1-1 (6-5[1])
2008-09	FC Barcelona (ESP)	Manchester United (ENG)	2-0

[1]Won in a penalty kick shoot-out.

UEFA European Championship

YEAR	WINNING TEAM	RUNNER-UP	SCORE
1960	USSR	Yugoslavia	2-1
1964	Spain	USSR	2-1
1968	Italy	Yugoslavia	2-0
1972	West Germany	USSR	3-0
1976	Czechoslovakia	West Germany	2-2
1980	West Germany	Belgium	2-1
1984	France	Spain	2-0
1988	The Netherlands	USSR	2-0
1992	Denmark	Germany	2-0
1996	Germany	Czech Republic	2-1
2000	France	Italy	2-1
2004	Greece	Portugal	1-0
2008	Spain	Germany	1-0

UEFA Cup

The UEFA Cup is considered Europe's second most important football competition. Established in the 1971–72 season, the Cup was restructured when the UEFA Cup Winners' Cup was abolished after the 1998–99 season. Originally played on an entirely two-legged basis, since 1998 the competition has concluded with a single match. The Cup competition is open to top- and second-ranked teams in each country's league as well as to the winners of domestic cups.

SEASON	WINNER (COUNTRY)	RUNNER-UP (COUNTRY)	SCORES
1971–72	Tottenham Hotspur FC (ENG)	Wolverhampton Wanderers FC (ENG)	2–1, 1–1
1972–73	Liverpool FC (ENG)	VfL Borussia Mönchengladbach (FRG)	3–0, 0–2
1973–74	Feyenoord (NED)	Tottenham Hotspur FC (ENG)	2–2, 2–0
1974–75	VfL Borussia Mönchengladbach (FRG)	FC Twente (NED)	0–0, 5–1
1975–76	Liverpool FC (ENG)	Club Brugge KV (BEL)	3–2, 1–1
1976–77	Juventus FC (ITA)	Athletic Club Bilbao (ESP)	1–0, 1–2
1977–78	PSV Eindhoven (NED)	SC Bastia (FRA)	0–0, 3–0
1978–79	VfL Borussia Mönchengladbach (FRG)	FK Crvena Zvezda Beograd (YUG)	1–1, 1–0
1979–80	Eintracht Frankfurt (FRG)	VfL Borussia Mönchengladbach (FRG)	2–3, 1–0
1980–81	Ipswich Town FC (ENG)	AZ Alkmaar (NED)	3–0, 2–4
1981–82	IFK Göteborg (SWE)	Hamburger SV (FRG)	1–0, 3–0
1982–83	RSC Anderlecht (BEL)	SL Benfica (POR)	1–0, 1–1
1983–84	Tottenham Hotspur FC (ENG)	RSC Anderlecht (BEL)	1–1, 1–1 (4–3[1])
1984–85	Real Madrid CF (ESP)	Videoton FCF (HUN)	3–0, 0–1
1985–86	Real Madrid CF (ESP)	1. FC Köln (FRG)	5–1, 0–2
1986–87	IFK Göteborg (SWE)	Dundee United FC (SCO)	1–0, 1–1
1987–88	Bayer 04 Leverkusen (FRG)	RCD Espanyol (ESP)	0–3, 3–0 (3–2[1])
1988–89	SSC Napoli (ITA)	VfB Stuttgart (FRG)	2–1, 3–3
1989–90	Juventus FC (ITA)	AC Fiorentina (ITA)	3–1, 0–0
1990–91	Internazionale FC (ITA)	AS Roma (ITA)	2–0, 0–1
1991–92	AFC Ajax (NED)	Torino Calcio (ITA)	2–2, 0–0
1992–93	Juventus FC (ITA)	BV Borussia Dortmund (GER)	3–1, 3–0
1993–94	Internazionale FC (ITA)	SV Austria Salzburg (AUT)	1–0, 1–0
1994–95	Parma AC (ITA)	Juventus FC (ITA)	1–0, 1–1
1995–96	FC Bayern München (GER)	FC Girondins de Bordeaux (FRA)	2–0, 3–1
1996–97	FC Schalke 04 (GER)	Internazionale FC (ITA)	1–0, 0–1 (4–1[1])
1997–98	Internazionale FC (ITA)	SS Lazio (ITA)	3–0
1998–99	Parma AC (ITA)	Olympique de Marseille (FRA)	3–0
1999–2000	Galatasaray SK (TUR)	Arsenal FC (ENG)	0–0 (4–1[1])
2000–01	Liverpool FC (ENG)	Deportivo Alavés (ESP)	5–4
2001–02	Feyenoord (NED)	BV Borussia Dortmund (GER)	3–2
2002–03	FC Porto (POR)	Celtic FC (SCO)	3–2[2]
2003–04	Valencia CF (ESP)	Olympique de Marseille (FRA)	2–0
2004–05	CSKA Moscow (RUS)	Sporting (POR)	3–1
2005–06	Sevilla FC (ESP)	Middlesbrough FC (ENG)	4–0
2006–07	Sevilla FC (ESP)	RCD Espanyol (ESP)	2–2 (3–1[1])
2007–08	FC Zenit St. Petersburg (RUS)	Rangers FC (SCO)	2–0
2008–09	Shakhtar Donetsk (UKR)	Werder Bremen (GER)	2–1[2]

[1]Won in a penalty kick shoot-out. [2]Won on "silver goal" in overtime.

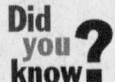

Orlando Cepeda, a star player in Major League Baseball for the Giants, Cardinals, and Braves from the late '50s to the early '70s, was superstitious about his bats, believing that every bat had only one good hit in it. Consequently, he used a different bat for each of his 2,351 lifetime hits.

Copa Libertadores de América

Held since 1960. Table shows results for the past 20 years.

YEAR	WINNER (COUNTRY)	RUNNER-UP (COUNTRY)	SCORES
1990	Olímpia (PAR)	Barcelona (ECU)	2–0, 1–1
1991	Colo Colo (CHI)	Olímpia (PAR)	0–0, 3–0
1992	São Paulo (BRA)	Newell's Old Boys (ARG)	0–1, 1–0 (3–2[1])
1993	São Paulo (BRA)	Universidad Católica (CHI)	5–1, 0–2
1994	Vélez Sársfield (ARG)	São Paulo (BRA)	1–0, 0–1 (5–4[1])
1995	Grêmio (BRA)	Atlético Nacional (COL)	3–1, 1–1
1996	River Plate (ARG)	América de Cali (COL)	0–1, 2–0

Copa Libertadores de América (continued)

YEAR	WINNER (COUNTRY)	RUNNER-UP (COUNTRY)	SCORES
1997	Cruzeiro (BRA)	Sporting Cristal (PER)	0-0, 1-0
1998	Vasco da Gama (BRA)	Barcelona (ECU)	2-0, 2-1
1999	Palmeiras (BRA)	Deportiva Cali (COL)	0-1, 2-1 (4-3[1])
2000	Boca Juniors (ARG)	Palmeiras (BRA)	2-2, 0-0 (4-2[1])
2001	Boca Juniors (ARG)	Cruz Azul (MEX)	1-0, 0-1 (3-1[1])
2002	Olímpia (PAR)	São Caetano (BRA)	0-1, 2-1 (4-2[1])
2003	Boca Juniors (ARG)	Santos (BRA)	2-0, 3-1
2004	Once Caldas (COL)	Boca Juniors (ARG)	0-0, 1-1 (2-0[1])
2005	São Paulo (BRA)	Atlético Paranaense (BRA)	1-1, 4-0
2006	Internacional (BRA)	São Paulo (BRA)	2-1, 2-2
2007	Boca Juniors (ARG)	Grêmio (BRA)	3-0, 2-0
2008	Liga de Quito (ECU)	Fluminense (BRA)	4-2, 1-3 (3-1[1])
2009	Estudiantes de la Plata (ARG)	Cruzeiro (BRA)	0-0, 2-1

[1]*Won in a penalty kick shoot-out.*

Copa América

Held since 1916. Table shows results for past 20 years. The cup was contested by rounds in 1989 and 1991 (scores are shown here as winner's wins/losses/draws in final round) and by a final championship match from 1993.

YEAR	WINNER	RUNNER-UP	SCORE	YEAR	WINNER	RUNNER-UP	SCORE
1989	Brazil	Uruguay	3/0/0	1999	Brazil	Uruguay	3-0
1991	Argentina	Brazil	4/0/0	2001	Colombia	Mexico	1-0
1993	Argentina	Mexico	2-1	2003	postponed until 2004		
1995	Uruguay	Brazil	1-1 (4-2[1])	2004	Brazil	Argentina	2-2 (2-0[1])
1997	Brazil	Bolivia	3-1	2007	Brazil	Argentina	3-0

[1]*Won in a penalty kick shoot-out.*

Asian Cup

Scored on a points (percentage of wins) system until 1972.

YEAR	WINNER	RUNNER-UP	SCORE	YEAR	WINNER	RUNNER-UP	SCORE
1956	Rep. of Korea	Israel	83.3	1984	Saudi Arabia	China	2-0
1960	Rep. of Korea	Israel	100	1988	Saudi Arabia	Rep. of Korea	0-0 (4-3[1])
1964	Israel	India	100	1992	Japan	Saudi Arabia	1-0
1968	Iran	Burma	100	1996	Saudi Arabia	United Arab Emirates	0-0 (4-2[1])
1972	Iran	Rep. of Korea	2-1	2000	Japan	Saudi Arabia	1-0
1976	Iran	Kuwait	1-0	2004	Japan	China	3-1
1980	Kuwait	Rep. of Korea	3-0	2007	Iraq	Saudi Arabia	1-0

[1]*Won in a penalty kick shoot-out.*

African Cup of Nations

YEAR	WINNER	RUNNER-UP	SCORE	YEAR	WINNER	RUNNER-UP	SCORE
1957	Egypt	Ethiopia	4-0	1984	Cameroon	Nigeria	3-1
1959	Egypt	The Sudan	2-1	1986	Egypt	Cameroon	0-0 (5-4[3])
1962	Ethiopia	Egypt	4-2	1988	Cameroon	Nigeria	1-0
1963	Ghana	The Sudan	3-0	1990	Algeria	Nigeria	1-0
1965	Ghana	Tunisia	3-2	1992	Côte d'Ivoire	Ghana	0-0 (11-10[3])
1968	Dem. Rep. of the Congo	Ghana	1-0	1994	Nigeria	Zambia	2-1
1970	The Sudan	Ghana	1-0	1996	South Africa	Tunisia	2-0
1972	Rep. of the Congo	Mali	3-2	1998	Egypt	South Africa	2-0
1974	Zaire	Zambia	2-2, 2-0[1]	2000	Cameroon	Nigeria	2-2 (4-3[3])
1976	Morocco	Guinea	1-1[2]	2002	Cameroon	Senegal	0-0 (3-2[3])
1978	Ghana	Uganda	2-0	2004	Tunisia	Morocco	2-1
1980	Nigeria	Algeria	3-0	2006	Egypt	Côte d'Ivoire	0-0 (4-2[3])
1982	Ghana	Libya	1-1 (7-6[3])	2008	Egypt	Cameroon	1-0

[1]*Game replayed.*   [2]*Won via group format.*   [3]*Won in a penalty kick shoot-out.*

Major League Soccer Cup

YEAR	WINNER	RUNNER-UP	SCORE	YEAR	WINNER	RUNNER-UP	SCORE
1996	DC United	Los Angeles Galaxy	3–2 (OT)	2003	San Jose Earthquakes	Chicago Fire	4–2
1997	DC United	Colorado Rapids	2–1	2004	DC United	Kansas City Wizards	3–2
1998	Chicago Fire	DC United	2–0				
1999	DC United	Los Angeles Galaxy	2–0	2005	Los Angeles Galaxy	New England Revolution	1–0 (OT)
2000	Kansas City Wizards	Chicago Fire	1–0				
2001	San Jose Earthquakes	Los Angeles Galaxy	2–1 (OT)	2006	Houston Dynamo	New England Revolution	4–3 (OT)
2002	Los Angeles Galaxy	New England Revolution	1–0	2007	Houston Dynamo	New England Revolution	2–1
				2008	Columbus Crew	New York Red Bulls	3–1

Golf

In individual events, three of the four major men's golf championships, the **British and US Open tournaments** and the **Professional Golfers' Association Championship**, are played annually at a variety of golf courses over 72 holes, and each is preceded by qualifying rounds. The fourth major, the invitational **Masters Tournament**, is held annually at the Augusta [GA] National Golf Course. Events for amateurs include the **US and British Amateur championships**. In 2007 the **Professional Golf Association** (PGA) inaugurated the **FedExCup**, a season-long competition in which players accumulate points based on their performances in various PGA events (including the major tournaments, which are weighted more heavily), participate in a four-week play-off, and determine the FedExCup champion at a final Tour Championship.

Women's golf has been around nearly as long as men's golf, but until the late 1940s, it was limited to amateurs. Thus, for women, the **British and US Amateur championships** were the major tournaments. The **US Women's Open Championship** was started in 1946, and the **Ladies Professional Golf Association** (LPGA) was formed in 1950. Since that time women's professional golf has flourished. In 1976 the **Women's British Open Championship** was added to the golf calendar.

In team events, the **Ryder Cup** was originally a biennial match between the US and Great Britain, but beginning in 1979 it was expanded into a biennial match between the United States and Europe. Teams of British and US women golfers compete every two years for the **Curtis Cup**, which since 1964 has involved two days' play of three 18-hole foursomes and six 18-hole singles. The **Solheim Cup**, the women's professional team tournament, had been played in even-numbered years since 1990 but was moved to odd-numbered years (beginning in 2003) following the rescheduling of the Ryder Cup because of the events of 11 Sep 2001.

Related Web sites: United States Golf Association: <www.usga.org>; Professional Golf Association: <www.pgatour.com>; Ladies Professional Golf Association: <www.lpga.com>.

FedExCup

In 2007 the PGA inaugurated the FedExCup, a season-long competition in which players accumulate points based on their performances in various PGA events throughout the year. In a standard (non-major) tournament, for instance, 3,513 points are awarded, with the winner receiving 500 points, a runner-up receiving 300 points, and so on. The four major tournaments award 3,776 points, with 600 going to the winner. The cumulative total of points each player has received during the regular season determines that player's seed going into a four-tournament play-off at the end of the year, for which the top 125 players are eligible. A progressive cut through the first three of these play-off events determines the players who qualify for the final competition, the Tour Championship, which determines the FedExCup champion. The winner of each of the play-offs receives 2,500 points, the second-place finisher 1,500, and so on. The points are reset for the Tour Championship, with the leader at the end of the first three play-offs starting with 2,500 points, the player in second place receiving 2,250, and so on. The player with the most points at the end of the Tour Championship becomes the FedExCup champion and is awarded US$10 million, US$1 million of which is deferred into a retirement fund, making this the largest single bonus payout in professional sports. (In 2007 the entire US$10 million awarded to the winner was deferred.) Tiger Woods was the inaugural FedExCup champion. Vijay Singh of Fiji won the cup in 2008.

Masters Tournament

Won by an American golfer except as indicated.

YEAR	WINNER	YEAR	WINNER	YEAR	WINNER
1934	Horton Smith	1937	Byron Nelson	1940	Jimmy Demaret
1935	Gene Sarazen	1938	Henry Picard	1941	Craig Wood
1936	Horton Smith	1939	Ralph Guldahl	1942	Byron Nelson

Masters Tournament (continued)

YEAR	WINNER	YEAR	WINNER	YEAR	WINNER
1943–45	*not held*	1967	Gay Brewer	1989	Nick Faldo (ENG)
1946	Herman Keiser	1968	Bob Goalby	1990	Nick Faldo (ENG)
1947	Jimmy Demaret	1969	George Archer	1991	Ian Woosnam (WAL)
1948	Claude Harmon	1970	Billy Casper	1992	Fred Couples
1949	Sam Snead	1971	Charles Coody	1993	Bernhard Langer (GER)
1950	Jimmy Demaret	1972	Jack Nicklaus	1994	José María Olazábal (ESP)
1951	Ben Hogan	1973	Tommy Aaron	1995	Ben Crenshaw
1952	Sam Snead	1974	Gary Player (RSA)	1996	Nick Faldo (ENG)
1953	Ben Hogan	1975	Jack Nicklaus	1997	Tiger Woods
1954	Sam Snead	1976	Raymond Floyd	1998	Mark O'Meara
1955	Cary Middlecoff	1977	Tom Watson	1999	José María Olazábal (ESP)
1956	Jack Burke	1978	Gary Player (RSA)	2000	Vijay Singh (FIJ)
1957	Doug Ford	1979	Fuzzy Zoeller	2001	Tiger Woods
1958	Arnold Palmer	1980	Seve Ballesteros (ESP)	2002	Tiger Woods
1959	Art Wall	1981	Tom Watson	2003	Mike Weir (CAN)
1960	Arnold Palmer	1982	Craig Stadler	2004	Phil Mickelson
1961	Gary Player (RSA)	1983	Seve Ballesteros (ESP)	2005	Tiger Woods
1962	Arnold Palmer	1984	Ben Crenshaw	2006	Phil Mickelson
1963	Jack Nicklaus	1985	Bernhard Langer (FRG)	2007	Zach Johnson
1964	Arnold Palmer	1986	Jack Nicklaus	2008	Trevor Immelman (RSA)
1965	Jack Nicklaus	1987	Larry Mize	2009	Ángel Cabrera (ARG)
1966	Jack Nicklaus	1988	Sandy Lyle (SCO)		

United States Open Championship—Men

Won by an American golfer except as indicated.

YEAR	WINNER	YEAR	WINNER	YEAR	WINNER
1895	Horace Rawlins	1933	John Goodman	1973	Johnny Miller
1896	James Foulis	1934	Olin Dutra	1974	Hale Irwin
1897	Joe Lloyd	1935	Sam Parks, Jr.	1975	Lou Graham
1898	Fred Herd	1936	Tony Manero	1976	Jerry Pate
1899	Willie Smith	1937	Ralph Guldahl	1977	Hubert Green
1900	Harry Vardon (ENG)	1938	Ralph Guldahl	1978	Andy North
1901	Willie Anderson	1939	Byron Nelson	1979	Hale Irwin
1902	Laurence Auchterlonie	1940	Lawson Little	1980	Jack Nicklaus
1903	Willie Anderson	1941	Craig Wood	1981	David Graham (AUS)
1904	Willie Anderson	1942–45	*not held*	1982	Tom Watson
1905	Willie Anderson	1946	Lloyd Mangrum	1983	Larry Nelson
1906	Alex Smith	1947	Lew Worsham	1984	Fuzzy Zoeller
1907	Alex Ross	1948	Ben Hogan	1985	Andy North
1908	Fred McLeod	1949	Cary Middlecoff	1986	Raymond Floyd
1909	George Sargent	1950	Ben Hogan	1987	Scott Simpson
1910	Alex Smith	1951	Ben Hogan	1988	Curtis Strange
1911	John J. McDermott	1952	Julius Boros	1989	Curtis Strange
1912	John J. McDermott	1953	Ben Hogan	1990	Hale Irwin
1913	Francis Ouimet	1954	Ed Furgol	1991	Payne Stewart
1914	Walter Hagen	1955	Jack Fleck	1992	Tom Kite
1915	Jerome D. Travers	1956	Cary Middlecoff	1993	Lee Janzen
1916	Chick Evans	1957	Dick Mayer	1994	Ernie Els (RSA)
1917–18	*not held*	1958	Tommy Bolt	1995	Corey Pavin
1919	Walter Hagen	1959	Billy Casper	1996	Steve Jones
1920	Edward Ray (ENG)	1960	Arnold Palmer	1997	Ernie Els (RSA)
1921	James M. Barnes	1961	Gene Littler	1998	Lee Janzen
1922	Gene Sarazen	1962	Jack Nicklaus	1999	Payne Stewart
1923	Bobby Jones	1963	Julius Boros	2000	Tiger Woods
1924	Cyril Walker	1964	Ken Venturi	2001	Retief Goosen (RSA)
1925	Willie MacFarlane, Jr.	1965	Gary Player (RSA)	2002	Tiger Woods
1926	Bobby Jones	1966	Billy Casper	2003	Jim Furyk
1927	Tommy Armour	1967	Jack Nicklaus	2004	Retief Goosen (RSA)
1928	Johnny Farrell	1968	Lee Trevino	2005	Michael Campbell (NZL)
1929	Bobby Jones	1969	Orville Moody	2006	Geoff Ogilvy (AUS)
1930	Bobby Jones	1970	Tony Jacklin (ENG)	2007	Ángel Cabrera (ARG)
1931	Billy Burke	1971	Lee Trevino	2008	Tiger Woods
1932	Gene Sarazen	1972	Jack Nicklaus	2009	Lucas Glover

British Open Tournament—Men

Won by an English golfer unless otherwise indicated.

YEAR	WINNER	YEAR	WINNER	YEAR	WINNER
1860	Willie Park, Sr. (SCO)	1907	Arnaud Massy (FRA)	1963	Bob Charles (NZL)
1861	Tom Morris, Sr. (SCO)	1908	James Braid (SCO)	1964	Tony Lema (USA)
1862	Tom Morris, Sr. (SCO)	1909	John H. Taylor	1965	Peter Thomson (AUS)
1863	Willie Park, Sr. (SCO)	1910	James Braid (SCO)	1966	Jack Nicklaus (USA)
1864	Tom Morris, Sr. (SCO)	1911	Harry Vardon (JEY)	1967	Roberto de Vicenzo (ARG)
1865	Andrew Strath (SCO)	1912	Ted Ray (JEY)	1968	Gary Player (RSA)
1866	Willie Park, Sr. (SCO)	1913	John H. Taylor	1969	Tony Jacklin
1867	Tom Morris, Sr. (SCO)	1914	Harry Vardon (JEY)	1970	Jack Nicklaus (USA)
1868	Tom Morris, Jr. (SCO)	1915–19 *not held*		1971	Lee Trevino (USA)
1869	Tom Morris, Jr. (SCO)	1920	George Duncan (SCO)	1972	Lee Trevino (USA)
1870	Tom Morris, Jr. (SCO)	1921	Jock Hutchison (USA)	1973	Tom Weiskopf (USA)
1871	*not held*	1922	Walter Hagen (USA)	1974	Gary Player (RSA)
1872	Tom Morris, Jr. (SCO)	1923	Arthur Havers	1975	Tom Watson (USA)
1873	Tom Kidd (SCO)	1924	Walter Hagen (USA)	1976	Johnny Miller (USA)
1874	Mungo Park (SCO)	1925	James Barnes (USA)	1977	Tom Watson (USA)
1875	Willie Park, Sr. (SCO)	1926	Bobby Jones (USA)	1978	Jack Nicklaus (USA)
1876	Bob Martin (SCO)	1927	Bobby Jones (USA)	1979	Seve Ballesteros (ESP)
1877	Jamie Anderson (SCO)	1928	Walter Hagen (USA)	1980	Tom Watson (USA)
1878	Jamie Anderson (SCO)	1929	Walter Hagen (USA)	1981	Bill Rogers (USA)
1879	Jamie Anderson (SCO)	1930	Bobby Jones (USA)	1982	Tom Watson (USA)
1880	Robert Ferguson (SCO)	1931	Tommy Armour (USA)	1983	Tom Watson (USA)
1881	Robert Ferguson (SCO)	1932	Gene Sarazen (USA)	1984	Seve Ballesteros (ESP)
1882	Robert Ferguson (SCO)	1933	Denny Shute (USA)	1985	Sandy Lyle (SCO)
1883	Willie Fernie (SCO)	1934	Henry Cotton	1986	Greg Norman (AUS)
1884	Jack Simpson (SCO)	1935	Alfred Perry	1987	Nick Faldo
1885	Bob Martin (SCO)	1936	Alfred Padgham	1988	Seve Ballesteros (ESP)
1886	David Brown (SCO)	1937	Henry Cotton	1989	Mark Calcavecchia (USA)
1887	Willie Park, Jr. (SCO)	1938	Reg A. Whitcombe	1990	Nick Faldo
1888	Jack Burns (SCO)	1939	Richard Burton	1991	Ian Baker-Finch (AUS)
1889	Willie Park, Jr. (SCO)	1940–45 *not held*		1992	Nick Faldo
1890	John Ball	1946	Sam Snead (USA)	1993	Greg Norman (AUS)
1891	Hugh Kirkaldy (SCO)	1947	Fred Daly (NIR)	1994	Nick Price (ZIM)
1892	Harold Hilton	1948	Henry Cotton	1995	John Daly (USA)
1893	William Auchterlonie (SCO)	1949	Bobby Locke (RSA)	1996	Tom Lehman (USA)
1894	John H. Taylor	1950	Bobby Locke (RSA)	1997	Justin Leonard (USA)
1895	John H. Taylor	1951	Max Faulkner	1998	Mark O'Meara (USA)
1896	Harry Vardon (JEY)	1952	Bobby Locke (RSA)	1999	Paul Lawrie (SCO)
1897	Harold Hilton	1953	Ben Hogan (USA)	2000	Tiger Woods (USA)
1898	Harry Vardon (JEY)	1954	Peter Thomson (AUS)	2001	David Duval (USA)
1899	Harry Vardon (JEY)	1955	Peter Thomson (AUS)	2002	Ernie Els (RSA)
1900	John H. Taylor	1956	Peter Thomson (AUS)	2003	Ben Curtis (USA)
1901	James Braid (SCO)	1957	Bobby Locke (RSA)	2004	Todd Hamilton (USA)
1902	Sandy Herd (SCO)	1958	Peter Thomson (AUS)	2005	Tiger Woods (USA)
1903	Harry Vardon (JEY)	1959	Gary Player (RSA)	2006	Tiger Woods (USA)
1904	Jack White (SCO)	1960	Kel Nagle (AUS)	2007	Padraig Harrington (IRL)
1905	James Braid (SCO)	1961	Arnold Palmer (USA)	2008	Padraig Harrington (IRL)
1906	James Braid (SCO)	1962	Arnold Palmer (USA)	2009	Stewart Cink (USA)

US Professional Golfers' Association (PGA) Championship

Won by an American golfer except as indicated.

YEAR	WINNER	YEAR	WINNER	YEAR	WINNER
1916	James M. Barnes	1931	Tom Creavy	1945	Byron Nelson
1917–18 *not held*		1932	Olin Dutra	1946	Ben Hogan
1919	James M. Barnes	1933	Gene Sarazen	1947	Jim Ferrier
1920	Jock Hutchison	1934	Paul Runyan	1948	Ben Hogan
1921	Walter Hagen	1935	Johnny Revolta	1949	Sam Snead
1922	Gene Sarazen	1936	Denny Shute	1950	Chandler Harper
1923	Gene Sarazen	1937	Denny Shute	1951	Sam Snead
1924	Walter Hagen	1938	Paul Runyan	1952	Jim Turnesa
1925	Walter Hagen	1939	Henry Picard	1953	Walter Burkemo
1926	Walter Hagen	1940	Byron Nelson	1954	Chick Harbert
1927	Walter Hagen	1941	Vic Ghezzi	1955	Doug Ford
1928	Leo Diegel	1942	Sam Snead	1956	Jack Burke
1929	Leo Diegel	1943	*not held*	1957	Lionel Hebert
1930	Tommy Armour	1944	Bob Hamilton	1958	Dow Finsterwald

US Professional Golfers' Association (PGA) Championship (continued)

YEAR	WINNER	YEAR	WINNER	YEAR	WINNER
1959	Bob Rosburg	1976	Dave Stockton	1993	Paul Azinger
1960	Jay Hebert	1977	Lanny Wadkins	1994	Nick Price (ZIM)
1961	Jerry Barber	1978	John Mahaffey	1995	Steve Elkington (AUS)
1962	Gary Player (RSA)	1979	David Graham (AUS)	1996	Mark Brooks
1963	Jack Nicklaus	1980	Jack Nicklaus	1997	Davis Love III
1964	Bobby Nichols	1981	Larry Nelson	1998	Vijay Singh (FIJ)
1965	Dave Marr	1982	Raymond Floyd	1999	Tiger Woods
1966	Al Geiberger	1983	Hal Sutton	2000	Tiger Woods
1967	Don January	1984	Lee Trevino	2001	David Toms
1968	Julius Boros	1985	Hubert Green	2002	Rich Beems
1969	Raymond Floyd	1986	Bob Tway	2003	Shaun Micheel
1970	Dave Stockton	1987	Larry Nelson	2004	Vijay Singh (FIJ)
1971	Jack Nicklaus	1988	Jeff Sluman	2005	Phil Mickelson
1972	Gary Player (RSA)	1989	Payne Stewart	2006	Tiger Woods
1973	Jack Nicklaus	1990	Wayne Grady (AUS)	2007	Tiger Woods
1974	Lee Trevino	1991	John Daly	2008	Padraig Harrington (IRL)
1975	Jack Nicklaus	1992	Nick Price (ZIM)	2009	Y.E. Yang (KOR)

Ladies Professional Golf Association (LPGA) Championship

Won by an American golfer except as indicated.

YEAR	WINNER	YEAR	WINNER	YEAR	WINNER
1955	Beverly Hanson	1974	Sandra Haynie	1993	Patty Sheehan
1956	Marlene Hagge	1975	Kathy Whitworth	1994	Laura Davies (ENG)
1957	Louise Suggs	1976	Betty Burfeindt	1995	Kelly Robbins
1958	Mickey Wright	1977	Chako Higuchi	1996	Laura Davies (ENG)
1959	Betsy Rawls	1978	Nancy Lopez	1997	Chris Johnson
1960	Mickey Wright	1979	Donna Caponi	1998	Pak Se Ri (KOR)
1961	Mickey Wright	1980	Sally Little	1999	Juli Inkster
1962	Judy Kimball	1981	Donna Caponi	2000	Juli Inkster
1963	Mickey Wright	1982	Jan Stephenson (AUS)	2001	Karrie Webb (AUS)
1964	Mary Mills	1983	Patty Sheehan	2002	Pak Se Ri (KOR)
1965	Sandra Haynie	1984	Patty Sheehan	2003	Annika Sörenstam (SWE)
1966	Gloria Ehret	1985	Nancy Lopez	2004	Annika Sörenstam (SWE)
1967	Kathy Whitworth	1986	Pat Bradley	2005	Annika Sörenstam (SWE)
1968	Sandra Post	1987	Jane Geddes	2006	Pak Se Ri (KOR)
1969	Betsy Rawls	1988	Sherri Turner	2007	Suzann Pettersen (NOR)
1970	Shirley Englehorn	1989	Nancy Lopez	2008	Yani Tseng (TPE)
1971	Kathy Whitworth	1990	Beth Daniel	2009	Anna Nordqvist (SWE)
1972	Kathy Ahern	1991	Meg Mallon		
1973	Mary Mills	1992	Betsy King		

United States Women's Open Championship

Won by an American golfer except as indicated.

YEAR	WINNER	YEAR	WINNER	YEAR	WINNER
1946	Patty Berg	1962	Murle Breer	1980	Amy Alcott
1947	Betty Jameson	1963	Mary Mills	1981	Pat Bradley
1948	Babe Didrikson Zaharias	1964	Mickey Wright	1982	Janet Anderson
1949	Louise Suggs	1965	Carol Mann	1983	Jan Stephenson (AUS)
1950	Babe Didrikson Zaharias	1966	Sandra Spuzich	1984	Hollis Stacy
1951	Betsy Rawls	1967	Catherine Lacoste (FRA)	1985	Kathy Baker
1952	Louise Suggs	1968	Susie Berning	1986	Jane Geddes
1953	Betsy Rawls	1969	Donna Caponi	1987	Laura Davies (ENG)
1954	Babe Didrikson Zaharias	1970	Donna Caponi	1988	Liselotte Neumann (SWE)
1955	Fay Crocker	1971	JoAnne Carner	1989	Betsy King
1956	Kathy Cornelius	1972	Susie Berning	1990	Betsy King
1957	Betsy Rawls	1973	Susie Berning	1991	Meg Mallon
1958	Mickey Wright	1974	Sandra Haynie	1992	Patty Sheehan
1959	Mickey Wright	1975	Sandra Palmer	1993	Lauri Merten
1960	Betsy Rawls	1976	JoAnne Carner	1994	Patty Sheehan
1961	Mickey Wright	1977	Hollis Stacy	1995	Annika Sörenstam (SWE)
		1978	Hollis Stacy	1996	Annika Sörenstam (SWE)
		1979	Jerilyn Britz	1997	Alison Nicholas (ENG)
				1998	Pak Se Ri (KOR)

United States Women's Open Championship (continued)

YEAR	WINNER	YEAR	WINNER	YEAR	WINNER
1999	Juli Inkster	2003	Hilary Lunke	2007	Cristie Kerr
2000	Karrie Webb (AUS)	2004	Meg Mallon	2008	Inbee Park (KOR)
2001	Karrie Webb (AUS)	2005	Birdie Kim (KOR)	2009	Ji Eun-Hee (KOR)
2002	Juli Inkster	2006	Annika Sörenstam (SWE)		

Women's British Open Championship

Won by an English golfer unless otherwise indicated.

YEAR	WINNER	YEAR	WINNER	YEAR	WINNER
1976	Jenny Lee-Smith	1988	Corinne Dibnah (AUS)	1999	Sherri Steinhauer (USA)
1977	Vivien Saunders	1989	Jane Geddes (USA)	2000	Sophie Gustafson (SWE)
1978	Janet Melville	1990	Helen Alfredsson (SWE)	2001	Pak Se Ri (KOR)
1979	Alison Sheard (RSA)	1991	Penny Grice-Whittaker	2002	Karrie Webb (AUS)
1980	Debbie Massey (USA)	1992	Patty Sheehan (USA)	2003	Annika Sörenstam (SWE)
1981	Debbie Massey (USA)	1993	Mardi Lunn (AUS)	2004	Karen Stupples
1982	Marta Figueras-Dotti (ESP)	1994	Liselotte Neumann (SWE)	2005	Jang Jeong (KOR)
1983	*not held*	1995	Karrie Webb (AUS)	2006	Sherri Steinhauer (USA)
1984	Okamoto Ayako (JPN)	1996	Emilee Klein (USA)	2007	Lorena Ochoa (MEX)
1985	Betsy King (USA)	1997	Karrie Webb (AUS)	2008	Ji Yai Shin (KOR)
1986	Laura Davies	1998	Sherri Steinhauer (USA)	2009	Catriona Matthew (SCO)
1987	Alison Nicholas				

Ryder Cup

YEAR	RESULT	YEAR	RESULT
1927	United States 9½, Britain 2½	1973	United States 19, Britain 13
1929	Britain 7, United States 5	1975	United States 21, Britain 11
1931	United States 9, Britain 3	1977	United States 12½, Britain 7½
1933	Britain 6½, United States 5½	1979	United States 17, Europe 11
1935	United States 9, Britain 3	1981	United States 18½, Europe 9½
1937	United States 8, Britain 4	1983	United States 14½, Europe 13½
1939–45	*not held*	1985	Europe 16½, United States 11½
1947	United States 11, Britain 1	1987	Europe 15, United States 13
1949	United States 7, Britain 5	1989	Europe 14, United States 14
1951	United States 9½, Britain 2½	1991	United States 14½, Europe 13½
1953	United States 6½, Britain 5½	1993	United States 15, Europe 13
1955	United States 8, Britain 4	1995	Europe 14½, United States 13½
1957	Britain 7½, United States 4½	1997	Europe 14½, United States 13½
1959	United States 8½, Britain 3½	1999	United States 14½, Europe 13½
1961	United States 14½, Britain 9½	2001	*postponed until 2002*
1963	United States 23, Britain 9	2002	Europe 15½, United States 12½
1965	United States 19½, Britain 12½	2004	Europe 18½, United States 9½
1967	United States 23½, Britain 8½	2006	Europe 18½, United States 9½
1969	United States 16, Britain 16	2008	United States 16½, Europe 11½
1971	United States 18½, Britain 13½		

Curtis Cup

YEAR	RESULT	YEAR	RESULT
1932	United States 5½, Britain and Ireland 3½	1966	United States 13, Britain and Ireland 5
1934	United States 6½, Britain and Ireland 2½	1968	United States 10½, Britain and Ireland 7½
1936	United States[1] 4½, Britain and Ireland 4½	1970	United States 11½, Britain and Ireland 6½
1938	United States 5½, Britain and Ireland 3½	1972	United States 10, Britain and Ireland 8
1940–46	*not held*	1974	United States 13, Britain and Ireland 5
1948	United States 6½, Britain and Ireland 2½	1976	United States 11½, Britain and Ireland 6½
1950	United States 7½, Britain and Ireland 2½	1978	United States 12, Britain and Ireland 6
1952	Britain and Ireland 5, United States 4	1980	United States 13, Britain and Ireland 5
1954	United States 6, Britain and Ireland 3	1982	United States 14½, Britain and Ireland 3½
1956	Britain and Ireland 5, United States 4	1984	United States 9½, Britain and Ireland 8½
1958	Britain and Ireland[1] 4½, United States 4½	1986	Britain and Ireland 13, United States 5
1960	United States 6½, Britain and Ireland 2½	1988	Britain and Ireland 11, United States 7
1962	United States 8, Britain and Ireland 1	1990	United States 14, Britain and Ireland 4
1964	United States 10½, Britain and Ireland 7½	1992	Britain and Ireland 10, United States 8

Curtis Cup (continued)

YEAR	RESULT	YEAR	RESULT
1994	Britain and Ireland[1] 9, United States 9	2002	United States 11, Britain and Ireland 7
1996	Britain and Ireland 11½, United States 6½	2004	United States 10, Britain and Ireland 8
1998	United States 10, Britain and Ireland 8	2006	United States 11½, Britain and Ireland 6½
2000	United States 10, Britain and Ireland 8	2008	United States 13, Britain and Ireland 7

[1]In case of a tie the defenders retain the cup.

United States Amateur Championship—Men

Won by an American golfer except as indicated. Table shows results for the past 20 years.

YEAR	WINNER	YEAR	WINNER	YEAR	WINNER
1990	Phil Mickelson	1997	Matt Kuchar	2004	Ryan Moore
1991	Mitch Voges	1998	Hank Kuehne	2005	Edoardo Molinari (ITA)
1992	Justin Leonard	1999	David Gossett	2006	Richie Ramsay (SCO)
1993	John Harris	2000	Jeff Quinney	2007	Colt Knost
1994	Tiger Woods	2001	Ben Dickerson	2008	Danny Lee (NZL)
1995	Tiger Woods	2002	Ricky Barnes	2009	Byeong-Hun An (KOR)
1996	Tiger Woods	2003	Nick Flanagan (AUS)		

British Amateur Championship—Men

Held since 1885. Table shows results for the past 20 years. Won by an English golfer except as indicated.

YEAR	WINNER	YEAR	WINNER	YEAR	WINNER
1990	Rolf Muntz (NED)	1997	Craig Watson (SCO)	2004	Stuart Wilson (SCO)
1991	Gary Wolstenholme	1998	Sergio García (ESP)	2005	Brian McElhinney (IRL)
1992	Stephen Dundas (SCO)	1999	Graeme Storm	2006	Julien Guerrier (FRA)
1993	Ian Pyman	2000	Mikko Ilonen (FIN)	2007	Drew Weaver (USA)
1994	Lee James	2001	Michael Hoey (NIR)	2008	Reinier Saxton (NED)
1995	Gordon Sherry (SCO)	2002	Alejandro Larrazábal (ESP)	2009	Matteo Manassero (ITA)
1996	Warren Bledon	2003	Gary Wolstenholme		

United States Women's Amateur Championship

Held since 1895. Table shows results for the past 20 years. Won by an American golfer except as indicated.

YEAR	WINNER	YEAR	WINNER	YEAR	WINNER
1990	Pat Hurst	1997	Silvia Cavalleri (ITA)	2004	Jane Park
1991	Amy Fruhwirth	1998	Grace Park	2005	Morgan Pressel
1992	Vicki Goetze	1999	Dorothy Delasin	2006	Kimberly Kim
1993	Jill McGill	2000	Marcy Newton	2007	María José Uribe (COL)
1994	Wendy Ward	2001	Meredith Duncan	2008	Amanda Blumenherst
1995	Kelli Kuehne	2002	Becky Lucidi	2009	Jennifer Song
1996	Kelli Kuehne	2003	Virada Nirapath-pongporn (THA)		

Ladies' British Amateur Championship

Held since 1893. Table shows results for the past 20 years. Won by an English golfer except as indicated.

YEAR	WINNER	YEAR	WINNER	YEAR	WINNER
1990	Julie Wade Hall	1997	Alison Rose (SCO)	2004	Louise Stahle (SWE)
1991	Valerie Michaud	1998	Kim Rostron	2005	Louise Stahle (SWE)
1992	Bernille Pedersen (DEN)	1999	Marine Monnet (FRA)	2006	Belén Mozo (ESP)
1993	Catriona Lambert (SCO)	2000	Rebecca Hudson	2007	Carlota Ciganda (ESP)
1994	Emma Duggleby	2001	Marta Prieto (ESP)	2008	Anna Nordqvist (SWE)
1995	Julie Wade Hall	2002	Rebecca Hudson	2009	Azahara Muñoz (ESP)
1996	Kelli Kuehne (USA)	2003	Elisa Serramia (ESP)		

Horse Racing

In the **oldest type** of horse racing, the rider sits astride the horse; in the other type of race, best known as **harness racing**, the driver sits in a sulky— a two-wheeled vehicle attached by shafts and traces to the horse. In the former type, a **Thoroughbred** horse is raced over either a track or a course of jumps

Horse Racing (continued)

and turns (**steeplechase**). Harness horses can be trotters or pacers and are Standardbred horses raced on a track.

The English Thoroughbred classics. The races are run by 3-year-old colts and fillies. **The Derby,** first run in 1780, is run at Epsom Downs, Surrey, over 1½ miles. **The Oaks** (for fillies only), also run at Epsom Downs, was first run in 1779; the oldest of the English races, however, is the **St. Leger** (1776). It is run over 1 mile 6½ furlongs at Doncaster, South Yorkshire. The **2,000 Guineas** (1809) is run over 1 mile at Newmarket, Suffolk. A horse that wins the Derby, the St. Leger, and the 2,000 Guineas all in one year is said to have won the **British Triple Crown.**

The American Thoroughbred classics. The **Kentucky Derby,** a **Triple Crown** event first run in 1875 and perhaps the best known of American horse races, is raced at Churchill Downs in Louisville KY, over a 10-furlong (1¼-mile) track. Another of the Triple Crown classics, the **Preakness Stakes,** was instituted in 1873; it is run over 9½ furlongs (1³⁄₁₆ miles) at Pimlico Race Track in Baltimore MD. The third Triple Crown event is the 12-furlong (1½-mile) **Belmont Stakes,** established in 1867. It is run at Belmont Park Race Track, Long Island NY. All three events are for 3-year-old horses.

Australian Thoroughbred racing. The Victoria Racing Club's **Melbourne Cup,** first run in 1861, is one of the world's great handicap races. The day on which it is held (the first Tuesday in November) is a public holiday in Melbourne, VIC.

Dubai World Cup, first run in 1996, is the world's richest horse race ($6 million in 2007). The 2,000-m (about 1¼-mi) race is held on the dirt track at the Nad Al Sheba Racecourse in Dubai, United Arab Emirates, and is open to four-year-old and older Thoroughbred horses.

The **Grand National,** the world's most significant and widely followed **steeplechase** race, has been run annually at Aintree Racecourse near Liverpool, England, since 1839. The race, which includes 30 jumps, is run over a traditional distance of 4 miles 4 furlongs.

Harness racing. In the United States, the **Hambletonian Trot** is probably the most prestigious of harness races. It was established in 1926, was raced in New York, Kentucky, and Illinois, and is now run at the Meadowlands in New Jersey.

Related Web sites: US National Thoroughbred Racing Association: <www.ntra.com>; Fédération Equestre Internationale: <www.horsesport.org>; *Thoroughbred Times:* <www.thoroughbredtimes.com>; and *Racing Post:* <www.racingpost.co.uk>.

Major Thoroughbred Race Winners, 2008–09

United States

DATE	RACE	WINNER	JOCKEY
2 Aug 2008	Test Stakes	Indian Blessing	John Velazquez
3 Aug 2008	Haskell Invitational Handicap	Big Brown	Kent Desormeaux
3 Aug 2008	John C. Mabee Handicap	Black Mamba	Garrett Gomez
9 Aug 2008	Arlington Million Stakes	Spirit One	Ioritz Mendizabal
9 Aug 2008	Beverly D. Stakes	Mauralakana	Kent Desormeaux
9 Aug 2008	Secretariat Stakes	Winchester	Rene Douglas
16 Aug 2008	Alabama Stakes	Proud Spell	Gabriel Saez
16 Aug 2008	Del Mar Oaks	Magical Fantasy	Alex Solis
16 Aug 2008	Sword Dancer Invitational Stakes	Grand Couturier	Alan Garcia
22 Aug 2008	Personal Ensign Stakes	Ginger Punch	Rafael Bejarano
23 Aug 2008	King's Bishop Stakes	Visionaire	Alan Garcia
23 Aug 2008	Travers Stakes	Colonel John	Garrett Gomez
24 Aug 2008	Pacific Classic Stakes	Go Between	Garrett Gomez
30 Aug 2008	Woodward Stakes	Curlin	Robby Albarado
31 Aug 2008	Spinaway Stakes	Mani Bhavan	Alan Garcia
1 Sep 2008	Del Mar Debutante Stakes	Stardom Bound	Mike Smith
1 Sep 2008	Hopeful Stakes	Vineyard Haven	Alan Garcia
3 Sep 2008	Del Mar Futurity	Midshipman	Tyler Baze
6 Sep 2008	Garden City Stakes	Backseat Rhythm	Javier Castellano
6 Sep 2008	Ruffian Handicap	Tough Tiz's Sis	Edgar Prado
13 Sep 2008	Gazelle Stakes	Music Note	Javier Castellano
27 Sep 2008	Ancient Title Stakes	Cost of Freedom	Tyler Baze
27 Sep 2008	Beldame Stakes	Cocoa Beach	Ramon Dominguez
27 Sep 2008	Flower Bowl Invitational Stakes	Dynaforce	Alan Garcia
27 Sep 2008	Goodwood Handicap Stakes	Well Armed	Aaron Gryder
27 Sep 2008	Jockey Club Gold Cup Stakes	Curlin	Robby Albarado
27 Sep 2008	Joe Hirsch Turf Classic Invitational Stakes	Grand Couturier	Alan Garcia
27 Sep 2008	Lady's Secret Stakes	Zenyatta	Mike Smith
27 Sep 2008	Vosburgh Stakes	Black Seventeen	Clinton Potts
27 Sep 2008	Yellow Ribbon Stakes	Wait a While	John Velazquez
28 Sep 2008	Norfolk Stakes	Street Hero	Alex Solis
3 Oct 2008	Darley Alcibiades Stakes	Dream Empress	Robby Albarado
3 Oct 2008	First Lady Stakes	Forever Together	Julien Leparoux
4 Oct 2008	Champagne Stakes	Vineyard Haven	Edgar Prado
4 Oct 2008	Frizette Stakes	Sky Diva	Ramon Dominguez
4 Oct 2008	Lane's End Breeders' Futurity	Square Eddie	Rafael Bejarano
4 Oct 2008	Shadwell Turf Mile Stakes	Thorn Song	Robby Albarado

Major Thoroughbred Race Winners, 2008–09 (continued)

United States (continued)

DATE	RACE	WINNER	JOCKEY
5 Oct 2008	Juddmonte Spinster Stakes	Carriage Trail	Kent Desormeaux
11 Oct 2008	Queen Elizabeth II Challenge Cup Stakes	Alwajeeha	John Velazquez
24 Oct 2008	Breeders' Cup Filly and Mare Turf	Forever Together	Julien Leparoux
24 Oct 2008	Breeders' Cup Juvenile Fillies	Stardom Bound	Mike Smith
24 Oct 2008	Breeders' Cup Ladies' Classic	Zenyatta	Mike Smith
25 Oct 2008	Breeders' Cup Classic	Raven's Pass	Frankie Dettori
25 Oct 2008	Breeders' Cup Juvenile	Midshipman	Garrett Gomez
25 Oct 2008	Breeders' Cup Mile	Goldikova	Olivier Peslier
25 Oct 2008	Breeders' Cup Sprint	Midnight Lute	Garrett Gomez
25 Oct 2008	Breeders' Cup Turf	Conduit	Ryan Moore
28 Nov 2008	Citation Handicap	Hyperbaric	Tyler Baze
29 Nov 2008	Cigar Mile Handicap	Tale of Ekati	Edgar Prado
30 Nov 2008	Hollywood Derby	Court Vision	Ramon Dominguez
30 Nov 2008	Matriarch Stakes	Cocoa Beach	Ramon Dominguez
6 Dec 2008	Hollywood Turf Cup Stakes	Champs Elysees	Jose Valdivia, Jr.
13 Dec 2008	Hollywood Starlet Stakes	Laragh	Edgar Prado
20 Dec 2008	CashCall Futurity	Pioneerof the Nile	Garrett Gomez
27 Dec 2008	La Brea Stakes	Indian Blessing	John Velazquez
31 Jan 2009	Donn Handicap	Albertus Maximus	Alan Garcia
1 Feb 2009	Gulfstream Park Turf Handicap	Kip Deville	Cornelio Velasquez
7 Mar 2009	Frank E. Kilroe Mile Handicap	Gio Ponti	Ramon Dominguez
7 Mar 2009	Santa Anita Handicap	Einstein	Julien Leparoux
7 Mar 2009	Santa Anita Oaks	Stardom Bound	Mike Smith
14 Mar 2009	Santa Margarita Invitational Handicap	Life Is Sweet	Garrett Gomez
28 Mar 2009	Florida Derby	Quality Road	John Velazquez
4 Apr 2009	Apple Blossom Handicap	Seventh Street	Rajiv Maragh
4 Apr 2009	Ashland Stakes	Hooh Why	Corey Lanerie
4 Apr 2009	Carter Handicap	Kodiak Kowboy	John Velazquez
4 Apr 2009	Santa Anita Derby	Pioneerof the Nile	Garrett Gomez
4 Apr 2009	Wood Memorial Stakes	I Want Revenge	Joseph Talamo
9 Apr 2009	Vinery Madison Stakes	Informed Decision	John Velazquez
10 Apr 2009	Maker's Mark Mile Stakes	Mr. Sidney	Kent Desormeaux
11 Apr 2009	Blue Grass Stakes	General Quarters	Eibar Coa
1 May 2009	Kentucky Oaks	Rachel Alexandra	Calvin Borel
2 May 2009	Humana Distaff Stakes	Informed Decision	Julien Leparoux
2 May 2009	Kentucky Derby[1]	Mine That Bird	Calvin Borel
2 May 2009	Turf Classic Stakes	Einstein	Julien Leparoux
16 May 2009	Preakness Stakes[1]	Rachel Alexandra	Calvin Borel
25 May 2009	Metropolitan Handicap	Bribon	Alan Garcia
25 May 2009	Shoemaker Mile Stakes	Thorn Song	Mike Smith
30 May 2009	Gamely Stakes	Magical Fantasy	Alex Solis
6 Jun 2009	Acorn Stakes	Gabby's Golden Gal	Javier Castellano
6 Jun 2009	Belmont Stakes[1]	Summer Bird	Kent Desormeaux
6 Jun 2009	Charles Whittingham Memorial Handicap	Midships	Victor Espinoza
6 Jun 2009	Just a Game Stakes	Diamondrella	Rajiv Maragh
6 Jun 2009	Manhattan Handicap	Gio Ponti	Garrett Gomez
13 Jun 2009	Ogden Phipps Handicap	Seattle Smooth	Ramon Dominguez
13 Jun 2009	Stephen Foster Handicap	Macho Again	Robby Albarado
27 Jun 2009	Mother Goose Stakes	Rachel Alexandra	Calvin Borel
27 Jun 2009	Vanity Handicap	Zenyatta	Mike Smith
4 Jul 2009	Prioress Stakes	Cat Moves	Ramon Dominguez
4 Jul 2009	United Nations Stakes	Presious Passion	Elvis Trujillo
5 Jul 2009	American Oaks Invitational Stakes	Gozzip Girl	Kent Desormeaux
5 Jul 2009	Triple Bend Handicap	Zensational	Victor Espinoza
11 Jul 2009	Hollywood Gold Cup Handicap	Rail Trip	Jose Valdivia, Jr.
11 Jul 2009	Man o' War Stakes	Gio Ponti	Ramon Dominguez
11 Jul 2009	Princess Rooney Handicap	Game Face	Edgar Prado
25 Jul 2009	Coaching Club American Oaks	Funny Moon	Alan Garcia
25 Jul 2009	Eddie Read Handicap	Global Hunter	Corey Nakatani

Canada

DATE	RACE	WINNER	JOCKEY
3 Aug 2008	Breeders' Stakes	Marlang	Richard Dos Ramos
7 Sep 2008	Woodbine Mile Stakes	Rahy's Attorney	Slade Callaghan
4 Oct 2008	Canadian International Stakes	Marsh Side	Javier Castellano
4 Oct 2008	E.P. Taylor Stakes	Folk Opera	Frankie Dettori
21 Jun 2009	Queen's Plate Stakes	Eye of the Leopard	Eurico Rosa da Silva
12 Jul 2009	Prince of Wales Stakes	Gallant	Corey Fraser

Major Thoroughbred Race Winners, 2008–09 (continued)

England

DATE	RACE	WINNER	JOCKEY
22 Aug 2008	Nunthorpe Stakes	Borderlescott	Pat Cosgrave
23 Aug 2008	Juddmonte International Stakes	Duke of Marmalade	Johnny Murtagh
13 Sep 2008	St. Leger Stakes[2]	Conduit	Frankie Dettori
27 Sep 2008	Queen Elizabeth II Stakes	Raven's Pass	Jimmy Fortune
2 May 2009	2,000 Guineas[2]	Sea The Stars	Mick Kinane
3 May 2009	1,000 Guineas	Ghanaati	Richard Hills
6 Jun 2009	The Derby[2]	Sea The Stars	Mick Kinane
18 Jun 2009	Ascot Gold Cup	Yeats	Johnny Murtagh
4 Jul 2009	Coral-Eclipse Stakes	Sea The Stars	Mick Kinane
25 Jul 2009	King George VI and Queen Elizabeth Stakes	Conduit	Ryan Moore
29 Jul 2009	Sussex Stakes	Rip Van Winkle	Johnny Murtagh

Ireland

DATE	RACE	WINNER	JOCKEY
7 Sep 2008	Irish Champion Stakes	New Approach	Kevin Manning
13 Sep 2008	Irish St. Leger	Septimus	Seamus Heffernan
23 May 2009	Irish 2,000 Guineas	Mastercraftsman	Johnny Murtagh
24 May 2009	Irish 1,000 Guineas	Again	Johnny Murtagh
28 Jun 2009	Irish Derby	Fame And Glory	Johnny Murtagh
12 Jul 2009	Irish Oaks	Sariska	Jamie Spencer

France

DATE	RACE	WINNER	JOCKEY
17 Aug 2008	Prix Jacques le Marois	Tamayuz	Davy Bonilla
5 Oct 2008	Prix de l'Arc de Triomphe	Zarkava	Christophe Soumillon
5 Oct 2008	Prix Jean-Luc Lagardère (Grand Critérium)	Naaqoos	Davy Bonilla
26 Oct 2008	Prix Royal-Oak	Yeats	Johnny Murtagh
26 Apr 2009	Prix Ganay	Vision d'État	Ioritz Mendizabal
10 May 2009	Poule d'Essai des Poulains	Silver Frost	Christophe Soumillon
10 May 2009	Poule d'Essai des Pouliches	Elusive Wave	Christophe Lemaire
17 May 2009	Prix Saint-Alary	Stacelita	Christophe Lemaire
7 Jun 2009	Prix du Jockey Club	Le Havre	Christophe Lemaire
14 Jun 2009	Prix de Diane	Stacelita	Christophe Lemaire
28 Jun 2009	Grand Prix de Saint-Cloud	Spanish Moon	Ryan Moore
14 Jul 2009	Grand Prix de Paris	Cavalryman	Maxime Guyon

Germany

DATE	RACE	WINNER	JOCKEY
7 Sep 2008	Grosser Preis von Baden	Kamsin	Johan Victoire
28 Sep 2008	Preis von Europa	Baila Me	Dominique Boeuf
5 Jul 2009	Deutsches Derby	Wiener Waltzer	Fredrik Johansson

Italy

DATE	RACE	WINNER	JOCKEY
9 May 2009	Derby Italiano	Mastery	Frankie Dettori

Australia

DATE	RACE	WINNER	JOCKEY
18 Oct 2008	Caulfield Cup	All The Good	Kerrin McEvoy
25 Oct 2008	Cox Plate	Maldivian	Michael Rodd
4 Nov 2008	Melbourne Cup	Viewed	Blake Shinn

United Arab Emirates

DATE	RACE	WINNER	JOCKEY
28 Mar 2009	Dubai Duty Free	Gladiatorus	Ahmad Ajtebi
28 Mar 2009	Dubai Golden Shaheen	Big City Man	Jose Verenzuela
28 Mar 2009	Dubai Sheema Classic	Eastern Anthem	Ahmad Ajtebi
28 Mar 2009	Dubai World Cup	Well Armed	Aaron Gryder
28 Mar 2009	Godolphin Mile	Two Step Salsa	Frankie Dettori
28 Mar 2009	UAE Derby	Regal Ransom	Alan Garcia

Japan

DATE	RACE	WINNER	JOCKEY
30 Nov 2008	Japan Cup	Screen Hero	Mirco Demuro

Hong Kong

DATE	RACE	WINNER	JOCKEY
14 Dec 2008	Hong Kong Cup	Eagle Mountain	Kevin Shea
22 Feb 2009	Hong Kong Gold Cup	Viva Pataca	Darren Beadman
26 Apr 2009	Queen Elizabeth II Cup	Presvis	Ryan Moore

Singapore

DATE	RACE	WINNER	JOCKEY
17 May 2009	International Cup	Gloria De Campeao	Tiago Josue Pereira

[1]*American Triple Crown race.*   [2]*British Triple Crown race.*

Kentucky Derby

YEAR	HORSE	JOCKEY	YEAR	HORSE	JOCKEY
1875	Aristides	Oliver Lewis	1940	Gallahadion	Carroll Bierman
1876	Vagrant	Bobby Swim	1941	Whirlaway	Eddie Arcaro
1877	Baden-Baden	William Walker	1942	Shut Out	Wayne D. Wright
1878	Day Star	Jimmy Carter	1943	Count Fleet	John Longden
1879	Lord Murphy	Charlie Shauer	1944	Pensive	Conn McCreary
1880	Fonso	George Garret Lewis	1945	Hoop Jr.	Eddie Arcaro
1881	Hindoo	James McLaughlin	1946	Assault	Warren Mehrtens
1882	Apollo	Babe Hurd	1947	Jet Pilot	Eric Guerin
1883	Leonatus	William Donohue	1948	Citation	Eddie Arcaro
1884	Buchanan	Isaac Murphy	1949	Ponder	Steve Brooks
1885	Joe Cotton	Erskine Henderson	1950	Middleground	William Boland
1886	Ben Ali	Paul Duffy	1951	Count Turf	Conn McCreary
1887	Montrose	Isaac Lewis	1952	Hill Gail	Eddie Arcaro
1888	Macbeth II	George Covington	1953	Dark Star	Henry Moreno
1889	Spokane	Thomas Kiley	1954	Determine	Raymond York
1890	Riley	Isaac Murphy	1955	Swaps	William Shoemaker
1891	Kingman	Isaac Murphy	1956	Needles	David Erb
1892	Azra	Alonzo Clayton	1957	Iron Liege	William Hartack
1893	Lookout	Eddie Kunze	1958	Tim Tam	Ismael Valenzuela
1894	Chant	Frank Goodale	1959	Tomy Lee	William Shoemaker
1895	Halma	James Perkins	1960	Venetian Way	William Hartack
1896	Ben Brush	Willie Simms	1961	Carry Back	John Sellers
1897	Typhoon II	Fred Garner	1962	Decidedly	William Hartack
1898	Plaudit	Willie Simms	1963	Chateaugay	Braulio Baeza
1899	Manuel	Fred Taral	1964	Northern Dancer	William Hartack
1900	Lieut. Gibson	Jimmy Boland	1965	Lucky Debonair	William Shoemaker
1901	His Eminence	James Winkfield	1966	Kauai King	Don Brumfield
1902	Alan-a-Dale	James Winkfield	1967	Proud Clarion	Robert Ussery
1903	Judge Himes	Harold Booker	1968	Forward Pass	Ismael Valenzuela
1904	Elwood	Frank Prior	1969	Majestic Prince	William Hartack
1905	Agile	Jack Martin	1970	Dust Commander	Mike Manganello
1906	Sir Huon	Roscoe Troxler	1971	Canonero II	Gustavo Avila
1907	Pink Star	Andy Minder	1972	Riva Ridge	Ron Turcotte
1908	Stone Street	Arthur Pickens	1973	Secretariat[1]	Ron Turcotte
1909	Wintergreen	Vincent Powers	1974	Cannonade	Angel Cordero, Jr.
1910	Donau	Fred Herbert	1975	Foolish Pleasure	Jacinto Vasquez
1911	Meridian	George Archibald	1976	Bold Forbes	Angel Cordero, Jr.
1912	Worth	Carroll Hugh Shilling	1977	Seattle Slew	Jean Cruguet
1913	Donerail	Roscoe Goose	1978	Affirmed	Steve Cauthen
1914	Old Rosebud	John McCabe	1979	Spectacular Bid	Ronnie Franklin
1915	Regret	Joe Notter	1980	Genuine Risk	Jacinto Vasquez
1916	George Smith	John Loftus	1981	Pleasant Colony	Jorge Velasquez
1917	Omar Khayyam	Charles Borel	1982	Gato del Sol	Eddie Delahoussaye
1918	Exterminator	William Knapp	1983	Sunny's Halo	Eddie Delahoussaye
1919	Sir Barton	John Loftus	1984	Swale	Laffit Pincay, Jr.
1920	Paul Jones	Ted Rice	1985	Spend a Buck	Angel Cordero, Jr.
1921	Behave Yourself	Charles Thompson	1986	Ferdinand	William Shoemaker
1922	Morvich	Albert Johnson	1987	Alysheba	Chris McCarron
1923	Zev	Earl Sande	1988	Winning Colors	Gary Stevens
1924	Black Gold	John D. Mooney	1989	Sunday Silence	Patrick Valenzuela
1925	Flying Ebony	Earl Sande	1990	Unbridled	Craig Perret
1926	Bubbling Over	Albert Johnson	1991	Strike the Gold	Chris Antley
1927	Whiskery	Linus McAtee	1992	Lil E. Tee	Pat Day
1928	Reigh Count	Charles Lang	1993	Sea Hero	Jerry Bailey
1929	Clyde Van Dusen	Linus McAtee	1994	Go for Gin	Chris McCarron
1930	Gallant Fox	Earl Sande	1995	Thunder Gulch	Gary Stevens
1931	Twenty Grand	Charles Kurtsinger	1996	Grindstone	Jerry Bailey
1932	Burgoo King	Eugene James	1997	Silver Charm	Gary Stevens
1933	Brokers Tip	Don Meade	1998	Real Quiet	Kent Desormeaux
1934	Cavalcade	Mack Garner	1999	Charismatic	Chris Antley
1935	Omaha	William Saunders	2000	Fusaichi Pegasus	Kent Desormeaux
1936	Bold Venture	Ira Hanford	2001	Monarchos	Jorge Chávez
1937	War Admiral	Charles Kurtsinger	2002	War Emblem	Victor Espinoza
1938	Lawrin	Eddie Arcaro	2003	Funny Cide	José Santos
1939	Johnstown	James Stout	2004	Smarty Jones	Stewart Elliott

Kentucky Derby (continued)

YEAR	HORSE	JOCKEY	YEAR	HORSE	JOCKEY
2005	Giacomo	Mike Smith	2008	Big Brown	Kent Desormeaux
2006	Barbaro	Edgar Prado	2009	Mine That Bird	Calvin Borel
2007	Street Sense	Calvin Borel			

[1]Fastest time—1 min 59⅖ sec.

Preakness Stakes

YEAR	HORSE	JOCKEY	YEAR	HORSE	JOCKEY
1873	Survivor	George Barbee	1932	Burgoo King	Eugene James
1874	Culpepper	William Donohue	1933	Head Play	Charles Kurtsinger
1875	Tom Ochiltree	Lloyd Hughes	1934	High Quest	Robert Jones
1876	Shirley	George Barbee	1935	Omaha	Willie Saunders
1877	Cloverbrook	Cyrus Holloway	1936	Bold Venture	George Woolf
1878	Duke of Magenta	Cyrus Holloway	1937	War Admiral	Charles Kurtsinger
1879	Harold	Lloyd Hughes	1938	Dauber	Maurice Peters
1880	Grenada	Lloyd Hughes	1939	Challedon	George Seabo
1881	Saunterer	T. Costello	1940	Bimelech	Fred A. Smith
1882	Vanguard	T. Costello	1941	Whirlaway	Eddie Arcaro
1883	Jacobus	George Barbee	1942	Alsab	Basil James
1884	Knight of Ellerslie	S. Fisher	1943	Count Fleet	John Longden
1885	Tecumseh	James McLaughlin	1944	Pensive	Conn McCreary
1886	The Bard	S. Fisher	1945	Polynesian	Wayne D. Wright
1887	Dunboyne	William Donohue	1946	Assault	Warren Mehrtens
1888	Refund	Fred Littlefield	1947	Faultless	Doug Dodson
1889	Buddhist	George Anderson	1948	Citation	Eddie Arcaro
1890	Montague	W. Martin	1949	Capot	Ted Atkinson
1891-93	not held		1950	Hill Prince	Eddie Arcaro
1894	Assignee	Fred Taral	1951	Bold	Eddie Arcaro
1895	Belmar	Fred Taral	1952	Blue Man	Conn McCreary
1896	Margrave	Henry Griffin	1953	Native Dancer	Eric Guerin
1897	Paul Kauvar	T. Thorpe	1954	Hasty Road	Johnny Adams
1898	Sly Fox	Willie Simms	1955	Nashua	Eddie Arcaro
1899	Half Time	R. Clawson	1956	Fabius	William Hartack
1900	Hindus	H. Spencer	1957	Bold Ruler	Eddie Arcaro
1901	The Parader	Fred Landry	1958	Tim Tam	Ismael Valenzuela
1902	Old England	L. Jackson	1959	Royal Orbit	William Harmatz
1903	Flocarline	W. Gannon	1960	Bally Ache	Robert Ussery
1904	Bryn Mawr	Eugene Hildebrand	1961	Carry Back	John Sellers
1905	Cairngorm	W. Davis	1962	Greek Money	John L. Rotz
1906	Whimsical	Walter Miller	1963	Candy Spots	William Shoemaker
1907	Don Enrique	G. Mountain	1964	Northern Dancer	William Hartack
1908	Royal Tourist	Eddie Dugan	1965	Tom Rolfe	Ron Turcotte
1909	Effendi	Willie Doyle	1966	Kauai King	Don Brumfield
1910	Layminster	Roy Estep	1967	Damascus	William Shoemaker
1911	Watervale	Eddie Dugan	1968	Forward Pass	Ismael Valenzuela
1912	Colonel Holloway	Clarence Turner	1969	Majestic Prince	William Hartack
1913	Buskin	James Butwell	1970	Personality	Eddie Belmonte
1914	Holiday	Andy Schuttinger	1971	Canonero II	Gustavo Avila
1915	Rhine Maiden	Douglas Hoffman	1972	Bee Bee Bee	Eldon Nelson
1916	Damrosch	Linus McAtee	1973	Secretariat	Ron Turcotte
1917	Kalitan	Everett Haynes	1974	Little Current	Miguel Rivera
1918[1]	War Cloud; Jack Hare, Jr.	John Loftus; Charles Peak	1975	Master Derby	Darrel McHague
1919	Sir Barton	John Loftus	1976	Elocutionist	John Lively
1920	Man o' War	Clarence Kummer	1977	Seattle Slew	Jean Cruguet
1921	Broomspun	Frank Coltiletti	1978	Affirmed	Steve Cauthen
1922	Pillory	Louis Morris	1979	Spectacular Bid	Ron Franklin
1923	Vigil	Benny Marinelli	1980	Codex	Angel Cordero, Jr.
1924	Nellie Morse	John Merimee	1981	Pleasant Colony	Jorge Velasquez
1925	Coventry	Clarence Kummer	1982	Aloma's Ruler	Jack Kaenel
1926	Display	John Maiben	1983	Deputed Testamony	Donald Miller
1927	Bostonian	Alf J. "Whitey" Abel	1984	Gate Dancer	Angel Cordero, Jr.
1928	Victorian	Raymond Workman	1985	Tank's Prospect[2]	Pat Day
1929	Dr. Freeland	Louis Schaefer	1986	Snow Chief	Alex Solis
1930	Gallant Fox	Earl Sande	1987	Alysheba	Chris McCarron
1931	Mate	George Ellis	1988	Risen Star	Eddie Delahoussaye
			1989	Sunday Silence	Patrick Valenzuela

Preakness Stakes (continued)

YEAR	HORSE	JOCKEY	YEAR	HORSE	JOCKEY
1990	Summer Squall	Pat Day	2000	Red Bullet	Jerry Bailey
1991	Hansel	Jerry Bailey	2001	Point Given	Gary Stevens
1992	Pine Bluff	Chris McCarron	2002	War Emblem	Victor Espinoza
1993	Prairie Bayou	Mike Smith	2003	Funny Cide	José Santos
1994	Tabasco Cat	Pat Day	2004	Smarty Jones	Stewart Elliott
1995	Timber Country	Pat Day	2005	Afleet Alex	Jeremy Rose
1996	Louis Quatorze	Pat Day	2006	Bernardini	Javier Castellano
1997	Silver Charm	Gary Stevens	2007	Curlin	Robby Albarado
1998	Real Quiet	Kent Desormeaux	2008	Big Brown	Kent Desormeaux
1999	Charismatic	Chris Antley	2009	Rachel Alexandra	Calvin Borel

[1]Run in two divisions in 1918 because of the large number of starters.   [2]Fastest time—1 min 53⅖ sec.

Belmont Stakes

YEAR	HORSE	JOCKEY	YEAR	HORSE	JOCKEY
1867	Ruthless	Gilbert Patrick	1918	Johren	Frank Robinson
1868	General Duke	Bobby Swim	1919	Sir Barton	John Loftus
1869	Fenian	Charley Miller	1920	Man o' War	Clarence Kummer
1870	Kingfisher	Edward Brown	1921	Grey Lag	Earl Sande
1871	Harry Bassett	W. Miller	1922	Pillory	C.H. Miller
1872	Joe Daniels	James Rowe	1923	Zev	Earl Sande
1873	Springbok	James Rowe	1924	Mad Play	Earl Sande
1874	Saxon	George Barbee	1925	American Flag	Albert Johnson
1875	Calvin	Bobby Swim	1926	Crusader	Albert Johnson
1876	Algerine	Billy Donohue	1927	Chance Shot	Earl Sande
1877	Cloverbrook	Cyrus Holloway	1928	Vito	Clarence Kummer
1878	Duke of Magenta	Lloyd Hughes	1929	Blue Larkspur	Mack Garner
1879	Spendthrift	George Evans	1930	Gallant Fox	Earl Sande
1880	Grenada	Lloyd Hughes	1931	Twenty Grand	Charles Kurtsinger
1881	Saunterer	T. Costello	1932	Faireno	Tom Malley
1882	Forester	James McLaughlin	1933	Hurryoff	Mack Garner
1883	George Kinney	James McLaughlin	1934	Peace Chance	Wayne D. Wright
1884	Panique	James McLaughlin	1935	Omaha	Willie Saunders
1885	Tyrant	Paul Duffy	1936	Granville	James Stout
1886	Inspector B	James McLaughlin	1937	War Admiral	Charles Kurtsinger
1887	Hanover	James McLaughlin	1938	Pasteurized	James Stout
1888	Sir Dixon	James McLaughlin	1939	Johnstown	James Stout
1889	Eric	W. Hayward	1940	Bimelech	Fred A. Smith
1890	Burlington	Shelby Barnes	1941	Whirlaway	Eddie Arcaro
1891	Foxford	Edward Garrison	1942	Shut Out	Eddie Arcaro
1892	Patron	W. Hayward	1943	Count Fleet	John Longden
1893	Comanche	Willie Simms	1944	Bounding Home	Gayle L. Smith
1894	Henry of Navarre	Willie Simms	1945	Pavot	Eddie Arcaro
1895	Belmar	Fred Taral	1946	Assault	Warren Mehrtens
1896	Hastings	Henry Griffin	1947	Phalanx	Ruperto Donoso
1897	Scottish Chieftain	J. Scherrer	1948	Citation	Eddie Arcaro
1898	Bowling Brook	Fred Littlefield	1949	Capot	Ted Atkinson
1899	Jean Bereaud	R. Clawson	1950	Middleground	William Boland
1900	Ildrim	Nash Turner	1951	Counterpoint	David Gorman
1901	Commando	H. Spencer	1952	One Count	Eddie Arcaro
1902	Masterman	John Bullman	1953	Native Dancer	Eric Guerin
1903	Africander	John Bullman	1954	High Gun	Eric Guerin
1904	Delhi	George Odom	1955	Nashua	Eddie Arcaro
1905	Tanya	Eugene Hildebrand	1956	Needles	David Erb
1906	Burgomaster	Lucien Lyne	1957	Gallant Man	William Shoemaker
1907	Peter Pan	G. Mountain	1958	Cavan	Pete Anderson
1908	Colin	Joe Notter	1959	Sword Dancer	William Shoemaker
1909	Joe Madden	Eddie Dugan	1960	Celtic Ash	William Hartack
1910	Sweep	James Butwell	1961	Sherluck	Braulio Baeza
1911–12	not held		1962	Jaipur	William Shoemaker
1913	Prince Eugene	Roscoe Troxler	1963	Chateaugay	Braulio Baeza
1914	Luke McLuke	Merritt Buxton	1964	Quadrangle	Manuel Ycaza
1915	The Finn	George Byrne	1965	Hail to All	John Sellers
1916	Friar Rock	Everett Haynes	1966	Amberoid	William Boland
1917	Hourless	James Butwell	1967	Damascus	William Shoemaker

Belmont Stakes (continued)

YEAR	HORSE	JOCKEY	YEAR	HORSE	JOCKEY
1968	Stage Door Johnny	Heliodoro Gustines	1989	Easy Goer	Pat Day
1969	Arts and Letters	Braulio Baeza	1990	Go and Go	Mick Kinane
1970	High Echelon	John Rotz	1991	Hansel	Jerry Bailey
1971	Pass Catcher	Walter Blum	1992	A.P. Indy	Eddie Delahoussaye
1972	Riva Ridge	Ron Turcotte	1993	Colonial Affair	Julie Krone
1973	Secretariat[1]	Ron Turcotte	1994	Tabasco Cat	Pat Day
1974	Little Current	Miguel Rivera	1995	Thunder Gulch	Gary Stevens
1975	Avatar	William Shoemaker	1996	Editor's Note	Rene Douglas
1976	Bold Forbes	Angel Cordero, Jr.	1997	Touch Gold	Chris McCarron
1977	Seattle Slew	Jean Cruguet	1998	Victory Gallop	Gary Stevens
1978	Affirmed	Steve Cauthen	1999	Lemon Drop Kid	José Santos
1979	Coastal	Ruben Hernandez	2000	Commendable	Pat Day
1980	Temperence Hill	Eddie Maple	2001	Point Given	Gary Stevens
1981	Summing	George Martens	2002	Sarava	Edgar Prado
1982	Conquistador Cielo	Laffit Pincay, Jr.	2003	Empire Maker	Jerry Bailey
1983	Caveat	Laffit Pincay, Jr.	2004	Birdstone	Edgar Prado
1984	Swale	Laffit Pincay, Jr.	2005	Afleet Alex	Jeremy Rose
1985	Creme Fraiche	Eddie Maple	2006	Jazil	Fernando Jara
1986	Danzig Connection	Chris McCarron	2007	Rags to Riches	John Velazquez
1987	Bet Twice	Craig Perret	2008	Da' Tara	Alan Garcia
1988	Risen Star	Eddie Delahoussaye	2009	Summer Bird	Kent Desormeaux

[1]Fastest time—2 min 24 sec.

Triple Crown Champions—United States

YEAR	HORSE	YEAR	HORSE	YEAR	HORSE	YEAR	HORSE
1919	Sir Barton	1937	War Admiral	1946	Assault	1977	Seattle Slew
1930	Gallant Fox	1941	Whirlaway	1948	Citation	1978	Affirmed
1935	Omaha	1943	Count Fleet	1973	Secretariat		

Horse of the Year

A Horse of the Year was selected by the *Daily Racing Form* from 1936 to 1970 and independently by the Thoroughbred Racing Association beginning in 1950. From 1971 these two organizations, plus the National Turf Writers Association, founded the Eclipse Awards, of which the Horse of the Year is the top among the 22 American prizes.

YEAR	HORSE	YEAR	HORSE	YEAR	HORSE	YEAR	HORSE
1936	Granville	1954	Native Dancer	1971	Ack Ack	1990	Criminal Type
1937	War Admiral	1955	Nashua	1972	Secretariat	1991	Black Tie Affair
1938	Seabiscuit	1956	Swaps	1973	Secretariat	1992	A.P. Indy
1939	Challedon	1957	Bold Ruler[1]; Dedicate[2]	1974	Forego	1993	Kotashaan
1940	Challedon			1975	Forego	1994	Holy Bull
1941	Whirlaway	1958	Round Table	1976	Forego	1995	Cigar
1942	Whirlaway	1959	Sword Dancer	1977	Seattle Slew	1996	Cigar
1943	Count Fleet	1960	Kelso	1978	Affirmed	1997	Favorite Trick
1944	Twilight Tear	1961	Kelso	1979	Affirmed	1998	Skip Away
1945	Busher	1962	Kelso	1980	Spectacular Bid	1999	Charismatic
1946	Assault	1963	Kelso	1981	John Henry	2000	Tiznow
1947	Armed	1964	Kelso	1982	Conquistador Cielo	2001	Point Given
1948	Citation	1965	Roman Brother[1]; Moccasin[2]	1983	All Along	2002	Azeri
1949	Capot[1]; Coaltown[2]			1984	John Henry	2003	Mineshaft
1950	Hill Prince	1966	Buckpasser	1985	Spend a Buck	2004	Ghostzapper
1951	Counterpoint	1967	Damascus	1986	Lady's Secret	2005	Saint Liam
1952	One Count[1]; Native Dancer[2]	1968	Dr. Fager	1987	Ferdinand	2006	Invasor
		1969	Arts and Letters	1988	Alysheba	2007	Curlin
1953	Tom Fool	1970	Fort Marcy[1]; Personality[2]	1989	Sunday Silence	2008	Curlin

[1]*Daily Racing Form.* [2]Thoroughbred Racing Association.

2,000 Guineas

Held since 1809. Table shows the winners for the past 20 years.

YEAR	HORSE	JOCKEY	YEAR	HORSE	JOCKEY
1990	Tirol	Mick Kinane	2000	King's Best	Kieren Fallon
1991	Mystiko	Michael Roberts	2001	Golan	Kieren Fallon
1992	Rodrigo de Triano	Lester Piggot	2002	Rock of Gibraltar	Johnny Murtagh
1993	Zafonic	Pat Eddery	2003	Refuse To Bend	Pat Smullen
1994	Mister Baileys	Jason Weaver	2004	Haafhd	Richard Hills
1995	Pennekamp	Thierry Jarnet	2005	Footstepsinthesand	Kieren Fallon
1996	Mark of Esteem	Frankie Dettori	2006	George Washington	Kieren Fallon
1997	Entrepreneur	Mick Kinane	2007	Cockney Rebel	Olivier Peslier
1998	King of Kings	Mick Kinane	2008	Henrythenavigator	Johnny Murtagh
1999	Island Sands	Frankie Dettori	2009	Sea The Stars	Mick Kinane

The Derby

Held since 1780. Table shows the winners for the past 20 years.

YEAR	HORSE	JOCKEY	YEAR	HORSE	JOCKEY
1990	Quest for Fame	Pat Eddery	2000	Sinndar	Johnny Murtagh
1991	Generous	Alan Munro	2001	Galileo	Mick Kinane
1992	Dr Devious	John Reid	2002	High Chaparral	Johnny Murtagh
1993	Commander in Chief	Mick Kinane	2003	Kris Kin	Kieren Fallon
1994	Erhaab	Willie Carson	2004	North Light	Kieren Fallon
1995	Lammtarra	Walter R. Swinburn	2005	Motivator	Johnny Murtagh
1996	Shaamit	Michael Hills	2006	Sir Percy	Martin Dwyer
1997	Benny the Dip	Willie Ryan	2007	Authorized	Frankie Dettori
1998	High Rise	Olivier Peslier	2008	New Approach	Kevin Manning
1999	Oath	Kieren Fallon	2009	Sea The Stars	Mick Kinane

The St. Leger

Held since 1776. Table shows the winners for the past 20 years.

YEAR	HORSE	JOCKEY	YEAR	HORSE	JOCKEY
1989	Michelozzo	Steve Cauthen	1999	Mutafaweq	Richard Hills
1990	Snurge	Richard Quinn	2000	Millenary	Richard Quinn
1991	Toulon	Pat Eddery	2001	Milan	Mick Kinane
1992	User Friendly	George Duffield	2002	Bollin Eric	Kevin Darley
1993	Bob's Return	Philip Robinson	2003	Brian Boru	Jamie Spencer
1994	Moonax	Pat Eddery	2004	Rule of Law	Kerrin McEvoy
1995	Classic Cliché	Frankie Dettori	2005	Scorpion	Frankie Dettori
1996	Shantou	Frankie Dettori	2006	Sixties Icon	Frankie Dettori
1997	Silver Patriarch	Pat Eddery	2007	Lucarno	Jimmy Fortune
1998	Nedawi	John Reid	2008	Conduit	Frankie Dettori

Triple Crown Champions—British

YEAR	WINNER	YEAR	WINNER	YEAR	WINNER	YEAR	WINNER
1853	West Australian	1891	Common	1900	Diamond Jubilee	1918	Gainsborough
1865	Gladiateur	1893	Isinglass	1903	Rock Sand	1935	Bahram
1866	Lord Lyon	1897	Galtee More	1915	Pommern	1970	Nijinsky
1886	Ormonde	1899	Flying Fox	1917	Gay Crusader		

Melbourne Cup

Held since 1861. Table shows the winners for the past 20 years.

YEAR	HORSE	JOCKEY	YEAR	HORSE	JOCKEY
1989	Tawrrific	Shane Dye	1999	Rogan Josh	John Marshall
1990	Kingston Rule	Darren Beadman	2000	Brew	Kerrin McEvoy
1991	Let's Elope	Steven King	2001	Ethereal	Scott Seamer
1992	Subzero	Greg Hall	2002	Media Puzzle	Damien Oliver
1993	Vintage Crop	Mick Kinane	2003	Makybe Diva	Glen Boss
1994	Jeune	Wayne Harris	2004	Makybe Diva	Glen Boss
1995	Doriemus	Damien Oliver	2005	Makybe Diva	Glen Boss
1996	Saintly	Darren Beadman	2006	Delta Blues	Yasunari Iwata
1997	Might and Power	Jim Cassidy	2007	Efficient	Michael Rodd
1998	Jezabeel	Chris Munce	2008	Viewed	Blake Shinn

Dubai World Cup

YEAR	HORSE	JOCKEY	YEAR	HORSE	JOCKEY
1996	Cigar	Jerry Bailey	2003	Moon Ballad	Frankie Dettori
1997	Singspiel	Jerry Bailey	2004	Pleasantly Perfect	Alex Solis
1998	Silver Charm	Gary Stevens	2005	Roses in May	John Velazquez
1999	Almutawakel	Richard Hills	2006	Electrocutionist	Frankie Dettori
2000	Dubai Millennium	Frankie Dettori	2007	Invasor	Fernando Jara
2001	Captain Steve	Jerry Bailey	2008	Curlin	Robby Albarado
2002	Street Cry	Jerry Bailey	2009	Well Armed	Aaron Gryder

Hambletonian Trot

YEAR	HORSE	DRIVER	YEAR	HORSE	DRIVER
1926	Guy McKinney	Nat Ray	1969	Lindy's Pride	Howard Beissinger
1927	Iosola's Worthy	Marvin Childs	1970	Timothy T.	John Simpson, Sr.
1928	Spencer	William H. Leese	1971	Speedy Crown	Howard Beissinger
1929	Walter Dear	Walter Cox	1972	Super Bowl	Stanley Dancer
1930	Hanover's Bertha	Thomas Berry	1973	Flirth	Ralph Baldwin
1931	Calumet Butler	Richard D. McMahon	1974	Christopher T.	William Haughton
1932	The Marchioness	William Caton	1975	Bonefish	Stanley Dancer
1933	Mary Reynolds	Ben White	1976	Steve Lobell	William Haughton
1934	Lord Jim	Hugh M. Parshall	1977	Green Speed	William Haughton
1935	Greyhound	Scepter F. Palin	1978	Speedy Somolli	Howard Beissinger
1936	Rosalind	Ben White	1979	Legend Hanover	George Sholty
1937	Shirley Hanover	Henry Thomas	1980	Burgomeister	William Haughton
1938	McLin Hanover	Henry Thomas	1981	Shiaway St. Pat	Ray Remmen
1939	Peter Astra	Hugh M. Parshall	1982	Speed Bowl	Tom Haughton
1940	Spencer Scott	Fred Egan	1983	Duenna	Stanley Dancer
1941	Bill Gallon	Lee Smith	1984	Historic Freight	Ben Webster
1942	The Ambassador	Ben White	1985	Prakas	William O'Donnell
1943	Volo Song	Ben White	1986	Nuclear Kosmos	Ulf Thoresen
1944	Yankee Maid	Henry Thomas	1987	Mack Lobell	John Campbell
1945	Titan Hanover	Harry Pownall, Sr.	1988	Armbro Goal	John Campbell
1946	Chestertown	Thomas Berry	1989	Park Avenue Joe;	Ronald Waples;
1947	Hoot Mon	Scepter F. Palin		Probe (tied)	William Fahy
1948	Demon Hanover	Harrison Hoyt	1990	Harmonious	John Campbell
1949	Miss Tilly	Fred Egan	1991	Giant Victory	Jack Moiseyev
1950	Lusty Song	Delvin Miller	1992	Alf Palema	Mickey McNichol
1951	Mainliner	Guy Crippen	1993	American Winner	Ron Pierce
1952	Sharp Note	Bion Shively	1994	Victory Dream	Michel Lachance
1953	Helicopter	Harry Harvey	1995	Tagliabue	John Campbell
1954	Newport Dream	Adelbert Cameron	1996	Continentalvictory	Michel Lachance
1955	Scott Frost	Joseph O'Brien	1997	Malabar Man	Malvern Burroughs
1956	The Intruder	Ned Bower	1998	Muscles Yankee	John Campbell
1957	Hickory Smoke	John Simpson, Sr.	1999	Self Possessed	Michel Lachance
1958	Emily's Pride	Flave Nipe	2000	Yankee Paco	Trevor Ritchie
1959	Diller Hanover	Frank Ervin	2001	Scarlet Knight	Stefan Melander
1960	Blaze Hanover	Joseph O'Brien	2002	Chip Chip Hooray	Eric Ledford
1961	Harlan Dean	James Arthur	2003	Amigo Hall	Michel Lachance
1962	A.C.'s Viking	Sanders Russell	2004	Windsong's Legacy	Trond Smedshammer
1963	Speedy Scot	Ralph Baldwin	2005	Vivid Photo	Roger Hammer
1964	Ayres	John Simpson, Sr.	2006	Glidemaster	John Campbell
1965	Egyptian Candor	Adelbert Cameron	2007	Donato Hanover	Ron Pierce
1966	Kerry Way	Frank Ervin	2008	Deweycheatumnhowe	Ray Schnittker
1967	Speedy Streak	Adelbert Cameron	2009	Muscle Hill	Brian Sears
1968	Nevele Pride	Stanley Dancer			

Ice Hockey

The **National Hockey League** (NHL), which was organized in Canada in 1917, welcomed the first US team, the Boston Bruins, in 1924. Since 1926 the symbol of supremacy in professional hockey has been the **Stanley Cup**, which is awarded to the winner of a play-off that concludes the NHL season. The Stanley Cup was presented to amateur champions from 1893 to 1925. The **World Hockey Championships**, contested by national teams and sponsored by the **International Ice Hockey Federation** (IIHF; founded 1908), have been held since 1930 for men and since 1990 for women.

Related Web sites: National Hockey League: <www.nhl.com>; International Ice Hockey Federation: <www.iihf.com>.

World Hockey Championship—Men

YEAR	WINNER	YEAR	WINNER	YEAR	WINNER	YEAR	WINNER
1920[1]	Canada	1953	Sweden	1973	USSR	1993	Russia
1924[1]	Canada	1954	USSR	1974	USSR	1994	Canada
1928[1]	Canada	1955	Canada	1975	USSR	1995	Finland
1930	Canada	1956[1]	USSR	1976	Czechoslovakia	1996	Czech Republic
1931	Canada	1957	Sweden	1977	Czechoslovakia	1997	Canada
1932[1]	Canada	1958	Canada	1978	USSR	1998	Sweden
1933	United States	1959	Canada	1979	USSR	1999	Czech Republic
1934	Canada	1960[1]	United States	1980	*not held*	2000	Czech Republic
1935	Canada	1961	Canada	1981	USSR	2001	Czech Republic
1936[1]	Great Britain	1962	Sweden	1982	USSR	2002	Slovakia
1937	Canada	1963	USSR	1983	USSR	2003	Canada
1938	Canada	1964[1]	USSR	1984	*not held*	2004	Canada
1939	Canada	1965	USSR	1985	Czechoslovakia	2005	Czech Republic
1940–46	*not held*	1966	USSR	1986	USSR	2006	Sweden
1947	Czechoslovakia	1967	USSR	1987	Sweden	2007	Canada
1948[1]	Canada	1968[1]	USSR	1988	*not held*	2008	Russia
1949	Czechoslovakia	1969	USSR	1989	USSR	2009	Russia
1950	Canada	1970	USSR	1990	Sweden		
1951	Canada	1971	USSR	1991	Sweden		
1952[1]	Canada	1972[2]	Czechoslovakia	1992	Sweden		

[1]*Olympic championships, recognized in this table as world championships.* [2]*In 1972 a separate world championship was held for the first time in an Olympic year.*

World Hockey Championship—Women

YEAR	WINNER	YEAR	WINNER	YEAR	WINNER	YEAR	WINNER
1990	Canada	1999	Canada	2003	*not held*	2007	Canada
1992	Canada	2000	Canada	2004	Canada	2008	United States
1994	Canada	2001	Canada	2005	United States	2009	United States
1997	Canada						

National Hockey League Final Standings, 2008–09

EASTERN CONFERENCE

Northeast Division

	WON	LOST	OTL[1]
Boston[2]	53	19	10
Montreal[2]	41	30	11
Buffalo	41	32	9
Ottawa	36	35	11
Toronto	34	35	13

Atlantic Division

	WON	LOST	OTL[1]
New Jersey[2]	51	27	4
Pittsburgh[2]	45	28	9
Philadelphia[2]	44	27	11
New York Rangers[2]	43	30	9
New York Islanders	26	47	9

Southeast Division

	WON	LOST	OTL[1]
Washington[2]	50	24	8
Carolina[2]	45	30	7
Florida	41	30	11
Atlanta	35	41	6
Tampa Bay	24	40	18

WESTERN CONFERENCE

Central Division

	WON	LOST	OTL[1]
Detroit[2]	51	21	10
Chicago[2]	46	24	12
St. Louis[2]	41	31	10
Columbus[2]	41	31	10
Nashville	40	34	8

Northwest Division

	WON	LOST	OTL[1]
Vancouver[2]	45	27	10
Calgary[2]	46	30	6
Minnesota	40	33	9
Edmonton	38	35	9
Colorado	32	45	5

Pacific Division

	WON	LOST	OTL[1]
San Jose[2]	53	18	11
Anaheim[2]	42	33	7
Dallas	36	35	11
Phoenix	36	39	7
Los Angeles	34	37	11

[1]*Overtime losses, worth one point.* [2]*Gained play-off berth.*

Stanley Cup

YEAR	WINNER	RUNNER-UP	RESULTS
1893	Montreal Amateur Athletic Association	*no challengers*	
1894	Montreal Amateur Athletic Association	Ottawa Generals	2–0
1895	Montreal Victorias	*no challengers*	

Stanley Cup (continued)

YEAR	WINNER	RUNNER-UP	RESULTS
1896	Winnipeg Victorias (Feb.); Montreal Victorias (Dec.)	Montreal Victorias (Feb.); Winnipeg Victorias (Dec.)	1-0; 1-0
1897	Montreal Victorias	Ottawa Capitals	1-0
1898	Montreal Victorias	no challengers	
1899	Montreal Victorias (Feb.); Montreal Shamrocks (March)	Winnipeg Victorias (Feb.); Queen's University (March)	2-0; 1-0
1900	Montreal Shamrocks	Winnipeg Victorias; Halifax Crescents	2-1; 2-0
1901	Winnipeg Victorias	Montreal Shamrocks	2-0
1902	Winnipeg Victorias (Jan.); Montreal Amateur Athletic Association (March)	Toronto Wellingtons (Jan.); Winnipeg Victorias (March)	2-0; 2-1
1903	Montreal Amateur Athletic Association (Feb.); Ottawa Silver Seven (March)	Winnipeg Victorias (Feb.); Montreal Victorias (March); Rat Portage Thistles (March)	2-1; 1-0; 2-0
1904	Ottawa Silver Seven	Winnipeg Rowing Club; Toronto Marlboros; Montreal Wanderers; Brandon Wheat Kings	2-1; 2-0; 0-0 (tie); 2-0
1905	Ottawa Silver Seven	Dawson City Nuggets; Rat Portage Thistles	2-0; 2-1
1906	Ottawa Silver Seven (Feb., March); Montreal Wanderers (March, Dec.)	Queen's University (Feb.); Smiths Falls (March); Ottawa Silver Seven (March); New Glasgow Cubs (Dec.)	2-0; 2-0; 1-1; 2-0
1907	Kenora Thistles (Jan.); Montreal Wanderers (March)	Montreal Wanderers (Jan.); Kenora Thistles (March)	2-0; 1-1
1908	Montreal Wanderers	Ottawa Victorias; Winnipeg Maple Leafs; Toronto Trolley Leaguers; Edmonton Eskimos	2-0; 2-0; 1-0; 1-1
1909	Ottawa Senators	no challengers	
1910	Ottawa Senators (Jan.); Montreal Wanderers (March)	Galt Professionals (Jan.); Edmonton Eskimos (Jan.); Berlin Union Jacks (March)	2-0; 2-0; 1-0
1911	Ottawa Senators	Port Arthur Bearcats; Galt Professionals	1-0; 1-0
1912	Quebec Bulldogs	Moncton Victorias	2-0
1913	Quebec Bulldogs[1]	Sydney Miners	2-0
1914	Toronto Blueshirts	Montreal Canadiens; Victoria Aristocrats	1-1; 3-0
1915	Vancouver Millionaires	Ottawa Senators	3-0
1916	Montreal Canadiens	Portland Rosebuds	3-2
1917	Seattle Metropolitans	Montreal Canadiens	3-1
1918	Toronto Arenas	Vancouver Millionaires	3-2
1919	no decision[2]		
1920	Ottawa Senators	Seattle Metropolitans	3-2
1921	Ottawa Senators	Vancouver Millionaires	3-2
1922	Toronto St. Patricks	Vancouver Millionaires	3-2
1923	Ottawa Senators	Edmonton Eskimos	2-0
1924	Montreal Canadiens	Calgary Tigers	2-0
1925	Victoria Cougars	Montreal Canadiens	3-1
1926	Montreal Maroons	Victoria Cougars	3-1
1927	Ottawa Senators	Boston Bruins	2-0
1928	New York Rangers	Montreal Maroons	3-2
1929	Boston Bruins	New York Rangers	2-0
1930	Montreal Canadiens	Boston Bruins	2-0
1931	Montreal Canadiens	Chicago Black Hawks	3-2
1932	Toronto Maple Leafs	New York Rangers	3-0
1933	New York Rangers	Toronto Maple Leafs	3-1
1934	Chicago Black Hawks	Detroit Red Wings	3-1
1935	Montreal Maroons	Toronto Maple Leafs	3-0
1936	Detroit Red Wings	Toronto Maple Leafs	3-1
1937	Detroit Red Wings	New York Rangers	3-2
1938	Chicago Black Hawks	Toronto Maple Leafs	3-1
1939	Boston Bruins	Toronto Maple Leafs	4-1
1940	New York Rangers	Toronto Maple Leafs	4-2
1941	Boston Bruins	Detroit Red Wings	4-0
1942	Toronto Maple Leafs	Detroit Red Wings	4-3
1943	Detroit Red Wings	Boston Bruins	4-0
1944	Montreal Canadiens	Chicago Black Hawks	4-0
1945	Toronto Maple Leafs	Detroit Red Wings	4-3
1946	Montreal Canadiens	Boston Bruins	4-1
1947	Toronto Maple Leafs	Montreal Canadiens	4-2
1948	Toronto Maple Leafs	Detroit Red Wings	4-0
1949	Toronto Maple Leafs	Detroit Red Wings	4-0

Stanley Cup (continued)

YEAR	WINNER	RUNNER-UP	RESULTS
1950	Detroit Red Wings	New York Rangers	4-3
1951	Toronto Maple Leafs	Montreal Canadiens	4-1
1952	Detroit Red Wings	Montreal Canadiens	4-0
1953	Montreal Canadiens	Boston Bruins	4-1
1954	Detroit Red Wings	Montreal Canadiens	4-3
1955	Detroit Red Wings	Montreal Canadiens	4-3
1956	Montreal Canadiens	Detroit Red Wings	4-1
1957	Montreal Canadiens	Boston Bruins	4-1
1958	Montreal Canadiens	Boston Bruins	4-2
1959	Montreal Canadiens	Toronto Maple Leafs	4-1
1960	Montreal Canadiens	Toronto Maple Leafs	4-0
1961	Chicago Black Hawks	Detroit Red Wings	4-2
1962	Toronto Maple Leafs	Chicago Black Hawks	4-2
1963	Toronto Maple Leafs	Detroit Red Wings	4-1
1964	Toronto Maple Leafs	Detroit Red Wings	4-3
1965	Montreal Canadiens	Chicago Black Hawks	4-3
1966	Montreal Canadiens	Detroit Red Wings	4-2
1967	Toronto Maple Leafs	Montreal Canadiens	4-2
1968	Montreal Canadiens	St. Louis Blues	4-0
1969	Montreal Canadiens	St. Louis Blues	4-0
1970	Boston Bruins	St. Louis Blues	4-0
1971	Montreal Canadiens	Chicago Black Hawks	4-3
1972	Boston Bruins	New York Rangers	4-2
1973	Montreal Canadiens	Chicago Black Hawks	4-2
1974	Philadelphia Flyers	Boston Bruins	4-2
1975	Philadelphia Flyers	Buffalo Sabres	4-2
1976	Montreal Canadiens	Philadelphia Flyers	4-0
1977	Montreal Canadiens	Boston Bruins	4-0
1978	Montreal Canadiens	Boston Bruins	4-2
1979	Montreal Canadiens	New York Rangers	4-1
1980	New York Islanders	Philadelphia Flyers	4-2
1981	New York Islanders	Minnesota North Stars	4-1
1982	New York Islanders	Vancouver Canucks	4-0
1983	New York Islanders	Edmonton Oilers	4-0
1984	Edmonton Oilers	New York Islanders	4-1
1985	Edmonton Oilers	Philadelphia Flyers	4-1
1986	Montreal Canadiens	Calgary Flames	4-1
1987	Edmonton Oilers	Philadelphia Flyers	4-3
1988	Edmonton Oilers	Boston Bruins	4-0
1989	Calgary Flames	Montreal Canadiens	4-2
1990	Edmonton Oilers	Boston Bruins	4-1
1991	Pittsburgh Penguins	Minnesota North Stars	4-2
1992	Pittsburgh Penguins	Chicago Blackhawks	4-0
1993	Montreal Canadiens	Los Angeles Kings	4-1
1994	New York Rangers	Vancouver Canucks	4-3
1995	New Jersey Devils	Detroit Red Wings	4-0
1996	Colorado Avalanche	Florida Panthers	4-0
1997	Detroit Red Wings	Philadelphia Flyers	4-0
1998	Detroit Red Wings	Washington Capitals	4-0
1999	Dallas Stars	Buffalo Sabres	4-2
2000	New Jersey Devils	Dallas Stars	4-2
2001	Colorado Avalanche	New Jersey Devils	4-3
2002	Detroit Red Wings	Carolina Hurricanes	4-1
2003	New Jersey Devils	Mighty Ducks of Anaheim	4-3
2004	Tampa Bay Lightning	Calgary Flames	4-3
2005	*not held*		
2006	Carolina Hurricanes	Edmonton Oilers	4-3
2007	Anaheim Ducks	Ottawa Senators	4-1
2008	Detroit Red Wings	Pittsburgh Penguins	4-2
2009	Pittsburgh Penguins	Detroit Red Wings	4-3

[1]*Though Victoria defeated Quebec in challenge games, Victoria's win was not officially recognized.* [2]*Series between Montreal Canadiens and Seattle Metropolitans called off because of flu epidemic.*

Marathon

The marathon is a long-distance footrace first held at the revival of the Olympic Games at Athens in 1896. It commemorates the legendary feat of a Greek soldier who, in 490 BC, is supposed to have run from Marathon to Athens, a distance of about 40 km (25 mi), to bring news of the Athenian victory over the Persians. Appropriately, the first modern marathon winner in 1896 was a Greek, Spyridon Louis. In 1924 the **Olympic marathon distance** was standardized at 42,195 m, or 26 mi 385 yd. This was based on a decision of the British Olympic Committee to start the 1908 Olympic race from Windsor Castle and finish it in front of the royal box in the stadium at London. The marathon was added to the **women's Olympic program** in 1984. Because marathon courses are not of equal diffi-

culty, the **International Association of Athletics Federations** (IAAF) does not list a world record for the event. After the Olympic Games championship, one of the most coveted honors in marathon running is victory in the **Boston Marathon**, held annually since 1897. It draws athletes from all parts of the world and in 1972 became the first marathon officially to allow women to compete. The **New York City Marathon** also attracts participants from many countries, as does the **Chicago Marathon**. Other popular marathons are held in London, Berlin, Dublin, and Rotterdam (The Netherlands).

Related Web sites:
Boston Marathon: <www.bostonmarathon.org>;
New York City Marathon: <www.ingnycmarathon.org>;
Chicago Marathon: <www.chicagomarathon.com>.

Boston Marathon

Times are given in hours:minutes:seconds.

men

YEAR	WINNER	TIME	YEAR	WINNER	TIME
1897	John J. McDermott (USA)	2:55:10	1942	Joe Smith (USA)	2:26:51
1898	Ronald J. McDonald (CAN)	2:42:00	1943	Gerard Cote (CAN)	2:28:25
1899	Lawrence J. Brignoli (USA)	2:54:38	1944	Gerard Cote (CAN)	2:31:50
1900	John J. Caffrey (CAN)	2:39:44	1945	John A. Kelley (USA)	2:30:40
1901	John J. Caffrey (CAN)	2:29:23	1946	Stylianos Kyriakides (GRE)	2:29:27
1902	Sammy A. Mellor (USA)	2:43:12	1947	Suh Yun Bok (KOR)	2:25:39
1903	John C. Lorden (USA)	2:41:29	1948	Gerard Cote (CAN)	2:31:02
1904	Michael Spring (USA)	2:39:04	1949	Karl G. Leandersson (SWE)	2:31:50
1905	Frederick Lorz (USA)	2:38:25	1950	Ham Kee Yong (KOR)	2:32:39
1906	Tim Ford (USA)	2:45:45	1951	Tanaka Shigeki (JPN)	2:27:45
1907	Thomas Longboat (CAN)	2:24:24	1952	Doroteo Flores (GUA)	2:31:53
1908	Thomas P. Morrissey (USA)	2:25:43	1953	Yamada Keizo (JPN)	2:18:51
1909	Henri Renaud (USA)	2:53:36	1954	Veikko L. Karanen (FIN)	2:20:39
1910	Fred L. Cameron (CAN)	2:28:52	1955	Hamamura Hideo (JPN)	2:18:22
1911	Clarence H. DeMar (USA)	2:21:39	1956	Antti Viskari (FIN)	2:14:14
1912	Michael J. Ryan (USA)	2:21:18	1957	John J. Kelley (USA)	2:20:05
1913	Fritz Carlson (USA)	2:25:14	1958	Franjo Mihalic (YUG)	2:25:54
1914	James Duffy (CAN)	2:25:01	1959	Eino Oksanen (FIN)	2:22:42
1915	Edouard Fabre (CAN)	2:31:41	1960	Paavo Kotila (FIN)	2:20:54
1916	Arthur V. Roth (USA)	2:27:16	1961	Eino Oksanen (FIN)	2:23:39
1917	William K. Kennedy (USA)	2:28:37	1962	Eino Oksanen (FIN)	2:23:48
1918	*not held*		1963	Aurele Vandendriessche (BEL)	2:18:58
1919	Carl W.A. Linder (USA)	2:29:13	1964	Aurele Vandendriessche (BEL)	2:19:59
1920	Peter Trivoulides (USA)	2:29:31	1965	Shigematsu Morio (JPN)	2:16:33
1921	Frank Zuna (USA)	2:18:57	1966	Kimihara Kenji (JPN)	2:17:11
1922	Clarence H. DeMar (USA)	2:18:10	1967	David McKenzie (NZL)	2:15:45
1923	Clarence H. DeMar (USA)	2:23:47	1968	Amby Burfoot (USA)	2:22:17
1924	Clarence H. DeMar (USA)	2:29:40	1969	Unetani Yoshiaki (JPN)	2:13:49
1925	Charles L. Mellor (USA)	2:33:06	1970	Ron Hill (GBR)	2:10:30
1926	John C. Miles (CAN)	2:25:40	1971	Alvaro Mejia (COL)	2:18:45
1927	Clarence H. DeMar (USA)	2:40:22	1972	Olavi Suomalainen (FIN)	2:15:30
1928	Clarence H. DeMar (USA)	2:37:07	1973	Jon Anderson (USA)	2:16:03
1929	John C. Miles (CAN)	2:33:08	1974	Neil Cusack (USA)	2:13:39
1930	Clarence H. DeMar (USA)	2:34:48	1975	Bill Rodgers (USA)	2:09:55
1931	James P. Hennigan (USA)	2:46:45	1976	Jack Fultz (USA)	2:20:19
1932	Paul DeBruyn (GER)	2:33:36	1977	Jerome Drayton (CAN)	2:14:46
1933	Leslie S. Pawson (USA)	2:31:01	1978	Bill Rodgers (USA)	2:10:13
1934	Dave Komonen (CAN)	2:32:53	1979	Bill Rodgers (USA)	2:09:27
1935	John A. Kelley (USA)	2:32:07	1980	Bill Rodgers (USA)	2:12:11
1936	Ellison M. Brown (USA)	2:33:40	1981	Seko Toshihiko (JPN)	2:09:26
1937	Walter Young (CAN)	2:33:20	1982	Alberto Salazar (USA)	2:08:51
1938	Leslie S. Pawson (USA)	2:35:34	1983	Greg A. Meyer (USA)	2:09:00
1939	Ellison M. Brown (USA)	2:28:51	1984	Geoff Smith (GBR)	2:10:34
1940	Gerard Cote (CAN)	2:28:28	1985	Geoff Smith (GBR)	2:14:05
1941	Leslie S. Pawson (USA)	2:30:38	1986	Robert de Castella (AUS)	2:07:51

Boston Marathon (continued)

men (continued)

YEAR	WINNER	TIME	YEAR	WINNER	TIME
1987	Seko Toshihiko (JPN)	2:11:50	1999	Joseph Chebet (KEN)	2:09:52
1988	Ibrahim Hussein (KEN)	2:08:43	2000	Elijah Lagat (KEN)	2:09:47
1989	Abebe Mekonnen (ETH)	2:09:06	2001	Lee Bong Ju (KOR)	2:09:43
1990	Gelindo Bordin (ITA)	2:08:19	2002	Rodgers Rop (KEN)	2:09:02
1991	Ibrahim Hussein (KEN)	2:11:06	2003	Robert Kipkoech Cheruiyot (KEN)	2:10:11
1992	Ibrahim Hussein (KEN)	2:08:14	2004	Timothy Cherigat (KEN)	2:10:37
1993	Cosmas N'Deti (KEN)	2:09:33	2005	Hailu Negussie (ETH)	2:11:45
1994	Cosmas N'Deti (KEN)	2:07:15	2006	Robert Kipkoech Cheruiyot (KEN)	2:07:14
1995	Cosmas N'Deti (KEN)	2:09:22	2007	Robert Kipkoech Cheruiyot (KEN)	2:14:13
1996	Moses Tanui (KEN)	2:09:16	2008	Robert Kipkoech Cheruiyot (KEN)	2:07:46
1997	Lameck Aguta (KEN)	2:10:34	2009	Deriba Merga (ETH)	2:08:42
1998	Moses Tanui (KEN)	2:07:34			

women

YEAR	WINNER	TIME	YEAR	WINNER	TIME
1972	Nina Kuscsik (USA)	3:10:26	1991	Wanda Panfil (POL)	2:24:18
1973	Jacqueline Hansen (USA)	3:05:59	1992	Olga Markova (RUS)	2:23:43
1974	Michiko Gorman (USA)	2:47:11	1993	Olga Markova (RUS)	2:25:27
1975	Liane Winter (FRG)	2:42:24	1994	Uta Pippig (GER)	2:21:45
1976	Kim Merritt (USA)	2:47:10	1995	Uta Pippig (GER)	2:25:11
1977	Michiko Gorman (USA)	2:46:22	1996	Uta Pippig (GER)	2:27:12
1978	Gayle S. Barron (USA)	2:44:52	1997	Fatuma Roba (ETH)	2:26:23
1979	Joan Benoit (USA)	2:35:15	1998	Fatuma Roba (ETH)	2:23:21
1980	Jacqueline Gareau (CAN)	2:34:28	1999	Fatuma Roba (ETH)	2:23:25
1981	Allison Roe (NZL)	2:26:46	2000	Catherine Ndereba (KEN)	2:26:11
1982	Charlotte Teske (FRG)	2:29:33	2001	Catherine Ndereba (KEN)	2:23:53
1983	Joan Benoit (USA)	2:22:42	2002	Margaret Okayo (KEN)	2:20:43
1984	Lorraine Moller (NZL)	2:29:28	2003	Svetlana Zakharova (RUS)	2:25:20
1985	Lisa Larsen (USA)	2:34:06	2004	Catherine Ndereba (KEN)	2:24:27
1986	Ingrid Kristiansen (NOR)	2:24:55	2005	Catherine Ndereba (KEN)	2:25:13
1987	Rosa Mota (POR)	2:25:21	2006	Rita Jeptoo (KEN)	2:23:38
1988	Rosa Mota (POR)	2:24:30	2007	Lidiya Grigoryeva (RUS)	2:29:18
1989	Ingrid Kristiansen (NOR)	2:24:33	2008	Dire Tune (ETH)	2:25:25
1990	Rosa Mota (POR)	2:25:23	2009	Salina Kosgei (KEN)	2:32:16

New York City Marathon

Times are given in hours:minutes:seconds.

YEAR	MEN	TIME	WOMEN	TIME
1970	Gary Muhrcke (USA)	2:31:38	no finisher	
1971	Norm Higgins (USA)	2:22:54	Beth Bonner (USA)	2:55:22
1972	Robert Karlin (USA)	2:27:52	Nina Kuscsik (USA)	3:08:41
1973	Tom Fleming (USA)	2:21:54	Nina Kuscsik (USA)	2:57:07
1974	Norbert Sander (USA)	2:26:30	Katherine Switzer (USA)	3:07:29
1975	Tom Fleming (USA)	2:19:27	Kim Merritt (USA)	2:46:14
1976	Bill Rodgers (USA)	2:10:09	Michiko Gorman (USA)	2:39:11
1977	Bill Rodgers (USA)	2:11:28	Michiko Gorman (USA)	2:43:10
1978	Bill Rodgers (USA)	2:12:12	Grete Waitz (NOR)	2:32:30
1979	Bill Rodgers (USA)	2:11:42	Grete Waitz (NOR)	2:27:33
1980	Alberto Salazar (USA)	2:09:41	Grete Waitz (NOR)	2:25:41
1981	Alberto Salazar (USA)	2:08:13	Allison Roe (NZL)	2:25:29
1982	Alberto Salazar (USA)	2:09:29	Grete Waitz (NOR)	2:27:14
1983	Rod Dixon (NZL)	2:08:59	Grete Waitz (NOR)	2:27:00
1984	Orlando Pizzolato (ITA)	2:14:53	Grete Waitz (NOR)	2:29:30
1985	Orlando Pizzolato (ITA)	2:11:34	Grete Waitz (NOR)	2:28:34
1986	Gianni Poli (ITA)	2:11:06	Grete Waitz (NOR)	2:28:06
1987	Ibrahim Hussein (KEN)	2:11:01	Priscilla Welch (GBR)	2:30:17
1988	Steve Jones (GBR)	2:08:20	Grete Waitz (NOR)	2:28:07
1989	Juma Ikangaa (TAN)	2:08:01	Ingrid Kristiansen (NOR)	2:25:30
1990	Douglas Wakiihuri (KEN)	2:12:39	Wanda Panfil (POL)	2:30:45
1991	Salvador Garcia (MEX)	2:09:28	Liz McColgan (GBR)	2:27:23
1992	Willie Mtolo (RSA)	2:09:29	Lisa Ondieki (AUS)	2:24:40
1993	Andrés Espinosa (MEX)	2:10:04	Uta Pippig (GER)	2:26:24
1994	German Silva (MEX)	2:11:21	Tegla Loroupe (KEN)	2:27:37

New York City Marathon (continued)

YEAR	MEN	TIME	WOMEN	TIME
1995	German Silva (MEX)	2:11:00	Tegla Loroupe (KEN)	2:28:06
1996	Giacomo Leone (ITA)	2:09:54	Anuta Catuna (ROM)	2:28:18
1997	John Kagwe (KEN)	2:08:12	Franziska Rochat-Moser (SUI)	2:28:43
1998	John Kagwe (KEN)	2:08:45	Franca Fiacconi (ITA)	2:25:17
1999	Joseph Chebet (KEN)	2:09:14	Adriana Fernández (MEX)	2:25:06
2000	Abdelkhader El Mouaziz (MAR)	2:10:09	Lyudmila Petrova (RUS)	2:25:45
2001	Tesfaye Jifar (ETH)	2:07:43	Margaret Okayo (KEN)	2:24:21
2002	Rodgers Rop (KEN)	2:08:07	Joyce Chepchumba (KEN)	2:25:56
2003	Martin Lel (KEN)	2:10:30	Margaret Okayo (KEN)	2:22:31
2004	Hendrik Ramaala (RSA)	2:09:28	Paula Radcliffe (GBR)	2:23:10
2005	Paul Tergat (KEN)	2:09:30	Jelena Prokopcuka (LAT)	2:24:41
2006	Marílson Gomes dos Santos (BRA)	2:09:58	Jelena Prokopcuka (LAT)	2:25:05
2007	Martin Lel (KEN)	2:09:04	Paula Radcliffe (GBR)	2:23:09
2008	Marílson Gomes dos Santos (BRA)	2:08:43	Paula Radcliffe (GBR)	2:23:56

Chicago Marathon

Times are given in hours:minutes:seconds.

YEAR	MEN	TIME	WOMEN	TIME
1977	Dan Cloeter (USA)	2:17:52	Dorothy Doolittle (USA)	2:50:47
1978	Mark Stanforth (USA)	2:19:20	Lynae Larson (USA)	2:59:25
1979	Dan Cloeter (USA)	2:23:20	Laura Michalek (USA)	3:15:45
1980	Frank Richardson (USA)	2:14:04	Sue Petersen (USA)	2:45:03
1981	Philip Coppess (USA)	2:16:13	Tina Gandy (USA)	2:49:39
1982	Greg Meyer (USA)	2:10:59	Nancy Conz (USA)	2:33:23
1983	Joseph Nzau (KEN)	2:09:44	Rosa Mota (POR)	2:31:12
1984	Steve Jones (GBR)	2:08:05	Rosa Mota (POR)	2:26:01
1985	Steve Jones (GBR)	2:07:13	Joan Benoit Samuelson (USA)	2:21:21
1986	Toshihiko Seko (JPN)	2:08:27	Ingrid Kristiansen (NOR)	2:27:08
1987	not held			
1988	Alejandro Cruz (MEX)	2:08:57	Lisa Weidenbach (USA)	2:29:17
1989	Paul Davis-Hale (GBR)	2:11:25	Lisa Weidenbach (USA)	2:28:15
1990	Martín Pitayo (MEX)	2:09:41	Aurora Cunha (POR)	2:30:11
1991	Joseildo Rocha (BRA)	2:14:33	Midde Hamrin-Senorski (SWE)	2:36:21
1992	José César de Souza (BRA)	2:16:14	Linda Somers (USA)	2:37:41
1993	Luiz Antônio dos Santos (BRA)	2:13:15	Ritva Lemettinen (FIN)	2:33:18
1994	Luiz Antônio dos Santos (BRA)	2:11:16	Kristy Johnston (USA)	2:31:34
1995	Eamonn Martin (GBR)	2:11:18	Ritva Lemettinen (FIN)	2:28:27
1996	Paul Evans (GBR)	2:08:52	Marian Sutton (GBR)	2:30:41
1997	Khalid Khannouchi (MAR)	2:07:10	Marian Sutton (GBR)	2:29:03
1998	Ondoro Osoro (KEN)	2:06:54	Joyce Chepchumba (KEN)	2:23:57
1999	Khalid Khannouchi (MAR)	2:05:42	Joyce Chepchumba (KEN)	2:25:59
2000	Khalid Khannouchi (USA)	2:07:01	Catherine Ndereba (KEN)	2:21:33
2001	Ben Kimondiu (KEN)	2:08:52	Catherine Ndereba (KEN)	2:18:47
2002	Khalid Khannouchi (USA)	2:05:56	Paula Radcliffe (GBR)	2:17:18
2003	Evans Rutto (KEN)	2:05:50	Svetlana Zakharova (RUS)	2:23:07
2004	Evans Rutto (KEN)	2:06:16	Constanţina Tomescu-Dita (ROM)	2:23:45
2005	Felix Limo (KEN)	2:07:02	Deena Kastor (USA)	2:21:25
2006	Robert Kipkoech Cheruiyot (KEN)	2:07:35	Berhane Adere (ETH)	2:20:42
2007	Patrick Ivuti (KEN)	2:11:11	Berhane Adere (ETH)	2:33:49
2008	Evans Cheruiyot (KEN)	2:06:25	Lidiya Grigoryeva (RUS)	2:27:17

Skiing

Although most of the events had been contested at the regional level since the mid-19th century, the first internationally organized skiing championships did not take place until 1924. From 1924 to 1931 only Nordic competition was involved; Alpine championship events were added to world competition in 1931 and to the Olympics in 1936. Except in Olympic years, the Nordic and Alpine championships are held separately and at different locations. Events include cross-country races, ski jumping, biathlon, and relay races (Nordic) and downhill and slalom skiing (Alpine). Since 1967, an Alpine World Cup has been presented to the competitor with the best combined downhill, slalom, giant slalom, and supergiant slalom (super-G) performance over a series of major contests. A Nordic World Cup for cross-country events has been awarded since 1979.

International Ski Federation (FIS) Web site:
<www.fis-ski.com>.

Alpine Skiing World Championships—Men
Held since 1931. Table shows results for the past 20 years.

DOWNHILL
1991 Franz Heinzer (SUI)
1992[1] Patrick Ortlieb (AUS)
1993 Urs Lehmann (SUI)
1994[1] Tommy Moe (USA)
1995 *not held*
1996 Patrick Ortlieb (AUS)
1997 Bruno Kernen (SUI)
1998[1] Jean-Luc Cretier (FRA)
1999 Hermann Maier (AUT)
2001 Hannes Trinkl (AUT)
2002[1] Fritz Strobl (AUT)
2003 Michael Walchhofer (AUT)
2005 Bode Miller (USA)
2006[1] Antoine Dénériaz (FRA)
2007 Aksel Lund Svindal (NOR)
2009 John Kucera (CAN)

COMBINED
1991 Stefan Eberharter (AUT)
1992[1] Josef Polig (ITA)
1993 Lasse Kjus (NOR)
1994[1] Lasse Kjus (NOR)
1995 *not held*
1996 Marc Girardelli (LUX)
1997 Kjetil André Aamodt (NOR)
1998[1] Mario Reiter (AUT)
1999 Kjetil André Aamodt (NOR)
2001 Kjetil André Aamodt (NOR)
2002[1] Kjetil André Aamodt (NOR)
2003 Bode Miller (USA)
2005 Benjamin Raich (AUT)
2006[1] Ted Ligety (USA)

COMBINED (CONTINUED)
2007 Daniel Albrecht (SUI)
2009 Aksel Lund Svindal (NOR)

SLALOM
1992[1] Finn Christian Jagge
        (NOR)
1993 Kjetil André Aamodt (NOR)
1994[1] Thomas Stangassinger
        (AUT)
1995 *not held*
1996 Alberto Tomba (ITA)
1997 Tom Stiansen (NOR)
1998[1] Hans Petter Buraas (NOR)
1999 Kalle Palander (FIN)
2001 Mario Matt (AUT)
2002[1] Jean-Pierre Vidal (FRA)
2003 Ivica Kostelic (CRO)
2005 Benjamin Raich (AUT)
2006[1] Benjamin Raich (AUT)
2007 Mario Matt (AUT)
2009 Manfred Pranger (AUT)

GIANT SLALOM
1991 Rudolf Nierlich (AUT)
1992[1] Alberto Tomba (ITA)
1993 Kjetil André Aamodt (NOR)
1994[1] Markus Wasmeier (GER)
1995 *not held*
1996 Alberto Tomba (ITA)
1997 Michael von Grünigen
        (SUI)
1998[1] Hermann Maier (AUT)
1999 Lasse Kjus (NOR)

GIANT SLALOM (CONTINUED)
2001 Michael von Grünigen
        (SUI)
2002[1] Stephan Eberharter (AUT)
2003 Bode Miller (USA)
2005 Hermann Maier (AUT)
2006[1] Benjamin Raich (AUT)
2007 Aksel Lund Svindal (NOR)
2009 Carlo Janka (SUI)

SUPERGIANT SLALOM
1991 Stephan Eberharter (AUT)
1992[1] Kjetil André Aamodt (NOR)
1993 *not held*
1994[1] Markus Wasmeier (GER)
1995 *not held*
1996 Atle Skårdal (NOR)
1997 Atle Skårdal (NOR)
1998[1] Hermann Maier (AUT)
1999 Lasse Kjus (NOR), Her-
        mann Maier (AUT) (*tied*)
2001 Daron Rahlves (USA)
2002[1] Kjetil André Aamodt
        (NOR)
2003 Stephan Eberharter (AUT)
2005 Bode Miller (USA)
2006[1] Kjetil André Aamodt (NOR)
2007 Patrick Staudacher (ITA)
2009 Didier Cuche (SUI)

[1]*Olympic champions, recognized in this table as world champions (though not by FIS).*

Alpine Skiing World Championships—Women
Held since 1931. Table shows results for the past 20 years.

DOWNHILL
1991 Petra Kronberger (AUT)
1992[1] Kerrin Lee-Gartner (CAN)
1993 Kate Pace (CAN)
1994[1] Katja Seizinger (GER)
1995 *not held*
1996 Picabo Street (USA)
1997 Hilary Lindh (USA)
1998[1] Katja Seizinger (GER)
1999 Renate Götschl (AUT)
2001 Michaela Dorfmeister
        (AUT)
2002[1] Carole Montillet (FRA)
2003 Mélanie Turgeon (CAN)
2005 Janica Kostelic (CRO)
2006[1] Michaela Dorfmeister
        (AUT)
2007 Anja Pärson (SWE)
2009 Lindsey Vonn (USA)

COMBINED
1991 Chantal Bournissen
        (SUI)
1992[1] Petra Kronberger (AUT)
1993 Miriam Vogt (GER)
1994[1] Pernilla Wiberg (SWE)
1995 *not held*

COMBINED (CONTINUED)
1996 Pernilla Wiberg (SWE)
1997 Renate Götschl (AUT)
1998[1] Katja Seizinger (GER)
1999 Pernilla Wiberg (SWE)
2001 Martina Ertl (GER)
2002[1] Janica Kostelic (CRO)
2003 Janica Kostelic (CRO)
2005 Janica Kostelic (CRO)
2006[1] Janica Kostelic (CRO)
2007 Anja Pärson (SWE)
2009 Kathrin Zettel (AUT)

SLALOM
1991 Vreni Schneider (SUI)
1992[1] Petra Kronberger (AUT)
1993 Karin Buder (AUT)
1994[1] Vreni Schneider (SUI)
1995 *not held*
1996 Pernilla Wiberg (SWE)
1997 Deborah Compagnoni
        (ITA)
1998[1] Hilde Gerg (GER)
1999 Zali Steggall (AUS)
2001 Anja Pärson (SWE)
2002[1] Janica Kostelic (CRO)
2003 Janica Kostelic (CRO)

SLALOM (CONTINUED)
2005 Janica Kostelic (CRO)
2006[1] Anja Pärson (SWE)
2007 Sarka Zahrobska (CZE)
2009 Maria Riesch (GER)

GIANT SLALOM
1991 Pernilla Wiberg (SWE)
1992[1] Pernilla Wiberg (SWE)
1993 Carole Merle (FRA)
1994[1] Deborah Compagnoni (ITA)
1995 *not held*
1996 Deborah Compagnoni (ITA)
1997 Deborah Compagnoni (ITA)
1998[1] Deborah Compagnoni (ITA)
1999 Alexandra Meissnitzer
        (AUT)
2001 Sonja Nef (SUI)
2002[1] Janica Kostelic (CRO)
2003 Anja Pärson (SWE)
2005 Anja Pärson (SWE)
2006[1] Julia Mancuso (USA)
2007 Nicole Hosp (AUT)
2009 Kathrin Hölzl (GER)

Alpine Skiing World Championships—Women (continued)

SUPERGIANT SLALOM
1991	Ulrike Maier (AUT)
1992[1]	Deborah Compagnoni (ITA)
1993	Katja Seizinger (GER)
1994[1]	Diann Roffe-Steinrotter (USA)
1995	not held
1996	Isolde Kostner (ITA)
1997	Isolde Kostner (ITA)
1998[1]	Picabo Street (USA)

SUPERGIANT SLALOM (CONTINUED)
1999	Alexandra Meissnitzer (AUT)
2001	Régine Cavagnoud (FRA)
2002[1]	Daniela Ceccarelli (ITA)
2003	Michaela Dorfmeister (AUT)
2005	Anja Pärson (SWE)

SUPERGIANT SLALOM (CONTINUED)
2006[1]	Michaela Dorfmeister (AUT)
2007	Anja Pärson (SWE)
2009	Lindsey Vonn (USA)

[1]Olympic champions, recognized in this table as world champions (though not by FIS).

Alpine World Cup

The winner is determined by the number of points awarded for finishes in various competitions during the season.

YEAR	MEN	WOMEN	YEAR	MEN	WOMEN
1967	Jean-Claude Killy (FRA)	Nancy Greene (CAN)	1987	Pirmin Zurbriggen (SUI)	Maria Walliser (SUI)
1968	Jean-Claude Killy (FRA)	Nancy Greene (CAN)	1988	Pirmin Zurbriggen (SUI)	Michela Figini (SUI)
1969	Karl Schranz (AUT)	Gertrude Gabl (AUT)	1989	Marc Girardelli (LUX)	Vreni Schneider (SUI)
1970	Karl Schranz (AUT)	Michele Jacot (FRA)	1990	Pirmin Zurbriggen (SUI)	Petra Kronberger (AUT)
1971	Gustavo Thöni (ITA)	Annemarie Pröll (AUT)	1991	Marc Girardelli (LUX)	Petra Kronberger (AUT)
1972	Gustavo Thöni (ITA)	Annemarie Pröll (AUT)	1992	Paul Accola (SUI)	Petra Kronberger (AUT)
1973	Gustavo Thöni (ITA)	Annemarie Pröll (AUT)	1993	Marc Girardelli (LUX)	Anita Wachter (AUT)
1974	Piero Gros (ITA)	Annemarie Moser-Pröll (AUT)	1994	Kjetil André Aamodt (NOR)	Vreni Schneider (SUI)
1975	Gustavo Thöni (ITA)	Annemarie Moser-Pröll (AUT)	1995	Alberto Tomba (ITA)	Vreni Schneider (SUI)
1976	Ingemar Stenmark (SWE)	Rosi Mittermaier (FRG)	1996	Lasse Kjus (NOR)	Katja Seizinger (GER)
1977	Ingemar Stenmark (SWE)	Lise-Marie Morerod (SUI)	1997	Luc Alphand (FRA)	Pernilla Wiberg (SWE)
1978	Ingemar Stenmark (SWE)	Hanni Wenzel (LIE)	1998	Hermann Maier (AUT)	Katja Seizinger (GER)
1979	Peter Luescher (SUI)	Annemarie Moser-Pröll (AUT)	1999	Lasse Kjus (NOR)	Alexandra Meissnitzer (AUT)
1980	Andreas Wenzel (LIE)	Hanni Wenzel (LIE)	2000	Hermann Maier (AUT)	Renate Götschl (AUT)
1981	Phil Mahre (USA)	Marie-Thérèse Nadig (SUI)	2001	Hermann Maier (AUT)	Janica Kostelic (CRO)
1982	Phil Mahre (USA)	Erika Hess (SUI)	2002	Stephan Eberharter (AUT)	Michaela Dorfmeister (AUT)
1983	Phil Mahre (USA)	Tamara McKinney (USA)	2003	Stephan Eberharter (AUT)	Janica Kostelic (CRO)
1984	Pirmin Zurbriggen (SUI)	Erika Hess (SUI)	2004	Hermann Maier (AUT)	Anja Pärson (SWE)
1985	Marc Girardelli (LUX)	Michela Figini (SUI)	2005	Bode Miller (USA)	Anja Pärson (SWE)
1986	Marc Girardelli (LUX)	Maria Walliser (SUI)	2006	Benjamin Raich (AUT)	Janica Kostelic (CRO)
			2007	Aksel Lund Svindal (NOR)	Nicole Hosp (AUT)
			2008	Bode Miller (USA)	Lindsey Vonn (USA)
			2009	Aksel Lund Svindal (NOR)	Lindsey Vonn (USA)

Nordic Skiing World Championships—Men

Held since 1924. Table shows results for the past 20 years.

INDIVIDUAL SPRINT
2001	Tor Arne Hetland (NOR)
2002[1]	Tor Arne Hetland (NOR)
2003	Thobias Fredriksson (SWE)
2005	Vassily Rochev (RUS)
2006[1]	Björn Lind (SWE)
2007	Jens Arne Svartedal (NOR)
2009	Ola Vigen Hattestad (NOR)

10-KM CROSS-COUNTRY[2]
1991	Terje Langli (NOR)
1992[1]	Vegard Ulvang (NOR)

10-KM CROSS-COUNTRY[2] (CONT.)
1993	Sture Sivertsen (NOR)
1994[1]	Bjørn Daehlie NOR)
1995	Vladimir Smirnov (KAZ)
1997	Bjørn Daehlie (NOR)
1998[1]	Bjørn Daehlie (NOR)
1999	Mika Myllylä (FIN)

15-KM CROSS-COUNTRY[2, 3]
1991	Bjørn Daehlie (NOR)
1992[1]	Bjørn Daehlie (NOR)
1993	Bjørn Daehlie (NOR)
1994[1]	Bjørn Daehlie (NOR)

15-KM CROSS-COUNTRY[2, 3] (CONT.)
1995	Vladimir Smirnov (KAZ)
1997	Bjørn Daehlie (NOR)
1998[1]	Thomas Alsgaard (NOR)
1999	Thomas Alsgaard (NOR)
2001	Per Elofsson (SWE)
2002[1]	Andrus Veerpalu (EST)
2003	Axel Teichmann (GER)
2005	Pietro Piller Cottrer (ITA)
2006[1]	Andrus Veerpalu (EST)
2007	Lars Berger (NOR)
2009	Andrus Veerpalu (EST)

Nordic Skiing World Championships—Men (continued)

COMBINED PURSUIT[2]

2001 Per Elofsson (SWE)
2002[1] Thomas Alsgaard (NOR),
  Frode Estil (NOR) (tied)
2003 Per Elofsson (SWE)
2005 Vincent Vittoz (FRA)
2006[1] Yevgeny Dementyev (RUS)
2007 Axel Teichmann (GER)
2009 Petter Northug, Jr. (NOR)

30-KM CROSS-COUNTRY

1991 Gunde Svan (SWE)
1992[1] Vegard Ulvang (NOR)
1993 Bjørn Daehlie (NOR)
1994[1] Thomas Alsgaard (NOR)
1995 Vladimir Smirnov (KAZ)
1997 Aleksey Prokurorov (RUS)
1998[1] Mika Myllylä (FIN)
1999 Mika Myllylä (FIN)
2001 Andrus Veerpalu (EST)
2002[1] Christian Hoffmann (AUT)
2003 Thomas Alsgaard (NOR)

50-KM CROSS-COUNTRY

1991 Torgny Mogren (SWE)
1992[1] Bjørn Daehlie (NOR)
1993 Torgny Mogren (SWE)
1994 Vladimir Smirnov (KAZ)
1995 Silvio Fauner (ITA)
1997 Mika Myllylä (FIN)
1998[1] Bjørn Daehlie (NOR)
1999 Mika Myllylä (FIN)
2001 Johann Mühlegg (ESP)
2002[1] Mikhail Ivanov (RUS)
2003 Martin Koukal (CZE)
2005 Frode Estil (NOR)
2006[1] Giorgio Di Centa (ITA)
2007 Odd-Bjørn Hjelmeset (NOR)
2009 Petter Northug, Jr. (NOR)

TEAM SPRINT

2005 Norway
2006[1] Sweden
2007 Italy
2009 Norway

RELAY[4]

1991 Norway
1992[1] Norway
1993 Norway
1994[1] Italy
1995 Norway
1997 Norway
1998[1] Norway
1999 Austria
2001 Norway
2002[1] Norway
2003 Norway
2005 Norway
2006[1] Italy
2007 Norway
2009 Norway

[1]Olympic champions, recognized in this table as world champions (though not by FIS). [2]From 1991 to 1999, the 10-km event was held in tandem with the 15-km event; one event featured classical and the other freestyle technique. Medals were awarded for both races. Beginning in 2001 this pursuit race (skiers competing directly against each other rather than against the clock) led to one medal being awarded upon winning. The 10-km was discontinued, and the 15-km became a stand-alone event featuring classical technique. In 2001–03 the pursuit race featured two 10-km races; since then, two 15-km races. [3]18-km cross-country through 1952; 15-km thereafter. [4]Military relay until 1939; 40-km relay in 1948 and thereafter.

Nordic Skiing World Championships—Women
Held since 1952. Table shows results for the past 20 years.

INDIVIDUAL SPRINT

2001 Pirjo Manninen (FIN)
2002[1] Yuliya Chepalova (RUS)
2003 Marit Bjørgen (NOR)
2005 Emilie Öhrstig (SWE)
2006[1] Chandra Crawford (CAN)
2007 Astrid Jacobsen (NOR)
2009 Arianna Follis (ITA)

5-KM CROSS-COUNTRY

1991 Trude Dybendahl (NOR)
1992[1] Marjut Lukkarinen (FIN)
1993 Larisa Lazutina (RUS)
1994[1] Lyubov Yegorova (RUS)
1995 Larisa Lazutina (RUS)
1997 Yelena Vyalbe (RUS)
1998[1] Larisa Lazutina (RUS)
1999 Bente Martinsen (NOR)

10-KM CROSS-COUNTRY[2]

1991 Yelena Vyalbe (URS)
1992[1] Lyubov Yegorova (UNT)
1993 Stefania Belmondo (ITA)
1994[1] Lyubov Yegorova (RUS)
1995 Larisa Lazutina (RUS)
1997 Stefania Belmondo (ITA)
1998[1] Larisa Lazutina (RUS)
1999 Stefania Belmondo (ITA)
2001 Bente Skari (NOR)
2002[1] Bente Skari (NOR)
2003 Bente Skari (NOR)
2005 Katerina Neumannova
  (CZE)
2006[1] Kristina Smigun (EST)

10-KM CROSS-COUNTRY[2] (CONT.)

2007 Katerina Neumannova (CZE)
2009 Aino-Kaisa Saarinen
  (FIN)

COMBINED PURSUIT[2]

2001 Virpi Kuitunen (FIN)
2002[1] Beckie Scott (CAN)
2003 Kristina Smigun (EST)
2005 Yuliya Chepalova (RUS)
2006[1] Kristina Smigun (EST)
2007 Olga Zavyalova (RUS)
2009 Justyna Kowalczyk (POL)

15-KM CROSS-COUNTRY

1991 Yelena Vyalbe (URS)
1992[1] Lyubov Yegorova (URS)
1993 Yelena Vyalbe (RUS)
1994[1] Manuela Di Centa (ITA)
1995 Larisa Lazutina (RUS)
1997 Yelena Vyalbe (RUS)
1998[1] Olga Danilova (RUS)
1999 Stefania Belmondo (ITA)
2001 Bente Skari (NOR)
2002[1] Stefania Belmondo (ITA)
2003 Bente Skari (NOR)

30-KM CROSS-COUNTRY

1991 Lyubov Yegorova (URS)
1992[1] Stefania Belmondo (ITA)
1993 Stefania Belmondo (ITA)
1994[1] Manuela Di Centa (ITA)
1995 Yelena Vyalbe (RUS)
1997 Yelena Vyalbe (RUS)

30-KM CROSS-COUNTRY (CONTINUED)

1998[1] Yulia Chepalova (RUS)
1999 Larisa Lazutina (RUS)
2001 not held
2002[1] Gabriella Paruzzi (ITA)
2003 Olga Savyalova (RUS)
2005 Marit Bjørgen (NOR)
2006[1] Katerina Neumannova (CZE)
2007 Virpi Kuitunen (FIN)
2009 Justyna Kowalczyk (POL)

TEAM SPRINT

2005 Norway
2006[1] Sweden
2007 Finland
2009 Finland

RELAY[3]

1991 USSR
1992[1] Unified Team
1993 Russia
1994[1] Russia
1995 Russia
1997 Russia
1998[1] Russia
1999 Russia
2001 Russia
2002[1] Germany
2003 Germany
2005 Norway
2006[1] Russia
2007 Finland
2009 Finland

Nordic Skiing World Championships—Women (continued)

SKI JUMP
2009   Lindsey Van

[1]Olympic champions, recognized in this table as world champions (though not by FIS).   [2]From 1991 to 1999, the 5-km event was held in tandem with the 10-km event; one event featured classical and the other freestyle technique. Medals were awarded for both races. Beginning in 2001 this pursuit race (skiers competing directly against each other rather than against the clock) led to one medal being awarded upon winning. The 5-km was discontinued, and the 10-km became a stand-alone event featuring classical technique. In 2001–03 the pursuit race featured two 5-km races; since then, two 7.5-km races.   [3]15-km relay until 1974; 20-km in 1976 and thereafter.

Nordic Skiing World Championships—Nordic Combined

The Nordic combined involves a 10-km cross-country race and ski jumping.
Held since 1925. Table shows results for the past 20 years.

YEAR	COMBINED (NORMAL HILL)[1]	YEAR	COMBINED (LARGE HILL)[3]	YEAR	TEAM (CONTINUED)
1991	Fred Børre Lundberg (NOR)	1999	Bjarte Engen Vik (NOR)	1993	Japan
1992[2]	Fabrice Guy (FRA)	2001	Marko Baacke (GER)	1994[2]	Japan
1993	Kenji Ogiwara (JPN)	2002[2]	Samppa Lajunen (FIN)	1995	Japan
1994[2]	Fred Børre Lundberg (NOR)	2003	Johnny Spillane (USA)	1997	Norway
1995	Fred Børre Lundberg (NOR)	2005	Ronny Ackermann (GER)	1998[2]	Norway
1997	Kenji Ogiwara (JPN)	2006[2]	Felix Gottwald (AUT)	1999	Finland
1998[2]	Bjarte Engen Vik (NOR)	2007	Hannu Manninen (FIN)	2001	Norway
1999	Bjarte Engen Vik (NOR)	2009	Bill Demong (USA)	2002[2]	Finland
2001	Bjarte Engen Vik (NOR)			2003	Austria
2002[2]	Samppa Lajunen (FIN)	YEAR	MASS START	2005	Norway
2003	Ronny Ackermann (GER)	2009	Todd Lodwick (USA)	2006[2]	Austria
2005	Ronny Ackermann (GER)			2007	Finland
2006[2]	Georg Hettich (GER)	YEAR	TEAM	2009	Japan
2007	Ronny Ackermann (GER)	1991	Austria		
2009	Todd Lodwick (USA)	1992[2]	Japan		

[1]15-km cross-country race until 2009.   [2]Olympic champions, recognized in this table as world champions (though not by FIS).   [3]7.5-km cross-country race until 2009.

Nordic Skiing World Championships—Ski Jump

Men's events only. Held since 1924. Table shows results for the past 20 years.

YEAR	NORMAL HILL[1]	YEAR	LARGE HILL[3] (CONTINUED)	YEAR	TEAM JUMP (LARGE HILL[3])
1991	Heinz Kuttin (AUT)	1994[2]	Jens Weissflog (GER)	1991	Austria
1992[2]	Ernst Vettori (AUT)	1995	Tommy Ingebrigtsen (NOR)	1992[2]	Finland
1993	Masahiko Harada (JPN)	1997	Masahiko Harada (JPN)	1993	Norway
1994[2]	Espen Bredesen (NOR)	1998[2]	Kazuyoshi Funaki (JPN)	1994[2]	Germany
1995	Takanobu Okabe (JPN)	1999	Martin Schmitt (GER)	1995	Finland
1997	Janne Ahonen (FIN)	2001	Martin Schmitt (GER)	1997	Finland
1998[2]	Jani Soininen (FIN)	2002[2]	Simon Ammann (SUI)	1998[2]	Japan
1999	Kazuyoshi Funaki (JPN)	2003	Adam Malysz (POL)	1999	Germany
2001	Adam Malysz (POL)	2005	Janne Ahonen (FIN)	2001	Germany
2002[2]	Simon Ammann (SUI)	2006[2]	Thomas Morgenstern (AUT)	2002[2]	Germany
2003	Adam Malysz (POL)	2007	Simon Ammann (SUI)	2003	Finland
2005	Rok Benkovic (SLO)	2009	Andreas Kuettel (SUI)	2005	Austria
2006[2]	Lars Bystøl (NOR)			2006[2]	Austria
2007	Adam Malysz (POL)	YEAR	TEAM JUMP (NORMAL HILL[1])	2007	Austria
2009	Wolfgang Loitzl (AUT)	2001	Austria	2009	Austria
		2002	*not held*		
YEAR	LARGE HILL[3]	2003	*not held*		
1991	Franci Petek (YUG)	2005	Austria		
1992[2]	Toni Nieminen (FIN)	2006	*not held*		
1993	Espen Bredesen (NOR)				

[1]The distance of the jump in the normal hill competition has varied over time; since 1992 it has been set at either 90 or 95 meters.   [2]Olympic champions, recognized in this table as world champions (though not by FIS).   [3]The distance of the jump in the large hill competition has varied over time; since 1992 it has been set at either 120 or 125 meters.

Nordic World Cup

*The winner is determined by the number of points awarded for finishes
in various competitions during the season.*

YEAR	MEN	WOMEN	YEAR	MEN	WOMEN
1979	Oddvar Braa (NOR)	Galina Kulakova (URS)	1996	Bjørn Daehlie (NOR)	Manuela Di Centa (ITA)
1980	not held		1997	Bjørn Daehlie (NOR)	Yelena Vyalbe (RUS)
1981	Aleksandr Zavyalov (URS)	Raisa Smetanina (URS)	1998	Thomas Alsgaard (NOR)	Larisa Lazutina (RUS)
1982	Bill Koch (USA)	Berit Aunli (NOR)	1999	Bjørn Daehlie (NOR)	Bente Martinsen (NOR)
1983	Aleksandr Zavyalov (URS)	Marja-Liisa Hämä-läinen (FIN)	2000	Johann Mühlegg (ESP)	Bente Skari-Martinsen (NOR)
1984	Gunde Svan (SWE)	Marja-Liisa Hämä-läinen (FIN)	2001	Per Elofsson (SWE)	Yuliya Chepalova (RUS)
1985	Gunde Svan (SWE)	Anette Boe (NOR)	2002	Per Elofsson (SWE)	Bente Skari (NOR)
1986	Gunde Svan (SWE)	Marjo Matikainen (FIN)	2003	Mathias Fredriksson (SWE)	Bente Skari (NOR)
1987	Torgny Mogren (SWE)	Marjo Matikainen (FIN)	2004	Rene Sommerfeldt (GER)	Gabriella Paruzzi (ITA)
1988	Gunde Svan (SWE)	Marjo Matikainen (FIN)	2005	Axel Teichmann (GER)	Marit Bjørgen (NOR)
1989	Gunde Svan (SWE)	Yelena Vyalbe (URS)			
1990	Vegard Ulvang (NOR)	Larisa Lazutina (URS)	2006	Tobias Angerer (GER)	Marit Bjørgen (NOR)
1991	Vladimir Smirnov (URS)	Yelena Vyalbe (URS)	2007	Tobias Angerer (GER)	Virpi Kuitunen (FIN)
1992	Bjørn Daehlie (NOR)	Yelena Vyalbe (RUS)	2008	Lukas Bauer (CZE)	Virpi Kuitunen (FIN)
1993	Bjørn Daehlie (NOR)	Lyudmila Yegorova (RUS)	2009	Dario Cologna (SUI)	Justyna Kowalczyk (POL)
1994	Vladimir Smirnov (KAZ)	Manuela Di Centa (ITA)			
1995	Bjørn Daehlie (NOR)	Yelena Vyalbe (RUS)			

Sled Dog Racing

Sled dog racing (or dogsled racing) is the sport of racing sleds pulled by sled dogs over snow-covered cross-country courses; it was developed from a principal **Eskimo** method of transportation. Dogsleds are still used for transportation and working purposes in some northern areas, although they largely have been replaced by aircraft and snowmobiles. The modern **racing sled** weighs about 30 lb (13.5 kg). Its frame (traditionally of ash) is lashed together with leather and its runners sheathed with steel or aluminum. **Dogs** usually are specially bred and trained Eskimo dogs, Siberian huskies, Samoyeds, or Alaskan Malamutes. The **teams** typically consist of 4–10 dogs, with more being used for longer races. They are driven in pairs in a gang hitch.

Control of the team is by voice, though drivers may carry whips as well. In open country, point-to-point races are held. In more populated areas, back roads form the course, with races usually varying in **length** from 12–30 mi (19–48 km). A team of dogs can pull the sled and its driver, called a **musher**, at speeds of more than 20 mph (32 km/hr). Teams start at intervals and race for time. Usually, all dogs must finish in the hitch order in which they started, and an injured dog must be carried on the sled.

A dogsled-racing event was included in the 1932 **Winter Olympics** program. The sport is popular in Norway, Canada, and the northern states of the contiguous United States. The **Iditarod Trail Sled Dog Race** has been held in Alaska since 1973.

Iditarod Trail Sled Dog Race

Men and women compete together in this annual race held in March between Anchorage and Nome AK. A short race of about 40 km (25 mi) organized in 1967 evolved in 1973 into the current race. The course, roughly 1,770 km (1,100 mi) long, partially follows the old Iditarod Trail dogsled mail route blazed from Knik to Nome in 1910. The course length and route vary slightly from year to year, and the middle third takes alternate routes in odd and even years. In 1976 the US Congress designated the original Iditarod Trail as a National Historic Trail.

Iditarod Web site: <www.iditarod.com>.

YEAR	WINNER	TIME	YEAR	WINNER	TIME
1973	Dick Wilmarth	20 days 49 min 41 sec	1985	Libby Riddles	18 days 20 min 17 sec
1974	Carl Huntington	20 days 15 hr 2 min 7 sec	1986	Susan Butcher	11 days 15 hr 6 min 0 sec
1975	Emmitt Peters	14 days 14 hr 43 min 45 sec	1987	Susan Butcher	11 days 2 hr 5 min 13 sec
1976	Gerald Riley	18 days 22 hr 58 min 17 sec	1988	Susan Butcher	11 days 11 hr 41 min 40 sec
1977	Rick Swenson	16 days 16 hr 27 min 13 sec	1989	Joe Runyan	11 days 5 hr 24 min 34 sec
1978	Dick Mackey	14 days 18 hr 52 min 24 sec	1990	Susan Butcher	11 days 1 hr 53 min 23 sec
1979	Rick Swenson	15 days 10 hr 37 min 47 sec	1991	Rick Swenson	12 days 16 hr 34 min 39 sec
1980	Joe May	14 days 7 hr 11 min 51 sec	1992	Martin Buser	10 days 19 hr 17 min 15 sec
1981	Rick Swenson	12 days 8 hr 45 min 2 sec	1993	Jeff King	10 days 15 hr 38 min 15 sec
1982	Rick Swenson	16 days 4 hr 40 min 10 sec	1994	Martin Buser	10 days 13 hr 5 min 39 sec
1983	Rick Mackey	12 days 14 hr 10 min 44 sec	1995	Doug Swingley	10 days 13 hr 2 min 39 sec
1984	Dean Osmar	12 days 15 hr 7 min 33 sec	1996	Jeff King	9 days 5 hr 43 min 13 sec

Iditarod Trail Sled Dog Race (continued)

YEAR	WINNER	TIME	YEAR	WINNER	TIME
1997	Martin Buser	9 days 8 hr 30 min 45 sec	2004	Mitch Seavey	9 days 12 hr 20 min 22 sec
1998	Jeff King	9 days 5 hr 52 min 26 sec	2005	Robert Sørlie	9 days 18 hr 39 min 31 sec
1999	Doug Swingley	9 days 14 hr 31 min 7 sec	2006	Jeff King	9 days 11 hr 11 min 36 sec
2000	Doug Swingley	9 days 58 min 6 sec	2007	Lance Mackey	9 days 5 hr 8 min 41 sec
2001	Doug Swingley	9 days 19 hr 55 min 50 sec	2008	Lance Mackey	9 days 11 hr 46 min 48 sec
2002	Martin Buser	8 days 22 hr 46 min 2 sec	2009	Lance Mackey	9 days 21 hr 38 min 46 sec
2003	Robert Sørlie	9 days 15 hr 47 min 36 sec			

Did you know? It is generally agreed that softball developed from a game called indoor baseball, first played in Chicago in 1887. It became known in the US by various names, such as kitten ball, mush ball, diamond ball, indoor-outdoor, and playground ball. The official softball is 12 inches in circumference; one variation, popular especially in Chicago, is played with a ball that is 16 inches in circumference.

Swimming

The **Fédération Internationale de Natation** (International Swimming Federation, FINA, still known by its French acronym that includes an "a" for "Amateur"; founded 1908) is the world governing body for amateur swimming. It held the first world swimming championships in 1973. After 1975 the FINA championships were held in non-Olympic, even-numbered years. (An exception was the 1991 championship that took place in Australia during the summer month of January.) Diving, synchronized (or synchro) swimming, and water polo events are included in the competition.

A distinction is made between **long-course** (50-m) and **short-course** (25-m) pools for purposes of record setting; world championships and other major contests were long held in 50-m pools, but now a separate short-course World Championship and World Cup take place.

International Swimming Federation Web site: <www.fina.org>.

World Swimming and Diving Championships—Men

swimming

50-M FREESTYLE
1986	Tom Jager (USA)
1991	Tom Jager (USA)
1994	Aleksandr Popov (RUS)
1998	Bill Pilczuk (USA)
2001	Anthony Ervin (USA)
2003	Aleksandr Popov (RUS)
2005	Roland Schoeman (RSA)
2007	Benjamin Wildman-Tobriner (USA)
2009	César Cielo Filho (BRA)

100-M FREESTYLE
1973	Jim Montgomery (USA)
1975	Andy Coan (USA)
1978	David McCagg (USA)
1982	Jörg Woithe (GDR)
1986	Matt Biondi (USA)
1991	Matt Biondi (USA)
1994	Aleksandr Popov (RUS)
1998	Aleksandr Popov (RUS)
2001	Anthony Ervin (USA)
2003	Aleksandr Popov (RUS)
2005	Filippo Magnini (ITA)
2007	Filippo Magnini (ITA)
2009	César Cielo Filho (BRA)

200-M FREESTYLE
1973	Jim Montgomery (USA)
1975	Tim Shaw (USA)
1978	Bill Forrester (USA)
1982	Michael Gross (FRG)
1986	Michael Gross (FRG)
1991	Giorgio Lamberti (ITA)

200-M FREESTYLE (CONTINUED)
1994	Antti Kasvio (FIN)
1998	Michael Klim (AUS)
2001	Ian Thorpe (AUS)
2003	Ian Thorpe (AUS)
2005	Michael Phelps (USA)
2007	Michael Phelps (USA)
2009	Paul Biedermann (GER)

400-M FREESTYLE
1973	Rick DeMont (USA)
1975	Tim Shaw (USA)
1978	Vladimir Salnikov (URS)
1982	Vladimir Salnikov (URS)
1986	Rainer Henkel (FRG)
1991	Jörg Hoffmann (GER)
1994	Kieren Perkins (AUS)
1998	Ian Thorpe (AUS)
2001	Ian Thorpe (AUS)
2003	Ian Thorpe (AUS)
2005	Grant Hackett (AUS)
2007	Park Tae Hwan (KOR)
2009	Paul Biedermann (GER)

800-M FREESTYLE
2001	Ian Thorpe (AUS)
2003	Grant Hackett (AUS)
2005	Grant Hackett (AUS)
2007	Przemyslaw Stanczyk (POL)
2009	Zhang Lin (CHN)

1,500-M FREESTYLE
1973	Steve Holland (AUS)
1975	Tim Shaw (USA)

1,500-M FREESTYLE (CONTINUED)
1978	Vladimir Salnikov (URS)
1982	Vladimir Salnikov (URS)
1986	Rainer Henkel (FRG)
1991	Jörg Hoffmann (GER)
1994	Kieren Perkins (AUS)
1998	Grant Hackett (AUS)
2001	Grant Hackett (AUS)
2003	Grant Hackett (AUS)
2005	Grant Hackett (AUS)
2007	Mateusz Sawrymowicz (POL)
2009	Oussama Mellouli (TUN)

50-M BACKSTROKE
2001	Randall Bal (USA)
2003	Thomas Rupprath (GER)
2005	Aristeidis Grigoriadis (GRE)
2007	Gerhard Zandberg (RSA)
2009	Liam Tancock (GBR)

100-M BACKSTROKE
1973	Roland Matthes (GDR)
1975	Roland Matthes (GDR)
1978	Bob Jackson (USA)
1982	Dirk Richter (GDR)
1986	Igor Polyansky (URS)
1991	Jeff Rouse (USA)
1994	Martin López-Zubero (ESP)
1998	Lenny Krayzelburg (USA)
2001	Matt Welsh (AUS)
2003	Aaron Peirsol (USA)
2005	Aaron Peirsol (USA)
2007	Aaron Peirsol (USA)
2009	Junya Koga (JPN)

World Swimming and Diving Championships—Men (continued)
swimming (continued)

200-M BACKSTROKE
1973	Roland Matthes (GDR)
1975	Zoltán Verrasztó (HUN)
1978	Jesse Vassallo (USA)
1982	Rick Carey (USA)
1986	Igor Polyansky (URS)
1991	Martin López-Zubero (ESP)
1994	Vladimir Selkov (RUS)
1998	Lenny Krayzelburg (USA)
2001	Aaron Peirsol (USA)
2003	Aaron Peirsol (USA)
2005	Aaron Peirsol (USA)
2007	Ryan Lochte (USA)
2009	Aaron Peirsol (USA)

50-M BREASTSTROKE
2001	Oleg Lisogor (UKR)
2003	James Gibson (GBR)
2005	Mark Warnecke (GER)
2007	Oleg Lisogor (UKR)
2009	Cameron van der Burgh (RSA)

100-M BREASTSTROKE
1973	John Hencken (USA)
1975	David Wilkie (GBR)
1978	Walter Kusch (FRG)
1982	Steve Lundquist (USA)
1986	Victor Davis (CAN)
1991	Norbert Rózsa (HUN)
1994	Norbert Rózsa (HUN)
1998	Fred Deburghgraeve (BEL)
2001	Roman Sloudnov (RUS)
2003	Kosuke Kitajima (JPN)
2005	Brendan Hansen (USA)
2007	Brendan Hansen (USA)
2009	Brenton Rickard (AUS)

200-M BREASTSTROKE
1973	David Wilkie (GBR)
1975	David Wilkie (GBR)
1978	Nick Nevid (USA)
1982	Victor Davis (CAN)
1986	József Szabó (HUN)
1991	Mike Barrowman (USA)
1994	Norbert Rózsa (HUN)
1998	Kurt Grote (USA)
2001	Brendan Hansen (USA)
2003	Kosuke Kitajima (JPN)
2005	Brendan Hansen (USA)
2007	Kosuke Kitajima (JPN)
2009	Daniel Gyurta (HUN)

50-M BUTTERFLY
2001	Geoff Huegill (AUS)
2003	Matt Welsh (AUS)

50-M BUTTERFLY (CONTINUED)
2005	Roland Schoeman (RSA)
2007	Roland Schoeman (RSA)
2009	Milorad Cavic (SRB)

100-M BUTTERFLY
1973	Bruce Robertson (CAN)
1975	Greg Jagenburg (USA)
1978	Joseph Bottom (USA)
1982	Matt Gribble (USA)
1986	Pablo Morales (USA)
1991	Anthony Nesty (SUR)
1994	Rafal Szukala (POL)
1998	Michael Klim (AUS)
2001	Lars Frölander (SWE)
2003	Ian Crocker (USA)
2005	Ian Crocker (USA)
2007	Michael Phelps (USA)
2009	Michael Phelps (USA)

200-M BUTTERFLY
1973	Robin Backhaus (USA)
1975	Bill Forrester (USA)
1978	Mike Bruner (USA)
1982	Michael Gross (FRG)
1986	Michael Gross (FRG)
1991	Melvin Stewart (USA)
1994	Denis Pankratov (RUS)
1998	Denys Silantyev (UKR)
2001	Michael Phelps (USA)
2003	Michael Phelps (USA)
2005	Pawel Korzeniowski (POL)
2007	Michael Phelps (USA)
2009	Michael Phelps (USA)

200-M INDIVIDUAL MEDLEY
1973	Gunnar Larsson (SWE)
1975	András Hargitay (HUN)
1978	Graham Smith (CAN)
1982	Aleksandr Sidorenko (URS)
1986	Tamás Darnyi (HUN)
1991	Tamás Darnyi (HUN)
1994	Jani Sievinen (FIN)
1998	Marcel Wouda (NED)
2001	Massimiliano Rosolino (ITA)
2003	Michael Phelps (USA)
2005	Michael Phelps (USA)
2007	Michael Phelps (USA)
2009	Ryan Lochte (USA)

400-M INDIVIDUAL MEDLEY
1973	András Hargitay (HUN)
1975	András Hargitay (HUN)
1978	Jesse Vassallo (USA)
1982	Ricardo Prado (BRA)

400-M INDIVIDUAL MEDLEY (CONT.)
1986	Tamás Darnyi (HUN)
1991	Tamás Darnyi (HUN)
1994	Tom Dolan (USA)
1998	Tom Dolan (USA)
2001	Alessio Boggiatto (ITA)
2003	Michael Phelps (USA)
2005	László Cseh (HUN)
2007	Michael Phelps (USA)
2009	Ryan Lochte (USA)

4 × 100-M FREESTYLE RELAY
1973	United States
1975	United States
1978	United States
1982	United States
1986	United States
1991	United States
1994	United States
1998	United States
2001	Australia
2003	Russia
2005	United States
2007	United States
2009	United States

4 × 200-M FREESTYLE RELAY
1973	United States
1975	West Germany
1978	United States
1982	United States
1986	East Germany
1991	Germany
1994	Sweden
1998	Australia
2001	Australia
2003	Australia
2005	United States
2007	United States
2009	United States

4 × 100-M MEDLEY RELAY
1973	United States
1975	United States
1978	United States
1982	United States
1986	United States
1991	United States
1994	United States
1998	Australia
2001	Australia
2003	United States
2005	United States
2007	Australia
2009	United States

diving

1-M SPRINGBOARD
1991	Edwin Jongejans (NED)
1994	Evan Stewart (ZIM)
1998	Yu Zhuocheng (CHN)
2001	Wang Feng (CHN)
2003	Xu Xiang (CHN)
2005	Alexandre Despatie (CAN)
2007	Luo Yutong (CHN)
2009	Qin Kai (CHN)

3-M SPRINGBOARD
1973	Philip Boggs (USA)
1975	Philip Boggs (USA)
1978	Philip Boggs (USA)
1982	Gregory Louganis (USA)
1986	Gregory Louganis (USA)
1991	Kent Ferguson (USA)
1994	Yu Zhuocheng (CHN)
1998	Dmitry Sautin (RUS)
2001	Dmitry Sautin (RUS)

3-M SPRINGBOARD (CONTINUED)
2003	Aleksandr Dobrosok (RUS)
2005	Alexandre Despatie (CAN)
2007	Qin Kai (CHN)
2009	He Chong (CHN)

PLATFORM
1973	Klaus Dibiasi (ITA)
1975	Klaus Dibiasi (ITA)
1978	Gregory Louganis (USA)

World Swimming and Diving Championships—Men (continued)

diving (continued)

PLATFORM (CONTINUED)
1982 Gregory Louganis (USA)
1986 Gregory Louganis (USA)
1991 Sun Shuwei (CHN)
1994 Dmitry Sautin (RUS)

PLATFORM (CONTINUED)
1998 Dmitry Sautin (RUS)
2001 Tian Liang (CHN)
2003 Alexandre Despatie (CAN)

PLATFORM (CONTINUED)
2005 Hu Jia (CHN)
2007 Gleb Galperin (RUS)
2009 Thomas Daley (GBR)

World Swimming and Diving Championships—Women
swimming

50-M FREESTYLE
1986 Tamara Costache (ROM)
1991 Zhuang Yong (CHN)
1994 Le Jingyi (CHN)
1998 Amy Van Dyken (USA)
2001 Inge de Bruijn (NED)
2003 Inge de Bruijn (NED)
2005 Lisbeth Lenton (AUS)
2007 Lisbeth Lenton (AUS)
2009 Britta Steffen (GER)

100-M FREESTYLE
1973 Kornelia Ender (GDR)
1975 Kornelia Ender (GDR)
1978 Barbara Krause (GDR)
1982 Birgit Meineke (GDR)
1986 Kristin Otto (GDR)
1991 Nicole Haislett (USA)
1994 Le Jingyi (CHN)
1998 Jenny Thompson (USA)
2001 Inge de Bruijn (NED)
2003 Hanna-Maria Seppälä (FIN)
2005 Jodie Henry (AUS)
2007 Lisbeth Lenton (AUS)
2009 Britta Steffen (GER)

200-M FREESTYLE
1973 Keena Rothhammer (USA)
1975 Shirley Babashoff (USA)
1978 Cynthia Woodhead (USA)
1982 Annemarie Verstappen (NED)
1986 Heike Friedrich (GDR)
1991 Hayley Lewis (AUS)
1994 Franziska van Almsick (GER)
1998 Claudia Poll (CRC)
2001 Giaan Rooney (AUS)
2003 Alena Popchanka (BLR)
2005 Solenne Figues (FRA)
2007 Laure Manaudou (FRA)
2009 Federica Pellegrini (ITA)

400-M FREESTYLE
1973 Heather Greenwood (USA)
1975 Shirley Babashoff (USA)
1978 Tracey Wickham (AUS)
1982 Carmela Schmidt (GDR)
1986 Heike Friedrich (GDR)
1991 Janet Evans (USA)
1994 Yang Aihua (CHN)
1998 Chen Yan (CHN)
2001 Yana Klochkova (UKR)
2003 Hannah Stockbauer (GER)
2005 Laure Manaudou (FRA)
2007 Laure Manaudou (FRA)
2009 Federica Pellegrini (ITA)

800-M FREESTYLE
1973 Novella Calligaris (ITA)
1975 Jenny Turrall (AUS)
1978 Tracey Wickham (AUS)
1982 Kim Linehan (USA)
1986 Astrid Strauss (GDR)
1991 Janet Evans (USA)
1994 Janet Evans (USA)
1998 Brooke Bennett (USA)
2001 Hannah Stockbauer (GER)
2003 Hannah Stockbauer (GER)
2005 Kate Ziegler (USA)
2007 Kate Ziegler (USA)
2009 Lotte Friis (DEN)

1,500-M FREESTYLE
2001 Hannah Stockbauer (GER)
2003 Hannah Stockbauer (GER)
2005 Kate Ziegler (USA)
2007 Kate Ziegler (USA)
2009 Alessia Filippi (ITA)

50-M BREASTSTROKE
2001 Luo Xuejuan (CHN)
2003 Luo Xuejuan (CHN)
2005 Jade Edmistone (AUS)
2007 Jessica Hardy (USA)
2009 Yuliya Yefimova (RUS)

100-M BREASTSTROKE
1973 Renate Vogel (GDR)
1975 Hannelore Anke (GDR)
1978 Yuliya Bogdanova (URS)
1982 Ute Geweniger (GDR)
1986 Sylvia Gerasch (GDR)
1991 Linley Frame (AUS)
1994 Samantha Riley (AUS)
1998 Kristy Kowal (USA)
2001 Luo Xuejuan (CHN)
2003 Luo Xuejuan (CHN)
2005 Leisel Jones (AUS)
2007 Leisel Jones (AUS)
2009 Rebecca Soni (USA)

200-M BREASTSTROKE
1973 Renate Vogel (GDR)
1975 Hannelore Anke (GDR)
1978 Lina Kachushite (URS)
1982 Svetlana Varganova (URS)
1986 Silke Hörner (GDR)
1991 Yelena Volkova (URS)
1994 Samantha Riley (AUS)
1998 Agnes Kovacs (HUN)
2001 Agnes Kovacs (HUN)
2003 Amanda Beard (USA)
2005 Leisel Jones (AUS)

200-M BREASTSTROKE (CONTINUED)
2007 Leisel Jones (AUS)
2009 Nadja Higl (SRB)

50-M BUTTERFLY
2001 Inge de Bruijn (NED)
2003 Inge de Bruijn (NED)
2005 Danni Miatke (AUS)
2007 Therese Alshammar (SWE)
2009 Marieke Guehrer (AUS)

100-M BUTTERFLY
1973 Kornelia Ender (GDR)
1975 Kornelia Ender (GDR)
1978 Joan Pennington (USA)
1982 Mary Meagher (USA)
1986 Kornelia Gressler (GDR)
1991 Qian Hong (CHN)
1994 Liu Limin (CHN)
1998 Jenny Thompson (USA)
2001 Petria Thomas (AUS)
2003 Jenny Thompson (USA)
2005 Jessicah Schipper (AUS)
2007 Lisbeth Lenton (AUS)
2009 Sarah Sjöström (SWE)

200-M BUTTERFLY
1973 Rosemarie Kother (GDR)
1975 Rosemarie Kother (GDR)
1978 Tracy Caulkins (USA)
1982 Ines Geissler (GDR)
1986 Mary T. Meagher (USA)
1991 Summer Sanders (USA)
1994 Liu Limin (CHN)
1998 Susie O'Neill (AUS)
2001 Petria Thomas (AUS)
2003 Otylia Jedrzejczak (POL)
2005 Otylia Jedrzejczak (POL)
2007 Jessicah Schipper (AUS)
2009 Jessicah Schipper (AUS)

50-M BACKSTROKE
2001 Haley Cope (USA)
2003 Nina Zhivanevskaya (ESP)
2005 Giaan Rooney (AUS)
2007 Leila Vaziri (USA)
2009 Zhao Jing (CHN)

100-M BACKSTROKE
1973 Ulrike Richter (GDR)
1975 Ulrike Richter (GDR)
1978 Linda Jezek (USA)
1982 Kristin Otto (GDR)
1986 Betsy Mitchell (USA)
1991 Krisztina Egerszegi (HUN)
1994 He Cihong (CHN)
1998 Lea Maurer (USA)

World Swimming and Diving Championships—Women (continued)
swimming (continued)

100-M BACKSTROKE (CONTINUED)
2001	Natalie Coughlin (USA)
2003	Antje Buschschulte (GER)
2005	Kirsty Coventry (ZIM)
2007	Natalie Coughlin (USA)
2009	Gemma Spofforth (GBR)

200-M BACKSTROKE
1973	Melissa Belote (USA)
1975	Birgit Treiber (GDR)
1978	Linda Jezek (USA)
1982	Cornelia Sirch (GDR)
1986	Cornelia Sirch (GDR)
1991	Krisztina Egerszegi (HUN)
1994	He Cihong (CHN)
1998	Roxana Maracineanu (FRA)
2001	Diana Mocanu (ROM)
2003	Katy Sexton (GBR)
2005	Kirsty Coventry (ZIM)
2007	Margaret Hoelzer (USA)
2009	Kirsty Coventry (ZIM)

200-M INDIVIDUAL MEDLEY
1973	Andrea Hubner (GDR)
1975	Kathy Heddy (USA)
1978	Tracy Caulkins (USA)
1982	Petra Schneider (GDR)
1986	Kristin Otto (GDR)
1991	Lin Li (CHN)
1994	Lu Bin (CHN)
1998	Wu Yanyan (CHN)
2001	Martha Bowen (USA)

200-M INDIVIDUAL MEDLEY (CONT.)
2003	Yana Klochkova (UKR)
2005	Katie Hoff (USA)
2007	Katie Hoff (USA)
2009	Ariana Kukors (USA)

400-M INDIVIDUAL MEDLEY
1973	Gudrun Wegner (GDR)
1975	Ulrike Tauber (GDR)
1978	Tracy Caulkins (USA)
1982	Petra Schneider (GDR)
1986	Kathleen Nord (GDR)
1991	Lin Li (CHN)
1994	Dai Guohong (CHN)
1998	Chen Yan (CHN)
2001	Yana Klochkova (UKR)
2003	Yana Klochkova (UKR)
2005	Katie Hoff (USA)
2007	Katie Hoff (USA)
2009	Katinka Hosszú (HUN)

4 × 100-M FREESTYLE RELAY
1973	East Germany
1975	East Germany
1978	United States
1982	East Germany
1986	East Germany
1991	United States
1994	China
1998	United States
2001	Germany

4 × 100-M FREESTYLE RELAY (CONT.)
2003	United States
2005	Australia
2007	Australia
2009	The Netherlands

4 × 200-M FREESTYLE RELAY
1986	East Germany
1991	Germany
1994	China
1998	Germany
2001	Great Britain
2003	United States
2005	United States
2007	United States
2009	China

4 × 100-M MEDLEY RELAY
1973	East Germany
1975	East Germany
1978	United States
1982	East Germany
1986	East Germany
1991	United States
1994	China
1998	United States
2001	Australia
2003	China
2005	Australia
2007	Australia
2009	China

diving

1-M SPRINGBOARD
1991	Gao Min (CHN)
1994	Chen Lixia (CHN)
1998	Irina Lashko (RUS)
2001	Blythe Hartley (CAN)
2003	Irina Lashko (AUS)
2005	Blythe Hartley (CAN)
2007	He Zi (CHN)
2009	Yuliya Pakhalina (RUS)

3-M SPRINGBOARD
1973	Christa Kohler (GDR)
1975	Irina Kalinina (URS)
1978	Irina Kalinina (URS)
1982	Megan Neyer (USA)

3-M SPRINGBOARD (CONT.)
1986	Gao Min (CHN)
1991	Gao Min (CHN)
1994	Tan Shuping (CHN)
1998	Yuliya Pakhalina (RUS)
2001	Guo Jingjing (CHN)
2003	Guo Jingjing (CHN)
2005	Guo Jingjing (CHN)
2007	Guo Jingjing (CHN)
2009	Guo Jingjing (CHN)

PLATFORM
1973	Ulrika Knape (SWE)
1975	Janet Ely (USA)
1978	Irina Kalinina (URS)

PLATFORM (CONT.)
1982	Wendy Wyland (USA)
1986	Chen Lin (CHN)
1991	Fu Mingxia (CHN)
1994	Fu Mingxia (CHN)
1998	Olena Zhupina (UKR)
2001	Xu Mian (CHN)
2003	Emilie Heymans (CAN)
2005	Laura Wilkinson (USA)
2007	Wang Xin (CHN)
2009	Paola Espinosa (MEX)

Swimming World Records—Long Course (50 m)
Some records are awaiting FINA ratification as of 21 Aug 2009.

men

EVENT	RECORD HOLDER (COUNTRY)	PERFORMANCE	DATE
50-m freestyle	Frédérick Bousquet (FRA)	20.94 sec	26 Apr 2009
100-m freestyle	César Cielo Filho (BRA)	46.91 sec	30 Jul 2009
200-m freestyle	Paul Biedermann (GER)	1 min 42.00 sec	28 Jul 2009
400-m freestyle	Paul Biedermann (GER)	3 min 40.07 sec	26 Jul 2009
800-m freestyle	Zhang Lin (CHN)	7 min 32.12 sec	29 Jul 2009
1,500-m freestyle	Grant Hackett (AUS)	14 min 34.56 sec	29 Jul 2001
50-m backstroke	Liam Tancock (GBR)	24.04 sec	2 Aug 2009
100-m backstroke	Aaron Peirsol (USA)	51.94 sec	8 Jul 2009
200-m backstroke	Aaron Peirsol (USA)	1 min 51.92 sec	31 Jul 2009
50-m breaststroke	Cameron van der Burgh (RSA)	26.67 sec	29 Jul 2009
100-m breaststroke	Brenton Rickard (AUS)	58.58 sec	27 Jul 2009

Swimming World Records—Long Course (50 m) (continued)

men (continued)

EVENT	RECORD HOLDER (COUNTRY)	PERFORMANCE	DATE
200-m breaststroke	Christian Sprenger (AUS)	2 min 07.31 sec	30 Jul 2009
50-m butterfly	Rafael Muñoz (ESP)	22.43 sec	5 Apr 2009
100-m butterfly	Michael Phelps (USA)	49.82 sec	1 Aug 2009
200-m butterfly	Michael Phelps (USA)	1 min 51.51 sec	29 Jul 2009
200-m individual medley	Ryan Lochte (USA)	1 min 54.10 sec	30 Jul 2009
400-m individual medley	Michael Phelps (USA)	4 min 03.84 sec	10 Aug 2008
4 × 100-m freestyle relay	United States (Michael Phelps, Garrett Weber-Gale, Cullen Jones, Jason Lezak)	3 min 08.24 sec	11 Aug 2008
4 × 200-m freestyle relay	United States (Michael Phelps, Ricky Berens, David Walters, Ryan Lochte)	6 min 58.55 sec	31 Jul 2009
4 × 100-m medley relay	United States (Aaron Peirsol, Eric Shanteau, Michael Phelps, David Walters)	3 min 27.28 sec	2 Aug 2009

women

EVENT	RECORD HOLDER (COUNTRY)	PERFORMANCE	DATE
50-m freestyle	Britta Steffen (GER)	23.73 sec	2 Aug 2009
100-m freestyle	Britta Steffen (GER)	52.07 sec	31 Jul 2009
200-m freestyle	Federica Pellegrini (ITA)	1 min 52.98 sec	29 Jul 2009
400-m freestyle	Federica Pellegrini (ITA)	3 min 59.15 sec	26 Jul 2009
800-m freestyle	Rebecca Adlington (GBR)	8 min 14.10 sec	16 Aug 2008
1,500-m freestyle	Kate Ziegler (USA)	15 min 42.54 sec	17 Jun 2007
50-m backstroke	Zhao Jing (CHN)	27.06 sec	30 Jul 2009
100-m backstroke	Gemma Spofforth (GBR)	58.12 sec	28 Jul 2009
200-m backstroke	Kirsty Coventry (ZIM)	2 min 04.81 sec	1 Aug 2009
50-m breaststroke	Yuliya Yefimova (RUS)	30.09 sec	2 Aug 2009
100-m breaststroke	Rebecca Soni (USA)	1 min 04.84 sec	27 Jul 2009
200-m breaststroke	Annamay Pierse (CAN)	2 min 20.12 sec	30 Jul 2009
50-m butterfly	Therese Alshammar (SWE)	25.07 sec	31 Jul 2009
100-m butterfly	Sarah Sjöström (SWE)	56.06 sec	27 Jul 2009
200-m butterfly	Jessicah Schipper (AUS)	2 min 03.41 sec	30 Jul 2009
200-m individual medley	Ariana Kukors (USA)	2 min 06.15 sec	27 Jul 2009
400-m individual medley	Stephanie Rice (AUS)	4 min 29.45 sec	10 Aug 2008
4 × 100-m freestyle relay	The Netherlands (Inge Dekker, Ranomi Kromowidjojo, Femke Heemskerk, Marleen Veldhuis)	3 min 31.72 sec	26 Jul 2009
4 × 200-m freestyle relay	China (Yang Yu, Zhu Qian Wei, Liu Jing, Pang Jiaying)	7 min 42.08 sec	30 Jul 2009
4 × 100-m medley relay	China (Zhao Jing, Chen Huijia, Jiao Liuyang, Li Zhesi)	3 min 52.19 sec	1 Aug 2009

Swimming World Records—Short Course (25 m)

Some records are awaiting FINA ratification as of 21 Aug 2009.

men

EVENT	RECORD HOLDER (COUNTRY)	PERFORMANCE	DATE
50-m freestyle	Roland Schoeman (RSA)	20.30 sec	8 Aug 2009
100-m freestyle	Amaury Leveaux (FRA)	44.94 sec	13 Dec 2008
200-m freestyle	Paul Biedermann (GER)	1 min 40.83 sec	16 Nov 2008
400-m freestyle	Grant Hackett (AUS)	3 min 34.58 sec	18 Jul 2002
800-m freestyle	Grant Hackett (AUS)	7 min 23.42 sec	19 Jul 2008
1,500-m freestyle	Grant Hackett (AUS)	14 min 10.10 sec	7 Aug 2001
50-m backstroke	Randall Bal (USA)	22.87 sec	16 Nov 2008
100-m backstroke	Aschwin Wildeboer (ESP)	49.20 sec	21 Dec 2008
200-m backstroke	Markus Rogan (AUT)	1 min 47.84 sec	13 Apr 2008
50-m breaststroke	Cameron van der Burgh (RSA)	25.43 sec	8 Aug 2009
100-m breaststroke	Cameron van der Burgh (RSA)	55.99 sec	9 Aug 2009
200-m breaststroke	Christian Sprenger (AUS)	2 min 01.98 sec	10 Aug 2009
50-m butterfly	Amaury Leveaux (FRA)	22.18 sec	14 Dec 2008
100-m butterfly	Ian Crocker (USA)	49.07 sec	26 Mar 2004
200-m butterfly	Nikolay Skvortsov (RUS)	1 min 50.53 sec	12 Feb 2009
100-m individual medley	Ryan Lochte (USA)	51.15 sec	13 Apr 2008
200-m individual medley	Ryan Lochte (USA)	1 min 51.56 sec	11 Apr 2008
400-m individual medley	László Cseh (HUN)	3 min 59.33 sec	14 Dec 2007
4 × 100-m freestyle relay	France (Gregory Mallet, Fabien Gilot, William Meynard, Frédérick Bousquet)	3 min 04.98 sec	20 Dec 2008

Swimming World Records—Short Course (25 m) (continued)

men (continued)

EVENT	RECORD HOLDER (COUNTRY)	PERFORMANCE	DATE
4 × 200-m freestyle relay	Canada (Colin Russell, Stefan Hirniak, Brent Hayden, Joel Greenshields)	6 min 51.05 sec	7 Aug 2009
4 × 100-m medley relay	Canada (Jake Tapp, Paul Kornfeld, Joe Bartoch, Brent Hayden)	3 min 23.33 sec	9 Aug 2009

women

EVENT	RECORD HOLDER (COUNTRY)	PERFORMANCE	DATE
50-m freestyle	Marleen Veldhuis (NED)	23.25 sec	13 Apr 2008
100-m freestyle	Lisbeth Trickett (AUS)	51.01 sec	10 Aug 2009
200-m freestyle	Federica Pellegrini (ITA)	1 min 51.85 sec	14 Dec 2008
400-m freestyle	Joanne Jackson (GBR)	3 min 54.92 sec	8 Aug 2009
800-m freestyle	Alessia Filippi (ITA)	8 min 04.53 sec	12 Dec 2008
1,500-m freestyle	Kate Ziegler (USA)	15 min 32.90 sec	12 Oct 2007
50-m backstroke	Sanja Jovanovic (CRO)	26.23 sec	13 Dec 2008
100-m backstroke	Shiho Sakai (JPN)	56.15 sec	22 Feb 2009
200-m backstroke	Kirsty Coventry (ZIM)	2 min 00.91 sec	11 Apr 2008
50-m breaststroke	Jessica Hardy (USA)	29.58 sec	10 Apr 2008
100-m breaststroke	Leisel Jones (AUS)	1 min 03.72 sec	25 Apr 2008
200-m breaststroke	Annamay Pierse (CAN)	2 min 16.83 sec	7 Aug 2009
50-m butterfly	Marieke Guehrer (AUS)	24.99 sec	16 Nov 2008
100-m butterfly	Jessicah Schipper (AUS)	55.68 sec	12 Aug 2009
200-m butterfly	Yuko Nakanishi (JPN)	2 min 03.12 sec	23 Feb 2008
100-m individual medley	Emily Seebohm (AUS)	58.54 sec	10 Aug 2009
200-m individual medley	Kirsty Coventry (ZIM)	2 min 06.13 sec	12 Apr 2008
400-m individual medley	Mireia Belmonte (ESP)	4 min 25.06 sec	14 Dec 2008
4 × 100-m freestyle relay	The Netherlands (Hinkelien Schreuder, Ranomi Kromowidjojo, Inge Dekker, Marleen Veldhuis)	3 min 28.22 sec	19 Dec 2008
4 × 200-m freestyle relay	The Netherlands (Inge Dekker, Femke Heemskerk, Marleen Veldhuis, Ranomi Kromowidjojo)	7 min 38.90 sec	9 Apr 2008
4 × 100-m medley relay	Canada (Katy Murdoch, Annamay Pierse, Audrey Lacroix, Victoria Poon)	3 min 49.45 sec	9 Aug 2009

Tennis

Four events dominate world championship tennis. The first of the traditional "Big Four," or "Grand Slam," events was the **All-England Lawn Tennis Championships** (better known as the **Wimbledon** Championships), founded in 1877. Its only event the first year was the men's singles championships; women first competed in 1884. Major tennis tournaments also sprang up in the **United States** (1881 for men; women's singles competition first officially added 1889), **France** (1891 for men; women's singles competition added 1897), and **Australia** (1905 for men; women's singles competition added 1922). Open tennis (open, that is, to both professionals and amateurs) became the rule in the Big Four tournaments in 1968. International team tennis was organized in 1900 with the institution of the **Davis Cup.** Men's teams competing for the Davis Cup play four singles matches and one doubles match in elimination rounds. The **Wightman Cup** was contested yearly between British and American women's teams from 1923 to 1989. The **International Tennis Federation** (ITF, formerly the International Lawn Tennis Federation; founded 1913) established the **Federation Cup** in 1963 (called the Fed Cup since 1994) for international women's team competition. It is decided by elimination rounds of two singles and one doubles contest.

Related Web sites: International Tennis Federation: <www.itftennis.com>; ATP (formerly Association of Tennis Professionals): <www.atptennis.com>; Women's Tennis Association: <www.wtatour.com>.

Australian Open Tennis Championships—Singles

YEAR	MEN	WOMEN
1905	Rodney Heath (AUS)	
1906	Tony Wilding (NZL)	
1907	Horace Rice (AUS)	
1908	Fred Alexander (USA)	
1909	Tony Wilding (NZL)	
1910	Rodney Heath (AUS)	
1911	Norman Brookes (AUS)	

Australian Open Tennis Championships—Singles (continued)

YEAR	MEN	WOMEN
1912	J. Cecil Parke (GBR)	
1913	E.F. Parker (AUS)	
1914	Pat O'Hara Wood (AUS)	
1915	Francis Lowe (GBR)	
1916–18	*not held*	
1919	A.R.F. Kingscote (GBR)	
1920	Pat O'Hara Wood (AUS)	
1921	Rhys Gemmell (AUS)	
1922	James Anderson (AUS)	Margaret Molesworth (AUS)
1923	Pat O'Hara Wood (AUS)	Margaret Molesworth (AUS)
1924	James Anderson (AUS)	Sylvia Lance (AUS)
1925	James Anderson (AUS)	Daphne Akhurst (AUS)
1926	John Hawkes (AUS)	Daphne Akhurst (AUS)
1927	Gerald Patterson (AUS)	Esna Boyd (AUS)
1928	Jean Borotra (FRA)	Daphne Akhurst (AUS)
1929	John Gregory (GBR)	Daphne Akhurst (AUS)
1930	Gar Moon (AUS)	Daphne Akhurst (AUS)
1931	Jack Crawford (AUS)	Coral Buttsworth (AUS)
1932	Jack Crawford (AUS)	Coral Buttsworth (AUS)
1933	Jack Crawford (AUS)	Joan Hartigan (AUS)
1934	Fred Perry (GBR)	Joan Hartigan (AUS)
1935	Jack Crawford (AUS)	Dorothy Round (GBR)
1936	Adrian Quist (AUS)	Joan Hartigan (AUS)
1937	Vivian McGrath (AUS)	Nancye Wynne (AUS)
1938	Don Budge (USA)	Dorothy Bundy (USA)
1939	John Bromwich (AUS)	Emily Westacott (AUS)
1940	Adrian Quist (AUS)	Nancye Wynne (AUS)
1941–45	*not held*	
1946	John Bromwich (AUS)	Nancye Wynne Bolton (AUS)
1947	Dinny Pails (AUS)	Nancye Wynne Bolton (AUS)
1948	Adrian Quist (AUS)	Nancye Wynne Bolton (AUS)
1949	Frank Sedgman (AUS)	Doris Hart (USA)
1950	Frank Sedgman (AUS)	Louise Brough (USA)
1951	Dick Savitt (USA)	Nancye Wynne Bolton (AUS)
1952	Ken McGregor (AUS)	Thelma Long (AUS)
1953	Ken Rosewall (AUS)	Maureen Connolly (USA)
1954	Mervyn Rose (AUS)	Thelma Long (AUS)
1955	Ken Rosewall (AUS)	Beryl Penrose (AUS)
1956	Lew Hoad (AUS)	Mary Carter (AUS)
1957	Ashley Cooper (AUS)	Shirley Fry (USA)
1958	Ashley Cooper (AUS)	Angela Mortimer (GBR)
1959	Alex Olmedo (PER)	Mary Carter-Reitano (AUS)
1960	Rod Laver (AUS)	Margaret Smith (AUS)
1961	Roy Emerson (AUS)	Margaret Smith (AUS)
1962	Rod Laver (AUS)	Margaret Smith (AUS)
1963	Roy Emerson (AUS)	Margaret Smith (AUS)
1964	Roy Emerson (AUS)	Margaret Smith (AUS)
1965	Roy Emerson (AUS)	Margaret Smith (AUS)
1966	Roy Emerson (AUS)	Margaret Smith (AUS)
1967	Roy Emerson (AUS)	Nancy Richey (USA)
1968	Bill Bowrey (AUS)	Billie Jean King (USA)
1969	Rod Laver (AUS)	Margaret Smith Court (AUS)
1970	Arthur Ashe (USA)	Margaret Smith Court (AUS)
1971	Ken Rosewall (AUS)	Margaret Smith Court (AUS)
1972	Ken Rosewall (AUS)	Virginia Wade (GBR)
1973	John Newcombe (AUS)	Margaret Smith Court (AUS)
1974	Jimmy Connors (USA)	Evonne Goolagong (AUS)
1975	John Newcombe (AUS)	Evonne Goolagong (AUS)
1976	Mark Edmondson (AUS)	Evonne Goolagong Cawley (AUS)
1977[1]	Roscoe Tanner (USA)	Kerry Reid (AUS)
1977[1]	Vitas Gerulaitis (USA)	Evonne Goolagong Cawley (AUS)
1978[2]	Guillermo Vilas (ARG)	Chris O'Neill (AUS)
1979[2]	Guillermo Vilas (ARG)	Barbara Jordan (USA)
1980[2]	Brian Teacher (USA)	Hana Mandlikova (TCH)
1981[2]	Johan Kriek (RSA)	Martina Navratilova (USA)
1982[2]	Johan Kriek (RSA)	Chris Evert Lloyd (USA)
1983[2]	Mats Wilander (SWE)	Martina Navratilova (USA)
1984[2]	Mats Wilander (SWE)	Chris Evert Lloyd (USA)

Australian Open Tennis Championships—Singles (continued)

YEAR	MEN	WOMEN
1985[2]	Stefan Edberg (SWE)	Martina Navratilova (USA)
1986	*not held*	
1987	Stefan Edberg (SWE)	Hana Mandlikova (TCH)
1988	Mats Wilander (SWE)	Steffi Graf (FRG)
1989	Ivan Lendl (TCH)	Steffi Graf (FRG)
1990	Ivan Lendl (TCH)	Steffi Graf (FRG)
1991	Boris Becker (GER)	Monica Seles (YUG)
1992	Jim Courier (USA)	Monica Seles (YUG)
1993	Jim Courier (USA)	Monica Seles (YUG)
1994	Pete Sampras (USA)	Steffi Graf (GER)
1995	Andre Agassi (USA)	Mary Pierce (FRA)
1996	Boris Becker (GER)	Monica Seles (USA)
1997	Pete Sampras (USA)	Martina Hingis (SUI)
1998	Petr Korda (CZE)	Martina Hingis (SUI)
1999	Yevgeny Kafelnikov (RUS)	Martina Hingis (SUI)
2000	Andre Agassi (USA)	Lindsay Davenport (USA)
2001	Andre Agassi (USA)	Jennifer Capriati (USA)
2002	Thomas Johansson (SWE)	Jennifer Capriati (USA)
2003	Andre Agassi (USA)	Serena Williams (USA)
2004	Roger Federer (SUI)	Justine Henin-Hardenne (BEL)
2005	Marat Safin (RUS)	Serena Williams (USA)
2006	Roger Federer (SUI)	Amélie Mauresmo (FRA)
2007	Roger Federer (SUI)	Serena Williams (USA)
2008	Novak Djokovic (SER)	Mariya Sharapova (RUS)
2009	Rafael Nadal (ESP)	Serena Williams (USA)

[1]*Tournament held in January and December.*   [2]*Tournament held in December rather than January.*

Australian Open Tennis Championships—Doubles

YEAR	MEN	WOMEN
1905	Tom Tachell, Randolph Lycett	
1906	Tony Wilding, Rodney Heath	
1907	Harry Parker, William Gregg	
1908	Fred Alexander, Alfred Dunlop	
1909	Ernie F. Parker, J.P. Keane	
1910	Horace Rice, Ashley Campbell	
1911	Rodney Heath, Randolph Lycett	
1912	J. Cecil Parke, Charles Dixon	
1913	Ernie F. Parker, Alf Hedemann	
1914	Ashley Campbell, Gerald Patterson	
1915	Horace Rice, Clarrie Todd	
1916–18	*not held*	
1919	Pat O'Hara Wood, Ron Thomas	
1920	Pat O'Hara Wood, Ron Thomas	
1921	S.H. Eaton-Rice, Rhys Gemmell	
1922	Gerald Patterson, John Hawkes	Esne Boyd, Marjorie Mountain
1923	Pat O'Hara Wood, Bert St. John	Esne Boyd, Sylvia Lance
1924	Norman Brookes, James Anderson	Daphne Akhurst, Sylvia Lance
1925	Gerald Patterson, Pat O'Hara Wood	Daphne Akhurst, Sylvia Lance Harper
1926	Gerald Patterson, John Hawkes	Meryl O'Hara Wood, Esne Boyd
1927	Gerald Patterson, John Hawkes	Meryl O'Hara Wood, Louise Bickerton
1928	Jean Borotra, Jacques Brugnon	Daphne Akhurst, Esne Boyd
1929	Jack Crawford, Harry Hopman	Daphne Akhurst, Louise Bickerton
1930	Jack Crawford, Harry Hopman	Margaret Molesworth, Emily Hood
1931	Charles Donohoe, Ray Dunlop	Daphne Akhurst Cozens, Louise Bickerton
1932	Jack Crawford, Gar Moon	Coral Buttsworth, Marjorie Cox Crawford
1933	Ellsworth Vines, Keith Gledhill	Margaret Molesworth, Emily Hood Westacott
1934	Fred Perry, George Hughes	Margaret Molesworth, Emily Hood Westacott
1935	Jack Crawford, Vivian McGrath	Evelyn Dearman, Nancy Lyle
1936	Adrian Quist, D.P. Turnbull	Thelma Coyne, Nancye Wynne
1937	Adrian Quist, D.P. Turnbull	Thelma Coyne, Nancye Wynne
1938	Adrian Quist, John Bromwich	Thelma Coyne, Nancye Wynne
1939	Adrian Quist, John Bromwich	Thelma Coyne, Nancye Wynne
1940	Adrian Quist, John Bromwich	Thelma Coyne, Nancye Wynne
1941–45	*not held*	
1946	Adrian Quist, John Bromwich	Joyce Fitch, Mary Bevis
1947	Adrian Quist, John Bromwich	Thelma Coyne Long, Nancye Wynne Bolton

Australian Open Tennis Championships—Doubles (continued)

YEAR	MEN	WOMEN
1948	Adrian Quist, John Bromwich	Thelma Coyne Long, Nancye Wynne Bolton
1949	Adrian Quist, John Bromwich	Thelma Coyne Long, Nancye Wynne Bolton
1950	Adrian Quist, John Bromwich	Louise Brough, Doris Hart
1951	Ken McGregor, Frank Sedgman	Thelma Coyne Long, Nancye Wynne Bolton
1952	Ken McGregor, Frank Sedgman	Thelma Coyne Long, Nancye Wynne Bolton
1953	Lew Hoad, Ken Rosewall	Maureen Connolly, Julia Sampson
1954	Rex Hartwig, Mervyn Rose	Mary Bevis Hawton, Beryl Penrose
1955	Vic Seixas, Tony Trabert	Mary Bevis Hawton, Beryl Penrose
1956	Lew Hoad, Ken Rosewall	Mary Bevis Hawton, Thelma Coyne Long
1957	Lew Hoad, Neale Fraser	Althea Gibson, Shirley Fry
1958	Ashley Cooper, Neale Fraser	Mary Bevis Hawton, Thelma Coyne Long
1959	Rod Laver, Robert Mark	Sandra Reynolds, Renee Schuurman
1960	Rod Laver, Robert Mark	Maria Bueno, Christine Truman
1961	Rod Laver, Robert Mark	Mary Reitano, Margaret Smith
1962	Roy Emerson, Neale Fraser	Robyn Ebbern, Margaret Smith
1963	Bob Hewitt, Fred Stolle	Robyn Ebbern, Margaret Smith
1964	Bob Hewitt, Fred Stolle	Judy Tegart, Lesley Turner
1965	John Newcombe, Tony Roche	Margaret Smith, Lesley Turner
1966	Roy Emerson, Fred Stolle	Carole Graebner, Nancy Richey
1967	John Newcombe, Tony Roche	Judy Tegart, Lesley Turner
1968	Dick Crealy, Allan Stone	Karen Krantzcke, Karrie Melville
1969	Roy Emerson, Rod Laver	Margaret Smith Court, Judy Tegart
1970	Bob Lutz, Stan Smith	Margaret Smith Court, Judy Tegart Dalton
1971	John Newcombe, Tony Roche	Margaret Smith Court, Evonne Goolagong
1972	Owen Davidson, Ken Rosewall	Kerry Harris, Helen Gourlay
1973	Mal Anderson, John Newcombe	Margaret Smith Court, Virginia Wade
1974	Ross Case, Geoff Masters	Evonne Goolagong, Peggy Michel
1975	John Alexander, Phil Dent	Evonne Goolagong, Peggy Michel
1976	John Newcombe, Tony Roche	Evonne Goolagong Cawley, Helen Gourlay
1977[1]	Arthur Ashe, Tony Roche	Dianne Fromholtz, Helen Gourlay
1977[1]	Allan Stone, Ray Ruffels	Evonne Goolagong Cawley, Helen Gourlay Cawley; Mona Guerrant, Kerry Reid[2]
1978[3]	Wojtek Fibak, Kim Warwick	Renata Tomanova, Betsy Nagelsen
1979[3]	Peter McNamara, Paul McNamee	Judy Chaloner, Dianne Evers
1980[3]	Kim Warwick, Mark Edmondson	Martina Navratilova, Betsy Nagelsen
1981[3]	Kim Warwick, Mark Edmondson	Kathy Jordan, Anne Smith
1982[3]	John Alexander, John Fitzgerald	Martina Navratilova, Pam Shriver
1983[3]	Mark Edmondson, Paul McNamee	Martina Navratilova, Pam Shriver
1984[3]	Mark Edmondson, Sherwood Stewart	Martina Navratilova, Pam Shriver
1985[3]	Paul Annacone, Christo van Rensburg	Martina Navratilova, Pam Shriver
1986	not held	
1987	Stefan Edberg, Anders Järryd	Martina Navratilova, Pam Shriver
1988	Rick Leach, Jim Pugh	Martina Navratilova, Pam Shriver
1989	Rick Leach, Jim Pugh	Martina Navratilova, Pam Shriver
1990	Pieter Aldrich, Danie Visser	Jana Novotna, Helena Sukova
1991	Scott Davis, David Pate	Patty Fendick, Mary Joe Fernández
1992	Todd Woodbridge, Mark Woodforde	Arantxa Sánchez Vicario, Helena Sukova
1993	Danie Visser, Laurie Warder	Gigi Fernández, Natasha Zvereva
1994	Jacco Eltingh, Paul Haarhuis	Gigi Fernández, Natasha Zvereva
1995	Jared Palmer, Richey Reneberg	Arantxa Sánchez Vicario, Jana Novotna
1996	Stefan Edberg, Petr Korda	Arantxa Sánchez Vicario, Chanda Rubin
1997	Todd Woodbridge, Mark Woodforde	Martina Hingis, Natasha Zvereva
1998	Jonas Björkman, Jacco Eltingh	Martina Hingis, Mirjana Lucic
1999	Jonas Björkman, Patrick Rafter	Martina Hingis, Anna Kournikova
2000	Ellis Ferreira, Rick Leach	Lisa Raymond, Rennae Stubbs
2001	Jonas Björkman, Todd Woodbridge	Venus Williams, Serena Williams
2002	Mark Knowles, Daniel Nestor	Martina Hingis, Anna Kournikova
2003	Michaël Llodra, Fabrice Santoro	Venus Williams, Serena Williams
2004	Michaël Llodra, Fabrice Santoro	Virginia Ruano Pascual, Paola Suárez
2005	Wayne Black, Kevin Ullyett	Alicia Molik, Svetlana Kuznetsova
2006	Bob Bryan, Mike Bryan	Yan Zi, Zheng Jie
2007	Bob Bryan, Mike Bryan	Cara Black, Liezel Huber
2008	Jonathan Erlich, Andy Ram	Alona Bondarenko, Kateryna Bondarenko
2009	Bob Bryan, Mike Bryan	Venus Williams, Serena Williams

[1]*Tournament held in January and December.*   [2]*Tie; finals rained out.*   [3]*Tournament held in December rather than January.*

French Open Tennis Championships—Singles

From 1891 to 1924, only members of French tennis clubs were eligible to play in the French Championships. The table shows the winners only since 1925, when the tournament was opened to international competition.

YEAR	MEN	WOMEN
1925	René Lacoste (FRA)	Suzanne Lenglen (FRA)
1926	Henri Cochet (FRA)	Suzanne Lenglen (FRA)
1927	René Lacoste (FRA)	Kornelia Bouman (NED)
1928	Henri Cochet (FRA)	Helen Wills (USA)
1929	René Lacoste (FRA)	Helen Wills (USA)
1930	Henri Cochet (FRA)	Helen Wills Moody (USA)
1931	Jean Borotra (FRA)	Cilly Aussem (GER)
1932	Henri Cochet (FRA)	Helen Wills Moody (USA)
1933	John Crawford (AUS)	Margaret Scriven (GBR)
1934	Gottfried von Cramm (GER)	Margaret Scriven (GBR)
1935	Fred Perry (GBR)	Hilde Sperling (DEN)
1936	Gottfried von Cramm (GER)	Hilde Sperling (DEN)
1937	Henner Henkel (GER)	Hilde Sperling (DEN)
1938	Don Budge (USA)	Simone Mathieu (FRA)
1939	Don McNeill (USA)	Simone Mathieu (FRA)
1940	*not held*	*not held*
1941	Bernard Destremau (FRA)	*not held*
1942	Bernard Destremau (FRA)	*not held*
1943	Yvon Petra (FRA)	*not held*
1944	Yvon Petra (FRA)	*not held*
1945	Yvon Petra (FRA)	*not held*
1946	Marcel Bernard (FRA)	Margaret Osborne (USA)
1947	Joseph Asboth (HUN)	Patricia Todd (USA)
1948	Frank Parker (USA)	Nelly Landry (BEL)
1949	Frank Parker (USA)	Margaret Osborne duPont (USA)
1950	Budge Patty (USA)	Doris Hart (USA)
1951	Jaroslav Drobny (TCH)	Shirley Fry (USA)
1952	Jaroslav Drobny (TCH)	Doris Hart (USA)
1953	Ken Rosewall (AUS)	Maureen Connolly (USA)
1954	Tony Trabert (USA)	Maureen Connolly (USA)
1955	Tony Trabert (USA)	Angela Mortimer (GBR)
1956	Lew Hoad (AUS)	Althea Gibson (USA)
1957	Sven Davidson (SWE)	Shirley Bloomer (GBR)
1958	Mervyn Rose (AUS)	Zsuzsi Kormoczi (HUN)
1959	Nicola Pietrangeli (ITA)	Christine Truman (GBR)
1960	Nicola Pietrangeli (ITA)	Darlene Hard (USA)
1961	Manuel Santana (ESP)	Ann Haydon (GBR)
1962	Rod Laver (AUS)	Margaret Smith (AUS)
1963	Roy Emerson (AUS)	Lesley Turner (AUS)
1964	Manuel Santana (ESP)	Margaret Smith (AUS)
1965	Fred Stolle (AUS)	Lesley Turner (AUS)
1966	Tony Roche (AUS)	Ann Haydon Jones (GBR)
1967	Roy Emerson (AUS)	Françoise Durr (FRA)
1968	Ken Rosewall (AUS)	Nancy Richey (USA)
1969	Rod Laver (AUS)	Margaret Smith Court (AUS)
1970	Jan Kodes (TCH)	Margaret Smith Court (AUS)
1971	Jan Kodes (TCH)	Evonne Goolagong (AUS)
1972	Andres Gimeno (ESP)	Billie Jean King (USA)
1973	Ilie Nastase (ROM)	Margaret Smith Court (AUS)
1974	Björn Borg (SWE)	Chris Evert (USA)
1975	Björn Borg (SWE)	Chris Evert (USA)
1976	Adriano Panatta (ITA)	Sue Barker (USA)
1977	Guillermo Vilas (ARG)	Mima Jausovec (YUG)
1978	Björn Borg (SWE)	Virginia Ruzici (ROM)
1979	Björn Borg (SWE)	Chris Evert Lloyd (USA)
1980	Björn Borg (SWE)	Chris Evert Lloyd (USA)
1981	Björn Borg (SWE)	Hana Mandlikova (TCH)
1982	Mats Wilander (SWE)	Martina Navratilova (USA)
1983	Yannick Noah (FRA)	Chris Evert Lloyd (USA)
1984	Ivan Lendl (TCH)	Martina Navratilova (USA)
1985	Mats Wilander (SWE)	Chris Evert Lloyd (USA)
1986	Ivan Lendl (TCH)	Chris Evert Lloyd (USA)
1987	Ivan Lendl (TCH)	Steffi Graf (FRG)
1988	Mats Wilander (SWE)	Steffi Graf (FRG)
1989	Michael Chang (USA)	Arantxa Sánchez Vicario (ESP)
1990	Andres Gómez (ECU)	Monica Seles (YUG)

French Open Tennis Championships—Singles (continued)

YEAR	MEN	WOMEN
1991	Jim Courier (USA)	Monica Seles (YUG)
1992	Jim Courier (USA)	Monica Seles (YUG)
1993	Sergi Bruguera (ESP)	Steffi Graf (GER)
1994	Sergi Bruguera (ESP)	Arantxa Sánchez Vicario (ESP)
1995	Thomas Muster (AUT)	Steffi Graf (GER)
1996	Yevgeny Kafelnikov (RUS)	Steffi Graf (GER)
1997	Gustavo Kuerten (BRA)	Iva Majoli (CRO)
1998	Carlos Moya (ESP)	Arantxa Sánchez Vicario (ESP)
1999	Andre Agassi (USA)	Steffi Graf (GER)
2000	Gustavo Kuerten (BRA)	Mary Pierce (FRA)
2001	Gustavo Kuerten (BRA)	Jennifer Capriati (USA)
2002	Albert Costa (ESP)	Serena Williams (USA)
2003	Juan Carlos Ferrero (ESP)	Justine Henin-Hardenne (BEL)
2004	Gastón Gaudio (ARG)	Anastasiya Myskina (RUS)
2005	Rafael Nadal (ESP)	Justine Henin-Hardenne (BEL)
2006	Rafael Nadal (ESP)	Justine Henin-Hardenne (BEL)
2007	Rafael Nadal (ESP)	Justine Henin (BEL)
2008	Rafael Nadal (ESP)	Ana Ivanovic (SRB)
2009	Roger Federer (SUI)	Svetlana Kuznetsova (RUS)

French Open Tennis Championships—Doubles

YEAR	MEN	WOMEN
1925	Jean Borotra, René Lacoste	Suzanne Lenglen, Didi Vlasto
1926	Vinnie Richards, Howard Kinsey	Suzanne Lenglen, Didi Vlasto
1927	Henri Cochet, Jacques Brugnon	Irene Peacock, Bobby Heine
1928	Jean Borotra, Jacques Brugnon	Phoebe Watson, Eileen Bennett
1929	Jean Borotra, René Lacoste	Lili de Alvarez, Kea Bouman
1930	Henri Cochet, Jacques Brugnon	Helen Wills Moody, Elizabeth Ryan
1931	George Lott, John Van Ryn	Eileen Whittingstall, Betty Nuthall
1932	Henri Cochet, Jacques Brugnon	Helen Wills Moody, Elizabeth Ryan
1933	Pat Hughes, Fred Perry	Simone Mathieu, Elizabeth Ryan
1934	Jean Borotra, Jacques Brugnon	Simone Mathieu, Elizabeth Ryan
1935	Jack Crawford, Adrian Quist	Margaret Scriven, Kay Stammers
1936	Jean Borotra, Marcel Bernard	Simone Mathieu, Billie Yorke
1937	Gottfried von Cramm, Henner Henkel	Simone Mathieu, Billie Yorke
1938	Bernard Destremau, Yvon Petra	Simone Mathieu, Billie Yorke
1939	Don McNeill, Charles Harris	Simone Mathieu, Jadwiga Jedrzejowska
1940–45	not held	
1946	Marcel Bernard, Yvon Petra	Louise Brough, Margaret Osborne
1947	Eustace Fannin, Eric Sturgess	Louise Brough, Margaret Osborne
1948	Lennart Bergelin, Jaroslav Drobny	Doris Hart, Patricia Todd
1949	Pancho Gonzáles, Frank Parker	Louise Brough, Margaret Osborne duPont
1950	Billy Talbert, Tony Trabert	Doris Hart, Shirley Fry
1951	Ken McGregor, Frank Sedgman	Doris Hart, Shirley Fry
1952	Ken McGregor, Frank Sedgman	Doris Hart, Shirley Fry
1953	Lew Hoad, Ken Rosewall	Doris Hart, Shirley Fry
1954	Vic Seixas, Tony Trabert	Maureen Connolly, Nell Hopman
1955	Vic Seixas, Tony Trabert	Beverly Fleitz, Darlene Hard
1956	Don Candy, Robert Perry	Angela Buxton, Althea Gibson
1957	Mal Anderson, Ashley Cooper	Shirley Bloomer, Darlene Hard
1958	Ashley Cooper, Neale Fraser	Rosie Reyes, Yola Ramirez
1959	Nicola Pietrangeli, Orlando Sirola	Sandra Reynolds, Renee Schuurman
1960	Roy Emerson, Neale Fraser	Maria Bueno, Darlene Hard
1961	Roy Emerson, Rod Laver	Sandra Reynolds, Renee Schuurman
1962	Roy Emerson, Neale Fraser	Sandra Reynolds Price, Renee Schuurman
1963	Roy Emerson, Manuel Santana	Ann Haydon Jones, Renee Schuurman
1964	Roy Emerson, Ken Fletcher	Margaret Smith, Lesley Turner
1965	Roy Emerson, Fred Stolle	Margaret Smith, Lesley Turner
1966	Clark Graebner, Dennis Ralston	Margaret Smith, Judy Tegart
1967	John Newcombe, Tony Roche	Françoise Durr, Gail Sherriff
1968	Ken Rosewall, Fred Stolle	Françoise Durr, Ann Haydon Jones
1969	John Newcombe, Tony Roche	Françoise Durr, Ann Haydon Jones
1970	Ilie Nastase, Ion Tiriac	Françoise Durr, Gail Chanfreau
1971	Arthur Ashe, Marty Riessen	Françoise Durr, Gail Chanfreau
1972	Bob Hewitt, Frew McMillan	Billie Jean King, Betty Stove
1973	John Newcombe, Tom Okker	Margaret Smith Court, Virginia Wade
1974	Dick Crealy, Onny Parun	Chris Evert, Olga Morozova

French Open Tennis Championships—Doubles (continued)

YEAR	MEN	WOMEN
1975	Brian Gottfried, Raúl Ramírez	Chris Evert, Martina Navratilova
1976	Fred McNair, Sherwood Stewart	Fiorella Bonicelli, Gail Lovera
1977	Brian Gottfried, Raúl Ramírez	Regina Marsikova, Pam Teeguarden
1978	Hank Pfister, Gene Mayer	Mima Jausovec, Virginia Ruzici
1979	Sandy Mayer, Gene Mayer	Wendy Turnbull, Betty Stove
1980	Victor Amaya, Hank Pfister	Kathy Jordan, Anne Smith
1981	Heinz Günthardt, Balázs Taróczy	Rosalyn Fairbank, Tanya Harford
1982	Sherwood Stewart, Ferdi Taygan	Martina Navratilova, Anne Smith
1983	Anders Järryd, Hans Simonsson	Rosalyn Fairbank, Candy Reynolds
1984	Henri Leconte, Yannick Noah	Martina Navratilova, Pam Shriver
1985	Kim Warwick, Mark Edmondson	Martina Navratilova, Pam Shriver
1986	John Fitzgerald, Tomas Smid	Martina Navratilova, Andrea Temesvari
1987	Robert Seguso, Anders Järryd	Martina Navratilova, Pam Shriver
1988	Emilio Sánchez, Andres Gómez	Martina Navratilova, Pam Shriver
1989	Jim Grabb, Patrick McEnroe	Larisa Savchenko, Natasha Zvereva
1990	Sergio Casal, Emilio Sánchez	Jana Novotna, Helena Sukova
1991	John Fitzgerald, Anders Järryd	Gigi Fernández, Jana Novotna
1992	Jacob Hlasek, Marc Rosset	Gigi Fernández, Natasha Zvereva
1993	Luke Jensen, Murphy Jensen	Gigi Fernández, Natasha Zvereva
1994	Byron Black, Jonathan Stark	Gigi Fernández, Natasha Zvereva
1995	Jacco Eltingh, Paul Haarhuis	Gigi Fernández, Natasha Zvereva
1996	Yevgeny Kafelnikov, Daniel Vacek	Lindsay Davenport, Mary Joe Fernández
1997	Yevgeny Kafelnikov, Daniel Vacek	Gigi Fernández, Natasha Zvereva
1998	Jacco Eltingh, Paul Haarhuis	Martina Hingis, Jana Novotna
1999	Mahesh Bhupathi, Leander Paes	Venus Williams, Serena Williams
2000	Todd Woodbridge, Mark Woodforde	Martina Hingis, Mary Pierce
2001	Mahesh Bhupathi, Leander Paes	Virginia Ruano Pascual, Paola Suárez
2002	Yevgeny Kafelnikov, Paul Haarhuis	Virginia Ruano Pascual, Paola Suárez
2003	Bob Bryan, Mike Bryan	Kim Clijsters, Ai Sugiyama
2004	Xavier Malisse, Olivier Rochus	Virginia Ruano Pascual, Paola Suárez
2005	Jonas Björkman, Max Mirnyi	Virginia Ruano Pascual, Paola Suárez
2006	Jonas Björkman, Max Mirnyi	Lisa Raymond, Samantha Stosur
2007	Mark Knowles, Daniel Nestor	Alicia Molik, Mara Santangelo
2008	Pablo Cuevas, Luis Horna	Anabel Medina Garrigues, Virginia Ruano Pascual
2009	Lukas Dlouhy, Leander Paes	Anabel Medina Garrigues, Virginia Ruano Pascual

All-England (Wimbledon) Tennis Championships—Singles

YEAR	MEN	WOMEN
1877	Spencer Gore (GBR)	
1878	Frank Hadow (GBR)	
1879	John Hartley (GBR)	
1880	John Hartley (GBR)	
1881	William Renshaw (GBR)	
1882	William Renshaw (GBR)	
1883	William Renshaw (GBR)	
1884	William Renshaw (GBR)	Maud Watson (GBR)
1885	William Renshaw (GBR)	Maud Watson (GBR)
1886	William Renshaw (GBR)	Blanche Bingley (GBR)
1887	Herbert Lawford (GBR)	Lottie Dod (GBR)
1888	Ernest Renshaw (GBR)	Lottie Dod (GBR)
1889	William Renshaw (GBR)	Blanche Bingley Hillyard (GBR)
1890	William Hamilton (GBR)	Lena Rice (GBR)
1891	Wilfred Baddeley (GBR)	Lottie Dod (GBR)
1892	Wilfred Baddeley (GBR)	Lottie Dod (GBR)
1893	Joshua Pim (GBR)	Lottie Dod (GBR)
1894	Joshua Pim (GBR)	Blanche Bingley Hillyard (GBR)
1895	Wilfred Baddeley (GBR)	Charlotte Cooper (GBR)
1896	Harold Mahony (GBR)	Charlotte Cooper (GBR)
1897	Reggie Doherty (GBR)	Blanche Bingley Hillyard (GBR)
1898	Reggie Doherty (GBR)	Charlotte Cooper (GBR)
1899	Reggie Doherty (GBR)	Blanche Bingley Hillyard (GBR)
1900	Reggie Doherty (GBR)	Blanche Bingley Hillyard (GBR)
1901	Arthur Gore (GBR)	Charlotte Cooper Sterry (GBR)
1902	Laurie Doherty (GBR)	Muriel Robb (GBR)
1903	Laurie Doherty (GBR)	Dorothea Douglass (GBR)
1904	Laurie Doherty (GBR)	Dorothea Douglass (GBR)

All-England (Wimbledon) Tennis Championships—Singles (continued)

YEAR	MEN	WOMEN
1905	Laurie Doherty (GBR)	May Sutton (USA)
1906	Laurie Doherty (GBR)	Dorothea Douglass (GBR)
1907	Norman Brookes (AUS)	May Sutton (USA)
1908	Arthur Gore (GBR)	Charlotte Cooper Sterry (GBR)
1909	Arthur Gore (GBR)	Dora Boothby (GBR)
1910	Tony Wilding (NZL)	Dorothea Lambert Chambers (GBR)
1911	Tony Wilding (NZL)	Dorothea Lambert Chambers (GBR)
1912	Tony Wilding (NZL)	Ethel Larcombe (GBR)
1913	Tony Wilding (NZL)	Dorothea Lambert Chambers (GBR)
1914	Norman Brookes (AUS)	Dorothea Lambert Chambers (GBR)
1915–18	*not held*	
1919	Gerald Patterson (AUS)	Suzanne Lenglen (FRA)
1920	Bill Tilden (USA)	Suzanne Lenglen (FRA)
1921	Bill Tilden (USA)	Suzanne Lenglen (FRA)
1922	Gerald Patterson (AUS)	Suzanne Lenglen (FRA)
1923	Bill Johnston (USA)	Suzanne Lenglen (FRA)
1924	Jean Borotra (FRA)	Kathleen McKane (GBR)
1925	René Lacoste (FRA)	Suzanne Lenglen (FRA)
1926	Jean Borotra (FRA)	Kathleen McKane Godfree (GBR)
1927	Henri Cochet (FRA)	Helen Wills (USA)
1928	René Lacoste (FRA)	Helen Wills (USA)
1929	Henri Cochet (FRA)	Helen Wills (USA)
1930	Bill Tilden (USA)	Helen Wills Moody (USA)
1931	Sidney Wood (USA)	Cilly Aussem (GER)
1932	Ellsworth Vines (USA)	Helen Wills Moody (USA)
1933	Jack Crawford (AUS)	Helen Wills Moody (USA)
1934	Fred Perry (GBR)	Dorothy Round (GBR)
1935	Fred Perry (GBR)	Helen Wills Moody (USA)
1936	Fred Perry (GBR)	Helen Jacobs (USA)
1937	Don Budge (USA)	Dorothy Round (GBR)
1938	Don Budge (USA)	Helen Wills Moody (USA)
1939	Bobby Riggs (USA)	Alice Marble (USA)
1940–45	*not held*	
1946	Yvon Petra (FRA)	Pauline Betz (USA)
1947	Jack Kramer (USA)	Margaret Osborne (USA)
1948	Bob Falkenburg (USA)	Louise Brough (USA)
1949	Ted Schroeder (USA)	Louise Brough (USA)
1950	Budge Patty (USA)	Louise Brough (USA)
1951	Dick Savitt (USA)	Doris Hart (USA)
1952	Frank Sedgman (AUS)	Maureen Connolly (USA)
1953	Vic Seixas (USA)	Maureen Connolly (USA)
1954	Jaroslav Drobny (TCH)	Maureen Connolly (USA)
1955	Tony Trabert (USA)	Louise Brough (USA)
1956	Lew Hoad (AUS)	Shirley Fry (USA)
1957	Lew Hoad (AUS)	Althea Gibson (USA)
1958	Ashley Cooper (AUS)	Althea Gibson (USA)
1959	Alex Olmedo (PER)	Maria Bueno (BRA)
1960	Neale Fraser (AUS)	Maria Bueno (BRA)
1961	Rod Laver (AUS)	Angela Mortimer (GBR)
1962	Rod Laver (AUS)	Karen Susman (USA)
1963	Chuck McKinley (USA)	Margaret Smith (AUS)
1964	Roy Emerson (AUS)	Maria Bueno (BRA)
1965	Roy Emerson (AUS)	Margaret Smith (AUS)
1966	Manuel Santana (ESP)	Billie Jean King (USA)
1967	John Newcombe (AUS)	Billie Jean King (USA)
1968	Rod Laver (AUS)	Billie Jean King (USA)
1969	Rod Laver (AUS)	Ann Jones (GBR)
1970	John Newcombe (AUS)	Margaret Smith Court (AUS)
1971	John Newcombe (AUS)	Evonne Goolagong (AUS)
1972	Stan Smith (USA)	Billie Jean King (USA)
1973	Jan Kodes (TCH)	Billie Jean King (USA)
1974	Jimmy Connors (USA)	Chris Evert (USA)
1975	Arthur Ashe (USA)	Billie Jean King (USA)
1976	Björn Borg (SWE)	Chris Evert (USA)
1977	Björn Borg (SWE)	Virginia Wade (GBR)
1978	Björn Borg (SWE)	Martina Navratilova (TCH)
1979	Björn Borg (SWE)	Martina Navratilova (TCH)
1980	Björn Borg (SWE)	Evonne Goolagong Cawley (AUS)

All-England (Wimbledon) Tennis Championships—Singles (continued)

YEAR	MEN	WOMEN
1981	John McEnroe (USA)	Chris Evert Lloyd (USA)
1982	Jimmy Connors (USA)	Martina Navratilova (USA)
1983	John McEnroe (USA)	Martina Navratilova (USA)
1984	John McEnroe (USA)	Martina Navratilova (USA)
1985	Boris Becker (FRG)	Martina Navratilova (USA)
1986	Boris Becker (FRG)	Martina Navratilova (USA)
1987	Pat Cash (AUS)	Martina Navratilova (USA)
1988	Stefan Edberg (SWE)	Steffi Graf (GDR)
1989	Boris Becker (FRG)	Steffi Graf (GDR)
1990	Stefan Edberg (SWE)	Martina Navratilova (USA)
1991	Michael Stich (GER)	Steffi Graf (GER)
1992	Andre Agassi (USA)	Steffi Graf (GER)
1993	Pete Sampras (USA)	Steffi Graf (GER)
1994	Pete Sampras (USA)	Conchita Martínez (ESP)
1995	Pete Sampras (USA)	Steffi Graf (GER)
1996	Richard Krajicek (NED)	Steffi Graf (GER)
1997	Pete Sampras (USA)	Martina Hingis (SUI)
1998	Pete Sampras (USA)	Jana Novotna (CZE)
1999	Pete Sampras (USA)	Lindsay Davenport (USA)
2000	Pete Sampras (USA)	Venus Williams (USA)
2001	Goran Ivanisevic (CRO)	Venus Williams (USA)
2002	Lleyton Hewitt (AUS)	Serena Williams (USA)
2003	Roger Federer (SUI)	Serena Williams (USA)
2004	Roger Federer (SUI)	Mariya Sharapova (RUS)
2005	Roger Federer (SUI)	Venus Williams (USA)
2006	Roger Federer (SUI)	Amélie Mauresmo (FRA)
2007	Roger Federer (SUI)	Venus Williams (USA)
2008	Rafael Nadal (ESP)	Venus Williams (USA)
2009	Roger Federer (SUI)	Serena Williams (USA)

All-England (Wimbledon) Tennis Championships—Doubles

YEAR	MEN	WOMEN
1879	L.R. Erskine, H. Lawford	
1880	William Renshaw, Ernest Renshaw	
1881	William Renshaw, Ernest Renshaw	
1882	J.T. Hartley, R.T. Richardson	
1883	C.W. Grinstead, C.E. Welldon	
1884	William Renshaw, Ernest Renshaw	
1885	William Renshaw, Ernest Renshaw	
1886	William Renshaw, Ernest Renshaw	
1887	Herbert Wilberforce, P.B. Lyon	
1888	William Renshaw, Ernest Renshaw	
1889	William Renshaw, Ernest Renshaw	
1890	Joshua Pim, F.O. Stoker	
1891	Wilfred Baddeley, Herbert Baddeley	
1892	E.W. Lewis, H.S. Barlow	
1893	Joshua Pim, F.O. Stoker	
1894	Wilfred Baddeley, Herbert Baddeley	
1895	Wilfred Baddeley, Herbert Baddeley	
1896	Wilfred Baddeley, Herbert Baddeley	
1897	Reggie Doherty, Laurie Doherty	
1898	Reggie Doherty, Laurie Doherty	
1899	Reggie Doherty, Laurie Doherty	
1900	Reggie Doherty, Laurie Doherty	
1901	Reggie Doherty, Laurie Doherty	
1902	Sidney Smith, Frank Riseley	
1903	Reggie Doherty, Laurie Doherty	
1904	Reggie Doherty, Laurie Doherty	
1905	Reggie Doherty, Laurie Doherty	
1906	Sidney Smith, Frank Riseley	
1907	Norman Brookes, Tony Wilding	
1908	Tony Wilding, M.J.G. Ritchie	
1909	Arthur Gore, H. Roper Barrett	
1910	Tony Wilding, M.J.G. Ritchie	
1911	André Gobert, Max Decugis	

All-England (Wimbledon) Tennis Championships—Doubles (continued)

YEAR	MEN	WOMEN
1912	H. Roper Barrett, Charles Dixon	
1913	H. Roper Barrett, Charles Dixon	Winifred McNair, Dora Boothby
1914	Norman Brookes, Tony Wilding	Elizabeth Ryan, Agatha Morton
1915-18	*not held*	
1919	R.V. Thomas, Pat O'Hara Wood	Suzanne Lenglen, Elizabeth Ryan
1920	Richard Williams, Chuck Garland	Suzanne Lenglen, Elizabeth Ryan
1921	Randolph Lycett, Max Woosnam	Suzanne Lenglen, Elizabeth Ryan
1922	James Anderson, Randolph Lycett	Suzanne Lenglen, Elizabeth Ryan
1923	Leslie Godfree, Randolph Lycett	Suzanne Lenglen, Elizabeth Ryan
1924	Frank Hunter, Vinnie Richards	Hazel Wightman, Helen Wills
1925	Jean Borotra, René Lacoste	Suzanne Lenglen, Elizabeth Ryan
1926	Henri Cochet, Jacques Brugnon	Mary Browne, Elizabeth Ryan
1927	Bill Tilden, Frank Hunter	Helen Wills, Elizabeth Ryan
1928	Henri Cochet, Jacques Brugnon	Peggy Saunders, Phoebe Watson
1929	Wilmer Allison, John Van Ryn	Peggy Saunders Michell, Phoebe Watson
1930	Wilmer Allison, John Van Ryn	Helen Wills Moody, Elizabeth Ryan
1931	George Lott, John Van Ryn	Phyllis Mudford, Dorothy Barron
1932	Jean Borotra, Jacques Brugnon	Doris Metaxa, Josane Sigart
1933	Jean Borotra, Jacques Brugnon	Simone Mathieu, Elizabeth Ryan
1934	George Lott, Lester Stoefen	Simone Mathieu, Elizabeth Ryan
1935	Adrian Quist, Jack Crawford	Freda James, Kay Stammers
1936	Pat Hughes, Raymond Tuckey	Freda James, Kay Stammers
1937	Don Budge, Gene Mako	Simone Mathieu, Billie Yorke
1938	Don Budge, Gene Mako	Sarah Palfrey Fabyan, Alice Marble
1939	Bobby Riggs, Elwood Cooke	Sarah Palfrey Fabyan, Alice Marble
1940-45	*not held*	
1946	Jack Kramer, Tom Brown	Louise Brough, Margaret Osborne
1947	Jack Kramer, Bob Falkenburg	Patricia Todd, Doris Hart
1948	John Bromwich, Frank Sedgman	Louise Brough, Margaret Osborne duPont
1949	Pancho Gonzáles, Frank Parker	Louise Brough, Margaret Osborne duPont
1950	Adrian Quist, John Bromwich	Louise Brough, Margaret Osborne duPont
1951	Ken McGregor, Frank Sedgman	Doris Hart, Shirley Fry
1952	Ken McGregor, Frank Sedgman	Doris Hart, Shirley Fry
1953	Lew Hoad, Ken Rosewall	Doris Hart, Shirley Fry
1954	Rex Hartwig, Mervyn Rose	Louise Brough, Margaret Osborne duPont
1955	Rex Hartwig, Lew Hoad	Angela Mortimer, Anne Shilcock
1956	Lew Hoad, Ken Rosewall	Angela Buxton, Althea Gibson
1957	Budge Patty, Gardnar Mulloy	Althea Gibson, Darlene Hard
1958	Sven Davidson, Ulf Schmidt	Maria Bueno, Althea Gibson
1959	Roy Emerson, Neale Fraser	Jeanne Arth, Darlene Hard
1960	Rafael Osuna, Dennis Ralston	Maria Bueno, Darlene Hard
1961	Roy Emerson, Neale Fraser	Karen Hantze, Billie Jean Moffitt
1962	Bob Hewitt, Fred Stolle	Karen Hantze Susman, Billie Jean Moffitt
1963	Rafael Osuna, Antonio Palafox	Maria Bueno, Darlene Hard
1964	Bob Hewitt, Fred Stolle	Margaret Smith, Leslie Turner
1965	John Newcombe, Tony Roche	Maria Bueno, Billie Jean Moffitt
1966	John Newcombe, Ken Fletcher	Maria Bueno, Nancy Richey
1967	Bob Hewitt, Frew McMillan	Billie Jean King, Rosemary Casals
1968	John Newcombe, Tony Roche	Billie Jean King, Rosemary Casals
1969	John Newcombe, Tony Roche	Margaret Smith Court, Judy Tegart
1970	John Newcombe, Tony Roche	Billie Jean King, Rosemary Casals
1971	Roy Emerson, Rod Laver	Billie Jean King, Rosemary Casals
1972	Bob Hewitt, Frew McMillan	Billie Jean King, Betty Stove
1973	Jimmy Connors, Ilie Nastase	Billie Jean King, Rosemary Casals
1974	John Newcombe, Tony Roche	Evonne Goolagong, Peggy Michel
1975	Vitas Gerulaitis, Sandy Mayer	Ann Kiyomura, Kazuko Sawamatsu
1976	Brian Gottfried, Raúl Ramírez	Chris Evert, Martina Navratilova
1977	Ross Case, Geoff Masters	Helen Gourlay Cawley, Joanne Russell
1978	Bob Hewitt, Frew McMillan	Kerry Reid, Wendy Turnbull
1979	John McEnroe, Peter Fleming	Billie Jean King, Martina Navratilova
1980	Peter McNamara, Paul McNamee	Kathy Jordan, Anne Smith
1981	John McEnroe, Peter Fleming	Martina Navratilova, Pam Shriver
1982	Peter McNamara, Paul McNamee	Martina Navratilova, Pam Shriver
1983	John McEnroe, Peter Fleming	Martina Navratilova, Pam Shriver
1984	John McEnroe, Peter Fleming	Martina Navratilova, Pam Shriver
1985	Heinz Günthardt, Balázs Taróczy	Kathy Jordan, Elizabeth Smylie
1986	Joakim Nyström, Mats Wilander	Martina Navratilova, Pam Shriver
1987	Robert Seguso, Ken Flach	Claudia Kohde-Kilsch, Helena Suková

All-England (Wimbledon) Tennis Championships—Doubles (continued)

YEAR	MEN	WOMEN
1988	Robert Seguso, Ken Flach	Steffi Graf, Gabriela Sabatini
1989	John Fitzgerald, Anders Järryd	Jana Novotna, Helena Sukova
1990	Rick Leach, Jim Pugh	Jana Novotna, Helena Sukova
1991	John Fitzgerald, Anders Järryd	Larisa Savchenko, Natasha Zvereva
1992	John McEnroe, Michael Stich	Gigi Fernández, Natasha Zvereva
1993	Todd Woodbridge, Mark Woodforde	Gigi Fernández, Natasha Zvereva
1994	Todd Woodbridge, Mark Woodforde	Gigi Fernández, Natasha Zvereva
1995	Todd Woodbridge, Mark Woodforde	Arantxa Sánchez Vicario, Jana Novotna
1996	Todd Woodbridge, Mark Woodforde	Helena Sukova, Martina Hingis
1997	Todd Woodbridge, Mark Woodforde	Gigi Fernández, Natasha Zvereva
1998	Jacco Eltingh, Paul Haarhuis	Martina Hingis, Jana Novotna
1999	Mahesh Bhupathi, Leander Paes	Lindsay Davenport, Corina Morariu
2000	Todd Woodbridge, Mark Woodforde	Venus Williams, Serena Williams
2001	Donald Johnson, Jared Palmer	Lisa Raymond, Rennae Stubbs
2002	Jonas Björkman, Todd Woodbridge	Venus Williams, Serena Williams
2003	Jonas Björkman, Todd Woodbridge	Kim Clijsters, Ai Sugiyama
2004	Jonas Björkman, Todd Woodbridge	Cara Black, Rennae Stubbs
2005	Stephen Huss, Wesley Moodie	Cara Black, Liezel Huber
2006	Bob Bryan, Mike Bryan	Yan Zi, Zheng Jie
2007	Arnaud Clément, Michaël Llodra	Cara Black, Liezel Huber
2008	Daniel Nestor, Nenad Zimonjic	Venus Williams, Serena Williams
2009	Daniel Nestor, Nenad Zimonjic	Venus Williams, Serena Williams

United States Open Tennis Championships—Singles

YEAR	MEN	WOMEN
1881	Richard Sears (USA)	
1882	Richard Sears (USA)	
1883	Richard Sears (USA)	
1884	Richard Sears (USA)	
1885	Richard Sears (USA)	
1886	Richard Sears (USA)	
1887	Richard Sears (USA)	Ellen Hansell (USA)
1888	Henry Slocum, Jr. (USA)	Bertha Townsend (USA)
1889	Henry Slocum, Jr. (USA)	Bertha Townsend (USA)
1890	Oliver Campbell (USA)	Ellen Roosevelt (USA)
1891	Oliver Campbell (USA)	Mabel Cahill (USA)
1892	Oliver Campbell (USA)	Mabel Cahill (USA)
1893	Robert Wrenn (USA)	Aline Terry (USA)
1894	Robert Wrenn (USA)	Helen Helwig (USA)
1895	Fred Hovey (USA)	Juliette Atkinson (USA)
1896	Robert Wrenn (USA)	Elisabeth Moore (USA)
1897	Robert Wrenn (USA)	Juliette Atkinson (USA)
1898	Malcom Whitman (USA)	Juliette Atkinson (USA)
1899	Malcom Whitman (USA)	Marion Jones (USA)
1900	Malcom Whitman (USA)	Myrtle McAteer (USA)
1901	William Larned (USA)	Elisabeth Moore (USA)
1902	William Larned (USA)	Marion Jones (USA)
1903	Laurie Doherty (GBR)	Elisabeth Moore (USA)
1904	Holcombe Ward (USA)	May Sutton (USA)
1905	Beals Wright (USA)	Elisabeth Moore (USA)
1906	Bill Clothier (USA)	Helen Homans (USA)
1907	William Larned (USA)	Evelyn Sears (USA)
1908	William Larned (USA)	Maud Barger-Wallach (USA)
1909	William Larned (USA)	Hazel Hotchkiss (USA)
1910	William Larned (USA)	Hazel Hotchkiss (USA)
1911	William Larned (USA)	Hazel Hotchkiss (USA)
1912	Maurice McLoughlin (USA)	Mary Browne (USA)
1913	Maurice McLoughlin (USA)	Mary Browne (USA)
1914	R. Norris Williams (USA)	Mary Browne (USA)
1915	Bill Johnston (USA)	Molla Bjurstedt (NOR)
1916	R. Norris Williams (USA)	Molla Bjurstedt (NOR)
1917	Lindley Murray (USA)	Molla Bjurstedt (NOR)
1918	Lindley Murray (USA)	Molla Bjurstedt (NOR)
1919	Bill Johnston (USA)	Hazel Hotchkiss Wightman (USA)

United States Open Tennis Championships—Singles (continued)

YEAR	MEN	WOMEN
1920	Bill Tilden (USA)	Molla Bjurstedt Mallory (USA)
1921	Bill Tilden (USA)	Molla Bjurstedt Mallory (USA)
1922	Bill Tilden (USA)	Molla Bjurstedt Mallory (USA)
1923	Bill Tilden (USA)	Helen Wills (USA)
1924	Bill Tilden (USA)	Helen Wills (USA)
1925	Bill Tilden (USA)	Helen Wills (USA)
1926	René Lacoste (FRA)	Molla Bjurstedt Mallory (USA)
1927	René Lacoste (FRA)	Helen Wills (USA)
1928	Henri Cochet (FRA)	Helen Wills (USA)
1929	Bill Tilden (USA)	Helen Wills (USA)
1930	John Doeg (USA)	Betty Nuthall (GBR)
1931	Ellsworth Vines (USA)	Helen Wills Moody (USA)
1932	Ellsworth Vines (USA)	Helen Jacobs (USA)
1933	Fred Perry (GBR)	Helen Jacobs (USA)
1934	Fred Perry (GBR)	Helen Jacobs (USA)
1935	Wilmer Allison (USA)	Helen Jacobs (USA)
1936	Fred Perry (GBR)	Alice Marble (USA)
1937	Don Budge (USA)	Anita Lizana (CHI)
1938	Don Budge (USA)	Alice Marble (USA)
1939	Bobby Riggs (USA)	Alice Marble (USA)
1940	Don McNeill (USA)	Alice Marble (USA)
1941	Bobby Riggs (USA)	Sarah Palfrey Cooke (USA)
1942	Ted Schroeder (USA)	Pauline Betz (USA)
1943	Joe Hunt (USA)	Pauline Betz (USA)
1944	Frank Parker (USA)	Pauline Betz (USA)
1945	Frank Parker (USA)	Sarah Palfrey Cooke (USA)
1946	Jack Kramer (USA)	Pauline Betz (USA)
1947	Jack Kramer (USA)	Louise Brough (USA)
1948	Pancho Gonzáles (USA)	Margaret du Pont (USA)
1949	Pancho Gonzáles (USA)	Margaret du Pont (USA)
1950	Arthur Larsen (USA)	Margaret du Pont (USA)
1951	Frank Sedgman (AUS)	Maureen Connolly (USA)
1952	Frank Sedgman (AUS)	Maureen Connolly (USA)
1953	Tony Trabert (USA)	Maureen Connolly (USA)
1954	Vic Seixas (USA)	Doris Hart (USA)
1955	Tony Trabert (USA)	Doris Hart (USA)
1956	Ken Rosewall (AUS)	Shirley Fry (USA)
1957	Mal Anderson (AUS)	Althea Gibson (USA)
1958	Ashley Cooper (AUS)	Althea Gibson (USA)
1959	Neale Fraser (AUS)	Maria Bueno (BRA)
1960	Neale Fraser (AUS)	Darlene Hard (USA)
1961	Roy Emerson (AUS)	Darlene Hard (USA)
1962	Rod Laver (AUS)	Margaret Smith (AUS)
1963	Rafael Osuna (MEX)	Maria Bueno (BRA)
1964	Roy Emerson (AUS)	Maria Bueno (BRA)
1965	Manuel Santana (ESP)	Margaret Smith (AUS)
1966	Fred Stolle (AUS)	Maria Bueno (BRA)
1967	John Newcombe (AUS)	Billie Jean King (USA)
1968[1]	Arthur Ashe (USA)	Virginia Wade (GBR); Margaret Smith Court (AUS)
1969[1]	Rod Laver (AUS); Stan Smith (USA)	Margaret Smith Court (AUS)
1970	Ken Rosewall (AUS)	Margaret Smith Court (AUS)
1971	Stan Smith (USA)	Billie Jean King (USA)
1972	Ilie Nastase (ROM)	Billie Jean King (USA)
1973	John Newcombe (AUS)	Margaret Smith Court (AUS)
1974	Jimmy Connors (USA)	Billie Jean King (USA)
1975	Manuel Orantes (ESP)	Chris Evert (USA)
1976	Jimmy Connors (USA)	Chris Evert (USA)
1977	Guillermo Vilas (ARG)	Chris Evert (USA)
1978	Jimmy Connors (USA)	Chris Evert (USA)
1979	John McEnroe (USA)	Tracy Austin (USA)
1980	John McEnroe (USA)	Chris Evert Lloyd (USA)
1981	John McEnroe (USA)	Tracy Austin (USA)
1982	Jimmy Connors (USA)	Chris Evert Lloyd (USA)
1983	Jimmy Connors (USA)	Martina Navratilova (USA)
1984	John McEnroe (USA)	Martina Navratilova (USA)
1985	Ivan Lendl (TCH)	Hana Mandlikova (TCH)
1986	Ivan Lendl (TCH)	Martina Navratilova (USA)

United States Open Tennis Championships—Singles (continued)

YEAR	MEN	WOMEN
1987	Ivan Lendl (TCH)	Martina Navratilova (USA)
1988	Mats Wilander (SWE)	Steffi Graf (FRG)
1989	Boris Becker (FRG)	Steffi Graf (FRG)
1990	Pete Sampras (USA)	Gabriela Sabatini (ARG)
1991	Stefan Edberg (SWE)	Monica Seles (YUG)
1992	Stefan Edberg (SWE)	Monica Seles (YUG)
1993	Pete Sampras (USA)	Steffi Graf (GER)
1994	Andre Agassi (USA)	Arantxa Sánchez Vicario (ESP)
1995	Pete Sampras (USA)	Steffi Graf (GER)
1996	Pete Sampras (USA)	Steffi Graf (GER)
1997	Patrick Rafter (AUS)	Martina Hingis (SUI)
1998	Patrick Rafter (AUS)	Lindsay Davenport (USA)
1999	Andre Agassi (USA)	Serena Williams (USA)
2000	Marat Safin (RUS)	Venus Williams (USA)
2001	Lleyton Hewitt (AUS)	Venus Williams (USA)
2002	Pete Sampras (USA)	Serena Williams (USA)
2003	Andy Roddick (USA)	Justine Henin-Hardenne (BEL)
2004	Roger Federer (SUI)	Svetlana Kuznetsova (RUS)
2005	Roger Federer (SUI)	Kim Clijsters (BEL)
2006	Roger Federer (SUI)	Mariya Sharapova (RUS)
2007	Roger Federer (SUI)	Justine Henin (BEL)
2008	Roger Federer (SUI)	Serena Williams (USA)
2009	Juan Martín Del Potro (ARG)	Kim Clijsters (BEL)

[1]In 1968 and 1969 both amateur and open championships were held. Ashe won both men's competitions in 1968; Smith won the amateur championship in 1969. Court won the women's amateur competition in 1968 and both championships in 1969. Thereafter the championships were open.

United States Open Tennis Championships—Doubles

YEAR	MEN	WOMEN
1881	Clarence Clark, Fred Taylor	
1882	Richard Sears, James Dwight	
1883	Richard Sears, James Dwight	
1884	Richard Sears, James Dwight	
1885	Richard Sears, Joseph Clark	
1886	Richard Sears, James Dwight	
1887	Richard Sears, James Dwight	
1888	Oliver Campbell, Valentine Hall	
1889	Henry Slocum, Howard Taylor	Bertha Townsend, Margarette Ballard
1890	Valentine Hall, Clarence Hobart	Ellen Roosevelt, Grace Roosevelt
1891	Oliver Campbell, Robert Huntington	Mabel Cahill, Mrs. W. Fellowes Morgan
1892	Oliver Campbell, Robert Huntington	Mabel Cahill, Adeline McKinley
1893	Clarence Hobart, Fred Hovey	Aline Terry, Hattie Butler
1894	Clarence Hobart, Fred Hovey	Helen Helwig, Juliette Atkinson
1895	Malcom Chace, Robert Wrenn	Helen Helwig, Juliette Atkinson
1896	Carr Neel, Samuel Neel	Elisabeth Moore, Juliette Atkinson
1897	Leo Ware, George Sheldon	Juliette Atkinson, Kathleen Atkinson
1898	Leo Ware, George Sheldon	Juliette Atkinson, Kathleen Atkinson
1899	Holcombe Ward, Dwight Davis	Jane Craven, Myrtle McAteer
1900	Holcombe Ward, Dwight Davis	Edith Parker, Hallie Champlin
1901	Holcombe Ward, Dwight Davis	Juliette Atkinson, Myrtle McAteer
1902	Reggie Doherty, Laurie Doherty	Juliette Atkinson, Marion Jones
1903	Reggie Doherty, Laurie Doherty	Elisabeth Moore, Carrie Neely
1904	Holcombe Ward, Beals Wright	Mary Sutton, Miriam Hall
1905	Holcombe Ward, Beals Wright	Helen Homans, Carrie Neely
1906	Holcombe Ward, Beals Wright	Mrs. L.S. Coe, Mrs. D.S. Platt
1907	Fred Alexander, Harold Hackett	Marie Weimer, Carrie Neely
1908	Fred Alexander, Harold Hackett	Evelyn Sears, Margaret Curtis
1909	Fred Alexander, Harold Hackett	Hazel Hotchkiss, Edith Rotch
1910	Fred Alexander, Harold Hackett	Hazel Hotchkiss, Edith Rotch
1911	Raymond Little, Gustave Touchard	Hazel Hotchkiss, Eleanora Sears
1912	Maurice McLoughlin, Thomas Bundy	Dorothy Green, Mary Browne
1913	Maurice McLoughlin, Thomas Bundy	Mary Browne, Mrs. R.H. Williams
1914	Maurice McLoughlin, Thomas Bundy	Mary Browne, Mrs. R.H. Williams
1915	William Johnston, Clarence Griffin	Hazel Hotchkiss Wightman, Eleanora Sears
1916	William Johnston, Clarence Griffin	Molla Bjurstedt, Eleanora Sears
1917	Fred Alexander, Harold Throckmorton	Molla Bjurstedt, Eleanora Sears

United States Open Tennis Championships—Doubles (continued)

YEAR	MEN	WOMEN
1918	Bill Tilden, Vinnie Richards	Marion Zinderstein, Eleanor Goss
1919	Norman Brookes, Gerald Patterson	Marion Zinderstein, Eleanor Goss
1920	William Johnston, Clarence Griffin	Marion Zinderstein, Eleanor Goss
1921	Bill Tilden, Vinnie Richards	Mary Browne, Mrs. R.H. Williams
1922	Bill Tilden, Vinnie Richards	Marion Zinderstein Jessup, Helen Wills
1923	Bill Tilden, Brian Norton	Kathleen McKane, Phyllis Covell
1924	Howard Kinsey, Robert Kinsey	Hazel Hotchkiss Wightman, Helen Wills
1925	Richard Williams, Vinnie Richards	Mary Browne, Helen Wills
1926	Richard Williams, Vinnie Richards	Elizabeth Ryan, Eleanor Goss
1927	Bill Tilden, Frank Hunter	Kathleen McKane Godfree, Ermyntrude Harvey
1928	George Lott, John Hennessey	Hazel Hotchkiss Wightman, Helen Wills
1929	George Lott, John Doeg	Phoebe Watson, Peggy Michell
1930	George Lott, John Doeg	Betty Nuthall, Sarah Palfrey
1931	Wilmer Allison, John Van Ryn	Betty Nuthall, Eileen Whittingstall
1932	Ellsworth Vines, Keith Gledhill	Helen Jacobs, Sarah Palfrey
1933	George Lott, Lester Stoefen	Betty Nuthall, Freda James
1934	George Lott, Lester Stoefen	Helen Jacobs, Sarah Palfrey
1935	Wilmer Allison, John Van Ryn	Helen Jacobs, Sarah Palfrey Fabyan
1936	Don Budge, Gene Mako	Marjorie Van Ryn, Carolin Babcock
1937	Gottfried von Cramm, Henner Henkel	Sarah Palfrey Fabyan, Alice Marble
1938	Don Budge, Gene Mako	Sarah Palfrey Fabyan, Alice Marble
1939	Adrian Quist, John Bromwich	Sarah Palfrey Fabyan, Alice Marble
1940	Jack Kramer, Ted Schroeder	Sarah Palfrey Fabyan, Alice Marble
1941	Jack Kramer, Ted Schroeder	Sarah Palfrey Cooke, Margaret Osborne
1942	Gardnar Mulloy, Billy Talbert	Louise Brough, Margaret Osborne
1943	Jack Kramer, Frank Parker	Louise Brough, Margaret Osborne
1944	Don McNeill, Bob Falkenburg	Louise Brough, Margaret Osborne
1945	Gardnar Mulloy, Billy Talbert	Louise Brough, Margaret Osborne
1946	Gardnar Mulloy, Billy Talbert	Louise Brough, Margaret Osborne
1947	Jack Kramer, Ted Schroeder	Louise Brough, Margaret Osborne
1948	Gardnar Mulloy, Billy Talbert	Louise Brough, Margaret Osborne du Pont
1949	John Bromwich, Billy Sidwell	Louise Brough, Margaret Osborne du Pont
1950	John Bromwich, Frank Sedgman	Louise Brough, Margaret Osborne du Pont
1951	Ken McGregor, Frank Sedgman	Doris Hart, Shirley Fry
1952	Mervyn Rose, Vic Seixas	Doris Hart, Shirley Fry
1953	Rex Hartwig, Mervyn Rose	Doris Hart, Shirley Fry
1954	Vic Seixas, Tony Trabert	Doris Hart, Shirley Fry
1955	Kosei Kamo, Atushi Miyagi	Louise Brough, Margaret Osborne du Pont
1956	Lew Hoad, Ken Rosewall	Louise Brough, Margaret Osborne du Pont
1957	Ashley Cooper, Neale Fraser	Louise Brough, Margaret Osborne du Pont
1958	Alex Olmedo, Hamilton Richardson	Jeanne Arth, Darlene Hard
1959	Roy Emerson, Neale Fraser	Jeanne Arth, Darlene Hard
1960	Roy Emerson, Neale Fraser	Maria Bueno, Darlene Hard
1961	Charles McKinley, Dennis Ralston	Darlene Hard, Lesley Turner
1962	Rafael Osuna, Antonio Palafox	Maria Bueno, Darlene Hard
1963	Charles McKinley, Dennis Ralston	Robyn Ebbern, Margaret Smith
1964	Charles McKinley, Dennis Ralston	Karen Susman, Billie Jean Moffitt
1965	Roy Emerson, Fred Stolle	Carole Caldwell Graebner, Nancy Richey
1966	Roy Emerson, Fred Stolle	Maria Bueno, Nancy Richey
1967	John Newcombe, Tony Roche	Billie Jean Moffitt King, Rosemary Casals
1968[1]	Robert Lutz, Stan Smith	Maria Bueno, Margaret Smith Court
1969[1]	Ken Rosewall, Fred Stolle; 　Dick Crealy, Allan Stone	Françoise Durr, Darlene Hard; 　Margaret Smith Court, Virginia Wade
1970	Pierre Barthes, Niki Pilic	Margaret Smith Court, Judy Dalton
1971	John Newcombe, Roger Taylor	Rosemary Casals, Judy Dalton
1972	Cliff Drysdale, Roger Taylor	Françoise Durr, Betty Stove
1973	Owen Davidson, John Newcombe	Margaret Smith Court, Virginia Wade
1974	Robert Lutz, Stan Smith	Billie Jean King, Rosemary Casals
1975	Jimmy Connors, Ilie Nastase	Margaret Smith Court, Virginia Wade
1976	Tom Okker, Marty Riessen	Delina Boshoff, Ilana Kloss
1977	Bob Hewitt, Frew McMillan	Martina Navratilova, Betty Stove
1978	Robert Lutz, Stan Smith	Billie Jean King, Martina Navratilova
1979	John McEnroe, Peter Fleming	Wendy Turnbull, Betty Stove
1980	Robert Lutz, Stan Smith	Billie Jean King, Martina Navratilova
1981	John McEnroe, Peter Fleming	Kathy Jordan, Anne Smith
1982	Kevin Curren, Steve Denton	Rosemary Casals, Wendy Turnbull
1983	John McEnroe, Peter Fleming	Martina Navratilova, Pam Shriver
1984	John Fitzgerald, Tomas Smid	Martina Navratilova, Pam Shriver

United States Open Tennis Championships—Doubles (continued)

YEAR	MEN	WOMEN
1985	Robert Seguso, Ken Flach	Claudia Kohde-Kilsch, Helena Sukova
1986	Andres Gómez, Slobodan Zivojinovic	Martina Navratilova, Pam Shriver
1987	Stefan Edberg, Anders Järryd	Martina Navratilova, Pam Shriver
1988	Sergio Casal, Emilio Sánchez	Gigi Fernández, Robin White
1989	John McEnroe, Mark Woodforde	Martina Navratilova, Hana Mandlikova
1990	Pieter Aldrich, Danie Visser	Martina Navratilova, Gigi Fernández
1991	John Fitzgerald, Anders Järryd	Pam Shriver, Natasha Zvereva
1992	Jim Grabb, Richey Reneberg	Gigi Fernández, Natasha Zvereva
1993	Ken Flach, Rick Leach	Arantxa Sánchez Vicario, Helena Sukova
1994	Jacco Eltingh, Paul Haarhuis	Arantxa Sánchez Vicario, Jana Novotna
1995	Todd Woodbridge, Mark Woodforde	Gigi Fernández, Natasha Zvereva
1996	Todd Woodbridge, Mark Woodforde	Gigi Fernández, Natasha Zvereva
1997	Yevgeny Kafelnikov, Daniel Vacek	Lindsay Davenport, Jana Novotna
1998	Sandon Stolle, Cyril Suk	Martina Hingis, Jana Novotna
1999	Sébastien Lareau, Alex O'Brien	Venus Williams, Serena Williams
2000	Lleyton Hewitt, Max Mirnyi	Julie Halard-Decugis, Ai Sugiyama
2001	Wayne Black, Kevin Ullyet	Lisa Raymond, Rennae Stubbs
2002	Mahesh Bhupathi, Max Mirnyi	Virginia Ruano Pascual, Paola Suárez
2003	Jonas Björkman, Todd Woodbridge	Virginia Ruano Pascual, Paola Suárez
2004	Mark Knowles, Daniel Nestor	Virginia Ruano Pascual, Paola Suárez
2005	Bob Bryan, Mike Bryan	Lisa Raymond, Samantha Stosur
2006	Martin Damm, Leander Paes	Nathalie Dechy, Vera Zvonareva
2007	Simon Aspelin, Julian Knowle	Nathalie Dechy, Dinara Safina
2008	Bob Bryan, Mike Bryan	Cara Black, Liezel Huber
2009	Lukas Dlouhy, Leander Paes	Venus Williams, Serena Williams

[1]In 1968 and 1969 both amateur and open championships were held. Lutz and Smith won both men's competitions in 1968; Crealy and Stone took the men's amateur championships in 1969. Bueno and Court won both women's competitions in 1968; Court and Wade took the women's amateur championships in 1969. Thereafter the championships were open.

Davis Cup

YEAR	WINNER	RUNNER-UP	RESULTS	YEAR	WINNER	RUNNER-UP	RESULTS
1900	United States	British Isles[1]	3-0	1936	Great Britain	Australia	3-2
1901	not held			1937	United States	Great Britain	4-1
1902	United States	British Isles[1]	3-2	1938	United States	Australia	3-2
1903	British Isles[1]	United States	4-1	1939	Australia	United States	3-2
1904	British Isles[1]	Belgium	5-0	1940-45	not held		
1905	British Isles[1]	United States	5-0	1946	United States	Australia	5-0
1906	British Isles[1]	United States	5-0	1947	United States	Australia	4-1
1907	Australasia[2]	British Isles[1]	3-2	1948	United States	Australia	5-0
1908	Australasia[2]	United States	3-2	1949	United States	Australia	4-1
1909	Australasia[2]	United States	5-0	1950	Australia	United States	4-1
1910	not held			1951	Australia	United States	3-2
1911	Australasia[2]	United States	5-0	1952	Australia	United States	4-1
1912	British Isles[1]	Australasia[2]	3-2	1953	Australia	United States	3-2
1913	United States	Great Britain	3-2	1954	United States	Australia	3-2
1914	Australasia[2]	United States	3-2	1955	Australia	United States	5-0
1915-18	not held			1956	Australia	United States	5-0
1919	Australasia[2]	Great Britain	4-1	1957	Australia	United States	3-2
1920	United States	Australasia[2]	5-0	1958	United States	Australia	3-2
1921	United States	Japan	5-0	1959	Australia	United States	3-2
1922	United States	Australasia[2]	4-1	1960	Australia	Italy	4-1
1923	United States	Australasia[2]	4-1	1961	Australia	Italy	5-0
1924	United States	Australia	5-0	1962	Australia	Mexico	5-0
1925	United States	France	5-0	1963	United States	Australia	3-2
1926	United States	France	4-1	1964	Australia	United States	3-2
1927	France	United States	3-2	1965	Australia	Spain	4-1
1928	France	United States	4-1	1966	Australia	India	4-1
1929	France	United States	3-2	1967	Australia	Spain	4-1
1930	France	United States	4-1	1968	United States	Australia	4-1
1931	France	Great Britain	3-2	1969	United States	Romania	5-0
1932	France	United States	3-2	1970	United States	West Germany	5-0
1933	Great Britain	France	3-2	1971	United States	Romania	3-2
1934	Great Britain	United States	4-1	1972	United States	Romania	3-2
1935	Great Britain	United States	5-0	1973	Australia	United States	5-0

Davis Cup (continued)

YEAR	WINNER	RUNNER-UP	RESULTS	YEAR	WINNER	RUNNER-UP	RESULTS
1974	South Africa	India	[3]	1991	France	United States	3–1
1975	Sweden	Czechoslovakia	3–2	1992	United States	Switzerland	3–1
1976	Italy	Chile	4–1	1993	Germany	Australia	4–1
1977	Australia	Italy	3–1	1994	Sweden	Russia	4–1
1978	United States	Great Britain	4–1	1995	United States	Russia	3–2
1979	United States	Italy	5–0	1996	France	Sweden	3–2
1980	Czecho-slovakia	Italy	4–1	1997	Sweden	United States	5–0
				1998	Sweden	Italy	4–1
1981	United States	Argentina	3–1	1999	Australia	France	3–2
1982	United States	France	4–1	2000	Spain	Australia	3–1
1983	Australia	Sweden	3–2	2001	France	Australia	3–2
1984	Sweden	United States	4–1	2002	Russia	France	3–2
1985	Sweden	West Germany	3–2	2003	Australia	Spain	3–1
1986	Australia	Sweden	3–2	2004	Spain	United States	3–2
1987	Sweden	India	5–0	2005	Croatia	Slovakia	3–2
1988	West Germany	Sweden	4–1	2006	Russia	Argentina	3–2
1989	West Germany	Sweden	3–2	2007	United States	Russia	4–1
1990	United States	Australia	3–2	2008	Spain	Argentina	3–1

[1]*Great Britain and Ireland.*   [2]*Australia and New Zealand.*   [3]*Won by forfeit; India withdrew from the final.*

Fed Cup

YEAR	WINNER	RUNNER-UP	RESULTS	YEAR	WINNER	RUNNER-UP	RESULTS
1963	United States	Australia	2–1	1986	United States	Czechoslovakia	3–0
1964	Australia	United States	2–1	1987	West Germany	United States	2–1
1965	Australia	United States	2–1	1988	Czechoslovakia	USSR	2–1
1966	United States	West Germany	3–0	1989	United States	Spain	3–0
1967	United States	Great Britain	2–0	1990	United States	USSR	2–1
1968	Australia	The Netherlands	3–0	1991	Spain	United States	2–1
1969	United States	Australia	2–1	1992	Germany	Spain	2–1
1970	Australia	West Germany	3–0	1993	Spain	Australia	3–0
1971	Australia	Great Britain	3–0	1994	Spain	United States	3–0
1972	South Africa	Great Britain	2–1	1995	Spain	United States	3–2
1973	Australia	South Africa	3–0	1996	United States	Spain	5–0
1974	Australia	United States	2–1	1997	France	The Netherlands	4–1
1975	Czechoslovakia	Australia	3–0	1998	Spain	Switzerland	3–2
1976	United States	Australia	2–1	1999	United States	Russia	4–1
1977	United States	Australia	2–1	2000	United States	Spain	5–0
1978	United States	Australia	2–1	2001	Belgium	Russia	2–1
1979	United States	Australia	3–0	2002	Slovakia	Spain	3–1
1980	United States	Australia	3–0	2003	France	United States	4–1
1981	United States	Great Britain	3–0	2004	Russia	France	3–2
1982	United States	West Germany	3–0	2005	Russia	France	3–2
1983	Czechoslovakia	West Germany	2–1	2006	Italy	Belgium	3–2
1984	Czechoslovakia	Australia	2–1	2007	Russia	Italy	4–0
1985	Czechoslovakia	United States	2–1	2008	Russia	Spain	4–0

Did you know? The Barbie doll was fashioned after a German doll that was sold as a gag gift for men. Mattel owner Ruth Handler was traveling in Germany where she encountered the Bild Lilli doll, which was sold there at tobacco shops and in bars. She bought a doll for her daughter, Barbie, and gave one to the designers at Mattel. Mattel acquired the rights to Bild Lilli, and shortly thereafter, in 1959, Barbie was introduced in the United States.

Track & Field

The world governing body for track and field, or athletics, is the **International Association of Athletics Federations** (IAAF), founded in 1912. The sport includes relay running, a number of individual running, jumping, and throwing events, and one event (the decathlon for men and the heptathlon for women) that includes all three activities. The best-known competition for most track-and-field athletics is the **Olympic Games** held every four years. In 1983 the first officially recognized non-Olympic world athletics championships were held.
IAAF Web site: <www.iaaf.org>.

World Track & Field Championships—Men

100 M
1983 Carl Lewis (USA)
1987 Carl Lewis (USA)
1991 Carl Lewis (USA)
1993 Linford Christie (GBR)
1995 Donovan Bailey (CAN)
1997 Maurice Greene (USA)
1999 Maurice Greene (USA)
2001 Maurice Greene (USA)
2003 Kim Collins (SKN)
2005 Justin Gatlin (USA)
2007 Tyson Gay (USA)
2009 Usain Bolt (JAM)

200 M
1983 Calvin Smith (USA)
1987 Calvin Smith (USA)
1991 Michael Johnson (USA)
1993 Frank Fredericks (NAM)
1995 Michael Johnson (USA)
1997 Ato Boldon (TRI)
1999 Maurice Greene (USA)
2001 Konstadinos Kederis (GRE)
2003 John Capel (USA)
2005 Justin Gatlin (USA)
2007 Tyson Gay (USA)
2009 Usain Bolt (JAM)

400 M
1983 Bert Cameron (JAM)
1987 Thomas Schoenlebe (GDR)
1991 Antonio Pettigrew (USA)
1993 Michael Johnson (USA)
1995 Michael Johnson (USA)
1997 Michael Johnson (USA)
1999 Michael Johnson (USA)
2001 Avard Moncur (BAH)
2003 Tyree Washington (USA)
2005 Jeremy Wariner (USA)
2007 Jeremy Wariner (USA)
2009 LaShawn Merritt (USA)

800 M
1983 Willi Wülbeck (FRG)
1987 Billy Konchellah (KEN)
1991 Billy Konchellah (KEN)
1993 Paul Ruto (KEN)
1995 Wilson Kipketer (DEN)
1997 Wilson Kipketer (DEN)
1999 Wilson Kipketer (DEN)
2001 André Bucher (SUI)
2003 Djabir Saïd-Guerni (ALG)
2005 Rashid Ramzi (BRN)
2007 Alfred Kirwa Yego (KEN)
2009 Mbulaeni Mulaudzi (RSA)

1,500 M
1983 Steve Cram (GBR)
1987 Abdi Bile (SOM)
1991 Noureddine Morceli (ALG)
1993 Noureddine Morceli (ALG)
1995 Noureddine Morceli (ALG)
1997 Hicham El Guerrouj (MAR)
1999 Hicham El Guerrouj (MAR)
2001 Hicham El Guerrouj (MAR)
2003 Hicham El Guerrouj (MAR)
2005 Rashid Ramzi (BRN)

1,500 M (CONTIINUED)
2007 Bernard Lagat (USA)
2009 Yusuf Saad Kamel (BRN)

5,000 M
1983 Eamonn Coghlan (IRL)
1987 Said Aouita (MAR)
1991 Yobes Ondieki (KEN)
1993 Ismael Kirui (KEN)
1995 Ismael Kirui (KEN)
1997 Daniel Komen (KEN)
1999 Salah Hissou (MAR)
2001 Richard Limo (KEN)
2003 Eliud Kipchoge (KEN)
2005 Benjamin Limo (KEN)
2007 Bernard Lagat (USA)
2009 Kenenisa Bekele (ETH)

10,000 M
1983 Alberto Cova (ITA)
1987 Paul Kipkoech (KEN)
1991 Moses Tanui (KEN)
1993 Haile Gebrselassie (ETH)
1995 Haile Gebrselassie (ETH)
1997 Haile Gebrselassie (ETH)
1999 Haile Gebrselassie (ETH)
2001 Charles Kamathi (KEN)
2003 Kenenisa Bekele (ETH)
2005 Kenenisa Bekele (ETH)
2007 Kenenisa Bekele (ETH)
2009 Kenenisa Bekele (ETH)

STEEPLECHASE
1983 Patriz Ilg (FRG)
1987 Francesco Panetta (ITA)
1991 Moses Kiptanui (KEN)
1993 Moses Kiptanui (KEN)
1995 Moses Kiptanui (KEN)
1997 Wilson Boit Kipketer (KEN)
1999 Christopher Koskei (KEN)
2001 Reuben Kosgei (KEN)
2003 Saif Saaeed Shaheen (QAT)
2005 Saif Saaeed Shaheen (QAT)
2007 Brimin Kiprop Kipruto (KEN)
2009 Ezekiel Kemboi (KEN)

110-M HURDLES
1983 Greg Foster (USA)
1987 Greg Foster (USA)
1991 Greg Foster (USA)
1993 Colin Jackson (GBR)
1995 Allen Johnson (USA)
1997 Allen Johnson (USA)
1999 Colin Jackson (GBR)
2001 Allen Johnson (USA)
2003 Allen Johnson (USA)
2005 Ladji Doucouré (FRA)
2007 Liu Xiang (CHN)
2009 Ryan Brathwaite (BAR)

400-M HURDLES
1983 Edwin Moses (USA)
1987 Edwin Moses (USA)
1991 Samuel Matete (ZAM)
1993 Kevin Young (USA)
1995 Derrick Adkins (USA)
1997 Stéphane Diagana (FRA)
1999 Fabrizio Mori (ITA)

400-M HURDLES (CONTINUED)
2001 Felix Sánchez (DOM)
2003 Felix Sánchez (DOM)
2005 Bershawn Jackson (USA)
2007 Kerron Clement (USA)
2009 Kerron Clement (USA)

MARATHON
1983 Robert de Castella (AUS)
1987 Douglas Wakiihuri (KEN)
1991 Hiromi Taniguchi (JPN)
1993 Mark Plaatjes (USA)
1995 Martín Fiz (ESP)
1997 Abel Antón (ESP)
1999 Abel Antón (ESP)
2001 Gezahegne Abera (ETH)
2003 Jaouad Gharib (MAR)
2005 Jaouad Gharib (MAR)
2007 Luke Kibet (KEN)
2009 Abel Kirui (KEN)

20-KM WALK
1983 Ernesto Canto (MEX)
1987 Maurizio Damilano (ITA)
1991 Maurizio Damilano (ITA)
1993 Valentí Massana (ESP)
1995 Michele Didoni (ITA)
1997 Daniel García (MEX)
1999 Ilya Markov (RUS)
2001 Roman Rasskazov (RUS)
2003 Jefferson Pérez (ECU)
2005 Jefferson Pérez (ECU)
2007 Jefferson Pérez (ECU)
2009 Valeriy Borchin (RUS)

50-KM WALK
1983 Ronald Weigel (GDR)
1987 Hartwig Gauder (GDR)
1991 Aleksandr Potashov (URS)
1993 Jesús Angel García (ESP)
1995 Valentin Kononen (FIN)
1997 Robert Korzeniowski (POL)
1999 Ivano Brugnetti (ITA)
2001 Robert Korzeniowski (POL)
2003 Robert Korzeniowski (POL)
2005 Sergey Kirdyapkin (RUS)
2007 Nathan Deakes (AUS)
2009 Sergey Kirdyapkin (RUS)

4 × 100-M RELAY
1983 United States
1987 United States
1991 United States
1993 United States
1995 Canada
1997 Canada
1999 United States
2001 South Africa
2003 United States
2005 France
2007 United States
2009 Jamaica

4 × 400-M RELAY
1983 USSR
1987 United States
1991 United Kingdom
1993 United States

World Track & Field Championships—Men (continued)

4 × 400-M RELAY (CONTINUED)
1995 United States
1997 United States
1999 United States
2001 United States
2003 France
2005 United States
2007 United States
2009 United States

HIGH JUMP
1983 Gennady Avdeyenko (URS)
1987 Patrik Sjöberg (SWE)
1991 Charles Austin (USA)
1993 Javier Sotomayor (CUB)
1995 Troy Kemp (BAH)
1997 Javier Sotomayor (CUB)
1999 Vyacheslav Voronin (RUS)
2001 Martin Buss (GER)
2003 Jacques Freitag (RSA)
2005 Yuri Krymarenko (UKR)
2007 Donald Thomas (BAH)
2009 Yaroslav Rybakov (RUS)

POLE VAULT
1983 Sergey Bubka (URS)
1987 Sergey Bubka (URS)
1991 Sergey Bubka (URS)
1993 Sergey Bubka (UKR)
1995 Sergey Bubka (UKR)
1997 Sergey Bubka (UKR)
1999 Maksim Tarasov (RUS)
2001 Dmitri Markov (AUS)
2003 Giuseppe Gibilisco (ITA)
2005 Rens Blom (NED)
2007 Brad Walker (USA)
2009 Steven Hooker (AUS)

LONG JUMP
1983 Carl Lewis (USA)
1987 Carl Lewis (USA)
1991 Mike Powell (USA)
1993 Mike Powell (USA)
1995 Iván Pedroso (CUB)
1997 Iván Pedroso (CUB)
1999 Iván Pedroso (CUB)

LONG JUMP (CONTINUED)
2001 Iván Pedroso (CUB)
2003 Dwight Phillips (USA)
2005 Dwight Phillips (USA)
2007 Irving Saladino (PAN)
2009 Dwight Phillips (USA)

TRIPLE JUMP
1983 Zdzislaw Hoffman (POL)
1987 Khristo Markov (BUL)
1991 Kenny Harrison (USA)
1993 Mike Conley (USA)
1995 Jonathan Edwards (GBR)
1997 Yoelbi Quesada (CUB)
1999 Charles Michael Friedek (GER)
2001 Jonathan Edwards (GBR)
2003 Christian Olsson (SWE)
2005 Walter Davis (USA)
2007 Nelson Évora (POR)
2009 Phillips Idowu (GBR)

SHOT PUT
1983 Edward Sarul (POL)
1987 Werner Günthör (SUI)
1991 Werner Günthör (SUI)
1993 Werner Günthör (SUI)
1995 John Godina (USA)
1997 John Godina (USA)
1999 C.J. Hunter (USA)
2001 John Godina (USA)
2003 Andrey Mikhnevich (BLR)
2005 Adam Nelson (USA)
2007 Reese Hoffa (USA)
2009 Christian Cantwell (USA)

DISCUS THROW
1983 Imrich Bugar (TCH)
1987 Jürgen Schult (GDR)
1991 Lars Riedel (GER)
1993 Lars Riedel (GER)
1995 Lars Riedel (GER)
1997 Lars Riedel (GER)
1999 Anthony Washington (USA)
2001 Lars Riedel (GER)
2003 Virgilijus Alekna (LTU)

DISCUS THROW (CONTINUED)
2005 Virgilijus Alekna (LTU)
2007 Gerd Kanter (EST)
2009 Robert Harting (GER)

HAMMER THROW
1983 Sergey Litvinov (URS)
1987 Sergey Litvinov (URS)
1991 Yury Sedykh (URS)
1993 Andrey Abduvaliyev (TJK)
1995 Andrey Abduvaliyev (TJK)
1997 Heinz Weis (GER)
1999 Karsten Kobs (GER)
2001 Szymon Ziolkowski (POL)
2003 Ivan Tikhon (BLR)
2005 Ivan Tikhon (BLR)
2007 Ivan Tikhon (BLR)
2009 Primoz Kozmus (SLO)

JAVELIN THROW
1983 Detlef Michel (GDR)
1987 Seppo Räty (FIN)
1991 Kimmo Kinnunen (FIN)
1993 Jan Zelezny (CZE)
1995 Jan Zelezny (CZE)
1997 Marius Corbett (RSA)
1999 Aki Parviainen (FIN)
2001 Jan Zelezny (CZE)
2003 Sergey Makarov (RUS)
2005 Andrus Varnik (EST)
2007 Tero Pitkämäki (FIN)
2009 Andreas Thorkildsen (NOR)

DECATHLON
1983 Daley Thompson (GBR)
1987 Torsten Voss (GDR)
1991 Dan O'Brien (USA)
1993 Dan O'Brien (USA)
1995 Dan O'Brien (USA)
1997 Tomas Dvorak (CZE)
1999 Tomas Dvorak (CZE)
2001 Tomas Dvorak (CZE)
2003 Tom Pappas (USA)
2005 Bryan Clay (USA)
2007 Roman Sebrle (CZE)
2009 Trey Hardee (USA)

World Track & Field Championships—Women

100 M
1983 Marlies Göhr (GDR)
1987 Silke Gladisch (GDR)
1991 Katrin Krabbe (GER)
1993 Gail Devers (USA)
1995 Gwen Torrence (USA)
1997 Marion Jones (USA)
1999 Marion Jones (USA)
2001 Zhanna Pintusevich (UKR)
2003 Torri Edwards (USA)
2005 Lauryn Williams (USA)
2007 Veronica Campbell (JAM)
2009 Shelly-Ann Fraser (JAM)

200 M
1983 Marita Koch (GDR)
1987 Silke Gladisch (GDR)

200 M (CONTINUED)
1991 Katrin Krabbe (GER)
1993 Merlene Ottey (JAM)
1995 Merlene Ottey (JAM)
1997 Zhanna Pintusevich (UKR)
1999 Inger Miller (USA)
2001 Marion Jones (USA)
2003 Anastasiya Kapachin-
      skaya (RUS)
2005 Allyson Felix (USA)
2007 Allyson Felix (USA)
2009 Allyson Felix (USA)

400 M
1983 Jarmila Kratochvilova (TCH)
1987 Olga Bryzgina (URS)
1991 Marie-José Pérec (FRA)

400 M (CONTINUED)
1993 Jearl Miles (USA)
1995 Marie-José Pérec (FRA)
1997 Cathy Freeman (AUS)
1999 Cathy Freeman (AUS)
2001 Amy Mbacke Thiam (SEN)
2003 Ana Guevara (MEX)
2005 Tonique Williams-Darling
      (BAH)
2007 Christine Ohuruogu (GBR)
2009 Sanya Richards (USA)

800 M
1983 Jarmila Kratochvilova (TCH)
1987 Sigrun Wodars (GDR)
1991 Liliya Nurutdinova (URS)
1993 Maria Mutola (MOZ)

World Track & Field Championships—Women (continued)

800 M (CONTINUED)
1995 Ana Quirot (CUB)
1997 Ana Quirot (CUB)
1999 Ludmila Formanova (CZE)
2001 Maria Mutola (MOZ)
2003 Maria Mutola (MOZ)
2005 Zulia Calatayud (CUB)
2007 Janeth Jepkosgei (KEN)
2009 Caster Semenya (RSA)

1,500 M
1983 Mary Decker (USA)
1987 Tatyana Samolenko (URS)
1991 Hassiba Boulmerka (ALG)
1993 Liu Dong (CHN)
1995 Hassiba Boulmerka (ALG)
1997 Carla Sacramento (POR)
1999 Svetlana Masterkova (RUS)
2001 Gabriela Szabo (ROM)
2003 Tatyana Tomashova (RUS)
2005 Tatyana Tomashova (RUS)
2007 Maryam Yusuf Jamal (BRN)
2009 Maryam Yusuf Jamal (BRN)

5,000 M[1]
1983 Mary Decker (USA)
1987 Tatyana Samolenko (URS)
1991 Tatyana Dorovskikh (URS)
1993 Qu Yunxia (CHN)
1995 Sonia O'Sullivan (IRL)
1997 Gabriela Szabo (ROM)
1999 Gabriela Szabo (ROM)
2001 Olga Yegorova (RUS)
2003 Tirunesh Dibaba (ETH)
2005 Tirunesh Dibaba (ETH)
2007 Meseret Defar (ETH)
2009 Vivian Cheruiyot (KEN)

10,000 M
1987 Ingrid Kristiansen (NOR)
1991 Liz McColgan (GBR)
1993 Wang Junxia (CHN)
1995 Fernanda Ribeiro (POR)
1997 Sally Barsosio (KEN)
1999 Gete Wami (ETH)
2001 Derartu Tulu (ETH)
2003 Berhane Adere (ETH)
2005 Tirunesh Dibaba (ETH)
2007 Tirunesh Dibaba (ETH)
2009 Linet Chepkwemoi Masai (KEN)

STEEPLECHASE
2005 Dorcus Inzikuru (UGA)
2007 Yekaterina Volkova (RUS)
2009 Marta Domínguez (ESP)

100-M HURDLES
1983 Bettine Jahn (GDR)
1987 Ginka Zagorcheva (BUL)
1991 Ludmila Narozhilenko (URS)
1993 Gail Devers (USA)
1995 Gail Devers (USA)
1997 Ludmila Engquist (SWE)
1999 Gail Devers (USA)
2001 Anjanette Kirkland (USA)
2003 Perdita Felicien (CAN)
2005 Michelle Perry (USA)

100-M HURDLES (CONTINUED)
2007 Michelle Perry (USA)
2009 Brigitte Foster-Hylton (JAM)

400-M HURDLES
1983 Yekaterina Fesenko (URS)
1987 Sabine Busch (GDR)
1991 Tatyana Ledovskaya (URS)
1993 Sally Gunnell (GBR)
1995 Kim Batten (USA)
1997 Nezha Bidouane (MAR)
1999 Daimí Pernía (CUB)
2001 Nezha Bidouane (MAR)
2003 Jana Pittman (AUS)
2005 Yuliya Pechonkina (RUS)
2007 Jana Rawlinson (AUS)
2009 Melanie Walker (JAM)

MARATHON
1983 Grete Waitz (NOR)
1987 Rosa Mota (POR)
1991 Wanda Panfil (POL)
1993 Asari Junko (JPN)
1995 Maria Machado (POR)
1997 Hiromi Suzuki (JPN)
1999 Jong Song Ok (PRK)
2001 Lidia Simon (ROM)
2003 Catherine Ndereba (KEN)
2005 Paula Radcliffe (GBR)
2007 Catherine Ndereba (KEN)
2009 Bai Xue (CHN)

10-KM WALK
1987 Irina Strakhova (URS)
1991 Alina Ivanova (URS)
1993 Sari Essayeh (FIN)
1995 Irina Stankina (RUS)
1997 Annarita Sidoti (ITA)

20-KM RACE WALK
1999 Liu Hongyu (CHN)
2001 Olimpiada Ivanova (RUS)
2003 Yelena Nikolayeva (RUS)
2005 Olimpiada Ivanova (RUS)
2007 Olga Kaniskina (RUS)
2009 Olga Kaniskina (RUS)

4 × 100-M RELAY
1983 East Germany
1987 United States
1991 Jamaica
1993 Russia
1995 United States
1997 United States
1999 Bahamas
2001 Germany
2003 France
2005 United States
2007 United States
2009 Jamaica

4 × 400-M RELAY
1983 East Germany
1987 East Germany
1991 USSR
1993 United States
1995 United States
1997 Germany

4 × 400-M RELAY (CONTINUED)
1999 Russia
2001 Jamaica
2003 United States
2005 Russia
2007 United States
2009 United States

HIGH JUMP
1983 Tamara Bykova (URS)
1987 Stefka Kostadinova (BUL)
1991 Heike Henkel (GER)
1993 Ioamnet Quintero (CUB)
1995 Stefka Kostadinova (BUL)
1997 Hanne Haugland (NOR)
1999 Inga Babakova (UKR)
2001 Hestrie Cloete (RSA)
2003 Hestrie Cloete (RSA)
2005 Kajsa Bergqvist (SWE)
2007 Blanka Vlasic (CRO)
2009 Blanka Vlasic (CRO)

POLE VAULT
1999 Stacy Dragila (USA)
2001 Stacy Dragila (USA)
2003 Svetlana Feofanova (RUS)
2005 Yelena Isinbayeva (RUS)
2007 Yelena Isinbayeva (RUS)
2009 Anna Rogowska (POL)

LONG JUMP
1983 Heike Daute (GDR)
1987 Jackie Joyner-Kersee (USA)
1991 Jackie Joyner-Kersee (USA)
1993 Heike Drechsler (GER)
1995 Fiona May (ITA)
1997 Ludmila Galkina (RUS)
1999 Niurka Montalvo (ESP)
2001 Fiona May (ITA)
2003 Eunice Barber (FRA)
2005 Tianna Madison (USA)
2007 Tatyana Lebedeva (RUS)
2009 Brittney Reese (USA)

TRIPLE JUMP
1993 Anna Biryukova (RUS)
1995 Inessa Kravets (UKR)
1997 Sarka Kasparkova (CZE)
1999 Paraskevi Tsiamita (GRE)
2001 Tatyana Lebedeva (RUS)
2003 Tatyana Lebedeva (RUS)
2005 Trecia Smith (JAM)
2007 Yargelis Savigne (CUB)
2009 Yargelis Savigne (CUB)

SHOT PUT
1983 Helena Fibingerova (TCH)
1987 Natalya Lisovskaya (URS)
1991 Huang Zhihong (CHN)
1993 Huang Zhihong (CHN)
1995 Astrid Kumbernuss (GER)
1997 Astrid Kumbernuss (GER)
1999 Astrid Kumbernuss (GER)
2001 Yanina Korolchik (BLR)
2003 Svetlana Krivelyova (RUS)
2005 Nadezhda Ostapchuk (BLR)
2007 Valerie Vili (NZL)
2009 Valerie Vili (NZL)

World Track & Field Championships—Women (continued)

DISCUS THROW
1983　Martina Opitz (GDR)
1987　Martina Hellmann (GDR)
1991　Tsvetanka Khristova (BUL)
1993　Olga Burova (RUS)
1995　Ellina Zvereva (BLR)
1997　Beatrice Faumuina (NZL)
1999　Franka Dietzsch (GER)
2001　Ellina Zvereva (BLR)
2003　Irina Yachenko (BLR)
2005　Franka Dietzsch (GER)
2007　Franka Dietzsch (GER)
2009　Dani Samuels (AUS)

HAMMER THROW
1999　Mihaela Melinte (ROM)
2001　Yipsi Moreno (CUB)

HAMMER THROW (CONTINUED)
2003　Yipsi Moreno (CUB)
2005　Olga Kuzenkova (RUS)
2007　Betty Heidler (GER)
2009　Anita Wlodarczyk (POL)

JAVELIN THROW
1983　Tiina Lillak (FIN)
1987　Fatima Whitbread (GBR)
1991　Xu Demei (CHN)
1993　Trine Hattestad (NOR)
1995　Natalya Shikolenko (BLR)
1997　Trine Hattestad (NOR)
1999　Mirela Tzelili (GRE)
2001　Osleidys Menéndez (CUB)
2003　Mirela Manjani (GRE)
2005　Osleidys Menéndez (CUB)

JAVELIN THROW (CONTINUED)
2007　Barbora Spotakova (CZE)
2009　Steffi Nerius (GER)

HEPTATHLON
1983　Ramona Neubert (GDR)
1987　Jackie Joyner-Kersee (USA)
1991　Sabine Braun (GER)
1993　Jackie Joyner-Kersee (USA)
1995　Ghada Shouaa (SYR)
1997　Sabine Braun (GER)
1999　Eunice Barber (FRA)
2001　Yelena Prokhorova (RUS)
2003　Carolina Klüft (SWE)
2005　Carolina Klüft (SWE)
2007　Carolina Klüft (SWE)
2009　Jessica Ennis (GBR)

[1]3,000 m until 1995.

Outdoor Track & Field World Records

men

EVENT	RECORD HOLDER (COUNTRY)	PERFORMANCE	DATE
100 m	Usain Bolt (JAM)[1]	9.58 sec	16 Aug 2009
200 m	Usain Bolt (JAM)[1]	19.19 sec	20 Aug 2009
400 m	Michael Johnson (USA)	43.18 sec	26 Aug 1999
800 m	Wilson Kipketer (DEN)	1 min 41.11 sec	24 Aug 1997
1,000 m	Noah Ngeny (KEN)	2 min 11.96 sec	5 Sep 1999
1,500 m	Hicham El Guerrouj (MAR)	3 min 26.00 sec	14 Jul 1998
1 mile	Hicham El Guerrouj (MAR)	3 min 43.13 sec	7 Jul 1999
3,000 m	Daniel Komen (KEN)	7 min 20.67 sec	1 Sep 1996
5,000 m	Kenenisa Bekele (ETH)	12 min 37.35 sec	31 May 2004
10,000 m	Kenenisa Bekele (ETH)	26 min 17.53 sec	26 Aug 2005
marathon[2]	Haile Gebrselassie (ETH)	2 hr 3 min 59 sec	28 Sep 2008
110-m hurdles	Dayron Robles (CUB)	12.87 sec	12 Jun 2008
400-m hurdles	Kevin Young (USA)	46.78 sec	6 Aug 1992
20-km walk	Vladimir Kanaykin (RUS)	1 hr 17 min 16 sec	29 Sep 2007
50-km walk	Denis Nizhegorodov (RUS)	3 hr 34 min 14 sec	11 May 2008
steeplechase	Saif Saaeed Shaheen (QAT)	7 min 53.63 sec	3 Sep 2004
4 × 100-m relay	Jamaica	37.10 sec	22 Aug 2008
4 × 400-m relay	United States	2 min 54.29 sec	22 Aug 1993
high jump	Javier Sotomayor (CUB)	2.45 m (8 ft ½ in)	27 Jul 1993
long jump	Mike Powell (USA)	8.95 m (29 ft 4½ in)	30 Aug 1991
triple jump	Jonathan Edwards (GBR)	18.29 m (60 ft ¼ in)	7 Aug 1995
pole vault	Sergey Bubka (UKR)	6.14 m (20 ft 1¾ in)	31 Jul 1994
shot put	Randy Barnes (USA)	23.12 m (75 ft 10¼ in)	20 May 1990
discus throw	Jürgen Schult (GDR)	74.08 m (243 ft)	6 Jun 1986
hammer throw	Yuriy Sedykh (URS)	86.74 m (284 ft 7 in)	30 Aug 1986
javelin throw	Jan Zelezny (CZE)	98.48 m (323 ft 1 in)	25 May 1996
decathlon	Roman Sebrle (CZE)	9,026 pt	27 May 2001

women

EVENT	RECORD HOLDER (COUNTRY)	PERFORMANCE	DATE
100 m	Florence Griffith-Joyner (USA)	10.49 sec	16 Jul 1988
200 m	Florence Griffith-Joyner (USA)	21.34 sec	29 Sep 1988
400 m	Marita Koch (GDR)	47.60 sec	6 Oct 1985
800 m	Jarmila Kratochvilova (TCH)	1 min 53.28 sec	26 Jul 1983
1,000 m	Svetlana Masterkova (RUS)	2 min 28.98 sec	23 Aug 1996
1,500 m	Qu Yunxia (CHN)	3 min 50.46 sec	11 Sep 1993
1 mile	Svetlana Masterkova (RUS)	4 min 12.56 sec	14 Aug 1996
3,000 m	Wang Junxia (CHN)	8 min 6.11 sec	13 Sep 1993
5,000 m	Tirunesh Dibaba (ETH)	14 min 11.15 sec	6 Jun 2008
10,000 m	Wang Junxia (CHN)	29 min 31.78 sec	8 Sep 1993
marathon[2]	Paula Radcliffe (GBR)	2 hr 15 min 25 sec	13 Apr 2003
100-m hurdles	Yordanka Donkova (BUL)	12.21 sec	20 Aug 1988
400-m hurdles	Yuliya Pechonkina (RUS)	52.34 sec	8 Aug 2003

Outdoor Track & Field World Records (continued)

women (continued)

EVENT	RECORD HOLDER (COUNTRY)	PERFORMANCE	DATE
20-km walk	Olimpiada Ivanova (RUS)	1 hr 25 min 41 sec	7 Aug 2005
steeplechase	Gulnara Samitova-Galkina (RUS)	8 min 58.81 sec	17 Aug 2008
4 × 100-m relay	East Germany	41.37 sec	6 Oct 1985
4 × 400-m relay	USSR	3 min 15.17 sec	1 Oct 1988
high jump	Stefka Kostadinova (BUL)	2.09 m (6 ft 10¼ in)	30 Aug 1987
long jump	Galina Chistyakova (URS)	7.52 m (24 ft 8¼ in)	11 Jun 1988
triple jump	Inessa Kravets (UKR)	15.50 m (50 ft 10¼ in)	10 Aug 1995
pole vault	Yelena Isinbayeva (RUS)[1]	5.06 m (16 ft 7¼ in)	28 Aug 2009
shot put	Natalya Lisovskaya (URS)	22.63 m (74 ft 3 in)	7 Jun 1987
discus throw	Gabriele Reinsch (GDR)	76.80 m (252 ft)	9 Jul 1988
hammer throw	Anita Wlodarczyk (POL)[1]	77.96 m (255 ft 9 in)	22 Aug 2009
javelin throw	Barbora Spotakova (CZE)	72.28 m (237 ft 2 in)	13 Sep 2008
heptathlon	Jackie Joyner-Kersee (USA)	7,291 pt	24 Sep 1988
decathlon	Austra Skujyte (LTU)	8,358 points	15 Apr 2005

[1]Awaiting IAAF ratification as of 1 Sep 2009.   [2]Not an officially ratified event; best performance on record.

Indoor Track & Field World Records

men

EVENT	RECORD HOLDER (COUNTRY)	PERFORMANCE	DATE
50 m	Donovan Bailey (CAN)	5.56 sec	9 Feb 1996
60 m	Maurice Greene (USA)	6.39 sec	3 Feb 1998
200 m	Frank Fredericks (NAM)	19.92 sec	18 Feb 1996
400 m	Kerron Clement (USA)	44.57 sec	12 Mar 2005
800 m	Wilson Kipketer (DEN)	1 min 42.67 sec	9 Mar 1997
1,000 m	Wilson Kipketer (DEN)	2 min 14.96 sec	20 Feb 2000
1,500 m	Hicham El Guerrouj (MAR)	3 min 31.18 sec	2 Feb 1997
1 mile	Hicham El Guerrouj (MAR)	3 min 48.45 sec	12 Feb 1997
3,000 m	Daniel Komen (KEN)	7 min 24.90 sec	6 Feb 1998
5,000 m	Kenenisa Bekele (ETH)	12 min 49.60 sec	20 Feb 2004
50-m hurdles	Mark McKoy (CAN)	6.25 sec	5 Mar 1986
60-m hurdles	Colin Jackson (GBR)	7.30 sec	6 Mar 1994
5,000-m walk	Mikhail Shchennikov (RUS)	18 min 07.08 sec	14 Feb 1995
4 × 200-m relay	Great Britain and Northern Ireland	1 min 22.11 sec	3 Mar 1991
4 × 400-m relay	United States	3 min 02.83 sec	7 Mar 1999
4 × 800-m relay	United States	7 min 13.94 sec	6 Feb 2000
high jump	Javier Sotomayor (CUB)	2.43 m (7 ft 11½ in)	4 Mar 1989
long jump	Carl Lewis (USA)	8.79 m (28 ft 10 in)	27 Jan 1984
triple jump	Aliecer Urrutia (CUB);	17.83 m (58 ft 6 in)	1 Mar 1997;
	Christian Olsson (SWE)		7 Mar 2004
pole vault	Sergey Bubka (UKR)	6.15 m (20 ft 2¼ in)	21 Feb 1993
shot put	Randy Barnes (USA)	22.66 m (74 ft 4¼ in)	20 Jan 1989
heptathlon	Dan O'Brien (USA)	6,476 pt	14 Mar 1993

women

EVENT	RECORD HOLDER (COUNTRY)	PERFORMANCE	DATE
50 m	Irina Privalova (RUS)	5.96 sec	9 Feb 1995
60 m	Irina Privalova (RUS)	6.92 sec	11 Feb 1993
200 m	Merlene Ottey (JAM)	21.87 sec	13 Feb 1993
400 m	Jarmila Kratochvilova (TCH)	49.59 sec	7 Mar 1982
800 m	Jolanda Ceplak (SLO)	1 min 55.82 sec	3 Mar 2002
1,000 m	Maria Mutola (MOZ)	2 min 30.94 sec	25 Feb 1999
1,500 m	Yelena Soboleva (RUS)	3 min 58.28 sec	18 Feb 2006
1 mile	Doina Melinte (ROM)	4 min 17.14 sec	9 Feb 1990
3,000 m	Meseret Defar (ETH)	8 min 23.72 sec	3 Feb 2007
5,000 m	Meseret Defar (ETH)	14 min 24.37 sec	18 Feb 2009
50-m hurdles	Cornelia Oschkenat (GDR)	6.58 sec	20 Feb 1988
60-m hurdles	Susanna Kallur (SWE)	7.68 sec	10 Feb 2008
3,000-m walk	Claudia Stef (ROM)	11 min 40.33 sec	30 Jan 1999
4 × 200-m relay	Russia	1 min 32.41 sec	29 Jan 2005
4 × 400-m relay	Russia	3 min 23.37 sec	28 Jan 2006
4 × 800-m relay	Russia	8 min 18.54 sec	11 Feb 2007
high jump	Kajsa Bergqvist (SWE)	2.08 m (6 ft 10 in)	4 Feb 2006
long jump	Heike Drechsler (GDR)	7.37 m (24 ft 2¼ in)	13 Feb 1988
triple jump	Tatyana Lebedeva (RUS)	15.36 m (50 ft 4¾ in)	6 Mar 2004

Indoor Track & Field World Records (continued)

women (continued)

EVENT	RECORD HOLDER (COUNTRY)	PERFORMANCE	DATE
pentathlon	Irina Belova (UNT)	4,991 pt	15 Feb 1992
pole vault	Yelena Isinbayeva (RUS)	5.00 m (16 ft 4¾ in)	15 Feb 2009
shot put	Helena Fibingerova (TCH)	22.50 m (73 ft 9¾ in)	19 Feb 1977

Volleyball

World volleyball championships for men were inaugurated in 1949. Women's competition began in 1952. These biennial championships are organized by the Fédération Internationale de Volleyball (FIVB; founded 1947). Indoor volleyball has been included in the Olympic Games since 1964 and beach volleyball since 1996.

FIVB Web site: <www.fivb.org>.

Volleyball World Championships

YEAR	MEN	WOMEN	YEAR	MEN	WOMEN
1949	USSR		1982	USSR	China
1952	USSR	USSR	1984[1]	United States	China
1956	Czechoslovakia	USSR	1986	United States	China
1960	USSR	USSR	1988[1]	United States	USSR
1962	USSR	Japan	1990	Italy	USSR
1964[1]	USSR	Japan	1992[1]	Brazil	Cuba
1966	Czechoslovakia	not held	1994	Italy	Cuba
1967	not held	Japan	1996[1]	The Netherlands	Cuba
1968[1]	USSR	USSR	1998	Italy	Cuba
1970	East Germany	USSR	2000[1]	Yugoslavia	Cuba
1972[1]	Japan	USSR	2002	Brazil	Italy
1974	Poland	Japan	2004[1]	Brazil	China
1976[1]	Poland	Japan	2006	Brazil	Russia
1978	USSR	Cuba	2008[1]	United States	Brazil
1980[1]	USSR	USSR			

[1]Olympic champions, recognized in this table as world champions (though not by FIVB).

Weight Lifting

World weight lifting is overseen by the International Weightlifting Federation (IWF; founded 1905). The first men's international weight lifting competition was held in London in 1891; the sport was also included in the first modern Olympic Games, in Athens in 1896. By the 1930s championship events consisted of the snatch, clean and jerk, and press (which was eliminated in 1972).

Women's world championships have been held since 1987, and women's competition was added to the Olympics in 2000. In 1998 the IWF established new weight classes (eight for men and seven for women) as well as a new world standard for each class in determining world records.

IWF Web site: <www.iwf.net>.

World Weight Lifting Champions, 2008

men

WEIGHT CLASS	WINNER (COUNTRY)	PERFORMANCE
56 kg (123 lb)	Long Qinquan (CHN)	292 kg (644 lb)
62 kg (137 lb)	Zhang Xiangxiang (CHN)	319 kg (703 lb)
69 kg (152 lb)	Liao Hui (CHN)	348 kg (767 lb)
77 kg (170 lb)	Sa Jae Hyouk (KOR)	366 kg (807 lb)
85 kg (187 lb)	Lu Yong (CHN)	394 kg (869 lb)
94 kg (207 lb)	Ilya Ilin (KAZ)	406 kg (895 lb)
105 kg (231 lb)	Andrei Aramnau (BLR)	436 kg (961 lb)
105+ kg (231+ lb)	Matthias Steiner (GER)	461 kg (1,016 lb)

World Weight Lifting Champions, 2008 (continued)

women

WEIGHT CLASS	WINNER (COUNTRY)	PERFORMANCE
48 kg (106 lb)	Chen Xiexia (CHN)	212 kg (467 lb)
53 kg (117 lb)	Prapawadee Jaroenrattanatarakoon (THA)	221 kg (487 lb)
58 kg (128 lb)	Chen Yanqing (CHN)	244 kg (538 lb)
63 kg (139 lb)	Pak Hyon Suk (KOR)	241 kg (531 lb)
69 kg (152 lb)	Liu Chunhong (CHN)	286 kg (631 lb)
75 kg (165 lb)	Cao Lei (CHN)	282 kg (622 lb)
75+ kg (165+ lb)	Jang Mi Ran (KOR)	326 kg (719 lb)

Weight Lifting World Records

Total weight for snatch and clean-and-jerk lifts.

men

WEIGHT CLASS	RECORD HOLDER (COUNTRY)	PERFORMANCE	DATE
56 kg (123 lb)	Halil Mutlu (TUR)	305 kg (672 lb)	16 Sep 2000
62 kg (137 lb)	Zhang Jie (CHN)	326 kg (719 lb)	28 Apr 2008
69 kg (152 lb)	Galabin Boevski (BUL)	357 kg (787 lb)	24 Nov 1999
77 kg (170 lb)	Plamen Zhelyazkov (BUL)	377 kg (831 lb)	27 Mar 2002
85 kg (187 lb)	Lu Yong (CHN);	394 kg (869 lb)	15 Aug 2008;
	Andrei Rybakov (BLR)		15 Aug 2008
94 kg (207 lb)	Akakios Kakiasvilis (GRE)	412 kg (908 lb)	27 Nov 1999
105 kg (231.5 lb)	Andrei Aramnau (BLR)	436 kg (961 lb)	18 Aug 2008
105+ kg (231.5+ lb)	Hossein Rezazadeh (IRI)	472 kg (1041 lb)	26 Sep 2000

women

WEIGHT CLASS	RECORD HOLDER (COUNTRY)	PERFORMANCE	DATE
48kg (106 lb)	Yang Lian (CHN)	217 kg (478 lb)	1 Oct 2006
53 kg (117 lb)	Qiu Hongxia (CHN)	226 kg (498 lb)	2 Oct 2006
58 kg (128 lb)	Chen Yanqing (CHN)	251 kg (553 lb)	3 Dec 2006
63 kg (139 lb)	Liu Haixia (CHN)	257 kg (567 lb)	23 Sep 2007
69 kg (152 lb)	Liu Chunhong (CHN)	286 kg (631 lb)	13 Aug 2008
75 kg (165 lb)	Svetlana Podobedova (RUS)	286 kg (631 lb)	2 Jun 2006
75+ kg (165+ lb)	Jang Mi Ran (KOR)	326 kg (719 lb)	16 Aug 2008

INDEX

Page numbers in **boldface** indicate main subject references; references in *italics* indicate illustrations.
Photographs are on plates 1–16 after page 480, flags of the world are on plates 17–22,
and maps of the world are on plates 23–32.